BRITAIN

BED & BREAKFAST

1997

Edited by Tim Stilwell

Publishing Ltd

Distributed in Great Britain & the Commonwealth by Bailey Distribution Ltd, Learoyd Road, New Romney, Kent, TN28 8XU (Tel: 01797 366905) and in the U.S.A. by Seven Hills Distributors, 49 Central Avenue, Cincinatti, Ohio, OH45202, (Tel: (513) 3813881.
Available from all good bookshops.

ISBN 0-9521909-7-4

Published by Stilwell Publishing Ltd,
59 Charlotte Road, Shoreditch, London, EC2A 3QT.
Tel: 0171 739 7179.

Editor: Tim Stilwell
Assistant Editor: Dean Conway
Design and Maps : Nigel Simpson
Cover Photograph: Viv Lawrence (0171 481 0717)

Front Cover: Wealden Hall House, Hunton, Kent is listed on page 218 of this Directory.

Special thanks go to my wife, Rosemarie McGoldrick (artist, lecturer and arbiter of good taste); to Nigel Simpson, who managed the production while moving house; to Charlotte, Zoë and Liz, who did all the repetitive work; to Wynne and Ruth, who sorted everything out; and to Dean Conway who missed football matches, beer sessions and girlfriends to work weekends on this book.

Printed in Great Britain by the Guernsey Press Company Ltd, Guernsey, Channel Islands.

STILWELL'S

Key to Entries

- Children welcome (from age shown in brackets, if specified)
- Off-street car parking (number of places shown in brackets)
- No smoking
- Television (either in every room or in a TV lounge)
- Pets accepted (by prior arrangement)
- Evening meal available (by prior arrangement)
- Special diets catered for (by prior arrangement - please check with owner to see if your particular requirements are catered for)
- Central heating throughout
- Suitable for disabled people (please check with owner to see what level of disability is provided for)
- Christmas breaks a speciality
- Coffee/Tea making facilities

The location heading - every hamlet, village, town and city mentioned in this directory is represented on the local county map at the head of each section.

Use the National Grid reference with Ordnance Survey maps and any atlas that uses the British National Grid. The letters refer to a 100 kilometre grid square. The first two numbers refer to a North/South grid line and the last two numbers refer to an East/West grid line. The grid reference indicates their intersection point.

Penny Hassett

National Grid Ref: PH2096.

Cat & Fiddle, The Bull

Local pubs - these are the names of nearby pubs that serve food in the evening, as suggested by local B&Bs

***The Old Rectory,** Main Street, Penny Hassett, Borchester, Borsetshire, BC2 3QT.*
C18th former rectory, lovely garden.
Grades: ETB 2 Cr, Comm.
Tel: **01676 512480.** Mrs Smythe.
Rates fr: *£14.00*-**£16.00**.
Open: All Year
Beds: 1F 1D 1T
Baths: 1 Private 2 Shared
(4) (2)

The figure in *italics* is the lowest 1997 double or twin rate per person per night. The figure in **bold** is the lowest 1997 single rate. Some establishments do not accept single bookings.

Bedrooms
F = Family
D = Double
T = Twin
S = Single

Grades - the English, Scottish and Welsh Tourist Boards (**ETB**, **STB** and **WTB**) have the national Crown rating (**Cr**), in which the range of facilities and services an establishment provides is indicated by "Listed" or 1 to 5 Crowns in ascending order of merit. Jersey in the Channel Islands uses Diamonds (**Di**). An optional quality grading, using the terms Approved (**Approv**), Commended (**Comm**), Highly Commended (**High Comm**) and De Luxe is also used. More details of the national Crown rating and the quality grading can be had from any Tourist Information Centre. The Automobile Association (**AA**) employs two grading systems: the one for hotels uses 1 to 5 Stars (**St**) in ascending order of merit; there is also a B&B rating that uses the letter **Q** (for quality) on a scale of 1 to 4; the highest have 4 Qs and a Selected award (**Select**). For more details, telephone the AA on 01256 20123. The Royal Automobile Club (**RAC**) also uses a Star (**St**) system for large hotels; small hotels and B&Bs obtain the ratings 'Listed' (**Listed**), 'Acclaimed' (**Acclaim**) or 'Highly Acclaimed' (**High Acclaim**). For more details, telephone the RAC on 0181-686 0088.

CURRENCY CONVERTER

Here is a quick dollar/sterling conversion table for our American readers, based on rates as we went to press in early November 1997 ($10 = £6.10 or £10 = $16.50). On these terms, the average price per person per night in this book is $25.

$20 = £12.20	£10 = $16.50
$30 = £18.30	£15 = $24.75
$40 = £24.40	£20 = $33.00
$50 = £30.50	£25 = $41.25

Please note: while it may be fine in some States to make advance bookings with several B&Bs for the same date, only to choose the final one later, it is certainly *not* acceptable practice in Britain. Owners who suffer at the hands of 'double-bookers' in this way are entitled to sue for compensation.

Contents

Introduction

This directory is really very straightforward. It sets out simply to list as many B&Bs in as many places in Britain as possible, so that wherever you go, you know there is one nearby. The book was actually born of frustration. My wife and I walked a long distance footpath over several weekends in the summer of 1991. As neither of us are born to camping or wished to stay in expensive hotels, we decided on B&Bs for our overnight stays. We encountered a problem straightaway. One could not find good value bed and breakfast accommodation along the route without going to a lot of trouble. Local libraries, directory enquiries, six different Tourist Information Centres and a large pile of brochures yielded nothing but a hotchpotch of B&B addresses, most of them miles out of our way. We abandoned the research and did the walk in one-day stretches, high-tailing it back to our London home each evening on the train. The memory stayed with us, however.

Earlier on that year I had needed to visit the National Exhibition Centre outside Birmingham, while working for a large publishing company. My colleagues and I had wished to stay in the area together and at short notice. Our office was typical of the times - the recession was in full swing and our budget did not stretch far. We asked for the local Tourist Information Centre's brochure, but it did not help us much - it arrived three days later, had no map and consisted mostly of hotels outside our price range. A 2-mile trek to the local reference library to trawl through through the Birmingham Yellow Pages yielded a list of local guest house telephone numbers. There was no way of knowing the kind of facilities they had or how much they cost - it was like blind man's buff. We were lucky. We got what we wanted after 20 calls - bed and breakfast in a thriving Coleshill pub, five miles from the Centre. We had booked it unseen, though, on the landlord's word only - an uninformed decision. In their small way, both experiences illustrated the need for a book such as Stilwell's Directory: Britain - Bed & Breakfast.

As the recession grew worse, I lost my job with the large publishing company. A year later, I set up a small publishing company myself and our first project was this directory. It has been rather successful. The reason must be that over the years many others have found themselves in similar straits - stuck for somewhere to stay overnight. For lack of information, they missed out on the good value offered by B&Bs. This is therefore a book to save the reader time and money: it suits anyone who wishes to plan a trip in Britain, who appreciates good value and who is open to ideas. The directory is quite deliberately *not* a guidebook. Its aim is that of any directory in any field: to be comprehensive, to offer the widest choice. By this definition, Stilwell's Directory outstrips any guidebook - we publish by far and away the largest number of B&Bs listed anywhere in this country. What we do not do is make up the reader's mind for them. There are plenty of other B&B books that push their particular premises as 'exclusive' or 'special'. We think that a simple glance over the salient details on any page and the reader will be his or her own guide.

We have two kinds of reader in mind. The first knows exactly where to go but not where to stay. The nearest B&B is the best solution; a quick look at the right county map gives the answer. The other reader is not so sure where to go. As they browse the pages, the short five-word descriptions provide good ideas.

All information here has been supplied by the B&B owners themselves. All are bona fide B&Bs; 99% are on the books of the local Tourist Information Centre. We should make it clear that inclusion in these pages does not imply personal recommendation. We have not visited them all individually; all we have done is write to them. The directory lists over 8,000 entries in over 4,500 locations throughout Britain. The vast majority were included because they offered B&B for under £25 per person per night (in fact the average double rate per person per night in this book is £16.00).

Owners were canvassed in the summer of 1996 and responded by the end of October. They were asked to provide their lowest rates per person per night for 1997. The rates are thus forecasts and are in any case always subject to seasonal fluctuation in demand. Some information may, of course, be out of date already. Grades may go up or down, or be removed altogether. British Telecom may alter exchange numbers. Proprietors may decide to sell up and move out of the business altogether. This is why the directory has to be a yearbook; in general, though, the information published here will be accurate, pertinent and useful for many a year. The pink highlight boxes are advertisements - the B&B has paid for some extra wordage and for their entry to stand out from the page a little more.

The main aim has been to provide details that are concise and easy to understand. The only symbols used are some conventional tourist symbols. There are some abbreviations, but it should be clear what they stand for without having to refer to the keys on the first and last pages. The grades are perhaps more difficult - each inspecting organisation has its own classification system with its own definition of merit. Once again, though, the reader will soon pick out the exceptional establishments -

many have high grades from each organisation. The general rule is that more facilities mean higher prices. Do not be misled into thinking that an ungraded establishment is inferior. Many B&B owners are locally registered but never apply for a grade or do not wish to pay for one. They thrive on business from guests who return again and again because the hospitality is excellent. My advice is: ring around. A simple telephone call and some judicious questions will give you an impression of your host very effectively. If you write to a B&B for more details, it is a good idea to enclose a stamped, addressed envelope for a quick reply. The largest number of British B&Bs is now laid out before you - the greatest choice available in the market. We think that your tastes and preferences will do the rest.

We have deliberately arranged the book by administrative county in alphabetical order (unless this would disrupt a perceived sequence such as East, North, South and West Yorkshire). There is an exception to prove the rule - County Durham appears perversely under D, as most people look for it under this heading. Merseyside is merged into the adjacent Greater Manchester section. South, West and Mid-Glamorgan appear together under the heading of 'The Glamorgans'. We also hope to delight the hearts of many who show pride in their native or adopted counties. Our government legislated to rename administrative counties and to revise many local government boundaries, as from April 1996. Out go many of the 1974 creations of the Heath government - Avon, Cleveland, Hereford & Worcester, Humberside, Dyfed, Clwyd, Gwynedd, Strathclyde, Grampian, Central and Tayside. In come older and more loved names, such as Argyll & Bute or Pembrokeshire. While this has undoubtedly served to make many people happier (hatred of the 1974 names was quite intense), it has proved rather a headache for travel book publishers. We are still stuck for a better name for North West Wales - Caernarfonshire & Merionethshire is horribly long and Aberconwy & Colwyn is as obscure as the Gwynedd it half replaces. Many of the new Scottish regions are too small to merit their own chapter and so we have merged them into neighbouring regions - hence 'Lothian & Falkirk' or 'Stirling & Clackmannan'. The Glasgow chapter mixes six new unitary authorities. The same goes for much of our Glamorgan and Monmouthshire chapters. We offer our commiserations to the aggrieved inhabitants of Powys, for they missed out on the reorganisation by a whisker. Those in Rutland are on the Leicestershire map as such, but do not have a heading or a chapter to themselves. The reason for the reorganisation is to provide 'unitary' as opposed to 'two-tier' authorities.

This, presumably, will cost the tax payer less. In perusing the map the dispassionate observer finds other, more cynical reasons. The major boundary changes occur along the Clyde and in the Welsh Valleys and seem calculated to help to neuter power in traditional Labour heartlands. Other long-sought name changes must provide a welcome fillip for shire Tories, whose power has recently been on the wane. In the end, the savings to be made in running these new unitary authorities will, hopefully, outweigh the general confusion caused to the average tourist. There is a pig in the sky outside my window.

Another feature of the book is that we insist on using the proper postal address. Many entries thus carry a county name different from the one they are listed under or show a 'post town' that is some miles from the village. These oddities arise from the Royal Mail's distribution system. They should not, under any circumstances, be used as a directional guide. In one case the village of Laid on Loch Eriboll is 67 miles from its quoted 'post town' - not a journey to make in error. Used on a letter though, it does speed the mail up. If you need directions to a B&B (especially if you are travelling at night), the best solution is to telephone the owner and ask the way.

The county maps are intended to act as a general reference. They present only the locations of each entry in the directory. For a more accurate idea of the location of a B&B, use the six-figure National Grid Reference published under each location's name. Used in tandem with an Ordnance Survey map (such as the excellent Landranger series) or any atlas that uses the National Grid, these numbers provide first-class route-planning references. The pubs that appear beneath each location heading are included on the recommendation of B&Bs themselves. The tankard and the knife and fork symbols show that they are local pubs where one can get a decent evening meal at a reasonable price.

Throughout the book you will find boxes offering peremptory advice to readers. These may seem of little consequence; some, we have been told, can annoy. We are sorry to tread upon delicate sensibilities, but the boxes fill up odd bits of space and neaten the page. Those that request courtesy and care for the customs of your hosts need no apology, however. Opening one's home to strangers, albeit for payment, requires a leap of faith for most people; B&B owners are no exceptions. We simply ask everyone to observe the usual house rules. In this way, other guests will continue to meet with a welcome when they, too, pass through.

The Editor,
Stoke Newington, November 1996.

GREAT BRITAIN
SHETLAND ISLANDS
ISLES OF ORKNEY
WESTERN ISLES
Wick
Stornoway
Inverness
Aberdeen
SCOTLAND
Fort William
Glasgow
EDINBURGH
Newcastle upon Tyne
Durham
NORTHERN
IRELAND
ISLE OF MAN
Kendal
York
Manchester
Liverpool
IRELAND
Norwich
Birmingham
Aberystwyth
ENGLAND
WALES
CARDIFF
Bristol
LONDON
Dover
Portsmouth
Exeter
Plymouth
ISLE OF WIGHT
ISLES OF SCILLY
CHANNEL ISLANDS
FRANCE

England & Wales *Regions*

ENGLAND

1	**Bedfordshire**
2	**Berkshire**
3	**Buckinghamshire**
4	**Cambridgeshire**
5	**Cheshire**
6	**Cornwall**
7	**Cumbria**
8	**Derbyshire**
9	**Devon**
10	**Dorset**
11	**County Durham**
12	**Essex**
13	**Gloucestershire**
14	**Greater Manchester & Merseyside**
15	**Hampshire**
16	**Herefordshire**
17	**Hertfordshire**
18	**Isle of Wight**
19	**Kent**
20	**Lancashire**
21	**Leicestershire**
22	**Lincolnshire**
23	**London** *inc. Greater London*
24	**Norfolk**
25	**Northamptonshire**
26	**Northumberland**
27	**Nottinghamshire**
28	**Oxfordshire**
29	**Shropshire**
30	**Somerset**
31	**Staffordshire**
32	**Suffolk**
33	**Surrey**
34	**East Sussex**
35	**West Sussex**
36	**Tyne & Wear**
37	**Warwickshire**
38	**West Midlands**
39	**Wiltshire**
40	**Worcestershire**
41	**East Yorkshire**
42	**North Yorkshire**
43	**South Yorkshire**
44	**West Yorkshire**
45	**Isle of Man**

WALES

46	**Anglesey**
47	**Cardiganshire**
48	**Carmarthenshire**
49	**Denbigh & Flint**
50	**The Glamorgans**
51	**Monmouthshire**
52	**North West Wales**
53	**Pembrokeshire**
54	**Powys**

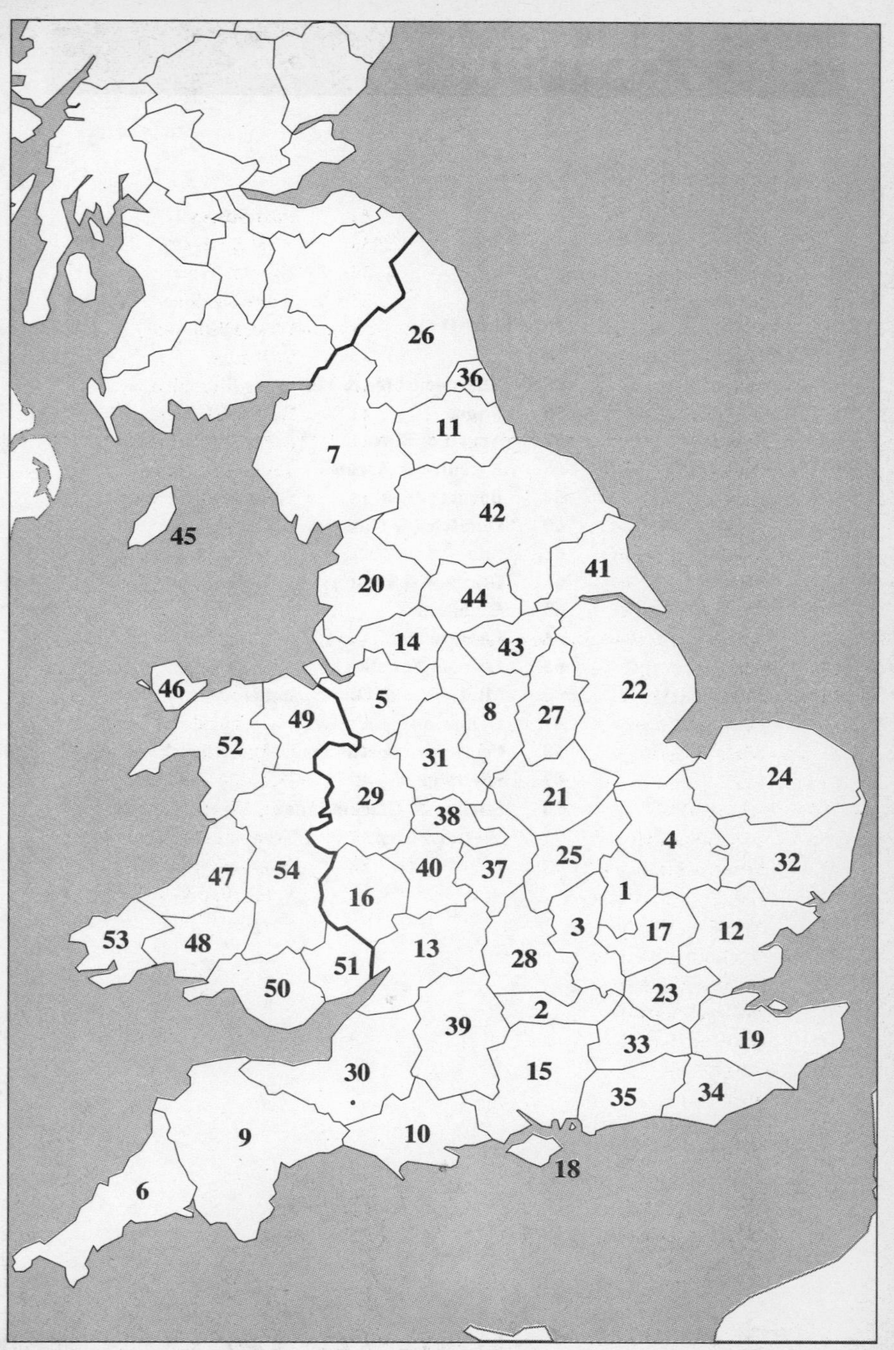
26
36
11
7
42
45
41
20
44
14
43
46
22
5
8
27
49
52
31
24
29
21
38
4
25
32
47
54
40
37
1
16
3
17
12
53
48
13
28
51
50
23
2
39
33
19
30
15
35
34
9
10
18
6

Scotland *Regions*

SCOTLAND

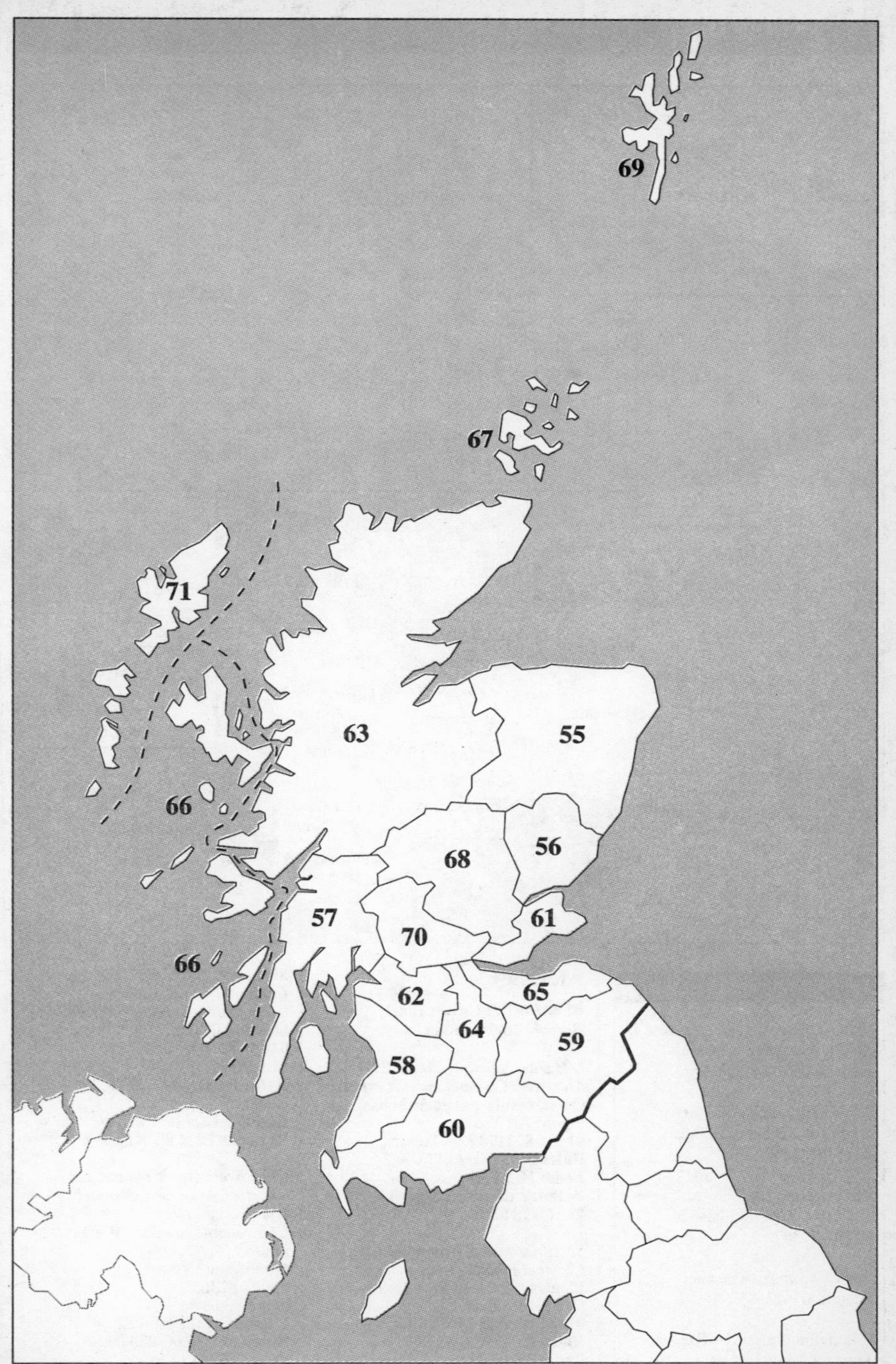
69
67
71
63
55
66
56
68
57
61
70
66
65
62
64
59
58
60

Channel Islands

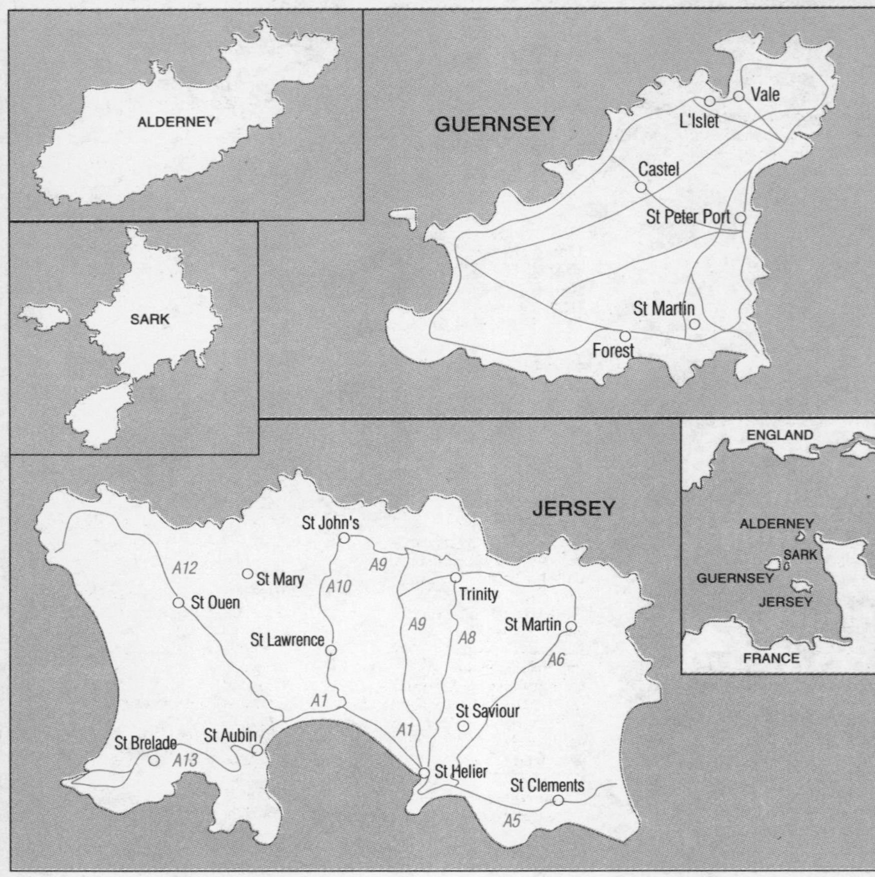

Tourist Information Centres

States Office, Queen Elizabeth II Street, **Alderney**, Channel Islands, 01481-822994.

Crown Pier, **St Peter Port**, Guernsey, Channel Islands, 01481-723552.

The Airport, La Villiaze, **Forest**, Guernsey, Channel Islands, 01481-37267.

Sark, Guernsey, Channel Islands, 01481-832345.

Liberation Square, **St Helier**, Jersey, Channel Islands, 01534-500777.

Alderney

Rose & Crown Hotel, Harbour Lights Hotel

L'Haras, *Newtown Road, Alderney, Channel Islands, GY9 3XP.*
Quiet, family-run guest house.
Open: All Year
01481 823174 Mrs Jansen
Rates fr: *£17.00*-**£17.00**.
Beds: 1F 2T 2S
Baths: 2 Ensuite 1 Shared
(10)

St Annes Guest House, *Alderney, Channel Islands, GY9 3TB.*
Elegant Victorian town house.
Open: All Year
01481 823145 Mrs Millan
Rates fr: *£19.00*-**£19.00**.
Beds: 2F 1T 1S
Baths: 2 Private 1 Shared

Simerock, *Les Velles, Alderney, Channel Islands, GY9 3TW.*
Large family-run guest bungalow.
Open: All Year
01481 823645
Mrs Lowe
Rates fr: *£16.00*-**£20.00**.
Beds: 4F
Baths: 2 Ensuite 2 Private
(10)

Chez Nous Guest House, *Les Venelles, Alderney, Channel Islands, GY9 3TW.*
Comfortable, traditional guest house.
Open: Mar to Nov
01481 823633
Mrs Matthews
Fax no: 01481 823732
Rates fr: *£19.00*-**£23.00**.
Beds: 1F 1D 1T
Baths: 3 Ensuite
(0)

***Les Quest,** Allee Es Fees, Alderney, Channel Islands, GY9 3XD.*
Modern comfortable bungalow with garden.
Open: Easter to Oct
01481 822809 Mrs Strick
Rates fr: *£20.00*-**£18.00**.
Beds: 1F
Baths: 1 Private
(3)

***Saye Farm Guest House,** Alderney, Channel Islands, GY9 3YJ.*
Comfortable peaceful old farmhouse.
Open: All Year
01481 82 2196 Mrs Hamon
Rates fr: *£16.00*-**£18.00**.
Beds: 1F 2D 2T 1S
Baths: 2 Private 1 Shared
(3) (15)

Guernsey — Castel

Fleurs Du Jardin

***Les Quatre Saisons,** Rue Des Tamaris, Castel, Guernsey, Channel Islands, GY5 7BA.*
Bright, comfortable and spacious room.
Open: Apr to Sep
01481 55653 Mrs Aslett
Rates fr: *£14.00*.
Beds: 1D
Baths: 1 Shared

Guernsey — Forest

The Venture Inn, The Mallard Hotel

***Mon Plaisir,** Rue des Landes, Forest, Guernsey, GY8 0DY.*
Delightful Guernsey farmhouse with garden.
Open: Jan to Nov
Grades: AA 3 Q
01481 64498 Mrs Torode
Fax no: 01481 63493
Rates fr: *£16.00*-**£21.00**.
Beds: 3D 2T
Baths: 5 Ensuite
(3) (5)

***Tudor Lodge Deer Farm,** Forest Road, Forest, Guernsey, Channel Islands, GY8 0A8.*
Farm guest house - it's different.
Open: Jan to Oct
01481 37849 Mrs Gallienne
Rates fr: *£20.00*-**£27.50**.
Beds: 2D 3T
Baths: 5 Private
(12) (12)

Always telephone to get directions to the B&B - you will save time!

Guernsey — St Martin

***Rosewood,** La Grand Rue, St Martin, Guernsey, Channel Islands, GY4 6RU.*
Large Victorian guest house.
Open: Easter to Oct
01481 38329
Mr Sinkinson
Rates fr: *£13.00*-**£16.00**.
Beds: 1F 2D 2T 1S
Baths: 2 Shared
(8)

***Woodlands Guest House,** Route des Blanches, St Martin, Guernsey, Channel Islands, GY4 6AF.*
Grade A, friendly guest house.
Open: All Year (not Xmas)
01481 37481 Mrs Carr
Rates fr: *£12.50*-**£15.00**.
Beds: 2D 3T 1S
(5) (9)

Guernsey — St Peter Port

Moore's Hotel, Mamma Rosa, Absolute End, La Collinette Hotel

***Marine Hotel,** Well Road, St Peter Port, Guernsey, Channel Islands, GY1 1WS.*
Open: All Year
Grades: ETB 2 Cr, AA 3 Q, Recomm, RAC High Acclaim
01481 724978 Mrs Clegg
Fax no: 01481 711729
Rates fr: *£15.50*-**£15.50**.
Beds: 3F 4D 3T 1S
Baths: 11 Ensuite
Comfortable owner-run friendly hotel, 5 minutes walk into town. Full breakfast with choice, cooked to order. Full CH, some rooms sea-view.

***Grisnoir,** Les Gravees, St Peter Port, Guernsey, Channel Islands, GY1 1RW.*
Good food, friendly, comfortable accommodation.
Open: All Year
01481 727267
Mrs Goodlass
Rates fr: *£12.50*-**£12.50**.
Beds: 2F 2D 4T 2S
Baths: 3 Shared

***Lindale Guest House,** Elm Grove, St Peter Port, Guernsey, Channel Islands, GY1 1XE.*
Open: All Year (not Xmas)
01481 722136
Mr & Mrs Gethings
Fax no: 01481 720266
Rates fr: *£15.00*-**£15.00**.
Beds: 2F 4D 2T 1S
Baths: 4 Ensuite 1 Shared
(3)
Heartbeat Award. Comfortable guest house run by owners. Easy walking distance of town, leisure centre, gardens and buses. Vegetarians catered for. Mostly free range products.

***Friends Vegetarian,** 20 Hauteville, St Peter Port, Guernsey, Channel Islands, GY1 1DG.*
Fairytale view of illuminated castle.
Open: Easter to Oct
01481 721146 Mr & Mrs Darling
Rates fr: *£16.00*-**£16.00**.
Beds: 3F 3D 2T 1S
Baths: 3 Shared

***Foresters Arms,** St Georges Esplanade, St Peter Port, Guernsey, Channel Islands, GY1 2BQ.*
Family-run pub.
Open: All Year (not Xmas)
01481 723583 Mrs Hillion
Rates fr: *£14.00*-**£16.00**.
Beds: 1D 1T

***St Clare Court Hotel,** Brock Road, St Peter Port, Guernsey, Channel Islands, GY1 1RS.*
Friendly central hotel.
Open: All Year
01481 723240
Mr McCusker
Rates fr: *£12.00*-**£12.00**.
Beds: 4F 10D 13T 3S
Baths: 30 Private
(10)

Guernsey — Vale

***Bordeaux Guest House,** Bordeaux Bay, Vale, Guernsey, Channel Islands, GY3 5LX.*
Family-run traditional Guernsey house.
Open: All Year (not Xmas)
Grades: ETB Listed
01481 47461
Mrs Ackrill
Rates fr: *£15.00*-**£15.00**.
Beds: 3F 4D 1T
Baths: 8 Private

***L'Ancresse View Guest House,** La Garenne, Vale, Guernsey, Channel Islands, GY3 5SQ.*
Victorian comfortable guest house.
Open: All Year
01481 43963
Mr Peacegood
Rates fr: *£10.00*-**£10.00**.
Beds: 2F 1D 2T

Jersey — St Aubin

***Peterborough House,** Rue du Croquet, High Street, St Aubin, Jersey, Channel Islands, JE3 8BR.*
C17th house, personally run, conservation area.
Open: Easter to Oct
Grades: ETB 3 Di, AA 4 Q, Select
01534 41568
Mrs Boyden
Fax no: 01534 46787
Rates fr: *£16.50*-**£16.50**.
Beds: 5D 5T 4S
Baths: 12 Private 2 Shared
(10)

Jersey — St Brelade

Smugglers, Old Portelet Inn

Three Bay View, *Route De Noirmont, St Brelade, Jersey, Channel Islands, JE3 8AJ.*
'Home from home' comfort.
Open: All Year (not Xmas)
01534 42028 Ms Somerville
Rates fr: *£16.00*-**£16.00**.
Beds: 1F 2D 2T 1S
Baths: 1 Ensuite 2 Shared
(7)

Au Caprice, *Route De La Haule, St Brelade, Jersey, Channel Islands, JE3 8BA.*
Modern sea front guest house.
Open: Apr to Oct
01534 22083 Mrs Deffains
Rates fr: *£17.00*-**£17.00**.
Beds: 1F 7D 4T 1S
Baths: 11 Private 1 Shared

Jersey — St Clements

Le Hocq Inn, Partners

Playa D'or, *Greve D'azette, St Clements, Jersey, Channel Islands, JE2 6SA.*
Family guest house, South Coast beachfront.
Open: Feb to Nov
Grades: ETB 3 Di
01534 22861 Mr Jeffery
Fax no: 01534 69668
Rates fr: *£15.00*-**£15.00**.
Beds: 5F 4D 4T 4S
Baths: 15 Ensuite
(14)

Rocqueberg View, *Rue De Samares, St Clements, Jersey, JE2 6LS.*
Friendly comfortable quality guest house.
Open: Mid-Jan to mid-Dec
Grades: ETB 2 Di
01534 852642 Monks
Fax no: 01534 851694
Rates fr: *£14.00*-**£14.00**.
Beds: 2F 5D 2T
Baths: 9 Private
(Any) (9)

Wavecrest Guest House, *Greve D'Azette, St Clements, Jersey, Channel Islands, JE2 6PT.*
Family house on sea front.
Open: Apr to Oct
01534 77185 Mr Downs
Rates fr: *£27.50*.
Beds: 2F 4D 2T
Baths: 8 Private
(12)

Please respect a B&B's wishes regarding children, animals & smoking.

National Grid References are for villages, towns and cities - *not* for individual houses.

Brookland, *Blanc Mondin, St Clements, Jersey, Channel Islands, JE2 6PR.*
Extended modern bungalow.
Open: May to Sep
01534 24705 Mrs Gavey
Rates fr: *£17.00*.
Beds: 3F 3D
Baths: 6 Private
(5) (2)

Jersey — St Helier

Nelson's Eye, The Admiral, Harvest Barn, Le Moulin de Lecq, St Marys Country Pub

Millbrook House, *Rue De Trachy, Millbrook, St Helier, Jersey, Channel Islands, JE2 3JN.*
Open: Apr to Oct
Grades: ETB 2 Cr, AA 3 Q, RAC Acclaim
01534 33036 Mr Pirouet
Fax no: 01534 24317
Rates fr: *£24.00*-**£24.00**.
Beds: 5F 9T 3S 10D
Baths: 27 Ensuite
(20)
C18th Listed building in 10 acres of gardens and parklands, offering exceptional standards at reasonable rates. Sea views, peace and quiet.

Alhambra Hotel, *Roseville Street, St Helier, Jersey, Channel Islands, JE2 4PL.*
Small privately run hotel with restaurant.
Open: Easter to Oct
01534 32128 Mrs Robertson
Rates fr: *£17.00*-**£17.00**.
Beds: 3F 9D 6T 1S
Baths: 19 Private 1 Shared

Glen Guest House, *Vallee Des Vaux, St Helier, Jersey, Channel Islands, JE2 3GB.*
Open: All Year (not Xmas)
Grades: ETB 3 Di
01534 32062
Mrs Cavicchia
Fax no: 01534 880738
Rates fr: *£18.50*-**£18.50**.
Beds: 2F 2D 2T 1S
Baths: 7 Private
(3) (8)
Calm, caring, comfortable Victorian home, in country 'Green Lane' just 1.5 miles from town centre. Rooms ensuite plus refrigerator. Ideal for motorist, cyclist and walker.

Shandene, *St Aubins Road, St Helier, Jersey, Channel Islands, JE2 3SF.*
Lovely old family home, sun patio, overlooking bay.
Open: Mar to Oct
01534 20386
Mrs Jayes
Fax no: 01534 23760
Rates fr: *£12.00*-**£12.00**.
Beds: 2F 4D 3T 2S
Baths: 8 Ensuite 3 Shared
(1) (5)

La Bonne Vie, *Roseville Street, St Helier, Jersey, Channel Islands, JE2 4PL.*
Open: All Year
Grades: ETB 3 Di
01534 35955
Mr Hetherington
Fax no: 01534 33357
Rates fr: *£17.00*-**£17.00**.
Beds: 1F 8D 1T 2S
Baths: 10 Private
(8)
Beautiful Victorian guest house 5 minutes walk from town, 1 minute walk from beach. All rooms ensuite, some having French four-poster beds, others antique brass beds.

Glenroyd, *26 Cleveland Road, St Helier, Jersey, Channel Islands, JE2 4PB.*
Comfortable Victorian guest house.
Open: All Year (not Xmas)
Grades: ETB 2 Di
01534 31578
Mrs Hill
Fax no: 01534 617367
Rates fr: *£10.00*-**£12.00**.
Beds: 1F 4D 2T 2S
Baths: 7 Ensuite 2 Shared

Bromlet Guest House, *7 Winchester Street, St Helier, Jersey, Channel Islands, JE2 4TH.*
Open: All Year
01534 25045
Mrs Schillaci
Fax no: 01534 69712
Rates fr: *£14.00*-**£15.00**.
Beds: 1F 4D 2S 2T
Baths: 7 Private 1 Shared
Comfortable, friendly guest house, centrally situated & open all year. B&B from £14-21, BB+EM from £20-26, according to season. Most rooms ensuite.

All details shown are as supplied by B&B owners in Autumn 1996.

De L'Etang, *33 Havre Des Pas, St Helier, Jersey, Channel Islands,* *JE2 4UQ.*
Homely guest house opposite seafront.
Open: All Year
Grades: ETB 2 Di
01534 21996
Mr Gavriel
Fax no: 01534 37829
Rates fr: *£12.00*-**£12.00**.
Beds: 1F 9D 2T 1S
Baths: 10 Private 3 Shared
(5)

Jersey — St Johns

Malta House Farm, *Route Du Mont Mado, St Johns, Jersey, Channel Islands,* *JE3 4DN.*
Comfortable farmhouse.
Open: Easter to Oct
01534 861678 Mrs Barlette
Rates fr: *£13.50*-**£13.50**.
Beds: 2F 1D
Baths: 1 Shared

Jersey — St Martin

Mont Orgueil House, *Gorey Pier, St Martin, Jersey, Channel Islands,* *JE3 6EW.*
Beach and harbourside location.
Open: Mar to Dec
01534 857736 Mr Thomas
Fax no: 01534 853777
Rates fr: *£16.00*-**£16.00**.
Beds: 2F 2D 1S
Baths: 4 Private 1 Shared
(2)

Jersey — St Mary

Roc Annick Guest House, *Rue A George, St Mary, Jersey, Channel Islands,* *JE3 3EQ.*
Quiet, modern, country guesthouse.
Open: Mar to Nov
Grades: AA 4 Q
01534 862272
Mrs Coote
Fax no: 01534 865709
Rates fr: *£12.50*-**£12.50**.
Beds: 2F 6D 2T 1S
Baths: 9 Private 2 Shared
(10)

Jersey — St Ouen

Lecq Farm, *Leoville, St Ouen, Jersey, Channel Islands,* *JE3 2BU.*
Comfortable old farmhouse in countryside.
Open: Easter to Oct
01534 481745
Mrs Renouf
Rates fr: *£15.00*-**£15.00**.
Beds: 1D 1T
Baths: 3 Ensuite 1 Shared
(6)

L'Etacquerel, *L'Etacq, St Ouen, Jersey, Channel Islands,* *JE3 2FB.*
Beachside - best views in Jersey.
Open: All Year
01534 482492
Mr Lamy
Rates fr: *£13.00*-**£13.00**.
Beds: 2F 7D 2T 3S
Baths: 2 Ensuite 3 Shared

The *lowest* **single** rate *is shown in* **bold.**

Jersey — Trinity

Trinity Arms

Les Avenues Farm, *Rue Du Nord, Trinity, Jersey, Channel Islands,* *JE3 5AH.*
Modern, comfortable, homely farmhouse.
Open: May to mid-Sept
01534 861093 Mrs Picot
Rates fr: *£14.50*-**£21.00**.
Beds: 2F **Baths:** 1 Shared
(3)

Undercliff, *Bouley Bay, Trinity, Jersey, Channel Islands,* *JE3 5AS.*
Olde worlde country guesthouse.
Open: Easter to Oct
01534 863058 Mr Huson
Rates fr: *£15.00*.
Beds: 2F 8T 8D **Baths:** 18 Ensuite
(5) (12)

All rates are subject to alteration at the owners' discretion.

Bedfordshire

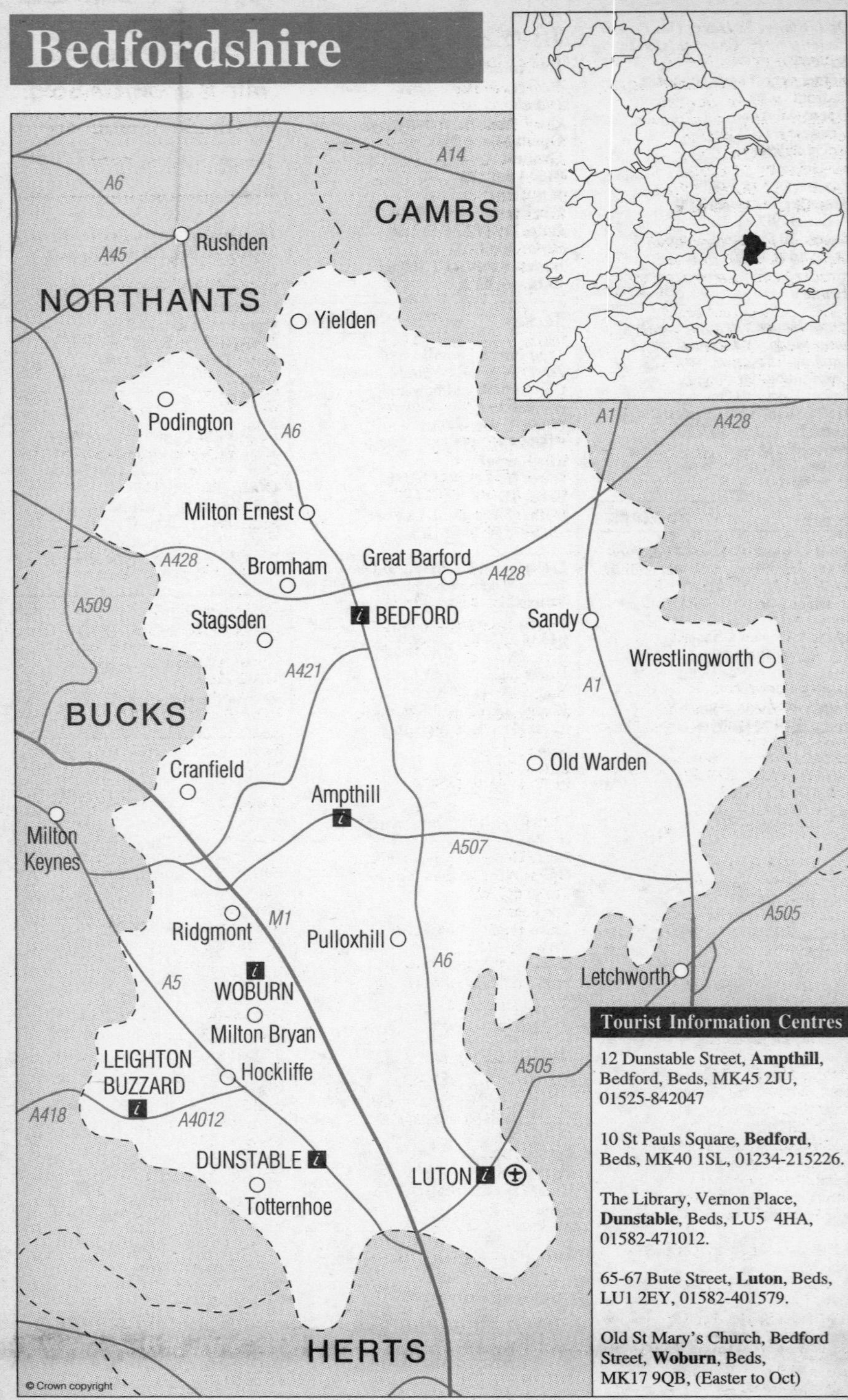

Tourist Information Centres

12 Dunstable Street, **Ampthill**, Bedford, Beds, MK45 2JU, 01525-842047

10 St Pauls Square, **Bedford**, Beds, MK40 1SL, 01234-215226.

The Library, Vernon Place, **Dunstable**, Beds, LU5 4HA, 01582-471012.

65-67 Bute Street, **Luton**, Beds, LU1 2EY, 01582-401579.

Old St Mary's Church, Bedford Street, **Woburn**, Beds, MK17 9QB, (Easter to Oct)

Ampthill

National Grid Ref: TL0337

***One-O-Five,** 105 Dunstable Street, Ampthill, Bedford, MK45 2NG.*
Delightful early Georgian town house. **Open:** All Year
01525 403778 Ms Carter
Rates fr: *£22.50*-**£30.00**.
Beds: 1D 1T **Baths:** 2 Private
(5) (2)

***Brookside Farm,** New Road, Ampthill, Bedford, MK45 2BG.*
Friendly family atmosphere, superb breakfast.
Open: All Year (not Xmas)
01525 405506 Mr & Mrs Sankey
Rates fr: *£17.50*-**£22.00**.
Beds: 2D 1T**Baths:** 3 Ensuite
(5)

Bedford

National Grid Ref: TL0549

Embankment Hotel

***Park View,** 11 Shaftesbury Avenue, Bedford, Beds, MK40 3SA.*
Central, riverside Victorian private house. **Open:** All Year (not Xmas)
01234 341376 Ms Sedgwick
Rates fr: *£16.00*-**£16.00**.
Beds: 1T 2S
Baths: 1 Private 2 Shared

***Bedford Park Hotel,** 59 De Parys Avenue, Bedford, Beds, MK40 2TR.*
Lovely Victorian house, quiet road.
Open: All Year
01234 215100 Mrs Butcher
Rates fr: *£17.50*-**£19.50**.
Beds: 4F 2D 2T 6S
Baths: 4 Ensuite
(6)

***Bedford Oak House,** 33 Shakespear Road, Bedford, Beds, MK40 2DX.*
Large mock-Tudor house.
Open: All Year
Grades: ETB 2 Cr, AA 2 Q
01234 266972 Mr Kemp
Rates fr: *£16.00*-**£29.50**.
Beds: 1F 8D 4T 2S
Baths: 11 Private 4 Shared
(8) (15)

***Victoria House,** 17 Shakespeare Road, Bedford, Beds, MK40 2DZ.*
Large Victorian house.
Open: All Year
01234 214135 Mrs O'Donnell
Rates fr: *£18.00*-**£25.00**.
Beds: 2F 1D 5T 5S
Baths: 3 Private 8 Shared

***20 Haylands Way,** Bedford, Beds, MK41 9BU.*
Semi-detached in residential area.
Open: Easter to Oct
01234 353272 Mrs Franklin
Rates fr: *£12.00*-**£12.00**.
Beds: 1T 1S
Baths: 1 Ensuite 1 Shared
(1)

Bromham

National Grid Ref: TL0051

Swan Pub

***Kerry Thatch,** 16 The Green, Bromham, Bedford, Beds, MK43 8JS.*
Attractive C16th thatched cottage.
Open: All Year (not Xmas)
01234 823287
Rates fr: *£12.50*-**£18.00**.
Beds: 1D 1T
Baths: 1 Private
(2)

Cranfield

National Grid Ref: SP9542

Cross Keys Pub

***14 Redlion Close,** Cranfield, Bedford, MK43 0JA.*
Modern private house.
Open: All Year
01234 750738 Mrs Last
Rates fr: *£12.00*-**£12.00**.
Beds: 1T 1S
(10)

Dunstable

National Grid Ref: TL0121

***Regent House Guest House,** 79a High Street North, Dunstable, Beds, LU6 1JF.*
Located in town centre.
Open: All Year
01582 660196 Mr Woodhouse
Rates fr: *£14.00*-**£16.00**.
Beds: 3T 2S
Baths: 2 Shared
(6)

***23 Priory Road,** Dunstable, Beds, LU5 4HR.*
Large Georgian private house.
Open: All Year (not Xmas)
01582 667396
Mrs Reavey
Rates fr: *£15.00*-**£20.00**.
Beds: 1F 1D 1T 1S
Baths: 1 Private 1 Shared
(4)

Great Barford

National Grid Ref: TL1252

***Anchor Hotel,** High Street, Great Barford, Bedford, Beds, MK44 3LF.*
Comfortable, traditional inn.
Open: All Year
01234 870364
Mrs Lloyd
Rates fr: *£15.00*-**£20.00**.
Beds: 1F 2D 1S
(30)

Bringing children with you? Always ask for any special rates.

Always telephone to get directions to the B&B - you will save time!

Hockliffe

National Grid Ref: SP9726

***The Red Lion,** Watling Street, Hockliffe, Leighton Buzzard, Beds, LU7 9LR.*
Village pub with large garden.
Open: All Year
01525 210240
Mrs Johnson
Rates fr: *£15.00*-**£20.00**.
Beds: 1F 5T 2S
Baths: 2 Shared
(20)

Luton

National Grid Ref: TL0921

Wigmore Arms, O'Sheas, Wardown Beefeater, Harvester

***Stockwood Hotel,** 41-43 Stockwood Crescent, Luton, Beds, LU1 3SS.*
Tudor-style town centre premises.
Open: All Year (not Xmas)
01582 21000
Mr Blanchard
Rates fr: *£20.00*-**£20.00**.
Beds: 1F 2D 6T 9S
Baths: 4 Private 3 Shared
(12)

***Belzayne,** 70 Lalleford Road, Luton, Beds, LU2 9JH.*
Small, friendly guest house, convenient airport.
Open: All Year (not Xmas)
01582 36591
Mrs Bell
Rates fr: *£11.00*-**£18.00**.
Beds: 1D 2T
Baths: 2 Shared
(6) (5)

***Hill House,** 93 London Road, Luton, Beds, LU1 3RG.*
In Luton, convenient for Airport.
Open: All Year
Grades: ETB Listed
01582 22725 Ms Stirling
Rates fr: *£15.00*-**£20.00**.
Beds: 2F 1D 1T 1S
Baths: 1 Ensuite 2 Shared
(5)

***Spinner's ,** 46 Hill Rise, Sundon Park, Luton, Beds, LU3 3EE.*
Immaculate, comfortable, convenient M1/trains.
Open: All Year (not Xmas)
01582 508327
Mrs Frances Spinner
Rates fr: *£13.00*-**£13.00**.
Beds: 1T 1S
Baths: 1 Shared
(2)

National Grid References are for villages, towns and cities - *not* for individual houses.

Milton Bryan

National Grid Ref: SP9730

Red Lion

Town Farm, *Milton Bryan, Milton Keynes, Bucks,* MK17 9HS.
Quiet, secluded farmhouse, good views.
Open: All Year (not Xmas)
Grades: ETB Listed
01525 210001 Mrs Harris
Rates fr: *£15.00*-**£18.00**.
Beds: 2T
(12) (4)

Milton Ernest

National Grid Ref: TL0156

Church Barn, *Churchgreen, Milton Ernest, Bedford, Beds,* MK44 1RH.
Quiet country converted stone barn.
Open: All Year (not Xmas)
01234 824097
Mrs Robson
Rates fr: *£12.50*-**£15.00**.
Beds: 2T
Baths: 2 Shared
(12)

Old Warden

National Grid Ref: TL1343

Hare & Hounds

Old Warden Guest House, *Shop & Post Office, Old Warden, Biggleswade, Beds,* SG18 9HQ.
Centre of quiet, picturesque village.
Open: All Year
01767 627201
Mr Bruton
Rates fr: *£17.00*-**£20.00**.
Beds: 1D 2T
Baths: 3 Ensuite
(5)

Podington

National Grid Ref: SP9462

Nags Head

Shepherds View, *4 Hinwick Road, Podington, Wellingborough, Northants,* NN9 7HU.
Converted house in small village.
Open: All Year
01933 315111 Mrs Turk
Rates fr: *£15.00*-**£15.00**.
Beds: 1D 2T
Baths: 1 Shared
(5)

Pulloxhill

National Grid Ref: TL0633

Pond Farm, *7 High Street, Pulloxhill, Bedford,* MK45 5NA.
C17th arable farm opposite the green in the middle of the village.
Open: All Year
Grades: ETB Listed
01525 712316
Mrs Tookey
Rates fr: *£15.00*-**£20.00**.
Beds: 1F 1D 1T
Baths: 2 Shared

Ridgmont

National Grid Ref: SP9736

Firs Guest House, *85 High Street, Ridgmont, Bedford,* MK43 0TY.
Large, comfortable, family-run guest house.
Open: All Year
01525 280279
Mr & Mrs Wright
Rates fr: *£16.00*-**£16.00**.
Beds: 2D 4T 4S
(1) (12)

Sandy

National Grid Ref: TL1649

Wheatsheaf (Tempsford)

Highfield Farm, *Sandy, Beds,* SG19 2AQ.
Tranquil and welcoming farmhouse.
Open: All Year
Grades: ETB 2 Cr, High Comm, AA 4 Q, Select
01767 682332
Mrs Codd
Fax no: 01767 692503
Rates fr: *£19.00*-**£20.00**.
Beds: 2F 2D 2T
Baths: 3 Private 1 Shared
(10)

Stagsden

National Grid Ref: SP9849

Slaters Arms

Firs Farm, *Stagsden, Bedford, Beds,* MK43 8TB.
Quiet, comfortable timber-framed farmhouse.
Open: All Year (not Xmas)
Grades: ETB 2 Cr, Comm
01234 822344 (also fax no)
Mrs Hutcheon
Rates fr: *£16.00*-**£18.50**.
Beds: 2D 1T
Baths: 1 Private 1 Shared
(2) (3)

The lowest *double* rate per person is shown in *italics*.

All details shown are as supplied by B&B owners in Autumn 1996.

Totternhoe

National Grid Ref: SP9821

Gower Cottage, *5 Brightwell Avenue, Totternhoe, Dunstable, Beds,* LU6 1QT.
Executive style, country position. Close M1.
Open: All Year (not Xmas)
01582 601287
Mrs Mardell
Rates fr: *£16.00*-**£16.00**.
Beds: 2D 1S
Baths: 1 Shared
(3)

Woburn

National Grid Ref: SP9433

Royal Oak

11 George Street, *Woburn, Milton Keynes, Bucks,* MK17 9PX.
Listed building of great charm.
Open: All Year
01525 290405
Mrs Tough
Rates fr: *£12.50*-**£12.50**.
Beds: 1D 3T 2S
Baths: 2 Shared

Copperfields, *15 Market Place, Woburn, Milton Keynes, Beds,* MK17 9PZ.
Friendly welcome in Georgian home.
Open: All Year (not Xmas)
01525 290464
Mrs Droy
Rates fr: *£16.00*-**£16.00**.
Beds: 1F 1D 1T
Baths: 1 Ensuite 1 Shared
(3)

Wrestlingworth

National Grid Ref: TL2547

The Chequers

Orchard Cottage, *1 High Street, Wrestlingworth, Sandy, Beds,* SG19 2EW.
Comfortable peaceful country cottage.
Open: All Year (not Xmas)
Grades: ETB 1 Cr, Comm
01767 631355
Mrs Strong
Rates fr: *£16.00*-**£16.00**.
Beds: 1F 1T 1S
Baths: 2 Shared
(6)

Berkshire

Tourist Information Centres

The Look Out, Nine Mile Ride, **Bracknell**, Berks, RG12 4QW, 01344 868196.

The Library, St Ives Road, **Maidenhead**, Berks, SL6 1QU, 01628 781110.

The Wharf, **Newbury**, Berks, RG14 5AS, 01635 30267.

Town Hall, Blagrave Street, **Reading**, Berks, RG1 1QH, 0188 956 6226.

Central Station, Thames Street, **Windsor**, Berks, SL4 1PJ, 01753-852010.

Ascot

National Grid Ref: SU9268

Old Manor, Crambourne Tavern

***Tanglewood,** Birch Lane, Off Longhill Road, Chavey Down, Ascot, Berks, SL5 8RF.*
Modern family home, large secluded garden.
Open: All Year (not Xmas)
Grades: ETB 2 Cr
01344 882528 Mrs Beer
Rates fr: *£20.00*-**£20.00**.
Beds: 2T 2S
Baths: 3 Private 1 Shared
(5)

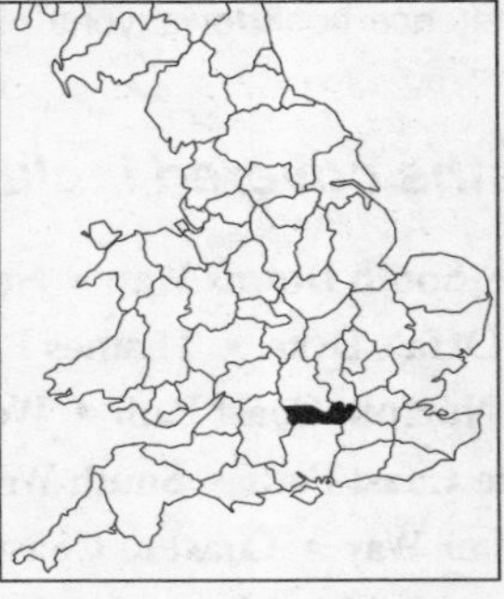

Bracknell

National Grid Ref: SU8688

Downshire Arms

***53 Swaledale, Wildridings,** Bracknell, Berks, RG12 7ET.*
Near station, M3, M4 & shops.
Open: All Year (not Xmas)
01344 421247 Mrs Webber
Rates fr: *£19.00*-**£20.00**.
Beds: 1T 1S
(2)

***8 Milman Close, Bullbrook,** Bracknell, Berks, RG12 2SN.*
Comfortable, peaceful modern home. **Open:** All Year
01344 52243 Mrs Harris
Rates fr: *£15.00*-**£14.00**.
Beds: 1T 1S

Burghfield Bridge

National Grid Ref: SU6870

***Boathouse,** Kennet House, Burghfield Bridge, Reading, Berks, RG30 3RA.*
Comfortable, traditional, canal house boat. **Open:** All Year
0118 957 1060 Mrs Ogden
Rates fr: *£14.00*-**£14.00**.
Beds: 2D 1S
(20)

Burghfield Common

National Grid Ref: SU6566

Hatch Gate Pub

***Highwoods,** Burghfield Common, Reading, Berks, RG7 3BG.*
Fine victorian house in extensive grounds with far reaching views.
Open: All Year
0118 983 2320 Mrs Steeds
Fax no: 01734 831070
Rates fr: *£21.00*-**£19.00**.
Beds: 1D 1S
Baths: 1 Ensuite 1 Shared
(6)

***Firlands,** Burghfield Common, Reading, Berks, RG7 3JN.*
Comfortable Victorian farmhouse in woods.
Open: All Year (not Xmas)
0118 983 2414 Mrs Stuckey
Rates fr: *£17.00*-**£17.00**.
Beds: 2D **Baths:** 1 Shared

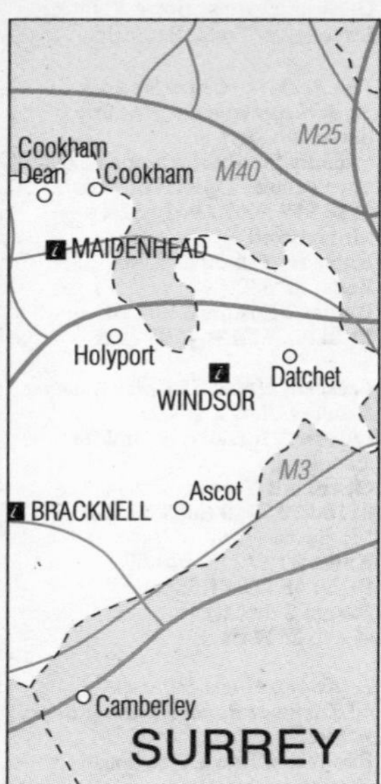

Chieveley

National Grid Ref: SU4773

Red Lion

The Old Farmhouse, *Downend Lane, Chieveley, Newbury, Berks, RG20 8TN.*
Old farmhouse in large grounds.
Open: All Year **Grades:** ETB 2 Cr
01635 248361 Mrs Pallett
Rates fr: *£20.00*-**£20.00**.
Beds: 1F **Baths:** 1 Private
(6)

Cookham

National Grid Ref: SU8985

Spencer Pub

Koala, *Vivien Close, Cookham, Maidenhead, Berks, SL6 9DQ.*
Modern comfortable family home.
Open: All Year
01628 523031 Mrs Gibbings
Rates fr: *£14.00*-**£15.00**.
Beds: 1F 1S **Baths:** 2 Shared
(3) (3)

Wylie Cottage, *School Lane, Cookham, Maidenhead, Berks, SL6 9QJ.*
Comfortable family home in village.
Open: All Year (not Xmas)
Grades: ETB Listed
01628 520106 Mrs Crowe
Rates fr: *£18.00*-**£22.00**.
Beds: 1D 1T **Baths:** 1 Shared
(2)

Cookham Dean

National Grid Ref: SU8684

Chequers, The Jolly Farmer

Primrose Hill, *Bradcutts Lane, Cookham Dean, Maidenhead, Berks, SL6 9TL.*
Easy access Heathrow. Rural location.
Open: All Year (not Xmas)
Grades: ETB Listed
01628 528179 Mrs Benson
Rates fr: *£17.50*-**£17.50**.
Beds: 1F 1S
Baths: 1 Shared
(3)

Cartlands Cottage, *Kings Lane, Cookham Dean, Maidenhead, Berks, SL6 9AY.*
Self-contained garden guest room, rural, quiet.
Open: All Year
Grades: ETB 1 Cr, Approv
01628 482196 Mr & Mrs Parkes
Rates fr: *£17.50*-**£19.50**.
Beds: 1F
Baths: 1 Private
(2)

Curridge

National Grid Ref: SU4871

Many Trees, *Curridge Road, Curridge, Thatcham, Berks, RG18 9DH.*
Picturesque hunting lodge.
Open: All Year (not Xmas)
01635 200872 Mrs Hendel
Rates fr: *£23.00*-**£25.00**.
Beds: 1D 1T 1S
Baths: 1 Ensuite 1 Private

Datchet

National Grid Ref: SU9877

Royal Stag

55 London Road, *Datchet, Slough, Berks, SL3 9JY.*
Conveniently located, near Windsor, Heathrow, M4/M25 motorways.
Open: All Year
01753 580401 Mrs Greenham
Fax no: 01753 540233
Rates fr: *£20.00*-**£28.50**.
Beds: 1F 2D 1T **Baths:** 2 Private

Hermitage

National Grid Ref: SU5173

Audley Cottage, *Slanting Hill, Hermitage, Thatcham, Berks, RG18 9QW.*
Country cottage in woods, log fires. **Open:** All Year
01635 200353 Ms Khan
Rates fr: *£20.00*-**£20.00**.
Beds: 2D 1S
Baths: 1 Ensuite 1 Private
1 Shared
(3) (y)

Holyport

National Grid Ref: SU8977

Moor Farm, *Holyport, Maidenhead, Berks, SL6 2HY.*
Mediaeval manor, near pretty village.
Open: All Year
Grades: ETB 2 Cr, High Comm
01628 33761 (also fax no)
Mrs Reynolds
Rates fr: *£20.00*-**£40.00**.
Beds: 1D 2T
Baths: 3 Private
(3)

Hungerford

National Grid Ref: SU3368

Three Swan Hotel

Wynbush, *135 Priory Road, Hungerford, Berks, RG17 0AP.*
Detached house, large garden, quiet.
Open: All Year
01488 682045 Mrs Simmonds
Rates fr: *£13.00*-**£15.00**.
Beds: 1D 1S
Baths: 1 Shared
(3)

15 Sanden Close, *Hungerford, Berks, RG17 0LA.*
Semi-detached bungalow in quiet close.
Open: All Year (not Xmas)
01488 682583
Mrs Hook
Rates fr: *£25.00*-**£14.00**.
Beds: 1D 1S
Baths: 1 Shared
(5) (3)

Hurley

National Grid Ref: SU8283

The Black Boy Inn, *Hurley, Maidenhead, Berks, SL6 5NQ.*
Famous C16th beamed rural inn.
Open: All Year (not Xmas)
01628 824212
Mr Wymark
Rates fr: *£20.00*-**£20.00**.
Beds: 1T 1S
(20)

Inkpen

National Grid Ref: SU3764

Beacon House, *Bell Lane, Upper Green, Inkpen, Hungerford, Berks, RG17 9QJ.*
Open: All Year
01488 668640
Mr & Mrs Cave
Rates fr: *£16.00*-**£16.00**.
Beds: 1T 2S
Baths: 2 Shared
(7)
A warm welcome 60 miles west of London. 1930s country house - peaceful rural setting. Excellent centre for walking, touring, exploring southern England. Delicious home cooking.

Kintbury

National Grid Ref: SU3866

***The Forbury,** Crossways, Kintbury, Hungerford, Berks, RG17 9SU.*
Extended C17th cottage.
Open: All Year (not Xmas)
01488 658377 Mr Cubitt
Rates fr: *£19.00*-**£19.50**.
Beds: 1D 1T 1S
Baths: 1 Private 1 Shared

Lambourn Woodlands

National Grid Ref: SU3175

***Lodge Down,** Lambourn Woodlands, Hungerford, Berks, RG17 7BJ.*
Ideal for touring Berkshire.
01672 540304 Mrs Cook
Rates fr: *£20.00*-**£20.00**.
Beds: 1F 2D 2T
Baths: 3 Ensuite
(10)

Maidenhead

National Grid Ref: SU8781

Boulter's Lock Inn

***Sheephouse Manor,** Sheephouse Road, Maidenhead, Berks, SL6 8HJ.*
Charming C16th farmhouse.
Open: All Year (not Xmas)
Grades: ETB 2 Cr, Comm
01628 776902 Mrs Street
Fax no: 01628 25138
Rates fr: *£21.50*-**£30.00**.
Beds: 2D 1T 2S
Baths: 5 Private
(5) (6)

***Copperfields Guest House,** 54 Bath Road, Maidenhead, Berks, SL6 4JY.*
Comfortable, clean and caring accommodation.
Open: All Year
01628 74941 Mrs Lindsay
Rates fr: *£17.50*-**£23.00**.
Beds: 2F 2D 2T 1S
Baths: 3 Private
(5)

***Clifton Guest House,** 21 Craufurd Rise, Maidenhead, Berks, SL6 7LR.*
Family-run, evening meals, fully licensed.
Open: All Year
Grades: ETB 3 Cr, RAC Listed
01628 23572 (also fax no)
Mr Arora
Rates fr: *£28.00*-**£45.00**.
Beds: 2F 4D 7T 3S
Baths: 7 Ensuite 3 Shared
(1) (11)

***4 Gables Close, Off Ray Lea Road,** Maidenhead, Berks, SL6 8QD.*
Modern comfortable house in quiet close. **Open:** All Year
01628 39630 Mrs Blight
Rates fr: *£17.00*-**£17.00**.
Beds: 1D 1S **Baths:** 1 Shared
(2)

***Laburnham Guest House,** 31 Laburnham Road, Maidenhead, Berks, SL6 4DB.*
A warm welcome assured.
Open: All Year
01628 76748 Mrs Stevens
Rates fr: *£20.00*-**£25.00**.
Beds: 1F 2D 1T 1S
Baths: 5 Private
(4)

Mortimer

National Grid Ref: SU6564

Red Lion

***35 The Avenue,** Mortimer, Reading, Berks, RG7 3QU.*
Comfortable detached house, in quiet location.
Open: All Year
01734 333166 Mrs Keast
Rates fr: *£15.00*-**£15.00**.
Beds: 1D 1T 1S
Baths: 1 Shared
(2) (8)

Newbury

National Grid Ref: SU4767

The Bunk (Curridge), Robin Hood, Toby Inn

***Mousefield Farm,** Long Lane, Shaw, Newbury, Berks, RG14 2TG.*
C17th comfortable, hospitable farm house.
Open: All Year (not Xmas)
Grades: ETB Listed
01635 40333 Mrs Houghton
Rates fr: *£18.00*-**£20.00**.
Beds: 1F 2T 2S
Baths: 3 Shared
(10)

***Tonayne House,** Oxford Road, Donnington, Newbury, Berks, RG14 2JD.*
Lovely red-brick Georgian private house.
Open: All Year (not Xmas)
01635 523138 Mrs Ritchie
Rates fr: *£17.00*-**£20.00**.
Beds: 1F 1T 1S
Baths: 1 Ensuite 1 Shared
(4)

***15 Shaw Road,** Newbury, Berks, RG14 1HG.*
Late-Georgian private house.
Open: All Year
01635 44962 Mrs Curtis
Rates fr: *£15.00*-**£15.00**.
Beds: 1D 1T **Baths:** 1 Shared
(1)

***Starwood,** 1 Rectory Close, Newbury, Berks, RG14 6DF.*
Close to town centre, stations, canal.
Open: All Year (not Xmas)
01635 49125 Mr Tillen
Rates fr: *£18.50*-**£19.00**.
Beds: 1F 1D 1T 2S
Baths: 1 Private 1 Shared
(5)

Reading

National Grid Ref: SU7173

The Mansion House, Gardeners Arms, Horse & Jockey, Sweeney & Todd, Beefeater

***The Berkeley Guest House,** 32 Berkeley Avenue, Reading, Berks, RG1 6JE.*
Friendly family-run home near town centre. **Open:** All Year
0118 959 5699 / 961 0329
Mr Hubbard
Rates fr: *£16.00*-**£18.00**.
Beds: 2F 3 T
Baths: 2 Ensuite 2 Shared
(6)

***Crescent Hotel,** 35 Coley Avenue, Reading, Berks, RG1 6LL.*
Licensed, friendly, central for amenities.
Open: All Year
0118 950 7980 (also fax no)
Ms Evans
Rates fr: *£19.00*-**£20.00**.
Beds: 6F 4D 1T 5S
Baths: 2 Private
(20)

***Dittisham Guest House,** 63 Tilehurst Road, Reading, Berks, RG3 2JL.*
Renovated Edwardian house.
Ensuite rooms.
Open: All Year
Grades: ETB Listed, Comm
0118 956 9483 Mr Harding
Rates fr: *£17.50*-**£20.00**.
Beds: 1F 1D 3S
Baths: 5 Ensuite

***10 Greystoke Road, Caversham,** Reading, Berks, RG4 5EL.*
Family home in private road.
Open: All Year (not Xmas)
Grades: ETB Listed, Comm
0118 947 5784 Mrs Tyler
Rates fr: *£17.00*-**£18.00**.
Beds: 1D 2S **Baths:** 2 Shared
(1)

Twyford

National Grid Ref: SU7975

***Chesham House,** 79 Wargrave Road, Twyford, Reading, Berks, RG10 9PE.*
Ensuite, beverage facilities, television, refrigerator.
Open: All Year (not Xmas)
0118 932 0428 Mr & Mrs Ferguson
Rates fr: *£18.00*-**£24.00**.
Beds: 1D 1T **Baths:** 2 Private
(6)

Bringing children with you? Always ask for any special rates.

Wargrave on Thames

National Grid Ref: SU7878

The Bull

Windy Brow, *204 Victoria Road, Wargrave on Thames, Reading, Berks, RG10 8AJ.*
Large Victorian house overlooking fields. **Open:** All Year
Grades: ETB Listed
0118 940 3336 Mrs Carver
Rates fr: *£20.00*-**£25.00**.
Beds: 1F 3D 3T 2S
Baths: 1 Private 2 Shared
(6)

Wash Water

National Grid Ref: SU4563

Cherry Tree Farm, *Horris Hill, Wash Water, Newbury, Berks, RG20 9DQ.*
Country cottage, beautiful quiet location.
Open: All Year (not Xmas)
01635 44789 Mrs Morris
Rates fr: *£17.00*-**£17.00**.
Beds: 1T 1S
(6)

Windsor

National Grid Ref: SU9676

Bexley Arms, The Windsor Lad, Harvester, Stag & Hounds, Red Lion, Vansittary Arms

1 Stovell Road, *Windsor, Berks, SL4 5JB.*
Open: All Year (not Xmas)
Grades: ETB Listed
01753 852055 Ms Sumner
Rates fr: *£20.00*-**£30.00**.
Beds: 1D 1T
Baths: 2 Private
(2)
Quiet, comfortable, self-contained ground floor flat, 100 yards to river and leisure centre. 7 minutes walk to castle, town centre and railway stations.

Elansey, *65 Clifton Rise, Windsor, Berks, SL4 5SX.*
Modern comfortable house, patio, garden.
Open: All Year (not Xmas)
Grades: ETB Listed
01753 864438 Mrs Forbutt
Rates fr: *£16.00*-**£16.00**.
Beds: 1D 1T 1S
Baths: 1 Ensuite 1 Shared
(2)

National Grid References are for villages, towns and cities - *not* for individual houses.

57 Grove Road, *Windsor, Berks, SL4 1JD.*
Private Victorian house, town centre.
Open: All Year (not Xmas)
Grades: ETB Listed
01753 853600 Mrs Ford
Rates fr: *£18.00*-**£25.00**.
Beds: 1F **Baths:** 1 Private

13 Keppel Spur, *Old Windsor, Windsor, Berks, SL4 2LU.*
Clean, comfortable, homely private house.
Open: All Year
01753 868757 Mr Wren
Rates fr: *£16.00*-**£18.00**.
Beds: 1F 1D 1T
Baths: 1 Shared
(4)

31 Upcroft, *Windsor, Berks, SL4 3NH.*
Semi-detached house, residential area.
Open: All Year (not Xmas)
01753 853371 Ms Horn
Rates fr: *£15.00*-**£16.00**.
Beds: 1T 1S
Baths: 1 Shared
(3) (2)

Tanglewood, *Oakley Green, Windsor, Berks, SL4 4PZ.*
Rural area, beautiful garden. Quiet.
Open: May to Sep
Grades: ETB Listed, High Comm
01753 860034 Mrs Salter
Rates fr: *£18.00*-**£22.00**.
Beds: 2T
Baths: 1 Shared
(2)

62 Buckland Crescent, *Windsor, Berks, SL4 5JS.*
Semi-detached house in quiet crescent.
Open: All Year (not Xmas)
01753 859109 Mrs Hutson
Rates fr: *£16.00*-**£16.00**.
Beds: 1T 1S **Baths:** 1 Shared
(0)

Trinity Guest House, *18 Trinity Place, Windsor, Berks, SL4 3AT.*
Large Victorian family guest house.
Open: All Year
Grades: ETB 2 Cr
01753 864186
Mrs Jackson
Fax no: 01753 862640
Rates fr: *£24.00*-**£29.00**.
Beds: 2F 3D 2T 1S
Baths: 5 Ensuite 1 Private 2 Shared
(4)

Halycon House, *131 Clarence Road, Windsor, Berks, SL4 5AR.*
Large comfortable home, off-street parking.
Open: All Year (not Xmas)
01753 863262 (also fax no)
Mr Golec
Rates fr: *£20.00*-**£30.00**.
Beds: 2D 2T
Baths: 3 Private
(5)

77 Whitehorse Road, *Windsor, Berks, SL4 4PG.*
Modern, comfortable private house.
Open: All Year (not Xmas)
01753 866803
Mrs Andrews
Rates fr: *£16.00*-**£20.00**.
Beds: 3D
(5) (3)

62 Queens Road, *Windsor, Berks, SL4 3BH.*
Excellent reputation,quiet and convenient.
Open: All Year
01753 866036 (also fax no)
Mrs Hughes
Rates fr: *£18.00*-**£20.00**.
Beds: 1F 1T
Baths: 2 Private

88 St Leonards Road, *Windsor, Berks, SL4 3DA.*
Centrally situated, elegant Victorian villa.
Open: All Year
01753 853984
Mrs Birch
Rates fr: *£16.50*-**£25.00**.
Beds: 2D 1T
Baths: 1 Private 1 Shared
(3)

Buckinghamshire

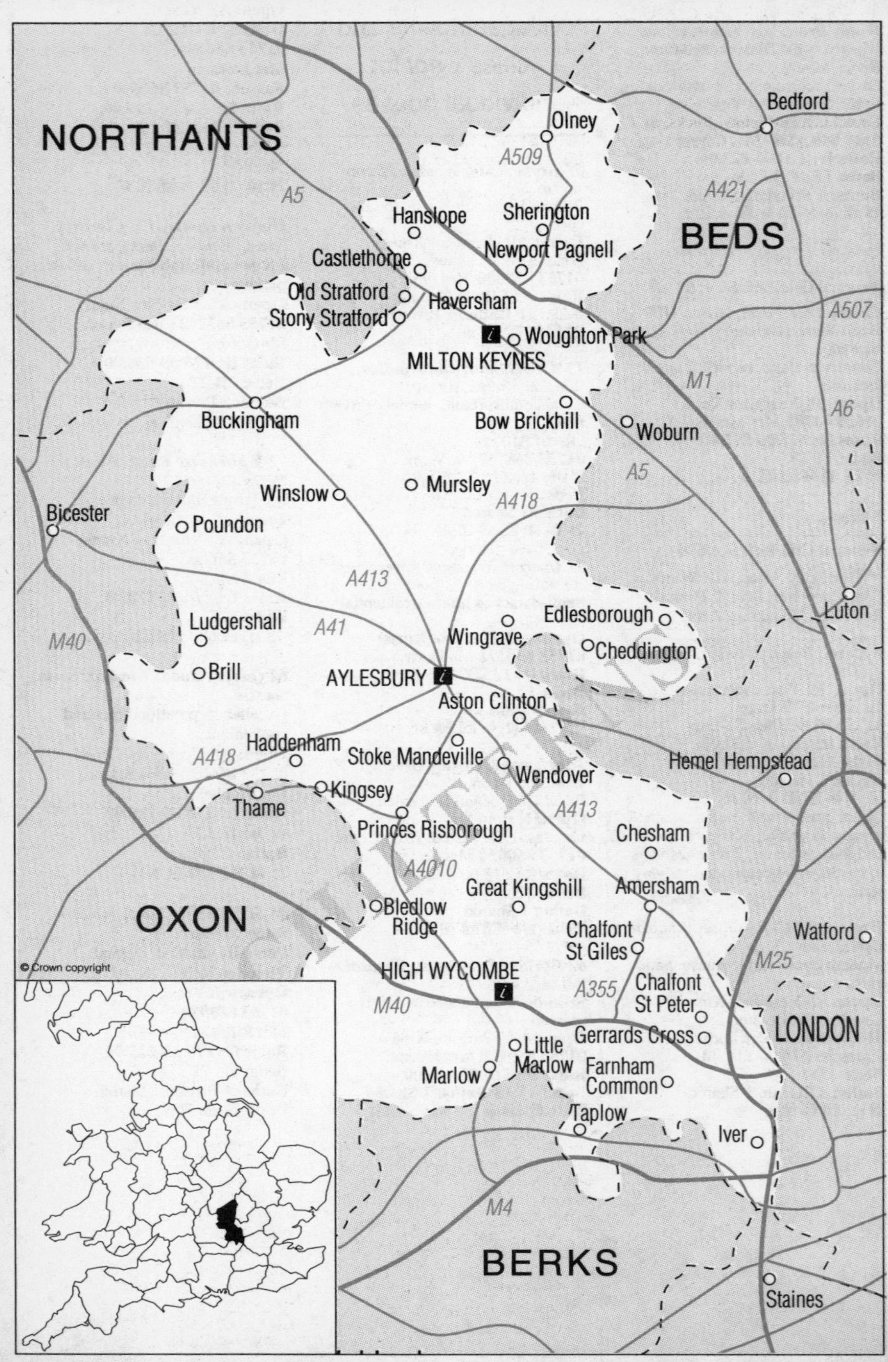

Tourist Information Centres

County Hall, Walton Street, **Aylesbury**, Bucks, HP20 1UA, 01296-382308, (Easter to Oct)

6 Cornmarket, **High Wycombe**, Bucks, HP11 2BW, 01494-28652.

Court Garden Leisure Complex, Pound Lane, **Marlow**, Bucks, SL7 2AE, 01628-483597, (Easter to Oct)

Saxon Court, 502 Avebury Boulevard, **Milton Keynes**, Bucks, MK9 3HS, 01908-691995.

The Clock Tower, **Wendover**, Bucks, HP22 6DU, 01296-623056.

Amersham

National Grid Ref: SU9698

Kings Head, Swan, Griffin, Plough (Winchmore Hill)

63 Hundred Acres Lane, *Amersham, Bucks, HP7 9BX.*
Comfortable semi, private house.
Open: All Year
Grades: ETB Listed
01494 433095 (also fax no)
Mrs Hurley **Rates fr:** -**£22.50**.
Beds: 1F 1D 1T 1S
Baths: 1 Private 1 Shared
(6) (3)

Glory Farm Cottage, *Fagnall Lane, Winchmore Hill, Amersham, Bucks, HP7 0PQ.*
Friendly and comfortable country cottage.
Open: All Year (not Xmas)
Grades: ETB Listed, High Comm
01494 727598 Mrs Olliver
Rates fr: *£20.00*-**£24.00**.
Beds: 1D 1T
Baths: 1 Private 1 Shared
(2)

The Old Barn, *Rectory Hill, Old Amersham, Amersham, Bucks, HP7 0BT.*
Warm, friendly, C17th tithe barn.
Open: All Year (not Xmas)
Grades: ETB Listed, High Comm
01494 722701 Mrs Meighan
Fax no: 01494 728826
Rates fr: *£25.00*-**£30.00**.
Beds: 1D 2T 1S **Baths:** 2 Shared
(8) (5)

Aston Clinton

National Grid Ref: SP8712

The Rising Sun

The Haven, *7 Lower Icknield Way, Aston Clinton, Aylesbury, Bucks, HP22 5JS.*
Friendly comfortable and homely.
Open: All Year (not Xmas)
01296 630751 Mrs Hall
Rates fr: *£17.00*-**£17.00**.
Beds: 1T 1S **Baths:** 1 Shared

Aylesbury

National Grid Ref: SP8113

Five Bells, Red Lion

The Seasons, *9 Ballard Close, Aylesbury, Bucks, HP21 9UY.*
Ideal business/holiday quality accommodation.
Open: All Year (not Xmas)
Grades: ETB 1 Cr, High Comm
01296 84465 Mrs Ion
Rates fr: *£17.50*-**£18.00**.
Beds: 1D 1T 1S **Baths:** 2 Shared
(10) (6)

66 Bierton Road, *Aylesbury, Bucks, HP20 1EJ.*
Comfortable central heating Victorian family house.
Open: All Year (not Xmas)
01296 435841 Mrs Moody
Rates fr: *£15.00*-**£15.00**.
(5)

27 Tindal Road, *Aylesbury, Bucks, HP20 1HT.*
Open: All Year
01296 84861 Mrs Nurse
Rates fr: *£12.50*-**£15.00**.
Beds: 1F 1D
(7) (1)

Bledlow Ridge

National Grid Ref: SU7899

Old Callow Down Farm, *Wigans Lane, Bledlow Ridge, High Wycombe, Bucks, HP14 4BH.*
Early C16th farmhouse, large garden.
Open: All Year
01844 344416 Mr & Mrs Gee
Rates fr: *£18.00*-**£20.00**.
Beds: 1T **Baths:** 1 Private

Bow Brickhill

National Grid Ref: SP9034

Plough House, *Church Road, Bow Brickhill, Milton Keynes, Bucks, MK17 9LH.*
Small Georgian house, once inn.
Open: All Year
Grades: ETB Listed
01908 372097 Mrs Drabble
Rates fr: *£25.00*-**£25.00**.
Beds: 1D 1S **Baths:** 1 Shared
(10) (2)

Brill

National Grid Ref: SP6513

Poletrees Farm, *Ludgershall Road, Brill, Aylesbury, Bucks, HP18 9TZ.*
Open: All Year
Grades: ETB Listed, Comm
01844 238276 (also fax no)
Ms Cooper
Rates fr: *£20.00*-**£25.00**.
Beds: 2D 1T **Baths:** 1 Shared
(12)
We provide spacious and comfortable accommodation in a C15th family home. NO SMOKING.

Buckingham

National Grid Ref: SP6933

Old Thatched Inn, The Wheatsheaf

Folly Farm, *Padbury, Buckingham, Bucks, MK18 2HS.*
Substantial comfortable farmhouse.
Open: All Year (not Xmas)
Grades: ETB 2 Cr, Comm, RAC Listed
01296 712413 Mrs Webb
Rates fr: *£17.00*-**£20.00**.
Beds: 3D
Baths: 3 Private
(4)

The Hall Farm, *Lillingstone Lovell, Buckingham, Bucks, MK18 5BL.*
Spacious farmhouse with character.
Open: All Year (not Xmas)
01280 860665
Mrs Culley
Rates fr: *£17.00*-**£17.00**.
Beds: 1D 2T
Baths: 3 Private 1 Shared
(6)

Castlethorpe

National Grid Ref: SP7944

Navigation Inn

Manor Farm House, *South Street, Castlethorpe, Milton Keynes, Bucks, MK19 7EL.*
Lovely Grade II Listed farmhouse.
Open: All Year
01908 510216
Mrs Tate
Rates fr: *£22.50*-**£18.00**.
Beds: 1F 1D 1T
Baths: 2 Private 1 Shared
(6)

Milford Leys Farm, *Castlethorpe, Milton Keynes, Bucks, MK19 7HH.*
Comfortable family farmhouse, working farm.
Open: All Year
01908 510153
Mrs Frost
Rates fr: *£15.00*-**£15.00**.
Beds: 2T 1S
Baths: 2 Shared
(4)

Chalfont St Giles

National Grid Ref: SU9893

Three Horse Shoes, Pheasant Inn, Seer Green

The Shieling, *81 Bottrells Lane, Chalfont St Giles, Bucks, HP8 4EH.*
Bungalow in half-acre garden.
Open: All Year (not Xmas)
Grades: ETB 1 Cr, Comm
01494 872147
Mrs Morris
Fax no: 01494 871431
Rates fr: *£17.50*-**£25.00**.
Beds: 2D 1T
Baths: 3 Private
(5)

National Grid References are for villages, towns and cities - *not* for individual houses.

***Gorelands Corner,** Gorelands Lane, Chalfont St Giles, Bucks,* HP8 4HQ.
Family house in own grounds.
Open: All Year
01494 872689 (also fax no)
Mrs Bickford
Rates fr: *£20.00*-**£20.00**.
Beds: 1F 1D 1T 1S
Baths: 1 Private 1 Shared
(0) (3)

Chalfont St Peter

National Grid Ref: SU9987

Jolly Farmer, Three Pigeons, The Greyhound

***Maytime,** 26 Eleanor Road, Chalfont St Peter, Bucks,* SL9 9LZ.
Cottage style house, beautiful garden.
Open: All Year
01753 890662 Mrs Hobley
Rates fr: *£14.00*-**£14.00**.
Beds: 2S **Baths:** 1 Shared
(5) (1)

***26 Eleanor Road,** Chalfont St Peter, Gerrards Cross, Bucks,* SL9 9LZ.
Modern bungalow, lovely garden, bath/shower.
Open: All Year (not Xmas)
01753 890662 Mrs Hobley
Rates fr: -**£14.00**.
Beds: 2S **Baths:** 2 Shared
(3) (4)

Cheddington

National Grid Ref: SP9217

Carpenters' Arms

***Rose Cottage,** 68 High Street, Cheddington, Leighton Buzzard, Beds,* LU7 0RQ.
Victorian house, garden N.G.S.
Open: All Year
Grades: ETB 1 Cr
01296 668693 Mrs Jones
Rates fr: *£18.00*-**£20.00**.
Beds: 1D 1T 1S
Baths: 2 Shared
(11) (3)

The lowest **single** *rate is shown in* **bold.**

Chesham

National Grid Ref: SP9601

***49 Lowndes Avenue,** Chesham, Bucks,* HP5 2HH.
Detached house, near town.
Open: All Year (not Xmas)
01494 792647 Mrs Orme
Rates fr: *£17.00*-**£17.00**.
Beds: 1T (6)

Edlesborough

National Grid Ref: SP9719

The Bell, Golden Rule

***Ridgeway End,** 5 Ivinghoe Way, Edlesborough, Dunstable, Beds,* LU6 2EL.
Bungalow set in quiet location.
Open: All Year (not Xmas)
01525 220405 Mrs Lloyd
Rates fr: *£18.00*-**£18.00**.
Beds: 1F 1D 1T 1S
Baths: 1 Private 3 Shared
(3)

Farnham Common

National Grid Ref: SU9685

Forresters

***Redwoods,** Foxhollow Drive, Templewood Lane, Farnham Common, Slough, Bucks,* SL2 3HB.
Lovely detached house, secluded gardens.
Open: All Year (not Xmas)
Grades: ETB 2 Cr, Comm
01753 642748 (also fax no)
Mrs Mearns
Rates fr: *£21.00*-**£25.00**.
Beds: 1D 2T
Baths: 2 Private 1 Shared
(3)

Gerrards Cross

National Grid Ref: SU9987

The Etorpe Hotel

***Tudor Acre,** South Park Crescent, Gerrards Cross, Bucks,* SL9 8HJ.
Large, modern, Tudor-style house.
Open: All Year (not Xmas)
01753 885874 Mrs Walker
Rates fr: *£20.00*-**£20.00**.
Beds: 1F 1D 1T 1S
Baths: 1 Private 1 Shared
(6) (6)

Great Kingshill

National Grid Ref: SU8798

The Red Lion

***Hatches Farm,** Hatches Lane, Great Kingshill, High Wycombe, Bucks,* HP15 6DS.
Quiet easily found comfortable farmhouse.
Open: All Year (not Xmas)
Grades: ETB Listed, Comm
01494 713125 Mrs Davies
Fax no: 01494 714666
Rates fr: *£14.00*-**£16.00**.
Beds: 1D 1T **Baths:** 1 Shared
(10) (10)

Haddenham

National Grid Ref: SP7408

***Haydon House,** 54 Churchway, Haddenham, Aylesbury, Bucks,* HP17 8HA.
Large Victorian private house.
Open: All Year (not Xmas)
01844 291067 Mrs Wright
Rates fr: *£16.00*-**£16.00**.
Beds: 1T 1D 2S
Baths: 2 Shared
(5)

Hanslope

National Grid Ref: SP8046

***Woad Farm,** Tathall End, Hanslope, Milton Keynes, Bucks,* MK19 7NE.
Comfortable farmhouse in own grounds.
Open: All Year
Grades: ETB Listed, Comm
01908 510985 Mr & Mrs Stacey
Fax no: 01908 510 985
Rates fr: *£16.00*-**£18.00**.
Beds: 1D 2T
Baths: 1 Shared
(6)

***Chantry Farm,** Pindon End, Hanslope, Milton Keynes, Bucks,* MK19 7HL.
Friendly C17th stone farmhouse.
Open: All Year (not Xmas)
01908 510269 Mrs Adams
Rates fr: *£16.00*-**£17.50**.
Beds: 1D 2T
Baths: 2 Shared
(8) (6)

Haversham

National Grid Ref: SP8243

The Greyhound

***Haversham Grange,** Haversham, Milton Keynes, Bucks,* MK19 7DX.
Large comfortable C14th grange, set in 10 acres.
Open: All Year (not Xmas)
Grades: ETB 2 Cr
01908 312389 (also fax no)
Mrs Smithers
Rates fr: *£23.00*-**£25.00**.
Beds: 3T **Baths:** 3 Private
(6) (5)

***Grange Barn,** Haversham, Milton Keynes, Bucks,* MK19 7DX.
Attractively converted period barn.
Open: All Year (not Xmas)
01908 313613 Mrs Kilby
Rates fr: *£17.00*-**£18.00**.
Beds: 1D 1T 1S
Baths: 1 Shared
(5) (6)

The lowest *double* rate per person is shown in *italics*.

High Wycombe

National Grid Ref: SU8693

***Wayside House**, 2 Hampden Road, High Wycombe, Bucks, HP13 6SX.*
Spacious; quiet, 5 minutes town centre.
Open: All Year
Grades: ETB Listed
01494 528463
Mrs Rifkin
Rates fr: *£16.00*-**£18.00**.
Beds: 1F 1D 1T 1S
Baths: 1 Shared
(2)

***The Masons Arms**, Saffron Road, High Wycombe, Bucks, HP13 6AB.*
Friendly family run traditional pub.
Open: All Year
Grades: ETB 1 Cr
01494 452204 (also fax no)
Rates fr: *£17.00*-**£18.50**.
Beds: 5T 3S
Baths: 3 Shared
(10)

Iver

National Grid Ref: TQ0381

Black Horse

***Oaklands**, Bangors Road South, Iver, Slough, Bucks, SL0 0BB.*
Large, comfortable, private house.
Open: All Year
01753 653003
Mrs Fowler
Rates fr: *£15.00*-**£15.00**.
Beds: 1D 2T 1S
Baths: 2 Shared
(4)

***The Old Vicarage**, 18 Thorney Lane North, Iver, Slough, Bucks, SL0 9JY.*
Beautiful modernised C18th vicarage.
Open: All Year (not Xmas)
01753 653924
Mrs Heywood
Rates fr: *£18.00*-**£22.00**.
Beds: 1F 2D
Baths: 2 Private 1 Shared
(3)

Kingsey

National Grid Ref: SP7406

Three Horse Shoes (Towersey)

***Foxhill**, Kingsey, Aylesbury, Bucks, HP17 8LZ.*
Large, comfortable C17th farmhouse.
Open: Feb to Nov
Grades: AA Listed, 3 Q
01844 291650
Mr Hooper
Rates fr: *£19.00*-**£23.00**.
Beds: 1D 2T
Baths: 1 Shared
(5) (20)

Little Marlow

National Grid Ref: SU8788

***Monkton Farm**, Little Marlow, Marlow, Bucks, SL7 3RF.*
C14th cruck farmhouse.
Open: All Year
01494 521082 Ms Kimber
Rates fr: *£20.00*-**£20.00**.
Beds: 1F 1T 1S
Baths: 1 Shared
(5) (3)

Ludgershall

National Grid Ref: SP6617

Bull & Butcher

***The Briars**, High Street, Ludgershall, Bucks, HP18 9PF.*
Large 5-bedroomed rural house.
Open: All Year (not Xmas)
Grades: ETB 1 Cr
01844 237721 Mrs Cross
Rates fr: *£17.00*-**£17.00**.
Beds: 1F 1D 1T
Baths: 1 Shared
(4)

Marlow

National Grid Ref: SU8488

The Three Horseshoes, Osbourne Arms, The Pegasus (Marlow Bottom)

***50a New Road, Marlow Bottom**, Marlow, Bucks, SL7 3NW.*
Open: All Year
Grades: ETB Listed
01628 472666 Mrs Parsons
Rates fr: *£19.00*-**£20.00**.
Beds: 1D 1T 1S
Baths: 3 Shared
(4)
Modern chalet-style house. Lounge with TV. Two miles from River Thames and Marlow. Four miles from Henley. Close to M40, London and Heathrow.

***Acha Pani**, Bovingdon Green, Marlow, Bucks, SL7 2JL.*
Modern private house, quiet garden.
Open: All Year
Grades: ETB Listed, Comm
01628 483435 (also fax no)
Mrs Cowling
Rates fr: *£15.00*-**£15.00**.
Beds: 1D 1T 1S
Baths: 1 Private 1 Shared
(10) (3)

Please respect a B&B's wishes regarding children, animals & smoking.

Always telephone to get directions to the B&B - you will save time!

***Merrie Hollow**, Seymour Court Hill, Marlow, Bucks, SL7 3DE.*
Secluded quiet country cottage.
Open: All Year
Grades: ETB Listed, Comm
01628 485663 Mr Wells
Rates fr: *£17.50*-**£20.00**.
Beds: 1D 1T **Baths:** 1 Shared
(4)

***The Venture**, Munday Dean Lane, Marlow, Bucks, SL7 3BU.*
'Home from home'. Quiet location.
Open: All Year
01628 472195 Mrs Whittle
Rates fr: *£12.50*-**£18.00**.
Beds: 2D **Baths:** 1 Shared
(10) (4)

***Sunnyside**, Munday Dean, Marlow, Bucks, SL7 3BU.*
Comfortable, friendly family home.
Open: All Year
01628 485701 Mrs O'Connor
Rates fr: *£12.50*-**£15.00**.
Beds: 2D 1T
(5)

***10 Lock Road**, Marlow, Bucks, SL7 1QP.*
Modern comfortable family house.
Open: All Year
01628 473875 Mrs Fry
Rates fr: *£16.00*-**£20.00**.
Beds: 1D 1S
Baths: 1 Private 1 Shared
(7) (2)

Milton Keynes

National Grid Ref: SP8537

Navigation Inn, Peartree Inn, The Black Horse (Great Linford)

***45 High Street, Great Linford**, Milton Keynes, Bucks, MK14 5AX.*
Modern comfortable village house.
Open: All Year (not Xmas)
01908 666139 Mrs Whyte
Rates fr: *£18.50*-**£18.50**.
Beds: 1D 1T 1S
Baths: 1 Private 1 Shared
(6) (2)

***Kingfishers**, 9 Rylstone Close, Heelands, Milton Keynes, Bucks, MK13 7QT.*
Modern luxurious house.
Open: All Year (not Xmas)
Grades: ETB Listed, Comm
01908 310231 Mrs Botterill
Rates fr: *£16.00*-**£18.00**.
Beds: 1F 1D 1S
Baths: 2 Private 1 Shared
(4)

Milford Leys Farm, *Castlethorpe, Milton Keynes, Bucks, MK19 7HH.*
Comfortable family farmhouse, working farm.
Open: All Year
01908 510153 Mrs Frost
Rates fr: *£15.00*-**£15.00**.
Beds: 2T 1S
Baths: 2 Shared
(4)

Vignoble, *2 Medland, Woughton Park, Milton Keynes, Bucks, MK6 3BH.*
Quiet, secluded, comfortable private house.
Open: All Year (not Xmas)
Grades: ETB Listed, Comm
01908 666804
Fax no: 01908 666626
Rates fr: *£21.00*-**£22.00**.
Beds: 1D 2T 1S
Baths: 1 Ensuite 1 Shared
(3)

All rates are subject to alteration at the owners' discretion.

Mursley

National Grid Ref: SP8128

The Bell (Winslow)

Richmond Hill Farm, *Stewkley Lane, Mursley, Milton Keynes, Bucks, MK17 0JD.*
Open: All Year
Grades: ETB Listed, High Comm
01296 720385 (also fax no)
Mrs Oldham
Rates fr: *£17.50*-**£20.00**.
Beds: 2T
Baths: 2 Private
Bedrooms overlook landscaped gardens, guests' lounge. Convenient for Woburn Abbey, Waddesdon Manor, Stowe and Silverstone. 40 minutes train to London. Local riding and trout fishing.

Newport Pagnell

National Grid Ref: SP8743

The White Hart

Mill Farm, *Gayhurst, Newport Pagnell, Bucks, MK16 8LT.*
Attractive C17th farmhouse, working farm.
Open: All Year
Grades: ETB 2 Cr, AA 3 St
01908 611489
Mrs Adams
Rates fr: *£17.50*-**£17.50**.
Beds: 1F 1T 1S
Baths: 1 Ensuite 1 Shared
(10)

Rectory Farm, *North Crawley, Newport Pagnell, Bucks, MK16 9HH.*
Traditional farmhouse offers warm welcome.
Open: All Year (not Xmas)
01234 391213
Mrs Hobbs
Rates fr: *£12.50*-**£15.00**.
Beds: 1D 1T
Baths: 1 Shared
(5)

Upstairs Downstairs, *38 High Street, Newport Pagnell, Bucks, MK16 8AQ.*
Modern comforts - old world charm.
Open: All Year (not Xmas)
01908 614096 Mrs Brown
Rates fr: *£16.00*-**£16.00**.
Beds: 1F 2D 1T
Baths: 1 Private 3 Shared
(10) (6)

Old Stratford

National Grid Ref: SP7741

Navigation Inn (Cosgrove)

Furtho Manor Farm, *Old Stratford, Milton Keynes, Bucks, MK19 6BA.*
Friendly, busy working farm.
Open: All Year
01908 542139 (also fax no)
Mrs Sansome
Rates fr: *£17.00*-**£20.00**.
Beds: 1D 2T
Baths: 2 Shared
(6)

Olney

National Grid Ref: SP8851

The Two Brewers

Longlands Farm, *Warrington Road, Olney, Bucks, MK46 4DU.*
Modern comfortable farmhouse overlooking Olney.
Open: All Year (not Xmas)
01234 712819 (also fax no)
Mr & Mrs Friedman
Rates fr: *£15.00*-**£15.00**.
Beds: 1D 2S
Baths: 1 Shared
(6)

Poundon

National Grid Ref: SP6425

Sow & Pigs

Manor Farm, *Poundon, Bicester, Oxon, OX6 0BB.*
Comfortable & Welcoming 17th farmhouse.
Open: All Year
Grades: ETB 1 Cr
01869 277212
Mrs Collett
Rates fr: *£18.00*-**£18.00**.
Beds: 1F 1D 1S
Baths: 2 Shared
(6)

Princes Risborough

National Grid Ref: SP8003

Three Crowns, Red Lion

The Bell House Barn, *Crowbrook Road, Askett, Princes Risborough, Bucks, HP27 9LS.*
Converted C18th barn.
Open: All Year (not Xmas)
01844 346107 Mrs Ramsay
Rates fr: *£14.00*-**£14.00**.
Beds: 2T 1S
Baths: 2 Shared

Pay B&Bs by cash or cheque. Be prepared to pay up front for one night stays.

The Red Lion, *Upper Icknield Way, Whiteleaf, Princes Risborough, Bucks, HP27 0LL.*
C17th olde worlde country inn.
Open: All Year
01844 344476
Mr Howard
Rates fr: *£19.75*-**£29.50**.
Beds: 2D 2T
Baths: 4 Ensuite
(12) (10)

Sherington

National Grid Ref: SP8846

White Hart, *1 Gun Lane, Sherington, Newport Pagnell, Bucks, MK16 9PE.*
Terraced house.
Open: All Year (not Xmas)
01908 617591
Mr Locke
Rates fr: *£15.00*-**£18.00**.
Beds: 1F 1D 2T 1S
(10)

Stoke Mandeville

National Grid Ref: SP8310

The Harrow

Marsh Hill Farm, *Marsh, Stoke Mandeville, Aylesbury, Bucks, HP17 8ST.*
Modern comfortable farmhouse. Excellent view.
Open: All Year
01296 613460 Mrs Mason
Rates fr: *£15.00*-**£15.00**.
Beds: 1D 1T

The lowest **single** *rate is shown in* **bold.**

Stony Stratford

National Grid Ref: SP7940

The Cock Hotel

Fegans View, *119 High Street, Stony Stratford, Milton Keynes, Bucks,* MK11 1AT.
C18th comfortable town house.
Open: All Year
Grades: ETB Listed
01908 562128 / 564246 Mrs Levitt
Rates fr: *£17.50*-**£17.50**.
Beds: 3T 1S
Baths: 3 Ensuite 1 Private
(5)

Telford House, *17 Wolverton Road, Stony Stratford, Milton Keynes, Bucks,* MK11 1EA.
Comfortable, large Victorian private house.
Open: All Year (not Xmas)
01908 564206 Mrs Pack
Rates fr: *£17.00*-**£18.00**.
Beds: 1F 1D 1T
Baths: 2 Private 1 Shared
(8)

Taplow

National Grid Ref: SU9182

Bridge Cottage Guest House, *Bath Road, Taplow, Maidenhead, Berks,* SL6 0AR.
Family-run, characteristic cottage, cosy rooms.
Open: All Year
01628 26805 Mrs Staszewski
Rates fr: *£18.00*-**£20.00**.
Beds: 3F 1T 2S
Baths: 2 Private 1 Shared
(6)

Wendover

National Grid Ref: SP8608

Red Lion

3 Lionel Avenue, *Wendover, Aylesbury, Bucks,* HP22 6LL.
Excellent accommodation, many facilities available.
Open: All Year
01296 624115 Mrs Bocca
Rates fr: *£15.00*-**£15.00**.
Beds: 2T 1S **Baths:** 1 Shared
(2)

46 Lionel Avenue, *Wendover, Aylesbury, Bucks,* HP22 6LP.
Private house with large garden.
Open: All Year (not Xmas)
01296 623426 Mr & Mrs MacDonald
Rates fr: *£18.00*-**£18.00**.
Beds: 1T 3S **Baths:** 1 Shared
(3)

26 Chiltern Road, *Wendover, Aylesbury, Bucks,* HP22 6DB.
Large Victorian private house.
Open: All Year
01296 622351 Mrs Condie
Rates fr: *£12.00*-**£12.00**.
Beds: 2F 1S
Baths: 1 Shared

Wingrave

National Grid Ref: SP8618

The Old Vicarage, *Leighton Road, Wingrave, Aylesbury, Bucks,* HP22 4PA.
Victorian vicarage overlooking village duckpond.
Open: All Year
Grades: ETB 2 Cr
01296 681235 Mrs Keighley
Rates fr: *£19.00*-**£22.00**.
Beds: 1D 1T
Baths: 2 Ensuite
(2)

Winslow

National Grid Ref: SP7627

Bell Hotel

Tuckey Farm, *Winslow, Buckingham, Bucks,* MK18 3ND.
C18th traditional farmhouse offering a warm welcome.
Open: Feb to Nov
01296 713208 Mrs Haynes
Rates fr: *£17.00*-**£17.00**.
Beds: 1F 1S
Baths: 1 Shared
(5) (3)

Woughton Park

National Grid Ref: SP8737

Peartree Inn

Vignoble, *2 Medland, Woughton Park, Milton Keynes, Bucks,* MK6 3BH.
Quiet, secluded, comfortable private house.
Open: All Year (not Xmas)
Grades: ETB Listed, Comm
01908 666804
Fax no: 01908 666626
Rates fr: *£21.00*-**£22.00**.
Beds: 1D 2T 1S
Baths: 1 Ensuite 1 Shared
(3)

Cambridgeshire

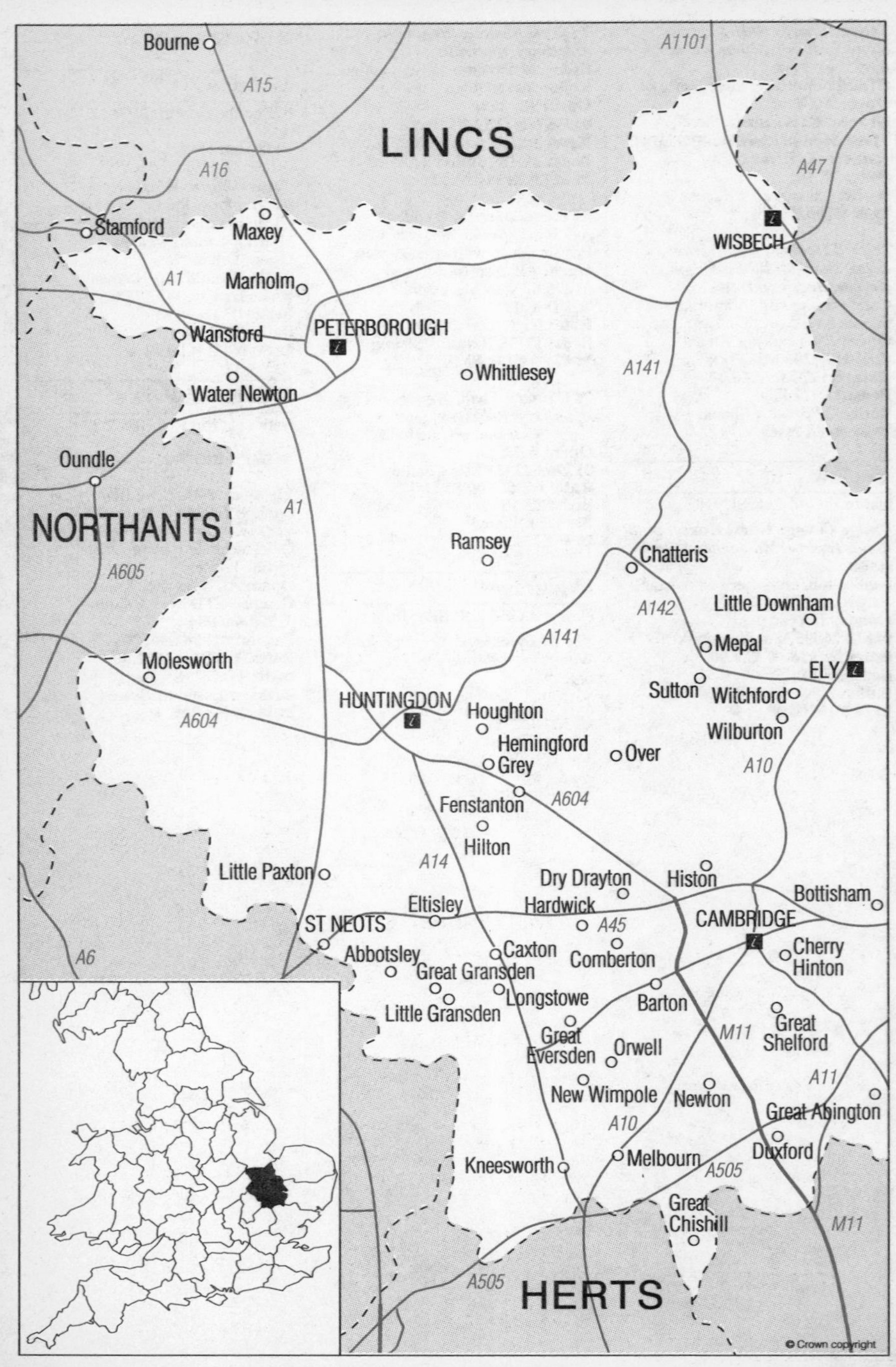

Tourist Information Centres

Wheeler Street, **Cambridge**, Cambs, CB2 3QB, 01223-322640

Oliver Cromwell's House, 29 St Mary's Street, **Ely**, Cambs, CB7 4HF, 01353-662062.

The Library, Princes Street, **Huntingdon**, Cambs, PE18 6PH, 01480-425831.

45 Bridge Street, **Peterborough**, Cambs, PE1 1HA, 01733-317336

District Library, Ely Place, **Wisbech**, Cambs, PE13 1EU, 01945-583263.

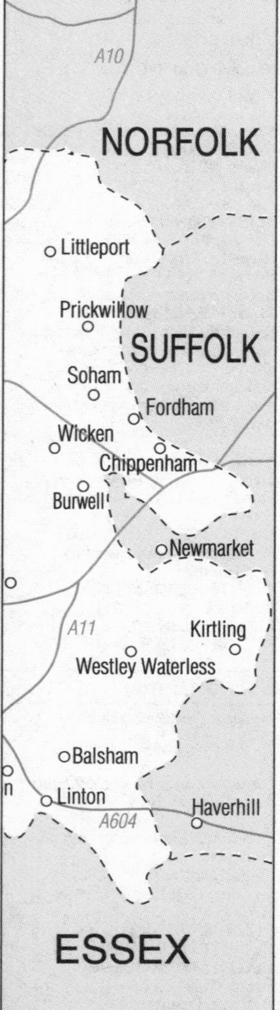

Abbotsley

National Grid Ref: TL2256

Eight Bells Pub

***Rectory Farm House,** Abbotsley, Huntingdon, Cambs, PE19 4UE.*
Quiet Victorian farmhouse.
Open: All Year (not Xmas)
01767 677282
Mr Hipwell
Rates fr: *£15.00*-**£15.00**.
Beds: 1D 2T 1S
Baths: 1 Shared
(6)

Balsham

National Grid Ref: TL5849

***Yole Farm,** Linton Road, Balsham, Cambridge, Cambs, CB1 6HB.*
Modern comfortable farmhouse, very quiet.
Open: All Year (not Xmas)
01223 893280
Mrs Kiddy
Rates fr: *£15.00*-**£15.00**.
Beds: 1D 1T
Baths: 1 Shared
(10) (6)

Barton

National Grid Ref: TL4055

Hoops, White Horse

***Leys Cottage,** 56 Wimpole Road, Barton, Cambridge, CB3 7AB.*
Part C17th thatched cottage, ensuite facilities.
Open: All Year
Grades: ETB 1 Cr, Approv
01223 262482
Mr & Mrs Brown
Fax no: 01223 264166
Rates fr: *£21.00*-**£25.00**.
Beds: 1F 1D 1T 1S
Baths: 2 Private 1 Shared
(10) (4)

Many rates vary according to season - the lowest are shown here.

***Kings Tithe,** 13a Comberton Road, Barton, Cambridge, CB3 7BA.*
Very comfortable family home overlooking open fields, quiet.
Open: Feb to Nov
Grades: ETB 1 Cr, High Comm
01223 263610 (also fax no)
Mr & Mrs Thorne
Rates fr: *£19.00*-**£26.00**.
Beds: 2T
Baths: 1 Shared
(8) (2)

Bottisham

National Grid Ref: TL5460

White Swan

***27 Beechwood Avenue,** Bottisham, Cambridge, CB5 9BG.*
Modern village house backing farmland.
Open: All Year (not Xmas)
01223 811493 (also fax no)
Mrs Knight
Rates fr: *£18.50*-**£18.50**.
Beds: 1D 2T 1S
Baths: 2 Shared
(12)

Burwell

National Grid Ref: TL5866

Five Bells

***The Meadow House,** 2a High Street, Burwell, Cambridge, CB5 0HB.*
Outstanding modern house, extensive grounds.
Open: All Year
Grades: ETB Listed
01638 741926 / 741354 Mrs Marsh
Fax no: 01638 741354
Rates fr: *£18.00*-**£20.00**.
Beds: 1F 2D 1T
Baths: 3 Private 1 Shared
(10)

Cambridge

National Grid Ref: TL4658

Sweeney Todd, India House, Robin Hood, Little Rose Restaurant, The Old Spring, Milton Arms, Isaac Newton

***53 Eltisley Avenue,** Cambridge, CB3 9JQ.*
Open: All Year (not Xmas)
01223 560466 Mrs Dathan
Rates fr: *£18.00*-**£19.00**.
Beds: 1F 1D 1S
Baths: 1 Shared
Situated close to city centre, but on edge of town near Grantchester Meadows. Close to University Departments, College Backs & Library. Quiet area. Warm welcome.

***39 Trumpington Street,** Cambridge, CB2 1QY.*
Old town centre college house.
Open: All Year (not Xmas)
01223 355439 Mrs Rowell
Rates fr: *£20.00*-**£20.00**.
Beds: 1D 1T 4S
Baths: 2 Shared
(6) (1)

Bringing children with you? Always ask for any special rates.

***Kings Tithe,** 13a Comberton Road, Barton, Cambridge, CB3 7BA.*
Open: Feb to Nov
Grades: ETB 1 Cr, High Comm
01223 263610 (also fax no)
Mr & Mrs Thorne
Rates fr: *£19.00*-**£26.00**.
Beds: 2T **Baths:** 1 Shared
(8) (2)
Very comfortable family home overlooking open fields, quiet. Outstanding attention. Excellent breakfasts. Rooms with basins & shaver points. Near pub. Very close to M11 Junction 12.

***264 Hills Road,** Cambridge, CB2 2QE.*
Elegant new accommodation in Cambridge. **Open:** All Year
Grades: ETB 1 Cr, High Comm
01223 248369 Mrs Owen
Fax no: 01223 441276
Rates fr: *£27.50*-**£35.00**.
Beds: 1D **Baths:** 1 Private
(2)

***Hamden Guest House,** 89 High Street, Cherry Hinton, Cambridge, CB1 4LU.*
Open: All Year
Grades: ETB Listed, Comm, AA 2 Q
01223 413263 Mr Casciano
Fax no: 01223 245960
Rates fr: *£19.00*-**£25.00**.
Beds: 1F 2D 1T 2S
Baths: 6 Ensuite
(10) (7)
Comfortable bedrooms with private facilities, situated on the outskirts of Cambridge within short distance of city centre, local shops, pubs & restaurant within walking distance.

***Home From Home,** 39 Milton Road, Cambridge, CB4 1XA.*
Non-smoking family-run B&B.
Open: All Year **Grades:** ETB 1 Cr
01223 323555 / 0850 538712
Mrs Fasano
Fax no: 01223 565660
Rates fr: *£17.50*-**£25.00**.
Beds: 2D 1T
Baths: 2 Ensuite 1 Private
(3)

***Victoria B&B,** 57 Arbury Road, Cambridge, CB4 2JB.*
Comfortable Victorian family house. **Open:** All Year
01223 350086 Mrs Fasano
Fax no: 01223 565660
Rates fr: *£17.50*-**£25.00**.
Beds: 1D 2T
Baths: 2 Ensuite 1 Private
(1)

***Ashtrees Guest House,** 128 Perne Road, Cambridge, Cambs, CB1 3RR.*
Comfortable suburban residence with garden.
Open: Mid-Jan to Xmas
Grades: ETB Listed, Comm, RAC Listed
01223 411233 Mrs Hill
Rates fr: *£17.50*-**£19.00**.
Beds: 1F 3D 1T 2S
Baths: 1 Private 6 Shared
(6)

***Arbury Lodge,** 82 Arbury Road, Cambridge, CB4 2JE.*
Comfortable, friendly guest house.
Open: All Year
Grades: ETB Listed, Comm, RAC Listed
01223 364319 Mrs Celentano
Fax no: 01223 566988
Rates fr: *£17.00*-**£18.00**.
Beds: 1F 2D 1T 1S
Baths: 2 Ensuite 1 Private 1 Shared
(9)

***Bon Accord House,** 20 St Margarets Square, Off Cherry Hinton Road, Cambridge, Cambs, CB1 4AP.*
Non-smokers only. Quiet situation.
Open: All Year (not Xmas)
Grades: ETB Listed, AA 2 Q, RAC Acclaim
01223 411188 Mrs Northrop
Rates fr: *£17.50*-**£20.50**.
Beds: 3D 1T 5S
Baths: 1 Private 2 Shared
(9)

***Tudor Cottage,** 292 Histon Road, Cambridge, CB4 3HF.*
Comfortable friendly private home.
Open: All Year
01223 565212 Mrs Celentano
Fax no: 01223 565660
Rates fr: *£19.00*-**£25.00**.
Beds: 1T **Baths:** 1 Ensuite
(2)

***153 Mowbray Road,** Cambridge, Cambs, CB1 4SP.*
Comfy, homely, near Addenbrookes Hospital.
Open: All Year (not Xmas)
01223 411051 Mrs Bradshaw
Rates fr: *£17.00*-**£18.00**.
Beds: 1D 1S **Baths:** 2 Private
(5) (3)

***Cristinas Guest House,** 47 St Andrews Road, Cambridge, CB4 1DL.*
15 minutes walk from city centre.
Open: All Year (not Xmas)
Grades: ETB 2 Cr, AA 3 Q, RAC Acclaim
01223 65855 Mrs Celentano
Fax no: 0223 365855 / 327700
Rates fr: *£20.00*-**£23.50**.
Beds: 2F 2D 2T 1S
Baths: 5 Private 2 Shared
(8)

***Double Two,** 22 St Margarets Road, Cambridge, CB3 0LT.*
Quiet, comfortable friendly home.
Open: All Year (not Xmas)
Grades: ETB Listed
01223 276103 Mrs Noble
Rates fr: *£17.00*-**£22.00**.
Beds: 1D 2T
Baths: 2 Private 1 Shared
(1)

***El Shaddai,** 41 Warkworth Street, Cambridge, Cambs, CB1 1EG.*
Centrally located, large quiet house.
Open: All Year
01223 327978 Mrs Droy
Rates fr: *£17.00*-**£18.00**.
Beds: 1F 2D 1T 1S
Baths: 1 Private 1 Shared

***Regency Guest House,** 7 Regent Terrace, Cambridge, Cambs, CB2 1AA.*
Comfortable, nicely located in Cambridge.
Open: Feb to Dec
01223 329626 Mrs Cappellaro
Fax no: 01223 871 816
Rates fr: *£22.50*-**£27.00**.
Beds: 4D 4S
Baths: 2 Private 2 Shared
(10) (4)

***Netley Lodge,** 112 Chesterton Road, Cambridge, CB4 1BZ.*
Comfortable, large Victorian private house.
Open: All Year (not Xmas)
01223 363 845 Mrs Mikolajczyk
Rates fr: *£19.00*-**£20.00**.
Beds: 1F 1T 1S
Baths: 1 Private 2 Shared
(5) (2)

Chatteris

National Grid Ref: TL3985

Cross Keys Hotel

***Cross Keys Hotel,** 12/16 Market Hill, Chatteris, Cambs, PE16 6BA.*
Open: All Year
Grades: ETB 3 Cr, Comm, AA 1 St, RAC 1 St
01354 693036 / 692644 Mr Skeggs
Fax no: 01354 693036
Rates fr: *£16.25*-**£21.00**.
Beds: 1F 3D 3T
Baths: 5 Private 2 Shared
(10)
Delightful C16th coaching inn, centre of town, overlooking the church. Oak-beamed lounge & inglenook fireplaces. Fine a la carte restaurant and bar meals available 7 days a week.

***North Bank Guest House,** 84 High Street, Chatteris, Cambs, PE16 6NN.*
Family-run, C18th Georgian guest house.
Open: All Year (not Xmas)
01354 695782 (also fax no)
Mrs Horsman
Rates fr: *£15.00*-**£17.00**.
Beds: 1T
Baths: 1 Shared
(0) (15)

Cherry Hinton

National Grid Ref: TL4856

Robin Hood

***Hamden Guest House,** 89 High Street, Cherry Hinton, Cambridge, CB1 4LU.*
Comfortable bedrooms with private facilities.
Open: All Year
Grades: ETB Listed, Comm, AA 2 Q
01223 413263 Mr Casciano
Fax no: 01223 245960
Rates fr: *£19.00*-**£25.00**.
Beds: 1F 2D 1T 2S
Baths: 6 Ensuite
(10) (7)

Please respect a B&B's wishes regarding children, animals & smoking.

Chippenham

National Grid Ref: TL6669

Maltings Yard Cottage, *20 High Street, Chippenham, Ely, Cambs, CB7 5PP.*
Listed cottages in picturesque village.
Open: All Year (not Xmas)
01638 720110 Mrs Blazey
Rates fr: *£20.00*-**£23.00**.
Beds: 2D 1T
Baths: 3 Ensuite
(5) (6)

Comberton

National Grid Ref: TL3658

Three Horseshoes

White Horse Cottage, *28 West Street, Comberton, Cambridge, CB3 7DS.*
Restored C17th cottage near Cambridge.
Open: All Year
01223 262914
Mrs Wright
Rates fr: *£17.00*-**£25.00**.
Beds: 1F 1D
Baths: 1 Private 1 Shared
(3)

Dry Drayton

National Grid Ref: TL3862

The Black Horse

Nimitabel, *St Neots Road (A 428), Dry Drayton, Cambridge, CB3 8AY.*
Comfortable bungalow with gardens/aviaries.
Open: All Year (not Xmas)
Grades: ETB 1 Cr
01954 210329
Mrs Maskell
Rates fr: *£18.00*-**£18.00**.
Beds: 1T 1S
Baths: 1 Shared
(10) (6)

Duxford

National Grid Ref: TL4745

The Old Vicarage, *The Green, Duxford, Cambridge, CB2 4RH.*
Comfortable period house.
Open: All Year (not Xmas)
01223 835795
Mrs Jonas
Rates fr: *£16.00*-**£18.00**.
Beds: 2T
Baths: 1 Private
(10) (2)

Eltisley

National Grid Ref: TL2759

The Leeds Arms, *The Green, Eltisley, Huntingdon, Cambs, PE19 4TG.*
C18th free house/motel.
Open: All Year (not Xmas)
Grades: ETB Listed
01480 880283 Mr Cottrell
Fax no: 01480 880379
Rates fr: *£17.50*-**£27.50**.
Beds: 3T 6S
Baths: 9 Ensuite
(20)

Ely

National Grid Ref: TL5480

Highflyer, The Cutter Inn (Annesdale)

The Nyton Hotel, *7 Barton Road, Ely, Cambs, CB7 4HZ.*
Comfortable family hotel.
Open: All Year
Grades: ETB 3 Cr, AA 1 St, RAC 1 St
01353 662459 Mr Setchell
Rates fr: *£25.00*-**£33.00**.
Beds: 3F 3D 2T 2S
Baths: 10 Ensuite

82 Broad Street, *Ely, Cambs, CB7 4BE.*
Comfortable, convenient, converted Victorian house.
Open: All Year (not Xmas)
01353 667609 Mr & Mrs Hull
Rates fr: *£14.00*-**£14.00**.
Beds: 1D 1T
Baths: 2 Shared

Annesdale Lodge, *8 Annesdale, Ely, Cambridge, CB7 4BN.*
Comfortable, riverside, converted Victorian cottages.
Open: All Year
01353 667533 Mrs Drage
Rates fr: *£20.00*-**£35.00**.
Beds: 2D
Baths: 2 Private
(2)

50 High Street, *Ely, Ely, Cambs, CB6 1HE.*
Large converted bungalow.
Open: All Year (not Xmas)
01353 861059
Mr & Mrs Bowditch
Rates fr: *£15.00*-**£15.00**.
Beds: 1F 1D 1T 2S
Baths: 5 Private
(2) (6)

Cathedral House, *17 St Mary's Street, Ely, Cambs, CB7 4ER.*
Grade II Listed house sympathetically restored.
Open: All Year (not Xmas)
01353 662124
Mr & Mrs Farndale
Rates fr: *£25.00*-**£35.00**.
Beds: 2D 1T
Baths: 3 Ensuite
(3)

Greenways, *Prickwillow Road, Queen Adelaide, Ely, Cambs, CB7 4TZ.*
Modern ground floor accommodation.
Open: All Year
01353 666706 Mr Dunlop-Hill
Rates fr: *£36.00*-**£18.00**.
Beds: 1F 1D 1T 1S
Baths: 2 Ensuite 2 Shared
(6)

Fenstanton

National Grid Ref: TL3168

Orchard House, *Hilton Road, Fenstanton, Huntingdon, Cambs, PE18 9LH.*
Family house, centre of village.
Open: All Year
01480 469208 Mrs Scarrow
Rates fr: *£13.00*-**£18.00**.
Beds: 1D 2T 1S
Baths: 2 Ensuite 1 Shared
(6)

Fordham

National Grid Ref: TL6270

The Crown

1 Carter Street, *Fordham, Ely, Cambs, CB7 5NG.*
Comfort in C16th private house.
Open: All Year (not Xmas)
01638 720363 Mrs Bycroft
Rates fr: *£20.00*-**£18.00**.
Beds: 1D 1T 1S
Baths: 3 Ensuite
(2)

Queensbury, *196 Carter Street, Fordham, Ely, Suffolk, CB7 5JU.*
Comfortable Georgian home - warm welcome.
Open: All Year
01638 720916 Mr & Mrs Roper
Fax no: 01638 720333
Rates fr: *£20.00*-**£20.00**.
Beds: 1D 1T 1S
Baths: 1 Ensuite 1 Private 1 Shared
(12)

Inglenook Guesthouse, *42 Carter Street, Fordham, Ely, Cambs, CB7 5NG.*
Motel-style, centre of village.
Open: All Year (not Xmas)
Grades: ETB 2 Cr, Approv
01638 720387 Mr Eccles
Fax no: 01638 720 387
Rates fr: *£17.00*-**£19.00**.
Beds: 1F 5T
Baths: 5 Ensuite 1 Private
(6)

Always telephone to get directions to the B&B - you will save time!

Great Chishill

National Grid Ref: TL4238

The Pheasant

***Hall Farm,** Great Chishill, Royston, Herts,* SG8 8SH.
Homely, comfortable, Georgian farmhouse. Working arable farm on edge of pretty village.
Open: All Year
Grades: ETB Listed, Comm
01763 838263 Mrs Wiseman
Rates fr: *£17.50*-**£20.00**.
Beds: 1F 1D 1T
Baths: 1 Shared
(4)

Great Eversden

National Grid Ref: TL3653

Hoops, Wheatsheaf (Harlton)

***The Moat House,** Great Eversden, Cambridge,* CB3 7HN.
Welcoming period family home.
Open: All Year (not Xmas)
01223 262836 Mr Webster
Rates fr: *£20.00*-**£20.00**.
Beds: 1T 1S **Baths:** 1 Private

Great Gransden

National Grid Ref: TL2755

***Chestnut House,** 7 Middle Street, Great Gransden, Sandy, Beds,* SG19 3AD.
Friendly, comfortable, interior designer's home.
Open: All Year
01767 677539 (also fax no)
Mrs Osborne
Rates fr: *£16.00*-**£15.00**.
Beds: 1D 2S
Baths: 1 Ensuite 1 Shared
(8) (4)

Great Shelford

National Grid Ref: TL4652

The Rose (Stapleford)

***Norfolk House,** 2 Tunwells Lane, Great Shelford, Cambridge, Cambs,* CB2 5LJ.
Comfortable elegant Victorian house.
Open: All Year (not Xmas)
01223 840287 Mrs Diver
Rates fr: *£18.50*-**£20.00**.
Beds: 2T
Baths: 1 Ensuite 1 Shared
(10) (2)

***Hunters Moon,** 31 Shelford Park Avenue, Great Shelford, Cambridge, Cambs,* CB2 5LU.
Modern ranch-style house.
Open: All Year (not Xmas)
01223 843934 (also fax no)
Ms Williams
Rates fr: *£18.00*-**£18.00**.
Beds: 1F 1T 2S
Baths: 1 Shared
(10) (4)

Hardwick

National Grid Ref: TL3759

Blue Lion

***Wallis Farm,** 98 Main Street, Hardwick, Cambridge,* CB3 7QU.
Open: All Year
Grades: ETB 2 Cr, High Comm
01954 210347 (also fax no)
Mrs Sadler
Rates fr: *£20.00*-**£25.00**.
Beds: 1F 1D 1T
Baths: 3 Ensuite
(6)
Traditional working farm in centre of peaceful village, close to university city of Cambridge. 3 comfortable ensuite rooms with colour TV and tea/coffee making facilities. Large gardens.

Hemingford Grey

National Grid Ref: TL2970

King William IV

***Willow Guest House,** 45 High Street, Hemingford Grey, Huntingdon, Cambs,* PE18 9BJ.
Large comfortable quiet guest-house.
Open: All Year
01480 494748 Mr Webster
Rates fr: *£19.00*-**£25.00**.
Beds: 2F 2D 2T 1S
Baths: 7 Ensuite
(11)

Histon

National Grid Ref: TL4363

The Boot

***Wynwyck,** 55 Narrow Lane, Histon, Cambridge,* CB4 4HD.
Modern, comfortable, quiet and peaceful.
Open: All Year (not Xmas)
01223 232496 Mrs Torrens
Rates fr: *£20.00*-**£24.00**.
Beds: 1F 1D 2T
Baths: 2 Ensuite 1 Shared
(4)

Houghton

National Grid Ref: TL2872

***Millside Cottage Guest House,** 9 Mill Street, Houghton, Huntingdon, Cambs,* PE17 2AZ.
Comfortable, licensed, converted Victorian alehouse.
Open: All Year
01480 464456 Mrs Woolford
Rates fr: *£16.00*-**£18.00**.
Beds: 1F 2D 2T 1S
Baths: 1 Private 2 Shared
(6)

The lowest **single** *rate is shown in* **bold.**

Huntingdon

National Grid Ref: TL2472

Victoria, Black Bull (Godmanchester)

***Braywood House,** 27 St Peters Road, Huntingdon, Cambs,* PE18 7AA.
Governor's House, formerly Huntingdon Gaol.
Open: All Year
01480 459782 (also fax no)
Mrs Knapp
Rates fr: *£18.75*-**£25.00**.
Beds: 2F 2D 2T 2S
Baths: 8 Ensuite
(10)

***Brecklyn Guest House,** 9 Euston Street, Huntingdon, Cambs,* PE18 6QR.
Family-run Victorian villa.
Open: All Year
Grades: ETB Listed, Approv
01480 455564
Rates fr: *£16.00*-**£16.00**.
Beds: 2T 2S
Baths: 1 Shared
(4)

Kirtling

National Grid Ref: TL6858

***Hill Farm Guest House,** Kirtling, Newmarket, Suffolk,* CB8 9HQ.
Comfortable old farmhouse.
Open: All Year
01638 730253 Mrs Benley
Rates fr: *£20.00*-**£22.00**.
Beds: 1D 1T 1S
Baths: 2 Ensuite
(4)

Kneesworth

National Grid Ref: TL3444

Queen Adelaide

***Fairhaven,** 102 Old North Road, Kneesworth, Royston, Herts,* SG8 5JR.
Comfortable well-appointed country home.
Open: All Year (not Xmas)
01763 249471 Mrs Watson
Rates fr: *£17.00*-**£19.00**.
Beds: 1D 1T
Baths: 1 Shared
(3)

Linton

National Grid Ref: TL5646

The Crown

***Linton Heights,** 36 Wheatsheaf Way, Linton, Cambridge, Cambs,* CB1 6XB.
Comfortable, friendly home, sharing lounge.
Open: All Year (not Xmas)
01223 892516 Mr & Mrs Peake
Rates fr: *£15.00*-**£15.00**.
Beds: 1T 1S
Baths: 1 Shared
(6) (2)

Springfield House, *14-16 Horn Lane, Linton, Cambridge, Cambs,* *CB1 6HT.*
Private, peaceful, riverside Regency residence.
Open: All Year
Grades: ETB 2 Cr
01223 891383
Mrs Rossiter
Rates fr: *£17.00*-**£18.50**.
Beds: 2D
Baths: 1 Ensuite 1 Private
(0) (4)

Little Downham

National Grid Ref: TL5283

Bury House, *11 Main Street, Little Downham, Ely, Cambs,* *CB6 2ST.*
Comfortable friendly home.
Open: All Year (not Xmas)
01353 699386
Mrs Ambrose
Rates fr: *£16.00*-**£16.00**.
Beds: 1F 1D 1T
Baths: 2 Shared
(2)

Little Gransden

National Grid Ref: TL2755

Golden Miller

Model Farm, *Little Gransden, Sandy, Beds,* *SG19 3EA.*
Comfortable, peaceful, working family farm.
Open: All Year
Grades: ETB Listed, Comm
01767 677361 Mrs Barlow
Rates fr: *£15.00*-**£18.00**.
Beds: 2D
Baths: 1 Ensuite 1 Shared
(10)

Elms Farm, *52 Main Road, Little Gransden, Sandy, Beds,* *SG19 3DL.*
Fully renovated comfortable farmhouse.
Open: All Year
01767 677459 Mrs Bygraves
Rates fr: *£15.00*-**£15.00**.
Beds: 1D 1T 1S
Baths: 1 Private 1 Shared

Gransden Lodge Farm, *Little Gransden, Sandy, Beds,* *SG19 3EB.*
Modern comfortable farmhouse, 10 miles Cambridge.
Open: All Year
Grades: ETB 2 Cr, High Comm, AA 3 Q, Recomm
01767 677365 Mrs Cox
Rates fr: *£15.00*-**£16.00**.
Beds: 2F 1D 1S
Baths: 2 Ensuite 1 Private 1 Shared
(6)

All rates are subject to alteration at tshe owners' discretion.

Little Paxton

National Grid Ref: TL1862

Soothoe Bell

Mill House, *Mill Lane, Little Paxton, St Neots, Huntingdon, Cambs,* *PE19 4LP.*
Victorian riverside house and lodge.
Open: All Year (not Xmas)
01480 215960 Mrs Roberts
Rates fr: *£17.50*-**£20.00**.
Beds: 1F 1D 1T
Baths: 1 Private 2 Shared
(5)

Littleport

National Grid Ref: TL5686

Black Horse

The Laurels, *104 Victoria Street, Littleport, Ely, Cambs,* *CB6 1LZ.*
Hospitality - comfort - excellent breakfast - parking.
Open: All Year (not Xmas)
01353 861972 / 01850 199299
Mrs Sicard
Rates fr: *£18.00*-**£36.00**.
Beds: 1D 2T **Baths:** 3 Ensuite
(4)

Longstowe

National Grid Ref: TL3055

Glebe House, *Park Lane, Longstowe, Cambridge,* *CB3 7UJ.*
Delightful Listed peaceful country house. **Open:** All Year (not Xmas)
01954 719509 Mrs Murray
Fax no: 01954 718033
Rates fr: *£18.50*-**£24.00**.
Beds: 1F 1D
Baths: 2 Private
(2)

Marholm

National Grid Ref: TF1402

Ancient Marholm Farm, *Woodcroft Road, Marholm, Peterborough, Cambs,* *PE6 7HU.*
Oak-beamed farmhouse in peaceful village. **Open:** All Year
01733 262824 Mrs Scott
Rates fr: *£20.00*-**£20.00**.
Beds: 1F 1T 1S **Baths:** 1 Shared
(20)

Maxey

National Grid Ref: TF1208

Golden Pheasant

Abbey House & Coach House, *West End Road, Maxey, Peterborough, Cambs,* *PE6 9EJ.*
Listed former vicarage, quiet location. **Open:** All Year
Grades: ETB 2 Cr, Comm, AA 3 Q
01778 344642 Mr & Mrs Fitton
Rates fr: *£22.00*-**£27.00**.
Beds: 1F 4D 4T 1S
Baths: 7 Ensuite 2 Private 1 Shared
(12)

Melbourn

National Grid Ref: TL3844

The Chequers (Fowlmere)

The Carlings, *Melbourn, Royston, Herts,* *SG8 6DX.*
Open: All Year (not Xmas)
01763 260686 Mrs Howard
Fax no: 01763 261988
Rates fr: *£19.00*-**£16.50**.
Beds: 1D 1T
Baths: 2 Ensuite
(3)
Luxurious rooms in delightful secluded setting. Separate entrance, conservatory, gardens. Ideal touring centre for Cambridge, Duxford, etc. Many good pubs in neighbourhood. Friendly welcome guaranteed.

Mepal

National Grid Ref: TL4480

The Three Pickerels, *19 The Bridge, Mepal, Ely, Cambs,* *CB6 2AT.*
Riverside inn and restaurant.
Open: All Year
01353 777777
Mr & Mrs Hammond
Rates fr: *£15.00*-**£22.50**.
Beds: 3T
Baths: 1 Shared
(8) (30)

Molesworth

National Grid Ref: TL0775

The Cross Keys, *Molesworth, Huntingdon, Cambs,* *PE18 0QF.*
Traditional village inn.
Open: All Year
Grades: ETB 2 Cr, RAC Acclaim
01832 710283 Mrs Peel
Fax no: 01832 710098
Rates fr: *£18.50*-**£27.50**.
Beds: 1F 2D 6T 1S
Baths: 10 Private
(40)

Molesworth Lodge Farm, *Molesworth, Huntingdon, Cambs,* *PE18 0PJ.*
Rural farmhouse, country lane, 0.75 off A14.
Open: All Year
01832 710309 Mrs Page
Rates fr: *£12.50*-**£15.00**.
Beds: 1F 1T **Baths:** 1 Shared
(3)

New Wimpole

National Grid Ref: TL3449

Royal Oak Barrington

Foxhounds, *71 Cambridge Road, New Wimpole, Royston, Herts,* *SG8 5QD.*
Family home with large garden.
Open: All Year (not Xmas)
Grades: ETB Listed
01223 207344 Mrs Parker
Rates fr: *£17.00*-**£17.00**.
Beds: 2T 1S **Baths:** 2 Shared
(3)

Newton (Cambridge)

National Grid Ref: TL4349

Queen's Head

***Manor Farm House,** Newton (Cambridge), Cambridge, CB2 5PE.*
Elegant, comfortable Georgian farmhouse. **Open:** All Year
01223 870260 Mrs Wightman
Rates fr: *£16.00*-**£20.00**.
Beds: 1T 1S
Baths: 1 Private 1 Shared
(6) (5)

Orwell

National Grid Ref: TL3650

Royal Oak (Barrington)

***Orchards End,** 9 Greenford Close, Orwell, Royston, Herts, SG8 5QA.*
Comfortable Tudor-style family home.
Open: All Year (not Xmas)
01223 207202 Mrs Sharman
Fax no: 01763 208865
Rates fr: *£17.00*-**£18.00**.
Beds: 1D 2S **Baths:** 1 Shared
(4)

Over

National Grid Ref: TL3770

***Charter Cottage,** Horseware, Church End, Over, Cambridge, CB4 5NX.*
Country cottage in peaceful location.
Open: All Year
01954 230056 Mr & Mrs Warden
Rates fr: *£13.50*-**£15.00**.
Beds: 1D 1T **Baths:** 1 Shared
(4) (6)

Peterborough

National Grid Ref: TL1999

Charters, Botolpn Arms

***Aragon House,** 75/77 London Road, Peterborough, Cambs, PE2 9BS.*
Conveniently situated quality accommodation.
Open: All Year (not Xmas)
Grades: ETB 2 Cr
01733 63718 (also fax no)
Mr & Mrs Spence
Rates fr: *£16.00*-**£19.00**.
Beds: 1F 3D 2T 6S
Baths: 3 Ensuite 2 Shared
(8)

***Longueville Guest House,** 411 Oundle Road, Orton Longueville, Peterborough, Cambs, PE2 7DA.*
Modern, newly-refurbished guest house.
Open: All Year (not Xmas)
Grades: ETB 2 Cr, Approv
01733 233442 Mr & Mrs Glover
Rates fr: *£17.50*-**£22.50**.
Beds: 1F 2D 2T
Baths: 5 Private
(6)

High season, bank holidays and special events mean low availability *anywhere*.

***Fern Villas Guest House,** 116 Broadway, Peterborough, Cambs, PE1 4DG.*
Comfortable Victorian family guesthouse.
Open: All Year (not Xmas)
01733 67158
Mr & Mrs Creedon
Rates fr: *£14.00*-**£16.00**.
Beds: 1D 2T 2S
Baths: 1 Shared
(5)

Prickwillow

National Grid Ref: TL5982

***The Old School,** Prickwillow, Ely, Cambs, CB7 4UN.*
Converted Victorian school, spacious rooms.
Open: All Year
01353 688325 Mrs Roberts
Rates fr: *£18.00*-**£22.00**.
Beds: 2F 2D 1T
Baths: 5 Private
(20)

Ramsey

National Grid Ref: TL2885

Three Horseshoes, Bow Windows

***The Leys,** 25 Bury Road, Ramsey, Huntingdon, Cambs, PE17 1NE.*
Large family home. Conveniently situated.
Open: All Year
Grades: ETB Listed
01487 813221 Pickard
Fax no: 01487 710053
Rates fr: *£15.00*-**£15.00**.
Beds: 2F 1T 1S
Baths: 2 Private 1 Shared
(8)

***Yesteryear Guest House,** 79/81 High Street, Ramsey, Huntingdon, Cambs, PE17 1BZ.*
C14th homely guest house.
Open: All Year
01487 815006 Grace
Rates fr: *£16.00*-**£19.00**.
Beds: 1D 1T 1S
Baths: 1 Private 1 Shared
(3)

The lowest *double* rate per person is shown in *italics*.

Planning a longer stay? Always ask for any special rates.

Soham

National Grid Ref: TL5973

***The Fountain,** 1 Churchgate Street, Soham, Ely, Cambs, CB7 5DS.*
Traditional and friendly public house.
Open: All Year
01353 720374 (also fax no)
Mr Hall Smith
Rates fr: *£14.00*-**£18.00**.
Beds: 2F 4T
Baths: 3 Private 1 Shared
(30)

***Greenbank,** 111 Brook Street, Soham, Ely, Cambs, CB7 5AE.*
Comfortable bungalow between Newmarket and Ely.
Open: All Year (not Xmas)
01353 720929 Mrs Rump
Rates fr: *£15.00*-**£15.00**.
Beds: 2D
(2)

St Neots

National Grid Ref: TL1860

The Chequers (Eynesbury)

***The Ferns,** Berkley Street, Eynesbury, St Neots, Huntingdon, Cambs, PE19 2NE.*
Friendly, picturesque C18th family home.
Open: All Year (not Xmas)
01480 213884 Mrs Raggatt
Rates fr: *£16.00*-**£18.00**.
Beds: 1F 1D
Baths: 1 Ensuite 1 Shared
(2)

***The Kings Head,** South Street, St Neots, Huntingdon, Cambs, PE19 2BW.*
Central location by Market Square, ideally placed.
Open: All Year
01480 474094 Mrs Hughes
Fax no: 01480 471006
Rates fr: *£20.00*-**£22.00**.
Beds: 1F 2D 2T 1S
Baths: 1 Ensuite 2 Shared

Sutton

National Grid Ref: TL4479

***2 Eastwood Close,** Sutton, Ely, Cambs, CB6 2RH.*
Modern house, quiet location.
Open: All Year (not Xmas)
01353 778423 Mrs Monk
Rates fr: *£15.00*-**£15.00**.
Beds: 1D
Baths: 1 Shared
(1)

Wansford

National Grid Ref: TL0799

Papermills, Haycock

Stoneacre, *Elton Road, Wansford, Peterborough, Cambs, PE8 6JT.*
Modern country house, large grounds.
Open: All Year
Grades: ETB 2 Cr
01780 783283 Mr Wilkinson
Rates fr: *£14.00*-**£22.00**.
Beds: 1F 4D 1T
Baths: 3 Private 1 Shared
(5) (12)

Water Newton

National Grid Ref: TL1097

Mill House, *Mill Lane, Water Newton, Peterborough, Cambs, PE8 6LY.*
Large, riverside C15th private house.
Open: All Year
01733 233096 Mrs Moody
Rates fr: *£18.00*-**£18.00**.
Beds: 1F 2T
Baths: 2 Shared
(12)

Westley Waterless

National Grid Ref: TL6256

Westley House, *Westley Waterless, Newmarket, Suffolk, CB8 0RQ.*
Spacious Georgian-style former rectory.
Open: All Year
Grades: ETB Listed
01638 508112 Mrs Galpin
Rates fr: *£20.00*-**£20.00**.
Beds: 2T 2S
Baths: 1 Private 1 Shared
(5) (6)

Whittlesey

National Grid Ref: TL2797

Cobwebs Guest House, *21 The Delph, Whittlesey, Peterborough, Cambs, PE7 1QH.*
Licensed, warm, friendly & relaxed.
Open: All Year (not Xmas)
Grades: ETB Listed
01733 350960 Mrs Ekins
Rates fr: *£15.00*.
Beds: 1F 3T 2S **Baths:** 2 Shared
(5)

The lowest *double* rate per person is shown in *italics.*

Wicken

National Grid Ref: TL5670

The Maids Head

Spinney Abbey, *Wicken, Ely, Cambs, CB7 5XQ.*
C18th farmhouse, large garden.
Open: All Year (not Xmas)
Grades: ETB 2 Cr, Comm
01353 720971
Mrs Fuller
Rates fr: *£19.00*-**£30.00**.
Beds: 1F 1D 1T
Baths: 3 Private
(5) (4)

Wilburton

National Grid Ref: TL4874

Sharps Farm, *Twenty Pence Road, Wilburton, Ely, Cambs, CB6 3PX.*
Comfortable countryside location, warm welcome.
Open: All Year
Grades: ETB 1 Cr
01353 740360
Mrs Peck
Rates fr: *£17.00*-**£20.00**.
Beds: 2F 1D 1T 1S
Baths: 1 Private
(10)

Willingham

National Grid Ref: TL4069

Belsar Lodge, *155 Rampton Road, Willingham, Cambridge, CB4 5JF.*
Open: All Year
01954 260359
Mrs Balaam
Rates fr: *£15.00*-**£15.00**.
Beds: 1F 1D 2T
Baths: 1 Shared 1 Shared Shower room
(6)
Detached house, H & C in bedrooms, edge of village. Access to Cambridge, Ely and St Ives. Horse riding locally. Golf courses nearby. Guest lounge. Warm welcome. W.I. member.

Wisbech

National Grid Ref: TF4609

Blackfriars, Red Lion

Algethi Guest House, *136 Lynn Road, Wisbech, Cambs, PE13 3DP.*
Small friendly-run guest house.
Open: All Year
01945 582278 Mrs McManus
Rates fr: *£14.00*-**£14.00**.
Beds: 2F 1D 2S
Baths: 1 Shared
(5)

Ravenscourt, *138 Lynn Road, Wisbech, Cambs, PE13 3DP.*
Edwardian house with original features.
Open: All Year
01945 585052 (also fax no)
Mr Parish
Rates fr: *£15.00*-**£15.00**.
Beds: 2F 1D 1T 1S
Baths: 5 Private

146 Lynn Road, *Wisbech, Cambs, PE13 3DP.*
Edwardian house, friendly atmosphere.
Open: All Year
01945 583121 Mr Potter
Rates fr: *£14.00*-**£14.00**.
Beds: 1F 1D 1T 2S
(6)

Holly Gap, *Mill Tree Lane, Wisbech, Cambs, PE13 4TR.*
Rural farm bungalow with horses.
Open: All Year (not Xmas)
Grades: ETB Listed
01945 63119
Mrs Fountain-Hoare
Rates fr: *£15.00*-**£16.50**.
Beds: 1D 1T
Baths: 1 Shared
(5)

Witchford

National Grid Ref: TL5078

Clare Farm House, *Main Street, Witchford, Ely, Cambs, CB6 2HQ.*
Modern, comfortable, arable farmhouse.
Open: All Year
01353 664135 Mrs Seymour
Rates fr: *£14.00*-**£15.00**.
Beds: 1F 1T 1S
Baths: 1 Private 1 Shared
(10)

Cheshire

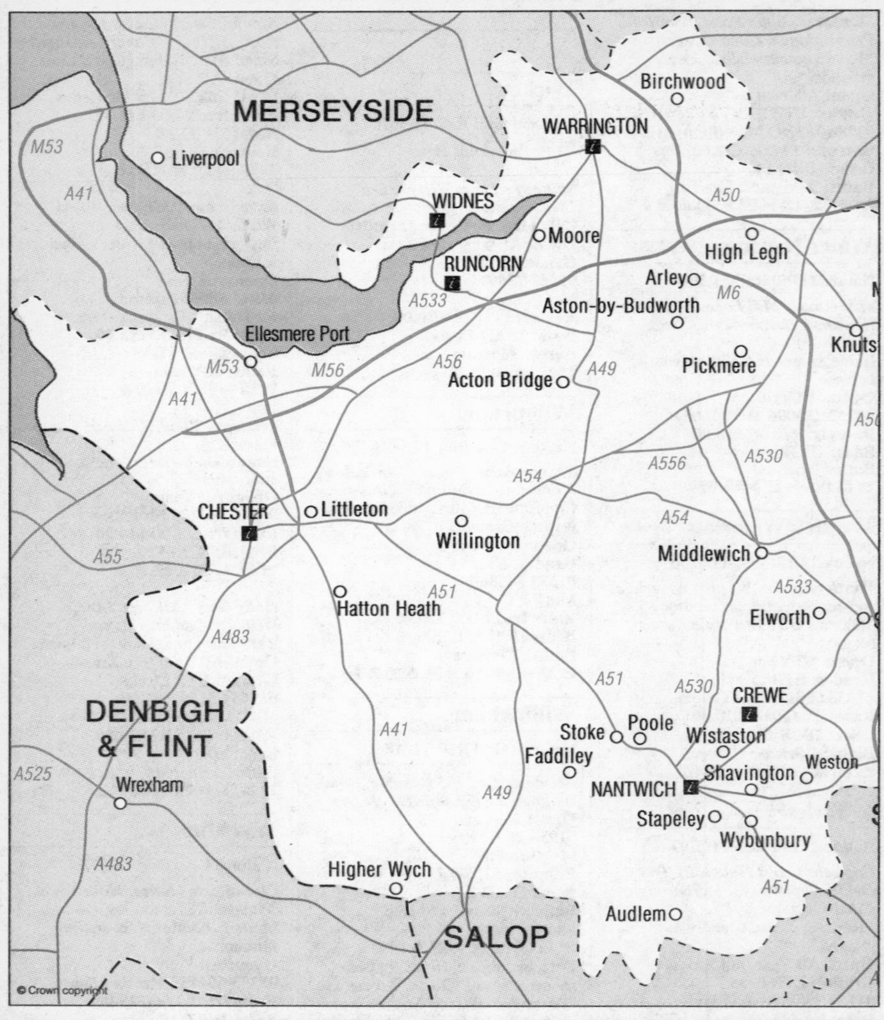

Tourist Information Centres

6 Station Road, **Cheadle Hulme**, Cheshire, SK8 5AE, 0161-486 0283

Town Hall, Northgate Street, **Chester**, Cheshire, CH1 2HJ, 01244-313126/317962

Town Hall, High Street, **Congleton**, Cheshire, CW12 1BN, 01260-271095.

The Market Hall, Earle Street, **Crewe**, Cheshire, CW1 2BJ, 01270-610983.

Council Offices, Toft Road, **Knutsford**, Cheshire, WA16 6TA, 01565-632611.

Town Hall, Market Place, **Macclesfield**, Cheshire, SK10 1HR, 01625-504114.

Beam Street, **Nantwich**, Cheshire, CW5 5LY, 01270-623914.

57-61 Church Street, **Runcorn**, Cheshire, WA7 1LG, 01928-576776

Graylaw House, Chestergate, **Stockport**, Cheshire, SK1 1SL, 0161-474 3320.

21 Rylands Street, **Warrington**, Cheshire, WA1 1EJ, 01925-36501.

Municipal Building, Kingsway, **Widnes**, Cheshire, WA8 7QF, 0151-424 2061.

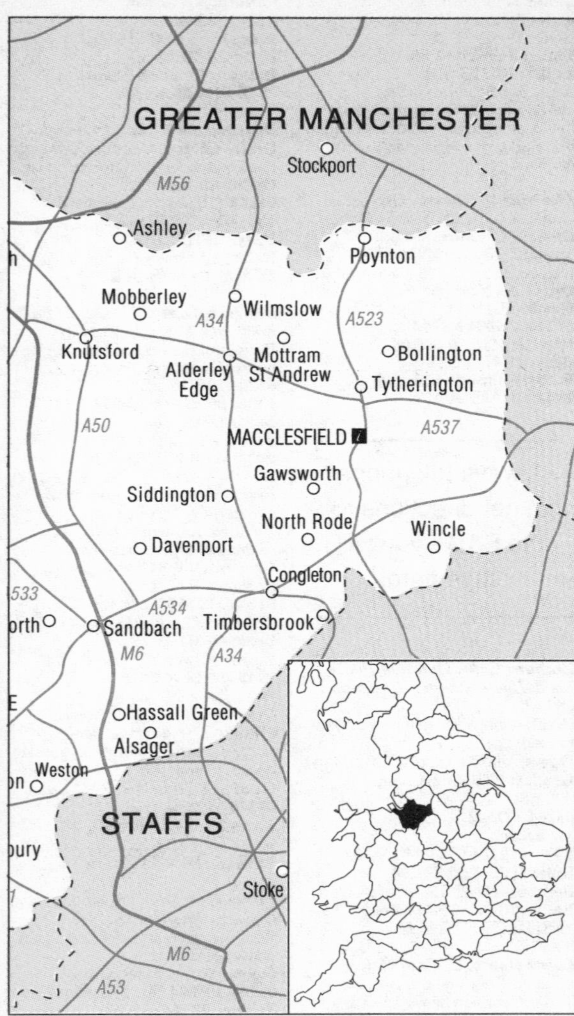

Acton Bridge

National Grid Ref: SJ5975

Horns Inn, *Warrington Road, Acton Bridge, Little Leigh, Northwich, Cheshire,* CW8 4QT.
Traditional country pub, friendly atmosphere.
Open: All Year
01606 852192
Mrs Redfern
Rates fr: *£17.50*-**£25.00**.
Beds: 1D 2T 1S
Baths: 2 Shared

Alderley Edge

National Grid Ref: SJ8478

Prospect House Hotel

Trafford House Farm, *Beswicks Lane, Row of Trees, Alderley Edge, Wilmslow, Cheshire,* SK9 7SN.
Set in beautiful Cheshire countryside. **Open:** All Year (not Xmas)
01625 582160 Mr/Mrs Blackmore
Fax no: 01625 584968
Rates fr: *£15.00*-**£20.00**.
Beds: 2F 1S **Baths:** 1 Shared
(0) (10)

Alsager

National Grid Ref: SJ7955

The Limes, *32 Sandbach Road South, Alsager, Stoke on Trent, Cheshire,* ST7 2LP.
Detached, Victorian private house.
Open: All Year (not Xmas)
01270 874659 Mrs Morgan
Rates fr: *£13.00*-**£13.00**.
Beds: 1T 1S
(3)

Arley

National Grid Ref: SJ6781

Smithy Farmhouse, *Arley Estate, Arley, Northwich, Cheshire,* CW9 6LZ.
Farmhouse, quiet country area.
Open: All Year
01565 777323 Mrs Walton
Rates fr: *£13.50*-**£13.50**.
Beds: 1T 1S **Baths:** 2 Shared
(4)

Ashley

National Grid Ref: SJ7784

The Greyhound

Castle Hill Farmhouse, *Castle Mill Lane, Ashley, Altrincham, Cheshire,* WA15 0RB.
Open: All Year
Grades: ETB 2 Cr, Comm
0161 929 0496 Mrs Lloyd
Fax no: 0161 929 4232
Rates fr: *£20.00*-**£25.00**.
Beds: 1F 2D 1T
Baths: 2 Ensuite 2 Shared
(0.5)
Set in 110 acres of Cheshire countryside and yet only minutes from the M56 and Manchester Airport. Guest lounge and large gardens. Transport provided to & from airport.

Ashley Mill, *Ashley Mill Lane, Ashley, Altrincham, Cheshire,* WA14 3PU.
Modernised miller's house.
Open: All Year
Grades: ETB 1 Cr, High Comm
0161 928 5751 Mr & Mrs Fox
Rates fr: *£20.00*-**£20.00**.
Beds: 2D 1T 1S **Baths:** 2 Shared
(10) (20)

Aston-by-Budworth

National Grid Ref: SJ6976

Cock-of-Budworth (Great Budworth), Red Lion (Pickmere)

Clock Cottage, *Hield Lane, Aston-by-Budworth, Northwich, Cheshire,* CW9 6LP.
Lovely C17th thatched country cottage. **Open:** All Year
Grades: ETB Listed
01606 891271 Mrs Tanner-Betts
Rates fr: *£16.50*-**£17.50**.
Beds: 1T 2S **Baths:** 1 Shared
(2) (6)

Bringing children with you? Always ask for any special rates.

Audlem

National Grid Ref: SJ6643

Little Heath Farm, *Audlem, Nantwich, Cheshire, CW3 0HE.*
Warm spacious beamed farmhouse.
Open: All Year
01270 811324 Mrs Bennion
Rates fr: *£14.50*-**£16.00**.
Beds: 2D 1T
Baths: 1 Private 1 Shared
(3)

Birchwood

National Grid Ref: SJ6492

The Noggin (Risley), The Horseshoe

14 Cadshaw Close, *Birchwood, Warrington, Cheshire, WA3 7LR.*
Friendly, family home set in pleasant, quiet area.
Open: All Year
01925 818108 Mrs Agarwal
Rates fr: *£17.00*-**£13.00**.
Beds: 1D 2S
Baths: 1 Private 1 Shared
(10) (3)

Chester

National Grid Ref: SJ4066

Miller's Kitchen, Kings Head, Faulkner Arms, Bensons, Red Lion (Dodleston), Spinning Wheel (Broughton)

Hamilton Court Hotel, *3/7 Hamilton Street, Hoole, Chester, CH2 3JG.*
Grades: ETB 3 Cr, Comm, AA Listed, RAC Listed
01244 345387
Mr & Mrs Finan
Fax no: 01244 317404
Rates fr: *£22.00*-**£30.00**.
Beds: 2F 2D 7T 1S
Baths: 10 Ensuite 2 Shared
(8)
Hamilton Court Hotel is a family-run hotel 10 minutes walk from city centre. We cater for both business people and tourists.

The Georgian House, *131 Boughton, Chester, Cheshire, CH3 5BH.*
Large Georgian town house.
Open: All Year (not Xmas)
Grades: ETB 2 Cr
01244 312186 Mr Chuter
Rates fr: *£17.00*-**£20.00**.
Beds: 1F 4D 1T 1S
Baths: 7 Private
(5) (7)

Glann Hotel, *2 Stone Place, Hoole, Chester, CH2 3NR.*
Open: All Year (not Xmas)
Grades: ETB 2 Cr, Comm
01244 344800 Mr Taylor
Rates fr: *£22.00*-**£22.00**.
Beds: 1F 5D 2T 2S
Baths: 8 Ensuite 2 Shared
(10)
Attractive hotel in a quiet cul-de-sac 10 minutes walk from city centre. Lounge with residential bar. Full size snooker table. Private car park.

Mitchells Of Chester, *Green Gables House, 28 Hough Green, Chester, Cheshire, CH4 8JQ.*
Tastefully restored Victorian residence.
Open: All Year (not Xmas)
Grades: ETB 2 Cr, High Comm
01244 679004 Mrs Mitchell
Rates fr: *£19.50*-**£25.00**.
Beds: 1F 1D 1T 1S
Baths: 4 Ensuite 1 Shared
(5)

Always telephone to get directions to the B&B - you will save time!

Leahurst Court Hotel, *74 Hoole Road, Hoole, Chester, Cheshire, CH2 3NL.*
Comfortable Victorian house. Own grounds.
Open: All Year (not Xmas)
Grades: ETB 3 Cr, Comm, AA 1 St
01244 327542
Mr Beech
Fax no: 01244 344889
Rates fr: *£18.00*-**£21.00**.
Beds: 5F 4D 3T 2S
Baths: 10 Private 4 Shared
(18)

Castle House, *23 Castle Street, Chester, Cheshire, CH1 2DS.*
Tudor/Georgian house 1590 & 1738.
Open: All Year
01244 350354 Marl
Rates fr: *£21.00*-**£22.00**.
Beds: 1F 1D 1T 2S
Baths: 3 Ensuite 1 Shared

Grosvenor Place Guest House, *2-4 Grosvenor Place, Chester, Cheshire, CH1 2DE.*
City centre guest house.
Open: All Year
01244 324455 Mrs Wood
Rates fr: *£15.00*-**£20.00**.
Beds: 2F 2D 3T 3S
Baths: 4 Private 2 Shared

Pear Tree, *69 Hoole Road, Hoole, Chester, Cheshire, CH2 3NJ.*
Large comfortable Victorian house.
Open: All Year
Grades: AA Listed
01244 323260
Rates fr: *£14.00*-**£16.00**.
Beds: 2F 5D 5T 3S
Baths: 4 Ensuite 5 Shared

Buckingham House, *38 Hough Green, Chester, Cheshire, CH4 8JQ.*
Family-run, large Victorian house.
Open: All Year
01244 678885 Ms Langmead
Rates fr: *£16.00*-**£18.00**.
Beds: 3F 1D 1T
Baths: 5 Ensuite
(6)

Dee Hills Lodge, *7 Dee Hills Park, Boughton, Chester, CH3 5AR.*
Delightful Edwardian private house. **Open:** All Year (not Xmas)
01244 325719
Rates fr: *£17.00*-**£20.00**.
Beds: 1F 1D 1T
Baths: 2 Ensuite 1 Private
(3) (3)

Eversley Hotel, *9 Eversley Park, Chester, Cheshire, CH2 2AJ.*
Victorian residential hotel, bar, restaurant. **Open:** All Year
Grades: ETB 3 Cr, AA Listed, Recomm, RAC Listed
01244 373744 Mr Povey
Rates fr: *£21.50*-**£23.00**.
Beds: 4F 3D 2T 2S
Baths: 9 Private 2 Shared
(17)

Devonia, *33-35 Hoole Road, Chester, Cheshire, CH2 3NH.*
Large Victorian family-run guest house. **Open:** All Year
Grades: ETB Listed, RAC Listed
01244 322236
Rates fr: *£14.50*-**£18.50**.
Beds: 4F 3D 3T 1S
(16)

Firbank, *64 Tarvin Road, Littleton, Chester, Cheshire, CH3 7DF.*
Welcoming comfortable Victorian house, gardens.
Open: All Year (not Xmas)
01244 335644 Mrs Shambler
Fax no: 01244 332068
Rates fr: *£16.00*-**£24.00**.
Beds: 2D **Baths:** 2 Ensuite
(2)

Green Gables Guest House, *11 Eversley Park, Chester, Cheshire, CH2 2AJ.*
Quietly situated, high standard throughout.
Open: All Year
Grades: AA 4 Q, RAC High Acclaim
01244 372243 Mrs Perruzza
Fax no: 01244 376352
Rates fr: *£17.00*-**£22.00**.
Beds: 1F 2D 1T 1S
Baths: 4 Ensuite 1 Private
(8)

***Laurels,** 14 Selkirk Road, Curzon Park, Chester, Cheshire, CH4 8AH.*
Private house, best residential area near racecourse.
Open: All Year (not Xmas)
01244 679682 Mrs Roberts
Rates fr: *£16.50*-**£17.00**.
Beds: 1F 1D 1S
Baths: 1 Private 2 Shared
(3)

***Ba Ba Guest House,** 65 Hoole Road, Hoole, Chester, Cheshire, CH2 3NJ.*
Large Victorian family house.
Open: All Year (not Xmas)
01244 315047 Mrs Smith
Rates fr: *£15.00*-**£20.00**.
Beds: 3F 2D
Baths: 3 Private 2 Shared
(5)

***Westminster Hotel,** City Road, Chester, Cheshire, CH1 3AF.*
Convenient for railway station & city centre.
Open: All Year
Grades: ETB 3 Cr
01244 317341
Mr Sadler
Fax no: 01244 325369
Rates fr: *£20.00*-**£25.00**.
Beds: 9F 17D 35T 13S
Baths: 74 Private

Congleton

National Grid Ref: SJ8663

***Cuttleford Farm,** Newcastle Road, Astbury, Congleton, Cheshire, CW12 4SD.*
160 acre mixed working farm.
Open: All Year
Grades: ETB 2 Cr
01260 272499
Mrs Downs
Rates fr: *£14.00*-**£17.00**.
Beds: 2D 1T
Baths: 1 Ensuite 1 Shared

***8 Cloud View,** Congleton, Cheshire, CW12 3TP.*
Lovely family home, edge of countryside.
Open: All Year (not Xmas)
01260 276048
Mrs Stewart
Rates fr: *£13.50*-**£15.00**.
Beds: 1T 1S 1D
Baths: 1 Ensuite 1 Shared
(1)

***Lion Swan Hotel,** Swan Bank, Congleton, Cheshire, CW12 1JR.*
C16th hotel (former coaching inn).
Open: All Year
Grades: ETB 4 Cr, AA 3 St, RAC 3 St
01260 273115
Mr Williams
Fax no: 01260 299270
Rates fr: *£26.00*-**£31.00**.
Beds: 1F 15D 1T 4S
Baths: 21 Private
(40)

Crewe

National Grid Ref: SJ7055

***Hunters Lodge Hotel,** Sydney Road, Sydney, Crewe, Cheshire, CW1 1LU.*
Quiet country-style location. Sports complex.
Open: All Year
Grades: AA 3 St
01270 583440 Mr Panayi
Rates fr: *£23.00*-**£26.00**.
Beds: 1F 27D 4T 10S
Baths: 42 Private
(180)

Davenport

National Grid Ref: SJ8065

***Copper Beech Hotel,** 198 Buxton Road, Davenport, Stockport, Cheshire, SK2 7AE.*
Homely large Victorian house.
0161 456 1183 Mrs Bailey
Rates fr: *£12.50*-**£18.00**.
Beds: 2F 2D 1S
Baths: 2 Ensuite 1 Shared
(11)

Elworth

National Grid Ref: SJ7461

***Poplar Mount Guest House,** 2 Station Road, Elworth, Sandbach, Cheshire, CW11 9JG.*
Large Victorian private house.
Open: All Year
Grades: ETB 2 Cr, Comm, AA 2 Q, Recomm, RAC Acclaim
01270 761268
Mrs McDonald
Rates fr: *£19.00*-**£19.00**.
Beds: 1F 3D 1T 2S
Baths: 4 Private 1 Shared
(9)

Faddiley

National Grid Ref: SJ5953

***Laburnum House Farm,** Hearns Lane, Faddiley, Nantwich, Cheshire, CW5 8JL.*
Spacious, warm, friendly comfortable farmhouse.
Open: All Year
01270 524378 Mrs Metcalfe
Rates fr: *£20.00*-**£15.00**.
Beds: 1D 1T
Baths: 2 Private
(6)

Gawsworth

National Grid Ref: SJ8969

***Rough Hey Farm,** Leek Road, Gawsworth, Macclesfield, Cheshire, SK11 0JQ.*
Quiet, historic, modernised farmhouse.
Open: All Year (not Xmas)
01260 252296 Mrs Worth
Rates fr: *£17.00*-**£17.00**.
Beds: 1D 1T 2S
Baths: 2 Private 1 Shared
(3) (4)

National Grid References are for villages, towns and cities - *not* for individual houses.

Hassall Green

National Grid Ref: SJ7858

***Canal Centre & Village Store,** Hassall Green, Sandbach, Cheshire, CW11 0YB.*
200-year-old centre.
Open: All Year
01270 762266
Mr & Mrs Paine
Rates fr: *£15.00*-**£15.00**.
Beds: 1F 2D 2T 1S
Baths: 2 Shared
(1) (6)

Hatton Heath

National Grid Ref: SJ4561

Grosvenor Arms

***Golborne Manor,** Platts Lane, Hatton Heath, Chester, Cheshire, CH3 9AN.*
Victorian, luxury, country manor house.
Open: All Year
Grades: ETB 2 Cr, Comm, AA 4 Cr
01829 770 310 / 0850 265425
Mrs Ikin
Fax no: 01244 318084
Rates fr: *£19.00*-**£25.00**.
Beds: 1F 1T 1D
Baths: 2 Ensuite 1 Private
(Any) (6)

High Legh

National Grid Ref: SJ7083

***Meadowpatch Cottage,** 10 Chollerton Close, High Legh, Knutsford, Cheshire, WA16 6TY.*
Family home in Cheshire countryside.
Open: All Year
01925 755161
Mrs Podmore
Rates fr: *£19.00*-**£20.00**.
Beds: 1D 1S
Baths: 1 Private
(2)

All details shown are as supplied by B&B owners in Autumn 1997.

The lowest *double* rate per person is shown in *italics*.

Higher Wych

National Grid Ref: SJ4943

Mill House, *Higher Wych, Malpas, Cheshire,* *SY14 7JR.*
Modernised mill house, rural setting.
Open: All Year (not Xmas)
Grades: ETB 3 Cr, High Comm
01948 780362 Mrs Smith
Fax no: 01948 780566
Rates fr: *£16.00*-**£16.00**.
Beds: 1D 1T
Baths: 1 Private 1 Shared
P (4)

Knutsford

National Grid Ref: SJ7578

Krakatoa, *Manor Park South, Knutsford, Cheshire,* *WA16 8AG.*
Large private house.
Open: All Year
01565 651157 Mrs Fisher
Rates fr: *£18.00*-**£23.00**.
Beds: 1D
Baths: 1 Private
P (3)

Littleton

National Grid Ref: SJ4466

Royal Oak (Mickle Trafford), Chester

Firbank, *64 Tarvin Road, Littleton, Chester, Cheshire,* *CH3 7DF.*
Welcoming comfortable Victorian house, gardens.
Open: All Year (not Xmas)
01244 335644 Mrs Shambler
Fax no: 01244 332068
Rates fr: *£16.00*-**£24.00**.
Beds: 2D **Baths:** 2 Ensuite
P (2)

Macclesfield

National Grid Ref: SJ9173

The Old Vicarage, *58 Blakelow Road, Macclesfield, Cheshire,* *SK11 7ED.*
Large Victorian family house.
Open: All Year (not Xmas)
01625 425575 (also fax no)
Mrs Russell
Rates fr: *£17.50*-**£17.50**.
Beds: 1D 1T
Baths: 1 Shared

The *lowest* **single** *rate is shown in* **bold.**

Middlewich

National Grid Ref: SJ7066

Big Lock

Sandhurst Guest House, *69 Chester Road, Middlewich, Cheshire,* *CW10 9EW.*
Open: All Year (not Xmas)
01606 834125 Mrs Fair
Fax no: 01606 833753
Rates fr: *£16.00*-**£21.00**.
Beds: 2F 3D 1T
Baths: 4 Private 2 Shared
P (8)
Set in the heart of rural Cheshire. Peak District, North Wales and Manchester Airport 0.5 hours. Large garden. Comfortable bedrooms. Off the road parking.

Mobberley

National Grid Ref: SJ7879

Bird In Hand

Laburnum Cottage, *Knutsford Road, Mobberley, Knutsford, Cheshire,* *WA16 7PU.*
Open: All Year
Grades: ETB 2 Cr, High Comm, AA Prem, Select
01565 872464
Mrs Foxwell
Rates fr: *£21.00*-**£30.00**.
Beds: 1D 2T 2S
Baths: 4 Private
P (8)
Country house close to historic Knutsford on B5085 overlooking Tatton Park. 1993 winner 'Britain in Bloom' and ETB 'Best B&B in North West' award. 4 miles M6 (J19), 15 mins airport. 1994 'Place to Stay' Award x 2 & Tourism & Environment Award.

Mottram St Andrew

National Grid Ref: SJ8778

Bulls Head

Woodlands, *Shaws Lane, Mottram St Andrew, Macclesfield, Cheshire,* *SK10 4RD.*
Luxury accommodation, beautiful location .
Open: All Year
01625 828166 Mrs Bell
Rates fr: *£18.00*-**£18.00**.
Beds: 2D
Baths: 1 Shared
P (4)

Goose Green Farm, *Oak Road, Mottram St Andrew, Macclesfield, Cheshire,* *SK10 4RA.*
Quiet farmhouse with beautiful views.
Open: All Year (not Xmas)
Grades: ETB 2 Cr, Comm
01625 828814 Mrs Hatch
Rates fr: *£18.00*-**£18.00**.
Beds: 1D 1T 2S
Baths: 1 Ensuite 1 Shared
(5) P (10)

Nantwich

National Grid Ref: SJ6552

Barbridge Inn, Jolly Tar, The Red Cow, Wilbraham Arms

Stoke Grange Farm, *Chester Road, Stoke, Nantwich, Cheshire,* *CW5 6BT.*
Canal-side farmhouse, 1838, mixed farm.
Open: All Year
Grades: ETB 2 Cr, Comm, RAC Listed
01270 625525 (also fax no)
Mrs West
Rates fr: *£17.50*-**£20.00**.
Beds: 1D 2T
Baths: 3 Ensuite
P (10)

Kiltearn House, *33 Hospital Street, Nantwich, Cheshire,* *CW5 5RL.*
Quiet, warm, comfortable period house.
Open: All Year
01270 628892 Mrs Pearson
Rates fr: *£24.00*-**£24.00**.
Beds: 1F 1D 1T
Baths: 1 Shared
P (3)

The Red Cow, *51 Beam Street, Nantwich, Cheshire,* *CW5 5NF.*
Real traditional pub. Wonderful food.
Open: All Year
01270 628581 Ms Casson
Rates fr: *£19.50*-**£19.50**.
Beds: 1D 2T
P (8)

The Wilbraham Arms, *Welsh Row, Nantwich, Cheshire,* *CW5 5EY.*
Family-run inn in market town.
Open: All Year
01270 626419 Mrs Merrick
Rates fr: *£16.00*-**£18.00**.
Beds: 1F 2D 2T 3S
Baths: 2 Private 2 Shared
P (15)

North Rode

National Grid Ref: SJ8866

Yew Tree Farm, *North Rode, Congleton, Cheshire,* *CW12 2PF.*
Cosy farmhouse in wooded parkland.
Open: All Year
Grades: ETB Listed, Comm
01260 223569 Mrs Kidd
Rates fr: *£17.00*-**£17.00**.
Beds: 1D 2T
Baths: 1 Private 2 Shared
P (10)

Planning a longer stay? Always ask for any special rates.

Oakmere

National Grid Ref: SJ5769

Fourways Inn

Springfield Guest House, *Chester Road, Oakmere, Northwich, Cheshire, CW8 2HB.*
Beautiful family run guest house.
Open: All Year
Grades: ETB 2 Cr, Comm
01606 882538 Mrs Mulholland
Rates fr: *£17.50*-**£19.00**.
Beds: 1F 2D 1T 3S
Baths: 2 Private 1 Shared
(8)

Pickmere

National Grid Ref: SJ6977

Pickmere House, *Park Lane, Pickmere, Knutsford, Cheshire, WA16 0JX.*
Open: All Year
Grades: ETB 2 Cr, AA 3 Q, RAC High Acclaim
01565 733433 Mrs Brown
Rates fr: *£19.50*-**£19.50**.
Beds: 4D 2T 3S
Baths: 6 Private 2 Shared
(10)
Highly Acclaimed Listed Georgian house. Spacious ensuite rooms overlooking farmlands. Convenient swift access to NW cities and tourist attractions. M6 - 2 miles. M56/M6 axis 7 miles. Airport 14 miles.

Poole

National Grid Ref: SJ6455

Poole Bank Farm, *Poole, Nantwich, Cheshire, CW5 6AL.*
C17th timbered farmhouse.
Open: All Year
01270 625169 Ms Hocknell
Rates fr: *£13.50*-**£16.00**.
Beds: 2D 1T
Baths: 1 Private 2 Shared

Poynton

National Grid Ref: SJ9283

Whitethorn, *1 Waters Reach, Poynton, Stockport, Cheshire, SK12 1XT.*
Modern detached house. Quiet cul-de-sac.
Open: All Year (not Xmas)
01625 871590 Mrs Williams
Rates fr: *£13.00*-**£15.00**.
Beds: 1D
Baths: 1 Private

Please respect a B&B's wishes regarding children, animals & smoking.

Runcorn

National Grid Ref: SJ5281

Fountains Hotel, *10 High Street, Runcorn, Cheshire, WA7 1AW.*
Converted town centre Victorian building.
Open: All Year
01928 569799 Mr & Mrs Gittins
Rates fr: *£15.00*-**£20.00**.
Beds: 2F 2D 3T 2S
Baths: 9 Private

16 Lime Grove, *Runcorn, Cheshire, WA7 5JZ.*
3-bedroom house.
Open: All Year
01928 572144 Mr Bratt
Rates fr: -**£14.00**.
Beds: 1D 1S **Baths:** 1 Shared
(10) (3)

16 Weymouth Close, Murdishaw, *Runcorn, Cheshire, WA7 6JJ.*
Modern semi-detached house.
Open: All Year (not Xmas)
01928 701064 Mrs Irwin
Rates fr: *£15.00*-**£15.00**.
Beds: 1D **Baths:** 1 Shared
(1)

Sandbach

National Grid Ref: SJ7560

East View, *104 Congleton Road, Sandbach, Cheshire, CW11 1HQ.*
Large comfortable Victorian private house.
Open: All Year (not Xmas)
01270 760056 Mrs Coulson
Rates fr: *£15.00*-**£17.00**.
Beds: 1F 2D 1T
Baths: 4 Ensuite
(3)

Shavington

National Grid Ref: SJ6951

Oakland House, *252 Newcastle Road, Blakelow, Shavington, Nantwich, Cheshire, CW5 7ET.*
All home comforts, ideally situated.
Open: All Year
Grades: ETB 2 Cr, High Comm, AA 4 Q
01270 67134 Mr & Mrs Wetton
Rates fr: *£16.00*-**£25.00**.
Beds: 1F 2D 2T
Baths: 5 Private
(14) (10)

Siddington

National Grid Ref: SJ8471

Golden Cross Farm, *Siddington, Macclesfield, Cheshire, SK11 9JP.*
Farmhouse in picturesque surroundings.
Open: All Year (not Xmas)
01260 224358 Mrs Rush
Rates fr: *£15.00*-**£15.00**.
Beds: 2D 2S
Baths: 2 Shared
(4)

Stapeley

National Grid Ref: SJ6749

Lamb Hotel

York Cottage, *82 Broad Lane, Stapeley, Nantwich, Cheshire, CW5 7QL.*
Attractive, modernised C19th country cottage.
Open: All Year (not Xmas)
01270 628867 Mrs Winfield
Rates fr: *£16.00*-**£17.00**.
Beds: 1D 1T 1S
Baths: 1 Shared
(3)

Stoke

National Grid Ref: SJ6552

Barbridge Inn, Jolly Tar, Royal Oak

Stoke Grange Farm, *Chester Road, Stoke, Nantwich, Cheshire, CW5 6BT.*
Canal-side farmhouse, 1838, mixed farm..
Open: All Year
Grades: ETB 2 Cr, Comm, RAC Listed
01270 625525 (also fax no)
Mrs West
Rates fr: *£17.50*-**£20.00**.
Beds: 1D 2T
Baths: 3 Ensuite
(10)

Timbersbrook

National Grid Ref: SJ8962

Pedley House Farm, *Pedley Lane, Timbersbrook, Congleton, Cheshire, CW12 3QD.*
Beamed farmhouse on traditional farm.
Open: All Year
01260 273650
Mrs Gilman
Rates fr: *£15.00*-**£15.00**.
Beds: 1F 1D
Baths: 1 Shared

Warrington

National Grid Ref: SJ6088

Brewers Fayre

22 Park Road, *Orford, Warrington, Cheshire, WA2 9AZ.*
Modern, comfortable.
Open: All Year (not Xmas)
01925 639464
Mrs Meredith
Rates fr: -**£16.00**.
Beds: 2S
(2) (2)

Bringing children with you? Always ask for any special rates.

The lowest *double* rate per person is shown in *italics*.

***The Hollies,** 1 Long Lane, Orford, Warrington, Cheshire, WA2 8PT.*
Homely clean and comfortable.
Open: All Year (not Xmas)
01925 635416 Mrs Holbrook
Rates fr: *£18.00*-**£18.00**.
Beds: 1F 2T 1S
Baths: 1 Shared
(5) (8)

***10 Hanover Street,** Warrington, Cheshire, WA1 1LZ.*
Large Victorian guest house.
Open: All Year
01925 418914 Mrs Harrington
Rates fr: *£17.50*-**£22.50**.
Beds: 1F 2D 1T
Baths: 1 Shared
(6)

***Laburnum House,** 106-112 Wilderspool Causeway, Warrington, Cheshire, WA4 6PU.*
Four large Victorian terraced houses.
Open: All Year
01925 575569 Mr Clarke
Rates fr: *£13.50*-**£16.50**.
Beds: 2F 5D 10T 5S
Baths: 4 Shared

Wervin

National Grid Ref: SJ4271

Wheatsheat Hotel

***Wervin New Hall,** Wervin, Chester, Cheshire, CH2 4BP.*
Tudor style mansion.
Open: All Year (not Xmas)
01244 372945 Mrs Warburton
Rates fr: *£16.00*-**£17.00**.
Beds: 1F 1D 1T
Baths: 1 Private 2 Shared
(0) (20)

Weston (Crewe)

National Grid Ref: SJ7352

***Snape Farm,** Snape Lane, Weston Crewe, Cheshire, CW2 5NB.*
Warm comfortable Victorian farm-house.
Open: All Year (not Xmas)
Grades: ETB 2 Cr, Comm
01270 820208 (also fax no)
Mrs Williamson
Rates fr: *£14.00*-**£16.00**.
Beds: 2T 1D
Baths: 1 Ensuite 1 Shared
(5)

Bringing children with you? Always ask for any special rates.

Widnes

National Grid Ref: SJ5185

***Mersey Hotel,** 148 Mersey Road, Widnes, Cheshire, WA8 0DT.*
Homely family-run public house.
Open: All Year
0151 424 2272
Mr Helps
Rates fr: *£12.50*-**£12.50**.
Beds: 1F 4T 1S
Baths: 2 Shared

Willington

National Grid Ref: SJ5366

The Boot Inn, Willington Hall

***Roughlow Farm,** Willington, Tarporley, Cheshire, CW6 0PG.*
Very comfortable quiet C18th farmhouse.
Open: All Year (not Xmas)
Grades: ETB 2 Cr, Comm
01829 751199 (also fax no)
Mrs Sutcliffe
Rates fr: *£25.00*-**£25.00**.
Beds: 3T
Baths: 3 Ensuite
(6)

Wilmslow

National Grid Ref: SJ8480

The Bulls Head, Wagon & Horses

***Rivendell,** 9 Cherington Close, Handforth, Wilmslow, Cheshire, SK9 3AS.*
Open: All Year
01625 526426
Mrs Huyshe
Fax no: 01625 539237
Rates fr: *£18.00*-**£24.00**.
Beds: 1F 1T
Baths: 1 Ensuite 1 Private
(4)
Friendly welcome to family-run quality accommodation, reasonable rates ensure our guests often return. Ensuite or standard rooms have colour TV and refreshments. Evening meals available. Courtesy car. On-site parking. Peaceful, with easy access to Manchester, Airport, Wilmslow, Cheadle, Handforth etc, all motorways, Intercity rail.

***Fernbank Guest House,** 188 Wilmslow Road, Handforth, Wilmslow, Cheshire, SK9 3JX.*
Large Victorian private house.
Open: All Year (not Xmas)
Grades: ETB 2 Cr, Comm, AA 3 Q, Recomm
01625 523729
Mr Wright
Fax no: 01625 539515
Rates fr: *£18.00*-**£25.00**.
Beds: 1F 1D 2T
Baths: 4 Private
(6)

Many rates vary according to season - the lowest are shown here.

***Heatherlea House,** 106 Lacey Green, Wilmslow, Cheshire, SK9 4BN.*
Open: All Year
01625 522872 (also fax no)
Mr Smidmore
Rates fr: *£19.50*-**£23.00**.
Beds: 1F 1D 2T 2S
(6)
Excellent accommodation, 10 mins walk Wilmslow town centre, Manchester Airport, local railway & bus stations served by 24 hour courtesy. Vacation car parking £14 per week.

***St Martins,** 35 Hawthorn Lane, Wilmslow, Cheshire, SK9 5DD.*
Close to town centre.
Open: All Year (not Xmas)
01625 535184 Mr & Mrs Taylor
Rates fr: *£17.50*-**£23.50**.
Beds: 2T 2S
(6)

***The Grange,** Clay Lane, Handforth, Wilmslow, Cheshire, SK9 3NR.*
Georgian building set in 10 acres.
Open: All Year
01625 523653 Mrs Godlee
Rates fr: *£20.00*-**£23.00**.
Beds: 1F 2T
Baths: 3 Ensuite
(6)

Wincle

National Grid Ref: SJ9566

The Ship Inn

***Hill Top Farm,** Wincle, Macclesfield, Cheshire, SK11 0QH.*
Peaceful and comfortable farm-house accommodation.
Open: All Year (not Xmas)
01260 227257 Mrs Brocklehurst
Rates fr: *£16.00*-**£18.00**.
Beds: 1T 1S
Baths: 1 Shared
(3) (3)

Right on the border? Look at the neighbouring county, too

Wistaston

National Grid Ref: SJ6853

The Woodside

Greenfields, *518 Crewe Road, Wistaston, Crewe, Cheshire, CW2 6PS.*
Comfortable family home. Pleasant area.
Open: All Year (not Xmas)
01270 69325
Mrs Gildea
Rates fr: *£15.00*-**£15.00**.
Beds: 1T 2S
Baths: 1 Shared
(4)

Wybunbury

National Grid Ref: SJ6949

Lea Farm, *Wrinehill Road, Wybunbury, Nantwich, Cheshire, CW5 7HS.*
Open: All Year (not Xmas)
Grades: ETB 2 Cr, Comm, AA Listed, RAC Listed
01270 841429 Mrs Callwood
Rates fr: *£14.50*-**£16.50**.
Beds: 1F 1D 1T
Baths: 2 Private 1 Shared
(22)
Charming farmhouse set in landscaped gardens where peacocks roam. Dairy farm. Pool/snooker table. Luxury guest lounge. Fishing available.

Red Lodge, *124 Stock Lane, Wybunbury, Nantwich, Cheshire, CW5 7HE.*
Large bungalow in private gardens.
Open: All Year (not Xmas)
01270 841561 Mrs Bottomley
Rates fr: *£15.00*-**£18.00**.
Beds: 1F 1D
Baths: 1 Shared
(4)

All rates are subject to alteration at the owners' discretion.

Cornwall

Tourist Information Centres

Shire House, Mount Folly Square, **Bodmin**, Cornwall, PL31 2DQ, 01208 76616.

The Crescent Car Park, **Bude**, Cornwall, EX2 8LE, 01288 354240.

North Cornwall Museum, The Clease, **Camelford**, Cornwall, PL32 9PL, 01840 212954, (Easter to Oct).

28 Killigrew Street, **Falmouth**, Cornwall, TR11 3PN, 01326 312300.

The Post Office, 4 Custom House Hill, **Fowey**, Cornwall, PL23 1AA, 01726 833616.

Flambards Theme Park, Culdrose, **Helston**, Cornwall, TR13 0GA, 01326 565431, (Easter to Oct).

Market House Arcade, Market Street, **Launceston**, Cornwall, PL15 8EP, 01566 772321.

The Guildhall, Fore Street, **Looe**, Cornwall, PL13 1AA, 01503 262072.

Lostwithiel Community Centre, Liddicoat Road, **Lostwithiel**, Cornwall, PL22 0HE, 01208 872207.

Municipal Offices, Marcus Hill, **Newquay**, Cornwall, TR7 1BD, 01637 871345.

The Quay, **Padstow,** Pl28 8AF 01841 533449

Station Road, **Penzance**, Cornwall, TR18 2NF, 01736 62207.

Polzeath, Wadebridge, 01208 862488

Mid-Cornwall Service Area (A30), Victoria, Roche, **St Austell**, Cornwall, PL26 8LQ, 01726 76333, (Easter to Oct).

The Guildhall, Street-an-Pol, **St Ives**, Cornwall, TR26 2DT, 01736 796297.

Municipal Buildings, Boscawen Street, **Truro**, Cornwall, TR1 2NE, 01872-74555.

The Town Hall, The Platt, **Wadebridge,** Pl27 7AQ, 01208 813725

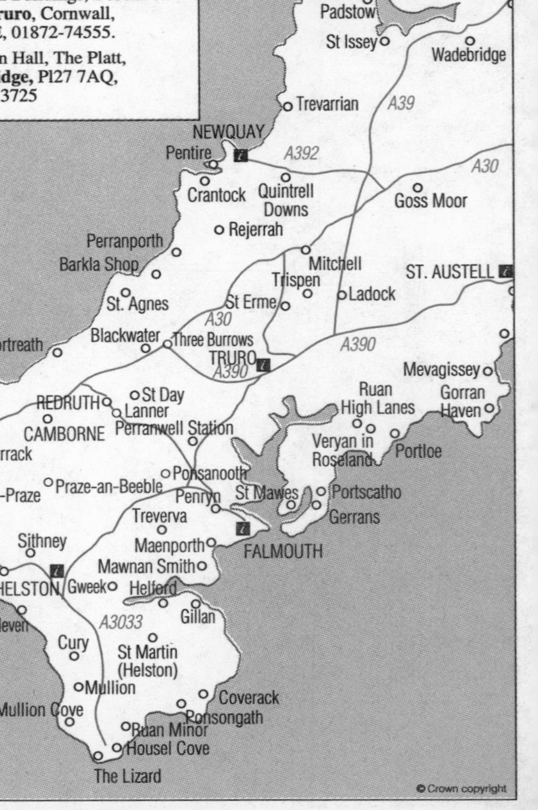

For **Isles of Scilly**
please see separate section

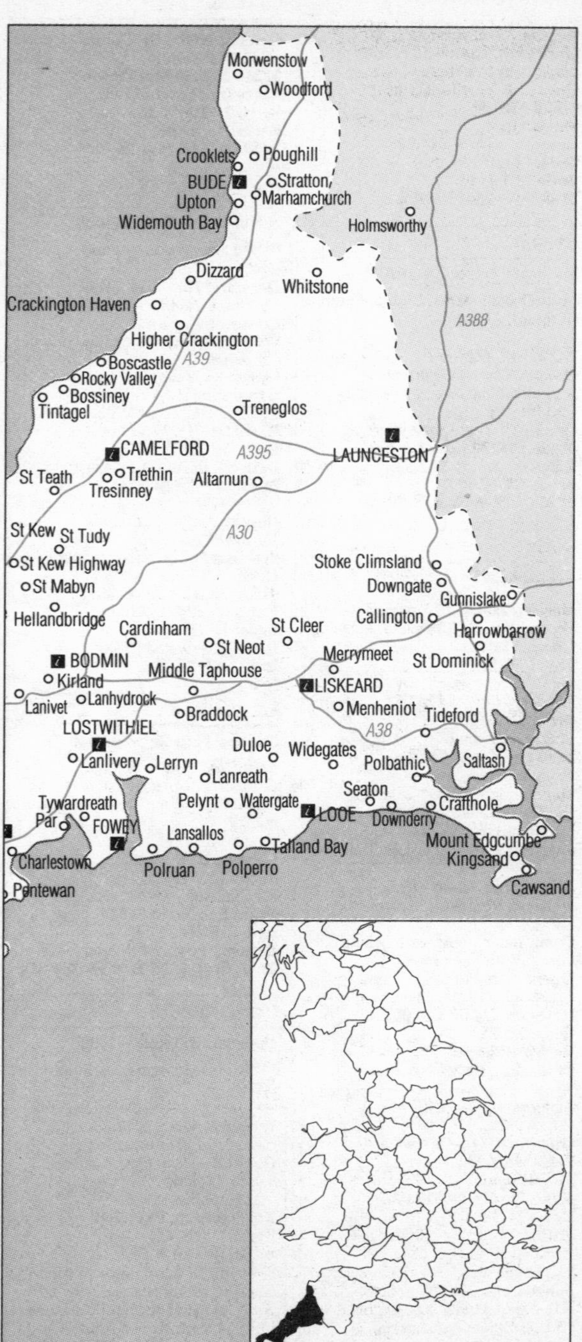

Altarnun

National Grid Ref: SX2281

Trecollas Farm, *Altarnun, Launceston, Cornwall, PL15 7SN.*
Open: Easter to Oct
01566 86386 Mrs Heath
Rates fr: *£12.00*-**£13.00**.
Beds: 1F 1D 1T
Baths: 2 Shared
Comfortable farmhouse set in beautiful Cornish countryside. Easily accessible to Devon/Cornwall. TV lounge, separate tables in flagstone dining room, scrumptious home cooking & friendly atmosphere.

Angarrack

National Grid Ref: SW5838

Byways, *22 Steamers Hill, Angarrack, Hayle, Cornwall, TR27 5JB.*
Bungalow in quiet pretty village.
Open: Easter to Oct
01736 753463 Mrs Pooley
Rates fr: *£12.00*-**£15.00**.
Beds: 1T 1D
Baths: 2 Private

Barkla Shop

National Grid Ref: SW7350

Plume of Feathers

The Grange Farm, *Barkla Shop, St Agnes, Cornwall, TR5 0XN.*
Comfortable, modern farmhouse. Warm welcome.
Open: All Year
01872 552332 Mrs Shine
Rates fr: *£17.50*-**£17.50**.
Beds: 1F 1D 1T
Baths: 2 Shared

Blackwater

National Grid Ref: SW8244

Rock Cottage, *Blackwater, Truro, Cornwall, TR4 8EU.*
C18th beamed schoolmaster's cottage.
Open: All Year
Grades: ETB 3 Cr, High Comm, AA 4 Q, Select, RAC Acclaim
01872 560252 (also fax no)
Mrs Wakeling
Rates fr: *£20.50*.
Beds: 2D 1T
Baths: 3 Ensuite

Right on the border?

Look at the neighbouring county, too

Bodmin

National Grid Ref: SX0677

Mount Pleasant Moorland Hotel, *Mount Village, Bodmin, Cornwall, PL30 4EX.*
Quiet, friendly, comfortable country hotel. **Open:** Easter to Sep
01208 821342 Mr & Mrs Capper
Rates fr: *£17.50*-**£15.00**.
Beds: 1F 3D 2T 1S
Baths: 6 Private 1 Shared
(5) (10)

Boscastle

National Grid Ref: SX0990

Napoleon Pub

Bottreaux House Hotel, *Boscastle, Cornwall, PL35 0BG.*
Open: All Year
Georgian hotel set in conservation area.
Grades: ETB 3 Cr, Comm
01840 250231 Mr Mee
Rates fr: *£18.00*-**£23.00**.
Beds: 1F 4D 2T **Baths:** 7 Ensuite
(7) (9)

The Old Coach House, *Boscastle, Cornwall, PL35 0AS.*
Beautiful former coach house all ensuite. **Open:** Mar to Oct
Grades: ETB 2 Cr, AA 3 Q, RAC Listed
01840 250398
Rates fr: *£16.00*-**£16.00**.
Beds: 1F 2D 2T 1S
Baths: 6 Ensuite
(6) (9)

Tolcarne House Hotel and Resturant, *Tintagel Road, Boscastle, Cornwall, PL35 0AS.*
Splendid walking with Hardy connections. **Open:** Jan to Oct
Grades: ETB 3 Cr, Comm, AA 4 Q, Select
01840 250654 Mr & Mrs Crown
Rates fr: *£20.00*-**£28.00**.
Beds: 6D 2T 1S
Baths: 8 Private 1 Shared
(12)

Bossiney

National Grid Ref: SX0688

Willapark Manor Hotel, *Bossiney, Tintagel, Cornwall, PL34 0BA.*
Open: All Year (not Xmas)
Grades: ETB 3 Cr, Comm
01840 770782 Mr Leeds
Rates fr: *£26.00*-**£26.00**.
Beds: 2F 7D 2T 3S
Baths: 14 Private
(20)
One of the most beautifully situated hotels in England set in 14 acre gardens & woodland overlooking one of the finest stretches of unspoilt coastline in Cornwall. Lovely rooms, excellent cuisine, well-stocked cocktail bar, friendly informal atmosphere. DIRECT ACCESS COASTAL PATH & BEACH.

Braddock

National Grid Ref: SX1662

Royal Oak, Halfway Inn

Wayton Barn, *Braddock, Lostwithiel, Cornwall, PL22 0RJ.*
Large converted barn.
Open: All Year (not Xmas)
01579 320700
Mrs Nottle
Rates fr: *£14.00*-**£14.00**.
Beds: 1F 1D
Baths: 1 Private
(4)

Breage

National Grid Ref: SW6128

Queens Arms, Lion & Lamb (Ashton)

Willavean, *Higher Road, Breage, Helston, Cornwall, TR13 9PL.*
Secluded bungalow, gardens. Children welcome.
Open: All Year (not Xmas)
01326 573732 (also fax no)
Rates fr: *£12.50*-**£12.50**.
Beds: 1D 1T 1S
(2)

Bude

National Grid Ref: SS2106

Mornish Hotel, *20 Summerleaze Crescent, Bude, Cornwall, EX23 8HJ.*
Open: Mar to Nov
01288 352972
Mr Hilder
Rates fr: *£18.75*-**£18.75**.
Beds: 3F 5D 2T
Baths: 10 Ensuite
(4)
On coastal path overlooking Summerleaze Beach, River Neet and Bude Canal. 400 yds level walking to the Golf club-house and town centre. Member Les Routiers.

Marhamrise Guest House, *50 Kings Hill, Bude, Cornwall, EX23 8QH.*
Comfortable house with beautiful views. With great food.
Open: Easter to Oct
01288 354713 Mrs Thornton
Rates fr: *£14.00*-**£14.00**.
Beds: 2D 2S
Baths: 1 Shared
(3) (3)

Kisauni, *4 Downs View, Bude, Cornwall, EX23 8.*
Open: All Year (not Xmas)
01288 352653
Mrs Kimpton
Rates fr: *£13.00*-**£13.00**.
Beds: 2F 3D 1T 1S
Baths: 1 Ensuite 2 Shared
(5)
Bright and airy Victorian house. 2 minutes to beach. A romantic four poster bed. Home cooking of course. Come as guests, go as friends.

Lower Northcott Farm, *Poughill, Bude, Cornwall, EX23 7EL.*
Georgian farmhouse with outstanding views 0.75 mile from Heritage Coastline.
Open: All Year
Grades: ETB 2 Cr, Comm, AA 3 Q, Recomm
01288 352350 Mrs Trewin
Rates fr: *£17.00*-**£17.00**.
Beds: 2F 2D 1T 1S
Baths: 5 Private
(4)

Callington

National Grid Ref: SX3669

Coachmakers Arms

Dozmary, *Tors View Close, Tavistock Road, Callington, Cornwall, PL17 7DY.*
Spacious dormer bungalow in quiet cul-de-sac.
Open: All Year (not Xmas)
Grades: ETB 1 Cr, Comm
01579 383677 Mrs Wills
Rates fr: *£15.00*-**£17.00**.
Beds: 1F 1D 1T
Baths: 2 Ensuite 1 Private
(4)

Dupath Farm, *Callington, Cornwall, PL17 8AD.*
Spacious 200-year-old farmhouse.
Open: All Year
01579 382197 Mrs Coombe
Rates fr: *£14.00*-**£14.00**.
Beds: 1F 1D
Baths: 2 Private
(6)

Camborne

National Grid Ref: SW6440

Erin Hall, *Bassett Road, Camborne, Cornwall, TR14 8SH.*
Tourist Board registered guest house.
Open: All Year
Grades: ETB Listed
01209 713911
Mr Simpson
Rates fr: *£13.50*-**£15.00**.
Beds: 1F 2D 2T 1S
Baths: 1 Private 1 Shared
(1) (7)

Camelford

National Grid Ref: SX1083

Masons Arms, Darlington Hotel

Trenarth, *Victoria Road, Camelford, Cornwall, PL32.*
Open: Easter to Oct
01840 213289
Mrs Hopkins
Rates fr: *£13.50*-**£13.50**.
Beds: 1F 1D 1T
(4)
Share my country home in friendly comfort. Enjoy beaches, rugged coast, moors, Du Maurier's Jamaica Inn, Tintagel, King Arthur's Castle, Port Isaac, Boscastle. Then relax.

Masons Arms, *Market Place, Camelford, Cornwall, PL32 9PD.*
Charming C18th public house.
Open: All Year
01840 213309
Mr Connolly
Rates fr: *£15.00*-**£15.00**.
Beds: 1F 2D 1T 2S
Baths: 2 Shared

Silvermoon, *Lane End, Camelford, Cornwall, PL32 9LE.*
Ensuite. Quietly situated, good walking.
Open: All Year
Grades: ETB Listed
01840 213736 Mrs Metters
Rates fr: *£14.00*-**£14.00**.
Beds: 1F 1D 1T
Baths: 1 Private
(4)

Carcade Farm, *Camelford, Cornwall, PL32 9XG.*
250-year-old comfortable farmhouse.
Open: All Year
01840 212288 Mrs Stiles
Rates fr: *£15.00*-**£15.00**.
Beds: 1F 1D 1T 1S
(4)

Canonstown

National Grid Ref: SW5335

Lamb & Flag

Colinden, *Canonstown, Hayle, Cornwall, TR27 6NB.*
Open: All Year (not Xmas)
01736 740344 Mrs Joseph
Rates fr: *£10.00*-**£12.00**.
Beds: 2D 1T 2S
Baths: 1 Ensuite 1 Private
(3)
Family-run herb farm and smallholding.

Carbis Bay

National Grid Ref: SW5238

Badger Inn

Fairfield Guest House, *Porthrepta Road, Carbis Bay, St Ives, Cornwall, TR26 2N.*
Family-run Victorian guesthouse.
Open: All Year
01736 796851
Mr & Mrs Sissons
Rates fr: *£15.00*-**£15.00**.
Beds: 3F 3D 2T 2S
Baths: 1 Ensuite
(10)

Monowai Hotel, *Headland Road, Carbis Bay, St Ives, Cornwall, TR26 2NR.*
Wonderful sea views, heated pool.
Open: Feb to Oct
Grades: ETB 2 Cr, Comm, AA 4 Q
01736 795733
Mr Whyte
Rates fr: *£16.00*-**£16.00**.
Beds: 2F 4D 1T 1S
Baths: 8 Ensuite
(5) (7)

Headland House, *Headland Road, Carbis Bay, St Ives, Cornwall, TR26 2NS.*
Charming Victorian private house.
Open: All Year
Grades: ETB 3 Cr
01736 796647
Mrs Antonini
Rates fr: *£14.00*-**£14.00**.
Beds: 3F 3D 1T
Baths: 5 Private 2 Shared
(Any) (10)

Cardinham

National Grid Ref: SX1268

London Inn

The Old School House, *Averys Green, Cardinham, Bodmin, Cornwall, PL30 4EA.*
Pretty, converted Victorian schoolhouse.
Open: All Year (not Xmas)
01208 821303
Mrs Pidcock
Rates fr: *£13.50*-**£15.00**.
Beds: 1D
Baths: 1 Private
(2)

The Stables, *Cardinham, Cardinham, Bodmin, Cornwall, PL30 4EG.*
Converted barn, rural, central Cornwall.
Open: All Year
01208 821316
Mr Moseley
Rates fr: *£13.50*-**£15.50**.
Beds: 2D 2T
Baths: 2 Private 2 Shared
(10) (2)

Charlestown

National Grid Ref: SX0352

Rashleigh Arms Hotel, *Charlestown, St Austell, Cornwall, PL25 3NJ.*
Pub-hotel, charming Cornish port.
Open: All Year
01726 73635
Mr Caithness
Rates fr: *£32.00*-**£24.00**.
Beds: 2D 2T 1S
Baths: 5 Private
(100)

Coverack

National Grid Ref: SW7818

Paris Hotel

Tamarisk Cottage, *North Corner, Coverack, Helston, Cornwall, TR12 6TG.*
Cottage overlooking bay, built 1720.
Open: Easter to Oct
01326 280638 Mrs Carey
Rates fr: *£14.00*-**£14.00**.
Beds: 1D 2S
Baths: 1 Shared
(8) (1)

Bakery Cottage, *Coverack, Helston, Cornwall, TR12 6TD.*
Comfortable accommodation in lovely fishing village.
Open: All Year (not Xmas)
01326 280474 Mrs Daw
Rates fr: *£13.80*-**£13.50**.
Beds: 1F 1D
Baths: 1 Shared
(3)

Crackington Haven

National Grid Ref: SX1496

Lower Tresmorn, *Crackington Haven, Bude, Cornwall, EX23 0NU.*
Mediaeval National Trust coastal farmhouse.
Open: All Year (not Xmas)
01840 230667 Mrs Crocker
Rates fr: *£15.00*-**£15.00**.
Beds: 2D 1T
Baths: 1 Ensuite 1 Shared
(4)

Hallagather, *Crackington Haven, Bude, Cornwall, EX23 0LA.*
C15th Listed farm house.
Open: All Year (not Xmas)
01840 230276 Mrs Anthony
Rates fr: *£13.00*-**£16.00**.
Beds: 1F 1D 1S
Baths: 3 Private
(6) (5)

Trevelyan, *Crackington Haven, St Gennys, Bude, Cornwall, EX23 0NP.*
Large, comfortable family home.
Open: All Year (not Xmas)
01840 230459 Mrs Eaton
Rates fr: *£14.00*-**£14.00**.
Beds: 3T
(4)

Crafthole

National Grid Ref: SX3654

Finnygook Inn

The Bungalow, *Cliff Road, Crafthole, Torpoint, Cornwall, PL11 3BY.*
Homely hospitality in superb setting.
Open: April to Oct
01503 230334 Mrs Harvey
Rates fr: *£15.00*-**£15.00**.
Beds: 1D 1T
Baths: 1 Shared

Crantock

National Grid Ref: SW7960

Old Albion

***The Malt House,** Crantock, Newquay, Cornwall, TR8 5RB.*
Open: All Year (not Xmas)
01637 830662 / 830015 Mrs Cann
Fax no: 01637 851891
Rates fr: *£18.00*-**£25.00**.
Beds: 1F 1D 1T
Baths: 3 Ensuite
(5) (3)
Crantock village surrounded by spectacular coastline is perfect for walking, surfing, relaxing. 8 minutes walk from magnificent beach. Warm welcome, total comfort, unbeatable breakfasts assured!

Crooklets

National Grid Ref: SS2006

***Inn On The Green,** Crooklets Beach, Crooklets, Bude, Cornwall, EX23 8NF.*
Comfortable family hotel, good food.
Open: All Year (not Xmas)
Grades: ETB 3 Cr, Comm
01288 356013 (also fax no)
Mr Bellward
Rates fr: *£16.00*-**£16.00**.
Beds: 2F 6D 9T 3S
Baths: 16 Ensuite 3 Shared
(1) (6)

Cury

National Grid Ref: SW6721

***Tregaddra Farmhouse,** Cury, Helston, Cornwall, TR12 7BB.*
Beautifully furnished farmhouse (working farm).
Open: All Year
Grades: ETB 3 Cr, High Comm, AA 4 Q, Select
01326 240235 (also fax no)
Mrs Lugg
Rates fr: *£18.50*-**£18.50**.
Beds: 1F 3D 1T 1S
Baths: 5 Private 1 Shared
(10)

***Cobblers Cottage,** Nantihet, Cury, Helston, Cornwall, TR12 7RB.*
Delightful C18th riverside cottage.
Open: All Year
Grades: ETB 2 Cr, High Comm
01326 241342 Mrs Lugg
Rates fr: *£18.00*-**£19.00**.
Beds: 3D
Baths: 3 Private
(12) (6)

***Nanplough Farm,** Cury, Whitecross, Helston, Cornwall, TR12 7BQ.*
Beautiful rooms, wonderful views. Luxury accommodation.
Open: All Year
01326 241088
Mrs Makin
Rates fr: *£20.00*-**£18.00**.
Beds: 3D 1T 1S
Baths: 3 Ensuite
(4)

Dizzard

National Grid Ref: SX1698

***Penrose,** Dizzard, St Gennys, Bude, Cornwall, EX23 0NX.*
Cosy, comfortable, clean, in NT area
Open: All Year
01840 230318 Mrs Joyner
Rates fr: *£17.00*-**£17.00**.
Beds: 3D
Baths: 2 Private 1 Shared
(3) (6Yes)

Downderry

National Grid Ref: SX3155

Smugglers Inn

***Cair,** Deviock, Downderry, Torpoint, Cornwall, PL11 3DN.*
Old farmhouse, large gardens, overlooking sea.
Open: Easter to Oct
01503 250320
Mrs Connell
Fax no: 01503 250272
Rates fr: *£16.00*-**£16.00**.
Beds: 1F 1D 1T
Baths: 3 Ensuite

Downgate

National Grid Ref: SX3672

***Niggles Nook Guest House,** Sandercock Close, Downgate, Callington, Cornwall, PL17 8JS.*
Ideal for family holidays.
Open: All Year
01579 370813 Mrs Bartlett
Rates fr: *£13.00*-**£13.00**.
Beds: 2D 1T
Baths: 1 Shared
(4)

Drift

National Grid Ref: SW4328

***Rose Farm,** Chyanhal, Drift, Penzance, Cornwall, TR19 6AN.*
Cosy, relaxing, old Cornish farm.
Open: All Year (not Xmas)
01736 731808
Mr & Mrs Lally
Rates fr: *£17.50*-**£22.00**.
Beds: 1F 2D
Baths: 3 Ensuite
(8)

Duloe

National Grid Ref: SX2358

***Carglonnon Farm,** Duloe, Liskeard, Cornwall, PL14 4QA.*
Georgian farmhouse in tranquil situation.
Open: All Year (not Xmas)
01579 320210
Mrs Bray
Rates fr: *£14.50*-**£17.00**.
Beds: 2D 1T
Baths: 2 Ensuite 1 Shared

Falmouth

National Grid Ref: SW8032

Warehouse Bistro, Quayside Inn, Pandora

***Telford Guest House,** 47 Melvill Road, Falmouth, Cornwall, TR11 4DG.*
Open: Mar to Oct
01326 314581
Ms Eschenauer
Rates fr: *£14.00*-**£14.00**.
Beds: 4D 1T 1S
Baths: 5 Private 1 Shared
(6)
Telford is a small registered guest house with ensuite rooms, CTV plus tea-making facilities. Convenient for town, beaches, station and as a touring base.

***The Grove Hotel,** Grove Place, Falmouth, Cornwall, TR11 4AU.*
Harbourside Georgian hotel, friendly atmosphere.
Open: All Year (not Xmas)
Grades: ETB 3 Cr, Approv
01326 319577
Mrs Cork
Rates fr: *£20.00*-**£20.00**.
Beds: 5F 5D 3T 2S
Baths: 13 Private 2 Shared

***Dolvean Hotel,** 50 Melvill Road, Falmouth, Cornwall, TR11 4DQ.*
Warm friendly family-run hotel.
Open: All Year (not Xmas)
Grades: AA 3 Q
01326 313658
Mrs Crocker
Fax no: 01326 313995
Rates fr: *£17.00*-**£17.00**.
Beds: 1F 4D 3T 4S
Baths: 9 Ensuite 3 Shared
(5) (10)

***Castleton Guest House,** 68 Killigrew Street, Falmouth, Cornwall, TR11 3PR.*
Clean, comfortable, with friendly atmosphere.
Open: All Year (not Xmas/New Year)
Grades: ETB Listed, Approv
01326 311072
Appleton
Rates fr: *£14.00*-**£18.00**.
Beds: 4F 2D
Baths: 4 Ensuite

Ambleside Guest House, *9 Marlborough Road, Falmouth, Cornwall, TR11 3LP.*
Victorian guesthouse. Relaxed & friendly.
Open: All Year
01326 319630 Mr Walker
Rates fr: *£14.00*-**£14.00**.
Beds: 1F 2D 1T 1S

Bosanneth, *Gyllyngvase Hill, Falmouth, Cornwall, TR11 4DW.*
Well-appointed, overlooking Falmouth Bay.
Open: All Year
Grades: RAC Acclaim
01326 314649 (also fax no)
Mrs McGonagle
Rates fr: *£19.00*-**£19.50**.
Beds: 1F 5D 1T 1S
Baths: 8 Private
(5) (8)

April Cottage, *The Praze, Penryn, Falmouth, Cornwall, TR10 8DH.*
Well recommended, friendly cottage accommodation.
Open: All Year
01326 372726 Mrs Williams
Rates fr: *£12.00*-**£12.00**.
Beds: 2D 1T
Baths: 2 Shared
(3)

20 Dracaena Avenue, *Falmouth, Cornwall, TR11 2EG.*
Friendly, comfortable, homely Victorian house.
Open: Easter to Oct
01326 211784 Mr Blowers
Rates fr: *£13.50*-**£15.00**.
Beds: 1D 2T
(3)

Selwood Cottage Guest House, *38 Melvill Road, Falmouth, Cornwall, TR11 4DQ.*
Excellent accommodation set in championship gardens.
Open: April - September (inc)
Grades: AA 3 Q
01326 314135 (also fax no)
Mr & Mrs Trezise
Rates fr: *£15.00*-**£18.00**.
Beds: 1F 1D 1T
Baths: 2 Ensuite 1 Private
(5) (6)

Tudor Court Hotel, *55 Melvill Road, Falmouth, Cornwall, TR11 4DF.*
Tudor style, modern family home.
Open: All Year
Grades: ETB 3 Cr
01326 312807 Mrs Swade
Rates fr: *£17.50*-**£18.50**.
Beds: 1F 6D 1T 3S
Baths: 9 Private 2 Shared
(6)

The lowest *double* rate per person is shown in *italics*.

Fowey

National Grid Ref: SX1251

Ship Inn

Trevanion, *70 Lostwithiel Street, Fowey, Cornwall, PL23 1BQ.*
Open: Mar to Dec
Grades: ETB Listed, Comm, AA 3 Q, Recomm
01726 832602
Mr Bullock
Rates fr: *£15.00*-**£18.00**.
Beds: 1F 3D 1S
Baths: 2 Ensuite 1 Shared
(4) (3)
Experience the unique character & comfort of this spacious C16th merchants house. All parts of the historic town of Fowey are within walking distance.

Fowey Hall, *Fowey, Cornwall, PL23 1ET.*
Grand Victorian manor house.
Open: All Year
01726 833104
Mrs Rayment
Rates fr: *£18.00*-**£18.00**.
Beds: 8F 22T 11S
(50)

11 Park Road, *Fowey, Cornwall, PL23 1EB.*
1930's private house. River views.
Open: Easter to Nov
01726 833559
Mrs Dorkins
Rates fr: *£12.50*-**£13.50**.
Beds: 1D 1T
Baths: 1 Shared
(2)

Coombe Farm, *Coombe, Fowey, Cornwall, PL23 1HW.*
Farmhouse overlooking sea, near Fowey.
Open: All Year
01726 833123
Mrs Paull
Rates fr: *£15.50*-**£17.50**.
Beds: 10D 1T
Baths: 1 Shared

Panorama, *Daglands Road, Fowey, Cornwall, PL23 1JY.*
Modern home with superb views.
Open: Easter to Oct
01726 833153
Rates fr: *£15.00*-**£15.00**.
Beds: 1D 1T 1S
Baths: 1 Shared
(3)

Carnethic House, *Lambs Barn, Fowey, Cornwall, PL23 1HQ.*
Regency house in 1.5 acre garden.
Open: Feb to Nov
Grades: ETB 3 Cr, Comm, AA 4 Q, RAC High Acclaim
01726 833336
Mr Hogg
Rates fr: *£23.00*-**£30.00**.
Beds: 2F 5D 1T
Baths: 7 Ensuite 1 Shared
(0) (20)

Gerrans

National Grid Ref: SW8739

Royal Standard, Plume of Feathers (Portscatho)

Harberton House, *Churchtown Road, Gerrans, Portscatho, Truro, Cornwall, TR2 5DZ.*
Large traditionally-built family home.
Open: Easter to Oct
01872 580598 Mr & Mrs Davis
Fax no: 01872 580789
Rates fr: *£16.00*-**£16.00**.
Beds: 1D 1T
Baths: 2 Shared
(3)

Gillan

National Grid Ref: SW7824

Porthvean, *Gillan, Manaccan, Helston, Cornwall, TR12 6HL.*
Self-contained annexe.
Open: All Year (not Xmas)
01326 231204 Mrs Whale
Rates fr: *£15.00*-**£15.00**.
Beds: 1T
Baths: 1 Private
(3)

Goonlaze

National Grid Ref: SW7137

Driftwood Spars

Jade Cottage, *Goonlaze, St Agnes, Cornwall, TR5 0XL.*
Beamed cottage. 0.5 sea, village.
Open: All Year (not Xmas)
01872 553558 Mrs Benson
Rates fr: *£13.50*-**£15.00**.
Beds: 1D 1T 1S
Baths: 1 Ensuite 1 Shared
(3)

Gorran Haven

National Grid Ref: SX0041

Barleysheaf, Llawnroc Inn

Piggys Pantry, *The Willows, Gorran Haven, St Austell, Cornwall, PL26 6JG.*
Family bungalow, beach 200 yards.
Open: All Year
01726 843545 Mrs Mott
Rates fr: *£16.00*-**£16.00**.
Beds: 1F 1D
Baths: 1 Shared

Llawnroc Inn, *Gorran Haven, St Austell, Cornwall, PL26 6NU.*
Family-run pub overlooking picturesque harbour.
Open: All Year
Grades: ETB 3 Cr, Comm, AA 3 St, Comm
01726 843461 Mr Gregory
Rates fr: *£18.00*-**£20.00**.
Beds: 1F 3D 3T
Baths: 6 Private 1 Shared
(40)

Goss Moor

National Grid Ref: SW9559

***Brentons Farm,** Goss Moor, St Columb, Cornwall, TR9 6HR.*
Warm & comfortable accommodation.
Open: All Year (not Xmas)
01726 860632 Mr & Mrs Hobson
Rates fr: *£11.50*-**£11.50**.
Beds: 1D 1T 1S
Baths: 1 Shared
(5)

Gulval

National Grid Ref: SW4831

***Chy-An-Ros,** Gulval, Penzance, Cornwall, TR18 3BG.*
Warm, friendly country house, own grounds.
Open: All Year
01736 61761 Mrs Taylor
Rates fr: *£16.00*-**£16.00**.
Beds: 2D 1T
Baths: 2 Private 1 Shared
(3)

Gunnislake

National Grid Ref: SX4371

***Sandhill House,** Tavistock Road, Gunnislake, Cornwall, PL18 9DR.*
Regency country manor house.
Open: Easter to Nov
01822 832442 Mrs Collins
Rates fr: *£18.00*-**£20.00**.
Beds: 4D 2T
Baths: 5 Private 1 Shared
(12) (12)

Gweek

National Grid Ref: SW7026

***Merther Uny Farm,** Treloquithack, Gweek, Helston, Cornwall, TR13 0NU.*
Listed traditional Cornish granite farmhouse. **Open:** All Year
01326 340342 Mrs Garrod
Rates fr: *£18.00*-**£20.00**.
Beds: 1D 1T
Baths: 2 Private
(8)

Harrowbarrow

National Grid Ref: SX3969

***The Divot,** Harrowbarrow, Callington, Cornwall, PL17 8JJ.*
Close National Trust, Golf. Quiet.
Open: All Year
01579 350910 Mr & Mrs Griffiths
Rates fr: *£15.00*-**£15.00**.
Beds: 1T
(1)

Planning a longer stay? Always ask for any special rates.

Hayle

National Grid Ref: SW5537

Cobbetts, Westray Grill

***54 Penpol Terrace,** Hayle, Cornwall, TR27 4BQ.*
Large Victorian terraced cottage.
Open: All Year (not Xmas)
01736 752855 Mrs Cooper
Rates fr: *£15.00*-**£15.00**.
Beds: 1D 2T 1S
Baths: 2 Shared
(2)

Helford

National Grid Ref: SW7526

Shipwrights Arms

***Pengwedhen,** Helford, Helston, Cornwall, TR12 6JZ.*
Wonderful views from 1920's verandahs.
Open: All Year
01326 231481 Mrs Davies
Rates fr: *£15.00*-**£15.00**.
Beds: 1F 1T
Baths: 1 Shared
(4)

***Heronsway,** Orchard Lane, Helford, Helston, Cornwall, TR12 6LA.*
Friendly modern bungalow, nice garden.
Open: All Year (not Xmas)
01326 231424
Mrs Chambers
Rates fr: *£15.00*-**£15.00**.
Beds: 1D 1T
Baths: 1 Private 1 Shared
(12) (4)

Hellandbridge

National Grid Ref: SX0671

***Lower Helland Farm,** Hellandbridge, Bodmin, Cornwall, PL30 4QP.*
Farmhouse - converted barn.
Open: All Year (not Xmas)
01208 72813 Mrs Coad
Rates fr: *£16.00*.
Beds: 1D 1T 1S
Baths: 2 Private

Helston

National Grid Ref: SW6627

New Inn

***Mandeley Guest House,** Clodgey Lane, Helston, Cornwall, TR13 8PJ.*
Friendly modern comfortable guest house.
Open: All Year
01326 572550
Mr Johns
Rates fr: *£15.00*-**£18.00**.
Beds: 2D 1T
Baths: 1 Shared
(4)

All rates are subject to alteration at the owners' discretion.

***Strathallan Guest House,** Monument Road, Helston, Cornwall, TR13 8EH.*
Beautiful Georgian house.
Open: All Year
01326 573683 Mr Griffin
Rates fr: *£17.00*-**£25.00**.
Beds: 6D 1T
Baths: 7 Private
(7)

***Lyndale Guest House,** Greenbank, Meneage Road, Helston, Cornwall, TR13 8JA.*
Comfortable Cornish cottage guest house.
Open: All Year
01326 561082
Mrs Tucker
Rates fr: *£14.50*-**£23.00**.
Beds: 1F 4D 1T
Baths: 3 Private 3 Shared
(8)

***Gwealdues Hotel,** Falmouth Road, Helston, Cornwall, TR13 8JX.*
Modern family-run licensed hotel.
Open: All Year
01326 572808
Mr & Mrs Murphy
Rates fr: *£20.00*-**£30.00**.
Beds: 6F 8D 1T 2S
Baths: 13 Ensuite 1 Private 3 Shared
(60)

Higher Crackington

National Grid Ref: SX1595

***5 Penkenna Close,** Higher Crackington, St Gennys, Bude, Cornwall, EX23 0PF.*
Private bungalow with sea view.
Open: All Year (not Xmas)
01840 230648 Mrs Short
Rates fr: *£11.50*-**£11.50**.
Beds: 2T
(2)

Housel Cove

National Grid Ref: SW7011

***Housel Bay Hotel,** Housel Cove, Helston, Cornwall, TR12 7PG.*
Elegant Victorian hotel.
Spectacular location.
Open: All Year
Grades: ETB 3 Cr, High Comm, AA 2 St, RAC 2 St
01326 290417 Mrs Oswald
Fax no: 01326 290359
Rates fr: *£30.00*-**£30.00**.
Beds: 1F 8D 8T 4S
Baths: 21 Ensuite
(25)

Kingsand

National Grid Ref: SX4350

Halfway House Inn

The Halfway House Inn, *Fore Street, Kingsand, Cawsand Bay, Torpoint, Cornwall, PL10 1NA.*
Family-run, comfortable coastal inn.
Open: All Year
Grades: ETB 3 Cr, High Comm
01752 822279 Mr Riggs
Fax no: 01752 823146
Rates fr: *£22.00*-**£22.00**.
Beds: 1F 3D 1S **Baths:** 5 Private
(200)

Cliff House, *Devon Port Hill, Kingsand, Torpoint, Cornwall, PL10 1NT.*
Open: All Year
01752 823110
Mrs Heasman
Rates fr: *£20.00*-**£25.00**.
Beds: 2D 1T
Baths: 3 Ensuite
(2)
Grade II Listed house in Rame Peninsula conservation area. Lovely sea and country views of Mount Edgcumbe on South Cornwall coastal footpath. Excellent wholefood cookery.

The Haven, *Market Street, Kingsand, Torpoint, Cornwall, PL10 1ND.*
Beautiful old house overlooking sea.
Open: All Year (not Xmas)
01752 823860
Mrs Taylor
Rates fr: *£16.00*-**£16.00**.
Beds: 1D 1T 1S
Baths: 1 Shared

Kirland

National Grid Ref: SX0665

Lidcutt Farm, *Kirland, Bodmin, Cornwall, PL30 5BD.*
Pretty, peaceful, traditionally converted barn.
Open: All Year (not Xmas)
01208 72033
Mrs Coad
Rates fr: *£12.50*-**£13.00**.
Beds: 1D
Baths: 1 Shared

Ladock

National Grid Ref: SW8950

Bissick Old Mill, *Ladock, Truro, Cornwall, TR2 4PG.*
Converted C17th water mill.
Open: All Year (not Xmas)
01726 882557
Mrs Henderson
Rates fr: *£27.00*-**£27.00**.
Beds: 2D 1T 2S
Baths: 3 Ensuite 1 Shared
(10) (9)

Lamorna

National Grid Ref: SW4425

Tremeneth Hotel, *Lamorna, Penzance, Cornwall, TR19 6XL.*
Area of Outstanding Batural Beauty.
Open: All Year
01736 731367 Mr & Mrs Richards
Rates fr: *£16.00*-**£18.00**.
Beds: 5D 3T 1S
Baths: 6 Private 1 Shared
(2) (8)

Lanhydrock

National Grid Ref: SX0863

Royal Oak

Treffry Farm, *Treffry Lane, Lanhydrock, Bodmin, Cornwall, PL30 5AF.*
C18th slate-hung Georgian farmhouse.
Open: All Year (not Xmas/New Year)
Grades: ETB 2 Cr, High Comm, AA 4 Q, Select
01208 74405
Mrs Smith
Rates fr: *£20.00*-**£20.00**.
Beds: 1D 2T
Baths: 3 Private
(6) (3)

Lanivet

National Grid Ref: SX0364

Tremeere Manor, *Lanivet, Bodmin, Cornwall, PL30 5BG.*
Spacious farmhouse in lovely surroundings.
Open: Easter to Oct
01208 831513
Mrs Oliver
Rates fr: *£13.00*-**£14.00**.
Beds: 2D 1T
Baths: 1 Ensuite 1 Shared
(4)

Bokiddick Farm, *Lanivet, Bodmin, Cornwall, PL30 5HP.*
Excellent farmhouse accommodation, warmest of welcome.
Open: Easter to Oct
Grades: ETB Listed, High Comm
01208 831481 (also fax no)
Mrs Hugo
Rates fr: *£19.00*-**£25.00**.
Beds: 2D
Baths: 2 Ensuite
(5) (3)

Tremorvah, *Rosehill, Lanivet, Bodmin, Cornwall, PL30 5ES.*
Comfortable home, superb views, beautiful countryside.
Open: All Year (not Xmas)
01208 831379
Mrs Wheeler
Rates fr: *£14.00*-**£15.00**.
Beds: 2D 1T 1S
Baths: 2 Ensuite 2 Shared
(4)

Lanlivery

National Grid Ref: SX0759

Crown Inn, Royal Oak

Lynnwood, *Lanlivery, Bodmin, Cornwall, PL30 5BX.*
Spacious in beautiful, tranquil gardens.
Open: All Year
01208 872326 Mrs Penk
Rates fr: *£13.00*-**£13.00**.
Beds: 1F 1D 1T
Baths: 2 Shared
(5)

Poltip Cottage, *Lanlivery, Bodmin, Cornwall, PL30 5BX.*
Modernised private wing, picturesque, quiet country village.
Open: All Year
01208 872715
Mrs Bromley-Fox
Rates fr: *£17.50*-**£17.50**.
Beds: 1D
Baths: 1 Private
(2)

Lanner

National Grid Ref: SW7140

Lanner Inn, *Lanner, Redruth, Cornwall, TR16 6EH.*
Open: All Year (not Xmas)
01209 215611 Mr Wilson
Rates fr: *£16.00*-**£16.00**.
Beds: 2F 1D 1T
Baths: 2 Ensuite 1 Shared
(15)
A warm welcome awaits you at a family-run traditional country pub. Real fire, real locals, comfortable rooms. The ideal centre to tour West Cornwall.

Lanreath

National Grid Ref: SX1856

Rowan Lodge & Cottages, *Lanreath, Looe, Cornwall, PL13 2NX.*
Modern guest house, home cooking, picturesque village.
Open: All Year (not Xmas)
01503 220289 Mrs Gamble
Rates fr: *£13.00*-**£13.00**.
Beds: 2D 2T
Baths: 2 Private 1 Shared
(6)

Lansallos

National Grid Ref: SX1751

Lansallos Barton Farm, *Lansallos, Polperro, Looe, Cornwall, PL13 2PU.*
C17th farmhouse with coastal views.
Open: All Year (not Xmas)
01503 272192 Mrs Talling
Rates fr: *£12.00*-**£14.00**.
Beds: 1F 1D
Baths: 1 Shared
(4)

Launceston

National Grid Ref: SX3384

Country Man

***Lower Dutson Farm,** Dutson, Launceston, Cornwall, PL15 9SP.*
Open: All Year
Grades: ETB 2 Cr, Comm, AA 3 Q
01566 776456
Mrs Broad
Rates fr: *£14.00*-**£16.00**.
Beds: 1F 1D 1S
Baths: 1 Ensuite 1 Shared
(6)
Listed C17th Cornish longhouse. Ideal touring spot. Guests' own TV lounge. Lake and riverside walks with fishing available. Also self-catering. Golf and riding 2 ml.

***Country Friends,** St Leonards House, Polson Bridge, Launceston, Cornwall, PL15 9QR.*
C16th Devon longhouse - gourmet food.
Open: All Year
01566 774479
Mr & Mrs Mardon
Rates fr: *£18.00*-**£18.00**.
Beds: 1D 2T
Baths: 3 Ensuite
(10)

***White Horse Inn,** 14 Newport Square, Launceston, Cornwall, PL15 8EL.*
Open: All Year
01566 772084
Mr Hairs
Fax no: 01566 772090
Rates fr: *£15.00*-**£15.00**.
Beds: 2D 3T
Baths: 2 Shared
(20)
A fine public house with accommodation. Two large bars, separate restaurant open all day every day, evenings only. B&B all year round.

***Bradbridge Farm,** Boyton, Launceston, Cornwall, PL15 9RL.*
Beautiful, peaceful 400 acre farm. Ideal for walks, wildlife, fishing.
Open: Easter to October
01409 271264
Mrs Strout
Rates fr: *£16.00*-**£16.00**.
Beds: 1D 1T 1S

***Trethorne Leisure Farm,** Kennards House, Launceston, Cornwall, PL15 8QE.*
Comfortable farmhouse, homely relaxed atmosphere.
Open: All Year (not Xmas)
Grades: ETB 2 Cr
01566 86324 / 01566 86992
Mrs Davey
Rates fr: *£18.00*-**£18.00**.
Beds: 3F 2D 1T
Baths: 6 Private
(10)

***Newport Villa Guest House,** 34 St Stephens Hill, Launceston, Cornwall, PL15 8HW.*
Comfortable historic house near town.
Open: All Year
Grades: ETB Listed
01566 775242
Mrs Ackroyd
Rates fr: *£13.50*-**£13.50**.
Beds: 1F 1D 1T 2S
Baths: 1 Ensuite 2 Shared
(4)

Lerryn

National Grid Ref: SX1456

Ship Inn

***Mixton Farm,** Lerryn, Lostwithiel, Cornwall, PL22 0DE.*
Modern farmhouse converted from thatch.
Open: All Year
01208 872545 Mrs Beard
Rates fr: *£15.00*-**£15.00**.
Beds: 1F 1T 1D
Baths: 1 Shared
(8)

Liskeard

National Grid Ref: SX2564

Fountain Hotel

***Hotel Nebula,** 27 Higher Lux Street, Liskeard, Cornwall, PL14 3JU.*
Comfortable Grade II Listed hotel.
Open: All Year
01579 343989
Mr Rogers
Rates fr: *£23.00*-**£23.00**.
Beds: 2F 1D 2T 1S
Baths: 6 Private
(22)

***Elnor Guest House,** 1 Russell Street, Liskeard, Cornwall, PL14 4BP.*
Friendly, family guest house.
Open: All Year (not Xmas)
Grades: ETB 2 Cr, Comm, AA 3 Q
01579 342472
Mrs Strudwick
Fax no: 01579 345673
Rates fr: *£16.50*-**£16.50**.
Beds: 2F 2D 1T 4S
Baths: 7 Private 2 Shared
(6)

***Hyvue House,** Barras Cross, Liskeard, Cornwall, PL14 6BN.*
Quiet location edge of town.
Open: All Year (not Xmas)
01579 348175 Mrs Demmer
Rates fr: *£15.00*-**£17.50**.
Beds: 2D 1T **Baths:** 3 Private
(5) (6)

Right on the border? Look at the neighbouring county, too

Looe

National Grid Ref: SX2553

Harbour Moon, Ship, Swan, Ye Olde Salutation, Double Decker, Tom Sawyers

***Marwinthy Guest House,** East Cliff, East Looe, Cornwall, PL13 1DE.*
Open: All Year
01503 264382 Mr & Mrs Mawby
Rates fr: *£15.00*-**£16.00**.
Beds: 1F 2D 1T
Baths: 2 Private 1 Shared
(4)
Small friendly family-run guesthouse on coastal footpath overlooking beach and harbour mouth. In the 'Which' Good Bed & Breakfast Guide. Some ensuite.

***Sea Breeze Guest House,** Lower Chapel Street, East Looe, Cornwall, PL13 1AT.*
Comfortable & friendly, centrally situated.
Open: All Year
01503 263131 Mr Miles
Rates fr: *£15.00*-**£17.00**.
Beds: 4D 1T
Baths: 3 Private 1 Shared
(7) (2)

***Woodlands Guest House,** St Martins Road, East Looe, Cornwall, PL13 1LP.*
Comfortable Victorian house overlooking river.
Open: All Year
Grades: AA 4 Q, Select
01503 264405 Mr Faulkner
Rates fr: *£18.00*-**£18.00**.
Beds: 3D 1T 1S
Baths: 4 Ensuite
(5)

***Killarney Hotel,** Shutta Road, East Looe, Cornwall, PL13 1HW.*
Victorian licensed hotel overlooking harbour.
Open: All Year (not Xmas)
01503 262307
Mr Charnock
Rates fr: *£15.00*-**£15.00**.
Beds: 2F 6D 1T 1S
Baths: 6 Ensuite 1 Shared
(7) (3)

***Coombe Farm,** Widegates, Looe, Cornwall, PL13 1QN.*
Open: Mar to Nov
Grades: ETB 3 Cr, High Comm, AA 5 Q, Prem Select, RAC High Acclaim
01503 240223 Mr Low
Fax no: 01503 240895
Rates fr: *£23.00*-**£23.00**.
Beds: 4F 3D 3T
Baths: 10 Private
(5) (20)
Lovely country house in wonderful setting and grounds. Superb views to the sea. Log fires. Good food. Candlelit dining. Warm, friendly, relaxed atmosphere. Seasonal bargain breaks. Johansens and Ashley Courtenay Recommended.

Kantara Guest House, *7 Trelawney Terrace, Looe, Cornwall, PL13 2AG.*
Comfortable Edwardian town house.
Open: All Year
Grades: ETB 1 Cr, Comm, AA 2 Q, Recomm
01503 262093
Mr & Mrs Storer
Rates fr: *£12.00*-**£12.00**.
Beds: 3F 1D 1T 1S
Baths: 2 Shared
(1)

The Duchy, *Top Of West Looe Hill, Portlooe Barton, Looe, Cornwall, PL13 2HY.*
Comfortable family-run guest house.
Open: All Year
01503 262664 Mrs Robinson
Rates fr: *£14.00*-**£14.00**.
Beds: 3F 1D 1T 1S
Baths: 2 Private 1 Shared
(10)

Schooner Point Guest House, *1 Trelawney Terrace, Polperro Road, Looe, Cornwall, PL13 2AG.*
Family guest house, river views.
Open: All Year (not Xmas)
01503 262670
Mr & Mrs Neaves
Rates fr: *£12.00*-**£12.00**.
Beds: 1F 3D 2S
Baths: 2 Private 1 Shared
(2)

Stonerock Cottage, *Portuan Road, Hannafore, Looe, Cornwall, PL13 2DN.*
Old world modernised cottage.
Open: Easter to Nov
Grades: ETB 2 Cr, Comm
01503 263651
Mrs Tymm
Rates fr: *£15.00*-**£15.00**.
Beds: 1F 2D 1S
Baths: 1 Private 2 Shared
(1) (4)

Bucklawren Farm, *St Martin, Looe, Cornwall, PL13 1NZ.*
Good farmhouse cooking, glorious countryside.
Open: Mar to Oct
Grades: ETB 3 Cr, High CommRAC Acclaim
01503 240738
Mrs Henly
Rates fr: *£18.00*.
Beds: 3F 1D 1T
Baths: 5 Private
(6 months) (6)

Trevanion Hotel, *Hannafore Road, Looe, Cornwall, PL13 2DE.*
Large Victorian private hotel.
Open: All Year (not Xmas)
Grades: ETB 3 Cr, Comm
01503 262003
Mr French
Fax no: 01503 265408
Rates fr: *£22.00*-**£27.00**.
Beds: 2F 6D 1T 2S
Baths: 11 Private

Lostwithiel

National Grid Ref: SX1059

Earl of Chatham

Benthams, *Grenville Road, Lostwithiel, Cornwall, PL22 0RA.*
Large house with home cooking.
Open: All Year (not Xmas)
01208 872472
Mrs Sanders
Rates fr: *£17.00*-**£18.00**.
Beds: 2D 1T 1S
Baths: 1 Ensuite 1 Private 1 Shared
(10) (6)

Barngate Farm, *Hillhead, Lostwithiel, Cornwall, PL22 0HU.*
Cosy farmhouse, panoramic countryside views.
Open: Easter to Oct
01208 872461
Mrs Hutchings
Rates fr: *£13.00*-**£13.00**.
Beds: 2D 1S **Baths:** 1 Shared
(5) (3)

Ludgvan

National Grid Ref: SW5033

Menwidden Farm, *Ludgvan, Penzance, Cornwall, TR20 8BN.*
Comfortable farmhouse, centrally situated.
Open: Mar to Oct
Grades: ETB Listed, Approv, AA Listed
01736 740415
Mrs Blewett
Rates fr: *£15.00*-**£15.00**.
Beds: 1F 3D 1T
Baths: 2 Shared
(6)

Maenporth

National Grid Ref: SW7929

Red Lion Inn

West Bay Hotel, *Maenporth, Falmouth, Cornwall, TR11 5HP.*
Family, licensed, coastal, small hotel.
Open: All Year
Grades: ETB Listed
01326 250447
Mr & Mrs Skelley
Rates fr: *£15.00*-**£17.50**.
Beds: 1F 4D 1T 1S
Baths: 5 Private 1 Shared
(14)

Marazion

National Grid Ref: SW5130

Cutty Sark Hotel, *Marazion, Cornwall, TR18.*
Situated in beautiful Marazion.
Open: All Year
01736 710334
Mrs Stevens
Rates fr: *£15.00*-**£20.00**.
Beds: 2F 4D 4T 1S
Baths: 11 Ensuite
(20)

National Grid References are for villages, towns and cities - *not* for individual houses.

Chymorvah Private Hotel, *Marazion, Cornwall, TR17 0DQ.*
Cheerful, coastal Victorian private house.
Open: All Year (not Xmas)
Grades: ETB 3 Cr, RAC High Acclaim
01736 710497
Mrs Bull
Rates fr: *£25.00*-**£25.00**.
Beds: 3F 4D 1T 1S
Baths: 9 Private
(0) (12)

Marhamchurch

National Grid Ref: SS2203

Bullers Arms

Cann Orchard, *Marhamchurch, Stratton, Bude, Cornwall, EX23 9TD.*
Open: Easter to Dec
01288 352098
Mr Crocker
Rates fr: *£16.00*-**£20.00**.
Beds: 2D 1T
Baths: 2 Ensuite 1 Shared
(5) (4)
Expect a very warm welcome at our old country house, idyllically surrounded by stunning gardens and orchard. Situated 2 miles from spectacular North Cornish coastline.

Mawnan Smith

National Grid Ref: SW7728

Red Lion, Guiseppes

The White House, *28 Castle View Park, Mawnan Smith, Falmouth, Cornwall, TR11 5HB.*
Guesthouse near village/beaches, coastal country walks.
Open: All Year
01326 250768
Mrs Grant
Rates fr: *£18.00*-**£18.00**.
Beds: 1F 1D 1T 1S
Baths: 1 Private 2 Shared
(5) (4)

Carwinion Vean, *Grove Hill, Mawnan Smith, Falmouth, Cornwall, TR11 5ER.*
Large comfortable country house.
Open: All Year (not Xmas)
01326 250513 Mrs Spike
Rates fr: *£17.50*-**£17.50**.
Beds: 2F 2D 1T
Baths: 1 Ensuite 2 Shared
(5) (7)

Menheniot

National Grid Ref: SX2862

Trewint Farm, *Menheniot, Liskeard, Cornwall, PL14 3RE.*
C17th comfortable farmhouse, working farm.
Open: All Year (not Xmas)
Grades: ETB 2 Cr, Comm, RAC Listed
01579 347155 Mrs Rowe
Fax no: 01579 341155
Rates fr: *£16.00*-**£20.00**.
Beds: 1F 2D **Baths:** 3 Ensuite
(6)

Merrymeet

National Grid Ref: SX2765

Butcher's Arms

Homer House, *Merrymeet, Liskeard, Cornwall, PL14 3LS.*
Beautiful converted farmhouse.
Open: All Year
01579 345378 Mrs Beer
Rates fr: *£15.00*-**£20.00**.
Beds: 2D 1T **Baths:** 3 Private
(5) (6)

Mevagissey

National Grid Ref: SX0145

Captains Table, End of Harbour

Honeycomb House, *Polkirt Hill, Mevagissey, St Austell, Cornwall, PL26 6UR.*
Victorian house with superb views.
Open: All Year (not Xmas)
01726 842200 Mrs Pannell
Rates fr: *£14.00*-**£16.00**.
Beds: 2D 1T
Baths: 1 Private 1 Shared

Polrudden Farm, *Mevagissey, St Austell, Cornwall, PL26 6BJ.*
Idyllic coastal & country setting.
Open: All Year
Grades: ETB 1 Cr, Comm
01726 843213 / 842051
Mrs Bainbridge & J Jackson
Rates fr: *£17.50*-**£18.00**.
Beds: 1D 3T
Baths: 2 Ensuite 1 Shared
(12) (12)

Auraville, *Trevarth, The Drive, Mevagissey, St Austell, Cornwall, PL26 6RX.*
Quiet, peaceful house near harbour.
Open: All Year (not Xmas)
01726 843293
Mr & Mrs Barritt
Rates fr: *£14.50*-**£14.50**.
Beds: 2D 1S
Baths: 2 Shared
(4)

The lowest *double* rate per person is shown in *italics*.

Please respect a B&B's wishes regarding children, animals & smoking.

Tregorran Guest House, *Cliff Street, Mevagissey, St Austell, Cornwall, PL26 6QW.*
Detached modern split level house.
Open: Easter to Oct
01726 842319
Mr Lawrence
Rates fr: *£16.50*-**£16.50**.
Beds: 3F 2D 1T
(6) (6)

Middle Taphouse

National Grid Ref: SX1763

Highfield, *Middle Taphouse, Liskeard, Cornwall, PL14 4NE.*
Large comfortable family home.
Open: All Year
01579 320633
Mrs Sheer
Rates fr: *£12.00*-**£13.00**.
Beds: 1F 1T

Mitchell

National Grid Ref: SW8654

Mitchell Farm, *Mitchell, Newquay, Cornwall, TR8 5AX.*
C19th stone-built farmhouse.
Open: All Year (not Xmas)
01872 510657 Mr Sessions
Rates fr: *£13.50*-**£13.50**.
Beds: 2F 2D
Baths: 1 Shared
(10)

Morwenstow

National Grid Ref: SS2015

Dene Farm, *Morwenstow, Bude, Cornwall, EX23 9SL.*
Comfortable farmhouse surrounded with gardens.
Open: All Year (not Xmas)
01288 331330
Mrs Heard
Rates fr: *£16.00*-**£17.00**.
Beds: 1F 3D
Baths: 1 Ensuite 1 Shared
(6)

Meadow Park, *Lee Barton, Morwenstow, Bude, Cornwall, EX23 9ST.*
Superb views on family farm.
Open: All Year (not Xmas)
01288 331499
Mrs Hobbs
Rates fr: *£15.00*-**£15.00**.
Beds: 1F 1D 1T
Baths: 1 Shared
(0) (4)

Mount Edgcumbe

National Grid Ref: SX4552

Friary Manor Hotel, *Maker Heights, Mount Edgcumbe, Millbrook, Torpoint, Cornwall, PL10 1JB.*
Open: All Year
Grades: ETB 3 Cr, Comm
01752 822112 Mr & Mrs Wood
Fax no: 01752 822804
Rates fr: *£22.50*-**£29.00**.
Beds: 3F 3D 3T 2S
Baths: 6 Ensuite 1 Private
(25)
C18th manor house in secluded location above Plymouth Sound and Cawsand Bay. Large rooms, log fires, cosy bar, fixed price & a la carte restaurant.

Mousehole

National Grid Ref: SW4630

Carn Du Hotel, *Mousehole, Penzance, Cornwall, TR19 6SS.*
Licensed hotel with magnificent views.
Open: All Year
Grades: ETB 3 Cr, AA 2 St
01736 731233
Mr Field
Rates fr: *£25.00*-**£25.00**.
Beds: 3D 3T 1S
Baths: 7 Private
(12)

The Old Coastguard Hotel, *Mousehole, Penzance, Cornwall, TR19 6PR.*
Lively pub & seafood restaurant.
Open: Feb to Dec
01736 731222
Rates fr: *£18.00*-**£18.00**.
Beds: 1F 7D 2T
Baths: 10 Ensuite
(12)

Mullion

National Grid Ref: SW6721

Old Inn, Mullion Cove Hotel

Tregaddra Farmhouse, *Cury, Mullion, Helston, Cornwall, TR12 7BB.*
Open: All Year
Grades: ETB 3 Cr, High Comm, AA 4 Q, Select
01326 240235 (also fax no)
Mrs Lugg
Rates fr: *£18.50*-**£18.50**.
Beds: 1F 3D 1T 1S
Baths: 5 Private 1 Shared
(10)
Beautifully furnished farmhouse (working farm). Pretty ensuite bedrooms, boot and clothes drying. Winter breaks, log fires, Aga cooking. Set in Area of Outstanding Natural Beauty.

Trenance Farmhouse, *Mullion, Helston, Cornwall, TR12 7HB.*
Victorian farmhouse 0.25 mile coastal footpath.
Open: Easter to Oct
Grades: ETB 2 Cr, Comm
01326 240639
Mr & Mrs Tyler-Street
Rates fr: *£16.00*-**£16.00**.
Beds: 3D 1T **Baths:** 4 Private
(8) (8)

Lower Meres, *Laflouder Lane, Mullion, Helston, Cornwall, TR12 7HT.*
Stunning views. Secluded cove. Relax! **Open:** All Year (not Xmas)
01326 240621 Mrs Wilkinson
Rates fr: *£15.00*-**£15.00**.
Beds: 1F 1D 1T
Baths: 2 Ensuite 1 Shared
(10) (5)

Mullion Cove Hotel, *Mullion Cove, Mullion, Helston, Cornwall, TR12 7EP.*
Stunning setting on coastal footpath. **Open:** All Year
Grades: ETB 3 Cr, RAC 2 St
01326 240328 Mrs Davis
Fax no: 01326 240998
Rates fr: *£25.00*-**£25.00**.
Beds: 1F 14D 10T 10S
Baths: 24 Private 6 Shared
(40)

Mullion Cove

National Grid Ref: SW6617

Criggan Mill, *Mullion Cove, Helston, Cornwall, TR12 7EU.*
Self-contained suites in timber lodge.
Open: Easter to Oct
Grades: ETB Listed
01326 240496 Mrs Storey
Rates fr: *£13.00*-**£15.00**.
Beds: 1F 1D 1T **Baths:** 3 Ensuite

Newquay

National Grid Ref: SW8161

Red Lion, The Harvester

Alicia, *136 Henver Road, Newquay, Cornwall, TR7 3EQ.*
Open: Easter to Nov
01637 874328 Mrs Limer
Rates fr: *£13.00*-**£16.00**.
Beds: 2F 3D 1T 1S
Baths: 2 Ensuite 1 Private1 Shared
(6)
Enjoy Mike and Alison's hospitality for a superb holiday. Excellent food and home comforts are our priority. Why not try the best in the west?

Stratford House, *31 Berry Road, Newquay, Cornwall, TR7 1AS.*
Large Victorian private house.
Open: All Year
01637 875603 Mrs Clark
Rates fr: *£12.00*-**£12.00**.
Beds: 1F 3D 1T 1S
Baths: 5 Ensuite 1 Shared
(2)

Chichester Guest House, *14 Bay View Terrace, Newquay, Cornwall, TR7 2LR.*
Comfortable, centrally situated guest house.
Open: All Year (not Xmas)
Grades: ETB Listed
01637 874216 Miss Harper
Rates fr: *£13.00*-**£13.00**.
Beds: 1F 2D 2T 2S
Baths: 5 Ensuite 1 Shared
(6)

Cotehele Lodge, *84 Tower Road, Newquay, Cornwall, TR7 1LY.*
Large detached guest house, car park.
Open: Mar to Oct
01637 873421
Rates fr: *£15.00*-**£20.00**.
Beds: 2F 4D
Baths: 4 Ensuite 2 Shared
(8)

Cotehele Lodge, *84 Tower Road, Newquay, Cornwall, TR7 1LY.*
Large guest house, own car park.
Open: All Year (not Xmas)
01637 873421 Mrs Drysdale
Rates fr: *£15.00*.
Beds: 2F 4D
Baths: 4 Ensuite 2 Shared
(8)

Cliffside Hotel, *The Crescent, Newquay, Cornwall, TR7 1DT.*
Comfortable modern family hotel.
Open: Easter to Jan
01637 872897 Mrs Machin
Rates fr: *£15.00*-**£15.00**.
Beds: 5F 15D 15T 5S
Baths: 37 Ensuite 1 Shared
(10)

Padstow

National Grid Ref: SW9175

Old Custon House

Cross House Hotel, *Church Street, Padstow, Cornwall, PL28 8BG.*
Comfortable, friendly, family-run hotel. **Open:** All Year
01841 532391 Miss Gidlow
Rates fr: *£22.00*-**£30.00**.
Beds: 1F 5D 1T
Baths: 4 Ensuite 3 Shared
(5) (4)

Newlands Hotel, *Trevone Bay, Padstow, Cornwall, PL28 8QJ.*
Small licensed hotel.
Open: All Year **Grades:** AA 3 Q
01841 520469 Mrs Philpott
Rates fr: *£18.50*-**£15.00**.
Beds: 1F 6D 3T 1S
Baths: 9 Private 1 Shared
(15)

Khandalla, *Sarahs Lane, Padstow, Cornwall, PL28 8.*
Large Victorian private house.
Open: All Year
01841 532961 Mrs Hair
Rates fr: *£16.00*-**£16.00**.
Beds: 1F 1D 1S
Baths: 2 Ensuite 1 Shared
(3)

Par

National Grid Ref: SX0753

Colwith Farm, *Par, Cornwall, PL24 2TU.*
200-acre family-run working farm.
Open: Easter to Sep
01208 872201
Mrs Dustow
Rates fr: *£14.00*-**£18.00**.
Beds: 2D 1T **Baths:** 1 Shared
(7)

Pelynt

National Grid Ref: SX2055

Jubilee Inn

Little Larnick Farm, *Pelynt, Looe, Cornwall, PL13 2NB.*
Spacious character farmhouse.
Open: Feb to Nov
Grades: ETB 2 Cr
01503 262837 (also fax no)
Mrs Eastley
Rates fr: *£17.00*-**£19.00**.
Beds: 1F 1D 1T
Baths: 3 Private
(3)

Colwells House, *Pelynt, Looe, Cornwall, PL13 2JX.*
Cornish family-run country house.
Open: All Year (not Xmas)
01503 220201 Mrs Harvey
Rates fr: *£13.50*.
Beds: 3D 1T
Baths: 1 Private 2 Shared
(6)

Pendeen

National Grid Ref: SW3834

North Inn

The Old Count House, *Boscaswell Downs, Pendeen, Penzance, Cornwall, TR19 7ED.*
Lovely old detatched house, quiet village. **Open:** Apr to Oct
01736 788058 Mrs Dymond
Rates fr: *£14.00*-**£14.00**.
Beds: 1F 1D **Baths:** 1 Shared
(2) (2)

Trewelland Manor Farm, *Pendeen, Penzance, Cornwall, TR19 7SU.*
Relaxed, friendly atmosphere. Comfortable farmhouse.
Open: All Year (not Xmas)
01736 788526 Mrs Bailey
Rates fr: *£16.00*-**£18.00**.
Beds: 2D 1T
Baths: 1 Ensuite 1 Shared

All rates are subject to alteration at the owners' discretion.

Pentewan

National Grid Ref: SX0147

Peruppa Farm, *Pentewan, St Austell, Cornwall, PL26 6EJ.*
Modern comfortable farmhouse near sea. **Open:** All Year
01726 843286 Mrs Nancarrow
Rates fr: *£15.00*-**£20.00**.
Beds: 1F 3D 1T **Baths:** 1 Shared
(6) (4)

Pentire

National Grid Ref: SW7881

Corisande Manor Hotel, *Riverside Avenue, Pentire, Newquay, Cornwall, TR7 1PL.*
Unique Victorian Austrian turreted design. **Open:** May to Oct
01637 872042 Mr Painter
Rates fr: *£20.00*-**£20.00**.
Beds: 3F 8D 3T 5S
Baths: 16 Ensuite 1 Private 2 Shared
(3) (30)

Penzance

National Grid Ref: SW4630

Bosuns Locker, Turks Head, Coalstreamer

Lynwood Guest House, *41 Morrab Road, Penzance, Cornwall, TR18 4EX.*
Open: All Year
Grades: ETB 2 CrRAC Listed
01736 65871 (also fax no)
Mrs Stacey
Rates fr: *£11.00*-**£11.00**.
Beds: 2F 2D 1T 1S
Baths: 2 Ensuite 3 Shared
Family-run Victorian guest house. Internationally recommended for good food, cleanliness. Close to all amenities. Ideally situated for visiting Lands End and St Michael Mount.

Kimberley House, *10 Morrab Rd, Penzance, Cornwall, TR18 4EZ.*
Large Victorian private house.
Open: All Year (not Xmas)
Grades: ETB Listed, AA Listed
01736 62727 Mr & Mrs Mudway
Rates fr: *£14.00*-**£14.00**.
Beds: 2F 2D 3T 2S **Baths:** 3 Shared
(5) (4)

Glencree Private Hotel, *2 Mennaye Road, Penzance, Cornwall, TR18 4NG.*
Open: Mar to Oct
Grades: ETB 2 Cr, Approv
01736 62026 (also fax no)
Mr Hodgetts
Rates fr: *£13.00*-**£16.00**.
Beds: 3F 4D 2S
Baths: 7 Private 1 Shared
(3)
Victorian Hotel 100 yards off seafront. Spacious rooms, some with sea views and four poster beds. Highly recommended for its comfort, cleanliness, excellent food and friendly personal service.

Carnson House Private Hotel, *East Terrace, Market Jew Street, Penzance, Cornwall, TR18 2TD.*
Centrally located, friendly small hotel. **Open:** All Year
Grades: ETB 2 Cr, RAC Listed
01736 65589 / 365589
Mr & Mrs Hilder
Rates fr: *£15.00*-**£16.00**.
Beds: 3D 2T 3S
Baths: 2 Private 1 Shared
(12)

Keigwin Hotel, *Alexandra Road, Penzance, Cornwall, TR18 4LZ.*
Open: All Year (not Xmas)
Grades: ETB 3 Cr, Approv, RAC Listed
01736 63930
Mr & Mrs Emons
Rates fr: *£13.00*-**£13.00**.
Beds: 1F 4D 1T 2S
Baths: 5 Private 1 Shared
Smoke free environment. Comfortable and quiet. Much recommended, family-run. Close to all amenities. Excellent cooking with fresh produce. On street parking.

Woodstock Guest House, *29 Morrab Road, Penzance, Cornwall, TR18 4EZ.*
On the Coastal footpath.
Open: All Year
Grades: ETB 2 Cr, AA 3 Q
01736 69049
Mr & Mrs Hopkins
Rates fr: *£11.00*-**£11.00**.
Beds: 2F 2D 2T 2S
Baths: 3 Private 2 Shared

Ocean View, *Chayndour Cliffe, Penzance, Cornwall, TR18 3LQ.*
Charming, comfortable seafront guest house.
Open: All Year (not Xmas)
01736 51770 Mrs Wenn
Rates fr: *£13.00*-**£17.00**.
Beds: 1F 1D 1T
Baths: 2 Shared
(3)

Trewella Guest House, *18 Mennaye Road, Penzance, Cornwall, TR18 4NG.*
Highly recommended friendly guesthouse.
Open: Mar to Oct
Grades: AA 3 Q
01736 63818
Mr & Mrs Glenn
Rates fr: *£12.50*-**£13.50**.
Beds: 2F 4D 2S
Baths: 4 Ensuite 1 Shared
(3)

Trevelyan Hotel, *16 Chapel Street, Penzance, Cornwall, TR18 4AN.*
Comfortable hotel, centrally situated. **Open:** All Year
01736 62494
Fitzgerald
Rates fr: *£15.00*-**£15.00**.
Beds: 3F 7D 3T 1S
Baths: 6 Private 2 Shared

Wymering Guest House, *15 Regent Square, Penzance, Cornwall, TR18 4BG.*
Regency guest house.
Open: All Year
01736 62126 Mrs Chinn
Rates fr: *£10.00*-**£10.00**.
Beds: 2F 2D 1T 1S **Baths:** 2 Shared

Menwidden Farm, *Ludgvan, Penzance, Cornwall, TR20 8BN.*
Comfortable farmhouse, centrally situated.
Open: Mar to Oct
Grades: ETB Listed, Approv, AA Listed
01736 740415
Mrs Blewett
Rates fr: *£15.00*-**£15.00**.
Beds: 1F 3D 1T **Baths:** 2 Shared
(6)

Penalva Guest House, *Alexandra Road, Penzance, Cornwall, TR18 4LZ.*
Large Victorian guest house.
Open: All Year
Grades: ETB 3 Cr, Approv, AA 3 Q
01736 69060
Mrs Buswell
Rates fr: *£11.00*-**£11.00**.
Beds: 1F 2D 1T 1S
Baths: 4 Private 1 Shared
(2)

Perranporth

National Grid Ref: SW7554

Bolingey Inn

Tremore, *Liskey Hill Crescent, Perranporth, Cornwall, TR6 0HP.*
Open: All Year (not Xmas)
01872 573537 M Crofts
Rates fr: *£15.00*-**£15.00**.
Beds: 3D 1T 2S
Baths: 2 Shared
(8) (6)
A warm welcome awaits in our well-established and highly recommended guest house. Off-road parking. Ideal for touring. Excellent value. Try us, you won't be disappointed.

The Morgans Of Perranporth, *Grannys Lane, Perranporth, Cornwall, TR6 0HB.*
Superior guest house overlooking Atlantic Ocean.
Open: All Year (not Xmas)
Grades: ETB 3 Cr, Comm
01872 573904 Mrs Morgan
Fax no: 01872 572425
Rates fr: *£12.50*-**£12.50**.
Beds: 2F 4D 2T 1S
Baths: 3 Private 1 Shared
(12) (6)

Cliffside Hotel, *Cliff Road, Perranporth, Cornwall, TR6 0DR.*
Small family hotel overlooking beach. **Open:** Mar to Oct
01872 573297
Rates fr: *£16.00*-**£14.50**.
Beds: 2F 2D 1T 3S

***Cellar Cove Hotel,** Droskyn Way, Perranporth, Cornwall, TR6 0DS.*
Family-run, friendly licensed hotel.
Open: All Year
01872 572110 (also fax no)
Mrs Hunley
Rates fr: *£15.00*-**£15.00**.
Beds: 7F 4D 1T 2S
Baths: 13 Ensuite
(0) (20)

Perranuthnoe

National Grid Ref: SW5329

Victorian Inn, Bertie Woosters Restaurant

***Ednovean House,** Perranuthnoe, Penzance, Cornwall, TR20 9LZ.*
Open: All Year
Grades: ETB 3 Cr, AA 3 Q
01736 711071
Mr & Mrs Compton
Rates fr: *£19.00*-**£21.00**.
Beds: 1F 4D 2T 2S
Baths: 6 Private 1 Shared
(7) (12)
Lovely Victorian house set in its own peaceful gardens with wonderful views over Mounts Bay and St Michaels Mount. Ideal for a very restful holiday.

***Ednovean Farm,** Perranuthnoe, Penzance, Cornwall, TR20 9LZ.*
Delightful C17th barn - flagstones, antiques. **Open:** All Year
Grades: AA 4 Q
01736 711883
Mr & Mrs Taylor
Rates fr: *£17.00*-**£20.00**.
Beds: 3D
Baths: 2 Private 1 Shared
(12) (6)

Perranwell Station

National Grid Ref: SW7839

Royal Oak

***Shepherds,** Greenwith Road, Perranwell Station, Truro, Cornwall, TR3 7RT.*
Quiet house in small village.
Open: All Year
01872 863828
Mrs James
Rates fr: *£15.00*-**£15.00**.
Beds: 2F
Baths: 1 Shared
(5)

Polbathic

National Grid Ref: SX3456

***Old Mill House,** Polbathic, Torpoint, Cornwall, PL11 3HA.*
300-year-old riverside mill.
Open: All Year
01503 230596
Mr Thompson
Rates fr: *£12.50*-**£12.50**.
Beds: 3F 4D 1T 2S
Baths: 3 Shared
(12)

Polperro

National Grid Ref: SX2050

Old Mill House, Lugger Inn, Russell Inn

***Penryn House Hotel,** The Coombes, Polperro, Looe, Cornwall, PL13.*
Open: All Year
Grades: ETB 3 Cr, RAC Listed
01503 272157 Ms Kay
Fax no: 01503 273055
Rates fr: *£19.00*-**£21.00**.
Beds: 10D 2T
Baths: 10 Ensuite 2 Shared
(0) (14)
Charming Victorian hotel in village centre; bedrooms ensuite, and car park. Relax in our comfortable lounge and candlelit restaurant. Peaceful setting, friendly atmosphere, personal service.

***Landaviddy Manor,** Landaviddy Lane, Polperro, Looe, Cornwall, PL13 2RT.*
C18th manor house in beautiful gardens.
Open: Mar to Sep
Grades: AA 4 Q, Select
01503 272210 (also fax no)
Mr Rowe
Rates fr: *£23.00*-**£30.00**.
Beds: 6D 1T
Baths: 5 Ensuite 2 Private
(14) (8)

***Claremont Hotel,** The Coombes, Polperro, Looe, Cornwall, PL13 2RG.*
Open: All Year
Grades: ETB 3 Cr, AA 1 St, RAC 1 St
01503 272241 Mr Couturier
Rates fr: *£17.00*-**£17.00**.
Beds: 2F 7D 1T 1S
Baths: 10 Private 1 Shared
(16)
Close to the harbour of this beautiful village. Hospitable and comfortable. Seafood restaurant open April - October. Secluded beaches, fishing, superb walks and places of interest nearby. Car park.

***Corner Ways,** Landaviddy Lane, Polperro, Looe, Cornwall, PL13 2RT.*
Modern comfortable guest house.
Open: All Year
Grades: ETB Listed
01503 272324 Mrs Puckey
Rates fr: *£15.00*-**£15.00**.
Beds: 1F 1D 1T **Baths:** 2 Shared

Polruan

National Grid Ref: SX1250

***Holly House,** 18 Fore Street, Polruan, Fowey, Cornwall, PL23 1PQ.*
4 minutes from passenger ferry to Fowey.
Open: All Year (not Xmas)
01726 870478 Mr & Mrs Blamey
Rates fr: *£13.50*-**£13.50**.
Beds: 3T **Baths:** 1 Shared
(2)

Polzeath

National Grid Ref: SW9378

***Pentire View,** Polzeath, Wadebridge, Cornwall, PL27 6TB.*
Large Victorian house near beach.
Open: All Year (not Xmas)
01208 862484 Mrs Pashley
Rates fr: *£13.00*-**£13.00**.
Beds: 1F 3T 2S **Baths:** 1 Shared

Ponsanooth

National Grid Ref: SW7536

Old Vicarage Stithians

***Gadles Farm,** Laity Moor, Ponsanooth, Truro, Cornwall, TR3 7HS.*
Comfortable farmhouse with Panoramic views.
Open: Apr to Oct
Grades: ETB Listed, AA Listed
01872 863214 Mrs Bennetts
Rates fr: *£13.00*-**£13.00**.
Beds: 2F 1D 1S **Baths:** 1 Shared
(4)

Ponsongath

National Grid Ref: SW7517

***Wych Elm,** Ponsongath, Helston, Cornwall, TR12 6SQ.*
Immaculate, pretty, country cottage with pool.
Open: All Year (not Xmas)
01326 280576 Mrs Whitaker
Rates fr: *£14.00*-**£16.00**.
Beds: 1T
Baths: 1 Ensuite
(2)

Port Isaac

National Grid Ref: SW9980

***St Andrews Hotel,** Port Isaac, Cornwall, PL29 3SG.*
Spectacular views over the Heritage Coast. **Open:** All Year
01208 880240 (also fax no)
Mr Slack
Rates fr: *£17.00*-**£17.00**.
Beds: 1F 4D 2T 2S
Baths: 9 Ensuite 1 Shared
(12) (8)

***The Homestead,** Tintagel Terrace, Port Isaac, Cornwall, PL29 3SE.*
Detached bungalow with sea views. **Open:** All Year
01208 880064 Mrs Corrigan
Rates fr: *£14.00*-**£14.00**.
Beds: 2D 1T **Baths:** 3 Ensuite
(4)

***Bay Hotel,** 1 The Terrace, Port Isaac, Cornwall, PL29 3SG.*
Purpose-built late-Victorian hotel.
Open: Easter to Oct
Grades: AA 2 Q, RAC Listed
01208 880380 Mr Andrews
Rates fr: *£18.00*-**£18.00**.
Beds: 4F 3D 1T 2S
Baths: 4 Private 2 Shared
(10)

Fairholme, *30 Trewetha Lane, Port Isaac, Cornwall,* *PL29 3RW.*
Large, immaculate, comfortable character property.
Open: All Year (not Xmas)
01208 880397 Mrs Von-Lintzgy
Rates fr: *£15.00*-**£15.00**.
Beds: 2F 3D 1T
Baths: 2 Private 2 Shared

Porthcurno

National Grid Ref: SW3822

Sea View House, *The Valley, Porthcurno, Penzance, Cornwall,* *TR19 6JX.*
Open: Easter to Oct
01736 810638 Mr & Mrs Christ
Rates fr: *£15.00*-**£22.00**.
Beds: 1F 3D 2T 1S
Baths: 1 Ensuite 2 Shared
Comfortable bedsits. All facilities. Near coast path and Minack Outdoor Theatre. Walkers welcome, including their dogs. Delicious cream teas available in tea room. Good home cooking.

Porthleven

National Grid Ref: SW6225

Seefar, *Peverell Terrace, Porthleven, Helston, Cornwall,* *TR13 9DZ.*
Traditional Cornish Victorian mine captain's house.
Open: All Year **Grades:** ETB 1 Cr
01326 573778 Mr & Mrs Hallam
Rates fr: *£14.00*-**£14.00**.
Beds: 3D 1T 2S **Baths:** 3 Shared

Portloe

National Grid Ref: SW7339

Tregain, *Portloe, Truro, Cornwall,* *TR2 5QU.*
Cottage accommodation, peaceful fishing village.
Open: All Year
01872 501252 (also fax no)
Mrs Holdsworth
Rates fr: *£19.00*-**£19.00**.
Beds: 1T 1S **Baths:** 1 Shared

Portreath

National Grid Ref: SW6545

Bassett Arms, Tabbs, Waterfront Inn

Portreath Sycamore Lodge, *Guest House, Primrose Terrace, Portreath, Redruth, Cornwall,* *TR16 4JS.*
Delightful old house, peaceful situation.
Open: All Year
01209 842784 Mr & Mrs Allen
Rates fr: *£16.00*-**£16.00**.
Beds: 1D 1T 1S **Baths:** 2 Shared

Suhaili, *14 Forth-an-Nance, Portreath, Redruth, Cornwall,* *TR16 4NQ.*
Friendly & comfortable accommodation.
Open: All Year (not Xmas)
01209 842110 Mrs Symonds
Rates fr: *£14.00*-**£16.00**.
Beds: 2D 1T **Baths:** 3 Private

Cliff House, *The Square, Portreath, Redruth, Cornwall,* *TR16 4LB.*
200-year-old whitewashed cottage.
Open: All Year (not Xmas)
Grades: AA 2 Q
01209 842008 Mrs Healan
Rates fr: *£17.50*-**£17.50**.
Beds: 1D 1T 2S
Baths: 2 Ensuite 2 Private

Bensons, *1 The Hillside, Portreath, Redruth, Cornwall,* *TR16 4LL.*
Beautiful accommodation - panoramic sea views.
Open: All Year
01209 842534 Mrs Benson
Rates fr: *£17.50*-**£25.00**.
Beds: 2D 2T **Baths:** 4 Ensuite

Portscatho

National Grid Ref: SW8735

Tregerein Guest House, *New Road, Portscatho, Truro, Cornwall,* *TR2 5HD.*
Large Victorian house.
Open: All Year
01872 580336 Mr Evans
Rates fr: *£14.00*-**£14.00**.
Beds: 1F 2D 2T **Baths:** 1 Private

Poughill

National Grid Ref: SS2207

Lower Northcott Farm, *Poughill, Bude, Cornwall,* *EX23 7EL.*
Georgian farmhouse with outstanding views 0.75 mile from Heritage Coastline.
Open: All Year
Grades: ETB 2 Cr, Comm, AA 3 Q, Recomm
01288 352350 Mrs Trewin
Rates fr: *£17.00*-**£17.00**.
Beds: 2F 2D 1T 1S
Baths: 5 Private

Praa Sands

National Grid Ref: SW5827

Wellow Rock Inn

Boslowen-Mor, *Castle Drive, Praa Sands, Penzance, Cornwall,* *TR20 9TF.*
Modern bungalow.
Open: June to Oct
01736 762223 Mrs Jennings
Rates fr: *£10.50*-**£12.00**.
Beds: 2D 1T
Baths: 1 Ensuite 1 Shared

Praze-an-Beeble

National Grid Ref: SW6335

St Michael Inn, Barripper

Halgarrack Farm, *Praze-an-Beeble, Camborne, Cornwall,* *TR14 0PH.*
Large rooms, quiet, open countryside.
Open: All Year (not Xmas)
01209 831254
Mrs Fowler
Rates fr: *£14.00*-**£20.00**.
Beds: 1D 1T
Baths: 1 Shared

Quintrell Downs

National Grid Ref: SW8460

Manuels Farm, *Quintrell Downs, Newquay, Cornwall,* *TR8 4NY.*
C17th traditional farmhouse.
Open: All Year (not Xmas)
Grades: ETB 2 Cr, High Comm, AA 4 Q
01637 873577 (also fax no)
Mrs Wilson
Rates fr: *£19.00*-**£19.00**.
Beds: 1F 2D 1S
Baths: 1 Private 2 Shared

Redruth

National Grid Ref: SW6942

Lansdowne House, *42 Clinton Road, Redruth, Cornwall,* *TR15 2QE.*
Architecturally unusual detached Victorian house.
Open: All Year
01209 216002 (also fax no)
Mrs Kilpatrick
Rates fr: *£16.50*-**£16.50**.
Beds: 2F 4D 3T 2S
Baths: 2 Ensuite 2 Shared

Lower Poldice Cottage, *St Day, Redruth, Cornwall,* *TR16 5PP.*
Modern, secluded, country cottage, central.
Open: All Year (not Xmas)
01209 820438
Mrs Oates
Rates fr: *£13.00*-**£13.00**.
Beds: 2D 1T
Baths: 1 Shared

Rejerrah

National Grid Ref: SW8056

Lower Treludderow Farm, *Rejerrah, Newquay, Cornwall,* *TR8 5QE.*
Comfortable, homely farmhouse.
Open: Jun to Sep
01637 830392
Rates fr: *£12.00*-**£16.00**.
Beds: 1F 1D **Baths:** 1 Shared

Rock

National Grid Ref: SW9476

Silvermead, *Rock, Wadebridge, Cornwall,* *PL27 6LB.*
Open: All Year
Grades: ETB 3 Cr, Comm
01208 862425
Mrs Martin
Rates fr: *£16.50*-**£16.50**.
Beds: 2F 2D 2T 3S
Baths: 5 Private 1 Shared
(9)
Ten bedroom family-run hotel overlooking Camel Estuary adjoining St Enodoc golf courses. 2 minutes walk to beach, sailing club. Most rooms ensuite. Licensed

Roskarnon House Hotel, *Rock, Wadebridge, Cornwall,* *PL27 6LD.*
Edwardian hotel, overlooking estuary.
Open: Easter to Oct
Grades: RAC 2 St
01208 862785
Mr Veall
Rates fr: *£19.50*-**£19.50**.
Beds: 3F 6D 2T 1S
Baths: 9 Private

Rocky Valley

National Grid Ref: SX0789

Trevillett Mill Trout Farm, *Rocky Valley, Tintagel, Cornwall,* *PL34 0BB.*
Interesting 1472 watermill beside river.
Open: All Year (not Xmas)
01840 770564
Mr Savage
Rates fr: *£15.00*.
Beds: 1F 3D

Ruan High Lanes

National Grid Ref: SW9039

Tregongon House, *Ruan High Lanes, Truro, Cornwall,* *TR2 5LD.*
Lovely Listed country house, panoramic views.
Open: Easter to Nov
01872 501708
Mrs Scullion
Rates fr: *£18.00*-**£20.00**.
Beds: 1D 1T
Baths: 2 Ensuite
(10) (4)

Trenestall Farm, *Ruan High Lanes, Truro, Cornwall,* *TR2 5LX.*
Family-run farm, beautiful countryside, close to sea.
Open: Feb to Nov
01872 501259
Mrs Palmer
Rates fr: *£14.00*-**£14.00**.
Beds: 1D 2T
Baths: 2 Shared
(6)

Ruan Minor

National Grid Ref: SW7115

Old Cellars Restaurant (Cadgwith)

Treworder Farm, *Ruan Minor, Helston, Cornwall,* *TR12 7JL.*
Open: May to Sep
01326 290970
Mr & Mrs Rosindale
Rates fr: *£15.00*-**£18.00**.
Beds: 1D
Baths: 1 Private
(5) (6)
Converted barn close to spectacular National Trust coastline. Spacious room overlooking garden with panoramic view. Excellent breakfast with homemade bread. 2 rooms available if required.

Saltash

National Grid Ref: SX4258

Notter Bridge Inn, Boatman Inn

The Old Cottage, *Barkers Hill, St Stephens, Saltash, Cornwall,* *PL12 4QA.*
Charming, old, beamed cottage.
Open: All Year
01752 845260
Mrs Plant
Rates fr: *£13.00*-**£13.00**.
Beds: 1D 2S
Baths: 1 Shared
(2)

Seaton

National Grid Ref: SX3054

Blue Haven Hotel, *Looe Hill, Seaton, Torpoint, Cornwall,* *PL11 3JQ.*
Small select hotel, panoramic sea-views.
Open: All Year
01503 250310
Mrs White
Rates fr: *£17.00*-**£20.00**.
Beds: 1F 2D 1T
Baths: 4 Private

Sennen

National Grid Ref: SW3525

Sunny Bank Hotel, *Seaview Hill, Sennen, Lands End, Penzance, Cornwall,* *TR19 7AR.*
Comfortable detached hotel, close beaches.
Open: Jan to Nov
Grades: AA Listed
01736 871278
Mr & Mrs Comber
Rates fr: *£13.00*-**£13.00**.
Beds: 2F 5D 2T 2S
Baths: 2 Ensuite 2 Shared
(20)

Lyonesse Guest House, *Sennen, Penzance, Cornwall,* *TR19 7AD.*
Large converted rectory. Superb views. **Open:** All Year
01736 871207 / 871564
Mrs Harrison
Rates fr: *£15.00*-**£15.00**.
Beds: 4F 2T 1D 1 S
Baths: 1 Shared
(20)

Sithney

National Grid Ref: SW6328

Parc-An-Ithan, *Sithney, Helston, Cornwall,* *TR13 0RN.*
Quiet, comfortable, country guest house. **Open:** All Year
01326 572565
Mrs Skeggs
Rates fr: *£17.00*-**£19.00**.
Beds: 4D
Baths: 7 Ensuite
(14)

St Agnes

National Grid Ref: SW7250

Driftwood Spars

Driftwood Spars Hotel, *Trevaunance Cove, St Agnes, Cornwall,* *TR5 0RT.*
Delightful old inn, enormous beams.
Open: All Year
Grades: ETB 3 Cr, Comm
01872 552428 / 553323 (also fax no)
Mrs Treleaven
Rates fr: *£29.00*-**£29.00**.
Beds: 1F 7D 1T
Baths: 9 Ensuite
(100)

Jade Cottage, *Goonlaze, St Agnes, Cornwall,* *TR5 0XL.*
Beamed cottage. 0.5 miles sea, village.
Open: All Year (not Xmas)
01872 553558
Mrs Benson
Rates fr: *£13.50*-**£15.00**.
Beds: 1D 1T 1S
Baths: 1 Ensuite 1 Shared
(3)

St Austell

National Grid Ref: SX0252

Polgooth Inn

Poltarrow Farm, *St Mewan, St Austell, Cornwall,* *PL26 7DR.*
Comfortable farmhouse, centrally positioned.
Open: All Year (not Xmas)
Grades: ETB 2 Cr, High Comm, AA 4 Q, Select
01726 67111 Mrs Nancarrow
Rates fr: *£19.00*-**£20.00**.
Beds: 1F 3D 1T
Baths: 5 Private

St Day

National Grid Ref: SW7342

Lower Poldice Cottage, *St Day, Redruth, Cornwall,* TR16 5PP.
Modern, secluded, country cottage, central.
Open: All Year (not Xmas)
01209 820438 Mrs Oates
Rates fr: *£13.00*-**£13.00**.
Beds: 2D 1T **Baths:** 1 Shared
(6)

St Dominick

National Grid Ref: SX4067

Who'd Have Thought It Inn

Burcombe Farm, *St Dominick, Saltash, Cornwall,* PL12 6SH.
Large farmhouse with wonderful views.
Open: Mar to Oct
Grades: RAC Listed
01579 350217 Mr & Mrs Batten
Fax no: 01579 50105
Rates fr: *£17.50*-**£20.00**.
Beds: 1D 2T
Baths: 2 Private 1 Shared
(5)

St Erme

National Grid Ref: SW8449

Trevispian Vean Farm Guest Hse, *St Erme, Truro, Cornwall,* TR4 9BL.
Secluded, comfortable farmhouse.
Open: Easter to Oct
01872 79514 Mr & Mrs Dymond
Rates fr: *£16.00*-**£18.00**.
Beds: 3F 6D 3T
Baths: 10 Private 2 Shared
(12)

St Erth-Praze

National Grid Ref: SW5735

Trengwyns, *12 Steppydowns Road, St Erth-Praze, Hayle, Cornwall,* TR27 6EF.
Friendly, comfortable, rural/coastal touring.
Open: All Year
01736 850505 Mrs Swift
Rates fr: *£14.00*-**£14.00**.
Beds: 1F 1D 1T 1S
Baths: 1 Private 2 Shared
(5)

St Issey

National Grid Ref: SW9271

Trevorrick Farm, *St Issey, Wadebridge, Cornwall,* PL27 7QH.
Most comfortable, scenically located farmhouse.
Open: All Year
Grades: ETB 2 Cr, Comm
01841 540574 Mr Mealing
Rates fr: *£17.50*-**£17.50**.
Beds: 2D 1T
Baths: 3 Ensuite
(10)

St Ives

National Grid Ref: SW5140

Sloop Inn, Queens Arms, The Croft, Moby's Table, Wellington

Chy-Roma Guest House, *2 Sea View Terrace, St Ives, Cornwall,* TR26 2DH.
Open: All Year
Grades: AA 2 Q, Recomm
01736 797539
Mrs Shackleton
Rates fr: *£13.00*-**£13.00**.
Beds: 2F 2D 1T 2S
Baths: 1 Ensuite 2 Shared
(6) (5)
Family guesthouse with superb sea views overlooking town/harbour 3-4 minutes bus, rail, beaches. Ideal base coastal walking/bird watching. Good home cooking.

Kandahar, *The Warren, St Ives, Cornwall,* TR26 2EA.
Water's edge, town centre location.
Open: All Year (not Xmas)
Grades: AA Listed, 3 Q
01736 796183
Mr & Mrs Mason
Rates fr: *£17.00*-**£19.00**.
Beds: 2F 5D 1T 2S
Baths: 3 Ensuite 1 Private 2 Shared
(6) (6)

Whitewaves, *4 Sea View, St Ives, Cornwall,* TR26 2DH.
Few minutes walk form train & coach station, Tate Gallery, town and beaches. Fabulous sea views. A warm and friendly welcome awaits you.
Open: All Year
Grades: ETB Listed
01736 796595
Mrs Webb
Rates fr: *£12.50*-**£12.50**.
Beds: 1F 2D 1T 3S
Baths: 2 Shared
(4)

Carlill, *9 Porthminster Terrace, St Ives, Cornwall,* TR26 2DQ.
Comfortable, friendly, licensed guest house.
Open: All Year
01736 796738
Mrs Bowden
Rates fr: *£14.00*-**£17.00**.
Beds: 2F 5D 1T 1S
Baths: 2 Shared
(6)

Rivendell, *7 Porthminster Terrace, St Ives, Cornwall,* TR26 2DQ.
Friendly hospitality, excellent food.
Open: All Year
Grades: ETB 1 Cr, Comm
01736 794923
Ms Walker
Rates fr: *£14.00*-**£14.00**.
Beds: 1F 4D 1T 2S
Baths: 1 Ensuite 1 Shared
(6)

The Old Vicarage Hotel, *Parc-An-Creet, St Ives, Cornwall,* TR26.
Large Victorian vicarage, beautifully converted. **Open:** Easter to Oct
Grades: AA 3 Q
01736 796124
Mr & Mrs Sykes
Rates fr: *£19.00*-**£22.00**.
Beds: 3F 4D 1T
Baths: 4 Private 2 Shared
(10)

St Just

National Grid Ref: SW3631

Bosavern House, *St Just, Penzance, Cornwall,* TR19 7RD.
Family-run guest house.
Open: Mar to Nov
Grades: ETB 2 Cr
01736 788301
Mr & Mrs Hartley
Rates fr: *£14.75*-**£16.25**.
Beds: 5F 2D 2T 1S
Baths: 5 ensuite 2 Shared
(15)

Boscean Country Hotel, *St Just, Penzance, Cornwall,* TR19 7QP.
Lovely quiet country hotel.
Open: Mar to Nov
Grades: ETB 3 Cr, Comm
01736 788748 Mr & Mrs Lee
Rates fr: *£20.00*-**£24.00**.
Beds: 4F 4D 4T
Baths: 12 Ensuite
(12)

Boswedden House Hotel, *Cape Cornwall, St Just, Penzance, Cornwall,* TR19 7NJ.
Georgian mine-captain's home.
Open: Mar to Dec
Grades: ETB 2 Cr
01736 788733 (also fax no)
Miss Stokes
Rates fr: *£18.00*-**£18.00**.
Beds: 1F 5D 1T 1S
Baths: 7 Private

St Kew

National Grid Ref: SX0177

St Kew Inn

Tregellist Farm, *Tregellist, St Kew, Bodmin, Cornwall,* PL30 3HG.
Beautiful Cornish countryside, good home cooking.
Open: Feb to Nov
Grades: ETB 2 Cr, Comm
01208 880537 Mrs Cleave
Rates fr: *£19.00*-**£21.00**.
Beds: 1F 1D 1T **Baths:** 3 Ensuite
(4)

All rates are subject to alteration at the owners' discretion.

St Kew Highway

National Grid Ref: SX0375

Hendra Country House, *St Kew Highway, Wadebridge, Cornwall, PL27 3EQ.*
Georgian manor house.
Open: Feb to Nov
Grades: ETB 3 Cr, RAC Acclaim
01208 841343
Mr & Mrs Jones
Fax no: 01208 841 343
Rates fr: *£18.50*-**£18.50**.
Beds: 1F 1D 2T 1S
Baths: 5 Private
(8)

St Levan

National Grid Ref: SW3722

Higher Bosistow, *St Levan, Penzance, Cornwall, TR19 6JJ.*
Tranquil, spacious residence, panoramic views.
Open: All Year (not Xmas)
01736 872269
Mrs Armitage
Rates fr: *£16.50*-**£16.50**.
Beds: 1D 1T 1S
Baths: 1 Shared
(5)

St Mabyn

National Grid Ref: SX0473

St Mabyn Inn

Cles Kernyk, *Wadebridge Rd, St Mabyn, Bodmin, Cornwall, PL30 3BH*
Open: All Year (not Xmas)
01208 841258
Mr & Mrs Jago
Rates fr: *£13.00*-**£13.00**.
Beds: 2F 1S
Baths: 1 Shared
(3)
Get away from it all & relax in this North Cornwall village, handy for beaches or moors. Friendly atmosphere, food hygiene certificate. Reductions for weekly bookings.

St Martin

National Grid Ref: SW7323

Prince of Wales (Newtown)

Lower Trenower Farm, *St Martin, Helston, Cornwall, TR12 6DP.*
Open: All Year
01326 231292
Mrs Blee
Rates fr: *£13.50*-**£13.50**.
Beds: 1F 1D 1T
Baths: 1 Shared
(6)
Working dairy farm situated close to Helford River. Ideal for exploring the picturesque Lizard Peninsula. Comfort, cleanliness and very warm welcome assured. Guest lounge and gardens.

St Mawes

National Grid Ref: SW8433

Old Watch House, Green Lantern

Braganza, *Grove Hill, St Mawes, Truro, Cornwall, TR2 5.*
Beautiful Regency house overlooking sea.
Open: Easter to Oct
01326 270281
Mrs Moseley-Kergorlay
Rates fr: *£21.00*-**£20.00**.
Beds: 3T 1S
Baths: 3 Ensuite 1 Shared

St Neot

National Grid Ref: SX1867

London Inn

18 Loveny Close, *St Neot, Liskeard, Cornwall, PL14 6NT.*
Modern bungalow quiet location.
Open: All Year (not Xmas)
01579 320392 Mrs Allen
Rates fr: *£13.00*-**£15.00**.
Beds: 1F **Baths:** 1 Shared

St Teath

National Grid Ref: SX0680

Tregarthen, *St Teath, Bodmin, Cornwall, PL30 3JX.*
Family accommodation. Good hospitality. **Open:** All Year
01208 850603 Mrs Jefferies
Rates fr: *£15.00*-**£15.00**.
Beds: 1F 1D 1T 1S
Baths: 1 Shared
(6)

St Tudy

National Grid Ref: SX0676

Old Inn (St Breward)

Hendra Farmhouse, *St Tudy, Bodmin, Cornwall, PL30 3PT.*
Charming farmhouse in beautiful countryside.
Open: All Year (not Xmas)
01208 841365 Mrs Kirkwood
Fax no: 01208 841699
Rates fr: *£15.00*-**£15.00**.
Beds: 2D 1T **Baths:** 1 Shared
(4) (3)

Stoke Climsland

National Grid Ref: SX3674

Penpill Farmhouse, *Stoke Climsland, Callington, Cornwall, PL17 8QE.*
Georgian farmhouse, gardens, home cooking. **Open:** All Year
Grades: ETB 2 Cr
01579 370540 Mr & Mrs Rae
Rates fr: *£18.00*-**£20.00**.
Beds: 2F 3D 2T
Baths: 7 Private

The Lizard

National Grid Ref: SW7012

Mounts Bay House Hotel, *The Lizard, Helston, Cornwall, TR12 7NP.*
Quiet, peaceful. Magnificent coastal scenery. **Open:** Dec to Oct
Grades: ETB 2 Cr, Comm
01326 290305 Mr Crossley
Rates fr: *£18.50*-**£18.50**.
Beds: 5D 1T 1S
Baths: 2 Private 1 Shared
(10)

The Most Southerly House, *Lizard Point, The Lizard, Helston, Cornwall, TR12 7NU.*
Detached cliff top house, fantastic views.
Open: All Year (not Xmas)
01326 290300 Mrs Sowden
Rates fr: *£15.00*-**£16.00**.
Beds: 2D **Baths:** 1 Shared
(7) (4)

Three Burrows

National Grid Ref: SW7447

Fox & Hounds (Scorrier)

Lands Vue Country House, *Lands Vue, Three Burrows, Truro, Cornwall, TR4 8JA.*
Superb views, very central country house.
Open: All Year (not Xmas/New Year)
Grades: ETB 2 Cr, AA 4 Q, Select
01872 560242 Mrs Hutchings
Rates fr: *£18.00*-**£22.00**.
Beds: 1D 2T
Baths: 2 Ensuite 1 Private
(4)

Tideford

National Grid Ref: SX3459

Kilna Guest House, *Tideford, Saltash, Cornwall, PL12 5AD.*
Detached country house, relaxed atmosphere.
Open: All Year (not Xmas)
01752 851236 Mrs Turner
Rates fr: *£15.00*-**£16.00**.
Beds: 2F 1D 1T 1S
Baths: 1 Shared
(6)

Tintagel

National Grid Ref: SX0588

Cornishman, Port William

The Old Borough House, *Bossiney, Tintagel, Cornwall, PL34 0AY.*
Open: All Year
01840 770475 Mrs Rayner
Rates fr: *£15.50*-**£25.50**.
Beds: 1F 3D 1T
Baths: 2 Private 2 Shared
(4) (10)
Charming licensed C17th guest house. Friendly atmosphere, excellent home-cooking, 4-course dinner. Safe bathing at Bossiney Cove 600 yards away.

All rates are subject to alteration at the owners' discretion.

The Old Malt House, *Fore Street, Tintagel, Cornwall,* *PL34 0DA.*
C14th hotel and licensed restaurant. **Open:** Easter to Oct
Grades: ETB 3 Cr, Comm
01840 770461 Mr & Mrs Ridgewell
Rates fr: *£15.50*-**£15.50**.
Beds: 5D 2T 1S
Baths: 5 Private 2 Shared
(5) (12)

Trevillett Mill Trout Farm, *Rocky Valley, Tintagel, Cornwall,* *PL34 0BB.*
Interesting 1472 watermill beside river.
Open: All Year (not Xmas)
01840 770564
Mr Savage
Rates fr: *£15.00*.
Beds: 1F 3D

Trewinnick Farm, *Tintagel, Cornwall,* *PL34 0HL.*
Comfortable farmhouse with good cooking.
Open: All Year (not Xmas)
01840 770738 (also fax no)
Mrs Reeves
Rates fr: *£16.00*-**£16.00**.
Beds: 1F 1T 1S
Baths: 1 Ensuite 1 Shared
(10)

Tintagel Arms Hotel, *Fore Street, Tintagel, Cornwall,* *PL34 0DB.*
Comfortable inn, ideally situated in centre of village.
Open: All Year **Grades:** AA 3 Q
01840 770780
Mr Hunter
Rates fr: *£17.50*-**£21.00**.
Beds: 1F 4D 2T **Baths:** 7 Private
(8)

Hallmoor House, *Bossiney Road, Tintagel, Cornwall,* *PL34 0AQ.*
A warm welcome awaits you.
Open: Easter to Oct
01840 770602 Mrs Bowker
Rates fr: *£14.00*-**£14.00**.
Beds: 2D 1T
Baths: 1 Ensuite 1 Shared
(3)

Treen

National Grid Ref: SW3923

Logan Rock Pub

Penver House Farm, *Treen, Penzance, Cornwall,* *TR19 6LG.*
Cornish home, countryside, sea-side. **Open:** All Year (not Xmas)
01736 810778 Mrs Jilbert
Rates fr: *£14.00*-**£14.00**.
Beds: 1D 1S **Baths:** 1 Shared

Treneglos

National Grid Ref: SX2088

The Old Vicarage, *Treneglos, Launceston, Cornwall,* *PL15 8UQ.*
Elegant Georgian vicarage, peaceful seclusion.
Open: Easter to Oct
Grades: ETB 3 Cr, High Comm
01566 781351 Mrs Fancourt
Rates fr: *£20.50*-**£25.00**.
Beds: 2D **Baths:** 2 Ensuite
(2) (10)

Tresinney

National Grid Ref: SX1081

Masons Arms

Higher Trezion, *Tresinney, Advent, Camelford, Cornwall,* *PL32 9QW.*
Modern comfortable farmhouse.
Open: All Year
01840 213761 Mr & Mrs Wood
Rates fr: *£14.00*-**£14.00**.
Beds: 1 D 1T **Baths:** 1 Private 1 Shared

Trethin

National Grid Ref: SX1083

Trethin Manor, *Advent, Trethin, Camelford, Cornwall,* *PL32 9QW.*
Comfortable C14th Cornish manor house. **Open:** Easter to Oct
01840 213522 Mr & Mrs Brocklehurst
Rates fr: *£17.00*-**£17.00**.
Beds: 3D 1S **Baths:** 4 Private
(20)

Trevarrian

National Grid Ref: SW8566

Double K Hotel, *Trevarrian, Mawgan Porth, Newquay, Cornwall,* *TR8 4AQ.*
Friendly licensed hotel, good food.
Open: All Year
01637 860422 Miss Allbutt
Rates fr: *£15.00*-**£15.00**.
Beds: 3F 3D 2T 1S
Baths: 5 Private 2 Shared

Treverva

National Grid Ref: SW7531

Trengilly Wartha Inn, Nancenoy, Constantine

Menallack Farm, *Treverva, Penryn, Falmouth, Cornwall,* *TR10 9BP.*
Relaxed working farm, lovely countryside. **Open:** Mar to Nov
01326 340333 (also fax no)
Rates fr: *£15.00*-**£16.00**.
Beds: 1D 2T **Baths:** 2 Shared

Bringing children with you? Always ask for any special rates.

Trevone Bay

National Grid Ref: SW8876

Well Parc Hotel, *Trevone Bay, Padstow, Cornwall,* *PL28 8QN.*
Small family-run hotel.
Open: All Year (not Xmas)
01840 520318
Mrs Mills
Rates fr: *£20.00*.
Beds: 4F 4D 1T 1S

Trispen

National Grid Ref: SW8450

Laniley House, *Newquay Road, Trispen, Truro, Cornwall,* *TR4 9AU.*
Large Victorian gentleman's residence.
Open: Easter to Nov
Grades: ETB Listed
01872 75201 Mrs Gartner
Rates fr: *£17.00*-**£24.00**.
Beds: 2D 1T
Baths: 1 Ensuite 1 Shared
(6)

Truro

National Grid Ref: SW8244

Country Arms, Fox & Hounds (Scorrier), Daniel Arms, County Arms

Lands Vue Country House, *Lands Vue, Three Burrows, Truro, Cornwall,* *TR4 8JA.*
Superb views, very central country house.
Open: All Year (not Xmas/New Year)
Grades: ETB 2 Cr, AA 4 Q, Select
01872 560242
Mrs Hutchings
Rates fr: *£18.00*-**£22.00**.
Beds: 1D 2T
Baths: 2 Ensuite 1 Private
(4)

The Fieldings, *35 Treyew Road, Truro, Cornwall,* *TR1 2BY.*
Spacious & comfortable Edwardian house. **Open:** All Year (not Xmas)
01872 262783
Mrs Inglefield
Fax no: 01872 72800
Rates fr: *£14.00*-**£18.00**.
Beds: 1F 1D 1T
Baths: 2 Shared
(3)

Rock Cottage, *Blackwater, Truro, Cornwall,* *TR4 8EU.*
C18th beamed schoolmaster's cottage. **Open:** All Year
Grades: ETB 3 Cr, High Comm, AA 4 Q, Select, RAC Acclaim
01872 560252 (also fax no)
Mrs Wakeling
Rates fr: *£20.50*.
Beds: 2D 1T
Baths: 3 Ensuite
(3)

Tywardreath

National Grid Ref: SX0854

Which Way Inn (Par)

Polbrean House, *Woodland Avenue, Tywardreath, Par, Cornwall, PL24 2PL.*
Lovely family home, comfortable rooms.
Open: All Year (not Xmas)
01726 812530 Mrs Ball
Rates fr: *£15.00*-**£18.00**.
Beds: 2D **Baths:** 1 Shared
(3)

Upton

National Grid Ref: SS2004

The Meva Gwin Hotel, *Upton, Crackington Haven, Bude, Cornwall, EX23 0LY.*
Family-run hotel, wonderful sea views. **Open:** Easter to Oct
01288 352347 Mrs Bull
Rates fr: *£18.00*-**£18.00**.
Beds: 7D 3T 3S
Baths: 13 Private

Veryan in Roseland

National Grid Ref: SW9139

The New Inn, *Veryan in Roseland, Truro, Cornwall, TR2 5QA.*
Open: All Year
01872 501362 Mr Gayton
Rates fr: *£15.50*-**£15.50**.
Beds: 1D 1T 2S **Baths:** 1 Shared
Unspoilt inn set in a beautiful village in the heart of the Roseland district, famed for its warm climate and safe sandy beaches. Real ale.

Wadebridge

National Grid Ref: SW9872

Trevanion House, *Trevanion Road, Wadebridge, Cornwall, PL27 7JY.*
C18th farmhouse - disabled welcomed. **Open:** Mar to Jan
01208 814903 Mrs Todd
Fax no: 01208 816268
Rates fr: *£16.00*-**£19.00**.
Beds: 7T 4S
Baths: 9 Private 2 Shared
(5) (8)

Watergate

National Grid Ref: SX2354

Harescombe Lodge Country, *Guest House, Watergate, Looe, Cornwall, PL13 2NE.*
Ex-shooting lodge, idyllic location.
Open: All Year (not Xmas)
01503 263158 Mr Wynn
Rates fr: *£17.00*.
Beds: 2D 1T 2D **Baths:** 3 Ensuite
(12) (10)

Whitstone

National Grid Ref: SX2698

Countryman

Langaton Farm, *Whitstone, Holsworthy, Cornwall, EX22 6TS.*
C18th comfortable farmhouse.
Open: Easter to Oct
01288 341 215 Mrs Short
Rates fr: *£12.00*-**£15.00**.
Beds: 1F **Baths:** 1 Shared
(10)

Widegates

National Grid Ref: SX2857

Copley Arms

Coombe Farm, *Widegates, Looe, Cornwall, PL13 1QN.*
Lovely country house in wonderful setting and grounds.
Open: Mar to Nov
Grades: ETB 3 Cr, High Comm, AA 5 Q, Prem Select, RAC High Acclaim
01503 240223 Mr Low
Fax no: 01503 240895
Rates fr: *£23.00*-**£23.00**.
Beds: 4F 3D 3T **Baths:** 10 Private
(5) (20)

Widemouth Bay

National Grid Ref: SS2002

Brocksmoor Hotel

The Bay View Inn, *Widemouth Bay, Bude, Cornwall, EX23 0AW.*
Family freehouse pub, overlooking sea. **Open:** All Year
Grades: ETB Listed
01288 361273 Mr Gooder
Rates fr: *£13.00*-**£13.00**.
Beds: 3F 3D 1T 2S
Baths: 4 Private 2 Shared
(30)

Penhalt Farm, *Widemouth Bay, Bude, Cornwall, EX23 0.*
Panoramic sea views, comfortable, welcoming. **Open:** Sep to Jun
01288 361210 Mrs Marks
Rates fr: *£12.50*-**£15.00**.
Beds: 1F 1T 1D
Baths: 2 Shared

Woodford

National Grid Ref: SS2113

Darzle Farm, *Woodford, Bude, Cornwall, EX23 9HY.*
Warm, homely welcome, quiet countryside.
Open: All Year
01288 331222 Mrs Cholwill
Rates fr: *£17.00*-**£17.00**.
Beds: 2F 1D
Baths: 3 Private
(10)

Zennor

National Grid Ref: SW4538

Tinners Arms, Gurnards Head Hotel (Treen)

Boswednack Manor, *Zennor, St Ives, Cornwall, TR26 3DD.*
Peaceful, organic gardens, sea sunsets.
Open: All Year (not Xmas)
01736 794183 Mr Gynn
Rates fr: *£15.00*-**£15.00**.
Beds: 3F 1T 1S
Baths: 2 Private 1 Shared
(10)

Trewey Farm, *Zennor, St Ives, Cornwall, TR26 3DA.*
Working farm. Peaceful attractive surroundings.
Open: Feb to Nov
01736 796936 Mrs Mann
Rates fr: *£16.00*-**£16.00**.
Beds: 2F 2D 1T 1S
Baths: 1 Shared
(10) (5)

Tregeraint House, *Zennor, St Ives, Cornwall, TR26 3DB.*
Traditional Cornish cottage overlooking sea.
Open: All Year (not Xmas)
01736 797061 (also fax no)
Mr & Mrs Wilson
Rates fr: *£15.50*-**£17.00**.
Beds: 1F 2D 1T **Baths:** 1 Shared
(4)

Cumbria

Langholm
DUMFRIES &
GALLOWAY
A7
Annan
Gretna
Hethersgill
Walton
Blackford
BRAMPTON
Bowness
on Solway
Rockcliffe
A69
Stanwix
Aglionby
CARLISLE
Warwick
Bridge
Blackwell
Brisco
Armathwaite
A596
Westnewton
Rosley
Ivegill
A595
Aspatria
Caldbeck
Newlands
M6
A6
Crosscanonby
Ireby
MARYPORT
Dearham
Ellonby
Newton Reigny
COCKERMOUTH
Dubwath
Bassenthwaite
Bassenthwaite
Greystoke
PENRITH
Skiddaw
Stainton
Yanwath
WORKINGTON
Threlkeld
A66
Dalemain
Dacre
Tirril
Lorton
Pardshaw
Thornthwaite
POOLEY BRIDGE
Keswick
Matterdale End
A5086
Helton
Loweswater
Braithwaite
Derwent Water
Watermillock
Butterwick
Glenridding
Ullswater
WHITEHAVEN
Grange-in-Borrowdale
Burnbanks
Ennerdale
Bridge
Borrowdale
Thirlmere
Patterdale
Haweswater
Sandwith
Ennerdale Water
Rosthwaite
Haweswater
Cleator
Helvellyn
St Bees
Ennerdale
Seatoller
EGREMONT
LAKE DISTRIC
A591
Scafell Pike
GRASMERE
Wast Water
Great Langdale
Skelwith
Bridge
AMBLESIDE
Kentmere
A6
Gosforth
Elterwater
Longsleddale
Nether Wasdale
Easedale
Boot
Troutbeck
Holmrook
High Wray
Eskdale Green
Ings
Staveley
Irton
Coniston
WINDERMERE
RAVENGLASS
Little Arrow
Hawkshead
Burneside
Torver
Near Sawrey
Bowness
© Crown copyright

Tourist Information Centres

The Railway Station, **Alston**, Cumbria, CA9 3JB, 01434 381696.

Old Courthouse, Church Street, **Ambleside**, Cumbria, LA22 0BT, 01539 432582.

Moot Hall, Boroughgate, **Appleby-in-Westmorland**, Cumbria, CA16 6XD, 01768 351177.

Town Hall, Duke Street, **Barrow-in-Furness**, Cumbria, LA14 2LD, 01229 870156.

Seatoller Barn, **Borrowdale**, Keswick, Cumbria, CA12 5XN, 01768 777294, (Easter to Oct).

Glebe Road, **Bowness-on-Windermere**, Windermere, Cumbria, LA23 3HJ, 01539 442895, (Easter to Oct)

Moot Hall, Market Place, **Brampton**, Cumbria, CA8 1AR, 016977-3433, (Easter to Oct).

Old Town Hall, Green Market, **Carlisle**, Cumbria, CA3 8JH, 01228 512444

Riverside Car Park, Market Street, **Cockermouth**, Cumbria, CA13 9NP, 01900 822634.

12 Main Street, **Egremont**, Cumbria, CA22 2DW, 01946 820693.

16 Yewdale Road, **Coniston**, Cumbria, LA21 8DU, 01539 441533, (Easter to Oct).

Victoria Hall, Main Street, **Grange-over-Sands**, Cumbria, LA11 6PT, 01539-534026, (Easter to Oct).

Redbank Road, **Grasmere**, Cumbria, LA22 9SW, 01539-435245, (Easter to Oct).

Town Hall, Highgate, **Kendal**, Cumbria, LA9 4DL, 01539-725758.

Moot Hall, Market Square, **Keswick**, Cumbria, CA12 4JR, 01768-772645.

Killington Lake Services (M6 South), **Killington**, Kendal, Cumbria, LA8 0NW, 01539-620138.

Market Street, **Kirkby Stephen**, Cumbria, CA17 4QN, 01768-371199.

Memorial Hall, Community Centre, **Longtown**, Carlisle, Cumbria, CA6 5SJ, 01228-791876.

1 Senhouse Street, **Maryport**, Cumbria, CA15 6AB, 01900-813738.

Millom Folk Museum, St Georges Road, **Millom**, Cumbria, LA18 4DQ, 01229-772555, (Easter to Oct).

Robinson's School, Middlegate, **Penrith**, Cumbria, CA11 7PT, 01768 867466

The Square, **Pooley Bridge**, Penrith, Cumbria, CA10 2NW, 01768 486530, (Easter to Oct).

Ravenglass & Eskdale Railway, **Ravenglass**,*(local information only)* Cumbria, CA18 1SW, 01229 717278, (Easter to Oct).

72 Main Street, **Sedbergh**, Cumbria, LA10 5AD, 01539 620125, (Easter to Oct).

The Green, **Silloth-on-Solway**, Carlisle, Cumbria, CA5 4QP, 01697 331944, (Easter to Oct).

M6 Service Area, **Southwaite**, Carlisle, Cumbria, CA4 0NS, 01697 473445.

Coronation Hall, County Square, **Ulverston**, Cumbria, LA12 7LZ, 01229 587120.

Civic Hall, Lowther Street, **Whitehaven**, Cumbria, CA28 7SH, 01946 695678.

Ullswater Main Car Park, **Glenridding**, Penrith, Cumbria, CA11 0PA, 01768 482414, (Easter to Oct)

Victoria Street, **Windermere**, Cumbria, LA23 1AD, 01539 446499.

Central Car Park, Washington Street, **Workington**, Cumbria, CA14 3AW, 01900 602923.

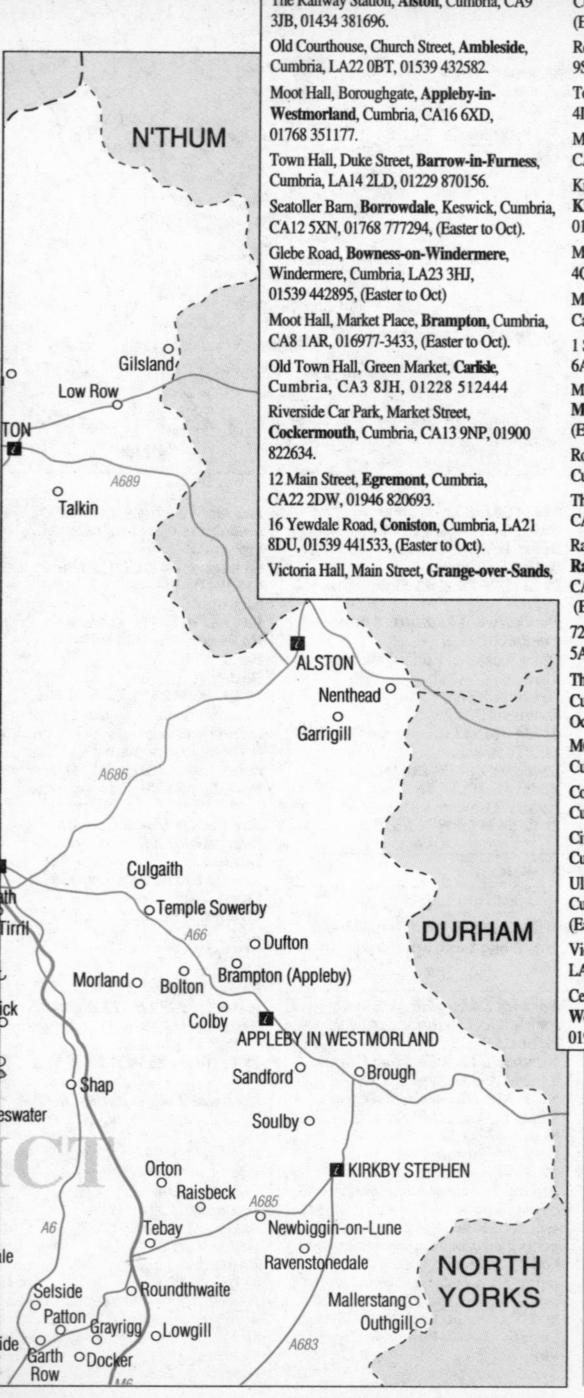

Aglionby

National Grid Ref: NY4456

***Beech Croft**, Aglionby, Carlisle, Cumbria, CA4 8AQ.*
Spacious modern house, rural setting.
Open: All Year (not Xmas)
Grades: ETB 2 Cr, Comm
01228 513762
Mrs Walne
Rates fr: *£19.00*-**£21.00**.
Beds: 1T 1D 1S
Baths: 1 Ensuite 2 Private
(3) (4)

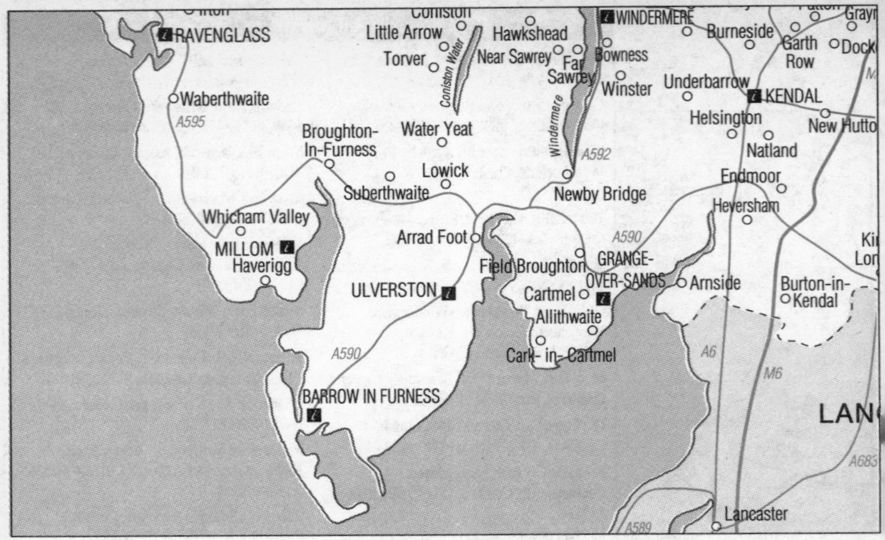

Allithwaite

National Grid Ref: SD3876

The Chateau, *Flookbrook Road, Allithwaite, Grange-over-Sands, Cumbria,* LA11 7JR.
Comfortable, modern family home.
Open: Feb to Nov
015395 32249
Mr Robinson
Rates fr: *£13.50*-**£13.50**.
Beds: 1D 2T
Baths: 1 Ensuite 2 Shared
P (4)

Alston

National Grid Ref: NY7146

Blue Bell Inn, Angel Inn

Harbut Law, *Brampton Road, Alston, Cumbria,* CA9 3BD.
Large Victorian former farmhouse.
Open: All Year
01434 381950
Mrs Younger
Rates fr: *£13.00*-**£13.00**.
Beds: 2D 1T
Baths: 1 Private 2 Shared
P (5)

Bridge End Farm, *Alston, Cumbria,* CA9 3BJ.
Warm, friendly, comfortable farmhouse.
Open: All Year
01434 381261 Mrs Williams
Rates fr: *£15.50*-**£17.50**.
Beds: 2D 1T
Baths: 1 Private 1 Shared
(1) P (4)

Middle Bayles Farm, *Penrith Road, Alston, Cumbria,* CA9 3BS.
C17th traditional farmhouse.
Open: All Year (not Xmas)
Grades: ETB 2 Cr, Comm
01434 381383 Mrs Dent
Rates fr: *£15.00*-**£18.00**.
Beds: 1F 1D
Baths: 2 Private
P (2)

Nentholme, The Butts, *Alston, Cumbria,* CA9 3JQ.
Quiet location, 1 min walk from town.
Open: All Year
Grades: ETB 2 Cr
01434 381523 (also fax no)
Mrs Thompson
Rates fr: *£14.00*-**£18.00**.
Beds: 1F 2D 3T 1S
Baths: 2 Ensuite 1 Private
P (6)

Ambleside

National Grid Ref: NY3704

Drunken Duck Inn, Outgate Inn, White Lion, Sportsman, Royal Oak

Borwick Lodge, *Hawkshead, Ambleside, Cumbria,* LA22 0PU.
Open: All Year
Grades: ETB 2 Cr, High Comm
015394 36332 (also fax no)
Mr & Mrs Bleasdale
Rates fr: *£18.00*-**£18.00**.
Beds: 2F 2D 2T
Baths: 6 Ensuite
(8) P (8)
Award-Winning 'Accommodation of the Highest Standards'. A rather special C17th country house with magnificent panoramic views. Quietly secluded yet ideally placed in the heart of the Lakes and close to restaurants and inns. Beautiful bedrooms, all ensuite. Also 'Special Occasions' and 'Romantic Breaks' king-size four poster rooms. Totally non-smoking.

The Old Vicarage, *Vicarage Road, Ambleside, Cumbria,* LA22 9DH.
Open: All Year
Grades: ETB 2 Cr, Comm
015394 33364
Mrs Burt
Fax no: 015394 34734
Rates fr: *£20.00*-**£28.00**.
Beds: 2F 6D 2T
Baths: 10 Ensuite
P (15)
Tranquil position in heart of village. Own car park. Quality ensuite accommodation with TV, clock radio, fridge, kettle, hairdryer. Friendly service. Pets welcome.

The Gables Hotel, *Compston Road, Ambleside, Cumbria,* LA22 9DJ.
Central situation. All ensuite.
Open: All Year
Grades: ETB 3 Cr, AA 1 St, RAC High Acclaim
015394 33272
Mr Burt
Fax no: 015394 34734
Rates fr: *£23.00*-**£23.00**.
Beds: 5F 5D 3S
Baths: 13 Ensuite
P (10)

Riverside Lodge, *Rothay Bridge, Ambleside, Cumbria,* LA22 0EH.
Open: All Year
Grades: ETB 2 Cr, Comm, AA 4 Q
015394 34208 Mr Rhone
Fax no: 015394 31884
Rates fr: *£21.00*.
Beds: 2F 2D 1T
Baths: 5 Private
P (10)
A superbly situated country house of immense charm and character in an idyllic riverside setting near the centre of Ambleside offering B&B accommodation.

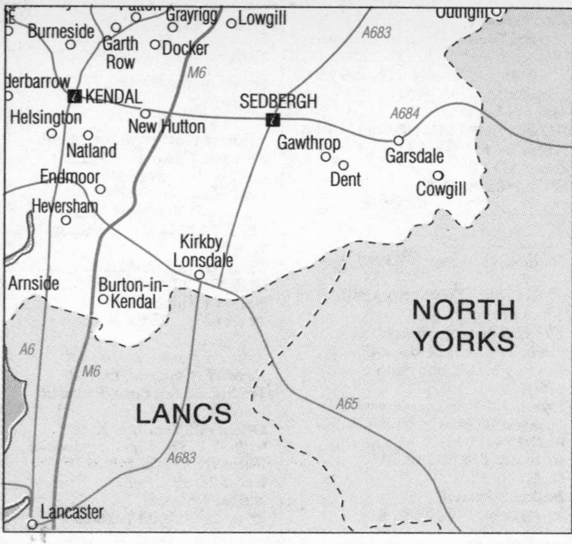

Windlehurst, *Millans Park, Ambleside, Cumbria, LA22 9AG.*
Open: All Year (not Xmas)
Grades: ETB 2 Cr
015394 33137 Mrs Boulton
Fax no: 015394 34570
Rates fr: *£15.00*-**£15.00**.
Beds: 3F 2D 1S
Baths: 2 Private 2 Shared
(1) (6)
Victorian house in quiet location but near to amenities. Commanding views of Loughrigg Fell. Comfortable rooms. Private parking. Dogs welcome. Totally non-smoking.

Old Fisherbeck, *Old Lake Road, Ambleside, Cumbria, LA22 0DH.*
C15th farmhouse. Centre Lake District.
Open: All Year (not Xmas)
015394 33540 Mrs Bingham
Fax no: 015394 33003
Rates fr: *£16.00*-**£16.00**.
Beds: 1D 2T **Baths:** 2 Shared
(8) (3)

Claremont House, *Compston Road, Ambleside, Cumbria, LA22 9DJ.*
Friendly family-run guest house.
Open: All Year
Grades: ETB 2 Cr, Approv
015394 33448
Rates fr: *£16.00*-**£17.00**.
Beds: 1F 4D 1T 2S
Baths: 6 Ensuite 1 Shared

Bringing children with you? Always ask for any special rates.

The lowest **single** *rate is shown in* **bold.**

Broadview, *Lake Road, Ambleside, Cumbria, LA22 0DN.*
Comfortable Victorian guest house.
Open: Feb to Nov
015394 32431 Mr Sunderland
Rates fr: *£17.50*-**£19.50**.
Beds: 2F 3D 1T
Baths: 2 Ensuite 2 Shared

Fisherbeck Cottage, *Lake Road, Low Fold, Ambleside, Cumbria, LA22 0DN.*
Quiet Lakeland country cottage.
Open: All Year (not Xmas)
Grades: ETB Listed
015394 33353 Mrs Dawson
Rates fr: *£12.00*-**£12.00**.
Beds: 2D 1T 1S
Baths: 1 Shared

Rowanfield Country House, *Kirkstone Road, Ambleside, Cumbria, LA22 9ET.*
Idyllic country setting, delightful rooms.
Open: Mar to Dec
Grades: ETB 2 Cr, High Comm, AA 5 Q, Prem Select, RAC High Acclaim
015394 33686
Mrs Butcher
Fax no: 015394 31569
Rates fr: *£25.00*-**£26.00**.
Beds: 1F 5D 1T
Baths: 7 Ensuite
(5) (7)

Appleby in Westmorland

National Grid Ref: NY6820

Royal Oak Inn

Bongate House, *Appleby in Westmorland, Cumbria, CA16 6UE.*
Open: All Year (not Xmas)
Grades: ETB 3 Cr, Comm, AA 3 Q
017683 51245 Mrs Dayson
Rates fr: *£17.00*-**£17.00**.
Beds: 2F 3D 2T 1S
Baths: 5 Private
(7) (8)
Large Georgian guest house in an acre of secluded gardens. Taste good food in a relaxed atmosphere. Ideal base to tour Lakes, Dales and Scottish Borders.

Limnerslease, *Bongate, Appleby in Westmorland, Cumbria, CA16 6UE.*
Family-run guest house 10 mins town centre.
Open: All Year (not Xmas)
017683 51578 Mrs Coward
Rates fr: *£14.00*.
Beds: 2D 1T **Baths:** 1 Shared
(3)

Church View, *Bongate, Appleby in Westmorland, Cumbria, CA16 6UN.*
C18th Listed character house.
Open: All Year (not Xmas)
017683 51792 (also fax no)
Mrs Kemp
Rates fr: *£15.00*-**£17.50**.
Beds: 1F 1D 1S **Baths:** 1 Shared
(1) (4)

Weymyss House, *48 Boroughgate, Appleby in Westmorland, Cumbria, CA16 6XG.*
Georgian house in small country town. **Open:** Easter to Nov
017683 51494 Mrs Hirst
Rates fr: *£14.00*-**£14.00**.
Beds: 1D 1T 1S **Baths:** 2 Shared
(3)

Howgill House, *Bongate, Appleby in Westmorland, Cumbria, CA16 6UW.*
Private house set in large garden.
Open: Easter to Oct
Grades: ETB 1 Cr, Comm
01768 351574 / 351240
Mrs Pigney
Rates fr: *£13.00*-**£14.50**.
Beds: 2F 1T 1S (6)

Armathwaite

National Grid Ref: NY5046

Dukes Head Hotel

Quarry House, *Armathwaite, Carlisle, Cumbria, CA4 9SL.*
Smallholding, homely, comfortable, open fire.
Open: All Year (not Xmas)
016974 72282 Mrs Brown
Rates fr: *£12.00*-**£12.50**.
Beds: 1F 1D 1T
Baths: 1 Private 1 Shared
(3)

Arnside

National Grid Ref: SD4578

Willowfield Hotel, *The Promenade, Arnside, Carnforth, Lancs, LA5 0AD.*
Non-smokers family-run hotel.
Open: All Year
Grades: ETB 3 Cr, Comm, AA 3 Q, RAC Listed
01524 761354 Mr Kerr
Rates fr: *£19.00*-**£19.00**.
Beds: 1F 4D 3T 2S
Baths: 7 Ensuite 2 Shared
(10)

Arrad Foot

National Grid Ref: SD3080

Armadale Hotel, *Arrad Foot, Ulverston, Cumbria, LA12 7SL.*
Small family-run country hotel.
Open: All Year (not Xmas)
01229 861257
Rates fr: *£20.00*-**£25.00**.
Beds: 3D 1S
Baths: 1 Ensuite
(30)

Aspatria

National Grid Ref: NY1441

Stoneleigh, *5 Beech Hill, Aspatria, Carlisle, Cumbria, CA5 2QA.*
2-acre smallholding.
Open: All Year
016973 21215 Mrs Cockburn
Rates fr: *£12.00*-**£12.00**.
Beds: 1T 1S
Baths: 1 Shared
(2)

Barrow-in-Furness

National Grid Ref: SD1969

Infield Hotel, *276 Abbey Road, Barrow-in-Furness, Cumbria, LA13 9JJ.*
Hotel standards, guest house prices.
Open: All Year
01229 831381 Mrs Parkin
Rates fr: *£16.00*-**£18.00**.
Beds: 3F 2D 2T 3S
Baths: 2 Private 2 Shared
(9)

Bassenthwaite

National Grid Ref: NY2332

Sun Inn

Chapel Farm, *Bassenthwaite Lake, Bassenthwaite, Keswick, Cumbria, CA12 4QH.*
Working family farm, friendly accommodation.
Open: All Year
017687 76495 Mrs Fell
Rates fr: *£13.00*-**£13.00**.
Beds: 1F 1D
Baths: 1 Shared

Bassenthwaite Hall Farm, *Bassenthwaite, Keswick, Cumbria, CA12 4QP.*
Charming, olde worlde, homely farmhouse.
Open: May to Oct
017687 76393 Mrs Trafford
Rates fr: *£15.00*-**£18.00**.
Beds: 1D 1T
(3)

Blackford

National Grid Ref: NY3969

Crown,Thistle Rockcliff

The Hill Cottage, *Blackford, Carlisle, Cumbria, CA6 4DU.*
Country house, one minute M6/A74.
Open: All Year (not Xmas)
Grades: ETB 1 Cr, High Comm
01228 74739 Mr & Mrs Martin
Rates fr: *£16.00*-**£18.50**.
Beds: 2D 1T
Baths: 2 Shared
(6) (4)

Blackwell

National Grid Ref: NY4053

Black Lion

Blackwell Farm, *Lowry Street, Blackwell, Carlisle, Cumbria, CA2 4SH.*
Comfortable farmhouse on working farm.
Open: All Year (not Xmas)
Grades: AA 2 Q
01228 24073
Ms Westmorland
Rates fr: *£14.00*-**£15.00**.
Beds: 1F 1T
(4)

Bolton

National Grid Ref: NY6323

Croft House, *Bolton, Appleby In Westmorland, Cumbria, CA16 6AW.*
C17th farmhouse in village.
Open: All Year (not Xmas)
017683 61264
Mrs Stockdale
Rates fr: *£15.00*-**£15.00**.
Beds: 2D 1T
Baths: 1 Shared
(6)

Boot

National Grid Ref: NY1701

Stanley Ghyll House, *Boot, Holmrook, Cumbria, CA19 1TF.*
Edwardian country house.
Open: All Year
019467 23327
Bryden
Rates fr: *£18.00*-**£18.00**.
Beds: 11F 9T 6S
Baths: 4 Shared
(30)

Borrowdale

National Grid Ref: NY2719

Langstrath, Dog & Gun (Keswick)

Ashness Cottage, *Borrowdale, Keswick, Cumbria, CA12 5UN.*
Cosy cottage overlooking Derwentwater.
Open: All Year (not Xmas)
017687 77244 Mrs Hamilton-Wright
Rates fr: *£15.00*-**£16.00**.
Beds: 2D 1T
Baths: 1 Shared
(10) (6)

Ashness Farm, *Borrowdale, Keswick, Cumbria, CA12 5UN.*
Traditional fell farm. Fantastic views.
Open: All Year (not Xmas)
017687 77361 Mrs Cornthwaite
Rates fr: *£15.50*-**£18.50**.
Beds: 2D 1T
Baths: 1 Shared
(0) (6)

Bowness

National Grid Ref: SD4096

Village Inn, Royal Oak, Sutherlands Restaurant, Spinnery

The Poplars, *Lake Road, Bowness, Windermere, CumbriaCumbria, LA23 2EQ.*
Open: Feb to Dec
Grades: ETB 2 Cr, Comm
015394 42325 (also fax no)
Mr & Mrs Riggs
Rates fr: *£18.50*-**£18.50**.
Beds: 4D 2T 1S
Baths: 6 Ensuite 1 Private
(5) (7)
Ideally situated midway between Bowness & Windermere. Superior ensuite accommodation coupled with the finest cuisine. Unique friendly atmosphere. Ideal base for walkers .

Virginia Cottage, *Kendal Road, Bowness, Windermere, Cumbria, LA23 3EJ.*
C18th cottage in heart of Bowness village, close to lake, shops, restaurants. Leisure facilities, private parking.
Open: All Year
Grades: ETB 2 Cr
015394 44891
Mr Tyler
Rates fr: *£14.00*-**£20.00**.
Beds: 2F 9D
Baths: 5 Private 3 Shared
(9)

The lowest *double* rate per person is shown in *italics*.

Fairfield Country House Hotel, *Brantfell Road, Bowness, Windermere, Cumbria, LA23 3AE.*
Open: All Year (not Xmas)
Grades: ETB 3 Cr, Comm, AA 4 Q, RAC High Acclaim
015394 46565 (also fax no)
Mr & Mrs Hood
Rates fr: *£24.00*-**£24.00**.
Beds: 2F 5D 1T 1S
Baths: 8 Ensuite 1 Private
(12)
Small friendly family-run hotel in Bowness at end of Dales Way. Ensuite rooms with colour TVs. Leisure facilities. Ideal venue to end your walk.

Above The Bay, *Brackenfield, Bowness, Windermere, Cumbria, LA23 3HL.*
Superb views of lake & fells .
Open: All Year
015394 88658
Mr Bell
Fax no: 015394 48007
Rates fr: *£17.50*-**£20.00**.
Beds: 1F 2D 1T 1S
Baths: 5 Private
(11) (10)

Brooklands, *Ferry View, Bowness, Windermere, Cumbria, LA23 3JB.*
Open: All Year (not Xmas)
Grades: ETB 2 Cr, Comm, AA 3 Q
015394 42344
Mrs Holland
Rates fr: *£16.00*-**£16.00**.
Beds: 3F 2D 1T 1S
Baths: 5 Ensuite 2 Private
(6)
Delightful Lakeland stone guest house in rural position. 15 minute walk lake. Restaurant, pubs, golf nearby. Comfortable rooms - hearty breakfasts. Very warm welcome.

The Old Rectory, *Bowness on Solway, Carlisle, Cumbria, CA5 5AF.*
Large former village rectory.
Open: All Year (not Xmas)
016973 51055
Mr Simpson
Rates fr: *£15.00*-**£17.00**.
Beds: 3D
Baths: 1 Shared

Cranleigh Hotel, *Kendal Road, Bowness, Windermere, Cumbria, LA23 3EW.*
Open: All Year
Grades: ETB 3 Cr, Comm, AA 2 St, RAC High Recomm
015394 43293
Mr Wigglesworth
Rates fr: *£18.00*-**£18.00**.
Beds: 3F 9D 3T
Baths: 15 Private
Clean, quiet, comfortable & convenient hotel only two minutes walk from Lake Windermere, village centre and free use of private leisure club. Parking, garden.

Lingwood, *Birkett Hill, Bowness, Windermere, Cumbria, LA23 3EZ.*
Friendly, comfortable, family guest house.
Open: All Year
Grades: ETB 2 Cr, Comm
015394 44680
Mrs Mossop
Rates fr: *£17.50*-**£21.00**.
Beds: 2F 3D 1T
Baths: 4 Ensuite 2 Private
(6)

Holmlea, *Kendal Road, Bowness, Windermere, Cumbria, LA23 3EW.*
Friendly, close to lake & amenites.
Open: All Year
Grades: ETB 2 Cr, Comm, RAC Listed
015394 42597 Mrs Goodacre
Rates fr: *£16.50*-**£16.50**.
Beds: 3D 1T 2S
Baths: 4 Private 2 Shared
(7)

Bowness on Solway

National Grid Ref: NY2262

Maia Lodge, *Bowness on Solway, Carlisle, Cumbria, CA5 5BH.*
Modern dormer bungalow. Drinks licence.
Open: All Year (not Xmas)
Grades: ETB Listed, Comm
016973 51955 Mrs Chettle
Rates fr: *£15.00*-**£15.00**.
Beds: 1F 1D 1T
Baths: 2 Shared
(5) (4)

Braithwaite

National Grid Ref: NY2323

Middle Ruddings Hotel

Cottage In The Wood Hotel, *Whinlatter Pass, Braithwaite, Keswick, Cumbria, CA12 5TW.*
Open: Mar to Nov
Grades: ETB 3 Cr, High Comm, AA 2 St, RAC 2 St
017687 78409
Mrs Littlefair
Rates fr: *£28.00*-**£28.00**.
Beds: 6D 1T
Baths: 7 Private
(5) (15)
Superb location in the Whinlatter Forest Park. Wonderful views. Excellent home cooking in idyllic surroundings. Log fires. Very well appointed bedrooms. 2 four poster rooms.

Thelmlea Country Guest House, *Braithwaite, Keswick, Cumbria, CA12 5TD.*
Victorian house in 1.75 acre grounds.
Open: All Year
Grades: ETB 3 Cr
017687 78305
Mrs Robinson
Rates fr: *£15.00*-**£15.00**.
Beds: 2D 1T
Baths: 3 Private
(2) (8)

Kendoon, *Braithwaite, Keswick, Cumbria, CA12 5RY.*
Panoramic views & good drying facilities.
Open: All Year (not Xmas)
017687 78430 Mrs Jackson
Rates fr: *£12.50*-**£13.50**.
Beds: 1D 2T
Baths: 2 Shared
(3)

Brampton

National Grid Ref: NY5261

White Lion Hotel

Beechwood, *Capon Tree Road, Brampton, Cumbria, CA8 1QL.*
Detached house in own grounds.
Open: All Year (not Xmas)
Grades: ETB Listed
01697 72239 Mrs Clark
Rates fr: *£14.00*-**£16.00**.
Beds: 1D 1T 1S
Baths: 1 Shared
(2) (10)

Cracrop Farm, *Brampton, Cumbria, CA8 2BW.*
High standard farmhouse.
Open: All Year (not Xmas)
Grades: ETB 3 St, High Comm, AA 4 Q, Select
016977 48245 Mrs Stobart
Fax no: 016977 48333
Rates fr: *£25.00*-**£25.00**.
Beds: 1D 1T 1S
Baths: 3 Private
(6)

Halidon, *Tree Road, Brampton, Cumbria, CA8 1TY.*
Comfortable, friendly, Edwardian terrace house.
Open: All Year
01697 72106 Mrs Streames
Rates fr: *£14.50*-**£15.00**.
Beds: 1F 1T
Baths: 1 Shared

Brampton (Appleby)

National Grid Ref: NY6723

New Inn, *Brampton (Appleby), Appleby in Westmorland, Cumbria, CA16 6JS.*
C18th traditional oak-beamed country pub.
Open: All Year (not Xmas)
017683 51231 Mrs Cranswick
Rates fr: *£18.00*-**£18.00**.
Beds: 1F 1D 1T
Baths: 2 Shared

The lowest *double* rate per person is shown in *italics*.

Brisco

National Grid Ref: NY4251

The Crown Inn (Broadfield), Black Lion (Durdar)

Crossroads House, *Brisco, Carlisle, Cumbria, CA4 0QZ.*
Charming country house, excellent breakfasts!
Open: All Year (not Xmas)
Grades: AA 3 Q, Recomm
01228 28994 Mr & Mrs Jennings
Rates fr: *£19.00*-**£20.00**.
Beds: 1F 2D 1T 1S
Baths: 1 Ensuite 2 Shared
(6)

Brough

National Grid Ref: NY7914

Golden Fleece Inn

Riverview, *Brough, Kirkby Stephen, Cumbria, CA17 4BZ.*
Open: All Year (not Xmas)
017683 41894 Mrs Holmes
Rates fr: *£14.00*-**£14.00**.
Beds: 1F 1D 1S
Baths: 1 Ensuite 1 Shared
(3)
Converted barn quietly located in village near A66. Ideal for touring Lakes, Dales and Northern Pennines. Friendly family home with clean, comfortable bedrooms. Excellent breakfasts.

Broughton-in-Furness

National Grid Ref: SD2187

Black Cock Inn

Cobblers Cottage, *Griffin Street, Broughton-in-Furness, Cumbria, LA20 6HH.*
Quaint C17th cottage.
Open: All Year (not Xmas)
01229 716413 Mr & Mrs Fletcher
Rates fr: *£17.50*-**£17.50**.
Beds: 2D 1T
Baths: 1 Private 1 Shared

Manor Arms Hotel, *The Square, Broughton-in-Furness, Cumbria, LA20 6GHJ.*
C18th inn, excellent traditional ales.
Open: All Year
01229 716286 Mr & Mrs Varty
Rates fr: *£14.00*-**£17.00**.
Beds: 2D 1T
Baths: 3 Private
(5)

Burnbanks

National Grid Ref: NY5016

Thornthwaite Hall, *Burnbanks, Bampton, Penrith, Cumbria, CA10 2RJ.*
C14th working sheep farm - former monastery.
Open: All Year
01931 713246 Mrs Lightburn
Rates fr: *£15.00*-**£15.00**.
Beds: 3D
Baths: 1 Shared

Burneside

National Grid Ref: SD5095

Gateside House Farm, *Windermere Road, Burneside, Kendal, Cumbria, LA9 5SE.*
Comfortable farm.
Open: All Year (not Xmas)
Grades: ETB Listed, Comm, AA 3 Q, RAC Acclaim
01539 722036 Mrs Ellis
Rates fr: *£17.00*-**£20.00**.
Beds: 1F 3D 1T
Baths: 3 Ensuite 2 Shared
(6)

Hill Fold Farm, *Burneside, Kendal, Cumbria, LA8 9AU.*
Warm friendly comfortable farmhouse.
Open: All Year
01539 722574
Mrs Bell
Rates fr: *£14.00*.
Beds: 1F 1D 1T
Baths: 1 Shared
(3)

Burton-in-Kendal

National Grid Ref: SD5376

The Rosary, *Heron Syke, Burton-in-Kendal, Carnforth, Lancs, LA6 1LG.*
Countryside tollhouse, families welcome.
Open: Mar to Oct
01524 781113 Mrs Jones
Rates fr: *£12.00*-**£16.00**.
Beds: 1F
Baths: 1 Private
(2)

Buttermere

National Grid Ref: NY1717

Bridge Hotel, Wheatsheaf (Lorton)

Trevene, *Buttermere, Cockermouth, Cumbria, CA13 9XA.*
Peaceful house, ideal for walkers.
Open: All Year (not Xmas)
017687 70210 Mrs Knight
Rates fr: *£16.00*-**£19.00**.
Beds: 1F 1D 1T
Baths: 1 Shared
(6) (4)

Cragg Farm, *Buttermere, Cockermouth, Cumbria, CA13 9XA.*
C17th cosy farmhouse.
Open: All Year (not Xmas)
017687 70204 Mrs Norman
Rates fr: *£14.50*-**£18.00**.
Beds: 2D 1T
Baths: 1 Shared
(3)

Dalegarth, *Buttermere, Cockermouth, Cumbria, CA13 9XA.*
Swiss chalet-style large house.
Open: Apr to Oct
017687 70233 Mr Parker
Rates fr: *£17.50*-**£22.00**.
Beds: 2F 3D 4T
Baths: 4 Private 2 Shared
(3) (20)

Butterwick

National Grid Ref: NY5119

St Patricks Well (Bampton)

Fell End Farm, *Butterwick, Penrith, Cumbria, CA10 2QQ.*
Quiet, comfortable, tastefully restored farmhouse.
Open: All Year
01931 713269 Mrs Sandells
Rates fr: *£18.00*-**£20.00**.
Beds: 1D 1T
Baths: 1 Shared
(2)

Caldbeck

National Grid Ref: NY3239

Oddfellows Arms

Swaledale Watch, *Whelpo, Caldbeck, Wigton, Cumbria, CA7 8HQ.*
Open: All Year (not Xmas)
Grades: ETB 2 Cr, High Comm, AA 4 Q, Select
016974 78409 Mrs Savage
Rates fr: *£16.00*-**£17.00**.
Beds: 2F 2D
Baths: 4 Ensuite
(10)
Enjoy great comfort, excellent home cooking, warm friendly farmhouse welcome. It's the little things that make the difference. Try us.

The Briars, *Caldbeck, Wigton, Cumbria, CA7 8DS.*
Modern farmhouse.
Open: Mar to Nov
016974 78633 Mrs Coulthard
Rates fr: *£18.00*-**£20.00**.
Beds: 1D 1T 1S
Baths: 1 Ensuite 1 Shared
(4)

Cark in Cartmel

National Grid Ref: SD3676

Rose & Crown

***Eeabank House,** 123 Station Road, Cark in Cartmel, Grange-over-Sands, Cumbria, LA11 7NY.*
Open: All Year
Grades: ETB 1 Cr
015395 58818 (also fax no)
Mr Worsley
Rates fr: *£16.50*-**£16.50**.
Beds: 2D 1T
Baths: 2 Ensuite 1 Private
A comfortable period house in village, colour TV all rooms. Ideal for touring South Lakelands' beautiful soft countryside avoiding main tourist centres.

Carlisle

National Grid Ref: NY3955

Lordy's, Casa Romana, Metal Bridge Inn

***Howard Lodge,** 90 Warwick Road, Carlisle, Cumbria, CA1 1JU.*
Open: All Year
Grades: ETB 1 Cr, AA 3 Q
01228 29842
Mr Hendrie
Rates fr: *£15.00*-**£15.00**.
Beds: 2F 1D 2T
Baths: 5 Ensuite 1 Shared
(6)
Large Victorian house on main road, 400 metres from city centre. Recently refurbished with ensuite facilities. Satellite TV and welcome tray in all rooms. Now with private parking.

***East View Guest House,** 110 Warwick Road, Carlisle, Cumbria, CA1 1JU.*
Victorian family-run guest house.
Open: All Year
Grades: ETB 1 Cr, AA 3 Q, RAC Acclaim
01228 22112
Mrs MacKin
Rates fr: *£16.00*-**£18.00**.
Beds: 3F 3D 1T 1S
Baths: 8 Ensuite
(4)

***Langleigh House,** 6 Howard Place, Carlisle, Cumbria, CA1 1HR.*
Open: All Year
Grades: ETB 2 Cr, High Comm, AA Listed
01228 30440
Rates fr: *£20.00*-**£25.00**.
Beds: 3D
Baths: 3 Ensuite
(10)
Number 6 has been restored to gracious comfortable home furnished with Victorian furniture. 5 minutes to city centre, very quiet. Private parking. 2 Cr, High Comm.

***Craighead,** 6 Hartington Place, Carlisle, Cumbria, CA1 1HL.*
Open: All Year (not Xmas)
Grades: ETB 2 Cr, Comm, AA 3 Q
01228 596767 Mrs Smith
Rates fr: *£15.50*-**£15.00**.
Beds: 1F 2D 1T 2S
Baths: 1 Ensuite 2 Shared
Grade II Listed spacious Victorian town house with comfortable rooms and original features. CTV, tea/coffee tray - all rooms. Minutes walk city centre, bus & rail station and all amenities. Friendly personal service.

***Marchmain Guest House,** 151 Warwick Road, Carlisle, Cumbria, CA1 1LU.*
Comfortable accommodation with friendly atmosphere.
Open: All Year
Grades: ETB 1 Cr, Comm
01228 29551 Mr Bertham
Rates fr: *£16.00*-**£15.00**.
Beds: 2F 2D 1T 1S
Baths: 1 Ensuite 2 Shared

***Courtfield Guest House,** 169 Warwick Road, Carlisle, Cumbria, CA1 1LP.*
Open: All Year
Grades: ETB 3 Cr, High Comm, RAC Acclaim
01228 22767
Mrs Dawes
Rates fr: *£15.00*-**£18.00**.
Beds: 1F 2D 1T
Baths: 4 Private
(4)
Highly recommended guest house, comfortable ensuite bedrooms with TV and welcome tray. Private parking. Short walk to city centre. Close to M6, J43.

***Chatsworth Guest House,** 22 Chatsworth Square, Carlisle, Cumbria, CA1 1HF.*
Large Victorian Listed town house.
Open: All Year (not Xmas)
Grades: ETB 2 Cr, Comm
01228 24023
Mrs Irving
Rates fr: *£14.00*-**£15.00**.
Beds: 2F 3T 1S
Baths: 2 Ensuite 1 Shared
(2)

***Avondale,** 3 St Aidans Road, Carlisle, Cumbria, CA1 1LT.*
Open: All Year (not Xmas)
Grades: ETB 2 Cr, High Comm, RAC Acclaim
01228 23012
Mr & Mrs Hayes
Rates fr: *£18.00*-**£20.00**.
Beds: 1D 2T
Baths: 1 Private 1 Shared
(3)
Attractive, comfortable Edwardian house in a quiet position, convenient for M6 (J43), city centre & amenities. Spacious well furnished rooms. Private parking.

***Crossroads House,** Brisco, Carlisle, Cumbria, CA4 0QZ.*
Charming country house, excellent breakfasts!
Open: All Year (not Xmas)
Grades: AA 3 Q, Recomm
01228 28994
Mr & Mrs Jennings
Rates fr: *£19.00*-**£20.00**.
Beds: 1F 2D 1T 1S
Baths: 1 Ensuite 2 Shared
(6)

***Metal Bridge House,** Metal Bridge, Rockcliffe, Carlisle, Cumbria, CA6 4HG.*
In country, close to M6/74.
Open: All Year
Grades: ETB 1 Cr
01228 74695
Mrs Rae
Rates fr: *£13.50*-**£18.00**.
Beds: 1D 2T
(4)

Cleator

National Grid Ref: NY0113

Grove Court Hotel

***Fell View,** 3 Cleator Gate, Cleator, Cumbria, CA23 3DN.*
Comfortable Georgian house. Home cooking.
Open: Apr to Oct
01946 813394
Mrs Fowler
Rates fr: *£15.00*-**£15.00**.
Beds: 1F 1T
Baths: 1 Shared
(2)

***Inglenook Cottage,** 37 Main Street, Cleator, Cumbria, CA23 3BU.*
Modernised clean, comfortable cottage. Every Facility.
Open: All Year (not Xmas)
01946 813156
Mrs Bradshaw
Rates fr: *£14.50*-**£14.50**.
Beds: 1D 1T 1S
Baths: 1 Shared
(2)

Cockermouth

National Grid Ref: NY1230

***Link House Hotel,** Dubwath, Bassenthwaite Lake, Cockermouth, Cumbria, CA13 9YD.*
Open: Feb to Nov
Grades: ETB 3 Cr, Comm, AA 4 Q, Select
017687 76291
Mr Tuppen
Fax no: 017687 76670
Rates fr: *£20.00*-**£20.00**.
Beds: 1F 3D 2T 2S
Baths: 8 Ensuite
(7) (10)
Family-run with excellent reputation for imaginative home cooking and inexpensive wine list. Friendly and relaxed atmosphere. Stunning scenery in quieter area. Leisure club membership.

The Castlegate Guest House, *6 Castlegate, Cockermouth, Cumbria, CA13 9EU.*
Grade II Listed Georgian town house.
Open: All Year
01900 826749 Miss Adams
Rates fr: *£16.00*-**£19.00**.
Beds: 2F 4D 1T
Baths: 4 Private 2 Shared

Globe Hotel, *Main Street, Cockermouth, Cumbria, CA13 9LE.*
C18th comfortable hotel.
Open: All Year (not Xmas)
Grades: ETB 4 Cr, RAC 2 St
01900 822126 Miss Greening
Rates fr: *£24.00*-**£25.00**.
Beds: 1F 11D 8T 5S
Baths: 20 Private 4 Shared
(10)

Colby

National Grid Ref: NY6620

Nether Hoff, *Colby, Appleby in Westmorland, Cumbria, CA16 6BD.*
Oak-beamed Westmorland stone farmhouse.
Open: All Year (not Xmas)
017683 52965 Mrs Thorburn
Rates fr: *£15.00*-**£15.00**.
Beds: 1D 1T
Baths: 2 Private
(5)

Coniston

National Grid Ref: SD3097

Sun Hotel, Black Bull, Yewdale Hotel, Church House Inn

Crown Hotel, *Coniston, Cumbria, LA21 8EA.*
Small village hotel.
Open: All Year
Grades: ETB 1 Cr, RAC Listed
015394 41243 Mr Tiidus
Rates fr: *£18.00*-**£20.00**.
Beds: 3F 3D 2T
Baths: 1 Private
(30)

Yewdale Hotel, *Coniston, Cumbria, LA21 8LU.*
Owners long distance walkers. Family-run.
Open: All Year
015394 41280 Mr Barrow
Fax no: 015394 41662
Rates fr: *£21.95*-**£28.70**.
Beds: 4F 3D 5T
Baths: 12 Ensuite
(6)

Lakeland House, *Tilberthwaite Avenue, Coniston, Cumbria, LA21 8ED.*
Friendly, family-run guest house.
Open: All Year (not Xmas)
Grades: ETB Listed
015394 41303 Mr Heywood
Rates fr: *£15.00*-**£15.00**.
Beds: 2F 2D 1T 1S
Baths: 1 Private 2 Shared
(2)

Orchard Cottage, *Yewdale Road, Coniston, Cumbria, LA21 8DU.*
Large modern bungalow of character.
Open: All Year (not Xmas/New Year)
Grades: ETB 2 Cr, Comm
015394 41373 Mrs Fawcett
Rates fr: *£16.50*-**£16.50**.
Beds: 2D 1T
Baths: 3 Ensuite
(3)

Arrowfield, *Little Arrow, Coniston, Cumbria, LA21 8AU.*
Style, comfort, home-made fare.
Open: Feb to Nov
Grades: ETB 2 Cr, High Comm
015394 41741 Mrs Walton
Rates fr: *£16.00*-**£18.00**.
Beds: 2D 2T 1S
Baths: 2 Ensuite 1 Shared
(3) (6)

Knipe Ground Farm, *Coniston, Cumbria, LA21 8AE.*
Secluded C16th farmhouse. Fabulous views.
Open: All Year (not Xmas)
015394 41221 Mrs Dutton
Rates fr: *£14.00*-**£13.00**.
Beds: 2D 2S
Baths: 1 Shared
(8) (4)

Cowgill

National Grid Ref: SD7587

Sportsman Inn

Scow Cottage, *Cowgill, Dent, Sedbergh, Cumbria, LA10 5RN.*
Open: All Year
015396 25445 Mrs Ferguson
Rates fr: *£16.00*-**£19.00**.
Beds: 1D 1T
Baths: 1 Shared
(12) (4)
Attractive and comfortable 250 year old Dales farmhouse, set in beautiful countryside. Near to Lakes and Yorkshire Dales. Pleasant gardens, near to river and quaint 'town' of Dent.

The Sportsman's Inn, *Cowgill, Dent, Sedbergh, Cumbria, LA10 5RG.*
300-year-old Dales inn, Listed building.
Open: All Year
015396 25282 Mr & Mrs Martin
Rates fr: *£19.00*.
Beds: 1F 3D 2T
Baths: 3 Shared

Crosscanonby

National Grid Ref: NY0739

Seychelles Restaurant (Allonby)

East Farm, *Crosscanonby, Maryport, Cumbria, CA15 6SJ.*
Modernised comfortable farmhouse. Traditional breakfast.
Open: All Year (not Xmas)
Grades: ETB Listed, Comm
01900 812153 Mrs Carruthers
Rates fr: *£15.00*-**£15.00**.
Beds: 1F 1D
Baths: 1 Shared
(2) (2)

Culgaith

National Grid Ref: NY6029

Black Swan

Elm Tree Barn, *Culgaith, Penrith, Cumbria, CA10 1QW.*
Tastefully converted C17th stone barn.
Open: All Year (not Xmas)
01768 88730 Mrs Wiedman
Rates fr: *£15.00*-**£20.00**.
Beds: 1D 2T
Baths: 1 Ensuite 1 Shared
(4)

Dacre

National Grid Ref: NY4526

Horse & Farrier

3 Rose Cottages, *Dacre, Penrith, Cumbria, CA11 0HJ.*
Warm, comfortable C18th Lakeland cottage.
Open: All Year (not Xmas)
017684 86569 Mrs Kinnersley
Rates fr: *£13.50*-**£13.50**.
Beds: 1T 1S
Baths: 1 Shared
(5) (2)

Dalemain

National Grid Ref: NY4726

Park House Farm, *Dalemain, Penrith, Cumbria, CA11 0HB.*
Wonderful views and peaceful tranquillity.
Open: Apr to Oct
Grades: ETB 1 Cr, Comm
017684 86212 Mrs Milburn
Rates fr: *£16.00*-**£17.00**.
Beds: 2F
Baths: 1 Private 2 Shared
(4)

Dearham

National Grid Ref: NY0736

Old Mill Inn, *Dearham, Maryport, Cumbria, CA15 7JP.*
Olde worlde family-run inn.
Open: All Year
01900 813148 Mrs Greenwood
Rates fr: *£12.50*-**£16.00**.
Beds: 1F 5D 1T
Baths: 2 Private 2 Shared
(1) (60)

Right on the border? Look at the neighbouring county, too

Dent

National Grid Ref: NY2518

George & Dragon

Dent Stores, *Dent, Sedbergh, Cumbria, LA10 5QL.*
Village centre, friendly family house.
Open: All Year (not Xmas)
015396 25209 Mrs Smith
Rates fr: *£15.00*-**£15.00**.
Beds: 2D 1T 1S
Baths: 1 Shared
P (3) TV V

Smithy Fold, *Whernside Manor, Dent, Sedbergh, Cumbria, LA10 5RE.*
Small C18th country house.
Open: All Year (not Xmas)
015396 25368 Mrs Cheetham
Rates fr: *£15.00*-**£15.00**.
Beds: 1F 1D 1T
Baths: 1 Shared
P (6) TV V

Rash House, *Dent Foot, Dent, Sedbergh, Cumbria, LA10 5SU.*
C18th farmhouse.
Open: All Year (not Xmas)
015396 20113 Mrs Hunter
Rates fr: *£16.00*-**£17.00**.
Beds: 1F 1D
Baths: 1 Shared
P (2) TV V

Stone Close Tea Shop, *Main Street, Dent, Sedbergh, Cumbria, LA10 5QL.*
C17th oak-beamed, stone-flagged tea-shop.
Open: Mar to Dec
015396 25231
Mr Hudson
Rates fr: *£15.50*-**£17.50**.
Beds: 1F 1D 1S
Baths: 1 Shared

Slack Cottage, *Dent, Sedbergh, Cumbria, LA10 5QU.*
Comfortable old cottage.
Open: All Year (not Xmas)
015396 25439
Mrs Gunson
Rates fr: *£13.00*-**£13.00**.
Beds: 1D 1S
Baths: 1 Shared
P TV

Derwent Water

National Grid Ref: NY2518

Mary Mount, *Country House Hotel, Derwent Water, Borrowdale, Keswick, Cumbria, CA12 5UU.*
Peaceful country house atmosphere & superb views.
Open: All Year
Grades: ETB 3 Cr
017687 77223
Mrs Mawdsley
Rates fr: *£23.00*-**£23.00**.
Beds: 3F 8D 2T 1S
Baths: 14 Private
P (25) TV V

Docker

National Grid Ref: SD5695

Myers Farm, *Docker, Grayrigg, Kendal, Cumbria, LA8 0DF.*
Working hill/sheep farm.
Open: All Year
01539 824610 Mrs Knowles
Rates fr: *£21.00 (inc dinner)*.
Beds: 1F 1D 1T
Baths: 1 Shared
P (2) TV

Dubwath

National Grid Ref: NY1931

Link House Hotel, *Dubwath, Bassenthwaite Lake, Cockermouth, Cumbria, CA13 9YD.*
Family-run with excellent reputation for imaginative home cooking and inexpensive wine list.
Open: Feb to Nov
Grades: ETB 3 Cr, Comm, AA 4 Q, Select
017687 76291 Mr Tuppen
Fax no: 017687 76670
Rates fr: *£20.00*-**£20.00**.
Beds: 1F 3D 2T 2S
Baths: 8 Ensuite
(7) P (10) TV V

Dufton

National Grid Ref: NY6825

Stag Inn

Dufton Hall Farm, *Dufton, Appleby in Westmorland, Cumbria, CA16 6DD.*
C18th farmhouse in village centre.
Open: Mar to Oct
Grades: ETB 1 Cr, Approv
017683 51573 Mrs Howe
Rates fr: *£16.00*-**£18.00**.
Beds: 1F 1D 1T
Baths: 2 Ensuite 1 Private
P (4) TV

Ghyll View, *Dufton, Appleby in Westmorland, Cumbria, CA16 6DF.*
Large Victorian private house.
Open: Easter to Oct
017683 51855 Mrs Hullock
Rates fr: *£14.00*-**£14.00**.
Beds: 3T 1S
Baths: 2 Shared
P (4) TV

Egremont

National Grid Ref: NY0110

Ghyll Farm Guest House, *Egremont, Cumbria, CA22 2UA.*
Large comfortable, clean friendly farmhouse.
Open: All Year (not Xmas)
01946 822256
Mrs Holliday
Rates fr: *£12.00*-**£12.00**.
Beds: 2F 2T
P (8) TV

Ellonby

National Grid Ref: NY4235

Greenfields, *Ellonby, Penrith, Cumbria, CA11 9SJ.*
Modern, comfortable rural house.
Open: Easter to Oct
Grades: ETB Listed, High Comm
01768 484671 Mrs Green
Rates fr: *£15.00*-**£15.00**.
Beds: 2D 1S
Baths: 2 Shared
(8) P (3) TV V

Elterwater

National Grid Ref: NY3204

Britannia Inn

Barnhowe, *Elterwater, Ambleside, Cumbria, LA22 9HU.*
Homemade bread. Quiet beautiful location.
Open: Feb to Nov
Grades: ETB 1 Cr, Comm
015394 37346
Mr & Mrs Riley
Rates fr: *£15.00*-**£15.00**.
Beds: 1D 1T 1S
Baths: 1 Shared
P (7) TV V

Endmoor

National Grid Ref: SD5385

Summerlands Tower, *Summerlands, Endmoor, Kendal, Cumbria, LA8 0ED.*
Fine Victorian country house in 9 acres.
Open: All Year (not Xmas)
015395 61081
Mr & Mrs Green
Rates fr: *£17.50*-**£22.50**.
Beds: 3T
Baths: 1 Ensuite 1 Shared
(13) P (4) TV V

Ennerdale

National Grid Ref: NY0515 to NY1015

Beckfoot, *Ennerdale, Cleator, Cumbria, CA23 3AU.*
Comfortable accommodation overlooking Ennerdale Lake.
Open: All Year (not Xmas)
01946 861235 (also fax no)
Mrs Loxham
Rates fr: *£16.00*-**£20.00**.
Beds: 1F 1D 1T
Baths: 1 Shared
(3) P (3) TV V

The Old Vicarage, *Ennerdale, Cleator, Cumbria, CA23 3AG.*
Lovely old former vicarage.
Open: All Year (not Xmas)
01946 861107
Mrs Lake
Rates fr: *£17.00*-**£17.00**.
Beds: 1F 1D 2T 1S
Baths: 2 Shared
P (6) TV V

How Hall Farm, *Ennerdale, Cleator, Cumbria, CA23 3AU.*
Traditional Lakeland farm. Peaceful location.
Open: Easter to Nov
01946 861266 Mrs Hardisty
Rates fr: *£15.00*-**£18.00**.
Beds: 1D 2T
Baths: 2 Shared
(4)

Ennerdale Bridge

National Grid Ref: NY0715

The Shepherds Arms Hotel, *Ennerdale Bridge, Cleator, Cumbria, CA23 3AR.*
Open: All Year
Grades: ETB 3 Cr, Approv
01946 861249 Mr Whitfield Bott
Rates fr: *£21.50*-**£21.50**.
Beds: 3D 2T 1S
Baths: 3 Ensuite 1 Shared
(6)
Family-owned and run. Traditional features include log fires & four poster beds. Varied menus feature local fish, game and home smoked salmon. Real ale.

Eskdale Green

National Grid Ref: NY1400

King George IV Inn

The Ferns, *Eskdale Green, Holmrook, Cumbria, CA19 1UA.*
Victorian residence of considerable character.
Open: All Year
019467 23217 Mrs Prestwood
Rates fr: *£16.50*-**£18.00**.
Beds: 1F 1D 1T
Baths: 1 Ensuite 2 Shared
(0) (4)

Far Sawrey

National Grid Ref: SD3795

West Vale Country Guest House, *Far Sawrey, Ambleside, Cumbria, LA22 0LQ.*
Peaceful, private, family-run accommodation.
Open: Mar to Oct
Grades: ETB 3 Cr, High Comm, AA 4 Q, Select, RAC High Acclaim
015394 42817 Mrs Forbes
Rates fr: *£22.50*-**£22.50**.
Beds: 1F 4D 2T
Baths: 6 Ensuite 1 Private
(7) (7)

Sawrey Hotel, *Far Sawrey, Ambleside, Cumbria, LA22 0LQ.*
C18th country inn.
Open: All Year (not Xmas)
Grades: ETB 3 Cr, Comm, RAC 2 St
015394 43425
Mr Brayshaw
Rates fr: *£23.00*-**£23.00**.
Beds: 6F 7D 5T 4S
Baths: 18 Private 1 Shared
(30)

The Glen, *Far Sawrey, Ambleside, Cumbria, LA22 0LQ.*
Comfortable old Lakeland country house. **Open:** All Year (not Xmas)
015394 43370 Mr Gardner
Rates fr: *£19.00*-**£26.00**.
Beds: 1F 3D 1T
Baths: 5 Ensuite
(7)

Field Broughton

National Grid Ref: SD3881

High Cark Cottage, *Field Broughton, Grange-over-Sands, Cumbria, LA11 6HS.*
Charming, peaceful, C16th stone cottage. **Open:** Easter to Sep
015395 36615 Mrs Wrigley
Rates fr: *£18.00*-**£15.00**.
Beds: 1D **Baths:** 1 Shared
(2)

Garrigill

National Grid Ref: NY7441

George & Dragon Hotel

The Post Office, *Garrigill, Alston, Cumbria, CA9 3DS.*
C17th village post office.
Open: Easter to Oct
01434 381257 Mrs Bramwell
Rates fr: *£14.00*-**£14.00**.
Beds: 2D 1T 1S **Baths:** 1 Shared

Sharon Cottage, *Garrigill, Alston, Cumbria, CA9 3DY.*
Comfortable family house, warm welcome.
Open: All Year (not Xmas)
01434 381570 Mrs Tucker
Rates fr: *£15.00*-**£15.00**.
Beds: 1T 1S **Baths:** 1 Shared
(3) (1)

High Windy Hall Hotel, *Middleton In Teesdale Road, Garrigill, Alston, Cumbria, CA9 3EZ.*
Panoramic views, good food, peaceful. **Open:** All Year
01434 381547 Mrs Platts
Fax no: 01434 382477
Rates fr: *£21.00*-**£30.00**.
Beds: 1F 2D 1T
Baths: 4 Private
(1) (5)

Garsdale

National Grid Ref: SD7389

Farfield Country Guest House, *Garsdale Road, Garsdale, Sedbergh, Cumbria, LA10 5LP.*
Beautiful Victorian house. Outstanding views.
Open: All Year (not Xmas)
015396 20537
Mr & Mrs clark
Rates fr: *£19.00*-**£20.00**.
Beds: 1F 3D 2T 1S
Baths: 4 Ensuite 1 Private
(10)

Garth Row

National Grid Ref: SD5395

Plough Inn

Hollin Root Farm, *Garth Row, Kendal, Cumbria, LA8 9AW.*
Peaceful farmhouse with warm welcome. **Open:** Easter to Nov
Grades: ETB Listed
01539 823638 Mrs Metcalfe
Rates fr: *£14.00*-**£16.00**.
Beds: 1F 1D 1T
Baths: 1 Ensuite 1 Shared
(6)

Gawthrop

National Grid Ref: SD6987

Ivy Dene, *Gawthrop, Dentdale, Sedbergh, Cumbria, LA10 5TA.*
Oak-beamed cottage.
Open: Mar to Oct
015396 25353 Mrs Williamson
Rates fr: *£16.00*.
Beds: 1F 2D **Baths:** 1 Shared

Gilsland

National Grid Ref: NY6366

Miller Hill Banks, *Gilsland, Carlisle, Cumbria, CA6 7DE.*
Comfortable farmhouse. Walls 52ins thick. **Open:** May to Oct
016977 47298 Mrs Graham
Rates fr: *£15.00*-**£15.50**.
Beds: 1F 1D

Alpha Mount House, *Gilsland, Carlisle, Cumbria, CA6 7EB.*
Large, comfortable family home.
Open: All Year
Grades: ETB 1 Cr, Comm
016977 47070 Mr Cole
Rates fr: *£13.00*-**£13.00**.
Beds: 1F 1D **Baths:** 1 Shared
(0) (2)

Howard House Farm, *Gilsland, Carlisle, Cumbria, CA6 7AN.*
Comfortable farmhouse on Roman wall. **Open:** All Year (not Xmas)
016977 47285 Mrs Woodmass
Rates fr: *£16.00*-**£20.00**.
Beds: 1F 1D 1T
Baths: 1 Ensuite 1 Private 1 Shared

Glenridding

National Grid Ref: NY3816

Travellers Rest

Grisedale Lodge, *Grisedale Bridge, Glenridding, Penrith, Cumbria, CA11 0PJ.*
Open: All Year (not Xmas)
017684 82084 Mrs Martin
Rates fr: *£15.00*-**£18.00**.
Beds: 1D 2T **Baths:** 1 Shared
Idyllically situated in quiet location set back off main road. Garden, excellent views from bedrooms and within easy walking distance of 2 villages and lake.

Gosforth

National Grid Ref: NY0603

Longacre Country Guest House, *Santon Bridge Road, Gosforth, Seascale, Cumbria, CA20 1JA.*
Detached house, gardens, West Lakeland.
Open: All Year
019467 25328
Mrs Moorhouse
Rates fr: *£14.00*-**£14.00**.
Beds: 1D 1T 1S
Baths: 2 Shared
(3) (5)

Grange-in-Borrowdale

National Grid Ref: NY2517

Swinside Inn, Riverside Inn

Scawdel, *Grange-in-Borrowdale, Keswick, Cumbria, CA12 5UQ.*
Modern, friendly, comfortable private house. **Open:** All Year
017687 77271 Mr Reinecke
Rates fr: *£16.50*-**£17.50**.
Beds: 3D
Baths: 2 Ensuite 1 Shared
(7) (4)

Grayrigg, *Grange-in-Borrowdale, Keswick, Cumbria, CA12 5UQ.*
Friendly, comfortable old school house. **Open:** All Year (not Xmas)
017687 77607 Mrs Figg
Rates fr: *£18.00*-**£18.00**.
Beds: 1F 1D 1T
Baths: 2 Ensuite 1 Private

Grange-over-Sands

National Grid Ref: SD4077

Mayfields, *3 Mayfield Terrace, Kents Bank Road, Grange-over-Sands, Cumbria, LA11 7DW.*
Well-appointed charming Edwardian town house.
Open: All Year (not Xmas)
Grades: ETB 3 Cr, Comm
015395 34730 Mr Thorburn
Rates fr: *£20.00*-**£18.50**.
Beds: 1D 1T 1S
Baths: 3 Ensuite 1 Shared
(3)

Holme Lea Guest House, *90 Kentsford Road, Kents Bank, Grange-over-Sands, Cumbria, LA11 7BB.*
Victorian house overlooking bay.
Open: Mar to Oct
015395 32545 Mrs Barton
Rates fr: *£17.00*-**£17.00**.
Beds: 1F 1D 1T 1S
Baths: 2 Ensuite 1 Shared
(4)

Grangeways, *6 Morecambe Bank, Grange-over-Sands, Cumbria, LA11 6DX.*
Excellent base for Lake District.
Open: Easter to Oct
Grades: ETB 1 Cr, Comm
015395 35329
Mr & Mrs Campbell
Rates fr: *£15.50*-**£15.50**.
Beds: 1F 1D 1T 1S
Baths: 1 Shared
(6) (2)

Grasmere

National Grid Ref: NY3307

Travellers Rest, Le Lac, Ruwan Tree

Undercrag, *Easedale Road, Grasmere, Ambleside, Cumbria, LA22 9QD.*
Open: All Year (not Xmas/New Year)
015394 35349 Mrs Nelson
Rates fr: *£17.50*-**£23.00**.
Beds: 1F 1D 1T
Baths: 2 Shared
(5)
Lovely room with mountain views in secluded yet centrally situated Victorian home. Delicious breakfasts with homemade bread, fresh fruit muesli and Cumberland sausage. No smoking!

Oak Lodge, *Easedale Road, Grasmere, Ambleside, Cumbria, LA22 9QJ.*
Quietly located, stone-built bungalow.
Open: Mar to Nov
Grades: ETB Listed
015394 35527 Mrs Dixon
Rates fr: *£16.00*-**£30.00**.
Beds: 1D 1T **Baths:** 1 Shared
(5) (3)

Crummock Cottage, *Keswick Road, Grasmere, Ambleside, Cumbria, LA22 9QY.*
Open: Mar to Dec
015394 35606 Mrs Hoare
Rates fr: *£18.00*-**£25.00**.
Beds: 2D **Baths:** 2 Ensuite
(2)
Small select establishment for non-smokers. Superb views. Excellent cuisine. Vegetarians welome. Dogs accepted.

St Oswalds, *Grasmere, Cumbria, LA22 9PX.*
English hospitality at its best.
Open: All Year (not Xmas)
015394 35705 (also fax no)
Mr Yates
Rates fr: *£23.00*-**£21.00**.
Beds: 1D 1T 1S **Baths:** 2 Private
(11) (2)

Titteringdales, *Pye Lane, Grasmere, Ambleside, Cumbria, LA22 9RQ.*
Quietly situated with good views.
Open: Feb to Dec
Grades: ETB 2 Cr, Comm
015394 35439 (also fax no)
Mr Scott
Rates fr: *£17.50*-**£22.50**.
Beds: 6D 1T 1S
Baths: 6 Private
(12) (8)

Eller Close House, *Grasmere, Ambleside, Cumbria, LA22 9RW.*
Delightfully secluded house and gardens.
Open: All Year
Grades: ETB Listed
015394 35786
Mr Greathead
Rates fr: *£14.50*-**£18.50**.
Beds: 1F 1D 1T
Baths: 2 Private 2 Shared
(0) (6)

Oak Bank Hotel, *Broadgate, Grasmere, Ambleside, Cumbria, LA22 9TA.*
Traditional Lakeland country house hotel. **Open:** Feb to Dec
Grades: ETB Listed , AA 2 St, RAC 2 St
015394 35217 Mrs Savasi
Fax no: 015394 35685
Rates fr: *£25.00*-**£25.00**.
Beds: 2F 5D 5T 2S
Baths: 14 Private
(14)

Grayrigg

National Grid Ref: SD5797

Punchbowl House, *Grayrigg, Kendal, Cumbria, LA8 9BU.*
Spacious Victorian house. Quiet area. **Open:** All Year
Grades: ETB 2 Cr, Comm
01539 824345 Mrs Johnson
Rates fr: *£16.00*-**£16.00**.
Beds: 2D 1T
Baths: 1 Ensuite 1 Shared
(5)

Grayrigg Hall Farm, *Grayrigg, Kendal, Cumbria, LA8 9BU.*
C18th comfortable farmhouse.
Open: Easter to Oct
01539 824689 Mrs Bindloss
Rates fr: *£14.00*-**£15.00**.
Beds: 1F 1D 1S
(2)

Great Langdale

National Grid Ref: NY3006

Baysbrown Farm, *Great Langdale, Ambleside, Cumbria, LA22 9JZ.*
C12th beautifully decorated farmhouse. **Open:** Mar to Oct
015394 37300 Mrs Rowand
Rates fr: *£17.50*-**£17.50**.
Beds: 1F 1D 1T **Baths:** 1 Shared
(6)

Greystoke

National Grid Ref: NY4430

Clickham Inn

Lattendales Farm, *Greystoke, Penrith, Cumbria, CA11 0UE.*
Comfortable C17th farmhouse.
Open: Mar to Oct
017684 83474 Mrs Ashburner
Rates fr: *£14.50*-**£15.00**.
Beds: 2D 1T
Baths: 1 Shared
(1) (4)

Haverigg

National Grid Ref: SD1578

Dunelm Cottage, *Main Street, Haverigg, Millom, Cumbria, LA18 4EX.*
Comfortable converted cottages. Superior accomodation, excellent cuisine. **Open:** Feb to Dec
Grades: AA 3 Q
01229 770097 Mrs Fairless
Rates fr: *£18.50*-**£20.00**.
Beds: 1D 2T (5)

Haweswater

National Grid Ref: NY4813

Haweswater Hotel, *Lakeside Road, Haweswater, Penrith, Cumbria, CA10 2RP.*
Open: Feb to Dec
01931 713235 Mr Weller
Fax no: 01931 713145
Rates fr: *£25.00*-**£25.00**.
Beds: 1F 4D 8T 3S
Baths: 7 Ensuite 4 Shared
(20)
Time to give yourself a treat? This is the place. Log fires, home cooking, enormous baths, comfy bar, friendly welcome, peace and quiet.

Hawkshead

National Grid Ref: SD3598

Drunken Duck Inn, Outgate Inn

Betty Fold Guest House, *Hawkshead Hill, Hawkshead, Ambleside, Cumbria, LA22 0PS.*
Large private house.
Open: All Year
Grades: ETB 2 Cr, High Comm
015394 36611 Mr Marsden
Rates fr: *£18.00*-**£24.00**.
Beds: 1F 1D 1T **Baths:** 3 Private
(8)

Borwick Lodge, *Hawkshead, Ambleside, Cumbria, LA22 0PU.*
Award-Winning 'Accommodation of the Highest Standards'. A rather special C17th country house.
Open: All Year
Grades: ETB 2 Cr, High Comm
015394 36332 (also fax no)
Mr & Mrs Bleasdale
Rates fr: *£18.00*-**£18.00**.
Beds: 2F 2D 2T **Baths:** 6 Ensuite
(8) (8)

Helton

National Grid Ref: NY5122

Helton Inn

Beckfoot Hotel, *Helton, Penrith, Cumbria, CA10 2QB.*
'Home from home' informal country house hotel. **Open:** Mar to Nov
01931 713241 Mrs White
Fax no: 01931 713391
Rates fr: *£25.00*-**£30.00**.
Beds: 2F 2D 1T 1S **Baths:** 6 Private
(12)

Holywell Country Guest House, *Helton, Penrith, Cumbria, CA10 2QA.*
Open: Easter to Nov
01931 712231 Mrs Hunt
Rates fr: *£20.00*-**£25.00**.
Beds: 2D 1T
Baths: 1 Ensuite 1 Shared
(12)
Need a break? Enjoy Cumbrian hospitality in our idyllically situated country house twixt Ullswater and Haweswater. Hearty breakfast. Superb views. Knowledgeable hosts. A little gem. Brochure.

Hethersgill

National Grid Ref: NY4767

New Pallyards, *Hethersgill, Carlisle, Cumbria, CA6 6HZ.*
National Gold Award Winner B&B.
Open: All Year
01228 577308 Mrs Elwen
Rates fr: *£17.50*-**£18.50**.
Beds: 1F 1D 1T 1S
Baths: 4 Ensuite

Heversham

National Grid Ref: SD4983

Blue Bell Hotel

Springlea, *Heversham, Milnthorpe, Cumbria, LA7 7EE.*
Comfortable house overlooking restful countryside.
Open: All Year
Grades: AA 3 Q, Recomm
015395 64026
Mrs Green
Rates fr: *£15.00*-**£18.50**.
Beds: 1F 2D 1T
Baths: 2 Ensuite 1 Private
(3)

High Wray

National Grid Ref: SD3799

Queens Head, Drunken Duck

Tock How Farm, *High Wray, Ambleside, Cumbria, LA22 0JF.*
Chrming, friendly farmhouse. Wonderful views.
Open: All Year (not Xmas)
Grades: ETB Listed, Comm
015394 36481 Mrs Benson
Rates fr: *£15.00*-**£17.00**.
Beds: 1F 1D
(4)

High Wray Farm, *High Wray, Ambleside, Cumbria, LA22 0JE.*
Charming C17th olde worlde farmhouse.
Open: All Year (not Xmas)
Grades: ETB Listed, Comm
015394 32280 Mrs Briggs
Rates fr: *£15.50*-**£16.00**.
Beds: 1F 1D 1T
Baths: 1 Private 1 Shared
(5)

Holmrook

National Grid Ref: SD0799

Horse & Groom

Hill Farm, *Holmrook, Cumbria, CA19 1UG.*
Comfortable farmhouse, excellent views.
Open: All Year (not Xmas)
Grades: ETB Listed
019467 24217 Mrs Leak
Rates fr: *£13.00*-**£13.00**.
Beds: 2F 1D **Baths:** 2 Shared

Low Holme, *Drigg Road, Holmrook, Cumbria, CA19 1YE.*
Bungalow with views of fells.
Open: All Year (not Xmas)
019467 24219 Mrs Skeen
Rates fr: *£10.50*-**£12.00**.
Beds: 1F **Baths:** 1 Shared
(1)

Ings

National Grid Ref: SD4498

A Badgers Rest, *Ings, Staveley, Kendal, Cumbria, LA8 9PY.*
Quaint 1901 Lakeland home, gourmet food. **Open:** All Year
01539 821135 Mr Badger
Rates fr: *£17.00*-**£20.00**.
Beds: 1F 2D
Baths: 1 Private 1 Shared
(4)

St Annes Farm, *Ings, Kendal, Cumbria, LA8 9QG.*
Very clean comfortable farmhouse.
Open: Easter to Oct
01539 821223 Mrs Allen
Rates fr: *£15.00*-**£20.00**.
Beds: 2D **Baths:** 1 Shared
(4)

Ireby

National Grid Ref: NY2338

Woodlands Country Hotel, *Ireby, Carlisle, Cumbria, CA5 1EX.*
Family-run Victorian country house.
Open: Mar to Nov
Grades: ETB 3 Cr, High Comm, RAC High Acclaim
016973 71791 Mr Bibby
Rates fr: *£22.50*-**£22.50**.
Beds: 2F 3D 2T 1S
Baths: 8 Ensuite
(5) (12)

Irton

National Grid Ref: NY1000

Cookson Place Farm, *Irton, Holmrook, Cumbria, CA19 1YQ.*
Comfortable farmhouse in quiet area. **Open:** All Year
01946 724286 Mrs Crayston
Rates fr: *£13.00*-**£13.00**.
Beds: 1D 1T
Baths: 1 Shared

Ivegill

National Grid Ref: NY4143

Crown Inn

Streethead Farm, *Ivegill, Carlisle, Cumbria, CA4 0NG.*
Open: Mar to Oct
Grades: ETB 2 Cr, Comm
016974 73327
Mrs Wilson
Rates fr: *£16.00*-**£16.00**.
Beds: 1F 1D
Baths: 1 Ensuite 1 Private
(7) (2)
Midway between Penrith & Carlisle. M6 10 minutes. Ideal for break enroute to Scotland. Real fires, homebaking. Choice of breakfasts. Brochure on request.

Kendal

National Grid Ref: SD5192

Punch Bowl, Castle Inn, Da Franco, The Moon

Brantholme, *7 Sedbergh Road, Kendal, Cumbria, LA9 6AD.*
Open: Feb to Nov
Grades: ETB Listed
01539 722340
Mrs Bigland
Rates fr: *£18.00*-**£25.00**.
Beds: 3T
Baths: 2 Ensuite 1 Private
(5)
Family-run guest house. Victorian house in large private garden. Excellent meals from fresh local produce. Friendly relaxing atmosphere. Ideal for a quiet restful holiday.

Higher House Farm, *Oxenholme Lane, Natland, Kendal, Cumbria, LA9 7QH.*
Tranquil Lakeland village, C17th farmhouse.
Open: All Year
Grades: ETB 3 Cr, Comm, AA 4 Q, Select
015395 61177
Mrs Sunter
Fax no: 015395 61520
Rates fr: *£18.00*-**£23.00**.
Beds: 2D 1T
Baths: 3 Private
(9)

Olde Peat Cotes, *Sampool Lane, Levens, Kendal, Cumbria, LA8 8EH.*
Open: All Year (not Xmas)
Grades: ETB Listed
015395 60096
Mrs Parsons
Rates fr: *£10.00*-**£10.00**.
Beds: 1F 1T
Baths: 1 Shared
(2)
Homely, modern bungalow, suitable wheelchairs. Ideal stopover south to Scotland. Edge of Lake District. Beautiful rural setting. Salmon fishing available. Personal service. Children welcome.

Newlands Guest House, *37 Milnthorpe Road, Kendal, Cumbria, LA9 5QG.*
Comfortable, friendly Victorian house. **Open:** All Year (not Xmas)
Grades: ETB 2 Cr, Approv
01539 725340 Mrs Horsley
Rates fr: *£15.00*-**£15.00**.
Beds: 1F 2D 1T 1S
Baths: 2 Private 1 Shared
(5)

West Mount, *39 Milnthorpe Road, Kendal, Cumbria, LA9 5QG.*
Open: All Year **01539 724621**
Keep **Rates fr:** *£16.00*-**£16.00**.
Beds: 1F 2D
(1) (3)
Ideally situated on outskirts of historic market town. Many good restaurants in vicinity. Excellent breakfast. Ensuite bedrooms. Friendly hosts offer warm welcome.

Bridge House, *65 Castle Street, Kendal, Cumbria, LA9 7AD.*
Beautiful Georgian Listed building.
Open: All Year **Grades:** ETB 1 Cr
01539 722041 Mrs Brindley
Rates fr: *£16.00*-**£18.00**.
Beds: 1F 1T **Baths:** 1 Shared
(1)

Fairways, *102 Windermere Road, Kendal, Cumbria, LA9 5EZ.*
Traditional Victorian guest house.
Open: All Year
Grades: ETB 2 Cr, Comm
01539 725564 Mrs Paylor
Rates fr: *£17.00*-**£18.00**.
Beds: 1F 2D **Baths:** 3 Ensuite
(2) (4)

Natland Mill Beck Farm, *Kendal, Cumbria, LA9 7LH.*
Open: Easter to Oct
Grades: AA 3 Q
01539 721122 Mrs Gardner
Rates fr: *£15.00*-**£16.00**.
Beds: 1D 1T 1S
Baths: 1 Ensuite 1 Private 1 Shared
(3)
Lake District. On working dairy farm. Hospitality recommended in C17th old farmhouse. English breakfast. 6 miles motorway.

Holmfield, *41 Kendal Green, Kendal, Cumbria, LA9 5PP.*
Superb accommodation, swimming pool, 4-poster. **Open:** All Year
Grades: ETB Listed, Deluxe
01539 720790 (also fax no)
Mrs Kettle
Rates fr: *£19.00*-**£20.00**.
Beds: 2D 1T **Baths:** 2 Shared
(12) (5)

Hillside Guest House, *4 Beast Banks, Kendal, Cumbria, LA9 4JW.*
Large Victorian guest house.
Open: All Year
Grades: ETB 2 Cr, Comm
01539 722836 Mrs Denison
Rates fr: *£18.00*-**£15.00**.
Beds: 4D 3S
Baths: 5 Ensuite 4 Private
(4) (4)

Kentmere

National Grid Ref: NY4504

Maggs Howe, *Kentmere, Kendal, Cumbria, LA8 9JP.*
Former farmhouse with old charm.
Open: All Year (not Xmas)
01539 821689
Mrs Foster
Rates fr: *£16.00*-**£16.00**.
Beds: 1F 1D
Baths: 1 Ensuite 1 Private
(4)

Keswick

National Grid Ref: NY2623

Skiddaw Hotel, Dog & Gun, Golden Lion

Dalkeith House, *1 Leonards Street, Keswick, Cumbria, CA12 4EJ.*
Open: All Year (not Xmas)
Grades: ETB 2 Cr
017687 72696 (also fax no)
Mr & Mrs Seymour
Rates fr: *£15.00*-**£15.00**.
Beds: 4D 2T 1S
Baths: 3 Ensuite 1 Shared
(5)
Family-run Victorian guest house serving home cooked, filling breakfasts and evening meals. Separate or group tables. Close to walking routes, Derwentwater, parks and shops.

Chaucer House Hotel, *Ambleside Road, Keswick, Cumbria, CA12 4DR.*
Friendly, comfortable country house hotel. **Open:** Feb to Nov
Grades: ETB 3 Cr, Comm, AA 2 St, RAC 2 St
017687 72318
Mr Pechartscheck
Rates fr: *£28.00*-**£29.00**.
Beds: 4F 14D 10T 7S
Baths: 32 Private 3 Shared
(27)

Greystoke House, *9 Leonard Street, Keswick, Cumbria, CA12 4EL.*
Traditional Lakeland townhouse.
Open: All Year
Grades: ETB 2 Cr, RAC Acclaim
017687 72603
Mrs Robinson
Rates fr: *£18.00*-**£16.00**.
Beds: 5D 1S
Baths: 4 Ensuite 1 Shared

Latrigg House, *St Herbert Street, Keswick, Cumbria, CA12 4DF.*
Quiet, convenient, friendly Victorian house.
Open: All Year
Grades: ETB 2 Cr
017687 73068
Mr & Mrs Townend
Rates fr: *£14.00*-**£15.00**.
Beds: 1F 1D 2T 1S
Baths: 3 Private 1 Shared

Goodwin House, *29 Southey Street, Keswick, Cumbria, CA12 4EE.*
Warm, comfortable and friendly guesthouse.
Open: All Year (not Xmas)
Grades: ETB 2 Cr, AA 3 Q
017687 74634 Mr Smith
Rates fr: *£15.00*-**£15.00**.
Beds: 3F 2D 1S
Baths: 3 Ensuite 1 Private 2 Shared
(7)

Clarence House, *14 Eskin Street, Keswick, Cumbria, CA12 4DQ.*
Quality large Victorian guest house.
Open: All Year (not Xmas)
Grades: ETB 3 Cr, Comm
017687 73186
Mrs Raine
Rates fr: *£19.00*-**£19.00**.
Beds: 1F 4D 3T 1S
Baths: 9 Private
(5)

Beckside, *5 Wordsworth Street, Keswick, Cumbria, CA12 4HU.*
Small, very comfortable guest house.
Open: All Year (not Xmas)
Grades: ETB 2 Cr, AA 3 Q, RAC High Acclaim
017687 73093
Mr & Mrs Helling
Rates fr: *£17.00*.
Beds: 3D 1T
Baths: 4 Private
(8)

Pitcairn House, *7 Blencathra Street, Keswick, Cumbria, CA12 4HW.*
Warm, comfortable B&B. Good value.
Open: All Year
017687 72453
Mrs Davies
Rates fr: *£13.00*-**£14.75**.
Beds: 2F 4D 1T
Baths: 2 Shared
(2)

Glaramara Guest House, *9 Acorn Street, Keswick, Cumbria, CA12 4EA.*
Large, comfortable Victorian private house.
Open: All Year (not Xmas)
017687 73216 / 75255
Mrs Harbage (BHSII)
Rates fr: *£15.00*-**£15.00**.
Beds: 1F 2D 1T 1S
Baths: 2 Private 2 Shared
(3)

Derwentdale Guest Hotel, *8 Blencathra Street, Keswick, Cumbria, CA12 4HP.*
Friendly, family-run guest house.
Open: All Year
Grades: ETB Listed, Comm
017687 74187
Mrs Riding
Rates fr: *£15.00*-**£15.00**.
Beds: 3D 1T 2S
Baths: 3 Ensuite
(10)

Dunsford Guest House, *16 Stanger Street, Keswick, Cumbria, CA12 5JU.*
Centrally situated, exclusively for non-smokers.
Open: All Year (not Xmas)
Grades: ETB Listed, Comm
017687 75059 Mrs Watson
Rates fr: *£18.50*.
Beds: 4D **Baths:** 4 Ensuite
(3)

Melbreak House, *29 Church Strett, Keswick, Cumbria, CA12 4DX.*
Comfortable, friendly atmosphere. Excellent value.
Open: All Year
Grades: ETB 2 Cr
017687 73398 Miss Watson
Rates fr: *£17.50*-**£17.50**.
Beds: 1F 5D 3T 1S
Baths: 10 Ensuite

Kirkby Lonsdale

National Grid Ref: SD6178
Snooty Fox

Green Lane End Farm, *Kirkby Lonsdale, Carnforth, Lancs, LA6 2PP.*
C17th farmhouse - working farm. M6 2 miles.
Open: Easter to Oct
01539 567236 Mrs Nicholson
Rates fr: *£15.00*-**£17.00**.
Beds: 1D 1T **Baths:** 1 Shared
(3)

Barnfield Farm, *Tunstall, Kirkby Lonsdale, Carnforth, Lancs, LA6 2QF.*
1702 working family farmhouse.
Open: All Year (not Xmas)
01524 274284 Mrs Stephenson
Rates fr: *£15.00*-**£16.00**.
Beds: 1F 1D
Baths: 2 Shared
(2)

Kirkby Stephen

National Grid Ref: NY7708
Old Forge Bistro

Jolly Farmers House, *63 High Street, Kirkby Stephen, Cumbria, CA17 4SH.*
Open: All Year
017683 71063 Mr Pepper
Rates fr: *£15.00*-**£15.00**.
Beds: 2F 2D 2T 1S
Baths: 3 Ensuite 4 Shared
(6)
Ideally situated on Coast to Coast Walk. Excellent home cooking: 4 course evening meal, home made biscuits & tea on arrival - warm friendly & informal atmosphere.

The lowest *double* rate per person is shown in *italics*.

Lyndhurst, *46 South Road, Kirkby Stephen, Cumbria, CA17 4SN.*
Delightful comfortable Victorian family home.
Open: Mar to Nov
017683 71448 Mrs Bell
Rates fr: *£15.00*-**£18.00**.
Beds: 1D 2T
Baths: 1 Private 1 Shared
(3)

Claremont, *Nateby Road, Kirkby Stephen, Cumbria, CA17 4AJ.*
Quiet setting near town centre.
Open: Easter to Oct
017683 71787 Mrs Rennison
Rates fr: *£14.00*-**£19.00**.
Beds: 1F 1T
Baths: 1 Shared
(2)

Cold Keld, *Fell End, Kirkby Stephen, Cumbria, CA17 4LN.*
Farmhouse offering guided walking holidays.
Open: All Year (not Xmas)
015396 23273 Mr & Mrs Trimmer
Rates fr: *£16.00*-**£19.00**.
Beds: 1F 3D 1T
Baths: 5 Private
(12)

Ing Hill Lodge, *Outhgill, Mallerstang Dale, Kirkby Stephen, Cumbria, CA17 4JT.*
Open: All Year
Grades: ETB 2 Cr, Comm
017683 71153 Mrs Sawyer
Rates fr: *£20.00*-**£25.00**.
Beds: 2D 1T
Baths: 3 Ensuite
(6)
Delightful Georgian country house in Mallerstang Valley, 4mls south Kirkby Stephen on B6259. Licensed. Glorious views, peace, quiet, open fires, home cooking, a warm welcome.

Lambrigg

National Grid Ref: SD5696

Holme Park Hall, *Lambrigg, Kendal, Cumbria, LA10 0SJ.*
Family-run. Large country house.
Open: Feb to Nov
Grades: ETB Listed
015394 84336 Mrs Boardley
Rates fr: *£14.00*-**£16.00**.
Beds: 3F
Baths: 1 Private 1 Shared
(10)

Langdale

National Grid Ref: NY3204
Britannia Inn

Barnhowe, *Elterwater, Langdale, Ambleside, Cumbria, LA22 9HU.*
Homemade bread. Quiet beautiful location. **Open:** Feb to Nov
Grades: ETB 1 Cr, Comm
015394 37346 Mr & Mrs Riley
Rates fr: *£15.00*-**£15.00**.
Beds: 1D 1T 1S **Baths:** 1 Shared
(7)

Lazonby

National Grid Ref: NY5439

Joiners Arms

Banktop House, *Lazonby, Penrith, Cumbria, CA10 1AQ.*
Early 1C17th yeoman farmer's residence .
Grades: ETB 2 Cr, Comm
01768 898268 Mrs Carlyle
Rates fr: *£18.50*-**£22.00**.
Beds: 1D 1T
Baths: 1 Ensuite 1 Private
(Any) (4)

Lea Yeat

National Grid Ref: SD7686

Sportsman's Inn

River View, *Lea Yeat, Cowgill, Sedbergh, Cumbria, LA10 5RF.*
Converted Quaker meeting house.
Open: All Year (not Xmas)
015396 25592 Mr & Mrs Playfoot
Rates fr: *£15.00*-**£15.00**.
Beds: 1D 1T **Baths:** 1 Shared
(12) (2)

Little Arrow

National Grid Ref: SD3197

Church House Inn

Arrowfield, *Little Arrow, Coniston, Cumbria, LA21 8AU.*
Style, comfort, home-made fare.
Open: Feb to Nov
Grades: ETB 2 Cr, High Comm
015394 41741 Mrs Walton
Rates fr: *£16.00*-**£18.00**.
Beds: 2D 2T 1S
Baths: 2 Ensuite 1 Shared
(3) (6)

Longsleddale

National Grid Ref: NY4903

Muirthwaite Farm, *Longsleddale, Kendal, Cumbria, LA8 9BA.*
C17th stone-built farmhouse on working farm.
Open: Mar to Oct
01539 823634 Mrs Waine
Rates fr: *£14.50*-**£14.50**.
Beds: 2D 1T
Baths: 2 Shared

Lorton

National Grid Ref: NY1525

Wheatsheaf Inn

Meadow Bank, *High Lorton, Lorton, Cockermouth, Cumbria, CA13 9UG.*
Modern comfortable private house.
Open: All Year (not Xmas)
01900 85315
Mrs Edmunds
Rates fr: *£14.00*-**£15.00**.
Beds: 1F 1D 1S **Baths:** 1 Shared
(4) (3)

The Old Vicarage, *Church Lane, Lorton, Cockermouth, Cumbria, CA13 9UN.*
Victorian house in wooded grounds.
Open: All Year
01900 85656 Mrs Dobbie
Rates fr: *£19.00*-**£19.00**.
Beds: 2D 1T
Baths: 2 Private 1 Shared
(12) (6)

Owl Brook, *Whinlatter Pass, High Lorton, Lorton, Cockermouth, Cumbria, CA13 9TX.*
Attractive greenslate bungalow.
Open: All Year
01900 85333 Mrs Roberts
Rates fr: *£16.50*-**£16.50**.
Beds: 3D
Baths: 1 Shared
(3) (3)

Low Row

National Grid Ref: NY5863

High Nook Farm, *Low Row, Brampton, Cumbria, CA8 2LU.*
Comfortable farmhouse built in 1857.
Open: May to Oct
Grades: ETB Listed
016977 46273 Mrs Foster
Rates fr: *£12.00*-**£14.00**.
Beds: 1F 1D
Baths: 1 Shared
(3)

Loweswater

National Grid Ref: NY1420

Kirkstile, Wheatsheaf

Brook Farm, *Loweswater, Cockermouth, Cumbria, CA13 0RP.*
Quiet comfortable farmhouse, working farm.
Open: May to Oct
Grades: ETB 1 Cr, Comm
01900 85606 Mrs Hayton
Rates fr: *£17.00*-**£17.00**.
Beds: 1F 1D **Baths:** 1 Shared
(3)

Greythwaite, *Loweswater, Cockermouth, Cumbria, CA13 0SU.*
Lovely home, North Loweswater.
Open: All Year (not Xmas)
01946 861555 Mrs Beebe
Rates fr: *£12.50*-**£18.00**.
Beds: 1D 1T
Baths: 1 Shared
(2)

Lowgill

National Grid Ref: SD6297

Tarnclose, *Beck Foot, Lowgill, Kendal, Cumbria, LA8 0BL.*
Old pay-master's cottage, large garden.
Open: Easter to Oct
01539 824658 Mrs Hogg
Rates fr: *£26.50 (inc dinner)*-**£16.50**.
Beds: 1D 1T **Baths:** 1 Shared

Lowick

National Grid Ref: SD2986

Red Lion

Garth Row, *Lowick Green, Lowick, Ulverston, Cumbria, LA12 8EB.*
Open: All Year (not Xmas)
Grades: ETB Listed
01229 885633 Mrs Wickens
Rates fr: *£14.00*-**£14.00**.
Beds: 1F 1D **Baths:** 1 Shared
(4)
Traditional Lakeland cottage in beautiful secluded setting amidst farmland in this lovely undiscovered corner of the Lakes. Comfortable and welcoming - perfect for a relaxing break.

Mallerstang

National Grid Ref: NY7800

Dalefoot, *Mallerstang, Kirkby Stephen, Cumbria, CA17 4JT.*
C17th farmhouse on working farm.
Open: All Year (not Xmas)
017683 72519 Mrs Halliday
Rates fr: *£15.00*-**£15.00**.
Beds: 1F 1S **Baths:** 1 Shared
(3)

Maryport

National Grid Ref: NY0739

Seychelles Restaurant (Allonby)

East Farm, *Crosscanonby, Maryport, Cumbria, CA15 6SJ.*
Modernised comfortable farmhouse. Traditional breakfast.
Open: All Year (not Xmas)
Grades: ETB Listed, Comm
01900 812153 Mrs Carruthers
Rates fr: *£15.00*-**£15.00**.
Beds: 1F 1D **Baths:** 1 Shared
(2) (2)

Ellenside Guest House, *17 Station Street, Maryport, Cumbria, CA15 6LS.*
Large Victorian comfortable house.
Open: All Year
Grades: ETB Listed
01900 815440 Mrs Kemp
Rates fr: *£12.00*-**£12.00**.
Beds: 1F 1D 1T 1S
Baths: 1 Shared

Matterdale End

National Grid Ref: NY3824

Troutbeck Inn, The Royal Dockray

Low Birch Close, *Matterdale, Matterdale End, Penrith, Cumbria, CA11 0RZ.*
Comfortable, 'home from home' farmhouse. **Open:** All Year
017684 83812 Mrs Edmondson
Rates fr: *£15.00*-**£15.00**.
Beds: 2D **Baths:** 1 Shared
(3)

Melmerby

National Grid Ref: NY6137

Shepherds Inn

Gale Hall Farm, *Melmerby, Penrith, Cumbria,* CA10 1HN.
Large comfortable farmhouse.
Open: Jun to Nov
01768 881254 Mrs Toppin
Rates fr: *£14.00*-**£14.00**.
Beds: 1F 1D 1S **Baths:** 1 Shared
(3)

Millom

National Grid Ref: SD1780

Station hotel

Fellview House, *Bay View, Millom, Cumbria,* LA18 5DF.
Large friendly family house.
Open: All Year (not Xmas)
01229 773325 Mrs Evison
Rates fr: *£15.00*-**£15.00**.
Beds: 2T 1S **Baths:** 2 Shared

Morland

National Grid Ref: NY5922

Hill Top Guest House, *Morland, Penrith, Cumbria,* CA10 3AX.
Georgian house with secluded garden.
Open: All Year (not Xmas)
01931 714561
Rates fr: *£19.00*-**£19.00**.
Beds: 1D 1T 1S
Baths: 2 Ensuite 1 Private
(7) (6)

Natland

National Grid Ref: SD5289

Punch Bowl - Barrons Green

Higher House Farm, *Oxenholme Lane, Natland, Kendal, Cumbria,* LA9 7QH.
Tranquil Lakeland village, C17th farmhouse. **Open:** All Year
Grades: ETB 3 Cr, Comm, AA 4 Q, Select
015395 61177 Mrs Sunter
Fax no: 015395 61520
Rates fr: *£18.00*-**£23.00**.
Beds: 2D 1T **Baths:** 3 Private
(9)

Near Sawrey

National Grid Ref: SD3795

High Green Gate Guest House, *Near Sawrey, Ambleside, Cumbria,* LA22 0LF.
Converted C18th farmhouse.
Open: Apr to Oct
Grades: ETB 2 Cr, Comm, AA 2 Q, RAC Acclaim
015394 36296 Miss Fletcher
Rates fr: *£20.00*-**£23.00**.
Beds: 4F 1D
Baths: 3 Private 1 Shared
(6)

The lowest *double* rate per person is shown in *italics*.

Buckle Yeat Guest House, *Near Sawrey, Hawkshead, Ambleside, Cumbria,* LA22 0LF.
Traditional & picturesque Lakeland cottage.
Open: All Year
015394 36446 (also fax no)
Mr Kirby
Rates fr: *£20.00*-**£20.00**.
Beds: 1F 4D 1T 1S
Baths: 6 Ensuite 1 Private
(8)

Beechmount, *Near Sawrey, Ambleside, Cumbria,* LA22 0JZ.
Spacious country house, superb views.
Open: All Year
015394 36356
Mrs Siddall
Rates fr: *£18.50*-**£24.00**.
Beds: 3D
Baths: 3 Private
(3)

Nenthead

National Grid Ref: NY7843

Miners Arms Nenthead

Cherry Tree, *Nenthead, Alston, Cumbria,* CA9 3PD.
Stone-built farm cottages with modern amenities.
Open: All Year (not Xmas)
01434 381434
Mrs Sherlock
Rates fr: *£15.00*-**£15.00**.
Beds: 2F 1D 1T
Baths: 1 Private
(13) (6)

The Miners Arms, *Nenthead, Alston, Cumbria,* CA9 3PF.
Homely family pub.
Open: All Year
01434 381427 Miss Clark
Rates fr: *£15.00*-**£15.00**.
Beds: 1F 1D 1T
Baths: 1 Shared

Nether Wasdale

National Grid Ref: NY1204

Own Bar

Low Wood Hall Hotel, *Nether Wasdale, Seascale, Cumbria,* CA20 1ET.
Victorian country house hotel.
Open: All Year (not Xmas)
Grades: ETB 4 Cr, Comm
019467 26289 Mr Brassington
Rates fr: *£28.50*-**£35.00**.
Beds: 4F 6D 7T 1S
Baths: 13 Ensuite 1 Private
(24)

New Hutton

National Grid Ref: SD5691

Station Inn

Cragg Farm, *New Hutton, Kendal, Cumbria,* LA8 0BA.
C17th farmhouse, tastefully modernised 3 miles M6, J37.
Open: Mar to Oct
Grades: ETB Listed
01539 721760 Mrs Knowles
Rates fr: *£15.50*-**£16.50**.
Beds: 1F 1D 1S
Baths: 1 Shared
(3)

Borrans, *New Hutton, Kendal, Cumbria,* LA8 0AT.
B&B in 1729 house.
Open: Easter to Oct
01539 722969 Ms Ellis
Rates fr: *£14.00*-**£14.00**.
Beds: 4D 1S
Baths: 2 Shared
(1) (8)

Newbiggin-on-Lune

National Grid Ref: NY7005

Kines Head

Tranna Hill, *Newbiggin-on-Lune, Kirkby Stephen, Cumbria,* CA17 4NY.
Warm welcome, Central fantastic views.
Open: All Year (not Xmas)
015396 23227
Mrs Boustead
Rates fr: *£16.00*-**£16.00**.
Beds: 10D 1T 1S
Baths: 1 Ensuite 1 Private 1 Shared
(6)

Bents Farm, *Newbiggin-on-Lune, Kirkby Stephen, Cumbria,* CA17 4NX.
Excellent walking & touring area.
Open: All Year (not Xmas)
015396 23681
Mrs Ousby
Rates fr: *£14.00*-**£13.00**.
Beds: 2F 1D
Baths: 1 Shared

Newby Bridge

National Grid Ref: SD3786

Swan hotel, Anglers Arms

Old Barn Farm, *Lake Windermere, Newby Bridge, Ulverston, Cumbria,* LA12 8NQ.
Delightfully situated C17th farmhouse.
Open: All Year (not Xmas)
Grades: ETB 2 St, Comm
015395 31842
Mrs Winton
Rates fr: *£17.00*-**£17.00**.
Beds: 1F 1D 1T 1S
Baths: 3 Ensuite 2 Private
(4)

Hill Crest, *Backbarrow, Newby Bridge, Ulverston, Cumbria, LA12 8QP.*
Set in quiet, picturesque Lakeland countryside.
Open: Mar to Nov
015395 31766 Mrs Jenkinson
Rates fr: *£16.00*-**£20.00**.
Beds: 1F 2D
Baths: 2 Private
(3)

Newlands

National Grid Ref: NY2320

Fish Hotel, Coaldale Inn

Keskadale Farm, *Newlands, Keswick, Cumbria, CA12 5TS.*
Friendly, comfortable farmhouse. Wonderful location.
Open: Mar to Dec
Grades: ETB 1 Cr, Comm
017687 78544 Mrs Harryman
Rates fr: *£15.00*-**£22.00**.
Beds: 2D 1T
Baths: 1 Shared
(6)

Newton Reigny

National Grid Ref: NY4731

The Sun Inn

Croft House, *Newton Reigny, Penrith, Cumbria, CA11 0AY.*
Open: Easter to Oct
Grades: ETB 2 Cr, Comm
01768 865535 Farncombe
Fax no: 01768 865435
Rates fr: *£18.00*-**£25.00**.
Beds: 1F 3D 1T
Baths: 2 Ensuite 1 Private
(8)
Georgian family house, 8 acres, horses, ducks, hens; overlooking Lakeland Fells. Beautiful ensuite rooms. Free leisure club indoor pool, jacuzzi, sauna, etc. Phone for availability/details.

The Sun Inn, *Newton Reigny, Penrith, Cumbria, CA11 0AP.*
Traditional village inn adjacent M6.
Open: All Year
01768 867055 Mr Watts
Rates fr: *£20.00*-**£18.00**.
Beds: 2D 1T 1S
Baths: 2 Ensuite 2 Shared

Orton

National Grid Ref: NY6208

The Vicarage, *Orton, Penrith, Cumbria, CA10 3RQ.*
Working vicarage, homemade bread.
Open: All Year
Grades: ETB Listed, Comm
015396 24873 (also fax no)
Mrs Levey
Rates fr: *£16.00*-**£16.00**.
Beds: 1D 2T
Baths: 1 Shared
(3)

Berwyn House, *Orton, Penrith, Cumbria, CA10 3RQ.*
Family home catering for walkers.
Open: All Year
015396 24345
Mrs Dunford
Rates fr: *£16.00*-**£16.00**.
Beds: 1D 2T **Baths:** 1 Shared
(8)

Outhgill

National Grid Ref: NY7801

Ing Hill Lodge, *Outhgill, Mallerstang Dale, Kirkby Stephen, Cumbria, CA17 4JT.*
Delightful Georgian country house in Mallerstang Valley.
Open: All Year
Grades: ETB 2 Cr, Comm
017683 71153 Mrs Sawyer
Rates fr: *£20.00*-**£25.00**.
Beds: 2D 1T
Baths: 3 Ensuite
(6)

Pardshaw

National Grid Ref: NY0924

Pardshaw Hall, *Pardshaw, Cockermouth, Cumbria, CA13 0SP.*
Warm comfortable farmhouse, lovely views.
Open: All Year
01900 822607 Mrs Richardson
Rates fr: *£14.00*-**£14.00**.
Beds: 1F 1D 1T 1S
Baths: 1 Shared
(4)

Patterdale

National Grid Ref: NY3915

Patterdale Hotel, *Patterdale, Penrith, Cumbria, CA11 0NN.*
Large comfortable hotel.
Open: Mar to Dec
Grades: ETB 3 Cr, AA 2 St, RAC 2 St
017684 82231
Mr Tonkin
Rates fr: *£23.00*-**£23.00**.
Beds: 3F 21D 21T 12S
Baths: 57 Ensuite
(50)

The White Lion Inn, *Patterdale, Penrith, Cumbria, CA11 0NN.*
Comfortable, family-run C17th inn.
Open: All Year (not Xmas)
017684 82214
Mrs McDowall
Rates fr: *£20.00*-**£20.00**.
Beds: 1F 2D 4T 1S
Baths: 1 Private 1 Shared

Home Farm, *Patterdale, Penrith, Cumbria, CA11 0PU.*
Working hill farm.
Open: Mar to Nov
017684 82370 Mrs Beatty
Rates fr: *£14.50*-**£14.50**.
Beds: 1D 1T
Baths: 1 Shared
(10)

Patton

National Grid Ref: SD5597

High Barn, *Shaw End, Patton, Kendal, Cumbria, LA8 9DU.*
Beautiful barn conversion, peaceful setting.
Open: All Year (not Xmas)
01539 824625 Mrs Sanderson
Rates fr: *£14.00*-**£14.00**.
Beds: 2D
Baths: 1 Ensuite 1 Private
(2) (6)

Penrith

National Grid Ref: NY5130

The Two Lions, Chataways, Royal Hotel, Cross Keys

Norcroft Guest House, *Graham Street, Penrith, Cumbria, CA11 9LQ.*
Open: All Year (not Xmas)
Grades: ETB 3 Cr, Comm
01768 862365 (also fax no)
Mr Bray
Rates fr: *£16.00*-**£21.50**.
Beds: 2F 2D 4T 1S
Baths: 6 Ensuite 1 Shared
(7)
A special welcome awaits you in our charming Victorian house. Large comfortable ensuite bedrooms with colour TV, beverage making facilities, spacious dining room. Secure parking.

Grosvenor House, *3 Lonsdale Terrace, Meeting House Lane, Penrith, Cumbria, CA11 7TS.*
Large, comfortable terraced house.
Open: Easter to Nov
Grades: ETB Listed, Approv
01768 863813 Mrs Fitzpatrick
Rates fr: *£13.00*-**£18.00**.
Beds: 1D 1T
Baths: 1 Shared

Brantwood Hotel, *Stainton, Penrith, Cumbria, CA11 0EP.*
Open: All Year
Grades: ETB 3 Cr, Comm, AA 2 St, RAC 2 St
01768 862748 Harvey
Fax no: 01768 890164
Rates fr: *£27.00*-**£36.00**.
Beds: 2F 8D 2T 2S
Baths: 11 Ensuite 3 Private
(40)
Pleasant country hotel in 3 acres secluded gardens. Family-run by Susan and John for 10 years. Comfortable ensuite rooms. Good food. Safe parking.

Corner House, *36 Victoria Road, Penrith, Cumbria, CA11 8HR.*
Relaxed, comfortable, homely atmosphere.
Open: Mar to Nov
01768 863566
Miss Robinson
Rates fr: *£15.00*-**£20.00**.
Beds: 2D 1T
Baths: 1 Shared
(3)

***The Friarage,** Friargate, Penrith, Cumbria, CA11 7XR.*
Ideal North/South, East/West.
Open: April to Sept
01768 863635 Mrs Clark
Rates fr: *£14.00*-**£17.00**.
Beds: 1D 1T 1S
Baths: 2 Shared
(8) (3)

***Barco House,** Carleton Road, Penrith, Cumbria, CA11 8LR.*
Victorian house with parking.
Open: All Year
01768 863176 Mrs Stockdale
Rates fr: *£16.00*-**£18.00**.
Beds: 2F 1T
(8)

Pooley Bridge

National Grid Ref: NY4724

***Ullswater House,** Pooley Bridge, Penrith, Cumbria, CA10 2NN.*
Licensed, detached village house.
Open: All Year
Grades: ETB 1 Cr, Comm
017684 86259 Mrs Booth
Rates fr: *£19.50*-**£27.50**.
Beds: 2D 1T **Baths:** 3 Private
(5)

Raisbeck

National Grid Ref: NY6407

***New House Farm,** Raisbeck, Orton, Penrith, Cumbria, CA10 3SD.*
Modern comfortable farmhouse.
Open: All Year
015396 24324 Mrs Winder
Rates fr: *£14.00*-**£14.00**.
Beds: 2T **Baths:** 1 Shared

Ravenglass

National Grid Ref: SD0896

Ratty Arms

***Muncaster Country Guest House,** Ravenglass, Cumbria, CA18 1RD.*
Open: All Year (not Xmas)
Grades: RAC Listed
01229 717693 (also fax no)
Mr Putnam
Rates fr: *£16.50*-**£17.00**.
Beds: 1F 3D 2T 3S
Baths: 2 Ensuite 2 Shared
(20)
Very comfortable licensed guest-house with attractive garden adjoining Muncaster Estate. Convenient for miniature railway and for walking in Eskdale and Wasdale. Guided walking by arrangement.

***Eskmeals House,** Eskmeal, Ravenglass, Cumbria, CA19 5YA.*
Listed secluded Georgian country house.
Open: All Year
01229 717151 Ms Stewart
Rates fr: *£15.00*-**£18.00**.
Beds: 1D 1T 1S
Baths: 2 Shared
(6)

***Muncaster Water Mill,** Ravenglass, Cumbria, CA18 1ST.*
Comfortable, welcoming C14th working flour-mill.
Open: All Year (not Xmas)
01229 717232
Mr & Mrs Park
Rates fr: *£17.00*-**£17.00**.
Beds: 1D 2T
Baths: 2 Shared
(5)

Ravenstonedale

National Grid Ref: NY7203

The King's Head

***The Book House,** Grey Garth, Ravenstonedale, Kirkby Stephen, Cumbria, CA17 4NQ.*
Secondhand bookshop in former vicarage.
Open: All Year (not Xmas)
015396 23634
Mrs Irwin
Fax no: 015396 23434
Rates fr: *£14.50*-**£14.50**.
Beds: 1F 1T 1S
Baths: 1 Shared
(4)

Rockcliffe

National Grid Ref: NY3955

Metal Bridge Inn

***Metal Bridge House,** Metal Bridge, Rockcliffe, Carlisle, Cumbria, CA6 4HG.*
In country, close to M6/74.
Open: All Year
Grades: ETB 1 Cr
01228 74695
Mrs Rae
Rates fr: *£13.50*-**£18.00**.
Beds: 1D 2T
(4)

Rosley

National Grid Ref: NY3245

***Causa Grange,** Rosley, Wigton, Cumbria, CA7 8DD.*
Charming period house, well-appointed.
Open: All Year (not Xmas)
016973 45358 Mrs Falck
Rates fr: *£20.00*-**£24.00**.
Beds: 1D 1T
Baths: 1 Ensuite 1 Private
(12) (6)

National Grid References are for villages, towns and cities - *not* for individual houses.

Rosthwaite

National Grid Ref: NY2514

Scatell Hotel

***Royal Oak Hotel,** Rosthwaite, Keswick, Cumbria, CA12 5XB.*
Open: All Year (not Xmas)
Grades: ETB 3 Cr, Comm
017687 77214 (also fax no)
Mr Dowie
Rates fr: *£17.00*-**£25.00**.
Beds: 4F 4D 2T 2S
Baths: 8 Ensuite 4 Shared
(12)
A traditional walkers' hotel set in the heart of Borrowdale. Cosy bar, open fire and home cooking. Brochure, tariff and special breaks available.

***Yew Craggs,** Rosthwaite, Borrowdale, Keswick, Cumbria, CA12 5XB.*
Central Borrowdale, spectacular views. Car park.
Open: Mar to Nov
Grades: ETB Listed
017687 77260 Mr & Mrs Crofts
Rates fr: *£15.00*-**£25.00**.
Beds: 2F 3D
Baths: 1 Shared
(6) (6)

***Gillercombe,** Stonethwaite Road End, Rosthwaite, Borrowdale, Keswick, Cumbria, CA12 5XG.*
Comfortable, homely, clean and good views.
Open: Feb to Nov
017687 77602 Mrs Dunkley
Rates fr: *£15.00*-**£15.00**.
Beds: 1D 3T 1S
Baths: 1 Shared
(5)

Roundthwaite

National Grid Ref: NY6003

***Beckside Farm,** Roundthwaite, Tebay, Penrith, Cumbria, CA10 3XD.*
Friendly accommodation, C17th farmhouse.
Open: Easter to Oct
015396 24628 Mrs Parsley
Rates fr: *£13.00*-**£14.00**.
Beds: 1D 1T
Baths: 1 Shared
(2)

Sandford

National Grid Ref: NY7216

***Sandford Arms,** Sandford, Appleby In Westmorland, Cumbria, CA16 6NR.*
Converted C17th farmhouse.
Open: All Year (not Xmas)
Grades: ETB 3 Cr, Comm
017683 51121
Mrs Dunwoodie
Rates fr: *£22.50*-**£30.00**.
Beds: 2F 2D 1T
Baths: 5 Private

Sandwith

National Grid Ref: NX9614

Dog & Partridge

***Aikbank Cottage**, Sandwith, Whitehaven, Cumbria, CA28 9UG.*
C17th Cottage and Post Office.
Open: All Year (not Xmas)
01946 695771 Mrs Urwin
Rates fr: *£14.00*-**£14.00**.
Beds: 1D 1S
Baths: 1 Shared
(2)

***Tarn Flatt Hall**, Sandwith, Whitehaven, Cumbria, CA28 9UX.*
Comfortable C18th working farmhouse.
Open: All Year
01946 692162 Mrs Telfer
Rates fr: *£13.50*-**£13.50**.
Beds: 2T
Baths: 1 Shared

Seatoller

National Grid Ref: NY2413

***Glaramara**, Seatoller, Keswick, Cumbria, CA12 5XQ.*
Ideally located country guest house.
Open: All Year
017687 77222 Baldwin
Rates fr: *£18.00*-**£18.00**.
Beds: 14T 19S
Baths: 10 Shared
(40)

Sedbergh

National Grid Ref: SD6592

Dalesman Inn

***Stable Antiques**, 15 Back Lane, Sedbergh, Cumbria, LA10 5AQ.*
C18th wheelwright's cottage.
Open: All Year
015396 20251 Miss Thurlby
Rates fr: *£16.00*-**£16.00**.
Beds: 1D 1T
Baths: 1 Shared
(10)

***Randall Hill**, Sedbergh, Cumbria, LA10 5HJ.*
Country house in 3 acres.
Open: All Year
015396 20633 Mrs Snow
Rates fr: *£15.00*-**£16.00**.
Beds: 1D 2T
Baths: 1 Shared
(6)

***Turvey House**, Sedbergh, Cumbria, LA10 5DJ.*
Stone-built large Victorian house.
Open: All Year
Grades: ETB Listed, Comm
015396 20841
Mr & Mrs Liddey-Smith
Rates fr: *£15.00*.
Beds: 1F 1D 1T
Baths: 2 Shared
(5)

***Sun Lea**, Joss Lane, Sedbergh, Cumbria, LA10 5AS.*
Spacious Victorian family house.
Open: All Year (not Xmas)
015396 20828 Mr & Mrs Ramsden
Rates fr: *£15.00*-**£15.00**.
Beds: 2D 1T
Baths: 2 Shared
(3)

Selside

National Grid Ref: SD5399

The Plough Inn

***Hollowgate**, Selside, Kendal, Cumbria, LA8 9LG.*
C16th comfortable farmhouse.
Open: All Year (not Xmas)
Grades: ETB 1 Cr, Comm
01539 823258
Mrs Knowles
Rates fr: *£15.50*-**£15.50**.
Beds: 2D 1S
(3)

***Low Jock Scar**, Selside, Kendal, Cumbria, LA8 9LE.*
Idyllic, comfortable, homely house.
Open: Mar to Nov
Grades: AA 5 Q
01539 823259 (also fax no)
Mr Midwinter
Rates fr: *£21.50*-**£28.50**.
Beds: 1D 1T
Baths: 3 Private
(6)

Shap

National Grid Ref: NY5615

Greyhound

***Fell House**, Shap, Penrith, Cumbria, CA10 3NY.*
Victorian house incorporating general store.
Open: All Year
01931 716343
Mr & Mrs Harrison
Rates fr: *£15.50*-**£17.50**.
Beds: 2F 2T 1S
Baths: 1 Shared
(5)

***Brookfield**, Shap, Penrith, Cumbria, CA10 3PZ.*
Good food. Comfortable. Personal attention.
Open: All Year (not Xmas)
Grades: AA 3 Q
01931 716397 Mrs Brunskill
Rates fr: *£16.50*-**£17.00**.
Beds: 3F 1D 1T
Baths: 1 Private 1 Shared
(20)

***1 The Rockery**, Shap, Penrith, Cumbria, CA10 3LY.*
C18th coaching inn.
Open: All Year (not Xmas)
01931 716340 Mrs Hicks
Rates fr: *£15.00*.
Beds: 1D 1T
Baths: 2 Shared
(4)

***New Ing Farm**, Shap, Penrith, Cumbria, CA10 3LX.*
Homely, spacious former coaching inn.
Open: Easter to October
01931 716661 Mrs Kirkby
Rates fr: *£16.00*-**£17.00**.
Beds: 2F 3D 3T
Baths: 3 Shared
(10) (10)

Skelwith Bridge

National Grid Ref: NY3403

Skelwith Bridge Hotel

***Greenbank**, Skelwith Bridge, Ambleside, Cumbria, LA22 9NW.*
Country comfort; home-baked bread!
Open: All Year
Grades: ETB 2 Cr, High Comm
015394 33236 Mr Green
Rates fr: *£19.00*-**£24.00**.
Beds: 2D 1T **Baths:** 3 Ensuite
(8) (5)

Soulby

National Grid Ref: NY7411

***Hutton Lodge**, Soulby, Kirkby Stephen, Cumbria, CA17 4PL.*
Georgain house, tranquil riverside setting.
Open: All Year (not Xmas)
017683 71396 Mrs March
Rates fr: *£16.50*-**£16.50**.
Beds: 1F 1T 1S **Baths:** 1 Shared
(3)

St Bees

National Grid Ref: NX9711

Queens Head, Manor House

***Stonehouse Farm**, Main Street, St Bees, Cumbria, CA27 0DE.*
Modern comfortable farmhouse, centre village. **Open:** All Year
Grades: ETB Listed, Approv
01946 822224 Mrs Smith
Rates fr: *£15.00*-**£18.00**.
Beds: 1F 2D 3T 1S
Baths: 1 Ensuite 3 Private
(10)

***Tomlin Guest House**, 1 Tomlin House, St Bees, Cumbria, CA27 0EN.*
Comfortable Victorian house.
Open: All Year (not Xmas)
Grades: ETB
01946 822284 Mrs Whitehead
Rates fr: *£14.00*-**£16.00**.
Beds: 1F 1D 2T
Baths: 2 Private 2 Shared
(2)

***Outrigg House**, St Bees, Cumbria, CA27 0AN.*
Large Georgian private house.
Open: All Year (not Xmas)
Grades: ETB Listed
01946 822348 Mrs Moffat
Rates fr: *£15.00*-**£15.00**.
Beds: 1D 1T 1S
Baths: 1 Shared
(4)

Stainton

National Grid Ref: NY4828

***Brantwood Hotel,** Stainton, Penrith, Cumbria, CA11 0EP.*
Pleasant country hotel in 3 acres secluded gardens.
Open: All Year
Grades: ETB 3 Cr, Comm, AA 2 St, RAC 2 St
01768 862748 Harvey
Fax no: 01768 890164
Rates fr: *£27.00*-**£36.00**.
Beds: 2F 8D 2T 2S
Baths: 11 Ensuite 3 Private
(40)

Stanwix

National Grid Ref: NY3957

***Angus Hotel,** 14 Scotland Road, Stanwix, Carlisle, Cumbria, CA3 9DG.*
Clean, comfortable Victorian town house.
Open: All Year
01228 23546 Mr Webster
Rates fr: *£18.00*-**£22.00**.
Beds: 4F 2D 4T 2S
Baths: 7 Ensuite 3 Shared
(6)

Staveley

National Grid Ref: SD4698

Railway Hotel, Duke William, Eagle & Child Hotel

***Stock Bridge Farm,** Staveley, Kendal, Cumbria, LA8 9LP.*
Modernised, comfortable C17th farmhouse.
Open: Mar to Oct
Grades: ETB Listed, Comm
01539 821580
Mrs Fishwick
Rates fr: *£15.00*-**£15.00**.
Beds: 1F 4D 1S **Baths:** 1 Shared
(6)

***17 Danes Road,** Staveley, Kendal, Cumbria, LA8 9PW.*
Attractive Victorian private country home.
Open: All Year
Grades: ETB Listed, Comm
01539 821148
Mrs Crawford
Rates fr: *£14.00*-**£20.00**.
Beds: 2F 1D **Baths:** 1 Shared

Storrs Park

National Grid Ref: SD4096

***Beech Tops,** Meadowcroft Lane, Storrs Park, Windermere, Cumbria, LA23 3JJ.*
Quality, spacious accommodation, near Lake.
Open: Mar to Nov
015394 45453 Mrs Lewthwaite
Rates fr: *£17.50*-**£25.00**.
Beds: 2F **Baths:** 2 Ensuite
(3) (4)

Subberthwaite

National Grid Ref: SD2687

***Crooked Birch Farm House,** Subberthwaite, Ulverston, Cumbria, LA12 8EP.*
Comfortable lakeland farmhouse.
Open: All Year (not Xmas)
01229 885317
Mrs Thorne
Rates fr: *£16.50*-**£18.00**.
Beds: 1F 1D 1T
Baths: 2 Ensuite 1 Shared
(4)

Talkin

National Grid Ref: NY5457

***Hare & Hounds,** Talkin, Brampton, Cumbria, CA8 1LE.*
Homely, friendly 200-year-old inn.
Open: All Year
01697 73456 Mr Goddard
Rates fr: *£10.00*-**£15.00**.
Beds: 1F 2D 2T 4S
Baths: 2 Ensuite 2 Shared
(20)

Tebay

National Grid Ref: NY6104

Cross Keys

***Primrose Cottage,** Orton Road, Tebay, Penrith, Cumbria, CA10 3TL.*
Spacious, scenic, adjacent J38, M6.
Open: All Year
Grades: ETB Listed, Comm
015396 24791 Mrs Jones
Rates fr: *£18.50*-**£20.00**.
Beds: 2D 1T
Baths: 1 Private 1 Shared
(6)

Temple Sowerby

National Grid Ref: NY6127

Kings Arms

***Barn Close,** Temple Sowerby, Penrith, Cumbria, CA10 1SB.*
Spacious comfortable accommodation, picturesque village.
Open: All Year (not Xmas)
017683 61383 Mrs Jephcott
Rates fr: *£15.00*-**£15.00**.
Beds: 1F 1T 1S **Baths:** 1 Shared
(0) (4)

Thornthwaite

National Grid Ref: NY2225

Swan hotel

***Jenkin Hill Cottage,** Thornthwaite, Keswick, Cumbria, CA12 5SG.*
Highly Commended country establishment.
Open: All Year (not Xmas)
Grades: ETB Listed, High Comm
017687 78443 Mr McMullan
Rates fr: *£18.00*-**£26.00**.
Beds: 2D 1T **Baths:** 3 Private
(13) (5)

Threlkeld

National Grid Ref: NY3125

***Scales Farm,** Threlkeld, Keswick, Cumbria, CA12 4SY.*
Picturesque, accessible, comfortable & welcoming.
Open: All Year (not Xmas)
Grades: ETB 3 Cr, High Comm
017687 79660 Mr Appleton
Rates fr: *£21.00*-**£26.00**.
Beds: 1F 3D 1T
Baths: 5 Ensuite
(6)

***Woodend,** Threlkeld, Keswick, Cumbria, CA12 4SU.*
Converted secluded detached farming steading.
Open: All Year (not Xmas)
017687 79686 Mrs Hume
Rates fr: *£14.00*-**£14.00**.
Beds: 1D 1T 1S
Baths: 2 Shared
(10)

Tirril

National Grid Ref: NY5026

***Sockbridge Mill Trout Farm,** Tirril, Penrith, Cumbria, CA10 2JT.*
Comfortable farmhouse on working trout farm.
Open: Easter to Oct
01768 865338 Mrs Claridge
Rates fr: *£13.00*-**£14.00**.
Beds: 2D 2T
Baths: 2 Shared
(6)

Torver

National Grid Ref: SD2894

***Old Rectory Hotel,** Torver, Coniston, Cumbria, LA21 8AX.*
Converted rectory, quiet country location.
Open: All Year
Grades: ETB 3 Cr, High Comm, AA 1 St
015394 41353 Mr Fletcher
Fax no: 015394 41156
Rates fr: *£20.00*-**£20.00**.
Beds: 1F 4D 2T
Baths: 7 Private
(10)

***Brigg House,** Torver, Coniston, Cumbria, LA21 8AY.*
Country house in beautiful setting.
Open: Easter to Nov
015394 41592 Mrs Newport
Rates fr: *£19.00*-**£21.00**.
Beds: 2D 1T
Baths: 3 Ensuite
(8) (4)

Bringing children with you? Always ask for any special rates.

Troutbeck

National Grid Ref: NY4002

Yew Grove, *Troutbeck, Windermere, Cumbria, LA23 1PG.*
Comfortable C18th house, beautiful village.
Open: All Year (not Xmas)
015394 33304 Mr Pratt
Rates fr: *£17.00*-**£19.00**.
Beds: 4D **Baths:** 1 Private 1 Shared
(3)

Stamp Howe, *Troutbeck, Windermere, Cumbria, LA23 1PL.*
Attractive lakeland house, beautiful gardens. **Open:** All Year
015394 33136 Mrs Evans
Rates fr: *£16.00*-**£18.00**.
Beds: 2D 1T **Baths:** 1 Shared
(8) (4)

Ulverston

National Grid Ref: SD2878

Rose & Crown

Church Walk House, *Church Walk, Ulverston, Cumbria, LA12 7EW.*
Comfortable and homely Georgian house. **Open:** All Year (not Xmas)
Grades: AA 3 Q, Recomm
01229 582211 Mr Chadderton
Rates fr: *£17.50*-**£15.00**.
Beds: 1F 2D 1T 1S
Baths: 3 Private 1 Shared

Sefton House , *Queen Street, Ulverston, Cumbria, LA12 7AF.*
Georgian town house.
Open: All Year (not Xmas)
01229 582190 Mrs Glaister
Rates fr: *£15.00*-**£20.00**.
Beds: 1F 2D **Baths:** 3 Ensuite
(15)

Rock House, *1 Alexander Road, Ulverston, Cumbria, LA12 0DE.*
Large well-established guest house, centrally situated.
Open: All Year (not Xmas)
Grades: ETB 1 Cr
01229 586879 Mr Ramsay
Rates fr: *£16.00*-**£16.00**.
Beds: 3F 1S **Baths:** 1 Shared

Underbarrow

National Grid Ref: SD4692

Punch Bowl

Tranthwaite Hall, *Underbarrow, Kendal, Cumbria, LA8 8HG.*
C11th farmhouse, beautiful oak beams/doors.
Open: All Year
Grades: ETB Listed, Comm, AA 3 Q
015395 68285
Mrs Swindlehurst
Rates fr: *£15.00*-**£17.00**.
Beds: 1F 2D 1T **Baths:** 4 Ensuite
(4)

Underloughrigg

National Grid Ref: NY3704

Foxghyll, *Lake Road, Underloughrigg, Ambleside, Cumbria, LA22 9LL.*
Large Listed country house.
Open: All Year (not Xmas)
015394 33292
Mrs Mann
Rates fr: *£21.00*.
Beds: 2D 1T
Baths: 3 Ensuite
(12) (7)

Underskiddaw

National Grid Ref: NY2328

The Sun Inn (Bassenthwaite)

Long Close Farm, *Underskiddaw, Keswick, Cumbria, CA12 4QD.*
Open: All Year
017687 72851 (also fax no)
Mrs Evers
Rates fr: *£17.00*-**£25.00**.
Beds: 1D 2T
Baths: 1 Ensuite 1 Shared
Period farmhouse enjoying exceptional Lake District views over mountains and Bassenthwaite Lake, close by river, hill and forest walks. Delightful accommodation; breakfasts until 11am.

Waberthwaite

National Grid Ref: SD1093

Glebe House, *Waberthwaite, Millom, Cumbria, LA19 5YN.*
Old comfortable farmhouse.
Open: All Year
01229 717268 Mrs Jones
Rates fr: *£14.50*-**£14.50**.
Beds: 1F 1D
Baths: 2 Shared
(3)

Walton

National Grid Ref: NY5264

Lane End Inn (Hayton)

Low Rigg Farm, *Walton, Brampton, Cumbria, CA8 2DX.*
Comfortable accommodation on working farm.
Open: All Year (not Xmas)
Grades: ETB Listed, Comm
01697 73233 Mrs Thompson
Rates fr: *£14.00*-**£18.00**.
Beds: 1F
Baths: 1 Shared
(6)

High Rigg Farm, *Walton, Brampton, Cumbria, CA8 2AZ.*
C17th Listed house - working farm.
Open: All Year (not Xmas)
01697 72117 Mrs Mounsey
Rates fr: *£14.00*-**£15.00**.
Beds: 1F
Baths: 1 Shared
(4)

Warwick Bridge

National Grid Ref: NY4756

Troutbeck Cottage, *Warwick Bridge, Carlisle, Cumbria, CA4 8RN.*
Individually-styled, detached family house.
Open: All Year
Grades: ETB Listed, Comm
01228 561929 Mrs Fraser
Rates fr: *£14.00*-**£15.00**.
Beds: 1F 1D 1T
Baths: 1 Private 1 Shared
(4)

Water Yeat

National Grid Ref: SD2889

Water Yeat Country Guest House, *Water Yeat, Ulverston, Cumbria, LA12 8DJ.*
Converted Lakeland farmhouse, fine cuisine.
Open: Feb to Dec
01299 885306 Mrs Labat
Rates fr: *£20.00*-**£20.50**.
Beds: 1F 2D 2T 2S
Baths: 3 Private 2 Shared
(4) (10)

Waterhead

National Grid Ref: SD3197

The Sun Hotel

Thwaite Cottage, *Waterhead, Coniston, Cumbria, LA21 8AJ.*
Beautiful peaceful C17th cottage.
Open: All Year (not Xmas)
015394 41367
Mrs Aldridge
Rates fr: *£17.00*.
Beds: 2D 1T
Baths: 1 Ensuite 2 Private
(3)

Watermillock

National Grid Ref: NY4422

Herdwick Inn

Rampsbeck Lodge on Ullswater, *Watermillock, Penrith, Cumbria, CA11 0LP.*
Lakeside residence. Private fishing, dinghy launching.
Open: All Year
01768 486647
Mrs Windle
Rates fr: *£17.50*-**£20.00**.
Beds: 2D 1T 1S
Baths: 1 Private 1 Shared
(6)

Waterside House, *Watermillock, Penrith, Cumbria, CA11 0JH.*
Beautiful Listed C18th statesman's house.
Open: All Year
017684 86038
Mrs Jenner
Rates fr: *£25.00*-**£25.00**.
Beds: 1F 4D 1T 1S
Baths: 4 Private 2 Shared

The lowest **single** *rate is shown in* **bold.**

Watermillock-on-Ullswater

National Grid Ref:

The Royal Hotel

Fair Place, *Watermillock-on-Ullswater, Penrith, Cumbria, CA11 0LR.*
Ullswater country guest house, non-smoking.
Open: Mar to Nov
017684 86235 Mr & Mrs Bewley
Fax no: 017684 86066
Rates fr: *£20.00*-**£25.00**.
Beds: 1F 1T **Baths:** 2 Private
(4)

Westnewton

National Grid Ref: NY1344

Swan Inn

Midtown House, *Westnewton, Carlisle, Cumbria, CA5 3NX.*
Comfortable accommodation in small village.
Open: All Year (not Xmas)
016973 20944 Mrs Walker
Rates fr: *£13.00*-**£13.00**.
Beds: 1F 1D **Baths:** 1 Shared
(2)

The Swan Inn, *Westnewton, Carlisle, Cumbria, CA5 3PQ.*
Cosy village inn.
Open: All Year (not Xmas)
016973 20627 Mr Hitchen
Rates fr: *£15.00*-**£18.00**.
Beds: 2F 2T 2S
Baths: 2 Private 2 Shared
(6)

Whicham Valley

National Grid Ref: SD1583

Miners Arms

Whicham Old School, *Whicham Valley, Millom, Cumbria, LA18 5LS.*
Tastefully converted C16th village school.
Open: All Year (not Xmas)
01229 773945 Mrs Woods
Rates fr: *£16.50*-**£16.50**.
Beds: 1D 2T
Baths: 2 Private 1 Shared
(4)

All rates are subject to alteration at the owners' discretion.

Whitehaven

National Grid Ref: NX9718

Bruno's Italian Restaurant, Ali Taj Indian, Chase Hotel, Waverly Hotel, Lamplighter

Corkickle Guest House, *1 Corkickle, Whitehaven, Cumbria, CA28 8AA.*
Superb Georgian house. Residential licence.
Open: All Year (not Xmas/New Year)
Grades: ETB 3 Cr, Comm
01946 692073 (also fax no)
Mrs Pearson
Rates fr: *£22.00*-**£24.50**.
Beds: 2D 2T 2S
Baths: 5 Ensuite 1 Private
(2)

The Cross Georgian Guest House, *Sneckyeat Road, Hensingham, Whitehaven, Cumbria, CA28 8JQ.*
In private ground, spectacular views.
Open: All Year
01946 63716
Mrs Bailey
Rates fr: *£15.00*-**£15.00**.
Beds: 2T 2S
Baths: 2 Private 1 Shared
(8)

Windermere

National Grid Ref: SD4198

Bruno's Italian Restaurant, Ali Taj Indian, Chase Hotel, Waverly Hotel, Lamplighter

Eastbourne Hotel, *Biskey Howe Road, Windermere, Cumbria, LA23 2JR.*
Open: All Year
Grades: ETB 2 Cr, Comm, AA 3 Q, Recomm, RAC High Acclaim
015394 43525
Mr Whitfield
Rates fr: *£17.50*-**£19.00**.
Beds: 2F 4D 2S
Baths: 6 Ensuite 2 Shared
(6)
A quiet family-run hotel. Easy walking distance to Lake and all amenities. Comfortable, spacious and well-furnished bedrooms with private facilities and colour TVs.

Haisthorpe Guest House, *Holly Road, Windermere, Cumbria, LA23 2AF.*
Friendly, comfortable, quiet, central, affordable.
Open: All Year
Grades: ETB 2 Cr, Comm, AA 3 Q, RAC High Acclaim
015394 43445 (also fax no)
Mr Brown
Rates fr: *£14.00*-**£16.00**.
Beds: 1F 4D 1T
Baths: 5 Ensuite 1 Private
(3)

Fayrer Garden House, *Lyth Valley Road, Storrs Park, Windermere, Cumbria, LA23 3JP.*
Open: All Year
Grades: ETB 4 Cr, AA 2 St
015394 88195 Mr Garside
Fax no: 015394 45986
Rates fr: *£27.50*-**£35.00**.
Beds: 18D
Baths: 18 Private
Beautiful country house overlooking lake. Superb restaurant, four posters, jacuzzis - your reward for completing Dales Way. Free leisure facilities. Special breaks. Ring for colour brochure.

Heatherbank, *13 Birch Street, Windermere, Cumbria, LA23 1EG.*
Open: All Year (not Xmas)
Grades: ETB 2 Cr, Comm
015394 46503 (also fax no)
Potter
Rates fr: *£16.00*.
Beds: 2D 3T
Baths: 5 Ensuite
(5)
Non-smoking Lakeland stone guest house, with private parking. Clean, comfortable, quiet location 5 minutes from rail/bus station in centre of village. Superb breakfasts.

Aaron Slack, *48 Ellerthwaite Road, Windermere, Cumbria, LA23 2BS.*
Stone-built Victorian terrace.
Open: All Year
Grades: ETB 1 Cr, Comm, AA 2 Q, RAC Acclaim
015394 44649
Ms Townsend
Rates fr: *£16.00*-**£16.00**.
Beds: 2D 1T
Baths: 2 Ensuite 1 Private
(12)

Cambridge House, *9 Oak Street, Windermere, Cumbria, LA23 1EN.*
Open: All Year (not Xmas)
Grades: ETB Listed, Comm
015394 43846
Mr Fear
Rates fr: *£15.00*-**£15.00**.
Beds: 5D 1T
Baths: 6 Private
(5)
Traditional Lakeland stone guest-house, conveniently situated in Windermere village centre. Modern comfortable rooms with ensuite facilities. Full English, Continental or vegetarian breakfast.

Greenriggs Guest House, *8 Upper Oak Street, Windermere, Cumbria, LA23 2LB.*
Quiet family-run guest house.
Open: All Year
Grades: ETB 2 Cr, Comm
015394 42265
Mr Fawcett
Rates fr: *£14.00*-**£13.00**.
Beds: 1F 3D 1T 2S
Baths: 4 Ensuite 1 Shared
(4)

***College House,** 15 College Road, Windermere, Cumbria, LA23 1BU.*
Open: All Year
Grades: ETB 2 Cr, Comm
015394 45767
Mrs Harvey
Fax no: 015394 88903
Rates fr: *£16.00*-**£21.00**.
Beds: 2D 1T
Baths: 2 Ensuite 1 Private
(3)
Warm, comfortable Victorian family house in quiet central location. Ensuite rooms with gorgeous mountain views. Sunny, secluded garden with patio. Private car park. Non-smoking.

***Osborne,** 3 High Street, Windermere, Cumbria, LA23 1AF.*
Open: All Year
Grades: ETB 2 Cr
015394 46452 Mr Harrison
Rates fr: *£14.50*.
Beds: 2F 2D
Baths: 3 Ensuite 1 Private
Traditional 1847 lakeland stone house. Central for transport, tours and walks. Clean, comfortable, warm. Full English breakfast - freshly cooked. Developed by present owners since 1982.

***Rockside,** Ambleside Road, Windermere, Cumbria, LA23 1AQ.*
Superb accommodation in Windermere village.
Open: All Year (not Xmas)
Grades: ETB 2 Cr, RAC Acclaim
015394 45343
Mrs Fowles
Rates fr: *£16.50*-**£16.50**.
Beds: 4F 5D 4T 2S
Baths: 10 Private 5 Shared
(12)

***Beaumont Hotel,** Holly Road, Windermere, Cumbria, LA23 2AF.*
Open: All Year
Grades: ETB 2 Cr, High Comm, AA 4 Q, Select, RAC High Acclaim
015394 47075 (also fax no)
Mr Cox
Rates fr: *£22.00*-**£27.00**.
Beds: 1F 7D 1T 1S
Baths: 10 Private
(6) (10)
Opened 1992. Victorian house hotel. Central location for touring Lake District. 10 luxury ensuite bedrooms. Tea-making facilities, colour TV, hairdryers, private parking. Warm sincere welcome.

National Grid References are for villages, towns and cities - *not* for individual houses.

***Kays Cottage,** 7 Broad Street, Windermere, Cumbria, LA23 2AB.*
Small guest house, comfortable, ensuite rooms.
Open: All Year (not Xmas)
Grades: ETB Listed, Comm
015394 44146
Mrs Hadfield
Rates fr: *£15.00*-**£18.00**.
Beds: 1F 2D 1T
Baths: 4 Private

***Rosemount,** Lake Road, Windermere, Cumbria, LA23 2EQ.*
Open: Feb to Dec
Grades: ETB 2 Cr, Comm, AA 3 Q, Recomm, RAC High Acclaim
015394 43739 (also fax no)
Mr & Mrs Fielding
Rates fr: *£18.50*-**£18.50**.
Beds: 5D 1T 2S
Baths: 8 Private
(8) (8)
Delightful guest house catering exclusively for non-smokers. Immaculate bedrooms, including single rooms, all with private facilities. 5 star service at affordable prices. Lovely breakfasts.

***Ivy Bank,** Holly Road, Windermere, Cumbria, LA23 3EW.*
Attractive Victorian family home - informal.
Open: All Year (not Xmas)
Grades: AA 2 Q
015394 42601 Clothier
Rates fr: *£13.50*-**£18.50**.
Beds: 2F 2D 1T 1S
Baths: 3 Ensuite 1 Shared
(8)

***Villa House,** 5 Victoria Street, Windermere, Cumbria, LA23 1AD.*
Comfortable, convenient friendly B&B.
Open: All Year (not Xmas)
015394 46041 Mrs Pearson
Rates fr: *£12.00*-**£17.00**.
Beds: 1D 1T 1S
(3) (3)

Workington

National Grid Ref: NX9927

Washington Central, Travellers' Rest

***The Boston,** 1 St Michael S Roadc, Workington, Cumbria, CA14 3EZ.*
Small guest house with big reputation.
Open: All Year
01900 603435 Mrs A Clarke
Rates fr: *£10.00*-**£15.00**.
Beds: 1F 1D 2T 2S
Baths: 1 Private 1 Shared
(3)

The lowest *double* rate per person is shown in *italics*.

All details shown are as supplied by B&B owners in Autumn 1996.

***Sandmans Guest House,** 123 John Street, Workington, Cumbria, CA14 3DD.*
Homely, comfortable accommodation, good food.
Open: All Year
01900 605763
Mrs McKenna
Rates fr: *£11.50*-**£15.00**.
Beds: 1F 3T
Baths: 1 Shared
(3)

***The Briery,** Stainburn Road, Stainburn, Workington, Cumbria, CA14 4UJ.*
Friendly, family-run hotel.
Open: All Year
01900 603395
Mr Lavelle
Rates fr: *£15.00*-**£20.00**.
Beds: 4T 1S
(60)

***Silverdale,** 17 Banklands, Workington, Cumbria, CA14 3EL.*
Large Victorian private house.
Open: All Year (not Xmas)
01900 61887 Mrs Hardy
Rates fr: *£11.00*-**£12.50**.
Beds: 2T 2S
Baths: 2 Shared

***Brampton House,** 29 Parkend Road, Workington, Cumbria, CA14 4DE.*
Large Victorian house.
Open: All Year
01900 603230 Mr D Harris
Rates fr: *£15.00*-**£17.00**.
Beds: 2F 2D 4T 4S
(4)

Yanwath

National Grid Ref: NY5128

Gate Inn

***Gate Farm,** Yanwath, Penrith, Cumbria, CA10 2LF.*
Comfortable C17th farmhouse. Good food.
Open: All Year
01768 864459
Mr & Mrs Donnelly
Rates fr: *£16.00*-**£16.00**.
Beds: 1F 2D 1T
Baths: 1 Ensuite
(0) (10)

The lowest **single** *rate is shown in* **bold.**

Derbyshire

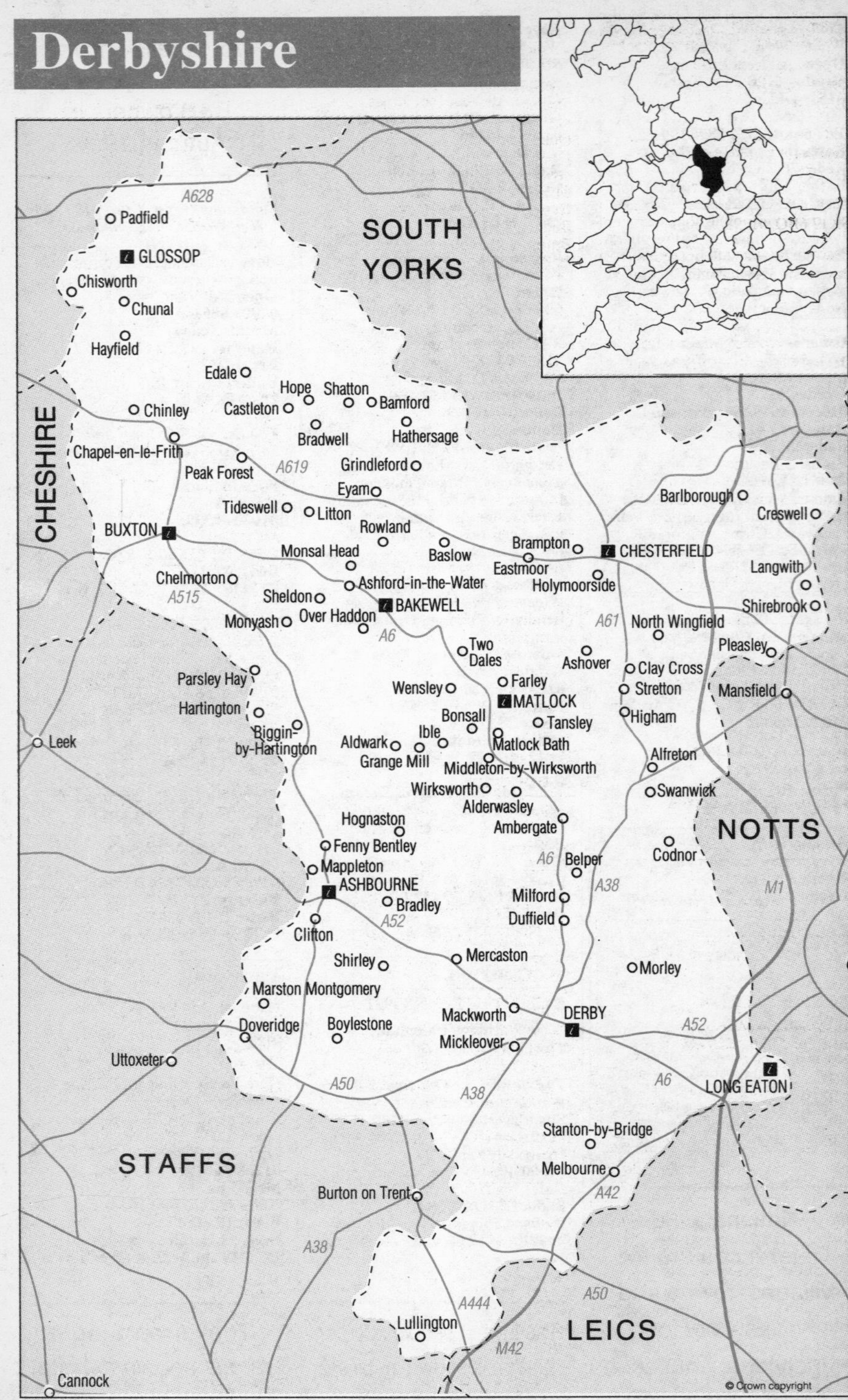

SOUTH YORKS
CHESHIRE
NOTTS
STAFFS
LEICS
A628
Padfield
GLOSSOP
Chisworth
Chunal
Hayfield
Edale
Hope
Shatton
Castleton
Bamford
Chinley
Bradwell
Hathersage
Chapel-en-le-Frith
Peak Forest
A619
Grindleford
Eyam
Tideswell
Litton
Rowland
BUXTON
Monsal Head
Baslow
Brampton
CHESTERFIELD
Eastmoor
Holymoorside
Chelmorton
Ashford-in-the-Water
A515
Sheldon
BAKEWELL
Monyash
Over Haddon
A6
A61
North Wingfield
Two Dales
Ashover
Clay Cross
Parsley Hay
Farley
Wensley
MATLOCK
Stretton
Hartington
Bonsall
Tansley
Higham
Biggin-by-Hartington
Ible
Aldwark
Matlock Bath
Grange Mill
Middleton-by-Wirksworth
Alfreton
Wirksworth
Alderwasley
Swanwick
Hognaston
Ambergate
Fenny Bentley
A6
Belper
Codnor
Mappleton
A38
ASHBOURNE
Bradley
Milford
A52
Duffield
Clifton
Mercaston
Shirley
Morley
Marston Montgomery
Mackworth
DERBY
Doveridge
Boylestone
Mickleover
A52
Uttoxeter
A50
A38
A6
LONG EATON
Stanton-by-Bridge
Melbourne
Burton on Trent
A42
A38
A444
A50
Lullington
M42
Cannock
Barlborough
Creswell
Langwith
Shirebrook
Pleasley
Mansfield
Leek
M1
© Crown copyright

Tourist Information Centres

13 Market Place, **Ashbourne**, Derbyshire, DE6 1EU, 01335-43666.

Old Market Hall, Bridge Street, **Bakewell**, Derbyshire, DE4 1DS, 01629-813227.

The Crescent, **Buxton**, Derbyshire, SK17 6BQ, 01298-25106.

Peacock Information Centre, Low Pavement, **Chesterfield**, Derbyshire, S40 1PB, 01246-207777.

Assembly Rooms, Market Place, **Derby**, Derbyshire, DE1 3AH, 01332-255802.

The Gatehouse, Victoria Street, **Glossop**, Derbyshire, SK13 8HT, 01457-855920.

The Pavilion, Matlock Bath, **Matlock**, Derbyshire, DE4 3NR, 01629-55082.

Alderwasley

National Grid Ref: SK3153

***Ye Olde Bear Inn,** Alderwasley, Belper, Derbyshire, DE56 2RD.*
Old coaching inn.
Open: All Year
01629 822585 Mrs Spencer
Rates fr: *£20.00*-**£20.00**.
Beds: 6D 2T 1S
Baths: 9 Private
(100)

Aldwark

National Grid Ref: SK2257

Old Bowling Green Inn

***Tidgate Farm,** Aldwark, Grangemill, Matlock, Derbyshire, DE4 4HW.*
Open: All Year
Grades: ETB Listed, Comm
01629 540250 Ms Lomas
Rates fr: *£18.00*-**£18.00**.
Beds: 1F 1D 1T
Baths: 2 Private
(3)
Grade II Listed farmhouse in old secluded Derbyshire hamlet. Stone mullions, oak beams and open fires. A warm friendly home waiting to make you welcome.

***The Farm,** Aldwark, Grangemill, Matlock, Derbyshire, DE4 4HX.*
Country guest house, home baking.
Open: Apr to Oct
Grades: ETB 2 Cr, Comm
01629 540263 Mrs Forsey
Rates fr: *£19.00*-**£24.00**.
Beds: 1F 1T
Baths: 2 Private

Alfreton

National Grid Ref: SK3961

***Ivy Beech,** Highstairs Lane, Stretton, Alfreton, Derbyshire, DE55 6FD.*
Quiet house with large garden.
Open: All Year (not Xmas)
Grades: ETB Listed, Comm
01246 863397 Mr Lardge
Rates fr: *£15.50*-**£15.50**.
Beds: 2T 1S
Baths: 1 Shared
(3)

Ambergate

National Grid Ref: SK3451

***Lawn Farm,** Whitewells Lane, Holly Lane, Ambergate, Belper, Derbyshire, DE56 2DN.*
Comfortable farmhouse on working farm.
Open: All Year (not Xmas)
01773 852352 Mrs Oulton
Rates fr: *£15.00*-**£20.00**.
Beds: 1F 1D
Baths: 1 Private 1 Shared
(3)

***The Canal Inn,** Bullbridge, Ambergate, Belper, Derbyshire, DE56 6EW.*
Friendly, welcoming, Derbyshire country pub.
Open: All Year
01773 852739 Mrs Peck
Rates fr: *£15.00*-**£15.00**.
Beds: 1F 1T
Baths: 1 Shared
(16)

Ashbourne

National Grid Ref: SK1846

White Hart

***The Coach House,** 52 The Firs, Ashbourne, Derbyshire, DE6 1HF.*
Open: All Year
Grades: ETB Listed, High Comm
01335 300145
Mrs Coker-Mayes
Rates fr: *£16.50*-**£20.00**.
Beds: 3D
Baths: 2 Ensuite 1 Shared
(3)
A private house, formerly a Victorian coach house, now offering its guests luxurious accommodation and warm hospitality in a quiet location near Ashbourne town centre. Our panelled four poster suite is very special indeed!

***Ye Olde Vaults,** Market Place, Ashbourne, Derbyshire, DE6 1EU.*
Centrally situated C18th public house.
Open: All Year (not Xmas)
01335 346127
Mr & Mrs Palmer
Rates fr: *£20.00*-**£20.00**.
Beds: 1F 1D 1T 1S
Baths: 4 Private
(5)

***Compton Guest House,** 27-31 Compton, Ashbourne, Derbyshire, DE6 1BX.*
3 terraced cottages, comfortably converted.
Open: All Year
Grades: ETB Listed
01335 343100 Mrs Maher
Rates fr: *£16.00*-**£18.00**.
Beds: 1F 4D 1T
Baths: 3 Ensuite 1 Shared
(6)

Ashford-in-the-Water

National Grid Ref: SK1969

Bull's Head

***Gritstone House,** Greaves Lane, Ashford-in-the-Water, Bakewell, Derbyshire, DE45 1QH.*
Open: All Year (not Xmas)
Grades: ETB 2 Cr, High Comm
01629 813563 (also fax no)
Mrs Lindsay
Rates fr: *£18.00*-**£28.00**.
Beds: 2D 1T
Baths: 1 Private 1 Shared
Listed Georgian house located in beautiful conservation village in Peak District National Park near to Bakewell, Chatsworth and Haddon. Choice dining out. Near to facilities.

***Chy-An-Dour,** Vicarage Lane, Ashford-in-the-Water, Bakewell, Derbyshire, DE45 1QL.*
Quality accommodation. Quiet picturesque position.
Open: All Year (not Xmas)
Grades: ETB 2 Cr, Comm
01629 813162 Mrs Rowland
Rates fr: *£18.00*-**£25.00**.
Beds: 2D 1T **Baths:** 3 Private
(5) (4)

***Arncliffe House,** Greaves Lane, Ashford-in-the-Water, Bakewell, Derbyshire, DE45 1QH.*
Spacious Victorian house, lovely views.
Open: All Year (not Xmas)
Grades: ETB Listed, Comm
01629 813121 Mrs Hunt
Rates fr: *£17.00*-**£18.00**.
Beds: 1D 1T 1S **Baths:** 1 Shared

Ashover

National Grid Ref: SK3463

White Horse Inn (Wooley Moor)

***Fairhaven,** Stone Rows Lane, Ashover Way, Ashover, Chesterfield, Derbyshire, S45 0HE.*
Clean, comfortable and homely cottage.
Open: All Year
01246 590405 Mrs Windle
Rates fr: *£16.00*-**£16.00**.
Beds: 1F 1D 1S
Baths: 1 Ensuite 1 Shared
(4)

***Greenhouse Farm,** Coach Road, Ashover, Chesterfield, Derbyshire, S45 0JN.*
Farmhouse with working farm.
Open: Easter to Nov
01246 590345 Mrs Taylor
Rates fr: *£15.00*-**£20.00**.
Beds: 1F 1D
(5)

Bakewell

National Grid Ref: SK2168
Red Lion Hotel

***Holly House,** The Avenue, Bakewell, Derbyshire, DE45 1EQ.*
Large comfortable quiet private house. **Open:** All Year (not Xmas)
Grades: AA Listed
01629 813207 Mrs Wright
Rates fr: *£18.00*-**£25.00**.
Beds: 1D 1T **Baths:** 1 Shared
(3) (4)

***Haddon House Farm,** Haddon Hall Estate, Bakewell, Derbyshire, DE45 1BN.*
Victorian farmhouse in valley setting. **Open:** All Year
Grades: ETB 2 Cr
01629 814024 Mrs Nichols
Fax no: 01629 812759
Rates fr: *£25.00*-**£30.00**.
Beds: 1F 1D **Baths:** 2 Ensuite
(2)

Bamford

National Grid Ref: SK2083
Derwent Hotel, Anglers Rest

***Apple Croft,** Fidlers Well, Bamford, Sheffield, S30 2AR.*
Large friendly, Victorian family house. **Open:** All Year (not Xmas)
01433 651495 Mrs Davies
Rates fr: *£16.00*-**£15.00**.
Beds: 1D 1T 1S **Baths:** 1 Shared
(5)

Barlborough

National Grid Ref: SK4777

***Stone Croft,** 15 Church Street, Barlborough, Chesterfield, Derbyshire, S43 4ER.*
Renovated stone-built house 1670.
Open: All Year
01246 810974 Mrs Widdowson
Rates fr: *£15.00*-**£15.00**.
Beds: 1F **Baths:** 1 Private
(6)

Baslow

National Grid Ref: SK2572

***Rose Hill Farm,** Over End, Baslow, Bakewell, Derbyshire, DE45 1RH.*
Modern comfortable farmhouse.
Open: Easter to November
01246 583280 Mrs White
Rates fr: *£13.00*-**£15.00**.
Beds: 1D 1T **Baths:** 1 Shared
(4)

***Bubnell Cliff Farm,** Wheatlands Lane, Baslow, Bakewell, Derbyshire, DE45 1RH.*
Working farm in scenic position.
Open: All Year
01246 582454 Mrs Mills
Rates fr: *£14.00*-**£20.00**.
Beds: 1F 1D
Baths: 1 Shared
(6)

Belper

National Grid Ref: SK3547
Hanging Gate, Railway, Cross Keys

***Chevin Green Farm,** Chevin Road, Belper, Derbyshire, DE56 2UN.*
Attractive farmhouse in picturesque scenery.
Open: All Year (not Xmas)
Grades: ETB 2 Cr, Comm
01773 822328 Mr Postles
Rates fr: *£16.00*-**£18.00**.
Beds: 1F 2D 1T 2S
Baths: 6 Ensuite
(6)

***Lumb Cottage,** Farnah Green, Belper, Derbyshire, DE56 2UP.*
Large comfortable cottage, own facilities.
Open: All Year
01773 822331 Mrs Ratcliffe
Rates fr: *£17.50*-**£18.50**.
Beds: 2D 1S
Baths: 1 Shared
(2)

Biggin-by-Hartington

National Grid Ref: SK1559

***Ivy House,** Newhaven, Biggin-by-Hartington, Buxton, Derbyshire, SK17 0DT.*
Elegant Listed Georgian country house.
Open: All Year
Grades: ETB 2 Cr
01298 84709 Mrs Flint
Rates fr: *£20.00*-**£20.00**.
Beds: 1F 2D 1T
Baths: 4 Private
(5) (7)

Bonsall

National Grid Ref: SK2758
Kings Head Inn

***Town Head Farmhouse,** 70 High Street, Bonsall, Matlock, Derbyshire, DE4 2AR.*
Open: All Year
Grades: ETB 2 Cr
01629 823762 Mrs Cordin
Rates fr: *£20.00*-**£22.00**.
Beds: 3D 1T
Baths: 4 Ensuite
(6)
C18th farmhouse, tastefully converted, set in quiet village. Guest lounge with log fire. Many local attractions including Chatsworth House and Dovedale. Ideal walking area.

***Sycamore House,** Bonsall, Matlock, Derbyshire, DE4 2AR.*
Attractive C18th stone house overlooking rolling hills.
Open: All Year
Grades: ETB 2 Cr, Comm, AA 3 Q, Recomm
01629 823903 (also fax no)
Mrs Sanders
Rates fr: *£21.00*-**£21.00**.
Beds: 1F 2D 2T
Baths: 4 Ensuite 1 Private
(7)

Boylestone

National Grid Ref: SK1835

***Lees Hall Farm,** Boylestone, Ashbourne, Derbyshire, DE6 5AA.*
Friendly farmhouse in quiet village.
Open: All Year (not Xmas)
01335 330259 Mrs Wilson
Rates fr: *£14.00*-**£16.00**.
Beds: 1F 1T **Baths:** 2 Private

Bradley

National Grid Ref: SK2246
Saracen's Head

***War Farm,** Bradley, Ashbourne, Derbyshire, DE6 1PH.*
Open: All Year (not Xmas)
01335 342104 Mrs Archer
Rates fr: *£14.00*-**£14.00**.
Beds: 1F 1T **Baths:** 1 Shared
(10)
Secluded family working farm, lake, grass tennis court. Ideal base to relax after visiting Ashbourne, Alton Towers, Peak District, Carsington Water, Matlock and local walks.

***Yeldersley Old Hall Farm,** Yeldersley Lane, Bradley, Ashbourne, Derbyshire, DE6 1PH.*
Peaceful farmhouse on dairy farm.
Open: Easter to Oct
Grades: ETB Listed, Comm
01335 344504 Mrs Hinds
Rates fr: *£16.00*-**£19.00**.
Beds: 2D 1T
Baths: 1 Ensuite 1 Shared
(4)

Bradwell

National Grid Ref: SK1781
Bowling Green Inn

***Stoney Ridge,** Granby Road, Bradwell, Sheffield, S30 2HU.*
Open: All Year
Grades: ETB 2 Cr, High Comm, AA 4 Q, Select
01433 620538 Mrs Plant
Rates fr: *£22.00*-**£23.00**.
Beds: 2D 1T
Baths: 2 Ensuite 1 Private
(10) (10)
Our lovely home is set in the beautiful Peak District. Enjoy a swim in our heated indoor pool followed by breakfast on the balcony.

Brampton

National Grid Ref: SK3670

75 Old Road, *Brampton, Chesterfield, Derbyshire, S40 2QU.*
Large Victorian private house.
Open: All Year
01246 276533 Mr Thompson
Rates fr: *£15.00*-**£15.00**.
Beds: 2F 1D 1T 1S
Baths: 3 Shared
(1) (6)

Buxton

National Grid Ref: SK0573

King's Head, Railway Hotel, Devonshire Arms (Fairfield)

Grosvenor House Hotel, *1 Broad Walk, Buxton, Derbyshire, SK17 6JE.*
Open: All Year
Grades: ETB 3 Cr, Comm, AA 4 Q, Select
01298 72439 (also fax no)
Mr & Mrs Fairbairn
Rates fr: *£25.00*-**£42.50**.
Beds: 2F 5D 1T **Baths:** 8 Ensuite
(8) (5)
Idyllically set in heart of historic spa town overlooking Pavilion Gardens/Opera House. Bedrooms ensuite/non-smoking. Excellent home-cooked cuisine. Ideal centre for exploring Peak District.

Lakenham, *11 Burlington Road, Buxton, Derbyshire, SK17 9AL.*
Centrally located elegant Victorian house. **Open:** All Year
Grades: ETB 3 Cr, Comm, AA 3 Q
01298 79209 Mrs Edge
Rates fr: *£20.00*-**£25.00**.
Beds: 2F 2D 2T
Baths: 6 Private
(8)

Buxton Wheelhouse Hotel, *19 College Road, Buxton, Derbyshire, SK17 9DZ.*
Elegant Victorian family-run hotel, central.
Open: All Year (not Xmas)
Grades: ETB 3 Cr, AA 4 Q, Select
01298 24869 (also fax no)
Ms Thompson Price
Rates fr: *£20.00*-**£25.00**.
Beds: 3F 3D 2T 1S
Baths: 9 Ensuite
(10)

Buxton View, *74 Corbar Road, Buxton, Derbyshire, SK17 6RJ.*
Open: All Year (not Xmas)
Grades: ETB 3 Cr, Comm, AA 3 Q, Recomm
01298 79222 Mr Howlett
Rates fr: *£18.00*-**£20.00**.
Beds: 1F 1D 2T 1S
Baths: 4 Ensuite 1 Private
(4)
A friendly home with delightful views over town and surrounding hills. Comfortable ensuite bedrooms and pleasing public rooms will make you wish you'd stayed longer.

Hawthorn Farm Guest House, *Fairfield Road, Buxton, Derbyshire, SK17 7ED.*
400-year-old ex-farmhouse.
Open: Mar to Oct
Grades: ETB 2 Cr, AA 2 Q, Recomm, RAC Acclaim
01298 23230 Mr Smith
Rates fr: *£20.00*-**£20.00**.
Beds: 4F 2D 2T 4S
Baths: 5 Private 2 Shared
(11)

Hilldeen, *97 Dale Road, Buxton, Derbyshire, SK17 6PD.*
Centrally situated, comfortable Victorian house.
Open: All Year (not Xmas)
Grades: ETB 2 Cr
01298 23015 Taylor
Rates fr: *£16.00*-**£16.00**.
Beds: 1F 1T 1S
Baths: 2 Ensuite 1 Private

Clifton Guest House, *2 Clifton Road, Silverlands, Buxton, Derbyshire, SK17 6QL.*
Clean, inexpensive, quiet guest house.
Open: All Year (not Xmas)
Grades: ETB Listed, Comm
01298 71671 Mrs Lowe
Rates fr: *£14.00*-**£14.00**.
Beds: 2T 2S
Baths: 1 Shared

The Victorian Guest House, *5 Wye Grove, Buxton, Derbyshire, SK17 9AJ.*
Tastefully furnished elegant Victorian home.
Open: All Year
Grades: ETB 3 Cr, Comm
01298 78759 Mrs Hames
Rates fr: *£19.00*-**£28.00**.
Beds: 1F 3D 1T 1S
Baths: 4 Private 1 Shared
(4)

Barms Farm, *Fairfield, Buxton, Derbyshire, SK17 7HW.*
Luxury accommodation, non-smoking farmhouse.
Open: All Year (not Xmas)
Grades: ETB 2 Cr, High Comm
01298 77723 Mrs Naden
Fax no: 01298 78692
Rates fr: *£19.00*-**£25.00**.
Beds: 2D 1T
Baths: 3 Ensuite
(10) (4)

Castleton

National Grid Ref: SK1582

George Hotel, Peak Hotel

Cryer House, *Castleton, Sheffield, S30 2WG.*
C17th rectory with cottage garden.
Open: All Year (not Xmas)
01433 620244 Mrs Skelton
Rates fr: *£16.00*.
Beds: 1F 1D
Baths: 1 Shared

Bargate Cottage, *Market Place, Castleton, Sheffield, S30 2WQ.*
Attractive old cottage in Castleton.
Open: All Year (not Xmas)
Grades: ETB 3 Cr, Comm
01433 620201
Mrs Newsome
Fax no: 01433 621739
Rates fr: *£19.50*-**£30.00**.
Beds: 2D 1T
Baths: 3 Private
(5) (4)

Myrtle Cottage, *Market Place, Castleton, Sheffield, S30 2WQ.*
Cottage situated near village green.
Open: All Year (not Xmas)
01433 620787
Mrs Johnson
Rates fr: *£19.00*.
Beds: 1F 3D 1T
Baths: 5 Private
(5)

The Ramblers Rest, *Mill Bridge, Back Street, Castleton, Sheffield, S30 2WR.*
Quietly situated, C17th guest house.
Open: All Year
Grades: ETB Listed, Comm
01433 620125
Mrs Gillott
Rates fr: *£15.00*-**£20.00**.
Beds: 1F 4D
Baths: 3 Private 2 Shared
(7)

Chapel-en-le-Frith

National Grid Ref: SK0580

Navigation

The Forge, *Ashbourne Lane, Chapel-en-le-Frith, Stockport, Cheshire, SK12 6UG.*
Open: All Year (not Xmas)
01298 815172
Mrs Howarth
Rates fr: *£15.00*-**£15.00**.
Beds: 2D 1T
Baths: 1 Ensuite 1 Shared
(4)
Converted Peak Forest canal and tramway workshop and forge (c.1797) in peaceful garden setting. Ideal for walking and touring Dales and National Park. Warm welcome guaranteed.

Chelmorton

National Grid Ref: SK1169

Church Inn

Shallow Grange, *Chelmorton, Buxton, Derbyshire, SK17 9SG.*
Luxury C17th farmhouse.
Open: All Year
Grades: ETB 2 Cr, High Comm
01298 23578
Ms Holland
Rates fr: *£19.50*-**£30.00**.
Beds: 3D
Baths: 3 Ensuite
(5) (10)

Chesterfield

National Grid Ref: SK3871

Abigails Guest House, *62 Brockwell Lane, Chesterfield, Derbyshire, S40 4EE.*
Overlooking Chesterfield & surrounding moorlands.
Open: All Year
01246 279391 Mrs Onza
Rates fr: *£19.00*-**£19.50**.
Beds: 3D 2T 2S
Baths: 7 Ensuite

138 Park Road, *Chesterfield, Derbyshire, S40 2LG.*
Quality, friendly accommodation opposite park.
Open: All Year (not Xmas)
01246 235985 Mr Appleyard
Rates fr: *£16.50*-**£16.50**.
Beds: 2T 1S
Baths: 1 Shared
(12) (1)

Shakespeare Villa, *3 St Margarets Drive, Saltergate, Chesterfield, Derbyshire, S40 4SY.*
Large Victorian detached house.
Open: All Year
01246 200704 Mrs Evans
Rates fr: *£15.00*-**£16.00**.
Beds: 1F 1T 1S
Baths: 2 Private 2 Shared

Chinley

National Grid Ref: SK0482

Crown & Mitre, Squirrel's Hotel

Craigside, *4 Buxton Road, Chinley, Stockport, Cheshire, SK12 6DJ.*
Comfortable family house, Chinley village.
Open: All Year (not Xmas)
01663 750604 Mrs Cameron
Rates fr: *£16.00*-**£16.00**.
Beds: 1D 1T
Baths: 1 Shared
(2)

Mosley House Farm, *Maynestone Road, Chinley, Stockport, Cheshire, SK12 6AH.*
Working farm, peaceful, attractive surroundings.
Open: All Year (not Xmas)
01663 750240 Mrs Goddard
Rates fr: *£15.00*-**£17.00**.
Beds: 1F 1D
Baths: 1 Shared
(3)

Always telephone to get directions to the B&B - you will save time!

Chisworth

National Grid Ref: SJ9992

Woodheys Restaurant, Rock Tavern

Shire Cottage Farmhouse, *Benches Lane, Chisworth, Broadbottom, Hyde, Cheshire, SK14 6RY.*
Real 'home from home', peaceful.
Open: All Year
Grades: ETB 2 Cr, Comm
01457 866536 Mrs Sidebottom
Rates fr: *£17.00*-**£18.00**.
Beds: 1F 1D 1T 1S
Baths: 2 Private 1 Shared
(5)

Chunal

National Grid Ref: SK0491

Stanley Farm, *Chunal, Glossop, Derbyshire, SK13 9JT.*
Private farmhouse on 26 acres.
Open: All Year (not Xmas)
01457 863727 Mrs Brown
Rates fr: *£15.00*-**£18.00**.
Beds: 1D 1T **Baths:** 1 Shared
(10)

Clay Cross

National Grid Ref: SK3963

Kingsfield Guest House, *23 High Street, Clay Cross, Chesterfield, Derbyshire, S45 9DX.*
Large Edwardian house with parking.
Open: All Year
Grades: ETB 1 Cr
01246 862547 Mr Wadd
Rates fr: *£15.50*-**£15.50**.
Beds: 2T 2S
Baths: 1 Shared
(6)

Clifton

National Grid Ref: SK1644

Queens Arms, Cock Inn, Royal Oak

Stone Cottage, *Green Lane, Clifton, Ashbourne, Derbyshire, DE6 1BX.*
Charming C19th cottage.
Open: All Year
Grades: ETB 2 Cr, Comm
01335 343377 Mrs Whittle
Rates fr: *£24.00*-**£25.00**.
Beds: 1F 1D 1T
Baths: 3 Private
(4)

Collycroft Farm, *Clifton, Ashbourne, Derbyshire, DE6 2GN.*
Comfortable farmhouse.
Open: All Year
Grades: ETB Listed, AA 3 Q, RAC Listed
01335 342187 Mrs Hollingsworth
Rates fr: *£17.00*-**£19.00**.
Beds: 1F 1D 1T
Baths: 1 Shared
(20)

Codnor

National Grid Ref: SK4149

Lupare, *13-15 Needham Street, Codnor, Ripley, Derbyshire, DE5 9RR.*
A warm welcome certain here.
Open: All Year
01773 742690 Mrs Sheldon
Rates fr: *£18.00*-**£20.00**.
Beds: 1D 1T 1S
Baths: 3 Private 2 Ensuite
(5)

Creswell

National Grid Ref: SK5274

Hazelmere Farm, *Hazelmere Road, Creswell, Worksop, Notts, S81 4RS.*
Large farmhouse on dairy farm.
Open: All Year
01909 721258 Mr & Mrs Platts
Fax no: 01909 721565
Rates fr: *£15.00*-**£15.00**.
Beds: 1F 1D 1T
Baths: 1 Shared

Derby

National Grid Ref: SK3535

Kingsway Restaurant

Dalby House Hotel, *100 Radbourne Street, off Windmill Hill Lane, Derby, Derbyshire, DE22 3BU.*
Private hotel in quiet residential area.
Open: All Year
Grades: AA 2 Q, Recomm
01332 342353 Mr Taylor
Rates fr: *£15.00*-**£17.00**.
Beds: 2F 1D 2T 4S
Baths: 2 Shared
(10)

Plews Guest House, *51-53 Uttoxeter New Road, Derby, Derbyshire, DE22 3NL.*
Small family-run guest house.
Open: All Year (not Xmas)
01332 344325 Mr Plews
Rates fr: *£13.00*-**£13.00**.
Beds: 2F 1T 6S
Baths: 1 Shared
(6)

48 Crompton Street, *Derby, Derbyshire, DE1 1NX.*
Family-run, city centre guest house.
Open: All Year
Grades: ETB Listed
01332 367193 Mrs Fraser
Rates fr: *£15.00*-**£15.00**.
Beds: 1D 1T 2S
Baths: 1 Shared

The lowest *double* rate per person is shown in *italics*.

Doveridge

National Grid Ref: SK1134

Cavendish ArmsThe Beeches

Dove Cottage, *Church Lane, Doveridge, Ashbourne, Derbyshire, DE6 5NN.*
Attractive family home, lovely views.
Open: All Year (not Xmas)
01889 563794 Mrs Aldabass
Rates fr: *£23.00*-**£23.00**.
Beds: 1D 1T 1S
Baths: 1 Private 1 Shared
(2) (3)

Duffield

National Grid Ref: SK3443

Burley Meadows Farm, *Duffield, Belper, Derbyshire, DE56 4FQ.*
Large Victorian farm house.
Open: All Year (not Xmas)
01332 840125 Mrs Foster
Rates fr: *£13.00*-**£15.00**.
Beds: 2F 1S **Baths:** 1 Shared
(1) (5)

Eastmoor

National Grid Ref: SK3071

Wheatsheaf

Sheeplea Cottage Farm, *Baslow Road, Eastmoor, Chesterfield, Derbyshire, S42 7DD.*
Friendly, comfortable, extended old farmhouse.
Open: Mar to Oct
01246 566785 Mrs Worrall
Rates fr: *£15.00*-**£20.00**.
Beds: 1D 1T **Baths:** 2 Shared
(10)

Edale

National Grid Ref: SK1285

Poachers Arms

Brookfield, *Edale, Sheffield, S30 2ZL.*
Beautiful quiet Victorian house.
Open: All Year (not Xmas)
01433 670227 Mrs Chapman
Rates fr: *£14.00*-**£16.00**.
Beds: 1F 1D 1T **Baths:** 1 Shared
(3)

The Old Parsonage, *Grindsbrook, Edale, Sheffield, S30 2ZD.*
Secluded C17th house & garden.
Open: Mar to Nov
01433 670232 Mrs Beney
Rates fr: *£14.00*-**£14.00**.
Beds: 1D 1T 1S
Baths: 1 Private 1 Shared
(2)

Stonecroft, *Grindsbrook, Edale, Sheffield, S30 2ZA.*
Lovely family home with pretty, well-equipped rooms.
Open: All Year (not Xmas)
01433 670262 Mrs Reid
Rates fr: *£21.00*-**£26.00**.
Beds: 1D 1T
Baths: 1 Ensuite 1 Private
(12) (5)

Eyam

National Grid Ref: SK2176

Miner's Arm Restaurant

Delf View House, *Church Street, Eyam, Sheffield, S30 1QW.*
Luxurious Listed Georgian country house.
Open: All Year
Grades: ETB 2 Cr, High Comm
01433 631533 Mr Lewis
Fax no: 01433 631972
Rates fr: *£23.00*-**£25.00**.
Beds: 1D 1T
(14) (4)

Farley

National Grid Ref: SK2961

Boat House

Robertswood, *Farley Hill, Farley, Matlock, Derbyshire, DE4 3LL.*
Comfortable, friendly Victorian house.
Open: All Year
Grades: ETB 3 Cr, High Comm, AA 4 Q, Select
01629 55642 (also fax no)
Mr Stuart
Rates fr: *£20.00*-**£35.00**.
Beds: 4D 3T
Baths: 7 Ensuite
(12) (7)

Fenny Bentley

National Grid Ref: SK1750

The Bentley Brook Inn, *Fenny Bentley, Ashbourne, Derbyshire, DE6 1LF.*
Peak District National Park traditional country inn.
Open: All Year
01335 350278 Mrs Allingham
Rates fr: *£23.75*-**£23.75**.
Beds: 1F 5D 2T 1S
Baths: 6 Private 2 Shared
(60)

Glossop

National Grid Ref: SK0394

Birds Nest Cottage, *40 Primrose Lane, Glossop, Derbyshire, SK13 8EW.*
Friendly and lots of home comforts.
Open: All Year (not Xmas)
01457 853478 Mills
Rates fr: *£14.00*-**£14.00**.
Beds: 1F 3T 1S
Baths: 3 Shared
(All)

Grangemill

National Grid Ref: SK2457

Holly Bush Inn, Bowling Green

Middle Hills Farm, *Grangemill, Matlock, Derbyshire, DE4 4HY.*
Comfortable modern farmhouse, magnificent views.
Open: All Year (not Xmas)
Grades: ETB 2 Cr, Comm
01629 650368 (also fax no)
Mrs Lomas
Rates fr: *£16.00*-**£20.00**.
Beds: 2F 1T
Baths: 2 Private 2 Shared
(5)

Avondale Farm, *Grangemill, Matlock, Derbyshire, DE4 4HT.*
Tastefully converted barn, ground-floor level.
Open: All Year (not Xmas)
Grades: ETB 2 Cr, Comm
01629 650820 Mrs Wragg
Rates fr: *£21.00*.
Beds: 1T
Baths: 1 Private
(1)

Grindleford

National Grid Ref: SK2477

Plough, Chequers

Yarncliff Lodge, *Upper Padley, Grindleford, Sheffield, S30 1HQ.*
Comfortable farmhouse amid moorland/woodland.
Open: All Year (not Xmas)
01433 631311 Mrs Hathaway
Rates fr: *£14.00*-**£14.00**.
Beds: 2D 1T
Baths: 1 Private 1 Shared
(4)

Hartington

National Grid Ref: SK1260

Devonshire Arms, Manifold Inn, Greyhound

Bank Top Farm, *Hartington, Buxton, Derbyshire, SK17 0AD.*
Farmhouse accommodation on working farm.
Open: All Year
Grades: ETB Listed, Comm
01298 84205 Pilkington
Rates fr: *£16.50*-**£18.00**.
Beds: 1F 1D 1T
Baths: 1 Private 1 Shared

Manifold House, *Hulme End, Hartington, Buxton, Derbyshire, SK17 0EZ.*
Beautiful stone house, perfect setting.
Open: All Year (not Xmas)
01298 84662 Mrs Baber
Rates fr: *£17.00*-**£17.00**.
Beds: 1F 1D 1S
Baths: 1 Shared
(3) (4)

Wolfscote Grange Farm, *Hartington, Buxton, Derbyshire, SK17 0AX.*
C15th farmhouse with character. Working farm.
Open: All Year (not Xmas)
Grades: ETB Listed, Comm
01298 84342
Mrs Gibbs
Rates fr: *£16.00*-**£17.00**.
Beds: 1F 1D 1T 1S

Hathersage

National Grid Ref: SK2381

Plough

Hillfoot Farm, *Castleton Road, Hathersage, Sheffield, S30 1AH.*
Open: All Year
Grades: ETB Listed, Comm
01433 651673
Mrs Wilcockson
Rates fr: *£17.00*-**£20.00**.
Beds: 1F 3D 2T 1S
Baths: 5 Private
(13)
Newly-built accommodation onto existing farmhouse offering comfortable well-appointed rooms with ensuite facilities. 2 ground floor rooms, 3 first floor rooms, carpark, telephone for guests. Fire-certificate.

Moorgate, *Castleton Road, Hathersage, Sheffield, S30 1AH.*
Victorian family house, in village.
Open: All Year (not Xmas)
01433 650293
Mrs Veevers
Rates fr: *£14.00*-**£16.00**.
Beds: 1D 1T 1S
Baths: 1 Shared
(3)

The Old Vicarage, *Church Bank, Hathersage, Sheffield, S30 1AB.*
Grade II Listed old vicarage.
Open: All Year (not Xmas)
01433 651099
Mrs Venning
Rates fr: *£16.50*-**£21.50**.
Beds: 2D 1T
Baths: 1 Private 2 Shared

Hayfield

National Grid Ref: SK0388

Packhorse

Stet Barn Farm, *Lane Head Road, Hayfield, Stockport, Cheshire, SK12 5NS.*
Attractive peaceful modernised farmhouse.
Open: Feb to Xmas
Grades: ETB Listed, Comm
01663 745970 (also fax no)
Mrs Isaacs
Rates fr: *£18.00*-**£18.00**.
Beds: 1D 1T
Baths: 1 Ensuite 1 Shared
(4)

The Old Bank House, *Hayfield, Stockport, Cheshire, SK12 5EP.*
Family home, beautiful decor.
Open: All Year
01663 747354 Mrs Collier-Johnson
Rates fr: *£18.50*-**£20.00**.
Beds: 1F 1D 1T **Baths:** 2 Shared

Higham

National Grid Ref: SK3959

Holly Tree Farm, *Higham, Alfreton, Derby, Derbyshire, DE55 6EF.*
C17th farmhouse, home cooking.
Open: All Year (not Xmas)
Grades: ETB Listed, Approv
01773 832614 Mrs Banham
Rates fr: *£16.00*-**£18.00**.
Beds: 2F 1D 1T 1S
Baths: 2 Private 3 Shared
(10)

Hognaston

National Grid Ref: SK2350

Ye Olde Forge, *Hognaston, Ashbourne, Derbyshire, DE6 1PU.*
Old forge. One mile Carsington Water.
Open: All Year
01335 370404
Mrs Wilkins
Rates fr: *£17.00*-**£20.00**.
Beds: 1D 1T
Baths: 1 Ensuite
(12) (5)

Holymoorside

National Grid Ref: SK3369

Eastview, *35 Holymoor Road, Holymoorside, Chesterfield, Derbyshire, S42 7EB.*
Quiet Peak District village. Stone-built family house.
Open: All Year
01246 566925
Ms Bentley
Rates fr: *£14.00*-**£14.50**.
Beds: 1D 1S
Baths: 1 Shared
(2)

Hope

National Grid Ref: SK1683

Old Blacksmiths Cottage, *18 Castleton Road, Hope, Sheffield, S30 2RD.*
Oak-beamed cottage, friendly atmosphere.
Open: All Year (not Xmas)
01433 612407 Lane
Rates fr: *£18.00*-**£21.00**.
Beds: 1F 2D 3T
Baths: 2 Ensuite 4 Shared
(6)

The lowest **single** *rate is shown in* **bold.**

Moorgate, *Edale Road, Hope, Sheffield, S30 2RF.*
Elegant country guest house.
Open: All Year
01433 621219
Rates fr: *£18.00*-**£18.00**.
Beds: 3D 16T 8S
Baths: 10 Private 5 Shared
(30)

Ible

National Grid Ref: SK2457

Home Farm, *Ible, Grangemill, Matlock, Derbyshire, DE4 4HS.*
Farmhouse quiet countryside in Peak Park.
Open: Jan to Nov
Grades: ETB 2 Cr, Comm
01629 650349 Ms Wain
Rates fr: *£14.50*-**£16.00**.
Beds: 1F 1D
Baths: 2 Ensuite

Langwith

National Grid Ref: SK5269

Little Loxley, *17 Langwith Drive, Langwith, Mansfield, Notts, NG20 9DJ.*
Small, friendly, family-run guest house.
Open: Easter to Dec
Grades: ETB Listed
01623 742568 Mrs Pepperday
Rates fr: *£16.00*-**£16.00**.
Beds: 1D 1T
Baths: 1 Shared
(10)

Blue Barn Farm, *Langwith, Mansfield, Notts, NG20 9JD.*
Warm, modernised Victorian farmhouse.
Open: All Year (not Xmas)
01623 742248 Mrs Ibbotson
Rates fr: *£16.00*-**£16.00**.
Beds: 1F 1D 1T
Baths: 1 Private 1 Shared
(6)

Litton

National Grid Ref: SK1675

George Hotel

Laurel House, *The Green, Litton, Buxton, Derbyshire, SK17 8QP.*
Victorian house in quiet village.
Open: Mar to Nov
Grades: ETB 2 Cr, Comm
01298 871971 Ms Harris
Rates fr: *£16.00*-**£20.00**.
Beds: 1D 1T
Baths: 1 Ensuite 1 Private

Beacon House, *Litton, Buxton, Derbyshire, SK17 8QP.*
Farm smallholding.
Open: All Year (not Xmas)
01298 871752 Mrs Parsons
Rates fr: *£17.50*.
Beds: 2D
Baths: 2 Private

Always telephone to get directions to the B&B - you will save time!

Long Eaton

National Grid Ref: SK4933

Half Crown, Manor

Clifton Hotel, *126 Nottingham Road, Long Eaton, Nottingham,* NG10 2BZ.
Large Victorian converted house.
Open: All Year
Grades: ETB 2 Cr
0115 973 4277 Fasey
Rates fr: *£13.50*-**£18.50**.
Beds: 10F 3D 2T 5S
Baths: 2 Ensuite 2 Shared
(20)

Millingtons, *47 Nottingham Road, Long Eaton, Nottingham, Notts,* NG10 2BN.
Spacious Edwardian home.
Open: All Year (not Xmas)
Grades: ETB Listed
0115 972 7238 Mr Millington
Rates fr: *£15.00*-**£16.50**.
Beds: 1D 1T 2S
Baths: 2 Shared
(4)

Lullington

National Grid Ref: SK2513

Great Man

The Old Post Office, *Main Street, Lullington, Swadlincote, Derbyshire,* DE12 8EG.
Georgian house in conservation village.
Open: All Year (not Xmas)
Grades: ETB Listed
01827 373314 Mrs Higgins
Rates fr: *£16.00*-**£20.00**.
Beds: 1T 1D
Baths: 2 Private

Mackworth

National Grid Ref: SK3137

Mundy Arms

Thames House, *6 Thames Close, Mackworth, Derby, Derbyshire,* DE22 4HT.
Large detached house, quiet cul-de-sac.
Open: All Year (not Xmas)
Grades: ETB 2 Cr, Comm
01332 513526 Mrs Swarbrooke
Rates fr: *£15.00*-**£15.00**.
Beds: 1F 1D
Baths: 2 Private
(4)

Mappleton

National Grid Ref: SK1647

Royal Oak (Mayfield)

Little Park Farm, *Mappleton, Ashbourne, Derbyshire,* DE6 2BR.
Open: Easter to Oct
Grades: ETB 1 Cr, Comm
01335 350341 Mrs Harrison
Rates fr: *£14.00*.
Beds: 2D 1T
Baths: 1 Shared
Enjoy the peace and quiet of this 300 year old Listed farmhouse situated in the beautiful Dove Valley. Ideal area for walking, cycling and National Trust properties.

Marston Montgomery

National Grid Ref: SK1337

Waldley Manor, *Marston Montgomery, Doveridge, Ashbourne, Derbyshire,* DE6 5LR.
C16th manor farmhouse.
Open: All Year (not Xmas)
01889 590287 Ms Whitfield
Rates fr: *£17.00*-**£18.00**.
Beds: 1F 1D
Baths: 2 Ensuite

Matlock

National Grid Ref: SK3060

Ritz Restaurant, Gate Hotel, Strand, Old Elizabethan, The Boat

Edgemount, *16 Edge Road, Matlock, Derbyshire,* DE4 3NH.
Open: All Year
Grades: ETB Listed, Approv
01629 584787 Mrs Allen
Rates fr: *£14.00*-**£14.00**.
Beds: 1F 1T 1S
Baths: 1 Shared
(5-12) (3)
Comfortable Edwardian house, with warm hospitality, in peaceful central location with country views. Convenient for public transport, rambling. Local holiday attractions Chatsworth House, Peak District.

Glendon, *Knowleston Place, Matlock, Derbyshire,* DE4 3BU.
Victorian house by the park.
Open: All Year (not Xmas)
Grades: ETB 1 Cr
01629 584732 Mrs Elliott
Rates fr: *£16.00*-**£17.00**.
Beds: 1F 1T 1D 1S
Baths: 2 Shared
(3) (6)

Planning a longer stay? Always ask for any special rates.

Kensington Villa, *84 Dale Road, Matlock, Derbyshire,* DE4 3LU.
Open: All Year (not Xmas)
Grades: AA 2 Q
01629 57627 Mrs Gorman
Rates fr: *£17.50*-**£17.50**.
Beds: 2D 1T
Baths: 1 Shared
You are assured of comfortable accommodation and a very warm welcome. Enjoy a substantial, leisurely breakfast and then experience the delights of the Peak District. Recommended by 'Which' Good Bed & Breakfast Guide.

Farley Farm, *Farley, Matlock, Derbyshire,* DE4 5LR.
Working farm, home-cooking, friendly.
Open: All Year (not Xmas)
Grades: ETB 2 Cr, Comm, AA 2 Q, Approv, RAC Listed
01629 582533
Mrs Brailsford
Rates fr: *£16.00*-**£18.00**.
Beds: 1F 1D 1T
Baths: 1 Ensuite 2 Shared
(10)

Bank House, *12 Snitterton Road, Matlock, Derbyshire,* DE4 3LZ.
Open: All Year
Grades: ETB 2 Cr
01629 56101
Mrs Donnell
Rates fr: *£17.00*-**£19.00**.
Beds: 1F 1D
Baths: 1 Ensuite 1 Private
(2)
Beamed C17th stone cottage. Centrally situated. Warm friendly welcome. Includes converted stable offering twin/family suite on 2 floors with fridge, bathroom and own entrance.

Tuckers Guest House, *48 Dale Road, Matlock, Derbyshire,* DE4 3NB.
Friendly, spacious home. Pets welcome.
Open: All Year
01629 583018
Mrs Martin
Rates fr: *£17.00*-**£20.00**.
Beds: 1F 1D 1T
Baths: 2 Shared
(3) (2)

Lane End House, *Green Lane, Tansley, Matlock, Derbyshire,* DE4 5FJ.
Open: All Year
Grades: ETB 2 Cr, AA 4 Q, Select, RAC High Acclaim
01629 583981 (also fax no)
Mrs Smith
Rates fr: *£22.00*-**£30.00**.
Beds: 3D 1T
Baths: 2 Ensuite 2 Private
(12) (6)
Georgian farmhouse c.1730, beautifully located rear of village. Delightful gardens, waterfalls, fish pond overlooking Riber Castle. Imaginative delicious foods, fresh products, extensive wine cellar.

***Sycamore House,** Bonsall, Matlock, Derbyshire, DE4 2AR.*
Open: All Year
Grades: ETB 2 Cr, Comm, AA 3 Q, Recomm
01629 823903 (also fax no)
Mrs Sanders
Rates fr: *£21.00*-**£21.00**.
Beds: 1F 2D 2T
Baths: 4 Ensuite 1 Private
(7)
Attractive C18th stone house overlooking rolling hills. Village situation, ensuite bedrooms, guests' lounge.Traditional English cuisine served. Ideal base to explore Derbyshire's attractions and Dales.

Matlock Bath

National Grid Ref: SK2958

Midland Hotel

***5 Clarence Terrace,** Holme Road, Matlock Bath, Matlock, Derbyshire, DE4 3NY.*
Comfortable accommodation in quiet surroundings.
Open: Easter to Nov
Grades: AA 1 Q
01629 55555
Ms Oldfield
Rates fr: *£13.00*-**£15.00**.
Beds: 1F 1D 1T
Baths: 2 Shared
(4)

***Ashdale Guest House,** 92 North Parade, Matlock Bath, Matlock, Derbyshire, DE4 3NS.*
Victorian house, monkey puzzle trees.
Open: All Year (not Xmas)
Grades: ETB Listed
01629 57826
Mrs Jackson
Rates fr: *£15.00*-**£20.00**.
Beds: 1F 2D
Baths: 1 Ensuite
(5)

***Beech Hurst,** 228 Dale Road, Matlock Bath, Matlock, Derbyshire, DE4 3RT.*
Comfortable Victorian house overlooking river.
Open: All Year (not Xmas)
Grades: ETB Listed
01629 56013
Mrs Swallow
Rates fr: *£15.00*-**£16.50**.
Beds: 1F 2D
Baths: 2 Shared
(1)

***1 Greenbank,** Matlock Bath, Matlock, Derbyshire, DE4 3NU.*
Victorian private house, scenic views.
Open: All Year (not Xmas)
Grades: ETB 1 Cr
01629 583909
Mrs Langston
Rates fr: *£15.00*-**£20.00**.
Beds: 2D 1T
Baths: 1 Shared
(10) (3)

***Cliffeside B & B,** Brunswood Road, Matlock Bath, Matlock, Derbyshire, DE4 3PA.*
Large friendly Victorian family home.
Open: All Year
01629 56981 Mrs Bowler
Rates fr: *£16.00*-**£16.00**.
Beds: 1F 1D
Baths: 2 Private
(2)

Melbourne

National Grid Ref: SK3825

***The Coach House,** 69 Derby Road, Melbourne, Derby, Derbyshire, DE73 1FE.*
Homely guest house, picturesque village.
Open: All Year
01332 862338 Mr Lee
Rates fr: *£20.00*-**£25.00**.
Beds: 2F 2D 2T
Baths: 6 Private
(8)

National Grid References are for villages, towns and cities - *not* for individual houses.

Mercaston

National Grid Ref: SK2643

***Mercaston Hall,** Mercaston, Brailsford, Ashbourne, Derbyshire, DE6 3BL.*
Friendly welcome in peaceful location.
Open: All Year (not Xmas)
Grades: ETB Listed
01335 360263
Mrs Haddon
Rates fr: *£16.00*-**£21.00**.
Beds: 2D 1T
Baths: 2 Ensuite 1 Private
(8) (6)

Mickleover

National Grid Ref: SK3033

***Bonehill Farm,** Etwall Road, Mickleover, Derby, Derbyshire, DE3 5DN.*
Comfortable Georgian farmhouse in countryside.
Open: All Year
Grades: ETB 2 Cr
01332 513553
Mrs Dicken
Rates fr: *£15.00*-**£15.00**.
Beds: 1F 1D 1T
Baths: 1 Ensuite 2 Shared
(6)

Middleton-by-Wirksworth

National Grid Ref: SK2756

Rising Sun Inn

***Rise End House,** 10 Rise End, Middleton-by-Wirksworth, Matlock, Derbyshire, DE4 4LS.*
Listed building with welcoming atmosphere.
Open: All Year (not Xmas)
01629 825359 Mrs Jennings
Rates fr: *£15.00*-**£18.00**.
Beds: 1F 1D **Baths:** 1 Shared
(5) (1)

***Newlands House,** 1 Duke Street, Middleton-by-Wirksworth, Matlock, Derbyshire, DE4 4NB.*
Detached house with beautiful garden.
Open: All Year (not Xmas)
01629 825292 Mrs Jackson
Rates fr: *£16.00*-**£18.50**.
Beds: 1F 2D 1S
(4)

Milford

National Grid Ref: SK3545

***King William IV,** The Bridge, Milford, Belper, Derbyshire, DE56 0RR.*
Imposing three-storey stone inn.
Open: All Year
01332 840842 Mr Hodgkison
Rates fr: *£16.00*-**£16.00**.
Beds: 3T 1D 1S **Baths:** 5 Ensuite

Monsal Head

National Grid Ref: SK1871

***Castle Cliffe Private Hotel,** Monsal Head, Bakewell, Derbyshire, DE45 1NL.*
Open: All Year
Grades: ETB 2 Cr, Comm, AA Listed, 3 Q
01629 640258 Mrs Gilbert
Rates fr: *£23.00*-**£30.00**.
Beds: 2F 3D 4T
Baths: 6 Ensuite 2 Shared
(11)
Victorian country house in the Peak National Park. Commended for its superb views, friendly atmosphere and home-made food. Near Chatsworth House. Ideal base for walkers.

Monyash

National Grid Ref: SK1566

***Sheldon House,** Chapel Street, Monyash, Bakewell, Derbyshire, DE45 1JJ.*
Recently renovated Grade II Listed house. **Open:** All Year (not Xmas)
Grades: ETB 2 Cr, High Comm
01629 813067 Mr & Mrs Tyler
Rates fr: *£19.00*-**£25.00**.
Beds: 3D **Baths:** 3 Ensuite
(8)

***Cheney Lodge,** Rowson Farm, Monyash, Bakewell, Derbyshire, DE45 1JH.*
Open: All Year
01629 815336 / 813521
Mr Mycock
Rates fr: *£14.00*-**£17.00**.
Beds: 1F 2D 1T
Baths: 2 Ensuite 1 Private 1 Shared
(3)
Fully modernised farm lodge, peacefully located. Lovely views across the White Peak. Log fires, Aga cooked breakfasts. Bargain breaks October to March. Photo on request.

***Shuttle Hill Cottage,** Chapel Street, Monyash, Bakewell, Derbyshire, DE45 1JJ.*
C18th Cruck-beam cottage.
Open: All Year
01629 813979 Mrs Allen
Rates fr: *£16.00*.
Beds: 2D
Baths: 1 Private 1 Shared

***Sheldon House,** Chapel Street, Monyash, Bakewell, Derbyshire, DE45 1JL.*
Comfortable, friendly C18th house.
Open: All Year (not Xmas)
Grades: ETB 2 Cr, High Comm
01298 813067 Mrs Tyler
Rates fr: *£18.50*-**£25.00**.
Beds: 3D **Baths:** 3 Private
(10) (3)

Morley

National Grid Ref: SK3940

Rose & Crown

***189 Main Road,** Morley On Smalley, Morley, Ilkeston, Derbyshire, DE7 6DG.*
Bungalow. Lovely garden; good home-cooking.
Open: All Year
Grades: ETB 2 Cr, Comm, AA 3 Q, Recomm
01332 780349 Mrs Green-Armytage
Rates fr: *£17.50*-**£20.00**.
Beds: 1F 1D 1T
Baths: 3 Private
(5)

North Wingfield

National Grid Ref: SK4165

Blue Bell Inn

***South View,** 95 Church Lane, North Wingfield, Chesterfield, Derbyshire, S42 5HR.*
Traditional breakfast. Victorian farmhouse, homely.
Open: All Year (not Xmas)
Grades: ETB Listed, Comm
01246 850091 Mrs Hopkinson
Rates fr: *£14.00*-**£14.00**.
Beds: 2D 1S
Baths: 1 Shared
(10) (3)

Over Haddon

National Grid Ref: SK2066

***Mandale House,** Haddon Grove, Over Haddon, Bakewell, Derbyshire, DE45 1JF.*
Peaceful farmhouse near Lathkill Dale.
Open: Mar to Oct
01629 812416 Mrs Finney
Rates fr: *£17.00*-**£25.00**.
Beds: 2D 1T
Baths: 3 Private

***Lathkill Cottage,** Over Haddon, Bakewell, Derbyshire, DE45 1JE.*
Self-contained room, adjacent country cottage.
Open: All Year (not Xmas)
01629 814518 Mrs Parker
Rates fr: *£18.00*-**£25.00**.
Beds: 1T
Baths: 1 Private

Padfield

National Grid Ref: SK0296

The Peels Arms

***Whitehouse Farm,** Padfield, Hyde, Cheshire, SK14 7ET.*
Comfortable working farmhouse.
Open: All Year
Grades: ETB Listed, Comm
01457 854695 Mrs Wynne
Rates fr: *£15.00*-**£18.00**.
Beds: 2T
(6)

Parsley Hay

National Grid Ref: SK1463

***Cotesfield Farm,** Parsley Hay, Buxton, Derbyshire, SK17 0BD.*
C18th Listed farmhouse.
Open: All Year
01298 83256 Mr Mckerrow
Rates fr: *£15.00*-**£17.50**.
Beds: 1F 1D
Baths: 1 Shared
(4)

Peak Forest

National Grid Ref: SK1179

***Dam Dale Farm,** Peak Forest, Buxton, Derbyshire, SK17 8EF.*
Comfortable, homely, wonderful views, quiet.
Open: Feb to Nov
01298 24104 Mrs Fletcher
Rates fr: *£16.00*-**£20.00**.
Beds: 1F 2D 1T **Baths:** 2 Shared
(10) (6)

Planning a longer stay? Always ask for any special rates.

Pleasley

National Grid Ref: SK5064

***Appleby Guesthouse,** Chesterfield Road, Pleasley, Mansfield, Notts, NG19 7PF.*
Large Victorian guest house.
Open: All Year (not Xmas)
01623 810508
Mrs Bloor
Rates fr: *£17.00*-**£18.00**.
Beds: 1F 2D 2T 2S
Baths: 2 Shared
(10)

Riddings

National Grid Ref: SK4252

***1 Peveril Drive,** Riddings, Alfreton, Derbyshire, DE55 4AP.*
Superb self-contained bungalow accommodation.
Open: All Year
01773 607712
Mrs Brown
Rates fr: *£16.00*-**£20.00**.
Beds: 1T 1S
Baths: 2 Private
(3)

Rowland

National Grid Ref: SK2172

Eyne Arms

***Holly Cottage,** Rowland, Bakewell, Derbyshire, DE45 1NR.*
Most attractive comfortable old cottage.
Open: Jan to Oct
01629 640624
Mrs Everard
Rates fr: *£19.00*-**£23.00**.
Beds: 2T
Baths: 1 Shared
(3)

***Jasmine Cottage,** Rowland, Bakewell, Derbyshire, DE45 1NR.*
Traditional cottage in peaceful hamlet.
Open: All Year (not Xmas)
Grades: ETB Listed
01629 640263
Mrs Mantell
Rates fr: *£17.50*-**£15.00**.
Beds: 1D 1S
Baths: 1 Private
(0) (2)

***Rowland Cottage,** Rowland, Great Longstone, Bakewell, Derbyshire, DE45 1NR.*
C17th cottage, quiet, relaxing, comfortable.
Open: All Year
Grades: ETB Listed, Approv
01629 640365
Mrs Scott
Rates fr: *£16.00*.
Beds: 1F 1D
Baths: 1 Private 1 Shared
(3)

Shatton

National Grid Ref: SK1982

Woodroffe Arms (Hope)

***The White House,** Shatton, Bamford, Sheffield, S30 2BG.*
Friendly, comfortable, private country house.
Open: All Year (not Xmas)
01433 651487 (also fax no)
Mrs Middleton
Rates fr: *£15.00*-**£15.00**.
Beds: 1D 1T 2S
Baths: 2 Shared
(4)

Sheldon

National Grid Ref: SK1768

***Barleycorn Croft,** Sheldon, Bakewell, Derbyshire, DE45 1QS.*
Independent ensuite apartment, quiet farming village.
Open: All Year
01629 813636 Mrs Spafford
Rates fr: *£14.00*-**£25.00**.
Beds: 1D 1T
(6) (3)

Please respect a B&B's wishes regarding children, animals & smoking.

Shirebrook

National Grid Ref: SK5267

***Old School Guest House,** Main Street, Shirebrook, Mansfield, Derbyshire, NG20 8DL.*
Converted C19th school & school-house.
Open: All Year
01623 744610 Mrs Miles
Rates fr: *£15.00*-**£15.00**.
Beds: 2F 1D 1T 1S
Baths: 4 Private
(12)

Shirley

National Grid Ref: SK2141

Saracens Head

***The Old Byre,** Shirley, Brailsford, Ashbourne, Derbyshire, DE6 3AS.*
Converted barn in tranquil village.
Open: All Year
Grades: ETB Listed
01335 360054
Mr Bradshaw
Rates fr: *£17.50*-**£17.50**.
Beds: 2D 2S
Baths: 2 Private
(4)

Stanton-by-Bridge

National Grid Ref: SK3727

Old Packhorse Inn

***Ivy House Farm,** Stanton-by-Bridge, Derby, Derbyshire, DE73 1HT.*
C18th farmhouse on working farm.
Open: All Year
01332 863152 Mrs Kidd
Rates fr: *£15.00*-**£15.00**.
Beds: 3D 2T 4S **Baths:** 5 Private
(10)

Stretton

National Grid Ref: SK3961

***Ivy Beech,** Highstairs Lane, Stretton, Alfreton, Derbyshire, DE55 6FD.*
Quiet house with large garden.
Open: All Year (not Xmas)
Grades: ETB Listed, Comm
01246 863397 Mr Lardge
Rates fr: *£15.50*-**£15.50**.
Beds: 2T 1S **Baths:** 1 Shared
(3)

Swanwick

National Grid Ref: SK4053

Excavator Pub

***The Spinney,** Derby Road, Swanwick, Alfreton, Derbyshire, DE55 1BG.*
Comfortable bungalow, TV, tea-making.
Open: All Year (not Xmas)
Grades: ETB Listed
01773 609020 Mrs Nunn
Rates fr: *£15.00*-**£15.50**.
Beds: 1D 2T **Baths:** 1 Shared
(6) (4)

Tansley

National Grid Ref: SK3259

***Lane End House,** Green Lane, Tansley, Matlock, Derbyshire, DE4 5FJ.*
Georgian farmhouse c.1730, beautifully located rear of village.
Open: All Year
Grades: ETB 2 Cr, AA 4 Q, Select, RAC High Acclaim
01629 583981 (also fax no)
Mrs Smith
Rates fr: *£22.00*-**£30.00**.
Beds: 3D 1T
Baths: 2 Ensuite 2 Private
(12) (6)

Tideswell

National Grid Ref: SK1575

***Poppies,** Bank Square, Tideswell, Buxton, Derbyshire, SK17 8LA.*
Comfortable rooms above small restaurant. **Open:** Feb to Dec
Grades: ETB Listed, Approv
01298 871083 Mrs Pinnegar
Rates fr: *£14.50*-**£14.50**.
Beds: 1F 1D 1T
Baths: 1 Private 2 Shared

Two Dales

National Grid Ref: SK2862

***Top o' the Hill,** Sydnope Hill, Two Dales, Matlock, Derbyshire, DE4 2FN.*
Modern house in country setting.
Open: All Year (not Xmas)
01629 734548 Mrs Bennett
Rates fr: *£14.00*-**£15.00**.
Beds: 2D 1T **Baths:** 1 Shared

Wensley

National Grid Ref: SK2661

Bowling Green

***Manor House,** Wensley, Matlock, Derbyshire, DE4 2LL.*
Picturesque C18th farm cottage.
Open: All Year
Grades: AA 2 Q
01629 734360
Mrs Elliott
Rates fr: *£17.50*-**£25.00**.
Beds: 2D 1T
Baths: 1 Shared
(6)

Wessington

National Grid Ref: SK3757

Three Horseshoes, Horse & Jockey

***Crich Lane Farm,** Moorwood Moor Lane, Wessington, Alfreton, Derbyshire, DE55 6DU.*
Open: All Year (not Xmas)
Grades: ETB Listed
01773 835186 Mrs Green
Rates fr: *£16.00*-**£16.00**.
Beds: 2F 3D 2T 1S
Baths: 5 Ensuite 1 Private 1 Shared
(10)
C17th farmhouse. Peaceful surroundings. Ideal base for local attractions including 'Peak Practice'. Enjoy a good farmhouse breakfast in a warm friendly atmosphere.

***Oaktree Farm,** Matlock Road, Oakerthorpe, Wessington, Alfreton Derbyshire, DE55 7NA.*
Modern comfortable farmhouse, lovely views.
Open: All Year (not Xmas)
Grades: AA 3 Q, Recomm
01773 832957 Mrs Prince
Rates fr: *£18.00*-**£20.00**.
Beds: 2D 1T **Baths:** 3 Ensuite
(10)

High season, bank holidays and special events mean low availability *anywhere*.

Whatstandwell

National Grid Ref: SK3354

Derwent Hotel

Robin Hood Cottage, *Robin Hood, Whatstandwell, Matlock, Derbyshire, DE4 5HF.*
Elevated woodland position for unrestricted views.
Open: All Year (not Xmas)
01773 856238 Mrs Hitchcock
Rates fr: *£16.50*-**£16.50**.
Beds: 1D 1T 1S
Baths: 1 Private 2 Shared
(4)

Winster

National Grid Ref: SK2460

Brae Cottage, *East Bank, Winster, Matlock, Derbyshire, DE4 2DT.*
Spacious cottage annexe. Picturesque village.
Open: All Year
01629 650375 Mrs Macbain
Rates fr: *£12.50*-**£15.00**.
Beds: 1F 1D
Baths: 1 Ensuite
(2)

Tearsall Farm, *Bonsall Lane, Winster, Matlock, Derbyshire, DE4 2PD.*
Private wing of large (non-working) farmhouse.
Open: Mar to Oct
01629 650602 Mrs Rigby
Rates fr: *£12.50*-**£15.00**.
Beds: 1D
Baths: 1 Private
(5)

Wirksworth

National Grid Ref: SK2853

Miner's Alms

Vaults Inn, *Coldwell Street, Wirksworth, Matlock, Derbyshire, DE4 4FB.*
Georgian family-run Peak District inn.
Open: All Year (not Xmas)
01629 822186
Mr Wildman
Rates fr: *£18.00*-**£24.00**.
Beds: 3F 1D
Baths: 4 Ensuite

Henmore Grange, *Wirksworth, Carsington, Matlock, Derbyshire, DE4 4DF.*
Converted barns. Good breakfast!
Open: All Year
Grades: AA 4 Q
01629 540420
Mrs Brassington
Rates fr: *£25*-**£31.00**.
Beds: 3F 4D 3T 1S
Baths: 11 Private
(1 month) (16)

Hareruns House, *9 Sough Lane, Cromford Road, Wirksworth, Matlock, Derbyshire, DE4 4FQ.*
Large Victorian private house.
Open: All Year (not Xmas)
01629 822418
Mrs Millar
Rates fr: *£14.00*-**£14.00**.
Beds: 2D 1S
Baths: 1 Shared
(7) (4)

Youlgreave

National Grid Ref: SK2164

Bulls Head, George Hotel, Farmyard Inn

Bankside Cottage, *Youlgreave, Bakewell, Derbyshire, DE45 1WD.*
Open: All Year
Grades: ETB Listed, Comm
01629 636689 Mr Blackburn
Rates fr: *£15.00*-**£15.00**.
Beds: 1D 1T
Baths: 1 Shared
Large stone cottage, unique off-road position, terrace garden overlooks secluded Bradford Dale, guest lounge. Relaxed friendly atmosphere. A house full of art and books.

The Old Bakery, *Church Street, Youlgreave, Bakewell, Derbyshire, DE45 1UR.*
Traditional property at heart of village.
Open: All Year
Grades: ETB 1 Cr, Comm
01629 636887 Ms Croasdell
Rates fr: *£14.00*-**£16.00**.
Beds: 2T **Baths:** 1 Shared
(1)

Planning a longer stay? Always ask for any special rates.

Devon

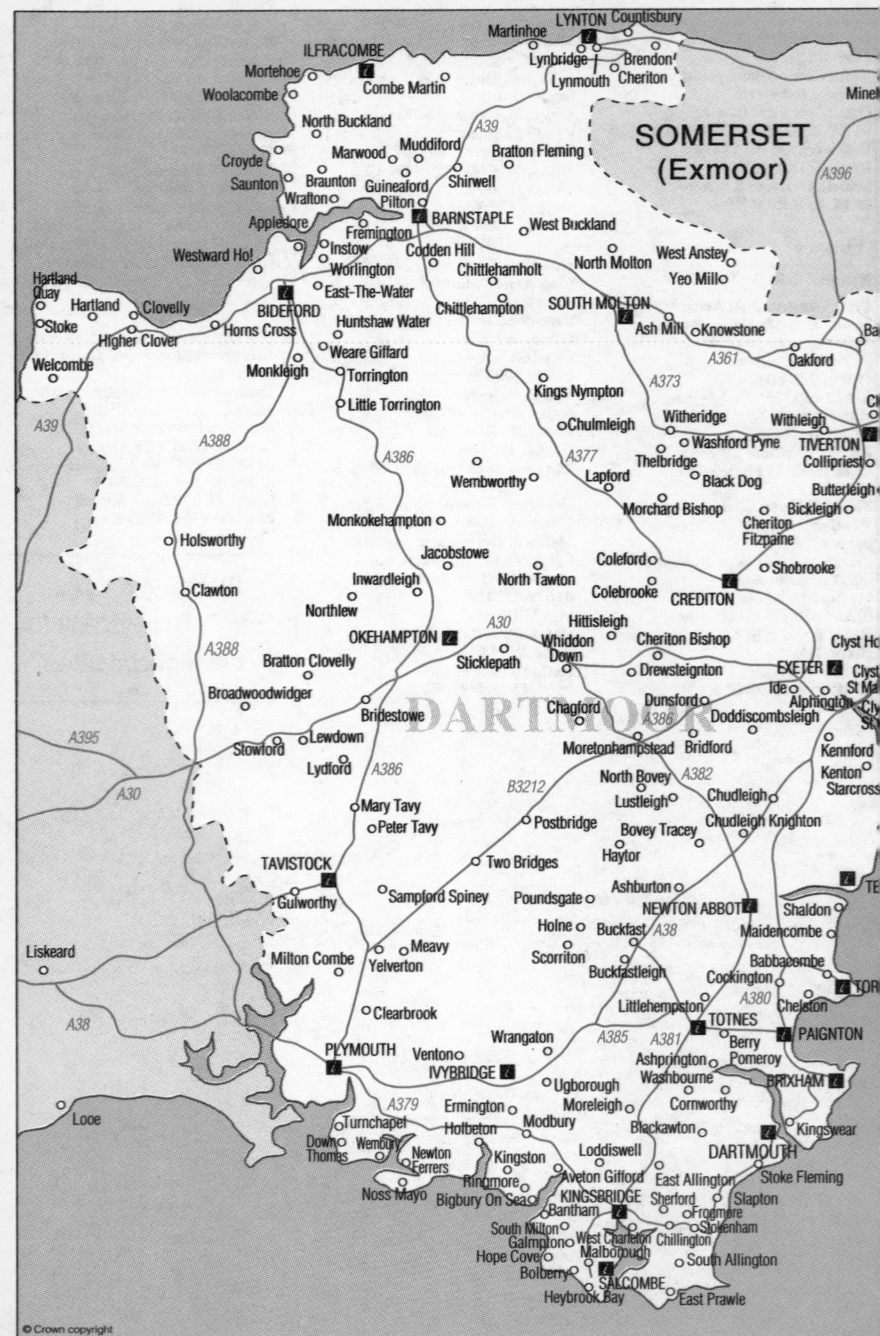
LYNTON
Countisbury
Martinhoe
ILFRACOMBE
Lynbridge
Brendon
Mortehoe
Lynmouth
Cheriton
Woolacombe
Combe Martin
A39
North Buckland
SOMERSET
(Exmoor)
Muddiford
Bratton Fleming
Croyde
Marwood
A396
Saunton
Braunton
Guineaford
Shirwell
Wrafton
Pilton
Appledore
BARNSTAPLE
West Buckland
Fremington
Westward Ho!
Instow
Codden Hill
West Anstey
North Molton
Worlington
Chittlehamholt
Yeo Mill
Hartland Quay
East-The-Water
Hartland
Clovelly
BIDEFORD
Chittlehampton
SOUTH MOLTON
Huntshaw Water
Stoke
Horns Cross
Ash Mill
Knowstone
Higher Clover
Weare Giffard
A361
Oakford
Welcombe
Monkleigh
Torrington
A373
Kings Nympton
Little Torrington
A39
Witheridge
Withleigh
Chulmleigh
A388
Washford Pyne
TIVERTON
A386
A377
Thelbridge
Collipriest
Wembworthy
Lapford
Black Dog
Butterleigh
Morchard Bishop
Bickleigh
Monkokehampton
Cheriton Fitzpaine
Holsworthy
Jacobstowe
Coleford
Shobrooke
Inwardleigh
North Tawton
Colebrooke
Clawton
CREDITON
Northlew
Hittisleigh
OKEHAMPTON
A30
Whiddon Down
Cheriton Bishop
A388
Bratton Clovelly
Sticklepath
Drewsteignton
EXETER
Ide
Broadwoodwidger
DARTMOOR
Dunsford
Alphington
Bridestowe
Chagford
A386
Doddiscombsleigh
A395
Lewdown
Stowford
Moretonhampstead
Bridford
Kennford
Lydford
A386
North Bovey
A382
Kenton
A30
B3212
Starcross
Lustleigh
Chudleigh
Mary Tavy
Peter Tavy
Postbridge
Chudleigh Knighton
Bovey Tracey
Haytor
Two Bridges
TAVISTOCK
Ashburton
Sampford Spiney
Poundsgate
NEWTON ABBOT
Shaldon
Gulworthy
Holne
Buckfast
A38
Maidencombe
Liskeard
Meavy
Scorriton
Milton Combe
Yelverton
Babbacombe
Buckfastleigh
Cockington
A380
Littlehempston
Chelston
A38
Clearbrook
TOTNES
A385
Wrangaton
A381
Berry Pomeroy
PAIGNTON
PLYMOUTH
Venton
Ashprington
IVYBRIDGE
Washbourne
BRIXHAM
Ugborough
Looe
A379
Ermington
Moreleigh
Cornworthy
Turnchapel
Modbury
Holbeton
Blackawton
Kingswear
Down Thomas
Wembury
Loddiswell
DARTMOUTH
Newton Ferrers
Kingston
Aveton Gifford
East Allington
Stoke Fleming
Noss Mayo
Ringmore
Bigbury On Sea
KINGSBRIDGE
Sherford
Slapton
Bantham
Frogmore
South Milton
West Charleton
Stokenham
Galmpton
Chillington
Malborough
Hope Cove
South Allington
Bolberry
SALCOMBE
Heybrook Bay
East Prawle
© Crown copyright

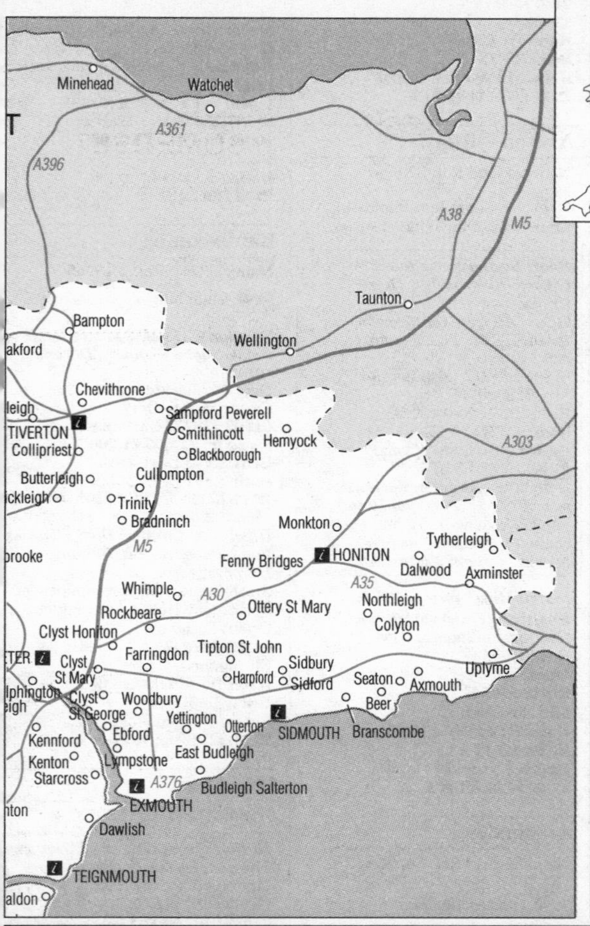

Tourist Information Centres

The Old Courthouse, Church Street, **Axminster**, Devon, EX13 5AQ, 01297 34386, (Easter to Oct).

North Devon Library, Tuly Street, **Barnstaple**, EX31 1TY, 01271 388583 / 388584.

The Pill, The Quay, **Bideford**, Devon, EX39 2QQ, 01237 477676.

The Bake House Centre, The Car Park **Braunton**, Devon, EX33 1AA, 01271 816400,

The Old Market House, The Quay, **Brixham**, Devon, TQ5 8TB, 01803-852861

Fore Street, **Budleigh Salterton**, Devon, EX9 6NG, 01395-445275.

Cross St, **Combe Martin**, Devon, EX34 0DH, 01271-883319, (Easter to Oct)

Market Street Car Park, Market Street, **Crediton**, Devon, EX17 2BN, 01363-772006, (Easter to Oct).

The Engine House, Mayor's Avenue, **Dartmouth**, Devon, TQ6 9PY, 01803 834224.

The Lawn, **Dawlish**, Devon, EX7 9AP, 01626-863589.

Civic Centre, Paris Street, **Exeter**, Devon, EX1 1JJ, 01392 265700.

Alexandra Terrace, **Exmouth**, Devon, EX8 1NZ, 01395 222299.

Dowell Street Car Park, **Honiton**, Devon, EX14 8LT, 01404-43716, (Easter to Oct).

Tourist Information Centres

The Promenade, **Ilfracombe**, Devon, EX34 9BX, 01271 863001.

Leonards Road, **Ivybridge**, Devon, PL21 0SL, 01752 897035.

Telegraph Hill, A380 (top), **Kennford**, Exeter, Devon, EX6 7YW, 01392 833559, (Easter to Oct).

The Quay, **Kingsbridge**, Devon, TQ7 1HS, 01548 853195.

Town Hall, Lee Road, **Lynton**, Devon, EX35 6BT, 01598 752225.

Poundwell Meadow Car Park, Modbury, **Ivybridge**, Devon, PL21 0QL, 01548-830159, (Easter to Oct).

The Old Town Hall, The Flexton, **Ottery St Mary**, Devon, EX11 1DJ, 01404 813964, (Easter to Oct).

3 West Street, **Okehampton**, Devon, EX20 1HQ, 01837 53020, (Easter to Oct)

The Esplanade, **Paignton**, Devon, TQ4 6BN, 01803 558383.

Island House, 9 The Barbican, **Plymouth**, Devon, PL1 2EW, 01752 264849.

Plymouth Discovery Centre, Crabtree, **Plymouth**, 01752 246030 / 266031.

Council Hall,Market Street, **Salcombe**, Devon, TQ8 8QL, 01548 842736, (Easter to Oct).

Tiverton Services, M5 Junction 7, Sampford Peverell, **Tiverton**, Devon, EX16 7SB, 01884 821242, (Easter to Oct)

The Esplanade, **Seaton**, Devon, EX12 2QQ, 01297 21660.

Ham Lane, **Sidmouth**, Devon, EX10 8XR, 01395 516441.

1 East Street, **South Molton**, Devon, EX36 3BU, 01769 574122, (Easter to Oct)

Town Hall, Bedford Square, **Tavistock**, Devon, PL19 0AE, 01822 612938, (Easter to Oct)

The Den, Sea Front, **Teignmouth**, Devon, TQ14 8BE, 01626 779769.

Phoenix Lane, **Tiverton**, Devon, EX16 6LU, 01884 255827.

Vaughan Parade, **Torquay**, Devon, TQ2 5JG, 01803 297428.

The Plains, **Totnes**, Devon, TQ9 5EJ, 01803 863168.

Red Barn Cafe, Car Park, Barton Road **Woolacombe**, Devon, EX34 7BT, 01271 870553, (Easter to Oct).

Alphington

National Grid Ref: SX9189

The New Inn, Admiral Vernon

The Old Mill, *Mill Lane, Alphington, Exeter, Devon, EX2 8SG.*
Historic mill in quiet area.
Open: All Year
01392 59977 Mrs Marchant
Rates fr: *£10.00*-**£10.00**.
Beds: 2F 1D 1T 1S
Baths: 1 Private 1 Shared
(8)

Appledore

National Grid Ref: SS4630

The Seagate Hotel, *The Quay, Appledore, Bideford, Devon, EX39 1QS.*
Open: All Year
01237 472589 (also fax no)
Mr & Mrs Gent
Rates fr: *£19.00*-**£19.00**.
Beds: 1F 5D 1T 2S
Baths: 9 Private
(10)
Ideally situated family-run English waterside hotel with independantly run authentic Chinese, Thai, Malaysian restaurant. Chinese feast, eat as much as you like £13.50.

Ashburton

National Grid Ref: SX7570

Rosary Mount House, *Ashburton, Newton Abbot, Devon, TQ13 7JL.*
Large country house, magnificently furnished.
Open: All Year (not Xmas)
01364 653900 Mr Stone
Rates fr: *£15.00*-**£20.00**.
Beds: 2D 1T **Baths:** 2 Shared
(9) (10)

Ashmill

National Grid Ref: SS7823

Kerscott Farm, *Ashmill, South Molton, Devon, EX36 4QG.*
Beautiful, unique old world break.
Open: All Year (not Xmas)
Grades: ETB 2 Cr, Comm, AA 5 Q, Prem Select
01769 550262 Mrs Sampson
Rates fr: *£17.50*-**£18.00**.
Beds: 2D 1T
Baths: 3 Ensuite
(6)

Ashprington

National Grid Ref: SX8157

The Watermans Arms, *Bow Bridge, Ashprington, Totnes, Devon, TQ9 7EG.*
Ancient riverside country residential inn.
Open: All Year **01803 732214**
Mr & Mrs Illingworth
Rates fr: *£24.00*-**£34.00**.
Beds: 10D 5T **Baths:** 15 Ensuite
(60)

Avenue Cottage, *Ashprington, Totnes, Devon, TQ9 7UT.*
House set in historic garden.
Open: All Year (not Xmas)
01803 732769
Mr Soans
Rates fr: *£20.00*.
Beds: 1T 1S
Baths: 1 Private 1 Shared
(3)

Aveton Gifford

National Grid Ref: SX6947

The Sloop Inn (Bantham), Churchhouse Inn (Churchstow)

Court Barton Farmhouse, *Aveton Gifford, Kingsbridge, Devon, TQ7 4LE.*
Open: All Year (not Xmas)
Grades: ETB 2 Cr, Comm, AA 3 Q
01548 550312 (also fax no)
Mrs Balkwill
Rates fr: *£16.00*-**£20.00**.
Beds: 2F 2D 2T 1S
Baths: 6 Ensuite 1 Shared
(10)
Delightful C16th farmhouse, peaceful setting 100 yds from village. Ensuite bedrooms. Perfect centre for coast and moors. You'll love our scrumptious breakfasts!

Marsh Mills, *Aveton Gifford, Kingsbridge, Devon, TQ7 4JW.*
Georgian millhouse, now a smallholding.
Open: All Year
01548 550549
Mrs Newsham
Rates fr: *£15.00*-**£15.00**.
Beds: 1D 1T 1S
Baths: 1 Shared
(6) (6)

Axminster

National Grid Ref: SY2998

Hunters Lodge

Mount House, *Lyme Road, Axminster, Devon, EX13 5BL.*
Large friendly Regency family house.
Open: All Year
01297 34630
Mrs Morrison
Rates fr: *£14.00*-**£14.00**.
Beds: 2F 1D
Baths: 2 Ensuite 1 Shared

Furzeleigh House, *Lyme Road, Axminster, Devon, EX13 5SW.*
House in 4 acre gardens.
Open: All Year (not Xmas)
01297 34448
Mr Berry
Rates fr: *£20.00*-**£25.00**.
Beds: 1F 2D 1T 1S
Baths: 4 Ensuite 1 Private
(4)

Axmouth

National Grid Ref: SY2591

Harbour Inn, Ship Inn

Stepps House, *Axmouth, Seaton, Devon, EX12 4AR.*
Beautifully preserved mediaeval hall house.
Open: All Year (not Xmas)
01297 20679 Mrs Trezise
Rates fr: *£15.00*-**£30.00**.
Beds: 1D 1T
Baths: 1 Shared
(10)

Babbacombe

National Grid Ref: SX9265

Churchills

Sandhurst Hotel, *8 Manor Road, Babbacombe, Torquay, Devon, TQ1 3XJ.*
Detached licensed hotel.
Open: May to Oct
01803 329722 Mr Proles
Rates fr: *£15.00*-**£15.00**.
Beds: 2F 10D 3T 1S
Baths: 12 Private 3 Shared
(6) (20)

Hotel Blue Conifer, *Higher Downs Road, Babbacombe, Torquay, Devon, TQ1 3LD.*
Small friendly hotel recommended by Torquay Hotels Association.
Open: Easter to Oct
01803 327637
Mr Ingram
Rates fr: *£19.00*-**£25.00**.
Beds: 3F 3D 1T
Baths: 7 Private
(5) (10)

Bampton

National Grid Ref: SS9522

Harton Farm, *Oakford, Bampton, Tiverton, Devon, EX16 9HH.*
Open: All Year (not Xmas)
Grades: ETB 1 Cr
01398 351209 Mrs Head
Rates fr: *£13.00*-**£13.00**.
Beds: 1F 1T **Baths:** 1 Shared
(4) (3)
Country lovers welcome on our traditional, non-intensive farm near Exmoor. Home baking and hearty meals using our own additive-free meat and vegetables.

Bantham

National Grid Ref: SX6643

Sloop Inn, *Bantham, Kingsbridge, Devon, TQ7 3AJ.*
Renowned C16th coastal village pub. **Open:** All Year
01548 560489
Mr Girling
Rates fr: *£25.50*.
Beds: 2F 3D 2T
Baths: 7 Private
(30)

Barnstaple

National Grid Ref: SS5633

Pyne Arms, Ring O Bells

Crossways, *Braunton Road, Barnstaple, Devon,* EX31 1JY.
Detached house - town centre 150 yds.
Open: All Year (not Xmas)
01271 79120
Mr & Mrs Capp
Rates fr: *£13.50*-**£15.50**.
Beds: 1F 1D 1T
Baths: 2 Private 1 Shared
(6)

Yeo Dale Hotel, *Pilton Bridge, Barnstaple, Devon,* EX31 1PG.
Spacious Georgian town house.
Open: All Year
Grades: AA Listed, RAC Acclaim
01271 42954
Mr Smith
Rates fr: *£19.00*-**£19.00**.
Beds: 3F 1D 3T 3S
Baths: 6 Private 2 Shared

West View, *Pilton Causeway, Barnstaple, Devon,* EX32 7AA.
Modernised Victorian property overlooking park.
Open: All Year
Grades: ETB Listed, Approv, AA Listed
01271 42079 (also fax no)
Mrs Rostock
Rates fr: *£16.00*-**£16.00**.
Beds: 3F 3D 10T 7S
Baths: 5 Ensuite 7 Shared
(15)

Moutn Sandford, *Mount Sandford Road, Barnstaple, Devon,* EX32 0HL.
Lovely Georgian house. Beautiful gardens.
Open: All Year
01271 42354 Mrs White
Rates fr: *£17.50*-**£17.50**.
Beds: 1F 1D 1T
Baths: 3 Ensuite
(3) (3)

The Spinney Country Guest Hse, *Shirwell, Barnstaple, Devon,* EX31 4JR.
Comfortable, spacious, former Regency rectory.
Open: All Year
Grades: ETB 2 Cr, Comm
01271 850282 Mrs Pelling
Rates fr: *£15.50*-**£15.50**.
Beds: 1F 2D 1T 1S
Baths: 1 Private 2 Shared
(8)

Beer

National Grid Ref: SY2289

Garlands, *Stovar Long Lane, Beer, Seaton, Devon,* EX12 3EA.
Open: All Year (not Xmas)
Grades: AA 3 Q, Recomm
01297 20958 Ms Harding
Rates fr: *£20.00*-**£20.00**.
Beds: 3F 2D 1T
Baths: 6 Ensuite
(10)
Edwardian character house in an acre of ground - superb views of sea and Devonshire countryside. Beer Beach and fishing village within easy walking distance.

Pamber House, *Clapps Lane, Beer, Seaton, Devon,* EX12 3HD.
Open: All Year
01297 20722 Mrs Cummins
Rates fr: *£16.00*.
Beds: 1F 4D
Baths: 2 Private 1 Shared
(7) (3)
Set in idyllic fishing village. Quiet positions, 2 minutes walk from village and beach, stunning views, food cooked to order. Winter rates, ideal base.

Berry Pomeroy

National Grid Ref: SX8261

Tally Ho (Littlehempston), Kingsbridge Inn Totnes

Berry Farm, *Berry Pomeroy, Totnes, Devon,* TQ9 6LG.
Welcome, spacious, clean and comfortable.
Open: All Year (not Xmas)
Grades: ETB Listed, Comm
01803 863231 Mrs Nicholls
Rates fr: *£15.00*-**£18.00**.
Beds: 1F 1D 1T
Baths: 1 Shared
(3) (4)

Bickleigh

National Grid Ref: SS9407

Bickleigh Cottage Hotel, *Bickleigh Bridge, Bickleigh, Tiverton, Devon,* EX16 8RS.
Thatched riverside hotel.
Open: Easter to Oct
Grades: RAC Recomm
01884 855230 Mr Cochrane
Rates fr: *£22.50*-**£21.50**.
Beds: 4D 4T 1S
Baths: 7 Private 2 Shared
(14) (9)

Bideford

National Grid Ref: SS4426

Tanton's Hotel

Sunset Hotel, *Landcross, Bideford, Devon,* EX39 5JA.
Open: Feb to Dec
Grades: ETB 3 Cr, AA 3 Q
01237 472962 Mrs Lamb
Rates fr: *£22.50*-**£25.00**.
Beds: 2F 2D 2T
Baths: 4 Private
(10)
Somewhere SPECIAL. Small country hotel, quiet peaceful location, overlooking spectacular scenery and Tarka Trail. Highly recommended quality accommodation. Superb food, everything homemade, special diets. Non-smoking establishment.

Ellerton, *Glenburnie Road, Bideford, Devon,* EX39 2LW.
Welcoming, comfortable house. Breakfast menu.
Open: All Year
01237 473352 Mrs Garnsey
Rates fr: *£13.50*-**£13.50**.
Beds: 1D 2T **Baths:** 2 Shared

The Mount Hotel, *Northdown Road, Bideford, Devon,* EX39 3LP.
Quiet, Georgian, edge-of-town hotel. **Open:** All Year (not Xmas)
Grades: ETB 3 Cr, AA 3 Q
01237 473748 Mr & Mrs Taylor
Rates fr: *£18.50*-**£21.00**.
Beds: 1F 3D 2T 2S
Baths: 7 Private 1 Shared
(4)

14 The Strand, *Bideford, Devon,* EX39 2ND.
Large, comfortable house.
Open: All Year (not Xmas)
01237 473722 Mrs Faulkner
Rates fr: *£14.00*-**£15.00**.
Beds: 1F 2D 1T 1S
Baths: 1 Shared

Bigbury on Sea

National Grid Ref: SX6544

Merrylees, *Ringmore Drive, Bigbury on Sea, Kingsbridge, Devon,* TQ7 4AU.
Delightful sea-view rooms, minutes beach. **Open:** All Year (not Xmas)
01548 810247 Mrs Evans
Rates fr: *£15.00*-**£15.00**.
Beds: 2D 1S **Baths:** 3 Shared
(3)

The Atlantic, *Marine Drive, Bigbury on Sea, Kingsbridge, Devon,* TQ7 4AS.
Licensed restaurants, spectacular sea views.
Open: Easter to Oct
01548 810682 Mrs Richardson
Rates fr: *£16.00*-**£18.00**.
Beds: 3D **Baths:** 3 Private

Black Dog

National Grid Ref: SS8009

Black Dog Inn

Oaklands, *Black Dog, Crediton, Devon, EX17 4RQ.*
Friendly accommodation in peaceful countryside. Central for coast and moors.
Open: All Year
01884 860645 Mrs Bradford
Rates fr: *£17.50*-**£15.00**.
Beds: 1F 1D 1T
Baths: 2 Ensuite 1 Private

Lower Brownstone Farm, *Black Dog, Crediton, Devon, EX17 4QE.*
Spacious Georgian comfortable farmhouse.
Open: All Year
01363 877256 Mrs Wedlake
Rates fr: *£12.00*-**£12.00**.
Beds: 1F 1D **Baths:** 2 Shared
(10)

Blackawton

National Grid Ref: SX8050

Normandy Arms, George Inn

Woodside Cottage, *Blackawton, Totnes, Devon, TQ9 7BL.*
Converted C18th gamekeeper's cottage.
Open: All Year (not Xmas)
01803 712375 Mrs Clark
Fax no: 01803 712605
Rates fr: *£16.00*-**£18.00**.
Beds: 3D 1T **Baths:** 3 Ensuite
(12) (6)

Seven Gates Farm, *Blackawton, Totnes, Devon, TQ9 7AJ.*
Modern, comfortable farm bungalow.
Open: All Year (not Xmas)
01803 712339 Mrs Dayment
Rates fr: *£12.50*-**£15.00**.
Beds: 1F 1D
Baths: 1 Shared
(3)

Wadstray House, *Blackawton, Dartmouth, Totnes, Devon, TQ9 7DE.*
Quiet village, warm & friendly.
Open: All Year
01803 712539 Mrs Smith
Rates fr: *£22.50*-**£25.00**.
Beds: 3D 3T
(6) (12)

Blackborough

National Grid Ref: ST0909

Catherine Wheel (Hemyock)

Hayne Farm, *Blackborough, Cullompton, Devon, EX15 2JD.*
C15th farmhouse, working farm.
Open: All Year (not Xmas)
01823 680337 Mrs Kittow
Rates fr: *£13.50*-**£14.00**.
Beds: 1F 1T
Baths: 1 Shared
(4)

Always telephone to get directions to the B&B - you will save time!

Bolberry

National Grid Ref: SX7039

Karrageen, *Bolberry, Malborough, Kingsbridge, Devon, TQ7 3DZ.*
Elegant country house (stay 2 nights).
Open: All Year (not Xmas)
01548 561230
Mrs Higgin
Rates fr: *£17.00*-**£16.00**.
Beds: 2D 1S
Baths: 2 Shared
(5) (6)

Bovey Tracey

National Grid Ref: SX8178

Cleave Inn (Lustleigh), White Hart Hotel (Moretonhampstead)

Lower Elsford Cottage, *Bovey Tracey, Newton Abbot, Devon, TQ13 9NY.*
Open: All Year (not Xmas)
Grades: ETB Listed, High Comm
01647 277408
Mrs Griffiths
Rates fr: *£18.00*-**£18.00**.
Beds: 1D 1S
Baths: 1 Ensuite 1 Shared
(8) (3)
A C17th stone cottage in woodland setting with spectacular views over glorious countryside within Dartmoor National Park. Complete peace and quiet, every home comfort.

Frost Farmhouse, *Hennock Road, Bovey Tracey, Newton Abbot, Devon, TQ13 9PP.*
Pretty, pink-washed thatched farmhouse.
Open: All Year (not Xmas)
Grades: ETB 1 Cr, Comm
01626 833266 Mrs Harvey
Rates fr: *£18.00*-**£18.00**.
Beds: 2D 1T
Baths: 2 Ensuite 1 Private

Bradninch

National Grid Ref: SS9903

Moorlands Farm, *Bradninch, Exeter, Devon, EX5 4NA.*
Large comfortable Georgian farmhouse.
Open: Apr to Oct
01392 881385 Mrs Selway
Rates fr: *£13.00*-**£13.50**.
Beds: 1F 1D **Baths:** 1 Shared
(6)

Branscombe

National Grid Ref: SY1988

Masons Arms, Fountain Head

Hole Mill, *Branscombe, Seaton, Devon, EX12 3BX.*
Open: All Year
01297 680314 Mr & Mrs Hart
Rates fr: *£16.00*-**£22.00**.
Beds: 2D 1T **Baths:** 2 Shared
(6) (6)
Old converted watermill providing comfortable accommodation in style of yesteryear. Beams, brass beds, inglenook lounge, garden, stream. No rush, no town noises - just peace/relaxation. Featured in 'Which? The Good Bed & Breakfast Guide' & 'Staying Off The Beaten Track'.

Bratton Clovelly

National Grid Ref: SX4691

The Old Rectory, *Bratton Clovelly, Okehampton, Devon, EX20 4LA.*
Open: All Year (not Xmas)
01837 871382 Mrs Arney
Rates fr: *£16.00*-**£16.00**.
Beds: 1F 1D 1T
Baths: 2 Shared
(4)
A charming old rectory set in beautiful countryside. With the moors & sea within easy reach. An ideal centre for a comfortable and relaxing holiday.

Bratton Fleming

National Grid Ref: SS6437

Haxton Down Farm, *Bratton Fleming, Barnstaple, Devon, EX32 7JL.*
Peaceful, comfortable working farm.
Open: Apr to Oct
Grades: ETB 2 Cr, Comm
01598 710275
Mrs Burge
Rates fr: *£15.00*-**£15.00**.
Beds: 1F 1D
Baths: 1 Ensuite 1 Private
(0) (3)

Braunton

National Grid Ref: SS4935

Williams Arms

Poyers Farm Hotel, *Wrafton, Braunton, Devon, EX33 2DN.*
Open: All Year (not Xmas)
Grades: ETB Listed, Approv
01271 812149
Mr & Mrs Gross
Rates fr: *£22.00*-**£25.00**.
Beds: 1F 3D 3T 2S
Baths: 9 Ensuite
(15)
Delightful C16th thatched Devon longhouse situated 4 miles from historic market town of Barnstaple & 2 miles from North Devon's glorious golden coast.

Denham Farm Country House, *North Buckland, Braunton, Devon,* EX33 1HY.
Open: All Year (not Xmas)
Grades: ETB 3 Cr, Comm, AA 3 Q, RAC Acclaim
01271 890297 (also fax no) Mrs Barnes
Rates fr: *£22.50*-**£27.50**.
Beds: 2F 6D 2T
Baths: 10 Private
(10)
Lovely farmhouse set amidst rolling hills & flower laden hedgerows. Pretty bedrooms, ensuite with TV. Delicious home cooking, and old fashioned courtesy. 3 Crowns, Commended.

Brendon

National Grid Ref: SS7647

Brendon House Hotel, *Brendon, Lynton, Devon,* EX35 6PS.
Small friendly country hotel.
Open: All Year (not Xmas)
01598 741206 Mrs Farthing
Rates fr: *£17.50*-**£17.50**.
Beds: 1F 2D 2T
Baths: 4 Private 1 Shared
(5)

Bridestowe

National Grid Ref: SX5189

The White Hart Inn, *Fore Street, Bridestowe, Okehampton, Devon,* EX20 4EL.
C17th country inn & restaurant.
Open: All Year **Grades:** ETB 2 Cr
01837 861318 Mr Owen
Rates fr: *£21.75*-**£26.00**.
Beds: 2D **Baths:** 2 Private
(20)

Bridford

National Grid Ref: SX8186

Bridford Inn

Horse-Engine House, *Lowton Farm, Bridford, Exeter, Devon,* EX6 7EN.
Secluded converted horse-engine house. **Open:** All Year
01647 252209 Mr Joslin
Rates fr: *£13.50*-**£15.50**.
Beds: 1D 1T
(4)

Brixham

National Grid Ref: SX9255

Smugglers Haunt Hotel, Blue Anchor

Sampford House, *57-59 King Street, Brixham, Devon,* TQ5 9TH.
Harbourside Georgian house, stunning views. **Open:** Mar to Nov
Grades: AA 2 Q
01803 857761 Mrs Hunter
Rates fr: *£15.00*-**£18.00**.
Beds: 5D
Baths: 4 Ensuite 1 Private
(2)

Smugglers Haunt Hotel, *& Restaurant, Church Hill, Brixham, Devon,* TQ5 8HH.
Open: All Year
01803 853050 Mr Hudson
Rates fr: *£14.00*-**£18.00**.
Beds: 2F 7D 4T 4S
Baths: 5 Private 4 Shared
Friendly, private 300-year-old hotel situated in the centre of old Brixham, only 400 metres from the 'old world' harbour. Very well known restaurant.

Mimosa Cottage, *75 New Road, Brixham, Devon,* TQ5 8NL.
Spacious, well-furnished Georgian house.
Open: All Year (not Xmas)
01803 855719 Mr Kershaw
Rates fr: *£14.00*-**£15.00**.
Beds: 2D 1T 1S
Baths: 2 Private 1 Shared
(2) (4)

Broadwoodwidger

National Grid Ref: SX4189

Harris Arms

Rexon Cross Farm, *Broadwoodwidger, Lifton, Devon,* PL16 0JJ.
Comfortable farmhouse, working farm.
Open: Easter to Oct
01566 784295 Mrs Worden
Rates fr: *£13.50*-**£13.50**.
Beds: 1D 1T
Baths: 1 Private
(2)

Buckfast

National Grid Ref: SX7367

Abbey Inn

Leat House, *Grange Road, Buckfast, Buckfastleigh, Devon,* TQ11 0EH.
Modern house near Abbey & Moors.
Open: All Year (not Xmas)
01364 642129 Mrs Nesbitt
Rates fr: *£20.00*-**£20.00**.
Beds: 1D 1T 1S
Baths: 1 Ensuite 1 Shared
(4)

Buckfastleigh

National Grid Ref: SX7366

Woodholme Guest House, *113 Plymouth Road, Buckfastleigh, Devon,* TQ11 0DB.
Spacious Victorian house.
Open: All Year (not Xmas)
01364 643350 Mr Flach
Rates fr: *£16.00*-**£22.00**.
Beds: 2D 1T
Baths: 1 Private 1 Shared

Budleigh Salterton

National Grid Ref: SY0682

Chapter House, *6 Westbourne Terrace, Budleigh Salterton, Devon,* EX9 6BR.
Victorian house near town. Sea and Coastal path.
Open: All Year
01395 444100 / 01421 49918 Ms Mrs Simmons
Rates fr: *£15.00*-**£16.50**.
Beds: 2D 2T
Baths: 1 Shared
(4)

Long Range Hotel, *Budleigh Salterton, Devon,* EX9 6HS.
Modern hotel in quiet location.
Open: All Year
Grades: RAC Acclaim
01395 443321 Mr & Mrs Morton
Rates fr: *£22.50*-**£35.00**.
Beds: 1F 2D 3T
Baths: 6 Ensuite
(6)

Butterleigh

National Grid Ref: SS9708

Fig Tree Farm, *Butterleigh, Cullompton, Devon,* EX15 1PQ.
Generous farmhouse hospitality, spectacular views.
Open: All Year
01884 855463 Mrs Chumbley
Rates fr: *£14.50*-**£16.00**.
Beds: 2F 1D
Baths: 1 Shared

Sunnyside Farmhouse, *Butterleigh, Cullompton, Devon,* EX15 1PP.
Convenient Victorian comfortable farmhouse.
Open: All Year (not Xmas)
01884 855322 Mrs Hill
Rates fr: *£14.00*-**£15.00**.
Beds: 1F 1D 1T
Baths: 3 Ensuite

Chagford

National Grid Ref: SX7087

Ring O' Bells, Bullers Arms, Sandy Park Inn

Lower Jurston, *Chagford, Newton Abbot, Devon,* TQ13 8EQ.
Open: All Year (not Xmas)
01647 433443 Mrs Evans
Rates fr: *£20.00*-**£20.00**.
Beds: 1D 1T 1S
Baths: 1 Ensuite 1 Private 1 Shared
(4)
One of Devon's last unspoilt mediaeval farmsteads. Luxury country house comfort, mellow, idyllic, Grade II Listed thatched C16th Devon longhouse. Inglenooks, log fires, oak beams. Peacefully situated on edge of open moor.

***Yellam Farm,** Chagford, Newton Abbot, Devon, TQ13 8JH.*
Country house B&B in 170 acres.
Open: All Year (not Xmas)
01647 432211 Mrs Prysor-Jones
Rates fr: *£17.95*-**£17.95**.
Beds: 2D 1T
Baths: 2 Shared

***St Johns West,** Chagford, Newton Abbot, Devon, TQ13 8HJ.*
Stunning granite house overlooking Dartmoor.
Open: All Year
01647 432468 Mr & Mrs West
Rates fr: *£20.00*-**£18.00**.
Beds: 1F 1D 1T 1S
Baths: 2 Ensuite
(12) (6)

***Glendarah House,** Lower Street, Chagford, Newton Abbot, Devon, TQ13 8BZ.*
Victorian house on village edge.
Open: All Year (not Xmas)
Grades: ETB 2 Cr, High Comm, AA 4 Q, Select
01647 433270 Mrs Bellenger
Fax no: 01647 433483
Rates fr: *£22.50*-**£25.00**.
Beds: 3D 3T
Baths: 6 Ensuite
(10) (7)

***Lawn House,** 24 Mill Street, Chagford, Newton Abbot, Devon, TQ13 7AW.*
C18th thatched house, centre of Chagford.
Open: Easter to Oct
01647 433329 Mrs Law
Rates fr: *£16.00*-**£20.00**.
Beds: 1F 2D
(8)

Chelston

National Grid Ref: SX8964

Chelston Manor

***Cedar Court Hotel,** 3 St Matthews Road, Chelston, Torquay, Devon, TQ2 6JA.*
Superior B&B in elegant Victorian Hotel.
Open: All Year
Grades: ETB 3 Cr
01803 607851 Mr Abbott
Rates fr: *£14.00*-**£18.00**.
Beds: 2F 6D 1T 1S
Baths: 10 Ensuite

Cheriton

National Grid Ref: SS7346

***South Cheriton Farm,** Cheriton, Lynton, Devon, EX35 6LJ.*
Happy C17th farmhouse, visitors' lounge, inglenook & beams.
Open: Easter to Oct
01598 753280 Mrs Tassell
Rates fr: *£18.00*-**£20.00**.
Beds: 2D 1T
Baths: 3 Ensuite
(6)

Cheriton Bishop

National Grid Ref: SX7793

***The Old Thatch Inn,** Cheriton Bishop, Exeter, Devon, EX6 6HS.*
Quality with value for money.
Open: All Year
01647 24204
Mr Bryon-Edmond
Rates fr: *£21.50*-**£32.00**.
Beds: 3D
Baths: 3 Private
(14) (25)

Cheriton Fitzpaine

National Grid Ref: SS8606

***Hayne Farm,** Cheriton Fitzpaine, Crediton, Devon, EX17 4HR.*
Large Victorian farmhouse, working farm.
Open: All Year (not Xmas)
01363 866392
Mrs Reed
Rates fr: *£15.00*-**£15.00**.
Beds: 1F 1D 1T
Baths: 1 Shared
(10)

***Brindiwell Farm,** Cheriton Fitzpaine, Crediton, Devon, EX17 4HR.*
Delightful old farmhouse with beams.
Open: All Year
01363 866357
Mrs Lock
Rates fr: *£15.00*-**£15.00**.
Beds: 1F 1D 1S
Baths: 1 Shared
(4)

Chevithorne

National Grid Ref: SS9715

Sea Horse (Bampton)

***Landrake Farm,** Chevithorne, Tiverton, Devon, EX16 7QN.*
Ideal for breaking journey south.
Open: Mar to Oct
Grades: ETB Listed
01398 331221
Mrs Kerslake
Rates fr: *£15.00*-**£15.00**.
Beds: 1F 1D 1T
Baths: 1 Shared
(4)

Chillington

National Grid Ref: SX7942

***Coleridge,** Chillington, Kingsbridge, Devon, TQ7 2JG.*
Georgian farmhouse on working farm.
Open: May to Oct
01548 580274 Mrs Darke
Rates fr: *£14.00*-**£14.00**.
Beds: 1F 1T
Baths: 1 Private 1 Shared
(3) (2)

Chittlehamholt

National Grid Ref: SS6520

Exeter Inn

***Farriers,** Chittlehamholt, Umberleigh, Devon, EX37 9NS.*
Open: All Year (not Xmas)
01769 540605 (also fax no)
Mr Campion
Rates fr: *£19.00*-**£22.00**.
Beds: 1D 1T
Baths: 2 Ensuite
(0) (6)
Double fronted family home, excellent facilities, acre garden, in unspoilt Devon village, close to Exmoor, Dartmoor and North Devon resorts. Between Rivers Taw and Mole.

Chittlehampton

National Grid Ref: SS6525

***Whitstone Farm,** Chittlehampton, Umberleigh, Devon, EX37 9RB.*
Attractive, spacious farmhouse, delicious food.
Open: Easter to Oct
01769 540410 Mrs Turner
Rates fr: *£14.50*-**£15.00**.
Beds: 2F 1S
Baths: 1 Shared
(10)

Chudleigh

National Grid Ref: SX8679

Coaching House

***Glen Cottage,** Rock Road, Chudleigh, Newton Abbot, Devon, TQ13 0JJ.*
Open: All Year (not Xmas)
01626 852209 Mrs Shears
Rates fr: *£14.00*-**£15.00**.
Beds: 1F 2D 2T
Baths: 1 Shared
(6)
Idyllically set in secluded glen, surrounded by woods, garden with river and open air swimming pool. Central for moors and sea. Tea-making facilities.

Chudleigh Knighton

National Grid Ref: SX8477

Claycutters Inn

***Church House,** Chudleigh Knighton, Newton Abbot, Devon, TQ13 0HE.*
Georgian home. Ideal touring centre.
Open: All Year
Grades: ETB 2 Cr, Comm
01626 852123 Mrs Brandon
Rates fr: *£16.00*-**£20.00**.
Beds: 1D 1T
Baths: 1 Ensuite 1 Shared
(10)

Chulmleigh

National Grid Ref: SS6814

Beara Farm, *Chulmleigh, Devon, EX18 7DU.*
Comfortable C17th Devon farmhouse.
Open: All Year (not Xmas)
01769 580282 Mrs Eastwood
Rates fr: *£14.50*-**£14.50**.
Beds: 1D 1T
Baths: 1 Private 1 Shared

Clawton

National Grid Ref: SX3599

Court Barn Country Hotel, *Clawton, Holsworthy, Devon, EX22 6PS.*
Large manor house in 5 acres.
Open: All Year
Grades: ETB 4 Cr, High Comm, AA 2 St, RAC 2 St
01409 271219
Rates fr: *£30.00*-**£35.00**.
Beds: 1F 3T 3D 1S
Baths: 8 Ensuite
(16)

Clearbrook

National Grid Ref: SX5265

Rosehill, *Clearbrook, Yelverton, Devon, PL20 6JD.*
Village house, edge of Dartmoor.
Open: All Year (not Xmas)
01822 852130 Mrs Wing
Rates fr: *£14.00*-**£14.00**.
Beds: 2D 1T **Baths:** 1 Private
(5) (6)

Clovelly

National Grid Ref: SS3124

New Inn, Red Lion

The Old Smithy, *Slerra Hill, Clovelly, Bideford, Devon, EX39 5ST.*
Cottage/converted C17th black-smith's forge. **Open:** All Year
01237 431202 Mrs Vanstone
Rates fr: *£14.50*.
Beds: 2F 1D 1T
Baths: 1 Private 2 Shared
(4)

The Boat House, *148 Slerra Hill, Clovelly, Bideford, Devon, EX39 5ST.*
C17th boathouse cottage.
Open: All Year
01237 431209 Mrs May
Rates fr: *£14.50*-**£16.00**.
Beds: 1F 1D 1T
Baths: 1 Shared
(2) (3)

Red Lion Hotel, *The Quay, Clovelly, Bideford, Devon, EX39 5TF.*
Sensitively renovated C18th har-bourside hotel.
Open: All Year
01237 431237 Mr Rous
Rates fr: *£35.00*-**£45.00**.
Beds: 2F 8D 2T **Baths:** 12 Private

New Inn Hotel, *Clovelly, Bideford, Devon, EX39 4TQ.*
Down the Cobbled Street.
Open: All Year (not Xmas)
01237 431303 Mr Cook
Fax no: 01237 431636
Rates fr: *£32.00*-**£32.00**.
Beds: 7D 1S **Baths:** 8 Ensuite
(200)

Clyst Honiton

National Grid Ref: SX9893

White Horse

Holbrook Farm, *Clyst Honiton, Exeter, Devon, EX5 2HR.*
Spacious modern farmhouse, beautiful views.
Open: All Year **Grades:** AA 4 Q
01392 367000 Mrs Glanvill
Rates fr: *£18.50*-**£20.00**.
Beds: 1F 1D 1T
Baths: 3 Ensuite
(0) (4)

Briar House, *Clyst Honiton, Exeter, Devon, EX5 2LZ.*
Large detached house in rural setting.
Open: All Year (not Xmas)
01392 367009 Mrs Barter
Rates fr: *£12.00*-**£12.00**.
Beds: 1D 1S 1T
Baths: 1 Private 1 Shared
(5)

Oaklee, *Clyst Honiton, Exeter, Devon, EX5 2DX.*
Secluded farmhouse in 7 acres.
Open: All Year (not Xmas)
01392 461253 Mrs Veysey
Rates fr: *£15.00*-**£17.00**.
Beds: 1D 1T 2S
Baths: 1 Ensuite 1 Shared
(2) (6)

Clyst St George

National Grid Ref: SX9888

George & Dragon

Marianne Pool Farm, *Clyst St George, Exeter, Devon, EX3 0NZ.*
Peacefully situated, thatched Devon longhouse. **Open:** Easter to Oct
Grades: ETB Listed
01392 874939 Mrs Bragg
Rates fr: *£16.00*-**£16.50**.
Beds: 1F 1T **Baths:** 1 Shared
(2)

Clyst St Mary

National Grid Ref: SX9791

White House

Old Mill House, *Oil Mill Lane, Clyst St Mary, Exeter, Devon, EX5 1AG*
Delightful accommodation in country setting. **Open:** All Year
01392 877733 Mrs Moore
Fax no: 01392 461278
Rates fr: *£19.50*-**£20.00**.
Beds: 2D 1T 1S
Baths: 1 Private 2 Shared
(10)

Shepherds Farm, *Oil Mill Lane, Clyst St Mary, Exeter, Devon, EX5 1AG.*
Comfortable farmhouse. Junction 30, M5.
Open: All Year (not Xmas)
01392 873095 Mrs Pike
Rates fr: *£12.00*-**£12.00**.
Beds: 1F 1D 1S
Baths: 2 Shared
(10)

Crealy Barton, *Clyst St Mary, Exeter, Devon, EX5 1DR.*
Delightful friendly well-appointed farmhouse.
Open: All Year
01395 232567 Mrs Prouse
Rates fr: *£18.00*-**£24.00**.
Beds: 2F 1D 1T 1S
Baths: 3 Private 1 Shared
(6)

Cockington

National Grid Ref: SX8964

Fairmount House Hotel, *Herbert Road, Cockington, Torquay, Devon, TQ2 6RW.*
Open: Mar to Oct
Grades: ETB 3 Cr, High Comm, AA 1 St, RAC 1 St
01803 605446 (also fax no)
Mrs Tolkien
Rates fr: *£23.00*-**£23.00**.
Beds: 1F 4D 2T 2S
Baths: 8 Ensuite
(8)
Treat yourself at our small, friendly hotel in peaceful setting near Cockington country park. Enjoy comfort, hospitality and delicious home cooking. Cosy bar. Dogs welcome

Courtlands Hotel & Cellar Bar, *Rawlyn Road, Cockington, Chelston, Torquay, Devon, TQ2 6PL.*
Large Victorian mansion. Public bar.
Open: All Year
01803 605506
Mr Cooper
Fax no: 01803 605970
Rates fr: *£14.15*-**£14.15**.
Beds: 7F 2D 6T 3S
Baths: 13 Private 1 Shared
(30)

Codden Hill

National Grid Ref: SS5829

Chichester Arms

Overton House, *Codden Hill, Bishops Tawton, Barnstaple, Devon, EX32 0DX.*
C15th house, valley views.
Open: All Year (not Xmas)
01271 42514
Mrs Bater
Fax no: 01271 75971
Rates fr: *£15.00*-**£15.00**.
Beds: 2D 1T
Baths: 1 Ensuite 1 Shared
(10)

Colebrooke

National Grid Ref: SS7700

New Inn (Coleford), Mare & Foal (Yeoford)

The Oyster, *Colebrooke, Crediton, Devon, EX17 5JQ.*
Modern bungalow. Central Devon, Colebrooke.
Open: All Year
01363 84576 Mrs Hockridge
Rates fr: *£15.00*-**£15.00**.
Beds: 2D 1T
Baths: 1 Ensuite 1 Private

Birchmans Farm, *Colebrooke, Crediton, Devon, EX17 5BL.*
All bedrooms ensuite, tea/coffee facilities.
Open: All Year (not Xmas)
Grades: ETB 2 Cr, Comm
01363 82393 Mrs Hill
Rates fr: *£15.00*-**£16.00**.
Beds: 2D 1T
Baths: 3 Ensuite

Coleford

National Grid Ref: SS7701

Coombe House Country Hotel, *Coleford, Crediton, Devon, EX17 5BY.*
Georgian country house hotel.
Open: All Year
01363 84487
Mr Wirrich
Rates fr: *£26.50*-**£30.00**.
Beds: 4F 4D 2T 2S
Baths: 12 Ensuite
(90)

Collipriest

National Grid Ref: SS9511

Little Holwell, *Collipriest, Tiverton, Devon, EX16 4PT.*
Set in rolling hills in the beautiful Exe Valley.
Open: All Year (not Xmas)
01884 257590 (also fax no)
Mrs Hill-King
Rates fr: *£16.00*-**£16.00**.
Beds: 1F 2D
Baths: 1 Ensuite 1 Shared
(6)

Colyton

National Grid Ref: SY2493

White Cottage Hotel, *Colyton, Devon, EX13 6NA.*
C15th hotel and holiday cottages.
Open: All Year
Grades: AA 4 Q, Comm, RAC 2 St
01297 552401
Mr Parker
Rates fr: *£29.90*-**£34.90**.
Beds: 1F 2D 2T
Baths: 5 Private
(16) (16)

The Grove, *South Street, Colyton, Devon, EX13 6ER.*
Victorian house, half acre garden.
Open: All Year (not Xmas)
01297 552438 Mr Hudson
Rates fr: *£15.50*-**£15.50**.
Beds: 3F 3D 1T
Baths: 4 Private 1 Shared
(10)

Combe Martin

National Grid Ref: SS5846

Dolphin Inn

Hillview Guest House, *Woodlands, Combe Martin, Ilfracombe, Devon, EX34 0AT.*
Comfortable, quiet position, pleasant gardens.
Open: Easter to Sep
01271 882331 Mrs Bosley
Rates fr: *£13.00*-**£14.00**.
Beds: 4D 1T
Baths: 2 Private 1 Shared
(6)

Glendower, *King Street, Combe Martin, Ilfracombe, Devon, EX34 0AL.*
Large Victorian private house.
Open: Easter to Nov
01271 883449 Mr & Mrs Barry
Rates fr: *£12.00*-**£15.00**.
Beds: 1F 1D 1T 1S
Baths: 1 Ensuite 1 Shared
(1) (3)

Cornworthy

National Grid Ref: SX8255

Hunters' Lodge

Black Ness Cottage, *East Cornworthy, Cornworthy, Totnes, Devon, TQ9 7HQ.*
Delightful cottage, idyllic rural setting. **Open:** All Year (not Xmas)
01803 722467 Mrs Bryant
Rates fr: *£15.00*-**£16.00**.
Beds: 1D 1T **Baths:** 1 Shared
(8) (4)

Gitcombe House, *Cornworthy, Totnes, Devon, TQ9 7HH.*
Grade II Listed Georgian manor.
Open: All Year
01803 712678 Mr Jolly
Rates fr: *£12.50*-**£25.00**.
Beds: 3D 1T **Baths:** 2 Private
(8)

Countisbury

National Grid Ref: SS7457

Staghunters Inn

Coombe Farm, *Countisbury, Lynton, Devon, EX35 6NF.*
C17th farmhouse.
Open: Mar to Nov
Grades: ETB 2 Cr, Comm, AA 3 Q
01598 741236 Mrs& Mrs Pile
Rates fr: *£16.00*-**£18.00**.
Beds: 2F 2D 1T
Baths: 2 Private 2 Shared
(6)

Crediton

National Grid Ref: SS8300

Libbetts Cottage, *Church Street, Crediton, Devon, EX17 2AQ.*
Central location, 'home from home'.
Open: All Year
01363 772709 Mrs Venn
Rates fr: *£17.00*-**£17.00**.
Beds: 1F
Baths: 1 Private
(5) (2)

Croyde

National Grid Ref: SS4439

The Thatch

West Winds Guest House, *Moor Lane, Croyde Bay, Croyde, Braunton, Devon, EX33 1PA.*
Open: All Year (not Xmas)
Grades: ETB 3 Cr, Comm, AA 3 Q, Recomm
01271 890489 (also fax no)
Mr & Mrs Gedling
Rates fr: *£21.00*-**£35.00**.
Beds: 3D 2T
Baths: 3 Private 2 Shared
(6)
Small family guest house on waters edge location, private steps onto beach. Magnificent views overlooking Croyde Bay. Adjacent to National Trust Baggy Point Coastal Path.

Combas Farm, *Croyde, Braunton, Devon, EX33 1PH.*
Welcoming C17th farmhouse, idyllic setting.
Open: Mar to Dec
Grades: ETB 2 Cr, Comm
01271 890398 Ms Adams
Rates fr: *£18.50*-**£18.50**.
Beds: 2F 2D 1S
Baths: 2 Ensuite 2 Private 1 Shared
(8)

Chapel Farm, *Hobbs Hill, Croyde, Braunton, Devon, EX33 1NE.*
C16th thatched farmhouse, 10 minutes to beach.
Open: Easter to Oct
01271 890429 Mrs Windsor
Rates fr: *£16.00*-**£18.00**.
Beds: 2D 1S
Baths: 1 Private 1 Shared
(0)

Cullompton

National Grid Ref: SS9708

Fig Tree Farm, *Butterleigh, Cullompton, Devon, EX15 1PQ.*
Open: All Year
01884 855463 Mrs Chumbley
Rates fr: *£14.50*-**£16.00**.
Beds: 2F 1D **Baths:** 1 Shared
Generous farmhouse hospitality with spectacular views overlooking the beautiful Burn Valley. Friendly family atmosphere. Ideal coast, moors, M5 (J28). Coarse fishing. Phone 'Free Wine, Free Children'.

Dalwood

National Grid Ref: ST2400

The Tuckers Arms, *Dalwood, Axminster, Devon, EX13 7EG.*
C12th thatched country inn.
Open: All Year
01404 881342 Mr Beck
Rates fr: *£20.00*-**£25.00**.
Beds: 1F 2D 3T
Baths: 6 Ensuite

Dartmouth

National Grid Ref: SX8751

The Cherub Inn, Wind Jammer, Royal Castle Hotel

The Captains House, *18 Clarence Street, Dartmouth, Devon, TQ6 9NW.*
Open: All Year
Grades: ETB 2 St, High Comm, AA 4 Q, Select, RAC Acclaim
01803 832133 Mr Jestico
Rates fr: *£20.00*-**£25.00**.
Beds: 1F 2D 1T 1S
Baths: 5 Ensuite
Georgian Listed house built 1730. Quiet street close town/river. All rooms TV, radio, tea/coffee, friedge, hairdryer, etc. Choice breakfasts with homemade produce.

Valley House, *46 Victoria Road, Dartmouth, Devon, TQ6.*
Comfortable small friendly guest house.
Open: All Year (not Xmas)
01803 834045
Mr & Mrs Ellis
Rates fr: *£18.00*-**£24.00**.
Beds: 2D 2T
Baths: 4 Ensuite

Townstal Farm House, *Townstal Road, Dartmouth, Devon, TQ6 9HY.*
Open: All Year
Grades: ETB 3 Cr, Comm, AA 3 Q, Recomm
01803 832300
Mr Edge
Rates fr: *£22.50*-**£20.00**.
Beds: 5F 9D 2T 1S
Baths: 14 Ensuite 3 Shared
Charming family-run C16th farmhouse, half a mile from village centre. Licensed bar, large car park and a very warm welcome. Off season bargain breaks.

Regency House, *30 Newcomen Road, Dartmouth, Devon, TQ6 9BN.*
Overlooking the beautiful River Dart.
Open: All Year (not Xmas)
01803 832714
Mrs Shalders
Rates fr: *£22.00*.
Beds: 1F 2D
Baths: 3 Ensuite

75 Victoria Road, *Dartmouth, Devon, TQ6 9RX.*
Large Victorian house.
Open: Easter to Jan
01803 833415
Mr Bruckner
Rates fr: *£14.00*-**£15.00**.
Beds: 2F 1D 1T 1S
Baths: 2 Shared

Victoria Cote, *105 Victoria Road, Dartmouth, Devon, TQ6 9DY.*
Detached, comfortable, Victorian private house.
Open: All Year (not Xmas)
01803 832997 Mr Fell
Rates fr: *£18.00*-**£23.00**.
Beds: 3D
Baths: 3 Private

Brenec House, *73 South Ford Road, Dartmouth, Devon, TQ6 9QT.*
Pleasant, comfortable small guest house.
Open: All Year (not Xmas)
01803 834788
Mr & Mrs Culley
Rates fr: *£13.50*-**£13.00**.
Beds: 1F 1D 1S
Baths: 1 Shared

Boringdon House, *1 Church Road, Dartmouth, Devon, TQ6 9HQ.*
Spacious, welcoming, elegant Georgian house.
Open: Mar to Dec
Grades: ETB 2 Cr, High Comm, AA 5 Q
01803 832235
Mr Green
Rates fr: *£22.50*-**£38.00**.
Beds: 1D 2T
Baths: 3 Ensuite

Three Feathers, *51 Victoria Road, Dartmouth, Devon, TQ6 9RX.*
Early Victorian town house.
Open: All Year (not Xmas)
01803 834694
Mrs George
Rates fr: *£14.50*-**£15.00**.
Beds: 4F 1T
Baths: 3 Ensuite 1 Shared

Dawlish

National Grid Ref: SX9676

Dawlish Grill

West Hatch Hotel, *34 West Cliff, Dawlish, Devon, EX7 9DN.*
Quality homely hotel near sea.
Open: All Year
Grades: ETB 2 Cr, High Comm, AA 4 Q, RAC Acclaim
01626 864211 / 862948
Mr & Mrs Badcock
Rates fr: *£20.00*-**£25.00**.
Beds: 2F 8D 1T
Baths: 10 Ensuite 1 Private

Doddiscombsleigh

National Grid Ref: SX8586

Nobody Inn

Whitemoor Farm, *Doddiscombsleigh, Exeter, Devon, EX6 7PU.*
C16th thatched farmhouse.
Open: All Year (not Xmas)
Grades: ETB 1 Cr, Comm, AA 2 Q
01647 252423
Mrs Lacey
Rates fr: *£16.50*-**£17.00**.
Beds: 1D 1T 2S
Baths: 1 Private 1 Shared

Down Thomas

National Grid Ref: SX5050

Langdon Hotel, Mussel Inn, Eddystone

Gabber Farm, *Down Thomas, Plymouth, Devon, PL9 0AW.*
Comfortable working farm, friendly welcome.
Open: All Year
Grades: ETB 2 Cr, Comm
01752 862269 Mrs MacBean
Rates fr: *£16.00*-**£18.00**.
Beds: 2F 1D 2T
Baths: 2 Ensuite 1 Shared

Drewsteignton

National Grid Ref: SX7390

Drewe Arms, Old Inn

The Old Rectory, *Drewsteignton, Exeter, Devon, EX6 6QT.*
Georgian house in two acres.
Open: All Year (not Xmas)
01647 281269
Mrs Emanuel
Rates fr: *£15.00*-**£18.00**.
Beds: 2D 1T
Baths: 1 Private 1 Shared

Dunsford

National Grid Ref: SX8189

Upperton Farm, *Dunsford, Exeter, Devon, EX6 7AQ.*
Large 400-year-old farmhouse.
Open: Mar to Oct
Grades: ETB 1 Cr, Comm
01647 24311
Mrs & Mrs Tripp
Rates fr: *£15.00*-**£15.00**.
Beds: 3D

Planning a longer stay? Always ask for any special rates.

East Allington

National Grid Ref: SX7648

Sir Walter Raleigh, Rolle Arms

Tor Cottage, *The Mounts, East Allington, Totnes, Devon, TQ9 7QJ.*
Modern rural cottage, friendly, comfortable.
Open: Mar to Oct
Grades: ETB 3 Cr, Comm
01548 521316 (also fax no)
Mr Nurthen
Rates fr: *£18.00*-**£26.00**.
Beds: 1F 1D 1T
Baths: 2 Ensuite 1 Private

East Budleigh

National Grid Ref: SYO684

Hill Farm, *East Budleigh, Budleigh Salterton, Devon, EX9 7DA.*
Thatched farmhouse in village.
Open: All Year (not Xmas)
01395 442761 Mrs Quick
Rates fr: *£14.00*-**£14.00**.
Beds: 1F 1S
Baths: 1 Shared
(3) (2)

Wynards Farm, *East Budleigh, Budleigh Salterton, Devon, EX9 7DQ.*
Best kept village in Devon.
Open: Easter to Sep
01395 443417 (also fax no)
Mrs Smith
Rates fr: *£14.00*-**£20.00**.
Beds: 1F 1D 1T
Baths: 1 Shared
(1) (3)

East Prawle

National Grid Ref: SX7836

Pigs Nose Inn, Milbrook Inn

Hines Hill, *East Prawle, Kingsbridge, Devon, TQ7 2BZ.*
Open: Mar to Oct
01548 511263 (also fax no)
Mrs Morris
Rates fr: *£20.00*-**£25.00**.
Beds: 2D 1T
Baths: 3 Ensuite
(12) (8)
Breathtaking panorama of Devon's southernmost coast from tranquil clifftop gardens, overlooking sandy beaches, coastal path, near Salcombe. Generous imaginative cooking, considerate hospitality. Sea views from every elegantly furnished room.

Stures Court, *East Prawle, Kingsbridge, Devon, TQ7 2BY.*
C17th thatched cottage, C20th comfort.
Open: All Year
Grades: ETB Listed, High Comm
01548 511261 Miss Benson
Rates fr: *£15.00*-**£15.00**.
Beds: 2D 2S
Baths: 1 Shared
(7)

The Forge on the Green, *East Prawle, Kingsbridge, South Devon, TQ7 2BU*
Open: All Year
Grades: ETB 1 Cr, High Comm
01548 511210 (also fax no)
Rates fr: *£20.00*-**£25.00**.
Beds: 2D
Baths: 1 Ensuite 1 Private
Acclaimed luxury cottage with picturesque views over Prawle Green to the sea. Ensuite spa bath plus all facilities. Fabulous buffet breakfast. Gourmet dinners by arrangement.

Migrants Rest, *East Prawle, Kingsbridge, Devon, TQ7 2DB.*
Bountiful wildlife & coastal paths.
Open: All Year
01548 511443 Mr Catt
Rates fr: *£14.00*-**£14.00**.
Beds: 1F 1D 1T
Baths: 1 Shared
(5)

Maelcombe House, *East Prawle, Kingsbridge, Devon, TQ7 2DE.*
Coastguard officer's house by the sea.
Open: Easter to Oct
01548 511300 Mr & Mrs Davies
Rates fr: *£15.50*-**£15.50**.
Beds: 3F 4D 1S
Baths: 5 Shared
(10)

East-The-Water

National Grid Ref: SS4626

Kumba, *Chudleigh Road, East-The-Water, Bideford, Devon, EX39 4AR.*
Detached Edwardian country house. Parking.
Open: All Year
01237 471526 Ms Doughty
Rates fr: *£17.50*-**£18.50**.
Beds: 3F 1D
Baths: 3 Ensuite 1 Shared
(2mth) (8)

Ebford

National Grid Ref: SX9887

Nutwell Lodge (Lympstone)

Ebford Court, *Ebford, Exeter, Devon, EX3 0RA.*
C15th peaceful thatched farm-house.
Open: All Year (not Xmas)
01392 875353 Mrs Howard
Rates fr: *£14.00*-**£20.00**.
Beds: 1D 1T
Baths: 1 Shared
(10) (4)

The lowest *double* rate per person is shown in *italics*.

Ermington

National Grid Ref: SX6453

First & Last

Waye Farm, *The Grange, Ermington, Ivybridge, Devon, PL21 9NU.*
Peaceful, idyllically situated, high standard.
Open: All Year
01752 830427
Mr & Mrs Livermore
Rates fr: *£16.00*-**£22.00**.
Beds: 1D 1T
Baths: 2 Ensuite
(4)

Exeter

National Grid Ref: SX9292

Mill-on-the-Exe, Papermakers, Chaucers Inn, Seven Stars

Clock Tower Hotel, *16 New North Road, Exeter, Devon, EX4 4HF.*
Open: All Year
Grades: ETB 2 Cr
01392 424545 Mr Morris
Fax no: 01392 218445
Rates fr: *£12.50*-**£15.00**.
Beds: 2F 6D 5T 3S
Baths: 8 Private 3 Shared
Central licensed hotel few minutes level walk cathedral, shops and station. Award winning patio garden. All modern facilities, ideal touring centre. Request brochure/information pack.

Meads Guest House, *2 St Davids Hill, Exeter, Devon, EX4 3RG.*
Attractive, comfortable accommodation near Cathedral.
Open: All Year
01392 274886 Mr Bodemeaid
Rates fr: *£14.00*-**£14.00**.
Beds: 2D 1T 1S
Baths: 2 Private 2 Shared

Highbury Guest House, *89 St Davids Hill, Exeter, Devon, EX4 4DW.*
Comfortable, central, close to station.
Open: All Year (not Xmas)
01392 434737
Mr & Mrs Morris
Fax no: 01392 218448
Rates fr: *£12.50*-**£12.50**.
Beds: 1F 3D 1T 1S
Baths: 4 Ensuite 2 Shared
(4)

The Old Mill, *Mill Lane, Alphington, Exeter, Devon, EX2 8SG.*
Historic mill in quiet area.
Open: All Year
01392 59977
Mrs Marchant
Rates fr: *£10.00*-**£10.00**.
Beds: 2F 1D 1T 1S
Baths: 1 Private 1 Shared
(8)

Ebford Court, *Ebford, Exeter, Devon, EX3 0RA.*
C15th peaceful thatched farmhouse.
Open: All Year (not Xmas)
01392 875353 Mrs Howard
Rates fr: *£14.00*-**£20.00**.
Beds: 1D 1T
Baths: 1 Shared
(10) (4)

Marianne Pool Farm, *Clyst St George, Exeter, Devon, EX3 0NZ.*
Peacefully situated, thatched Devon longhouse.
Open: Easter to Oct
Grades: ETB Listed
01392 874939 Mrs Bragg
Rates fr: *£16.00*-**£16.50**.
Beds: 1F 1T
Baths: 1 Shared
(2)

Claremont, *36 Wonford Road, Exeter, Devon, EX2 4LD.*
Clean, quiet, near city centre.
Open: All Year
01392 274699
Mrs Self
Rates fr: *£19.00*-**£26.00**.
Beds: 1F 1D 1T
Baths: 3 Private
(5) (1)

Janbri Guest House, *102 Alphington Road, Exeter, Devon, EX2 8HZ.*
Large Victorian private house.
Open: All Year
01392 77346 Mr Prest
Rates fr: *£14.00*-**£15.00**.
Beds: 2F 2T 1S

Park View Hotel, *8 Howell Road, Exeter, Devon, EX4 4LG.*
Family-run hotel overlooking park.
Open: All Year (not Xmas)
Grades: ETB 2 Cr, Comm, AA 3 Q, RAC Acclaim
01392 71772
Mrs Batho
Rates fr: *£17.50*-**£20.00**.
Beds: 2F 7D 3T 3S
Baths: 10 Ensuite 2 Shared
(6)

Killarney Guest House, *Alphington Street, Exeter, Devon, EX2 8AT.*
Comfortable, friendly, family guest house.
Open: All Year (not Xmas)
01392 76932 Mrs Flint
Rates fr: *£14.00*-**£15.00**.
Beds: 1F 3D 2T 3S
Baths: 3 Shared

Hillcrest Corner, *1 Hillcrest Park, Exeter, Devon, EX4 4SH.*
Vegetarian, adjacent university, quiet, views.
Open: All Year (not Xmas)
01392 77443 Mr & Mrs Bligh
Rates fr: *£14.00*-**£14.00**.
Beds: 1D 1T 1S
Baths: 1 Shared
(2)

Crossmead, *Dunsford Hill, Exeter, Devon, EX4 1TF.*
Comfortable rooms within tranquil grounds.
Open: All Year
01392 422 594 Mrs Snow
Rates fr: *£12.50*-**£12.50**.
Beds: 1F 24D 15T 54S
Baths: 26 Ensuite 63 Shared
(0) (110)

Exmouth

National Grid Ref: SY0081

Pendennis Guest House, *84 St Andrews Road, Exmouth, Devon, EX8 1AS.*
Comfortable family-run guest house.
Open: All Year (not Xmas)
Grades: ETB 1 Cr
01395 271458 Mr & Mrs Field
Rates fr: *£14.00*-**£14.00**.
Beds: 2F 2D 1T 2S
Baths: 2 Shared
(5)

Blenheim Guest House, *39 Morton Road, Exmouth, Devon, EX8 1BA.*
Comfortable house near beach & shops.
Open: All Year (not Xmas)
01395 223123
Mr Dormer
Rates fr: *£13.50*-**£16.00**.
Beds: 2F 3D 2T
Baths: 1 Shared
(2)

Moorfield, *Foxholes Hill, Exmouth, Devon, EX8 2DF.*
Unique, spacious sea-side home.
Open: All Year (not Xmas)
01395 272660 Ms Delany
Rates fr: *£15.00*-**£15.00**.
Beds: 2F 1S
Baths: 1 Private 1 Shared
(2)

Sandrevin, *59 Salterton Road, Exmouth, Devon, EX8 2EQ.*
Large detached Victorian house.
Open: All Year (not Xmas)
01395 266898
Mr & Mrs Cooper
Rates fr: *£16.00*-**£16.00**.
Beds: 1F 1D 1T 1S
Baths: 2 Ensuite 1 Shared
(10)

Farringdon

National Grid Ref: SY0191

White Horse Inn

Wood Barton, *Farringdon, Exeter, Devon, EX5 2HY.*
Quiet C17th farmhouse, near Exeter.
Open: All Year
01395 233407
Mrs Bolt
Rates fr: *£15.00*-**£18.00**.
Beds: 1F 1D 1T
Baths: 3 Private
(6)

Home Farm, *Farringdon, Exeter, Devon, EX5 2HY.*
Large comfortable warm farmhouse.
Open: All Year (not Xmas)
01395 232293 Mrs Thompson
Rates fr: *£18.00*-**£20.00**.
Beds: 1D 2T
Baths: 1 Ensuite 2 Shared
(7) (12)

Fenny Bridges

National Grid Ref: SY1198

Olter Inn

Little Ash Farm, *Fenny Bridges, Honiton, Devon, EX14 0BL.*
Comfortable farmhouse with large garden.
Open: All Year
01404 850271 Mrs Reid
Rates fr: *£12.50*-**£15.00**.
Beds: 1F 1D 1T 1S
Baths: 2 Shared
(4)

Skinners Ash Farm, *Fenny Bridges, Honiton, Devon, EX14 0BH.*
Working rare breeds farm. Also self-catering.
Open: All Year
Grades: ETB Listed, High Comm
01404 850231 Mrs Godfrey
Rates fr: *£15.50*.
Beds: 1F 1T **Baths:** 1 Shared
(Any) (7)

Fremington

National Grid Ref: SS5132

Kneesworth Nurseries, *Penhill, Fremington, Barnstaple, Devon, EX31 2NG.*
Private house on working nursery.
Open: All Year (not Xmas)
01271 73816 Mr & Mrs Broad
Rates fr: *£12.00*-**£12.00**.
Beds: 1D 1T

Oakwood, *34 Yelland Road, Fremington, Barnstaple, Devon, EX31 3DS.*
Run like a family home - very friendly.
Open: All Year
01271 73884 Mrs George
Rates fr: *£11.00*-**£11.00**.
Beds: 1F 2D
Baths: 1 Shared
(3)

Frogmore

National Grid Ref: SX7742

The Globe Inn, *Frogmore, Kingsbridge, Devon, TQ7 2NR.*
Picturesque country, creekside village inn.
Open: All Year
Grades: ETB 2 Cr, AA 2 Q
01548 531351 Mr & Mrs Johnston
Rates fr: *£16.00*-**£17.50**.
Beds: 2F 3D 1T
Baths: 3 Private 2 Shared
(0) (20)

Galmpton

National Grid Ref: SX6840

Burton Farm, *Galmpton, Kingsbridge, Devon, TQ7 3EY.*
Open: All Year (not Xmas)
Grades: ETB 2 Cr, High Comm
01548 561210 Ms Rossiter
Rates fr: *£19.75*-**£20.00**.
Beds: 3F 2D 2T 2S
Baths: 5 Ensuite 1 Private 1 Shared
(15)
Working farm in valley near Hope Cove beaches and Salcombe. Comfortably furnished rooms with tea-making and TV. Farmhouse cooking. Children's play area. Warm welcome. Self-catering available.

Guineaford

National Grid Ref: SS5437

Valley View, *Guineaford, Marwood, Barnstaple, Devon, EX31 4EA.*
Farm bungalow in peaceful area.
Open: All Year
01271 43458 Mrs Chugg
Rates fr: *£12.00*-**£12.00**.
Beds: 1F 1T
Baths: 1 Private
(2)

Gulworthy

National Grid Ref: SX4572

Bistro 19

Rubbytown Farm, *Gulworthy, Tavistock, Devon, PL19 8PA.*
Charming C17th farmhouse, wonderful views.
Open: All Year (not Xmas)
Grades: ETB 2 Cr, High Comm
01822 832493 Mrs Steer
Rates fr: *£18.00*.
Beds: 3T
Baths: 3 Ensuite
(5) (6)

Harpford

National Grid Ref: SY0990

Peeks House, *Harpford, Sidmouth, Devon, EX10 0NH.*
Elegant C16th accommodation - C20th comforts.
Open: All Year
Grades: ETB 3 Cr, High Comm, AA 4 Q
01395 567664 Mr Somerfield
Rates fr: *£23.00*-**£28.00**.
Beds: 3D 2T
Baths: 5 Private
(5) (6)

Bringing children with you? Always ask for any special rates.

Hartland

National Grid Ref: SS2524

Hartland Quay Hotel, Manor Inn

West Titchberry Farm, *Hartland, Bideford, Devon, EX39 6AU.*
Comfortable, renovated C18th coastal farmhouse. Also self catering cottage.
Open: All Year (not Xmas)
01237 441287 Mrs Heard
Rates fr: *£14.00*-**£14.00**.
Beds: 1F 1D 1T **Baths:** 1 Shared
(0) (Lots)

Anchor Inn, *Fore Street, Hartland, Bideford, Devon, EX39 6BD.*
Friendly C16th inn.
Open: All Year
01237 441414 Mr Hodges
Rates fr: *£15.00*-**£17.00**.
Beds: 2F 4D 2T 1S
Baths: 5 Private 1 Shared
(15)

Hartland Quay

National Grid Ref: SS2224

Hartland Quay Hotel, The Manor Inn

Hartland Quay Hotel, *Hartland Quay, Hartland, Bideford, Devon, EX39 6DU.*
Former Corn Exchange, family home. **Open:** Easter to Nov
Grades: ETB 2 Cr
01237 441218 Mrs Johns
Rates fr: *£20.00*-**£22.00**.
Beds: 2F 6D 6T 2S
Baths: 10 Private 3 Shared

Haytor

National Grid Ref: SX7777

Egryn House, *Haytor, Newton Abbot, Devon, TQ13 9XU.*
Comfortable, homely, countryside house. **Open:** All Year (not Xmas)
01364 661254 Ms Barrett
Rates fr: *£14.00*-**£16.00**.
Beds: 2D 1T
Baths: 1 Ensuite 2 Shared
(2)

Hemyock

National Grid Ref: ST1313

Catherine Wheel

Brook House, *The Square, Hemyock, Cullompton, Devon, EX15 3RG*
Open: All Year
01823 680811 Mr & Mrs Eldridge
Rates fr: *£16.00*-**£15.00**.
Beds: 1D 2T 1S
Baths: 3 Ensuite 1 Private
(2)
Small family guest house in the 'Blackdowns' Area of Outstanding Natural Beauty. Location ideal for moors and coast or enjoy cycling, riding and walking locally.

Hayne Farm, *Blackborough, Hemyock, Cullompton, Devon, EX15 2JD.*
C15th farmhouse, working farm.
Open: All Year (not Xmas)
01823 680337
Mrs Kittow
Rates fr: *£13.50*-**£14.00**.
Beds: 1F 1T
Baths: 1 Shared
(4)

Heybrook Bay

National Grid Ref: SX4948

Eddyston Inn, Mossell Inn (Down Thomas)

Heybrook Bay Private Hotel, *Beach Road, Heybrook Bay, Plymouth, Devon, PL9 0BS.*
Comfortable, friendly 1920's hotel.
Open: All Year (not Xmas)
01752 862345
Rates fr: *£14.00*-**£16.00**.
Beds: 6D
Baths: 2 Shared
(12)

Higher Clovelly

National Grid Ref: SS3124

Farmers Arms

Burnstone Farm, *Higher Clovelly, Bideford, Devon, EX39 5RX.*
Refurbished old farmhouse with central heating.
Open: All Year
Grades: AA 3 Q
01237 431219 (also fax no)
Mrs Symons
Rates fr: *£17.00*-**£18.00**.
Beds: 1F 1D 1T
Baths: 1 Shared

Dyke Green Farm, *Higher Clovelly, Bideford, Devon, EX39 5RU.*
Beautiful converted barn, every comfort.
Open: All Year (not Xmas)
01237 431699 (also fax no)
Mrs Johns
Rates fr: *£15.50*-**£18.50**.
Beds: 2D 1T
Baths: 2 Private 1 Shared
(6)

Hittisleigh

National Grid Ref: SX7395

Hill Farm, *Hittisleigh, Exeter, Devon, EX6 6LQ.*
C17th farmhouse - heated pool - seclusion.
Open: All Year (not Xmas)
01647 24149
Mrs Howell
Rates fr: *£15.00*-**£15.00**.
Beds: 1D 1T
Baths: 1 Shared
(10)

Holbeton

National Grid Ref: SX6150

The Mildmay Colours Inn, *Holbeton, Plymouth, Devon,* *PL8 1NA.*
Traditional village inn with brewery.
Open: All Year
01752 830248 Mrs Martin
Rates fr: *£20.00*-**£20.00**.
Beds: 1F 1D 6T
Baths: 8 Private
(25)

Holne

National Grid Ref: SX7069

Church House Inn, Tradesman's Arms (Scorriton)

Mill Leat Farm, *Holne, Ashburton, Newton Abbot, Devon,* *TQ13 7RZ.*
Off the beaten track.
Open: All Year (not Xmas)
Grades: ETB 1 Cr, Approv
01364 631283 Mrs Cleave
Rates fr: *£16.00*-**£18.00**.
Beds: 2F
Baths: 1 Ensuite 1 Shared
(2)

Wellpritton Farm, *Holne, Ashburton, Newton Abbot, Devon,* *TQ13 7RX.*
Farmhouse, farmfood, lovely setting.
Open: All Year
Grades: ETB 2 Cr, High Comm, AA 4 Q, Select
01364 631273 Ms Gifford
Rates fr: *£18.00*-**£18.00**.
Beds: 2F 1T 1D 1S
Baths: 5 Ensuite
(10)

Hunters Reach, *Michelcombe Lane, Holne, Newton Abbot, Devon,* *TQ13 7WR.*
Modern comfortable bungalow. Peaceful location.
Open: All Year (not Xmas)
01364 631300 Mr & Mrs Dance
Rates fr: *£14.00*-**£15.00**.
Beds: 2D 1S
Baths: 1 Shared
(4)

Hazelwood, *Holne, Newton Abbot, Devon,* *TQ13 7SJ.*
Panoramic views, personal service, homemade bread.
Open: All Year (not Xmas)
01364 631235 Mrs Mortimore
Rates fr: *£16.00*-**£16.00**.
Beds: 1D 1S

Middle Leat, *Holne, Ashburton, Newton Abbot, Devon,* *TQ13 7SJ.*
Modern, comfortable farmhouse.
Open: All Year
01364 631413 Mrs Torr
Rates fr: *£13.00*-**£16.00**.
Beds: 1F 1D
Baths: 1 Private

Middle Stoke Farm, *Holne, Ashburton, Devon,* *TQ13 7SS.*
Lovely peaceful location on Dartmoor.
Open: All Year (not Xmas)
01364 631444 Miss Neal
Rates fr: *£16.00*-**£16.00**.
Beds: 1D
Baths: 1 Private
(0) (2)

Holsworthy

National Grid Ref: SS3403

Leworthy Farm, *Holsworthy, Devon,* *EX22 6SJ.*
Friendly, hospitable farmhouse.
Open: All Year
01409 253488 Mr & Mrs Cornish
Fax no: 01409 254671
Rates fr: *£16.50*-**£16.50**.
Beds: 4F 2D 1T 2S
Baths: 3 Private 2 Shared
(20)

Honiton

National Grid Ref: ST1600

Red Cow Pub

Monkton Court Inn, *Monkton, Honiton, Devon,* *EX14 9QH.*
Open: All Year
Grades: ETB 3 Cr, AA 2 St
01404 42309 Mrs Taylor
Rates fr: *£22.50*-**£27.50**.
Beds: 2F 4D 1T 1S
Baths: 6 Private 1 Shared
(80)
C17th former manor house. Freehouse with quality rooms - most ensuite. Beamed bars and log fires. Bar and restaurant meals every evening. Gardens and ample parking.

Westgate, *Parsonage Lane, Honiton, Devon,* *EX14 8TF.*
Peaceful and friendly country house.
Open: Easter to Oct
01404 41494 Mrs Sturley
Rates fr: *£17.00*-**£20.00**.
Beds: 1F 1D
Baths: 2 Shared
(2)

Cabernem, *Bowling Green Lane, Honiton, Devon,* *EX14 8DP.*
Detached family house.
Open: All Year
01404 41370
Mrs van Halteren
Rates fr: *£15.00*-**£15.00**.
Beds: 1D 1T
Baths: 2 Shared
(4)

The Heathfield Inn, *Walnut Road, Honiton, Devon,* *EX14 8UG.*
C16th thatched Devon longhouse.
Open: All Year
Grades: AA 4 Q
01404 45321 Mr Ford
Rates fr: *£25.00*-**£32.50**.
Beds: 3D 4T 1S
(40)

Hope Cove

National Grid Ref: SX6739

Hope & Anchor

Fern Lodge Guest House, *Hope Cove, Kingsbridge, Devon,* *TQ7 3HF.*
Open: Easter to Oct
01548 561326 Mrs Lonsdale
Rates fr: *£22.00*-**£22.00**.
Beds: 2F 2D 2T
Baths: 6 Ensuite
(5) (8)
Friendly guesthouse. Pets free. All rooms ensuite, colour TVs, beverage making facilities. Own keys. 3 mins sandy beaches. Please ring for brochure: 01548 561326.

Cove Cottage, *Hope Cove, Kingsbridge, Devon,* *TQ7 3HG.*
Detached cottage 100 yds from sea.
Open: All Year (not Xmas)
01548 561446 Mrs Guymer
Rates fr: *£13.50*-**£13.50**.
Beds: 1D 1T 1S
Baths: 1 Shared
(3)

Hope Cove Hotel, *Hope Cove, Hope Cove, Kingsbridge, Devon,* *TQ7 3HH.*
Spectacular sea views.
Open: Easter to Oct
01548 561233 Mr Clarke
Rates fr: *£22.50*-**£32.50**.
Beds: 2T 5D
Baths: 7 Ensuite
(6) (15)

Rockcliffe, *Hope Cove, Kingsbridge, Devon,* *TQ7 3HE.*
Detached house, 75 yards from sea.
Open: All Year (not Xmas)
01548 560061 Mrs Hewitt
Rates fr: *£16.50*-**£21.50**.
Beds: 1F 2D
Baths: 3 Private
(4)

Horns Cross

National Grid Ref: SS3823

Hoops Inn, Bell Inn

The Hoops Inn, *Horns Cross, Bideford, Devon,* *EX39 5DL.*
C13th historic thatched inn/hotel.
Open: All Year
Grades: ETB 3 Cr, Comm, RAC 2 St
01237 451222 Mrs Marriott
Rates fr: *£26.00*-**£35.00**.
Beds: 8D 4T 4S
Baths: 12 Ensuite 2 Shared
(10) (100)

Acorn House, *Horns Cross, Bideford, Devon,* *EX39 5D.*
Family house opposite heritage coast.
Open: Easter to Oct
01237 451402 Mrs Stacey
Rates fr: *£13.00*-**£15.00**.
Beds: 1F 1D 1T
Baths: 1 Shared
(6) (2)

Northway House, *Horns Cross, Bideford, Devon,* EX39 5EA.
C17th farmhouse. Overlooking Bideford bay.
Open: All Year
01237 451899 Mr Sanders
Rates fr: *£15.00*-**£18.00**.
Beds: 2F 2D 1T
Baths: 2 Shared
(8)

The Holt, *(on A39), Horns Cross, Bideford, Devon,* EX39 5DW.
Breathtaking views across Bideford Bay to Lundy Island.
Open: All Year
01237 451342 Mrs McNeil
Rates fr: *£12.00*-**£12.00**.
Beds: 1F 1D 1T
Baths: 1 Shared
(6)

Huntshaw Water

National Grid Ref: SS5023

Hunters Inn

The Roundhouse, *Guscott, Huntshaw Water, Torrington, Devon,* EX38 7HE.
Splendid converted roundhouse barn.
Open: All Year
01271 858626
Mrs Smith
Rates fr: *£15.00*-**£15.00**.
Beds: 1F 2D
Baths: 3 Private
(8)

Ide

National Grid Ref: SX9292

Huntsman

Drakes Farm House, *Ide, Exeter, Devon,* EX2 9RQ.
Characterful house, coffee/tea making facilities.
Open: All Year
01392 256814 / 495564
Mrs Easterbrook
Rates fr: *£15.00*-**£16.50**.
Beds: 1F 1D 1T
Baths: 2 Ensuite 1 Private
(6)

Ilfracombe

National Grid Ref: SS5147

Britannia Inn

Sunnymeade Hotel, *Dean Cross, West Down, Ilfracombe, Devon,* EX34 8NT.
Comfortable country house hotel.
Open: All Year
Grades: ETB 3 Cr, Approv
01271 863668
Mr & Mrs Hunt
Rates fr: *£18.50*-**£20.50**.
Beds: 2F 6D 1T
Baths: 8 Ensuite 1 Private
(19)

Cairn House Hotel, *43 St Brannocks Road, Ilfracombe, Devon,* EX34 8EH.
Comfortable family hotel. Super views.
Open: All Year
Grades: ETB 3 Cr, RAC 1 St
01271 863911 Mrs Tupper
Rates fr: *£18.00*-**£20.00**.
Beds: 3F 6D 1S
(2)

Westwell Hall, *Torrs Park, Ilfracombe, Devon,* EX34 8AZ.
Elegant Victorian gentleman's residence.
Open: All Year
Grades: ETB 3 Cr, RAC Acclaim
01271 862792 (also fax no)
Lomas
Rates fr: *£18.00*-**£18.00**.
Beds: 1F 5D 2T 1S
Baths: 9 Ensuite

2 Capstone Place, *Ilfracombe, Devon,* EX34 9BT.
Converted fisherman's cottage near harbour.
Open: Easter to Oct
01271 865201 Mrs Howard
Rates fr: *£13.50*-**£13.50**.
Beds: 1D 1T
Baths: 1 Shared
(3)

The Epchris Hotel, *Torrs Park, Ilfracombe, Devon,* EX34 8AZ.
Family hotel with pool, grounds.
Open: Feb to Dec
Grades: ETB 3 Cr, Approv, RAC Listed
01271 862751 Mrs Barleycorn
Rates fr: *£19.00*-**£19.00**.
Beds: 7F 1S
Baths: 8 Ensuite 1 Private
(8)

Instow

National Grid Ref: SS4426

Pilton Cottage, *Victoria Terrace, Marine Parade, Instow, Bideford, Devon,* EX39 4JW.
Victorian house, beautiful estuary view.
Open: Easter to Oct
01271 860202 Mrs Gardner
Rates fr: *£16.00*-**£16.00**.
Beds: 1F 2D 1T 1S
Baths: 1 Private 1 Shared
(3)

Inwardleigh

National Grid Ref: SX5699

Lower Oak Farm, *Inwardleigh, Okehampton, Devon,* EX20 3AS.
Modern, comfortable C16th farmhouse.
Open: Easter to Oct
01837 810412 Mrs Banbury
Rates fr: *£13.50*-**£14.00**.
Beds: 1F 1D 1T
Baths: 1 Shared
(3) (3)

Ivybridge

National Grid Ref: SX6356

Sportsmans Inn

The Toll House, *Exeter Road, Ivybridge, Devon,* PL21 0DE.
1850s house with beautiful gardens.
Open: All Year
01752 893522 Mrs Hancox
Rates fr: *£14.00*-**£18.00**.
Beds: 2T 1S
Baths: 1 Ensuite 1 Shared
(5)

Venn Farm, *Ugborough, Ivybridge, Devon,* PL21 0PE.
Situated amidst peaceful rural surroundings.
Open: Jan to Nov
Grades: ETB 2 Cr, Comm
01364 73240
Mr Stephens
Rates fr: *£19.00*-**£19.00**.
Beds: 2F 2T
Baths: 3 Ensuite 1 Shared
(5) (6)

East Highlands, *Blachford Road, Ivybridge, Devon,* PL21 0AD.
Georgian mansion in large gardens.
Open: All Year (not Xmas)
01752 893121
Mr & Mrs Lucas
Rates fr: *£14.00*-**£14.00**.
Beds: 1F 1D 1T 1S
Baths: 1 Ensuite 1 Private 1 Shared
(6)

Jacobstowe

National Grid Ref: SS5801

Higher Cadham Farm, *Jacobstowe, Okehampton, Devon,* EX20 3RB.
Open: All Year (not Xmas)
Grades: ETB 3 Cr, Comm, AA 4 Q, Select
01837 851647 Mrs King
Rates fr: *£17.00*-**£17.00**.
Beds: 2F 1D 3T 1S
Baths: 5 Ensuite 1 Shared
(6)
Superb accommodation set in idyllic countryside. All meals available in our licensed restaurant. Fax/public telephone. 3 lounges & bar.

Kennford

National Grid Ref: SX9186

Fairwinds Hotel, *Kennford, Exeter, Devon,* EX6 7UD.
Cosy modern hotel, excellent value.
Open: All Year (not Xmas)
01392 832911 Mr Price
Rates fr: *£22.00*-**£22.00**.
Beds: 1F 4D 2T 2S
Baths: 8 Private
(9)

Kenton

National Grid Ref: SX9583

Mill Farm, *Kenton, Exeter, Devon, EX6 8JR.*
Pleasing accommodation, lovely farmhouse.
Open: All Year (not Xmas)
01392 832471 Mrs Lambert
Rates fr: *£14.00*-**£14.00**.
Beds: 2F 2D 1T
Baths: 2 Ensuite 2 Shared
(10)

Kings Nympton

National Grid Ref: SS6819

Great Oakwell Farm, *Kings Nympton, Umberleigh, Devon, EX37 9TE.*
Join us in our friendly, comfortable, relaxing old farmhouse.
Open: All Year (not Xmas)
01769 572810 Mr & Mrs Cole
Rates fr: *£14.00*-**£14.00**.
Beds: 2D 1S **Baths:** 2 Shared
(5)

Kingsbridge

National Grid Ref: SX7334

Church House Inn, Crabshell Inn, The Globe (Frogmore)

Centry Farm, *Kingsbridge, Devon, TQ7 2HF.*
Extremely comfortable farmhouse, beautiful setting.
Open: Easter to Oct
01548 852037 Mrs Lidstone
Rates fr: *£16.00*-**£22.00**.
Beds: 1D 1T **Baths:** 2 Ensuite
(8)

Riverside House, *Kingsbridge, Devon, TQ7 2NR.*
Comfortable converted village cottage. **Open:** Easter to Oct
01548 531617 (also fax no)
Mr & Mrs Parrish
Rates fr: *£15.00*-**£15.00**.
Beds: 1T

Rockwood Hotel, *Embankment Road, Kingsbridge, Devon, TQ7 1JZ.*
Completely refurbished hotel.
Open: All Year
01548 852480
Rates fr: *£20.00*-**£25.00**.
Beds: 5D 2T 1S
Baths: 8 Private

Kingston

National Grid Ref: SX6347

The Dolphin

Torr House, *Kingston, Kingsbridge, Devon, TQ7 4PT.*
Georgian house in coastal village.
Open: All Year
01548 810723 Mr & Mrs Kies
Rates fr: *£16.00*-**£16.00**.
Beds: 2D 1T 1S **Baths:** 2 Shared
(2)

Trebles Cottage Hotel, *Kingston, Kingsbridge, Devon, TQ7 4PT.*
Converted 1801 country cottage.
Open: All Year
Grades: AA 4 Q, Select, RAC Acclaim
01548 810268 (also fax no)
Mr Kinder
Rates fr: *£25.00*-**£36.00**.
Beds: 3D 2T
Baths: 5 Private
(12) (12)

Kingswear

National Grid Ref: SX8851

Carlton House, *Higher Street, Kingswear, Dartmouth, Devon, TQ6 0AG.*
Magnificent views over Dartmouth Harbour.
Open: All Year
01803 752244
Mr & Mrs Congdon
Rates fr: *£14.00*-**£15.00**.
Beds: 2F 2D 1T 1S
Baths: 2 Shared

Knowstone

National Grid Ref: SS8223

Masons Arms

The Masons Arms Inn, *Knowstone, South Molton, Devon, EX36 4RY.*
Open: All Year (not Xmas)
01398 341231 / 341582 Mr & Mrs Todd
Rates fr: *£21.00*-**£21.00**.
Beds: 4D
Baths: 4 Ensuite
(12)
Classic early C17th thatched & cob inn. Picturesque village, Exmoor foothills. Quality home made food, charming bedrooms, real ales traditionally served. Garden with Exmoor view. Children & pets welcome.

The Old Chapel, *Knowstone, South Molton, Devon, EX36 4RY.*
Converted Methodist chapel, centrally heated.
Open: All Year (not Xmas)
01398 341404 Mrs Jones
Rates fr: *£15.00*-**£15.00**.
Beds: 1T 1S
Baths: 1 Shared
(8) (4)

Lapford

National Grid Ref: SS7308

Lower Bridge Farm, *Lapford, Crediton, Devon, EX17 6AE.*
C15th thatched farmhouse, working farm.
Open: All Year (not Xmas)
01363 83342 Mr & Mrs Squance
Rates fr: *£15.00*-**£15.00**.
Beds: 1F 1D
Baths: 1 Ensuite 1 Private
(0) (4)

Parsonage Farm, *Lapford, Crediton, Devon, EX17 6LX.*
Comfortable farmhouse on working farm.
Open: All Year
01363 83784 Mrs John
Rates fr: *£10.00*-**£12.00**.
Beds: 1F 1D
Baths: 1 Shared
(3)

Lewdown

National Grid Ref: SX4486

Ramplins Barn, *Middle Raddon Farm, Lewdown, Okehampton, Devon, EX20 4PW.*
Easily accessible comfortable working farmhouse.
Open: Easter to Oct
01566 783276
Mrs Meakin
Rates fr: *£14.00*-**£14.00**.
Beds: 1D 1T 1S
Baths: 1 Shared
(6)

Little Torrington

National Grid Ref: SS4916

Smytham Manor, *Little Torrington, Torrington, Devon, EX38 8PU.*
C17th manor house.
Open: Easter to Oct
01805 622110
Mrs Crowe
Rates fr: *£14.00*-**£14.00**.
Beds: 1F 3D 3T
Baths: 5 Private 1 Shared
(10)

Littlehempston

National Grid Ref: SX8162

Buckyette Farm, *Littlehempston, Totnes, Devon, TQ9 6ND.*
Victorian farm house in commanding position in Devon Valley.
Open: Mar to Oct
01803 762638
Mrs Miller
Rates fr: *£17.50*-**£17.50**.
Beds: 4F 1D 1T
Baths: 6 Ensuite
(8)

Loddiswell

National Grid Ref: SX7148

Riverleigh, *Topsham Bridge, Loddiswell, Kingsbridge, Devon, TQ7 4DR.*
C18th cottage with gardens & woodlands.
Open: Apr to Sept
01548 550372
Mrs Betts
Rates fr: *£15.00*-**£17.50**.
Beds: 1F 1T
Baths: 1 Ensuite 1 Shared
(1) (2)

Lustleigh

National Grid Ref: SX7881

Cleave Hotel

Lustleigh Mill, *Lustleigh, Newton Abbot, Devon, TQ13 9SS.*
Beautiful riverside C15th millhouse.
Open: All Year
Grades: ETB Listed
01647 277357 Mrs Rowe
Rates fr: *£18.50*-**£19.50**.
Beds: 3D
Baths: 1 Ensuite 2 Shared
(10) (4)

Lydford

National Grid Ref: SX5184

Castle Inn & Hotel, *Lydford, Okehampton, Devon, EX20 4BH.*
Romantic, award-winning mediaeval inn.
Open: All Year
Grades: ETB Listed, Comm
01822 820242 Mr Walker
Fax no: 01822 820454
Rates fr: *£21.25*-**£28.75**.
Beds: 1F 2T 4D 1S
Baths: 6 Ensuite 1 Shared
(12)

Lympstone

National Grid Ref: SX9984

Saddlers' Arms, Swan Inn

Gulliford Farm, *Lympstone, Exmouth, Devon, EX8 5AQ.*
Charming farmhouse. Large rooms. Garden.
Open: All Year
01392 873067 Mrs Hallett
Rates fr: *£18.00*-**£18.00**.
Beds: 1F 1T 1S
Baths: 1 Ensuite 1 Shared
(6)

Wotton Farm, *Lympstone, Exmouth, Devon, EX8 5AY.*
Old farmhouse, lovely gardens.
Open: All Year
01395 264401 Mrs Harding
Rates fr: *£16.00*-**£16.00**.
Beds: 1F 1D 1T
Baths: 1 Shared
(4)

Lynbridge

National Grid Ref: SS7248

Top of the World, *Lynbridge, Lynton, Devon, EX35 6BE.*
Character Victorian cottage on high ground.
Open: Feb to Oct
01598 753693 Mrs Champion
Rates fr: *£14.50*-**£17.00**.
Beds: 1D 1T
Baths: 1 Shared
(2)

Lynmouth

National Grid Ref: SS7249

Rising Sun Inn, Golden Hind Bistro, Staghunters Inn

Tregonwell Guest House, *1 Tors Road, Lynmouth, Devon, EX35 6ET.*
Open: All Year (not Xmas)
Grades: ETB 2 Cr, Approv
01598 753369
Mrs Parker
Rates fr: *£17.50*-**£17.50**.
Beds: 2F 3D 1T 1S
Baths: 3 Ensuite 3 Shared
(5)
Tranquil, romantic riverside guesthouse alongside waterfalls, cascades, enchanting harbour, England's highest clifftops, 'olde worlde' smugglers village. Nature lovers/walkers paradise. Pretty ensuite bedrooms, garaged parkings.

Glenville House, *2 Tors Road, Lynmouth, Devon, EX35 6ET.*
Charming, licensed riverside Victorian house.
Open: Mar to Nov
01598 752202
Mr & Mrs Francis
Rates fr: *£16.50*-**£16.50**.
Beds: 1F 4D 1T 1S
Baths: 3 Ensuite 1 Private 2 Shared
(7)

Ferndale House, *Watersmeet Road, Lynmouth, Devon, EX35 6EP.*
Large Victorian house (sea views).
Open: Easter to Nov
01598 753431
Mr Burns
Rates fr: *£16.50*-**£20.00**.
Beds: 1F 2D
Baths: 3 Ensuite
(5)

East Lyn House, *Lynmouth, Devon, EX35 6.*
Riverside location, four posters, home cooking.
Open: Mar to Nov
Grades: ETB 3 Cr, Comm, RAC High Acclaim
01598 752540 (also fax no)
Mrs Price
Rates fr: *£26.00*.
Beds: 6D 2T
Baths: 8 Ensuite
(8) (10)

Lynton

National Grid Ref: SS7149

Gable Lodge Hotel, *Lee Road, Lynton, Devon, EX35 6BS.*
Large Victorian Listed private house.
Open: All Year
01598 752367 (also fax no)
Mr Bowman
Rates fr: *£15.00*-**£15.00**.
Beds: 1F 5D 1T 1S
Baths: 6 Ensuite 1 Shared
(8)

The Denes Guest House, *Longmead, Lynton, Devon, EX35 6DQ.*
Quiet comfortable, friendly Victorian home.
Open: All Year (not Xmas)
01598 753573 Mr & Mrs Gay
Rates fr: *£16.00*-**£16.00**.
Beds: 3F 2D 2S
Baths: 2 Shared
(7)

Sylvia House Hotel, *Lydiate Lane, Lynton, Devon, EX35 6HE.*
Delightful Georgian house.
Open: Feb to Dec
Grades: ETB 3 Cr, Comm
01598 752391 Mr Channing
Rates fr: *£17.00*-**£15.00**.
Beds: 1F 5D 1T 1S
Baths: 6 Private 1 Shared

Castle Hill House Hotel, *Castle Hill, Lynton, Devon, EX35 6JA.*
Friendly family hotel, super views.
Open: All Year
Grades: ETB 3 Cr, Comm, AA 3 Q
01598 752291
Mr & Mrs Dodwell
Rates fr: *£19.00*-**£25.00**.
Beds: 2F 5D 2T
Baths: 9 Private
(0) (4)

Alford House Hotel, *3 Alford Terrace, Lynton, Devon, EX35 6AT.*
Elegant Georgian House. Spectacular views.
Open: Closed Mid Nov - Mid Feb Open Xmas & New Year
Grades: ETB 3 Cr, AA 4 Q
01598 752359
Rates fr: *£22.00*-**£22.00**.
Beds: 2T 6D
Baths: 8 Ensuite

Victoria Lodge, *Lee Road, Lynton, Devon, EX35 6BP.*
An elegant Victorian house.
Open: Feb to Dec
Grades: ETB 3 Cr, High Comm, AA 5 Q, Prem Select, RAC High Recomm
01598 753203
Freephone: 0500 30 30 26
Mr & Mrs Bennett
Fax no: 01598 753203
Rates fr: *£22.00*-**£25.00**.
Beds: 1F 7D 1T
Baths: 9 Private 1 Shared
(Any) (8)

National Grid References are for villages, towns and cities - *not* for individual houses.

Waterloo House Hotel, Lynton, Devon, EX35 6AJ.
Home cooking. Bargain breaks all year.
Open: All Year
Grades: ETB 3 Cr, AA 4 Q, Select, RAC High Acclaim
01598 753391 Mrs Mountis
Rates fr: *£18.50*-**£20.00**.
Beds: 2F 5D 3T 2S
(3)

Maidencombe

National Grid Ref: SX9268

Parkfield Hotel, Claddon Lane, Maidencombe, Torquay, Devon, TQ1 4TB.
Friendly, comfortable family-run hotel.
Open: Easter to Oct
01803 328952 Mrs Jones
Rates fr: *£12.50*-**£12.50**.
Beds: 4F 6D
Baths: 10 Private

Malborough

National Grid Ref: SX7039

Royal Oak, Old Inn, Lodge Hotel

Bolberry View, 5 Well Hill Close, Malborough, Kingsbridge, Devon, TQ7 3SS.
Lovely views, quiet, near Salcombe.
Open: All Year (not Xmas)
01548 560793 Mrs Hilditch
Rates fr: *£13.50*-**£15.00**.
Beds: 1D 1T
Baths: 1 Shared
(3) (2)

Higher Collaton House, Collaton, Malborough, Kingsbridge, Devon, TQ7 3D.
Idyllic, peaceful, relax in luxury.
Open: Easter to Mid Oct
01548 560826 Mrs Hernaiz
Rates fr: *£16.00*-**£15.00**.
Beds: 2D 1T 1S
Baths: 2 Ensuite 2 Private
(7) (4)

Martinhoe

National Grid Ref: SS6648

Mannacott Farm, Martinhoe, Parracombe, Barnstaple, Devon, EX31 4QS.
Bar meals obtainable nearby inn.
Open: Apr to Nov
01598 763227 Mrs Dallyn
Rates fr: *£13.00*-**£14.00**.
Beds: 1D 1T
Baths: 1 Shared
(2)

The lowest **single** *rate is shown in* **bold.**

Marwood

National Grid Ref: SS5437

Ring O' Bells

Lee House, Marwood, Barnstaple, Devon, EX31 4DZ.
Family-run Elizabethan manor house.
Open: Apr to Oct
01271 74345 Mrs Darling
Rates fr: *£16.00*-**£20.00**.
Beds: 1T
Baths: 2 Ensuite 1 Private
(12) (6)

The Old Rectory, Marwood, Barnstaple, Devon, EX31 4EB.
Friendly, elegantly furnished Georgian home.
Open: Easter to Sep
Grades: ETB Listed
01271 44433 Mrs Pover
Rates fr: *£19.00*-**£17.00**.
Beds: 2D 1T 2S
Baths: 2 Ensuite 1 Private 1 Shared
(12) (6)

Mary Tavy

National Grid Ref: SX5079

Mary Tavy Inn

Wringworthy Farm, Mary Tavy, Tavistock, Devon, PL19 9LT.
Open: Easter to Nov
Grades: AA 3 Q
01822 810434 (also fax no)
Mrs Anning
Rates fr: *£16.00*-**£16.00**.
Beds: 2D 1T
Baths: 2 Shared
(1) (4)
Elizabethan farmhouse, edge of Dartmoor, entrance on A386. Working beef/sheep. Retaining old features, spiral stairs, panelling with modern comforts. Quiet valley, ideal walking country.

Meavy

National Grid Ref: SX5467

Greenwell Farm, Meavy, Yelverton, Devon, PL20 6PY.
Period farmhouse on Dartmoor.
Open: All Year (not Xmas)
Grades: ETB 3 Cr, Comm, AA 3 Q
01822 853563 Mrs Cole
Rates fr: *£19.50*-**£23.00**.
Beds: 1F 1D 1T
Baths: 3 Ensuite 1 Private
(8)

Milton Combe

National Grid Ref: SX4865

Blowiscombe Barton, Milton Combe, Yelverton, Devon, PL20 6HR.
Modernised secluded farmhouse. Swimming pool.
Open: All Year (not Xmas)
Grades: ETB 3 Cr, Comm
01822 854853 Mrs Fisk
Rates fr: *£17.50*-**£22.00**.
Beds: 2D 1T
Baths: 3 Private
(6)

Modbury

National Grid Ref: SX6551

First & Last (Ermington), Mildmay Colours (Houberton)

Goutsford, Modbury, Ivybridge, South Devon, PL21 9NY.
Private cottage in peaceful woodland setting.
Open: All Year (not Xmas)
01548 830633 Mrs Ewen
Rates fr: *£17.00*-**£20.00**.
Beds: 1D 2T
Baths: 3 Private
(10) (4)

Monkleigh

National Grid Ref: SS4520

Petticombe Manor, Monkleigh, Bideford, Devon, EX39.
Large manor, 35 acres parkland.
Open: All Year
01237 475605 Mr Wilson
Rates fr: *£22.50*.
Beds: 1F 2D
Baths: 3 Shared

Horwood Barton, Monkleigh, Bideford, Devon, EX39 5LF.
Large, impressive country farmhouse.
Open: Easter to Nov
01805 623174 Mrs Beer
Rates fr: *£15.00*-**£16.00**.
Beds: 1F 1D 1S
Baths: 2 Private
(8)

Monkokehampton

National Grid Ref: SS5805

Seldon Farm, Monkokehampton, Winkleigh, Devon, EX19 8RX.
Peaceful C17th farmhouse.
Open: Easter to Nov
01837 810312 Mrs Case
Rates fr: *£15.00*-**£15.00**.
Beds: 1F 2D

Monkton

National Grid Ref: ST1600

Monkton Court Inn, Monkton, Honiton, Devon, EX14 9QH.
C17th former manor house.
Open: All Year
Grades: ETB 3 Cr, AA 2 St
01404 42309 Mrs Taylor
Rates fr: *£22.50*-**£27.50**.
Beds: 2F 4D 1T 1S
Baths: 6 Private 1 Shared
(80)

Morchard Bishop

National Grid Ref: SS7607

London Inn

Oldborough Fishing Retreat, *Morchard Bishop, Crediton, Devon,* *EX17 6JQ.*
Modern house by lakes/woods.
Open: All Year (not Xmas)
01363 877437 Mrs Wilshaw
Rates fr: *£16.00*-**£16.00**.
Beds: 1F 2T
Baths: 1 Shared
(10)

Wigham, *Morchard Bishop, Crediton, Devon,* *EX17 6RJ.*
C16th thatched longhouse, luxurious.
Open: All Year
01363 877350
Mr & Mrs Chilcott
Rates fr: *£25.50*-**£25.50**.
Beds: 1F 2D 2T
Baths: 5 Ensuite
(8) (5)

Moretonhampstead

National Grid Ref: SX7586

White Hart

Great Sloncombe Farm, *Moretonhampstead, Devon,* *TQ13 8QF.*
C13th Dartmoor farmhouse.
Open: All Year
Grades: ETB 3 Cr, High Comm, AA 4 Q, Select
01647 440595
Mrs Merchant
Rates fr: *£20.00*-**£20.00**.
Beds: 2D 1T
Baths: 3 Private 1 Shared
(8) (3)

Yarningale, *Exeter Road, Moretonhampstead, Newton Abbot, Devon,* *TQ13 8QA.*
Excellent accommodation, superb Dartmoor views.
Open: All Year
Grades: ETB 2 Cr
01647 440560 (also fax no)
Mrs Radcliffe
Rates fr: *£15.00*-**£15.00**.
Beds: 2F
Baths: 2 Ensuite
(3)

Mortehoe

National Grid Ref: SS4545

The Chichester

Harrold Lodge, *Chapel Hill, Mortehoe, Woolacombe, N. Devon,* *EX34 7EA.*
Stunning location. Short stroll beach/coastal path.
Open: All Year
01271 870036 Mrs Keenan
Rates fr: *£17.50*-**£25.00**.
Beds: 1D
Baths: 1 Private
(4)

Lundy House Hotel, *Chapel Hill, Mortehoe, Woolacombe, Devon,* *EX34 7RZ.*
Licensed hotel in peaceful location, overlooking secluded beach.
Open: Feb to Dec
Grades: ETB 3 Cr, Comm
01271 870372
Mr Cole
Fax no: 01271 871001
Rates fr: *£17.50*-**£17.50**.
Beds: 5F 2D 2S
Baths: 6 Private 1 Shared
(6) (10)

Muddiford

National Grid Ref: SS5638

Home Park Farm, *Lower Blakewell, Muddiford, Barnstaple, Devon,* *EX31 4ET.*
Paradise for the country garden lover.
Open: Easter to Nov
Grades: ETB 2 Cr, Comm, AA 4 Q, RAC Acclaim
01271 42955
Mrs Lethaby
Rates fr: *£17.50*-**£18.50**.
Beds: 1F 1D 1T
Baths: 3 Private
(3)

Newton Abbot

National Grid Ref: SX8671

Bulleigh Park Farm, *Ipplepen, Newton Abbot, Devon,* *TQ12 5UA.*
Beautiful farmhouse and surroundings.
Open: All Year
Grades: AA 3 Q
01803 872254
Mrs Dallyn
Rates fr: *£15.00*-**£18.00**.
Beds: 1F 1D 1S
Baths: 1 Ensuite 1 Private
(6)

Newton Ferrers

National Grid Ref: SX5448

Dolphin Inn, Swan Inn, Ship Inn, Bistro Ferrers

Crown Yealm, *Bridgend Hill, Newton Ferrers, Plymouth, Devon,* *PL8 1AW.*
Open: All Year
Grades: ETB Listed
01752 872365 (also fax no)
Mrs Johnson
Rates fr: *£16.00*-**£21.00**.
Beds: 1F 1D 1T
Baths: 1 Ensuite 1 Shared
(9)
Beautiful riverside country house. All guest rooms overlook garden to waters edge. Comfortable beds, good breakfasts, private off road parking. Between Dartmoor and South Devon Coast on River Yealm Estuary.

Melbury, *Church Park Road, Newton Ferrers, Plymouth, Devon,* *PL8 1AZ.*
South-facing comfortable bungalow.
Open: All Year
01752 872755
Mrs Hemming
Rates fr: *£15.00*-**£17.00**.
Beds: 2D 2T
Baths: 2 Ensuite 1 Shared

Maywood Cottage, *Bridgend, Newton Ferrers, Plymouth, Devon,* *PL8 1AW.*
Modernised cottage in estuary village.
Open: All Year
01752 872372
Mrs Cross
Rates fr: *£15.00*-**£17.00**.
Beds: 1F 2T
Baths: 1 Ensuite 1 Private
(2)

North Bovey

National Grid Ref: SX7383

Gatehouse, *North Bovey, Moretonhampstead, Devon,* *TQ13 8RB.*
Beautiful mediaeval Devon longhouse.
Open: All Year
Grades: AA 5 Q
01647 440479 Mrs Williams
Rates fr: *£24.00*-**£29.00**.
Beds: 3D
Baths: 3 Private
(3)

North Buckland

National Grid Ref: SS4836

Denham Farm Country House, *North Buckland, Braunton, Devon,* *EX33 1HY.*
Lovely farmhouse set amidst rolling hills and flower laden hedgerows.
Open: All Year (not Xmas)
Grades: ETB 3 Cr, Comm, AA 3 Q, RAC Acclaim
01271 890297 (also fax no)
Mrs Barnes
Rates fr: *£22.50*-**£27.50**.
Beds: 2F 6D 2T
Baths: 10 Private
(10)

North Molton

National Grid Ref: SS7329

Zeales, *East Street, North Molton, South Molton, Devon,* *EX36 3JQ.*
Spacious comfortable Exmoor village home.
Open: All Year (not Xmas)
01598 740356
Mr & Mrs Stratta
Rates fr: *£18.00*-**£18.00**.
Beds: 1D 2T **Baths:** 3 Ensuite
(12)

Crangs Heasleigh, *North Molton, South Molton, Devon,* EX36 3LE.
Comfortable accommodation. Convenient for Moors.
Open: All Year
01598 740268 Mrs Yendell
Rates fr: *£13.50*-**£13.50**.
Beds: 1F 1D 1T 1S
Baths: 1 Shared

North Tawton

National Grid Ref: SS6601

Higher Nichols Nymett, *North Tawton, Devon,* EX20 2BP.
Thatched C15th hall house.
Open: All Year (not Xmas)
01837 82181 Mrs Jordan
Rates fr: *£16.50*-**£16.50**.
Beds: 2D 1T **Baths:** 3 Ensuite

Oaklands Farm, *North Tawton, Devon,* EX20 4PZ.
Comfortable farmhouse, views, good cooking.
Open: All Year (not Xmas)
01837 82340 Mrs Headon
Rates fr: *£15.00*-**£15.00**.

Northleigh

National Grid Ref: SY1996

The Old Rectory, *Northleigh, Colyton, Axminster, Devon,* EX13 6BS.
Large early Victorian Gothic rectory. **Open:** All Year
01404 871300 Mrs Cohen
Rates fr: *£17.50*-**£17.50**.
Beds: 1D 1T
Baths: 1 Ensuite 1 Private

Northlew

National Grid Ref: SX5099

Crossroads (Folly Gate)

Lower Gorhuish Farm, *Northlew, Okehampton, Devon,* EX20 3BU.
Modern farmhouse, ideal for touring.
Open: All Year (not Xmas)
Grades: ETB 2 Cr
01837 810272 Mrs Bryan
Rates fr: *£17.50*-**£20.00**.
Beds: 1F 1D 1T **Baths:** 3 Private

Noss Mayo

National Grid Ref: SX5477

Swan Inn, Old Ship Inn

Higher Shippen, *Worswell Barton Fr., Noss Mayo, Plymouth, Devon,* PL8 1HB.
5 mins from coastal path.
Open: All Year
01752 872977 Mrs Rogers
Rates fr: *£16.50*.
Beds: 1D

Rowden House, *Stoke Road, Noss Mayo, Plymouth, Devon,* PL8 1JG.
Listed Victorian farmhouse.
Open: Apr to Oct
01752 872153 Mrs Hill
Rates fr: *£15.00*-**£17.50**.
Beds: 1F 1T **Baths:** 1 Private

Brookindale, *Noss Mayo, Plymouth, Devon,* PL8 1EN.
Heavenly little spot in countryside.
Open: All Year
01752 872665 Mrs Sherell
Rates fr: *£13.00*-**£13.00**.
Beds: 2D 1T

Oakford

National Grid Ref: SS9021

Masons Arms

Higher Western Restaurant, *Oakford, Tiverton, Devon,* EX16 9JE.
Licensed country restaurant, excellent food.
Open: All Year (not Xmas)
01398 341210 Mr & Mrs Cook
Rates fr: *£14.00*-**£16.00**.
Beds: 2D 1T **Baths:** 3 Ensuite

Newhouse Farm, *Oakford, Tiverton, Devon,* EX16 9JE.
Comfortable farmhouse, home-baked bread.
Open: All Year (not Xmas)
Grades: ETB 2 Cr, Comm, AA 4 Q
01398 351347 Mrs Boldry
Rates fr: *£16.00*-**£19.00**.
Beds: 2D 1T
Baths: 2 Ensuite 1 Private

Harton Farm, *Oakford, Tiverton, Devon,* EX16 9HH.
Country lovers welcome on our traditional, non-intensive farm near Exmoor.
Open: All Year (not Xmas)
Grades: ETB 1 Cr
01398 351209 Mrs Head
Rates fr: *£13.00*-**£13.00**.
Beds: 1F 1T **Baths:** 1 Shared

Okehampton

National Grid Ref: SX5895

Cellars Restaurant, Crossroads (Folly Gate)

Fairway Lodge Guest House, *Thorndon Cross, Okehampton, Devon,* EX20 4ND.
Open: All Year
Grades: AA 3 Q, Recomm
01837 52827 (also fax no)
Mrs Burgoine
Rates fr: *£19.50*-**£20.00**.
Beds: 1F 1D 1T **Baths:** 3 Ensuite
On the Northern slopes of Dartmoor a modern stone built farmhouse set on 10 acre organic smallholding with herd of ponies, golf and horse-riding nearby.

Heathfield House, *Okehampton, Devon,* EX20 1EW.
Open: All Year (not Xmas)
Grades: ETB 3 Cr, Comm
01837 54211 (also fax no)
Mrs Seigal
Rates fr: *£23.00*-**£25.00**.
Beds: 1F 2D 1T
Baths: 4 Private
Victorian stationmaster's house. Tucked away location. Small with the personal touch, safe car parking. Famed cuisine, wonderful conservatory and heated pool. Phone Jane: 01837 54211.

Lower Gorhuish Farm, *Northlew, Okehampton, Devon,* EX20 3BU.
Modern farmhouse, ideal for touring.
Open: All Year (not Xmas)
Grades: ETB 2 Cr
01837 810272
Mrs Bryan
Rates fr: *£17.50*-**£20.00**.
Beds: 1F 1D 1T
Baths: 3 Private

Otterton

National Grid Ref: SY0885

Kings Arms

Spinning Wheel Cottage, *Fore Street, Otterton, Budleigh Salterton, Devon,* EX9 7HB.
Traditional thatched village cottage.
Open: Easter to Sep
01395 568893
Rates fr: *£17.50*-**£17.50**.
Beds: 1F 1D 1T 1S
Baths: 1 Private 1 Shared

Ottery St Mary

National Grid Ref: SY1095

Hare & Hounds

The Otters, *1 Kings Avenue, Ottery St Mary, Devon,* EX11 1TA.
Quiet, friendly, comfortable accommodation.
Open: All Year (not Xmas)
01404 812108
Mrs Broadley
Rates fr: *£15.00*-**£15.00**.
Beds: 2D 1S
Baths: 1 Shared

Keepers Lodge, *Strete Raleigh, Whimple, Ottery St Mary, Devon,* EX5 2PS.
Delightful country home, beautiful views.
Open: All Year (not Xmas)
01404 822980
Mrs Rudham
Rates fr: *£12.50*-**£12.50**.
Beds: 1F 1D 1T 1S
Baths: 1 Shared

Paignton

National Grid Ref: SX8960

Talk of the Town, Inn on the Green

South Sands Hotel, *Alta Vista Road, Paignton, Devon, TQ4 6BZ.*
Open: Mar to Oct
Grades: ETB 3 Cr, Comm, AA 1 St
01803 557231 Mr Cahill
Fax no: 01803 529947
Rates fr: *£20.00*-**£20.00**.
Beds: 12F 3D 2T 2S
Baths: 19 Private
(18)
Licensed family-run hotel in peaceful location overlooking beach/park. Close harbour. Superb cuisine. Outstanding value for money. All rooms ensuite with televisions, telephones, teamakers.

Mandalay Hotel, *Cleveland Road, Paignton, Devon, TQ4 6EN.*
Comfortable family-run licensed hotel.
Open: All Year
Grades: ETB 2 Cr
01803 525653 Mr & Mrs Davis
Fax no: 01803 525196
Rates fr: *£16.00*-**£20.00**.
Beds: 2F 6D 2T
Baths: 5 Ensuite 2 Shared
(9)

Bruce Lodge Guest House, *2 Elmsleigh Road, Paignton, Devon, TQ4 5AU.*
A small, friendly guest house.
Open: Easter to Oct
Grades: ETB 1 Cr, Comm
01803 550972 Mrs Kingdon
Rates fr: *£14.00*-**£14.00**.
Beds: 2F 2D 1T 1S
Baths: 3 Shared
(5)

The Barbican, *5 Beach Road, Paignton, Devon, TQ4 6AY.*
Spacious, homely, family-run hotel.
Open: All Year
Grades: ETB Listed
01803 551332 Mr & Mrs Bunting
Rates fr: *£12.00*-**£15.00**.
Beds: 4F 3D 2T 1S
Baths: 2 Shared
(0)

Adelphi Hotel, *14 Queens Road, Paignton, Devon, TQ4 6AT.*
Large homely run hotel.
Open: All Year (not Xmas)
01803 558022 Mr Elnor
Rates fr: *£10.00*-**£10.00**.
Beds: 5F 3D 1T 2S
Baths: 5 Ensuite 2 Shared
(1)

Arden House Licensed Hotel, *10 Youngs Park Road, Paignton, Devon, TQ4 6BU.*
Homely, family-run, seaside hotel.
Open: Easter to Oct
01803 558443 (also fax no)
Mr Tyler
Rates fr: *£12.00*-**£12.00**.
Beds: 6F 2D 1T 1S
Baths: 2 Shared
(0) (6)

The Look Out Hotel, *Marine Parade, Paignton, Devon, TQ3 2NU.*
Friendly seafront hotel.
Open: Easter to Oct
01803 525638
Rates fr: *£15.00*-**£15.00**.
Beds: 1F 5D 2T 2S
Baths: 10 Ensuite
(4) (8)

Norbeck Guest House, *35 New Street, Paignton, Devon, TQ3 3HL.*
Large comfortable guest house.
Open: All Year
01803 558033
Mr & Mrs Edworthy
Rates fr: *£10.00*-**£10.00**.
Beds: 5F 1D 1T 1S
Baths: 2 Private 2 Shared

Sunnybank Private Hotel, *2 Cleveland Road, Paignton, Devon, TQ4 6EN.*
Modern, comfortable hotel.
Open: All Year
Grades: RAC Listed
01803 525540 (also fax no)
Mr Blount
Rates fr: *£13.00*-**£13.00**.
Beds: 4F 4D 1T 3S
Baths: 3 Private 2 Shared
(3) (8)

Peter Tavy

National Grid Ref: SX5177

Churchtown, *Peter Tavy, Tavistock, Devon, PL19 9NP.*
Large Victorian house, large garden.
Open: All Year (not Xmas)
01822 810477
Mrs Lane
Rates fr: *£13.00*-**£13.00**.
Beds: 2D 2S
Baths: 2 Ensuite 1 Shared
(10) (6)

Pilton

National Grid Ref: SS5534

Bradiford Cottage, *Halls Mill Lane, Pilton, Barnstaple, Devon, EX31 4DP.*
Open: All Year (not Xmas/New Year)
Grades: ETB 1 Cr, Comm
01271 45039 (also fax no)
Mrs Hare
Rates fr: *£15.00*-**£15.00**.
Beds: 1D 1T 1S
Baths: 1 Shared
(8) (4)
Family-run C17th cottage. Tranquil surroundings. Ideally placed for exploring Atlantic Coast, moors, South West Way/Tarka Trail. Outstanding welcome; lovely rooms, every home comfort.

Plymouth

National Grid Ref: SX4756

Sippers, Frog & Frigate, Waterfront, Walrus

Sea Breezes, *28 Grand Parade, West Hoe, Plymouth, Devon, PL1 3DJ.*
Open: All Year
01752 667205 Mr & Mrs Lake
Rates fr: *£15.00*-**£15.00**.
Beds: 3F 2D 2T 1S
Baths: 2 Ensuite 2 Private 2 Shared
A warm welcome assured in our elegant Victorian town-house on sea front. Theatres, shopping centre, historic Hoe and Barbican close by. Ideal touring centre for South-West Peninsula.

Morwenna Guest House, *112 North Road East, Plymouth, Devon, PL4 6AW.*
Friendly, family-run guest house.
Open: All Year
01752 663540
Mrs Jones
Rates fr: *£13.00*-**£13.50**.
Beds: 2F 2D 1T 2S
Baths: 2 Shared

Allington House, *6 St James Place East, The Hoe, Plymouth, Devon, PL1 3AS.*
Open: All Year
01752 221435
Mrs Budziak
Rates fr: *£15.00*-**£16.00**.
Beds: 4D 1T 1S
Baths: 3 Ensuite
(2)
Victorian town house in conservation area. Secluded square. On Plymouth Hoe close to historic Barbican and city centre. Comfortable rooms and an excellent English breakfast.

Rusty Anchor, *30 Grand Parade, West Hoe, Plymouth, Devon, PL1 3DJ.*
Seafront large Victorian property.
Open: All Year
01752 663924 (also fax no)
Ms Turner
Rates fr: *£12.50*-**£12.50**.
Beds: 4F 1D 2T 2S
Baths: 3 Ensuite 2 Private 2 Shared

The Elizabethan, *223 Citadel Road, The Hoe, Plymouth, Devon, PL1 2NG.*
Open: All Year
01752 661672
Rates fr: *£12.50*-**£18.00**.
Beds: 1F 4D 2T
Baths: 1 Ensuite 2 Shared
(3)
Small well-run family guest house adjacent to Plymouth's historic Barbican & Hoe, 600 yards from city centre, coach station & marina.

*Tountbatten Hotel, 52 Exmouth
oad, Stoke, Plymouth, Devon,
LA 4QH.*
pen: All Year
rades: ETB 2 Cr
1752 563843 Mr Hendy
ax no: 01752 606014
ates fr: *£16.00*-**£16.50**.
eds: 3F 6D 2T 4S
aths: 6 Ensuite 2 Shared
(4)
mall family-owned licensed hotel tuated in conservation area. Close city centre, ferry port with good ccess to Cornwall. Extensive enus. Garage/free street parking.

***he Dudley,** 42 Sutherland Road,
Iutley, Plymouth, Devon, PL4 6BN.*
mall comfortable family-run hotel
pen: All Year
rades: ETB 3 Cr, Comm,
A 3 Q, RAC Listed
1752 668322 Mr Folland
ates fr: *£14.00*-**£15.00**.
eds: 2F 3D 2S
aths: 5 Ensuite 1 Shared
(3)

***eviot Guest House,** 20 North
oad East, Plymouth, Devon,
L4 6AS.*
omfort, quality in Victorian wnhouse.
pen: All Year (not Xmas)
rades: ETB Listed, High Comm
1752 262656 Mrs Fisher
ates fr: *£16.00*-**£18.00**.
eds: 2F 2D 1T 1S
aths: 2 Ensuite 3 Private
Shared
(10) (2)

***rillium Guest House,** 4 Alfred
treet, The Hoe, Plymouth, Devon,
L1 2RP.*
omfortable, central Hoe,
arbican. **Open:** All Year
1752 670452 (also fax no)
Irs Cross
ates fr: *£17.00*-**£20.00**.
eds: 2F 1D 2T 2S
aths: 3 Private 1 Shared
(3)

***smond Guest House,** 42 Pier
treet, West Hoe, Plymouth,
evon, PL1 3BT.*
eafront Edwardian house.
Valking distance to all attractions.
pen: All Year (not Xmas)
rades: ETB 2 Cr, High Comm
1752 229705 Mrs Richards
ates fr: *£14.00*-**£15.00**.
eds: 1F 2D 2T 1S
aths: 2 Private 2 Shared
(2)

***unray Hotel,** 3/5 Alfred Street,
he Hoe, Plymouth, Devon, PL1 2RP.*
arge Victorian centrally located
otel. **Open:** All Year
1752 669113 Mr Sutton
ax no: 01752 268969
ates fr: *£16.50*-**£16.80**.
eds: 3F 10D 3T 3S
aths: 13 Ensuite
(6)

***Olivers Hotel & Restaurant,**
33 Sutherland Road, Plymouth,
Devon, PL4 6BN.*
Former Victorian merchant's house.
Open: All Year (not Xmas)
Grades: ETB 3 Cr, Comm,
RAC Listed
01752 663923 Mrs Purser
Rates fr: *£13.50*-**£14.50**.
Beds: 1F 2D 1T 2S
Baths: 4 Ensuite 1 Shared
(12) (2)

***The Churston,** 1 Apsley Road,
Plymouth, Devon, PL4 6PJ.*
Arrive guests. Depart friends.
Open: All Year (not Xmas)
01752 664850 Tiley
Rates fr: *£16.00*-**£16.00**.
Beds: 1F 2D 2T 3S
Baths: 2 Private 2 Shared

***Berkeleys Of St James,** 4 St James
Place East, The Hoe, Plymouth,
Devon, PL1 3AS.*
Large Victorian town house.
Open: All Year
Grades: ETB Listed
01752 221654 Mrs Coon
Rates fr: *£16.00*-**£16.00**.
Beds: 1F 1D 2T 1S
Baths: 3 Ensuite 1 Shared
(2)

Postbridge

National Grid Ref: SX6579

Old Inn, Warren Inn

***Hartyland,** Postbridge, Yelverton,
Devon, PL20 6SZ.*
Large, warm, comfortable
Dartmoor house.
Open: All Year (not Xmas)
01822 880210 Mr & Mrs Bishop
Rates fr: *£17.00*-**£17.00**.
Beds: 1F 2T 1S
Baths: 2 Shared
(4)

Poundsgate

National Grid Ref: SX7072

Tavistock Inn

***Lower Aish Guest House,**
Poundsgate, Ashburton, Newton
Abbot, Devon, TQ13 7NY.*
C17th house on Dartmoor.
Open: Easter to Oct
01364 631229 Mrs Wilkinson
Rates fr: *£15.00*-**£18.00**.
Beds: 1F 3D
(8)

***New Cott Farm,** Poundsgate,
Newton Abbot, Devon, TQ13 7PD.*
Working farm with modern bungalow.
Open: All Year
01364 631421 Mrs Phipps
Rates fr: *£17.00*-**£21.00**.
Beds: 1F 2D 1T
Baths: 4 Ensuite
(3) (4)

Ringmore

National Grid Ref: SX6545

Journeys End

***Cliff Path,** Ringmore, Kingsbridge,
Devon, TQ7 4HR.*
Bungalow on Coast Path link.
Open: All Year (not Xmas)
01548 810654 Mrs Brunskill
Rates fr: *£13.00*-**£13.00**.
Beds: 1T **Baths:** 1 Shared
(1)

Rockbeare

National Grid Ref: SY0294

Jack in the Green

***Lyndale,** London Road, Rockbeare,
Exeter, Devon, EX5 2PH.*
A personal friendly welcome
awaits.
Open: All Year
01404 822304 Mrs Granger
Rates fr: *£15.00*-**£16.00**.
Beds: 1F 1D 1T
(6)

Salcombe

National Grid Ref: SX7339

The Fortescue

***Widdecombe,** Herbert Road,
Salcombe, Devon, TQ8 8HN.*
Country style home, panoramic
views.
Open: All Year (not Xmas)
01548 842127 Mrs MacDonald
Rates fr: *£18.50*.
Beds: 1D 1T
Baths: 2 Ensuite
(10)

***Suncroft,** Fortescue Road,
Salcombe, Devon, TQ8 8AP.*
Spacious home, spectacular coastal
views.
Open: All Year (not Xmas)
01548 843975 Sherlock
Rates fr: *£20.00*-**£30.00**.
Beds: 3D
Baths: 1 Ensuite 1 Shared
(3)

***Lyndhurst Hotel,** Bonaventure
Road, Salcombe, Devon, TQ8 8BG.*
Edwardian harbour-master's
residence.
Open: Feb to Oct
Grades: ETB 3 Cr, Comm, AA 4
Q, Select, RAC High Acclaim
01548 842481 (also fax no)
Mr & Mrs Sharp
Rates fr: *£20.00*-**£20.00**.
Beds: 1F 3D 4T
Baths: 8 Private
(5) (4)

The lowest *double* rate per person is shown in *italics*.

***Dell House,** Dell Court, Onslow Road, Salcombe, Devon, TQ8 8BW.*
Large family home. 8 mins walk from town.
Open: Feb to Nov
01548 843215 Mrs Pritchard
Rates fr: *£12.50*-**£12.50**.
Beds: 1F 1D 1T 1S
Baths: 2 Shared
(3)

Sampford Peverell

National Grid Ref: ST0314
Globe Inn

***Challis,** 12 Lower Town, Sampford Peverell, Tiverton, Devon, EX16 7BJ.*
Superb accommodation, convenient to motorway.
Open: All Year (not Xmas)
01884 820620 Mrs Isaac
Rates fr: *£15.00*-**£15.00**.
Beds: 1D 1T 1S
Baths: 1 Ensuite 2 Shared
(6)

Sampford Spiney

National Grid Ref: SX5372
Walkhampton Inn

***Eggworthy Farm,** Sampford Spiney, Yelverton, Devon, PL20 6LJ.*
Relaxing Dartmoor farmhouse, quiet location.
Open: All Year
Grades: ETB 1 Cr, Comm
01822 852142 Mrs Landick
Rates fr: *£15.00*-**£16.00**.
Beds: 2D 1S
Baths: 1 Shared
(6)

Saunton

National Grid Ref: SS4537

***2 Linksview,** Saunton, Braunton, Devon, EX33.*
Very comfortable, homely welcome.
Open: All Year (not Xmas)
01271 812233 Mrs Dale
Rates fr: *£12.50*-**£12.50**.
Beds: 1F 1D 1T
Baths: 1 Shared

Scorriton

National Grid Ref: SX7068

***Scorriton Down Farm,** Scorriton, Buckfastleigh, Devon, TQ11 0JB.*
Dartmoor farmhouse with panoramic views.
Open: All Year (not Xmas)
01364 644236 Mrs Batt
Rates fr: *£15.00*-**£15.00**.
Beds: 1F 1D 1T
Baths: 1 Private
(6)

***Newcombe Farm,** Scorriton, Buckfastleigh, Devon, TQ11 0JE.*
Modern comfortable farmhouse.
Open: All Year (not Xmas)
01364 643734 Mr Pearse
Rates fr: *£18.00*-**£15.00**.
Beds: 1D 1T 1S
Baths: 2 Ensuite
(6)

Seaton

National Grid Ref: SY2490
Rosswi's, Harbour Inn, Ship Inn (Axmouth)

***The Kettle Restaurant,** 15 Fore Street, Seaton, Devon, EX12 2LE.*
Comfrotable, friendly and great food.
Open: All Year (not Xmas)
01297 20428 Mr Thomas
Rates fr: *£15.00*-**£18.00**.
Beds: 1F 1D 1T
Baths: 2 Ensuite

***Tors Guest House,** 55 Harbour Road, Seaton, Devon, EX12 2LX.*
Comfortable rooms. Excellent hearty breakfast.
Open: All Year (not Xmas)
01297 20531 Mrs Tawse
Rates fr: *£18.50*-**£18.50**.
Beds: 4D 2T 2S
Baths: 8 Ensuite
(6)

***The Harbour House,** 1 Trevelyan Road, Seaton, Devon, EX12 2NL.*
Spacious terraced house, harbour-side setting.
Open: All Year
01297 21797 Mr Sandbrook
Rates fr: *£15.00*-**£20.00**.
Beds: 1F 2D
Baths: 2 Shared
(1) (4)

***Eyre Court Hotel,** Queen Street, Seaton, Devon, EX12 2NY.*
Hotel, ideal for exploring.
Open: All Year (not Xmas)
01297 21455 Mr While
Fax no: 01297 625491
Rates fr: *£20.00*-**£25.00**.
Beds: 2F 5D 2T
Baths: 9 Private
(9)

***Mariners Hotel,** Esplanade, Seaton, Devon, EX12 2NP.*
Friendly comfortable hotel.
Open: All Year
01297 20560 Mr Christopher
Rates fr: *£19.00*-**£23.00**.
Beds: 1F 4D 4T 1S
Baths: 10 Private
(10)

Shaldon

National Grid Ref: SX9372

***Glenside Hotel,** Ringmore Road, Shaldon, Teignmouth, Devon, TQ14 0EP.*
Olde worlde waterside cottage hotel.
Open: All Year
01626 872448 Mr Underwood
Rates fr: *£18.00*-**£18.00**.
Beds: 1F 6D 3T
Baths: 8 Private 1 Shared
(5) (10)

Sherford

National Grid Ref: SX7744

***Sherford Down,** Sherford, Kingsbridge, Devon, TQ7 2BA.*
Beautiful Georgian house, working farm.
Open: Easter to Oct
01548 531208 Mrs Peters
Rates fr: *£18.50*-**£30.00**.
Beds: 1F 1D
Baths: 1 Ensuite 1 Private
(5) (6)

Shirwell

National Grid Ref: SS5937
Pyne Arms

***The Spinney Country Guest Hse,** Shirwell, Barnstaple, Devon, EX31 4JR.*
Comfortable, spacious, former Regency rectory.
Open: All Year
Grades: ETB 2 Cr, Comm
01271 850282 Mrs Pelling
Rates fr: *£15.50*-**£15.50**.
Beds: 1F 2D 1T 1S
Baths: 1 Private 2 Shared
(8)

***Waytown Farm,** Shirwell, Barnstaple, Devon, EX31 4JN.*
Comfortable C17th spacious farm-house.
Open: All Year (not Xmas)
Grades: ETB 2 Cr, Comm
01271 850396 Mrs Kingdon
Rates fr: *£16.00*-**£18.00**.
Beds: 1F 1D 1T 1S
Baths: 2 Private 1 Shared
(6)

Shobrooke

National Grid Ref: SS8600

***The Red Lion,** Shobrooke, Crediton, Devon, EX17 1AT.*
Friendly, comfortable, C17th village inn.
Open: All Year
01363 772340 Mr Raven
Rates fr: *£12.50*-**£20.00**.
Beds: 1F 3D
Baths: 1 Shared
(1) (20)

Sidbury

National Grid Ref: SY1391

***Bovetts Farm,** Roncombe Lane, Sidbury, Sidmouth, Devon, EX10 0QN.*
Idyllically set in peaceful valley, five miles from sea.
Open: All Year (not Xmas)
01395 597456 Mrs Hopkinson
Rates fr: *£18.00*-**£18.00**.
Beds: 2D 1T
Baths: 3 Ensuite
(10) (5)

Sidford

National Grid Ref: SY1390

The Blue Ball Inn, *Sidford, Sidmouth, Devon, EX10 9QL.*
C14th thatched inn.
Open: All Year
01395 514062 Mr Newton
Rates fr: *£18.00*-**£22.00**.
Beds: 3T

Sidmouth

National Grid Ref: SY1287

King's Arms, Blue Ball, Kings Arms (Otterton)

Barrington Villa Guest House, *Salcombe Road, Sidmouth, Devon, EX10 8PU.*
Open: Jan to Oct
Grades: ETB 2 Cr, Comm
01395 514252 Mr & Mrs Carr
Rates fr: *£13.00*-**£13.00**.
Beds: 1F 3D 1T 3S
Baths: 4 Private 1 Shared
(10)
A charming Regency Gothic Villa, set in beautiful gardens on the bank of the River Sid in the heart of glorious East Devon.

Canterbury Guest House, *Salcombe Road, Sidmouth, Devon, EX10 8PR.*
Charming detached Georgian guest house. **Open:** Mar to Nov
Grades: ETB 2 Cr, AA Listed, RAC Listed
01395 513373 Mr & Mrs Lever
Rates fr: *£17.00*-**£17.00**.
Beds: 3F 3D 2T
Baths: 7 Private 1 Shared
(6)

Cheriton Guest House, *Vicarage Road, Sidmouth, Devon, EX10 8UQ.*
Open: All Year
01395 513810 Mrs Lee
Rates fr: *£17.00*-**£17.00**.
Beds: 1F 6D 1T 2S
Baths: 10 Ensuite
(10)
Large town house. National Trust parkland at rear. Famous for fine cooking. Parking for all guests' cars. Secluded garden.

Enstone Guest House, *Lennox Avenue, Sidmouth, Devon, EX10 8TX.*
Delightful, quietly situated guest house.
Open: Easter to Sep
01395 514444 Mrs Osswald
Rates fr: *£14.00*.
Beds: 1F 3D 1T
Baths: 1 Shared
(3) (5)

Sidling Field, *105 Peaslands Road, Sidmouth, Devon, EX10 8XE.*
Large bungalow, outskirts of town.
Open: Jan to Nov
01395 513859 Mrs Shenfield
Rates fr: *£13.00*-**£15.50**.
Beds: 1D 1T **Baths:** 1 Shared
(8) (3)

Burnthouse Farm, *Sidmouth, Devon, EX10 0NL.*
Open: Easter to Sep
01395 568304 Mrs Hill
Rates fr: *£15.00*-**£15.00**.
Beds: 1F 1T 1S **Baths:** 1 Shared
(3)
Farmhouse Bed & Breakfast on a working farm, set in the beautiful Otter Valley, with plenty of good walks. A warm welcome awaits you.

Lower Pinn Farm, *Peak Hill, Sidmouth, Devon, EX10 0NN.*
Comfortable, spacious rooms. Substantial breakfast.
Open: All Year
Grades: ETB 2 Cr, Comm
01395 513733 Mrs Tancock
Rates fr: *£16.00*-**£16.00**.
Beds: 2D 1T
Baths: 2 Ensuite 1 Shared
(3)

Silverton

National Grid Ref: SS9502

Lamb Inn

New Park Farm, *Silverton, Exeter, Devon, EX5 4DH.*
Modern farmhouse - 'home from home'.
Open: All Year (not Xmas)
Grades: ETB Listed
01392 861182
Mrs Hawkins
Rates fr: *£15.00*-**£15.00**.
Beds: 3D 1S
Baths: 1 Shared
(2) (6)

Slapton

National Grid Ref: SX8245

Queens Arms, Tower Inn

Start House, Start, *Slapton, Kingsbridge, Devon, TQ7 2QD.*
Open: All Year (not Xmas)
Grades: ETB 2 Cr, Comm
01548 580254
Mrs Ashby
Rates fr: *£18.00*-**£17.00**.
Beds: 2D 1T 1S
Baths: 2 Private 1 Shared
(4)
Situated in quiet hamlet 1 mile from Slapton. Comfortable Georgian house overlooking beautiful valley. 2 acre attractive partly-terraced garden. Ideal for wildlife and walking.

Old Walls, *Slapton, Kingsbridge, Devon, TQ7 2QN.*
Listed C18th house.
Open: All Year (not Xmas)
01548 580516
Mrs Mercer
Rates fr: *£15.00*-**£15.00**.
Beds: 2D 1T 1S
Baths: 2 Shared

Smithincott

National Grid Ref: ST0611

Gaddon Leaze, *Smithincott, Uffculme, Cullompton, Devon, EX15 3DL.*
Welcoming Georgian family house, lovely garden.
Open: All Year (not Xmas)
01884 840267 Mr & Mrs Bancroft
Rates fr: *£18.00*-**£18.00**.
Beds: 1F 1D 1T **Baths:** 2 Private
(6) (4)

South Allington

National Grid Ref: SX7938

South Allington House, *Chivelstone, South Allington, Kingsbridge, Devon, TQ7 2NB.*
Set in four acres of mature gardens.
Open: All Year
01548 511272 Mrs Baker
Rates fr: *£17.00*-**£18.00**.
Beds: 2F 4D 3T 1S
Baths: 5 Private 5 Shared
(15)

South Milton

National Grid Ref: SX6942

Shute Farm, *South Milton, Kingsbridge, Devon, TQ7 3JL.*
C16th oak-beamed farmhouse.
Open: Mar to Oct
01548 560680 Mrs Luscombe
Rates fr: *£14.00*-**£16.00**.
Beds: 1F 2D
Baths: 2 Private 1 Shared
(6)

South Molton

National Grid Ref: SS7125

West Down, *Whitechapel, South Molton, Devon, EX36 3EQ.*
Quiet house in 30 acres.
Open: All Year
01769 550373 Mrs Savery
Rates fr: *£20.00*-**£20.00**.
Beds: 1F 2D 1T **Baths:** 4 Private
(10)

Starcross

National Grid Ref: SX9781

Anchor Inn, Ship Inn, Courtenay Arms

The Croft Guest House, *Cockwood Harbour,, Starcross, Exeter, Devon, EX6 8QY.*
Open: All Year (not Xmas)
Grades: ETB 2 Cr
01626 890282 Mr Stewart
Fax no: 01626 891768
Rates fr: *£15.50*-**£18.50**.
Beds: 2F 3D 4T 1S
Baths: 6 Ensuite 1 Shared
(14)
Set in an acre of secluded gardens, overlooking Cockwood Harbour and River Exe. 2 minutes walk to 2 of Devon's finest seafood/pub restaurants. Discount card available for our guests.

The Old Vicarage, *Starcross, Exeter, Devon, EX6 8PX.*
Character, comfort, charm. Ideal location. **Open:** All Year
Grades: ETB 2 Cr, Comm
01626 890206 Mr & Mrs Hayes
Rates fr: *£15.00*-**£19.00**.
Beds: 1F 2D 2T
Baths: 3 Ensuite 1 Shared
(5)

Sticklepath

National Grid Ref: SX6394

Rising Sun Inn, *Sticklepath, Okehampton, Devon, EX20 2PD.*
Friendly inn on Dartmoor.
Open: All Year (not Xmas)
Grades: ETB 1 Cr
01837 840215 Mr Manley
Rates fr: *£17.00*-**£17.00**.
Beds: 1D 1T 1S
(30)

Stoke

National Grid Ref: SS2324

The Bar

Homeleigh, *Stoke, Hartland, Bideford, Devon, EX39 6DU.*
Secluded dormer bungalow, warm welcome. **Open:** Mar to Oct
01237 441465 Mrs Slee
Rates fr: *£14.50*-**£15.00**.
Beds: 1D 1T **Baths:** 1 Shared
(10) (2)

Stoke Fleming

National Grid Ref: SX8648

Green Dragon, Endsleigh Hotel, Flemings

Southfield House, *Stoke Fleming, Dartmouth, Devon, TQ6 0NR.*
Open: All Year (not Xmas)
01803 770359 Mrs Nixon
Rates fr: *£16.00*-**£20.00**.
Beds: 1D 2T
Baths: 2 Ensuite 1 Private
(3)
A very warm welcome in elegant Georgian house. Central but peaceful coastal village. Walk to pubs, restaurants, church, beautiful Blackpool Sands Beach. 10 minutes drive from Dartmouth.

Stokenham

National Grid Ref: SX8042

Trademan's Arms, Church House Inn, Globe Inn

Woodland View, *Kiln Lane, Stokenham, Kingsbridge, Devon, TQ7 2SQ.*
Modern comfortable, quiet guest house. **Open:** Easter to end-Sept
Grades: ETB 2 Cr, Comm
01548 580542 Mrs Cadman
Rates fr: *£15.15*-**£16.50**.
Beds: 2D 2T 1S
Baths: 2 Ensuite 2 Private
(0) (8)

Stowford

National Grid Ref: SX4386

Stowford House Hotel, *Stowford, Lewdown, Okehampton, Devon, EX20 4BZ.*
Open: Mar to Nov
01566 783415 Mr & Mrs Irwin
Rates fr: *£22.00*-**£22.00**.
Beds: 3D 2T 1S
Baths: 4 Ensuite 1 Shared
(6)
Charming former rectory in peaceful gardens. Beautifully appointed guest rooms. Outstanding good food. Everything is home cooked from fresh ingredients.

Tavistock

National Grid Ref: SX4874

Cornish Arms, Carpenters Arms, Ordulph Arms

Westward, *15 Plymouth Road, Tavistock, Devon, PL19 8AU.*
Open: All Year (not Xmas)
Grades: ETB 2 Cr, Comm
01822 612094 Ms Parkin
Rates fr: *£13.00*-**£13.00**.
Beds: 1F 1D 1S
Baths: 1 Ensuite 1 Shared
(3)
Listed Victorian house. Alongside river walks and park. In centre of small historic town with charm and character. Ideally situated for touring nearby moors and coast.

Eko Brae, *4 Bedford Villas, Springhill, Tavistock, Devon, PL19 8LA.*
Georgian villa overlooking Tavistock.
Open: All Year (not Xmas)
Grades: ETB 2 Cr, Comm
01822 614028 Mrs Rodgers
Rates fr: *£19.00*-**£16.00**.
Beds: 3F 1D 1S
Baths: 3 Ensuite 2 Shared
(6)

Hele Farm, *Tavistock, Devon, PL19 8PA.*
Open: Easter to Nov
Grades: ETB 2 Cr
01822 833084 Mrs Steer
Rates fr: *£16.00*-**£20.00**.
Beds: 2D **Baths:** 2 Private
(4)
Welcome cup of tea in architecturally Listed 1780 farmhouse. Dartmoor within 10 minutes and many National Trust properties. Good facilities with old features retained.

April Cottage, *Mount Tavy Road, Vigo Bridge, Tavistock, Devon, PL19 9JB.*
Riverside character cottage, 150m town.
Open: All Year (not Xmas)
Grades: ETB 2 Cr, High Comm
01822 613280 Mrs Bacon
Rates fr: *£15.00*-**£18.00**.
Beds: 2D 1T **Baths:** 3 Ensuite
(1) (4)

Teignmouth

National Grid Ref: SX9473

Trade Winds

Seafield Guest House, *21 Higher Brimley Road, Teignmouth, Devon, TQ14 8JS.*
Open: All Year
01626 773550 Mrs Field
Rates fr: *£12.00*-**£12.00**.
Beds: 2F 3D 1T 2S
Baths: 5 Ensuite 2 Private 2 Shared
(1.5) (4)
Warm welcome with full facilities, ensuites, televisions, seaviews. Conveniently placed, very attractive sun terrace. Private car park. Access all times, own keys. Open all year.

Leicester House, *2 Winterbourne Road, Teignmouth, Devon, TQ14 8JT.*
Imposing Edwardian non-smoking town house.
Open: Easter to Sep
Grades: ETB Listed
01626 773043 Mrs Pickup
Rates fr: *£12.00*.
Beds: 1F 3D 2T
Baths: 3 Private 1 Shared
(3)

Beachley Guest House, *3 Brunswick Street, Teignmouth, Devon, TQ14 8AE.*
Ideal for touring coast.
Open: All Year (not Xmas)
Grades: ETB Listed
01626 774249
Rates fr: *£14.00*-**£14.00**.
Beds: 3F 2D 1T 1S
Baths: 3 Shared

Thelbridge

National Grid Ref: SS7911

Thelbridge Cross Inn

Marchweeke Farm, *Thelbridge, Witheridge, Crediton, Devon, EX16 8NY.*
Old modernised farmhouse. Good food. **Open:** April to Nov
Grades: ETB 2 Cr, Comm, AA 4 Q, Select
01884 860418 Ms Webber
Rates fr: *£16.00*-**£16.00**.
Beds: 1D 1T
Baths: 1 Ensuite 1 Private
(10) (2)

Hele Barton, *Thelbridge Cross, Thelbridge, Black Dog, Crediton, Devon, EX17 4QJ.*
Lovely thatched farmhouse, many recommendations.
Open: All Year (not Xmas)
Grades: ETB 2 Cr, Comm, AA 3 Q
01884 860278 Mrs Gillbard
Rates fr: *£15.00*-**£16.00**.
Beds: 1F 1D 1T
Baths: 1 Ensuite 1 Shared
(6)

The lowest **single** *rate is shown in* **bold.**

Thorndon Cross

National Grid Ref: SX5393

Crossways Inn (Folly Gate), Cellars Restaurant (Okehampton)

Fairway Lodge Guest House, *Thorndon Cross, Okehampton, Devon, EX20 4ND.*
On the Northern slopes of Dartmoor.
Open: All Year
Grades: AA 3 Q, Recomm
01837 52827 (also fax no)
Mrs Burgoine
Rates fr: *£19.50*-**£20.00**.
Beds: 1F 1D 1T
Baths: 3 Ensuite
(8)

Tipton St John

National Grid Ref: SY0991

Golden Lion

Higher Coombe Farm, *Tipton St John, Sidmouth, Devon, EX10 0AX.*
Edwardian farmhouse, sheep & beef farm.
Open: All Year (not Xmas)
Grades: ETB 1 Cr, Comm
01404 813385
Mrs Farmer
Rates fr: *£19.00*-**£19.00**.
Beds: 1F 2D 1S
Baths: 1 Shared
(3)

Tiverton

National Grid Ref: SS9512

Sea Horse (Bampton)

Little Holwell, *Collipriest, Tiverton, Devon, EX16 4PT.*
Open: All Year (not Xmas)
01884 257590 (also fax no)
Mrs Hill-King
Rates fr: *£16.00*-**£16.00**.
Beds: 1F 2D
Baths: 1 Ensuite 1 Shared
(6)
A warm welcome awaits you in our home, set in rolling hills in the beautiful Exe Valley, 1.5 miles south of Tiverton.

Bridge Guest House, *23 Angel Hill, Tiverton, Devon, EX16 6PE.*
Imposing Victorian riverside town house.
Open: All Year
Grades: ETB 3 Cr, Comm, AA 3 Q, Recomm, RAC Acclaim
01884 252804
Ms Coxall
Rates fr: *£17.50*-**£18.50**.
Beds: 2F 2D 1T 4S
Baths: 5 Ensuite 2 Shared
(6)

Angel Guest House, *13 St Peter Street, Tiverton, Devon, EX16 6NU.*
Comfortable licensed Georgian guesthouse.
Open: All Year
Grades: ETB 2 Cr
01884 253392
Mr & Mrs Evans
Rates fr: *£14.50*-**£14.50**.
Beds: 2F 3D 1T 1S
Baths: 2 Private 2 Shared
(4)

Landrake Farm, *Chevithorne, Tiverton, Devon, EX16 7QN.*
Ideal for breaking journey south.
Open: Mar to Oct
Grades: ETB Listed
01398 331221 Mrs Kerslake
Rates fr: *£15.00*-**£15.00**.
Beds: 1F 1D 1T
Baths: 1 Shared
(4)

Torquay

National Grid Ref: SX9165

Old Coach House Inn, Marina Restaurant, Bay Tree Bistro, Churchills, Farmhouse Tavern

Shirley Hotel, *Braddons Hill Road East, Torquay, Devon, TQ1 1HF.*
Open: All Year
Grades: ETB 3 Cr, RAC Acclaim
01803 293016
Mrs Stephens
Rates fr: *£16.00*-**£16.00**.
Beds: 2F 9D 1T 2S
Baths: 11 Private 1 Shared
(5) (4)
Elegant, detached, licensed Victorian hotel. Quiet location yet close to harbour, shops, restaurants, theatres. Enjoy the relaxing sauna, jacuzzi & outdoor heated swimming pool.

Clovelly Guest House, *91 Avenue Road, Torquay, Devon, TQ2 5LH.*
Good food & choice of menu.
Open: All Year
Grades: ETB 1 Cr, AA 2 Q
01803 292286
Mr & Mrs Ledward
Rates fr: *£12.00*-**£12.00**.
Beds: 2F 2D 1T 2S
Baths: 1 Ensuite 1 Private 1 Shared
(4)

Mount Edgcombe Hotel, *23 Avenue Road, Torquay, Devon, TQ2 5LB.*
Open: Mar to Dec
Grades: ETB 3 Cr
01803 292310 Mr Ford
Rates fr: *£13.50*-**£16.00**.
Beds: 4F 5D 1T
Baths: 10 Ensuite
(12)
Friendly, family-run licensed hotel with well-equipped rooms for your comfort. Level walk to the sea front, conference/leisure centre & Abbey gardens. Discounts available for senior citizens & children.

Athina, *8 Vansittart Road, Torquay, Devon, TQ2 5BT.*
Open: Easter to Oct
01803 297547
Mrs Smith
Rates fr: *£10.00*.
Beds: 2D 1T
Baths: 1 Shared
(4)
Friendly welcome awaits you at Athina. In residential area, approx 800 yards from sea front, Riviera Centre and all amenities. Finest food, private parking, highly recommended.

Beauly Guest House, *503 Babbacombe Road, Torquay, Devon, TQ1 1HL.*
Warm hospitality, offering quality, value.
Open: All Year
Grades: ETB 1 Cr, Comm, AA 2 Q, Recomm
01803 296993 (also fax no)
Mrs Farrell
Rates fr: *£16.00*-**£18.00**.
Beds: 2F 1D 2T 1S
Baths: 6 Ensuite

Hotel Blue Conifer, *Higher Downs Road, Babbacombe, Torquay, Devon, TQ1 3LD.*
Open: Easter to Oct
01803 327637
Mr Ingram
Rates fr: *£19.00*-**£25.00**.
Beds: 3F 3D 1T
Baths: 7 Private
(5) (10)
Small friendly hotel recommended by Torquay Hotels Association. Quietly situated on Babbacombe seafront yet close to all amenities. Lovely coastal walks. Phone for colour brochure.

Garway Lodge, *79 Avenue Road, Torquay, Devon, TQ2 5LL.*
Comfortable friendly guest house.
Open: All Year
01803 293126
Mr Robinson
Rates fr: *£10.00*-**£10.00**.
Beds: 2F 4D 1T 1S
Baths: 5 Private 3 Shared
(7)

Hantwell Guest House, *487 Babbacombe Road, Torquay, Devon, TQ1 1HL.*
Open: All Year
01803 293990
Mrs Williams
Rates fr: *£12.00*-**£12.00**.
Beds: 3F 1S
Baths: 1 Ensuite 1 Shared
Torquay Hotels Association Inspected. Homely, friendly, Victorian guest house. Tastefully decorated & furnished, 700 yards from harbour, rooms colour TV, tea/coffee, families, groups welcome. Open all year. No VAT. Some ensuite.

Palm Tree House, *93 Avenue Road, Torquay, Devon, TQ2 5LH.*
Comfortable family guest house.
Open: All Year (not Xmas)
01803 299141 Ms Barnett
Rates fr: *£13.00*-**£13.00**.
Beds: 2F 3D 1T **Baths:** 1 Shared
(3) (3)

Cranborne Hotel, *58 Belgrave Road, Torquay, Devon, TQ2 5HY.*
Comfortable, friendly family-run hotel.
Open: All Year (not Xmas)
Grades: ETB 3 Cr, Comm, AA 3 Q, RAC Acclaim
01803 298046 (also fax no)
Mrs Dawkins
Rates fr: *£16.00*-**£16.00**.
Beds: 6F 4D 1T 1S
Baths: 11 Private 1 Shared
(3)

Beau Vista, *14 Ash Hill Road, Torquay, Devon, TQ1 3HZ.*
Close to all amenities. Sea views.
Open: All Year (not Xmas)
Grades: ETB 1 Cr, Approv
01803 297202 Mrs Wiggins
Rates fr: *£12.00*-**£18.00**.
Beds: 4F
Baths: 3 Private 1 Shared
(4)

Hotel Fiesta, *St Marychurch Road, Torquay, Devon, TQ1 3JE.*
Georgian hotel in spacious grounds.
Open: All Year (not Xmas)
01803 292388 Mr James
Rates fr: *£14.00*-**£14.00**.
Beds: 3F 4D 1T 1S
Baths: 6 Private 3 Shared
(10)

Sunleigh Hotel, *Livermead Hill, Torquay, Devon, TQ2 6QY.*
Family hotel overlooking sea.
Open: Easter to Oct
Grades: ETB 3 Cr, AA 1 St, RAC 1 St
01803 607137 Mr & Mrs Smith
Rates fr: *£17.00*-**£17.00**.
Beds: 3F 11D 4T 2S
Baths: 20 Ensuite
(14)

Craig Court Hotel, *10 Ash Hill Road, Torquay, Devon, TQ1 3HZ.*
Detached villa, quiet position. Detached Hotel, wellcoming, service excellent.
Open: All year
Grades: ETB 2 Cr, Comm, AA 3 Q, Listed
01803 294400 Mrs Box
Rates fr: *£16.50*-**£16.50**.
Beds: 2F 4D 2T 2S
Baths: 5 Private 3 Shared
(0) (6)

Hotel Fluela, *15-17 Hatfield Road, Torquay, Devon, TQ1 3BW.*
Award winning, family-run hotel.
Open: All Year
Grades: ETB 3 Cr, AA 1 St, RAC 1 St
01803 297512 Mrs Jarvis
Fax no: 01803 296261
Rates fr: *£16.50*-**£16.50**.
Beds: 3F 9D 1T
Baths: 1 Shared
(20)

Maple Lodge, *36 Ash Hill Road, Torquay, Devon, TQ1 3JD.*
Detached lodge with lovely views.
Open: Easter to Oct
Grades: ETB 2 Cr, Comm
01803 297391 Mrs Bridges
Rates fr: *£15.00*-**£15.00**.
Beds: 2F 3D 1T 1S
Baths: 5 Ensuite 1 Private
(5)

Torrington

National Grid Ref: SS4919

Tarka Country Guest House, *6 Halsdon Terrace, Torrington, Devon, EX38 8DY.*
Comfortable, friendly B&B.
Open: All Year
01805 622948 Mrs Wye
Rates fr: *£17.00*-**£17.50**.
Beds: 1F 3D 1T **Baths:** 4 Ensuite

Totnes

National Grid Ref: SX8060

Church House Inn, Kingsbridge Inn

2 Antrim Terrace, *Totnes, Devon, TQ9 5QA.*
Elegant Edwardian house overlooking castle.
Open: All Year (not Xmas)
01803 862638 Mrs Allen
Rates fr: *£16.00*-**£16.00**.
Beds: 1D 1T 2S
Baths: 1 Ensuite 2 Shared

Great Court Farm, *Weston Lane, Totnes, Devon, TQ9 6LB.*
Victorian farmhouse, spacious comfortable rooms.
Open: All Year
Grades: ETB Listed, High Comm
01803 862326 Mrs Hooper
Rates fr: *£15.00*-**£17.00**.
Beds: 1F 1D 1T **Baths:** 2 Shared
(3)

Lower Blakemore Farm, HR. *Plymouth Road, Totnes, Devon, TQ9 6DN.*
Comfortable farmhouse on working farm.
Open: All Year
Grades: ETB 2 Cr
01803 863718 Mrs Anning
Rates fr: *£14.00*-**£14.00**.
Beds: 1F 1T
Baths: 2 Ensuite
(6)

Royal Seven Stars Hotel, *The Plains, Totnes, Devon, TQ9 5DD.*
Former coaching inn, c.1660.
Open: All Year
Grades: ETB 3 Cr, AA 2 St, RAC 2 St
01803 862125 Mr Stone
Rates fr: *£27.00*-**£40.00**.
Beds: 2F 12D 3T 1S
Baths: 12 Private 3 Shared
(20)

Trinity

National Grid Ref: ST0207

Wishay, *Trinity, Cullompton, Devon, EX15 1PE.*
Spacious, comfortable farmhouse.
Open: Easter to Oct
01884 33223 Mrs Baker
Rates fr: *£14.00*-**£14.00**.
Beds: 1F 1D
Baths: 1 Ensuite 1 Private
(2)

Turnchapel

National Grid Ref: SX4952

Boringdon Arms, *Boringdon Terrace, Turnchapel, Plymouth, Devon, PL9 9TQ.*
Award-winning real ale pub.
Open: All Year
Grades: ETB Listed
01752 402053 Mrs Rayne
Rates fr: *£14.00*-**£20.00**.
Beds: 2F 2D 2T
Baths: 1 Ensuite 1 Shared

Two Bridges

National Grid Ref: SX6075

Two Bridges Hotel, *Two Bridges, Princetown, Yelverton, Devon, PL20 6SW.*
C18th riverside Dartmoor inn.
Open: All Year
01822 890581 Mrs Frazer
Rates fr: *£21.25*-**£24.50**.
Beds: 3F 14D 7T 1S
Baths: 23 Private 2 Shared
(10)

Tytherleigh

National Grid Ref: ST3103

Higher Courtfield House, *Tytherleigh, Axminster, Devon, EX13 7BG.*
Outstanding views, sea close by.
Open: All Year
01460 220709 Mrs Bedford
Rates fr: *£17.50*-**£17.00**.
Beds: 2D 1T
Baths: 1 Private 1 Shared
(3)

All details shown are as supplied by B&B owners in Autumn 1996.

Ugborough

National Grid Ref: SX6356

Hillhead Farm, *Ugborough, Ivybridge, Devon, PL21 0HQ.*
Comfortable family home, working farm.
Open: All Year (not Xmas)
Grades: ETB 1 Cr, Comm
01752 892674 Mrs Johns
Rates fr: *£17.00*-**£17.00**.
Beds: 2D 1T **Baths:** 1 Shared
(5)

Venn Farm, *Ugborough, Ivybridge, Devon, PL21 0PE.*
Situated amidst peaceful rural surroundings.
Open: Jan to Nov
Grades: ETB 2 Cr, Comm
01364 73240 Mr Stephens
Rates fr: *£19.00*-**£19.00**.
Beds: 2F 2T
Baths: 3 Ensuite 1 Shared
(5) (6)

Uplyme

National Grid Ref: SY3293

Pilot Boat

Hill Barn, *Gore Lane, Uplyme, Lyme Regis, Dorset, DT7 3RJ.*
Beautifully converted stone barn.
Open: All Year (not Xmas)
01297 445185 Mrs Wyon-Brown
Rates fr: *£16.00*-**£16.00**.
Beds: 1F 1D 1T
Baths: 2 Shared

Venton

National Grid Ref: SX5956

New Country Inn (Smithaleigh)

Flora House, *Venton, Sparkwell, Plymouth, PL7 5DR.*
Open: All Year (not Xmas)
01752 837239 Mrs Laid
Rates fr: *£13.00*-**£13.00**.
Beds: 1D 1T
Baths: 1 Shared
(2)
Warm welcome, quiet hamlet south of Dartmoor with beautiful views. Meals prepared with home produce when available. Early morning tea & evening drink included.

Right on the border? Look at the neighbouring county, too

Washbourne

National Grid Ref: SX7954

Penny Rowden, *Washbourne, Dartmouth, Totnes, Devon, TQ9 7DN.*
Open: All Year (not Xmas)
Grades: ETB 2 Cr
01803 712485 (also fax no)
Mrs Parsons
Rates fr: *£17.00*-**£18.00**.
Beds: 1F 1D 1T 1S
Baths: 4 Ensuite
(10)
Beautiful, secluded property peacefully located in a tranquil valley 'twixt Dartmouth and Totnes. Friendly relaxing atmosphere. All rooms ensuite. E/M optional. Brochure available.

Newhouse Farm, *Washbourne, Totnes, Devon, TQ9 7UD.*
Secluded, peaceful, superb setting, welcoming.
Open: All Year
01803 732546 Mrs Todd
Rates fr: *£13.50*-**£15.00**.
Beds: 1D 1T
(10) (4)

Washford Pyne

National Grid Ref: SS8111

Cobscombe Farm, *Washford Pyne, Black Dog, Crediton, Devon, EX17 4QJ.*
Chris and Merv welcome you to their lovely home, on a working farm. Set in a very picturesque area - central Devon good touring base.
Open: Easter to Oct
01884 860075 Mrs Ayre
Rates fr: *£15.00*-**£15.00**.
Beds: 1F 1D 1T 1S
(1) (6)

Weare Giffard

National Grid Ref: SS4721

Bracken Haven, *Weare Giffard, Bideford, Devon, EX39 4QR.*
Spacious bungalow, overlooking scenic valley.
Open: May to Oct
01237 472918 Mrs Curtis
Rates fr: *£11.00*-**£11.50**.
Beds: 2D 1S
Baths: 1 Ensuite
(3)

Welcombe

National Grid Ref: SS2218

Old Smithy Inn, *Welcombe, Bideford, Devon, EX39 6HG.*
C13th thatched country inn.
Open: All Year
01288 331305
Mr Marshall
Rates fr: *£17.50*-**£20.00**.
Beds: 2F 1D 1T 1S
Baths: 1 Ensuite 2 Shared
(50)

Wembury

National Grid Ref: SX5248

Odd Wheel

Willowhayes, Near Post Office, *Ford Road, Wembury, Plymouth, Devon, PL9 0JA.*
Comfortable house, sea/country views. **Open:** All Year (not Xmas)
01752 862581 Mrs Mills
Rates fr: *£12.50*-**£12.50**.
Beds: 1F 2D 1T
Baths: 1 Ensuite 1 Shared
(4)

Bay Cottage, *150 Church Road, Wembury, Plymouth, Devon, PL9 0HR.*
Victorian cottage by the sea.
Open: All Year (not Xmas)
01752 862559 (also fax no)
Mrs Farrington
Rates fr: *£22.00*-**£22.00**.
Beds: 2D 1T
Baths: 3 Private 1 Shared
(2)

Wembworthy

National Grid Ref: SS6609

Bankland Farm, *Wembworthy, Chulmleigh, Devon, EX18 7SN.*
Dairy farm in beautiful countryside. **Open:** May to Sep
01837 82343 Mrs Bragg
Rates fr: *£15.00*-**£20.00**.
Beds: 1F 1D **Baths:** 1 Shared
(2)

West Anstey

National Grid Ref: SS8426

The Old Vicarage, *West Anstey, South Molton, Devon, EX36 3PE.*
Manor house, peaceful, all comforts. **Open:** All Year
01398 341529 Mr & Mrs Moss
Rates fr: *£18.00*-**£15.00**.
Beds: 1D 4S
Baths: 1 Ensuite 2 Shared
(7)

Lands Farm, *West Anstey, South Molton, Devon, EX36 3PD.*
Comfortable farmhouse.
Open: All Year
01398 341309 Mrs Maude
Rates fr: *£12.50*-**£12.50**.
Beds: 2D

West Buckland

National Grid Ref: SS6531

Huxtable Farm, *West Buckland, Barnstaple, Devon, EX32 0SR.*
Mediaeval longhouse, farm walks & wildlife.
Open: All Year (not Xmas)
Grades: ETB 3 Cr, Comm
01598 760254 (also fax no)
Mrs Payne
Rates fr: *£22.00*-**£23.00**.
Beds: 2F 3D 1T
Baths: 5 Ensuite 1 Private
(0)

West Charleton

National Grid Ref: SX7542

Ashburton Arms, Globe Inn (Frogmore)

***West Charleton Grange,** West Charleton, Kingsbridge, Devon, TQ7 2AD.*
Open: Feb to Oct
01548 531779 Mr & Mrs Fowles
Fax no: 01548 531100
Rates fr: *£19.00*-**£24.00**.
Beds: 1D 2T
Baths: 2 Ensuite 1 Private
(10) (14)
Old rectory, in 11 acre secluded valley. Wild life lake. Approached down 0.25 mile private drive. 30ft indoor heated pool. Gamesroom. Large guest breakfast room/lounge.

Westward Ho!

National Grid Ref: SS4329

Elizabethan

***Brockenhurst,** 11 Atlantic Way, Westward Ho!, Bideford, Devon, EX39 1NX.*
Warm, clean, comfortable, detached house.
Open: All Year (not Xmas)
Grades: ETB 2 Cr, Comm
01237 423346 Mrs Snowball
Rates fr: *£19.50*-**£24.00**.
Beds: 2D 1T
Baths: 3 Ensuite
(4)

***Buckleigh Lodge,** 135 Bay View Road, Westward Ho!, Bideford, Devon, EX39 1BJ.*
Large Victorian house, sea views.
Open: All Year (not Xmas)
01237 475988 Mr & Mrs Kivell
Rates fr: *£18.00*-**£18.00**.
Beds: 1F 2D 2T 1S
Baths: 6 Ensuite
(7)

***72 Atlantic Way,** Westward Ho!, Bideford, Devon, EX39 1JG.*
Victorian private house. Comfortable, friendly.
Open: All Year
01237 421174 Ms Michalak
Rates fr: *£13.00*-**£13.00**.
Beds: 2F 1T **Baths:** 1 Shared

Whiddon Down

National Grid Ref: SX6892

Post Inn

***Tor View,** Whiddon Down, Okehampton, Devon, EX20 2PR.*
Peaceful, Dartmoor accommodation. Panoramic views.
Open: All Year (not Xmas)
01647 231447 Mrs Knox
Fax no: 01647 231623
Rates fr: *£15.00*-**£15.00**.
Beds: 1D 1T **Baths:** 1 Shared
(2)

Whimple

National Grid Ref: SY0495

Hungry Fox, New Inn, Red Lion

***Down House,** Whimple, Exeter, Devon, EX5 2QR.*
Open: All Year
Grades: ETB 2 Cr, Comm, AA 4 Q
01404 822860 Sanders
Rates fr: *£20.00*-**£18.00**.
Beds: 1F 2D 2T 1S
Baths: 4 Ensuite 2 Private
(10)
Edwardian country house set in 6 acres of gardens, orchard and paddocks. Fine views of Tiverton Hills and Dartmoor. Exeter, Honiton, Sidmouth all within 7 miles.

***Keepers Lodge,** Strete Raleigh, Whimple, Exeter, Devon, EX5 2PS.*
Delightful country home, beautiful views.
Open: All Year (not Xmas)
01404 822980 Mrs Rudham
Rates fr: *£12.50*-**£12.50**.
Beds: 1F 1D 1T 1S
Baths: 1 Shared
(6)

***Saundercroft,** Whimple, Exeter, Devon, EX5 2PF.*
Comfortable C19th farmhouse.
Open: All Year (not Xmas)
01404 822380 Mrs Darbey
Rates fr: *£14.00*-**£14.00**.
Beds: 1F 1T
Baths: 1 Private 1 Shared
(0) (20)

Witheridge

National Grid Ref: SS8014

The Mitre

***Hole Farm,** Witheridge, Tiverton, Devon, EX16 8QD.*
Grade II Listed Devon longhouse.
Open: All Year (not Xmas)
01884 860265 Mrs Knapton
Rates fr: *£18.00*-**£12.00**.
Beds: 1F 1D 2S
Baths: 2 Ensuite 2 Shared
(3)

***Hope House,** 6 The Square, Witheridge, Tiverton, Devon, EX16 8AE.*
Spacious Victorian rectory in village.
Open: All Year
01884 860012 Mr & Mrs Childs
Rates fr: *£14.00*-**£14.00**.
Beds: 1F 2D 1T 1S
Baths: 2 Shared
(3)

All rates are subject to alteration at the owners' discretion.

Withleigh

National Grid Ref: SS9012

***Great Bradley Farm,** Withleigh, Tiverton, Devon, EX16 8JL.*
Delicious farmhouse fare. Comfortable beds.
Open: Mar to Oct
Grades: ETB 2 Cr, High Comm
01884 256946 Mrs Hann
Rates fr: *£17.50*-**£20.00**.
Beds: 1D 1T
Baths: 2 Private
(2)

Woodbury

National Grid Ref: SY0187

***Cottles Farm,** Woodbury, Exeter, Devon, EX5 1ED.*
Picturesque thatched farmhouse.
Open: All Year (not Xmas)
01395 232547 Mrs Brown
Rates fr: *£16.00*-**£18.00**.
Beds: 1F 1D 1T
Baths: 1 Private 2 Shared
(3)

Woolacombe

National Grid Ref: SS4543

Chichester Arms, The Mill, Michael's Restaurant, Stables Restaurant, Jubilee Bar, Golden Hind

***Clyst House,** Rockfield Road, Woolacombe, Devon, EX34 7DH.*
Open: Mar to Nov
01271 870220 Mrs Braund
Rates fr: *£17.00*-**£17.00**.
Beds: 1F 1D 1T
Baths: 1 Shared
(7)
Friendly, comfortable guest house close to excellent beach. Delicious English breakfast. Tea/coffee facilities, TV lounge, ideal touring centre beautiful walks and surfing.

***Sunny Nook,** Beach Road, Woolacombe, Devon, EX34 7AA.*
Friendly home with superb views.
Open: All Year (not Xmas)
01271 870964
Mr Fenn
Rates fr: *£15.00*-**£16.00**.
Beds: 2F 2D 1S
Baths: 2 Ensuite 1 Shared
(6) (5)

***Lundy House Hotel,** Chapel Hill, Mortehoe, Woolacombe, Devon, EX34 7RZ.*
Open: Feb to Dec
Grades: ETB 3 Cr, Comm
01271 870372 Mr Cole
Fax no: 01271 871001
Rates fr: *£17.50*-**£17.50**.
Beds: 5F 2D 2S
Baths: 6 Private 1 Shared
(6) (10)
Licensed hotel in peaceful location, overlooking secluded beach. Coastal walks and views of Lundy Island. TV and tea making facilities in all rooms.

Barton Lea, *Beach Road, Woolacombe, Devon, EX34 7BT.*
On North Devon Coastal Footpath.
Open: Easter to Oct
01271 870928 Mrs Vickery
Rates fr: *£14.50*-**£19.50**.
Beds: 1F 1D 1T
Baths: 3 Private
(7)

Headlands Hotel, *Beach Road, Woolacombe, Devon, EX34 7BT.*
Small, friendly, comfortable family hotel.
Open: Easter to Oct
Grades: ETB 3 Cr, RAC 2 St
01271 970320
Mr Millichope
Rates fr: *£24.00*-**£24.00**.
Beds: 2F 8D 3T 1S
Baths: 10 Private 2 Shared
(1) (16)

Ivycott Mews, *Woolacombe, Devon, EX34 7.*
Comfortable Converted victorian barn.
Open: Easter to Sep
01271 871048
Mrs Collis
Rates fr: *£14.00*-**£15.00**.
Beds: 1F 1T
Baths: 2 Ensuite 1 Shared
(0) (3)

Camberley, *Beach Road, Woolacombe, Woolacombe, Devon, EX34 7AA.*
Large Victorian private house.
Open: All Year
Grades: ETB 2 Cr, Comm, AA 3 Q
01271 870231
Mr & Mrs Riley
Rates fr: *£15.00*-**£16.00**.
Beds: 1F 3D 2T
Baths: 6 Ensuite
(6)

Ocean View, *The Esplanade, Woolacombe, Devon, EX34 7DJ.*
Detached gentleman's residence.
Open: Easter to Nov
01271 870359
Mrs Gyles
Rates fr: *£15.00*-**£17.00**.
Beds: 2F 4D 1T 3S
Baths: 10 Ensuite

Worlington

National Grid Ref: SS4830

Hensley Farm, *Worlington, Crediton, Devon, EX17 4TG.*
Open: All Year (not Xmas)
01884 860346 (also fax no)
Ms Webber
Rates fr: *£14.00*-**£15.00**.
Beds: 1F 1D
(6)
Just unwind and relax on a working dairy farm with a beautiful thatched farmhouse overlooking one of the prettiest valleys in Devon.

Wrafton

National Grid Ref: SS4935

Williams Arms

Poyers Farm Hotel, *Wrafton, Braunton, Devon, EX33 2DN.*
Delightful C16th thatched Devon longhouse.
Open: All Year (not Xmas)
Grades: ETB Listed, Approv
01271 812149 Mr & Mrs Gross
Rates fr: *£22.00*-**£25.00**.
Beds: 1F 3D 3T 2S
Baths: 9 Ensuite
(15)

Wrangaton

National Grid Ref: SX6757

West Cannamore Farm, *Wrangaton, South Brent, Devon, TQ10 9HA.*
Spacious farm bungalow.
Open: All Year
01364 72250 Mrs Wakeham
Rates fr: *£12.50*-**£13.00**.
Beds: 1F 1D **Baths:** 1 Shared
(4)

Yelverton

National Grid Ref: SX5267

Rock Inn

Waverley Guest House, *5 Greenbank Terrace, Yelverton, Devon, PL20 6DR.*
Family-run Victorian guest house.
Open: All Year
01822 854617 Mrs Gent
Rates fr: *£19.00*-**£19.00**.
Beds: 2F 1D 1T 1S
Baths: 5 Private
(4)

Peek Hill Farm, *Yelverton, Yelverton, Devon, PL20 6PD.*
Comfortable, easy-going, working farmhouse.
Open: All Year (not Xmas)
Grades: ETB 2 Cr, Comm
01822 854 408 (also fax no)
Mrs Colton
Rates fr: *£17.00*-**£20.00**.
Beds: 1F 1D
Baths: 2 Ensuite
(6)

Yeo Mill

National Grid Ref: SS8426

Partridge Arms Farm, *Yeo Mill, West Anstey, South Molton, Devon, EX36 3NU.*
Licensed olde worlde farmhouse. Formerly country inn.
Open: All Year (not Xmas)
Grades: ETB 2 Cr, Comm
01398 341217
Mrs Milton
Fax no: 01398 341569
Rates fr: *£18.00*-**£18.00**.
Beds: 2F 3D 2T
Baths: 4 Ensuite 1 Shared
(10)

Yettington

National Grid Ref: SY0585

Sir Walter Raleigh

Lufflands, *Yettington, Budleigh Salterton, Devon, EX9 7BP.*
Friendly welcome in comfortable farmhouse.
Open: All Year (not Xmas)
01395 568422
Mrs Lovett
Rates fr: *£16.00*-**£16.00**.
Beds: 1F 1D 1S
Baths: 1 Private 1 Shared
(6)

Dorset

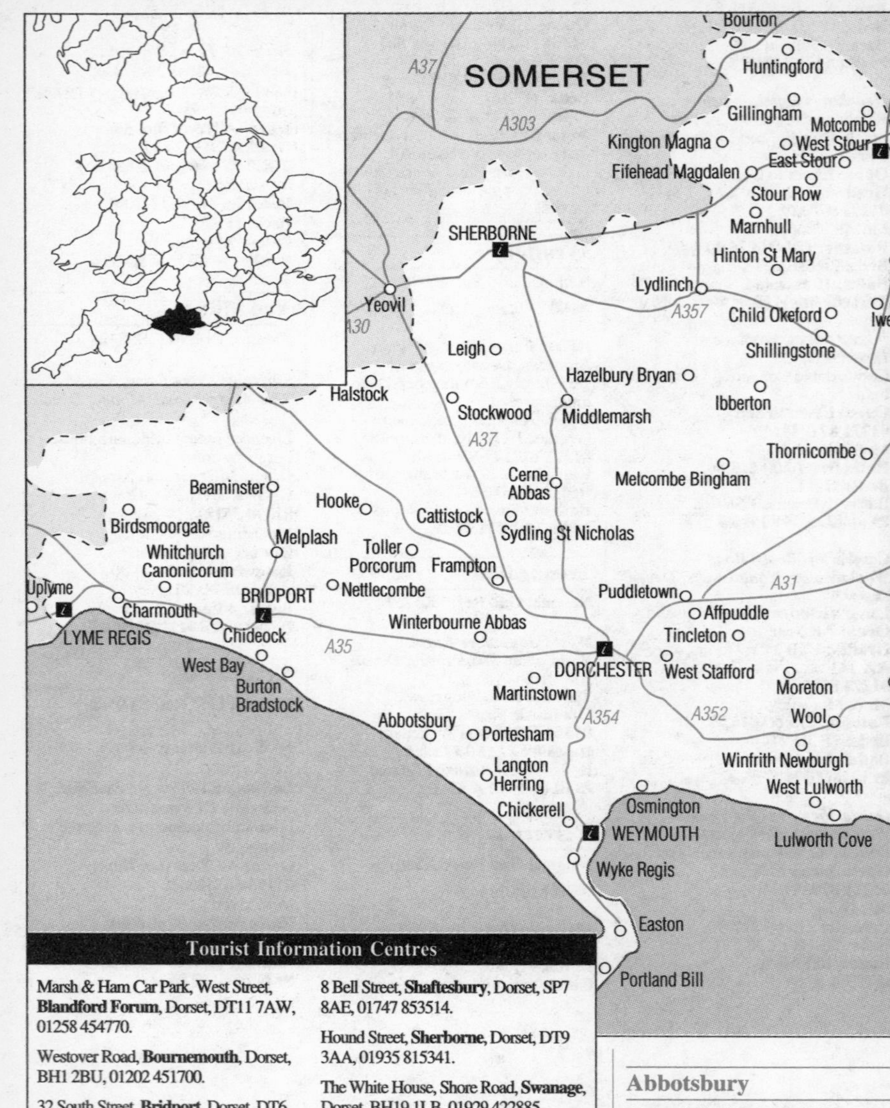

Tourist Information Centres

Marsh & Ham Car Park, West Street, **Blandford Forum**, Dorset, DT11 7AW, 01258 454770.

Westover Road, **Bournemouth**, Dorset, BH1 2BU, 01202 451700.

32 South Street, **Bridport**, Dorset, DT6 3NQ, 01308 424901.

23 High Street, **Christchurch**, Dorset, BH23 1AB, 01202 471780.

1 Acland Road, **Dorchester**, Dorset, DT1 1JW, 01305-267992.

Guildhall Cottage, Church Street, **Lyme Regis**, Dorset, DT7 3DA, 01297 442138.

The Quay, **Poole**, Dorset, BH15 1HE, 01202 253253.

8 Bell Street, **Shaftesbury**, Dorset, SP7 8AE, 01747 853514.

Hound Street, **Sherborne**, Dorset, DT9 3AA, 01935 815341.

The White House, Shore Road, **Swanage**, Dorset, BH19 1LB, 01929 422885.

Town Hall, East Street, **Wareham**, Dorset, BH20 4NG, 01929 552740.

Pavilion Complex, The Esplanade, **Weymouth**, Dorset, DT4 8ED, 01305 765221.

29 High Street, **Wimborne**, Dorset, BH21 1HR, 01202 886116.

Abbotsbury

National Grid Ref: SY5785

***Swan Lodge**, Abbotsbury, Weymouth, Dorset, DT3 4JL.*
Modern guest house.
Open: All Year
Grades: ETB 2 Cr, Comm
01305 871249 (also fax no)
Mr Roper
Rates fr: *£20.00*-**£28.00**.
Beds: 2F 4D 2T
Baths: 2 Private 3 Shared

Linton Cottage, Abbotsbury, Weymouth, Dorset, DT3 4JL.
Victorian cottage in picturesque setting.
Open: All Year (not Xmas)
Grades: ETB Listed, Comm
01305 871339
Mrs Harman
Rates fr: *£18.00*-**£28.50**.
Beds: 2D 1T
Baths: 1 Ensuite 1 Shared
(4)

Affpuddle

National Grid Ref: SY8093

Royal Oak

***Appletrees,** Affpuddle, Dorchester, Dorset, DT2 7HH.*
Modern farm cottage. Splendid views. **Open:** Easter to Oct
01929 471300 Mr Howell
Rates fr: *£14.00*-**£14.00**.
Beds: 2T 1S**Baths:** 1 Shared
(1) (2)

Alderholt

National Grid Ref: SU1212

Churchill Arms

***Hillbury Guest House,** 2 Fir Tree Hill, Camel Green, Alderholt, Fordingbridge, Hants, SP6 3AY.*
Large modern bungalow. Quiet situation.
Open: All Year
Grades: ETB Listed
01425 652582 Mrs Sillence
Fax no: 01425 657587
Rates fr: *£16.00*-**£16.00**.
Beds: 1F 1T 1S
Baths: 1 Shared
(4)

Beaminster

National Grid Ref: ST4701

Pickwicks

***Beam Cottage,** 16 North Street, Beaminster, Dorset, DT8 3DZ.*
Very attractive Listed (Grade II) cottage.
Open: All Year (not Xmas)
Grades: ETB 1 Cr
01308 863639 Mrs Standeven
Rates fr: *£17.50*-**£20.00**.
Beds: 2D 1T
Baths: 2 Ensuite
(3)

***Kitwhistle Farm,** Beaminster Down, Beaminster, Dorset, DT8 3SG.*
Comfortable farmhouse, quiet location.
Open: Easter to Oct
Grades: ETB 2 Cr
01308 862458 Mrs Hasell
Rates fr: *£15.00*-**£18.00**.
Beds: 1D 1T
Baths: 1 Private

Birdsmoorgate

National Grid Ref: ST3900

***Rose & Crown,** Birdsmoorgate, Marshwood, Bridport, Dorset, DT6 5QG.*
Country pub.
Open: All Year
01297 678527 Mr Cornock
Rates fr: *£12.50*-**£12.50**.
Beds: 3F 1D 1T 1S
Baths: 1 Shared
(20)

Blandford Forum

National Grid Ref: ST8806

***Fortune House,** 19 Bayfran Way, Blandford Forum, Dorset, DT11 7RZ.*
Modern private house near town.
Open: All Year
01258 455154 Ms Billam
Rates fr: *£14.00*-**£14.00**.
Beds: 1D 1T 2S **Baths:** 2 Shared

Methuen, *25 Whitecliff Mill Street, Blandford Forum, Dorset, DT11 7BQ.*
Large Victorian private house.
Open: All Year
01258 452834
Mrs Atkins
Rates fr: *£14.00*-**£16.00**.
Beds: 1D 1T 1S
(2)

Sutcombe Knap, *The Lane, Durweston, Blandford Forum, Dorset, DT11 0QA.*
Private country home, 2 miles Blandford.
Open: All Year (not Xmas)
01258 450600
Mrs Munro
Rates fr: *£17.50*-**£17.50**.
Beds: 2D 1S
Baths: 1 Shared
(8) (6)

Bournemouth

National Grid Ref: SZ0891

Durley Inn, Spyglass & Kettle, Neptune, Moon in the Square

Balincourt Hotel, *58 Christchurch Road, Bournemouth, Dorset, BH1 3PF.*
Open: All Year
01202 552962
Mr & Mrs Budd
Rates fr: *£18.00*-**£18.00**.
Beds: 3F 7D 3S
Baths: 10 Ensuite 1 Shared
(5) (14)
Balincourt Hotel. Comfortable family-run hotel. Offering four night breaks Winter, Spring, Autumn. Tinsel & Turkey Christmas Break. Separate tables. Licensed bar. Car parking.

Chilterns Hotel, *44 Westby Road, Bournemouth, Dorset, BH5 1HD.*
Excellent location, licensed, highly recommended.
Open: All Year
Grades: ETB Listed, AA Listed, RAC Listed
01202 396539 (also fax no)
Mr & Mrs Andrews
Rates fr: *£15.00*-**£15.00**.
Beds: 6F 9D 9T 2S
Baths: 8 Ensuite 8 Private 3 Shared
(15)

Kingsley Hotel, *20 Glen Road, Boscombe, Bournemouth, Dorset, BH5 1HR.*
Open: Mar to Sep
01202 398683 (also fax no)
Mr & Mrs Smith
Rates fr: *£18.00*-**£18.00**.
Beds: 3F 5D 1T 1S
Baths: 10 Ensuite
(6)
No smoking throughout. Small hotel situated on quiet road but close to award winning sandy beaches and shops. Ideal for touring New Forest and Dorset.

Gervis Court Hotel, *38 Gervis Road, Eastcliff, Bournemouth, Dorset, BH1 3DH.*
Open: All Year
01202 556871 Mrs Edwards
Rates fr: *£18.00*-**£20.00**.
Beds: 2F 8D 3T **Baths:** 12 Ensuite
(20)
Centrally located for all Bournemouth's amenities including shops, BIC, beach and nightclubs. Ample parking, TV, tea/coffee. Please ask about our special activity breaks.

West Cliff Sands Hotel, *9 Priory Road, West Cliff, Bournemouth, Dorset, BH2 5DF.*
Minutes walk beach, town, theatres. **Open:** All Year (not Xmas)
Grades: ETB 3 Cr
01202 557013 Mr & Mrs Pannell
Rates fr: *£19.00*-**£26.00**.
Beds: 1F 11D 4T **Baths:** 16 Ensuite
(16)

Albrightleigh Guest House, *4 Burnaby Road, Alum Chine, Bournemouth, Dorset, BH4 8JF.*
Open: All Year (not Xmas)
01202 764054 Mr & Mrs Knight
Rates fr: *£14.00*-**£14.00**.
Beds: 2F 3D 1T **Baths:** 6 Ensuite
(5)
Ideally situated close to sandy beach and the beautiful Chines. Entertainment & shops within easy reach. Reductions for OAPs and children. Full English breakfast.

Westover Gardens Hotel, *5-7 Westover Road, Bournemouth, Dorset, BH1 2BY.*
Family-run hotel. Town centre.
Open: Easter to Oct
01202 556380 (also fax no)
Mr Irvins
Rates fr: *£16.00*-**£16.00**.
Beds: 2F 3D 18T 3S
Baths: 6 Private

Shearwater Hotel, *61 Grand Avenue, Southbourne, Bournemouth, Dorset, BH6 3TA.*
Open: Jan to Oct
Grades: ETB 2 Cr
01202 423396 Mr Edwards
Rates fr: *£15.00*-**£15.00**.
Beds: 3F 2D 1T 1S
Baths: 2 Ensuite 2 Shared
(5)
Attractive Edwardian dwelling situated in a pleasant tree-lined avenue, 100 metres from cliff-top walks & Blue Flag beach. New Forest nearby. Brochure on request.

Audmore Hotel, *3 Cecil Road, Boscombe, Bournemouth, Dorset, BH5 1DU.*
Friendly, licensed, family-run hotel. **Open:** Mar to Nov
Grades: ETB 2 Cr, Comm
01202 395166 Mrs Lane
Rates fr: *£15.00*-**£14.00**.
Beds: 5F 2D 1T 2S
Baths: 7 Private 3 Shared
(4)

St Michaels Friendly Guest House, *42 St Michaels Road, Westcliffe, Bournemouth, Dorset, BH2 5DY.*
Small, friendly guesthouse.
Open: All Year
01202 557386 (also fax no)
Mrs Davies
Rates fr: *£13.00*-**£16.00**.
Beds: 1F 2D 2T 1S
Baths: 1 Shared

Sydney House Hotel, *6 West Cliff Road, Bournemouth, Dorset, BH2 5EY.*
Seaside, central, special, comfortable.
Open: All Year
Grades: ETB 2 Cr, Comm
01202 555536 Mr & Mrs Mcveigh
Rates fr: *£15.00*-**£25.00**.
Beds: 3F 6D 4T 2S
Baths: 13 Ensuite 2 Private
(14)

Tall Pine Hotel, *3 Wolpole Road, Boscombe, Bournemouth, Dorset, BH1 4EZ.*
Small, comfortable, family-run hotel.
Open: All Year (not Xmas)
01202 397131
Mr & Mrs Lunn
Rates fr: *£16.00*-**£16.00**.
Beds: 3F 3D 1T 3S
Baths: 4 Private 2 Shared
(3)

Golden Sovereigns Hotel, *97 Alumhurst Road, Alum Chine, Bournemouth, Dorset, BH4 8HR.*
Welcoming, attractive hotel near beach.
Open: All Year
Grades: ETB 3 Cr
01202 762088
Mrs Hamill
Rates fr: *£15.0*-**£15.00**.
Beds: 4F 2D 1T 1S
Baths: 5 Ensuite 1 Private 1 Shared
(9)

Victoria, *120 Parkwood Road, Southbourne, Bournemouth, Dorset, BH5 2BN.*
Friendly, comfortable private house.
Open: May to Oct
01202 423179
Mrs Rising
Rates fr: *£11.00*-**£11.00**.
Beds: 1D 1T
Baths: 1 Shared
(7) (2)

Tenby House Hotel, *23 Pinecliffe, Southbourne, Bournemouth, Dorset, BH6 3PY.*
Delightful Edwardian-style private hotel.
Open: All Year (not Xmas)
01202 423696
Mrs Rudland
Rates fr: *£14.00*-**£14.00**.
Beds: 2F 7D 1T 2S
Baths: 4 Ensuite 3 Shared
(3) (6)

Chedworth Hotel, *45 Westby Road, Bournemouth, Dorset, BH5 1HB.*
Homely, comfortable, friendly hotel.
Open: All Year
Grades: ETB 3 Cr
01202 395848 Mr Dehgham
Rates fr: *£18.00*-**£25.00**.
Beds: 6F 3T 8D
Baths: 9 Ensuite 2 Private
P (14) TV V

The Cottage, *12 Southern Road, Southbourne, Bournemouth, Dorset, BH6 3SR.*
Enchanting, small, cottage-style hotel.
Open: Feb to Nov
Grades: ETB 3 Cr, Comm
01202 422764 Mr Halliwell
Rates fr: *£17.50*-**£17.50**.
Beds: 3F 1D 2T 1S
Baths: 5 Private 2 Shared
(4) P (8) TV V

Beach Hotel, *18 Undercliff Road, Boscombe, Bournemouth, Dorset, BH5 1BL.*
Seafront hotel.
Open: April - Nov.
01202 394577 (also fax no)
Mr Walls
Rates fr: *£16.00*-**£16.00**.
Beds: 2F 4D 1T 1S
Baths: 2 Shared
P (5) TV

Inverness Hotel, *26 Tregonwell Road, Westcliffe, Bournemouth, Dorset, BH2 5NS.*
Five minutes from town and sea.
Open: All Year
Grades: ETB 3 Cr
01202 554968 Mr Brown
Rates fr: *£16.00*-**£16.00**.
Beds: 1F 5D 3T 1S
Baths: 1 Private
P TV

Acorns Hotel, *14 Southwood Avenue, Southbourne, Bournemouth, Dorset, BH6 3QA.*
Family-run, close to beach.
Open: All Year (not Xmas)
Grades: ETB 3 Cr
01202 422438 Mr & Mrs Cokayne
Rates fr: *£15.00*-**£15.00**.
Beds: 2F 3D 1T 1S
Baths: 7 Private
(4) P (5) TV

Ambleside Hotel, *27 Southern Road, Southbourne, Bournemouth, Dorset, BH6 3SR.*
Friendly hotel, quiet residential area. **Open:** All Year
01202 423713 Mr & Mrs Benham
Rates fr: *£14.00*-**£14.00**.
Beds: 1F 4D 3T 1S
Baths: 6 Private 1 Shared
P (5) TV V

Bramdean Hotel, *30 Westbourne Park Road, Westbourne, Bournemouth, Dorset, BH4 8HG.*
Spacious, comfortable, quiet family hotel.
Open: All Year (not Xmas)
01202 764095 Mr Marshall
Rates fr: *£12.00*-**£12.00**.
Beds: 5F 1T
Baths: 3 Private 1 Shared
(4) P (4) TV

Highlin Hotel, *14 Knole Road, Bournemouth, Dorset, BH1 4DQ.*
Service with a smile.
Open: All Year (not Xmas)
01202 393758 Mr Sanday
Rates fr: *£13.50*-**£13.50**.
Beds: 3F 4D 2T 2S
Baths: 3 Shared
(1) P (7) TV V

Bourton

National Grid Ref: ST7630

Snape Cottage, *Chaffeymoor, Bourton, Gillingham, Dorset, SP8 5BY.*
Country cottage with plantsman's garden.
Open: All Year (not Xmas)
01747 840330 Mrs Whinfield
Rates fr: *£18.50*-**£18.50**.
Beds: 1D 1T **Baths:** 1 Shared
TV

Bridport

National Grid Ref: SY3693

Britmead House, *West Bay Road, Bridport, Dorset, DT6 4EG.*
Open: All Year
Grades: ETB 3 Cr, High Comm, AA 4 Q, Select, RAC Acclaim
01308 422941 Mr Walker
Fax no: 01308 422516
Rates fr: *£20.00*-**£25.00**.
Beds: 1F 4D 2T
Baths: 7 Private
(5) P (8) TV V
Treat yourself, stay at Britmead - the ideal base for discovering Dorset. We offer you many thoughtful extras you'll appreciate, delicious meals, and put your comfort first.

Ashdell, *85 Dunyeats Road, Broadstone, Dorset, BH18 8AF.*
Central, comfortable, secluded. Breakfast choice.
Open: All Year
01202 692032 Mrs Critchley
Rates fr: *£12.00*-**£14.00**.
Beds: 1D 2T
Baths: 1 Shared
(6) P (3) V

Bull Hotel, *34 East Street, Bridport, Dorset, DT6 3LF.*
Open: All Year
Grades: ETB 3 Cr
01308 422878 (also fax no)
Mr Buzza
Rates fr: *£19.50*-**£24.50**.
Beds: 4F 8D 4T 4S
Baths: 12 Ensuite 2 Shared
(0) P (20) TV V
C16th coaching inn, centre historic rope making and market town. Close Dorset Coastal Path, countryside, attractions. Hardy's Port Brealy. Cask ales - *à la carte* - bar meals. Log fires.

The Mill House, *East Road, Bridport, Dorset, DT6 4AG.*
Pretty water garden. Excellent cuisine.
Open: Mar to Oct
01308 425147 Mr Shatford-Butcher
Rates fr: *£13.50*-**£14.00**.
Beds: 2D 1S
Baths: 1 Private 1 Shared
(10) P (6) TV V

144 West Bay Road, *Bridport, Dorset, DT6 4AZ.*
Quality accommodation. Quiet, beautiful location.
Open: All Year
01308 422577 Mrs Loving
Rates fr: *£13.00*-**£16.00**.
Beds: 1F 1T
Baths: 1 Shared
P (3) TV V

107 South Street, *Bridport, Dorset, DT6 3PA.*
Cosy, Listed Victorian terraced cottage.
Open: All Year (not Xmas)
01308 420907
Rates fr: *£14.00*-**£15.50**.
(5) TV V

Broadstone

National Grid Ref: SZ0095

Stepping Stones

Tarven, *Corfe Lodge Road, Broadstone, Dorset, BH18 9NF.*
Quiet woodland area, near Poole.
Open: All Year
01202 694338 Mrs Browning
Rates fr: *£14.00*-**£14.00**.
Beds: 1F 1T 1S
Baths: 2 Shared
(4) P (6) TV V

Bucknowle

National Grid Ref: SY9481

Bucknowle House, *Bucknowle, Wareham, Dorset, BH20 5PQ.*
Large Victorian country house.
Open: All Year (not Xmas)
01929 480352 Mr Harvey
Rates fr: *£20.00*-**£25.00**.
Beds: 2D 1T
Baths: 3 Ensuite
P (3)

Burton Bradstock

National Grid Ref: SY4889

Burton Cliff Hotel, *Cliff Road, Burton Bradstock, Bridport, Dorset, DT6 4RB.*
Friendly, relaxed hotel, spectacular views.
Open: Mar to Dec
Grades: ETB 3 Cr, Approv
01308 897205 Mr Barnikel
Rates fr: *£19.00*-**£19.00**.
Beds: 14D 3S
Baths: 14 Private 3 Shared
P (40) TV V

Cattistock

National Grid Ref: SY5999

***Sandhills Cottage,** Cattistock, Dorchester, Dorset, DT2 0HQ.*
Comfortable country cottage.
Open: All Year (not Xmas)
01300 321146 Mrs Willis
Rates fr: *£18.00*.
Beds: 1F 1D 1T
Baths: 1 Ensuite 2 Private

Cerne Abbas

National Grid Ref: ST6601

***New Inn,** 14 Long Street, Cerne Abbas, Dorchester, Dorset, DT2 7JF.*
Historic C13th converted abbey.
Open: All Year
01300 341274 Mr Parsons
Rates fr: *£15.00*-**£25.00**.
Beds: 4D 1T
(12)

Charmouth

National Grid Ref: SY2693

***Newlands House,** Stonebarrow Lane, Charmouth, Bridport, Dorset, DT6 6RA.*
Comfortable, relaxing and delicious food.
Open: Mar to Oct
Grades: ETB 3 Cr, Comm, AA 4 Q, Select, RAC Acclaim
01297 560212
Mrs Vear
Rates fr: *£23.00*-**£21.00**.
Beds: 2F 4D 3T 3S
Baths: 2 Ensuite 1 Private
(6) (15)

***Hensleigh Hotel,** Lower Sea Lane, Charmouth, Bridport, Dorset, DT6 6P.*
Comfortable, Georgian-style house, large conservatory.
Open: Mar to Oct
Grades: ETB 3 Cr, High Comm, AA 2 St, RAC 2 St
01297 560830
Mrs Macnair
Rates fr: *£23.00*-**£23.00**.
Beds: 2F 3D 4T 2S
Baths: 11 Ensuite

***Fernhill Hotel,** Charmouth, Bridport, Dorset, DT6 6BX.*
14 acres of countryside.
Open: Easter to Oct
01297 560492 Mr Bridges
Rates fr: *£22.50*-**£22.50**.
Beds: 3F 6D 3T 2S
Baths: 14 Ensuite

The lowest **single** *rate is shown in* **bold.**

Chickerell

National Grid Ref: SY6480

Turks Head

***Stonebank,** West Street, Chickerell, Weymouth, Dorset, DT3 4DY.*
Comfortable C17th former farmhouse. **Open:** Apr to Sept
Grades: ETB 2 Cr, High Comm
01305 760120 Mrs Westcott
Fax no: 01305 760871
Rates fr: *£17.50*-**£25.00**.
Beds: 2D **Baths:** 2 Ensuite
(2)

Chideock

National Grid Ref: SY4292

***Park Farmhouse,** Main Street, Chideock, Bridport, Dorset, DT6 6JD.*
C17th thatched farmhouse & converted barn.
Open: All Year
Grades: ETB 3 Cr, Comm, AA 4 Q, Select, RAC Acclaim
01297 489157 Mrs Balchin
Rates fr: *£19.50*-**£25.00**.
Beds: 1F 4D 1T **Baths:** 6 Ensuite
(0) (12)

***Betchworth House,** Chideock, Bridport, Dorset, DT6 6JW.*
Lovely C17th cottage in gardens.
Open: All Year
01297 489478 Mr & Mrs Wagstaff
Rates fr: *£15.00*-**£15.00**.
Beds: 1F 2D 2T 1S
Baths: 3 Private 2 Shared
(15)

Child Okeford

National Grid Ref: ST8312

Cricketers Arms

***Gold Hill Bed & Breakfast,** Gold Hill Organic Farm, Child Okeford, Blandford Forum, Dorset, DT11 8HB.*
Open: All Year
Grades: ETB 2 Cr
01258 860293 Mr & Mrs Cross
Rates fr: *£17.00*-**£18.00**.
Beds: 1F 1T **Baths:** 2 Private
(5) (4)
Relaxing holiday in charming farmhouse. Lovely garden - organic vegetable farm with shire horses and rare breed cattle. Ideal for walking, riding, National Trust Properties. Brochures. Charming s/c ground-floor annexe. Sleeps 2 or 3.

Christchurch

National Grid Ref: SZ1592

Globe Inn, Lamb Inn

***Holfleet Cottage,** 2 Bockhampton Road, Winkton, Christchurch, Dorset, BH23 7AE.*
Rural cottage near New Forest.
Open: Apr to Sep
01425 672560 Mrs Snelling
Rates fr: *£15.00*-**£15.00**.
Beds: 2T 1S **Baths:** 1 Private
(4)

***Bure Farmhouse,** 107 Bure Lane, Friar's Cliff, Christchurch, Dorset, BH23 4DN.*
Open: All Year (not Xmas)
01425 270436
Mrs Erhardt
Rates fr: *£15.00*-**£17.00**.
Beds: 1F 1D 1T
Baths: 1 Ensuite 2 Private
Warm welcome to our early 1900s farmhouse of character. Few minutes' walk from award-winning beach. New Forest 10 minute drive. Excellent restaurants within walking distance.

***Hazeldene,** 62 Hurn Road, Christchurch, Dorset, BH23 2RW.*
Warm welcome. Comfortable chalet bungalow.
Open: All Year (not Xmas)
01202 486299 Mrs Cook
Rates fr: *£13.50*-**£15.00**.
Beds: 1D 1T
Baths: 1 Shared
(0) (4)

***Cockneys,** 8 Stanley Road, Highcliffe, Christchurch, Dorset, BH23 5HL.*
Bungalow near sea and shops.
Open: All Year (not Xmas)
01425 279896
Rates fr: *£12.00*-**£12.00**.
Beds: 1D **Baths:** 1 Ensuite
(1)

***Ivy Lea,** 120 Stony Lane, Burton, Christchurch, Dorset, BH23 7LD.*
Friendly, cosy atmosphere.
Open: All Year
01202 499517 Mrs Sandison
Rates fr: *£15.00*-**£17.50**.
Beds: 2D 1T
(4)

***Beverly Glen,** 1 Stuart Road, Highcliffe, Christchurch, Dorset, BH23 5JS.*
Village location, close to sea.
Open: All Year (not Xmas)
01425 273811 Mr Bourn
Rates fr: *£17.50*-**£18.00**.
Beds: 3D 2T 1S
Baths: 5 Ensuite 1 Private
(7)

***The Beech Tree,** 2 Stuart Road, Highcliffe, Christchurch, Dorset, BH23 5JS.*
Above average, warm, comfortable, homely.
Open: All Year
01425 272038
Mr Stephens
Rates fr: *£17.00*-**£17.00**.
Beds: 5D 1T 1S
Baths: 6 Private 1 Shared
(7)

Planning a longer stay? Always ask for any special rates.

Church Knowle

National Grid Ref: SY9381

New Inn

Bradle Farmhouse, *Church Knowle, Corfe Castle, Wareham, Dorset, BH20 5NU.*
Picturesque Victorian farmhouse, splendid views. **Open:** All Year
Grades: ETB 2 Cr, Comm
01929 480712 Mrs Hole
Fax no: 01929 481144
Rates fr: *£18.50*-**£20.00**.
Beds: 2D 1T **Baths:** 3 Ensuite
(5) (3)

Compton Abbas

National Grid Ref: ST8617

Cricketers (Shroton)

The Old Forge, *Fanners Yard, Chapel Hill, Compton Abbas, Shaftesbury, Dorset, SP7 0NQ.*
Open: All Year
Grades: ETB Listed, High Comm
01747 811881 (also fax no)
Mrs Kerridge
Rates fr: *£22.50*-**£25.00**.
Beds: 1F 1D 1S
Baths: 1 Ensuite 1 Private
(4)
Charming C18th converted wheelwrights. Lovely village with views and walks to NT downland. Ideal for relaxing, walking, wildlife, etc. Traditional farmhouse organic breakfast served.

Corfe Castle

National Grid Ref: SY9381

New Inn (Church Knowle)

Bradle Farmhouse, *Church Knowle, Corfe Castle, Wareham, Dorset, BH20 5NU.*
Picturesque Victorian farmhouse, splendid views. **Open:** All Year
Grades: ETB 2 Cr, Comm
01929 480712 Mrs Hole
Fax no: 01929 481144
Rates fr: *£18.50*-**£20.00**.
Beds: 2D 1T **Baths:** 3 Ensuite
(5) (3)

Cranborne

National Grid Ref: SU0513

The Fleur De Lys Hotel, *Cranborne, Wimborne, Dorset, BH21 5PP.*
Open: All Year (not Xmas)
01725 517282 Mr Hancock
Rates fr: *£18.00*-**£26.00**.
Beds: 1F 3D 3T 1S
Baths: 4 Ensuite 3 Private 1 Shared
(30)
Charming creeper-clad inn, idyllically set in small village. Friendly hospitality and cosy atmosphere. Restaurant/bar with excellent menu. Superb ensuite accommodation. Convenient New Forest & coast.

La Fosse Restaurant, *London House, The Square, Cranborne, Wimborne, Dorset, BH21 5PR.*
Superb food in quiet village.
Open: All Year (not Xmas)
Grades: ETB 3 Cr, Comm
01725 517604 Mr La Fosse
Fax no: 01725 517778
Rates fr: *£22.50*-**£25.00**.
Beds: 2D 1T **Baths:** 3 Ensuite

Sheaf Of Arrows, *4 The Square, Cranborne, Wimborne, Dorset, BH21 5PR.*
Village coaching inn, family-run.
Open: All Year
01725 517456 Mrs Tuppen
Rates fr: *£17.50*-**£27.50**.
Beds: 1F 2D 1T **Baths:** 4 Private
(10)

Dorchester

National Grid Ref: SY6890

Cornwall Hotel, Old Ship, Blue Raddle

Churchview Guest House, *Winterbourne Abbas, Dorchester, Dorset, DT2 9LS.*
Open: All Year (not Xmas)
Grades: ETB 3 Cr, Comm, AA 3 Q
01305 889296 Mr Deller
Rates fr: *£18.00*-**£18.00**.
Beds: 1F 4D 3T 1S
Baths: 7 Private 1 Shared
(3) (10)
Delightful C17th guest house. Delicious evening meals, character bedrooms, 2 comfortable lounges & bar. Your hosts will give every assistance to ensure a memorable stay.

Castleview, *8 Edward Road, Dorchester, Dorset, DT1 2HJ.*
Comfortable, friendly Edwardian family house.
Open: All Year
Grades: ETB Listed, Comm
01305 263507 Mr West
Rates fr: *£17.00*-**£15.00**.
Beds: 1D 1T 1S
Baths: 2 Private 1 Shared
(3)

Maiden Castle Farm, *Dorchester, Dorset, DT2 9PR.*
Large Victorian farmhouse, working farm.
Open: All Year
Grades: ETB 2 Cr, High Comm, AA 3 St
01305 262356 Mrs Hoskin
Fax no: 01305 251085
Rates fr: *£18.00*-**£18.00**.
Beds: 1F 2D 1T 1S
Baths: 5 Private 3 Ensuite
(10)

The lowest **single** *rate is shown in* **bold.**

Fujimar, *54 London Road, Dorchester, Dorset, DT1 1NE.*
Comfortable, family-run private house.
Open: All Year (not Xmas)
01305 265295 Mrs Ring
Rates fr: *£15.00*.
Beds: 1D 1T
Baths: 1 Ensuite 1 Private
(4)

Riverhill House, *7 East Hill, Charminster, Dorchester, Dorset, DT2 9QL.*
Superb accommodation in C18th house in Hardy country.
Open: All Year
01305 265614 Mr & Mrs Woods
Rates fr: *£18.00*-**£20.00**.
Beds: 2d 1T
Baths: 3 Ensuite
(6)

Timsgarry, *32 Culliford Road South, Dorchester, Dorset, DT1 2AT.*
Pleasant Victorian house, spacious rooms.
Open: All Year
01305 262717 Mrs Lee
Rates fr: *£13.50*-**£15.00**.
Beds: 1F 1T
Baths: 1 Shared

East Stoke

National Grid Ref: SY8786

Luckford Wood Farm House, *East Stoke, Wareham, Dorset, BH20 6AW.*
Peaceful family farmhouse, excellent views.
Open: All Year
01929 463098 Mrs Barnes
Rates fr: *£15.00*-**£18.00**.
Beds: 1F 1D 1T
Baths: 2 Private 1 Shared
(4)

East Stour

National Grid Ref: ST7922

Aysgarth, *Back Street, East Stour, Gillingham, Dorset, SP8 5JY.*
Chalet bungalow.
Open: Easter to Oct
01747 838351 Mrs Dowding
Rates fr: *£13.50*-**£15.00**.
Beds: 2D 1T
Baths: 1 Shared
(3)

Easton

National Grid Ref: SY6971

Alessandria Hotel, *71 Wakeham, Easton, Portland, Weymouth, Dorset, DT5 1HW.*
C18th building. Italy on Portland!
Open: All Year
Grades: ETB 3 Cr, High Comm, AA Listed
01305 822270 Mr Bisogno
Rates fr: *£20.00*-**£25.00**.
Beds: 4F 4D 4T 4S
Baths: 12 Private 4 Shared
(16)

Ferndown

National Grid Ref: SU0700

Whincroft

Smugglers Cottage, *577 Wimborne Road East, Ferndown, Dorset, BH22 9NW.*
Open: All Year
01202 870738
Mr Marshall
Rates fr: *£20.00*-**£25.00**.
Beds: 2D 1T 1S
Baths: 2 Ensuite 2 Shared
(10)
Former refuge for smugglers. Was featured in 'Homes & Garden' magazine. It is built from the timbers of Spanish galleon. Large garden, licensed bar.

73 Beaufoys Avenue, *Ferndown, Dorset, BH22 9RN.*
Large house in woodland garden.
Open: All Year (not Xmas)
01202 876729
Mrs Davies
Rates fr: *£17.00*-**£17.00**.
Beds: 2D 1T
Baths: 2 Ensuite 1 Private
(6)

Cirendell, *155 Golf Links Road, Ferndown, Dorset, BH22 8BX.*
Luxurious B&B adjacent golf course.
Open: All Year
01202 875356
Mrs Craddock
Rates fr: *£15.00*-**£15.00**.
Beds: 2T 1S
Baths: 2 Shared
(10) (6)

Fifehead Magdalen

National Grid Ref: ST7821

Stapleton Arms (Buckhorn Weston)

Manor Farm, *Fifehead Magdalen, Gillingham, Dorset, SP8 5RR.*
Beautiful C16th manor farmhouse.
Open: Mar to Oct
01258 820717
Mrs Denning
Rates fr: *£15.00*-**£15.00**.
Beds: 1F 1D 1T
Baths: 1 Ensuite 1 Private 1 Shared
(5) (6)

Frampton

National Grid Ref: SY6295

Ashdell, *85 Dunyeats Road, Broadstone, Dorset, BH18 8AF.*
Central, comfortable, secluded. Breakfast choice.
Open: All Year
01202 692032
Mrs Critchley
Rates fr: *£12.00*-**£14.00**.
Beds: 1D 2T
Baths: 1 Shared
(6) (3)

The Stables, *Hyde Crook, Frampton, Dorchester, Dorset, DT2 9NW.*
Friendly modern comfortable equestrian property.
Open: All Year
Grades: ETB 2 Cr, Comm
01300 320075
Mrs Langley
Rates fr: *£19.00*-**£18.00**.
Beds: 1D 1T 1S
Baths: 1 Ensuite 1 Private
(6) (8)

Hyde Farm House, *Frampton, Dorchester, Dorset, DT2 9NG.*
Secluded, luxurious country house.
Open: All Year (not Xmas)
01300 320272
Mr Saunders
Rates fr: *£27.50*-**£27.50**.
Beds: 1D 2T
Baths: 3 Ensuite
(13) (10)

Gillingham

National Grid Ref: ST8026

Dolphin, Peacemarsh

Barley Cottage, *Wyke Road, Gillingham, Dorset, SP8 4NW.*
Modern, welcoming house overlooking fields.
Open: Easter to Oct
01747 824771
Mrs Jacobs
Rates fr: *£13.00*-**£13.00**.
Beds: 1D 1T
Baths: 1 Shared
(10) (2)

Cole Street Farmhouse, *Cole Street Lane, Gillingham, Dorset, SP8 5JQ.*
300-year-old stone farmhouse.
Open: All Year (not Xmas)
01747 822691
Mrs Hawkett
Rates fr: *£16.00*-**£16.00**.
Beds: 2F 1D 1T
Baths: 2 Private 1 Shared
(6)

Halstock

National Grid Ref: ST5308

Halstock Mill, *Halstock, Yeovil, Somerset, BA22 9SJ.*
Secluded, C17th converted water mill.
Open: All Year (not Xmas)
Grades: ETB 3 Cr, Comm, AA 3 Q
01935 891278 Mrs Spender
Rates fr: *£24.00*-**£29.00**.
Beds: 2D 2T
Baths: 4 Private
(5) (20)

The lowest *double* rate per person is shown in *italics*.

Hamworthy

National Grid Ref: SZ0191

Yachtsman

53 Branksea Avenue, *Hamworthy, Poole, Dorset, BH15 4DP.*
Open: All Year (not Xmas)
Grades: ETB 2 Cr, High Comm
01202 673419 Mrs Wadham
Fax no: 01202 667260
Rates fr: *£20.50*-**£26.00**.
Beds: 1D 1T **Baths:** 2 Ensuite
(3)
Select accommodation for those seeking something special. Large bedroom/lounge. Magnificent harbour views. Own balcony, quiet location, close to town. Colour TV, tea-making facilities.

Hazelbury Bryan

National Grid Ref: ST7408

Droop Farm, *Hazelbury Bryan, Sturminster Newton, Dorset, DT10 2ED*
Charming, comfortable C15th thatched farmhouse.
Open: All Year
01258 817244 Mrs Kirby
Fax no: 01258 817806
Rates fr: *£20.00*-**£20.00**.
Beds: 1D 1T
Baths: 1 Private 1 Shared
(4)

The Antelope Hotel, *Hazelbury Bryan, Sturminster Newton, Dorset, DT10 2EB.*
Old country inn.
Open: All Year (not Xmas)
01258 817295 Mr & Mrs Bennett
Rates fr: *£11.00*-**£11.00**.
Beds: 1F 2D **Baths:** 1 Shared
(10)

Hinton St Mary

National Grid Ref: ST7816

Old Post Office, *Marnhull Road, Hinton St Mary, Sturminster Newton, Dorset, DT10 1NG.*
Interesting old country house in pretty village. **Open:** All Year
01258 472366 Mrs Sofield
Fax no: 01258 472173
Rates fr: *£15.00*-**£17.00**.
Beds: 1F 1D 1T
Baths: 1 Ensuite 1 Shared
(5)

Hooke

National Grid Ref: ST5300

Winyards Gap Inn

Hooke Court, *Hooke, Beaminster, Dorset, DT8 3NY.*
Listed C17th manor house, in 14-acre grounds.
Open: All Year (not Xmas)
01308 862260 Mrs Cooper
Rates fr: *£18.00*-**£20.00**.
Beds: 5F 5T 2S
Baths: 9 Ensuite 3 Shared
(30)

***atermeadow House,** Bridge
'arm, Hooke, Beaminster, Dorset,*
T8 3PD.
)pen: Mar to Oct
rades: ETB 2 Cr, High Comm
1308 862619 Mrs Wallbridge
Rates fr: *£18.00*-**£24.00**.
Beds: 1F 1D 1T
Baths: 2 Ensuite 1 Private
(6)
et in tiny Dorset village amidst
eautiful countryside. Breakfast is
erved in a lovely sun lounge.
'erfect for those seeking peace and
uiet.

Iuntingford

National Grid Ref: ST8029

***Iuntingford Oak,** Huntingford,
Gillingham, Dorset, SP8 5QH.*
Modern house on working farm.
Open: All Year (not Xmas)
Grades: ETB 2 Cr, High Comm
1747 860574 Mrs James
Rates fr: *£19.00*-**£21.00**.
Beds: 1F 1D 1T
Baths: 3 Private
(15)

Hyde

National Grid Ref: SY8790

***Iyde Wood Guest House,** Hyde,
Bere Regis, Wareham, Dorset,
H20 7NT.*
Country house. Riding, fishing,
golf.
Open: All Year
1929 471087 Mr William
Rates fr: *£19.50*-**£26.00**.
Beds: 2F 2D 5T
Baths: 4 Private 1 Shared
(100)

bberton

National Grid Ref: ST7807

Crown Inn

***Manor House Farm,** Ibberton,
Blandford Forum, Dorset, DT11 0EN.*
C16th comfortable farmhouse.
Open: All Year
1258 817349 Mrs Old
Rates fr: *£13.00*-**£15.00**.
Beds: 2D 1T
Baths: 1 Private 1 Shared
(4)

werne Courtney

National Grid Ref: ST8512

Cricketers

***'oxhangers,** 4 Old Mill Cottages,
werne Courtney, Blandford
'orum, Dorset, DT11 8TW.*
Friendly, well appointed cottage
style.
Open: All Year (not Xmas)
1258 861049 Mrs Moss
Rates fr: *£17.50*-**£20.00**.
Beds: 1D
Baths: 1 Ensuite
(1)

Iwerne Minster

National Grid Ref: ST8614

***The Talbot Hotel,** Blandford Road,
Iwerne Minster, Blandford Forum,
Dorset, DT11 8QN.*
Set in beautiful Dorset countryside.
Open: All Year
01747 811269 Mr & Mrs
Richardson
Rates fr: *£11.50*-**£16.50**.
Beds: 2F 2D 1T 1S
Baths: 2 Private 2 Shared
(30)

Kimmeridge

National Grid Ref: SY9179

***Kimmeridge Farmhouse,**
Kimmeridge, Wareham, Dorset,
BH20 5PE.*
Large attractive C16th farmhouse.
Open: All Year (not Xmas)
Grades: ETB Listed
01929 480990
Mrs Hole
Rates fr: *£17.00*-**£20.00**.
Beds: 2D 1T
Baths: 1 Private 1 Shared
(3)

Kington Magna

National Grid Ref: ST7623

Ship Inn (West Stour), Stapleton Arms (Buckhorn Weston)

***Kington Manor Farm,** Church
Hill, Kington Magna, Gillingham,
Dorset, SP8 5EG.*
Attractive, comfortable, quiet
working farm.
Open: All Year (not Xmas)
01747 838371
Mrs Gosney
Rates fr: *£16.00*-**£16.00**.
Beds: 1F 1D 1T
Baths: 2 Private
(3)

Langton Herring

National Grid Ref: SY6182

Elm Tree Inn

***Foxbarrow House,** Langton
Herring, Weymouth, Dorset,
DT3 4HT.*
Open: All Year (not Xmas/New
Year)
Grades: ETB 2 Cr, Comm
01305 871463 (also fax no)
Mrs Andrews
Rates fr: *£18.00*-**£18.00**.
Beds: 2D 1T 1S
Baths: 2 Ensuite 1 Private 1
Shared
(7) (3)
Lovingly restored former Victorian
farmhouse - located in idyllic con-
servation village on Heritage Coast
- friendly, welcoming, hospitable &
comfortable accommodation with
'home from home' atmosphere.

***Lower Farmhouse,** Langton
Herring, Weymouth, Dorset,
DT3 4JB.*
Homely C16th character
farmhouse.
Open: All Year (not Xmas)
01305 871187 Ms Mayo
Rates fr: *£15.00*-**£20.00**.
Beds: 1D 2T
Baths: 3 Private
(6)

Langton Matravers

National Grid Ref: SY9978

King's Arms

***Maycroft,** Old Malthouse Lane,
Langton Matravers, Swanage,
Dorset, BH19 3HH.*
Victorian home in lovely garden.
Open: Feb to Nov
01929 424305 Mrs Bjorkstrand
Rates fr: *£15.00*-**£20.00**.
Beds: 1D 1T
Baths: 1 Shared
(3) (4)

Leigh

National Grid Ref: ST6108

***Frampton Farm,** Chetnole Road,
Leigh, Sherborne, Dorset, DT9 6HJ.*
Listed C17th farmhouse in quiet
village.
Open: Easter to Oct
Grades: ETB Listed, Comm
01935 872269 Mrs Tuke
Rates fr: *£16.00*-**£20.00**.
Beds: 1D 2T
Baths: 2 Shared
(7) (3)

Lulworth Cove

National Grid Ref: SY8279

Castle Inn

***Lulworth Cove Hotel,** Main Road,
West Lulworth, Lulworth Cove,
Wareham, Dorset, BH20 5RQ.*
100m from Cove, on Coastal Path.
Open: All Year
Grades: ETB 2 Cr
01929 400333
Mr Foote
Fax no: 01929 400534
Rates fr: *£19.00*-**£19.00**.
Beds: 1F 12D
Baths: 9 Private 2 Shared
(13)

***The Old Barn,** Lulworth Cove,
West Lulworth, Wareham, Dorset,
BH20 5RL.*
Picturesque converted barn.
Coastal village.
Open: All Year
Grades: ETB Listed
01929 400305 Mr Else
Rates fr: *£17.00*-**£17.00**.
Beds: 2F 2D 2T 2S
Baths: 3 Shared
(8)

Lydlinch

National Grid Ref: ST7413

Warr Barn, *Lydlinch, Sturminster Newton, Dorset, DT10 2JP.*
Cosy character Saxon barn conversion.
Open: All Year
01258 473174 Mrs Rattle
Rates fr: *£14.00*-**£20.00**.
Beds: 1D 2T
Baths: 1 Shared
(4)

Lyme Regis

National Grid Ref: SY3492

Pilot Boat, Smugglers, Volunteer Inn, Cliff Cottage Fish Restaurant, Harbour Inn

The Old Monmouth, *12 Church Street, Lyme Regis, Dorset, DT7 3BS.*
Open: All Year
01297 442456 Mr Brown
Rates fr: *£16.00*-**£16.00**.
Beds: 1F 6D 1T
Baths: 5 Private 1 Shared
Family-run hotel, established 1630. 100 yards from the sea, close to coastal paths and town's amenities. Excellent breakfast, menu including vegetarian. Axminster station transport.

Charnwood Guest House, *21 Woodmead Road, Lyme Regis, Dorset, DT7.*
Colonial style, with sea views.
Open: All Year
01297 445281
Mrs Turner
Rates fr: *£17.00*-**£17.00**.
Beds: 2F 3D 1T 1S
Baths: 2 Shared
(7)

Willow Cottage, *Ware Lane, Lyme Regis, Dorset, DT7 3EL.*
Open: Mar to Nov
01297 443199 Mr Griffin
Rates fr: *£22.00*-**£20.00**.
Beds: 1D 1S
Baths: 1 Private
(8) (1)
Overlooking pastureland & Coast Path. Bedrooms (single adjacent main bedroom for third member of party) command sea views. Main room opens onto private balcony.

Coverdale Guest House, *Woodmead Road, Lyme Regis, Dorset, DT7 3AB.*
Spacious comfortable non-smoking guest house.
Open: Feb to Nov
Grades: ETB 2 Cr, Comm, AA 3 Q, Recomm
01297 442882
Mr & Mrs Harding
Rates fr: *£15.00*-**£15.00**.
Beds: 1F 3D 2T 2S
Baths: 6 Private 1 Shared
(8) (9)

New Haven Hotel, *1 Pound Street, Lyme Regis, Dorset, DT7 3HZ.*
C18th town house.
Open: All Year
01297 442499 Mrs Petitt
Rates fr: *£15.50*-**£17.50**.
Beds: 1F 3D 1T 2S
Baths: 2 Private 2 Shared

Southernhaye, *Pound Road, Lyme Regis, Dorset, DT7 3HX.*
Edwardian house with sea views.
Open: All Year (not Xmas)
Grades: ETB 1 Cr, Comm
01297 443077 (also fax no)
Mr Garrard
Rates fr: *£16.00*-**£18.00**.
Beds: 1D 1T
Baths: 1 Shared
(14) (2)

Haye Farm, *Haye Lane, Lyme Regis, Dorset, DT7 3UD.*
Large, modern, comfortable farmhouse.
Open: All Year (not Xmas)
Grades: ETB Listed
01297 442400 Mr Anderson
Rates fr: *£13.00*-**£15.50**.
Beds: 2D 1T 1S
Baths: 1 Shared
(1) (8)

Coombe House, *41 Coombe Street, Lyme Regis, Dorset, DT7 3PY.*
C19th stone house. Sea 100 metres.
Open: All Year
01297 443849 (also fax no)
Mrs Duncan
Rates fr: *£16.00*-**£18.00**.
Beds: 1D 1T **Baths:** 2 Ensuite
(2)

Rotherfield Guest House, *View Road, Lyme Regis, Dorset, DT7 3AA.*
Beautiful guest house, panoramic views.
Open: All Year
Grades: ETB 2 Cr, Comm
01297 445585
Rates fr: *£16.50*-**£18.50**.
Beds: 1F 2T 4D
Baths: 3 Ensuite 1 Private 2 Shared
(0) (7)

Ilex Cottage Guest House, *View Road, Lyme Regis, Dorset, DT7 3AA.*
Modern comfortable guest house.
Open: All Year
Grades: ETB 2 Cr, Approv
01297 442891 Mrs Forrester
Rates fr: *£15.00*-**£15.00**.
Beds: 2F 3D 1T **Baths:** 6 Ensuite
(6)

The Red House, *Sidmouth Road, Lyme Regis, Dorset, DT7 3ES.*
Enchanting house, magnificent coastal views.
Open: Mar to Nov
Grades: ETB 2 Cr, High Comm
01297 442055 (also fax no)
Mr & Mrs Norman
Rates fr: *£20.00*-**£30.00**.
Beds: 1D 2T **Baths:** 3 Ensuite
(8) (3)

Whitsbury, *38 Silver Street, Lyme Regis, Dorset, DT7 3HS.*
Victorian house, magnificent sea views.
Open: All Year
01297 443753 Mr Jones
Rates fr: *£16.00*-**£16.00**.
Beds: 1D 1T
Baths: 2 Private
(4)

Marnhull

National Grid Ref: ST7718

Crown Inn, The Bull, White Horse

Wisteria House, *New Street, Marnhull, Sturminster Newton, Dorset, DT10 1PZ.*
Spacious Georgian former rectory.
Open: All Year
Grades: ETB Listed
01258 820778 Mrs Gillett
Rates fr: *£18.00*-**£18.00**.
Beds: 2D
Baths: 2 Private
(4)

Moorcourt Farm, *Moorside, Marnhull, Sturminster Newton, Dorset, DT10 1HH.*
Friendly, welcoming, happy farmhouse.
Open: Easter to Nov
01258 820271 Mrs Martin
Rates fr: *£13.00*-**£13.00**.
Beds: 2D 1T
Baths: 2 Shared
(10) (6)

Old Lamb House, *Walton Elm, Marnhull, Sturminster Newton, Dorset, DT10 1QG.*
C18th country house. Large rooms.
Open: All Year (not Xmas)
01258 820491 Mrs Chilcott
Fax no: 01258 821464
Rates fr: *£17.00*-**£20.00**.
Beds: 1F 1D **Baths:** 1 Shared
(4)

Martinstown

National Grid Ref: SY6488

The Old Post Office, *Martinstown, Dorchester, Dorset, DT2 9LF.*
Georgian, stone & slate cottage.
Open: All Year
Grades: ETB Listed, Approv
01305 889254 Mrs Rootham
Rates fr: *£16.00*-**£20.00**.
Beds: 1D 2T **Baths:** 1 Shared
(3)

Melbury Abbas

National Grid Ref: ST8820

Melbury Mill, *Melbury Abbas, Shaftesbury, Dorset, SP7 0BD.*
Working mill in rural surroundings.
Open: All Year (not Xmas)
01747 852163
Mr & Mrs Bradley-Watson
Rates fr: *£17.50*-**£27.50**.
Beds: 1F 1D 1T **Baths:** 3 Private
(6)

Melcombe Bingham

National Grid Ref: ST7602

Badgers Sett, *Cross Lanes, Melcombe Bingham, Dorchester, Dorset, DT2 7NY.*
Converted C17th cottages.
Open: All Year (not Xmas)
Grades: ETB 1 Cr, Comm
01258 880697 (also fax no)
Ms Dowsett
Rates fr: *£19.00*-**£19.00**.
Beds: 1F 1T **Baths:** 2 Private
(4)

Melplash

National Grid Ref: SY4898

Hare & Hounds

Mount Meadow Farm, *The Mount, Melplash, Bridport, Dorset, DT6 3TU.*
Modern farmhouse in lovely countryside.
Open: All Year (not Xmas)
Grades: ETB 2 Cr
01308 488524 Mrs Groves
Rates fr: *£14.00*-**£17.50**.
Beds: 1F 1D
Baths: 1 Ensuite 1 Private
(6)

Middlemarsh

National Grid Ref: ST6707

White Horse Farm, *Middlemarsh, Sherborne, Dorset, DT9 5QN.*
Open: All Year (not Xmas)
01963 210222 Mr O'Neill
Rates fr: *£15.00*-**£20.00**.
Beds: 1F 1D 1T
Baths: 2 Ensuite 1 Private
(10)
Middlemarsh, set in beautiful Thomas Hardy country, is within easy reach of the South Coast. Comfortable pine-furnished rooms. Noted for good, ample breakfasts. Also S/C cottages - pets welcome.

Moreton

National Grid Ref: SY8089

Frampton Arms, *Moreton, Dorchester, Dorset, DT2 8BB.*
Very attractive country pub.
Open: All Year
01305 852253 Mr Paulson
Fax no: 01305 854586
Rates fr: *£17.50*-**£25.00**.
Beds: 1F 2D
(40)

Motcombe

National Grid Ref: ST8425

Culverhouse Farm, *Motcombe, Shaftesbury, Dorset, SP7 9HU.*
Large comfortable Victorian farmhouse.
Open: Apr to Oct
01747 852273 Mrs Menlove
Rates fr: *£16.00*-**£16.00**.
Beds: 3T
Baths: 1 Private 1 Shared
(5)

Nettlecombe

National Grid Ref: SY5195

Marquis of Lorne, *Nettlecombe, Bridport, Dorset, DT6 3SY.*
Delightful C16th country inn.
Open: All Year (not Xmas)
01308 485236 Mr Barrett
Rates fr: *£25.00*-**£30.00**.
Beds: 4D 2T **Baths:** 6 Ensuite
(10) (50)

Organford

National Grid Ref: SY9392

The Old Farmhouse, *Organford, Lytchett Minster, Poole, Dorset, BH16 6EU.*
Large Listed Georgian farmhouse.
Open: All Year (not Xmas)
01202 622233 Mrs Palmer
Rates fr: *£12.00*-**£12.00**.
Beds: 1D 1T
Baths: 1 Shared
(5) (2)

Osmington

National Grid Ref: SY7283

Sunray Hotel

Rosedale, *Church Lane, Osmington, Weymouth, Dorset, DT3 6EW.*
Very attractive cottage. Large comfortable rooms, warm friendly atmosphere.
Open: Mar to Nov
Grades: ETB Listed
01305 832056 Mrs Legg
Rates fr: *£14.00*.
Beds: 1D 1T
Baths: 2 Private
(5) (3)

Upton Farm, *Ringstead, Osmington, Weymouth, Dorset, DT2 8NE.*
Award-winning luxurious converted C17th barn.
Open: All Year (not Xmas)
01305 853970 Mr & Mrs Davis
Rates fr: *£18.00*-**£18.00**.
Beds: 1D 1T
Baths: 1 Private 1 Shared
(6)

Poole

National Grid Ref: SZ0191

Yachtsman, Crown Hotel, Shah of Persia, Red Lion, Grasshopper, Conjurer's Half Crown

Shalimar, *14 Burngate Road, Hamworthy, Poole, Dorset, BH15 4HS.*
Modern house, quiet cul-de-sac.
Open: All Year (not Xmas)
01202 680070
Mrs Batten
Rates fr: *£15.00*-**£15.00**.
Beds: 1F 1T 1S
Baths: 2 Shared
(1) (2)

The Laurels, *60 Britannia Road, Lower Parkstone, Poole, Dorset, BH14 8BB.*
Open: All Year (not Xmas)
01202 723369 Mrs North
Rates fr: *£16.00*-**£16.00**.
Beds: 1T **Baths:** 1 Private
(2)
High standard accommodation awaits you in large Victorian home. Ideally situated for watersports, beaches, park & local restaurants. Ferry passengers welcome. Family room with child discounts.

Heathwood Guest House, *266 Wimborne Road, Poole, Dorset, BH15 3EF.*
Friendly establishment. All catered for. **Open:** All Year
Grades: ETB 2 Cr, Comm
01202 679176 (also fax no)
Mrs Dobson
Rates fr: *£17.00*-**£20.00**.
Beds: 2F 2D 2T 2S
Baths: 8 Ensuite

53 Branksea Avenue, *Hamworthy, Poole, Dorset, BH15 4DP.*
Open: All Year (not Xmas)
Grades: ETB 2 Cr, High Comm
01202 673419 Mrs Wadham
Fax no: 01202 667260
Rates fr: *£20.50*-**£26.00**.
Beds: 1D 1T **Baths:** 2 Ensuite
(3)
Select accommodation for those seeking something special. Large bedroom/lounge. Magnificent harbour views. Own balcony, quiet location, close to town. Colour TV, tea-making facilities.

Rosemount Hotel, *167 Bournemouth Road, Parkstone, Poole, Dorset, BH14 9HT.*
Fairly large early 1920's building.
Open: All Year (not Xmas)
Grades: ETB Listed
01202 732138 Mrs Standhaft
Rates fr: *£16.00*-**£16.00**.
Beds: 1F 3D 1D 1S
Baths: 2 Ensuite 1 Private 2 Shared

South Rising Guest House, *86 Parkstone Road, Poole, Dorset, BH15 2QE.*
Adjacent park, town & beaches.
Open: All Year (not Xmas)
Grades: ETB Listed, Comm
01202 240766 Mr Keller
Rates fr: *£16.00*-**£18.00**.
Beds: 3F 3D **Baths:** 2 Shared
(3) (6)

Little Haven Guest House, *126 Sandbanks Road, Parkstone, Poole, Dorset, BH14 8DA.*
Friendly, small, comfortable, good value.
Open: All Year (not Xmas)
Grades: ETB Listed, Comm
01202 746 944 Mr & Mrs Daunt
Rates fr: *£15.00*-**£15.50**.
Beds: 1F 2D 1T **Baths:** 2 Shared
(5) (5)

***Ashdell,** 85 Dunyeats Road, Poole, Broadstone, Dorset, BH18 8AF.*
Central, comfortable, secluded. Breakfast choice.
Open: All Year
01202 692032 Mrs Critchley
Rates fr: *£12.00*-**£14.00**.
Beds: 1D 2T
Baths: 1 Shared
(6) (3)

***Annelise,** 41 Danecourt Road, Lower Parkstone, Poole, Dorset, BH14 0PG.*
Comfortable accommodation, homely atmosphere.
Open: All Year (not Xmas)
Grades: ETB 1 Cr
01202 744833 Mrs Vincent
Rates fr: *£14.00*-**£15.00**.
Beds: 2F 1D **Baths:** 2 Shared
(3)

***Melbury Guest House,** 101 Parkstone Road, Poole, Dorset, BH15 2NZ.*
Large, wholesome, happy Edwardian home. **Open:** All Year
Grades: ETB Listed, Comm
01202 749015 Mrs Lloyd
Rates fr: *£15.00*-**£16.00**.
Beds: 1F 1D 1T 1S
Baths: 2 Shared
(5) (4)

***St Leonards Hotel,** Ringwood Road, Poole, Dorset, BH24 2NP.*
Modern country hotel.
Open: All Year
01425 471220 Mrs Cross
Rates fr: *£25.00*-**£30.00**.
Beds: 5F 20D 8T
Baths: 33 Private
(96)

***Seacourt Guest House,** 249 Blandford Road, Hamworthy, Poole, Dorset, BH15 4AZ.*
Guest house 'Simply the Best'.
Open: All Year
Grades: ETB 2 Cr, Comm, AA 3 Q
01202 674995 Ms Hewitt
Rates fr: *£19.00*-**£25.00**.
Beds: 1F 2D 2T **Baths:** 5 Private
(5)

***Fleetwater Guest House,** 161 Longfleet Road, Poole, Dorset, BH15 2HS.*
Clean, friendly, with personal service. **Open:** All Year
Grades: ETB 2 Cr, Comm
01202 682509 Mr Hewitt
Rates fr: *£18.00*-**£20.00**.
Beds: 1F 2D 1T **Baths:** 4 Ensuite
(5)

***Quay House,** Thames Street, Poole, Dorset, BH15 1JN.*
Poole Old Town, quay, harbour views.
Open: All Year (not Xmas)
Grades: ETB Listed, Comm
01202 686335 Mrs Goodey
Rates fr: *£16.50*-**£19.00**.
Beds: 1D **Baths:** 1 Private
(1)

***Southern Comfort Guest House,** 192 Bournemouth Road, Poole, Dorset, BH14 9HZ.*
Modern detached guest house.
Open: All Year
01202 722250 Mrs Richmond
Rates fr: *£18.00*-**£18.00**.
Beds: 3F 2D 1T 1S
Baths: 2 Private 3 Shared
(6)

***Acorns,** 264 Wimborne Road, Poole, Dorset, BH15 3EF.*
Well-established, close to town centre.
Open: All Year (not Xmas/New Year)
01202 672901 Mrs Haines
Rates fr: *£20.00*-**£19.00**.
Beds: 2D 2T 2S
Baths: 4 Ensuite 2 Private
(6)

***St Christophers,** 7 Flaghead Road, Canford Cliffs, Poole, Dorset, BH13 7JN.*
Lovely bright welcoming house.
Open: All Year
01202 701160 Mrs Blagrave
Rates fr: *£17.00*. **Beds:** 2D
Baths: 1 Ensuite 1 Private
(4)

Portesham

National Grid Ref: SY6085
Kings Arms

***The Old Vicarage,** 2 Church Lane, Portesham, Weymouth, Dorset, DT3 4HB.*
Georgian house in village centre.
Open: Easter to Nov
01305 871296 Mr & Miss Saunders
Rates fr: *£11.50*-**£11.50**.
Beds: 1F 1D 1T **Baths:** 1 Shared
(3)

Portland Bill

National Grid Ref: SY6874

***The Old Higher Lighthouse,** Portland Bill, Portland, Dorset, DT5 2JT.*
C18th restored lighthouse, breath-taking views.
Open: All Year (not Xmas)
01305 822300 Mrs Lockyer
Rates fr: *£20.00*-**£25.00**.
Beds: 2F 2D 2T
Baths: 1 Private 2 Shared
(12)

Puddletown

National Grid Ref: SY7594
Prince of Wales, Blue Vinney, Martyres

***Zoar House,** Puddletown, Dorchester, Dorset, DT2 8SR.*
Large Victorian private house.
Open: All Year
01305 848498 Mrs Stephens
Rates fr: *£14.00*-**£15.00**.
Beds: 1F 1T **Baths:** 1 Ensuite
(6)

Sandford

National Grid Ref: SY9289
Woods Edge Restaurant

***Glen Ness,** 1 The Merrows, Sandford, Wareham, Dorset, BH20 7AX.*
Cedar/stone bungalow, secluded surroundings.
Open: All Year (not Xmas)
01929 552313 Mrs Gegg
Rates fr: *£15.00*-**£15.00**.
Beds: 3D 3S
Baths: 1 Shared
(4)

Shaftesbury

National Grid Ref: ST8622
The Talbot, Grove Arms, Rising Sun, Two Brewers

***Charnwood Cottage,** Charlton, Shaftesbury, Dorset, SP7 9LZ.*
C17th thatched cottage.
Open: All Year (not Xmas)
01747 828310 Mr & Mrs Morgan
Rates fr: *£15.00*-**£20.00**.
Beds: 1F 1D
Baths: 1 Shared
(5) (2)

***5 Ivy Cross,** Shaftesbury, Dorset, SP7 8DW.*
Large Victorian private house.
Open: Easter to Oct
01747 853734 Mrs Keating
Rates fr: *£15.00*-**£15.00**.
Beds: 1F 1D 1T 1S
Baths: 1 Shared
(4)

***Carraig,** 14 Old Boundary Road, Shaftesbury, Dorset, SP7 8ND.*
Welcoming family home in Hardy country.
Open: Mar to Oct
01747 852681 Mr & Mrs Hartshorne
Rates fr: *£14.50*-**£14.50**.
Beds: 1F 1T 1S
Baths: 2 Shared
(All) (3)

***19 Old Boundary Road,** Shaftesbury, Dorset, SP7 8ND.*
Comfortable house in quiet location.
Open: All Year
01747 852087 Mrs Jones
Rates fr: *£13.00*-**£13.00**.
Beds: 1D 2S
Baths: 1 Shared
(4)

***Saxon Rise Farm,** Lower Blandford Road, Cann, Shaftesbury, Dorset, SP7 0BH.*
Modern comfortable with wonderful views.
Open: All Year (not Xmas)
01747 854515 Mrs Buckley
Rates fr: *£16.00*-**£18.00**.
Beds: 1F 1D 1T 1S
Baths: 1 Ensuite 2 Shared
(6)

Sherborne

National Grid Ref: ST6316

Britannia Inn, *Sherborne, Dorset, DT9 3EH.*
C18th inn.
Open: All Year (not Xmas)
Grades: ETB 1 Cr
01935 813300 Mr Spicer
Rates fr: *£16.00*-**£17.50**.
Beds: 2F 1D 3T 1S
Baths: 2 Private 2 Shared
(8)

Frampton Farm, *Chetnole Road, Leigh, Sherborne, Dorset, DT9 6HJ.*
Listed C17th farmhouse in quiet village.
Open: Easter to Oct
Grades: ETB Listed, Comm
01935 872269 Mrs Tuke
Rates fr: *£16.00*-**£20.00**.
Beds: 1D 2T
Baths: 2 Shared
(7) (3)

The Antelope Hotel, *Greenhill, Sherborne, Dorset, DT9 4EP.*
C17th 3 Star hotel.
Open: All Year
01935 812077
Rates fr: *£20.00*-**£35.00**.
Beds: 1F 10D 3T 5S
Baths: 14 Private

Quinns, *Marston Road, Sherborne, Dorset, DT9 4BL.*
Well-appointed, modern, detached house.
Open: All Year
01935 815008 Mrs Quinn
Rates fr: *£22.50*-**£25.50**.
Beds: 3D **Baths:** 3 Private
(5) (4)

Shillingstone

National Grid Ref: ST8211

The Willows Tea Rooms, *5 Blandford Road, Shillingstone, Blandford Forum, Dorset, DT11 0SG.*
C18th cottage & tearooms.
Open: Feb to Xmas
01258 861167 Mr & Mrs Auckland
Rates fr: *£15.00*-**£20.00**.
Beds: 1D
Baths: 1 Ensuite
(6)

Bere Marsh House, *Shillingstone, Blandford Forum, Dorset, DT11 0QY.*
Large open-fired farmhouse.
Open: Feb to Dec
01258 861133 Mrs Roe
Rates fr: *£16.00*-**£18.00**.
Beds: 1D 1T
Baths: 1 Private
(6) (12)

Bringing children with you? Always ask for any special rates.

Shroton

National Grid Ref: ST8512

Cricketers

Lattemere, *Frog Lane, Shroton, Blandford Forum, Dorset, DT11 8QL.*
Comfortable house in picturesque village.
Open: All Year
01258 860115 Mrs Wright
Rates fr: *£16.00*-**£17.00**.
Beds: 1D 1T
Baths: 1 Private 1 Shared
(3)

Sixpenny Handley

National Grid Ref: ST9918

The Barleycorn House, *Sixpenny Handley, Salisbury, Wilts, SP5 5PD.*
Converted C17th country inn.
Open: All Year
Grades: ETB 2 Cr
01725 552583 Mrs Howes
Rates fr: *£18.50*-**£18.50**.
Beds: 1D 2T **Baths:** 3 Private
(4)

Spetisbury

National Grid Ref: ST9102

Drax Arms

Copper Beech House, *Spetisbury, Blandford Forum, Dorset, DT11 9DF.*
Country residence, balcony, acre garden.
Open: Easter to October
01258 452901 Mr & Mrs Young
Rates fr: *£14.00*-**£14.00**.
Beds: 1D 1T 1S
Baths: 1 Shared
(4)

St Leonards

National Grid Ref: SU1103

Hotspur House, *12 Wayside Road, St Leonards, Ringwood, Hants, BH24 2SH.*
Detached house & two chalets.
Open: Mar to Dec
01202 896226 Mrs Roberts
Rates fr: *£13.00*.
Beds: 1F 1D 1T 1S
Baths: 2 Private 1 Shared
(10)

Stockwood

National Grid Ref: ST5806

Chetnole Inn

Church Farm, *Stockwood, Evershot, Dorchester, Dorset, DT2 0NG.*
Beautiful Georgian house on family farm.
Open: All Year
Grades: ETB 2 Cr, High Comm
01935 83221 Mrs House
Fax no: 01935 83771
Rates fr: *£18.00*-**£20.00**.
Beds: 2D 1T**Baths:** 3 Private
(3)

Stour Row

National Grid Ref: ST8221

Blackmore Vale

Beechmead, *Stour Row, Shaftesbury, Dorset, SP7 0QF.*
Quiet bungalow, garden & views.
Open: All Year
01747 838405 Mrs Slingerland
Rates fr: *£12.50*-**£16.00**.
Beds: 1D 1T
Baths: 1 Private 1 Shared 1 Private Shower
(2)

Studland

National Grid Ref: SZ0382

Purbeck Down Guest House, *The Glebe, Studland, Swanage, Dorset, BH19 3AS.*
Spacious/secluded, with 40ft pool.
Open: Feb to Dec
01929 450257 Mrs Rose
Rates fr: *£17.50*-**£22.00**.
Beds: 1F 1D1T
Baths: 2 Ensuite 1 Private
(5) (3)

Sturminster Marshall

National Grid Ref: SY9400

Kilvey, *26b Churchill Close, Sturminster Marshall, Wimborne, Dorset, BH21 4BQ.*
Modern comfortable friendly home.
Open: All Year
01258 857057 Mrs Hopkins
Rates fr: *£15.00*-**£17.00**.
Beds: 1D 1T
Baths: 1 Ensuite 1 Shared
(5) (4)

Swanage

National Grid Ref: SZ0278

Tawnys Wine Bar

Burlington House Hotel, *Highcliffe Road, Swanage, Dorset, BH19 1LW.*
Open: All Year
Grades: ETB 3 Cr
01929 422422 Mr Mitchell
Rates fr: *£16.00*-**£16.00**.
Beds: 5F 2D 1T 1S
Baths: 7 Ensuite 1 Shared
(9)
Delightfully situated small licensed hotel with own cliff top garden. Fantastic sea views stretching from the sea front to the Isle of Wight. Phone for brochure.

The Corner House, *4 Manor Road, Swanage, Dorset, BH19 2BJ.*
Large private house near beach.
Open: Easter to Oct
01929 424410
Mrs Preston
Rates fr: *£14.00*.
Beds: 1F 1T
Baths: 1 Shared
(1) (2)

Hermitage Guest House, *1 Manor Road, Swanage, Dorset, BH19 2BH.*
Bay views, comfortable, friendly, central.
Open: Easter to Nov
01929 423014 Mrs Pickering
Rates fr: *£15.50*-**£15.50**.
Beds: 4F 2D 1T
Baths: 2 Shared
(0) (7)

Pennyfarthings, *124 Kings Road West, Swanage, Dorset, BH19 1HS.*
Lovely friendly house, beautiful garden.
Open: All Year
01929 422256 Mr & Mrs Davison
Rates fr: *£15.00*-**£16.00**.
Beds: 1F 1D 1T
Baths: 2 Private 1 Shared
(2) (2)

Easter Cottage, *9 Eldon Terrace, Swanage, Dorset, BH19 1HA.*
Cosy cottage, close beach and amenities.
Open: All Year
Grades: ETB 2 Cr
01929 427782
Mrs Needham
Rates fr: *£13.00*-**£18.00**.
Beds: 2D
Baths: 2 Ensuite
(5)

Ingleston Hotel, *2 Victoria Road, Swanage, Dorset, BH19 1LY.*
Large Victorian house, 3 minutes beach.
01929 422391 Mrs McLintic
Rates fr: *£17.00*-**£17.00**.
Beds: 4F 2D 2T 2S
Baths: 3 Private 2 Shared
(9)

The Haven Hotel, *Victoria Road, Swanage, Dorset, BH19 1LY.*
Attractive detached hotel near beach.
Open: All Year (not Xmas)
01929 423088 Mrs Goodman
Rates fr: *£15.75*-**£15.75**.
Beds: 4F 3D 1T 1S
Baths: 5 Ensuite 1 Private 2 Shared
(3) (8)

Verulam Lodge, *26 Cluny Crescent, Swanage, Dorset, BH19 2BT.*
Detached house near town & sea.
Open: Easter to Oct
01929 422079
Mrs Willey
Rates fr: *£14.00*-**£14.00**.
Beds: 2F 1D
Baths: 2 Shared
(4)

Cluny Croft Hotel, *19 Cluny Crescent, Swanage, Dorset, BH19 2BP.*
Friendly, family-run private hotel.
Open: All Year (not Xmas)
01929 424322 Mr Dack
Rates fr: *£17.50*-**£17.50**.
Beds: 3F 3D 1T
Baths: 3 Private 2 Shared
(1) (6)

Skelmorlie House, *50 Queens Road, Swanage, Dorset, BH19 2EU.*
Beautiful sea views & delicious home cooking.
Open: Apr to Sep
01929 424643 Mrs Rudd
Rates fr: *£17.00*-**£15.00**.
Beds: 1F 1D 2S
Baths: 2 Private 1 Shared
(5) (2)

Fermain Hotel, *12 Rempstone Road, Swanage, Dorset, BH19 1DW.*
Close to sea-front, town, railway.
Open: All Year (not Xmas)
01929 423271 Mrs Pettitt
Rates fr: *£19.50*-**£19.50**.
Beds: 1F 3D 1T 1S
Baths: 5 Ensuite 1 Private
(4) (11)

Sydling St Nicholas

National Grid Ref: SY6399

Greyhound

Lamperts Cottage, *Sydling St Nicholas, Dorchester, Dorset, DT2 9NU.*
Grade II thatched C16th cottage.
Open: All Year
Grades: ETB Listed, AA 3 Q
01300 341659
Mr Wills
Fax no: 01300 341699
Rates fr: *£19.00*-**£21.00**.
Beds: 2D 1T
Baths: 2 Shared
(8) (3)

City Cottage, *Sydling St Nicholas, Dorchester, Dorset, DT2 9NX.*
Comfortable country cottage.
Open: All Year (not Xmas)
01300 341300
Mrs Wareham
Rates fr: *£15.00*-**£15.00**.
Beds: 1D 1S
Baths: 1 Shared
(2)

Magiston Farm, *Sydling St Nicholas, Dorchester, Dorset, DT2 9NR.*
Old comfortable farmhouse.
Open: All Year (not Xmas)
Grades: ETB Listed
01300 320295
Mrs Barraclough
Rates fr: *£16.50*-**£16.50**.
Beds: 1D 1T 2S
Baths: 1 Private 1 Shared
(10) (10)

Lamperts Farmhouse, *11 Dorchester Road, Sydling St Nicholas, Dorchester, Dorset, DT2 9NU.*
C17th thatched Listed farmhouse.
Open: All Year
Grades: ETB 2 Cr
01300 341790
Mrs Bown
Rates fr: *£18.00*-**£20.00**.
Beds: 1F 1D
Baths: 2 Ensuite
(4)

Thornicombe

National Grid Ref: ST8703

Gorcombe Farm, *Thornicombe, Blandford Forum, Dorset, DT11 9AG.*
Secluded, comfortable, modern farmhouse.
01258 452219 Mrs Meaden
Rates fr: *£16.00*-**£18.00**.
Beds: 2D
Baths: 2 Shared
(6)

Tincleton

National Grid Ref: SY7791

Timber Lodge, *Clyffe, Tincleton, Dorchester, Dorset, DT2 8QR.*
Superb woodland location.
Open: All Year (not Xmas)
01305 848461
Rates fr: *£17.00*-**£18.00**.
Beds: 1F 1D **Baths:** 2 Ensuite
(4)

Toller Porcorum

National Grid Ref: SY5698

Colesmoor Farm, *Toller Porcorum, Dorchester, Dorset, DT2 0DU.*
Small family farm, quiet setting.
Open: May to Nov
Grades: ETB 1 Cr. Comm
01300 320812 (also fax no)
Mrs Geddes
Rates fr: *£15.00*-**£18.00**.
Beds: 1D 1T
Baths: 1 Ensuite 1 Private
(0) (3)

The Kingcombe Centre, *Toller Porcorum, Dorchester, Dorset, DT2 0EQ.*
Converted riverside farm buildings.
Open: All Year
01300 320684 Mr Spring
Rates fr: *£15.00*-**£15.00**.
Beds: 1F 6T 4S
Baths: 11 Shared
(20)

Uplyme

National Grid Ref: SY3492

Lydwell House, *Lyme Road , Uplyme, Lyme Regis, Dorset, DT7 3TJ.*
Charming Edwardian house with gardens.
Open: All Year
01297 443522 Mrs Greenhalgh
Rates fr: *£14.50*-**£15.50**.
Beds: 2F 1D 1T 1S
Baths: 2 Private 1 Shared
(7)

Pitt White, *Mill Lane, Uplyme, Lyme Regis, Dorset, DT7 3TZ.*
Country house, bamboo gardens, River Lym. **Open:** All Year
01297 442094 Mrs Gear
Rates fr: *£17.50*-**£16.00**.
Beds: 1F 4D 4T 2S
Baths: 4 Private
(12)

Verwood

National Grid Ref: SU0808

Monmoth Ash

Verwood Farmhouse, *Margards Lane, Verwood, Dorset, BH31 6JQ.*
Architect-designed home in peaceful location.
Open: All Year
01202 822083 Mrs Lancy
Rates fr: *£15.00*-**£15.00**.
Beds: 2D 1T 1S
Baths: 1 Ensuite 2 Shared
(5) (4)

Pear Tree Cottage, *93 Ringwood Road, Verwood, Dorset, BH31 7AD.*
C17th cottage. Comfort is our business.
Open: All Year (not Xmas)
01202 826734 Mrs Marcantonio
Rates fr: *£15.00*-**£15.00**.
Beds: 1F 2T 1S
Baths: 1 Private 1 Shared
(5)

Red Cedars, *86 Dewlands Road, Verwood, Dorset, BH31 6PN.*
Quiet, secluded, Canadian cedarwood bungalow.
Open: All Year
01202 822585 Mrs Saville
Rates fr: *£16.50*-**£18.50**.
Beds: 1D
Baths: 1 Private

Wareham

National Grid Ref: SY9287

Granary Restaurant

Ashcroft Bed & Breakfast, *64 Furzebrook Road, Wareham, Dorset, BH20 5AX.*
Comfortable friendly 'home from home'.
Open: All Year (not Xmas)
01929 552392 (also fax no)
Mrs Cake
Rates fr: *£15.00*-**£15.00**.
Beds: 1F 1D 1T
Baths: 2 Private 1 Shared
(3) (6)

The Maltings, *2 Abbots Quay, Wareham, Dorset, BH20 4LW.*
Character house in riverside position.
Open: All Year (not Xmas)
01929 552092 Mrs Wheeldon
Rates fr: *£20.00*-**£30.00**.
Beds: 2T
Baths: 2 Private
(2)

Dorothea Bed & Breakfast, *10 Sandford Road, Wareham, Dorset, BH20 4DH.*
1930s cottage with garden railway.
Open: All Year (not Xmas)
01929 553869 Mrs Holland
Rates fr: *£14.00*-**£14.00**.
Beds: 1F 2D 1T 1S
Baths: 2 Shared
(4)

Greenacres, *Bere Road, Wareham, Dorset, BH20 7PA.*
Large private house.
Open: All Year
01929 553821 Mrs Jacobs
Rates fr: *£19.00*-**£22.00**.
Beds: 1F 2D 1S
Baths: 2 Ensuite 1 Private
(2) (8)

West Bay

National Grid Ref: SY4690

Egdon, *Third Cliff Walk, West Bay, Bridport, Dorset, DT6 4HX.*
Quiet house, panoramic views.
Open: All Year
Grades: ETB Listed
01308 422542 Mrs Vallard
Rates fr: *£14.00*.
Beds: 1F 1D 1T **Baths:** 2 Shared
(4)

West Lulworth

National Grid Ref: SY8280

Castle Inn

Shirley Hotel, *West Lulworth, Wareham, Dorset, BH20 5RL.*
Open: Feb to Nov
Grades: ETB 3 Cr, High Comm, AA 2 St
01929 400358 Tony Williams
Rates fr: *£27.50*-**£27.50**.
Beds: 3F 8D 4T 3S
Baths: 18 Ensuite
(22)
Magnificent coastal path & inland walks from hotel. Family-run serving delicious food, we have a heated indoor pool & fully equipped rooms. Dogs welcome.

Lulworth Cove Hotel, *Main Road, West Lulworth, Wareham, Dorset, BH20 5RQ.*
100m from Cove, on Coastal Path.
Open: All Year
Grades: ETB 2 Cr
01929 400333 Mr Foote
Fax no: 01929 400534
Rates fr: *£19.00*-**£19.00**.
Beds: 1F 12D
Baths: 9 Private 2 Shared
(13)

Elads Nevar Guest House, *West Road, West Lulworth, Wareham, Dorset, BH20 5RZ.*
Modern private house.
Open: All Year (not Xmas)
01929 400467 Mrs Ravensdale
Rates fr: *£13.00*.
Beds: 1F 1D 1T **Baths:** 1 Shared
(4) (3)

Tewkesbury Cottage, *28 Main Road, West Lulworth, Wareham, Dorset, BH20 5RL.*
Converted C16th thatched cottage.
Open: All Year
01929 400561 Mrs Laing
Rates fr: *£15.00*-**£18.00**.
Beds: 2D 1T
Baths: 1 Ensuite 2 Shared
(12) (8)

Graybank Guest House, *Main Road, West Lulworth, Wareham, Dorset, BH20 5RL.*
Comfortable Victorian guest house - excellent breakfast.
Open: Feb to Nov
01929 400256 Mr & Mrs Burrill
Rates fr: *£17.00*-**£17.00**.
Beds: 2F 2D 2T 1S
Baths: 3 Shared
(4) (7)

West Stafford

National Grid Ref: SY7289

Church Cottage, *2 Church Cottages, West Stafford, Dorchester, Dorset, DT2 8AB.*
Self-contained Grade II Listed conversion.
Open: All Year
Grades: ETB 1 Cr
01305 269287 (also fax no)
Rates fr: *£10.00*.
Beds: 1D
Baths: 1 Ensuite
(1)

West Stour

National Grid Ref: ST7822

Ship Inn

Stour Cross Farm, *West Stour, Gillingham, Dorset, SP8 5SE.*
Scandinavian farmhouse overlooking Blackmore Vale.
Open: All Year (not Xmas)
01747 838183 (also fax no)
Ms Trim
Rates fr: *£17.00*-**£22.00**.
Beds: 1D 1T
Baths: 2 Private
(6)

Weymouth

National Grid Ref: SY6769

Golden Bay Restaurant, Hamiltons, Cork & Bottle, Sailors' Return

Warwick Court Hotel, *20 Abbotsbury Road, Weymouth, Dorset, DT4 0AE.*
Family hotel. Close sea, amenities.
Open: All Year (not Xmas)
Grades: AA 3 Q, Recomm
01305 783261 Mr Flitney
Rates fr: *£15.00*-**£15.00**.
Beds: 5F 2D 2T 2S
Baths: 6 Ensuite 2 Shared
(6)

Kimberley Guest House, *16 Kirtleton Avenue, Weymouth, Dorset, DT4 7PT.*
'Home from home' atmosphere, excellent home cooked food.
Open: All Year
01305 783333
Mr Smith & Miss L Archer
Rates fr: *£14.00*-**£14.00**.
Beds: 2F 3D 1T
Baths: 1 Ensuite 2 Shared
(8)

Birchfields Hotel, *22 Abbotsbury Road, Weymouth, Dorset, DT4 0AE.*
Attractive hotel, a warm welcome guaranteed. **Open:** Easter to Oct
Grades: AA 2 Q, RAC Listed
01305 773255 Mr & Mrs Dutton
Rates fr: *£16.00*-**£16.00**.
Beds: 4F 2D 1T 2S
Baths: 3 Private 1 Shared
(3)

Hazeldene Guest House, *16 Abbotsbury Road, Weymouth, Dorset, DT4 0AE.*
A cosy seaside guest house.
Open: All Year
Grades: ETB 1 Cr, AA 2 Q, RAC Listed
01305 782579 Mr & Mrs Dyer
Fax no: 01305 761022
Rates fr: *£13.00*-**£13.00**.
Beds: 2F 3D 1T 1S
Baths: 1 Ensuite 3 Shared
(6)

Golden Bay Hotel, *54-55 The Esplanade, Weymouth, Dorset, DT4 8DG.*
Friendly service, great value & good food. **Open:** Easter to Oct
01305 760868 Mr Lam
Rates fr: *£17.50*-**£23.00**.
Beds: 2F 7D 2T 1S
Baths: 12 Private
(1)

Morven Hotel, *Westerhall Road, Weymouth, Dorset, DT4 7SZ.*
Conveniently situated, family-run hotel. **Open:** All Year (not Xmas)
01305 785075 Mr Lambley
Rates fr: *£17.00*-**£17.00**.
Beds: 8D 2T
Baths: 5 Ensuite 1 Shared
(12)

Brunswick Guest House, *9 Brunswick Terrace, Weymouth, Dorset, DT4 7RW.*
Beach view across Weymouth Bay.
Open: All Year
01305 785408 Mr Sherriff
Rates fr: *£14.00*-**£14.00**.
Beds: 2F 1T 3D 1S
Baths: 5 Ensuite
(5)

Valentines Hotel, *1 Waterloo Place, Weymouth, Dorset, DT4 7NS.*
Seafront Listed Georgian building.
Open: All Year
01305 771597 Mrs Simcox
Rates fr: *£14.00*-**£14.00**.
Beds: 2F 1D 3T 1S
Baths: 4 Private 3 Shared

Anchorage, *23 Stavordale Road, Weymouth, Dorset, DT4 0AB.*
Victorian haven, close harbour, beach.
Open: All Year (not Xmas)
01305 785719 Mrs Wakefield
Fax no: 01305 771501
Rates fr: *£15.00*-**£17.00**.
Beds: 2D 1T
Baths: 2 Ensuite 1 Shared
(4)

Lilac Villa, *124 Dorchester Road, Weymouth, Dorset, DT4 7JR.*
Friendly guest house.
Open: All Year (not Xmas)
Grades: ETB Listed
01305 782670 Mr & Mrs Taylor
Rates fr: *£20.00*-**£25.00**.
Beds: 1F 6D 1T
Baths: 8 Private
(9) (8)

Hotel Fairhaven, *37 The Esplanade, Weymouth, Dorset, DT4 8DH.*
Victorian seafront RAC 2 Star Hotel.
Open: Easter to Nov
Grades: RAC 2 St
01305 760200 Mr Thwaite
Fax no: 01605 760300
Rates fr: *£28.00*-**£30.00**.
Beds: 19F 16D 26T 15S
Baths: 76 Private
(20)

Hardwick House, *23 Hardwick Street, Weymouth, Dorset, DT4 7HU.*
Comfortable family-run house, very friendly.
Open: All Year (not Xmas)
01305 784303
Rates fr: *£13.00*-**£13.00**.
Beds: 4F 2D 2T 1S
Baths: 3 Ensuite 1 Private

Newbridge House, *7 Commercial Road, Weymouth, Dorset, DT4 7DW.*
Victorian house, close all amenities.
Open: All Year (not Xmas)
01305 787010 Mr & Mrs Allen
Rates fr: *£13.00*-**£13.00**.
Beds: 3D 2T 1S **Baths:** 2 Shared
(2)

Sou West Winds Hotel, *215 Dorchester Road, Weymouth, Dorset, DT3 5EQ.*
Nice, quality friendly accommodation.
Open: All Year (not Xmas)
01305 782362 Mrs Waring
Rates fr: *£15.00*-**£16.00**.
Beds: 2F 2D 2T
Baths: 3 Ensuite 2 Shared
(3) (6)

Whitchurch Canonicorum

National Grid Ref: SY3995

Five Bells

Cardsmill Farm, *Whitchurch Canonicorum, Bridport, Dorset, DT6 6RP.*
Comfortable farmhouse on working family farm.
Open: Feb to Nov
Grades: ETB 2 Cr, Approv
01297 489375 Mrs Johnson
Fax no: 01297 489 375
Rates fr: *£15.00*-**£16.00**.
Beds: 1F 1D
Baths: 1 Ensuite 1 Private
(6)

Wimborne Minster

National Grid Ref: SU0100

Puddine & Pye, Rising Sun

Sunnysides, *18 Victoria Road, Wimborne, Dorset, BH21 1EW.*
Warm, friendly, good touring centre.
Open: All Year
01202 886953
Mrs Randall
Rates fr: *£14.00*-**£14.00**.
Beds: 1D 1T
Baths: 1 Shared
(5) (2)

Hetherlands, *13 Wimborne Road, Colehill, Wimborne, Dorset, BH21 2RS.*
Large, friendly, Victorian family house.
Open: All Year (not Xmas)
01202 882032 Mrs Gibbs
Rates fr: *£12.50*-**£12.50**.
Beds: 2F 1T
Baths: 1 Shared
(3)

Acacia House, *2 Oakley Road, Wimborne, Dorset, BH21 1QJ.*
Nobody does it better.
Open: All Year (not Xmas)
01202 883958
Rates fr: *£20.00*-**£17.00**.
Beds: 1F 1T 1D 1S
Baths: 2 Ensuite 2 Shared
(1) (3)

Turi, *21 Grove Road, Wimborne Minster, Dorset, BH21 1BN.*
Near Minster, market & river.
Open: All Year
01202 884818
Mrs Joyner
Rates fr: *£14.00*-**£14.00**.
Beds: 1F 1T
Baths: 2 Shared

Winfrith Newburgh

National Grid Ref: SY8084

Sailors Return

The Manor House, *Winfrith Newburgh, Dorchester, Dorset, DT2 8JR.*
Historic manor house with luxury rooms.
Open: All Year
01305 852988
Mr & Mrs Smith
Fax no: 01305 854988
Rates fr: *£21.00*.
Beds: 1D 1T
Baths: 2 Private
(5)

The lowest *double* rate per person is shown in *italics*.

Winterborne Zelston

National Grid Ref: SY8997

Botany Bay Inn

Brook Farm, *Winterborne Zelston, Blandford Forum, Dorset, DT11 9EU.*
Friendly farmhouse, quiet, pretty village.
Open: All Year (not Xmas)
01929 459267 Mrs Kerley
Rates fr: *£16.00*-**£20.00**.
Beds: 2F 1T
Baths: 2 Ensuite 1 Private
(4)

Winterbourne Abbas

National Grid Ref: SY6190

Churchview Guest House, *Winterbourne Abbas, Dorchester, Dorset, DT2 9LS.*
Delightful C17th guest house.
Open: All Year (not Xmas)
Grades: ETB 3 Cr, Comm, AA 3 Q
01305 889296 Mr Deller
Rates fr: *£18.00*-**£18.00**.
Beds: 1F 4D 3T 1S
Baths: 7 Private 1 Shared
(3) (10)

Witchampton

National Grid Ref: ST9806

Hemsworth Farm, *Witchampton, Wimborne Minster, Dorset, BH21 5BN.*
Spacious manor farmhouse, peaceful located.
Open: All Year (not Xmas)
01258 840216 Mrs Tory
Rates fr: *£18.50*-**£20.00**.
Beds: 1F 1D 1T
Baths: 2 Ensuite 1 Private

Wool

National Grid Ref: SY8486

Black Beck, Ship Inn

Long Coppice, *Bindon Lane, Wool, Wareham, Dorset, BH20 6AS.*
Comfortable family bungalow in 8 acres.
Open: All Year (not Xmas)
01929 463123
Ms Lowman
Rates fr: *£17.50*-**£20.00**.
Beds: 1F 1D 1T
Baths: 2 Private 1 Shared
(10)

High Tor, *Frome Avenue, Wool, Wareham, Dorset, BH20 6ER.*
Large detached house. Country setting.
Open: All Year
01929 462467 / 463395
Mrs Foggon
Fax no: 01929 462467
Rates fr: *£12.50*-**£15.00**.
Beds: 2D 1S
Baths: 1 Shared
(12)

Worth Matravers

National Grid Ref: SY9777

Belros, *Winspit Road, Worth Matravers, Swanage, Dorset, BH19 3LW.*
Spacious, comfortable, friendly family house.
Open: All Year (not Xmas)
01929 439259
Mrs Prior
Rates fr: *£18.00*-**£18.50**.
Beds: 3D 1T
Baths: 1 Ensuite 2 Shared
(8) (10)

Bringing children with you? Always ask for any special rates.

Sunnydown Farm, *Worth Matravers, Swanage, Dorset, BH19 3JP.*
Modern comfortable farmhouse.
Open: All Year (not Xmas)
01929 439385
Mrs Notley
Rates fr: *£16.00*-**£15.00**.
Beds: 1F 1D 1T
Baths: 1 Shared
(4)

Wyke Regis

National Grid Ref: SY6677

The Old Wyke Bakehouse, *100 Portland Road, Wyke Regis, Weymouth, Dorset, DT4 9AB.*
Converted bakery, original features.
Open: All Year
01305 772580
Mrs Wild
Rates fr: *£16.00*-**£16.00**.
Beds: 3F 3D 1S
Baths: 7 Private
(4)

All details shown are as supplied by B&B owners in Autumn 1996.

County Durham

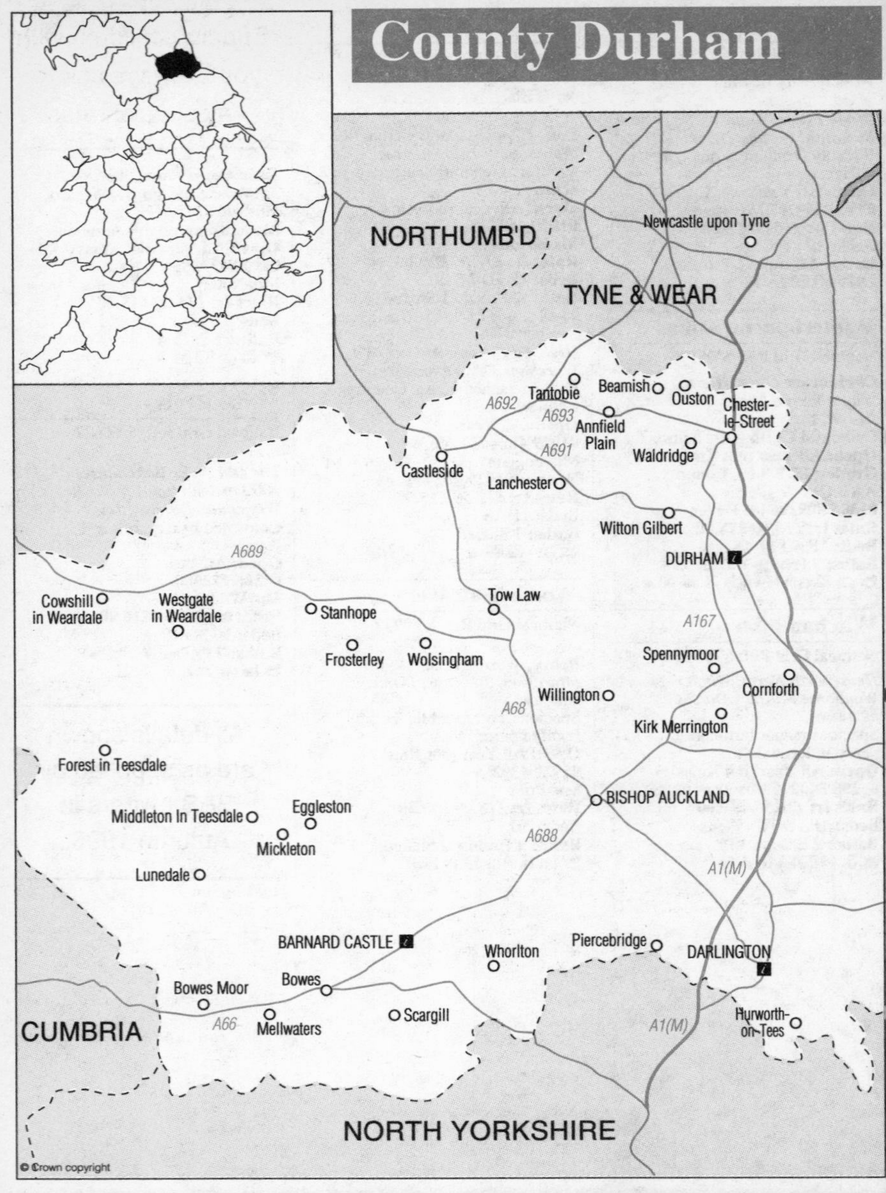

Tourist Information Centres

43 Galgate, **Barnard Castle,**
County Durham,
DL12 8EL,
01833-690909.

13 Horsemarket, **Darlington,**
County Durham,
DL1 5PW,
01325 388666.

Durham Dales Centre, Market
Place, Weardale, **Stanhope,**
County Durham, DL13 2FJ,
01388-527650.

Tourist Information Centre,
Beamish,.
0191-370 2533.

20 The Upper Chare,
Peterlee, County Durham,
SR8 5TE,
0191-586 4450.

North of England Open Air
Museum, Beamish, **Stanley,**
County Durham, DH9 0RG,
01207 231811

Annfield Plain

National Grid Ref: NZ1751

***Hvam,** St Aidans, Annfield Plain, Stanley, Co Durham, DH9 7XF.*
Well-appointed detached house.
Open: All Year
01207 234414 Mrs Robertson
Rates fr: *£15.00*-**£15.00**.
Beds: 1F 1T
Baths: 1 Shared
(2)

Barnard Castle

National Grid Ref: NZ0314

Ancient Unicorn (Bowes)

***Old Well Inn,** 21 The Bank, Barnard Castle, Co Durham, DL12 8PH.*
Historic coaching Inn. Superb food.
Open: All Year
Grades: ETB 3 Cr, Comm
01833 690130 Mrs Carter
Fax no: 01833 690140
Rates fr: *£22.50*-**£32.00**.
Beds: 2F 3D 1T 1S
Baths: 7 Ensuite

***West Roods,** Barnard Castle, Barnard Castle, Co Durham, DL12 9SW.*
Geordie hospitality, Teesdale working farm.
Open: April to Oct
Grades: ETB 3 Cr, AA 1 Q, RAC Listed
01833 690116 Mrs Lowson
Rates fr: *£18.00*-**£18.00**.
Beds: 1F 1D 1S
Baths: 2 Private 1 Shared
(0) (6)

Beamish

National Grid Ref: NZ2253

The Beamish Mary Inn

***No Place House,** Beamish, Stanley, Co Durham, DH9 0QH.*
Open: All Year
Grades: ETB 2 Cr, Comm
0191 370 0891 Mr & Mrs Wood
Rates fr: *£17.00*-**£17.00**.
Beds: 2D 1T
Baths: 2 Ensuite 1 Shared
(3) (5)
Converted co-operative store, half a mile from Beamish Museum. Beautiful spacious rooms, ensuites with steam/showers. 6 miles from Durham, Metro Centre. Friendly warm welcome.

***Mount Escob Farm,** Beamish Woods, Beamish, Stanley, Co Durham, DH9 0SA.*
Country house in tranquil historic setting.
Open: All Year (not Xmas)
0191 370 0289 Mrs Bovill
Rates fr: *£15.00*-**£17.00**.
Beds: 1F 1D
(5) (6)

Bishop Auckland

National Grid Ref: NZ1928

***Albion Cottage Guest House,** Albion Terrace, Bishop Auckland, Co Durham, DL14 6EL.*
Detached early Victorian house.
Open: All Year (not Xmas)
01388 602217 Miss Gordon
Rates fr: *£15.00*-**£15.00**.
Beds: 1D 1T 2S
Baths: 2 Shared
(6)

Bowes

National Grid Ref: NY9913

Ancient Unicorn

***West End Farm,** Bowes, Barnard Castle, Co Durham, DL12 9LH.*
Traditional old working farm.
Open: May to Oct
01833 628239
Mrs Foster
Rates fr: *£12.00*.
Beds: 1F
Baths: 1 Shared

Bowes Moor

National Grid Ref: NY9211

Ancient Unicorn (Bowes)

***Bowes Moor Hotel,** Bowes Moor, Barnard Castle, Co Durham, DL12 9RH.*
300-year-old former shooting lodge.
Open: All Year
01833 628331
Mrs Luscombe(SHL Partnership)
Rates fr: *£17.00*-**£19.50**.
Beds: 5D 2T 3S
Baths: 9 Private
(60)

Castleside

National Grid Ref: NZ0848

***Bee Cottage Farm,** Castleside, Consett, Co Durham, DH8 9HW.*
Working farm in lovely surroundings.
Open: All Year
Grades: ETB 2 Cr, High Comm
01207 508224
Mrs Lawson
Rates fr: *£22.00*-**£25.00**.
Beds: 3F 3D 2T 1S
Baths: 3 Ensuite 4 Shared
(20)

***Castlenook Guest House,** 18 Front Street, Castleside, Consett, Co Durham, DH8 9AR.*
C16th hostelry, castleside village centre.
Open: All Year (not Xmas)
01207 506634
Mrs Stafford
Rates fr: *£15.00*-**£20.00**.
Beds: 1D 2T 1S
Baths: 3 Private
(5)

Always telephone to get directions to the B&B - you will save time!

Chester-le-Street

National Grid Ref: NZ2751

***16 St Cuthberts Avenue,** Holmlands Park, Chester-le-Street, Co Durham, DH3 3PS.*
Private house near Lumley Castle. Extremely close to cricket grounds.
Open: All Year (not Xmas)
0191 387 3071 Mrs McCann
Rates fr: *£34.00*-**£17.00**.
Beds: 1D 1S
Baths: 1 Shared
(8) (2)

Cornforth

National Grid Ref: NZ3134

Old Mill, Poachers Pocket

***Ash House,** 24 The Green, Cornforth, Co Durham, DL17 9JH.*
Victorian house on quiet village green.
Open: All Year
01740 654654 Mrs Slack
Rates fr: *£18.00*-**£22.00**.
Beds: 1F 1T
Baths: 1 Shared
(3) (5)

Cowshill

National Grid Ref: NY8540

***Low Cornriggs Farm,** Cowshill, Wearhead, Bishop Auckland, Co Durham, DL13 1AQ.*
Restored 200-year-old beamed farmhouse. **Open:** All Year
Grades: ETB 3 Cr, Comm
01388 537600 Ms Ellis
Rates fr: *£18.00*-**£20.00**.
Beds: 1F 1D 1T 1S
Baths: 4 Private

Darlington

National Grid Ref: NZ2814

Railway Tavern

***Aberlady Guest Hotel,** 51 Corporation Road, Darlington, Co Durham, DL3 6AD.*
Victorian house close to town centre.
Open: All Year
Grades: ETB 1 Cr, Approv
01325 461449 Ms Chaplin
Rates fr: *£13.50*-**£13.50**.
Beds: 2F 3T 2S
(2)

***Woodlands Guest House,** 63 Woodland Road, Darlington, Co Durham, DL3 7BQ.*
Beautiful Victorian town house on A68.
Open: All Year
Grades: ETB 2 Cr, Comm, AA 3 Q
01325 461908 Mr Hawke
Rates fr: *£18.00*-**£20.00**.
Beds: 2F 1D 2T 3S
Baths: 2 Private 2 Shared

***Bernia House,** 56 Vane Terrace, Darlington, Co Durham, DL3 7RB.*
Victorian town house, quiet location.
Open: All Year
Grades: ETB 1 Cr
01325 461493
Mr & Mrs Weyman-Fellows
Rates fr: *£15.00*-**£16.00**.
Beds: 1F 1D 1T 1S

***Alba House,** 51 Swinburne Road, Darlington, Co Durham, DL3 7TD.*
Large Victorian private house.
Open: All Year
01325 489690 Mrs MacKay
Rates fr: *£18.00*-**£18.00**.
Beds: 1F 1S
Baths: 2 Private
(5)

Durham

National Grid Ref: NZ2742

Duke of Wellington, Court Inn

***14 Gilesgate,** Durham, DH1 1QW.*
Central spacious C18th town house.
Open: All Year (not Xmas)
Grades: ETB 1 Cr
0191 384 6485 (also fax no)
Mr Nimmins
Rates fr: *£15.00*-**£15.00**.
Beds: 2F 2D 2T 1S
Baths: 2 Shared
(1)

***Castle View Guest House,** 4 Crossgate, Durham, DH1 4PS.*
City centre Georgian guest house.
Open: All Year (not Xmas)
Grades: ETB 2 Cr, Comm, AA 3 Q
0191 386 8852
Mrs Williams
Rates fr: *£20.00*-**£25.00**.
Beds: 1F 2D 2T 1S
Baths: 3 Ensuite 3 Shared
(2)

***26 St Johns Road,** Nevilles Cross, Durham, DH1 4NU.*
Late Victorian house - quiet area.
Open: All Year (not Xmas)
0191 384 8329
Mrs Burton
Rates fr: *£17.00*-**£20.00**.
Beds: 1D 1T
Baths: 1 Shared

***The Pink House,** 16 Gilesgate, Durham, DH1 1QW.*
Small Georgian house. Homely, central.
Open: All Year
Grades: ETB Listed
0191 386 7039
Mrs Miles
Rates fr: *£14.00*-**£17.50**.
Beds: 1F 1T
Baths: 1 Shared

***Collingwood College,** South Road, Durham, DH1 3LT.*
Beautifully modern comfortable accommodation.
Open: Jun to Sep
Grades: ETB Listed
0191 374 4565 Mr Hewlett
Fax no: 0191 374 4595
Rates fr: *£22.00*-**£17.00**.
Beds: 16T 514S
Baths: 213 Ensuite
(130)

***Park View,** 1 Allergate Terrace, Durham, DH1 4ES.*
Large central town house.
Open: All Year (not Xmas)
Grades: ETB Listed
0191 386 7034 Mrs Buxton
Rates fr: *£19.00*-**£19.00**.
Beds: 2D 1T
Baths: 3 Ensuite
(5)

***Castledene,** 37 Nevilledale Terrace, Durham, DH1 4QG.*
Clean, comfortable, Victorian terrace house.
Open: All Year
0191 384 8386 Mrs Byrne
Rates fr: *£17.00*-**£17.00**.
Beds: 2T 1S **Baths:** 1 Shared
(7) (5)

***Pension Montez,** 6 Providence Close, Durham, DH1 1XG.*
City centre location, friendly management.
Open: All Year
0191 383 0186 Mr Ralte
Rates fr: *£10.00*-**£15.00**.
Beds: 1D
Baths: 1 Shared
(2)

***Bees Cottage Guest House,** Bridge Street, Durham, DH1 4RT.*
Durham's oldest cottage, city location.
Open: All Year (not Xmas)
0191 384 5775 Mrs Heslop
Rates fr: *£20.00*-**£27.00**.
Beds: 1F 2D 2T
Baths: 5 Private
(4)

***Green Grove,** 99 Gilesgate, Durham, DH1 1JA.*
Large Victorian town house.
Open: All Year (not Xmas)
0191 384 4361 Mrs Cummings
Rates fr: *£16.00*-**£18.00**.
Beds: 2F 2D 4T
Baths: 1 Private 1 Shared
(8)

National Grid References are for villages, towns and cities - *not* for individual houses.

Always telephone to get directions to the B&B - you will save time!

Eggleston

National Grid Ref: NZ0023

Moorcock Inn, *Hill Top, Gordon Bank, Eggleston, Co Durham, DL12 0AU.*
Country inn with panoramic view.
Open: All Year
01833 650395
Mr & Mrs Zacharias
Fax no: 01833 650052
Rates fr: *£16.00*-**£20.00**.
Beds: 1F 3D 1T
Baths: 1 Ensuite
(50)

Forest in Teesdale

National Grid Ref: NY8629

High Force Hotel

High Force Hotel, *Forest in Teesdale, Barnard Castle, Co Durham, DL12 0XH.*
Warm, comfortable converted shooting lodge.
Open: All Year
Grades: ETB 3 Cr
01833 22222
Mrs Baxter
Fax no: 01833 622264
Rates fr: *£21.00*-**£21.00**.
Beds: 3F 1T 2S

High Force Training Centre, *The Old Vicarage, Forest in Teesdale, Barnard Castle, Co Durham, DL12 0HA.*
Stay in England's last wilderness.
Open: All Year
01833 622302
Mr Hosey
Rates fr: *£15.00*-**£15.00**.
Beds: 8F 2D 2S
Baths: 1 Private 3 Shared
(30)

High season, bank holidays and special events mean low availability *anywhere.*

National Grid References are for villages, towns and cities - *not* for individual houses.

Langdon Beck Hotel, *Forest in Teesdale, Barnard Castle, Co Durham, DL12 0XP.*
Warm welcome with traditional home-cooked food.
Open: All Year (not Xmas)
01833 622267
Mrs Collin
Rates fr: *£22.00*-**£19.00**.
Beds: 1F 2D 1T 3S
Baths: 2 Private 2 Shared
(12)

Frosterley

National Grid Ref: NZ0237

Lime Tree House, *7 Osborne Terrace, Frosterley, Bishop Auckland, Co Durham, DL13 2RD.*
Small, comfortable, centrally-heated house.
Open: All Year
01388 527139
Miss Robson
Rates fr: *£14.00*-**£15.00**.
Beds: 1D 1T
Baths: 1 Shared
(3) (2)

Hartlepool

National Grid Ref: NZ5032

Durham House Hotel, *38/39 The Front, Seaton Carew, Hartlepool, TS25 1DA.*
Family hotel, sea front location.
Open: All Year
01429 236502
Mrs Bell
Rates fr: *£13.00*-**£14.00**.
Beds: 3F 5D 3T 3S
Baths: 3 Private

York Hotel, *185-187 York Road, Hartlepool, TS26 9EE.*
Luxurious accommodation, Pennicks Restaurant.
Open: All Year
01429 867373
Mr Pennick
Rates fr: *£20.00*-**£30.00**.
Beds: 8D 6S

The lowest **single** *rate is shown in* **bold.**

Haswell Plough

National Grid Ref: NZ3742

The Gables Hotel, *Haswell Plough, Durham, DH6 2EW.*
Open: All Year
Grades: AA Listed
0191 526 2982 Mr Milner
Rates fr: *£16.00*-**£22.00**.
Beds: 1F 2D 2T
Baths: 2 Shared
(30)
Small family-run hotel in the heart of Geordieland. Laugh, sing & be merry - you'll never forget The Gables (east of Durham city on B1283).

Hurworth-on-Tees

National Grid Ref: NZ3010

Black Bull (Moulton)

Hill Top Farm, *Hurworth-on-Tees, Darlington, Co Durham, DL2 2EG.*
Rustic farmhouse, ample parking, stables.
Open: All Year (not Xmas)
Grades: ETB Listed
01325 721064 Mrs Emery
Rates fr: *£16.00*-**£16.00**.
Beds: 1F 1S
Baths: 1 Shared
(5)

Kirk Merrington

National Grid Ref: NZ2631

Fox & Hounds, *Cameron Terrace, Kirk Merrington, Spennymoor, Co Durham, DL16 9HS.*
Country village inn.
Open: All Year
01388 814043
Rates fr: *£17.50*-**£25.00**.
Beds: 2D 1T
Baths: 3 Private
(50)

Lanchester

National Grid Ref: NZ1647

Kings Head Hotel, *Station Road, Lanchester, Durham, DH7 0EX.*
Delightful public house.
Open: All Year
01207 520054 Mr Batista
Rates fr: *£20.00*-**£25.00**.
Beds: 1D 3T 1S
Baths: 2 Shared
(200)

Partridge Close Stud Farm, *Lanchester, Durham, DH7 0SZ.*
Small country house in lovely setting.
Open: All Year
01207 520896 Mrs Alexander
Rates fr: *£23.50*-**£25.00**.
Beds: 1D 1T 1S
Baths: 2 Private
(8)

The lowest *double* rate per person is shown in *italics*.

Lunedale

National Grid Ref: NY9221

***Grassholme Farm,** Lunedale, Middleton in Teesdale, Barnard Castle, Co Durham, DL12 0PR.*
Open: Easter to Sep
01833 640494 Mrs Sayer
Rates fr: *£13.00*-**£13.00**.
Beds: 1T
Baths: 1 Shared
(3)
A warm welcome awaits you at our family-run farm, overlooking Grassholme Reservoir. Good farmhouse food in our cosy restaurant with open fires.

***Wythes Hill Farm,** Lunedale, Middleton in Teesdale, Barnard Castle, Co Durham, DL12 0NX.*
Farmhouse with panoramic views.
Open: Easter to Oct
01833 640349 Mrs Dent
Rates fr: *£15.00*-**£15.00**.
Beds: 1F 1T
Baths: 1 Ensuite 1 Shared
(3)

Mellwaters

National Grid Ref: NY9612

***East Mellwaters Farm,** Mellwaters, Bowes, Barnard Castle, Co Durham, DL12 9RH.*
Modernised comfortable C17th farmhouse.
Open: All Year (not Xmas)
01833 628269 Mrs Milner
Rates fr: *£17.50*-**£18.00**.
Beds: 1F 2D 1T 1S
Baths: 5 Private
(10)

Mickleton

National Grid Ref: NY9623

***Rose & Crown Inn,** Mickleton, Barnard Castle, Co Durham, DL12 0JZ.*
Friendly family-run pub.
Open: All Year
01833 640381 Carter
Rates fr: *£16.00*-**£16.00**.
Beds: 1F 2D 2T
(10)

The lowest **single** *rate is shown in* **bold.**

Middleton in Teesdale

National Grid Ref: NY9425

Chatter Box, Talbot Hotel

***Brunswick House,** 55 Market Place, Middleton in Teesdale, Barnard Castle, Co Durham, DL12 0QH.*
Charming C18th guesthouse, excellent food.
Open: All Year
Grades: ETB 3 Cr, Comm, AA 3 Q
01833 640393 Mr & Mrs Milnes
Rates fr: *£21.00*-**£21.00**.
Beds: 1F 2D 1T
Baths: 4 Private
(4)

***25 Bridge Street,** Middleton in Teesdale, Barnard Castle, Co Durham, DL12 0QB.*
Victorian private house.
Open: All Year
01833 640549 Mrs Sowerby
Rates fr: *£17.00*-**£17.00**.
Beds: 1D 4T 1S
Baths: 2 Shared
(10)

***Kingsway Adventure Centre,** Alston Road, Middleton in Teesdale, Barnard Castle, Co Durham, DL12 0UU.*
Family-run outdoor centre.
Open: All Year
01833 640881
Mr Hearn
Rates fr: *£10.00*-**£12.00**.
Beds: 3F 2T
Baths: 2 Ensuite 2 Shared
(0) (50)

***Lonton South,** Middleton in Teesdale, Barnard Castle, Co Durham, DL12 0PL.*
Old, comfortable farmhouse.
Open: Mar to Oct
Grades: ETB Listed
01833 640409 Mrs Watson
Rates fr: *£15.00*-**£15.00**.
Beds: 1D 1T 1S
Baths: 1 Shared

***Talbot Hotel,** Market Place, Middleton in Teesdale, Barnard Castle, Co Durham, DL12 0.*
Converted C17th house.
Open: All Year
01833 640273 Mr Parker
Rates fr: *£13.50*-**£13.50**.
Beds: 1F 1T
Baths: 1 Ensuite

***Ivy House,** Stanhope Road, Middleton in Teesdale, Bishop Auckland, Co Durham, DL12 0RT.*
Large Victorian private house.
Open: All Year
01833 640603 Mrs Ebdon
Rates fr: *£15.00*-**£14.00**.
Beds: 1D 1T 1S
Baths: 1 Private 1 Shared

Ouston

National Grid Ref: NZ2554

***Low Urpeth Farmhouse,** Ouston, Chester-le-Street, Co Durham, DH2 1BD.*
Relax in our traditional farmhouse.
Open: All Year
0191 410 2901 Mrs Johnson
Rates fr: *£16.00*-**£20.00**.
Beds: 1D 2T
Baths: 2 Ensuite 1 Shared
(6)

Piercebridge

National Grid Ref: NZ2015

George Hotel

***The Bridge House,** Piercebridge, Darlington, Co Durham, DL2 3SG.*
C18th, spacious riverside cottage.
Open: All Year (not Xmas)
01325 374727
Mrs Waller
Rates fr: *£17.50*-**£22.00**.
Beds: 1D 2T
Baths: 1 Ensuite 1 Shared

Scargill

National Grid Ref: NZ0411

Morritt Arms (Greta Bridge)

***Lodge Farm,** Scargill, Barnard Castle, Co Durham, DL12 9SY.*
Dales stock rearing farm.
Open: All Year (not Xmas)
01833 621238
Mrs Jeffrey
Rates fr: *£15.00*-**£20.00**.
Beds: 1D

Seaham

National Grid Ref: NZ4149

***2 Bath Terrace,** Seaham, Co Durham, SR7 7EZ.*
Large Victorian house on clifftop with views 40 miles down coast.
Open: All Year
0191 581 3284 Mr Bond
Rates fr: *£16.00*-**£16.00**.
Beds: 1D 2T
Baths: 1 Shared

Shotley Bridge

National Grid Ref: NZ0852

***Crown & Crossed Swords Hotel,** Shotley Bridge, Consett, Co Durham, DH8 0NH.*
Historical country hotel.
Open: All Year
01207 502006 Mrs Suddick
Rates fr: *£18.00*-**£23.00**.
Beds: 1F 4D 4T 1S
Baths: 4 Private 2 Shared
(40)

Redwell Hall Farm, *Shotley Bridge, Consett, Co Durham, DH8 9TS.*
Accommodation in cottage, farmhouse annexe.
Open: All Year
01207 255216 Mrs Ward
Rates fr: *£15.50*-**£18.50**.
Beds: 1F 1D 1T 1S
Baths: 1 Shared

Spennymoor

National Grid Ref: NZ2533

Thinford Inn, Fox & Hounds

Idsley House, *4 Green Lane, Spennymoor, Co Durham, DL16 6HD.*
Detached Victorian house, quiet location.
Open: All Year (not Xmas)
Grades: ETB 2 Cr. High Comm
01388 814237 Mrs Dartnall
Rates fr: *£19.00*-**£28.00**.
Beds: 1F 1D 2T 1S
Baths: 4 Private 1 Shared
(3) (8)

The Gables, *10 South View, Middlestone Moor, Spennymoor, Co Durham, DL16 7DF.*
Spacious Victorian detached house.
Open: All Year
Grades: ETB 3 Cr, Comm
01388 817544 Mr Shortman
Rates fr: *£14.00*-**£17.00**.
Beds: 2D 4T
Baths: 3 Private 2 Shared
(0) (7)

Ye Olde Station Guest House, *1 Whitworth Terrace, Spennymoor, Co Durham, DL16 7LD.*
Family-run guest house.
Open: All Year
01388 814455 Mr Murray
Rates fr: *£12.00*-**£12.00**.
Beds: 2F 4T 1S
Baths: 1 Private 2 Shared
(1) (8)

Staindrop

National Grid Ref: NZ1220

Gazebo House, *4 North Green, Staindrop, Co Durham, DL2 3JN.*
Queen Anne house, Listed gazebo.
Open: All Year (not Xmas)
01833 660222 Mrs Shingler
Rates fr: *£19.00*-**£18.00**.
Beds: 1D 1T
Baths: 2 Private

Pay B&Bs by cash or cheque. Be prepared to pay up front for one night stays.

Stanhope

National Grid Ref: NY9939

Queens Head, Stanhope Old Hall

Redlodge Cottage, *2 Market Place, Stanhope, Bishop Auckland, Co Durham, DL13 2UN.*
Well-appointed guest house.
Open: All Year
01388 527851
Mr & Mrs Hamilton
Rates fr: *£17.00*-**£22.50**.
Beds: 2F 1D 1T
Baths: 1 Private 1 Shared
(2)

Stockton-on-Tees

National Grid Ref: NZ4320

Stonyroyd Hotel, *187 Oxbridge Lane, Stockton-on-Tees, TS18 4JB.*
Large detached Victorian house.
Open: All Year (not Xmas)
01642 607734 Mrs Povey
Rates fr: *£20.00*-**£24.00**.
Beds: 3F 6D 2T 4S
Baths: 1 Private 1 Shared

Windsor Hotel, *47-49 Norton Road, Stockton-on-Tees, TS18 2BZ.*
Warm, friendly, centrally situated hotel. **Open:** All Year
01642 612143
Mr Stoddart
Rates fr: *£16.50*-**£16.50**.
Beds: 6T 6S

Tantobie

National Grid Ref: NZ1754

Oak Tree Inn, *Tantobie, Stanley, Co Durham, DH9 9RF.*
Victorian inn with good restaurant.
Open: All Year
Grades: ETB 3 Cr, AA 3 Q
01207 235445 Mrs Hurst
Rates fr: *£20.00*-**£20.50**.
Beds: 3D 1T 1S
Baths: 5 Ensuite 1 Shared
(2) (10)

Tow Law

National Grid Ref: NZ1138

Bay Horse (Wolsingham)

Greenwell Farm, *Tow Law, Wolsingham, Bishop Auckland, Co Durham, DL13 4PH.*
Converted barn in tranquil setting.
Open: All Year (not Xmas)
Grades: ETB 3 Cr, Comm
01388 527248
Mrs Vickers
Fax no: 01388 526735
Rates fr: *£18.50*-**£20.00**.
Beds: 1F 2D 1T 1S
Baths: 5 Ensuite
(6)

Right on the border? Look at the neighbouring county, too

Waldridge

National Grid Ref: NZ2550

Waldridge Fell House, *Waldridge Lane, Waldridge, Chester-le-Street, Co Durham, DH2 3RY.*
Converted village chapel.
Open: All Year (not Xmas)
0191 389 1908 Mrs Sharratt
Rates fr: *£18.00*-**£22.00**.
Beds: 5F
Baths: 1 Private 1 Shared
(8)

Westgate in Weardale

National Grid Ref: NY9038

Lands Farm, *Westgate in Weardale, Bishop Auckland, Co Durham, DL13 1SN.*
Peaceful farmhouse with high standards.
Open: Easter to Oct
Grades: ETB 2 Cr, High Comm
01388 517210 Mrs Reed
Rates fr: *£20.00*-**£25.00**.
Beds: 1F 1D
Baths: 2 Private
(4)

Breckon Hill Country Guest House, *Westgate in Weardale, Bishop Auckland, Co Durham, DL13 1PD.*
Breathtaking views in tranquil surroundings.
Open: All Year (not Xmas)
01388 517228
Mrs Say
Rates fr: *£20.00*-**£27.00**.
Beds: 3D 3T
Baths: 6 Ensuite
(6)

Wingate House Farm, *Westgate in Weardale, Bishop Auckland, Co Durham, DL13 1LP.*
Beautiful Victorian farmhouse. Working farm.
Open: Easter to Oct
01388 517281 Mrs Peart
Rates fr: *£16.00*-**£15.00**.
Beds: 1F 1T
Baths: 1 Private 1 Shared
(6)

Westgate House, *Westgate in Weardale, Bishop Auckland, Co Durham, DL13 1LW.*
Victorian country home.
Open: Easter to Oct
01388 517564 Mrs Williams
Rates fr: *£20.00*-**£20.00**.
Beds: 1D 2T
Baths: 2 Private 1 Shared

Wheatley Hill

National Grid Ref: NZ3739

Castle Eaden Inn

***Lynngarth Guest House,** Lynn Terrace, Wheatley Hill, Durham, DH6 3QN.*
Open: All Year (not Xmas)
01429 821198 Hughes
Rates fr: *£16.00*-**£17.00**.
Beds: 1F 3D 3T
Baths: 2 Ensuite 2 Shared
(10)
Friendly family-run detached Georgian-style guest house. Coal fire. Quiet location on edge of village with country views. 8 miles east of Durham City.

Whorlton

National Grid Ref: NZ1014

***The Coach House,** Whorlton, Barnard Castle, Co Durham, DL12 8XQ.*
Converted stables.
Open: Apr to Feb
01833 627237 Mrs Calder
Rates fr: *£17.50*-**£17.50**.
Beds: 1D 1T **Baths:** 1 Shared
(14) (2)

Willington

National Grid Ref: NZ1935

***Kensington Hall Hotel,** Kensington Terrace, Willington, Crook, Co Durham, DL15 0PJ.*
Very comfortable family-run hotel.
Open: All Year
Grades: ETB 2 Cr, Comm, AA 2 St
01388 745071 Mr Smeaton
Rates fr: *£22.50*-**£32.50**.
Beds: 4F 2D 4T **Baths:** 10 Private

Witton Gilbert

National Grid Ref: NZ2346

Travellers Rest

***Lothlorien,** Front Street, Witton Gilbert, Durham, DH7 6SY.*
Comfortable period cottage.
Open: All Year (not Xmas)
Grades: ETB 1 Cr, Comm, AA 3 Q, Recomm, RAC Listed
0191 371 0067 Mrs Milne
Rates fr: *£17.00*-**£17.00**.
Beds: 1D 1T 1S
Baths: 2 Shared
(4)

Wolsingham

National Grid Ref: NZ0737

Bay Horse, Mill Race

***Friarside Farm,** Wolsingdale, Wolsingham, Weardale, Bishop Auckland, Co Durham, DL13 3BH.*
Well worth holydaying here.
Open: All Year (not Xmas)
Grades: ETB 1 Cr, Comm
01388 527361 Mrs Anderson
Rates fr: *£16.00*-**£16.00**.
Beds: 2D
Baths: 1 Shared
(5) (2)

***Holywell Farm,** Wolsingham, Bishop Auckland, Co Durham, DL13 3HB.*
Grade II Listed old farmhouse.
Open: Apr to Nov
Grades: ETB Listed
01388 527249 Mrs Love
Rates fr: *£12.50*-**£15.00**.
Beds: 2D
Baths: 1 Shared
(All) (2)

***Chapman House,** 52 Front Street, Wolsingham, Bishop Auckland, Co Durham, DL13 3DD.*
Interesting end-of-terrace house.
Open: All Year (not Xmas)
01388 528918
Mrs Bushell
Rates fr: *£14.00*-**£14.00**.
Beds: 1D 1T
Baths: 1 Private 1 Shared

***Hill Race Hotel,** 8 West End, Wolsingham, Bishop Auckland, Co Durham, DL13 3AP.*
Comfortable and friendly atmosphere.
Open: All Year
01388 526551 Mrs Walker
Rates fr: *£15.00*-**£17.50**.
Beds: 1F 1D 1T 1S
Baths: 1 Private 1 Shared

***Bay Horse Hotel,** Upper Town, Wolsingham, Bishop Auckland, Co Durham, DL13 3EX.*
Real pub food & beer.
Open: All Year
01388 527220 Mrs Ellila
Rates fr: *£15.00*-**£18.00**.
Beds: 4D 3T
Baths: 5 Private 1 Shared
(20)

Please respect a B&B's wishes regarding children, animals & smoking.

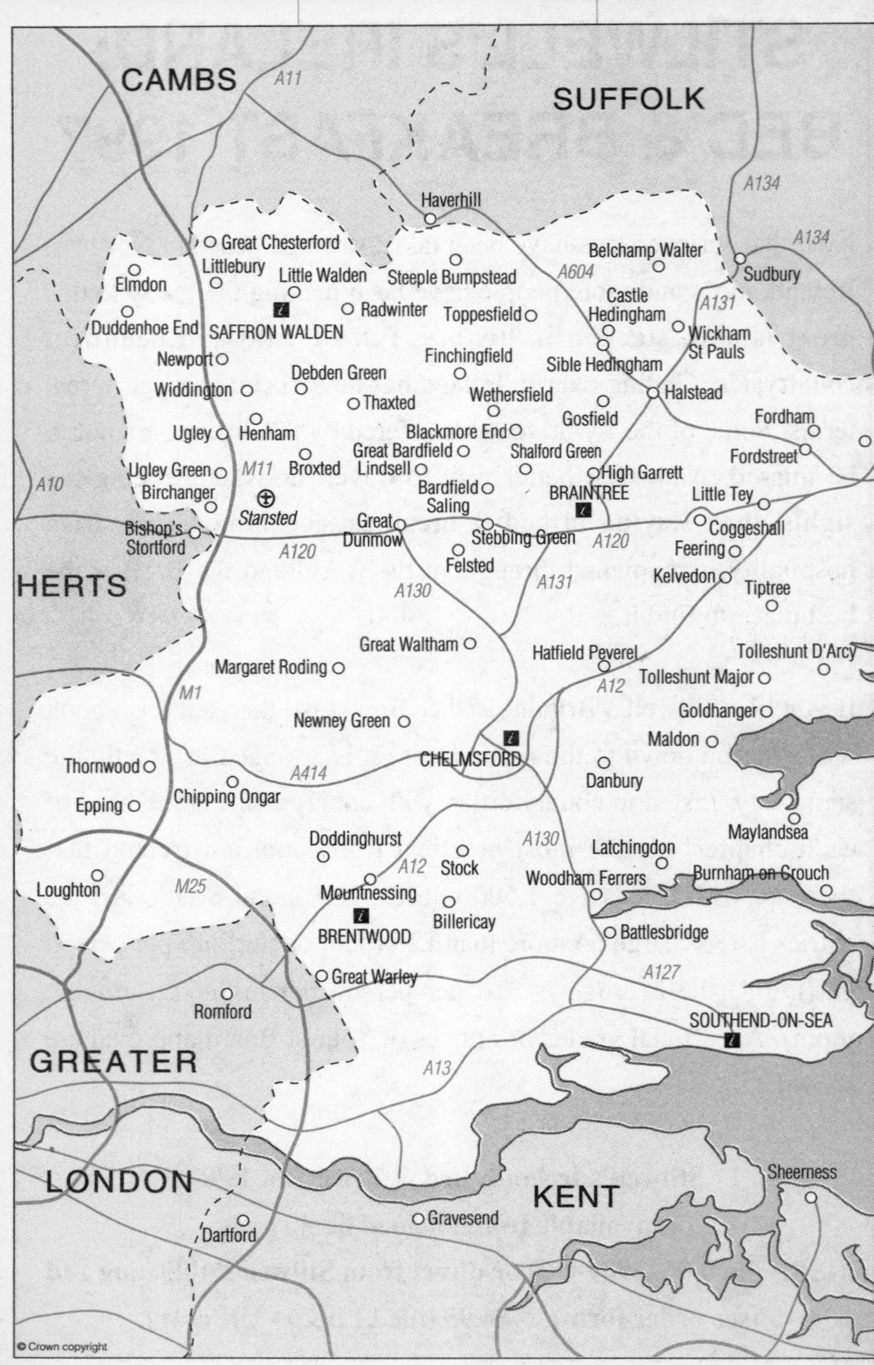

CAMBS
SUFFOLK
HERTS
GREATER
LONDON
KENT
A11
A134
A604
A131
A10
M11
A120
A130
A12
M1
A414
M25
A127
A13
Haverhill
Great Chesterford
Littlebury
Elmdon
Little Walden
Steeple Bumpstead
Belchamp Walter
Sudbury
Castle Hedingham
Wickham St Pauls
Duddenhoe End
SAFFRON WALDEN
Radwinter
Toppesfield
Newport
Finchingfield
Sible Hedingham
Halstead
Widdington
Debden Green
Thaxted
Wethersfield
Gosfield
Fordham
Ugley
Henham
Blackmore End
Great Bardfield
Shalford Green
Fordstreet
Ugley Green
Broxted
Lindsell
High Garrett
Birchanger
Bardfield Saling
BRAINTREE
Little Tey
Stansted
Bishop's Stortford
Great Dunmow
Stebbing Green
Coggeshall
Feering
Felsted
Kelvedon
Tiptree
Great Waltham
Hatfield Peverel
Tolleshunt D'Arcy
Margaret Roding
Tolleshunt Major
Goldhanger
Newney Green
Maldon
CHELMSFORD
Thornwood
Danbury
Chipping Ongar
Epping
Maylandsea
Doddinghurst
Latchingdon
Stock
Woodham Ferrers
Burnham on Crouch
Loughton
Mountnessing
Billericay
BRENTWOOD
Battlesbridge
Great Warley
Romford
SOUTHEND-ON-SEA
Sheerness
Gravesend
Dartford

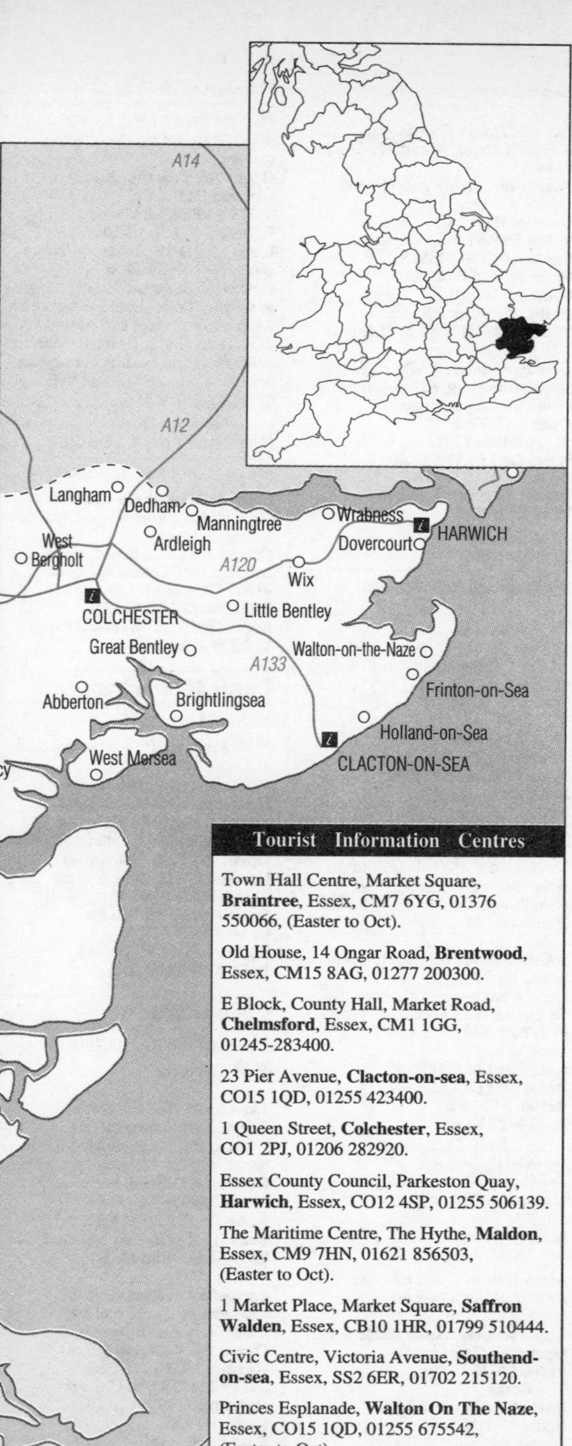

Tourist Information Centres

Town Hall Centre, Market Square, **Braintree**, Essex, CM7 6YG, 01376 550066, (Easter to Oct).

Old House, 14 Ongar Road, **Brentwood**, Essex, CM15 8AG, 01277 200300.

E Block, County Hall, Market Road, **Chelmsford**, Essex, CM1 1GG, 01245-283400.

23 Pier Avenue, **Clacton-on-sea**, Essex, CO15 1QD, 01255 423400.

1 Queen Street, **Colchester**, Essex, CO1 2PJ, 01206 282920.

Essex County Council, Parkeston Quay, **Harwich**, Essex, CO12 4SP, 01255 506139.

The Maritime Centre, The Hythe, **Maldon**, Essex, CM9 7HN, 01621 856503, (Easter to Oct).

1 Market Place, Market Square, **Saffron Walden**, Essex, CB10 1HR, 01799 510444.

Civic Centre, Victoria Avenue, **Southend-on-sea**, Essex, SS2 6ER, 01702 215120.

Princes Esplanade, **Walton On The Naze**, Essex, CO15 1QD, 01255 675542, (Easter to Oct).

Abberton

National Grid Ref: TM0019

The Maltings, *Mersea Road, Abberton, Colchester, Essex, CO5 7NR.*
Attractive C15th country house.
Open: All Year
Grades: ETB Listed
01206 735780 Mrs Cox
Rates fr: *£15.00*-**£15.00**.
Beds: 1F 1T 1S
Baths: 1 Private 1 Shared
(10)

Ardleigh

National Grid Ref: TM0529

Wooden Fender Inn

Dundas Place, *Colchester Road, Ardleigh, Colchester, Essex, CO7 7NP.*
Friendly, comfortable C17th cottage.
Open: All Year (not Xmas)
Grades: ETB 2 Cr, Comm
01206 230625 Mrs Le May
Rates fr: *£17.00*-**£20.00**.
Beds: 1D 2T
Baths: 1 Ensuite 1 Shared
(12) (3)

Crockleford Grange, *Bromley Road, Crockleford Heath, Ardleigh, Colchester, Essex, CO7 7SE.*
Peaceful, thatched farmhouse, superior accommodation.
Open: All Year
01206 864405 Mrs Harrington
Rates fr: *£16.00*-**£20.00**.
Beds: 2D 1T
Baths: 2 Private 1 Shared
(1) (10)

Bardfield Saling

National Grid Ref: TL6826

White Hart

Taborsfield, *Woolpits Road, Bardfield Saling, Braintree, Essex, CM7 5EA.*
Detached house, attractive rural setting.
Open: All Year (not Xmas)
Grades: ETB Listed
01371 850391 Mrs Smith
Rates fr: *£15.50*-**£15.00**.
Beds: 1F 1D 1S
Baths: 1 Ensuite 1 Shared
(8)

Battlesbridge

National Grid Ref: TQ7794

The Cottages Guest House, *Beeches Road, Battlesbridge, Wickford, Essex, SS11 8TJ.*
Rural, cosy, licensed guest house.
Open: All Year (not Xmas)
Grades: ETB Listed
01702 232105 Miss Carr
Rates fr: *£17.50*-**£20.00**.
Beds: 1F 1D 3T 1S
(10)

Belchamp Walter

National Grid Ref: TL8140

***St Mary Hall,** Belchamp Walter, Sudbury, Suffolk, CO10 7BB.*
Lovely mediaeval country house.
Open: All Year
01787 237202 Mr Morse
Rates fr: *£25.00*-**£28.00**.
Beds: 1D 1T 1S
Baths: 3 Private

Billericay

National Grid Ref: TQ6794

Kings Head, The Hoop

***Badgers Restaurant,** 2 Mountview, Billericay, Essex, CM11 1HB.*
Modern detached house, excellent accommodation.
Open: All Year
Grades: ETB Listed, Comm
01277 625384 / 0378 444169
Mr & Mrs Parker
Fax no: 01277 633912
Rates fr: *£17.50*-**£17.50**.
Beds: 1D 3S
Baths: 2 Shared
(6)

***Banavie,** 5 Bluebell Wood, Off Mountnessing Road, Billericay, Essex, CM12 0ES.*
Bungalow in large country garden.
Open: All Year (not Xmas)
Grades: ETB Listed, Comm
01277 622939 Mrs Burcham
Rates fr: *£16.00*-**£17.50**.
Beds: 1T
Baths: 1 Private
(1)

Birchanger

National Grid Ref: TL5122

Three Willows

***The Cottage Guest House,** 71 Birchanger Lane, Birchanger, Bishops Stortford, Essex, CM23 5QA.*
Listed building, gardens, quiet village.
Open: All Year (not Xmas)
Grades: ETB 2 Cr, High Comm, AA 4 Q, Select, RAC Acclaim
01279 812349 Mr Jones
Rates fr: *£24.00*-**£30.00**.
Beds: 1F 5D 6T 3S
Baths: 13 Ensuite 1 Shared

Blackmore End

National Grid Ref: TL7330

***School Green Farm,** Blackmore End, Braintree, Essex, CM7 4DS.*
C17th farmhouse. Warm welcome guaranteed.
Open: All Year
01371 850679 Mrs Deacon
Rates fr: *£15.00*-**£15.00**.
Beds: 2D
Baths: 1 Shared
(15)

Braintree

National Grid Ref: TL7623

***The Old House Guesthouse,** 11 Bradford Street, Braintree, Essex, CM7 9AS.*
Family-run, C16th guest house.
Open: All Year
Grades: ETB 2 Cr
01376 550457 Mrs Hughes
Fax no: 01376 343863
Rates fr: *£16.00*-**£20.00**.
Beds: 2F 3D 1T
Baths: 4 Private 2 Shared
(10)

***Gantway House,** 77-79 High Street, Braintree, Essex, CM7 7JS.*
C14th town centre house.
Open: All Year
01376 349044 Mr Galpin
Rates fr: *£18.50*-**£18.50**.
Beds: 1F 1D 2T 5S
Baths: 3 Private 3 Shared

Brentwood

National Grid Ref: TQ6093

Artichoke

***77 Rose Valley,** Brentwood, Essex, CM14 4HJ.*
Open: All Year
01277 262713
Mr & Mrs Corbo
Fax no: 01277 211146
Rates fr: *£20.00*-**£20.00**.
Beds: 4F 6D 4T 2S
Baths: 4 Private 3 Shared
(10)
Two minute walk to Brentwood Station, 30 minutes by rail to the centre of London. Relaxed & friendly atmosphere. Pleasant & comfortable rooms.

***2 Kensington Road,** Brentwood, Essex, CM15 9LG.*
Family-run house, very friendly.
Open: All Year (not Xmas)
01277 229668
Mrs Colley
Rates fr: *£16.00*-**£20.00**.
Beds: 1F 1T 1S
Baths: 1 Shared

Brightlingsea

National Grid Ref: TM0817

Red Lion

***Birch House,** Church Road, Brightlingsea, Colchester, Essex, CO7 0QT.*
Large, modern, comfortable home.
Open: All Year
01206 302877
Mrs Bragg
Rates fr: *£19.00*-**£22.50**.
Beds: 1F 2D 2T
Baths: 3 Ensuite 1 Shared
(6)

Broxted

National Grid Ref: TL5726

***The Old Post Office,** Church End, Broxted, Great Dunmow, Essex, CM6 2BU.*
Open: All Year (not Xmas)
Grades: ETB 2 Cr
01279 850050 Mrs Haigh
Rates fr: *£23.50*-**£20.00**.
Beds: 1F 1D 1S **Baths:** 3 Private
(5) (4)
Converted & extended old cottage in village. Comfortable and pretty rooms. Convenient to Stansted Airport and M11. Broxted Church contains Beirut hostages commemorative windows. WARM WELCOME ASSURED.

Burnham on Crouch

National Grid Ref: TQ9596

***Cromwell House Guesthouse,** 42 High Street, Burnham on Crouch, Essex, CM0 8AA.*
Central Victorian house, clean, comfortable. **Open:** All Year
01621 783654 Ms Lewis
Rates fr: *£17.50*-**£19.00**.
Beds: 1F 1D 1T **Baths:** 3 Private

Castle Hedingham

National Grid Ref: TL7835

Moot House Restaurant Bell

***Pannells Ash Farm,** Castle Hedingham, Halstead, Essex, CO9 3AD.*
Period furnished C15th farmhouse.
Open: All Year (not Xmas)
Grades: ETB Listed, Comm
01787 460364 Mrs Redgewell
Rates fr: *£15.50*-**£16.50**.
Beds: 1F 1D 1T 1S
Baths: 1 Private 1 Shared
(6)

Chelmsford

National Grid Ref: TL7006

The Ship

***The Copse,** Cedar Avenue West, Chelmsford, Essex, CM1 2XA.*
Comfortable, well-situated, family home. **Open:** All Year (not Xmas)
Grades: ETB Listed
01245 358976 Mrs Coates
Rates fr: *£17.50*-**£16.50**.
Beds: 1T 1S **Baths:** 1 Shared
(5) (6)

***Aarandale,** 9 Roxwell Road, Chelmsford, Essex, CM1 2LY.*
Large Victorian private house.
Open: All Year (not Xmas)
Grades: ETB 1 Cr, Comm
01245 251713 Mrs Chivers
Rates fr: *£19.00*-**£20.00**.
Beds: 1D 4S
Baths: 1 Private 1 Shared
(6)

Chipping Ongar

National Grid Ref: TL5103

The Black Bull

***Bumbles,** Moreton Road, Chipping Ongar, Essex, CM5 0EZ.*
Open: All Year (not Xmas)
Grades: ETB Listed, Comm
01277 362695 Mrs Withey
Fax no: 01277 365245
Rates fr: *£18.00*-**£18.00**.
Beds: 3T
Baths: 2 Shared
(12) (6)
Large, comfortable country cottage, centrally heated, also log fires in winter. Within easy reach M11 (Junction 7), M25, London, East Anglia. Tea/coffee always available.

Clacton on Sea

National Grid Ref: TM1715

Nookes & Crannies

***The Chantry Hotel,** 2-4 Orwell Road, Clacton on Sea, Essex, CO15 1PR.*
Family-run atmosphere & diets.
Open: All Year
01255 421846 (also fax no)
Rates fr: *£24.00*-**£12.00**.
Beds: 6D 8T 6S
Baths: 7 Ensuite 2 Private 2 Shared
(10)

***Brunton House,** 15 Carnarvon Road, Clacton on Sea, Essex, CO15 6PH.*
Nice rooms for nice people.
Open: All Year
01255 420431 Mrs Walton
Rates fr: *£12.50*-**£15.00**.
Beds: 1F 4D 1S
Baths: 1 Ensuite 1 Private 1 Shared
(6)

Coggeshall

National Grid Ref: TL8522

Woolpack

***White Heather Guest House,** 19 Colchester Road, Coggeshall, Colchester, Essex, CO6 1RP.*
Modern, family-run guesthouse.
Open: All Year
01376 563004 Mrs Shaw
Rates fr: *£20.00*-**£20.00**.
Beds: 2D 1T 3S
Baths: 2 Ensuite 1 Shared
(8)

The lowest *double* rate per person is shown in *italics*.

Colchester

National Grid Ref: TL9925

Forresters, Rovers Tye, Siege House

***The Old Manse,** 15 Roman Close, Colchester, Essex, CO1 1UR.*
Open: All Year (not Xmas)
Grades: ETB Listed, AA 2 Q
01206 45154 Ms Anderson
Rates fr: *£18.00*-**£25.00**.
Beds: 1D 1T
Baths: 1 Private 2 Shared
(3) (1)
Quiet town centre location beside Castle Park. 3 minutes walk to bus station, town, castle, Leisure World. Large ground-floor double-bedded room. Guaranteed warm welcome.

***Globe Hotel,** 71 North Station Road, Colchester, Essex, CO1 1RQ.*
Recently modernised Victorian pub/hotel. **Open:** All Year
01206 573881 Mr Higgins
Rates fr: *£25.00*-**£30.00**.
Beds: 3F 3D 3T 3S
Baths: 12 Private

***St John's Guest House,** 330 Ipswich Road, Colchester, Essex, CO4 4ET.*
Well situated, close to town.
Open: All Year
Grades: ETB Listed
01206 852 288 Mrs Knight
Rates fr: *£17.00*-**£22.00**.
Beds: 1F 1D 2T 1S
Baths: 2 Ensuite 1 Shared
(10)

***The Vines,** 42 Military Road, Colchester, Essex, CO1 2AN.*
Large Georgian private house.
Open: All Year
Grades: ETB Listed
01206 767301
Rates fr: *£16.50*-**£19.00**.
Beds: 1D 1T
Baths: 1 Ensuite 1 Private
(0) (1)

Danbury

National Grid Ref: TL7705

Bell, Griffin

***3 Millfields,** Danbury, Chelmsford, Essex, CM3 4LE.*
Good quality, comfortable, quiet, friendly.
Open: All Year
Grades: ETB Listed
01245 224946 Mrs Law
Rates fr: *£18.00*-**£18.00**.
Beds: 1F 1D 1T
Baths: 1 Ensuite 1 Shared
(3)

***Southways,** Copt Hill, Danbury, Chelmsford, Essex, CM3 4NN.*
Quiet house in the country.
Open: All Year (not Xmas)
Grades: ETB Listed
01245 223428 Mrs Deavin
Rates fr: *£16.00*-**£18.00**.
Beds: 2T
Baths: 1 Shared
(2)

Debden Green

National Grid Ref: TL5732

***Wigmores Farm,** Debden Green, Saffron Walden, Essex, CB11 3LX.*
C16th thatched farmhouse.
Open: All Year
Grades: ETB Listed, Comm
01371 830050 Mr & Mrs Worth
Rates fr: *£18.00*-**£20.00**.
Beds: 2D 1T
Baths: 2 Shared
(8)

Dedham

National Grid Ref: TM0533

Anchor, Marlborough Head

***Mays Barn Farm,** Mays Lane, Dedham, Colchester, Essex, CO7 6EW.*
Secluded, comfortable old farmhouse.
Open: All Year (not Xmas)
Grades: ETB 2 Cr, High Comm
01206 323191 Mrs Freeman
Rates fr: *£19.00*-**£22.00**.
Beds: 1D 1T
Baths: 2 Private
(12) (4)

Doddinghurst

National Grid Ref: TQ5998

***Red House Farm,** Warren Lane, Doddinghurst, Brentwood, Essex, CM15 0JD.*
C16th comfortable farmhouse.
Open: All Year (not Xmas)
01277 372336 Mrs Porter
Rates fr: *£15.00*-**£20.00**.
Beds: 2T 1S
Baths: 1 Shared
(4)

Dovercourt

National Grid Ref: TM2531

***154 Fronks Road,** Dovercourt, Harwich, Essex, CO12 4EF.*
Detached house in tree-lined boulevard.
Open: Dec to Jan
01255 503081 (also fax no)
Mrs Cullen
Rates fr: *£13.00*-**£15.00**.
Beds: 1F 1T **Baths:** 1 Shared
(4)

***Swyncombe Guest House,** 19 Cliff Road, Dovercourt, Harwich, Essex, CO12 3PP.*
Warm family-run guest house.
Open: All Year (not Xmas)
01255 551245 Mr Cheney
Rates fr: *£14.00*-**£14.00**.
Beds: 1F 1D 1S
Baths: 2 Shared

Duddenhoe End

National Grid Ref: TL4636

The Woopman

***Duddenhoe End Farm, Saffron Walden,** Duddenhoe End, Saffron Walden, Essex, CB11 4UU.*
Delightful C17th farmhouse.
Open: All Year (not Xmas)
Grades: ETB 2 Cr, Comm
01763 838258 Mrs Foster
Rates fr: *£18.00*-**£22.00**.
Beds: 2D 1T
Baths: 3 Private
(12) (3)

***Rockells Farm,** Duddenhoe End, Saffron Walden, Essex, CB11 4UY.*
Georgian farmhouse with lake view.
Open: All Year
01763 838053 Mrs Westerhuis
Rates fr: *£18.00*-**£18.00**.
Beds: 1F 1T 1S
Baths: 3 Ensuite
(4)

Elmdon

National Grid Ref: TL4639

***Elmdon Bury,** Elmdon, Saffron Walden, Essex, CB11 4NF.*
Spacious comfortable renovated Essex farmhouse.
Open: All Year (not Xmas)
Grades: ETB 2 Cr, High Comm
01763 838220 Mrs Pearson
Fax no: 01763 838504
Rates fr: *£25.00*-**£30.00**.
Beds: 2D 1T
Baths: 3 Private
(10) (12)

Epping

National Grid Ref: TL4502

Duke of Wellington

***Uplands,** 181a Lindsey Street, Epping, Essex, CM16 6RF.*
Rural private house, near London.
Open: All Year
Grades: ETB Listed, Approv
01992 573733 Mrs Stacy
Rates fr: *£16.00*-**£16.00**.
Beds: 2F 2S
Baths: 2 Shared
(6)

Feering

National Grid Ref: TL8719

***The Old Anchor,** 132 Feering Hill, Feering, Colchester, Essex, CO5 9PY.*
A large welcoming public house.
Open: All Year
01376 570684 Mr Baldry
Rates fr: *£18.50*-**£18.50**.
Beds: 3D 3T 3S
Baths: 2 Shared
(70)

Felsted

National Grid Ref: TL6720

The Swan, Yew Tree

***Potash Farm House,** Causeway End Road, Cobblers Green, Felsted, Great Dunmow, Essex, CM6 3LX.*
Half moated farmhouse, quietly situated.
Open: All Year
Grades: ETB 1 Cr, Comm, AA 4 Q
01371 820510 (also fax no)
Mr & Mrs Smith
Rates fr: *£17.00*-**£20.00**.
Beds: 1D 2T **Baths:** 1 Shared
(5)

***Yarrow,** Felsted, Great Dunmow, Essex, CM6 3HD.*
Large Edwardian house close to village.
Open: All Year
Grades: ETB 2 Cr, Comm
01371 820878 Mr & Mrs Bellingham Smith
Rates fr: *£16.00*-**£15.00**.
Beds: 2D 1T
Baths: 1 Ensuite 1 Shared
(6)

***Hyfield,** Bannister Green, Felsted, Great Dunmow, Essex, CM6 3ND.*
C13th beamed country house.
Open: All Year (not Xmas)
01371 820372 Mrs Shaw
Rates fr: *£17.00*-**£17.00**.
Beds: 2D 2S
Baths: 1 Shared
(6)

Finchingfield

National Grid Ref: TL6832

The Fox

***Finchingfield House,** Bardfield Road, Finchingfield, Braintree, Essex, CM7 4JS.*
Magnificent historic Tudor country house.
Open: All Year
Grades: ETB 2 Cr, Comm, AA 3 Q, RAC Listed
01371 810289 (also fax no)
Mrs Patient
Rates fr: *£20.00*-**£28.00**.
Beds: 2D 1T
Baths: 1 Ensuite 1 Shared
(6)

Fordham

National Grid Ref: TL9228

***Kings Vineyard,** Fordham, Colchester, Essex, CO6 3NY.*
Warm hospitality in peaceful farmhouse, panoramic views.
Open: All Year
Grades: ETB 2 Cr, Comm
01206 240377 Mrs Tweed
Rates fr: *£16.00*-**£20.00**.
Beds: 1F 1D 1T
Baths: 1 Private 1 Shared
(1) (6)

Fordstreet

National Grid Ref: TL9226

Coopers Arms, Queens Head

***Old House,** Fordstreet, Aldham, Colchester, Essex, CO6 3PH.*
Historic C14th 'old hall house'.
Open: All Year
Grades: ETB 1 Cr, Comm
01206 240456 Mrs Mitchell
Rates fr: *£17.50*-**£22.50**.
Beds: 1F 1T 1S
Baths: 1 Ensuite 2 Private
(8)

Frinton on Sea

National Grid Ref: TM2319

***Uplands Guest House,** 41 Hadleigh Road, Frinton on Sea, Essex, CO13 9HQ.*
Quiet, comfortable. No smoking. Ample parking.
Open: All Year (not Xmas)
Grades: ETB Listed
01255 674889 Mrs Creates
Rates fr: *£21.00*-**£21.00**.
Beds: 2D 2T 3S
Baths: 4 Ensuite 2 Shared
(5)

Goldhanger

National Grid Ref: TL9008

***The Chequers Inn,** The Square, Goldhanger, Maldon, Essex, CM9 8AS.*
C15th inn & restaurant.
Open: All Year
01621 788203 Mr Jones
Rates fr: *£15.00*-**£20.00**.
Beds: 1D 3T
Baths: 1 Shared
(30)

***Pinelodge,** Head Street, Goldhanger, Maldon, Essex, CM9 8AY.*
Comfortably furnished modern village house.
Open: All Year (not Xmas)
01621 788481
Mr & Mrs Marigold
Rates fr: *£16.00*-**£16.00**.
Beds: 1D 1T
Baths: 1 Ensuite 1 Shared
(3)

Gosfield

National Grid Ref: TL7829

***Gosfield Lake Resort,** Church Road, Gosfield, Halstead, Essex, CO9 1UE.*
Modern detached bungalow.
Open: All Year
01787 475043
Mr Turp
Rates fr: *£15.00*-**£18.50**.
Baths: 3 Private

Great Bardfield

National Grid Ref: TL6730

The Vine

Bell Cottage, *Bell Lane, Great Bardfield, Braintree, Essex,* CM7 4TH.
Pretty C16th thatched cottage.
Open: All Year (not Xmas)
Grades: ETB Listed
01371 810149 (also fax no)
Mrs Mason
Rates fr: *£16.00*-**£16.00**.
Beds: 1T 1S
Baths: 1 Shared

Great Bentley

National Grid Ref: TM1121

Cherrywoods, *Great Bentley, Colchester, Essex,* CO7 8QF.
Modern, detached private house.
Open: All Year (not Xmas)
01206 250271 Mrs Buckles
Rates fr: *£14.00*-**£16.00**.
Beds: 1D 1S
Baths: 1 Shared
(2) (2)

Great Chesterford

National Grid Ref: TL5042

Crown & Thistle, Plough

The Delles, *Carmen Street, Great Chesterford, Saffron Walden, Essex,* CB10 1NR.
Open: All Year
Grades: ETB 2 Cr, High Comm
01799 530256 (also fax no)
Mrs Chater
Rates fr: *£21.00*-**£25.00**.
Beds: 2D 1T
Baths: 1 Ensuite 2 Private
(2) (5)
Beautiful old farmhouse dating from 1520, furnished to the highest standard with many fine antiques and paintings. Surrounded by 2 acre garden with tennis court.

Mill House, *Great Chesterford, Saffron Walden, Essex,* CB10 1NS.
Large, welcoming family house.
Open: All Year
Grades: ETB Listed, Comm
01799 530493 Mrs King
Fax no: 01799 531531
Rates fr: *£17.00*-**£17.00**.
Beds: 4D 1T 1S
Baths: 2 Shared
(8)

July Cottage, *Carmel Street, Great Chesterford, Saffron Walden, Essex,* CB10 1PH.
Attractive, quiet, modernised period cottage.
Open: All Year (not Xmas)
01799 530315 Mrs Dey
Rates fr: *£16.50*-**£16.50**.
Beds: 2T
Baths: 1 Shared
(3) (2)

Great Dunmow

National Grid Ref: TL6221

Kicking Dickey, Sailing Oak

Mallards, *Star Lane, Great Dunmow, Essex,* CM6 1AY.
Modern farmhouse-style home, in town. **Open:** All Year
Grades: ETB 2 Cr
01371 872641 Mrs Miller
Rates fr: *£17.50*-**£17.50**.
Beds: 1D 1T
Baths: 2 Ensuite 1 Private
(0) (10)

Homelye Farm, *Homelye Chase, Braintree Road, Great Dunmow, Essex,* CM6 3AW.
Motel-style chalets.
Open: All Year
Grades: ETB Listed
01371 872127 Mrs Pickford
Rates fr: *£20.00*-**£20.00**.
Beds: 1D 1T 1S **Baths:** 3 Private
(5)

Great Waltham

National Grid Ref: TL6013

Windmill

Wildingtree, *South Street, Great Waltham, Chelmsford, Essex,* CM3 1EE.
Non-smoking, traditional, comfortable house.
Open: All Year (not Xmas)
Grades: ETB Listed, High Comm
01245 362369 Mrs Pyne
Rates fr: *£20.00*-**£20.00**.
Beds: 1D 2S
Baths: 1 Private 1 Shared
(12) (3)

Great Warley

National Grid Ref: TQ5890

Thatchers Arms

Chestnut Tree Cottage, *Great Warley Street, Great Warley, Brentwood, Essex,* CM13 3JF.
Village cottage. Convenient London/M25. **Open:** All Year
Grades: ETB Listed
01277 221727 Mrs Malyon
Rates fr: *£19.00*-**£24.00**.
Beds: 2D 1T 1S
Baths: 3 Private 1 Shared
(5) (6)

Halstead

National Grid Ref: TL8130

White Hart

The Woodman Inn, *Colchester Road, Halstead, Essex,* CO9 2DY.
Comfortable mock-Tudor public house. **Open:** All Year
01787 476218 (also fax no)
Mr Redsell
Rates fr: *£18.00*-**£18.00**.
Beds: 1F 1D 1T 1S
(12)

Harwich

National Grid Ref: TM2431

The Billy

Reids of Harwich, *3 West Street, Harwich, Essex,* CO12 3DA.
Spacious Victorian property - historic location.
Open: April to Oct
01255 506796 Mr Reid
Rates fr: *£16.00*-**£16.00**.
Beds: 1D 1T 1S
Baths: 2 Shared
(12)

Queens Hotel, *119 High Street, Dovercourt, Harwich, Essex,* CO12 3AP.
Public house/hotel.
Open: All Year
Grades: ETB Listed, Approv
01255 502634 Mrs Skinner
Rates fr: *£15.00*-**£15.00**.
Beds: 1F 4T 2S
Baths: 2 Shared
(15)

Hatfield Peverel

National Grid Ref: TL7811

Square & Compasses

The Wick, *Terling Hall Road, Hatfield Peverel, Chelmsford, Essex,* CM3 2EZ.
C16th farmhouse - comfortable and interesting.
Open: All Year (not Xmas)
01245 380705 Mrs Tritton
Rates fr: *£19.50*-**£19.50**.
Beds: 2T
(10) (4)

Henham

National Grid Ref: TL5428

Bacons Cottage, *Crow Street, Henham, Bishops Stortford, Herts,* CM22 6AG.
Picturesque village setting near Stansted Airport.
Open: All Year (not Xmas)
01279 850754 Mrs Philpot
Rates fr: *£15.00*-**£16.00**.
Beds: 2D 1S
Baths: 1 Ensuite
(1)

High Garrett

National Grid Ref: TL7726

Hare & Hounds, *High Garrett, Braintree, Essex,* CM7 5NT.
Comfortable country inn, 'home cooking'.
Open: All Year
01376 324430 Mr & Mrs Page
Rates fr: *£17.00*-**£24.00**.
Beds: 1F 1D 2T 1S
Baths: 3 Ensuite 1 Private
(20)

Holland on Sea

National Grid Ref: TM2016

***Kudu,** 24 Norman Road, Holland on Sea, Clacton on Sea, Essex, CO15 5XS.*
Quiet, comfortable, in seaside village.
Open: All Year
01255 812285 Mrs Hazell
Rates fr: *£16.50*-**£25.00**.
Beds: 3D
Baths: 2 Ensuite 1 Private
(4)

Kelvedon

National Grid Ref: TL9925

The Sun

***Highfields Farm,** Kelvedon, Colchester, Essex, CO5 9BJ.*
Comfortable, quiet farmhouse, convenient A12.
Open: All Year
Grades: ETB 2 Cr, Comm
01376 570334 (also fax no)
Mrs Bunting
Rates fr: *£18.00*-**£20.00**.
Beds: 3T
Baths: 2 Ensuite 1 Private
(10)

Langham

National Grid Ref: TM0231

Shepherd & Dog

***Oak Apple Farm,** Greyhound Hill, Langham, Colchester, Essex, CO4 5QF.*
Comfortable farmhouse with large attractive garden.
Open: All Year (not Xmas)
Grades: ETB Listed
01206 272234 Mrs Helliwell
Rates fr: *£18.50*-**£19.00**.
Beds: 2T 1S **Baths:** 1 Shared
(6)

Latchingdon

National Grid Ref: TL8800

***Neptune Cafe Motel,** Burnham Road, Latchingdon, Chelmsford, Essex, CM3 6EX.*
Open: All Year (not Xmas)
Grades: ETB Listed, Approv
01621 740770 Mr Lloyd
Rates fr: *£15.00*-**£20.00**.
Beds: 2F 6D 3T 4S
Baths: 10 Ensuite 1 Shared
(40)
Motel with adjoining cafe. Set in village in the Dengie Peninsula. Close to boating & fishing areas. Large garden. Beautiful outlook.

Bringing children with you? Always ask for any special rates.

Lindsell

National Grid Ref: TL6427

***Cowels Cottage,** Lindsell, Great Dunmow, Essex, CM6 3QG.*
Quiet rural situation. Handy for Stansted Airport.
Open: All Year
01371 870454 Mrs Gray
Rates fr: *£18.00*-**£18.00**.
Beds: 1D 2S
Baths: 1 Ensuite 2 Private

Little Bentley

National Grid Ref: TM1125

***Bentley Manor,** Little Bentley, Colchester, Essex, CO7 8SE.*
C16th manor house.
Open: All Year (not Xmas)
01206 250622 Mrs Dyson
Rates fr: *£17.00*-**£22.00**.
Beds: 1F 1D 1T

Little Tey

National Grid Ref: TL8923

***Knaves Farmhouse,** Great Tey Road, Little Tey, Colchester, Essex, CO6 1JA.*
Victorian farmhouse in rural surroundings.
Open: All Year
01206 211039 Mrs Carr
Rates fr: *£30.00*-**£20.00**.
Beds: 1D 1T
Baths: 1 Ensuite 1 Shared
(2) (4)

Little Walden

National Grid Ref: TL5438

The Crown, Eight Bells

***Rowley Hill Lodge,** Little Walden Road, Little Walden, Saffron Walden, Essex, CB10 1UZ.*
Attractive Victorian farm lodge with large secluded garden.
Open: All Year (not Xmas)
Grades: ETB 2 Cr, Comm, AA 3 Q
01799 525975 Mr & Mrs Haslam
Fax no: 01799 516622
Rates fr: *£19.50*-**£22.00**.
Beds: 1D 1T
Baths: 2 Private
(4)

Littlebury

National Grid Ref: TL5139

***The Queens Head Inn,** High Street, Littlebury, Saffron Walden, Essex, CB11 4TD.*
Family-run C15th coaching house.
Open: All Year
01799 522251
Mr & Mrs O'Gorman
Rates fr: *£22.50*-**£29.95**.
Beds: 1F 2D 1T 2S
Baths: 6 Private
(30)

Loughton

National Grid Ref: TQ4396

***61 York Hill,** Loughton, Essex, IG10 1HZ.*
Picturesque Edwardian family home.
Open: All Year (not Xmas)
Grades: ETB Listed, Comm
0181 508 9834 Mrs Catterall
Rates fr: *£15.00*-**£20.00**.
Beds: 1F 1T 1S
Baths: 2 Shared
(0) (3)

Maldon

National Grid Ref: TL8407

***Hillypool House,** 14 North Street, Maldon, Essex, CM9 7HL.*
Comfortable family home near quay.
Open: All Year (not Xmas)
Grades: ETB Listed, Comm
01621 853885 Mr & Mrs Knox
Rates fr: *£15.00*-**£18.00**.
Beds: 1D 1T 1S
Baths: 2 Shared
(0) (3)

Manningtree

National Grid Ref: TM1031

***Aldhams,** Bromley Road, Lawford, Manningtree, Essex, CO11 2NE.*
Open: All Year (not Xmas)
Grades: ETB 2 Cr, Comm, AA 3 Q
01206 393210 Mrs McEwen
Fax no: 01255 870722
Rates fr: *£20.00*-**£25.00**.
Beds: 2D 1T 1S
Baths: 2 Private 1 Shared
(6)
Converted farmhouse in Lutyens style set in 3 acres and surrounded by fields. Wonderfully peaceful yet only a short drive to Harwich, Colchester and Dedham.

Margaret Roding

National Grid Ref: TL5912

***Greys,** Ongar Road, Margaret Roding, Great Dunmow, Essex, CM6 1QR.*
Comfortable country cottage, pleasant situation.
Open: All Year (not Xmas)
Grades: ETB Listed, Comm, AA 2 Q
01245 231509 Mrs Matthews
Rates fr: *£18.00*-**£18.50**.
Beds: 2D 1T
Baths: 1 Shared
(10) (3)

Planning a longer stay? Always ask for any special rates.

Mountnessing

National Grid Ref: TQ6297

George & Dragon

***Millers,** Thoby Lane, Mountnessing, Brentwood, Essex, CM15 0TD.*
Modern comfortable house situated in farmland.
Open: All Year
01277 354595 Mrs Stacey
Rates fr: *£18.00*-**£25.00**.
Beds: 3T **Baths:** 1 Shared
(6)

Newney Green

National Grid Ref: TL6507

The Duck

***Moor Hall,** Newney Green, Writtle, Chelmsford, Essex, CM1 3SE.*
Mediaeval timber-framed farmhouse.
Open: All Year (not Xmas)
Grades: ETB Listed
01245 420814 Mrs Gemmill
Rates fr: *£19.00*-**£21.00**.
Beds: 2F
(10)

Newport

National Grid Ref: TL5234

***The Manse,** Wicken Road, Newport, Saffron Walden, Essex, CB11 3QH.*
Attractive Edwardian family house.
Open: Feb to Nov
01799 540411 Mr Hargreaves
Rates fr: *£17.50*-**£17.50**.
Beds: 1D **Baths:** 1 Ensuite
(2)

Radwinter

National Grid Ref: TL6037

The Plough Inn

***Saxons,** Water Lane, Radwinter, Saffron Walden, Essex, CB10 2TX.*
C16th thatched cottage in peaceful setting.
Open: All Year (not Xmas)
Grades: ETB 1 Cr, Comm
01799 599565 Mr & Mrs Hordern
Rates fr: *£19.50*-**£19.50**.
Beds: 1T 1S
Baths: 2 Private
(12) (2)

Saffron Walden

National Grid Ref: TL5438

The Crown, Eight Bells

***27 South Road,** Saffron Walden, Essex, CB11 3DW.*
Pretty, double-fronted Victorian cottage.
Open: All Year
01799 525425 Mrs McBride
Rates fr: *£18.00*-**£18.00**.
Beds: 2T 1S **Baths:** 1 Shared

***Rowley Hill Lodge,** Little Walden Road, Little Walden, Saffron Walden, Essex, CB10 1UZ.*
Open: All Year (not Xmas)
Grades: ETB 2 Cr, Comm, AA 3 Q
01799 525975
Mr & Mrs Haslam
Fax no: 01799 516622
Rates fr: *£19.50*-**£22.00**.
Beds: 1D 1T
Baths: 2 Private
(4)
Attractive Victorian farm lodge with large secluded garden. Both rooms ensuite. Only 1.5 miles from historic Saffron Walden. Close to Duxford Aircraft Museum & Cambridge.

***1 Gunters Cottage,** Thaxted Road, Saffron Walden, Essex, CB10 2UT.*
Quiet comfortable accommodation. Friendly welcome.
Open: All Year (not Xmas)
Grades: ETB 2 Cr
01799 522091 Mrs Goddard
Rates fr: *£16.00*-**£14.00**.
Beds: 2D 1S
Baths: 1 Private 1 Shared
(3)

***10 Victoria Avenue,** Saffron Walden, Essex, CB11 3AE.*
Comfortable detached house, friendly atmosphere.
Open: All Year
Grades: ETB Listed
01799 525923 Mrs Gilder
Rates fr: *£14.00*-**£14.00**.
Beds: 1T 3S
Baths: 1 Shared

***Ashleigh House,** 7 Farmadine Grove, Saffron Walden, Essex, CB11 3DR.*
Comfortable house in quiet location.
Open: All Year
Grades: ETB 2 Cr, Comm
01799 513611 Mrs Gilder
Rates fr: *£15.00*-**£16.00**.
Beds: 1D 1T 2S
Baths: 1 Private 1 Shared
(5) (5)

***30 Lambert Cross,** Saffron Walden, Essex, CB10 2DP.*
Modern, comfortable, detached, friendly house.
Open: All Year (not Xmas)
01799 527287 Mrs Chapman
Rates fr: *£15.00*-**£16.00**.
Beds: 1T 2S **Baths:** 1 Shared
(2)

Shalford Green

National Grid Ref: TL7127

***Corkers,** Shalford Green, Braintree, Essex, CM7 5AZ.*
Comfortable C16th cottage.
Open: All Year
01371 850376 Mrs Willey
Rates fr: *£15.00*-**£15.00**.
Beds: 1D 2S **Baths:** 2 Shared
(4)

Pay B&Bs by cash or cheque. Be prepared to pay up front for one night stays.

Sible Hedingham

National Grid Ref: TL7734

White Horse

***Hedingham Antiques,** 100 Swan Street, Sible Hedingham, Halstead, Essex, CO9 3HP.*
Large Victorian house/shop combined.
Open: All Year (not Xmas)
Grades: ETB 1 Cr
01787 460360 Mrs Patterson
Rates fr: *£17.50*-**£20.00**.
Beds: 1F 1D **Baths:** 2 Private
(0) (4)

Southend-on-Sea

National Grid Ref: TQ8786

Hamlet, Last Post

***Retreat Guest House,** 12 Canewdon Road, Westcliff-on-Sea, Southend-on-Sea, Essex, SS0 7NE.*
Open: All Year
Grades: ETB 2 Cr
01702 348217 / 337413
Mr & Mrs Bartholomew
Fax no: 01702 391179
Rates fr: *£18.00*-**£18.00**.
Beds: 1F 4D 3S
Baths: 5 Private 2 Shared
(1) (5)
Close to Cliffs Pavilion, Palace Theatre, Westcliff Station and near to the seafront. Leading to Southend's main attractions & shopping centre. Celebrating our tenth year.

***Argyle Hotel,** 12 Clifftown Parade, Southend-on-Sea, Essex, SS1 1DP.*
Situated on cliff, in a conservation area.
Open: All Year (not Xmas)
Grades: ETB Listed, AA Listed, RAC Listed
01702 339483 Mrs Burdett
Rates fr: *£17.50*-**£17.50**.
Beds: 6D 3T 2S
(5)

***Regency Hotel,** 18 Royal Terrace, Southend-on-Sea, Essex, SS1 1DU.*
Easy access to seaside facilities.
Open: All Year (not Xmas)
Grades: ETB Listed
01702 340747 Mr Fidgeon
Rates fr: *£12.50*-**£18.00**.
Baths: 8 Ensuite

***The Norman Guest House,** 191 Eastern Esplanade, Southend-on-Sea, Essex, SS1 3AA.*
Cosy, large Victorian seafront house.
Open: All Year
Grades: ETB 2 Cr
01702 585212 Mr & Mrs Carr
Rates fr: *£18.00*-**£18.00**.
Beds: 3F 3D 3T 2S
Baths: 4 Ensuite 1 Shared

***Terrace Hotel,** 8 Royal Terrace, Southend-on-Sea, Essex, SS1 1DY.*
Clean, highly recommended, overlooking estuary.
Open: All Year
Grades: ETB 2 Cr, AA 2 Q, RAC Listed
01702 348143 Mr & Mrs Beck
Rates fr: *£16.00*-**£20.00**.
Beds: 2F 2D 2T 3S
Baths: 3 Private 6 Shared
(5)

***Arosa Guest House,** 184 Eastern Esplande, Southend-on-Sea, Essex, SS1 3AA.*
Beautiful sea front guest-house.
Open: All Year (not Xmas)
01702 585416 Miss Grundy
Rates fr: *£18.00*-**£18.00**.
Beds: 1F 2D 3T 1S
Baths: 7 Ensuite
(100)

Stebbing Green

National Grid Ref: TL6723

***Holly Cottage,** Stebbing Green, Dunmow, Essex, CM6 3TE.*
Gardeners delight in beautiful countryside.
Open: All Year (not Xmas)
Grades: ETB Listed, Comm
01371 856637 / 811009 Mr Barrett
Fax no: 01371 810631
Rates fr: *£16.50*-**£16.50**.
Beds: 2T 1S
Baths: 1 Shared
(12) (5)

Steeple Bumpstead

National Grid Ref: TL6841

***Yew Tree House,** 15 Chapel Street, Steeple Bumpstead, Haverhill, Suffolk, CB9 7DQ.*
Victorian home offering superior accommodation.
Open: All Year
Grades: ETB 1 Cr, Comm
01440 730364 (also fax no)
Mrs Stirling
Rates fr: *£14.00*-**£14.00**.
Beds: 1D 1T 1S
Baths: 1 Ensuite 1 Shared
(2) (2)

The lowest *double* rate per person is shown in *italics*.

Stock

National Grid Ref: TQ6899

***Eibiswald,** 85 Mill Road, Stock, Ingatestone, Essex, CM4 9LR.*
First class Anglo-Austrian hospitality. **Open:** All Year (not Xmas)
01277 840631 Mrs Bates
Rates fr: *£17.00*-**£24.00**.
Beds: 3D 3S
Baths: 1 Ensuite 1 Shared
(10) (4)

Thaxted

National Grid Ref: TL6231

***Folly House,** Watling Lane, Thaxted, Great Dunmow, Essex, CM6 2QY.*
Historic village, views, attentive service. **Open:** All Year
01371 830618 Mrs King
Rates fr: *£20.00*-**£25.00**.
Beds: 1D 1T
Baths: 2 Private 1 Shared
(10)

Thornwood

National Grid Ref: TL4704

King's Head

***Marshalls,** Woodside, Thornwood, Epping, Essex, CM16 6LQ.*
Converted barn opposite Epping Forest.
Open: All Year (not Xmas)
01992 574344 (also fax no)
Mrs Potter
Rates fr: *£25.00*-**£25.00**.
Beds: 1D 1T **Baths:** 2 Ensuite
(7) (4)

Tiptree

National Grid Ref: TL8916

New Times

***Linden,** 8 Clarkesmead, Maldon Road, Tiptree, Colchester, Essex, CO5 0BX.*
Modern detached house.
Open: All Year (not Xmas)
Grades: ETB Listed, High Comm
01621 819737 (also fax no)
Mrs Wilson
Rates fr: *£19.00*-**£22.00**.
Beds: 1D 2T 1S
Baths: 2 Private 1 Shared
(4)

Tolleshunt D'Arcy

National Grid Ref: TL9211

Queen's Head

***The Limes,** 10 Kelvedon Road, Tolleshunt D'Arcy, Maldon, Essex, CM9 8TE.*
Old house, modern luxury annexe.
Open: All Year
Grades: ETB Listed
01621 860219 Mrs Fairbanks
Rates fr: *£14.00*-**£18.00**.
Beds: 2T **Baths:** 1 Shared
(2)

Tolleshunt Major

National Grid Ref: TL9011

Bell, Compasses

***Mill Lodge,** Mill Lane, Tolleshunt Major, Maldon, Essex, CM9 7LD.*
Large, ultra modern house.
Open: All Year (not Xmas)
Grades: ETB Listed
01621 860311 Mrs Frost
Rates fr: *£12.00*-**£15.00**.
Beds: 1F 2D 1T 1S
Baths: 1 Ensuite 1 Shared
(1) (12)

***Wicks Manor Farm,** Witham Road, Tolleshunt Major, Maldon, Essex, CM9 8JU.*
Comfortable C17th moated farmhouse.
Open: All Year (not Xmas)
Grades: AA Listed
01621 860629
Mrs Howie
Rates fr: *£12.50*-**£15.00**.
Beds: 1D 1T
Baths: 1 Shared
(4)

Toppesfield

National Grid Ref: TL7337

***Olivers Farm,** Toppesfield, Halstead, Essex, CO9 4LS.*
C17th, quiet idyllic location.
Open: All Year (not Xmas)
01787 237642
Mrs Blackie
Rates fr: *£18.00*-**£18.00**.
Beds: 2D 1T
Baths: 1 Ensuite 1 Shared
(10) (4)

Ugley

National Grid Ref: TL5228

Three Willows, Chequers

***The Thatch,** Cambridge Road, Ugley, Bishops Stortford, Herts, CM22 6HZ.*
Convenient airport/M11. Warm, friendly atmosphere.
Open: All Year (not Xmas)
Grades: ETB Listed, High Comm
01799 543440
Mrs Hawkes
Rates fr: *£18.00*-**£20.00**.
Beds: 1F 2D 1T
Baths: 2 Ensuite 2 Shared
(10)

***Pargets,** Cambridge Road, Ugley, Bishops Stortford, Herts, CM22 6HZ.*
Well-appointed, detached modern house.
Open: All Year (not Xmas)
01799 543354
Mrs Daniels
Rates fr: *£18.00*-**£18.00**.
Beds: 2D 1S
Baths: 1 Private 1 Shared

Ugley Green

National Grid Ref: TL5227

The Thatched Cottage, *Snakes Lane, Ugley Green, Bishops Stortford, Herts,* CM22 6HW.
Beautiful, extensive quiet gardens.
Open: All Year (not Xmas)
01279 812341 Mrs Hilton
Rates fr: *£17.50*-**£20.00**.
Beds: 3T
Baths: 2 Shared
(10)

West Bergholt

National Grid Ref: TL9627

The Old Post House, *10 Colchester Road, West Bergholt, Colchester, Essex,* CO6 3JG.
Large Victorian private house.
Open: All Year (not Xmas)
Grades: ETB 2 Cr
01206 240379 Mrs Brown
Rates fr: *£16.00*-**£20.00**.
Beds: 1F 1D 1T
Baths: 1 Ensuite 1 Shared
(3)

West Mersea

National Grid Ref: TM0112

Willow Lodge

Hazel Oak, *28 Seaview Avenue, West Mersea, Colchester, Essex,* CO5 8HE.
Quiet, residential, tree-lined avenue.
Open: All Year
Grades: ETB 2 Cr, Comm
01206 383030 Mrs Blackmore
Rates fr: *£20.00*-**£20.00**.
Beds: 1D 1T
Baths: 1 Ensuite 1 Private
(2)

Wethersfield

National Grid Ref: TL7131

Dog Inn

Spicers Farm, *Rotten End, Wethersfield, Braintree, Essex,* CM7 4AL.
Farmhouse, quiet area, lovely views.
Open: All Year (not Xmas)
01371 851021 Mrs Douse
Rates fr: *£15.00*-**£18.00**.
Beds: 1D 2T
Baths: 3 Private
(6)

Wethersfield Arts Centre, *Hedingham Road, Wethersfield, Braintree, Essex,* CM7 4EQ.
Open: All Year
01371 851054 Mrs Bryant
Rates fr: *£20.00*-**£20.00**.
Beds: 1D 2T 1S
Baths: 2 Private 1 Shared
(12)
Converted Tudor barn of great character. Comfortable, calming & friendly. Superb four poster, excellent breakfasts & lovely gardens. Paintings for sale & art courses available.

Wickham St Pauls

National Grid Ref: TL8336

The Victory Inn, *The Green, Wickham St Pauls, Halstead, Essex,* CO9 2PT.
Friendly, homely atmosphere.
Open: All Year
01787 269364 Mr Bush
Rates fr: *£14.00*-**£17.50**.
Beds: 2D 1T 1S
Baths: 1 Shared
(20)

Widdington

National Grid Ref: TL5331

Pond Mead, *Widdington, Saffron Walden, Essex,* CB11 3SB.
Large converted farmhouse on edge of picturesque village.
Open: All Year
Grades: ETB 2 Cr, Approv
01799 540201 Mr Geen
Rates fr: *£17.00*-**£20.00**.
Beds: 1F 1S
Baths: 1 Private
(0) (5)

Wix

National Grid Ref: TM1628

Village Maid

Dairy House Farm, *Bradfield Road, Wix, Manningtree, Essex,* CO11 2SR.
Spacious, comfortable, peaceful setting.
Open: All Year (not Xmas)
Grades: ETB 2 Cr, Comm, AA 4 Q
01255 870322 Mrs Whitworth
Fax no: 01255 870186
Rates fr: *£17.00*-**£22.00**.
Beds: 1F 1T**Baths:** 2 Private
(2) (10)

New Farm House, *Spinnells Lane, Wix, Manningtree, Essex,* CO11 2UJ.
Country guest house with warmest welcome.
Open: All Year
Grades: ETB 3 Cr, Comm, AA 3 Q, RAC Listed, Acclaim
01255 870365
Mrs Mitchell
Fax no: 0255 870837
Rates fr: *£20.00*-**£21.00**.
Beds: 5F 1D 3T 3S
Baths: 7 Private 1 Shared
(20)

Woodham Ferrers

National Grid Ref: TQ7999

Chandler's Restaurant, The Bell

Woolfes Cottage, *The Street, Woodham Ferrers, Chelmsford, Essex,* CM3 5RG.
Large converted Victorian cottage.
Open: All Year
Grades: ETB Listed
01245 320037
Ms Oliver
Rates fr: *£15.00*-**£16.00**.
Beds: 1D 2T
Baths: 1 Shared
(2)

Wrabness

National Grid Ref: TM1731

Wheatsheaf Inn

Dimbols Farm, *Station Road, Wrabness, Manningtree, Essex,* CO11 2TH.
Georgian farmhouse, peaceful environment.
Open: All Year (not Xmas)
Grades: ETB 1 Cr, Comm
01255 880328 (also fax no)
Mrs Macaulay
Rates fr: *£15.00*-**£20.00**.
Beds: 1F 1D
Baths: 1 Shared
(4)

All rates are subject to alteration at the owners' discretion.

Gloucestershire

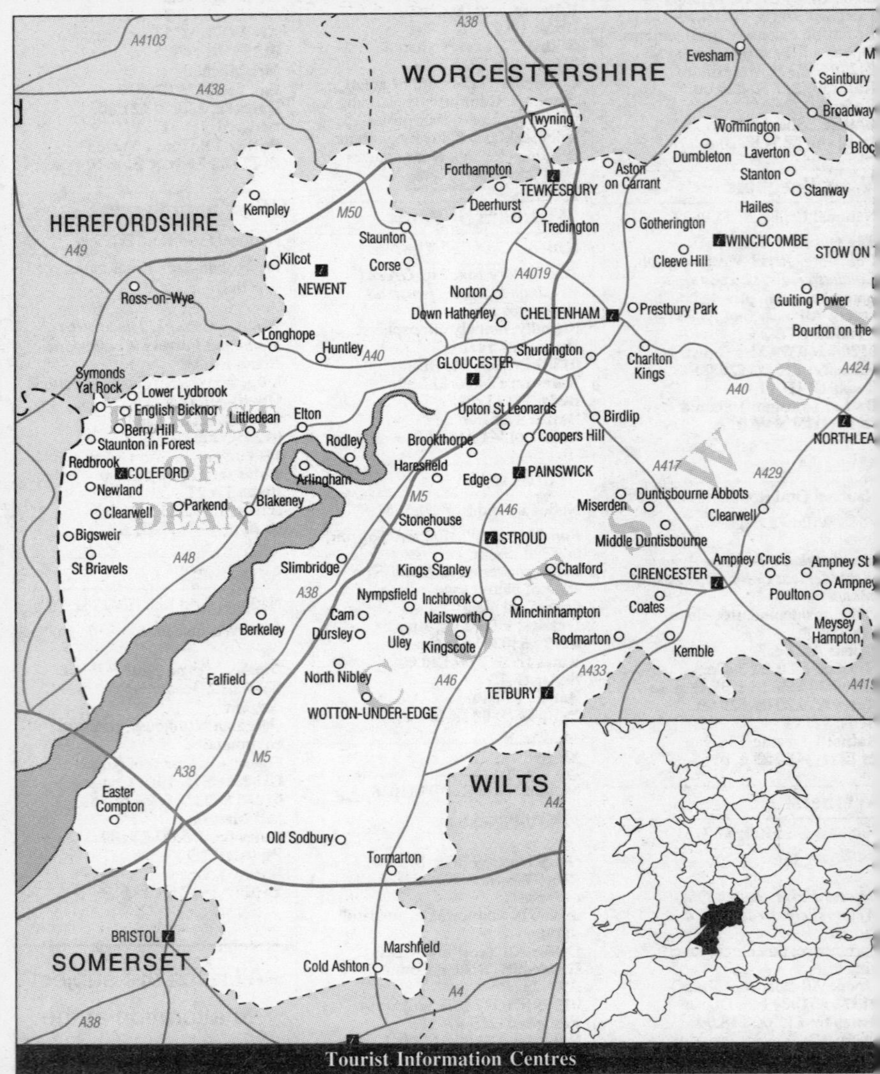

Tourist Information Centres

77 Promenade, **Cheltenham**, Glos, GL50 1PP, 01242 522878.

Hollis House, The Square, **Stow-on-the-Wold**, Glos, GL54 1AF, 01451 31082.

Town Hall, High Street, **Winchcombe**, Glos, GL54 5LJ, 01242 602925, (Easter to Oct).

Town Hall, High St, **Chipping Campden**, Glos, GL55 6AT, 01386 840101, (Easter to Oct)

Corn Hall, Market Place, **Cirencester**, Glos, GL7 2NW, 01285 654180.

27 Market Place, **Coleford**, Glos, GL16 8AE, 01594 836307.

St Michaels Tower, The Cross, **Gloucester**, Glos, GL1 1PD, 01452 421188.

The Library, High Street, **Newent**, Glos, GL18 1AS, 01531 822145.

Cotswold Countryside Collection, **Northleach**, Glos, GL54 3JH, 01451 860715, (Easter to Oct).

The Library, Stroud Road, **Painswick**, Glos, GL6 6DT, 01452 813552, (Easter to Oct).

Subscription Rooms, George Street, **Stroud**, Glos, GL5 1AE, 01543 765768.

The Old Court House, 63 Long Street, **Tetbury**, Glos, GL8 8AA, 01666 503552, (Easter to Oct).

64 Barton Street, **Tewkesbury**, Glos, GL20 5PX, 01684 295027.

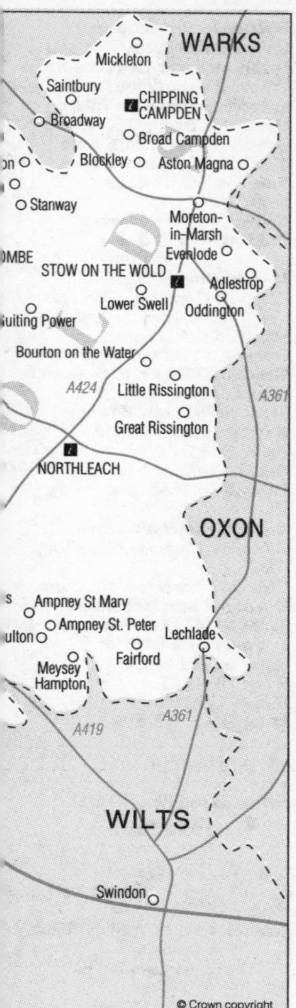

Adlestrop

National Grid Ref: SP2427

Fox Inn

***Honeybrook Cottage,** 2 Main Street, Adlestrop, Moreton in Marsh, Glos, GL56 0YN.*
Tranquil village setting, fine views.
Open: Feb to Nov
Grades: ETB 2 Cr, Comm
01608 658884 (also fax no)
Mrs Warrick
Rates fr: *£18.50*-**£22.00**.
Beds: 1D 1T
Baths: 1 Ensuite 1 Private
(12) (2)

Ampney Crucis

National Grid Ref: SP0601

***Waterton Gardens Cottage,** Ampney Crucis, Cirencester, Glos, GL7 5RX.*
Converted stables. Victorian walled gardens.
Open: All Year (not Xmas)
01285 851303 Mr Cassidy
Rates fr: *£22.50*-**£25.00**.
Beds: 2D 1S
Baths: 3 Private
(8)

Ampney St Mary

National Grid Ref: SP0802

Catherine Wheel

***College Farm,** Ampney St Mary, Cirencester, Glos, GL7 5SW.*
Working Cotswold dairy farm.
Open: April - End October
Grades: ETB 2 Cr
01285 851382 Mrs Bennett
Rates fr: *£15.00*-**£15.00**.
Beds: 1D 1T
Baths: 1 Private 1 Shared
(5)

Ampney St Peter

National Grid Ref: SP0201

Crown of Crucis

***Chantry Cottage,** Ampney St Peter, Cirencester, Glos, GL7 5SL.*
C16th Grade II family home.
Open: All Year (not Xmas)
Grades: ETB 2 Cr
01285 851358 Mrs Mills
Rates fr: *£20.00*-**£25.00**.
Beds: 1T
Baths: 1 Ensuite
(1)

Arlingham

National Grid Ref: SO7010

***Horseshoe View,** Overton Lane, Arlingham, Gloucester, GL2 7JJ.*
Modern house, lovely views of river.
Open: All Year
Grades: ETB Listed, Comm
01452 740293 Mrs Turrell
Rates fr: *£12.00*-**£12.50**.
Beds: 1D 1T 1S
Baths: 1 Private 1 Shared
(5)

Aston Magna

National Grid Ref: SP1935

***Bran Mill Cottage,** Aston Magna, Moreton in Marsh, Glos, GL56 9QP.*
Cotswold cottage in peaceful spot.
Open: All Year (not Xmas)
Grades: ETB Listed
01386 593517 Mrs Baggaley
Rates fr: *£16.50*-**£17.00**.
Beds: 1D 1T 1S
Baths: 2 Shared
(2)

Aston on Carrant

National Grid Ref: SO9434

Fox & Hounds

***Wistaria Cottage,** Aston on Carrant, Tewkesbury, Glos, GL20 8HL*
C17th cottage.
Open: Apr to Oct
01684 772357 Mrs Allen
Rates fr: *£17.00*-**£19.00**.
Beds: 1D 1T
Baths: 1 Private 1 Shared
(3) (2)

Berkeley

National Grid Ref: ST6899

Black Horse

***Pickwick Farm,** Berkeley, Glos, GL13 9EU.*
C18th inn, now comfortable farmhouse.
Open: All Year (not Xmas)
Grades: ETB Listed, Comm, RAC Listed, Comm
01453 810241 Mrs Jordan
Rates fr: *£16.00*-**£16.00**.
Beds: 1D 2T
Baths: 1 Shared
(3)

Berry Hill

National Grid Ref: SO5712

***Westlands House,** 20 Grove Road, Berry Hill, Coleford, Glos, GL16 8QY.*
Cottage close to forest walks.
Open: All Year (not Xmas)
01594 837143 Mrs Atherley
Rates fr: *£15.00*-**£15.00**.
Beds: 1D 1T **Baths:** 1 Shared
(2)

Bigsweir

National Grid Ref: SO8628

***Florence Country Hotel,** Bigsweir, St Briavels, Lydney, Glos, GL15 6QQ.*
The picturesque lower Wye Valley.
Open: All Year
Grades: ETB 3 Cr
01594 530830 Mr Sabin
Rates fr: *£23.00*-**£25.00**.
Beds: 3D 2T **Baths:** 5 Private
(13)

Birdlip

National Grid Ref: SO9214

***Beechmount,** Birdlip, Gloucester, GL4 8JH.*
Open: All Year
Grades: ETB 2 Cr, Comm
01452 862262 Mrs Carter
Rates fr: *£14.00*-**£14.50**.
Beds: 2F 2D 2T 1S
Baths: 2 Private 1 Shared
(7)
A warm welcome in this family-run guest house. Personal attention. Ideal centre for walking, touring the Cotswolds. Home cooking, choice of menu for breakfast.

Blakeney

National Grid Ref: SO6606

New Inn

***Upper Viney Farmhouse,** Viney Hill, Blakeney, Glos, GL15 4LT.*
Open: All Year (not Xmas)
Grades: ETB 2 Cr, Comm
01594 516672 Mrs Litten
Rates fr: *£18.00*-**£20.00**.
Beds: 1F 1D 1T
Baths: 2 Ensuite 1 Private
(6)
The Littens offer a warm welcome to their C16th home which features oak beams & inglenook fireplaces, character bedrooms with modern facilities and wonderful views.

***Viney Hill Country Guesthouse,** Blakeney, Glos, GL15 4LT.*
Open: All Year
Grades: ETB 3 Cr, Comm, RAC High Acclaim
01594 516000 Mr Humphreys
Fax no: 01594 516018
Rates fr: *£22.00*-**£30.00**.
Beds: 4D 2T **Baths:** 6 Private
(6)
Set in half an acre of lawns and gardens in the beautiful Gloucestershire countryside. Adjacent to the Royal Forest of Dean & Wye Valley.

***Treetops,** Viney Hill, Blakeney, Glos, GL15 4LZ.*
Spacious modern home, beautiful garden.
Open: All Year (not Xmas)
Grades: ETB 2 Cr, High Comm
01594 516149 Mrs Holding
Rates fr: *£18.00*-**£18.00**.
Beds: 1D 1T 1S
Baths: 1 Ensuite 1 Private
(3)

Blockley

National Grid Ref: SP1634

Great Western Arms

***Park Farm,** Blockley, Moreton in Marsh, Glos, GL56 9TA.*
Modernised C16th farmhouse, idyllic surroundings.
Open: Mar to Sept
Grades: ETB Listed
01386 700266 Mr & Mrs Dee
Rates fr: *£17.00*-**£17.00**.
Beds: 1D 1T 2S
Baths: 1 Shared
(6)

***Tudor House,** High Street, Blockley, Moreton in Marsh, Glos, GL56 9EX.*
Welcoming house, lovely unspoilt village.
Open: All Year (not Xmas)
01386 700356 Mrs Thompson
Rates fr: *£18.00*-**£20.00**.
Beds: 1D 1T
Baths: 1 Shared
(10) (2)

Bourton on the Water

National Grid Ref: SP1620

The Plough, Mouse Trap Inn

***Lansdowne House,** Lansdowne, Bourton on the Water, Cheltenham, Glos, GL54 2AT.*
Tastefully furnished period stone house.
Open: All Year (not Xmas)
Grades: ETB 1 Cr, Comm
01451 820812
Mrs Garwood
Rates fr: *£15.00*-**£24.00**.
Beds: 1F 1D 1T
Baths: 3 Private
(5)

***Fosseside,** Lansdowne, Bourton on the Water, Cheltenham, Glos, GL54 2AT.*
Comfortable accommodation in lovely location.
Open: All Year (not Xmas)
Grades: ETB 2 Cr, High Comm
01451 820574
Mrs Waterworth
Rates fr: *£16.50*-**£27.50**.
Beds: 3D
Baths: 2 Ensuite 1 Private
(8) (4)

***Farncombe,** Clapton On The Hill, Bourton on the Water, Cheltenham, Glos, GL54 2LG.*
Peace, tranquillity guaranteed. Superb views.
Open: All Year (not Xmas)
Grades: ETB 2 Cr
01451 820120
Mrs Wright
Rates fr: *£18.00*-**£18.00**.
Beds: 2D 1T
Baths: 1 Ensuite 2 Shared
(3)

***Lansdowne Villa Guest House,** Bourton on the Water, Cheltenham, Glos, GL54 2AT.*
Spacious rooms, completely refurbished.
Open: All Year
Grades: ETB 3 Cr, High Comm, AA 4 Q
01451 820673
Mr & Mrs Baker
Fax no: 01451 822099
Rates fr: *£21.50*-**£26.00**.
Beds: 8D 2T 2S
Baths: 12 Ensuite
(14)

***Windrush Farm,** Bourton on the Water, Cheltenham, Glos, GL54 3BY.*
Traditional Cotswold stone farmhouse, near Bourton-on-the-Water.
Open: Mar to Dec
Grades: ETB 2 Cr, High Comm
01451 820419
Mrs Burrough
Rates fr: *£19.00*-**£28.00**.
Beds: 1D 1T
Baths: 2 Private
(4)

Broad Campden

National Grid Ref: SP1537

Bakers Arms Inn

***Wyldlands,** Broad Campden, Chipping Campden, Glos, GL55 6UR.*
Highly recommended comfortable Cotswold stone house in picturesque conservation village.
Open: All Year (not Xmas)
Grades: ETB Listed, Comm
01386 840478 Mrs Wadey
Rates fr: *£18.00*-**£22.00**.
Beds: 2D 1T
Baths: 2 Ensuite 1 Private
(4)

***Marnic,** Broad Campden, Chipping Campden, Glos, GL55 6UR.*
Comfortable, friendly & well furnished family home.
Open: All Year (not Xmas)
Grades: ETB 2 Cr, High Comm, AA 4 Q, Select
01386 840014 Mrs Rawlings
Rates fr: *£20.00*-**£20.00**.
Beds: 2D 1T
Baths: 2 Ensuite 1 Private
(8) (4)

***Orchard Hill House,** Broad Campden, Chipping Campden, Glos, GL55 6UU.*
Charming farmhouse with character.
Open: All Year (not Xmas)
01386 841473 Mrs Ashmore
Fax no: 01386 841030
Rates fr: *£22.00*-**£35.00**.
Beds: 1F 2D 1T
Baths: 3 Ensuite 1 Private
(6) (6)

Brookthorpe

National Grid Ref: SO8312

Four Mile House

***Gilberts,** Gilberts Lane, Brookthorpe, Gloucester, GL4 0UH.*
Open: All Year
Grades: ETB 2 Cr, High Comm, RAC High Acclaim
01452 812364 (also fax no)
Mrs Beer
Rates fr: *£23.00*-**£23.00**.
Beds: 2D 1T 1S **Baths:** 4 Private
(6)
An updated Listed gem lying beneath the Cotswolds in organic grounds (guaranteeing superb breakfasts) and fantastic countryside. Central to Gloucester, Cheltenham, Stroud, Oxford, Bath, Stratford.

Cam

National Grid Ref: ST7499

***Green Street Farm,** Cam Green, Cam, Dursley, Glos, GL11 5HW.*
1680 farmhouse with indoor pool.
Open: All Year (not Xmas)
01453 542845 Mrs Purnell
Rates fr: *£17.00*-**£18.50**.
Beds: 1F **Baths:** 1 Private
(5)

Chalford

National Grid Ref: SO8902

***Beechcroft,** Brownshill, Chalford, Stroud, Glos, GL6 8AG.*
Quietly situated Edwardian house.
Open: All Year
Grades: ETB 1 Cr, Comm
01453 883422 Mrs Salt
Rates fr: *£16.00*-**£20.00**.
Beds: 1D 1T **Baths:** 1 Shared

***Ashleigh House,** Bussage, Chalford, Stroud, Glos, GL6 8AZ.*
Peaceful village location. Warm welcome.
Open: All Year (not Xmas)
Grades: ETB 2 Cr, Comm
01453 883944 Mr Dunsford
Fax no: 01453 886931
Rates fr: *£25.00*-**£30.00**.
Beds: 3F 3D 3T **Baths:** 9 Ensuite
(9)

***Green Court,** The High Street, Chalford, Stroud, Glos, GL6 8DS.*
Fine Georgian house, fascinating village. **Open:** All Year
01453 883234 Mrs Bateman
Rates fr: *£15.00*-**£18.00**.
Beds: 1F 1T **Baths:** 1 Shared
(4)

Charlton Kings

National Grid Ref: SO9620

Reservior Inn

***Old Stables,** 239a London Road, Charlton Kings, Cheltenham, Glos, GL52 6YE.*
Former coach house and stables.
Open: All Year
01242 583660 Mr Seeley
Rates fr: *£14.00*-**£15.00**.
Beds: 1F 1D 1T
Baths: 1 Private 1 Shared
(3)

***Langett,** Dowdeswell Reservoir, Charlton Kings, Cheltenham, Glos, GL54 4HG.*
Large bungalow, rural setting.
Open: All Year (not Xmas)
01242 820192 Cox
Rates fr: *£17.00*-**£20.00**.
Beds: 1D 1T
Baths: 2 Shared
(5) (10)

Cheltenham

National Grid Ref: SO9422

Montpellier Wine Bar, Beaumont Arms, Flynn's Bistro

***Orchard Leigh,** Hayden Road, Cheltenham, Glos, GL51 0SN.*
Modern comfortable house. Close to Cheltenham.
Open: All Year
01242 690415 (also fax no)
Mr & Mrs Parsons
Rates fr: *£20.00*-**£20.00**.
Baths: 2 Ensuite 1 Private

***Lonsdale House,** Montpellier Drive, Cheltenham, Glos, GL50 1TX.*
Open: All Year (not Xmas)
Grades: ETB 2 Cr, Comm, AA 2 Q
01242 232379 (also fax no)
Mr Duesbury
Rates fr: *£18.00*-**£18.00**.
Beds: 3F 2D 1T 5S
Baths: 3 Private 4 Shared
(2) (6)
Listed Regency house situated five minutes walk from town hall, town centre, parks and theatres. Easy access to Cotswolds and all main routes. Car parking.

***The Bowler Hat Hotel,** 130 London Road, Cheltenham, Glos, GL52 6HJ.*
Regency house close to town.
Open: All Year
Grades: ETB 2 Cr
01242 523614 Mr Barton
Fax no: 01242 577362
Rates fr: *£16.50*-**£19.00**.
Beds: 1F 2D 1T 2S
Baths: 2 Ensuite 1 Shared
(8) (8)

***Parkview,** 4 Pittville Crescent, Cheltenham, Glos, GL52 2QZ.*
Open: All Year
01242 575567 Mrs Sparrey
Rates fr: *£16.50*-**£16.50**.
Beds: 2F 1S
Beautiful Regency house in Cheltenham's nicest area. Cotswolds handy for touring, while Prestbury, England's most haunted village, is nearby. TV and tea-making in all rooms.

***St Michaels Guest House,** 4 Montpellier Drive, Cheltenham, Glos, GL50 1TX.*
Elegant Edwardian guest house - central.
Open: All Year
Grades: ETB 2 Cr, Comm
01242 513587 Mrs Perkin
Rates fr: *£19.00*-**£23.00**.
Beds: 3F 2D
Baths: 3 Ensuite 1 Shared
(4)

***North Hall Hotel,** Pittville Circus Road, Cheltenham, Glos, GL52 2PZ.*
Comfortable early Victorian town house.
Open: All Year (not Xmas)
Grades: ETB 3 Cr, Comm, AA Listed, RAC Listed
01242 520589 Mr Lancaster
Rates fr: *£21.75*-**£18.00**.
Beds: 6D 6T 8S
Baths: 16 Private 4 Shared
(20)

Bringing children with you? Always ask for any special rates.

Chipping Campden

National Grid Ref: SP1539

Kings Arms, Butchers Arms, Bakers Arms Inn, Badgers

***The Bank House,** Mickleton, Chipping Campden, Glos, GL55 6RX.*
Open: All Year (not Xmas)
Grades: ETB 2 Cr, Comm
01386 438302 Mrs Billington
Rates fr: *£18.00*-**£27.00**.
Beds: 1D 2T
Baths: 1 Ensuite 2 Private
(3)
Period Cotswold house with tranquil old world garden in heart of historic village, which contains excellent pubs serving good food. Hidcote, Broadway and Stratford nearby.

***Bran Mill Cottage,** Aston Magna, Chipping Campden, Moreton in Marsh, Glos, GL56 9QP.*
Cotswold cottage in peaceful spot.
Open: All Year (not Xmas)
Grades: ETB Listed
01386 593517 Mrs Baggaley
Rates fr: *£16.50*-**£17.00**.
Beds: 1D 1T 1S
Baths: 2 Shared
(2)

***Wyldlands,** Broad Campden, Chipping Campden, Glos, GL55 6UR.*
Open: All Year (not Xmas)
Grades: ETB Listed, Comm
01386 840478 Mrs Wadey
Rates fr: *£18.00*-**£22.00**.
Beds: 2D 1T
Baths: 2 Ensuite 1 Private
(4)
Highly recommended comfortable Cotswold stone house in picturesque conservation village. Beautiful garden with lovely views. Ideal touring, walking, gardens. Traditional inn nearby. Relaxed friendly atmosphere.

***Weston Park Farm,** Dovers Hill, Chipping Campden, Glos, GL55 6UW.*
Farmhouse in magnificent setting.
Open: All Year (not Xmas)
Grades: ETB 2 Cr
01386 840835 Mr Whitehouse
Rates fr: *£19.00*.
Beds: 1F
Baths: 1 Private

***Sandalwood House,** Back Ends, Chipping Campden, Glos, GL55 6AU.*
Open: All Year (not Xmas)
Grades: ETB 2 Cr, Comm
01386 840091 Mrs Bendall
Rates fr: *£20.00*-**£25.00**.
Beds: 1F 1T
Baths: 2 Private
(6) (6)
Comfortable quality accommodation for non-smokers peacefully located 5 minutes from centre of town. Central base for Cotswold holidays. Large rooms, every facility, private bathrooms. Large garden. Parking.

***The Eight Bells Inn,** Church Street, Chipping Campden, Glos, GL55 6JG.*
C14th Cotswold Inn, idyllic town.
Open: All Year
01386 840371 Mr Dare
Fax no: 01386 841 669
Rates fr: *£22.00*-**£38.00**.
Beds: 1F 1D 1T **Baths:** 1 Ensuite

***Marnic,** Broad Campden, Chipping Campden, Glos, GL55 6UR.*
Open: All Year (not Xmas)
Grades: ETB 2 Cr, High Comm, AA 4 Q, Select
01386 840014 Mrs Rawlings
Rates fr: *£20.00*-**£20.00**.
Beds: 2D 1T
Baths: 2 Ensuite 1 Private
(8) (4)
Comfortable, friendly and well furnished family home. Peacefully situated, scenic views. Ideal base for touring the Cotswolds. Bedrooms have full facilities. Non-smoking, private parking.

***Brymbo,** Mickleton, Chipping Campden, Glos, GL55 6PU.*
Friendly, comfortable, farm building conversion.
Open: All Year
Grades: ETB Listed
01386 438890 Mrs Jeffrey
Fax no: 01386 438113
Rates fr: *£15.00*-**£15.00**.
Beds: 1F 1D 1T
Baths: 2 Ensuite 2 Shared
(5)

***Haydon House,** Church Street, Chipping Campden, Glos, GL55 6JG.*
Converted dairy/bakehouse round courtyard. **Open:** Apr to Oct
01386 840275 Mrs Gilmour
Rates fr: *£22.00*-**£22.00**.
Beds: 1D 1T 1S
Baths: 2 Ensuite 1 Private
(10)

Cirencester

National Grid Ref: SP0201

Crown of Crucis, The Falcon, Wagon & Horses, Odd Fellows, Plough

***The Ivy House,** 2 Victoria Road, Cirencester, Glos, GL7 1EN.*
Large Victorian residence near town centre.
Open: All Year (not Xmas)
01285 656626 Mrs Goldsbury
Rates fr: *£20.00*-**£26.00**.
Beds: 3D 1T **Baths:** 4 Ensuite
(8) (4)

***Sprucewood,** Elf Meadow, Poulton, Cirencester, Glos, GL7 5HQ.*
Quiet, comfortable, homely, open views.
Open: All Year (not Xmas)
Grades: ETB 1 Cr, High Comm
01285 851351 Mr & Mrs Walker
Rates fr: *£16.00*-**£16.00**.
Beds: 1D 1T 1S **Baths:** 1 Shared
(4)

***The Golden Cross Inn,** Black Jack Street, Cirencester, Glos, GL7 2AA.*
Early C18th inn.
Open: All Year
Grades: ETB 1 Cr, Approv
01285 652137
Mr & Mrs Smith
Rates fr: *£15.00*-**£18.00**.
Beds: 1F 1T **Baths:** 1 Shared

***Sunset,** Baunton Lane, Cirencester, Glos, GL7 2NQ.*
Small, friendly guest house.
Open: Easter to Oct
Grades: ETB Listed, Comm
01285 654822 Mrs Castle
Rates fr: *£13.50*-**£13.50**.
Beds: 1T 2S
Baths: 1 Shared
(5) (4)

***The Leauses,** 101 Victoria Road, Cirencester, Glos, GL7 1EU.*
Attractive, comfortable, Victorian private house.
Open: All Year
Grades: ETB 2 Cr, Comm
01285 653643 Mrs Richens
Rates fr: *£16.50*.
Beds: 1F 2D 1T
Baths: 4 Private
(6)

***Clonsilla Guest House,** 7 Victoria Road, Cirencester, Glos, GL7 1EN.*
Five minutes from town centre.
Open: All Year
Grades: ETB Listed
01285 652621 Mr Sullivan
Rates fr: *£15.00*-**£18.00**.
Beds: 1F 3D 3T 1S
Baths: 4 Private 2 Shared
(5)

***Chesil Rocks,** Baunton Lane, Cirencester, Glos, GL7 2LL.*
Pleasant friendly home, quiet lane.
Open: All Year
Grades: ETB Listed, Comm
01285 655031
Mrs Clayton
Rates fr: *£15.00*-**£15.00**.
Beds: 1T 2S
Baths: 1 Shared
(2)

***58 Queen Elizabeth Road,** Cirencester, Glos, GL7 1DJ.*
Modern comfortable house, rural outlook.
Open: All Year (not Xmas)
01285 652782
Mrs Biggs
Rates fr: *£13.00*-**£15.00**.
Beds: 1D 1T 2S
Baths: 2 Shared
(5) (2)

***26 Victoria Road,** Cirencester, Glos, GL7 1ES.*
Large Victorian private house.
Open: All Year (not Xmas)
01285 656440 Mrs Cremin
Rates fr: *£11.00*-**£15.00**.
Beds: 1F 1D 1T
Baths: 1 Private 1 Shared
(2)

Clearwell

National Grid Ref: SO5708

***Scatterford Cottage,** The Butts, Lowercross, Clearwell, Coleford, Glos, GL16 8PW.*
Detached modern character cottage.
Open: All Year (not Xmas)
Grades: ETB Listed, Comm
01594 835527
Mrs Simpson
Rates fr: *£14.00*-**£15.00**.
Beds: 1D 1T **Baths:** 1 Shared
(10) (4)

Cleeve Hill

National Grid Ref: SP9826

Rising Sun Hotel

***Inglecroft,** Post Office Lane, Cleeve Hill, Cheltenham, Glos, GL52 3PS4*
Large Edwardian private house.
Open: All Year
01242 673558 Mrs Carter
Rates fr: *£15.00*-**£15.00**.
Beds: 2F 1T **Baths:** 1 Shared
(4)

***Cleyne Hage,** Southam Lane, Cleeve Hill, Cheltenham, Glos, GL52 3NY.*
Cotswold stone house in tranquil village.
Open: All Year
Grades: ETB 1 Cr, Approv
01242 518569 / 0850 285338
Mrs Blankenspoor
Rates fr: *£16.00*-**£18.00**.
Beds: 1F 1D 1T 1S
Baths: 2 Ensuite 1 Private 1 Shared
(6)

Coates

National Grid Ref: SO9800

***The Sleight,** Coates, Cirencester, Glos, GL7 6NH.*
Comfortable modern house, welcome assured.
Open: All Year
01285 770654
Mrs Hyland
Rates fr: *£14.00*-**£15.00**.
Beds: 2T
Baths: 1 Ensuite 1 Shared
(4)

Cold Ashton

National Grid Ref: ST7472

White Hart

***High Lanes,** Cold Ashton, Chippenham, Wilts, SN14 8JU.*
C17th Cotswold Way cottage.
Open: Feb to Nov
Grades: ETB Listed
01225 891255
Mrs Williamson
Rates fr: *£18.50*-**£20.50**.
Beds: 1T 1S
Baths: 1 Shared
(8)

***Vhittington Farmhouse,** Cold ,shton, Chippenham, Wilts, SN14 8JS.*
, peaceful Cotswold farmhouse :.1700) on the Cotswold Way.
)pen: Feb to Nov
;rades: ETB 2 Cr, High Comm
1225 891628
1rs Hacker
:ates fr: *£17.50*-**£25.00**.
;eds: 2D
:aths: 1 Ensuite
(10)

***'oghill House Farm,** Cold Ashton, Vick, Bristol, BS15 5RT.*
Varm & cosy C17th farmhouse.
)pen: All Year
;rades: ETB Listed
1225 891261
1rs Bishop
:ates fr: *£19.50*-**£25.00**.
;eds: 2F 1D
:aths: 3 Private
(0) (20)

***Vhiteways,** Tormarton Road, Cold shton, Chippenham, Wilts, SN14 8JY*
lodern comfortable smallholding.
)pen: All Year (not Xmas)
1225 891333 Mrs Pike
:ates fr: *£17.00*-**£20.00**.
;eds: 1F 1D 1T
:aths: 2 Shared

:oleford

[N]ational Grid Ref: SO5710

Montague Inn

***Iarefold,** Gorsty Knoll, Coleford, 'los, GL16 7LR.*
[Q]uiet, C18th family country house.
)pen: All Year (not Xmas)
1594 833969
1rs Webb
:ates fr: *£16.00*-**£16.00**.
;eds: 1T 1S
:aths: 1 Private 1 Shared
(2)

:oopers Hill

[N]ational Grid Ref: SO8914

***he Haven Tea Garden,** Coopers 'ill, Brockworth, Gloucester, L3 4SB.*
Vooden bungalow along Cotswold [W]ay.
)pen: Easter to Oct
1452 863213
1rs Hellerman
:ates fr: *£15.00*-**£15.00**.
;eds: 1F 1T
:aths: 1 Shared
(2)

Always telephone to get directions to the B&B - you will save time!

Corse

National Grid Ref: SO7826

***Kilmorie Guest House,** Gloucester Road, Corse, Staunton, Gloucester, GL19 3RQ.*
Open: All Year (not Xmas)
Grades: ETB 2 Cr, Approv
01452 840224 Ms Barnfield
Rates fr: *£14.00*-**£14.00**.
Beds: 2F 3D 1T 1S
Baths: 2 Private 2 Shared
(5) (8)
Modernised Victorian smallholding, all ground floor. Tea-trays, colour TVs, hot & cold all rooms, excellent accommodation, at reasonable rates. Tour Cotswolds, Forest of Dean, Malvern Hills.

Deerhurst

National Grid Ref: SO8729

***Deerhurst House,** Deerhurst, Gloucester, GL19 4BX.*
Beautiful classical Georgian country house.
Open: All Year (not Xmas)
01684 292135 Ms Leeke
Rates fr: *£20.00*-**£25.00**.
Beds: 1D 1T **Baths:** 2 Ensuite
(10)

Down Hatherley

National Grid Ref: SO8622

King's Head (Norton)

***Frog Furlong Cottage,** Frog Furlong Lane, Down Hatherley, Gloucester, GL2 9QE.*
Exclusive, tranquil accommodation for one couple.
Open: All Year (not Xmas)
01452 730430 Mrs Rooke
Rates fr: *£17.00*-**£18.00**.
Beds: 1D **Baths:** 1 Ensuite

Dumbleton

National Grid Ref: SP0136

Hobnails (Alderton)

***Raymeadow Farm,** Dumbleton, Evesham, Worcs, WR11 6TR.*
C17th Cotswold stone farm house.
Open: Mar to Oct
01242 621215 Ms Alvis
Rates fr: *£15.00*-**£15.00**.
Beds: 1F 1T 1S **Baths:** 1 Shared

Duntisbourne Abbots

National Grid Ref: SO9707

***Dixs Barn,** Duntisbourne Abbots, Cirencester, Glos, GL7 7NJ.*
Converted barn with lovely views.
Open: All Year
01285 821249 Mrs Wilcox
Rates fr: *£16.00*-**£16.00**.
Beds: 1D 1T
Baths: 1 Ensuite 1 Private

Dursley

National Grid Ref: ST7698

The Kings Head, Bunters Restaurant

***The Old Malthouse,** 19 Woodmancote , Dursley, Glos, GL11 4AF.*
Listed Cotswold stone malthouse.
Open: May to Sep
01453 545105 Mrs Trump
Rates fr: *£17.50*-**£20.00**.
Beds: 1T
Baths: 1 Ensuite
(1)

***Claremont House,** 66 Kingshill Road, Dursley, Glos, GL11 4EG.*
Victorian family house, views of Cotswold Escarpment.
Open: All Year (not Xmas/New Year)
Grades: ETB 2 Cr, Comm
01453 542018 Mrs Williams
Rates fr: *£17.50*-**£17.50**.
Beds: 1F 2D 1T
Baths: 2 Private 1 Shared
(8)

Easter Compton

National Grid Ref: ST5782

***Firwood House,** Mains Road, Easter Compton, Bristol, BS12 3RA.*
Self-contained, family-run guest house.
Open: All Year
01454 633394
Mr & Mrs Griffiths
Rates fr: *£16.00*-**£18.00**.
Beds: 1F 2T
Baths: 2 Shared
(5)

Edge

National Grid Ref: SO8509

***Wild Acre,** Back Edge Lane, Edge, Stroud, Glos, GL6 6PE.*
Large bungalow overlooking Painswick.
Open: Easter to Oct
01452 813077
Mrs Sanders
Rates fr: *£15.00*-**£18.00**.
Beds: 1D 1T
Baths: 1 Private 1 Shared
(3)

Elton

National Grid Ref: SO6913

***Upper Hall,** Elton, Newnham, Glos, GL14 1JJ.*
C17th stone country house.
Open: All Year (not Xmas)
01452 760243 Mrs Tucker
Rates fr: *£17.50*-**£20.00**.
Beds: 1D 1T
Baths: 2 Private
(6)

English Bicknor

National Grid Ref: SO5815

***Oak Farm,** Ross Road, English Bicknor, Coleford, Glos, GL16 7PA.*
Open: All Year (not Xmas)
Grades: ETB Listed
01594 860606 Mr & Mrs Edwards
Rates fr: *£13.00*-**£14.00**.
Beds: 1D 1T 1S
Baths: 2 Private 1 Shared
(5)
Modern farmhouse with superb views from all rooms. Ideally situated for exploring the magnificent Forest of Dean & the grandeur of the Wye Valley.

***Lower Tump Farm,** Eastbach, English Bicknor, Coleford, Glos, GL16 7EU.*
C16th farmhouse on working farm.
01594 860253 / 0836 536674
Ms Davis
Rates fr: *£13.50*-**£16.50**.
Beds: 1F 1D 1T 1S
Baths: 4 Ensuite
(10)

***Upper Tump Farm,** East Bach, English Bicknor, Coleford, Glos, GL16 7EU.*
C15th stone farmhouse.
Open: All Year
01594 860072
Mrs Merrett
Rates fr: *£16.50*-**£16.50**.
Beds: 1F 2D
Baths: 2 Private
(6)

Evenlode

National Grid Ref: SP2229

Red Lion (Little Compton)

***Journeys End,** Evenlode, Moreton in Marsh, Glos, GL56 0NN.*
Gabled Cotswold house in undiscovered quiet village.
Open: All Year
Grades: ETB 2 Cr, Comm
01608 650786
Miss Woolley
Rates fr: *£18.00*-**£20.00**.
Beds: 1F 3D 1T
Baths: 5 Private
(5)

Fairford

National Grid Ref: SP1500

***Waiten Hill Farm,** Mill Lane, Fairford, Glos, GL7 4JG.*
Imposing farmhouse overlooking River Coln.
Open: All Year
Grades: ETB 2 Cr, Approv
01285 712652
Mrs Rymer
Rates fr: *£15.00*-**£20.00**.
Beds: 1F 1D 1T
Baths: 1 Ensuite 2 Private 1 Shared

Falfield

National Grid Ref: ST6893

***Green Farm Guest House,** Falfield, Wotton-under-Edge, GL12 8DL.*
C16th farmhouse. Access M4 & M5. **Open:** All Year
Grades: ETB Listed, AA 2 Q, RAC Listed
01454 260319 Mr Burrell
Rates fr: *£16.00*-**£20.00**.
Beds: 1F 4D 2T 1S
Baths: 3 Private 1 Shared
(10)

Forthampton

National Grid Ref: SO8532

Duke of York

***Downend Farm,** Long Green, Forthampton, Tewkesbury, Gloucester, GL19 4QJ.*
Large, bright, well-furnished farmhouse. **Open:** Easter to Autumn
01684 833371 Mrs Bloxham
Rates fr: *£16.00*-**£16.00**.
Beds: 2T 2S **Baths:** 2 Shared
(6)

Gloucester

National Grid Ref: SO8318

***Rotherfield House Hotel,** 5 Horton Road, Gloucester, GL1 3PX.*
Immaculate, extended detached Victorian property.
Open: All Year (not Xmas)
Grades: ETB 3 Cr, Comm, AA 1 St, RAC High Acclaim
01452 410500 Mr Eacott
Rates fr: *£22.00*-**£21.00**.
Beds: 2F 2D 1T 8S
Baths: 8 Private 5 Shared
(9)

***Notley House,** 93 Hucclecote Road, Gloucester, GL3 3TR.*
Old, beamed property, four posters.
Open: All Year (not Xmas)
Grades: ETB 3 Cr, Comm
01452 611584 Mr George
Fax no: 01452 371229
Rates fr: *£19.00*-**£23.50**.
Beds: 2F 3D 2T 1S
Baths: 5 Private 2 Shared
(8)

***Gemini Guest House,** 83a Innsworth Lane, Longlevens, Gloucester, GL2 0TT.*
Spacious, modern, comfortable detached house.
Open: All Year (not Xmas)
01452 415849 Mrs Burby
Rates fr: *£15.00*-**£15.00**.
Beds: 1F 1D 1T 1S
Baths: 1 Shared
(6)

***31 Spa Road,** Gloucester, GL1 1UY.*
Large house overlooking bowling green. **Open:** All Year
Grades: ETB 1 Cr
01452 306034 Mr Powell
Rates fr: *£15.00*-**£15.00**.
Beds: 1F 2D 1T 4S
Baths: 2 Private 1 Shared
(4)

Gotherington

National Grid Ref: SO9629

Royal Oak (Gretton)

***Pardon Hill Farm,** Prescott, Gotherington, Cheltenham, Glos, GL52 4RD.*
Modern, comfortable farmhouse, lovely views.
Open: All Year (not Xmas)
Grades: ETB 2 Cr, Comm, AA 3 Q
01242 672468 (also fax no)
Mrs Newman
Rates fr: *£20.00*-**£25.00**.
Beds: 1D 1T 1S **Baths:** 3 Ensuite
(10)

***Moat Farm,** Gotherington, Cheltenham, Glos, GL52 4ET.*
Old farmhouse with moat.
Open: All Year (not Xmas)
01242 676807 Mrs Tilley
Rates fr: *£16.00*-**£16.00**.
Beds: 2D 1S

Great Rissington

National Grid Ref: SP1917

Lamb Inn

***Lower Farmhouse,** Great Rissington, Bourton on the Water, Cheltenham, Glos, GL54 2LH.*
Child-friendly converted Cotswold barn.
Open: All Year
Grades: ETB Listed, Approv
01451 810163 Mr & Mrs Fleming
Rates fr: *£16.00*-**£16.00**.
Beds: 1D 1T
Baths: 1 Shared
(3)

Guiting Power

National Grid Ref: SP0924

***The Old Vicarage,** Tally Ho Lane, Guiting Power, Cheltenham, Glos, GL54 5TY.*
Comfortable Edwardian private house. **Open:** Mar to Oct
01451 850596 Mrs Burrough
Rates fr: *£23.00*-**£14.00**.
Beds: 2T **Baths:** 2 Private
(5) (2)

Hailes

National Grid Ref: SP0430

***Pilgrim House,** Hailes, Winchcombe, Cheltenham, Glos, GL54 5PB.*
Early C18th Cotswold stone farmhouse.
Open: All Year (not Xmas)
01242 603011 Mrs Cooper
Rates fr: *£15.00*-**£20.00**.
Beds: 2T **Baths:** 1 Shared
(6)

Haresfield

National Grid Ref: SO8110

Beacon Hotel

Lower Green Farmhouse, *Haresfield, Stonehouse, Glos, GL10 3DS.*
C18th Cotswold stone farmhouse.
Open: All Year (not Xmas)
Grades: ETB 1 Cr
01452 728264 (also fax no)
Mrs Reed
Rates fr: *£16.50*-**£19.00**.
Beds: 1F 1T
Baths: 2 Shared
(6)

Huntley

National Grid Ref: SO7219

Red Lion

Forest Gate, *Huntley, Gloucester, GL19 3EU.*
Large Victorian former rectory.
Open: All Year (not Xmas)
Grades: ETB 2 Cr
01452 831192
Mr Blakemore
Rates fr: *£19.00*-**£19.00**.
Beds: 1F 1D 1S
Baths: 1 Private 1 Shared
(0) (6)

Inchbrook

National Grid Ref: SO8400

The Laurels, *Inchbrook, Nailsworth, Stroud, Glos, GL5 5HA.*
Lovely C18th house, food, hospitality.
Open: All Year
Grades: ETB 3 Cr
01453 834021
Mrs Williams-Allen
Fax no: 01453 834004
Rates fr: *£18.00*-**£24.00**.
Beds: 1F 2D 1T
Baths: 4 Ensuite
(6)

Kemble

National Grid Ref: ST9897

Thames Head

Smerrill Barns, *Kemble, Cirencester, Glos, GL7 6BW.*
Open: All Year
Grades: ETB 2 Cr, Comm, AA 3 Q, RAC Acclaim
01285 770907
Mrs Benson
Fax no: 01285 770706
Rates fr: *£22.50*-**£30.00**.
Beds: 1F 4D 1T 1S
Baths: 7 Private 1 Shared
(3) (8)
C18th converted barn, all rooms ensuite. Guest lounge with log fires in winter, drinks licence. Enjoy the heart of the Cotswolds with us.

Kempley

National Grid Ref: SO6729

Lower House Farm, *Kempley, Dymock, Newent, Glos, GL18 2BS.*
Idyllic comfortable farmhouse, wonderful food.
Open: All Year
Grades: ETB 3 Cr, Approv
01531 890301 (also fax no)
Mrs Bennett
Rates fr: *£16.00*-**£18.00**.
Beds: 1D 2T
Baths: 2 Ensuite

Kilcot

National Grid Ref: SO6925

The Roadmaker (Gorsley)

Cherry Grove B&B, *Mill Lane, Kilcot, Newent, Glos, GL18 1NY.*
Modern house, peaceful rural situation.
Open: All Year (not Xmas)
Grades: ETB Listed
01989 720126 Mr & Mrs Inwood
Rates fr: *£15.00*-**£16.00**.
Beds: 1F 2D
Baths: 1 Ensuite 1 Shared
(5) (6)

Kings Stanley

National Grid Ref: SO8103

Nurashell, *Bath Road, Kings Stanley, Stonehouse, Glos, GL10 3JG.*
Victorian private house. Village centre.
Open: All Year (not Xmas)
01453 823642 Mrs Rollins
Rates fr: *£16.00*-**£16.00**.
Beds: 1D 1T
Baths: 1 Shared

Old Chapel House, *Broad Street, Kings Stanley, Stonehouse, Glos, GL10 3PN.*
Converted chapel on Cotswold Way.
Open: All Year (not Xmas)
01453 826289 Mrs Richards Hanna
Rates fr: *£20.00*-**£20.00**.
Beds: 1F 1D 2T 1S
Baths: 2 Private 1 Shared
(3) (4)

Kingscote

National Grid Ref: ST8196

Hunters Hall

Bumpers Island Farm, *Kingscote, Tetbury, Glos, GL8 8YQ.*
Comfortable, friendly Cotswold farmhouse.
Open: Apr to Oct
01453 860498
Mrs Bateman
Rates fr: *£16.00*-**£16.00**.
Beds: 1F 1T 2S
Baths: 2 Private 1 Shared
(6)

Laverton

National Grid Ref: SP0735

Gunners Orchard, *Laverton, Broadway, Glos, WR12 7NA.*
Comfortable private house, personal attention.
Open: All Year (not Xmas)
01386 584213
Mrs Stephenson
Rates fr: *£16.00*-**£25.00**.
Beds: 1D 1T
Baths: 1 Shared
(10) (6)

Lechlade

National Grid Ref: SU2199

Swan, Red Lion, Black Cat, New Inn, Trout Inn

Cambrai Lodge Guest House, *Oak Street, Spring Gardens, Lechlade, Glos, GL7 3AH.*
Modern comfortable house off the road.
Open: All Year
Grades: ETB Listed, Comm
01367 253173 / 0860 150467
Mr Titchener
Rates fr: *£16.00*-**£20.00**.
Beds: 1F 1D 1T 1S
Baths: 2 Private 1 Shared
(9)

The New Inn Hotel, *Market Square, Lechlade, Glos, GL7 3AB.*
C17th fully modernised coaching inn.
Open: All Year
Grades: ETB 3 Cr
01367 252296
Mr Sandhu
Fax no: 01367 252315
Rates fr: *£20.00*-**£40.00**.
Beds: 2F 10D 10T 4S
Baths: 26 Ensuite
(40)

Apple Tree House, *Lechlade, Lechlade, Oxon, SN7 8DA.*
Listed property - National Trust village.
Open: All Year
Grades: ETB 2 Cr
01367 252592 Mrs Reay
Rates fr: *£17.00*-**£22.00**.
Beds: 2D 1T
Baths: 1 Ensuite 2 Shared
(8)

Little Rissington

National Grid Ref: SP1919

Hill Farm, *Little Rissington, Bourton on the Water, Cheltenham, Glos, GL54 2ND.*
Large Cotswold farmhouse, quiet position.
Open: All Year
01451 820330 Mrs Sweeting
Rates fr: *£15.00*-**£18.00**.
Beds: 1F 1D 1T
Baths: 1 Private 1 Shared
(6)

Littledean

National Grid Ref: SO6713

***Littledean House Hotel,** Littledean, Cinderford, Glos, GL14 3JT.*
Open: Mar to Nov
01594 822106 Mrs Felton
Fax no: 01594 823696
Rates fr: *£19.95*-**£19.95**.
Beds: 10F 15T 15S
Baths: 4 Private 10 Shared
(20)
Rambling, informal, friendly country hotel in Forest of Dean. Large gardens, tennis. Bar, lounges, conservatory, games room. Ideal for walkers, cyclists, families.

Longhope

National Grid Ref: SO6818

***New House Farm,** Aston Ingham Lane, Longhope, Glos, GL17 0LS.*
Unique house and owners, serendipity.
Open: All Year (not Xmas)
Grades: ETB 2 Cr
01452 830484 Mrs Beddows
Rates fr: *£18.00*-**£20.00**.
Beds: 1F 1D 1T
Baths: 1 Ensuite 1 Shared
(10)

Lower Lydbrook

National Grid Ref: SO5916

***Courtfields Arms Hotel,** Lower Lydbrook, Glos, GL17 9NU.*
Country inn/restaurant overlooking river. **Open:** All Year
01594 860207
Rates fr: *£12.50*-**£15.00**.
Beds: 2F 1D
Baths: 1 Ensuite 1 Private

Lower Swell

National Grid Ref: SP1725

***Wendover,** 2 Rectory Close, Lower Swell, Stow On The Wold, Cheltenham, Glos, GL54 1LH.*
Modern Cotswold stone house.
Open: All Year (not Xmas)
Grades: ETB Listed, Comm
01451 831310 Mrs Worker
Rates fr: *£16.00*-**£19.00**.
Beds: 1F 1D 1S **Baths:** 1 Shared
(7) (3)

Marshfield

National Grid Ref: ST7773

Catherine Wheel, Nelson. Crown

***Knowle Hill Farm,** Beeks Lane, Marshfield, Chippenham, Wilts, SN14 8AA.*
Modern, comfortable farmhouse.
Open: All Year (not Xmas)
01225 891503 Mrs Bond
Rates fr: *£16.00*-**£16.00**.
Beds: 1F 1D 1T **Baths:** 1 Shared
(3)

Meysey Hampton

National Grid Ref: SU1199

***The Masons Arms,** High Street, Meysey Hampton, Cirencester, Glos, GL7 5JT.*
Traditional C17th village inn.
Open: All Year
01285 850164 Mr Gent
Rates fr: *£22.00*-**£28.00**.
Beds: 1F 5D 1T 1S
Baths: 9 Private
(10)

Mickleton

National Grid Ref: SP1643

Kings Arms, Butchers Arms

***Old Barn House,** Mill Lane, Mickleton, Chipping Campden, Glos, GL55 6RT.*
Open: All Year (not Xmas)
Grades: ETB 2 Cr
01386 438668 (also fax no)
Mrs Lodge
Rates fr: *£18.00*-**£20.00**.
Beds: 1D 1T
Baths: 2 Private
(10) (3)
Quiet centrally situated in village conservation area 1 mile from Hidcote Gardens and Kiftsgate Court Gardens, ideal for Cotswolds, Shakespeare Country, Malverns & Vale of Evesham.

Middle Duntisbourne

National Grid Ref: SO9806

Bear Inn, Perrotts Brook

***Manor Farm,** Middle Duntisbourne, Cirencester, Glos, GL7 7AR.*
Farmhouse set in beautiful Duntisbourne.
Open: All Year (not Xmas)
Grades: ETB 2 Cr
01285 658145 Mrs Barton
Rates fr: *£14.00*-**£20.00**.
Beds: 1D 1T
Baths: 1 Ensuite 1 Private
(8)

***The Coach House,** Middle Duntisbourne, Cirencester, Glos, GL7 7AR.*
C17th Cotswold farmhouse.
Open: All Year (not Xmas)
01285 653058 Mrs Barton
Rates fr: *£15.00*-**£16.00**.
Beds: 1D 1T **Baths:** 2 Private
(14) (8)

Minchinhampton

National Grid Ref: SO8600

Old Lodge, Ram Inn

***Hunters Lodge,** Dr Browns Road, Minchinhampton, Stroud, Glos, GL6 9BT.*
Cotswold stone house overlooking common.
Open: All Year (not Xmas)
Grades: ETB 2 Cr, High Comm, AA 4 Q
01453 883588 Mrs Helm
Fax no: 01453 731449
Rates fr: *£19.00*-**£25.00**.
Beds: 1F 1D 1T
Baths: 1 Ensuite 2 Private
(6)

Miserden

National Grid Ref: SO9308

***Bidfield Farmhouse,** B4070, The Camp, Miserden, Stroud, Glos, GL6 7ET.*
Large comfortable C17th Cotswold farmhouse.
Open: Mar to Nov
01285 821263 Mrs Baird
Rates fr: *£15.00*-**£18.00**.
Beds: 1F 1T
Baths: 2 Ensuite
(10)

Moreton in Marsh

National Grid Ref: SP2032

***Treetops,** London Road, Moreton in Marsh, Glos, GL56 0HE.*
Open: All Year
Grades: ETB 2 Cr, Comm
01608 651036 Mrs Dean
Rates fr: *£21.00*-**£30.00**.
Beds: 1F 3D 2T
Baths: 6 Private
(8)
Family-run guest house set in secluded gardens yet only 5 minutes walk to village centre. Ideal for exploring the Cotswolds.

***Moreton House,** High Street, Moreton in Marsh, Glos, GL56 0LQ.*
100-year-old family-run guest house. **Open:** All Year
Grades: ETB 2 Cr, AA 2 Q, RAC Acclaim
01608 650747 Mr & Mrs Dempster
Fax no: 01608 652747
Rates fr: *£21.00*-**£22.00**.
Beds: 1F 6D 2T 3S
Baths: 7 Private 4 Shared
(5)

***Dorn Priory,** Dorn, Moreton in Marsh, Glos, GL56 9NS.*
Quiet, comfortable non-working farmhouse.
Open: Easter to Nov
01608 650152 Mrs Clifford
Rates fr: *£15.00*.
Beds: 1F 1D 1T **Baths:** 1 Shared
(8)

Nailsworth

National Grid Ref: ST8499

***The Vicarage,** Nailsworth, Stroud, Glos, GL6 0BS.*
Large, comfortable Victorian vicarage, garden.
Open: All Year (not Xmas)
01453 832181 Mrs Strong
Rates fr: *£18.00*-**£20.00**.
Beds: 1T 2S
Baths: 1 Private 1 Shared
(2) (4)

Windsoredge House, *Windsoredge Lane, Nailsworth, Stroud, Glos, GL6 0NP.*
Open: All Year
01453 833626 Mrs Butcher
Rates fr: *£14.00*-**£20.00**.
Beds: 1F 1D 1T **Baths:** 3 Private
(3)
Clean comfortable accommodation. Widely acclaimed hospitality and home cooking. Set in a quiet secluded hamlet with wonderful views over Woodchester Park and the Nailsworth Valley.

Aaron Farm, *Nympsfield Road, Nailsworth, Stroud, Glos, GL6 0ET.*
Modernised former farmhouse. Panoramic views.
Open: All Year
Grades: ETB 2 Cr, Comm
01453 833598 Mrs Mulligan
Fax no: 01453 836737
Rates fr: *£17.00*-**£24.00**.
Beds: 1D 2T **Baths:** 3 Ensuite
(3)

Newent

National Grid Ref: SO7225

George HotelBlack Bag

5 Onslow Road, *Newent, Glos, GL18 1TL.*
Modern 4 bedroom house. Quiet on edge of Newent. **Open:** All Year
01531 821677 Miss Bayley
Rates fr: *£13.50*-**£13.50**.
Beds: 1D 1T 1S
Baths: 1 Private 1 Shared
(10) (2)

Newland

National Grid Ref: SO5509

Ostrich Inn

Cherry Orchard Farm, *Newland, Coleford, Glos, GL16 8NP.*
Large, welcoming, comfortable Victorian farmhouse.
Open: All Year (not Xmas)
01594 832212 Mrs Blanch
Rates fr: *£15.00*-**£15.00**.
Beds: 1D 1T **Baths:** 1 Shared
(2)

The Ostrich Inn, *Newland, Coleford, Glos, GL16 8NP.*
Traditional village pub.
Open: All Year (not Xmas)
01594 833260 Mrs Dewe
Rates fr: *£20.00*-**£25.00**.
Beds: 1D 1T **Baths:** 1 Shared

North Nibley

National Grid Ref: ST7395

Nibley House, *North Nibley, Dursley, Glos, GL11 6DL.*
Spacious C17th Georgian manor house. **Open:** All Year (not Xmas)
01453 543108 Mrs Eley
Rates fr: *£16.00*-**£16.00**.
Beds: 1F 1D 1T **Baths:** 1 Shared
(12)

Black Horse Inn, *North Nibley, Dursley, Glos, GL11 6DT.*
Traditional Cotswold country inn.
Open: All Year
01453 546841
Mr & Mrs Hamston
Rates fr: *£20.00*-**£27.50**.
Beds: 1F 2D 3T
Baths: 4 Ensuite 1 Shared

Northleach

National Grid Ref: SP1114

Wheatsheaf Hotel

Market House, *The Square, Northleach, Cheltenham, Glos, GL54 3EJ.*
400-year-old Cotswold house.
Open: All Year (not Xmas)
Grades: ETB 2 Cr
01451 860557 Mr Eastman
Rates fr: *£17.00*-**£20.00**.
Beds: 1D 1T 2S
Baths: 1 Private 1 Shared
(12)

Norton

National Grid Ref: SO8524

Kings Head

Merrivale, *Tewkesbury Road, Norton, Gloucester, GL2 9LQ.*
Clean friendly house, pleasant garden.
Open: All Year
Grades: ETB 1 Cr, Comm
01452 730412 Mrs Price
Rates fr: *£15.50*-**£15.50**.
Beds: 1F 2D 3T
Baths: 2 Private 1 Shared
(8)

Nympsfield

National Grid Ref: SO8000

Rose & Crown Inn, *Nympsfield, Stonehouse, Glos, GL10 3TU.*
C17th Cotswold stone inn.
Open: All Year
Grades: ETB 3 Cr, Comm, AA 3 Q, RAC Listed, Comm
01453 860240 (also fax no)
Mr Smith
Rates fr: *£24.00*-**£14.50**.
Beds: 3F 1D
Baths: 4 Private

Oddington

National Grid Ref: SP2225

Orchard Cottage, *Back Lane, Oddington, Moreton in Marsh, Glos, GL56 0XL.*
Attractive stone cottage, log fires, pretty garden.
Open: Mar to Nov
01451 830785 Ms Beynon
Rates fr: *£17.50*-**£24.00**.
Beds: 1D 1T
Baths: 2 Private
(5) (2)

Old Sodbury

National Grid Ref: ST7581

Dog Inn

1 The Green, *Old Sodbury, Bristol, BS17 6LY.*
Converted C18th Cotswold cottages.
Open: All Year (not Xmas)
01454 314688 Mr & Mrs Rees
Rates fr: *£19.00*-**£19.00**.
Beds: 2D 1T 3S
Baths: 1 Ensuite 1 Shared
(4)

Crofton, *8 Chapel Lane, Old Sodbury, Bristol, BS17 6NG.*
Artist's C18th cottage.
Open: Easter to October
01454 314288 Mrs Ford
Rates fr: *£16.00*-**£17.50**.
Beds: 1F 1D **Baths:** 1 Shared
(8)

Dornden Guest House, *Church Lane, Old Sodbury, Bristol, BS17 6NB.*
Former vicarage, beautiful setting, quiet.
Open: All Year (not Xmas)
Grades: ETB 2 Cr
01454 313325 Mrs Paz
Fax no: 01454 312263
Rates fr: *£22.00*-**£25.00**.
Beds: 5F 2T 2S
Baths: 5 Ensuite 2 Shared
(15)

Elmgrove, *Badminton Road, Old Sodbury, Bristol, BS17 6LL.*
Private house in own grounds.
Open: All Year (not Xmas)
01454 313276 Mrs Arney
Rates fr: *£13.00*-**£13.00**.
Beds: 2T 2S **Baths:** 1 Shared
(8)

Dog Inn, *Old Sodbury, Bristol, BS17 6LZ.*
Large cottage. **Open:** All Year
01454 317053 Mr & Mrs Harris
Rates fr: *£15.00*-**£17.50**.
Beds: 2F 1D 1T
Baths: 1 Ensuite 2 Shared

Painswick

National Grid Ref: SO8609

Royal Oak, Falcon Inn

Hambutts Mynd, *Edge Road, Painswick, Stroud, Glos, GL6 6UP.*
Open: All Year
Grades: ETB 2 Cr, Comm, RAC Acclaim
01452 812352 Mr Warland
Rates fr: *£19.50*-**£21.00**.
Beds: 1D 1T 1S
Baths: 1 Ensuite 1 Shared
(8) (3)
Superb views. Close to village (2 blocks). Quiet location. Central heating. Near M5, M4. Ideal centre for Bath & North Cotswolds.TV in all rooms.

Upper Doreys Mill, *Edge, Painswick, Stroud, Glos, GL6 6NF.*
C18th cloth mill by stream.
Open: All Year
Grades: ETB 2 Cr
01452 812459
Mrs Marden
Rates fr: *£20.00*-**£28.00**.
Beds: 2D 1T
Baths: 3 Private
(6)

Armany, *Golf Course Road, Painswick, Stroud, Glos, GL6 6TJ.*
Quiet, comfortable, modern family house.
Open: All Year (not Xmas)
01452 812242 Mrs Dean
Rates fr: *£18.00*-**£20.00**.
Beds: 1D 1T
Baths: 1 Private 1 Shared
(1) (5)

Thorne, *Friday Street, Painswick, Stroud, Glos, GL6 6QJ.*
Grade II Listed Tudor cloth merchant's house.
Open: Easter to Oct
Grades: ETB 2 Cr
01452 812476
Mrs Blatchley
Rates fr: *£18.00*-**£22.00**.
Beds: 2T
Baths: 2 Private

Castle Lodge, *The Beacon, Painswick, Stroud, Glos, GL6 6TU.*
Traditional manor house. Charming position.
Open: All Year
01452 813603
Mr Cooke
Rates fr: *£20.00*-**£25.00**.
Beds: 1F 1D 1T
Baths: 5 Private

Parkend

National Grid Ref: SO6108

The Fountain Inn

The Fountain Inn, *Parkend, Lydney, Glos, GL15 4JD.*
Comfortable village pub, rural setting, real ales.
Open: All Year
01594 562189
Mr Powell
Rates fr: *£23.00*-**£27.00**.
Beds: 4D 2T 2S
Baths: 8 Private
(0) (30)

Edale House, *Folly Road, Parkend, Lydney, Glos, GL15 4JF.*
Elegant Georgian house, every facility.
Open: All Year
01594 562835
Mr Reid
Rates fr: *£17.50*-**£27.00**.
Beds: 4D 1T
Baths: 5 Private
(5)

Poulton

National Grid Ref: SP1001

Crown of Crucis, Falcon

Sprucewood, *Elf Meadow, Poulton, Cirencester, Glos, GL7 5HQ.*
Quiet, comfortable, homely, open views.
Open: All Year (not Xmas)
Grades: ETB 1 Cr, High Comm
01285 851351 Mr & Mrs Walker
Rates fr: *£16.00*-**£16.00**.
Beds: 1D 1T 1S **Baths:** 1 Shared
(4)

Prestbury Park

National Grid Ref: SO9524

Hunters Lodge, *Cheltenham Race Course, Prestbury Park, Cheltenham, Glos, GL50 4SH.*
Open: May to Sep
01242 513345 Ms Clark
Fax no: 01242 224227
Rates fr: *£17.50*-**£23.00**.
Beds: 30F
A friendly hotel within the grounds of Cheltenham Race Course. An ideal base for groups & families, offering comfortable & economical accommodation. Advanced booking necessary.

Redbrook

National Grid Ref: SO5310

Boat Inn

Tresco, *Redbrook, Monmouth, NP5 4LY.*
All ground floor bedrooms.
Open: All Year
01600 712325 Mrs Evans
Rates fr: *£14.50*-**£14.50**.
Beds: 1D 1T 2S
Baths: 2 Shared

Rodley

National Grid Ref: SO7411

Cowleys Elm Farm, *Rodley, Westbury on Severn, Glos, GL14 1QZ.*
C17th farmhouse on dairy farm.
Open: All Year (not Xmas)
01452 760284 Ms Davies
Rates fr: *£14.00*-**£16.00**.
Beds: 2D
Baths: 1 Private
(10)

Rodmarton

National Grid Ref: ST9497

The Old Rectory, *Rodmarton, Cirencester, Glos, GL7 6PE.*
Former C17th Cotswold village rectory.
Open: All Year (not Xmas)
01285 841246 Mrs Fitzgerald
Rates fr: *£17.50*-**£20.00**.
Beds: 1D 1T
Baths: 2 Ensuite
(6)

Saintbury

National Grid Ref: SPO943

Bell Inn (Willersey), Fleece (Bretforton)

The Pond House, *Lower Fields, Weston Road, Bretforton, Saintbury, Evesham, Worcs, WR11 5QA.*
Open: All Year
Grades: ETB 2 Cr, High Comm, AA 4 Q, Select
01386 831687 Mrs Payne
Rates fr: *£18.00*-**£35.00**.
Beds: 2D 1T
Baths: 3 Ensuite
(4) (10)
Superb country home. Peaceful secluded position 500m off road. Wonderful views. Friendly relaxed atmosphere with high standards of comfort & service. The perfect base, near Broadway, Chipping Campden, Stratford Upon Avon.

Shurdington

National Grid Ref: SO9218

Allards Hotel & Reataurant, *Shurdington, Cheltenham, Glos, GL51 5XA.*
Hotel with restaurant in 3 acres on A46.
Open: All Year
Grades: AA 2 St, RAC 2 St
01242 862498
Mr Castle
Fax no: 01242 863017
Rates fr: *£27.50*-**£38.00**.
Beds: 2F 5D 4T 1S
Baths: 12 Ensuite
(50)

Slimbridge

National Grid Ref: SO7303

Old Hurst Farm Guest House, *Slimbridge, Gloucester, GL2 7DJ.*
Secluded C17th farmhouse, full facilities.
Open: All Year
01453 890524
Mrs Gallop
Rates fr: *£12.50*-**£12.50**.
Beds: 2F 1S
Baths: 1 Private 2 Shared
(7)

St Briavels

National Grid Ref: SO5604

The George

Woodcroft, *Lower Meend, St Briavels, Lydney, Glos, GL15 6RW.*
Small farm surrounded by woods.
Open: All Year
01594 530083
Mrs Allen
Rates fr: *£16.00*-**£16.00**.
Beds: 2F
Baths: 2 Ensuite
(7)

Blue Barn, *The Hudnalls, St Briavels, Lydney, Glos, GL15 6RT.*
Wye Valley Area of Oustanding Natural Beauty.
Open: All Year
01594 530252 / 0589 373192
Mrs Parker
Rates fr: *£19.00*-**£19.00**.
Beds: 3D 3T 2S
Baths: 8 Ensuite
(15)

Tyersall, *St Briavels, Lydney, Glos, GL15 6RT.*
Secluded wisteria-clad period house.
Open: Mar to Nov
01594 530215
Mrs Morgan
Rates fr: *£16.00*-**£16.00**.
Beds: 1D 1T 1S
Baths: 1 Ensuite 2 Shared
(2) (4)

Ghyll House Farm, *St Briavels, Lydney, Glos, GL15 6UQ.*
Attractive, Grade II Listed octagonal farmhouse.
Open: Easter to Oct
01594 530341
Mrs Price
Rates fr: *£15.00*-**£15.00**.
Beds: 1F 1D
Baths: 1 Shared
(3) (3)

Offas Mead, *The Fence, St Briavels, Lydney, Glos, GL15 6QG.*
Spacious country house, superb views.
Open: All Year (not Xmas)
Grades: ETB 1 Cr
01594 530229
Mrs Lacey
Rates fr: *£15.00*-**£17.00**.
Beds: 1D 2T
Baths: 2 Private 1 Shared
(8) (5)

Stanton

National Grid Ref: SP0634

Mount Inn

Shenberrow Hill, *Stanton, Broadway, Worcs, WR12 7NE.*
Charming country house, peaceful, comfortable.
Open: All Year (not Xmas)
01386 584468
Mrs Neilan
Rates fr: *£18.00*-**£25.00**.
Beds: 1F 1D 1T
Baths: 3 Private
(5) (6)

The Vine, *Stanton, Broadway, Worcs, WR12 7NE.*
Cotswold farmhouse set in the heart of Stanton.
Open: All Year
01386 584250
Mrs Gabb
Fax no: 01368 584385
Rates fr: *£18.00*.
Beds: 2F 3D 2T

Stanway

National Grid Ref: SP0632

The Old Bakehouse, *Stanway, Cheltenham, Glos, GL54 5PH.*
Lovely family home. Outstanding views.
Open: All Year (not Xmas)
01386 584204
Mrs Garwood
Rates fr: *£15.00*-**£17.00**.
Beds: 2D 1T
Baths: 1 Shared
(12)

Staunton

National Grid Ref: SO7829

Mayfield Cottage, *Moat Lane, Staunton, Gloucester, GL19 3QA.*
Converted C18th cottage, rural location.
Open: All Year (not Xmas)
Grades: ETB 2 Cr
01452 840673
Mrs Clayton
Rates fr: *£16.00*-**£16.00**.
Beds: 1D 1T 1S
Baths: 3 Private
(5)

Staunton in Forest

National Grid Ref: SO5512

White Horse

Assisi, *The Buckstone, Staunton in Forest, Coleford, Glos, GL16 8PD.*
Country home on private lane.
Open: All Year (not Xmas)
01594 836900 Hockey
Fax no: 01594 836991
Rates fr: *£13.50*-**£13.50**.
Beds: 1D 1T 1S
Baths: 1 Shared
(3)

Stonehouse

National Grid Ref: SO8005

Ryfond Carvery

Merton Lodge, *8 Ebley Road, Stonehouse, Glos, GL10 2LQ.*
Spacious, impressive 100-year-old house.
Open: All Year (not Xmas)
Grades: ETB 2 Cr
01453 822018 Mrs Hodge
Rates fr: *£15.00*-**£15.00**.
Beds: 1F 1D
Baths: 1 Ensuite 1 Shared

Tiled House Farm, *Oxlynch, Stonehouse, Glos, GL10 3DF.*
C16th half-timbered farmhouse.
Open: All Year (not Xmas)
01453 822363 Mrs Jeffrey
Rates fr: *£16.00*-**£15.00**.
Beds: 1D 1T 1S
Baths: 1 Private 1 Shared
(10) (2)

Stow on the Wold

National Grid Ref: SP1925

Horse & Groom, Queens Head, Farmers Lodge

The Limes, *Evesham Road, Stow on the Wold, Cheltenham, Glos, GL54 1EN.*
Large Victorian house, attractive garden.
Open: All Year (not Xmas)
Grades: AA Listed, RAC Listed, Acclaim
01451 830034 Mr Keyte
Rates fr: *£16.50*-**£16.50**.
Beds: 1F 3D 1T
Baths: 3 Private 2 Shared
(6)

Fifield Cottage, *Fosse Lane, Stow on the Wold, Cheltenham, Glos, GL54 1EH.*
Cottage, close to town, peaceful situation.
Open: All Year (not Xmas)
01451 831056 Mrs Keyte
Rates fr: *£16.50*-**£18.50**.
Beds: 1F 1D 1T
Baths: 2 Ensuite 1 Private
(5)

Corsham Field Farmhouse, *Bledington Road, Stow on the Wold, Cheltenham, Glos, GL54 1JH.*
Homely farmhouse with breathtaking views. **Open:** All Year
Grades: ETB 2 Cr, AA 2 Q
01451 831750 Mr Smith
Rates fr: *£15.00*-**£15.00**.
Beds: 3F 2D 2T
Baths: 5 Ensuite 1 Shared
(10)

South Hill Farmhouse, *Fosseway, Stow on the Wold, Cheltenham, Glos, GL54 1JU.*
Only the best will do!
Open: All Year (not Xmas)
Grades: ETB 2 Cr
01451 831219 Mrs Kenneally
Fax no: 01451 831554
Rates fr: *£19.00*. **Beds:** 1F 3D 1T
Baths: 4 Private 1 Shared
(6)

Old Farmhouse Hotel, *Lower Swell, Stow on the Wold, Cheltenham, Glos, GL54 1LF.*
Quiet, unpretentious, converted Cotswold farmhouse.
Open: All Year
0500 657842 Mr Burger
Rates fr: *£22.00*-**£22.00**.
Beds: 1F 9D 4T
Baths: 12 Private 1 Shared
(25)

Pear Tree Cottage, *High Street, Stow on the Wold, Cheltenham, Glos, GL54 1DL.*
Period cottage near town square.
Open: All Year
Grades: ETB 1 Cr
01451 831210 Mr Henderson
Rates fr: *£18.00*-**£25.00**.
Beds: 2D **Baths:** 2 Private
(Yes) (2)

Stroud

National Grid Ref: SO8405

Imperial Hotel

***Cairngall Guest House,** 65 Bisley Old Road, Stroud, Glos, GL5 1NF.*
Large, comfortable, Georgian Listed house.
Open: Feb to Dec
Grades: ETB 1 Cr, Approv
01453 764595
Mrs Thacker
Rates fr: *£16.00*-**£16.00**.
Beds: 1F 1T
Baths: 1 Shared
(3)

***Court Farm,** Randwick, Stroud, Glos, GL6 6HH.*
C17th beamed Cotswold farmhouse.
Open: All Year
01453 764210
Mr Taylor
Rates fr: *£16.00*-**£16.00**.
Beds: 1F 1D 2T
Baths: 2 Shared
(6)

***Downfield Hotel,** Cainscross Road, Stroud, Glos, GL5 4HN.*
Imposing Victorian hotel. Comfortable, friendly.
Open: All Year (not Xmas)
Grades: ETB 3 Cr, AA 3 Q, RAC Acclaim
01453 764496
Fax no: 01453 753 155
Rates fr: *£16.50*-**£20.00**.
Beds: 3F 7D 7T 4S
Baths: 11 Ensuite 3 Shared

***New Inn House,** The Camp, Stroud, Glos, GL6 7HL.*
Period cottage, unspoilt Cotswold countryside.
Open: Easter to Nov
01285 821336
Miss Macswiney
Rates fr: *£14.00*-**£16.00**.
Beds: 1T 1S
Baths: 1 Shared
(10) (2)

***Fern Rock House,** 72 Middle Street, Stroud, Glos, GL5 1EA.*
Near to town centre.
Open: All Year (not Xmas)
01453 757307
Mr Evans
Rates fr: *£13.50*-**£14.00**.
Beds: 1D 1T 1S
(5)

***1 Highfield,** Dudbridge Hill, Stroud, Glos, GL5 3HN.*
Large comfortable Georgian house.
Open: All Year (not Xmas)
Grades: ETB 2 Cr
01453 752214 Mrs Eames
Rates fr: *£15.00*-**£22.00**.
Beds: 2D
Baths: 2 Private
(2)

Symonds Yat Rock

National Grid Ref: SO5614

***The Rock Inn,** Hillersland, Symonds Yat Rock, Coleford, Glos, GL16 7NY.*
Country inn with outstanding views.
Open: All year
01594 832367 Mrs Matthews
Rates fr: *£18.00*.
Beds: 2D 2S
Baths: 4 Private
(20)

Tetbury

National Grid Ref: ST8993

Crown Inn

***Conifers,** Northfield Road, Tetbury, Glos, GL8 8HQ.*
Warm welcome, charming character home.
Open: All Year
01666 502510 Mrs Waters
Rates fr: *£17.00*-**£19.00**.
Beds: 2D 1S
Baths: 1 Ensuite 1 Shared
(9) (3)

***Crown Inn,** Gumstool Hill, Tetbury, Glos, GL8 8DG.*
C17th coaching inn.
Open: All Year (not Xmas)
01666 502469 Mr Wainwright
Rates fr: *£16.00*-**£19.00**.
Beds: 1F 2D 1S
Baths: 2 Shared
(4)

***Folly Farm Cottages,** Malmesbury Road, Tetbury, Glos, GL8 8XA.*
Queen Anne farmhouse & C18th cottages.
Open: All Year (not Xmas)
01666 502475 Mr Benton
Fax no: 01666 502358
Rates fr: *£16.00*-**£20.00**.
Beds: 2D 2T
Baths: 1 Shared

Tewkesbury

National Grid Ref: SO8933

Woody's

***Carrant Brook House,** Rope Walk, Tewkesbury, Glos, GL20 5DS.*
Quietly situated Victorian family house.
Open: All Year
01684 290355 Mr Dickenson
Rates fr: *£18.50*-**£19.50**.
Beds: 1D 1T 1S **Baths:** 3 Ensuite
(3)

***Hoo Farm,** Tewkesbury, Glos, GL20 7DD.*
Peaceful family farmhouse, in 6 acres.
Open: All Year
01684 292185 Mrs Mitchell
Rates fr: *£17.00*-**£17.00**.
Beds: 2T 1S
Baths: 1 Private 1 Shared
(0) (10)

***Willow Cottages,** Shuthonger Common, Tewkesbury, Glos, GL20 6ED.*
Peaceful former farmhouse, large garden.
Open: All Year
01684 298599 Mr Bird
Rates fr: *£15.00*-**£15.00**.
Beds: 1F 2T
Baths: 2 Shared
(6)

***The Bali Hai,** 5 Barton Road, Tewkesbury, Glos, GL20 5QG.*
Large Georgian house.
Open: All Year
01684 292049
Rates fr: *£14.00*-**£20.00**.
Beds: 4F 1T
Baths: 2 Shared
(4)

Tormarton

National Grid Ref: ST7678

***Chestnut Farm,** Tormarton, Badminton, GL9 1HS.*
Small Georgian farmhouse.
Open: All Year
01454 218563
Ms Cadei
Rates fr: *£19.50*-**£25.00**.
Beds: 2D 3T
Baths: 3 Private
(8)

Tredington

National Grid Ref: SO9029

***Gothic Farm,** Tredington, Tewkesbury, Glos, GL20 7BS.*
Friendly, comfortable, character farmhouse.
Open: All Year (not Xmas)
Grades: ETB Listed
01684 293360
Mr Coleman
Rates fr: *£18.00*-**£20.00**.
Beds: 1D 1T
Baths: 2 Shared
(5) (8)

Uley

National Grid Ref: ST7898

***Hill House,** Crawley Hill, Uley, Dursley, Glos, GL11 5BH.*
Quiet beautiful views, Cotswold stone house.
Open: All Year (not Xmas)
01453 860267 Mr & Mrs Kent
Rates fr: *£16.50*-**£15.00**.
Beds: 1F 1D 1S
Baths: 2 Ensuite 1 Shared
(5) (y)

The Old Crown Inn, *Uley, Dursley, Glos, GL11 5SN.*
Comfortable Cotswold C17th village inn.
Open: All Year (not Xmas)
01453 860502 Mrs Barrell
Rates fr: *£20.00*-**£25.00**.
Beds: 1F 2D **Baths:** 3 Private
(30)

Upton St Leonards

National Grid Ref: SO8614

Kings Head, Royal William

Bullens Manor Farm, *Portway, Upton St Leonards, Gloucester, GL4 8DL.*
Comfortable C17th farmhouse.
Open: All Year
Grades: ETB 2 Cr, High Comm
01452 616463 Mrs Warner
Rates fr: *£16.50*-**£20.00**.
Beds: 1D 2T **Baths:** 3 Private
(6) (10)

Winchcombe

National Grid Ref: SP0228

White Hart, Plaisterers Arms, Harvest Home, Royal Oak

Almsbury Farm, *Vineyard Street, Winchcombe, Cheltenham, Glos, GL54 5LP.*
Open: Feb to Nov
Grades: ETB 2 Cr, High Comm
01242 602403 Mrs Hitch
Rates fr: *£22.50*-**£26.50**.
Beds: 1F 1D
Baths: 2 Ensuite
(10) (10)
Luxury accommodation in a peaceful C17th Cotswold farmhouse in an Area of Outstanding Natural Beauty on the Cotswold Way only 150 yards pubs, shops, etc.

Gower House, *16 North Street, Winchcombe, Cheltenham, Glos, GL54 5LH.*
C18th town house near shops.
Open: All Year (not Xmas)
Grades: ETB 2 Cr, Comm
01242 602616 Mrs Simmonds
Rates fr: *£16.00*-**£20.00**.
Beds: 1D 2T
Baths: 2 Shared
(3)

The Plaisterers Arms, *Abbey Terrace, Winchcombe, Cheltenham, Glos, GL52 5LL.*
Open: All Year
Grades: ETB 2 Cr, Approv
01242 602358 (also fax no)
Mr Gould
Rates fr: *£17.50*-**£22.50**.
Beds: 1F 2D 1T 1S
Baths: 5 Ensuite
Traditional stone Cotswold inn with beautiful garden; extensive menu of barsnacks, pub lunches & evening meals; comfortable ensuite accommodation & range of traditional ales.

The Dairy Farm House, *Rushley Lane, Winchcombe, Cheltenham, Glos, GL54 5JE.*
Comfortable converted C18th Cotswold farmhouse.
Open: All Year (not Xmas)
Grades: ETB Listed
01242 603496 Mrs Fisher
Rates fr: *£16.50*-**£17.50**.
Beds: 2T **Baths:** 2 Private
(5) (4)

Mercia, *Hailes Street, Winchcombe, Cheltenham, Glos, GL54 5HU.*
C15th black-and-white cottage.
Open: All Year (not Xmas)
Grades: ETB 2 Cr, High Comm
01242 602251 Mrs Upton
Rates fr: *£18.00*-**£20.00**.
Beds: 2D 1T **Baths:** 3 Private
(3)

The Homestead, *Smithy Lane, Greet, Winchcombe, Cheltenham, Glos, GL54 5BP.*
C16th country house.
Open: All Year (not Xmas)
01242 603808 Mrs Bloom
Rates fr: *£16.00*-**£20.00**.
Beds: 1F 2D 1T
Baths: 2 Private 1 Shared
(8) (4)

Sudeley Hill Farm, *Winchcombe, Cheltenham, Glos, GL54 5JB.*
Comfortably furnished C15th farmhouse.
Open: All Year (not Xmas)
Grades: ETB 2 Cr, High Comm, AA 4 Q, Select
01242 602344 Mrs Scudamore
Rates fr: *£21.00*-**£26.00**.
Beds: 1F 1D 1T **Baths:** 3 Private
(10)

Manor Farm, *Winchcombe, Cheltenham, Glos, GL54 5BJ.*
Cotswold manor on working farm.
Open: All Year (not Xmas)
Grades: ETB 2 Cr, High Comm
01242 602423 Mr & Mrs Day
Rates fr: *£20.00*-**£20.00**.
Beds: 2D 1T **Baths:** 3 Ensuite
(50)

Great House, *Castle Street, Winchcombe, Cheltenham, Glos, GL54 5JA.*
500-year-old Listed building.
Open: All Year
01242 602490 Mrs Saunders
Rates fr: *£18.00*-**£20.00**.
Beds: 1F 1D 1T
Baths: 1 Shared
(6) (3)

Blair House, *41 Gretton Road, Winchcombe, Cheltenham, Glos, GL54 5EG.*
Friendly, comfortable Georgian town house.
Open: All Year
01242 603626 Mrs Chisholm
Fax no: 01242 604214
Rates fr: *£16.00*-**£17.50**.
Beds: 1F 1T 2S **Baths:** 2 Shared
(1)

Wormington

National Grid Ref: SP0336

Manor Farm, *Wormington, Broadway, Worcs, WR12 7NL.*
Black-and-white Tudor farmhouse.
Open: All Year
01386 584302
Mrs Russell
Rates fr: *£16.00*-**£18.00**.
Beds: 2D 1T
Baths: 3 Ensuite
(5) (4)

Wotton-under-Edge

National Grid Ref: ST7692

Royal Oak

The Thatched Cottage, *Wortley, Wotton-under-Edge, Glos, GL12 7QP.*
Open: All Year (not Xmas)
01453 842776 (also fax no)
Mr & Mrs Cory
Rates fr: *£16.00*-**£19.00**.
Beds: 1D 2T
Baths: 1 Private 1 Shared
(6)
Quiet hamlet situated in beautiful Cotswold countryside. Walkers, historians and naturalists' paradise. Places of interest in abundance. Secluded garden, complete with Roman villa under excavation.

Under-the-Hill-House, *Adeys Lane, Wotton-under-Edge, Glos, GL12 7LY.*
C18th Listed period house.
Open: Easter to Oct
01453 842557
Mrs Forster
Rates fr: *£16.50*-**£16.50**.
Beds: 1D 1T
Baths: 1 Shared
(13) (2)

Coombe Lodge, *Wotton-under-Edge, Glos, GL12 7NB.*
Georgian country house, south Cotswolds.
Open: All Year (not Xmas)
Grades: ETB 1 Cr, High Comm
01453 845057
Mrs Mayo
Rates fr: *£19.00*-**£25.00**.
Beds: 2D 1T
Baths: 1 Shared
(6)

The Old Repository, *3 Church Street, Old Town, Wotton-under-Edge, Glos, GL12 7HB.*
C16th Listed accommodation.
Open: All Year
01453 843272 / 521650
Mrs McIlroy
Rates fr: *£19.00*-**£28.00**.
Beds: 1D 2T
Baths: 2 Shared

Greater Manchester & Merseyside

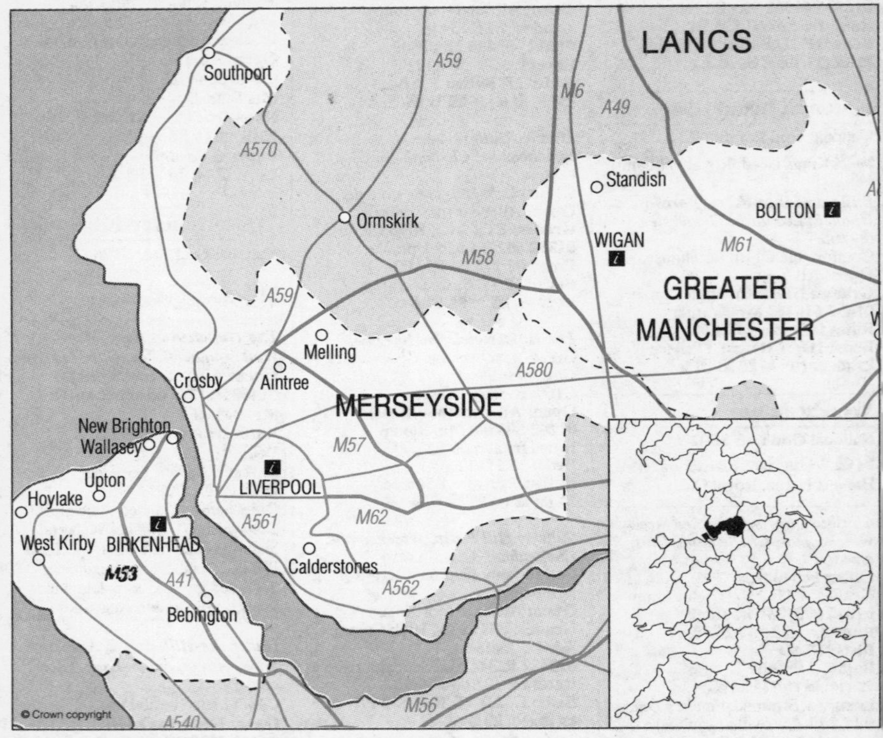

Tourist Information Centres

Stamford New Road, **Altrincham**, Cheshire, WA14 1EJ, 0161912 5931

Woodside Ferry Terminal, Woodside, **Birkenhead**, Merseyside, L41 1EQ, 0151 647 6780.

Town Hall, Victoria Square, Bolton, **Lancashire**, BL1 1RU, 01204 364333.

6 Station Road, **Cheadle Hulme**, Cheshire, SK8 5AE, 0161 486 0283.

Municipal Buildings, Cherry Tree Drive, **Kirkby**, Merseyside, L32 1TX, 0151 709 3631.

Merseyside Welcome Centre, Clayton Square Shopping Centre, **Liverpool**, Merseyside, L1 1QR, 0151 709 3631.

Town Hall Extension, Lloyd Street, **Manchester**, M60 2LA, 0161 234 3157.

International Arrivals Hall, **Manchester Airport**, Terminal 2, M22 5NY, 0161 489 6412.

11 Albion Street, **Oldham**, Lancashire, OL1 1DN, 0161 627 1024.

The Clock Tower, Town Hall, **Rochdale**, Lancs, OL16 1AB, 01706 356592.

112 Lord Street, **Southport**, Merseyside, PR8 1NY, 01704 533333.

9 Princes Street, **Stockport**, Cheshire, SK1 1SL, 0161 474 3320.

Saddleworth Museum, High Street, Uppermill, **Oldham**, Lancashire, OL3 6HS, 01457 874093.

Trencherfield Mill, Wigan Pier, **Wigan**, Lancashire, WN3 4EL, 01942-825677.

Aintree

National Grid Ref: SJ3798

Church View, *7 Church Avenue, Aintree, Liverpool, L9 4SG.*
Small award-winning guest house.
Open: All Year
Grades: ETB 1 Cr, Comm
0151 525 8166
Mrs Martin
Rates fr: *£13.00*-**£14.00**.
Beds: 3T
(4)

Altrincham

National Grid Ref: SJ7687

Marron Guesthouse, *15 Manchester Road, Altrincham, Cheshire, WA14 4RG.*
Large Victorian guest house.
Open: All Year
0161 941 5603
Mr Bartle
Rates fr: *£20.00*-**£25.00**.
Beds: 2F 3D 3T 4S
Baths: 2 Shared
(4)

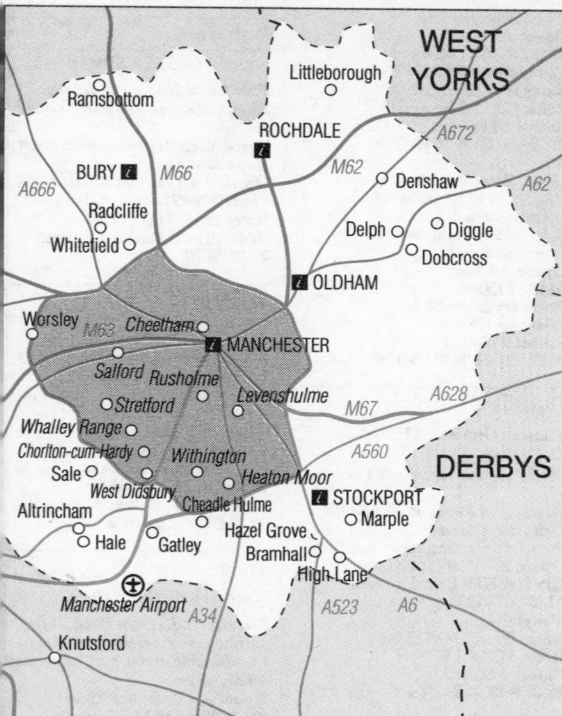

Belvedere Guest House, *58 Barrington Road, Altrincham, Cheshire, WA14 1HY.*
Large Victorian private house.
Open: All Year
0161 941 5996
Mr Kelly
Rates fr: *£16.0*-**£20.00**.
Beds: 1F 1D 2T
Baths: 4 Private
(5)

Bebington

National Grid Ref: SJ3383

Bebington Hotel, *24 Town Lane, Bebington, Wirral, Merseyside, L63 5JG.*
Converted, large Victorian private house.
Open: All Year (not Xmas)
0151 645 0608 (also fax no)
Mrs Smith
Rates fr: *£17.50*-**£19.50**.
Beds: 3F 2D 1T 3S
Baths: 9 Ensuite
(10)

Birkenhead

National Grid Ref: SJ3088

The Mersey Clipper

Mount Road Guest House, *31 Mount Road, Higher Tranmere, Birkenhead, Merseyside, L42 6PN.*
Friendly homely-run guest house.
Open: All Year
0151 644 9687 Mrs Hammett
Rates fr: *£15.00*-**£16.50**.
Beds: 1T 2S
Baths: 1 Private 1 Shared
(4)

Bolton

National Grid Ref: SD7108

Farmers Arms

Heyesleigh, *98 Castle Road, Bolton, Lancs, BL2 1JL.*
A warm welcome awaits you.
Open: All Year (not Xmas)
01204 523647 Mrs Longworth
Rates fr: *£13.00*-**£14.00**.
Beds: 3F 1D 1T 3S
Baths: 5 Private 1 Shared

Glengarry Guest House, *79 Bradford Street, Bolton, Lancs, BL2 1JY.*
Small family-run guest house.
Open: All Year
Grades: ETB Listed, Comm
01204 534299 Mrs Hope
Rates fr: *£16.00*-**£16.00**.
Beds: 1F 1D 4T 2S
Baths: 1 Private 1 Shared

Broomfield Hotel, *33/35 Wigan Road, Deane, Bolton, Lancs, BL1 5PX.*
Family-run hotel.
Open: All Year
Grades: ETB 3 Q, AA Listed, RAC Listed
01204 61570 Mrs Hydes
Rates fr: *£19.00*-**£26.50**.
Beds: 1F 4D 3T 7S
Baths: 15 Private
(15)

Bradfort Park Guest House, *44 Bradford Street, Bolton, Lancs, BL2 1JJ.*
Very homely atmosphere.
Open: All Year
01204 525480 Mrs Lowe
Rates fr: *£14.00*-**£15.00**.
Beds: 2F 1D 6T
Baths: 2 Shared
(6)

Bramhall

National Grid Ref: SJ8984

1 Walmer Drive, *Bramhall, Stockport, Cheshire, SK7 3AT.*
Pleasant, traditional detached house.
Open: All Year
0161 439 9413 Mrs Heller
Rates fr: *£12.00*-**£12.00**.
Beds: 1D 2S
Baths: 1 Shared
(2)

Bury

National Grid Ref: SD8010

Rostrevor Hotel, *148 Manchester Road, Bury, Lancs, BL9 0TL.*
Open: All Year
Grades: ETB 3 Cr, Comm
0161 764 3944 Mr Fletcher
Fax no: 0161 764 8266
Rates fr: *£21.00*-**£29.00**.
Beds: 5D 4T 5S
Baths: 14 Ensuite
(14)
A warm friendly family-run hotel offering Northern hospitality, superb food & accommodation only 8 miles from Manchester city centre & close to motorway network.

The lowest **single** *rate is shown in* **bold.**

***The White Lion,** 6 Bolton Street, Bury, Lancs, BL9 0LQ.*
Central town centre, near Metro Line.. **Open:** All Year
Grades: ETB 3 Cr
0161 764 2641 (also fax no)
Ms Farrand
Rates fr: *£18.80*-**£21.15**.
Beds: 4T 2S
Baths: 1 Ensuite 2 Shared
(20)

***Woolfield House,** Wash Lane, Bury, Lancs, BL9 6BJ.*
Large detached hotel near motorway. **Open:** All Year
0161 797 9775 Mrs Stafford
Rates fr: *£22.50*-**£22.00**.
Beds: 5D 4T 7S
Baths: 10 Private 2 Shared
(3) (30)

Calderstones

National Grid Ref: SJ4087

***Annas,** 65 Dudlow Lane, Calderstones, Liverpool, L18 2EY.*
Comfortable 1920s house, Beatles' area.
Open: All Year (not Xmas/New Year) **0151 722 3708**
Rates fr: *£16.50*-**£18.50**.
Beds: 4T **Baths:** 1 Shared
(3)

Cheadle Hulme

National Grid Ref: SJ8786

Wesketh Tavern

***Spring Cottage,** 60 Hulme Hall Road, Cheadle Hulme, Cheadle, Cheshire, SK8 6JZ.*
Beautifuly furnished Victorian house. **Open:** All Year
Grades: ETB Listed, High Comm
0161 485 1037 Mr Stent
Rates fr: *£16.25*-**£18.50**.
Beds: 1D 4T 1S
Baths: 3 Private 1 Shared
(6)

***Butterfly Guest House,** 115 Grove Lane, Cheadle Hulme, Cheadle, Cheshire, SK8 7NE.*
1920s detached private house.
Open: All Year
0161 439 3154 Ms Basuik
Rates fr: *£16.00*-**£18.00**.
Beds: 2T 2D 2S
Baths: 4 Ensuite 1 Shared
(8)

Crosby

National Grid Ref: SJ3198

***Lakeview Guest House,** 19 Adelaide Terrace, Waterloo, Crosby, Liverpool, L22 8QD.*
Victorian house, overlooking lake & seafront.
Open: All Year
0151 920 9754
Mrs Davies
Rates fr: *£14.00*-**£15.00**.
Beds: 3T 4S
Baths: 2 Shared
(5)

Delph

National Grid Ref: SD9807

***Old Bell Inn Hotel,** Delph, Oldham, Lancs, OL3 5EG.*
C18th coaching inn.
Open: All Year
01457 870130 Mr Grew
Fax no: 01457 876597
Rates fr: *£22.50*-**£35.00**.
Beds: 6D 1T 3S
Baths: 10 Private
(25)

***Globe Farm Bunkhouse,** Huddersfield Road, Standedge, Delph, Oldham, Lancs, OL3 5LU.*
Independent youth hostel. Self-catering/catered.
Open: All Year
01457 873040
Rates fr: *£6.50*-**£6.50**.
Beds: 4F 1D
Baths: 2 Shared
(20)

Denshaw

National Grid Ref: SD9710

Junction Inn, Black Horse

***Boothstead Farm,** Rochdale Road, Denshaw, Oldham, Lancs, OL3 5UE.*
Pretty, C18th farmhouse, log fires.
Open: All Year (not Xmas)
Grades: ETB Listed, Comm
01457 878622
Mrs Hall
Rates fr: *£17.00*-**£18.00**.
Beds: 1D 1T 1S
Baths: 1 Shared

Diggle

National Grid Ref: SE0008

Church Inn, Diggle Hotel, Navigation Inn, Floating Light

***New Barn,** Harrop Green Farm, Diggle, Oldham, Lancs, OL3 5LW.*
Modern farmhouse on working sheep farm.
Open: All Year (not Xmas)
01457 873937 Mr Rhodes
Rates fr: *£15.00*-**£15.00**.
Beds: 1F 1D 1T 1S
Baths: 1 Private 1 Shared
(10)

***Sunfield,** Diglea, Diggle, Saddleworth, Oldham, Lancs, OL3 5LA.*
High standard ensuite farmhouse accommodation.
Open: All Year
01457 874030 Mr & Mrs Francis
Rates fr: *£12.50*-**£20.00**.
Beds: 3D 3T **Baths:** 6 Ensuite
(8)

***Hillcrest,** 9 Harrop Green, Diggle, Oldham, Lancs, OL3 5LW.*
Large Victorian modernised private house. With views of the Pennines.
Open: All Year
01457 875286 Mrs Castle
Rates fr: *£13.00*-**£13.00**.
Beds: 1D 1T
Baths: 1 Shared

Dobcross

National Grid Ref: SD9906

***Fold Guest House,** 18 Woods Lane, Dobcross, Oldham, Lancs, OL3. 5AN*
Friendly, family-run village guest house & stores.
Open: All Year (not Xmas)
01457 876491 Mr Hodgkinson
Rates fr: *£17.00*-**£17.00**.
Beds: 2D 1T **Baths:** 1 Shared

Gatley

National Grid Ref: SJ8488

***7 Motcombe Grove,** Gatley, Cheadle, Cheshire, SK8 3TL.*
Ideally situated for North West travel.
Open: All Year
Grades: ETB 2 Cr, Comm
0161 436 4732 Mr Slater
Rates fr: *£17.50*-**£25.00**.
Beds: 1D 1T **Baths:** 2 Private

Hale

National Grid Ref: SJ7686

***Merton,** 12 Egerton Road, Hale, Altrincham, Cheshire, WA15 8EE.*
Comfortable, quiet, well-appointed 1920s house.
Open: All Year (not Xmas)
0161 980 6618 Mrs Schorah
Rates fr: *£18.00*-**£18.00**.
Beds: 1T 1S **Baths:** 1 Shared
(2)

Hazel Grove

National Grid Ref: SJ9286

***The Birches,** Birch Drive, Bramhall Moor Lane, Hazel Grove Stockport, Cheshire, SK7 5AT.*
Healthy, multi-featured guesthouse
Open: All Year
0161 483 1422 Mr Winstanley
Rates fr: *£16.50*-**£20.00**.
Beds: 1F 1T 1D 1S
Baths: 1 Ensuite 1 Private
(5)

High Lane

National Grid Ref: SJ9585

***The Red Lion Inn,** 112 Buxton Road, High Lane, Stockport, Cheshire, SK6 8ED.*
Comfortable friendly inn.
Open: All Year
01663 765227 Mrs Brown
Rates fr: *£22.00*-**£25.50**.
Beds: 3D 1T 2S
Baths: 6 Private
(100)

Hoylake

National Grid Ref: SJ2188

Rockland, *70 Birkenhead Road, Hoylake, Wirral, Merseyside, L47 OLA.*
Large Victorian house friendly atmosphere. **Open:** All Year
0151 632 4249 Mrs Hardman
Rates fr: *£20.00.* **Beds:** 3F 3T
Baths: 1 Ensuite
(10)

Littleborough

National Grid Ref: SD9316

Stubley Old Hall

16 Laburnum Way, *Littleborough, Lancs, OL15 8LS.*
Modern semi-detached bungalow.
Open: All Year (not Xmas)
01706 379170 Mrs Hill
Rates fr: -**£14.00**.
Beds: 1S **Baths:** 1 Shared
(3)

Kenmoor House, *Smithybridge Road, Hollingworth Lake, Littleborough, Lancs, OL15 0BQ.*
Tastefully decorated rooms in annexe. **Open:** All Year
01706 378203 Mr Craven
Rates fr: *£17.50*-**£30.00**.
Beds: 1F 1D 2T **Baths:** 4 Private
(6)

Liverpool

National Grid Ref: SJ3791

Devonshire House

Embassie Youth Hostel, *1 Falkner Square, Liverpool, L8 7NU.*
Set in beautiful Georgian square - townhouse. **Open:** All Year
0151 707 1089 Mr Murphy
Rates fr: £9.50.
Beds: 20S **Baths:** 5 Shared
(12)

Marie & Tony's, *98 Edge Lane, Liverpool, L7 1QZ.*
Large Victorian house near city.
Open: All Year
0151 263 2882 Mr Lemos
Rates fr: *£15.00*-**£15.00**.
Beds: 2F 6D 2T 3S
Baths: 2 Shared

Manchester Cheetham

National Grid Ref: SD8400

New Central Hotel, *144-146 Heywood Street, Cheetham, Manchester, M8 7PD.*
Small, comfortable, friendly hotel.
Open: All Year
Grades: ETB 1 Cr, AA 2 Q, RAC Listed
0161 205 2169 Mrs Greenwood
Rates fr: *£16.50*-**£20.00**.
Beds: 1D 2T 7S
Baths: 5 Private 2 Shared
(2) (7)

Manchester Chorlton-cum-Hardy

National Grid Ref: SJ8193

Sabre D'Or Hotel, *392 Wilbraham Road, Chorlton-cum-Hardy, Manchester, M21 1UH.*
Open: All Year
0161 881 5055 Mr Sinclair
Fax no: 0161 881 1546
Rates fr: *£25.00*-**£30.00**.
Beds: 3F 5D 4T 4S
Baths: 6 Private 4 Shared
(15)
All our rooms are spacious & range from singles, twins, doubles, family rooms & even the famous four poster. Short or long stay, try us.

Lyndhurst Hotel, *22-24 Whitelow Road, Chorlton-cum-Hardy, Manchester, M21 1HQ.*
Large Victorian private house.
Open: All Year
Grades: ETB 2 Cr
0161 862 9001
Mrs Bottomley
Fax no: 0161 881 3556
Rates fr: *£20.50*-**£25.00**.
Beds: 2F 2D 2T 7S
Baths: 6 Private 3 Shared
(14)

Manchester Didsbury

National Grid Ref: SJ8491

Bird in Hand, Old Cock Pub

Didsbury Lodge Service Flats, *The Village House, 132 Palatine Road, Didsbury, Manchester, M20 3ZA.*
Ideal for Manchester city centre.
Open: All Year
0161 445 9997 Mr Majid
Rates fr: *£12.50*-**£25.00**.
Beds: 6F 4D 4T 1S
Baths: 4 Private 2 Shared
(30)

13 Lynway Drive, *Didsbury, Manchester, M20 4TS.*
Large homely modern private house.
Open: All Year (not Xmas)
0161 434 2542 Mrs Turner
Rates fr: *£18.00*-**£18.00**.
Beds: 1F 2D 1S **Baths:** 1 Ensuite
(3)

26 Highbank Drive, *Didsbury, Manchester, M20 5QR.*
Comfortable family house, convenient location.
Open: All Year
0161 448 9053 Mrs Matiz
Rates fr: *£13.00*-**£15.00**.
Beds: 2F 1T 1S **Baths:** 1 Shared
(0) (2)

Bringing children with you? Always ask for any special rates.

Bourneville Hotel, *148 Barlow Moor Road, Didsbury, Manchester, M20 8UT.*
Ideally located for airport/city centre.
Open: All Year
0161 434 6733
Ms Fareed
Rates fr: *£14.00*-**£18.00**.
Beds: 1F 4D 2T 8S
Baths: 6 Private 2 Shared
(10)

Manchester Heaton Moor

National Grid Ref: SJ8791

Heatons Tandoori, Rudyard Hotel

Heathfield Guest House, *24 Broomfield Road, Heaton Moor, Stockport, Cheshire, SK4 4ND.*
Edwardian, leafy area, near city.
Open: All Year
0161 431 7531 Ms Gray
Rates fr: *£15.00*-**£19.00**.
Beds: 1F 1D 1T
Baths: 2 Private 1 Shared
(3)

Appleton Lodge Hotel, *15 Brownsville Road, Heaton Moor, Stockport, Cheshire, SK4 4PE.*
Suburban, detached Victorian private house.
Open: All Year (not Xmas)
0161 432 8198 / 432 3818
Mrs Pilling
Rates fr: *£18.00*-**£17.00**.
Beds: 3F 2D 8T 2S
Baths: 11 Private 1 Shared
(18)

Manchester Levenshulme

National Grid Ref: SJ8794

Kingsway Hotel

191 Slade Lane, *Levenshulme, Manchester, M19 2AE.*
Victorian private house.
Open: All Year
0161 224 7753
Ms Hepworth-Smith
Rates fr: *£12.00*-**£12.00**.
Beds: 1F 1D 2T 2S
Baths: 3 Private 1 Shared
(4)

Manchester Rusholme

National Grid Ref: SJ8695

Verdene Hotel, *454 Moss Lane East, Rusholme, Manchester, M14 4PW.*
Large Victorian house.
Open: All Year
0161 224 1576
Mr & Mrs Gallagher
Rates fr: *£18.00*-**£19.00**.
Beds: 3F 3D 6T
Baths: 5 Private 2 Shared

Manchester — Salford

National Grid Ref: SJ8098

White Lodge Hotel, *89 Great Cheetham Street West, Salford,* M7 9JA.
Small comfortable hotel.
Open: All Year
0161 792 3047 Mr Byrne
Rates fr: *£16.00*-**£18.00**.
Beds: 3T 3D 3S **Baths:** 2 Shared
(2) (6)

Manchester — Stretford

National Grid Ref: SJ8095

Lloyds Hotel

Greatstone Hotel, *843-845 Chester Road, Gorse Hill, Stretford, Manchester,* M32 0RN.
Open: All Year
0161 865 1640 Mr Sill
Rates fr: *£18.00*-**£20.00**.
Beds: 2F 6T 5D 12S
Baths: 6 Ensuite 1 Private 2 Shared
Family-run hotel established since 1955. Close to Manchester United's ground as well as Old Trafford Cricket ground.

Parkside Guest House, *58 Cromwell Roadoff Edge Lane, Stretford, Manchester,* M32 8QT.
Convenient for all major venues.
Open: All Year (not Xmas)
0161 685 2860 Mr Meadowcroft
Rates fr: *£18.00*-**£19.00**.
Beds: 1F 1D 1T 2S
Baths: 3 Private 2 Shared
(7) (3)

Manchester — Whalley Range

National Grid Ref: SJ8294

Cornelius Hotel

Polex Hotel, *70-78 Dudley Road, Off Withington Road, Whalley Range, Manchester,* M16 8DE.
Close to city centre, Manchester Airport.
Open: All Year
0161 881 4038 Mr Klocek
Fax no: 0161 881 1567
Rates fr: *£20.00*-**£22.00**.
Beds: 16D 5T 4S
Baths: 25 Ensuite
(6) (18)

Marple

National Grid Ref: SJ9588

The Pineapple Inn, *45 Market Street, Marple, Stockport, Cheshire,* SK6 7AA.
Friendly traditional inn.
Open: All Year (not Xmas)
Grades: ETB 1 Cr, Approv
0161 427 3935 Mrs Beecham
Rates fr: *£18.00*-**£18.00**.
Beds: 2T
Baths: 1 Shared
(10)

Melling

National Grid Ref: SJ3791

Merlin Guest House, *Bank Lane, Melling, Liverpool,* L31 1AX.
C16th farmhouse. Traditional cooked breakfasts.
Open: All Year (not Xmas)
0151 548 8608 Ms Welsh
Rates fr: *£16.00*-**£16.00**.
Beds: 2F 1T 2S
Baths: 1 Private 1 Shared
(6)

New Brighton

National Grid Ref: SJ3093

Wellington House Hotel, *65 Wellington Road, New Brighton, Wirral, Merseyside,* L45 2NE.
Views over Irish Sea, enclosed car park.
Open: All Year
0151 639 6594 Mr Edwards
Rates fr: *£14.00*-**£15.50**.
Beds: 2F 4D 3T 2S
Baths: 6 Ensuite 2 Shared
(14)

Oldham

National Grid Ref: SD9204

Park Road Guest House, *389 Park Road, Oldham, Lancs,* OL4 1SQ.
Warm, comfortable guest house.
Open: All Year
0161 626 2322 Mr Taylor
Rates fr: *£12.50*-**£15.00**.
Beds: 1F 2T 3S
(2)

Radcliffe

National Grid Ref: SD7807

Hawthorn Hotel, *143 Stand Lane, Radcliffe, Manchester,* M26 1JR.
Comfortable, friendly family-run hotel.
Open: All Year (not Xmas)
Grades: ETB 2 Cr
0161 723 2706
Mr Smith
Rates fr: *£19.75*-**£29.50**.
Beds: 2F 6T 5D 1S
Baths: 14 Ensuite
(9)

Ramsbottom

National Grid Ref: SD7816

Edwardia, *416 Bolton Road West, Ramsbottom, Bury, Lancs,* BL0 9RY.
Spacious, relaxed ambience - tourist business.
Open: All Year
01204 888061
Ms Matheson
Rates fr: *£16.00*-**£18.00**.
Beds: 1D 2T 2S
Baths: 1 Private 1 Shared
(5) (4)

Rochdale

National Grid Ref: SD8913

Egerton Arms, Owd Bets

Leaches Farm, *Ashworth Valley, Rochdale, Lancs,* OL11 5UN.
C17th farm. Wonderful views.
Open: All Year (not Xmas)
Grades: AA 2 Q
01706 41116 / 41117 Mrs Neave
Fax no: 01706 228520
Rates fr: *£17.00*-**£18.00**.
Beds: 1D 1T 1S
Baths: 1 Shared
(6)

Harridge End Homestay, *Shawclough Road, Rochdale, Lancs,* OL12 7HL.
Large, comfortable, friendly, quiet house.
Open: All Year
01706 45272 Mrs Whiteley
Rates fr: *£20.00*-**£20.00**.
Beds: 1D 1T 1S
Baths: 2 Shared
(1) (6)

Britannia Inn, *4 Lomax Street, Rochdale, Lancs,* OL12 0DN.
Friendly local public house.
Open: All Year
01706 46391 Mr Ainsworth
Rates fr: *£14.00*-**£18.00**.
Beds: 3T **Baths:** 1 Shared

Sale

National Grid Ref: SJ7891

Little 'B' Pub, Station Hotel

136 Woodhouse Lane, *Sale, Cheshire,* M33 4LL.
Open: All Year
0161 962 1151 Mrs O' Reilly
Rates fr: *£15.00*-**£15.00**.
Beds: 1T 1S **Baths:** 1 Private
Clean up-to-date accommodation in modern, detached four-bedroomed house with large garden. Home cooking a speciality.

Brooklands Luxury Lodge, *208 Marsland Road, Sale, Greater Manchester,* M33 3NE.
Charming residence with carpark on A6144 Road.
Open: All Year
Grades: AA 4 Q, Select
0161 973 3283 Mr Bowker
Rates fr: *£21.00*-**£25.00**.
Beds: 2F 2D 1T 3S
Baths: 5 Ensuite 2 Shared
(1) (6)

Karinya Hotel, *13 Barkers Lane, Sale, Cheshire,* M33 6RP.
Friendly family-run Victorian house. **Open:** All Year
0161 973 7786 Mr & Mrs Wallace
Rates fr: *£16.50*-**£16.50**.
Beds: 1F 1D 1T 5S
Baths: 2 Shared
(6)

Newjoy Guest House, *21 Poplar Grove, Sale, Cheshire, M33 3AX.*
Family-run guest house conveniently situated.
Open: All Year (not Xmas)
0161 973 7125 (also fax no)
Mrs Pollard
Rates fr: *£12.50*-**£15.00**.
Beds: 2T 2S
Baths: 2 Shared
(16) (5)

Southport

National Grid Ref: SD3620

Metropole Hotel, *Portland Street, Southport, Merseyside, PR8 1LL.*
Elegant Victorian building.
Open: All Year
01704 536836 Mr Rogers
Rates fr: *£24.00*-**£34.00**.
Beds: 3F 3D 5T 13S
Baths: 21 Private
(1) (12)

Standish

National Grid Ref: SD5610

52 Bentham Road, *Standish, Wigan, Lancs, WN6 0ND.*
Large garden & sun lounge.
Open: All Year (not Xmas)
01257 422750 Mrs Hutchinson
Rates fr: *£10.00*-**£12.00**.
Beds: 1T
Baths: 1 Private
(3)

Stockport

National Grid Ref: SJ8990

Bamford Arms, Red Lion

Northumbria House, *35 Corbar Road, Stockport, Cheshire, SK2 6EP.*
Edwardian house in lovely garden.
Open: All Year (not Xmas)
Grades: ETB 1 Cr, Comm
0161 483 4000 Mrs Kennington
Rates fr: *£16.00*-**£17.00**.
Beds: 1D 1T
Baths: 1 Shared
(2)

Upton

National Grid Ref: SJ2788

Field House, *71 Saughall Massie Lane, Upton, Wirral, Merseyside, L49 6LZ.*
Modern detached house.
Open: All Year (not Xmas)
0151 606 9458 Mr Bagley
Rates fr: *£12.00*-**£14.00**.
Beds: 1D 1S
Baths: 2 Shared
(4)

Wallasey

National Grid Ref: SJ2992

The Lighthouse

St Nicholas Vicarage, *22 Groveland Road, Wallasey, Merseyside, L45 8JY.*
Large homely Anglican Vicarage.
Open: All Year (not Xmas)
Grades: ETB Listed
0151 639 3589 Mrs Bentley
Rates fr: *£10.00*-**£10.00**.
Beds: 1F 2D 1T 2S
Baths: 1 Ensuite 1 Shared
(0) (2)

West Kirby

National Grid Ref: SJ2186

Hilbre Court, Surfers, Ring O' Bells

26 North Road, *West Kirby, Wirral, Merseyside, L48 4DF.*
Large Victorian private home.
Open: All Year (not Xmas)
0151 625 2327 Mrs Dempsey
Rates fr: *£14.00*-**£14.00**.
Beds: 1T
(1)

Maconachie Guest House, *1 Victoria Road, West Kirby, Wirral, Merseyside, L48 3HL.*
Edwardian house overlooking Dee estuary.
Open: All Year
0151 625 1915 Mrs Hicks
Rates fr: *£18.00*-**£20.00**.
Beds: 2D 1T
Baths: 2 Private
(1)

Warren Cottage, *42 Caldy Road, West Kirby, Wirral, Merseyside, L48 2HQ.*
Spectacular river views.
Exceptional accommodation.
Open: All Year (not Xmas)
0151 625 8740 Mrs Graves
Rates fr: *£20.00*-**£25.00**.
Beds: 1D 1T 1S
Baths: 2 Ensuite 1 Shared
(2)

La Petite Paix, *12 Gorse Lane, West Kirby, Wirral, Merseyside, L48 8BH.*
Delightful English country garden setting.
Open: All Year
0151 625 7538
Mrs Corfe
Rates fr: *£18.00*-**£18.00**.
Beds: 1D 1S
Baths: 1 Shared
(3)

Whitefield

National Grid Ref: SD8106

122 Radcliffe New Road, *Whitefield, Manchester, M25 7RW.*
Close to M62, J17.
Open: All Year (not Xmas)
0161 766 5161 Mr Burke
Rates fr: *£15.00*-**£15.00**.
Beds: 1D 1T 1S
Baths: 2 Shared

Wigan

National Grid Ref: SD5805

Charles Dickens, Bellingham Hotel, Royal Oak Pub

The Maple Hotel, *35 Upper Dicconson Street, Wigan, Lancs, WN1 2AG.*
Near the town centre, warm hospitality.
Open: All Year
01942 243537 (also fax no)
Rates fr: *£12.00*-**£14.00**.
Beds: 1F 3T 3S
Baths: 2 Shared
(0) (1)

Hotel Bel-Air, *236 Wigan Lane, Wigan, Lancs, WN1 2ND.*
Superior RAC award-winning hotel & restaurant.
Open: All Year (not Xmas)
01942 241410 Mr Owen
Rates fr: *£20.00*-**£25.00**.
Beds: 12F
Baths: 12 Ensuite
(12)

Worsley

National Grid Ref: SD7401

Oaks Pub

Postmans Cottage, *26 Roe Green, Worsley, Manchester, M28 2RF.*
Pretty C18th cottage.
Open: All Year (not Xmas)
0161 790 2645 Mrs Merryweather
Rates fr: *£18.00*-**£18.00**.
Beds: 1D 1T
Baths: 1 Shared

Bringing children with you? Always ask for any special rates.

Hampshire

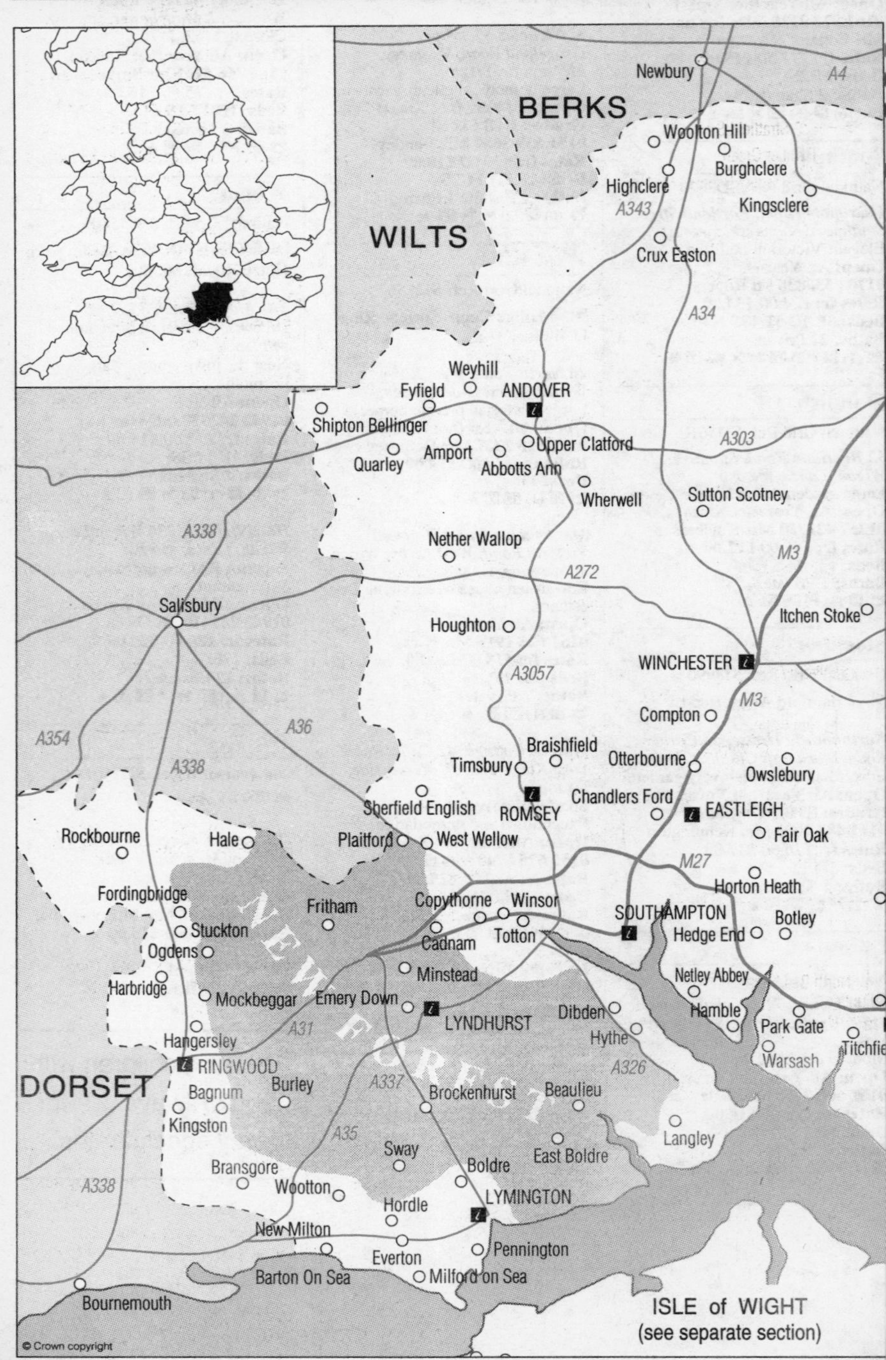
BERKS
WILTS
DORSET
NEW FOREST
Newbury
A4
Woolton Hill
Burghclere
Highclere
Kingsclere
A343
Crux Easton
A34
Weyhill
Fyfield
ANDOVER
Shipton Bellinger
Amport
Upper Clatford
Quarley
Abbotts Ann
A303
Wherwell
Sutton Scotney
A338
Nether Wallop
M3
A272
Salisbury
Itchen Stoke
Houghton
WINCHESTER
A3057
M3
Compton
A354
A36
Braishfield
A338
Timsbury
Otterbourne
Owslebury
Chandlers Ford
Sherfield English
ROMSEY
EASTLEIGH
Rockbourne
Hale
Plaitford
West Wellow
Fair Oak
M27
Horton Heath
Fordingbridge
Fritham
Copythorne
Winsor
SOUTHAMPTON
Stuckton
Totton
Botley
Cadnam
Hedge End
Ogdens
Minstead
Netley Abbey
Harbridge
Mockbeggar
Emery Down
Hamble
Dibden
LYNDHURST
Park Gate
Hythe
Hangersley
A31
Titchfie
Warsash
RINGWOOD
A326
A337
Bagnum
Burley
Brockenhurst
Beaulieu
Kingston
A35
Langley
Sway
East Boldre
Bransgore
Boldre
A338
Wootton
LYMINGTON
Hordle
New Milton
Pennington
Everton
Barton On Sea
Milford on Sea
Bournemouth
ISLE of WIGHT
(see separate section)
© Crown copyright

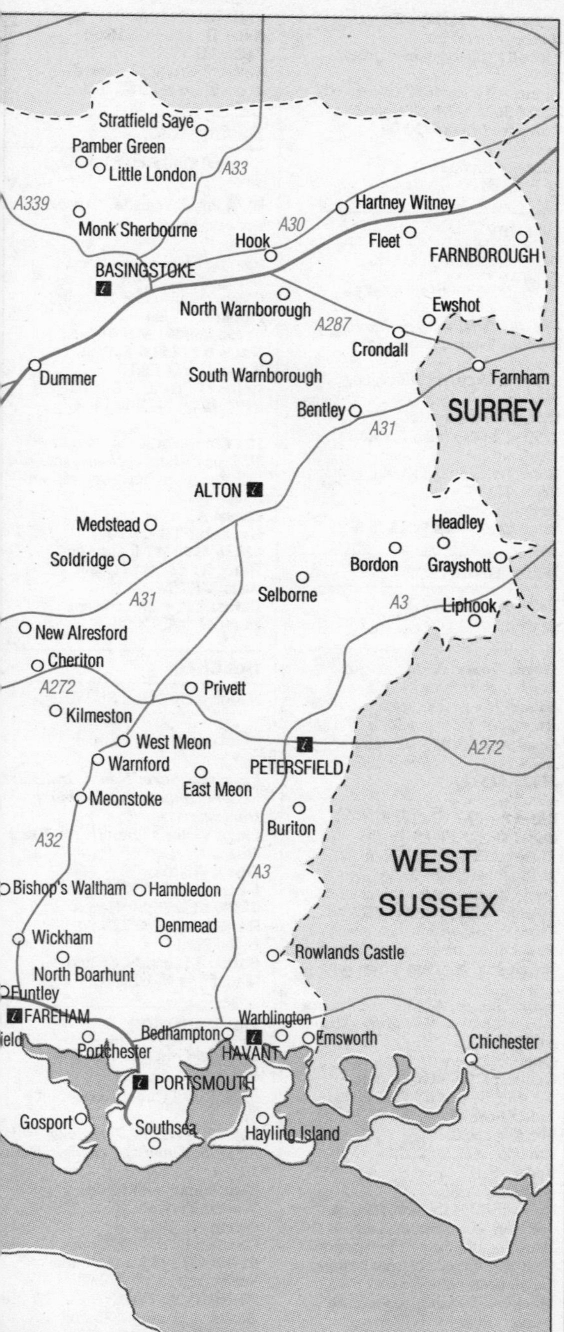

Tourist Information Centres

Military Museum, Queens Avenue, **Aldershot**, Hants, GU11 2LG, 01252 20968.

7 Cross & Pillory Lane, **Alton**, Hants, GU34 1HL, 01420 88448.

Bridge Street, **Andover**, Hants, SP10 1BL, 01264 324320.

Willis Museum, Old Town Hall, Market Place, **Basingstoke**, Hants, RG21 1QD, 01256 817618

Town Hall Centre, Leigh Road, **Eastleigh**, Hants, SO5 4DE, 01703 641261.

Westbury Manor, West Street, **Fareham**, Hants, PO16 0JJ, 01329 221342.

Hartington Centre, Fleet Road, **Fleet**, Hants, GU13 8BY, 01252 811151.

Salisbury Street, **Fordingbridge**, Hants, SP6 1AB, 01425 654560, (Easter to Oct).

1 Park Road South, **Havant**, Hants, PO9 1HA, 01705 480024.

Beachlands Seafront, **Hayling Island**, Hants, PO11 0AS, 01705 467111, (Easter to Oct).

Saint Barb, New Street, **Lymington**, Hants, SO41 9NB, 01590 672422, (Easter to Oct).

New Forest Museum & Visitor Centre, Main Car Park, **Lyndhurst**, Hants, SO43 7NY, 01703 282269.

County Library, 27 The Square, **Petersfield**, Hants, GU32 3HH, 01730 268829.

102 Commercial Road, **Portsmouth**, Hants, PO1 1EJ, 01705 838382.

The Furlong, **Ringwood**, Hants, BH24 1AZ, 01425 470896, (Easter to Oct).

1 Latimore Street, Broadwater Road, **Romsey**, Hants, SO51 8DF, 01794 512987.

Rownhams M27 Services (Westbound), **Southampton**, Hants, SO1 8AW, 01703 730345.

9 The Civic Centre, **Southampton**, Hants, SO9 4XF, 01703 221106.

Guildhall, The Broadway, **Winchester**, Hants, SO14 7LP, 01962 840500.

Abbotts Ann

National Grid Ref: SU3243

Virginia Lodge, *Salisbury Road, Abbotts Ann, Andover, Hants,* SP11 7NX.
Modern comfortable bungalow, beautiful gardens. **Open:** All Year
01264 710713 Mrs Stuart
Rates fr: *£16.00*-**£20.00**.
Beds: 1D 2T
Baths: 1 Ensuite 1 Shared
(5) (6)

Alton

National Grid Ref: SU7139

The Royal Oak , Three Horseshoes, French Horn

Glen Derry, *52 Wellhouse Road, Beech, Alton, Hants,* GU34 4AG.
Open: All Year
Grades: ETB Listed, Comm
01420 83235 / 0378 406084
Mrs Griffiths
Rates fr: *£15.00*-**£20.00**.
Beds: 1F 1D 1T
Baths: 1 Private 1 Shared
(10)
Peaceful, secluded family home. Large spacious rooms, extensive gardens. Beautiful mature trees. Winchester, Portsmouth, New Forest nearby. Heathrow/Gatwick Airports 45 miles. Warm welcome assured.

East Worldham Vicarage, *Alton, Hants,* GU34 3AS.
Typically quiet country vicarage.
Open: All Year (not Xmas)
01420 82392 Mrs Bradford
Rates fr: *£17.00*-**£16.00**.
Beds: 1D 1S 1T **Baths:** 2 Shared
(3)

Amport

National Grid Ref: SU2944

White Horse

Broadwater, *Amport, Andover, Hants,* SP11 8AY.
Thatched cottage, convenient Stonehenge & West Country.
Open: All Year
Grades: ETB 2 St, Comm, AA 3 Q
01264 772240 (also fax no)
Mrs Mallam
Rates fr: *£22.00*-**£25.00**.
Beds: 1F 2T **Baths:** 3 Private
(3)

Andover

National Grid Ref: SU3645

Folly Inn

Amarylan, *20 Junction Road, Andover, Hants,* SP10 3QU.
A family 'home from home'.
Open: All Year (not Xmas)
Grades: ETB Listed
01264 355362 (also fax no)
Mrs Daws
Rates fr: *£16.50*-**£16.50**.
Beds: 1F 1T 1S
Baths: 1 Ensuite 1 Shared
(10) (4)

99 Salisbury Road, *Andover, Hants,* SP10 2LN.
Virtually self-contained ground floor.
Open: All Year (not Xmas)
01264 362638 Mrs Targett
Rates fr: *£15.00*-**£20.00**.
Beds: 1F
Baths: 1 Private

Bartley

National Grid Ref: SU4213

Haywain Restaurant

Dreyfus Release, *New Inn Road, Bartley, Southampton, Hants,* SO40 2LR.
Quiet, converted cottage, edge New Forest.
Open: All Year
01703 813483 (also fax no)
Mrs Tottle
Rates fr: *£15.00*-**£18.00**.
Beds: 1D 1T
Baths: 1 Shared
(2) (2)

Barton-on-Sea

National Grid Ref: SZ2393

Rising Sun, The Rydal

Cleeve House, *58 Barton Court Avenue, Barton-on-Sea, New Milton, Hants,* BH25 7HG.
Open: All Year (not Xmas)
Grades: ETB 2 Cr, Comm, AA 4 Q
01425 615211
Mrs Carter
Rates fr: *£17.00*-**£17.00**.
Beds: 1F 1D 1T 1S
Baths: 2 Private 1 Shared
(10)
Large, comfortable, character family home with beautiful gardens. Close to sea, within easy reach of New Forest, beaches, cliffs, golf and sailing. Non-smoking house.

Laurel Lodge, *48 Western Avenue, Barton-on-Sea, New Milton, Hants,* BH25 7PZ.
Open: All Year
Grades: ETB 3 Cr, Comm, AA 4 Q, Select, RAC Acclaim
01425 618309
Mrs Copeland
Rates fr: *£17.00*-**£22.00**.
Beds: 1F 1D 1T
Baths: 3 Ensuite
(8) (3)
Peaceful, comfortable, friendly, charming, the best of both worlds. Near panoramic clifftop, beaches & the glorious New Forest. Thoughtfully equipped ensuite rooms. Great food. Warm welcome.

Sunnycroft, *35 Becton Lane, Barton-on-Sea, New Milton, Hants,* BH25 7AB.
Detached. Between sea & town.
Open: All Year
01425 622075 Mrs Burridge
Rates fr: *£16.00*-**£16.00**.
Beds: 1D 1T 1S
Baths: 1 Private 1 Shared
(5) (4)

Basingstoke

National Grid Ref: SU6352

Pig & Whistle, Harvester, Brewers Fare

Fordyce, *Hackwood Road, Basingstoke, Hants,* RG21 3AF.
Clean, comfortable & friendly.
Open: All Year
01256 468461 Mrs Cooke
Rates fr: *£15.00*-**£20.00**.
Beds: 1F 3D 1T 1S
Baths: 1 Private 2 Shared
(8) (4)

104 Gershwin Road, Brighton Hill, *Basingstoke, Hants,* RG22 4HJ.
Family atmosphere, homely surroundings.
Open: All Year
Grades: ETB Listed
01256 410024 Mr Carroll
Rates fr: *£17.00*-**£17.50**.
Beds: 2T 2S
Baths: 1 Private 1 Shared
(5) (3)

Beaulieu

National Grid Ref: SU3802

Royal Oak, Hilltop

Leygreem Farm House, *Lyndhurst Road, Beaulieu, Brockenhurst, Hants,* SO42 7YP.
Large Victorian farmhouse. Rural area.
Open: All Year
Grades: ETB 2 Cr, Comm
01590 612355 Mr Helyer
Rates fr: *£15.00*-**£18.00**.
Beds: 2D 1T
Baths: 3 Private 1 Shared
(6)

Bedhampton

National Grid Ref: SU7006

Rusty Cutter Restaurant

High Towers, *14 Portsdown Hill Road, Bedhampton, Havant, Hants* PO9 3JY.
Near Portsmouth ferries & Wayfarer's Walk.
Open: All Year
Grades: ETB 2 Cr, Comm
01705 471748 Mrs Boulton
Rates fr: *£18.00*-**£20.00**.
Beds: 1F 2D 1T 1S
Baths: 4 Ensuite 1 Shared
(5) (6)

Bentley

National Grid Ref: SU7844

Hen & Chicken, Jolly Farmer, Anchor, Prince of Wales

Vine Farmhouse, *Isington, Bentley, Alton, Hants, GU34 4PW.*
Attractive, recently converted comfortable farmhouse.
Open: All Year (not Xmas)
01420 23262 Mrs Sinclair
Fax no: 01589 396533
Rates fr: *£15.00*-**£15.00**.
Beds: 1F 1D 1S
Baths: 1 Ensuite 1 Shared
(10)

Pittersfield, *Hole Lane, Bentley, Farnham, Surrey, GU10 5LT.*
Delightful village house in rural setting.
Open: All Year
Grades: ETB Listed, High Comm
01420 22414 Mrs Coulton
Rates fr: *£20.00*-**£20.00**.
Beds: 1D 2T
Baths: 2 Private 1 Shared
(3)

Bishop's Waltham

National Grid Ref: SU5517

Barleycorn Inn

Anchor Cottage, *Bank Street, Bishop's Waltham, Southampton, Hampshire, SO32 1AN.*
Modern comforts, attractive village setting.
Open: All Year
01489 894935 Mrs Fairhurst
Rates fr: *£16.00*-**£16.00**.
Beds: 1D 1T
Baths: 1 Shared
(11) (2)

Boldre

National Grid Ref: SZ3298

Four Winds, *Sandy Down, Boldre, Lymington, Hants, SO41 8PN.*
Beautiful country house bordering Forest.
Open: All Year
01590 622057 Mrs Ling
Rates fr: *£19.00*-**£25.00**.
Beds: 2D 1T
Baths: 3 Ensuite
(12) (10)

Bordon

National Grid Ref: SU7838

Cricketers (Kingsley)

30 Churchfields, Kingsley, *Bordon, Hants, GU35 9PJ.*
Modern comfortable house by commonland.
Open: All Year
01420 472271 Mrs Clack
Rates fr: *£15.00*-**£17.50**.
Beds: 1D 1S
Baths: 1 Shared
(10) (4)

Botley

National Grid Ref: SU5113

Steeple Court Farm, *Church Lane, Botley, Southampton, Hants, SO30 2EQ.*
Modern comfortable farmhouse.
Open: All Year (not Xmas)
01489 788738 Mrs King
Rates fr: *£18.00*-**£18.00**.
Beds: 1D 2T
Baths: 1 Shared
(8) (6)

Braishfield

National Grid Ref: SU3725

Springwood, *Crook Hill, Braishfield, Romsey, Hants, SO51 0QB.*
Bungalow garden/copse. Adjacent arboretum.
Open: All Year
01794 368134 Mrs Dickens
Rates fr: *£15.00*-**£16.00**.
Beds: 1D
Baths: 1 Private

Bransgore

National Grid Ref: SZ1897

Three Tuns

Wiltshire House, *West Road, Bransgore, Christchurch, Dorset, BH23 8BD.*
Comfortable secluded Victorian family residence.
Open: All Year
Grades: ETB 2 Cr, High Comm, AA 4 Q, Select
01425 672450 Mr Hooper
Rates fr: *£16.00*-**£18.00**.
Beds: 1F 1D 1S
Baths: 2 Ensuite
(3)

Brockenhurst

National Grid Ref: SU2902

Foresters

Seraya Guest House, *8 Grigg Lane, Brockenhurst, Hants, SO42 7RE.*
Central forest, friendly family home.
Open: All Year
01590 622426 Mrs Ward
Rates fr: *£14.00*-**£14.00**.
Beds: 1F 1D 1T 1S
Baths: 1 Shared
(4)

Rose & Crown, *Lyndhurst Road, Brockenhurst, Hants, SO42 7RH.*
Comfortable C18th inn.
Open: All Year
01590 622225 Mr Parkin
Fax no: 01590 623056
Rates fr: *£19.50*-**£21.00**.
Beds: 2F 6D 1T 2S
Baths: 5 Private 6 Shared
(50)

Burghclere

National Grid Ref: SU4761

Adbury Holt House, *Burghclere, Newbury, Berks, RG20 9BW.*
Large, comfortable, secluded Victorian house.
Open: All Year (not Xmas)
01635 42846
Mrs Cooper
Fax no: 01635 35777
Rates fr: *£19.75*-**£18.50**.
Beds: 1F 2D 2T 1S
Baths: 1 Private 2 Shared
(20)

Buriton

National Grid Ref: SU7320

Pilmead House, *North Lane, Buriton, Petersfield, Hants, GU31 5RS.*
Stone-built Victorian family house.
Open: All Year
01730 266795
Mrs Moss
Rates fr: *£18.50*-**£20.00**.
Beds: 1D 1T
(3)

Burley

National Grid Ref: SU2103

White Buck, Toad Hall

Bay Tree House, *1 Clough Lane, Burley, Ringwood, Hants, BH24 4AE.*
Open: All Year
01425 403215 (also fax no)
Mrs Allen
Rates fr: *£18.00*-**£18.00**.
Beds: 1F 1S
Baths: 1 Shared
(4)
Friendly family home in heart of the 'New Forest'. Riding, golf, fishing, badger-watching close by. Lovely walks, maps provided. Home-produced honey for breakfast.

Charlwood, *Longmead Road, Burley, Ringwood, Hants, BH24 4BY.*
Quiet, rural, off main road.
Open: Jan to Nov
01425 403242
Mrs Russell
Rates fr: *£17.00*.
Beds: 1D 1T
Baths: 1 Shared
(3)

The Vicarage, *Church Lane, Burley, Ringwood, Hants, BH24 4AP.*
Secluded, comfortable New Forest cottage.
Open: All Year
01425 402303
Mrs Clarkson
Fax no: 01425 403753
Rates fr: *£17.50*-**£17.50**.
Beds: 1D 1T
Baths: 1 Shared
(4)

***Holmans,** Bisterne Close, Burley, Ringwood, Hants, BH24 4AZ.*
Charming country family house.
Open: All Year
Grades: ETB Listed, High Comm
01425 402307 Mr & Mrs Ford
Rates fr: *£20.00*-**£30.00**.
Beds: 1D 2T
Baths: 2 Ensuite
(4)

Cadnam

National Grid Ref: SU2913

Compass Inn, Haywain, White Hart

***Bushfriers,** Winsor Road, Winsor, Cadnam, Southampton, Hants, SO40 2HF.*
Character beamed cottage; fine views.
Open: All Year (not Xmas)
01703 812552 Mrs Wright
Rates fr: *£15.00*-**£18.00**.
Beds: 1F 1D
Baths: 1 Shared
(2)

***Dreyfus Release,** New Inn Road, Bartley, Cadnam, Southampton, Hants, SO40 2LR.*
Quiet, converted cottage, edge New Forest.
Open: All Year
01703 813483 (also fax no)
Mrs Tottle
Rates fr: *£15.00*-**£18.00**.
Beds: 1D 1T
Baths: 1 Shared
(2) (2)

Chandlers Ford

National Grid Ref: SU4320

Hot Hotel, Clump Inn

***St Lucia,** 68 Shaftesbury Avenue, Chandlers Ford, Eastleigh, Hants, SO53 3BP.*
Open: All Year
Grades: ETB Listed, Comm
01703 262995 (also fax no)
Mrs Willis
Rates fr: *£15.00*-**£14.00**.
Beds: 1D 1T 2S
(7) (5)
Family home in large mature gardens, within half a mile of M3/M27. Easy access - Winchester, Southampton, Salisbury, Portsmouth & Bournemouth. Home-grown produce in season.

***133 Bournemouth Road,** Chandlers Ford, Eastleigh, Hants, SO53 3HA.*
Comfortable detached family home.
Open: All Year
01703 254801 Mr Lanham
Rates fr: *£15.00*-**£16.00**.
Beds: 1D 1S
Baths: 1 Shared
(2)

Cheriton

National Grid Ref: SU5828

***Brandy Lea,** Cheriton, Alresford, Hants, SO24 0QQ.*
Friendly semi-detached next to pub.
Open: All Year
01962 771534 Mrs Hoskings
Rates fr: *£13.50*-**£13.50**.
Beds: 1T
Baths: 1 Private

Compton

National Grid Ref: SU4625

The Bridge

***Old Orchard,** Compton Street, Compton, Winchester, Hants, SO21 2AT.*
Sitting room ensuite, peaceful, large gardens.
Open: All Year (not Xmas)
01962 712460 Mrs Case
Rates fr: *£16.50*.
Beds: 1T
Baths: 1 Private
(3)

***The Manor House,** Place Lane, Compton, Winchester, Hants, SO21 2BA.*
C17th private house.
Open: All Year
Grades: ETB Listed
01962 712162 Mrs Neyroud
Rates fr: *£11.50*-**£12.00**.
Beds: 1D
Baths: 1 Shared

Copythorne

National Grid Ref: SU3014

***The Old Well Restaurant,** Romsey Road, Copythorne, Southampton, Hants, SO40 2PE.*
Restaurant with rooms above.
Open: All Year
01703 812321 Mr Martin
Rates fr: *£17.00*-**£22.00**.
Beds: 2F 4D
Baths: 3 Ensuite
(3) (8)

Crondall

National Grid Ref: SU7948

Plume of Feathers, Hampshire, Horns

***Potters Hill,** Well Road, Crondall, Farnham, Surrey, GU10 5PN.*
Secluded, peaceful cottage-style house.
Open: All Year (not Xmas)
01252 850444 Mrs Chilton
Rates fr: *£20.00*-**£25.00**.
Beds: 1D 1T 1S
Baths: 3 Private
(6)

***Peperstiche,** Itchel Lane, Crondall, Farnham, Surrey, GU10 5PT.*
Beautiful family house overlooking farmland.
Open: All Year (not Xmas)
01252 850156 Mr & Mrs Thomas
Rates fr: *£17.00*-**£17.00**.
Beds: 2D 1S
Baths: 2 Shared
(5) (8)

Crux Easton

National Grid Ref: SU4256

Furze Bush

***Manor House,** Crux Easton, Newbury, Hants, RG20 9QF.*
Comfortable historic farmhouse.
Open: All Year (not Xmas)
01635 254314 (also fax no)
Mrs O'Shaughnessy
Rates fr: *£16.50*-**£16.50**.
Beds: 3T
Baths: 2 Shared
(6)

Denmead

National Grid Ref: SU6511

White Hart

***Forest Gate,** Hambledon Road, Denmead, Waterlooville, Hants, PO7 6EX.*
Large Georgian private house.
Open: All Year (not Xmas)
Grades: ETB Listed
01705 255901 Mrs Cox
Rates fr: *£18.00*-**£22.00**.
Beds: 2T
Baths: 2 Ensuite
(10) (2)

Dibden

National Grid Ref: SU4008

***Dale Farm Guest House,** Manor Road, Applemore Hill, Dibden, Southampton, Hants, SO45 5TJ.*
Converted C18th comfortable farmhouse.
Open: All Year (not Xmas)
01703 849632 Mrs Archdeacon
Rates fr: *£16.00*-**£18.00**.
Beds: 1F 2D 2T 1S
Baths: 1 Private 2 Shared

Dummer

National Grid Ref: SU5845

Sun Inn

***Oakdown Farm,** Dummer, Basingstoke, Hants, RG23 7LR.*
Secluded modern farm bungalow.
Open: All Year
Grades: ETB 1 Cr, Comm
01256 397218 Mrs Hutton
Rates fr: *£15.00*-**£15.00**.
Beds: 1D 2T
Baths: 1 Shared
(12) (4)

East Boldre

National Grid Ref: SU3700

Turf Cutters

***Coolderry Cottage,** Masseys Lane, East Boldre, Beaulieu, Brockenhurst, Hants, SO42 7WE.*
Cosy Forest cottage, quiet location.
Open: All Year (not Xmas)
01590 612428 Mr & Mrs Reeves
Rates fr: *£15.00*-**£17.50**.
Beds: 2D
Baths: 1 Shared
(0) (2)

East Meon

National Grid Ref: SU6822

George, Issac Walton

***Drayton Cottage,** East Meon, Petersfield, Hants, GU32 1PW.*
Beamed cottage overlooking River Meon.
Open: All Year
Grades: ETB Listed, High Comm
01730 823472
Mrs Rockett
Rates fr: *£18.00*-**£20.00**.
Beds: 1T 1D
Baths: 1 Ensuite 1 Private
(9) (3)

***Coombe Cross House,** Coombe Road, East Meon, Petersfield, Hants, GU32 1HQ.*
Georgian country house, stunning views.
Open: All Year (not Xmas)
01730 823298
Mrs Bulmer
Fax no: 01730 823515
Rates fr: *£20.00*-**£20.00**.
Beds: 1D 2T
Baths: 2 Private 1 Shared
(8) (12)

Eastleigh

National Grid Ref: SU4519

Crickets Arms

***Willow End,** 60 Ruskin Road, Eastleigh, Hants, SO50 4JX.*
Quiet, homely, near station, Airport.
Open: All Year (not Xmas)
01703 617317 Mrs Dyer
Rates fr: *£16.00*-**£18.00**.
Beds: 2T 1S
Baths: 1 Shared
(4) (1)

***Park Farm,** Stoneham Lane, Eastleigh, Hants, SO50 3HS.*
Rural setting, close New Forest.
Open: All Year
Grades: ETB Listed, Comm
01703 612960
Mrs Fright
Rates fr: *£16.00*-**£17.50**.
Beds: 2F 1T
Baths: 1 Ensuite 1 Shared
(6)

Emery Down

National Grid Ref: SU2808

***Stable End Guest House,** Mill Lane, Emery Down, Lyndhurst, Hants, SO43 7FJ.*
Converted Victorian stables, Edwardian house.
Open: All Year
01703 282504 Mrs Dibben
Rates fr: *£17.00*-**£20.00**.
Beds: 1D 1T
Baths: 1 Ensuite 1 Private
(4)

Everton

National Grid Ref: SZ2994

The Crown, The Oak

***Efford Cottage,** Milford Road, Everton, Lymington, Hants, SO41 0JD.*
Friendly, spacious, part-Georgian family home.
Open: All Year
Grades: ETB 3 Cr, Comm, AA 4 Q, Select, RAC Acclaim
01590 642315 / 0374 703075
Mrs Ellis
Fax no: 01590 642315
Rates fr: *£19.00*-**£20.00**.
Beds: 1F 3D 1T
Baths: 3 Ensuite
(12) (4)

***Harts Lane Nurseries,** 242 Everton Road, Everton, Lymington, Hants, SO41 0HE.*
Friendly comfortable accommodation. Quiet location.
Open: All Year
01590 645902 Mrs Sque
Rates fr: *£17.00*-**£20.00**.
Beds: 1F 2D
Baths: 3 Private
(5)

Ewshot

National Grid Ref: SU8149

***Oak Mead,** Heath Lane, Ewshot, Farnham, Surrey, GU9 5AW.*
Quiet, rural, pleasant views.
Open: All Year
01252 850392 Mrs Joy
Rates fr: *£15.00*-**£17.00**.
Beds: 1D 1T
Baths: 1 Private 1 Shared
(3)

Fair Oak

National Grid Ref: SU4918

River Inn

***13 Camelia Grove,** Fair Oak, Eastleigh, Hants, SO50 7GZ.*
Modern open plan house.
Open: All Year
01703 692822 Mrs Williams
Rates fr: *£12.50*-**£12.50**.
Beds: 1T 1S
Baths: 1 Shared
(2)

Fareham

National Grid Ref: SU5606

Seagull, Cormorant

***36 Romsey Avenue,** Fareham, Hants, PO16 9TA.*
Clean, comfortable home farm views.
Open: All Year (not Xmas)
01329 231520 Mrs Cartwright
Rates fr: *£15.00*-**£15.00**.
Beds: 1D 1S **Baths:** 1 Shared
(5)

***Beaulieu,** 67 Portchester Road, Fareham, Hants, PO16 8AP.*
Comfortable home in pleasant surroundings.
Open: All Year
01329 232461 Mrs Wycherley
Rates fr: *£17.50*-**£17.50**.
Beds: 1D 1T 1S
Baths: 1 Shared
(3)

Farnborough

National Grid Ref: SU8754

***21 Tay Close,** Cove, Farnborough, Hants, GU14 9NB.*
Modern comfortable private home.
Open: All Year
01252 513691 Mrs Raynsford
Fax no: 0252 513691
Rates fr: *£13.00*-**£15.00**.
Beds: 1D 1T
Baths: 1 Shared
(1)

***11 Hurst Road,** Hawley Estate, Farnborough, Hants, GU14 8HE.*
Widow with three bedroom house.
Open: All Year
01252 373982 Mrs Abel
Rates fr: -**£10.00**.
Beds: 1S
Baths: 1 Shared

Fleet

National Grid Ref: SU8054

***12 Warren Close,** Fleet, Hants, GU13 9LT.*
Friendly comfortable in quiet location.
Open: All Year
01252 615063 Mrs Webb
Rates fr: *£17.00*-**£17.00**.
Beds: 1F 2S
(2)

Fordingbridge

National Grid Ref: SU1414

***Alderholt Mill,** Sandleheath Road, Fordingbridge, Hants, SP6 1PU.*
Comfortable cottage beside picturesque watermill.
Open: All Year (not Xmas)
01425 653130 Mrs Harte
Rates fr: *£19.00*-**£15.00**.
Beds: 3D 1T 1S
Baths: 4 Ensuite
(10)

The Ship Inn, *High Street, Fordingbridge, Hants, SP6.*
Comfortable town centre inn.
Open: All Year
01425 652776 Mr Smith
Rates fr: *£15.00*-**£18.00**.
Beds: 2F 1D 3T 1S
Baths: 2 Shared
(7)

Fritham

National Grid Ref: SU2314

Bell Inn

Chapel Lane Cottage, *Fritham, Lyndhurst, Hants, SO43 7HL.*
Self contained, quiet. Direct access to Forest.
Open: Mar to Oct
01703 812359 Mrs Borrelli
Rates fr: *£17.00*.
Beds: 1D
Baths: 1 Private
(1)

Primrose Cottage, *Fritham, Lyndhurst, Hampshire, SO43 7HH.*
Private suite of three rooms.
Open: Easter to Oct
01703 812272 Mrs Penfound
Rates fr: *£15.00*-**£18.00**.
Beds: 1D
Baths: 1 Private
(3) (2)

Funtley

National Grid Ref: SU5608

Miner's Arms

17 Lakeside, *Funtley, Fareham, Hants, PO17 5EP.*
Modern country house, overlooking lake.
Open: All Year (not Xmas)
01329 236128 Ms Moore
Rates fr: *£14.00*-**£14.00**.
Beds: 1D 3S
Baths: 1 Shared
(6)

Fyfield

National Grid Ref: SU2946

Spring Meadow, *Fyfield, Andover, Hants, SP11 8EL.*
Good comfortable country home, welcoming.
Open: All Year (not Xmas)
01264 773487 Mrs Smith
Rates fr: *£15.00*-**£18.00**.
Beds: 2T
(15) (2)

The lowest *double* rate per person is shown in *italics.*

Gosport

National Grid Ref: SU5900

North Star

Raysal, *90a Fareham Road, Gosport, Hants, PO13 0AG.*
On main Fareham-Gosport highway.
Open: All Year (not Xmas)
01329 280093 Mrs Rolls
Rates fr: *£15.00*-**£16.00**.
Beds: 1F 1D 1T
Baths: 3 Shared
(1) (5)

Grayshott

National Grid Ref: SU8735

Fox & Pelican

The Valleys, *School Road, Grayshott, Hindhead, Surrey, GU26 6LR.*
Hospitable, beautifully situated quiet house.
Open: All Year
01428 606987 Mrs Burgess
Rates fr: *£19.50*-**£19.50**.
Beds: 1D 1S
Baths: 1 Shared
(4)

Hale

National Grid Ref: SU1919

Forest Cottage, *Hatchet Green, Hale, Fordingbridge, Hants, SP6 2NE.*
Pretty cottage on village green.
Open: All Year
01725 510529 Ms Sutherland
Rates fr: *£17.00*-**£17.00**.
Beds: 2D 1S
Baths: 1 Private 1 Shared
(7) (6)

Hamble

National Grid Ref: SU4706

Braymar, *35 Westfield Close, Hamble, Southampton, Hants, SO31 4LG.*
Comfortable home, quiet, near sea.
Open: All Year
01703 453831 Mrs Welsh
Rates fr: *£14.00*-**£14.00**.
Beds: 1D 2T 1S
Baths: 1 Shared
(2) (4)

Hambledon

National Grid Ref: SU6414

Vine & George

Cams, *Hambledon, Waterlooville, Hants, PO7 4SP.*
Comfortable C17th house.
Open: All Year (not Xmas)
Grades: ETB 2 Cr
01705 632865 Mrs Fawcett
Rates fr: *£16.00*-**£17.00**.
Beds: 1D 2T
Baths: 1 Ensuite 1 Shared
(10) (6)

Mornington House, *Hambledon, Waterlooville, Hants, PO7 4RU.*
Comfortable, attractive, Georgian family home.
Open: All Year
Grades: ETB Listed
01705 632704 (also fax no)
Mr & Mrs Lutyens
Rates fr: *£15.00*-**£20.00**.
Beds: 2T
Baths: 1 Shared
(6)

Harbridge

National Grid Ref: SU1410

North Plumley Farmhouse, *Harbridge, Ringwood, Hants, BH24 3QA.*
Farmhouse 1.5 miles off road.
Open: All Year (not Xmas)
Grades: ETB Listed, Comm
01202 826393 Mrs Crome
Rates fr: *£15.00*-**£18.00**.
Beds: 1F 2D 1S
Baths: 1 Ensuite 1 Private
(5)

Hartley Wintney

National Grid Ref: SU7656

4 Campion Way, *Hartley Wintney, Hook, Hants, RG27 8TL.*
Open: Easter to Oct
01252 843826 (also fax no)
Mr & Mrs Fitzgerald
Rates fr: *£15.00*-**£12.50**.
Beds: 1D 1T 1S
Baths: 1 Ensuite 1 Shared
(5)
Situated in Hampshire village modern Georgian house with easy access to train station - London 1 hour. Local places of interest - Winchester (Jane Austen's house), Windsor.

Hayling Island

National Grid Ref: SU7201

Yew Tree, Barley Mow

Marley Cottage, *112 Havant Road, Hayling Island, Hants, PO11 0LJ.*
Comfortable family home, ample parking.
Open: All Year (not Xmas)
01705 464928
Mr & Mrs Wilson
Rates fr: *£14.00*-**£16.00**.
Beds: 3D
Baths: 1 Shared
(3)

Anns Cottage, *45 St Andrews Road, Hayling Island, Hants, PO11 9JN.*
Detached comfortable bungalow, close seafront.
Open: All Year (not Xmas)
01705 467048 Mrs Jay
Rates fr: *£12.50*-**£12.50**.
Beds: 1F 2D 1S
Baths: 1 Private 1 Shared
(5)

Broad Oak Hotel, *Copse Lane, Hayling Island, Hants, PO11 0QB.*
Small country hotel. Superb location.
Open: All Year
Grades: ETB 3 Cr, Comm
01705 462333 (also fax no)
Mrs Millins (managing)
Rates fr: *£18.00*-**£22.50**.
Beds: 2F 7D 2T 2S
Baths: 13 Ensuite
(0) (30)

Headley

National Grid Ref: SU8236

Sleepy Hollow, *Pond Road, Headley, Bordon, Hants, GU35 8NN.*
Charming thatched cottage in woodland.
Open: All Year (not Xmas)
01428 712473 Mrs Hall
Rates fr: *£19.00*-**£20.00**.
Beds: 2D 1S
Baths: 1 Private 1 Shared
(3)

Hedge End

National Grid Ref: SU4912

Montana Guest House, *90 Lower Northam Road, Hedge End, Southampton, Hants, SO30 4FT.*
Comfortable, friendly, family guest house.
Open: All Year
01489 782797 Mr & Mrs Cooper
Rates fr: *£17.00*-**£18.00**.
Beds: 1F 1D 2T 4S
Baths: 3 Private 2 Shared
(7)

Highclere

National Grid Ref: SU4360

Red House, Yew Tree

Westridge Open Centre, *Andover Road, Highclere, Newbury, Berks, RG20 9PJ.*
Country house with gardens. Bookings essential.
Open: All Year (not Xmas or public holidays)
01635 253322 Miss Gribble
Rates fr: *£10.00*-**£10.00**.
Beds: 2T 2S
Baths: 2 Shared
(2)

Hook

National Grid Ref: SU7254

Leather Bottle

Cherry Lodge, *Reading Road, Hook, Basingstoke, Hants, RG27 9DB.*
Friendly family-run guesthouse.
Open: All Year
Grades: AA Listed, RAC Listed
01256 762532 (also fax no)
Mrs Phillips
Rates fr: *£18.00*-**£25.00**.
Beds: 2F 3D 4T 2S
Baths: 11 Private
(30)

Cedar Court Country Guest Hse, *Reading Road, Hook, Basingstoke, Hants, RG27 9DB.*
Quiet setting in beautiful gardens.
Open: All Year
Grades: ETB 2 Cr, AA 2 Q, RAC Listed
01256 762178 Mrs Jennions
Fax no: 01256 762 178
Rates fr: *£18.00*-**£22.00**.
Beds: 1F 3D 1T 1S
Baths: 5 Private 1 Shared
(0) (6)

Hordle

National Grid Ref: SZ2795

Royal Oak

Shamrox Guest House, *96 Everton Road, Hordle, Lymington, Hants, SO41 0FD.*
Comfortable, secluded, adjacent Forest & sea.
Open: All Year (not Xmas)
01425 615123 Mr Hoy
Rates fr: *£13.00*-**£13.00**.
Beds: 1D 1T 1S **Baths:** 1 Shared
(3)

Horton Heath

National Grid Ref: SU4916

Fox & Hounds

Sandelwood, *Knowle Lane, Horton Heath, Eastleigh, Hants, SO50 7DZ.*
Quiet country house, friendly atmosphere. **Open:** All Year
01703 693726 Mrs Phipp
Rates fr: *£18.00*-**£18.50**.
Beds: 1F 1D **Baths:** 2 Ensuite
(4)

Houghton

National Grid Ref: SU3432

John of Gaunt Inn, Boot Inn

Rowans, *South End, Houghton, Stockbridge, Hants, SO20 6LT.*
C16th Listed cottages, modernised & enlarged.
Open: All Year
01794 388551 Mrs Shea
Rates fr: *£24.00*-**£22.00**.
Beds: 1D 1T 2S
Baths: 1 Private 1 Shared
(3) (3)

Hythe

National Grid Ref: SU4207

The Croft

Four Seasons Hotel, *Hamilton Road, Hythe, Southampton, Hants, SO45 3PD.*
Friendly family-run licensed hotel.
Open: All Year
01703 845151 (also fax no)
Mr & Mrs Robinson
Rates fr: *£17.50*-**£17.50**.
Beds: 3F 2D 3T 2S
Baths: 4 Private 3 Shared
(10)

Itchen Stoke

National Grid Ref: SU5532

The Parsonage, *Itchen Stoke, Alresford, Hants, SO24 0QU.*
Modern house, quiet rural setting.
Open: All Year
01962 732123 Mrs Pitt
Rates fr: *£14.00*-**£14.00**.
Beds: 1T
Baths: 1 Shared
(20)

Kilmeston

National Grid Ref: SU5926

Dean Farm, *Kilmeston, Alresford, Hants, SO24 0NL.*
Peaceful & comfortable C18th farmhouse.
Open: All Year (not Xmas)
01962 771286 Mrs Warr
Rates fr: *£17.00*-**£17.00**.
Beds: 1F 2D
Baths: 1 Shared
(10) (3)

Kingsclere

National Grid Ref: SU5258

Swan

Cleremede, *Foxs Lane, Kingsclere, Newbury, Hants, RG15 8SL.*
Secluded house with large garden.
Open: All Year
Grades: ETB 2 Cr, Comm
01635 297298 Mrs Salm
Rates fr: *£20.00*-**£21.00**.
Beds: 2T 1S
Baths: 2 Ensuite 1 Private
(10) (7)

Kingston

National Grid Ref: SU1402

Woolpack

Greenacres Farmhouse, *Christchurch Road, Kingston, Ringwood, Hants, BH24 3BJ.*
Large Victorian private house.
Open: All Year
01425 480945
Mrs Armstrong
Rates fr: *£15.00*-**£15.00**.
Beds: 1D 2T
Baths: 2 Shared
(7)

Langley

National Grid Ref: SU4400

Langley Tavern

Langley Village Restaurant and Guest House, *Lepe Road, Langley, Southampton, Hants, SO45 1XR.*
On edge of New Forest.
Open: All Year (not Xmas)
01703 891667 Mrs McEvoy
Rates fr: *£16.50*-**£16.50**.
Beds: 1D 1T 2S
Baths: 1 Shared
(12) (10)

Liphook

National Grid Ref: SU8431

Black Fox, Prince of Wales

***The Bailiffs Cottage,** Home Farm, Hollycombe, Liphook, Hants, GU30 7LR.*
Open: All Year
01428 722171 Mrs Jenner
Rates fr: *£16.50*-**£16.50**.
Beds: 1T 1S
Baths: 1 Shared
(3)
Welcoming, attractive cottage & garden on arable & sheep farm. Beautiful views. Within easy reach London, Chichester, Portsmouth. Own choice of breakfast from good menu.

***Old Barn Farm,** Hewshott Lane, Liphook, Hants, GU30 7SY.*
C18th comfortable farmhouse, friendly atmosphere.
Open: All Year
01428 722644 Mr Gilbert
Rates fr: *£19.00*-**£19.00**.
Beds: 2D 2S
Baths: 2 Private 1 Shared
(14) (10)

Little London

National Grid Ref: SU6259

***Bangla,** Silchester Road, Little London, Basingstoke, Hants, RG26 5EP.*
Comfortable & homely chalet bungalow.
Open: All Year
01256 850735 Mrs Baker
Rates fr: *£15.00*-**£13.50**.
Beds: 1D 1T 1S
Baths: 2 Shared
(4)

Lymington

National Grid Ref: SZ3295

Wagon & Horses, Mayflower Hotel, Crown Inn. Fishermans Rest, The Kings Head

***Ferrypoint House,** Lymington, Hants, SO41 8SB.*
Open: All Year
01590 675665 Mrs Nineham
Rates fr: *£19.00*-**£20.00**.
Beds: 4F 4D 2T
Baths: 4 Ensuite
(20)
Riverside location with superb views of river, marinas, the Solent & Isle of Wight. On edge of New Forest in busy market town.

Always telephone to get directions to the B&B - you will save time!

***The White Lyon,** 113 High Street, Lymington, Hants, SO41 9AP.*
Open: All Year
01590 672276 Mrs Baddock
Rates fr: *£20.00*-**£25.00**.
Beds: 2D 2T
Baths: 4 Ensuite
(5)
Lymington town's only freehouse & oldest pub. Recently refurbished, situated in the New Forest and a short walk from the marinas. Secluded, walled garden.

***Our Bench Guest House,** 9 Lodge Road, Pennington, Lymington, Hants, SO41 8HH.*
Edge of Forest, heated pool/jacuzzi.
Open: All Year (not Xmas)
Grades: ETB 3 Cr, Comm, AA 4 Q, Select, RAC Acclaim
01590 673141 Mrs Lewis
Rates fr: *£20.00*-**£20.00**.
Beds: 2D 1T **Baths:** 3 Ensuite
(14) (5)

***Jevington Guest House,** 47 Waterford Lane, Lymington, Hants, SO41 9PT.*
Open: All Year
01590 672148 Mr & Mrs Carruthers
Rates fr: *£17.00*-**£25.00**.
Beds: 1F 1D 1T **Baths:** 3 Ensuite
(3)
Idealy located between marinas and old market town, convenient for the Isle of Wight, New Forest, Coastal Walks. Good pups, restaurants, within walking distance.

***Admiral House,** 5 Stanley Road, Lymington, Hants, SO41 3SJ.*
Victorian semi. Owner next door.
Open: All Year
Grades: ETB Listed
01590 674339 Mrs Wild
Rates fr: *£11.00*-**£11.00**.
Beds: 2F 1T **Baths:** 1 Shared
(1)

***Efford Cottage,** Milford Road, Everton, Lymington, Hants, SO41 0JD.*
Open: All Year
Grades: ETB 3 Cr, Comm, AA 4 Q, Select, RAC Acclaim
01590 642315 / 0374 703075
Mrs Ellis **Fax no: 01590 642315**
Rates fr: *£19.00*-**£20.00**.
Beds: 1F 3D 1T **Baths:** 3 Ensuite
(12) (4)
Friendly, spacious, part-Georgian family home. Four course, multi-choice breakfast. Homemade bread, preserves. Traditional country cooking, by professional chef, using homegrown produce. Good touring location. Parking.

***Hideaway,** Middle Common Road, Pennington, Lymington, Hants, SO41 8LE.*
Quiet chalet house. Private parking.
Open: All Year (not Xmas)
Grades: ETB Listed
01590 676974 Mrs Pickford
Rates fr: *£18.00*-**£25.00**.
Beds: 1F 1D 1T **Baths:** 3 Ensuite
(3)

***Wheatsheaf House,** 25 Gosport Street, Lymington, Hants, SO41 9BG.*
Converted C17th coaching inn.
Open: All Year (not Xmas)
01590 679208
Mrs Cutmore
Rates fr: *£25.00*-**£28.00**.
Beds: 3F
Baths: 2 Ensuite 1 Private
(2)

Lyndhurst

National Grid Ref: SU2908

New Forest Inn, Mailmans Arms

***Furzey Lawn,** Romsey Road, Lyndhurst, Hants, SO43 7FL.*
Comfortable Victorian house of character.
Open: Mar to Oct
01703 282011
Mrs Green
Rates fr: *£16.00*-**£16.00**.
Beds: 1D 1S
Baths: 1 Shared
(2)

***Rose Cottage Guest House,** Chapel Lane, Lyndhurst, Hants, SO43 7FG.*
Charming C17th cottage - quiet position.
Open: All Year
01703 283413 (also fax no)
Mrs Hiscock
Rates fr: *£16.00*-**£20.00**.
Beds: 1F 2D
Baths: 1 Ensuite 1 Shared
(8) (5)

***Laurels Guest House,** 9 Wellands Road, Lyndhurst, Hants, SO43 7AB.*
Comfortable home in New Forest.
Open: All Year (not Xmas)
01703 282545
Rates fr: *£16.00*-**£20.00**.
Beds: 1F 1D 1T
Baths: 1 Private
(2) (1)

***Little Hayes Guest House,** 43 Romsey Road, Lyndhurst, Hants, SO43 7AR.*
Beautifully restored Victorian family home.
Open: Mar to Oct
Grades: ETB 2 Cr, High Comm
01703 283000
Mr Robinson
Rates fr: *£17.00*-**£22.00**.
Beds: 2D 1T
Baths: 1 Private 1 Shared
(10) (3)

***Forest Cottage,** High Street, Lyndhurst, Hants, SO43 7BH.*
Charming 300-year-old cottage.
Open: All Year (not Xmas)
Grades: ETB Listed, Comm
01703 283461
Mrs Rowland
Rates fr: *£17.00*-**£18.00**.
Beds: 1D 1T 1S
Baths: 2 Shared
(14) (3)

Medstead

National Grid Ref: SU6537

French Horn, New Tree
Lower Wield

***Ramjaks,** High Street, Medstead, Alton, Hants, GU34 5LW.*
Modern private house in village.
Open: All Year (not Xmas)
01420 562601 Mrs Williams
Rates fr: *£14.00*-**£15.00**.
Beds: 1D 1T
Baths: 1 Shared
(2)

***East Barrow,** Wield Road, Medstead, Alton, Hants, GU34 5NJ.*
Modern house. Wonderful views.
Open: All Year (not Xmas)
01420 564148 Mrs Davies
Rates fr: *£15.50*.
Beds: 2T 1D
Baths: 1 Shared
(3)

Meonstoke

National Grid Ref: SU6119

***Harvestgate Farm,** Stocks Lane, Meonstoke, Southampton, Hants, SO32 3NQ.*
Modernised farmhouse in beautiful countryside.
Open: All Year
01489 877675 Mrs Allan
Rates fr: *£18.00*-**£18.00**.
Beds: 1D 2T
Baths: 1 Ensuite 2 Private
(15) (5)

Milford on Sea

National Grid Ref: SZ2891

***Compton Hotel,** 59 Keyhaven Road, Milford on Sea, Lymington, Hants, SO41 0QX.*
Private hotel comfortable & friendly.
Open: All Year (not Xmas)
Grades: ETB 2 Cr
01590 643117 Mr Emberson
Rates fr: *£18.00*-**£18.00**.
Beds: 1F 6D
Baths: 4 Private 2 Shared
(8)

Minstead

National Grid Ref: SU2811

Trusty Servant, New Forest Inn

***Grove House,** Minstead, Lyndhurst, Hants, SO43 7GG.*
Comfortable, quiet, New Forest farmhouse.
Open: All Year
Grades: ETB Listed
01703 813211 Mrs Dixon
Rates fr: *£15.00*-**£18.00**.
Beds: 1F
Baths: 1 Private

***Lyngs,** Seamans Lane, Minstead, Lyndhurst, Hants, SO43 7FU.*
Excellent facilities, DIY stabling paddock.
Open: All Year (not Xmas)
01703 813428 Mrs Sizer
Rates fr: *£17.50*.
Beds: 1D 1T
Baths: 1 Private
(6)

Mockbeggar

National Grid Ref: SU1609

Tudor Rose

***Plantation Cottage,** Mockbeggar, Ringwood, Hants, BH24 3NQ.*
Charming 200-year-old cottage.
Open: All Year
Grades: ETB 2 Cr, High Comm
01425 477443 Mrs Yates
Rates fr: *£17.50*-**£20.00**.
Beds: 2D
Baths: 2 Private

Monk Sherbourne

National Grid Ref: SU6056

***Manor Farm,** Monk Sherbourne, Basingstoke, Hants, RG26 5HW.*
Farmhouse in rural setting.
Open: All Year (not Xmas)
01256 850889 Mrs Dalgarno
Rates fr: *£15.00*-**£20.00**.
Beds: 2D 1T
Baths: 1 Shared
(10)

Nether Wallop

National Grid Ref: SU3036

Tally Ho

***The Great Barn,** Five Bells Lane, Nether Wallop, Stockbridge, Hants, SO20 8EN.*
Converted C16th Hampshire barn.
Open: All Year (not Xmas)
Grades: ETB 2 Cr, High Comm
01264 782142 Mrs Quaife
Rates fr: *£18.00*-**£26.00**.
Beds: 1D 1T
Baths: 2 Ensuite
(2)

Netley Abbey

National Grid Ref: SU4508

***La Casa Blanca,** 48 Victoria Road, Netley Abbey, Southampton, Hants, SO31 5DQ.*
Small, licensed family hotel.
Open: All Year
Grades: ETB 2 Cr, Comm, AA 3 Q, Recomm
01703 453718 (also fax no)
Mr Poole
Rates fr: *£23.00*-**£26.00**.
Beds: 1F 2D 2T 4S
Baths: 9 Private
(4)

***Garland Villa Guest House,** 59 New Road, Netley Abbey, Southampton, Hants, SO31 5AD.*
Spacious, friendly, comfortable Victorian dwelling.
Open: All Year (not Xmas)
01703 453419 Mrs Rockell
Rates fr: *£14.00*-**£14.00**.
Beds: 3D 3T 1S
Baths: 2 Shared
(1) (4)

New Alresford

National Grid Ref: SU5832

***Hunters Restaurant,** 32 Broad Street, New Alresford, Hants, SO24 9AQ.*
Georgian building with guide listed restaurant.
Open: All Year (not Xmas)
01962 732468 (also fax no)
Mr Birmingham
Rates fr: *£23.75*-**£37.50**.
Beds: 2D 1T
Baths: 3 Ensuite

New Forest

National Grid Ref: SU2719

***Pyesmead Farm,** Salisbury Road, New Forest, Romsey, Hants, SO51 6EE.*
Farmhouse on family stock farm.
Open: All Year (not Xmas)
Grades: ETB Listed, Comm
01794 323386 Mrs Pybus
Rates fr: *£15.00*-**£17.00**.
Beds: 2D 1T
Baths: 1 Ensuite 1 Shared
(0)

New Milton

National Grid Ref: SZ2395

Speckled Trout, La Dolce Vita

***Saint Ursula,** 30 Hobart Road, New Milton, Hants, BH25 6EG.*
Ideal for New Forest/coast.
Open: All Year
Grades: AA 4 Q
01425 613515 Mrs Pearce
Rates fr: *£17.00*-**£17.00**.
Beds: 1F 1D 2T 2S
Baths: 2 Private 2 Shared
(4)

North Boarhunt

National Grid Ref: SU6010

***Brackenside,** Tampers Lane, North Boarhunt, Fareham, Hants, PO17 6BX.*
Modern house in country setting.
Open: All Year (not Xmas)
01329 833874 Mr Bishop
Rates fr: *£15.00*-**£15.00**.
Beds: 1F 1D 1S
Baths: 1 Ensuite 1 Shared
(1) (3)

North Warnborough

National Grid Ref: SU7351

***The Jolly Miller,** North Warnborough, Basingstoke, Hants, RG25 1ET.*
Half-timbered building, next to canal.
Open: All Year
01256 702085 Mr Metcalfe
Rates fr: *£21.00*-**£31.00**.
Beds: 1F 2D 3T 2S
Baths: 4 Private 2 Shared
(60)

Ogdens

National Grid Ref: SU1812

***Sandy Corner,** Ogdens North, Ogdens, Fordingbridge, Hants, SP6 2QD.*
Very quiet New Forest location.
Open: All Year
01425 657295
Rates fr: *£18.00*-**£20.00**.
Beds: 2D 1T
Baths: 2 Ensuite 1 Private
(4)

Otterbourne

National Grid Ref: SU4623

***Rose Cottage,** Winchester Road, Otterbourne, Winchester, Hants, SO21 2EQ.*
Old English cottage, lovely bedrooms.
Open: All Year
01962 713926 Mrs Mayle
Rates fr: *£16.50*-**£27.50**.
Beds: 1F 1D
Baths: 1 Private 1 Shared
(5) (3)

Owslebury

National Grid Ref: SU4829

Ship Inn, Milburys

***Mays Farmhouse,** Longwood Dene, Owslebury, Winchester, Hants, SO21 1JR.*
Lovely C16th farmhouse, beautiful countryside.
Open: All Year
01962 777486 Mrs Ashby
Rates fr: *£18.00*-**£23.00**.
Beds: 1F 1D 1T
Baths: 3 Private
(7) (5)

Pamber Green

National Grid Ref: SU6059

***The Old House,** Pamber Green, Basingstoke, Hants, RG26 6AE.*
Well-established guest house since 1976.
Open: All Year (not Xmas)
01734 814681 Mrs Lelliott
Rates fr: *£13.00*-**£18.00**.
Beds: 1D 1S 1S
Baths: 1 Private
(4)

Park Gate

National Grid Ref: SU5108

Village Inn, Tallishaw Inn

***Four Winds Guest House,** 17 Station Road, Park Gate, Southampton, Hants, SO31 7GJ.*
Near Junction 9, M27.
Open: All Year
Grades: ETB Listed, Approv
01489 584433 Mr & Mrs Yates
Rates fr: *£18.00*-**£22.00**.
Beds: 1F 4T 1S
Baths: 1 Private 2 Shared
(6)

***60 Southampton Road,** Park Gate, Southampton, Hants, SO31 6AF.*
Friendly welcome. Quiet, convenient location.
Open: All Year (not Xmas)
Grades: ETB Listed
01489 573994 Mrs White
Rates fr: *£15.00*-**£15.00**.
Beds: 1F 1D 1S
Baths: 1 Shared
(4)

Pennington

National Grid Ref: SZ3194

Hare & Hounds

***Restormel,** Sway Road, Pennington, Lymington, Hants, SO41 8LJ.*
Character country 'home from home'.
Open: All Year (not Xmas)
01590 673875
Mrs Morgan
Rates fr: *£16.00*-**£20.00**.
Beds: 1F 1T
Baths: 1 Ensuite 1 Private
(3)

Petersfield

National Grid Ref: SU7423

Five Bells, Good Intent

***Heath Farmhouse,** Sussex Road, Petersfield, Hants, GU31 4HU.*
Pretty Georgian farmhouse near town.
Open: All Year (not Xmas)
Grades: ETB 2 Cr, Comm
01730 264709
Mrs Scurfield
Rates fr: *£17.00*-**£17.00**.
Beds: 1D 1T
Baths: 1 Ensuite 1 Shared
(4)

***Ridgefield,** Station Road, Petersfield, Hants, GU32 3DE.*
Family atmosphere, near town centre.
Open: All Year (not Xmas)
01730 261402 Mrs West
Rates fr: *£18.00*-**£18.00**.
Beds: 1D 2T
Baths: 2 Shared
(4)

***Forge Cottage,** Village Street, Sheet, Petersfield, Hants, GU32 2AQ.*
C16th cottage on village green.
Open: All Year (not Xmas)
01730 268568
Ms Mathiot
Rates fr: *£13.50*-**£19.50**.
Beds: 1D 1T 1S
Baths: 1 Shared
(2)

Plaitford

National Grid Ref: SU2719

Red Rover

***Southernwood,** Plaitford Common, Salisbury Road, Plaitford, Romsey, Hants, SO51 6EE.*
Easy reach Salisbury, Winchester, continental ferries.
Open: All Year
Grades: ETB Listed
01794 323255 Mrs Hocking
Rates fr: *£13.00*-**£20.00**.
Beds: 2F 3D 1T**Baths:** 2 Private
(0) (6)

Portchester

National Grid Ref: SU6105

The Cormorant

***Appletrees,** 144 Castle Street, Portchester, Fareham, Hants, PO16 9QH.*
Quiet location near Portchester Castle. **Open:** All Year
01705 370376 Mrs Jones
Rates fr: *£15.00*-**£15.00**.
Beds: 1T 1S**Baths:** 2 Shared
(3)

Portsmouth

National Grid Ref: SU6501

Rusty Cutter, Seafarers

***Hamilton House,** 95 Victoria Road North, Portsmouth, Southsea, Hants, PO5 1PS.*
Open: All Year
Grades: ETB 2 Cr, Comm, AA 3 Q, Recomm, RAC Acclaim
01705 823502 (also fax no)
Mr & Mrs Tubb
Rates fr: *£17.00*-**£17.00**.
Beds: 3F 3D 2T 1S
Baths: 4 Private 2 Shared
Delightful AA/RAC Victorian townhouse, many original features, bright modern rooms. 5 minutes - continental & IoW ferry terminals, tourist attractions, city centre, university, Guildhall and stations.

The lowest **single** *rate is shown in* **bold.**

Hillside Lodge, *1 Blake Road, Farlington, Portsmouth, Hants,* *PO6 1ET.*
Comfortable house near continental ferries.
Open: All Year
Grades: ETB Listed, Comm
01705 372687
Mrs Wood
Rates fr: *£13.00*-**£13.00**.
Beds: 1D 1T 1S
Baths: 1 Private 1 Shared

Privett

National Grid Ref: SU6726

Thatched Cottage Farm, *Filmore Hill, Privett, Alton, Hants,* *GU34 3NX.*
C16th thatched, beamed drovers cottage. **Open:** All Year
Grades: ETB Listed, High Comm
01730 828278 Mr Thorne
Rates fr: *£20.00*-**£20.00**.
Beds: 1T 1S
Baths: 1 Shared
(5) (5)

Quarley

National Grid Ref: SU2743

Plough Inn

Lains Cottage, *Quarley, Andover, Hants,* *SP11 8PX.*
Comfortable thatched house in country setting.
Open: All Year
Grades: ETB Listed, Comm
01264 889697 Mrs Hicks
Rates fr: *£20.00*-**£25.00**.
Beds: 2T 1D
Baths: 3 Ensuite
(8) (8)

Ringwood

National Grid Ref: SU1505

Fish Inn, Old Beams Inn, Woolpack, Fish Inn

Picket Hill House, *Picket Hill, Ringwood, Hants,* *BH24 3HH.*
New Forest - large country house.
Open: All Year (not Xmas)
Grades: ETB 2 Cr, Comm
01425 476173
Mrs Pocock
Fax no: 01425 470022
Rates fr: *£17.00*-**£25.00**.
Beds: 2D 1T
Baths: 2 Ensuite 1 Private
(10) (6)

National Grid References are for villages, towns and cities - *not* for individual houses.

Greenacres Farmhouse, *Christchurch Road, Kingston, Ringwood, Hants,* *BH24 3BJ.*
Large Victorian private house.
Open: All Year
01425 480945
Mrs Armstrong
Rates fr: *£15.00*-**£15.00**.
Beds: 1D 2T
Baths: 2 Shared
(7)

Maybridge, *Bickerley, Ringwood, Hants,* *BH24 1EQ.*
Attractive, comfortable home. Riverside garden.
Open: Easter to Oct
01425 472657 Mrs Hiscock
Rates fr: *£15.00*-**£15.00**.
Beds: 1D 1T 1S
Baths: 1 Private 1 Shared
(6)

Highdene Guest House, *Warren Lane, Hurn Road, Ringwood, Hants,* *BH24 2AR.*
Comfortable family home.
Open: All Year (not Xmas)
01425 472758 Ms Evans
Rates fr: *£15.00*-**£15.00**.
Beds: 1D 1T 1S
Baths: 1 Ensuite 1 Private 1 Shared
(3)

Rockbourne

National Grid Ref: SU1118

Rose & Thistle

Shearings, *Rockbourne, Fordingbridge, Hants,* *SP6 3NA.*
C16th timber framed thatched cottage. **Open:** Feb to Dec
01725 518256 Mr & Mrs Watts
Fax no: 01725 518255
Rates fr: *£23.00*-**£23.00**.
Beds: 1D 1T 1S **Baths:** 3 Private
(12) (5)

Romsey

National Grid Ref: SU3521

Abbey Hotel, Hatchet Inn, Luzborough House

Wessex Guest House, *5 Palmerston Street, Romsey, Hants,* *SO51 8FL.*
Georgian, Grade II Listed building.
Open: All Year (not Xmas)
01794 512038 Mrs Edwards
Rates fr: *£18.00*-**£18.00**.
Beds: 2F 4D 1T 1S
Baths: 3 Shared
(8)

Woodlands Guest House, *Bunny Lane, Sherfield English, Romsey, Hants,* *SO51 6FT.*
Close Salisbury, ferries, Forest, Southampton.
01794 884840 Mrs Hayter
Rates fr: *£14.00*-**£15.00**.
Beds: 1F 1D 1T
Baths: 1 Ensuite 1 Shared
(6)

Chalet Guest House, *105 Botley Road, Romsey, Hants,* *SO51 5RQ.*
Small family run guest house.
Open: All Year
01794 517299 Mrs Male
Rates fr: *£16.00*-**£16.00**.
Beds: 2F 1D
Baths: 2 Ensuite 1 Shared
(4)

Rowlands Castle

National Grid Ref: SU7310

Three Coins Restaurant

The Fountain Inn, *34 The Green, Rowlands Castle, Havant, Hants,* *PO9 6AB.*
Coaching inn on village green.
Open: All Year
Grades: ETB Listed, Approv
01705 412291 Mr Hargest
Fax no: 01705 413945
Rates fr: *£18.00*-**£24.00**.
Beds: 2F 4D 1T 1S
Baths: 3 Private 1 Shared
(20)

Selborne

National Grid Ref: SU7433

The Queens & The Limes, *High Street, Selborne, Alton, Hants,* *GU34 3JH.*
Comfortable family-run establishments. **Open:** All Year
01420 511454 Mr Paton
Rates fr: *£20.00*-**£28.00**.
Beds: 2F 6T 2S
Baths: 6 Private 2 Shared
(30)

Sherfield English

National Grid Ref: SU2922

Hatchet Inn

Woodlands Guest House, *Bunny Lane, Sherfield English, Romsey, Hants,* *SO51 6FT.*
Close Salisbury, ferries, forest, Southampton.
01794 884840 Mrs Hayter
Rates fr: *£14.00*-**£15.00**.
Beds: 1F 1D 1T
Baths: 1 Ensuite 1 Shared
(6)

Shipton Bellinger

National Grid Ref: SU2345

Boot Inn

Parsonage Farm, *Shipton Bellinger, Tidworth, Hants,* *SP9 7UF.*
Open: All Year (not Xmas)
Grades: ETB 1 Cr, Comm
01980 842404 Col & Mrs Peecock
Rates fr: *£17.50*-**£20.00**.
Beds: 1F 2T
Baths: 1 Private 1 Shared
(10) (6)
A comfortable family home in a former farmhouse in a quiet Salisbury Plain village. Attractive walled garden, stables, paddocks. A303 1.5 miles.

Shootash

National Grid Ref: SU3222

The Hatchet

Kintail, *Salisbury Road, Shootash, Romsey, Hants, SO51 6GA.*
Quiet, friendly bungalow close forest.
Open: Feb to Nov
Grades: ETB 1 Cr, Comm
01794 513849
Ms Mansbridge
Rates fr: *£17.00*-**£20.00**.
Beds: 1D 1T
Baths: 2 Private
(6)

Soldridge

National Grid Ref: SU6534

The Ship

Stoney Croft, *Grosvenor Road, Soldridge, Alton, Hants, GU34 5JE.*
Peaceful smallholding in 4 acres.
Open: All Year
01420 562691 Mrs Ringrose
Rates fr: *£15.00*-**£15.00**.
Beds: 1D 1T
Baths: 2 Shared
(4)

South Warnborough

National Grid Ref: SU7247

Royal Oak, Chequers, Hollington Arms

Street Farm House, *The Street, South Warnborough, Basingstoke, Hants, RG29 1RS.*
Open: All Year
Grades: ETB 2 Cr, Comm
01256 862225 (also fax no)
Mrs Turner
Rates fr: *£15.00*-**£26.00**.
Beds: 1F 2T
Baths: 1 Private 1 Shared
(9)
Charming Jacobean farmhouse in village setting. Restored to offer extremely comfortable accommodation. Heated outdoor pool in season, walks. English breakfast. 5 minutes M3, Junction 5.

Southampton

National Grid Ref: SU4213

The Cowherds, Bellemoor Inn

55 The Polygon, *Southampton, Hants, SO15 2BP.*
Family-run guest house.
Open: All Year (not Xmas)
Grades: ETB Listed
01703 333331 Mrs Gilligan
Rates fr: *£12.50*-**£13.00**.
Beds: 2F 1D 1T 2S
Baths: 1 Shared
(5)

Ashelee Lodge, *36 Atherley Road, Shirley, Southampton, Hants, SO15 5DQ.*
Open: All Year
Grades: ETB Listed, Comm, AA Listed
01703 222095 (also fax no)
Mrs Ward
Rates fr: *£14.00*-**£15.00**.
Beds: 1F 1D 1T 1S
Baths: 1 Shared
Homely guest house. Dip pool, garden, TV lounge, home-cooking. Base for historic areas Salisbury, Stonehenge, New Forest. Easy reach Southampton Docks, Stenaline ferries, station. 0.5 mile city. Pat Ward.

Beacon Guest House, *49 Archers Road, Southampton, Hants, SO15 2NF.*
Convenient city life, countryside, ferries. **Open:** All Year (not Xmas)
Grades: ETB Listed
01703 225910 (also fax no)
Mrs Clark
Rates fr: *£13.50*-**£14.50**.
Beds: 3F 2D 1T 1S
Baths: 2 Shared
(4)

Pages Place Guest House, *14 Porchester Road, Southampton, Hants, SO19 2LD.*
Quiet, friendly, yet near town.
Open: All Year
Grades: ETB Listed
01703 421275 Mrs Smith
Rates fr: *£14.00*-**£14.50**.
Beds: 1D 1T 1S **Baths:** 1 Shared

Alcantara Guest House, *20 Howard Road, Shirley, Southampton, Hants, SO15 5BN.*
Quality accommodation in central location. **Open:** All Year
Grades: ETB Listed, Comm
01703 332966 Mr & Mrs Rose
Rates fr: *£16.00*-**£17.00**.
Beds: 2F 2D 1T 4S
Baths: 3 Private 1 Shared
(2) (7)

Banister House Hotel, *Banister Road, Southampton, Hants, SO15 2JJ.*
Large central town house.
Open: All Year (not Xmas)
Grades: ETB 2 Cr, Comm
01703 221279 Mr Parkinson
Rates fr: *£14.75*-**£21.50**.
Beds: 3F 4D 3T 13S
Baths: 13 Private 4 Shared
(14)

Fenland Guest House, *79 Hill Lane, Southampton, Hants, SO15 5AD.*
Friendly family-run guest house.
Open: All Year (not Xmas)
Grades: ETB Listed, Comm
01703 220360
Rates fr: *£16.00*-**£17.00**.
Beds: 1F 2D 2T 2S
Baths: 3 Ensuite 1 Shared
(6)

Madison House, *137 Hill Lane, Southampton, Hants, SO15 5AF.*
Spacious Victorian house, family atmosphere.
Open: All Year (not Xmas)
Grades: ETB 2 Cr, AA Listed
01703 333374 Mrs Foley
Rates fr: *£15.00*-**£15.50**.
Beds: 2F 3D 2T 2S
Baths: 3 Private 2 Shared
(6)

Southsea

National Grid Ref: SZ6499

Town House, Seafarers, Wine Vaults, Coastguard Tavern

Amberly Guest House, *37 Castle Road, Southsea, Hants, PO5 3DE.*
Open: All Year
01705 830563 Mr Pullen
Rates fr: *£18.00*-**£19.00**.
Beds: 3F 2D 2T 1S
Baths: 3 Private 1 Shared
(2)
Central to all arrival/departure terminals. Most tourist attractions within walking distance. Substantial evening meals available. Ideal flat walking area. Junction 12 off M27 (M275).

Norfolk Hotel, *25 Granada Road, Southsea, Hants, PO4 0RD.*
Small friendly close to sea-front.
Open: All Year (not Xmas)
Grades: ETB 3 Cr, Comm
01705 824162 Mr Pilkington
Rates fr: *£16.00*-**£24.00**.
Beds: 2F 5D 2T 2S
Baths: 11 Private
(8)

Lamorna Guest House, *23 Victoria Road South, Southsea, Hants, PO5 2BX.*
Charming Victorian guest house.
Open: All Year
Grades: ETB 1 Cr
01705 811157 Mrs Barratt
Rates fr: *£14.50*-**£16.00**.
Beds: 3F 1D 1T **Baths:** 2 Shared

Woodville Hotel, *6 Florence Road, Southsea, Hants, PO5 2NE.*
Comfortable family-run hotel.
Open: All Year
Grades: ETB 3 Cr
01705 823409 Mr Chaffer
Rates fr: *£17.00*-**£17.00**.
Beds: 2F 3D 2T 3S
Baths: 7 Private 1 Shared
(12)

Aquarius Court Hotel, *34 St Ronans Road, Southsea, Hants, PO4 0PT.*
Comfortable family-run Victorian hotel.
Open: All Year
Grades: ETB 2 Cr, RAC Listed
01705 822872 Mrs Ryder
Rates fr: *£17.00*-**£17.00**.
Beds: 3F 4D 2T 3S
Baths: 4 Ensuite 2 Shared
(6)

Bembell Court Hotel, *69 Festing Road, Southsea, Portsmouth, Hants, PO4 0NQ.*
Friendly family-run licensed hotel.
Open: All Year
Grades: ETB 3 Cr, AA 3 Q, Recomm, RAC Acclaim
01705 735915 Mr Irwin
Rates fr: *£20.00*-**£20.00**.
Beds: 3F 7D 5T 2S
Baths: 10 Private

Newleaze Guest House, *11 St Edwards Road, Southsea, Hants, PO5 3DH.*
Comfortable family-run guest house.
Open: All Year (not Xmas)
Grades: ETB Listed, Approv
01705 832735 Mrs Inkpen
Rates fr: *£15.00*-**£20.00**.
Beds: 1F 1D 3T 1S
Baths: 1 Ensuite 1 Private 1 Shared
(1)

Hamilton House, *95 Victoria Road North, Southsea, Hants, PO5 1PS.*
Delightful AA/RAC Victorian townhouse, many original features.
Open: All Year
Grades: ETB 2 Cr, Comm, AA 3 Q, Recomm, RAC Acclaim
01705 823502 (also fax no)
Mr & Mrs Tubb
Rates fr: *£17.00*-**£17.00**.
Beds: 3F 3D 2T 1S
Baths: 4 Private 2 Shared

Oakleigh Guest House, *48 Festing Grove, Southsea, Hants, PO4 9QD.*
family-run guest house.
Open: All Year
Grades: ETB Listed
01705 812276 Mr Willett
Rates fr: *£14.00*-**£14.00**.
Beds: 2F 2D 1T 2S
Baths: 1 Shared

Abbey Lodge, *30 Waverley Road, Southsea, Hants, PO5 2PW.*
Large guest house.
Open: All Year (not Xmas)
Grades: ETB 2 Cr, Comm, AA 2 Q
01705 828285 Mrs Forbes
Fax no: 01705 877943
Rates fr: *£15.00*-**£16.00**.
Beds: 2F 2D 2T 3S
Baths: 3 Private 6 Shared

The Elms Guest House, *48 Victoria Road South, Southsea, Hants, PO5 2BT.*
Small guest house. Warm welcome assured.
Open: All Year
Grades: ETB 2 Cr, AA 2 Q
01705 823924 (also fax no)
Mrs Erskine
Rates fr: *£18.00*-**£18.00**.
Beds: 1F 2D 2T 1S
Baths: 2 Ensuite 1 Shared
(2)

The Solent Hotel, *14-17 South Parade, Southsea, Hants, PO5 2JB.*
Very comfortable, family seaside hotel.
Open: All Year
Grades: ETB 4 Cr
01705 875566 Mr De Lara
Rates fr: *£23.75*-**£35.00**.
Beds: 10F 16D 9T 14S
Baths: 50 Private
(5)

Briona Lodge, *16 Herbert Road, Southsea, Hants, PO4 0QA.*
Large Victorian private house.
Open: All Year (not Xmas)
01705 814030
Ms Cross
Rates fr: *£14.00*-**£14.00**.
Beds: 1F 3D 1T 3S
Baths: 2 Shared
(2)

Britannia Guest House, *8 Outram Road, Southsea, Hants, PO5 1QU.*
Large Victorian family rooms.
Open: All Year
Grades: ETB 2 Cr, Comm
01705 814234 Mrs Mitchell
Rates fr: *£16.00*-**£17.00**.
Beds: 4F 1D
Baths: 1 Ensuite 2 Shared

Glenroy Guest House, *28 Waverley Road, Southsea, Hants, PO5 2PW.*
Ideal for touring Hampshire coast.
Open: All Year
Grades: ETB 2 Cr, Approv
01705 814922 Mrs Willis
Rates fr: *£12.00*-**£13.00**.
Beds: 2F 2D 2T 2S

Stratfield Saye

National Grid Ref: SU6861

Parsons Farm, *Stratfield Saye, Reading, Berks, RG7 2DX.*
Self-catering & B&B in beautiful farmhouse.
Open: All Year
01734 333607 Mrs Floyd
Rates fr: *£20.00*-**£30.00**.
Beds: 1D
Baths: 1 Private
(6)

Stuckton

National Grid Ref: SU1613

Three Lions

The Old Posthouse, *Stuckton Road, Stuckton, Fordingbridge, Hants, SP6 2HE.*
Large, comfortable friendly house.
Open: All Year (not Xmas)
01425 657477 Mrs Troy
Fax no: 01425 657963
Rates fr: *£16.00*-**£16.00**.
Beds: 1D 1T 1S
Baths: 2 Shared

Sutton Scotney

National Grid Ref: SU4639

The Swan, Coach & Horses

Dever View, *17 Upper Bullington, Sutton Scotney, Winchester, Hants, SO21 3RB.*
Open: All Year (not Xmas)
Grades: ETB 2 Cr, Comm
01962 760566 Mrs Somerton
Rates fr: *£18.00*-**£25.00**.
Beds: 1D 2T
Baths: 1 Ensuite 2 Shared
(4)
Comfortable warm country cottage in rural setting offering quality B&B. Lots to see and do locally. Only 0.5 mile from main roads, A34, A303.

Sway

National Grid Ref: SZ2798

White Rose Hotel, Hare & Hounds

Squirrels, *Broadmead, Sway, Lymington, Hants, SO41 6DH.*
Friendly comfortable secluded modern home.
Open: All Year (not Xmas)
Grades: ETB 1 Cr, Comm
01590 683163 Mrs Kilford
Rates fr: *£17.00*-**£17.00**.
Beds: 1F 1D 1S
Baths: 2 Private 1 Shared
(8) (6)

Kingfishers, *Coombe Lane, Sway, Lymington, Hampshire, SO41 6BP.*
Comfortable New Forest home.
Open: Easter to End-Oct
01590 682414 Mrs Smith
Fax no: 01590 683460
Rates fr: *£20.00*-**£25.00**.
Beds: 1D 1T
Baths: 2 Private
(6) (4)

Redwing Farm, *Pitmore Lane, Sway, Lymington, Hants, SO41 6BW.*
Beamed cottage farmhouse. Beautifully situated.
Open: All Year
01590 683319 Mrs Dowson
Rates fr: *£20.00*-**£20.00**.
Beds: 2D 2S
Baths: 3 Ensuite
(6)

Timsbury

National Grid Ref: SU3425

The Morthouse, Dukes Head

The Herons, *Heron Lane, Timsbury, Romsey, Hampshire, SO51 0ND.*
Spacious, secluded, country ground floor flat.
Open: All Year
01794 368355 Mrs Murphy
Rates fr: *£20.00*.
Beds: 1D 1T **Baths:** 1 Private
(6)

Titchfield

National Grid Ref: SU5305

***Half Acre,** Brownwich Lane, Titchfield, Fareham, Hants, PO14 4NZ.*
Private house near conservation area.
Open: All Year (not Xmas)
01329 845128 Mr & Mrs Darwent
Rates fr: *£15.00*-**£15.00**.
Beds: 1D 1T
Baths: 1 Private
(10) (3)

Totton

National Grid Ref: SU3513

***Brimar Guest House,** 12-14 High Street, Totton, Southampton, Hants, SO40 4HN.*
Large, comfortable, homely guest house.
Open: All Year
01703 862950
Rates fr: *£15.00*-**£15.00**.
Beds: 2F 2D 6T 2S
Baths: 3 Shared
(7)

***Jubilee Cottage,** 303 Salisbury Road, Totton, Southampton, Hants, SO40 3LZ.*
Large sympathetically modernised Victorian cottage.
Open: All Year
01703 862397 Mrs Hucker
Rates fr: *£16.00*-**£16.00**.
Beds: 1F 1T
Baths: 1 Ensuite 1 Private
(2)

Upper Clatford

National Grid Ref: SU3543

Mayfly Inn

***Malt Cottage,** Upper Clatford, Andover, Hants, SP11 7QL.*
Country house in beautiful grounds.
Open: All Year (not Xmas)
Grades: ETB 2 Cr, High Comm
01264 323469 Mrs Mason
Fax no: 01264 334100
Rates fr: *£20.00*-**£25.00**.
Beds: 1D 1T 1S
Baths: 1 Ensuite 2 Private
(3)

Warblington

National Grid Ref: SU7206

***Warblers Rest,** 11 Castle Avenue, Warblington, Havant, Hants, PO9 2RY.*
Modern detached house.
Open: All Year
01705 486748
Mrs Chessell
Rates fr: *£17.00*-**£17.50**.
Beds: 1D
Baths: 1 Private
(2)

Warnford

National Grid Ref: SU6223

***Hayden Barn Cottage,** Warnford, Southampton, Hants, SO32 3LF.*
Real hospitality, stunning country location.
Open: All Year (not Xmas)
01730 829454 Mrs Broadbent
Rates fr: *£18.50*-**£18.50**.
Beds: 2T 1S
Baths: 1 Ensuite 1 Private 1 Shared
(5)

Warsash

National Grid Ref: SU4906

***1 Wightway Mews,** Warsash, Southampton, Hants, SO31 9AF.*
Modern house close by River Hamble. **Open:** All Year
01489 575684 Mrs Stokes
Rates fr: *£15.00*-**£15.00**.
Beds: 1D 1T
Baths: 1 Private 1 Shared
(2)

West Meon

National Grid Ref: SU6424

***Brocklands Farm,** West Meon, Petersfield, Hants, GU32 1JG.*
Modern light, comfortable farmhouse. **Open:** All Year
01730 829228 Mrs Wilson
Rates fr: *£17.50*-**£17.50**.
Beds: 2D 1T **Baths:** 1 Shared
(6)

West Wellow

National Grid Ref: SU2919

***St Lawrence,** Salisbury Road, West Wellow, Romsey, Hants, SO51 6AP.*
Interesting New Forest cottage, garden. **Open:** All Year
01794 322086 Mrs Rawlings
Rates fr: *£15.00*-**£15.00**.
Beds: 1D 1T **Baths:** 2 Shared
(10) (5)

Weyhill

National Grid Ref: SU3146

***Station House,** Weyhill, Andover, Hants, SP11 8DU.*
Victorian station-master's house, pretty gardens.
Open: All Year (not Xmas)
01264 773430 Mrs Rooke
Rates fr: *£17.50*-**£20.00**.
Beds: 1D 1S **Baths:** 2 Shared
(2)

Wherwell

National Grid Ref: SU3840

***The White Lion,** Wherwell, Andover, Hants, SP11 7JF.*
Large bedrooms with standard fittings.
Open: All Year (not Xmas)
01264 860317 Mr Stent
Rates fr: *£18.00*-**£18.00**.
Beds: 1F 1D 3T **Baths:** 1 Shared
(20)

Wickham

National Grid Ref: SU5711

Kings Head, Greens, White Lion, Old House Hotel, Black Dog

***Montrose,** Shirrell Heath, Wickham, Southampton, Hants, SO32 2HU.*
Open: All Year
Grades: ETB 2 Cr, High Comm
01329 833345 (also fax no)
Mrs Chivers
Rates fr: *£21.00*-**£23.00**.
Beds: 2D 1T
Baths: 1 Private 1 Shared
(4)
Attractive Victorian country house offering accommodation of a high standard in pleasant surroundings. Comfort, personal attention & a warm welcome assured.

***Wickhaven,** 23 School Road, Wickham, Fareham, Hants, PO17 5AA.*
Comfortable rural house, TV lounge.
Open: All Year (not Xmas)
01329 832457 Mrs Toogood
Rates fr: *£14.00*-**£14.00**.
Beds: 1F 1D 1T 1S
Baths: 1 Shared
(1)

***Chiphall Acre,** Droxford Road, Wickham, Fareham, Hants, PO17 5AY.*
Super food - families welcome.
Open: All Year (not Xmas)
01329 833188 Mr & Mrs Stevens
Rates fr: *£17.00*-**£20.00**.
Beds: 1F 1D 1T
Baths: 1 Private 1 Shared
(4)

Winchester

National Grid Ref: SU4829

Bell Inn, Wykeham Arms, Kings Head, Stanhore Hotel, Roebuck, The Queen, Cart & Horses

***5 Ranelagh Road,** Winchester, Hants, SO23 9TA.*
Open: All Year (not Xmas)
Grades: ETB 2 Cr, Comm
01962 869555 Mr Farrell
Rates fr: *£16.00*-**£18.00**.
Beds: 1F 1D 1T 1S
Baths: 2 Private 2 Shared
(5) (2)
Turn of the century Victorian villa, furnished in that style. We are close to the Cathedral and like to share our love of Winchester with our guests.

The lowest *double* rate per person is shown in *italics*.

***Shawlands,** 46 Kilham Lane, Winchester, Hants, SO22 5QD.*
Open: All Year
Grades: ETB 2 Cr, Comm, AA 4 Q, RAC Acclaim
01962 861166 (also fax no)
Mrs Pollock
Rates fr: *£18.0*-**£23.00**.
Beds: 2F 1D 2T
Baths: 1 Private 2 Shared
(5)
Attractive house & beautiful garden in peaceful area. 1 mile from centre of Winchester. Excellent English breakfast including home-made bread and preserves. Payphone.

***85 Christchurch Road,** Winchester, Hants, SO23 9QY.*
Comfortable detached Victorian family house.
Open: All Year (not Xmas)
Grades: ETB 2 Cr, Comm
01962 868661 (also fax no)
Mrs Fetherston-Dilke
Rates fr: *£18.00*-**£18.00**.
Beds: 1D 1T 1S
Baths: 2 Ensuite 1 Shared
(3)

***Acacia,** 44 Kilham Lane, Winchester, Hants, SO22 5PT.*
Open: All Year (not Xmas)
Grades: ETB 2 Cr, Comm
01962 852259 / 0585 462993
Mrs Buchanan
Rates fr: *£19.00*-**£24.00**.
Beds: 1D 2T
Baths: 2 Ensuite 1 Private
(10) (4)
Acacia is a peaceful country home in beautiful gardens, 5 minutes drive to Cathedral, city centre & railway station (London one hour). Portsmouth, Stonehenge 3/4 hour.

***32 Hyde Street,** Winchester, Hants, SO23 7DX.*
Attractive C18th town house.
Open: All Year (not Xmas)
01962 851621 Mrs Tisdall
Rates fr: *£16.00*-**£19.00**.
Beds: 1F 1D **Baths:** 1 Shared
(3)

***The Lilacs,** 1 Harestock Close, Off Andover Road North, Winchester, Hants, SO22 6NP.*
Attractive Georgian-style family home.
Open: All Year (not Xmas)
01962 884122 Mrs Pell
Rates fr: *£16.00*-**£18.00**.
Beds: 1F 1D 1T
Baths: 1 Private 1 Shared
(2)

***Ivy House,** 45 Vernham Road, Winchester, Hants, SO22 6BF.*
Open: All Year (not Xmas)
Grades: ETB High Comm, Listed
01962 855512 Mrs Lampard
Rates fr: *£17.50*-**£17.50**.
Beds: 1D 1T 1S
Baths: 1 Shared
(12) (3)
Situated in quiet residential road, 5 minutes drive city centre. Rooms comfortably furnished, guest lounge, garden & friendly welcome. Special weekend breaks. Phone for brochure.

***Sycamores,** 4 Bereweeke Close, Winchester, Hants, SO22 6AR.*
1930s house, peaceful suburban area.
Open: All Year
Grades: ETB Listed, Comm
01962 867242 Mrs Edwards
Fax no: 01962 620300
Rates fr: *£18.00*.
Beds: 2D 1T
Baths: 3 Private
(3)

***54 St Cross Road,** Winchester, Hants, SO23 9PS.*
Victorian family house, near water meadows.
Open: All Year
Grades: ETB Listed, Comm
01962 852073 (also fax no)
Mrs Blockley
Rates fr: *£17.00*-**£18.00**.
Beds: 1D 1T 1S
Baths: 1 Shared
(5) (2)

***Brambles,** Northbrook Avenue, Winchester, Hants, SO23 0JW.*
Delightful self-contained studio flat.
Open: All Year
Grades: ETB Listed, High Comm
01962 856387 Mrs Meadows
Rates fr: *£18.00*-**£25.00**.
Beds: 1F
Baths: 1 Private
(2)

***Dellbrook,** Hubert Road, St Cross, Winchester, Hants, SO23 9RG.*
Spacious welcoming Edwardian family home.
Open: All Year
Grades: ETB Listed, AA 2 Cr, Comm
01962 865093 (also fax no)
Mrs Leonard
Rates fr: *£19.00*-**£26.00**.
Beds: 1F 2T
Baths: 2 Ensuite 1 Shared
(4)

Winsor

National Grid Ref: SU3114

Compass Inn, Haywain, White Hart

***Bushfriers,** Winsor Road, Winsor, Southampton, Hants, SO40 2HF.*
Character beamed cottage; fine views.
Open: All Year (not Xmas)
01703 812552
Mrs Wright
Rates fr: *£15.00*-**£18.00**.
Beds: 1F 1D
Baths: 1 Shared
(2)

***Budds Farm Guest House,** Winsor Road, Winsor, Southampton, Hants, SO40 2HN.*
Charming, comfortable, modernised thatched farmhouse.
Open: Easter to Oct
01703 812381 Mrs Dawe
Rates fr: *£16.00*-**£16.00**.
Beds: 1F 1D
Baths: 1 Ensuite 1 Private
(3)

Woolton Hill

National Grid Ref: SU4261

Rampany Cat

***Tile Barn House,** Woolton Hill, Newbury, Berks, RG15 9UZ.*
Part large Victorian country house.
Open: All Year
01635 254677
Mrs Mitchell
Rates fr: *£16.00*-**£16.00**.
Beds: 1F 1D
Baths: 1 Ensuite 1 Shared
(0) (10)

Wootton

National Grid Ref: SZ2498

***Valesmoor Farm,** Holmsley Road, Wootton, New Milton, Hants, BH25 5TW.*
Comfortable family home, horsey environment.
Open: Easter to Oct
01425 614487
Mrs Marshallsay
Rates fr: *£14.00*-**£15.00**.
Beds: 1F 1D 1S
Baths: 1 Shared
(3)

Herefordshire

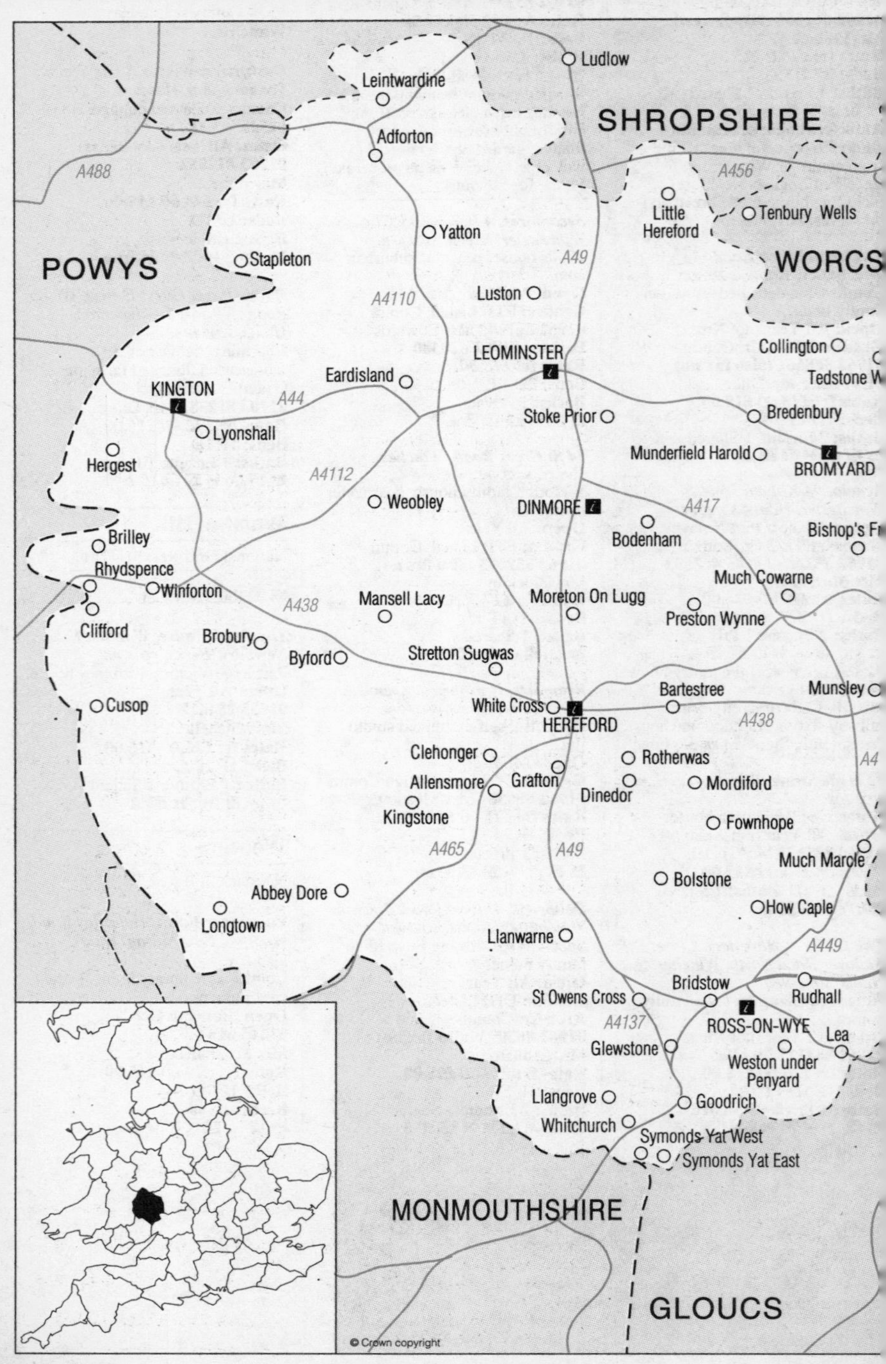

Tourist Information Centres

1 Rowberry Street, **Bromyard**, Herefordshire, HR7 4DX, 01885 482308

Queens Wood, (Nr Leominster), Queens Wood Country Park,**Dinmore**, Herefordshire, HR6 OPY, 01568 797842

1 Kings Street, St Owens Street, **Hereford**, Herefordshire, HR4 9BW, 01432-268430.

2 Mill Street, **Kington**, HR5 3BQ, 01544 230778

3 The Home End, **Ledbury**, Herefordshire, HR8 1BN, 01531 636147.

1 Corn Square, **Leominster**, Herefordshire, HR6 8LR, 01568 616460.

Edde Cross Street, **Ross-on-Wye**, Herefordshire, HR9 7BZ, 01989 562768.

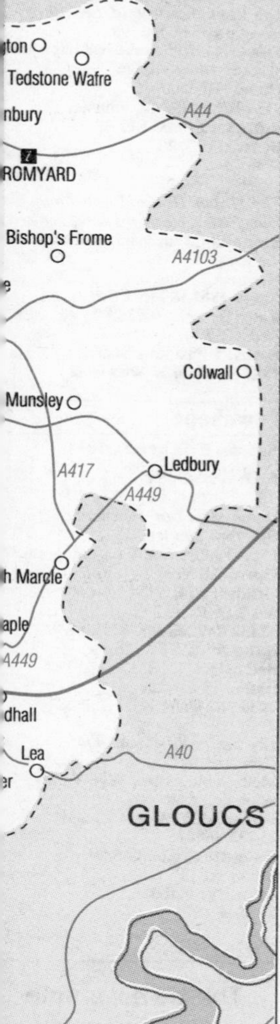

Abbey Dore

National Grid Ref: SO3830

Heavenly House, *Golden Valley, Abbey Dore, Hereford, HR2 0AJ.*
Spacious family home, magical countryside.
Open: All Year (not Xmas)
01981 240841 Miss Cholmondeley
Rates fr: *£16.50*-**£16.50**.
Beds: 1T 1S
Baths: 2 Shared
(10) (2)

Adforton

National Grid Ref: SO4071

Lower House, ***Adforton, Leintwardine, Craven Arms, Shropshire,*** *SY7 0NF.*
Small C17th country guest house.
Open: All Year
01568 770223 Mrs Cutler
Rates fr: *£22.00*-**£22.00**.
Beds: 2D 2T
Baths: 4 Private
(12) (10)

Allensmore

National Grid Ref: SO4635

Three Horseshoes

Holly House, *Allensmore, Hereford, HR2 9BH.*
Elegant farmhouse surrounded by horses.
Open: All Year (not Xmas)
Grades: ETB 2 Cr, Comm
01432 277294 Mrs Sinclair
Rates fr: *£18.00*-**£18.00**.
Beds: 1D 1T
Baths: 1 Ensuite 1 Private

Bartestree

National Grid Ref: SO5641

Lower Bartestree Farm, *Bartestree, Hereford, HR1 4DT.*
Welcoming country farmhouse, wonderful views.
Open: All Year (not Xmas)
Grades: ETB 1 Cr, Approv
01432 851005 Mrs Erskine
Rates fr: *£16.00*-**£20.00**.
Beds: 1F 1T
Baths: 1 Shared
(4)

Bishops Frome

National Grid Ref: SO6648

The Chase Inn, *Bishops Frome, Worcester, Worcs, WR6 5BP.*
Homely country inn with character.
Open: All Year
01885 490234 Mr Ashley
Rates fr: *£18.00*-**£18.00**.
Beds: 3D 2T
Baths: 3 Ensuite 1 Shared
(30)

Bodenham

National Grid Ref: SO5351

Three Crowns (Ullingswick), The Crozens (Felton)

Maund Court, *Bodenham, Hereford, HR1 3JA.*
Open: Mar to Nov
Grades: ETB 2 Cr, High Comm
01568 797282 Mrs Edwards
Rates fr: *£18.00*-**£22.00**.
Beds: 2D 1T
Baths: 3 Ensuite
(6)
Charming C15th farmhouse with large garden, swimming pool and croquet. Golf & pleasant walks nearby. Ideal centre for touring.

Bolstone

National Grid Ref: SO5532

Owls Hoot, *Bolstone, Hereford, HR2 6NB.*
Modern country bungalow. Wildlife / conservation.
Open: All Year
01432 870616 Mrs Kingston
Rates fr: *£16.00*.
Beds: 1D
Baths: 1 Private
(4)

Bredenbury

National Grid Ref: SO6056

Barneby Arms

Red Hill Farm, *Bredenbury, Bromyard, Herefordshire, HR7 4SY.*
Open: All Year (not Xmas)
Grades: ETB Listed
01885 483255 / 483535 Mrs Evans
Fax no: 01885 483535
Rates fr: *£15.00*-**£17.00**.
Beds: 1F 2D 1T
Baths: 1 Shared
(10)
C17th comfortable farmhouse. Peaceful unspoilt countryside, panoramic views. Central for Malvern, Hereford, Worcester, Ledbury, Ludlow. Children & pets welcome. 'Home from home'. On A44 road.

Munderfield Harold, *Bredenbury, Bromyard, Herefordshire, HR7 4SZ.*
Farmhouse Bed & Breakfast with day fishing.
Open: Mar to Dec
01885 482231
Rates fr: *£14.00*-**£14.00**.
Beds: 1F 1D 1T
(7) (10)

Bringing children with you? Always ask for any special rates.

Bridstow

National Grid Ref: SO6024

Lavender Cottage, *Bridstow, Ross-on-Wye, Herefordshire, HR9 6QB.*
Friendly part-C17th family home.
Open: All Year
Grades: ETB Listed
01989 562836 Mrs Nash
Rates fr: *£16.00*-**£16.00**.
Beds: 1D 2T
Baths: 2 Private
(10) (3)

Brilley

National Grid Ref: SO2248

Pentwyn Farm, *Brilley, Hereford, HR3 6HW.*
Working farm.
Open: All Year (not Xmas)
01497 831337 Mrs Price
Rates fr: *£15.00*-**£15.00**.
Beds: 2D 2S
Baths: 1 Shared

Brobury

National Grid Ref: SO3444

Magdalen, *Brobury, Hereford, HR3 6DX.*
C13th chancel & glazed octagon.
Open: All Year
01981 500470 Mrs Phillips
Rates fr: *£18.00*-**£20.00**.
Beds: 2D 2P
Baths: 2 Private
(4)

Bromyard

National Grid Ref: SO6554

Goodships Relaxation Farm, *Avenbury, Bromyard, Herefordshire, HR7 4EZ.*
Private relaxation farm, swimming school.
Open: All Year (not Xmas)
01885 482735 Mrs Setters
Rates fr: *£25.00*-**£25.00**.
Beds: 2D 1T 1S
Baths: 1 Private
(20)

Byford

National Grid Ref: SO3943

Portway Hotel

The Old Rectory, *Byford, Hereford, HR4 7LD.*
Large Georgian rectory, lovely views.
Open: March to Nov
01981 590218 Mrs Mayson
Fax no: 01981 590499
Rates fr: *£19.00*-**£25.00**.
Beds: 2D 1T
Baths: 3 Ensuite

National Grid References are for villages, towns and cities - *not* for individual houses.

Clifford

National Grid Ref: SO2445

Cottage Farm, *Middlewood, Clifford, Hereford, HR3 5SX.*
Working modernised farmhouse. Families welcome.
Open: All Year (not Xmas)
01497 831496 Mrs Jones
Rates fr: *£13.50*-**£14.00**.
Beds: 1F 1T **Baths:** 1 Shared
(4)

Collington

National Grid Ref: SO6460

Granary Licenced Restaurant, *Church House Farm, Collington, Bromyard, Herefordshire, HR7 4NA.*
Converted granary & farm buildings.
Open: All Year
01885 410345 Mrs Naiden
Rates fr: *£19.00*-**£19.00**.
Beds: 1D 4T **Baths:** 5 Private
(40)

Colwall

National Grid Ref: SO7342

Hacketts, *Mathon Road, Colwall, Malvern, Worcs, WR13 6EW.*
Friendly farm house.
Open: Easter to Oct
01684 540261 Mrs Bevan
Rates fr: *£16.00*-**£16.00**.
Beds: 1F 1D 1T 1S
Baths: 1 Shared
(6)

Sunfold, *Walwyn Road, Colwall, Malvern, Worcs, WR13 6PZ.*
Castellated house beneath Malvern Hills.
Open: All Year (not Xmas)
01684 540604
Rates fr: *£21.50*-**£26.50**.
Beds: 1F 3D 1T 1S
Baths: 6 Ensuite
(20)

Cusop

National Grid Ref: SO2341

Swan Hotel, Old Black Lion

Fernleigh, *Hardwick Road, Cusop, Hay-on-Wye, Hereford, HR3 5QX.*
Large Victorian private house.
Open: Easter to Oct
01497 820459 Mr Hughes
Rates fr: *£14.00*-**£18.00**.
Beds: 2D 1T
Baths: 1 Shared

Dinedor

National Grid Ref: SO5336

Crown Inn, Woolhope

Dinedor Court, *Dinedor, Hereford, HR2 6LG.*
Rambling C16th farmhouse; peaceful location.
Open: Easter to Oct
Grades: ETB Listed
01432 870481 Mrs Price
Rates fr: *£18.00*-**£20.00**.
Beds: 1D 1T
Baths: 1 Shared
(10) (4)

Eardisland

National Grid Ref: SO4158

The Elms, *Eardisland, Leominster, Herefordshire, HR6 9BN.*
Spacious farmhouse in picturesque black & white village.
Open: All Year
01544 388405 Mrs Johnson
Rates fr: *£16.00*-**£17.00**.
Beds: 1D 1T 2S

The Manor House, *Eardisland, Leominster, Herefordshire, HR6 9BN.*
Beautiful C17th manor house, log fires.
Open: All Year
01544 388138 Mrs Lowry
Rates fr: *£17.50*-**£25.00**.
Beds: 2D 1T
Baths: 1 Ensuite 1 Shared
(6)

Fownhope

National Grid Ref: SO5834

Green Man

Green Man Inn, *Fownhope, Hereford, HR1 4PE.*
15th Century B&W coaching inn.
Open: All Year
Grades: ETB 3 Cr, Comm, AA 2 St, RAC 2 St
01432 860243 Mr Williams
Rates fr: *£25.00*-**£25.50**.
Beds: 4F 12D 2T 1S
Baths: 19 Ensuite
(70)

The Squirrels, *Fownhope, Hereford, HR1 4PB.*
Modern bungalow, Wye Valley Walk.
Open: All Year (not Xmas)
01432 860413
Rates fr: *£15.00*-**£15.00**.
Beds: 1D 1T
Baths: 1 Shared

The lowest **single** *rate is shown in* **bold.**

Glewstone

National Grid Ref: SO5522

The Skates, *Glewstone, Ross-on-Wye, Herefordshire, HR9 6AZ.*
Comfortable old former farmhouse.
Open: All Year
01989 770456 Mr Williams
Fax no: 01989 770781
Rates fr: *£17.00*-**£22.00**.
Beds: 4D 2T 2S
Baths: 4 Private 3 Shared
(10) (7)

Goodrich

National Grid Ref: SO5719

Jollys, *Goodrich, Ross-on-Wye, Herefordshire, HR9 6HX.*
Above old-fashioned village shop.
Open: All Year (not Xmas)
01600 890135 Mrs Danby
Rates fr: *£18.50*-**£22.00**.
Beds: 2D 1T
Baths: 1 Ensuite 2 Private
(4)

Grafton

National Grid Ref: SO4937

Grafton Inn

Grafton Villa Farm, *Grafton, Hereford, HR2 8ED.*
Superbly appointed character farmhouse.
Open: All Year (not Xmas)
Grades: ETB 2 Cr, High Comm, AA 4 Q, Select
01432 268689 Mrs Layton
Rates fr: *£18.00*-**£20.00**.
Beds: 2D 1T **Baths:** 3 Ensuite
(5)

Hereford

National Grid Ref: SO5140

Chelsey House, *9 Southbank Road, Hereford, HR1 2TJ.*
Open: All Year
Grades: ETB 2 Cr, Comm
01432 274800 Mr Jones
Rates fr: *£18.00*-**£20.00**.
Beds: 1D 2T
Baths: 3 Ensuite
(6)
This comfortable family-run guest house (est. 1984) in a former Victorian vicarage is surrounded by a lovely walled garden & located in a quiet residential road 0.75 mile east of the city centre (bus/train stations 5 mins walk). Full ensuite rooms with colour TV and coffee/tea making facilities. Write or phone for brochure.

The lowest *double* rate per person is shown in *italics*.

The lowest *double* rate per person is shown in *italics*.

Somerville Hotel, *Bodenham Road, Hereford, HR1 2TS.*
Comfortable privately owned quiet hotel.
Open: All Year (not Xmas)
Grades: ETB 2 Cr, Comm, AA 2 St
01432 273991 Mr Westwood
Rates fr: *£15.00*-**£18.00**.
Beds: 2F 4D 2T 4S
Baths: 6 Private 2 Shared
(12)

Sink Green Farm, *Rotherwas, Hereford, HR2 6LE.*
Open: All Year (not Xmas)
Grades: ETB 2 Cr, Comm, AA 4 Q, Select
01432 870223 Mr Jones
Rates fr: *£18.00*-**£19.00**.
Beds: 2D 1T
Baths: 3 Private
(10)
C16th farmhouse overlooking the peaceful, picturesque River Wye, yet only 3 miles from the cathedral city of Hereford. Superior ensuite rooms, four poster available.

Hergest

National Grid Ref: SO2753

Bucks Head House, *Upper Hergest, Hergest, Kington, Herefordshire, HR5 3EW.*
Modern, comfortable farmhouse, central heating.
Open: All Year
01544 231063 Mrs Protheroe
Rates fr: *£16.00*-**£17.00**.
Beds: 2F 2D 1T 1S
Baths: 2 Shared
(6)

Empton Farm, *Lower Hergest, Hergest, Kington, Herefordshire, HR5 3ES.*
Peaceful old black-and-white farmhouse.
Open: Easter to Oct
01544 230153 Mrs James
Rates fr: *£15.00*-**£15.00**.
Beds: 1F 1D
Baths: 1 Shared

How Caple

National Grid Ref: SO6030

White House, *How Caple, Hereford, HR1 4SR.*
Comfortable farmhouse, also cottage.
Open: All Year (not Xmas)
01989 740644 Mrs Edwards
Rates fr: *£15.00*-**£15.00**.
Beds: 1D 1T **Baths:** 1 Shared
(3)

Kingstone

National Grid Ref: SO4235

Madley Arms, Red Lion

Webton Court Farmhouse, *Kingstone, Hereford, HR2 9NF.*
Open: All Year (not Xmas)
Grades: ETB 2 Cr
01981 250220
Mrs Andrews
Rates fr: *£14300*-**£15.00**.
Beds: 3F 2D 3T 1S
Baths: 2 Private 2 Shared
(0) (10)
Large Grade II Listed Georgian black-and-white farm house, set in quiet location. Open all year (not Xmas). Home cooking a speciality.

Kington

National Grid Ref: SO2956

Royal Oak, Swan Inn

Bucks Head House, *Upper Hergest, Hergest, Kington, Herefordshire, HR5 3EW.*
Modern, comfortable farmhouse, central heating.
Open: All Year
01544 231063
Mrs Protheroe
Rates fr: *£16.00*-**£17.00**.
Beds: 2F 2D 1T 1S
Baths: 2 Shared
(6)

Church House, *Church Road, Kington, Herefordshire, HR5 3AG.*
Sodden walkers always welcome here! Large Georgian family house.
Open: All Year (not Xmas)
01544 230534
Mrs Darwin
Fax no: 01544 231100
Rates fr: *£20.00*-**£20.00**.
Beds: 1D 1T
Baths: 1 Shared
(2)

Royal Oak Inn, *Church Street, Kington, Herefordshire, HR5 3BE.*
Traditional friendly family-run inn.
Open: All Year
01544 230484
Mrs Thompson
Rates fr: *£18.00*-**£18.00**.
Beds: 1F 1D 1T 1S
Baths: 1 Shared
(5) (4)

2 Bradnor View Close, *Kington, Herefordshire, HR5 3UA.*
Modern bungalow with lovely views.
Open: All Year (not Xmas)
01544 231208 Mrs Condon
Rates fr: *£11.50*-**£11.50**.
Beds: 1D 1T 1S
Baths: 1 Private 1 Shared
(10) (1)

The lowest **single** *rate is shown in* **bold.**

Cambridge Cottage, *19 Church Street, Kington, Herefordshire, HR5 3BE.*
C17th cottage; Offa's Dyke Path.
Open: All Year (not Xmas)
01544 231300
Mr & Mrs Hooton
Rates fr: *£13.50*-**£13.50**.
Beds: 1F 1S
Baths: 1 Ensuite 1 Shared
(2)

Lea

National Grid Ref: SO6521

Farmers Boy, Pennyfarthing

Brook House, *Lea, Ross-on-Wye, Herefordshire, HR9 7JZ.*
Listed, Queen Anne village house.
Open: All Year
01989 750710
Rates fr: *£20.00*-**£25.00**.
Beds: 2D 1T
Baths: 3 Ensuite 1 Shared
(7) (4)

Ledbury

National Grid Ref: SO7037

The Royal Oak Hotel, *The South End, Ledbury, Herefordshire, HR8 2EY.*
C15th coaching inn.
Open: All Year
01531 632110 Mr Riga
Rates fr: *£18.50*-**£19.50**.
Beds: 2F 3D 5T 9S
Baths: 7 Private 3 Shared
(20)

Leintwardine

National Grid Ref: SO4074

Millfield House, *Leintwardine, Ludlow, Shropshire, SY7 0LB.*
Comfortable country house, large gardens.
Open: All Year (not Xmas)
01547 540356 Mrs Wixted
Rates fr: *£13.50*-**£13.50**.
Beds: 1D 1T 1S
Baths: 1 Shared
(10) (10)

Leominster

National Grid Ref: SO4959

Stockton Cross Inn, Barons Cross Inn, Royal Oak

Woonton Court Farm, *Leysters, Leominster, Herefordshire, HR6 0HL.*
Comfortable Tudor farmhouse, own produce.
Open: All Year (not Xmas)
Grades: ETB 1 Cr, Approv, AA 1 Q, Recomm
01568 750232 Mrs Thomas
Rates fr: *£16.00*-**£16.50**.
Beds: 1D 1T
Baths: 1 Ensuite 1 Private
(3)

Bramlea, *Barons Cross Road, Leominster, Herefordshire, HR6 8RW.*
Very comfortable, spacious, extended bungalow.
Open: All Year
Grades: ETB 1 Cr, Comm
01568 613406
Mr & Mrs Longworth
Rates fr: *£17.00*-**£17.00**.
Beds: 1F 1T 1S **Baths:** 1 Shared
(3)

Black Swan Hotel, *West Street, Leominster, Herefordshire, HR6 8EP.*
Small, family-run town hotel.
Open: All Year
01568 612020 Mr Bond
Rates fr: *£18.00*.
Beds: 1F 1D 1T 4S
Baths: 1 Private 2 Shared

Highfield, *Ivington Road, Newtown, Leominster, Herefordshire, HR6 8QD.*
Attractive Edwardian house, large garden.
Open: All Year (not Xmas)
Grades: ETB 2 Cr, Comm
01568 613216
Misses Fothergill
Rates fr: *£18.50*-**£18.50**.
Beds: 1D 2T
Baths: 1 Ensuite 2 Private
(3)

Copper Hall, *South Street, Leominster, Herefordshire, HR6 8JN.*
Large C17th private house.
Open: All Year (not Xmas)
Grades: ETB 1 Cr, Comm
01568 611622 Mrs Blackburn
Rates fr: *£17.50*-**£20.00**.
Beds: 1F 1D 2T **Baths:** 1 Shared
(5)

Lingen

National Grid Ref: SO3667

Royal George

Brook Cottage, *Lingen, Bucknell, Shropshire, SY7 0DY.*
Delightful C18th cottage. Garden, brook.
Open: Feb to Nov
01544 267990 Mrs Phillips
Rates fr: *£15.00*-**£15.00**.
Beds: 1D 1S **Baths:** 1 Private
(3) (5)

Little Hereford

National Grid Ref: SO5568

Temeside

Red Roofs, *Little Hereford, Ludlow, Shropshire, SY8 4AT.*
Luxury accommodation in lovely surroundings.
Open: All Year (not Xmas)
Grades: ETB 2 Cr, AA 4 Q
01584 711439 Mrs Lanman
Rates fr: *£18.00*.
Beds: 1D 1T
Baths: 1 Ensuite 1 Private
(6)

Haynall Villa, *Haynall Lane, Little Hereford, Ludlow, Shropshire, SY8 4BG.*
Early C17th comfortable farmhouse.
Open: All Year (not Xmas) & Jan
Grades: ETB 2 Cr, Comm
01584 711589 Mrs Edwards
Rates fr: *£16.00*-**£16.00**.
Beds: 1F 1D 1T **Baths:** 1 Private
(6) (4)

Llangrove

National Grid Ref: SO5219

Royal Arms

Prospect Place, *Llangrove, Ross-on-Wye, Herefordshire, HR9 6ET.*
Recently renovated house & views.
Open: All Year
Grades: ETB 2 Cr, Comm
01989 770596 Mr Powell
Rates fr: *£17.50*.
Beds: 5T **Baths:** 5 Ensuite
(8) (8)

Llanwarne

National Grid Ref: SO5028

Fountain Inn

The Lawns, *Llanwarne, Hereford, HR2 8EN.*
Spacious, elegant home, unique experience.
Open: All Year (not Xmas)
Grades: ETB 2 Cr, High Comm
01981 540351 Mrs Howard
Rates fr: *£20.00*-**£25.00**.
Beds: 1D 2T
Baths: 2 Ensuite 1 Shared
(9) (10)

Longtown

National Grid Ref: SO3228

Crown Inn

Olchon Cottage Farm, *Turnant Road, Longtown, Hereford, HR2 0NS.*
Small working farm.
Open: All Year (not Xmas)
Grades: ETB 2 Cr, Comm
01873 860233 (also fax no)
Mrs Pritchard
Rates fr: *£18.00*-**£18.00**.
Beds: 2F
Baths: 1 Ensuite 1 Private

Luston

National Grid Ref: SO4863

Balance Inn

Ladymeadow Farm, *Luston, Leominster, Herefordshire, HR6 0AS.*
Large, spacious, comfortable C17th farmhouse.
Open: Easter to Oct
Grades: ETB 1 Cr
01568 780262 Mrs Ruell
Rates fr: *£16.00*-**£16.00**.
Beds: 1F 1D 1T **Baths:** 1 Shared
(10)

Lyonshall

National Grid Ref: SO3355

Church House, *Lyonshall, Kington, Herefordshire, HR5 3HR.*
Period house set in beautiful countryside.
Open: All Year (not Xmas)
01544 340350 Mr & Mrs Dilley
Rates fr: *£15.00*-**£20.00**.
Beds: 3D
Baths: 1 Ensuite 1 Shared
(8)

Mansell Lacy

National Grid Ref: SO4245

Dog & Duck (Wormsley)

Apple Tree Cottage, *Mansell Lacy, Hereford, HR4 7HH.*
C15th cottage, warm, quiet, friendly.
Open: All Year
01981 590688 Mrs Barker
Rates fr: *£14.00*-**£14.00**.
Beds: 1D 2T 1S
Baths: 1 Private 1 Shared
(0) (4)

Mordiford

National Grid Ref: SO5737

Green Man (Townhope)

Orchard Farm House, *Mordiford, Hereford, HR1 4EJ.*
C17th farmhouse overlooking beautiful valley.
Open: All Year (not Xmas)
Grades: ETB 2 Cr, Comm
01432 870253
Mrs James
Rates fr: *£16.50*-**£18.00**.
Beds: 2D 1T
Baths: 1 Private 1 Shared

Moreton on Lugg

National Grid Ref: SO5045

Tall Trees Country House Hotel, *Moreton on Lugg, Hereford, HR4 8AH.*
Unspoilt former rectory. Attractive gardens.
Open: All Year
01432 760277
Mr Riches
Rates fr: *£19.50*-**£25.00**.
Beds: 1F 1D 2T 1S
Baths: 3 Ensuite 2 Shared
(10)

Many rates vary according to season - the lowest are shown here.

Much Cowarne

National Grid Ref: SO6247

Paunceford Court, *Much Cowarne, Bromyard, Herefordshire, HR7 4JQ.*
Delightful old farmhouse.
Open: All Year (not Xmas)
01432 820208 Mr & Mrs Keenan
Rates fr: *£15.00*-**£16.00**.
Beds: 1F 1D 1T
Baths: 1 Shared
(10)

Much Marcle

National Grid Ref: SO6532

New House Farm, *Much Marcle, Ledbury, Herefordshire, HR8 2PH.*
Cosy farmhouse with fine views.
Open: All Year
Grades: ETB Listed
01531 660604 Mrs Jordan
Rates fr: *£15.00*-**£15.00**.
Beds: 1D 1T
(6) (6)

Munderfield Harold

National Grid Ref: SO6254

Home Farm, *Munderfield Harold, Bredenbury, Bromyard, Herefordshire, HR7 4SZ.*
Farmhouse B&B with coarse fishing.
Open: All Year (not Xmas)
01885 483231 Mrs Morgan
Rates fr: *£13.00*-**£13.00**.
Beds: 1F 1D 1T
(10) (6)

Munsley

National Grid Ref: SO6640

Munsley Acre Guest House, *Munsley, Ledbury, Herefordshire, HR8 2SH.*
Peaceful with super rural views.
Open: Easter to Oct
01531 670568 Mrs Brazier
Rates fr: *£15.00*-**£20.00**.
Beds: 2F 1D 1S
Baths: 2 Ensuite 1 Shared
(5)

Preston Wynne

National Grid Ref: SO5546

Crozen Pub

New House Farm, *Preston Wynne, Hereford, HR1 3PE.*
Open: All Year (not Xmas)
Grades: ETB Listed, High Comm
01432 820621 / 01589 107696
Mrs Rogers
Fax no: 01432 820621
Rates fr: *£18.00*-**£19.00**.
Beds: 1F 1S **Baths:** 1 Private
(0) (4)
Peaceful tranquil farmhouse with wealth of old beams. Beautiful views, we offer leisure room with jacuzzi, sailing, gym, pool table. Garden, patio, pets corner. Pony rides.

Rhydspence

National Grid Ref: SO2447

Rhydspence Inn

Rhydspence Cottage, *Rhydspence, Whitney-on-Wye, Hereford, HR3 6EU.*
Traditional stone-built cottage, wonderful views.
Open: All Year (not Xmas)
01497 831595
Mrs Phillips
Rates fr: *£14.50*-**£12.00**.
Beds: 1T 1S
Baths: 1 Shared
(3)

Ross-on-Wye

National Grid Ref: SO6024

Castle Lodge, Hanwood End, Kings Head, Man of Ross

The Skates, *Glewstone, Ross-on-Wye, Herefordshire, HR9 6AZ.*
Open: All Year
01989 770456
Mr Williams
Fax no: 01989 770781
Rates fr: *£17.00*-**£22.00**.
Beds: 4D 2T 2S
Baths: 4 Private 3 Shared
(10) (7)
Comfortable old former farmhouse in an acre of gardens, and surrounded by unspoilt Wye Valley countryside. Well-equipped bedrooms and cosy licensed lounges. Dinner available.

Radcliffe Guest House, *Wye Street, Ross-on-Wye, Herefordshire, HR9 7BS.*
C17th guest house.
Open: All Year (not Xmas)
Grades: ETB 2 Cr, RAC Listed
01989 563895 Mrs Sivill
Rates fr: *£17.00*-**£20.00**.
Beds: 1F 4D 1S
Baths: 6 Ensuite

Rosswyn Hotel, *High Street, Ross-on-Wye, Herefordshire, HR9 5BZ.*
C15th free house, off market square.
Open: All Year
01989 562733
Mrs Livesey
Rates fr: *£25.00*-**£35.00**.
Beds: 2T 6D
Baths: 7 Ensuite 1 Private
(6)

Broadlands, *Ledbury Road, Ross-on-Wye, Herefordshire, HR9 7BG.*
Modern comfortable home.
Open: All Year (not Xmas)
01989 563663
Mrs Ryder
Rates fr: *£15.00*-**£15.00**.
Beds: 2D 2S
Baths: 1 Shared
(6)

Copperfield House, *Copperfield, Wilton Lane, Ross-on-Wye, Herefordshire,* *HR9 6AH.*
Large comfortable house overlooking river meadows.
Open: All Year
01989 764379 Mrs Brown
Rates fr: *£15.00*-**£20.00**.
Beds: 2D 1T
Baths: 1 Shared
(5)

The Arches Country House, *Walford Road, Ross-on-Wye, Herefordshire,* *HR9 5PT.*
Georgian style, set in 0.5 acre lawns.
Open: All Year (not Xmas)
Grades: AA 4 Q, RAC Acclaim
01989 563348 Mrs Jones
Rates fr: *£17.00*-**£17.00**.
Beds: 1F 4D 1T 1S
Baths: 4 Private 2 Shared
(8)

Rotherwas

National Grid Ref: SO5338

The Moon (Mordiford)

Sink Green Farm, *Rotherwas, Hereford,* *HR2 6LE.*
C16th farmhouse overlooking the peaceful, picturesque River Wye.
Open: All Year (not Xmas)
Grades: ETB 2 Cr, Comm, AA 4 Q, Select
01432 870223 Mr Jones
Rates fr: *£18.00*-**£19.00**.
Beds: 2D 1T
Baths: 3 Private
(10)

Rudhall

National Grid Ref: SO6225

Penny Farthing Moody Cow

Rudhall Farm, *Rudhall, Ross-on-Wye, Herefordshire,* *HR9 7TL.*
Elegant farmhouse, luxury accommodation.
Open: All Year (not Xmas)
Grades: ETB 2 Cr, High Comm
01989 780240 Mrs Gammond
Rates fr: *£18.50*-**£20.00**.
Beds: 2D
Baths: 1 Shared
(10)

St Owen's Cross

National Grid Ref: SO5324

New Inn, Red Lion

Aberhall Farm, *St Owen's Cross, Hereford,* *HR2 8LL.*
Palatial new farmhouse, panoramic views.
Open: All Year (not Xmas)
Grades: ETB 2 Cr, Comm
01989 730256 Ms Davies
Rates fr: *£17.50*-**£20.00**.
Beds: 1D 1T
Baths: 1 Ensuite 1 Private
(10) (2)

Stapleton

National Grid Ref: SO3265

Hat Shop (Presteigne), Riverside Inn (Aymestry), Bakers Arms (Shobden)

Carters Croft, *Ford Street, Stapleton, Presteigne, Powys,* *LD8 2LS.*
Midiaeval cottage beneath ruined castle.
Open: All Year (not Xmas)
01544 260331 Mr Holmes
Rates fr: *£15.00*-**£17.50**.
Beds: 1D 1T
Baths: 1 Shared
(2)

Stoke Prior

National Grid Ref: SO5256

Wheelbarrow Castle

Heath House, *Stoke Prior, Leominster, Herefordshire,* *HR6 0NF.*
Comfortable stone farmhouse, peaceful countryside.
Open: Mar to Nov
Grades: ETB 2 Cr, High Comm, AA 4 Q
01568 760385 Mrs Neal
Rates fr: *£20.00*-**£22.00**.
Beds: 1D 2T
Baths: 2 Ensuite 1 Private
(9) (6)

Stretton Sugwas

National Grid Ref: SO4642

New Priory Hotel, *Stretton Sugwas, Hereford,* *HR4 7AR.*
Comfortable, converted former vicarage.
Open: All Year
Grades: ETB 3 Cr, Approv
01432 760264 Mr Benjamin
Fax no: 01432 761809
Rates fr: *£20.00*-**£25.00**.
Beds: 1F 4D 2T 2S
Baths: 8 Ensuite
(100)

Symonds Yat East

National Grid Ref: SO5516

Saracens Head, Wye Knot

Rose Cottage, *Symonds Yat East, Ross-on-Wye, Herefordshire,* *HR9 6JL.*
Luxury accommodation in riverside cottage.
Open: Mar to Oct
Grades: ETB Listed
01600 890514
Mrs Whyberd
Fax no: 01600 890498
Rates fr: *£16.50*.
Beds: 3D
Baths: 3 Private
(3)

Symonds Yat West

National Grid Ref:

Walnut Tree Cottage Hotel, *Symonds Yat West, Ross-on-Wye, Herefordshire,* *HR9 6BN.*
Good value - charming idyllic cottage.
Open: Mar to Oct
Grades: ETB 3 Cr
01600 890828 Mrs Baker
Rates fr: *£24.00*-**£24.00**.
Beds: 2F 3D
Baths: 4 Private
(10)

Woodlea Hotel, *Symonds Yat West, Ross-on-Wye, Herefordshire,* *HR9 6BL.*
Licensed Victorian country house hotel.
Open: All Year
Grades: ETB 3 Cr, Comm, AA 3 Q, RAC Acclaim
01600 890206 (also fax no)
Mrs Blunt
Rates fr: *£24.00*-**£24.00**.
Beds: 2F 2T 4D 1S
Baths: 6 Ensuite 2 Shared
(9)

Mountain Daisy Guest House, *Symonds Yat West, Ross-on-Wye, Herefordshire,* *HR9 6BL.*
Quiet cottage, superb river view.
Open: All Year (not Xmas)
Grades: ETB Listed
01600 890507 Mr Smith
Rates fr: *£18.00*-**£18.00**.
Beds: 1D
Baths: 1 Ensuite
(2)

Tedstone Wafre

National Grid Ref: SO6759

Littlebridge, *Tedstone Wafre, Bromyard, Herefordshire,* *HR7 4PN.*
Large elegant Victorian gentlemans' residence.
Open: All Year
01885 482471 Mrs Williams
Rates fr: *£17.50*-**£22.50**.
Beds: 1F 2D
(6)

Weobley

National Grid Ref: SO4051

Mellington House, *Broad Street, Weobley, Hereford,* *HR4 8SA.*
Comfortable Tudor house.
Open: All Year (not Xmas)
01544 318537 Mr & Mrs Saunders
Rates fr: *£16.50*-**£16.50**.
Beds: 1D 1T 1S
Baths: 1 Private 1 Shared
(3)

Planning a longer stay? Always ask for any special rates.

Weston under Penyard

National Grid Ref: SO6223

Moody Cow

Wharton Farm, *Weston under Penyard, Ross-on-Wye, Herefordshire, HR9 5SX.*
Comfortable farmhouse, excellent bedrooms.
Open: All Year (not Xmas)
Grades: ETB Listed, Comm
01989 750255 (also fax no)
Mrs Savidge
Rates fr: *£19.00*-**£22.00**.
Beds: 2D 1T
Baths: 1 Ensuite 2 Private
(0) (4)

The Hill, *Weston under Penyard, Ross-on-Wye, Herefordshire, HR9 7PZ.*
Comfortable farmhouse in wonderful surroundings.
Open: All Year (not Xmas)
01989 750225 Mrs Evans
Rates fr: *£14.00*-**£15.00**.
Beds: 1D 1T
Baths: 1 Ensuite

Hown Hall, *Weston under Penyard, Ross-on-Wye, Herefordshire, HR9 5SU.*
Large Edwardian private house.
Open: Easter to Oct
01989 750271 Mrs Roberts
Rates fr: *£18.00*.
Beds: 1F 2D
Baths: 2 Ensuite 1 Shared

The lowest **single** *rate is shown in* **bold.**

Whitchurch

National Grid Ref: SO5417

The Cedars Guest House, *Llangrove Road, Whitchurch, Ross-on-Wye, Herefordshire, HR9 6DQ.*
Elegant, comfortable Georgian house.
Open: All Year
01600 890351 Ms Wormser
Rates fr: *£16.00*-**£17.00**.
Beds: 4D 2T 2S
Baths: 4 Private 1 Shared
(8)

White Cross

National Grid Ref: SO4940

Imperial

Cedar Guest House, *123 White Cross Road, White Cross, Hereford, HR4 0LS.*
Friendly, family-run guest house.
Open: All Year
Grades: ETB 1 Cr
01432 267235 Mr & Mrs Burrough
Rates fr: *£16.00*-**£20.00**.
Beds: 3F 1T
Baths: 1 Shared
(10)

Winforton

National Grid Ref: SO2949

Sun Inn

Winforton Court, *Winforton, Winforton, Hereford, HR3 6EA.*
C16th country house overlooking Black Mountains.
Open: All Year (not Xmas)
01544 328498 Mrs Kingdon
Rates fr: *£17.00*-**£22.00**.
Beds: 3D
Baths: 1 Ensuite 1 Shared 1 Private
(10) (8)

Yatton

National Grid Ref: SO4266

Rocks Place Country Hotel, *Rocks Place, Yatton, Ross-on-Wye, Herefordshire, HR9 7RD.*
Beautifully converted half-timbered barn. **Open:** All Year
01531 660218 Mr & Mrs Cotton
Rates fr: *£25.00*-**£35.00**.
Beds: 1F 2D 3T 1S
Baths: 7 Private

Always telephone to get directions to the B&B - you will save time!

Hertfordshire

Tourist Information Centres

The Library, Kings Road, **Berkhamsted**, Herts, HP4 3BD, 01442 877638, (Easter to Oct).

The Old Monastery, Windhill **Bishops Stortford**, Herts, CM23 2ND, 01279 655261.

Civic Offices, Elstree Way, **Borehamwood**, Herts, WD6 1WA, 0181 207 7496.

Pavilion Box Office, Marlowes, **Hemel Hempstead**, Herts, HP1 1HA, 01442 234222.

The Castle, **Hertford**, Herts, SG14 1HR, 01992 584322.

Hitchin Library, Paynes Park, **Hitchin**, Herts, SG5 1EW, 01462 434738 / 450133.

M25 Motorway Services, South Mimms, **Potters Bar**, Herts, EN6 3QQ, 01707 643233.

Three Rivers House, Northway, **Rickmansworth**, Herts, WD3 1RL, 01923 776611.

Town Hall, Market Place, **St Albans**, Herts, AL3 5DJ, 01727 864511.

Central Library, Southgate, **Stevenage**, Herts, SG1 1HD, 01438 369441.

Campus West, The Campus, **Welwyn Garden City**, Herts, AL8 6BX, 01707 390653.

Bishops Stortford

National Grid Ref: TL4921

Nags Head

***High Willows Guest House,** 91 Dunmow Road, Bishops Stortford, Herts, CM23 5HF.*
Modern, comfortable, private town house. **Open:** All Year
01279 659780 Mr & Mrs Bircham
Rates fr: *£17.50*-**£23.00**.
Beds: 1F 1D 1T 1S
Baths: 3 Private 1 Shared
(7)

Borehamwood

National Grid Ref: TQ1977

***84 Stevenage Crescent,** Borehamwood, Herts, WD6 4NS.*
Luxury, modern private house.
Open: All Year
0181 207 3320 Mrs Copley
Rates fr: *£12.50*-**£15.00**.
Beds: 1T 1S **Baths:** 1 Shared
(2)

***9 Ranskill Road,** Borehamwood, Herts, WD6 5EU.*
Full use of our home.
Open: All Year
0181 386 1858 Mrs Hall
Rates fr: -**£13.50**.
Beds: 2S

Chorleywood

National Grid Ref: TQ0296

***Kennels Cottage,** Common Road, Chorleywood, Herts, WD3 5LW.*
Converted buildings in conservation area.
Open: All Year (not Xmas)
01923 282927 Mrs Smethurst
Rates fr: *£17.00*-**£18.00**.
Beds: 1D 1T 2S **Baths:** 1 Shared
(4)

Cuffley

National Grid Ref: TL3003

The Plough, The Cuffley

***52 Brookside Crescent,** Cuffley, Potters Bar, Herts, EN6 4QN.*
Private house, convenient major roads. **Open:** All Year (not Xmas)
01707 874016 Mrs Shelton
Rates fr: *£14.00*-**£14.00**.
Beds: 1D 1T **Baths:** 1 Shared
(3)

Elstree

National Grid Ref: TQ1795

***North Medburn Farm,** Watlin Street, Elstree, Herts, WD6 3AA.*
Easy access to London.
Open: All Year
Grades: ETB Listed
0181 953 1522 Mrs Williams
Rates fr: *£17.50*-**£17.50**.
Beds: 1F 2D 1S **Baths:** 1 Private
(4)

Goffs Oak

National Grid Ref: TL3203

Goffs Oak Inn

***329 Goffs Lane,** Goffs Oak, Cheshunt, Herts, EN7 5QH.*
Large detached house near countryside. **Open:** All Year
01992 628524 Mrs Morgan
Rates fr: *£20.00*-**£25.00**.
Beds: 1F 1D 4T 1S
Baths: 5 Ensuite 1 Shared
(7)

Great Offley

National Grid Ref: TL1426

Green Man, Red Lion, Prince Henry

***Beechlea,** Kings Walden Road, Great Offley, Hitchin, Herts, SG5 3DU.*
Quiet, comfortable, opposite village church.
Open: All Year (not Xmas)
01462 768703 Mr & Mrs Clarke
Rates fr: *£16.00*-**£18.00**.
Beds: 1D 1T 1S
Baths: 1 Private 1 Shared
(5) (6)

Harpenden

National Grid Ref: TL1314

Old Bell, The Harrow

***2 Longfield Oad,** Harpenden, Herts, AL5 1QE.*
Small comfortable friendly private house. **Open:** All Year (not Xmas)
01582 769852 Mrs Bellew
Rates fr: -**£14.00**.
Beds: 2S **Baths:** 1 Shared

***The Old Cottage,** 417 Luton Road, Harpenden, Herts, AL5 3QE.*
Comfortable C18th cottage.
Open: All Year (not Xmas)
01582 762257 Mr & Mrs Horn
Rates fr: *£15.00*-**£16.00**.
Beds: 1F 1D 1S
Baths: 1 Private 1 Shared

***Heritage Halt,** 235 Luton Road, Harpenden, Herts, AL5 3DE.*
Private house with pleasant outlook. **Open:** Apr to Oct
01582 713524 Mrs Woodward
Rates fr: *£15.00*-**£25.00**.
Beds: 1D 1T **Baths:** 1 Shared
(5) (2)

***Milton Hotel,** 25 Milton Road, Harpenden, Herts, AL5 5LA.*
Clean, quiet, friendly, comfortable hotel. **Open:** All Year
Grades: ETB 1 Cr
01582 762914 Mr Gray
Rates fr: *£16.50*-**£21.00**.
Beds: 2D 1T 5S
Baths: 3 Private 5 Shared
(8)

Hemel Hempstead

National Grid Ref: TL0607

Bell at Two Waters

***47 Alexandra Road,** Hemel Hempstead, Herts, HP2 4AQ.*
Pleasant Victorian house town centre. **Open:** All Year
Grades: ETB Listed
01442 246611 Mrs Kelly
Rates fr: *£15.00*-**£16.50**.
Beds: 1T 2S
Baths: 1 Shared

***Southville Private Hotel,** 9 Charles Street, Hemel Hempstead, Herts, HP1 1JH.*
Detached town centre hotel.
Open: All Year
Grades: ETB Listed, RAC Listed
01442 251387 Mr Davis
Rates fr: *£16.50*-**£20.00**.
Beds: 2F 1D 6T 10S
(8)

Hertford

National Grid Ref: TL3212

Golden Griffin

***89 Ware Road,** Hertford, Herts, SG13 7EE.*
Large Victorian family house.
Open: All Year (not Xmas)
01992 582302 Mrs Kingwell
Rates fr: *£19.25*-**£27.50**.
Beds: 1D 1T
Baths: 2 Ensuite
(3)

***Bengeo Hall,** St Leonards Road, Hertford, Herts, SG14 3JN.*
C17th manor, something very special. **Open:** All Year
01992 505897 Mrs Savory
Rates fr: *£20.00*-**£25.00**.
Beds: 1D 2T
Baths: 2 Private 1 Shared
(10) (10)

***5 Hollycroft,** Sele Farm Estate, Hertford, Herts, SG14 2DR.*
Modern, comfortable private house. **Open:** All Year (not Xmas)
Grades: ETB Listed
01992 552807 Mrs Harding
Rates fr: -**£15.00**.
Beds: 2S
Baths: 1 Shared
(1)

Hitchin

National Grid Ref: TL1930

***64 Fishponds Road,** Hitchin, Herts, SG5 1NU.*
Edwardian house opposite swimpool. **Open:** All Year (not Xmas)
Grades: ETB Listed
01462 458050 Mr Rollason
Rates fr: *£15.00*-**£17.00**.
Beds: 1F 1T 1S
Baths: 1 Shared

Kings Langley

National Grid Ref: TL0702

The Eagle, Cricketers Inn

***Woodcote House,** 7 The Grove, Chipperfield Road, Kings Langley, Herts, WD4 9JF.*
Large timber-framed detached house. **Open:** All Year (not Xmas)
Grades: ETB 2 Cr, Comm
01923 262077
Mr & Mrs Leveridge
Rates fr: *£18.00*-**£20.00**.
Beds: 1D 1T 2S
Baths: 4 Private
(1) (6)

***The Eagle,** 127 Hempstead Road, Kings Langley, Herts, WD4 8AJ.*
Coaching inn dating back to 1740.
Open: All Year
01923 262563
Rates fr: *£19.00*-**£21.50**.
Beds: 1F 1T 1S
Baths: 1 Shared
(30)

Markyate

National Grid Ref: TL0616

Waggon & Horses, Frog & Rhubab, Half Moon

***High Winds,** Hicks Road, Markyate, St Albans, Herts, AL3 8EW.*
Modern, self-contained, in farmhouse.
Open: All Year (not Xmas)
Grades: ETB 1 Cr
01582 841198
Rates fr: *£15.00*-**£18.00**.
Beds: 1D 1T 1S
Baths: 1 Shared
(4) (10)

Much Hadham

National Grid Ref: TL4219

***Sidehill House,** Much Hadham, Herts, SG10 6DS.*
Pretty C16th timbered house.
Open: All Year
Grades: ETB 2 Cr
01279 843167 Mrs Stephens
Rates fr: *£19.00*-**£22.00**.
Beds: 1T 1S
Baths: 1 Private 1 Shared

Nasty

National Grid Ref: TL3524

The Plough, Sword in Hand

***Chequers,** Nasty, Great Munden, Ware, Herts, SG11 1HP.*
Self-sufficient small holding.
Open: All Year (not Xmas)
01920 438280 Mrs Ingham
Rates fr: *£13.00*-**£15.00**.
Beds: 1D 1T
Baths: 2 Ensuite
(2)

Piccotts End

National Grid Ref: TL0509

Marchmont Arms, Red Lion, Boards Head

***Eight Mill Close,** Piccotts End, Hemel Hempstead, Herts, HP1 3AX.*
Modern, sunny house. Country views. **Open:** All Year (not Xmas)
01442 236573 Mrs Johnson
Rates fr: *£15.00*-**£17.50**.
Beds: 1T 1S
Baths: 1 Shared
(10) (3)

Potters Bar

National Grid Ref: TL2501

The Bridge, Cask & Stellago

***The Wildings,** 58 Cranborne Crescent, Potters Bar, Herts, EN6 3AG.*
10 minutes to London by fast train.
Open: All Year (not Xmas)
01707 650533 Ms Wilding
Rates fr: *£14.50*-**£14.50**.
Beds: 1F 1D 1T
Baths: 1 Shared
(7) (4)

Redbourn

National Grid Ref: TL1012

Chequers Inn

***Broomsticks,** 106 High Street, Redbourn, St Albans, Herts, AL3 7BD.*
Small, modern, comfy Victorian cottage. **Open:** All Year (not Xmas) **Grades:** ETB Listed
01582 792882 Mrs Simpson
Rates fr: *£15.00*-**£15.00**.
Beds: 1T 1S **Baths:** 1 Shared

Rickmansworth

National Grid Ref: TQ0494

Coach & Horses, Two Bridges, Red Horse, Sportsman, Duke of York

***The Old Ale House,** Batchworth Hill, 1 London Road, Rickmansworth, Herts, WD3 1JL.*
Charactful C16th listed cottage.
Open: All Year
01923 775824 Mrs Dinsmore
Rates fr: *£17.00*-**£17.00**.
Beds: 1T **Baths:** 1 Private

***30 Hazelwood Road,** Croxley Green, Rickmansworth, Herts, WD3 3EB.*
Quiet, homely. Pleasant canalside location. **Open:** All Year
Grades: ETB Listed
01923 226666 Mrs Millward
Rates fr: *£16.00*-**£18.00**.
Beds: 3T 1S
Baths: 2 Shared
(2)

***6 Swallow Close,** Nightingale Road, Rickmansworth, Herts, WD3 2DZ.*
Detached house in quiet cul-de-sac.
Open: All Year
Grades: ETB Listed
01923 720069 Mrs Childerhouse
Rates fr: *£18.00*-**£18.00**.
Beds: 1F 1D 2S
Baths: 2 Shared
(5) (4)

Ringshall

National Grid Ref: SP9814

Bridgwater Arms

***12/13 Ringshall,** Ringshall, Berkhamsted, Herts, HP4 1ND.*
200-year-old country cottage, home produce.
Open: All Year (not Xmas)
01442 843396 Mrs Martin
Rates fr: *£13.00*-**£13.00**.
Beds: 1F 1T
Baths: 1 Private 1 Shared
(1 Month)

Royston

National Grid Ref: TL3541

Jockey Inn, Old Bull Inn, White Bear

***Jockey Inn,** 31-33 Baldock Street, Royston, Herts, SG8 5BD.*
Traditional, friendly public house.
Open: All Year (not Xmas)
01763 243377 Mrs Critchell
Rates fr: *£24.50*-**£24.50**.
Beds: 1F 2T 1S
Baths: 4 Ensuite
(8) (10)

***Greenlawns,** 39 Market Hill, Royston, Herts, SG8 9JU.*
Large comfortable Victorian private house.
Open: All Year (not Xmas)
01763 242619 Mrs Little
Rates fr: *£18.00*-**£18.00**.
Beds: 1F 1D 1T
Baths: 1 Shared
(3)

***Middle Brooklands,** 44 Kneesworth Street, Royston, Herts, SG8 5AQ.*
Early Victorian town house.
Open: Easter to Oct
01763 245750 Mrs King
Rates fr: *£15.00*-**£15.00**.
Beds: 1D 1T 1S
Baths: 1 Shared
(1)

***White Bear Lodge,** 53 Kneesworth Street, Royston, Herts, SG8 5AQ.*
Victorian house adjoining pub/restaurant.
Open: All Year
01763 242458
Rates fr: *£19.00*-**£20.00**.
Beds: 4F 3T 1D 4S
Baths: 3 shared
(30)

South Mimms

National Grid Ref: TL2201

White Hart

***The Black Swan,** 62-64 Blanche Lane, South Mimms, Potters Bar, Herts, EN6 3PD.*
Former inn, also self-catering.
Open: All Year (not Xmas)
Grades: ETB Listed
01707 644180 Mr Marsterson
Rates fr: *£17.50*-**£25.00**.
Beds: 1F 1D
Baths: 1 Private 1 Shared
(5)

St Albans

National Grid Ref: TL1507

Robin Hood, The Baton, Garibaldi, Goat, Portland Arms, Tudor Tavern, Three Hammers, Six Bell, Ancient Briton, Cricketers, King William IV

***Amaryllis,** 25 Ridgmont Road, St Albans, Herts, AL1 3AG.*
Friendly comfortable family home.
Open: All Year
Grades: ETB Listed
01727 862755 Mrs Burroughes
Rates fr: *£16.00*-**£15.00**.
Beds: 1F 1T 1S **Baths:** 1 Shared
(1)

***24 Kingshill Avenue,** St Albans, Herts, AL4 9QD.*
3 bed semi-detached.
Open: All Year
Grades: ETB Listed
01727 852647 Mrs Thwaites
Rates fr: *£15.00*-**£15.00**.
Beds: 1D 2S **Baths:** 1 Shared
(2)

***2 The Limes, Spencer Gate,** St Albans, Herts, AL1 4AT.*
Modern, comfortable home, quiet cul-de-sac. **Open:** All Year (not Xmas) **Grades:** ETB Listed
01727 831080 Mrs Mitchell
Rates fr: *£15.00*-**£15.00**.
Beds: 1T 1S **Baths:** 1 Shared
(3) (2)

***The Squirrels,** 74 Sandridge Road, St Albans, Herts, AL1 4AR.*
Edwardian house near town centre.
Open: All Year (not Xmas)
Grades: ETB Listed, Approv
01727 840497 Mr & Mrs Dawtry
Rates fr: *£12.50*-**£15.00**.
Beds: 1T 1S
Baths: 1 Ensuite 1 Shared

***5 Cunningham Avenue,** St Albans, Herts, AL1 1JJ.*
Large house, exclusive residential area. **Open:** All Year (not Xmas)
Grades: ETB Listed
01727 857388 Mrs Cullingford
Rates fr: *£16.00*-**£16.00**.
Beds: 1D 1T 1F
Baths: 1 Ensuite 2 Shared
(2)

***35 Chestnut Drive,** St Albans, Herts, AL4 0ER.*
Comfortable room on quiet road.
Open: All Year
Grades: ETB Listed
01727 833401 Mrs Redgrave
Rates fr: *£14.00*-**£14.00**.
Beds: 1D
Baths: 1 Shared
(1)

***32 Gurney Court Road,** St Albans, Herts, AL1 4RL.*
Large semi, convenient station and town. **Open:** All Year
Grades: ETB Listed
01727 835819 Mrs Salisbury
Rates fr: *£15.00*-**£18.00**.
Beds: 1T 1S
Baths: 1 Shared
(5)

***7 Marlborough Gate,** St Albans, Herts, AL1 3TX.*
Detached house close to station.
Open: All Year (not Xmas)
Grades: ETB Listed
01727 865498 Mrs Jameson
Rates fr: *£14.00*-**£14.00**.
Beds: 2T **Baths:** 1 Private
(1)

Thundridge

National Grid Ref: TL3517

Sow & Pigs

***Downfield Gallery,** Poles Lane, Thundridge, Ware, Herts, SG12 0SG.*
Secluded converted Victorian generating station. **Open:** All Year (not Xmas) **Grades:** ETB Listed
01920 461625
Mr & Mrs Spielman
Rates fr: *£16.50*-**£16.50**.
Beds: 2D
Baths: 1 Shared
(4)

Tring

National Grid Ref: SP9211

Crows Nest

***Terriers End,** Tring, Herts, HP23 6JT.*
C17th country cottage.
Open: All Year (not Xmas)
01442 822274 Mrs Dixon
Rates fr: *£16.00*-**£15.00**.
Beds: 1D 1T 1S
Baths: 1 Shared
(10)

Ware

National Grid Ref: TL3614

***Ashridge,** 3 Belle Vue Road, Ware, Herts, SG12 7BD.*
Comfortable Edwardian residence. Quiet road. **Open:** All Year (not Xmas) **Grades:** ETB 1 Cr, Comm
01920 463895 Mrs Atkins
Rates fr: *£16.50*-**£16.50**.
Beds: 1D 1T 2S
Baths: 2 Shared
(3)

***Timber Hall,** Ware, Ware, Herts, SG12 7SN.*
Quiet, warm, friendly and comfortable. **Open:** All Year (not Xmas)
01920 466086 Mrs Shand
Rates fr: *£17.50*-**£20.00**.
Beds: 2T 2S
Baths: 2 Shared
(10) (5)

Watford

National Grid Ref: TQ1097

The Hare,The Two Bridges, The Red Horse, The Sportsman, The Duke of York.

***33 Courtlands Drive,** Watford, Herts, WD1 3HU.*
Near M25, M1 and A41.
Open: All Year
01923 220531 Mrs Troughton
Rates fr: *£15.00*-**£15.00**.
Beds: 2T **Baths:** 1 Shared
(3) (7)

***30 Hazelwood Road,** Croxley Green, Watford, Herts, WD3 3EB.*
Quiet, homely. Pleasant canalside location. **Open:** All Year
Grades: ETB Listed
01923 226666 Mrs Millward
Rates fr: *£16.00*-**£18.00**.
Beds: 3T 1S **Baths:** 2 Shared
(2)

Welwyn Garden City

National Grid Ref: TL2413

The Cottage, White Horse

***The Seven Bees,** 76 Longcroft Lane, Welwyn Garden City, Herts, AL8 6EF.*
Central, quiet, pleasant, artist's home. **Open:** All Year (not Xmas)
01707 333602 Mrs Bunyan
Rates fr: *£17.50*-**£20.00**.
Beds: 1T 1S
(2)

***1 Redwoods,** Welwyn Garden City, Herts, AL8 7NR.*
Private house close to A1(M).
Open: All Year (not Xmas)
01707 322724 Mrs Cook
Rates fr: *£14.00*-**£20.00**.
Beds: 1T 1S **Baths:** 1 Shared
(1)

***10 Blakemere Road,** Welwyn Garden City, Herts, AL8 7PJ.*
Private house. Good area.
Open: All Year
01707 335294 Mrs O'Donoghue
Rates fr: *£15.00*-**£15.00**.

***73 Attimore Road,** Welwyn Garden City, Herts, AL8 6LG.*
Private house.
Open: All Year
Grades: ETB Listed
01707 323868 Mrs Densham
Rates fr: *£15.00*-**£17.50**.
Beds: 2D 2S **Baths:** 2 Shared
(6)

Isle of Wight

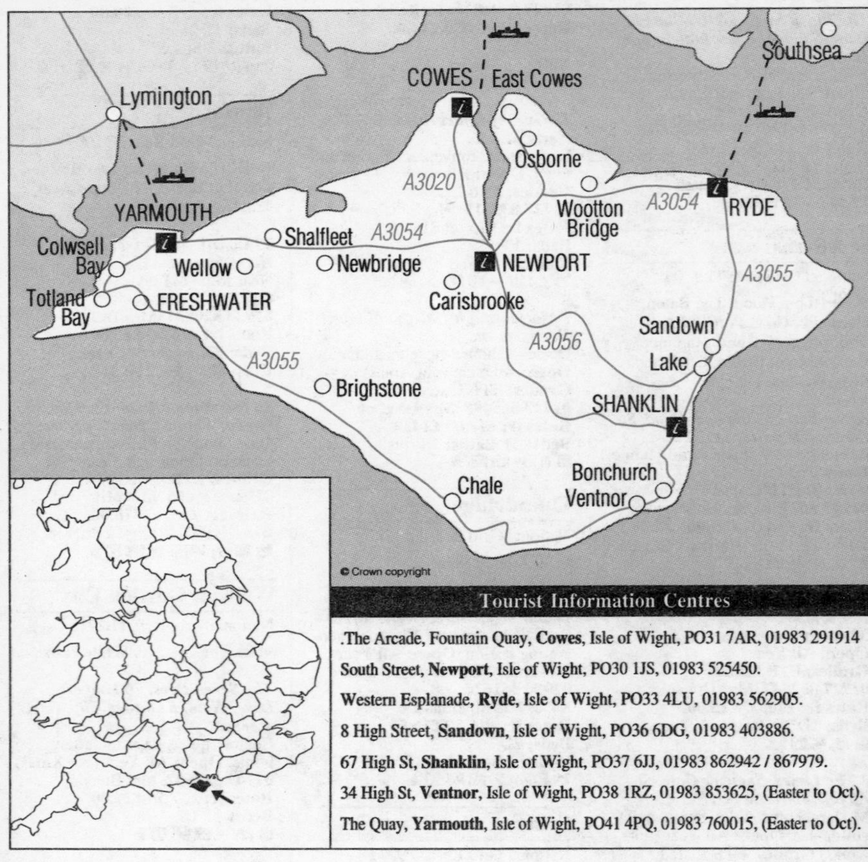

Tourist Information Centres

.The Arcade, Fountain Quay, **Cowes**, Isle of Wight, PO31 7AR, 01983 291914

South Street, **Newport**, Isle of Wight, PO30 1JS, 01983 525450.

Western Esplanade, **Ryde**, Isle of Wight, PO33 4LU, 01983 562905.

8 High Street, **Sandown**, Isle of Wight, PO36 6DG, 01983 403886.

67 High St, **Shanklin**, Isle of Wight, PO37 6JJ, 01983 862942 / 867979.

34 High St, **Ventnor**, Isle of Wight, PO38 1RZ, 01983 853625, (Easter to Oct).

The Quay, **Yarmouth**, Isle of Wight, PO41 4PQ, 01983 760015, (Easter to Oct).

Bonchurch

National Grid Ref: SZ5777

The Lake Hotel, *Shore Road, Bonchurch, Ventnor, Isle of Wight, PO38 1LF.*
Good value country house hotel.
Open: Mar to Nov
01983 852613 Mr Wyatt
Rates fr: *£21.00*-**£21.00**.
Beds: 7F 6D 6T 1S
Baths: 21 Private
(3) (20)

All details shown are as supplied by B&B owners in Autumn 1996.

Brighstone

National Grid Ref: SZ4382

Country Man Inn, Three Bishops

Buddlebrook Guest House, *Moortown Lane, Brighstone, Newport, Isle of Wight, PO30 4AN.*
Open: All Year (not Xmas)
Grades: ETB 1 Cr, Comm
01983 740381
Mr & Mrs Woodford
Rates fr: *£18.00*-**£20.00**.
Beds: 2D 1T
Baths: 3 Ensuite
(3)
Peaceful country guest house with warm welcome. Non-smoking. Adults only. Rooms ensuite. C/TV. C/H. Hospitality trays. Car park. 1 acre grounds. Good breakfast.

Carisbrooke

National Grid Ref: SZ4888

Eight Bells

The Mount, *1 Calbourne Road, Carisbrooke, Newport, Isle of Wight, PO30 5AP.*
Large Victorian private house.
Open: All Year (not Xmas)
01983 522173 / 524359 Mrs Skeats
Rates fr: *£15.00*-**£16.00**.
Beds: 1F 1D 1T **Baths:** 3 Shared
(3)

Chale

National Grid Ref: SZ4877

Cortina, *Gotten Lane, Chale, Ventnor, Isle of Wight, PO38 2HQ.*
Modern comfortable bungalow.
Open: All Year (not Xmas)
01983 551292 Mrs Whittington

Rates fr: *£15.00*-**£17.00**.
Beds: 1D 1T
Baths: 1 Shared
(6)

National Grid Ref: SZ3288

Ontario, *Colwell Common Road, Colwell Bay, Totland, Isle of Wight, PO39 0DD.*
Well-established private family hotel.
Open: All Year (not Xmas)
01983 753237 Mrs Blandford
Rates fr: *£19.00*-**£19.00**.
Beds: 3F 2D 1T 1S
Baths: 3 Ensuite 2 Shared
(9)

National Grid Ref: SZ4995

Duke of York, Anchor Inn

Caledon Guest House, *59 Mill Road, Cowes, Isle of Wight, PO31 7EG.*
Open: All Year (not Xmas)
01983 293599 Mrs Finch
Rates fr: *£15.00*-**£15.00**.
Beds: 2F 1D 1T 2S
Baths: 2 Shared

Ryde

National Grid Ref: SZ5992

White Hart, Telf's

Rodborough, *25 Queens Road, Ryde, Isle of Wight, PO33 3BG.*
Established quality accommodation, excellent breakfast.
Open: Mar to Oct
Grades: ETB 2 Cr, Comm
01983 565370 Mrs Davis
Rates fr: *£16.00*-**£18.00**.
Beds: 2D 1T **Baths:** 3 Ensuite
(3)

Sandown

National Grid Ref: SZ5984

Silverdale Guest House, *69 Grove Road, Sandown, Isle of Wight, PO36 8HH.*
Open: All Year (not Xmas)
01983 405382 Mr & Mrs Pocock
Rates fr: *£15.00*-**£15.00**.
Beds: 2F 2D 1T 1S
Baths: 2 Shared
(5) (3)
Glorious Isle of Wight for sun, sea and country. Warm welcome assured. Central all amenities. Home cooking, TVs all bedrooms, payphone, parking. Telephone for brochure.

Cliff Lodge, *13 Cliff Path, Sandown, Isle of Wight, PO36 8PL.*
Large Edwardian house & gardens.
Open: Feb to Nov
Grades: ETB 2 Cr
01983 402963 Mrs Grinstead
Rates fr: *£15.00*-**£15.00**.
Beds: 2F 5D 1T 2S
Baths: 9 Ensuite
(2) (8)

St Michaels Hotel, *33 Leed Street, Sandown, Isle of Wight, PO36 8JE.*
Good comfortable family-run hotel.
Open: All Year
Grades: ETB 2 Cr, Approv
01983 403636 Mr De Boise
Rates fr: *£14.00*-**£14.00**.
Beds: 3F 8D 2T 1S
Baths: 7 Private 1 Shared
(8)

Hazelwood Hotel, *19 Carter Street, Sandown, Isle of Wight, PO36 8BL.*
Family-run private licensed hotel.
Open: All Year
Grades: ETB Listed, Approv
01983 402536 Mrs Wright
Rates fr: *£14.00*-**£14.00**.
Beds: 4F 1D 2T
(8)

Denlin Guest House, *45 Ranlagh Road, Sandown, Isle of Wight, PO36 8NT.*
Come and relax at 'Denlin'.
Open: Easter to Oct
Grades: ETB Listed, Comm
01983 402821 Mrs Ling
Rates fr: *£13.00*-**£13.00**.
Beds: 4F 2D 1S **Baths:** 3 Shared
(5)

Carisbrooke House Hotel, *11 Beachfield Road, Sandown, Isle of Wight, PO36 8NA.*
Licensed family hotel.
Open: All Year (not Xmas)
Grades: ETB 3 Q
01983 402257 Mr & Mrs McHugh
Rates fr: *£15.00*-**£15.00**.
Beds: 5F 3D 2T 2S
Baths: 7 Private 3 Shared
(0)

Royal Pier Hotel, *Esplanade, Sandown, Isle of Wight, PO36 8JP.*
Magnificently positioned Victorian seafront hotel.
Open: Mar to Nov
01983 403187 Mr Maddocks
Rates fr: *£15.00*-**£16.00**.
Beds: 8F 25D 18T
Baths: 49 Private 2 Shared
(12)

St Ninans Guest House, *19 Avenue Road, Sandown, Isle of Wight, PO36 8BN.*
Perfect for touring.
Open: Easter to Oct
01983 402755 Mrs Ryan
Rates fr: *£12.00*-**£12.00**.
Beds: 4F 1D 1S
Baths: 2 Private 1 Shared
(2)

Sands Hotel, *Seafront, Sandown, Isle of Wight, PO36 8AT.*
Family-run seafront hotel.
Open: All Year
01983 402305 Mrs Hedges
Rates fr: *£18.00*-**£18.00**.
Beds: 9F 13D 4T 8S
Baths: 26 Private 3 Shared
(14)

Shalfleet

National Grid Ref: SZ4189

New Inn

The Old Malthouse, *1 Mill Road, Shalfleet, Newport, Isle of Wight, PO30 4NE.*
Open: All Year (not Xmas)
01983 531329 Mrs Young
Rates fr: *£15.00*-**£15.00**.
Beds: 1F 1D 1S
Baths: 3 Private
(1)

Shanklin

National Grid Ref: SZ5881

Billy Bunters

Hambledon Hotel, *Queens Road, Shanklin, Isle of Wight, PO37 6AW.*
Central position, open all year.
Open: All Year
Grades: ETB 3 Cr, Comm, AA 3 Q, RAC High Acclaim
01983 862403
Mr Birch
Rates fr: *£17.00*-**£17.00**.
Beds: 4F 5D 1T 1S
Baths: 11 Private
(8)

Culham Lodge Hotel, *31 Lanfguard Manor Road, Shanklin, Isle of Wight, PO37 7HZ.*
Open: All Year
Grades: ETB 3 Cr, Comm, AA 3 Q, Recomm
01983 862880 (also fax no)
Mr Metcalf
Rates fr: *£20.00*-**£20.00**.
Beds: 5D 4T 1S
Baths: 10 Ensuite
(12) (8)
This delightful small hotel perfect for breaks is well known for good value, with lovely gardens, heated swimming-pool, conservatory. All rooms SKY TV, hairdryers, teamakers. Ferries booked.

Dene Court, *Crescent Road, Shanklin, Isle of Wight, PO37 6DH.*
Country house set in lawned gardens. **Open:** Easter to Oct
01983 862903 Mr Rhind
Fax no: 01983 866337
Rates fr: *£17.50*-**£17.50**.
Beds: 1F 2D **Baths:** 3 Ensuite
(6)

Overstrand Hotel, *Howard Road, Shanklin, Isle of Wight, PO37 6HD.*
Open: All Year
Grades: ETB 3 Cr
01983 862100 Mr & Mrs Vale
Rates fr: *£17.50*-**£17.50**.
Beds: 5F 4D 3T 3S
Baths: 13 Ensuite 2 Shared
(20)
Building full of character. Beautiful sea views. Free parking, huge 3 acre garden. Free use of local leisure centre. Fantastic food incredible value. Children most welcome.

The Glen Hotel, *4 Avenue Road, Shanklin, Isle of Wight, PO37 7BG.*
Converted large Victorian house.
Open: Easter to Oct
Grades: RAC Acclaim
01983 862154 Mr & Mrs James
Rates fr: *£14.00*-**£14.00**.
Beds: 4D 2T
Baths: 2 Ensuite 1 Shared
(5) (3)

Ryedale, *3 Atherley Road, Shanklin, Isle of Wight, PO37 7AT.*
Small, friendly private hotel near station. **Open:** Easter to Oct
Grades: ETB 2 Cr, Comm
01983 862375 Mrs Carney
Rates fr: *£14.50*-**£14.50**.
Beds: 4F 2D 2S
Baths: 4 Private 2 Shared

Hazelwood Hotel, *14 Clarence Rd, Shanklin, Isle of Wight, PO37 7BH.*
Large detached Victorian private house. **Open:** All Year
Grades: ETB 3 Cr, Comm, RAC Acclaim
01983 862824 (also fax no)
Mr & Mrs Tubbs
Rates fr: *£16.00*-**£16.00**.
Beds: 3F 3D 3T 1S
Baths: 8 Private 2 Shared
(1) (5)

The Edgecliffe Hotel, *Clarence Gardens, Shanklin, Isle of Wight, PO37 6HA.*
A haven for non-smokers.
Open: All Year
Grades: ETB 3 Cr, Comm, AA 3 Q, Recomm
01983 866199 (also fax no)
Mr Bateson
Rates fr: *£16.00*-**£16.00**.
Beds: 2F 5D 2T 1S
Baths: 6 Private 1 Shared
(3) (2)

Cliftonville Hotel, *6 Hope Road, Shanklin, Isle of Wight, PO37 6EA.*
Friendly, comfortable family-run hotel.
Open: All Year (not Xmas)
01983 862197 Mrs Brown
Rates fr: *£12.00*-**£12.00**.
Beds: 3F 5D 2T 2S
Baths: 4 Private 4 Shared
(3) (12)

Keats Cottage, *Hotel & Tea Rooms, 76 High Street, Shanklin, Isle of Wight, PO37 6NJ.*
Small family-run licensed hotel.
Open: All Year (not Xmas)
01983 866351 Mr & Mrs Nickless
Rates fr: *£13.50*-**£13.50**.
Beds: 3F 2D 1T
Baths: 2 Private 1 Shared

Mayfair Hotel, *Eastcliffe Promenade, Shanklin, Isle of Wight, PO37 6EJ.*
Large hotel overlooking sea.
Open: Easter to Oct
01983 862168 Mrs Bolwell
Rates fr: *£15.00*-**£20.00**.
Beds: 4F 20D 20T 4S
Baths: 48 Ensuite

The Lindens Private Hotel, *6 Clarence Road, Shanklin, Isle of Wight, PO37 7BH.*
Friendly, small family private hotel. **Open:** All Year
01983 862172 Mrs Cottington
Rates fr: *£14.00*-**£14.00**.
Beds: 4F 4D 1T 1S
Baths: 8 Ensuite 1 Shared
(6)

Atholl Court, *1 Atherley Road, Shanklin, Isle of Wight, PO37 7AT.*
Quiet, comfortable, friendly guest house. **Open:** Mar to Oct
01983 862414 Mr & Mrs Bland
Rates fr: *£13.00*-**£13.00**.
Beds: 3D 4T 3S
Baths: 2 Ensuite 1 Shared
(6)

Scotgrove Guest House, *4 Sandy Lane, Shanklin, Isle of Wight, PO37 7DT.*
Charming, detached guest house.
Open: Easter to Oct
01983 862565 Mr & Mrs Andrew
Rates fr: *£14.00*-**£14.00**.
Beds: 2F 5D 1T 1S
Baths: 2 Private 2 Shared
(9)

Totland Bay

National Grid Ref: SZ3186

Sandford Lodge Hotel, *The Avenue, Totland Bay, Isle of Wight, PO39 0DN.*
Very comfortable Edwardian house.
Open: All Year (not Xmas)
01983 753478 Mr Malt
Rates fr: *£16.00*-**£16.00**.
Beds: 1F 3D 1T 1S
Baths: 5 Private 1 Shared
(5) (5)

Littledene Lodge, *Granville Road, Totland Bay, Isle of Wight, PO39 0AX.*
Charming small hotel. Friendly atmosphere.
Open: Mar to Nov
01983 752411 Mrs Wright
Rates fr: *£18.00*-**£22.00**.
Beds: 2F 2D 2T
Baths: 6 Ensuite
(3) (5)

The Nodes Country Hotel, *Alum Bay Old Road, Totland Bay, Isle of Wight, PO39 0HZ.*
Character country hotel.
Open: All Year
01983 752859 Mr Harris
Rates fr: *£22.50*-**£24.50**.
Beds: 4F 4D 3T
Baths: 11 Private
(15)

Ventnor

National Grid Ref: SZ5677

The Brunswick Hotel, *Victoria Street, Ventnor, Isle of Wight, PO38 1ET.*
Friendly, family-run, licensed hotel.
Open: All Year (not Xmas)
Grades: RAC Listed
01983 852656
Rates fr: *£15.50*-**£15.50**.
Beds: 4F 2D 1T
Baths: 4 Private 1 Shared

Cornerways Hotel, *39 Medeira Road, Ventnor, Isle of Wight, PO38 1QS.*
Beautiful sea & Downs views.
Open: Mar to Oct
Grades: ETB 3 Cr, Comm
01983 852323
Mr Malcolm
Rates fr: *£17.00*-**£17.00**.
Beds: 5F 3D 1T 2S
Baths: 8 Private 1 Shared
(6)

Medina House Hotel, *Alma Road, Ventnor, Isle of Wight, PO38 1JU.*
Small 1860 Victorian hotel.
Open: All Year
01983 852424 Mrs Berry
Rates fr: *£16.00*-**£15.00**.
Beds: 1F 3D 2S
Baths: 6 Ensuite
(4)

Wellow

National Grid Ref: SZ3888

Mattingley Farm, *Wellow, Yarmouth, Isle of Wight, PO41 0SZ.*
C17th country island stone farmhouse.
Open: All Year (not Xmas)
01983 760503 Mrs McMullan
Rates fr: *£16.00*-**£16.00**.
Beds: 1F 1T 1S
Baths: 1 Shared
(10)

Wootton Bridge

National Grid Ref: SZ5491

Ashlake Farmhouse, *Ashlake Farm Lane, Wootton Creek, Wootton Bridge, Ryde, Isle of Wight, PO33 4LF.*
Cosy C17th waterside farmhouse.
Open: All Year
01983 882124 Ms Pearce
Rates fr: *£15.00*-**£20.00**.
Beds: 1F 1D 1T 1S
Baths: 1 Private 1 Shared
(6) (4)

Briddlesford Lodge Farm, *Wootton Bridge, Ryde, Isle of Wight, PO33 4RY.*
Comfortable old farmhouse.
Open: All Year (not Xmas)
01983 882239 Mrs Griffin
Rates fr: *£15.00*-**£17.00**.
Beds: 2D 1T
Baths: 1 Shared
(3)

Island Charters Barge, *Barge Lane, Wootton Bridge, Ryde, Isle of Wight, PO33 4LB.*
Luxury cabins on beautiful Wootton Creek.
Open: Easter to Oct
01983 525728 / 01983 882315
Mr Gallop
Rates fr: *£14.00*-**£14.00**.
Beds: 10T 10D 10S
Baths: 3 Shared

Yarmouth

National Grid Ref: SZ3589

New Inn (Shalfleet)

Quinces, *Cranmore Avenue, Yarmouth, Isle of Wight, PO41 0XS.*
Open: All Year (not Xmas)
Grades: ETB Listed, Comm
01983 760080 Mrs Poulter
Rates fr: *£17.00*-**£18.00**.
Beds: 1D 1T
(0) (4)
An attractive cedar house & lovely garden, peacefully set in an Area of Outstanding Natural Beauty, in its own 6 acres.

The lowest **single** *rate is shown in* **bold.**

Isles of Scilly

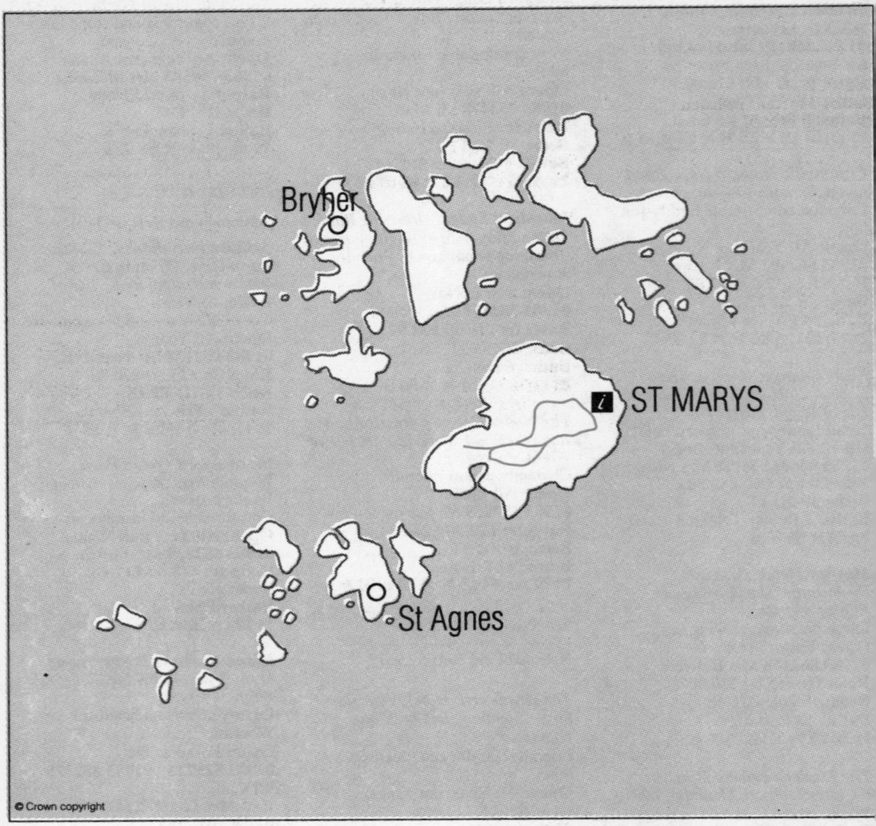

Bryher

ST MARYS

St Agnes

Tourist Information Centre

Porthcressa Bank, **St Mary's**, Isles of Scilly, TR21 0JY, 01720 422536

Bryher

National Grid Ref: SV8715

***Soleil D'Or**, Bryher, Isles of Scilly, TR23 0PR.*
Modern, comfortable bungalow.
Open: Easter to Nov
Grades: ETB 2 Cr, Comm
01720 422003
Mrs Coysh
Rates fr: *£22.00*-**£28.00**.
Beds: 2D 1T
Baths: 3 Private
(3)

St Agnes

National Grid Ref: SV8807

42 Covean Cottage, *St Agnes, Isles of Scilly, TR22 0PL.*
Island cottage overlooking sea.
Open: Easter to Nov
01720 422620 Mrs Sewell
Rates fr: *£20.00*-**£20.00**.
Beds: 2D 1T
Baths: 2 Private 1 Shared
(12)

St Marys

National Grid Ref: SV9111

Lyonnesse House, *The Strand, St Marys, Isles of Scilly, TR21 0PT.*
Listed building, magnificent sea views. **Open:** Feb to Oct
Grades: ETB 1 Cr, Comm
01720 422458 Mrs Woodcock
Rates fr: *£20.00*-**£20.00**.
Beds: 1F 3D 3T 2S
Baths: 5 Shared
(5)

Pieces Of Eight, *Porthcressa Road, St Marys, Isles of Scilly, TR21 0JL.*
Comfortable, modern family home.
Open: All Year (not Xmas)
Grades: ETB Listed, Comm
01720 422163
Mr Lawson
Rates fr: *£16.00*.
Beds: 1T
Baths: 1 Private

Carnwethers Country House, *Pelistry, St Marys, Isles of Scilly, TR21 0NX.*
Secluded country house. Private hotel.
Open: Apr to Oct
Grades: ETB 3 Cr, Comm, RAC High Acclaim
01720 422415
Mr & Mrs Graham
Rates fr: *£34.00*-**£46.00**.
Beds: 1F 4D 3T 1S
Baths: 9 Private
(7) (6)

Carn Warvel, *Church Road, St Marys, Isles of Scilly, TR21 0NA.*
Farmhouse of character and charm.
Open: All Year
Grades: ETB 3 Cr, High Comm, AA 4 Q, Select
01720 422111 Mr Hedges
Rates fr: *£20.00*-**£20.00**.
Beds: 2D 2T 1S
Baths: 9 Private
(8) (2)

Buckingham House, *Bank, St Marys, Isles of Scilly, TR21 0HY.*
Small friendly guest house.
Open: Mar to Nov
Grades: ETB 1 Cr
01720 422543 Mr Malec
Rates fr: *£17.00*-**£17.00**.
Beds: 3F 1D 1T 1S
Baths: 2 Shared

The lowest **single** *rate is shown in* **bold.**

Kent

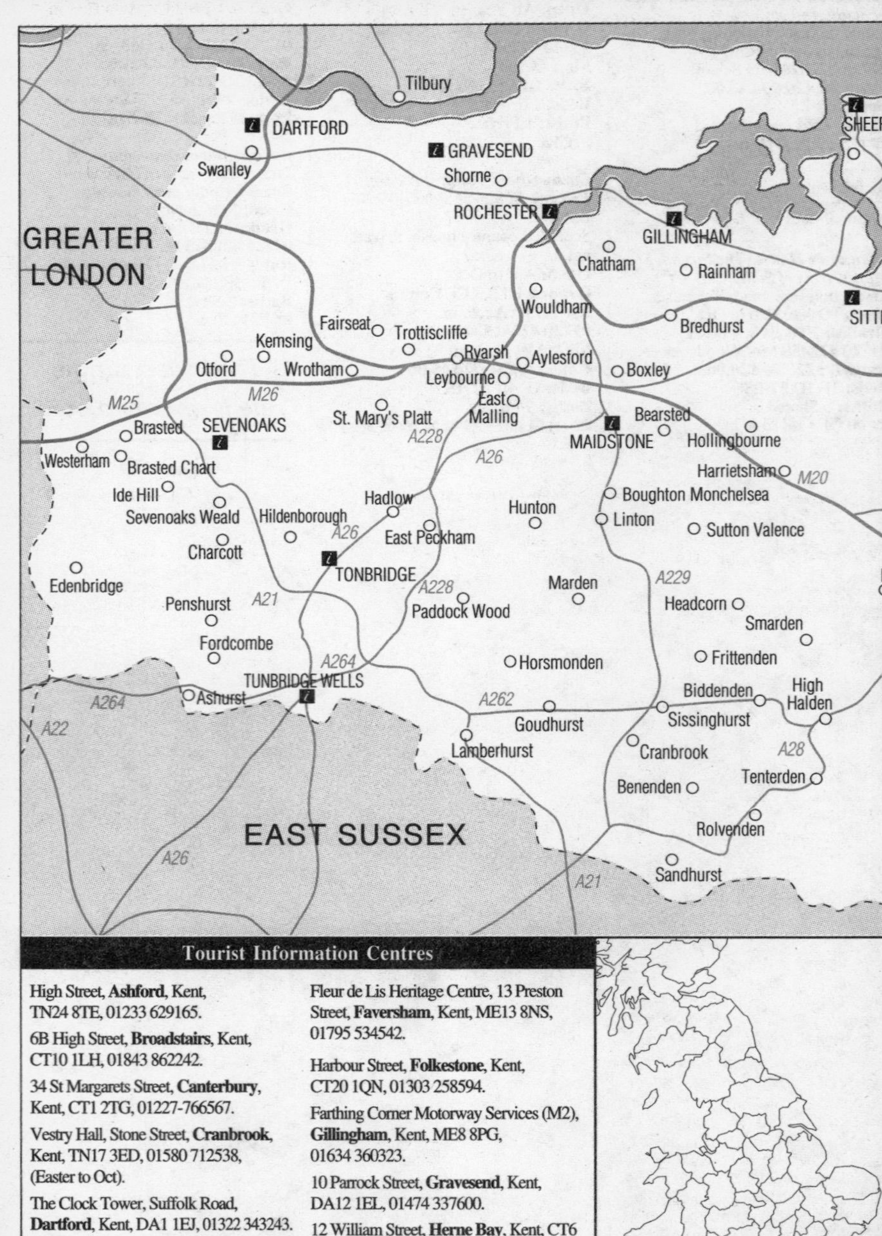

Tourist Information Centres

High Street, **Ashford**, Kent, TN24 8TE, 01233 629165.

6B High Street, **Broadstairs**, Kent, CT10 1LH, 01843 862242.

34 St Margarets Street, **Canterbury**, Kent, CT1 2TG, 01227-766567.

Vestry Hall, Stone Street, **Cranbrook**, Kent, TN17 3ED, 01580 712538, (Easter to Oct).

The Clock Tower, Suffolk Road, **Dartford**, Kent, DA1 1EJ, 01322 343243.

Town Hall, High Street, **Deal**, Kent, CT14 6BB, 01304 369576.

Townwall Street, **Dover**, Kent, CT16 1JR, 01304 205108.

Fleur de Lis Heritage Centre, 13 Preston Street, **Faversham**, Kent, ME13 8NS, 01795 534542.

Harbour Street, **Folkestone**, Kent, CT20 1QN, 01303 258594.

Farthing Corner Motorway Services (M2), **Gillingham**, Kent, ME8 8PG, 01634 360323.

10 Parrock Street, **Gravesend**, Kent, DA12 1EL, 01474 337600.

12 William Street, **Herne Bay**, Kent, CT6 5EJ, 01227 361911

Enroute Travel, Red Lion Square, **Hythe**, Kent, CT21 5AV, 01303 267799, (Easter toOct).

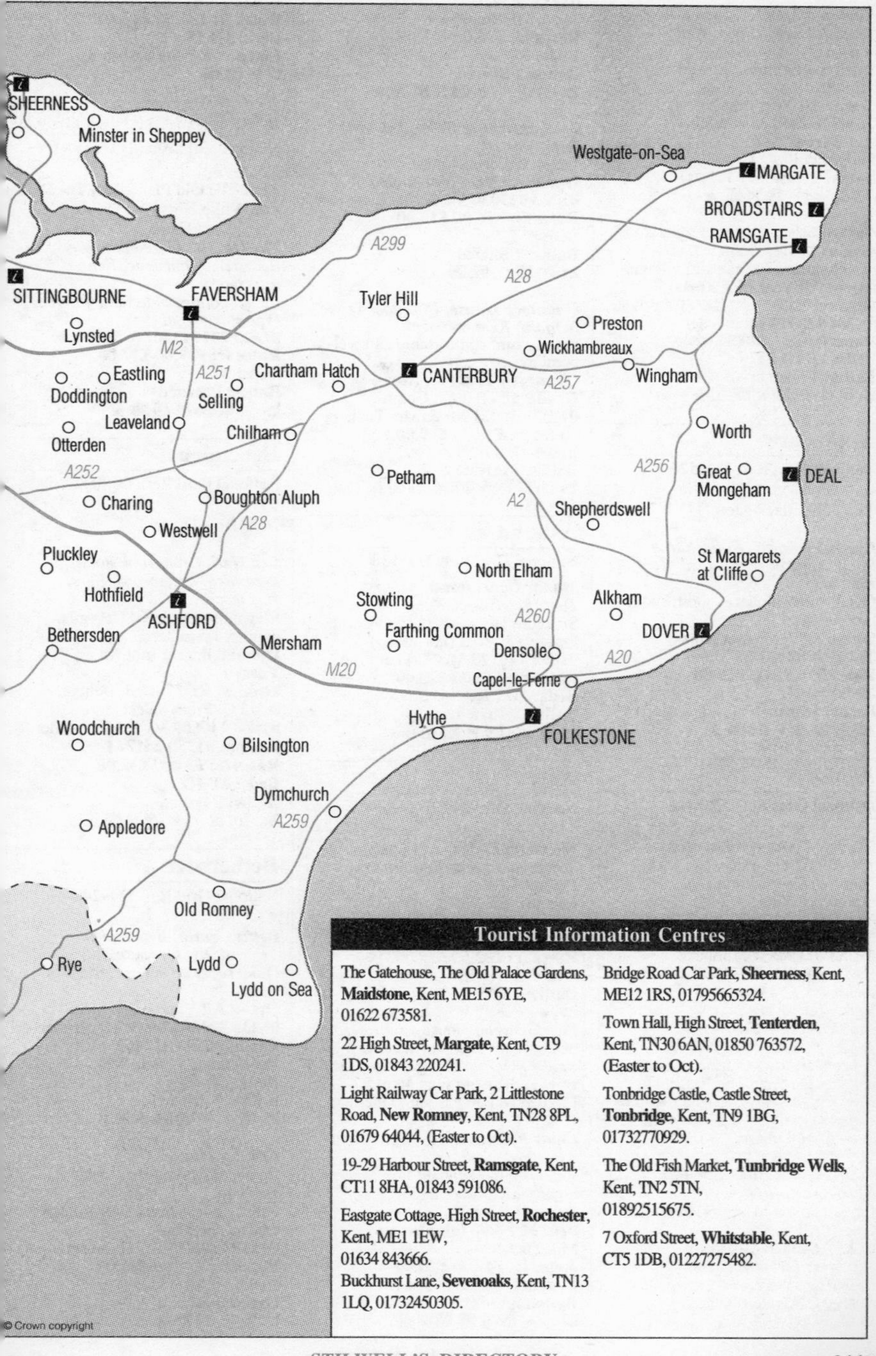

Tourist Information Centres

The Gatehouse, The Old Palace Gardens, **Maidstone**, Kent, ME15 6YE, 01622 673581.

22 High Street, **Margate**, Kent, CT9 1DS, 01843 220241.

Light Railway Car Park, 2 Littlestone Road, **New Romney**, Kent, TN28 8PL, 01679 64044, (Easter to Oct).

19-29 Harbour Street, **Ramsgate**, Kent, CT11 8HA, 01843 591086.

Eastgate Cottage, High Street, **Rochester**, Kent, ME1 1EW, 01634 843666.

Buckhurst Lane, **Sevenoaks**, Kent, TN13 1LQ, 01732450305.

Bridge Road Car Park, **Sheerness**, Kent, ME12 1RS, 01795665324.

Town Hall, High Street, **Tenterden**, Kent, TN30 6AN, 01850 763572, (Easter to Oct).

Tonbridge Castle, Castle Street, **Tonbridge**, Kent, TN9 1BG, 01732770929.

The Old Fish Market, **Tunbridge Wells**, Kent, TN2 5TN, 01892515675.

7 Oxford Street, **Whitstable**, Kent, CT5 1DB, 01227275482.

Alkham

National Grid Ref: TR2542

Marquis of Granby

Hopton Manor, *Alkham Valley Road, Alkham, Dover, Kent,* CT15 7EL.
Small manor house in Alkham hamlet.
Open: All Year (not Xmas)
01303 892481 Mrs Walk
Rates fr: *£18.00*.
Beds: 2D 1T
Baths: 2 Ensuite 1 Private
(12) (6)

Owler Lodge, *Alkham Valley Road, Alkham, Dover, Kent,* CT15 7DF.
Lovely house in beautiful village.
Open: All Year (not Xmas)
Grades: ETB 3 Cr, High Comm
01304 826375 Mrs Owler
Rates fr: *£21.00*-**£30.00**.
Beds: 1F 1D 1T
Baths: 3 Ensuite
(6)

Appledore

National Grid Ref: TQ9529

The Black Lion

Lavender Farm, *Woodchurch Road, Appledore, Ashford, Kent,* TN26 2BJ.
Quiet, rural, modern, comfortable farmhouse.
Open: All Year (not Xmas)
01233 758232 Mrs Mann
Rates fr: *£15.00*-**£18.00**.
Beds: 1F 1D
Baths: 1 Shared
(2) (2)

Ashford

National Grid Ref: TR0042

Warren Cottage Guest House, *136 The Street, Willesborough, Ashford, Kent,* TN24 0NB.
Open: All Year
Grades: ETB 3 Cr, AA 3 Q, RAC 3 St
01233 621905 Mrs Jones
Fax no: 01233 623400
Rates fr: *£20.50*-**£18.50**.
Beds: 1D 1T 2S
Baths: 4 Private
(20)
A privately-owned hotel set in 2 acres of gardens. The Warren's bedrooms all have private facilities complete with TVs. Restaurant open 6.30-8.00pm.

Vickys Guest House, *38 Park Road North, Ashford, Kent,* TN24 8LY.
Large converted Victorian house.
Open: All Year
01233 640420 Mrs Ford
Rates fr: *£17.00*-**£17.00**.
Beds: 1F 1D 1T 1S
Baths: 2 Private 2 Shared

Stone House, *Faversham Road, Kennington, Ashford, Kent,* TN25 4PQ.
Jacobean-style Listed building.
Open: All Year (not Xmas)
01233 623776
Mr & Mrs Buckler
Rates fr: *£16.00*-**£18.00**.
Beds: 3T
Baths: 2 Shared
(5) (4)

2-4 Canterbury Road, *Ashford, Kent,* TN24 8JX.
Large Victorian house.
Open: All Year (not Xmas)
01223 623030 Mr & Mrs Lavender
Rates fr: *£16.00*-**£16.00**.
Beds: 2T 2S
Baths: 1 Shared
(5) (5)

Quantock House, *Quantock Drive, Ashford, Kent,* TN24 8QH.
Family run, comfortable and welcoming.
Open: All Year (not Xmas)
Grades: ETB 2 Cr, Comm
01233 638921 Mr & Mrs Tucker
Rates fr: *£18.00*-**£19.00**.
Beds: 1D 1T 1S
Baths: 3 Private
(5) (3)

Ashurst

National Grid Ref: TQ5138

Manor Court Farm, *Ashurst, Tunbridge Wells, Kent,* TN3 9TB.
Spacious Georgian farmhouse.
Open: All Year (not Xmas)
01892 740279 Mrs Soyke
Rates fr: *£18.00*-**£18.00**.
Beds: 1D 2T
Baths: 2 Shared
(10)

Aylesford

National Grid Ref: TQ7258

Wickham Lodge, *The Quay, High Street, Aylesford, Kent,* ME20 7AY.
Open: All Year
Grades: ETB 3 Cr, Comm
01622 717267 (also fax no)
Mrs Kelsey Bourne
Rates fr: *£22.50*-**£25.00**.
Beds: 1F 1D 1S
Baths: 2 Ensuite 1 Private
(3)
Fine Georgian house on the banks of the River Medway near the historic Aylesford Bridge. Lawns to river at the front with an old English walled garden to the rear.

Court Farm, *Village High Street, Aylesford, Kent,* ME20 7AZ.
Beautiful old beamed farmhouse, quality accommodation.
Open: All Year
01622 717293 (also fax no)
Mrs Tucker
Rates fr: *£17.50*-**£20.00**.
Beds: 1D 1T 1S
Baths: 2 Ensuite 1 Private
(6)

15 Birch Crescent, *Aylesford, Kent,* ME20 7QE.
Modern comfortable detached house.
Open: All Year (not Xmas)
01622 717481 Mr & Mrs Newton
Rates fr: *£17.50*-**£17.50**.
Beds: 1D 1S
Baths: 1 Private 1 Shared

Bearsted

National Grid Ref: TQ7955

The Old Plantation, The Bell, The White Horse

The Hazels, *13 Yeoman Way, Bearsted, Maidstone, Kent,* ME15 8PQ.
Large, comfortable family home.
Open: All Year
01622 737943 Mr & Mrs Buse
Rates fr: *£17.00*-**£17.00**.
Beds: 2T
Baths: 1 Shared
(2) (2)

Benenden

National Grid Ref: TQ8032

Royal Oak

Crit Hall, *Cranbrook Road, Benenden, Cranbrook, Kent,* TN17 4EU.
Elegantly appointed Georgian country house.
Open: All Year (not Xmas/New Year)
Grades: ETB Listed, Deluxe, AA 5 Q, Prem Select
01580 240609 Mr & Mrs Bruder
Fax no: 01580 241743
Rates fr: *£25.00*-**£32.00**.
Beds: 2T 1D
Baths: 3 Private
(10) (6)

Bethersden

National Grid Ref: TQ9240

Potters Farm, *Bethersden, Ashford, Kent,* TN26 3JX.
Quiet separate annexe, friendly farm.
Open: All Year
01233 820341 Mr & Mrs Anderson
Fax no: 0233 820469
Rates fr: *£15.00*-**£17.50**.
Beds: 2T
Baths: 1 Private
(6)

Brimley House, *The Street, Bethersden, Ashford, Kent,* TN26 3AG.
Family home in friendly village.
Open: All Year
01233 820397 Mrs Hunnisett
Rates fr: *£14.00*-**£14.00**.
Beds: 1D 1T 1S
Baths: 1 Shared
(1)

Biddenden

National Grid Ref: TQ8438

Three Chimneys, Red Lion

***Bettmans Oast,** Hareplain Road, Biddenden, Ashford, Kent, TN27 8LJ.*
Converted oasthouse near Sissinghurst Gardens.
Open: All Year (not Xmas)
Grades: ETB 2 Cr, High Comm
01580 291463 Mrs Pickup
Rates fr: *£17.50*-**£20.00**.
Beds: 2D 1S
Baths: 1 Private 1 Shared
(4)

***Drayton House Farm,** Stede Quarter, Biddenden, Ashford, Kent, TN27 8JQ.*
Small friendly farmhouse.
Open: Mar to Oct
01580 291931 Mrs Lidgett
Rates fr: *£11.00*.
Beds: 1D 2T
Baths: 2 Shared
(4)

***Frogs Hole Oast,** Sissinghurst Road, Biddenden, Ashford, Kent, TN27 8LW.*
C18th converted oast house.
Open: Mar to Oct
01580 291935 Mrs Hartley
Rates fr: *£18.00*-**£25.00**.
Beds: 1D 2T
Baths: 2 Private 1 Shared
(5)

Bilsington

National Grid Ref: TR0434

White Horse

***Willow Farm,** Stone Cross, Bilsington, Ashford, Kent, TN25 7JJ.*
Organic smallholding in rural setting.
Open: All Year (not Xmas)
01233 720484 Mrs Hopper
Rates fr: *£16.25*-**£17.50**.
Beds: 1F 1D 2S
Baths: 2 Shared
(6)

Boughton

National Grid Ref: TR0659

Queens Head, White Horse Inn

***Queens Head Inn,** 111 The Street, Boughton, Faversham, Kent, ME13 9BH.*
Open: All Year (not Xmas)
Grades: ETB Listed, Approv
01227 751369 (also fax no)
Ms Sabey
Rates fr: *£17.50*-**£25.00**.
Beds: 1F 2D 1T 1S
Baths: 2 Shared
(25)
C16th village inn, landscaped gardens. Home cooked meals speciality. 2 miles - Canterbury. Location Exit 7 - M2 Motorway.).

***Tenterden House,** 209 The Street, Boughton, Faversham, Kent, ME13 9BL.*
Self-contained cottage to C16th house.
Open: All Year (not Xmas)
01227 751593
Mrs Latham
Rates fr: *£18.00*-**£25.00**.
Beds: 1D 1T
Baths: 1 Shared
(5)

Boughton Aluph

National Grid Ref: TR0348

Flying Horse Inn

***Warren Cottage,** Boughton Aluph, Ashford, Kent, TN25 4HS.*
Quiet cottage with garden, fantastic view!
Open: All Year (not Xmas)
01233 740483
Mrs Fearne
Rates fr: *£13.50*-**£15.00**.
Beds: 2D
Baths: 1 Shared
(5) (6)

***Flying Horse Inn,** Boughton Aluph, Ashford, Kent, TN25 4HS.*
Open fires, beams, comfortable, friendly reception.
Open: All Year (not Xmas)
01233 620914 Ms Smith
Rates fr: *£17.50*-**£20.00**.
Beds: 3D 1T
Baths: 2 Shared
(14) (60)

Boughton Monchelsea

National Grid Ref: TQ7651

Cock Inn

***Bramleys,** Church Street, Boughton Monchelsea, Maidstone, Kent, ME17 4HN.*
Detached house in quiet village.
Open: All Year (not Xmas)
Grades: ETB Listed
01622 747453 Mrs Knight
Rates fr: *£14.00*-**£15.00**.
Beds: 1D 1S
Baths: 1 Shared
(0) (2)

Boxley

National Grid Ref: TQ7757

Kings Arms

***Barn Cottage,** Harbourland, Boxley, Maidstone, Kent, ME14 3DN.*
Listed converted C16th barn.
Open: All Year (not Xmas)
01622 675891
Mrs Munson
Rates fr: *£15.00*-**£15.00**.
Beds: 3T
Baths: 1 Shared
(5)

Brasted

National Grid Ref: TQ4755

Bull Inn

***Holmesdale House,** High Street, Brasted, Westerham, Kent, TN16 1HS.*
Delightful Victorian house (part C17th).
Open: All Year
01959 564834 Mr Jinks
Rates fr: *£19.00*-**£22.00**.
Beds: 1F 1D 1T
Baths: 3 Ensuite 1 Private
(6)

Brasted Chart

National Grid Ref: TQ4653

Bull Inn (Brasted)

***The Orchard House,** Brasted Chart, Westerham, Kent, TN16 1LR.*
Family home, quiet, rural surroundings.
Open: All Year (not Xmas)
01959 563702 Mrs Godsal
Rates fr: *£17.50*-**£18.00**.
Beds: 2T 1S **Baths:** 2 Shared
(4)

Bredhurst

National Grid Ref: TQ7962

The Bell

***Condor House,** The Street, Bredhurst, Gillingham, Kent, ME7 3JY.*
Convenient Kent ports, Rochester, London. **Open:** All Year
Grades: ETB Listed, Comm
01634 232988 Mrs Field
Rates fr: *£15.00*-**£18.00**.
Beds: 3T
Baths: 1 Private 1 Shared
(10)

Broadstairs

National Grid Ref: TR3967

The Crown

***Devonhurst Hotel,** Eastern Esplanade, Broadstairs, Kent, CT10 1DR.*
Seafront hotel. All ensuite.
Open: All Year
Grades: ETB 3 Cr, AA 3 Q, RAC Acclaim
01843 863010 Mr & Mrs Payne
Fax no: 01843 868940
Rates fr: *£20.00*-**£22.00**.
Beds: 1F 4D 4T **Baths:** 9 Ensuite
(5)

Please respect a B&B's wishes regarding children, animals & smoking.

Oakfield Private Hotel, *11 The Vale, Broadstairs, Kent,* *CT10 1RB.*
Comfortable licensed hotel.
Open: All Year
Grades: ETB 3 Cr, AA 3 Q, RAC High Acclaim
01843 862506 Mr & Mrs Keightley
Rates fr: *£22.00*-**£22.00**.
Beds: 2F 5D 2T 2S
Baths: 10 Private 1 Shared
(12)

The White House Hotel, *Kingsgate Avenue, Kingsgate, Broadstairs, Kent,* *CT10 3LW.*
Small select licensed hotel.
Open: All Year
01843 863315 Mrs Harcus
Rates fr: *£20.00*-**£20.00**.
Beds: 1F 3D 3T 1S
Baths: 4 Ensuite 1 Shared
(8) (8)

Canterbury

National Grid Ref: TR1457

Black Horse, Bishops Finger, The Old City, White Hart, Canterbury Tales

Anns House, *63 London Road, Canterbury, Kent,* *CT2 8JZ.*
Open: All Year
Grades: ETB 2 Cr
01227 768767
Mrs Dellaway
Fax no: 01227 768172
Rates fr: *£18.00*-**£20.00**.
Beds: 4F 8D 4T 3S
Baths: 18 Ensuite 1 Shared
(12)
A splendid Victorian house, restored with love and care to accommodate those wishing to step back in time and explore the ancient city centre or beautiful countryside.

London Guest House, *14 London Road, Canterbury, Kent,* *CT2 8LR.*
Spacious Grade II Listed period house.
Open: All Year
Grades: ETB Listed, Comm
01227 765860 Mrs Harris
Rates fr: *£17.50*-**£18.00**.
Beds: 1F 1D 2T 2S
Baths: 2 Shared

Clare Ellen Guest House, *9 Victoria Road, Canterbury, Kent,* *CT1 3SG.*
Open: All Year
Grades: ETB 2 Cr, High Comm
01227 760205 Mr Williams
Fax no: 01227 784482
Rates fr: *£22.00*-**£22.00**.
Beds: 1F 2D 2T 1S
Baths: 6 Ensuite
(8)
Large elegant ensuite rooms with TV, hairdryer, tea/coffee facilities. Cosy lounge. Five minutes walk to town centre, train station. Parking/garage available. Credit cards accepted.

Oriel Lodge, *3 Queens Avenue, Canterbury, Kent,* *CT2 8AY.*
Residential area near city centre.
Open: All Year
Grades: ETB 2 Cr, High Comm, AA 3 Q, RAC Acclaim
01227 462845 Mr & Mrs Rishworth
Rates fr: *£18.00*-**£20.00**.
Beds: 1F 3D 1T 1S
Baths: 2 Private 2 Shared
(6) (6)

Acacia Lodge, *39 London Road, Canterbury, Kent,* *CT2 8LF.*
Small, central, friendly guest house.
Open: All Year
01227 769955 Mrs Cain
Rates fr: *£14.25*-**£20.00**.
Beds: 2D 1T **Baths:** 3 Private

Castle Court Guest House, *8 Castle Street, Canterbury, Kent,* *CT1 2QF.*
Grade II Listed Georgian house.
Open: All Year
Grades: ETB Listed, AA Listed
01227 463441 (also fax no)
Mrs Noble
Rates fr: *£17.00*-**£18.00**.
Beds: 2F 4D 3T 1S
Baths: 4 Private 3 Shared
(3)

Milton House, *9 South Canterbury Road, Canterbury, Kent,* *CT1 3LH.*
Quiet, comfortable, friendly family house.
Open: All Year (not Xmas)
01227 765531 Mrs Wright
Rates fr: *£15.00*-**£17.00**.
Beds: 1D 1T **Baths:** 1 Shared

Abbey Lodge Guest House, *8 New Dover Road, Canterbury, Kent,* *CT1 3AP.*
Large private home near city.
Open: All Year (not Xmas)
01227 462878 Mr Gardner
Rates fr: *£16.00*-**£19.00**.
Beds: 1F 1T 1S
Baths: 2 Ensuite 1 Shared
(10)

Maynard Cottage, *106 Wincheap, Canterbury, Kent,* *CT1 3RS.*
Scrumptiously clean, friendly, excellent food.
Open: All Year
Grades: ETB Listed
01227 454991 / 0850 315558
Miss Banks
Rates fr: *£17.50*-**£20.00**.
Beds: 1F 1D 1T **Baths:** 1 Shared

Courtney Guest House, *4 London Road, Canterbury, Kent,* *CT2 8LR.*
Elegant Georgian town house.
Open: All Year
Grades: ETB 1 Cr, Comm
01227 769668 Mr Broadbridge
Rates fr: *£15.00*-**£20.00**.
Beds: 2F 2D 1T
Baths: 4 Private 1 Shared
(3)

Raemore House, *33 New Dover Road, Canterbury, Kent,* *CT1 3AS.*
Comfortable, family-run house.
Open: All Year (not Xmas)
Grades: ETB Listed, Comm
01227 769740 Mr Gardener
Rates fr: *£16.00*-**£20.00**.
Beds: 1F 3D 1T 1S
Baths: 3 Private 3 Shared
(6)

Capel-le-Ferne

National Grid Ref: TR2538

Valiant Sailor

Xaipe, *18 Alexandra Road, Capel-le-Ferne, Folkestone, Kent,* *CT18 7LD.*
Modern comfortable bungalow.
Open: Mar to Oct
01303 257956 Mrs Strutt
Rates fr: *£12.50*-**£13.50**.
Beds: 1D 1T **Baths:** 1 Shared
(2)

Charcott

National Grid Ref: TQ5247

Charcott Farmhouse, *Charcott, Leigh, Tonbridge, Kent,* *TN11 8LG.*
Listed farmhouse in peaceful surroundings. **Open:** All Year
01892 870024 Mr & Mrs Morris
Rates fr: *£17.50*-**£22.00**.
Beds: 3T
Baths: 2 Ensuite 1 Private
(4)

Charing

National Grid Ref: TQ9549

Arketts Farm, *Charing, Ashford, Kent,* *TN27 0HH.*
Comfortable period farm house. Log fires.
Open: All Year (not Xmas)
Grades: ETB Listed
01233 712893 Mrs Okell
Rates fr: *£15.00*-**£16.00**.
Beds: 1D 1T **Baths:** 1 Shared
(3) (4)

Old Hill Lodge, *The Hill, Charing, Ashford, Kent,* *TN27 0LU.*
Friendly, Comfortable house and lovely garden.
Open: All Year (not Xmas)
01233 712812 Mrs Graham
Rates fr: *£16.00*-**£16.00**.
Beds: 1D 1T 1S **Baths:** 1 Shared
(4)

Chartham Hatch

National Grid Ref: TR1056

The Willows, *Howfield Lane, Chartham Hatch, Canterbury, Kent,* *CT4 7HG.*
Welcoming, quiet, comfortable. Gardener's delight.
Open: All Year
01227 738442 Mrs Gough
Rates fr: *£21.00*-**£17.00**.
Beds: 1D 1T 1S **Baths:** 2 Ensuite
(5)

Chatham

National Grid Ref: TQ7665

Holmwood Hotel, *158 Maidstone Road, Chatham, Kent, ME4 6EN.*
Private converted Victorian house.
Open: Feb to Dec
Grades: ETB 2 Cr
01634 842849 Mr Cheeseman
Fax no: 01634 832 905
Rates fr: *£16.50*-**£20.50**.
Beds: 1D 4T 7S
Baths: 8 Private 4 Shared
(16)

Chilham

National Grid Ref: TR0653

The George (Molash)

Cutlers Farmhouse, *Chilham, Canterbury, Kent, CT4 8EU.*
Quiet, rural, flintstone farmhouse.
Open: April to Oct
01233 740349 Mrs Dixon
Rates fr: *£16.00*-**£20.00**.
Beds: 1F 1D 1T **Baths:** 1 Shared

Bagham Cross, *Chilham, Canterbury, Kent, CT4 8DU.*
Country cottage.
Open: Easter to Oct
01227 730264 Mrs Wood
Rates fr: *£15.00*-**£20.00**.
Beds: 1D 1T **Baths:** 1 Shared
(10) (2)

Jullieberrie House, *Canterbury Road, Chilham, Canterbury, Kent, CT4 8DX.*
Luxury modern house. Lovely views.
Open: All Year
01227 730488 Mrs Hooker
Rates fr: *£16.00*-**£20.00**.
Beds: 1F 1D 1S
Baths: 2 Ensuite 1 Shared
(4)

Cranbrook

National Grid Ref: TQ7736

White Horse,The Windmill

The White Horse Inn, *High Street, Cranbrook, Kent, TN17 3EX.*
Victorian inn in small town centre.
Open: All Year (not Xmas)
Grades: ETB 1 Cr
01580 712615 Mr Strutt
Rates fr: *£17.00*-**£24.00**.
Beds: 1F 1D 1T
Baths: 1 Shared
(8)

Cordons, *Round Green Lane, Cranbrook, Cranbrook, Kent, TN17 2NB.*
Quiet country house near Sissinghurst.
Open: All Year
01580 211633 Mrs Johnstone
Rates fr: *£20.00*-**£25.00**.
Beds: 1D 1T 1S
Baths: 2 Private
(3) (3)

The Hollies, *Old Angley Road, Cranbrook, Kent, TN17 2PN.*
Well-appointed comfortable bungalow, close town centre.
Open: All Year (not Xmas)
01580 713106 Mrs Waddoup
Rates fr: *£18.00*-**£18.00**.
Beds: 1T 1S
Baths: 1 Ensuite 1 Private
(2)

Hillview Cottage, *Starvenden Lane, Sissinghurst, Cranbrook, Kent, TN17 2AN.*
Peaceful country house, gloriously situated.
Open: All Year (not Xmas)
Grades: ETB Listed
01580 712823 / 0850 909838
Mrs Lloyd Jones
Rates fr: *£17.00*-**£20.00**.
Beds: 2D 1T
(6)

Dartford

National Grid Ref: TQ5273

Rosedene Guest House, *284-286 Lowfield Street, Dartford, Kent, DA1 1LH.*
Convenient, comfortable, caring catering.
Open: All Year (not Xmas)
01322 277042 Mrs Rose
Rates fr: *£16.00*-**£22.00**.
Beds: 1F 3T 2S
Baths: 2 Shared
(2)

Deal

National Grid Ref: TR3752

Prince Albert, Kings Head , Zetland Arms

Kingsdown Country Hotel, *Cliffe Road, Deal, Kent, CT14 8AJ.*
Quiet seaside village location near Deal.
Open: All Year
Grades: ETB 3 Cr, AA 3 Q
01304 373755 (also fax no)
Mr Thompson
Rates fr: *£22.00*-**£25.00**.
Beds: 2D 2S **Baths:** 4 Ensuite
(8)

Hardicot Guest House, *Kingsdown Road, Deal, Kent, CT14 8AW.*
Detached Victorian house overlooking Channel.
Open: All Year
Grades: ETB 2 Cr, Comm
01304 373867 Mrs Stacey
Rates fr: *£17.00*-**£18.00**.
Beds: 1D 2T
Baths: 1 Ensuite 1 Shared
(5) (3)

The lowest **single** *rate is shown in* **bold.**

The Prince Albert, *187-189 Middle Street, Deal, Kent, CT14 6LW.*
Family run inn located in conservation area. **Open:** All Year
01304 375425 Mr & Mrs Hopkin
Fax no: 01304 369950
Rates fr: *£17.00*-**£20.00**.
Beds: 1F 1D 1T
Baths: 1 Private 1 Shared

Densole

National Grid Ref: TR2141

Garden Lodge, *324 Canterbury Road, Densole, Folkestone, Kent, CT18 7BB.*
Attractive family run guest house.
Open: All Year
Grades: ETB 2 Cr, High Comm
01303 893147 (also fax no)
Mrs Cooper, MCFA
Rates fr: *£20.00*-**£21.00**.
Beds: 3F 1D 2S
Baths: 2 Shared
(12)

Doddington

National Grid Ref: TQ9357

Palace Farmhouse, *Chequers Hill, Doddington, Sittingbourne, Kent, ME9 0AU.*
Early Victorian farmhouse.
Open: All Year
Grades: ETB 2 Cr
01795 886820 Mr & Mrs Leake
Rates fr: *£16.00*-**£14.00**.
Beds: 1F 2D 1T 2S
Baths: 2 Private 2 Shared
(0) (6)

Dover

National Grid Ref: TR3141

White Horse Inn, The Britannia, The Plough, The Swingate

Hubert House, *9 Castle Hill Road, Dover, Kent, CT16 1QW.*
Open: All Year
Grades: ETB 2 Cr, AA 3 Q, RAC Acclaim
01304 202253 Mr Hoynes
Rates fr: *£17.00*-**£26.00**.
Beds: 2F 2D 3T 1S
Baths: 8 Private
(6)
Comfortable Georgian house with parking; ideally situated for local attractions and ferries. Eurotunnel 10 minutes. All rooms ensuite, spacious family rooms. Credit cards accepted.

Number One Guest House, *1 Castle Street, Dover, Kent, CT16 1QH.*
Centrally located Georgian town house convenient for port and tunnel, garage parking.
Open: All Year
Grades: AA 3 Q, High Acclaim
01304 202007 Mr Reidy
Rates fr: *£18.00*.
Beds: 3F 2D 2T **Baths:** 4 Ensuite
(4)

***Bleriot's**, Belper House, 47 Park Avenue, Dover, Kent, CT16 1HE.*
Victorian residence in quiet location.
Open: All Year (not Xmas)
Grades: ETB 2 Cr
01304 211394 Mrs Casey
Rates fr: *£13.00*-**£15.00**.
Beds: 5F 1D 1T 3S
Baths: 5 Ensuite 5 Shared
(8)

***Elmo Guest House,** 120 Folkestone Road, Dover, Kent, CT17 9SP.*
Family run guest house.
Open: All Year
Grades: ETB 1 Cr, RAC Listed
01304 206236 Mr Christo
Rates fr: *£24.00*-**£12.00**.
Beds: 3F 2D 1S **Baths:** 2 Shared
(7)

***Conifers Guest House,** 241 Folkestone Road, Dover, Kent, CT17 9LL.*
Clean, comfortable, friendly accommodation.
Open: All Year (not Xmas)
01304 205609 Mr Andrews
Rates fr: *£14.00*-**£15.00**.
Beds: 2F 2D 1T 1S
Baths: 2 Private 2 Shared

***Esther House,** 55 Barton Road, Dover, Kent, CT16 2NF.*
Christian, non-smoking, 15 mins Channel Tunnel.
Open: All Year
Grades: ETB Listed, Comm
01304 241332 (also fax no)
Mrs Roberts
Rates fr: *£13.00*-**£13.00**.
Beds: 1F 1T 1S **Baths:** 1 Shared

***Pennyfarthing,** 109 Maison Dieu Road, Dover, Kent, CT16 1RT.*
Victorian house, privately owned, close to ferries.
Open: All Year
Grades: ETB 2 Cr, RAC Acclaim
01304 205563 Ms McPherson
Rates fr: *£20.00*-**£20.00**.
Beds: 2F 2D 1T 1S
Baths: 4 Ensuite
(6)

***Castle House,** 10 Castle Hill Road, Dover, Kent, CT16 1QW.*
Foothills of Dover Castle; non-smoking.
Open: All Year **Grades:** AA 3 Q
01304 201656 Mrs Dimech
Fax no: 01304 210197
Rates fr: *£16.00*-**£22.00**.
Beds: 1F 4D 1T **Baths:** 6 Private

***Owler Lodge,** Alkham Valley Road, Alkham, Dover, Kent, CT15 7DF.*
Lovely house in beautiful village.
Open: All Year (not Xmas)
Grades: ETB 3 Cr, High Comm
01304 826375 Mrs Owler
Rates fr: *£21.00*-**£30.00**.
Beds: 1F 1D 1T **Baths:** 3 Ensuite
(6)

***Linden Guest House,** 231 Folkestone Road, Dover, Kent, CT17 9SL.*
Elegantly decorated, immaculately clean.
Open: All Year (not Xmas)
01304 205449 Mr & Mrs Walkden
Rates fr: *£14.00*-**£15.00**.
Beds: 3F 1D 1S
Baths: 2 Ensuite 1 Private
1 Shared
(4)

***Restover Guest House,** 69 Folkestone Road, Dover, Kent, CT17 9RZ.*
Victorian house opposite train station. **Open:** All Year
Grades: ETB 1 Cr
01304 206031 Mrs Adamou
Rates fr: *£13.00*-**£16.00**.
Beds: 1F 4D 1T 1S
Baths: 1 Ensuite 1 Shared
(2)

***Tower Guest House,** 98 Priory Hill, Dover, Kent, CT17 0AD.*
Converted old water tower.
Open: All Year (not Xmas)
Grades: ETB 2 Cr, RAC Recomm
01304 208212 Mrs Wraight
Rates fr: *£16.00*-**£22.00**.
Beds: 2F 1D 2T
Baths: 3 Private 1 Shared
(2)

***Talavera House,** 275 Folkestone Road, Dover, Kent, CT17 9LL.*
Excellent value accommodation. High standards.
Open: All Year
Grades: ETB 1 Cr, Comm
01304 206794 Mrs Swain
Fax no: 0171 827 6267
Rates fr: *£13.00*.
Beds: 1D 2T **Baths:** 1 Shared
(3)

***The Haven Guest House,** 46 Salisbury Road, Dover, Kent, CT16 1EY.*
Victorian house close to ferries.
Open: All Year
Grades: ETB 1 Cr, High Comm
01304 203317 (also fax no)
Mrs Corby
Rates fr: *£14.00*-**£15.00**.
Beds: 3F 1S
Baths: 2 Shared
(3)

Dymchurch

National Grid Ref: TR1029

Ship Inn, Corner House, Ocean Inn

***Burwood House,** 2 Eastbridge Road, Dymchurch, Romney Marsh, Kent, TN29 0PD.*
Comfortable family home. Friendly atmosphere.
Open: All Year (not Xmas)
01303 873398 Mrs Apps
Rates fr: *£15.00*-**£15.00**.
Beds: 2D 1S
Baths: 1 Shared
(4)

***24 Mill Road,** Dymchurch, Romney Marsh, Kent, TN29 0NY.*
C18th Listed building.
Open: All Year
01303 873159 Mr Steele
Rates fr: *£16.00*-**£16.00**.
Beds: 1F 1D 1T 1S
Baths: 2 Shared
(5) (20)

***Waterside Guest House,** 15 Hythe Road, Dymchurch, Romney Marsh, Kent, TN29 0LN.*
Guest house overlooking Romney Marsh.
Open: All Year
Grades: ETB 2 Cr, Comm, AA 3 Q
01303 872253 Mrs Tinklin
Rates fr: *£14.00*-**£15.00**.
Beds: 1F 3D 2T 1S
Baths: 2 Private 2 Shared
(7)

***The Ship Inn,** 118 High Street, Dymchurch, Romney Marsh, Kent, TN29 0LD.*
Large C15th village inn.
Open: All Year
01303 872122 Mr Sharp
Rates fr: *£10.25*-**£15.50**.
Beds: 2F 1D 3T
Baths: 2 Shared
(50)

East Malling

National Grid Ref: TQ7057

King & Queen

***Blacklands House,** Blacklands, East Malling, Kent, ME19 6DS.*
Large Georgian house. Quiet. Family-run.
Open: All Year
01732 844274 Mr Leonard
Rates fr: *£17.50*-**£22.00**.
Beds: 1F 2D 1T 1S
Baths: 1 Private 2 Shared
(1) (10)

East Peckham

National Grid Ref: TQ6648

The Red Fort

***Roydon Hall,** East Peckham, Tonbridge, Kent, TN12 5NH.*
C16th Manor, peaceful, extensive gardens.
Open: All Year
01622 812121 Mr Cowan
Fax no: 01622 813959
Rates fr: *£15.00*-**£19.00**.
Beds: 3F 2D 7T 14S
Baths: 8 Ensuite 1 Private
6 Shared
(70)

Bringing children with you? Always ask for any special rates.

astling

ational Grid Ref: TQ9656

Carpenters Arms

he Carpenters Arms, *The Street, astling, Faversham, Kent,* ME13 0AZ.
14th inn, candlelit restaurant.
pen: All Year (not Xmas)
795 890234 Mrs O'Regan
ates fr: *£22.50*-**£35.00**.
eds: 3D 3S **Baths:** 3 Private
(12) (20)

denbridge

ational Grid Ref: TQ4446

The Four Elms, The /heatsheaf

nowlands, *Four Elms, denbridge, Kent,* TN8 6NA.
pacious Victorian private country ouse, non-smoking.
pen: All Year (not Xmas)
rades: AA 3 Q
1732 700314 Mr & Mrs Haviland
ates fr: *£25.00*-**£35.00**.
eds: 2D 1S
(3)

airseat

ational Grid Ref: TQ6261

he Old Post House, *Fairseat, evenoaks, Kent,* TN15 7LU.
retty C18th house, lovely gardens.
pen: All Year (not Xmas)
rades: ETB Listed
1732 822444 Mrs Gray
ates fr: *£16.00*-**£16.00**.
eds: 1D 1T **Baths:** 2 Shared
(3)

arthing Common

lational Grid Ref: TR1340

Drum Inn

outhfields, *Farthing Common, yminge, Folkestone, Kent,* CT18 8DH.
pen: Mar to Oct
1303 862391 Ms Wadie
ates fr: *£17.50*-**£17.50**.
eds: 1F 1T **Baths:** 1 Shared
(6)
amily home set in 8 acres of pasure on the North Downs. anoramic views across countryide to the channel. Historic Kent asily reached by car.

aversham

lational Grid Ref: TR0161

White Lion, Chimney Boy

4 London Road, *Faversham, Kent,* ME13 8CX.
arge Victorian private house.
pen: All Year
1795 537175 Mrs Best
ates fr: *£13.00*-**£14.00**.
eds: 1F 1T **Baths:** 1 Shared

Owens Court Farm, *Selling, Faversham, Kent,* ME13 9QN.
Open: All Year
Grades: ETB 1 Cr, Comm
01227 752247 (also fax no)
Mrs Higgs
Rates fr: *£17.00*-**£17.00**.
Beds: 1F 1T 1S
Baths: 2 Shared
(6)
Gracious Georgian farmhouse set amongst hop-gardens and orchards. Large, comfortable rooms. Lovely garden. Canterbury and Channel Ports and Tunnel within easy reach.

Tanners Cottage, *37 Tanner Street, Faversham, Kent,* ME13 7JP.
Small attractive old cottage.
Open: All Year (not Xmas)
01795 536698
M Jameson
Rates fr: *£12.00*-**£12.00**.
Beds: 1D 1T
Baths: 1 Shared
(5)

Folkestone

National Grid Ref: TR2136

The Carpenters, East Kent Arms

Abbey House Hotel, *5-6 Westbourne Gardens, Off Sandgate Road, Folkestone, Kent,* CT20 2JA.
Friendly licensed hotel.
Unrestricted parking.
Open: All Year (not Xmas)
Grades: ETB 2 Cr
01303 255514
Mr Donoghue
Rates fr: *£17.00*-**£18.00**.
Beds: 4F 4D 4T 3S
Baths: 3 Ensuite 4 Shared

Sunny Lodge Guest House, *85 Cheriton Road, Folkestone, Kent,* CT20 2QL.
The place to stay with lovely garden.
Open: All Year (not Xmas)
Grades: ETB 1 Cr
01303 251498
Mrs Young
Rates fr: *£15.00*-**£16.00**.
Beds: 2F 2D 2T 2S
Baths: 2 Shared
(5) (5)

Normandie Guest House, *39 Cheriton Road, Folkestone, Kent,* CT20 1DD.
Comfortable family-run guest house.
Open: All Year (not Xmas)
Grades: ETB Listed
01303 256233
Mrs Watts
Rates fr: *£14.50*-**£14.50**.
Beds: 2F 1D 2T 1S
Baths: 1 Shared
(4)

Fordcombe

National Grid Ref: TQ5240

The Chafford Arms

Lockerbie, *Chafford Lane, Fordcombe, Tunbridge Wells, Kent,* TN3 0SH.
Modern comfortable private house.
Open: All Year
01892 740278 Mrs McRow
Rates fr: *£16.00*-**£18.00**.
Beds: 1D
Baths: 1 Private
(2)

Frittenden

National Grid Ref: TQ8141

Tolehurst Barn, *Knoxbridge, Cranbrook Road, Frittenden, Cranbrook, Kent,* TN17 2BP.
Comfortable, newly-converted barn.
Open: All Year (not Xmas)
01580 714385 Mrs Tresilian
Rates fr: *£17.50*-**£17.50**.
Beds: 1F 2D
Baths: 3 Private
(6)

Gillingham

National Grid Ref: TQ7767

Queens Head

178 Bredhurst Road, *Wigmore, Gillingham, Kent,* ME8 0QX.
Large chalet bungalow 4 minutes M2. **Open:** All Year
01634 233267 Mrs Penn
Rates fr: *£16.00*-**£18.00**.
Beds: 1F 1T **Baths:** 2 Private
(2)

Abigails, *17 The Maltings, Rainham, Gillingham, Kent,* ME8 8JL.
Modern friendly atmosphere, countryside views.
Open: All Year
01634 365427 Ms Nielsen
Rates fr: *£13.50*-**£13.50**.
Beds: 1F 1D 2T 2S
(4)

The Post Office, *17 Gads Hill, Gillingham, Kent,* ME7 2RU.
Friendly family home.
Open: All Year
01634 851214 Mrs Fountain
Rates fr: *£16.00*-**£16.00**.
Beds: 1D 1T 2S

Condor House, *The Street, Bredhurst, Gillingham, Kent,* ME7 3JY.
Convenient Kent ports, Rochester, London.
Open: All Year
Grades: ETB Listed, Comm
01634 232988 Mrs Field
Rates fr: *£15.00*-**£18.00**.
Beds: 3T
Baths: 1 Private 1 Shared
(10)

Goudhurst

National Grid Ref: TQ7237

Green Cross Inn

West Winchet, *Winchet Hill, Goudhurst, Cranbrook, Kent, TN17 1JX.*
Large Victorian house, secluded position.
Open: All Year (not Xmas)
01580 212024 Mrs Parker
Rates fr: *£18.00*-**£25.00**.
Beds: 1D 1T
Baths: 2 Private
(5) (6)

The Green Cross Inn, *Goudhurst, Cranbrook, Kent, TN17 1HA.*
Small family-run inn.
Open: All Year
01580 211200 Mr Collings
Rates fr: *£20.00*-**£25.00**.
Beds: 1F 1D 1T 1S
Baths: 1 Shared
(20)

Great Mongeham

National Grid Ref: TR3451

Beaconhill Cottage, *Beaconhill, Great Mongeham, Deal, Kent, CT14 0HW.*
Comfortable, secluded farmhouse, nature reserve.
Open: All Year
01304 372809 Mr & Mrs Wiggins
Rates fr: *£16.00*-**£18.00**.
Beds: 4T
Baths: 3 Shared
(20)

Hadlow

National Grid Ref: TQ6350

The Harrow Inn

Smithers House, *The Terrace, Hadlow, Tonbridge, Kent, TN11 0DL.*
Architecturally Listed building, converted smithy.
Open: All Year
01732 850256 Mrs Hawkins
Rates fr: *£22.50*-**£22.50**.
Beds: 1D **Baths:** 1 Private

Dunsmore, *Hadlow Park, Hadlow, Tonbridge, Kent, TN11 0HX.*
Private park, ground floor accommodation.
Open: All Year (not Xmas)
01732 850611 Mrs Tubbs
Rates fr: *£17.00*-**£20.00**.
Beds: 1T **Baths:** 1 Private

The lowest *double* rate per person is shown in *italics*.

Harrietsham

National Grid Ref: TQ8752

The Roebuck

Mannamead, *Pilgrims Way, Harrietsham, Maidstone, Kent, ME17 1BT.*
Friendly atmosphere, quiet, comfortable accommodation.
Open: All Year (not Xmas)
Grades: ETB 2 Cr, Comm
01622 859336 Mrs Atkins
Rates fr: *£16.00*-**£18.00**.
Beds: 1D 1T 1S
Baths: 1 Private 1 Shared
(2) (4)

Headcorn

National Grid Ref: TQ8344

Three Chimneys

Vine Farm, *Waterman Quarter, Headcorn, Ashford, Kent, TN27 9JJ.*
Peaceful C16th beamed farmhouse.
Open: All Year (not Xmas)
Grades: ETB 2 Cr
01622 890203 Mrs Harman
Fax no: 01622 891819
Rates fr: *£22.50*-**£25.00**.
Beds: 2D 1T **Baths:** 3 Private
(12) (6)

High Halden

National Grid Ref: TQ8937

Monarch House, *Ashford Road, High Halden, Ashford, Kent, TN26 3NA.*
Comfortable private house.
Open: All Year (not Xmas)
01233 850316 Mrs Paxton
Rates fr: *£14.00*-**£15.00**.
Beds: 1D 1T 1S **Baths:** 1 Shared
(6)

Hildenborough

National Grid Ref: TQ5648

150 Tonbridge Road, *Hildenborough, Tonbridge, Kent, TN11 9HW.*
Spacious Victorian house.
Open: All Year (not Xmas)
01732 838894 Mrs Romney
Rates fr: *£12.50*-**£15.00**.
Beds: 1T 1S **Baths:** 1 Shared
(2)

Hollingbourne

National Grid Ref: TQ8455

Sugar Loaves, Windmill

Woodhouses, *49 Eyhorne Street, Hollingbourne, Maidstone, Kent, ME17 1TR.*
Two inter-connected C17th cottages. **Open:** All Year
Grades: ETB 2 Cr
01622 880594 (also fax no)
Mr & Mrs Woodhouse
Rates fr: *£17.00*-**£18.00**.
Beds: 3T **Baths:** 3 Ensuite
(10) (4)

The Limes, *53 Eyhorne Street, Hollingbourne, Maidstone, Kent, ME17 1TS.*
Beautiful Georgian house, walled garden.
Open: Feb to Nov
01622 880554 Mrs Reed
Rates fr: *£16.00*-**£16.00**.
Beds: 1D 1S
Baths: 1 Private
(10) (5)

Horsmonden

National Grid Ref: TQ7040

The Gun & Spit Roast

Forge House, *Brenchley Road, Horsmonden, Tonbridge, Kent, TN12 8DN.*
Friendly house, ideal touring base.
Open: All Year
01892 723584 Mrs Brett
Rates fr: *£14.00*-**£14.00**.
Beds: 1D 1T 1S
Baths: 1 Shared
(5)

Hothfield

National Grid Ref: TQ9744

The Coach House, *Chapel Road, Hothfield, Ashford, Kent, TN25 4LN.*
Large, detached, oak-beamed house.
Open: All Year
01233 713878 (also fax no)
Mr Cooke
Rates fr: *£13.00*-**£15.00**.
Beds: 2D
Baths: 1 Shared
(3)

Hunton

National Grid Ref: TQ7149

Stilebridge Inn

Wealden Hall House, *East Street, Hunton, Maidstone, Kent, ME15 0RB.*
Open: Feb to Dec
Grades: ETB 2 Cr, High Comm
01622 820246
Mrs Horrocks
Rates fr: *£20.00*-**£25.00**.
Beds: 2D 1T 1S
Baths: 2 Ensuite 1 Shared
(12) (4)
Set in one acre of beautiful landscape watergardens with waterfowl. All rooms have TV & tea/coffee-making facilities. 9 miles to Leeds & Sissinghurst Castles.

The Woolhouse, *Grove Lane, Hunton, Maidstone, Kent, ME15 0SE.*
Converted C16th Listed brick barn.
Open: All Year (not Xmas)
01622 820778 Mrs Wetton
Rates fr: *£20.00*-**£22.00**.
Beds: 1D 1T 2S
Baths: 4 Private
(12)

Hythe

National Grid Ref: TR1634

Nyanza Lodge Hotel, *87 Seabrook Road, Hythe, Kent, CT21 5RB.*
Large Edwardian, one acre, parking, seaviews.
Open: All Year (not Xmas)
01303 267315 Rates fr: *£20.00*-**£25.00**.
Beds: 2F 3D 1T
Baths: 4 Ensuite 2 Shared
(6)

Ide Hill

National Grid Ref: TQ4851

The Wheatsheaf, Castle Inn

Winkhurst Green, *Ide Hill, Sevenoaks, Kent, TN14 6LD.*
Comfortable farmhouse with excellent cuisine.
Open: All Year (not Xmas)
01732 750257 (also fax no)
Mrs Cohen
Rates fr: *£20.00*-**£20.00**.
Beds: 2D 1S
Baths: 1 Private
(10) (20)

Kemsing

National Grid Ref: TQ5558

16 Copperfields, *Kemsing, Sevenoaks, Kent, TN15 6QG.*
Quiet, comfortable Kentish barn-style house.
Open: All Year (not Xmas)
01732 761607
Mr & Mrs Swales
Rates fr: *£15.00*-**£12.00**.
Beds: 1T 1D
Baths: 1 Private
(5) (2)

Lamberhurst

National Grid Ref: TQ6736

Chequers Oast, *Lamberhurst, Tunbridge Wells, Kent, TN3 8DB.*
Oast house in village centre.
Open: All Year (not Xmas)
01892 890579
Mrs Harrison
Rates fr: *£15.00*-**£17.50**.
Beds: 1D 1T
Baths: 1 Private 1 Shared
(10) (2)

Owls Castle Cottage, *Hoghole Lane, Lamberhurst, Tunbridge Wells, Kent, TN3 8BN.*
Beautiful C17th farmhouse in AONB.
Open: Easter to Oct
01892 890510
Mrs Marchant
Rates fr: *£15.00*-**£20.00**.
Beds: 1T 1P
Baths: 1 Private
(2)

Leaveland

National Grid Ref: TR0053

White Lion

Leaveland Court, *Leaveland, Faversham, Kent, ME13 0NP.*
Open: Feb - Nov
Grades: ETB 2 Cr, High Comm
01233 740596 Mrs Scutt
Rates fr: *£20.00*-**£25.00**.
Beds: 2D 1T
Baths: 3 Ensuite 1 Private
(4)
Enchanting C15th timbered farmhouse with delightful gardens and heated outdoor swimming pool. Close to Canterbury and Channel ports. All rooms ensuite with colour TVs.

Leybourne

National Grid Ref: TQ6858

20 Rectory Lane South, *Leybourne, West Malling, Kent, ME19 5HB.*
Comfortable, secluded bungalow, private sitting-room.
Open: All Year (not Xmas)
01732 848020 Mrs Pragnell
Rates fr: *£18.00*-**£20.00**.
Beds: 1D **Baths:** 1 Private
(2)

Linton

National Grid Ref: TQ7549

The Bull, The Stilebridge

Hill Place, *Linton, Maidstone, Kent, ME17 4AL.*
Open: All Year (not Xmas)
01622 743834 Mrs Johnston
Rates fr: *£19.00*-**£19.00**.
Beds: 2D 1T
Baths: 2 Ensuite 1 Shared
(7) (6)
Grade II Listed family home dating from C17th, with panoramic views across the Weald of Kent. Spacious bedrooms. Mature gardens. Tennis court. Swimming pool.

The White Lodge, *Loddington Lane, Linton, Maidstone, Kent, ME17 4AG.*
Elegant country house in parkland.
Open: All Year (not Xmas)
01622 743129 Mrs Boorman
Rates fr: *£20.00*-**£20.00**.
Beds: 1F 1D 2T 2S
Baths: 1 Private 1 Shared

Always telephone to get directions to the B&B - you will save time!

Lydd

National Grid Ref: TR0420

The George

George Hotel, *11 High Street, Lydd, Kent, TN29 9AJ.*
Family-run pub, good food.
Open: All Year
01797 320134 Ms Smith
Rates fr: *£15.00*-**£20.00**.
Beds: 2F 4D 3T **Baths:** 3 Shared
(20)

Lydd on Sea

National Grid Ref: TR0820

Fairwind, *133 Coast Drive, Lydd on Sea, Romney Marsh, Kent, TN29 9NS.*
Modern detached bungalow on coast.
Open: All Year
01797 321219 Mr Gilbert
Rates fr: *£15.00*-**£17.00**.
Beds: 1F 1D 1T 1S
Baths: 1 Shared
(4)

Lynsted

National Grid Ref: TQ9460

Black Lion Inn

Forge Cottage, *Lynsted, Sittingbourne, Kent, ME9 0RH.*
Converted C17th forge and cottage.
Open: All Year (not Xmas)
01795 521273 Mrs Bage
Rates fr: *£14.00*-**£20.00**.
Beds: 1F 1D 1T
Baths: 2 Shared
(10)

Maidstone

National Grid Ref: TQ7655

Grangemoor Hotel, The Old Plantation, Railway Hotel , The Victory

Court Farm, *Village High Street, Maidstone, Aylesford, Kent, ME20 7AZ.*
Open: All Year
01622 717293 (also fax no)
Mrs Tucker
Rates fr: *£17.50*-**£20.00**.
Beds: 1D 1T 1S
Baths: 2 Ensuite 1 Private
(6)
Beautiful old beamed farmhouse offering quality accommodation. Antiques, four poster bed. Equipped bedrooms. Ensuite. Close M20/M2. Parking. Relaxed, quiet. Sorry no children. Ideal business or pleasure.

51 Bower Mount Road, *Maidstone, Kent, ME16 8AX.*
Large comfortable Edwardian semi. **Open:** All Year (not Xmas)
01622 762948 Mrs Haddow
Rates fr: *£15.00*-**£17.00**.
Beds: 1D 1T 1S **Baths:** 1 Shared
(9)

Willington Court, *Willington Street, Maidstone, Kent, ME15 8JW.*
Charming listed building. Lovely accomodation.
Open: All Year
Grades: ETB 2 Cr, High Comm, AA 4 Q
01622 738885 Mrs Waterman
Rates fr: *£20.00*-**£26.00**.
Beds: 2D 1T
Baths: 3 Private
(6)

Wits End Guest House, *78 Bower Mount Road, Maidstone, Kent, ME16 8AT.*
Quiet Edwardian Licensed guest house.
Open: All Year
Grades: ETB 3 Cr, Comm
01622 752684 Mrs King
Rates fr: *£19.00*-**£19.00**.
Beds: 2F 1D 1T 2S
Baths: 3 Private 2 Shared
(0) (8)

Conway House, *12 Conway Road, Allington, Maidstone, Kent, ME16 0HD.*
Quality accommodation in friendly family-home.
Open: All Year
01622 688287 Mrs Backhouse
Rates fr: *£17.50*-**£20.00**.
Beds: 1F 1T 1S
Baths: 1 Ensuite
(7)

Fairlawn, *Whiterock Place, Terrace Road, Maidstone, Kent, ME16 8HX.*
Detached bungalow in private road.
Open: All Year (not Xmas)
01622 763642 Mrs Outlaw
Rates fr: *£16.00*-**£15.00**.
Beds: 1D 1T 1S
(3)

10 Fant Lane, *Maidstone, Kent, ME16 8NL.*
Quiet Victorian cottage.
Open: All Year
01622 729883 Mrs Layton
Rates fr: *£12.50*-**£12.50**.
Beds: 1F 1S 1T
Baths: 2 Shared
(2)

Raigersfeld House, *Mote Park, Ashford Road, Maidstone, Kent, ME14 4AE.*
400-year-old hall house.
Open: All Year
01622 685211
Mr & Mrs Carpenter
Rates fr: *£15.00*-**£18.00**.
Beds: 1F 1D 1T 1S
Baths: 1 Private 2 Shared
(6)

The lowest **single**
rate is shown in **bold.**

25 Holland Road, *Maidstone, Kent, ME14 1UN.*
Victorian town house, warm welcome.
Open: All Year (not Xmas)
01622 678606 Ms Davies-Wheeler
Rates fr: *£15.00*-**£16.00**.
Beds: 1D 2T

Marden

National Grid Ref: TQ7444

Tanner House, *Tanner Farm, Goudhurst Road, Marden, Tonbridge, Kent, TN12 9ND.*
Large, comfortable Tudor farmhouse.
Open: All Year (not Xmas)
01622 831214 Mrs Mannington
Rates fr: *£18.00*-**£28.00**.
Beds: 1D 2T
Baths: 3 Private
(5) (3)

Margate

National Grid Ref: TR3570

Malvern Hotel, *Eastern Esplanade, Cliftonville, Margate, Kent, CT9 2HL.*
Open: All Year
Grades: ETB 2 Cr, Comm
01843 290192
Rates fr: *£18.00*-**£21.00**.
Beds: 1F 6D 2T 1S
Baths: 8 Ensuite 1 Shared
Small seafront hotel, close indoor bowls, winter gardens, etc. Canterbury, Dover, Ramsgate within easy reach. French/Belgian daytrips arranged. All rooms TV. Dining room non-smoking. Access/Visa.

Carnforth, *103 Norfolk Road, Cliftonville, Margate, Kent, CT9 2HX.*
Friendly, family-run private hotel.
Open: All Year
01843 292127 Mr Clark
Rates fr: *£15.50*-**£15.50**.
Beds: 2F 5D 2T 2S
Baths: 3 Ensuite 3 Shared
(3)

9 Dalby Square, *Margate, Kent, CT9 2ER.*
Large, elegantly furnished Victorian hotel.
Open: All Year
Grades: ETB 3 Cr
01843 290598 Mr Irani
Rates fr: *£20.00*-**£28.00**.
Beds: 3F 7D 2T 1S
Baths: 13 Private
(4)

Crescent House, *24 Fort Crescent, Cliftonville, Margate, Kent, CT9 1HX.*
Grade II Listed seafront house.
Open: All Year
01843 223092 Mr & Mrs Fish
Rates fr: *£15.00*-**£15.00**.
Beds: 2F 3D 1T 2S
Baths: 2 Private 2 Shared

Mersham

National Grid Ref: TR0539

Gill Farm, *Gill Lane, Mersham, Ashford, Kent, TN25 7HZ.*
Luxurious farmhouse in secluded grounds.
Open: All Year
01233 720345 Mrs Bowman
Rates fr: *£22.00*-**£25.00**.
Beds: 1D 1T 2S
Baths: 2 Private 1 Shared
(10)

Minster in Sheppey

National Grid Ref: TQ9573

Lady Hamilton

Cherry Tree Lodge, *451 Minster Road, Minster in Sheppey, Sheerness, Kent, ME12 3NS.*
Modern, comfortable detached house.
Open: All Year (not Xmas)
01795 874958 Mrs Girt
Rates fr: *£15.00*-**£20.00**.
Beds: 3T
Baths: 1 Private 1 Shared
(5)

Kenstowe House, *177 Wards Hill, Minster in Sheppey, Sheerness, Kent, ME12 2JZ.*
Detached bungalow, large garden, quiet close to sea front .
Open: Easter to Oct
01795 872234 Mrs Lester
Rates fr: *£13.50*-**£15.50**.
Beds: 1F 2D
Baths: 1 Shared
(3)

North Elham

National Grid Ref: TR1844

Kings Arms

Hillbrook House, *North Elham, Canterbury, Kent, CT4 6UY.*
Large Victorian country house, beautiful valley.
Open: All Year
Grades: ETB Listed
01303 840220 Mrs Sisk
Rates fr: *£18.00*-**£25.00**.
Beds: 1F 1D 1T
Baths: 1 Private 1 Shared
(7)

Old Romney

National Grid Ref: TR0325

Rose & Crown

Rose & Crown Inn, *Old Romney, Romney Marsh, Kent, TN29 9SQ.*
C17th inn with modern chalets.
Open: All Year (not Xmas)
Grades: ETB Listed
01797 367500 Mr Carter
Rates fr: *£19.00*-**£25.00**.
Beds: 5T
Baths: 5 Private
(1)

Otford

National Grid Ref: TQ5159

***Darenth Dene,** Shoreham Road, Otford, Sevenoaks, Kent, TN14 5RP.*
Quiet comfortable private house.
Open: All Year (not Xmas)
01959 522293 Mrs Reid
Rates fr: *£16.00*-**£18.00**.
Beds: 2T 2S
Baths: 1 Shared
(10) (4)

***25 Hillydeal Road,** Otford, Sevenoaks, Kent, TN14 5RT.*
Detached house in private road.
Open: Mar to Oct
01959 523528 Mrs Knight
Rates fr: *£17.50*.
Beds: 1T
Baths: 1 Private
(3)

Otterden

National Grid Ref: TQ9454

***Frith Farm House,** Otterden, Faversham, Kent, ME13 0DD.*
Elegant Georgian house in 6-acre garden.
Open: All Year
01795 890701 Mr & Mrs Chesterfield
Fax no: 01795 890009
Rates fr: *£23.50*-**£25.00**.
Beds: 2D 1T
Baths: 3 Ensuite
(12) (6)

Paddock Wood

National Grid Ref: TQ6744

George & Dragon

***Mascalls Oast,** Badsell Road, Paddock Wood, Tonbridge, Kent, TN12 6LR.*
Converted Kentish oasthouse.
Open: All Year (not Xmas)
01892 832747 Mrs Weston
Rates fr: *£15.00*-**£20.00**.
Beds: 1D 1T 1S
Baths: 1 Private 1 Shared
(7) (4)

Penshurst

National Grid Ref: TQ5243

***2 Keymer Court,** Penshurst, Tonbridge, Kent, TN11 8BU.*
Large double room, village centre.
Open: All Year (not Xmas)
01892 870280 Mrs Day
Rates fr: *£17.50*-**£35.00**.
Beds: 1T
Baths: 1 Shared
(1)

Petham

National Grid Ref: TR1351

***Upper Ansdore,** Duckpit Lane, Petham, Canterbury, Kent, CT4 5QB.*
Tudor farmhouse overlooking nature reserve.
Open: All Year (not Xmas)
Grades: AA 3 Q
01227 700672 Mr & Mrs Linch
Rates fr: *£18.00*-**£25.00**.
Beds: 1F 4D 1T
Baths: 4 Private
(5)

Pluckley

National Grid Ref: TQ9245

Dering Arms, Rose & Crown, The Chequers

***Arden,** Forge Hill, Pluckley, Ashford, Kent, TN27 0SN.*
Large country house with pool.
Open: Easter to Oct
Grades: ETB 2 Cr
01233 840330 Mrs Hummerson
Rates fr: *£17.00*-**£20.00**.
Beds: 1D 1T 1S
Baths: 1 Ensuite 2 Private
(3) (10)

***The Dering Arms,** Pluckley, Ashford, Kent, TN27 0RR.*
Relaxed, C17th hunting lodge.
Open: All Year (not Xmas)
01233 840371 Mr Buss
Rates fr: *£18.00*-**£28.00**.
Beds: 1F 2D
Baths: 1 Shared
(15)

Preston

National Grid Ref: TR2561

***Forstal House,** The Forstal, Preston, Canterbury, Kent, CT3 1DT.*
Open: All Year (not Xmas)
01227 722282 (also fax no)
Mrs Scott
Rates fr: *£18.00*-**£20.00**.
Beds: 1D 1T
Baths: 1 Ensuite 1 Private
(4)
Secluded C18th country house near river and orchards. Beautiful walled garden with water features and spinney. Superb home grown produce in season. Comfortable TV room.

Rainham

National Grid Ref: TQ8165

***Irwin Grange,** Meresborough Road, Rainham, Gillingham, Kent, ME8 8PN.*
Farmhouse set in 13 acres.
Open: All Year (not Xmas)
01634 232801 Mrs Knight
Rates fr: *£17.50*-**£20.00**.
Beds: 1F 2T
Baths: 1 Private 1 Shared
(20)

Ramsgate

National Grid Ref: TR3864

Churchill Tavern, The Royal Harbour

***Spencer Court Hotel,** 37 Spencer Square, Ramsgate, Kent, CT11 9LD.*
Grade II Listed Regency hotel.
Open: All Year
Grades: ETB 2 Cr, Comm
01843 594582 Mr & Mrs Jordan
Rates fr: *£15.00*-**£17.00**.
Beds: 2F 3D 2T 2S
Baths: 4 Private 2 Shared

***York House,** 7 Augusta Road, Eastcliff, Ramsgate, Kent, CT11 8JP.*
Homely guest house near sea.
Open: All Year (not Xmas)
01843 596775 Mr & Mrs Rhodes
Rates fr: *£13.00*-**£13.00**.
Beds: 2F 2D 2T 1S
Baths: 2 Shared

***The Royale Guest House,** 7 Royal Road, Ramsgate, Kent, CT11 9LE.*
Friendly, family run guest house.
Open: All Year
01843 594712 Mrs Barry
Rates fr: *£14.00*-**£14.00**.
Beds: 1F 2D 2T 4S
Baths: 2 Shared
(2)

***Goodwin View,** 19 Wellington Crescent, Ramsgate, Kent, CT11 8JD.*
Comfortable, licensed, Regency seafront hotel.
Open: All Year
Grades: ETB 2 Cr, Approv, RAC Listed
01843 591419
Mr & Mrs Denne
Rates fr: *£16.00*-**£19.00**.
Beds: 4F 3D 2T 4S
Baths: 4 Ensuite 3 Shared
(0)

Rochester

National Grid Ref: TQ7268

King's Head, Royal Oak

***255 High Street,** Rochester, Kent, ME1 1HQ.*
Victorian family house near station.
Open: All Year (not Xmas)
01634 842737 Mrs Thomas
Rates fr: *£13.00*-**£15.00**.
Beds: 1F 1D 1T
Baths: 1 Private 1 Shared
(1)

***St Martin,** 104 Borstal Road, Rochester, Kent, ME1 3BD.*
Comfortable Victorian home overlooking river.
Open: All Year (not Xmas)
01634 848192 Mrs Colvin
Rates fr: *£14.00*-**£15.00**.
Beds: 2T 1S

19 Roebuck Road, *Rochester, Kent, ME1 1UE.*
Central quiet Victorian house. Modern comforts.
Open: All Year (not Xmas)
01634 827153
Mrs Smithwhite
Rates fr: *£15.00*-**£17.00**.
Beds: 1F 1D
Baths: 1 Shared
(1)

The Old Priory, *Mill Road, Rochester, Kent, ME2 3BT.*
Large victorian private house.
Open: All Year
01634 714053
Mr & Mrs Phillips
Fax no: 01634 717716
Rates fr: *£13.00*-**£13.00**.
Beds: 2T 2S
(10)

Rolvenden

National Grid Ref: TQ8431

Another Hooden House

Little Halden Farm, *Rolvenden, Cranbrook, Kent, TN17 4JL.*
Open: Easter to Sep
01580 241254 Mrs Hilder
Rates fr: *£15.00*.
Beds: 2D 1T
Baths: 2 Shared
(3)
This working hop and livestock farm is situated in an area of outstanding natural beauty. Guests are welcome to wander around the farm and garden.

Ryarsh

National Grid Ref: TQ6759

Heavers Farm, *Ryarsh, West Malling, Kent, ME19 5JU.*
Open: All Year (not Xmas)
Grades: ETB 2 Cr
01732 842074 (also fax no)
Mrs Edwards
Rates fr: *£15.00*-**£20.00**.
Beds: 1D 2T
Baths: 2 Shared
(Birth) (3)
Set in countryside surrounded by woods and fields. 250 year old cottage, large garden. 2.5 miles M20, easy reach of airports, London, Canterbury and Dover.

Sandhurst

National Grid Ref: TQ7928

Hoads Farm, *Crouch Lane, Sandhurst, Cranbrook, Kent, TN18 5PA.*
C17th farmhouse on working farm.
Open: All Year
01580 850296 Mrs Nicholas
Rates fr: *£17.00*-**£17.00**.
Beds: 3T
Baths: 2 Shared

Planning a longer stay? Always ask for any special rates.

Selling

National Grid Ref: TR0456

White Lion

Owens Court Farm, *Selling, Faversham, Kent, ME13 9QN.*
Gracious Georgian farmhouse, hop-gardens, orchards.
Open: All Year
Grades: ETB 1 Cr, Comm
01227 752247 (also fax no)
Mrs Higgs
Rates fr: *£17.00*-**£17.00**.
Beds: 1F 1T 1S
Baths: 2 Shared
(6)

Parkfield House, *Hogbens Hill, Selling, Faversham, Kent, ME13 9QU.*
Large detached house with garden.
Open: All Year (not Xmas)
01227 752898 Mrs Hogben
Rates fr: *£16.00*-**£16.00**.
Beds: 1F 1D 2T 1S
Baths: 2 Shared
(6)

Sevenoaks

National Grid Ref: TQ5255

White Hart

40 Robyns Way, *Sevenoaks, Kent, TN13 3EB.*
Quiet house, station 10 minutes.
Open: All Year
01732 452401 Mrs Ingram
Rates fr: *£18.00*-**£20.00**.
Beds: 1F
Baths: 1 Ensuite
(1)

Green Tiles, *46 The Rise, Sevenoaks, Kent, TN13 1RJ.*
Quiet ground floor garden annexe.
Open: All Year (not Xmas)
01732 451522 (also fax no)
Mrs Knoops
Rates fr: *£16.00*-**£22.00**.
Beds: 1F**Baths:** 1 Private
(2)

Sevenoaks Weald

National Grid Ref: TQ5250

Lambarde Hill, *Glebe Road, Sevenoaks Weald, Sevenoaks, Kent, TN14 6PD.*
Quietly situated former vicarage.
Open: Jan to Nov
Grades: ETB 2 Cr, Comm
01732 463635 Mrs Conacher
Rates fr: *£19.00*-**£20.00**.
Beds: 1D 1T 1S
Baths: 3 Private
(3)

Laural Cottage, *Morleys Road, Sevenoaks Weald, Sevenoaks, Kent, TN14 6QY.*
Picturesque chalet bungalow, rural, views.
Open: All Year
01732 463500 Mrs Townsend
Rates fr: *£17.50*-**£20.00**.
Beds: 1F 1T
Baths: 2 Ensuite
(12) (2)

Sheerness

National Grid Ref: TQ9175

Victoriana Hotel, *103-109 Alma Road, Sheerness, Kent, ME12 2PD.*
Converted Victorian houses.
Open: All Year
Grades: RAC Listed
01795 665555 Mr Taylor
Fax no: 01795 580633
Rates fr: *£15.50*-**£16.00**.
Beds: 2F 6D 6T 6S
Baths: 8 Private 3 Shared
(8)

42 St Agnes Gardens, *Sheerness, Kent, ME12 1XN.*
Open: All Year
01795 665426 Mr & Mrs Harman
Rates fr: *£10.00*-**£10.00**.
Beds: 1T
Baths: 1 Private

Shepherdswell

National Grid Ref: TR2547

Sunshine Cottage, *The Green, Shepherdswell, Dover, Kent, CT15 7LQ.*
C17th cottage on village green.
Open: All Year
Grades: ETB 2 Cr, Comm
01304 831359 / 831218
Mrs Popple
Rates fr: *£19.00*-**£25.00**.
Beds: 1F 4D 1T
Baths: 2 Private 4 Shared

Shorne

National Grid Ref: TQ6970

Rose & Crown

Gardeners Cottage, *Puckle Hill, Shorne, Gravesend, Kent, DA12 3LB.*
Woodland cottage, woodburners and beam.
Open: All Year (not Xmas)
Grades: ETB Listed
01474 823269 Mrs Peters
Rates fr: *£21.00*-**£22.00**.
Beds: 1D 1T 1S
(6)

All rates are subject to alteration at the owners' discretion.

Sissinghurst

National Grid Ref: TQ7937

The Bull Inn, Three Chimneys (Biddenden)

Hillview Cottage, *Starvenden Lane, Sissinghurst, Cranbrook, Kent, TN17 2AN.*
Peaceful country house, gloriously situated..
Open: All Year (not Xmas)
Grades: ETB Listed
01580 712823 / 0850 909838 Mrs Lloyd Jones
Rates fr: *£17.00*-**£20.00**.
Beds: 2D 1T
(6)

Briar Knoll, *Chapel Lane, Sissinghurst, Cranbrook, Kent, TN17 2JN.*
Villa-style bungalow with land.
Open: All Year (not Xmas)
01580 713 497 Mrs Winter
Fax no: 01580 713419
Rates fr: *£17.50*-**£22.00**.
Beds: 2D
Baths: 2 Private
(10)

Sittingbourne

National Grid Ref: TQ9063

Old School Club, Dover Castle

Yew Trees, *132 London Road, Sittingbourne, Kent, ME10 1QB.*
Recently renovated, near ferry ports.
Open: All Year
01795 471526 Mrs Montgomery
Rates fr: *£15.00*-**£20.00**.
Beds: 1F 1D 1T
Baths: 2 Shared
(2)

8 The Crescent, *Sittingbourne, Kent, ME9 9EL.*
Comfortable modern home.
Open: All Year
01795 522398 Mrs Waltz
Rates fr: *£11.25*-**£12.00**.
Beds: 1T
Baths: 1 Shared

Smarden

National Grid Ref: TQ8842

Chequers Inn, The Bell

Munk Farm, *Smarden, Ashford, Kent, TN27 8PN.*
Elegant oak-beamed Georgian farmhouse.
Open: All Year (not Xmas) and New Year
Grades: ETB Listed, High Comm
01233 770265 Mrs Scott
Rates fr: *£22.00*-**£27.00**.
Beds: 2T
Baths: 2 Private
(3)

St Margarets at Cliffe

National Grid Ref: TR3644

Merzenich Guest House, *Station Road, St Margarets at Cliffe, Dover, Kent, CT15 6AY.*
Modern, comfortable, friendly guest house. **Open:** All Year
01304 852260 Mr & Mrs Claringbould
Fax no: 01304 852167
Rates fr: *£14.00*-**£21.00**.
Beds: 3D 1T **Baths:** 4 Private
(4)

Woodpeckers, *Chapel Lane, St Margarets at Cliffe, Dover, Kent, CT15 6BQ.*
Modern, comfortable quiet, near Dover.
Open: All Year (not Xmas)
01304 852761 Mrs Swan
Rates fr: *£17.00*-**£20.00**.
Beds: 1F 1T **Baths:** 2 Private
(4)

St Mary's Platt

National Grid Ref: TQ6057

George & Dragon (Ightham)

Holmes, *Boneashe Lane, St Mary's Platt, Borough Green, Sevenoaks, Kent, TN15 8NW.*
Beautiful C15th spacious, convenient farmhouse.
Open: Apr to Oct
Grades: ETB Listed
01732 882502 Mrs Hickey
Rates fr: *£15.00*.
Beds: 1D 1T **Baths:** 1 Shared
(12) (4)

Stowting

National Grid Ref: TR1241

The Tiger Inn, Five Bells

Water Farm, *Stowting, Ashford, Kent, TN25 6BA.*
Lakeside farm, homely and comfortable.
Open: All Year (not Xmas)
01303 862401 Mrs Cole
Rates fr: *£18.00*-**£18.00**.
Beds: 1F 1T
Baths: 1 Ensuite 2 Private
(8) (2)

Sutton Valence

National Grid Ref: TQ8149

The Kings Head

West Belringham, *Chart Road, Sutton Valence, Maidstone, Kent, ME17 3AW.*
Large bungalow with panoramic views.
Open: All Year (not Xmas)
Grades: ETB 1 Cr, Comm
01622 843995 Mrs King
Rates fr: *£18.00*-**£22.00**.
Beds: 1F 1T
Baths: 1 Shared
(3) (6)

Coppins, *Maidstone Road, Sutton Valence, Maidstone, Kent, ME17 3LW.*
Spacious detached chalet bungalow.
Open: Mar to Oct
01622 842600 Mrs Wilding
Rates fr: *£15.00*.
Beds: 1D 1T
(7) (2)

Swanley

National Grid Ref: TQ5168

Alice Dene, *Beechenlea Lane, Swanley, Kent, BR8 7PR.*
Beautiful 1820 Georgian country house.
Open: All Year (not Xmas)
Grades: ETB 1 Cr, AA 4 Q
01322 664420 Mr Crush
Rates fr: *£20.00*-**£20.00**.
Beds: 1D 2T
(8) (4)

Tenterden

National Grid Ref: TQ8833

Eight Bells

The White Cottage, *London Beach, Tenterden, Kent, TN30 6SR.*
Rural house with garden.
Open: All Year
Grades: ETB 2 Cr
01233 850583 Mrs Matthews
Rates fr: *£15.50*-**£15.50**.
Beds: 2D 1T
Baths: 1 Private 2 Shared
(3)

The Hollies, *Appledore Road, Tenterden, Kent, TN30 7BE.*
Modern Georgian house.
Open: All Year (not Xmas)
01580 763069 Mrs Wilkinson
Rates fr: *£17.00*-**£17.00**.
Beds: 1T 2S
Baths: 1 Shared
(5) (3)

Tonbridge

National Grid Ref: TQ5946

Chaser Inn (Shipbourne)

Starvecrow Place, *Shipbourne Road, Tonbridge, Kent, TN11 9NL.*
Luxury accommodation set in woodlands.
Open: All Year (not Xmas)
01732 356863 Mrs Batson
Rates fr: *£18.00*-**£25.00**.
Beds: 1D 1T 1S
Baths: 2 Ensuite 1 Private
(14) (6)

61 The Ridgeway, *Tonbridge, Kent, TN10 4NL.*
Comfortable and convenient modern house.
Open: All Year (not Xmas)
01732 353530 Mrs Bohan
Rates fr: *£15.00*-**£18.00**.
Beds: 1T 1D 1S

4 Redwood Park, *Five Oak Green, Tonbridge, Kent,* *TN12 6WB.*
New house, rural district.
Open: All Year (not Xmas/New Year)
01892 838200
Mrs Prance
Fax no: 01732 810312
Rates fr: *£15.00*-**£15.00**.
Beds: 1D 1S
Baths: 1 Shared
(3)

Trottiscliffe

National Grid Ref: TQ6460

The Plough

Bramble Park, *Church Lane, Trottiscliffe, West Malling, Kent,* *ME19 5EB.*
Secluded, tranquil, Victorian rectory.
Open: All Year
01732 822397
Mrs Towler
Rates fr: *£18.00*-**£18.00**.
Beds: 1F 1T 1S
Baths: 1 Private 2 Shared
(6)

Tunbridge Wells

National Grid Ref: TQ5839

Brecknock Arms, The Barn , Brokers Arms

10 Modest Corner, *Southborough, Tunbridge Wells, Kent,* *TN4 0LS.*
Open: All Year
01892 522450
Ms Leemhuis
Rates fr: *£18.00*-**£20.00**.
Beds: 1F 2T 1S
Baths: 2 Shared
(3)
Situated in picturesque hamlet away from traffic. In easy reach of mainline station. Excellent walking facilities. Homely, warm welcome. Good food, breakfast outside (weather permitting).

45 Stone Street, *Tunbridge Wells, Kent,* *TN1 2QU.*
Victorian house in town centre.
Open: All Year
01892 522651
Mr & Mrs Katz
Rates fr: *£15.00*-**£15.00**.
Beds: 1F 1T 1D 1S
Baths: 1 Shared
(2)

17 Claremont Road, *Tunbridge Wells, Kent,* *TN1 1SY.*
Comfortable Victorian house, centrally situated.
Open: All Year (not Xmas)
Grades: ETB Listed
01892 538938
Mrs Maurer
Rates fr: *£17.00*-**£17.00**.
Beds: 1D 1T 1S
Baths: 1 Shared
(4)

Hawkenbury Farm, *Hawkenbury Road, Tunbridge Wells, Kent,* *TN3 9AD.*
Comfortable accommodation, small working farm.
Open: All Year (not Xmas)
01892 536977 Mrs Wright
Rates fr: *£18.00*-**£25.00**.
Beds: 1D 1T
Baths: 2 Private
(6)

6 Arundel Road, *Tunbridge Wells, Kent,* *TN1 1TB.*
Spacious Victorian private house.
Open: All Year
01892 525675 Mrs Bowen
Rates fr: *£18.00*-**£18.00**.
Beds: 1F 1T 1S
Baths: 1 Private 1 Shared

Highlands, *Nevill Court, Tunbridge Wells, Kent,* *TN4 8NJ.*
Large house in quiet park.
Open: All Year
01892 512680 Mrs Legon
Rates fr: *£20.00*-**£20.00**.
Beds: 1F 2D
Baths: 1 Shared
(3)

Park End, *82 Upper Grosvenor Road, Tunbridge Wells, Kent,* *TN1 2EU.*
Town centre large Victorian home.
Open: All Year (not Xmas)
01892 522404
Mrs Huggett
Rates fr: *£15.00*-**£15.00**.
Beds: 2T
Baths: 1 Private 1 Shared
(2)

Tyler Hill

National Grid Ref: TR1460

Olde Beverlie

York Cottage, *57 Hackington Road, Tyler Hill, Canterbury, Kent,* *CT2 9NF.*
Open: All Year
Grades: ETB Listed
01227 471253 / 0860 175151
Mr Bryden
Rates fr: *£16.00*-**£25.00**.
Beds: 2D
Baths: 1 Shared
(10) (4)
Delightful cottage offering warm welcome in village 2 miles from Canterbury. Pretty garden and attractive guest rooms. Ideal location for city break, walking and coast.

Always telephone to get directions to the B&B - you will save time!

The Bield, *2 Canterbury Hill, Tyler Hill, Canterbury, Kent,* *CT2 9SL.*
Spacious modern house.
Open: Feb to Dec
01227 464621 Mrs Wilkins
Rates fr: *£15.00*-**£16.00**.
Beds: 1D 1T 1S
Baths: 1 Shared
(4)

Westerham

National Grid Ref: TQ4454

The Orchard House, *Brasted Chart, Westerham, Kent,* *TN16 1LR.*
Family home, quiet, rural surroundings.
Open: All Year (not Xmas)
01959 563702 Mrs Godsal
Rates fr: *£17.50*-**£18.00**.
Beds: 2T 1S
Baths: 2 Shared
(4)

Corner Cottage, *Toys Hill, Westerham, Kent,* *TN16 1PY.*
Beautifully positioned C15th cottage.
Open: All Year
Grades: ETB Listed
01732 750362 Mrs Olszowska
Rates fr: *£18.50*-**£25.00**.
Beds: 1F
(2)

Westgate-on-Sea

National Grid Ref: TR3270

White Lodge Guest House, *12 Domneva Road, Westgate-on-Sea, Kent,* *CT8 8PE.*
Detached house, 100 yards Sandy Bay.
Open: All Year
Grades: ETB 3 Cr, Comm, AA 3 Q
01843 831828 Mr & Mrs Cutler
Rates fr: *£18.00*-**£18.00**.
Beds: 2F 2D 2T 1S
Baths: 5 Private 1 Shared
(3)

Westwell

National Grid Ref: TQ9847

Royal Oak (Charing)

Dean Court Farm, *Challock Lane, Westwell, Ashford, Kent,* *TN25 4NH.*
Period farmhouse with modern comforts.
Open: All Year
01233 712924 Mrs Lister
Rates fr: *£16.00*-**£17.00**.
Beds: 2T
Baths: 1 Shared
(5)

Bringing children with you? Always ask for any special rates.

Wickhambreaux

National Grid Ref: TR2258

Rose Inn

The Old Stone House, *The Green, Wickhambreaux, Canterbury, Kent, CT3 1RQ.*
Historical, medieval village green house. **Open:** All Year
Grades: ETB Listed, Comm
01227 728591 Mrs Knight
Rates fr: *£18.00*-**£18.00**.
Beds: 1F 1D 1T 1S
Baths: 2 Private 2 Shared
(6)

Wingham

National Grid Ref: TR2357

Tanner of Wingham Restaurant, *44 High Street, Wingham, Canterbury, Kent, CT3 1AB.*
Open: All Year
Grades: ETB Listed, Approv
01227 720532 (also fax no)
Mr & Mrs Martin
Rates fr: *£17.50*-**£20.00**.
Beds: 2F 2D 1S
Baths: 2 Ensuite 1 Shared
(2)
Situated midway between Canterbury and Sandwich in historic village. Ideal for touring East Kent or stopover for Continent. Friendly, homely atmosphere. Phone for brochure.

Planning a longer stay? Always ask for any special rates.

Woodchurch

National Grid Ref: TQ9434

Bonny Cravat

Hornbrook Oast, *Appledore Road, Woodchurch, Ashford, Kent, TN26 3TJ.*
Delightful rural setting. Very Peaceful.
Open: All Year (not Xmas/New Year)
01233 860484 / 860686
Mrs Mathews & Mobbs
Rates fr: *£17.50*-**£17.50**.
Beds: 1D 1T
Baths: 2 Ensuite

Four Winds, *Shirkoak, Woodchurch, Ashford, Kent, TN26 3QP.*
Warm welcome, log-fire, quiet garden.
Open: All Year (not Xmas)
01233 860530 Mrs Barlow
Rates fr: *£18.00*-**£18.00**.
Beds: 1D 1T 1S
Baths: 2 Ensuite 1 Private
(5)

Worth

National Grid Ref: TR3355

Ilex Cottage, *Temple Way, Worth, Deal, Kent, CT14 0DA.*
Secluded peaceful C18th cottage.
Open: All Year (not Xmas)
Grades: ETB 2 Cr
01304 617026 Mrs Stobie
Rates fr: *£16.00*-**£20.00**.
Beds: 1F 1D 1T
Baths: 3 Ensuite
(6)

Wouldham

National Grid Ref: TQ7164

Wouldham Court Farmhouse, *246 High Street, Wouldham, Rochester, Kent, ME1 3TY.*
Beamed farmhouse, Grade II, inglenook fireplace.
Open: All Year (not Xmas)
01634 683271
Ms Parnell
Rates fr: *£17.00*-**£17.00**.
Beds: 1F 1D 1S
Baths: 2 Shared
(1)

Wrotham

National Grid Ref: TQ6059

The Bull

Hillside House, *Gravesend Road, Wrotham, Sevenoaks, Kent, TN15 7JH.*
Ideal touring, walking, channel ports..
Open: All Year (not Xmas)
01732 822564
Mrs Thomas
Rates fr: *£16.00*-**£16.00**.
Beds: 1D 1T 1S
Baths: 1 Shared

Green Hill House, *High Street, Wrotham, Sevenoaks, Kent, TN15 7AH.*
Comfortable family home in historic village.
Open: All Year
01732 883069 Mrs Jolliffe
Rates fr: *£16.00*-**£20.00**.
Beds: 1D 1T
Baths: 1 Shared

Lancashire

Tourist Information Centres

Gothic House, St James Street, **Accrington**, Lancashire, BB5 1NT, 01254 386807.

King George's Hall, Northgate, **Blackburn**, Lancashire, BB2 1AA, 01254 53277.

1 Clifton Street, **Blackpool**, Lancashire, FY1 1LY, 01253 403223

Burnley Mechanics, Manchester Road, **Burnley**, Lancashire, BB11 1JA, 01282 455485.

Charnock Richard Service Area, M6 (Northbound), **Chorley**, PR7 5NG, 01257 793773, (Easter to Oct).

12-14 Market Place, **Clitheroe**, Lancashire, BB7 2DA, 01200 425566.

Ferry Office, Ferry Dock, The Esplanade, **Fleetwood**, Lancashire, FY7 6DN, 01253 773953

Discovery Centre, Council Offices, High Street, **Garstang**, Lancashire, PR3 1FU, 01995 602125.

29 Lancaster Hill, **Lancaster**, Lancashire, LA1 1YN, 01524 32878.

The Square, **Lytham St Annes**, Lancashire, FY8 1LW, 01253 725610.

Station Buildings, Central Promenade, **Morecambe**, LA4 4DB, 01524 582808.

20a Scotland Road, **Nelson**, Lancashire, BB9 7UU, 01282 692890.

The Guildhall, Lancaster Road, **Preston**, PR1 1HT, 01772 253731.

15 Burnley Road, **Todmorden**, Lancashire, OL14 7BU, 01706 818181.

Accrington

National Grid Ref: SD7528

Wendys B&B, *139 Whalley Road, Accrington, Lancs,* BB5 1BX.
'Home from home', modern accommodation.
Open: All Year
Grades: ETB Listed, Comm
01254 871060 Mrs Walsh
Rates fr: *£14.00*-**£15.00**.
Beds: 1F 1D 1T 1S
Baths: 1 Shared

Adlington

National Grid Ref: SD6013

Appenzell, *Babylon Lane, Heath Charnock, Adlington, Chorley, Lancs,* PR6 9EJ.
Elegant Victorian manor house.
Open: All Year
01257 480418 Mrs Tolen
Rates fr: *£20.00*-**£30.00**.
Beds: 2F 2D 2T 2S
Baths: 8 Private
(80)

Alston

National Grid Ref: SD6033

White Bull

Greyfriars, *Alston Lane, Alston, Preston, Lancs,* PR3 3BN.
Country house with large garden.
Open: All Year (not Xmas)
01772 782309
Mr Wallbank
Rates fr: *£15.00*-**£15.00**.
Beds: 1F 1D 1T 1S
Baths: 1 Shared
(5)

Anglezarke

National Grid Ref: SD6317

Jepsons Farm, *Moor Road, Anglezarke, Chorley, Lancs,* PR6 9DQ.
Beautiful C17th stone farmhouse.
Open: All Year (not Xmas)
01257 481691 Mrs Hilton
Rates fr: *£16.00*-**£16.00**.
Beds: 1F 1D 1T 1S
Baths: 2 Shared
(6)

Aughton

National Grid Ref: SD3905

Thorn Tree Farm, *Prescot Road, Aughton, Ormskirk, Lancs,* L39 6RS.
Farmhouse set in rural surroundings.
Open: All Year
Grades: ETB Listed, Comm
01695 422109 R & W Pemberton
Rates fr: *£20.00*-**£20.00**.
(Any) (5)

Bacup

National Grid Ref: SD8622

Pasture Bottom Farm, *Bacup, Lancs,* OL13 0UZ.
Comfortable farmhouse bed & breakfast.
Open: All Year (not Xmas)
Grades: ETB 1 Cr, Approv
01706 873790 Ms Isherwood
Rates fr: *£13.50*-**£13.50**.
Beds: 2T
Baths: 1 Shared
(4)

Bamber Bridge

National Grid Ref: SD5626

Hob Inn

Anvil Guest House, *321 Station Road, Bamber Bridge, Preston, Lancs,* PR5 6EE.
Comfortable, friendly, near M6/J29, M61/J9.
Open: All Year (not Xmas)
01772 39022 Mrs Arkwright
Rates fr: *£12.00*-**£13.50**.
Beds: 2F 1D 6T
Baths: 2 Shared

Barnoldswick

National Grid Ref: SD8746

Monks House, *5 Manchester Road, Barnoldswick, Colne, Lancs,* BB8 5NZ.
Centrally situated Georgian house.
Open: All Year
01282 814423 Mrs Robinson
Rates fr: *£15.00*-**£15.00**.
Beds: 2T 2S
Baths: 2 Shared

Barton

National Grid Ref: SD5137

Old Nells

Ratcliffe Farm, *White Horse Lane, Barton, Preston, Lancs,* PR3 5AH.
Comfortable friendly farmhouse.
Open: All Year (not Xmas)
01995 640536 Mrs Worden
Rates fr: *£15.00*-**£15.00**.
Beds: 1F 1D
Baths: 1 Shared
(4)

Bay Horse

National Grid Ref: SD4953

Bay Horse Hotel

Saltoke South, *Bay Horse, Galgate, Lancaster,* LA2 0HL.
Family home in rural setting.
Open: All Year (not Xmas)
01524 752313 Mrs Robin
Rates fr: *£15.00*-**£20.00**.
Beds: 1F 1D 1T
(4)

Stanley Lodge Farmhouse, *Cockerham Road, Bay Horse, Lancaster,* LA2 0HE.
Farmhouse conveniently situated in rural area.
Open: All Year (not Xmas)
01524 791863
Rates fr: *£16.00*-**£16.00**.
Beds: 1F 2D
Baths: 1 Shared
(4)

Bilsborrow

National Grid Ref: SD5139

Olde Duncombe House, *Garstang Road, Bilsborrow, Preston, Lancs,* PR3 0RE.
Converted C17th cottages.
Open: All Year
01995 640336 Mr Bolton
Rates fr: *£22.50*-**£32.50**.
Beds: 2F 5D 2T 2S
Baths: 11 Private
(20)

The Gables, *Bilsborrow Lane, Bilsborrow, Preston, Lancs,* PR3 0RN.
A comfortable, friendly home.
Open: All Year (not Xmas)
01995 640683 Mrs Biscomb
Rates fr: *£14.00*-**£14.00**.
Beds: 1D 1T 1S
Baths: 1 Shared
(5)

Blackburn

National Grid Ref: SD6827

Counting House, The Washington

Ellerbeck Guest House, *37 Wellington Street, St Johns, Blackburn, Lancs,* BB1 8AF.
Centrally placed Victorian private hotel.
Open: All Year
01254 55010 Mr Elvin
Rates fr: *£15.00*-**£20.00**.
Beds: 4F 1D 3T 2S
Baths: 7 Private 3 Shared
(10)

Woodlands Hotel, *361 Preston Road, Blackburn, Lancs,* BB2 7AA.
Popular happening disco pub.
Open: All Year
01254 681 368 Mr McEnery
Rates fr: *£16.25*-**£25.00**.
Beds: 1F 1T 4D 1S
Baths: 4 Ensuite 1 Shared
(4) (60)

The Woodlands Hotel (b), *361 Preston New Road, Blackburn, Lancs,* BB2 7AA.
Well-appointed Victorian house hotel.
Open: All Year
01254 681368 Mr Nelson
Rates fr: *£16.25*-**£27.50**.
Beds: 8D
Baths: 4 Private 4 Shared
(40)

Blackpool

National Grid Ref: SD3136

***Fairway Hotel,** 34/36 Hull Road, Blackpool, Lancs, FY1 4QB.*
Open: All Year
01253 23777 Mr Hodges
Fax no: 01253 27751
Rates fr: *£18.00*-**£30.00**.
Beds: 9F 7D 2T
Baths: 18 Private
Family-run licensed hotel, close to Tower, Winter Gardens, shops and night life. No hidden extras. Deposit refundable if not satisfied on arrival.

***The Arncliffe Hotel,** 24 Osborne Road, South Shore, Blackpool, Lancs, FY4 1HJ.*
Small, friendly, near promenade, pleasurebeach.
Open: All Year
01253 345209 Mr Wood
Rates fr: *£12.00*-**£12.00**.
Beds: 2F 5D 1S
Baths: 5 Ensuite 1 Shared
(2)

***The Carlis Private Hotel,** 34 Charnley Road, Blackpool, Lancs, FY1 4PF.*
Open: All Year
01253 22586 Ms Boyd
Rates fr: *£12.00*-**£15.00**.
Beds: 5F 9D 3T 2S
Baths: 12 Ensuite 7 Shared
Licensed, good food and cleanliness assured. Central to beach, shops, shows, winter gardens. TV lounge, pool table. Hygiene certificate. Weekly rates from £79 BBed, E/S extra.

***Glenview Private Hotel,** 18 Vance Road, Blackpool, Lancs, FY1 4QD.*
Two minutes from town centre.
Open: Xmas to Oct
01253 24954
Mr & Mrs Stewart
Rates fr: *£12.00*-**£13.00**.
Beds: 3F 8D 2T 1S

***Holme Lea Private Hotel,** 93 Lord Street, Blackpool, Lancs, FY1 2DJ.*
Hotel commended by Tourist Board.
Open: All Year
01253 25766 Mr Foster
Rates fr: *£13.00*-**£16.00**.
Beds: 2F 9D 1T
Baths: 5 Private
(4)

***St Ives Hotel,** 10 King George Avenue, North Shore, Blackpool, Lancs, FY2 9SN.*
Small, friendly, clean, comfortable hotel.
Open: All Year
01253 352122 Mrs Dempsey
Rates fr: *£17.00*-**£18.00**.
Beds: 2F 4D 2T 1S
Baths: 5 Private 4 Shared
(2)

***The Marina,** 30 Gynn Avenue, Blackpool, Lancs, FY1 2LD.*
Home cooking and comfortable surroundings.
Open: Easter to Nov
01253 352833 Mrs Lockhart
Rates fr: *£12.00*-**£12.00**.
Beds: 3F 2D 2S **Baths:** 1 Shared
(5)

***Westcliffe Private Hotel,** 46 King Edward Avenue, Blackpool, Lancs, FY2 9TA.*
Homely, hotel in select area.
Open: All Year
01253 352943 Mr Carter
Rates fr: *£17.00*-**£17.00**.
Beds: 2F 2D 2T 4S
Baths: 8 Ensuite 1 Shared
(7)

***The Ambleside,** 89 Palatine Road, Blackpool, Lancs, FY1 4BX.*
Large Victorian semi-detached house. **Open:** All Year (not Xmas)
01253 24035 Mr Lapsins
Rates fr: *£9.50*-**£12.00**.
Beds: 3F 3D 2T
Baths: 3 Private 1 Shared
(1)

***The Tudor Rose Original,** 5 Withnell Road, Blackpool, Lancs, FY4 1HF.*
Lovely small hotel, 3 Crown.
Open: All Year
01253 343485 Mrs Thompson
Rates fr: *£15.00*-**£15.00**.
Beds: 9D 2T 1S **Baths:** 11 Ensuite

***Charter House,** 31 Blundell Street, Blackpool, Lancs, FY1 5DB.*
Family-run, comfortable and fun.
Open: All Year (not Xmas)
01253 26942 Mrs Parker
Rates fr: *£10.00*-**£10.00**.
Beds: 3F 3D 1T **Baths:** 1 Shared
(2)

***South View Hotel,** 205 Central Promenade, Blackpool, Lancs, FY1 5DL.*
Sea front hotel.
Open: All Year
01253 26980 Mrs Creighton
Rates fr: *£17.00*-**£17.00**.
Beds: 9F 8D 1T **Baths:** 18 Private

***Brentwood,** 50 Egerton Road, Blackpool, Lancs, FY1 2NW.*
Corner position, no back rooms.
Open: Easter to Nov
01253 23612 Mr & Mrs Bohannon
Rates fr: *£12.00*.
Beds: 2F 4D 1T
Baths: 1 Shared
(5) (7)

***Alma Guest House,** 112 High Street, Blackpool, Lancs, FY1 2DL.*
Family-run homely guest house.
Open: All Year
01253 21985 Miss Marsh
Rates fr: *£10.00*-**£10.00**.
Beds: 3F 5D 1S **Baths:** 1 Shared
(3)

***Normoss House Hotel,** 13 Reads Avenue, Blackpool, Lancs, FY1 4BW.*
Small, friendly, clean, comfortable guest house.
Open: Easter to Dec
01253 21137 Mrs Brown
Rates fr: *£11.00*-**£11.00**.
Beds: 3F 7D 1T 1S
Baths: 2 Shared

***Lynton House,** 24 St Bedes Avenue, Blackpool, Lancs, FY4 1AQ.*
Family-run guest house.
Open: All Year
01253 345784 Mrs Halloran
Rates fr: *£10.00*-**£10.00**.
Beds: 1F 7D 1T
Baths: 1 Ensuite 1 Shared

***Hotel Royale,** 31-33 Lord Street, Blackpool, Lancs, FY1 2BD.*
Private licensed hotel.
Open: All Year
01253 295954
Mr Davies
Rates fr: *£12.00*-**£12.00**.
Beds: 10F 6D 7T
Baths: 23 Private

***The Royal Vincent Hotel,** 22-30 Hull Road, Blackpool, Lancs, FY1 4QB.*
Centrally situated, close all ameneties.
Open: All Year
01253 22530
Fax no: 01253 28711
Rates fr: *£13.00*-**£13.00**.
Beds: 10F 40D 10T
Baths: 15 Ensuite 10 Shared

Bolton-le-Sands

National Grid Ref: SD4868

Blue Anchor

***The Blue Anchor Hotel,** Main Street, Bolton-le-Sands, Carnforth, Lancs, LA5 8DN.*
Open: All Year
Grades: ETB 3 Cr, Approv
01524 823241
Mr Duncan
Fax no: 01524 824745
Rates fr: *£20.00*-**£22.00**.
Beds: 3D 1T
Baths: 4 Private
(4)
C18th coaching house. Ideally situated for Lancaster, Morecambe & lakes. Special rates for 2 or more nights stay. Home cooking a speciality.

***Row-Bar,** 4 Whin Grove, Bolton-le-Sands, Carnforth, Lancs, LA5 8DD.*
Friendly family-run private home.
Open: All Year (not Xmas)
01524 735369
Mrs Udall
Rates fr: *£15.00*-**£20.00**.
Beds: 1F 1D
Baths: 2 Ensuite
(2)

Bankside Cottage, *21 Whin Grove, Bolton-le-Sands, Carnforth, Lancs,* *LA5 8DD.*
Canalside, village location, picturesque quiet.
Open: All Year (not Xmas)
01524 735078 Mrs Addy
Rates fr: *£15.00*-**£17.50**.
Beds: 3T
Baths: 2 Ensuite 1 Shared
(12) (1)

Burnley

National Grid Ref: SD8332

Reedley Hallows Hotel, The Forest Inn, The Cellar

18 Healdwood Drive, *Reedley Hallows, Burnley, Lancs, BB12 0EA.*
Private detached house. Country views.
Open: All Year (not Xmas)
01282 453985 Mrs Forman
Rates fr: *£12.00*-**£12.00**.
Beds: 1D 2S
Baths: 1 Shared
(2)

Windsor House, *71 Church Street, Padiham, Burnley, Lancs, BB12 8JH.*
Large friendly Victorian private house.
Open: All Year (not Xmas)
01282 773271
Mrs Stinton
Rates fr: *£16.00*-**£16.00**.
Beds: 2D 3T 2S
Baths: 2 Shared
(8)

Eaves Barn Farm, *Hapton, Burnley, Lancs, BB12 7LP.*
Traditional farmhouse, very high standard.
Open: All Year (not Xmas)
Grades: ETB 2 Cr, High Comm
01282 771591 (also fax no)
Mrs Butler
Rates fr: *£19.50*-**£20.00**.
Beds: 2D 1S
Baths: 2 Ensuite 1 Private
(10) (15)

Cedars Lodge, *66 Westgate, Burnley, Lancs, BB11 1RY.*
Large Victorian private house.
Open: All Year (not Xmas)
01282 458501
Mr Phillips
Rates fr: *£15.00*-**£17.00**.
Beds: 1F 1D 1T 2S
Baths: 2 Shared
(3)

Ormerod Hotel, *123 Ormerod Road, Burnley, Lancs, BB11 3QW.*
All ensuite, refurbished guest house.
Open: All Year
01282 423255
Ms Whitehead
Rates fr: *£18.00*-**£20.00**.
Beds: 2F 3D 2T 4S
Baths: 11 Ensuite

Carnforth

National Grid Ref: SD4970

Eagles Head (Over Kellet), Bay Horse (Arkholme)

Capernwray House, *Capernwray, Carnforth, Lancs, LA6 1AE.*
Open: All Year (not Xmas)
Grades: ETB 2 Cr, Comm
01524 732363 (also fax no)
Mrs Smith
Rates fr: *£20.00*-**£17.00**.
Beds: 2D 1T 1S
Baths: 3 Private
(5) (8)
Beautiful country house. Panoramic views. Tastefully decorated throughout. No smoking. Close Lakes, Dales, Lancaster. Excellent stopover South - Scotland. Warm welcome our speciality! Phone for brochure.

Cotestone Farm, *Sand Lane, Warton, Carnforth, Lancs, LA5 9NH.*
Warm welcome awaits you.
Open: All Year (not Xmas)
01524 732418 Mrs Close
Rates fr: *£14.00*-**£15.00**.
Beds: 1F 1D 1T
Baths: 2 Shared
(3)

26 Victoria Street, *Carnforth, Lancs, LA5 9ED.*
Comfortable home, good food, clean.
Open: All Year (not Xmas)
01524 732520 Mr Dickinson
Rates fr: *£12.00*-**£13.00**.
Beds: 1F 1D 1T
Baths: 1 Shared
(2)

Chipping

National Grid Ref: SD6243

Carrside Farm, *Chipping, Preston, Lancs, PR3 2TS.*
C18th farmhouse, patchwork bedrooms.
Open: All Year (not Xmas)
01995 61590 Mrs Cowgill
Rates fr: *£17.50*-**£20.00**.
Beds: 2D 1T
Baths: 2 Private 1 Shared
(3) (6)

Clayton-le-Dale

National Grid Ref: SD6733

Royal Oak, Bay Horse

2 Rose Cottage, *Longsight Road (A59), Clayton-le-Dale, Blackburn, Lancs, BB1 9EX.*
Picturesque well-equipped 100-year-old cottage.
Open: All Year
01254 813223 Mrs Adderley
Fax no: 01254 813831
Rates fr: *£17.00*-**£20.00**.
Beds: 1D 2T
Baths: 3 Private
(0) (3)

Clayton-le-Moors

National Grid Ref: SD7431

Hynburn Bridge Hotel

Red House Cottage, *Off Burnley Road, Clayton-le-Moors, Accrington, Lancs, BB5 5UD.*
Quiet, delightful olde worlde cottage.
Open: All Year (not Xmas)
01254 301163 Mrs Stephenson
Rates fr: *£15.00*-**£18.00**.
Beds: 1T **Baths:** 1 Private
(3)

Clitheroe

National Grid Ref: SD7441

Swan with Two Necks, Edisford Bridge Inn

Brooklands, *9 Pendle Road, Clitheroe, Lancs, BB7 1JQ.*
Ribble Valley. Comfortable Victorian home.
Open: All Year
Grades: ETB Listed, Comm
01200 422797 (also fax no)
Mrs Lord
Rates fr: *£15.00*-**£15.00**.
Beds: 1D 2T
Baths: 1 Ensuite 2 Shared
(5)

Selborne House, *Back Commons, Clitheroe, Lancs, BB7 2DX.*
Quiet lane, short walk to town.
Open: All Year
01200 423571 / 422236
Mrs Barnes
Rates fr: *£15.00*-**£17.50**.
Beds: 1F 2D 1T
Baths: 1 Private 1 Shared
(6)

Springfield Cottage, *18 Nelson Street, Low Moor, Clitheroe, Lancs, BB7 2NQ.*
Home of character, Ribble Way.
Open: All Year
01200 442237 Mr Whitfield
Rates fr: *£16.00*-**£16.00**.
Beds: 1F 1D
Baths: 1 Shared
(0)

Colne

National Grid Ref: SD8940

Alma Inn

148 Keightley Road, *Colne, Lancs, BB8 0PJ.*
Open: Mar to Dec (not Xmas)
Grades: ETB 2 Cr, High Comm
01282 862002 Mrs Etherington
Rates fr: *£16.00*-**£16.00**.
Beds: 2D 1S
Baths: 1 Private 1 Shared
(11) (1)
Edwardian town house with many original features. Comfortable, attractive bedrooms. Friendly, helpful hosts. Situated on the outskirts of Colne, close to open countryside.

Higher Wanless Farm, *Red Lane, Colne, Lancs,* BB8 7JP.
Ideally situated, luxuriously furnished farmhouse.
Open: Feb to Nov
Grades: ETB 2 Cr, High Comm, AA 4 Q, Select
01282 865301 Ms Mitson
Rates fr: *£19.00*-**£22.00**.
Beds: 1F 1T
Baths: 1 Ensuite 1 Shared
(4) (4)

Conder Green

National Grid Ref: SD4656
The Stork

Stork Hotel, *Conder Green, Lancaster,* LA2 0AN.
Traditional country inn.
Open: All Year
Grades: ETB 3 Cr, Comm
01524 751234 Mr Cragg
Rates fr: *£18.00*-**£22.50**.
Beds: 1F 2D 1T 1S
Baths: 7 Private
(20)

Coppull

National Grid Ref: SD5614
Oak Tree

Oak Tree Hotel, *130 Preston Road, Coppull, Chorley, Lancs,* PR7 5ED.
Village pub, homely, comfortable, clean.
Open: All Year
01257 791217 Mr Le Marinel
Rates fr: *£15.00*-**£15.00**.
Beds: 1D 3T 1S
Baths: 1 Ensuite 4 Private
(2) (30)

Earby

National Grid Ref: SD9046

Grange Fell, *Skipton Road, Earby, Colne, Lancs,* BB8 6JL.
Apartment-style accommodation in Edwardian home.
Open: Easter to Oct
01282 843621 Mrs Eden
Rates fr: *£15.00*-**£17.00**.
Beds: 1F
Baths: 1 Shared

Fence

National Grid Ref: SD8237

Lower White Lee Farm, *Barrowford Road, Fence, Burnley, Lancs,* BB12 9ER.
Beautifully furnished farmhouse, gourmet food.
Open: All Year (not Xmas)
01282 613563 Mrs Boothman
Rates fr: *£17.00*-**£17.00**.
Beds: 2T
Baths: 1 Shared
(2) (4)

Fleetwood

National Grid Ref: SD3247
Strawberry Gardens

Chavock Guest House, *116 London Street, Fleetwood, Lancs,* FY7 6EU.
Licensed guest house.
Open: All Year
01253 771196 Mr McEvoy
Rates fr: *£12.00*-**£12.00**.
Beds: 3F 3D 1S **Baths:** 2 Shared

Mount Pleasant Guest House, *111 London Street, Fleetwood, Lancs,* FY7 6EU.
Family-run guest house with good breakfast.
Open: All Year
01253 873641 Mrs Richardson
Rates fr: *£12.50*-**£12.50**.
Beds: 5F 2D 1T 1S
Baths: 1 Shared

Fulwood

National Grid Ref: SD5431

Whitburn House Hotel, *111 Garstang Road, Fulwood, Preston, Lancs,* PR2 3EB.
Comfortable family-run hotel.
Open: All Year
01772 717973 Mrs Murch
Rates fr: *£20.00*-**£20.00**.
Beds: 1F 6D 1T 5S
Baths: 1 Shared
(12)

Garstang

National Grid Ref: SD4945
Crofters Hotel, Guys Thatched Hamlet

Sandbriggs, *Lancaster Road, Garstang, Preston, Lancs,* PR3 1JA.
Comfortable, convenient, secluded private house.
Open: All Year
01995 603080 (also fax no)
Mr Wilkinson
Rates fr: *£13.50*-**£14.00**.
Beds: 2D 1T
Baths: 1 Private 2 Shared
(4) (10)

Calderbank Country Lodge, *Garstang, Preston, Lancs,* PR3 1UL.
Beautifully situated. Full English breakfast. **Open:** All Year
01995 604384 Mrs Jackson
Rates fr: *£17.00*-**£19.50**.
Beds: 1D 1T 1S
Baths: 1 Private 2 Shared

Ashdene, *Parkside Lane, A6, Garstang, Preston, Lancs,* PR3 0JA.
Warm, friendly, family home.
Open: All Year
01995 602676 Mrs Wrathall
Rates fr: *£15.00*-**£17.00**.
Beds: 1D 2T **Baths:** 3 Private
(5)

Lucas Farm, *Garstang, Preston, Lancs,* PR3 1QJ.
C18th oak-beamed farmhouse.
Open: All Year (not Xmas)
01995 603135 Mrs Tait
Rates fr: *£13.00*-**£14.00**.
Beds: 1D 1T
Baths: 1 Shared
(4)

Guys Thatched Hamlet, *Canal Side, Garstang, Preston, Lancs,* PR3 0RS.
Thatched canalside inn and hotel.
Open: All Year
01995 640010 Mr Wilkinson
Rates fr: *£21.50*-**£38.00**.
Beds: 10F 11D 32T
Baths: 53 Private

Gisburn

National Grid Ref: SD8248

The Stirk House Hotel, *Gisburn, Clitheroe, Lancs,* BB7 4LJ.
C16th manor house. Leisure facilities. **Open:** All Year
01200 445581 Mr MacMillan
Rates fr: *£25.00*-**£30.00**.
Beds: 1F 4D 30T 13S
Baths: 48 Ensuite
(70)

Goosnargh

National Grid Ref: SD5536
Ye Horns Inn

Isles Field Barn, *Syke House Lane, Goosnargh, Preston, Lancs,* PR3 2EN.
Open: All Year
Grades: ETB Listed
01995 640398 Mr McHugh
Rates fr: *£17.00*-**£17.00**.
Beds: 2F 1S
Baths: 2 Ensuite 1 Shared
(6)
Spacious ensuite accommodation in barn conversion (5 miles Junction 32, M6). Surrounded by beautiful countryside. Hearty breakfast. Friendly welcome. Good eating places nearby.

Great Mitton

National Grid Ref: SD7138

Mitton Green Barn, *Church Lane, Great Mitton, Clitheroe, Lancs,* BB7 9PJ.
Newly-converted barn offering luxury accommodation.
Open: All Year
01245 826673 Mrs Hargreaves
Rates fr: *£17.00*-**£22.00**.
Beds: 2D 1T
Baths: 2 Private 1 Shared
(6)

The lowest *double* rate per person is shown in *italics*.

Grindleton

National Grid Ref: SD7545

Fellside Farm, *Grindleton, Clitheroe, Lancs, BB7 4RX.*
Beautiful farmhouse with fantastic views.
Open: All Year (not Xmas)
01200 441359 Mrs MacGregor
Rates fr: *£13.00*-**£20.00**.
Beds: 1D
Baths: 1 Private
(6)

Hapton

National Grid Ref: SD7931

Eaves Barn Farm, *Hapton, Burnley, Lancs, BB12 7LP.*
Traditional farmhouse, very high standard.
Open: All Year (not Xmas)
Grades: ETB 2 Cr, High Comm
01282 771591 (also fax no)
Mrs Butler
Rates fr: *£19.50*-**£20.00**.
Beds: 2D 1S
Baths: 2 Ensuite 1 Private
(10) (15)

Hawkshaw

National Grid Ref: SD7515

Loe Farm Country House, *Redisher Lane, Hawkshaw, Bury, Lancs, BL8 4HX.*
Lovely situation. Beamed, modernised farmhouse.
Open: All Year
01204 883668 Mr &Mrs Baxter
Rates fr: *£20.00*-**£25.00**.
Beds: 2D
Baths: 2 Private
(12)

Holden

National Grid Ref: SD7749

Baygate Farm, *Holden, Bolton-By-Bowland, Clitheroe, Lancs, BB7 4PQ.*
Family-run farm in Trough of Bowland.
Open: All Year (not Xmas)
01200 447643 Ms Townson
Rates fr: *£14.00*-**£14.00**.
Beds: 3T
Baths: 1 Shared
(6)

Hurst Green

National Grid Ref: SD6838

Shireburn Arms Hotel, *Whalley Road, Hurst Green, Clitheroe, Lancs, BB6 9QJ.*
C16th family-run hotel.
Open: All Year
01254 826518 Mr Alcock
Rates fr: *£24.50*-**£39.00**.
Beds: 2F 5D 6T 3S
Baths: 16 Private
(100)

Hutton

National Grid Ref: SD4926

The Anchor, *Liverpool Road, Hutton, Preston, Lancs, PR4 5SL.*
Clean, comfortable, pub accommodation.
Open: All Year
01772 612962 Mrs Mccarthy
Rates fr: *£15.00*-**£18.00**.
Beds: 1F 2D 2T 3S
Baths: 4 Shared

Lancaster

National Grid Ref: SD4761

White Cross

Victoria House, *35 West Road, Lancaster, LA1 5NU.*
Open: All Year (not Xmas)
01524 381489
Mrs Buckingham
Rates fr: *£18.50*-**£25.00**.
Beds: 1D 1T
Baths: 2 Ensuite
(5)
Large, beautifully restored Victorian house full of original features, large garden within easy walking distance city centre, castle and railway station. Big breakfasts with home produce.

Shakespeare Hotel, *96 St Leonardgate, Lancaster, LA1 1NN.*
N.W.T.B. 'Place to Stay' Award Winner.
Open: All Year (not Xmas)
Grades: ETB 2 Cr, RAC Acclaim
01524 841041 Mr Sylvester
Rates fr: *£17.50*-**£18.00**.
Beds: 2F 3D 2T 2S
Baths: 9 Ensuite
(1) (4)

Elsinore House, *76 Scotforth Road, Lancaster, LA1 4SF.*
Large detached private house.
Open: All Year (not Xmas)
01524 65088 Mrs Moorhouse
Rates fr: *£15.00*-**£30.00**.
Beds: 2D
Baths: 2 Ensuite
(12) (3)

West View Farm, *Langthwaite Road, Lancaster, LA1 3JJ.*
200-year-old farmhouse. Organic working.
01524 841336 Mrs Holmes
Rates fr: *£15.00*-**£18.00**.
Beds: 2D 1T
Baths: 1 Shared
(0) (10)

50 West Road, *Lancaster, LA1 5NU.*
Large Victorian house.
Open: Apr to Sep
01524 67602 Mrs Gardner
Rates fr: *£16.00*-**£20.00**.
Beds: 1D 1T 1S
Baths: 1 Shared
(2)

Longridge

National Grid Ref: SD6037

Alston Arms

14 Whittingham Road, *Longridge, Preston, Lancs, PR3 2AA.*
Homely, caring accommodation. Scenic area.
Open: All Year
01772 783992 Mrs Morley
Rates fr: *£15.50*-**£15.50**.
Beds: 1F 1T 1S
Baths: 1 Shared
(3)

Jenkinsons Farmhouse, *Longridge, Alston, Preston, Lancs, PR3 3BD.*
Old worlde farmhouse, outstanding countryside.
Open: All Year (not Xmas)
01772 782624 Mrs Ibison
Rates fr: *£20.00*-**£20.00**.
Beds: 2D 3T 1S
Baths: 1 Private 3 Shared
(12) (8)

Lytham-St-Annes

National Grid Ref: SD3327

Monarch Hotel, *29 St Annes Road East, Lytham-St-Annes, Lancs, FY8 1TA.*
Clean, comfortable hotel. Great food. **Open:** All Year
01253 720464 Mr Churchill
Rates fr: *£16.00*-**£16.00**.
Beds: 1F 5D 1T 2S
Baths: 5 Private 4 Shared
(7)

Sandpiper Hotel, *35 South Promenade, Lytham-St-Annes, Lancs, FY8 1LS.*
Licensed, seafront, family-run.
Open: Mar to Nov
Grades: ETB 3 Cr, Comm
01253 724271 Mrs Perry
Rates fr: *£21.00*-**£21.00**.
Beds: 5F 4D 3T 2S
Baths: 14 Ensuite
(10)

Melrose Hotel, *37 South Promenade, Lytham-St-Annes, Lancs, FY8 1LS.*
Promenade hotel, overlooking gardens & beach.
Open: Mar to Nov
Grades: ETB 3 Cr, Comm
01253 725117 Mrs Bennet
Rates fr: *£22.50*-**£22.50**.
Beds: 4F 4D 2T 2S 3T
Baths: 13 Private 1 Shared
(12)

Seacroft, *5 Eastbank Road, Lytham-St-Annes, Lancs, FY8 1ND.*
Friendly, family-run, licensed hotel. **Open:** All Year
Grades: ETB 3 Cr, Comm
01253 721806 I A Taylor
Rates fr: *£15.00*-**£16.00**.
Beds: 5F 1T 3S
Baths: 8 Private 2 Shared
(0) (5)

Craigavon, *299-301 Clifton Drive South, Lytham-St-Annes, Lancs, FY8 1HN.*
Two minutes to shops/beach.
Open: All Year
01253 725801 Mr Clare
Rates fr: *£20.00*-**£22.00**.
Beds: 4F 13D 7T 2S
Baths: 23 Private 3 Shared
(18)

Gaydon Hotel, *33 Derbe Road, Lytham-St-Annes, Lancs, FY8 1NJ.*
Private hotel and personal service.
Open: Easter to Nov
01253 722082 Mrs Dawson
Rates fr: *£16.00*-**£16.00**.
Beds: 2F 4D 1T 2S
Baths: 4 Shared
(1) (5)

Morecambe

National Grid Ref: SD4364

Westleigh Licensed Hotel, *9 Marine Road, Morecambe, Lancs, LA3 1BS.*
Seafront hotel. Views of Morecambe Bay.
Open: All Year (not Xmas)
Grades: ETB 3 Cr
01524 418352 Mr & Mrs Harrison
Rates fr: *£15.00*-**£15.00**.
Beds: 6D 5T 2S **Baths:** 14 Private

Delmae Private Hotel, *48 West End Rd, Morecambe, Lancs, LA4 4DL*
Friendly family-run licensed hotel.
Open: All Year **Grades:** ETB Listed
01524 410819 Mrs Couper
Rates fr: *£13.00*-**£13.00**.
Beds: 3F 5D 3T 2S
Baths: 1 Private 4 Shared

Silverwell Christian Hotel, *20 West End Road, Morecambe, Lancs, LA4 4DL.*
Family-run Christian hotel.
Open: All Year
01524 410532 Mr Last
Rates fr: *£13.50*-**£15.00**.
Beds: 4F 1S 7D 3T
Baths: 1 Ensuite 3 Shared

Ballantrae Guest House, *26 Westminster Road, Morecambe, Lancs, LA4 4JB.*
Small comfortable modernised guest house.
Open: All Year (not Xmas)
01524 419963 Mrs Mcgee
Rates fr: *£12.00*-**£12.00**.
Beds: 1F 2D 1T 1S

Lakeland View Guest House, *130 Clarendon Road, Morecambe, Lancs, LA3 1SD.*
'Home-from-home', good food.
Open: All Year (not Xmas)
01524 415873
Rates fr: *£11.00*-**£11.00**.
Beds: 3F 1T 3D 2S
Baths: 1 Private 4 Shared

The Durham Guest House, *73 Albert Road, Morecambe, Lancs, LA4 4HY.*
Clean, friendly, small but comfortable.
Open: All Year (not Xmas)
01524 424790
P & Morrison
Rates fr: *£11.00*-**£12.00**.
Beds: 1F 3D 2T
Baths: 2 Shared

Nelson

National Grid Ref: SD8637

Lovett House, *6 Howard Street, Off Carr Road, Nelson, Lancs, BB9 7SZ.*
Excellent hospitality, quiet central location.
Open: All Year
01282 697352
Mrs Helm
Rates fr: *£13.50*-**£13.50**.
Beds: 1F 1T
Baths: 1 Shared

Padiham

National Grid Ref: SD7933

The Cellar

Windsor House, *71 Church Street, Padiham, Burnley, Lancs, BB12 8JH.*
Large friendly Victorian private house.
Open: All Year (not Xmas)
01282 773271
Mrs Stinton
Rates fr: *£16.00*-**£16.00**.
Beds: 2D 3T 2S
Baths: 2 Shared
(8)

Preston

National Grid Ref: SD5329

Butler's Guest House, *(Formerly Stanley House Hotel), 6 Stanley Terrace, Off Fishergate Hill, Preston, Lancs, PR1 8JE.*
Grade II Listed Georgian house.
Open: All Year
01772 254486
Mrs Reynolds-Butler
Fax no: 01772 257407
Rates fr: *£15.00*-**£17.00**.
Beds: 3F 1D 1T 3S
Baths: 1 Private
(5)

County Hotel, *1 Fishergate Hill, Preston, Lancs, PR1 8UL.*
Listed Victorian building, 120 yds from station.
Open: All Year
01772 253188
Mr Hunt
Rates fr: *£17.00*-**£20.00**.
Beds: 1F 3D 4T 6S
Baths: 7 Private 2 Shared
(7)

Ribchester

National Grid Ref: SD6435

Black Bull, White Bull, Hall's Arms

New House Farm, *Preston Road, Ribchester, Preston, Lancs, PR3 3XL.*
Old renovated farmhouse, rare breeds.
Open: All Year
Grades: ETB Listed, Comm
01254 878954 Mr & Mrs Bamber
Rates fr: *£18.00*-**£22.00**.
Beds: 1F 1D 1T
Baths: 3 Ensuite
(3) (6)

Smithy Farm, *Huntingdon Hall Lane, Dutton, Ribchester, Preston, Lancs, PR3 2ZT.*
Comfortable, homely, helpful.
Open: All Year (not Xmas)
Grades: ETB Listed
01254 878250 Mrs Jackson
Rates fr: *£12.50*-**£15.00**.
Beds: 1F 1D 1T
Baths: 1 Shared

Rimington

National Grid Ref: SD8045

Asheton Arms, Moorcock Inn

Wytha Farm, *Rimington, Clitheroe, Lancs, BB7 4EQ.*
Working farmhouse with fantastic views.
Open: All Year (not Xmas)
01200 445295
Mrs Oliver
Rates fr: *£13.50*-**£16.00**.
Beds: 1F 1D 1T
(3)

Rufford

National Grid Ref: SD4515

Rufford Arms Hotel, *380 Liverpool Road, Rufford, Ormskirk, Lancs, L40 1SG.*
Modern country hotel.
Open: All Year
01704 822040 Mr Lockwood
Rates fr: *£17.50*-**£19.95**.
Beds: 2F 15D
Baths: 15 Private
(49)

Silverdale

National Grid Ref: SD4675

The Limes Village Guest House, *23 Stankelt Road, Silverdale, Carnforth, Lancs, LA5 0TF.*
Exceptionally good food.
Open: All Year
01524 701454 (also fax no)
Mrs Livesey
Rates fr: *£17.54*-**£24.50**.
Beds: 1F 1D 1T
Baths: 3 Private
(3)

Stacksteads

National Grid Ref: SD8421

Glen Heights, *190 Booth Road, Stacksteads, Bacup, Lancs, OL13 0TH.*
Comfortable family guest house.
Open: All Year
01706 875459 Mrs Graham
Rates fr: *£15.00*-**£18.50**.
Beds: 1D 1T 1S
Baths: 1 Shared
(12) (3)

Thornton-Cleveleys

National Grid Ref: SD3442

The Oakwood Guest House, *11 Cambridge Road, Thornton-Cleveleys, Lancs, FY5 1EP.*
Clean, small, friendly guest house.
Open: Easter to Nov
01253 853401 Mrs Oakley
Rates fr: *£13.00*-**£13.00**.
Beds: 5D
Baths: 1 Shared
(2)

Beacholme Guest House, *38 Beach Road, Thornton-Cleveleys, Lancs, FY5 1EQ.*
Small, homely guest house.
Open: All Year
01253 855350 Mrs Edwards
Rates fr: *£12.00*-**£12.00**.
Beds: 1F 2D 1T 1S
Baths: 2 Private 3 Shared
(3)

Esperance Villa Guest House, *30 Ellerbeck Road, Thornton-Cleveleys, Lancs, FY5 1DH.*
Quiet family-run guest house.
Open: All Year (not Xmas)
01253 853513 Mrs Duckett
Rates fr: *£12.00*-**£15.00**.
Beds: 1F 4D 2T 1S
Baths: 2 Shared
(2)

Trawden

National Grid Ref: SD9138

Sun Inn

Middle Beardshaw Head Farm, *Trawden, Colne, Lancs, BB8 8PP.*
C18th beamed farmhouse - wonderful setting.
Open: All Year (not Xmas)
Grades: ETB Listed
01282 865257 Mr & Mrs Mann
Rates fr: *£17.50*-**£17.50**.
Beds: 1F 1D 2S
Baths: 1 Private 1 Shared
(10)

High season, bank holidays and special events mean low availability *anywhere*.

Tunstall

National Grid Ref: SD6073

Lunesdale Arms Hotel

Barnfield Farm, *Tunstall, Kirkby Lonsdale, Carnforth, Lancs, LA6 2QF.*
1702 working family farmhouse.
Open: All Year (not Xmas)
01524 274284 Mrs Stephenson
Rates fr: *£15.00*-**£16.00**.
Beds: 1F 1D **Baths:** 2 Shared
(2)

Waddington

National Grid Ref: SD7243

Moorcock Inn

Peter Barn Country House, *Cross Lane, Waddington, Clitheroe, Lancs, BB7 3JH.*
Luxurious peaceful accommodation, beautiful garden.
Open: All Year (not Xmas)
01200 428585 Mrs Smith
Rates fr: *£18.50*-**£25.00**.
Beds: 2D 1T **Baths:** 3 Private
(12) (6)

Moorcock Inn, *Slaidburn Road, Waddington, Clitheroe, Lancs, BB7 3AA.*
Country inn with panoramic views.
Open: All Year
01200 422333 Mrs Fillary
Rates fr: *£25.00*-**£33.00**.
Beds: 5T 2D
Baths: 6 Ensuite 1 Private
(150)

Backfold Cottage, *The Square, Waddington, Clitheroe, Lancs, BB7 3JA.*
Luxury country guest house.
Open: All Year
01200 422367 Mrs Forbes
Rates fr: *£20.00*-**£20.00**.
Beds: 1F 1D 1T 1S
Baths: 4 Private
(10) (10)

Lower Buck Inn, *Church Road, Waddington, Clitheroe, Lancs, BB7 3HU.*
Superbly furnished Victorian house. **Open:** All Year (not Xmas)
01200 428705 Mrs Brown
Rates fr: *£18.50*-**£18.50**.
Beds: 1D 2T **Baths:** 2 Private

Warton

National Grid Ref: SD5072

Eagles Head

Kiln Croft, *Main Street, Warton, Carnforth, Lancs, LA5 9NR.*
Edwardian guest house and restaurant.
Open: All Year
01524 735788 Mrs Holmes
Rates fr: *£18.00*-**£22.00**.
Beds: 3F 1D **Baths:** 4 Ensuite
(8)

Cotestone Farm, *Sand Lane, Warton, Carnforth, Lancs, LA5 9NH.*
Warm welcome awaits you.
Open: All Year (not Xmas)
01524 732418 Mrs Close
Rates fr: *£14.00*-**£15.00**.
Beds: 1F 1D 1T
Baths: 2 Shared
(3)

West Bradford

National Grid Ref: SD7444

Three Millstones

Old Hall, *Back Lane, West Bradford, Clitheroe, Lancs, BB7 4SN.*
Spacious manor house in AONB.
Open: All Year (not Xmas)
01200 423 282
Mr & Mrs Gretton
Rates fr: *£14.00*-**£16.00**.
Beds: 1D 2T
Baths: 1 Private 1 Shared
(10)

Whalley

National Grid Ref: SD7336

Monk Hall, *78 Mitton Road, Whalley, Clitheroe, Lancs, BB7 9JN.*
Small, friendly guest house.
Open: All Year
Grades: ETB 3 Cr, High Comm
01254 822501
Mr Hollin
Rates fr: *£17.50*-**£17.50**.
Beds: 2D 1T 1S
Baths: 4 Ensuite

Wrightington

National Grid Ref: SD5313

Tudor Inn

95 Mossy Lea Road, *Wrightington, Wigan, Lancs, WN6 9RD.*
Modern bungalow near M6 (J27).
Open: All Year
01257 421929
Mr & Mrs Sutton
Rates fr: *£12.00*-**£12.50**.
Beds: 1D 2T
Baths: 1 Shared
(2) (6)

Wycoller

National Grid Ref: SD9339

Alma Inn

Wycoller Cottage, *Wycoller, Colne, Lancs, BB8 8SY.*
C17th cottage with exposed beams.
Open: All Year
01282 867336
Mrs Houlker
Rates fr: *£20.00*-**£20.00**.
Beds: 1D 1T 1S
Baths: 2 Private
(2)

Leicestershire

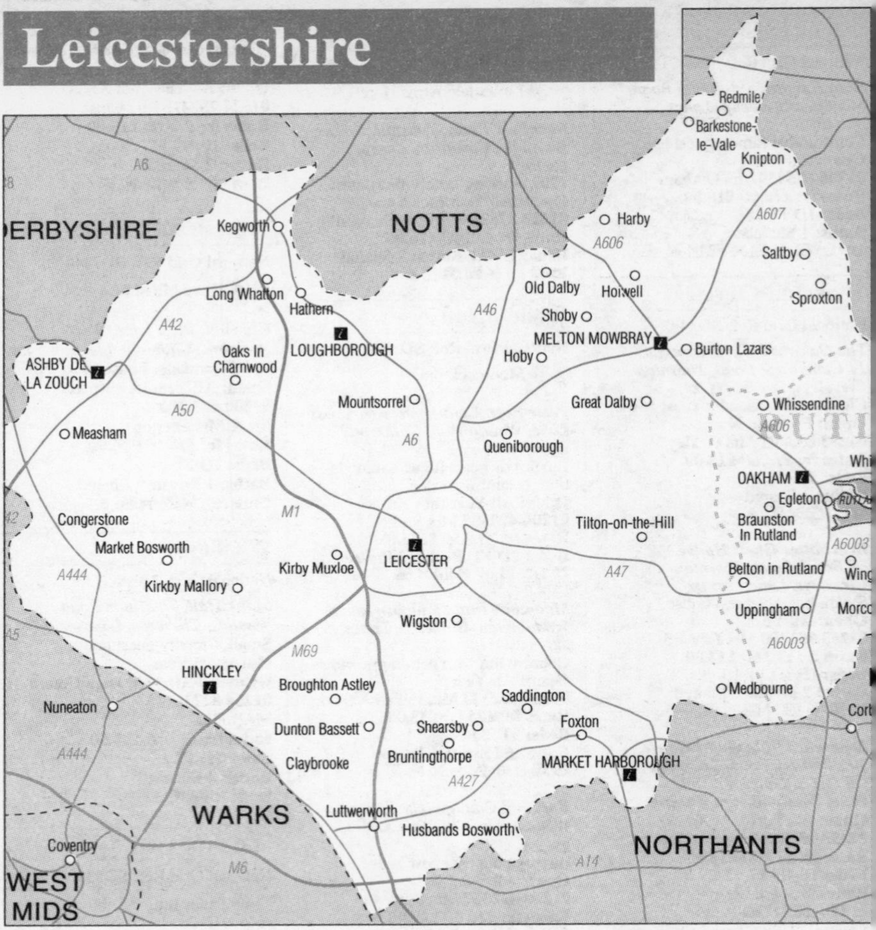

Tourist Information Centres

North Street, **Ashby de la Zouch**, Leics, LE6 5AB, 01530 411767.

Snibson Discovery Park, Ashby Road, **Coalville**, Leics, LE6 3LN, 01455 813608.

Hinckley Library, Lancaster Road, **Hinckley**, Leicestershire, LE10 0AT, 01455 635106.

7-9 Every Street, Town Hall Square, **Leicester**, Leicestershire, LE1 6AG, 0116 265 0355.

John Storer House, Wards End, **Loughborough**, Leicestershire, LE11 3HA, 01509 218113.

Pen Lloyd Library, Adam and Eve Street, **Market Harborough**, Leicestershire, LE16 7LT, 01858 468106.

Melton Carnegie Museum, Thorpe End, **Melton Mowbray**, Leics, LE13 1RB, 01664 480992.

Oakham Library, Catmos Street, **Oakham**, Leicestershire, LE15 6HW, 01572 724329.

Sykes Lane, **Empingham**, Oakham, Leicestershire, LE15 8PX, 01780 460321, (Easter to Oct).

Ashby de la Zouch

National Grid Ref: SK3516

The Cedars Guest House, *60 Burton Road, Ashby de la Zouch, Leicester, Leics, LE65 2LN.*
Victorian house close to town.
Open: All Year (not Xmas)
01530 412017
Mrs Sedgley
Rates fr: *£15.00*-**£16.00**.
Beds: 4F 1D 3T 3S
Baths: 7 Private 2 Shared
(10)

The Bungalow, *10 Trinity Close, Ashby de la Zouch, Leicester, Leics, LE65 2GQ.*
Private family home.
Open: All Year
01530 560698 Ms Chapman
Rates fr: *£15.00*-**£15.00**.
Beds: 1T
Baths: 1 Shared

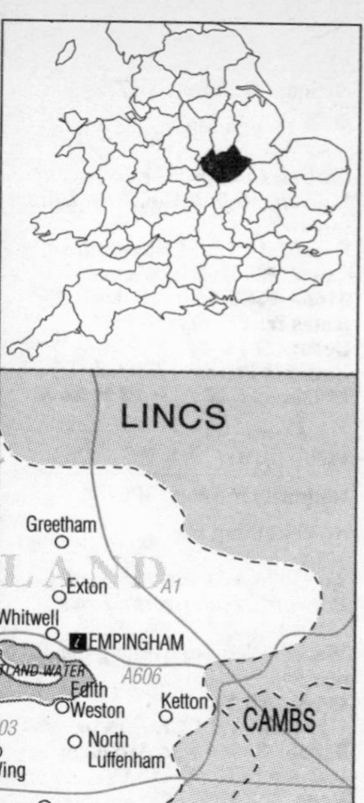

Barkestone-le-Vale

National Grid Ref: SK7834

Windmill, The Haven

Little Orchard, *Chapel Street, Barkestone-le-Vale, Nottingham, Notts,* *NG13 0HE.*
Bungalow, picturesque village, near Belvoir Castle.
Open: All Year (not Xmas)
01949 842698 Mrs Fisher
Rates fr: *£15.00*-**£15.00**.
Beds: 1F 1D 1T 1S
Baths: 1 Shared
(3) (4)

The Dairies, *22 The Green, Barkestone-le-Vale, Nottingham, Notts,* *NG13 0HH.*
Farmhouse in small village.
Open: All Year (not Xmas)
Grades: ETB Listed
01949 842495 Mrs Watchorn
Rates fr: *£13.00*-**£15.00**.
Beds: 1F 1D 1T
Baths: 1 Private 2 Shared

Planning a longer stay? Always ask for any special rates.

Belton in Rutland

National Grid Ref: SK8101

Bewicke Arms, Salisbury Arms

The Old Rectory, *4 New Road, Belton in Rutland, Oakham, Leics,* *LE15 9LE.*
Large country house with guest annexe.
Open: All Year
Grades: ETB 2 Cr, Comm, RAC Listed
01572 717279 Mr Peach
Rates fr: *£16.00*-**£23.00**.
Beds: 2F 3D 2T 1S
Baths: 7 Private 1 Shared
(0) (10)

College Farm, *College Farm Road, Belton in Rutland, Oakham, Leics,* *LE15 9AF.*
Idyllic C18th farmhouse and s/c cottage.
Open: All Year (not Xmas)
01572 717440 Mrs Brown
Rates fr: *£15.00*-**£15.00**.
Beds: 1D 1T
Baths: 2 Private
(10)

Braunston in Rutland

National Grid Ref: SK8306

Rutland Cottages, *5 Cedar Street, Braunston in Rutland, Oakham, Leics,* *LE15 8QS.*
Charming cottages in conservation village. **Open:** All Year
01572 722049 Mr Beadman (John & Connie Beadman)
Rates fr: *£18.00*-**£18.00**.
Beds: 2D 2T 2S
Baths: 2 Private 4 Shared
(3)

Broughton Astley

National Grid Ref: SP5292

The Old Farm House, *Old Mill Road, Broughton Astley, Leicester, Leics,* *LE9 6PQ.*
Open: All Year
Grades: ETB Listed
01455 282254 Mrs Cornelius
Rates fr: *£18.00*-**£18.00**.
Beds: 3D 1S
Baths: 2 Shared
(6)
Quietly situated farmhouse in well served village, good local pubs/shops. Easy access M1 J20/21, M69J1 and A1/M1 link. Evening meal by arrangement. Advance booking please.

Bruntingthorpe

National Grid Ref: SP6089

White House Farm, *Main Street, Bruntingthorpe, Lutterworth, Leics,* *LE17 5QF.*
C16th comfortable farmhouse.
Open: All Year (not Xmas)
0116 247 8543 Mrs Percival
Rates fr: *£16.00*-**£18.50**.
Beds: 1T
(2)

Burton Lazars

National Grid Ref: SK7519

Hillside House, *27 Melton Road, Burton Lazars, Melton Mowbray, Leics,* *LE14 2UR.*
Charming converted C19th farm buildings.
Open: All Year (not Xmas)
01664 66312 Mrs Goodwin
Rates fr: *£16.50*-**£22.00**.
Beds: 1D 2T
Baths: 2 Ensuite 1 Private
(10) (3)

Congerstone

National Grid Ref: SK3605

Black Horse Inn

Church House Farm, *Shadows Lane, Congerstone, Nuneaton, Warks,* *CV13 6NA.*
Spacious, comfortable, former farmhouse.
Open: All Year (not Xmas)
Grades: ETB 2 Cr
01827 880402 Mrs Martin
Rates fr: *£17.00*-**£17.00**.
Beds: 1D 1T 1S
Baths: 1 Ensuite 1 Shared
(12) (6)

The Old Barn, *Shadows Lane, Congerstone, Nuneaton, Warks,* *CV13 6NF.*
Converted barn in walled garden.
Open: All Year (not Xmas)
01827 880431 Mrs Savage
Rates fr: *£15.00*.
Beds: 1T 1S
(12) (6)

Dunton Bassett

National Grid Ref: SP5490

Dunton Bassett Arms

Ivydene Farmhouse, *The Mount, Dunton Bassett, Lutterworth, Leics,* *LE17 5JL.*
Family farmhouse, warm welcome.
Open: All Year
01455 202246 Mr Tebbutt
Rates fr: *£15.00*-**£15.00**.
Beds: 1D 1T 1S
Baths: 1 Private 1 Shared

Edith Weston

National Grid Ref: SK9305

10 Church Lane, *Edith Weston, Oakham, Leics,* *LE15 8EY.*
Private house near Rutland Water.
Open: All Year (not Xmas)
01780 720710 Mr Phillips
Rates fr: *£16.00*-**£16.00**.
Beds: 2T 1S
Baths: 1 Shared
(6)

Egleton

National Grid Ref: SK8707

Barnetts Farm, *7 Church Road, Egleton, Oakham, Leics, LE15 8AD.*
C17th Grade II Listed farmhouse.
Open: All Year
01572 756630 Mrs Thwaites
Rates fr: *£19.50*-**£22.00**.
Beds: 1F 1T
Baths: 1 Shared
(10)

The Old Bakehouse, *Hambleton Road, Egleton, Oakham, Leics, LE15 8AE.*
C17th thatched former bakehouse.
Open: All Year (not Xmas)
01572 770612 Mrs Walker
Rates fr: *£21.50*-**£25.00**.
Beds: 1D 2T **Baths:** 3 Private
(12) (5)

Exton

National Grid Ref: SK9211

Fox & Hounds

Fox & Hounds, *Exton, Oakham, Leics, LE15 8AP.*
C17th inn. **Open:** All Year
Grades: ETB Listed
01572 812403 D Hillier
Rates fr: *£18.00*-**£22.00**.
Beds: 1D 1T 1S
(8) (2)

Church Farmhouse, *5 Oakham Road, Exton, Oakham, Leics, LE15 8AX.*
Listed homely farmhouse, beautiful village. **Open:** All Year
01572 813435 Mr & Mrs Hudson
Rates fr: *£15.00*-**£15.00**.
Beds: 1D 1T **Baths:** 1 Private
(5) (2)

Foxton

National Grid Ref: SP7089

The Old Manse, *Swingbridge Street, Foxton, Market Harborough, Leics, LE16 7RH.*
Period house in large gardens.
Open: All Year (not Xmas)
Grades: ETB 2 Cr
01858 545456 Mrs Pickering
Rates fr: *£19.50*-**£23.00**.
Beds: 1D
Baths: 2 Ensuite
(5)

Great Dalby

National Grid Ref: SK7414

Royal Oak

Glebe Farm, *Nether End, Great Dalby, Melton Mowbray, Leics, LE14 2EY.*
C17th house, stables and paddock.
Open: All Year
01664 61548 Mrs Byrne
Rates fr: *£16.00*-**£18.00**.
Beds: 1F 1D **Baths:** 1 Shared
(0) (6)

Dairy Farm, *8 Burrough End, Great Dalby, Melton Mowbray, Leics, LE14 2EW.*
Comfortable friendly farmhouse, pretty village.
Open: All Year
01664 62783 Mrs Parker
Rates fr: *£15.00*-**£15.00**.
Beds: 1D 1T 1S
Baths: 1 Private 1 Shared
(5)

Greetham

National Grid Ref: SK9214

Priestwells, *Main Street, Greetham, Oakham, Leics, LE15 7HU.*
Modern house in peaceful surroundings.
Open: All Year
01572 812660 Mrs Wilson
Rates fr: *£14.00*-**£14.00**.
Beds: 1F 1D 1S
Baths: 2 Shared
(6)

Harby

National Grid Ref: SK7431

Peacock Inn, Red Lion

Box House, *Dickmans Lane, Harby, Melton Mowbray, Leics, LE14 4BG.*
Victorian farmhouse in the Vale of Belvoir.
Open: Mar to Nov
01949 860248 Mrs Fox
Rates fr: *£18.00*-**£16.00**.
Beds: 1T
Baths: 1 Ensuite
(1)

Hathern

National Grid Ref: SK5022

Leys Guest House, *Loughborough Road, Hathern, Loughborough, Leics, LE12 5JB.*
Small, family-run guest house.
Open: All Year (not Xmas)
Grades: ETB 1 Cr
01509 844373
Mrs Hudson
Rates fr: *£15.00*-**£17.00**.
Beds: 1F 1D 2T 2S
Baths: 2 Shared
(8)

Hoby

National Grid Ref: SK6617

Wreake Cottage, *Lower Lane, Hoby, Melton Mowbray, Leics, LE14 3DT.*
Warm, welcoming cottage. Lovely views.
Open: All Year (not Xmas)
01664 434326 Mrs Draper
Rates fr: *£13.50*-**£13.50**.
Beds: 1T 1S
Baths: 1 Shared
(2)

Holwell

National Grid Ref: SK7323

Plough Inn

Church Cottage, *The Green, Holwell, Melton Mowbray, Leics, LE14 4SZ.*
Beautiful C18th Listed cottage.
Open: All Year (not Xmas)
01664 444255 Mrs Bailey
Rates fr: *£17.00*-**£18.00**.
Beds: 1D 1T
Baths: 1 Private 1 Shared
(3months) (2)

Husbands Bosworth

National Grid Ref: SP6484

Bell Inn

31-33 High Street, *Husbands Bosworth, Lutterworth, Leics, LE17 6LJ.*
Warm welcome. Evening meals nearby.
Open: All Year
Grades: ETB 1 Cr, Approv
01858 880066 Mrs Armitage
Rates fr: *£15.00*-**£15.00**.
Beds: 3T
(6)

Kegworth

National Grid Ref: SK4826

Kegworth Lantern Hotel, *1 Market Place, Kegworth, Derby, DE74 2EE.*
Family-run hotel of high standard.
Open: All Year
01509 673989 Mr & Mrs Bilson
Fax no: 01509 670725
Rates fr: *£20.00*-**£18.50**.
Beds: 1F 1D 6T 2S
Baths: 4 Private 3 Shared
(20)

Ketton

National Grid Ref: SK9704

Peverick, *7 Sand Furrows, Ketton, Stamford, Lincs, PE9 3SS.*
Bungalow between Stamford & Rutland Water.
Open: All Year (not Xmas)
01780 721310 Mrs Grace
Rates fr: *£15.00*-**£15.00**.
Beds: 1D 1T 1S
Baths: 1 Shared
(2)

Kirby Muxloe

National Grid Ref: SK5104

Faith Cottage, *400 Ratby Lane, Kirby Muxloe, Leicester, Leics, LE9 9AQ.*
Old world cottage.
Open: All Year (not Xmas)
0116 238 7435 Mrs Saunders
Rates fr: *£17.50*-**£17.50**.
Beds: 1T 1S
Baths: 1 Private 1 Shared
(7) (6)

Knipton

National Grid Ref: SK8231

Red House

The Red House, *Knipton, Grantham, Lincs,* *NG32 1RH.*
C18th ex-hunting lodge near Belvoir Castle.
Open: All Year (not Xmas)
01476 870352 Mr Newport
Rates fr: *£16.25*-**£18.00**.
Beds: 1F 6D 2S
Baths: 3 Private 1 Shared

Leicester

National Grid Ref: SK5804

Backpackers Hostel, *157 Wanlip Lane, Birstall, Leicester,* *LE4 4GL.*
Small, cosy, backpacker's hostel.
0116 267 3107 Mr Allen
Rates fr: *£10.50*-**£10.50**.
Beds: 1F 1T **Baths:** 1 Shared

Westerby House, *161 Uppingham Road, Leicester,* *LE5 4BP.*
Edwardian house, east of city.
Open: All Year
0116 276 3906 Mrs Morgan
Rates fr: *£14.00*-**£18.00**.
Beds: 1F 1D 1T 1S **Baths:** 1 Shared
(11) (6)

Aylestone Park Hotel, *69 Belvoir Drive, Leicester,* *LE2 8PB.*
Large privately-owned property.
Open: All Year
0116 283 3637 (also fax no)
Mr Davies **Rates fr:** *£18.00*-**£20.00**
Beds: 3F 2D 2T 10S
Baths: 7 Private 2 Shared
(5) (14)

Long Whatton

National Grid Ref: SK4823

The Falcon

Uplands Farm, *West End, Long Whatton, Loughborough, Leics,* *LE12 5DW.*
Converted C17th farmhouse.
Open: All Year
01509 842244 Mrs Wilds
Rates fr: *£15.00*-**£15.00**.
Beds: 5F 2D 1T 2S
Baths: 1 Shared
(20)

Loughborough

National Grid Ref: SK5319

Peachnook Guest House, *154 Ashby Road, Loughborough, Leics,* *LE11 3AG.*
Friendly, family-run Victorian villa. **Open:** All Year
Grades: ETB Listed
01509 264390 Ms Wood
Rates fr: *£14.00*-**£12.00**.
Beds: 2F 1D 1T 1S
Baths: 1 Ensuite 1 Private 1 Shared
(5)

De Montfort Hotel, *88 Leicester Rd, Loughborough, Leics,* *LE11 2AQ.*
Open: All Year
Grades: ETB 3 Cr, Comm, RAC Acclaim
01509 216061 Mrs Charwat
Rates fr: *£17.50*-**£23.00**.
Beds: 4F 4D 4T 2S
Baths: 7 Private 2 Shared
One of the town's longest established hotels. Friendly family-run hotel with Victorian flavour. English/German speaking, close to town centre, steam trust, university and beautiful countryside of Charnwood Forest.

The Highbury Guest House, *146 Leicester Rd, Loughborough, Leicestershire,* *LE12 2AQ.*
Comfortable, spacious, modern guest house. **Open:** All Year
Grades: ETB 3 Cr, Approv, AA Listed
01509 230545 Mr Cunningham
Rates fr: *£17.50*-**£19.00**.
Beds: 3F 4D 4S
(0.25) (12)

Garendon Park Hotel, *92 Leicester Road, Loughborough, Leics,* *LE11 2AQ.*
Open: All Year (not Xmas)
Grades: ETB 3 Cr, Comm, AA 3 Q, Recomm, RAC Acclaim
01509 236557 Mrs Hassall
Fax no: 01509 265559
Rates fr: *£18.00*-**£23.00**.
Beds: 2F 4D 3T 2S
Baths: 7 Private 2 Shared
Large Victorian residence close to town centre, steam railway and university offering high standard 'B&B' in bright comfortable surroundings. Also renown for a helpful friendly atmosphere.

Lutterworth

National Grid Ref: SP5484

Highcross House, *Highcross, Lutterworth, Leics,* *LE17 5AT.*
Unique use type C.
Open: All Year
Grades: ETB 3 Cr, High Comm
01455 220840 (also fax no)
Miss Galliford
Rates fr: *£17.50*-**£20.00**.
Beds: 1F 3D 2T 1S
Baths: 3 Private 3 Shared

Market Bosworth

National Grid Ref: SK4003

Bosworth Firs, *Bosworth Road, Market Bosworth, Nuneaton, Warks,* *CV13 0DW.*
Comfortable, clean, friendly. Home cooking. **Open:** All Year
Grades: ETB 2 Cr, Comm
01455 290727 Mrs Christian
Rates fr: *£17.00*-**£17.00**.
Beds: 2D 1T 2S
Baths: 1 Ensuite 2 Private 1 Shared
(6)

11 Stanley Road, *Market Bosworth, Nuneaton, Warks,* *CV13 0NB.*
Small homely private home.
Open: All Year
01455 290196
Mrs Caldwell
Rates fr: *£15.00*-**£15.00**.
Baths: 1 Shared
(Yes)

Ye Olde Red Lion Hotel, *Park Street, Market Bosworth, Nuneaton, Warks,* *CV13 0LL.*
Olde worlde public house.
Open: All Year (not Xmas)
01455 291713
Rates fr: *£23.50*-**£23.50**.
Beds: 2D 1T 1S
Baths: 2 Ensuite 1 Shared

Market Harborough

National Grid Ref: SP7387

Millstones Guest House, *138 Northampton Road, Market Harborough, Leics,* *LE16 9HF.*
Large Victorian house with extension.
Open: All Year (not Xmas)
01858 465441 Mrs Blackburn
Rates fr: *£15.00*-**£16.00**.
Beds: 1F 3D 2T 2S
Baths: 3 Shared

Measham

National Grid Ref: SK3312

The Swan

Laurels Guest House, *17 Ashby Road, Measham, Swadlincote, Derbyshire,* *DE12 7JR.*
Modern guest house, rural pleasant surroundings.
Open: All Year
Grades: ETB 2 Cr
01530 272567 Mrs Evans
Rates fr: *£20.00*-**£18.00**.
Beds: 1D 1T 1S
Baths: 2 Ensuite 1 Private
(1) (8)

Medbourne

National Grid Ref: SP7993

Nevill Arms

Medbourne Grange, *Nevill Holt, Medbourne, Market Harborough, Leics,* *LE16 8EF.*
Comfortable farmhouse with breathtaking views.
Open: All Year (not Xmas)
01858 565249
Mrs Beaty
Fax no: 01858 565257
Rates fr: *£16.00*-**£16.00**.
Beds: 1D 1T 2S
Baths: 2 Shared
(0) (6)

Melton Mowbray

National Grid Ref: SK7519

The Crown

Shoby Lodge Farm, *Shoby, Melton Mowbray, Leics, LE14 3PF.*
Open: All Year (not Xmas)
Grades: ETB Listed
01664 812156 Mrs Lomas
Rates fr: *£15.00*-**£20.00**.
Beds: 3D
Baths: 1 Ensuite 1 Private
Comfortable spacious farmhouse set in attractive gardens with beautiful views of surrounding countryside. Generous Aga cooked breakfast. Ideally situated for Leicestershire & Nottinghamshire.

Cherry Tree Cottage, *Main Street, Wartnaby, Melton Mowbray, Leics, LE14 3HY.*
Attractive cottage, quiet hamlet.
Open: All Year (not Xmas)
01664 822524 Mrs Spicer
Rates fr: *£15.00*-**£15.00**.
Beds: 1D 1T
Baths: 1 Shared
(2) (4)

Burton Road Guest House, *86 Burton Road, Melton Mowbray, Leics, LE13 1DL.*
Large comfortable Victorian terraced house.
Open: All Year
01664 60188 Mrs Sayles
Rates fr: *£15.00*-**£15.00**.
Beds: 1F 1T 2S
Baths: 1 Shared
(2)

Bricklayers Arms, *16 Timber Hill, Melton Mowbray, Leics, LE13 1RF.*
Town centre public house.
Open: All Year
01664 60188 Mrs Sayles
Rates fr: *£13.00*-**£13.00**.
Beds: 3T
Baths: 1 Shared

The Noel Arms, *31 Burton Street, Melton Mowbray, Leics, LE13 1AE.*
Clean and friendly.
Open: All Year
01664 62363 Mrs Ling
Rates fr: *£15.00*-**£15.00**.
Beds: 2F 2T 2S
Baths: 2 Shared

Morcott

National Grid Ref: SK9200

5 Church Lane, *Morcott, Uppingham, Oakham, Leics, LE15 9DH.*
Cosy home, well-kept garden.
Open: All Year
01572 747829 Mrs Martin
Rates fr: *£15.00*-**£15.00**.
Beds: 1T 1D
Baths: 1 Shared

Mountsorrel

National Grid Ref: SK5814

Swan Inn

Barley Loft Guest House, *33a Hawcliffe Road, Mountsorrel, Loughborough, Leics, LE12 7AQ.*
Open: All Year
01509 413514 Mrs Pegg
Rates fr: *£15.00*-**£16.00**.
Beds: 2F 3D 1S
Baths: 2 Shared
(12)
Spacious bungalow, quiet rural location. Close A6 between Leicester and Loughborough. Outstanding riverside walking, local beauty spots. Traditional hearty breakfast. EM by arrangement. Suitable disabled.

The Swan Inn, *Loughborough Road, Mountsorrel, Loughborough, Leics, LE12 7AT.*
C17th riverside coaching inn.
Open: All Year (not Xmas)
0116 230 2340 Miss Gosnall
Fax no: 0116 237 6115
Rates fr: *£16.00*-**£20.00**.
Beds: 1D 1T 1S
Baths: 1 Shared
(10)

North Luffenham

National Grid Ref: SK9303

Pinfold House, *6 Pinfold Lane, North Luffenham, Oakham, Rutland, LE15 8LE.*
C18th cottage with large garden.
Open: All Year (not Xmas)
01780 720175 Mrs Cook
Rates fr: *£13.50*-**£16.00**.
Beds: 1F 2D 1T 2S
Baths: 1 Shared
(4)

Oakham

National Grid Ref: SK8509

White Lion

Westgate Lodge, *9 Westgate, Oakham, Leics, LE15 6BH.*
Spacious and friendly family home.
Open: All Year
Grades: ETB Listed
01572 757370
Mrs Addison & Mrs D Davey
Rates fr: *£18.50*-**£18.50**.
Beds: 1F 1D 1T
Baths: 3 Ensuite
(5) (3)

27 Northgate, *Oakham, Leics, LE15 6QR.*
Victorian private house. Very homely.
Open: All Year (not Xmas)
01572 755057 Mrs George
Rates fr: *£13.00*-**£13.00**.
Beds: 1F 1D 1T
Baths: 1 Shared

The Merry Monk, *12 Church Street, Oakham, Leics, LE15 6AA.*
Close to Rutland Water.
Open: All Year
01572 722094 Mr Riordan
Rates fr: *£14.00*-**£18.00**.
Beds: 3T
Baths: 1 Shared
(5)

Angel House, *20 Northgate, Oakham, Leics, LE15 6QS.*
Large Victorian private house.
Open: All Year
01572 756153 Mrs Weight
Rates fr: *£12.50*-**£15.50**
Beds: 1D 2T
Baths: 3 Ensuite

Oaks in Charnwood

National Grid Ref: SK4716

Jolly Farmer

St Josephs, *Abbey Road, Oaks in Charnwood, Coalville, Leics, LE67 4UA.*
Old country house, welcoming hosts.
Open: Easter to Oct
01509 503943 Mrs Havers
Rates fr: *£17.00*-**£17.00**.
Beds: 1D 2T 2S
Baths: 2 Shared
(4)

Old Dalby

National Grid Ref: SK6723

Crown Inn

Home Farm, *Church Lane, Old Dalby, Melton Mowbray, Leics, LE14 3LB.*
Warm, comfortable, quiet Victorian farmhouse.
Open: All Year (not Xmas)
Grades: AA 3 Q, Recomm, RAC Listed
01664 822622 Mr & Mrs Anderson
Rates fr: *£17.50*-**£21.00**.
Beds: 1D 2T 2S
Baths: 4 Ensuite 1 Private
(5)

Queniborough

National Grid Ref: SK6412

Britannia Inn, Horse & Groom

Three Ways Farm, *Melton Road, Queniborough, Leicester, Leics, LE7 3FN.*
Modern, comfortable, peaceful farm bungalow.
Open: All Year (not Xmas)
Grades: ETB Listed, Comm
0116 260 0472 Mrs Clarke
Rates fr: *£15.00*-**£17.00**.
Beds: 1D 1T 1S
Baths: 1 Shared
(20)

Redmile

National Grid Ref: SK7935

Peacock Farm Restaurant, *& Guest House, Redmile, Vale of Belvoir, Nottingham, Notts, NG13 0GQ.*
Great atmosphere, great food.
Open: All Year
01949 842475 Miss Need
Fax no: 01949 843127
Rates fr: *£18.00*-**£19.50**.
Beds: 5F 2D 2T 1S
Baths: 6 Private 1 Shared
(4)

Saddington

National Grid Ref: SP6591

The Queen's Head

Breach Farm, *Shearsby Road, Saddington, Leicester, Leics, LE8 0QU*
Modern, comfortable farmhouse with open views.
Open: All Year (not Xmas)
0116 240 2539 Mrs Thornton
Rates fr: *£15.00*-**£16.00**.
Beds: 2D 1T **Baths:** 1 Shared
(4)

Saltby

National Grid Ref: SK8526

Nags Head Inn

The Nags Head Inn, *1 Back Street, Saltby, Melton Mowbray, Leics, LE14 4QD.*
200-year-old inn, open fires.
Open: All Year (not Xmas)
01476 860491 Mr Mannion
Rates fr: *£16.00*-**£16.00**.
Beds: 2D 2T
Baths: 2 Private 1 Shared

Shearsby

National Grid Ref: SP6290

Shearsby Bath

The Greenway, *Knaptoft House Farm, Bruntingthorpe Road, Shearsby, Lutterworth, Leics, LE17 6PR.*
Spacious bungalow/farmhouse with lovely views.
Open: All Year (not Xmas)
Grades: ETB 2 Cr, AA 4 Q, Select
0116 247 8388 (also fax no)
Mr Hutchinson
Rates fr: *£18.00*-**£22.00**.
Beds: 2D 1T
Baths: 2 Private 1 Shared
(6) (5)

Please respect a B&B's wishes regarding children, animals & smoking.

Shoby

National Grid Ref: SK6820

Shoby Lodge Farm, *Shoby, Melton Mowbray, Leics, LE14 3PF.*
Comfortable spacious farmhouse, attractive gardens.
Open: All Year (not Xmas)
Grades: ETB Listed
01664 812156 Mrs Lomas
Rates fr: *£15.00*-**£20.00**.
Beds: 3D
Baths: 1 Ensuite 1 Private

Sproxton

National Grid Ref: SK8524

Crown Inn

Appletree Cottage, *Sproxton, Melton Mowbray, Leics, LE14 4QS.*
Self-catering (2 Key, High Comm) also available. **Open:** All Year
01476 860435 Mrs Slack
Rates fr: *£18.00*-**£19.00**.
Beds: 1D 1S **Baths:** 1 Shared
(1)

Tilton-on-the-Hill

National Grid Ref: SK7405

Knebworth House, *Loddington Lane, Launde, Tilton-on-the-Hill, Leicester, Leics, LE7 9DE.*
Comfortable accommodation in secluded countryside.
Open: All Year (not Xmas)
0116 259 7257 Miss Layton
Rates fr: *£15.00*-**£15.00**.
Beds: 1D 1T 1S
Baths: 1 Shared
(4)

Uppingham

National Grid Ref: SP8699

George & Dragon, White Hart

8 Main Street, *Uppingham, Oakham, Leics, LE15 9HU.*
Modern cottage.
Open: All Year (not Xmas)
01572 747358 Mrs Warburton
Rates fr: *£15.00*-**£15.00**.
Beds: 1D 1S **Baths:** 1 Shared
(2)

The White Hart, *High Street West, Uppingham, Oakham, Leics, LE15 9QB.*
C16th coaching inn.
Open: All Year
01572 822229
Rates fr: *£14.25*-**£18.50**.
Beds: 1D 1T 2S
Baths: 1 Shared

Whissendine

National Grid Ref: SK8214

Noel Arms (Langham)

Pickwell Grange, *Whissendine, Oakham, Leics, LE15 7ET.*
Comfortable farmhouse. Large garden.
Open: All Year (not Xmas)
Grades: ETB Listed
01664 474274
Mrs Bailey
Rates fr: *£12.50*-**£15.00**.
Beds: 1F 1D 1T 1S
Baths: 1 Ensuite 1 Shared

Whitwell

National Grid Ref: SK9208

Noel Arms

Noel Arms, *Main Street, Whitwell, Oakham, Leics, LE15 8BW.*
Farmhouse and public house.
Open: All Year
01780 460334 Mr Healey
Rates fr: *£19.00*-**£17.50**.
Beds: 1F 3D 9T 1S
Baths: 4 Private 2 Shared

Wing

National Grid Ref: SK8903

4 Westhorpe Close, *Wing, Oakham, Rutland, LE15 8RJ.*
Detached house with walled garden.
Open: All Year (not Xmas)
01572 737508 Mrs Martin-Pope
Rates fr: *£12.50*-**£15.00**.
Beds: 1D 1T **Baths:** 1 Shared
(12) (2)

Always telephone to get directions to the B&B - you will save time!

Lincolnshire

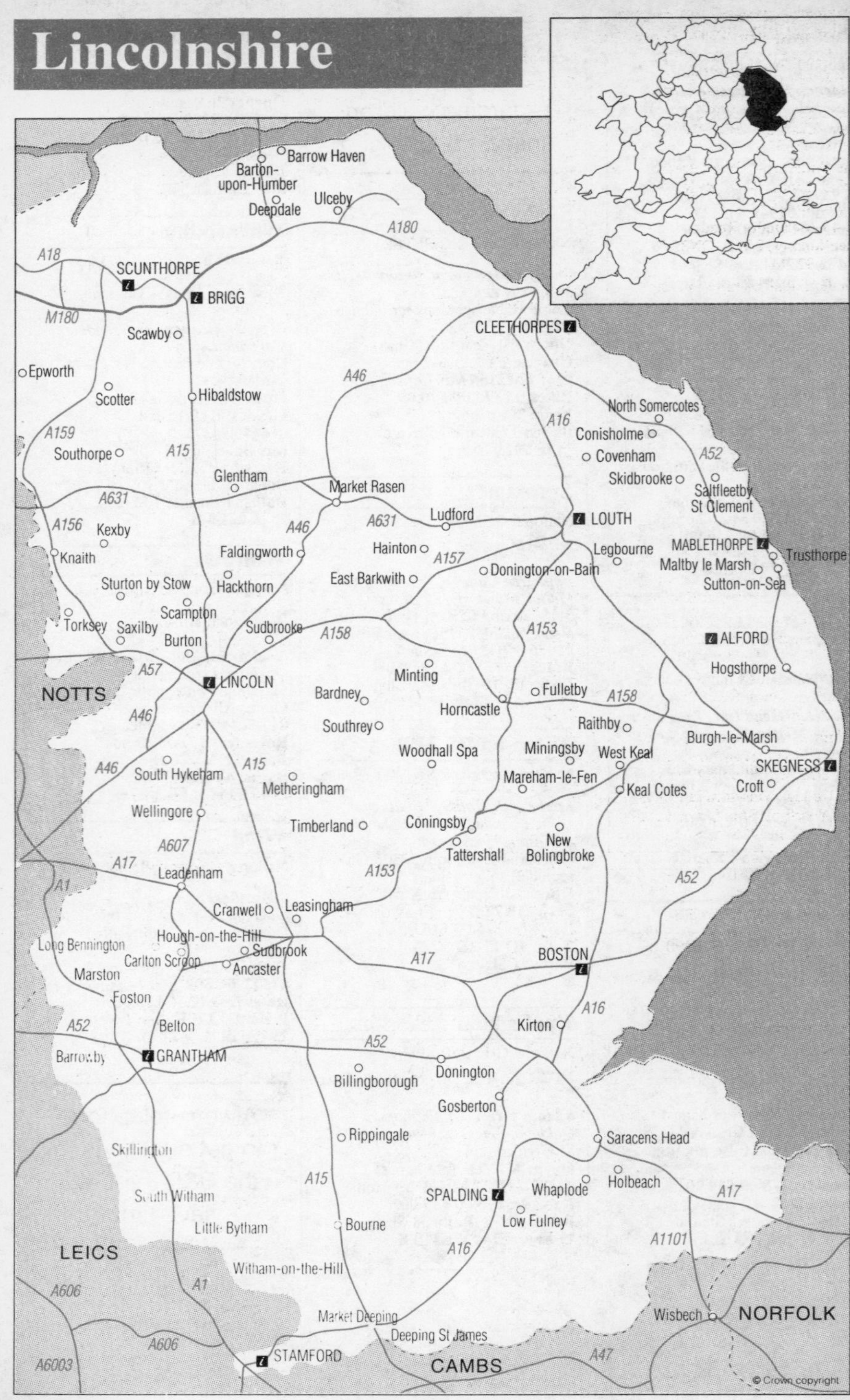

Tourist Information Centres

'he Manor House, West Street, **Alford**, Lincs, LN13 9DJ, 1507 609289, (Easter to Oct).
Blackfriars Arts Centre, Spain Lane, **Boston**, Lincs, PE21 6HP, 1205-356656,
'he Buttercross, Marketplace, **Brigg**, Lincs, DN20 8ER, 1652 657053
2-43 Alexandra Road, **Cleethorpes**, Lincs, DN35 8LE, 1472 323111
'he Guildhall Centre, St Peter's Hill, **Grantham**, Lincs, NG31 6PZ, 01476-66444.
National Fishing Heritage Centre, Alexandra Dock, **Grimsby**, Lincs, DN31 IUF, 01472 323222
Castle Hill, **Lincoln**, Lincs, LN1 3AA, 01522 529828.
outh Town Hall, Cannon Street, **Louth**, Lincs, LN11 9NW, 1507 609289.
Dunes Family Entertainment Centre, Central Promenade, **Mablethorpe**, Lincs, LN12 1RG, 1507 472496.
Embassy Centre, Grand Parade, **Skegness**, PE25 2UP, 01754 764821
'he Mill, Money's Yard, Carre Street, **Sleaford**, Lincs, NG34 7TW, 01529 414294.
Ayscoughfee Hall, Churchgate, **Spalding**, Lincs, PE11 2RA, 1775 725468.
Stamford Arts Centre, 27 St Mary's Street, **Stamford**, Lincs, PE9 2DL, 01780 55611.
'he Cottage Museum, Iddesleigh Rd, **Woodhall Spa**, Lincs, LN10 SH, 01526 53775, (Easter to Oct)

Alford

National Grid Ref: TF4575

alton House, *50 East Street, Alford, Lincs, LN13 9EH.*
Comfortable relaxing accommodation.
Open: All Year (not Xmas)
1507 462058 Mrs Mackey
Rates fr: *£15.00*-**£15.00**.
Beds: 1D 1T
Baths: 1 Shared
(3)

Ancaster

National Grid Ref: SK9643

Woodlands, *West Willoughby, Ancaster, Grantham, Lincs, NG32 3SH.*
Peaceful Victorian farmhouse.
Open: Easter to Dec
1400 230340 Mrs Mival
Rates fr: *£16.00*-**£18.00**.
Beds: 1F 1T
Baths: 1 Shared
(1) (6)

Bardney

National Grid Ref: TF1169

Railway Inn, *Station Road, Bardney, Lincoln, Lincs, LN3 5UF.*
Riverside pub.
Open: All Year (not Xmas)
01526 398313
Rates fr: *£12.50*-**£12.50**.
Beds: 2D 1S **Baths:** 1 Shared

Barnetby

National Grid Ref: TA0509

Holcombe Guest House, *34 Victoria Road, Barnetby, DN38 6JR.*
Very comfortable, modern, guest house. **Open:** All Year
Grades: ETB 3 Cr, Comm
01850 764002 Mrs Vora
Rates fr: *£15.00*-**£17.50**.
Beds: 2F 1D 2T 6S
Baths: 4 Private 2 Shared
(7)

Barrow Haven

National Grid Ref: TA0622

Barrow Haven Inn

Castle House, *Barrow Haven, Barton-upon-Humber, Lincs, DN19 7EY*
C18th farmhouse near Norman castle. **Open:** All Year (not Xmas)
01469 530040 Mrs Rawlings
Rates fr: *£12.50*-**£12.50**.
Beds: 1D 2S **Baths:** 1 Shared
(2)

Barrowby

National Grid Ref: SK8836

Welby Arms

Old Timbers, *Low Rd, Barrowby, Grantham, Lincs, NG32 1DJ.*
Comfortable cottage style village house. **Open:** All Year (not Xmas)
01476 576609 Mrs Fowler
Rates fr: *£15.00*-**£15.00**.
Beds: 1D 1T 1S **Baths:** 1 Shared
(4)

Barton-upon-Humber

National Grid Ref: TA0322

Southgarth Guest House, *2 Caistor Road, Barton-upon-Humber, Lincs, DN18 5AH.*
Originally a gatekeepers lodge.
Open: All Year (not Xmas)
01652 632833 Mrs Havercroft
Rates fr: *£14.00*-**£16.00**.
Beds: 3T **Baths:** 2 Shared
(5) (5)

Belton-by-Grantham

National Grid Ref: SK9239

Coach House, *Belton-by-Grantham, Grantham, Lincs, NG32 2LS.*
Idyllically set in National Trust village. **Open:** All Year
01476 573636 Mrs Norton
Rates fr: *£17.00*-**£18.50**.
Beds: 1F 1D 2S **Baths:** 4 Private
(12)

Billingborough

National Grid Ref: TF1134

Saint Boswells, *10 Vine Street, Billingborough, Sleaford, Lincs, NG34 0QE.*
Large Victorian house, large garden.
Open: All Year (not Xmas)
01529 240413
Rates fr: *£15.00*-**£15.00**.
Beds: 1D 2T **Baths:** 1 Shared
(4)

Boston

National Grid Ref: TF3344

Four Crossroads Inn

Bramley House, *267 Sleaford Road, Boston, Lincs, PE21 7PQ.*
Comfortable former farmhouse; large garden.
Open: All Year (not Xmas)
Grades: ETB Listed, Comm
01205 354538 Mrs Tilke
Rates fr: *£15.00*-**£18.50**.
Beds: 4D 2T 4S
Baths: 3 Ensuite 2 Shared
(15)

Lochiel Guest House, *69 Horncastle Road, Boston, Lincs, PE21 9HY.*
Comfortable, friendly, picturesque waterside setting.
Open: All Year (not Xmas)
Grades: ETB Listed
01205 363628 Mr & Mrs Lynch
Rates fr: *£15.00*-**£17.00**.
Beds: 1D 1T 1S
Baths: 1 Private 1 Shared
(2) (3)

90 Pilleys Lane, *Boston, Lincs, PE21 9RB.*
Modern, large, comfortable bungalow.
Open: All Year
01205 360723 Mrs Claridge
Rates fr: *£14.00*-**£15.00**.
Beds: 1F
(4)

The Chestnuts, *117 London Road, Boston, Lincs, PE21 7EZ.*
Late Victorian three-storey house.
Open: All Year
01205 354435 Mrs Clarke
Rates fr: *£15.00*-**£17.50**.
Beds: 1D 2T **Baths:** 3 Private
(5)

Park Lea Guest House, *85 Norfolk Street, Boston, Lincs, PE21 6PE.*
Comfortable accommodation, friendly service.
Open: All Year
01205 356309 Mrs Cockburn
Rates fr: *£15.00*-**£17.00**.
Beds: 4F 1T **Baths:** 3 Private
(5)

Bourne

National Grid Ref: TF0920

Kings Head

***The Mullions,** 123 North Road, Bourne, Lincs, PE10 9BU.*
Comfortable relaxed atmosphere.
Open: All Year
Grades: ETB 2 Cr, Comm
01778 393978 Mrs Essex
Fax no: 01778 393990
Rates fr: *£18.00*-**£23.00**.
Beds: 2D 1T
Baths: 2 Ensuite 1 Private
(6) (6)

Brigg

National Grid Ref: TA0007

Sutton Arms

***Olivers of Scawby,** Church Street, Scawby, Brigg, Lincs, DN20 9AH.*
200 year-old house, lovely village.
Open: All Year
01652 650446 Mrs Oliver
Rates fr: *£17.50*-**£25.00**.
Beds: 3T
Baths: 1 Private
(10) (5)

***Arties Mill,** Wressle Road, Castlethorpe, Brigg, Lincs, DN20 9LF.*
Old mill with separate lodge.
Open: All Year
Grades: ETB 3 Cr, Comm
01652 652094 Mr Briggs & Mrs J Ibbetson
Fax no: 01652 657107
Rates fr: *£22.50*-**£32.50**.
Beds: 2F 7D 16T
Baths: 22 Private 3 Shared
(0) (90)

Burgh-le-Marsh

National Grid Ref: TF5064

Burgh Inn

***The Old Mill,** West End, Burgh-le-Marsh, Skegness, Lincs, PE24 5EA.*
Converted windmill with beautiful views.
Open: All Year (not Xmas)
Grades: ETB Listed
01754 810081 (also fax no)
Mr & Mrs Southward
Rates fr: *£12.00*-**£20.00**.
Beds: 1F 1D 1T
Baths: 2 Private 1 Shared
(8)

Burton

National Grid Ref: SK9674

Woodcocks

***New Farm,** Burton, Lincoln, Lincs, LN1 2RD.*
Modern bungalow on working farm.
Open: Mar to Oct
Grades: ETB 2 Cr
01522 527326 Mrs Russon
Rates fr: *£17.50*-**£22.00**.
Beds: 2T
Baths: 1 Private 1 Shared
(5) (3)

Carlton Scroop

National Grid Ref: SK9545

***Stonehorse Farm,** Hough Lane, Carlton Scroop, Grantham, Lincs, NG32 3BB.*
Farmhouse in quiet country area.
Open: All Year (not Xmas)
01400 250147 Mrs Hutchins
Rates fr: *£13.00*-**£15.00**.
Beds: 1D 1T
Baths: 1 Shared

Cleethorpes

National Grid Ref: TA3008

Punchbowl, Swashbuckle

***Gladson Guest House,** 43 Isaacs Hill, Cleethorpes, Lincs, DN35 8JT.*
Licensed family guest house.
Open: All Year
01472 694858 Mrs Pearce
Rates fr: *£12.50*-**£14.00**.
Beds: 2F 1D 2S

***Holmhirst Hotel,** 3 Alexandra Road, Cleethorpes, Lincs, DN35 8LQ.*
Family-run seafront hotel.
Open: All Year (not Xmas)
01472 692656 Mr Barrs
Rates fr: *£18.00*-**£18.00**.
Beds: 2D 1T 5S
Baths: 4 Private 4 Shared
(3)

***Aavon Court,** 4 Isaacs Hill, Cleethorpes, Lincs, DN35 8JR.*
Modern, refurbished, comfortable guest house.
Open: All Year
01472 698706 Mrs Marriott
Rates fr: *£12.00*-**£14.00**.
Beds: 2F 5D 5T 3S
Baths: 3 Private 1 Shared

***Abbeydale Guest House,** 39 Isaacs Hill, Cleethorpes, Lincs, DN35 8JT.*
Clean comfortable accomodation, friendly atmosphere.
Open: All Year
Grades: ETB Listed, Approv
01472 692248 Mr Inskip
Rates fr: *£12.50*-**£14.00**.
Beds: 1F 1D 1T 3S
(0)

***Shellys Guest House,** 15 Princes Road, Cleethorpes, Lincs, DN35 8AW.*
Warm, modern, seaside guest house.
Open: All Year
01472 690153 Mrs Reid
Rates fr: *£13.00*-**£16.00**.
Beds: 1F 2D 1T 1S
Baths: 2 Shared
(0) (6)

***Albany Guest House,** 23 Isaacs Hill, Cleethorpes, Lincs, DN35 8JU.*
Large Victorian guest house.
Open: All Year
01472 602223 Mrs Walsh
Rates fr: *£13.00*-**£14.00**.
Beds: 2F 2T 2S

***The Carisbrook Guest House,** 57 Queens Parade, Cleethorpes, Lincs, DN35 0DQ.*
Situated on the A1098.
Open: All Year
01472 693302 Ms Hibbard
Rates fr: *£9.00*-**£11.70**.
Beds: 2F 1D 1S
Baths: 1 Shared
(4)

Coningsby

National Grid Ref: TF2258

White Bull

***The White Bull,** High Street, Coningsby, Lincoln, Lincs, LN4 4RB.*
Open: All Year
Grades: ETB 3 Cr
01526 342439 Mr & Mrs Gordon
Rates fr: *£13.00*-**£14.00**.
Beds: 2D 2S
Baths: 2 Ensuite 2 Shared
(60)
Family Pub of the Year finalist 1995. Children's Certificate. 0.5 mile RAF Coningsby, home to Battle of Britain Memorial flight. Open all day. Food available every day.

Conisholme

National Grid Ref: TF4095

***Wickham House,** Church Lane, Conisholme, Louth, Lincs, LN11 7LX.*
C18th cottage (was 3 cottages) near Louth.
Open: All Year (not Xmas)
01507 358465 Mr & Mrs Painter
Rates fr: *£18.50*.
Beds: 1D 1T 1S
Baths: 3 Private
(8) (4)

Covenham

National Grid Ref: TF3394

The Mill House

The Grange, *Grange Lane, Covenham, Louth, Lincs, LN11 0PD.*
Peaceful, comfortable old farmhouse.
Open: All Year (not Xmas)
Grades: ETB Listed
01507 363678 Mrs Shaw
Rates fr: *£15.00*-**£13.50**.
Beds: 1F 3D 2S **Baths:** 1 Shared

The Anchorage, *Cold Harbour Lane, Covenham, Louth, Lincs, LN11 0PQ.*
Excellent ground floor accommodation.
Open: All Year (not Xmas)
01507 363681 Mrs Woodward
Rates fr: *£15.00*-**£15.00**.
Beds: 1D 1S **Baths:** 1 Private
(3)

Cranwell

National Grid Ref: TF0349

Byards Leap Cottage, *Cranwell, Sleaford, Lincs, NG34 8EY.*
Comfortable country cottage, beautiful garden.
Open: All Year (not Xmas)
01400 261537 Mrs Wood
Rates fr: *£15.00*-**£15.00**.
Beds: 1F 1T **Baths:** 1 Shared
(6)

Croft

National Grid Ref: TF5061

Top Yard Farm, *Croft Bank, Croft, Skegness, Lincs, PE24 4RL.*
Old comfortable farmhouse, near Skegness.
Open: All Year (not Xmas)
Grades: ETB 2 Cr
01754 880189 Mrs Bell
Rates fr: *£12.50*-**£15.00**.
Beds: 1F 1D 1T
Baths: 1 Private 1 Shared
(6)

Deepdale

National Grid Ref: TA0418

West Wold Farmhouse, *Deepdale, Barton-upon-Humber, DN18 6ED.*
C19th comfortable family farmhouse.
Open: All Year
01652 633293 Mrs Atkin
Rates fr: *£15.00*-**£16.00**.
Beds: 1D 1T
Baths: 1 Private 1 Shared
(All)

The lowest *double* rate per person is shown in *italics*.

Deeping St James

National Grid Ref: TF1509

The Rose, Ruddy Duck.

Horseshoe Cottage, *The Old Forge, Bridge Street, Deeping St James, Peterborough, Cambs, PE6 8HA.*
C17th riverside cottage.
Open: All Year
01778 342230 Ms Aveling
Rates fr: *£20.00*-**£25.00**.
Beds: 1F 3D 3T
Baths: 2 Ensuite 2 Private 3 Shared
(10)

Donington

National Grid Ref: TF2135

Black Swan

Cooks, *19 Quadring Road, Donington, Spalding, Lincs, PE11 4TB.*
1920's comfortable family house.
Open: All Year (not Xmas)
Grades: ETB Listed, Comm
01775 820478 Mrs Silverton
Rates fr: *£16.00*-**£18.00**.
Beds: 2D 1T
Baths: 1 Ensuite 1 Shared
(4)

Red Cow Hotel, *High Street, Donington, Spalding, Lincs, PE11 4TA.*
Cosy, comfortable C16th coaching inn.
Open: All Year
01775 820298 Mrs Hallas
Rates fr: *£20.00*-**£20.00**.
Beds: 3F 5D 1T
Baths: 1 Ensuite 2 Shared
(12)

Donington-on-Bain

National Grid Ref: TF2382

Black Horse

The Black Horse, *Donington-on-Bain, Louth, Lincs, LN11 9TJ.*
C18th inn and motel.
Open: All Year
01507 343640
Mrs Pacey
Rates fr: *£20.00*-**£30.00**.
Beds: 4F 8T
Baths: 8 Private
(200)

East Barkwith

National Grid Ref: TF1681

Bodkin Lodge, *Torrington Lane, East Barkwith, Lincoln, Lincs, LN3 5RY.*
Lodge on family farm, quiet countryside.
Open: All Year (not Xmas/New Year)
01673 858249 Mrs Stamp
Rates fr: *£20.00*-**£25.00**.
Beds: 1D 1T **Baths:** 2 Ensuite
(10) (6)

Epworth

National Grid Ref: SE7803

Red Lion Hotel, Mowbray Arms

Epworth Old Rectory, *Epworth, Doncaster, DN9 1HX.*
Reverend John Wesley's boyhood home. **Open:** Mar to Oct
Grades: AA 2 Q
01427 872268 Mr Barton
Rates fr: *£20.00*-**£27.50**.
Beds: 2T **Baths:** 1 Shared
(12)

Faldingworth

National Grid Ref: TF0785

East Farm House, *Mill Lane, Middle Rasen Road, Faldingworth, Buslingthorpe, Market Rasen, Lincs, LN3 5AQ.*
Spacious C18th house overlooking farmland. **Open:** All Year
01673 842283 Mrs Grant
Rates fr: *£19.00*-**£21.00**.
Beds: 1D 1T **Baths:** 2 Private
(5) (5)

Folkingham

National Grid Ref: TF0733

Three Kings

6 Sleaford Road, *Folkingham, Sleaford, Lincs, NG34 0SB.*
Comfortable family home.
Open: All Year (not Xmas)
01529 497277 Mr Lack
Rates fr: *£14.00*-**£15.00**.
Beds: 3T **Baths:** 2 Shared
(3)

Foston

National Grid Ref: SK8542

Hillcrest, *Foston, Grantham, Lincs, NG31 2LF.*
Large detached house.
Open: All Year (not Xmas)
01400 281339 Mrs Cooper
Rates fr: *£11.00*-**£15.00**.
Beds: 2D 2S **Baths:** 1 Shared
(4)

Fulletby

National Grid Ref: TF2973

Tho Old Rectory, *Fulletby, Horncastle, Lincs, LN9 6JX.*
Open: All Year
01507 533533 (also fax no)
Mr Swan
Rates fr: *£20.00*-**£20.00**.
Beds: 2D 1T
Baths: 3 Ensuite
(8)
Lovely country house, nestling in idyllic Wolds. Undiscovered, rural tranquillity, yet near to historic Lincoln and the coast. Walking, cycling, golf, antiques, local history, or just relaxing. Superior ensuite accommodation. A real gem ....

Glentham

National Grid Ref: TF0090

Glendower Guest House, *High Street, Glentham, Lincoln, Lincs,* LN2 3EQ.
Recently refurbished friendly guest house.
Open: All Year
01673 878660 Mr & Mrs Turner
Rates fr: *£15.00*-**£15.00**.
Beds: 1D 2T **Baths:** 2 Shared
(6)

Gosberton

National Grid Ref: TF2431

Elm Tree Farm, *Gosberton Bank, Gosberton, Spalding, Lincs,* PE11 4PB.
Beautiful Georgian farmhouse. Pets accepted.
Open: All Year
01775 840767 Mrs Devaney
Rates fr: *£15.00*-**£20.00**.
Beds: 1D 1T
Baths: 1 Private 1 Shared
(25)

Grantham

National Grid Ref: SK9136

Tollemache Inn, Orangery, Kings Hotel, Five Bells

Roberts Roost, *82 Harrowby Road, Grantham, Lincs,* NG31 9DS.
Large Victorian private house.
Open: All Year (not Xmas)
Grades: ETB 1 Cr, AA 2 Q
01476 560719 Mrs Roberts
Rates fr: *£14.00*-**£15.00**.
Beds: 1F 2T 1S
Baths: 2 Shared
(3)

Hawthorne Guest House, *51 Cambridge Street, Grantham, Lincs,* NG31 6EZ.
Spacious Victorian house, centrally situated.
Open: All Year
01476 573644 Mrs Holliday
Rates fr: *£17.00*-**£18.00**.
Beds: 1F 1D 2T 1S
Baths: 1 Shared
(5)

Laburnum House, *35 Gladstone Terrace, Grantham, Lincs,* NG31 8BW.
Large Victorian town house.
Open: All Year (not Xmas)
01476 566623 Mr Dixon
Rates fr: *£14.00*-**£14.00**.
Beds: 1T 1S
Baths: 1 Shared

Planning a longer stay? Always ask for any special rates.

Lanchester Guest House, *84 Harrowby Road, Grantham, Lincs,* NG31 9DS.
Large homely Edwardian guest house.
Open: All Year
Grades: ETB 2 CrRAC Acclaim
01476 574169 Ms Standish
Rates fr: *£15.00*-**£15.00**.
Beds: 1D 2T
Baths: 1 Private 1 Shared
(3)

Hackthorn

National Grid Ref: SK9982

Honeyholes, *South Farm, Hackthorn, Lincoln, Lincs,* LN2 3PW.
Comfortable farmhouse, traditional cooking.
Open: All Year (not Xmas)
01673 861868 Mrs Greenfield
Rates fr: *£16.00*-**£16.00**.
Beds: 2D 1T
Baths: 1 Shared
(5)

Hainton

National Grid Ref: TF1884

Black Horse

The Old Vicarage, *School Lane, Hainton, Lincoln, Lincs,* LN3 6LW.
Charming house in peaceful Wolds.
Open: All Year
Grades: ETB Listed, Comm, AA 3 Q
01507 313660 Mr Slater
Rates fr: *£16.00*-**£16.00**.
Beds: 1D 2T 1S
Baths: 2 Shared
(12) (6)

Hibaldstow

National Grid Ref: SE9702

Red Lion

Brookside, *Beck Lane, Hibaldstow, Brigg,* DN20 9EQ.
Very central excellent country accommodation.
Open: All Year (not Xmas)
01652 654347 Mrs Walton
Rates fr: *£15.00*-**£18.00**.
Beds: 1D 1T 1S
Baths: 1 Private
(4)

Hogsthorpe

National Grid Ref: TF5372

Mill House, *West End, Hogsthorpe, Skegness, Lincs,* PE24 5PA.
Old Lincolnshire rural house. Modernised.
Open: Easter to Oct
01754 872977 Mrs MacDonald
Rates fr: *£13.00*-**£14.00**.
Beds: 1F 1D 2T
Baths: 2 Shared
(10)

Holbeach

National Grid Ref: TF3625

Bull's Neck, Crown Hotel, Black Bull

Cackle Hill House, *Cackle Hill Lane, Holbeach, Spalding, Lincs,* PE12 8BS.
Modern comfortable farmhouse. Rural position.
Open: All Year (not Xmas)
01406 426721 Mrs Biggadike
Fax no: 01406 424659
Rates fr: *£20.00*-**£22.00**.
Beds: 1D 2T
Baths: 2 Ensuite 1 Private
(10) (5)

Barrington House, *Barrington Gate, Holbeach, Spalding, Lincs,* PE12 7LB.
Spacious Georgian house, near town centre.
Open: All Year
01406 425178 (also fax no)
Mrs Symonds
Rates fr: *£17.50*-**£20.00**.
Beds: 2D 1T 1S
Baths: 1 Ensuite 3 Private
(5)

Horncastle

National Grid Ref: TF2669

Fighting Cocks, *West Street, Horncastle, Lincs,* LN9 5JF.
Traditional C17th inn.
Open: All Year (not Xmas)
01507 527307 Mr Butler
Rates fr: *£17.50*-**£17.50**.
Beds: 2F 1T
Baths: 1 Shared

The Admiral Rodney Hotel, *North Street, Horncastle, Lincs,* LN9 5DX.
Central location.
Open: All Year
01507 523131 Mrs Young
Rates fr: *£24.00*-**£35.50**.
Beds: 3F 16D 12T
Baths: 31 Ensuite
(70)

Hough-on-the-Hill

National Grid Ref: SK9246

Brownlow Arms, *Hough-on-the-Hill, Grantham, Lincs,* NG32 2AZ.
Lovely C17th stone-built country inn.
Open: All Year (not Xmas)
01400 250234 Mrs Willoughby
Rates fr: *£21.00*-**£30.00**.
Beds: 2D 1T 1S
Baths: 64 Private
(5)

The lowest **single** *rate is shown in* **bold.**

Keal Coates

National Grid Ref: TF3661

Holly Lodge, *Hagnaby Lane, Keal Coates, Spilsby, Lincs,* PE23 4AJ.
Victorian private house, rural outlook.
Open: All Year (not Xmas)
01790 763206 Ms Tuley
Rates fr: *£17.00*-**£17.00**.
Beds: 1F
Baths: 1 Private
(4)

Village Post Office, *Main Road 'A16), Keal Coates, Spilsby, Lincs,* PE23 4AG.
Friendly, comfortable with huge breakfasts.
Open: All Year (not Xmas)
01790 763200 Mr Angove
Rates fr: *£18.00*-**£19.00**.
Beds: 1F 1D 1T
Baths: 1 Shared
(9)

Kexby

National Grid Ref: SK8785

Stags Head, Rose & Crown

Kexby Grange, *Kexby, Gainsborough, Lincs,* DN21 5PJ.
Victorian farmhouse in pleasant countryside.
Open: All Year (not Xmas)
Grades: ETB Listed
01427 788265
Mrs Edwardson
Rates fr: *£14.00*-**£14.00**.
Beds: 1D 1S
Baths: 1 Private 1 Shared
(4)

Kirton

National Grid Ref: TF3038

Westfield House, *31 Willington Road, Kirton, Boston, Lincs,* PE20 1EP.
Victorian house.
Open: All Year
01205 722221 Mrs Duff
Rates fr: *£15.00*-**£15.00**.
Beds: 1F 1D 1S
Baths: 1 Shared
(5)

Knaith

National Grid Ref: SK8284

Stags Head

Laundry Cottage, *Knaith Hill, Knaith, Gainsborough, Lincs,* DN21 5PF.
Comfortable converted old laundry.
Open: All Year (not Xmas)
01427 613248 Mrs Steadman
Rates fr: *£14.50*-**£14.50**.
Beds: 1D 2T
Baths: 2 Private
(6)

Leadenham

National Grid Ref: SK9552

The George

George Hotel, *High Street, Leadenham, Lincoln, Lincs,* LN5 0PP.
Old country coaching inn.
Open: All Year **Grades:** ETB 3 Cr
01400 272251 Mr Willgoose
Fax no: 01400 272091
Rates fr: *£12.50*-**£18.00**.
Beds: 2D 3T 2S
Baths: 2 Private 2 Shared
(100)

Leasingham

National Grid Ref: TF0548

Duke of Wellington

Manor Farm, *Leasingham, Sleaford, Lincs,* NG34 8JN.
Comfortable farmhouse overlooking spacious garden.
Open: All Year
Grades: ETB 1 Cr, Approv
01529 302671 Mrs Franks
Fax no: 01529 414946
Rates fr: *£15.00*-**£18.00**.
Beds: 2D **Baths:** 1 Shared

Legbourne

National Grid Ref: TF3684

Gordon House, *Legbourne, Louth, Lincs,* LN11 8LH.
Detached country house, homely atmosphere.
Open: All Year
01507 607568 Mr Norman
Rates fr: *£15.50*-**£15.50**.
Beds: 1D 1T
Baths: 1 Private
(2)

Lincoln

National Grid Ref: SK9771

Lord Tennyson, Sun Inn, The Barge, Royal William

Ridgeways Guest House, *243 Burton Road, Lincoln,* LN1 3UB.
Open: All Year
01522 546878 Mr Barnes
Rates fr: *£15.00*-**£20.00**.
Beds: 2F 1D 1T
Baths: 3 Ensuite 1 Private
(4)
A modern detached house within ten minutes walking distance of the historic heart of Lincoln. Spacious, ensuite rooms, off-street private car park.

Westlyn House, *67 Carholme Road, Lincoln,* LN1 1RT.
Victorian town house with garden.
Open: All Year (not Xmas)
01522 537468 Mrs Kaye
Rates fr: *£16.00*-**£17.00**.
Beds: 1F 2T 1D 1S
Baths: 3 Shared
(3)

The Cottage Guest House, *17 Bridge Street, Saxilby, Lincoln, Lincs,* LN1 2PZ.
Open: All Year (not Xmas)
Grades: ETB 2 Cr, Comm
01522 702834 (also fax no)
Mrs Williams
Rates fr: *£16.00*-**£20.00**.
Beds: 1F 1D 1T
Baths: 1 Ensuite 1 Shared
(3)
Truly peaceful beamed cottage overlooking waterfront. Pretty, fully equipped bedrooms with ensuite facilities. Easy access to Lincoln Cathedral and Castle and many other places of interest.

Edward King House, *The Old Palace, Minster Yard, Lincoln,* LN2 1PU.
By Cathedral and Old Palace.
Open: All Year (not Xmas)
01522 528778
Rev Adkins
Rates fr: *£17.50*-**£18.00**.
Beds: 1F 11T 5S
Baths: 7 Shared
(12)

Admiral Guest House, *16 Nelson Street, Lincoln,* LN1 1PJ.
Old-type Nelson's cottages.
Open: All Year
01522 544467
Mr Robertson
Rates fr: *£13.00*-**£13.00**.
Beds: 4F 2D 1T 2S
Baths: 6 Private 2 Shared

The Old Rectory, *19 Newport, Lincoln,* LN1 3DQ.
Large Edwardian house near cathedral.
Open: All Year (not Xmas)
01522 514774
Mr Downes
Rates fr: *£17.50*-**£18.00**.
Beds: 1F 3D 1T 1S
Baths: 4 Private 1 Shared
(8)

Mayfield Guest House, *213 Yarborough Road, Lincoln,* LN1 3NQ.
Comfortable, convenient for tourist attractions.
Open: All Year (not Xmas)
Grades: ETB 2 Cr, Comm
01522 533732 (also fax no)
Mr Benson
Rates fr: *£17.50*-**£17.00**.
Beds: 2F 1D 1T 1S
Baths: 4 Ensuite 1 Private
(5) (5)

Alder Hotel, *2 Hamilton Road, St Catherines, Lincoln,* LN5 8ED.
Converted Victorian house. Licensed.
Open: All Year
01522 528243
Mr Green
Rates fr: *£13.50*-**£14.50**.
Beds: 2F 1D 4T 1S
Baths: 3 Private 2 Shared
(8)

10 Neustadt Court, *Danes Terrace, Lincoln, LN2 1PG.*
Close to shops, tourist attractions.
Open: All Year (not Xmas)
01522 531831 Mr Todd
Rates fr: *£15.00*-**£20.00**.
Beds: 1T
(3) (1)

Pines Guest House, *104 Yarborough Road, Lincoln, LN1 1HR.*
Comfortable, clean, friendly, good value. **Open:** All Year
01522 532985 Mrs Morgan
Rates fr: *£14.00*-**£15.00**.
Beds: 5F
Baths: 4 Ensuite 2 Shared

Little Bytham

National Grid Ref: SK9818

The Mallard Inn, *Little Bytham, Grantham, Lincs, NG33 4PP.*
C16th inn. Good food, beers.
Open: All Year (not Xmas)
01780 410470 (also fax no)
Mr & Mrs Winspear
Rates fr: *£17.50*-**£20.00**.
Beds: 1F 1D 1T **Baths:** 3 Ensuite
(32)

Long Bennington

National Grid Ref: SK8344

Springfield, *15 Main Road, Long Bennington, Newark, Lincs, NG23 5EH.*
Quiet homely. 3/4 acre garden.
Open: All Year
01400 281445
Mrs Richardson
Rates fr: *£12.50*-**£12.50**.
Beds: 1F 2D 2T 1S
(6)

Rest A While, *9 Witham Road, Long Bennington, Newark, Notts, NG23 5DS.*
Quiet private house. Large garden.
Open: All Year
01400 281082 Mrs Kirton
Rates fr: *£12.50*-**£12.00**.
Beds: 1T 1S
Baths: 1 Shared
(3)

Louth

National Grid Ref: TF3387

Plough Inn

The Plough Inn, *Upgate, Louth, Lincs, LN11 9HG.*
Comfortable family-run public house.
Open: All Year
Grades: ETB Listed
01507 603551
Mrs Symons
Rates fr: *£17.50*-**£17.50**.
Beds: 2F 1D 2T 2S
Baths: 2 Shared
(2) (10)

Butterfield's Guest House, *63 Legbourne Road, Louth, Lincs, LN11 8ES.*
3-bed semi with large extension.
Open: All Year
01507 606719 Mrs Butterfield
Rates fr: *£17.00*-**£17.00**.
Beds: 1D 2T 2S
Baths: 2 Shared
(7)

Kings Head Hotel, *10 Mercer Row, Louth, Lincs, LN11 9JQ.*
Town centre coaching inn.
Open: All Year
01507 602965 Mr Maguire
Rates fr: *£17.50*-**£18.50**.
Beds: 1F 6D 6T 6S
Baths: 6 Private 4 Shared
(40)

Masons Arms, *Cornmarket, Louth, Lincs, LN11 9PY.*
Sympathetically refurbished C18th posting inn.
Open: All Year (not Xmas)
01507 609525 Mr Harrison
Rates fr: *£17.50*-**£20.00**.
Beds: 5D 2T 3S
Baths: 5 Ensuite 5 Shared

Low Fulney

National Grid Ref: TF2621

Pindsvin, *17 Swindlers Drove, Low Fulney, Spalding, Lincs, PE12 6BS.*
Homely accommodation in rural location.
Open: All Year (not Xmas)
01775 768629
Miss Stoner
Rates fr: *£13.00*.
Beds: 1D
(10)

Ludford

National Grid Ref: TF1989

White Hart

The White Hart, *Ludford, Lincoln, Lincs, LN3 6.*
Open: All Year
01507 313489 Mrs Johnson
Rates fr: *£17.50*-**£20.00**.
Beds: 1D 3T
Baths: 4 Ensuite
(30)
Delightful C18th coaching inn on Viking Way in the heart of the picturesque Lincolnshire Wolds. Warm friendly atmosphere, excellent food, real ales, log fires.

Hainton Walk Farm, *Ludford, Lincoln, Lincs, LN3 6AP.*
Large comfortable farmhouse, very peaceful.
Open: All Year (not Xmas)
01507 313242
Mr Thornalley
Rates fr: *£14.15*-**£14.00**.
Beds: 1F 1D 1S
Baths: 1 Shared
(6)

Mablethorpe

National Grid Ref: TF5085

White Heather, *114 Victoria Road, Mablethorpe, Lincs, LN12 2AJ.*
Comfortable established guest-house.
Open: All Year (not Xmas)
01507 472626 Mrs Harvey
Rates fr: *£13.50*-**£13.50**.
Beds: 3F 3D 1T 2S
Baths: 2 Shared

Leicester House, *61 Victoria Road, Mablethorpe, Lincs, LN12 2AF.*
Friendly family run guest house.
Open: All Year
01507 472406 Mrs Allen
Rates fr: *£16.00*-**£18.00**.
Beds: 3F 5D 2T
Baths: 10 Private
(6)

Glenveagh Guest House, *17 Waterloo Road, Mablethorpe, Lincs, LN12 1JR.*
Large Victorian private house.
Open: All Year
01507 473277 Mr Allen
Rates fr: *£11.00*-**£11.00**.
Beds: 1F 3D 1T
Baths: 1 Shared

Maltby-le-Marsh

National Grid Ref: TF4681

Crown Inn

The Poplars, *Beesby Road, Maltby-le-Marsh, Alford, Lincs, LN13 0JJ.*
Open: All Year
01507 450788 Mrs Chapman
Fax no: 01507 450966
Rates fr: *£19.00*-**£22.00**.
Beds: 2D 1S
Baths: 3 Ensuite
(4)
Warm, comfortable ensuite accommodation in rural 1720s country house. Convenient for Georgian Louth, antiques centres, golfing, beach walks. Unspoiled village pub offers excellent fare.

Grange Farm, *Maltby-le-Marsh, Alford, Lincs, LN13 0JP.*
Converted stable block - private fishing.
Open: All Year (not Xmas)
01507 450267 Mrs Graves
Fax no: 01507 450180
Rates fr: *£15.00*-**£16.00**.
Beds: 3F 1D 3T
Baths: 3 Shared
(30)

The lowest *double* rate per person is shown in *italics*.

Mareham-le-Fen

National Grid Ref: TF2761

Barn Croft, *Main Street, Mareham-le-Fen, Boston, Lincs,* PE22 7QJ.
Ensuite facilities in rural setting.
Open: All Year
01507 568264 Mrs Shaw
Rates fr: *£17.00*-**£20.00**.
Beds: 2D 1T
Baths: 3 Private
(5)

Market Deeping

National Grid Ref: TF1310

Deeping Stage Hotel

Deeping Stage Hotel, *Market Place, Market Deeping, Peterborough, Cambs,* PE6 8EA.
Riverside coaching inn.
Open: All Year
01778 343234
Mrs Ryan
Rates fr: *£15.00*-**£17.50**.
Beds: 1F 4D 5T 1S
Baths: 5 Ensuite 3 Private 2 Shared

Market Rasen

National Grid Ref: TF1089

White Swan

The Waveney Guest House, *Willingham Road, Market Rasen, Lincs,* LN8 3DN.
Family size Tudor-style cottage.
Open: All Year
01673 843236
Mrs Dawson-Margrave
Rates fr: *£15.00*-**£17.00**.
Beds: 1F 2T
Baths: 3 Private
(6)

White Swan Hotel, *Queen Street, Market Rasen, Lincs,* LN8 3.
Main street, market town, inn.
Open: All Year
01673 843356
Rates fr: *£12.50*-**£15.00**.
Beds: 1F 1D 1T 2S
Baths: 1 Shared

Marston

National Grid Ref: SK8943

Thorrold Arms

Thorrold Arms, *Marston, Grantham, Lincs,* NG32 2HH.
Large Victorian pub.
Open: All Year
Grades: ETB Listed, Comm
01400 250899
Mr Bryan
Fax no: 01400 251030
Rates fr: *£25.00*-**£25.00**.
Beds: 1F 1D
Baths: 2 Ensuite
(14)

All rates are subject to alteration at the owners' discretion.

Gelston Grange, *Marston, Grantham, Lincs,* NG32 2AQ.
Quiet, comfortable, working farm.
Open: All Year (not Xmas)
01400 250281 Mrs Sharman
Rates fr: *£16.00*-**£16.00**.
Beds: 2D 1T
Baths: 1 Private 1 Shared

The Pinfold, *Pinfold Lane, Marston, Grantham, Lincs,* NG32 2.
Large house, site of old pinfold.
Open: All Year (not Xmas)
01400 250571 Mrs Hartwell
Rates fr: *£15.00*-**£15.00**.
Beds: 1D
Baths: 1 Private

Metheringham

National Grid Ref: TF0661

Lincolnshire Poacher

Lincolnshire Poacher, *High Street, Metheringham, Lincoln, Lincs,* LN4 3DZ.
Pretty stone-built village pub.
Open: All Year
01526 320556 Mr Burns
Rates fr: *£12.50*-**£14.50**.
Beds: 1D 1T 1S
Baths: 1 Shared
(5) (20)

Miningsby

National Grid Ref: TF3264

Stamford House, *Miningsby, Boston, Lincs,* PE22 7NW.
Breakfast as early or late as you wish.
Open: All Year
01507 588682 Mrs Morris
Rates fr: *£16.50*-**£18.50**.
Beds: 3T
Baths: 3 Private
(6)

Minting

National Grid Ref: TF1873

The Midge, The Sebastopol

Greenfield Farm, *Mill Lane, Cow Lane, Minting, Horncastle, Lincs,* LN9 5RX.
Quiet farmhouse, ensuite facilities.
Open: All Year (not Xmas)
Grades: ETB 2 Cr, High Comm, AA 4 Q, Select
01507 578457 Mrs Bankes-Price
Rates fr: *£19.00*-**£22.00**.
Beds: 2D 1T
Baths: 3 Ensuite
(0) (6)

New Bolingbroke

National Grid Ref: TF3057

Fairoaks Cottage, *Main Road, New Bolingbroke, Boston, Lincs,* PE22 7LN.
Old worlde Victorian country cottage.
Open: Mar to Oct
01205 480075
Mrs Hurd
Rates fr: *£15.00*-**£15.00**.
Beds: 2D 1T 1S
Baths: 2 Shared
(8) (3)

North Somercotes

National Grid Ref: TF4296

Bay Horse

Mount Pleasant, *Churchill Road, North Somercotes, Louth, Lincs,* LN11 7QS.
Lovely C18th farmhouse. Large rooms.
Open: All Year (not Xmas)
01507 358761
Mr Woodward
Rates fr: *£18.00*-**£18.00**.
Beds: 2T 1S
(6)

Raithby

National Grid Ref: TF3767

Red Lion Inn

Red Lion Inn, *Raithby, Spilsby, Lincs,* PE23 4DS.
Open: All Year
Grades: ETB 2 Cr
01790 753727 Mrs Smith
Rates fr: *£15.00*-**£19.00**.
Beds: 2D 2T
Baths: 3 Private
(20)
Olde worlde inn, traditional and continental food. Comfortable rooms. Real ales. Micro-brewery.

Rippingale

National Grid Ref: TF0928

Brook Cottage, *Middle Street, Rippingale, Bourne, Lincs,* PE10 0SU.
Converted cottage.
Open: All Year (not Xmas)
01778 440328 Mrs Wellman
Rates fr: *£14.00*-**£14.00**.
Beds: 1D 1T 1S
Baths: 1 Shared

Right on the border?

Look at the neighbouring county, too

Saltfleetby St Clement

National Grid Ref: TF4591

***Elm House,** Saltfleetby St Clement, Louth, Lincs, LN11 7TP.*
Manor house cottage, self-contained.
Open: All Year
01507 338230 Mrs Ellis
Rates fr: *£10.00*-**£10.00**.
Beds: 2D 1S
Baths: 1 Private
(2)

Saracen's Head

National Grid Ref: TF3427

The Chequers

***Pipewell Manor,** Washaway Road, Saracen's Head, Holbeach, Spalding, Lincs, PE12 8AL.*
C18th Georgian manor house.
Open: All Year (not Xmas)
Grades: ETB 2 Cr, High Comm, AA 4 Q, Select
01406 423119 Mrs Honnor
Rates fr: *£19.00*-**£25.00**.
Beds: 2D 1T 1S
Baths: 2 Ensuite 2 Private
(6)

***Whaplode Manor,** Saracen's Head, Holbeach, Spalding, Lincs, PE12 8AZ.*
C18th manor house and mews.
Open: All Year
01406 422837 Mrs Wood
Rates fr: *£17.00*-**£20.00**.
Beds: 1F 3T 6D
Baths: 9 Ensuite 1 Private

Saxilby

National Grid Ref: SK8975

Sun Inn

***The Cottage Guest House,** 17 Bridge Street, Saxilby, Lincoln, Lincs, LN1 2PZ.*
Truly peaceful beamed cottage overlooking waterfront.
Open: All Year (not Xmas)
Grades: ETB 2 Cr, Comm
01522 702834 (also fax no)
Mrs Williams
Rates fr: *£16.00*-**£20.00**.
Beds: 1F 1D 1T
Baths: 1 Ensuite 1 Shared
(3)

Scampton

National Grid Ref: SK9479

***The Copse,** Brigg Road, Scampton, Lincoln, Lincs, LN1 2SY.*
Lovely views and garden conservatory.
Open: All Year
01522 543870
Rates fr: *£15.00*-**£15.00**.
Beds: 1D 1T 1S
(3)

Scawby

National Grid Ref: SE9605

Sutton Arms

***Olivers of Scawby,** Church Street, Scawby, Brigg, Lincs, DN20 9AH.*
200 year-old house, lovely village.
Open: All Year
01652 650446 Mrs Oliver
Rates fr: *£17.50*-**£25.00**.
Beds: 3T **Baths:** 1 Private
(10) (5)

Scotter

National Grid Ref: SE8800

***Ivy Lodge Hotel & Tea Room,** 4 Messingham Road, Scotter, Gainsborough, Lincs, DN21 3UQ.*
Open: All Year
Grades: ETB 2 Cr, Comm
01724 763723
Mrs Mewis
Fax no: 01724 763770
Rates fr: *£21.00*-**£25.00**.
Beds: 1F 1D 1T 2S
Baths: 5 Ensuite
(8)
Family-run, situated in picturesque village, relaxing atmosphere, large garden, attractively furnished ensuite rooms. Delicious home cooked meals, varied menu, good base for touring and business.

Scunthorpe

National Grid Ref: SE8910

***Downs Guest House,** 33 Deyne Avenue, Scunthorpe, Lincs, DN15 7PZ.*
Clean comfortable guesthouse in quiet location.
Open: All Year
Grades: ETB Listed
01724 850710 Mrs Neal
Rates fr: *£14.00*-**£16.00**.
Beds: 1F 2D 2T 3S
(3)

Skegness

National Grid Ref: TF5663

***Mickleton Guest House,** 6 North Parade Extention, Skegness, Lincs, PE25 1BX.*
On sea front.
Open: All Year
01754 763862 Mrs White
Rates fr: *£13.50*-**£15.50**.
Beds: 4F 2D 2T 1S
Baths: 3 Private 2 Shared
(9)

***Hamewith,** 12 Cecil Avenue, Skegness, Lincs, PE25 2BX.*
Clean, comfortable, friendly guest house.
Open: All Year
01754 766770 Mr Gunner
Rates fr: *£15.00*-**£15.00**.
Beds: 2F 3D 1T 1S

***Glynvale Hotel,** 101 Drummond Road, Skegness, Lincs, PE25 3EH.*
Small, friendly, family-run hotel.
Open: All Year
01754 767190 Mrs Wood
Rates fr: *£12.00*-**£12.00**.
Beds: 4F 2D 3T 1S
Baths: 2 Shared
(5)

***The Singlecote Hotel,** 34 Drummond Road, Skegness, Lincs, PE25 3EB.*
Homely coastal hotel.
Open: Easter to Oct
Grades: ETB Listed
01754 764698 Mr Shaw
Rates fr: *£14.50*-**£14.50**.
Beds: 1F 6D 2T 3S
Baths: 9 Private 2 Shared
(10)

***Craigside Hotel,** 26 Scarborough Avenue, Skegness, Lincs, PE25 2SY.*
'Craigside' for comfort and enjoyment .
Open: All Year
01754 763307 Mrs Milner
Rates fr: *£19.00*-**£19.00**.
Beds: 5F 5D 3T 3S
Baths: 12 Ensuite 16 Private 1 Shared
(0) (10)

***Linroy Guest House,** 26 Lumley Avebue, Skegness, Lincs, PE25 2AT.*
Family-run guest house.
Open: All Year
01754 763924 Mr Spence
Rates fr: *£13.00*-**£15.00**.
Beds: 3F 2T 4D 1S
Baths: 2 Shared
(5)

***White Lodge Guest House,** 129 Drummond Road, Skegness, Lincs, PE25 3DW.*
'Home from home'. Non-smoking.
Open: All Year
01754 764120 Mr Cartwright
Rates fr: *£14.00*-**£14.00**.
Beds: 1F 5D 3T 2S
Baths: 2 Private 1 Shared

***Rufford Hotel,** 5 Saxby Avenue, Skegness, Lincs, PE25 3JZ.*
Quiet residential avenue, near Promenade.
Open: All Year
01754 763428
Mr & Mrs Smith
Rates fr: *£16.00*-**£17.00**.
Beds: 3F 5D 2T 1S
Baths: 11 Ensuite 2 Shared
(6)

***Maryland Hotel,** Prince Alfred Avenue, Grand Parade, Skegness, Lincs, PE25 2UH.*
Quiet hotel, relaxed, friendly atmosphere.
Open: All Year
01754 764465 Mrs Golby
Rates fr: *£13.00*-**£13.00**.
Beds: 4F 10D 4T 5S
Baths: 1 Private 4 Shared

Skillington

National Grid Ref: SK8925

Beeches, *Park Lane, Skillington, Grantham, Lincs, NG33 5HH.*
New bungalow, well appointed.
Open: All Year (not Xmas)
01476 860271 Mrs Black
Rates fr: *£16.00*-**£16.00**.
Beds: 1D 1T 2S
Baths: 2 Private 1 Shared
(5) (6)

Sproxton Lodge, *Skillington, Grantham, Lincs, NG33 5HJ.*
Quiet family farm.
Open: All Year (not Xmas)
01476 860307 Mrs Whatton
Rates fr: *£15.00*-**£15.00**.
Beds: 1F 1D 1S
Baths: 1 Shared
(4)

South Hykeham

National Grid Ref: SK9364

The Hall, *Meadow Lane, South Hykeham, Lincoln, Lincs, LN6 9PF.*
Large Victorian farmhouse.
Open: All Year
01522 686432
Mrs Phillips
Fax no: 01522 696496
Rates fr: *£19.00*-**£19.00**.
Beds: 1F 1D
Baths: 2 Private
(4)

South Witham

National Grid Ref: SK9219

Rose Cottage, *7 High Street, South Witham, Grantham, Lincs, NG33 5QB.*
C18th stone cottage in 2 acres.
Open: All Year
Grades: ETB Listed
01572 767757 Mrs Van Kimmenade
Rates fr: *£15.50*-**£15.50**.
Beds: 1T
Baths: 1 Private

Corner Cottage, *Water Lane, South Witham, Grantham, Lincs, NG33 5PH.*
Old stone cottage in 1 acre.
Open: All Year (not Xmas)
01572 767258 Mrs Williamson
Rates fr: *£12.50 (inc dinner)*-**£12.50**.
Beds: 1D **Baths:** 1 Shared

Southorpe

National Grid Ref: SK8995

Midstone Farm House, *Midstone House, Southorpe, Stamford, Lincs, PE9 3BX.*
Comfortable farmhouse in quiet location.
Open: All Year (not Xmas)
01780 740136 Mrs Harrison Smith
Rates fr: *£17.50*-**£20.00**.
Beds: 1F 1D 1T
Baths: 2 Shared

Southrey

National Grid Ref: TF1366

Riverside Inn

Riverside Inn, *Ferry Road, Southrey, Lincoln, Lincs, LN3 5TA.*
Peaceful country inn by river.
Open: All Year
Grades: ETB Listed
01526 398374 Mrs Walley
Rates fr: *£15.00*-**£18.00**.
Beds: 1F
Baths: 1 Shared
(10)

Spalding

National Grid Ref: TF2422

White Horse, Red Lion, Crystal Inn, Bull Inn, Lincolnshire Poacher

88 Winsover Road, *Spalding, Lincs, PE11 1HA.*
Victorian family house.
Open: All Year
01775 725661 Mrs Rae
Rates fr: *£12.50*-**£12.50**.
Beds: 2T
(1)

Bedford Court Guest House, *10 London Road, Spalding, Lincs, PE11 2TA.*
Large Georgian town house.
Open: All Year
01775 722377 Mr & Mrs Herd
Rates fr: *£25.00*-**£25.00**.
Beds: 1D 2T 1S
Baths: 1 Private

National Grid References are for villages, towns and cities - *not* for individual houses.

The Bull Inn, *Knight Street, Spalding, Lincs, PE11 3GA.*
Village free house/restaurant.
Open: All Year
01775 723022 Ms Gardner
Rates fr: *£17.50*-**£19.50**.
Beds: 1D 3T
(50)

High Bridge House, *9 London Road, Spalding, Lincs, PE11 2TA.*
Large Victorian house by river.
Open: All Year (not Xmas)
01775 725810
Mrs Marshall
Rates fr: *£16.50*-**£16.50**.
Beds: 2T 4S
Baths: 3 Shared
(10)

Lincolnshire Poacher, *11 Double Street, Spalding, Lincs, PE11 2AA.*
Ancient riverside pub, free house.
Open: All Year (not Xmas)
01775 766490
Mr & Mrs Wainwright-Bateman
Rates fr: *£17.50*-**£20.00**.
Beds: 2D 2T 1S
Baths: 2 Shared

Barrington House, *28 Holbeach Road, Spalding, Lincs, PE11 2HQ.*
Welcoming modern house, overlooking river.
Open: All Year
01775 713468
Mrs Harman
Rates fr: *£12.50*-**£14.00**.
Beds: 2D 2T
(1) (5)

Stamford

National Grid Ref: TF0207

Falstaffs, Danish Invader, St Peters Inn

St Georges, *16 St Georges Square, Stamford, Lincs, PE9 2BN.*
Open: All Year (not Xmas)
01780 482099 Mrs Swithinbank
Rates fr: *£15.00*-**£20.00**.
Beds: 2T
Baths: 2 Shared
Situated in the original BBC Middlemarch Square overlooking C14th church. Luxury and elegance, space and history in a comfortable family atmosphere. Delicious home cooking.

10 Stirling Road, *Stamford, Lincs, PE9 2XG.*
Quiet area. Handy for A1/A606.
Open: All Year
Grades: ETB Listed
01780 63065 Mrs Nichols
Rates fr: *£14.00*-**£14.00**.
Beds: 1F 1T 1S 1D
Baths: 1 Shared
(1)

Stukeley House, *9 Barn Hill, Stamford, Lincs, PE9 2AE.*
Large historic comfortable C18th house.
Open: All Year (not Xmas)
01780 57939 Mrs Walker
Rates fr: *£15.00*-**£17.00**.
Beds: 1D 1T 1S
Baths: 2 Shared
(1)

Highfields, *31 Main Road, Collyweston, Stamford, Lincs, PE9 3PF.*
Village location. Ground floor rooms.
Open: All Year
Grades: ETB Listed
01780 444339 Mrs Hindley
Rates fr: *£18.00*-**£17.00**.
Beds: 1D 1T 1S
Baths: 2 Shared
(4) (4)

Cringleford, *7 Exeter Gardens, Stamford, Lincs, PE9 2RN.*
Updated private house.
Open: All Year (not Xmas)
01780 62136 Mrs Webster
Rates fr: *£16.00*-**£16.00**.
Beds: 1D 1S
Baths: 1 Shared
(2)

Birch House, *4 Lonsdale Road, Stamford, Lincs, PE9 2RW.*
Established well-presented family-run house.
Open: All Year (not Xmas)
Grades: ETB Listed, Comm
01780 54876 Mrs Headland
Rates fr: *£16.00*-**£16.00**.
Beds: 1D 1T 2S
Baths: 1 Shared
(5) (2)

38 Exeter Gardens, *Stamford, Lincs, PE9 2RN.*
Detached private house.
Open: All Year (not Xmas)
01780 64769 Mrs Johnson
Rates fr: *£16.00*-**£16.00**.
Beds: 1T 1S
Baths: 1 Shared
(3)

10 Luffenham Close, *Stamford, Lincs, PE9 2SE.*
Large, modern, comfortable bungalow, parking.
Open: All Year
01780 63354 Mrs McKittrick
Rates fr: *£12.00*-**£12.00**.
Beds: 2D **Baths:** 1 Shared

The Green Man, *29 Scotgate, Stamford, Lincs, PE9 2YQ.*
C18th Georgian public house.
Open: All Year
01780 53598 Mr Shilling
Rates fr: *£17.00*-**£17.00**.
Beds: 2D 1T
Baths: 3 Ensuite
(2)

2 North Street, *Stamford, Lincs, PE9 2YN.*
Late Georgian town house.
Open: All Year (not Xmas)
01780 65946 Mrs Kingston
Rates fr: *£13.00*-**£13.00**.
Beds: 2T 1S

Sturton-by-Stow

National Grid Ref: SK8980

Red Lion, Plough

Gallows Dale Farm, *Stow Park Road, Sturton-by-Stow, Lincoln, Lincs, LN1 2AH.*
Tastefully refurbished Georgian farmhouse.
Open: All Year
Grades: AA 4 Q, Select
01427 788387 Mrs Williams
Rates fr: *£14.00*-**£15.00**.
Beds: 1F 1D 1T 1S
Baths: 1 Ensuite 2 Shared
(6)

Sudbrook

National Grid Ref: SK9744

Willoughby Lodge, *Sudbrook, Grantham, Lincs, NG32 3SQ.*
Truly off the beaten track.
Open: All Year (not Xmas)
01400 230258 Ms Bagnald
Rates fr: *£14.00*-**£14.00**.
Beds: 1D 1T
Baths: 1 Shared
(12) (6)

Sudbrooke

National Grid Ref: TF0376

Bottle & Glass, White Hart

Westwood House, *Wragby Road, Sudbrooke, Lincoln, Lincs, LN2 2QU.*
Spacious luxury accommodation, lovely gardens.
Open: All Year (not Xmas)
01522 751903 (also fax no)
Mrs Weaver
Rates fr: *£17.00*-**£17.00**.
Beds: 1D 1T
(12) (6)

Sutton on Sea

National Grid Ref: TF5281

Wharncliffe Private Hotel, *24 Trusthorpe Road, Sutton on Sea, Mablethorpe, Lincs, LN12 2LT.*
Hotel adjacent to beautiful beach.
Open: Easter to Sep
01507 441510 Mrs Massey
Rates fr: *£15.00*-**£17.50**.
Beds: 2F 2D 3T 2S
Baths: 2 Shared
(5)

Tattershall

National Grid Ref: TF2158

Ratty's

Lodge House, *Market Place, Tattershall, Lincoln, Lincs, LN4 4LQ.*
C18th town house - comfortable.
Open: All Year
01526 342575 Mr Palethorpe
Rates fr: *£12.00*-**£12.00**.
Beds: 2D 2S
Baths: 2 Private 1 Shared
(3)

6 High Street, *Tattershall, Lincoln, Lincs, LN4 4LE.*
Comfortable Victorian house near castle.
Open: All Year
01526 342689 Mrs Garth
Rates fr: *£11.00*-**£12.00**.
Beds: 1F 1D
Baths: 1 Shared

The lowest **single** *rate is shown in* **bold.**

Please respect a B&B's wishes regarding children, animals & smoking.

Timberland

National Grid Ref: TF1258

Penny Farthing Inn

The Penny Farthing Inn, *Station Road, Timberland, Lincoln, Lincs, LN4 3SA.*
Relaxed C18th beamed inn.
Open: All Year
01526 378359
Mr Dobson
Rates fr: *£22.00*-**£25.00**.
Beds: 2D 4T
Baths: 2 Shared
(40)

Torksey

National Grid Ref: SK8378

Castle Inn

Castle Inn, *Torksey, Lincoln, Lincs, LN1 2EQ.*
Friendly, comfortable public house.
Open: All Year
01427 718212 Mr Jones
Rates fr: *£15.00*-**£15.00**.
Beds: 1F 3D
Baths: 1 Private 1 Shared
(20)

Trusthorpe

National Grid Ref: TF5183

Ramblers Hotel, *Sutton Road, Trusthorpe, Mablethorpe, Lincs, LN12 2PY.*
Detached hotel, large front garden.
Open: All Year (not Xmas)
Grades: ETB 2 Cr
01507 441171
Mr McGonigle
Rates fr: *£16.50*-**£19.50**.
Beds: 2F 3D 1T
Baths: 6 Ensuite
(10)

Ulceby

National Grid Ref: TA1014

Gillingham Guest House, *Spruce Lane, Ulceby, Lincs, DN39 6UL.*
Large Spanish-style villa.
Open: All Year
01469 588427 Mrs Stranix
Rates fr: *£18.00*-**£19.50**.
Beds: 2T 2S
Baths: 2 Shared
(12) (8)

Wellingore

National Grid Ref: SK9856

Marquis of Granby

Marquis of Granby, *High Street, Wellingore, Lincoln, Lincs, LN5 0HW.*
Friendly village inn just off A607.
01522 810442
Rates fr: *£17.50*-**£20.00**.
Beds: 1F 1D 3T 1S
Baths: 3 Ensuite

West Keal

National Grid Ref: TF3663

Red Lion

De Cavell House, *Main Road, West Keal, Spilsby, Lincs, PE23 4BE.*
Modern house. Lincolnshire Wolds view.
Open: Easter to Oct
01790 752482 Mrs Rose
Rates fr: *£16.50*-**£16.50**.
Beds: 2D 1T
Baths: 2 Ensuite 1 Shared
(6)

The lowest *double* rate per person is shown in *italics*.

Whaplode

National Grid Ref: TF3224

Guy Wells Farm, *Whaplode, Spalding, Lincs, PE12 6TZ.*
Spacious Queen Anne farmhouse and garden.
Open: All Year (not Xmas)
01406 422239 Mrs Thompson
Rates fr: *£17.00*-**£20.00**.
Beds: 2D 1T
Baths: 1 Private 1 Shared
(10) (5)

Tevinly, *Eastgate, Whaplode, Spalding, Lincs, PE12 6TT.*
Modern detached private house.
Open: All Year (not Xmas)
01406 422479 Mrs Peachman
Rates fr: *£16.00*-**£15.00**.
Beds: 2D
Baths: 1 Shared
(4)

Witham on the Hill

National Grid Ref: TF0516

Ragrose, *Bottom Street, Witham on the Hill, Bourne, Lincs, PE10 0JP.*
Secluded private house in village.
Open: All Year (not Xmas)
01778 590438 Mrs Ray
Rates fr: *£20.00*-**£20.00**.
Beds: 1F 1D
Baths: 1 Shared
(8)

Woodhall Spa

National Grid Ref: TF1963

The Mall

Claremont Guest House, *9-11 Witham Road, Woodhall Spa, Lincs, LN10 6RW.*
Homely unspoilt Victorian guest house. **Open:** All Year
Grades: ETB 2 Cr, AA 2 Q
01526 352000 Mrs Brennan
Rates fr: *£15.00*-**£15.00**.
Beds: 2F 3D 2T 2S
Baths: 2 Ensuite 2 Shared
(3)

Dower House Hotel, *Manor Estate, Woodhall Spa, Lincs, LN10 6PY.*
Large Victorian dower house.
Open: All Year
01526 352588 Mr Plumb
Rates fr: *£32.00*-**£42.00**.
Beds: 1F 6T
Baths: 6 Private 1 Shared
(40)

Pitchaway Guest House, *The Broadway, Woodhall Spa, Lincs, LN10 6SQ.*
Friendly family-run guest house.
Open: All Year
01526 352969 Miss Leggate
Rates fr: *£15.00*-**£15.00**.
Beds: 2F 1D 2T 2S
Baths: 2 Private 1 Shared
(1) (10)

London

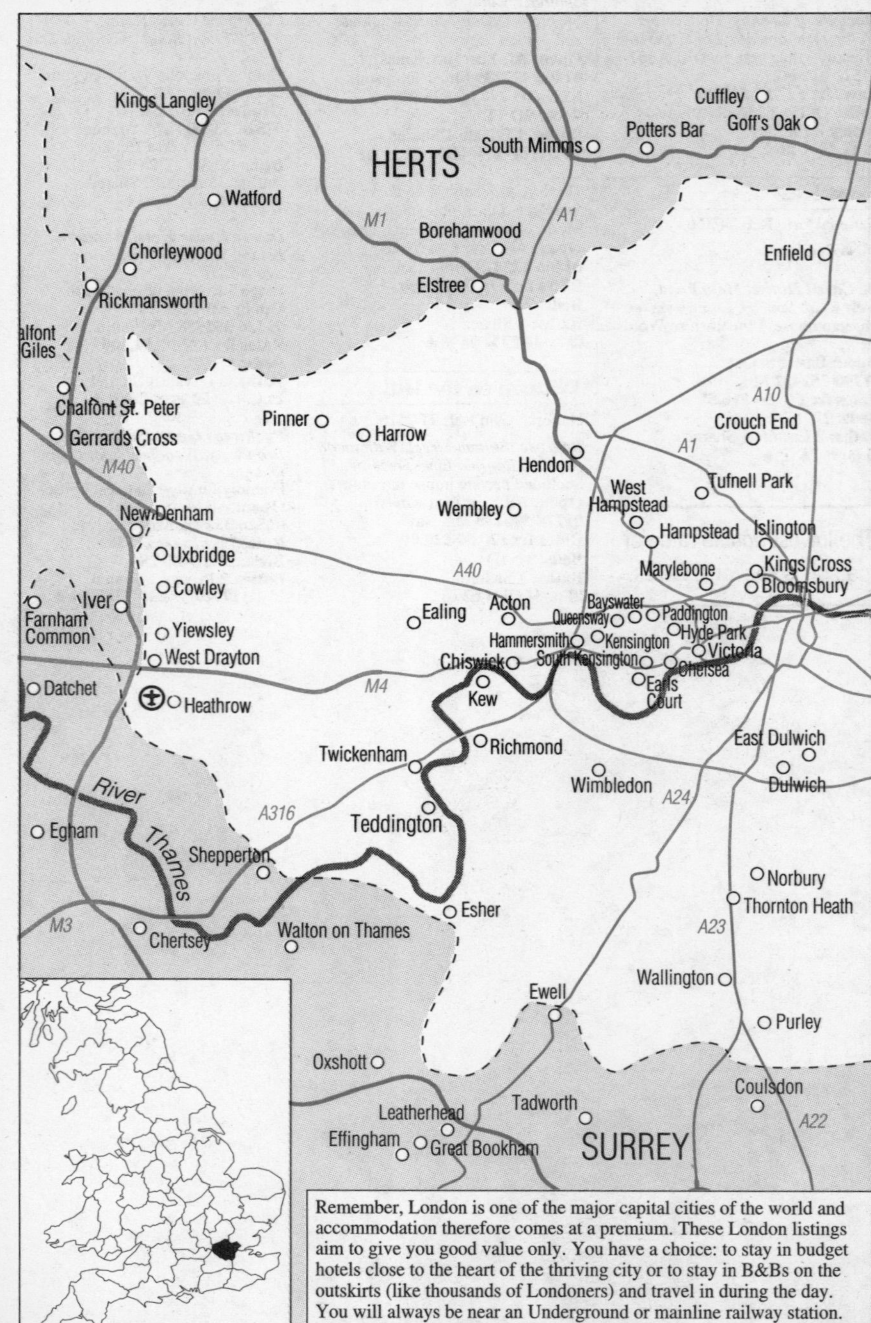

Remember, London is one of the major capital cities of the world and accommodation therefore comes at a premium. These London listings aim to give you good value only. You have a choice: to stay in budget hotels close to the heart of the thriving city or to stay in B&Bs on the outskirts (like thousands of Londoners) and travel in during the day. You will always be near an Underground or mainline railway station.

Tourist Information Centres

Victoria Station, London, SW1.

46 Greenwich Church St, **Greenwich**, London, SE10 9BL, 0181 858 6376.

44 Duncan Street, **Islington**, London N1 8BL, 0171 278 8787.

199-201 **Lewisham** High St, London, SE13 6LG, 0181 297 8317.

Civic Centre, Station Road, **Harrow**, Middx, HA1 2UJ, 0181 424 1103.

Heathrow Station (Terminals 1,2,3), Middx, TW6 2JA, 0893 123456.

The Old Town Hall, Whittaker Ave, **Richmond**, Surrey, TW9 1TP, 0181 940 9125.

44 York St, **Twickenham**, Middx, TW1, 081 891 1411.

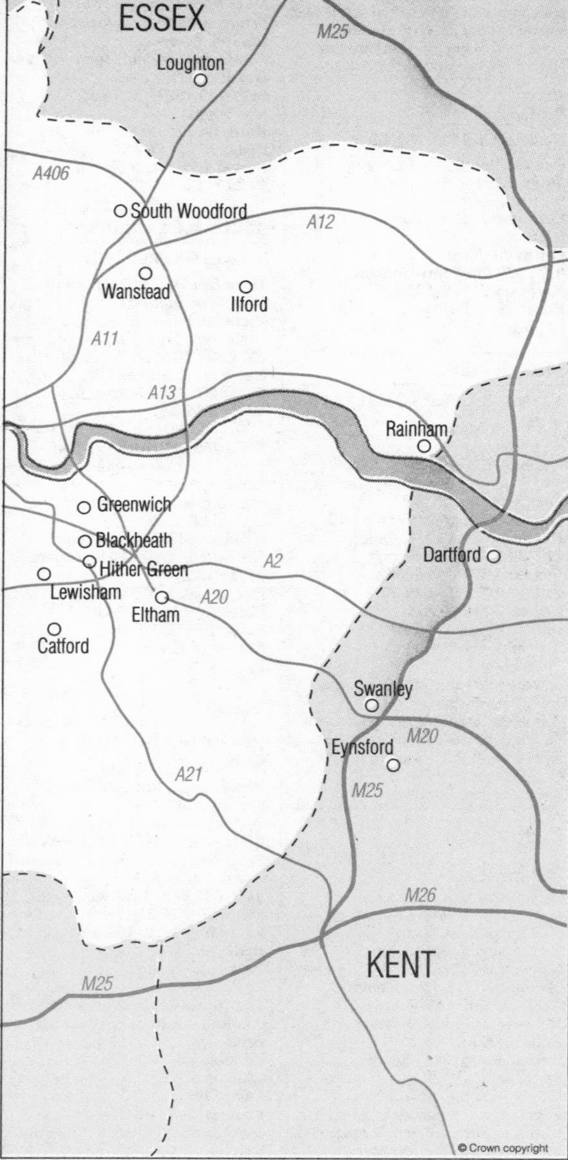

INNER LONDON (Central)

Bayswater

National Grid Ref: TQ2580

***Allandale Hotel,** 3 Devonshire Terrace, Bayswater, London, W2 3DN.*
Small, select family hotel.
Open: All Year
0171 723 8311 Fax no: 0171 723 8311 / 0181 905 4891
Rates fr: *£25.00*-**£35.00**.
Beds: 5F 5T 10D 2S
Baths: 21 Ensuite

Bloomsbury

National Grid Ref: TQ3082

Museum Tavern

***Bedford House Hotel,** 1 Bloomsbury Place, Bloomsbury, London, WC1A 2RA.*
Friendly, family-run hotel.
Open: All Year
Grades: ETB Listed
0171 636 4661 Mr Fitzgerald
Fax no: 0171 636 0577
Rates fr: *£20.00*-**£27.00**.
Beds: 5F 10D 10T 10S
Baths: 8 Shared

***St Athans Hotel,** 20 Tavistock Place, Bloomsbury, London, WC1H 9RE.*
Comfortable family-run bed & breakfast.
Open: All Year
0171 837 9140 Mr Geyer
Rates fr: *£18.00*-**£26.00**.
Beds: 4F 15D 16T 16S
Baths: 6 Private 12 Shared

Chelsea

National Grid Ref: TQ2777

***Magnolia Hotel, Chelsea,** 104 - 105 Oakley Street, Chelsea, London, SW3 5NT.*
Small family-owned B&B hotel.
Open: All Year
0171 352 0187 Ms Marovic
Rates fr: *£20.00*-**£25.00**.
Beds: 5D **Baths:** 2 Shared

Earl's Court

National Grid Ref: TQ2578

Angus Steak House

***Lord Jim Hotel,** 23-25 Penywern Road, Earls Court, London, SW5 9TT.*
Well-positioned, clean, comfortable hotel.
Open: All Year
Grades: ETB Listed
0171 370 6071 Mr Tayeb
Rates fr: *£12.00*-**£20.00**.
Beds: 10F 10D 7T 8S
Baths: 18 Private 15 Shared

Merlyn Court Hotel, *2 Barkston Gardens, Earl's Court, London, SW5 0EN.*
Open: All Year **Grades:** ETB 2 Cr
0171 370 1640 Mr Ishani
Fax no: 0171 370 4986
Rates fr: *£18.00*-**£25.00**.
Beds: 4F 4D 8T 4S
Baths: 10 Private 5 Shared
Very central, good value, friendly family-run in a quiet garden square in Kensington. Handy for Earls Court & Olympia Exhibition Halls, museums & City. Direct links to Heathrow, Gatwick & train stations.

Rasool Court Hotel, *19 - 21 Penywern Road, Earls Court, London, SW5 9TT.*
Open: All Year
Grades: ETB Listed
0171 373 4893 Mr Younis
Rates fr: *£18.00*-**£26.00**.
Beds: 7F 16D 7D 27S
Rasool Court Hotel is situated close to Earl's Court Exhibition and Underground station. Within easy reach of the West End, Marble Arch, Piccadilly & Heathrow.

Ramsees Hotel, *32-36 Hogarth Road, Earls Court, London, SW5 0PU.*
Open: All Year
0171 370 1445 Mr Younis
Fax no: 0171 244 6835
Rates fr: *£16.00*-**£18.00**.
Beds: 33D 6T 18S
Ramsees Hotel is situated close to Earls Court Exhibition Centre and Underground station. Within easy reach of the West End, Marble Arch, Piccadilly & Heathrow.

Hyde Park

National Grid Ref: TQ2780

Barry House Hotel, *12 Sussex Place, Hyde Park, London, W2 2TP.*
Open: All Year
Grades: ETB 1 Cr, Approv, RAC Listed
0171 723 7340 Mr Bhasin
Fax no: 0171 723 9775
Rates fr: *£29.00*-**£29.00**.
Beds: 6F 3D 6T 3S
Baths: 14 Ensuite 3 Shared
'We believe in family-like care.' Comfortable B&B with ensuite bedrooms. Central London location close to Paddington Station. Ideal for sightseeing, shopping or theatre breaks.

sun + mon

The lowest **single** *rate is shown in* **bold.**

Kensington

National Grid Ref: TQ2579-

Demetriou Guest House, *9 Strathmore Gardens, Kensington, London, W8 4RZ.*
Open: All Year (not Xmas)
0171 229 6709 Mr & Mrs Demetriou
Rates fr: *£25.00*-**£30.00**.
Beds: 2F 1D 2T 1S
Baths: 3 Ensuite 3 Shared
A small privately owned B&B which provides a personal service situated at the heart of London, close to Kensington Gardens and Hyde Park, reasonable prices.

Kings Cross

National Grid Ref: TQ3083

Central Hotel, *16 - 18 Argyle Street, Kings Cross, London, WC1H 8EJ.*
Convenient, clean, family-run B&B.
Open: All Year
0171 837 9008 Mrs Caruana
Rates fr: *£15.00*-**£22.00**.
Beds: 2F 16T 10D 5S

Marylebone

National Grid Ref: TQ2881

The Aristocrats

Lincoln House Hotel, *33 Gloucester Place, Marylebone, London, W1H 3PD.*
Open: All Year
Grades: ETB 1 Cr, Comm
0171 486 7630 Mr Sheriff
Fax no: 0171 486 0166
Rates fr: *£29.50*-**£39.00**.
Beds: 3F 7D 4T 8S
Baths: 17 Ensuite 2 Private 3 Shared
Attractively refurbished Georgian hotel with ensuite rooms. Admirable standard of services and facilities. Superb location in the heart of London's West End. Commended by world distinguished guide books.

Paddington

National Grid Ref: TQ2681

Swan

Ruddimans, *160 Sussex Gardens, Paddington, London, W2 1UD.*
Open: All Year
Grades: ETB Listed, Comm
0171 723 1026 Mr Petrides
Rates fr: *£19.00*-**£25.00**.
Beds: 15F 15D 6T 5S
Baths: 32 Private 3 Shared
(1) (18)
C19th Victorian town house. Highly recommended for its friendly atmosphere, service & generous traditional full English breakfast.

Albro House Hotel, *155 Sussex Gardens, Paddington, London, W2 2RY.*
Central, comfortable, safe.
Open: All Year
0171 724 2931 Mr Caruso
Rates fr: *£14.00*-**£18.00**.
Beds: 4F 6D 6T 2S
Baths: 14 Ensuite 4 Shared
(4) (1)

Queensway

National Grid Ref: TQ3169

Hyde Park House, *48 St Petersburgh Place, Queensway, London, W2 4LD.*
Central for London. **Open:** All Year
Grades: ETB Listed
0171 229 1687 / 229 9652
Mrs Toygar
Rates fr: *£15.00*-**£20.00**.
Beds: 3F 4D 4T 4S
Baths: 1 Private 5 Shared

South Kensington

National Grid Ref: TQ2678

More House, *53 Cromwell Road, South Kensington, London, SW7 2EH.*
Victorian building, central London attractions. **Open:** Jul to Aug
0171 584 2040 Mr Mitchell
Rates fr: *£19.00*-**£23.00**.
Beds: 20T 40S **Baths:** 12 Shared
(1)

Swiss House Hotel, *171 Old Brompton Road, South Kensington, London, SW5 0AN.*
Excellent value for money.
Open: All Year
Grades: ETB Listed, Comm, AA Listed, RAC Listed, Comm
0171 373 2769
Fax no: 0171 373 4983
Rates fr: *£36.00*-**£56.00**.
Beds: 16F 6D 6T 4S
Baths: 16 Ensuite

Victoria

National Grid Ref: TQ2878

Chimes, Marquis of Westminster, Princess Royal, Constitution

Alexander Hotel, *13 Belgrave Road, Victoria, London, SW1V 1RB.*
Open: All Year
0171 834 9738 Mr Montagnani
Fax no: 0171 630 9630
Rates fr: *£22.50*-**£30.00**.
Beds: 3F 7D 2T 1S
Baths: 13 Ensuite
The Alexander Hotel is a clean, comfortable, affordable Bed & Breakfast situated in the centre of London. We are within easy walking distance of London's major tourist attractions & only two minutes' walk from Victoria's coach, train, bus and Underground stations.

NO

Marne Hotel, *34 Belgrave Road, Victoria, London,* SW1V 1RG.
Open: All Year
0171 834 51950850 657226
Mr Montagnani
Fax no: 0171 976 6180
Rates fr: *£17.50*-**£25.00**.
Beds: 3F 4D 2T 3S
Baths: 7 Ensuite 2 Shared
Marne Hotel is a small, clean, friendly, family-run establishment situated just 3 minutes walk from Victoria tube station; a full English breakfast is included.

Stanley House Hotel, *19-21 Belgrave Road, Victoria, London,* SW1V 1RB.
Clean, comfortable accommodation. Perfect location. Budget rates.
Open: All Year
Grades: ETB 2 Cr, AA 2 St
0171 834 5042 Mr Shah
Fax no: 0171 834 8439
Rates fr: *£20.25*-**£26.35**.
Beds: 6F 22D 18T 11S
Baths: 28 Ensuite 6 Shared

Kirness Inn, *29 Belgrave Road, Victoria, London,* SW1V 1RB.
Small, friendly, satisfaction guaranteed.
Open: All Year
0171 834 0030 Mrs Walker
Rates fr: *£17.50*-**£25.00**.
Beds: 2D 2T

St George's Hotel, *25 Belgrave Road, Victoria, London,* SW1V 1RB.
Comfortable, clean, spacious bright rooms.
Open: All Year
Grades: ETB 2 Cr
0171 828 2061 / 828 3605
Mr Zaidi
Fax no: 0171 834 8439
Rates fr: *£22.00*-**£24.00**.
(15)

Melbourne House, *79 Belgrave Road, Victoria, London,* SW1V 2BJ.
Family-run hotel.
Open: All Year
Grades: ETB Listed, Comm
0171 828 3516 Mr Desira
Rates fr: *£35.00*-**£38.00**.
Beds: 2F 5D 7T 2S
Baths: 16 Private 1 Shared

Edward House B&B, *5 St George's Drive, Victoria, London,* SW1V 4DP.
Modern Comfortable Rooms.
Open: All Year
0171 834 5207 Fax no: 0171 976 5428
Rates fr: *£25.00*-**£32.00**.
Beds: 8F 5D 5T 2S
Baths: 10 Ensuite 10 Shared

Georgian House Hotel, *35 St Georges Drive, Victoria, London,* SW1V 4DG.
Friendly service, excellent English breakfast.

Open: All Year
Grades: ETB Listed
0171 834 1438 Mrs Von der Heyde
Fax no: 0171 976 6085
Rates fr: *£16.00*-**£19.00**.
Beds: 4F 7D 15T 8S
Baths: 21 Private 3 Shared
(0)

Melta House Hotel, *35 Charlwood Street, Victoria, London,* SW1V 2DU.
Economic, central, friendly, long established.
Open: All Year
Grades: ETB Listed
0171 828 0471 / 834 1387
Mrs Gabrielle
Rates fr: *£19.00*-**£26.00**.
Beds: 3F 6D 5T 5S
Baths: 11 Ensuite 4 Private 4 Shared

INNER LONDON (East)

Wanstead

National Grid Ref: TQ4388

The George

71 Grosvenor Road, *Wanstead, London,* E11 2ES.
Large, quiet, comfortable, Edwardian house.
Open: All Year (not Xmas)
0181 530 6970 (also fax no)
Mrs Foster
Rates fr: *£16.00*-**£16.00**.
Beds: 1F 1D 1T
Baths: 2 Ensuite 1 Shared

Sunningdale Guest House, *35 Lonsdale Road, Wanstead, London,* E11 2PH.
C18th hotel, hospitable, friendly.
Open: All Year
0181 989 3435 Mrs Novlis
Rates fr: *£17.50*-**£23.00**.
Beds: 1F 5D 1T 1S
Baths: 3 Shared
(4)

INNER LONDON (North)

Crouch End

National Grid Ref: TQ3089

Banners, Hungry Horse

Mount View, *31 Mount View Road, Crouch End, London,* N4 4SS.
Open: All Year
Grades: AA 4 Q, Select
0181 340 9222 Mrs Hendrickx
Fax no: 0181 342 8494
Rates fr: *£20.00*-**£26.00**.
Beds: 2D 1T**Baths:** 1 Ensuite
Friendly, clean, privately owned B&B in quiet area, tastefully decorated bedrooms. Finsbury Park Station (Picadilly & Victoria lines). No parking restrictions. Access M1, A1.

Parkland Walk Guest House, *12 Hornsey Rise Gardens, Crouch End, London,* N19 3PR.
Beautiful, award-winning Victorian guest house.
Open: All Year (not Xmas)
Grades: ETB Listed, Comm, AA 3 Q, RAC Acclaim
0171 263 3228 Mr Solomons
Fax no: 0171 831 9489
Rates fr: *£21.00*-**£24.00**.
Beds: 1F 1D 1T 2S
Baths: 2 Private 1 Shared

Aber Hotel, *89 Crouch Hill, Crouch End, London,* N8 9EG.
Family-run, friendly guest house.
Open: All Year
Grades: AA 2 Q, RAC Listed
0181 340 2847 Mr & Mrs Jenkins
Rates fr: *£17.00*-**£20.00**.
Beds: 3F 2D 2T 2S
Baths: 2 Shared

Hampstead

National Grid Ref: TQ2685

Belsize Tavern

Dillons Hotel, *21 Belsize Park, Hampstead, London,* NW3 4DU.
Fairly centrally-located economy hotel. **Open:** All Year (not Xmas)
Grades: ETB Listed
0171 794 3360 Mr Dillon
Fax no: 0171 586 1104
Rates fr: *£18.00*-**£26.00**.
Beds: 3F 1D 5T 4S
Baths: 7 Ensuite 3 Shared

Islington

National Grid Ref: TQ3184

Kandara Guest House, *68 Ockendon Road, Islington, London,* N1 3NW.
Large Victorian house.
Open: All Year
Grades: ETB Listed
0171 226 5721 / 226 3379
Mrs Harmon
Rates fr: *£18.00*-**£26.00**.
Beds: 1F 2D 1T 4S
Baths: 2 Shared

Tufnell Park

National Grid Ref: TQ2986

Boston Bar

Five Kings Guest House, *59 Anson Road, Tufnell Park, London,* N7 0AR.
Open: All Year **Grades:** ETB 1 Cr
0171 607 3996 / 607 6466
Mr Poulacheris
Rates fr: *£15.00*-**£20.00**.
Beds: 4F 3D 3T 6S
Baths: 7 Ensuite 7 Private 3 Shared
(3)
Five Kings is a family-run guest house in a quiet residential area. Only 15 minutes to Central London and tourist attractions. No parking restrictions in Anson Road.

Queens Mansions, *33 Anson Road, Tufnell Park, London, N7 0RB.*
Large Victorian house near Regents Park.
Open: All Year
0171 607 4725 Mr Stavrou
Rates fr: *£18.00*-**£20.00**.
Beds: 5F 10D 10T 11S
Baths: 16 Ensuite 20 Shared
(7)

West Hampstead

National Grid Ref: TQ2585

Charlotte Guest House, *221 West End Lane, West Hampstead, London, NW6 1XJ.*
Open: All Year
Grades: ETB Listed
0171 794 6476 Mr Koch
Fax no: 0171 431 3584
Rates fr: *£17.50*-**£25.00**.
Beds: 2F 10D 10T 10S
Baths: 10 Private 10 Shared
Free London Travelcard for 7 nights stay. Access to the West End or City in 10-15 minutes.

INNER LONDON (South)

Blackheath

National Grid Ref: TQ3976

135 Shooters Hill Road, *Blackheath, London, SE3 8UQ.*
Large Victorian private family house. **Open:** All Year
0181 858 1420 Mr & Mrs Poole
Rates fr: *£17.50*-**£17.50**.
Beds: 1F **Baths:** 1 Private
(1)

Catford

National Grid Ref: TQ3873

Black Horse, Harrow, George, Rising Sun

Hazeldene, *75 Brownhill Road (South Circular Road), Catford, London, SE6 2HF.*
Open: All Year
0181 697 2436 Mrs Holben
Fax no: 0181 473 9601
Rates fr: *£15.50*-**£17.50**.
Beds: 1F 1D 2T 2S
Baths: 2 Shared
(6) (1)
Exceptionally clean and comfortable English Bed & Breakfast. Cable television in each bedroom. Tea/coffee-making facilities. Excellent breakfasts. Guests' telephone. 15 minutes to city centre.

All details shown are as supplied by B&B owners in Autumn 1996.

31 & 33 Ringstead Road, *Catford, London, SE6 2BU.*
A small, family 'Bed and Breakfast'.
Open: All Year
Grades: ETB Listed
0181 461 0146 Mrs Broughton
Rates fr: *£17.00*-**£25.00**.
Beds: 2F 1D 2T 1S
Baths: 2 Private 3 Shared
(8)

East Dulwich

National Grid Ref: TQ3474

Crown & Greyhound

Bedknobs, *58 Glengarry Road, East Dulwich, London, SE22 8QD.*
Open: All Year
Grades: ETB Listed, Comm, AA 3 Q, RAC Listed
0181 299 2004 Mrs Jenkins
Rates fr: *£18.00*-**£20.00**.
Beds: 2D 2T 3S
Baths: 1 Ensuite 3 Shared
Carefully restored Victorian family-run house offering many home comforts, modern facilities, excellent service & a warm welcome. BTA London B&B Award 1992.

Greenwich

National Grid Ref: TQ3977

Greenwich Parkhouse Hotel, *1 & 2 Nevada Street, Greenwich, London, SE10 9JL.*
Small hotel facing Greenwich Park.
Open: All Year (not Xmas)
0181 305 1478 Mrs Bryan
Rates fr: *£17.50*-**£27.50**.
Beds: 2F 3D 1T 3S
Baths: 3 Private 2 Shared
(8)

78 Vanbrugh Park, Blakheath, *Greenwich, London, SE3 7JQ.*
Beautiful Victorian house, near Blackheath.
Open: All Year
Grades: ETB Listed
0181 858 0338 Mrs Mattey
Rates fr: *£18.00*-**£20.00**.
Beds: 1F 2T **Baths:** 2 Private
(3)

4 Egerton Drive, *Greenwich, London, SE10 8JS.*
Listed building (1829), conservation area.
Open: All Year
0181 691 5587 Mrs Courtney
Rates fr: *£18.00*-**£18.00**.
Beds: 1F 2T 3S
Baths: 2 Shared

132 Old Woolwich Road, *Greenwich, London, SE10 9PR.*
200-year-old character home.
Open: All Year
0181 858 2391 Mrs Price
Rates fr: *£15.00*-**£15.00**.
Beds: 1D 1S

Lewisham

National Grid Ref: TQ3875

Maggie's Cafe & Restaurant

8 Yeats Close, Eliot Park, *Lewisham, London, SE13 7EG.*
Homely base for Greenwich & London.
Open: All Year
0181 318 3421 (also fax no)
Ms Hutton
Rates fr: *£17.50*-**£16.00**.
Beds: 1D 1T 1S
Baths: 1 Shared

Baileys, *77 Belmont Hill, Lewisham, London, SE13 5AX.*
Refurbished Victorian house near Greenwich.
Open: All Year (not Xmas)
0181 852 7373 Mrs Bailey
Fax no: 0181 473 7777
Rates fr: *£15.00*-**£15.00**.
Beds: 1F 2T 1S
Baths: 1 Shared

Norbury

National Grid Ref: TQ3169

The Konyots, *95 Pollards Hill South, Norbury, London, SW16 4LS.*
Quiet area, parking space.
Open: All Year
0181 764 0075 Mrs Konyot
Rates fr: *£15.00*-**£15.00**.
Beds: 1F 1T 1S
Baths: 1 Shared

St Johns

National Grid Ref: TQ3875

Dauys Wine Vaults

4 Cliff Terrace, *St Johns, London, SE8 4DZ.*
Charming, self catering/B&B garden flat.
Open: All Year
01378 280515
Mrs Wellings-Longmore
Fax no: 0171 727 1672
Rates fr: *£19.50*-**£26.00**.
Beds: 2D
Baths: 2 Private
(4)

Wimbledon

National Grid Ref: TQ2471

Fox & Grapes

3 Oakhill Court, Edge Hill, *Wimbledon, London, SW19 4NR.*
Favoured by Wimbledon tennis stars!
Open: All Year (not Xmas)
0181 946 6039
Mrs Patterson
Rates fr: *£18.00*-**£20.00**.
Beds: 1T
Baths: 1 Shared
(1)

***2 Mayfield Road,** Wimbledon,*
ondon, *SW19 3NF.*
rtist's detached home. Warm
elcome.
pen: All Year
181 543 2607 Mr & Mrs Daglish
ates fr: *£18.00*-**£18.00**.
eds: 1T 1S
aths: 1 Private
(1)

INNER LONDON (West)

Chiswick

ational Grid Ref: TQ2078

The Windmill

***oubert's Hotel,** 162-166 Chiswick*
igh Road, Chiswick, London,
4 1PR.
amily-run hotel, continental
mosphere.
pen: All Year
rades: ETB Listed
181 994 5202
r Lodico
ates fr: *£22.50*-**£25.00**.
eds: 3F 4D 2T 12S
aths: 21 Private 4 Shared

***lliott Private Hotel,** 62 Elliott*
oad, Chiswick, London, *W4 1PE.*
urnham Green station 120 metres.
pen: All Year (not Xmas)
181 995 9794
rs Reluga
ates fr: *£15.00*-**£20.00**.
eds: 1F 2D 4T 6S
aths: 2 Shared
(5) (1)

Ealing

ational Grid Ref: TQ1780

***8 Cleveland Road,** Ealing,*
ondon, *W13 8AJ.*
pen: All Year
181 991 5142 Mrs McHugh
ax no: 0181 998 2872
ates fr: *£20.00*-**£25.00**.
eds: 2F 2D 1S
aths: 2 Private
(5) (3)
arge luxury house overlooking
rkland. Friendly atmosphere.
elicious English breakfasts. Easy
cess to Heathrow & central
ondon. Tea/coffee facilities &
irdryers supplied. Pretty garden.

***bbey Lodge Hotel,** 51 Grange*
ark, Ealing, London, *W5 3PR.*
ictorian outside; modern comfort-
ble inside.
pen: All Year (not Xmas)
rades: ETB 2 C, rRAC Listed
81 567 7914
r Grindrod
ax no: 0181 579 5350
ates fr: *£22.00*-**£33.00**.
eds: 3F 3D 1T 9S
aths: 16 Ensuite

Hammersmith

National Grid Ref: TQ2279

***67 Rannoch Road,** Hammersmith, London,* *W6 9SS.*
Open: All Year
0171 385 4904
Mr & Mrs Armanios
Rates fr: *£20.00*.
Beds: 1F 1D 1T
Baths: 1 Shared
Central, quiet. Close river, pubs, restaurants. 3 minutes to bus, 12 minutes Underground. Direct links to shopping, Harrods, museums, theatres, Earls Court/Olympia exhibition centres, Heathrow, Gatwick. Continental breakfast.

Kew

National Grid Ref: TQ1977

Coach & Horses

***1 Chelwood Gardens,** Kew, Richmond, Surrey,* *TW9 4JG.*
Large Edwardian, friendly family house.
Open: All Year
0181 876 8733
Mrs Gray
Rates fr: *£20.00*-**£20.00**.
Beds: 2T 2S
Baths: 2 Shared
(5) (8)

***179 Mortlake Road,** Kew, Richmond, Surrey,* *TW9 4AW.*
Large Georgian private house.
Open: All Year
0181 876 0584 Mrs Butt
Rates fr: *£20.00*.
Beds: 1T
Baths: 1 Private
(2)

***8 Taylor Avenue,** Kew, Richmond, Surrey,* *TW9 4ED.*
Spacious, modernised period family home.
Open: All Year (not Xmas)
0181 876 3930
Mrs Allen
Rates fr: *£20.00*-**£20.00**.
Beds: 1T 1S
Baths: 1 Private
(2)

Shepperton

National Grid Ref: TQ0767

The Harrow

***Old Manor House,** Squires Bridge Road, Littleton, Shepperton, Middx,* *TW17 0QG.*
An historic house dating from the reign of Henry VII.
Open: All Year
01932 571293
Mrs Bouwens
Rates fr: *£23.00*-**£25.00**.
Beds: 1D 1T 1S
Baths: 1 Ensuite 1 Shared
(5)

Twickenham

National Grid Ref: TQ1573

Popes Grotto

***3 Waldegrave Gardens,** Twickenham, Middx,* *TW1 4PQ.*
Large Victorian private house.
Open: All Year
0181 892 3523 Mrs Park
Rates fr: *£16.00*-**£16.00**.
Beds: 1F 1D 1S
Baths: 1 Shared

***11 Spencer Road,** Twickenham, Middx,* *TW2 5TH.*
Elegant Edwardian private house.
Open: All Year
Grades: ETB Listed
0181 894 5271 Mrs Duff
Rates fr: *£17.00*-**£17.00**.
Beds: 1D 1T
Baths: 1 Shared
(12) (all)

OUTER LONDON

Borehamwood

National Grid Ref: TQ1977

***84 Stevenage Crescent,** Borehamwood, Herts,* *WD6 4NS.*
Luxury, modern private house.
Open: All Year
0181 207 3320
Mrs Copley
Rates fr: *£12.50*-**£15.00**.
Beds: 1T 1S
Baths: 1 Shared
(2)

Chalfont St Giles

National Grid Ref: SU9893

Three Horse Shoes, Pheasant Inn, Seer Green

***Gorelands Corner,** Gorelands Lane, Chalfont St Giles, Bucks,* *HP8 4HQ.*
Family house in own grounds.
Open: All Year
01494 872689 (also fax no)
Mrs Bickford
Rates fr: *£20.00*-**£20.00**.
Beds: 1F 1D 1T 1S
Baths: 1 Private 1 Shared
(0) (3)

Chalfont St Peter

National Grid Ref: SU9987

***Maytime,** 26 Eleanor Road, Chalfont St Peter, Bucks,* *SL9 9LZ.*
Cottage style house, beautiful garden.
Open: All Year
01753 890662
Mrs Hobley
Rates fr: *£14.00*-**£14.00**.
Beds: 2S
Baths: 1 Shared
(5) (1)

Chorleywood

National Grid Ref: TQ0296

Rose & Crown

***Kennels Cottage,** Common Road, Chorleywood, Herts, WD3 5LW.*
Converted buildings in conservation area.
Open: All Year (not Xmas)
01923 282927 Mrs Smethurst
Rates fr: *£17.00*-**£18.00**.
Beds: 1D 1T 2S **Baths:** 1 Shared
(4)

Coulsdon

National Grid Ref: TQ3058

***512 Chipstead Valley Road,** Coulsdon, Surrey, CR5 2BN.*
Modern, homely, comfortable.
Open: All Year (not Xmas)
01737 553155 Mrs Bateman
Rates fr: *£17.50*-**£17.00**.
Beds: 1D 1S **Baths:** 1 Shared

Cuffley

National Grid Ref: TL3003

The Oak

***52 Brookside Crescent,** Cuffley, Potters Bar, Herts, EN6 4QN.*
Private house, convenient major roads.
Open: All Year (not Xmas)
01707 874016 Mrs Shelton
Rates fr: *£14.00*-**£14.00**.
Beds: 1T
Baths: 1 Shared
(3)

Dartford

National Grid Ref: TQ5273

***Rosedene Guest House,** 284-286 Lowfield Street, Dartford, Kent, DA1 1LH.*
Convenient, comfortable, caring catering.
Open: All Year (not Xmas)
01322 277042 Mrs Rose
Rates fr: *£16.00*-**£22.00**.
Beds: 1F 3T 2S
Baths: 2 Shared
(2)

Datchet

National Grid Ref: SU9877

Royal Stag

***55 London Road,** Datchet, Slough, Berks, SL3 9JY.*
Conveniently located, near Windsor, Heathrow, M4/M25 motorways.
Open: All Year
01753 580401
Mrs Greenham
Fax no: 01753 540233
Rates fr: *£20.00*-**£28.50**.
Beds: 1F 2D 1T
Baths: 2 Private

Effingham

National Grid Ref: TQ1153

Plough, Sir Douglas

***Chalklands,** Beech Avenue, Effingham, Surrey, KT24 5PJ.*
Large, detached house overlooking golfcourse.
Open: All Year (not Xmas)
01372 454936 Mrs Reilly
Rates fr: *£20.00*-**£25.00**.
Beds: 1F 1D 1T
Baths: 2 Ensuite 1 Private
(8)

***Crosslands Guest House,** Guildford Road, Effingham, Surrey, KT24 5PE.*
Large ex-pub. C13th & C16th.
Open: All Year (not Xmas)
01372 453479 Mrs Gifford
Rates fr: *£17.00*-**£17.00**.
Beds: 1F 5T 1S **Baths:** 1 Private

Egham

National Grid Ref: TQ0071

***The Old Parsonage,** 2 Parsonage Road, Englefield Green, Egham, Surrey, TW20 0JW.*
Georgian parsonage, old-fashioned gardens.
Open: All Year (not Xmas)
01784 436706 (also fax no)
Mr & Mrs Clark
Rates fr: *£25.00*-**£25.00**.
Beds: 1F 1D 1T 1S
Baths: 1 Ensuite 1 Private1 Shared
(3)

***Beau Villa,** 44 Grange Road, Egham, Surrey, TW20 9QP.*
Friendly, clean, comfortable family house.
Open: All Year (not Xmas)
01784 435115 Mrs Wilding
Rates fr: *£17.00*-**£20.00**.
Beds: 1D 1S **Baths:** 1 Ensuite
(14) (4)

Elstree

National Grid Ref: TQ1795

***North Medburn Farm,** Watlin Street, Elstree, Herts, WD6 3AA.*
Easy access to London.
Open: All Year
0181 953 1522 Mrs Williams
Rates fr: *£17.50*-**£20.00**.
Beds: 1F 2D 1S **Baths:** 1 Private
(4)

Enfield

National Grid Ref: TQ3396

Plough Inn

***42 Mapleton Crescent, Off Hoe Lane,** Enfield, Middx, EN3 5RD.*
Comfortable accommodation, 3 mins M25. **Open:** All Year
0181 804 6907 Mrs Gibbins
Rates fr: *£17.50*-**£17.50**.
Beds: 1F 1D 1S **Baths:** 1 Shared
(2)

***Oak Lodge Hotel,** 80 Village Road, Enfield, Middx, EN1 2EU.*
Exclusive country house, hotel/restaurant.
Open: All Year
0181 360 7082
Mr Brown
Rates fr: *£27.50*-**£40.00**.
Beds: 1F 1D 2T 1S
Baths: 5 Private
(5)

Esher

National Grid Ref: TQ1565

Swan Inn (Claygate)

***Lilac Cottage,** 14 Greenways, Hinchley Wood, Esher, Surrey, KT10 0QD.*
Luxury friendly family home.
Open: All Year (not Xmas)
0181 398 7546 (also fax no)
Mrs Evans
Rates fr: *£20.00*-**£25.00**.
Beds: 1T
Baths: 1 Ensuite
(2)

Ewell

National Grid Ref: TQ2162

***Tuum,** Epsom Road, Ewell, Epsom, Surrey, KT17 1LJ.*
Comfortable house with own parking.
Open: All Year
0181 393 1682
Mrs Rosa
Rates fr: *£12.50*-**£15.00**.
Beds: 1F 4T
Baths: 2 Shared
(7)

Gerrards Cross

National Grid Ref: SU9987

Etorpe Hotel

***Tudor Acre,** South Park Crescent, Gerrards Cross, Bucks, SL9 8HJ.*
Large, modern, Tudor-style house.
Open: All Year (not Xmas)
01753 885874 Mrs Walker
Rates fr: *£20.00*-**£20.00**.
Beds: 1F 1D 1T 1S
Baths: 1 Private 1 Shared
(6) (6)

Goff's Oak

National Grid Ref: TL3203

***329 Goffs Lane,** Goff's Oak, Cheshunt, Herts, EN7 5QH.*
Large detached house near countryside.
Open: All Year
01992 628524
Mrs Morgan
Rates fr: *£20.00*-**£25.00**.
Beds: 1F 1D 4T 1S
Baths: 5 Ensuite 1 Shared
(7)

Great Bookham

National Grid Ref: TQ1354

The Lodge, *2 Park Green, Great Bookham, Leatherhead, Surrey, KT23 3NL.*
Quiet location, easy parking.
Open: All Year (not Xmas)
01372 459642 Mrs Dawson
Rates fr: *£16.00*-**£16.00**.
Beds: 1D 1T
Baths: 1 Shared

Harrow

National Grid Ref: TQ1488

Crescent Hotel, *58-60 Welldon Crescent, Harrow, Middlesex, HA1 1QR.*
Open: All Year
Grades: ETB 3 Cr, Comm, AA 3 Q, RAC Acclaim
0181 863 5491 Mr Jivraj
Fax no: 0181 427 5965
Rates fr: *£25.00*-**£35.00**.
Beds: 2F 2D 7T 10S
Baths: 13 Ensuite 3 Shared
(7)
Modern friendly hotel with full facilities within the heart of Harrow. Easy access to Wembley, West End, Heathrow & all major motorways.

Hindes Hotel, *8 Hindes Road, Harrow, Middlesex, HA1 1SJ.*
Clean, near motorway & Wembley, Underground train 8 minutes walk.
Open: All Year
Grades: ETB 3 Cr, AA 2 Q, RAC Acclaim
0181 427 7468 Mr Ahluwalia
Rates fr: *£20.00*-**£37.00**.
Beds: 2F 4D 4T 4S
Baths: 7 Ensuite 7 Shared
(25)

Central Hotel, *6 Hindes Road, Harrow, Middlesex, HA1 1SJ.*
Friendly hotel, 20 mins from West End.
Open: All Year (not Xmas)
0181 427 0893 Mr Ryan
Rates fr: *£17.50*-**£28.00**.
Beds: 2F 2T 2D 3S
Baths: 3 Ensuite 3 Shared
(1) (12)

Heathrow

National Grid Ref: TQ0980

Shepiston Lodge, *31 Shepiston Lane, Heathrow, Middlesex, UB3 1LJ.*
Character house near Heathrow.
Open: All Year
Grades: ETB 1 Cr, AA 1 Q, RAC Listed
0181 573 0266 Mr Dhawan
Fax no: 0181 569 2536
Rates fr: *£21.75*-**£27.50**.
Beds: 3F 7T 3S
Baths: 6 Private 2 Shared
(15)

The lowest **single rate is shown in bold.**

Hendon

National Grid Ref: TQ2389

Rilux House, *1 Lodge Road, Hendon, London, NW4 4DD.*
High standard, all private facilities.
Open: All Year
0181 203 0933 Mrs Weissman
Rates fr: *£22.50*-**£27.00**.
Beds: 1F 1D 1T 1S
Baths: 4 Private
(2)

Hither Green

National Grid Ref: TQ3974

51 Manor Park, *Hither Green, London, SE13 5RA.*
Large, friendly, Victorian private house.
Open: All Year
0181 318 6474 Mr McMurray
Rates fr: *£15.00*-**£16.00**.
Beds: 2T 1S
Baths: 1 Shared
(10)

53 Manor Park, *Hither Green, London, SE13 5RA.*
Small, private, Victorian guest house.
Open: All Year
0181 318 5590
Mr Clegg
Fax no: 0181 244 4196
Rates fr: *£17.50*-**£18.50**.
Beds: 1F 3D 1T 3S
Baths: 2 Private 2 Shared
(6)

Ilford

National Grid Ref: TQ4486

Woodville Guest House, *10/12 Argyle Road, Ilford, Essex, IG1 3BQ.*
Family-run comfortable & friendly.
Open: All Year
0181 478 3779
Mrs Murray
Rates fr: *£15.00*-**£21.00**.
Beds: 2F 4D 6T 3S
Baths: 4 Ensuite 4 Shared
(14)

Iver

National Grid Ref: TQ0381

Black Horse

Oaklands, *Bangors Road South, Iver, Slough, Bucks, SL0 0BB.*
Large, comfortable, private house.
Open: All Year
01753 653003
Mrs Fowler
Rates fr: *£15.00*-**£15.00**.
Beds: 1D 2T 1S
Baths: 2 Shared
(4)

The Old Vicarage, *18 Thorney Lane North, Iver, Slough, Bucks, SL0 9JY.*
Beautiful modernised C18th vicarage.
Open: All Year (not Xmas)
01753 653924
Mrs Heywood
Rates fr: *£18.00*-**£22.00**.
Beds: 1F 2D
Baths: 2 Private 1 Shared
(3)

Kings Langley

National Grid Ref: TL0702

The Eagle

Woodcote House, *7 The Grove, Chipperfield Road, Kings Langley, Herts, WD4 9JF.*
Large timber-framed detached house.
Open: All Year (not Xmas)
Grades: ETB 2 Cr, Comm
01923 262077
Mr & Mrs Leveridge
Fax no: 01923 266198
Rates fr: *£18.00*-**£20.00**.
Beds: 1D 1T 2S
Baths: 4 Private
(1) (6)

The Eagle, *127 Hempstead Road, Kings Langley, Herts, WD4 8AJ.*
Coaching inn dating back to 1740.
Open: All Year
01923 262563
Rates fr: *£21.50*-**£21.50**.
Beds: 1F 1T 1S
Baths: 1 Shared
(30)

Leatherhead

National Grid Ref: TQ1656

20 Melvinshaw, *Leatherhead, Surrey, KT22 8SX.*
Clean, comfortable family house.
Open: All Year
01372 373786 Mrs Pearce
Rates fr: *£17.50*-**£17.50**.
Beds: 1T 1S
Baths: 1 Shared

Loughton

National Grid Ref: TQ4396

61 York Hill, *Loughton, Essex, IG10 1HZ.*
Picturesque Edwardian family home.
Open: All Year (not Xmas)
Grades: ETB Listed, Comm
0181 508 9834 Mrs Catterall
Rates fr: *£15.00*-**£20.00**.
Beds: 1F 1T 1S
Baths: 2 Shared
(0) (3)

The lowest *double* rate per person is shown in *italics*.

Bringing children with you? Always ask for any special rates.

Oxshott

National Grid Ref: TQ1460

Apple Tree Cottage, *Oakshade Road, Oxshott, Leatherhead, Surrey,* KT22 0LF.
Quietly located cottage, modernised accommodation.
Open: All Year (not Xmas)
Grades: ETB Listed
01372 842087 Mrs Crowhurst
Fax no: 01372 842101
Rates fr: *£27.50*-**£49.50**.
Beds: 1D 1T 1S
Baths: 1 Shared
(3)

Pinner

National Grid Ref: TQ1189

11 Meadow Road, *Pinner, Middx,* HA5 1EB.
Modern, comfortable, family home.
Open: All Year
0181 868 1074 Mrs Goodman
Rates fr: *£15.00*-**£15.00**.
Beds: 2T **Baths:** 2 Shared
(3) (1)

Potters Bar

National Grid Ref: TL2501

The Wildings, *58 Cranborne Crescent, Potters Bar, Herts,* EN6 3AG.
10 minutes to London by fast train.
Open: All Year (not Xmas)
01707 650533
Ms Wilding
Rates fr: *£14.50*-**£14.50**.
Beds: 1F 1D 1T
Baths: 1 Shared
(7) (4)

Purley

National Grid Ref: TQ3161

Foxley Hatchet

51 Selcroft Road, *Purley, South East London,* CR8 1AJ.
Within weekly distance to Station.
Open: Jan to Nov
0181 660 3054 (also fax no)
Mr Stock
Rates fr: *£20.00*-**£20.00**.
Beds: 1D 1S 1T
Baths: 1 Private 1 Shared
(3)

The Nook, *12 Grasmere Road, Purley, Surrey,* CR8 1DU.
Edwardian private house.
Open: All Year (not Xmas)
0181 660 1742 Mrs Andrews
Rates fr: *£16.00*-**£15.00**.
Beds: 1D 2S **Baths:** 1 Shared

Rainham

National Grid Ref: TQ5282

Harbledown House, *150 Edwin Road, Rainham, Essex,* RM13.
Large detached house close to all amenities.
Open: All Year
01634 389266 Mrs Flynn
Rates fr: *£16.5016.50*.
Beds: 3D 1S
(10) (6)

Richmond

National Grid Ref: TQ1874

4 Church Road, *Richmond, Surrey,* TW9 2QA.
Open: All Year
0181 948 5852 Mrs Bird
Rates fr: *£23.00*-**£36.00**.
Beds: 2F
Baths: 2 Ensuite
Bright, spacious, all ensuite rooms in comfortable Victorian house. Two minutes' walk from Underground & station. Family of 3 - £56, of 4 - £66. Handy for Kew Gardens, Hampton Court, etc.

136 Sheen Road, *Richmond, Surrey,* TW9 1UR.
Great value, great service.
Open: All Year (not Xmas)
0181 948 5608
Mrs Bates
Rates fr: *£17.50*-**£25.00**.
Beds: 2T
Baths: 3 Shared
(11)

Rickmansworth

National Grid Ref: TQ0494

Duke of York

30 Hazelwood Road, *Croxley Green, Rickmansworth, Herts,* WD3 3EB.
Quiet, homely. Pleasant canalside location.
Open: All Year
01923 226666
Mrs Millward
Fax no: 01923 494137
Rates fr: *£18.00*-**£20.00**.
Beds: 3T 1S
Baths: 2 Shared
(2)

6 Swallow Close, *Nightingale Road, Rickmansworth, Herts,* WD3 2DZ.
Detached house in quiet cul-de-sac.
Open: All Year
Grades: ETB Listed
01923 720069
Mrs Childerhouse
Rates fr: *£18.00*-**£18.00**.
Beds: 1F 1D 2S
Baths: 2 Shared
(5) (4)

South Mimms

National Grid Ref: TL2201

The Black Swan, *62-64 Blanche Lane, South Mimms, Potters Bar, Herts,* EN6 3PD.
Former inn, also self-catering.
Open: All Year (not Xmas)
01707 644180 Mr Marsterson
Rates fr: *£17.50*-**£25.00**.
Beds: 1F 1D
Baths: 1 Private 1 Shared
(5)

Swanley

National Grid Ref: TQ5168

Alice Dene, *Beechenlea Lane, Swanley, Kent,* BR8 7PR.
Beautiful 1820 Georgian country house.
Open: All Year (not Xmas)
Grades: ETB 1 Cr, AA 4 Q
01322 664420 Mr Crush
Rates fr: *£20.00*-**£20.00**.
Beds: 1D 2T
(8) (4)

Tadworth

National Grid Ref: TQ2256

Hand in Hand

57 Ashurst Road, *Tadworth, Surrey,* KT20 5EY.
Congenial, modern, comfortable terraced house.
Open: All Year (not Xmas)
01737 812644 Mrs Cheal
Rates fr: **-£15.00**.
Beds: 1S
Baths: 1 Shared
(1)

Merrow, *Box Hill Road, Tadworth, Surrey,* KT20 7PS.
Modern comfortable chalet bungalow.
Open: All Year (not Xmas)
01737 842855
Mrs Durant
Fax no: 01731 842855
Rates fr: *£15.00*-**£18.00**.
Beds: 2D 1S
Baths: 1 Ensuite 1 Shared
(3)
National Grid Ref: TQ1573

Uxbridge

National Grid Ref: TQ0583

Cleveland Hotel, *4 Cleveland Road, Uxbridge, Middlesex,* UB8 2DW.
Large early Victorian detached property.
Open: All Year
01895 257618
Mrs Tindale
Rates fr: *£17.00*-**£22.00**.
Beds: 2F 3D 4T 5S
Baths: 4 Ensuite 5 Shared
(10`)

Wallington

National Grid Ref: TQ2964

Whispering Moon

17 Osmond Gardens, *Wallington, Surrey, SM6 8SX.*
London 11 miles, easy transport.
Open: All Year
0181 647 1943 Mrs Dixon
Rates fr: *£18.00.*
Beds: 1F 1T
Baths: 1 Private 1 Shared

Walton-on-Thames

National Grid Ref: TQ1066

The Swan

Beech Tree Lodge, *7 Rydens Avenue, Walton-on-Thames, Surrey, KT12 3JB.*
Large Edwardian private house, friendly, languages.
Open: All Year
Grades: ETB Listed
01932 242738 / 886667
Mrs Spiteri
Rates fr: *£17.00*-**£17.00**.
Beds: 1F 2T
Baths: 2 Shared
(6)

Oak Tree Lodge, *11 Hersham Road, Walton-on-Thames, Surrey, KT12 1LQ.*
Mock-Tudor family home.
Open: All Year
01932 221907 Mrs Hall
Rates fr: *£16.00*-**£17.00**.
Beds: 1F 1D
Baths: 1 Shared
(4)

Watford

National Grid Ref: TQ1097

The Hare, Duke of York

33 Courtlands Drive, *Watford, Herts, WD1 3HU.*
Near M25, M1 & A41.
Open: All Year
01923 220531 Mrs Troughton
Rates fr: *£16.00*-**£18.00**.
Beds: 2T **Baths:** 1 Shared
(3) (7)

30 Hazelwood Road, *Croxley Green, Rickmansworth, Watford, Herts, WD3 3EB.*
Quiet, homely. Pleasant canalside location.
Open: All Year
01923 226666 Mrs Millward
Fax no: 01923 494137
Rates fr: *£18.00*-**£20.00**.
Beds: 3T 1S **Baths:** 2 Shared
(2)

Wembley

National Grid Ref: TQ1785

J J Moon

Elm Hotel, *1 - 7 Elm Road, Wembley, Middlesex, HA9 7JA.*
Open: All Year (not Xmas)
Grades: ETB 2 Cr, Comm, RAC Listed
0181 902 1764 Mr Gosden
Fax no: 0181 903 8365
Rates fr: *£24.00*-**£35.00**.
Beds: 2F 10D 10T 5S
Baths: 24 Ensuite 1 Shared
(8)
Get into hot water with your wife! Jacuzzi jet spa baths in some doubles. Wembley Stadium, Arena & Conference Centre 1200 yds.

Wembley Park Guest House, *8 Forty Lane, Wembley, Middlesex, HA9 9EB.*
Large converted Georgian house.
Open: All Year
0181 904 6329
Mr **Rates fr:** *£20.00*-**£25.00**.
Beds: 3F 2D 1T 2S
Baths: 8 Shared
(11)

West Drayton

National Grid Ref: TQ0679

Elmcroft, *33 The Green, West Drayton, Middx, UB7 7PN.*
Twin C18th cottages - quiet.
Open: All Year
01895 442933 Mr & Mrs Nailard
Rates fr: *£12.50*-**£15.00**.
Beds: 1D 1T 2S
Baths: 2 Shared
(5) (2)

Yiewsley

National Grid Ref: TQ0680

70 Royal Lane, *Yiewsley, West Drayton, Middx, UB7 8DN.*
'Home from home', private house.
Open: All Year
Grades: ETB Listed, Approv
01895 447458 Mrs Gear
Rates fr: *£17.00*-**£19.00**.
Beds: 1T 1S
Baths: 1 Private, 1 Shared
(2)

The lowest **single** *rate is shown in* **bold.**

Norfolk

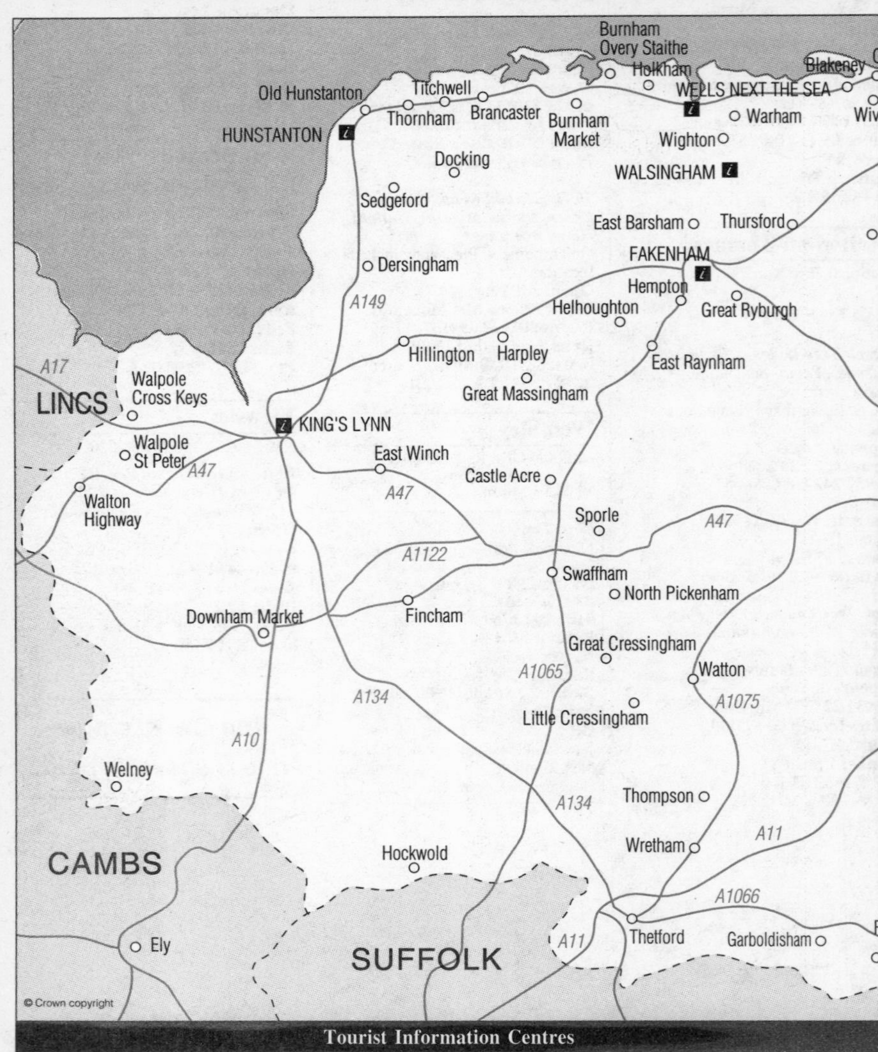

Tourist Information Centres

Bus Station, Prince of Wales Road, **Cromer**, Norfolk, NR27 9HS, 01263-512497, (Easter to Oct).

Meres Mouth, Mere Street, **Diss**, Norfolk, IP22 3AG, 01379-650523, (Easter to Oct).

Red Lion House, Market Place, **Fakenham**, Norfolk, NR21 9BY, 01328-851981, (Easter to Oct).

Marine Parade, **Great Yarmouth**, Norfolk, NR30 2EJ, 01493-842195, (Easter to Oct).

Town Hall, Hall Quay, **Great Yarmouth**, Norfolk, NR30 2PX, 01493-846345.

Town Hall, The Green, **Hunstanton**, Norfolk, PE36 5AH, 01485-532610.

The Old Gaol House, Saturday Market Place, **King's Lynn**, Norfolk, PE30 5DQ, 01553-763044.

Station Road, **Hoveton**, Norwich, Norfolk, NR12 8EU, 01603-782281, (Easter to Oct).

2a Station Road, **Mundesley**, Norwich, Norfolk, NR11 8JH, 01263-721070, (Easter to Oct).

The Guildhall, Gaol Hill, **Norwich**, Norfolk, NR2 1NF, 01603-666071.

The Staithe, **Ranworth**, Norwich , NR13 6HY, 01605 49 453, (Easter to Oct)

Station Approach, **Sheringham**, Norfolk, NR26 8RA, 01263-824329, (Easter to Oct).

Shirehall Museum, Common Place, Little Walsingham, **Walsingham**, Norfolk, NR22 6BP, 01328-820510, (Easter to Oct).

Staithe Street, **Wells-next-the-Sea**, Norfolk, NR23 1AN, 01328-710885.

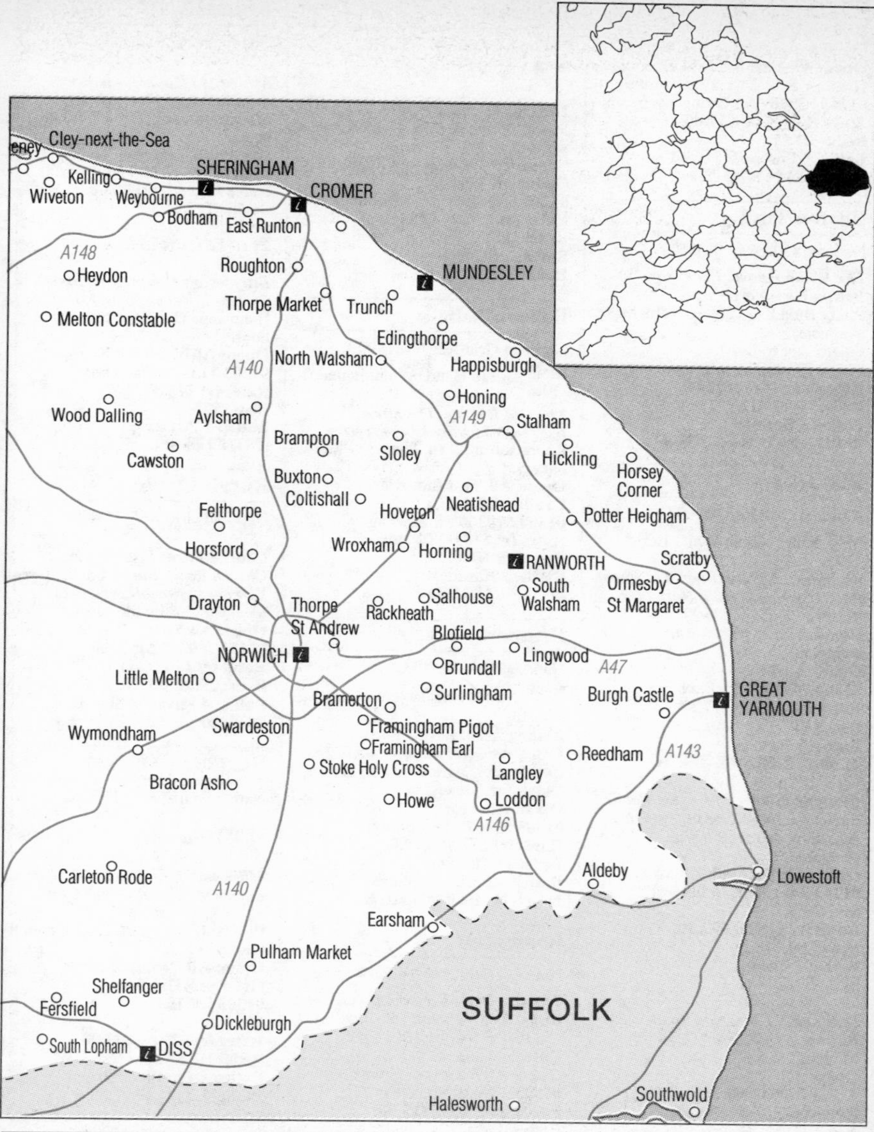

Aldeby

National Grid Ref: TM4493

Waveney Inn

The Old Vicarage, *Rectory Road, Aldeby, Beccles, Suffolk,* NR34 0BJ.
Spacious vicarage, large tranquil surroundings.
Open: May to Sep
01502 678229 Mr Butler
Rates fr: *£14.00*-**£14.00**.
Beds: 1F 3T
Baths: 1 Ensuite 2 Shared
(1) (5)

Aylsham

National Grid Ref: TG1927

Walpole Arms (Itteringham)

The Old Bank House, *3 Norwich Road, Aylsham, Norwich,* NR11 6BN.
Historic private bank, period features. **Open:** All Year
Grades: ETB 2 Cr, High Comm, AA 3 Q, Recomm
01263 733843 Mrs Parry
Rates fr: *£17.00*-**£20.00**.
Beds: 1F 1D 1T
Baths: 1 Ensuite 2 Shared
(3)

Birchdale, *Blickling Road, Aylsham, Norwich,* NR11 6ND.
Quiet house in conservation area.
Open: All Year (not Xmas)
01263 734827 Mrs Cross
Rates fr: *£16.00*-**£16.00**.
Beds: 1D 1T 1S
Baths: 1 Ensuite 1 Shared
(4)

The lowest **single** *rate is shown in* **bold.**

The Old Pump House, *Holman Road, Aylsham, Norwich, NR11 6BY.*
Creature comforts in 1750s home.
Open: All Year (not Xmas)
Grades: ETB 2 Cr, High Comm
01263 733789 Ms Stringer
Rates fr: *£17.00*-**£17.00**.
Beds: 3D 2T
Baths: 3 Ensuite 2 Shared

Barton Turf

National Grid Ref: TG3522

The White House, *Pennygate, Barton Turf, Norwich, NR12 8BG.*
Pretty Broadland cottage (dinghy available).
Open: Apr to Dec
01692 536057 Mr Morgan
Rates fr: *£18.00*-**£22.00**.
Beds: 1F 1T 1D
Baths: 3 Ensuite
(4)

Blakeney

National Grid Ref: TG0243

Kings Arms, White Horse

Springers, *55 New Road, Off Coast Road, Blakeney, Holt, Norfolk, NR25 7PA.*
Non-smoking, with warm welcome.
Open: All Year
01263 740103 Mrs Buckey
Rates fr: *£16.00*-**£17.50**.
Beds: 1T
Baths: 1 Ensuite
(6)

Bramble Lodge, *3 Morston Road, Blakeney, Holt, Norfolk, NR25 7PF.*
Accommodation of a high standard.
Open: All Year (not Xmas)
01263 740191 (also fax no)
Mrs Gray
Rates fr: *£18.00*-**£23.00**.
Beds: 1D 2T
Baths: 3 Ensuite
(3)

Dallinga, *71 Morston Road, Blakeney, Holt, Norfolk, NR25 7BD.*
Modern deluxe, ensuite.
Open: All Year
01263 740943 Mr & Mrs Ward
Rates fr: *£15.00*-**£20.00**.
Beds: 1D 1T
Baths: 2 Ensuite
(13) (6)

Blofield

National Grid Ref: TG3309

Pine Trees, *Holly Lane, Blofield, Norwich, NR13 4BY.*
Large, modern country house.
Open: All Year (not Xmas)
01603 713778 Mrs Eldred
Rates fr: *£15.00*-**£20.00**.
Beds: 1D 1T
Baths: 1 Private
(10)

Bodham

National Grid Ref: TG1240

The Wheatsheaf

The Old Foundry House, *The Street, Bodham, Holt, Norfolk, NR25 6NP.*
Converted 250-year-old foundry.
Open: All Year
01263 588449 Mr & Mrs Gimbrere
Rates fr: *£16.00*-**£18.00**.
Beds: 1D 1T
Baths: 1 Shared

Bracon Ash

National Grid Ref: TM1899

Bird in Hand (Wrenningham)

The Old Bakery, *The Street, Bracon Ash, Norwich, NR14 8EL.*
Characterful C18th former village bakery.
Open: All Year (not Xmas)
Grades: ETB 2 Cr
01508 570360 Mr Starling
Rates fr: *£18.00*-**£20.00**.
Beds: 1F 1D 1T
Baths: 3 Ensuite
(5)

Bramerton

National Grid Ref: TG2905

Woods End Tavern

Rolling Acre, *Woods End, Bramerton, Norwich, NR14 7ED.*
Comfortable period country house. Quiet, fine view.
Open: All Year
01508 538529 Mrs Barton
Rates fr: *£17.50*-**£19.00**.
Beds: 1F 1D
Baths: 1 Ensuite 1 Shared
(12) (6)

Brampton

National Grid Ref: TG2224

The Old Inn, *Marsham Road, Brampton, Norwich, NR10 5HN.*
Converted inn, walled garden. Quiet location.
Open: All Year (not Xmas)
01603 279438 Mrs Galer
Rates fr: *£15.00*-**£15.00**.
Beds: 1D 1T 1S
Baths: 1 Shared
(3)

Brancaster

National Grid Ref: TF7743

Barmstone House, *Brancaster, Kings Lynn, Norfolk, PE31 8AZ.*
Large 3-storey Victorian house.
Open: All Year (not Xmas)
01485 210501 Mrs Townshend
Rates fr: *£17.50*-**£20.00**.
Beds: 2D 1T 1S
Baths: 2 Shared
(3)

Brundall

National Grid Ref: TG3208

Ashlea, *30 Holmesdale Road, Brundall, Norwich, NR13 5LX.*
Modern house in Broadland village.
Open: All Year (not Xmas)
01603 714247 Mrs Solomon
Rates fr: *£16.00*-**£20.00**.
Beds: 1D 1T
Baths: 1 Shared
(7) (2)

Braydeston House, *The Street, Brundall, Norwich, NR13 5JY.*
Handsome Georgian country house.
Open: All Year (not Xmas)
01603 713123 Mrs Knox
Rates fr: *£18.50*.
Beds: 1T
Baths: 1 Private
(1)

Burgh Castle

National Grid Ref: TG4804

Church Farm Free House, *Church Road, Burgh Castle, Great Yarmouth, Norfolk, NR31 9QG.*
Ideal for touring the coast.
Open: All Year
01493 780251 Mr Snell
Rates fr: *£18.00*-**£18.00**.
Beds: 2F 2D 1T 1S
Baths: 4 Private 2 Shared
(600)

Burnham Market

National Grid Ref: TF8342

Hoste Arms

Millwood, *Herrings Lane, Burnham Market, Kings Lynn, Norfolk, PE31 8DW.*
Peaceful, luxurious, coastal country house.
Open: All Year (not Xmas)
Grades: ETB Listed
01328 730152
Mrs Leftley
Rates fr: *£20.00*-**£25.00**.
Beds: 1D 1T 1S
Baths: 1 Ensuite 1 Shared
(8) (8)

Burnham Overy

National Grid Ref: TF8442

Ostrich House, *Burnham Overy, Kings Lynn, Norfolk, PE31 8HU.*
300-year-old Listed end-of-terrace cottage.
Open: All Year (not Xmas)
Grades: ETB Listed
01328 738517
Mrs O'Connor
Rates fr: *£16.00*-**£16.00**.
Beds: 1D 1T 1S
Baths: 2 Shared
(3)

Burnham Overy Staithe

National Grid Ref: TF8444

***Domville Guest House,** Glebe Lane, Burnham Overy Staithe, Kings Lynn, Norfolk, PE31 8JQ.*
Quietly situated, family-run guest house.
Open: All Year (not Xmas)
Grades: ETB 1 Cr, Comm
01328 738298 Mr & Mrs Smith
Rates fr: *£17.00*-**£17.00**.
Beds: 2D 2T 4S
Baths: 2 Private 2 Shared
(6) (10)

Buxton

National Grid Ref: TG2322

***Birds Place Farm,** Back Lane, Buxton, Norwich, NR10 5HD.*
C17th picturesque farmhouse.
Open: All Year
Grades: ETB 2 Cr, Comm
01603 279585
Rates fr: *£22.00*-**£25.00**.
Beds: 2F 1S **Baths:** 2 Private
(5) (3)

Carleton Rode

National Grid Ref: TM1193

***Upgate Farm,** Carleton Rode, Norwich, NR16 1NJ.*
Comfortable farmhouse in rural Norfolk.
Open: All Year (not Xmas)
Grades: ETB Listed
01953 860300 Mr Wright
Rates fr: *£15.50*-**£15.50**.
Beds: 1D 1T **Baths:** 1 Shared
(2)

Castle Acre

National Grid Ref: TF8115

Ostrich Inn

***The Old Red Lion,** Bailey Street, Castle Acre, Kings Lynn, Norfolk, PE32 2AG.*
Exclusively wholefood; also self catering. Sleeps 20.
Open: All Year
01760 755557 Mrs Loughlin
Rates fr: *£12.50*-**£15.00**.
Beds: 2F 1D 2T **Baths:** 3 Shared
(9)

***Gemini House,** Pyes Lane, Castle Acre, Kings Lynn, Norfolk, PE32 2XB.*
Well-situated for all Norfolk sights.
Open: All Year
01760 755375 Mrs Clark
Rates fr: *£15.00*-**£15.00**.
Beds: 2D 2T **Baths:** 1 Private 2 Shared
(4)

***Willow Cottage,** Stocks Green, Castle Acre, Swaffham, Kings Lynn, Norfolk, PE32 2AE.*
Picturesque flint cottage, village green.
Open: Easter to Dec
01760 755551 Mrs Johnson
Rates fr: *£15.00*-**£18.00**.
Beds: 2D 2T **Baths:** 1 Shared

Cawston

National Grid Ref: TG1323

***Grey Gables Hotel,** Norwich Road, Cawston, Norwich, NR10 4EY.*
Open: All Year (not Xmas)
Grades: ETB 3 Cr, AA 1 St, RAC Listed
01603 871259 Mr Snaith
Rates fr: *£21.00*-**£21.00**.
Beds: 1F 4D 2T 2S
Baths: 7 Private 1 Shared
(15)
Former rectory in rural setting, convenient for Norwich, Coast, & Broads. Elegant candlelit dining-room serving home prepared food. Award-winning wine list. Log fires.

Cley-next-the-Sea

National Grid Ref: TG0544

George & Dragon

***Cley Windmill,** Cley-next-the-Sea, Holt, Norfolk, NR25 7NN.*
Open: All Year
01263 740209 (also fax no)
Mr Buisseret
Rates fr: *£33.00*-**£33.00**.
Beds: 5D 3T
Baths: 6 Private 1 Shared
(6)
Built in 1713, the Mill has been converted into a comfortable guest house with stunning views, and a licensed residential restaurant for dinners. Ideal for walkers & bird watchers.

***Marshlands,** High Street, Cley-next-the-Sea, Holt, Norfolk, NR25 7RB.*
Victorian old town hall house.
Open: All Year (not Xmas)
01263 740284 Mr & Mrs Kinsella
Rates fr: *£15.00*-**£25.00**.
Beds: 1D 2T
Baths: 2 Ensuite 1 Private
(5)

Coltishall

National Grid Ref: TG2720

Kings Head

***Broadgates,** 1 Wroxham Road, Coltishall, Norwich, NR12 7DU.*
Comfortable accommodation in Broadland village.
Open: All Year (not Xmas)
Grades: ETB Listed
01603 737598 Mrs Dack
Rates fr: *£19.50*-**£19.50**.
Beds: 2T 1S
Baths: 1 Ensuite 1 Shared
(8)

The lowest **single** *rate is shown in* **bold.**

***Kings Head,** Wroxham Road, Coltishall, Norwich, NR12 7EA.*
C17th public house by riverside.
Open: All Year
01603 737426
Ms Gardner
Rates fr: *£18.50*-**£18.50**.
Beds: 4D 2T
Baths: 4 Ensuite 1 Shared
(20)

Cromer

National Grid Ref: TG2142

Red Lion

***Cambridge House,** Sea Front, East Cliff, Cromer, Norfolk, NR27 9HD.*
Charming Victorian house overlooking sea.
Open: All Year
Grades: ETB 2 Cr, Comm
01263 512085 Mrs Wass
Rates fr: *£19.00*-**£19.00**.
Beds: 2F 1D 2S
Baths: 2 Ensuite 2 Shared
(5)

***The Pleasaunce,** Overstrand, Cromer, Norfolk, NR27 0PN.*
Christian holiday centre.
Open: All Year
01263 579212 Mrs Powell
Rates fr: *£16.00*-**£16.00**.
Beds: 12F 8D 10T 6S
Baths: 2 Private
(60)

***Crowmere Guest House,** 4 Vicarage Road, Cromer, Norfolk, NR27 9DQ.*
Large Victorian house near sea.
Open: All Year
Grades: ETB Listed, Comm
01263 513056
Ms Marriott
Rates fr: *£16.00*-**£18.00**.
Beds: 2F 3D 2T
Baths: 5 Private 1 Shared
(6)

***The Knoll Guest House,** 23 Alfred Road, Cromer, Norfolk, NR27 9AN.*
Licensed, family-run, near sea.
Open: All Year
01263 512753 Mrs Nuthall
Rates fr: *£16.00*-**£16.00**.
Beds: 2F 1D 2S
Baths: 1 Shared
(1)

Dersingham

National Grid Ref: TF6830

***Meadow Vale,** 63 Manor Road, Dersingham, Kings Lynn, Norfolk, PE31 6LH.*
Modern comfortable house, friendly atmosphere.
Open: Easter to Oct
01485 540769
Mr & Mrs Williams
Rates fr: *£14.0014.00*.
Beds: 1D 1T 1S
Baths: 1 Shared
(8) (4)

The White House, *44 Hunstanton Road, Dersingham, Kings Lynn, Norfolk,* PE31 6HQ.
Comfortable, warm welcome, good breakfast. **Open:** All Year
01485 541895 Ms Nightingale
Rates fr: *£15.50*-**£15.50**.
Beds: 2D 2T 1S
Baths: 1 Private 2 Shared
(5)

Dicklebrugh

National Grid Ref: TM1682

Old Barn, Half Moon, Crown

Low Brook Farm, *Semere Green Lane, Dickleburgh, Diss, Norfolk,* IP21 4NT.
C18th barn conversion. Peaceful setting. **Open:** All Year (not Xmas)
Grades: ETB 1 Cr, High Comm
01379 741265 (also fax no)
Mr Hill
Rates fr: *£20.00*-**£20.00**.
Beds: 1D 1T
(8) (4)

Diss

National Grid Ref: TM1180

Old Barn, The Half Moon, Crown

Low Brook Farm, *Semere Green Lane, Dickleburgh, Diss, Norfolk,* IP21 4NT.
Open: All Year (not Xmas)
01379 741265 (also fax no)
Mr Hill
Rates fr: *£20.00*-**£20.00**.
Beds: 1D 1T
(8) (4)
Peaceful setting near Norfolk/Suffolk attractions. C18th barn conversion. Spacious beamed rooms. Guest lounge. Local/home produce. Water garden, ample parking. High priority: Guests' comfort!

Hollies, *33 Croft Lane, Diss, Norfolk,* IP22 3NA.
Large comfortable twin: private bathroom. **Open:** All Year
Grades: ETB Listed
01379 652031 Mrs Robinson
Rates fr: *£16.00*-**£18.00**.
Beds: 1T **Baths:** 1 Private

The Strenneth, *Airfield Road, Fersfield, Diss, Norfolk,* IP22 2BP.
Open: All Year
Grades: ETB 2 Cr, Comm
01379 688182 Mr Webb
Fax no: 01379 688260
Rates fr: *£18.00*-**£25.00**.
Beds: 4D 2T 1S
Baths: 7 Private
(10)
Family-run, C17th house with a newer single storey courtyard wing. Executive and four poster, all ensuite. Licensed, pets welcome. Close Bressingham Gardens. Credit cards accepted.

Docking

National Grid Ref: TF7637

Haddin, *Ringstead Road, Docking, Kings Lynn, Norfolk,* PE31 8PL.
Dormer bungalow in large garden.
Open: All Year (not Xmas)
01485 518701 Mr Thomas
Rates fr: *£15.00*-**£15.00**.
Beds: 2T
Baths: 1 Shared
(3)

Downham Market

National Grid Ref: TF6103

Crown Hotel

Park House, *74 London Road, Downham Market, Norfolk,* PE38 9AT.
Welcoming 1833 farmhouse in town.
Open: All Year (not Xmas)
01366 387035 Mrs Johnson
Rates fr: *£14.00*-**£15.00**.
Beds: 1F 1D 1T
Baths: 1 Shared
(6)

The Dial House, *12 Railway Road, Downham Market, Norfolk,* PE38 9EB.
Comfortable C18th family home.
Open: All Year
Grades: ETB 3 Cr, Comm, AA 3 Q
01366 388358 Mrs Murray
Fax no: 01366 384844
Rates fr: *£16.00*-**£22.00**.
Beds: 1D 2T
Baths: 2 Ensuite 1 Shared
(6)

Drayton

National Grid Ref: TG1813

Red Lion

The Chestnuts, *27 Fakenham Road, Drayton, Norwich,* NR8 6PS.
High standard accommodation in bungalow.
Open: All Year
01603 868860 Mrs Howard
Rates fr: *£16.00*-**£16.00**.
Beds: 2D 1T
Baths: 1 Ensuite 1 Shared
(3) (10)

Earsham

National Grid Ref: TM3289

Park Farm, *Harleston Road, Earsham, Bungay, Norfolk,* NR35 2AQ.
Quiet, delightful, spacious Victorian farmhouse.
Open: All Year
Grades: ETB 2 Cr, High Comm, AA 3 Q
01986 892180 Mrs Watchorn
Rates fr: *£18.50*-**£23.00**.
Beds: 2D 1T
Baths: 3 Ensuite
(8)

East Barsham

National Grid Ref: TF9133

White Horse Inn, *Fakenham Road, East Barsham, Fakenham, Norfolk,* NR21 0LH.
Refurbished C17th country inn.
Open: All Year
01328 820645 (also fax no)
Mrs Baines
Rates fr: *£24.00*-**£30.00**.
Beds: 1F 3T
Baths: 3 Private
(50)

Fieldview, *West Barsham Road, East Barsham, Fakenham, Norfolk,* NR21 0AR.
Central, comfortable, modern flint house.
Open: All Year
01328 820083 Ms Marcus
Rates fr: *£19.00*-**£19.00**.
Beds: 2D 3T
Baths: 1 Ensuite 2 Shared
(7) (5)

East Raynham

National Grid Ref: TF8825

Hardlands, *East Raynham, Fakenham, Norfolk,* NR21 7EQ.
Comfortable private house in country.
Open: All Year (not Xmas)
Grades: ETB Listed, High Comm
01328 862567 Mrs Walpole
Rates fr: *£16.00*.
Beds: 1D 1T
Baths: 2 Shared
(10) (10)

East Runton

National Grid Ref: TG1942

Dalkeith, *Lower Green, East Runton, Cromer, Norfolk,* NR27 9PG.
Comfortable, friendly, family home.
Open: All Year (not Xmas)
01263 514803 Mr & Mrs Slater
Rates fr: *£16.50*-**£22.00**.
Beds: 2D 1T
Baths: 2 Shared
(5)

East Winch

National Grid Ref: TF6916

Carpenters Arms

Field Cottage, *Station Road, East Winch, Kings Lynn, Norfolk,* PE32 1NR.
Small cottage. Views overlooking village, fields.
Open: Easter to Oct
01553 841231 Miss Bass
Rates fr: *£13.00*-**£13.00**.
Beds: 2D 1S
Baths: 1 Shared
(5)

Edingthorpe

National Grid Ref: TG3232

***The Old Hall,** Edingthorpe, North Walsham, Norfolk, NR28 9TJ.*
Historic Elizabethan hall, candle-light dinners.
Open: All Year
Grades: ETB Listed, High Comm
01692 650189
Mrs Brooke-Lander
Rates fr: *£18.00*-**£18.00**.
Beds: 1F 1D 1T
Baths: 1 Ensuite 1 Private 1 Shared
(0) (10)

***Forest Edge,** Mill Road, Edingthorpe, North Walsham, Norfolk, NR28 9SJ.*
Imposing modern quiet country residence.
Open: All Year
01692 500350
Mr & Mrs Hoey
Rates fr: *£18.00*-**£25.00**.
Beds: 2D 1T
Baths: 3 Ensuite
(8) (10)

Felthorpe

National Grid Ref: TG1618

Marsham Arms, Ratcatchers

***Spinney Ridge,** Hall Lane, Felthorpe, Norwich, NR10 4BX.*
Open: All Year (not Xmas)
Grades: ETB Listed
01603 754833
Mr & Mrs Thompson
Rates fr: *£17.00*-**£15.00**.
Beds: 1F 1D 1T 1S
Baths: 2 Private 2 Shared
(5) (4)
Charactered, warm and friendly house in quiet setting, just off the A1149, centres us for Norwich, North Norfolk and the Broads. Convenient to recommended restaurants.

***Lodge Farmhouse,** The Street, Felthorpe, Norwich, NR10 4BY.*
Comfortable accommodation, friendly service.
Open: All Year (not Xmas)
01603 754896
Mrs Howe
Rates fr: *£14.00*-**£14.00**.
Beds: 1D 1T
(4)

***Flitcham Cottage,** Fir Covert Road, Felthorpe, Norwich, NR10 4DT.*
Well-appointed converted farm cottage.
Open: All Year (not Xmas)
Grades: ETB Listed, Comm
01603 867493
Mr Smith
Rates fr: *£15.00*-**£15.00**.
Beds: 2D 1T
Baths: 1 Shared
(9)

Fersfield

National Grid Ref: TM0683

***The Strenneth,** Airfield Road, Fersfield, Diss, Norfolk, IP22 2BP.*
Family-run, C17th house.
Open: All Year
Grades: ETB 2 Cr, Comm
01379 688182 Mr Webb
Fax no: 01379 688260
Rates fr: *£18.00*-**£25.00**.
Beds: 4D 2T 1S **Baths:** 7 Private
(10)

Fincham

National Grid Ref: TF6806

The Swan

***Rose Cottage,** Downham Road, Fincham, Kings Lynn, Norfolk, PE33 9HF.*
Comfortable, friendly, traditional Georgian house.
Open: All Year (not Xmas)
Grades: ETB , AA 3 Q
01366 347426
Mrs Vaughan Arbuckle
Rates fr: *£15.00*-**£17.00**.
Beds: 2T
Baths: 1 Private 1 Shared
(6)

Framingham Earl

National Grid Ref: TG2702

***Oakfield,** Yelverton Road, Framingham Earl, Norwich, NR14 7SD.*
Peaceful, superior accommodation, excellent breakfast.
Open: All Year (not Xmas)
Grades: ETB Listed, High Comm
01508 492605 Mrs Thompson
Rates fr: *£16.00*-**£17.00**.
Beds: 1D 1T 1S
Baths: 1 Private 1 Shared
(12) (4)

Framingham Pigot

National Grid Ref: TG2703

Old Feather's Restaurant

***The Old Rectory,** Rectory Lane, Framingham Pigot, Norwich, NR14 7QQ.*
Comfortable Victorian rectory, large garden.
Open: All Year (not Xmas)
01508 493082 Mrs Thurman
Rates fr: *£18.00*-**£18.00**.
Beds: 1F 1D 1T
Baths: 2 Ensuite 1 Shared
(6)

Garboldisham

National Grid Ref: TM0081

White Horse

***Ingleneuk Lodge,** Hopton Road, Garboldisham, Diss, Norfolk, IP22 2RQ.*
Modern home in peaceful surroundings.
Open: All Year (not Xmas)
Grades: ETB 3 Cr, Comm, AA 3 Q, RAC High Acclaim
01953 681541
Mr Boreham & Mrs B Fry
Rates fr: *£18.75*-**£23.00**.
Beds: 1F 2D 2T 2S
Baths: 6 Private 1 Shared
(20)

***Swan House Bed and Breakfast,** Hopton Road, Garboldisham, Diss, Norfolk, IP22 2RQ.*
Comfortable C17th former coaching house.
Open: All Year (not Xmas)
Grades: ETB Listed, Comm
01953 688221
Miss May and Eldridge
Rates fr: *£17.00*-**£22.00**.
Beds: 1D 1T 1S
Baths: 1 Shared
(12) (6)

Great Cressingham

National Grid Ref: TF8501

Windmill

***The Vines,** The Street, Great Cressingham, Thetford, Norfolk, IP25 6NL.*
Comfortable, friendly, C16th house.
Open: All Year (not Xmas)
01760 756303
Mrs Wymer
Rates fr: *£15.00*-**£15.00**.
Beds: 2D 1T
Baths: 1 Shared

Great Massingham

National Grid Ref: TF7922

Rose & Crown

***Bramble Cottage,** Station Road, Great Massingham, King's Lynn, Norfolk, PE32 2HW.*
Modern cottage, overlooking village green.
Open: All Year (not Xmas)
01485 520076
Mrs Leening
Rates fr: *£15.00*-**£15.00**.
Beds: 1D 1T 1S
Baths: 1 Private
(5) (3)

Great Ryburgh

National Grid Ref: TF9527

***Highfield Farm,** Great Ryburgh, Fakenham, Norfolk, NR21 7AL.*
Beautiful large farmhouse, peaceful location.
Open: All Year (not Xmas)
01328 829249
Mrs Savory
Rates fr: *£16.00*-**£21.00**.
Beds: 1D 2T
Baths: 1 Ensuite
(12) (10)

Always telephone to get directions to the B&B - you will save time!

Great Yarmouth

National Grid Ref: TG5207

Holland House, *13 Apsley Road, Great Yarmouth, Norfolk,* *NR30 2HG.*
Good food, minute from beach.
Open: All Year (not Xmas)
01493 859534
Mr & Mrs Simmons
Rates fr: *£10.00*-**£10.00**.
Beds: 2F 4D 1S
Baths: 1 Shared

Concorde Private Hotel, *84 North Denes Road, Great Yarmouth, Norfolk,* *NR30 4LW.*
Highly recommended family-run hotel.
Open: All Year
01493 843709
Mrs Sexton
Rates fr: *£10.00*-**£10.00**.
Beds: 4F 8D 2T
Baths: 8 Ensuite 2 Shared
(9)

Belvedere, *90 North Deves Road, Great Yarmouth, Norfolk,* *NR30 4LN.*
Large semi-detached good decoratively.
Open: All Year (not Xmas)
01493 844200
Mrs Holden
Rates fr: *£11.50*-**£11.50**.
Beds: 2F 5D 2T 1S
(2) (7)

Senglea Lodge, *7 Euston Road, Great Yarmouth, Norfolk,* *NR30 1DX.*
Family-run, comfortable guest house.
Open: All Year (not Xmas)
01493 859632
Mrs Formosa
Rates fr: *£12.00*-**£12.00**.
Beds: 2F 4D 1T
Baths: 4 Private 3 Shared

Beaumont House, *52 Wellesley Road, Great Yarmouth, Norfolk,* *NR30 1EX.*
Victorian pleasant area accessable amenities.
Open: June to Sept
01493 843957
Mrs Albone
Rates fr: *£15.00*-**£16.00**.
Beds: 3F 4D 1T 2S
Baths: 2 Shared
(8)

Happisburgh

National Grid Ref: TG3830

Cliff House Guest House, *And Tea Shop, Beach Road, Happisburgh, Norwich,* *NR12 0PP.*
Tea shop and guesthouse. Home baking.
Open: All Year (not Xmas)
01692 650775 Ms Wrightson
Rates fr: *£14.50*-**£14.50**.
Beds: 1D 1T 2S
Baths: 2 Shared
(4)

Harpley

National Grid Ref: TF7825

Rose & Crown

Manor Farm Barn, *11 Rudham Road, Harpley, Kings Lynn, Norfolk,* *PE31 6TJ.*
Lovely converted barn, quiet, picturesque.
Open: All Year (not Xmas)
Grades: ETB Listed
01485 520708 Mrs Thomas
Rates fr: *£18.00*-**£18.00**.
Beds: 2D 1T
Baths: 1 Ensuite 2 Shared
(0) (4)

Helhoughton

National Grid Ref: TF8626

Greenlea, *Raynham Road, Helhoughton, Fakenham, Norfolk,* *NR21 7BH.*
Large comfortable bungalow - rural setting.
Open: All Year
01485 528547 Mrs Curtis
Rates fr: *£17.00*-**£22.00**.
Beds: 2D 1T
Baths: 2 Shared
(5)

Hempton

National Grid Ref: TF9129

Yew Tree House, *2 East View, Hempton, Fakenham, Norfolk,* *NR21 7LW.*
Modern comfortable friendly accommodation.
Open: All Year
01328 851450 Mr Beales
Rates fr: *£14.00*-**£14.00**.
Beds: 2F 1D 1T 1S
Baths: 2 Shared
(5)

Heydon

National Grid Ref: TG1137

Cropton Hall, *Heydon, Norwich,* *NR11 6RX.*
Jacobean country hall. Quiet location.
Open: All Year
01263 587869 Mrs Easy
Rates fr: *£13.95*-**£13.95**.
Beds: 3F 2D 2T 1S
Baths: 8 Ensuite
(20)

Hickling

National Grid Ref: TG4123

Greyhound

Paddock Cottage, *Staithe Road, Hickling, Norwich,* *NR12 0YJ.*
Comfortable modern cottage, quiet location.
Open: All Year (not Xmas)
01692 598259 Mrs Parry
Rates fr: *£16.00*-**£17.00**.
Beds: 1F 1D 1T
Baths: 1 Ensuite 2 Private
(4)

Hillington

National Grid Ref: TF7125

Seven Folks Arms

Gatton Waters, *Hillington, Sandringham, Kings Lynn, Norfolk,* *PE31 6BJ.*
Open: Easter to Oct
01485 600643
Mr & Mrs Donaldson
Rates fr: *£15.00*-**£18.00**.
Beds: 1D 1T
Baths: 1 Shared
Converted Norfolk barn set in 24 acres. Bedrooms overlooking private lake (coarse fishing). Sandringham House 2.5 miles. Norfolk Coast 20 mins. Evening meal in high season.

Hockwold

National Grid Ref: TL7388

New Inn, Red Lion

Junipers, *18 South Street, Hockwold, Thetford, Norfolk,* *IP26 4JG.*
Spacious bungalow in quiet village.
Open: All Year
01842 827370 Mrs Waddington
Rates fr: *£17.50*-**£17.50**.
Beds: 2T 1S
Baths: 2 Shared
(5)

Holkham

National Grid Ref: TF8943

Victoria Hotel, *Holkham, Wells-next-the-Sea, Norfolk,* *NR23 1RG.*
Comfortable Victorian family-run hotel.
Open: All Year (not Xmas)
01328 710469 Mr Hoskins
Rates fr: *£25.00*-**£27.50**.
Beds: 4D 2T 1S
Baths: 7 Private
(50)

The lowest **single** *rate is shown in* **bold.**

Honing

National Grid Ref: TG3227

Ferry Pub

Chandlers, *Honing, North Walsham, Norfolk, NR28 9QW.*
Large, Victorian country house.
Open: All Year (not Xmas)
01692 536504 Mr White
Rates fr: *£14.00*-**£14.00**.
Beds: 1F 1T **Baths:** 1 Shared
(3)

Horning

National Grid Ref: TG3417

Keppelgate, *Upper Street, Horning, Norwich, NR12 8NG.*
Open countryside near Broads coast.
Open: All Year (not Xmas)
01692 630610 Mrs Freeman
Rates fr: *£15.00*-**£18.00**.
Beds: 1F 1D 1T
Baths: 1 Ensuite 1 Shared
(3) (4)

Horsey Corner

National Grid Ref: TG4523

The Old Chapel, *Horsey Corner, Norfolk, NR29 4EH.*
Converted chapel in rural splendour! **Open:** All Year
Grades: ETB Listed, Comm
01493 393498 Miss Webster
Rates fr: *£13.00*-**£19.00**.
Beds: 1F 1D 1T
Baths: 1 Ensuite 1 Shared
(4)

Horsford

National Grid Ref: TG1916

The Yeast, Feast Inn

Church Farm Guest House, *Church Street, Horsford, Norwich, NR10 3DB.*
Modern comfortable farmhouse, large garden.
Open: All Year
Grades: ETB 2 Cr, Comm, AA 3 Q
01603 898020 Mrs Hinchley
Fax no: 01603 891649
Rates fr: *£18.00*-**£20.00**.
Beds: 2F 3D
Baths: 5 Private 1 Shared
(20)

Hoveton

National Grid Ref: TG3018

Kings Head

The Vineries, *72 Stalham Road, Hoveton, Norwich, NR12 8DU.*
Private annexe, own living room.
Open: All Year
01603 782514 Mrs Meacock
Rates fr: *£19.50*-**£25.00**.
Beds: 1D
Baths: 1 Private
(2)

Howe

National Grid Ref: TG2700

Wildebeast Arms

Church Farm House, *Howe, Norwich, NR15 1HD.*
Peaceful C16th farmhouse 6 miles Norwich.
Open: All Year
Grades: ETB 2 Cr
01508 550565 Ms Michie
Rates fr: *£18.00*-**£18.00**.
Beds: 2D 1T
Baths: 1 Ensuite 1 Private
(6)

Hunstanton

National Grid Ref: TF6740

Ancient Mariner Inn

Kiama Cottage, *23 Austin Street, Hunstanton, Norfolk, PE36 6AN.*
Friendly small family guest house.
Open: Easter to Oct
Grades: ETB 2 Cr, Comm
01485 533615 Mr & Mrs Flowerdew
Rates fr: *£16.00*-**£19.00**.
Beds: 1F 2D 1T
Baths: 4 Private
(1)

Caltofts, *15 Austin Street, Hunstanton, Norfolk, PE36 6AJ.*
Family-run guest house.
Open: All Year
01485 533759 Mr & Mrs Vass
Rates fr: *£15.00*-**£15.00**.
Beds: 2F 2D 1T 1S
Baths: 2 Private 1 Shared
(3)

Burleigh Hotel, *7 Cliff Terrace, Hunstanton, Norfolk, PE36 6DY.*
'Home-from-home', friendly atmosphere.
Open: All Year
Grades: ETB 3 Cr, Comm
01485 533080 Mr & Mrs Abos
Rates fr: *£21.00*-**£23.00**.
Beds: 4F 4D 2T 1S
Baths: 9 Ensuite 2 Private
(5)

Sutton House Hotel, *24 Northgate, Hunstanton, Norfolk, PE36 6AP.*
Edwardian house near town/sea.
Open: All Year
Grades: AA Listed, 3 Q
01485 532552 (also fax no)
Mr Emsden
Rates fr: *£20.00*-**£25.00**.
Beds: 2F 4D 2T
Baths: 8 Private
(1) (6)

Deepdene Hotel & Leisure Club, *29 Avenue Road, Hunstanton, Norfolk, PE36 5BW.*
Large Victorian house.
Open: All Year
01485 532460 Mrs Brunt
Rates fr: *£25.00*-**£25.00**.
Beds: 3F 3D 3S **Baths:** 1 Private
(6)

Kelling

National Grid Ref: TG0942

The Pheasant Hotel, *Weybourne Road (A 149), Kelling, Holt, Norfolk, NR25 7EG.*
Outstanding value, friendly country hotel.
Open: All Year
01263 588382 Mr Percival
Rates fr: *£22.00*-**£28.00**.
Beds: 1F 15D 13T
Baths: 29 Private
(10) (80)

King's Lynn

National Grid Ref: TF6120

Fairlight Lodge, *79 Goodwins Road, King's Lynn, Norfolk, PE30 5PE.*
Lovely Victorian home, warm welcome.
Open: All Year (not Xmas)
Grades: ETB 2 Cr, High Comm, AA 4 Q
01553 762234
Mrs Rowe
Fax no: 01553 770280
Rates fr: *£16.00*-**£20.00**.
Beds: 2D 3T 2S
Baths: 4 Ensuite 2 Shared
(6)

Guanock Hotel, *Southgates, London Road, King's Lynn, Norfolk, PE30 5JG.*
Adjacent to historic Southgates.
Open: All Year
Grades: AA Listed, RAC Listed
01553 772959 (also fax no)
Mr Parchment
Rates fr: *£17.00*-**£21.00**.
Beds: 5F 4D 3T 5S
Baths: 5 Shared
(1) (12)

Maranatha Guest House, *115 Gaywood Road, King's Lynn, Norfolk, PE30 2PU.*
Large Victorian guesthouse with garden, parking.
Open: All Year
Grades: ETB 2 Cr, Approv, AA 2 Q, RAC Listed
01553 774596
Mr Bastone
Rates fr: *£14.00*-**£17.00**.
Beds: 2F 2D 2T 3S
Baths: 2 Ensuite 1 Private
(8)

Havana Guest House, *117 Gaywood Road, King's Lynn, Norfolk, PE30 2PU.*
Large comfortable Victorian house.
Open: All Year (not Xmas)
Grades: ETB 2 Cr, Comm, AA 3 Q, Recomm, RAC Acclaim
01553 772 331
Mr & Mrs Breed
Rates fr: *£15.00*-**£17.00**.
Beds: 1F 2D 3T 1S
Baths: 4 Private 1 Shared
(2) (8)

Langley

National Grid Ref: TG3601

Staithe Farm, *Langley, Loddon, Norwich, NR14 6AD.*
C16th farmhoue. Country/river views.
Open: All Year (not Xmas)
01508 528518 Mrs Baird
Rates fr: *£16.50*-**£16.50**.
Beds: 1F 1D 1S
Baths: 1 Shared
(3)

Lingwood

National Grid Ref: TG3608

The Station House, *Station Road, Lingwood, Norwich, NR13 4AZ.*
Peaceful, restored Victorian station house.
Open: All Year
01603 715872 Mrs Meo
Rates fr: *£14.00*-**£14.00**.
Beds: 1D 2T
Baths: 1 Shared
(6)

Little Cressingham

National Grid Ref: TF8700

White Horse Inn

Sycamore House, *Little Cressingham, Thetford, Norfolk, IP25 6NE.*
Large modern family house.
Open: All Year
01953 881887 Mrs Wittridge
Rates fr: *£16.00*-**£17.00**.
Beds: 2D 1T 1S
Baths: 1 Ensuite 1 Private 1 Shared
(8)

Little Melton

National Grid Ref: TG1606

Kings Head

The Old Rectory, *Watton Road, Little Melton, Norwich, NR9 3PB.*
Victorian country house in grounds.
Open: All Year (not Xmas)
Grades: ETB 2 Cr, Deluxe
01603 812121 Mr Turner
Fax no: 01603 812521
Rates fr: *£26.00*-**£38.00**.
Beds: 3D
Baths: 2 Ensuite 1 Private
(10) (10)

Loddon

National Grid Ref: TM3698

Mornington House, *33 Church Plain, Loddon, Norwich, NR14 6EX.*
Delightful C16th house in town centre.
Open: All Year (not Xmas)
01508 528572 Mrs Earp
Rates fr: *£16.00*-**£20.00**.
Beds: 1D 1T
Baths: 1 Shared
(2)

Melton Constable

National Grid Ref: TG0433

Burgh Parva Hall, *Melton Constable, Norfolk, NR24 2PU.*
Listed C16th farmhouse, large bedrooms.
Open: All Year
01263 860797 Mrs Heal
Rates fr: *£17.00*-**£17.00**.
Beds: 1D 1T
Baths: 1 Shared
(0) (2)

Mundesley

National Grid Ref: TG3136

Overcliff Lodge, *46 Cromer Road, Mundesley, Norwich, NR11 8DB.*
Large Victorian guest house.
Open: All Year
Grades: ETB 2 Cr, Comm
01263 720016 (also fax no)
Mrs Gilburt
Rates fr: *£17.00*-**£15.00**.
Beds: 3D 2T 2S
Baths: 4 Private 1 Shared
(8) (7)

Neatishead

National Grid Ref: TG3420

White Horse, Barton Angler

Regency Guest House, *The Street, Neatishead, Norwich, NR12 8AD.*
C18th house, serves generous breakfasts. **Open:** All Year
Grades: ETB 2 Cr, Comm, AA 3 Q, Recomm
01692 630233 Mrs Wrigley
Rates fr: *£19.50*-**£20.00**.
Beds: 1F 2D 2T
Baths: 3 Private 2 Shared
(8)

White Horse Inn, *The Street, Neatishead, Norwich, NR12 8AD.*
Broadland village pub.
Open: All Year (not Xmas)
01692 630828 Mr Potts
Rates fr: *£17.50*-**£17.50**.
Beds: 2T **Baths:** 1 Shared
(20)

The Rowans, *Hollygrove Farm, School Road, Neatishead, Norwich, NR12 8XW.*
Attractive converted Norfolk barn.
Open: All Year (not Xmas)
01692 631475 Mrs Angel
Rates fr: *£20.00*-**£25.00**.
Beds: 1D 1T **Baths:** 1 Shared
(2)

North Pickenham

National Grid Ref: TF8606

Riverside House, *Meadow Lane, North Pickenham, Swaffham, Norfolk, PE37 8LE.*
Flintstone cottage by River Wissey.
Open: Easter to Sep
01760 440219 Mrs Norris
Rates fr: *£15.00*-**£15.00**.
Beds: 2T

North Walsham

National Grid Ref: TG2830

Beechwood Hotel

Green Ridges, *104 Cromer Road, North Walsham, Norfolk, NR28 0HE.*
Clean, friendly, modern comfortable accommodation.
Open: All Year (not Xmas)
01692 402448 Mrs Mitchell
Rates fr: *£17.00*-**£18.00**.
Beds: 1D 1T
Baths: 1 Ensuite 1 Shared
(5)

Norwich

National Grid Ref: TG2308

The Pickwick, Kings Head, Bawburgh, Falcon

Chiltern House, *2 Trafford Road, Norwich, NR1 2QW.*
Open: All Year
Grades: ETB Listed
01603 663033
Mrs Harrison
Rates fr: *£16.50*-**£16.50**.
Beds: 1F 1D 5S
Baths: 1 Ensuite 1 Shared
Good home cooking. 5 minutes city centre and bus station. All rooms have colour TV and tea/coffee facilities. Celia and Ken Harrison welcome you all year round.

The Old Rectory, *Watton Road, Little Melton, Norwich, NR9 3PB.*
Victorian country house in grounds.
Open: All Year (not Xmas)
Grades: ETB 2 Cr, Deluxe
01603 812121
Mr Turner
Fax no: 01603 812521
Rates fr: *£26.00*-**£38.00**.
Beds: 3D
Baths: 2 Ensuite 1 Private
(10) (10)

Trebeigh House, *16 Brabazon Road, Hellesdon, Norwich, NR6 6SY.*
Friendly private house. Non-smoking.
Open: All Year (not Xmas)
01603 429056 Mrs Jope
Fax no: 01603 414247
Rates fr: *£15.00*-**£17.00**.
Beds: 1D 1T
Baths: 1 Shared
(2)

Alpha Hotel, *82 Unthank Road, Norwich, NR2 2RW.*
Comfortable Victorian rectory with character.
Open: All Year (not Xmas)
Grades: ETB 2 Cr
01603 621105 (also fax no)
Mr Downton
Rates fr: *£20.00*-**£22.00**.
Beds: 6D 6T 9S
Baths: 10 Ensuite 4 Shared
(10) (16)

Edmar Lodge, *64 Earlham Road, Norwich, NR2 3DF.*
City guest house with parking.
Open: All Year
Grades: ETB 2 Cr, Comm
01603 615599 Mrs Lovatt
Fax no: 01603 632977
Rates fr: *£16.50*-**£23.00**.
Beds: 2F 1D 1T 1S
Baths: 3 Private 2 Shared
(6)

Old Hunstanton

National Grid Ref: TF6842

Lakeside, *Waterworks Road, Old Hunstanton, Norfolk, PE36 6JE.*
Converted waterworks, overlooking private lake.
Open: All Year
Grades: ETB 3 Cr
01485 533763 Mr Diamant
Rates fr: *£18.00*-**£17.50**.
Beds: 3D 1T 2S
Baths: 4 Private 1 Shared
(13) (10)

Ormesby St Margaret

National Grid Ref: TG4915

Grange Hotel & Freehouse

The Grange Hotel & Freehouse, *Ormesby St Margaret, Great Yarmouth, Norfolk, NR29 3QG.*
Listed Georgian property.
Open: All Year
01493 731877 Mr Smith
Rates fr: *£22.50*-**£32.50**.
Beds: 3F 4D
Baths: 7 Private

Potter Heigham

National Grid Ref: TG4119

Falgate

Red Roof Farmhouse, *Ludham Road, Potter Heigham, Great Yarmouth, Norfolk, NR29 5NB.*
Modern, friendly, comfortable centrally-heated farmhouse.
Open: All Year
01692 670604 Mrs Playford
Fax no: 01692 670065
Rates fr: *£15.00*-**£20.00**.
Beds: 1F 1D 1T
Baths: 1 Shared
(10)

Pulham Market

National Grid Ref: TM1986

The Old Bakery, *Church Walk, Pulham Market, Diss, Norfolk, IP21 4SJ.*
Listed oak-beamed C16th house.
Open: All Year
Grades: ETB 2 Cr, High Comm
01379 676492 Mr Croft
Rates fr: *£20.00*-**£35.00**.
Beds: 1F 1D 1T
Baths: 3 Private
(3)

Rackheath

National Grid Ref: NG2814

Green Man

Barn Court, *Back Lane, Rackheath, Norwich, NR13 6NN.*
Traditional Norfolk barn conversion.
Open: All Year (not Xmas)
Grades: ETB Listed, Approv
01603 782536 (also fax no)
Mrs Simpson
Rates fr: *£17.00*-**£17.00**.
Beds: 2D 1T
Baths: 1 Ensuite 2 Shared
(3)

Manor Barn House, *Back Lane, Rackheath, Norwich, NR13 6NN.*
Traditional C17th Norfolk barn, exposed beams.
Open: All Year
Grades: ETB 2 Cr, Comm
01603 783543
Mrs Lebbell
Rates fr: *£17.00*-**£18.00**.
Beds: 3D 2T 1S
Baths: 5 Ensuite 1 Private
(3) (6)

Reedham

National Grid Ref: TG4201

Railway Tavern, Ferry Inn

The Railway Tavern, *17 The Havaker, Reedham, Norwich, NR13 3HG.*
Norfolk Broads - free house - CAMRA.
Open: All Year
Grades: ETB Listed, Comm
01493 700340 (also fax no)
Mrs Swan
Rates fr: *£25.00*-**£30.00**.
Beds: 1F 1D 1T
Baths: 3 Ensuite
(8)

Briars, *Riverside, Reedham, Norwich, NR13 3TF.*
Riverside location with fabulous views.
Open: All Year (not Xmas)
Grades: ETB 2 Cr, AA 3 Q, Recomm
01493 700054 (also fax no)
Mr Monk
Rates fr: *£22.50*-**£30.00**.
Beds: 3D
Baths: 3 Ensuite
(6)

'The Old Post Office', *26 The Hills, Reedham, Norwich, NR13 3AR.*
Self-contained converted village post office.
Open: All Year
01493 701262
Mrs Blanche
Rates fr: *£20.00*-**£25.00**.
Beds: 1D
Baths: 1 Ensuite

Roughton

National Grid Ref: TG2137

New Inn

Chalden Cottage, *Felbrigg Road, Roughton, Norwich, NR11 8PA.*
Homely old cottage, lovely gardens.
Open: All Year (not Xmas)
01263 513353 Mrs Varden
Rates fr: *£15.00*-**£20.00**.
Beds: 2D
Baths: 1 Shared
(12) (4)

Salhouse

National Grid Ref: TG3114

Bell Inn

Brooksbank, *Lower Street, Salhouse, Norwich, NR13 6RW.*
C18th house in heart of Broads.
Open: All Year
Grades: ETB 2 Cr, Comm
01603 720420 Mr & Mrs Coe
Rates fr: *£17.00*-**£20.00**.
Beds: 2D 1T
Baths: 3 Private
(4)

Scratby

National Grid Ref: TG5015

Grove Lodge, *18 The Promenade, Scratby, Great Yarmouth, Norfolk, NR29 3PA.*
Olde worlde decorated period bungalow.
Open: All Year (not Xmas)
01493 731950 (also fax no)
Mr Walker
Rates fr: *£11.00*-**£15.00**.
Beds: 1F 2D
Baths: 2 Shared
(5)

Sedgeford

National Grid Ref: TF7136

King William

Dove Hill Cottage, *Cole Green, Sedgeford, Hunstanton, Norfolk, PE36 5LS.*
Family house in conservation area.
Open: All Year (not Xmas)
01485 571642 Mrs Lyle
Rates fr: *£16.00*-**£16.00**.
Beds: 1F 1T
Baths: 1 Shared
(3) (4)

All rates are subject to alteration at the owners' discretion.

Shelfanger

National Grid Ref: TM1083

Shelfanger Hall, *Shelfanger, Diss, Norfolk, IP22 2DE.*
C16th moated farmhouse, peaceful surroundings.
Open: Mar to Oct
01379 642094 Mrs Butler
Rates fr: *£18.00*-**£20.00**.
Beds: 1F 1D 1T **Baths:** 3 Private
(9) (10)

Sheringham

National Grid Ref: TG1543

Red Lion, Crown, Two Lifeboats

Holly Cottage, *14a The Rise, Sheringham, Norfolk, NR26 8QB.*
Sea view, warm welcome, beamed cottage..
Open: All Year (not Xmas)
01263 822807 Mrs Perkins
Rates fr: *£15.00*-**£18.00**.
Beds: 2F 1D
Baths: 1 Ensuite 2 Shared
(3)

The Bay-Leaf Guest House, *10 St Peters Road, Sheringham, Norfolk, NR26 8QY.*
Charming Victorian licensed guesthouse. **Open:** All Year
Grades: ETB 1 Cr, Comm
01263 823779 Mr Pigott
Rates fr: *£17.00*-**£17.00**.
Beds: 4F 1D 2T
Baths: 7 Ensuite
(4)

Beacon Hotel, *1 Nelson Road, Sheringham, Norfolk, NR26 8BT.*
Quiet hotel near the sea.
Open: Easter to Oct
Grades: ETB 2 Cr
01263 822019 Mr Gausden
Rates fr: *£19.00*-**£19.00**.
Beds: 2D 2T 2S
Baths: 3 Ensuite 1 Private 2 Shared
(5)

Camberley Guest House, *62 Cliff Road, Sheringham, Norfolk, NR26 8BJ.*
Comfortable spacious, ideally situated, quiet.
Open: All Year (not Xmas)
Grades: ETB 2 Cr, Comm
01263 823101 Mr & Mrs Simmons
Rates fr: *£17.00*-**£17.00**.
Beds: 2F 4D 2T
Baths: 6 Private
(8)

The Old Vicarage, *Sheringham, Norfolk, NR26 8NH.*
Attractive turn-of-century house. Bed-sitting rooms. Lovely pine staircase.
Open: All Year (not Xmas)
01263 822627 Mrs O'Connor
Rates fr: *£21.00*.
Beds: 1F 1D 1T **Baths:** 3 Ensuite
(5)

Pay B&Bs by cash or cheque. Be prepared to pay up front for one night stays.

Beeston Hills Lodge, *64 Cliff Road, Sheringham, Norfolk, NR26 8BJ.*
Edwardian lodge, superb sea views.
01263 825936 Ms Rowan
Fax no: 01263 821900
Rates fr: *£16.50*-**£24.00**.
Beds: 1F 1D 1S
Baths: 1 Private 1 Shared
(5)

The Birches, *27 Holway Road, Sheringham, Norfolk, NR26 8HW.*
Late Victorian private house.
Open: Easter to Oct
01263 823550 Ms Pearce
Rates fr: *£20.00*-**£25.00**.
Beds: 1D 1T
Baths: 2 Ensuite
(12) (2)

Sloley

National Grid Ref: TG2924

Crown

Sloley Farm, *High Street, Sloley, Norwich, NR12 8HJ.*
Comfortable farmhouse on working farm.
Open: All Year (not Xmas/New Year)
Grades: ETB 2 Cr, Comm
01692 536281 Mrs Jones
Fax no: 01692 535162
Rates fr: *£17.50*-**£17.50**.
Beds: 1F 1D 1S
Baths: 1 Ensuite 1 Shared
(4) (3)

Cubitt Cottage, *Low Street, Sloley, Norwich, NR12 8HD.*
Comfortable, modernised C19th cottage. **Open:** All Year
01692 538295 Mrs Foulkes
Rates fr: *£20.00*-**£23.00**.
Beds: 3T
Baths: 2 Private 1 Shared

South Lopham

National Grid Ref: TM0481

Malting Farm, *Blo Norton Road, South Lopham, Diss, Norfolk, IP22 2HT.*
Dairy farm. Patchwork & quilting.
Open: All Year (not Xmas)
Grades: ETB 2 Cr, Comm
01379 687201 Mrs Huggings
Rates fr: *£17.00*-**£25.00**.
Beds: 2D 1T
Baths: 1 Ensuite 1 Shared

South Walsham

National Grid Ref: TG3613

Ship Inn, King's Arms

Old Hall Farm, *South Walsham, Norwich, NR13 6DT.*
Thatched farmhouse in Broadland village.
Open: Easter to Oct
Grades: ETB 2 Cr
01603 270271 Mrs Dewing
Rates fr: *£15.00*-**£20.00**.
Beds: 2D 1T
Baths: 1 Ensuite 2 Shared
(4)

Sporle

National Grid Ref: TF8411

Cambridge Cottage, *Love Lane, Sporle, Kings Lynn, Norfolk, PE32 2EP.*
Quiet country cottage.
Open: All Year
01760 723718 Mr & Mrs Anderson
Rates fr: *£15.00*-**£15.00**.
Beds: 2T
Baths: 1 Ensuite

Corfield House, *Sporle, Swaffham, Norfolk, PE32 2EA.*
Family-run country guest house.
Open: Apr to Dec
Grades: ETB 3 Cr, High Comm, AA 4 Q, Select
01760 723636 Mr & Mrs Hickey
Rates fr: *£18.50*-**£23.00**.
Beds: 2D 2T 1S
Baths: 5 Private

Stalham

National Grid Ref: TG3725

The Old Surgery, *137 High Street, Stalham, Norwich, NR12 9BB.*
Georgian private house.
Open: All Year (not Xmas)
01692 581248
Mrs Durrell Walsh
Rates fr: *£18.00*-**£18.00**.
Beds: 1D 1T 1S
Baths: 1 Private 1 Shared
(3)

Stoke Holy Cross

National Grid Ref: TG2301

Salamanca Farm Guest House, *Stoke Holy Cross, Norwich, NR14 8QJ.*
Real experience of English hospitality.
Open: All Year (not Xmas/New Year)
01508 492322 Mrs Harrold
Rates fr: *£18.00*-**£20.00**.
Beds: 3D 1T
Baths: 3 Ensuite 1 Private
(6) (10)

Surlingham

National Grid Ref: TG3106

Goldham Hall

***The Hermitage,** Chapel Loke, Surlingham, Norwich, NR14 7AQ.*
Peaceful C18th delightful country home.
Open: All Year (not Xmas)
01508 538431 Mr Pinder
Rates fr: *£16.00*-**£16.00**.
Beds: 1D 1T 1S
Baths: 1 Ensuite 1 Shared
(12) (8)

Swaffham

National Grid Ref: TF8109

Red Lion, Horse & Groom, George Hotel

***Purbeck House,** Whitsands Road, Swaffham, Norfolk, PE37 7BJ.*
Comfortable, family-run guest house.
Open: All Year (not Xmas)
01760 721805 / 725345
Mrs Webster
Rates fr: *£16.00*-**£16.00**.
Beds: 2F 2T 2S
Baths: 1 Private 2 Shared
(3)

***Hill View,** 15 Norwich Road, Swaffham, Norfolk, PE37 8DF.*
Large comfortable house, warm welcome.
Open: All Year (not Xmas)
01760 723306 Mrs Johnstone
Rates fr: *£14.00*-**£14.00**.
Beds: 1D 2T 1S
Baths: 1 Shared
(8)

Swardeston

National Grid Ref: TG2002

King's Head

***Gavell House,** Swardeston, Norwich, NR14 8DZ.*
Historic small Georgian farmhouse.
Open: All Year
Grades: ETB Listed
01508 578195 Mrs Harris
Rates fr: *£15.00*-**£10.00**.
Beds: 1D 1T 1S
Baths: 1 Private 1 Shared
(10)

Thetford

National Grid Ref: TL8783

Black Horse, Anchor Hotel

***3 Magdalen Street,** Thetford, Norfolk, IP24 2BP.*
00-year-old cottage, near station.
Open: All Year (not Xmas)
01842 764564
Mrs Findlay
Rates fr: *£17.00*-**£17.00**.
Beds: 2T 1S
Baths: 1 Shared

***The Wilderness,** Earls Street, Thetford, Norfolk, IP24 2AF.*
Tudor-style house, landscaped garden.
Open: All Year (not Xmas)
01842 764646
Mrs Pomorski
Rates fr: *£17.00*-**£19.00**.
Beds: 3D 1S
Baths: 1 Shared
(6) (6)

Thompson

National Grid Ref: TL9196

***The Thatched House,** Pockthorpe Corner, Thompson, Thetford, Norfolk, IP24 1PJ.*
400-year-old thatched house.
Open: All Year (not Xmas)
01953 483577 Mrs Mills
Rates fr: *£18.00*-**£25.00**.
Beds: 2D 2T
Baths: 2 Shared
(10) (10)

***College Farm,** Thompson, Thetford, Norfolk, IP24 1QG.*
Converted C14th college of priests.
Open: All Year
01953 483318 Mrs Garnier
Rates fr: *£18.00*-**£18.00**.
Beds: 1D 2T 1S
Baths: 2 Private 2 Shared
(7) (10)

Thornham

National Grid Ref: TF7343

King's Head

***Kings Head Hotel,** High Street, Thornham, Hunstanton, Norfolk, PE36 6LY.*
C16th inn, open log fires.
Open: All Year (not Xmas)
01485 512213 Mrs John
Rates fr: *£18.00*-**£18.00**.
Beds: 2D 1T
Baths: 1 Shared

***Rush Meadow,** Main Road, Thornham, Hunstanton, Norfolk, PE36 6LZ.*
Comfortable home, marsh\sea views.
Open: All Year (not Xmas)
01485 512372 Mr Wyett
Rates fr: *£20.00*-**£30.00**.
Beds: 1F 1D
Baths: 1 Ensuite 1 Private
(5)

***Ilex Cottage,** High Street, Thornham, Hunstanton, Norfolk, PE36 6QY.*
Fully modernised traditional-style property.
Open: All Year
01485 512310 Miss Leary
Rates fr: *£17.50*-**£20.00**.
Beds: 1D 2T
Baths: 2 Private 1 Shared
(8) (5)

Thorpe Market

National Grid Ref: TG2435

***Green Farm Restaurant & Hotel,** North Walsham Road, Thorpe Market, Norwich, NR11 8TH.*
C16th farmhouse inn.
Open: All Year
01263 833602
Mr Lomax & D D Lomax
Rates fr: *£25.00*-**£45.00**.
Beds: 7D 2T
Baths: 9 Ensuite
(30)

Thorpe St Andrew

National Grid Ref: TG2609

***Yew Tree Guest House,** 79 Yarmouth Road, Thorpe St Andrew, Norwich, NR7 0HF.*
Idyllic house opposite river and boats.
Open: All Year (not Xmas)
01603 300448
Mrs Legg
Rates fr: *£16.50*-**£20.00**.
Beds: 2D 1T 1S
Baths: 4 Ensuite
(10) (5)

***Raeburn,** 83 Yarmouth Road, Thorpe St Andrew, Norwich, NR7 0HE.*
Semi detached house, near river.
Open: All Year (not Xmas)
01603 439177
Mrs Hawkins
Rates fr: *£16.00*-**£15.00**.
Beds: 1D 1T 1S
(4)

Thursford

National Grid Ref: TF9734

The Crawfish

***The Heathers,** Hindringham Road, Thursford, Fakenham, Norfolk, NR21 0BL.*
Luxury accommodation, country location.
Open: All Year
01328 878352
Mrs Brangwyn
Rates fr: *£18.00*-**£25.00**.
Beds: 2D 1T
Baths: 3 Ensuite
(5)

***Old Coach House,** Thursford, Fakenham, Norfolk, NR21 0BD.*
C17th farmhouse in 60 acre park-land.
Open: All Year
01328 878273
Mrs Green
Rates fr: *£16.00*-**£18.00**.
Beds: 1D 2T
Baths: 1 Ensuite 2 Shared
(4)

Titchwell

National Grid Ref: TF7543

Three Horseshoes

Three Horseshoes, *Titchwell, Kings Lynn, Norfolk,* PE31 8BB.
Traditional village inn, near bird reserve.
Open: All Year
01485 210202 Mr Sverdloff
Rates fr: *£23.00*-**£28.00**.
Beds: 1F 4D 2T **Baths:** 7 Ensuite
(5) (50)

Trunch

National Grid Ref: TG2834

Brewery House, *Brewery Road, Trunch, North Walsham, Norfolk,* NR28 0PU.
Charming C17th country house.
Open: All Year (not Xmas)
01263 720327 Mrs Neville
Rates fr: *£16.00*-**£18.00**.
Beds: 2D 1T **Baths:** 3 Private
(10)

Walpole Cross Keys

National Grid Ref: TF5119

Woolpack Inn

St Helens, *Sutton Road, Walpole Cross Keys, Kings Lynn, Norfolk,* PE34 4HE.
Converted Victorian church.
Open: All Year
01553 828852 (also fax no)
Mr & Mrs Judd
Rates fr: *£15.00*-**£15.00**.
Beds: 1D 1T
(5) (6)

Walpole St Peter

National Grid Ref: TF5116

King of Hearts

Twnsend, Walnut Road, Walpole St Peter, Wisbech, Cambs, PE14 7NR
Elegant Listed Georgian country house.
Open: All Year (not Xmas)
01945 780881 Mrs Couroy
Rates fr: *£16.00*-**£16.00**.
Beds: 1F 1D 1T 1S **Baths:** 4 Ensuite

Walsingham

National Grid Ref: TF9437

White Horse

Knights Gate Guest House, *Knights Street, Little Walsingham, Walsingham, Norfolk,* NR22 6DP.
Open: All Year (not Xmas)
01328 820200 Mr & Mrs Brooks
Rates fr: *£21.00*-**£26.00**.
Beds: 3T **Baths:** 3 Private
(6)
Walsingham is known as 'England's Nazareth', more than 500,000 people visit the village every year. Sandy beaches and the unspoilt Norfolk coast 5 miles away.

St Davids House, *Friday Market, Walsingham, Norfolk,* NR22 6BY.
Tudor house in mediaeval village.
Open: All Year
01328 820633 Mrs Renshaw
Rates fr: *£17.00*-**£17.00**.
Beds: 3F 1D 1T
Baths: 1 Ensuite 2 Shared

The Old Bakehouse, *33 High Street, Walsingham, Norfolk,* NR22 6BZ.
Restaurant with rooms. Small, friendly.
Open: All Year (not Xmas)
01328 820454 Mrs Padley
Rates fr: *£20.00*-**£25.00**.
Beds: 2D 1T
Baths: 1 Private 1 Shared

Vicarage Cottage, *Great Walsingham, Walsingham, Norfolk,* NR22 6DS.
Historic house in historic village.
Open: Easter to Oct
01328 820381 Mrs Dyson
Rates fr: *£21.00*-**£25.00**.
Beds: 1F **Baths:** 1 Ensuite

Foundry Farm House, *Hindringham Road. Great Walsingham, Norfolk,* NR22 6DR.
Modern, comfortable farmhouse.
Open: Easter to Nov
01328 820316 Mr Fox
Rates fr: *£17.00*-**£15.00**.
Beds: 2T 2S **Baths:** 2 Shared
(4)

Walton Highway

National Grid Ref: TF4912

Homeleigh Guest House, *Lynn Road, Walton Highway, Wisbech, Cambs,* PE14 7DE.
Large Victorian private house.
Open: All Year
01945 582356 Mrs Wiseman
Rates fr: *£15.00*-**£15.00**.
Beds: 1F 2D 1T 2S
(10)

Warham

National Grid Ref: TF9441

The Three Horseshoes / The Old Post Office, *69 Bridge Street, Warham, Wells-next-the-Sea, Norfolk,* NR23 1NL.
Dream country cottage.
Open: All Year (not Xmas)
01328 710547 Mr Salmon
Rates fr: *£20.00*-**£20.00**.
Beds: 3D 1S
Baths: 1 Private 1 Shared
(14) (20)

Bringing children with you? Always ask for any special rates.

Watton

National Grid Ref: TF9100

The Hare & Barrel, *80 Brandon Road, Watton, Thetford, Norfolk,* IP25 6LB.
Converted Victorian house and outhouses.
Open: All Year
01953 882752 Mr Green
Rates fr: *£18.00*-**£23.00**.
Beds: 2F 2D 12T 2S
Baths: 18 Private
(40)

Wells-next-the-Sea

National Grid Ref: TF9143

Edinburgh, Crown Hotel

Eastdene Guest House, *Northfield Lane, Wells-next-the-Sea, Norfolk,* NR23 1LH.
Comfortable guest house.
Open: All Year
01328 710381 Mrs Court
Rates fr: *£18.00*-**£20.00**.
Beds: 1D 2T 1S
Baths: 3 Private 1 Shared
(9) (5)

The Normans Guest House, *Invaders Court, Standard Road, Wells-next-the-Sea, Norfolk,* NR23 1JW.
Elegant Georgian house within courtyard.
Open: All Year (not Xmas)
Grades: ETB 2 Cr
01328 710657 Mrs MacDonald
Fax no: 01328 710468
Rates fr: *£23.50*-**£30.00**.
Beds: 6D 1T **Baths:** 7 Ensuite
(10)

The Warren, *Warham Road, Wells-next-the-Sea, Norfolk,* NR23 1NE.
Comfortable bungalow - outskirts of Wells.
Open: All Year (not Xmas)
01328 710273 Mrs Wickens
Rates fr: *£18.00*-**£20.00**.
Beds: 1D 1T
Baths: 1 Ensuite 1 Private
(2)

Hideaway, *Red Lion Yard, Wells-next-the-Sea, Norfolk,* NR23 1AX.
Annexe on to private house.
Open: Jan to Nov
Grades: ETB 2 Cr, Comm
01328 710524 Miss Higgs
Rates fr: *£17.00*-**£20.00**.
Beds: 1D 2T **Baths:** 3 Ensuite
(3)

Brooklands, *31 Burnt Street, Wells-next-the-Sea, Norfolk,* NR23 1HP.
Charming beamed 200-year-old house.
Open: All Year (not Xmas)
01328 710768 Mrs Wykes
Rates fr: *£14.00*-**£16.00**.
Beds: 1F 1D **Baths:** 1 Shared
(7) (2)

East House, *East Quay, Wells-next-the-Sea, Norfolk, NR23 1LE.*
Old house overlooking coastal marsh.
Open: All Year (not Xmas)
01328 710408 Mrs Scott
Rates fr: *£18.50*-**£22.00**.
Beds: 2T
Baths: 2 Ensuite
(7) (2)

Mill House, *Northfield Lane, Wells-next-the-Sea, Norfolk, NR23 1JZ.*
Former Mill owner's house.
Open: All Year
01328 710739 Mr Downey
Rates fr: *£17.00*-**£17.50**.
Beds: 1F 3D 2T 2S
Baths: 6 Ensuite 2 Private
(8) (10)

West End House, *Dogger Lane, Wells-next-the-Sea, Norfolk, NR23 1BE.*
Small friendly guest house.
Open: All Year
01328 711190 Mr Cox
Rates fr: *£14.00*-**£14.00**.
Beds: 1F 1T 1D 1S
Baths: 2 Shared
(4)

Welney

National Grid Ref: TL5294

Lamb & Flag

Stockyard Farm, *Wisbech Road, Welney, Wisbech, Cambs, PE14 9RQ.*
Comfortable former Fenland farmhouse.
Open: All Year (not Xmas)
01354 610433 Mrs Bennett
Rates fr: *£16.00*-**£20.00**.
Beds: 1D 1T
Baths: 1 Shared
(5) (2)

Welney House, *Wisbech Road, Welney, Wisbech, Cambs, PE14 9QA.*
Classic Georgian farmhouse, beautiful garden.
Open: All Year (not Xmas)
01354 610207 Mrs Gerrard Wright
Rates fr: *£17.00*-**£17.00**.
Beds: 2T
(4)

The lowest *double* rate per person is shown in *italics*.

Weybourne

National Grid Ref: TG1142

The Maltings Hotel, *The Street, Weybourne, Holt, Norfolk, NR25 7SY.*
Open: All Year
01263 588731 Mr Mears
Rates fr: *£25.00*-**£28.00**.
Beds: 3F 8D 7T 2S
Baths: 20 Ensuite
(150)

Wighton

National Grid Ref: TF9439

Sandpiper Inn

The Sandpiper Inn, *57 High Street, Wighton, Wells-next-the-Sea, Norfolk, NR23 1PF.*
Modernised C18th country inn.
Open: All Year
01328 820752 Mrs Bridge
Rates fr: *£15.00*-**£20.00**.
Beds: 1D 2T **Baths:** 1 Shared
(7) (30)

Wiveton

National Grid Ref: TG0443

Flintstones Guest House, *Wiveton, Holt, Norfolk, NR25 7TL.*
Peaceful, comfortable guest house.
Open: All Year (not Xmas)
Grades: ETB Listed, Comm, AA 3 Q, RAC Acclaim
01263 740337 Mr Ormerod
Rates fr: *£17.00*-**£22.00**.
Beds: 3F 1D 1S
Baths: 5 Private
(5)

Rosemeade, *The Street, Wiveton, Holt, Norfolk, NR25 7TH.*
Tranquil 1930's bungalow, plus chalet.
Open: All Year (not Xmas)
01263 740747 Mrs Sayers
Rates fr: *£15.00*-**£18.00**.
Beds: 2D 1T **Baths:** 2 Shared

Wood Dalling

National Grid Ref: TG0927

Westwood Barn, *Wood Dalling, Norwich, NR11 6SW.*
Outstanding C15th barn, idyllic location.
Open: All Year
Grades: ETB 2 Cr, High Comm
01263 584108 Mrs Westwood
Rates fr: *£21.00*-**£28.00**.
Beds: 2D 1T **Baths:** 3 Private
(12) (6)

Wretham

National Grid Ref: TL9190

Dog & Partridge, *Watton Road, Wretham, Thetford, Norfolk, IP24 1QS.*
C18th flint public house.
Open: All Year
01953 498245
Mrs Nicholls
Rates fr: *£14.00*-**£16.00**.
Beds: 1F 3D

Wroxham

National Grid Ref: TG3017

The Mount, *93 Norwich Road, Wroxham, Norwich, NR12 8RX.*
Delightful Broads guest house.
Open: All Year (not Xmas)
Grades: ETB 2 Cr, Comm
01603 783909
Mrs Leeming
Rates fr: *£18.00*-**£22.00**.
Beds: 2D 1T
Baths: 1 Ensuite 2 Shared
(3)

Wymondham

National Grid Ref: TM1196

Three Boars, Crossed Keys

Willow Farm, *Wattlefield, Wymondham, Norfolk, NR18 9PA.*
Peaceful farmhouse, relaxing atmosphere.
Open: All Year (not Xmas)
Grades: ETB Listed, Comm
01953 604679
Mrs Highton
Rates fr: *£17.00*-**£17.00**.
Beds: 1D 1T 1S
Baths: 2 Shared

Turret House, *27 Middleton Street, Wymondham, Norfolk, NR18 0AB.*
Large central Victorian private house.
Open: All Year (not Xmas)
Grades: ETB Listed, Approv
01953 603462
Mrs Morgan
Rates fr: *£15.00*-**£15.00**.
Beds: 1F 1T
Baths: 1 Shared
(2)

Northamptonshire

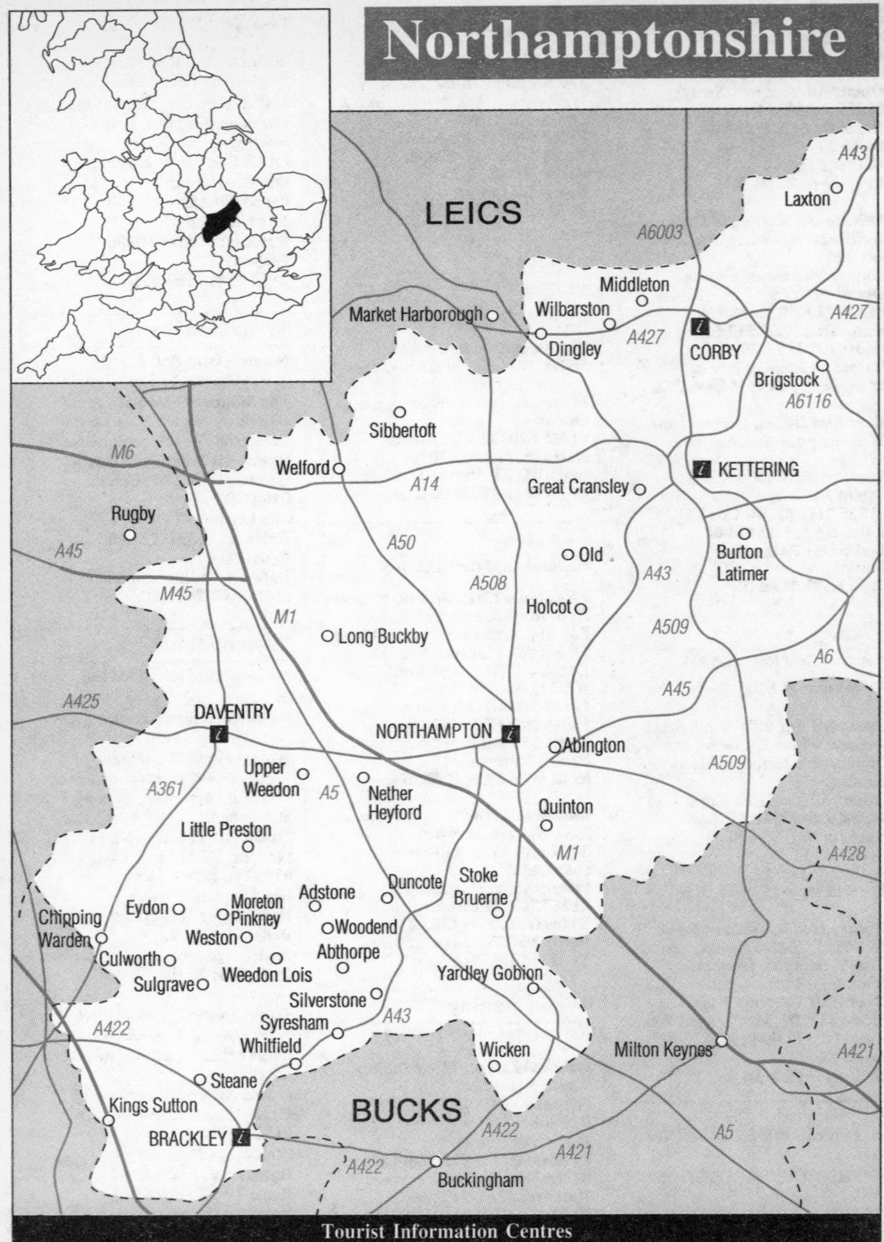

Tourist Information Centres

2 Bridge St, **Brackley**, Northants, NN13 5EP, 01280 700111.

Civic Centre, George Street, **Corby**, Northants, NN17 1QB, 01536 407507.

Moot Hall, Market Square, **Daventry**, Northants, NN11 4BH, 01327 300277.

The Coach House, Sheep Street, **Kettering**, Northants, NN16 0AN, 01536 534212.

Mr Grant's House, 10 St Giles Square, **Northampton**, Northants, NN1 1DA, 01604 22677.

Market Hall, Market Place, **Oundle**, Northants, PE8 4BA, 01832 274333.

Wellingborough Library, Pebble Lane, **Wellingborough**, Northants, NN8 1AS, 01933 228101.

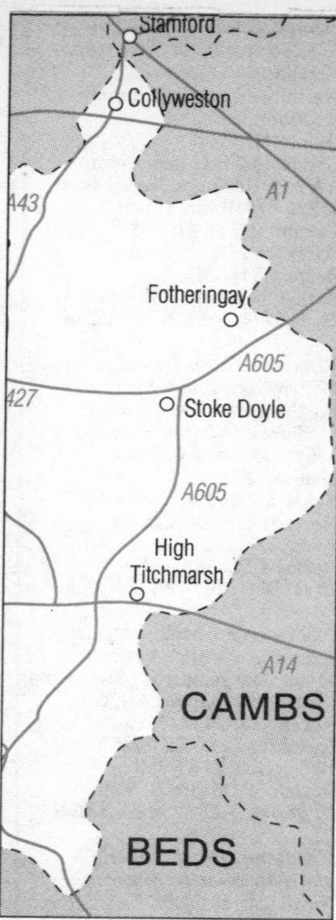

Abington

National Grid Ref: SP7761

Pembroke House, *36 Garrick Road, Abington, Northampton, Northants,* NN1 5ND.
Large Victorian comfortable private house.
Open: All Year
01604 21858 Mr Thomas
Rates fr: *£14.50*-**£16.00**.
Beds: 1D 1T 1S
Baths: 1 Shared

Abthorpe

National Grid Ref: SP6446

Stone Cottage, *Main Street, Abthorpe, Towcester, Northants,* NN12 8QN.
Pretty cottage with extensive grounds.
Open: All Year
01327 857544 Mrs Brodie
Rates fr: *£18.00*-**£20.00**.
Beds: 1F 1T 1S
(4)

The lowest **single** rate is shown in **bold.**

Adstone

National Grid Ref: SP5951

Red Lion (Farthingstone)

Stone Dene, *The Green, Adstone, Towcester, Northants,* NN12 8DY.
Open: All Year (not Xmas)
Grades: ETB Listed, Comm
01327 860434 Mrs Snook
Rates fr: *£13.25*-**£12.00**.
Beds: 1D 1T
Baths: 1 Shared
(10) (6)
A stone house set in a quiet hamlet of Northants, within easy reach of Warwick, Stratford & Silverstone, offering a warm welcome with good food.

Brackley

National Grid Ref: SP5837

The Fox

Walltree House Farm, *Steane, Brackley, Northants,* NN13 5NS.
Warm farmhouse, ground-floor courtyard rooms.
Open: All Year (not Xmas)
Grades: ETB 3 Cr, Comm
01295 811235 Mrs Harrison
Fax no: 01295 811147
Rates fr: *£20.00*-**£30.00**.
Beds: 3F 2D 3T **Baths:** 8 Private

Brigstock

National Grid Ref: SP9485

Bridge House, *3 Grafton Road, Brigstock, Kettering, Northants,* NN14 3EY.
Modern, comfortable family home.
Open: All Year (not Xmas)
01536 373297
Rates fr: *£16.50*-**£16.50**.
Beds: 1T 1S **Baths:** 1 Shared
(3)

Burton Latimer

National Grid Ref: SP8974

Olde Victoria

The Wold, *34 Church Street, Burton Latimer, Kettering, Northants,* NN15 5LU.
Detached house of generous proportions.
Open: All Year (not Xmas)
Grades: ETB 1 Cr, Comm
01536 722685 Mrs Baggaley
Rates fr: *£15.50*-**£17.50**.
Beds: 1D 1T 1S **Baths:** 3 Ensuite
(4)

Chipping Warden

National Grid Ref: SP4948

Hogg End House, *Hogg End Lane, Chipping Warden, Banbury, Oxon,* OX17 1LY.
4 converted farm cottages.
Open: Easter to Oct
01295 660669 Mrs Prince
Rates fr: *£26.00*-**£26.00**.
Beds: 1D 1T
Baths: 1 Ensuite 1 Private
(8)

Collyweston

National Grid Ref: SK9902

Highfields, *31 Main Road, Collyweston, Stamford, Lincs,* PE9 3PF.
Village location. Ground floor rooms.
Open: All Year
Grades: ETB Listed
01780 444339 Mrs Hindley
Rates fr: *£18.00*-**£17.00**.
Beds: 1D 1T 1S
Baths: 2 Shared
(4) (4)

The Manor Cottage, *Collyweston, Stamford, Lincs,* PE9 3PN.
Georgian house with panoramic views. **Open:** All Year
01780 444209 Mr & Mrs Mitchell
Rates fr: *£15.00*-**£20.00**.
Beds: 1F 1D 2T
Baths: 2 Private 2 Shared
(15)

Corby

National Grid Ref: SP8889

Spread Eagle

49 Dolver Close, *Corby, Northants,* NN18 8NB.
Comfortable family house overlooking countryside.
Open: All Year (not Xmas)
01536 747151 Mr & Mrs Campbell
Rates fr: *£13.00*-**£15.00**.
Beds: 1T 2S
Baths: 1 Ensuite 1 Shared
(5) (1)

Macallan Guest House, *18-20 Lundy Avenue, Corby, Northants,* NN18 8BU.
Comfortable, friendly family-run house.
Open: All Year (not Xmas)
01536 261848 Mrs MacLeod
Rates fr: *£12.50*-**£15.00**.
Beds: 2T 2S
Baths: 3 Shared

28 Denmark Close, *Corby, Northants,* NN18 9EH.
Detached house in residential area.
Open: All Year
01536 743247 Mrs Christie
Rates fr: *£15.00*-**£15.00**.
Beds: 2T 1S
Baths: 1 Shared
(4)

65 Rockingham Road, *Corby, Northants,* NN17 1AH.
Detached modern bungalow.
Open: All Year (not Xmas)
01536 262084 Mrs Haas
Rates fr: *£12.50*-**£12.50**.
Beds: 1T 1S **Baths:** 1 Shared
(5)

Culworth

National Grid Ref: SP5447

Red Lion

Ivy Cottage, *Culworth, Banbury, Oxfordshire, OX17 2AP.*
Comfortable cottage in delightful setting.
Open: All Year (not Xmas)
Grades: ETB Listed, Comm
01295 768131 Mrs McKenzie
Rates fr: *£18.00*-**£18.00**.
Beds: 1F 1D 1S
(4)

Dingley

National Grid Ref: SP7787

Dingley Lodge, *Harborough Road, Dingley, Market Harborough, Leics, LE16 8PJ.*
Restored Victorian private country house.
Open: All Year (not Xmas)
01858 535365 Mrs Kirkman
Rates fr: *£19.00*-**£25.00**.
Beds: 1F 2T 3D 1S
Baths: 7 Ensuite
(20)

Duncote

National Grid Ref: SP6750

Butchers

Ulmustilia, *Duncote, Towcester, Northants, NN12 8AH.*
Large private house in half acre ground.
Open: All Year (not Xmas)
01327 350392 Mrs Swaddle
Rates fr: *£12.50*-**£18.00**.
Beds: 2D
Baths: 1 Shared

Eydon

National Grid Ref: SP5450

Wheelwrights, *30 Lime Avenue, Eydon, Daventry, Northants, NN11 6PG.*
Modern, comfortable stone house.
Open: All Year (not Xmas)
01327 260983 Mr & Mrs Billing
Rates fr: *£19.00*-**£26.00**.
Beds: 1D 1T
Baths: 2 Private
(2)

Fotheringhay

National Grid Ref: TL0593

Castle Farm, *Fotheringhay, Oundle, Peterborough, Cambs, PE8 5HZ.*
First class accommodation, river frontage.
Open: All Year
Grades: ETB 3 Cr, Comm
01832 226200 Ms Gould
Rates fr: *£17.50*-**£24.00**.
Beds: 1F 1D 2T 1S
Baths: 5 Ensuite 1 Private

Great Cransley

National Grid Ref: SP8376

Three Cranes

Cransley Hall, *Church Lane, Great Cransley, Kettering, Northants, NN14 1PX.*
Queen Anne mansion.
Open: All Year (not Xmas)
01536 790259 Mrs Perkins
Rates fr: *£25.00*-**£30.00**.
Beds: 2T 2S
Baths: 4 Private
(9)

High Titchmarsh

National Grid Ref: TL0279

Chapter House, *High Titchmarsh, Kettering, Northants, NN14 3DF.*
Four-bedroom detached house.
Open: All Year (not Xmas)
01832 732927
Mr Hankins
Rates fr: *£14.00*-**£15.00**.
Beds: 2D
Baths: 1 Shared

Holcot

National Grid Ref: SP7969

White Swan

White Swan Inn, *Main Street, Holcot, Northampton, Northants, NN6 9SP.*
Thatched village inn.
Open: All Year
01604 781263 (also fax no)
Mr Buckler
Rates fr: *£17.50*-**£20.00**.
Beds: 2T 2S
Baths: 2 Shared
(5) (10)

Kettering

National Grid Ref: SP8778

Hawthorn House Private Hotel, *2 Hawthorn Road, Kettering, Northants, NN15 7HS.*
Victorian town house private hotel.
Open: All Year
Grades: ETB 3 Cr
01536 82513 / 525166
Mrs McQuade
Fax no: 01536 513121
Rates fr: *£17.00*-**£24.00**.
Beds: 1D 4T
Baths: 3 Ensuite 2 Private
(4)

South View Guest House, *79 Reservoir Road, Kettering, Northants, NN16 9QU.*
Homely, quiet, friendly, comfortable accommodation.
Open: All Year
01536 520291 Mrs Pell
Rates fr: *£14.00*-**£14.00**.
Beds: 2T 2S
Baths: 1 Ensuite
(3)

Pennels Guest House, *175 Beatrice Road, Kettering, Northants, NN16 9QR.*
Warm, welcoming & quality accommodation.
Open: All Year
Grades: ETB Listed, Comm, AA 3 Q, Recomm, RAC Listed
01536 81940 Mrs Green
Fax no: 01536 410798
Rates fr: *£18.00*-**£17.00**.
Beds: 1F 1D 3T 2S
Baths: 5 Ensuite 2 Shared
(0) (4)

Tennyson Guest House, *42 Tennyson Road, Kettering, Northants, NN16 0DD.*
Modern, comfortable private house. **Open:** All Year
Grades: ETB 1 St
01536 515868 Mr Jones
Rates fr: *£14.00*-**£14.00**.
Beds: 1F 1D 2T 1S
Baths: 1 Shared
(1) (6)

The George Hotel, *Sheep Street, Kettering, Northants, NN16 4AD.*
Traditional standards of upkeeping maintained. **Open:** All Year
01536 518620 Mr Farrar
Rates fr: *£15.00*-**£19.75**.
Beds: 1F 28D 4T 20S
Baths: 32 Private 20 Shared
(40)

Headlands Private Hotel, *49-51 Headlands, Kettering, Northants, NN15 7ET.*
Attractively converted Victorian villa. **Open:** All Year (not Xmas)
01536 524624 Mrs Barnett
Rates fr: *£18.00*-**£19.00**.
Beds: 4F 2D 2T 4S
Baths: 6 Private 6 Shared

Kings Sutton

National Grid Ref: SP5036

College Farm House, *Kings Sutton, Banbury, Oxon, OX17 3PS.*
Exceptionally comfortable. Warm welcome guaranteed.
Open: All Year (not Xmas)
01295 811473 Mrs Allday
Rates fr: *£24.00*-**£24.00**.
Beds: 3T **Baths:** 3 Private

Laxton

National Grid Ref: SP9446

White Swan

The Old Vicarage, *Laxton, Corby, Northants, NN17 3AT.*
Splendid Regency vicarage, beautiful gardens.
Open: All Year
01780 450248 Mrs Hill-Brookes
Fax no: 01780 450398
Rates fr: *£15.00*-**£15.00**.
Beds: 3F 1D 1T 1S
Baths: 1 Private 1 Shared
(3)

Little Preston

National Grid Ref: SP5854

Kings Arms (Farthingstone)

***Bee Close House,** Little Preston, Daventry, Northants, NN11 3TF.*
Modern detached house, rural situation.
Open: All Year (not Xmas)
Grades: ETB Listed
01327 361641 (also fax no)
Mrs Maclaren
Rates fr: *£15.50*-**£16.00**.
Beds: 1D 1T 1S
Baths: 1 Ensuite 2 Shared

Long Buckby

National Grid Ref: SP6267

***Murcott Mill,** Murcott, Long Buckby, Northampton, Northants, NN6 7QR.*
Recently renovated Georgian mill house.
Open: All Year
Grades: ETB 2 Cr, Comm
01327 842236 Mrs Hart
Rates fr: *£17.00*-**£18.00**.
Beds: 1F 2T
Baths: 3 Private
(8)

Middleton

National Grid Ref: SP8390

Red Lion

***Valley View,** 3 Camsdale Walk, Middleton, Market Harborough, Leics, LE16 8YR.*
Panoramic views of the Welland Valley.
Open: All Year (not Xmas)
Grades: ETB 1 Cr
01536 770874 Mrs Randle
Rates fr: *£15.00*-**£15.00**.
Beds: 1D 1T
Baths: 1 Shared
(2)

Moreton Pinkney

National Grid Ref: SP5749

***Barewell Fields,** Prestidge Row, Moreton Pinkney, Daventry, Northants, NN11 3NJ.*
Peaceful setting in conservation village.
Open: All Year (not Xmas)
Grades: ETB Listed, High Comm
01295 760754 Mrs Lainchbury
Rates fr: *£16.00*-**£16.00**.
Beds: 1D 1T 1S
Baths: 1 Shared
(7) (3)

Nether Heyford

National Grid Ref: SP6658

***27 Church Street,** Nether Heyford, Northampton, Northants, NN7 3LH.*
Junction 16, M1 (1 mile).
Open: All Year
Grades: ETB Listed
01327 340872 Mrs Clements
Rates fr: *£12.50*-**£15.00**.
Beds: 1D 1T 1S
Baths: 1 Private 1 Shared
(6)

Northampton

National Grid Ref: SP7561

Rose & Crown

***Arrandale Regent Hotel,** 6-8 Royal Terrace, Barrack Road (A508), Northampton, Northants, NN1 3RF.*
Open: All Year (not Xmas)
Grades: ETB 1 Cr
01604 31096 Mrs Allsop
Fax no: 01604 21035
Rates fr: *£17.50*-**£22.00**.
Beds: 4F 6D 6T 4S
(1) (14)
Situated within easy walking distance of town centre, theatres, bus & rail stations. Handy for all major events at Silverstone Circuit & Billing Aquadrome.

***Hollington Guest House,** 22 Abington Grove, Northampton, Northants, NN1 4QW.*
Small, comfortable guest house.
Open: All Year (not Xmas)
Grades: ETB Listed, AA Listed
01604 32584
Mrs Taylor
Rates fr: *£15.00*-**£16.00**.
Beds: 2F 2D 1T 2S
Baths: 2 Shared
(5)

***Birchfields Guest House,** 17 Hester Street, Northampton, Northants, NN2 6AP.*
Very comfortable, friendly.
Open: All Year (not Xmas)
01604 28199 Mrs Darmanin
Rates fr: *£14.00*-**£16.50**.
Beds: 1D 4T 1S
Baths: 1 Shared

***Quinton Green Farm,** Quinton, Northampton, Northants, NN7 2EG.*
Rambling comfortable C17th farmhouse.
Open: All Year
Grades: ETB 2 Cr, AA 4 Q
01604 863685
Mrs Turney
Fax no: 01604 862230
Rates fr: *£20.00*-**£20.00**.
Beds: 1D 1T 1S
Baths: 3 Ensuite

***Castilian House,** 34 Park Avenue North, Northampton, Northants, NN3 2JE.*
Large, privately-run C19th house.
Open: All Year
Grades: ETB Listed
01604 712863
Mrs Smith
Rates fr: *£16.50*-**£16.50**.
Beds: 1D 1S
Baths: 1 Shared
(6)

Old

National Grid Ref: SP7873

***Wold Farm,** Old, Northampton, Northants, NN6 9RJ.*
C18th farmhouse & converted barn. **Open:** All Year (not Xmas)
01604 781258 Mrs Engler
Rates fr: *£19.00*-**£19.00**.
Beds: 3D 1T 2S
Baths: 3 Private 1 Shared
(7)

Quinton

National Grid Ref: SP7754

Rose & Crown (Hartwell)

***Quinton Green Farm,** Quinton, Northampton, Northants, NN7 2EG.*
Rambling comfortable C17th farmhouse. **Open:** All Year
Grades: ETB 2 Cr, AA 4 Q
01604 863685 Mrs Turney
Fax no: 01604 862230
Rates fr: *£20.00*-**£20.00**.
Beds: 1D 1T 1S **Baths:** 3 Ensuite

Sibbertoft

National Grid Ref: SP6882

Red Lion

***The Wrongs,** Sibbertoft, Market Harborough, Leics, LE16 9UJ.*
Modern farmhouse, also carp fishing. **Open:** All Year
Grades: ETB Listed
01858 880886 (also fax no)
Mrs Hart
Rates fr: *£15.00*-**£15.00**.
Beds: 1D 2S **Baths:** 1 Shared
(4)

Silverstone

National Grid Ref: SP6644

White Horse

***Silverthorpe Farm,** Abthorpe Road, Silverstone, Towcester, Northants, NN12 8TW.*
Spacious, family-run, rural bungalow.
Open: All Year (not Xmas)
Grades: ETB Listed, Comm, AA 3 Q
01327 858020 Mrs Branch
Fax no: 01327 858406
Rates fr: *£18.00*-**£20.00**.
Beds: 1F 3T
Baths: 1 Private 1 Shared
(8)

***The Walnut,** 9 High Street, Silverstone, Towcester, Northants, NN12 8US.*
C16th village farmhouse with C20th amenities.
Open: All Year (not Xmas)
01327 858595 Mrs Cox
Rates fr: *£16.00*-**£16.00**.
Beds: 1D 1T 2S
Baths: 2 Private 2 Shared
(12) (6)

Steane

National Grid Ref: SP5539

The Fox (Farthinghoe)

***Walltree House Farm,** Steane, Brackley, Northants, NN13 5NS.*
Warm farmhouse, ground-floor courtyard rooms.
Open: All Year (not Xmas)
Grades: ETB 3 Cr, Comm
01295 811235 Mrs Harrison
Fax no: 01295 811147
Rates fr: *£20.00*-**£30.00**.
Beds: 3F 2D 3T
Baths: 8 Private

Stoke Bruerne

National Grid Ref: SP7449

Boat Inn, Navigation

***Waterways Cottage,** Stoke Bruerne, Towcester, Northants, NN12 7SD.*
Picturesque canalside cottage opposite pub.
Open: All Year (not Xmas)
Grades: ETB Listed, High Comm
01604 863865 Mrs Cox
Rates fr: *£15.00*-**£18.00**.
Beds: 1D 2T
Baths: 1 Private 1 Shared
(6)

***Rookery Lane Bed & Breakfast,** Stoke Bruerne, Towcester, Northants, NN12 7SJ.*
Modern Georgian house. Pretty gardens.
Open: All Year (not Xmas)
01604 863397 (also fax no)
Rates fr: *£18.00*-**£18.00**.
Beds: 1T 2S
Baths: 1 Shared
(4)

Stoke Doyle

National Grid Ref: TL0286

Shuckburgh Arms

***The Shuckburgh Arms,** Stoke Doyle, Peterborough, Cambs, PE8 5TG.*
C16th stone built rural inn.
Open: All Year (not Xmas)
Grades: ETB 3 Cr, Comm
01832 272339 Mr Kirkby
Rates fr: *£22.00*-**£27.50**.
Beds: 1D 2T 2S
Baths: 5 Ensuite
(40)

Sulgrave

National Grid Ref: SP5545

***Rectory Farm,** Little Street, Sulgrave, Banbury, Oxon, OX17 2SG.*
C17th thatched farmhouse.
Open: All Year (not Xmas)
Grades: ETB Listed, Comm
01295 760261 Mrs Smyth-Osbourne
Fax no: 01295 760089
Rates fr: *£17.50*-**£20.00**.
Beds: 1F 1D 2T
Baths: 2 Shared
(10)

Upper Weedon

National Grid Ref: SP6258

Globe Hotel

***Mullions,** 9 Oak Street, Upper Weedon, Northampton, Northants, NN7 4RQ.*
C17th stone cottage, quiet location.
Open: All Year (not Xmas)
Grades: ETB 2 Cr
01327 341439 Mrs Piercey
Rates fr: *£16.00*-**£16.00**.
Beds: 1D **Baths:** 1 Private
(2)

Weedon Lois

National Grid Ref: SP6047

***Green Farm,** Weedon Lois, Towcester, Northants, NN12 8PL.*
Comfortable C18th farmhouse, working farm.
Open: All Year (not Xmas)
01327 860249 Mrs Elkington
Rates fr: *£17.00*-**£17.00**.
Beds: 2D 1T
Baths: 1 Private 1 Shared
(4)

Welford

National Grid Ref: SP6480

Shoulder of Moulton

***West End Farm,** 5 West End, Welford, Northampton, Northants, NN6 6HJ.*
Comfortable 1848 farmhouse. Quiet street. **Open:** All Year
Grades: ETB 1 Cr, Comm
01858 575226 Mrs Bevin
Rates fr: *£15.00*-**£15.00**.
Beds: 1D 1T **Baths:** 1 Shared
(4)

Weston

National Grid Ref: SP5847

Star Inn

***4 Helmdon Road,** Weston, Towcester, Northants, NN12 8PX.*
Farmhouse, built 1585.
Open: All Year
Grades: ETB Listed
01295 760667 Mrs Wild
Rates fr: *£15.00*-**£15.00**.
Beds: 1D 2T 1S **Baths:** 1 Shared

Whitfield

National Grid Ref: SP6039

The Sun

***Chestnut View,** Mill Road, Whitfield, Brackley, Northants, NN13 5TQ.*
Country, Silverstone, Oxford, Cotswold area.
Open: All Year (not Xmas)
01280 850246 Mrs James
Rates fr: *£15.00*-**£18.00**.
Beds: 1D 1S
Baths: 1 Private
(0) (2)

***Hill House,** Whitfield, Brackley, Northants, NN13 5TQ.*
Early C19th stone farmhouse.
Open: All Year (not Xmas)
01280 850332 Mrs Digby
Rates fr: *£17.50*-**£17.50**.
Beds: 2T 1S
Baths: 1 Shared
(4)

Wicken

National Grid Ref: SP7439

***Halcyon,** 3 Pound Close, Wicken, Milton Keynes, Bucks, MK19 6BN.*
Large Canadian-style house.
Open: All Year
01908 571237 Mrs Preston
Rates fr: *£18.00*-**£18.00**.
Beds: 2S
Baths: 2 Shared
(7) (Yes)

Wilbarston

National Grid Ref: SP8188

Fox Inn

***The Fox Inn,** Church Street, Wilbarston, Market Harborough, Leics, LE16 8QG.*
Friendly, comfortable village inn.
Open: All Year (not Xmas)
Grades: ETB 2 Cr, Comm
01536 771270 Mr McHarg
Rates fr: *£15.00*-**£20.00**.
Beds: 1F 2D 1T
Baths: 4 Private
(10)

Woodend

National Grid Ref: SP6149

***Rose Cottage,** Top Green, Woodend, Towcester, Northants, NN12 8RZ.*
Rebuilt Country cottage. Quietly situated.
Open: All Year (not Xmas)
01327 860968 (also fax no)
Mrs Davey-Turner
Rates fr: *£20.00*-**£25.00**.
Beds: 1D 1T
Baths: 1 Ensuite 1 Private
(7) (4)

Yardley Gobion

National Grid Ref: SP7644

***Old Wharf Farm,** Yardley Gobion, Towcester, Northants, NN12 7UE.*
Historic Listed canalside working wharf.
Open: All Year (not Xmas)
01908 542293 / 542844 Mr Bowen
Rates fr: *£16.00*-**£18.00**.
Beds: 1F 1D 1T 1S
Baths: 2 Shared
(10)

Northumberland

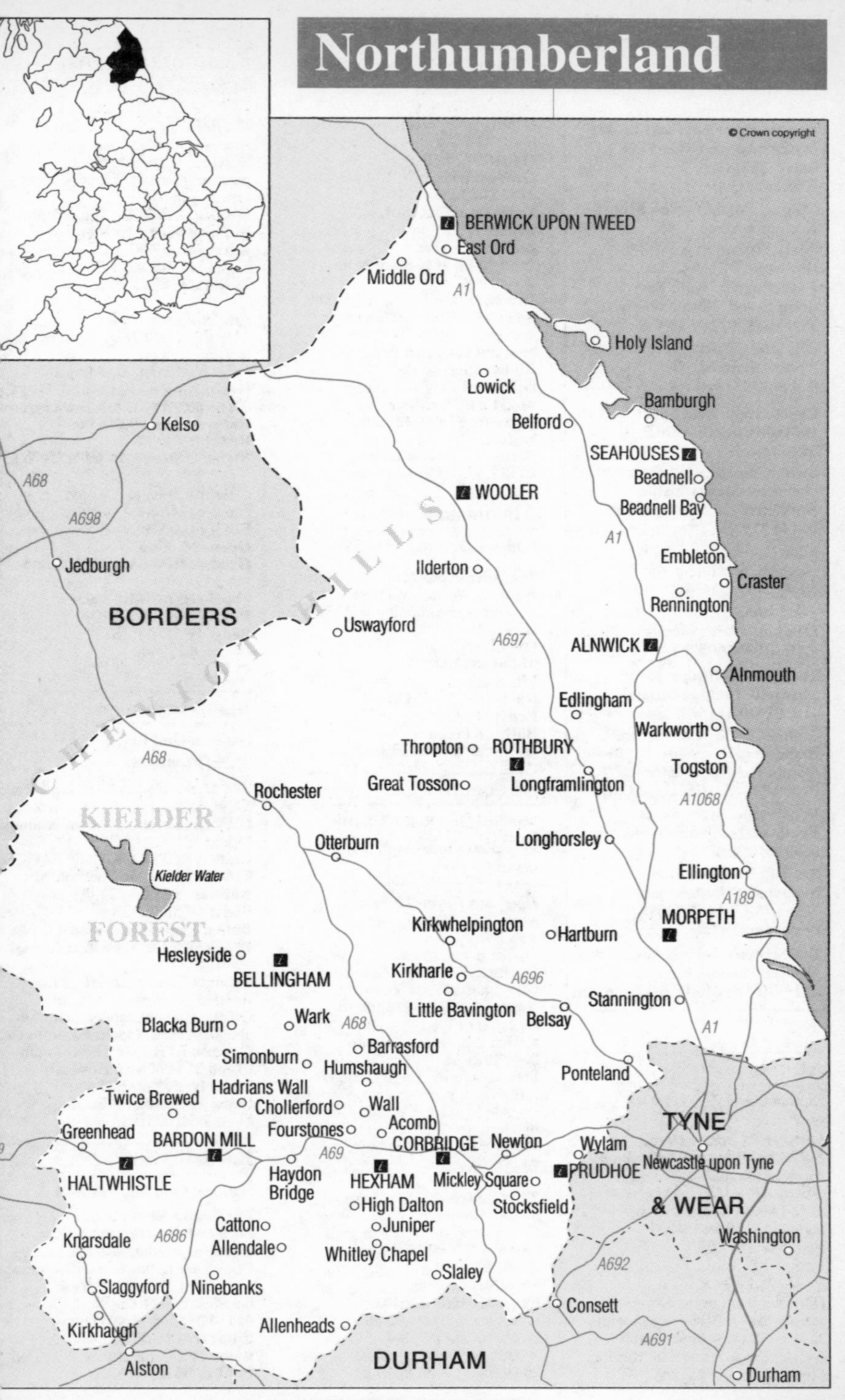

Tourist Information Centres

The Shambles, **Alnwick**, Northumberland, NE66 1TN, 01665 510665.

Queens Street Car Park, **Amble**, Northumberland, NE65 0DQ, 01665 712313, (Easter to Oct).

Military Road, **Bardon Mill**, Northumberland, NE47 7AN, 01434 344396, (Easter to Oct).

Castlegate Car Park, **Berwick-upon-tweed**, Northumberland, TD15 1JS, 01289 330733.

Hill Street, **Corbridge**, Northumberland, NE45 5AA, 01434 632815, (Easter to Oct).

Church Hall, Main Street, **Haltwhistle,** NE49 0BE, 01434 322002

Swimming and Leisure Centre, Greencroft, **Haltwhistle**, Northumberland, NE49 9DP, 01434 322002, (Nov to Easter).

Main Street, **Bellingham**, Hexham, Northumberland, NE48 2BQ, 01434 220616.

The Manor Office, Hallgate, **Hexham**, Northumberland, NE46 1XD, 01434 605225.

The Chantry, Bridge Street, **Morpeth**, Northumberland, NE61 1PJ, 01670 511323.

Church House, Church Street, **Rothbury**, Morpeth, Northumberland, NE65 7UP, 01669 620887, (Easter to Oct).

Waterworld, Front Street, **Prudhoe**, Northumberland, NE42 5DQ, 01661 833144.

Seafield Road Car Park, **Seahouses**, Northumberland, NE68 7SR, 01665 720884, (Easter to Oct).

Bus Station Car Park, High Street, **Wooler**, Northumberland, NE71 8LD, 01668 281602, (Easter to Oct)

Acomb

National Grid Ref: NY9366

Mariner's Cottage Hotel, *Fallowfield Dene Road, Acomb, Hexham, Northd, NE46 4RP.*
Open: All Year
01434 603666 Mrs Darling
Rates fr: *£18.00*-**£17.00**.
Beds: 1F 1D 1T 2S
Baths: 3 Private 2 Shared
(60)
Hotel set in country, 3 miles from market town of Hexham & within easy reach of Hadrian's Wall, Kielder Water, Beamish Museum, Metro Shopping Centre.

Allendale

National Grid Ref: NY8355

Thornley House, *Allendale, Hexham, Northd, NE47 9NH.*
Comfortable, luxurious country house.
Open: Dec to Nov
Grades: ETB 3 Cr, High Comm
01434 683255 Mr Finn
Rates fr: *£17.50*-**£21.00**.
Beds: 1D 2T
Baths: 3 Private
(9)

Manor House Farm, *Allendale, Allendale, Hexham, Northd, NE47 8DA.*
Peaceful Georgian farmhouse. All facilities.
Open: All Year (not Xmas)
01434 345236 Mrs Lee
Rates fr: *£15.50*-**£17.00**.
Beds: 2F 1T
Baths: 1 Private 1 Shared
(3)

Allenheads

National Grid Ref: NY8545

The Allenheads Inn, *Allenheads, Hexham, Northd, NE47 9HJ.*
Eccentric, entertaining and high standards.
Open: All Year
01434 685200
Mrs Stenson
Rates fr: *£21.50*-**£21.50**.
Beds: 5D 3T
Baths: 8 Private
(10)

Alnmouth

National Grid Ref: NU2410

Red Lion, Topsy Turvey (Warkworth)

Hipsburn Farm, *Lesbury, Alnmouth, Alnwick, Northd, NE66 3PY.*
Open: Easter to Oct
Grades: ETB 1 Cr, High Comm
01665 830206 Ms Tulip
Rates fr: *£20.00*-**£20.00**.
Beds: 2D 1T
Baths: 2 Ensuite 1 Private
Stay on a farm. Large Georgian farmhouse, superv views overlooking Aln Estuary. Centrally located on Heritage Coast Line. Excellent location for bird-watchers, golfers, walkers.

The Grange, *Northumberland Street, Alnmouth, Northd, NE66 2RJ.*
C18th stone-built former granary.
Open: All Year (not Xmas)
01665 830 401
Mr &Mrs Cossins
Fax no: 01665 830401
Rates fr: *£22.00*-**£22.00**.
Beds: 1F 2D 1T 1S
Baths: 2 Private 2 Shared
(5) (5)

Alnwick

National Grid Ref: NU1813

Plough

Rooftops, *14 Blakelaw Road, Alnwick, Northd, NE66 1AZ.*
Spacious accommodation, panoramic views, friendly.
Open: Feb to Nov
Grades: ETB 2 Cr, High Comm
01665 604201 Mrs Blair
Rates fr: *£17.50*.
Beds: 1D **Baths:** 1 Ensuite
(1)

Eradell Guest House, *1 Beaconsfield Terrace, Alnwick, Northd, NE66 1XB.*
Quiet Victorian guest house.
Open: All Year **Grades:** ETB 1 Cr
01665 602617 Mr & Mrs Richardson
Rates fr: *£16.00*-**£16.00**.
Beds: 3F 2D 1T 2S
Baths: 2 Shared

Charlton House, *2 Aydon Gardens, Alnwick, Northd, NE66 2NT.*
Family-run Victorian town house.
Open: All Year
Grades: ETB 3 Cr, High Comm, AA 3 Q
01665 605185 Mrs Jones
Rates fr: *£18.00*-**£20.00**.
Beds: 1F 2D 1T 1S
Baths: 4 Private
(2)

Bamburgh

National Grid Ref: NU1734

Greenhouse

The Mizen Head Hotel, *Lucker Road, Bamburgh, Northd, NE69 7BS.*
Fully licensed hotel - own grounds.
Open: All Year
Grades: ETB 3 Cr, AA 2 St, RAC 2 St
01668 214254 Mr Charlton
Rates fr: *£21.00*-**£21.00**.
Beds: 4F 5D 4T 2S
Baths: 11 Private 2 Shared
(30)

Squirrel Cottage, *1 Friars Court, Bamburgh, Northd, NE69 7AE.*
Quietly situated, modern, comfortable bungalow. **Open:** Easter to Oct
Grades: ETB 2 Cr, High Comm
01668 214494 Mrs Turnbull
Rates fr: *£18.00*-**£22.00**.
Beds: 2D **Baths:** 2 Ensuite
(4)

Bardon Mill

National Grid Ref: NY7864

The Craws Nest, *East Twice Brewed Farm, Bardon Mill, Hexham, Northd, NE47 7AL.*
Converted farmhouse with spectacular views. **Open:** All Year
Grades: ETB 1 Cr
01434 344348 Mrs Wanless
Rates fr: *£16.00*-**£17.00**.
Beds: 2F 1D 1T **Baths:** 1 Shared

Barrasford

National Grid Ref: NY9173

Elwood, *Barrasford, Hexham, Northd, NE48 4AN.*
Open: All Year
01434 681421 Mrs Towle
Fax no: 01434 681026
Rates fr: *£15.00*-**£18.00**.
Beds: 1F 1T 1D 4S
Baths: 2 Ensuite 1 Shared
(5) (10)
Secluded Georgian country house with extensive grounds. Uninterrupted views. Premier touring location. Very warm welcome. Our URL is **http://www.northumbria.com/business/elwood.html**

Barrasford Arms, *Barrasford, Hexham, Northd, NE48 4AA.*
Stone built C18th country inn.
Open: All Year
Grades: ETB 2 Cr, Approv
01434 681237 (also fax no)
Mr Milburn
Rates fr: *£17.00*-**£26.00**.
Beds: 2F 1D 3T
Baths: 5 Ensuite 1 Shared
(30)

Beadnell

National Grid Ref: NU2329

Craster Alms

Beach Court, *Harbour Road, Beadnell, Chathill, Northd, NE67 5BJ.*
Magnificent turreted beachside home. **Open:** All Year
Grades: ETB 3 Cr, High Comm
01665 720225 Mrs Field
Fax no: 01665 721499
Rates fr: *£24.50*-**£39.50**.
Beds: 2D 1T **Baths:** 3 Private
(5) (4)

Beadnell Bay

National Grid Ref: NU2327

Craster Alms (Beadnell)

Low Dover, *Harbour Road, Beadnell Bay, Chathill, Northd, NE67 5BH.*
Luxurious, quiet suites, beach 20 yards. **Open:** All Year (not Xmas)
Grades: ETB 1 Cr, High Comm
01665 720291 / 0860 370866
Mrs Thompson **Rates fr:** *£22.50*.
Beds: 1F 1D **Baths:** 2 Ensuite
(8) (2)

Belford

National Grid Ref: NU1033

Black Swan

Rosebank, *5 Cragside Avenue, Belford, Northd, NE70 7NA.*
Dutch bungalow, lovely views. Private parking. **Open:** Easter to Sep
Grades: ETB Listed, Approv
01668 213762 Mrs Godtschailk
Rates fr: *£15.00*-**£18.00**.
Beds: 1F 1T **Baths:** 1 Shared
(2)

Blue Bell Farm House, *West Street, Belford, Northd, NE70 7QE.*
Large modern comfortable house.
Open: All Year (not Xmas)
01668 213890 Mrs Mosley
Rates fr: *£12.00*-**£12.00**.
Beds: 1F 1D 1T 1S
Baths: 1 Ensuite 1 Shared
(5)

Bellingham

National Grid Ref: NY8383

Rose & Crown, Coach House

Crofters End, *The Croft, Bellingham, Hexham, Northd, NE48 2JY.*
Family house overlooking beautiful countryside. **Open:** Easter to Oct
01434 220034 Mrs Forster
Rates fr: *£14.00*-**£14.00**.
Beds: 2F 1D 1S **Baths:** 1 Shared
(4) (3)

Lynn View, *Bellingham, Hexham, Northd, NE48 2BL.*
Comfortable friendly accommodation in village.
Open: All Year (not Xmas)
01434 220344 (also fax no)
Mrs Batey
Rates fr: *£16.00*-**£17.00**.
Beds: 1F 2D **Baths:** 1 Shared
(2) (3)

Lyndale Guest House, *Off The Square, Bellingham, Kielderwater, Hexham, Northd, NE48 2AW.*
Panoramic views. Walkers welcome. Delicious home-cooking.
Open: All Year
Grades: ETB 3 Cr, High Comm, RAC Acclaim
01434 220361 Mrs Gaskin
Rates fr: *£22.00*-**£25.00**.
Beds: 1F 2D 1T 1S
Baths: 2 Ensuite 1 Private 1 Shared
(10) (5)

Bank Cottage, *Off The Square, Bellingham, Hexham, Northd, NE48 2AW.*
Superb comfortable. Situated for fells & River Dene.
Open: Jan to Nov
Grades: ETB 3 Cr, High Comm, RAC Acclaim
01434 220361 Mrs Gaskin
Rates fr: *£22.00*-**£30.00**.
Beds: 1D 1T
Baths: 1 Shared
(10) (5)

Belsay

National Grid Ref: NZ1078

Bounder House, *Belsay, Newcastle-upon-Tyne, NE20 0JR.*
Quiet farmhouse in beautiful surroundings.
Open: All Year
01661 881267 Mrs Fearns
Rates fr: *£17.00*-**£20.00**.
Beds: 1F 2D 1T
Baths: 2 Private 1 Shared
(12)

Berwick-upon-Tweed

National Grid Ref: NT9952

Foxtons Wine Bar, Magnus, Cobbled Yard

Tree Tops, *The Village Green, East Ord, Berwick-upon-Tweed, TD15 2NS.*
Open: Apr to Oct
Grades: ETB 2 Cr, Deluxe
01289 330679 Mr Nicholls
Rates fr: *£24.00*-**£30.00**.
Beds: 1D 1T
Baths: 2 Ensuite
(4)
ETB 'England for Excellence' National Awards 1995, Winner: B&B of the Year. Which? Hotel Guide 1997, Northumberland's Hotel of the Year. Be pampered in this spacious, single-storey home in peaceful village 1.5 miles Berwick. Superb home cooking, candle-lit dinners, licensed. Residents' lounge, 0.75 acre garden.

The Castle, *103 Castlegate, Berwick-upon-Tweed, TD15 1LF.*
Friendly convenient family-run accommodation.
Open: All Year (not Xmas)
Grades: ETB Listed, Comm
01289 307900 / 306471 (also fax no)
Mr & Mrs Thompson
Rates fr: *£20.00*-**£30.00**.
Beds: 1F 7D 4T 2S
Baths: 10 Ensuite 1 Shared

Rob Roy Pub & Restaurant, *Dock Road, Tweedmouth, Berwick-upon-Tweed, TD15 2BQ.*
Open: All Year (not Xmas)
01289 306428 Mr Wilson
Rates fr: *£17.00*-**£21.00**.
Beds: 1D 1T
Baths: 2 Shared
Stone-built cosy riverside pub with open coal fire. Bar/restaurant menus offer Tweed salmon/trout, Northumbrian lobster, Lindisfarne oysters, North Sea scallops. 2 mins Berwick centre.

Milestone House, *109 Etal Road, Tweedmouth, Berwick-upon-Tweed, TD15 2DU.*
Warm, welcoming, superior guest house.
Open: All Year (not Xmas)
01289 304404 Mrs Sanderson
Rates fr: *£15.00*-**£15.00**.
Beds: 1D 1T **Baths:** 1 Shared
(4) (2)

8 Ravensdowne, *Berwick-upon-Tweed, TD15 1HX.*
Sally Duke offers year-round welcome.
Open: All Year (not Xmas)
Grades: ETB 2 Cr, High Comm
01289 307883 Mrs Duke
Rates fr: *£17.00*-**£17.00**.
Beds: 1F 1D 2T 2S
Baths: 2 Ensuite 2 Shared

Tweedview, *1 Blakewell RoadTweedmouth, Berwick-upon-Tweed, TD15 2HG.*
Small guest house with excellent views .
Open: All Year (not Xmas)
Grades: ETB 1 Cr, High Comm
01289 303317 Mrs Robson
Rates fr: *£15.00*-**£15.00**.
Beds: 1D 1T 1S
Baths: 1 Shared
(2)

Wallace Guest House, *1 Wallace Green, Berwick-upon-Tweed, TD15 1EB.*
Centrally situated, comfortable guest house.
Open: All Year (not Xmas)
Grades: ETB Listed, Comm
01289 306539 (also fax no)
Mrs Hoggan
Rates fr: *£15.50*-**£19.00**.
Beds: 3F 1D 1T
Baths: 3 Private 2 Shared
(5)

Harberton Guest House, *181 Main Street, Spittal, Berwick-upon-Tweed, TD15 1RP.*
Victorian house, magnificent sea views.
Open: All Year (not Xmas)
01289 308813 Mrs Winters
Rates fr: *£20.00*-**£16.50**.
Beds: 3D 2T 1S
Baths: 3 Ensuite 3 Shared
(6)

Alletsa Guest House, *66 Ravensdowne, Berwick-upon-Tweed, TD15 1DQ.*
Georgian townhouse within ramparts.
Open: All Year (not Xmas)
Grades: ETB 2 Cr, Comm
01289 308199 Mrs Weeks
Rates fr: *£16.00*-**£16.00**.
Beds: 5D 2T 1S
Baths: 2 Private 2 Shared
(9)

The Old Vicarage Guest House, *Church Road, Tweedmouth, Berwick-upon-Tweed, TD15 2AN.*
Attractive C19th detached house.
Open: All Year (not Xmas)
Grades: ETB 2 Cr, High Comm, AA 4 Q, Select
01289 306909
Mrs Richardson
Rates fr: *£14.00*-**£14.00**.
Beds: 1F 4D 1T 1S
Baths: 4 Ensuite 1 Shared
(5)

91 Castlegate, *Berwick-upon-Tweed, TD15 1LF.*
Converted old inn, near town centre.
Open: Mar to Oct
Grades: ETB 1 Cr
01289 302225
Mr & Mrs Stevens
Rates fr: *£17.50*-**£20.00**.
Beds: 1D 1T 1S
Baths: 1 Private 1 Shared

Blacka Burn

National Grid Ref: NY8677

Battlestead's Hotel

Hetherington Farm, *Blacka Burn, Wark, Hexham, Northd, NE48 3DR.*
Very comfortable farmhouse in country.
Open: Easter to Nov
01434 230260 Mrs Nichol
Rates fr: *£14.00*-**£14.00**.
Beds: 2D 1T 1S
Baths: 1 Shared
(10) (3)

Catton

National Grid Ref: NY8257

Crown Inn

The Old Hostel, *1 Allen View, Catton, Hexham, Northd, NE47 9QQ.*
Comfortable, friendly house. Lovely views.
Open: All Year
01434 683780 Mrs Coulson
Fax no: 01434 683037
Rates fr: *£15.00*-**£15.00**.
Beds: 1F 1D 1T 2S
Baths: 2 Shared
(0) (4)

Chollerford

National Grid Ref: NY9170

Brunton Water Mill, *Chollerford, Hexham, Northd, NE46 4EL.*
Beautifully converted water mill.
Open: All Year (not Xmas)
01434 681002 Mrs Pesarra
Rates fr: *£20.00*-**£25.00**.
Beds: 2D 1T
Baths: 2 Ensuite 1 Shared
(12) (8)

Corbridge

National Grid Ref: NY9964

Black Bull, Angel

The Hayes Guest House, *Newcastle Road, Corbridge, Northd, NE45 5LP.*
Peaceful house, spacious, lovely views.
Open: All Year (not Xmas)
Grades: ETB 1 Cr
01434 632010 Mr Matthews
Rates fr: *£16.00*-**£16.00**.
Beds: 2F 2D 2T 3S
Baths: 2 Shared
(12)

Fellcroft, *Station Road, Corbridge, Northd, NE45 5AY.*
Comfortable Edwardian house.
Open: All Year
Grades: ETB Listed
01434 632384 Mr & Mrs Brown
Rates fr: *£15.00*-**£19.00**.
Beds: 2T
Baths: 1 Ensuite 1 Private
(2)

Priorfield, *Hippingstones Lane, Corbridge, Northd, NE45 5JA.*
Elegant Edwardian house, peaceful location.
Open: All Year (not Xmas)
Grades: ETB 2 Cr, High Comm, AA 3 Q
01434 633179 Mrs Steenberg
Fax no: 01434 633077
Rates fr: *£18.00*-**£25.00**.
Beds: 1D 1T
Baths: 1 Ensuite 1 Private
(5) (2)

Craster

National Grid Ref: NU2519

Cottage Inn, Masons Arms

Stonecroft, *Craster, Alnwick, Northd, NE66 3SZ.*
Spacious detached bungalow, peaceful location.
Open: All Year
Grades: ETB Listed, High Comm
01665 576433 Mrs Stafford
Rates fr: *£15.00*.
Beds: 2D
Baths: 1 Private 1 Shared
(1) (4)

Howick Scar Farm, *Craster, Alnwick, Northd, NE66 3SU.*
Comfortable farmhouse on Heritage coast.
Open: May to Nov
Grades: ETB Listed, Comm
01665 576665 Mrs Curry
Rates fr: *£15.00*-**£18.00**.
Beds: 2D
Baths: 1 Shared
(5) (4)

4 South Acres, *Craster, Alnwick, Northd, NE66 3TN.*
Modern, comfortable house, 50 metres from sea.
Open: All Year (not Xmas)
01665 576374 Mrs Lumsden
Rates fr: *£15.00*-**£15.00**.
(2)

Edlingham

National Grid Ref: NU1108

Lumbylaw Farm, *Edlingham, Alnwick, Northd, NE66 2BW.*
Panoramic views all round.
Open: Easter to Oct
01665 574277 Mrs Lee
Rates fr: *£17.00*-**£17.00**.
Beds: 1D 2T
Baths: 1 Shared
(12) (3)

Ellington

National Grid Ref: NZ2791

Hagg Farmhouse, *Ellington, Morpeth, Northd, NE61 5JW.*
Converted C17th farmhouse.
Open: All Year
01670 860514 Mrs Nixon
Rates fr: *£12.50*-**£15.00**.
Beds: 1F 1D 1T 1S
Baths: 2 Ensuite 1 Shared
(10)

Embleton

National Grid Ref: NU2322

Brunton House, *Embleton, Alnwick, Northd, NE66 3HQ.*
Fine, spacious, well-furnished country house.
Open: All Year (not Xmas)
Grades: ETB 2 Cr, Comm
01665 589238 Mr Robson
Rates fr: *£17.00*-**£17.00**.
Beds: 2D 3T 2S
Baths: 3 Ensuite 2 Shared
(7)

Fourstones

National Grid Ref: NY8967

Thistlerigg Farm, *High Warden, Fourstones, Hexham, Northd, NE46 4SR.*
Comfortable farmhouse, warm welcome awaits.
Open: Easter to Nov
01434 602041 Mrs Mitchell
Rates fr: *£13.50*-**£14.00**.
Beds: 2D 1T
(4)

Great Tosson

National Grid Ref: NU0200

Three Wheat Heads

Tosson Tower Farm, *Great Tosson, Rothbury, Morpeth, Northd, NE65 7NW.*
Traditional working farm guest house. **Open:** Jan to Nov
Grades: ETB 2 Cr, High Comm
01669 620228 Mrs Foggin
Rates fr: *£18.50*-**£18.50**.
Beds: 1F 1D 1T **Baths:** 3 Ensuite
(4)

Greenhead

National Grid Ref: NY6665

Milecastle Inn, Greenhead Hotel

Holmhead Farm, *Licensed Guesthouse, Hadrians Wall, Greenhead, Carlisle, Cumbria, CA6 7HY.*
Former farm on Hadrians Wall.
Open: All Year (not Xmas)
Grades: ETB 3 Cr, Comm, AA 3 Q
016977 47402 (also fax no)
Mr & Mrs Staff
Rates fr: *£23.50*-**£33.00**.
Beds: 1F 1D 2T
Baths: 4 Ensuite
(6)

Hadrians Wall

National Grid Ref: NY7969

Milecastle Inn

Sewingshields Farm, *Hadrians Wall, Haydon Bridge, Hexham, Northd, NE47 6NW.*
On Hadrian's Wall - breathtaking views.
Open: All Year (not Xmas)
Grades: ETB Listed, Comm
01434 684418 Mrs Murray
Rates fr: *£15.00*-**£15.00**.
Beds: 1F 1D 1T
Baths: 2 Shared
(4)

Crindledykes Farm, *Hadrians Wall, Housesteads, Hexham, Northd, NE47 7AP.*
Well maintained C17th farmhouse.
Open: All Year (not Xmas)
Grades: ETB Listed, High Comm, AA 3 Q
01434 344316 Mrs Davidson
Rates fr: *£14.00*-**£20.00**.
Beds: 1D 1T
Baths: 1 Shared

Haltwhistle

National Grid Ref: NY7064

Grey Bull Hotel, Milecastle Inn

Grey Bull Hotel, *Main Street, Haltwhistle, Northd, NE49 0DL.*
Open: All Year
Grades: ETB 1 Cr, Approv
01434 321991 Mr & Mrs Morpeth
Rates fr: *£12.50*-**£15.00**.
Beds: 2F 3D 1T 1S
Baths: 3 Shared
(20)
Perfectly situated for easy access to the most important sites of Hadrians Wall. Close to golf course. Local walks. All local amenities.

Hall Meadows, *Main Street, Haltwhistle, Northd, NE49 0AZ.*
Large C19th private house.
Open: All Year
Grades: ETB 1 Cr, Comm
01434 321021 Mrs Humes
Rates fr: *£16.00*-**£16.00**.
Beds: 1D 1T 1S
Baths: 1 Shared
(3)

Riverway House, *4 Wydon Avenue, Haltwhistle, Northd, NE49 0AS.*
Comfortable C18th riverside farmhouse.
Open: All Year
01434 320378 Mrs Dawson
Rates fr: *£15.00*-**£17.00**.
Beds: 1D 1T
Baths: 1 Shared
(3)

White Craig, *Nr Hadrian's Wall, Shield Hill, Haltwhistle, Northd, NE49 9NW.*
Snug old rambling single storey farmhouse.
Open: All Year
Grades: ETB 2 Cr, High Comm, AA 4 Q, Select
01434 320565 (also fax no)
Ms Laidlow
Rates fr: *£19.25*-**£25.00**.
Beds: 2D 1T **Baths:** 3 Private
(3)

Hartburn

National Grid Ref: NZ0886

The Bakers Chest, *Hartburn, Morpeth, Northd, NE61 4JB.*
Large comfortable house. Quiet village.
Open: All Year (not Xmas)
01670 772214 Mrs Cansdale
Rates fr: *£15.00*-**£25.00**.
Beds: 1D 1T
Baths: 2 Shared
(3)

Haydon Bridge

National Grid Ref: NY8464

Railway Hotel, *Church Street, Haydon Bridge, Northd, NE47 6JG.*
Friendly-run pub/hotel.
Open: All Year
01434 684254 Miss Bell
Rates fr: *£17.50*-**£17.50**.
Beds: 1F 1D 2T **Baths:** 1 Shared

Geeswood House, *Whittis Road, Haydon Bridge, Hexham, Northd, NE47 6AQ.*
Early Victorian spacious stone-built house.
Open: All Year (not Xmas)
01434 684220 Mr & Mrs Easton
Rates fr: *£16.00*-**£20.00**.
Beds: 1D 2T **Baths:** 2 Shared
(10)

Hesleyside

National Grid Ref: NY8183

Mantle Hill, *Hesleyside, Bellingham, Hexham, Northd, NE48 2LB.*
Luxury licensed country house B&B.
Open: All Year (not Xmas)
01434 220428 Mrs Loyd
Rates fr: *£19.00*-**£20.00**.
Beds: 1T 1D
Baths: 1 Ensuite 1 Private
(3) (8)

Hexham

National Grid Ref: NY9363

Coach & Horses, Dipton Mill, Rat Inn, Daniella's Bistro, Harlequin's

West Close House, *Hextol Terrace, Hexham, Northd, NE46 2AD.*
Open: All Year
Grades: ETB 2 Cr, High Comm
01434 603307
Ms Graham-Tomlinson
Rates fr: *£17.50*-**£17.50**.
Beds: 1F 1D 2S
Baths: 1 Private 1 Shared
(10) (4)
Charming, secluded detached 1920s villa. Immaculately maintained. Lovely gardens with revolving summerhouse. Quiet private cul-de-sac 10 minute stroll from town centre. Warm, friendly, relaxing ambience.

Dukeslea, *32 Shaws Park, Hexham, Northd,* *NE46 3BJ.*
Comfortable, modern, detached family home.
Open: All Year (not Xmas)
Grades: ETB 2 Cr, High Comm, AA 3 Q, Recomm
01434 602947 Mrs Theobald
Rates fr: *£17.00*-**£19.00**.
Beds: 2D **Baths:** 2 Private
(1) (4)

Middlemarch, *Hencotes, Hexham, Northd,* *NE46 2EB.*
Beautiful award-winning Georgian house. **Open:** All Year
Grades: AA 4 Q, Select
01434 605003 Mrs Elliott
Rates fr: *£21.00*-**£26.00**.
Beds: 1F 1D 1T
Baths: 2 Private 1 Shared
(10) (4)

Topsy Turvy, *9 Leazes Lane, Hexham, Northd,* *NE46 3BA.*
Cosy, pretty, chalet-type home.
Open: All Year (not Xmas)
Grades: ETB Listed, High Comm
01434 603152 Ms McCormick
Rates fr: *£15.00*.
Beds: 2D 1T
Baths: 1 Private 1 Shared
(3)

18 Hextol Terrace, *Hexham, Northd,* *NE46 2DF.*
Comfortable, spacious, private town house.
Open: All Year (not Xmas)
01434 602265 Mrs Boaden
Rates fr: *£14.00*-**£14.00**.
Beds: 1F 1D 1S **Baths:** 1 Shared

Rose & Crown Inn, *Slaley, Hexham, Northd,* *NE47 0AA.*
Warm, friendly family-run inn.
Open: All Year
Grades: ETB 3 Cr, High Comm, AA 3 Q, Recomm, RAC Acclaim
01434 673263 Mr & Mrs Pascoe
Fax no: 01434 673305
Rates fr: *£19.50*-**£19.50**.
Beds: 1F 2D 1S
Baths: 3 Private
(10) (30)

High Dalton

National Grid Ref: NY9158

Dipton Mill

High Dalton Farm, *High Dalton, Hexham, Northd,* *NE46 2LB.*
Comfortable family farmhouse, children welcome.
Open: All Year
01434 673320 Mrs Stobbs
Rates fr: *£15.00*-**£15.00**.
Beds: 1F 1D 1S **Baths:** 2 Shared
(2)

The lowest **single** *rate is shown in* **bold.**

Holy Island

National Grid Ref: NU1241

North View Lodge, *Marygate, Holy Island, Berwick-upon-Tweed, Northd,* *TD15 2SD.*
Open: All Year (not Xmas)
Grades: ETB 3 Cr, High Comm
01289 389222 Mrs Richardson
Rates fr: *£23.00*-**£30.00**.
Beds: 2D 1T
(6)
450-year-old Listed building on beautiful unspoilt island. Ideal for history & nature enthusiasts and as a base for exploring the glories of Northumberland.

Britannia House, *Holy Island, Berwick-upon-Tweed, Northd,* *TD15 2RX.*
Excellent cosy accommodation.
Open: Mar to Oct
01289 389218 Mrs Patterson
Rates fr: *£14.00*-**£16.00**.
Beds: 2D 1T
Baths: 1 Ensuite 1 Shared

Humshaugh

National Grid Ref: NY9171

Crown Inn, *Humshaugh, Hexham, Northd,* *NE46 4AG.*
Old fashioned country inn.
Open: All Year (not Xmas)
01434 681231 Miss Buck
Rates fr: *£15.00*-**£15.00**.
Beds: 1F 1D 1S
Baths: 1 Shared

Ilderton

National Grid Ref: NU0121

Station House

West Cottage, *Ilderton, Alnwick, Northd,* *NE66 4YD.*
Comfortable cottage in Cheviot foothills.
Open: All Year
01668 217360
Ms Chute
Rates fr: *£15.00*-**£15.00**.
Beds: 1D
Baths: 1 Shared
(10) (3)

Juniper

National Grid Ref: NY9358

Rose & Crown

Dene House, *Juniper, Hexham, Northd,* *NE46 1SJ.*
Stone farmhouse with beamed ceilings.
Open: All Year (not Xmas)
Grades: ETB 2 Cr, High Comm, AA 4 Q, Select
01434 673413 Mrs Massey
Rates fr: *£18.00*-**£15.00**.
Beds: 1D 1T 1S **Baths:** 2 Private
(0) (3)

Peth Head Cottage, *Juniper, Hexham, Northd,* *NE47 0LA.*
Traditional country cottage, pretty garden.
Open: All Year (not Xmas)
Grades: ETB 2 Cr, High Comm
01434 673286
Mrs Liddle
Fax no: 01434 673038
Rates fr: *£18.00*-**£18.00**.
Beds: 1D 1T
Baths: 2 Private

Kirkharle

National Grid Ref: NZ0182

Shieldhall, *Kirkharle, Morpeth, Northd,* *NE61 4AQ.*
The best accommodation in Northumberland.
Open: Mar to Nov
Grades: ETB 3 Cr, High Comm
01830 540387 (also fax no)
Mr Gay
Rates fr: *£17.50*-**£26.00**.
Beds: 2F 2D 2T 2S
Baths: 4 Private
(10) (10)

Kirkhaugh

National Grid Ref: NY6949

Barhaugh Hall, *Kirkhaugh, Alston, Cumbria,* *CA9 3NJ.*
Victorian manor in own grounds.
Open: All Year
01434 381978
Mr Brack
Rates fr: *£18.75*-**£18.75**.
Beds: 2F 5D 18T 5S
(40)

Kirkwhelpington

National Grid Ref: NY9984

Tone Inn

Cornhills, *Kirkwhelpington, Newcastle-upon-Tyne,* *NE19 2RE.*
Large Victorian farmhouse, working farm.
Open: All Year (not Xmas)
Grades: ETB Listed, High Comm
01830 540232 Ms Thornton
Rates fr: *£17.50*-**£20.00**.
Beds: 1F 1T
Baths: 2 Shared
(10)

Knarsdale

National Grid Ref: NY6753

Stonehall Farm, *Knarsdale, Slaggyford, Carlisle, Cumbria,* *CA6 7PB.*
C18th farmhouse.
Open: All Year (not Xmas)
01434 381349 Mrs Graham
Rates fr: *£15.00*-**£15.00**.
Beds: 2F 1T
Baths: 1 Private 1 Shared

Little Bavington

National Grid Ref: NY9878

Old Post Office Cottage, *Little Bavington, Capheaton, Newcastle-upon-Tyne, NE19 2BB.*
Spacious, beamed C19th cottage.
Open: All Year (not Xmas)
01830 530331 Mrs Rodger
Rates fr: *£15.00*-**£18.00**.
Beds: 1F 1T
(3)

Longframlington

National Grid Ref: NU1300

The Lee Farm, *Longframlington, Morpeth, Northd, NE65 8JQ.*
Attractive farmhouse in beautiful countryside.
Open: All Year (not Xmas)
Grades: ETB 2 Cr, High Comm
01665 570257 Mrs Aynsley
Rates fr: *£16.00*-**£22.00**.
Beds: 1F 1D 1T
Baths: 1 Ensuite 1 Shared
(4)

West Raw Farm, *Longframlington, Morpeth, Northd, NE65 8JF.*
Very warm welcome awaits.
Open: All Year
01665 570227 Ms Gibson
Rates fr: *£13.00*-**£13.50**.
Beds: 1F 1D 1T
Baths: 1 Shared

Longhorsley

National Grid Ref: NZ1494

Baronial Restaurant & Guest House, *Cross Cottage, Longhorsley, Morpeth, Northd, NE65 8TD.*
Traditional oak-beamed house, warm welcome. **Open:** All Year
01670 788378 Mrs Glenwright
Rates fr: *£16.50*-**£20.00**.
Beds: 2F **Baths:** 1 Shared

Lowick

National Grid Ref: NU0139

The Old Manse, *5 Cheviot View, Lowick, Berwick-upon-Tweed, TD15 2TY.*
Georgian former church manse.
Open: Mar to Nov
01289 388264 Mrs Huddart
Rates fr: *£18.50*-**£22.50**.
Beds: 2D 1T **Baths:** 3 Private

Mickley Square

National Grid Ref: NZ0762

Riverside, *Mickley Square, Stocksfield, Northd, NE43 7DF.*
Peaceful retreat for country lovers.
Open: All Year
01661 842887 Mrs Henderson
Rates fr: *£15.00*-**£16.00**.
Beds: 1D 1T **Baths:** 2 Shared
(6)

Middle Ord

National Grid Ref: NT9650

Canty's Brig

Middle Ord Manor House Farm, *Middle Ord, Berwick-upon-Tweed, TD15 2XQ.*
Open: Easter to Oct
Grades: ETB 2 Cr, Deluxe
01289 306323 Mrs Gray
Rates fr: *£25.00*-**£28.00**.
Beds: 2D 1T **Baths:** 3 Ensuite
(3)
Award winning gracious Georgian farmhouse on working farm. Spacious ensuite rooms - 4 posters if desired. Sorry no children or pets. Phone for brochure.

Morpeth

National Grid Ref: NZ2085

Sun Inn

Carlisle House, *St Marys Field, Morpeth, Northd, NE61 2QS.*
Large, elevated, Victorian house.
Open: All Year (not Xmas)
01670 513591 Mrs Smith
Rates fr: *£15.00*-**£16.50**.
Beds: 1F 1D 1T

Elder Cottage, *High Church, Morpeth, Northd, NE61 2QT.*
C18th Cottage with garden and sunroof.
Open: All Year (not Xmas)
01670 517664 Mrs Cook
Rates fr: *£15.00*-**£15.00**.
Beds: 2D 1T
Baths: 1 Shared
(3)

Newton

National Grid Ref: NZ0364

Robin Hood

Crookhill Farm, *Newton, Stocksfield, Northd, NE43 7UX.*
Comfortable, welcoming farmhouse.
Open: Easter to Oct
Grades: ETB Listed, Comm, AA Listed
01661 843117 Mrs Leech
Rates fr: *£15.00*-**£17.00**.
Beds: 1F 1T 1S
Baths: 1 Shared
(4)

Ninebanks

National Grid Ref: NY7853

Taylor Burn, *Ninebanks, Hexham, Northd, NE47 8DE.*
Large, comfortable farmhouse, excellent food.
Open: All Year
01434 345343 Mrs Ostler
Rates fr: *£14.00*-**£14.00**.
Beds: 2D 1S **Baths:** 1 Shared
(6) (6)

Otterburn

National Grid Ref: NY8893

Tower Hotel

Brown Rigg Cottage, *Otterburn, Newcastle-upon-Tyne, NE19 1LG.*
Open: All Year
01830 520541 Mrs Boon
Rates fr: *£18.00*-**£18.00**.
Beds: 1F 1D
Baths: 1 Private
(6)
Relax in Northumberland wind-powered cottage with panoramic views. Home cooking. Also available 3 day breaks, 2 people sharing only £149, bed, breakfast, evening meal.

Blakehope Farm, *Otterburn, Newcastle-upon-Tyne, NE19 1LQ.*
Open: All Year
01830 520266 Mrs Anderson
Rates fr: *£13.00*-**£15.00**.
Beds: 1F 1T 1S **Baths:** 1 Shared
(1) (3)
Typical 200-year-old Northumbrian farmhouse - working farm. On A68. Built on site of Roman camp. Ideal touring centre. Adjacent Pennine Way.

Ponteland

National Grid Ref: NZ1673

Highlander Inn

7 Collingwood Cottages, *Limestone Lane, Ponteland, Newcastle-upon-Tyne, NE20 0DD.*
Quiet countryside home. Lovely views. **Open:** All Year
Grades: ETB Listed
01661 825967 Mrs Baxter
Rates fr: *£15.00*-**£20.00**.
Beds: 1F 1D **Baths:** 1 Shared
(4)

Rennington

National Grid Ref: NU2118

Masons Arms, *Rennington, Alnwick, Northd, NE66 3RX.*
Country inn serving good food & real ale.
Open: All Year (not Xmas)
01665 577275 Mr Sloan
Rates fr: *£23.50*-**£37.50**.
Beds: 2F 2D 1T **Baths:** 5 Private
(14) (40)

Rochester

National Grid Ref: NY8398

Redesdale Arms Hotel, *Rochester, Otterburn, Newcastle-upon-Tyne, NE19 1TA.*
600-year-old coaching inn.
Open: All Year
Grades: ETB 3 Cr, Comm
01830 520668 Mrs Wright
Fax no: 01830 520063
Rates fr: *£25.00*-**£25.00**.
Beds: 10 **Baths:** 10 Ensuite
(20)

The lowest **single** *rate is shown in* **bold.**

Rothbury

National Grid Ref: NU0501

Three Wheat Heads

***Tosson Tower Farm,** Great Tosson, Rothbury, Morpeth, Northd, NE65 7NW.*
Traditional working farm guest house.
Open: Jan to Nov
Grades: ETB 2 Cr, High Comm
01669 620228 Mrs Foggin
Rates fr: *£18.50*-**£18.50**.
Beds: 1F 1D 1T
Baths: 3 Ensuite
(4)

***The Lee Farm,** Longframlington, Rothbury, Morpeth, Northd, NE65 8JQ.*
Attractive farmhouse in beautiful countryside.
Open: All Year (not Xmas)
Grades: ETB 2 Cr, High Comm
01665 570257
Mrs Aynsley
Rates fr: *£16.00*-**£22.00**.
Beds: 1F 1D 1T
Baths: 1 Ensuite 1 Shared
(4)

***Well Strand,** Rothbury, Morpeth, Northd, NE65 7UD.*
Small friendly, central for Northumberland.
Open: All Year (not Xmas)
01669 620794
Mr & Mrs Edes
Rates fr: *£13.50*-**£13.50**.
Beds: 1D 1T 1S
Baths: 1 Shared
(2)

***Thropton Demesne Farmhouse,** Rothbury, Morpeth, Northd, NE65 7LT.*
Comfortable Victorian farmhouse, spectacular views.
Open: All Year (not Xmas)
Grades: ETB 2 Cr, High Comm
01669 620196
Mr & Mrs Giles
Rates fr: *£19.00*-**£25.00**.
Beds: 1F 1D 1T
Baths: 2 Ensuite 1 Private
(6)

Seahouses

National Grid Ref: NU2132

The Viking, Silk Bar

***Drumoyne,** 4 James Street, Seahouses, Northd, NE68 7YB.*
Large detached house.
Open: Easter to Oct
01665 720809 Ms Stevens
Rates fr: *£15.00*-**£16.00**.
Beds: 1F 1D 1T 1S
Baths: 1 Shared
(2)

***Rowena,** 99 Main Street, Seahouses, Northd, NE68 7TS.*
Open: All Year (not Xmas)
01665 721309
Mrs Hodgson
Rates fr: *£15.00*-**£15.00**.
Beds: 1F 1T 1S
Baths: 1 Private
(4)
Comfortable accommodation within walking distance to harbour for boats to Farne Islands. Beautiful beaches, castles, golf courses. Ideal for out of season breaks.

***The Lodge,** Main Street, Seahouses, Northd, NE68 7UA.*
Small, stone hotel with log fires.
Open: All Year
Grades: ETB 3 Cr, Comm
01665 720158 Mr & Mrs Brown
Rates fr: *£25.00*-**£25.00**.
Beds: 1F 4D **Baths:** 5 Private
(8) (5)

Slaggyford

National Grid Ref: NY6752

***Crianlarich,** Slaggyford, Carlisle, Cumbria, CA6 7NJ.*
Stone-built detached private house.
Open: All Year
01434 381329 Mrs Galilee
Rates fr: *£13.00*-**£13.00**.
Beds: 2D 1T **Baths:** 2 Shared
(2) (3)

Slaley

National Grid Ref: NY9757

***Rye Hill Farm,** Slaley, Hexham, Northd, NE47 0AH.*
Working farm, all rooms ensuite.
Open: All Year
Grades: ETB 3 Cr, Comm, AA 3 Q
01434 673259 Ms Courage
Fax no: 01434 673608
Rates fr: *£20.00*-**£25.00**.
Beds: 2F 2D 2T **Baths:** 6 Private
(6)

***Rose & Crown Inn,** Slaley, Hexham, Northd, NE47 0AA.*
Warm, friendly family-run inn.
Open: All Year
Grades: ETB 3 Cr, High Comm, AA 3 Q, Recomm, RAC Acclaim
01434 673263
Mr & Mrs Pascoe
Fax no: 01434 673305
Rates fr: *£19.50*-**£19.50**.
Beds: 1F 2D 1S **Baths:** 3 Private
(10) (30)

Stagshaw Bank

National Grid Ref: NY9964

***Fox & Hounds Hotel,** Stagshaw Bank, Corbridge, Northd, NE45 5QW.*
3 Crown Commended 400-year-old inn. **Open:** All Year
Grades: ETB 3 Cr, Comm
01434 633024 Mr & Mrs Clark
Rates fr: *£20.00*-**£25.00**.
Beds: 1F 4D 3T 1S
Baths: 9 Ensuite
(50)

Stannington

National Grid Ref: NZ2179

Ridley Arms

***30 Station Road,** Stannington, Morpeth, Northd, NE61 6DX.*
Country house just off A1.
Open: All Year
Grades: ETB Listed
01670 789536
Mrs Parker
Rates fr: *£15.00*-**£18.00**.
Beds: 1F 1D 1T
Baths: 2 Private 1 Shared
(6)

Stocksfield

National Grid Ref: NZ0561

Blue Bell

***Old Ridley Hall,** Stocksfield, Northd, NE43 7RU.*
Large private house. Listed building.
Open: All Year
Grades: ETB Listed
01661 842816
Mrs Aldridge
Rates fr: *£17.50*-**£17.50**.
Beds: 2F 3T 1S
Baths: 1 Private 1 Shared
(14)

***Runswick House,** Main Road, Stocksfield, Northd, NE43 7JT.*
Large, detached, comfortable house.
Open: All Year
01661 844355 Mr Millar
Rates fr: *£19.00*-**£20.00**.
Beds: 2D 1T
Baths: 3 Private
(3)

***The Dene,** 11 Cade Hill Road, Stocksfield, Northd, NE43 7PB.*
Large Edwardian house - beautiful gardens.
Open: All Year (not Xmas)
01661 842025
Mrs Mitchell
Rates fr: *£19.00*-**£19.00**.
Beds: 2T 1S
Baths: 2 Ensuite 1 Private
(4)

***Bluebell Cottage,** Stocksfield, Northd, NE43 7LP.*
Beautiful cottage in rural hamlet.
Open: All Year (not Xmas)
01661 843415
Mr Yates
Rates fr: *£15.00*-**£15.00**.
Beds: 1F 1T
Baths: 1 Private 1 Shared
(3) (2)

Bringing children with you? Always ask for any special rates.

Thropton

Vational Grid Ref: NU0202

Three Wheat Heads

Carbottle, West Steads, Thropton, Morpeth, Northd, NE65 7JT.
Open: May to end-Oct
Grades: ETB Listed, Comm
01665 574672 Mrs Farr
Rates fr: *£14.50*-**£14.50**.
Beds: 1D 1T 1S
(3)
Nestling in the quiet peaceful Whittingham Vale. Spacious farmhouse overlooking the Simonside Hills, Coquet Valley, Cheviot Hills. Rothbury 5 miles. Central for walking, cycling, sightseeing Northumbria.

Three Wheat Heads, *Thropton, Rothbury, Morpeth, Northd,* NE65 7LR.
Old coaching inn overlooking Simonside. **Open:** All Year
01669 620262 Mrs Breakwell
Rates fr: *£22.95*.
Beds: 1F 4D 2T
Baths: 1 Ensuite 5 Shared

Twice Brewed

National Grid Ref: NY7567

Vallum Lodge Hotel, *Military Road, Twice Brewed, Bardon Mill, Hexham, Northd,* NE47 7AN.
Country hotel by Hadrian's Wall.
Open: Mar to Nov
Grades: ETB 2 Cr, Comm, AA 3 Q
01434 344248 Mr & Mrs Wright
Fax no: 01434 344488
Rates fr: *£21.00*-**£24.00**.
Beds: 3D 3T 1S
Baths: 2 Private 2 Shared
(25)

Uswayford

National Grid Ref: NT8814

Uswayford Farm, *Uswayford, Harbottle, Morpeth, Northumberland,* NE65 7BU.
Open: All Year
01669 650237 Mrs Buglass
Rates fr: *£14.00*-**£14.00**.
Beds: 1F 1D 1T
Baths: 1 Shared

Wall

National Grid Ref: NY9168

Hadrian Hotel

St Oswalds Farm, *Wall, Hexham, Northd,* NE46 4HB.
Working farm on Hadrians Wall.
Open: Feb to Nov
Grades: ETB Listed
01434 681307 Mrs Reay
Rates fr: *£13.50*-**£13.50**.
Beds: 1D 1T 1S
Baths: 1 Shared
(4)

Wark

National Grid Ref: NY8677

Woodpark Farm, *Wark, Hexham, Northd,* NE48 3PZ.
Listed farmhouse.
Open: May to Oct
01434 230259 Mrs Bell
Rates fr: *£14.00*-**£17.00**.
Beds: 1F 1D
Baths: 1 Shared
(3)

Battlesteads Hotel, *Wark, Hexham, Northd,* NE48 3LS.
Converted C17th farm, tastefully modernised.
Open: All Year
01434 230209 Mr & Mrs Rowland
Rates fr: *£20.00*-**£20.00**.
Beds: 1F 4D 4T 1S
Baths: 10 Ensuite
(30)

Warkworth

National Grid Ref: NU2406

Black Bull, Mason's Arms

Beck N Call, *Birling West Cottage, Warkworth, Morpeth, Northd,* NE65 0XS.
Open: All Year (not Xmas)
Grades: ETB 2 Cr, High Comm
01665 711653
Mr Halliday
Rates fr: *£19.00*-**£19.00**.
Beds: 1F 2D
Baths: 3 Ensuite
(4)
Country cottage set in 0.5 acre terraced gardens with stream. Ideal base for exploring Northumberland's magnificent coastline & many attractions. 5 mins walk from village & beach.

Aulden, *9 Watershaugh Road, Warkworth, Morpeth, Northd,* NE65 0TT.
Comfortable & welcoming, quiet surroundings.
Open: Easter to Oct
01665 711583
Mrs Lillico
Rates fr: *£15.00*-**£20.00**.
Beds: 1D 1T
Baths: 1 Shared

Bide A While, *4 Beal Croft, Warkworth, Morpeth, Northd,* NE65 0XL.
Open: All Year
Grades: ETB Listed, Comm
01665 711753
Mrs Graham
Rates fr: *£15.50*-**£17.50**.
Beds: 1F 1D 1T
Baths: 2 Private 1 Shared
(3)
Modern comfortable bungalow in cul-de-sac. Full traditional breakfast served, good base for touring historic Northumberland, bird-watching, etc.

Planning a longer stay? Always ask for any special rates.

Whitley Chapel

National Grid Ref: NY9257

Rose & Crown

Gairshield Farm, *Whitley Chapel, Hexham, Northd,* NE47 0HS.
Comfortable, peaceful C17th farmhouse.
Open: Mar to Nov
Grades: ETB Listed, High Comm
01434 673562 Mrs Kristensen
Rates fr: *£17.00*-**£20.00**.
Beds: 1F
Baths: 1 Private
(6) (10)

Wooler

National Grid Ref: NT9928

St Hilliers, *6 Church Street, Wooler, Northd,* NE71 6DA.
Stone-built village house.
Open: All Year
Grades: ETB Listed, Comm
01668 281340
Mrs Hugall
Rates fr: *£14.00*-**£15.00**.
Beds: 1F 1D 2T
Baths: 1 Shared

Millvale Cottage, *14 South Road, Wooler, Northd,* NE71 6NL.
C18th country cottage.
Open: All Year
01668 282057
Ms Witson
Rates fr: *£13.00*-**£16.00**.
Beds: 1D
(1)

Wylam

National Grid Ref: NZ1164

Fox & Hounds

Wormald House, *Main Street, Wylam, Northd,* NE41 8DN.
Very welcoming, pleasant country home.
Open: All Year (not Xmas)
Grades: ETB 2 Cr, High Comm
01661 852529
Mr & Mrs Craven
Rates fr: *£17.00*-**£17.50**.
Beds: 1D 1T
Baths: 2 Ensuite
(3)

The lowest *double* rate per person is shown in *italics*.

Nottinghamshire

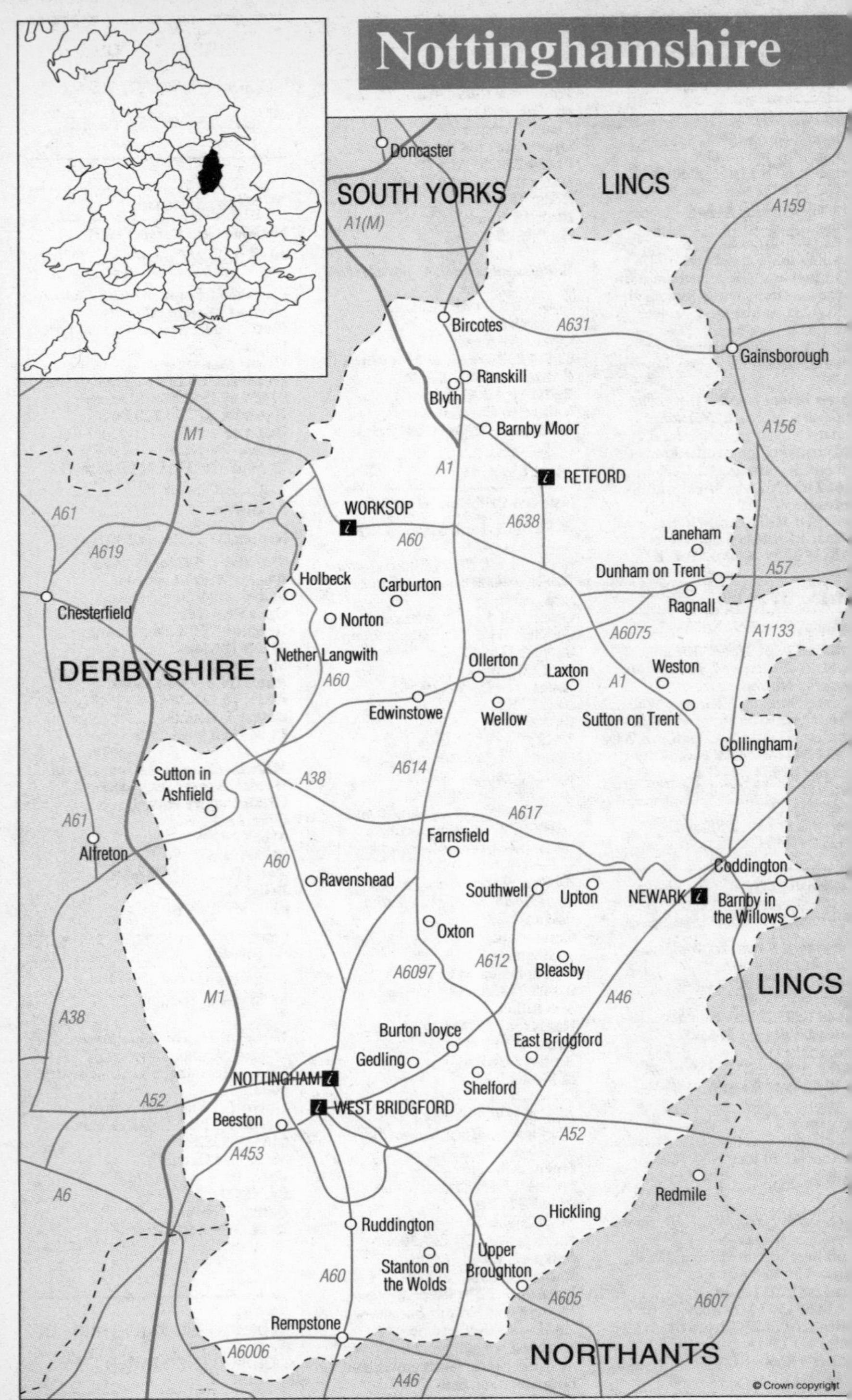

Tourist Information Centres

Sherwood Forest Visitor Centre, Edwinstowe, **Mansfield**, Nottinghamshire, NG21 9HN, 01623 824490.

Old Town Hall, Market Place, **Mansfield**, NG18 1HX, 01623 427770

The Gilstrap Centre, Castlegate, **Newark**, Nottinghamshire, NG24 1BG, 01636 78962.

Sherwood Heath, Ollerton Roundabout, **Newark**, Nottinghamshire, NG22 9DR, 01623 824545.

1-2 Smithy Row, **Nottingham**, Nottinghamshire, NG1 2BY, 0115 947 0661.

40 Grove Street, **Retford**, Nottinghamshire, DN22 6LD, 01777 860780.County Hall, Loughborough Road,

West Bridgford, Nottingham, Nottinghamshire, NG2 7QP, 01215 9773558

Worksop Library, Memorial Avenue, **Worksop**, Notts, S80 2BP, 01909 501148.

Barnby Moor

National Grid Ref: SK6684

White Horse Inn

White Horse Inn (Barnby Moor), *Le Cheval Blanc Restaurant, Great North Road, Barnby Moor, Retford, Notts, DN22 8QS.*
200-year-old country inn, French restaurant.
Open: All Year (not Xmas)
Grades: ETB 2 Cr
01777 707721 Miss Phillips
Rates fr: *£16.00*-**£20.00**.
Beds: 1D 2T
Baths: 2 Ensuite 1 Private
(30)

Beeston

National Grid Ref: SK5236

Hylands Hotel, *307 Queens Road, Beeston, Nottingham, Notts, NG9 1JA.*
Victorian hotel with home cooking.
Open: All Year
0115 925 5472
Rates fr: *£16.00*-**£16.00**.
Beds: 4F 10T 11D 17S
Baths: 20 Ensuite 6 Shared
(30)

The lowest *double* rate per person is shown in *italics*.

Bircotes

National Grid Ref: SK6391

The Flowers, *13 Galway Road, Bircotes, Doncaster, DN11 8BJ.*
Nice corner house with lovely garden. **Open:** All Year
01302 750759 Mrs Hill-Morris
Rates fr: *£14.50*-**£14.50**.
Beds: 1D 1T
Baths: 1 Shared
(2)

Bleasby

National Grid Ref: SK7149

Red Lion (Thurgarton)

Little Rudsey Farm, *Bleasby, Nottingham, Notts, NG14 7FR.*
Comfortable old farmhouse, views, garden.
Open: All Year (not Xmas)
Grades: ETB Listed
01636 830249 Mrs Norman
Rates fr: *£14.00*-**£14.00**.
Beds: 1F 1T
Baths: 1 Shared
(4) (3)

Blyth

National Grid Ref: SK6287

Priory Farm Guest House, *Hodsock Priory Estate, Blyth, Worksop, Notts, S81 0TY.*
C18th secluded farmhouse, log fire.
Open: All Year (not Xmas)
Grades: ETB 2 Cr, Approv
01909 591515 Mrs Hambleton
Fax no: 01427 890611
Rates fr: *£17.50*-**£17.50**.
Beds: 1F 1D 1T 2S
Baths: 2 Ensuite 2 Shared
(6)

Burton Joyce

National Grid Ref: SK6443

Wheatsheaf

Owston, *32 Main Street, Burton Joyce, Nottingham, Notts, NG14 5DZ.*
Welcoming comfort in village centre.
Open: All Year
0115 931 3398 Mrs Sturgeon
Rates fr: *£17.00*-**£17.00**.
Beds: 2T 1S
Baths: 1 Shared
(1)

Carburton

National Grid Ref: SK6073

Duncan Wood Lodge Guest House, *Carburton, Worksop, Notts, S80 3BP.*
C19th stone lodge house.
Open: All Year
Grades: ETB 2 Cr, Comm
01909 483614 Mrs Beevers
Rates fr: *£18.00*-**£23.00**.
Beds: 1F 2D 3T
Baths: 4 Private 1 Shared
(7)

Coddington

National Grid Ref: SK8354

Hungry Horse

3 Old Hall Gardens, *Coddington, Newark, Notts, NG24 2QJ.*
Quiet location, easy access A1 & showground.
Open: All Year (not Xmas)
01636 79417 Mrs Goodman
Rates fr: *£15.00*-**£16.00**.
Beds: 1D 1S **Baths:** 1 Shared
(2)

Collingham

National Grid Ref: SK8361

Lime Tree Farm, *Lunn Lane, Collingham, Newark, Notts, NG23 7LP.*
Attractive converted barn.
Open: All Year (not Xmas)
01636 892044 Mrs Glenny
Rates fr: *£15.00*-**£17.00**.
Beds: 1F 1D 1T **Baths:** 3 Private
(6)

Cotgrave

National Grid Ref: SK6435

Neville Arms

Jerico Farm, *Fosse Way, Cotgrave, Nottingham, Notts, NG12 3HG.*
Quality farmhouse accommodation. Working farm.
Open: All Year (not Xmas)
Grades: ETB 2 Cr, Comm
01949 81733 Mrs Herrick
Rates fr: *£18.00*-**£20.00**.
Beds: 1D 1T 1S
Baths: 1 Private 1 Shared
(3)

Dunham on Trent

National Grid Ref: SK8174

Bridge Inn

Wilmot House, *Church Walk, Dunham on Trent, Newark, Notts, NG22 0TX.*
Large Georgian house near river.
Open: All Year
01777 228226 Mrs East
Rates fr: *£16.00*-**£16.00**.
Beds: 2D 1T 1S
Baths: 1 Private 2 Shared
(14) (8)

East Bridgford

National Grid Ref: SK6943

Reindeer Inn

Barn Farm Cottage, *Kneeton Road, East Bridgford, Nottingham, Notts, NG13 8PH.*
A warm welcome. Beautiful cottage.
Open: All Year
01949 20196 Mrs Shouls
Rates fr: *£15.50*-**£15.50**.
Beds: 1F 3T 1S **Baths:** 2 Shared
(8)

East Retford

National Grid Ref: SK7080

New Queen's Head, King & Miller

The Black Boy, *14 Moorgate, East Retford, Notts, DN22 6RH.*
'Local' pub in historic area.
Open: All Year (not Xmas)
01777 702758 Mrs Cliff
Rates fr: *£14.00*-**£14.00**.
Beds: 2T 1S
Baths: 2 Private 1 Shared
(7) (20)

Tanamara Guest House, *167 Moorgate Cottage, East Retford, Notts, DN22 6TL.*
Comfortable friendly guesthouse.
Open: All Year
01777 706447 Mrs Craig
Rates fr: *£18.50*-**£18.50**.
Beds: 2D 2T 3S
Baths: 4 Ensuite 1 Private
(10)

Edwinstowe

National Grid Ref: SK6266

Friars Lodge Guest House, *3 Mill Lane, Edwinstowe, Mansfield, Notts, NG21 9QY.*
Guest house full of character.
Open: All Year
01623 823405 Mrs Bott
Rates fr: *£16.00*-**£18.00**.
Beds: 1F 1D 2T 1S
Baths: 3 Ensuite 2 Private
(6)

Farnsfield

National Grid Ref: SK6357

Dower Country House, *Lower Hexgreave Farm, Farnsfield, Newark, Notts, NG22 8LT.*
Open: All Year
Grades: ETB 3 Cr, Comm
01623 882020 Mrs Winward
Fax no: 01623 882100
Rates fr: *£16.00*-**£22.00**.
Beds: 4D 1T
Baths: 5 Ensuite
(10)
Do come & stay in our fine Georgian farmhouse where all rooms are ensuite. A varied *table de'hôte'* menu & wines are available.

Gedling

National Grid Ref: SK6142

Red Lion

25 Vernon Avenue, *Gedling, Nottingham, Notts, NG4 3FX.*
Comfortable, quiet, friendly, private house.
Open: All Year
0115 961 2830 Mrs Riley
Rates fr: *£14.00*-**£14.00**.
Beds: 1D 1S
Baths: 1 Shared
(10)

Holbeck

National Grid Ref: SK5473

Browns, *The Old Orchard Cottage, Holbeck, Worksop, Notts, S80 3NF.*
Stone cottage in large garden.
Open: All Year (not Xmas)
01909 720659
Mrs Brown
Rates fr: *£19.00*-**£30.00**.
Beds: 1F 1D
Baths: 2 Private
(8) (6)

Laneham

National Grid Ref: SK8076

Butchers' Arms

Laneham, *The Old Cottage, Laneham, Retford, Notts, DN22 0NA.*
Comfortable accommodation in quiet location.
Open: All Year (not Xmas)
01777 228555 Mrs Hardman
Fax no: 01777 228 900
Rates fr: *£17.50*-**£22.00**.
Beds: 1F 1T 2S **Baths:** 4 Private
(3) (8)

Laxton

National Grid Ref: SK7267

Dovecote Inn

Manor Farm, *Moorhouse Road, Laxton, Newark, Notts, NG22 0NU.*
Old comfortable farmhouse.
Open: All Year (not Xmas)
Grades: ETB Listed, Comm
01777 870417 Mrs Haigh
Rates fr: *£15.00*-**£15.00**.
Beds: 2F 1D
Baths: 1 Shared
(4)

Lilac Farm, *Laxton, Newark, Notts, NG22 0NX.*
C17th farmhouse.
Open: All Year (not Xmas)
Grades: ETB 1 Cr
01777 870376
Mrs Rose
Rates fr: *£15.00*-**£15.00**.
Beds: 1F 1D 1T
Baths: 1 Shared
(6)

Nether Langwith

National Grid Ref: SK5370

Boon Hills Farm, *Nether Langwith, Mansfield, Notts, NG20 9JQ.*
Large, comfortable farmhouse.
Open: Mar to Oct
01623 743862
Mrs Palmer
Rates fr: *£14.00*-**£15.00**.
Beds: 1F 1D
Baths: 1 Shared
(3)

Newark-on-Trent

National Grid Ref: SK8151

Aandacht, *54 Boundary Road, Newark-on-Trent, Notts, NG24 4AL.*
Modern, comfortable guest house.
Open: All Year (not Xmas)
Grades: ETB Listed
01636 703321 Mrs Watkins
Rates fr: *£12.00*-**£12.00**.
Beds: 1F 1S
Baths: 1 Shared
(2) (3)

Albert House, *76 Albert Street, Newark-on-Trent, Notts, NG24 4BB.*
Large private house. 5 mins from town centre.
Open: All Year
01636 705525 Mr Hall
Rates fr: *£16.00*-**£16.00**.
Beds: 1F 2T 2S
(12) (6)

Norton

National Grid Ref: SK5772

Norton Grange Farm, *Norton, Cuckney, Mansfield, Notts, NG20 9LP.*
Listed Georgian stone farmhouse.
Open: All Year (not Xmas)
Grades: ETB 1 Cr, Comm
01623 842666 Mr Palmer
Rates fr: *£16.00*-**£16.00**.
Beds: 1F 1D 1T
Baths: 1 Shared
(6)

Nottingham

National Grid Ref: SK5839

Limekiln, Fellows, Ferry Inn

Adams' Castle View Guest House, *85 Castle Boulevard, Nottingham, NG7 1FE.*
Refurbished late-Victorian city centre house.
Open: All Year
Grades: ETB Listed
0115 950 0022 Mr Adams
Rates fr: *£15.00*-**£16.00**.
Beds: 1T 3S **Baths:** 1 Shared

63 Coppice Road, Arnold, *Nottingham, NG5 7GR.*
Conveniently situated. Warm friendly atmosphere.
Open: All Year (not Xmas)
Grades: ETB Listed, Comm
0115 926 3686 Mr & Mrs Neill
Rates fr: *£15.50*-**£18.50**.
Beds: 1F 1D 2T 1S
Baths: 5 Ensuite
(6) (4)

The Conifers, *14 Helm Close, Sellers Wood, Nottingham, NG6 7FU.*
Modern house, one mile M1.
Open: All Year (not Xmas)
0115 976 4849 (also fax no)
Mrs Floyd
Rates fr: *£14.00*-**£16.00**.
Beds: 1D 1T **Baths:** 2 Private
(2)

Greenwood Lodge, *5 Third Avenue, Sherwood Rise, Nottingham,* *NG7 6JH.*
Large Victorian house, warm welcome.
Open: All Year
0115 962 1206 (also fax no)
Mr Spratt
Rates fr: *£20.00*-**£27.00**.
Beds: 1F 2D 1T 1S
Baths: 5 Ensuite
(1) (5)

Ollerton

National Grid Ref: SK6567

Durham Ox

Longmynd Guest House, *Wellow Road, Ollerton, Newark, Notts,* *NG22 9AX.*
Comfortable, family-run.
Open: All Year
01623 863493 Ms Keegan
Rates fr: *£16.50*-**£16.50**.
Beds: 5F
Baths: 3 Private 1 Shared
(5)

Oxton

National Grid Ref: SK6351

Pilgrim Cottage, *Water Lane, Oxton, Southwell, Notts,* *NG25 0SH.*
C18th cottage, tranquillity, glorious garden.
Open: All Year
0115 965 2913 Mrs Walker
Rates fr: *£21.00*-**£23.00**.
Beds: 1D
Baths: 1 Shared
(4)

Ragnall

National Grid Ref: SK8073

Bridge Inn

Ragnall House, *Ragnall, Newark, Notts,* *NG22 0UR.*
Period residence in large grounds.
Open: All Year
Grades: ETB 2 Cr, Comm
01777 228575 Mrs Hatfield
Rates fr: *£15.00*-**£15.00**.
Beds: 1F 1D 1T 1S
Baths: 1 Ensuite 1 Private 1 Shared
(6)

Ranskill

National Grid Ref: SK6587

Blue Bell

Tirl House, *Mattersey Road, Ranskill, East Retford, Notts,* *DN22 8ND.*
Small family guest house.
Open: All Year (not Xmas)
01777 818940 Mrs Key
Rates fr: *£14.50*-**£14.50**.
Beds: 2T 1S
Baths: 1 Shared
(5) (3)

Ravenshead

National Grid Ref: SK5554

Little John Inn, The Hutt

Westlands, *12 Cambourne Gardens, Ravenshead, Nottingham, Notts,* *NG15 9FU.*
Welcoming house near Newstead Abbey.
Open: All Year (not Xmas)
01623 793419 Mrs Hawkins
Rates fr: *£15.00*-**£15.00**.
Beds: 1D 1T 1S
Baths: 1 Private
(3)

Jacqmar, *18 Lea Road, Ravenshead, Nottingham, Notts,* *NG15 9EG.*
Comfortable accommodation, Nottingham 10 miles.
Open: All Year (not Xmas)
01623 793253 Mr & Mrs Thorpe
Rates fr: *£15.00*-**£15.00**.
Beds: 1F 2S
Baths: 2 Shared
(0) (3)

Rempstone

National Grid Ref: SK5724

The Thatch, *Main Street, Rempstone, Loughborough, Leics,* *LE12 6RH.*
C17th thatched cottage.
Open: All Year
01509 881512 Revd Fisher
Rates fr: *£15.00*-**£15.00**.
Beds: 1T
Baths: 1 Private
(8)

Retford

National Grid Ref: SK7080

Elms Hotel

Bolham Hall, *Bolham, Retford, Notts,* *DN22 9JQ.*
Georgian house in rural surroundings.
Open: All Year
01777 705875 Mrs Turner
Rates fr: *£15.00*-**£15.00**.
Beds: 1F 2S
Baths: 1 Shared
(4)

Shelford

National Grid Ref: SK6642

Tom Browns

Fox Cottage Guest House, *Main Street, Shelford, Nottingham, Notts,* *NG12 1ED.*
Quiet cottage in delightful gardens.
Open: All Year
0115 933 5741 Mrs Lewis
Rates fr: *£16.00*-**£17.00**.
Beds: 2D 1T 1S
Baths: 2 Private 1 Shared
(6)

Southwell

National Grid Ref: SK7053

Bramley Apple

Barn Lodge, *Duckers Cottage, Brinkley, Southwell, Notts,* *NG25 0TP.*
Converted barn in rural setting.
Open: All Year
Grades: ETB Listed, Comm
01636 813435 Mrs Hanbury
Rates fr: *£20.00*-**£20.00**.
Beds: 1F 1D 1T
Baths: 3 Private
(6)

Stanton on the Wolds

National Grid Ref: SK6330

Pullman Inn

Laurel Farm, *Browns Lane, Stanton on the Wolds, Keyworth, Nottingham, Notts,* *NG12 5BL.*
Open: All Year
0115 937 3488 Mrs Moffat
Rates fr: *£16.50*-**£16.50**.
Beds: 1F 1D 2T
Baths: 3 Ensuite 1 Private
(8)
Spacious old farmhouse in 4 acres. Many pets. Guests may use garden. Golf & horse-riding nearby. Children welcome. All-day access to rooms.

Sutton in Ashfield

National Grid Ref: SK4958

Fox & Crown

Dalestorth Guest House, *Skegby Lane, Skegby, Sutton in Ashfield, Notts,* *NG17 3DH.*
Clean friendly accommodation, hotel standards.
Open: All Year
01623 551110 Mr Jordan
Rates fr: *£12.00*-**£12.00**.
Beds: 1F 2D 5T 5S
Baths: 7 Shared
(100)

Central Hotel & Restuarant, *1 Station Road, Sutton in Ashfield, Notts,* *NG17 5FF.*
Clean, friendly, privately owned hotel.
Open: All Year
01623 552373 Mr Freeman
Rates fr: *£18.00*-**£19.50**.
Beds: 4D 7T 3S
Baths: 10 Private 7 Shared
(17)

Please respect a B&B's wishes regarding children, animals & smoking.

Sutton on Trent

National Grid Ref: SK7965

The Leylands, *Old Great North Road, Sutton on Trent, Newark, Notts, NG23 6QN.*
Friendly atmosphere, charming comfortable accommodation.
Open: All Year (not Xmas)
01636 821710 Mrs Walton
Rates fr: *£18.00*-**£17.50**.
Beds: 1F 2D 1T 1S
Baths: 2 Ensuite 2 Shared
(6)

Upper Broughton

National Grid Ref: SK6826

Golden Fleece, Crown Inn (Old Dalby)

Sulney Fields, *Colonels Lane, Upper Broughton, Melton Mowbray, Leics, LE14 3BD.*
Large country house, spectacular views.
Open: All Year (not Xmas)
01664 822204 (also fax no)
Mrs Dowson
Rates fr: *£17.50*-**£20.00**.
Beds: 2D 2T 1S
Baths: 1 Private 2 Shared
(12)

Upton

National Grid Ref: SK7354

High Barn, *Main Street, Upton, Newark, Notts, NG23 5TE.*
Converted barn in conservation village.
Open: All Year (not Xmas)
01636 813444 Mrs Searle
Rates fr: *£14.00*-**£15.00**.
Beds: 1D 1T 1S **Baths:** 1 Shared
(4)

Wellow

National Grid Ref: SK6766

Durham Ox, Old Red Lion

Krefeld Bed & Breakfast, *Eakring Road, Wellow, Newark, Notts, NG22 0ED.*
Modern house with groundfloor bedrooms.
Open: All Year (not Xmas)
Grades: ETB Listed
01623 861112 Mrs Haggett
Rates fr: *£11.00*-**£14.00**.
Beds: 1D 1T 1S **Baths:** 1 Shared
(2)

West Bridgford

National Grid Ref: SK5836

Nottingham Knight

Forest Hills Hotel & Ingrid's German Restaurant, *102 Musters Road, West Bridgford, Nottingham, NG2 7PS.*
Open: All Year
0115 981 1133 Mrs Grenville
Fax no: 0115 981 1488
Rates fr: *£19.75*-**£19.95**.
Beds: 3F 7D 2T 7S
Baths: 16 Ensuite 3 Shared
(15)
With prices from as low as £19.95 per night, we feel we offer the very best value for money in Nottinghamshire. Friendly staff, excellent bar, recently opened 50 seater German restaurant with emphasis on home cooking.

Gallery Hotel, *8-10 Radcliffe Road, West Bridgford, Nottingham, NG2 5FW.*
Large Victorian house. Large car park.
Open: All Year
Grades: ETB 2 Cr, AA 3 Q
0115 981 3651 Mr & Mrs Masson
Fax no: 0115 981 3732
Rates fr: *£19.00*-**£25.00**.
Beds: 3F 4D 5T 4S
Baths: 4 Ensuite 15 Private
(45)

Talbot House Hotel, *18-20 Bridgford Road, West Bridgford, Nottingham, NG2 6AB.*
Open: All Year
0115 981 1123 / 0500 413341 (free) Fax no: 0115 981 3545
Rates fr: *£17.50*-**£20.00**.
Beds: 8F 8D 8T 8S
Baths: 18 Private 6 Shared
(30)
Central position, opposite Trent Bridge Cricket Ground. Large car park. 1 mile to Holme Pierrepoint water sports. 1 minute from Notts Forest & County football grounds. Licensed bar.

Rushcliffe Guest House, *104 Radcliffe Road, West Bridgford, Nottingham, NG2 5HG.*
Family-run comfortable guest house. **Open:** All Year
0115 981 1413 Mrs Nurse
Rates fr: *£12.00*-**£15.00**.
Beds: 1F 1D 2T **Baths:** 2 Shared
(5)

Croft Hotel, *6-8 North Road, West Bridgford, Nottingham, NG2 7NH.*
Charming quiet Victorian private hotel.
Open: All Year (not Xmas)
Grades: ETB Listed
0115 981 2744 Mr & Mrs Kennedy
Rates fr: *£15.00*-**£20.00**.
Beds: 3F 3D 2T 8S
Baths: 5 Shared
(12)

Riverside Guest House, *42 Holme Road, West Bridgford, Nottingham, NG2 5AA.*
Highly recommended. Close to Trent Bridge.
Open: All Year (not Xmas)
0115 982 0915 Mrs Clarke
Rates fr: *£13.00*-**£14.00**.
Beds: 1F 4T 3S **Baths:** 2 Shared
(3)

11 Bridgford Road, *West Bridgford, Nottingham, NG2 6AN.*
Victorian family home.
Open: All Year
0115 981 9531 Mrs Nunn
Rates fr: *£12.00*-**£12.00**.
Beds: 1F 2D 2T 2S
Baths: 1 Private 3 Shared
(5)

Worksop

National Grid Ref: SK5879

Newcastle Inn

Sherwood Guest House, *57 Carlton Road, Worksop, Notts, S80 1PP.*
Large, centrally placed Edwardian house.
Open: All Year
Grades: ETB 2 Cr, Comm
01909 474209 / 478214 Mrs Hunt
Rates fr: *£18.00*-**£18.00**.
Beds: 1F 5T 1S
Baths: 2 Private 2 Shared
(2)

Oxfordshire

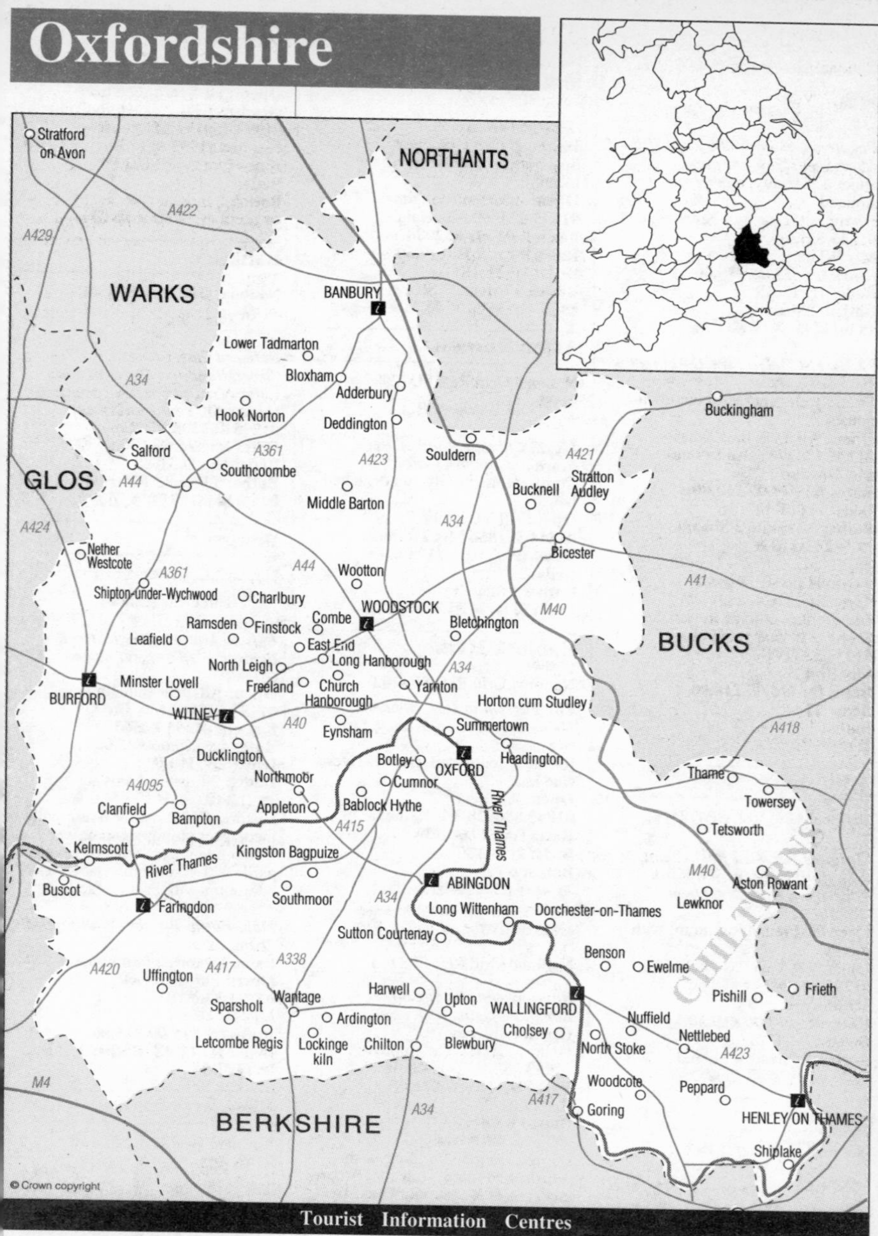

Tourist Information Centres

25 Bridge Street, **Abingdon**, Oxon, OX14 3XN, 01235 522711.

Banbury Museum, 8 Horsefair, **Banbury**, Oxfordshire, OX16 0AA, 01295-259855.

The Brewery, Sheep Street, **Burford**, Oxfordshire, OX8 4LP, 01993 823558.

The Guildhall, **Chipping Norton**, Oxon, OX7 5NH, 01608 644379.

7 Market Place, **Faringdon**, Oxfordshire, SN7 7HL, 01367 242191, (Easter to Oct).

Town Hall, Market Place, **Henley-on-Thames**, Oxfordshire, RG9 2AQ, 01491 578034, (Easter to Oct).

The Old School, Gloucester Green, **Oxford**, Oxfordshire, OX1 2DA, 01865 726871.

Town Hall, **Thame**, Oxfordshire, OX9 3DP, 01844 212834.

Town Hall, Market, **Wallingford**, Oxfordshire, OX10 0EG, 01491 826972.

Town Hall, Market Square, **Witney**, Oxon, OX8 6AG, 01993 775802.

Hensington Rd, **Woodstock**, Oxon, OX7 1JQ, 01993-811038, (Easter to Oct).

Abingdon

National Grid Ref: SU4997

The Plough, The Parasol

Pastures Green, *46 Picklers Hill, Abingdon, Oxon,* *OX14 2BB.*
Quiet & friendly, conveniently situated.
Open: All Year (not Xmas)
01235 521369
Mrs White
Rates fr: *£15.00*-**£16.00**.
Beds: 1D 1T 1S
Baths: 2 Shared
(4) (3)

22 East St Helen Street, *Abingdon, Oxon,* *OX14 5EB.*
Friendly elegant Georgian town house.
Open: All Year (not Xmas)
01235 533278 (also fax no)
Mrs Howard
Rates fr: *£14.00*-**£17.00**.
Beds: 1D 1T 1S
Baths: 1 Ensuite 2 Shared

9 Gravel Lane, *Drayton, Abingdon, Oxon,* *OX14 14HY.*
Old groom's cottage in village.
Open: All Year (not Xmas)
01235 533194
Mrs Bird
Rates fr: *£16.00*-**£18.00**.
Beds: 2T
Baths: 1 Shared
(2)

Adderbury

National Grid Ref: SP4735

Morgans Orchard Restaurant, *9 Twyford Gardens, Twyford, Adderbury, Banbury, Oxon,* *OX17 3JA.*
Licensed French restaurant with rooms.
Open: All Year
01295 812047
Mr Morgan
Rates fr: *£18.00*-**£19.50**.
Beds: 1D 3T 1S
Baths: 1 Private 4 Shared

Appleton

National Grid Ref: SP4401

Eight Bells (Eaton), The Vine (Cumnor)

West Farm, *Eaton, Appleton, Abingdon, Oxon,* *OX13 5PR.*
Warm, comfortable farmhouse - very quiet.
Open: Apr to Dec
01865 862908
Mrs Gow
Rates fr: *£20.00*-**£20.00**.
Beds: 1F 1D 1S
Baths: 1 Private 1 Shared
(10)

Ardington

National Grid Ref: SU4087

Boars Head

Orpwood House, *Ardington, Wantage, Oxon,* *OX12 8PN.*
Spacious farmhouse in village location.
Open: All Year (not Xmas)
01235 833300 Mrs Haigh
Fax no: 01235 862088
Rates fr: *£19.50*-**£19.50**.
Beds: 1F 2T 1S
Baths: 1 Private 2 Shared
(15)

Aston Rowant

National Grid Ref: SU7298

Old Heathern Bottle

Libra, *Chinnor Road, Aston Rowant, Chinnor, Oxford,* *OX9 5SH.*
Comfortable, family-run detached house.
Open: All Year (not Xmas)
01844 351856 Mrs Trotman
Rates fr: *£16.00*-**£17.00**.
Beds: 2T
Baths: 1 Shared
(8) (4)

Bablock Hythe

National Grid Ref: SP4202

The Ferryman Inn, *Bablock Hythe, Northmoor, Witney, Oxon,* *OX8 1BL.*
Recently renovated Thames riverside inn.
Open: All Year
01865 880028 Mr Kelland
Rates fr: *£20.00*-**£30.00**.
Beds: 2F 3D 1T
Baths: 6 Private

Bampton

National Grid Ref: SP3103

Romany Inn, *Bridge Street, Bampton, Oxon,* *OX18 2HA.*
Open: All Year
Grades: ETB 2 Cr, Approv
01993 850237 Mr Booth
Rates fr: *£15.00*-**£21.00**.
Beds: 2F 6D 4T
Baths: 8 Private
(7)
C17th Georgian building, just refurbished family-run chef proprietor. Inn & Restaurant, Good Beer Guide, Good Pub Guide, Sunday Times Recommended. Quiet village location - Brochures.

The lowest *double* rate per person is shown in *italics*.

Morar, *Weald Street, Bampton, Oxon,* *OX18 2HL.*
Keen gardeners, bellringers = much laughter!
Open: All Year (not Xmas)
Grades: ETB 2 Cr, High Comm
01993 850162 Ms Rouse
Fax no: 01993 851738
Rates fr: *£21.00*-**£21.00**.
Beds: 2D 1T
Baths: 2 Ensuite 1 Private
(6) (5)

Banbury

National Grid Ref: SP4540

Swan Inn

Belmont Guest House, *34 Crouch Street, Banbury, Oxon,* *OX16 9PR.*
Large Victorian house (detached).
Open: All Year (not Xmas)
01295 262308 Mr Raby
Rates fr: *£15.00*-**£20.00**.
Beds: 1F 2D 3T 2S
Baths: 5 Private 1 Shared
(7) (6)

Benson

National Grid Ref: SU6191

Three Horseshoes

Fyfield Manor, *Brook Street, Benson, Wallingford, Oxon,* *OX10 6HA.*
Open: All Year (not Xmas)
01491 835184 Mrs Brown
Fax no: 01491 825635
Rates fr: *£20.00*-**£25.00**.
Beds: 1F 1D 1T
Baths: 2 Ensuite 1 Private
(10) (10)
Historic C12th manor house with mediaeval dining-room & many C18th features. 8 acres of beautiful gardens. Large, comfortable period bedrooms with ensuite facilities.

Hale Farm, *Benson, Wallingford, Oxon,* *OX10 6NE.*
Large Victorian farmhouse.
Open: Easter to Oct
01491 836818
Mrs Belcher
Rates fr: *£15.00*-**£15.00**.
Beds: 1D 1T 1S **Baths:** 1 Shared

Bicester

National Grid Ref: SP5822

Red Lion (Stratton Audley), Trigger Pond

The Old School, *Stratton Audley, Bicester, Oxon,* *OX6 9BJ.*
Open: All Year
01869 277371 Mrs Wertheimer
Rates fr: *£20.00*-**£20.00**.
Beds: 3T 1S **Baths:** 2 Shared
(6)
Interesting old school in pretty village. Pleasant garden & tennis court. Guests' own drawing room. Tea & home-made cake. Everyone sleeps well - so peaceful.

Trigger Pond Cottage, *33 Bicester Road, Bucknell, Bicester, Oxon,* *OX6 9LP.*
C17th stone cottage in village.
Open: All Year (not Xmas)
Grades: ETB Listed
01869 245560 Mrs Hemsley
Rates fr: *£19.00*-**£22.00**.
Beds: 1D 1S **Baths:** 1 Shared
(3)

Bletchingdon

National Grid Ref: SP5018

Stonehouse Farm, *Weston Road, Bletchingdon, Kidlington, Oxon,* *OX5 3EA.*
C17th farmhouse.
Open: All Year (not Xmas)
01869 350585 Mrs Hedges
Rates fr: *£16.00*-**£20.00**.
Beds: 1F 1D 1T 1S
Baths: 2 Shared
(6)

Blewbury

National Grid Ref: SU5385

The Load of Mischief, *South Street, Blewbury, Didcot, Oxon,* *OX11 9PX.*
Comfortable C17th village inn.
Open: All Year (not Xmas)
01235 850281 Mrs Welch
Rates fr: *£17.50*-**£17.50**.
Beds: 2F 1S **Baths:** 1 Shared
(20)

Bloxham

National Grid Ref: SP4236

Red Lion, Joiners Arms

The Knoll Guest House, *Little Bridge Road, Bloxham, Banbury, Oxon,* *OX15 4PU.*
Lovely Geogian private village house. **Open:** All Year (not Xmas)
Grades: ETB Listed
01295 720843 Mr Woodward
Rates fr: *£17.50*-**£20.00**.
Beds: 2D 1T 1S
Baths: 2 Ensuite 2 Shared
(Yes)

Botley

National Grid Ref: SP5106

Conifer Lodge, *159 Eynsham Road, Corner Nobles Lane, Botley, Oxford, Oxon,* *OX2 9NE.*
Modern luxury stone house, peaceful surroundings.
Open: All Year (not Xmas)
01865 862280 Mr Underwood
Rates fr: *£20.00*-**£22.00**.
Beds: 2D 1T 1S
Baths: 2 Private 2 Shared

The lowest **single** *rate is shown in* **bold.**

Bucknell

National Grid Ref: SP5625

Trigger Pond

Trigger Pond Cottage, *33 Bicester Road, Bucknell, Bicester, Oxon,* *OX6 9LP.*
C17th stone cottage in village.
Open: All Year (not Xmas)
Grades: ETB Listed
01869 245560
Mrs Hemsley
Rates fr: *£19.00*-**£22.00**.
Beds: 1D 1S
Baths: 1 Shared
(3)

Burford

National Grid Ref: SP2512

Mermaid, Cotswold Arms, Royal Oak

Highway Hotel, *Inc Burford Needlecraft, 117 High Street, Burford, Oxon,* *OX18 4RG.*
Open: All Year
Grades: ETB 2 Cr
01993 822136 (also fax no)
Mr Cohen
Rates fr: *£20.00*-**£30.00**.
Beds: 2F 7D 2T
Baths: 9 Private 1 Shared
Guest house and needlecraft shop. Built in 1520, perfectly situated as a base for your Cotswold visit. Wonderful walking, golf, cycling on our doorstep, plus Burford's ancient beautiful High Street.

Providence Cottage, *26 High Street, Burford, Oxon,* *OX18 4RR.*
Elegant C15th traditional stone cottage.
Open: All Year (not Xmas)
Grades: ETB 2 Cr, High Comm
01993 823310
Mrs Theodorou
Rates fr: *£20.00*.
Beds: 1D 1T
Baths: 1 Ensuite 1 Private
(14)

Buscot

National Grid Ref: SU2397

Trout Inn

Apple Tree House, *Buscot, Faringdon, Oxon,* *SN7 8DA.*
Listed property - National Trust village.
Open: All Year
Grades: ETB 2 Cr
01367 252592
Mrs Reay
Rates fr: *£17.00*-**£22.00**.
Beds: 2D 1T
Baths: 1 Ensuite 2 Shared
(8)

Charlbury

National Grid Ref: SP3619

The Crown (Enstone)

Banbury Hill Farm, *Enstone Road, Charlbury, Chipping Norton, Oxon,* *OX7 3JH.*
Comfortable family farmhouse, all mod-cons.
Open: All Year (not Xmas)
Grades: ETB 2 Cr, Comm
01608 810314 Ms Widdows
Fax no: 01608 811891
Rates fr: *£16.00*-**£16.00**.
Beds: 1T 1S
Baths: 2 Ensuite
(10 +)

Chilton

National Grid Ref: SU4885

The Workshop, *South Road, Chilton, Didcot, Oxon,* *OX11 0RT.*
Large modern bungalow set in 1.75 acres.
Open: All Year (not Xmas)
01235 834130 Mrs Young
Rates fr: *£20.00*-**£25.00**.
Beds: 2T
Baths: 2 Private

Cholsey

National Grid Ref: SU5886

Red Lion, Walnut Tree

Old Blackalls, *Old Blackalls Drive, Cholsey, Wallingford, Oxon,* *OX10 9HD.*
Friendly, family house in rural position.
Open: All Year (not Xmas)
01491 652864
Mrs Robson
Rates fr: *£17.50*-**£17.50**.
Beds: 1D
Baths: 1 Ensuite
(5)

Church Hanborough

National Grid Ref: SP4212

Hand & Shears

1 Mansell Close, *Church Hanborough, Witney, Oxon,* *OX8 8AU.*
Open: All Year (not Xmas)
Grades: ETB Listed, High Comm
01993 881914
Mr & Mrs Gould
Rates fr: *£19.00*-**£23.00**.
Beds: 2D
Baths: 2 Private
(2)
In a small, attractive village conveniently located for Oxford, Witney & Woodstock (Blenheim Palace). Ideal too for the Cotswolds & Thames Valley. Very warm welcome.

Clanfield

National Grid Ref: SP2801

Chestnut Grove, *Clanfield, Bampton, Oxon, OX18 2RG.*
Modern, newly-built house.
Open: All Year
01367 810249 Miss Pocock
Rates fr: *£15.00*-**£15.00**.
Beds: 1D 2S
Baths: 1 Private
(3)

The Granary, *Clanfield, Bampton, Oxon, OX18 2SH.*
One ground-floor room, ensuite.
Open: All Year (not Xmas)
01367 810266 Mrs Payne
Rates fr: *£15.00*-**£15.00**.
Beds: 1D 1T 1S
Baths: 1 Private 1 Shared
(4)

Combe

National Grid Ref: SP4115
Cock Inn

Mayfield Cottage, *West End, Combe, Witney, Oxon, OX8 8NP.*
Comfortable stone cottage, quiet location.
Open: Feb to Nov
Grades: ETB Listed, High Comm
01993 898298 Mrs Fox
Rates fr: *£16.00*-**£18.00**.
Beds: 1T 1S 1D
Baths: 1 Shared
(12) (2)

Cumnor

National Grid Ref: SP4604
The Vine

Cumnor Bed & Breakfast, *Beinn Bheag, 96 Oxford Road, Cumnor, Oxford, Oxon, OX2 9PQ.*
Spacious bungalow, garden, peaceful rural environment.
Open: All Year (not Xmas)
Grades: ETB Listed, Comm
01865 864020 Mrs Tricker
Rates fr: *£21.00*-**£20.00**.
Beds: 1F 1D 1S
Baths: 2 Ensuite 1 Shared
(3)

Ceres, *50 Norreys Road, Cumnor, Oxford, OX2 9PT.*
Family home on outskirts of Oxford. Vegetarian specialities.
Open: All Year (not Xmas)
01865 865004 Mrs Matthews
Rates fr: *£12.50*-**£15.00**.
Beds: 1T 1S
Baths: 1 Ensuite 1 Shared
(3)

The lowest *double* rate per person is shown in *italics*.

Deddington

National Grid Ref: SP4631

Hillbarn, *Milton Gated Road, Deddington, Banbury, Oxon, OX15 0TS.*
Peaceful farmhouse accommodation. Beautiful views.
Open: All Year
Grades: ETB Listed
01869 338631 Mrs White
Rates fr: *£16.00*-**£20.00**.
Beds: 1F 1D 1T
Baths: 1 Shared
(6)

Dorchester-on-Thames

National Grid Ref: SU5794

Willowmour, *24 Martins Lane, Dorchester-on-Thames, Wallingford, Oxon, OX10 7JE.*
Quiet, modern detached house.
Open: All Year (not Xmas)
01865 340444 Mrs Taylor
Rates fr: *£21.00*-**£21.00**.
Beds: 1T
Baths: 1 Private

Ducklington

National Grid Ref: SP3507

Walnut Tree Cottage, *Back Lane, Ducklington, Witney, Oxon, OX8 7UE.*
Cotswold stone house. River frontage.
Open: All Year (not Xmas)
01993 774430 Mrs Burns
Rates fr: *£15.00*-**£25.00**.
Beds: 2D
Baths: 1 Shared
(2)

East End

National Grid Ref: SP3914

Forge Cottage, *East End, North Leigh, Witney, Oxon, OX8 6PZ.*
Quiet, informal C17th stone cottage.
Open: All Year
01993 881120 Mrs French
Rates fr: *£18.00*-**£20.00**.
Beds: 2D
Baths: 1 Private 1 Shared
(4)

Ewelme

National Grid Ref: SU6491

May's Farm, *Turner's Court, Ewelme, Wallingford, Oxon, OX10 6QF.*
Working stock farm, fabulous views. Quiet.
Open: All Year (not Xmas)
01491 641294 Mrs Passmore
Rates fr: *£17.50*-**£18.00**.
Beds: 1D 1T
Baths: 1 Private 1 Shared
(10)

Eynsham

National Grid Ref: SP4309
Talbot Inn

Swinford Park, *Eynsham, Witney, Oxon, OX8 1BY.*
Modern, comfortable country house.
Open: All Year (not Xmas)
01865 881212 Mrs Tapper
Rates fr: *£13.00*-**£15.00**.
Beds: 1D 1T 1S
Baths: 1 Private 1 Shared
(3) (3)

Faringdon

National Grid Ref: SU2895
Fox & Hounds

Bowling Green Farm, *Stanford Road, Faringdon, Oxon, SN7 8EZ.*
Attractive C18th period farmhouse.
Open: All Year
Grades: ETB 2 Cr
01367 240229 Mr Barnard
Rates fr: *£20.00*-**£25.00**.
Beds: 2F **Baths:** 2 Ensuite
(6)

Finstock

National Grid Ref: SP3616
Plough Inn

Well Cottage, *High Street, Finstock, Chipping Norton, Oxon, OX7 3BY.*
C17th cottage in small village.
Open: All Year (not Xmas)
01993 868201 Mrs Breakell
Rates fr: *£15.00*-**£15.00**.
Beds: 1D 1S **Baths:** 1 Shared
(1)

Freeland

National Grid Ref: SP4112

Shepherds Hall Inn, *Witney Road, Freeland, Witney, Oxon, OX8 8HQ.*
Open: All Year (not Xmas)
Grades: ETB 2 Cr
01993 881256 Mr Fyson
Rates fr: *£20.00*-**£25.00**.
Beds: 2D 2T 1S **Baths:** 5 Ensuite
(50)
Attractive inn with excellent well-appointed accommodation. Wide selection of appetising meals available lunch times & evenings. Ideally situated for Oxford, Woodstock - Blenheim Palace - and Cotswolds. On A4095 Woodstock-Witney Road.

High season, bank holidays and special events mean low availability *anywhere*.

Wrestler's Mead, *35 Wroslyn Road, Freeland, Witney, Oxon,* OX8 8HJ.
Use us as a base for sightseeing.
Open: All Year
01993 882003
Mrs Taphouse
Rates fr: *£16.00*-**£17.00**.
Beds: 1F 1D 1S
Baths: 1 Ensuite 1 Shared
(3)

Goring

National Grid Ref: SU6081

Catherine Wheel, John Barley Corn, Miller of Mansfield

14 Mountfield, *Wallingford Road, Goring, Reading, Berks,* RG8 0BE.
Modern home in riverside village.
Open: All Year
01491 872029
Mrs Ewen
Rates fr: *£17.50*-**£20.00**.
Beds: 1D 1T 1S
Baths: 1 Shared
(4)

Queens Arms, *Reading Road, Goring, Reading, Berks,* RG8 0ER.
200-year-old country pub.
Open: All Year (not Xmas)
01491 872825 Mrs Carter
Rates fr: *£19.00*-**£19.00**.
Beds: 1T 2S
Baths: 1 Shared
(30)

The John Barleycorn, *Manor Road, Goring, Reading, Berks,* RG8 9DP.
C17th inn near Thames.
Open: All Year
01491 872509 Mr Fincham
Rates fr: *£20.00*-**£23.00**.
Beds: 1F 1D 1T 1S
Baths: 1 Shared

Harwell

National Grid Ref: SU4989

The Old Brewery, *High Street, Harwell, Didcot, Oxon,* OX11 0EQ.
Coverted C17th village brewery.
Open: All Year
01235 832880
Mrs Howes
Rates fr: *£20.00*-**£22.00**.
Beds: 2T 2S
Baths: 4 Private
(6)

Kings Farm House, *Townsend, Harwell, Didcot, Oxon,* OX11 0DX.
Modernised former farmhouse character abounds.
Open: All Year (not Xmas)
01235 832833
Mrs Buff
Rates fr: *£21.00*-**£24.00**.
Beds: 2D 1S
Baths: 2 Shared

Headington

National Grid Ref: SP5407

White Horse

Sandfield House, *19 London Road, Headington, Oxford, Oxon,* OX3 7RE.
Close hospitals, Oxford Brookes University, M40.
Open: All Year (not Xmas)
Grades: ETB 2 Cr, Comm
01865 62406 Mrs Anderson
Rates fr: *£22.50*-**£25.00**.
Beds: 2D 2S
Baths: 3 Ensuite 1 Private
(4)

Henley-on-Thames

National Grid Ref: SU7682

Anchor , Cork Talk, Old Bell, Bottle & Glass

Ledard, *Rotherfield Road, Henley-on-Thames, Oxon,* RG9 1NN.
Large well-appointed Victorian house.
Open: All Year (not Xmas)
01491 575611 Mrs Howard
Rates fr: *£16.00*-**£16.00**.
Beds: 1F 1D **Baths:** 1 Private
(4)

Alftrudis, *8 Norman Avenue, Henley-on-Thames, Oxon,* RG9 1SG.
Victorian house in town centre.
Open: All Year
Grades: ETB 1 Cr, High Comm
01491 573099 Mrs Lambert
Rates fr: *£17.00*-**£25.00**.
Beds: 2D 1T
Baths: 2 Ensuite 1 Shared
(8) (2)

Mervyn House, *4 St Marks Road, Henley-on-Thames, Oxon,* RG9 1LJ.
Victorian house, very close town centre.
Open: All Year (not Xmas)
Grades: ETB 1 Cr, Comm
01491 575331 Mrs Ely
Fax no: 01491 411747
Rates fr: *£17.00*-**£23.00**.
Beds: 2D 1T
Baths: 1 Ensuite 1 Shared
(12)

Mervyn House, *4 St Marks Road, Henley-on-Thames, Oxon,* RG9 1LJ.
Comfortable, friendly Victorian house close to town/river.
Open: All Year (not Xmas)
Grades: ETB 1 Cr
01491 575 331 Mrs Ely
Fax no: 01491 411747
Rates fr: *£17.00*-**£23.00**.
Beds: 2D 1T
Baths: 1 Ensuite 1 Shared
(12)

Lenwade, *3 Western Road, Henley-on-Thames, Oxon,* RG9 1JL.
Victorian house close to river.
Open: All Year
Grades: ETB 2 Cr, High Comm, AA 3 Q
01491 573468 (also fax no)
Mrs Williams
Rates fr: *£17.00*-**£20.00**.
Beds: 1D 2T
Baths: 2 Private 2 Shared
(2)

Old Bell House, *Northfield End, Henley-on-Thames, Oxon,* RG9 2JG.
Large attractive Georgian town house.
Open: All Year
01491 574350 Mrs Duckett
Rates fr: *£20.00*-**£20.00**.
Beds: 1F 1T
Baths: 1 Private
(2)

The Laurels, *107 St Marks Road, Henley-on-Thames, Oxon,* RG9 1LP.
Large, comfortable house in quiet location.
Open: All Year
01491 572982
Mrs Bridekirk
Rates fr: *£16.00*-**£18.00**.
Beds: 1F 1D 1T
Baths: 1 Private 1 Shared
(2)

New Lodge, *Henley Park, Henley-on-Thames, Oxon,* RG9 6HU.
Small Victorian lodge cottage.
Open: All Year
Grades: ETB 1 Cr
01491 576340 Mrs Warner
Rates fr: *£16.00*-**£22.00**.
Beds: 2D
Baths: 2 Private
(7)

Hook Norton

National Grid Ref: SP3533

Pear Tree Inn, *Scotland End, Hook Norton, Banbury, Oxon,* OX15 5NU.
Quiet country pub near brewery.
Open: All Year (not Xmas)
Grades: ETB 2 Cr, Comm
01608 737482 Mrs Tindsley
Rates fr: *£17.50*-**£20.00**.
Beds: 1D
Baths: 1 Private
(15)

Horton cum Studley

National Grid Ref: SP5912

Kings Arms Hotel, *Horton cum Studley, Oxford,* OX33 1AY.
Friendly, relaxed country village hotel.
Open: All Year
Grades: ETB 3 Cr, Comm
01865 351235
Mr Balfour-Morrison
Rates fr: *£27.50*-**£35.00**.
Beds: 1F 5D 2T 2S
Baths: 10 Ensuite
(4) (20)

Kelmscott

National Grid Ref: SU2599

The Plough Inn, *Kelmscott, Lechlade, Glos, GL7 3HG.*
Comfortable, well appointed inn.
Open: All Year
Grades: ETB 3 St
01367 253543 Mr Pardoe
Rates fr: *£22.50*-**£30.00**.
Beds: 1F 4D 3T
Baths: 8 Private
(12)

Kingston Bagpuize

National Grid Ref: SU4098

Court Close, *Southmoor, Kingston Bagpuize, Abingdon, Oxon, OX13 5HS.*
Secluded, picturesque C17th Cotswold farmhouse.
Open: All Year (not Xmas)
01865 820186
Countess Tolstoy
Rates fr: *£20.00*-**£25.00**.
Beds: 1D
Baths: 1 Ensuite
(2)

Leafield

National Grid Ref: SP3115

The Swan (Swinbrook)

Langley Farm, *Leafield, Witney, Oxon, OX8 5QD.*
Ideal for touring the Cotswolds.
Open: May to Oct
01993 878686 Mrs Greves
Rates fr: *£14.00*-**£20.00**.
Beds: 2D 1T
Baths: 1 Private 1 Shared
(8) (8)

Pond View, *10 Fairspear Road, Leafield, Witney, Oxon, OX8 5NT.*
Quiet house with lovely views.
Open: All Year
01993 878133 Mrs Wiggins
Rates fr: *£15.00*-**£15.00**.
Beds: 1D 1T 2S
Baths: 1 Private 2 Shared
(3)

The Spindleberry Inn, *Leafield, Witney, Oxon, OX8 5QG.*
C17th inn.
Open: All Year
01993 878277 Mr Steer
Rates fr: *£14.50*-**£20.00**.
Beds: 1D 1T
Baths: 1 Shared
(14) (30)

Greenside Cottage, *The Ridings, Leafield, Witney, Oxon, OX8 5NN.*
Stone cottage. Cotswold village green.
Open: All Year
01993 878368
Mrs Martin-Doyle
Rates fr: *£16.00*-**£16.00**.
Beds: 1D 1T 1S
Baths: 1 Private 1 Shared
(7) (3)

The lowest **single** *rate is shown in* **bold.**

Letcombe Regis

National Grid Ref: SU3886

The Sparrow, The Lamb

Quince Cottage, *Letcombe Regis, Wantage, Oxon, OX12 9J.*
Spacious C18th thatched house.
Open: All Year
01235 763652 Mrs Boden
Rates fr: *£17.00*-**£17.50**.
Beds: 1T 1S
Baths: 1 Private
(1) (2)

The Greyhound, *Main Street, Letcombe Regis, Wantage, Oxon, OX12 9JL.*
C18th historic village pub.
Open: All Year (not Xmas)
01235 770905 Mr Smithard
Rates fr: *£17.50*-**£17.50**.
Beds: 2T
Baths: 1 Shared
(1) (30)

Lewknor

National Grid Ref: SU7197

Peel Guest House, *London Road, Lewknor, Watlington, Oxon, OX9 5SA.*
Detached house overlooking Chiltern escarpment.
Open: All Year (not Xmas)
01844 351310 Ms Hunt
Rates fr: *£18.00*-**£20.00**.
Beds: 5T 1S
Baths: 3 Private 1 Shared
(10) (7)

Little Wittenham

National Grid Ref: SU5693

The Vine, The Plough

Rooks Orchard, *Little Wittenham, Abingdon, Oxon, OX14 4QY.*
C17th Listed house, beams, inglenooks.
Open: All Year (not Xmas)
Grades: ETB 2 Cr, High Comm
01865 407765 Mrs Welfare
Rates fr: *£19.00*-**£24.00**.
Beds: 1D 1T
Baths: 1 Ensuite 1 Private
(4)

All details shown are as supplied by B&B owners in Autumn 1996.

Lockinge Kiln

National Grid Ref: SU4283

Lockinge Kiln Farm, *Lockinge Kiln, Wantage, Oxon, OX12 8PA.*
Comfortable farmhouse, working mixed farm.
Open: All Year (not Xmas)
01235 763308 (also fax no)
Mrs Cowan
Rates fr: *£16.00*-**£17.00**.
Beds: 2T 1S
Baths: 3 Shared
(10) (3)

Long Hanborough

National Grid Ref: SP4114

George & Dragon, The Bell

Gorselands Farmhouse Auberge, *Boddington Lane, Long Hanborough, Woodstock, Oxon, OX8 6PU.*
Old Cotswold stone farmhouse.
Open: All Year
Grades: ETB 2 CrRAC Listed
01993 881895
Mrs Jones
Rates fr: *£18.00*-**£28.00**.
Beds: 1F 2D 1T
Baths: 4 Ensuite

Wynford House, *79 Main Road, Long Hanborough, Witney, Oxon, OX8 8BX.*
Comfortable detached family house.
Open: All Year
01993 881402
Mrs Ellis
Rates fr: *£18.00*-**£22.00**.
Beds: 1F 1D 1T
Baths: 1 Private 1 Shared

Old Farmhouse, *Station Hill, Long Hanborough, Witney, Oxon, OX8 8JZ.*
Charming C17th house near Oxford.
Open: All Year (not Xmas)
01993 882097
Mrs Maundrell
Rates fr: *£17.50*-**£23.00**.
Beds: 2D
Baths: 1 Private 1 Shared
(12) (4)

Lower Tadmarton

National Grid Ref: SP4037

Mill Barn, *Lower Tadmarton, Banbury, Oxon, OX15 5SU.*
Converted barn offering spacious accommodation.
Open: All Year
01295 780349
Mrs Lee
Rates fr: *£17.50*-**£25.00**.
Beds: 1F 1D
Baths: 2 Private
(2)

Middle Barton

National Grid Ref: SP4325
Fox

Cottage By The Ford, *Mill Lane, Middle Barton, Chipping Norton, Oxon, OX7 7BT.*
Detached cottage accommodation by stream.
Open: All Year
Grades: ETB 1 Cr, Comm
01869 347150 Mrs Brooks
Rates fr: *£18.00*-**£20.00**.
Beds: 1T
Baths: 1 Ensuite
(1)

Minster Lovell

National Grid Ref: SP3110
White Hart, Old Swan

Hill Grove Farm, *Minster Lovell, Witney, Oxon, OX8 5NA.*
Comfortable farmhouse overlooking Windrush River.
Open: All Year (not Xmas)
Grades: ETB 2 Cr, High Comm, AA 3 Q
01993 703120
Mrs Brown
Fax no: 01993 700528
Rates fr: *£19.00*-**£18.00**.
Beds: 1D 1T
Baths: 1 Ensuite 1 Private
(6)

Nether Westcote

National Grid Ref: SP2220

Cotswold View Guest House, *Nether Westcote, Chipping Norton, Oxon, OX7 6SD.*
Converted farmyard house.
Open: All Year (not Xmas)
01993 830699
Mr Gibson
Rates fr: *£17.50*-**£20.00**.
Beds: 4D 2T 2S
Baths: 6 Ensuite 2 Private
(8)

Nettlebed

National Grid Ref: SU6986
Crown Inn

Park Corner Farm House, *Nettlebed, Henley-on-Thames, Oxon, RG9 6DX.*
Queen Anne brick-and-flint farmhouse.
Open: All Year (not Xmas)
01491 641450
Mrs Rutter
Rates fr: *£16.00*-**£18.00**.
Beds: 2T
Baths: 1 Shared

The lowest *double* rate per person is shown in *italics*.

North Leigh

National Grid Ref: SP3812

North Leigh Guest House, *28 Common Road, North Leigh, Witney, Oxon, OX8 6RA.*
Comfortable family home. Warm welcome.
Open: All Year
Grades: ETB 2 Cr, High Comm
01993 881622
Mrs Perry
Rates fr: *£19.00*-**£25.00**.
Beds: 1F 1T
Baths: 2 Ensuite
(6)

The Leather Bottel, *East End, North Leigh, Witney, Oxon, OX8 3PX.*
Warm C16th inn full of character.
Open: All Year
Grades: ETB 2 Cr, Comm
01993 882174
Mr Purcell
Rates fr: *£18.00*-**£25.00**.
Beds: 1F 2D 1S
Baths: 3 Private
(50)

North Stoke

National Grid Ref: SU6186

Footpath Cottage, *The Street, North Stoke, Wallingford, Oxon, OX10 6BJ.*
C18th cottage, exquisite village.
Open: All Year
01491 839763
Mrs Tanner
Rates fr: *£17.00*-**£18.00**.
Beds: 2D 1S
Baths: 1 Private 1 Shared

The Old Farm House, *North Stoke, Wallingford, Oxon, OX10 6BL.*
C17th farmhouse in Oxfordshire village.
Open: All Year
01491 837079
Mrs Lucey
Rates fr: *£17.00*-**£18.00**.
Beds: 2T 1S
Baths: 1 Shared
(4)

Northmoor

National Grid Ref: SP4202
Harcourt Arms

Rectory Farm, *Northmoor, Witney, Oxon, OX8 1SX.*
C16th farmhouse, peaceful.
Open: Feb to Nov
Grades: ETB 2 Cr, High Comm
01865 300207 Mrs Florey
Rates fr: *£19.50*-**£30.00**.
Beds: 1D 1T
Baths: 2 Private

Nuffield

National Grid Ref: SU6687

The Rectory, *Nuffield, Henley-on-Thames, Oxon, RG9 5SN.*
Working rural Rectory.
Open: All Year (not Xmas)
01491 641305 Mr Shearer
Rates fr: *£18.00*-**£20.00**.
Beds: 1D,1T,1S
Baths: 1 Private
(0) (4)

Oxford

National Grid Ref: SP5106
The Ox, Boundary House, Duke of Monmouth, Fox & Hounds, Brown's Restaurant

West Farm, *Eaton, Appleton, Oxford, Oxon, OX13 5PR.*
Open: Apr to Dec
01865 862908
Mrs Gow
Rates fr: *£20.00*-**£20.00**.
Beds: 1F 1D 1S
Baths: 1 Private 1 Shared
(10)
Warm, comfortable farmhouse - very quiet but only 1 mile from A420, 6 miles Oxford & Abingdon. TV, tea/coffee facilities all rooms. Good pubs & excellent location.

Highfield West, *188 Cumnor Hill, Oxford, OX2 9PJ.*
Comfortable home in residential area.
Open: All Year
Grades: ETB 2 Cr, High Comm
01865 863007
Mrs Barrett
Rates fr: *£19.50*-**£20.00**.
Beds: 1F 1D 1T 2S
Baths: 3 Private 1 Shared
(3) (5)

Green Gables, *326 Abingdon Road, Oxford, OX1 4TE.*
Open: All Year
Grades: ETB 2 Cr, Comm, AA 3 Q
01865 725870
Mrs Ellis
Rates fr: *£18.00*-**£22.00**.
Beds: 3F 4D 1T 1S
Baths: 6 Private 1 Shared
(8)
Characterful, detached, Edwardian house shielded by trees. Bright spacious rooms with TV & beverage facilities. Ensuite rooms. 1.25 miles to city centre, on bus routes. Ample off-street parking.

Combermere House, *11 Polstead Road, Oxford, OX2 6TW.*
Victorian house in quiet road.
Open: All Year
Grades: ETB Listed, AA Listed
01865 56971 (also fax no)
Mr & Mrs Welding
Rates fr: *£20.00*-**£22.00**.
Beds: 2F 1D 2T 4S
(3)

***Cumnor Bed and Breakfast,** Beinn Bheag, 96 Oxford Road, Cumnor, Oxford, Oxon, OX2 9PQ.*
Open: All Year (not Xmas)
Grades: ETB Listed, Comm
01865 864020 Mrs Tricker
Rates fr: *£21.00*-**£20.00**.
Beds: 1F 1D 1S
Baths: 2 Ensuite 1 Shared
(3)
Situated in the attractive village of Cumnor, just outside Oxford. Spacious bungalow & garden in peaceful rural environment. Homely atmosphere & excellent pub food locally.

***Acorn Guest House,** 260 Iffley Road, Oxford, OX4 1SE.*
Modern comfort in Victorian house.
Open: All Year (not Xmas)
Grades: ETB Listed, AA Listed, RAC Listed
01865 247998 Mrs Lewis
Rates fr: *£17.00*-**£22.00**.
Beds: 3F 1T 2S
Baths: 2 Shared
(5)

***Gables Guest House,** 6 Cumnor Hill, Oxford, OX2 9HA.*
Open: All Year (not Xmas)
Grades: ETB 2 Cr, High Comm, AA 3 Q, Recomm, RAC High Acclaim
01865 862153 Mrs Tompkins
Fax no: 01865 864054
Rates fr: *£20.00*-**£24.00**.
Beds: 1F 2D 1T 2S
Baths: 5 Ensuite 1 Private
(6)
Situated in a perfect location only 5 minutes from bus, railway stations & city centre. A warm & friendly welcome awaits you. Ample car parking.

***The Garden House,** 10 Red Copse Lane, Oxford, OX1 5ER.*
Peaceful, quite residential area.
Open: All Year
Grades: ETB 2 Cr, Comm
01865 739006 Mrs Morrison
Rates fr: *£20.00*-**£25.00**.
Beds: 2T
Baths: 2 Private

***Arden Lodge,** 34 Sunderland Avenue, Oxford, OX2 8DX.*
Select, spacious, modern detached house.
Open: All Year
Grades: ETB Listed
01865 552076 Mr & Mrs Price
Rates fr: *£20.00*-**£25.00**.
Beds: 1D 1T 1S
Baths: 3 Private
(7)

All rates are subject to alteration at the owners' discretion.

***Cornerways Guest House,** 282 Abingdon Road, Oxford, OX1 4TA.*
Friendly establishment near City centre.
Open: All Year (not Xmas)
Grades: ETB 2 Cr, Comm
01865 240135
Mrs Jeakings
Rates fr: *£21.00*-**£26.00**.
Beds: 1F 1D 1T 1S
(2)

***5 Galley Field,** Radley Road, Oxford, OX14 3RU.*
Detached 1960 house in quiet cul-de-sac.
Open: All Year
01235 521088 Mrs Bird
Rates fr: *£16.0017.00*-**£18.00**.
Beds: 3T
Baths: 2 Shared
(12) (2)

***58 St John Street,** Oxford, OX1 2QR.*
Tall Victorian house.
Open: All Year
01865 515454 Mrs Old
Rates fr: *£17.00*-**£17.00**.
Beds: 1F 1T 1S
Baths: 2 Shared
(12)

***Pine Castle Hotel,** 290 Iffley Road, Oxford, OX4 4AE.*
Comfortable family-run Victorian house.
Open: All Year (not Xmas)
Grades: ETB 3 Cr, High Comm, AA 4 Q, Select
01865 241497 / 728887
Mrs Morris
Rates fr: *£28.00*-**£48.00**.
Beds: 1F 5D 2T
Baths: 8 Ensuite
(3)

***Guest House,** 103-105 Woodstock Road, Oxford, OX2 6HL.*
5 mins walk to city centre.
Open: All Year
Grades: ETB 2 Cr
01865 552 579 Mr Pal
Fax no: 01865 311244
Rates fr: *£20.00*-**£25.00**.
Beds: 2F 3D 4T 4S
Baths: 4 Ensuite 4 Shared
(1) (12)

Peppard

National Grid Ref: SU7081

Greyhound, Unicorn, Red Lion, Grouse & Claret

***The Elms,** Gallowstree Road, Peppard, Henley-on-Thames, Oxon, RG9 5HT.*
Spacious Victorian house, swimming pool.
Open: All Year
Grades: ETB 2 Cr, Comm
01734 723164
Mrs Storch
Rates fr: *£15.00*-**£15.50**.
Beds: 1F 1D 1T 1S
Baths: 2 Private 1 Shared
(6) (8)

***Pennyford House,** Peppard, Henley-on-Thames, Oxon, RG9 5JE.*
Large, centrally-heated house, pretty garden.
Open: All Year
Grades: ETB 2 Cr
01491 628272 (also fax no)
Mrs Howden-Ferme
Rates fr: *£17.50*-**£20.00**.
Beds: 2F 1D 1T 1S
Baths: 4 Private 1 Shared
(10)

***Slaters Farm,** Peppard, Henley-on-Thames, Oxon, RG9 5JL.*
Quiet C18th country cottage.
Open: All Year (not Xmas)
Grades: AA 3 Q
01491 628675 (also fax no)
Mrs Howden
Rates fr: *£22.50*-**£25.00**.
Beds: 1D 2T
Baths: 1 Private 1 Shared
(4)

Pishill

National Grid Ref: SU7289

Crown Inn, Five Horseshoes

***Bank Farm,** Pishill, Henley-on-Thames, Oxon, RG9 6HJ.*
Quiet comfortable farmhouse, beautiful countryside.
Open: All Year
01491 638601 Mrs Lakey
Rates fr: *£15.00*-**£12.00**.
Beds: 1F 1S
Baths: 1 Ensuite 1 Shared
(10)

***Old Rectory,** Pishill, Henley-on-Thames, Oxon, RG9 6HJ.*
Comfortable Victorian family home.
Open: All Year (not Xmas)
01491 638243 Mrs Godfrey
Rates fr: *£17.50*-**£20.00**.
Beds: 1T
Baths: 1 Ensuite
(6)

Ramsden

National Grid Ref: SP3515

***Anns Cottage,** Ramsden, Oxon, OX7 3AZ.*
Cottage in pretty Cotswold village.
Open: All Year
Grades: ETB Listed, Approv
01993 868592 Mrs Foxwood
Rates fr: *£16.00*-**£16.00**.
Beds: 1T 1S
Baths: 1 Private
(10) (2)

High season, bank holidays and special events mean low availability *anywhere.*

Salford

National Grid Ref: SP2828

Black Horse, Red Lion

Kingsmoor Cottage, *Chapel Lane, Salford, Chipping Norton, Oxon, OX7 5YN.*
Quiet Cotswold village, traditional comfort.
Open: All Year
Grades: ETB Listed
01608 643276
Mrs Barnard
Rates fr: *£13.50*-**£13.50**.
Beds: 1T
Baths: 1 Shared
(1)

Shiplake

National Grid Ref: SU7678

Baskerville Arms, White Hart (Binfield Heath)

Crowsley House, *Crowsley Road, Shiplake, Henley-on-Thames, Oxon, RG9 3JT.*
Attractive house in Thameside village.
Open: All Year (not Xmas)
Grades: ETB Listed
01189 403197 Mrs Spedding
Rates fr: *£19.00*-**£19.00**.
Beds: 1D 2T
Baths: 1 Private 1 Shared
(3) (4)

Shipton-under-Wychwood

National Grid Ref: SP2717

Shaven Crown, Lamb Inn

Courtlands Road, *Shipton-under-Wychwood, Chipping Norton, Oxon, OX7 6DF.*
Friendly, quiet, comfortable house/garden.
Open: All Year
Grades: ETB Listed, Comm
01993 830551
Mr & Mrs Fletcher
Rates fr: *£17.50*-**£20.00**.
Beds: 2D 1T
Baths: 2 Ensuite 1 Private
(3)

Souldern

National Grid Ref: SP5231

The Fox

The Fox Inn, *Souldern, Bicester, Oxon, OX6 9JN.*
C18th stone village inn.
Open: All Year
Grades: ETB Listed
01869 345284 Mr MacKay
Rates fr: *£16.00*-**£19.50**.
Beds: 1T 3D
Baths: 2 Ensuite 1 Shared
(10)

Towerfields, *Tusmore Road, Souldern, Bicester, Oxon, OX6 9HY.*
Renovated farmhouse, smallholding, rare breeds.
Open: All Year (not Xmas)
Grades: ETB 2 Cr, Comm
01869 346554
Mrs Hamilton Gould
Fax no: 01869 345157
Rates fr: *£20.00*-**£20.00**.
Beds: 1D 1T 1S
Baths: 3 Ensuite
(4)

Southcoombe

National Grid Ref: SP3327

Southcombe Lodge Guest House, *Southcoombe, Chipping Norton, Oxon, OX7 5QH.*
Modern, comfortable guest house.
Open: All Year
Grades: ETB 2 Cr, RAC Listed
01608 643068 Mrs Findlay
Rates fr: *£18.00*-**£20.00**.
Beds: 1F 2D 4T
Baths: 2 Private 2 Shared
(10)

Southmoor

National Grid Ref: SU3998

Hinds Head, Rose Revived (Newbridge)

Alpenhaus, *Faringdon Road, Southmoor, Abingdon, Oxon, OX13 5AF.*
Large private house. Lovely garden.
Open: All Year (not Xmas)
01865 820666 Mrs Curtis
Rates fr: *£16.00*-**£23.00**.
Beds: 1D 2T
Baths: 2 Shared
(12) (3)

Sparsholt

National Grid Ref: SU3487

Westcot Lodge, *Westcot, Sparsholt, Wantage, Oxon, OX12 9QA.*
Comfortable modern country house.
Open: All Year (not Xmas)
01235 751251 Mrs Upton
Rates fr: *£20,00*-**£20.00**.
Beds: 1D 1T
Baths: 1 Shared

Stratton Audley

National Grid Ref: SP6026

Red Lion

The Old School, *Stratton Audley, Bicester, Oxon, OX6 9BJ.*
Interesting old school in pretty village.
Open: All Year
01869 277371 Mrs Wertheimer
Rates fr: *£20.00*-**£20.00**.
Beds: 3T 1S
Baths: 2 Shared
(6)

Summertown

National Grid Ref: SP5108

Adam's Guest House, *302 Banbury Road, Summertown, Oxford, OX2 7ED.*
B&B close to city centre.
Open: All Year
01865 56118 Mr Strange
Rates fr: *£19.00*-**£25.00**.
Beds: 2F 2D 2T
Baths: 3 Shared
(5)

Sutton Courtenay

National Grid Ref: SU5093

Bekynton House, *7 The Green, Sutton Courtenay, Abingdon, Oxon, OX14 4AE.*
Period house on village green.
Open: All Year (not Xmas)
01235 848630 Ms Cornwall
Fax no: 01235 848436
Rates fr: *£20.00*-**£25.00**.
Beds: 1D 1T 1S
Baths: 2 Shared
(2)

Tetsworth

National Grid Ref: SP6802

The Lion on the Green, *Tetsworth, Thame, Oxon, OX9 7AS.*
Open: All Year
01844 281274 Mr Hodgkinson
Rates fr: *£17.50*-**£25.00**.
Beds: 2T 1F
Baths: 1 Shared
(20)
Privately owned country inn & restaurant. We specialise in top quality home-cooked food at affordable prices. Your pleasure is our business!

Little Acre, *4 High Street, Tetsworth, Thame, Oxon, OX9 7AT.*
Country house retreat offering every comfort.
Open: All Year
01844 281423 Mr Tanner
Rates fr: *£13.00*-**£15.00**.
Beds: 1F 1D 2T
Baths: 2 Private
(5) (4)

Thame

National Grid Ref: SP7005

Royal Oak

Vine Cottage, *Moreton, Thame, Oxon, OX9 2HX.*
Novelist's enchanting cottage near Oxford.
Open: All Year (not Xmas)
01844 216910 Ms Blumenthal
Rates fr: *£19.00*-**£18.00**.
Beds: 1D 1S
Baths: 1 Shared
(10) (6)

Towersey

National Grid Ref: SP7308

***Upper Green Farm,** Manor Road, Towersey, Thame, Oxon, OX9 3QR.*
C15th thatched farmhouse.
Open: All Year
01844 212496 Ms Aitken
Rates fr: *£20.00*-**£30.00**.
Beds: 7D 2T 1S
Baths: 10 Private
(13) (10)

Uffington

National Grid Ref: SU3089

Fox & Hounds, White Horse

***Norton House,** Broad Street, Uffington, Faringdon, Oxon, SN7 7RA.*
Friendly C18th family home.
Open: All Year
01367 820230 (also fax no)
Mrs Oberman
Rates fr: *£16.00*-**£17.00**.
Beds: 1F 1D 1S
Baths: 2 Private
(3)

***Sower Hill Farm,** Uffington, Faringdon, Oxon, SN7 7QH.*
Modern farmhouse with brilliant views.
Open: All Year (not Xmas)
Grades: ETB Listed
01367 820758 Mrs Cox
Rates fr: *£18.00*-**£18.00**.
Beds: 1F 1D 1T
Baths: 2 Shared
(10) (6)

***The Craven,** Uffington, Faringdon, Oxon, SN7 7RD.*
C17th thatched, beamed farmhouse/hotel.
Open: All Year
01367 820449 Mrs Wadsworth
Rates fr: *£20.00*-**£25.00**.
Beds: 1F 3D 2T 2S
Baths: 2 Private 2 Shared
(9)

***Shotover House,** Uffington, Faringdon, Oxon, SN7 7RH.*
Traditonal chalkstone cottage, stylishly decorated.
Open: All Year (not Xmas)
01367 820351 Mrs Shaw
Rates fr: *£25.00*-**£25.00**.
Beds: 1D 1T 1S
Baths: 2 Ensuite 1 Private
(3)

National Grid References are for villages, towns and cities - *not* for individual houses.

Bringing children with you? Always ask for any special rates.

Upton

National Grid Ref: SU5186

***Prospect House,** Station Road, Upton, Didcot, Oxon, OX11 9HU.*
Late-Georgian farmhouse, lovely garden.
Open: All Year (not Xmas)
01235 850268 Mrs Powell
Rates fr: *£20.00*-**£20.00**.
Beds: 1D 2T
Baths: 1 Shared

Wallingford

National Grid Ref: SU6089

Chillingford Bridge Hotel

***North Farm,** Shillingford Hill, Wallingford, Oxon, OX10 8ND.*
Quiet farmhouse near River Thames.
Open: All Year (not Xmas)
Grades: ETB 2 Cr, High Comm
01865 858406 Mrs Warburton
Fax no: 01865 858519
Rates fr: *£20.00*-**£25.00**.
Beds: 1D 1T
Baths: 2 Private
(8)

***3 Aston Close,** Wallingford, Oxon, OX10 9AY.*
Modern, quiet private house.
Open: All Year (not Xmas)
01491 836434 Mrs Holmes
Rates fr: *£15.00*-**£17.50**.
Beds: 1D 1T
Baths: 1 Private 1 Shared
(5) (3)

***The Nook,** 2 Thames Street, Wallingford, Oxon, OX10 0BH.*
Character house close to river/town.
Open: All Year
01491 834214 Mrs Colclough
Rates fr: *£19.00*-**£28.00**.
Beds: 1D 2T
Baths: 1 Shared

Wantage

National Grid Ref: SU4087

Bell Inn

***Ormond Guest House,** 23 Ormond Road, Wantage, Oxon, OX12 8EG.*
Victorian house near town centre.
Open: All Year
01235 762409 Mr & Mrs Mudway
Rates fr: *£18.00*-**£20.00**.
Beds: 2F 4T
Baths: 3 Private 2 Shared
(8)

Witney

National Grid Ref: SP3509

Three Horse Shoes

***Quarrydene,** Dene Rise, off Moorland Road, Witney, Oxon, OX8 5LU.*
Quiet, friendly, detached 1930s house.
Open: All Year
01993 772152 / 0850 054786
Mrs Marshall
Rates fr: *£17.00*-**£17.00**.
Beds: 1D 1T 2S
Baths: 1 Private 2 Shared

***The Witney Hotel,** 7 Church Green, Witney, Oxon, OX8 6AZ.*
Grade II Listed building.
Open: All Year (not Xmas)
Grades: ETB 2 Cr
01993 702137 Mrs Dawson
Rates fr: *£20.00*-**£25.00**.
Beds: 2F 4D 3T 1S
Baths: 10 Private

***Field View,** Woodgreen, Witney, Oxon, OX8 6DE.*
Stone house in secluded setting.
Open: All Year
01993 705485 Mrs Simpson
Rates fr: *£20.00*-**£25.00**.
Beds: 1D 2T
Baths: 3 Ensuite
(6)

***The Court Inn,** Bridge Street, Witney, Oxon, OX8 6DA.*
Modernised, heated, welcoming coach house.
Open: All Year
01993 703228 Mr & Mrs Kendall
Rates fr: *£16.00*-**£20.00**.
Beds: 2F 2D 3T 3S
Baths: 5 Private 1 Shared
(10)

***The Old Coach House,** 9f West End, Witney, Oxon, OX8 6NG.*
Converted C18th coach house.
Open: All Year
01993 705586 Mrs Smith
Rates fr: *£18.00*.
Beds: 1D
Baths: 1 Ensuite
(1)

Woodcote

National Grid Ref: SU6481

Red Lion

***Hedges,** South Stoke Road, Woodcote, Reading, Berks, RG8 0PL.*
Area of Outstanding Natural Beauty.
Open: All Year (not Xmas)
01491 680461
Mrs Howard-Allen
Rates fr: *£15.00*-**£15.00**.
Beds: 2T 2S
Baths: 2 Shared
(2) (4)

Voodstock

Vational Grid Ref: SP4416

Kings Head

lane Tree House B & B, 15 High treet, Woodstock, Oxon, OX20 1TE.
pen: All Year (not Xmas)
rades: ETB 1 Cr
1993 813075
Miss Drewett
ates fr: *£15.00.*
eds: 1F 1D 1T
aths: 1 Shared
otswold stone town house, over 00 years old, in Woodstock's pret- High Street, only minutes walk om Blenheim Palace & its eautiful lake and parkland.

orselands Farmhouse Auberge, oddington Lane, Long anborough, Woodstock, Oxon, X8 6PU.
ld Cotswold stone farmhouse.
pen: All Year
rades: ETB 2 Cr, RAC Listed
1993 881895
Irs Jones
ates fr: *£18.00*-**£28.00.**
eds: 1F 2D 1T
aths: 4 Ensuite

unchbowl Inn, 12 Oxford Street, Voodstock, Oxon, OX20 1TR.
eal for Blenheim & Oxford.
pen: All Year
993 811218 Mr Vidgen
ates fr: *£17.50*-**£25.00.**
eds: 2F 4D 2T 2S
aths: 3 Private 3 Shared
(12)

Bringing children with you? Always ask for any special rates.

Pine Trees, *44 Green Lane, Woodstock, Oxon, OX20 1JZ.*
House surrounded by landscaped gardens.
Open: All Year
01993 813333
Mrs Marshall
Rates fr: *£18.00*-**£25.00.**
Beds: 2F 1T
Baths: 1 Private 2 Shared
(2)

14 Hensington Road, *Woodstock, Oxon, OX20 1JL.*
Family home of textile artist.
Open: All Year (not Xmas)
01993 812051
Mrs MacCabe
Rates fr: *£16.00*-**£18.00.**
Beds: 2D 1S
Baths: 1 Shared
(1)

Regent House, *Oxford Street, Woodstock, Oxon, OX20 1TQ.*
Centrally positioned Georgian guest house.
Open: All Year
01993 811004
Mrs Gosling
Rates fr: *£20.00*-**£30.00.**
Beds: 3D 1T
Baths: 3 Ensuite 1 Private

Wootton

National Grid Ref: SP4319

The Kings Head

8 Manor Court, *Wootton, Woodstock, Oxon, OX20 1EU.*
Friendly, comfortable village house.
Open: All Year (not Xmas)
01993 811186
Mrs Fletcher
Rates fr: *£16.00*-**£16.00.**
Beds: 1D 2S
Baths: 1 Private 1 Shared
(12) (2)

Killingworth Castle, *Wootton, Woodstock, Oxon, OX20 1EJ.*
300-year-old coaching inn.
Open: All Year
01993 811401
Mr Brooks
Rates fr: *£17.50*-**£25.00.**
Beds: 2D 1T
Baths: 1 Private 2 Shared
(50)

The Manor Farm, *Wootton, Woodstock, Oxon, OX20 1DX.*
1639 farm house, beautiful village.
Open: All Year
01993 811479 Mrs Lamb
Rates fr: *£20.00*-**£30.00.**
Beds: 2F 3D 1T
Baths: 7 Private 2 Shared
(10)

Yarnton

National Grid Ref: SP4712

The Square Bassett

Kings Bridge Guest House, *Woodstock Road, Yarnton, Kidlington, Oxon, OX5 1PH.*
Friendly welcome in modern bungalow.
Open: All Year
Grades: ETB 2 Cr
01865 841748 Ms Shaw
Rates fr: *£17.50*-**£25.00.**
Beds: 1F 1D 1T
Baths: 3 Ensuite
(6)

Eltham Villa, *148 Woodstock Road, Yarnton, Kidlington, Oxon, OX5 1PW.*
Renovated old house - modern facilities.
Open: All Year (not Xmas)
01865 376037 Mrs Willoughby
Fax no: 01685 376037
Rates fr: *£15.00*-**£20.00.**
Beds: 2F 2D 1T 2S
Baths: 7 Ensuite
(7)

Shropshire

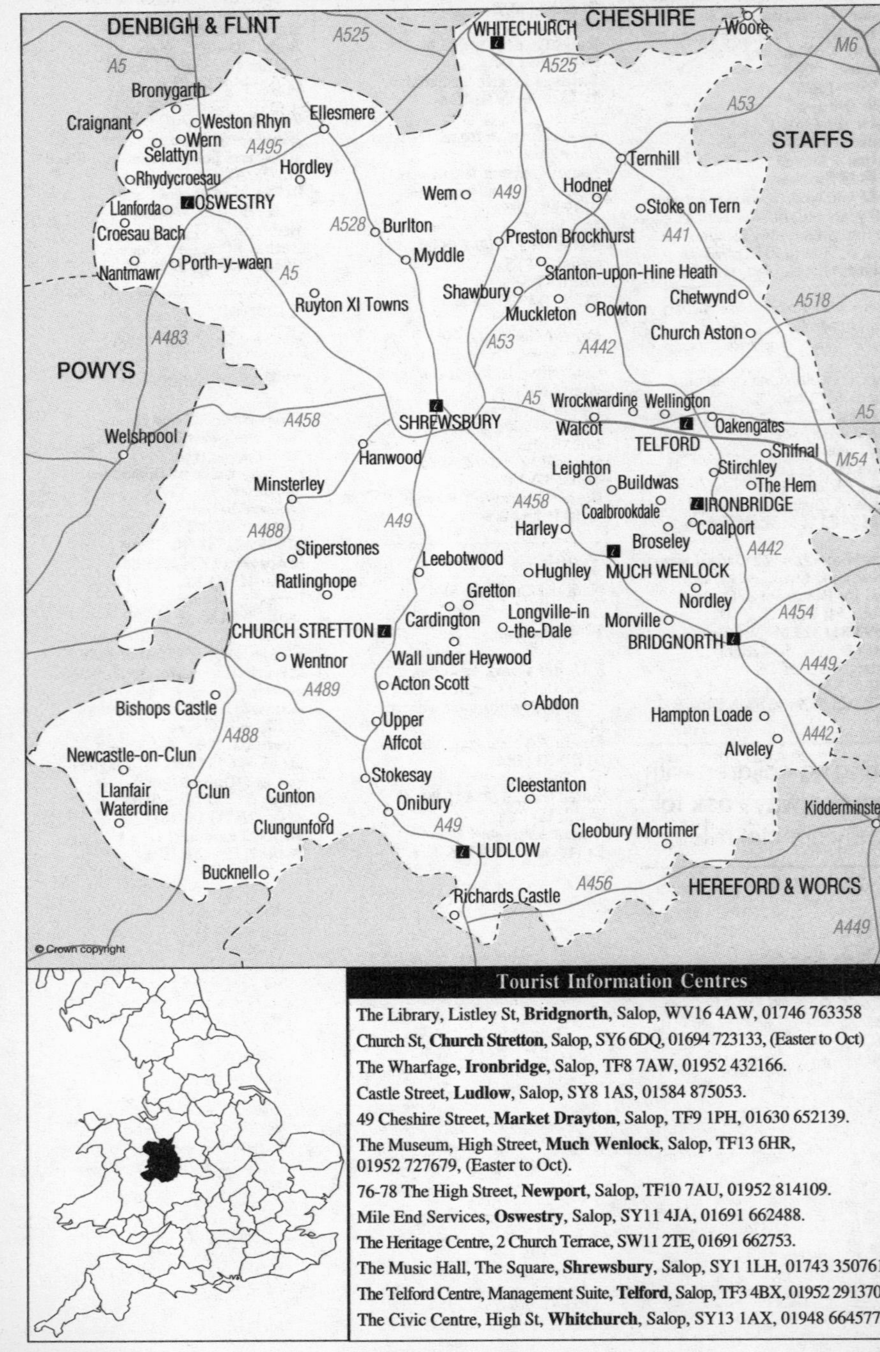

Tourist Information Centres

The Library, Listley St, **Bridgnorth**, Salop, WV16 4AW, 01746 763358

Church St, **Church Stretton**, Salop, SY6 6DQ, 01694 723133, (Easter to Oct)

The Wharfage, **Ironbridge**, Salop, TF8 7AW, 01952 432166.

Castle Street, **Ludlow**, Salop, SY8 1AS, 01584 875053.

49 Cheshire Street, **Market Drayton**, Salop, TF9 1PH, 01630 652139.

The Museum, High Street, **Much Wenlock**, Salop, TF13 6HR, 01952 727679, (Easter to Oct).

76-78 The High Street, **Newport**, Salop, TF10 7AU, 01952 814109.

Mile End Services, **Oswestry**, Salop, SY11 4JA, 01691 662488.

The Heritage Centre, 2 Church Terrace, SW11 2TE, 01691 662753.

The Music Hall, The Square, **Shrewsbury**, Salop, SY1 1LH, 01743 350761

The Telford Centre, Management Suite, **Telford**, Salop, TF3 4BX, 01952 291370.

The Civic Centre, High St, **Whitchurch**, Salop, SY13 1AX, 01948 664577.

Abdon

National Grid Ref: SO5786

Spring Cottage, *Cockshutford Road, Abdon, Craven Arms, Shropshire, SY7 9HU.*
Country house in idyllic hillside location.
Open: All Year (not Xmas)
Grades: ETB 2 Cr, High Comm
01746 712551 Mrs Langham
Fax no: 01746 712001
Rates fr: *£18.00*-**£23.00**.
Beds: 1D 1T 1S
Baths: 3 Ensuite
(10) (5)

Acton Scott

National Grid Ref: SO4589

Plough Inn

Acton Scott Farm, *Acton Scott, Church Stretton, Shropshire, SY6 6QN.*
Lovely C17th farmhouse, working farm.
Open: Feb to Nov
Grades: ETB 2 Cr, Comm
01694 781260 Mrs Jones
Rates fr: *£14.00*-**£16.00**.
Beds: 1F 1D 1T
Baths: 1 Private 1 Shared
(6)

Alveley

National Grid Ref: SO7684

Astley Farm, *Alveley, Bridgnorth, Shropshire, WV15 6ER.*
Friendly comfortable farm house.
Open: All Year
01746 780227 Mr Thompson
Rates fr: *£15.00*-**£15.00**.
Beds: 3D
Baths: 2 Private 1 Shared
(10)

Bishop's Castle

National Grid Ref: SO3288

Boar's head

Old Brick Guest House, *7 Church Street, Bishop's Castle, Shropshire, SY9 5AA.*
C18th guest house in historic town.
Open: All Year (not Xmas)
Grades: ETB 2 Cr, AA 3 Q
01588 638471 Mr Hutton
Rates fr: *£20.00*-**£25.00**.
Beds: 1F 2D 1T
Baths: 4 Ensuite
(5)

Always telephone to get directions to the B&B - you will save time!

The lowest **single** *rate is shown in* **bold.**

Bridgnorth

National Grid Ref: SO7193

Golden Lion, Shakespeare

The Golden Lion, *83 High Street, Bridgnorth, Shropshire, WV16 4DS.*
Open: All Year
Grades: ETB 1 Cr
01746 762016 (also fax no)
Mr Watkins
Rates fr: *£16.00*-**£18.50**.
Beds: 4F
Baths: 1 Ensuite 2 Shared
(15)
Only Bed & Breakfast on Bridgnorth's historic High Street, by the Northgate. Fully licensed C17th town centre inn with car park at rear.

Wyndene Guest House, *57 Innage Lane, Bridgnorth, Shropshire, WV16 4HS.*
Comfortable family guest house.
Open: All Year
Grades: ETB 1 Cr
01746 764369
Mrs Morse
Rates fr: *£18.00*-**£18.00**.
Beds: 1D 1T 2S
Baths: 1 Shared
(6)

Bronygarth

National Grid Ref: SJ2637

Swan

Old School, *Bronygarth, Oswestry, Shropshire, SY10 7NB.*
Recently converted Victorian schoolhouse.
Open: All Year (not Xmas)
01691 772546
Mr & Mrs Bampfield
Rates fr: *£15.00*-**£15.00**.
Beds: 2T 1S **Baths:** 2 Shared
(10) (2)

Broseley

National Grid Ref: SJ6701

Brewery Inn

Lord Hill Guest House, *Duke Street, Broseley, Shropshire, TF12 5LU.*
Renovated public house, comfortable, friendly.
Open: All Year
Grades: ETB Listed
01952 884270 / 580792
Mr Ryan
Rates fr: *£15.00*-**£15.00**.
Beds: 1D 4T 2S
Baths: 3 Private 1 Shared
(9)

Orchard House, *40 King Street, Broseley, Shropshire, TF12 5NA.*
Georgian house, large warm bedrooms.
Open: All Year (not Xmas)
Grades: ETB 2 Cr, Comm
01952 882684
Mrs Kaiser
Rates fr: *£15.00*-**£16.00**.
Beds: 1F 1D 1T
Baths: 1 Ensuite 2 Shared
(4)

Annscroft, *25 King Street, Broseley, Shropshire, TF12 5NA.*
Large converted Victorian shop.
Open: All Year (not Xmas)
01952 882670
Mrs Beddow
Rates fr: *£16.00*-**£18.00**.
Beds: 1D 2T
Baths: 2 Shared

Bucknell

National Grid Ref: SO3573

Barron of Beef

The Hall, *Bucknell, Shropshire, SY7 0AA.*
Open: All Year (not Xmas)
Grades: ETB 2 Cr, Comm
01547 530249
Mrs Price
Rates fr: *£17.00*-**£17.00**.
Beds: 2D 1T
Baths: 1 Private 1 Shared
(7) (6)
Relax in our Georgian farmhouse and garden. Ideal for exploring the Welsh Borderlands, towns & castles, also the black-and-white villages of North Herefordshire.

Buildwas

National Grid Ref: SJ6304

Meadow Inn

Bridge House, *Buildwas, Telford, Shropshire, TF8 7BN.*
Half-timbered C17th period residence.
Open: All Year (not Xmas)
Grades: ETB 2 Cr, High Comm
01952 432105
Mrs Hedges
Rates fr: *£19.00*-**£28.00**.
Beds: 1F 1D 1T
Baths: 1 Ensuite 2 Shared
(8)

Grove Farm House, *Leighton Road, Buildwas, Ironbridge, Shropshire, TF8 7DF.*
Comfortably restored C18th farmhouse.
Open: All Year (not Xmas)
Grades: ETB 1 Cr, High Comm
01952 433572
Mrs Pygott
Rates fr: *£16.00*-**£20.00**.
Beds: 1D 1T 1S
Baths: 1 Shared
(10) (4)

***Hill View Farm,** Buildwas, Ironbridge, Telford, Shropshire, TF8 7BP.*
Comfortable farmhouse, convenient Ironbridge Museums.
Open: All Year (not Xmas)
01952 432228 Mrs Hawkins
Rates fr: *£15.00*-**£16.00**.
Beds: 2D 1T
Baths: 1 Private 1 Shared

Burlton

National Grid Ref: SJ4526

***The Grove,** Burlton, Shrewsbury, Shropshire, SY4 5SZ.*
C17th Listed farmhouse, comfortable, welcoming.
Open: All Year (not Xmas)
01939 270310 Mrs Martin
Rates fr: *£16.00*-**£19.00**.
Beds: 1F 1T **Baths:** 1 Private

Cardington

National Grid Ref: SO5095

Plough

***Grove Farm,** Cardington, Church Stretton, Shropshire, SY6 7JZ.*
Comfortable oak-beamed farmhouse in village.
Open: All Year
Grades: ETB Listed, Approv
01694 771451 Mrs Pennington
Rates fr: *£12.00*-**£14.00**.
Beds: 1F 1T
Baths: 1 Shared

Chetwynd

National Grid Ref: SJ7321

***Lane End Farm,** Chester Road, Chetwynd, Newport, Shropshire, TF10 8BN.*
Friendly farmhouse in wonderful countryside.
Open: All Year
Grades: ETB 2 Cr, Comm
01952 550337 Mrs Park
Rates fr: *£18.00*-**£18.00**.
Beds: 1F 1D
Baths: 2 Ensuite

Church Aston

National Grid Ref: SJ7417

***White Gables,** 16 The Close, Church Aston, Newport, Shropshire, TF10 9JL.*
Close to National Sports Centre & Telford town centre.
Open: All Year
01952 810365
Mr & Mrs Leicester
Rates fr: *£13.00*-**£15.00**.
Beds: 2T
Baths: 1 Ensuite 1 Private

Church Stretton

National Grid Ref: SO4593

***Belvedere Guest House,** Burway Road, Church Stretton, Shropshire, SY6 6DP.*
Open: All Year (not Xmas)
Grades: ETB 3 Cr, Comm, AA 4 Q, Select, RAC Acclaim
01694 722232 (also fax no)
Mr Rogers
Rates fr: *£22.00*-**£22.00**.
Beds: 3F 4D 2T 3S
Baths: 6 Private 3 Shared
Beautiful surroundings, situated on the edge of 6,000 acres of National Trust hill country, yet convenient for town. Very peaceful, two guest lounges, drying facilities.

***Highcliffe,** Madeira Walk, Church Stretton, Shropshire, SY6 6JQ.*
Large Edwardian hillside family home.
Open: All Year (not Xmas)
01694 722908
Mr & Mrs Wren
Rates fr: *£14.50*-**£14.50**.
Beds: 1F 1D 1S
Baths: 1 Shared

***Littlebrook,** 38 Ludlow Road, Church Stretton, Shropshire, SY6 6AB.*
Scenic, quiet, comfortable Christian home.
Open: All Year (not Xmas)
01694 722307 Mrs Dancy
Rates fr: *£15.00*-**£17.50**.
Beds: 2D 1T

***Dalesford,** Carding Mill Valley, Church Stretton, Shropshire, SY6 6JF.*
Large, Edwardian private house.
Open: All Year
01694 723228 Mrs Wharton
Rates fr: *£16.00*-**£18.00**.
Beds: 2D 1T
Baths: 1 Private 1 Shared

Cleestanton

National Grid Ref: SO5779

***The Bank Farm,** Cleestanton, Ludlow, Shropshire, SY8 3EL.*
Modernised Victorian farmhouse near Ludlow.
Open: Easter to Oct
01584 823368 Mrs Campbell
Rates fr: *£12.00*-**£12.00**.
Beds: 1F 1T 1S
Baths: 1 Ensuite 1 Private 1 Shared

The lowest **single** *rate is shown in* **bold.**

Cleobury Mortimer

National Grid Ref: SO6775

***Coxs Barn,** Bagginswood, Cleobury Mortimer, Kidderminster, Worcs, DY14 8LS.*
Converted, warm, comfortable, spacious barn.
Open: All Year
Grades: ETB 1 Cr
01746 718415 / 718277
Mrs Thompson
Rates fr: *£17.00*-**£17.00**.
Beds: 2D 1T
Baths: 3 Private

Clun

National Grid Ref: SO3080

Sun Inn, White Horse

***New House Farm,** Mainstone, Clun, Craven Arms, Shropshire, SY7 8NJ.*
Open: Feb to Oct
Grades: ETB 2 Cr, High Comm, AA 4 Q, Select, RAC Listed
01588 638314
Mr & Mrs Ellison
Rates fr: *£20.00*-**£27.00**.
Beds: 1F 1D 1T
Baths: 1 Ensuite 2 Private
Isolated farmhouse set high in Clun Hills. Walks from doorstep. Books and more books to browse in an English country garden. Ring for brochure.

***Clun Farm,** High Street, Clun, Craven Arms, Shropshire, SY7 8JB.*
C16th double cruck farmhouse.
Open: All Year
Grades: ETB Listed
01588 640432
Mrs Lewis
Rates fr: *£16.00*-**£16.00**.
Beds: 1F 1T 2S
Baths: 1 Private 1 Shared

***Crown House,** Church Street, Clun, Craven Arms, Shropshire, SY7 8JW.*
Self-contained Georgian stable conversion.
Open: All Year (not Xmas)
Grades: ETB 2 Cr
01588 640780
Mrs Bailey & Mr R Maund
Rates fr: *£16.50*-**£16.50**.
Beds: 1D 1T
Baths: 1 Ensuite 1 Private

***Llanhedric Farm,** Clun, Craven Arms, Shropshire, SY7 8NG.*
Vantastic views from all rooms.
Open: Easter to Nov
Grades: ETB Listed
01588 640203
Mrs Jones
Rates fr: *£14.00*-**£15.00**.
Beds: 1F 1D

The Old Farmhouse, *Woodside, Clun, Clunton, Craven Arms, Shropshire, SY7 0JB.*
300-year-old stone farmhouse.
Open: Mar to Oct
Grades: ETB 1 Cr, Comm
01588 640695 Mr Wall
Rates fr: *£15.00*-**£15.00**.
Beds: 1F 1D
Baths: 1 Shared
(3)

Clungunford

National Grid Ref: SO3978

Engine & Tender, Kangaroo, Hundred House

North Barn, *Abcott Manor, Clungunford, Craven Arms, Shropshire, SY7 0PX.*
Converted barn, views, ideal touring centre.
Open: All Year (not Xmas)
Grades: ETB Listed
01588 660596 Mrs Mattison
Rates fr: *£14.50*-**£15.00**.
Beds: 1D 2S
Baths: 1 Private
(8) (4)

Clunton

National Grid Ref: SO3381

Hurst Mill Farm, *Clunton, Craven Arms, Shropshire, SY7 0JA.*
Attractive riverside farmhouse.
Open: All Year
Grades: ETB 2 Cr, Comm, AA 3 Q, Recomm
01588 640224 Mrs Williams
Rates fr: *£14.50*-**£15.00**.
Beds: 1F 1D 1T
(6)

Coalbrookdale

National Grid Ref: SJ6604

Meadow Inn, Coalbrookdale Inn, Grove

Paradise House, *Coalbrookdale, Telford, Shropshire, TF8 7NR.*
Large comfortable Georgian family house.
Open: Feb to Nov
Grades: ETB 1 Cr, Approv
01952 433379 Mrs Gilbride
Rates fr: *£20.00*-**£20.00**.
Beds: 1F 1D 1T
Baths: 2 Ensuite 1 Shared
(1)

All details shown are as supplied by B&B owners in Autumn 1996.

Springhill, *2 School Road, Coalbrookdale, Telford, Shropshire, TF8 7DY.*
Large Georgian private house.
Open: All Year
Grades: ETB 2 Cr
01952 432210 Mrs Clegg
Rates fr: *£18.00*-**£25.00**.
Beds: 1F 1D 1T
Baths: 3 Private
(3)

Coalport

National Grid Ref: SJ6902

Willow Brook, *Sutton Bank, Coalport, Telford, Shropshire, TF8 7JB.*
Luxury home, woodland setting.
Open: Mar to Dec
Grades: ETB Listed
01952 583934
Mrs Brookes
Rates fr: *£20.00*.
Beds: 1F
Baths: 1 Ensuite
(3)

Croesau Bach

National Grid Ref: SJ2428

Pant Hir, *Croesau Bach, Oswestry, Shropshire, SY10 9BH.*
Pretty country house on Shropshire/Welsh border.
Open: Feb to Nov
01691 791457
Mrs Werry
Rates fr: *£16.00*-**£24.00**.
Beds: 1F 1D 1T
Baths: 3 Private

Ellesmere

National Grid Ref: SJ3934

The Grange, *Grange Road, Ellesmere, Shropshire, SY12 0DE.*
Georgian house in ten acres.
Open: Mar to Oct
01691 623495
Mrs Ward
Rates fr: *£18.50*-**£22.50**.
Beds: 2F 1D 8T 2S
Baths: 13 Private

Gretton

National Grid Ref: SO5195

Court Farm, *Gretton, Church Stretton, Shropshire, SY6 7HU.*
Large C17th farmhouse.
Open: Feb to Nov
Grades: ETB 3 Cr, High Comm, RAC Acclaim
01694 771219
Mrs Norris
Rates fr: *£20.00*-**£25.00**.
Beds: 1D 3T
Baths: 4 Ensuite
(14) (6)

Hampton Loade

National Grid Ref: SO7486

Lion Inn

The Old Forge House, *Hampton Loade, Bridgnorth, Shropshire, WV15 6HD.*
Peaceful, homely. Woods and pub.
Open: All Year (not Xmas)
Grades: ETB Listed
01746 780338 Ms Ibberson
Rates fr: *£14.00*-**£16.00**.
Beds: 1F 1D 1T
Baths: 2 Private 1 Shared
(6)

Hanwood

National Grid Ref: SJ4409

The White House, *Hanwood, Shrewsbury, Shropshire, SY5 8LP.*
Lovely C16th guesthouse, 2-acre gardens.
Open: All Year
01743 860414 (also fax no)
Mrs Mitchell
Rates fr: *£22.50*-**£22.50**.
Beds: 4D 1T 1S
Baths: 3 Ensuite 1 Shared
(10)

Harley

National Grid Ref: SJ5901

Plume of Feathers

The Plume of Feathers, *Harley, Shrewsbury, Shropshire, SY5 6LP.*
C17th inn, excellent food.
Open: All Year
Grades: ETB 3 Cr, Comm, AA 3 Q
01952 727360
Mr & Mrs Hitchin
Rates fr: *£19.00*-**£28.00**.
Beds: 3F 4D 2T
Baths: 9 Private
(76)

Rowley Farm, *Harley, Shrewsbury, Shropshire, SY5 6LX.*
Farmhouse in secluded area with lots of views.
Open: Easter to Oct
01952 727348
Ms Munslow
Rates fr: *£14.50*-**£20.00**.
Beds: 1D 2S
Baths: 1 Shared
(8)

National Grid References are for villages, towns and cities - *not* for individual houses.

Hodnet

National Grid Ref: SJ6128

Bear Hotel

***The Heath Farm,** Hodnet, Market Drayton, Shropshire, TF9 3JJ.*
Open: All Year (not Xmas)
Grades: ETB Listed
01630 685570 Mrs Drysdale
Rates fr: *£15.00*-**£15.00**.
Beds: 1D 2T 1S
Baths: 1 Shared
(5) (4)
Working farm, conveniently situated for Hawkestone Follies, golf course & Hawkestone Hall, Hodnet Hall Gardens, Ironbridge Gorge Museum & Bridgemere Garden World.

Hordley

National Grid Ref: SJ3830

***Hordley Hall,** Hordley, Ellesmere, Shropshire, SY12 9BB.*
Attractive Georgian family house. Comfortable accomodation in homely atmosphere.
Open: All Year
Grades: ETB Listed
01691 622772
Mrs Rodenhurst
Rates fr: *£15.00*-**£15.00**.
Beds: 2F 1D
Baths: 1 Shared
(5)

Hughley

National Grid Ref: SO5697

***Mill Farm,** Hughley, Shrewsbury, Shropshire, SY5 6NT.*
Victorian farmhouse.
Open: All Year (not Xmas)
01746 785645
Mrs Bosworth
Rates fr: *£15.00*-**£20.00**.
Beds: 1F 1D
Baths: 2 Private

Ironbridge

National Grid Ref: SJ6703

Old Vaults

***Post Office House,** 6 The Square, Ironbridge, Telford, Shropshire, TF8 7AQ.*
Open: All Year
Grades: ETB 1 Cr, Comm
01952 433201 Mrs Jones
Rates fr: *£17.50*-**£25.00**.
Beds: 1F 2D
Baths: 1 Ensuite 1 Shared
(2)
Ann Jones offers you a warm welcome at Post Office House. This elegant C18th house has warm & spacious accommodation overlooking the famous Ironbridge.

Always telephone to get directions to the B&B - you will save time!

Leebotwood

National Grid Ref: SO4798

Pound Inn

***Rectory Farm,** Leebotwood, Church Stretton, Shropshire, SY6 6NN.*
Half-timbered farm house 1620.
Open: All Year (not Xmas) & Jan
Grades: AA 5 Q, Prem Select
01694 751306
Mrs Davies
Rates fr: *£20.00*-**£25.00**.
Beds: 1D 2T
Baths: 3 Private
(12) (10)

Leighton

National Grid Ref: SJ6105

Plume & Feathers

***Eye Manor,** Leighton, Ironbridge, Shrewsbury, Shropshire, SY5 6SQ.*
Manor house listed in Domesday Book.
Open: All Year
Grades: ETB 2 Cr
01952 510066 / 610061
Mrs Chillcott
Fax no: 01952 610066
Rates fr: *£18.00*-**£20.00**.
Beds: 1T
Baths: 1 Ensuite

Llanfair Waterdine

National Grid Ref: SO2476

Lloyney Inn, Red Lion

***The Mill,** Lloyney, Llanfair Waterdine, Knighton, Powys, LD7 1RG.*
Cosy old mill.
Open: All Year
01547 528049
Mr & Mrs Davies
Rates fr: *£13.50*-**£13.50**.
Beds: 1F 1D 2T
Baths: 1 Ensuite 2 Shared
(6)

***Cwm Cole,** Llanfair Waterdine, Knighton, Powys, LD7 1TU.*
Comfortable cottage amid peaceful hills.
Open: All Year (not Xmas)
01547 520357 Ms Lewis
Rates fr: *£16.00*-**£16.00**.
Beds: 2D 1T
Baths: 2 Shared

Llanforda

National Grid Ref: SJ2528

Old Llanforda Mill Inn

***The Old Llanforda Mill Inn,** Candy, Llanforda, Oswestry, Shropshire, SY10 9AZ.*
Picturesque pub with excellent food.
Open: All Year
Grades: ETB 1 Cr, Comm, AA 2 Q
01691 657058 Mrs Atkinson
Rates fr: *£17.00*-**£17.00**.
Beds: 1D 2T 2S
Baths: 1 Shared
(3) (100)

Longville-in-the-Dale

National Grid Ref: SO5393

***Stanway Cottage,** Longville-in-the-Dale, Much Wenlock, Shropshire, TF13 6DS.*
Beautifully located large country house.
Open: All Year (not Xmas)
Grades: ETB Listed
01694 771317 Ms Strachan
Fax no: 01694 771333
Rates fr: *£16.00*-**£16.00**.
Beds: 1D 1T
Baths: 1 Shared
(4)

Ludlow

National Grid Ref: SO5174

***Arran House,** 42 Gravel Hill, Ludlow, Shropshire, SY8 1QR.*
Comfortable Victorian private house.
Open: All Year (not Xmas)
Grades: ETB 1 Cr
01584 873764 Mrs Bowen
Rates fr: *£15.00*-**£16.00**.
Beds: 1D 1T 2S
Baths: 1 Shared
(5) (5)

***Cecil Guest House,** Sheet Road, Ludlow, Shropshire, SY8 1LR.*
Modern, comfortable, clean guest house.
Open: All Year (not Xmas)
Grades: ETB 2 Cr, Comm, AA 3 Q, RAC Acclaim
01584 872442 (also fax no)
Mrs Phillips
Rates fr: *£19.00*-**£19.00**.
Beds: 1F 1D 5T 3S
Baths: 4 Private 2 Shared
(8)

Many rates vary according to season - the lowest are shown here.

Right on the border?

Look at the neigh-

bouring county, too

Minsterley

National Grid Ref: SJ3705

Stables Inn

***Cricklewood Cottage,** Plox Green, Minsterley, Shrewsbury, Shropshire, SY5 0HT.*
C18th cottage with lovely garden.
Open: All Year
Grades: ETB 2 Cr, High Comm, AA 4 Q, Select
01743 791229
Mr & Mrs Costello
Rates fr: *£19.00*-**£19.00**.
Beds: 2D 1T
Baths: 3 Private
(8) (3)

Morville

National Grid Ref: SO6694

***Hannigans Farm,** Morville, Bridgnorth, Shropshire, WV16 4RN.*
Converted barn, glorious views of rolling country.
Open: All Year
01746 714332
Mrs Thompson
Rates fr: *£17.00*-**£34.00**.
Beds: 1T
Baths: 1 Ensuite

Much Wenlock

National Grid Ref: SO6299

George & Dragon

***31 Oakfield Park,** Much Wenlock, Shropshire, TF13 6HH.*
Modern 3-bedroom bungalow.
Open: All Year
01952 727473 Mrs Stevenson
Rates fr: *£13.00*-**£12.00**.
Beds: 2D 1S
Baths: 1 Shared
(5) (3)

Muckleton

National Grid Ref: SJ5921

***New Farm,** Muckleton, Shawbury, Telford, Shropshire, TF6 6RJ.*
Modern farmhouse. Beautiful, peaceful surroundings.
Open: All Year (not Xmas)
Grades: ETB 2 Cr, Comm
01939 250358 Mr Evans
Rates fr: *£16.00*-**£18.00**.
Beds: 1F 1D 1T 1S
Baths: 3 Private 1 Shared
(10)

Myddle

National Grid Ref: SJ4723

Red Lion

***Oakfields,** Myddle, Shrewsbury, Shropshire, SY4 3RX.*
Open: All Year
Grades: ETB 1 Cr, Comm
01939 290823 Mrs Frost
Rates fr: *£15.00*-**£16.00**.
Beds: 1F 1D 1T
Baths: 2 Shared
(10)
Friendly welcome at large comfortable Oakfields in the historic vilage of Myddle. Extensive, well-kept garden with fine views over farmland. Traditional home cooked breakfast.

Nantmawr

National Grid Ref: SJ2424

***April Spring Cottage,** Nantmawr, Oswestry, Shropshire, SY10 9HL.*
Comfortable cottage amidst peaceful countryside.
Open: All Year (not Xmas)
01691 828802 Mrs Richardson
Rates fr: *£15.50*-**£31.00**.
Beds: 1D 1T
(8) (6)

Newcastle-on-Clun

National Grid Ref: SO2482

***The Quarry House,** Newcastle-on-Clun, Craven Arms, Shropshire, SY7 8QJ.*
Converted barn, fantastic views, peaceful.
Open: All Year (not Xmas)
01588 640774 Mr Woodward
Rates fr: *£17.00*-**£17.00**.
Beds: 2T 1S
Baths: 1 Private 1 Shared
(20)

Nordley

National Grid Ref: SO6996

***The Albynes,** Nordley, Bridgnorth, Shropshire, WV16 4SX.*
Beautiful country house in large gardens.
Open: All Year (not Xmas)
01746 762261 Mrs Woolley
Rates fr: *£17.50*-**£20.00**.
Beds: 1D 1T 1S
Baths: 3 Private
(5) (10)

Oakengates

National Grid Ref: SJ7011

***Sunnymede Guest House,** Leonard Street, Oakengates, Telford, Shropshire, TF2 6EU.*
Homely atmosphere, comfortable rooms.
Open: All Year (not Xmas)
01952 612980 Mrs Hume
Rates fr: *£16.00*-**£18.00**.
Beds: 1D 1T 2S **Baths:** 2 Shared
(12)

Onibury

National Grid Ref: SO4579

***Fairview,** Green Lane, Onibury, Craven Arms, Shropshire, SY7 9BL.*
300-year-old smallholding in south Shropshire hills.
Open: Apr to Oct
01584 856505
Mrs Coates
Rates fr: *£16.50*-**£17.00**.
Beds: 2D 1T
Baths: 1 Private 1 Shared
(14) (6)

Oswestry

National Grid Ref: SJ2929

The Bear

***Brownhill House,** Brownhill, Ruyton-XI-Towns, Oswestry, Shropshire, SY4 1LR.*
Open: All Year
Grades: ETB 2 Cr, Comm
01939 260626 (also fax no)
Mrs Brown
Rates fr: *£17.0*-**£19.00**.
Beds: 1D 1T 1S
Baths: 3 Ensuite
(0) (5)
First class accommodation, all ensuite. 5 Star service. Good food, good conversation. Bring your own wine. Extensive breakfast menu. Unique hillside garden. Phone, fax or email for details.

***Montrose,** Weston Lane, Oswestry, Shropshire, SY11 2BG.*
Large Victorian private house.
Open: All Year
Grades: ETB Listed
01691 652063
Mrs Leggatt
Rates fr: *£14.00*-**£14.00**.
Beds: 2T
Baths: 1 Shared
(4)

***Elgar House,** 16 Elgar Close, Oswestry, Shropshire, SY11 2LZ.*
Modern, comfortable elevated guest house.
Open: All Year
Grades: ETB 2 Cr, High Comm
01691 661323
Mr Harding
Rates fr: *£17.50*-**£20.00**.
Beds: 2F 3D 3S
Baths: 1 Private 1 Shared
(3)

***18 Hampton Road,** Oswestry, Shropshire, SY11 1SJ.*
Quiet house near town centre.
Open: All Year (not Xmas)
Grades: ETB Listed, Comm
01691 652184
Mrs Willetts
Rates fr: *£14.00*-**£14.00**.
Beds: 1D 1T 2S
(5) (4)

Bear Hotel, *Salop Road, Oswestry, Shropshire, SY11 2NR.*
Family-run, town-centre hotel.
Open: All Year (not Xmas)
Grades: ETB 3 Cr, Comm
01691 652093 Mr & Mrs Lucks
Rates fr: *£20.00*-**£24.00**.
Beds: 1F 4D 2T 3S
Baths: 5 Private 1 Shared
(25)

The Hawthorns, *Weston Lane, Oswestry, Shropshire, SY11 2BG.*
Large, comfortable, Victorian private house.
Open: All Year
01691 657678 Mr Roberts
Rates fr: *£17.00*-**£18.50**.
Beds: 1D 1T
Baths: 2 Ensuite
(4)

Porth-y-waen

National Grid Ref: SJ2623

Red Lion Inn, *Porth-y-waen, Oswestry, Shropshire, SY10 8LX.*
Traditional old country pub.
Open: All Year (not Xmas)
01691 830219 Mrs Jones
Rates fr: *£15.00*-**£15.00**.
Beds: 2D 2T
Baths: 1 Shared

Preston Brockhurst

National Grid Ref: SJ5324

Grove Farm, *Preston Brockhurst, Shrewsbury, Shropshire, SY4 5QA.*
Comfortable traditionally furnished C17th farmhouse.
Open: All Year (not Xmas)
01939 220223 Mrs Jones
Rates fr: *£18.50*-**£16.50**.
Beds: 1F 1D 1T 1S
Baths: 1 Shared
(5)

Ratlinghope

National Grid Ref: SO4096

Lower Stitt Farm, *Ratlinghope, Shrewsbury, Shropshire, SY5 0SN.*
Scenic countryside. Friendly comfortable farmhouse.
Open: All Year (not Xmas)
Grades: ETB 1 Cr, Comm
01588 650640 Mrs Betton
Rates fr: *£15.00*-**£15.00**.
Beds: 1D 1T
Baths: 1 Shared
(2)

Please respect a B&B's wishes regarding children, animals & smoking.

All rates are subject to alteration at the owners' discretion.

Richards Castle

National Grid Ref: SO4969

Longlands, *Woodhouse Lane, Richards Castle, Ludlow, Shropshire, SY8 4EU.*
Farmhouse set in rural landscape.
Open: All Year (not Xmas)
01584 831636
Mrs Kemsley
Rates fr: *£17.00*-**£18.00**.
Beds: 1D 1T
Baths: 1 Ensuite 1 Private
(3)

Rowton

National Grid Ref: SJ6119

Church Farm, *Rowton, Wellington, Telford, Shropshire, TF6 6QY.*
Comfortable farmhouse. Large country breakfast.
Open: All Year
01952 770381
Mrs Evans
Rates fr: *£15.00*-**£18.50**.
Beds: 1F 2D 2T 1S
Baths: 2 Private 1 Shared
(8)

Ruyton-XI-Towns

National Grid Ref: SJ3922

Brownhill House, *Brownhill, Ruyton-XI-Towns, Shrewsbury, Shropshire, SY4 1LR.*
First class accommodation, all ensuite.
Open: All Year
Grades: ETB 2 Cr, Comm
01939 260626 (also fax no)
Mrs Brown
Rates fr: *£17.0*-**£19.00**.
Beds: 1D 1T 1S
Baths: 3 Ensuite
(0) (5)

Ryton

National Grid Ref: SJ4903

The Old House, *Ryton, Dorrington, Shrewsbury, Shropshire, SY5 7LY.*
C16th manor house, oak-beamed rooms.
Open: All Year (not Xmas)
01743 718585
Mr Paget-Brown
Rates fr: *£18.00*-**£28.00**.
Beds: 1D 1T
Baths: 2 Private
(7) (6)

Selattyn

National Grid Ref: SJ2633

The Old Rectory, *Selattyn, Oswestry, Shropshire, SY10 7DH.*
Attractive period stone house, secluded grounds.
Open: All Year (not Xmas)
Grades: ETB 2 Cr
01691 659708 Mrs Barnes
Rates fr: *£16.00*-**£16.00**.
Beds: 1F 1D 1T
Baths: 2 Ensuite 1 Private
(0) (6)

Carreg Y Big, *Selattyn, Oswestry, Shropshire, SY10 7HX.*
Stone building, luxuriously converted.
Open: Sep to Jun
01691 654754 Mrs Brown
Rates fr: *£12.50*-**£12.50**.
Beds: 3T
Baths: 2 Private
(4) (20)

Shawbury

National Grid Ref: SJ5521

Unity Lodge, *Moreton Mill, Shawbury, Shrewsbury, Shropshire, SY4 4ES.*
Comfortable, homely accommodation, spacious house.
Open: All Year
Grades: ETB Listed
01939 250831 Mrs Woodcock
Rates fr: *£15.00*-**£16.00**.
Beds: 1F 1D 1T 1S
Baths: 2 Shared
(8)

New Farm, *Muckleton, Shawbury, Telford, Shropshire, TF6 6RJ.*
Modern farmhouse. Beautiful, peaceful surroundings.
Open: All Year (not Xmas)
Grades: ETB 2 Cr, Comm
01939 250358 Mr Evans
Rates fr: *£16.00*-**£18.00**.
Beds: 1F 1D 1T 1S
Baths: 3 Private 1 Shared
(10)

Shifnal

National Grid Ref: SJ7407

Beech House, *Wolverhampton Road, Shifnal, Shropshire, TF11 9HA.*
Quiet country house, large garden.
Open: All Year (not Xmas)
01952 460261 Mrs Foster
Rates fr: *£16.00*-**£17.50**.
Beds: 2T
Baths: 1 Shared
(4)

Drayton Lodge, *Shifnal, Shropshire, TF11 8QW.*
Large Georgian farmhouse.
Open: All Year (not Xmas)
01952 460244 Mrs Minton
Rates fr: *£14.00*-**£14.00**.
Beds: 1D 2T 1S
Baths: 1 Ensuite 1 Shared
(6)

Shrewsbury

National Grid Ref: SJ4912

Boathouse Inn, Traitors Gate, Old Bell Abbey, Three Fishes

***Avonlea,** 33 Coton Crescent, Coton Hill, Shrewsbury, SY1 2NZ.*
Open: All Year (not Xmas)
Grades: ETB Listed, Approv
01743 359398
Mrs O'Keefe
Rates fr: *£14.00*-**£15.00**.
Beds: 2T 1S
Baths: 1 Ensuite 1 Shared
(11)
Victorian home outskirts of medi-aeval town of 'Brother Cadfael' fame. Close to all public transport. Full English breakfast & comfort in tasteful surroundings.

***Bancroft Guest House,** 17 Coton Crescent, Shrewsbury, Shropshire, SY1 2NY.*
Comfortable, clean, friendly guest-house.
Open: All Year (not Xmas)
Grades: ETB Listed
01743 231746
Mrs Oldham-Malcolm
Rates fr: *£16.00*-**£17.00**.
Beds: 1F 1T 2S
Baths: 2 Shared
(4)

***Merevale House,** 66 Ellesmere Road, Shrewsbury, Shropshire, SY1 2QP.*
Comfortable Victorian house, 10 minutes from town.
Open: All Year
Grades: ETB Listed, Comm
01743 243677
Mrs Spooner
Rates fr: *£16.00*-**£16.00**.
Beds: 3D 1S
Baths: 1 Shared
(4)

***Anton House,** 1 Canon Street, Monkmoor, Shrewsbury, Shropshire, SY2 5HG.*
Comfortable, large Victorian private house.
Open: All Year (not Xmas)
Grades: ETB 1 Cr, Comm
01743 359275
Mrs Sandford
Rates fr: *£17.00*-**£20.00**.
Beds: 1F 2D 1T
Baths: 2 Shared
(3)

High season, bank holidays and special events mean low availability *anywhere*.

***Abbey Court House,** 134 Abbey Foregate, Shrewsbury, Shropshire, SY2 6AU.*
Substantial well-appointed guest house.
Open: All Year (not Xmas)
Grades: ETB 2 Cr
01743 364416 Mrs Turnock
Rates fr: *£17.00*-**£19.00**.
Beds: 21F 3D 3T 2S
Baths: 4 Private 2 Shared
(10) (10)

***Castlecote Guesthouse,** 77 Monkmoor Road, Shrewsbury, Shropshire, SY2 5AT.*
Family-run. Comfortable Victorian house.
Open: All Year (not Xmas)
01743 245473 Mrs Tench
Rates fr: *£15.50*-**£15.50**.
Beds: 1F 3D 1T 1S
Baths: 1 Private 3 Shared
(4)

***The Stiperstones,** 18 Coton Crescent, Coton Hill, Shrewsbury, Shropshire, SY1 2NZ.*
Very clean & comfortable. Warm welcome.
Open: All Year
Grades: ETB 1 Cr, Comm, AA 3 Q
01743 246720 / 350303
Mrs Coomby
Fax no: 01743 350303
Rates fr: *£15.30*-**£16.20**.
Beds: 1F 3D 1T 1S
Baths: 3 Shared
(7)

***Roseville,** 12 Berwick Road, Shrewsbury, Shropshire, SY1 2LN.*
Comfortable,Victorian,family house.
Open: Feb to Dec
Grades: ETB 2 Cr, High Comm, AA 3 Q
01743 236470
Mr & Mrs Stening-Rees
Rates fr: *£21.00*-**£21.00**.
Beds: 1D 1T 1S
Baths: 3 Private
(12) (3)

***Shorthill Lodge,** Shorthill, Lea Cross, Shrewsbury, Shropshire, SY5 8JE.*
Large, luxury, country home.
Open: All Year (not Xmas)
Grades: ETB 2 Cr, High Comm
01743 860864 Ms Spring
Rates fr: *£16.00*-**£20.00**.
Beds: 1D 1T
Baths: 2 Ensuite
(4)

***Hillsboro,** 1 Port Hill Gardens, Shrewsbury, Shropshire, SY3 8SH.*
Quiet Edwardian house near park.
Open: All Year (not Xmas)
Grades: ETB Listed, Comm
01743 231033
Mrs Davey
Rates fr: *£16.00*-**£16.00**.
Beds: 1D 1T
Baths: 1 Shared
(8) (2)

Stanton upon Hine Heath

National Grid Ref: SJ5624

***The Sett,** Stanton upon Hine Heath, Shrewsbury, Shropshire, SY4 4LR.*
Farmhouse in converted barn.
Open: All Year (not Xmas)
01939 250391 Mr Grumdey
Rates fr: *£20.00*-**£20.00**.
Beds: 3D
Baths: 3 Ensuite
(3)

Stiperstones

National Grid Ref: SO3599

Stiperstones Inn

***Tankerville Lodge,** Stiperstones, Minsterley, Shrewsbury, Shropshire, SY5 0NB.*
Breathtaking scenery in Welsh borderland.
Open: All Year
Grades: ETB 1 Cr, Comm, AA 2 Q, Recomm
01743 791401 Mr & Mrs Anderson
Rates fr: *£15.95*-**£18.45**.
Beds: 1D 3T
Baths: 2 Shared
(5) (4)

Stirchley

National Grid Ref: SJ7006

***The Old Rectory,** Stirchley, Telford, Shropshire, TF3 1DY.*
Large & secluded, convenient for town centre.
Open: All Year (not Xmas)
Grades: ETB 2 Cr
01952 596308 Mrs Miller
Rates fr: *£17.50*-**£23.00**.
Beds: 1F 1D 2T 2S
Baths: 6 Ensuite 1 Private 2 Shared
(6)

Stokesay

National Grid Ref: SO4381

***Castle View B & B,** Stokesay, Craven Arms, Shropshire, SY7 9AL.*
Large comfortable Victorian stone-built house.
Open: All Year
Grades: ETB Listed, High Comm
01588 673712 Mrs Grizzell
Fax no: 01588 672466
Rates fr: *£16.00*-**£16.00**.
Beds: 1D 1T 1S
Baths: 1 Ensuite 1 Private
(3) (4)

Bringing children with you? Always ask for any special rates.

Telford

National Grid Ref: SJ6909

Church Farm, *Wrockwardine, Wellington, Telford, Shropshire, TF6 5DG.*
Splendid Georgian farmhouse, 1 mile M54/A5.
Open: All Year
Grades: ETB 3 Cr, High Comm, AA 4 Q, Select
01952 244917 Mrs Savage
Rates fr: *£19.00*-**£25.00**.
Beds: 3D 3T
Baths: 3 Private 1 Shared
(5) (20)

Stone House, *Shifnal Road, Priorslee, Telford, Shropshire, TF2 9NN.*
Warm & friendly guesthouse.
Open: All Year
Grades: ETB 3 Cr
01952 290119 Mrs Silcock
Rates fr: *£19.00*-**£24.00**.
Beds: 1F 2D 2T
Baths: 5 Ensuite
(5)

The Cock Hotel, *148 Holyhead Road, Wellington, Telford, Shropshire, TF1 2ED.*
Comfortable C18th former coaching inn.
Open: All Year (not Xmas)
Grades: AA 2 Q
01952 244954 Fax no: 01952 248965
Rates fr: *£18.00*-**£20.00**.
Beds: 1F 2D 6T
Baths: 2 Ensuite 2 Shared
(30)

Ternhill

National Grid Ref: SJ6332

Willow House, *Shrewsbury Road, Ternhill, Market Drayton, Shropshire, TF9 3PX.*
Modern comfortable farmhouse.
Open: All Year (not Xmas)
01630 638326 Mrs Roberts
Rates fr: *£15.00*-**£16.00**.
Beds: 1D 1T
Baths: 1 Shared
(8) (6)

Mickley House, *Faulsgreen, Ternhill, Market Drayton, Shropshire, TF9 3QW.*
Luxury farmhouse accommodation, beautiful garden.
Open: All Year (not Xmas)
01630 638505 Mrs Williamson
Rates fr: *£18.00*-**£18.00**.
Beds: 1D 1T 1S
Baths: 3 Ensuite
(6)

Planning a longer stay? Always ask for any special rates.

The Hem

National Grid Ref: SJ7407

TreeTops, *The Hem, Shifnal, Shropshire, TF11 9PS.*
C18th cottage with friendly atmosphere.
Open: All Year
01952 460566 Mrs Bell
Rates fr: *£16.50*-**£20.00**.
Beds: 1D 1T 1S
Baths: 2 Shared
(9) (4)

Upper Affcot

National Grid Ref: SO4486

Travellers Rest Inn

Travellers Rest Inn, *Upper Affcot, Church Stretton, Shropshire, SY6 6RL.*
Traditional inn with warm welcome.
Open: All Year (not Xmas)
Grades: ETB 2 Cr, Approv
01694 781275 Mr Allison
Fax no: 01694 781555
Rates fr: *£20.00*-**£20.00**.
Beds: 3F 2D 3T 2S
Baths: 4 Private 1 Shared
(30)

Walcot

National Grid Ref: SJ5911

Alscott Inn

Alscott Inn, *Walcot, Wellington, Telford, Shropshire, TF6 5EQ.*
Friendly country inn.
Open: All Year
Grades: ETB 3 Cr
01952 248484 Ms Young
Rates fr: *£16.00*-**£20.00**.
Beds: 1F 1D 2T
Baths: 2 Ensuite 1 Shared
(40)

Wall under Heywood

National Grid Ref: SO5092

Oakbrook, *Wall under Heywood, Church Stretton, Shropshire, SY6 7DP.*
Peaceful location, wonderful views.
Open: All Year (not Xmas)
01694 723819 Mrs Hartley
Rates fr: *£12.50*-**£12.50**.
Beds: 2D 1T
Baths: 2 Shared
(10)

Gilberries Farm Cottage, *Wall under Heywood, Church Stretton, Shropshire, SY6 7HZ.*
Country cottage, joining family farm.
Open: All Year (not Xmas)
01694 771400 Mrs Griffiths
Rates fr: *£16.00*-**£20.00**.
Beds: 1D 1T
Baths: 1 Shared
(3) (8)

Wellington

National Grid Ref: SJ6411

The Cock Hotel, *148 Holyhead Road, Wellington, Telford, Shropshire, TF1 2ED.*
Comfortable C18th former coaching inn.
Open: All Year (not Xmas)
Grades: AA 2 Q
01952 244954
Fax no: 01952 248965
Rates fr: *£18.00*-**£20.00**.
Beds: 1F 2D 6T
Baths: 2 Ensuite 2 Shared
(30)

Arleston Inn Hotel, *Arleston Lane, Wellington, Telford, Shropshire, TF1 2LA.*
Tudor-style building, warm friendly atmosphere.
Open: All Year
01952 501881
Mrs Southgate
Rates fr: *£20.50*-**£31.00**.
Beds: 4D 1T 2S
Baths: 7 Ensuite
(40)

Wem

National Grid Ref: SJ5129

The Raven, Dicken Arms

Foxleigh House, *Foxleigh Drive, Wem, Shrewsbury, Shropshire, SY4 5BP.*
Comfortable elegant C18th private house.
Open: All Year (not Xmas)
Grades: ETB 2 Cr, Comm, AA 4 Q
01939 233528
Mrs Barnes
Rates fr: *£18.00*-**£18.00**.
Beds: 1F 1T
Baths: 2 Private
(12) (4)

Forncet, *Soulton Road, Wem, Shrewsbury, Shropshire, SY4 5HR.*
Large Victorian private house.
Open: All Year (not Xmas)
Grades: ETB Listed, Comm
01939 232996
Mr & Mrs James
Rates fr: *£15.00*-**£15.00**.
Beds: 1D 1T 1S
Baths: 2 Shared
(4)

Lowe Hall Farm, *The Lowe, Wem, Shrewsbury, Shropshire, SY4 5UE.*
Historically famous C16th farmhouse.
Open: All Year
Grades: ETB 2 Cr, Comm
01939 232236
Mrs Jones
Rates fr: *£17.00*-**£18.00**.
Beds: 1F 1D 1T
Baths: 1 Private 1 Shared
(6)

Wentnor

National Grid Ref: SO3892

The Crown, The Inn on the Green

The Green Farm, *Wentnor, Bishops Castle, Shropshire, SY9 5EF.*
Open: All Year (not Xmas)
Grades: ETB Listed
01588 650394
Mrs Allbuary
Rates fr: *£15.50*-**£22.50**.
Beds: 1D 1T
Baths: 2 Ensuite
(8) (3)
Quietly situated in picturesque South Shropshire hills between the Long Mynd and Stiperstones. Horse-riding on premises. 2 village inns within easy walking distance.

Wern

National Grid Ref: SJ2734

Spring Cottage, *Wern, Weston Rhyn, Oswestry, Shropshire, SY10 7LH.*
Detached modernised country cottage.
Open: All Year
01691 650293
Mr & Mrs Andrews
Rates fr: *£15.00*-**£15.00**.
Beds: 4D 1T
Baths: 1 Shared
(2)

Weston Rhyn

National Grid Ref: SJ2835

Plough

Rhoswiel Lodge, *Weston Rhyn, Oswestry, Shropshire, SY10 7TG.*
Pleasantly situated Victorian country house.
Open: All Year (not Xmas)
Grades: ETB 2 Cr
01691 777609
Mrs Plunkett
Fax no: 01691 774952
Rates fr: *£16.00*-**£18.00**.
Beds: 1D 1T
Baths: 2 Private
(6)

Whitchurch

National Grid Ref: SJ5441

Stoneleigh, *16 Sedgeford, Whitchurch, Shropshire, SY13 1EX.*
Friendly happy 'home from home'.
Open: All Year (not Xmas)
01948 664618 Mrs Gibson
Rates fr: *£11.00*-**£11.00**.
Beds: 1D 1T 1S
Baths: 2 Shared
(3)

The lowest *double* rate per person is shown in *italics*.

Bradley Green Farm, *Tarporley Rd, Whitchurch, Shropshire, SY13 4HD.*
Spacious comfortable Georgian farmhouse.
Open: All Year (not Xmas)
01948 663442 Ms Mulliner
Rates fr: *£18.00*-**£18.00**.
Beds: 1D 2T
Baths: 2 Ensuite 1 Private
(6)

Woore

National Grid Ref: SJ7342

Herriotts Guest House, *London Rd, Woore, Crewe, Cheshire, CW3 9SF.*
Quiet location, complimented home cooking. **Open:** All Year
Grades: ETB 2 Cr, High Comm
01630 647556 Mr King
Rates fr: *£15.00*-**£22.00**.
Beds: 1F 1D 1T
Baths: 2 Private 1 Shared
(4)

Wrockwardine

National Grid Ref: SJ6211

Church Farm, *Wrockwardine, Wellington, Telford, Shropshire, TF6 5DG.*
Splendid Georgian farmhouse, 1 mile M54/A5. **Open:** All Year
Grades: ETB 3 Cr, High Comm, AA 4 Q, Select
01952 244917 Mrs Savage
Rates fr: *£19.00*-**£25.00**.
Beds: 3D 3T
Baths: 3 Private 1 Shared
(5) (20)

Somerset

Tourist Information Centres

Somerset Visitor Centre, M5 South, Sedgemoor Services, **Axbridge**, Somerset, BS26 2UF, 01934 750833, (Easter to Oct).

Abbey Chambers, Abbey Chyrchyard, **Bath**, BA1 1LY, 01225 462831.

Town Hall, 50 High Street, **Bridgwater**, Somerset, TA6 3ES, 01278 427652, (Easter to Oct).

St Nicholas Church, Nicholas Street **Bristol**, BS1 1VE,0117 9260767

South Esplanade, **Burnham-on-Sea**, Somerset, TA8 1BB, 01278 787852

The Guildhall, Fore Street, **Chard**, Somerset, TA20 1PP, 01460 67463

The Gorge, **Cheddar**, Somerset, BS27 3QE, 01934 744071, (Easter to Oct).

The Tribunal, 9 High Street, **Glastonbury**, Somerset, BA6 9DP, 01458 832954, (Easter to Oct)

South Wansdyke Sports Centre, Rackvernal Road, **Midsomer Norton**, Avon, BA3 2UG, 01761 412221.

17 Friday Street, **Minehead**, Somerset, TA24 5UB, 01643 702624.

Paul Street, **Taunton**, Somerset, TA1 3PF, 01823 336344.

The Museum, 28 Fore Street, **Wellington**, Somerset, TA21 8AQ, 01823 664747 (Easter to Oct).

Town Hall, Market Place, **Wells**, Somerset, BA5 2RB, 01749 672552.

Beach Lawns, **Weston-super-Mare**, BS23 1AT, 01934 888800.

Trusthouse Forte Services (A303), Podimore, **Yeovil**, Somerset, BA22 8JG, 01935 841302, (Easter to Oct).

Petter's House, Petter's Way, **Yeovil**, Somerset, BA20 1SH, 01935 71279.

Fleet Air Arm Museum Car Park, **Yeovilton**, Yeovil, Somerset, BA22 8HT, 01935 841083, (Easter to Oct)

The Round Tower, The Black Swan, 2 Bridge Street, **Frome,** BA11 1BB, 01373 467271

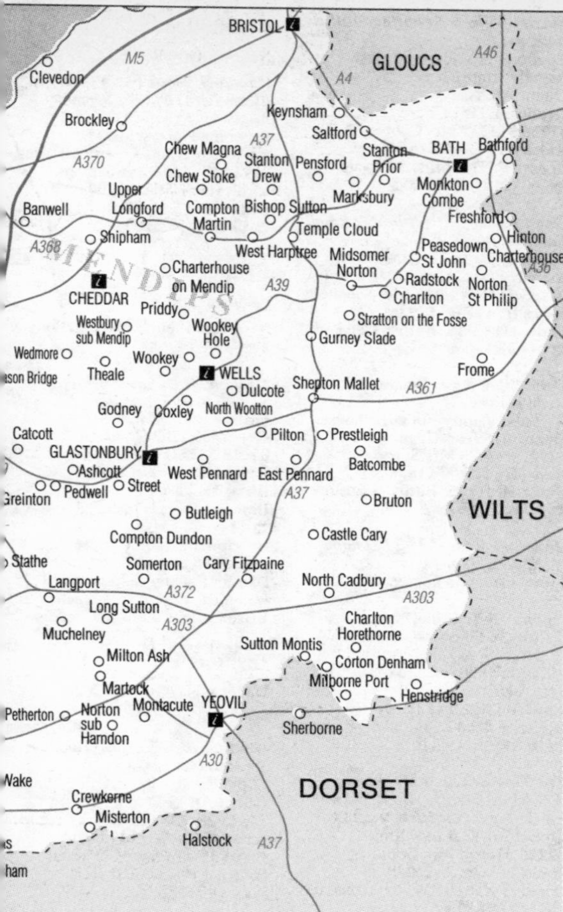

Banwell

National Grid Ref: ST3959

Banwell Castle, *Banwell, Weston-Super-Mare, Somerset, BS24 6NX.*
Tranquil, romantic Victorian Gothic castle.
Open: All Year
Grades: ETB 2 Cr
01934 822263 Mr Parsons
Fax no: 01934 823946
Rates fr: *£22.50*-**£22.50**.
Beds: 1F 8D **Baths:** 9 Private
(40)

Bason Bridge

National Grid Ref: ST3445

Watchfield, White Horse

Churchland Farm, *Newmans Lane, Bason Bridge, Highbridge, Somerset, TA9 4RJ.*
Old, beamed, remote gentle house.
Open: All Year
01278 783754 (also fax no)
Rates fr: *£15.00*-**£16.00**.
Beds: 1T **Baths:** 1 Ensuite

Batcombe

National Grid Ref: ST6837

Batcombe Vale, *Batcombe, Shepton Mallet, Somerset, BA4 6BW.*
Own secluded valley of lakes.
Open: Mar to Nov
01749 830246 Mrs Sage
Rates fr: *£14.00*-**£17.00**.
Beds: 3T
(6)

Bath

National Grid Ref: ST7464

The Beat, Old Crown, The Huntsman, Park Tavern, Harvester, Horseshoe

Membland & The Gardens Guest House, *7 Pulteney Gardens, Bath, BA2 4HG.*
Open: All Year
Grades: ETB Listed
01225 337642 Mr & Mrs Moore
Rates fr: *£17.00*-**£20.00**.
Beds: 1F 3D 3T
Baths: 7 Ensuite
(2)
2 establishments situated 30 seconds apart, 5 minutes level walk to city centre, Roman baths, train/coach stations. Showers ensuite, generous breakfasts & private parking.

Fyfield, *Ralph Allen Drive, Combe Down, Bath, BA2 5AE.*
Attractive 1950s house,large garden.
Open: All Year (not Xmas)
01225 833561 Mrs Waterman
Rates fr: *£17.00*-**£17.00**.
Beds: 1D 1T 1S
Baths: 1 Shared
(4)

llerford

Vational Grid Ref: SS9047

'ern Cottage, *Allerford, Minehead, Somerset, TA24 8HN.*
.arge C16th cottage.
)pen: All Year
;rades: ETB 3 Cr, Comm
1643 862215 Mr Hamilton
Rates fr: *£25.00*-**£28.50**.
Beds: 2D 2T 1S
Baths: 4 Private
(5)

Hillside, *Higher Allerford, Allerford, Minehead, Somerset, TA24 8HS.*
)elightful West Country thatched ottage.
)pen: All Year
1643 862831 Ms Bickerstaff
ax no: 01643 862447
Rates fr: *£16.00*-**£16.00**.
Beds: 1D 1T
Baths: 1 Shared
(4) (3)

Ashbrittle

National Grid Ref: ST0521

Lower Westcott Farm, *Ashbrittle, Wellington, Somerset, TA21 0HZ.*
Working family farm, superb views. **Open:** All Year (not Xmas)
Grades: ETB 2 Cr
01398 361296 Mrs Heard
Rates fr: *£14.00*-**£15.00**.
Beds: 1F 1D 1T
Baths: 2 Private 1 Shared
(3)

Ashcott

National Grid Ref: ST4337

Little Whitley, *Stagman Lane, Ashcott, Bridgwater, Somerset, TA7 9QW*
Secluded 'home from home'.
Open: All Year
01458 210050 Mrs Frampton
Rates fr: *£12.50*-**£12.50**.
Beds: 1F 1D
Baths: 1 Private 1 Shared
(4)

Wentworth House Hotel, *106 Bloomfield Road, Bath,* *BA2 2AP.*
Open: All Year (not Xmas)
Grades: ETB 3 Cr, AA 2 St, RAC Acclaim
01225 339193 Mrs Kitching
Fax no: 01225 310460
Rates fr: *£23.00*-**£30.00**.
Beds: 2F 11 D 5T
Baths: 16 Ensuite 2 Private
(5) (20)
Elegant Victorian mansion in secluded gardens with stunning views. Quietly situated. Free car park. Walking distance Bath - the Georgian city.

Joanna House, *5 Pulteney Avenue, Bath,* *BA2 4HH.*
Quiet, city centre Victorian house.
Open: All Year
01225 335246 Mr House
Rates fr: *£14.00*-**£15.00**.
Beds: 1F 2D 1T 2S

Sarnia, *19 Combe Park, Weston, Bath,* *BA1 3NR.*
Open: All Year (not Xmas/New Year)
Grades: ETB 2 Cr, High Comm, AA 4 Q, Select
01225 424159 Mr & Mrs Fradley
Rates fr: *£20.00*-**£25.00**.
Beds: 1F 1D 1T
Baths: 2 Ensuite 1 Private
(3)
Superb Bed & Breakfast in large Victorian home. Spacious bedrooms, comfortable lounge, secluded gardens. English, Continental and vegetarian breakfasts. Frequent bus service. Warm welcome, friendly atmosphere.

Wellsway Guest House, *51 Wellsway, Bath,* *BA2 4RS.*
Walking distance to city. Clean, comfortable. **Open:** All Year
Grades: ETB 1 Cr
01225 423434 Mrs Strong
Rates fr: *£14.00*-**£18.00**.
Beds: 1F 1D 1T 1S
Baths: 1 Shared
(2)

14 Dunsford Place, Bathwick Hill, *Bath,* *BA2 6HF.*
Open: All Year (not Xmas)
Grades: ETB 2 Cr
01225 464134 Mrs Smith
Rates fr: *£19.00*-**£30.00**.
Beds: 1D 1T **Baths:** 2 Private
Widely travelled hosts offer a warm welcome in their comfortable home within 15 minutes walk of Bath's city centre. Unrestricted street parking.

Orchard Cottage, *Dovers Lane, Bathford, Bath,* *BA1 7SU.*
Delightful detached period country cottage.**Open:** All Year (not Xmas)
Grades: ETB 2 Cr, Comm
01225 858649 Mr Hartley
Rates fr: *£20.00*-**£24.00**.
Beds: 2D **Baths:** 2 Ensuite
(2)

Flaxley Villa, *9 Newbridge Hill, Bath,* *BA1 3PW.*
Comfortable Victorian house, friendly atmosphere.
Open: All Year
Grades: ETB 1 Cr
01225 313237 Mrs Cooper
Rates fr: *£17.00*-**£16.00**.
Beds: 1F 2D **Baths:** 3 Private
(0.5) (5)

Guest House, *21 Newbridge Road, Bath,* *BA1 3HE.*
Spacious house, informative, friendly hosts. **Open:** All Year
01225 314694 Mr & Mrs Shepherd
Rates fr: *£17.00*-**£19.00**.
Beds: 1D 1T 1S **Baths:** 1 Shared

Dene Villa, *5 Newbridge Hill, Bath,* *BA1 3PW.*
Victorian family-run guest house.
Open: All Year **Grades:** ETB 2 Cr
01225 427676 Mrs Surry
Rates fr: *£19.00*-**£18.00**.
Beds: 1F 1D 1S **Baths:** 3 Ensuite
(3) (4)

Bailbrook Lodge, *35-37 London Road West, Bath,* *BA1 7HZ.*
Listed Georgian house, original features.
Open: All Year (not Xmas)
Grades: ETB 3 Cr, Comm, AA 4 Q, Select, RAC High Acclaim
01225 859090 (also fax no)
Mrs Addison
Rates fr: *£24.00*-**£32.00**.
Beds: 4F 4D 4T **Baths:** 12 Ensuite
(14)

The Terrace Guest House, *3 Pulteney Terrace, Bath,* *BA2 4HJ.*
Small house close to city centre.
Open: All Year (not Xmas)
01225 316578 Mrs Gould
Rates fr: *£16.00*-**£20.00**.
Beds: 1F 1D 1S **Baths:** 2 Shared
(6)

14 Raby Place, *Bathwick Hill, Bath,* *BA2 4EH.*
Georgian terrace house. Fine views. **Open:** All Year
Grades: ETB 1 Cr
01225 465120 Mrs Guy
Fax no: 01225 465283
Rates fr: *£20.00*-**£20.00**.
Beds: 1F 2D 2T 1S
Baths: 2 Private 2 Shared

Bathford

National Grid Ref: ST7966

Crown Inn

Orchard Cottage, *Dovers Lane, Bathford, Bath,* *BA1 7SU.*
Delightful detached period country cottage.
Open: All Year (not Xmas)
Grades: ETB 2 Cr, Comm
01225 858649 Mr Hartley
Rates fr: *£20.00*-**£24.00**.
Beds: 2D **Baths:** 2 Ensuite
(2)

Bicknoller

National Grid Ref: ST1139

Quantock Moor Farm Cottage, *Bicknoller, Taunton, Somerset,* *TA4 4ER.*
Panoramic views, ideal walking/touring. **Open:** All Year
01984 656626 Mrs Seamons
Rates fr: *£14.00*-**£14.00**.
Beds: 1D 1T 1S **Baths:** 1 Shared

Bishop Sutton

National Grid Ref: ST5859

Red Lion, Stoke Inn, Pony & Trap

Centaur, *Ham Lane, Bishop Sutton, Bristol,* *BS18 4TZ.*
Open: All Year (not Xmas)
Grades: ETB 2 Cr, Comm
01275 332321 Mrs Warden
Rates fr: *£15.00*-**£16.00**.
Beds: 1F 1T
Baths: 1 Private 1 Shared
(4)
Comfortable family house in peaceful Chew Valley. Close to lake for fishing, sailing & bird watching. Within easy reach of Bristol, Bath, Wells & Cheddar.

Bishops Hull

National Grid Ref: ST2024

Old Inn

Old Inn, *Bishops Hull, Taunton, Somerset,* *TA1 5EG.*
C16th country inn in quiet village.
Open: All Year (not Xmas)
01823 284728 Mr & Mrs Redrup
Rates fr: *£17.00*-**£17.00**.
Beds: 3F 4T 2S
Baths: 1 Private 2 Shared
(20)

Bishops Lydeard

National Grid Ref: ST1629

Slimbridge Station Farm, *Bishops Lydeard, Taunton, Somerset,* *TA4 3BX.*
Victorian house beside W.S.R.
Open: All Year (not Xmas)
01823 432223 Mrs Pattemore
Rates fr: *£16.00*-**£16.00**.
Beds: 1D 1T 1S
(3) (4)

Bishopswood

National Grid Ref: ST2512

Candlelight Inn

Hawthorne House, *Bishopswood, Chard, Somerset,* *TA20 3RS.*
Comfortable C19th house in A.O.N.B. **Open:** All Year
Grades: ETB 2 Cr, Comm
01460 234482
Mr & Mrs Newman-Coburn
Rates fr: *£19.50*-**£22.50**.
Beds: 2D 1T
Baths: 2 Ensuite 1 Private
(12) (4)

Bridgwater

National Grid Ref: ST3037

Malt Shovel Inn, Kings Head, Crossways Inn

Admirals Rest Guest House, *5 Taunton Road, Bridgwater, Somerset,* TA6 3LW.
Elegant Victorian house, centrally situated.
Open: All Year
Grades: ETB 2 Cr, Comm
01278 458580 Mrs Parker
Rates fr: *£15.00*-**£17.00**.
Beds: 2F 1D 1T
Baths: 3 Ensuite 1 Private
(5)

Cokerhurst Farm, *87 Wembdon Hill, Bridgwater, Somerset,* TA6 7QA.
Friendly, comfortable, peaceful, pleasant outlook.
Open: All Year
Grades: ETB 2 Cr, High Comm
01278 422330 / 0850 692065
Mr & Mrs Chappell
Rates fr: *£17.00*-**£17.00**.
Beds: 1F 1D 1T
Baths: 1 Private 1 Shared
(62)

Chinar Guest House, *17 Oakfield Road, Bridgwater, Somerset,* TA6 7LX.
Good beds, imaginative breakfasts, peaceful.
Open: All Year (not Xmas)
Grades: ETB Listed, AA 3 Q, Recomm
01278 458639
Mr & Mrs Bret
Rates fr: *£19.00*-**£18.00**.
Beds: 1D 1S
Baths: 2 Ensuite
(6) (2)

The Acorns, *61 Taunton Road, Bridgwater, Somerset,* TA6 3LP.
Large guest house with modern facilities.
Open: All Year (not Xmas)
01278 445577
Rates fr: *£15.00*-**£15.00**.
Beds: 3F 2D 5T 3S
Baths: 5 Ensuite 3 Shared
(15)

Nevys House, *Old Main Road, Pawlett, Bridgwater, Somerset,* TA6 4RY.
Comfortable C17th ex-farmhouse.
Open: All Year
Grades: ETB 1 Cr
01278 683779
Mrs Weatherhead
Rates fr: *£16.00*-**£16.00**.
Beds: 1F 2D 1S
Baths: 1 Shared
(3)

The lowest *double* rate per person is shown in *italics*.

Bristol

National Grid Ref: ST6075

Engineers Arms

40 Eldon Terrace, *Windmill Hill, Bedminster, Bristol,* BS3 4PA.
Victorian terrace close to centre.
Open: All Year
Grades: ETB 1 Cr
0117 966 4361 (also fax no)
Mrs Green
Rates fr: *£15.00*-**£16.00**.
Beds: 1D 1T 1S
Baths: 1 Shared

Norfolk House, *577 Gloucester Road, Horfield, Bristol,* BS7 0BW.
Pleasant Victorian house overlooking park.
Open: All Year (not Xmas)
Grades: ETB 1 Cr
0117 951 3191
Mr Thomas
Rates fr: *£16.00*-**£18.00**.
Beds: 2D 1T
Baths: 1 Ensuite 2 Shared

Alcove Guest House, *508-510 Fishponds Road, Bristol,* BS16 3DT.
Easy access, M32 half mile.
Open: All Year
0117 965 3886 (also fax no)
Mr & Mrs Newman
Rates fr: *£20.00*-**£20.00**.
Beds: 2F 3D 3T 1S
Baths: 4 Private 4 Shared
(1) (8)

Brockley

National Grid Ref: ST4666

Manor Farm, *Brockley, Backwell, Bristol,* BS19 3AQ.
Attractive Victorian stone-built family farmhouse.
Open: All Year (not Xmas)
01275 462313
Mr & Mrs Ridge
Rates fr: *£17.50*-**£17.50**.
Beds: 1F 1T 1S
Baths: 1 Private 1 Shared
(5)

Broomfield

National Grid Ref: ST2232

Travellers Rest, Swan, Tynte Arms

Waterpitts Farm, *Broomfield, Bridgwater, Somerset,* TA5 1AT.
Smallholding in fabulous Quantock countryside.
Open: All Year (not Xmas)
01823 451679
Mrs Jordan
Rates fr: *£14.00*-**£16.00**.
Beds: 1F 1D
Baths: 1 Private 1 Shared
(10)

Bruton

National Grid Ref: ST6834

Royal Oak Inn

The Old Forge, *89 High Street, Bruton, Somerset,* BA10 0AL.
High-quality accommodation in family home.
Open: All Year (not Xmas)
01749 812585 Mr Dunn
Rates fr: *£16.00*-**£17.00**.
Beds: 1F 1D 1T
Baths: 2 Private 1 Shared
(3)

The Royal Oak Inn, *Coombe Street, Bruton, Somerset,* BA10 0EN.
Sympathetically refurbished C18th Inn. **Open:** All Year
01749 812215 Mrs Winstanley
Rates fr: *£20.00*-**£30.00**.
Beds: 1F 1D 1T 1S
Baths: 4 Private
(4)

Burnham-on-Sea

National Grid Ref: ST3049

Red Cow

Sandhills, *3 Poplar Road, Burnham-on-Sea, Somerset,* TA8 2HD.
Spacious, well-appointed Edwardian building.
Open: All Year (not Xmas)
Grades: ETB 1 Cr
01278 781208 Mrs Trett
Rates fr: *£14.00*-**£16.50**.
Beds: 1F 2D 2T **Baths:** 2 Shared
(6)

Priorsmead, *23 Rectory Road, Burnham-on-Sea, Somerset,* TA8 2BZ.
Edwardian house with peaceful gardens. **Open:** All Year (not Xmas)
Grades: ETB 2 Cr
01278 782116 / 0860 573018
Mrs Alexander
Rates fr: *£15.00*-**£18.00**.
Beds: 2D 1T
Baths: 1 Ensuite 2 Private
(10) (3)

Butleigh

National Grid Ref: ST5233

Rose & Portcullis

Court Lodge, *Butleigh, Glastonbury, Somerset,* BA6 8SA.
Attractive, modernised lodge, built 1850s. **Open:** All Year (not Xmas)
Grades: RAC Listed
01458 50575 Mrs Atkinson
Rates fr: *£12.50*-**£12.50**.
Beds: 1D 1T 2S

Twelve Hides, *Quarry Lane, Butleigh, Glastonbury, Somerset,* BA6 8TE.
Peaceful C18th cottage - wonderful situation. **Open:** All Year (not Xmas)
01458 850380 Mrs Dodds
Rates fr: *£15.00*-**£15.00**.
Beds: 1D 1T **Baths:** 1 Shared
(2)

Cary Fitzpaine

National Grid Ref: ST5427

Cary Fitzpaine Farmhouse, *Cary Fitzpaine, Yeovil, Somerset, BA22 8JB.*
Georgian manor farmhouse, peaceful location.
Open: All Year
01458 223250 Mrs Crang
Rates fr: *£14.50*-**£14.50**.
Beds: 1F 1D 1T 1S
Baths: 1 Private
(6)

Castle Cary

National Grid Ref: ST6231

Orchard Farm, *Castle Cary, Castle Cary, Somerset, BA7 7NY.*
Comfortable farmhouse in large gardens.
Open: All Year
Grades: ETB 2 Cr, Comm
01963 350418 Mrs Boyer
Rates fr: *£18.00*-**£18.00**.
Beds: 1F 1D
Baths: 2 Private
(4)

Castle Cary

National Grid Ref: ST6332

South Court, *South Street, Castle Cary, Somerset, BA7 7ET.*
Spacious, friendly Georgian guest house.
Open: All Year
01963 351440 Mrs Ovland
Rates fr: *£15.00*-**£17.50**.
Beds: 1D 1T 1S
Baths: 2 Private 1 Shared
(6)

Catcott

National Grid Ref: ST3939

King William Inn

Pear Tree, *16 Manor Road, Catcott, Bridgwater, Somerset, TA7 9HF.*
Comfortable touring base for Somerset.
Open: Easter to Nov
01278 722390 Mrs Hill
Rates fr: *£15.00*-**£15.00**.
Beds: 1D 1T
Baths: 1 Shared
(2)

Chard

National Grid Ref: ST3208

WIndwhistle Inn, Thatchers Pond, Bath House

Ammonite Lodge, *43 High Street, Chard, Somerset, TA20 1QL.*
Comfortable large C17th cottage.
Open: All Year (not Xmas)
01460 63839 Mrs Fortescue
Rates fr: *£14.00*.
Beds: 4D
Baths: 3 Private 1 Shared
(3)

Charlton

National Grid Ref: ST6852

Somerset Wagon

Melon Cottage Vineyard, *Charlton, Radstock, Bath, BA3 5TN.*
Sandstone farmhouse, acre garden/vineyard.
Open: All Year
01761 435090 Mrs Pountney
Rates fr: *£15.00*-**£15.00**.
Beds: 2F 1S
Baths: 1 Ensuite 2 Shared
(4)

Charlton Horethorne

National Grid Ref: ST6623

Ashclose Farm, *Charlton Horethorne, Sherborne, Dorset, DT9 4PG.*
Modern comfortable farmhouse, delightful views.
Open: All Year (not Xmas)
01963 220360 Mrs Gooding
Rates fr: *£14.00*-**£14.00**.
Beds: 3F 1T 1S
Baths: 2 Shared

Charterhouse-on-Mendip

National Grid Ref: ST5055

New Inn (Blagdon)

Warren Farm, *Charterhouse-on-Mendip, Blagdon, Bristol, BS18 6XR.*
1,000 acre sheep farm.
Open: All Year (not Xmas)
01761 462674 Mrs Small
Rates fr: *£16.00*-**£16.00**.
Beds: 1F 1D 1S
Baths: 1 Shared

Cheddar

National Grid Ref: ST4553

Rodney Stole Inn, Edelweiss Restaurant

Tor Farm Guest House, *Nyland, Cheddar, Somerset, BS27 3UD.*
Working farm on Somerset Levels.
Open: All Year
Grades: ETB 1 Cr, High Comm, AA 4 Q, Select
01934 743710 Mrs Ladd
Rates fr: *£17.50*-**£19.00**.
Beds: 1F 4D 1T 2S
Baths: 5 Private 3 Shared
(10)

The Forge, *Cliff Street, Cheddar, Somerset, BS27 3PL.*
Comfortable old stone cottage.
Open: All Year (not Xmas)
01934 742345 Mr Phillips
Rates fr: *£14.50*-**£20.00**.
Beds: 1F 1D
Baths: 1 Shared
(4) (4)

Chew Magna

National Grid Ref: ST5763

Woodbarn Farm, *Denny Lane, Chew Magna, Bristol, BS18 8SZ.*
Friendly farmhouse in picturesque setting.
Open: Mar to Dec
01275 332599 Mrs Hasell
Rates fr: *£17.00*-**£18.00**.
Beds: 1F 1D
Baths: 2 Ensuite
(3) (6)

Chew Stoke

National Grid Ref: ST5561

Stoke Inn

Orchard House, *Bristol Road, Chew Stoke, Bristol, BS18 8UB.*
Family-run, 'home from home'.
Open: All Year
Grades: ETB 2 Cr, Comm
01275 333143 Mrs Hollomon
Fax no: 01275 333754
Rates fr: *£17.00*-**£17.00**.
Beds: 1F 2D 3T 1S
Baths: 5 Private 2 Shared
(8)

Churchstanton

National Grid Ref: ST1914

White Lion, Lamb & Flag

Pear Tree Cottage, *Stapley, Churchstanton, Taunton, Somerset, TA3 7QB.*
Picturesque thatched private country cottage.
Open: All Year
01823 601224 (also fax no)
Mrs Parry
Rates fr: *£13.00*-**£20.00**.
Beds: 1F 1D 1S
Baths: 2 Private
(4)

Strawbridges Farm, *Churchstanton, Taunton, Somerset, TA3 7DP.*
Country house amidst peaceful countryside.
Open: All Year (not Xmas)
Grades: ETB 2 Cr
01823 601591 Mrs Slipper
Rates fr: *£16.00*-**£15.00**.
Beds: 2D 2T 1S
Baths: 2 Private 1 Shared
(5) (10)

Clevedon

National Grid Ref: ST3971

5 Sunnyside Road, *Clevedon, BS21 7TE.*
Modern, comfortable, family accommodation.
Open: All Year
01275 873315 Mrs Potter
Rates fr: *£17.00*-**£17.00**.
Beds: 1F 1T
Baths: 1 Shared
(2)

Combe Florey

National Grid Ref: ST1531

***ectory Cottage,** Combe Florey, aunton, Somerset, TA4 3JD.*
Character cottage in conservation rea. **Open:** All Year
1823 432349 Mr Berry
ates fr: *£16.00*-**£16.00**.
eds: 1F 1T 1S **Baths:** 1 Shared
(8) (2)

Compton Dundon

ational Grid Ref: ST4933

***hurch Farm Guest House,** Compton Dundon, Somerton, omerset, TA11 6PE.*
elightful part-thatched house, eautiful countryside.
pen: All Year (not Xmas)
rades: AA 3 Q
458 272927 Mr & Mrs Middle
ates fr: *£18.50*-**£22.00**.
eds: 2F 3D 2T 1S
aths: 8 Ensuite
(5) (5)

Compton Martin

ational Grid Ref: ST5457

Ring of Bells

***erons Green Farm,** Compton artin, Bristol, BS18 6NL.*
ttractive farmhouse by Chew alley Lake. **Open:** Mar to Oct
275 333372 Mrs Hasell
ates fr: *£16.00*-**£20.00**.
eds: 1F 1D **Baths:** 1 Shared
(3)

Corton Denham

ational Grid Ref: ST6322

***heatsheaf House,** Corton enham, Sherborne, Dorset, DT9 4LQ*
arge country house, lovely ounds. **Open:** Mar to Nov
963 220207 Mrs Hall
ates fr: *£18.00*-**£18.00**.
eds: 1F 2D **Baths:** 1 Ensuite
(10)

Coxley

ational Grid Ref: ST5343

Riverside Restaurant

***ome Farm,** Stoppers Lane, oper Coxley, Coxley, Wells, merset, BA5 1QS.*
d cider house, converted pre-war.
pen: All Year (not Xmas)
rades: ETB 2 Cr, AA 2 Q
749 672434 Ms Higgs
ates fr: *£18.50*-**£18.50**.
ds: 2F 2D 2T 1S
ths: 2 Ensuite 1 Private 4 Shared
(10) (7)

***ollow Tree Farm,** Launcherley, xley, Wells, Somerset, BA5 1QJ.*
odern, comfortable farm ngalow. Friendly, Good food, nderful views.

Open: Easter to Oct
01749 673715 Mrs Coombes
Rates fr: *£14.00*-**£15.00**.
Beds: 1F 1D **Baths:** 1 Shared
(5) (5)

Crewkerne

National Grid Ref: ST4409

***Merefield House,** East Street, Crewkerne, Somerset, TA18 7AB.*
Large Georgian historic house.
Open: All Year
01460 73112 Ms McQue
Rates fr: *£16.00*-**£20.00**.
Beds: 1D 2T
Baths: 1 Private 1 Shared
(12) (3)

Cricket St Thomas

National Grid Ref: ST3708

Windwhistle Inn

***The Firs,** Crewkerne Road, Cricket St Thomas, Nr Chard, Somerset, TA20 4BU.*
Pretty rooms - first class service!
Open: All Year
01460 65646 Mrs Bright
Rates fr: *£16.00*-**£17.50**.
Beds: 1F 1D 1T
Baths: 1 Ensuite 2 Shared
(8)

Cross

National Grid Ref: ST4154

***Brewery Farm,** Cross, Axbridge, Somerset, BS26 2EM.*
C17th farmhouse.
Open: All Year (not Xmas)
01934 732451 Mr Cooper
Rates fr: *£15.00*-**£15.00**.
Beds: 1D 1T **Baths:** 1 Private
(4)

Culbone

National Grid Ref: SS8448

***Silcombe Farm,** Culbone, Porlock, Minehead, Somerset, TA24 8JN.*
Secluded Exmoor farmhouse overlooking sea.
Open: All Year (not Xmas)
Grades: ETB Listed
01643 862248 Mrs Richards
Rates fr: *£16.00*-**£15.00**.
Beds: 2D 1T 1S
Baths: 1 Private 2 Shared
(4) (10)

Dowlish Wake

National Grid Ref: ST3712

New Inn

***Beam Ends,** Mill Lane, Dowlish Wake, Ilminster, Somerset, TA19 0NY.*
Pretty village, cider mill nearby.
Open: All Year (not Xmas)
01460 57530 Mrs Wicks
Rates fr: *£17.00*-**£20.00**.
Beds: 1T **Baths:** 1 Ensuite
(3)

Dulcote

National Grid Ref: ST5644

***The Willows,** Dulcote, Wells, Somerset, BA5 3PZ.*
Comfortable cottage, four course breakfast.
Open: All Year
01749 676151 / 674747 Mrs Adams
Rates fr: *£15.00*-**£20.00**.
Beds: 1F 1D 1S
Baths: 2 Shared
(6)

Dulverton

National Grid Ref: SS9128

Crispings Restaurant

***Highercombe Farm,** Dulverton, Somerset, TA22 9PT.*
Open: Mar to Nov
Grades: ETB 1 Cr, Comm
01398 323616 (also fax no)
Mrs Humphrey
Rates fr: *£18.00*-**£20.00**.
Beds: 2D 1T
Baths: 3 Ensuite
(4)
A 450-acre farm with an abundance of wildlife in a spectacular, peaceful setting on Exmoor. Enjoy exceptional hospitality. Explore unspoilt coast & countryside.

***Exton House Hotel,** Exton, Dulverton, Somerset, TA22 9JT.*
Delicious home-made dinners, idyllic scenery.
Open: All Year
Grades: ETB 3 Cr, High Comm
01643 851365 Mr Glaister
Fax no: 01643 851213
Rates fr: *£23.50*-**£27.50**.
Beds: 3F 3D 2T 1S
Baths: 8 Ensuite 1 Private
(9)

Dunster

National Grid Ref: SS9943

Luttrell Arms, Stables Restaurant, Castle Hotel, Notley

***Woodville House,** 25 West Street, Dunster, Minehead, Somerset, TA24 6SN.*
Georgian house with rear courtyard. **Open:** Mar to Nov
Grades: ETB Listed, Comm
01643 821228 Mrs Tymms
Rates fr: *£17.00*-**£16.00**.
Beds: 1D 1T 1S **Baths:** 1 Shared
(12) (4)

***Burnells Farm,** Knowle Lane, Dunster, Minehead, Somerset, TA24 6UU.*
Modern comfortable farmhouse.
Open: Easter to Oct
01643 821841
Mr & Mrs Greenfield
Rates fr: *£16.00*-**£16.00**.
Beds: 1D 1T 1S
Baths: 2 Shared
(8) (4)

***The Old Nunnery,** 6 Church Street, Dunster, Minehead, Somerset, TA24 6SH.*
Mediaeval house in ancient village.
Open: All Year (not Xmas)
01643 821711 Mr Frost
Rates fr: *£17.00*-**£19.00**.
Beds: 1D 1T
Baths: 1 Private 1 Shared
(16)

***Exmoor House Hotel,** 12 West Street, Dunster, Minehead, Somerset, TA24 6SN.*
Historic C17th Listed building.
Open: All Year
Grades: ETB 3 Cr, High Comm, AA 2 St, RAC 2 St
01643 821268 Mr Lally
Rates fr: *£27.50*-**£27.50**.
Beds: 4D 3T
Baths: 7 Private 1 Shared
(12)

***Buttercross,** St Georges Street, Dunster, Minehead, Somerset, TA24 6RS.*
Private family house. Quiet location.
Open: All Year (not Xmas)
Grades: ETB Listed, High Comm
01643 821413 Mrs Buck
Rates fr: *£15.00*-**£16.00**.
Beds: 2D
Baths: 1 Private 1 Shared
(6)

***Spears Cross Hotel,** 1 West Street, Dunster, Minehead, Somerset, TA24 6SN.*
Charming C15th small hotel.
Open: Feb to Dec
Grades: ETB 2 Cr, AA 4 Q
01643 821439 (also fax no)
Mrs Rathbone
Rates fr: *£21.00*-**£21.00**.
Beds: 1F 1D 1T **Baths:** 3 Ensuite
(5) (4)

***Dollons House,** Church Street, Dunster, Minehead, Somerset, TA24 6SH.*
Mediaeval Dunster inside Exmoor National Park.
Open: All Year (not Xmas)
Grades: ETB 2 Cr, High Comm, AA 5 Q, Select
01643 821880
Major & Mrs Bradshaw
Rates fr: *£20.50*.
Beds: 2D 1T **Baths:** 3 Private

East Pennard

National Grid Ref: ST5937

***Pennard Hill Farm,** Stickleball Hill, East Pennard, Shepton Mallet, Somerset, BA4 6UG.*
Luxurious house overlooking Somerset Levels.
Open: All Year
01749 890221 Mrs Judah
Fax no: 01749 890665
Rates fr: *£20.00*-**£20.00**.
Beds: 2D 2S
Baths: 2 Ensuite 1 Private 1 Shared

Exford

National Grid Ref: SS8538

White Horse Inn, Crown Hotel (Exmoor)

***Edgcott House,** Exford, Minehead, Somerset, TA24 7QG.*
Peaceful spacious C17th country house.
Open: All Year
Grades: ETB 2 Cr, Comm
01643 831495 Ms Lamble
Rates fr: *£18.00*-**£18.00**.
Beds: 1D1T 1S
Baths: 1 Ensuite 1 Private 1 Shared
(4)

***Court Farmhouse,** Exford, Minehead, Somerset, TA24 7LY.*
Lovely C16th farmhouse.
Open: All Year
01643 831207 Mrs Mole
Rates fr: *£17.00*-**£17.00**.
Beds: 1F 2D 1T **Baths:** 2 Shared
(10) (10)

***Ashcott Barton Farm,** Exford, Minehead, Somerset, TA24 7NG.*
Devon longhouse lots of character & comfort. **Open:** All Year
01643 831294 Mrs Thorne
Rates fr: *£17.00*-**£17.00**.
Beds: 1T 1D

Exton

National Grid Ref: SS9233

***Exton House Hotel,** Exton, Dulverton, Somerset, TA22 9JT.*
Delicious home-made dinners, idyllic scenery.
Open: All Year
Grades: ETB 3 Cr, High Comm
01643 851365 Mr Glaister
Fax no: 01643 851213
Rates fr: *£23.50*-**£27.50**.
Beds: 3F 3D 2T 1S
Baths: 8 Ensuite 1 Private
(0) (9)

Fiddington

National Grid Ref: ST2140

***Keenthorne Farm,** Fiddington, Bridgwater, Somerset, TA5 1HZ.*
Modern comfortable farmhouse.
Open: All Year (not Xmas)
01278 732215 Mrs Hancoac
Rates fr: *£15.00*-**£15.00**.
Beds: 1F 1D 1T
Baths: 1 Private 1 Shared

Freshford

National Grid Ref: ST7860

The Inn, Old Coaching Inn

***Long Acre,** 17 Staples Hill, Freshford, Bath, BA3 6EL.*
Magnificent southerly views, own 3 acres.
Open: All Year
01225 723254 Mrs Cameron
Rates fr: *£14.00*-**£16.00**.
Beds: 2D 1T
Baths: 2 Ensuite 1 Shared

***Tyning House,** Freshford, Bath, BA3 6DR.*
Great hospitality in beautiful surroundings!
Open: All Year
01225 723288 Mrs Harward
Rates fr: *£15.00*-**£20.00**.
Beds: 1D 1T
Baths: 1 Shared
(6)

Frome

National Grid Ref: ST7747

Mason's Arms, Fox & Hounds

***Kensington Lodge Hotel,** The Butts, Frome, Somerset, BA11 4AA.*
Modern country-house style hotel.
Open: All Year
01373 463935 (also fax no)
Mr Salimi
Rates fr: *£18.50*-**£25.00**.
Beds: 1F 2D 3T 1S
Baths: 7 Ensuite
(40)

***Gioia,** 2 Vallis Farm Cottages, Egford, Frome, Somerset, BA11 3JQ.*
Private house, rural, beautiful views.
Open: All Year
01373 463545 Mrs Allen
Rates fr: *£12.50*-**£16.00**.
Beds: 1T
Baths: 1 Shared
(4) (2)

***Old Ford House,** Frome, Somerse BA11 2NF.*
Delightful, caring, comfortable family home.
Open: All Year
01373 462142
Mrs Jelly
Rates fr: *£17.00*-**£17.00**.
Beds: 1T
Baths: 1 Ensuite
(9) (3)

Glastonbury

National Grid Ref: ST5039

Mitre Inn, George & Pilgrim The Lion

***Blake House,** 3 Bove Town, Glastonbury, Somerset, BA6 8JE.*
Open: All Year (not Xmas)
01458 831680
Mrs Hankins
Rates fr: *£16.00*-**£16.00**.
Beds: 2D 1T
Baths: 3 Ensuite
Welcome to our Grade II Listed C17th stone house. Two minutes t town centre. Vegetarians welcome Easy walking distance to Abbey, Tor and Chalice Well.

Wick Hollow House, *8 Wick Hollow, Glastonbury, Somerset, BA6 8JJ.*
Open: All Year (not Xmas)
Grades: ETB 2 Cr
01458 833595 Mrs Evans
Rates fr: *£19.00*-**£28.00**.
Beds: 1F **Baths:** 1 Private
(2)
Outstanding accommodation in self-contained ground floor annexe. Private sitting room. Peaceful location with wonderful views of the Tor & Chalice Hill. Children half price.

Pippin, *4 Ridgeway Gardens, Glastonbury, Somerset, BA6 8ER.*
Peace, comfort, value for money.
Open: All Year (not Xmas)
Grades: ETB Listed, Approv
01458 834262 Mrs Slater
Rates fr: *£12.50*-**£12.50**.
Beds: 1D 1T 1S
Baths: 1 Private 1 Shared
(2)

191a Wells Road, *Glastonbury, Somerset, BA6 9AW.*
Ground floor detached cottage.
Open: All Year (not Xmas)
01458 834733 Mrs Bressey
Rates fr: *£12.00*-**£12.00**.
Beds: 1T **Baths:** 1 Private
(1)

Meadow Barn, *Middlewick Farm, Wick Lane, Glastonbury, Somerset, BA6 8JW.*
Accommodation with indoor heated pool.
Open: All Year (not Xmas)
Grades: ETB 2 Cr
01458 832351 Mrs Coles
Rates fr: *£18.00*-**£22.00**.
Beds: 2D 1T **Baths:** 3 Private

46 High Street, *Glastonbury, Somerset, BA6 9DX.*
Good centre for touring Somerset.
Open: All Year
01458 832214 Mr & Mrs Allen
Rates fr: *£15.00*-**£17.50**.
Beds: 1D 1T **Baths:** 2 Private
(1)

Huna House Healing Sanctuary, *51 Benedict Street, Glastonbury, Somerset, BA6 9NB.*
Self-development healing holidays. Hawaiian massage.
Open: All Year
01458 834451 Ms Samet
Rates fr: *£13.00*-**£20.00**.
Beds: 2D **Baths:** 2 Shared

Court Lodge, *Butleigh, Glastonbury, Somerset, BA6 8SA.*
Attractive, modernised lodge, built 1850's.
Open: All Year (not Xmas)
Grades: RAC Listed
01458 50575 Mrs Atkinson
Rates fr: *£12.50*-**£12.50**.
Beds: 1D 1T 2S

Godney

National Grid Ref: ST4842

Sheppey Inn

Double Gate Farm, *Godney, Wells, Somerset, BA5 1RZ.*
Listed Georgian farmhouse, working farm.
Open: Feb to Nov
Grades: ETB 2 Cr, Comm, AA 3 Q, RAC Acclaim
01458 832217 Mrs Millard
Fax no: 01585 443336
Rates fr: *£18.00*-**£18.00**.
Beds: 1F 1D 1T
Baths: 3 Ensuite
(0) (6)

Greenham

National Grid Ref: ST1018

Globe Inn (Appley)

Greenham Hall, *Greenham, Wellington, Somerset, TA21 0JJ.*
Open: All Year
01823 672603 Mrs Ayre
Fax no: 01823 672307
Rates fr: *£17.50*-**£22.50**.
Beds: 2F 3D 2T
Baths: 3 Ensuite 1 Private 3 Shared
(10)
Large turreted Victorian family home surrounded by beautiful garden in rural location. Ideal base for touring, walking & just relaxing. Excellent pub nearby.

Greinton

National Grid Ref: ST4136

Red Tile

Greinton House, *Greinton, Bridgwater, Somerset, TA7 9BW.*
Beautiful Listed old rectory.
Open: All Year
01458 210307
Mrs Tingey
Rates fr: *£15.00*-**£20.00**.
Beds: 2D 1T
Baths: 3 Private
(10) (4)

Gurney Slade

National Grid Ref: ST6249

Somerset Wagon

Cockhill Farm, *Marchants Hill, Gurney Slade, Bath, BA3 4TY.*
Tastefully furnished comfortable Victorian farmhouse.
Open: All Year (not Xmas)
01749 840125
Mrs Hawkins
Rates fr: *£14.00*-**£15.00**.
Beds: 1D 1T
Baths: 1 Shared
(4)

Hawkridge

National Grid Ref: SS8530

Tarr Steps Hotel, *Hawkridge, Dulverton, Somerset, TA22 9PY.*
Superbly situated country house hotel.
Open: All Year
01643 851293 Ms Blackmore
Fax no: 01643 851218
Rates fr: *£30.00*-**£40.00**.
Beds: 6D 4T 3S
Baths: 8 Ensuite 1 Private 4 Shared
(20)

Henlade

National Grid Ref: ST2623

The Barn, *Henlade, Taunton, Somerset, TA3 5NB.*
Delightful character barn conversion.
Open: All Year (not Xmas)
01823 442531 Mr & Mrs Harrison
Rates fr: *£18.00*-**£27.00**.
Beds: 3D**Baths:** 3 Ensuite

Henstridge

National Grid Ref: ST7219

Virginia Ash, Fountain Inn Motel

Quiet Corner Farm, *Henstridge, Somerset, BA8 0RA.*
The name says it all!
Open: All Year (not Xmas)
Grades: ETB 2 Cr, Comm
01963 363045 Mrs Thompson
Fax no: 01963 363400
Rates fr: *£19.00*-**£25.00**.
Beds: 1F 2D
Baths: 1 Private 1 Shared
(5) (8)

Fountain Inn Motel, *High Street, Henstridge, Templecombe, Somerset, BA8 0RA.*
Village inn with modern accommodation.
Open: All Year
Grades: ETB 2 Cr
01963 362722 (also fax no)
Mr Petts
Rates fr: *£13.50*-**£15.00**.
Beds: 6D **Baths:** 6 Private
(30)

Highercombe

National Grid Ref: SS9128

Crispins

Highercombe, *Highercombe, Dulverton, Somerset, TA22 9PT.*
Former hunting lodge, C14th.
Open: All Year
Grades: ETB 2 Cr, High Comm, AA 4 Q
01398 323451 Mrs Marchant
Rates fr: *£18.00*-**£23.00**.
Beds: 2D 1T
Baths: 2 Ensuite 1 Private
(0) (Any)

Hinam

National Grid Ref: SS8829

Scatterbrook Farm, *Hinam, Dulverton, Somerset, TA22 9QQ.*
Working farm, beautiful countryside. **Open:** All Year
Grades: ETB Listed, Approv
01398 323857 Ms Aldridge
Rates fr: *£12.50*-**£15.00**.
Beds: 2D 1T **Baths:** 1 Ensuite
(4)

Hinton Charterhouse

National Grid Ref: ST7758

The Stag

Green Lane House, *1 Green Lane, Hinton Charterhouse, Bath, BA3 6BL.*
Tastefully renovated, comfortably furnished C18th house.
Open: All Year
Grades: AA 3 Q, Recomm
01225 723631 Mr Davies
Fax no: 01225 723773
Rates fr: *£18.00*-**£24.00**.
Beds: 2D 2T
Baths: 2 Ensuite 1 Shared

Holford

National Grid Ref: ST1541

Quantock House, *Holford, Bridgwater, Somerset, TA5 1RY.*
C17th thatched country house.
Open: All Year (not Xmas)
01278 741439 Mrs Laidler
Rates fr: *£18.00*-**£22.00**.
Beds: 1F 1D 1T **Baths:** 3 Private
(4)

Howley

National Grid Ref: ST2609

Howley Tavern

Howley Tavern, *Howley, Chard, Somerset, TA20 3DX.*
C16th village inn.
Open: All Year (not Xmas)
01460 62157 Mr Leaf
Rates fr: *£20.00*-**£29.50**.
Beds: 1F 1D 1T **Baths:** 3 Ensuite
(50)

Ilminster

National Grid Ref: ST3614

Lamb Inn, The Crown, The Nelson

Westerholme, *33 Station Road, Ilminster, Somerset, TA19 9BG.*
Open: All Year (not Xmas)
01460 54566 Mrs Wensley
Rates fr: *£15.00*-**£15.00**.
Beds: 1D 2T
Baths: 1 Private 1 Shared
(4)
Georgian house close to town centre, 8 miles from Cricket St Thomas. Elegant and homely, safe parking, TV in rooms. Pleasant gardens. Come & be spoilt.

Hermitage, *29 Station Road, Ilminster, Somerset, TA19 9BE.*
Open: All Year
01460 53028 Mrs Phillips
Rates fr: *£15.00*-**£17.00**.
Beds: 1D 1T **Baths:** 1 Shared
(2)
Friendly C17th Listed house, beams, inglenooks, four-poster beds. 2.5 acres delightful gardens, ideal touring centre for coast, country, picturesque villages, Wells, Glastonbury, National Trust houses & gardens.

Hylands, *22 New Road, Ilminster, Somerset, TA19 9AF.*
Attractive Edwardian end-of-terrace. Friendly atmosphere.
Open: All Year (not Xmas)
01460 52560 Mrs Hayter
Rates fr: *£10.50*-**£12.50**.
Beds: 1F 1T **Baths:** 2 Shared

Keynsham

National Grid Ref: ST6568

Fiorita, *91 Bath Road, Keynsham, Bristol, BS18 1SR.*
Warm welcome, comfortable family home.
Open: All Year (not Xmas)
0117 986 3738 Mrs Poulter
Rates fr: *£12.50*-**£14.00**.
Beds: 1D 1T **Baths:** 1 Shared
(4)

Langford Budville

National Grid Ref: ST1122

Orchard Haven, *Langford Budville, Wellington, Somerset, TA21 0QZ.*
Country house in lovely peaceful location. **Open:** Easter to Oct
01823 672116 Mrs Perry Jones
Rates fr: *£18.00*-**£21.00**.
Beds: 2D **Baths:** 1 Shared
(5) (4)

Langport

National Grid Ref: ST4226

Tuckers Hill, *Frog Lane, Langport, Somerset, TA10 0NE.*
Wonderful views, secluded, acclaimed cooking.
Open: All Year (not Xmas)
Grades: ETB 2 Cr, High Comm
01458 250413 Mrs Patterson
Rates fr: *£16.50*-**£17.50**.
Beds: 1F 1D 1T
Baths: 2 Private 1 Shared
(5) (4)

Long Sutton

National Grid Ref: ST4625

Devonshire Arms

The Old Mill, *Knole, Long Sutton, Langport, Somerset, TA10 9HY.*
Old watermill - centrally yet idyllically located.
Open: All Year (not Xmas)
Grades: ETB 2 Cr, Comm
01458 241599 Mrs Barber
Fax no: 01458 241710
Rates fr: *£20.00*-**£25.00**.
Beds: 2D 1T 1S
Baths: 2 Private 1 Shared
(8) (6)

Lopen

National Grid Ref: ST4214

Poulett Arms

September House, *Lopen, South Petherton, Somerset, TA13 5JU.*
Open: All Year (not Xmas)
Grades: ETB Listed, Comm
01460 240647 Mrs Hepworth
Rates fr: *£15.00*-**£15.00**.
Beds: 2D 1T
Baths: 1 Ensuite 1 Shared
(5) (3)
Comfortable hamstone brick house in rural village. Ideal touring centre for Somerset & Dorset. 18 miles from coast. Many local attractions. Very warm, friendly welcome.

Marksbury

National Grid Ref: ST6662

Wansdyke Cottage, *Marksbury Gate, Bath, BA2 9HE.*
Georgian cottage in country garden.
Open: All Year
Grades: ETB Listed, Comm
01225 873674 (also fax no)
Mrs Damrel
Rates fr: *£16.00*-**£16.00**.
Beds: 2D 1T 1S
Baths: 1 Private 2 Shared
(6)

Martock

National Grid Ref: ST4619

George Inn

Wychwood, *7 Bearley Road, Martock, Somerset, TA12 6PG.*
Close to 10 'Classic' Gardens.
Open: All Year (not Xmas)
Grades: ETB 2 Cr, High Comm, AA 4 Q, Select, RAC Acclaim
01935 825601 Mrs Turton
Rates fr: *£18.00*-**£26.00**.
Beds: 2D 1T
Baths: 3 Private
(3)

Midsomer Norton

National Grid Ref: ST6654

Ellsworth, *Fosseway, Midsomer Norton, Bath, BA3 4AU.*
Homely, comfortable & friendly house.
Open: All Year (not Xmas)
01761 412305 Mrs Gentle
Rates fr: *£16.00*-**£16.00**.
Beds: 2F 1D 1S
(2) (4)

Milborne Port

National Grid Ref: ST6718

Queens Head

The Queens Head, *High Street, Milborne Port, Sherborne, Dorset, DT9 5DQ.*
Grade II Listed village freehouse.
Open: All Year
01963 250314 Mr Fitzgerald
Rates fr: *£17.50*-**£21.00**.
Beds: 1F 2D
Baths: 1 Shared
(12)

Milton Ash

National Grid Ref: ST4621

Falconers Farm, *Milton Ash, Martock, Somerset, TA12 6AL.*
Georgian house set in 320 acres.
Open: All Year
01935 823363 Mrs Peach
Rates fr: *£13.00*-**£13.00**.
Beds: 1F 1T 1S
Baths: 1 Shared
(5)

Milverton

National Grid Ref: ST1225

Globe Inn

Lovelynch Farm, *Milverton, Taunton, Somerset, TA4 1NR.*
Open: All Year (not Xmas)
01823 400268 Mrs Loram
Rates fr: *£17.00*-**£20.00**.
Beds: 1F 1D 1T 1S
Baths: 2 Shared
Quiet C15th farm. Easy access Exmoor. Good English breakfast with good views. Furnished with antiques. Brochure available.

Minehead

National Grid Ref: SS9646

Queens Head, Kildare Lodge, Wellington Parade

The Parks Hotel, *26 The Parks, Minehead, Somerset, TA24 8BT.*
Close Exmoor, coast, town centre.
Open: All Year
01643 703547 Mr & Mrs Gibson
Rates fr: *£15.00*-**£18.00**.
Beds: 4F 1D 1T
Baths: 4 Ensuite 1 Shared
(0) (10)

Kildare Lodge, *Townsend Road, Minehead, Somerset, TA24 5RQ.*
Outstanding Lutyens-style period inn.
Open: All Year
Grades: ETB 3 Cr, Comm, AA 3 Q, Recomm
01643 702009 Mr Beckett
Fax no: 01643 706516
Rates fr: *£17.00*-**£20.00**.
Beds: 2F 4D 2T 1S
Baths: 9 Ensuite
(26)

Fernside, *The Holloway, Minehead, Somerset, TA24 5PB.*
Comfortable 200-year-old -cottage.
Open: All Year (not Xmas)
Grades: ETB 2 Cr, Comm
01643 707594
Mrs Smith
Rates fr: *£14.00*-**£15.00**.
Beds: 1F 2D
Baths: 1 Ensuite 1 Shared
(3)

Glen View, *39 Summerland Road, Minehead, Somerset, TA24 5BS.*
Quiet house. Near town and sea.
Open: Easter to Nov
01643 705025 Miss Tame
Rates fr: *£12.50*-**£13.50**.
Beds: 1F 1D 1S
Baths: 1 Shared
(5) (1)

Misterton

National Grid Ref: ST4508

White Swan

Field House, *Unity Lane, Misterton, Crewkerne, Somerset, TA18 8NA.*
Interesting house, quiet village setting.
Open: All Year (not Xmas)
01460 72619 Mrs Clark
Rates fr: *£16.00*-**£16.00**.
Beds: 1D
Baths: 1 Ensuite
(2)

Yew Tree Cottage, *Silver Street, Misterton, Crewkerne, Somerset, TA18 8NB.*
Warm, friendly, comfortable quiet cottage.
Open: All Year (not Xmas)
01460 77192 Mr & Mrs Clifton
Rates fr: *£16.00*-**£16.00**.
Beds: 1D 1T 1S
Baths: 1 Shared
(8) (3)

Dryclose, *Newbery Lane, Misterton, Crewkerne, Somerset, TA18 8NE.*
C16th Listed former farmhouse.
Open: All Year (not Xmas)
01460 73161 Mr & Mrs Gregory
Rates fr: *£16.00*-**£16.50**.
Beds: 2T 1S
Baths: 1 Private 1 Shared
(8) (6)

Monkton Combe

National Grid Ref: ST7762

Hop Pole

Dundas Lock Cottage, *Monkton Combe, Bath, BA2 7BN.*
Canalside lock-keeper's cottage.
Open: All Year (not Xmas)
01225 723890 Mrs Wheeldon
Rates fr: *£22.50*-**£21.00**.
Beds: 1D 1T 1S
Baths: 2 Private
(4)

Montacute

National Grid Ref: ST4916

Phelips Arms

Mad Hatters Tea Shop, *1 South Street, Montacute, Somerset, TA15 6XD.*
Listed Georgian property in village. **Open:** Easter to Dec
01935 823024 Mrs Hicken
Rates fr: *£15.00*-**£20.00**.
Beds: 1D **Baths:** 1 Private

Muchelney

National Grid Ref: ST4324

Wyndham Arms

Gothic House, *Muchelney, Langport, Somerset, TA10 0DW.*
Peaceful & comfortable Victorian farmhouse.
Open: All Year (not Xmas)
Grades: ETB 2 Cr
01458 250626 Ms Thorne
Rates fr: *£14.00*-**£20.00**.
Beds: 3D **Baths:** 2 Private 1 Shared
(6)

North Cadbury

National Grid Ref: ST6327

Catash Inn

The Catash Inn, *North Cadbury, Yeovil, Somerset, BA22 7DH.*
200-year-old country inn.
Open: All Year (not Xmas)
01963 440248 Mr & Mrs Robinson
Rates fr: *£22.50*-**£20.00**.
Beds: 1F 1D 1T
Baths: 1 Ensuite 1 Shared
(30)

North Wootton

National Grid Ref: ST5641

Crossways Inn

Riverside Grange, *Tanyard Lane, North Wootton, Wells, Somerset, BA4 4AE.*
Converted tannery on river's edge.
Open: All Year (not Xmas)
01749 890761 Mrs English
Rates fr: *£17.50*-**£22.00**.
Beds: 1D 1T **Baths:** 2 Private
(3)

Norton St Philip

National Grid Ref: ST7755

The George, Flur de Lye

The Place, *Norton St Philip, Bath, Somerset, BA3 6LH.*
C16th Grade II Listed guest house.
Open: All Year (not Xmas)
Grades: ETB 2 Cr, High Comm, AA 4 Q, Select
01373 834723 Mrs Gazzard
Rates fr: *£25.00*-**£35.00**.
Beds: 3D **Baths:** 3 Ensuite
(5)

Norton-sub-Hamdon

National Grid Ref: ST4715

Lord Nelson

Courtfield, *Norton-sub-Hamdon, Stoke-sub-Hamdon, Somerset, TA14 6SG.*
Beautiful family home & gardens.
Open: All Year (not Xmas)
01935 881246 Mrs Constable
Rates fr: ***£25.00*-£25.00.**
Beds: 1D 1T **Baths:** 2 Private
(8) (4)

Pawlett

National Grid Ref: ST2942

Crossways Inn

Nevys House, *Old Main Road, Pawlett, Bridgwater, Somerset, TA6 4RY.*
Comfortable C17th ex-farmhouse.
Open: All Year
Grades: ETB 1 Cr
01278 683779 Mrs Weatherhead
Rates fr: ***£16.00*-£16.00.**
Beds: 1F 2D 1S
Baths: 1 Shared
(3)

Peasedown St John

National Grid Ref: ST7057

Prince of Wales, Wheatsheaf

Eastfield Farm & Guest House, *Dunkerton Hill, Peasedown St John, Bath, BA2 8PF.*
Peaceful, panoramic views, near Bath.
Open: Feb to Nov
Grades: ETB 1 Cr
01761 432161 Mrs Newland
Rates fr: ***£14.00*-£20.00.**
Beds: 1F 1D 1T **Baths:** 2 Shared
(5)

Peasmarsh

National Grid Ref: ST3412

Graden, *Peasmarsh, Donyatt, Ilminster, Somerset, TA19 0SG.*
Comfortable home in peaceful location.
Open: All Year
01460 52371 Mrs Bond
Rates fr: ***£15.00*-£16.00.**
Beds: 2F 1D 1T **Baths:** 2 Shared
(4)

Pedwell

National Grid Ref: ST4236

Ring O' Bells

Barncroft, *20a Taunton Road, Pedwell, Street, Somerset, TA7 9BG.*
Converted stone barn, very quiet.
Open: All Year
01458 210294 Mrs Pitman
Rates fr: ***£14.50*-£15.50.**
Beds: 2D 1T **Baths:** 1 Shared
(5) (4)

Pensford

National Grid Ref: ST6263

The Hollies Guest House, *Pensford Hill, Pensford, Bristol, BS18 4AA.*
Large old Victorian private bakery.
Open: All Year
01761 490456 Mr & Mrs Jones
Rates fr: ***£10.00*-£12.00.**
Beds: 1F 1T **Baths:** 2 Shared
(3)

Pilton

National Grid Ref: ST5940

Crown Inn

Uphill Lodge, *Conduit Square, Pilton, Shepton Mallet, Somerset, BA4 4EA.*
Converted C19th cider-house. Quiet village.
Open: All Year
01749 890306
Mrs London
Rates fr: ***£16.00*-£20.00.**
Beds: 1D 1T
Baths: 2 Private
(7) (2)

The Long House, *Mount Pleasant, Pilton, Shepton Mallet, Somerset, BA4 4BP.*
Picturesque village, care, comfort, wholefoods.
Open: All Year
01749 890701
Mr & Mrs Case
Rates fr: ***£17.50*-£22.00.**
Beds: 1F 2D 2T 1S
Baths: 5 Private
(8)

Porlock

National Grid Ref: SS8846

Royal Oak, Culbone Inn

Silcombe Farm, *Culbone, Porlock, Minehead, Somerset, TA24 8JN.*
Secluded Exmoor farmhouse overlooking sea.
Open: All Year (not Xmas)
Grades: ETB Listed
01643 862248
Mrs Richards
Rates fr: ***£16.00*-£15.00.**
Beds: 2D 1T 1S
Baths: 1 Private 2 Shared
(4) (10)

Lorna Doone Hotel, *High Street, Porlock, Minehead, Somerset, TA24 8PS.*
Attractive village - superb walking country.
Open: All Year
Grades: ETB 3 Cr, AA 3 Q, RAC Acclaim
01643 862404
Mr Thornton
Rates fr: ***£19.50*-£22.50.**
Beds: 5D 6T 4S
Baths: 15 Ensuite
(7)

Myrtle Cottage, *High Street, Porlock, Minehead, Somerset, TA24 8PU.*
C17th thatched cottage.
Open: All Year
01643 862978 Mr & Mrs Thorne
Rates fr: ***£16.00*-£17.00.**
Beds: 2D 1T **Baths:** 1 Shared
(6) (4)

Leys, *The Ridge, Bossington Lane, Porlock, Minehead, Somerset, TA24 8HA.*
Peaceful comfortable home, lovely views.
Open: All Year (not Xmas)
01643 862477 Mrs Stiles-Cox
Rates fr: ***£16.00*-£16.00.**
Beds: 1D 2S **Baths:** 1 Shared
(4)

West Porlock House, *Country House Hotel, West Porlock, Porlock, Minehead, Somerset, TA24 8NX.*
Superbly set in woodland garden.
Open: Feb to Nov
Grades: ETB 2 Cr, High Comm
01643 862880 Mrs Dyer
Rates fr: ***£23.00*-£28.00.**
Beds: 1F 2D 2T
Baths: 2 Ensuite 3 Private
(10) (8)

Hurlstone, *Sparkhayes Lane, Porlock, Minehead, Somerset, TA24 8NE.*
Quiet house near village centre.
Open: All Year (not Xmas)
01643 862650 Mrs Commbs
Rates fr: ***£15.00*-£15.00.**
Beds: 1D 1T **Baths:** 1 Shared

Prestleigh

National Grid Ref: ST6340

Manor House Farm, *Prestleigh, Shepton Mallet, Somerset, BA4 4NJ.*
C18th farmhouse with Victorian addition. **Open:** Feb to Dec
01749 830385
Mr Masson
Rates fr: ***£16.00*-£18.00.**
Beds: 1F 2D
Baths: 1 Ensuite 1 Shared
(6)

Priddy

National Grid Ref: ST5251

Miners Arms, New Inn

The Miners Arms, *Priddy, Wells, Somerset, BA5 3DB.*
Open: All Year (not Xmas)
01749 870217
Mr & Mrs Reynolds
Rates fr: ***£22.00*-£32.00.**
Beds: 1F 1D 1T
Baths: 3 Ensuite
(30)
Small, long established country restaurant, specialising in fresh food, with a few letting rooms & situated in the heart of the beautiful Mendip Hills.

Highcroft, *Wells Road, Priddy, Wells, Somerset, BA5 3AU.*
Comfortable spacious modern county house.
Open: All Year (not Xmas)
Grades: ETB 2 Cr, Comm
01749 673446
Mrs Hares
Rates fr: *£17.00*-**£18.00**.
Beds: 1F 1D 1T 1S
Baths: 2 Ensuite

Puriton

National Grid Ref: ST3241

Rockfield House, *Puriton Hill, Puriton, Bridgwater, Somerset, TA7 8AG.*
H&C as well as TV all rooms.
Open: All Year (not Xmas)
01278 683561
Mrs Pipkin
Rates fr: *£14.00*-**£15.00**.
Beds: 1F 1D 1T 1S
Baths: 1 Ensuite 1 Private 1 Shared
(5)

Radstock

National Grid Ref: ST6854

The Rookery, *Wells Road, Radstock, Bath, BA3 3RS.*
Homely family-run guest house.
Open: All Year
Grades: ETB 3 Cr
01761 432626 (also fax no)
Mrs Sims
Rates fr: *£19.00*-**£20.00**.
Beds: 3F 3D 3T
Baths: 10 private

Roadwater

National Grid Ref: ST0338

Valiant Soldier, Royal Oak

Orchard House, *Roadwater, Watchet, Somerset, TA23 0QH.*
Modern house with river frontage.
Open: All Year
01984 641011 Ms Martin
Rates fr: *£13.00*-**£13.00**.
Beds: 2D 1T 2S
Baths: 2 Shared
(10) (6)

Saltford

National Grid Ref: ST6866

Prospect Villa, *570 Bath Road, Saltford, Bristol, BS18 3JN.*
Pleasant, friendly, Victorian guest house.
Open: All Year
01225 873211 Mrs Bryan
Rates fr: *£15.00*-**£17.00**.
Beds: 2F 4D 3T 2S
Baths: 1 Private 2 Shared

Sampford Arundel

National Grid Ref: ST1018

Pinksmoor Millhouse, *Pinksmoor Farm, Sampford Arundel, Wellington, Somerset, TA21 0HD.*
C13th millhouse with C20th facilities.
Open: All Year (not Xmas)
01823 672361 Mrs Ash
Rates fr: *£18.5021.00*-**£20.50**.
Beds: 1F 1D 1T
Baths: 3 Private

Shepton Mallet

National Grid Ref: ST6143

Bowlish House Restaurant, *Wells Road, Shepton Mallet, Somerset, BA4 5JD.*
Georgian restaurant with rooms.
Open: All Year
01749 342022 Mr Morley
Rates fr: *£24.00*-**£48.00**.
Beds: 1F 2D 1T
Baths: 3 Private
(10)

Shipham

National Grid Ref: ST4457

Herongates, *Horseleaze Lane, Shipham, Winscombe, BS25 1UQ.*
Noted for quality, peaceful location.
Open: All Year (not Xmas)
Grades: ETB 2 Cr
01934 843280 Mrs Stickland
Rates fr: *£14.50*-**£14.50**.
Beds: 1D 2T
Baths: 3 Private
(3)

Simonsbath

National Grid Ref: SS7739

Moorland Cottage, *Simonsbath, Minehead, Somerset, TA24 7LQ.*
Comfortable renovated character farm cottage.
Open: All Year (not Xmas)
01643 831458 Mrs Pile
Rates fr: *£15.00*-**£15.00**.
Beds: 1D 2S
Baths: 1 Private
(4)

Warren Farm, *Simonsbath, Minehead, Somerset, TA24 7LN.*
Traditional, comfortable farmhouse. Warm welcome.
Open: All Year
01643 831283 Mrs Hawkins
Rates fr: *£15.00*-**£18.00**.
Beds: 1F 1T
(4)

Bringing children with you? Always ask for any special rates.

Somerton

National Grid Ref: ST4828

Halfway House Inn

Etsome Dairy Farm, *Etsome Hill, Somerton, Somerset, TA11 6JD.*
Hospitality. Peaceful. Fantastic scenery.
Open: All Year
01458 274500 (also fax no)
Ms Cooper
Rates fr: *£14.50*-**£16.00**.
Beds: 1D 1T
Baths: 1 Private

South Petherton

National Grid Ref: ST4316

Bake House Restaurant, Royal Oak

St James's Cottage, *31 St James's Street, South Petherton, Somerset, TA13 5BN.*
Open: All Year
01460 240460
Mr & Mrs Sheridan
Rates fr: *£25.00*-**£25.00**.
Beds: 1D 1T
Baths: 1 Ensuite 1 Private
(10) (1)
Grade II Listed C16th thatched cottage, centre of attractive village. Private sitting room. Log fires. Generous English breakfast. Good restaurants & pubs nearby. Trains met.

Kings Pleasure, *24 Silver Street, South Petherton, Somerset, TA13 5BZ.*
C17th Listed hamstone house.
Open: All Year
Grades: ETB 2 Cr, High Comm
01460 241747
Mr & Mrs Veit
Rates fr: *£20.00*-**£27.00**.
Beds: 1D 1T
Baths: 2 Private
(2)

Spaxton

National Grid Ref: ST2237

Malt Shovel (Cannington)

Gatesmoor, *Hawkridge, Spaxton, Bridgwater, Somerset, TA5 1AL.*
Open: All Year (not Xmas/New Year)
Grades: AA 4 Q, Select
01278 671353 Mrs Harvey
Rates fr: *£16.50*-**£21.50**.
Beds: 1D 1T
Baths: 1 Shared
(10) (4)
Lakeside C17th cottage, gardens to water's edge. National Trust & interesting gardens nearby. Log fires, old beams and cosy rooms complement the friendly atmosphere. M5 15 minutes.

Stanton Drew

National Grid Ref: ST5963

Auden House, *Stanton Drew, Bristol, BS18 4DS.*
Large modern house.
Open: All Year (not Xmas)
01275 332232 Mrs Smart
Rates fr: *£11.00*-**£11.00**.
Beds: 2F 1D 1T 1S
(6)

Valley Farm, *Sandy Lane, Stanton Drew, Bristol, BS18 4EL.*
Modern farmhouse, quiet location, old village.
Open: All Year (not Xmas)
01275 332723 Mrs Keel
Rates fr: *£15.00*-**£20.00**.
Beds: 1F
Baths: 2 Ensuite
(3)

Stanton Prior

National Grid Ref: ST6762

Hunters Rest (Clutton)

Poplar Farm, *Stanton Prior, Bath, BA2 9HX.*
Idyllically set in village near Bath.
Open: All Year (not Xmas)
Grades: ETB Listed, Comm
01761 470382 (also fax no)
Mrs Hardwick
Rates fr: *£15.00*-**£18.00**.
Beds: 1F 1D 1T
Baths: 2 Private 1 Shared
(3) (4)

Staplegrove

National Grid Ref: ST2126

Cross Keys (Norton Fitzwarren)

Yallands Farmhouse, *Staplegrove, Taunton, Somerset, TA2 6PZ.*
Delightful C16th farmhouse. Friendly atmosphere.
Open: All Year
01823 278979 (also fax no)
Mr & Mrs Kirk
Rates fr: *£24.00*-**£25.00**.
Beds: 1F 1D 1T 1S
Baths: 4 Ensuite
(4)

Stathe

National Grid Ref: ST3728

Black Smock Inn

Black Smock Inn, *Stathe, Bridgwater, Somerset, TA7 0JN.*
Panoramic views, home made food, welcoming.
Open: All Year
Grades: ETB Listed, Comm
01823 698352 (also fax no)
Mr Horsham
Rates fr: *£16.50*-**£24.00**.
Beds: 3T 1S
Baths: 2 Ensuite 1 Shared
(40)

Stratton on the Fosse

National Grid Ref: ST6550

Somerset Wagons (Chilcompton)

Oval House, *Stratton on the Fosse, Bath, Somerset, BA3 4RB.*
C17th house of character.
Open: All Year (not Xmas)
Grades: ETB Listed
01761 232183 Mrs Mellotte
Rates fr: *£15.00*-**£15.00**.
Beds: 1T 1S
Baths: 2 Shared
(5)

Street

National Grid Ref: ST4836

Pipers Inn

Marshalls Elm Farm, *Street, Somerset, BA16 0TZ.*
Comfortable, 450-year-old characterful farmhouse.
Open: All Year (not Xmas)
01458 442878 Mrs Tucker
Rates fr: *£14.50*-**£15.00**.
Beds: 1D 1T **Baths:** 1 Shared

Sutton Montis

National Grid Ref: ST2324

Red Lion, Mitre, Sandford Orcas

Parsonage Farm, *Sutton Montis, Yeovil, Somerset, BA22 7HE.*
C17th farmhouse on working farm.
Open: Easter to Oct
01963 220256 Mrs Kerton
Rates fr: *£15.00*-**£16.00**.
Beds: 1D 2T **Baths:** 2 Shared
(3)

Taunton

National Grid Ref: ST2324

Cross Keys

Yallands Farmhouse, *Staplegrove, Taunton, Somerset, TA2 6PZ.*
Open: All Year
01823 278979 (also fax no)
Mr & Mrs Kirk
Rates fr: *£24.00*-**£25.00**.
Beds: 1F 1D 1T 1S
Baths: 4 Ensuite
(4)
Delightful C16th farmhouse. Town centre 1.5 miles. Comfortable, attractive ensuite rooms. Warm welcome. Friendly atmosphere. Pub meals within easy walking distance. Autumn/Winter breaks. Brochure available.

The lowest *double* rate per person is shown in *italics*.

Old Manor Farmhouse, *Norton Fitzwarren, Taunton, Somerset, TA2 6RZ.*
Modernised former Edwardian farmhouse.
Open: All Year (not Xmas)
Grades: ETB 3 Cr, Comm, AA 3 Q, RAC Acclaim
01823 289801 (also fax no)
Mr & Mrs Foley
Rates fr: *£23.00*-**£34.00**.
Beds: 4D 2T 1S
Baths: 7 Ensuite
(1) (12)

73 St Augustine Street, *Taunton, Somerset, TA1 1QH.*
Friendly, homely, modern, TV, teamaker.
Open: All Year (not Xmas)
01823 272905
Mrs Jones
Rates fr: *£15.00*-**£15.00**.
Beds: 2T 1S
Baths: 1 Shared

Temple Cloud

National Grid Ref: ST6257

Old Station Hotel

Temple Bridge Farm, *Temple Cloud, Bristol, BS18 5AA.*
Halfway between Bath & Wells.
Open: All Year (not Xmas)
Grades: ETB 1 Cr, Comm, AA 3 Q
01761 452377 Mrs Wyatt
Rates fr: *£17.00*-**£18.00**.
Beds: 2F
Baths: 1 Shared
(2) (3)

Theale

National Grid Ref: ST4646

Barrows Farm, *Theale, Wedmore, Somerset, BS28 4SR.*
Beautiful old farmhouse in 4-acre garden.
Open: All Year
01934 712582
Mrs Dromgoole
Rates fr: *£18.00*-**£18.00**.
Beds: 1F 1D 1T 1S
Baths: 2 Ensuite 1 Shared
(4)

Thorne St Margaret

National Grid Ref: ST0921

Thorne Manor, *Thorne St Margaret, Wellington, Somerset, TA21 0EQ.*
Jacobean manor house.
Open: Easter to Oct
01823 672954
Mrs Hasell
Rates fr: *£18.00*-**£20.00**.
Beds: 1F
(2)

Timberscombe

National Grid Ref: SS9542

Lion Inn

The Dell, *Cowbridge, Timberscombe, Minehead, Somerset,* TA24 7TD.
Open: All Year (not Xmas)
Grades: ETB Listed, Comm
01643 841564
Mr & Mrs Crawford
Rates fr: *£14.50*-**£14.50**.
Beds: 2D 1T 1S
Baths: 1 Shared
(8) P (4) TV V
Exmoor excellence in comfortable farmhouse situated in Exmoor National Park affording visitors an ideal centre from which to enjoy many attractions & interesting places.

Wellum, *Brook Street, Timberscombe, Minehead, Somerset,* TA24 7TG.
Lovely old house, spectacular views.
Open: Mar to Nov
Grades: ETB 1 Cr, Comm
01643 841234 Mrs Kelsey
Rates fr: *£15.00*-**£18.00**.
Beds: 1D 1T 1S
Baths: 1 Private 1 Shared
TV V

Wanneroo Farm, *Timberscombe, Minehead, Somerset,* TA24 7TU.
Modern, comfortable farmhouse.
Open: All Year
01643 841493 Mrs Webber
Rates fr: *£15.00*-**£15.00**.
Beds: 1F 2D 1S
P (10) TV V

Upper Langford

National Grid Ref: ST4659

Burrington Arms, Seymour Arms

Holly Cottage, *Langford Green, Upper Langford, Bristol,* BS18 7DG.
Lovely hillside, & wood views.
Open: April to October
01934 852557 Mrs Wade
Rates fr: *£15.00*-**£18.00**.
Beds: 1D 1T
Baths: 1 Private
P (4) TV

Vellow

National Grid Ref: ST0938

Curdon Mill, *Vellow, Williton, Taunton, Somerset,* TA4 4LS.
Quiet country water mill.
Open: All Year
Grades: AA 1 St
01984 656522 Mrs Criddle
Fax no: 01984 656197
Rates fr: *£25.00*-**£30.00**.
Beds: 3D 3T
Baths: 6 Ensuite
(10) P (100) TV V

Washford

National Grid Ref: ST0441

Green Bay Guest House, *Washford, Watchet, Somerset,* TA23 0NN.
Double fronted stone built cottage close Exmoor/Sea.
Open: Easter to Nov
Grades: ETB 2 Cr, Comm
01984 640303 Mrs Brown
Rates fr: *£15.00*-**£15.00**.
Beds: 1D 2T
Baths: 2 Ensuite 1 Private
(5) P (3) TV V

Steps Farmhouse, *Bilbrook, Washford, Minehead, Somerset,* TA24 6HE.
Charming, family-run, C16th farmhouse.
Open: Mar to Oct
01984 640974 Mrs Cox
Rates fr: *£16.00*-**£16.00**.
Beds: 2D 1T
Baths: 3 Private
(10) P (6) TV V

Waterrow

National Grid Ref: ST0525

The Rock Inn, *Waterrow, Taunton, Somerset,* TA4 2AX.
400-year-old inn.
Open: All Year (not Xmas)
01984 623293 Mr Broughall
Rates fr: *£20.00*-**£20.00**.
Beds: 1F 4D 2T
Baths: 7 Private
P (22) TV V

Wedmore

National Grid Ref: ST4347

Sexey's Arms, George Hotel

Upper Farm, *Sand, Wedmore, Somerset,* BS28 4XF.
Large, quiet, historic stone farmhouse.
Open: All Year
01934 712595 Mr Hicks
Rates fr: *£17.00*-**£17.00**.
Beds: 2D 1T
Baths: 2 Private 1 Shared
(1) P (3) TV V

The George Hotel, *Church Street, Wedmore, Somerset,* BS28 4AB.
C17th coaching inn.
Open: All Year
01934 712124 Mr Hodge
Rates fr: *£17.50*-**£20.00**.
Beds: 2F 2D 4T 1S
Baths: 3 Ensuite 2 Shared
P (30) TV V

Bringing children with you? Always ask for any special rates.

Wells

National Grid Ref: ST5445

Fountain Inn, Vence Club, Riverside Restaurant, New Inn

17 Priory Road, *Wells, Somerset,* BA5 1SU.
Large Victorian house. Homemade bread.
Open: All Year (not Xmas)
01749 677300 Mrs Winter
Rates fr: *£15.00*-**£15.00**.
Beds: 3F 3S
Baths: 2 Shared
P (5) TV V

Bekynton House, *7 St Thomas Street, Wells, Somerset,* BA5 2UU.
Near Cathedral & City Centre.
Open: All Year (not Xmas)
Grades: ETB 2 Cr, Comm, AA 4 Q, RAC Acclaim
01749 672222 (also fax no)
Mr & Mrs Gripper
Rates fr: *£20.00*-**£22.00**.
Beds: 1F 4D 2T 1S
Baths: 6 Private 2 Shared
(5) P (6) TV V

Burcott Mill Guest House, *Burcott, Wookey, Wells, Somerset,* BA5 1NJ.
Comfortable, rural working water mill. **Open:** All Year
Grades: ETB 2 Cr, Comm
01749 673118
Mr & Mrs Grimstead
Rates fr: *£16.00*-**£20.00**.
Beds: 2F 2D 2T 1S
Baths: 7 Private
P (20) TV V

Home Farm, *Stoppers Lane, Upper Coxley, Wells, Somerset,* BA5 1QS.
Old cider house, converted pre-war.
Open: All Year (not Xmas)
Grades: ETB 2 Cr, AA 2 Q
01749 672434 Ms Higgs
Rates fr: *£18.50*-**£18.50**.
Beds: 2F 2D 2T 1S
Baths: 2 Ensuite 1 Private 4 Shared
(10) P (7) TV

Highcroft, *Wells Road, Priddy, Wells, Somerset,* BA5 3AU.
Comfortable spacious modern county house.
Open: All Year (not Xmas)
Grades: ETB 2 Cr, Comm
01749 673446 Mrs Hares
Rates fr: *£17.00*-**£18.00**.
Beds: 1F 1D 1T 1S
Baths: 2 Ensuite
P TV V

30 Mary Road, *Wells, Somerset,* BA5 2NF.
Small, friendly family home.
Open: Feb to Nov
01749 674031 (also fax no)
Mrs Bailey
Rates fr: *£15.00*-**£15.00**.
Beds: 2D 2S **Baths:** 1 Shared
(3) P (7) TV V

***Manor Farm,** Old Bristol Road, Upper Milton, Wells, Somerset, BA5 3AH.*
Elizabethan manor house, lovely views.
Open: All Year (not Xmas)
Grades: ETB 1 Cr, AA 3 Q
01749 673394 Mrs Gould
Rates fr: *£15.00*-**£17.00**.
Beds: 1F 1D 1T **Baths:** 1 Shared
(4)

West Harptree

National Grid Ref: ST5656

King's Arms (Litton)

***Vicarage Lawns,** Bristol Road, West Harptree, Bristol, Somerset, BS18 6HF.*
Open: All Year
Grades: ETB 2 Cr
01761 221668 Mrs Rowell
Rates fr: *£16.00*-**£18.00**.
Beds: 1F 2D 2T
Baths: 3 Private 1 Shared
(8)
In Mendip Hills village. In an acre of walled garden, close to Chew Valley Lake, sailing, birdwatching, walking. 20 minutes from Bristol, Bath, Wells.

West Monkton

National Grid Ref: ST2628

Merry Monk, Monkton

***Prockters Farm,** West Monkton, Taunton, Somerset, TA2 8QN.*
Lovely, quiet, comfortable farmhouse.
Open: All Year
Grades: ETB 2 Cr
01823 412269 (also fax no)
Mrs Besley
Rates fr: *£18.00*-**£18.00**.
Beds: 1F 2D 2T
Baths: 2 Private 3 Shared
(6)

West Pennard

National Grid Ref: ST5438

Lion

***Orchard House,** Church Lane, West Pennard, Glastonbury, Somerset, BA6 8NT.*
Grade II Listed house. Quiet cul-de-sac.
Open: Easter to Sep
01458 832838 Mrs Sadler
Rates fr: *£15.00*-**£15.00**.
Beds: 1D 1T
Baths: 1 Shared
(2)

Planning a longer stay? Always ask for any special rates.

***Middle Farm,** West Pennard, Glastonbury, Somerset, BA6 8NQ.*
Modern farmhouse in landscaped gardens.
Open: All Year
01749 890753 Mr & Mrs Stephens
Rates fr: *£15.00*-**£18.00**.
Beds: 2D 1T
Baths: 3 Private
(6)

Westbury-sub-Mendip

National Grid Ref: ST5048

Westbury Inn, The Lamb

***Box Tree House,** Westbury-sub-Mendip, Wells, Somerset, BA5 1HA.*
Delightful converted C17th farmhouse.
Open: All Year
Grades: AA 4 Q
01749 870777 Mrs White
Rates fr: *£18.00*-**£20.00**.
Beds: 1F 1D 1T
Baths: 1 Ensuite 2 Private
(4)

***The Old Stores,** Westbury-sub-Mendip, Wells, Somerset, BA5 1HA.*
300-year-old cottage with many features.
Open: All Year (not Xmas)
01749 870567 Ms Harris
Rates fr: *£17.00*-**£17.00**.
Beds: 2D 2S
(5)

Weston-Super-Mare

National Grid Ref: ST3261

***Conifers,** 63 Milton Road, Weston-Super-Mare, BS23 2SP.*
Open: All Year (not Xmas)
Grades: ETB 2 Cr, Comm, AA 2 Q, Recomm
01934 624404 Mrs Bowley
Rates fr: *£16.00*-**£18.00**.
Beds: 1D 1T 1S
Baths: 1 Private 1 Shared
(13) (3)
High class Bed & Breakfast establishment. 26th year. Parking in own grounds. Many guests return year after year. Close all amenities. Warm welcome assured.

***Vaynor,** 346 Locking Road, Weston-Super-Mare, Somerset, BS22 8PD.*
Comfortable, friendly guesthouse.
Open: All Year (not Xmas)
Grades: RAC Listed
01934 632332 Mrs Monk
Rates fr: *£12.00*-**£12.00**.
Beds: 1F 2D **Baths:** 1 Shared
(3)

***Almond Lodge Guest House,** 42 Clevedon Road, Weston-Super-Mare, BS23 1DQ.*
Small, quiet, 'home from home'.
Open: All Year (not Xmas)
01934 625113 Mr & Mrs Hall
Rates fr: *£12.00*-**£14.00**.
Beds: 2F 2D **Baths:** 1 Shared
(4)

***Parasol,** 49 Walliscote Road, Weston-Super-Mare, BS23 1EE.*
Small, friendly. Near sea-front & town.
Open: All Year
01934 636409 Mrs Warren
Rates fr: *£16.00*-**£18.00**.
Beds: 2F 1D 1T
Baths: 4 Private
(2) (2)

***L'Arrivee Guest House,** 75 Locking Road, Weston-Super-Mare, BS23 3DW.*
Spacious, comfortable, friendly Victorian house.
Open: All Year
Grades: ETB 3 Cr, RAC Acclaim
01934 625328 (also fax no)
Rates fr: *£18.50*-**£22.50**.
Beds: 4F 5D 3T
Baths: 10 Private 2 Shared
(12)

Wheddon Cross

National Grid Ref: SS9238

Rest & Be Thankful Inn

***Rest & Be Thankful Inn,** Wheddon Cross, Exmoor, Minehead, Somerset, TA24 7DR.*
Old coaching inn, ideal Exmoor location.
Open: All Year (not Xmas)
Grades: ETB 3 Cr, High Comm, AA 4 Q, RAC Acclaim
01643 841222 Mr Weaver
Fax no: 01643 841222 / 841230
Rates fr: *£26.00*-**£26.00**.
Beds: 3D 1T 1S
Baths: 5 Private 1 Shared
(11) (50)

***Little Quarme Farm,** Wheddon Cross, Exmoor, Minehead, Somerset, TA24 7EA.*
Lovely old farmhouse, outstanding location.
Open: Easter to Oct
Grades: ETB Listed, High Comm
01643 841249 Mr Cody-Boutcher
Fax no: 01643 841 249
Rates fr: *£17.00*-**£19.00**.
Beds: 2D 1T **Baths:** 2 Shared
(4)

***Exmoor House,** Wheddon Cross, Exmoor , Minehead, Somerset, TA24 7DU.*
Elegant spacious accommodation in Edwardian house.
Open: Mar to Dec
01643 841432 Mrs Vosper
Rates fr: *£19.00*-**£29.00**.
Beds: 3D 3T
Baths: 4 Private 2 Shared
(10) (10)

Right on the border? Look at the neighbouring county, too

***utthorne Farm,** Luckwell Bridge, /heddon Cross, Minehead, omerset, TA24 7EW.*
eautifully secluded Exmoor ountry house.
pen: Feb to Dec
1643 831255
Irs Durbin
ates fr: *£20.00*-**£20.00**.
eds: 2D 1T
aths: 3 Ensuite
(12) (10)

Villiton

lational Grid Ref: ST0741

Foresters Arms Hotel

***oresters Arms Hotel,** 55 Long treet, Williton, Taunton, Somerset, A4 4QY.*
:17th coaching inn.
)pen: All Year
1984 632508
Ir Goble
ates fr: *£15.00*-**£15.00**.
eds: 3F 3D 1T 2S
aths: 5 Private 1 Shared
(24)

Vinsford

lational Grid Ref: SS9034

***unning Waters,** East, The Hebes, Winsford, Minehead, omerset, TA24 7JF.*
:omfortable house, large park-like arden.
)pen: Apr to Nov
1643 851250
Irs Butler
ates fr: *£20.00*-**£20.00**.
eds: 1D 1T 1S
aths: 1 Private 1 Shared
(3)

Vinsham

lational Grid Ref: ST3706

Windwhistle Inn

***ast Whatley Farm,** Winsham, Chard, Somerset, TA20 4JS.*
:omfortable thatched C17th armhouse.
)pen: All Year (not Xmas)
)1460 30312
Irs Goodlet
Rates fr: *£15.00*-**£15.00**.
Beds: 1D 1S 1T
Baths: 2 Shared
(6)

High season, bank holidays and special events mean low availability *anywhere.*

Withypool

National Grid Ref: SS8435

***The Old Rectory,** Withypool, Minehead, Somerset, TA24 7QP.*
Large comfortable bungalow. Lovely views.
Open: All Year
01643 831553
Mr Clatworthy
Rates fr: *£15.00*-**£15.00**.
Beds: 1D 1T 1S
Baths: 1 Shared
(3)

Wiveliscombe

National Grid Ref: ST0827

***Clerkspool,** 1 Ford Road, Wiveliscombe, Taunton, Somerset, TA4 2NJ.*
Rambling family house, large garden.
Open: All Year (not Xmas)
01984 623364
Mr & Mrs Pearce
Rates fr: *£16.00*-**£16.00**.
Beds: 1F 1T
Baths: 1 Shared
(8)

***Watercombe House,** Huish Champflower, Wiveliscombe, Taunton, Somerset, TA4 2EE.*
Secluded country home, warm welcome.
Open: Easter to Nov
01984 623725
Mrs Garner-Richards
Rates fr: *£19.00*-**£30.00**.
Beds: 1D 1T 1S
Baths: 1 Private 1 Shared
(10) (6)

Wookey

National Grid Ref: ST5145

***Burcott Mill Guest House,** Burcott, Wookey, Wells, Somerset, BA5 1NJ.*
Comfortable, rural working water mill.
Open: All Year
Grades: ETB 2 Cr, Comm
01749 673118
Mr & Mrs Grimstead
Rates fr: *£16.00*-**£20.00**.
Beds: 2F 2D 2T 1S
Baths: 7 Private
(20)

***Cross Farm,** Yarley, Wookey, Wells, Somerset, BA5 1PA.*
Comfortable, well-furnished C15th Somerset longhouse.
Open: Easter to Nov
01749 678925
Mr & Mrs Alcock
Rates fr: *£13.50*-**£15.00**.
Beds: 1F 2D
Baths: 1 Private 1 Shared
(6)

Wookey Hole

National Grid Ref: ST5347

Pheasant

***Ganymede,** Hurst Batch, Wookey Hole, Wells, Somerset, BA5 1BE.*
Comfortable stone cottage.
Open: Jan to Nov
01749 677250 Mrs Baddeley
Rates fr: *£13.00*-**£13.00**.
Beds: 2D
Baths: 1 Shared
(8) (2)

***Whitegate Cottage,** Milton Lane, Wookey Hole, Wells, Somerset, BA5 1DG.*
Large country cottage on farmland.
Open: All Year
01749 675326 Mr & Mrs Lee
Rates fr: *£12.50*-**£15.00**.
Beds: 2D 1S
(4)

Yeovil

National Grid Ref: ST5516

Quick Silver Mail, Coopers Mill, Royal Marine

***Greystones Guest House,** 152 Hendford Hill, Yeovil, Somerset, BA20 2RG.*
Comfortable Georgian guest house.
Open: All Year
Grades: ETB 1 Cr
01935 26124 Mr & Mrs Hector
Rates fr: *£16.00*-**£19.00**.
Beds: 3F 1D 1T 1S
Baths: 3 Private 2 Shared
(7)

***1 Alondale Gardens,** Yeovil, Somerset, BA20 1QU.*
Spacious bungalow adjacent town/amenities.
Open: All Year (not Xmas)
01935 23184 Mrs Poulton
Rates fr: *£15.50*-**£17.00**.
Beds: 2F 1D
Baths: 2 Shared
(3)

***Mallans,** 62 West Coker Road, Yeovil, Somerset, BA20 2JA.*
Warm, comfortable, excellent English breakfast.
Open: All Year (not Xmas)
01935 24053 Mr Dare
Rates fr: *£17.00*-**£19.00**.
Beds: 2D
Baths: 2 Ensuite
(3)

***Wyndham Guest House,** 142 Sherborne Road, Yeovil, Somerset, BA21 4HQ.*
Large, comfortable Victorian guest house.
Open: All Year (not Xmas)
Grades: ETB Listed
01935 21468 Mrs Smith
Rates fr: *£17.00*-**£17.00**.
Beds: 1F 2D 2T 1S
Baths: 1 Shared
(8)

Staffordshire

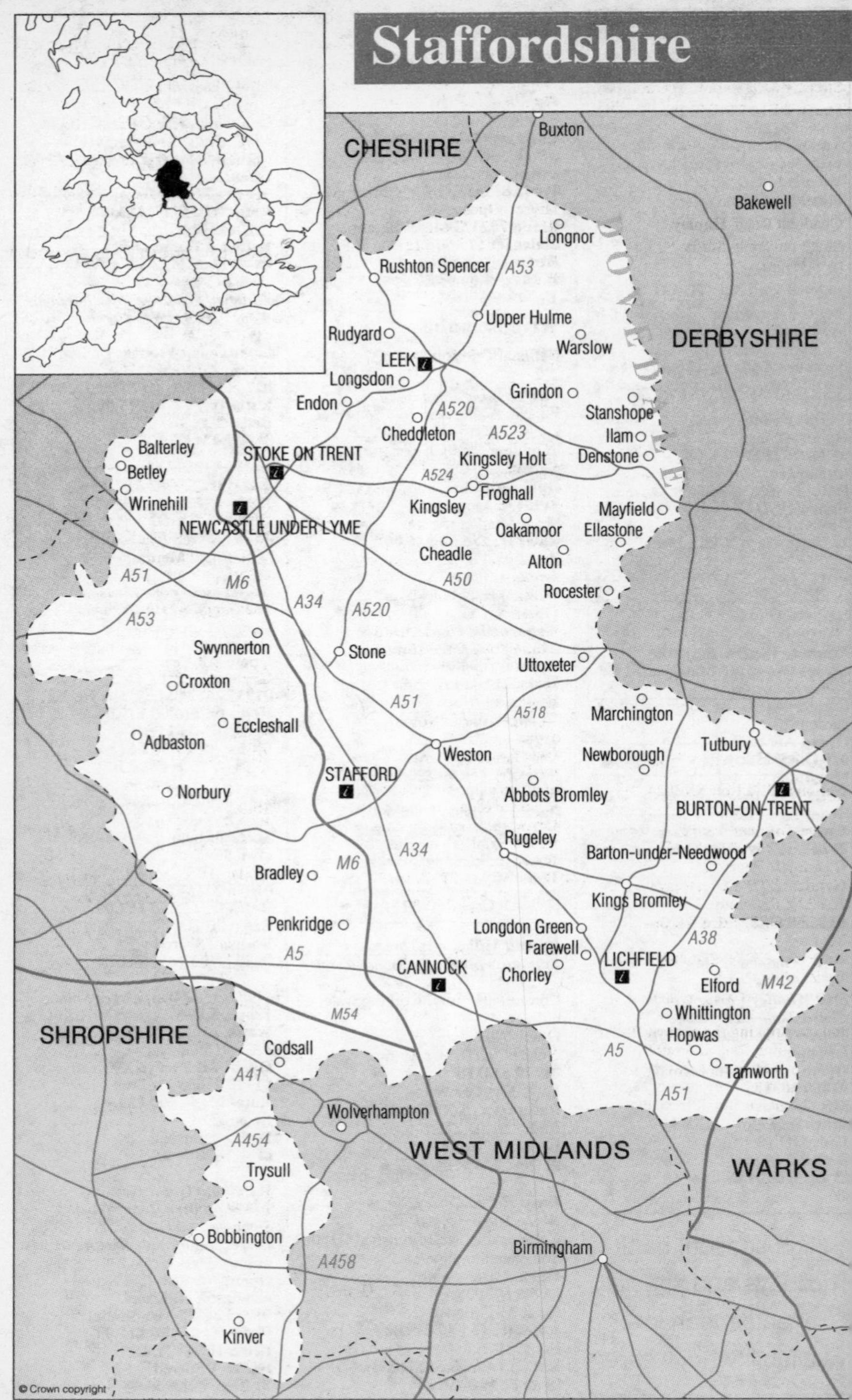

Tourist Information Centres

Unit 40, Octagon Centre, New Street, **Burton-upon-Trent**, Staffs, DE14 3TN, 01283 516609.

Valley Heriatge Centre Cannock, Staffs, WS12 5 TD, 01543 877666.

Potteries Shopping Centre, Quadrant Road, **Hanley**, Stoke-on-Trent, Staffs, ST1 1RZ, 01782 284600.

Market Place, **Leek**, Staffs, ST13 5HH, 01538 381000.

Donegal House, Bore Street, **Lichfield**, Staffs, WS13 6NE, 01543 252109.

Area Reference Library, Ironmarket, **Newcastle-under-Lyme**, Staffs, ST5 1AT, 01782 297314.

The Ancient High House, Greengate Street, **Stafford**, Staffs, ST16 2JA, 01785 240204.

Town Hall, Market Street, **Tamworth**, B79 7LY, 01827 59134

Abbots Bromley

National Grid Ref: SK0824

Crown Inn, *Market Place, Abbots Bromley, Rugeley, Staffs, WS15 3BS.*
Open: All Year
Grades: ETB 1 Cr, Approv, AA 2 Q, Recomm
01283 840227 (also fax no) Mr Barford
Rates fr: *£20.00*-**£20.00**.
Beds: 1F 2D 2T 1S
Baths: 2 Shared
(40)
Inn overlooking the ancient Butter Cross, home cooked food, fine ales & warm welcome. Adjacent to Snugborough, Burton-upon-Trent and Alton Towers. Phone for brochure.

Adbaston

National Grid Ref: SJ7627

Offley Grove Farm, *Adbaston, Eccleshall, Stafford, Staffs, ST20 0QB.*
You'll consider this a good find!
Open: All Year (not Xmas)
01785 280205 Mrs Hiscoe James
Rates fr: *£15.00*-**£15.00**.
Beds: 1D 2T
(4)

Alton

National Grid Ref: SK0742

Blacksmiths Arms, Talbot Arms

Crescent House, *Smithy Bank, Alton, Stoke on Trent, Staffs, ST10 4AD.*
Personal attention: Victorian guest house. **Open:** All Year
01538 702377 Mrs Whitefoot
Rates fr: *£15.00*-**£15.00**.
Beds: 1F 1D 1T
Baths: 2 Private

The Hawthorns, *8 Tythe Barn, Alton, Stoke on Trent, Staffs, ST10 4AZ.*
Friendly, homely private house.
Open: All Year (not Xmas)
Grades: ETB 1 Cr
01538 702197 Mrs Callear
Rates fr: *£15.00*-**£20.00**.
Beds: 1F 1D
Baths: 1 Private 1 Shared
(5) (4)

Bulls Head Inn, *High Street, Alton, Stoke on Trent, Staffs, ST10 4AR.*
C18th village inn.
Open: All Year
Grades: ETB 3 Cr, AA 2 St
01538 702307 Mr Harvey
Rates fr: *£20.00*-**£30.00**.
Beds: 2F 3D 1T
Baths: 6 Ensuite
(15)

Dale Farm, *The Dale, Alton, Stoke on Trent, Staffs, ST10 4BG.*
Upgraded period farmhouse - secluded location.
Open: All Year (not Xmas)
01538 702012 Mrs Gregory
Rates fr: *£14.50*-**£20.00**.
Beds: 1F 1D 1T **Baths:** 1 Shared
(5) (6)

Balterley

National Grid Ref: SJ7650

Broughton Arms

Balterley Hall, *Balterley, Crewe, Cheshire, CW2 5QG.*
C17th farmhouse, convenient for pottery factories.
Open: All Year (not Xmas)
Grades: ETB 2 Cr, High Comm, AA 4 Q, Select
01270 820206 Mrs Edwards
Rates fr: *£15.00*-**£18.00**.
Beds: 3D
Baths: 2 Private 1 Shared
(5)

Bringing children with you? Always ask for any special rates.

High season, bank holidays and special events mean low availability *anywhere.*

Barton-under-Needwood

National Grid Ref: SK1818

The Bell, Shoulder of Lamb, Three Horseshoes

Threeway Cottage, *2 Wales Lane, Barton-under-Needwood, Burton-upon-Trent, Staffs, DE13 8JF.*
C17th charming beamed cottage.
Open: All Year
Grades: ETB 2 Cr, Comm
01283 713572 Mrs Jakeman
Rates fr: *£17.00*-**£17.00**.
Beds: 2T 1S
Baths: 2 Ensuite 1 Private
(0) (4)

Betley

National Grid Ref: SJ7548

Crown Inn

Betley Court Farm, Betley, Crewe, *Cheshire, CW3 9BH.*
Large Victorian traditional working farm.
Open: All Year
Grades: ETB 2 Cr, High Comm, AA 3 Q
01270 820229 Mrs Speed
Rates fr: *£18.00*-**£22.0**.
Beds: 1F 1D 1S **Baths:** 3 Ensuite

Adderley Green Farm, *Heighley Castle Lane, Betley, Crewe, Cheshire, CW3 9BA.*
'Laura Ashley'-style Georgian farmhouse.
Open: All Year (not Xmas/New Year)
Grades: ETB 2 Cr, High CommRAC
01270 820203 Ms Berrisford
Rates fr: *£15.00*-**£20.00**.
Beds: 2D 1T 1S
Baths: 3 Ensuite
(4)

Bobbington

National Grid Ref: SO8090

Blakelands, *Halfpenny Green, Bobbington, Stourbridge, Staffs, DY7 5DP.*
Queen Anne country house set in 7 acres.
Open: All Year
01384 221464 Mrs Morgan
Rates fr: *£20.00*-**£30.00**.
Beds: 6D 2T
Baths: 8 Private
(50)

The lowest *double* rate per person is shown in *italics*.

Bradley

National Grid Ref: SJ8717

Red Lion

Littywood Farm, *Bradley, Stafford, ST18 9DW.*
Open: All Year (not Xmas)
Grades: ETB 2 Cr
01785 780234 Mrs Busby
Fax no: 01785 780770
Rates fr: *£17.00*-**£20.00**.
Beds: 1D 1T
Baths: 1 Ensuite 1 Shared
(10)
Beautiful double moated C14th manor house set in own grounds, on a mixed working farm. Secluded position yet easily accessible from the M6. Centrally heated.

Burton-upon-Trent

National Grid Ref: SK2422

Edgecote Hotel, *179 Ashby Road, Burton-upon-Trent, Staffs, DE15 0LB.*
Relaxed, family-run Edwardian hotel. Some romantic, brass-bedded rooms.
Open: All Year (not Xmas)
Grades: ETB Listed, Comm
01283 568966
Mr McCabe
Fax no: 01283 740118
Rates fr: *£23.00*-**£22.00**.
Beds: 4F 2D 6S
Baths: 5 Private 2 Shared
(8)

Westlake Guest House, *204 Ashby Road, Burton-upon-Trent, Staffs, DE15 0LB.*
Large Victorian private house.
Open: All Year (not Xmas)
01283 546717
Mr Westlake
Rates fr: *£13.00*-**£15.00**.
Beds: 4F 3T 3S
Baths: 3 Shared
(6)

Cannock

National Grid Ref: SJ9810

Mill Farm Restaurant

Mill Farm Cottage, *Adj Mill Farm Restaurant, Lichfield Road, Cannock, Staffs, WS11 3EE.*
Converted C17th mill farm barn.
Open: All Year
01543 573310
Mr & Mrs Payne
Fax no: 01543 467873
Rates fr: *£15.00*-**£20.00**.
Beds: 1F 2D 2T
Baths: 3 Ensuite 1 Private
(6)

Cheadle

National Grid Ref: SK0143

Leyfields Farm, *Leek Road, Cheadle, Stoke on Trent, Staffs, ST10 2EF.*
High standard accommodation, dairy farm.
Open: All Year (not Xmas)
Grades: ETB 3 Cr, Comm
01538 752875
Mrs Clowes
Rates fr: *£17.00*-**£18.00**.
Beds: 2F 1D
Baths: 3 Private
(4)

Cheddleton

National Grid Ref: SJ9752

Choir Cottage, *Ostlers Lane, Cheddleton, Leek, Staffs, ST13 7HS.*
C17th former ostlers' resting place.
Open: All Year (not Xmas)
Grades: ETB 3 Cr, High Comm, AA 4 Q, RAC High Acclaim
01538 360561
Mr & Mrs Sutcliffe
Rates fr: *£22.00*-**£35.00**.
Beds: 1F 1D
Baths: 2 Private
(5) (6)

Chorley

National Grid Ref: SK0710

The Windmill

The Stone House, *Farewell, Chorley, Lichfield, Staffs, WS13 8DS.*
400-year-old stone cottage.
Open: All Year (not Xmas)
Grades: AA 3 Q
01543 682575
Mrs Cowell
Rates fr: *£15.00*-**£15.00**.
Beds: 2D 1S
Baths: 2 Shared
(Unlimited)

Codsall

National Grid Ref: SJ8703

Moors Farm & Country Restaurnt, *Chillington Lane, Codsall, Wolverhampton, Staffs, WV8 1QF.*
Open: All Year
Grades: ETB 3 Cr, AA 3 Q, RAC Acclaim
01902 842330
Mrs Moreton
Fax no: 01902 847878
Rates fr: *£20.00*-**£25.00**.
Beds: 2F 2D 2T
Baths: 3 Private 2 Shared
(4) (20)
Picture a cosy farmhouse in a quiet, picturesque valley. Your comfortable bedroom has wonderful views. Tea/coffee, radio, TV etc. Superb cuisine with home grown produce.

Croxton

National Grid Ref: SJ7831

Glenwood, *Croxton, Eccleshall, Staffs, ST21 6PF.*
C16th timber-framed cottage.
Open: All Year
01630 620238
Mrs Thorpe
Rates fr: *£15.00*-**£16.00**.
Beds: 1F 1D 1T
Baths: 1 Private 1 Shared
(4)

Denstone

National Grid Ref: SK0940

Blacksmith's Arms

Hillside Farm, *Denstone, Uttoxeter, Staffs, ST14 5HG.*
Victorian farmhouse adjacent Alton Towers.
Open: Mar to Nov
Grades: ETB Listed
01889 590760 Mrs Johnson
Rates fr: *£15.00*-**£17.00**.
Beds: 2F 2D
Baths: 2 Shared

Denstone Hall Farm, *Denstone, Uttoxeter, Staffs, ST14 5HF.*
Acton Towers is 10 mins away.
Open: Easter to Nov
01889 590253
Mrs Boden
Rates fr: *£14.00*-**£16.00**.
Beds: 1F 1T
Baths: 1 Shared
(3)

Eccleshall

National Grid Ref: SJ8329

Kings Arms

Cobblers Cottage, *Kerry Lane, Eccleshall, Staffs, ST21 6EJ.*
Tastefully refurbished 1850s cottage.
Open: All Year (not Xmas)
Grades: ETB 2 Cr
01785 850116
Mrs Pimble
Rates fr: *£17.00*-**£22.00**.
Beds: 1F 1D
Baths: 2 Ensuite
(2)

Elford

National Grid Ref: SK1910

The Hawthorns, *The Square, Elford, Tamworth, Staffs, B79 9DB.*
Modern cottage-style house.
Open: All Year (not Xmas)
01827 383487
Mr & Mrs Robotham
Rates fr: *£13.25*-**£15.00**.
Beds: 1D 1S
Baths: 1 Shared
(3)

Ellastone

National Grid Ref: SK1143

Churchfields Cottage, *Church Lane, Ellastone, Ashbourne, Derbyshire,* DE6 2HB.
C17th cottage, lovely views.
Open: All Year (not Xmas)
01335 324431 Mrs Chown
Fax no: 01335 324478
Rates fr: *£15.00*-**£15.00**.
Beds: 2D
Baths: 1 Shared
(2)

Endon

National Grid Ref: SJ9253

Plough, Travellers Rest

The Hollies, *Clay Lake, Endon, Stoke on Trent, Staffs,* ST9 9DD.
Spacious comfortable Victorian family home.
Open: All Year (not Xmas)
Grades: ETB 2 Cr, Comm, AA 3 Q
01782 503252 Mrs Hodgson
Rates fr: *£18.00*-**£22.00**.
Beds: 2F 1D 2T
Baths: 4 Ensuite 1 Private
(2) (5)

Farewell

National Grid Ref: SK0811

Little Pipe Farm, *Little Pipe Lane, Farewell, Lichfield, Staffs,* WS13 8BS.
Old comfortable farmhouse, superb views.
Open: All Year
01543 683066 Mrs Clewley
Rates fr: *£15.00*-**£15.00**.
Beds: 1F 1D 1S
Baths: 2 Shared
(10)

Froghall

National Grid Ref: SK0247

The Railway Inn, *Froghall, Cheadle, Stoke on Trent, Staffs,* ST10 2HE.
Comfortable family-run public house.
Open: All Year
Grades: ETB 3 Cr, Comm
01538 754782 Mrs Ruscoe
Rates fr: *£22.00*-**£26.00**.
Beds: 2F 2D 1T
Baths: 5 Ensuite
(30)

Grindon

National Grid Ref: SK0854

Summerhill Farm, *Grindon, Leek, Staffs,* ST13 7TT.
Farmhouse in Peak District. 15 mins Alton Towers.
Open: All Year (not Xmas)
01538 304264 Mrs Simpson
Rates fr: *£16.00*-**£18.30**.
Beds: 2D 2T
Baths: 3 Private
(6) (4)

Hopwas

National Grid Ref: SK1705

Red Lion, Chequers

Oak Tree Farm, *Hints Road, Hopwas, Tamworth, Staffs,* B79 3AA.
Luxuriously renovated farmhouse; all comforts.
Open: All Year
Grades: ETB 2 Cr, High Comm, AA 4 Q, Select
01827 56807 Mrs Purkis
Rates fr: *£21.00*-**£28.50**.
Beds: 3F 3D 1T
Baths: 7 Ensuite
(5) (10)

Ilam

National Grid Ref: SK1350

Throwley Hall Farm, *Ilam, Ashbourne, Derbyshire,* DE6 2BB.
Large, rural Georgian farmhouse.
Open: All Year (not Xmas)
Grades: ETB 2 Cr, Comm
01538 308202 Mrs Richardson
Rates fr: *£16.00*-**£18.00**.
Beds: 1F 2D 1T
Baths: 2 Private 1 Shared

Beechenhill Farm, *Ilam, Ashbourne, Derbyshire,* DE6 2BD.
Warm C17th farmhouse. Delicious breakfasts.
Open: All Year (not Xmas)
01335 310274 Mrs Prince
Rates fr: *£17.50*-**£20.00**.
Beds: 1F 1D
Baths: 1 Ensuite 1 Private
(4)

Air Cottage Farm, *Ilam, Ashbourne, Derbyshire,* DE6 2BD.
Large Victorian limestone shooter's lodge.
Open: Mar to Nov
01335 350475 Mrs Wain
Rates fr: *£14.00*-**£16.00**.
Beds: 1D 1T 1S
Baths: 1 Shared

King's Bromley

National Grid Ref: SK1216

Royal Oak

5 Manor Road, *King's Bromley, Burton-on-Trent, Staffs,* DE13 7HZ.
Early C19th manor cottage.
Open: All Year (not Xmas)
01543 472769 Mr & Mrs Hodges
Rates fr: *£13.50*-**£14.50**.
Beds: 1D 1T
Baths: 1 Shared
(1)

The lowest **single** *rate is shown in* **bold.**

Kingsley

National Grid Ref: SK0046

The Church Farm, *Holt Lane, Kingsley, Stoke on Trent, Staffs,* ST10 2BA.
Traditionally furnished C18th farmhouse.
Open: All Year (not Xmas)
01538 754759 Mrs Clowes
Rates fr: *£14.50*-**£18.00**.
Beds: 2D 1T
Baths: 1 Shared
(6)

Kingsley Holt

National Grid Ref: SK0246

The Holt Guest House, *Churnet Valley Road, Kingsley Holt, Stoke on Trent, Staffs,* ST10 2BQ.
Small, homely guest house.
Open: All Year
Grades: ETB Listed, Comm
01538 757221
Mr & Mrs Barrow
Rates fr: *£15.00*-**£15.00**.
Beds: 1F 1D
Baths: 1 Shared
(2)

Kinver

National Grid Ref: SO8483

The Old Vicarage, *Vicarage Drive, Kinver, Stourbridge, W. Mids,* DY7 6HJ.
Quiet postion in own grounds.
Open: All Year (not Xmas)
01384 872784
Mr & Mrs Harris
Rates fr: *£17.50*-**£17.50**.
Beds: 2T
Baths: 2 Shared
(1) (10)

Anchor Hotel, *Dark Lane, Kinver, Stourbridge, W. Mids,* DY7 6NR.
Converted pub & cottages.
Open: All Year (not Xmas)
01384 872085
Mr Olivieri
Rates fr: *£17.00*-**£21.00**.
Beds: 1F 4D 3T 2S
Baths: 10 Ensuite
(20)

Leek

National Grid Ref: SJ9856

Raymonde's

The Hatcheries, *Church Lane, Mount Pleasant, Leek, Staffs,* ST13 5ET.
Secluded position, yet only 2 minutes from town centre.
Open: All Year
01538 383073 / 399552
Mr Birchall
Rates fr: *£17.50*-**£21.00**.
Beds: 1F 2D 2T 2S
Baths: 1 Private 2 Shared
(1) (12)

***The Abbey Inn,** Abbey Green Road, Leek, Staffs, ST13 8SA.*
Pub with converted barn.
Open: All Year
01538 382865 Mrs O'Hagan
Rates fr: *£21.00*-**£27.00**.
Beds: 5D 2S
Baths: 7 Private
(14) (60)

***Warrington House,** 108 Buxton Road, Leek, Staffs, ST13 6EJ.*
For lovers of good food.
Open: All Year
01538 399566 Mr Whone
Rates fr: *£14.00*-**£16.00**.
Beds: 1F 2T
Baths: 1 Shared
(1)

Lichfield

National Grid Ref: SK1109

Little Barrow, Greyhound, Shoulder of Mutton, Pig & Truffle

***Old Rectory Cottage,** 21 Gaia Lane, Lichfield, Staffs, WS13 7LW.*
C18th black/cream beamed cottage.
Open: All Year
01543 254941 Mrs Zavou
Rates fr: *£17.50*-**£22.00**.
Beds: 1D 1T
Baths: 1 Shared
(5) (2)

***Altair House,** 21 Shakespeare Avenue, Lichfield, Staffs, WS14 9BE.*
Comfortable house, near bus/rail stations.
Open: All Year (not Xmas)
01543 252900 Ms Hattersley
Rates fr: *£16.00*-**£16.00**.
Beds: 2T 1S
Baths: 2 Shared
(5) (4)

***20 Beacon Street,** Lichfield, Staffs, WS13 7AD.*
Large elegant Georgian townhouse near Cathedral.
Open: All Year
Grades: ETB Listed, Comm
01543 262338 Mrs Knapman
Rates fr: *£18.00*-**£20.00**.
Beds: 2D 1T 1S
Baths: 2 Ensuite 1 Shared
(4)

***Moat Cottage,** 29 Gaia Lane, Lichfield, Staffs, WS13 7LW.*
Ground-floor accommodation. Fine cathedral views.
Open: All Year (not Xmas)
01543 264591 Mrs Simmonds
Rates fr: *£18.00*-**£22.00**.
Beds: 1T
Baths: 1 Ensuite

Bringing children with you? Always ask for any special rates.

***Park View,** Shaw Lane, Lichfield, Staffs, WS13 7AG.*
Bungalow near cathedral, town, park.
Open: All Year (not Xmas)
01543 256166 Mrs Stokes
Rates fr: *£16.50*-**£22.00**.
Beds: 2T **Baths:** 2 Ensuite
(6)

***Copper's End,** Walsall Road, Muckley Corner, Lichfield, Staffs, WS14 0BG.*
Attractive, comfortable, rural, detached house.
Open: All Year (not Xmas)
01543 372910 Mr Lumb
Rates fr: *£17.50*-**£20.00**.
Beds: 2D 3T 1S
Baths: 1 Private 1 Shared
(8)

***Netherstowe House North,** Netherstowe Lane, Off Eastern Avenue, Lichfield, Staffs, WS13 6AY.*
Grade II Listed Georgian house.
Open: All Year (not Xmas)
01543 254631 Mrs Marshall
Rates fr: *£18.00*-**£16.00**.
Beds: 1F 1T
Baths: 1 Private 1 Shared
(1) (6)

Longdon Green

National Grid Ref: SK0813

***Rookery Field Cottage,** Longdon Green, Rugeley, Staffs, WS13 4QF.*
Large Victorian private country house. **Open:** All Year (not Xmas)
01543 492026 Mr Popp
Rates fr: *£15.00*-**£15.00**.
Beds: 1D 1T **Baths:** 1 Shared
(4)

Longnor

National Grid Ref: SK0864

Black Lion (Butterton)

***Mount Pleasant Farm,** Elkstone, Longnor, Buxton, Derbyshire, SK17 0LU.*
Peaceful farmhouse in idyllic setting. **Open:** Mar to Nov
Grades: ETB 2 Cr, Comm
01538 300380 Mrs Faulkner
Rates fr: *£20.00*-**£26.00**.
Beds: 1D 1T
Baths: 1 Ensuite 1 Private
(6) (4)

Longsdon

National Grid Ref: SJ9655

***Micklea Farm,** Micklea Lane, Longsdon, Stoke on Trent, Staffs, ST9 9QA.*
C17th farmhouse with spacious gardens.
Open: All Year (not Xmas)
Grades: ETB Listed, Comm
01538 385006 Mrs White
Fax no: 01538 382882
Rates fr: *£15.00*-**£15.00**.
Beds: 2D 2S **Baths:** 2 Shared
(4)

Marchington

National Grid Ref: SK1330

***Forest Hills,** Moisty Lane, Marchington, Uttoxeter, Staffs, ST14 8JY.*
Edwardian house, rural, friendly, comfortable.
Open: All Year (not Xmas)
Grades: ETB 2 Cr
01283 820447
Mrs Brassington
Rates fr: *£17.00*-**£19.00**.
Beds: 1D 2T
Baths: 1 Ensuite 2 Shared
(5) (6)

Mayfield

National Grid Ref: SK1545

Royal Oak

***Lichfield Guest House,** Bridgeview, Mayfield, Ashbourne, Derbyshire, DE6 2HN.*
Open: All Year (not Xmas)
Grades: ETB 2 Cr, High Comm, AA 4 Q, Select, RAC High Acclaim
01335 344422 (also fax no)
Mr & Mrs Mellor
Rates fr: *£19.00*-**£20.00**.
Beds: 1F 1D 1T 1S
Baths: 2 Private 2 Shared
(10)
Family-run Georgian house, standing in two acres of grounds on the Derbyshire/Staffordshire border, overlooking the River Dove & valleys beyond. Self-catering cottage available.

Newborough

National Grid Ref: SK1325

***Gospel Oak,** Thorney Lanes, Newborough, Burton-upon-Trent, Staffs, DE13 8RX.*
Beautiful beamed C18th cottage.
Open: All Year (not Xmas)
01283 575588
Mrs Averill
Rates fr: *£15.00*-**£20.00**.
Beds: 1D
Baths: 1 Private
(3)

Newcastle-under-Lyme

National Grid Ref: SJ8546

***Durlston Guest House,** Kimberley Road (off A34), Newcastle-under-Lyme, Staffs, ST5 9EG.*
Large Victorian town house.
Open: All Year (not Xmas)
Grades: ETB 1 Cr, Comm, AA 2 Q
01782 611708 Mr Stott
Rates fr: *£17.00*-**£19.00**.
Beds: 2F 1D 1T 3S
Baths: 2 Shared

layhanger Guest House Hotel, *2 King Street, Newcastle-under-yme, Staffs, ST5 1HX.*
Welcoming restored period town ouse.
Open: All Year
01782 714428 (also fax no)
Mr Tams
Rates fr: *£16.00*-**£17.00**.
Beds: 1F 2D 4S
Baths: 1 Ensuite 1 Shared
(5) (20)

Norbury

National Grid Ref: SJ7823

Bridge Inn

Oulton House Farm, *Norbury, Stafford, Staffs, ST20 0PG.*
Open: All Year
Grades: ETB 2 Cr, High Comm
01785 284264 (also fax no)
Mrs Palmer
Rates fr: *£19.50*-**£19.50**.
Beds: 2D 1T
Baths: 3 Private
(3)
Visit our warm, comfortable Victorian farmhouse with marvellous countryside views, attractive rooms, hearty breakfasts. Ideally situated for Ironbridge, Shrewsbury, Weston Park, Alton Towers & potteries.

Oakamoor

National Grid Ref: SK0544

Talbot Inn

Bank House, *Farley Road, Oakamoor, Stoke on Trent, Staffs, ST10 3BD.*
Luxurious, elegant country home.
Open: All Year
Grades: ETB 2 Cr, High Comm, AA 5 Q, Prem Select
01538 702810 (also fax no)
Mrs Orme
Rates fr: *£25.00*-**£39.00**.
Beds: 2F 1D 1S
Baths: 2 Ensuite 1 Shared
(8)

Ribden Farm, *Oakamoor, Stoke on Trent, Staffs, ST10 3BW.*
Built 1748, set in open country.
Open: All Year (not Xmas)
01538 702830
Mrs Shaw
Rates fr: *£18.00*-**£25.00**.
Beds: 1F 1D 1T
Baths: 3 Private
(6)

Tenement Farm, *Ribden, Oakamoor, Stoke on Trent, Staffs, ST10 3BW.*
Modern guest house, Staffordshire Moorlands.
Open: Easter to November
01538 702333 Ms Miller
Rates fr: *£17.50*-**£25.00**.
Beds: 3F 3T 2D 8S
Baths: 8 Ensuite
(5) (10)

Old Furnace Farm, *Greendale, Oakamoor, Stoke on Trent, Staffs, ST10 3AP.*
Beautiful Victorian farmhouse in superb setting.
Open: All Year
01538 702442 Mrs Wheeler
Rates fr: *£19.00*-**£25.00**.
Beds: 1F 1D 1T
Baths: 3 Private
(4)

Penkridge

National Grid Ref: SJ9213

Bickford Grange, *Bickford, Penkridge, Stafford, ST19 5QJ.*
Large, family-run Georgian country house.
Open: All Year (not Xmas)
01785 840257
Mrs Bryant
Rates fr: *£18.00*-**£18.00**.
Beds: 1F 1D 2T 2S
Baths: 1 Ensuite 1 Private 2 Shared
(10)

Rocester

National Grid Ref: SK1039

The Leeze Guest House, *63 High Street, Rocester, Uttoxeter, Staffs, ST14 5JU.*
Good home-cooking, relaxed atmosphere.
Open: All Year
Grades: ETB 2 Cr
01889 591146 (also fax no)
Mr Venn
Rates fr: *£15.00*-**£17.00**.
Beds: 2F 1D 2T
Baths: 1 Private 2 Shared
(6)

Rudyard

National Grid Ref: SJ9458

Fairboroughs Farm, *Rudyard, Leek, Staffs, ST13 8PR.*
Large peaceful C17th stone farmhouse.
Open: Easter to Nov
01260 226341 Mrs Lowe
Rates fr: *£15.00*-**£15.00**.
Beds: 1F 1D
(4)

Rugeley

National Grid Ref: SK0418

Ash Tree

Parks Farm, *Hawksyard, Armitage Lane, Rugeley, Staffs, WS15 1ED.*
Old comfortable farmhouse, very quiet.
Open: All Year
Grades: ETB 1 Cr, Comm
01889 583477 Mrs Lewis
Rates fr: *£16.00*-**£16.00**.
Beds: 2F 1T
Baths: 2 Private 1 Shared
(8)

The Cedar Tree Hotel, *Main Road, Brereton, Rugeley, Staffs, WS15 1DY.*
Centrally situated, comfortable historic building.
Open: All Year (not Xmas)
01889 584241 Mrs Elderkin
Rates fr: *£22.00*-**£29.00**.
Beds: 1F 10D 10T 9S
Baths: 15 Private 4 Shared

Rushton Spencer

National Grid Ref: SJ5864

Barnswood Farm, *Rushton Spencer, Macclesfield, Cheshire, SK11 0RA.*
Large comfortable farmhouse.
Open: All Year (not Xmas)
01260 226261
Mrs Brown
Rates fr: *£14.00*-**£16.00**.
Beds: 1F 3D

Stanton

National Grid Ref: SK1346

Royal Oak

Ivy Cottage, *Stanton, Ashbourne, Derbyshire, DE6 2BZ.*
Beautiful C17th stone cottage.
Open: All Year
Grades: ETB Listed
01335 324209
Mr Lewis
Rates fr: *£16.50*-**£13.00**.
Beds: 2D
Baths: 1 Ensuite 1 Shared
(3)

Homesclose House, *Stanton, Ashbourne, Derbyshire, DE6 2DA.*
Modern comfortable home magnificent views.
Open: Mar to Nov
Grades: ETB 3 Q
01335 324475
Mrs Tomlinson
Rates fr: *£30.00*-**£18.00**.
Beds: 1F 1D 1S
(Any) (6)

Stafford

National Grid Ref: SJ9223

Sun Inn, Crown Inn

Aviemore Hotel, *4a Lloyd Street, Stafford, ST16 3AS.*
Open: All Year (not Xmas)
Grades: ETB 3 Cr
01785 211986
Mr Sale
Fax no: 01785 226143
Rates fr: *£16.00*-**£18.00**.
Beds: 2F 2D 2T 7S
Baths: 4 Private 3 Shared
(12)
Friendly family-run hotel conveniently situated for visiting Alton Towers, Shugborough Hall, County Show Ground, Wedgewood, Stafford University, etc. Close to M6, Junction 14.

***The Albany Guest House,** 49 Lichfield Road, Stafford, ST17 4LL.*
Comfortable family-run guest house.
Open: All Year (not Xmas)
01785 256285 Mr & Mrs Bradley
Rates fr: *£14.00*-**£14.00**.
Beds: 1F 1D 1T 1S
Baths: 1 Shared
(4)

***Bailey Hotel,** 63 Lichfield Road, Stafford, ST17 4LL.*
Modern detached hotel.
Open: All Year (not Xmas)
Grades: ETB 2 Cr, AA Listed
01785 214133 Mr & Mrs Ayres
Rates fr: *£16.50*-**£17.00**.
Beds: 1F 5D 3T 3S
Baths: 3 Ensuite 2 Shared
(11)

***Park Farm,** Weston Road, Stafford, ST18 0BD.*
Period farmhouse with lovely views.
Open: All Year
01785 240257 Mrs Williams
Rates fr: *£15.00*-**£20.00**.
Beds: 1F 1T **Baths:** 2 Private
(4)

***Furtherhill Guest House,** 55 Lichfield Road, Stafford, ST17 4LL.*
Clean & friendly family home.
Open: All Year (not Xmas)
01785 258723
Mrs Payne
Rates fr: *£14.00*-**£18.00**.
Beds: 2F 2D 2T 1S
Baths: 1 Private 1 Shared
(1) (7)

***Vine Hotel,** Salter Street, Stafford, ST16 2JU.*
Warm, friendly, comfortable hotel.
Open: All Year
01785 244112
Mr Austin
Fax no: 01785 246612
Rates fr: *£21.00*-**£34.50**.
Beds: 1F 11D 3T 11S
Baths: 26 Private 1 Shared
(20)

***Furtherhill Guest House,** 55 Lichfield Road, Stafford, ST17 4LL.*
Large clean comfortable house.
Open: All Year (not Xmas)
01785 58723
Mrs Payne
Rates fr: *£14.00*-**£16.00**.
Beds: 1F 1D 2T 1S
Baths: 1 Ensuite 1 Shared
(1) (6)

***The Abbey Hotel & Windsor,** Suite, 65-69 Lichfield Road, Stafford, ST11 4LW.*
Comfortably furnished, family-run hotel.
Open: All Year (not Xmas)
01785 258531 Mr Rust
Rates fr: *£15.00*-**£18.00**.
Beds: 3F 9D 2T 10S
Baths: 10 Private 3 Shared
(40)

***Leonards Croft Hotel,** 80 Lichfield Road, Stafford, ST17 4LP.*
Large Victorian private house.
Open: All Year (not Xmas)
01785 223676 Mrs Johnson
Rates fr: *£18.00*-**£18.00**.
Beds: 2F 3D 3T 4S
Baths: 4 Ensuite 4 Shared
(12)

Stanshope

National Grid Ref: SK1254

***Stanshope Hall,** Stanshope, Ashbourne, Derbyshire, DE6 2AD.*
Open: All Year (not Xmas)
Grades: ETB 2 Cr, Comm, AA 4 Q, Select
01335 310278 Miss Chambers
Fax no: 01335 310470
Rates fr: *£21.00*-**£21.00**.
Beds: 2D 1T
Baths: 3 Ensuite
(3)
Ensuite accommodation in beautifully furnished, centrally heated C18th hall. Peaceful setting near Dovedale with lovely views. Home cooking with vegetables from our garden. Recommended by The Times and The Independent.

Stoke on Trent

National Grid Ref: SJ8747

Plough, Travellers Rest, Rendezvous

***The Hollies,** Clay Lake, Endon, Stoke on Trent, Staffs, ST9 9DD.*
Spacious comfortable Victorian family home.
Open: All Year (not Xmas)
Grades: ETB 2 Cr, Comm, AA 3 Q
01782 503252 Mrs Hodgson
Rates fr: *£18.00*-**£22.00**.
Beds: 2F 1D 2T
Baths: 4 Ensuite 1 Private
(2) (5)

***The Corrie Guest House,** 13 Newton Street, Basford, Stoke on Trent, Staffs, ST4 6JN.*
Superb Victorian house, privately-run. **Open:** All Year
Grades: ETB 2 Cr
01782 614838 Mr & Mrs Burton
Rates fr: *£17.00*-**£18.00**.
Beds: 2F 2D 2T 2S
Baths: 2 Private 3 Shared
(3) (7)

***White Gables Hotel,** Trentham Road, Blurton, Stoke on Trent, Staffs, ST3 3DT.*
Large 'country house'-style hotel.
Open: All Year
Grades: ETB 2 Cr, AA 3 Q
01782 324882
Mr Worrall
Fax no: 01782 598302
Rates fr: *£17.00*-**£20.00**.
Beds: 2F 2D 4T 1S
Baths: 4 Private 2 Shared
(12)

Stone

National Grid Ref: SJ9034

Granvilles, Butchers

***Couldreys,** 8 Airdale Road, Stone, Staffs, ST15 8DW.*
Victorian house, quiet, residential outskirts.
Open: All Year (not Xmas)
Grades: ETB 2 Cr, Comm
01785 812500
Mrs Couldrey
Fax no: 01785 811761
Rates fr: *£17.00*-**£22.00**.
Beds: 1D 1T
Baths: 1 Ensuite 1 Private
(2)

***Norton Farm,** Eccleshall Road, Stone, Staffs, ST15 0NS.*
Georgian farmhouse.
Open: Easter to
01785 760224
Mrs Brown
Rates fr: *£15.00*-**£20.00**.
Beds: 1F 1D 1T
Baths: 1 Shared
(6)

***Lock House,** 74 Newcastle Road, Stone, Staffs, ST15 8LB.*
Canalside residence, comfortable, friendly accommodation.
Open: All Year
Grades: ETB 2 Cr
01785 814822 / 811551
Mrs Heath
Fax no: 01785 814822
Rates fr: *£18.50*-**£25.00**.
Beds: 2D
Baths: 2 Ensuite
(4)

***The Boat House,** Newcastle Road, Stone, Staffs, ST15 8LD.*
Converted C18th canalside inn.
Open: All Year (not Xmas)
Grades: ETB 2 Cr
01785 815389
Mrs Adams
Rates fr: *£18.50*-**£23.00**.
Beds: 1T
Baths: 1 Private
(2)

Swynnerton

National Grid Ref: SJ8535

Fitzherbert Arms

***Home Farm,** Swynnerton, Stone, Staffs, ST15 0RA.*
Modernised Elizabethan family-run farmhouse.
Open: All Year
Grades: ETB Listed
01782 796241
Mrs Cope
Rates fr: *£15.00*-**£16.00**.
Beds: 2F 2D 3T 2S
Baths: 2 Ensuite 3 Shared
(10)

Tamworth

National Grid Ref: SK2203

The Shrubberies Hotel, *42 Victoria Road, Tamworth, Staffs, B79 7HU.*
Private hotel with Italian restaurant.
Open: All Year
01827 64698 Mrs Morlini
Rates fr: *£17.50*-**£22.00**.
Beds: 2F 3D 4S
Baths: 5 Private 1 Shared
(20)

Trysull

National Grid Ref: SO8594

Park Farm, *Trysull, Wolverhampton, W. Mids, WV5 7HT.*
Old farmhouse in quiet countryside.
Open: All Year
01902 324797 Mrs Baker
Rates fr: *£13.00*-**£14.00**.
Beds: 1F 1D 1T
Baths: 2 Shared
(10)

Tutbury

National Grid Ref: SK2028

Ye Old Dog & Partridge

Robinia House, *21 High Street, Tutbury, Burton-upon-Trent, Staffs, DE13 9LS.*
Very comfortable Victorian private house.
Open: All Year (not Xmas)
01283 814051 Mrs Johnston
Rates fr: *£17.00*-**£17.00**.
Beds: 1F 1D 1T
Baths: 1 Shared
(3)

All rates are subject to alteration at the owners' discretion.

Upper Hulme

National Grid Ref: SK0160

Keekork Lodge Farm, *Upper Hulme, Leek, Staffs, ST13 8UA.*
Secluded, peaceful, comfortable, charming farmhouse.
Open: Easter to Nov
01538 300218
Ms Lomas
Rates fr: *£16.00*-**£20.00**.
Baths: 1 Shared
(2)

Uttoxeter

National Grid Ref: SK0933

Old Royd Guest House, *18-20 Bridge Street, Uttoxeter, Staffs, ST14 8AP.*
Open: All Year
01889 562763
Mrs Butterworth
Rates fr: *£15.00*-**£15.00**.
Beds: 4F 4D 1T 2S
Baths: 3 Ensuite
(14)
A very comfortable family-run guest house offering first class accommodation and excellent food. Ideally situated for the Staffordshire Way & the Peak District.

White Hart Hotel, *Carter Street, Uttoxeter, Staffs, ST14 8EU.*
Charming C16th coaching Inn.
Open: All Year
01889 562437
Mrs McGirr
Fax no: 01889 565099
Rates fr: *£25.50*-**£45.00**.
Beds: 3F 6T 9D 3S
Baths: 21 Ensuite
(40)

West Lodge, *Bramshall, Uttoxeter, Staffs, ST14 5BG.*
Private residence, one acre garden.
Open: All Year
01889 566000
Mr & Mrs Udall
Rates fr: *£15.00*-**£20.00**.
Beds: 1F 1D 1T

Warslow

National Grid Ref: SK0858

Sea Trout

The Greyhound Inn, *Warslow, Buxton, Derbyshire, SK17 0JN.*
Charming old stone coaching inn.
Open: All Year (not Xmas)
Grades: ETB 2 Cr
01298 84249 Mr Mullarkey
Rates fr: *£16.50*-**£22.00**.
Beds: 2D 2S **Baths:** 1 Shared
(10) (30)

Weston

National Grid Ref: SJ9727

Common Farm Motel, *Pasturefields, Weston, Stafford, Staffs, ST18 0RB.*
140-year-old converted barns.
Open: All Year
Grades: ETB Listed
01889 270209 Mrs Pickard
Rates fr: *£14.75*-**£17.50**.
Beds: 3F 5D 2T 4S
Baths: 12 Ensuite 1 Shared
(1) (16)

Whittington

National Grid Ref: SK1608

Hawthorns House, *44a Church Street, Whittington, Lichfield, Staffs, WS14 9JX.*
Large Victorian house, pretty village.
Open: All Year (not Xmas)
01543 432613 Mrs Christie
Rates fr: *£18.00*-**£18.50**.
Beds: 1F 2T 1S **Baths:** 1 Shared

Wrinehill

National Grid Ref: SJ7547

The Hand & Trumpet, *Main Road, Wrinehill, Crewe, Cheshire, CW3 9BJ.*
Rural family-run village inn.
Open: All Year
01270 820048
Rates fr: *£15.00*-**£25.00**.
Beds: 2F 2D 2T **Baths:** 6 Private
(60)

Suffolk

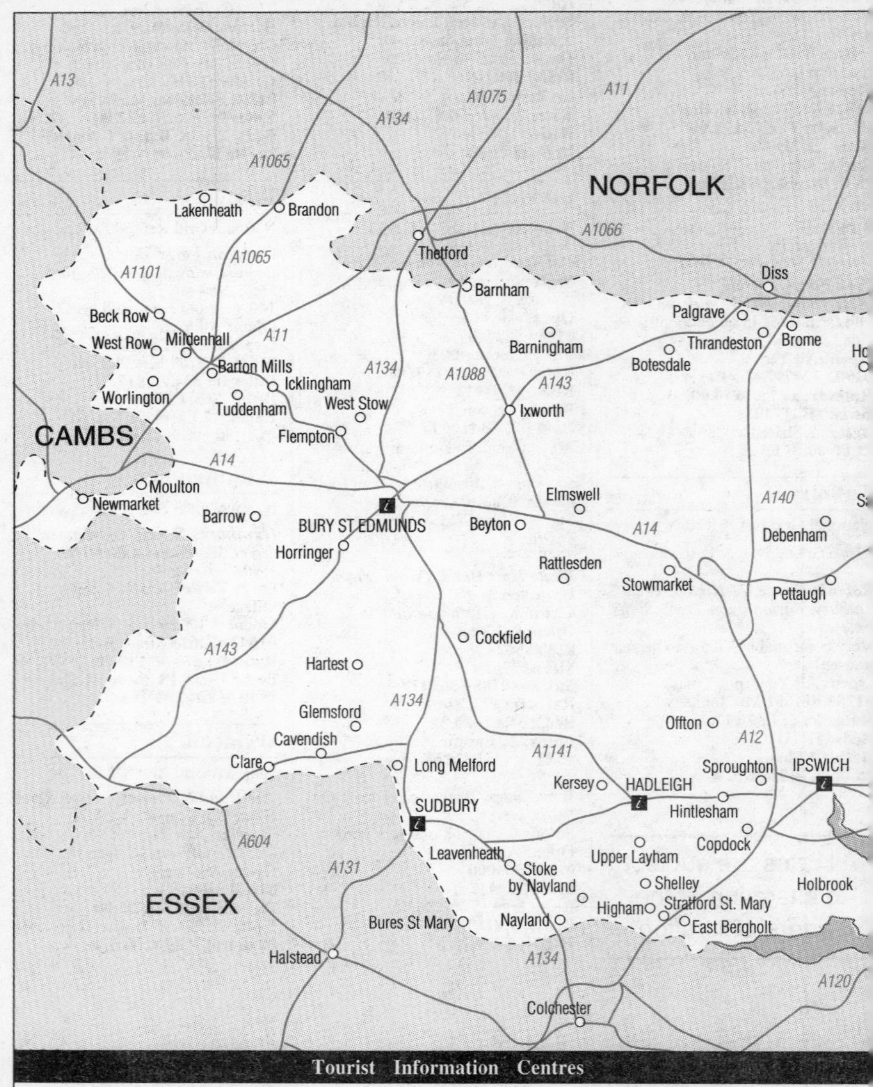

Tourist Information Centres

The Cinema, High Street, **Aldeburgh**, Suffolk, IP15 5AU, 01728 453637, (Easter to Oct).

The Quay, Fen Lane, **Beccles**, Suffolk, NR34 9BH, 01502 713196, (Easter to Oct).

The Athenaeum, Angel Hill, **Bury St Edmunds**, Suffolk, IP33 1LY, 01284 764667.

Leisure Centre, Undercliff Road West, **Felixstowe**, Suffolk, IP11 8AB, 01394 276770.

Toppesfield Hall, **Hadleigh**, Ipswich, Suffolk, IP7 5DN, 01473 823824.

St Stephen's Church, **Ipswich**, St Stephen's Lane. Suffolk, IP1 1DP, 01473 258070.

The Guildhall , Market Place, **Lavenham**, Suffolk, CO10 9QZ, 01787 248207, (Easter to Oct).

The Esplanade, **Lowestoft**, Suffolk, NR33 0QF, 01502 523000 (Easter to Oct).

Town Hall, Market Place, **Southwold**, Suffolk, IP18 6EF, 01502 724729, (Easter to Oct).

Wilkes Way, **Stowmarket**, Suffolk, IP14 1DE, 01449 676800

Town Hall Met Hill, **Sudbury**, Suffolk, CO10 6TL, 01787 881320, (Easter to Oct).

Aldeburgh

National Grid Ref: TM4656

Cross Keys, Mill Inn

Ocean House, *25 Crag Path, Aldeburgh, Suffolk, IP15 5BS.*
Elegant family house, unsurpassed seaviews.
Open: All Year
Grades: ETB Listed
01728 452094 Mr & Mrs Brereton
Rates fr: *£25.00*-**£40.00**.
Beds: 1D 1T
Baths: 2 Ensuite
(2)

Margarets, *50 Victoria Road, Aldeburgh, Suffolk, IP15 5EJ.*
Family-run Victorian guest house.
Open: All Year (not Xmas)
Grades: ETB 1 Cr, Comm
01728 453239 Mrs Testoni
Rates fr: *£16.00*-**£16.00**.
Beds: 4D 2T
Baths: 2 Shared
(10)

Badingham

National Grid Ref: TM3068

White Horse, Queens Head

Colston Hall, *Badingham, Woodbridge, Suffolk, IP13 8LB.*
C16th farmhouse, wonderful setting, quiet.
Open: All Year (not Xmas)
Grades: ETB 2 Cr, Comm
01728 638375 Mrs Bellefontaine
Rates fr: *£20.00*-**£25.00**.
Beds: 1F 1D 1T
Baths: 3 Private
(Many)

Barnham

National Grid Ref: TL8779

Grafton Arms

East Farm, *Barnham, Thetford, Norfolk, IP24 2PB.*
Large, warm, comfortable farm house.
Open: All Year (not Xmas)
Grades: ETB 1 Cr, Comm
01842 890231 Mrs Heading
Rates fr: *£20.00*-**£23.00**.
Beds: 1D 1T
Baths: 2 Ensuite
(4)

Barningham

National Grid Ref: TL9676

College House Farm, *Bardwell Road, Barningham, Bury St Edmunds, Suffolk, IP31 1DF.*
Jacobean country house.
Open: All Year (not Xmas)
01359 221512 Mrs Brightwell
Rates fr: *£22.00*-**£25.00**.
Beds: 2F 2D 1S
Baths: 1 Private 1 Shared
(5) (7)

Barrow

National Grid Ref: TL7663

Horseshoe, Weeping Willow

Apex House, *Barrow, Bury St Edmunds, Suffolk, IP29 5AP.*
Comfortable non-smoking accommodation.
Open: All Year (not Xmas)
Grades: ETB Listed
01284 811493 Mrs Howlett
Rates fr: *£17.00*-**£17.00**.
Beds: 1T 1D 1S **Baths:** 1 Private
(5) (3)

Barton Mills

National Grid Ref: TL7173

Apple Lodge, *Bell Lane, Barton Mills, Mildenhall, Bury St Edmunds, Suffolk, IP28 6AJ.*
Modern, comfortable, traditional village house.
Open: All Year (not Xmas)
01638 717868 Mrs Smith
Rates fr: *£15.00*-**£18.00**.
Beds: 1D **Baths:** 1 Ensuite

Beeches Moat, *The Street, Barton Mills, Mildenhall, Bury St Edmunds, Suffolk, IP28 6AA.*
Quiet country residence.
Open: All Year (not Xmas)
01638 714791 Mrs Smith
Rates fr: *£14.00*-**£18.00**.
Beds: 2D 1T
(3)

Beccles

National Grid Ref: TM4289

Catherine House, *2 Ringsfield Road, Beccles, Suffolk, NR34 9PQ.*
Comfortable family home, excellent facilities. **Open:** All Year
Grades: ETB 2 Cr, Comm
01502 716428 Mrs Renilson
Rates fr: *£16.50*-**£16.50**.
Beds: 1F 1D 1S
Baths: 1 Ensuite 1 Shared
(5)

St Peters House, *Old Market, Beccles, Suffolk, NR34 9AP.*
Converted fisherman's chapel. Gothic style.
Open: All Year
Grades: ETB 1 St, Comm
01502 713203 (also fax no)
Mrs Broome
Rates fr: *£20.00*-**£25.00**.
Beds: 1D 1T 1S
Baths: 1 Shared
(1) (4)

Riverview House, *29 Ballygate, Beccles, Suffolk, NR34 9ND.*
Large Georgian house. Former rectory.
Open: All Year (not Xmas)
01502 713519 Miss Shirley
Rates fr: *£16.50*-**£16.50**.
Beds: 1F 6D 2T 2S
Baths: 4 Private 3 Shared

Beck Row

National Grid Ref: TL6977

Bird in Hand

Fairleigh Guest House, *69 The Street, Beck Row, Mildenhall, Bury St Edmunds, Suffolk, IP28 8DH.*
Private semi-detached house.
Open: All Year
01638 714240 Mr Sheridan
Rates fr: *£15.00*-**£15.00**.
Beds: 1T 4D 1S **Baths:** 6 Ensuite
(20)

Beyton

National Grid Ref: TL8564

White Horse, Gardeners Arms

Manorhouse, *The Green, Beyton, Bury St Edmunds, Suffolk, IP30 9AF.*
C16th farmhouse overlooking village green.
Open: All Year (not Xmas)
Grades: ETB 2 Cr, High Comm, AA 4 Q, Select
01359 270960 Mrs Dewsbury
Rates fr: *£19.00*-**£25.00**.
Beds: 1D 1T 1S **Baths:** 3 Private
(4)

Botesdale

National Grid Ref: TM0475

Virginia Cottage, *The Street, Botesdale, Diss, Norfolk, IP22 1BZ.*
Comfortable, beamed inglenook house & garden.
Open: All Year (not Xmas)
01379 890128 Mrs Webbe
Rates fr: *£16.50*-**£17.50**.
Beds: 1F 1D 1T
Baths: 1 Ensuite 1 Private
(3)

Bramfield

National Grid Ref: TM4073

Queens Head

Broad Oak Farm, *Bramfield, Halesworth, Suffolk, IP19 9AB.*
Carefully modernised C16th farmhouse. Peaceful situation.
Open: All Year
Grades: ETB 2 Cr, Comm, AA 4 Q
01986 784232 Mrs Kemsley
Rates fr: *£15.00*-**£18.00**.
Beds: 1F 1D 1T
Baths: 2 Private 1 Shared

Brandon

National Grid Ref: TL7886

Bridge House Hotel, *79 High Street, Brandon, Suffolk, IP27 0AX.*
Privately owned Victorian riverside hotel. **Open:** All Year
01842 813137 Mrs Gordon
Rates fr: *£25.00*-**£25.00**.
Beds: 1F 1T 1D 1S
Baths: 4 Ensuite
(15)

Bredfield

National Grid Ref: TM2652

Moat Farmhouse, *Dallinghoo Road, Bredfield, Woodbridge, Suffolk, IP13 6BD.*
Converted farm building. Self-contained.
Open: Mar to Oct
Grades: ETB Listed
01473 737475 Mrs Downing
Rates fr: *£15.00*-**£15.00**.
Beds: 1D 1T
Baths: 1 Shared
(1) (4)

Moat Barn, *Bredfield, Woodbridge, Suffolk, IP13 6BD.*
Beautiful converted timbered Suffolk barn.
Open: All Year
01473 737520 Mr Allen
Rates fr: *£15.00*-**£20.00**.
Beds: 1F 1D 1T 1S
Baths: 1 Private 2 Shared
(15)

Brome

National Grid Ref: TM1376

The Chestnuts, *Rectory Road, Brome, Eye, Suffolk, IP23 8AH.*
Peaceful modern luxurious family house.
Open: All Year
01379 870690
Mrs Crouch
Rates fr: *£20.00*-**£20.00**.
Beds: 1T 1S
Baths: 2 Private
(3)

Brundish

National Grid Ref: TM2669

Kings Head

Woodlands Farm, *Brundish, Woodbridge, Suffolk, IP13 8BP.*
Old timber framed farmhouse.
Open: All Year (not Xmas)
Grades: ETB 2 Cr, High Comm, AA 4 Q
01379 384444
Mrs Graham
Rates fr: *£17.00*-**£20.00**.
Beds: 2D 1T
Baths: 2 Ensuite 1 Private
(10) (3)

Bungay

National Grid Ref: TM3389

Hillside House, *Hillside Road West, Bungay, Suffolk, NR35 1PJ.*
Edwardian house in superb gardens.
Open: All Year
01986 893690 Mrs Niblett
Rates fr: *£11.00*-**£12.00**.
Beds: 1F 2D
Baths: 2 Shared
(4)

***Kings Hotel,** Market Place, Bungay, Suffolk, NR35 1AF.*
C16th freehouse in charming market town. **Open:** All Year
01986 893583 Mrs Parker
Rates fr: *£17.50*-**£18.00**.
Beds: 1F 3D 5T 6S
Baths: 9 Private 6 Shared
(20)

Bures St Mary

National Grid Ref: TL9034

***Queens House,** Church Square, Bures St Mary, Suffolk, CO8 5AB.*
C16th country house, licensed restaurant.
Open: All Year (not Xmas)
Grades: ETB 2 Cr
01787 227760 Mrs Gordon
Fax no: 01787 227903
Rates fr: *£20.00*-**£22.00**.
Beds: 1F 2D 2T
Baths: 4 Ensuite 1 Private
(2)

Bury St Edmunds

National Grid Ref: TL8564

***Oak Cottage,** 54 Guildhall Street, Bury St Edmunds, Suffolk, IP33 1QF.*
Listed Tudor cottage - town centre.
Open: All Year
Grades: ETB Listed
01284 762745 Ms Keeley
Rates fr: *£13.00*-**£13.00**.
Beds: 1F 1D 1T 1S
Baths: 1 Ensuite 1 Private 1 Shared

***Hilltop,** 22 Bronyon Close, Bury St Edmunds, Suffolk, IP33 3XB.*
Family home with ground floor bedroom.
Open: All Year (not Xmas)
Grades: ETB Listed
01284 767066 Mrs Hanson
Rates fr: *£16.00*-**£16.00**.
Beds: 1F 1T 1S
Baths: 1 Private 1 Shared
(2)

***The Leys,** 113 Fornham Road, Bury St Edmunds, Suffolk, IP32 6AT.*
Large detached Victorian private house.
Open: All Year
01284 760225 Mrs Lee
Rates fr: *£17.00*-**£20.00**.
Beds: 1F 1D 1T
Baths: 1 Private 1 Shared
(6)

Cavendish

National Grid Ref: TL8046

Bull

***The Red House,** Stour Street, Cavendish, Sudbury, Suffolk, CO10 8BH.*
C16th country home, delightful garden.
Open: All Year (not Xmas)
Grades: ETB 2 Cr, High Comm
01787 280611 Mrs Theaker
Fax no: 01787 280 611
Rates fr: *£21.00*-**£25.00**.
Beds: 2T
Baths: 1 Ensuite 1 Private
(2)

***The Grape Vine,** The Green, Cavendish, Sudbury, Suffolk, CO10 8BB.*
Comfortable C16th house, facing green.
Open: All Year
01787 280423 Mr & Mrs Morley
Rates fr: *£15.00*-**£17.50**.
Beds: 1D 1T **Baths:** 2 Private

Clare

National Grid Ref: TL7645

Swan Inn, Bell Hotel

***Cobwebs,** 26 Nethergate, Clare, Sudbury, Suffolk, CO10 8NP.*
Delightful, welcoming, beamed period cottage.
Open: All Year
01787 277539 Mrs Tuffill
Rates fr: *£18.00*-**£18.00**.
Beds: 2T 1S
Baths: 1 Private 1 Shared
(12)

***Ship Stores,** 22 Callis Street, Clare, Sudbury, Suffolk, CO10 8PX.*
C16th Listed building.
Open: All Year
Grades: ETB 3 Cr, Comm
01787 277834 Mrs Bowles
Rates fr: *£18.50*-**£26.00**.
Beds: 1F 3D 1T
Baths: 5 Private
(3)

Cockfield

National Grid Ref: TL9054

Three Horseshoes

***Craufurd House,** Cockfield, Bury St Edmunds, Suffolk, IP30 0HA.*
Open: Easter to Oct
Grades: ETB 2 Cr
01284 828216 Mr & Mrs Bowen
Rates fr: *£17.50*-**£17.50**.
Beds: 1D
Baths: 1 Private
(2)
Detached country house. Self-contained unit consisting of double bedroom, sitting room & bathroom. Overlooking miles of farmland. Situated 4 miles from historic village of Lavenham & 7 miles Bury St Edmunds.

***Holly Cottage,** Great Green, Cockfield, Bury St Edmunds, Suffolk, IP30 0HQ.*
Period cottage in country area.
Open: All Year (not Xmas)
Grades: ETB Listed, Comm
01284 828682 Mrs Golding
Rates fr: *£15.50*-**£16.00**.
Beds: 2D
Baths: 1 Ensuite 1 Private
(1) (4)

Copdock

National Grid Ref: TM1141

***Westhill,** Elm Lane, Copdock, Ipswich, Suffolk, IP6 3ET.*
Attractive rural Georgian private house.
Open: All Year (not Xmas)
Grades: ETB Listed
01473 730259 (also fax no)
Mrs Winship
Rates fr: *£16.00*-**£17.00**.
Beds: 2T 1S
Baths: 1 Shared
(10) (4)

Cransford

National Grid Ref: TM3164

***High House Farm,** Cransford, Woodbridge, Suffolk, IP13 9PD.*
Beautiful oak-beamed C15th farmhouse.
Open: All Year (not Xmas)
01728 663461 Mrs Kindred
Rates fr: *£17.00*-**£18.00**.
Beds: 1F 1D
Baths: 2 Private
(4)

Dallinghoo

National Grid Ref: TM2655

Three Horseshoes, Castle

***Old Rectory,** Dallinghoo, Woodbridge, Suffolk, IP13 0LA.*
Restful rural retreat, regularly revisited.
Open: All Year (not Xmas)
Grades: ETB Listed, Comm
01473 737700 Mrs Quinlan
Rates fr: *£15.00*.
Beds: 1D 1T
Baths: 1 Private 1 Shared
(6)

Darsham

National Grid Ref: TM4169

***Priory Farm,** Priory Lane, Darsham, Saxmundham, Suffolk, IP17 3QD.*
Comfortable C17th farmhouse ideal for exploring Suffolk.
Open: Easter to Oct
01728 668459 Mrs Bloomfield
Rates fr: *£18.50*-**£20.00**.
Beds: 1D 1T
Baths: 2 Private
(8)

Debenham

National Grid Ref: TM1763

***Kenton Hall,** Debenham, Stowmarket, Suffolk, IP14 6JU.*
Beautiful moated Tudor hall.
Open: All Year (not Xmas)
01728 860279 Mrs McVeigh
Rates fr: *£16.50*-**£19.50**.
Beds: 1F 1D
Baths: 2 Ensuite
(6)

East Bergholt

National Grid Ref: TM0735

Red Lion, Carriers Arms, Kings Head, Hare & Hounds

***Wren Cottage,** The Street, East Bergholt, Colchester, Essex, CO7 6SE.*
C16th cottage in middle of village, easy walk to Flatford.
Open: Easter to Sep
Grades: ETB Listed
01206 298327 Mrs Commercial
Rates fr: *£20.00*-**£22.00**.
Beds: 1F 1T
Baths: 2 Ensuite

Elmswell

National Grid Ref: TL9863

***Kiln Farm Guest House,** Kiln Lane, Elmswell, Bury St Edmunds, Suffolk, IP30 9QR.*
Victorian farmhouse and converted barns.
Open: All Year
Grades: ETB 2 Cr, Comm
01359 240442 Mr & Mrs Knights
Rates fr: *£16.00*-**£18.00**.
Beds: 1F 1D 1T 1S
Baths: 4 Private
(10)

Felixstowe

National Grid Ref: TM3034

***Elm House,** 32 Undercliff Road West, Felixstowe, Suffolk, IP11 8AJ.*
Detached, friendly, small guest house.
Open: All Year (not Xmas)
01394 282292 Mrs Nelmes
Rates fr: *£13.00*-**£13.00**.
Beds: 1D 1T 1S
Baths: 1 Shared
(3)

***The Norfolk Hotel,** Holland Road, Felixstowe, Suffolk, IP11 8BA.*
Comfortable friendly Christian hotel.
Open: Easter to October
Grades: ETB 1 Cr
01394 283160
Rates fr: *£15.00*-**£15.00**.
Beds: 1F 3D 3T 3S
Baths: 2 Shared
(5)

Flempton

National Grid Ref: TL8169

***School House,** Flempton, Bury St Edmunds, Suffolk, IP28 6EG.*
Converted Victorian school & house.
Open: All Year
01284 728792 Mrs Lindsay
Rates fr: *£11.50*-**£12.00**.
Beds: 1F 1T
(6)

Framlingham

National Grid Ref: TM2863

Queen's Head, Crown

***Shimmens Pightle,** Dennington Road, Framlingham, Woodbridge, Suffolk, IP13 9JT.*
Open: All Year (not Xmas)
Grades: ETB Listed, Comm
01728 724036 Mrs Collett
Rates fr: *£18.00*-**£20.00**.
Beds: 1F 1D 1T
Baths: 1 Shared
(6) (5)
Comfortable family home set in an acre of landscaped garden, overlooking fields. Ground floor rooms with wash basins. Local cured bacon & home preserves.

***Boundary Farm,** Off Saxmundham Road, Framlingham, Woodbridge, Suffolk, IP13 9NU.*
C17th farmhouse,open countryside.
Open: All Year
Grades: ETB 1 Cr, Comm
01728 723401
Mrs Cook
Rates fr: *£16.00*-**£20.00**.
Beds: 2D 1T
Baths: 1 Private 2 Shared
(8)

Fressingfield

National Grid Ref: TM2677

***Elm Lodge,** Chippenhall Green, Fressingfield, Eye, Suffolk, IP21 5SL.*
Victorian farmhouse on working farm.
Open: Easter to Oct
Grades: ETB 2 Cr, Comm, AA 3 Q
01379 586249 Mrs Webster
Rates fr: *£15.00*-**£15.00**.
Beds: 1D 1T
Baths: 1 Shared
(10) (4)

Glemsford

National Grid Ref: TL8248

***Mill Hill Cottage,** Plum Street, Glemsford, Sudbury, Suffolk, CO10 7PU.*
Peaceful C17th cottage, home cooking.
Open: All Year
01787 280721 Miss Cundy
Rates fr: *£19.50*-**£19.50**.
Beds: 1T
Baths: 1 Private
(6)

Bringing children with you? Always ask for any special rates.

Grundisburgh

National Grid Ref: TM2250

The Dog Pub

***Hawthorn Cottage,** Lower Road, Grundisburgh, Woodbridge, Suffolk, IP13 6UQ.*
Superb detached barn conversion (one third to Oxfam).
Open: All Year
01473 738199 Mrs Hutchison
Rates fr: *£16.00*-**£16.00**.
Beds: 1D 1T
Baths: 1 Private
(5)

Hacheston

National Grid Ref: TM3059

White Horse

***Cherry Tree House,** Hacheston, Woodbridge, Suffolk, IP13 0DR.*
Large C17th farmhouse, large garden. **Open:** All Year
01728 746371 Mrs Hall
Rates fr: *£15.00*-**£16.00**.
Beds: 1F 1T 2S
Baths: 2 Shared
(3)

Hadleigh

National Grid Ref: TM0242

Marquis of Cornwallis

***Spider Hall,** Lower Raydon, Shelley, Hadleigh, Ipswich, Suffolk, IP7 5QN.*
Lovely Grade II Listed C15th farmhouse.
Open: All Year (not Xmas)
Grades: ETB Listed
01473 822585 Mrs Pyman
Fax no: 01473 824820
Rates fr: *£18.00*-**£18.00**.
Beds: 1D 1T **Baths:** 1 Shared
(6)

***Howells,** 93 Angel Street, Hadleigh, Ipswich, Suffolk, IP7 5EY.*
Friendly, welcoming, comfortable private home.
Open: All Year
01473 828117 Mrs Howell
Rates fr: *£15.00*-**£18.00**.
Beds: 1D **Baths:** 1 Private
(1)

Halesworth

National Grid Ref: TM3877

Queens Head

***Broad Oak Farm,** Bramfield, Halesworth, Suffolk, IP19 9AB.*
Carefully modernised C16th farmhouse. Peaceful situation.
Open: All Year
Grades: ETB 2 Cr, Comm, AA 4 Q
01986 784232 Mrs Kemsley
Rates fr: *£15.00*-**£18.00**.
Beds: 1F 1D 1T
Baths: 2 Private 1 Shared

Fen Way, *School Lane, Halesworth, Suffolk, IP19 8BW.*
Bungalow set in peaceful meadowland.
Open: All Year
01986 873574 Mrs George
Rates fr: *£14.00*-**£16.00**.
Beds: 2D 1T
Baths: 1 Shared
(8) (5)

Hartest

National Grid Ref: TL8352

Crown

Pear Tree Farm, *Brockley Road, Hartest, Bury St Edmunds, Suffolk, IP29 4EG.*
Open: Easter to Nov
Grades: ETB 2 Cr, Comm
01284 830217 Mrs White
Rates fr: *£19.00*-**£22.00**.
Beds: 1D 1T
Baths: 2 Ensuite
(10)
Warm welcome in excellent accommodation. All rooms ensuite. TV, coffee/tea facilities. Ideally situated for exploring Lavenham, Bury St Edmunds, Long Melford for antiques, 'Constable Country'.

Giffords Hall, *Hartest, Bury St Edmunds, Suffolk, IP29 4EX.*
Spacious Georgian farmhouse with vineyard.
Open: All Year (not Xmas)
01284 830464 Mr Kemp
Rates fr: *£17.00*-**£21.00**.
Beds: 1D 2T
Baths: 3 Private

Higham

National Grid Ref: TM0335

The Bauble, *Higham, Colchester, Essex, CO7 6LA.*
Peaceful old country home.
Open: All Year
Grades: ETB 2 Cr, High Comm, AA 4 Q, Recomm
01206 337254 Mrs Watkins
Fax no: 01206 337263
Rates fr: *£20.00*-**£22.00**.
Beds: 2T 1S
Baths: 3 Ensuite
(12) (5)

Hintlesham

National Grid Ref: TM0843

The Bell

Birch Farm, *Hintlesham, Ipswich, Suffolk, IP8 3NJ.*
Picturesque, quiet country farmhouse.
Open: All Year
Grades: ETB 2 Cr
01473 652249 Mrs Bryce
Rates fr: *£17.50*-**£20.00**.
Beds: 2D 1S
Baths: 2 Ensuite
(2)

College Farm, *Hintlesham, Ipswich, Suffolk, IP8 3NT.*
C15th beamed farmhouse in Idyllic surroundings.
Open: Mid-Jan to mid-Dec
Grades: ETB 2 Cr, High Comm
01473 652253 (also fax no)
Mrs Bryce
Rates fr: *£17.50*-**£17.00**.
Beds: 1F 1D 1S 1T
Baths: 1 Private 1 Shared
(10) (6)

Holbrook

National Grid Ref: TM1636

Compasses

Highfield, *Harkstead Road, Holbrook, Ipswich, Suffolk, IP9 2RA.*
Friendly quiet country house.
Open: All Year (not Xmas)
Grades: ETB 2 Cr, High Comm
01473 328250 Mr & Mrs Morris
Rates fr: *£17.50*-**£27.00**.
Beds: 3D
Baths: 2 Private 1 Shared
(4)

Holton

National Grid Ref: TM4077

Gavelcroft, *Harrisons Lane, Holton, Halesworth, Suffolk, IP19 8LY.*
Listed C16th farmhouse in tranquil surroundings.
Open: All Year (not Xmas)
01986 873117 Mrs Hart
Rates fr: *£18.00*-**£22.00**.
Beds: 1F 1T
Baths: 2 Private
(8)

Horham

National Grid Ref: TM2072

Queens Head (Stradbroke)

Thick Thorn Farm, *Horham, Eye, Suffolk, IP21 5ER.*
Comfortable part-Tudor farmhouse.
Open: All Year (not Xmas)
01379 384005 Mrs Cudmore
Rates fr: *£15.00*-**£17.00**.
Beds: 1T 2S
Baths: 1 Private 1 Shared
(10) (3)

Horringer

National Grid Ref: TL8261

Beehive, Six Bells

12 The Elms, *Horringer, Bury St Edmunds, Suffolk, IP29 5SE.*
Modern, comfortable, friendly private house.
Open: All Year
01284 735400 Ms Pemberton
Rates fr: *£15.00*-**£18.00**.
Beds: 1D 1T 1S

Icklingham

National Grid Ref: TL7772

Weatherhill Farm, *Icklingham, Bury St Edmunds, Suffolk, IP28 6PP.*
C18th farmhouse on working arable farm.
Open: All Year
01284 728839 Mr Browning
Rates fr: *£12.50*-**£12.50**.
Beds: 1F 1T 2S
Baths: 2 Shared
(8)

Ilketshall St Margaret

National Grid Ref: TM3585

Tally Ho

Shoo-Devil Farmhouse, *Ilketshall St Margaret, Bungay, Suffolk, NR35 1QU.*
Comfortable, secluded thatched C16th farmhouse.
Open: Easter to Oct
Grades: ETB 2 Cr, Comm
01986 781303 Mrs Lewis
Rates fr: *£16.50*-**£18.50**.
Beds: 1D 1T **Baths:** 2 Ensuite
(6)

Ipswich

National Grid Ref: TM1644

Westerfield Swan, Greyhound, Ram

107 Hatfield Road, *Ipswich, Suffolk, IP3 9AG.*
Large Victorian guest house, modern facilities. **Open:** All Year
01473 723172 Mrs Debenham
Fax no: 01473 270876
Rates fr: *£14.00*-**£15.00**.
Beds: 1D 2T
Baths: 1 Private 2 Shared

Frenchs Farm, *Ipswich, Suffolk, IP7 5PQ.*
Large Victorian Private farmhouse.
Open: All Year **Grades:** ETB 2 Cr
01473 824215 Mrs Stringer
Rates fr: *£19.00*-**£20.00**.
Beds: 2F 4D 1T 1S
Baths: 1 Private
(30)

Craigerne, *Cauldwell Avenue, Ipswich, Suffolk, IP4 4DZ.*
Tastefully restored Victorian, gardens, parking.
Open: All Year (not Xmas)
01473 718200 Mrs Krotunas
Rates fr: *£15.00*-**£15.00**.
Beds: 1D 1T 3S
Baths: 3 Ensuite 1 Shared
(10)

Maple House, *114 Westerfield Road, Ipswich, Suffolk, IP4 2XW.*
Attractive private house near park.
Open: All Year (not Xmas)
01473 253797 Mrs Seal
Rates fr: *£11.00*-**£15.00**.
Beds: 1D 1S **Baths:** 1 Shared
(3)

***Orwell View,** 24 Vermont Road, Ipswich, Suffolk, IP4 2SR.*
Peaceful, close to centre, easy parking.
Open: All Year (not Xmas)
01473 211451 Mrs Carroll
Rates fr: *£12.50*-**£12.50**.
Beds: 1T 1S
Baths: 1 Shared
(4)

Ixworth

National Grid Ref: TL9270

Pykerell

***Robert Peel House,** Ixworth, Bury St Edmunds, Suffolk, IP31 2HH.*
Comfortable, converted Victorian police station.
Open: All Year (not Xmas)
01359 230555
Mr Dew
Fax no: 01359 232553
Rates fr: *£15.75*-**£17.50**.
Beds: 1F 6T
Baths: 3 Ensuite 2 Shared
(6) (6)

Kersey

National Grid Ref: TM0044

***Red House Farm,** Kersey, Ipswich, Suffolk, IP7 6EY.*
Comfortable farmhouse (c.1840).
Open: All Year
01787 210245
Mrs Alleston
Rates fr: *£18.00*-**£20.00**.
Beds: 1D 1T
Baths: 1 Private 1 Shared
(4)

Kessingland

National Grid Ref: TM5286

***The Old Rectory,** 157 Church Road, Kessingland, Lowestoft, Suffolk, NR33 7SQ.*
Beautiful, secluded, late-Georgian house.
Open: Easter to Sep
01502 740020 Mr Halton
Rates fr: *£20.00*-**£22.00**.
Beds: 2D 1T
Baths: 2 Private 1 Shared
(8) (6)

Lakenheath

National Grid Ref: TL7182

Bell Inn

***Bell Inn,** 20 High Street, Lakenheath, Brandon, Suffolk, IP27 9DS.*
Old coaching house.
Open: All Year
01842 860308
Rates fr: *£10.00*-**£15.00**.
Beds: 3F 2T 3D 1S
Baths: 2 Shared
(20)

Leavenheath

National Grid Ref: TL9536

***Leavenheath Farm,** Locks Lane, Leavenheath, Colchester, Essex, CO6 4PF.*
Open: All Year (not Xmas)
Grades: ETB Listed, High Comm
01206 262322 Mrs Warren Thomas
Rates fr: *£18.00*-**£20.00**.
Beds: 1F 1D 2T 1S
Baths: 3 Ensuite 1 Private
(4) (8)
Welcoming period farmhouse, in quiet setting within its own 30 acre orchards with pony & pedigree sheep. Located in 'Constable Country', convenient for Sudbury, Colchester, Lavenham & 40 minutes drive from ports of Felixstowe & Harwich.

Levington

National Grid Ref: TM2339

Ship Inn

***Redhouse,** Bridge Road, Levington, Ipswich, Suffolk, IP10 0LZ.*
Edge of tiny village, magnificent views. **Open:** Easter to Nov
Grades: ETB Listed, Approv
01473 659670 Mrs Matthews
Rates fr: *£17.00*-**£17.00**.
Beds: 2F 2T **Baths:** 1 Shared
(0) (5)

Long Melford

National Grid Ref: TL8645

The Bull

***High Street Farm House,** Long Melford, Sudbury, Suffolk, CO10 9BD.*
Partly beamed, comfortable old farmhouse.
Open: All Year (not Xmas)
Grades: ETB Listed
01787 375765 Mrs Westlake
Rates fr: *£17.50*-**£17.50**.
Beds: 2T **Baths:** 1 Private 1 Shared
(10) (4)

***Holly Cottage,** 3 Borley Road, Long Melford, Sudbury, Suffolk, CO10 9HH.*
Comfortable C18th country cottage.
Open: All Year
01787 379848 Mrs Dixon
Rates fr: *£15.00*-**£16.00**.
Beds: 1F 1T **Baths:** 2 Private
(3)

Lowestoft

National Grid Ref: TM5292

***Acorn Guest House,** 336 London Rd South, Lowestoft, Suffolk, NR33 0BG.*
Friendly family-run guest house.
Open: All Year
01502 513332 (also fax no)
Mrs Matthews
Rates fr: *£17.00*-**£17.00**.
Beds: 1F 1D 1T 2S
Baths: 2 Shared
(2)

***Coventry Guest House,** 8 Kirkley Cliff, Lowestoft, Suffolk, NR33 0BY.*
Large seafront Victorian private house.
Open: All Year (not Xmas)
01502 573865 Mrs Alden
Rates fr: *£15.00*-**£17.00**.
Beds: 2F 2D 1T 2S
Baths: 3 Private 1 Shared

***Fairways Guest House,** 398 London Road South, Lowestoft, Suffolk, NR33 0BQ.*
Welcoming comfortable guest house.
Open: All Year (not Xmas)
Grades: ETB 2 Cr, Comm, AA 2 Q
01502 572659 Mrs Montali
Rates fr: *£16.00*-**£17.00**.
Beds: 2F 2D 1T 2S
Baths: 4 Ensuite 2 Shared

***Somerton Hotel,** Kirkley Cliff, Lowestoft, Suffolk, NR33 0BY.*
Large Victorian seafront house.
Open: All Year (not Xmas)
Grades: ETB 3 Cr, Comm, AA 3 Q
01502 565665 Mr Crocker
Fax no: 01502 501176
Rates fr: *£18.00*-**£25.00**.
Beds: 3F 5D 3T 3S
Baths: 4 Private 1 Shared
(0)

Mendham

National Grid Ref: TM2782

***Weston House Farm,** Mendham, Harleston, Norfolk, IP20 0PB.*
C17th Grade II Listed farmhouse.
Open: Mar to Nov
Grades: ETB 2 Cr, AA 3 Q, Recomm
01986 782206
Mrs Holden
Rates fr: *£17.00*-**£19.50**.
Beds: 1F 2T
Baths: 3 Ensuite
(6)

Middleton

National Grid Ref: TM4367

Middleton Bell

***Rose Villa,** The Street, Middleton, Saxmundham, Suffolk, IP17 3NJ.*
Private house, close to Minsmere.
Open: All Year
01728 648489 Mrs Crowden
Rates fr: *£15.00*-**£13.00**.
Beds: 1D 1T
Baths: 1 Shared
(3)

The lowest **single** *rate is shown in* **bold.**

Mildenhall

National Grid Ref:TL7074

White Hart Hotel, *21 High Street, Mildenhall, Bury St Edmunds, Suffolk, IP28 7EA.*
Home-cooked food by home-loving people.
Open: All Year
01638 713894 Mr Moore
Rates fr: *£20.00*-**£30.00**.
Beds: 1F 3D 2T 5S
Baths: 11 Ensuite
(1) (20)

Moulton

National Grid Ref: TL6964

Handsell House, *The Street, Moulton, Newmarket, Suffolk, CB8 8RZ.*
Attractively unique & artistic home.
Open: All Year (not Xmas)
01638 751803 Mrs Perry
Rates fr: *£18.50*-**£18.50**.
Beds: 1D 1T 2S
Baths: 2 Shared
(14) (4)

Flint End House, *6 The Street, Moulton, Newmarket, Suffolk, CB8 8RZ.*
Comfortable Victorian private house.
Open: All Year (not Xmas)
01638 750966 Mrs Bolus
Rates fr: *£18.50*-**£18.50**.
Beds: 1D 1S
Baths: 1 Private
(2)

Mutford

National Grid Ref: TM4888

Ash Farm, *Dairy Lane, Mutford, Beccles, Suffolk, NR34 7QJ.*
C16th farmhouse, quiet countryside. **Open:** All Year
01502 476892 Mrs Warnes
Rates fr: *£15.00*-**£20.00**.
Beds: 1F
Baths: 1 Private 1 Shared
(4)

Nayland

National Grid Ref: TL9734

White Hart, Angel

Gladwins Farm, *Harpers Hill, Nayland, Colchester, Essex, CO6 4NU.*
Open: All Year (not Xmas)
01206 262261 Mrs Dossor
Fax no: 01206 263001
Rates fr: *£25.00*-**£20.00**.
Beds: 1F 1D 1T 1S
Baths: 2 Private 1 Shared
Suffolk farmhouse with self-catering cottages in 22 acres 'Constable Country'. Beautiful views, trout lake, tennis court, heated indoor pool. Colour brochure from resident owners.

Hill House, *Gravel Hill, Nayland, Colchester, Essex, CO6 4JB.*
C16th village hall house.
Open: All Year (not Xmas)
Grades: ETB Listed, Comm, AA 3 Q
01206 262782 Mrs Heigham
Rates fr: *£19.00*-**£20.00**.
Beds: 1D 1T 1S
Baths: 1 Ensuite 1 Shared
(10) (3)

Newmarket

National Grid Ref: TL6463

Westley House, *Westley Waterless, Newmarket, Suffolk, CB8 0RQ.*
Spacious Georgian-style former rectory.
Open: All Year
Grades: ETB Listed
01638 508112 Mrs Galpin
Rates fr: *£20.00*-**£20.00**.
Beds: 2T 2S
Baths: 1 Private 1 Shared
(5) (6)

Falmouth House, *Falmouth Avenue, Newmarket, Suffolk, CB8 0NB.*
Large, comfortable, modern, detached house.
Open: All Year (not Xmas)
01638 660409 Mrs Shaw
Rates fr: *£18.00*-**£24.00**.
Beds: 1D 2T
Baths: 1 Shared
(10) (6)

Derby House, *27 Exeter Road, Newmarket, Suffolk, CB8 8LL.*
Large Victorian villa, sympathetically restored.
Open: All Year (not Xmas)
01638 662887 Mr & Mrs Kay
Rates fr: *£17.50*-**£22.50**.
Beds: 1F 3T 1D
Baths: 2 Shared
(12)

Offton

National Grid Ref: TM0649

Mount Plesant Farm, *Offton, Ipswich, Suffolk, IP8 4RP.*
Secluded, comfortable C16th farmhouse.
Open: All Year
01473 658896 Mrs Redman
Rates fr: *£14.00*-**£18.00**.
Beds: 2D 1T
Baths: 3 Private
(10)

Palgrave

National Grid Ref: TM1178

3 The Paddocks, *Palgrave, Diss, Norfolk, IP22 1AG.*
Comfortable, friendly in pretty village.
Open: All Year (not Xmas)
01379 642098 Mrs Jones
Rates fr: *£15.00*-**£14.00**.
Beds: 1F 1D 1T 1S
Baths: 1 Private 1 Shared
(6)

Pettaugh

National Grid Ref: TM1659

Doberman, Bell

Old Rectory, *Pettaugh, Stowmarket, Suffolk, IP14 6DR.*
Superb house, swimming pool (one third to Oxfam).
Open: All Year
01473 890615 Mrs Underhill
Rates fr: *£17.00*-**£17.00**.
Beds: 1D 1T 1S
Baths: 2 Private
(3)

Rattlesden

National Grid Ref: TL9759

Brewers Arms

Barkers Farm, *Brettenham Road, Rattlesden, Bury St Edmunds, Suffolk, IP30 0ST.*
Secluded C16th farmhouse, two acres. **Open:** All Year
Grades: ETB Listed
01449 736257 Ms Wright
Rates fr: *£17.00*-**£18.00**.
Beds: 1D 1T **Baths:** 1 Shared
(3)

Saxmundham

National Grid Ref: TM3863

White Hart

White Hart Hotel, *High Street, Saxmundham, Suffolk, IP17 1DD.*
Family-run comfortable inn.
Open: All Year (not Xmas)
01728 602009 Mr Banks
Rates fr: *£18.50*-**£18.50**.
Beds: 2F 2D 1T 1S
Baths: 2 Shared
(40)

Saxstead

National Grid Ref: TM2664

Bantry, *Chapel Road, Saxstead, Woodbridge, Suffolk, IP13 9RB.*
Open: All Year
01728 685578 Mrs Jones
Rates fr: *£19.00*-**£25.00**.
Beds: 2D 1T
Baths: 3 Ensuite
(4)
Purpose-built comfortable self-contained private ensuite apartments, separate from house. Each with own dining room/lounge. Open countryside, near historic Framlingham & Heritage Coast.

National Grid References are for villages, towns and cities - *not* for individual houses.

Shelley

National Grid Ref: TM0338

Marquis of Cornwallis

Spider Hall, *Lower Raydon, Shelley, Ipswich, Suffolk, IP7 5QN.*
Lovely Grade II Listed C15th farmhouse.
Open: All Year (not Xmas)
Grades: ETB Listed
01473 822585 Mrs Pyman
Fax no: 01473 824820
Rates fr: *£18.00*-**£18.00**.
Beds: 1D 1T
Baths: 1 Shared
(6)

Sibton

National Grid Ref: TM3669

Sibton White Horse

Sibton White Horse, *Halesworth Road, Sibton, Saxmundham, Suffolk, IP17 2JJ.*
C16th inn with large secluded grounds.
Open: All Year
Grades: ETB Listed
01728 660337 Mr Waddingham
Rates fr: *£16.00*-**£19.00**.
Beds: 3D 3T 3S
Baths: 7 Ensuite 2 Private
(60)

Snape

National Grid Ref: TM3959

Golden Key, Crown

Flemings Lodge, *Gromford Lane, Snape, Saxmundham, Suffolk, IP17 1RG.*
Modern bungalow, overlooking open farmland.
Open: All Year (not Xmas)
Grades: ETB Listed, Comm
01728 688502
Mrs Edwards
Rates fr: *£17.00*-**£25.00**.
Beds: 1D 1T
Baths: 1 Shared
(3)

Southwold

National Grid Ref: TM5076

Lord Nelson, Sutherland Restaurant, Hamiltons Restaurant

Saxon House, *86 Pier Avenue, Southwold, Suffolk, IP18 6BL.*
Comfortable family-run guest-house.
Open: All Year (not Xmas)
Grades: ETB 2 Cr, Comm
01502 723651
Mr & Mrs Whiting
Rates fr: *£22.00*-**£25.00**.
Beds: 1F 4D 2T
Baths: 6 Ensuite 1 Private
(1) (6)

Northcliffe Guesthouse, *20 North Parade, Southwold, Suffolk, IP18 6LT.*
Charming Victorian terrace - overlooking beach.
Open: All Year
01502 724074
Mrs Henshaw
Rates fr: *£20.00*-**£22.00**.
Beds: 5D 1T 2S
Baths: 6 Ensuite 2 Shared

Shanklin House, *6 Chester Road, Southwold, Suffolk, IP18 6LN.*
Victorian town house. Recently converted.
Open: All Year (not Xmas)
01502 724748 Mr & Mrs Ratcliff
Rates fr: *£20.00*-**£25.00**.
Beds: 1F 1D 1T
Baths: 3 Ensuite

20 North Parade, *Southwold, Suffolk, IP18 6LT.*
Comfortable seafront guest house.
Open: All Year (not Xmas)
01502 724074 Mrs Henshaw
Rates fr: *£20.00*-**£20.00**.
Beds: 2F 6D 2T 3S
Baths: 3 Private 3 Shared

Acton Lodge, *18 South Green, Southwold, Suffolk, IP18 6HB.*
Magnificent Victorian house with turret.
Open: All Year
Grades: ETB Listed
01502 723217 Ms Smith
Rates fr: *£22.00*-**£22.00**.
Beds: 1F 1D 1T 1S
Baths: 2 Private 2 Shared
(6) (3)

Sproughton

National Grid Ref: TM1244

Finjaro Guest House, *Valley Farm Drive, Hadleigh Road, Sproughton, Ipswich, Suffolk, IP8 3EL.*
Set in quiet countryside, home cooking.
Open: All Year (not Xmas)
01473 652581 Mrs Finbow
Rates fr: *£15.00*-**£17.00**.
Beds: 2D 2S
Baths: 2 Shared
(5) (8)

Stoke by Nayland

National Grid Ref: TL9836

Black Horse, Angel Inn

Ryegate House, *Stoke by Nayland, Colchester, Essex, CO6 4RA.*
Cheerful house in village setting.
Open: All Year (not Xmas)
Grades: ETB 2 Cr, High Comm
01206 263679 Mr & Mrs Geater
Rates fr: *£17.00*-**£23.00**.
Beds: 2D 1T
Baths: 3 Ensuite
(10) (5)

Thorington Hall, *Stoke by Nayland, Colchester, Essex, CO6 4SS.*
Beautiful C17th house, warm welcome.
Open: Easter to Oct
Grades: ETB Listed, Approv
01206 337329 Mrs Wollaston
Rates fr: *£20.00*-**£17.50**.
Beds: 1F 2D 1T 1S
Baths: 3 Private 1 Shared
(4)

Stowmarket

National Grid Ref: TM0558

Cherry Tree Farm, *Mendlesham Green, Stowmarket, Suffolk, IP14 5RQ.*
Superb atmosphere in tranquil setting.
Open: All Year (not Xmas)
Grades: ETB 2 Cr, High Comm
01449 766376 Mr Ridsdale
Rates fr: *£21.00*.
Beds: 3D
Baths: 3 Private
(3)

Stratford St Mary

National Grid Ref: TM0434

Marlborough Head, Sun Hotel, Swan, Black Horse

Teazles, *Stratford St Mary, Colchester, Essex, CO7 6LU.*
Comfortable old merchant weavers' house.
Open: All Year
01206 323148 Mrs Clover
Rates fr: *£18.00*-**£18.00**.
Beds: 1F 1D 1T 1S
Baths: 1 Ensuite 1 Shared

Sudbourne

National Grid Ref: TM4153

Long Meadow, *Gorse Lane, Sudbourne, Woodbridge, Suffolk, IP12 2BD.*
Quiet traditonal bungalow, show garden.
Open: All Year (not Xmas)
01394 450269 Mrs Wood
Rates fr: *£14.00*-**£14.00**.
Beds: 1D 1T 1S
Baths: 1 Private 1 Shared
(12) (4)

Sudbury

National Grid Ref: TL8741

The Old Bull & Trivets, *Church Street, Ballingdon, Sudbury, Suffolk, CO10 6BL.*
C16th beamed hotel.
Open: All Year
01787 374120 Mr Taylor
Rates fr: *£18.00*-**£20.00**.
Beds: 4F 3D 1T 1S
Baths: 7 Private 2 Shared

Thrandeston

National Grid Ref: TM1176

The Swan, Black Bull, Cornwall Arms, Scole Inn

***Abbey Farm,** Great Green, Thrandeston, Diss, Norfolk, IP21 4BN.*
Elizabethan farmhouse, peaceful secluded setting.
Open: All Year **Grades:** ETB 2 Cr
01379 783422 Mrs Carlisle
Rates fr: *£20.00*-**£20.00**.
Beds: 1D 1T 1S
Baths: 1 Ensuite 1 Shared
(4)

Tuddenham

National Grid Ref: TL7371

White Hart

***Oakdene,** Higham Road, Tuddenham, Bury St Edmunds, Suffolk, IP28 6SG.*
Very comfortable home from home.
Open: All Year (not Xmas)
Grades: ETB Listed
01638 718822 Mrs Titcombe
Rates fr: *£16.50*-**£18.50**.
Beds: 2F 1T
Baths: 1 Ensuite 1 Shared
(3)

Tunstall

National Grid Ref: TM3655

***Lucerne,** Mill Lane, Tunstall, Woodbridge, Suffolk, IP12 2JR.*
Quiet location (one third to Oxfam). **Open:** All Year
01728 688429 Mr Read
Rates fr: *£12.00*-**£12.00**.
Beds: 1D 1T **Baths:** 1 Shared
(2)

Uggeshall

National Grid Ref: TM4480

Plough Inn

***Pears Old Barn,** Stoven Road, Uggeshall, Beccles, Suffolk, NR34 8EW.*
Converted barn, landscaped garden.
Open: Easter to Oct
01502 578423 Mr & Mrs Bartlett
Rates fr: *£18.00*-**£18.00**.
Beds: 1D 1T **Baths:** 1 Shared
(5) (8)

Upper Layham

National Grid Ref: TM0340

Marquis Of Cornwallis

***Marquis Of Cornwallis,** Upper Layham, Ipswich, Suffolk, IP7 5JZ.*
Heavily beamed old country inn.
Open: All Year
01473 822051 Mr Abbott
Rates fr: *£19.50*-**£27.00**.
Beds: 3D
Baths: 1 Private
(22)

West Row

National Grid Ref: TL6775

Judes Ferry

***Airview Guest House,** 34 Beeches Road, West Row, Mildenhall, Bury St Edmunds, Suffolk, IP28 8NY.*
Excellent views of aerial activity.
Open: All Year (not Xmas)
01638 715502 Mr & Mrs Hitt
Rates fr: *£12.50*-**£15.00**.
Beds: 2F 2T 1S
Baths: 1 Ensuite 3 Shared
(7)

West Stow

National Grid Ref: TL8564

***Eastleigh,** West Stow, Bury St Edmunds, Suffolk, IP28 6EZ.*
Cottage in village. Homely welcome. **Open:** All Year
01284 728264 Mrs Cooke
Rates fr: *£13.00*-**£13.00**.
Beds: 1D 1S **Baths:** 1 Shared

Westleton

National Grid Ref: TM4469

White Horse, Crown, Monets Restaurant

***Barn Cottage,** Mill Street, Westleton, Saxmundham, Suffolk, IP17 3BD.*
Interesting cottage home, residents' lounge. Close RSPB Minsmere.
Open: All Year (not Xmas)
01728 648437 Mr & Mrs Allen
Rates fr: *£17.00*-**£17.00**.
Beds: 1D 2T **Baths:** 2 Shared
(3)

High season, bank holidays and special events mean low availability *anywhere.*

Woodbridge

National Grid Ref: TM2649

Crown, Cherry Tree

***19 Saxon Way, Bury Hill,** Woodbridge, Suffolk, IP12 1LG.*
Wooded location (one third to Oxfam).
Open: All Year
01394 387931
Mrs Mummery
Rates fr: *£15.00*-**£15.00**.
Beds: 1T
Baths: 1 Private
(2)

***Fen House,** Fen Walk, Woodbridge, Suffolk, IP12 4BG.*
Comfortable house (one third to Oxfam) in quiet location.
Open: All Year
01394 387343
Mrs Thubron
Rates fr: *£16.00*-**£15.00**.
Beds: 1T 1S
Baths: 1 Shared
(4)

Worlington

National Grid Ref: TL6973

Walnut Tree

***The Old Forge,** Newmarket Road, Worlington, Bury St Edmunds, Suffolk, IP28 8RZ.*
Charming C18th country cottage.
Open: All Year
01638 718014
Mrs Wilson
Rates fr: *£17.50*-**£25.00**.
Beds: 1D 1T
Baths: 1 Shared
(2)

Surrey

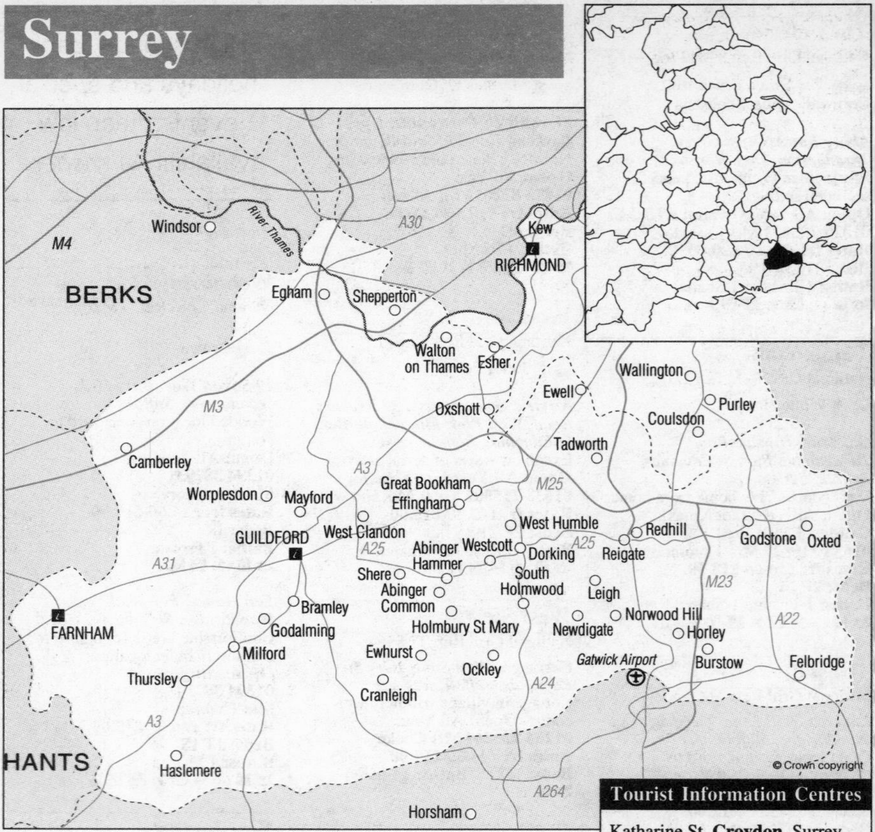

Tourist Information Centres

Katharine St, **Croydon**, Surrey , CR9 1ET, 0181 253 1009 (Easter to Oct).

Vernon House, 28 West Street, **Farnham**, Surrey, GU9 7BR, 01252-715109.

14 Tunsgate, **Guildford**, Surrey, GU1 3QT, 01483 444333.

Old Town Hall, Whittaker Avenue, **Richmond**, Surrey, TW 91TP, 0181-940 9125.

Abinger Common

National Grid Ref: TQ1145

Stephan Langton

Leylands Farm, *Sheephouse Lane, Abinger Common, Dorking, Surrey, RH56JU.*
Self-contained annexe of period farmhouse
Open: All Year (not Xmas)
Grades: ETB Listed, High Comm
01306 730115 Mrs Eshelby
Fax no: 01306 881287
Rates fr: *£20.00*-**£35.00**.
Beds: 2F **Baths:** 1 Ensuite
(4)

Abinger Hammer

National Grid Ref: TQ0947

Wootton Hatch

Crossways Farm, *Raikes Lane, Abinger Hammer, Dorking, Surrey, RH5 6PZ.*
Listed C17th farmhouse.
Open: Mar to Nov
01306 730173 Mrs Hughes
Rates fr: *£17.00*-**£21.00**.
Beds: 1F 1D 1T
Baths: 1 Private 1 Shared
(3)

Bramley

National Grid Ref: TQ0044

Beevers Farm, *Chinthurst Lane, Bramley, Guildford, Surrey, GU5 0DR*
Modern comfortable farmhouse.
Open: Easter to Nov
01483 898764 Mr Cook
Rates fr: *£14.00*-**£20.00**.
Beds: 1F 2T
Baths: 1 Private 1 Shared
(10)

Burstow

National Grid Ref: TQ3041

Burstow Park, *Antlands Lane, Burstow, Horley, Surrey, RH6 9TF.*
Converted farmhouse, now family home. **Open:** All Year
01293 785936 Mrs Puttock
Fax no: 01293 774694
Rates fr: *£18.00*-**£18.00**.
Beds: 2T 1S
Baths: 1 Shared
(10)

Camberley

National Grid Ref: SU8860

Toby One Oak, Royal Standard

Loganberry Lodge, *6 Mytchett Road, Camberley, Surrey, GU14 6EZ.*
Next door to homely, local pub.
Open: All Year (not Xmas)
Grades: ETB Listed, Approv
01252 544603 Mrs Wiltshire
Rates fr: *£15.00*-**£20.00**.
Beds: 1D 1T 1S
Baths: 1 Private
(3)

***Youlden Lodge,** 12 Youlden Drive, Camberley, Surrey, GU15 1AL.*
Spacious Tudor-style private house.
Open: All Year
01276 61793 Mrs Bennie
Rates fr: *£17.50*-**£18.00**.
Beds: 1D 1T 2S
Baths: 2 Shared
(5)

***Railway Corner,** 1 James Road, Camberley, Surrey, GU15 2RG.*
Near Windsor, Thorpe Park, Wentworth & Sunningdale Golf Course.
Open: All Year (not Xmas)
01276 65880 Mrs Toone
Fax no: 01276 685063
Rates fr: *£17.50*-**£17.50**.
Beds: 1D 1T 1S **Baths:** 1 Shared
(5)

***11 Holly Avenue,** Camberley, Surrey, GU16 5QX.*
Comfortable well-appointed private house.
Open: All Year (not Xmas)
01276 25406 Mrs Holland
Rates fr: *£17.50*-**£17.50**.
Beds: 1D 1T
Baths: 2 Private 1 Shared
(6)

Coulsdon

National Grid Ref: TQ3058

***512 Chipstead Valley Road,** Coulsdon, Surrey, CR5 2BN.*
Modern, homely, comfortable.
Open: All Year (not Xmas)
01737 553155 Mrs Bateman
Rates fr: *£17.50*-**£17.00**.
Beds: 1D 1S **Baths:** 1 Shared

Cranleigh

National Grid Ref: TQ0638

Wheatsheaf

***Dalkeith,** Horsham Road, Cranleigh, Surrey, GU6 8DW.*
Guest's Comments: Unbeatable, Gold Star.
Open: All Year
01483 272730 (also fax no)
Mrs Addison
Rates fr: *£20.00*-**£25.00**.
Beds: 2D 1T
Baths: 1 Shared
(6)

Croydon

National Grid Ref: TQ3364

Black Horse (Addiscombe)

***Iverna,** 1 Annandale Road, Croydon, Surrey, CR0 7HP.*
Large house in quiet road.
Open: All Year (not Xmas)
0181 654 8639 Mrs Able
Rates fr: *£20.00*-**£20.00**.
Beds: 1T 3S
Baths: 1 Shared
(1)

Dorking

National Grid Ref: TQ1649

King William, The Bush

***Shrub Hill,** 3 Calvert Road, Dorking, Surrey, RH4 1LT.*
Convenient, comfortable, quiet family home.
Open: All Year (not Xmas)
01306 885229 Mrs Scott Kerr
Rates fr: *£17.50*-**£18.00**.
Beds: 1T 1S 1D
Baths: 1 Shared
(5) (2)

***The Waltons,** 5 Rose Hill, Dorking, Surrey, RH4 2EG.*
Listed Victorian house, conservation area.
Open: All Year
Grades: ETB Listed
01306 883127 Mrs Walton
Rates fr: *£15.00*-**£17.50**.
Beds: 2F 1D 1T
(3)

***Highbank,** 1 Townfield Road, Dorking, Surrey, RH4 2HX.*
Family home - central - lovely views.
Open: All Year
01306 888135 Mrs Paul
Rates fr: *£17.50*-**£17.50**.
Beds: 1T 1S
Baths: 1 Private 1 Shared

***Torridon Guest House,** Longfield Road, Dorking, Surrey, RH4 3DF.*
Large chalet bungalow - quiet location.
Open: All Year
Grades: ETB Listed
01306 883724 Mrs Short
Fax no: 01306 880759
Rates fr: *£17.50*-**£20.00**.
Beds: 1D 1T 1S
Baths: 1 Shared
(2)

Effingham

National Grid Ref: TQ1153

Plough, Sir Douglas

***Chalklands,** Beech Avenue, Effingham, Surrey, KT24 5PJ.*
Large, detached house overlooking golf course.
Open: All Year (not Xmas)
01372 454936 Mrs Reilly
Rates fr: *£20.00*-**£25.00**.
Beds: 1F 1D 1T
Baths: 2 Ensuite 1 Private
(8)

***Crosslands Guest House,** Guildford Road, Effingham, Surrey, KT24 5PE.*
Large ex-pub. C13th & C16th.
Open: All Year (not Xmas)
01372 453479 Mrs Gifford
Rates fr: *£17.00*-**£17.00**.
Beds: 1F 5T 1S
Baths: 1 Private

Egham

National Grid Ref: TQ0071

***The Old Parsonage,** 2 Parsonage Road, Englefield Green, Egham, Surrey, TW20 0JW.*
Georgian parsonage, old-fashioned gardens.
Open: All Year (not Xmas)
01784 436706 (also fax no)
Mr & Mrs Clark
Rates fr: *£25.00*-**£25.00**.
Beds: 1F 1D 1T 1S
Baths: 1 Ensuite 1 Private 1 Shared
(3)

***Beau Villa,** 44 Grange Road, Egham, Surrey, TW20 9QP.*
Friendly, clean, comfortable family house.
Open: All Year (not Xmas)
01784 435115 Mrs Wilding
Rates fr: *£17.00*-**£20.00**.
Beds: 1D 1S
Baths: 1 Ensuite
(14) (4)

Esher

National Grid Ref: TQ1565

Swan Inn (Claygate)

***Lilac Cottage,** 14 Greenways, Hinchley Wood, Esher, Surrey, KT10 0QD.*
Luxury friendly family home.
Open: All Year (not Xmas)
0181 398 7546 (also fax no)
Mrs Evans
Rates fr: *£20.00*-**£25.00**.
Beds: 1T
Baths: 1 Ensuite
(2)

Ewell

National Grid Ref: TQ2162

***Tuum,** Epsom Road, Ewell, Epsom, Surrey, KT17 1LJ.*
Comfortable house with own parking.
Open: All Year
0181 393 1682 Mrs Rosa
Rates fr: *£12.50*-**£15.00**.
Beds: 1F 4T
Baths: 2 Shared
(7)

Ewhurst

National Grid Ref: TQ0940

Scarlett Arms

***High Edser,** Shere Road, Ewhurst, Cranleigh, Surrey, GU6 7PQ.*
C16th family home.
Open: All Year (not Xmas)
Grades: ETB Listed, Comm
01483 278214
Mrs Franklin-Adams
Rates fr: *£20.00*-**£22.00**.
Beds: 2D 1T
Baths: 1 Shared
(6)

Malricks, *The Street, Ewhurst, Cranleigh, Surrey, GU6 7RH.*
Modern centrally-heated detached house. **Open:** All Year
01483 277575 Mrs Budgen
Rates fr: *£16.50*-**£16.50**.
Beds: 1F 1T
Baths: 1 Private 2 Shared
(3)

Yard Farm, *North Breache Road, Ewhurst, Cranleigh, Surrey, GU6 7SN.*
Comfortable farmhouse.
Open: All Year (not Xmas)
01483 276649 (also fax no)
Mrs Nutting
Rates fr: *£20.00*-**£20.00**.
Beds: 1D 2T 1S
Baths: 2 Ensuite 1 Shared
(12) (6)

Farnham

National Grid Ref: SU8446

Bat & Ball, Prince of Wales, Anchor, Hare & Hound

Heathfield, *44 Sandrock Hill Road, Farnham, Surrey, GU10 4RJ.*
Comfortable large Victorian private house.
Open: All Year (not Xmas)
Grades: ETB 1 Cr, Comm
01252 793200 Mrs Graham Smith
Fax no: 01252 793000
Rates fr: *£16.50*-**£17.50**.
Beds: 1T 1S **Baths:** 1 Shared
(2)

High Wray / Audubon House, *73 Lodge Hill Road, Farnham, Surrey, GU10 3RB.*
Family home with wing for disabled. **Open:** All Year (not Xmas)
Grades: ETB Listed, Comm
01252 715589 Mrs Crawford
Rates fr: *£20.00*-**£16.00**.
Beds: 1D 3T 2S
Baths: 1 Private 3 Shared
(6)

Pittersfield, *Hole Lane, Bentley, Farnham, Surrey, GU10 5LT.*
Delightful village house in rural setting. **Open:** All Year
Grades: ETB Listed, High Comm
01420 22414 Mrs Coulton
Rates fr: *£20.00*-**£20.00**.
Beds: 1D 2T
Baths: 2 Private 1 Shared
(3)

The Croft, *2 Trebor Avenue, Farnham, Surrey, GU9 8JH.*
Large comfortable 'home from home'. **Open:** All Year
01252 715054 Mr Rose
Fax no: 01252 715391
Rates fr: *£20.00*-**£20.00**.
Beds: 1T 2S
Baths: 1 Private 1 Shared
(3)

Orchard House, *13 Applelands Close, Farnham, Surrey, GU10 4TL.*
Peaceful, homely, countryside views.
Open: All Year (not Xmas)
01252 793813 Mrs Warburton
Rates fr: *£17.50*-**£17.50**.
Beds: 1T 1S
Baths: 1 Shared
(3)

Hawkridge, *20 Upper Old Park Road, Farnham, Surrey, GU9 0AT.*
Large family house.
Open: All Year
01252 722068 Mr & Mrs Ackland
Rates fr: *£17.50*-**£17.50**.
Beds: 1D 1T 1S **Baths:** 1 Shared

Felbridge

National Grid Ref: TQ3639

Toads Croak House, *30 Copthorne Road, Felbridge, East Grinstead, West Sussex, RH19 2NS.*
Quiet, beautiful house, gardens. Non-smoking.
Open: All Year
01342 328524
Rates fr: *£16.50*-**£17.00**.
Beds: 1F 1T 1D 1S
Baths: 2 Ensuite 1 Shared
(7)

Gatwick

National Grid Ref: TQ2843

Foreseters, Six Bells

Melville Lodge Guest House, *15 Brighton Road, Gatwick, Horley, Surrey, RH6 7HH.*
Open: All Year
Grades: ETB 2 Cr, Approv, RAC Listed
01293 784951 Mrs Brooks
Fax no: 01293 785669
Rates fr: *£17.50*-**£20.00**.
Beds: 1F 3D 2T 1S
Baths: 3 Ensuite 2 Shared
(1)
Family-run Edwardian guest house. Gatwick Airport 5 miles drive. Courtesy transport by arrangement. Restaurant, pubs, London & Brighton train walking distance. French spoken. Ground floor room.

Rosemead Guest House, *19 Church Road, Gatwick, Horley, Surrey, RH6 7EY.*
Small guest house, convenient Gatwick.
Open: All Year (not Xmas)
Grades: ETB Listed, Comm, AA 2 Q, Recomm
01293 784965 / 430546 Mr Wood
Fax no: 01293 430547
Rates fr: *£17.50*-**£23.00**.
Beds: 1F 2D 1T 2S
Baths: 2 Private 2 Shared
(8)

Godalming

National Grid Ref: SU9643

Meads Hotel, *65 Meadrow, Godalming, Surrey, GU7 3HS.*
Charming elegant & comfortable hotel.
Open: All Year
Grades: ETB Listed, AA Listed
01483 421800 Mr Smith
Rates fr: *£21.00*-**£26.00**.
Beds: 3F 4D 3T 5S
Baths: 6 Private 3 Shared

Rosemary Cottage, *Guildford Road, Godalming, Surrey, GU7 3BU.*
Pretty Victorian cottage. Semi-rural.
Open: All Year (not Xmas)
01483 421083 Mrs Smith
Rates fr: *£18.00*-**£25.00**.
Beds: 1T 1D 1S
Baths: 1 Ensuite 1 Private 1 Shared
(4)

Godstone

National Grid Ref: TQ3551

Godstone Hotel, *The Green, Godstone, Surrey, RH9 8DT.*
C16th coaching house, original timbers, inglenook fireplaces.
Open: All Year
01883 742461 Mr Howe
Rates fr: *£22.50*-**£32.00**.
Beds: 1F 5D 2T
Baths: 8 Private

Great Bookham

National Grid Ref: TQ1354

The Lodge, *2 Park Green, Great Bookham, Leatherhead, Surrey, KT23 3NL.*
Quiet location, easy parking.
Open: All Year (not Xmas)
01372 459642 Mrs Dawson
Rates fr: *£16.00*-**£16.00**.
Beds: 1D 1T
Baths: 1 Shared

Guildford

National Grid Ref: SU9949

Kings Head, Jolly Farmer

Atkinsons Guest House, *129 Stoke Road, Guildford, Surrey, GU1 1ET.*
Open: All Year
01483 38260
Mrs Atkinson
Rates fr: *£17.50*-**£20.00**.
Beds: 1F 1D 1T 1S
Baths: 2 Ensuite 1 Shared
(6) (2)
Small comfortable family-run guest house close to town centre & all local amenities. All rooms with colour TV, hairdriers etc. Some ensuites available.

Weybrook House, *113 Stoke Road, Guildford, Surrey, GU1 1ET.*
Quiet & friendly atmosphere.
Open: All Year (not Xmas)
01483 302394
Mr & Mrs Bourne
Rates fr: *£14.00*-**£18.00**.
Beds: 1F 1D 1S
Baths: 2 Shared
(2)

Westbury Cottage, *Waterden Road, Guildford, Surrey, GU1 2AN.*
Cottage-style house in large secluded garden,
Open: All Year (not Xmas)
Grades: ETB Listed
01483 822602
Mrs Smythe
Rates fr: *£20.00*-**£22.00**.
Beds: 1D 2T
Baths: 1 Shared
(12) (3)

Greyfriars, *Castle Hill, Guildford, Surrey, GU1 3SY.*
Large Victorian private house in conservation area.
Open: All Year
01483 61795 Mr Parsons
Rates fr: *£15.00*-**£15.00**.
Beds: 1F 1D 2T 2S
Baths: 3 Shared
(0) (4)

Haslemere

National Grid Ref: SU8932

Wheatsheaf Inn

Town House, *High Street, Haslemere, Surrey, GU27 2JY.*
Elegant historic Listed Georgian house.
Open: Feb to Dec
Grades: ETB Listed, High Comm
01428 643310
Mrs Smyrk
Fax no: 01428 641080
Rates fr: *£19.00*-**£25.00**.
Beds: 2D 1T
Baths: 3 Private
(4) (3)

Quoins, *Museum Hill, Haslemere, Surrey, GU27 2JR.*
Elegant, comfortable Edwardian home.
Open: All Year
01428 658540
Mrs Bell
Rates fr: *£18.00*-**£20.00**.
Beds: 1D 1T **Baths:** 2 Private
(3)

Holmbury St Mary

National Grid Ref: TQ1144

Royal Oak, Parrot Inn

Woodhill Cottage, *Holmbury St Mary, Dorking, Surrey, RH5 6NL.*
Comfortable country family home.
Open: All Year
01306 730498
Mrs McCann
Rates fr: *£17.00*-**£20.00**.
Beds: 1F 1D 1T
Baths: 1 Ensuite 2 Shared
(3)

Bulmer Farm, *Holmbury St Mary, Dorking, Surrey, RH5 6LG.*
Quiet modernised C17th farmhouse/barn.
Open: All Year
Grades: ETB 2 Cr, Comm
01306 730210 Mrs Hill
Rates fr: *£18.00*-**£19.00**.
Beds: 3D 5T
Baths: 5 Private 2 Shared
(12) (12)

Horley

National Grid Ref: TQ2843

Air Balloon, Six Old Bell

Oakdene Guest House, *32 Massetts Road, Horley, Surrey, RH6 7DS.*
Large Victorian guest house.
Open: All Year (not Xmas)
01293 772047 Mr Ali
Fax no: 01293 771586
Rates fr: *£16.00*-**£20.00**.
Beds: 1F 1D 1T 3S
Baths: 3 Shared
(10)

Chalet Guest House, *77 Massetts Road, Horley, Surrey, RH6 7EB.*
Modern. Close town - Gatwick Airport.
Open: All Year (not Xmas)
Grades: ETB 2 Cr, Comm, AA 3 Q, RAC Acclaim
01293 821666 Mr Shortland
Fax no: 01293 821619
Rates fr: *£22.00*-**£26.00**.
Beds: 1F 1D 1T 4S
Baths: 5 Private 1 Shared
(12)

Yew Tree, *31 Massetts Road, Horley, Surrey, RH6 7DQ.*
Tudor-style house, 0.5 acre garden.
Open: All Year
01293 785855 Mr Stroud
Rates fr: *£15.00*-**£15.00**.
Beds: 1F 2D 1T 2S
Baths: 2 Shared
(1) (10)

Prinsted Guest House, *Oldfield Road, Horley, Surrey, RH6 7EP.*
Large Victorian private house.
Open: All Year (not Xmas)
Grades: ETB Listed
01293 785233 Mrs Kendall
Rates fr: *£17.50*-**£30.00**.
Beds: 1F 2D 2T 2S
Baths: 4 Ensuite

Felcourt Guest House, *79 Massetts Road, Horley, Surrey, RH6 7EB.*
Airport 3 minutes, close to town.
Open: All Year
Grades: ETB Listed
01293 78265101293 776255
Mr Ahmed
Fax no: 01293 782651
Rates fr: *£15.00*-**£18.00**.
Beds: 3F 4D 2T 2S
Baths: 4 Private 3 Shared
(12)

The Corner House, *72 Massetts Road, Horley, Surrey, RH6 7ED.*
Quality accommodation, Gatwick 5 minutes.
Open: All Year
Grades: ETB 2 Cr
01293 784574 Mrs Smith
Rates fr: *£18.00*-**£23.00**.
Beds: 3F 3D 2T 5S
Baths: 4 Private 3 Shared
(30)

Copperwood Guest House, *Massetts Road, Horley, Surrey, RH6 7DJ.*
Gatwick Airport 5 minutes.
Open: All Year
Grades: ETB 2 Q, Comm, AA 3 Q
01293 783388 Mrs Hooks
Fax no: 01293 420156
Rates fr: *£17.00*-**£23.00**.
Beds: 1F 1D 1T 2S
Baths: 1 Private 2 Shared
(5)

Rawbones House, *Norwood Hill, Horley, Surrey, RH6 0ET.*
Elegant C20th parkland country house.
Open: All Year (not Xmas)
01293 862087 Mrs Grant
Fax no: 01293 862396
Rates fr: *£19.00*-**£22.00**.
Beds: 1D 2S
Baths: 1 Private
(10)

Kew

National Grid Ref: TQ1977

Coach & Horses

1 Chelwood Gardens, *Kew, Richmond, Surrey, TW9 4JG.*
Large Edwardian, friendly family house.
Open: All Year
0181 876 8733 Mrs Gray
Rates fr: *£20.00*-**£20.00**.
Beds: 2T 2S
Baths: 2 Shared
(5) (8)

179 Mortlake Road, *Kew, Richmond, Surrey, TW9 4AW.*
Large Georgian private house.
Open: All Year
0181 876 0584 Mrs Butt
Rates fr: *£20.00*.
Beds: 1T
Baths: 1 Private
(2)

8 Taylor Avenue, *Kew, Richmond, Surrey, TW9 4ED.*
Spacious, modernised period family home.
Open: All Year (not Xmas)
0181 876 3930 Mrs Allen
Rates fr: *£20.00*-**£20.00**.
Beds: 1T 1S **Baths:** 1 Private
(2)

Leatherhead

National Grid Ref: TQ1656

20 Melvinshaw, *Leatherhead, Surrey, KT22 8SX.*
Clean, comfortable family house.
Open: All Year
01372 373786 Mrs Pearce
Rates fr: *£17.50*-**£17.50**.
Beds: 1T 1S
Baths: 1 Shared

Leigh

National Grid Ref: TQ2246

Barn Cottage, *Church Road, Leigh, Reigate, Surrey, RH2 8RF.*
Converted C17th barn, beautiful gardens. **Open:** All Year
Grades: ETB Listed
01306 611347 Mrs Comer
Rates fr: *£22.00*-**£25.00**.
Beds: 1D 1T **Baths:** 2 Shared
(3)

Mayford

National Grid Ref: SU9956

Mayford Arms

East House, *Beech Hill, Mayford, Woking, Surrey, GU22 0SB.*
Quiet, traditional, restful family house.
Open: All Year
01483 763218 Dr Moss
Rates fr: *£15.00*-**£18.00**.
Beds: 2T
Baths: 1 Shared
(2)

Milford

National Grid Ref: SU9442

Coturnix House, *Rake Lane, Milford, Godalming, Surrey, GU8 5AB.*
Modern house,friendly family atmosphere. **Open:** All Year
01483 416897 Mrs Bell
Rates fr: *£17.00*-**£17.00**.
Beds: 1D 2T
Baths: 1 Private 1 Shared
(1) (6)

Newdigate

National Grid Ref: TQ1942

Surrey Oaks, Six Bells

Sturtwood Farm, *Partridge Lane, Newdigate, Dorking, Surrey, RH5 5EE.*
Comfortable, friendly farmhouse.
Open: All Year (not Xmas)
Grades: ETB 2 Cr, Comm
01306 631308 Mrs MacKinnon
Fax no: 01306 631908
Rates fr: *£17.50*-**£20.00**.
Beds: 1T 1S 1D
Baths: 1 Ensuite 1 Shared
(10)

Norwood Hill

National Grid Ref: TQ2443

Fox Revived

Latchetts Cottage, *Ricketts Wood Road, Norwood Hill, Horley, Surrey, RH6 0ET.*
Cosy country cottage.
Open: All Year (not Xmas)
Grades: ETB Listed
01293 862831 Mrs Lees
Rates fr: *£18.50*-**£20.00**.
Beds: 2D 1S **Baths:** 1 Shared
(5)

Ockley

National Grid Ref: TQ1440

Hazels, *Walliswood, Ockley, Dorking, Surrey, RH5 5PL.*
Private, secluded & off the 'beaten track'. **Open:** All Year
01306 627228 Mrs Floud
Rates fr: *£17.50*-**£20.00**.
Beds: 1D **Baths:** 1 Ensuite
(2)

Oxshott

National Grid Ref: TQ1460

Apple Tree Cottage, *Oakshade Road, Oxshott, Leatherhead, Surrey, KT22 0LF.*
Quietly located cottage, modernised accommodation.
Open: All Year (not Xmas)
Grades: ETB Listed
01372 842087 Mrs Crowhurst
Fax no: 01372 842101
Rates fr: *£27.50*-**£49.50**.
Beds: 1D 1T 1S **Baths:** 1 Shared
(3)

Oxted

National Grid Ref: TQ3852

Royal Oak, George

Old Forge House, *Merle Common, Oxted, Surrey, RH8 0JB.*
Comfortable home in rural surroundings.
Open: All Year (not Xmas)
01883 715969 Mrs Mills
Rates fr: *£16.00*-**£18.00**.
Beds: 1D 1T 1S **Baths:** 1 Shared
(3)

Pinehurst Grange Guest House, *East Hill (Part of A25), Oxted, Surrey, RH8 9AE.*
Comfortable, homely, refurbished, Victorian ex-farmhouse.
Open: All Year (not Xmas/New Year)
01883 716413 Mr Rodgers
Rates fr: *£19.50*-**£24.00**.
Beds: 1D 1T 1S **Baths:** 1 Shared
(5) (3)

The Croft, *Quarry Road, Oxted, Surrey, RH8 9HE.*
Substantial Edwardian house - peaceful location. **Open:** All Year
01883 713605 Mrs Todd
Rates fr: *£19.50*-**£21.00**.
Beds: 1F 1T 1D **Baths:** 1 Shared
(5) (8)

Purley

National Grid Ref: TQ3161

Foxley Hatchet

51 Selcroft Road, *Purley, London, CR8 1AJ.*
Within walking distance to a station.
Open: Jan to Nov
0181 660 3054 (also fax no)
Mr Stock
Rates fr: *£20.00*-**£20.00**.
Beds: 1D 1S 1T
Baths: 1 Private 1 Shared
(3)

The Nook, *12 Grasmere Road, Purley, Surrey, CR8 1DU.*
Edwardian private house.
Open: All Year (not Xmas)
0181 660 1742 Mrs Andrews
Rates fr: *£16.00*-**£15.00**.
Beds: 1D 2S **Baths:** 1 Shared

Redhill

National Grid Ref: TQ2750

Home Cottage

Arun Lodge Guest House, *37 Redstone Hill, Redhill, Surrey, RH1 4AW.*
Open: All Year
Grades: ETB Listed
01737 761933 (also fax no)
Ms Metcalfe
Rates fr: *£22.00*-**£26.00**.
Beds: 1F 1D 1T 1S
Baths: 2 Ensuite 1 Shared
(8)
Beautifully decorated Edwardian house, set just 2 minutes walk Redhill centre. Close to station, open countryside, local walks, quaint villages. All facilities & warm welcome.

Lynwood Guest House, *50 London Road, Redhill, Surrey, RH1 1LN.*
Large Victorian modernised house.
Open: All Year **Grades:** AA 3 Q
01737 766894 Mrs Rao
Rates fr: *£18.00*-**£23.00**.
Beds: 4F 1D 2T 2S
Baths: 3 Ensuite 1 Shared
(7)

Reigate

National Grid Ref: TQ2649

Norfolk Lodge Hotel, *23-25 London Road, Reigate, Surrey, RH2 9PY.*
Very comfortable, licensed family hotel. **Open:** All Year
01737 248702 Mr Bowley
Rates fr: *£15.00*-**£24.00**.
Beds: 3F 2D 5T 6S
Baths: 2 Shared
(50)

Richmond

National Grid Ref: TQ1874

4 Church Road, *Richmond, Surrey, TW9 2QA.*
Open: All Year
0181 948 5852 Mrs Bird
Rates fr: *£23.00*-**£36.00**.
Beds: 2F
Baths: 2 Ensuite
Bright, spacious, all ensuite rooms in comfortable Victorian house. Two minutes' walk from Underground & station. Family of 3 - £56, of 4 - £66. Handy for Kew Gardens, Hampton Court, etc.

'36 Sheen Road, *Richmond, urrey,* *TW9 1UR.*
ìreat value, great service.
)pen: All Year (not Xmas)
·181 948 5608 Mrs Bates
Rates fr: *£17.50*-**£25.00**.
Beds: 2T **Baths:** 3 Shared
(11)

Shepperton

National Grid Ref: TQ0767

The Harrow

)ld Manor House, *Squires Bridge Road, Littleton, Shepperton, Middx,* *TW17 0QG.*
Historic house dating from Henry VII's reign. **Open:** All Year
·1932 571293 Mrs Bouwens
Rates fr: *£23.00*-**£25.00**.
Beds: 1D 1T 1S
Baths: 1 Ensuite 1 Shared
(5)

Shere

National Grid Ref: TQ0847

White Horse

Cherry Trees, *Gomshall, Shere, Guildford, Surrey,* *GU5 9HE.*
Quiet comfortable home, beautiful garden. **Open:** Jan to Nov
·1483 202288 Mrs Warren
Rates fr: *£18.50*-**£18.50**.
Beds: 1D 2T 1S
Baths: 2 Private 1 Shared
(4)

Manor Cottage, *Shere, Guildford, Surrey,* *GU5 9JE.*
16th cottage in beautiful village.
Open: Easter to Oct
Grades: ETB Listed
·1483 202979 Mrs James
Rates fr: *£16.00*-**£18.00**.
Beds: 1D 1S
Baths: 1 Shared
(6) (2)

South Holmwood

National Grid Ref: TQ1745

Steyning Cottage, *Horsham Road, South Holmwood, Dorking, Surrey,* *RH5 4NE.*
Comfortable Edwardian house. French spoken.
Open: All Year (not Xmas)
Grades: ETB Listed
·1306 888481 Mrs Treays
Rates fr: *£17.00*-**£16.00**.
Beds: 1T 1S **Baths:** 1 Shared
(4)

Tadworth

National Grid Ref: TQ2256

Hand in Hand

57 Ashurst Road, *Tadworth, Surrey,* *KT20 5EY.*
Congenial, modern, comfortable terraced house.
Open: All Year (not Xmas)
01737 812644 Mrs Cheal
Rates fr: -**£15.00**.
Beds: 1S **Baths:** 1 Shared
(1)

Merrow, *Box Hill Road, Tadworth, Surrey,* *KT20 7PS.*
Modern comfortable chalet bungalow.
Open: All Year (not Xmas)
01737 842855 Mrs Durant
Fax no: 01731 842855
Rates fr: *£15.00*-**£18.00**.
Beds: 2D 1S
Baths: 1 Ensuite 1 Shared
(3)

Thursley

National Grid Ref: SU9643

Three Horse Shoes

Hindhead Hill Farm, *Portsmouth Road, Thursley, Godalming, Surrey,* *GU8 6NN.*
Modern farmhouse, family-run farm.
Open: All Year (not Xmas)
01428 684727 Mrs Roe
Fax no: 01428 685004
Rates fr: *£14.50*-**£14.50**.
Beds: 1F 1T
Baths: 1 Ensuite 1 Shared
(5) (4)

Little Cowdray Farm, *Thursley, Godalming, Surrey,* *GU8 6QJ.*
Quiet, homely, modern, comfortable farmhouse.
Open: All Year
01428 605016 Mrs Goble
Rates fr: *£16.00*-**£16.00**.
Beds: 1T **Baths:** 1 Shared

Wallington

National Grid Ref: TQ2964

Whispering Moon

17 Osmond Gardens, *Wallington, Surrey,* *SM6 8SX.*
London 11 miles, easy transport.
Open: All Year
0181 647 1943 Mrs Dixon
Rates fr: *£18.00*.
Beds: 1F 1T
Baths: 1 Private 1 Shared

Walton-on-Thames

National Grid Ref: TQ1066

Swan

Beech Tree Lodge, *7 Rydens Avenue, Walton-on-Thames, Surrey,* *KT12 3JB.*
Large Edwardian private house, friendly, languages.
Open: All Year
Grades: ETB Listed
01932 242738 / 886667 Mrs Spiteri
Rates fr: *£17.00*-**£17.00**.
Beds: 1F 2T
Baths: 2 Shared
(6)

Oak Tree Lodge, *11 Hersham Road, Walton-on-Thames, Surrey,* *KT12 1LQ.*
Mock-Tudor family home.
Open: All Year
01932 221907 Mrs Hall
Rates fr: *£16.00*-**£17.00**.
Beds: 1F 1D
Baths: 1 Shared
(4)

West Clandon

National Grid Ref: TQ0452

Ways Cottage, *Lime Grove, West Clandon, Guildford, Surrey,* *GU4 7UT.*
Detached, rural family home.
Open: All Year
Grades: ETB Listed, Comm
01483 222454 Mrs Hughes
Rates fr: *£16.50*-**£17.00**.
Beds: 2T 1S
Baths: 1 Ensuite 2 Shared
(3)

Westcott

National Grid Ref: TQ1448

Crown, Prince of Wales, Wotton Hatch

The Dene, *Hole Hill, Westcott, Dorking, Surrey,* *RH4 3LS.*
Large country house in seven acres.
Open: All Year (not Xmas)
01306 885595 Mrs King
Rates fr: *£15.00*-**£20.00**.
Beds: 1F 1D 2T
Baths: 2 Shared
(10)

Westhumble

National Grid Ref: TQ1651

Stepping Stones

Treetops, *Pilgrims Way, Westhumble, Dorking, Surrey,* *RH5 6AP.*
Quiet, friendly, detached house overlooking Boxhill.
Open: All Year (not Xmas)
01306 883905
Miss Wood
Rates fr: *£15.00*-**£23.00**.
Beds: 1D 1S
Baths: 1 Private 1 Shared

Worplesdon

National Grid Ref: SU9753

Beefeater

The Old Malt House, *Worplesdon, Guildford, Surrey,* *GU3 3PT.*
Country house, extensive grounds, Guildford - 4m.
Open: All Year
Grades: ETB 1 Cr
01483 232152 Mrs Millar
Rates fr: *£16.00*-**£20.00**.
Beds: 1D 1S 2T
Baths: 3 Shared
(5)

East Sussex

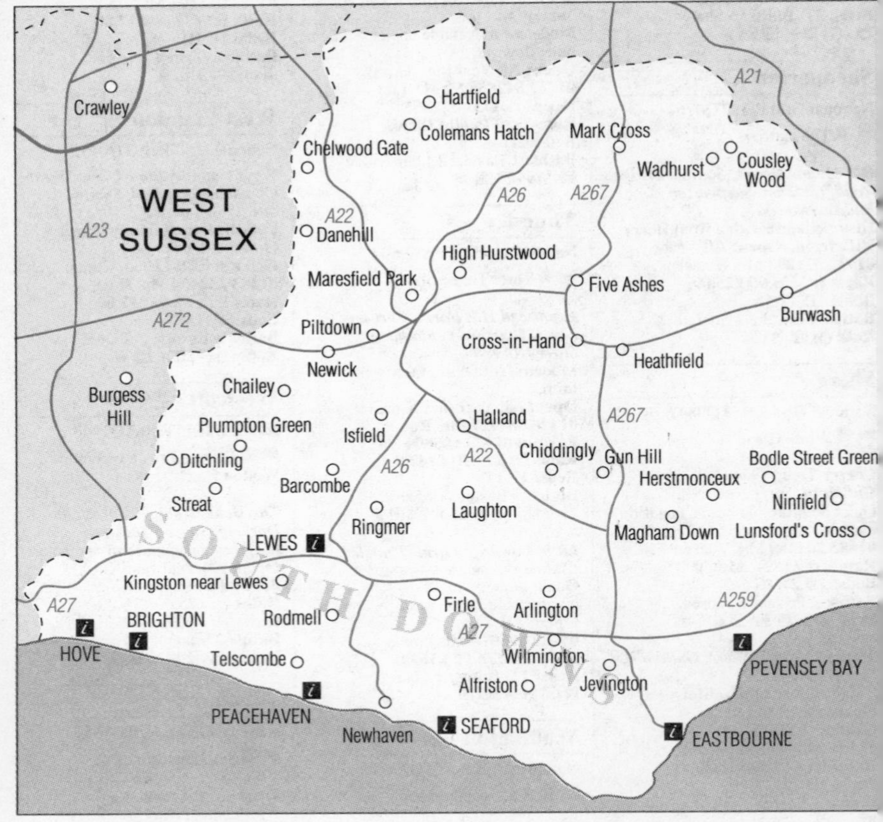

Tourist Information Centres

88 High Street, **Battle**, East Sussex, TN33 0AQ, 01424 773721.

De La Warr Pavilion, Marina, **Bexhill-on-Sea**, East Sussex, TN40 1DP, 01424 212023.

10 Bartholemew Square, **Brighton**, East Sussex, BN1 1JS, 01273 323755.

Cornfield Road, **Eastbourne**, East Sussex, BN21 4QL, 01323 411400

Lower Dicker, Boship, **Hailsham**, East Sussex, BN27 4DP, 01323 442667.

The Library, Western Road, **Hailsham**, East Sussex, BN27 3DN, 01323 844426.

4 Robertson Terrace, **Hastings**, East Sussex, TN34 1EZ, 01424 781111.

King Alfred Leisure Centre, Kingsway, **Hove**, East Sussex, BN3 2WW, 01273-746100.

Church Road, **Hove**, BN3 3BQ, 01273 778087

187 High Street, **Lewes**, East Sussex, BN7 2PE, 01273 483448.

Meridian Centre, Roderick Avenue, **Peacehaven**, East Sussex, BN10 8BB, 01273 582668.

Pevensey Castle, High Street, **Pevensey**, East Sussex, BN24 5LE, 01323 761444, (Easter to Oct).

The Heritage Centre, Strand Quay, **Rye**, East Sussex, TN31 7AY, 01797 226696.

Station Approach, **Seaford**, East Sussex, BN25 2AR, 01323 897426

Alfriston

National Grid Ref: TQ5103

Market Cross, George Inn, Smugglers Inn

Winton Street Farm Cottage, *Winton Street, Alfriston, Polegate, E. Sussex, BN26 5UH.*
Comfy beds, substantial breakfasts
Open: All Year
01323 870118 Mrs Fitch
Rates fr: *£15.00*-**£15.00**.
Beds: 1F 1D 1T 1S
Baths: 2 Shared
(5) (2)

Pleasant Rise Farm, *Alfriston, Polegate, E. Sussex, BN26 5TN.*
Very quiet, beautiful house - lovely views.
Open: All Year (not Xmas)
01323 870545 Mrs Savage
Rates fr: *£17.50*-**£17.50**.
Beds: 2D 1T 1S **Baths:** 2 Private
(7) (4)

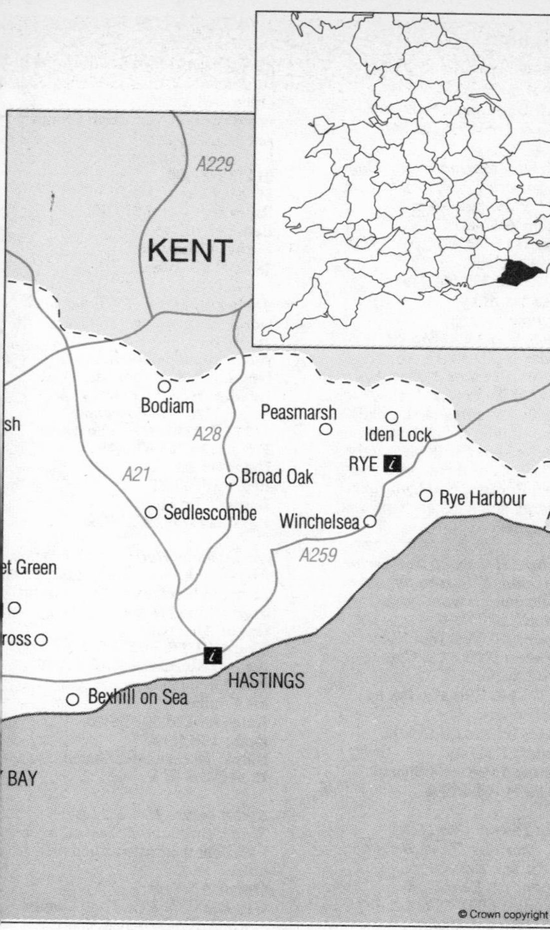

Arlington

National Grid Ref: TQ5407

Old Oak, Yew Tree

Bates Green, *Arlington, Polegate, E. Sussex, BN26 6SH.*
Tile-hung farmhouse, plantsmans' tranquil garden.
Open: All Year (not Xmas)
Grades: AA 5 Q, RAC High Acclaim
01323 482039 (also fax no)
Mrs McCutchan
Rates fr: *£22.00*-**£30.00**.
Beds: 1D 2T **Baths:** 3 Private
(3)

Barcombe

National Grid Ref: TQ4114

Holroyds, *High Street, Barcombe Cross, Barcombe, Lewes, E. Sussex, BN8 5DH.*
Old house in village centre.
Open: All Year (not Xmas)
01273 400256 Mrs Ashdown
Rates fr: *£15.00*-**£20.00**.
Beds: 2D 1T
Baths: 1 Private 1 Shared
(10) (4)

Bexhill on Sea

National Grid Ref: TQ7308

Wheatsheaf, Kings Arms (Ninfield)

Slepe House, *135 Dorset Road, Bexhill on Sea, E. Sussex, TN40 2HU.*
Open: All Year
01424 220589
Mrs Godfrey
Rates fr: *£14.00*-**£28.00**.
Beds: 1D 2T
Baths: 1 Ensuite 2 Private
(2)
Large Edwardian house in quiet seaside town. All bedrooms with their own bathroom, television & tea/coffee facilities. Ensuite available. Strictly non-smoking.

Buenos Aires, *24 Albany Road, Bexhill on Sea, East Sussex, TN40 1BZ.*
Open: All Year
01424 212269
Mr & Mrs Lax
Rates fr: *£15.00*-**£18.00**.
Beds: 2F 1D 1T 1S
Baths: 2 Shared
(5)
Well-established guest house offering comfortable accommodation in a warm & friendly atmosphere. Adjacent to seafront & close to town centre.

16 Magdalen Road, *Bexhill on Sea, E. Sussex, TN40 1SB.*
Large friendly family home.
Open: All Year (not Xmas)
01424 218969
Mrs Barker
Rates fr: *£15.00*-**£15.00**.
Beds: 1F 1D 1T 2S
Baths: 2 Shared

Sunshine Guest House, *Sandhurst Lane, Little Common, Bexhill on Sea, E. Sussex, TN39 4RH.*
Open: All Year
01424 842009
Mrs Sands
Rates fr: *£17.00*-**£18.50**.
Beds: 1F 2T
(20)
Family home, in country lane, 2 miles form beach. Easy parking with practice bowls green, tuition given. Lounge, TV, tea/coffee available in rooms.

Bedford Lodge Hotel, *Cantelupe Road, Bexhill on Sea, E. Sussex, TN40 1PR.*
Comfortable Victorian residence, close to sea.
Open: All Year
Grades: ETB 3 Cr, Comm, AA 3 Q, Recomm
01424 730097
Mr Gebbie
Fax no: 01424 212500
Rates fr: *£20.00*-**£20.00**.
Beds: 1F 1D 2T 2S
Baths: 3 Private 2 Shared
(10)

Manor Barn, *Lunsford's Cross, Bexhill on Sea, E. Sussex, TN39 5JJ.*
Ensuite chalets in rural setting.
Open: All Year
01424 893018 (also fax no)
Mrs Gillingham
Rates fr: *£13.50*-**£18.00**.
Beds: 1F 1D 1T 1S
Baths: 4 Private
(5) (6)

14 Wilton Road, *Bexhill on Sea, E. Sussex, TN40 1HY.*
Large Victorian private house.
Open: All Year (not Xmas)
01424 210250 / 01976 216411
Miss Halls
Rates fr: *£12.50*-**£12.50**.
Beds: 1F 3T 1S
Baths: 1 Shared

Myosotis Guest House, *11 Egerton Road, Bexhill on Sea, E. Sussex, TN39 3HH.*
Comfortable Victorian terraced house.
Open: All Year (not Xmas)
01424 215600 Mrs Walder
Rates fr: *£14.00*-**£14.00**.
Beds: 1F 1D 2T

Selsdon House, *23 Jameson Road, Bexhill on Sea, E. Sussex, TN40 1EG.*
Edwardian family house with parking.
Open: All Year
01424 221191 Mrs Jeffrey
Rates fr: *£14.00*-**£19.00**.
Beds: 1F 2D 1T 1S
Baths: 2 Ensuite 1 Shared
(3)

Bodiam

National Grid Ref: TQ7825

Kitchenham Farm, *Bodiam, Robertsbridge, E. Sussex, TN32 5UN.*
Comfortable C14th farmhouse.
Open: All Year (not Xmas)
01580 850357
Mrs Daws
Rates fr: *£12.50*-**£12.50**.
Beds: 1D 1T
Baths: 1 Shared
(12) (6)

Bodle Street Green

National Grid Ref: TQ6514

White Horse

The Stud Farm, *Bodle Street Green, Hailsham, E. Sussex, BN27 4RJ.*
Peaceful, rural, comfortable farmhouse.
Open: All Year (not Xmas)
Grades: ETB Listed, AA 2 Q
01323 833201 (also fax no)
Mr & Mrs Gentry
Rates fr: *£17.00*-**£20.00**.
Beds: 1D 2T
Baths: 1 Private 1 Shared
(4)

Hole Farm, *Bodle Street Green, Hailsham, E. Sussex, BN27 4QJ.*
C17th farmhouse, 0.5 mile private drive.
Open: All Year (not Xmas)
01323 833254
Mr Harding
Rates fr: *£15.00*-**£15.00**.
Beds: 2T 2S
Baths: 1 Shared
(8)

Always telephone to get directions to the B&B - you will save time!

Brighton

National Grid Ref: TQ3106

Burlington, Hand in Hand, Lion & Lobster, The Stag

Brighton Marina House Hotel, *8 Charlotte Street, Brighton, E. Sussex, BN2 1AG.*
Open: All Year
Grades: ETB 3 Cr, AA 3 Q, RAC Acclaim
01273 605349 / 679484 (also fax no)
Mr Jung
Rates fr: *£15.00*-**£15.00**.
Beds: 3F 7D 4T 3S
Baths: 7 Private 1 Shared
Highly recommended, clean, comfortable, caring family-run licensed hotel with pleasantly furnished, well equipped rooms in quiet Regency Brighton street leading down to beach, near all amenities.

Fyfield House, *26 New Steine, Brighton, E. Sussex, BN2 1PD.*
Welcoming, clean, 'home from home'.
Open: All Year (not Xmas)
Grades: ETB 3 Cr, Comm, RAC Acclaim
01273 602770 (also fax no)
Mr Culpeck
Rates fr: *£16.00*-**£16.00**.
Beds: 2F 3D 4S
Baths: 5 Private 4 Shared

The Twenty One Hotel, *21 Charlotte Street, Brighton, E. Sussex, BN2 1AG.*
Open: All Year
Grades: ETB 3 Cr, AA 4 Q, RAC High Acclaim
01273 686450
Mr Jung
Fax no: 01273 695560
Rates fr: *£27.50*-**£35.00**.
Beds: 4D 2T
Baths: 7 Ensuite
(1)
All rooms are exquisitely furnished, ensuite & fully equipped for business & leisure - offering brass & 4-poster beds with a mouthwatering breakfast!

Diana House, *25 St Georges Terrace, Brighton, E. Sussex, BN2 1JJ.*
Friendly run guest house. Close to seafront.
Open: All Year
Grades: ETB Listed
01273 605797
Ms Burgess
Fax no: 01273 600533
Rates fr: *£18.00*-**£20.00**.
Beds: 1F 3D 1T 2S
Baths: 4 Ensuite

Arlanda Hotel, *20 New Steine, Brighton, E. Sussex, BN2 1PD.*
The highest graded private hotel in Brighton!
Open: All Year
Grades: ETB 3 Cr, High Comm, AA 4 Q, Select, RAC High Acclaim
01273 699300
Mr Mathews
Rates fr: *£22.00*-**£25.00**.
Beds: 4F 4D 4S
Baths: 12 Ensuite

Amblecliff Hotel, *35 Upper Rock Gardens, Brighton, E. Sussex, BN2 1QF.*
A non-smoking hotel.
Open: All Year (not Xmas)
Grades: ETB 3 Cr, AA 4 Q, Select, RAC High Acclaim
01273 681161 Mr Kelman
Fax no: 01273 676945
Rates fr: *£20.00*-**£25.00**.
Beds: 3F 3D 2T
Baths: 8 Private
(5) (3)

Ambassador Hotel, *22 New Steine, Brighton, E. Sussex, BN2 1PD.*
Licensed hotel, excellent location, overlooking the sea.
Open: All Year
Grades: ETB 3 Cr, AA 3 Q, Recomm, RAC Listed
01273 676869
Mr Koullas
Rates fr: *£20.00*-**£25.00**.
Beds: 10F 5D 6S
Baths: 18 Ensuite 2 Shared

Ascott House Hotel, *21 New Steine, Brighton, E. Sussex, BN2 1PD.*
Excellent well-established private hotel.
Open: All Year
Grades: ETB 3 Cr, High Comm, AA 4 Q, RAC High Acclaim
01273 688085
Mr Strong
Rates fr: *£25.00*-**£25.00**.
Beds: 8F 4S
Baths: 10 Private 1 Shared

Orient Hotel, *9 Oriental Place, Brighton, E. Sussex, BN1 2LL.*
By the sea.
Open: All Year
01273 325082
Rates fr: *£30.00*-**£15.00**.
Beds: 8D 4S
Baths: 8 Ensuite 2 Shared

Paskins Hotel, *19 Charlotte Street, Brighton, E. Sussex, BN2 1AG.*
Organic vegetarian food, stylish.
Open: All Year
Grades: ETB 3 Cr, AA 3 Q, RAC 3 St
01273 601203
Rates fr: *£17.50*-**£20.00**.
Beds: 2F 10D 2T 6S
Baths: 17 Ensuite 3 Shared
(0)

The Langham Guest House, *16 Charlotte Street, Brighton, E. Sussex, BN2 1AG.*
Small cosy, family-run period guest house.
Open: All Year
01273 682843 Mrs Jung
Rates fr: *£12.50*-**£12.50**.
Beds: 4F 5D 5T 2S
Baths: 2 Shared

Broad Oak

National Grid Ref: TQ8220

Rainbow Trout

Arndale Cottage, *Northiam Road, Broad Oak, Brede, Rye, E. Sussex, TN31 6EP.*
Charming comfortable country cottage.
Open: All Year
Grades: ETB Listed
01424 882813 Mrs Smith
Rates fr: *£17.00*-**£18.00**.
Beds: 1F 1D 1T **Baths:** 3 Ensuite
(8)

Furnace Lane Oast, *Broad Oak, Brede, Rye, E. Sussex, TN31 6ET.*
Tastefully converted double oast-house. **Open:** All Year
01424 882407 Mr Sevastopulo
Rates fr: *£20.00*-**£25.00**.
Beds: 1F 2D 1T
Baths: 4 Private
(10)

Burwash

National Grid Ref: TQ6724

The Wheel

Woodlands Farm, *Heathfield Road, Burwash, Etchingham, E. Sussex, TN19 7LA.*
Comfortable, quiet, friendly C16th farmhouse.
Open: Easter to Dec
Grades: ETB Listed, AA 2 Q
01435 882794 Mrs Sirrell
Rates fr: *£16.50*-**£18.50**.
Beds: 2D 2T
Baths: 2 Private 2 Shared

Chailey

National Grid Ref: TQ3919

Wayside Cottage, *North Common, Chailey, Lewes, E. Sussex, BN8 4DR.*
Country cottage, overlooking common. **Open:** All Year
01825 722955 L Hartley
Rates fr: *£15.00*-**£18.00**.
Beds: 1F 2T
Baths: 2 Shared
(3) (6)

The lowest **single** *rate is shown in* **bold.**

Chelwood Gate

National Grid Ref: TQ4229

Holly House, *Beaconsfield Road, Chelwood Gate, Haywards Heath, West Sussex, RH17 7LF.*
Warm welcome, comfortable, scenic garden.
Open: All Year
Grades: ETB 2 Cr, Comm
01825 740484 Mrs Birchell
Rates fr: *£20.00*-**£20.00**.
Beds: 2D 2T 1S
Baths: 3 Ensuite 1 Shared
(5)

Chiddingly

National Grid Ref: TQ5414

Six Bells

Holmes Hill, *Chiddingly, Lewes, E. Sussex, BN8 6JA.*
Cosy modernised C18th cottage.
Open: All Year (not Xmas)
01825 872746 Mr & Mrs Farrier
Rates fr: *£18.00*-**£18.00**.
Beds: 1D 1S 1T
Baths: 1 Private
(2)

Colemans Hatch

National Grid Ref: TQ4533

Gospel Oak, *Sandy Lane, Colemans Hatch, Hartfield, E. Sussex, TN7 4ER.*
Converted C17th crofters cottage.
Open: All Year
01342 823840
Mrs Hawker
Rates fr: *£17.00*-**£18.00**.
Beds: 1D 1T
Baths: 1 Ensuite 1 Shared
(5)

Cousley Wood

National Grid Ref: TQ6533

Cheviots, *Cousley Wood, Wadhurst, E. Sussex, TN5 6HD.*
Modern house, large delightful garden.
Open: Easter to October
01892 782952 Mr Field
Rates fr: *£25.00*-**£20.00**.
Beds: 2T 1D 1S
Baths: 2 Ensuite 1 Shared
(5)

Cross-in-Hand

National Grid Ref: TQ5521

Old Corner Cottage, *Little London Road, Cross-in-Hand, Heathfield, E. Sussex, TN21 0LT.*
Pretty period cottage.
Open: All Year
01435 863787 Mrs Brown
Rates fr: *£18.00*-**£19.00**.
Beds: 2D 1T
Baths: 2 Private 1 Shared
(10)

Danehill

National Grid Ref: TQ4027

Coach & Horses

Sliders Farmhouse, *Furners Green, Danehill, Uckfield, E. Sussex, TN22 3RT.*
Lovely Tudor farmhouse, mature gardens.
Open: All Year (not Xmas)
Grades: AA 4 Q
01825 790258 Mr Salmon
Rates fr: *£19.00*-**£28.00**.
Beds: 2D 1T **Baths:** 3 Ensuite
(10)

Ditchling

National Grid Ref: TQ3215

White Horse, Blacksmiths Arms (Offham)

South Cottage, *2 The Drove, Ditchling, Hassocks, W. Sussex, BN6 8TR.*
Welcoming, comfortable, quiet. Lovely views.
Open: All Year (not Xmas)
01273 846636 Mrs Stock
Rates fr: *£20.00*-**£20.00**.
Beds: 1D 1T 1S **Baths:** 1 Shared

Longcroft, *Beacon Road, Ditchling, Hassocks, W. Sussex, BN6 8UZ.*
Beautiful South Downs country house. **Open:** All Year
01273 842740 Mr & Mrs Scull
Rates fr: *£21.00*-**£26.00**.
Beds: 2D 1T
Baths: 2 Ensuite 1 Private
(7) (10)

Eastbourne

National Grid Ref: TQ5900

Marine Pub, The Lamb

Heatherdene Hotel, *26-28 Elms Avenue, Eastbourne, E. Sussex, BN21 3DN.*
Open: All Year
Grades: ETB 2 Cr
01323 723598 Mrs Mockford
Fax no: 01323 722338
Rates fr: *£16.00*-**£16.00**.
Beds: 1F 3D 8T 3S
Baths: 5 Private 4 Shared
Licensed hotel close to seafront & town centre. Home cooked meals served in our pleasant dining room. Friendly helpful service.

Arden Hotel, *17 Burlington Place, Eastbourne, E. Sussex, BN21 4AR.*
Non-smoking, Victorian, family-run hotel.
Open: All Year (not Xmas)
Grades: ETB 3 Cr
01323 639639 Mr Jones
Rates fr: *£20.00*-**£20.00**.
Beds: 2F 5D 5T 2S
Baths: 9 Private 1 Shared
(4)

Edelweiss Hotel, *10-12 Elms Avenue, Eastbourne, E. Sussex, BN21 3DN.*
Open: All Year
Grades: ETB 2 Cr, Approv
01323 732071 (also fax no)
Mr & Mrs Butler
Rates fr: *£13.50*-**£13.50**.
Beds: 1F 6D 5T 2S
Baths: 3 Private 4 Shared
Small family-run hotel set in picturesque avenue close to seafront. Rooms with TV & tea-making. Guests' lounge, bar, evening meals available. Excellent value.

Bay Lodge Hotel, *61 62 Royal Parade, Eastbourne, E. Sussex, BN20.*
Small seafront Victorian hotel.
Open: Mar to Oct
Grades: ETB 3 Cr, Comm, AA 3 Q, Recomm, RAC Acclaim
01323 732515
Mr Hunt
Fax no: 01323 735009
Rates fr: *£19.00*-**£19.00**.
Beds: 5D 4T 3S
Baths: 9 Ensuite
(7)

Ambleside Private Hotel, *24 Elms Avenue, Eastbourne, E. Sussex, BN21 3DN.*
Open: All Year
01323 724991
Mr Pattenden
Rates fr: *£17.00*-**£17.00**.
Beds: 4D 4T 2S
Baths: 2 Shared
Small hotel situated on quiet period avenue, adjacent to the seafront, pier, town centre, theatres. Central for railway & coach stations. Close to car park.

Cromwell Private Hotel, *23 Cavendish Place, Eastbourne, E. Sussex, BN21 3EJ.*
Friendly family run. Central position.
Open: All Year
Grades: ETB 2 Cr
01323 725288 (also fax no)
Mr & Mrs Millar
Rates fr: *£16.00*-**£16.00**.
Beds: 2F 3D 3T 3S
Baths: 5 Private 2 Shared

National Grid References are for villages, towns and cities - *not* for individual houses.

Courtlands Hotel, *68 Royal Parade, Eastbourne, E. Sussex, BN22 7AQ.*
Seafront position, business/touring base.
Open: All Year
Grades: ETB 2 Cr, RAC Listed, Acclaim
01323 721068
Rates fr: *£17.00*-**£17.00**.
Beds: 3F 2D 1T 2S
Baths: 3 Ensuite 1 Private
(2)

Cherry Tree Hotel, *15 Silverdale Road, Eastbourne, E. Sussex, BN20 7AJ.*
Small family-run quality hotel.
Open: All Year
Grades: ETB 3 Cr, Comm
01323 722406
Mr Clarke
Rates fr: *£23.00*-**£23.00**.
Beds: 2F 3D 3T 2S
Baths: 10 Private
(7)

Pevensey Lodge, *27 Pevensey Road, Eastbourne, E. Sussex, BN21 3HR.*
Family-run licensed guest house.
Open: Feb to Nov
Grades: ETB 2 Cr
01323 649539
Mrs Chapman
Rates fr: *£14.50*-**£14.50**.
Beds: 2F 1D 1T 2S
Baths: 6 Private
(3)

Adrian House Hotel, *24 Selwyn Road, Eastbourne, E. Sussex, BN21 2LR.*
Family-run hotel. Quiet area.
Open: All Year
Grades: ETB 3 Cr
01323 720372
Mr & Mrs Miles
Rates fr: *£17.00*-**£17.00**.
Beds: 1F 5D 1T 3S
Baths: 5 Private 2 Shared
(10)

Southcroft Private Hotel, *15 South Cliff Avenue, Eastbourne, E. Sussex, BN20 7AH.*
Elegant Edwardian town house.
Open: All Year (not Xmas)
Grades: ETB 3 Cr, Comm
01323 729071
Mr Ellis
Rates fr: *£21.00*-**£21.00**.
Beds: 3D 2T 1S
Baths: 6 Ensuite

Seagulls Guest House, *12 South Cliff Avenue, Eastbourne, E. Sussex, BN20 7AH.*
Edwardian, welcoming, near sea & South Downs.
Open: Mar to Oct
01323 737831
Mrs Rogers
Rates fr: *£17.50*-**£17.50**.
Beds: 3D 2T 1S
Baths: 2 Ensuite 2 Shared
(4)

Firle

National Grid Ref: TQ4607

Gibraltar Farm, *Firle, Lewes, E. Sussex, BN8 6NB.*
Large comfortable C17th farmhouse.
Open: All Year
01273 858225
Mrs Yallowley
Rates fr: *£20.00*-**£15.00**.
Beds: 1D 1T
Baths: 2 Private
(12)

Five Ashes

National Grid Ref: TQ5525

Five Ashes Inn

Edstone Cottage, *Five Ashes, Mayfield, E. Sussex, TN20 6HS.*
Large house in the country.
Open: All Year (not Xmas)
01825 830605
Mrs Edwards
Rates fr: *£15.00*-**£16.00**.
Beds: 2T
Baths: 1 Shared
(5) (5)

Gun Hill

National Grid Ref: TQ5614

The Gun

The Gun, *Gun Hill, Horam, Heathfield, E. Sussex, TN21 0JU.*
Idyllic C16th inn, excellent food.
Open: All Year (not Xmas)
01825 872361
Mr Bear
Rates fr: *£16.00*-**£25.00**.
Beds: 1F 1D 1T
Baths: 1 Ensuite 1 Shared
(0)

Pedlars Cottage, *Gun Hill, Horam, Heathfield, E. Sussex, TN21 0JS.*
C18th country cottage.
Open: Apr to Oct
01825 873107
Mrs Winter
Rates fr: *£15.50*-**£15.50**.
Beds: 2D
Baths: 1 Shared

Halland

National Grid Ref: TQ5016

Black Lion

Black Lion, *Lewes Road, Halland, Lewes, E. Sussex, BN8 6PN.*
Open: All Year
01825 840304
Mrs Sumers
Rates fr: *£15.00*-**£19.50**.
Beds: 1F 2D 1T 2S
Baths: 4 Ensuite 2 Shared
(40)

Always telephone to get directions to the B&B - you will save time!

Hartfield

National Grid Ref: TQ4735

Anchor Inn

***Stairs Farm House,** & Tea Room, High Street, Hartfield, E. Sussex, TN7 4AB.*
Spacious comfortable C17th farmhouse. **Open:** All Year
Grades: ETB Listed, Comm
01892 770793 (also fax no)
Mrs Pring
Rates fr: *£20.00*-**£25.00**.
Beds: 1F 1D 1T **Baths:** 2 Shared
(8)

***Anchor Inn,** Church Street, Hartfield, E. Sussex, TN7 4AG.*
C16th inn, friendly atmosphere.
Open: All Year
01892 770424 Mr Thompson
Rates fr: *£17.50*-**£20.00**.
Beds: 1D 1T
Baths: 2 Ensuite

Hastings

National Grid Ref: TQ8110

Bo Peep, Plough Inn, Churchills

***The Pines,** 50 Baldslow Road, Hastings, E. Sussex, TN34 2EY.*
Open: All Year (not Xmas)
01424 435838 (also fax no)
Mrs Piper
Rates fr: *£15.00*-**£18.00**.
Beds: 1F 2D 1T 1S
Baths: 2 Private 1 Shared
Lovely Victorian house, quiet location, 15 minutes walk to town centre, seafront, station, 5 minutes to beautiful Alexandra Park. No smoking throughout. Parking available.

***Gainsborough Hotel,** 5 Carlisle Parade, Hastings, E. Sussex, TN34 1JG.*
Centrally situated seafront hotel.
Open: All Year (not Xmas)
01424 434010 Mrs Moules
Rates fr: *£17.00*.
Beds: 2F 3D 3T 4S
Baths: 8 Private 2 Shared

The lowest *double* rate per person is shown in *italics*.

***Woodhurst Lodge,** Ivyhouse Lane, Hastings, E. Sussex, TN35 4NN.*
Large modern farmhouse. Quiet grounds.
01424 754147 Mr Turner
Rates fr: *£18.00*-**£17.00**.
Beds: 2D 3T
Baths: 1 Ensuite 1 Private 1 Shared
(10) (10)

***The Sherwood Guest House,** 15 Grosvenor Crescent, St Leonards on Sea, Hastings, E. Sussex, TN38 0AA.*
Guest house on seafront.
Open: All Year (not Xmas)
01424 433331 (also fax no)
Mr Aldridge
Rates fr: *£15.00*-**£15.00**.
Beds: 3F 4D 1T 4S
Baths: 3 Private 2 Shared
(5)

***Millifont Guest House,** 8/9 Cambridge Gardens, Hastings, E. Sussex, TN34 1EH.*
Centrally situated 15 bedroomed guest house.
Open: All Year (not Xmas)
Grades: ETB 2 Cr
01424 425645
Mr Main
Rates fr: *£15.00*-**£15.00**.
Beds: 2F 5D 4T 4S
Baths: 2 Ensuite 2 Private 2 Shared

***Marina Lodge Guest House,** 123 Marina, St Leonards on Sea, Hastings, E. Sussex, TN38 0BN.*
Large, sea-front, family guest house.
Open: All Year
01424 715067
Mrs Snell
Rates fr: *£13.00*-**£13.00**.
Beds: 3D 1F 2S

***Grand Hotel,** Grand Parade, St Leonards On Sea, Hastings, E. Sussex, TN38 0DD.*
Seafront family, some non-smoking rooms.
Open: All Year
Grades: ETB 2 Cr
01424 428510
Mr & Mrs Mann
Fax no: 01424 722387
Rates fr: *£14.00*-**£15.00**.
Beds: 6F 12D 13T 11S
Baths: 8 Private

***Westwood Farm,** Stonestile Lane, Hastings, E. Sussex, TN35 4PG.*
Peaceful rural location, outstanding views.
Open: All Year (not Xmas)
01424 751038
Mr York
Rates fr: *£15.00*-**£22.00**.
Beds: 1F 1D 1T
Baths: 1 Ensuite 1 Shared
(5) (8)

***Argyle Guest House,** 32 Cambridge Gardens, Hastings, E. Sussex, TN34 1EN.*
Late Victorian city centre guest-house.
Open: All Year
Grades: ETB 2 Q, Comm
01424 421294 Mr Jacob
Rates fr: *£14.00*-**£15.00**.
Beds: 2F 2D 2T 2S
Baths: 3 Ensuite 2 Shared
(4)

Heathfield

National Grid Ref: TQ5821

***Risingholme,** High Street, Heathfield, E. Sussex, TN21 8LS.*
Large secluded Victorian private house.
Open: All Year
01435 864645 Mrs Farmer
Rates fr: *£17.50*-**£25.00**.
Beds: 1D 2T
Baths: 2 Private
(10) (4)

***Alma Villa,** Cross in Hand, Heathfield, E. Sussex, TN21 0SR.*
Small country home.
Open: Easter to Oct
01435 864109 Mr Ashdown
Rates fr: *£13.50*-**£13.50**.
Beds: 2D
Baths: 1 Shared
(2)

Herstmonceux

National Grid Ref: TQ6312

***Cleavers Lyng Country Hotel,** Church Road, Herstmonceux, Hailsham, E. Sussex, BN27 1QJ.*
C16th family-run country hotel.
Open: All Year
01323 833131 Mr Simpson
Rates fr: *£21.50*-**£30.00**.
Beds: 4D 3T
Baths: 7 Ensuite
(20)

High Hurstwood

National Grid Ref: TQ4926

Crown & Gate

***Chillies Granary,** High Hurstwood, Crowborough, E. Sussex, TN6 3TB.*
Beautifully situated converted granary. Cheerful!
Open: Mar to Dec
01892 655560 Mr & Mrs Peck
Rates fr: *£16.00*-**£20.00**.
Beds: 1F 1D 1T **Baths:** 2 Shared
(8)

Planning a longer stay? Always ask for any special rates.

Pay B&Bs by cash or cheque. Be prepared to pay up front for one night stays.

Hove

National Grid Ref: TQ2805

Iron Duke

***Lichfield House,** 30 Waterloo Street, Hove, E. Sussex, BN3 1AN.*
Close to seafront & main shopping areas. **Open:** All Year
01273 777740 Mr Baker
Fax no: 01273 732970
Rates fr: *£15.00*-**£15.00**.
Beds: 2F 2D 3T 2S
Baths: 2 Shared
(2)

***Griffon Guest House,** 59 Montifiore Road, Hove, E. Sussex, BN3 6EP.*
Edwardian terrace near cricket ground.
Open: All Year
01273 732760
Rates fr: *£16.00*-**£16.00**.
Beds: 2T 1S **Baths:** 1 Shared

***Kingsway Hotel,** 2 St Aubyns, Hove, E. Sussex, BN3 2TB.*
Comfortable hotel overlooking sea.
Open: All Year
01273 732575 Mrs Williams
Rates fr: *£25.00*-**£17.50**.
Beds: 5F 11D 2T 2S
Baths: 12 Ensuite 2 Private 2 Shared
(5)

Iden Lock

National Grid Ref: TQ9123

***Cliff Farm,** Military Road, Iden Lock, Rye, E. Sussex, TN31 7QE.*
Established comfortable farmhouse.
Open: Mar to Oct
01797 280331 Mr Sullivan
Rates fr: *£13.50*-**£15.50**.
Beds: 1F 1D 1T
(5)

Isfield

National Grid Ref: TQ4517

***Farm Place,** Isfield, Uckfield, E. Sussex, TN22 5TY.*
Attractive, white weather-boarded country house.
Open: Mar to Nov
01825 750485 Mrs Houchen
Rates fr: *£20.00*-**£25.00**.
Beds: 1D 1T **Baths:** 2 Ensuite
(5)

Jevington

National Grid Ref: TQ5601

***Ash Farm,** Filching, Jevington, Polegate, E. Sussex, BN26 5QA.*
150-year-old Downland farmhouse.
Open: All Year
01323 487335 Mr Steer
Fax no: 01323 484474
Rates fr: *£16.50*-**£18.50**.
Beds: 1F 1D 1T
Baths: 2 Private 1 Shared
(20)

Kingston near Lewes

National Grid Ref: TQ3908

The Juggs

***Nightingales,** The Avenue, Kingston near Lewes, Lewes, E. Sussex, BN7 3LL.*
Marvellous breakfast, lovely garden, quiet.
Open: All Year
Grades: AA 4 Q, Select
01273 475673
Mr Hudson
Rates fr: *£20.00*-**£30.00**.
Beds: 1D 1T
Baths: 1 Ensuite 1 Private
(2)

***Hyde Cottage,** The Street, Kingston near Lewes, Lewes, E. Sussex, BN7 3PB.*
C18th oak-beamed flint cottage.
Open: All Year (not Xmas)
01273 472709
Mrs Maddock
Rates fr: *£20.00*-**£16.00**.
Beds: 2T 1S
Baths: 1 Ensuite 1 Shared
(2)

Laughton

National Grid Ref: TQ5013

The Bluebell

***Spencers Farm,** Laughton, Lewes, E. Sussex, BN8 6BX.*
Picturesque farmhouse in peaceful setting.
Open: All Year (not Xmas)
01825 840489
Mrs Gosling
Rates fr: *£17.50*-**£17.50**.
Beds: 1F 1T 1S
Baths: 1 Shared
(6)

***Holly Cottage,** Lewes Road, Laughton, Lewes, E. Sussex, BN8 6BL.*
Charming C18th Listed country cottage.
Open: All Year (not Xmas)
01323 811309
Mrs Clarke
Rates fr: *£17.50*-**£20.00**.
Beds: 1F 1T
Baths: 2 Private
(4)

Lewes

National Grid Ref: TQ4110

Royal Oak, Pelham Arms

***Hillside,** Rotten Row, Lewes, E. Sussex, BN7 1TN.*
Central, beautiful views, quiet road.
Open: All Year
01273 473120 Miss Hollins
Rates fr: *£21.00*-**£20.00**.
Beds: 1D 1T 1S
Baths: 1 Ensuite
(1) (3)

***Felix Gallery,** 2 Sun Street, Lewes, E. Sussex, BN7 2QB.*
Modernised period house, town centre.
Open: All Year
01273 472668 Mrs Whitehead
Rates fr: *£18.00*-**£25.00**.
Beds: 1T 1S
Baths: 1 Shared
(8)

***Number Four,** Castle Bank, Lewes, E. Sussex, BN7 1UZ.*
Large, comfortable room, central, quiet.
Open: All Year
01273 476291 Mrs Wigglesworth
Rates fr: *£20.00*-**£20.00**.
Beds: 1T 1S
Baths: 1 Shared

***Grey Tiles,** 12 Gundreda Road, Lewes, E. Sussex, BN7 1PX.*
Quiet location, excellent facilities.
Open: All Year
01273 471805 Mr Fuller
Rates fr: *£18.00*.
Beds: 2T
(7) (3)

***Crink House,** Barcombe Mills, Lewes, E. Sussex, BN8 5BJ.*
Welcoming rural family home.
Open: All Year (not Xmas)
01273 400625 Mrs Gaydon
Rates fr: *£20.00*-**£25.00**.
Beds: 2D 1T
Baths: 3 Private
(10)

***Ousedale House,** Offham, Lewes, E. Sussex, BN7 3QF.*
Victorian country house.
Open: All Year
01273 478680 Mr & Mrs Gough
Fax no: 01273 486510
Rates fr: *£22.00*-**£24.00**.
Beds: 1F 1D 1T
Baths: 2 Ensuite 1 Private
(17)

Please respect a B&B's wishes regarding children, animals & smoking.

All details shown are as supplied by B&B owners in Autumn 1996.

Lunsford's Cross

National Grid Ref: TQ7210

Kings Arms (Ninfield)

***Manor Barn,** Lunsford's Cross, Bexhill on Sea, E. Sussex, TN39 5JJ.*
Ensuite chalets in rural setting.
Open: All Year
01424 893018 (also fax no) Mrs Gillingham
Rates fr: *£13.50*-**£18.00**.
Beds: 1F 1D 1T 1S
Baths: 4 Private
(5) (6)

***Wakeford House,** Potmans Lane, Lunsford's Cross, Bexhill on Sea, E. Sussex, TN39 5JL.*
Edwardian house in country setting.
Open: All Year
01424 892013 Mrs Skinner
Rates fr: *£17.50*.
Beds: 1F 1D 1S
Baths: 2 Shared
(5)

Magham Down

National Grid Ref: TQ6011

Red Lion, Merry Harriers

***Sandy Bank,** Old Road, Magham Down, Hailsham, E. Sussex, BN27 1PW.*
Well-appointed, comfortable rooms.
Open: All Year (not Xmas)
Grades: ETB 2 Cr, Comm
01323 842488 (also fax no) Miss Burridge
Rates fr: *£18.50*-**£22.00**.
Beds: 3T
Baths: 3 Private
(3)

Maresfield Park

National Grid Ref: TQ4624

***South Paddock,** Maresfield Park, Uckfield, E. Sussex, TN22 2HA.*
Country house set in 3.5 acres.
Open: All Year
01825 762335 Mr Allt
Rates fr: *£25.00*-**£24.00**.
Beds: 1D 2T 1S
Baths: 2 Shared
(10) (6)

Mark Cross

National Grid Ref: TQ5831

***Houndsell Cottage,** Wadhurst Road, Mark Cross, Crowborough, E. Sussex, TN6 3PF.*
Quiet, comfortable country cottage.
Open: Jan to Nov
01892 782292 Mrs Sears
Rates fr: *£17.50*-**£16.00**.
Beds: 2T 2S
Baths: 1 Shared
(5) (6)

Newhaven

National Grid Ref: TQ4401

***Newhaven Lodge,** 12 Brighton Road, Newhaven, E. Sussex, BN9 9NB.*
Licensed family-run guest house.
Open: All Year
01273 513736 Mrs Jones
Rates fr: *£16.00*-**£15.00**.
Beds: 3F 1S
Baths: 1 Private
(6)

Newick

National Grid Ref: TQ4121

***Greenacre,** Station Road (A272), Newick, Lewes, E. Sussex, BN8 4HE.*
Open: All Year
Grades: ETB 3 Cr, Comm, AA 3 Q
01825 723712 Mrs Bostel
Rates fr: *£15.00*-**£20.00**.
Beds: 3F 4D 3T 2S
Baths: 2 Private 1 Shared
(12)
Large country house on A272. Convenient for Glyndebourne, the Newhaven Port, Gatwick Airport, & the International East Sussex Golf Course. Family rooms ensuite, doubles & singles.

Ninfield

National Grid Ref: TQ7012

United Friends Inn, Kings Arms

***Marshwood House,** Lewes Road, Ninfield, Battle, E. Sussex, TN33 9JR.*
Period country house, beautiful gardens.
Open: All Year (not Xmas)
01424 892469 Miss Smithson
Rates fr: *£17.00*.
Beds: 1F 1D
Baths: 1 Shared
(7)

***The United Friends Inn,** The Green, Ninfield, Battle, E. Sussex, TN33 9JL.*
Friendly village inn.
Open: All Year (not Xmas)
01424 892462 Mr & Mrs Fillingham
Rates fr: *£15.00*-**£15.00**.
Beds: 3D 1T 2S
Baths: 2 Private 4 Shared
(20)

Peasmarsh

National Grid Ref: TQ8723

***Kimblee,** Main Street, Peasmarsh, Rye, E. Sussex, TN31 6UL.*
5 minutes drive to historic Rye.
Open: All Year
01797 230514 Mr Griffin
Rates fr: *£17.00*-**£18.00**.
Beds: 3D 1S
Baths: 3 Private
(4)

Pevensey Bay

National Grid Ref:

The Moorings

***Montana,** The Promenade, Pevensey Bay, Pevensey, E. Sussex, BN24 6HD.*
Victorian house, on the beach.
Open: All Year (not Xmas)
01323 764651 Mr & Mrs Scales
Rates fr: *£13.00*-**£14.00**.
Beds: 2T 1S
Baths: 1 Shared
(4)

***Napier House,** The Promenade, Pevensey Bay, E. Sussex, BN24 6HD.*
Guest house with beach garden.
Open: Easter to Nov
Grades: AA 2 Q
01323 768875 Mrs Silver
Rates fr: *£16.00*-**£16.00**.
Beds: 2F 5D 2T 1S
Baths: 5 Private 2 Shared
(1) (7)

***Driftwood,** 36 Eastbourne Road, Pevensey Bay, Pevensey, E. Sussex, BN24 6HJ.*
Comfortable family home, village centre.
Open: All Year
01323 768530 Ms McKeever
Rates fr: *£13.00*-**£16.00**.
Beds: 1F 1D 1T
Baths: 1 Shared
(5)

Piltdown

National Grid Ref: TQ4422

The Peacock

***Holly Farm,** Piltdown, Uckfield, E. Sussex, TN22 3XB.*
Well situated converted Victorian cottages.
Open: All Year
01825 722592 (also fax no) Ms Mayes
Rates fr: *£20.50*-**£20.50**.
Beds: 2T 1S
Baths: 1 Private 1 Shared
(5)

The lowest *double* rate per person is shown in *italics*.

Plumpton Green

National Grid Ref: TQ3616

Farthings, *Station Road, Plumpton Green, Lewes, E. Sussex, BN7 3BY.*
Chalet bungalow in village setting.
Open: All Year (not Xmas)
01273 890415 Mrs Baker
Rates fr: *£18.50*-**£20.00**.
Beds: 2D 1T
Baths: 1 Ensuite 1 Shared
(11) (5)

Ringmer

National Grid Ref: TQ4412

Green Man, Anchor Inn

Gote Farm, *Gote Lane, Ringmer, Lewes, E. Sussex, BN8 5HX.*
Traditional Sussex farmhouse near Glyndebourne.
Open: All Year (not Xmas)
01273 812303 (also fax no)
Mrs Craig
Rates fr: *£16.50*-**£16.50**.
Beds: 1D 1T 1S
Baths: 2 Shared
(4)

Sundown Cottage, *53 Sadlers Way, Ringmer, Lewes, E. Sussex, BN8 5HG.*
Quiet modern cottage near Glyndebourne.
Open: All Year
01273 813640
Mrs Arnold
Rates fr: *£16.00*-**£22.00**.
Beds: 1D
Baths: 1 Ensuite
(2)

Rodmell

National Grid Ref: TQ4105

Barn House, *Rodmell, Lewes, E. Sussex, BN7 3HE.*
Converted C18th barn.
Open: Mar to Jan
01273 477865 Mr Fraser
Rates fr: *£20.00*-**£25.00**.
Beds: 4D 3T 1S
Baths: 8 Private
(10)

Bankside, *Rodmell, Lewes, E. Sussex, BN7 3EZ.*
Comfortable, converted cart lodge.
Open: All Year (not Xmas)
01273 477058 Mrs Burnaby Davies
Rates fr: *£16.50*-**£20.00**.
Beds: 1F
Baths: 1 Private

Right on the border?

Look at the neighbouring county, too

Bringing children with you? Always ask for any special rates.

Rye

National Grid Ref: TQ9120

Aviemore Guest House, *28/30 Fishmarket Road, Rye, E. Sussex, TN31 7LP.*
Genuinely warm welcome, excellent breakfast.
Open: All Year
Grades: ETB 2 Cr, Approv, RAC Listed
01797 223052 (also fax no)
Mrs Keay
Rates fr: *£16.00*-**£19.50**.
Beds: 4D 3T 1S
Baths: 4 Ensuite 2 Shared

Camber Sands Lodge, *Lydd Road, Rye, E. Sussex, TN31 7RS.*
Motel in Camber Sands Leisure Park.
Open: Mar to Oct
Grades: ETB 4 Cr
01797 225555
Mr Baron
Fax no: 01797 225756
Rates fr: *£20.00*-**£30.00**.
Beds: 1F 4D 4T

The Old Vicarage, *66 Church Square, Rye, E. Sussex, TN31 7HF.*
Splendid Georgian house, peaceful setting.
Open: All Year
Grades: AA 5 Q, Prem Select
01797 222119
Mr Masters
Fax no: 01797 227466
Rates fr: *£20.00*-**£32.00**.
Beds: 1F 4D 1T
Baths: 6 Private
(8) (5)

Jeakes House, *Mermaid Street, Rye, E. Sussex, TN31 7ET.*
C17th award-winning B&B hotel in cobbled mediaeval town centre
Open: All Year
01797 222828
Mr & Mrs Hadfield
Fax no: 01797 222 828
Rates fr: *£20.50*-**£35.00**.
Beds: 2F 8D 1T 1S
Baths: 10 Ensuite 2 Shared

Western House, *113 Winchelsea Road, Rye, E. Sussex, TN31 7EL.*
Charming C18th Listed house.
Open: All Year
01797 223419 Mrs Dellar
Rates fr: *£18.00*-**£25.00**.
Beds: 2D 1T
Baths: 3 Ensuite
(10) (3)

Rye Harbour

National Grid Ref: TQ9313

Inkerman Arms

The Old Vicarage, *Rye Harbour, Rye, E. Sussex, TN31 7TT.*
Quietly situated, close Nature Reserve.
Open: All Year
Grades: ETB Listed, Comm
01797 222088 Mr Bosher
Rates fr: *£16.00*-**£19.50**.
Beds: 1D 1T
Baths: 1 Shared
(3) (2)

Seaford

National Grid Ref: TV4899

Silverdale, *21 Sutton Park Road, Seaford, E. Sussex, BN25 1RH.*
Outstanding hospitality & service.
Open: All Year
Grades: ETB 3 Cr, Comm, AA 3 Q, Recomm
01323 491849 Mr Cowdrey
Fax no: 01323 891131
Rates fr: *£13.00*-**£13.00**.
Beds: 3F 4D 2T 1S
Baths: 5 Private 2 Shared
(6)

Sedlescombe

National Grid Ref: TQ7818

White Hart

Sedlescombe Vineyard, *Sedlescombe, Robertsbridge, E. Sussex, TN32 5SA.*
Organic vineyard, self-build timber-frame house.
Open: All Year
01580 830715 Mrs Cook
Rates fr: *£16.00*-**£17.00**.
Beds: 2F 2D
Baths: 1 Shared
(0) (10)

Streat

National Grid Ref: TQ3515

North Acres, *Streat, Hassocks, W. Sussex, BN6 8RX.*
Large, quiet Victorian country house.
Open: All Year (not Xmas)
01273 890278 Mr & Mrs Eastwood
Rates fr: *£15.00*-**£15.00**.
Beds: 1F 2T
Baths: 2 Shared

Telscombe

National Grid Ref: TQ4003

Stud Farm House, *Telscombe, Lewes, E. Sussex, BN7 3HZ.*
Large C16th stud farm house.
Open: All Year (not Xmas)
01273 302486 Mrs Armour
Rates fr: *£16.50*-**£18.50**.
Beds: 1F 1D 2T
Baths: 1 Shared
(20)

Wadhurst

National Grid Ref: TQ6431

Best Beech Inn

***Kirkstone,** Mayfield Lane, Wadhurst, E. Sussex, TN5 6HX.*
Open: All Year
01892 783204
Mr & Mrs Inman
Rates fr: *£18.00*-**£20.00**.
Beds: 1F 1T
Baths: 2 Shared
(3)
Large Victorian house with fine views in rural East Sussex. Convenient for London (1 hour), South Coast (45 minutes) & many historic sites & gardens.

***Spring Cottage,** Best Beech Hill, Wadhurst, E. Sussex, TN5 6JH.*
Modern family house, stunning views.
Open: All Year (not Xmas)
01892 783896 Ms Bones
Rates fr: *£17.00*-**£18.00**.
Beds: 1F 1D
Baths: 1 Private 1 Shared
(4)

***The Best Beech Inn,** Mayfield Lane, Wadhurst, E. Sussex, TN5 6JH.*
Close to Kent/Sussex border, near Bewl Water.
Open: All Year (not Xmas)
01892 782046 Mr & Mrs Peel
Rates fr: *£17.50*-**£25.00**.
Beds: 1F 3D 2T 1S
Baths: 3 Ensuite 1 Private 3 Shared
(20)

Wilmington

National Grid Ref: TQ5804

Giants Rest

***Crossways Hotel,** Wilmington, Polegate, E. Sussex, BN26 5SG.*
Georgian house in two acres.
Open: All Year (not Xmas)
Grades: AA 4 Q
01323 482455
Mr Stott
Fax no: 01323 487811
Rates fr: *£34.00*-**£44.00**.
Beds: 3D 2T 2S
Baths: 7 Ensuite
(20)

***Fairview,** Wilmington, Polegate, E. Sussex, BN26 5SQ.*
Small country cottage.
Open: Apr to Oct
01323 870210
Mrs Forrest
Rates fr: *£14.00*-**£14.00**.
Beds: 2T
Baths: 1 Shared
(2)

***The Giants Rest,** Wilmington, Polegate, E. Sussex, BN26 5SQ.*
Country freehouse in Downland village.
Open: All Year (not Xmas)
01323 870207
Mr Jones
Rates fr: *£16.00*-**£16.00**.
Beds: 2F
Baths: 1 Shared
(20)

Winchelsea

National Grid Ref: TQ9017

New Inn, Bridge Inn

***The Strand House,** Tanyard Lane, Winchelsea, Rye, E. Sussex, TN36 4JT.*
Open: All Year
Grades: ETB 3 Cr, Comm, AA 4 Q, Select, RAC Acclaim
01797 226276 Mr & Mrs Roche
Fax no: 01797 224806
Rates fr: *£20.00*-**£28.00**.
Beds: 1F 8D 1T
Baths: 8 Ensuite 1 Shared
(12)
C15th house of charm & character with oak beams & inglenooks. Individual, well-appointed rooms. Pretty gardens. Ideal base for exploring Kent & Sussex.

***Chestnut Cottage,** Hihamrd, Winchelsea, E. Sussex, TN36 4HG.*
Pretty cottage, tranquil historic setting.
Open: All Year (not Xmas)
01797 226533 Mrs Allen
Rates fr: *£20.00*-**£30.00**.
Beds: 1D
Baths: 1 Private
(1)

Please respect a B&B's wishes regarding children, animals & smoking.

West Sussex

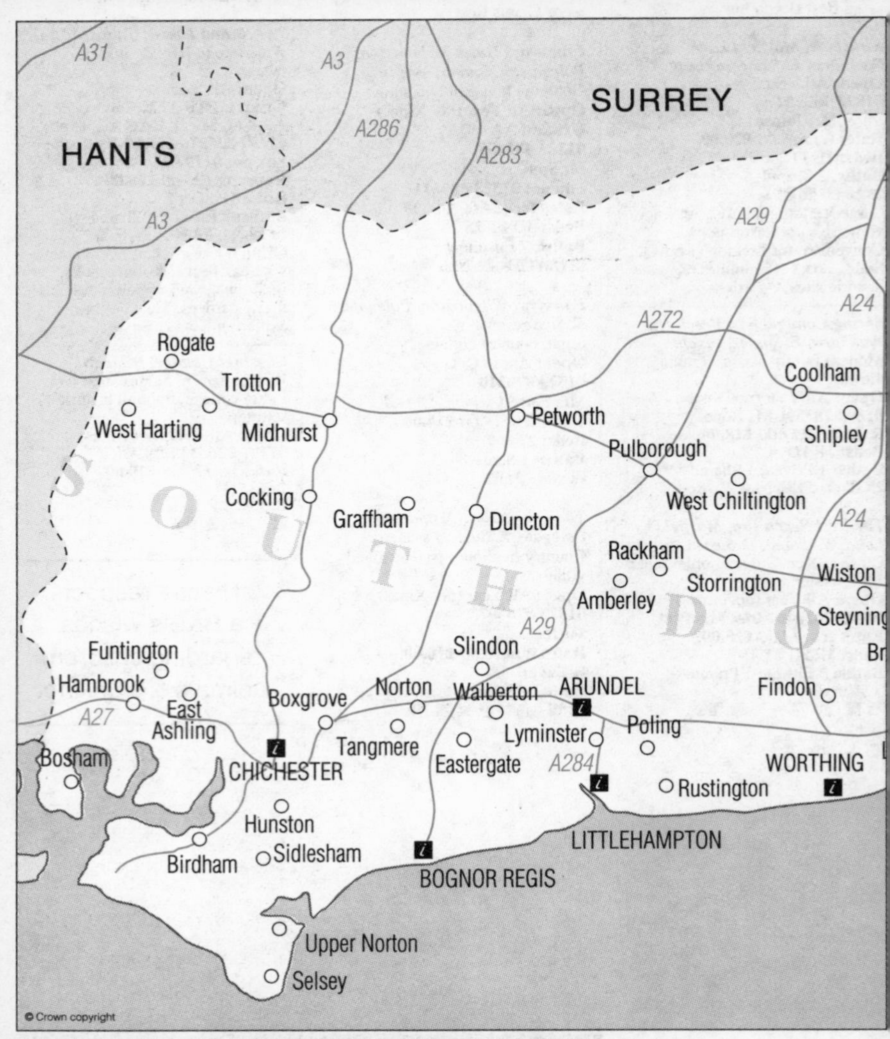

Tourist Information Centres

61 High Street, **Arundel**, West Sussex, BN18 9AJ, 01903 882268.

Little Chef Complex, **Fontwell**, Arundel, West Sussex, BN18 0SD, 01243 543269.

Belmont Street, **Bognor Regis**, W Sussex, PO21 1BJ, 01243 823140.

St Peter's Market, West Street, **Chichester**, West Sussex, PO19 1AH, 01243 775888.

International Arrivals, The Concourse, South Terminal, Gatwick Airport, **Gatwick**, West Sussex, RH6 0NP, 01293 560108.

9 The Causeway, **Horsham**, West Sussex, RH12 1HE, 01403 211661.

Windmill Complex, Coastguard Road, **Littlehampton**, West Sussex, BN17 5LH, 01903 713480, (Easter to Oct).

Chapel Road, **Worthing**, West Sussex, BN11 1HQ, 01903 210022.

Amberley

National Grid Ref: TQ0313

Bacons, *Amberley, Arundel, W. Sussex,* BN18 9NJ.
Pretty old cottage.
Open: All Year (not Xmas)
01798 831234
Mrs Jollands
Rates fr: *£17.00*-**£17.00**.
Beds: 2T
Baths: 1 Shared

Ardingly

National Grid Ref: TQ3429

Gardener's Arms

***Coneybury,** Hook Lane, West Hoathly, Ardingly, East Grinstead, W. Sussex, RH19 4PX.*
Open: All Year (not Xmas)
Grades: ETB 2 Cr, High Comm
01342 810200
Mrs Day
Fax no: 01342 810887
Rates fr: *£20.00*-**£30.00**.
Beds: 1D 1T
Baths: 1 Private 1 Shared
(4)
Secluded unique cedarwood country house.

Arundel

National Grid Ref: TQ0107

Spur, Six Bells, White Hart

***Beam Ends,** Hedgers Hill, Walberton, Arundel, W. Sussex, BN18 0LR.*
Thatched C16th cottage. Superb views. **Open:** Feb to Dec
01243 551254 Mr Botteley
Rates fr: *£19.00*-**£25.00**.
Beds: 1F 1D
Baths: 2 Ensuite
(20)

The lowest **single** *rate is shown in* **bold.**

***Arundel Vineyard,** Church Lane, Lyminster, Arundel, W. Sussex, BN17 7QF.*
Modern farmhouse, peaceful English vineyard.
Open: All Year (not Xmas)
Grades: ETB 2 Cr, Comm
01903 883393
Mrs Rankin
Rates fr: *£18.00*-**£24.00**.
Beds: 1D 1T
Baths: 2 Private
(6) (4)

***Portreeves Acre,** The Causeway, Arundel, W. Sussex, BN18 9JL.*
Modern house beside River Arun.
Open: All Year (not Xmas)
01903 883277 Mr Rogers
Rates fr: *£18.00*-**£20.00**.
Beds: 2D 1T
Baths: 3 Private
(8) (7)

***Kingfishers,** The Slipe, Arundel, W. Sussex, BN18 9DU.*
Modern house, rooms overlooking River Arun.
Open: Easter to Sep
Grades: ETB Listed, Approv
01903 883443
Rates fr: *£15.00*-**£15.00**.
Beds: 1D 1T
Baths: 1 Shared
(3)

***Bridge House,** 18 Queen Street, Arundel, W. Sussex, BN18 9JG.*
C18th family-run guest house.
Open: All Year (not Xmas)
Grades: ETB 3 Cr, Comm
01903 882142
Freecall: 0500 323 224
Mr Hutchinson
Fax no: 01903 883600
Rates fr: *£15.00*-**£20.00**.
Beds: 6F 9D 2T 2S
Baths: 15 Private 4 Shared
(10)

***The Meadows,** 64 Ford Road, Arundel, W. Sussex, BN18 9EX.*
Historic town views, easy walk.
Open: All Year (not Xmas)
01903 884895
Mrs Gimson
Rates fr: *£12.50*-**£15.00**.
Beds: 1D 1T 1S
Baths: 1 Private 1 Shared
(3)

Balcombe

National Grid Ref: TQ3130

Half Moon

***Rocks Lane Cottage,** Rowhill Lane, Balcombe, Haywards Heath, West Sussex, RH17 6JG.*
Stone cottage with glorious views.
Open: All Year (not Xmas)
01444 811245
Mrs Parry
Rates fr: *£20.00*-**£25.00**.
Beds: 1D
Baths: 1 Private
(1)

National Grid References are for villages, towns and cities - *not* for individual houses.

Birdham

National Grid Ref: SU8200

Bell Inn

Seldens, *Bell Lane, Birdham, Chichester, W. Sussex, PO20 7HY.*
Listed C18th thatched cottage.
Open: All Year
01243 512358 Mrs Hepburn
Rates fr: *£20.00*-**£20.00**.
Beds: 1D 1S
Baths: 1 Ensuite 1 Private
(4)

Bognor Regis

National Grid Ref: SZ9399

Tanngry Llannrwst

Selwood Lodge, *93 Victoria Drive, Bognor Regis, W. Sussex, PO21 2DZ.*
Large detached house. Licensed bar. **Open:** All Year
01243 865071 Mrs Bodle
Rates fr: *£15.00*-**£17.00**.
Beds: 2F 2D 1T
Baths: 2 Shared
(3)

Regis Lodge, *Gloucester Road, Bognor Regis, W. Sussex, PO21 1NU.*
Family-run guest house.
Open: All Year (not Xmas)
Grades: ETB 3 Cr, High Comm
01243 827110 Mr Rider
Rates fr: *£16.00*-**£18.00**.
Beds: 3F 3D 2T
Baths: 6 Ensuite 2 Private
(5) (9)

Lorna Doone, *58 Sandymount Avenue,, Bognor Regis, W. Sussex, PO22 9EP.*
Bungalow, usual facilities, quiet area. **Open:** All Year
01243 822203 Mr & Mrs Robinson
Rates fr: *£15.00*-**£20.00**.
Beds: 1F 1D 1T
Baths: 2 Ensuite 1 Private
(10) (3)

Please respect a B&B's wishes regarding children, animals & smoking.

Bosham

National Grid Ref: SU8004

Memories of India, The Swan

Kenwood, *Off A259 Coast Road, Bosham, Chichester, W. Sussex, PO18 8PH.*
Harbour views from Victorian country house. **Open:** All Year
Grades: AA 5 Q, Prem Select
01243 572727 Mrs Godden
Fax no: 01243 572738
Rates fr: *£22.50*-**£15.00**.
Beds: 1F 3D 2T 1S
Baths: 7 Ensuite
(20)

Good Hope, *Delling Lane, Old Bosham, Bosham, Chichester, W. Sussex, PO18 8NR.*
Comfortably furnished, friendly private home.
Open: All Year (not Xmas)
01243 572487 Mrs Jones
Rates fr: *£20.00*-**£20.00**.
Beds: 1T **Baths:** 1 Ensuite
(2)

White Barn, *Crede Lane, Bosham, Chichester, W. Sussex, PO18 8NX.*
Unique modern house.
Open: All Year (not Xmas)
01243 573113 Mrs Trotman
Rates fr: *£25.00*-**£25.00**.
Beds: 1D 2T **Baths:** 3 Private
(4)

Barford, *Bosham Lane, Bosham, Chichester, West Sussex, PO18 8HL.*
Attractive cottage style bungalow.
Open: All Year
01243 573393 Mr & Mrs Flanagan
Rates fr: *£17.00*-**£20.00**.
Beds: 2D 1T
(1)

Boxgrove

National Grid Ref: SU9007

Olde Cottage Inn

66 The Street, *Boxgrove, Chichester, W. Sussex, PO18 0EE.*
Quiet annexe with own entrance.
Open: All Year
Grades: ETB Listed, Comm
01243 774085 Mrs Bruford
Rates fr: *£20.00*-**£30.00**.
Beds: 1D 1T **Baths:** 2 Private
(3)

Bramber

National Grid Ref: TQ1810

Castle Hotel

Castle Hotel, *The Street, Bramber, Steyning, W. Sussex, BN44 3WE.*
Spacious, characterful, romantic, friendly inn. **Open:** All Year
01903 812102 Mr & Mrs Mitchell
Fax no: 01903 816711
Rates fr: *£17.00*-**£22.00**.
Beds: 2F 4D 2T
Baths: 6 Ensuite 4 Shared
(20)

The lowest **single** *rate is shown in* **bold.**

Burgess Hill

National Grid Ref: TQ3119

Well House, *Well House Lane, Burgess Hill, West Sussex, RH15 0BN.*
Large mock-Tudor detached house.
Open: All Year (not Xmas)
01444 233231 Mr & Mrs Allen
Rates fr: *£20.00*-**£18.00**.
Beds: 2D 1T 1S
Baths: 1 Ensuite 1 Shared
(5)

Roselands, *3 Upper St Johns Road, Burgess Hill, West Sussex, RH15 8HB.*
Comfortable family home.
Open: All Year
01444 870491 Mr & Mrs Tancred
Rates fr: *£17.50*-**£17.50**.
Beds: 1T 1D 2S
Baths: 2 Shared
(4)

Chichester

National Grid Ref: SU8604

Crown Inn, Nags Head, Royal Oak (Lavant)

Bayleaf, *16 Whyke Road, Chichester, W. Sussex, PO19 2HN.*
Open: All Year
01243 774330 Mrs Easton
Rates fr: *£22.00*-**£20.00**.
Beds: 1D 1T 2S
Baths: 1 Ensuite
Historical Cathedral city set between South Downs and sea. Chichester Festival Theatre, Fishbourne Roman Palace, Glorious Goodwood, Weald & Woodland Open Museum, beautiful gardens and houses open to public. City centre, restaurants & pubs within easy walking distance. Freshly cooked breakfast in large room overlooking garden. A very warm welcome waiting for all our guests.

5a Little London, *Chichester, W. Sussex, PO19 1PH.*
Town centre house, second floor.
Open: All Year (not Xmas)
01243 788405 Mrs Campbell White
Rates fr: *£17.50*-**£17.50**.
Beds: 1T
Baths: 1 Shared

Bringing children with you? Always ask for any special rates.

Always telephone to get directions to the B&B - you will save time!

Litten House, *148 St Pancras, Chichester, W. Sussex, PO19 1SH.*
Open: All Year (not Xmas)
01243 774503 (also fax no)
Mrs Steward
Rates fr: *£17.00*-**£17.00**.
Beds: 1F 1D 1T
Baths: 2 Shared
(4)
Characterful Georgian house central for all city amenities & theatre. Wash-basins in all rooms, kingsize bed, garden rooms. Restaurants & public car park in our street.

White Lodge, *First House, Lavant Road, Chichester, W. Sussex, PO19 4QY.*
Large 1920s private house & beautiful garden.
Open: All Year (not Xmas)
01243 527495 Mrs Wingfield Hayes
Rates fr: *£20.00*-**£20.00**.
Beds: 1D 1T 1S
Baths: 1 Ensuite 1 Private 1 Shared
(4)

Hedgehogs, *45 Whyke Lane, Chichester, W. Sussex, PO19 2JT.*
Open: All Year
Grades: ETB Listed, Comm
01243 780022 Mrs Hosking
Rates fr: *£16.00*-**£21.00**.
Beds: 1D 1T
Baths: 2 Shared
(3)
Quiet family house about 0.5 miles from city centre, stations, theatre. Secluded garden. Tea/coffee facilities. Cyclists & hikers welcome. Non-smoking.

Whyke House, *13 Whyke Lane, Chichester, W. Sussex, PO19 2JR.*
Convenient house and S/C flat.
Open: All Year
01243 788767 Mr Hollis
Rates fr: *£17.50*-**£20.00**.
Beds: 1F 1D 1T
Baths: 3 Private
(4)

Please respect a B&B's wishes regarding children, animals & smoking.

Riverside Lodge, *7 Market Avenue, Chichester, W. Sussex, PO19 1JU.*
Traditional brick & flint house.
Open: All Year (not Xmas)
01243 783164 Mrs Tregear
Rates fr: *£18.00*-**£20.00**.
Beds: 3D
Baths: 2 Ensuite 1 Private
(1)

Marias, *47 Birdham Road, Chichester, W. Sussex, PO19 2TB.*
Delightful detached house & garden.
Open: All Year
01243 783452 Mrs O'Flinn
Rates fr: *£18.00*-**£17.00**.
Beds: 1D 1T 1S
Baths: 1 Ensuite 1 Shared
(5)

5 Willowbed Avenue, *Chichester, W. Sussex, PO19 2JD.*
Friendly house. Walking distance to city centre.
Open: All Year
01243 786366 Mrs Pring
Rates fr: *£16.00*-**£17.00**.
Beds: 1T 2S
Baths: 1 Private 1 Shared
(10) (2)

Clayton

National Grid Ref: TQ3014

Jack & Jill

Dower Cottage, *Underhill Lane, Clayton, Hassocks, W. Sussex, BN6 9PL.*
Open: All Year (not Xmas)
01273 843363 Mrs Bailey
Fax no: 01273 846836
Rates fr: *£20.00*-**£25.00**.
Beds: 1F 3D 1T 1S
Baths: 2 Ensuite 1 Shared
(8)
Lovely country house in peaceful location near South Downs Way, wonderful views from all rooms. Guest library. Brighton 15 minutes. Gatwick & Newhaven within 30 minutes.

Cocking

National Grid Ref: SU8717

Cocking Village Tea Rooms, *Chichester Road, Cocking, Midhurst, W. Sussex, GU29 0HN.*
1815 house with tea garden.
Open: All Year (not Xmas)
01730 813336 Mrs Thomas
Rates fr: *£18.00*-**£24.00**.
Beds: 2D 1T
Baths: 1 Shared
(5)

Coolham

National Grid Ref: TQ1222

Blue Idol Guest House, *Coolham, Horsham, W. Sussex, RH13 8QP.*
Historic house, peaceful, rural setting.
Open: All Year
01403 741241 D Curtis
Rates fr: *£16.00*-**£18.00**.
Beds: 2D 1T 2S
Baths: 2 Shared
(12) (15)

Copsale

National Grid Ref: TQ0814

The Bridge

Copsale Farm, *Copsale, Horsham, W. Sussex, RH13 6QU.*
Open: All Year (not Xmas)
01403 731114 (also fax no)
Mrs Churcher
Rates fr: *£18.00*-**£18.00**.
Beds: 2D
Baths: 1 Shared
(16)
C16th beamed farmhouse rurally situated amidst own 4 acres. Next to Downs Link, Bridle Path. Walking distance country pub. Ideal touring holidays. 0.75 hour airport/seaport.

Cuckfield

National Grid Ref: TQ3024

Stonecroft, *Broad Street, Cuckfield, Haywards Heath, West Sussex, RH17 5DY.*
Victorian private house, large gardens.
Open: All Year (not Xmas)
01444 455275 Mrs Skelton
Rates fr: *£17.00*-**£17.00**.
Beds: 1F 1T 1S
Baths: 1 Shared
(4)

Duncton

National Grid Ref: SU9517

Drifters, *Duncton, Petworth, W. Sussex, GU28 0JZ.*
Lovely, friendly modern house.
Open: All Year
01798 342706 Mrs Folkes
Rates fr: *£16.00*-**£20.00**.
Beds: 1D 2T 1S
Baths: 1 Ensuite 1 Shared

East Ashling

National Grid Ref: SU8207

Horse & Groom

Englewood, *East Ashling, Chichester, W. Sussex, PO18 9AS.*
Comfortable, cottage-style bungalow, 1/3 acre gardens.
Open: All Year (not Xmas)
01243 575407 Mrs Jones
Rates fr: *£16.50*-**£28.00**.
Beds: 1D 1T
Baths: 2 Ensuite
(4)

The lowest **single** *rate is shown in* **bold.**

East Grinstead

National Grid Ref: TQ3938

Ship Inn, Dunnings Mill Restaurant

Ship Inn, *Ship Street, East Grinstead, W. Sussex,* *RH19 4EG.*
Open: All Year
01342 323197 / 312089
Mr Connor
Rates fr: *£17.50*-**£20.00**.
Beds: 7T
Baths: 2 Ensuite 1 Shared
(12)
Very friendly, family-run freehouse within easy reach of stations & Gatwick Airport. 8 real ales, 6 international lagers, 2 stouts. Very friendly atmosphere.

Brentridge, *24 Portland Road, East Grinstead, W. Sussex,* *RH19 4EA.*
Central & quiet. Beautiful garden.
Open: All Year
01342 322004
Mrs Greenwood
Fax no: 01342 324145
Rates fr: *£15.00*-**£20.00**.
Beds: 1D 1T 1S
Baths: 2 Shared
(2)

Cranston House, *Cranston Road, East Grinstead, W. Sussex,* *RH19 3HW.*
House with parking near Gatwick.
Open: All Year
01342 323609
Mr Linacre
Rates fr: *£16.00*-**£20.00**.
Beds: 1F 1T 1S
Baths: 1 Ensuite 1 Shared
(6) (4)

Cranfield Lodge Hotel, *Maypole Road, East Grinstead, W. Sussex,* *RH19 1HW.*
Quiet position near town & Gatwick.
Open: All Year
01342 321251
Mr Sandhu
Rates fr: *£15.00*-**£15.00**.
Beds: 4F 9D 1T 5S
Baths: 10 Ensuite 9 Shared
(1) (15)

Eastergate

National Grid Ref: SU9405

Wilkes Head

Greenfields Farm, *Fontwell Avenue, Eastergate, Chichester, W. Sussex,* *PO20 6RU.*
Modern comfortable farmhouse, warm welcome.
Open: All Year (not Xmas)
01243 542815
Mrs Bland
Rates fr: *£16.00*-**£18.00**.
Beds: 1F 1D 1T
Baths: 1 Shared
(0) (3)

High season, bank holidays and special events mean low availability *anywhere.*

Findon

National Grid Ref: TQ1208

Village House

Findon Tower, *Cross Lane, Findon, Worthing, W. Sussex,* *BN14 0UG.*
Elegant Edwardian country house.
Open: All Year (not Xmas)
Grades: ETB 2 Cr, Comm
01903 873870 Mr & Mrs Smith
Rates fr: *£17.50*-**£25.00**.
Beds: 2D 1T
Baths: 2 Ensuite 1 Private
(10)

Racehorse Cottage, *Nepcote, Findon, Worthing, W. Sussex,* *BN14 0SN.*
Comfortable cottage under Cissbury Ring.
Open: All Year (not Xmas)
01903 873783 Mr Lloyd
Rates fr: *£16.00*-**£20.00**.
Beds: 2T
Baths: 1 Shared
(5) (2)

Fulking

National Grid Ref: TQ2411

Shepherd & Dog, Royal Oak (Poynings)

Downers Vineyard, *Clappers Lane, Fulking, Henfield, W. Sussex,* *BN5 9NH.*
Panoramic views, Brighton 8 miles.
Open: All Year (not Xmas)
Grades: ETB Listed, Approv
01273 857484 Mrs Downer
Fax no: 01273 857068
Rates fr: *£16.50*-**£19.00**.
Beds: 1D 1T
Baths: 2 Shared
(6)

Funtington

National Grid Ref: SU8008

Fox & Hounds

Stanes Farm, *Funtington, Chichester, W. Sussex,* *PO18 9DW.*
Converted Sussex barn in country.
Open: All Year (not Xmas)
01243 575558 Mrs Jones
Fax no: 01243 575701
Rates fr: *£18.00*-**£18.00**.
Beds: 1D 1T
Baths: 1 Shared
(4)

Gatwick

National Grid Ref: TQ2537

Brooklyn Manor Hotel, *Bonnetts Lane, Gatwick, Crawley, W. Sussex,* *RH11 0NY.*
Large Victorian house, convenient for airport.
Open: All Year (not Xmas)
01293 546024 Mr Davis
Rates fr: *£17.50*-**£20.00**.
Beds: 2F 4D 4T 1S
Baths: 4 Private 3 Shared
(100)

Graffham

National Grid Ref: SU9217

Eastwood Farm, *Graffham, Petworth, W. Sussex,* *GU28 0QF.*
Large country house, lovely surroundings.
Open: All Year
01798 867317 Mrs Allen
Rates fr: *£19.00*-**£19.00**.
Beds: 1D 1T 2S
Baths: 1 Private 1 Shared
(5) (6)

Hambrook

National Grid Ref: SU7806

Fox & Hounds

14 The Avenue, *Hambrook, Chichester, W. Sussex,* *PO18 8TY.*
Quiet comfortable country home.
Open: All Year (not Xmas)
01243 573199 Mrs Bailey
Rates fr: *£16.00*-**£16.00**.
Beds: 1D 1T **Baths:** 1 Shared
(3)

Hassocks

National Grid Ref: TQ3015

26 Keymer Gardens, *Hassocks, W. Sussex,* *BN6 8QZ.*
Quiet, friendly, views to Downs.
Open: All Year (not Xmas)
01273 844537 Mrs Davies
Rates fr: *£12.00*-**£13.50**.
Beds: 1F 1D **Baths:** 1 Shared

Haywards Heath

National Grid Ref: TQ3324

The Wheatsheaf, Snowdrop, Sergison Arms, Bent Arms, Fox & Hounds

Pinehurst, *Tylers Green, Haywards Heath, W. Sussex,* *RH16 4BW.*
Open: All Year
01444 456578 Mrs O'Riordan
Rates fr: *£16.00*-**£22.00**.
Beds: 1F 1D 2T 1S
Baths: 2 Ensuite 2 Private
(8) (4)
Beamed country house set in 1 acre of gardens backing onto mature reserve. One mile to restaurants & shops. 20 minutes to Gatwick & Brighton.

The lowest *double* rate per person is shown in *italics*.

***12 Petlands Road,** Haywards Heath, West Sussex, RH16 4HH.*
Homely, cottage atmosphere.
Open: All Year
01444 454473 Mrs Hartley
Rates fr: *£17.00*-**£17.00**.
Beds: 1D 1T 1S
Baths: 1 Shared
(3)

***Mattagami,** 61 Franklynn Road, Haywards Heath, West Sussex, RH16 4DS.*
Modern, smoke-free, warm, panoramic view.
Open: All Year
01444 453506
Mrs Pettitt
Rates fr: *£16.00*-**£18.00**.
Beds: 2T 2S
Baths: 1 Private 1 Shared
(0) (4)

Henfield

National Grid Ref: TQ2116

Plough Inn

***Beeches,** West End Lane, Henfield, West Sussex, BN5 9RG.*
Tudor farmhouse with swimming pool.
Open: All Year (not Xmas)
01273 492495 Mrs Abbott
Fax no: 01273 493000
Rates fr: *£18.50*-**£25.00**.
Beds: 1D 2T
Baths: 2 Ensuite 1 Private
(3)

***Little Oreham Farm,** Oreham Common, Woods Mill, Henfield, W. Sussex, BN5 9SB.*
Beautiful 300-year-old farmhouse, convenient Gatwick.
Open: All Year (not Xmas)
01273 492931 Mrs Forbes
Rates fr: *£17.50*-**£20.00**.
Beds: 2D 1T
Baths: 2 Ensuite 1 Private

Horsham

National Grid Ref: TQ1731

***...ton House,** 29 Rusper Road, Horsham, West Sussex, RH12 4BA.*
Small, high standard guest house.
Open: All Year
01403 211825 Mrs Ashton
Rates fr: *£17.50*-**£25.00**.
Beds: 1D 2T
Baths: 3 Private 1 Shared
(1) (4)

Hunston

National Grid Ref: SU8601

***2 Meadow Close,** Hunston, Chichester, W. Sussex, PO20 6PB.*
Warm welcome to our home.
Open: All Year
01243 788504 Mrs Parfoot
Rates fr: *£16.00*.
Beds: 1F 1D 1T
Baths: 1 Private
(2)

Hurstpierpoint

National Grid Ref: TQ2816

***Bankyfield,** 21 Hassocks Road, Hurstpierpoint, Hassocks, W. Sussex, BN6 9QH.*
Georgian house in Downland village.
Open: All Year
Grades: ETB Listed
01273 833217 Mrs Norris
Rates fr: *£16.00*-**£16.00**.
Beds: 1T
Baths: 1 Shared
(1)

***Wickham Place,** Wickham Drive, Hurstpierpoint, Hassocks, W. Sussex, BN6 9AP.*
Ideally situated in a pretty village.
Open: All Year (not Xmas)
01273 832172 Mrs Moore
Rates fr: *£18.50*-**£22.00**.
Beds: 1D 2T
Baths: 1 Shared
(5)

Ifield

National Grid Ref: TQ2537

***Waterhall Country House,** Prestwood Lane, Ifield Wood, Ifield, Crawley, West Sussex, RH11 0LA.*
Luxury accommodation in open countryside.
Open: All Year (not Xmas)
01293 520002
Mr & Mrs Dawson
Rates fr: *£20.00*-**£20.00**.
Beds: 1F 2D 2T 1S
Baths: 5 Ensuite 1 Private

Lancing

National Grid Ref: TQ1804

***The Moorings,** 71 Brighton Road, Lancing, W. Sussex, BN15 8RB.*
1930s house on seafront.
Open: All Year (not Xmas)
01903 755944
Mr Stuart
Rates fr: *£15.00*-**£15.00**.
Beds: 1F 1D 1T 1S
Baths: 1 Shared

The lowest *double* rate per person is shown in *italics*.

Lindfield

National Grid Ref: TQ3425

Gardeners Arms

***Little Lywood,** Ardingly Road, Lindfield, Haywards Heath, West Sussex, RH16 2QX.*
Beautiful C16th cottage & setting.
Open: All Year (not Xmas)
01444 892571 Mrs Leadsom
Rates fr: *£20.00*-**£25.00**.
Beds: 1D
Baths: 1 Private
(2)

***2 Hickmans Close,** Lindfield, Haywards Heath, West Sussex, RH16 2PS.*
Modern, detached, comfortable village house.
Open: All Year
01444 482006 Mr & Mrs Robinson
Rates fr: *£13.00*-**£16.00**.
Beds: 1D 2T
Baths: 2 Shared
(6) (4)

Littlehampton

National Grid Ref: TQ0202

***The Lucknow,** 86 South Terrace, Littlehampton, W. Sussex, BN17 5LJ.*
Edwardian house - premier seafront position.
Open: All Year
01903 715092
Mrs Wakefield
Rates fr: *£13.50*-**£17.50**.
Beds: 1F 1D 1T
Baths: 2 Ensuite 1 Private

***Amber Guest House,** 5 Selborne Road, Littlehampton, W. Sussex, BN17 5NN.*
Small, homely guest house.
Open: All Year
01903 717456 Mrs Kelly
Rates fr: *£13.00*-**£17.00**.
Beds: 1F 1D 1T
Baths: 2 Private 1 Shared

***Amberley House,** 74 Arundel Road, Littlehampton, W. Sussex, BN17 7DF.*
Large family-run guest house.
Open: All Year (not Xmas)
01903 721627
Mrs Latter
Rates fr: *£11.00*-**£15.00**.
Beds: 2F 2D 2T 1S
Baths: 2 Private 2 Shared
(5)

***6 Selborne Road,** Littlehampton, W. Sussex, BN17 5NN.*
Large Edwardian private house.
Open: Jan to Nov
01903 716387
Mrs Pay
Rates fr: *£13.00*-**£14.00**.
Beds: 1F 1T 1S
Baths: 1 Shared
(2)

All details shown are as supplied by B&B owners in Autumn 1996.

Littleworth

National Grid Ref: TQ1920

Windmill, Green Man, Horse & Groom

The Bushes, *Littleworth, Partridge Green, Horsham, W. Sussex,* RH13 8JF.
Edwardian country house in hamlet.
Open: All Year
Grades: ETB 2 Cr, Comm
01403 710495 Mrs Bolt
Rates fr: *£16.00*-**£17.00**.
Beds: 2D 1T 1S
Baths: 1 Ensuite 1 Shared
(7)

Lower Beeding

National Grid Ref: TQ2128

Wheatsheaf Inn, Plummers Plain

Village Pantry, *Handcross Road, Plummers Plain, Lower Beeding, Horsham, W. Sussex,* RH13 6NU.
Comfortable family home, lovely garden.
Open: All Year (not Xmas)
01403 891319 Mrs Jays
Rates fr: *£16.50*-**£23.00**.
Beds: 1F 1D 1T 1S
Baths: 2 Private 2 Shared
(6)

The Old Posthouse, *Plummers Plain, Lower Beeding, Horsham, W. Sussex,* RH13 6NU.
C19th lovely garden. Cactus collection.
Open: All Year
01403 891776 Mrs Murby
Rates fr: *£20.00*-**£20.00**.
Beds: 1F 2D 1T 2S
Baths: 3 Private 2 Shared
(5)

Brookfield Farm Hotel, *Winterpit Lane, Plummers Plain, Lower Beeding, Horsham, W. Sussex,* RH13 6LY.
Situated midst beautiful country side.
Open: All Year
Grades: ETB 3 Cr
01403 891568 Mr Christian
Fax no: 01403 891499
Rates fr: *£24.00*-**£35.00**.
Beds: 2F 6D 6T 9S
Baths: 23 Ensuite
(Yes) (Yes)

Lyminster

National Grid Ref: TQ0204

Six Bells

Sandfield House, *Lyminster, Littlehampton, W. Sussex,* BN17 7PG.
Large Victorian private house.
Open: All Year
Grades: ETB 1 Cr, Comm
01903 724129 Mrs Farrer-Brown
Fax no: 01903 715041
Rates fr: *£17.00*-**£32.00**.
Beds: 1D **Baths:** 1 Shared
(3)

Arundel Vineyard, *Church Lane, Lyminster, Arundel, W. Sussex,* BN17 7QF.
Modern farmhouse, peaceful English vineyard.
Open: All Year (not Xmas)
Grades: ETB 2 Cr, Comm
01903 883393 Mrs Rankin
Rates fr: *£18.00*-**£24.00**.
Beds: 1D 1T **Baths:** 2 Private
(6) (4)

Midhurst

National Grid Ref: SU8821

Crown Inn

The Crown Inn, *Edinburgh Square, Midhurst, W. Sussex,* GU29 9NL.
C16th free house.
Open: All Year
Grades: ETB Listed
01730 813462 Mr Stevens
Rates fr: *£15.00*-**£17.50**.
Beds: 1D 1T 1S
Baths: 1 Shared

Norton

National Grid Ref: SU9206

Old Cottage Inn

Five Acres, *Norton Lane, Norton, Chichester, W. Sussex,* PO20 6NH.
Tranquil country setting, relaxing atmosphere.
Open: All Year
01243 543294 Mrs Underwood
Rates fr: *£18.00*-**£18.00**.
Beds: 1D 1T 2S
Baths: 1 Ensuite 1 Private 1 Shared
(6)

Petworth

National Grid Ref: SU9721

Welldiggers Arms

Grove House, *Grove Street, Petworth, W. Sussex,* GU28 0BD.
C16th historic Tudor town house.
Open: All Year
01798 342563 Mrs Houghton Connell
Rates fr: *£17.00*-**£25.00**.
Beds: 1D 1T **Baths:** 2 Shared

Rectory Cottage, *Rectory Lane, Petworth, W. Sussex,* GU28 0DB.
C18th, quiet, close town centre.
Open: Easter to Sep
01798 342380 Mrs Craddock
Rates fr: *£16.00*-**£20.00**.
Beds: 1D 1S
Baths: 1 Shared
(1) (2)

Poling

National Grid Ref: TQ0107

Plough & Sail

Medlar Cottage, *Poling, Arundel, W. Sussex,* BN18 9PT.
Very comfortable accomodation. Lovely countryside.
Open: All Year (not Xmas)
01903 883106
Mr & Mrs Mercer
Rates fr: *£18.00*-**£18.00**.
Beds: 1T 1S 1D
Baths: 1 Shared
(3)

Poynings

National Grid Ref: TQ2612

Manor Farm, *Poynings, Brighton, E. Sussex,* BN45 7AG.
Comfortable farmhouse on working farm.
Open: Mar to Dec
01273 857371 Mrs Revell
Rates fr: *£18.50*-**£22.00**.
Beds: 1D 2T
Baths: 2 Shared
(8)

Pulborough

National Grid Ref: TQ0418

Chequers Hotel, *Church Place, Pulborough, W. Sussex,* RH20 1AD.
Country hotel in glorious Sussex countryside.
Open: All Year
Grades: ETB 4 Cr, High Comm, AA 2 St, RAC 2 St
01798 872486
Mr Searancke
Fax no: 01798 872715
Rates fr: *£38.50*-**£49.50**.
Beds: 3F 5D 3T
Baths: 10 Ensuite 1 Private
(14)

Rackham

National Grid Ref: TQ0413

Sparright Farm, *Rackham, Pulborough, W. Sussex,* RH20 2EY.
C17th, peacefully situated, homel
Open: All Year (not Xmas)
01798 872132
Mrs West
Rates fr: *£15.00*-**£16.00**.
Beds: 1F 1D
Baths: 2 Shared
(2)

ɩogate

ational Grid Ref: SU8023

Three Horse Shoes

***íizzards Farm,** Rogate, etersfield, Hants, GU31 5HS.*
onverted farmhouse, spacious & ecluded.
pen: All Year (not Xmas)
rades: AA 5 Q, Prem Select
1730 821656 Mrs Francis
ax no: 01730 821655
ates fr: *£25.00*-**£30.00**.
eds: 3D **Baths:** 3 Ensuite
(8) (20)

ɩustington

ational Grid Ref: TQ0502

***enmore Guest House,** Claigmar oad, Rustington, Littlehampton, /. Sussex, BN16 2NL.*
etached Edwardian guest house ose to sea. **Open:** All Year
rades: ETB 3 Cr, High Comm, A 4 Q, Select, RAC High cclaim
1903 784634 Mrs Dobbs
ates fr: *£22.50*-**£16.50**.
eds: 3F 2D 1T 2S
aths: 7 Private 1 Shared
(8)

ɩelsey

ational Grid Ref: SZ8593

***t Andrews Lodge**, Chichester oad, Selsey, Chichester, W. ussex, PO20 0LX.*
pen: All Year (not Xmas)
rades: ETB 3 Cr, Comm, A 4 Q, Select
1243 606899 Mrs Kennedy
ax no: 01243 607826
ates fr: *£20.00*-**£20.00**.
eds: 2F 4D 2T 1S
aths: 9 Private
(15)
warm welcome awaits you at our amily-run establishment situated n the Manhood Peninsula. riendly relaxed atmosphere. Cosy og-fires. Home cooked food.

ɩharpthorne

ational Grid Ref: TQ3732

Vinols Cross, Cat Inn (West loathly)

***he Middle House,** Cookhams, harpthorne, East Grinstead, West ussex, RH19 4HU.*
pen: All Year (not Xmas)
rades: ETB 1 Cr, Comm
1342 810566 (also fax no)
Ars Long
ates fr: *£20.00*-**£30.00**.
eds: 1D 1T 1S
aths: 1 Ensuite 2 Shared
(4)
entral portion of 100-year-old ountry house on Sussex Weald. eaceful rural setting. Outstanding iews. Comfortable spacious ooms. Good village inn 0.75 mile.

Pay B&Bs by cash or cheque. Be prepared to pay up front for one night stays.

***Saxons,** Horsted Lane, Sharpthorne, East Grinstead, W. Sussex, RH19 4HY.*
Detached country house. Beautiful countryside!
Open: All Year
01342 810821
Mrs Smith
Rates fr: *£16.00*-**£20.00**.
Beds: 2D 2S
Baths: 2 Ensuite 1 Shared
(6)

Shipley

National Grid Ref: TQ1421

***Goffsland Farm,** Shipley, Horsham, W. Sussex, RH13 7BQ.*
C16th farmhouse working farm.
Open: All Year
Grades: ETB 2 Cr, Comm
01403 730434 Mrs Liverton
Rates fr: *£16.00*-**£18.00**.
Beds: 1F
Baths: 1 Private

Shoreham-by-Sea

National Grid Ref: TQ2205

The Crabtree

***The Crabtree,** 6 Buckingham Road, Shoreham-by-Sea, W. Sussex, BN43 5UA.*
Friendly traditional pub with garden.
Open: All Year (not Xmas)
01273 463508 Mr & Mrs Jones
Rates fr: *£17.50*-**£17.50**.
Beds: 1F 1D
Baths: 1 Shared
(10)

Sidlesham

National Grid Ref: SU8598

Blacksmiths Arms

***Meadowview,** Jury Lane, Sidlesham, Chichester, W. Sussex, PO20 7PX.*
Quiet country bungalow in acre of garden.
Open: All Year
01243 641316 Mrs Shepherd
Rates fr: *£20.00*.
Beds: 3D
Baths: 3 Ensuite
(4)

The lowest *double* rate per person is shown in *italics*.

Slindon

National Grid Ref: SU9608

***Mill Lane House,** Mill Lane, Slindon, Arundel, W. Sussex, BN18 0RP.*
C17th house, National Trust village.
Open: All Year
Grades: ETB 2 Cr, Comm
01243 814440 Mrs Fuente
Rates fr: *£19.25*-**£25.00**.
Beds: 2F 2D 2T 1S
Baths: 7 Ensuite
(7)

Steyning

National Grid Ref: TQ1711

Wine Bar, Star Inn

***Buncton Manor Farm,** Steyning Road, Wiston, Steyning, W. Sussex, BN44 3DD.*
C15th farmhouse on working farm.
Open: All Year
01903 812736 Mrs Rowland
Rates fr: *£16.00*-**£20.00**.
Beds: 1F 1T
Baths: 1 Shared
(6)

***5 Coxham Lane,** Steyning, W. Sussex, BN44 3LG.*
Comfortable house in quiet lane.
Open: All Year (not Xmas)
01903 812286 Mrs Morrow
Rates fr: *£14.00*-**£14.00**.
Beds: 2T 1S
Baths: 1 Shared
(4)

***The Old Museum House,** 93 High Street, Steyning, W. Sussex, BN44 3RE.*
Comfortable Georgian house, home produce.
Open: All Year (not Xmas)
01903 812317 Mrs Dawson
Rates fr: *£17.00*-**£20.00**.
Beds: 1D 1T
Baths: 2 Shared
(3)

High season, bank holidays and special events mean low availability *anywhere*.

Milestones, *25 High Street, Steyning, W. Sussex, BN44 3YE.*
Located on edge of South Downs.
Open: All Year (not Xmas)
01903 812338 Mrs Wood
Rates fr: *£19.00*-**£16.00**.
Beds: 1D 1T 1S **Baths:** 3 Private
(1)

Storrington

National Grid Ref: TQ0814

Anchor Inn, Old Forge

No 1, Lime Chase (Off Fryern Road), *Storrington, Pulborough, W. Sussex, RH20 4LX.*
Secluded luxury in Area of Outstanding Natural Beauty.
Open: All Year (not Xmas)
Grades: ETB Listed, High Comm
01903 740437 (also fax no)
Mrs Warton
Rates fr: *£20.00*-**£20.00**.
Beds: 1F 1T 1S
Baths: 1 Ensuite 1 Shared
(10) (5)

Willow Tree Cottage, *Washington Road, Storrington, Pulborough, W. Sussex, RH20 4AF.*
Open: All Year (not Xmas)
01903 740835 Mrs Smith
Fax no: 01903 262277
Rates fr: *£20.00*.
Beds: 2D 1T **Baths:** 4 Private
(10)
Welcoming, friendly, quiet. All rooms ensuite. Colour TV, tea-making facilities. Situated at foot of Sussex Downs. Arundel, Worthing 10 minutes. Children & dogs welcome.

Oakfield House, *Merrywood Lane, Thakeham, Storrington, Pulborough, W. Sussex, RH20 3HD.*
Modern, comfortable, delightful countryside home.
Open: All Year (not Xmas)
01903 740843 Mrs Arter
Rates fr: *£18.00*-**£17.00**.
Beds: 1D 2S
Baths: 1 Private 1 Shared
(3)

Tangmere

National Grid Ref: SU9006

Hill Farm House, *Chestnut Walk, Tangmere, Chichester, W. Sussex, PO20 6HH.*
C16th timber-framed, thatched cottage.
Open: Easter to Oct
01243 775104 Mrs Wood
Fax no: 01903 237378
Rates fr: *£16.00*.
Beds: 1D 1T **Baths:** 1 Shared
(5) (2)

All rates are subject to alteration at the owners' discretion.

The lowest *double* rate per person is shown in *italics*.

Upper Norton

National Grid Ref: SZ8695

Norton Lea Guest House, *Chichester Road, Upper Norton, Chichester, W. Sussex, PO20 9EA.*
Comfortable country house, warm welcome.
Open: All Year (not Xmas)
01243 605454 Mrs Halfacre
Rates fr: *£16.00*-**£16.00**.
Beds: 1F 2T
Baths: 1 Shared
(6)

Walberton

National Grid Ref: SU9705

The Spur (Slindon)

Beam Ends, *Hedgers Hill, Walberton, Arundel, W. Sussex, BN18 0LR.*
Thatched C16th cottage. Superb views.
Open: Feb to Dec
01243 551254 Mr Botteley
Rates fr: *£19.00*-**£25.00**.
Beds: 1F 1D
Baths: 2 Ensuite
(20)

Warninglid

National Grid Ref: TQ2623

Timbers Edge, *Longhouse Lane, off Spronketts Lane, Warninglid, Haywards Heath, West Sussex, RH17 5TE.*
Beautiful traditional Sussex country house.
Open: All Year (not Xmas)
01444 461456
Mr & Mrs Earlam
Rates fr: *£20.00*-**£20.00**.
Beds: 1D 1T 2S
Baths: 1 Ensuite 1 Shared
(12) (6)

West Chiltington

National Grid Ref: TQ0918

New House Farm, *Broadford Bridge Road, West Chiltington, Pulborough, W. Sussex, RH20 2LA.*
C15th Listed beamed farmhouse.
Open: Jan to Nov
01798 812215 Ms Steele
Rates fr: *£18.00*-**£25.00**.
Beds: 1D 2T
Baths: 3 Private
(10) (6)

West Harting

National Grid Ref: SU7821

3 Quebec, *West Harting, Petersfield, Hants, GU31 5PG.*
Peaceful, secluded private country house. **Open:** All Year
01730 825386 Mrs Stevens
Rates fr: *£15.00*-**£17.00**.
Beds: 1F 1S
Baths: 1 Ensuite 1 Private
(2)

West Hoathly

National Grid Ref: TQ3632

Cat Inn, Gardener's Arms (Ardingly)

Coneybury, *Hook Lane, West Hoathly, East Grinstead, W. Sussex, RH19 4PX.*
Secluded unique cedarwood country house.
Open: All Year (not Xmas)
Grades: ETB 2 Cr, High Comm
01342 810200
Mrs Day
Fax no: 01342 810887
Rates fr: *£20.00*-**£30.00**.
Beds: 1D 1T
Baths: 1 Private 1 Shared
(4)

Wineham

National Grid Ref: TQ2320

Wheatsheaf

Great Wapses Farm, *Wineham, Henfield, W. Sussex, BN5 9BJ.*
Peaceful attractive Tudor/Georgian farmhouse.
Open: All Year
01273 492544
Mr & Mrs Wilkin
Rates fr: *£18.00*-**£22.00**.
Beds: 3D 1T
Baths: 3 Private
(5)

Frylands Farm, *Wineham, Henfield, W. Sussex, BN5 9BP.*
Secluded C16th farmhouse, swimming, fishing.
Open: All Year (not Xmas)
01403 710214 Mr & Mrs Fowler
Rates fr: *£18.00*-**£20.00**.
Beds: 1F 1D 1T
Baths: 1 Private 2 Shared
(0) (6)

Wiston

National Grid Ref: TQ1414

Buncton Manor Farm, *Steyning Road, Wiston, Steyning, W. Sussex, BN44 3DD.*
C15th farmhouse on working farm.
Open: All Year
01903 812736
Mrs Rowland
Rates fr: *£16.00*-**£20.00**.
Beds: 1F 1T **Baths:** 1 Shared
(6)

Worthing

National Grid Ref: TQ1303

The Cricketers

Wolsey Hotel, *179-181 Brighton Road, Worthing, W. Sussex,* *BN11 2EX.*
Family-run, overlooking the sea.
Open: All Year (not Xmas)
Grades: AA 2 Q
01903 236149 Mr Price
Fax no: 01903 235875
Rates fr: *£21.00*-**£21.00**.
Beds: 2F 2D 3T 6S
Baths: 3 Private 2 Shared

Merton Guest House, *96 Broadwater Road, Worthing, W. Sussex,* *BN14 8AW.*
Family-run, comfortable & friendly.
Open: All Year
01903 238222 Mr Smith
Rates fr: *£20.00*-**£19.00**.
Beds: 4D 1T
Baths: 5 Ensuite
(8) (5)

The Beacons, *18 Shelley Road, Worthing, W. Sussex,* *BN11 1TU.*
Small, centrally situated, private hotel.
Open: All Year
Grades: ETB 3 Cr, Comm
01903 230948 Mrs Beckett
Rates fr: *£18.00*-**£25.00**.
Beds: 1F 3D 4T **Baths:** 8 Ensuite
(8)

Northview Guest House, *43 Wenban Road, Worthing, W. Sussex,* *BN11 1HY.*
Large Victorian house.
Open: All Year
01903 231350 Mrs Strudwick
Rates fr: *£14.00*-**£15.00**.
Beds: 1F 3T
(2) (4)

New Eversley Hotel Restaurant, *121-123 Brighton Road, Worthing, W. Sussex,* *BN11 2ES.*
Victorian licensed hotel & restaurant. **Open:** All Year
01903 239827 Mr Baker
Rates fr: *£17.50*-**£17.50**.
Beds: 2F 4D 3T 4S
Baths: 5 Private 2 Shared

Aspen House, *13 Winchester Road, Worthing, W. Sussex,* *BN11 4DJ.*
Quiet, tastefully furnished Edwardian house.
Open: All Year (not Xmas)
Grades: ETB 2 Cr, High Comm, AA 4 Q
01903 230584 Mrs Taylor
Rates fr: *£24.00*-**£26.00**.
Beds: 2D 1T 1S **Baths:** 3 Private
(3)

Williton Guest House, *10 Windsor Road, Worthing, W. Sussex,* *BN11 2LX.*
Large Victorian private house.
Open: All Year (not Xmas)
01903 237974
Mrs Leeds
Rates fr: *£15.50*-**£15.50**.
Beds: 1D 3T 2S
Baths: 1 Shared
(2)

12 Bath Road, *Worthing, W. Sussex,* *BN11 3NU.*
Large Victorian private house.
Open: All Year
01903 233181
Mrs Nightingale
Rates fr: *£18.00*-**£18.00**.
Beds: 1F 1D 1T 1S
Baths: 4 Ensuite

Marcroft Guest House, *17 St Georges Road, Worthing, W. Sussex,* *BN11 2DS.*
Comfortable guest house.
Open: All Year
01903 233626
Mr Pacy
Rates fr: *£16.00*.
Beds: 3D 2T
Baths: 5 Private

Tyne & Wear

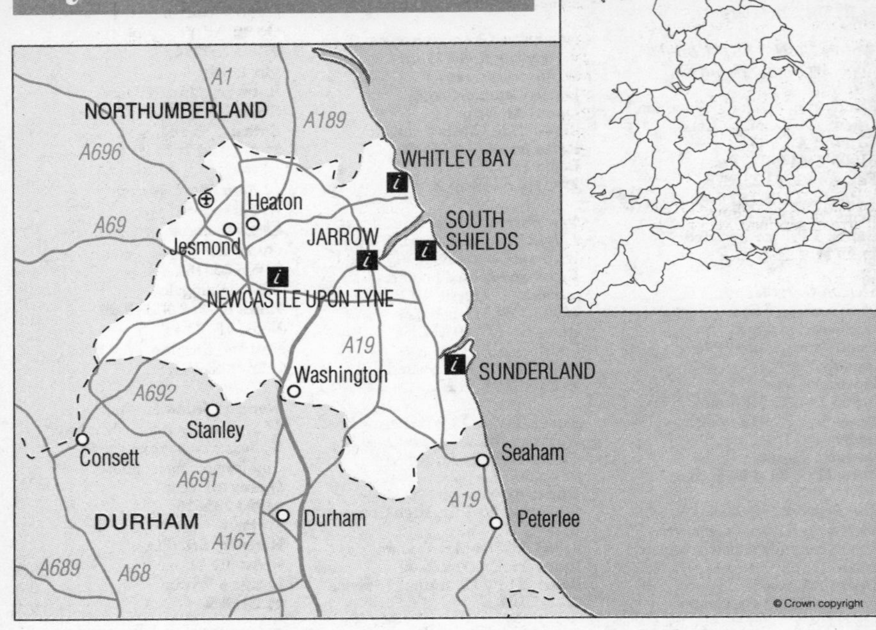

Tourist Information Centres

Central Library, Prince Consort Road, **Gateshead**, Tyne & Wear, NE8 4LN, 0191-477 3478.

Bede's World, The Museum, Church Bank, **Jarrow**, Tyne & Wear, NE32 3DY, 0191-489 2106.

Newcastle Airport, Woolsington, **Newcastle-upon-Tyne**, Tyne & Wear, NE13 8BZ, 0191-214 4422.

Central Library, Princess Square, **Newcastle-upon-Tyne**, Tyne & Wear, NE99 1DX, 0191-261 0610.

Ferry Terminal, Royal Quays, **North Shields**, Tyne & Wear, NE29 6EN, 0191-200 5895, (Easter to Oct)

Ampitheatre, Sea Road, **South Shields**, Tyne & Wear, NE33 2LD, 0191-455 7411.

Unit 3, Crowtree Road, **Sunderland**, Tyne & Wear, SR1 3EL, 0191-533 2000.

Park Road, **Whitley Bay**, Tyne & Wear, NE26 1EJ, 0191-200 8535.

Byrness

National Grid Ref: NT7602

The Redesdale

Low Byrness Farm, *Byrness, Otterburn, Newcastle-upon-Tyne, NE19 1TF.*
Comfortable country cottage. Lovely views.
Open: All Year (not Xmas)
Grades: ETB Listed
01830 520648 Mrs Cranston
Rates fr: *£18.00*-**£18.00**.
Beds: 1F 3D
Baths: 2 Ensuite 1 Shared
(Yes)

Heaton

National Grid Ref: NZ2766

Corner House

Holly Guesthouse, *188 Heaton Park Road, Heaton, Newcastle-upon-Tyne, NE6 5AP.*
Comfortable family-run guest house.
Open: All Year
Grades: ETB Listed
0191 265 6933
Mrs Richardson
Rates fr: *£16.00*-**£16.50**.
Beds: 1F 1T 1S
Baths: 1 Shared
(3)

Ann Stratford Guesthouse, *47 Stratford Road, Heaton, Newcastle-upon-Tyne, NE6 5PB.*
Warm, friendly, comfortable guest house.
Open: All Year
0191 265 6219
Mr Scott
Rates fr: *£15.00*-**£15.00**.
Beds: 1F 1D 1T 1S
Baths: 2 Shared
(4)

Jarrow

National Grid Ref: NZ3465

The Queens Arms, *7-9 Union Street, Jarrow, Tyne & Wear, NE32 3PD.*
Clean comfortable public house.
Open: All Year
0191 489 7503
Mrs Gallagher
Rates fr: *£14.00*-**£14.00**.
Beds: 1F 1D 4T 1S
Baths: 2 Shared

Always telephone to get directions to the B&B - you will save time!

Jesmond

National Grid Ref: NZ2566

Dene Hotel, *38-42 Grosvenor Road, Jesmond, Newcastle-upon-Tyne, NE2 2RP.*
Open: All Year
Grades: ETB 3 Cr, Comm
0191 281 1502 Mr Venayak
Rates fr: *£23.75*-**£25.50**.
Beds: 3F 5D 3T 12S
Baths: 11 Ensuite 12 Private
Pleasantly situated in quiet residential area of Jesmond, yet only 4 minutes from city centre, University and huge Eldon Square Shopping Precinct.

Osborne Hotel, *Osborne Road, Jesmond, Newcastle-upon-Tyne, NE2 2AL.*
Ideal for exploring Newcastle.
Open: All Year
0191 281 3385 Mr Curry
Rates fr: *£20.00*-**£20.00**.
Beds: 3T 4D 18S
Baths: 13 Ensuite 4 Shared

Hansen Hotel, *131 Sandyford Road, Jesmond, Newcastle-upon-Tyne, NE2 1QR.*
Homely family business near town.
Open: All Year (not Xmas)
0191 281 0289
Miss Hansen
Rates fr: *£17.00*-**£18.00**.
Beds: 2F 1T 8S
Baths: 4 Shared

Newcastle-upon-Tyne

National Grid Ref: NZ2564

Chirton House Hotel, *46 Clifton Road, Newcastle-upon-Tyne, NE4 6SH.*
Large Victorian private house.
Open: All Year
Grades: ETB 3 Cr, AA 3 Q, RAC Acclaim
0191 273 0407
Mr Hagerty
Rates fr: *£17.00*-**£23.00**.
Beds: 3F 2D 3T 3S
Baths: 5 Ensuite 2 Shared

South Shields

National Grid Ref: NZ3666

Sea Hotel

Ocean House, *107 Ocean Road, South Shields, Tyne & Wear, NE33 2JL.*
Large guest house. Rooms with private shower.
Open: All Year
0191 455 3339
Mrs Ruiz
Rates fr: *£15.00*-**£16.00**.
Beds: 3F 3D 2T 2S

Sea Crest Guest House, *34 Lawe Road, South Shields, Tyne & Wear, NE33 2EU.*
Large Victorian house with seaviews.
Open: All Year
0191 427 1447
Mrs Bass
Rates fr: *£14.00*-**£16.00**.
Beds: 3F 1T 3S
Baths: 2 Shared
(2)

Dunlin Guest House, *11 Urfa Terrace, South Shields, Tyne & Wear, NE33 2ES.*
Near beach & town centre.
Open: All Year (not Xmas)
Grades: ETB 1 Cr
0191 456 7442 Mrs Wilson
Rates fr: *£14.00*-**£14.00**.
Beds: 1F 2D 1T 2S
Baths: 1 Private 1 Shared

Marina Guest House, *32 Seaview Terrace, South Shields, Tyne & Wear, NE33 2NW.*
Comfortable guest house with panoramic seaviews.
Open: All Year (not Xmas)
Grades: ETB 2 Cr
0191 456 1998 Mrs Johnson
Rates fr: *£19.00*-**£18.00**.
Beds: 2F 2T 2S
Baths: 4 Private 2 Shared
(3)

Saraville Guest House, *103 Ocean Road, South Shields, Tyne & Wear, NE33 2JL.*
Family-run & centrally located.
Open: All Year
0191 454 1169 Mrs Taylor
Rates fr: *£14.00*-**£18.00**.
Beds: 1F 2D 1T 2S
Baths: 2 Ensuite 2 Private 2 Shared
(6)

Sunderland

National Grid Ref: NZ3959

Bed & Breakfast Stop, *183 Newcastle Road, Fulwell, Sunderland, Tyne & Wear, SR5 1NR.*
Tudor-style, semi-detached.
Open: All Year
Grades: ETB 1 Cr, Comm
0191 548 2291 Mrs Starr
Rates fr: *£13.00*-**£15.00**.
Beds: 1F 1T 1S
Baths: 1 Shared
(3) (3)

Felicitations Guest House, *94 Ewesley Road, High Barnes, Sunderland, Tyne & Wear, SR4 7RJ.*
Warm, airy, with lovely atmosphere.
Open: All Year (not Xmas)
0191 522 0960
Mrs Lindsay
Rates fr: *£18.00*-**£18.00**.
Beds: 1F 1D 1S
(5) (1)

The lowest *double* rate per person is shown in *italics*.

Washington

National Grid Ref: NZ3157

Poachers Pocket

Village Farmhouse, *Village Lane, Washington, Tyne & Wear, NE38 7HS.*
Comfortable & hospitable converted farmhouse.
Open: All Year
Grades: ETB 3 Cr, Comm
0191 415 3355 Mr Bloss
Rates fr: *£18.00*-**£22.00**.
Beds: 3F 4D 1T 2S
Baths: 4 Ensuite 1 Private 2 Shared
(10)

Whitley Bay

National Grid Ref: NZ3572

Fitzgeralds, Rex Hotel

Cherrytree House, *35 Brook Street, Whitley Bay, Tyne & Wear, NE26 1AF.*
Edwardian town-house near sea front. **Open:** All Year
Grades: ETB 2 Cr, AA 3 Q
0191 251 4306 Mr Coleman
Rates fr: *£16.00*-**£16.00**.
Beds: 1D 1T 1S
Baths: 3 Ensuite 1 Shared
(1)

Shan-Gri-La, *29 Esplanade, Whitley Bay, Tyne & Wear, NE26 2AL.*
Town & seafront 200 yds.
Open: All Year **Grades:** ETB 1 Cr
0191 253 0230 Mrs Longton
Rates fr: *£14.00*-**£15.00**.
Beds: 2F 4T 4S

Parkholme Guest House, *8 Ocean View, Whitley Bay, Tyne & Wear, NE26 1AL.*
Comfortable Edwardian terraced house.
Open: All Year (not Xmas)
0191 253 0370 Mr Mood
Rates fr: *£14.00*-**£14.00**.
Beds: 2F 1D 1T 2S
Baths: 1 Ensuite 1 Private 2 Shared

Always telephone to get directions to the B&B - you will save time!

Warwickshire

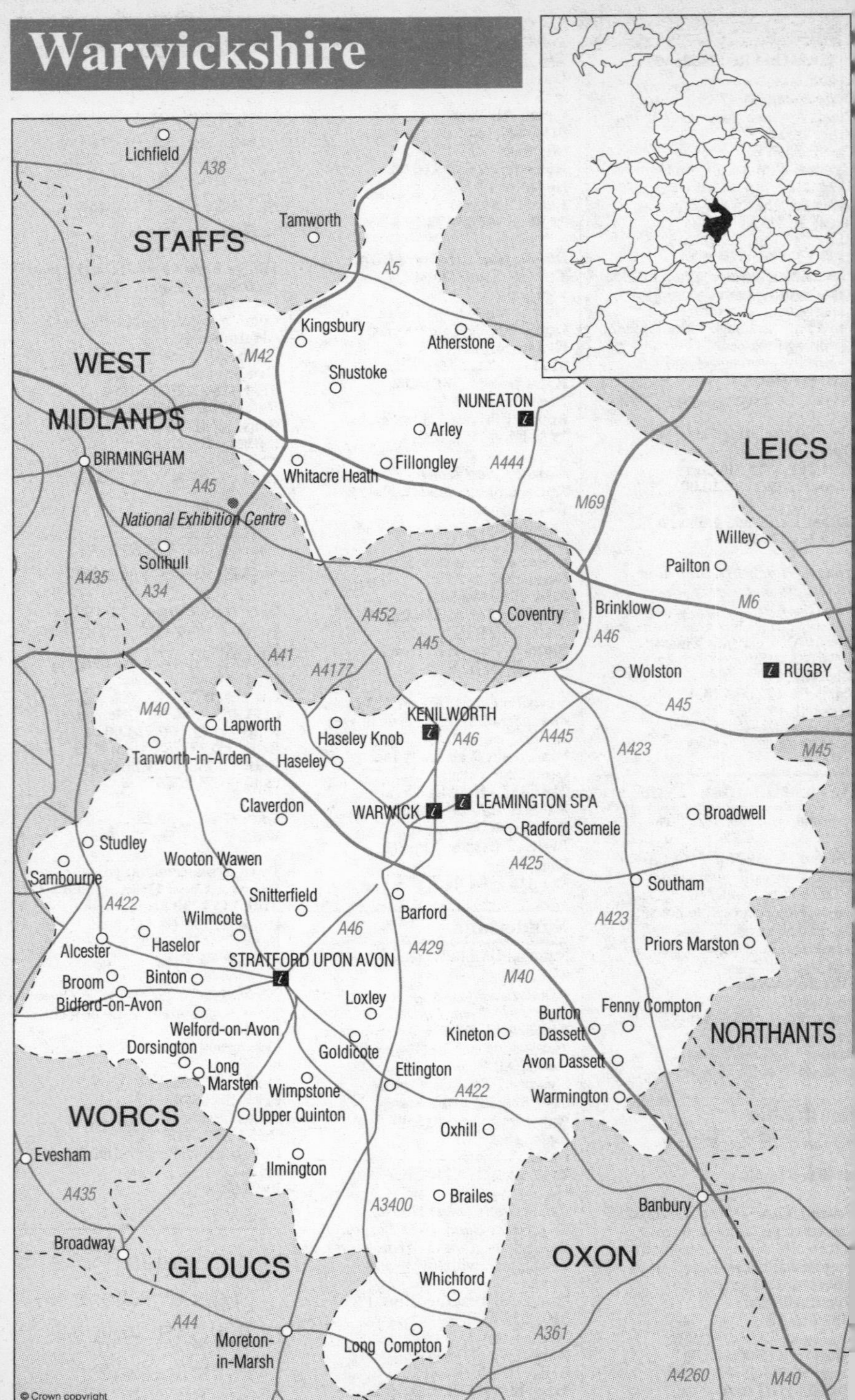

Tourist Information Centres

The Library, 11 Smalley Place, **Kenilworth**, Warks, CV8 1QG, 01926 852595.

Jephson Lodge, Jephson Gardens, The Parade, **Leamington Spa**, Warks, CV32 4AB, 01926 311470

Bosworth Battlefield Visitor Centre, **Sutton Cheney**, Nuneaton, Warks, CV13 0AD, 01455 292239, (Easter to Oct).

Nuneaton Library, Church Street, **Nuneaton**, Warks, CV11 4DR, 01203 384027.

The Library, St Matthew's Street, **Rugby**, Warks, CV21 3BZ, 01788 535348.

Bridgefoot, **Stratford-upon-Avon**, Warks, CV37 6GW, 01789 293127.

The Court House, Jury Street, **Warwick**, Warks, CV34 4EW, 01926 492212.

Alcester

National Grid Ref: SP0857

Roebuck Inn, *Birmingham Road, Alcester, Warks, B49 5QA.*
C18th country inn.
Open: All Year
01789 762410
Fax no: 01789 765794
Rates fr: *£17.50*-**£25.00**.
Beds: 1F 5D 4T 1S

Arley

National Grid Ref: SP2790

Stillwaters, *Stonehouse Lane, Arley, Coventry, W. Mids, CV7 8GB.*
Large country house, lovely garden.
Open: All Year
01676 540944
Mrs Bonner
Rates fr: *£17.00*-**£17.00**.
Beds: 1F 1D 2T
(20)

Atherstone

National Grid Ref: SP3197

Blue Lion

Abbey Farm, *Merevale Lane, Atherstone, Warks, CV9 2LA.*
Period farmhouse in attractive surroundings.
Open: All Year (not Xmas)
01827 713119
Mrs Noble
Rates fr: *£18.00*-**£18.00**.
Beds: 2T
Baths: 1 Shared
(8) (3)

Avon Dassett

National Grid Ref: SP4150

Prince Rupert Inn, Butchers Arms

Crandon House, *Avon Dassett, Leamington Spa, Warks, CV33 0AA.*
Comfortable, warm, spacious farmhouse.
Open: All Year (not Xmas)
Grades: ETB 2 Cr, High Comm
01295 770652 (also fax no)
Miss Lea
Rates fr: *£18.50*-**£25.00**.
Beds: 1D 2T
Baths: 2 Ensuite 1 Private
(12) (8)

Barford

National Grid Ref: SP2760

Kings Head (Wellesbourne)

Lower Watchbury Farm, *Wasperton Lane, Barford, Warwick, CV35 8DH.*
Beautifully situated rural farmhouse. **Open:** All Year
Grades: ETB 2 Cr, Comm
01926 624772 Mrs Eykyn
Rates fr: *£18.50*-**£21.50**.
Beds: 1F 1D 1T **Baths:** 3 Private
(3)

Bidford-on-Avon

National Grid Ref: SP1257

Fosbroke House, *4 High Street, Bidford-on-Avon, Alcester, Warks, B50 4BU.*
Grade II Listed Georgian house.
Open: Feb to Nov
Grades: ETB 2 Cr, Comm
01789 772327 Mr Newbury
Rates fr: *£18.00*-**£20.00**.
Beds: 1F 2D 1T 1S
Baths: 5 Ensuite
(8)

Huit Barn, *Tower Croft, Tower Hill, Bidford-on-Avon, Alcester, Warks, B50 4DY.*
Delightful Victorian barn conversion. **Open:** All Year (not Xmas)
01789 778516 Mrs Pugh
Rates fr: *£17.50*-**£16.00**.
Beds: 1D 1S
Baths: 1 Ensuite 1 Shared
(5) (4)

Binton

National Grid Ref: SP1454

Blue Boar

Gravelside Barn, *The Gravels, Binton, Stratford upon Avon, Warks, CV37 9TU.*
A truly peaceful country retreat.
Open: All Year (not Xmas)
Grades: ETB 2 Cr, High Comm
01789 750502 Mr Belchambers
Rates fr: *£20.00*-**£30.00**.
Beds: 2D 1T **Baths:** 3 Ensuite
(14) (6)

Brailes

National Grid Ref: SP3039

New House Farm, *Brailes, Banbury, Oxon, OX15 5BD.*
Quietly situated, comfortable Georgian farmhouse.
Open: All Year (not Xmas)
01608 686239 Ms Taylor
Rates fr: *£17.00*-**£18.00**.
Beds: 2D 1T
Baths: 2 Ensuite 1 Shared
(10)

Brinklow

National Grid Ref: SP4379

The White Lion, *Broad Street, Brinklow, Rugby, Warks, CV23 0LN.*
Country inn. Courtesy vehicle available.
Open: All Year (not Xmas)
01788 832579 Mr Yeend
Rates fr: *£17.50*-**£22.50**.
Beds: 1D 3T
Baths: 4 Ensuite

Broadwell

National Grid Ref: SP4565

Boat Inn (Stockton)

High House, *The Green, Broadwell, Rugby, Warks, CV23 8HD.*
Peaceful, comfy old country house.
Open: All Year (not Xmas)
01926 812687 Mr Pickering
Rates fr: *£14.00*-**£15.00**.
Beds: 1F
Baths: 1 Private
(4)

Broom

National Grid Ref: SP0953

Broom Hall Inn, *Bidford Road, Broom, Alcester, Warks, B50 4HE.*
C16th country inn.
Open: All Year
01789 773757 Mrs Tavener
Rates fr: *£20.00*-**£20.00**.
Beds: 2F 2D 4T 4S
Baths: 12 Ensuite
(100)

Burton Dassett

National Grid Ref: SP3847

Butchers Arms (Farnborough)

Grove Farm, *Burton Dassett, Leamington Spa, CV33 0AB.*
C16th local stone farmhouse.
Open: All Year
01295 770204 Mrs Thompstone
Rates fr: *£15.00*-**£20.00**.
Beds: 1F 1D 1T 1S
Baths: 2 Shared

Claverdon

National Grid Ref: SP1964

Woodside, *Langley Road, Claverdon, Warwick, Warks, CV35 8PJ.*
Comfortable, country dormer-style bungalow.
Open: All Year (not Xmas)
01926 842446 Mrs Bromilow
Rates fr: *£18.22*-**£21.00**.
Beds: 1F 1D 2T 1S
Baths: 2 Shared
(12)

Dorsington

National Grid Ref: SP1349

Church Farm, *Dorsington, Stratford upon Avon, Warks, CV37 8AX.*
Friendly Georgian farmhouse. Quiet, peaceful.
Open: All Year
01789 720471 / 0831 504194
Mrs Walters
Fax no: 01831 504194
Rates fr: *£14.50*-**£18.00**.
Beds: 2F 3D 2T
Baths: 4 Ensuite 3 Shared
(12)

Ettington

National Grid Ref: SP2648

Hounds Hill, Chequers Inn, Bell (Alderminster)

Thornton Manor, *Ettington, Stratford upon Avon, Warks, CV37 7PN.*
C16th peaceful manor house.
Open: Easter to Nov
Grades: ETB 2 Cr
01789 740210
Mrs Hutsby
Rates fr: *£18.00*-**£21.00**.
Beds: 2D 1T
Baths: 3 Private
(5) (5)

The Leys, *64 Banbury Road, Ettington, Stratford-upon-Avon, Warks, CV37 7SU.*
Friendly family, modern village house.
Open: All Year (not Xmas)
01789 740365 / 0836 366615
Mrs Brewer
Fax no: 01789 740365
Rates fr: *£15.00*-**£18.00**.
Beds: 1D 1T
Baths: 2 Private
(8) (2)

Please respect a B&B's wishes regarding children, animals & smoking.

Fenny Compton

National Grid Ref: SP4152

Willow Cottage, *Brook Street, Fenny Compton, Leamington Spa, Warks, CV33 0YH.*
Character cottage in delightful gardens.
Open: All Year (not Xmas)
01295 770429 Mrs Fielder
Rates fr: *£15.00*-**£15.00**.
Beds: 1T 1S
Baths: 1 Shared
(2)

The Granary, *Fenny Compton Wharf, Fenny Compton, Leamington Spa, Warks, CV33 0XE.*
Modern, quiet, canal-side house.
Open: Feb to Nov
01295 770214 Mrs Cotterill
Rates fr: *£16.50*-**£18.00**.
Beds: 2D 1T
Baths: 3 Private
(10)

Fillongley

National Grid Ref: SP2887

Mill Farmhouse, *Mill Lane, Fillongley, Coventry, W. Mids, CV7 8EE.*
Beautiful, tranquil farmhouse, rooms/stone chalets.
Open: All Year
01676 541898 Mrs Chamberlain
Rates fr: *£20.00*-**£17.00**.
Beds: 1F 1D 2T 3S
Baths: 3 Private 2 Shared
(5)

Goldicote

National Grid Ref: SP2452

Bell (Alderminster)

Park Leys Farmhouse, *Banbury Road, Goldicote, Stratford upon Avon, Warks, CV37 7ND.*
Old & comfortable farmhouse, fabulous views!
Open: All Year
01789 740691 Mr Starley
Fax no: 01789 740501
Rates fr: *£17.00*-**£15.00**.
Beds: 1F 2D 1T 2S
Baths: 4 Ensuite 1 Shared
(8)

Haseley

National Grid Ref: SP2367

Falcon Inn

Shrewley Pools Farm, *Haseley, Warwick, CV35 7HB.*
Beautiful, traditional farmhouse. Glorious gardens.
Open: All Year
Grades: ETB Listed, comm
01926 484315 Mrs Dodd
Rates fr: *£22.50*-**£25.00**.
Beds: 1F 1T
Baths: 2 Ensuite
(8)

Haseley Knob

National Grid Ref: SP2371

Croft Guest House, *The Croft, Haseley Knob, Warwick, CV35 7NL.*
Friendly, family country guest house.
Open: All Year (not Xmas)
Grades: ETB 2 Cr, Comm, AA 4 Q, RAC Acclaim
01926 484447 (also fax no)
Mr Clapp
Rates fr: *£20.00*-**£19.00**.
Beds: 2F 2D 2T 1S
Baths: 5 Private 2 Shared
(8)

The Elms Bungalow, *Drum Lane, Haseley Knob, Warwick, CV35 7NL.*
Cosy, friendly, picturesque bungalow.
Open: All Year
01926 484377 Mrs Turner
Rates fr: *£16.50*-**£17.50**.
Beds: 1D 1T
Baths: 1 Shared
(4)

Haselor

National Grid Ref: SP1257

Blue Boar

Walcote Farm, *Walcote, Haselor, Alcester, Warks, B49 6LY.*
Open: All Year (not Xmas)
Grades: ETB 2 Cr, Comm
01789 488264 (also fax no)
Mr & Mrs Finnemore
Rates fr: *£18.00*-**£23.00**.
Beds: 1D 1T
Baths: 2 Ensuite
(6)
Comfortable C16th oak-beamed farmhouse with inglenook fire-places in a tranquil picturesque hamlet. Ideal location for Shakespeare's birthplace & theatre, Warwick Castle & the Cotswolds.

Ilmington

National Grid Ref: SP2143

Howard Arms

Meadow Hill, *Mickleton Road, Ilmington, Shipston on Stour, Warks, CV36 4JQ.*
Quiet, detached, Cotswold stone house.
Open: All Year
01608 682456 Mrs Murray White
Rates fr: *£16.00*-**£20.00**.
Beds: 2D
Baths: 1 Shared
(6myh) (2)

Folly Farm Cottage, *Ilmington, Shipston on Stour, Warks, CV36 4LJ.*
Country cottage, four-posters.
Open: All Year (not Xmas)
01608 682425 Mrs Lowe
Rates fr: *£22.50*.
Beds: 3D
Baths: 3 Ensuite

Kenilworth

National Grid Ref: SP2971

Anchor Pub, Earl of Clarendon

***The Cottage Inn**, 36 Stoneleigh Road, Kenilworth, Warks, CV8 2GD.*
Open: All Year
Grades: ETB 2 Cr, Approv
01926 853900
Mr & Mrs English
Rates fr: *£20.00*-**£29.00**.
Beds: 2D 2T 1S
Baths: 5 Ensuite
(12)
Friendly family-run freehouse serving fine traditional ales & fine home cooked meals. Happy hour, car park, golf courses nearby. Most major motorways 5-20 minutes.

***Hollyhurst Guest House**, 47 Priory Road, Kenilworth, Warks, CV8 1LL.*
High standard, family-run guest house.
Open: All Year
Grades: ETB 2 Cr, Comm, AA 3 Q
01926 853882 (also fax no)
Ms Millar
Rates fr: *£20.00*-**£19.00**.
Beds: 2F 1D 3T 1S
Baths: 3 Private 2 Shared
(9)

***Nightingales Hotel**, 95-97 Warwick Road, Kenilworth, Warks, CV8 1HP.*
Lovely hotel with excellent restaurant.
Open: All Year (not Xmas)
Grades: ETB 2 Cr
01926 53594 / 853594
Fax no: 01926 853594
Rates fr: *£15.00*-**£19.50**.
Beds: 1F 2D 4T 4S
Baths: 4 Ensuite 2 Shared
(50)

***Banner Hill Farm**, Rouncil Lane, Kenilworth, Warks, CV8 1NN.*
Listed Georgian farmhouse. Homely atmosphere.
Open: All Year (not Xmas)
01926 52850
Mr Snelson
Rates fr: *£16.00*-**£17.50**.
Beds: 1F 1D 1T 1S
Baths: 2 Ensuite 1 Private 2 Shared
(20)

***Enderley Guest House**, 20 Queens Road, Kenilworth, Warks, CV8 1JQ.*
Comfortable large Edwardian house.
Open: All Year
Grades: ETB 2 Cr, Approv
01926 55388
Mr & Mrs Lumsden
Rates fr: *£18.50*-**£24.00**.
Beds: 1F 2D 1T
Baths: 4 Private
(0) (2)

***Abbey Guest House**, 41 Station Road, Kenilworth, Warks, CV8 1JD.*
Comfortable Victorian house, central, quiet.
Open: All Year
01926 512707 Mrs Jefferies
Rates fr: *£17.00*-**£19.00**.
Beds: 1F 2D 3T 1S
Baths: 3 Private 1 Shared
(2)

Kineton

National Grid Ref: SP3351

***Willowbrook Farmhouse**, Lighthorne Road, Kineton, Warwick, CV35 0JL.*
Very comfortable house in country.
Open: All Year (not Xmas)
Grades: AA 3 Q
01926 640475 Ms Howard
Fax no: 01926 641747
Rates fr: *£16.00*.
Beds: 2D 1T
Baths: 1 Private 2 Shared
(6)

Kingsbury

National Grid Ref: SP2196

***67 Tamworth Road**, Kingsbury, Tamworth, Staffs, B78 2HH.*
Modern bungalow in country village.
Open: All Year
01827 873880
Mrs Painter
Rates fr: *£15.00*-**£15.00**.
Beds: 1F 1D 1S
Baths: 1 Shared
(5) (2)

Lapworth

National Grid Ref: SP1671

***Lapworth Lodge**, Bushwood Lane, Lapworth, Solihull, W. Mids, B94 5PJ.*
Georgian country house near NEC.
Open: All Year
01564 783038
Ms Boucher
Rates fr: *£22.50*-**£35.00**.
Beds: 2F 2D 3T
Baths: 7 Ensuite
(20)

Leamington Spa

National Grid Ref: SP3166

Rugby Tavern

***The Orchard**, 3 Sherbourne Terrace, Clarendon Street, Leamington Spa, Warks, CV32 5SP.*
Victorian house. Town 5 mins walk.
Open: All Year
Grades: ETB Listed, Approv
01926 428198 Mrs Thacker
Rates fr: *£16.00*-**£16.00**.
Beds: 1F 1T 1S
Baths: 2 Shared

***Charnwood Guest House**, 47 Avenue Road, Leamington Spa, Warks, CV31 3PF.*
Comfortable, informal atmosphere.
Open: All Year (not Xmas)
01926 831074 Mr Booth
Rates fr: *£17.00*-**£17.00**.
Beds: 1F 2D 2T 1S
Baths: 2 Private 2 Shared
(5)

***11 St Andrews Road**, Leamington Spa, Warks, CV32 7EU.*
Family home, quiet, pleasant room.
Open: All Year (not Xmas)
Grades: ETB Listed
01926 428864
Mrs Poultney
Rates fr: *£15.00*.
Beds: 1D
Baths: 1 Ensuite
(1)

***Eaton Court Hotel**, 1-7 St Marks Road, Leamington Spa, Warks, CV32 6DL.*
Family-run large Victorian house.
Open: All Year (not Xmas)
Grades: ETB 3 Cr, Comm
01926 885848 (also fax no)
Mr Gregory
Rates fr: *£27.50*-**£30.00**.
Beds: 3F 11D 12T 10S
Baths: 36 Private
(60)

Long Compton

National Grid Ref: SP2832

Red Lion, Gate Hangs High

***Archways**, Crockwell Street, Long Compton, Shipston on Stour, Warks, CV36 5JN.*
Charming C17th Cotswold cottage.
Open: All Year (not Xmas)
Grades: ETB 1 Cr
01608 684358
Mrs Cunnington
Rates fr: *£16.00*-**£17.00**.
Beds: 2D 1T
Baths: 2 Shared
(0) (4)

Long Marston

National Grid Ref: SP1548

***Church Farm**, Long Marston, Stratford upon Avon, Warks, CV37 8RH.*
Comfortable C17th farmhouse, high standards.
Open: All Year (not Xmas)
01789 720275 Mrs Taylor
Rates fr: *£17.00*-**£25.00**.
Beds: 1F 1T
Baths: 2 Private
(6)

The lowest *double* rate per person is shown in *italics*.

Always telephone to get directions to the B&B - you will save time!

Loxley

National Grid Ref: SP2552

Fox Inn

Elm Cottage, *Stratford Road, Loxley, Warks, CV35 9JW.*
Private house, rural, large gardens.
Open: All Year (not Xmas)
Grades: ETB 1 Cr, Comm
01789 840609
Mrs Brocklehurst
Rates fr: *£17.00*-**£20.00**.
Beds: 1D 1T
Baths: 1 Shared
(10) (8)

Nuneaton

National Grid Ref: SP3691

La Tavola Calda, *68 & 70 Midland Road, Nuneaton, Warks, CV11 5DY.*
Family-run hotel & restaurant.
Open: All Year
Grades: ETB 1 Cr, Comm, RAC Recomm
01203 383195 / 381303
Mr Emanuele
Fax no: 01203 381816
Rates fr: *£12.50*-**£15.00**.
Beds: 2F 5T 1S
Baths: 8 Private
(2) (50)

Oxhill

National Grid Ref: SP3145

Royal Oak (Whatcote)

Nolands Farm & Country, *Restaurant, Oxhill, Warwick, CV35 0RJ.*
Open: All Year (not Xmas)
Grades: ETB 2 Cr, AA 4 Q, Select, RAC Acclaim
01926 640309
Mrs Hutsby
Fax no: 01926 641662
Rates fr: *£18.00*-**£20.00**.
Beds: 7D 1T 1S
Baths: 9 Ensuite
(7) (10)
Working farm situated in tranquil valley. Romantic four poster bedrooms in converted stables. Fishing, clay pigeon shooting, bike hire, riding nearby. Peace & quiet for discerning country lovers!

Pailton

National Grid Ref: SP4781

White Lion Inn, *Coventry Road, Pailton, Rugby, Warks, CV23 0QD.*
Modernised C17th public house.
Open: All Year
Grades: ETB Listed
01788 832359
Mr Brindley
Fax no: 01788 832 359
Rates fr: *£18.50*-**£18.50**.
Beds: 2F 7T
(60)

Radford Semele

National Grid Ref: SP3464

White Hart (Upton)

Hill Farm, *Lewis Road, Radford Semele, Leamington Spa, Warks, CV31 1UX.*
Comfortable, friendly farmhouse. Attractive rooms.
Open: All Year (not Xmas)
Grades: ETB 2 Cr, Comm, AA 3 Q
01926 337571 Ms Gibbs
Rates fr: *£16.00*-**£20.00**.
Beds: 3D 2T
Baths: 3 Ensuite 2 Shared
(12) (6)

Rugby

National Grid Ref: SP5075

The Bull

Manor Farm, *Buckwell Lane, Clifton-upon-Dunsmore, Rugby, Warks, CV23 0BJ.*
Converted granary barn.
Open: All Year
01788 544016
Mrs Walters
Rates fr: *£17.50*-**£20.00**.
Beds: 1D 1T 2S
Baths: 4 Ensuite
(12) (6)

The Imperial Hotel, *165 Oxford Street, Rugby, Warks, CV21 3LY.*
Public house with B&B.
Open: All Year (not Xmas)
01788 543627
Mr Cox
Rates fr: *£12.50*-**£16.50**.
Beds: 2F 2D 4T 1S
Baths: 3 Private 6 Shared
(20)

Murray Road Cafe and Guesthouse, *178 Murray Road, Rugby, Warks, CV21 3JU.*
Welcoming, comfortable, convenient for all facilities.
Open: All Year
01788 578134
Mrs Whale
Rates fr: *£12.00*-**£13.50**.
Beds: 2T 1S

Sambourne

National Grid Ref: SP0662

Sambourne Hall Farm, *Sambourne, Alcester, Warks, B96 6NZ.*
Beautiful C16th farmhouse. Idyllic setting.
Open: All Year (not Xmas)
01527 852151
Mrs Hammersley
Rates fr: *£17.50*-**£22.00**.
Beds: 1F 1D 1T
Baths: 1 Ensuite 1 Private
(6)

Shustoke

National Grid Ref: SP2290

The Old Vicarage, *Shustoke, Coleshill, Birmingham, Warks, B46 2LA.*
Large Georgian private house.
Open: All Year (not Xmas)
01675 481331
Mrs Hawkins
Rates fr: *£19.50*-**£19.50**.
Beds: 2D 1S
Baths: 2 Shared
(4)

Snitterfield

National Grid Ref: SP2159

Foxhunter, Snitterfield Arms

The Hill Cottage, *Kings Lane, Snitterfield, Stratford upon Avon, Warks, CV37 0QA.*
Country house with glorious views.
Open: All Year (not Xmas)
01789 731 830
Mrs Waldron
Rates fr: *£18.00*-**£20.00**.
Beds: 1D 1T 1S
Baths: 1 Ensuite 1 Shared
(2)

Avoncroft Farmhouse, *The Green, Snitterfield, Stratford-upon-Avon, CV37 0JE.*
Self-contained family unit in character barn. Beautiful grounds.
Open: All Year
01789 731302
Mrs Cox
Rates fr: *£20.00*-**£25.00**.
Beds: 1F
Baths: 1 Ensuite
(4)

High season, bank holidays and special events mean low availability *anywhere.*

Southam

National Grid Ref: SP4162

Bridge House, *Warwick Street, Southam, Leamington Spa, Warks, CV33 0HD.*
Converted C17th tannery.
Open: All Year (not Xmas)
01926 814787 Mrs Carr
Rates fr: *£15.00*-**£17.00**.
Beds: 2T 1S
Baths: 1 Shared
(3)

Stratford upon Avon

National Grid Ref: SP1955

Thatcher Tavern, Masons' Arms, Encore, Red Lion, Slug & Lettuce

Arden Park Hotel, *6 Arden Street, Stratford upon Avon, Warks, CV37 6PA.*
Open: All Year
Grades: ETB Listed
01789 296072 (also fax no)
Mr Morgan
Rates fr: *£16.00*-**£20.00**.
Beds: 2F 3D 2T 2S
Baths: 9 Private
(8)
Old Victorian house, architectural interest. Guest accom. Tourist Board Listed. Fire, hygiene, & public liability certificates. Ensuite facilities, TVs, Tea/coffee. Town centre near train, bus.

Compton House, *22 Shipston Road, Stratford upon Avon, Warks, CV37 7LP.*
Family guest house, 5 mins theatre.
Open: All Year
Grades: ETB Listed
01789 205646 Mrs Bealing
Rates fr: *£15.00*-**£17.00**.
Beds: 3F 1D 1S
Baths: 1 Shared
(7)

Penshurst, *34 Evesham Place, Stratford upon Avon, Warks, CV37 6HT.*
Open: All Year
Grades: ETB Listed, Comm
01789 205259 Mrs Cauvin
Fax no: 01789 295322
Rates fr: *£14.00*-**£15.00**.
Beds: 4F 1D 1T 2S
Baths: 2 Private 2 Shared
A pretty refurbished Victorian townhouse 5 minutes walk from centre. Totally non-smoking. Delicious breakfasts served from 7.00 am right up until 10.30 am. Excellent value for money. Brochure available.

All rates are subject to alteration at the owners' discretion.

Cadle Pool Farm, *The Ridgeway, Stratford upon Avon, Warks, CV37 9RE.*
Open: All Year (not Xmas)
01789 292494
Mrs Turney
Rates fr: *£20.00*-**£25.00**.
Beds: 1F 1D 1T
Baths: 1 Ensuite 1 Private
(10) (10)
Beautiful period farmhouse, with delightful grounds. 2 miles from Stratford-on-Avon. 8 minutes by car to theatre & Shakespeare attractions. Reductions for stays over 3 nights.

Park Leys Farmhouse, *Banbury Road, Goldicote, Stratford upon Avon, Warks, CV37 7ND.*
Old and comfortable farmhouse, fabulous views!
Open: All Year
01789 740691
Mr Starley
Fax no: 01789 740501
Rates fr: *£17.00*-**£15.00**.
Beds: 1F 2D 1T 2S
Baths: 4 Ensuite 1 Shared
(8)

East Bank House, *19 Warwick Road, Stratford upon Avon, Warks, CV37 6YW.*
Open: All Year
Grades: ETB 2 Cr, Comm, AA 3 St
01789 292758 (also fax no)
Mr Marshall
Rates fr: *£17.50*-**£28.00**.
Beds: 2F 5D 3T 1S
Baths: 6 Ensuite 2 Shared
(5)
This fine Victorian house stands in private grounds within a conservation area just 3 minutes walk from the town centre. Booking is advisable but not compulsory.

Quilt & Croissants Guest House, *33 Evesham Plave, Stratford upon Avon, Warks, CV37 6HT.*
Well-appointed, late-Victorian house.
Open: All Year (not Xmas)
Grades: ETB Listed
01789 267629
Mr Stanway
Rates fr: *£17.50*-**£19.00**.
Beds: 3F 3D 1T 1S
Baths: 4 Private 1 Shared
(2)

Avoncroft Farmhouse, *The Green, Snitterfield, Stratford upon Avon, CV37 0JE.*
Open: All Year
01789 731302
Mrs Cox
Rates fr: *£20.00*-**£25.00**.
Beds: 1F
Baths: 1 Ensuite
(4)
Self-contained family unit in character barn. Beautiful grounds, swimming pool, ducks, horses, etc. 3 miles to Stratford. 7 miles to Warwick. Children welcome.

Broadlands Guest House, *23 Evesham Place, Stratford upon Avon, Warks, CV37 6HT.*
Walking distance theatre, town centre.
Open: All Year (not Xmas)
Grades: ETB Listed, RAC Listed
01789 299181
Mr Griffith
Rates fr: *£14.00*-**£14.00**.
Beds: 1F 4D 1S
Baths: 4 Ensuite 2 Shared
(2) (5)

Aidan Guest House, *11 Evesham Place, Stratford upon Avon, Warks, CV37 6HT.*
Close to theatre & town centre.
Open: All Year (not Xmas)
01789 292824 (also fax no)
Mr & Mrs Thompson
Rates fr: *£17.00*-**£25.00**.
Beds: 1F 4D 1T
Baths: 6 Private
(3)

35 Evesham Place, *Stratford upon Avon, Warks, CV37 6HT.*
Central large Victorian guest house.
Open: All Year
Grades: ETB Listed
01789 292879
Ms Tallis
Rates fr: *£13.00*-**£13.00**.
Beds: 3F 2D 3T 1S
Baths: 2 Private 6 Shared

Willowdale, *192 Evesham Road, Stratford upon Avon, Warks, CV37 9BS.*
Homely large house, comfortable bedrooms.
Open: All Year (not Xmas)
01789 205416
Mrs Willey
Rates fr: *£15.00*-**£16.00**.
Beds: 4F 1D
Baths: 2 Shared
(1) (5)

Windfall, *118 Alcester Road, Stratford upon Avon, Warks, CV37 9DP.*
Private house.
Open: All Year (not Xmas)
01789 266880
Mrs Allard
Rates fr: *£15.00*-**£15.00**.
Beds: 1D 1T 1S
Baths: 2 Ensuite 1 Private 1 Shared
(3)

Parkfield Guest House, *3 Broad Walk, Stratford upon Avon, Warks, CV37 6HS.*
Elegant Victorian house, central location.
Open: All Year
Grades: ETB 2 Cr, AA 3 Q, RAC Listed
01789 293313
Mr Pettitt
Rates fr: *£18.00*-**£18.00**.
Beds: 2F 3D 1T 1S
Baths: 5 Private 1 Shared
(5) (7)

Arrandale Guest House, *208 Evesham Road, Stratford upon Avon, Warks,* CV37 9AS.
Comfortable, double-glazed, family-run.
Open: All Year (not Xmas)
01789 267112
Mrs Mellor
Rates fr: *£15.00*-**£17.50**.
Beds: 3D 1T
Baths: 2 Private 1 Shared
(1) (3)

Studley

National Grid Ref: SP0763

Barley Now

Field Farm, *Hardwick Lane, Studley, Warks,* B80 7AE.
Friendly, relaxed, 'home from home'.
Open: All Year (not Xmas)
01527 852032
Mrs Vale
Rates fr: *£13.00*-**£13.00**.
Beds: 1F 1T
Baths: 1 Shared
(10)

Tanworth-in-Arden

National Grid Ref: SP1170

Bell Inn

Mungunyah, *Poolhead Lane, Tanworth-in-Arden, Solihull, Warks,* B94 5EH.
Attractive, peaceful, rural family home.
Open: All Year (not Xmas or new year day)
01564 742437
Mrs Palser
Rates fr: *£20.00*-**£30.00**.
Beds: 2T
Baths: 1 Shared
(12) (6)

Upper Quinton

National Grid Ref: SP1746

Winton House, *The Green, Upper Quinton, Stratford upon Avon, Warks,* CV37 8SX.
Victorian farmhouse in rural setting.
Open: All Year
01789 720500 / 0831 485483
Mrs Lyon
Rates fr: *£21.00*-**£30.00**.
Beds: 1F 1D 1T
Baths: 3 Private
(5)

Please respect a B&B's wishes regarding children, animals & smoking.

Warmington

National Grid Ref: SP4147

The Plough

Pond Cottage, *The Green, Warmington, Banbury, Oxon,* OX17 1BU.
Picturesque cottage overlooking village green.
Open: Apr to Oct
Grades: ETB
01295 690682 Mrs Viljoen
Rates fr: *£18.00*-**£18.50**.
Beds: 1D 1S
Baths: 2 Private
(2)

Warwick

National Grid Ref: SP2865

Tudor House, Crown Hotel, Ricochet, Snitterfield Arms

The Seven Stars, *Friars Street, Warwick,* CV34 6HD.
Friendly C16th beamed inn.
Open: All Year (not Xmas)
Grades: ETB 1 Cr, Comm
01926 492658
Mrs Flynn
Rates fr: *£17.50*-**£20.00**.
Beds: 3D 1T
Baths: 2 Ensuite 1 Shared
(8) (11)

Ashburton Guest House, *74 Emscote Road, Warwick,* CV34 5QG.
Extremely high standard of accommodation.
Open: All Year
Grades: ETB 2 Cr, Comm
01926 401082
Mrs Whitelaw
Rates fr: *£17.00*-**£17.00**.
Beds: 2F 1D 1T 3S
Baths: 5 Private 2 Shared
(3)

Lower Watchbury Farm, *Wasperton Lane, Barford, Warwick,* CV35 8DH.
Beautifully situated rural farmhouse.
Open: All Year
Grades: ETB 2 Cr, Comm
01926 624772
Mrs Eykyn
Rates fr: *£18.50*-**£21.50**.
Beds: 1F 1D 1T
Baths: 3 Private
(3)

Croft Guest House, *The Croft, Haseley Knob, Warwick,* CV35 7NL.
Friendly, family country guest house.
Open: All Year (not Xmas)
Grades: ETB 2 Cr, Comm, AA 4 Q, RAC Acclaim
01926 484447 (also fax no)
Mr Clapp
Rates fr: *£20.00*-**£19.00**.
Beds: 2F 2D 2T 1S
Baths: 5 Private 2 Shared
(8)

Agincourt Lodge Hotel, *36 Coten End, Warwick,* CV34 4NP.
Pleasant family-run hotel, walk to Castle.
Open: All Year
Grades: ETB 3 Cr, AA 1 St
01926 499399 (also fax no)
Mr & Mrs Black-Band
Rates fr: *£22.50*-**£26.50**.
Beds: 1F 3D 1T 2S
Baths: 6 Ensuite 1 Shared
(0) (9)

Hillcrest Guest House, *Sherbourne Hill, Stratford Road, Warwick,* CV35 8AG.
C18th country cottage.
Open: All Year
Grades: ETB 1 Cr, Approv
01926 624386
Mrs Twigger
Rates fr: *£17.00*-**£25.00**.
Beds: 1D 1T 1S
Baths: 1 Shared
(3) (6)

Pageant Lodge, *2 Castle Lane, Warwick,* CV34 4BU.
Period house next to Castle .
Open: All Year
Grades: ETB 2 Cr, Comm
01926 491244
Mrs King
Rates fr: *£20.00*-**£25.00**.
Beds: 2D 1T
Baths: 3 Private
(30)

Welford-on-Avon

National Grid Ref: SP1451

Bell Inn

Springfields Farm, *Welford Road, Welford-on-Avon, Stratford upon Avon, Warks,* CV37 8RA.
Farmhouse - walk in Shakespeare's paths.
Open: Feb to Oct
Grades: ETB Listed
01789 720136
Mrs Reid
Fax no: 01789 720885
Rates fr: *£18.00*-**£18.00**.
Beds: 1F 1D 2T 1S
Baths: 2 Ensuite 1 Private
(6) (10)

One Acre Guest House, *Barton Road, Welford-on-Avon, Stratford upon Avon, Warks,* CV37 8EZ.
Rural village, large gardens.
01789 750477
Ms Clifton
Rates fr: *£16.00*-**£20.00**.
Beds: 1F 2D
Baths: 4 Private
(6)

The lowest **single** *rate is shown in* **bold.**

Whichford

National Grid Ref: SP3134

The Gate

Ascott House Farm, *Whichford, Long Compton, Shipston on Stour, Warks, CV36 5PP.*
Cotswold farmhouse, area of natural beauty.
Open: All Year
Grades: ETB 2 Cr
01608 684655 (also fax no)
Mrs Haines
Rates fr: *£16.00*-**£18.00**.
Beds: 1F 1D 1T
Baths: 2 Ensuite 1 Shared
(12)

Whitacre Heath

National Grid Ref: SP2192

Swan Inn

Heathland Farm, *Birmingham Road, Whitacre Heath, Coleshill, W. Mids, B46 2ER.*
Quiet, secluded, comfortable farmhouse.
Open: All Year (not Xmas)
Grades: ETB 2 Cr
01675 462129 Rates fr: *£19.00*-**£21.00**.
Beds: 4T 2S
Baths: 4 Ensuite 1 Private
(10)

Always telephone to get directions to the B&B - you will save time!

Willey

National Grid Ref: SP4984

Sarah Mansfield

Manor Farm, *Willey, Rugby, Warks, CV23 0SH.*
Open: All Year (not Xmas)
01455 553143 Mrs Sharpe
Rates fr: *£18.00*-**£22.00**.
Beds: 1D 2T
Baths: 1 Private 2 Shared
An oasis of peace & tranquillity tucked within the Midlands Motorway network & easy to find. Our repeat bookings are our testimony. Non-smoking.

Wilmcote

National Grid Ref: SP1658

Masons Arms

Dosthill Cottage, *The Green, Wilmcote, Stratford upon Avon, Warks, CV37 9XJ.*
Cottage overlooking Mary Arden's house. **Open:** All Year
Grades: ETB 2 Cr, Comm, AA 3 Q
01789 266480 Mr Stevenson
Fax no: 01789 266 480
Rates fr: *£20.00*-**£29.00**.
Beds: 2D 1T **Baths:** 3 Private
(3)

Wimpstone

National Grid Ref: SP2148

Howard Arms (Ilmington)

Whitchurch Farm, *Wimpstone, Stratford upon Avon, Warks, CV37 8NS.*
Lovely Georgian farmhouse on edge of Cotswolds.
Open: All Year
Grades: ETB 2 Cr, Approv, AA 2 Q
01789 450275
Mrs James
Fax no: 01789 450359
Rates fr: *£17.00*-**£18.00**.
Beds: 2D 1T
Baths: 3 Private
(3)

Wolston

National Grid Ref: SP4175

Queens Head

The Byre, *Lords Hill Farm, Wolston, Coventry, Warks, CV8 3GB.*
Comfortable farmhouse accommodation.
Open: All Year (not Xmas)
Grades: ETB 1 Cr, Comm
01203 542098
Mrs Gibbs
Rates fr: *£15.00*-**£15.00**.
Beds: 2D 1T
Baths: 1 Ensuite 2 Shared
(5) (6)

Wootton Wawen

National Grid Ref: SP1563

Wootton Park Farm, *Alcester Road, Wootton Wawen, Solihull, W. Mids, B95 6HJ.*
Delightful C16th half-timbered farmhouse.
Open: All Year (not Xmas)
01564 792673
Mrs McCall
Rates fr: *£19.00*-**£24.00**.
Beds: 2F 1D
Baths: 1 Private 1 Shared
(6)

West Midlands

Balsall Common

National Grid Ref: SP2377

Blythe Paddocks, *Barston Lane, Balsall Common, Coventry, W. Midlands,* CV7 7BT.
Detached house in four acres.
Open: All Year
01676 533050 Mrs Marshall
Rates fr: *£18.00*-**£18.00**.
Beds: 1D 1T 2S
Baths: 1 Shared
(10)

Barston

National Grid Ref: SP2078

Malt Shovel, Bulls Head

The Gatehouse, *Barston Lane, Barston, Solihull, W. Mids,* B92 0JN.
Large, comfortable, welcoming family home.
Open: All Year
Grades: ETB Listed, AA 3 Q
01675 443274 Mr Emmett
Rates fr: *£20.00*-**£20.00**.
Beds: 1D 2T
Baths: 2 Private 1 Shared
(20)

Berkswell

National Grid Ref: SP2479

Elmcroft Country Guest House, *Hodgetts Lane, Berkswell, Coventry, W. Mids,* CV7 7DH.
Charming C18th country cottage.
Open: All Year (not Xmas)
01676 535204
Mrs Weston
Rates fr: *£20.00*-**£20.00**.
Beds: 2D 1T
Baths: 3 Private
(6)

Bilston

National Grid Ref: SO9497

Haven Hotel & Restaurant, *15 Claremont Street, Bilston, W. Midlands,* WV14 6BA.
Clean friendly with bars/restaurant.
Open: All Year (not Xmas)
01902 491661
Mr Poster
Rates fr: *£16.00*-**£18.00**.
Beds: 3F 7T 5S
Baths: 9 Ensuite 6 Shared

Birmingham Acocks Green

National Grid Ref: SP1183

Westley Arms

Pineway, *5 Elmdon Road, Acocks Green, Birmingham, W. Mids,* B27 6LJ.
Large Victorian, clean, comfortable house.
Open: All Year (not Xmas)
Grades: ETB Listed, Approv, RAC Acclaim
0121 708 2177 Mr McCoy
Rates fr: *£17.00*-**£17.00**.
Beds: 1F 1D 2T 3S
Baths: 2 Shared
(6)

Atholl Lodge, *16 Elmdon Road, Acocks Green, Birmingham, W. Mids,* B27 6LH.
Friendly house near NEC & city.
Open: All Year
Grades: ETB 2 Cr
0121 707 4417 Mr Hardy
Rates fr: *£15.00*-**£16.00**.
Beds: 1F 1D 4T 4S
Baths: 2 Private 3 Shared
(10)

Tourist Information Centres

Convention & Visitor Bureau, 2 City Arcade, **Birmingham**, West Midlands, B2 4TX, 0121 643 2514.

Convention & Visitor Bureau, National Exhibition Centre, **Birmingham**, West Midlands, B40 1NT, 0121 780 4321.

Management Suite, Merry Hill Centre, Pedmore Road, **Brierley Hill**, West Mids, DY5 1SY, 01384 481141

Bayley Lane, **Coventry**, West Midlands, CV1 5RN, 01203-832303.

39 Churchill Precinct, **Dudley**, West Midlands, DY2 7BL, 01384 457494.

Central Library, Horner Road, **Solihull**, West Midlands, B91 3RG, 0121 704 6130.

Travellers Joy, 47 High Street, Kinver, **Stourbridge**, West Midlands, DY7 6HE, 01384-872940.

18 Queen Square, **Wolverhampton**, West Midlands, WV1 1TQ, 01902-312051.

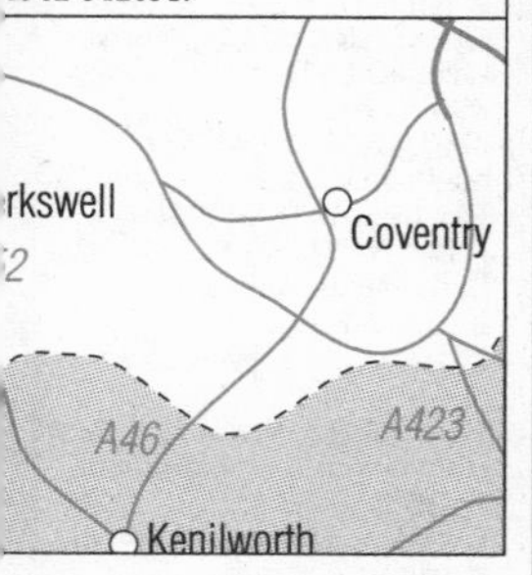

Birmingham Edgbaston

National Grid Ref: SP0584

***Woodville House,** 39 Portland Road, Edgbaston, Birmingham, W. Mids,* B16 9HN.
Open: All Year (not Xmas)
0121 454 0274 Mr Desousa
Rates fr: *£15.00*-**£15.00**.
Beds: 2F 3D 5T 6S
Baths: 4 Ensuite 3 Private
(12)
First class accommodation just one mile from city centre. All rooms colour TV, tea/coffee making facilities. Ensuite bedrooms available. Car parking. Full English breakfast.

***Kennedy Guest House,** 38 York Road, Edgbaston, Birmingham, W. Mids,* B16 9JB.
Large Victorian private house.
Open: All Year
Grades: ETB Listed
0121 454 1284
Mr & Mrs Kennedy
Rates fr: *£14.00*-**£15.00**.
Beds: 1F 1D 4T 5S
Baths: 2 Shared
(3)

Birmingham Hall Green

National Grid Ref: SP1181

***Bilthoven,** 1253 Stratford Road, Hall Green, Birmingham, W. Mids,* B28 9AJ.
Large, detached house on A34.
Open: All Year (not Xmas)
0121 777 3324 Mrs Lankester
Rates fr: *£22.00*-**£22.00**.
Beds: 1D 1T 2S
Baths: 1 Shared
(5) (6)

Birmingham Harborne

National Grid Ref: SP0284

Michelle Restaurant

***Grasmere,** 37 Serpentine Road, Harborne, Birmingham, W. Midlands,* B17 9RD.
Clean tidy & homely.
Open: All Year
Grades: ETB Listed, Approv
0121 427 4546 Mr Baker
Rates fr: *£12.00*-**£12.00**.
Beds: 2T 1S
Baths: 3 Ensuite
(0)

Birmingham Marston Green

National Grid Ref: SP1785

***17 Land Lane,** Marston Green, Birmingham, W. Mids,* B37 7DE.
Welcoming, traditional comfortable family home.
Open: All Year (not Xmas)
0121 779 2445 Mrs Simpson
Rates fr: *£15.00*-**£15.00**.
Beds: 2D
Baths: 1 Shared
(5) (2)

***Dagmar Guest House,** 85 Elmdon Road, Marston Green, Birmingham, W. Mids,* B37 7DR.
Detached family house, friendly welcome.
Open: All Year (not Xmas)
0121 779 2335
Mrs Brooks
Rates fr: *£15.00*-**£14.00**.
Beds: 1D 1T 2S
Baths: 1 Shared
(3) (3)

Birmingham Selly Park

National Grid Ref: SP0582

***Awentsbury Hotel,** 21 Serpentine Road, Selly Park, Birmingham, W. Mids,* B29 7HU.
Open: All Year
0121 472 1258 Mr Kerr
Rates fr: *£19.50*-**£26.00**.
Beds: 1F 2D 8T 5S
Baths: 6 Private 2 Shared
(12)
Victorian country house set in own gardens, close to Birmingham University, BBC Pebble Mill, Queen Elizabeth/Selly Oak Hospitals. ICC, NIA, and only 2 miles from City Centre.

***Kensington Guest House,** 785 Pershore Road, Selly Park, Birmingham, W. Midlands,* B29 2LJ.
Open: All Year
Grades: ETB 3 Cr, Comm
0121 472 7086
Mr Price
Rates fr: *£17.50*-**£28.00**.
Beds: F 14T 7D 4S
Baths: 18 Ensuite 5 Shared
(30)
Family-run hotel where you will be assured a warm welcome, friendly atmosphere. Close to city centre, ICC, NIA, NEC, M5, M42, M6.

Birmingham Sheldon

National Grid Ref: SP1584

Wheatsheaf Inn

***Fairways,** No 1 Shepheard Road, Sheldon, Birmingham, W. Mids,* B26 3RN.
Friendly, comfortable, near NEC/airport.
Open: All Year
Grades: ETB 2 Cr
0121 743 4292 Mrs Thompson
Rates fr: *£16.00*-**£20.00**.
Beds: 1F 1D 2T 1S
Baths: 2 Private 3 Shared
(7) (5)

***Homelea,** 2399 Coventry Road, Sheldon, Birmingham, W. Mids,* B26 3PN.
5 minutes Birmingham Airport/NEC.
Open: All Year
Grades: ETB 2 Cr, Comm
0121 742 0017 Mrs Read
Fax no: 0121 688 1879
Rates fr: *£25.00*-**£19.00**.
Beds: 1D 1T 1S
Baths: 2 Ensuite 1 Shared
(1) (4)

***Elmdon Guest House,** 2369 Coventry Road, Sheldon, Birmingham, W. Mids,* B26 3PN.
Modern family-run guest house.
Open: All Year (not Xmas)
0121 742 1626
Mr Gardner
Rates fr: *£17.00*-**£19.00**.
Beds: 2F 2D 3T 1S
Baths: 5 Private 2 Shared
(8)

Birmingham Yardley

National Grid Ref: SP1285

***Olton Cottage,** School Lane, Yardley, Birmingham, W. Mids,* B33 8PD.
Country cottage in the city.
Open: All Year (not Xmas)
Grades: ETB 2 Cr, High Comm
0121 783 9249 Mr Crofts
Fax no: 0121 789 6545
Rates fr: *£16.00*-**£18.00**.
Beds: 1F 1D 2T 3S
Baths: 2 Private
(2) (2)

Brierley Hill

National Grid Ref: SO9286

Saltwells Inn

***Saltwells Inn,** Saltwells Lane, Brierley Hill, W. Mids, DY5 1AX.*
Situated in a nature reserve.
Open: All Year
01384 569224 Mrs Stewart
Rates fr: *£16.00*-**£20.00**.
Beds: 3F 1D 5T 7S
Baths: 8 Ensuite 1 Private 3 Shared

Coventry

National Grid Ref: SP3378

Bear Inn, White Lion, New Varsity, Cottage Bistro, Bourbons

***Abigail Guest House,** 39 St Patricks Road, Coventry, W. Mids, CV1 2LP.*
Small, comfortable, convenient, city-centre.
Open: All Year (not Xmas)
Grades: ETB Listed
01203 221378 Mrs Griffiths
Rates fr: *£15.00*-**£16.00**.
Beds: 1F 1D 1T 2S
Baths: 2 Shared

***Acorn Lodge Guest House,** Pond Farm, Upper Eastern Green Lane, Coventry, W. Mids, CV5 7DP.*
C16th farmhouse. Quiet location.
Open: All Year (not Xmas)
Grades: ETB 2 Cr, Comm
01203 465182 Mrs Allsop
Rates fr: *£16.00*-**£16.00**.
Beds: 1D 1T 3S
Baths: 1 Private 2 Shared

***Chester House,** 3 Chester Street, Coventry, W. Mids, CV1 4DH.*
Family-run. Warm friendly atmosphere. **Open:** All Year
Grades: ETB Listed
01203 223857 Mrs Saunders
Rates fr: *£14.00*-**£14.00**.
Beds: 1F 1D 2T 1S
Baths: 1 Ensuite 1 Shared

***Northanger House,** 35 Westminster Road, Coventry, W. Mids, CV1 3GB*
Large friendly Victorian family house.
Open: All Year (not Xmas)
Grades: ETB 1 Cr, Approv
01203 226780 Ms Beccham
Rates fr: *£14.00*-**£16.00**.
Beds: 2F 2D 3T 2S
Baths: 3 Shared

***Woodlands Guest House,** Oak Lane, Allesley, Coventry, W. Mids, CV5 9BX.*
Near NEC, quiet, friendly, comfortable.
Open: All Year (not Xmas)
Grades: ETB 2 Cr
01676 522688 Mr & Mrs Laban
Rates fr: *£16.00*-**£17.00**.
Beds: 1F 1D 3T 1S
Baths: 1 Private 1 Shared

***Lodge Farm House,** Westwood Heath Road, Coventry, W. Mids, CV4 8AA.*
Country house in rural setting.
Open: All Year (not Xmas)
Grades: ETB 2 Cr
01203 466786 (also fax no)
Mrs Hall
Rates fr: *£17.50*-**£20.00**.
Beds: 1D 1T 1S
Baths: 3 Private

***Gilcrist Guest House,** 106 St James Lane, Coventry, W. Mids, CV3 3GS.*
Modern, comfortable, friendly establishment. **Open:** All Year
Grades: ETB Listed
01203 302001 Mrs Howes
Rates fr: *£15.00*-**£15.00**.
Beds: 1T 1S

***Mount Guest House,** 9 Coundon Road, Coventry, W. Mids, CV1 4AR.*
Friendly family-run guest house.
Open: All Year
Grades: ETB Listed
01203 225998 (also fax no)
Mrs Whitehead
Rates fr: *£14.00*-**£14.00**.
Beds: 2F 2D 4T 2S
Baths: 2 Shared

***Almar Lodge,** 37 Mount Nod Way, Coventry, W. Mids, CV5 7GY.*
Detached dormer bungalow, quiet location.
Open: All Year (not Xmas)
01203 468841 Mrs Bastock
Rates fr: *£14.00*-**£15.00**.
Beds: 1D 1T 1S
Baths: 1 Private 1 Shared

***Arlon Guest House,** 25 St Patricks Road, Coventry, W. Mids, CV1 2LP.*
Detached central. All amenities parking.
Open: All Year (not Xmas)
01203 225942 Mrs Walker
Rates fr: *£16.00*-**£16.00**.
Beds: 2F 1T 1S
Baths: 1 Private 2 Shared

Dudley

National Grid Ref: SO9293

***Merdeka,** 16 Dawlish Road, Woodsetton, Dudley, W. Mids, DY1 4LU.*
Detached, facing landscaped open area.
Open: All Year (not Xmas)
01902 884775 Mrs Green
Rates fr: *£15.00*-**£15.00**.
Beds: 1T 1S
Baths: 1 Shared

Great Barr

National Grid Ref: SP0494

The Towers

***Grants Guest House,** 643 Walsall Road, Great Barr, Walsall, Birmingham, W. Mids, B42 1EH.*
Small, friendly guest house, well located.
Open: All Year
Grades: ETB 1 Cr
0121 357 4826 Mrs Grant
Fax no: 0121 604 5910
Rates fr: *£18.00*-**£19.00**.
Beds: 2T 2S
Baths: 2 Shared

Hampton in Arden

National Grid Ref: SP2081

The Bear, Saracens Lievad

***The Hollies Guest House,** Kenilworth Road, Hampton in Arden, Solihull, W. Mids, B92 0LW.*
A family-run guest house.
Open: All Year (not Xmas)
Grades: ETB 2 Cr, Comm, RAC Listed
01675 442941 / 442681
Mr Fitzpatrick
Fax no: 01675 442941
Rates fr: *£18.00*-**£25.00**.
Beds: 2F 3D 4T 1S
Baths: 6 Private 1 Shared

***The Cottage,** Kenilworth Road, Hampton in Arden, Solihull, W. Mids, B92 0LW.*
Excellent accommodation in charming cottage.
Open: All Year
Grades: AA 3 Q, Recomm
01675 442323 Mr Howles
Rates fr: *£18.00*-**£20.00**.
Beds: 2F 2D 1T 4S
Baths: 8 Private 1 Shared

Kingswinford

National Grid Ref: SO8789

***Prince Albert,** High Street, Wall Heath, Kingswinford, W. Mids, DY6 0HB.*
Urban pub with guest rooms.
Open: All Year (not Xmas)
01384 287411 Mr Fereday
Rates fr: *£15.00*-**£17.00**.
Beds: 1F 1T 3S
Baths: 1 Shared

Always telephone to get directions to the B&B - you will save time!

nowle

ational Grid Ref: SP1876

Black Boy

***vy House,** Warwick Road, nowle, Solihull, W. Mids, B93 0EB.*
arge rural country house.
pen: All Year
rades: ETB 2 Cr, Comm, A 3 Q
1564 770247
Ir & Mrs Townsend
ates fr: *£22.00*-**£28.00**.
eds: 1F 2D 2T 2S
aths: 8 Private
(20)

leriden

ational Grid Ref: SP2482

***ooperage Farm B & B,** Old oad, Meriden, Coventry, W. Mids, V7 7JP.*
n the attractive village of Meriden n Heart of England Way.
pen: All Year (not Xmas)
rades: ETB 1 Cr, Approv
1676 523493 Mrs Simonds
ates fr: *£22.50*-**£25.00**.
eds: 2F 2D 2T
aths: 4 Ensuite 2 Shared

edmore

ational Grid Ref: SO9182

***he Limes Hotel,** 260 Hagley oad, Pedmore, Stourbridge, /. Midlands, DY9 0RW.*
onmfortable, quiet Victorian roperty. **Open:** All Year
1562 882689 Mr Rix
ates fr: *£18.25*-**£28.50**.
eds: 1F 3D 5T 1S
aths: 5 Ensuite 3 Shared

enn

ational Grid Ref: SO8996

Old Stags Head

***encroft Guest House,** 100 oalway Road, Penn, Volverhampton, W. Mids, WV3 7NB.*
mall homely, with beautiful ardens.
pen: All Year (not Xmas)
1902 340906 Mrs Macey
ates fr: *£15.00*-**£17.00**.
eds: 1F 2D 2T 2S
aths: 1 Shared
(5)

The lowest **single** rate is shown in **bold.**

Shirley

National Grid Ref: SP1279

Shelly Barn

***8 Felgate Close,** Shirley, Solihull, W. Mids, B90 4XU.*
Modern comfortable C/H house.
Open: All Year (not Xmas)
0121 745 8121 Mrs Wood
Rates fr: *£16.00*-**£17.00**.
Beds: 1T 2S
(2)

Solihull

National Grid Ref: SP1579

Pierre Victoire, Fats Cats

***Acorn Guest House,** 29 Links Drive, Solihull, W. Mids, B91 2DJ.*
Homely service in private house.
Open: All Year (not Xmas)
0121 705 5241 Mrs Wood
Rates fr: *£18.00*-**£18.00**.
Beds: 1D 1T 3S
Baths: 1 Private 2 Shared
(5)

***Ravenhurst Guest House,** 56 Lode Lane, Solihull, W. Mids, B91 2AW.*
Beautiful, large Victorian guest house.
Open: All Year
0121 705 5754 Mr Keppy
Rates fr: *£17.50*-**£20.00**.
Beds: 1F 1D 1T 1S
Baths: 2 Private 2 Shared
(4)

***Ammonds,** 11 Clifton Crescent, Solihull, W. Mids, B91 3LG.*
Friendly, modern, detached private house.
Open: All Year (not Xmas)
0121 704 9399 Mrs Hammond
Rates fr: *£14.00*-**£15.00**.
Beds: 1T 2S
Baths: 1 Shared
(5) (3)

***104 Silhill Hall Road,** Solihull, W. Mids, B91 1JS.*
Convenient for town centre.
Open: All Year
0121 705 2275 Mrs Nicol
Rates fr: *£17.50*-**£20.00**.
Beds: 1F 1D 1T 1S
Baths: 1 Private 2 Shared
(5)

***251 Rowood Drive,** Solihull, W. Mids, B92 9LG.*
Modern house, private, 4 miles NEC.
Open: All Year
0121 704 9458 Ms Cettler
Rates fr: *£15.00*-**£15.00**.
Beds: 1T 1S
Baths: 1 Shared

***27 Rectory Gardens,** Solihull, W. Mids, B91 3RL.*
Quiet home in town centre.
Open: All Year (not Xmas)
0121 705 1602 Mrs Pullinger
Rates fr: *£17.50*-**£17.50**.
Beds: 1D 1T
Baths: 1 Shared
(5)

***52 Seven Star Road,** Solihull, W. Mids, B91 2BY.*
Modern 4-bedroom detached house.
Open: All Year (not Xmas)
0121 705 5197 Mrs Iles
Rates fr: *£15.00*-**£15.00**.
Beds: 2T 1S
Baths: 1 Shared
(4)

Tipton

National Grid Ref: SO9592

Golden Cup

***Golden Cup,** 48 Toll End Road, Tipton, W. Mids, DY4 0HE.*
Comfortable, clean, warm, with parking.
Open: All Year
0121 557 1573 Mr Kalirai
Rates fr: *£10.00*-**£12.00**.
Beds: 3D 1T 1S
Baths: 2 Private
(3)

Walsall

National Grid Ref: SP0199

Towers

***Grants Guest House,** 643 Walsall Road, Great Barr, Walsall, Birmingham, W. Mids, B42 1EH.*
Small, friendly guesthouse, well located.
Open: All Year
Grades: ETB 1 Cr
0121 357 4826 Mrs Grant
Fax no: 0121 604 5910
Rates fr: *£18.00*-**£19.00**.
Beds: 2T 2S
Baths: 2 Shared
(2)

Wolverhampton

National Grid Ref: SO9198

Ship, Press Wine Bar

***The Wheatsheaf,** Market Street, Wolverhampton, W. Mids, WV1 3AE.*
Friendly town centre inn serving Bank's best beers.
Open: All Year (not Xmas)
01902 24446 Mrs Hall
Rates fr: *£15.00*-**£16.00**.
Beds: 1D 4T 7S
Baths: 3 Shared
(10)

***Wulfrun Hotel,** 37 Pipers Row, Wolverhampton, W. Mids, WV1 3JY.*
Town centre, comfortable homely hotel.
Open: All Year
01902 24017 Mr Perry
Rates fr: *£18.00*-**£22.00**.
Beds: 4F 4D 4T 4S
(3)

Wiltshire

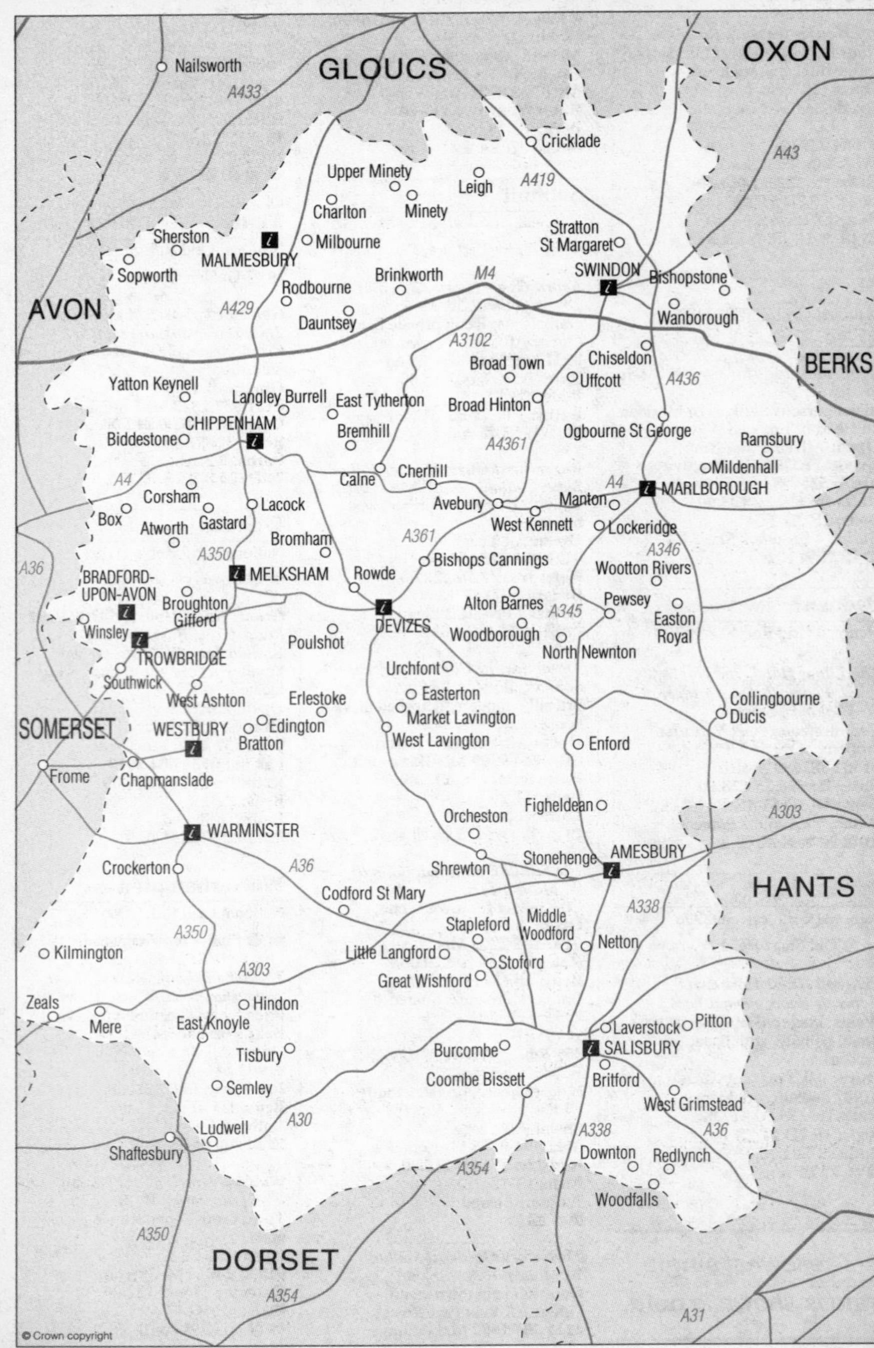

GLOUCS
OXON
AVON
BERKS
SOMERSET
HANTS
DORSET
Nailsworth
A433
Cricklade
A419
A43
Upper Minety
Leigh
Charlton
Minety
Stratton St Margaret
Sherston
Milbourne
MALMESBURY
Sopworth
Brinkworth
M4
SWINDON
Bishopstone
Rodbourne
A429
Dauntsey
Wanborough
A3102
Chiseldon
Broad Town
Uffcott
A436
Yatton Keynell
Langley Burrell
East Tytherton
Broad Hinton
CHIPPENHAM
Biddestone
Bremhill
Ogbourne St George
A4361
Ramsbury
Mildenhall
A4
Calne
Cherhill
MARLBOROUGH
Corsham
Manton
Box
Lacock
Avebury
Atworth
Gastard
West Kennett
Lockeridge
Bromham
A361
A346
A350
Bishops Cannings
Wootton Rivers
A36
MELKSHAM
Rowde
BRADFORD-UPON-AVON
Broughton Gifford
Alton Barnes
Pewsey
A345
Easton Royal
DEVIZES
Winsley
Woodborough
Poulshot
North Newnton
TROWBRIDGE
Urchfont
Southwick
West Ashton
Easterton
Collingbourne Ducis
Erlestoke
Market Lavington
WESTBURY
Edington
Bratton
West Lavington
Enford
Frome
Chapmanslade
Figheldean
A303
Orcheston
WARMINSTER
Stonehenge
AMESBURY
Shrewton
Crockerton
A36
Codford St Mary
A338
Stapleford
Middle Woodford
A350
Netton
Kilmington
Little Langford
Stoford
A303
Great Wishford
Zeals
Hindon
Mere
East Knoyle
Laverstock
Pitton
Tisbury
Burcombe
SALISBURY
Coombe Bissett
Britford
Semley
West Grimstead
A30
A338
A36
Ludwell
Shaftesbury
Downton
Redlynch
A354
Woodfalls
A350
A354
A31
© Crown copyright

Tourist Information Centres

The Great Barn, **Avebury**, Wilts, SN8 1RF, 01672 539425, (Easter to Oct).

The Library, Silver Street, **Bradford-on-Avon**, Wilts, BA15 IJX, 01225 865797.

The Citadel, Bath Road, **Chippenham**, Wilts, SN15 ZAA, 01249 657733.

39 St John's Street, **Devizes**, Wilts, SN10 1BN, 01380 729408.

Town Hall, Market Lane, **Malmesbury**, Wilts, SN16 9BZ, 01666 823748.

George Lane, **Marlborough**, Wilts, SN8 4BS, 01672 513989.

The Roundhouse, Church Street, **Melksham**, Wilts, SN12 6LS, 01225 707424.

Redworth House, Flower Lane, **Amesbury**, Salisbury, Wilts, SP4 7HG, 01980 622833.

Fish Row, **Salisbury**, Wilts, SP1 1EJ, 01722 334956.

Regent Street, **Swindon**, Wilts, SN1 1JL, 01793 530328.

St Stephens Place, **Trowbridge**, Wilts, BA14 8AH, 01225 777054.

The Square, **Mere**, Warminster, Wilts, BA12 6JJ, 01747 861211.

Central Car Park, **Warminster**, Wilts, BA12 9BT, 01985 218548.

The Library, Edward Street, **Westbury**, Wilts, BA13 3BD, 01373 827158.

Alton Barnes

National Grid Ref: SU1062

Newtown House, *Alton Barnes, Marlborough, Wilts, SN8 4LB.*
Comfortable farmhouse with beautiful views.
Open: All Year (not Xmas)
01672 851391 Mr & Mrs Shutter
Rates fr: *£22.50*-**£25.00**.
Beds: 2D 1T
Baths: 1 Ensuite 2 Shared
(14) (10)

Amesbury

National Grid Ref: SU1541

Church Cottage, *Church Street, Amesbury, Salisbury, Wilts, SP4 7EY.*
Beautiful bedrooms with ensuite/private bathrooms.
Open: All Year (not Xmas)
Grades: ETB 1 Cr, High Comm
01980 624650 Mr & Mrs Jeffrey
Rates fr: *£19.00*-**£29.00**.
Beds: 3D
Baths: 3 Private
(10)

Mandalay Guest House, *15 Stonehenge Road, Amesbury, Salisbury, Wilts, SP4 7BA.*
Elegantly furnished, ensuite bedrooms.
Open: All Year
01980 623733 Mr Courtney
Rates fr: *£18.00*-**£25.00**.
Beds: 1F 1D 1T
Baths: 3 Private
(4)

Atworth

National Grid Ref: ST8665

The Forresters

Church Farm, *Atworth, Melksham, Wilts, SN12 8JA.*
Working dairy farm, large garden.
Open: Easter to Oct
01225 702215 Mrs Hole
Rates fr: *£15.00*-**£18.00**.
Beds: 1F 1D
Baths: 1 Shared
(4)

Avebury

National Grid Ref: SU1069

Red Lion, Waggon & Horses (Beckhampton)

6 Beckhampton Road, *Avebury, Marlborough, Wilts, SN8 1QT.*
Semi-detached house near the Stones.
Open: All Year (not Xmas)
01672 539588 Mrs Dixon
Rates fr: *£16.00*-**£20.00**.
Beds: 1D 1T
Baths: 1 Shared
(6)

Biddestone

National Grid Ref: ST8673

White Horse, Biddestone Arms

Home Farm, *Biddestone, Chippenham, Wilts, SN14 7DQ.*
Working farm in picturesque village.
Open: All Year
Grades: ETB 2 Cr, Comm, AA 3 Q
01249 714475
Mr & Mrs Smith
Rates fr: *£17.50*-**£20.00**.
Beds: 1F 1D
Baths: 1 Ensuite 1 Private
(4)

Elm Farm House, *The Green, Biddestone, Chippenham, Wilts, SN14 7DG.*
Picturesque C17th stylish farmhouse.
Open: All Year
Grades: ETB 2 Cr, Comm
01249 713354 Mrs Sexton
Rates fr: *£17.50*-**£20.00**.
Beds: 1F 1D 1T
Baths: 1 Ensuite 1 Private 1 Shared
(4)

Bishops Cannings

National Grid Ref: SU0364

Crown Inn, Bridge Inn

Partacre, *Horton, Bishops Cannings, Devizes, Wilts, SN10 3NB.*
Welcoming family house. Relaxing.
Open: All Year
01380 860261 Mrs Jones
Rates fr: *£14.00*-**£14.00**.
Beds: 1D 1T 1S
Baths: 1 Shared
(2) (3)

Blackwells Farm, *Bishops Cannings, Devizes, Wilts, SN10 2JZ.*
C16th comfortable thatched house.
Open: All Year (not Xmas)
01380 860438 Mrs Quinlan
Rates fr: *£17.50*-**£20.00**.
Beds: 1F 1D 1S
Baths: 1 Private 1 Shared
(8)

Bishopstone

National Grid Ref: SU2483

Prebendal Farm, *Bishopstone, Swindon, Wilts, SN6 8PT.*
Farmhouse in beautiful downland village.
Open: All Year (not Xmas)
01793 790485
Mrs Selbourne
Rates fr: *£19.00*-**£20.00**.
Beds: 2D 1T 1S
Baths: 2 Shared
(12)

Bridge House, *The Alley, Bishopstone, Salisbury, Wilts,* *SP5 4DB.*
Large old village house.
Open: All Year
01722 780671
Mrs Stimpson
Rates fr: *£16.00*-**£28.00**.
Baths: 1 Ensuite 1 Shared
(2)

Box

National Grid Ref: ST8268

Northey Arms, Quarrymans Arms

Cheney Cottage, *Ditteridge, Box, Corsham, Wilts,* *SN14 9QF.*
Open: All Year (not Xmas)
Grades: ETB 2 Cr, Comm, AA 3 Q, Recomm
01225 742346 (also fax no)
Mrs Evans
Rates fr: *£17.50*-**£25.00**.
Beds: 1F 2D 2T 1S
Baths: 4 Ensuite 2 Shared
(7)
Very warm welcome to our pretty thatched cottage, beautiful peaceful location. Excellent breakfasts. Ideal touring base Bath - 5 miles.

Saltbox Farm, *Drewetts Mill Lane, Box, Corsham, Wilts,* *SN13 8PT.*
Idyllic retreat in conservation area.
Open: All Year (not Xmas)
Grades: ETB 1 Cr, Comm
01225 742608
Mrs Gregory
Rates fr: *£16.00*-**£18.00**.
Beds: 1D 1T
Baths: 1 Shared
(3)

Bradford-on-Avon

National Grid Ref: ST8261

Barge Inn, Cross Guns, Kings Arms, Bear Inn, Beehive

The Barge Inn, *17 Frome Road, Bradford-on-Avon, Wilts,* *BA15 2EA.*
Grade II Listed building.
Open: All Year
01225 863403
Ms Maytom-Jones
Rates fr: *£22.50*-**£22.50**.
Beds: 2D 1T
Baths: 1 Private 1 Shared
(0) (40)

National Grid References are for villages, towns and cities - *not* for individual houses.

Avonvilla, *Avoncliff, Bradford-on-Avon, Wilts,* *BA15 2HD.*
River & canalside private fishing.
Open: All Year
01225 863867 Mrs Mumford
Rates fr: *£15.00*-**£15.00**.
Beds: 1D 1T 1S
Baths: 1 Private 1 Shared
(5) (3)

Fern Cottage, *74 Monkton Farleigh, Bradford-on-Avon, Wilts,* *BA15 2QJ.*
C17th cottage in conservation village.
Open: All Year
Grades: ETB 2 Cr, High Comm, AA Prem, Select, RAC High Acclaim
01225 859412 Mrs Valentine
Fax no: 01225 859018
Rates fr: *£25.00*-**£30.00**.
Beds: 1F 2D
Baths: 2 Ensuite 1 Private
(5)

Bear Inn, *26 Silver Street, Bradford-on-Avon, Wilts,* *BA15 1JY.*
Town centre, Napoleonic, traditional inn.
Open: All Year
01225 866632
Mr Borland
Rates fr: *£19.00*-**£28.00**.
Beds: 1F 1D
Baths: 2 Private

Great Ashley House, *Ashley Lane, Bradford-on-Avon, Wilts,* *BA15 2PP.*
Quiet country house. Pool table. Jacuzzi .
Open: All Year (not Xmas)
01225 863381 Mrs Rawlings
Rates fr: *£12.50*-**£12.50**.
Beds: 2D 1T
Baths: 1 Shared
(Any) (3)

The Locks, *265 Trowbridge Road, Bradford-on-Avon, Wilts,* *BA15 1UA.*
Private house alongside restored canal.
Open: All Year
01225 863358
Mrs Benjamin
Rates fr: *£15.00*-**£15.00**.
Beds: 1F 2T
Baths: 1 Ensuite 1 Shared
(4)

Bratton

National Grid Ref: ST9152

Duke Hotel

The Duke Hotel, *Melbourne Street, Bratton, Westbury, Wilts,* *BA13 4RW.*
Traditional oak-beamed village inn.
Open: All Year
01380 830242
Mr Overend
Rates fr: *£20.00*-**£25.00**.
Beds: 2T 2D
Baths: 2 Shared
(14) (30)

Bremhill

National Grid Ref: ST9773

Lowbridge Farm, *Bremhill, Calne, Wilts,* *SN11 9HE.*
Thatched farmhouse with scenic views.
Open: All Year
01249 815889 Miss Sinden
Rates fr: *£15.50*-**£16.50**.
Beds: 1F 1D 1T
Baths: 1 Shared

Brinkworth

National Grid Ref: SU0184

B & B, *Bella Pais, Barnes Green, Brinkworth, Chippenham, Wilts,* *SN15 5AG.*
Comfortable friendly village house.
Open: All Year (not Xmas)
Grades: ETB Listed, Comm
01666 510204 Mrs Bennett
Fax no: 01666 510520
Rates fr: *£15.00*-**£15.00**.
Beds: 2D 1S
Baths: 1 Shared
(4)

Britford

National Grid Ref: SU1628

Bridge Farm, *Britford, Salisbury, Wilts,* *SP5 4DY.*
Listed C18th farmhouse in beautiful gardens.
Open: All Year
01722 332376 Mrs Hunt
Rates fr: *£18.00*-**£18.00**.
Beds: 2D 1T
Baths: 1 Shared
(4)

Broad Hinton

National Grid Ref: SU1076

Crown Inn

Damar Guest House, *Post Office Lane, Broad Hinton, Swindon, Wilts,* *SN4 9PB.*
Large modern house, lovely views.
Open: All Year (not Xmas)
01793 731442 Mrs Baker
Rates fr: *£15.00*-**£17.50**.
Beds: 1F 1T 1S
Baths: 1 Shared
(8) (5)

Broad Town

National Grid Ref: SU0977

Little Cotmarsh Farm, *Broad Town, Wootton Bassett, Swindon, Wilts,* *SN4 7RA.*
Superb accommodation in peaceful hamlet.
Open: All Year (not Xmas)
01793 731322 Mrs Richards
Rates fr: *£16.00*-**£16.00**.
Beds: 1F 1D 1T
Baths: 1 Private 2 Shared
(10)

Bromham

Vational Grid Ref: ST9665

***Vayside,** Chittoe Heath, Bromham, Chippenham, Wilts, SN15 2EH.*
Modern country chalet.
Open: All Year
Grades: ETB 3 Cr, Comm
1380 850458 Mr Collins
Rates fr: *£18.00*-**£20.00**.
Beds: 1F 1D
Baths: 2 Private
(12)

Broughton Gifford

Vational Grid Ref: ST8763

Bell on the Common

***Frying Pan Farm,** Broughton Gifford, Melksham, Wilts, SN12 8LL.*
Comfortable C17th farmhouse.
Open: All Year (not Xmas)
Grades: ETB 2 Cr, Comm
1225 702343 Mrs Pullen
Rates fr: *£17.00*-**£18.00**.
Beds: 1D 1T
Baths: 1 Ensuite 1 Shared
(2) (3)

Burcombe

Vational Grid Ref: SU0730

Ship Inn, Emblems

***Manor Farm,** Burcombe, Salisbury, Wilts, SP2 0EJ.*
Comfortable farmhouse in pretty village.
Open: Mar to Dec
Grades: ETB Listed, Comm
1722 742177 Mrs Combes
Fax no: 01722 744 600
Rates fr: *£16.00*-**£16.00**.
Beds: 1D 1T 1S
Baths: 1 Shared
(4)

Calne

National Grid Ref: ST9971

***Lower Sands Farm,** Calne, Wilts, SN11 8TR.*
Quiet, friendly, comfortable farmhouse.
Open: All Year
Grades: ETB Listed, Approv
1249 812402 Mrs Henly
Rates fr: *£16.00*-**£16.00**.
Beds: 1T 1D 1S
Baths: 1 Shared
(10)

Chapmanslade

National Grid Ref: ST8348

***Spinney Farmhouse,** Thoulstone, Chapmanslade, Westbury, Wilts, BA13 4AQ.*
C17th Listed farmhouse.
Open: All Year
1373 832412 Mrs Hoskins
Rates fr: *£16.00*-**£17.00**.
Beds: 1F 1D 1T
Baths: 2 Shared
(8)

Charlton

National Grid Ref: ST9688

Horse & Groom, The Talbot, Grove Arms, Rising Sun

***Stonehill Farm,** Charlton, Malmesbury, Wilts, SN16 9DY.*
Welcoming, comfortable beds, delicious breakfasts.
Open: All Year
Grades: ETB Listed, Comm, AA 2 Q
01666 823310 Mr & Mrs Edwards
Rates fr: *£16.00*-**£16.00**.
Beds: 1D 2T
Baths: 1 Private 1 Shared
(4)

***Charnwood Cottage,** Charlton, Shaftesbury, Dorset, SP7 9LZ.*
C17th thatched cottage.
Open: All Year (not Xmas)
01747 828310
Mr & Mrs Morgan
Rates fr: *£15.00*-**£20.00**.
Beds: 1F 1D **Baths:** 1 Shared
(5) (2)

Cherhill

National Grid Ref: SU0370

Black Horse

***Poachers Croft,** Yatesbury Hill, Cherhill, Calne, Wilts, SN11 8XY.*
Open: All Year
Grades: ETB Listed
01249 812587 Mrs Trafford
Rates fr: *£17.00*-**£25.00**.
Beds: 1F 1D 2T **Baths:** 2 Shared
(12)
Charming bungalow nestling alone below Cherhill's White Horse and monument, in Area of Outstanding Natural Beauty. Easy access Avebury, Marlborough, Bath, etc. - ideal friendly base.

Chippenham

National Grid Ref: ST9173

Hungry Horse, White Horse (Biddestone)

***Bramleys,** 73 Marshfield Road, Chippenham, Wilts, SN15 1JR.*
Large Victorian house, Grade II Listed. **Open:** All Year
Grades: ETB Listed, Comm
01249 653770 Mrs Swatton
Rates fr: *£14.00*-**£14.00**.
Beds: 1F 3T 1S
Baths: 1 Shared
(4)

***Frogwell House,** 132 Hungerdown Lane, Chippenham, Wilts, SN14 0BD.*
Attractive, stone-built guest house.
Open: All Year
Grades: ETB 3 Cr
01249 650328 (also fax no)
Mrs Burgess
Rates fr: *£16.00*-**£22.00**.
Beds: 1D 2T 1S
Baths: 2 Ensuite 1 Shared
(6)

***Home From Home,** Grathie Cottage, 72 Marshfield Road, Chippenham, Wilts, SN15 1JR.*
Modernised dolls house like cottage.
Open: All Year
Grades: ETB 1 Cr
01249 650306
Mrs Hicks
Rates fr: *£15.00*-**£20.00**.
Beds: 1F 1T 1S
Baths: 1 Shared
(4)

***Elm Farm House,** The Green, Biddestone, Chippenham, Wilts, SN14 7DG.*
Picturesque C17th stylish farmhouse.
Open: All Year
Grades: ETB 2 Cr, Comm
01249 713354
Mrs Sexton
Rates fr: *£17.50*-**£20.00**.
Beds: 1F 1D 1T
Baths: 1 Ensuite 1 Private 1 Shared
(4)

Chiseldon

National Grid Ref: SU1879

Old Crown

***Courtleigh House,** 40 Draycott Road, Chiseldon, Swindon, Wilts, SN4 0LS.*
Large, well appointed country home.
Open: All Year (not Xmas)
01793 740246
Ms Hibberd
Rates fr: *£15.00*-**£18.00**.
Beds: 2T
Baths: 1 Ensuite 1 Private
(4)

***Norton House,** 46 Draycott Road, Chiseldon, Swindon, Wilts, SN4 0LT.*
Executive countryside house, peaceful surroundings.
Open: All Year (not Nov/Xmas)
01793 741210
Mrs Dixon
Rates fr: *£18.00*-**£20.00**.
Beds: 2D 1T 1S
Baths: 1 Ensuite 1 Private 1 Shared
(5) (4)

Codford St Mary

National Grid Ref: ST9739

***The Old School House,** Codford St Mary, Warminster, Wilts, BA12 0NA.*
Converted Victorian school.
Open: Easter to Nov
01985 850673
Mrs Bradley
Rates fr: *£15.00*-**£15.00**.
Beds: 1D 1T 1S
Baths: 1 Shared
(8) (3)

Bringing children with you? Always ask for any special rates.

Collingbourne Ducis

National Grid Ref: SU2453

The Shears, School House

Hougoumont Farm, *Collingbourne Ducis, Marlborough, Wilts, SN8 3ET.*
Spacious, comfortable & peaceful.
Open: All Year (not Xmas)
01264 850260 Mrs Carter
Rates fr: *£16.00*-**£16.00**.
Beds: 2D 2T **Baths:** 2 Shared

Manor Farm, *Collingbourne Ducis, Marlborough, Wilts, SN8 3SD.*
Comfortable farmhouse with period character. **Open:** All Year
01264 850251 Mrs May
Rates fr: *£17.50*-**£15.00**.
Beds: 2T 1S
Baths: 1 Ensuite 1 Shared
(50)

Coombe Bissett

National Grid Ref: SU1026

Fox & Goose

Two Bridges, *Homington Road, Coombe Bissett, Salisbury, Wilts, SP5 4LR.*
Riverside home in pretty village.
Open: All Year (not Xmas)
Grades: ETB 2 Cr, Comm
01722 718531 Mrs Germain
Rates fr: *£19.00*-**£25.00**.
Beds: 2T
Baths: 1 Ensuite 1 Private
(5) (2)

Swaynes Firs Farm, *Grimsdyke, Coombe Bissett, Salisbury, Wilts, SP5 5RF.*
Spacious farmhouse on working farm.
Open: All Year (not Xmas)
Grades: AA 2 Q, Recomm
01725 519240 Mr Shering
Rates fr: *£20.00*-**£20.00**.
Beds: 1F 2T
Baths: 3 Private
(6)

Cross Farm, *Coombe Bissett, Salisbury, Wilts, SP5 4LY.*
Comfortable farmhouse on working farm.
Open: All Year
01722 718293
Mrs Kittermaster
Rates fr: *£16.00*-**£16.00**.
Beds: 1F 1T 1S
Baths: 2 Shared
(4)

Corsham

National Grid Ref: ST8670

White Horse Inn, Hare & Hounds (Pickwick)

Halfway Firs, *5 Halfway Firs, Corsham, Wilts, SN13 0PJ.*
Comfortable converted farm cottage.
Open: All Year (not Xmas)
Grades: ETB Listed
01225 810552 Mr & Mrs Fisher
Rates fr: *£14.00*-**£16.00**.
Beds: 1F 1D 1S
Baths: 1 Shared
(8) (3)

Spiders Barn, *Cross Keys, Corsham, Wilts, SN13 0DT.*
Converted C18th barn, ensuite rooms.
Open: All Year
Grades: ETB 2 Cr, Comm
01249 712012 Ms Thornton-Norris
Rates fr: *£17.50*-**£25.00**.
Beds: 2D 1T
Baths: 3 Ensuite
(6)

75 High Street, *Corsham, Wilts, SN13 0HA.*
Listed C18th stone house.
Open: All Year
Grades: ETB Listed, Comm
01249 713366 Mrs Rodger
Rates fr: *£16.00*-**£18.00**.
Beds: 1F 1D 1T
Baths: 1 Shared

Pickwick Lodge Farm, *Corsham, Wilts, SN13 0PS.*
Spacious well-furnished farmhouse, half mile off A4.
Open: All Year (not Xmas)
01249 712207 Mrs Stafford
Fax no: 01249 701904
Rates fr: *£17.00*-**£22.00**.
Beds: 2D 1T
Baths: 1 Ensuite 1 Private 1 Shared
(4)

Thurlestone Lodge, *13 Prospect, Corsham, Wilts, SN13 9AD.*
Spacious elegant Victorian family home.
Open: All Year
01249 713397 Mrs Ogilvie-Robb
Rates fr: *£16.00*-**£18.00**.
Beds: 1F 1D
Baths: 1 Shared
(6)

Cricklade

National Grid Ref: SU0993

Chelworth Farm, *Chelworth, Cricklade, Swindon, Wilts, SN6 6HD.*
Former farmhouse, large garden.
Open: All Year (not Xmas)
01793 750440 Mrs Hopkins
Rates fr: *£15.00*-**£20.00**.
Beds: 1F 2D 1T 3S
Baths: 6 Private 1 Shared
(5) (10)

Crockerton

National Grid Ref: ST8642

Bath Arms

Tanhouse Cottage, *Crockerton, Warminster, Wilts, BA12 8AU.*
C16th farmhouse, log fires, beams.
Open: All Year (not Xmas)
01985 214816 Mrs Dickinson
Rates fr: *£17.00*-**£17.00**.
Beds: 1F 1D 1T 1S
Baths: 2 Shared
(6)

Springfield House, *Crockerton, Warminster, Wilts, BA12 8AU.*
A special place to stay; C17th country house.
Open: All Year
01985 213696 Mrs Singer
Rates fr: *£22.00*-**£26.00**.
Beds: 2D 1T **Baths:** 3 Ensuite
(5)

Dauntsey

National Grid Ref: ST9982

Three Crowns, Wellesley Arms

Olivemead Farm, *Olivemead Lane Dauntsey, Chippenham, Wilts, SN15 4JQ.*
Delightful farmhouse, relaxed friendly atmosphere.
Open: All Year (not Xmas)
Grades: ETB 1 Cr, Comm
01666 510205 Mrs Candy
Rates fr: *£15.00*-**£17.00**.
Beds: 1F 1D 1T
Baths: 1 Shared
(6)

Scots Smith Farm Bungalow, *Sodom Lane, Dauntsey, Chippenham, Wilts, SN15 4JA.*
Modern, comfortable family home
Open: All Year
01249 890345
Mrs Denyer
Rates fr: *£15.00*-**£15.00**.
Beds: 1D 1T
Baths: 1 Shared
(4)

Devizes

National Grid Ref: SU0061

Bear Hotel, Royal Oak, Moonrakers, Four Seasons

Pinecroft, *Potterne Road (A360), Devizes, Wilts, SN10 5DA.*
Spacious Georgian home, exquisite garden.
Open: All Year
Grades: ETB 2 Cr, Comm, AA 3 Q, RAC Listed
01380 721433
Mr & Mrs Linton
Fax no: 01380 721229
Rates fr: *£16.00*-**£20.00**.
Beds: 1F 2D 2T
Baths: 4 Private
(7)

Craven House, *Station Road, Devizes, Wilts,* SN10 1BZ.
Victorian house in town centre.
Open: All Year
01380 723514
Mrs Shaw
Rates fr: *£16.00*-**£18.00**.
Beds: 1D 2T
Baths: 3 Ensuite

Eastcott Manor, *Easterton, Devizes, Wilts,* SN10 4PL.
Elizabethan manor house in own grounds.
Open: All Year (not Xmas)
01380 813313 Mrs Firth
Rates fr: *£21.00*-**£18.00**.
Beds: 1D 2T 1S
Baths: 2 Ensuite 2 Private
(20)

Gate House, *Wick Lane, Devizes, Wilts,* SN10 5DW.
Peaceful, spacious, detached house. Large garden.
Open: All Year (not Xmas)
01380 725283 (also fax no)
Mr Stratton
Rates fr: *£17.50*-**£14.50**.
Beds: 1D 1T 1S
Baths: 1 Ensuite 1 Shared
(8)

Traquair, *2 Bricksteed Avenue, Devizes, Wilts,* SN10 3AE.
Comfortable house, good parking. Quiet situaton.
Open: All Year (not Xmas)
01380 722014
Mr Forbes Peebles
Rates fr: *£15.00*-**£15.00**.
Beds: 1T 1S
Baths: 1 Ensuite 1 Shared
(12) (3)

Asta, *66 Downlands Road, Devizes, Wilts,* SN10 5EF.
Friendly, comfortable, modern town house.
Open: All Year
01380 722546
Mrs Milne-Day
Rates fr: *£12.50*-**£12.50**.
Beds: 1D 2S
Baths: 1 Shared
(2)

Kenavon, *London Road, Devizes, Wilts,* SN10 2DS.
Guest house overlooking Kennet/Avon canal.
Open: All Year
01380 721494 Mr Fry
Rates fr: *£16.00*-**£17.00**.
Beds: 1F 2D 2T 1S
Baths: 2 Private 1 Shared
(5)

The lowest *double* rate per person is shown in *italics*.

Rathlin Guest House, *Wick Lane, Devizes, Wilts,* SN10 5DP.
Elegantly furnished. All ensuite. Quiet.
Open: All Year (not Xmas)
01380 721999 Mr Fletcher
Rates fr: *£20.00*-**£25.00**.
Beds: 2D 2T
Baths: 4 Private
(6)

Eastfield House, *London Road, Devizes, Wilts,* SN10 2DW.
Comfortable canal-side house.
Open: All Year
01380 721562 Mr & Mrs Lamb
Rates fr: *£15.00*.
Beds: 1T 1D
Baths: 1 Private
(12) (4)

Downton

National Grid Ref: SU1821

The Warren, *15 High Street, Downton, Salisbury, Wilts,* SP5 3PG.
Grade II Listed Georgian house.
Open: All Year (not Xmas)
Grades: AA 3 Q, RAC Acclaim
01725 510263 Mrs Baxter
Rates fr: *£20.00*-**£27.00**.
Beds: 1F 3D 2T
Baths: 2 Private 2 Shared
(5) (8)

East Knoyle

National Grid Ref: ST8830

Swainscombe, *The Green, East Knoyle, Salisbury, Wilts,* SP3 6BN.
Beautiful period thatched country house.
Open: All Year (not Xmas)
01747 830224 (also fax no)
Mrs Orman
Rates fr: *£19.00*-**£22.50**.
Beds: 2D 1T 2S
Baths: 1 Ensuite 2 Private 1 Shared
(10) (6)

Moors Farmhouse, *East Knoyle, Salisbury, Wilts,* SP3 6BU.
C17th farmhouse, self-contained suite.
Open: All Year (not Xmas)
01747 830385 Mrs Reading
Rates fr: *£20.00*-**£25.00**.
Beds: 1T
Baths: 1 Ensuite
(8)

East Tytherton

National Grid Ref: ST9674

Barnbridge, *East Tytherton, Chippenham, Wilts,* SN15 4LT.
Spacious country farmhouse, beautiful views.
Open: All Year
01249 740280
Mrs Giffard-Taylor
Rates fr: *£15.00*-**£15.00**.
Beds: 2T 1S
Baths: 2 Shared
(10)

Easterton

National Grid Ref: SU0255

Royal Oak

Eastcott Manor, *Easterton, Devizes, Wilts,* SN10 4PL.
Elizabethan manor house in own grounds.
Open: All Year (not Xmas)
01380 813313 Mrs Firth
Rates fr: *£21.00*-**£18.00**.
Beds: 1D 2T 1S
Baths: 2 Ensuite 2 Private
(20)

Easton Royal

National Grid Ref: SU2060

Follets, *Easton Royal, Pewsey, Wilts,* SN9 5LZ.
Comfortable, detached house, tranquil surroundings.
Open: All Year
01672 810619
Mrs Landless
Rates fr: *£17.50*-**£20.00**.
Beds: 1F 1D 1T
Baths: 1 Ensuite 1 Shared
(4)

Hook Cottage, *Easton Royal, Pewsey, Wilts,* SN9 5LY.
Quiet, comfortable & wonderful views.
Open: All Year
Grades: ETB 2 Cr
01672 810 275 / 0589 144862
Mrs McNaught
Fax no: 01672 810275
Rates fr: *£17.50*-**£20.00**.
Beds: 1F 1T 1S
Baths: 1 Ensuite 1 Private
(5)

Edington

National Grid Ref: ST9253

Hillside Farm, *Edington, Westbury, Wilts,* BA13 4PG.
Secluded farmhouse with delightful gardens.
Open: Feb to Dec
01380 830437 (also fax no)
Mrs Mussell
Rates fr: *£15.00*-**£16.00**.
Beds: 1F 1T
Baths: 1 Shared
(3)

Enford

National Grid Ref: SU1351

The Swan

Enford House, *Enford, Pewsey, Wilts,* SN9 6DJ.
Village rectory. Very quiet.
Open: All Year (not Xmas)
Grades: ETB 1 Cr
01980 670414 Mr Campbell
Rates fr: *£15.00*-**£17.00**.
Beds: 1D 2T
Baths: 3 Shared
(6)

Erlestoke

National Grid Ref: ST9653

***Longwater,** Lower Road, Erlestoke, Devizes, Wilts, SN10 5UE.*
Peaceful comfortable farmhouse. All ensuite.
Open: All Year (not Xmas)
Grades: ETB 3 Cr, Comm, AA 3 Q
01380 830095 (also fax no)
Mrs Hampton
Rates fr: *£21.00*-**£28.00**.
Beds: 1F 2D 2T
Baths: 5 Private
(6)

Figheldean

National Grid Ref: SU1547

Dog & Gun

***Vale House,** Figheldean, Salisbury, Wilts, SP4 8JJ.*
Comfortable family house. Centre village.
Open: All Year (not Xmas)
Grades: ETB 2 Cr, Comm
01980 670713
Mrs Strefford
Rates fr: *£14.50*-**£14.50**.
Beds: 2T 1S
Baths: 1 Ensuite 1 Shared
(3)

Gastard

National Grid Ref: ST8868

***Boyds Farm,** Gastard, Corsham, Wilts, SN13 9PT.*
Listed C16th farmhouse.
Open: All Year
01249 713146
Mrs Robinson
Rates fr: *£15.00*-**£18.00**.
Beds: 1F 1D 1T
Baths: 1 Private 1 Shared
(6)

Great Wishford

National Grid Ref: SU0735

Royal Oak

***Wishford Farmhouse,** Great Wishford, Salisbury, Wilts, SP2 0NN.*
Quiet farmhouse in pretty village.
Open: Mar to Nov
01722 790235
Mrs Thatcher
Rates fr: *£15.00*-**£16.00**.
Beds: 2T 1S
Baths: 1 Private 1 Shared
(2)

Planning a longer stay? Always ask for any special rates.

Hindon

National Grid Ref: ST9132

***Chicklade Lodge,** Chicklade, Hindon, Salisbury, Wilts, SP3 5SU.*
Spacious Victorian cottage, large walled garden.
Open: All Year
01747 820389 Mrs Jerram
Rates fr: *£15.00*-**£16.00**.
Beds: 2T
Baths: 1 Shared
(5)

Kilmington

National Grid Ref: ST7736

***The Red Lion Inn,** On B3092 (Mere to Frome road), Kilmington, Warminster, Wilts, BA12 6RP.*
Traditional country inn, modern accommodation.
Open: All Year
01985 844263 Mr Gibbs
Rates fr: *£15.00*-**£20.00**.
Beds: 1D 1T
Baths: 1 Shared
(4) (25)

Lacock

National Grid Ref: ST9168

George, Red Lion, Carpenters Arms, The Angel

***The Old Rectory,** Lacock, Chippenham, Wilts, SN15 2LX.*
Large country house, mature gardens.
Open: All Year (not Xmas)
Grades: ETB 2 Cr, Comm
01249 730335 Mrs Addison
Rates fr: *£22.50*-**£45.00**.
Beds: 2D 1T
Baths: 3 Ensuite
(10) (6)

***Lacock Pottery,** The Tan Yard, Lacock, Chippenham, Wilts, SN15 2LB.*
Beautiful, comfortable, working pottery, mediaeval village.
Open: All Year (not Xmas)
Grades: ETB 2 Cr, Comm
01249 730266 Mrs McDowell
Rates fr: *£23.00*-**£26.00**.
Beds: 2T 1D
Baths: 1 Ensuite 1 Shared 1 Private
(6)

Langley Burrell

National Grid Ref: ST9375

***Old Brewery House,** Langley Burrell, Chippenham, Wilts, SN15 4LQ.*
Comfortable Georgian home. 12 miles Bath.
Open: All Year (not Xmas)
01249 652694 Mrs Payne
Rates fr: *£12.50*-**£15.00**.
Beds: 1D 2T 1S
Baths: 2 Shared
(5) (6)

Laverstock

National Grid Ref: SU1530

Duck Inn

***Pasket House,** 57 Church Road, Laverstock, Salisbury, Wilts, SP1 1QY.*
Spacious, detached, quiet comfortable house.
Open: All Year (not Xmas)
Grades: ETB 2 Cr
01722 327651 Mrs Naish
Rates fr: *£15.00*-**£18.00**.
Beds: 1D 2T
Baths: 3 Private
(3) (4)

***Daheim,** 3 Willow Close, Laverstock, Salisbury, Wilts, SP1 1QF.*
Unique riverside bungalow near city.
Open: Easter to Dec
Grades: ETB 1 Cr, Comm
01722 334536 Mrs Lavers
Rates fr: *£14.00*-**£14.00**.
Beds: 1T 1S
Baths: 1 Shared
(6) (2)

Leigh

National Grid Ref: SU0692

Foresters Inn

***Waterhay Farm,** Leigh, Cricklade, Swindon, Wilts, SN6 6QY.*
Working farm in peaceful surroundings.
Open: All Year
Grades: ETB 2 Cr, Comm
01285 861253 Mrs Rumming
Rates fr: *£17.00*-**£17.00**.
Beds: 1F 1D 1T
Baths: 3 Private
(5) (4)

Little Langford

National Grid Ref: SU0436

***Little Langford Farmhouse,** Little Langford, Salisbury, Wilts, SP3 4NR.*
Beautiful, spacious Victorian farmhouse.
Open: All Year (not Xmas)
01722 790205 Mrs Helyer
Rates fr: *£17.50*-**£22.00**.
Beds: 1F 1D 1T
Baths: 2 Shared
(3)

National Grid References are for villages, towns and cities - *not* for individual houses.

Lockeridge

National Grid Ref: SU1467

Who'd A Thought It

The Taffrail, *Rhyls Lane, Lockeridge, Marlborough, Wilts, SN8 4ED.*
Open: Jan to Nov
01672 861266
Mrs Spencer
Rates fr: *£17.50*-**£20.00**.
Beds: 1D 1T 1S
Baths: 1 Shared
(8) (3)
Delightful modern house in mature garden. Lovely views over the Marlborough Downs. Guest lounge with snooker table. Form comfortable beds & a very friendly welcome.

Lower Wanborough

National Grid Ref: SU2082

Iris Cottage, *Lower Wanborough, Swindon, Wilts, SN4 0AP.*
Close to Ridgeway, excellent walking.
Open: All Year
01793 790591
Mrs Rosier
Rates fr: *£19.00*-**£19.00**.
Beds: 1D 1S
Baths: 1 Shared
(2)

Ludwell

National Grid Ref: ST9122

Birdbush Farm, *Ludwell, Shaftesbury, Dorset, SP7 9NH.*
Comfortable farmhouse in quiet position.
Open: Easter to Oct
01747 828252
Mrs Rossiter
Rates fr: *£15.50*-**£16.00**.
Beds: 1D 1S
Baths: 1 Shared
(6)

Malmesbury

National Grid Ref: ST9387

Plough Inn, White Horse Inn, Old Inn, Vintage, Horse & Groom

Angrove Farm, *Rodbourne, Malmesbury, Wilts, SN16 0ET.*
Open: Feb to Nov
Grades: AA 3 Q
01666 822982 Mrs Parfitt
Rates fr: *£14.00*-**£16.00**.
Beds: 2D 1T
Baths: 1 Ensuite 2 Private
Peacefully secluded. Working beef farm. Breakfast menu choice. Lounge TV. Drink making. Trout & coarse fishing. Central for Lacock, Castle Combe, Bath, Costwolds. Personal attention.

Flisteridge Cottage, *Flisteridge Road, Upper Minety, Minety, Malmesbury, Wilts, SN16 9PS.*
Open: All Year
Grades: ETB Listed, Comm
01666 860343 Mrs Toop-Rose
Rates fr: *£16.00*-**£15.00**.
Beds: 1D 1T 1S
Baths: 1 Private 1 Shared
(11) (5)
Idyllic countryside retreat. Warm welcome, friendly atmosphere. Beautiful secluded gardens. Choice of delicious breakfasts. Home-made preserves. Ideal touring base Cotswolds, National Trust properties, etc.

Stonehill Farm, *Charlton, Malmesbury, Wilts, SN16 9DY.*
Welcoming, comfortable beds, delicious breakfasts.
Open: All Year
Grades: ETB Listed, Comm, AA 2 Q
01666 823310 Mr & Mrs Edwards
Rates fr: *£16.00*-**£16.00**.
Beds: 1D 2T
Baths: 1 Private 1 Shared
(4)

Bremilham House, *Bremilham Road, Malmesbury, Wilts, SN16 0DQ.*
Open: All Year
Grades: ETB Listed
01666 822680 Mrs Ball
Rates fr: *£15.00*-**£17.50**.
Beds: 2D 1T 1S
Baths: 2 Shared
(3)
Delightful, recently renovated Edwardian house in historic Malmesbury. Central for Bath, Cheltenham, Salisbury & the glorious Cotswolds. Traditional English breakfast. Delicious home cooked evening meals. Residential licence.

Kings Arms Hotel, *High Street, Malmesbury, Wilts, SN16 9AA.*
400-year-old coaching inn.
Open: All Year
01666 823383 Mr Timms
Rates fr: *£16.00*-**£18.00**.
Beds: 1F 4D 2T 1S
Baths: 2 Shared
(30)

Whychurch Farm, *Malmesbury, Wilts, SN16 9JL.*
C17th farmhouse, central for Bath/Cotswolds.
Open: All Year (not Xmas)
01666 822156 Mr & Mrs Weaver
Rates fr: *£13.00*-**£17.50**.
Beds: 1D 1T
Baths: 2 Ensuite 2 Shared
(8)

All details shown are as supplied by B&B owners in Autumn 1996.

Manton

National Grid Ref: SU1768

Junipers, Up The Garden Path, Oddfellows Arms

Sunrise Farm, *Manton, Marlborough, Wilts, SN8 4HL.*
Quietly situated, restful home, panoramic views.
Open: Easter to Sep
01672 512878 (also fax no)
Mrs Couzens
Rates fr: *£16.00*-**£20.00**.
Beds: 1D 2T
Baths: 1 Private 1 Shared
(4)

Market Lavington

National Grid Ref: SU0154

Green Dragon

The Old Coach House, *21 Church Street, Market Lavington, Devizes, Wilts, SN10 4DU.*
Comfortable, spacious C18th house.
Open: All Year
Grades: ETB 2 Cr, Comm, AA 3 Q
01380 812879 Mr & Mrs Mattingly
Rates fr: *£21.00*-**£25.00**.
Beds: 1D 2T
Baths: 3 Ensuite
(3)

Marlborough

National Grid Ref: SU1869

Junipers Up the Garden Path, The Oddfellows Arms, Bear, Wellington Arms, Roeback Inn

Redlands, *Elcot Lane, Marlborough, Wilts, SN8 2BA.*
Warm welcome, excellent food.
Open: All Year (not Xmas)
01672 515477 (also fax no)
Mrs Camm
Rates fr: *£15.00*-**£20.00**.
Beds: 2D 1T
Baths: 1 Ensuite 1 Shared
(2)

Sunrise Farm, *Manton, Marlborough, Wilts, SN8 4HL.*
Quietly situated, restful home, panoramic views.
Open: Easter to Sep
01672 512878 (also fax no)
Mrs Couzens
Rates fr: *£16.00*-**£20.00**.
Beds: 1D 2T
Baths: 1 Private 1 Shared
(4)

Kennet Beeches, *54 George Lane, Marlborough, Wilts, SN8 4BY.*
Comfortable modern house, riverside garden.
Open: All Year
01672 512579 Mr & Mrs Young
Rates fr: *£16.00*-**£16.00**.
Beds: 2T 1S **Baths:** 1 Shared
(2)

***Cartref,** 63 George Lane, Marlborough, Wilts, SN8 4BY.*
Family home near country town.
Open: All Year (not Xmas)
01672 512771 Mrs Harrison
Rates fr: *£16.00*-**£16.00**.
Beds: 1F 1D 1T
Baths: 1 Shared
(1) (2)

***5 Reeds Ground,** London Road, Marlborough, Wilts, SN8 2AW.*
Modern clean comfortable private house.
Open: All Year (not Xmas)
01672 513926 Mrs Waite
Rates fr: *£16.00*-**£20.00**.
Beds: 1D
Baths: 1 Private
(2)

***Paddocks,** Cardigan Road, Marlborough, Wilts, SN8 1LB.*
Large house - two private suites.
Open: All Year (not Xmas)
01672 515280 Mrs Brockwell
Rates fr: *£17.50*.
Beds: 2D **Baths:** 2 Ensuite
(4)

Melksham

National Grid Ref: ST9064

Kings Arms, Barge Inn

***Longhope Guest House,** 9 Beanacre Road, Melksham, Wilts, SN12 8AG.*
Large comfortable Victorian guest house.
Open: All Year
Grades: ETB 2 Cr
01225 706737 Mrs Hyatt
Rates fr: *£17.50*-**£24.00**.
Beds: 2F 2D 1T 1S
Baths: 6 Ensuite
(10)

***Craycroft,** 402 The Spa, Spa Road, Melksham, Wilts, SN12 6QL.*
Large Georgian house, excellent value.
Open: All Year
01225 707984 Mrs Pavey
Rates fr: *£13.00*-**£15.00**.
Beds: 1F 1D 1T
Baths: 2 Private 1 Shared
(4)

***36 Church Walk,** Melksham, Wilts, SN12 6LY.*
Small Georgian townhouse, town centre.
Open: All Year (not Xmas)
01225 790018 Mrs Clark
Rates fr: *£13.00*-**£15.00**.
Beds: 1F 1T
Baths: 1 Shared
(10)

All rates are subject to alteration at the owners' discretion.

The lowest **single** *rate is shown in* **bold.**

Mere

National Grid Ref: ST8132

Talbot Inn, Butt & Sherry, Ship Hotel

***Norwood House,** Mere, Warminster, Wilts, BA12 6LA.*
Large family house, rural setting.
Open: All Year
01747 860992 Mrs Tillbrook
Rates fr: *£14.00*-**£16.00**.
Beds: 1F
Baths: 1 Ensuite
(3)

***Downleaze,** North Street, Mere, Warminster, Wilts, BA12 6HH.*
Comfortable in quiet area.
Open: All Year (not Xmas)
01747 860876
Mrs Lampard
Rates fr: *£14.00*-**£14.00**.
Beds: 1D 1T
Baths: 1 Shared
(3)

***Meltone House, The Causeway,** Shaftesbury Road, Mere, Warminster, Wilts, BA12 6BW.*
Modern house outskirts of town.
Open: All Year (not Xmas)
01747 861383
Mr & Mrs Parfitt
Rates fr: *£15.00*-**£15.00**.
Beds: 1D 1S
Baths: 1 Private
(8)

Middle Woodford

National Grid Ref: SU1136

Wheatsheaf, Bridge Inn

***Great Croft,** Middle Woodford, Salisbury, Wilts, SP4 6NR.*
Situated between Salisbury & Stonehenge.
Open: All Year (not Xmas)
01722 782357 Mrs Cates
Rates fr: *£16.00*-**£20.00**.
Beds: 1T
Baths: 1 Ensuite
(2)

Milbourne

National Grid Ref: ST9487

***Southfields Cottage,** Milbourne, Malmesbury, Wilts, SN16 9JB.*
Pretty C17th cottage, quiet, friendly.
Open: All Year
01666 823168 Mrs Meller
Rates fr: *£17.00*-**£20.00**.
Beds: 1D 1T
Baths: 2 Private
(12) (4)

Mildenhall

National Grid Ref: TL7174

Horseshoe

***Watersedge,** Werg Lane, Mildenhall, Marlborough, Wilts, SN8 2LY.*
Riverside position in beautiful Kennet Valley.
Open: All Year (not Xmas)
01672 511590 Mrs Hodder
Rates fr: *£16.50*-**£17.00**.
Beds: 1D 1S
Baths: 1 Shared
(11) (3)

Minety

National Grid Ref: SU0091

Plough Inn, White Horse Inn, Old Inn

***Flisteridge Cottage,** Flisteridge Road, Upper Minety, Minety, Malmesbury, Wilts, SN16 9PS.*
Idyllic countryside retreat. Warm welcome, friendly atmosphere.
Open: All Year
Grades: ETB Listed, Comm
01666 860343
Mrs Toop-Rose
Rates fr: *£16.00*-**£15.00**.
Beds: 1D 1T 1S
Baths: 1 Private 1 Shared
(11) (5)

Netton

National Grid Ref: SU1336

***Thorntons,** Netton, Salisbury, Wilts, SP4 6AW.*
Friendly comfortable quiet village house.
Open: All Year (not Xmas)
01722 782535
Mrs Bridger
Rates fr: *£15.00*-**£16.50**.
Beds: 1F 1T
Baths: 2 Shared
(3)

***The Old Bakery,** Netton, Salisbury, Wilts, SP4 6AW.*
Pleasantly modernised, former village bakery.
Open: All Year (not Xmas)
01722 782351
Mrs Dunlop
Rates fr: *£14.00*-**£14.00**.
Beds: 1D 1T 1S
Baths: 1 Shared
(5) (3)

***Avonbank,** Netton, Salisbury, Wilts, SP4 6AW.*
Comfortable friendly, in small village.
Open: All Year (not Xmas)
01722 782331
Mrs Vincent
Rates fr: *£16.00*-**£20.00**.
Beds: 1D 3T
Baths: 1 Ensuite 2 Shared
(3)

North Newnton

National Grid Ref: SU1257

Woodbridge Inn

Woodbridge Inn, *North Newnton, Pewsey, Wilts, SN9 6JZ.*
Comfortable cottage, cosy in C16th inn.
Open: All Year (not Xmas)
Grades: ETB Listed, AA 2 Q, RAC Acclaim
01980 630266 (also fax no)
Mr Vertessy
Rates fr: *£16.25*-**£27.00**.
Beds: 1F 1T 1D
Baths: 1 Ensuite 1 Shared
(60)

Ogbourne St George

National Grid Ref: SU2074

Old Crown

The Parklands Hotel, *Ogbourne St George, Marlborough, Wilts, SN8 1SL.*
Open: All Year
Grades: ETB 3 Cr, Comm
01672 841555 Mrs Naffine
Rates fr: *£30.00*-**£30.00**.
Beds: 2D 6T 2S
Baths: 10 Ensuite
(20)
Just minutes from the Ridgeway Trail in charming village location, this well appointed hotel & restaurant offers excellent ensuite accommodation, superb restaurant & real ale bar.

Laurel Cottage, *Southend, Ogbourne St George, Marlborough, Wilts, SN8 1SG.*
Picturesque C16th thatched cottage.
Open: Easter to Oct
Grades: ETB 2 Cr, High Comm, AA 5 Q
01672 841288 Mrs Francis
Rates fr: *£22.50*-**£35.00**.
Beds: 1F 2T
Baths: 3 Private
(8) (5)

The Old Crown, *Marlborough Road, Ogbourne St George, Marlborough, Wilts, SN8 1SQ.*
C18th coaching inn with restaurant.
Open: Easter to Sep
01672 841445
Mr & Mrs Shaw
Rates fr: *£15.00*-**£25.00**.
Beds: 2T
Baths: 2 Private
(5) (15)

All rates are subject to alteration at the owners' discretion.

Orcheston

National Grid Ref: SU0546

Crown Inn

Cozens House Cottage, *Orcheston, Salisbury, Wilts, SP3 4RW.*
Secluded comfortable Georgian farmhouse.
Open: All Year (not Xmas)
01980 620257 Mrs Smith
Rates fr: *£15.00*-**£15.00**.
Beds: 1F 1T
Baths: 1 Shared
(3)

Pewsey

National Grid Ref: SU1660

Alfreds of Pewsey

Alfreds of Pewsey, *70 High Street, Pewsey, Wilts, SN9 5AQ.*
Friendly, comfortable village free house.
Open: All Year
01672 563414
Mrs Goddard
Rates fr: *£20.00*-**£20.00**.
Beds: 1D 2T 2S
Baths: 2 Private 1 Shared
(12)

Pitton

National Grid Ref: SU2131

The Homestead, *Stockbottom, Pitton, Salisbury, Wilts, SP5 1SU.*
C18th farmhouse & converted barn.
Open: All Year (not Xmas)
01980 611160 (also fax no)
Mr & Mrs Lodge
Rates fr: *£21.00*-**£21.00**.
Beds: 2F 2D 2T 1S
Baths: 3 Private 1 Shared
(7)

Poulshot

National Grid Ref: ST9659

Raven

Higher Green Farm, *Poulshot, Devizes, Wilts, SN10 4RW.*
Peaceful Picturesque C17th timbered farmhouse.
Open: All Year (not Xmas)
Grades: ETB Listed, Comm
01380 828355 Mrs Nixon
Rates fr: *£16.00*-**£16.00**.
Beds: 1D 1T 2S
Baths: 2 Shared

Townsend Farmhouse, *Poulshot, Devizes, Wilts, SN10 1SD.*
Spacious, comfortable farmhouse with garden.
Open: All Year
01380 828221 Mrs Young
Rates fr: *£15.00*-**£13.50**.
Beds: 2D
Baths: 1 Private 1 Shared
(4) (3)

Ramsbury

National Grid Ref: SU2771

Marridge Hill House, *Ramsbury, Marlborough, Wilts, SN8 2HG.*
Comfortable, relaxed home with warm welcome.
Open: All Year (not Xmas)
01672 520237
Mrs Davies
Fax no: 01672 520053
Rates fr: *£17.00*-**£22.00**.
Beds: 3T
Baths: 1 Ensuite 1 Shared
(5) (6)

Redlynch

National Grid Ref: SU2020

Kings Head, Apple Tree

Saddlers, *Princes Hill, Redlynch, Salisbury, Wilts, SP5 2HF.*
Delightful village house, lovely garden.
Open: All Year (not Xmas)
01725 510571 (also fax no)
Mrs Sanders
Rates fr: *£16.00*-**£16.00**.
Beds: 1D 1T
Baths: 1 Shared
(2)

Yew Tree Cottage, *Grove Lane, Redlynch, Salisbury, Wilts, SP5 2NR.*
Spacious country cottage and smallholding.
Open: All Year (not Xmas)
01725 511730
Mr & Mrs Churchill
Rates fr: *£17.00*-**£17.00**.
Beds: 1D 1T 1S
Baths: 1 Shared
(5) (6)

Templemans Old Farmhouse, *Redlynch, Salisbury, Wilts, SP5 2JS.*
Large, gracious peaceful country house.
Open: Apr to Oct
Grades: ETB 1 Cr, Comm
01725 510331
Mrs Dabell
Rates fr: *£18.00*-**£20.00**.
Beds: 1D 1T 1S
Baths: 1 Shared
(5) (6)

Rodbourne

National Grid Ref: ST9383

Vintage

Angrove Farm, *Rodbourne, Malmesbury, Wilts, SN16 0ET.*
Peacefully secluded. Working beef farm.
Open: Feb to Nov
Grades: AA 3 Q
01666 822982 Mrs Parfitt
Rates fr: *£14.00*-**£16.00**.
Beds: 2D 1T
Baths: 1 Ensuite 2 Private

Salisbury

National Grid Ref: SU1430

Fox & Goose Inn, George & Dragon, Avon Inn, Bell Inn, Castle Inn

***Swaynes Firs Farm,** Grimsdyke, Coombe Bissett, Salisbury, Wilts, SP5 5RF.*
Open: All Year (not Xmas)
Grades: AA 2 Q, Recomm
01725 519240 Mr Shering
Rates fr: *£20.00*-**£20.00**.
Beds: 1F 2T
Baths: 3 Private
(6)
Spacious farmhouse on working farm with horses, cattle, poultry, geese & duck ponds. All rooms ensuite with colour TV & nice views.

***Avonlee,** 231 Castle Road, Salisbury, Wilts, SP1 3RY.*
Spacious, detached house, comfortable rooms.
Open: All Year
Grades: ETB Listed, Comm
01722 338351 Mrs Tottem
Rates fr: *£16.00*-**£18.00**.
Beds: 1D 1T 1S
Baths: 1 Shared
(5) (2)

***Rokeby Guest House,** 3 Wain-A-Long Road, Salisbury, Wilts, SP1 1LJ.*
Open: All Year (not Xmas)
Grades: ETB 3 Cr, Comm, AA 3 Q, Recomm, RAC Acclaim
01722 329800 (also fax no)
Mrs Rogers
Rates fr: *£18.00*-**£26.00**.
Beds: 5F 1D 3T
Baths: 5 Ensuite 2 Private 2 Shared
(12) (8)
Beautiful, nostalgic, Edwardian guest house quietly situated 10 minutes walk city/cathedral. Large landscaped gardens with summerhouse, ornamental pond/fountain. Gymnasium, elegant conservatory, licensed restaurant. Brochure available.

***Gerrans House,** 91 Castle Road, Salisbury, Wilts, SP1 3RW.*
Comfortable detached house, private facilities.
Open: Easter to Nov
Grades: ETB 2 Cr, High Comm, AA 4 Q, Select
01722 334394 Mrs Robins
Rates fr: *£18.00*-**£25.00**.
Beds: 1D 1T
Baths: 2 Ensuite
(7) (2)

The lowest *double* rate per person is shown in *italics*.

***The Gallery,** 36 Wyndham Road, Salisbury, Wilts, SP1 3AB.*
Open: All Year
Grades: ETB Listed, Comm
01722 324586 / 500956
Mrs Musslewhite
Fax no: 01722 324586
Rates fr: *£16.00*-**£22.00**.
Beds: 1D 2T
Baths: 2 Ensuite 1 Private
(12)
Experience our warm hospitality & delicious breakfasts in a non-smoking environment. Well-situated for exploring Salisbury & the many attractions in the area.

***48 Wyndham Road,** Salisbury, Wilts, SP1 3AB.*
Tastefully restored Edwardian family home.
Open: All Year
01722 327757 Mrs Jukes
Rates fr: *£15.00*-**£15.00**.
Beds: 2D 1T
Baths: 1 Ensuite 1 Shared

***Cricket Field Cottage House,** Wilton Road, Salisbury, Wilts, SP2 7NS.*
Open: All Year
Grades: AA 4 Q, RAC Acclaim
01722 322595 (also fax no)
Mrs James
Rates fr: *£22.00*-**£32.00**.
Beds: 4F 5D 2T 3S
Baths: 14 Ensuite
(5) (14)
Cricket Field Cottage is an ideal base for excursions to Sonehenge, Salisbury Cathedral, the historic cities of Bath & Winchester. Situated close to city centre & railway station.

***Leenas Guest House,** 50 Castle Road, Salisbury, Wilts, SP1 3RL.*
Attractive & comfortable family house.
Open: All Year
01722 335419 Mrs Street
Rates fr: *£18.50*-**£19.00**.
Beds: 1F 2D 2T 1S
Baths: 5 Ensuite 1 Shared
(6)

***Hillside,** 72 St Marks Avenue, Salisbury, Wilts, SP1 3DW.*
Comfortable home in secluded surroundings.
Open: All Year (not Xmas)
01722 335474 Mrs Browning
Rates fr: *£16.00*-**£16.00**.
Beds: 1D 1T **Baths:** 2 Shared
(7) (4)

***Daheim,** 3 Willow Close, Laverstock, Salisbury, Wilts, SP1 1QF.*
Unique riverside bungalow near city.
Open: Easter to Dec
Grades: ETB 1 Cr, Comm
01722 334536 Mrs Lavers
Rates fr: *£14.00*-**£14.00**.
Beds: 1T 1S **Baths:** 1 Shared
(6) (2)

***The Bell Inn,** Warminster Road, Salisbury, Salisbury, Wilts, SP2 0QD..*
Village pub on main road.
Open: All Year
Grades: ETB 2 Cr
01722 743336 Mr Elmer
Rates fr: *£18.00*-**£20.00**.
Beds: 1D 1T 1S
Baths: 3 Private
(10) (50)

***The Old Bakery,** 35 Bedwin Street, Salisbury, Wilts, SP1 3UT.*
C15th house - cosy oak-beamed bedrooms.
Open: All Year (not Xmas)
Grades: ETB 1 Cr
01722 320100
Mr & Mrs Bunce
Rates fr: *£16.00*-**£17.00**.
Beds: 1D 1T 1S
Baths: 2 Private 1 Shared

***Richburn Guest House,** 23-35 Estcourt Road, Salisbury, Wilts, SP1 3AP.*
Comfortable, homely, Victorian house.
Open: All Year (not Xmas)
Grades: ETB 2 Cr, Approv, AA 1 Q, RAC Listed
01722 325189
Mr & Mrs Loader
Rates fr: *£15.00*-**£17.50**.
Beds: 2F 4D 2T 2S
Baths: 2 Private 2 Shared
(10)

***Glenlyn Guest House,** 6 Bellamy Lane, Milford Hill, Salisbury, Wilts, SP1 2SP.*
Large elegant Victorian guest house.
Open: All Year
Grades: ETB 2 Cr, Comm, AA 3 Q, Recomm, RAC Acclaim
01722 327880 Mr Stuart
Rates fr: *£20.00*-**£22.00**.
Beds: 9D
Baths: 4 Ensuite 2 Shared
(12) (7)

***Beulah,** 144 Britford Lane, Salisbury, Wilts, SP2 8AL.*
Bungalow at end of cul-de-sac.
Open: All Year
Grades: ETB Listed
01722 333517
Mr & Mrs Bath
Rates fr: *£15.00*-**£15.00**.
Beds: 1F 1S
Baths: 1 Shared
(2) (4)

Pay B&Bs by cash or cheque. Be prepared to pay up front for one night stays.

***Michaelas Cottage,** 1 Guilder Lane, Salisbury, Wilts, SP1 1HW.*
Pretty, oak-beamed cottage 400 yds old.
Open: Easter to Oct
01722 329580 Mrs Robinson
Rates fr: *£16.00.*
Beds: 1D
Baths: 1 Shared

***20 Queens Road,** Salisbury, Wilts, SP1 3AJ.*
Private house, 10 mins from town.
Open: Easter to Oct
01722 336024 Mrs Jerred
Rates fr: *£12.00*-**£12.00**.
Beds: 1T 1S
Baths: 1 Shared
(5)

***Clovelly Guest House,** 17-19 Mill Road, Salisbury, Wilts, SP2 7RT.*
Open: All Year
Grades: ETB Listed, Comm, AA 3 Q
01722 322055
Rates fr: *£20.00*-**£21.00**.
Beds: 2F 2D 4T 6S
Baths: 6 Private 7 Shared
(14)

***Castleavon,** 15 Wyndham Road, Salisbury, Wilts, SP1 3AA.*
Large, comfortable Victorian house, antiques.
Open: All Year
01722 339087 Mrs Coppack
Rates fr: *£14.00*-**£15.00**.
Beds: 1D 1T 1S
Baths: 1 Shared

***17 Guilder Lane,** Salisbury, Wilts, SP1 1HW.*
Comfortable C14th cottage, city centre.
Open: All Year (not Xmas)
01722 325335 Mrs Lyons
Rates fr: *£16.00*-**£20.00**.
Beds: 1D **Baths:** 1 Shared
(1)

Semley

National Grid Ref: ST8926

Benett Arms

***Whitebridge Farm,** Semley, Shaftesbury, Dorset, SP7 9JT.*
Pretty Victorian farmhouse plus cottages.
Open: All Year
01747 830462 Mr Cornell
Rates fr: *£18.00*-**£22.00**.
Beds: 3D 2T
Baths: 5 Private
(10)

Right on the border?

Look at the neighbouring county, too

***The Benett Arms,** Semley, Shaftesbury, Dorset, SP7 9AS.*
Traditional C16th inn.
Open: All Year
01747 830221 Mr Duthie
Rates fr: *£22.00*-**£29.00**.
Beds: 4D 1T
(40)

Sherston

National Grid Ref: ST8586

Rattlebone Inn

***The Old Swan House,** Swan Barton, Sherston, Malmesbury, Wilts, SN16 0LH.*
C16th Cotswold stone, former coaching inn.
Open: All Year (not Xmas)
01666 840995 Mrs Harris
Rates fr: *£20.00*-**£20.00**.
Beds: 1D 1T
Baths: 1 Private 1 Shared
(2)

***Widleys Farm,** Sherston, Malmesbury, Wilts, SN16 0PY.*
300-acre working farm.
Open: Jan to Nov
01666 840213 Mrs Hibbard
Rates fr: *£18.00.*
Beds: 1F 1D 1T **Baths:** 2 Shared

Shrewton

National Grid Ref:

The George

***Ashwick House,** Upper Backway, Shrewton, Salisbury, Wilts, SP3 4DE.*
Village house, 2 miles Stonehenge.
Open: All Year
Grades: ETB 2 Cr, Comm
01980 621138 Mrs Barnes
Fax no: 01980 620152
Rates fr: *£14.00*-**£14.00**.
Beds: 2T 1S
Baths: 1 Private 1 Shared
(5)

***Maddington House,** Shrewton, Salisbury, Wilts, SP3 4JD.*
Beautiful Listed C17th house.
Open: All Year
01980 620406 Mrs Robothan
Rates fr: *£16.00*-**£17.50**.
Beds: 1F 1D 1T
Baths: 1 Private 1 Shared
(4)

Sopworth

National Grid Ref: ST8286

Rattlebone Inn

***Manor Farm,** Sopworth, Chippenham, Wilts, SN14 6PR.*
Quietly situated, traditional Cotswold farmhouse.
Open: Easter to Oct
01454 238676 Mrs Barker
Rates fr: *£15.00*-**£16.00**.
Beds: 2F
Baths: 1 Private 1 Shared
(4)

Southwick

National Grid Ref: ST8355

Hunserford Arms, Poplars Wingfield

***Brooksfield House,** Vaggs Hill, Southwick, Trowbridge, Wilts, BA14 9NA.*
Delightful converted country barn.
Open: All Year (not Xmas)
01373 830615 Mrs Parry
Rates fr: *£17.00*-**£15.00**.
Beds: 2D 1T
Baths: 1 Ensuite 1 Private 1 Shared
(20)

Stapleford

National Grid Ref: SU0737

***Elm Tree Cottage,** Stapleford, Salisbury, Wilts, SP3 4LH.*
C17th cottage. Large garden.
Open: Easter to Oct
01722 790507 Mrs Sykes
Rates fr: *£22.00*-**£22.00**.
Beds: 1F 2D **Baths:** 3 Private
(4)

Stoford

National Grid Ref: SU0835

Swan Inn

***The Swan Inn,** A36 Warminster Road, Stoford, Salisbury, Wilts, SP2 0PR.*
Main road family-run country inn.
Open: All Year (not Xmas)
01722 790236 Mr Ringwood
Rates fr: *£20.00*-**£25.00**.
Beds: 1F 2D 3T **Baths:** 6 Ensuite
(6) (50)

Stratton St Margaret

National Grid Ref: SU1787

***Treetops,** 8 Marshfield Way, Stratton St Margaret, Swindon, Wilts, SN3 4PS.*
Tastefully extended, quiet, next to fishing lake.
Open: All Year
01793 822954 Mr Lewis
Rates fr: *£17.00*-**£20.00**.
Beds: 3D 2S
Baths: 2 Private 1 Shared
(10)

Swindon

National Grid Ref: SU1685

The Savoy

***County View Guest House,** 31/33 County Road, Swindon, Wilts, SN1 2EG.*
5 minutes drive M4 Junctions 15 and 16. **Open:** All Year
Grades: ETB Listed
01793 610434 Mr Chaudhry
Rates fr: *£14.00*-**£18.00**.
Beds: 1F 4D 7T 3S
Baths: 4 Private
(10)

Acorn Guest House, *41 Victoria Road, Old Town, Swindon, Wilts, SN1 3AJ.*
Very central.
Open: All Year (not Xmas)
Grades: ETB Listed
01793 614870 Mr Zukowski
Rates fr: *£13.00*-**£13.00**.
Beds: 2D 1T 1S
Baths: 1 Ensuite 1 Private
(2)

Bradford Guest House, *40 Devizes Road, Old Town, Swindon, Wilts, SN1 4BG.*
Small friendly guest house.
Open: All Year
01793 642427 Ms McCalla
Rates fr: *£15.00*-**£20.00**.
Beds: 2F 3T 2S
Baths: 2 Shared
(8)

Tisbury

National Grid Ref: ST9429

South Western Hotel, *Station Road, Tisbury, Salisbury, Wilts, SP3 6JT.*
Country pub opposite main-line railway.
Open: All Year
01747 870160 Ms Evans
Rates fr: *£14.50*-**£14.50**.
Beds: 1F 1D 1S **Baths:** 2 Ensuite
(10)

Trowbridge

National Grid Ref: ST8557

44 Wingfield Road, *Trowbridge, Wilts, BA14 9ED.*
Fine victorian house. 'Home from home'.
Open: All Year
01225 761455 Mr & Mrs Dobbin
Rates fr: *£15.00*-**£15.00**.
Beds: 1F 1D 1T 1S
(0)

62 Bradley Road, *Trowbridge, Wilts, BA14 0QY.*
Conveniently situated family home.
Open: All Year (not Xmas)
01225 760424 Mrs Sawle
Rates fr: *£17.50*-**£18.50**.
Beds: 1F 4S
Baths: 2 Shared
(3)

26 The Beeches, *Hilperton Road, Trowbridge, Wilts, BA14 7HG.*
Small modern house large welcome.
Open: All Year
01225 760760 Mrs Staples
Rates fr: *£15.00*-**£13.50**.
Beds: 1D 1S
Baths: 1 Shared
(2)

The lowest **single** *rate is shown in* **bold.**

Magnolia Lodge, *46 Wingfield Road, Trowbridge, Wilts, BA14 9EN.*
Fine Victorian private house.
Open: All Year
01225 763093
Mr & Mrs Harris
Rates fr: *£18.00*-**£19.00**.
Beds: 1F 1D 1T 1S
Baths: 1 Private 1 Shared
(4)

Uffcott

National Grid Ref: SU1278

Crown Inn, Bell Inn

Uffcott House, *Uffcott, Swindon, Wilts, SN4 9NB.*
Spacious period farmhouse, superb views.
Open: All Year (not Xmas)
01793 731207 (also fax no)
Mr & Mrs Hussey
Rates fr: *£17.00*-**£24.00**.
Beds: 1D 2T
Baths: 1 Private 1 Shared
(8) (6)

Upper Minety

National Grid Ref: SU0091

Wheatsheave

Oakwood Farm, *Upper Minety, Malmesbury, Wilts, SN16 9PY.*
Spacious farmhouse set in landscaped gardens.
Open: All Year
Grades: ETB Listed, Comm
01666 860286 Mrs Gallop
Rates fr: *£15.00*-**£15.00**.
Beds: 2D 1T
Baths: 1 Shared
(Any) (6)

Urchfont

National Grid Ref: SU0457

Mulberry House, *Urchfont, Devizes, Wilts, SN10 4QP.*
Attractive Queen Anne house.
Open: All Year (not Xmas)
01380 840357 Mrs Courtney
Rates fr: *£15.00*-**£15.00**.
Beds: 1D 1S
(2)

Wanborough

National Grid Ref: SU2082

Brewers Arms, Cross Keys

Ducksbridge, *Bury Croft, Wanborough, Swindon, Wilts, SN4 0AP.*
Large house, lawns and lake.
Open: All Year (not Xmas)
01793 790338 Mr & Mrs Sadler
Rates fr: *£18.00*-**£20.00**.
Beds: 1D 1T 2S
Baths: 1 Ensuite 1 Shared

Warminster

National Grid Ref: ST8745

Yew Tree

Yew Tree, *Boreham Road, Warminster, Wilts, BA12 9NG.*
C18th village inn.
Open: All Year
01985 212335 Mrs Downs
Rates fr: *£20.00*-**£20.00**.
Beds: 1F 1D 1S
Baths: 2 Ensuite 1 Shared
(5) (10)

West Ashton

National Grid Ref: ST8755

Lamb on the Strand

Aston Hill Farm, *Yarnbrook Road, West Ashton, Trowbridge, Wilts, BA14 6AR.*
Working family farm, home cooked food.
Open: All Year (not Xmas)
01225 760359 (also fax no)
Mrs Awdry
Rates fr: *£17.00*-**£17.50**.
Beds: 1F 1D
Baths: 1 Private 1 Shared

West Grimstead

National Grid Ref: SU2126

Old Brickwood Farm, *West Grimstead, Salisbury, Wilts, SP5 3RN.*
Modern, comfortable, farmhouse, rural setting.
Open: All Year
01722 712701 Mrs Wheildon
Rates fr: *£15.00*-**£15.00**.
Beds: 1D 1T
Baths: 1 Private 1 Shared
(4)

West Kennett

National Grid Ref: SU1168

Silbury Hill Cottage, *West Kennett, Marlborough, Wilts, SN8 1QH.*
Charming thatched cottage, unique location.
Open: All Year (not Xmas)
01672 539416 Mr & Mrs Rendle
Rates fr: *£15.00*-**£18.00**.
Beds: 1D 1T
Baths: 1 Shared
(3)

West Lavington

National Grid Ref: SU0052

Parsonage House, *West Lavington, Devizes, Wilts, SN10 4LT.*
Comfortable, welcoming C17th former parsonage.
Open: All Year (not Xmas)
01380 813345 Mrs West
Rates fr: *£15.00*-**£17.50**.
Beds: 1F 1T
Baths: 1 Shared
(5)

Westbury

National Grid Ref: ST8650

Full Moon, Kicking Donkey

Brokerswood House, *Brokerswood, Westbury, Wilts, BA13 4EH.*
Situated in woodland park.
Open: All Year (not Xmas)
01373 823428
Mrs Phillips
Rates fr: *£14.00*-**£14.00**.
Beds: 1F 1T 1S
Baths: 1 Ensuite 1 Shared
(1) (6)

Glenmore Farm, *The Ham, Westbury, Wilts, BA13 4HQ.*
Comfortable friendly farmhouse.
Open: All Year
01373 865022
Mrs Painter
Rates fr: *£15.00*-**£18.00**.
Beds: 1F 1T
Baths: 1 Private
(20)

Winsley

National Grid Ref: ST7961

Seven Stars

Serendipity, *19f Bradford Road, Winsley, Bradford-on-Avon, Wilts, BA15 2HW.*
Beautiful bungalow, between Bath & Bradford-on-Avon.
Open: All Year
Grades: ETB Listed
01225 722380
Mrs Shepherd
Rates fr: *£16.00*-**£16.00**.
Beds: 1F 1D 1S
Baths: 2 Ensuite 1 Shared
(0) (0)

Woodborough

National Grid Ref: SU1159

Well Cottage, *Honey Street, Woodborough, Pewsey, Wilts, SN9 5PS.*
Picturesque thatched cottage, warm welcome.
Open: All Year
01672 851577
Mrs Trowbridge
Rates fr: *£16.00*-**£20.00**.
Beds: 2D 1T **Baths:** 3 Ensuite
(2)

Woodfalls

National Grid Ref: SU1920

Woodfalls Inn

The Woodfalls Inn, *The Ridge, Woodfalls, Salisbury, Wilts, SP5 2LN.*
Award-winning inn, superbly furnished.
Open: All Year
01725 513222
Mr Elvis
Rates fr: *£19.95*-**£19.95**.
Beds: 1F 8D 2T
Baths: 11 Ensuite
(30)

Wootton Rivers

National Grid Ref: SU1869

Royal Oak

The Royal Oak, *Wootton Rivers, Marlborough, Wilts, SN8 4NQ.*
C16th free house.
Open: All Year
01672 810322 Mr Jones
Rates fr: *£20.00*-**£25.00**.
Beds: 1F 4D 1T 1S
Baths: 3 Private 1 Shared

Yatton Keynell

National Grid Ref: ST8676

Bell Inn, Salutation Inn

Mermaids Barn, *Yatton Keynell, Chippenham, Wilts, SN14 7BA.*
Modernised, quiet country property.
Open: All Year (not Xmas)
01249 782326 (also fax no)
Mrs Doughty
Rates fr: *£16.50*-**£20.00**.
Beds: 1T **Baths:** 1 Private
(3)

Oakfield Farm, *Easton Piercy Lane, Yatton Keynell, Chippenham, Wilts, SN14 6JU.*
Modern farmhouse. Quiet, beautiful location.
Open: Mar to Oct
01249 782355 Mrs Read
Rates fr: *£16.00*-**£18.00**.
Beds: 1F 1D 1T
Baths: 1 Private 1 Shared
(10)

Zeals

National Grid Ref: ST7831

Cornerways Cottage, *Zeals, Longcross, Warminster, Wilts, BA12 6LL.*
Open: All Year (not Xmas/New Year)
Grades: ETB 2 Cr, Comm
01747 840477 (also fax no)
Mrs Snook
Rates fr: *£17.00*-**£19.00**.
Beds: 2D 1T
Baths: 2 Ensuite 1 Private
(8) (6)
Cornerways is a C18th cottage offering a high standard of accommodation with a lovely 'cottagey' feel, complemented by excellent breakfasts in the old dining room.

Worcestershire

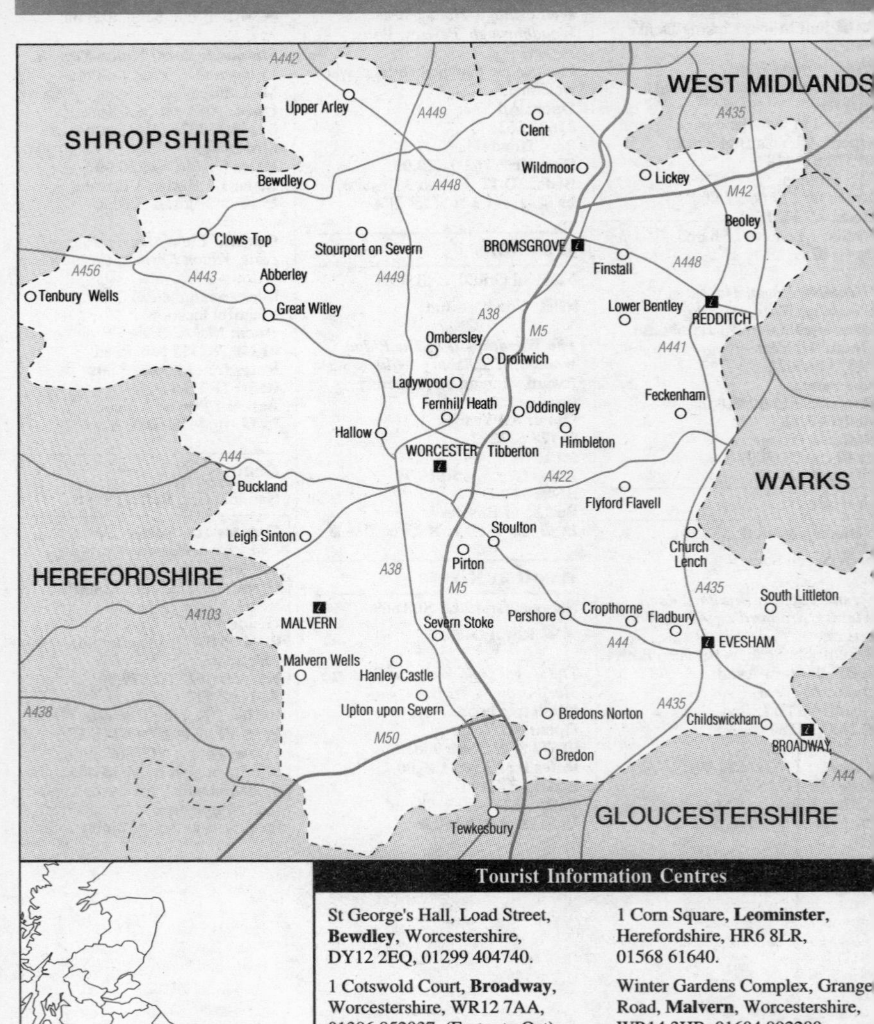

Tourist Information Centres

St George's Hall, Load Street, **Bewdley**, Worcestershire, DY12 2EQ, 01299 404740.

1 Cotswold Court, **Broadway**, Worcestershire, WR12 7AA, 01386 852937, (Easter to Oct).

26 Birmingham Road, **Bromsgrove**, Worcestershire, B61 ODD, 01527 831809.

St Richard's House, Victoria Square, **Droitwich**, Worcestershire, WR9 8DS, 01905 774312.

Almonry Museum, Abbey Gate, **Evesham**, Worcestershire, WR11 4BG, 01386 446944.

Severn Valley Railway Station, Comberton Hill, **Kidderminster**, Worcestershire, DY10 1QX, 01562 829400, (Easter to Oct).

1 Corn Square, **Leominster**, Herefordshire, HR6 8LR, 01568 61640.

Winter Gardens Complex, Grange Road, **Malvern**, Worcestershire, WR14 3HB, 01684 892289.

19 High Street, **Pershore**, Worcestershire, WR10 1AA, 01386 554262.

Civic Square, Alcester Street, **Redditch**, Worcestershire, B98 8AH, 01684 594200.

4 High Street, **Upton upon Severn**, Worcestershire, WR8 OHB,.016846 4200, (Easter to Oct).

The Guildhall, High Street, **Worcester**, Worcestershire, WR1 2EY, 01905 726311.

Abberley

National Grid Ref: SO7467

Hill Farm, *Wynniatts Way, Abberley, Worcester, Worcs,* *WR6 6BZ.*
Part-C16th farmhouse. Magnificent views.
Open: Apr to Oct
01299 896415 Mr & Mrs Reece
Rates fr: *£16.00*-**£16.00**.
Beds: 3T
Baths: 2 Private 1 Shared
(6)

Beoley

National Grid Ref: SP0669

Village Inn

Windmill Hill, *Cherry Pit Lane, Beoley, Redditch, Worcs,* *B98 9DH.*
Cottage adjoining C15th style house.
Open: All Year (not Xmas)
01527 62284 Mr & Mrs Cotton
Fax no: 0121 627 4417
Rates fr: *£17.50*-**£20.00**.
Beds: 1T
Baths: 1 Ensuite
(10)

Bewdley

National Grid Ref: SO7875

James's, Little Pack Horse

Lightmarsh Farm, *Crundalls Lane, Bewdley, Worcs,* *DY12 1NE.*
C18th comfortable farmhouse, outstanding views.
Open: All Year
Grades: ETB 2 Cr, High Comm
01299 404027 Mrs Grainger
Rates fr: *£18.00*-**£22.00**.
Beds: 1D 1T
Baths: 1 Ensuite 1 Private
(10) (4)

Bank House, *14 Lower Park, Bewdley, Worcs,* *DY12 2DP.*
Warm family atmosphere, memorable breakfasts.
Open: All Year (not Xmas)
01299 402652 Mrs Nightingale
Rates fr: *£16.00*-**£16.00**.
Beds: 1F 1T 1S
Baths: 2 Shared
(1)

Alton Guest House & Tea Rooms, *Long Bank, Bewdley, Worcs,* *DY12 2UL.*
Welcome walkers, adjacent Wyre Forest.
Open: All Year
01299 266733 Miss Evans
Rates fr: *£16.00*-**£16.00**.
Beds: 1D 1T 1S
Baths: 3 Private
(10)

Severn Valley Guest House, *240 Westbourne Street, Bewdley, Worcs,* *DY12 1BS.*
450-year-old coaching inn.
Open: All Year
01299 402192 Mr George
Rates fr: *£17.00*-**£17.0**.
Beds: 2F 2D 2 T
Baths: 2 Ensuite 1 Shared
(5)

Bredon

National Grid Ref: SO9236

Appledram, *Church Street, Bredon, Tewkesbury, Glos,* *GL20 7LA.*
Modern, comfortable, detached house. **Open:** All Year
01684 772471 Ms Hardwick
Rates fr: *£15.00*-**£15.00**.
Beds: 2D

Bredons Norton

National Grid Ref: SO9339

Fox & Hound

Home Farm, *Bredons Norton, Tewkesbury, Glos,* *GL20 7HA.*
Comfortably furnished C18th farmhouse.
Open: All Year (not Xmas)
Grades: ETB 2 Cr, Comm
01684 772322 Mrs Meadows
Rates fr: *£18.00*-**£20.00**.
Beds: 1F 1D 1T
Baths: 2 Ensuite 1 Private

Broadway

National Grid Ref: SP0937

Childswickham Arms, Crown & Trumpet, Bell Inn, Horse & Hounds

Crown & Trumpet Inn, *Church Street, Broadway, Worcs,* *WR12 7AE.*
Open: All Year
Grades: ETB 3 Cr, Approv
01386 853202 Mr Scott
Rates fr: *£20.00*.
Beds: 3D 1T
Baths: 4 Ensuite
(6)
C17th Cotswold inn in picturesque village (also on the Cotswold Way). Specialising in homemade local & seasonal dishes. Ideal base for touring & walking.

Mill Hay Cottage, *Bury End, Broadway, Worcs,* *WR12 7JS.*
House in large beautiful garden.
Open: All Year (not Xmas)
Grades: ETB Listed, Comm
01386 858241 Mrs Payne
Rates fr: *£20.00*-**£24.00**.
Beds: 1D 1T **Baths:** 1 Private
(2) (12)

Whiteacres Guest House, *Station Road, Broadway, Worcs,* *WR12 7DE.*
Tastefully decorated, spacious Victorian house.
Open: Mar to Oct
Grades: ETB 2 Cr, High Comm
01386 852320 Mrs Richardson
Rates fr: *£19.00*.
Beds: 5D 1T **Baths:** 6 Ensuite
(8)

The Driffold, *Murcot Turn, A44, Broadway, Worcs,* *WR12 7HT.*
Open: All Year (not Xmas)
01386 830825 Mr Reohorn
Rates fr: *£18.00*-**£18.00**.
Beds: 1F 2D 1T 2S
Baths: 3 Ensuite 1 Shared
(15)
Detached country house. Large garden, friendly atmosphere. Swimming pool. Broadway. Evesham Golf Clubs. Riding stables. Historic houses. Museums, country walks. Gardens. Boating.

Pennylands, *Evesham Road, Broadway, Worcs,* *WR12 7DG.*
Edwardian house, large comfortable rooms.
Open: All Year (not Xmas)
Grades: AA 3 Q, Recomm
01386 858437 Mrs Brazier
Rates fr: *£16.00*.
Beds: 2D 1T **Baths:** 3 Private
(5)

The Pond House, *Lower Fields, Weston Road, Bretforton, Broadway, Evesham, Worcs,* *WR11 5QA.*
Open: All Year
Grades: ETB 2 Cr, High Comm, AA 4 Q, Select
01386 831687 Mrs Payne
Rates fr: *£18.00*-**£35.00**.
Beds: 2D 1T
Baths: 3 Ensuite
(4) (10)
Superb country home. Peaceful secluded position 500 m off road. Wonderful views. Friendly relaxed atmosphere with high standards of comfort & service. The perfect base, near Broadway, Chipping Campden, Stratford upon Avon.

Bourne House, *Leamington Road, Broadway, Worcs,* *WR12 7DZ.*
Quiet comfortable home, friendly atmosphere.
Open: All Year
Grades: ETB 2 Cr, Comm
01386 853486 (also fax no)
Mrs Tarte
Rates fr: *£22.50*-**£28.00**.
Beds: 1D 1T
(10) (2)

Bromsgrove

National Grid Ref: SO9570

Golden Cross, Shoulder of Mutton

The Grahams, *95 Old Station Road, Bromsgrove, Worcs,* *B60 2AF.*
Open: All Year (not Xmas)
Grades: ETB Listed, Comm
01527 874463 Mrs Graham
Rates fr: *£16.00*-**£16.00**.
Beds: 1T 2S
Baths: 1 Shared
(2) (2)
Modern house, quiet pleasant location, near A38, 3 miles from M5, 1.5 miles from M42 within easy reach of NEC, Worcester, Birmingham & Stratford.

***Cherry Tree Cottage,** 49 The Flats, Santridge Lane, Bromsgrove, Worcs, B61 8LB.*
Comfortable modernised cottage, friendly welcome.
Open: Jan to Dec
01527 875413 / 872085 Mrs Fincham
Fax no: 01527 875413
Rates fr: *£16.00*-**£15.00**.
Beds: 1T 1S
Baths: 1 Shared
(2) (2)

***Home Farm,** Mill Lane, Wildmoor, Bromsgrove, Worcs, B61 0BX.*
Modern comfortable extension of farmhouse.
Open: All Year
01527 874964 Mr Lees
Rates fr: *£12.50*-**£15.00**.
Beds: 3T 2S **Baths:** 3 Shared
(7) (10)

***Korners,** 1 Willow Close, Bromsgrove, Worcs, B61 8RG.*
Modern house near town centre.
Open: All Year
01527 832832 Mrs Hunt
Rates fr: *£17.50*-**£20.00**.
Beds: 1F 1T **Baths:** 1 Shared
(2)

Buckland

National Grid Ref: SO5556

Snowshill Arms

***Garretts Farm,** Buckland, Broadway, Glos, WR12 7LY.*
Victorian farmhouse in pretty village.
Open: All Year (not Xmas)
01386 852091 / 858699
Rates fr: *£17.00*-**£20.00**.
Beds: 1D **Baths:** 1 Private
(1) (1)

Childswickham

National Grid Ref: SP0738

***Mount Pleasant Farm,** Childswickham, Broadway, Worcs, WR12 7HZ.*
Farmhouse set in 350 acres, near Broadway.
Open: All Year
01386 853424 Mrs Perry
Rates fr: *£17.50*-**£22.00**.
Beds: 2D 1T 1S
Baths: 4 Private
(5) (12)

Church Lench

National Grid Ref: SP0251

***Hill Barn Orchard,** Evesham Road, Church Lench, Evesham, Worcs, WR11 4UB.*
Stylishly modern, comfortable farmhouse, views.
Open: All Year (not Xmas)
01386 871035 Mr & Mrs Badger
Rates fr: *£15.00*-**£20.00**.
Beds: 2T 1D
Baths: 1 Private 1 Shared
(4)

Clent

National Grid Ref: SO9279

Woodman Inn

***The Barn,** Woodman Lane, Clent, Stourbridge, W. Mids, DY9 9PX.*
Converted barn on smallholding.
Open: All Year
Grades: ETB 2 Cr, Comm
01562 885879 Mrs Hobbs
Fax no: 01384 401977
Rates fr: *£25.00*-**£25.00**.
Beds: 1F 1D
Baths: 1 Private

***Adam House,** Adams Hill, Clent, Stourbridge, W. Mids, DY9 9PS.*
Victorian country house.
Open: All Year
01562 883297 Mr & Mrs Taylor
Rates fr: *£12.50*-**£15.00**.
Beds: 2T

Clows Top

National Grid Ref: SO7171

Colliers Arms

***Clay Farm,** Clows Top, Kidderminster, Worcs, DY14 9NN.*
Modern comfortable farmhouse, wonderful views.
Open: All Year (not Xmas)
Grades: ETB 2 Cr, High Comm
01299 832421 Mrs Grinnall
Rates fr: *£17.00*-**£20.00**.
Beds: 2D 1T
Baths: 2 Private 1 Shared
(2) (6)

Cropthorne

National Grid Ref: SO9944

***Cedars Guest House,** Evesham Road, Cropthorne, Pershore, Worcs, WR10 3JU.*
Ideal for business or pleasure visits.
Open: All Year
Grades: ETB 2 Cr
01386 860219 Mrs Faulkner
Rates fr: *£15.00*-**£15.00**.
Beds: 2F 1D 2T 1S
Baths: 2 Private 2 Shared
(6)

Droitwich

National Grid Ref: SO8963

The Castle

***Merrivale,** 216 Worcester Road, Droitwich, Worcs, WR9 8AY.*
Four poster beds. Friendly welcome.
Open: All Year
Grades: ETB Listed
01905 778213
Mrs Goodwin
Rates fr: *£14.00*-**£16.00**.
Beds: 2D 1T
Baths: 1 Private 1 Shared
(3)

Evesham

National Grid Ref: SP0343

Round of Grass, The Kings Arms, Falconry

***Far Horizon,** Long Hyde Road, South Littleton, Evesham, Worcs, WR11 5TH.*
Elegant home with fine views.
Open: All Year (not Xmas)
Grades: ETB 2 Cr, Comm
01386 831691 Mr & Mrs Rowe
Rates fr: *£17.50*-**£17.50**.
Beds: 1D 1T 1S
Baths: 1 Ensuite 2 Private
(10) (4)

***Fircroft,** 84 Greenhill, Evesham, Worcs, WR11 4NH.*
Elegant house in attractive gardens.
Open: Mar to Oct
Grades: ETB 2 Cr, Comm
01386 45828 Ms Greenwood
Rates fr: *£17.50*-**£25.00**.
Beds: 1F 1D 1T
Baths: 1 Ensuite 2 Shared
(6)

***Agebury House,** 42 Merstow Green, Evesham, Worcs, WR11 4BB.*
Georgian Grade II Listed building.
Open: All Year
01386 41664 Mr & Mrs Message
Rates fr: *£15.00*-**£15.00**.
Beds: 2F 1T
Baths: 1 Shared

***Park View Hotel,** Waterside, Evesham, Worcs, WR11 6BS.*
Friendly, family-run riverside hotel.
Open: All Year (not Xmas)
Grades: ETB 1 CrRAC Listed
01386 442639 Mr & Mrs Spires
Rates fr: *£17.50*-**£19.50**.
Beds: 2F 4D 10T 10S
Baths: 7 Shared
(40)

Feckenham

National Grid Ref: SP0061

***The Steps Guest House,** 6 High Street, Feckenham, Redditch, Worcs, B96 6HS.*
Lovely, comfortable Georgian village house.
Open: All Year
Grades: ETB 2 Cr, Comm
01527 892678 Mrs Thomas
Rates fr: *£17.00*-**£20.00**.
Beds: 1D 1T 1S
Baths: 1 Private 1 Shared
(0) (3)

Planning a longer stay? Always ask for any special rates.

Fernhill Heath

National Grid Ref: SO8659

Heathside, *Droitwich Road, Fernhill Heath, Worcester, Worcs,* WR3 7UA.
Victorian house, extension, high standards.
Open: All Year
Grades: ETB 3 Cr, Comm
01905 458245 Mr Lewis
Rates fr: *£19.00*-**£21.00**.
Beds: 1D 3T 5S
Baths: 6 Ensuite
(13)

Finstall

National Grid Ref: SO9870

Stoke Cross Farm, *Dusthouse Lane, Finstall, Bromsgrove, Worcs,* B60 3AE.
Comfortable, modern farmhouse.
Open: All Year
01527 876676 Mrs Orford
Rates fr: *£15.00*-**£18.00**.
Beds: 2D 1T
Baths: 2 Shared
(6)

Fladbury

National Grid Ref: SO9946

Field House, *Fladbury Cross, Fladbury, Pershore, Worcs,* WR10 2QR.
Victorian house in 1.5 acres.
Open: All Year
01386 860533 Mrs Buxton
Rates fr: *£17.00*-**£17.00**.
Beds: 1D 2T
Baths: 1 Shared
(6)

Flyford Flavell

National Grid Ref: SO9854

Flyford Arms

Flyford Arms Inn, *Flyford Flavell, Worcester, Worcs,* WR7 4DA.
Traditional family-run country inn.
Open: All Year (not Xmas)
01905 381890 Mrs Stephens
Rates fr: *£20.00*-**£35.00**.
Beds: 1D 1T
Baths: 2 Private

Great Witley

National Grid Ref: SO7566

Southleigh, *Great Witley, Worcester, Worcs,* WR6 6HX.
Chalet bungalow ideal for rambling/touring.
Open: All Year
01299 896312
Mr & Mrs Hutcheson-France
Rates fr: *£15.00*-**£15.00**.
Beds: 1F 1D 1S
Baths: 2 Shared
(100)

Hallow

National Grid Ref: SO8258

Wagon Wheel Inn, Hunters Lodge

Ivy Cottage, *Sinton Green, Hallow, Worcester, Worcs,* WR2 6NP.
Charming cottage in quiet village.
Open: All Year (not Xmas)
Grades: ETB 2 Cr, Comm
01905 641123 Mrs Rendle
Rates fr: *£18.00*-**£25.00**.
Beds: 1D 1T 1S
Baths: 2 Private
(4)

Hanley Castle

National Grid Ref: SO8341

Three Kings Inn, The Swan

Three Kings Inn, *Hanley Castle, Worcester, Worcs,* WR8 0BL.
Traditional C15th village inn.
Open: All Year (not Xmas)
01684 592686 Mrs Roberts
Rates fr: *£22.50*-**£27.50**.
Beds: 1T
Baths: 1 Private

Four Hedges, *The Rhydd, Hanley Castle, Worcester, Worcs,* WR8 0AD.
Friendly, family house, spacious garden.
Open: All Year (not Xmas)
Grades: ETB Listed, Approv
01684 310405 Mrs Cooper
Rates fr: *£16.00*-**£15.00**.
Beds: 1D 1T 2S
Baths: 1 Private 1 Shared
(4)

Himbleton

National Grid Ref: SO9458

The Firs

Phepson Farm, *Himbleton, Droitwich, Worcs,* WR9 7JZ.
Comfortable C17th farmhouse & converted granary.
Open: All Year (not Xmas)
Grades: ETB 2 Cr, Comm, AA 4 Q, Select
01905 391205 Mrs Havard
Rates fr: *£19.00*-**£23.00**.
Beds: 1F 2D 1T
Baths: 4 Private
(6)

Ladywood

National Grid Ref: SO8761

Caulin Court, *Ladywood, Droitwich, Worcs,* WR9 OAL.
Country house set in 20 acres.
Open: All Year
01905 756382 Mrs Harfield
Rates fr: *£20.00*-**£17.50**.
Beds: 1D 1T 1S
Baths: 1 Private 1 Shared
(5) (4)

Leigh Sinton

National Grid Ref: SO7750

Chirkenhill, *Leigh Sinton, Malvern, Worcs,* WR13 5DE.
Old farmhouse in picturesque location.
Open: All Year
Grades: ETB 2 Cr, Comm
01886 832205 Mrs Wenden
Rates fr: *£17.00*-**£18.00**.
Beds: 1F 1D 1T
Baths: 3 Private

Lickey

National Grid Ref: SO9975

Honeypot, *305 Old Birmingham Road, Lickey, Bromsgrove, Worcs,* B60 1HQ.
Attractive modern detached house.
Open: All Year (not Xmas)
0121 445 2580 Mrs Stanworth
Rates fr: *£18.80*-**£18.80**.
Beds: 2D 1T
Baths: 1 Shared
(4)

Lower Bentley

National Grid Ref: SO9865

Lower Bentley Farm, *Lower Bentley Lane, Lower Bentley, Bromsgrove, Worcs,* B60 4JB.
Close to M5, M42 & Birmingham.
Open: All Year
Grades: ETB 2 Cr, AA 3 Q, Recomm
01527 821286 Mrs Gibbs
Rates fr: *£17.50*-**£20.00**.
Beds: 2D 1T **Baths:** 3 Private
(5)

Malvern

National Grid Ref: SO7846

Bluebell Inn, Seven Stairs, Railway Inn

The Red Gate, *32 Avenue Road, Malvern, Worcs,* WR14 3BJ.
Open: All Year (not Xmas)
Grades: ETB 3 Cr, High CommRAC High Acclaim
01684 565013 (also fax no)
Mr & Mrs Rowan
Rates fr: *£25.00*-**£28.00**.
Beds: 4D 2T 1S
Baths: 7 Private
(8) (7)
Friendly, Victorian hotel praised for comfort, friendliness & decor. Seven non-smoking, ensuite bedrooms. Traditional or vegetarian breakfast. Great walking area. Convenient for M5.

All rates are subject to alteration at the owners' discretion.

***Kylemore,** 30 Avenue Road, Malvern, Worcs, WR14 3BJ.*
Large Victorian family house.
Open: All Year (not Xmas)
Grades: ETB 1 Cr
01684 563753 Mrs Bell
Rates fr: *£14.00*-**£14.00**.
Beds: 1D 1T 1S
Baths: 1 Shared
(3)

***Nether Green Farm,** Ridge Way Cross, Malvern, Worcs, WR13 5JS.*
Beautifully positioned comfortable homely farmhouse.
Open: All Year (not Xmas)
01886 880387 Mrs Orford
Rates fr: *£14.00*-**£14.00**.
Beds: 1D 1T 1S
Baths: 1 Shared
(4)

***Elm Bank Guest House,** 52 Worcester Road, Malvern, Worcs, WR14 4AB.*
Grade II Listed building, unrivalled views.
Open: All Year
Grades: ETB 2 Cr, Comm
01684 566051 Mr Mobbs
Rates fr: *£19.00*-**£30.00**.
Beds: 2F 3D 1T
Baths: 5 Ensuite 1 Private
(7)

***Ashford Cottage,** 32 North Malvern Road, Malvern, Worcs, WR14 4LT.*
Homely & very friendly.
Open: All Year
Grades: ETB 1 Cr, Approv
01684 565350
Rates fr: *£14.50*-**£17.00**.
Beds: 2T 1D
Baths: 1 Shared
(5)

***Priory Holme,** 18 Avenue Road, Malvern, Worcs, WR14 3AR.*
Spacious Victorian family home.
Grades: ETB 2 Cr
01684 568455 Mrs Emuss
Rates fr: *£20.00*-**£18.00**.
Beds: 1F 1D 1T 1S
Baths: 3 Ensuite 1 Shared
(5)

***Cowleigh Park Farm,** Cowleigh Road, Malvern, Worcs, WR13 5HJ.*
Peacefully situated C17th timbered farmhouse.
Open: All Year (not Xmas)
Grades: ETB 2 Cr, High Comm
01684 556750 Mrs Stringer
Rates fr: *£21.00*-**£30.00**.
Beds: 1D 2T
Baths: 3 Private
(7) (6)

Right on the border? Look at the neighbouring county, too

Malvern Wells

National Grid Ref: SO7742

Railway Inn, Hawthorn Inn

***The Dell House,** Green Lane, Malvern Wells, Worcs, WR14 4HU.*
Idyllic period country house luxury.
Open: All Year
Grades: ETB 2 Cr, Comm
01684 564448 Mrs Knight
Fax no: 01684 893974
Rates fr: *£19.00*-**£25.00**.
Beds: 2D 1T
Baths: 2 Ensuite 1 Shared
(3)

***The Hawthorn Inn,** Upper Welland Road, Malvern Wells, Malvern, Worcs, WR14 4LB.*
Open: All Year (not Xmas)
01684 575340
Rates fr: *£15.00*-**£18.50**.
Beds: 1F 1T
Baths: 2 Shared
(20)

Oddingley

National Grid Ref: SO9059

Firs Inn

***Wessex House Farm,** Trench Lane, Oddingley, Droitwich, Worcs, WR9 7NB.*
Modern comfortable farmhouse.
Open: Easter to Oct
01905 772826 Mrs Jackson
Rates fr: *£16.00*-**£16.00**.
Beds: 1F 1D
Baths: 1 Shared
(3) (3)

Ombersley

National Grid Ref: SO8463

Hadley Bowling Green Inn, Kings Arms

***The Old Farmhouse,** Hadley Heath, Ombersley, Droitwich, Worcs, WR9 0AR.*
Attractive farmhouse, mature gardens, tennis.
Open: All Year (not Xmas)
Grades: ETB 1 Cr, High Comm
01905 620837 (also fax no)
Mrs Lambe
Rates fr: *£25.00*-**£25.00**.
Beds: 1D 2T
Baths: 3 Ensuite 1 Private
(7)

***Greenlands,** Ombersley, Worcester, Droitwich, Worcs, WR9 0JP.*
Convenient to Worcester, good eating places.
Open: All Year
Grades: ETB 2 Cr, High Comm
01905 620873 Mrs Crossland
Rates fr: *£15.00*-**£18.00**.
Beds: 1F 1D 1T 1S
Baths: 1 Private 2 Shared
(6)

Pershore

National Grid Ref: SO9445

Old Mill Inn

***Pensham Hill House,** Pensham Hill, Pershore, Worcs, WR10 3HA.*
Superior barn conversion, wonderful views.
Open: All Year
Grades: ETB 2 Cr, High Comm
01386 555270 Mrs Horton
Rates fr: *£21.00*-**£29.00**.
Beds: 2D 1T
Baths: 3 Ensuite
(6)

***Ayron House,** 6 Bridge Street, Pershore, Worcs, WR10 1AT.*
Large Tudor town house.
Open: All Year (not Xmas)
01386 556449 Mr Brighton
Rates fr: *£15.00*-**£15.00**.
Beds: 1D 2T
Baths: 1 Shared

Pirton

National Grid Ref: SO8747

***The Old Smithy,** Pirton, Worcester, WR8 9EJ.*
C17th black-and-white country house.
Open: All Year
Grades: ETB Listed, High Comm
01905 820482 Mrs Wynn
Rates fr: *£16.00*-**£18.50**.
Beds: 1D 1T
Baths: 1 Private 1 Shared
(4)

Redditch

National Grid Ref: SPO669

***Cherrypit,** Cherrypit Lane, Redditch, Worcs, B98 9DH.*
Quiet, secluded, convenient to motorways.
Open: All Year
01527 62454 Mrs Howles
Rates fr: *£17.00*-**£17.00**.
Beds: 2T 2S
Baths: 1 Private 1 Shared
(8)

***Walcote,** Dagnell End Road, Bordesley, Redditch, Worcs, B98 9BH.*
Cottage, 2 acres garden.
Open: All Year
01527 68784 Mrs Smith
Rates fr: *£12.00*-**£12.00**.
Beds: 2T 1S
Baths: 1 Shared
(y) (7)

Bringing children with you? Always ask for any special rates.

Severn Stoke

National Grid Ref: SO8544

Madge Hill House, *Severn Stoke, Worcester, Worcs,* *WR8 9JN.*
Georgian country house peaceful setting.
Open: All Year (not Xmas)
01905 371362 Mrs Ellis
Rates fr: *£17.00*-**£17.00**.
Beds: 1D 1T
(3)

South Littleton

National Grid Ref: SP0746

Round of Grass, Kings Arms

Far Horizon, *Long Hyde Road, South Littleton, Evesham, Worcs,* *WR11 5TH.*
Elegant home with fine views.
Open: All Year (not Xmas)
Grades: ETB 2 Cr, Comm
01386 831691 Mr & Mrs Rowe
Rates fr: *£17.50*-**£17.50**.
Beds: 1D 1T 1S
Baths: 1 Ensuite 2 Private
(10) (4)

Stoulton

National Grid Ref: SO9049

Plough & Harrow

Caldewell, *Stoulton, Worcester, Worcs,* *WR7 4RL.*
Georgian mansion in parkland setting.
Open: Mar to Dec
Grades: ETB 2 Cr
01905 840894 Mrs Booth
Rates fr: *£17.50*-**£20.00**.
Beds: 1F 1D 1T
Baths: 2 Ensuite 2 Shared

Stourport on Severn

National Grid Ref: SO8171

Baldwin House, *8 Lichfield Street, Stourport on Severn, Worcs,* *DY13 9EU.*
Grade II Listed Georgian town house.
Open: All Year
Grades: ETB 3 Cr
01299 877221 Mrs Barclay
Rates fr: *£17.00*-**£18.00**.
Beds: 2F 3D 2T 2S
Baths: 6 Private

Tenbury Wells

National Grid Ref: SO5967

Peacock

Hunt House Farm, *Frith Common, Tenbury Wells, Worcs,* *WR15 8JY.*
C16th farmhouse, bedrooms ensuite, breathtaking views.
Open: All Year (not Xmas)
Grades: ETB 2 Cr, High Comm
01299 832277 Mrs Keel
Rates fr: *£17.50*-**£22.00**.
Beds: 1F 1D 1T
Baths: 3 Private
(8) (4)

Redgate House, *Bromyard Road, Tenbury Wells, Worcs,* *WR15 8BS.*
Large Victorian private house.
Open: Easter to Nov
01584 810574 Mrs Picton
Rates fr: *£15.00*-**£15.00**.
Beds: 2T
Baths: 1 Private 1 Shared
(4)

Tibberton

National Grid Ref: SO9058

Old Chequers Inn (Crowle)

Old House Farm, *Tibberton, Droitwich, Worcs,* *WR9 7NP.*
Tastefully furnished farmhouse near M5.
Open: All Year (not Xmas)
Grades: ETB 1 Cr, Comm
01905 345247 Mrs Chilman
Rates fr: *£18.00*-**£20.00**.
Beds: 1D 1T 1S
Baths: 1 Shared
(0) (4)

Upper Arley

National Grid Ref: SO7680

Shades of Green B&B, Vegetarian Restaurant, *Upper Arley, Bewdley, Worcs,* *DY12 1XA.*
Formerly C17th vicarage, Severn Valley.
Open: All Year (not Xmas)
01299 861311
Mr & Mrs Maynard-Rollings
Rates fr: *£13.50*-**£13.50**.
Beds: 2D
Baths: 1 Shared
(1) (2)

Upton upon Severn

National Grid Ref: SO8540

Kings Head, Anchor Pub

Lockeridge Farm, *Upton upon Severn, Worcester,* *WR8 0RP.*
Comfortable accommodation, home-cooking, large rooms.
Open: All Year
01684 592193 Mrs Albert
Rates fr: *£15.00*-**£12.00**.
Beds: 2F 1T 1S
Baths: 1 Shared
(3)

Jasmin, *21 School Lane, Upton upon Severn, Worcester, Worcs,* *WR8 0LD.*
Modern comfortable bungalow.
Open: All Year
Grades: ETB Listed
01684 593569 Mrs Leighton
Rates fr: *£16.00*-**£18.00**.
Beds: 1D 1T
Baths: 1 Shared
(10) (2)

Wildmoor

National Grid Ref: SO9575

Home Farm, *Mill Lane, Wildmoor, Bromsgrove, Worcs,* *B61 0BX.*
Modern comfortable extension of farmhouse.
Open: All Year
01527 874964 Mr Lees
Rates fr: *£12.50*-**£15.00**.
Beds: 3T 2S
Baths: 3 Shared
(7) (10)

Worcester

National Grid Ref: SO8555

Ye Old Talbot, The Retreat

Burgage House, *4 College Precincts, Worcester,* *WR1 2LG.*
Open: All Year (not Xmas)
Grades: ETB Listed, AA 3 Q
01905 25396 (also fax no)
Mrs Ratcliffe
Rates fr: *£19.00*-**£26.00**.
Beds: 1F 1D 1T 1S
Baths: 1 Ensuite 2 Private
Elegant Georgian mews house in cobbled street next to Cathedral. Attractive curved stone staircase leading to comfortable colour co-ordinated rooms. Quaint lounge with inglenook fireplace.

Beacon Lodge, *84 Victoria Avenue, Worcester, Worcs,* *WR5 1ED.*
Quiet, convenient to M5, J7.
Open: All Year (not Xmas)
01905 763098
Mr & Mrs Baldock
Rates fr: *£14.00*-**£14.00**.
Beds: 2T 1S
Baths: 1 Ensuite 1 Shared

The Old Smithy, *Pirton, Worcester,* *WR8 9EJ.*
C17th black-and-white country house.
Open: All Year
Grades: ETB Listed, High Comm
01905 820482
Mrs Wynn
Rates fr: *£16.00*-**£18.50**.
Beds: 1D 1T
Baths: 1 Private 1 Shared
(4)

Wood View, *High Park, Whittington, Worcester, Worcs,* *WR5 2RS.*
200-year-old bed & breakfast country house near Junction 7 M5.
Open: All Year (not Xmas)
Grades: ETB 1 Cr, Approv
01905 351893
Mrs Wheeler
Rates fr: *£16.00*-**£19.00**.
Beds: 1D 2T
Baths: 1 Ensuite 2 Shared
(0) (4)

East Yorkshire

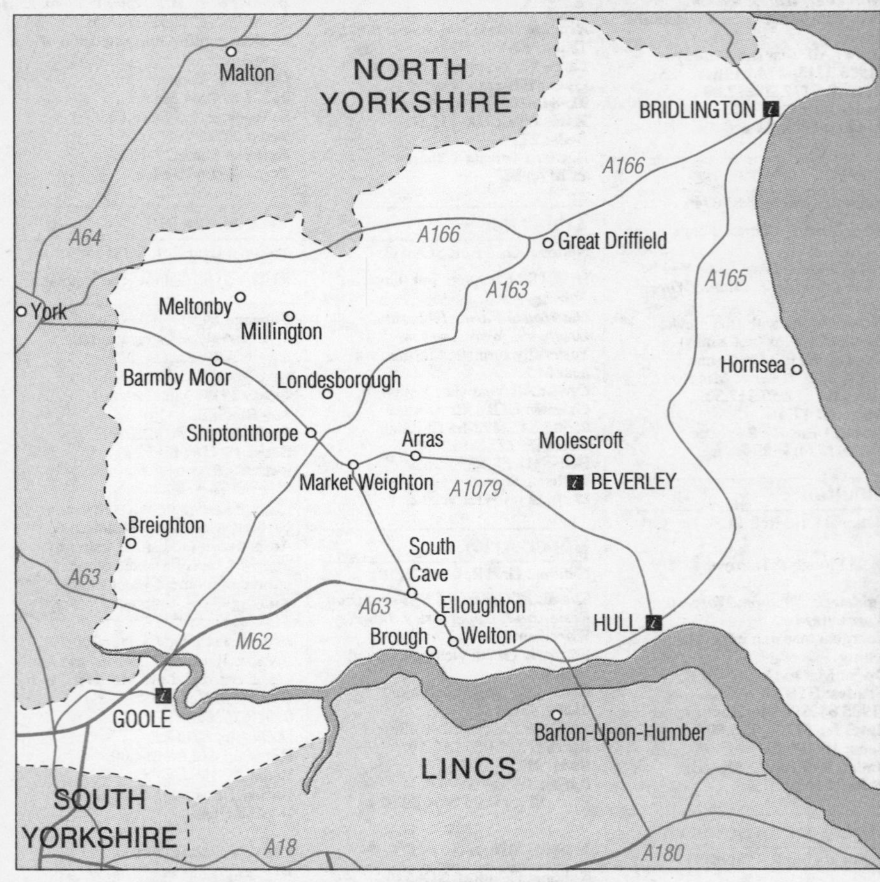

Tourist Information Centres

The Guildhall, Register Square, **Beverley**, North Humberside, HU17 9AU, 01482 867430.

Museum of Army Transport, **Flemingate**, Beverley, North Humberside, HU17 0NG, 01482 865263.

25 Prince Street, **Bridlington**, North Humberside, YO15 2NP, 01262673474.

The Buttercross, Marketplace, **Brigg**, South Humberside, DN20 8ER, 01652 657053.

42-43 Alexandra Road, **Cleethorpes**, South Humberside, DN35 8LE, 01472 200220.

Goole Library, Carlisle Street, **Goole**, South Humberside, DN14 5AA, 01405 762187.

National Fishing Heritage Centre, Alexandra Dock, **Grimsby**, South Humberside, DN31 1UF, 01472 342422.

Humber Bridge Viewing Area, North Bank, Ferriby Road, **Hessle**, North Humberside, HU13 0LN, 01482 640852.

75-76 Carr Lane, **Hull**, North Humberside, HU1 3RQ, 01482 223559.

Central Library, Carlton Street, **Scunthorpe**, South Humberside, DN15 6TX, 01724 282301.

Arras

National Grid Ref: SE9241

***Arras Farmhouse**, Arras, Market Weighton, York, E. Yorks,* YO4 3RN.
Large, traditional family farmhouse.
Open: All Year
Grades: ETB Listed
01430 872404 Mrs Stephenson
Rates fr: *£17.00*-**£19.00**.
Beds: 2D 1T
Baths: 2 Private 1 Shared
(5)

Bringing children with you? Always ask for any special rates.

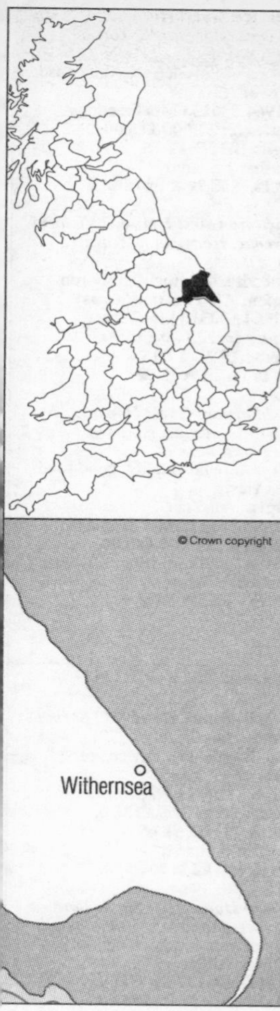

Barmby Moor

National Grid Ref: SE7748

Wellington Oak

***Alder Carr House**, York Road, Barmby Moor, York, E. Yorks, YO4 5HU.*
Comfortable Georgian-style country house.
Open: All Year (not Xmas)
01759 380566 Mrs Steel
Rates fr: *£16.00*-**£18.00**.
Beds: 1F 1D 1T
Baths: 3 Ensuite
(6)

The lowest *double* rate per person is shown in *italics*.

Always telephone to get directions to the B&B - you will save time!

Beverley

National Grid Ref: TA0440

Rose & Crown, Mokescroft Inn, Tudor Rose

***Northumbria**, 13 The Croft, Molescroft, Beverley, E. Yorks, HU17 7HT.*
Quiet area. Delightful market town.
Open: All Year
01482 872254
Mrs Whitelaw
Rates fr: *£15.00*-**£16.00**.
Beds: 1F 1D
Baths: 1 Private 1 Shared
(3)

***Tudor Rose**, Wednesday Market, Beverley, E. Yorks, HU17 0DG.*
Public house, restaurant & hotel.
Open: All Year
01482 882028
Rates fr: *£18.00*-**£18.00**.
Beds: 5D 1T 2S
Baths: 4 Ensuite 2 Shared

***Cairnlite**, 60 Wood Lane, Beverley, E. Yorks, HU17 8BS.*
Victorian family house. Quiet, central.
Open: All Year (not Xmas)
01482 867494
Mrs Holwell
Rates fr: *£14.00*-**£16.00**.
Beds: 1F 3D 2T
Baths: 1 Private 2 Shared
(5)

***Number One**, 1 Woodlands, Beverley, E. Yorks, HU17 8BT.*
Intriguing Victorian house. Walled garden.
Open: All Year
01482 862752
Mrs King
Rates fr: *£16.00*-**£15.00**.
Beds: 1F 1D 1T 1S
Baths: 1 Ensuite 1 Shared
(2)

***Crow Tree Farm**, Arram, Beverley, E. Yorks, HU17 7NR.*
Tranquil, historic, well-appointed farmhouse.
Open: All Year (not Xmas)
01964 550167
Mr Hart
Rates fr: *£14.00*-**£15.00**.
Beds: 1F 1D 1T
Baths: 1 Shared

The lowest **single** *rate is shown in* **bold.**

***Cross Keys Hotel**, 8 Lairgate, Beverley, E. Yorks, HU17 8EE.*
Old Georgian coaching inn.
Open: All Year
01482 882573
Mrs Brooks
Rates fr: *£12.00*-**£12.00**.
Beds: 3F 2D 2S
Baths: 3 Private 1 Shared

Breighton

National Grid Ref: SE7134

***Manor House**, Breighton, Selby, E. Yorks, YO8 7DH.*
Large Victorian private house.
Open: All Year (not Xmas)
01757 288273
Mrs Davies
Rates fr: *£15.00*-**£15.00**.
Beds: 2F 1D
Baths: 2 Private 1 Shared
(5)

Bridlington

National Grid Ref:

***Rags Hotel & Restaurant**, South Pier, Bridlington, E. Yorks, YO15 3AN.*
Open: All Year
Grades: ETB 3 Cr
01262 674729
Ms Shackleton
Rates fr: *£22.50*-**£35.00**.
Beds: 3D 3T
Baths: 6 Ensuite
(15)
Harbour view rooms all ensuite with corner baths, colour television & tea/coffee making facilities. Harbour view restaurant & bar.

***Marton Grange**, Sewerby, Bridlington, E. Yorks, YO15 1DT.*
Listed Georgian house. 5 mins sea.
Open: All Year
Grades: AA 3 Q
01262 602034
Mrs Goodall
Rates fr: *£14.00*.
Beds: 1F 4D 3T
(3) (8)

National Grid References are for villages, towns and cities - *not* for individual houses.

Springfield Private Hotel, *12 Trinity Road, Bridlington, E. Yorks, YO15 2EY.*
Open: All Year
01262 672896 Mrs Fielding
Rates fr: *£14.00*-**£14.00**.
Beds: 3F 1D 1T 2S
Baths: 1 Shared
Centrally situated, near all amenities. All rooms have showers, TVs and teamakers. Licensed bar & comfy lounge. A warm welcome awaits you at the 'Springfield'.

Oaklea Guest House, *26 Marshall Avenue, Bridlington, E. Yorks, YO15 2DS.*
Homely, comfortable, friendly guest house.
Open: All Year (not Xmas)
01262 675186 Ms Baker
Fax no: 01262 609494
Rates fr: *£14.00*-**£14.00**.
Beds: 4F 3D 1T 1S
Baths: 2 Private 2 Shared

Waverley Hotel, *105 Cardigan Road, Bridlington, E. Yorks, YO15 3LP.*
Quiet, close to South Beach.
Open: All Year
01262 671040 Mrs Britton
Rates fr: *£17.50*-**£22.50**.
Beds: 4F 1T
Baths: 5 Private

Winston House Hotel, *South Street, Bridlington, E. Yorks, YO15 3BY.*
Licensed, friendly, excellent home cooking.
Open: All Year
01262 670216 (also fax no)
Mr & Mrs Botham
Rates fr: *£16.00*-**£16.00**.
Beds: 1F 7D 2T 2S
Baths: 6 Private 1 Shared

Coleraine Guest House, *10 Horsforth Avenue, Bridlington, E. Yorks, YO15 3DF.*
Clean & comfortable guest house.
Open: All Year (not Xmas)
01262 676407 Mrs Tilley
Rates fr: *£13.50*-**£13.50**.
Beds: 4F 1D 1S
Baths: 1 Shared

Brough

National Grid Ref: SE9326

Elloughton Mount Guest House, *62 Elloughton Road, Brough, E. Yorks, HU15 1AL.*
Large Victorian house, great views.
Open: All Year (not Xmas)
01482 667941 Mrs Floyd
Rates fr: *£16.00*-**£16.00**.
Beds: 1F 1T 1S
Baths: 1 Shared

Elloughton

National Grid Ref: SE9427

Chat Moss, *16 Larchmont Close, Elloughton, Brough, E. Yorks, HU15 1AW.*
Large, peaceful, comfortable modern house.
Open: All Year
01482 666514
Mrs Dixon
Rates fr: *£16.00*-**£16.00**.
Beds: 1D 2T
Baths: 1 Shared

Goole

National Grid Ref: SE7423

Clifton Hotel, *155 Boothferry Road, Goole, DN14 6AL.*
Small, family-run comfortable hotel.
Open: All Year (not Xmas)
Grades: ETB 3 Cr, Approv, AA 2 St
01405 761336
Mr Hope
Rates fr: *£19.50*-**£26.00**.
Beds: 1F 3D 1T 4S
Baths: 9 Private

Briarcroft Hotel, *49-51 Clifton Gardens, Goole, DN14 6AR.*
Comfortable, friendly, pleasant hotel - licensed.
Open: All Year
01405 767317
Mrs Elborough
Rates fr: *£19.00*-**£19.50**.
Beds: 2F 11D 4T 5S
Baths: 15 Private 6 Shared

Great Driffield

National Grid Ref: TA0258

The Charles Dickens, *57 Middle Street North, Great Driffield, E. Yorks, YO25 7SS.*
Large public house.
Open: All Year (not Xmas)
01377 252289
Rates fr: *£15.00*-**£18.00**.
Beds: 1F 1D 4T

Hornsea

National Grid Ref: TA2047

Southfield Guest House, *61 Eastgate, Hornsea, E. Yorks, HU18 1NB.*
Comfortable, homely Victorian house.
Open: All Year
Grades: ETB Listed, Comm
01964 534961 Mr Hornby
Rates fr: *£14.00*-**£14.00**.
Beds: 1F 2D 1T 1S
Baths: 1 Shared

Seaview Guest House, *6 Victoria Avenue, Hornsea, E. Yorks, HU18 1NH.*
Elegant seafront Victorian house.
Open: All Year
01964 536133 Mrs Freedman
Rates fr: *£13.00*-**£15.00**.
Beds: 1F 2D 1T 1S
Baths: 1 Shared

Victoria Guest House, *2 Victoria Avenue, Hornsea, E. Yorks, HU18 1NH.*
Friendly, sea-front family-run.
Open: All Year (not Xmas)
01964 533310 Mrs Turner
Rates fr: *£13.00*-**£13.00**.
Beds: 2F 2D 1T 1S

Ashburnam Guest House, *1 Victoria Avenue, Hornsea, E. Yorks, HU18 1NH.*
Yorkshire hospitality, good food, sea views.
Open: All Year
01964 535118 Mrs Scamans
Rates fr: *£13.00*-**£13.00**.
Beds: 2F 2D 1T 1S
Baths: 3 Shared

Hull

National Grid Ref: TA0929

Marlborough Hotel, *232 Spring Bank, Hull, HU3 1LU.*
Family run near city centre.
Open: All Year
01482 224479 Mr Stonehouse
Rates fr: *£13.00*-**£15.00**.
Beds: 3F 2D 5T 6S
Baths: 3 Shared

Town House, *102 Sunny Bank, Spring Bank West, Hull, HU3 1LF.*
Guest house, quiet location.
Open: All Year
01482 446177 Mr Hogg
Rates fr: *£14.00*-**£15.00**.
Beds: 1D 2T 4S
Baths: 1 Shared

Beck House Hotel, *628 Beverley High Road, Hull, HU6 7LL.*
Elegant, Victorian town house hotel.
Open: All Year
01482 445468 Mrs Aylwin
Rates fr: *£19.00*-**£19.00**.
Beds: 1F 3D 6S
Baths: 6 Private

Please respect a B&B's wishes regarding children, animals & smoking.

Acorn Guest House, *719 Beverley High Road, Hull, HU6 7JN.*
Friendly guest house with large garden.
Open: All Year
01482 853248 Mrs Langton
Rates fr: *£18.00*-**£18.00**.
Beds: 2T 2S
Baths: 3 Ensuite 1 Shared
(6)

Windmill House, *56 Witham, Hull, HU9 1AT.*
Friendly Victorian inn with entertainment.
Open: All Year (not Xmas)
01482 324623 Mr Binns
Rates fr: *£12.00*-**£12.00**.
Beds: 3D 1T 3S
Baths: 1 Shared

Londesborough

National Grid Ref: SE8645

Towthorpe Grange, *Towthorpe Lane, Londesborough, York, YO4 3LB.*
Comfortable working farm.
Open: All Year (not Xmas)
01430 873814 Mrs Rowlands
Rates fr: *£14.50*-**£14.50**.
Beds: 1F 2D
Baths: 1 Shared

Market Weighton

National Grid Ref: SE8741

Black Horse Inn

The Gables, *38 Londesborough Road, Market Weighton, York, E. Yorks, YO4 3HS.*
Friendly, comfortable country house.
Open: All Year (not Xmas)
01430 872255 Mr Green
Rates fr: *£13.50*-**£16.00**.
Beds: 2D 1T 2S
Baths: 2 Shared
(5)

Planning a longer stay? Always ask for any special rates.

Meltonby

National Grid Ref: SE7952

Meltonby Hall Farm, *Meltonby, Pocklington, York, E. Yorks, YO4 2PW.*
Modernised comfortable farmhouse, peaceful surroundings.
Open: Easter to oct
Grades: AA Listed
01759 303214 Mr Pearson
Rates fr: *£14.00*-**£16.00**.
Beds: 1D 1T
Baths: 1 Shared

Millington

National Grid Ref: SE8351

Gate Inn

Laburnum Cottage, *Millington, York, E. Yorks, YO4 2TX.*
Comfortable cottage with large garden.
Open: Feb to Oct
Grades: ETB Listed
01759 303055 Mrs Dykes
Rates fr: *£15.00*-**£18.00**.
Beds: 1F 1T
Baths: 1 Shared
(5)

Molescroft

National Grid Ref: TA0440

Plot 39, *The Bungalow, Wainholmes Site, Woodhall Way, Molescroft, Beverley, E. Yorks, HU17 9BL.*
Detached bungalow in quiet area of Beverley.
Open: All Year (not Xmas)
01482 861120 Mrs Stow
Rates fr: *£14.00*-**£14.00**.
Beds: 2S
Baths: 2 Shared
(2)

Shiptonthorpe

National Grid Ref: SE8543

Robeanne House Farm & Stables, *Driffield Lane, Shiptonthorpe, York, E. Yorks, YO4 3LB.*
Modern comfortable farmhouse.
Open: All Year
01430 873312 Mrs Wilson
Rates fr: *£16.50*-**£16.50**.
Beds: 3F 2D 1T
Baths: 6 Private
(10)

South Cave

National Grid Ref: SE9231

Tunstall, *2 Cleaves Avenue, South Cave, Brough, E. Yorks, HU15 2BA.*
Quiet, friendly Christian home.
Open: All Year
01430 422456 Mrs Watson
Rates fr: *£15.00*-**£16.50**.
Beds: 1T 1S **Baths:** 1 Shared
(0) (2)

Welton

National Grid Ref: SE9627

Hemingford House, *Church Street, Welton, Brough, E. Yorks, HU15 1NH.*
Large, friendly, comfortable Georgian house.
Open: All Year (not Xmas)
01482 668405 Mr Kiddle
Rates fr: *£18.00*-**£26.00**.
Beds: 1D 2T 1S **Baths:** 4 Private
(7) (6)

Withernsea

National Grid Ref: TA3427

Hildyard Arms

Take 5 Guest House, *5 Young Street, Withernsea, E. Yorks, HU19 2DX.*
Small & friendly coastal accommodation. **Open:** All Year
01964 613716 Mrs Redfearn
Rates fr: *£12.50*-**£15.00**.
Beds: 1F 2D 1T 1S
Baths: 2 Shared

Vista Mar Guest House, *48 Promenade, Withernsea, E. Yorks, HU19 2DW.*
Central for all amenities.
Open: All Year
Grades: ETB Listed
01964 612858 Mr & Mrs Hirst
Rates fr: *£12.50*-**£12.50**.
Beds: 1F 1D 4T 1S
Baths: 2 Private 2 Shared

Sefton Guest House, *6 Bannister Street, Withernsea, E. Yorks, HU19 2DU.*
Clean comfortable family-run house. **Open:** All Year (not Xmas)
01964 613523 Mrs Wealthy
Rates fr: *£12.50*-**£13.00**.
Beds: 1F 1D 1T 1S
Baths: 1 Shared

North Yorkshire

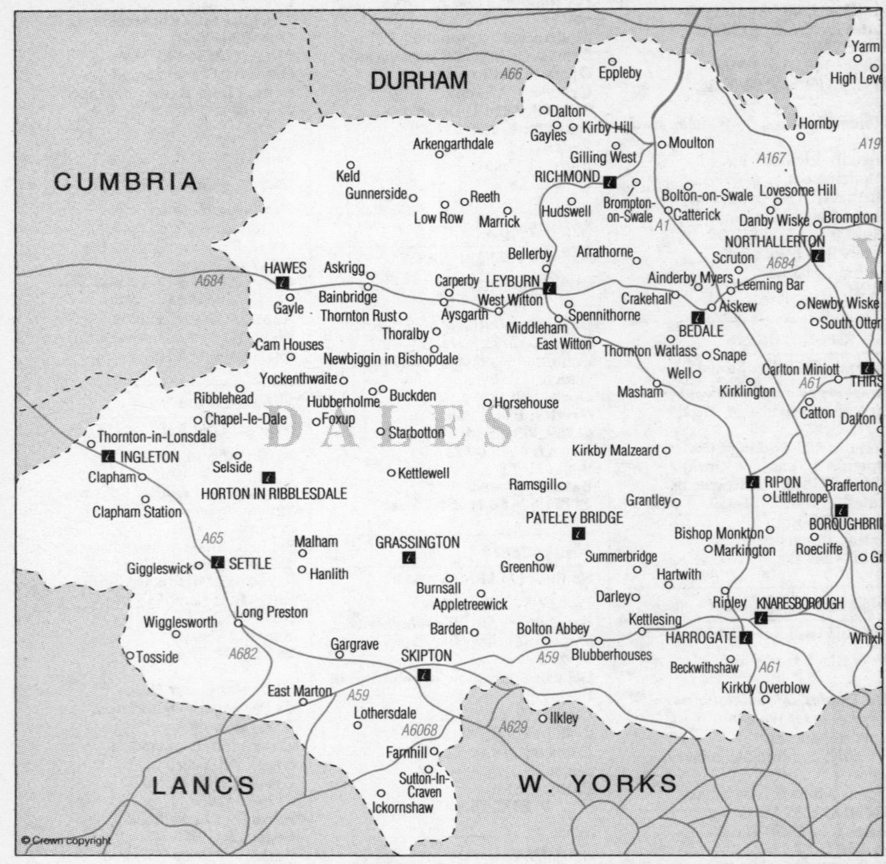

Tourist Information Centres

Bedale Hall, **Bedale**, N.Yorks, DL8 1AA, 01677 424604, (Easter to Oct).

National Park Centre, Hebden Road, **Grassington**, Skipton, N.Yorks, BD23 5LB, 01756 752774, (Easter to Oct)

Royal Baths Assembly Rooms, Crescent Road, **Harrogate**, N.Yorks, HG1 2RR, 01423 537300.

Dales Countryside Museum, Station Yard, **Hawes**, N.Yorks, DL8 3NT, 01969 667450, (Easter to Oct).

Pen-y-Ghent Cafe, **Horton-in-Ribblesdale**, Settle, N.Yorks, BD24 0HE, 01729 860333.

35 Market Place, **Knaresborough**, N.Yorks, HG5 8AL, 01423-866886, (Easter to Oct).

Thornborough Hall, **Leyburn**, N.Yorks, DL8 5AB, 01969 623069.

14 High Street, **Paley Bridge**, Harrogate, N.Yorks, HG3 5AP, 01423 711147, (Easter to Oct)

Friary Gardens, Victoria Road, **Richmond**, N.Yorks, DL10 4AJ, 01325 377677.

Minster Road, **Ripon**, N.Yorks, HG4 1LT, 01765 604625, (Easter to Oct)

Town Hall, Cheapside, **Settle**, N.Yorks, BD24 9EJ, 01729 825192.

Sheep Street, **Skipton**, N.Yorks, BD23 1JH, 01756 792809.

Fishergate, **Boroughbridge**, York, N.Yorks, YO5 9AL, 01423 323373, (Easter to Oct).

The Moors Centre, Danby Lodge, **Danby**, Whitby, N.Yorks, YO21 2NB, 01287 660654, (Easter to Oct).

Town Hall, Market Place, **Helmsley**, York, N.Yorks, YO6 5BL, 01439 770173, (Easter to Oct).

The Old Town hall, Market Place, **Malton**, N.Yorks, YO17 0LH, 01653-600048.

The Applegarth Car Park, **Northallerton**, N.Yorks, DL7 8LZ, 01609-776864

Eastgate Car Park, **Pickering**, N.Yorks, YO18 7DP, 01751 473791.

St Nicholas Cliff, **Scarborough**, N.Yorks, YO11 2EP, 01723-373333.

Park Street, **Selby**, N.Yorks, YO8 0AA, 01757-703263.

Sutton Bank Visitor Centre, Sutton Bank, N.Yorks, YO7 2EK, 01845-597426.

14 Kirkgate, **Thirsk**, N.Yorks, YO7 1PQ, 01845-522755.

Langborne Road, **Whitby**, N.Yorks, YO21 1YN, 01947-602674.

De Grey Rooms, Exhibition Sq, **York**, N.Yorks, YO1 2HB, 01904-621756.

Acaster Malbis

National Grid Ref: SE5845

Ship Inn

Field House, *Acaster Malbis, York,* *YO2 1UL.*
Riverside bungalow, indoor pool.
Open: All Year (not Xmas)
01904 706834 Mrs Wormald
Rates fr: *£18.00*-**£20.00**.
Beds: 2D 1T
Baths: 3 Private 1 Shared

Ainderby Myers

National Grid Ref: SE2688

Ainderby Myers Farm, *Ainderby Myers, Bedale, N. Yorks,* *DL8 1PF.*
Ancient manor house in 'Herriot Country'.
Open: All Year
Grades: ETB 1 Cr, Comm
01609 748668 Mrs Anderson
Rates fr: *£17.00*-**£20.00**.
Beds: 1F 1D 1S
Baths: 1 Private 2 Shared
(All)

Ainthorpe

National Grid Ref: NZ7008

Fox & Hounds Inn

Rowantree Farm, *Ainthorpe, Danby, Whitby, N. Yorks,* *YO21 2LE.*
Old, stone farmhouse (mod cons).
Open: All Year (not Xmas)
01287 660396
Mrs Tindall
Rates fr: *£13.00*-**£12.50**.
Beds: 1F 1D 1T
(4)

***Fox & Hounds Inn,** Ainthorpe, Danby, Whitby, N. Yorks, YO21 2LD.*
C16th coaching inn.
Open: All Year
01287 660218 Mrs Dickinson
Rates fr: *£17.00*-**£17.00**.
Beds: 2F 4D 2T 1S
Baths: 2 Shared
(40)

Aiskew

National Grid Ref: SE2788

Fox & Hounds

***Bobbie's B&B,** XVII Century Cottage, Aiskew, Bedale, N. Yorks, DL8 1DD.*
Grade II Listed C17th cottage.
Open: All Year (not Xmas)
01677 423385
Ms Bauer
Rates fr: *£16.00*-**£18.00**.
Beds: 1D 2T
Baths: 2 Shared
(5)

Aislaby

National Grid Ref: SE7785

Blacksmiths Arms

***Blacksmiths Arms,** Aislaby, Pickering, N. Yorks, YO18 8PE.*
Olde worlde, former blacksmith's.
Open: All Year
Grades: ETB 2 Cr, Comm
01751 472182
Mrs Bullock
Rates fr: *£19.00*-**£20.00**.
Beds: 1F 3D 1T 1S
Baths: 3 Private 2 Shared
(25)

Allerston

National Grid Ref: SE7984

***Rains Farm,** Allerston, Pickering, N. Yorks, YO18 7PQ.*
Farm nestles in peaceful picturesque location.
Open: All Year
Grades: ETB 2 Cr
01723 859333 (also fax no)
Mrs Allanson
Rates fr: *£18.50*-**£18.50**.
Beds: 2D 2T 1S
Baths: 5 Ensuite
(10)

Ampleforth

National Grid Ref: SE5878

Abbey In, White Swan, Wombwell Arms

***Spring Cottage,** Ampleforth, York, YO6 4DA.*
Can't be bettered, magnificent views.
Open: All Year (not Xmas)
01439 788579
Mr Benson
Rates fr: *£19.00*-**£19.00**.
Beds: 1F 1D
(6)

***Carr House Farm,** Shallowdale, Ampleforth, York, YO6 4ED.*
C16th farmhouse. Romantic 4-poster bedrooms.
Open: All Year (not Xmas)
Grades: ETB 2 Cr, Comm
01347 868526 Mrs Lupton
Rates fr: *£15.00*-**£15.00**.
Beds: 3D
Baths: 3 Private
(7) (3)

***Ampleforth Lodge Country House,** Ampleforth, York, YO6 4DA.*
In scenic National Park village.
Open: All Year (not Xmas)
01439 788789
Mr Johnson
Rates fr: *£19.00*-**£25.00**.
Beds: 1F 1D 1T
Baths: 3 Private
(7)

Appleton Roebuck

National Grid Ref: SE5542

***Holly House,** Broad Lane, Appleton Roebuck, York, YO5 7DS.*
Modern, comfortable guest house, indoor pool/spa.
Open: All Year (not Xmas)
01904 744314 Mr Whitehead
Rates fr: *£18.75*-**£30.00**.
Beds: 1F 2D 2T
Baths: 3 Private 1 Shared
(6)

Appletreewick

National Grid Ref: SE0560

Craven Arms

***Blundellstead,** Appletreewick, Skipton, N. Yorks, BD23 6DB.*
Comfortable, quiet, Dales country home.
Open: All Year (not Xmas)
01756 720632 Ms Coney
Rates fr: *£17.00*-**£17.00**.
Beds: 1D 2S
Baths: 1 Shared
(2)

Arkengarthdale

National Grid Ref: NZ0002

***The White House,** Arkle Town, Arkengarthdale, Richmond, N. Yorks, DL11 6RB.*
Open: Jan to Nov
Grades: ETB 2 Cr, Comm
01748 884203 Mrs Whitworth
Rates fr: *£18.50*-**£26.00**.
Beds: 2D 1T
Baths: 2 Private 1 Shared
(10) (4)
Family-run guest house with panoramic views of this secluded dale. Close to Richmond & Barnard Castle and 3 miles from Reeth in Swaledale. Ideal touring & walking centre. Reduced rates for 2 or more nights dinner, bed & breakfast.

Arrathorne

National Grid Ref: SE2093

***Elmfield Country House,** Arrathorne, Bedale, N. Yorks, DL8 1NE.*
Country house in rural settings.
Open: All Year
Grades: ETB 3 Cr, Comm, AA 4 Q, Select, RAC High Acclaim
01677 450558 Mrs Lillie
Fax no: 01677 450557
Rates fr: *£19.50*-**£25.00**.
Beds: 2F 4D 3T **Baths:** 9 Ensuite
(12)

Askrigg

National Grid Ref: SD9491

Crown Inn

***Milton House,** Askrigg, Leyburn, N. Yorks, DL8 3HJ.*
Lovely comfortable family home.
Open: All Year
Grades: ETB 2 Cr, Comm
01969 650217 Mrs Percival
Rates fr: *£19.00*-**£30.00**.
Beds: 3D **Baths:** 3 Private
(10) (3)

***Whitfield,** Helm, Askrigg, Leyburn, N. Yorks, Dl8 3JF.*
Tranquil environment with spectacular views.
Open: All Year (not Xmas)
Grades: ETB 2 Cr, Comm
01969 650565 (also fax no)
Mr Empsall
Rates fr: *£15.00*-**£17.00**.
Beds: 1T
Baths: 1 Ensuite 1 Shared
(2)

***Thornsgill House,** Moor Road, Askrigg, Leyburn, N. Yorks, DL8 3HH.*
Very attractive Victorian guest house. **Open:** All Year
Grades: ETB 2 Cr, Comm
01969 650617 Mrs Gilyeat
Rates fr: *£21.00*.
Beds: 2D 1T **Baths:** 3 Private
(10) (3)

***Lucys House,** Askrigg, Leyburn, N. Yorks, DL8 3HT.*
C17th cottage. Lovely views & garden.
Open: All Year (not Xmas)
01969 650586 Mrs Hartley
Rates fr: *£17.00*-**£17.00**.
Beds: 1T **Baths:** 1 Private

Aysgarth

National Grid Ref: SE0088

George & Dragon

***Wensleydale Farmhouse,** Aysgarth, Leyburn, N. Yorks, DL8 3SR.*
Ex-farmhouse above famous waterfalls. **Open:** All Year
01969 663534 Mr & Mrs Massa
Rates fr: *£16.00*. **Beds:** 2D 1T
Baths: 2 Ensuite 1 Private
(3) (3)

***Thorngarth,** Home Farm, Aysgarth, Leyburn, N. Yorks, DL8 3AG.*
Modern farmhouse with open views.
Open: Mar to Oct
01969 663519 Mrs Spence
Rates fr: *£14.00*-**£15.00**.
Beds: 1F 1D **Baths:** 1 Shared
(4)

***Marlbeck,** Aysgarth, Leyburn, N. Yorks, DL8 3AH.*
Attractive village home near waterfalls.
Open: Feb to Nov
Grades: ETB Listed
01969 663610 Mrs Hairsine
Rates fr: *£15.00*-**£16.00**.
Beds: 1D 1T 1S
Baths: 1 Ensuite 1 Shared
(5) (12)

***Low Gill Farm,** Aysgarth, Leyburn, N. Yorks, DL8 3AL.*
Warm welcome on working farm.
Open: Mar to Oct
01969 663554 Mrs Dinsdale
Rates fr: *£14.00*-**£15.00**.
Beds: 1F 1D **Baths:** 1 Shared
(3)

***Palmer Flatt Hotel,** Aysgarth, Leyburn, N. Yorks, DL8 3SR.*
Hotel/public house by Aysgarth Falls.
Open: All Year
01969 663228 Mrs Hansard
Rates fr: *£22.50*-**£27.50**.
Beds: 1F 7D 2T **Baths:** 10 Private

Bainbridge

National Grid Ref: SD9390

***High Force Farm,** Bainbridge, Leyburn, N. Yorks, DL8 3DL.*
Warm welcome, relaxed atmosphere.
Open: Jan to Nov
01969 650379 Mrs Iveson
Rates fr: *£13.00*.
Beds: 1F 1D **Baths:** 2 Shared
(5) (2)

***Rose & Crown Hotel,** Bainbridge, Wensleydale, Leyburn, N. Yorks, DL8 3EE.*
500-year-old coaching inn.
Open: All Year
Grades: ETB 4 Cr, Comm, AA 2 St, RAC 2 St
01969 650225 Mr Collins
Fax no: 01969 650735
Rates fr: *£26.30*-**£30.00**.
Beds: 1F 9D 2T
Baths: 12 Private
(65)

***Riverdale House,** Bainbridge, Leyburn, N. Yorks, DL8 3BW.*
Converted traditional stone-built Dales house.
Open: Mar to Nov
01969 650311 Ms Harrison
Rates fr: *£25.00*-**£25.00**.
Beds: 2F 4T 8D **Baths:** 10 Private
(4)

***Syke Cottage,** Bainbridge, Leyburn, N. Yorks, DL8 3EL.*
Small & friendly family cottage.
Open: All Year (not Xmas)
01969 650607 Mrs Punchard
Rates fr: *£16.50*.
Beds: 1F **Baths:** 1 Shared

Barden

National Grid Ref: SE0557

***Howgill Lodge,** Barden, Skipton, N. Yorks, BD23 6DJ.*
Converted C17th barn, magnificent views. **Open:** All Year
01756 720655 Mrs Foster
Rates fr: *£25.00*-**£31.00**.
Beds: 1F 2D 1T **Baths:** 4 Ensuite

Beckwithshaw

National Grid Ref: SE2653

Smiths Arms

***Garden Cottage,** Moor Park, Beckwithshaw, Harrogate, N. Yorks, HG3 1QN.*
Country estate - luxury gourmet B&B. Evening meal by arrangement.
Open: Nov to Sep
01423 530197 Mrs Harrison
Rates fr: *£22.50*-**£25.00**.
Beds: 2T **Baths:** 2 Ensuite
(2)

Bedale

National Grid Ref: SE2688

Green Dragon, Castle Arms Inn, Swaledale Arms

***Southfield,** 96 South End, Bedale, N. Yorks, DL8 2DS.*
Open: All Year
01677 423510 Mrs Keighley
Rates fr: *£16.00*-**£16.00**.
Beds: 1F 1D 1T 1S
Baths: 1 Private
(4)
Now 'Which' Recommended. One mile from A1. Ideal North/South stopover. Pot of tea on arrival, free supper. Private off road parking. Genuine welcome.

***Hyperion House,** 88 South End, Bedale, N. Yorks, DL8 2DS.*
Large attractive detached Victorian house.
Open: All Year (not Xmas)
Grades: ETB 2 Cr, High Comm
01677 422334 Mrs Dean
Rates fr: *£18.00*-**£25.00**.
Beds: 2D 1T **Baths:** 1 Ensuite
(12) (4)

***Waggon & Horses,** 20 Market Place, Bedale, N. Yorks, DL8 1EQ.*
Cosy traditional pub.
Open: All Year
01677 422747 Mr Young
Rates fr: *£19.00*-**£22.00**.
Beds: 1F 1D 2T **Baths:** 4 Private
(12)

Bellerby

National Grid Ref: SE1192

Cross Keys Inn

***Hilltop House,** Bellerby, Leyburn, N. Yorks, DL8 5QN.*
Centrally heated stone-built farmhouse.
Open: All Year (not Xmas)
01969 622596 Mrs Munro
Rates fr: *£14.50*-**£14.50**.
Beds: 1D 1T
Baths: 1 Shared
(12) (2)

Bickerton

National Grid Ref: SE4550

Anchor Inn

***The Old Post Office,** Tom Cat Lane, Bickerton, Wetherby, W. Yorks, LS22 5ER.*
Convenient for York & Dales.
Open: All Year
01423 358261 Mrs Thompson
Fax no: 01423 359013
Rates fr: *£16.00*-**£16.00**.
Beds: 1D 1S
Baths: 1 Private
(2)

Bishop Monkton

National Grid Ref: SE3266

Masons Arms

***Masons Arms,** Bishop Monkton, Harrogate, N. Yorks, HG3 3QY.*
Family-run, cosy country inn.
Open: All Year
Grades: ETB 2 Cr
01765 677427 Mrs Pawson
Rates fr: *£20.00*-**£25.00**.
Beds: 2D 1T
Baths: 3 Ensuite

Blakey Ridge

National Grid Ref: SE6897

***The Lion Inn,** Blakey Ridge, Kirkbymoorside, York, YO6 6LQ.*
C16th inn. Breathtaking views.
Open: All Year
01751 417320 Mr Crossland
Rates fr: *£16.50*-**£16.50**.
Beds: 3F 6D 1T
Baths: 7 Private 3 Shared
(150)

***High Blakey House,** Blakey Ridge, Kirkbymoorside, York, YO6 6LQ.*
Unique stone-built house - restored ruin.
Open: Mar to Nov
01751 417641 Mrs Ellerington
Rates fr: *£19.00*-**£19.00**.
Beds: 1D 2T
Baths: 2 Shared
(2)

Blubberhouses

National Grid Ref: SE1655

***Scaife Hall Farm**, Blubberhouses, Otley, N. Yorks, LS21 2PL.*
Working farm, peaceful, comfortable farmhouse.
Open: All Year (not Xmas)
01943 880354 Mrs Ryder
Rates fr: *£20.00*-**£22.00**.
Beds: 2D 1T
Baths: 3 Ensuite
(5)

Boltby

National Grid Ref: SE4986

***Town Pasture Farm**, Boltby, Thirsk, N. Yorks, YO7 2DY.*
Comfortable farmhouse in beautiful village.
Open: All Year
Grades: ETB Listed, Approv
01845 537298 Mrs Fountain
Rates fr: *£15.50*-**£15.50**.
Beds: 1F 1D 1T
Baths: 3 Ensuite
(3)

***Lower Paradise Farm**, Boltby, Thirsk, N. Yorks, YO7 2HS.*
Recently refurbished C17th farmhouse.
Open: Apr to Oct
01845 537253 Mrs Todd
Rates fr: *£16.00*-**£18.00**.
Beds: 1F 1D 1T **Baths:** 1 Shared
(5) (6)

Bolton Abbey

National Grid Ref: SE0753

***Hesketh House**, Bolton Abbey, Skipton, N. Yorks, BD23 6HA.*
Large working hill/sheep farm.
Open: March to Nov
01756 710332 Mrs Heseltine
Rates fr: *£15.00*-**£20.00**.
Beds: 2D 1T **Baths:** 2 Shared

Bolton Percy

National Grid Ref: SE5341

Shoulder of Mutton

***Beckside House**, Bolton Percy, York, YO5 7AQ.*
Very peaceful village near York.
Open: All Year (not Xmas)
01904 744246 Mrs Rhodes
Rates fr: *£15.00*-**£17.00**.
Beds: 1T **Baths:** 1 Private
(1)

Bolton-on-Swale

National Grid Ref: SE2599

***School House**, Bolton-on-Swale, Richmond, N. Yorks, DL10 6AQ.*
Stone-built converted school.
Open: Mar to Oct
01748 818532 Mrs Robinson
Rates fr: *£15.00*-**£15.00**.
Beds: 2T **Baths:** 1 Shared

High season, bank holidays and special events mean low availability *anywhere.*

Boroughbridge

National Grid Ref: SE3966

Black Bull

***Heaton House**, York Road, Boroughbridge, York, YO5 9HE.*
Elegant Georgian farmhouse - landscaped gardens.
Open: All Year (not Xmas)
01423 323777
Mr & Mrs Rhodes
Rates fr: *£17.50*-**£20.00**.
Beds: 2D 1T
Baths: 2 Shared
(14)

Boulby

National Grid Ref: NZ7619

***Old Stables**, Boulby, Saltburn-by-the-Sea, TS13 4UR.*
Peaceful surroundings, stunning coastal views.
Open: All Year
01287 641109
Mrs Yeomans
Rates fr: *£13.50*-**£15.00**.
Beds: 1F 3D 1T
Baths: 3 Ensuite 2 Private
(3) (5)

Brackenholme

National Grid Ref: SE7030

***Hagthorpe House**, Selby Road, Brackenholme, Selby, N. Yorks, YO8 7EL.*
Beautiful country house, large garden.
Open: All Year
01757 638867
Mrs Jackson
Rates fr: *£15.00*-**£16.00**.
Beds: 1D 1T
Baths: 1 Shared
(3)

Brafferton

National Grid Ref: SE4370

Farmers Inn

***The Farmers Inn**, Raskelf Road, Brafferton, Helperby, York, YO6 2PQ.*
Charming rustic 360-year-old inn.
Open: All Year (not Xmas)
01423 360477
Mrs Hewitt
Rates fr: *£18.00*-**£20.00**.
Beds: 2D 1T
Baths: 3 Private
(5)

Brawby

National Grid Ref: SE7378

***Brawby Grange**, Brawby, Malton, N. Yorks, YO17 0PZ.*
Comfortable farmhouse.
Open: All Year (not Xmas)
01653 668245 Mrs Fairweather
Rates fr: *£13.00*-**£15.00**.
Beds: 2D 1T **Baths:** 1 Shared
(10)

Brayton

National Grid Ref: SE6132

***West Cottage**, Mill Lane, Brayton, Selby, N. Yorks, YO8 9LB.*
Comfortable country cottage, all ensuite.
Open: All Year
Grades: ETB 2 Cr, Comm, AA Listed
01757 213318 Mrs Fletcher
Rates fr: *£18.00*-**£24.00**.
Beds: 1F 1D
Baths: 2 Ensuite
(12) (10)

Brompton

National Grid Ref: SE3796

Green Tree, Three Tune

***Hallikeld House**, Brompton, Northallerton, N. Yorks, DL6 2UE.*
Comfortable country setting.
Open: Easter to Oct
01609 773613
Mrs Saxby
Rates fr: *£14.00*-**£14.00**.
Beds: 1F 1D 1S
Baths: 1 Shared
(2)

Brompton-on-Swale

National Grid Ref: SE2199

***Holly Villa**, Gatherley Road, Brompton-on-Swale, Richmond, N. Yorks, DL10 7JF.*
Refurbished, comfortable Georgian farmhouse.
Open: All Year
01748 811183
Mr Coventry
Rates fr: *£16.00*-**£20.00**.
Beds: 2T
Baths: 2 Private
(5) (6)

Brotherton

National Grid Ref: SE4825

***Crosshill Guest House**, High Street, Brotherton, Knottingley, W. Yorks, WF11 9EY.*
C18th old farm buildings.
Open: All Year
01977 672741 Mr & Mrs Hughes
Rates fr: *£12.50*-**£13.00**.
Beds: 2F 1T 2S
Baths: 2 Shared
(15)

uckden

ational Grid Ref: SD9477

***eck Cottage,** Buckden, Skipton, . Yorks,* BD23 5JA.
ales cottage. Central. Peaceful tuation.
pen: All Year (not Xmas)
1756 760340 Mr & Mrs Leach
ates fr: *£15.00*-**£20.00**.
(2)

ulmer

ational Grid Ref: SE6967

Bay Horse Inn, Highwayman

***ower Barn,** Wandales Lane, ulmer, York,* YO6 7ES.
00-year-old converted barn.
pen: Easter to Oct
rades: ETB 1 Cr, Comm
1653 618575 Mrs Hall
ates fr: *£15.00*-**£15.00**.
eds: 2D 1T
aths: 2 Shared
(5) (10)

urniston

ational Grid Ref: TA0193

***herry Tree Cottage,** South End, urniston, Scarborough, N. Yorks,* O13 0HP.
ld comfortable cottage - odernised.
pen: All Year
1723 870407 Mrs Rimington
ates fr: *£12.00*-**£12.00**.
eds: 1D 1S
aths: 1 Shared
(1)

urnsall

ational Grid Ref: SE0361

***ed Lion Hotel,** Burnsall, Skipton, . Yorks,* BD23 6BU.
pen: All Year
rades: AA 2 St, RAC 2 St
1756 720204
rs Grayshon
ax no: 01756 720292
ates fr: *£32.00*-**£32.00**.
eds: 2F 4D 4T 1S
aths: 12 Ensuite
(40)
16th ferryman's inn on River harfe overlooking fell & village reen. Traditional Dales bar, xcellent restaurant (AA rosette), g fires, lovely characterful ccommodation. Brass beds. alking & fishing.

***olly Tree Farm,** Thorpe, urnsall, Skipton, N. Yorks,* D23 6BJ.
uiet, homely Dales sheep farm.
pen: All Year
1756 720604 Mrs Hall
ates fr: *£16.00*-**£16.00**.
eds: 1D 1S
aths: 1 Shared

Please respect a B&B's wishes regarding children, animals & smoking.

***Conistone House,** Burnsall, Skipton, N. Yorks,* BD23 6BN.
Comfortable, friendly, family house.
Open: Easter to Oct
01756 720650 Mrs Mason
Rates fr: *£18.00*-**£23.00**.
Beds: 1D 2T
Baths: 1 Shared
(3)

Cam Houses

National Grid Ref: SD8282

***Cam Farm,** Cam Houses, Oughtershaw, Skipton, N. Yorks,* BD23 5JT.
Typical Dales hill farm.
Open: All Year
01860 648045 Mrs Smith
Rates fr: *£16.00*-**£16.00**.
Beds: 3T
Baths: 1 Shared
(6)

Carlton

National Grid Ref: SE6424

***Norden Alpine Nursery,** Hirst Road, Carlton, Goole,* DN14 9PX.
Modern, comfortable bungalow.
Open: All Year (not Xmas)
01405 861348 Mrs Walton
Rates fr: *£13.00*.
Beds: 3T
(10)

Carlton Miniott

National Grid Ref: SE3981

Dog & Gun

***Carlton House Farm,** Carlton Miniott, Thirsk, N. Yorks,* YO7 4NJ.
Old very comfortable farmhouse.
Open: All Year
Grades: ETB Listed
01845 524139
Mrs Lee
Rates fr: *£12.50*-**£15.00**.
Beds: 2D
Baths: 1 Shared
(10) (2)

***Grove Farm,** Carlton Miniott, Thirsk, N. Yorks,* YO7 4NJ.
Modern bungalow, comfortable friendly farmhouse.
Open: All Year
01845 524257
Mrs Corner
Rates fr: *£12.50*-**£15.00**.
Beds: 2T
Baths: 1 Shared
(6)

Carlton-in-Cleveland

National Grid Ref: NZ3921

***Hill Rise,** Carlton-in-Cleveland, Stokesley, Middlesbrough,* TS9 7DD.
Modernn comfortable farmhouse.
Open: Easter to Nov
01642 712212 Mrs Leng
Rates fr: *£14.00*-**£14.00**.
Beds: 1D 1T
Baths: 1 Shared
(3) (3)

Carperby

National Grid Ref: SE0089

Kings Arms

***The Old Stables,** Carperby, Leyburn, N. Yorks,* DL8 4DA.
Converted stables, Peaceful, scenic Wensleydale.
Open: All Year (not Xmas)
Grades: ETB 2 Cr, High Comm
01969 663590 (also fax no)
Mrs Nicholson
Rates fr: *£20.00*-**£25.00**.
Beds: 2D 1T **Baths:** 3 Ensuite
(5)

***Wheatsheaf Hotel,** Carperby, Leyburn, N. Yorks,* DL8 4DF.
Charming Dales hotel.
Open: All Year
01969 663216 Mr & Mrs MacKay
Rates fr: *£25.00*-**£26.00**.
Beds: 5D 2T 1S
Baths: 8 Ensuite
(12) (25)

***The Grayford Private Hotel,** Carperby, Leyburn, N. Yorks,* DL8 4DW.
Quiet family-run country hotel, home cooking. **Open:** All Year
01969 663517 Mr Knowles
Rates fr: *£10.00*-**£13.00**.
Beds: 4D
Baths: 1 Private 2 Shared
(12)

Castle Howard

National Grid Ref: SE6967

Crown & Cushion, Bay Horse Inn

***Grange Farm,** Castle Howard, Bulmer, York,* YO6 7BN.
A warm Yorkshire welcome awaits at our comfortable farmhouse on family farm.
Open: Easter to Nov
Grades: ETB Listed
01653 618376 (also fax no)
Mrs Foster
Rates fr: *£15.00*-**£15.00**.
Beds: 1F 1D 1T 1S
Baths: 1 Shared
(6)

The lowest **single** *rate is shown in* **bold.**

Lower Barn, *Wandales Lane, Castle Howard, Bulmer, York,* YO6 7ES.
200-year-old converted barn.
Open: Easter to Oct
Grades: ETB 1 Cr, Comm
01653 618575 Mrs Hall
Rates fr: *£15.00*-**£15.00**.
Beds: 2D 1T **Baths:** 2 Shared
(5) (10)

Catterick

National Grid Ref: SE2497

Rose Cottage Guest House, *26 High Street, Catterick , Richmond, N. Yorks,* DL10 7LJ.
Small, cosy, stone-built cottage.
Open: All Year (not Xmas)
Grades: ETB Listed
01748 811164 Mrs Archer
Rates fr: *£17.50*-**£20.00**.
Beds: 1D 2T 1S
Baths: 2 Private 1 Shared
(4)

The Angel, *Catterick , Richmond, N. Yorks,* DL10 7LL.
Friendly, comfortable, family-run inn. **Open:** All Year (not Xmas)
01748 818490
Rates fr: *£15.00*-**£20.00**.
Beds: 1F 1D 1T 2S **Baths:** 1Shared
(5)

Catton

National Grid Ref: SE3778

Angel

The Old Smithy, *Catton, Thirsk, N. Yorks,* YO7 4SQ.
C16th house with modern additions. **Open:** All Year
01845 578250 Mrs Parks
Rates fr: *£15.00*-**£10.00**.
Beds: 1F **Baths:** 1 Ensuite
(6) (2)

Chapel-le-Dale

National Grid Ref: SD7377

Broadrake Farm, *Chapel-le-Dale, Ingleton, Carnforth, Lancs,* LA6 3AX.
Comfortable friendly family farm-house. **Open:** All Year
015242 41623 Mr & Mrs Hawes
Rates fr: *£15.00*-**£15.00**.
Beds: 1F 1D 1S **Baths:** 1 Shared
(6)

Chop Gate

National Grid Ref: SE5599

Buck Inn

Hill End Farm, *Chop Gate, Bilsdale, North Yorkshre,* TS9 7JR.
Comfortable, North Yorkshire Moors farmhouse.
Open: Easter to Nov
Grades: ETB 2 Cr, Comm
01439 798278 Mrs Johnson
Rates fr: *£20.00*-**£25.00**.
Beds: 1F 1D **Baths:** 2 Ensuite
(5) (3)

1 Foresters Cottage, *Chop Gate, Stokesley, Middlesbrough,* TS9 7JD.
Semi-detached forester's cottage.
Open: All Year (not Xmas)
01642 778368 Mrs Cook
Rates fr: *£14.00*-**£14.00**.
Beds: 1F 1D
Baths: 1 Shared
(2)

Buck Inn Hotel, *Chop Gate, Stokesley, Middlesbrough,* TS9 7JL.
Friendly inn with restaurant.
Open: All Year (not Xmas)
01642 778334 Mrs Stewart
Rates fr: *£21.00*-**£28.00**.
Beds: 1F 1D 4T
Baths: 6 Private
(60)

Clapham

National Grid Ref: SD7469

Goat Gap Inn

Goat Gap Inn, *Newby, Clapham, Lancaster,* LA2 8JB.
Open: All Year
015242 41230 Mr & Mrs Willis
Rates fr: *£24.00*-**£35.00**.
Beds: 1F 4D 1T
Baths: 4 Ensuite 2 Shared
(80)
Goat Gap Inn, famous C17th hostelry, detached with incredible 360 degree views across the Moors. Real ales, bar & restaurant, meals, ensuite rooms, four poster, colour TV, tea/coffee making facilities.

Clapham Station

National Grid Ref: SD7367

Flying Horseshoe Hotel, *Clapham Station, Clapham, Lancaster,* LA2 8ES.
Idyllic spot - panoramic views.
Open: All Year
015242 51229 Mr & Mrs Harris
Rates fr: *£20.00*-**£25.00**.
Beds: 3D 1T
Baths: 4 Ensuite
(40)

Clay Bank Top

National Grid Ref: NZ5701

Maltkiln House, *Clay Bank Top, Bilsdale, Middlesbrough,* TS9 7HZ.
Stone farmhouse in magnificent location.
Open: All Year
01642 778216 Mr & Mrs Broad
Rates fr: *£16.00*-**£16.00**.
Beds: 1D 2T
Baths: 2 Shared
(8) (3)

The lowest *double* rate per person is shown in *italics*.

Cloughton

National Grid Ref: TA0094

Gowland Farm, *Gowland Lane, Cloughton, Scarborough, N. Yorks* YO13 0DU.
Warm, friendly, peaceful, beautiful views.
Open: Easter to Oct
01723 870924 Mrs Martin
Rates fr: *£14.00*-**£14.00**.
Beds: 1D 1T 1S
Baths: 1 Shared
(3) (6)

Coulton

National Grid Ref: SE6374

Swathgill, *Coulton, Hovingham, York,* YO6 4NG.
Secluded country house with beautiful gardens.
Open: All Year (not Xmas)
01347 888675 Mrs Kibble
Rates fr: *£20.00*-**£25.00**.
Beds: 1D 1T
Baths: 2 Private
(15) (2)

Coxwold

National Grid Ref: SE5377

Fauconberg Arms

School House, *Coxwold, York,* YO6 4AD.
Open: All Year (not Xmas)
01347 868356 Mr & Mrs Richardson
Rates fr: *£17.00*-**£18.50**.
Beds: 1F 1D 1T
Baths: 2 Shared
(5)
Coxwold is a charming village 18 miles north of York, on the edge of the North York Moors. A good base for touring this lovely area.

Crakehall

National Grid Ref: SE2489

The Old Vicarage, *Crakehall, Bedale, N. Yorks,* DL8 1HE.
Elegant family home, log fires.
Open: All Year (not Xmas)
01677 422967 Mrs Young
Rates fr: *£20.00*-**£25.00**.
Beds: 3D 2T
Baths: 2 Private 3 Shared
(7) (8)

Crambe

National Grid Ref: SE7364

Ryders Corner, *Crambe, York,* YO6 7JR.
Friendly, warm, comfortable, old cottage.
Open: All Year (not Xmas)
01653 618359 Mrs Hewitt
Rates fr: *£15.00*-**£20.00**.
Beds: 1D 1T
Baths: 1 Shared
(4)

Crayke

National Grid Ref: SE5670

Durham Ox

***Durham Ox,** Crayke, York, YO6 4TE.*
Open: All Year
01347 821506 Mrs Chadwick
Rates fr: *£17.50*-**£25.00**.
Beds: 1D 2T
Baths: 1 Shared
Stylish C18th family-run freehouse in pictuesque & historic village 12 miles north of York. Inglenook, log fires. Traditional ales. Bar meals & restaurant.

Cringle Moor

National Grid Ref: SE5599

***Beakhills Farm,** Cold Moor, Cringle Moor, Chop Gate, Stokesley, Middlesbrough, TS9 7JJ.*
Comfortable farmhouse.
Open: All Year (not Xmas)
01642 778371 Mrs Cook
Rates fr: *£14.00*-**£14.00**.
Beds: 1F 1T

Cropton

National Grid Ref: SE7589

New Inn

***Burr Bank Cottage,** Cropton, Pickering, N. Yorks Moors, YO18 8HL.*
Comfortable, spacious, luxury, personal service.
Open: All Year
Grades: ETB 3 Cr, High Comm
01751 417777
Ms Richardson
Fax no: 01759 417789
Rates fr: *£21.00*-**£21.00**.
Beds: 1D 1T
Baths: 2 Ensuite

***High Farm,** Cropton, Pickering, N. Yorks, YO18 8HL.*
Beautiful Victorian Farmhouse, well-situated.
Open: All Year
Grades: ETB 2 Cr, Comm
01751 417461
Mrs Feaster
Rates fr: *£18.00*-**£25.00**.
Beds: 3D
Baths: 3 Ensuite
(10) (10)

***The New Inn,** Cropton, Pickering, N. Yorks, YO18 8HH.*
Old established country inn/brewery.
Open: All Year
01751 417330 Mrs Lee
Rates fr: *£22.50*-**£35.00**.
Beds: 2F 4D 2T
Baths: 8 Private
(30)

Dalton (Richmond)

National Grid Ref: NZ1108

Travellers Rest

***Dalton Hall,** Dalton (Richmond), Richmond, N. Yorks, DL11 7HU.*
Grade II Listed country house.
Open: All Year (not Xmas)
01833 621339 Mrs Freeman
Rates fr: *£16.00*-**£19.00**.
Beds: 1F 1D
Baths: 2 Private
(3)

Dalton (Thirsk)

National Grid Ref: SE4376

***Garth House,** Dalton (Thirsk), Thirsk, N. Yorks, YO7 3HY.*
Working stock farm, friendly welcome.
Open: All Year (not Xmas)
Grades: ETB Listed
01845 577310
Mrs Ramshay
Rates fr: *£12.00*-**£12.00**.
Beds: 1F 1T
Baths: 1 Shared
(6)

Danby

National Grid Ref: NZ7008

Duke of Wellington

***Sycamore House,** Danby, Whitby, N. Yorks, YO21 2NW.*
C17th farmhouse. Stunning views.
Open: All Year (not Xmas)
01287 660125 Mr Lowson
Rates fr: *£16.00*-**£16.00**.
Beds: 1F 1D 1T 1S
Baths: 2 Shared
(6)

***Botton Grove Farm,** Danby Head, Danby, Whitby, N. Yorks, YO21 2NH.*
Large, comfortable, stone-built farmhouse.
Open: May to Feb
01287 660284 Mrs Tait
Rates fr: *£15.00*-**£15.00**.
Beds: 1D 1T 2S
Baths: 1 Shared
(3)

Danby Wiske

National Grid Ref: SE3398

White Swan, Oakdene Tea Rooms

***Middle Brockholme Farm,** Streetlam, Danby Wiske, Northallerton, N. Yorks, DL7 0AJ.*
Quiet, comfortable farmhouse, good food.
Open: Easter to Oct
01609 780456 Mrs Robertshaw
Rates fr: *£16.00*-**£16.00**.
Beds: 1D 2T
Baths: 1 Shared
(4)

***The Manor House,** Danby Wiske, Northallerton, N. Yorks, DL7 0LZ.*
C17th hand-made brick long house.
Open: All Year (not Xmas)
01609 774662 Mrs Sanders
Rates fr: *£16.00*-**£16.00**.
Beds: 1D 1T 2S
Baths: 2 Ensuite 1 Shared
(4)

Darley

National Grid Ref: SE2059

***Brimham Guest House,** Silverdale Close, Darley, Harrogate, N. Yorks, HG3 2PQ.*
Modern, comfortable village guest house.
Open: All Year (not Xmas)
01423 780948 Mrs Barker
Rates fr: *£15.00*-**£20.00**.
Beds: 3D
Baths: 3 Private
(1) (4)

Dunnington

National Grid Ref: SE6652

Windmill Inn, Cross Keys

***Brookland House,** Hull Road, Dunnington, York, YO1 5LW.*
Open: Mar to Oct
01904 489548 Mrs Foster
Rates fr: *£15.00*-**£17.00**.
Beds: 1D 1T 1S
Baths: 1 Shared
(5) (3)
Attractive detached house, country area. Dining room separate tables overlooking delightful garden. Near to many interesting places to visit. Excellent park & ride nearby. Non-smoking.

***Moonlight Cottage,** 8 Greencroft Court, Dunnington, York, YO1 5QJ.*
A traditional home.
Open: All Year
01904 489369 Mrs McNab
Rates fr: *£15.00*.
Beds: 1D
Baths: 1 Private 1 Shared
(2)

Dunsley

National Grid Ref: NZ8511

***Low Farm,** Dunsley, Whitby, N. Yorks, YO21 3TL.*
Working dairy farm. Sea views.
Open: Jun to Oct
01947 893218 Mrs Hodgson
Rates fr: *£14.00*-**£14.00**.
Beds: 1D 1T
Baths: 1 Shared

***Dunsley Hall,** Dunsley, Whitby, N. Yorks, YO21 3TL.*
C19th country hall, two miles Whitby.
Open: All Year
01947 893437 Mr Ward
Rates fr: *£36.50*-**£36.50**.
Beds: 11T
Baths: 11 Ensuite
(30)

Easingwold

National Grid Ref: SE5369

The Garth

Alderside, *Thirsk Road, Easingwold, York,* YO6 3HJ.
Peacefully dream in gardens serene.
Open: Mar to Nov
01347 822132 Mrs Tanner Smith
Rates fr: *£17.50*-**£25.00**.
Beds: 2D
Baths: 1 Ensuite 1 Private
(12) (3)

East Heslerton

National Grid Ref: SE9276

Snooty Fox Inn

The Snooty Fox Inn, *East Heslerton, Malton, N. Yorks,* YO17 8EN.
Motel, pub, restaurant, camping.
Open: All Year
01944 710554 Mrs Bland
Rates fr: *£19.00*-**£25.00**.
Beds: 1F 3D 1T
Baths: 5 Ensuite
(30)

East Marton

National Grid Ref: SD9050

Cross Keys

Sawley House, *East Marton, Skipton, N. Yorks,* BD23 3LP.
Ideally situated for touring Dales.
Open: All Year
01282 843207 Mrs Pilling
Rates fr: *£17.00*-**£17.00**.
Beds: 2T 1S
Baths: 1 Shared
(10)

East Witton

National Grid Ref: SE1486

Blue Lion

Dale View, *38 East Witton, East Witton, Leyburn, N. Yorks,* DL8 4SH.
Beautifully refurbished, traditional Dales cottage.
Open: All Year (not Xmas)
Grades: ETB Listed
01969 624113
Mr Dunthorne
Rates fr: *£21.00*-**£35.00**.
Beds: 1D 1T
Baths: 2 Ensuite
(6)

11 East Witton Village, *East Witton, Leyburn, N. Yorks,* DL8 4SH.
Comfortable cottage, beautiful quiet village.
Open: Mar to Oct
01969 623210 Mrs Sunter
Rates fr: *£14.50*-**£20.00**.
Beds: 1F 1D
Baths: 2 Shared
(2)

Ebberston

National Grid Ref: SE8982

Grapes Inn, Foxholme Hotel

Studley House, *67 Main Street, Ebberston, Scarborough, N. Yorks,* YO13 9NR.
Open: All Year (not Xmas)
Grades: ETB 2 Cr, Comm
01723 859285 Mrs Hodgson
Rates fr: *£17.00*-**£17.00**.
Beds: 1D 1T 1S
Baths: 2 Ensuite 1 Private
(10) (3)
Quiet picturesque village with stone cottages & running stream. Excellent breakfast served in friendly atmosphere. Cleanliness assured in spacious bedrooms. Your comfort is our concern.

Eddlethorpe

National Grid Ref: SE7866

Blacksmiths Arms

Kennels Farm, *Eddlethorpe, Malton, N. Yorks,* YO17 9QT.
Beautiful old farmhouse.
Open: Easter to Oct
01653 658213 Mrs Hodsman
Rates fr: *£12.00*-**£15.00**.
Beds: 1F 1D 1T
Baths: 1 Shared
(3)

Egton Bridge

National Grid Ref: NZ8005

Horseshoe Hotel, *Egton Bridge, Whitby, N. Yorks,* YO21 1XE.
Comfortable, family-run riverside hotel.
Open: All Year (not Xmas)
01947 895245 Mr & Mrs Mullins
Rates fr: *£19.00*-**£26.00**.
Beds: 4D 2T
Baths: 3 Private 3 Shared

Postgate Inn, *Egton Bridge, Whitby, N. Yorks,* YO21 1UX.
As seen in 'Heartbeat' on TV!
Open: All Year
01947 895241 Mr Mead
Rates fr: *£18.00*-**£18.00**.
Beds: 1F 4D 1T 1S
Baths: 1 Private 2 Shared

Ellerby

National Grid Ref: NZ7914

Ellerby Hotel

Ellerby Hotel, *Ellerby, Saltburn-by-the-Sea,* TS13 5LP.
Residential country inn.
Open: All Year
01947 840342 Mr Alderson
Rates fr: *£23.00*-**£31.00**.
Beds: 2F 5D 2T
Baths: 9 Private
(50)

Eppleby

National Grid Ref: NZ1713

The George

Thornfield House, *Eppleby, Richmond, N. Yorks,* DL11 7AR.
Large, modern, comfortable private house.
Open: All Year (not Xmas)
01325 718765 Mrs Davidson
Rates fr: *£16.00*-**£16.00**.
Beds: 1T
Baths: 1 Private
(3)

Faceby

National Grid Ref: NZ4903

Four Wynds, *Whorl Hill, Faceby, Middlesbrough,* TS9 7BZ.
Modern, comfortable farmhouse - ideally situated.
Open: All Year
01642 701315 Mr Barnfather
Rates fr: *£15.00*-**£15.00**.
Beds: 1F 1D 1T
Baths: 1 Ensuite 1 Shared
(8)

Fadmoor

National Grid Ref: SE6789

Plough Inn

The Plough Inn, *Fadmoor, Kirkbymoorside, York,* YO6 6HY.
C18th country inn.
Open: All Year (not Xmas)
01751 431515 Mr O'Connell
Rates fr: *£14.50*-**£14.50**.
Beds: 1D 1T 2S
Baths: 1 Shared
(12) (15)

Farndale

National Grid Ref: SE6697

Royal Oak

Olive House Farm, *Farndale, Kirkbymoorside, York,* YO6 6JY.
Homely accommodation, working farm.
Open: Easter to Oct
01751 433207 Mrs Blacklock
Rates fr: *£12.00*-**£14.00**.
Beds: 2F
(4)

Keysbeck Farm, *Farndale, Kirkbymoorside, York,* YO6 6UZ.
Old oak-beamed farmhouse.
Open: All Year (not Xmas)
01751 433221 Mrs Featherstone
Rates fr: *£12.00*-**£12.00**.
Beds: 2D 1T 1S
Baths: 1 Shared

The lowest *double* rate per person is shown in *italics*.

Farnhill

National Grid Ref: SE0046

White Lion, Bull Inn

Kirkgate House, *1 Kirkgate, Farnhill, Keighley, W. Yorks,* BD20 9BA.
C18th former coaching inn.
Open: All Year
01535 636448 Mrs Barwick
Rates fr: *£16.00*-**£16.00**.
Beds: 1F 1D 1T 2S
Baths: 1 Shared
(2)

Filey

National Grid Ref: TA1180

Abbots Leigh Guest House, *7 Rutland Street, Filey, N. Yorks,* YO14 9JA.
Victorian terrace house.
Open: All Year (not Xmas)
Grades: ETB 3 Cr, Comm, AA 3 Q
01723 513334 Mr & Mrs Carter
Rates fr: *£18.00*-**£20.00**.
Beds: 2F 2D 2T
Baths: 6 Private
(3) (4)

Flixton

National Grid Ref: TA0379

Foxhounds

Ariston House, *Flixton Main Street, Flixton, Flixton, Scarborough, N. Yorks,* YO11 3UB.
Beautiful location between Wolds and Coast.
Open: All Year (not Xmas)
01723 891 851 Mrs Wright
Rates fr: *£16.00*-**£17.00**.
Beds: 1F 1T
Baths: 1 Ensuite 1 Shared
(2)

Foxup

National Grid Ref: SD8676

Bridge Farm, *Foxup, Arncliffe, Skipton, N. Yorks,* BD23 5QP.
Working Dales farm.
Open: Easter to Oct
01756 770249 Mrs Lund
Rates fr: *£15.00*-**£16.00**.
Beds: 1T 1D
Baths: 1 Shared
(4)

Fylingthorpe

National Grid Ref: NZ9404

Croft Farm, *Fylingthorpe, Whitby, N. Yorks,* YO22 4PW.
Farmhouse & cottage. Panoramic views.
Open: Easter to Oct
01947 880231 Mrs Featherstone
Rates fr: *£16.00*-**£16.00**.
Beds: 1F 1D 1S
Baths: 1 Private 1 Shared
(5) (4)

Ganthorpe

National Grid Ref: SE6870

Gate Farm, *Ganthorpe, Terrington, York,* YO6 4QD.
Traditional working dairy farm.
Open: Easter to Oct
Grades: ETB 2 Cr, Comm
01653 648269
Mrs Miller
Rates fr: *£14.00*-**£15.00**.
Beds: 1F 1D 1T
Baths: 1 Ensuite 1 Private
(6)

Gargrave

National Grid Ref: SD9354

2 Westville Gardens, *Eshton Road, Gargrave, Skipton, N. Yorks,* BD23 3SG.
New comfortable bungalow.
Open: All Year (not Xmas)
01756 748084
Mrs Moorhouse
Rates fr: *£15.00*-**£15.00**.
Beds: 1D 1T
Baths: 1 Shared

Gateforth

National Grid Ref: SE5628

Lund Farm, *Gateforth, Selby, N. Yorks,* YO8 9LE.
C18th farmhouse on working farm.
Open: All Year
Grades: ETB 1 Cr, High Comm
01757 228775
Mr & Mrs Middleton
Rates fr: *£18.00*-**£18.00**.
Beds: 1F 1T
Baths: 2 Ensuite
(4)

Gayle

National Grid Ref: SD8789

Board Hotel, Fountain Hotel, Crown Hotel

Gayle Laithe, *Gayle, Hawes, N. Yorks,* DL8 3RR.
Modern, comfortable, converted barn.
Open: Mar to Nov
01969 667397 Mrs McGregor
Rates fr: *£15.00*-**£15.00**.
Beds: 1D 1T 1S
Baths: 1 Shared
(2)

East House, *Gayle, Hawes, N. Yorks,* DL8 3RZ.
Spacious comfortable country house.
Open: Easter to October
Grades: ETB 2 Cr, Comm
01969 667405 Mrs Ward
Rates fr: *£16.00*-**£16.00**.
Beds: 1F 1T 1D 1S
Baths: 1 Ensuite 1 Shared
(5) (3)

Ivy House, *Gayle, Hawes, N. Yorks,* DL8 3RZ.
Quiet, comfortable house, beautiful views.
Open: All Year (not Xmas)
01969 667476 Mrs Chapman
Rates fr: *£13.00*-**£14.00**.
Beds: 1F 1D
Baths: 1 Shared

Rookhurst Hotel, *West End, Gayle, Hawes, N. Yorks,* DL8 3RT.
Family-run hotel beside Pennine Way.
Open: Feb to Dec
Grades: AA 2 St
01969 667454 (also fax no)
Mrs Vandersteen
Rates fr: *£30.00*-**£30.00**.
Beds: 4D 1T
Baths: 5 Private
(12) (10)

Gayles

National Grid Ref: NZ1207

Slip Inn Farm, *East Street, Gayles, Richmond, N. Yorks,* DL11 7JQ.
C16th comfortable family home.
Open: Easter to Oct
01833 621386 Mrs Fava
Rates fr: *£14.00*-**£14.00**.
Beds: 1D 1T 1S
Baths: 2 Shared

Giggleswick

National Grid Ref: SD8164

Yorkshire Dales Field Centre, *Church Street, Giggleswick, Settle, N. Yorks,* BD24 0BE.
Famous for cooking, groups only.
Open: All Year
01729 824180 Mrs Barbour
Rates fr: *£8.50*-**£8.50**.
Beds: 6F 2S
Baths: 5 Shared
(7)

Gilling West

National Grid Ref: NZ1805

Mack & Spade, White Swan

Crabtree House Farm, *Gilling West, Richmond, N. Yorks,* DL10 5JD.
Victorian farmhouse with peaceful surroundings.
Open: All Year (not Xmas)
01748 850158 Mrs Willis
Rates fr: *£14.00*-**£18.00**.
Beds: 1D 1T
Baths: 1 Shared

The White Swan Inn, *Gilling West, Richmond, N. Yorks,* DL10 5JG.
C17th inn, traditional ales.
Open: All Year
01748 822778 Mrs Kirk
Rates fr: *£16.00*-**£16.00**.
Beds: 1F 2D 1T 2S
Baths: 1 Shared
(6) (5)

Glaisdale

National Grid Ref: NZ7603

Anglers Rest

***Red House Farm**, Glaisdale, Whitby, N. Yorks, YO21 2PZ.*
Listed Georgian farmhouse, tastefully refurbished.
Open: All Year
01947 897242
Mr Spashett
Rates fr: *£18.00*-**£18.00**.
Beds: 1F 2D 1T
Baths: 4 Private 1 Shared
(5) (4)

***The Grange**, Glaisdale, Whitby, N. Yorks, YO21 2QW.*
Country manor house.
Open: Feb to Nov
01947 897241 Mrs Kelly
Rates fr: *£15.00*-**£15.00**.
Beds: 2D 1T
Baths: 1 Ensuite 2 Private 1 Shared
(10) (6)

***Hollins Farm**, Glaisdale, Whitby, N. Yorks, YO21 2PZ.*
Comfortable C16th farmhouse, all day access.
Open: All Year (not Xmas)
01947 897516
Mr Mortimer
Rates fr: *£13.00*-**£13.00**.
Beds: 1F 1D 1T 1S

***The Railway Station**, Glaisdale, Whitby, N. Yorks, YO21 2QL.*
Converted railway station, Esk Valley.
Open: All Year (not Xmas)
01947 897533
Mr & Mrs Silkstone
Rates fr: *£15.00*.
Beds: 1T
Baths: 1 Ensuite
(2)

***Sycamore Dell**, Glaisdale, Whitby, N. Yorks, YO21 2PZ.*
Comfortable converted C17th barn.
Open: Mar to Oct
01947 897345
Mr & Mrs Hogben
Rates fr: *£14.00*-**£14.00**.
Beds: 1F 2D 1S
Baths: 1 Shared
(11) (3)

Goathland

National Grid Ref: NZ8301

Mallyan Spout

***1 The Orchards**, Goathland, Whitby, N. Yorks, YO22 5JU.*
Quiet situation in popular village.
Open: All Year (not Xmas)
01947 896300
Mrs Turford
Rates fr: *£14.00*-**£14.00**.
Beds: 1D 1T
Baths: 1 Shared
(2)

***Dale End Farm**, Green End, Goathland, Whitby, N. Yorks, YO22 5LJ.*
500-year-old working farm.
Open: All Year
01947 895371 Mrs Cockrem
Rates fr: *£15.00*-**£15.00**.
Beds: 2F 1D
Baths: 1 Shared
(6)

***Glendale House**, Goathland, Whitby, N. Yorks, YO22 5AN.*
Picturesque village, beautiful views.
Open: All Year (not Xmas)
01947 896281 Mrs Simmonds
Rates fr: *£18.00*-**£25.00**.
Beds: 2F 1D
Baths: 1 Shared

Grafton

National Grid Ref: SE4163

Ye Olde Punch Bowl Inn

***Primrose Cottage**, Grafton, York, YO5 9QJ.*
Warm hospitality in country cottage.
Open: All Year
Grades: ETB 1 Cr, High Comm
01423 322835 / 322711 Mrs Styan
Fax no: 01423 323985
Rates fr: *£16.00*-**£20.00**.
Beds: 1D 2T
Baths: 1 Private 1 Shared
(8)

Grantley

National Grid Ref: SE2369

***St Georges Court**, Old Home Farm, Grantley, Ripon, N. Yorks, HG4 3EU.*
Peace and tranquillity. Beautifully situated.
Open: All Year (not Xmas)
Grades: ETB 2 Cr, Comm
01765 620618 Mrs Gordon
Rates fr: *£19.00*.
Beds: 1F 3D 1T
Baths: 5 Ensuite
(12)

Grassington

National Grid Ref: SE0064

Black Horse, Devonshire, Old Hall Inn

***Town Head Guest House**, 1 Low Lane, Grassington, Skipton, N. Yorks, BD23 5AU.*
Modern comfortable guest house.
Open: All Year (not Xmas)
Grades: ETB 2 Cr, Comm
01756 752811
Mrs Lister
Rates fr: *£21.00*-**£30.00**.
Beds: 3D 1T
Baths: 4 Ensuite
(7) (3)

***3 Wharfeside Avenue**, Grassington, Skipton, N. Yorks, BD23 5BS.*
Large, comfortable, warm family house.
Open: Easter to Nov
Grades: ETB 2 Cr
01756 752115 Mr & Mrs Cahill
Rates fr: *£18.00*-**£18.00**.
Beds: 1F 1T 1S
Baths: 1 Private
(3)

***Mayfield Bed & Breakfast**, Low Mill Lane, Grassington, Skipton, N. Yorks, BD23 5BX.*
Riverside Dales long house.
Open: All Year
01756 753052 Mr & Mrs Trewartha
Rates fr: *£18.00*-**£20.00**.
Beds: 1F 1T 1D
Baths: 1 Ensuite 1 Shared
(10)

***Springroyd House**, 8a Station Road, Grassington, Skipton, N. Yorks, BD23 5NQ.*
Conveniently situated, friendly family home.
Open: All Year
01756 752473 Mr Berry
Rates fr: *£16.50*-**£20.00**.
Beds: 1D 1T
Baths: 2 Shared
(5) (2)

Great Ayton

National Grid Ref: NZ5611

Royal Oak Hotel, Buck Hotel

***Petch's**, 1 Park Rise, Great Ayton, Middlesbrough, N. Yorks, TS9 6HD.*
Comfortable, modern, quiet bungalow - central.
Open: All Year (not Xmas)
Grades: ETB 2 Cr, Comm
01642 722436 Mrs Petch
Rates fr: *£16.00*-**£18.00**.
Beds: 1F 1T **Baths:** 2 Private
(2)

Great Broughton

National Grid Ref: NZ5406

Bay Horse, Jet Miners, The Wainstones

***Red Hall**, Great Broughton, Middlesbrough, N. Yorks, TS9 7ET.*
Open: All Year
01642 712300 (also fax no)
Mr Richmond
Rates fr: *£20.00*-**£28.00**.
Beds: 1F 2D
Baths: 3 Ensuite
(10)
Our welcoming, elegant C17th Grade II Listed country house, completely modernised, stands in own tranquil meadowland on fringe of North Yorks Moors National Park. Exquisite far-reaching views, ideal walking & touring base. Stabling, excellent local leisure facilities, including tennis.

The Hollies, 98 High Street, Great Broughton, Middlesbrough, N. Yorks, TS9 7HA.
Open: All Year
01642 710592 (also fax no) Mrs Scott
Rates fr: *£15.00*-**£15.00**.
Beds: 1F 1D **Baths:** 1 Shared
(2)
Set in picturesque village close to national park, Captain Cook country. Easy travel to Whitby, Scarborough, York & 'Herriot Country'. Guest lounge & friendly welcome.

***Ingle Hill,** Ingleby Road, Great Broughton, Middlesbrough, N. Yorks, TS9 7ER.*
Modern, comfortable, detached dormer bungalow.
Open: All Year (not Xmas)
01642 712449 Mrs Sutcliffe
Rates fr: *£16.00*-**£17.50**.
Beds: 1F 2D 1T
Baths: 1 Private 2 Shared
(2) (3)

***Hilton House,** 52 High Street, Great Broughton, Middlesbrough, N. Yorks, TS9 7EG.*
Open: All Year (not Xmas)
01642 712526 Mrs Mead
Rates fr: *£17.00*-**£17.00**.
Beds: 1D 2T
Baths: 2 Ensuite 1 Shared
(3)
Attractive C18th detached sandstone house set back from High Street. Very comfortable. Home made teas on arrival, packed lunches, drying, lifts to footpath, extensive collection of walking books.

Green Hammerton

National Grid Ref: SE4556

Bay Horse Inn

***Bay Horse Inn,** York Road, Green Hammerton, York, YO5 8BN.*
Traditional village inn, modern motel. **Open:** All Year
Grades: AA 3 Q
01423 330338 Mrs Whitelegg
Fax no: 01423 331279
Rates fr: *£22.50*-**£30.00**.
Beds: 1F 3D 4T 2S
Baths: 10 Private
(40)

Greenhow

National Grid Ref: SE1064

Miner's Arms

***Mole End,** Greenhow, Pateley Bridge, Harrogate, N. Yorks, HG3 5JQ.*
Comfortable stone-built private house.
Open: All Year
01423 712565 Mr & Mrs Knowles
Rates fr: *£16.00*-**£20.00**.
Beds: 1D 2T
Baths: 1 Private 1 Shared
(12) (5)

Grosmont

National Grid Ref: NZ8205

Wheatsheaf

***Eskdale,** Grosmont, Whitby, N. Yorks, YO22 5PT.*
Detached Georgian house.
Open: Easter to Nov
Grades: ETB Listed, Comm
01947 895385 Mrs Counsell
Rates fr: *£16.00*-**£16.00**.
Beds: 2D 2S **Baths:** 1 Shared
(4)

***Woodside,** Front Street, Grosmont, Whitby, N. Yorks, YO22 5PF.*
Friendly family home. Delightful views.
Open: All Year
01947 895205 Mrs Beesley
Rates fr: *£16.00*-**£20.00**.
Beds: 2T **Baths:** 1 Shared
(2)

***Hazelwood House,** Front Street, Grosmont, Whitby, N. Yorks, YO22 5QE.*
Large Victorian private house.
Open: All Year
01947 895292 Mr Atha
Rates fr: *£16.00*-**£16.00**.
Beds: 2D 2T 1S **Baths:** 2 Shared
(4)

Guisborough

National Grid Ref: NZ6115

***Three Fiddles Hotel,** 34 Westgate, Guisborough, TS14 6ND.*
Bed & Breakfast & pub.
Open: All Year (not Xmas)
01287 632417
Rates fr: *£19.50*-**£19.50**.
Beds: 2D 3T

Gunnerside

National Grid Ref: SD9598

***Rogans Country House,** Gunnerside, Richmond, N. Yorks, DL11 6JW.*
Exceptional accommodation for the discerning.
Open: All Year (not Xmas)
01748 886414 Mrs Trafford
Rates fr: *£20.00*-**£25.00**.
Beds: 2D 1T **Baths:** 3 Private
(6)

Hanlith

National Grid Ref: SD9061

Buck

***Coachmans Cottage,** Hanlith, Malham, Skipton, N. Yorks, BD23 4BP.*
Tranquil C17th cottage, every comfort.
Open: All Year (not Xmas)
01729 830538 Mrs Jenkins
Rates fr: *£20.00*-**£25.00**.
Beds: 2D 1T 1S
Baths: 4 Private
(10) (3)

Harrogate

National Grid Ref: SE3055

Empress, Greyhound, Dragon, Queens Head, Smiths Arms

***Ashley House Hotel,** 36-40 Franklin Road, Harrogate, N. Yorks, HG1 5EE.*
Open: All Year
Grades: ETB 3 Cr, Comm, AA 4 Q, Select, RAC Acclaim
01423 507474 Mr & Mrs Thomas
Fax no: 01423 560858
Rates fr: *£24.00*-**£27.50**.
Beds: 2F 5D 5T 5S
Baths: 17 Ensuite
(6)
Friendly hotel close to town centre. Delicious home cooking. Cosy bar with extensive collection of single malts. Play golf or tour the Yorkshire Dales.

***Madeira House,** 117 Franklin Road, Harrogate, N. Yorks, HG1 5EN.*
Comfortable Victorian semi, quiet surroundings.
Open: All Year (not Xmas)
Grades: ETB Listed, Approv
01423 505752 Mr Bennett
Rates fr: *£19.00*-**£20.00**.
Beds: 1D 1T 2S **Baths:** 4 Ensuite
(2)

***Daryl House Hotel,** 42 Dragon Parade, Harrogate, N. Yorks, HG1 5DA*
Open: All Year (not Xmas)
01423 502775 Mrs Young
Rates fr: *£16.00*-**£16.00**.
Beds: 2F 2T 2S **Baths:** 2 Shared
Small, friendly, family-run hotel. Personal attention is the hallmark of Daryl House. Tea/coffee & colour TV in all rooms, home-cooked food.

***Spring Lodge,** 22 Spring Mount, Harrogate, N. Yorks, HG1 2HX.*
Comfortable, central, family, Edwardian house.
Open: All Year (not Xmas)
01423 506036 Mr Vinter
Rates fr: *£16.00*-**£20.00**.
Beds: 1F 3D 1S
Baths: 2 Ensuite 1 Shared
(2)

***Acacia Lodge,** 21 Ripon Road, Harrogate, N. Yorks, HG1 2JL.*
Open: All Year
Grades: ETB 2 Cr, High Comm, AA 4 Q, Select
01423 560752 Mr & Mrs Bateson
Rates fr: *£24.00*-**£38.00**.
Beds: 1F 1D 3T
Baths: 5 Private
(7) (7)
Warm, lovingly restored Victorian family-run hotel in select central area. Fine furnishings/antiques. All bedrooms luxuriously ensuite. Entirely 'non-smoking'. Delicious breakfasts. Private parking. Phone for brochure.

***Anro,** 90 Kings Road, Harrogate, N. Yorks, HG1 5JX.*
Open: All Year (not Xmas)
Grades: ETB 2 Cr, Comm, AA 3 Q, Recomm, RAC Listed
01423 503087
Mr & Mrs Joyner
Rates fr: *£20.00*-**£20.00**.
Beds: 1F 1D 2T 3S
Baths: 4 Private 3 Shared
(7)
Near town, bus/rail. Close to Valley Gardens. 2 minutes Conference Centre. Ideal for touring Dales. Some ensuite rooms. Four course dinner if required. Highly recommended.

***Eton House,** 3 Eton Terrace, Knareborough Road, Harrogate, N. Yorks, HG2 7SU.*
Standing on the edge of open parkland.
Open: All Year (not Xmas)
Grades: ETB 2 Cr
01423 886850 Mrs Wyatt
Rates fr: *£18.00*-**£18.00**.
Beds: 2F 2D 2T 1S
Baths: 2 Ensuite 2 Shared
(10)

***Knox Mill House,** Knox Mill Lane, Harrogate, N. Yorks, HG3 2AE.*
Converted C18th mill house.
Open: All Year (not Xmas)
Grades: ETB 2 Cr, Comm, AA 3 Q, Recomm
01423 560650 (also fax no)
Mrs Thomson
Rates fr: *£20.00*-**£20.00**.
Beds: 1D 2T
Baths: 3 Private
(4)

***Barkers,** 204 Kings Road, Harrogate, N. Yorks, HG1 5JG.*
Homely character Edwardian town house.
Grades: ETB 2 Cr
01423 568494 Mr Barker
Rates fr: *£19.00*-**£25.00**.
Beds: 1F 1D 1S
Baths: 1 Ensuite 1 Shared
(2)

***Imbercourt Hotel,** 57 Valley Drive, Harrogate, N. Yorks, HG2 0JW.*
Huge breakfasts, well-stocked bar.
Open: All Year
01423 502513
Mr Leatherdale
Rates fr: *£20.00*-**£25.00**.
Beds: 2F 5T 1D 2S
Baths: 5 Ensuite 2 Shared
(Nil)

***The Dales Hotel,** 101 Valley Drive, Harrogate, N. Yorks, HG2 0JP.*
A warm welcome awaits you!
Open: All Year
Grades: ETB 3 Cr, Comm, AA 4 Q, Select
01423 507248 (also fax no)
Mrs Burton
Rates fr: *£24.00*-**£35.00**.
Beds: 1F 3D 2T 2S
Baths: 8 Private
(1)

***Knabbs Ash,** Skipton Road, Kettlesing, Felliscliffe, Harrogate, N. Yorks, HG3 2LT.*
Tranquil, beautiful views. Award winning.
Open: All Year
Grades: ETB 2 Cr, High Comm
01423 771040 Mrs Smith
Rates fr: *£20.00*-**£25.00**.
Beds: 2D 1T
Baths: 3 Private
(10) (6)

***Garden Cottage,** Moor Park, Beckwithshaw, Harrogate, N. Yorks, HG3 1QN.*
Country estate - luxury gourmet B&B. Evening meal by arrangement.
Open: Nov to Sep
01423 530197 Mrs Harrison
Rates fr: *£22.50*-**£25.00**.
Beds: 2T
Baths: 2 Ensuite
(2)

Hartwith

National Grid Ref: SE2161

Joiners' Arms, Bay horse

***Holly Cottage,** Mill Lane, Hartwith, Harrogate, N. Yorks, HG3 3EU.*
200-year-old cottage, overlooking dale. **Open:** All Year
01423 770746 Mrs Drake
Rates fr: *£17.50*-**£25.00**.
Beds: 2D 1T **Baths:** 3 Private
(3)

Hawes

National Grid Ref: SD8789

White Hart Inn, Wensleydale Pantry

***Old Station House,** Hawes, N. Yorks, DL8 3NL.*
Open: All Year (not Xmas)
Grades: ETB 2 Cr, High Comm
01969 667785
Mr & Mrs Watkinson
Rates fr: *£19.00*-**£26.00**.
Beds: 1D 2T
Baths: 2 Ensuite 1 Private
(4)
Former stationmaster's house with large garden. Comfortable lounge with large selection of books and maps. Open fire. Friendly welcome.

***Pry House,** Hawes, N. Yorks, DL8 3LP.*
Working farm in 'Herriot country'.
Open: Easter to Nov
01969 667241 Mrs Fawcett
Rates fr: *£15.00*-**£16.00**.
Beds: 1F 2D **Baths:** 1 Shared
(3)

***Halfway House,** Hawes, N. Yorks, DL8 3LL.*
Small homely Dales farmhouse.
Open: Easter to Nov
01969 667442 Mrs Guy
Rates fr: *£16.00*-**£20.00**.
Beds: 1D 1T
Baths: 1 Shared
(4)

***Ebor House,** Burtersett Road, Hawes, N. Yorks, DL8 3NT.*
Family-run, central, friendly.
Open: All Year (not Xmas)
Grades: ETB 2 Cr
01969 667337 Mrs Clark
Rates fr: *£16.00*-**£16.00**.
Beds: 2D 1T 1S
Baths: 2 Private 1 Shared
(4)

***Tarney Fors,** Hawes, N. Yorks, DL8 3LS.*
Country guest house.
Open: Mar to Nov
Grades: ETB 3 Cr, Comm
01969 667475 Mrs Harpley
Rates fr: *£19.00*-**£30.00**.
Beds: 2D 1T **Baths:** 3 Private

***The Green Dragon Inn,** Hardraw, Hawes, N. Yorks, DL8 3.*
Olde worlde inn/hotel, fully modernised.
Open: All Year (not Xmas)
01969 667392 Mr Stead
Rates fr: *£17.00*-**£18.00**.
Beds: 1F 11D 1T 3S
Baths: 16 Private

***Gayle Laithe,** Gayle, Hawes, N. Yorks, DL8 3RR.*
Modern, comfortable, converted barn.
Open: Mar to Nov
01969 667397 Mrs McGregor
Rates fr: *£15.00*-**£15.00**.
Beds: 1D 1T 1S
Baths: 1 Shared
(2)

Hawnby

National Grid Ref: SE5489

Hawnby Hotel

***Laskill Farm,** Hawnby, Helmsley, York, YO6 5NB.*
Warm, comfortable, lovingly cared-for farmhouse.
Open: All Year
Grades: ETB Listed
01439 798268 Mrs Smith
Rates fr: *£17.50*-**£17.50**.
Beds: 4D 3T 1S
Baths: 6 Private 1 Shared

Helmsley

National Grid Ref: SE6184

The Feathers

***Buckingham House,** 33 Bridge Street, Helmsley, York, YO6 5DX.*
Listed Georgian town house.
Open: All Year (not Xmas)
01439 770613 Mrs Wood
Rates fr: *£14.00*-**£14.00**.
Beds: 1D 1T 1S **Baths:** 1 Shared
(2)

Stilworth House, 1 Church Street, Helmsley, York, YO6 5AD.
Elegant Georgian town house.
Open: All Year (not Xmas)
Grades: ETB 2 Cr, Comm
01439 771072 Mrs Swift
Rates fr: *£17.50*-**£30.00**.
Beds: 1F 2D 1T
Baths: 3 Private 1 Shared
(4)

Ashdale Road, Helmsley, York, YO6 5DD.
Quiet private house.
Open: All Year (not Xmas)
01439 770375 Mrs Barton
Rates fr: *£13.00*-**£14.00**.
Beds: 1D 1T
Baths: 1 Shared
(2)

4 Elmslac Road, Helmsley, York, YO6 5AP.
Pleasant situation, quiet house.
Open: All Year
01439 770287 Mrs Holding
Rates fr: *£11.50*-**£12.50**.
Beds: 1D
Baths: 1 Private
(8)

Helperby

National Grid Ref: SE0481

Golden Lion Inn

Treble Sykes Farm, Helperby, York, YO6 2SB.
Quiet, panoramic view over Vale of York.
Open: Mar to Oct
Grades: ETB 1 Cr
01423 360667 Mrs Sowray
Rates fr: *£16.00*-**£16.00**.
Beds: 1F 2T
Baths: 2 Shared

High Hawsker

National Grid Ref: NZ9207

Hare & Hounds

York House Private Hotel, High Hawsker, Whitby, N. Yorks, YO22 4LW.
Small modernised Edwardian private hotel.
Open: Easter to Oct
Grades: ETB 3 Cr, Comm, RAC High Acclaim
01947 880314 Mr & Mrs Walley
Rates fr: *£22.00*-**£22.00**.
Beds: 4T
Baths: 4 Ensuite
(6)

Old Blacksmiths Arms, High Hawsker, Whitby, N. Yorks, YO22 4LH.
Converted C17th village pub.
Open: Mar to Oct
01947 880800 Mrs Stubbs
Rates fr: *£16.00*-**£16.00**.
Beds: 1T 1D 1S
Baths: 2 Shared
(10) (3)

High Leven

National Grid Ref: NZ4412

Leven Close Farm, High Leven, Yarm, TS15 9JP.
C17th farmhouse on 250-acre mixed farm.
Open: All Year
Grades: ETB 1 Cr
01642 750114 Mrs Simpson
Rates fr: *£15.00*-**£15.00**.
Beds: 2F 2T **Baths:** 1 Shared
(10)

Hornby

National Grid Ref: NZ3605

Staindale Grange Farm, Hornby, Great Smeaton, Northallerton, N. Yorks, DL6 2JE.
Pleasantly situated farmhouse, good food. **Open:** Mar to Oct
01609 881346 Mrs Robinson
Rates fr: *£14.00*-**£14.00**.
Beds: 1F 1D 1T
(4)

Horsehouse

National Grid Ref: SE0481

Thwaite Arms

The Thwaite Arms, Horsehouse, Leyburn, N. Yorks, DL8 4TS.
Traditional unspoilt Dales inn.
Open: All Year (not Xmas)
01969 640206 Mrs Powell
Rates fr: *£16.50*-**£16.50**.
Beds: 1D 1T **Baths:** 1 Shared
(8)

Horton in Ribblesdale

National Grid Ref: SD8072

Crown Hotel

Middle Studfold Farm, Horton in Ribblesdale, Settle, N. Yorks, BD24 0ER.
Delightfully relaxing C18th farmhouse. **Open:** All Year
01729 860236 Mr Pilkington
Rates fr: *£16.00*-**£16.00**.
Beds: 1F 1D **Baths:** 1 Shared
(8)

Townend Cottage, Townend, Horton in Ribblesdale, Settle, N. Yorks, BD24 0EX.
Quietly situated converted barn/farm. **Open:** All Year
01729 860320 Mrs Wagstaff
Rates fr: *£18.00*-**£20.00**.
Beds: 1D 2T
Baths: 1 Private 1 Shared
(6)

Studfold House, Horton in Ribblesdale, Settle, N. Yorks, BD24 0ER.
Georgian house in own grounds.
Open: All Year (not Xmas)
01729 860200 Mr & Mrs Horsfall
Rates fr: *£16.00*-**£20.00**.
Beds: 1F 2D 1T **Baths:** 2 Shared
(0) (6)

The Willows, Horton in Ribblesdale, Settle, N. Yorks, BD24 0HT.
Large detached house, luxurious bedrooms.
Open: Easter to Sep
01729 860373
Mrs Barker
Rates fr: *£16.00*-**£17.00**.
Beds: 1F 1D 1T
(5)

Hovingham

National Grid Ref: SE6675

Royal Oak, Manor Shovel

Spa House, Hovingham, York, YO6 4LP.
Open: All Year (not Xmas)
01653 628824
Mr Allen
Rates fr: *£22.00*-**£22.00**.
Beds: 1D 1T
Baths: 2 Ensuite
(4)
Secluded & tranquil Victorian spa convenient for country walks, North York Moors, York, Castle Howard. All rooms overlook garden and countryside. Log fires, warm welcome.

Beckside Cottage, Hovingham, York, YO6 4LG.
Fine Georgian oak-beamed cottage.
Open: All Year (not Xmas)
01653 628352 Mrs Lucas
Rates fr: *£14.00*-**£14.00**.
Beds: 1D 1T 1S
Baths: 3 Shared
(0) (2)

Sedgwick Country Guest House, Park Street, Hovingham, York, YO6 4JZ.
Large Victorian country house.
Open: All Year
01653 628740 (also fax no)
Mr Smurthwaite
Rates fr: *£19.50*-**£24.00**.
Beds: 2F 2D 2T 1S
Baths: 1 Ensuite 1 Private
(7)

Hubberholme

National Grid Ref: SD9278

George Inn

The George Inn, Hubberholme, Skipton, N. Yorks, BD23 5JE.
Open: All Year
Grades: RAC Listed
01756 760223 (also fax no)
Mr Lanchbury
Rates fr: *£18.50*-**£25.00**.
Beds: 3D 3T
Baths: 3 Ensuite 2 Shared
(8)
An original & unspoilt C16th Dales country inn. Stone flagged floors. Copper topped tables. Excellent food, wines and beers. J B Priestley's favourite watering hole.

Church Farm, *Hubberholme, Skipton, N. Yorks, BD23 5JE.*
Comfortable farmhouse bed & breakfast.
Open: All Year
01756 760240 Mrs Huck
Rates fr: *£15.00*-**£15.00**.
Beds: 1F 1T **Baths:** 1 Shared

Kirkgill Manor Guest House, *Hubberholme, Skipton, N. Yorks, BD23 5JE.*
Comfortable detached converted old vicarage.
Open: All Year
01756 760800 Mrs Jowsey
Rates fr: *£23.00*-**£28.00**.
Beds: 1F 3D 2T **Baths:** 6 Private
(10)

Huby

National Grid Ref: SE5665

New Inn

New Inn Motel, *Main Street, Huby, York, YO6 1HQ.*
Open: All Year (not Xmas)
Grades: AA 2 Q, Recomm
01347 810219 Mrs Birkinshaw
Rates fr: *£22.50*-**£27.00**.
Beds: 4F 2D 1T 1S
Baths: 8 Ensuite
(8)
The motel is an ideal centre for York, Coast, Moors, Dales, Herriot and 'Heartbeat' country. 8 ensuite bungalows, hospitality tray, colour TV & central heating. Special 2/3 night breaks throughout the year, AA listed, pets welcome.

Hudswell

National Grid Ref: NZ1400

George & Dragon

Holme Farm Cottage, *Hudswell, Richmond, N. Yorks, DL11 6BJ.*
Peaceful country cottage. Richmond 2.5 miles.
Open: All Year
01748 824514 Mrs Farrar
Rates fr: *£15.00*-**£16.00**.
Beds: 1D 1T 1S
Baths: 2 Shared
(3)

Hunmanby

National Grid Ref: TA0977

White Swan

Paddock Lodge, *25 Northgate, Hunmanby, Filey, N. Yorks, YO14 0NT.*
Comfortable guest house, farmhouse breakfast.
Open: All Year (not Xmas)
01723 890581 Mr & Mrs Randerson
Rates fr: *£13.00*-**£16.00**.
Beds: 1F 1D 1T
Baths: 1 Shared
(4)

Wrangham House, *10 Stonegate, Hunmanby, Filey, N. Yorks, YO14 0NS.*
Georgian vicarage in own grounds.
Open: All Year
01723 891333 Miss Shaw
Rates fr: *£27.00*-**£27.00**.
Beds: 7D 4T 2S
Baths: 13 Ensuite
(20)

Husthwaite

National Grid Ref: SE5175

Throstle Nest, *Husthwaite, York, YO6 3SH.*
Comfortable country farmhouse.
Open: All Year (not Xmas)
01347 821291 Mrs Clark
Rates fr: *£12.00*-**£12.00**.
Beds: 1D 1T

Hutton-le-Hole

National Grid Ref: SE7089

The Barn Hotel, *Hutton-le-Hole, York, YO6 6UA.*
Converted and extended stone barn.
Open: All Year (not Xmas)
Grades: ETB 2 Cr, Comm, AA 2 Q
01751 417311 Mrs Fairhurst
Rates fr: *£22.00*-**£22.00**.
Beds: 1F 4D 1T 2S
Baths: 3 Private 2 Shared
(0) (10)

Hammer & Hand Country Guest Hs, *Hutton-le-Hole, York, YO6 6UA.*
Former beerhouse 1784, character features.
Open: All Year (not Xmas)
01751 417300 Mr Wilkins
Rates fr: *£18.00*-**£25.00**.
Beds: 2D 1T
Baths: 3 Private
(5)

Huttons Ambo

National Grid Ref: SE7667

Bar Farm, *Huttons Ambo, York, YO6 7HZ.*
C18th toll house, York 15 minutes.
Open: Easter to October
01653 693267 Mrs Monkman
Rates fr: *£14.00*-**£14.00**.
Beds: 1F 1D
Baths: 1 Private
(6)

Ickornshaw

National Grid Ref: SD9642

The Hawthorns, *Ickornshaw, Cowling, Keighley, W. Yorks, BD22 0DH.*
Bungalow 'Hilton of Ickornshaw'.
Open: All Year (not Xmas)
01535 633299 Mrs Sawley
Rates fr: *£14.50*-**£20.00**.
Beds: 1F 2D 1T
Baths: 2 Private 1 Shared
(5) (6)

Ingleby Arncliffe

National Grid Ref: NZ4400

Monks House, *Ingleby Arncliffe, Northallerton, N. Yorks, DL6 3ND.*
Unique, comfortable, atmospheric C14th residence.
Open: Easter to Oct
01609 882294 Mrs Backhouse
Rates fr: *£15.00*-**£15.00**.
Beds: 1D 1S
Baths: 1 shared
(8)

Ingleby Cross

National Grid Ref: NZ4500

Blue Bell Inn

North York Moors Adventure Ctr, *Park House, Ingleby Cross, Northallerton, N. Yorks, DL6 3PE.*
Comfortable sandstone farmhouse in woodland.
Open: All Year (not Xmas)
01609 882571 Mr Bennett
Rates fr: *£12.00*-**£12.00**.
Beds: 2F 1D 1T 2S
Baths: 2 Shared
(1) (10)

Blue Bell Inn, *Ingleby Cross, Northallerton, N. Yorks, DL6 3NF.*
Friendly village inn.
Open: All Year
01609 882272 Mrs Kinsella
Rates fr: *£15.00*-**£15.00**.
Beds: 2D 3T
(20)

Ingleton

National Grid Ref: SD6973

Bridge Hotel, Craven Heifer, Marton Arms

Springfield Hotel, *Main Street, Ingleton, Carnforth, Lancs, LA6 3HJ.*
Open: All Year (not Xmas)
Grades: ETB 3 Cr, Approv, AA 3 Q, RAC Acclaim
015242 41280
Mr Thornton
Rates fr: *£20.00*-**£20.00**.
Beds: 1F 3D 1T
Baths: 5 Private 1 Shared
(12)
Detached Victorian villa in own grounds. Large garden, car park, patios. Central for Lakes and Dales. Private fishing, home cooking, panoramic views. All rooms ensuite, colour TV.

Stackstead Farm, *Ingleton, Carnforth, Lancs, LA6 3DT.*
Comfortable farmhouse in Yorkshire Dales.
Open: All Year (not Xmas)
Grades: AA 2 Q, Recomm
015242 41386
Mrs Charlton
Fax no: 015242 42407
Rates fr: *£16.00*-**£16.00**.
Beds: 2D 1T
Baths: 2 Ensuite
(6)

Gatehouse Farm, Far West House, ngleton, Carnforth, Lancs, LA6 3NR.
Open: All Year (not Xmas)
Grades: ETB 2 Cr, Comm
015242 41458 / 41307
Mrs Lund
Rates fr: *£16.00*-**£20.00**.
Beds: 1F 1D 1T
Baths: 3 Ensuite
(4)
Oak-beamed working farm built in 1740 in Yorkshire Dales National Park enjoying panoramic views over open countryside. 15 miles from exit 34 M6.

Keld

National Grid Ref: NY8901

Tan Hill Inn

***Frith Lodge,** Keld, Richmond, N. Yorks, DL11 6EB.*
Family-run farmhouse accommodation.
Open: All Year
01748 886489
Mrs Pepper
Rates fr: *£14.00*-**£14.00**.
Beds: 2T
Baths: 1 Shared

***Tan Hill Inn,** Keld, Richmond, N. Yorks, DL11 6ED.*
Highest inn in Great Britain.
Open: All Year (not Xmas)
01833 628246 Mrs Baines
Rates fr: *£18.50*-**£25.00**.
Beds: 2D 5T
Baths: 7 Private
(20)

Kettleness

National Grid Ref: NZ8315

***The Anchorage,** Kettleness, Whitby, N. Yorks, YO21 3RY.*
C17th cliff-top cottage.
Open: Easter to Oct
01947 893386 Mrs Radford
Rates fr: *£13.50*-**£13.50**.
Beds: 1F 1D
Baths: 1 Shared
(3)

Kettlesing

National Grid Ref: SE2256

Queens Head

***Knabbs Ash,** Skipton Road, Kettlesing, Felliscliffe, Harrogate, N. Yorks, HG3 2LT.*
Tranquil, beautiful views. Award winning.
Open: All Year
Grades: ETB 2 Cr, High Comm
01423 771040 Mrs Smith
Rates fr: *£20.00*-**£25.00**.
Beds: 2D 1T
Baths: 3 Private
(10) (6)

Kettlewell

National Grid Ref: SD9772

Race Horses, Bluebell, Fox & Hounds

***The Elms,** Middle Lane, Kettlewell, Skipton, N. Yorks, BD23 5QX.*
Open: All Year (not Xmas)
Grades: ETB 2 Cr, High Comm
01756 760224 Mr Cuthbert
Fax no: 01756 760380
Rates fr: *£20.00*-**£28.00**.
Beds: 2D 1T
Baths: 3 Ensuite
(3)
Warm friendly accommodation in our roomy Victorian home, with a secluded garden, in this typical Yorkshire Dales village. Panoramic views accross & up Upper Wharfedale.

***Lynburn,** Kettlewell, Skipton, N. Yorks, BD23 5RF.*
Comfortable Dales cottage, superb position. **Open:** Easter to Oct
01756 760803 Mrs Thornborrow
Rates fr: *£18.00*-**£25.00**.
Beds: 1D 1T **Baths:** 1 Shared
(2)

***High Fold,** Kettlewell, Skipton, N. Yorks, BD23 5RJ.*
Open: Feb to Dec
Grades: ETB 3 Cr, Deluxe
01756 760390 Mr Earnshaw
Rates fr: *£25.00*-**£30.00**.
Beds: 1F 2D 1T
Baths: 4 Ensuite
(2) (4)
Dales barn recently converted to high standard offering elegant yet relaxing surroundings in quiet picturesque location. Imaginative cuisine. Ground floor rooms for disabled/elderly guests.

Kexby

National Grid Ref: SE7051

Windmill

***Ivy House Farm,** Kexby, York, YO4 5LQ.*
Clean, modern, comfortable farmhouse.
Open: All Year
Grades: AA Listed, RAC Listed
01904 489368 Mrs Daniel
Rates fr: *£14.00*-**£16.00**.
Beds: 1F 1D 1T **Baths:** 1 Shared
(10)

Kilburn

National Grid Ref: SE5179

***Village Farmhouse,** Kilburn, York, YO6 4AG.*
Comfortable farmhouse in picturesque village.
Open: All Year (not Xmas)
01347 868562 Mrs Thompson
Rates fr: *£14.00*.
Beds: 1F 1D **Baths:** 1 Shared

Kildale

National Grid Ref: NZ6009

***Bankside Cottage,** Kildale, Whitby, N. Yorks, YO21 2RT.*
Homely country cottage, beautiful views.
Open: All Year (not Xmas)
01642 723259 Mrs Addison
Rates fr: *£15.00*-**£15.00**.
Beds: 1F 1D 1T
Baths: 1 Shared
(2)

Kirby Hill

National Grid Ref: NZ1306

Shoulder of Mutton Inn

***The Shoulder of Mutton Inn,** Kirby Hill, Richmond, N. Yorks, DL11 7JH.*
Family-run village inn near Richmond, magnificent views.
Open: All Year
Grades: ETB 2 Cr
01748 822772 Mr & Mrs Burns
Rates fr: *£19.50*-**£25.00**.
Beds: 1F 4D **Baths:** 5 Ensuite
(40)

Kirby Misperton

National Grid Ref: SE7779

***Beansheaf Restaurant & Hotel,** Malton Road, Kirby Misperton, Malton, N. Yorks, YO17 0UE.*
Part-C17th house, new hotel extension.
Open: All Year
Grades: ETB 3 Cr, Comm, AA 2 Q
01653 668614 Mrs Sardone
Rates fr: *£20.50*-**£25.00**.
Beds: 2F 7D 4T 7S
Baths: 20 Private
(30)

Kirby-in-Cleveland

National Grid Ref: NZ5208

***Dromonby Hall Farm,** Busby Lane, Kirby-in-Cleveland, Stokesley, Middlesbrough, TS9 7AP.*
Spacious modern farmhouse.
Open: All Year (not Xmas)
01642 712312 Mrs Weighell
Rates fr: *£15.00*-**£17.50**.
Beds: 1D 2T **Baths:** 1 Shared
(2) (6)

Kirkby Malzeard

National Grid Ref: SE2374

Galphay

***Yew Tree Farm,** Kirkby Malzeard, Ripon, N. Yorks, HG4 3SE.*
Converted farm property by farmhouse.
01765 658474 (also fax no)
Mrs Atkinson
Rates fr: *£16.00*-**£20.00**.
Beds: 1F 1D 2T 1S
Baths: 2 Private 1 Shared
(5)

Kirkby Overblow

National Grid Ref: SE3249

Star Garter, Shoulder of Mutton

Barrowby Ripon Diocesan House, *Kirkby Overblow, Harrogate, N. Yorks, HG3 1HY.*
Delightful holiday & conference centre.
Open: All Year (not Xmas)
0113 288 6240 Mr Hewitson
Rates fr: *£17.50*-**£17.50**.
Beds: 2F 2D 9T 8S
Baths: 1 Private 7 Shared

Kirkbymoorside

National Grid Ref: SE6986

Sinnington Common Farm, *Kirkbymoorside, York, YO6 6NX.*
Recently built stone annexe.
Open: All Year (not Xmas)
Grades: ETB 3 Cr
01751 431719 Mrs Wiles
Rates fr: *£16.00*-**£20.00**.
Beds: 1F 1D 1T **Baths:** 3 Private
(4)

Kirklington

National Grid Ref: SE3181

Freemasons Arms, Boot & Shoe

Upsland Farm, *Lime Lane, Well, Kirklington, Bedale, N. Yorks, DL8 2PA.*
Moated site, lovely farmhouse. Brass beds.
Open: All Year (not Xmas)
Grades: ETB 2 Cr, High Comm
01845 567709 Mrs Hodgson
Rates fr: *£20.00*-**£22.00**.
Beds: 3F **Baths:** 3 Ensuite
(4)

Knaresborough

National Grid Ref: SE3557

Mother Shipton Inn

Newton House Hotel, *York Place, Knaresborough, N. Yorks, HG5 0AD.*
Charming C17th former coaching inn.
Open: All Year
Grades: ETB 2 Cr, Comm, AA 3 Q, Recomm, RAC Acclaim
01423 863539 Mr & Mrs Elliott
Fax no: 01423 869748
Rates fr: *£25.00*-**£32.50**.
Beds: 2F 6D 3T 1S
Baths: 11 Ensuite 1 Private
(10)

Planning a longer stay? Always ask for any special rates.

Ebor Mount, *18 York Place, Knaresborough, N. Yorks, HG5 0AA.*
Charming C18th town house.
Open: All Year (not Xmas)
Grades: ETB 2 Cr, Comm, RAC Listed
01423 863315 (also fax no)
Mrs Kneeshaw
Rates fr: *£19.00*-**£25.00**.
Beds: 2F 4D 1T 1S **Baths:** 8 Private
(8)

Leeming Bar

National Grid Ref: SE2890

Little Holtby, *Leeming Bar, Northallerton, N. Yorks, DL7 9LH.*
Open: All Year (not Xmas)
Grades: ETB 2 Cr, High Comm
01609 748762 Mrs Hodgson
Rates fr: *£17.50*-**£20.00**.
Beds: 2D 1T
Baths: 2 Ensuite 1 Private
(10)
Beautiful old farmhouse. Polished wood floors, beams, log fires and furnished with antiques. Lovely bedrooms with wonderful views of the Dales. Large Yorkshire breakfasts!

Nursery Cottage, *Leeming Bar, Northallerton, N. Yorks, DL7 9BG.*
Said to be the best!
Open: Easter to Oct
01677 422861 Mrs Braithwaite
Rates fr: *£17.00*-**£25.00**.
Beds: 1F 1D **Baths:** 1 Shared
(12) (y)

Leyburn

National Grid Ref: SE1190

Sandpiper Inn, Golden Lion

Secret Garden House, *Grove Square, Leyburn, N. Yorks, DL8 5AE.*
Open: All Year (not Xmas)
Grades: ETB 3 Cr, Comm
01969 623589 Mr Digges
Rates fr: *£20.0*-**£18.00**.
Beds: 2D 3T
Baths: 5 Ensuite 1 Shared
(10) (10)
Secluded walled garden & conservatory. Filmed in Herriot series. Off street parking. Ideal for walking & touring. Genealogy weekends. Self catering also available.

Wensley House, *Grove Square, Leyburn, N. Yorks, DL8 5AG.*
Converted terraced Georgian stone farmhouse.
Open: All Year (not Xmas)
01969 623792 Mr Mitchell
Rates fr: *£14.00*-**£14.00**.
Beds: 2D 1T **Baths:** 1 Shared

Cliff Lodge, *Harmby Road, Leyburn, N. Yorks, DL8 5NS.*
Secluded country house, swimming, tennis. **Open:** All Year
01969 623766 Mr & Mrs Childs
Rates fr: *£20.00*-**£25.00**.
Beds: 2D 1T **Baths:** 3 Private
(10)

Littlethorpe

National Grid Ref: SE3269

Moor End Farm, *Knaresborough Road, Littlethorpe, Ripon, N. Yorks, HG4 3LU.*
Comfortable farmhouse. Friendly welcome.
Open: All Year (not Xmas)
Grades: ETB 2 Cr
01765 677419 Mrs Spensley
Rates fr: *£15.50*-**£21.00**.
Beds: 2D 1T
Baths: 1 Ensuite 1 Shared
(5)

Lockton

National Grid Ref: SE8489

Horseshoe Inn, Fox & Rabbit Inn

Ivy Cottage, *Lockton, Pickering, N. Yorks, YO18 7PY.*
Cosy, oak beamed C17th cottage.
Open: All Year (not Xmas)
01751 460325 Mr & Mrs Fisk
Rates fr: *£15.00*-**£18.00**.
Beds: 1F 1D **Baths:** 1 Shared
(5) (4)

Loftus

National Grid Ref: NZ7118

Station Hotel, *Station Road, Loftus, Saltburn-by-the-Sea, TS13 4QB.*
North Yorks-Cleveland border.
Open: All Year
01287 640373 Mr Fitzpatrick
Rates fr: *£11.00*-**£14.00**.
Beds: 2F 3T 2S
Baths: 2 Ensuite 3 Shared

Long Marston

National Grid Ref: SE5051

Gill House Farm, *Tockwith Road, Long Marston, York, YO5 8PJ.*
Peaceful period working family farm. **Open:** All Year
Grades: ETB 3 Cr, High Comm
01904 738379 Mrs Barnitt
Rates fr: *£22.00*-**£30.00**.
Beds: 2F 1D 1T **Baths:** 4 Ensuite

Long Preston

National Grid Ref: SD8358

Maypole Inn

Maypole Inn, *Long Preston, Skipton, N. Yorks, BD23 4PH.*
Open: All Year (not Xmas)
Grades: ETB 3 Cr, Comm
01729 840219 Mr & Mrs Palmer
Rates fr: *£19.50*-**£26.00**.
Beds: 3F 2D 1S **Baths:** 6 Ensuite
(25)
C17th inn on village green. Home-cooked food, real ales, open fires. Direct access to many attractive walks in the surrounding Dales.

Lothersdale

National Grid Ref: SD9645

***Burlington House,** Lothersdale, Keighley, W. Yorks, BD20 8EL.*
Old mill-owner's house.
Open: All Year (not Xmas)
01535 634635 Mrs Wood
Rates fr: *£14.00*-**£14.00**.
Beds: 1D 1T
Baths: 1 Shared
(2)

Lovesome Hill

National Grid Ref: SE3599

***Lovesome Hill Farm,** (off A167), Lovesome Hill, Northallerton, N. Yorks, DL6 2PB.*
Lovely farmhouse with camping barn.
Open: Easter to Nov
01609 772311 Mrs Pearson
Rates fr: *£18.00*-**£20.00**.
Beds: 1F 1D 1T 1S
Baths: 4 Private

Low Row

National Grid Ref: SD9897

Punch Bowl Inn

***Punch Bowl Inn,** Low Row, Richmond, N. Yorks, DL11 6PF.*
Informal, hospitable C17th inn.
Open: All Year
01748 886233 Mr Roe
Rates fr: *£15.00*-**£19.00**.
Beds: 4F 3D 5T 2S
Baths: 5 Private

***Glory Be,** Blades, Low Row, Richmond, N. Yorks, DL11 6PS.*
Luxury, period accommodation, magnificent views.
Open: All Year (not Xmas)
01748 886361 Mrs Jutsum
Rates fr: *£18.00*-**£24.00**.
Beds: 1T 1S
Baths: 1 Ensuite 1 Shared

Malham

National Grid Ref: SD9062

***Miresfield Farm,** Malham, Skipton, N. Yorks, BD23 4DA.*
Open: All Year
Grades: ETB 3 Cr
01729 830414 Mrs Sharp
Rates fr: *£20.00*-**£30.00**.
Beds: 2F 6D 6T 1S
Baths: 12 Private 2 Shared
Listed farmhouse in landscaped garden. All home cooking. Two well furnished lounges with TV & log fires. Groups catered for.

***Eastwood House,** Malham, Skipton, N. Yorks, BD23 4DA.*
Comfortable large semi-detached country house.
Open: All Year
01729 830409 Mr Calvert
Rates fr: *£16.00*-**£18.00**.
Beds: 3F 2D 1T 1S
Baths: 3 Shared
(3)

Malton

National Grid Ref: SE7871

The George

***The Brow,** York Road, Malton, N. Yorks, YO17 0AX.*
Beautiful house with riverside views.
Open: All Year (not Xmas)
01653 693402 Mrs Hopkinson
Rates fr: *£15.00*-**£16.00**.
Beds: 1F 2D 1T 1S
Baths: 3 Ensuite 1 Shared
(8)

***Ivy Chimneys,** 12 East Mount, Malton, N. Yorks, YO17 0EX.*
Victorian house with large garden.
Open: All Year (not Xmas)
Grades: ETB Listed, Comm
01653 693856 Mr & Mrs Rennard
Rates fr: *£14.00*-**£14.00**.
Beds: 2T
Baths: 1 Shared
(3)

Markington

National Grid Ref: SE2865

Drovers, Chequers

***Dole Bank Farm,** Dole Bank, Markington, Harrogate, N. Yorks, HG3 3PJ.*
C14th Listed farmhouse, beautiful setting.
Open: All Year (not Xmas)
01423 771289 (also fax no)
Rates fr: *£17.00*-**£17.00**.
Beds: 2T
Baths: 1 Private 1 Shared
(4)

Marrick

National Grid Ref: SE0798

***Helmsley House,** Marrick, Richmond, N. Yorks, DL11 7LQ.*
Quiet C18th Dales farmhouse.
Open: All Year (not Xmas)
01748 884351 Mrs Sutcliffe
Rates fr: *£15.00*-**£20.00**.
Beds: 2F 1D 1T
Baths: 1 Shared
(4)

Masham

National Grid Ref: SE2280

***Bank Villa Guest House,** Masham, Ripon, N. Yorks, HG4 4DB.*
Stone-built Georgian house.
Open: Easter to Oct
Grades: AA 4 Q
01765 689605 Mr Gill
Rates fr: *£18.00*-**£26.00**.
Beds: 3D 3T
Baths: 1 Shared
(5)

***Lamb Hill Farm,** Masham, Ripon, N. Yorks, HG4 4OJ.*
Spacious old farmhouse on working farm.
Open: Mar to Nov
01765 689274 Mrs Robinson
Rates fr: *£16.00*-**£30.00**.
Beds: 1F 1D 1T
Baths: 3 Private
(8) (4)

Middleham

National Grid Ref: SE1287

Black Swan Hotel

***The Priory Guest House,** Middleham, Leyburn, N. Yorks, DL8 4QC.*
Tastefully restored Georgian house.
Open: Mar to Nov
Grades: ETB 3 Cr, Approv
01969 23279 Mrs Robinson
Rates fr: *£20.00*-**£20.00**.
Beds: 1F 3D 1T 2S
Baths: 4 Ensuite 2 Shared
(6) (8)

***The Priory Guest House,** Middleham, Leyburn, N. Yorks, DL8 4QC.*
Tastefully restored Georgian House.
Open: Mar to Nov
Grades: ETB 3 Cr, Approv
01969 623279 Mrs Robinson
Rates fr: *£19.00*-**£20.00**.
Beds: 3D 2T 2S
Baths: 4 Ensuite 2 Shared
(6) (7)

Moulton

National Grid Ref: NZ1701

***Moulton Manor,** Moulton, Richmond, N. Yorks, DL10 6QG.*
Historic C16th manor house.
Open: All Year (not Xmas/New Year)
01325 377228 Mr & Mrs Vaux
Rates fr: *£16.50*-**£16.50**.
Beds: 1D 2T
Baths: 2 Shared
(10)

Nether Silton

National Grid Ref: SE4592

Gold Cup Inn

***The Gold Cup Inn,** Nether Silton, Thirsk, N. Yorks, YO7 2JZ.*
Quiet country inn.
Open: All Year
01609 883416 Mr Makin
Rates fr: *£17.50*-**£17.50**.
Beds: 1D
Baths: 1 Ensuite

The lowest **single** *rate is shown in* **bold.**

Newbiggin in Bishopdale

National Grid Ref: SD9985

Street Head Inn

Newbiggin House, *Newbiggin in Bishopdale, Leyburn, N. Yorks, DL8 3TD.*
Comfortable house in quiet hamlet.
Open: Feb to Nov
Grades: ETB 1 Cr, Comm
01969 663583
Mrs Proctor
Rates fr: *£13.00*-**£13.00**.
Beds: 1T 1S 1D **Baths:** 2 Shared
(6)

The Street Head Inn, *Newbiggin in Bishopsdale, Leyburn, N. Yorks, DL8 3TE.*
Inn in heart of Dales.
Open: All Year (not Xmas)
01969 663282 (also fax no)
Mr White
Rates fr: *£20.00*. **Beds:** 2D 1T
Baths: 2 Ensuite 1 Private
(20)

Newby Wiske

National Grid Ref: SE3688

Black Swan

Well House, *Newby Wiske, Northallerton, N. Yorks, DL7 9EX.*
Victorian private house, lovely gardens.
Open: All Year (not Xmas)
Grades: ETB Listed.
01609 772253 (also fax no)
Mrs Smith
Rates fr: *£15.00*-**£15.00**.
Beds: 1F 1D **Baths:** 1 Shared
(0)

Newton-on-Rawcliffe

National Grid Ref: SE8190

Swan Hotel

Swan Cottage, *Newton-on-Rawcliffe, Pickering, N. Yorks, YO18 8QA.*
Comfortable, homely C18th cottage. **Open:** All Year
01751 472502
Mrs Heaton
Rates fr: *£14.00*-**£14.00**.
Beds: 1D 1T 1S
Baths: 1 Shared
(2)

North Grimston

National Grid Ref: SE8467

Middleton Arms, *North Grimston, Malton, N. Yorks, YO17 8AX.*
Country pub, at foot of escarpment.
Open: All Year (not Xmas)
01944 768255
Mrs Grayston
Rates fr: *£17.50*-**£22.50**.
Beds: 2D 1T
Baths: 1 Private 1 Shared

Northallerton

National Grid Ref: SE3794

Potto Grange, *Northallerton, N. Yorks, DL6 3HH.*
Open: May to Nov
Grades: ETB 1 Cr, High Comm
01642 700212 (also fax no)
Major & Mrs Kynge
Rates fr: *£22.00*-**£22.00**.
Beds: 2D 1T
Baths: 2 Ensuite 1 Private
(4)
Serene Georgian farmhouse in own parkland on the edge of the National Park. Lovely gardens, spacious sunny bedrooms, comfort, tranquillity, good food. Tennis, croquet. Brochure.

Alverton Guest House, *26 South Parade, Northallerton, N. Yorks, DL7 8SG.*
Modernised Victorian town house.
Open: All Year (not Xmas)
Grades: ETB 3 Cr, AA 3 Q, RAC Acclaim
01609 776207 Mr Longley
Rates fr: *£18.50*-**£18.00**.
Beds: 1F 1D 1T 2S
Baths: 3 Private 1 Shared
(4)

Norton

National Grid Ref: SE7971

Harvest Mouse Bed & Breakfast, *Norton Parks, Norton, Malton, N. Yorks, YO17 8EE.*
Working farm, central Ryedale attractions.
Open: Easter to Nov
01653 692738
Mrs Monkman
Rates fr: *£13.50*-**£13.50**.
Beds: 1D 1T **Baths:** 1 Shared
(4)

Grange Guest House, *33 Grange Road, Norton, Stockton-on-Tees, N. Yorks, TS20 2NS.*
Home cooking, clean and very friendly.
Open: All Year
01642 552541
Mrs Chesworth
Rates fr: *£18.00*-**£18.00**.
Beds: 4T 5S
Baths: 2 Ensuite 1 Shared

Osmotherley

National Grid Ref: SE4597

Queen Catherine Hotel

Foxton Mill, *Osmotherley, Northallerton, N. Yorks, DL6 3PZ.*
Converted C17th corn mill.
Open: All Year (not Xmas)
01609 883377
Mrs Russell
Rates fr: *£20.00*-**£20.00**.
Beds: 1D 1T
Baths: 1 Private 1 Shared
(10) (6)

Quintana House, *Back Lane, Osmotherley, Northallerton, N. Yorks, DL6 3BJ.*
Detached stone cottage, National Park.
Open: All Year (not Xmas)
Grades: ETB Listed, Comm
01609 883258 Dr Bainbridge
Rates fr: *£16.50*.
Beds: 1D 1T **Baths:** 1 Shared
(6) (4)

The Queen Catherine Hotel, *Osmotherley, Northallerton, N. Yorks, DL6 3AG.*
Comfortable friendly, value for money. **Open:** All Year
01609 883209 Mrs Bell
Rates fr: *£17.00*-**£17.00**.
Beds: 1D 3T 1S **Baths:** 1 Shared
(y)

Over Silton

National Grid Ref: SE4593

Gold Cup Inn

Thistle Garth, *Over Silton, Thirsk, N. Yorks, YO7 2LJ.*
Large family country house.
Open: All Year (not Xmas)
01609 883495 Mrs Martin
Rates fr: *£14.00*-**£15.00**.
Beds: 2D 1T **Baths:** 1 Shared
(10) (4)

Pateley Bridge

National Grid Ref: SE1565

Grassfields Country Hotel, *Wath Road, Pateley Bridge, Harrogate, N. Yorks, HG3 5HL.*
Open: All Year
Grades: ETB 3 Cr, Comm, AA 2 St
01423 711412 Mrs Garforth
Rates fr: *£19.00*-**£25.00**.
Beds: 2F 2D 4T 1S
Baths: 9 Ensuite
(20)
Georgian mansion in private grounds. Wholesome meals prepared from local produce in this friendly family-run hotel set in an Area of Outstanding Natural Beauty.

Woodlands, *Bewerley, Pateley Bridge, Harrogate, N. Yorks, HG3 5HS.*
Comfortable Victorian house. Wonderful views.
Open: All Year (not Xmas)
01423 711175 Mrs Shaw
Rates fr: *£16.00*-**£20.00**.
Beds: 1D 1T **Baths:** 2 Private
(2)

Roslyn Hotel, *9 King Street, Pateley Bridge, Harrogate, N. Yorks, HG3 5AT.*
Large Victorian house.
Open: All Year
01423 711374 Mr Briggs
Rates fr: *£19.00*-**£23.50**.
Beds: 2F 3D 1T **Baths:** 6 Private
(5) (6)

Pickering

National Grid Ref: SE7984

Forest & Vale Hotel, India Garden Restaurant

Sunnyside, *Carr Lane, Middleton, Pickering, N. Yorks, YO18 8PD.*
Open: Easter to Nov
Grades: ETB 2 Cr, High Comm
01751 476104 (also fax no)
Mr Whitaker
Rates fr: *£18.00*-**£24.00**.
Beds: 1F 1D 1T
Baths: 3 Ensuite
(3)
Large comfortable chalet bungalow. South facing over countryside. 2 ground floor rooms. All rooms ensuite. Ideal centre 'Heartbeat' country, coast, Moors, York & steam railway.

Grindale House, *123 Eastgate, Pickering, N. Yorks, YO18 7DW.*
Open: All Year
Grades: ETB 2 Cr, Comm
01751 476636 Mrs Dawson
Rates fr: *£20.00*-**£25.00**.
Beds: 2D 1T
Baths: 3 Ensuite
(6)
We hope you'll love our C18th stone townhouse. Antique bedsteads, country-style rooms, beamed lounge. Friendly informal place with large car park, bicycle storage.

Kirkham Garth, *Whitby Road, Pickering, N. Yorks, YO18 7AT.*
Quiet, private, homely residence.
Open: All Year (not Xmas)
01751 474931 Mrs Rayner
Rates fr: *£15.00*-**£17.00**.
Beds: 1F 1D 1T 1S
(3)

Rains Farm, *Allerston, Pickering, N. Yorks, YO18 7PQ.*
Open: All Year
Grades: ETB 2 Cr
01723 859333 (also fax no)
Mrs Allanson
Rates fr: *£18.50*-**£18.50**.
Beds: 2D 2T 1S
Baths: 5 Ensuite
(10)
Farm nestles in peaceful picturesque location, close Moors, coast, forest, steam railway, York. High standards of comfort, excellent food. Warm welcome. Set in open countryside.

Eden House, *120 Eastgate, Pickering, N. Yorks, YO18 7DW.*
Charming, comfortable, Listed Yorkshire cottage.
Open: All Year (not Xmas)
Grades: ETB 2 Cr, Comm
01751 472289 (also fax no)
Mr Smith
Rates fr: *£16.00*-**£20.00**.
Beds: 2D 1T
Baths: 1 Ensuite 1 Private 1 Shared
(3)

Port Mulgrave

National Grid Ref: NZ7917

Ship Inn

The Ship Inn, *Port Mulgrave, Hinderwell, Saltburn-by-the-Sea, TS13 5JZ.*
Traditional family run village pub.
Open: All Year
01947 840303 Mrs Nedley
Rates fr: *£15.00*-**£15.00**.
Beds: 2F 2S
Baths: 2 Shared
(10)

Ramsgill

National Grid Ref: SE1171

Yorke Arms

Longside House, *Ramsgill, Pateley Bridge, N. Yorks, HG3 5RH.*
Open: Mar to Nov
Grades: ETB Listed
01423 755207 Mrs Crosse
Rates fr: *£21.00*-**£25.00**.
Beds: 1F 1D 1T
Baths: 2 Ensuite 1 Private
(4)
Former shooting lodge 6 miles from Pateley Bridge on the 53 miles Nidderdale Way. A.O.N.B. Superb views towards Gouthwaite Reservoir & its bird sanctuary.

Raskelf

National Grid Ref: SE4971

Old Farmhouse, *Raskelf, York, YO6 3LF.*
Former farmhouse now comfortable hotel.
Open: Feb to 20th Dec.
Grades: ETB 3 Cr, High Comm, AA 4 Q, Select
01347 821971 Mr Frost
Fax no: 01347 822392
Rates fr: *£24.00*-**£27.00**.
Beds: 2F 6D 2T
Baths: 10 Private
(10)

Ravenscar

National Grid Ref: NZ9801

Bide A While Guest House, *3 Loring Road, Ravenscar, Scarborough, N. Yorks, YO13 4LY.*
Small family guest house.
Open: All Year
Grades: ETB Listed, Approv
01723 870643 Mr & Mrs Leach
Rates fr: *£16.50*-**£18.50**.
Beds: 2F 2D
Baths: 1 Shared

All rates are subject to alteration at the owners' discretion.

Smugglers Rock, *Country Guest House, Ravenscar, Scarborough, N. Yorks, YO13 0ER.*
Old smuggling inn, refurbished & restored.
Open: Mar to Nov
01723 870044 Mr Greenfield
Rates fr: *£19.00*-**£19.00**.
Beds: 1F 3D 2T 2S
Baths: 8 Private
(3) (12)

Dunelm, *Raven Hall Road, Ravenscar, Scarborough, N. Yorks, YO13 0NA.*
Comfortable accommodation, splendid view.
Open: All Year (not Xmas)
01723 870430 Ms Bartlet
Rates fr: *£13.00*-**£13.00**.
Beds: 1D 1T 2S
Baths: 2 Shared

Redcar

National Grid Ref: NZ6124

3 Newcomen Terrace, *Redcar, TS10 1AT.*
Centrally located, sea views available.
Open: All Year
01642 472767 Mrs Heinze
Rates fr: *£10.00*-**£11.00**.
Beds: 2F 4T 3S
Baths: 2 Shared

Tudor Lodge, *7 Turner Street, Redcar, TS10 1AT.*
Family-run private hotel.
Open: All Year
01642 474883 Mr Noble
Rates fr: *£10.50*-**£12.50**.
Beds: 1F 3D 3T 7S
Baths: 3 Shared

Reeth

National Grid Ref: SE0499

Kings Arms Hotel, Bridge Inn

Springfield House, *Quaker Close, Reeth, Richmond, N. Yorks, DL11 6UY.*
Comfortable stone built private house.
Open: All Year (not Xmas)
Grades: ETB Listed, Comm
01758 84634 Mrs Guy
Rates fr: *£16.00*-**£16.00**.
Beds: 1D 1T 1S
Baths: 1 Shared
(9) (5)

2 Bridge Terrace, *Reeth, Richmond, N. Yorks, DL11 6TP.*
A welcoming, friendly home.
Open: Easter to Oct
01748 884572
Mrs Davies
Rates fr: *£14.50*-**£17.00**.
Beds: 1D 1T
Baths: 1 Shared

Arkle House, *Mill Lane, Reeth, Richmond, N. Yorks,* *DL11 6SJ.*
Large Georgian private house.
Open: All Year (not Xmas)
01748 884815 Mr Simpson
Rates fr: *£15.00*-**£20.00**.
Beds: 1F 1T 1D
Baths: 2 Ensuite 1 Shared
(11) (3)

Ribblehead

National Grid Ref: SD7880

Station Inn

Gearstones Farm, *Ribblehead, Ingleton, Carnforth, Lancs,* *LA6 3AS.*
Old Dales farm cottage.
Open: Easter to Oct
015242 41405 Mrs Timmins
Rates fr: *£14.00*-**£14.00**.
Beds: 1F 1D 1T **Baths:** 1 Shared

Station Inn, *Ribblehead, Ingleton, Carnforth, Lancs,* *LA6 3AS.*
Comfortable country inn, fantastic views. **Open:** All Year
015242 41274 Mr Coates
Rates fr: *£17.50*-**£16.00**.
Beds: 1F 3D 1T
Baths: 3 Ensuite 1 Shared
(50)

Riccall

National Grid Ref: SE6237

South Newlands Farm, *Selby Road, Riccall, York,* *YO4 6QR.*
Comfortable converted barn, family-run.
Open: All Year
01757 248203 Mrs Swann
Rates fr: *£14.00*-**£16.00**.
Beds: 1F 1D 1T
Baths: 2 Private 1 Shared

Richmond

National Grid Ref: NZ1701

Black Lion, Shoulder of Mutton Inn, Holly Hill

The Buck Inn, *Newbiggin, Richmond, N. Yorks,* *DL10 4DX.*
Open: All Year
01748 822259 Mrs Fluen
Rates fr: *£22.00*-**£25.00**.
Beds: 2F 2D 1T 1S
Baths: 6 Ensuite
Beautiful olde inn with grand views of Castle, Swale Valley and Colloden Folly. All rooms ensuite. Beautiful beer garden & friendly inn.

Bringing children with you? Always ask for any special rates.

58 Frenchgate, *Richmond, N. Yorks,* *DL10 7AG.*
Open: Easter to Oct
Grades: ETB Listed
01748 823227 Mrs Fifoot
Rates fr: *£18.00*.
Beds: 1D 1T
Baths: 1 Ensuite 1 Private
(1)
Beautiful Georgian house in elegant Frenchgate. Spacious room, comfortable brass bed with cotton sheets. Delicious breakfast served in the conservatory. Breathtaking views & lovely gardens.

The Castle Tavern, *Market Place, Richmond, N. Yorks,* *DL10 4HU.*
Grade II Listed building of great character. **Open:** All Year
01748 823187 Mrs Chaplin
Rates fr: *£16.00*-**£16.00**.
Beds: 1D 1T 1S **Baths:** 2 Shared

The Shoulder of Mutton Inn, *Kirby Hill, Richmond, N. Yorks,* *DL11 7JH.*
Open: All Year
Grades: ETB 2 Cr
01748 822772 Mr & Mrs Burns
Rates fr: *£19.50*-**£25.00**.
Beds: 1F 4D **Baths:** 5 Ensuite
(40)
Family-run village inn near Richmond, holding an elevated position giving magnificent views. Two bars, dining room, log fires, home cooking.

Hillcrest, *Sleegill, Richmond, N. Yorks,* *DL10 4RH.*
Country home overlooking castle.
Open: Easter to Sep
01748 823280 Mrs Irwin
Rates fr: *£15.00*-**£15.00**.
Beds: 1D 1T 1S
Baths: 1 Shared
(6) (3)

Rievaulx

National Grid Ref: SE5785

Barn Close Farm, *Rievaulx, Helmsley, York,* *YO6 5LH.*
'Daily Telegraph' recommended, quiet, comfortable.
Open: All Year
Grades: ETB 3 Cr, High Comm
01439 798321 Mrs Milburn
Rates fr: *£16.00*-**£18.00**.
Beds: 1F 1D
Baths: 1 Ensuite 1 Private
(Any)

Ripley

National Grid Ref: SE2860

Newton Hall Farm, *Ripley, Harrogate, N. Yorks,* *HG3 3DZ.*
Friendly, peaceful countryside views.
Open: All Year
01423 770166 Mrs Iveson
Rates fr: *£18.00*-**£25.00**.
Beds: 2D 1T**Baths:** 1 Shared

Slate Rigg Farm, *Birthwaite Lane, Ripley, Harrogate, N. Yorks,* *HG3 3JQ.*
Quiet, rural, working farm.
Open: All Year (not Xmas)
01423 770135 Mrs Bowes
Rates fr: *£15.00*-**£22.00**.
Beds: 1F 1T
Baths: 2 Shared
(4)

Ripon

National Grid Ref: SE3171

Golden Lion, Mr Beaujangles

St Georges Court, *Old Home Farm, Grantley, Ripon, N. Yorks,* *HG4 3EU.*
Open: All Year (not Xmas)
Grades: ETB 2 Cr, Comm
01765 620618 Mrs Gordon
Rates fr: *£19.00*.
Beds: 1F 3D 1T
Baths: 5 Ensuite
(12)
Peace & tranquillity. Beautifully situated, comfortable ground floor rooms in renovated farm buildings. Delicious breakfasts served in our charming Listed farmhouse. Let us charm you.

Beech House, *7 South Crescent, Ripon, N. Yorks,* *HG4 1SW.*
Large Victorian private house.
Open: Easter to Oct
01765 603294 Mrs Darbyshire
Rates fr: *£16.00*-**£16.00**.
Beds: 1D 1T 1S
Baths: 1 Private 1 Shared
(3)

Bishopton Grove House, *Ripon, N. Yorks,* *HG4 2QL.*
Large comfortable quiet Georgian house.
Open: All Year
Grades: ETB 1 Cr, Comm
01765 600888 Mrs Wimpress
Rates fr: *£17.50*-**£20.00**.
Beds: 1F 1D 1T
Baths: 1 Ensuite 2 Shared

The Coopers, *36 College Road, Ripon, N. Yorks,* *HG4 2HA.*
Large, comfortable, Victorian private house.
Open: All Year (not Xmas)
Grades: ETB 2 Cr
01765 603708 Mr Cooper
Rates fr: *£14.00*-**£16.00**.
Beds: 1F 1T 1S
Baths: 1 Private 1 Shared
(0) (2)

Please respect a B&B's wishes regarding children, animals & smoking.

***Kingstonia,** 109 Harrogate Road, Ripon, N. Yorks, HG4 1TB.*
Lovely house, garden, swimming pool.
Open: All Year
01765 600395 Mrs Pope
Rates fr: *£20.00*-**£20.00**.
Beds: 1F 1S 1D1T
Baths: 1 Shared
(2) (6)

Robin Hood's Bay

National Grid Ref: NZ9504

Bay Hotel, Dolphin Hotel, Grosvenor Hotel, Victoria Hotel

***Meadowfield,** Mount Pleasant North, Robin Hood's Bay, Whitby, N. Yorks, YO22 4RE.*
Victorian house, in quiet road.
Open: All Year
01947 880564 Mrs Luker
Rates fr: *£14.00*-**£18.00**.
Beds: 3D 2T 1S
Baths: 1 Private 1 Shared

***The White Owl,** Station Road, Robin Hood's Bay, Whitby, N. Yorks, YO22 4RL.*
Large private house, central location.
Open: All Year
01947 880879 Mr & Mrs Higgins
Rates fr: *£15.50*-**£15.50**.
Beds: 1F 1D 1T **Baths:** 3 Private
(3)

***Gilders Green,** Raw, Robin Hood's Bay, Whitby, N. Yorks, YO22 4PP.*
C17th farm cottage on working farm.
Open: Easter to Oct
01947 880025 Mrs Reynolds
Rates fr: *£14.00*-**£15.00**.
Beds: 1F **Baths:** 1 Shared

***Rosegarth,** Thorpe Lane, Robin Hood's Bay, Whitby, N. Yorks, YO22 4RN.*
Modern comfortable semi detached house. **Open:** Easter to Oct
Grades: ETB Listed
01947 880578 Mrs Stubbs
Rates fr: *£15.00*-**£17.00**.
Beds: 1D 1T 1S
Baths: 1 Shared
(11) (4)

Roecliffe

National Grid Ref: SE3765

Crown Inn

***The Crown Inn,** Roecliffe, York, YO5 9LY.*
Luxurious rooms in C17th inn.
Open: All Year
Grades: AA 4 Q, RAC 2 St
01423 322578 Mr Barker
Fax no: 01423 324060
Rates fr: *£25.00*-**£35.00**.
Beds: 1F 7D 5T 1S
Baths: 12 Ensuite 2 Shared

Rosedale Abbey

National Grid Ref: SE7295

Milburn Arms Hotel

***Low Bell End Farm,** Rosedale Abbey, Pickering, N. Yorks, YO18 8RE.*
Comfortable accommodation on working farm.
Open: All Year (not Xmas)
01751 417451 Mrs Brayshaw
Rates fr: *£13.00*-**£14.00**.
Beds: 1F 1D 1T
Baths: 1 Shared
(4)

***The White Horse Farm Hotel,** Rosedale Abbey, Pickering, N. Yorks, YO18 8SA.*
Converted C17th farmhouse.
Open: All Year (not Xmas)
Grades: ETB 3 Cr, Comm, AA 2 St
01751 417239 Mrs Proctor
Rates fr: *£30.00*-**£34.00**.
Beds: 2F 11D 2T
Baths: 15 Private 1 Shared
(50)

***Sevenford House,** Rosedale Abbey, Pickering, N. Yorks, YO18 8SE.*
Victorian vicarage, 3 acres of grounds.
Open: All Year (not Xmas)
01751 417283 Ms Sugars
Rates fr: *£18.0*-**£18.00**.
Beds: 1F 1D 1T
Baths: 3 Ensuite
(9)

Roxby

National Grid Ref: NZ7818

Fox Inn

***Fox Inn,** Roxby, Staithes, Saltburn-by-the-Sea, N. Yorks, TS13 5EB.*
Small friendly village inn.
Open: All Year (not Xmas)
01947 840335
Mrs Stevenson
Rates fr: *£18.00*-**£20.00**.
Beds: 1F 1D
Baths: 1 Shared
(12)

Rufforth

National Grid Ref: SE5251

Buckles Inn, Tankard Inn

***Rosedale Guest House,** Wetherby Road, Rufforth, York, YO2 3QB.*
Comfortable village guest house.
Open: All Year (not Xmas)
Grades: ETB 2 Cr, Comm
01904 738297
Mrs Smith
Rates fr: *£17.50*-**£16.00**.
Beds: 1F 2D 1T 1S
Baths: 1 Ensuite 2 Shared
(2) (6)

***Wellgarth House,** Rufforth, York, YO2 3QB.*
Quietly situated, large detached house.
Open: All Year (not Xmas)
Grades: ETB 2 Cr, Comm, AA 4 Q, Listed
01904 738592 Mrs Cundall
Rates fr: *£15.00*-**£17.00**.
Beds: 1F 3D 2T 1S
Baths: 5 Private 2 Shared
(2) (10)

Runswick Bay

National Grid Ref: NZ8016

Royal Hotel

***Cockpit House,** The Old Village, Runswick Bay, Saltburn-by-the-Sea, TS13 5HU.*
Large seafront cottage, sea views.
Open: All Year (not Xmas)
01947 840504 / 603047 Mrs Smith
Rates fr: *£15.00*-**£15.00**.
Beds: 2T
Baths: 1 Shared
(5)

Salton

National Grid Ref: SE7180

***Low Northolm Farm,** Salton, Kirkbymoorside, York, YO6 6RP.*
Lovely Georgian farmhouse. Tranquil location.
Open: Mar to Oct
01751 432321 Ms Pierson
Rates fr: *£18.00*-**£18.00**.
Beds: 1F 1T
Baths: 2 Ensuite
(5) (4)

Sandsend

National Grid Ref: NZ8612

***Estbek House,** Sandsend, Whitby, N. Yorks, YO21 3SU.*
Tastefully furnished stone Georgian house.
Open: Easter to Oct
01947 893424 Mr Cooper
Rates fr: *£20.00.*
Beds: 3D 1T
Baths: 4 Private

Scalby

National Grid Ref: TA0190

Rosette Inn

***Wrea Head House,** Wrea Head Farm, Barmoor Lane, Scalby, Scarborough, N. Yorks, YO13 0PG.*
Lovely country house. Y.H.T.B. B&B of the Year.
Open: Easter to Oct
01723 375844 Mrs Wood
Fax no: 01723 500274
Rates fr: *£25.00*-**£27.50**.
Beds: 2D 1T
Baths: 3 Ensuite
(6)

Scarborough

National Grid Ref: TA0388

Crescent Hotel Bar, Rosette Inn, Scarborough Arms

Stewart Hotel, *St Nicholas Cliff, Scarborough, N. Yorks, YO11 2ES.*
Open: All Year
Grades: ETB Listed
01723 361095 Mr Pummell
Rates fr: *£20.00*-**£20.00**.
Beds: 3F 10D 2T
Baths: 15 Ensuite
Close to the Cleveland Way on the cliff. Beach & shopping nearby. Good beer & food yards away. Start the day with a good breakfast.

Highbank Hotel, *5 Givendale Road, Scarborough, N. Yorks, YO12 6LE.*
Non-smoking hotel, quiet area.
Open: All Year
01723 365265 Mr Marsh
Rates fr: *£18.00*-**£18.00**.
Beds: 1F 3D 1T 2S
Baths: 7 Ensuite
(5) (10)

Boundary Hotel, *124-126 North Marine Road, Scarborough, N. Yorks, YO12 7HZ.*
Open: All Year
01723 376737 / 0500 543224
Mr & Mrs Fenton
Rates fr: *£16.00*-**£16.00**.
Beds: 7F 2D 1T 2S
Baths: 12 Private
(1)
Comfortable hotel, all en-suite. Ideally situated for North & South Bays town centre, cricket ground, Peaseholme Park Swimming Pools, Kinderland and Mr Marvel's Amusement Park.

Dodsworth Hotel, *41 Albemarle Crescent, Scarborough, N. Yorks, YO11 1XX.*
Friendly hotel, vegetarians, children, pets welcome.
Open: All Year
01723 372861
Mrs Williams
Rates fr: *£14.50*-**£14.50**.
Beds: 2F 3D 1T 2S
Baths: 2 Shared

Lonsdale Villa Hotel, *Lonsdale Road, South Cliff, Scarborough, N. Yorks, YO11 2QY.*
Open: Feb to Nov
Grades: ETB 2 Cr, Comm
01723 363383
Mr & Mrs Wilson
Rates fr: *£18.00*-**£18.00**.
Beds: 2F 5D 1T 1S
Baths: 9 Ensuite
Friendly family-run licensed South Cliff hotel. All rooms ensuite. Excellent home cooked meals with choice of menu. Vegetarians catered for. Weekly rates. Brochure available.

Glenderry Non-Smoking Guest House, *26 The Dene, Scarborough, N. Yorks, YO12 7NJ.*
Quiet residential area. Small & friendly.
Open: All Year (not Xmas)
Grades: ETB 2 Cr, Comm
01723 362546
Mr & Mrs Harrison
Rates fr: *£14.00*-**£14.00**.
Beds: 3F 1D 1S
Baths: 2 Private 1 Shared
(2)

The Girvan Hotel, *61 Northstead Manor Drive, Scarborough, N. Yorks, YO12 6AF.*
Charming detached hotel overlooking park.
Open: All Year
01723 364518 Mrs Hurrell
Rates fr: *£14.00*-**£15.00**.
Beds: 4F 2D 1T 5S
Baths: 12 Ensuite
(12)

Wrea Head House, *Wrea Head Farm, Barmoor Lane, Scalby, Scarborough, N. Yorks, YO13 0PG.*
Open: Easter to Oct
01723 375844 Mrs Wood
Fax no: 01723 500274
Rates fr: *£25.00*-**£27.50**.
Beds: 2D 1T
Baths: 3 Ensuite
(6)
Lovely country house. Y.H.T.B. B& B of the Year - commended 1992. Luxury ensuite bedrooms. Non-smoking, private parking & sea views. Indoor swimming pool, jacuzzi & sauna.

Brincliffe Edge Hotel, *105 Queens Parade, Scarborough, N. Yorks, YO12 7HY.*
Family-run hotel overlooking sea.
Open: Easter to Oct
01723 364834
Mr & Mrs Sutcliffe
Rates fr: *£17.00*-**£17.00**.
Beds: 2F 7D 1T 1S
Baths: 9 Ensuite 2 Shared
(7)

Kenilworth Hotel, *90 North Marine Road, Scarborough, N. Yorks, YO12 7JA.*
Small, select, friendly & comfortable.
Open: Feb to Nov
01723 374611 Mr Ellis
Rates fr: *£15.00*-**£15.00**.
Beds: 1F 5D 1S
Baths: 3 Ensuite 2 Shared
(5)

Argo Hotel, *134 North Marine Road, Scarborough, N. Yorks, YO12 7HZ.*
Friendly, family-run, licensed hotel.
Open: All Year
01723 375745
Mr & Mrs Sugden
Rates fr: *£13.00*-**£13.00**.
Beds: 3F 2D 1T 2S
Baths: 2 Ensuite 1 Shared

Wheatcroft Motel, *156 Filey Road, Scarborough, N. Yorks, YO11 3AA.*
Modern facilities, old fashioned courtesy.
Open: All Year (not Xmas)
01723 374613 Mrs Batty
Rates fr: *£17.50*-**£17.50**.
Beds: 2F 3D 1T 1S
Baths: 7 Ensuite
(7)

Howdale Hotel, *121 Queens Parade, Scarborough, N. Yorks, YO12 7HU.*
Comfortable hotel, panoramic sea views.
Open: All Year (not Xmas)
01723 372696
Mr & Mrs Abbott
Rates fr: *£15.00*.
Beds: 1F 11D 2T 1S
Baths: 13 Ensuite 2 Shared
(9)

Villa Marina Hotel, *59 Northstead Manor Drive, Scarborough, N. Yorks, YO12 6AF.*
Modern detached hotel overlooking park.
Open: Easter to Oct
Grades: ETB 3 Cr
01723 361088 Mr & Mrs Pearson
Rates fr: *£20.00*-**£20.00**.
Beds: 4F 5D 2T
Baths: 11 Private
(3) (9)

Scruton

National Grid Ref: SE3092

Swaledale Arms

Richmond House, *6 Beech Close, Scruton, Northallerton, N. Yorks, DL7 0TU.*
Superb accommodation in delightful village.
Open: Apr to Oct
01609 748369
Mr & Mrs Coppin
Rates fr: *£13.00*-**£15.00**.
Beds: 1D
Baths: 1 Shared
(1)

Selby

National Grid Ref: SE6132

Abbey Vaults, Londesborough Hotel, Grey Horse

Hazeldene Guest House, *32-34 Brook Street, Selby, N. Yorks, YO8 0AR.*
Large Victorian town house.
Open: All Year (not Xmas)
Grades: ETB Listed, Approv, AA Listed, Recomm, RAC Listed, Acclaim
01757 704809
Mr Leake
Fax no: 01757 709300
Rates fr: *£15.00*-**£17.00**.
Beds: 1F 2D 2T 2S
Baths: 1 Ensuite 2 Shared
(2) (5)

Selside

Vational Grid Ref: SD8072

***outh House Farm,** Selside, Settle, V. Yorks, BD24 0HU.*
Modern, comfortable farmhouse.
)pen: All Year (not Xmas)
1729 860271 Ms Kenyon
tates fr: *£15.00*-**£15.00**.
Beds: 1F 2D 1T
Baths: 1 Shared
(1) (6)

Sessay

Vational Grid Ref: SE4575

***)owne House Farm,** Sessay, Thirsk, N. Yorks, YO7 3BE.*
Large, Grade II Listed Victorian ouse.
)pen: All Year (not Xmas)
1845 501221
Mrs Seaman
tates fr: *£12.50*-**£12.50**.
Beds: 1D 1T
Baths: 1 Shared

Settle

Vational Grid Ref: SD8163

***angcliffe Lodge,** Langcliffe Road, ettle, N. Yorks, BD24 9LT.*
Attractive cosy Victorian country odge.
)pen: All Year
1729 823362 Mrs Westall
tates fr: *£16.50*-**£16.50**.
Beds: 1D 1T
Baths: 2 Ensuite
(4)

***Vhitebeam Croft,** Duke Street, ettle, N. Yorks, BD24 9AN.*
Modern comfortable house, warm velcome.
)pen: All Year (not Xmas)
1729 822824
Mrs Houlton
tates fr: *£15.00*-**£15.00**.
Beds: 1F 1T
Baths: 2 Shared
(3)

***iverpool House,** Chapel Square, ettle, N. Yorks, BD24 9HR.*
Mid C18th town house.
)pen: All Year
1729 822247
Mrs Duerden
tates fr: *£16.00*-**£16.00**.
Beds: 2D 3T 3S
Baths: 2 Shared
(8)

***halimbana Cottage,** 3 Ribble errace, Settle, N. Yorks, BD24 9DE.*
Homely accommodation in private ouse.
)pen: All Year (not Xmas)
1729 823988 Mrs Jarvis
tates fr: *£14.50*-**£16.00**.
Beds: 1F 1D 1T
Baths: 1 Shared

Sherburn

National Grid Ref: SE9577

Station Inn

***Pigeon Pie,** Sherburn, Malton, N. Yorks, YO17 8QB.*
Old coaching inn.
Open: All Year (not Xmas)
01944 710383
Rates fr: *£17.00*-**£19.50**.
Beds: 1D 1T 2S
Baths: 1 Shared
(100)

Sherburn in Elmet

National Grid Ref: SE4933

Half Moon Inn

***Wheelgate Guest House,** 7 Kirkgate, Sherburn in Elmet, Leeds, N Yorks, LS25 6BH.*
Olde worlde cottage-style house.
Open: All Year (not Xmas)
01977 682231
Mrs Tomlinson
Rates fr: *£16.00*-**£23.00**.
Beds: 1D 3T
Baths: 1 Ensuite 2 Shared
(1) (7)

Skelton

National Grid Ref: NZ6518

Holy Bush Hotel, Blacksmiths Arms, Ship Inn

***Westerlands Guest House,** 27 East Parade, Skelton, Saltburn-by-the-Sea, N. Yorks, TS12 2BJ.*
Modern, large detached country house.
Open: Mar to Oct
01287 650690
Mr Bull
Rates fr: *£14.00*-**£14.00**.
Beds: 3D 3S
Baths: 2 Private 4 Shared
(5)

***Wharton Arms Hotel,** High Street, Skelton, Saltburn-by-the-Sea, N. Yorks, TS12 2DY.*
Old coaching inn.
Open: All Year
01287 650618
Miss Cummings
Rates fr: *£17.50*-**£18.50**.
Beds: 2F 2T
Baths: 4 Ensuite
(20)

***Grange Farmhouse,** Orchard View, Skelton, York, YO3 6YQ.*
Peaceful, ensuite accommodation near York.
Open: All Year (not Xmas)
01904 470780
Mr & Mrs Appleton
Rates fr: *£18.00*-**£25.00**.
Beds: 1F 3D 2T 2S
Baths: 8 Ensuite
(1) (8)

The lowest **single** *rate is shown in* **bold.**

Skipton

National Grid Ref: SD9851

Slater's Arms

***Low Skibeden Farmhouse,** Skibeden Road, Skipton, N. Yorks, BD23 6AB.*
Detached C16th farmhouse.
Luxury accommodation.
Open: All Year
Grades: ETB 2 Cr, Comm
01756 793849 / 0831 126473
Mrs Simpson
Rates fr: *£16.00*-**£30.00**.
Beds: 3F 1D 1T
Baths: 3 Ensuite 2 Shared
(12) (5)

***Syke House,** 103 Raikes Road, Skipton, N. Yorks, BD23 1LS.*
Set in quiet residential area.
Open: All Year (not Xmas)
01756 793460 Mrs Lambert
Rates fr: *£15.00*-**£17.50**.
Beds: 1T 1D
Baths: 1 Ensuite 1 Shared
(0) (2)

***Peace Villas,** 69 Gargrave Road, Skipton, N. Yorks, BD23 1QN.*
Large converted Victorian private house.
Open: All Year
01756 790672
Mr & Mrs Feather
Rates fr: *£13.50*-**£13.50**.
Beds: 3D 2T 1S
Baths: 6 Ensuite
(3)

Sleights

National Grid Ref: NZ8607

The Plough

***Ryedale House,** 154-8 Coach Road, Sleights, Whitby, N. Yorks, YO22 5EQ.*
Relaxing home with high standards, private facilities.
Open: Mar to Nov
01947 810534 Mrs Beale
Rates fr: *£16.00*.
Beds: 2D 1T
Baths: 2 Private 1 Shared
(3)

***Inkwells Guest House,** 1 Eskdaleside, Sleights, Whitby, N. Yorks, YO22 5EP.*
Stone-built converted village school.
Open: All Year
01947 810959 (also fax no)
Mrs Thompson
Rates fr: *£16.50*-**£16.50**.
Beds: 2D 1T 1S
Baths: 1 Shared
(5) (3)

***Fernbank,** 11 Carr Hill Lane, Sleights, Whitby, N. Yorks, YO21 1RS.*
Large family home, superb surroundings.
Open: All Year (not Xmas)
01947 811320 Mrs Grindle
Rates fr: *£15.00*-**£20.00**.
Beds: 2D
Baths: 2 Ensuite
(2)

Slingsby

National Grid Ref: SE6975

***Lowrys Restaurant,** Malton Road, Slingsby, York, YO6 7AF.*
Licensed restaurant & guest house.
Open: All Year
01653 628417 (also fax no)
Ms Hinds
Rates fr: *£16.00*-**£18.00**.
Beds: 1F 1D 2T
Baths: 2 Private 2 Shared
(10)

Snape

National Grid Ref: SE2684

Castle Arms Inn

***The Castle Arms Inn,** Snape, Bedale, N. Yorks, DL8 2TB.*
Countryside inn.
Open: All Year (not Xmas)
01677 470270
Mr & Mrs Kennedy
Rates fr: *£15.00*-**£16.00**.
Beds: 1D 1T
Baths: 1 Shared
(20)

South Milford

National Grid Ref: SE4931

Swan Hotel

***Swan Hotel,** Low Street, South Milford, Leeds, LS25 5AR.*
Friendly country inn.
Open: All Year
01977 682783
Mr Roberts
Rates fr: *£25.00*-**£36.00**.
Beds: 2D 2T 1S
Baths: 5 Private
(50)

South Otterington

National Grid Ref: SE3787

Otterington Shorthorn Inn

***Otterington Shorthorn Inn,** South Otterington, Northallerton, N. Yorks, DL7 9HP.*
Charming, traditional village inn.
Open: All Year
01609 773816
Mrs Nasby
Rates fr: *£14.00*-**£14.00**.
Beds: 3D 2T
Baths: 1 Shared
(12)

Spaunton

National Grid Ref: SE7387

Blacksmiths Arms

***Holywell House,** Spaunton Bank Foot, Spaunton, Appleton Le Moors, York, YO6 6TR.*
C18th beamed cottage with large garden.
Open: All Year (not Xmas)
Grades: ETB Listed, High Comm
01751 417624 Mrs Makepeace
Rates fr: *£16.00*-**£16.00**.
Beds: 1D 1T
(5)

Spennithorne

National Grid Ref: SE1389

***Garden House,** Spennithorne, Leyburn, N. Yorks, DL8 5PR.*
Delightful country cottage beautiful gardens.
Open: All Year
01969 622092 Mrs Lofthouse
Rates fr: *£15.00*-**£15.00**.
Beds: 1D 1T 1S**Baths:** 1 Shared
(2)

Sproxton

National Grid Ref: SE6181

***Sproxton Hall,** Sproxton, Helmsley, York, YO6 5EQ.*
Tranquil C17th Grade II farmhouse.
Open: All Year (not Xmas)
01439 770225 Mrs Wainwright
Fax no: 01439 771373
Rates fr: *£19.50*-**£23.50**.
Beds: 2D 2T
Baths: 1 Ensuite 1 Private 1 Shared
(10) (10)

Staintondale

National Grid Ref: SE9998

***Tofta Farm,** Staintondale, Scarborough, N. Yorks, YO13 0EB.*
Modernised C17th farmhouse.
Open: All Year (not Xmas)
01723 870298 Mrs Dobson
Rates fr: *£16.00*-**£16.00**.
Beds: 1F 3D
Baths: 1 Private 1 Shared

Staithes

National Grid Ref: NZ7818

***Endeavour Restaurant,** 1 High Street, Staithes, Saltburn-by-the-Sea, N. Yorks, TS13 5BH.*
Seafood restaurant with accommodation.
Open: Mar to Jan
01947 840825 Ms Chapman
Rates fr: *£19.00*-**£18.50**.
Beds: 1D 1T 1S
Baths: 1 Private 1 Shared

***Harbour Side Guest House,** Staithes, Saltburn-by-the-Sea, N. Yorks, TS13 5.*
Friendly seafront guest house.
Open: All Year (not Xmas)
01947 841296 Mrs Wilkinson
Rates fr: *£19.50*-**£25.00**.
Beds: 1F 1D 1T
Baths: 2 Shared
(0)

***Black Lion Hotel,** High Street, Staithes, Saltburn-by-the-Sea, N. Yorks, TS13 5BQ.*
Refurbished Georgian period hotel inn.
Open: All Year
01947 841132 Mr Stead
Rates fr: *£19.0*-**£19.00**.
Beds: 3F 7D **Baths:** 10 Ensuite

Stape

National Grid Ref: SE7993

***Grange Farm Guest House,** Stape, Pickering, N. Yorks, YO18 8HZ.*
Open: All Year
01751 473805 Mrs Peacock
Fax no: 01751 477805
Rates fr: *£17.50*-**£17.50**.
Beds: 1F 2D 3T
Baths: 3 Ensuite 2 Shared
(10)
Beautifully appointed accommodation set in 5 acres of grounds, amid glorious forest and moorland scenery. Friendly welcome. Large rooms. Good food. Colour brochure available.

***Seavy Slack Farm,** Stape, Pickering, N. Yorks, YO18 8HZ.*
Comfortable farmhouse on working farm.
Open: Easter to Oct
Grades: ETB Listed, Approv
01751 473131 Mrs Barrett
Rates fr: *£14.00*-**£16.00**.
Beds: 1F 1D **Baths:** 1 Shared
(4)

***Rawcliffe House Farm,** Newton-upon-Rawcliffe, Stape, Pickering, N. Yorks, YO18 8JA.*
Luxurious tranquil oasis, warm welcome.
Open: Feb to Oct
01751 473292 Mrs Ducat
Rates fr: *£17.50*-**£22.50**.
Beds: 2D 1T **Baths:** 3 Ensuite
(8)

Starbotton

National Grid Ref: SD9574

The Fox

***Fox & Hounds Inn,** Starbotton, Skipton, N. Yorks, BD23 5HY.*
Traditional cosy Dales inn.
Open: Mid-Feb to Dec
01756 760269
Mr & Mrs McFadyen
Rates fr: *£22.00*-**£30.00**.
Beds: 1D 1T **Baths:** 2 Private
(10)

Hill Top Country Guest House, *Starbotton, Skipton, N. Yorks,* *BD23 5HY.*
C17th Listed farmhouse.
Open: Easter to Nov
Grades: ETB 2 Cr, High Comm, AA 5 Q, Prem Select
01756 760321
Mr Rathmell
Rates fr: *£25.00*-**£32.00**.
Beds: 1F 3D 1T
Baths: 5 Ensuite
(6) (6)

Cleveliot House, *Starbotton, Skipton, N. Yorks, BD23 5HY.*
Modern comfortable house.
Open: All Year (not Xmas)
01756 760825
Mrs Madin
Rates fr: *£15.50*-**£15.50**.
Beds: 1D 1T 1S
(3)

Stillington

National Grid Ref: SE5867

Roseberry View, *Easingwold Road, Stillington, York, YO6 1LR.*
Warm, comfortable bungalow.
Good breakfast choice.
Open: All Year (not Xmas)
01347 810795 Mrs Knowles
Rates fr: *£15.00*-**£18.00**.
Beds: 1D 1T
Baths: 1 Private 1 Shared
(3)

Stockton-on-the-Forest

National Grid Ref: SE6555

Orillia House, *89 The Village, Stockton-on-the-Forest, York, YO3 9UP.*
Open: All Year
Grades: ETB 2 Cr
01904 400600
Mrs Cundal
Rates fr: *£18.00*-**£22.00**.
Beds: 2F 2D 1T
Baths: 5 Private
(20)
Comfortable sympathetically renovated 300-year-old farmhouse in village location 3m York. All rooms ensuite with CTV and tea/coffee facilities. ETB 2 Crowns.

Stokesley

National Grid Ref: NZ5209

Red Hall, *Great Broughton, Stokesley, Middlesbrough, N. Yorks, TS9 7ET.*
Welcoming,elegant C17th Grade II Listed country house.
Open: All Year
01642 712300 (also fax no)
Mr Richmond
Rates fr: *£20.00*-**£28.00**.
Beds: 1F 2D
Baths: 3 Ensuite
(10)

Suffield

National Grid Ref: SE9890

Rosette Inn, Gatehouse

Suffield Farm, *Suffield, Scarborough, N. Yorks, YO13 0BJ.*
Attractive farmhouse.
Open: May to Oct
01723 369532
Mrs Lockey
Rates fr: *£12.50*-**£12.50**.
Beds: 1T 1D
Baths: 1 Shared
(1) (2)

Summerbridge

National Grid Ref: SE2062

Clifton House, *Summerbridge, Harrogate, N. Yorks, HG3 4HP.*
Small village, panoramic views.
Open: All Year
01423 780482
Mr Somerville
Rates fr: *£12.00*-**£12.00**.
Beds: 1F 1D 1S
Baths: 1 Shared

Sutton Bank

National Grid Ref: SE5182

Hambleton Inn

Cote Faw, *Hambleton Cottages, Sutton Bank, Thirsk, N. Yorks, YO7 2EZ.*
Comfortable cottage in National Park.
Open: All Year (not Xmas)
01845 597363 Mrs Jeffray
Rates fr: *£14.00*-**£14.00**.
Beds: 1F 1D 1S
Baths: 1 Shared
(3)

High House Farm, *Sutton Bank, Thirsk, N. Yorks, YO7 2HA.*
Comfortable with home produced food.
Open: Easter to Nov
Grades: ETB 1 Cr
01845 597557 Mrs Hope
Rates fr: *£18.00*-**£36.00**.
Beds: 1F 1D
Baths: 1 Shared
(4)

Sutton in Craven

National Grid Ref: SE0043

Ravenshill, *Holme Lane, Sutton in Craven, Keighley, W. Yorks, BD20 7LN.*
Detached house opposite village park.
Open: All Year (not Xmas)
01535 633276 (also fax no)
Mrs Barwick-Nicholson
Rates fr: *£16.00*-**£16.00**.
Beds: 1T 1S **Baths:** 1 Shared
(5) (2)

Sutton-under-Whitestonecliffe

National Grid Ref: SE4883

Hambleton Inn, Whitestonecliffe Inn

High Cleaves, *Sutton-under-Whitestonecliffe, Thirsk, N. Yorks, YO7 2QD.*
Open: All Year
01845 597612 (also fax no)
Mrs Haggas
Rates fr: *£25.00*-**£35.00**.
Beds: 1F 1D
Baths: 2 Ensuite
(20)
Magnificent views of York Vale, adjacent North York Moors National Park & Gormire Lake. Local walks. Modernised farmhouse combining accommodation with a friendly welcome. Phone for details.

Thirsk

National Grid Ref: SE4282

Golden Fleece

Town Pasture Farm, *Boltby, Thirsk, N. Yorks, YO7 2DY.*
Comfortable farmhouse in beautiful village.
Open: All Year
Grades: ETB Listed, Approv
01845 537298
Mrs Fountain
Rates fr: *£15.50*-**£15.50**.
Beds: 1F 1D 1T
Baths: 3 Ensuite
(3)

Doxford House, *73 Front Street, Sowerby, Thirsk, N. Yorks, YO7 1JP.*
Spacious Georgian house - rooms ensuite.
Open: All Year (not Xmas)
Grades: ETB 2 Cr, Approv
01845 523238 Mrs Proudley
Rates fr: *£16.00*-**£21.00**.
Beds: 2F 1D 1T
Baths: 4 Ensuite
(4)

Thornborough House Farm, *South Kilvington, Thirsk, N. Yorks, YO7 2NP.*
Comfortable 200-year-old farmhouse.
Open: All Year
Grades: ETB 2 Cr, Comm, AA 3 Q
01845 522103 (also fax no)
Mrs Williamson
Rates fr: *£14.00*-**£14.00**.
Beds: 1D 1T 1S **Baths:** 3 Private
(4)

Bringing children with you? Always ask for any special rates.

Thixendale

National Grid Ref: SE8461

Cross Keys

Manor Farm, *Thixendale, Malton, N. Yorks, YO17 9TG.*
Private accommodation in large Victorian farmhouse.
Open: All Year (not Xmas)
01377 288315 Mrs Brader
Rates fr: *£16.00*-**£16.00**.
Beds: 1F 1D
Baths: 1 Private
(6)

Tholthorpe

National Grid Ref: SE4766

New Inn

The New Inn, *Tholthorpe, York, YO6 2JL.*
Character village inn.
Open: All Year
01347 838329
Mr Bentley
Rates fr: *£18.00*-**£22.00**.
Beds: 1F 1D 1T
Baths: 2 Private

Thoralby

National Grid Ref: SE0086

Scarr House, *Thoralby, Leyburn, N. Yorks, DL8 3SU.*
Ultimate Unwind! Rest, relax, recharge!
Open: All Year
01969 663654 Mr Carter
Rates fr: *£23.50*-**£23.50**.
Beds: 2D 1T
Baths: 3 Ensuite
(10) (3)

Low Green House, *Thoralby, Leyburn, N. Yorks, DL8 3SZ.*
Comfortable stone-built Dales house.
Open: All Year
Grades: ETB 3 Cr, High Comm
01969 663623
Mr & Mrs Philpott
Rates fr: *£20.00*-**£24.00**.
Beds: 3D 1T
Baths: 4 Ensuite
(5)

Thorgill

National Grid Ref: SE7096

Rosedale View, *Thorgill, Rosedale, Pickering, N. Yorks, YO18 8SG.*
Centre of National Park.
Open: All Year (not Xmas)
01751 417318
Miss Langthorne
Rates fr: *£16.00*-**£16.00**.
Beds: 1D 1T
Baths: 1 Shared
(3)

Thormanby

National Grid Ref: SE4794

Carlton Inn

Thormanby Hill Farm, *Thormanby, Easingwold, York, YO6 3HY.*
Open: Easter to Oct
01845 501224 Mrs Williamson
Rates fr: *£13.50*.
Beds: 2D 1T
Baths: 1 Shared
Thormanby Hill Farm is set in the heart of North Yorkshire with outstanding views of the Pennines, Yorkshire Dales and the famous White Horse at Kilburn Thirsk.

The Old Rectory, *Thormanby, Easingwold, York, YO6 3NN.*
Early C18th rectory.
Open: All Year (not Xmas)
Grades: ETB Listed
01845 501417 Mrs Ritchie
Rates fr: *£16.00*-**£19.00**.
Beds: 1F 2D 1T
Baths: 2 Private 1 Shared
(6)

Thornton le Dale

National Grid Ref: SE8382

The Hall, Buck

Nabgate, *Wilton Road, Thornton le Dale, Pickering, N. Yorks, YO18 7QP.*
Open: All Year
Grades: ETB 1 Cr, Approv
01751 474279 Mrs Pickering
Rates fr: *£14.00*-**£17.00**.
Beds: 2D 1T
Baths: 1 Ensuite 1 Shared
(4)
Clean friendly home, close to Moors, Coast & Steam Railway. Hot & cold in all rooms. Good Yorkshire breakfast. Food hygiene certificate. TVs in rooms.

Tangalwood, *Roxby Road, Thornton le Dale, Pickering, N. Yorks, YO18 7SX.*
Friendly comfortable accommodation, quietly situated.
Open: Easter to Oct
01751 474688 Mrs Wardell
Rates fr: *£13.50*-**£20.00**.
Beds: 2D 1T
Baths: 1 Ensuite 1 Shared
(7) (3)

Thornton Rust

National Grid Ref: SD9788

Penny Acre, *Thornton Rust, Leyburn, N. Yorks, DL8 3AN.*
Comfortable family home, large garden.
Open: Easter to Oct
01969 663293 Mrs Hudson
Rates fr: *£19.00*-**£23.00**.
Beds: 1D 2T
Baths: 3 Private
(12) (4)

Thornton Watlass

National Grid Ref: SE2385

Buck Inn

Buck Inn, *Thornton Watlass, Ripon, N. Yorks, HG4 4AH.*
Country inn overlooking cricket green.
Open: All Year (not Xmas)
Grades: ETB 3 Cr, Comm, AA 1 St
01677 422461
Mr & Mrs Fox
Fax no: 01677 422447
Rates fr: *£22.00*-**£30.00**.
Beds: 1F 3D 2T 1S
Baths: 5 Ensuite 1 Shared
(10)

The Old Rectory, *Thornton Watlass, Ripon, N. Yorks, HG4 4AH.*
Georgian country rectory. Listed building.
Open: All Year
01677 423456 Mrs Farnell
Rates fr: *£32.50*-**£45.00**.
Beds: 1D 1T
Baths: 2 Private
(12) (8)

Thornton-in-Lonsdale

National Grid Ref: SD6873

Marton Arms Hotel

Marton Arms Hotel, *Thornton-in-Lonsdale, Ingleton, Carnforth, Lancs, LA6 3PB.*
Centuries old inn, bedrooms modernised.
Open: All Year
015242 41281 Mr Elsdon
Rates fr: *£20.00*-**£20.00**.
Beds: 3T 3D 2S
Baths: 7 Ensuite 1 Shared
(10)

Thorpe Bassett

National Grid Ref: SE8673

The Old School House, *Thorpe Bassett, Rillington, Malton, N. Yorks, YO17 8LU.*
C18th converted school.
Open: Easter to Oct
01944 758797
Mrs Baron
Rates fr: *£16.00*-**£16.00**.
Beds: 1D 1S
Baths: 1 Shared

National Grid References are for villages, towns and cities - *not* for individual houses.

Tosside

National Grid Ref: SD9048

***Sandy Laithe**, Tosside, Skipton, N. Yorks, BD23 3TU.*
Spacious detatched barn conversion.
Open: All Year (not Xmas)
01729 840482 Mrs Davey
Rates fr: *£17.00*-**£19.00**.
Beds: 1D
Baths: 2 Shared
(0) (5)

Weaverthorpe

National Grid Ref: SE9670

Star Inn

***The Star Inn**, Weaverthorpe, Malton, N. Yorks, YO17 8EY.*
Renowned high quality food & drink.
Open: All Year (not Xmas)
01944 738273 Mr Richardson
Rates fr: *£16.00*-**£17.50**.
Beds: 1F 2D 1T 1S
Baths: 3 Ensuite 2 Shared
(5) (30)

Well

National Grid Ref: SE2682

Freemasons Arms, Boot & Shoe

***Upsland Farm**, Lime Lane, Well, Bedale, N. Yorks, DL8 2PA.*
Moated site, lovely farmhouse. Brass beds.
Open: All Year (not Xmas)
Grades: ETB 2 Cr, High Comm
01845 567709
Mrs Hodgson
Rates fr: *£20.00*-**£22.00**.
Beds: 3F
Baths: 3 Ensuite
(4)

West Witton

National Grid Ref: SE0688

***The Old Vicarage**, West Witton, Leyburn, N. Yorks, DL8 4LX.*
Comfortable Georgian house, lovely views.
Open: Easter to Oct
01969 622108 Mrs Coates
Rates fr: *£18.00*-**£22.00**.
Beds: 2D 1T
Baths: 2 Ensuite 1 Private
(6)

***Ivy Dene Country House**, West Witton, Leyburn, N. Yorks, DL8 4LP.*
C17th licensed country house.
Open: All Year (not Xmas)
01969 622785
Mr & Mrs Dickinson
Rates fr: *£18.00*-**£30.00**.
Beds: 2F 2D 1T
Baths: 5 Private
(5) (5)

Bringing children with you? Always ask for any special rates.

Westow

National Grid Ref: SE7565

Blacksmiths Arms

***Blacksmiths Arms Inn**, Main Street, Westow, York, YO6 7NE.*
Open: All Year (not Xmas)
Grades: ETB 2 Cr, Comm, AA 3 Q
01653 618365 / 618343 (also fax no)
Mr Greenwood
Rates fr: *£21.00*-**£21.00**.
Beds: 1F 1D 2T 2S
Baths: 6 Ensuite
Westow, set in the Yorkshire Wolds, is an ideal base to see both York & the North Yorkshire Moors & coast.

Wharram le Street

National Grid Ref: SE8666

***Red House**, Wharram le Street, Malton, N. Yorks, YO17 9TL.*
Spacious country house, family-run.
Open: All Year (not Xmas)
Grades: RAC Acclaim
01944 768455 Mr Scott
Rates fr: *£20.70*-**£20.70**.
Beds: 1F 1D 1T
Baths: 3 Ensuite
(8)

Whitby

National Grid Ref: NZ8910

Shepherds Purse, The Plough, Granby Inn

***The Shepherds Purse**, Sanders Yard, Church Street, Whitby, N. Yorks, YO22 4DU.*
Open: All Year
01947 820228 Mr Budd
Fax no: 01947 601670
Rates fr: *£16.00*-**£20.00**.
Beds: 1F 6D 1T 1S
Baths: 7 Ensuite 2 Shared
Shepherd's Purse, Whitby. Vegetarian restaurant with galleried courtyard of ensuite rooms. Four poster & brass beds. In the old town close to Abbey and harbour.

High season, bank holidays and special events mean low availability *anywhere.*

***Inkwells Guest House**, 1 Eskdaleside, Sleights, Whitby, N. Yorks, YO22 5EP.*
Stone-built converted village school.
Open: All Year
01947 810959 (also fax no)
Mrs Thompson
Rates fr: *£16.50*-**£16.50**.
Beds: 2D 1T 1S
Baths: 1 Shared
(5) (3)

***Haven Guest House**, 4 East Crescent, Whitby, N. Yorks, YO21 3HD.*
Comfortable, homely house, overlooking sea.
Open: Mar to Oct
Grades: AA 3 Q
01947 603842
Mrs Smith
Rates fr: *£16.00*-**£19.00**.
Beds: 1F 5D 2S
Baths: 5 Private 1 Shared
(5)

Whixley

National Grid Ref: SE4458

***Princes Lodge**, Whixley, York, YO5 8EE.*
Modern, comfortable farmhouse. Swimming - bar.
Open: All Year (not Xmas)
01423 330168
Mr Bielby
Rates fr: *£16.00*-**£28.00**.
Beds: 1F 2D
Baths: 3 Ensuite
(20)

Wigglesworth

National Grid Ref: SD8056

Plough Inn

***The Plough Inn**, Wigglesworth, Skipton, N. Yorks, BD23 4RJ.*
Dales country inn.
Open: All Year
01729 840243
Mr Goodhall
Rates fr: *£22.50*-**£31.50**.
Beds: 2F 7D 3T
Baths: 12 Private
(50)

Wrelton

National Grid Ref: SE7686

***The Huntsman**, Main Street, Wrelton, Pickering, N. Yorks, YO18 8PG.*
Converted village farmhouse. Quiet location.
Open: All Year
01751 472530
Mr Lower
Rates fr: *£20.00*-**£24.00**.
Beds: 3D
(2)

Always telephone to get directions to the B&B - you will save time!

Yarm

National Grid Ref: NZ4112

Black Bull, New Cross Keys

Bank View, *2 West End Gardens, Yarm, TS15 9QX.*
Modern dormer bungalow overlooking river.
Open: All Year
01642 888803 Mrs Stredwick
Rates fr: *£18.00*-**£18.00**.
Beds: 1T 1D
(2)

2 Valley Close, *Yarm, TS15 9SE.*
Friendly, comfortable, modern, detached house.
Open: All Year
01642 780633 Mrs Bond
Rates fr: *£18.00*-**£18.00**.
Beds: 1D 2S
Baths: 1 Shared
(2)

Yedingham

National Grid Ref: SE8976

The Old Vicarage, *Yedingham, Malton, N. Yorks, YO17 8SL.*
Delightful C18th former vicarage.
Open: All Year (not Xmas)
Grades: ETB 2 Cr
01944 728426
Mrs Rayment
Rates fr: *£15.00*-**£15.00**.
Beds: 2D 1T
Baths: 1 Ensuite 1 Shared
(5) (3)

Yockenthwaite

National Grid Ref: SD9079

Low Raisgill Cottage, *Yockenthwaite, Hubberholme, Skipton, N. Yorks, BD23 5JQ.*
Quietly situated in unspoilt Longshortdale.
Open: All Year
01756 760351
Mrs Middleton
Rates fr: *£17.00*-**£17.00**.
Beds: 1F 1D 1T **Baths:** 3 Private

The lowest *double* rate per person is shown in *italics*.

York

National Grid Ref: SE5951

Wagon & Horses, Royal Oak, Ye Olde Punch Bowl Inn, Exhibition Pub, Tankard Inn

The Hazelwood, *24-25 Portland Street, Gillygate, York, YO3 7EH.*
Open: All Year
Grades: ETB 2 Cr, Comm, AA 4 Q, Select, RAC Acclaim
01904 626548 Mr McNabb
Fax no: 01904 628032
Rates fr: *£16.00*-**£19.50**.
Beds: 2F 7D 3T 2S
Baths: 11 Ensuite 3 Shared
(11)
Situated in centre of York only 400 yards from York Minster in extremely quiet location & with private car park. An elegant Victorian townhouse with comfortable ensuite bedrooms offering excellent value for money - wide choice of quality breakfasts, catering for all tastes including vegetarian. Non-smoking.

Cornerways Guest House, *16 Murton Way, Osbaldwick, York, YO1 3UN.*
Comfortable detached friendly guest house.
Open: All Year
01904 645544 / 413366
Mr White
Rates fr: *£16.00*-**£14.00**.
Beds: 1F 1D 1S
Baths: 2 Ensuite 1 Private
(4)

Linden Lodge, *6 Nunthorpe Avenue, Scarcroft Road, York, YO2 1PF.*
Open: All Year (not Xmas)
Grades: ETB 2 Cr, Comm, AA 3 Q, RAC Listed
01904 620107
Mr Wharton
Fax no: 01904 620985
Rates fr: *£18.50*-**£18.00**.
Beds: 2F 5D 2T 2S
Baths: 9 Private 2 Shared
Quality accommodation 10 minutes walk to rail station, city centre. Quiet location. Unrestricted parking. Licensed. CTVs. Tea & coffee in rooms. Ensuite/standard. Rates 18-30 pppn B&B.

Holly Lodge, *206 Fulford Road, York, YO1 4DD.*
Open: All Year (not Xmas)
Grades: ETB 2 Cr, Approv
01904 646005
Mr Gallagher
Rates fr: *£18.00*-**£30.00**.
Beds: 1F 3D 1T
Baths: 5 Ensuite
(5)
Ideally located 10 minutes riverside walk from the city centre, convenient for all York's amenites. This fine Georgian property, with walled garden & car park, offers a warm welcome.

Feversham Lodge, *Feversham Crescent, York, YO3 7HQ.*
Open: All Year
Grades: ETB 2 Cr, Approv
01904 623882
Mr & Mrs Peacock
Rates fr: *£20.00*-**£16.00**.
Beds: 1F 6D 2T 1S
Baths: 6 Private
(8)
We are situated just a pleasant ten minutes walk from city & attractions with moors and Dales a short ride away. Bowling green & park opposite.

Dairy Wholefood Guest House, *3 Scarcroft Road, York, YO2 1ND.*
Tasteful in many ways!
Open: Feb to Dec
01904 639367
Mr Jackman
Rates fr: *£17.00*.
Beds: 2F 2D 1T
Baths: 2 Private 1 Shared

Newton Guest House, *Neville Street, Haxby Road, York, YO3 7NP.*
Open: All Year (not Xmas)
Grades: ETB 1 Cr
01904 635627
Mrs Tindall
Rates fr: *£15.00*-**£18.00**.
Beds: 1F 2D 1T 1S
Baths: 4 Ensuite 1 Private
(5)
Friendly, family-run, few minutes walk to city centre. Non-smoking, choice of breakfast menu. Private parking. Your comfort our first priority. Personal attention. Bowling green opposite.

York Lodge Guest House, *64 Bootham Crescent, Bootham, York, YO3 7AH.*
Comfortable, relaxing accommodation, friendly service.
Open: All Year
Grades: ETB Listed
01904 654289
Mr Moore
Rates fr: *£15.00*-**£14.50**.
Beds: 3F 3D 1T 1S
Baths: 4 Ensuite 4 Shared

St Raphael Guest House, *44 Queen Annes Road, Bootham, York, YO3 7AF.*
Open: All Year
Grades: ETB Listed, Approv, AA 2 Q, RAC Listed
01904 645028
Mrs Farrell
Fax no: 01904 658788
Rates fr: *£14.00*-**£15.00**.
Beds: 1F 5D 2T
Baths: 5 Ensuite 1 Shared
(2)
A family-run guest house. Rooms are tastefully decorated. We boast a good, healthy, traditional English breakfast. Five minute walk to city centre & York Minster.

Bowen House, *4 Gladstone Street, Huntington Road, York, YO3 7RF.*
Open: All Year
Grades: ETB 2 Cr
01904 636881 (also fax no)
Mrs Wood
Rates fr: *£16.00*-**£20.00**.
Beds: 1F 2D 1T 1S
Baths: 2 Ensuite 1 Shared
(4)
Victorian family-run guest house, with high-quality facilities & old-style charm. Short stroll to city centre. Private carpark. Non-smoking. Traditional or vegetarian breakfasts.

Byron House Hotel, *7 Driffield Terrace, The Mount, York, YO2 2DD.*
Late Georgian, spacious & welcoming.
Open: All Year (not Xmas)
Grades: ETB 3 Cr, Comm, AA 3 Q, Recomm, RAC High Acclaim
01904 632525 Mr Tyson
Fax no: 01904 638904
Rates fr: *£25.00*-**£24.00**.
Beds: 4F 2D 1T 3S
Baths: 7 Private 3 Shared
(6)

Cumbria House, *2 Vyner Street, Haxby Road, York, YO3 7HS.*
Open: All Year
Grades: ETB Listed, Comm, AA 3 Q
01904 636817 Mrs Curtis
Rates fr: *£16.00*-**£17.00**.
Beds: 2F 2D 1S
Baths: 3 Private 1 Shared
(4)
Beautifully decorated family-run guest house. Private carpark. Ideal for city centre & all attractions. (12 minute walk). Warm friendly welcome assured.

City Guest House, *68 Monkgate, York, YO3 7PF.*
Five minutes walk to Minster.
Open: All Year (not Xmas)
Grades: ETB 2 Cr, AA 3 Q
01904 622483 Mr Leigh
Rates fr: *£15.00*-**£15.00**.
Beds: 1F 4D 1T 1S
Baths: 5 Ensuite 1 Shared
(4)

Coppers Lodge, *15 Alma Terrace, Fulford Road, York, YO1 4DQ.*
Homely, comfortable, full English breakfast. **Open:** All Year
Grades: ETB Listed, AA Listed
01904 639871 Mrs Grima
Rates fr: *£15.00*-**£15.00**.
Beds: 5F 2D 1S
Baths: 1 Private 3 Shared
(5)

Bridge House, *181 Haxby Road, York, YO3 7JL.*
Open: All Year (not Xmas)
Grades: ETB 2 Cr
01904 636161 (also fax no)
Mrs Parker
Rates fr: *£14.00*-**£16.00**.
Beds: 2F 3D 2T 2S
Baths: 7 Private 2 Shared
Valerie Harry and son, Grant, welcome you to their friendly guest house. 12 minutes walk city centre, also ideal for touring moors, Dales & coast.

Georgian Guest House, *35 Bootham, York, YO3 7BT.*
City centre family-run guest house.
Open: All Year (not Xmas)
Grades: ETB Listed, AA Listed, RAC Listed
01904 622874 Mr Semple
Rates fr: *£15.00*-**£18.00**.
Beds: 9D 3T 3S
Baths: 6 Ensuite 3 Shared
(5) (10)

Nunmill House, *85 Bishopthorpe Road, York, YO2 1NX.*
Open: Feb to Nov
Grades: ETB 2 Cr, High Comm, AA 4 Q, Select
01904 634047
Mr & Mrs Whitbourn-Hammond
Fax no: 01904 655879
Rates fr: *£18.00*-**£25.00**.
Beds: 1F 6D 1T
Baths: 7 Ensuite 1 Private
(4)
Splendid Victorian house, lovingly furnished & smoke-free, for those looking for comfortable yet affordable accommodation. Easy walk to all attractions. SAE for brochure.

White Doves, *20 Claremont Terrace, Off Gillygate, York, YO3 7EJ.*
Victorian house in cul-de-sac near Minster.
Open: All Year (not Xmas)
Grades: ETB 2 Cr
01904 625957 Mr Pearce
Rates fr: *£15.00*-**£30.00**.
Beds: 3D 1T
Baths: 3 Ensuite 1 Private
(5) (4)

Grange Lodge, *52 Bootham Crescent, Bootham, York, YO3 7AH.*
Small family-run guest house, near city centre. **Open:** All Year
Grades: ETB 2 Cr
01904 621137 Mrs Robinson
Rates fr: *£15.00*-**£16.00**.
Beds: 2F 2D 2T 1S
Baths: 4 Private 3 Shared

Dalescroft Guest House, *10 Southlands Road, Bishopthorpe Road, York, YO2 1NP.*
Open: All Year
Grades: ETB Listed
01904 626801
Mrs Blower
Rates fr: *£12.00*-**£12.00**.
Beds: 2F 2D 2T 1S
Baths: 2 Ensuite 1 Private 2 Shared
In a quiet side street, 10 mins from city & race course, you will be sure of a warm welcome in our family-run guest house.

Park View Guest House, *34 Grosvenor Terrace, Bootham, York, YO3 7AG.*
Friendly, comfortable Victorian house.
Open: All Year
Grades: ETB Listed, Comm
01904 620437 (also fax no)
Mrs Ashton
Rates fr: *£15.00*-**£16.00**.
Beds: 1F 3D 2T 1S
Baths: 3 Private 1 Shared

Primrose Cottage, *Grafton, York, YO5 9QJ.*
Open: All Year
Grades: ETB 1 Cr, High Comm
01423 322835 / 322711
Mrs Styan
Fax no: 01423 323985
Rates fr: *£16.00*-**£20.00**.
Beds: 1D 2T
Baths: 1 Private 1 Shared
(8)
Warm hospitality in country cottage set in 0.75 acres in picturesque village 1 mile east of A1. Comfortable bedrooms, spacious television lounge & sheltered garden.

Rosedale Guest House, *Wetherby Road, Rufforth, York, YO2 3QB.*
Comfortable village guest house.
Open: All Year (not Xmas)
Grades: ETB 2 Cr, Comm
01904 738297
Mrs Smith
Rates fr: *£17.50*-**£16.00**.
Beds: 1F 2D 1T 1S
Baths: 1 Ensuite 2 Shared
(2) (6)

The lowest *double* rate per person is shown in *italics*.

South Yorkshire

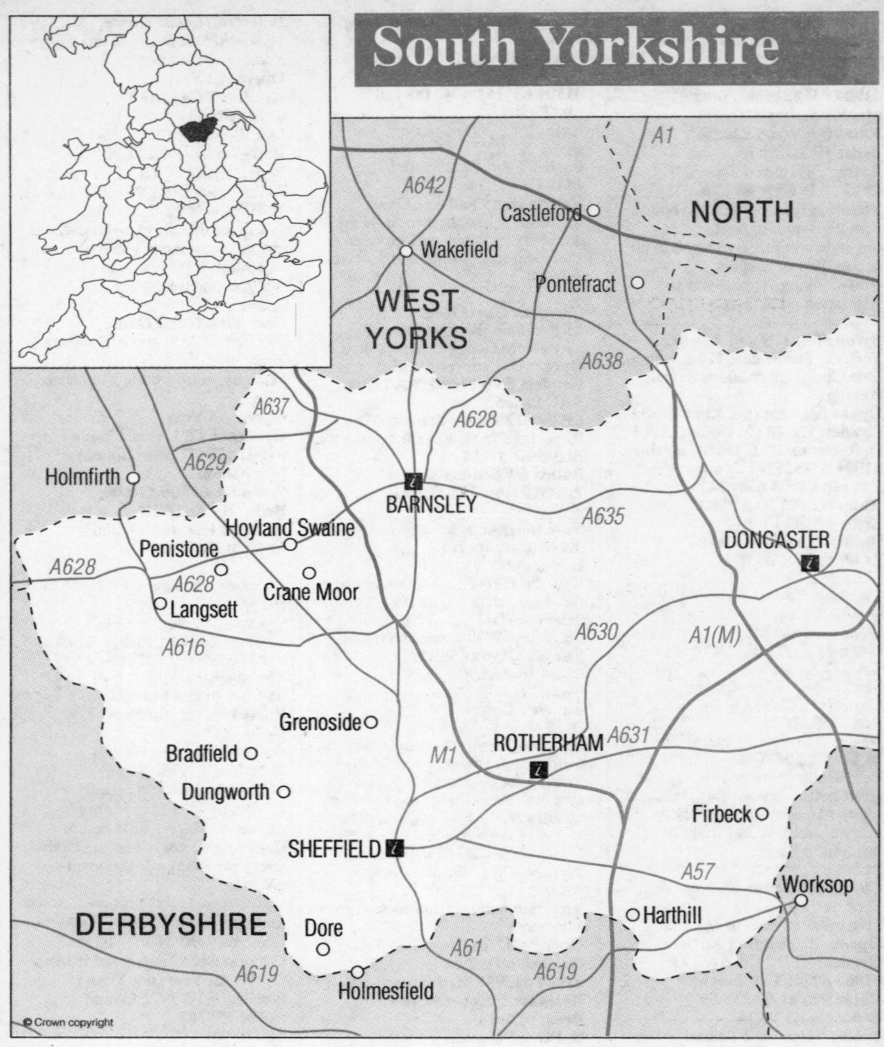

Tourist Information Centres

56 Eldon Street, **Barnsley**, S.Yorks, S70 2JL, 01226 206757.

Central Library, Waterdale, **Doncaster**, S.Yorks, DN1 3JE, 01302 734309.

Central Library, Walker Place, **Rotherham**, S.Yorks, S65 1JH, 01709 823611.

Peace Garden, **Sheffield**, S.Yorks, S1 2HH, 01142 273 4671

Barnsley

National Grid Ref: SE3406

Keresforth Hall

Park View Guest House, *2 Beech Grove, Kingstone, Barnsley, S. Yorks, S70 6NG.*
Large detached Georgian style house.
Open: All Year (not Xmas)
01226 297268
Mrs Banks
Rates fr: *£12.00*-**£13.00**.
Beds: 5F 3D 3S
Baths: 3 Private 4 Shared
(20)

Bradfield

National Grid Ref: SK2692

Woodseats Farm, *Bradfield, Sheffield, S6 6LE.*
C17th working sheep farm.
Open: All Year (not Xmas)
0114 285 1429 Mrs Robinson
Rates fr: *£17.00*-**£17.00**.
Beds: 1F 1D
Baths: 2 Private

The lowest **single** *rate is shown in* **bold.**

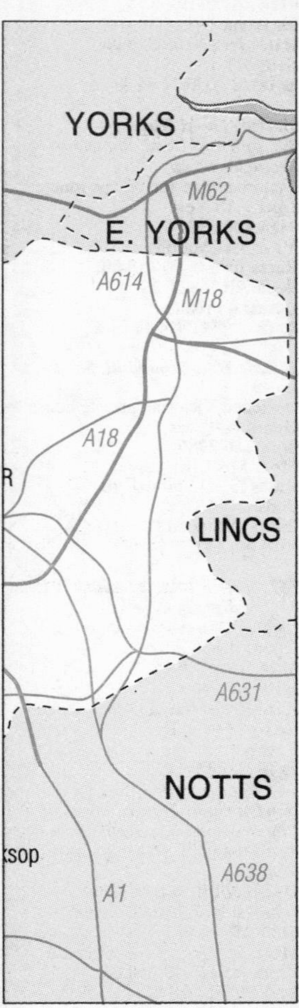

Crane Moor

National Grid Ref: SE3001

Poplar Cottage, *Crane Moor, Sheffield,* S30 7AT.
Converted cottages, quiet rural village.
Open: All Year
0114 288 8317 Mrs Moate
Rates fr: *£20.00*-**£22.00**.
Beds: 1F 3D
Baths: 3 Ensuite

The lowest *double* rate per person is shown in *italics*.

Doncaster

National Grid Ref: SE5702

Nags Head

Lyntone, *24 Avenue Road, Wheatley, Doncaster, S. Yorks,* DN2 4AQ.
Good value for your money.
Open: All Year
Grades: ETB 2 Cr
01302 361586 Ms Holbrey
Rates fr: *£13.00*-**£15.00**.
Beds: 2F 3D 2T 4S
Baths: 3 Shared
(8)

Earlesmere Guest House, *84 Thorne Road, Doncaster, S. Yorks,* DN2 5SL.
Modern, comfortable, family guest house.
Open: All Year
01302 368532 Mrs Barnes
Rates fr: *£13.00*-**£15.00**.
Beds: 2F 2T
Baths: 1 Private
(6)

Dore

National Grid Ref: SK3181

Critchleys, *6 Causeway Head Road, Dore, Sheffield,* S17 3DJ.
Modern well-furnished guest house.
Open: All Year
0114 236 4328
Mr Critchleys
Rates fr: *£16.00*-**£17.50**.
Beds: 1F 3D 2T 1S
Baths: 6 Ensuite 2 Private
(12) (4)

Dungworth

National Grid Ref: SK2889

Plough Inn

Sykehouse Farm, *Dungworth, Sheffield,* S6 6HG.
Comfortable farmhouse.
Open: All Year (not Xmas)
0114 285 1216 Mrs Gray
Rates fr: *£16.00*-**£17.00**.
Beds: 1D 1T
(4)

Firbeck

National Grid Ref: SK5688

Yews Farm, *Firbeck, Worksop, Notts,* S81 8JW.
Comfortable & spacious. Peaceful with lovely views.
Open: Mar to Oct
01909 731458 (also fax no)
Mrs Stewart-Smith
Rates fr: *£25.00*-**£32.00**.
Beds: 2T
Baths: 2 Ensuite
(10) (4)

Grenoside

National Grid Ref: SK3393

Red Lion

Middleton Green Farm, *Cinder Hill Lane, Grenoside, Sheffield, South Yorkshire,* S30 3NH.
Luxurious farmhouse.
Open: All Year
0114 245 3279 Ms Mennell
Rates fr: *£20.00*-**£25.00**.
Beds: 1D 1T 1S
Baths: 3 Private
(10)

Harthill

National Grid Ref: SK4980

57 Firvale, *Harthill, Sheffield,* S31 8XP.
Delightful cottage, warm conservatory.
Open: All Year
01909 773605 Mrs Stevens
Rates fr: *£15.00*-**£18.00**.
Beds: 2D
Baths: 1 Private

Hoyland Swaine

National Grid Ref: SE2604

Fell House, *354 Barnsley Road, Hoylandswaine, Sheffield,* S30 6JA.
1830s cottage, guests' private suite.
Open: All Year (not Xmas)
01226 790937 Ms Sykes
Rates fr: *£17.00*-**£22.00**.
Beds: 1F
Baths: 1 Private
(3)

Langsett

National Grid Ref: SE2100

Aldermans Head Manor, *Hartcliffe Hill Road, Lanssett, Holmfirth, Sheffield,* S30 5GY.
Historic manor house, dramatic views.
Open: All Year (not Xmas/New Year)
Grades: ETB 3 Cr, High Comm, AA 4 Q
01226 766209 Mrs Unitt
Rates fr: *£22.50*-**£30.00**.
Beds: 2D 2T
Baths: 4 Private
(12) (12)

Penistone

National Grid Ref: SE2403

Millhouse Guest Centre, *Carr House Farm, Royd Lane, Penistone, Sheffield,* S30 6NY.
Converted barn adjacent to farmhouse.
Open: All Year
01226 762917 Mr Worboys
Rates fr: *£10.00*-**£15.00**.
Beds: 2F 1D 2T
Baths: 2 Shared
(4)

Old Vicarage Guest House, *Shrewsbury Road, Penistone, Sheffield, S30 6DZ.*
Large Victorian vicarage.
Open: All Year (not Xmas)
01226 370607 Mrs Clibbens
Rates fr: *£19.00*-**£22.00**.
Beds: 2F 2D 3S
Baths: 1 Private 3 Shared
(6)

Rotherham

National Grid Ref: SK4392

Regis Court Guest House, *1 Hall Road, Rotherham, S. Yorks, S60 2BP.*
Large detached private house.
Open: All Year
01709 376666 Mr & Mrs Womble
Rates fr: *£12.50*-**£18.00**.
Beds: 1F 2D 6T 2S
Baths: 4 Private 2 Shared
(6)

Sheffield

National Grid Ref: SK3587

The Priory, The Fox, Wagon & Horses, Robin Hood, Cross Pool Tavern, Cross Pool Tavern

Tyndale, *164 Millhouses Lane, Sheffield, S7 2HE.*
Open: All Year
0114 236 1660
Mr & Mrs Wilmshurst
Rates fr: *£16.00*-**£16.00**.
Beds: 1F 1D 1S
Baths: 1 Shared
(3)
Comfortable home in leafy suburb. 3 miles from Peak District & Derbyshire Dales. Universities, hospitals, shops (including Meadowhall) and nightlife all within easy reach.

Laurels Guest House, *592 Barnsley Road, Sheffield, S5 6UA.*
Large private house on A6135.
Open: All Year
Grades: ETB Listed
0114 249 2596 Mr & Mrs Byne
Rates fr: *£15.00*-**£15.00**.
Beds: 1D 1T 1S
Baths: 1 Shared

The lowest **single** *rate is shown in* **bold.**

484 Ecclesall Road, *Sheffield, S11 8PX.*
Convenient for City & Universities.
Open: All Year (not Xmas)
0114 266 7426 Mr & Mrs Williams
Rates fr: *£15.00*-**£15.00**.
Beds: 1F 1D 1S **Baths:** 1 Shared
(5)

Peace Guest House, *92 Brocco Bank, Hunters Bar, Sheffield, S11 8RS.*
Open: All Year
Grades: ETB Listed
0114 268 5110 / 267 0760
Mr Manavi
Rates fr: *£15.00*-**£18.00**.
Beds: 1F 1D 1T 4S
Baths: 3 Private 2 Shared
(5)
Conveniently situated close to university, hospitals. Enroute to Peak District, 1 mile from city centre. Good hospitality & service. Discounts for block bookings.

Ivory House Hotel, *34 Wostenholm Road, Nether Edge, Sheffield, S7 1LJ.*
Small, friendly, family-run hotel.
Open: All Year (not Xmas)
0114 255 1853 Mrs Nur
Rates fr: *£15.00*-**£18.00**.
Beds: 1F 1D 1T 5S
Baths: 2 Ensuite 3 Shared
(8)

Greensleeves Cottage, *183 Foxhill Road, Sheffield, S6 1HF.*
Detached cottage, leisure, shops nearby.
Open: All Year (not Xmas)
0114 232 1107
Mrs Atkin
Rates fr: *£16.00*-**£17.00**.
Beds: 1D 1S
Baths: 1 Shared
(1)

Beech House, *44 Broomgrove Road, Sheffield, S10 2NA.*
Large homely Victorian house.
Open: All Year (not Xmas)
0114 266 2537
Miss Boler
Rates fr: *£19.00*-**£21.00**.
Beds: 3D 4T 1S
Baths: 2 Shared
(2) (2)

Mile Ash House, *4 Hartington Road, Millhouses, Sheffield, S7 2LE.*
Large Victorian house. Residential area.
Open: All Year
0114 236 6666 Mrs Palmer
Rates fr: *£15.00*-**£15.00**.
Beds: 2T **Baths:** 1 Shared
(10)

Crown Inn, *21 Meadowhall Road, Sheffield, S9 1BS.*
Modern family-run inn.
Open: All Year
0114 243 1319
Mr Layne
Rates fr: *£20.00*-**£20.00**.
Beds: 4T 1S
(8) (8)

Martins Guest House, *397 Fulwood Road, Ranmoor, Sheffield, S10 3GE.*
Victorian mansion on bus route.
Open: All Year
0114 230 8588
Mr & Mrs Martins
Rates fr: *£15.00*-**£18.00**.
Beds: 2F 3D 2T 2S
Baths: 4 Private
(12)

17 Sale Hill, Broomhill, *Sheffield, S10 5BX.*
Detached Victorian private house.
Open: All Year
0114 266 2986
Mr & Mrs Chambers
Rates fr: *£16.00*-**£18.00**.
Beds: 1D 1S
Baths: 1 Shared

167 Ecclesall Road South, *Sheffield, S11 9PN.*
Large Victorian private house.
Open: All Year
0114 262 0729
Mrs Gulliver
Rates fr: *£15.00*-**£15.00**.
Beds: 1F 1D 1T
Baths: 1 Shared
(3)

Newlyn Guest House, *9 Newlyn Place, Woodseats, Sheffield, S8 8ST.*
Victorian villa. Stylish interior design .
Open: All Year (not Xmas)
Grades: ETB Listed, Comm
0114 258 3484
Mrs Kirk
Rates fr: *£17.50*-**£18.00**.
Beds: 1D 1T 1S
Baths: 1 Shared
(8)

The Queens Hotel, *85 Scotland Street, Sheffield, S3 7BX.*
City centre hotel, public house.
Open: All Year
0114 272 6909
Rates fr: *£17.50*-**£17.50**.
Beds: 2F 1D 2T
Baths: 1 Shared

West Yorkshire

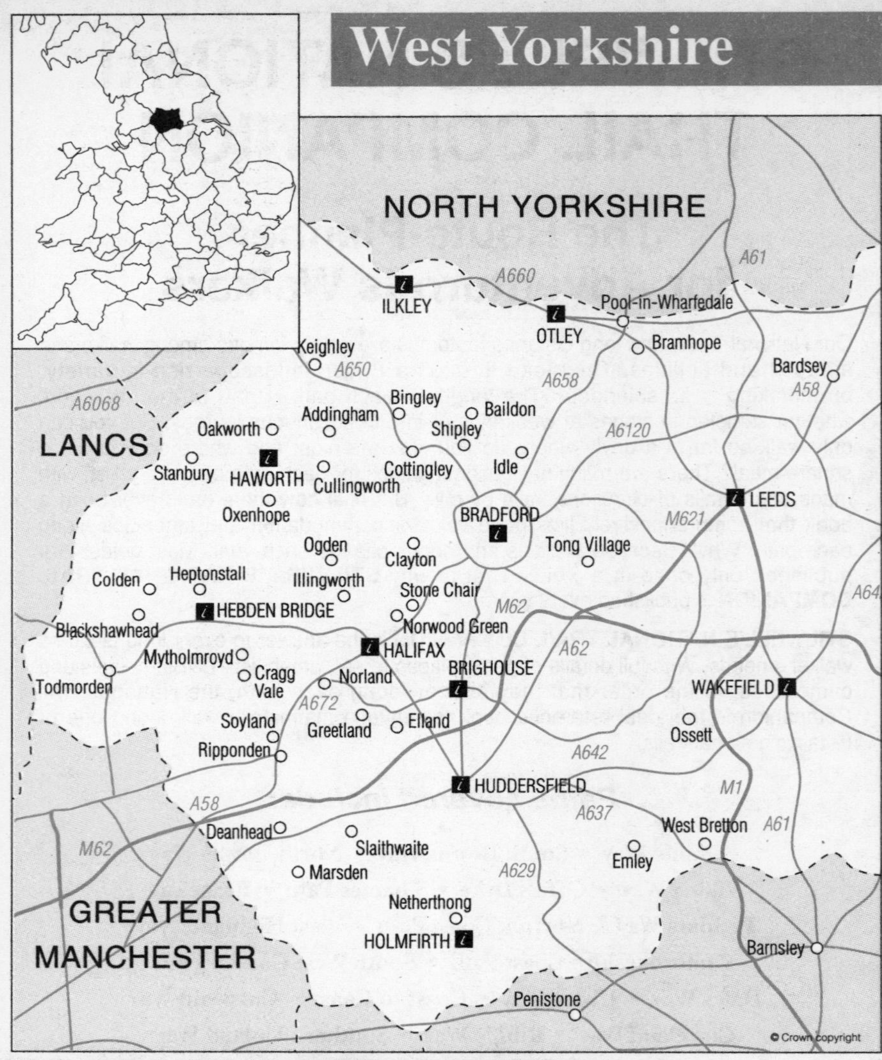

Tourist Information Centres

National Museum of Photography, Film & TV, Princes View, **Bradford**, W. Yorks, BD5 0TR, 01274 753678.

Hartshead Moor M62 Service Area, Clifton, **Brighouse**, W. Yorks, HD6 4JX, 01274 869167.

Piece Hall, **Halifax**, W. Yorks, HX1 1RE, 01422 368725.

1 Bridge Gate,**Hebden Bridge**, W. Yorks, HX7 8EX, 01422 843831.

49-51 Huddersfield Road, **Holmfirth**, Huddersfield, W. Yorks, HD7 1JP, 01484 687603.

3-5 Albion Street, **Huddersfield**, W. Yorks, HD1 2NW, 01484 223200.

Station Road, **Ilkley**, W. Yorks, LS29 8HA, 01943 602319.

2-4 West Lane, **Haworth**, Keighley, W. Yorks, BD22 8EF, 01535 642329.

Gateway Yorkshire, The Arcade, P.O Box 244, City Station, **Leeds**, LS1 1PL, 0113 242 5242

Council Offices, 8 Boroughgate, **Otley**, W. Yorks, LS21 3AH, 0113 247 7707

Town Hall, Wood Street, **Wakefield**, W. Yorks, WF1 2HQ, 01924 305000.

Council Offices, 24 Westgate, **Wetherby**, W. Yorks, LS22 4NL, 01937 582706.

Addingham

National Grid Ref: SE0749

Sailor, Craven Heifer

Ghyll House Farm, *Straight Lane, Moorside, Addingham, Ilkley, W. Yorks, LS29 9JY.*
Peaceful C17th working farm.
Open: All Year
01943 830370 Mrs Flesher
Rates fr: *£14.00*-**£14.00**.
Beds: 1F 1D 1S
(4)

The lowest **single** *rate is shown in* **bold.**

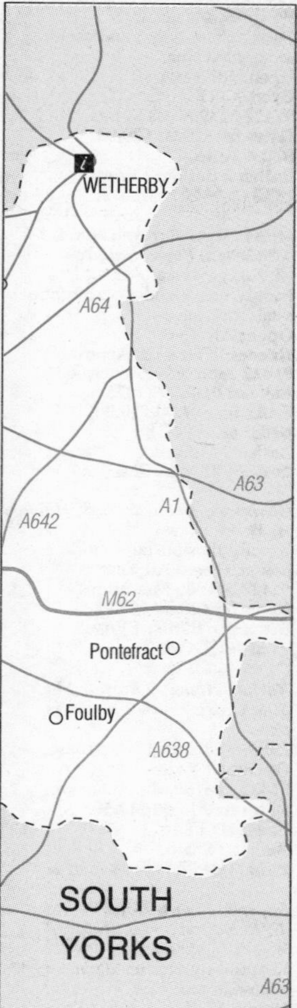

***Olicana Cottage,** High Mill Lane, Addingham, Ilkley, W. Yorks, LS29 0RD.*
Olde worlde riverside cottage.
Open: All Year (not Xmas)
01943 830500 Mrs Pape
Rates fr: *£15.50*-**£16.00**.
Beds: 2D 2S
Baths: 1 Shared
(3)

Bringing children with you? Always ask for any special rates.

Baildon

National Grid Ref: SE1539

***3 Belmont Rise,** Baildon, Shipley, W. Yorks, BD17 5AN.*
Comfortable private house, quiet area.
Open: All Year (not Xmas)
01274 590558 Mrs Thompson
Rates fr: *£16.00*-**£16.00**.
Beds: 1T 1S
Baths: 1 Shared
(2)

Bardsey

National Grid Ref: SE3643

Bingley Arms

***The Ferns,** Tithe Barn Lane, Bardsey, Leeds, LS17 9DX.*
Detached country house - large garden.
Open: Easter to Sep
01937 572357 Mrs Hill
Rates fr: *£18.00*-**£20.00**.
Beds: 2T
Baths: 1 Shared
(2)

Bingley

National Grid Ref: SE1139

Fishermans Inn, Dick Hudsons

***Ashley End,** 22 Ashley Road, off Ashfield Crescent, Bingley, W. Yorks, BD16 1DZ.*
Warm welcome into our home.
Open: All Year (not Xmas)
01274 569679 Mrs Robertson
Rates fr: *£15.00*-**£15.00**.
Beds: 1T 2S
Baths: 1 Shared
(4)

Blackshawhead

National Grid Ref: SD9527

Shoulder of Mutton

***Higher Earnshaw,** Blackshawhead, Hebden Bridge, W. Yorks, HX7 7JB.*
Family smallholding in lovely countryside.
Open: All Year (not Xmas)
01422 844117 Mr & Mrs Redmond
Rates fr: *£15.00*-**£16.00**.
Beds: 1F 1D 1S
Baths: 1 Shared
(4)

***Badger Fields Farm,** Badger Lane, Blackshawhead, Hebden Bridge, W. Yorks, HX7 7JX.*
Modern, comfortable farmhouse.
Open: Apr to Oct
Grades: ETB Listed, Comm
01422 845161 Mrs Whitaker
Rates fr: *£15.00*-**£15.00**.
Beds: 1F 1D
Baths: 1 Shared
(3)

Bradford

National Grid Ref: SE1632

Dick Hudsons

***Carnoustie,** 8 Park Grove, Bradford, W. Yorks, BD9 4JY.*
Detached Victorian private house.
Open: All Year
Grades: ETB 1 Cr
01274 490561 Mr Sugden
Rates fr: *£16.00*-**£20.00**.
Beds: 1D 1T
Baths: 2 Ensuite
(2)

***New Beehive Inn,** Westgate, Bradford, W. Yorks, BD1 3AA.*
Unique gas lit Edwardian inn.
Open: All Year
Grades: ETB 3 Cr
01274 721784 Mr Wagstaff
Rates fr: *£15.00*-**£20.00**.
Beds: 3F 3D 6T 1S
Baths: 9 Ensuite 2 Shared
(18)

***Ivy Guest House,** 3 Melbourne Place, Bradford, W. Yorks, BD5 0HZ.*
Detached Victorian house near centre.
Open: All Year
Grades: ETB Listed
01274 727060 Mr Baggio
Fax no: 01274 411428
Rates fr: *£15.00*-**£18.00**.
Beds: 1F 2D 3T 3S
Baths: 3 Shared
(10)

***Marriners,** 241 Keighley Road, Heaton, Bradford, W. Yorks, BD9 4JU.*
Large Victorian private house.
Open: All Year (not Xmas)
01274 543586 Mrs Murphy
Rates fr: *£14.00*-**£16.00**.
Beds: 1F 2T 1S
Baths: 2 Shared

***Norland House,** 695 Gt Horton Road, Bradford, W. Yorks, BD7 4DU.*
Friendly, family-run guest house.
Open: All Year
01274 571698 Mrs Dawson
Rates fr: *£16.00*-**£19.50**.
Beds: 1F 2D 3T 2S
(8)

Bramhope

National Grid Ref: SE2543

Korks Wine Bar, White Hart

***The Cottages,** Moor Road, Bramhope, Leeds, LS16 9HH.*
Renovated cottages, fringe of village.
Open: All Year (not Xmas)
Grades: ETB 2 Cr, High Comm
0113 284 2754 Mrs Adams
Rates fr: *£21.00*-**£28.00**.
Beds: 4D 1T
Baths: 5 Ensuite
(10) (5)

Bretton

National Grid Ref: SE3320

Station Pub

***Birch Laithes Farm,** Bretton Lane, Bretton, Wakefield, W. Yorks, WF4 4LF.*
C18th house in countryside, 4 miles from Wakeland.
Open: All Year
Grades: ETB 1 Cr, Comm
01924 252129 Mr Hoyland
Rates fr: *£15.00*-**£17.00**.
Beds: 1F 1T 1D

Brighouse

National Grid Ref: SE1423

Lakeside Lodge

***Lakeside Lodge,** Elland Road, Brighouse, W. Yorks, HD6 2RG.*
Black-and-white house, lakeside location. **Open:** All Year
Grades: ETB 3 Cr
01484 713049 Mrs Mitchell
Rates fr: *£20.75*-**£15.50**.
Beds: 1F 7D 1T 3S
Baths: 10 Private 2 Shared
(40)

***16 Daisy Road,** Brighouse, W. Yorks, HD6 3SX.*
Comfortable bungalow with conservatory.
Open: All Year (not Xmas)
01484 720257 Mr & Mrs Darwin
Rates fr: *£15.00*-**£15.00**.
Beds: 1F 1S
(1)

Clayton

National Grid Ref: SE1231

***Brow Top Farm,** Baldwin Lane, Clayton, Bradford, W. Yorks, BD14 6PS.*
Working farm in rural setting.
Open: All Year (not Xmas)
01274 882178 Mrs Priestley
Rates fr: *£15.00*-**£20.00**.
Beds: 1F 1D 1T **Baths:** 3 Private
(6)

Colden

National Grid Ref: SD9628

***New Delight Inn,** Jack Bridge, Colden, Hebden Bridge, W. Yorks, HX7 7HT.*
Ideal for the Pennine Way.
Open: All Year
01422 842795 Mr Marigold
Rates fr: *£13.00*-**£13.00**.
Baths: 3 Ensuite
(50)

Cottingley

National Grid Ref: SE1137

***March Cote Farm,** Off Woodside Avenue, Cottingley, Bingley, W. Yorks, BD16 1UB.*
Top quality farmhouse cooking.
Open: All Year (not Xmas)
01274 487433 Mrs Warin
Rates fr: *£16.00*-**£17.00**.
Beds: 1F 1D 1T
Baths: 1 Private 1 Shared
(8)

Cragg Vale

National Grid Ref: SE0023

***Springfield,** Cragg Road, Cragg Vale, Hebden Bridge, W. Yorks, HX7 5SR.*
Peaceful, modern stone-built house. **Open:** All Year (not Xmas)
01422 882029 Mrs Nelson
Rates fr: *£16.00*-**£16.00**.
Beds: 1D 1T 2S
Baths: 1 Private 1 Shared
(4)

Deanhead

National Grid Ref: SE0214

***The Old School,** Deanhead, Barkisland, Halifax, W. Yorks, HX4 0EA.*
Converted Pennine school, quiet, comfortable. **Open:** All Year
01422 824117 Mr Bancroft
Rates fr: *£15.00*-**£20.00**.
Beds: 1D 1T **Baths:** 2 Ensuite
(3)

Elland

National Grid Ref: SE1121

***Pinfold Hotel,** Dewsbury Road, Elland, W. Yorks, HX5 9JU.*
Former 1840 coaching inn.
Open: All Year (not Xmas)
01422 372645 Mr Coleman
Rates fr: *£16.00*-**£20.00**.
Beds: 1F 1D 2T 3S
Baths: 7 Ensuite
(7)

Emley

National Grid Ref: SE2413

Green Dragon

***White Cross Farm,** Ash Lane, Emley, Huddersfield, W. Yorks, HD8 9QU.*
Comfortable C16th farmhouse.
Open: All Year
01924 848339 Mrs Gill
Rates fr: *£16.00*-**£16.00**.
Beds: 1F 1D 1S
Baths: 1 Ensuite 1 Shared
(4)

Greetland

National Grid Ref: SE0821

***Crawstone Knowl Farm,** Rochdale Road, Greetland, Halifax, W. Yorks, HX4 8PX.*
Large, comfortable Pennine farmhouse.
Open: All Year
Grades: ETB 2 Cr, Comm
01422 370470 Mrs Shackleton
Rates fr: *£15.00*-**£16.00**.
Beds: 1F 1D 1S **Baths:** 3 Ensuite
(6)

Halifax

National Grid Ref: SE0925

***Heathleigh Guest House,** 124 Skircoat Road, Halifax, W. Yorks, HX1 2RE.*
Town centre, luxurious ensuite accommodation.
Open: All Year
Grades: ETB 1 Cr
01422 323957 Ms Eccles
Rates fr: *£20.00*-**£20.00**.
Beds: 2F 1S
Baths: 2 Ensuite 1 Private
(2)

***Milans Wine Bar And Hotel,** 6/8 Carlton Place, Halifax, W. Yorks, HX1 2SB.*
Family-run, friendly town centre establishment.
Open: All Year
Grades: ETB 4 Cr, Approv
01422 330539 Mr Reenwood
Fax no: 01422 381873
Rates fr: *£21.00*-**£30.00**.
Beds: 6F 4D 4T 8S
Baths: 22 Ensuite
(Any)

***Glenmore,** 19 Savile Park, Halifax, W. Yorks, HX1 3EA.*
Beautifully situated Victorian house. **Open:** All Year
01422 341500 Mrs Briggs
Rates fr: *£20.00*-**£25.00**.
Beds: 2D **Baths:** 1 Private

***Norfolk House,** 7 Norfolk Place, King Cross, Halifax, W. Yorks, HX1 3JY.*
Large Victorian private house.
Open: All Year
01422 366100 Mrs Auton
Rates fr: *£15.00*-**£17.50**.
Beds: 1D 1T
Baths: 2 Shared
(4)

***Imperial Crown Hotel,** 42/46 Horton Street, Halifax, W. Yorks, HX1 1BR.*
Luxuriously appointed renovated Victorian residence.
Open: All Year
01422 342342 Mrs Turczak
Rates fr: *£25.00*-**£40.00**.
Beds: 2F 6T 7D 27S
Baths: 42 Ensuite
(60)

Haworth

National Grid Ref: SE0337

Old White Lion

***Moorfield Guest House,** 80 West Lane, Haworth, Keighley, W. Yorks, BD22 8EN.*
Large Victorian private house.
Open: All Year (not Xmas)
01535 643689 Mrs Hargreaves
Rates fr: *£18.00*-**£18.00**.
Beds: 1F 2D 2T 1S
Baths: 5 Private 1 Shared
(6)

***Woodlands Drive Guest House,** Woodlands Grange, Belle Isle, Haworth, Keighley, W. Yorks, BD22 8PB.*
Open: All Year
Grades: ETB 2 Cr, Comm
01535 646814 Ms Harker
Rates fr: *£16.00*-**£22.00**.
Beds: 2F 3D 1T **Baths:** 6 Private
(15)
Haworth (Brontë Country), secluded detatched guest house overlooking Worth Valley Steam Railway close to Yorkshire Dales. Family-run, enjoy Yorkshire hospitality. A warm welcome assured.

***Cobwebs Guest House,** 11 West Lane, Haworth, Keighley, W. Yorks, BD22 8DU.*
Victorian house overlooking Brontë parsonage.
Open: All Year
01535 642501 Mrs Walton
Rates fr: *£17.50*-**£17.50**.
Beds: 1F 2D 1S
Baths: 3 Ensuite 1 Private
(2)

***Meltham House,** 3 Belle Isle Road, Haworth, Keighley, W. Yorks, BD22 8QQ.*
Modern comfortable detached house.
Open: All Year
01535 645282 Mrs Ingham
Rates fr: *£15.00*-**£15.00**.
Beds: 1D 1T 1S
Baths: 1 Private 1 Shared
(5) (3)

***The Manor House,** Changegate, Haworth, Keighley, W. Yorks, BD22 8EB.*
C17th manor house, like parsonage.
Open: Easter to Dec
01535 642911
Mrs Lambert
Rates fr: *£17.00*.
Beds: 2D 1T
Baths: 3 Private
(3)

***Bridgehouse Private Hotel,** Bridgehouse Lane, Haworth, Keighley, W. Yorks, BD22 8PA.*
Mill-owner's Georgian residence. Licensed parking.
Open: All Year (not Xmas)
01535 642372
Mrs Waddington
Rates fr: *£16.00*-**£16.00**.
Beds: 1F 1D 2T 2S
Baths: 3 Ensuite 3 Shared
(0) (8)

***Bronte Cottage,** 4 Park Top Row, Main Street, Haworth, Keighley, W. Yorks, BD22 8DN.*
Modern terrace cottage with view.
Open: All Year
Grades: ETB Listed
01535 647012 Mrs Gray
Rates fr: *£12.50*-**£12.50**.
Beds: 1F 1D 1S
Baths: 3 Ensuite
(10) (3)

***Roos Cottage,** 1 Belle Isle Road, Haworth, Keighley, W. Yorks, BD22 8QQ.*
A warm welcome awaits our guests.
Open: All Year
01535 642594 Mrs Dickson
Rates fr: *£15.00*-**£15.00**.
Beds: 1F 1D 1S **Baths:** 1 Shared
(1)

***Ye Sleeping House,** 8 Main Street, Haworth, Keighley, W. Yorks, BD22 8DA.*
Warm welcome, comfortable, relaxed atmosphere.
Open: All Year
01535 645992 Mr Hutchinson
Rates fr: *£14.00*-**£28.00**.
Beds: 1F 1D 1S **Baths:** 1 Shared
(1) (1)

***Hoyle Farm Cottage,** Dimples Lane, Haworth, Keighley, W. Yorks, BD22 8QT.*
Detached 1854 stone cottage.
Open: All Year
01535 646809 Miss Williams
Rates fr: *£18.00*-**£20.00**.
Beds: 2D 1T **Baths:** 3 Private
(4)

Hebden Bridge

National Grid Ref: SD9927

White Lion, Packhorse

***Redacre House,** Redacre, Mytholmroyd, Hebden Bridge, W. Yorks, HX7 5DQ.*
Open: Mar to Oct
Grades: ETB 2 Cr, High Comm
01422 883019 Mr & Mrs Mawson
Rates fr: *£18.00*-**£22.00**.
Beds: 1D 1T
Baths: 2 Ensuite
(6)
Charming C17th Listed house with inglenook fireplace & mullion windows. Featured on 'Wish You Were Here'. Situated in secluded position with pretty gardens. Homely & relaxed atmosphere. Guests own lounge.

***Prospect End,** 8 Prospect Terrace, Savile Road, Hebden Bridge, W. Yorks, HX7 6NA.*
Ensuite B&B - heart of South Pennines.
Open: All Year
Grades: ETB 1 Cr, Comm
01422 843586 (also fax no)
Mrs Anthon
Rates fr: *£15.00*-**£18.00**.
Beds: 1D 1T **Baths:** 2 Ensuite

***29 Slack Top,** Heptonstall, Hebden Bridge, W. Yorks, HX7 7HA.*
Guest wing to private house.
Open: All Year
01422 843636 Mrs Morley
Fax no: 01422 845621
Rates fr: *£16.00*-**£20.00**.
Beds: 1F 1D
Baths: 2 Ensuite
(4)

***Higher Earnshaw,** Blackshawhead, Hebden Bridge, W. Yorks, HX7 7JB.*
Family smallholding in lovely countryside.
Open: All Year (not Xmas)
01422 844117
Mr & Mrs Redmond
Rates fr: *£15.00*-**£16.00**.
Beds: 1F 1D 1S
Baths: 1 Shared
(4)

***1 Primrose Terrace,** Hebden Bridge, W. Yorks, HX7 6HN.*
Stonebuilt house with canalside location.
Open: All Year
Grades: ETB Listed
01422 844747
Ms McNamee
Rates fr: *£13.00*-**£13.00**.
Beds: 2D 1S
Baths: 1 Shared
(1)

***8 Birchcliffe, (off Sandy Gate),** Hebden Bridge, W. Yorks, HX7 8JA.*
Large, stone weaver's cottage.
Open: All Year
01422 844777
Ms Handley
Rates fr: *£12.50*-**£15.00**.
Beds: 1D
Baths: 1 Private
(1)

***Old Civic Hall Hotel,** Crown Street, Hebden Bridge, W. Yorks, HX7 8EH.*
Small town centre private hotel.
Open: All Year
01422 842814
Mr Midgley
Rates fr: *£17.00*-**£17.00**.
Beds: 2F 2D 4T 1S
Baths: 9 Private

Heptonstall

National Grid Ref: SD9927

White Lion Hotel

***29 Slack Top,** Heptonstall, Hebden Bridge, W. Yorks, HX7 7HA.*
Guest wing to private house.
Open: All Year
01422 843636
Mrs Morley
Fax no: 01422 845621
Rates fr: *£16.00*-**£20.00**.
Beds: 1F 1D
Baths: 2 Ensuite
(4)

***White Lion Hotel,** 58 Towngate, Heptonstall, Hebden Bridge, W. Yorks, HX7 7NB.*
C17th village inn.
Open: All Year (not Xmas)
01422 842027
Rates fr: *£18.00*-**£18.00**.
Beds: 2F 1D
Baths: 3 Ensuite
(4) (4)

Holmfirth

National Grid Ref: SE1408

Valley Guest House, *97 Huddersfield Road, Holmfirth, Huddersfield, W. Yorks, HD7 1JA.*
Comfortable, homely Georgian guest house.
Open: All Year (not Xmas)
01484 681361 Mrs Kilner
Rates fr: *£15.00*-**£20.00**.
Beds: 2D 1T
Baths: 2 Private 1 Shared
(3)

29 Woodhead Road, *Holmfirth, Huddersfield, W. Yorks, HD7 1JU.*
Comfortable Georgian family home.
Open: All Year (not Xmas)
Grades: ETB 1 Cr, Comm
01484 683962 Mrs Beck
Rates fr: *£15.00*-**£15.00**.
Beds: 1T **Baths:** 1 Private

Springfield House, *95 Huddersfield Road, Holmfirth, Huddersfield, W. Yorks, HD7 1JA.*
Centrally situated, comfortable Victorian house.
Open: All Year
01484 683031 Mr Brook
Rates fr: *£15.00*-**£19.00**.
Beds: 1F 2D 1T
Baths: 2 Private 1 Shared
(3)

Holme Castle Country Hotel, *Holmfirth, Huddersfield, W. Yorks, HD7 1QG.*
Conservation area. BBC Green Award. **Open:** All Year
Grades: AA 4 Q
01484 686764 Ms Hayfield
Fax no: 01484 687775
Rates fr: *£20.00*-**£20.00**.
Beds: 2F 3D 2T 1S
Baths: 5 Private 3 Shared
(0) (12)

Shoulder of Mutton, *2 Dunford Road, Holmfirth, Huddersfield, W. Yorks, HD7 1DP.*
Pub in 'Summer Wine' country.
Open: All Year
01484 684414 Mr Messenger
Rates fr: *£15.00*-**£15.00**.
Beds: 2F
Baths: 1 Shared
(4)

Huddersfield

National Grid Ref: SE1016

Scapehouse Inn

14 Grandstand, *Scapegoat Hill, Huddersfield, W. Yorks, HD7 4NQ.*
Converted weaver's cottage, stunning location.
Open: All Year (not Xmas)
Grades: ETB Listed
01484 658342 Mrs West
Rates fr: *£16.00*-**£16.00**.
Beds: 1D 1T **Baths:** 2 Shared
(2)

Idle

National Grid Ref: SE1737

Glengarry Guest House, *175 Albion Road, Idle, Bradford, W. Yorks, BD10 9QP.*
200-year-old house, cosy, quaint.
Open: All Year
01274 613781 Mr Swain
Rates fr: *£13.00*-**£15.00**.
Beds: 2T 1S
Baths: 2 Shared
(4)

Ilkley

National Grid Ref: SE1147

Wharfedale Gate

Riverside Hotel, *Bridge Lane, Ilkley, W. Yorks, LS29 9HN.*
Open: All Year
01943 607338 Mrs Dobson
Rates fr: *£25.00*-**£30.00**.
Beds: 1F 4D 3T 2S
Baths: 10 Ensuite
(30)
Recommended family owned licensed hotel. Ensuite - newly refurbished. TV/Sky, tea/coffee, lounge bar with log fire. Food & drink available on the patio overlooking the river.

The Grove Hotel, *66 The Grove, Ilkley, W. Yorks, LS29 9PA.*
Spacious, well-appointed Victorian townhouse.
Open: All Year (not Xmas)
Grades: ETB 3 Cr, Comm, AA 1 St
01943 600298 Mr Emslie
Rates fr: *£20.00*-**£30.00**.
Beds: 2F 1D 2T 1S
Baths: 6 Private 1 Shared
(5)

Belvedere, *2 Victoria Avenue, Ilkley, W. Yorks, LS29 9BL.*
Large Victorian house overlooking valley. **Open:** All Year
01943 607598 Mrs Terry
Rates fr: *£13.50*-**£14.00**.
Beds: 1F 1D 1T 1S
Baths: 1 Shared
(1)

63 Skipton Road, *Ilkley, W. Yorks, LS29 9BH.*
Modern family-run detached house. Pleasant garden.
Open: All Year
01943 817542
Mrs Roberts
Rates fr: *£16.00*-**£15.00**.
Beds: 1F 1D 1S
Baths: 2 Shared
(5)

The lowest *double* rate per person is shown in *italics*.

Hollygarth House, *293 Leeds Road, Ilkley, W. Yorks, LS29 8LL.*
Comfortable house by River Wharfe. **Open:** All Year
01943 609223 Mrs Taylor
Rates fr: *£14.00*-**£14.00**.
Beds: 1F 1D 1T **Baths:** 1 Shared
(5) (5)

Archway Cottage, *24 Skipton Road, Ilkley, W. Yorks, LS29 9EP.*
Modernised comfortable accommodation in central Ilkley.
Open: All Year (not Xmas)
01943 603399 Mrs Below
Rates fr: *£15.00*-**£15.00**.
Beds: 2D 2T (2)

Illingworth

National Grid Ref: SE0728

The Elms, *Keighley Road, Illingworth, Halifax, W. Yorks, HX2 8HT.*
Large Victorian detached house.
Open: All Year (not Xmas)
Grades: ETB 2 Cr
01422 244430 Mrs Davis-Crowther
Rates fr: *£18.00*-**£18.00**.
Beds: 1F 2D 2S
Baths: 2 Private 1 Shared
(8)

Keighley

National Grid Ref: SE0541

Currer Laithe Farm, *Moss Carr Road, Long Lee, Keighley, W. Yorks, BD21 4SL.*
C16th 'Brontë Country' working farm. **Open:** All Year (not Xmas)
01535 604387 Miss Brown
Rates fr: *£12.00*-**£12.00**.
Beds: 2F 1D 3T 1S **Baths:** 3 Shared
(10)

Leeds

National Grid Ref: SE3034

Old Red Lion, The Wrens, Korks Wine, Deer Park, Lawnswood Arms

High Bank Private & Commercial Hotel, *83 Harehills Lane, Leeds, West Yorkshire, LS7 4HA.*
Convenient, affordable, comfortable modern hotel.
Open: All Year
Grades: ETB 2 Cr
0113 262 2164 Mr Butt
Fax no: 0113 237 4436
Rates fr: *£17.78*-**£21.00**.
Beds: 4F 4D 5T 8S
Baths: 8 Ensuite 3 Shared
(30)

The Old Lamb Guest House, *997 York Road, Seacroft, Leeds, West Yorkshire, LS14 6HP.*
Originally 200-year-old coaching inn. **Open:** All Year
0113 260 5844 Mrs Spink
Fax no: 0113 260 3119
Rates fr: *£10.00*-**£16.00**.
Beds: 2F 1D 1T
Baths: 1 Private 2 Shared
(10)

Central Hotel, *35 New Briggate, Leeds, West Yorkshire, LS2 8JD.*
30 bedrooms, licensed, city centre.
Open: All Year
Grades: ETB Listed
0113 294 1456 Mrs Scriven
Fax no: 0113 294 1551
Rates fr: *£18.50*-**£18.50**.
Beds: 6D 10T 9S
Baths: 11 Ensuite 3 Shared
(10) (6)

The Cottages, *Moor Road, Bramhope, Leeds, LS16 9HH.*
Renovated cottages, fringe of village.
Open: All Year (not Xmas)
Grades: ETB 2 Cr, High Comm
0113 284 2754 Mrs Adams
Rates fr: *£21.00*-**£28.00**.
Beds: 4D 1T **Baths:** 5 Ensuite
(10) (5)

18 Moor Allerton Drive, Off Street Lane, *Moortown, Leeds, West Yorkshire, LS17 6RZ.*
Modern comfortable guest house.
Open: All Year
0113 293 5469 Mr & Mrs Gibb
Fax no: 0113 275 3300
Rates fr: *£16.00*-**£20.00**.
Beds: 2F 3D 2T 1S
Baths: 1 Private 1 Shared
(4)

Abbey Guest House, *44 Vesper Road, Kirkstall, Leeds, West Yorkshire, LS5 3NX.*
Large Victorian house near Abbey.
Open: All Year (not Xmas)
Grades: ETB 3 Cr, Comm
0113 225 6700 Mrs Nicol
Rates fr: *£20.00*-**£26.00**.
Beds: 1F 1D 2T 1S
Baths: 5 Private
(2) (5)

Merevale Hotel, *16 Wetherby Road, Oakwood, Leeds, West Yorkshire, LS8 2QD.*
Elegant (Victorian) hotel, quiet, friendly atmosphere.
Open: All Year
Grades: AA 3 Q, Recomm
0113 265 8933 Mr Jeynes
Rates fr: *£18.00*-**£20.00**.
Beds: 1F 3D 2T 8S
Baths: 6 Private 2 Shared
(9)

Aragon Hotel, *250 Stainbeck Lane, Leeds, West Yorkshire, LS7 2PS.*
Large Victorian private house.
Open: All Year (not Xmas)
Grades: ETB 3 Cr, AA 1 St, RAC Acclaim
0113 275 7166 Mr Heaton
Rates fr: *£20.00*-**£26.00**.
Beds: 1F 4D 3T 5S
Baths: 11 Private 2 Shared
(24)

The Ascot Grange Hotel, *126-130 Otley Road, Leeds, West Yorkshire, LS16 5JX.*
Newly refurbished, Edwardian city house. **Open:** All Year
0113 293 4444
Fax no: 0113 293 5555
Rates fr: *£22.50*-**£35.00**.
Beds: 7F 11D 4T 4S
Baths: 26 Ensuite
(50)

6 South Parade, North Lane, *Headingley, Leeds, West Yorkshire, LS6 3LF.*
Internationally recommended, friendly home cuisine.
Open: All Year (not Xmas)
0113 278 9789 Mr Pitts
Fax no: 0133 2745745
Rates fr: *£16.00*-**£19.00**.
Beds: 1F 1D 1T
Baths: 1 Shared
(8)

Ashfield Hotel, *44 Cardigan Road, Leeds, West Yorkshire, LS6 3AG.*
Converted large victorian house.
Open: All Year (not Xmas)
0113 275 8847
Fax no: 0113 275 7991
Rates fr: *£20.00*-**£27.00**.
Beds: 1F 4D 2T 5S
Baths: 3 Ensuite 3 Shared
(9)

17 Cottage Road, Headingley, *Leeds, West Yorkshire, LS6 4DD.*
Traditional Yorkshire stone detached house.
Open: All Year (not Xmas)
0113 275 5575 Mr & Mrs Hood
Rates fr: *£16.00*-**£16.00**.
Beds: 1T 2S **Baths:** 1 Shared
(6 months)

The Coach House, *North Grove Approach, Leeds, West Yorkshire, LS22 7GA.*
Tranquil coach house, own entrance. 0.5 acre garden.
Open: All Year
Grades: ETB Listed, Approv
01937 586100 Mrs Hobson
Fax no: 01937 587773
Rates fr: *£17.50*-**£25.00**.
Beds: 1F **Baths:** 1 Ensuite
(1) (4)

Beechwood Private Hotel, *34 Street Lane, Leeds, West Yorkshire, LS8 2ET.*
User-friendly, suburban, licensed hotel.
Open: All Year (not Xmas)
0113 266 2578 Ms Jackson
Fax no: 01132 662578
Rates fr: *£22.00*-**£26.00**.
Beds: 4F 5D 3T 7S
Baths: 7 Private 12 Shared

Marsden

National Grid Ref: SE0411

Forest Farm, *Mount Road, Marsden, Huddersfield, W. Yorks, HD7 6NN.*
300-year-old farmhouse.
Open: All Year (not Xmas)
01484 842687 Mrs Fussey
Rates fr: *£15.00*-**£15.00**.
Beds: 1F 1D 1T
Baths: 2 Shared
(6)

Mytholmroyd

National Grid Ref: SE0126

Shoulder of Mutton

Reedacres, *Mytholmroyd, Hebden Bridge, W. Yorks, HX7 5DQ.*
Detached modern house.
Open: All Year (not Xmas)
01422 884423 Mr & Mrs Boggis
Rates fr: *£16.00*-**£25.00**.
Beds: 1F 1S **Baths:** 1 Private

Redacre House, *Redacre, Mytholmroyd, Hebden Bridge, W. Yorks, HX7 5DQ.*
Charming C17th Listed house, inglenook fireplace.
Open: Mar to Oct
Grades: ETB 2 Cr, High Comm
01422 883019 Mr & Mrs Mawson
Rates fr: *£18.00*-**£22.00**.
Beds: 1D 1T **Baths:** 2 Ensuite
(6)

Rogergate, *Mytholmroyd, Hebden Bridge, W. Yorks, HX7 5AP.*
Large bungalow in landscaped gardens. **Open:** All Year (not Xmas)
01422 883355 Mrs Cooper
Rates fr: *£14.50*-**£17.00**.
Beds: 2D
Baths: 1 Ensuite 1 Private
(1) (3)

Netherthong

National Grid Ref: SE1309

Westwood, *7 St Marys Crescent, Netherthong, Holmfirth, W. Yorks, HD7 2XP.*
Detached bungalow with swimming pool. **Open:** All Year
01484 685695 Mrs Dickinson
Rates fr: *£16.00*-**£16.00**.
Beds: 1T 1S
Baths: 1 Private 1 Shared
(2)

Norland

National Grid Ref: SE0722

The Hobbit Hotel, *Hob Lane, Norland, Sowerby Bridge, W. Yorks, HX6 3QL.*
Country hotel, pub/bistro, restaurant. **Open:** All Year
01422 832202 Mr Gomersall
Rates fr: *£21.50*-**£29.00**.
Beds: 2F 11D 6T 3S
Baths: 22 Private
(1) (100)

Norwood Green

National Grid Ref: SE1326

Ruby

5 Mayfield, *Norwood Green, Halifax, W. Yorks, HX3 8QT.*
Pretty village cottage.
Open: All Year
01274 679856 Mrs Beddoe
Rates fr: *£14.00*-**£14.00**.
Beds: 1T 1S

Oakworth

National Grid Ref: SE0338

Railway Cottage, *59 Station Road, Oakworth, Keighley, W. Yorks, BD22 0DZ.*
Cottage of 'Railway Children' film.
Open: All Year (not Xmas)
01535 642693 Mrs Cope
Rates fr: *£12.00*-**£14.50**.
Beds: 3D 2S **Baths:** 5 Private
(5)

Greenways, *30 Goose Cote Lane, Oakworth, Keighley, W. Yorks, BD22 7NQ.*
Large house with large gardens.
Open: All Year
01535 667959 Mrs Cowling
Rates fr: *£16.00*-**£11.00**.
Beds: 1D 1S **Baths:** 1 Private
(3)

Newsholme Manor Hotel, *Slaymaker Lane, Slack Lane, Oakworth, Keighley, W. Yorks, BD22 0RQ.*
Delightful country hotel, panoramic views.
Open: All Year
01535 642964 Mr Sexton
Rates fr: *£16.50*-**£19.50**.
Beds: 1F 3D 1T 1S
Baths: 6 Private
(40)

Ogden

National Grid Ref: SE0631

Windmill Court Hotel, *Ye Olde Golden Egg Restaurant, Ogden, Halifax, W. Yorks, HX2 8YB.*
Beautiful rural views.
Open: All Year
01422 244941 Mrs Ginley
Rates fr: *£35.00*-**£25.00**.
Beds: 3F 6D 3S
Baths: 12 Private
(30)

Ossett

National Grid Ref: SE2820

Crown Cottage, *18 Horbury Road, Ossett, W. Yorks, WF5 0BN.*
Open: All Year (not Xmas)
01924 272495 Mr Mellor
Rates fr: *£18.00*-**£18.00**.
Beds: 2D 2T 3S **Baths:** 2 Shared
(20)

Otley

National Grid Ref: SE2045

Three Horseshoes, Spite Inn, Jewel of India

18 Harecroft Road, *Otley, W. Yorks, LS21 2BQ.*
Homely private residence, quiet location.
Open: All Year
01943 463643 Mrs Mandy
Rates fr: *£15.00*-**£15.00**.
Beds: 1T 2S **Baths:** 2 Shared
(1) (2)

11 Newall Mount, *Otley, W. Yorks, LS21 2DY.*
Comfortable, friendly, quietly-situated house.
Open: All Year (not Xmas)
01943 462898 Mrs Davison
Rates fr: *£13.50*-**£13.50**.
Beds: 1F 1D 1T 1S
Baths: 2 Shared
(2)

Oxenhope

National Grid Ref: SE0337

The Three Sister, Dog & Gun

West View, *Jew Lane, Oxenhope, Haworth, Keighley, W. Yorks, BD22 9HS.*
Large Victorian semi in countryside.
Open: Easter to Nov
01535 642779 Mrs Pawson
Rates fr: *£14.00*-**£16.00**.
Beds: 2T
Baths: 1 Shared
(8) (2)

Springfield Guest House, *Shaw Lane, Oxenhope, Keighley, W. Yorks, BD22 9QL.*
Large Victorian house.
Open: All Year
01535 643951
Mrs Hargreaves
Rates fr: *£15.00*-**£16.00**.
Beds: 2F 1D 1T
Baths: 1 Private 2 Shared
(6)

Pontefract

National Grid Ref: SE4521

Carlton Hotel

Tudor Guest House, *18 Tudor Close, Pontefract, W. Yorks, WF8 4NJ.*
Private house in residential area.
Open: All Year (not Xmas)
01977 701007
Mrs Kilby
Rates fr: *£17.50*-**£25.00**.
Beds: 2D
Baths: 2 Private
(2)

Pool-in-Wharfedale

National Grid Ref: SE2445

Half Moon Inn

Half Moon Inn, *Main Street, Pool-in-Wharfedale, Otley, W. Yorks, LS21 1LH.*
Friendly inn with home cooking.
Open: All Year
Grades: ETB 3 Cr, Approv
0113 284 2878
Mr Regan
Rates fr: *£20.00*-**£30.00**.
Beds: 1D 4T
Baths: 5 Ensuite
(8)

Ripponden

National Grid Ref: SE0319

Blue Ball Inn, *Blue Ball Lane, Ripponden, Sowerby Bridge, W. Yorks, HX6 4LR.*
C18th moorland inn, good food.
Open: All Year
01422 823603 Mrs Foster
Rates fr: *£17.60*-**£17.60**.
Beds: 3D 1T
Baths: 1 Private 1 Shared

Dove Dale, *14 Small Lees, Ripponden, Sowerby Bridge, W. Yorks, HX6 4DZ.*
Modern, detached house, splendid views. **Open:** All Year
01422 823611 Mr & Mrs Sands
Rates fr: *£15.00*-**£15.50**.
Beds: 2D 1T **Baths:** 1 Shared

Shipley

National Grid Ref: SE1437

Southgate House, *145 Bradford Road, Shipley, W. Yorks, BD18 3TH.*
Large Victorian house.
Open: All Year
Grades: RAC Listed
01274 585549 Mrs Hainsworth
Rates fr: *£16.00*-**£16.00**.
Beds: 2T 1D
Baths: 1 Ensuite 2 Shared
(3)

Cliffwood Guest House, *1 Cliffwood Avenue, Shipley, W. Yorks, BD18 3DD.*
Friendly, family-run, clean, comfortable.
Open: All Year (not Xmas)
01274 591664 Mrs Steel
Rates fr: *£15.00*-**£15.00**.
Beds: 1F 1D 2T 3S
Baths: 2 Private 1 Shared

Slaithwaite

National Grid Ref: SE0813

Oakmere, *44 Longlands Road, Slaithwaite, Huddersfield, W. Yorks, HD7 5DR.*
Motorway network within easy reach.
Open: All Year (not Xmas)
01484 843323 Mrs Campbell
Rates fr: *£16.00*-**£16.00**.
Beds: 1D 1T **Baths:** 2 Private
(1)

Soyland Town

National Grid Ref: SE0320

Wood End, *Lighthazels Road, Soyland Town, Ripponden, Sowerby Bridge, W. Yorks, HX6 4NP*
C17th converted farmhouse, idyllic setting. **Open:** All Year (not Xmas
01422 822135 Mrs Eccles
Rates fr: *£20.00*-**£15.00**.
Beds: 1F 2D 1S
Baths: 3 Ensuite 1 Shared
(4)

Stanbury

National Grid Ref: SE0037

Wuthering Heights Inn

Ponden Hall, *Stanbury, Haworth, Keighley, W. Yorks, BD22 0HR.*
Welcoming relaxed Elizabethan farmhouse.
Open: All Year (not Xmas)
01535 644154 Mrs Taylor
Rates fr: *£17.00*-**£15.00**.
Beds: 1F 1D 1T

Buckley Green, *Stanbury, Haworth, Keighley, W. Yorks, BD22 0HL.*
Large Bronte moorland farmhouse.
Open: All Year (not Xmas)
01535 645095 (also fax no)
Mrs Archer
Rates fr: *£14.00*-**£15.00**.
Beds: 2D 1T
Baths: 1 Shared
(6)

Wuthering Heights Inn, *26 Main Street, Stanbury, Keighley, W. Yorks, BD22 0HB.*
Warm & friendly country pub.
Open: All Year
01535 643332 Mrs Mitchell
Rates fr: *£14.00*-**£15.00**.
Beds: 1F 1D 1T 1S
Baths: 2 Shared
(20)

Stone Chair

National Grid Ref: SE1127

Duke of York Inn

The Duke of York Inn, *Denholmegate Road, Stone Chair, Halifax, W. Yorks, HX3 7SB.*
C17th former coaching inn.
Open: All Year
01422 202056 Mr Whitaker
Rates fr: *£19.00*-**£28.00**.
Beds: 2F 6D 6T 4S
Baths: 18 Private
(10) (20)

Todmorden

National Grid Ref: SD9424

Calder Bank House, *Shaw Wood Road, Todmorden, W. Yorks, OL14 6DA.*
Millowner's house set in 1.5 acres.
Open: All Year
01706 816188 Ms Wardroper
Rates fr: *£19.00*-**£17.00**.
Beds: 1F 1D 2T 2S
Baths: 1 Private
(10)

Tong Village

National Grid Ref: SE2230

Greyhound Inn, Tong Village Hotel

Keeper Cottage, *Keeper Lane, Tong Village, Bradford, W. Yorks, BD4 0RS.*
Charming, welcoming, comfortable country cottage.
Open: All Year (not Xmas)
0113 285 2566
Mrs Fearnside
Rates fr: *£17.50*-**£18.50**.
Beds: 1T 1S
Baths: 1 Shared
(2)

Wakefield

National Grid Ref: SE3220

The Poppies, *8 Cobbler Hall, West Bretton, Wakefield, W. Yorks, WF4 4LJ.*
Modern comfortable detached house West Bretton, Wakefield.
01924 830317
Mr & Mrs Harbourne
Rates fr: *£16.00*-**£16.00**.
Beds: 2T 1S
Baths: 2 Shared
(3)

Stanley View Guesthouse, *226/228 Stanley Road, Wakefield, W. Yorks, WF1 4AE.*
2 large Victorian houses.
Open: All Year
Grades: AA 4 Q
01924 376803 Mr Heppinstall
Rates fr: *£17.00*-**£18.00**.
Beds: 5F 5D 5T 4S
Baths: 7 Ensuite 2 Private 1 Shared
(10)

Harlequin Hotel, *165 Westgate, Wakefield, W. Yorks, WF2 9SA.*
Clean, caring, friendly, private hotel.
Open: All Year
01924 372500 Mrs Taylor
Rates fr: *£16.00*-**£20.00**.
Beds: 3F 2D 4T 5S
Baths: 5 Ensuite 3 Shared
(3)

The lowest **single** *rate is shown in* **bold.**

Always telephone to get directions to the B&B - you will save time!

West Bretton

National Grid Ref: SE2813

The Poppies, *8 Cobbler Hall, West Bretton, Wakefield, W. Yorks, WF4 4LJ.*
Modern comfortable detached house in West Bretton, Wakefield.
01924 830317 Mr & Mrs Harbourne
Rates fr: *£16.00*-**£16.00**.
Beds: 2T 1S
Baths: 2 Shared
(3)

Wetherby

National Grid Ref: SE4048

Swan & Talbot, Angel Hotel, Windmill

14 Woodhill View, *Wetherby, W. Yorks, LS22 4PP.*
Quiet area near town centre.
Open: All Year
Grades: ETB Listed, Comm
01937 581200 / 0374 220304
Mr Green
Rates fr: *£15.50*-**£18.50**.
Beds: 1F 1T
Baths: 1 Shared
(3)

Glendales, *Muddy Lane, Off Northgate Lane, Wetherby, W. Yorks, LS22 4HW.*
Detached Georgian house, overlooking green.
Open: All Year
Grades: ETB 2 Cr
01937 585915 Mrs Smith
Rates fr: *£18.00*-**£18.00**.
Beds: 1D 2T 1S
Baths: 1 Private 2 Shared
(10) (6)

2 Wharfe Grove, *Wetherby, W. Yorks, LS22 6HA.*
Fine, peaceful stone manor-style house.
Open: All Year (not Xmas)
01937 582711 Mrs Silcox
Rates fr: *£18.50*-**£25.00**.
Beds: 1F 1D
Baths: 1 Ensuite 1 Shared
(2)

Isle of Man

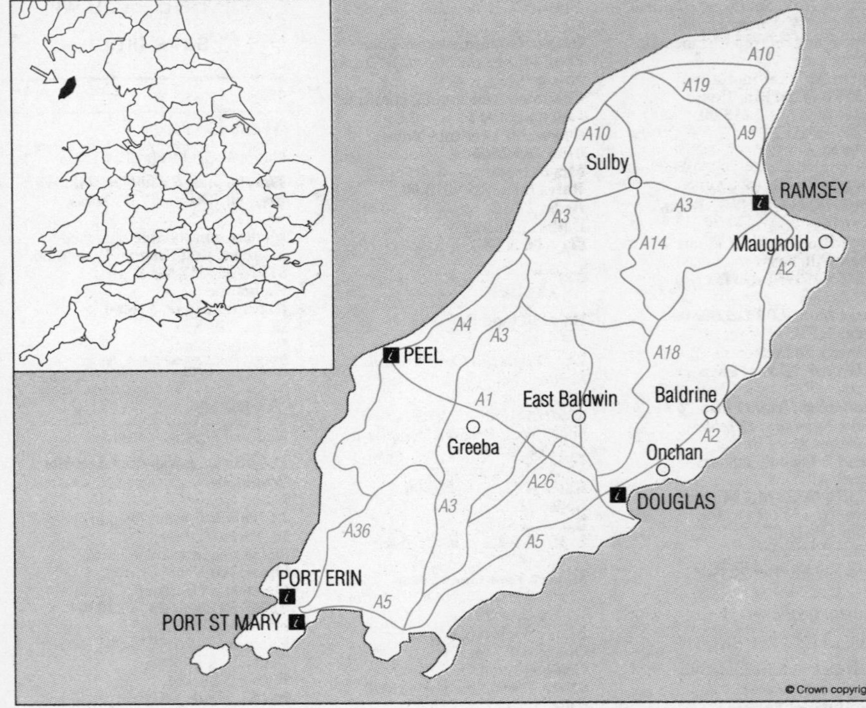

Tourist Information Centres

Airport Information Desk, **Ronaldsway**, Ballasalla, Isle of Man, 01624 823311.

Commissioners Office, Civic Centre, Farrants Way, **Castletown**, Isle of Man, 01624 823518.

Harris Promenade, **Douglas**, Isle of Man, 01624 686766.

Laxey Heritage Trust, Old Fire House, **Laxey Wheel**, Isle of Man, 01624 862007, (Easter to Oct)

Commissioners Office, Town Hall, Derby Road, **Peel**, Isle of Man, 01624 842341.

Commissioners Office, Station Road, **Port Erin**, Isle of Man, 01624 832298.

Commissioners Office, Town Hall, **Port St Mary**, Isle of Man, 01624 832101.

The Library, Town Hall, **Ramsey**, Isle of Man, 01624 812228.

Baldrine

National Grid Ref: SC4281

High Standing, *Main Road, Baldrine, Isle of Man, IM4 6DU.*
Quiet, country & sea view.
Open: All Year (not Xmas)
01624 861220 Mrs Kelly
Rates fr: *£18.00*-**£18.00**.
Beds: 2D 1T
Baths: 3 Private
(8) (3)

Douglas

National Grid Ref: SC3875

Bentlea, *8 The Esplanade, Douglas, Isle of Man, IM2 4LR.*
Open: All Year
Grades: ETB 2 Cr, Comm
01624 673879 Ms Myers
Rates fr: *£16.00*-**£16.00**.
Beds: 3D 2T
Baths: 5 Ensuite
(2)
Family-run guest house on central promenade. With 40 years of experience in tourist industry. Good home cooking & friendly welcome assured. Highly recommended!

All Seasons, *Broadway, Douglas, Isle of Man, IM2 3HX.*
Inclusive low-cost travel arranged.
Open: All Year (not Xmas)
Grades: ETB 3 Cr, AA 2 Q
01624 676323 Mr & Mrs Hanson
Rates fr: *£18.50*-**£18.50**.
Beds: 3D 2T 1S **Baths:** 6 Private

Mitre Hotel, *Central Promenade, Douglas, Isle of Man, IM2 4LT.*
Private licensed hotel, sea views.
Open: Easter to Oct
Grades: ETB 3 Cr, Comm
01624 629232 (also fax no)
Mr & Mrs Lowry
Rates fr: *£19.00*-**£19.00**.
Beds: 5F 5D 4T **Baths:** 14 Ensuite

Midland Hotel, *Loch Promenade, Douglas, Isle of Man, IM1 2LY.*
Very comfortable Victorian seafront hotel.
Open: Easter to Sep
Grades: ETB 1 Cr
01624 674990 (also fax no)
Mr & Mrs Akerman
Rates fr: *£18.00*-**£18.00**.
Beds: 5F 6D 2T 3S
Baths: 4 Shared

The Rio, 42 Loch Promenade, Douglas, Isle of Man, IM1 2LY.
Modern hotel, seafront, well-run.
Open: Jan to Oct
Grades: RAC Listed
01624 676698
Mr & Mrs Ireton
Rates fr: *£18.00*-**£20.00**.
Beds: 3F 2D 4T 3S
Baths: 11 Ensuite
(1)

Edelweiss, Queens Promenade, Douglas, Isle of Man, IM2 4NF.
Featured on BBC2 Travel Show.
Open: All Year (not Xmas)
01624 675115 Mr Fleming
Rates fr: *£17.84*-**£23.09**.
Beds: 4F 8D 7T 1S
Baths: 20 Private

Rangemore, 12 Derby Square, Douglas, Isle of Man, IM1 3LS.
Quiet central Victorian square.
Open: All Year (not Xmas)
Grades: ETB 3 Cr, Comm
01624 674892 Mrs Quirk
Rates fr: *£15.00*-**£15.00**.
Beds: 1F 2D 1T 1S
Baths: 3 Ensuite 5 Private 3 Shared
(5)

East Baldwin

National Grid Ref: SC3682

Booilshuggel Farm, East Baldwin, Braddan, Douglas, Isle of Man, IM4 5ER.
Modern, comfortable farmhouse, picturesque scenery.
Open: Easter to Oct
Grades: ETB 1 Cr, High Comm
01624 851235
Mrs Caley
Rates fr: *£16.00*-**£16.00**.
Beds: 2D
Baths: 1 Shared
(3)

Greeba

National Grid Ref: SC3080

Farmers Arms

Kerrow Garrow Farm, Greeba, St Johns, Isle of Man, IM4 3LG.
Quiet farm, centrally positioned.
Open: Easter to Sep
01624 801871 Mrs Jackson
Rates fr: *£15.00*-**£15.00**.
Beds: 1F 1D
Baths: 1 Shared
(2)

Bringing children with you? Always ask for any special rates.

Maughold

National Grid Ref: SC4991

Glen Mona

Thalloo-Ree, Dhoon, Maughold, Ramsey, Isle of Man, IM7 1HP.
Modern comfortable bungalow. Excellent location.
Open: Easter to Oct
Grades: ETB 1 Cr, High Comm
01624 861450 Mrs Lace
Rates fr: *£16.50*-**£16.50**.
Beds: 1T **Baths:** 1 Ensuite
(20)

Onchan

National Grid Ref: SC3978

Hillberry Manor, Little Mill Road, Onchan, Douglas, Isle of Man, IM4 5BE.
Open: All Year
Grades: ETB 3 Cr, Comm
01624 661660
Mr & Mrs Leventhorpe
Rates fr: *£23.00*-**£28.00**.
Beds: 1D 3T
Baths: 3 Private 1 Shared
(10) (5)
Substantial Victorian country house in extensive grounds. Some guests' comments 'Most comfortable stay - wonderful hospitality', 'couldn't have chosen a better place to stay. Excellent food'.

Peel

National Grid Ref: SC2484

Fernleigh Private Hotel, Marine Parade, Peel, Isle of Man, IM5 1PB.
Excellent service, modern, comfortable, popular.
Open: All Year (not Xmas)
Grades: ETB 2 Cr, Comm
01624 842435 Mr & Mrs Pownall
Rates fr: *£17.00*-**£17.00**.
Beds: 1F 3D 2T 6S
Baths: 4 Private 2 Shared

The Haven, 10 Peveril Avenue, Peel, Isle of Man, IM5 1QB.
Homely guest house, superior accommodation.
Open: All Year
01624 842585 Mrs Breakey
Rates fr: *£15.00*-**£17.00**.
Beds: 1F 1D 1T **Baths:** 3 Private

Port Erin

National Grid Ref: SC1969

Cherry Orchard Hotel

Regent House, The Promenade, Port Erin, Isle of Man, IM9 6LE.
Comfortable guest house.
Open: Easter to Oct
01624 833454 Mrs Renton
Rates fr: *£21.50*-**£18.00**.
Beds: 3D 3T 2S
Baths: 6 Private 1 Shared

Port Erin Hotels, The Promenade, Port Erin, Isle of Man, IM6 6LH.
Overlooking beautiful Port Erin Bay.
Open: Mar to Oct
01624 833558 Mr Schmidtke
Fax no: 01624 835402
Rates fr: *£23.95*-**£30.45**.
Beds: 60F 70D 70T 20S
Baths: 220 Ensuite
(100)

Brobourne House, The Promenade, Port Erin, Isle of Man, IM9 6LA.
Friendly, clean, comfortable guest house.
Open: All Year
01624 832369 Mr Mordaunt
Rates fr: *£13.00*-**£13.00**.
Beds: 4F 6D 4T 2S
Baths: 3 Private 3 Shared
(2)

Port St Mary

National Grid Ref: SC2067

Albert Hotel

The Albert Hotel, Athol Street, Port St Mary, Isle of Man, IM9 5DS.
Clean, comfortable, friendly atmosphere.
Open: All Year
01624 832118 Mr Holt
Rates fr: *£15.00*-**£20.00**.
Beds: 2D 2T 1S
Baths: 2 Shared
(6)

Ramsey

National Grid Ref: SC4594

Viking Apart Hotel

Whitestones, The Vollan, Ramsey, Isle of Man, IM8 3UJ.
Quiet, seafront location, homely atmosphere.
Open: All Year
Grades: ETB 1 Cr, High Comm
01624 813824 Miss Gaskell
Rates fr: *£16.00*-**£16.00**.
Beds: 1D 1S
Baths: 2 Private
(8) (3)

Sulby

National Grid Ref: SC3894

Sulby Glen Hotel

Sulby Glen Hotel, Main Road, Sulby, Isle of Man, IM7 2HR.
Traditional real ale country inn.
Open: All Year (not Xmas)
Grades: ETB 2 Cr, AA Listed
01624 897240 Mrs Sayle
Fax no: 01624 898100
Rates fr: *£21.00*-**£21.00**.
Beds: 3D 6T 2S
Baths: 3 Ensuite 2 Private 7 Shared

Aberdeenshire & Moray

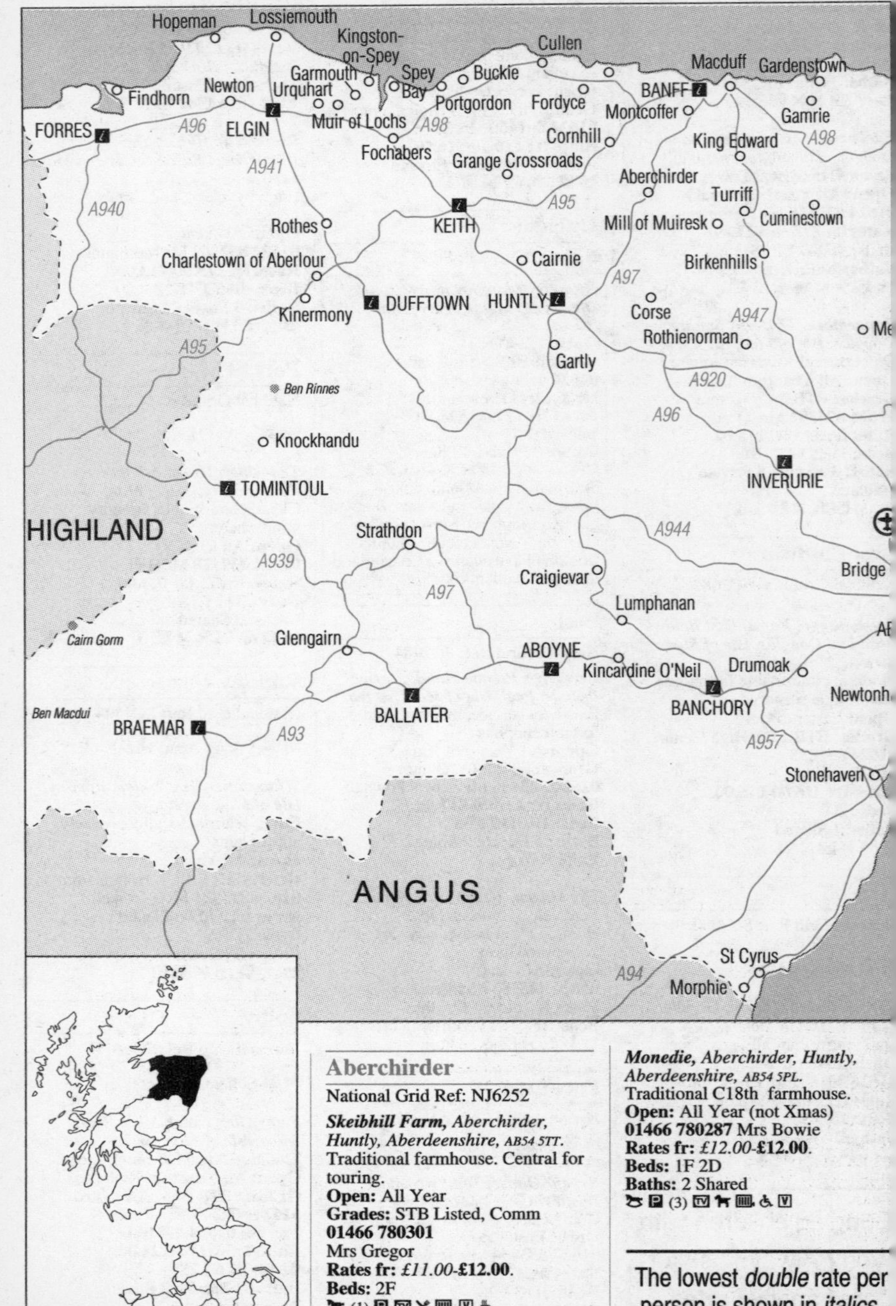

Aberchirder

National Grid Ref: NJ6252

Skeibhill Farm, *Aberchirder, Huntly, Aberdeenshire,* AB54 5TT.
Traditional farmhouse. Central for touring.
Open: All Year
Grades: STB Listed, Comm
01466 780301
Mrs Gregor
Rates fr: *£11.00*-**£12.00**.
Beds: 2F
(1)

Monedie, *Aberchirder, Huntly, Aberdeenshire,* AB54 5PL.
Traditional C18th farmhouse.
Open: All Year (not Xmas)
01466 780287 Mrs Bowie
Rates fr: *£12.00*-**£12.00**.
Beds: 1F 2D
Baths: 2 Shared
(3)

The lowest *double* rate per person is shown in *italics*.

Tourist Information Centres

St Nicholas House, Broad Street, **Aberdeen**, Aberdeenshire, AB9 1GZ, 01224 632727.

Ballater Road Car Park, **Aboyne**, Aberdeenshire, AB34 5HY, 01339 886060, (Easter to Oct).

Railway Museum, Station Yard, **Alford**, Aberdeenshire, AB33 8AD, 01975 562052, (Easter to Oct).

Grampian Road, **Aviemore**, Invernessshire, PH22 1RH, 01479 810363.

Station Square, **Ballater**, Aberdeenshire, AB35 5QB, 01339 755306, (Easter to Oct).

Bellfield Car Park, **Banchory**, Kincardineshire, AB31 3SR, 01330 22000, (Easter to Oct).

Collie Lodge, Low Street, **Banff**, Banffshire, AB45 1AU, 01261 812419, (Easter to Oct).

Balnellan Road, **Braemar**, Ballater, Aberdeenshire, AB35 5YE, 01339 741600, (Easter to Oct)

Car Park, **Crathie**, Ballater, Aberdeenshire, AB35 5TT, 01339 742414, (Easter to Oct).

20 Seafield Street, Portknockie, **Buckie**, Banffshire, AB56 2LX, 01542 40757, (Easter to Oct).

The Clock Tower, The Square, Dufftown, **Keith**, Banffshire, AB55 4AD, 01340 20501, (Easter to Oct)

17 High Street, **Elgin**, Moray, IV30 1EE, 01343 542666.

Market Street Car Park, **Ellon**, Aberdeenshire, AB41 9JD, 01358 20730, (Easter to Oct).

Falconer Museum, Tolbooth Street, **Forres**, Moray, IV36 0PH, 01309 72938, (Easter to Oct).

Saltoun Square, **Fraserburgh**, Aberdeenshire, AB43 5DB, 01346 28315, (Easter to Oct).

7a The Square, **Huntly**, Aberdeenshire, AB54 5AE, 01466 792255, (Easter to Oct).

Town Hall, Market Place, **Inverurie**, Aberdeenshire, AB51 9SN, 01467 20600, (Easter to Oct).

Church Rd, **Keith**, Banffshire, AB55 3BR, 01542 22634, (Easter to Oct).

Aden Country Park, **Mintlaw**, Peterhead, Aberdeenshire, AB54 5AE, (Easter to Oct).

54 Broad Street, **Peterhead**, Aberdeenshire, AB42 6BY, 01779 471904, (Easter to Oct).

The Square, **Tomintoul**, Ballindalloch, Banffshire, AB37 9ET, 01807 580285, (Easter to Oct).

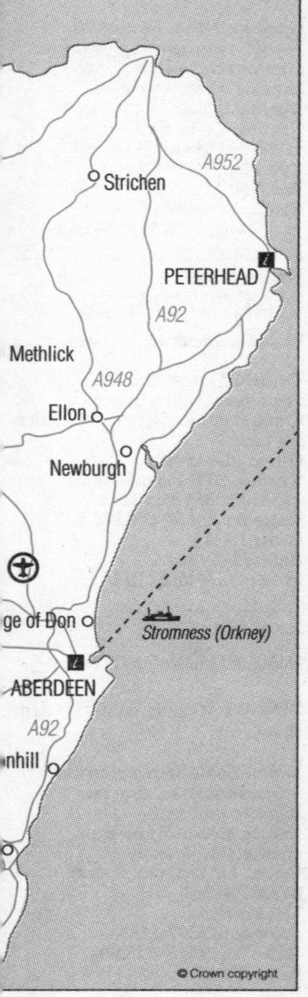

Aberdeen

National Grid Ref: NJ9206

Brent Wood Hotel, Highland Hotel, Atholl Hotel, Ashvale Fish Restaurant, Northern Hotel, Malacca, Inn at the Park

***Hamilton Guest House,** 22 Hamilton Place, Aberdeen, AB2 4BH.*
Open: All Year (not Xmas)
Grades: STB Listed, Comm
01224 644619 Mr Robertson
Rates fr: *£15.00*-**£20.00**.
Beds: 2F 1D 2T 2S
Baths: 1 Ensuite 2 Shared
(1)
Comfortable and friendly, family-run. All modern amenities but retaining many original Victorian features. Situated in quiet West End street. Convenient for city centre.

***Crown Private Hotel,** 10 Spring Bank Terrace, Aberdeen, AB1 2LS.*
Small family-run private hotel.
Open: All Year
Grades: STB 2 Cr, Comm
01224 586842 Mr Buthlay
Fax no: 01224 573787
Rates fr: *£15.00*-**£20.00**.
Beds: 2F 4T 2S
Baths: 4 Private 3 Shared

***Beeches Private Hotel,** 193 Great Western Road, Aberdeen, AB10 6PS.*
Friendly atmosphere, private car park.
Open: All Year
Grades: STB 2 Cr, Comm
01224 586413
Mr Sandison
Fax no: 01224 596919
Rates fr: *£16.00*-**£20.00**.
Beds: 2F 2D 2T 2S
Baths: 4 Private 2 Shared
(12)

***St Elmo,** 64 Hilton Drive, Aberdeen, AB24 4NP.*
Granite family home with parking.
Open: All Year
Grades: STB Listed, Comm
01224 483065 Mrs Watt
Rates fr: *£14.00*-**£17.00**.
Beds: 1D 2T
Baths: 1 Shared
(1) (1)

***Roselodge Guest House,** 3 Springbank Terrace, Aberdeen, AB11 6LS.*
Central, comfortable Victorian guesthouse.
Open: All Year
Grades: STB Listed, Comm
01224 586794 Mrs Wink
Rates fr: *£14.00*-**£18.00**.
Beds: 3F 2T **Baths:** 2 Shared
(3)

***Haven Guest House,** 62 Albergeldie Road, Aberdeen, AB1 6EN.*
Comfortable and friendly accommodation.
Open: All Year (not Xmas)
Grades: STB Listed, Comm
01224 585659 Mrs Hay
Rates fr: *£14.00*-**£16.00**.
Beds: 1F 1D 2T 1S
Baths: 2 Shared

***Fourways Guest House,** 435 Great Western Road, Aberdeen, AB1 6NJ.*
Small, family-run guest house.
Open: All Year
Grades: STB 2 Cr, Comm, AA 3 Q, RAC Acclaim
01224 310218 Mr Milne
Rates fr: *£20.00*-**£25.00**.
Beds: 3F 2D 2T
Baths: 6 Private
(6)

Allan Guest House, *56 Polmuir Road, Aberdeen,* *AB11 7RT.*
Friendly, comfortable. Extensive breakfast menu.
Open: All Year
Grades: STB Listed, Comm
01224 584484 Mr & Mrs Sherriffs
Rates fr: *£17.00*-**£17.00**.
Beds: 2F 2D 1T 2S
Baths: 3 Shared

Aberdeen Springbank Guesthouse, *6 Springbank Terrace, Aberdeen,* *AB1 2LS.*
Family-run, central location.
Open: All Year
Grades: STB Listed, Approv
01224 592048 / 587503
Mr & Mrs Robertson
Fax no: 01224 592048
Rates fr: *£14.00*-**£18.00**.
Beds: 5F 2D 2T 2S
Baths: 4 Private 5 Shared

Klibreck Guest House, *410 Great Western Road, Aberdeen,* *AB1 6NR.*
Comfortable large tradtional granite house.
Open: All Year (not Xmas)
Grades: STB 1 Cr, Comm, AA 2 Q, RAC Listed
01224 316115
Mrs Ramsay
Rates fr: *£15.00*-**£19.00**.
Beds: 2D 3T 1S
Baths: 2 Shared

Aboyne

National Grid Ref: NO5298

Arbor Lodge, *Ballater Road, Aboyne, Aberdeenshire,* *AB34 5HY.*
Luxury accommodation in large garden.
Open: Mar to Nov
Grades: STB 2 Cr, Deluxe, AA 5 Q
01339 886951 (also fax no)
Mrs Buchan
Rates fr: *£24.00*-**£24.00**.
Beds: 3T
Baths: 3 Ensuite
(12) (5)

Ballater

National Grid Ref: NO3695

Inverdeen House B&B, *Bridge Square, Ballater, Royal Deeside,* *AB35 5QJ.*
Open: All Year
013397 55759
Mr & Mrs Munroe
Rates fr: *£15.00*-**£15.00**.
Beds: 1F 2D
Baths: 2 Shared
100% non-smoking, next River Dee. Warm 1820 Listed building, period furnishings, kingsize beds. Superb Scottish, Canadian & special diet breakfasts. Many outdoor activities. Brochure.

Auld Kirk Hotel, *Braemar Road, Ballater, Aberdeenshire,* *AB35 5RQ.*
Open: All Year (not Xmas)
Grades: STB 3 Cr, Comm
013397 55762 Mrs Chivas
Fax no: 013397 55707
Rates fr: *£18.00*-**£28.00**.
Beds: 3D 3T
Baths: 6 Private
(10)
Small friendly hotel with reputable good home cooking. All rooms with extra comforts. Close by Balmoral Castle, Whisky Trail, golfing, walking, etc.

Netherley Guest House, *2 Netherley Place, Ballater, Aberdeenshire,* *AB35 5QE.*
Traditional, stone-built private house.
Open: Mar to Oct
013397 55792 Mrs Stewart
Rates fr: *£16.00*-**£18.00**.
Beds: 3F 2D 2T 2S
Baths: 4 Private 2 Shared
(4)

Deeside Hotel, *Braemar Road, Ballater, Aberdeenshire,* *AB35 5RQ.*
Quiet, comfortable Victorian villa.
Open: Feb to Nov
Grades: STB 3 Cr, Comm
013397 55420
Mr Brooker
Fax no: 013397 35357
Rates fr: *£19.00*-**£20.00**.
Beds: 1F 4D 4T
Baths: 9 Private
(15)

Banchory

National Grid Ref: NO6995

Burnett Arms

Towerbank House, *93 High Street, Banchory, Kincardineshire,* *AB31 3XT.*
Centrally situated Victorian house.
Open: All Year
Grades: STB 2 Cr, High Comm
01330 824798 Ms Balsamo
Rates fr: *£19.00*-**£22.00**.
Beds: 2T
Baths: 2 Ensuite
(2)

Banff

National Grid Ref: NJ6864

Royal Oak Hotel, *Bridge Street, Banff,* *AB45 1HB.*
Open: All Year
01261 812494
Mr Hancock
Rates fr: *£14.00*-**£16.50**.
Beds: 1F 1D 2T 1S
Baths: 1 Shared
Centrally situated for shopping and very close to local beaches. Surrounded by championship golf courses, fine walks and wonderful fishing. We offer a warm welcome.

Birkenhills

National Grid Ref: NJ7445

Devoran Country House (Turriff)

Lendrum Farm, *Birkenhills, Turriff, Aberdeenshire,* *AB53 8HA.*
Comfortable historic farmhouse,warm welcome.
Open: All Year (not Xmas)
Grades: STB 2 Cr, Comm
01888 544285 Mrs Roebuck
Rates fr: *£18.00*-**£18.00**.
Beds: 1F 1T
Baths: 1 Private 1 Shared
(5) (5)

Blackdam

National Grid Ref: NJ7502

Garmouth Hotel (Garmouth)

Castlehill Farm, *Blackdam, Fochabers, Moray,* *IV32 7LJ.*
Comfortable farmhouse, ideal touring base.
Open: Mar to Nov
Grades: STB Listed, Comm
01343 820351 Mrs Shand
Rates fr: *£13.00*-**£15.00**.
Beds: 1F 1D
Baths: 1 Shared
(6 +)

Braemar

National Grid Ref: NO1292

The Wishing Well, Fife Arms Hotel

Robert Louis Stephenson Cottage, *3 Glenshee Road, Braemar, Ballater,* *AB35 5YQ.*
Unique historical house, comfortable, friendly.
Open: All Year (not Xmas)
013397 41207
Mrs Corrigan
Fax no: 013397 41330
Rates fr: *£15.00*-**£18.00**.
Beds: 1D 1T
Baths: 1 Shared
(2)

Balnellan House, *Braemar, Ballater, Aberdeenshire,* *AB35 5YQ.*
Tastefully renovated Victorian house.
Open: All Year (not Xmas)
013397 41474 Mrs Sharp
Rates fr: *£20.00*-**£30.00**.
Beds: 2D 1T
Baths: 3 Private
(0-12) (4)

Morningside, *Kindrochit Drive, Braemar, Ballater, Aberdeenshire,* *AB35 5YQ.*
Modern, cosy, personally run house.
Open: Jan to Nov
013397 41370 Mrs McKellar
Rates fr: *£16.00*-**£19.00**.
Beds: 1D 1T
(3)

Birchwood, *Chapel Brae, Braemar, Ballater, Aberdeenshire, AB35 5YT.*
Birchwood is located in a very beautiful and quiet area.
Open: All Year
Grades: STB 1 Cr, Comm
013397 41599 Mrs MacKinnon
Rates fr: *£15.00*-**£17.50**.
Beds: 1F 1D 1S
Baths: 1 Private 2 Shared

Bridge of Don

National Grid Ref: NJ9206

White Horse Inn

Blackdog Heights, *Bridge of Don, Aberdeen, AB23 8BT.*
Modern bungalow in large garden.
Open: All Year (not Xmas)
Grades: STB Listed, Comm
01224 704287 Mrs Goudriaan
Rates fr: *£16.00*-**£17.00**.
Beds: 1D 1T 2S **Baths:** 1 Shared
(6)

Buckie

National Grid Ref: NJ8916

Rosemount, *62 East Church Street, Buckie, Banffshire, AB56 1ER.*
Large Victorian house overlooking Moray Firth. **Open:** All Year
Grades: STB 2 Cr, High Comm
01542 833434 Mrs Pirie
Rates fr: *£18.00*-**£25.00**.
Beds: 1D 2T
Baths: 2 Ensuite 1 Private
(4)

Highlander Hotel, *75 West Church Street, Buckie, Banffshire, AB56 1BQ.*
Family-run, fully licensed hotel.
Open: All Year
01542 834008 Mr Sharp
Rates fr: *£15.00*-**£18.00**.
Beds: 2F 1D 1T **Baths:** 1 Shared

Cairnie

National Grid Ref: NJ4844

Huntly hotel

Broadland Farm, *Cairnie, Huntly, Aberdeenshire, AB54 4UU.*
Victorian farmhouse in lovely surroundings. **Open:** Apr - Oct
Grades: STB Listed, Comm
01466 760330 Mrs Bailie
Rates fr: *£15.00*-**£18.00**.
Beds: 1D 1T **Baths:** 1 Shared
(4) (8)

Charlestown of Aberlour

National Grid Ref: NJ2642

83 High Street, *Charlestown of Aberlour, Banffshire, AB38 9QB.*
Attatched to leather craft shop.
Open: All Year
01340 871319 Mrs Gammack
Rates fr: *£12.00*-**£12.50**.
Beds: 1F 1D 1S **Baths:** 2 Shared
(2)

Kinermony Farm, *Kinermony, Charlestown of Aberlour, Banffshire, AB38 9LX.*
Open: All Year (not Xmas)
01340 871818 Mrs Thom
Rates fr: *£12.50*-**£12.50**.
Beds: 3T **Baths:** 1 Shared
200-year-old farmhouse. Black and white.

Cornhill

National Grid Ref: NJ5858

Castle of Park, *Cornhill, Banff, AB45 2AX.*
Historic castle in peaceful setting.
Open: All Year
Grades: STB 3 Cr, High Comm
01466 751667 (also fax no)
Mrs Duncan
Rates fr: *£25.00*-**£25.00**.
Beds: 2F 2D **Baths:** 4 Private

Corse

National Grid Ref: NJ6040

Mains of Corse, *Corse, Huntly, Aberdeenshire, AB54 6ES.*
Modern, comfortable farmhouse.
Open: All Year (not Xmas)
01466 684249 Mrs Stewart
Rates fr: *£12.00*-**£12.00**.
Beds: 2D **Baths:** 1 Shared

Craigievar

National Grid Ref: NJ5609

Craigievar Schoolhouse, *Craigievar, Alford, Aberdeenshire, AB33 8JE.*
Traditional rural schoolhouse, scenic location. **Open:** Easter to Oct
Grades: STB Listed, Comm
019755 81343 Mrs Young
Rates fr: *£14.00*-**£16.00**.
Beds: 1F 1T **Baths:** 2 Shared
(3)

Cullen

National Grid Ref: NJ5167

Royal Oak, Waverley Hotel

The Elms Guest House, *2 Seafield Place, Cullen, Buckie, Banffshire, AB56 2UU.*
Open: All Year (not Xmas)
01542 841271 Mrs Welford
Rates fr: *£14.00*-**£16.00**.
Beds: 1F 2D 2T 1S
Baths: 1 Private 2 Shared
(4)
Comfortable accommodation in friendly family atmosphere. Lovely coastal walks close to Whisky & Castle Trails. 10 golf courses in 18 mile radius.

The lowest **single** rate is shown in **bold.**

Waverley Hotel, *12 Blantyre Street, Cullen, Buckie, Banffshire, AB56 4RP.*
Situated near excellent golf courses. **Open:** All Year
01542 840210 Mrs Finnie
Rates fr: *£14.00*-**£14.00**.
Beds: 3F 2T 2S **Baths:** 2 Shared
(5)

Torrach, *147 Seatown, Cullen, Buckie, Banffshire, AB56 2SL.*
Traditional house, near golf course & beach. **Open:** Easter to Oct
Grades: STB 1 Cr, Comm
01542 840724 Mrs Mair
Rates fr: *£14.00*-**£16.00**.
Beds: 1F 1D
(2)

Cuminestown

National Grid Ref: NJ8050

East Balthangie Farm, *Cuminestown, Turriff, Aberdeenshire, AB53 7XY.*
Traditional farm with homely atmosphere.
Open: All Year (not Xmas)
01888 544261 Mrs Burdon
Rates fr: *£12.00*-**£12.00**.
Beds: 1D 1T 1S **Baths:** 1 Shared
(10)

Drumoak

National Grid Ref: NO7898

Mains Of Drum, *Drum Castle Road, Drumoak, Banchory, Aberdeenshire, AB31 5AE.*
Modernised farmhouse, convenient for Aberdeen. **Open:** All Year
01330 811335 Mrs Brebner
Rates fr: *£15.00*-**£17.00**.
Beds: 3F 1T **Baths:** 4 Private

Dufftown

National Grid Ref: NJ3239

Taste of Speyside Restaurant, Fife Arms Hotel, Commercial Hotel, The Croft Inn

Fife Arms Hotel, *2 The Square, Dufftown, Keith, Banffshire, AB55 4AD.*
Small modern town centre hotel.
Open: All Year
Grades: STB 1 Cr, Approv, AA 2 Q, Recomm
01340 820220 Mr Widdowson
Fax no: 01340 821137
Rates fr: *£21.00*-**£26.00**.
Beds: 1F 2D 3T **Baths:** 6 Ensuite
(1) (8)

Nashville, *8a Balvenie Street, Dufftown, Keith, Banffshire, AB55 4AB*
A family-run B&B, relaxed atmosphere. **Open:** All Year
Grades: STB 1 Cr, Comm
01340 820553 Mrs Morrison
Rates fr: *£12.00*-**£12.00**.
Beds: 1F 1D 1T
Baths: 1 Shared

Elgin

National Grid Ref: NJ2162

Harry's Restaurant, High Spirits

***Belleville,** 14 South College Street, Elgin, Moray,* IV30 1EP.
Open: All Year
Grades: STB Listed, Comm, AA 3 Q, Recomm
01343 541515 Mr & Mrs McMillan
Rates fr: *£15.00*-**£18.00**.
Beds: 1D 1T **Baths:** 2 Private
(2)
Centrally situated within walking distance of cathedral, park, library and town centre. Ideal base for golf, fishing, Whisky Trail, castles and gardens. Warm welcome guaranteed.

***Torr House Hotel,** 8 Moss Street, Elgin, Moray,* IV30 1LU.
Homely, with good home cooking.
Open: All Year
Grades: STB 3 Cr, Comm
01343 542661 Mrs Sheridan
Fax no: 01343 548200
Rates fr: *£30.00*-**£35.00**.
Beds: 2F 2D 3T 1S
Baths: 3 Ensuite 1 Private

***Carronvale,** 18 South Guildry Street, Elgin, Moray,* IV30 1QN.
Open: All Year
Grades: STB 1 Cr, Approv
01343 546864 Mrs Munn
Rates fr: *£14.50*-**£18.00**.
Beds: 2D 1T **Baths:** 1 Shared
(3)
Quiet artist's residence and gallery. Dine amongst paintings and sculptures. Painting tuition offered. Scenes of architectural interest. Old fishing harbours, beaches, golf courses, fishing, etc.

***Non-Smokers Haven,** 37 Duff Avenue, Elgin, Morayshire,* IV30 1QS.
Bungalow with heather, conifer garden. **Open:** All Year (not Xmas)
01343 541993 Mrs McGowan
Rates fr: *£14.00*-**£14.00**.
Beds: 1D 1T **Baths:** 1 Shared
(3)

***The Bungalow,** 7 New Elgin Road, Elgin, Moray,* IV30 3BE.
Lovely house run by family.
Open: All Year
Grades: STB 1 Cr, Comm
01343 542035 Mr Ross
Rates fr: *£14.00*-**£14.00**.
Beds: 1F 1D 1T 1S
Baths: 2 Shared
(5)

Ellon

National Grid Ref: NJ9530

***Station Hotel,** Station Brae, Ellon, Aberdeenshire,* AB4 9BD.
Warm, welcoming family-run hotel. **Open:** All Year
01358 720209 Mrs Keith
Rates fr: *£20.00*-**£30.00**.
Beds: 1F 3D 3T 1S
Baths: 8 Ensuite

Findhorn

National Grid Ref: NJ0464

***Crown & Anchor Inn,** Findhorn, Forres, Moray,* IV36 0YF.
Harbourside coaching inn c.1739.
Open: All Year
01309 690243 Mr Burrell
Rates fr: *£16.00*-**£18.00**.
Beds: 1F 3D 2T **Baths:** 6 Ensuite
(30)

Fochabers

National Grid Ref: NJ3458

Garmouth Hotel (Garmouth)

***Castlehill Farm,** Blackdam, Fochabers, Moray,* IV32 7LJ.
Comfortable farmhouse, ideal touring base.
Open: Mar to Nov
Grades: STB Listed, Comm
01343 820351 Mrs Shand
Rates fr: *£13.00*-**£15.00**.
Beds: 1F 1D **Baths:** 1 Shared
(6 +)

Fordyce

National Grid Ref: NJ5563

***Academy House,** School Road, Fordyce, Portsoy, Banffshire,* AB45 2SJ.
Stylish Victorian country house.
Open: All Year
Grades: STB Listed, Deluxe
01261 842743 Mrs Leith
Rates fr: *£15.00*-**£18.00**.
Beds: 2D 1T
Baths: 2 Shared
(7)

Forres

National Grid Ref: NJ0358

Ramnee Hotel

***Scania,** Forres, Moray,* IV36 0RE.
Architect's country house, spacious grounds.
Open: Apr to Nov
01309 672583 Mrs Shewan
Rates fr: *£18.00*-**£20.00**.
Beds: 1D 2T
Baths: 1 Shared
(6)

Gamrie

National Grid Ref: NJ7963

***Bankhead Croft,** Gamrie, Banff,* AB45 3HN.
Beautiful peaceful, modern country cottage.
Open: All Year
01261 851584 Mrs Smith
Rates fr: *£12.50*-**£15.00**.
Beds: 1F 1D 1T 1S
Baths: 1 Shared
(6)

***Roughwards,** Gamrie, Gardenstown, Banff,* AB45 3HA.
Good food, warm, comfortable accommodation.
Open: All Year (not Xmas)
01261 851758 Mrs Hawick
Rates fr: *£12.00*-**£13.00**.
Beds: 1D 1T **Baths:** 1 Shared
(3)

Gardenstown

National Grid Ref: NJ8064

***The Palace Farm,** Gardenstown, Banff,* AB45 3HS.
Picturesque landscape, C18th farmhouse. **Open:** Easter to Oct
Grades: STB 3 Cr, Comm
01261 851261 Mrs Duncan
Rates fr: *£18.00*-**£18.00**.
Beds: 1F 1D 1T
Baths: 2 Ensuite 1 Private
(6)

Garmouth

National Grid Ref: NJ3364

Garmouth Hotel

***Rowan Cottage,** Station Road, Garmouth, Fochabers, Moray,* IV32 7LZ
C18th 'bool-and-clay' cottage.
Open: Jan to Nov
01343 870267 Mrs Bingham
Fax no: 01343 870621
Rates fr: *£11.00*-**£11.00**.
Beds: 1D 1S **Baths:** 1 Shared
(5)

Gartly

National Grid Ref: NJ5232

***Faich Hill,** Gartly, Huntly, Aberdeenshire,* AB54 4RR.
'Farmhouse of Year' award-winner (repeatedly). **Open:** Easter to Oct
01466 720240 Mrs Grant
Rates fr: *£18.00*-**£25.00**.
Beds: 1D 1T
Baths: 1 Ensuite 1 Private
(5)

Glengairn

National Grid Ref: NJ2900

***Gairnshiel Lodge,** Glengairn, Ballater, Aberdeenshire,* AB35 5UQ.
Victorian hunting lodge.
Open: All Year
013397 55582 Mrs Debremaeker
Rates fr: *£16.50*-**£16.50**.
Beds: 8F 2D
Baths: 6 Private 2 Shared

Glenlivet

National Grid Ref: NJ2028

***Deepdale,** Glenlivet, Ballindalloch, Banffshire,* AB37 9EJ.
Warm, comfortable, farming family hospitality.
Open: All Year (not Xmas)
Grades: STB 1 Cr, Comm
01807 590364 Mrs Durno
Rates fr: *£15.00*-**£15.00**.
Beds: 1D 1T **Baths:** 1 Shared
(3)

Grange Crossroads

National Grid Ref: NJ4754

Chapelhill Croft, *Grange Crossroads, Keith, Banffshire,* *AB55 3LQ.*
Comfortable working rural croft.
Open: All Year
Grades: STB Listed, Comm
01542 870302 Mrs Fleming
Rates fr: *£13.00*-**£13.00**.
Beds: 1D 1T
Baths: 1 Ensuite 1 Shared
(4)

Hopeman

National Grid Ref: NJ1469

Station hotel

Ardent House, *43 Forsyth Street, Hopeman, Elgin, Moray,* *IV30 2SY.*
Renowned hospitality: Be pampered - GUARANTEED.
Open: All Year (not Xmas)
Grades: STB 2 Cr, Comm, AA 3 Q
01343 830694 Mrs McPherson
Rates fr: *£14.00*-**£18.00**.
Beds: 2D 1T
Baths: 1 Ensuite 1 Private 1 Shared
(5)

Huntly

National Grid Ref: NJ5240

Gordon Arms Hotel

Braeside, *Provost Street, Huntly, Aberdeenshire,* *AB54 8BB.*
Modern chalet bungalow, quiet location.
Open: All Year
Grades: STB 1 Cr, Comm
01466 793825 / 0831 706754
Mr & Mrs Calcraft
Rates fr: *£15.00*-**£15.00**.
Beds: 1F 1T 1S
Baths: 1 Private 1 Shared
(5)

Southview, *Victoria Road, Huntly, Banffshire,* *AB56 5AH.*
Large Victorian private house.
Open: All Year
Grades: STB 1 Cr, Comm
01466 792456
Mrs Thomson
Rates fr: *£14.00*-**£14.00**.
Beds: 1F 2D 1T
Baths: 2 Shared
(4)

Castle Hotel, *Huntly, Aberdeenshire,* *AB54 4SH.*
Large former C17th hunting lodge.
Open: All Year
Grades: STB 4 Cr, Comm, AA 2 St
01466 792696 Mr Duncan
Fax no: 01466 792641
Rates fr: *£34.25*-**£48.00**.
Beds: 4F 5D 11T
Baths: 20 Private
(35)

Inverurie

National Grid Ref: NJ7721

Bugles Cafe bar

Glenburnie Guest House, *Blackhall Road, Inverurie, Aberdeenshire,* *AB51 9JE.*
Comfortable detached house.
Open: All Year
Grades: STB Listed, Comm
01467 623044 Mrs Christie
Rates fr: *£13.00*-**£15.00**.
Beds: 1D 5T **Baths:** 2 Shared
(3)

Keith

National Grid Ref: NJ4250

The Haughs, *Keith, Banffshire,* *AB55 6QN.*
Large comfortable farmhouse. Lovely view.
Open: Easter to Oct
Grades: STB 3 Cr, Comm, AA 4 Q
01542 882238 Mrs Jackson
Rates fr: *£16.00*-**£22.00**.
Beds: 1F 2D 1T
Baths: 3 Ensuite 1 Private
(2) (6)

73 Mid Street, *Keith, Banffshire,* *AB55 3AF.*
Large friendly townhouse.
Open: All Year
01542 886401 Mrs Grant
Rates fr: *£13.50*-**£13.50**.
Beds: 2D 1T

Kincardine O'Neil

National Grid Ref: NO5899

Gordon Arms Hotel, *Kincardine O'Neil, Aboyne, Aberdeenshire,* *AB34 5AA.*
Open: All Year
Grades: STB 3 Cr
01339 884236 Mr Wayte
Fax no: 013398 84401
Rates fr: *£16.00*-**£30.00**.
Beds: 3F 2D 2T
Baths: 6 Ensuite 2 Private
(1) (6)
Family-run hotel in oldest village on Royal Deeside. Extensive menus including vegetarian and vegan, real ales, organic wines. Short breaks and DBB terms available.

Kinermony

National Grid Ref: NJ2541

Kinermony Farm, *Kinermony, Charlestown of Aberlour, Banffshire,* *AB38 9LX.*
200-year-old farmhouse. Black and white.
Open: All Year (not Xmas)
01340 871818 Mrs Thom
Rates fr: *£12.50*-**£12.50**.
Beds: 3T
Baths: 1 Shared

King Edward

National Grid Ref: NJ7157

Blackton Farm, *King Edward, Banff,* *AB45 3NJ.*
Comfortable farmhouse on working farm.
Open: Easter to Oct
Grades: STB 2 Cr, Approv
01888 551205 Mrs Elrick
Rates fr: *£14.50*-**£14.50**.
Beds: 3D
Baths: 1 Ensuite 1 Shared

Kingston-on-Spey

National Grid Ref: NJ3365

Sunnybank, *Lein Road, Kingston-on-Spey, Fochabers, Moray,* *IV32 7NW.*
Large family house near sea.
Open: All Year
01343 870362
Mrs Anderson
Rates fr: *£12.00*-**£12.00**.
Beds: 1F 1D
Baths: 1 Shared
(2)

Knockandhu

National Grid Ref: NJ2123

Pole Inn, *Auchnarrow, Knockandhu, Glenlivet, Ballindalloch, Banffshire,* *AB37 9JN.*
Traditional Scottish pub.
Open: All Year (not Xmas)
01807 590252
Mr Shewan
Rates fr: *£12.50*-**£12.50**.
Beds: 1D 1T
Baths: 1 Shared

Lossiemouth

National Grid Ref: NJ2370

The 1629 Seafood Restaurant, Lossie Inn

Lossiemouth House, *33 Clifton Road, Lossiemouth, Moray,* *IV31 6DP.*
200-year-old dower house.
Open: All Year (not Xmas)
Grades: STB 2 Cr, Comm, AA 3 Q
01343 813397 Ms Reddy
Rates fr: *£14.00*-**£15.00**.
Beds: 1F 1D 1T 1S
Baths: 2 Ensuite 2 Shared
(5)

Skerryhill, *63 Dunbar Street, Lossiemouth, Moray,* *IV31 6AN.*
Modern, comfortable bungalow.
Open: All Year (not Xmas)
01343 813035 Mrs Stewart
Rates fr: *£14.00*-**£15.00**.
Beds: 1F 1D 1T
Baths: 1 Shared

Moray View, *1 Seatown Road, Lossiemouth, Moray, IV31 6JL.*
350 year old house, sea views.
Open: All Year (not Xmas)
Grades: STB 1 Cr, Comm
01343 813915
Mrs MacKenzie
Rates fr: *£15.00*-**£20.00**.
Beds: 2D 1T
Baths: 2 Shared

Lumphanan

National Grid Ref: NJ5804

Macbeth Arms Hotel, *Lumphanan, Banchory, Kincardineshire, AB31 4TE.*
Open: All Year
Grades: STB 3 Cr, Comm
013398 83236 Mrs Keir
Fax no: 013398 83421
Rates fr: *£16.00*-**£16.00**.
Beds: 2F 1T
Baths: 2 Ensuite 1 Shared
(8)
Small friendly family-run village pub, 10 minutes from Royal Deeside Castle and Trail. Good food. Local golf course. Shooting and fishing may be arranged.

Macduff

National Grid Ref: NJ7064

11 Gellymill Street, *Macduff, Banffshire, AB44 1TN.*
Comfortable family-run Bed & Breakfast.
Open: All Year (not Xmas)
01261 833314
Mrs Greig
Rates fr: *£12.00*-**£13.00**.
Beds: 1D 1T
Baths: 1 Shared

The Highland Haven, *Shore Street, Macduff, Banffshire, AB44 1UB.*
Warm friendly hotel with magnificent views.
Open: All Year
01261 832408 Mr Alcock
Rates fr: *£20.00*-**£25.00**.
Beds: 3F 8D 10T 3S
Baths: 24 Ensuite

Methlick

National Grid Ref: NJ8537

Gight House Hotel

Sunnybrae Farm, *Gight, Methlick, Ellon, Aberdeenshire, AB41 7JA.*
Comfortable, traditional farmhouse.
Open: All Year
Grades: STB 2 Cr, Approv
01651 806456 Mrs Staff
Rates fr: *£16.50*-**£16.50**.
Beds: 1D 1T 1S
Baths: 2 Private

Mill of Muiresk

National Grid Ref: NJ6948

Carlotta Cottage, *Mill of Muiresk, Turriff, Aberdeenshire, AB53 7HE.*
Pretty, detached country cottage.
Open: All Year
01888 562025 Mrs Strong
Rates fr: *£12.50*-**£15.00**.
Beds: 1F 1D
Baths: 1 Shared
(2) (2)

Montcoffer

National Grid Ref: NJ6861

Montcoffer House, *Montcoffer, Banff, AB45 3LJ.*
C17th mansion. Walled garden.
Open: All Year (not Xmas)
01261 812979 Mr & Mrs Clark
Rates fr: *£16.00*-**£16.00**.
Beds: 1F 1D 1T 1S
Baths: 3 Private
(6)

Muir of Lochs

National Grid Ref: NJ3062

Carriages, *Muir of Lochs, Fochabers, IV32 7LG.*
Malt Whisky country, peaceful country village.
Open: Mar to Dec
01343 842258 Mrs Campbell
Rates fr: *£13.50*-**£13.00**.
Beds: 1F 1S
Baths: 1 Shared
(3) (2)

Newburgh

National Grid Ref: NJ9925

Udny Arms Hotel

Southlea House, *Newburgh, Ellon, Aberdeenshire, AB41 0AU.*
Secluded former manse near Aberdeen.
Open: All Year
Grades: STB 2 Cr, Comm
01358 789055 Mrs McDonald
Rates fr: *£21.00*-**£26.00**.
Beds: 2D 1T
Baths: 3 Ensuite
(10) (6)

Newton

National Grid Ref: NJ1663

Crooked Inn

Foresters House, *Newton, Elgin, Morayshire, IV30 3XW.*
Open: All Year
Grades: STB 1 Cr, Comm
01343 552862 Mrs Goodwin
Rates fr: *£14.00*-**£16.00**.
Beds: 2F
Baths: 1 Shared
Situated on B9013, 3 miles west of Elgin, near sandy beaches and Whisky Trail. Bedrooms with Toilets and W.H.B. Guest lounge with TV. Book now.

Newtonhill

National Grid Ref: NO9193

Cammach Hotel

3 Greystone Place, *Newtonhill, Stonehaven, Kincardineshire, AB3 2PW.*
House in beautiful coastal village.
Open: All Year (not Xmas)
Grades: STB Listed, Approv
01569 730391 Mrs Allen
Rates fr: *£15.00*-**£15.00**.
Beds: 2F
Baths: 2 Shared
(2)

Peterhead

National Grid Ref: NK1346

Palace Hotel

Carrick Guest House, *16 Merchant Street, Peterhead, Aberdeenshire, AB42 1DU.*
Open: All Year
Grades: STB 2 Cr, Comm
01779 470610 Mrs Mroczek
Rates fr: *£17.00*-**£17.00**.
Beds: 2F 3T 2S
Baths: 7 Ensuite
(4)
Comfortable accommodation, centrally situated 2 minutes walk from main shopping centre, harbour and beach. Ensuite bedrooms with central heating, colour TV, hospitality tray, hairdryer, trouser-press.

Portgordon

National Grid Ref: NJ3964

Sea Breezes Guest House, *28 Gordon Street, Portgordon, Buckie, Banffshire, AB56 2QR.*
Warm, comfortable, welcoming seaside cottage.
Open: All Year
01542 833681
Mrs Fielding
Rates fr: *£12.50*-**£12.50**.
Beds: 1T 1D
Baths: 1 Ensuite 1 Shared
(4)

Rothes

National Grid Ref: NJ2749

Eastbank Hotel, *15/17 High Street, Rothes, Banffshire, AB38 7AU.*
Open: All Year
Grades: STB 3 Cr, Comm
01340 831564 (also fax no)
Mrs Humphreys
Rates fr: *£17.50*-**£18.250**.
Beds: 2F 3D 3T 2S
Baths: 4 Private 3 Shared
(10)
Friendly comfortable 'Whisky Trail' hotel, family-run, situated centre of Rothes Speyside. A941, parking available. Good food and atmosphere, friendly bar. Disabled facilities. Pets welcome.

Rothienorman

National Grid Ref: NJ7235

***Rothie Inn,** Main Street, Rothienorman, Inverurie, Aberdeenshire, AB51 8UD.*
Family-run village inn.
Open: All Year (not Xmas)
Grades: STB Listed
01651 821206 Miss Thompson
Rates fr: *£18.00*-**£20.00**.
Beds: 1D 1T 1S
Baths: 1 Shared
(20)

Spey Bay

National Grid Ref: NJ3564

***Spey Bay Hotel,** Spey Bay, Fochabers, Moray, IV32 7PY.*
Comfortable, popular seaside golfing hotel. **Open:** All Year
01343 820362 Mr Christie
Rates fr: *£24.00*-**£27.00**.
Beds: 10F 3D 2T 2S
Baths: 17 Private

St Cyrus

National Grid Ref: NO7464

Bush Hotel

***Burnmouth House,** St Cyrus, Montrose, Angus, DD10 0DL.*
Open: Mar to Nov
Grades: STB Listed, Comm
01674 850430 Mrs Coates
Rates fr: *£16.00*-**£17.00**.
Beds: 1F 2D 1T 1S
Baths: 2 Ensuite 1 Private 1 Shared
(10) (4)
Country seaside guest house 200 years old. Situated on Smugglers Coast. Golf courses, glens, fishing villages, home cooking, TV lounge. Warm welcome, car essential.

Stonehaven

National Grid Ref: NO8786

***Arduthie House,** Ann Street, Stonehaven, Kincardineshire, AB3 2DA.*
Open: All Year (not Xmas)
Grades: STB 2 Cr, Comm
01569 762381 (also fax no)
Mrs Marr
Rates fr: *£18.00*-**£19.0**.
Beds: 2F 1D 1T
Baths: 3 Ensuite
Large detached Victorian Guest House, set in a lovely garden in the centre of Stonehaven. Guests' lounge and sun lounge in which to relax.

The lowest *double* rate per person is shown in *italics*.

National Grid References are for villages, towns and cities - *not* for individual houses.

Strathdon

National Grid Ref: NJ3512

Kildrummy Inn, Glenkindie Arms Hotel

***Buchaam Farm,** Strathdon, Aberdeenshire, AB36 8TN.*
Open: May to Oct
Grades: STB Listed, Comm
019756 51238 Mrs Ogg
Rates fr: *£14.00*-**£14.00**.
Beds: 1F 1D 1T
Baths: 2 Shared
(3)
A previous 'Farmhouse of the Year' award winner, our 600-acre family-run farm is in an area of unspoilt beauty, on the Castle Trail and the Highland tourist route.

***Colquhonnie Hotel,** Strathdon, Aberdeenshire, AB36 8UN.*
Modernised C18th drovers' inn.
Open: All Year (not Xmas)
019756 51210 Mrs Young
Rates fr: *£25.00*-**£25.00**.
Beds: 2F 3D 3T 1S
Baths: 9 Ensuite
(20)

Strichen

National Grid Ref: NJ9455

***Findon House,** Strichen, Fraserburgh, Aberdeenshire, AB43 4SR.*
Edwardian town house in rural village. **Open:** All Year
01771 637831 Mrs Bruce
Rates fr: *£15.00*-**£15.00**.
Beds: 1F 1T
Baths: 2 Private
(2)

Tomintoul

National Grid Ref: NJ1618

Glenhaven Hotel (Tomintoul)

***Milton Farm,** Tomintoul, Ballindalloch, Banffshire, AB37 9EQ.*
Open: All Year (not Xmas)
01807 580288 Mrs McIntosh
Rates fr: *£13.00*-**£15.00**.
Beds: 2D
Baths: 1 Shared
(3)
Situated on a small working farm, this modernised C18th home offers visitors a warm friendly welcome. Ideal base for touring, cycling, walking, Whisky Trail.

***Findron Farm,** Braemar Road, Tomintoul, Ballindalloch, Banffshire, AB37 9ER.*
Modern, comfortable farmhouse.
Open: All Year
Grades: STB 2 Cr, High Comm
01807 580382 Mrs Turner
Rates fr: *£14.00*-**£14.00**.
Beds: 1F 2D
Baths: 2 Ensuite 1 Private

***Glenavon Hotel,** The Square, Tomintoul, Ballindalloch, Banffshire, AB37 9ET.*
Friendly informal comfortable hotel.
Open: All Year
01807 580218
Mr Kennedy
Rates fr: *£18.00*-**£18.00**.
Beds: 2F 2D 1T 2S
Baths: 5 Ensuite 1 Shared

Turriff

National Grid Ref: NJ7250

Devoran Country House

***Meikle Colp,** Turriff, Aberdeenshire, AB53 8DT.*
Working farm, 0.5 mile from Turriff.
Open: All Year (not Xmas)
Grades: STB 1 Cr, Comm
01888 562728
Mrs Beattie
Rates fr: *£15.00*-**£15.00**.
Beds: 1F 1T **Baths:** 1 Shared

***Lendrum Farm,** Birkenhills, Turriff, Aberdeenshire, AB53 8HA.*
Comfortable historic farmhouse,warm welcome.
Open: All Year (not Xmas)
Grades: STB 2 Cr, Comm
01888 544285
Mrs Roebuck
Rates fr: *£18.00*-**£18.00**.
Beds: 1F 1T
Baths: 1 Private 1 Shared
(5) (5)

Urquhart

National Grid Ref: NJ2862

Garmouth Hotel (Garmouth)

***Glenlossie,** Urquhart, Elgin, Moray, IV30 3LG.*
Modern comfortable house. Rural location.
Open: All Year
01343 842289 (also fax no)
Mrs Milne
Rates fr: *£12.00*-**£12.00**.
Beds: 1D 1T **Baths:** 1 Shared
(3)

The lowest *double* rate per person is shown in *italics*.

Angus

Tourist Information Centres

Market Place, **Arbroath**, Angus, DD11 1HR, 01241 872609.

St Ninian's Place, **Brechin**, Angus, DD9 7AH, 01356 623050, (Easter to Oct).

The Library, 1, High St, **Carnoustie**, Angus, DD7 6AG, 01241 852258, (Easter to Oct).

4 City Square, **Dundee**, Angus, DD1 3BA, 01382 227723.

The Library, West High St, **Forfar**, Angus, DD8 1AA, 01307 467876, (Easter to Oct).

Bank Street, **Kirriemuir**, Angus, DD8 4BE, 01575 574097, (Easter to Oct)

The Library, 214 High St, **Montrose**, Angus, DD10 8PJ, 01674 872000, (Easter to Oct).

Aberlemno

National Grid Ref: NO5555

The Stables (Brechin)

Wood of Auldbar, *Aberlemno, Brechin, Angus, DD9 6SZ.*
Excellent accommodation, food. Warm welcome.
Open: All Year
Grades: STB Listed, Comm
01307 830218 Mrs Stewart
Rates fr: *£14.50*-**£16.00**.
Beds: 1F 1T 1S **Baths:** 2 Shared

The lowest *double* rate per person is shown in *italics.*

The lowest **single** *rate is shown in* **bold.**

Airlie

National Grid Ref: NO3150

Lismore, *Airlie, Kirriemuir, Forfar, Angus, DD8 5NP.*
Comfortable rural bungalow. Home cooking.
Open: Easter to Sep
01575 530213
Mrs Grimmond
Rates fr: *£14.00*-**£14.00**.
Beds: 1D 1T
Baths: 1 Shared
(2)

Arbroath

National Grid Ref: NO6441

Old Brewhouse

Scurdy Guest House, *33 Marketgate, Arbroath, Angus, DD11 1AU.*
Family-run guest house & restaurant.
Open: All Year
Grades: STB 2 Cr, Comm, AA Listed, RAC Acclaim
01241 872417 (also fax no)
Mr & Mrs Henderson
Rates fr: *£13.50*-**£16.00**.
Beds: 2F 4D 3T
Baths: 3 Ensuite 2 Private 5 Shared
(2)

Kingsley Guest House, *29-31 Marketgate, Arbroath, Angus, DD11 1AU.*
Centrally located comfortable town house. **Open:** All Year
Grades: STB 2 Cr, Comm, AA 2 Q, RAC Recomm
01241 873933 (also fax no)
Mr Giacomini
Rates fr: *£13.50*-**£16.00**.
Beds: 3F 6D 5T 2S
Baths: 8 Ensuite

Brechin

National Grid Ref: NO6059

The Stables

Doniford, *26 Airlie Street, Brechin, Angus, DD9 6JX.*
Large stone-built detached villa.
Open: All Year (not Xmas/New Year)
Grades: STB 2 Cr, High Comm, AA 4 Q
01356 622361 Mrs Stewart
Rates fr: *£17.50*-**£20.00**.
Beds: 2T **Baths:** 2 Ensuite
(4)

Blibberhill Farmhouse, *Brechin, Angus, DD9 6TH.*
C18th well-appointed farmhouse.
Open: All Year (not Xmas)
Grades: STB 2 Cr, Comm
01307 830323 Mrs Stewart
Rates fr: *£15.00*-**£17.50**.
Beds: 1F 1D 1T
Baths: 3 Ensuite 1 Shared
(4)

Broughty Ferry

National Grid Ref: NO4630

Ship Inn

Mossburn, *363 King St, Broughty Ferry, Dundee, Angus, DD5 2HA.*
Open: All Year (not Xmas)
01382 477331 Mrs Young
Rates fr: *£15.00*-**£16.00**.
Beds: 1D 1T
(2)
Victorian house, overlooking castle and harbour. Variety of restaurants within walking distance. Choice of golf courses, including St Andrews and Carnoustie. Warm Scottish hospitality.

Auchenean, *177 Hamilton Street, Broughty Ferry, Dundee, Angus, DD5 2RE.*
Detached house in quiet cul-de-sac.
Open: Mar to Oct
Grades: STB Listed, High Comm
01382 774782 Mrs Laing
Rates fr: *£14.50*-**£14.50**.
Beds: 1T 1S
Baths: 1 Shared
(4)

Invermark Hotel, *23 Monifieth Road, Broughty Ferry, Dundee, Angus, DD5 2RN.*
Smoke-free, modernised Victorian family hotel.
Open: All Year
01382 739430 Mrs Metcalf
Rates fr: *£20.00*-**£25.00**.
Beds: 1F 3T
Baths: 4 Private
(14)

Carnoustie

National Grid Ref: NO5634

Cairds Hotel

Kinloch Arms Hotel, *27 High Street, Carnoustie, Angus, DD7 6AN.*
Small, fully licensed family hotel.
Open: All Year
Grades: STB 2 Cr
01241 853127
Mrs Ross
Rates fr: *£20.00*-**£25.00**.
Beds: 1F 1D 5T
Baths: 7 Private
(30)

Morven House, *28 West Path, Carnoustie, Angus, DD7 7SN.*
Georgian house bed & breakfast.
Open: All Year
01241 852385
Mrs Ireland
Fax no: 01241 856125
Rates fr: *£20.00*-**£25.00**.
Beds: 1F 2D 3T
Baths: 5 Ensuite 1 Private
(16)

The Two Bs, *13 Queen Street, Carnoustie, Angus, DD7 7AX.*
Comfortable, relaxing accommodation near seaside.
Open: All Year
01241 852745
Mrs Burgess
Rates fr: *£16.00*-**£20.00**.
Beds: 2D 1T
Baths: 2 Ensuite 1 Private
(2)

Balhousie Farm, *Carnoustie, Angus, DD7 6LG.*
Comfortable farmhouse with spacious rooms.
Open: All Year (not Xmas)
Grades: STB Listed, Comm
01241 853533 (also fax no)
Mrs Watson
Rates fr: *£15.00*-**£15.00**.
Beds: 3D
Baths: 1 Shared

National Grid References are for villages, towns and cities - *not* for individual houses.

Dundee

National Grid Ref: NO3632

Laings, Antonio's, Russells Restaurant, Raffles Wine Bar, Hogs Head, Park Hotel, Roseangle

Auld Steeple Guest House, *94 Nethergate, Dundee, Angus, DD1 4EL.*
Open: All Year
01382 200302 (also fax no)
Rates fr: *£16.50*-**£18.50**.
Beds: 3F 1D 3T 5S
Baths: 4 Shared
Central, near railway and bus station. Tea and coffee making facilities and TV in all rooms. Excellent for the business traveller or tourist.

Ardmoy, *359 Arbroath Road, Dundee, Angus, DD4 7SQ.*
Welcoming, comfortable, homely, detached house.
Open: All Year
Grades: STB Listed, Comm
01382 453249 Mrs Taylor
Rates fr: *£17.00*-**£22.00**.
Beds: 1F 1D 1T 1S
Baths: 2 Shared
(4)

Bruce Hotel, *39 Roseangle, Dundee, Angus, DD1 4LZ.*
Open: All Year (not Xmas)
Grades: STB Listed, Approv
01382 203203
Ms Malkin
Fax no: 01382 204866
Rates fr: *£16.50*-**£19.00**.
Beds: 1F 1D 4T 14S
Baths: 2 Ensuite 2 Shared
(6)
Situated quiet area west end of city - close university, Ninewells Hospital, airport. City centre 10 minutes walk, local golf courses. Privately owned tourist/commercial hotel.

Monifieth Hotel Ltd, *Albert Street, Dundee, Angus, DD5 4JS.*
Large Victorian private house.
Open: All Year
Grades: STB 3 Cr, Comm
01382 532630 (also fax no)
Mr Harrow
Rates fr: *£19.00*-**£23.00**.
Beds: 1F 2D 3T
Baths: 4 Ensuite 1 Shared
(50)

National Grid References are for villages, towns and cities - *not* for individual houses.

Craigtay Hotel, *101 Broughty Ferry Road, Tayside, Dundee, Angus, DD4 6JE.*
Modern, friendly atmosphere & pub.
Open: All Year (not Xmas)
01382 451142 Mr Carson
Rates fr: *£19.00*-**£25.00**.
Beds: 2F 3D 13T
Baths: 18 Private
(28)

Auchenean, *177 Hamilton Street, Broughty Ferry, Dundee, Angus, DD5 2RE.*
Detached house in quiet cul-de-sac.
Open: Mar to Oct
Grades: STB Listed, High Comm
01382 774782
Mrs Laing
Rates fr: *£14.50*-**£14.50**.
Beds: 1T 1S
Baths: 1 Shared
(4)

Errolbank Guest House, *9 Dalgleish Road, Dundee, Angus, DD4 7JN.*
Large Victorian house near river.
Open: All Year
Grades: STB 2 Cr, Comm, AA 3 Q
01382 462118 (also fax no)
Mr Wilson
Rates fr: *£17.50*-**£22.00**.
Beds: 2D 3T 1S
Baths: 5 Private 1 Shared
(5) (6)

Kemback Guest House, *8 McGill Street, Dundee, Angus, DD4 6PH.*
Modern family atmosphere, friendly, central car park. All rooms have central heating.
Open: All Year
01382 461273
Mr Bissett
Rates fr: *£15.00*-**£17.00**.
Beds: 1F 2D 3T 1S
Baths: 2 Ensuite 2 Private 2 Shared
(7)

Ash Villa, *216 Arbroath Road, Dundee, Angus, DD4 7RZ.*
Large, comfortable, detached villa.
Open: All Year
Grades: STB 1 Cr, Comm
01382 450831
Mrs Hill
Rates fr: *£15.00*-**£15.00**.
Beds: 1F 1T 1S
Baths: 1 Shared
(4)

Elm Lodge, *49 Seafield Road, Dundee, Angus, DD1 4NW.*
Large Victorian Listed private house.
Open: All Year (not Xmas)
01382 228402 Mrs McDowall
Rates fr: *£14.00*-**£14.00**.
Beds: 1D 1T 1S
Baths: 1 Shared
(4)

Cloisterbank, *8 Coupar Angus Road, Dundee, Angus, DD2 3HN.*
Homely, comfortable, Lochee area. Golf.
Open: All Year
01382 622181 Mrs Black
Rates fr: *£14.50*-**£16.50**.
Beds: 1F 4T 1S
Baths: 2 Shared
(5)

Carlton House Hotel, *2 Dalgleish Road, Dundee, Angus, DD4 7JR.*
Friendly home. Homely atmosphere.
Open: All Year (not Xmas)
01382 462056 Mr Larson
Rates fr: *£15.00*-**£20.00**.
Beds: 6D 7T 4S
Baths: 6 Shared
(10)

Strathdon Hotel, *277 Perth Road, Dundee, Angus, DD2 1JS.*
Elegant Edwardian terrace.
Open: All Year (not Xmas)
Grades: STB 3 Cr
01382 665648
Mr & Mrs Hornsby
Rates fr: *£24.00*-**£25.00**.
Beds: 3F 2D 3T 2S
Baths: 10 Private

Aberlaw Guest House, *230 Broughty Ferry Road, Dundee, Angus, DD4 7JP.*
Victorian villa (Listed), overlooking river.
Open: All Year
Grades: STB 2 Cr, Comm
01382 456929
Mrs McGlashan
Rates fr: *£18.00*-**£16.00**.
Beds: 1F 1T 2S
Baths: 3 Private
(6)

Edzell

National Grid Ref: NO6068

Glenesk Hotel, Luck Inn

The Gorse, *Dunlappie Road, Edzell, Brechin, Angus, DD9 7UB.*
Attractive, detached house, overlooking golf course.
Open: All Year
Grades: STB 1 Cr, Comm
01356 648207
Mrs Myles
Fax no: 01356 648265
Rates fr: *£14.00*-**£14.00**.
Beds: 2T 1S
Baths: 2 Shared

The lowest *double* rate per person is shown in *italics.*

Central Hotel, *18-20 Church Street, Edzell, Brechin, Angus, DD9 7TQ.*
Comfortable family-run hotel.
Open: All Year
Grades: STB 3 Cr, Approv
01356 648218 (also fax no)
Mr Lawson
Rates fr: *£20.00*-**£15.00**.
Beds: 1F 5D 5T
Baths: 11 Ensuite 2 Shared
(0) (60)

Forfar

National Grid Ref: NO4550

West Mains Of Turin, *Forfar, Angus, DD8 2TE.*
Farmhouse with panoramic view o Loch.
Open: Easter to Oct
Grades: STB 2 Cr, Comm
01307 830229 (also fax no)
Mrs Jolly
Rates fr: *£16.00*-**£18.00**.
Beds: 1F 1D 1S
Baths: 1 Ensuite 1 Private 1 Shared

Wemyss Farm, *Montrose Road, Forfar, Angus, DD8 2TB.*
Friendly, welcoming family, comfortable farmhouse.
Open: All Year
Grades: STB Listed, Comm
01307 462887
Mrs Lindsay
Rates fr: *£15.00*-**£18.00**.
Beds: 1F 1D
Baths: 2 Shared

Glenisla

National Grid Ref: NO1967

Glenmarkie Farmhouse, *Glenisla Blairgowrie, Perthshire, PH11 8QB.*
Friendly farmhouse in secluded glen.
Open: All Year (not Xmas)
Grades: STB 2 Cr, Comm
01575 582341 (also fax no)
Mr Evans
Rates fr: *£17.50*-**£17.50**.
Beds: 2D 1T
Baths: 1 Private 1 Shared
(20)

Planning a longer stay? Always ask for any special rates.

Justinhaugh

National Grid Ref: NO4657

***Glencoul House,** Justinhaugh, Forfar, Angus, DD8 3SF.*
Quiet Victorian private country house.
Open: All Year (not Xmas)
01307 860248 Mrs Kirby
Rates fr: *£14.00*-**£14.00**.
Beds: 1F 1T
Baths: 2 Shared
(3)

Kirkton of Glenisla

National Grid Ref: NO2160

***Kirkside House Hotel,** Kirkton of Glenisla, Blairgowrie, Perthshire, PH11 8PH.*
Converted C18th manse.
Open: All Year
01575 582278 Mr Mayward
Rates fr: *£16.00*-**£17.00**.
Beds: 1F 2D 1T 1S
Baths: 1 Shared
(20)

Kirriemuir

National Grid Ref: NO3853

Thrums Hotel, Woodville Inn

***Crepto,** Kinnordy Place, Kirriemuir, Forfar, Angus, DD8 4JW.*
Comfortable, welcoming, near town centre.
Open: All Year
Grades: STB Listed, Comm
01575 572746 Mrs Lindsay
Rates fr: *£13.50*-**£13.50**.
Beds: 1D 1T 1S
Baths: 2 Shared
(3)

All rates are subject to alteration at the owners' discretion.

***63 The Roods,** Kirriemuir, Forfar, Angus, DD8 4HP.*
Large comfortable private house.
Open: Apr to Sep
01575 574229 Mrs Scott
Rates fr: *£14.00*.
Beds: 2D 1T
Baths: 1 Shared

Leysmill

National Grid Ref: NO6047

Colliston Inn

***The Old Inn,** Leysmill, Arbroath, Angus, DD11 4RR.*
200-year-old former inn.
Open: All Year (not Xmas)
01241 828436 Mrs Storey
Rates fr: *£15.00*-**£15.00**.
Beds: 1F 1D
Baths: 1 Shared
(2)

Lunan

National Grid Ref: NO6851

***Lunan Lodge,** Lunan, Montrose, Angus, DD10 9TG.*
C18th manse overlooking beach.
Open: April to Oct
01241 830267 Mrs Mackintosh
Rates fr: *£16.00*-**£20.00**.
Beds: 1F 2T
Baths: 2 Shared
(10)

Montrose

National Grid Ref: NO7157

Park Hotel

***Muirshade of Gallery Farm,** Montrose, Angus, DD10 9JU.*
Modern, comfortable farmhouse.
Open: All Year (not Xmas)
Grades: STB 2 Cr, Comm
01674 840209 Mrs Ruxton
Rates fr: *£16.00*.
Beds: 2D 1T
Baths: 2 Ensuite 1 Private

Planning a longer stay? Always ask for any special rates.

***Cranes Meadow Guest House,** 28 The Mall, Montrose, Angus, DD10 8NW.*
Redbrick house, some downstairs rooms.
Open: All Year
01674 672296 Mrs Bruce
Rates fr: *£14.00*-**£16.00**.
Beds: 2F 2D 2T 1S
Baths: 3 Shared

***The Carlton Hotel,** 139 High Street, Montrose, Angus, DD10 8QN.*
Well-situated for many places of interest.
Open: All Year
01674 677237
Mr Strachan
Rates fr: *£20.00*-**£25.00**.
Beds: 1F 2D 3T 1S
Baths: 5 Ensuite 1 Shared
(14)

Nether Finlarg

National Grid Ref: NO4241

***Nether Finlarg Farm,** Nether Finlarg, Forfar, Angus, DD8 1XQ.*
Open: All Year (not Xmas)
01307 820250
Mr & Mrs Rymer
Fax no: 01307 820386
Rates fr: *£17.00*-**£20.00**.
Beds: 1D 1T 1S
Baths: 2 Shared
(6)
This conservation awarded farm is within 10 minutes of Dundee and Forfar, 1 mile off A90. Quiet and secluded with beautifully layed out gardens set amongst the Sidlaw Hills. Glamis Castle 6 miles, golfing and glens closeby.

Argyll & Bute

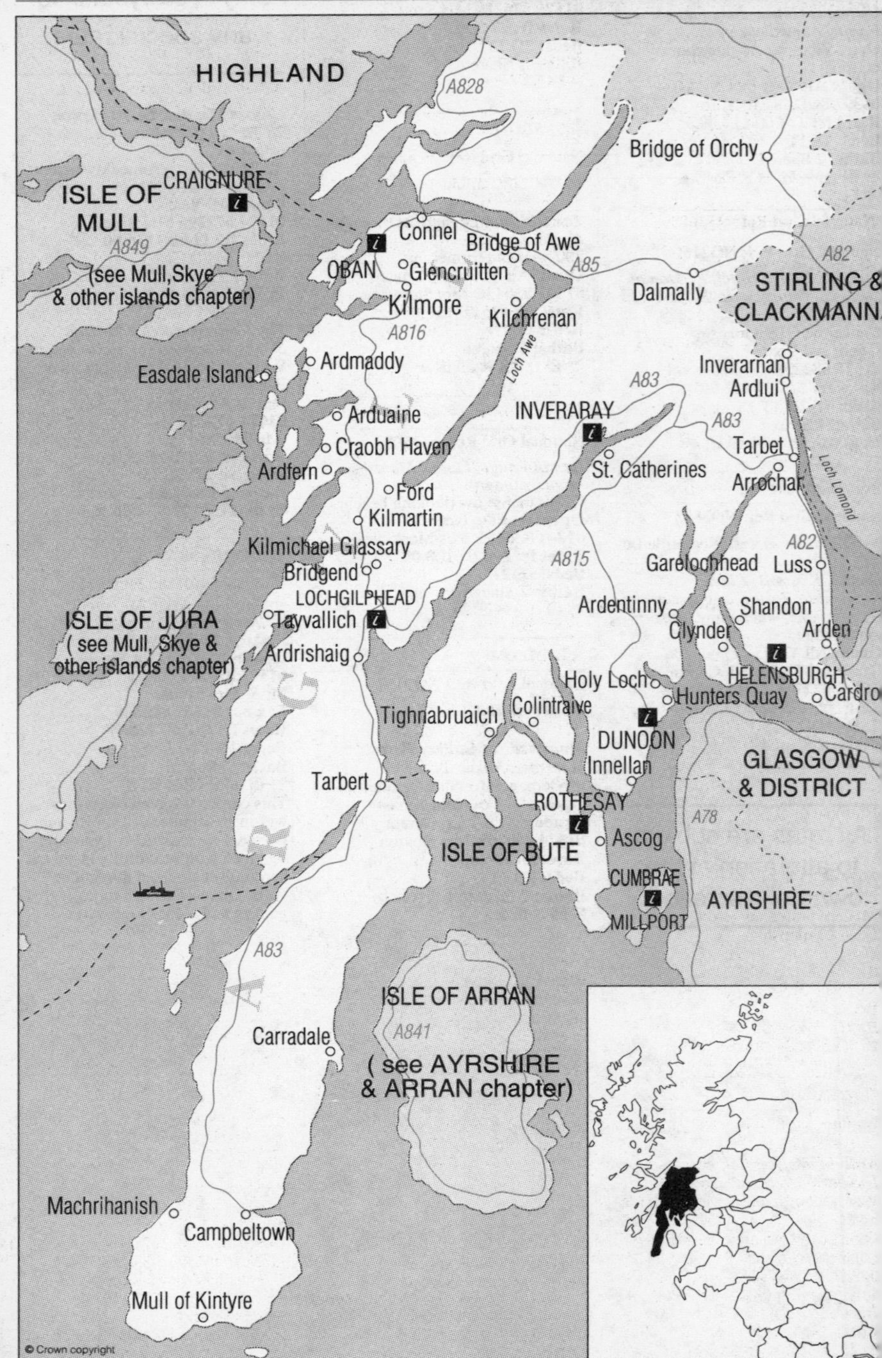

HIGHLAND
A828
Bridge of Orchy
ISLE OF MULL
CRAIGNURE
A849
(see Mull, Skye & other islands chapter)
Connel
OBAN
Bridge of Awe
Glencruitten
A85
A82
Dalmally
STIRLING & CLACKMANN
Kilmore
Kilchrenan
A816
Ardmaddy
Easdale Island
Loch Awe
Inverarnan
Ardlui
A83
INVERARAY
Arduaine
Craobh Haven
Tarbet
Ardfern
St. Catherines
Arrochar
Loch Lomond
Ford
Kilmartin
Kilmichael Glassary
A815
Bridgend
Garelochhead
Luss
LOCHGILPHEAD
Ardentinny
Shandon
ISLE OF JURA
(see Mull, Skye & other islands chapter)
Tayvallich
Clynder
Arden
Ardrishaig
HELENSBURGH
Holy Loch
Hunters Quay
Cardro
Tighnabruaich
Colintraive
DUNOON
GLASGOW & DISTRICT
Innellan
Tarbert
ROTHESAY
A78
Ascog
ISLE OF BUTE
CUMBRAE
MILLPORT
AYRSHIRE
A83
ISLE OF ARRAN
A841
Carradale
(see AYRSHIRE & ARRAN chapter)
Machrihanish
Campbeltown
Mull of Kintyre
© Crown copyright

Tourist Information Centres

7 Alexandra Parade, **Dunoon**, Argyll, PA23 8AB, 01369 703785

The Clock Tower, **Helensburgh**, Dunbartonshire, G84 7DD, 01436 672642, (Easter to Oct).

Front Street, **Inveraray**, Argyll, PA32 8UY,01499 302063

Lochnell Street, **Lochgilphead**, Argyll, PA31 8JN, 01546 602344, (Easter to Oct).

Boswell House, Argyll Square, **Oban**, Argyll, PA34 4AT, 01631 563122

15 Victoria Street, **Rothesay**, Isle of Bute, PA20 0AJ, 01700 502151

Arden

National Grid Ref: NS3684

***Waters Edge Cottage,** Duck Bay, Arden, Loch Lomond, Dunbartonshire,* G83 8QZ.
Quaint 1830's lochside cottage.
Open: All Year
01389 850629 Mrs Robertson
Rates fr: *£20.00*.
Beds: 2D
Baths: 2 Private
(12) (2)

Ardentinny

National Grid Ref: NS1887

Glenfinart Hotel

***Drynain Cottage,** Ardentinny, Dunoon, Argyll,* PA23 8TT.
Peaceful large gardened traditional cottage.
Open: Easter to Oct
01369 810232 Mrs Mathison
Rates fr: *£14.00*-**£14.00**.
Beds: 1F 1D
Baths: 1 Private
(1)

Ardfern

National Grid Ref: NM8004

Galley of Lorne

***Herons Cottage,** Ardfern, Lochgilphead, Argyll,* PA31 8QN.
Modern bungalow overlooking Loch Craignish.
Open: Easter to Oct
01852 500255 Mrs Thorgrimsson
Rates fr: *£15.00*-**£15.00**.
Beds: 1D 1T
Baths: 1 Shared
(1) (2)

Ardlui

National Grid Ref: NN3115

***Ardlui Hotel,** Ardlui, Arrochar, Dunbartonshire,* G83 7EB.
Warm, comfortable friendly family hotel.
Open: All Year (not Xmas)
Grades: STB Listed
01301 704243 Mrs Squires
Rates fr: *£28.00*-**£33.00**.
Beds: 2F 7D 4T
Baths: 7 Private
(50)

Ardmaddy

National Grid Ref: NM7816

Tigh-An Truish Inn, Willowburn Hotel

***Ardshellach Farm,** Ardmaddy, Oban, Argyll,* PA34 4QY.
Open: May to Oct
01852 300218 Mrs Gilbert
Rates fr: *£14.00*-**£14.50**.
Beds: 1F
Baths: 1 Shared
(2)
Quiet farmhouse on working farm 400 yds from sea near Atlantic Bridge on Easdale Road, overlooking Isles of Luing and Scarba. Meals and gardens nearby.

Ardrishaig

National Grid Ref: NR8585

***Allt-Na-Craig,** Tarbert Road, Ardrishaig, Lochgilphead, Argyll,* PA30 8EP.
Large Victorian house.
Open: All Year (not Xmas)
01546 603245 Mrs McKay
Rates fr: *£24.00*-**£24.00**.
Beds: 1F 2D 2T 1S
Baths: 6 Private
(10)

Arduaine

National Grid Ref: NM8010

Chartroom Bar, Galley of Lorne, Crafty Kitchen

***Asknish Cottage,** Arduaine, Oban, Argyll,* PA34 4XQ.
Open: All Year
01852 200247 Miss Campbell
Rates fr: *£15.50*-**£15.50**.
Beds: 2D 1T **Baths:** 1 Shared
(4)
Warm welcome in hillside cottage overlooking islands. National Trust Gardens 0.5 mile. Opportunities locally for a variety of inside/outside activities. Wild garden, tame owner.

Arrochar

National Grid Ref: NN2904

***Fascadail Country Guest House,** Arrochar, Dunbartonshire,* G83 7AB.
Much loved mansion and grounds.
Open: All Year
Grades: STB 3 Cr, Comm
01301 702344 Mrs Dornbrack
Rates fr: *£15.00*. **Beds:** 5D 2T
Baths: 6 Ensuite 1 Private
(9)

***Ferry Cottage,** Ardmay, Arrochar, Dunbartonshire,* G83 7AH.
Original ferryman's cottage, beautifully renovated.
Open: All Year (not Xmas)
01301 702428 Mrs Bennetton
Fax no: 01301 270269
Rates fr: *£16.00*-**£25.00**.
Beds: 1F 2D 1T
Baths: 3 Private 1 Shared
(9)

***Oak Bank,** Arrochar, Dunbartonshire,* G83 7AA.
Large Victorian private house.
Open: All Year (not Xmas)
01301 702400 Mrs Nicolson
Rates fr: *£13.00*-**£17.00**.
Beds: 2D 1T
Baths: 1 Ensuite 2 Shared
(5) (6)

Bridge of Awe

National Grid Ref: NN0329

***Brookscroft,** Bridge of Awe, Taynuilt, Argyll,* PA35 1HT.
Happy and comfortable family bungalow.
Open: All Year (not Xmas)
01866 822484 Mrs Kirkham
Rates fr: *£10.00*-**£10.00**.
Beds: 1D 1T **Baths:** 1 Shared
(6)

Bridge of Orchy

National Grid Ref: NN2939

***Glen Orchy Farm,** Glen Orchy, Bridge of Orchy, Argyll,* PA33 1BD.
Friendly welcome on remote hill farm. **Open:** Mar to mid-Nov
01838 200221 Mrs MacLennan
Rates fr: *£13.00*-**£13.00**.
Beds: 2F **Baths:** 1 Shared

Bridgend

National Grid Ref: NR8592

***Kintra,** 3 Bridgend, Bridgend, Kilmichael Glassary, Lochgilphead, Argyll,* PA31 8QA.
Modern comfortable bungalow.
Open: Easter to Oct
01546 605294 Mrs Gillie
Rates fr: *£15.00*.
Beds: 2D
(2)

Campbeltown

National Grid Ref: NR7220

***Dellwood Hotel,** Drummore, Campbeltown, Argyll,* PA28 6HD.
Excellent family-run hotel.
Open: All Year (not Xmas)
Grades: STB 3 Cr, Comm
01586 552465 Ms Strang
Rates fr: *£21.00*-**£17.00**.
Beds: 6F 1D 6T
Baths: 6 Ensuite 4 Private 3 Shared

The lowest **single** *rate is shown in* **bold.**

Sandiway, *Fort Argyll Road, Low Askomil, Campbeltown, Argyll, PA28 6SN.*
Welcoming, homely, modern, comfortable bungalow.
Open: All Year (not Xmas)
Grades: STB 1 Cr, Comm
01586 552280 Mrs Bell
Rates fr: *£16.00*-**£19.00**.
Beds: 2T
Baths: 1 Private 1 Shared
(4)

Cardross

National Grid Ref: NS3477

Kirkton House, *Darleith Road, Cardross, Dumbarton, G82 5EZ.*
Open: All Year (not Xmas)
Grades: STB 3 Cr, High Comm, AA 4 Q, Select, RAC High Acclaim
01389 841951
Mr & Mrs Macdonald
Fax no: 01389 841868
Rates fr: *£27.00*-**£37.50**.
Beds: 4F 2T **Baths:** 6 Private
(12)
Converted farmstead. Tranquil country location. Magnificent Clyde views. Home-cooked 'Taste of Scotland' dinners by oil lamp-light. Residential licence. Rustic open fire. Two rooms downstairs.

Lea Farm, *Cardross, Dumbarton, G82 5EW.*
Comfortable farmhouse with panoramic views.
Open: All Year (not Xmas)
01389 763035 Mrs Russell
Rates fr: *£15.00*-**£17.00**.
Beds: 1F 1T **Baths:** 1 Shared

Carradale

National Grid Ref: NR8138

The Mains Farm, *Carradale, Campbeltown, Argyll, PA28 6QG.*
Traditional, comfortable farmhouse near beach.
Open: Easter to Oct
Grades: STB Listed, Comm
01583 431216 Mrs MacCormick
Rates fr: *£14.50*-**£14.50**.
Beds: 1F 1D 1S
Baths: 1 Shared

Kiloran Guest House, *Carradale, Campbeltown, Argyll, PA28 6QG.*
Family-run Victorian guest house.
Open: All Year
Grades: STB Listed, Comm
01583 431795 Mrs Nicholson
Rates fr: *£16.00*-**£17.00**.
Beds: 1F 2D 2T
Baths: 2 Ensuite 1 Private 1 Shared
(5)

Ashbank Hotel, *Carradale, Campbeltown, Argyll, PA28 6RY.*
Comfortable village-centre hotel.
Open: All Year
01583 431650 Mrs Cook
Rates fr: *£17.50*-**£21.00**.
Beds: 1F 1D 3T 1S
Baths: 3 Private 1 Shared
(6)

Clynder

National Grid Ref: NS2484

Glengair House, *Shore Road, Clynder, Helensburgh, Dunbartonshire, G84 0QN.*
Listed country house. Quiet, picturesque setting.
Open: All Year (not Xmas)
01436 831786 Mrs McEwan
Rates fr: *£18.00*-**£20.00**.
Beds: 1F 1D 1S **Baths:** 3 Private
(2) (8)

Colintraive

National Grid Ref: NS0374

Colintraive Hotel, *Colintraive, Argyll, PA22 3AS.*
Victorian hunting lodge.
Open: All Year
Grades: STB 3 Cr
01700 841207 Mr Williamson
Rates fr: *£18.00*-**£18.00**.
Beds: 1F 1D 2T **Baths:** 4 Private

Connel

National Grid Ref: NM9134

Falls of Lora Hotel

Ach Na Craig, *Grosvenor Crescent, Connel, Oban, Argyll, PA37 1PQ.*
Modern house in woodland glade.
Open: All Year
Grades: STB 3 Cr, Comm
01631 710588 Mrs Craig
Rates fr: *£17.00*.
Beds: 1D 2T **Baths:** 3 Ensuite
(6)

Falls Of Lora Hotel, *Connel Ferry, Connel, Oban, Argyll, PA37 1PB.*
Victorian hotel with modern extension.
Open: Feb to Dec
Grades: STB 3 Cr, Comm, AA 2 St, RAC 2 St
01631 710483 Miss Innes
Fax no: 01631 710694
Rates fr: *£19.50*-**£29.50**.
Beds: 4F 6D 14T 6S
Baths: 30 Private
(40)

Loch Etive House Hotel, *Connel, Oban, Argyll, PA37 1PH.*
Modernised Victorian house, own grounds.
Open: May to Oct
01631 710400 Mr Mossman
Rates fr: *£17.50*. **Beds:** 2F 2D 2T
Baths: 4 Private 2 Shared
(7)

Ronebhal Guest House, *Connel, Oban, Argyll, PA37 1PJ.*
Large Victorian private house.
Open: Easter to Oct
01631 710310 Mr & Mrs Strachen
Rates fr: *£17.00*-**£17.00**.
Beds: 1F 4D 1T 1S
Baths: 6 Private
(6) (6)

Craobh Haven

National Grid Ref: NM7907

Buidhe Lodge, *Craobh Haven, Lochgilphead, Argyll, PA31 8UA.*
Lodge in idyllic lochside setting.
Open: All Year (not Xmas)
Grades: STB 3 Cr, Comm
01852 500291 Mr & Mrs Twinn
Rates fr: *£21.00*-**£29.00**.
Beds: 2D 4T
Baths: 6 Private
(8)

Dalmally

National Grid Ref: NN1627

Orchy Bank Guest House, *Dalmally, Argyll, PA33 1AS.*
Large Victorian house on river.
Open: All Year
Grades: STB Listed, Comm
01838 200370
Mr Burke
Rates fr: *£17.00*-**£25.00**.
Beds: 2F 2D 2T 2S
Baths: 2 Shared
(8)

Craig Villa Guest House, *Dalmally, Argyll, PA33 1AX.*
Converted farmhouse amidst Highland scenery.
Open: Easter to Oct
Grades: STB 3 Cr, Comm
01838 200255
Mr Cressey
Rates fr: *£19.00*-**£25.00**.
Beds: 2F 2D 2T
Baths: 6 Private
(10)

Dunoon

National Grid Ref: NS1776

Royal Marine Hotel, Hunters Quay Hotel

The Anchorage, *Shore Road, Holy Loch, Dunoon, Argyll, PA23 8QG.*
Open: All Year
Grades: AA 5 Q, RAC High Acclaim
01369 705108
Mr & Mrs Hancock
Rates fr: *£21.50*-**£34.00**.
Beds: 5D
Baths: 5 Private
(14)
Idyllically set on shore road by Holy Loch, north of Dunoon. Conservatory Restaurant, restricted licence. STB Highly Commended. AA QQQQQ Selected. RAC Highly Acclaimed.

Craigieburn Hotel, *Alexandra Parade, East Bay, Dunoon, Argyll, PA23 8AN.*
Friendly family-run private hotel.
Open: All Year (not Xmas)
01369 702048 Mrs Hutchinson
Rates fr: *£14.00*-**£14.00**.
Beds: 3F 2D 2T 2S
Baths: 4 Shared
(10)

Lyall Cliff Hotel, *Alexandra Parade, East Bay, Dunoon, Argyll, PA23 8AW.*
Family hotel, sea front location.
Open: All Year (not Xmas)
Grades: STB 3 Cr, Comm
01369 702041
Mr & Mrs Greenshields
Fax no: 01369 702 041
Rates fr: *£19.00*-**£22.00**.
Beds: 2F 4D 4T
Baths: 10 Private
(3) (12)

Clifton Guest House, *Marine Parade, Hunters Quay, Dunoon, Argyll, PA23 8HJ.*
Large Victorian private house.
Open: All Year (not Xmas)
01369 702623 Mr & Mrs Smith
Rates fr: *£14.00*-**£14.00**.
Beds: 1F 2D 1T 1S
Baths: 2 Shared
(6)

Easdale Island

National Grid Ref: NM7317

Number 22, *Easdale Island, Oban, Argyll, PA34 4TB.*
Open: All Year (not Xmas)
01852 300438 Mrs Baldock
Rates fr: *£13.00*.
Beds: 1D 1T
Baths: 1 Shared
(10)
Homely cottage, small quiet island, slate industry museum, pub and cafe. Passenger ferry, three minute crossing, local walks and shops. Interesting places within travelling distance.

Ford

National Grid Ref: NM8603

Tigh An Lodan, *Ford, Lochgilphead, Argyll, PA31 8RH.*
Comfortable modern house, scenic splendour.
Open: Easter to Oct
01546 810287 Mrs Bannister
Rates fr: *£18.00*-**£20.00**.
Beds: 1D 2T
Baths: 3 Private
(12) (3)

The lowest *double* rate per person is shown in *italics*.

Garelochhead

National Grid Ref: NS2391

Glenmallon House, *Loch Long, Garelochhead, Helensburgh, Dunbartonshire, G84 0EZ.*
Lochside Georgian house - comfortable rooms.
Open: All Year
01436 810293 Mrs Eyles
Rates fr: *£17.00*-**£20.00**.
Beds: 2D 1T 1S
Baths: 2 Private
(3)

Glencruitten

National Grid Ref: NM8630

Barranrioch Farm, *Glencruitten, Oban, Argyll, PA34 4QD.*
Farmhouse, 2.5 miles from Oban.
Open: May to Mar
01631 770223
Ms Davidson
Rates fr: *£14.50*-**£15.00**.
Beds: 1F 1D
Baths: 2 Private
(20)

Helensburgh

National Grid Ref: NS2982

Toby Commodore Hotel, Pinewood, Upper Crust, Bonner's

Ravenswood, *32 Suffolk Street, Helensburgh, Dunbartonshire, G84 9PA.*
Large red sandstone Victorian home.
Open: All Year
01436 672112 (also fax no)
Mrs Richards
Rates fr: *£22.50*-**£22.50**.
Beds: 1D 1T 2S
Baths: 2 Private 1 Shared
(4)

Longleat, *39 East Argyle Street, Helensburgh, Dunbartonshire, G84 7EN.*
Comfortable home, quiet residential area.
Open: All Year (not Xmas)
Grades: STB 1 Cr, Comm
01436 672465
Mrs Blackwell
Rates fr: *£17.00*-**£17.00**.
Beds: 2D 1T
Baths: 1 Shared
(3)

Eastbank, *10 Hanover Street, Helensburgh, Dunbartonshire, G84 7AW.*
Upper flat of Victorian house.
Open: All Year (not Xmas)
Grades: STB Listed, Approv
01436 673665 (also fax no)
Mrs Ross
Rates fr: *£16.00*-**£16.00**.
Beds: 1F 1T 1S
Baths: 1 Ensuite 1 Shared
(3) (4)

Thorndean, *64 Colquhoun Street, Helensburgh, Dunbartonshire, G84 9NF.*
Warm, spacious Victorian private house.
Open: All Year
Grades: STB 2 Cr, Comm, AA 3 Q
01436 674922 Mrs Urquhart
Fax no: 01436 679913
Rates fr: *£20.00*-**£20.00**.
Beds: 1F 1D 1T
Baths: 2 Ensuite 1 Private
(6)

Garemount Lodge, *Helensburgh, Dunbartonshire, G84 8NP.*
Architect designed house, overlooking Gareloch.
Open: All Year (not Xmas)
Grades: STB 2 Cr, Comm
01436 820780 (also fax no)
Mrs Cowie
Rates fr: *£19.00*-**£23.00**.
Beds: 1F 1D
Baths: 1 Ensuite 1 Private
(4)

Holy Loch

National Grid Ref: NS1776

The Anchorage, *Shore Road, Holy Loch, Dunoon, Argyll, PA23 8QG.*
Idyllically set on shore road by Holy Loch.
Open: All Year
Grades: AA 5 Q, RAC High Acclaim
01369 705108
Mr & Mrs Hancock
Rates fr: *£21.50*-**£34.00**.
Beds: 5D
Baths: 5 Private
(14)

Hunters Quay

National Grid Ref: NS1879

Larkfield, *41 George Street, Hunters Quay, Dunoon, Argyll, PA23 8JT.*
Comfortable family home.
Open: Easter to Oct
01369 702247 Mrs Glass
Rates fr: *£12.50*-**£12.50**.
Beds: 1D 1T
Baths: 1 Shared
(2)

Innellan

National Grid Ref: NS1469

Osborne Hotel

Ashgrove Guest House, *Wyndham Road, Innellan, Dunoon, Argyll, PA23 7SH.*
Quiet country house, outstanding scenery.
Open: All Year (not Xmas)
01369 830306 Ms Kohls
Fax no: 01369 830776
Rates fr: *£17.00*-**£17.00**.
Beds: 1F 1D 1T
Baths: 3 Ensuite

Inveraray

National Grid Ref: NN0908

Fernpoint Hotel

***The Bank House,** Church Square, Inveraray, Argyll, PA32 8TX.*
Beautiful Georgian house. Prime situation.
Open: Mar to Nov
01499 302170 Mrs Smith
Rates fr: *£16.00*-**£20.00**.
Beds: 1F 3D
Baths: 2 Ensuite 2 Private
(12)

***Creag Dhubh,** Inveraray, Argyll, PA32 8XF.*
Beautiful views across Loch Fyne.
Open: Mar to Nov
Grades: STB 2 Cr, Comm, RAC Recomm
01499 302430 Mrs MacLugash
Rates fr: *£14.00*.
Beds: 1F 2D 1T
Baths: 1 Private 2 Shared
(5)

***The Old Rectory,** Inveraray, Argyll, PA32 8UH.*
Georgian house overlooking Loch Fyne.
Open: All Year (not Xmas)
01499 302280 Mrs Maclaren
Rates fr: *£13.50*-**£13.50**.
Beds: 4F 4D 1S
(9)

***Breagha Lodge,** The Avenue, Inveraray, Argyll, PA32 8YX.*
Modern villa in secluded avenue.
Open: All Year (not Xmas)
01499 302061 Mr Campbell
Rates fr: *£18.00*-**£36.00**.
Beds: 1F 2D 1T
Baths: 4 Ensuite
(4)

Isle of Bute — Ascog

National Grid Ref: NS1063

Black Bull

***Ascog Farm,** Ascog, Rothesay, Isle of Bute, PA20 9LL.*
Well-appointed farmhouse with character.
Open: All Year (not Xmas)
01700 503372 Mrs Watson
Rates fr: *£15.00*-**£15.00**.
Beds: 2D 1S **Baths:** 2 Shared
(6)

Isle of Bute — Rothesay

National Grid Ref: NS0864

Black Bull Inn

***Avon,** 16 Argyle Place, Rothesay, Isle of Bute, PA20 0BA.*
Warm, friendly, family, seafront home.
Open: All Year
01700 505897
Rates fr: *£16.00*-**£16.00**.
Beds: 1F 1S
(0)

***Ardyne Private Hotel,** 38 Mountstuart Road, Rothesay, Isle of Bute, PA20 9EB.*
Licensed seafront hotel, magnificent views.
Open: All Year
Grades: STB 3 Cr, Comm, RAC High Acclaim
01700 502052 Fax no: 01700 505129
Rates fr: *£18.00*-**£20.00**.
Beds: 3F 2D 3T 2S
Baths: 10 Ensuite

***The Commodore,** 12 Battery Place, Rothesay, Isle of Bute, PA20 9DP.*
Ideal island holiday base.
Open: All Year
Grades: STB 2 Cr, Comm
01700 502178 Mr Spear
Rates fr: *£18.00*-**£20.00**.
Beds: 1F 3D 2S
Baths: 6 Ensuite

Kilchrenan

National Grid Ref: NN0322

Kilchrenan Inn

***Innisfree,** Kilchrenan, Taynuilt, Argyll, PA35 1HG.*
Quiet location overlooking Loch Awe.
Open: All Year (not Xmas)
Grades: STB Listed, High Comm
01866 833352
Mrs Wright
Rates fr: *£15.00*-**£15.00**.
Beds: 1D 1T 1S
Baths: 2 Shared
(4)

Kilmartin

National Grid Ref: NR8398

The Cairn

***Tibertich,** Kilmartin, Lochgilphead, Argyll, PA31 8RQ.*
Working farm nestling among hills.
Open: Mar to Nov
01546 810281 Mrs Caulton
Rates fr: *£14.00*-**£14.00**.
Beds: 1D 1T 1S
Baths: 1 Shared
(4)

Kilmichael Glassary

National Grid Ref: NR8593

***Edmundsbury,** Dunadd View, Kilmichael Glassary, Lochgilphead, Argyll, PA31 8QE.*
Convenient for ferries, home cooking.
Open: All Year (not Xmas)
Grades: ETB Listed, Comm
01546 605309
Mrs Shuttlewood
Rates fr: *£15.00*-**£15.00**.
Beds: 1D 1T
Baths: 1 Shared
(2)

Lochgilphead

National Grid Ref: NR8688

Stag Hotel

***Kilmory House,** Paterson Street, Lochgilphead, Argyll, PA31 8JP.*
Comfortable family-run guest house.
Open: All Year
01546 603658 Mr Moore
Rates fr: *£14.00*-**£18.00**.
Beds: 3D 4T
Baths: 1 Ensuite 2 Shared
(10) (16)

***Empire Travellers Lodge,** Union Street, Lochgilphead, Argyll, PA31 8JS.*
Recently converted cinema.
Open: All Year (not Xmas)
01546 602381 Mr Haysom
Rates fr: *£20.00*-**£20.00**.
Beds: 2F 5D 2T
Baths: 9 Ensuite
(9)

Luss

National Grid Ref: NS3592

***Doune of Glen Douglas Farm,** Luss, Inverbeg, Alexandria, Dunbartonshire, G83 8PD.*
Open: Easter to Oct
Grades: STB 2 Cr, High Comm
01301 702312 Mrs Robertson
Rates fr: *£18.00*-**£24.00**.
Beds: 2D 1T
Working hill sheep farm extending to over 6,000 acres of unspoilt mountainside to which guests are offered free access for hill walking and observing wildlife.

***Shantron Farm,** Shantron Cottage, Luss, Alexandria, Dunbartonshire, G83 8N.*
5000-acre farm overlooking Loch Lomond.
Open: Mar to Nov
Grades: STB 2 Cr, Comm
01389 850231 / 0468 378400
Mrs Lennox
Fax no: 01389 850231
Rates fr: *£16.00*-**£20.00**.
Beds: 1F 1D 1T
Baths: 2 Ensuite 1 Shared
(1) (3)

Machrihanish

National Grid Ref: NR6320

Machrihanish Golf Club, Beachcomber Restaurant

***Ardell House,** Machrihanish, Campbeltown, Argyll, PA28 6PT.*
Large Victorian private house.
Open: Feb to Oct
Grades: AA 3 Q
01586 810235 Mr Baxter
Rates fr: *£20.00*-**£25.00**.
Beds: 1F 2D 8T
Baths: 9 Private
(10)

Mull of Kintyre

National Grid Ref: NR6908

***Ormsary Farm,** Mull of Kintyre, Campbeltown, Argyll, PA28 6RN.*
Comfortable farmhouse in rural area. **Open:** Easter to Sep
Grades: STB 2 Cr, Comm
01586 830665 Mrs Ronald
Rates fr: *£16.00*-**£17.00**.
Beds: 1F 1D 1T
Baths: 2 Private 1 Shared

Oban

National Grid Ref: NM8630

The Step Inn, Soroba House Hotel, The Barn Bar, Studio Restaurant

***Drumriggend,** Drummore Road, Oban, Argyll, PA34 4JL.*
Open: All Year
Grades: STB 3 Cr, High Comm, AA 4 Q, Select, RAC Acclaim
01631 563330 (also fax no)
Mr & Mrs Ledwidge
Rates fr: *£15.00*.
Beds: 1F 1D 1T **Baths:** 3 Private
(6)
Drumriggend is situated in a quiet residential setting 10-15 minutes walk from the town centre. Private parking. All bedrooms ensuite, colour TV, tea/coffee, central heating.

***Harbour View Guest House,** Shore Street, Oban, Argyll, PA34 4LQ.*
Centrally situated town house.
Open: All Year (not Xmas)
01631 563462 Mrs McDougall
Rates fr: *£15.00*.
Beds: 3F 2T **Baths:** 2 Shared

***Ferndale,** Pulpit Hill, Oban, Argyll, PA34 4LX.*
Modern comfortable and welcoming home. **Open:** All Year
Grades: STB Listed
01631 566284 Mrs Stark
Rates fr: *£14.00*.
Beds: 1D 1T **Baths:** 1 Shared
(12) (2)

***Elmbank Guest House,** Croft Road, Oban, Argyll, PA34 5JN.*
Friendly atmosphere. Quiet residential area.
Open: Easter to Oct
01631 562545 Mrs Douglas
Rates fr: *£15.00*-**£15.00**.
Beds: 4D 2T 1S
Baths: 2 Private 2 Shared

***Duncarden,** Rowan Road, Oban, Argyll, PA34 5TQ.*
Modern detached villa, large garden.
Open: Easter to Sep
01631 564947 Mrs MacCalman
Rates fr: *£17.00*-**£21.00**.
Beds: 1D 1T
Baths: 2 Private
(5) (3)

***Kathmore,** Soroba Road, Oban, Argyll, PA34 4JF.*
Family-run guest house.
Open: All Year
01631 562104 Mrs Wardhaugh
Rates fr: *£14.00*-**£18.00**.
Beds: 1F 3D 1T
Baths: 4 Private 1 Shared
(9)

***Kenmore,** Soroba Road, Oban, Argyll, PA34 4JF.*
Typical Highland home.
Open: All Year
01631 563592 Mrs Griffin
Rates fr: *£14.00*-**£16.00**.
Beds: 1F 1D 1T 1S
(10)

***1 Lonan Drive,** Oban, Argyll, PA34 4NN.*
Bungalow, quite residential area, easily located from A816 Local knowledge assured, Spanish spoken fluently.
Open: All Year (not Xmas)
Grades: STB Listed, Comm
01631 563164
Mrs Cooper
Rates fr: *£16.00*-**£18.00**.
Beds: 1D 1T
Baths: 1 Ensuite 1 Private
(11) (3)

***Glenburnie Private Hotel,** Esplade, Oban, Argyll, PA34 5AQ.*
Comfortable Victorian seafront hotel.
Open: Easter to Oct
Grades: STB 2 Cr, High Comm
01631 562089 Mr Strachan
Fax no: 01631 562 089
Rates fr: *£20.00*-**£20.00**.
Beds: 7D 5T 2S
Baths: 10 Private 6 Shared
(5) (10)

***Ard Struan,** Croft Road, Oban, Argyll, PA34 5JN.*
Well appointed private house.
Open: All Year
Grades: STB 2 Cr, Comm
01631 563689 Mrs McQuade
Rates fr: *£13.00*.
Beds: 3D 1T
Baths: 4 Private
(5)

St Catherines

National Grid Ref: NN1207

***Thistle House,** St Catherines, Cairndow, Argyll, PA25 8AZ.*
Comfortable Victorian country house in large garden.
Open: Easter to Oct
01499 302209 Mrs Cameron
Rates fr: *£18.50*-**£24.00**.
Beds: 1F 2D 2T
Baths: 3 Ensuite 2 Shared
(10)

Tarbet

National Grid Ref: NN3104

Weavers Rest

***Lochview,** Tarbet, Arrochar, Dunbartonshire, G83 7DD.*
200-year-old Georgian house.
Open: All Year (not Xmas)
Grades: STB Listed, Approv
01301 702200 Mrs Fairfield
Rates fr: *£13.50*-**£15.00**.
Beds: 1F 1D 1T
Baths: 1 Shared

***Blairannaich,** Tarbet, Arrochar, Dunbartonshire, G83 7DN.*
Old lodge, magnificent views of loch.
Open: All Year
01301 702257 Mr & Mrs Handy
Rates fr: *£17.00*-**£25.00**.
Beds: 1D 2T
Baths: 3 Ensuite
(6)

Tighnabruaich

National Grid Ref: NR9773

Royal Hotel

***Ardeneden,** Tighnabruaich, Argyll, PA21 2BD.*
Large Victorian villa. Sea views.
Open: All Year
01700 811354 Mrs Mansey
Rates fr: *£14.00*-**£16.00**.
Beds: 1F 3D 4T
Baths: 3 Shared

***Ferguslie,** Seafront, Tighnabruaich, Argyll, PA21 2BE.*
Victorian villa with attractive garden.
Open: Easter to Oct
01700 811414 Mrs McLachlan
Rates fr: *£15.00*-**£16.00**.
Beds: 2D 1S
Baths: 1 Shared
(3)

Ayrshire & Arran

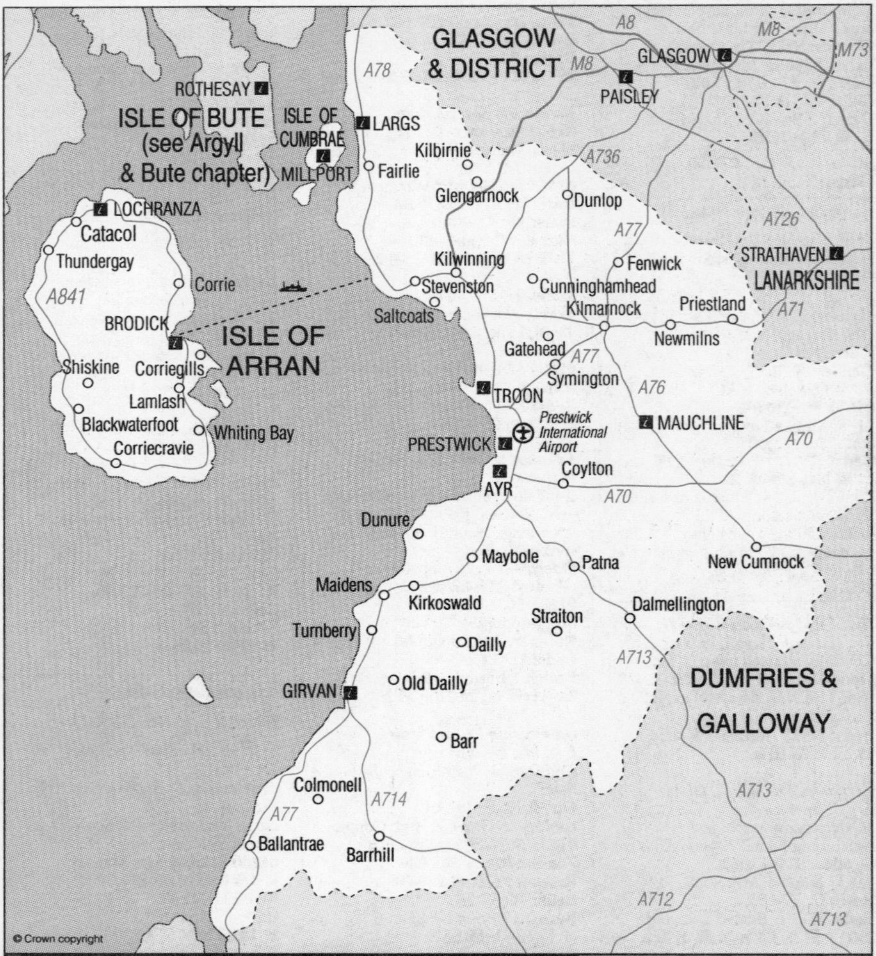

GLASGOW & DISTRICT
GLASGOW
PAISLEY
ROTHESAY
ISLE OF BUTE (see Argyll & Bute chapter)
ISLE OF CUMBRAE
MILLPORT
LARGS
Fairlie
Kilbirnie
Glengarnock
Dunlop
LOCHRANZA
Catacol
Thundergay
Corrie
A841
BRODICK
ISLE OF ARRAN
Shiskine
Corriegills
Lamlash
Blackwaterfoot
Whiting Bay
Corriecravie
Kilwinning
Stevenston
Saltcoats
Cunninghamhead
Fenwick
Kilmarnock
Priestland
Newmilns
STRATHAVEN
LANARKSHIRE
Gatehead
Symington
TROON
Prestwick International Airport
PRESTWICK
MAUCHLINE
AYR
Coylton
Dunure
Maybole
Patna
New Cumnock
Maidens
Kirkoswald
Turnberry
Straiton
Dalmellington
Dailly
Old Dailly
GIRVAN
DUMFRIES & GALLOWAY
Barr
Colmonell
Ballantrae
Barrhill
A8
M8
M73
A78
A736
A726
A77
A71
A76
A70
A713
A714
A712

Tourist Information Centres

Burns House, Burns Statue Square,**Ayr**, Ayrshire, KA7 1UP, 01292 288688.

The Pier, **Brodick**, Isle of Arran, KA27 8AU, 01770 302140.

Bridge Street, **Girvan**, Ayrshire, KA26 9HH, 01465 714950, (Easter to Oct).

The Promenade, **Largs**, Ayrshire, KA30 8BG, 01475 673765.

National Burns Memorial Tower, Kilmarnock Road, **Mauchline**, Ayrshire, KA5 5TT, 01290 551916.

Stuart St, **Millport**, Isle of Cumbrae, KA28 0AN, 01475 530753, (Easter to Oct).

Boydfield Gardens, **Prestwick**, Ayrshire, KA9 2JL, 01292 79946, (Easter to Oct).

15 Victoria Street, **Rothesay**, Isle of Bute, PA20 0AJ, 01700 502151.

Municipal Buildings, South Beach, **Troon**, Ayrshire, KA10 6EF, 01292 317696, (Easter to Oct).

Ayr

National Grid Ref: NS3422

Kylestrome Hotel, Finlay's Bar, Burrofield's Bar, Carrick Lodge, Durward Hotel, Hollybush Inn

Belmont Guest House, *15 Park Circus, Ayr, KA7 2DJ.*
Open: All Year (not Xmas)
Grades: STB 2 Cr, Approv
01292 265588 Mr Hillhouse
Rates fr: *£16.00*-**£18.00**.
Beds: 2F 2D 1T
Baths: 5 Private
(5)
Warm, comfortable hospitality assured in this Victorian town house, situated in a quiet residential area within easy walking distance of the town centre and beach. Ground floor bedroom with en-suite available.

Kilkerran, *15 Prestwick Road, Ayr, KA8 8LD.*
Family-run guest house.
Open: All Year
01292 266477 Ms Ferguson
Rates fr: *£14.00*-**£14.00**.
Beds: 1F 1D 2T 1S
Baths: 2 Private 1 Shared
(5)

13 Forest Way, *Ayr, KA7 3ST.*
Quiet bungalow in suburbs.
Open: Easter to Nov
01292 267100 Ms Murdoch
Rates fr: *£15.00*-**£16.00**.
Beds: 1F 1D **Baths:** 1 Shared
(3) (3)

38 Forehill Road, *Ayr, KA7 3DT.*
Comfortable bungalow, homely atmosphere.
Open: All Year
01292 286686 Mrs Stewart
Rates fr: *£14.50*-**£16.50**.
Beds: 1F 1D 1T **Baths:** 1 Shared
(3)

Deanbank, *44 Ashgrove Street, Ayr, KA7 3BG.*
Excellent B&B accommodation.
Open: All Year
Grades: STB 1 Cr, High Comm
01292 263745 Ms Wilson
Rates fr: *£16.00*-**£18.00**.
Beds: 1F 1D **Baths:** 1 Shared
(1)

Ferguslea, *98 New Road, Ayr, KA8 8JG*
Traditional Scottish hospitality.
Open: All Year
Grades: STB 2 Cr, Comm
01292 268551 Mrs Campbell
Rates fr: *£13.00*-**£13.00**.
Beds: 2T 1S
Baths: 1 Private 2 Shared
(3)

Iona, *27 St Leords Road, Ayr, KA7 2PS*
Modernised Victorian semi-villa.
Open: Feb to Nov
Grades: STB 2 Cr, Comm
01292 269541 Mr & Mrs Gibson
Rates fr: *£15.00*-**£15.00**.
Beds: 1D 1T 2S
Baths: 2 Ensuite 1 Shared
(4)

Malcolmston Farm, *Hollybush, Ayr, KA6 6EZ.*
Farmhouse near Turnberry and Troon.
Open: May to Oct
01292 560238 Mrs Drummond
Rates fr: *£15.00*-**£15.00**.
Beds: 3D 1T
Baths: 1 Ensuite 2 Shared
(4)

Inverewe Guest House, *45 Bellevue Crescent, Ayr, KA7 2DP.*
Home form home. Central location.
Open: All Year
01292 265989 Mr & Mrs Taylor
Rates fr: *£15.00*-**£18.00**.
Beds: 1F 2D 1T 1S
Baths: 2 Ensuite 1 Shared
(2)

Windsor Hotel, *6 Alloway Place, Ayr, KA7 2AA.*
Comfortable, private, family-run hotel.
Open: All Year (not Xmas)
Grades: STB 3 Cr, Comm, AA 2 Q, RAC High Recomm
01292 264689 Mrs Hamilton
Rates fr: *£22.00*-**£22.00**.
Beds: 4F 3D 1T 2S
Baths: 7 Ensuite 1 Private 2 Shared

The Elms Court Hotel, *Miller Road, Ayr, KA7 2AX.*
Comfortable town centre hotel.
Open: All Year
Grades: STB 4 Cr, Comm, AA 2 St
01292 264191 Mr & Mrs Gregor
Fax no: 01292 610254
Rates fr: *£30.00*-**£30.00**.
Beds: 3F 7D 6T 4S
Baths: 20 Ensuite 20 Private

Ballantrae

National Grid Ref: NX1998

Laggan Farm, *Ballantrae, Girvan, Ayrshire, KA26 0JZ.*
Comfortable farmhouse in coastal area.
Open: May to Oct
01465 831402 Mrs Mckinley
Rates fr: *£14.00*-**£16.00**.
Beds: 1F 1D
Baths: 1 Private 1 Shared

Ardstinchar Cottage, *81 Main Street, Ballantrae, Girvan, Ayrshire, KA26 0NA.*
Beautiful cottage in magnificent countryside.
Open: All Year
Grades: STB 1 Cr, Comm
01465 831343 Mrs Drummond
Rates fr: *£13.00*-**£15.00**.
Beds: 2D 1T
Baths: 1 Private
(3)

Balkissock Lodge, *Ballantrae, Girvan, Ayrshire, KA26 0LP.*
Modernised C19th shooting lodge.
Open: Dec to Oct
Grades: AA 3 Q
01465 831537 (also fax no)
Mr & Mrs Beale
Rates fr: *£22.50*-**£32.50**.
Beds: 1F 1D 1T **Baths:** 3 Private
(6)

Barr

National Grid Ref: NX2794

Glengennet Farm, *Barr, Girvan, Ayrshire, KA26 9TY.*
Original shooting lodge, lovely views. **Open:** April to Oct
Grades: STB Listed
01465 861220 Ms Dunlop
Rates fr: *£18.50*-**£23.50**.
Beds: 1D 1T 1S **Baths:** 2 Ensuite
(5) (3)

Barrhill

National Grid Ref: NX2382

Blair Farm, *Barrhill, Girvan, Ayrshire, KA26 0RD.*
Delightful farmhouse on working farm. **Open:** Easter to Oct
Grades: STB 2 Cr, Comm
01465 821247 Mrs Hughes
Rates fr: *£15.00*-**£15.00**.
Beds: 2D 1T
Baths: 1 Ensuite 1 Shared

14 Main Street, *Barrhill, Girvan, Ayrshire, KA26 0PQ.*
Comfortable family home.
Open: All Year (not Xmas)
01465 821344 Mrs Hegarty
Rates fr: *£14.00*-**£14.00**.
Beds: 1F 1T
Baths: 1 Private 1 Shared

Colmonell

National Grid Ref: NX1485

Boars Head

The Yett, *4 Manse Road, Colmonell, Girvan, Ayrshire, KA26 0SA*
Very comfortable old house.
Open: Easter to Oct
Grades: STB Listed
01465 881223 Mrs Fergusson
Rates fr: *£12.50*-**£12.50**.
Beds: 1D 2T

Coylton

National Grid Ref: NS4219

Kyle Hotel, Finlayson Arms

Strathcoyle, *Coylton, Ayr, KA6 6JR.*
Excellent location, golf, Burns, Ayr.
Open: All Year (not Xmas)
01292 570366
Mrs Hepher
Rates fr: *£15.00*-**£18.00**.
Beds: 1D 1T **Baths:** 1 Shared
(3)

The Kyle Hotel, *Main Street, Coylton, Ayr, Scotland, KA6 6JW.*
Deluxe Scottish country hotel.
Open: All Year **Grades:** STB
01292 570312 Mr Henderson
Rates fr: *£15.00*-**£18.00**.
Beds: 2F 2T **Baths:** 2 Private 1Shared
(0)

Cunninghamhead

National Grid Ref: NS3741

The Stables, *Fairliecrevoch Farm, Cunninghamhead, Kilmarnock, Ayrshire, KA2 3PD.*
Converted C18th stable block.
Open: All Year (not Xmas)
01294 850333 Mrs Mckay
Rates fr: *£14.00*-**£14.00**.
Beds: 1F **Baths:** 1 Private
(6)

Dailly

National Grid Ref: NS2701

Maxwelston Farm, *Dailly, Girvan, Ayrshire, KA26 9RH.*
Homely, friendly, comfortable, spacious farmhouse.
Open: Easter to Oct
01465 811210 Mrs Whiteford
Rates fr: *£18.00*-**£22.00**.
Beds: 1D 1T **Baths:** 2 Shared
(3)

Dalmellington

National Grid Ref: NS4806

Benbain, *Cummock Road, Dalmellington, Ayr, KA6 7PS.*
C16th cottage, 1000 ft above sea level
Open: All Year
01292 550556 Mrs Taveren
Rates fr: *£14.50*-**£14.50**.
Beds: 1D 1T 1S **Baths:** 2 Shared
(5) (6)

Dunlop

National Grid Ref: NS4049

Struther Farmhouse, *17 Newmill Road, Dunlop, Kilmarnock, Ayrshire, KA3 4BA.*
Country house with large garden.
Open: All Year
01560 484946 Mrs Leggat
Rates fr: *£16.00*-**£18.00**.
Beds: 2F 1D 1T **Baths:** 2 Shared
(16)

Dunure

National Grid Ref: NS2515

The Anchorage

Dunduff Farm, *Dunure, Ayr, KA7 4LH.*
Farmhouse overlooking Firth of Clyde.
Open: Easter to Oct
Grades: STB 2 Cr, High Comm, AA 4 Q, Select
01292 500225 Mrs Gemmell
Fax no: 01292 500222
Rates fr: *£18.00*-**£20.00**.
Beds: 1F 2D 1T **Baths:** 3 Private
(10)

Fisherton Farm, *Dunure, Ayr, KA7 4LF*
Delightfully situated traditional Scottish farmhouse.
Open: Mar to Nov
Grades: STB 1 Cr, Comm
01292 500223
Mrs Wilcox
Rates fr: *£15.00*-**£17.50**.
Beds: 2T
Baths: 1 Shared

Fairlie

National Grid Ref: NS2055

Beachview, *8 Bay Street, Fairlie, Largs, Ayrshire, KA29 0AL.*
Conventional sandstone house.
Open: Apr to Oct
01475 568389
Mrs Reid
Rates fr: *£14.00*-**£14.00**.
Beds: 2T
Baths: 1 Shared

Fenwick

National Grid Ref: NS4643

King's Arms

Mansefield, *10 Kirkton Road, Fenwick, Kilmarnock, Ayrshire, KA3 6DH.*
Victorian house near country pub.
Open: All Year
01560 600834
Mrs MacNab
Rates fr: *£14.00*-**£16.00**.
Beds: 1D 2T
Baths: 1 Shared
(3)

Gatehead

National Grid Ref: NS4237

Muirhouse Farm, *Gatehead, Kilmarnock, Ayrshire, KA2 0BT.*
Comfortable farmhouse.
Convenient to town.
Open: All Year (not Xmas)
Grades: STB 2 Cr, Comm
01563 523975
Mrs Love
Rates fr: *£15.00*-**£16.00**.
Beds: 1F 1D 1T
Baths: 2 Ensuite 1 Private
(6)

Girvan

National Grid Ref: NX1998

Southfield hotel

Sands Private Hotel, *20 Louisa Drive, Girvan, Ayrshire, KA26 9AH.*
Friendly comfortable seafront panoramic view.
Open: All Year (not Xmas)
01465 712178
Mrs Johnstone
Rates fr: *£16.00*-**£17.00**.
Beds: 4F 3D 2T
Baths: 7 Ensuite 1 Shared
(3)

Thistleneuk Guest House, *19 Louisa Drive, Girvan, Ayrshire, KA26 9AH.*
Large Victorian seafront house.
Open: Easter to October
Grades: STB 3 Cr, Comm
01465 712137
Mr & Mrs Lacey
Rates fr: *£19.00*-**£19.00**.
Beds: 2F 2D 2T 1S
Baths: 7 Private

St Edmunds, *Stair Park, Girvan, Ayrshire, KA26 9AN.*
Large Victorian private house.
Centre of town.
Open: Easter to Sep
01465 713421
Mrs Sneddon
Rates fr: *£15.00*-**£15.00**.
Beds: 2D 1T

Appin Cottage, *27-29 Ailsa Street West, Girvan, Ayrshire, KA26 9AD.*
Converted fisherman's cottages, central, quiet.
Open: Easter to Oct
01465 713214
Mr & Mrs Mulholland
Rates fr: *£16.00*-**£25.00**.
Beds: 1D 1T
Baths: 2 Ensuite

Glengarnock

National Grid Ref: NS3253

Meikle Auchengree, *Glengarnock, Beith, Ayrshire, KA14 3BU.*
Modern comfortable farmhouse.
Open: All Year
01294 832205
Mrs Workman
Rates fr: *£15.00*-**£16.00**.
Beds: 2D 1T
Baths: 1 Private 2 Shared
(3)

Isle of Arran Blackwaterfoot

National Grid Ref: NR8928

Morvern, *Blackwaterfoot, Brodick, Isle of Arran, KA27 8EU.*
Comforable, spacious, ex-bank manager's house.
Open: All Year (not Xmas)
Grades: STB 2 Cr, Approv
01770 860254
Ms Sherwood
Rates fr: *£15.50*-**£15.50**.
Beds: 1F 1D 1T
Baths: 1 Ensuite 1 Shared

Parkhouse, *Blackwaterfoot, Brodick, Isle of Arran, KA27 8HE.*
Converted farm house and buildings.
Open: Apr to Oct
01770 860392
Mrs Faulkner
Rates fr: *£14.00*-**£14.00**.
Beds: 2D 1T
Baths: 2 Shared

Isle of Arran — Brodick

National Grid Ref: NS0136

Ormidale Hotel Bar, Brodick Bar

Belvedere, *Alma Road, Brodick, Isle of Arran, KA27 8AZ.*
Semi-villa with panoramic views.
Open: Easter to Oct
01770 302397 Mrs Hendry
Rates fr: *£13.50*-**£13.50**.
Beds: 2D 1T **Baths:** 1 Shared
(2)

Cala Sona, *Alma Park, Brodick, Isle of Arran, KA27 8AT.*
Modern bungalow, views sea and mountains.
Open: All Year (not Xmas)
01770 302828 Mrs Wilkie
Rates fr: *£14.00*-**£14.00**.
Beds: 1D 1T **Baths:** 1 Shared
(2)

Carrick Lodge, *Brodick, Isle of Arran, KA27 8BH.*
Victorian sandstone building, panoramic views.
Open: Feb to Oct
Grades: STB 3 Cr, Comm
01770 302550 (also fax no)
Mr Thompson
Rates fr: *£20.00*-**£20.00**.
Beds: 1F 2D 2T 1S
Baths: 5 Ensuite 1 Private
(6)

Quivive, *Corriegills, Brodick, Isle of Arran, KA27 8BL.*
Modern bungalow, scenic views, walks. **Open:** All Year (not Xmas)
01770 302843 Ms Cresswell
Rates fr: *£16.00*-**£18.00**.
Beds: 3T **Baths:** 1 Shared
(4)

Tigh Na Mara, *Seafront, Brodick, Isle of Arran, KA27 8AJ.*
Tigh Na Mara overlooks beach and hills. **Open:** Easter to Oct
Grades: STB 2 Cr, Comm
01770 302538 Miss Smith
Fax no: 01770 302340
Rates fr: *£16.50*-**£17.00**.
Beds: 1F 3D 3T
Baths: 2 Private 4 Shared
(4) (2)

Isle of Arran — Catacol

National Grid Ref: NR9149

Catacol Bay Hotel, *Catacol, Brodick, Isle of Arran, KA27 8HN.*
Open: All Year
01770 830231 Mr Ashcroft
Fax no: 01770 830350
Rates fr: *£17.50*-**£17.50**.
Beds: 2F 1D 1T 2S
Baths: 2 Shared
(30)
Small, friendly, fully licensed hotel, nestling in hills at the picturesque north end of Arran. Situated on the seashore, overlooking the Kilbrannan Sound and Kintyre.

Fairhaven, *Catacol, Brodick, Isle of Arran, KA27 8HN.*
Family-run guest house.
Open: All Year
01770 830237 Mrs Bannatyne
Rates fr: *£15.00*-**£15.00**.
Beds: 1F 3D 3T 2S
Baths: 7 Ensuite 2 Shared

Isle of Arran — Corrie

National Grid Ref: NS0243

Blackrock Guest House, *Corrie, Brodick, Isle of Arran, KA27 8JP.*
Comfortable, friendly guest house.
Open: Mar to Nov
01770 810282 Mr Wilkinson
Rates fr: *£19.00*-**£19.00**.
Beds: 4F 1D 1T 2S
Baths: 2 Shared
(10)

Isle of Arran — Corriegills

National Grid Ref: NS0435

Quivive, *Corriegills, Brodick, Isle of Arran, KA27 8BL.*
Modern bungalow, scenic views, walks.
Open: All Year (not Xmas)
01770 302843 Ms Cresswell
Rates fr: *£16.00*-**£18.00**.
Beds: 3T **Baths:** 1 Shared
(4)

Isle of Arran — Lamlash

National Grid Ref: NS0230

Westfield Guest House, *Lamlash, Brodick, Isle of Arran, KA27 8NN.*
Typical island red sandstone villa.
Open: All Year (not Xmas)
01770 600428 Mrs Marr
Rates fr: *£16.00*-**£16.00**.
Beds: 1D 1T 2S
Baths: 2 Shared
(1) (4)

Lilybank Hotel, *Shore Road, Lamlash, Brodick, Isle of Arran, KA27 8LS.*
Award-winning hotel and restaurant.
Open: Mar to Dec
01770 600230 Mrs Berry
Rates fr: *£25.00*-**£25.00**.
Beds: 3D 3T 1S
Baths: 7 Ensuite
(7)

Isle of Arran — Lochranza

National Grid Ref: NR9349

Apple Lodge Hotel, *Lochranza, Brodick, Isle of Arran, KA27 8HL.*
Highly Commended luxury hotel, spectacular views.
Open: All Year (not Xmas)
Grades: STB 3 Cr, High Comm, AA Listed , RAC Listed
01770 830229 (also fax no)
Rates fr: *£25.00*-**£40.00**.
Beds: 3D 1T
Baths: 3 Ensuite 1 Private
(12) (4)

Isle of Arran — Shiskine

National Grid Ref: NR9129

Road End Christian Guest House, *Shiskine, Brodick, Isle of Arran, KA27 8EW.*
Traditional Scottish country house.
Open: All Year
Grades: STB 1 Cr, Comm
01770 860448 Mrs Mills
Rates fr: *£16.00*-**£16.00**.
Beds: 1F 1D **Baths:** 1 Shared
(2)

Isle of Arran — Whiting Bay

National Grid Ref: NS0425

Kiscadale Hotel

Rowallan, *School Road, Whiting Bay, Brodick, Isle of Arran, KA27 8PZ.*
Detached house overlooking the sea.
Open: Apr to Nov
Grades: STB 2 Cr, Comm
01770 700377 Miss White
Fax no: 01770 700640
Rates fr: *£15.00*-**£15.00**.
Beds: 1F 1D 1T 1S
Baths: 1 Ensuite 1 Shared
(12) (3)

Norwood, Smiddy Brae, *Whiting Bay, Brodick, Isle of Arran, KA27 8PR.*
Comfortable family house overlooking sea.
Open: All Year (not Xmas)
Grades: STB 1Cr, Comm
01770 700536 Mrs McCormack
Rates fr: *£14.00*-**£14.00**.
Beds: 1D 2T **Baths:** 2 Shared
(3)

Invermay Hotel, *Whiting Bay, Brodick, Isle of Arran, KA27 8PZ.*
Private hotel of outstanding character.
Open: Easter to Oct
Grades: STB 3 Cr, Comm, AA 3 Q, RAC Acclaim
01770 700431 Mr Watterson
Rates fr: *£23.00*-**£23.00**.
Beds: 3D 2T 2S
Baths: 5 Ensuite 3 Shared
(9)

Isle of Cumbrae — Millport

National Grid Ref: NS1655

Denmark Cottage, *8 Ferry Road, Millport, Isle of Cumbrae, KA28 0DZ.*
Modern comfortable detached house. **Open:** All Year
01475 530958 Mrs Carruthers
Rates fr: *£13.50*-**£13.50**.
Beds: 2F 1D 2T **Baths:** 2 Shared

Craig Ard Guest House, *1 Craig Street, Millport, Isle of Cumbrae, KA28 0DR.*
Ideally situated on Millport's seafront. **Open:** Mar to Oct
01475 530532 Mr Barry
Rates fr: *£14.00*-**£14.00**.
Beds: 3F 2D 2T 1S
Baths: 2 Shared

Kilbirnie

National Grid Ref: NS3154

Alpenrose, *113 Herriot Avenue, Kilbirnie, Ayrshire, KA25 7JB.*
'Home from home' Scottish villa.
Open: All Year
01505 683122 Mrs Cameron
Rates fr: *£11.00*-**£11.00**.
Beds: 1D 1T 1S
Baths: 1 Shared
(4)

Kilmarnock

National Grid Ref: NS4237

Coffee Club, Blair Tavern

Hillhouse Farm, *Grassyards Road, Kilmarnock, Ayrshire, KA3 6HG*
Open: All Year
Grades: STB 2 Cr, Comm
01563 523370
Mrs Howie
Rates fr: *£15.00*-**£16.00**.
Beds: 2F 1T
Baths: 1 Private 2 Shared
(8)
Large comfortable friendly farmhouse with lounge, dining room, safe parking. Ideal location for coast, Glasgow, golf. High standard assured with real farmhouse breakfeasts. S/C cottages available.

Birken Shaw, *61 Irvine Road, Kilmarnock, Ayrshire, KA1 2JP.*
Well equipped rooms, lovely home.
Open: Easter to Oct
01563 528392
Mrs Hannah
Rates fr: *£16.50*-**£20.00**.
Beds: 1D 1T
Baths: 1 Private 1 Shared
(2)

Burnside Hotel, *18 London Road, Kilmarnock, Ayrshire, KA3 7AQ.*
Open: All Year
Grades: STB 3 Cr, High Comm, AA 4 Q, Select
01563 522952
Mr & Mrs Dye
Fax no: 01563 573381
Rates fr: *£17.50*-**£17.50**.
Beds: 3F 2D 2T 3S
Baths: 5 Ensuite 5 Shared
(12)
Fine sandstone family owned hotel in town's conservation area with private parking. Relaxed atmosphere for business or pleasure. Palace Theatre, golf courses, Prestwick Airport nearby.

Muirhouse Farm, *Gatehead, Kilmarnock, Ayrshire, KA2 0BT.*
Comfortable farmhouse. Convenient to town.
Open: All Year (not Xmas)
Grades: STB 2 Cr, Comm
01563 523975
Mrs Love
Rates fr: *£15.00*-**£16.00**.
Beds: 1F 1D 1T
Baths: 2 Ensuite 1 Private
(6)

Kilwinning

National Grid Ref: NS3043

Claremont Hotel

Tarcoola, *Montgreenan, Kilwinning, Ayrshire, KA13 7QZ.*
Open: All Year
01294 850379
Mrs Melville
Fax no: 01294 850249
Rates fr: *£14.00*-**£13.00**.
Beds: 1D 1S
Baths: 1 Shared
(3)
Attractive country setting. Convenient for Arran ferry, Ayrshire golf and Glasgow City attractions. Local pub food. Near A736 Irvine to Glasgow. Friendly welcome. Languages spoken.

Claremont Guest House, *27 Howgate, Kilwinning, Ayrshire, KA13 6EW.*
Friendly family-run guest house.
Open: All Year
01294 553905 Mrs Filby
Rates fr: *£15.00*-**£15.00**.
Beds: 1F 1S
Baths: 2 Shared

Woodburn Cottage, *Woodwynd, Kilwinning, Ayrshire, KA13 7DD.*
Delightful converted C19th farmhouse.
Open: All Year (not Xmas)
Grades: STB Listed, Comm
01294 551657 Mrs Harris
Fax no: 01294 558297
Rates fr: *£15.00*-**£15.00**.
Beds: 2T 1S
Baths: 2 Shared
(3)

Kirkoswald

National Grid Ref: NS2407

Kirkton Jeans Hotel, *47 Main Street, Kirkoswald, Maybole, Ayrshire, KA19 8HY.*
Comfortable accommodation, renowned for food.
Open: All Year
01655 760220
Mrs Appleyard
Rates fr: *£17.50*-**£25.00**.
Beds: 2F 7T **Baths:** 9 Private

Largs

National Grid Ref: NS2059

Morris's

Rutland Guest House, *22 Charles Street, Largs, Ayrshire, KA30 8HJ.*
Comfortable, family-run guest house.
Open: All Year
Grades: STB 2 Cr, Comm
01475 675642 Mrs Russell
Rates fr: *£15.00*-**£16.00**.
Beds: 1F 1D 1T 1S
Baths: 1 Ensuite 1 Private 2 Shared

South Whittleburn Farm, *Brisbane Glen, Largs, Ayrshire, KA30 8SN.*
Superb farmhouse accommodation, friendly hospitality.
Open: All Year (not Xmas)
Grades: STB 2 Cr, High Comm, AA 3 Q, RAC Listed
01475 675881 Mrs Watson
Rates fr: *£16.50*-**£17.00**.
Beds: 1F 1D 1T **Baths:** 3 Ensuite
(10)

Queens Hotel, *North Promendade, Largs, Ayrshire, KA30 8QW.*
Traditional seafront hotel.
Open: All Year
Grades: RAC 2 St
01475 675311 Mr & Mrs Boyle
Rates fr: *£30.00*-**£30.00**.
Beds: 2F 7D 2T 1S
Baths: 12 Ensuite
(30)

Ardmore Guest House, *16 Aubery Crescent, Largs, Ayrshire, KA30 8PR.*
Victorian terrace house on seafront.
Open: Easter to Oct
01475 672516 Mr & Mrs Capocchi
Rates fr: *£16.00*-**£17.00**.
Beds: 2F 2D 2T **Baths:** 2 Shared
(6)

Maidens

National Grid Ref: NS2107

Barley Bree Pub

Jameston Farmhouse, *Maidens, Girvan, Ayrshire, KA26 9MF.*
Open: All Year
01655 331286 Ms Kennedy
Rates fr: *£17.00*-**£20.00**.
Beds: 1F 1D 1T
Baths: 1 Ensuite 2 Shared
Farmhouse in lovely setting, stylishly decorated, TV, HC, comfortable beds, great breakfast. Near Culzean Castle & Turnberry Golf Course. Open all year. From £17.00-£20.00.

Maybole

National Grid Ref: NS2909

Anchorage Hotel (Dunure)

Homelea, *62 Culzean Road, Maybole, Ayrshire, KA19 8AH.*
Victorian house near Culzean Castle. **Open:** Mar to Oct
Grades: STB Listed, Comm
01655 882736 Mrs McKellar
Rates fr: *£14.00*-**£16.00**.
Beds: 1F 1D **Baths:** 2 Shared

Garpin, *Maybole, Ayrshire, KA19 7PX.*
Traditional, comfortable farmhouse.
Open: All Year (not Xmas)
01655 740214 / 740381 Mrs Young
Rates fr: *£12.00*-**£16.00**.
Beds: 1F 1T

New Cumnock

National Grid Ref: NS6113

Low Polquheys Farm, *New Cumnock, Cumnock, Ayrshire, KA18 4NX.*
Modern farmhouse, very friendly and central.
Open: Easter to Oct
01290 338307 Mrs Caldwell
Rates fr: *£12.00*-**£12.00**.
Beds: 1F 1T **Baths:** 1 Shared
(2)

Fernbank, *Boig Road, New Cumnock, Cumnock, Ayrshire, KA18 4QE.*
Large, comfortable house.
Open: All Year
01290 338493 Mrs McTurk
Rates fr: *£11.00*-**£11.00**.
Beds: 2F **Baths:** 1 Shared

Newmilns

National Grid Ref: NS5237

The Maxwood

Whatriggs Farm, *Newmilns, Ayrshire, KA16 9LJ.*
Very comfortable large farmhouse.
Open: All Year (not Xmas)
01560 700279 Mrs Mitchell
Rates fr: *£12.50*-**£12.50**.
Beds: 2F **Baths:** 1 Shared

Old Dailly

National Grid Ref: NX2299

Kings Arms, Wildings

Hawkhill Farm, *Old Dailly, Girvan, Ayrshire, KA26 9RD.*
Delightful farmhouse with good food.
Open: Easter to October
01465 871232 Mrs Kyle
Rates fr: *£20.00*-**£25.00**.
Beds: 2D 1T
Baths: 3 Private
(3)

Patna

National Grid Ref: NS4110

Parsons Lodge, *Patna, Ayr, KA6 7LN.*
Ballochmyle sandstone former manse.
Open: All Year
Grades: STB 3 Cr, Comm
01292 531306
Mrs Campbell
Rates fr: *£15.00*-**£17.50**.
Beds: 1F 1D 1T 1S
Baths: 3 Private
(5)

The lowest *double* rate per person is shown in *italics*.

Prestwick

National Grid Ref: NS3425

North Beach Hotel

66 Adamton Road, *Prestwick, Ayrshire, KA9 2HD.*
Homely, quiet B&B.
Open: All Year
01292 470399 Mrs Auld
Rates fr: *£14.00*-**£14.00**.
Beds: 1D 1T 1S
Baths: 2 Shared

Ardbeg, *6 Ayr Road, Prestwick, Ayrshire, KA9 1PZ.*
Large comfortable private house.
Open: All Year (not Xmas)
01292 479316 Mrs Smith
Rates fr: *£14.00*-**£15.00**.
Beds: 1D 2T
Baths: 1 Private 2 Shared
(6)

Golf View Hotel, *17 Links Road, Prestwick, Ayrshire, KA9 1QG.*
Victorian house, overlooking golf course.
Open: All Year
01292 671234
Mr & Mrs McKerrigan
Rates fr: *£24.00*-**£24.00**.
Beds: 1F 2D 2T 1S
Baths: 6 Private
(10)

Crookside Farm, *Kerrix Road, Monkton, Prestwick, Ayrshire, KA9 2QU.*
Comfortable farmhouse on working farm.
Open: All Year (not Xmas)
01563 830266
Mrs Gault
Rates fr: *£11.00*-**£11.00**.
Beds: 1F 1D
Baths: 1 Shared

Priestland

National Grid Ref: NS5737

Auchenbart Farm, *Priestland, Darvel, Ayrshire, KA17 0LS.*
Farmhouse with panoramic views.
Open: Easter to Nov
01560 320392
Mrs Seton
Rates fr: *£16.00*-**£16.00**.
Beds: 1F 1D

Saltcoats

National Grid Ref: NS2441

50 Caledonia Road, *Saltcoats, Ayrshire, KA21 5AL.*
Large family private house.
Open: All Year (not Xmas)
01294 601465
Mrs Darling
Rates fr: *£16.00*-**£18.00**.
Beds: 1D 1T **Baths:** 2 Shared
(4) (2)

Stevenston

National Grid Ref: NS2642

Lochcraigs Farm, *Stevenston, Ayrshire, KA20 4LB.*
Modern, comfortable farmhouse, central heating.
Open: All Year
01294 465288 Mrs Thomson
Rates fr: *£14.00*-**£14.00**.
Beds: 1D 1T 1S
Baths: 1 Shared
(6)

Straiton

National Grid Ref: NS3804

Heid Inn, Kirkmichael Arms, Black Bull

Three Thorns Farm, *Straiton, Maybole, Ayrshire, KA19 7QR.*
C18th upgraded cosy farmhouse.
Open: All Year (not Xmas)
Grades: STB 2 Cr, Comm
01655 770221 Mrs Henry
Rates fr: *£18.00*-**£20.00**.
Beds: 1F 2D 1T
Baths: 2 Ensuite 2 Private
(10)

Symington

National Grid Ref: NS3831

Wheatsheaf Inn

Muirhouse, *Symington, Kilmarnock, Ayrshire, KA1 5PA.*
Traditional, comfortable farmhouse excellent food.
Open: All Year
Grades: STB 1 Cr, Comm
01563 830218
Mrs Howie
Rates fr: *£16.00*-**£18.00**.
Beds: 1D 1T
Baths: 1 Shared
(20)

Troon

National Grid Ref: NS3230

The Bruce Inn

The Cherries, *50 Ottoline Drive, Troon, Ayrshire, KA10 7AW.*
Beautiful home on golf course.
Open: All Year (not Xmas)
Grades: STB 2 Cr, Comm
01292 313312
Mrs Tweedie
Rates fr: *£17.00*-**£16.00**.
Beds: 1F 1T 1S
Baths: 1 Private 2 Shared
(5)

Bringing children with you? Always ask for any special rates.

Borders

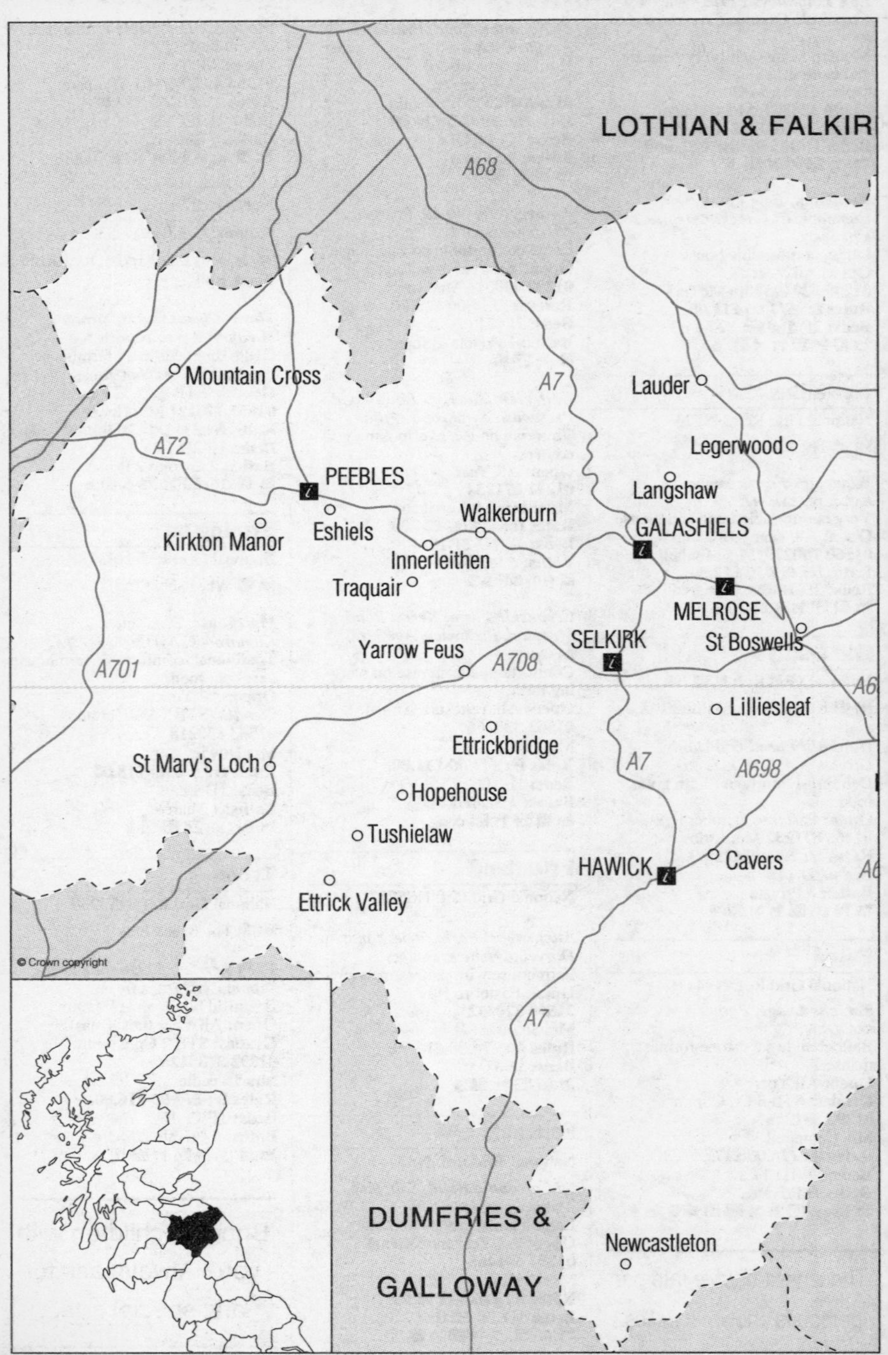
LOTHIAN & FALKIR
A68
A7
Mountain Cross
Lauder
Legerwood
A72
PEEBLES
Langshaw
Walkerburn
GALASHIELS
Kirkton Manor
Eshiels
Innerleithen
Traquair
MELROSE
SELKIRK
St Boswells
Yarrow Feus
A708
A701
Lilliesleaf
Ettrickbridge
St Mary's Loch
A7
A698
Hopehouse
Tushielaw
Cavers
HAWICK
Ettrick Valley
© Crown copyright
A7
DUMFRIES &
GALLOWAY
Newcastleton

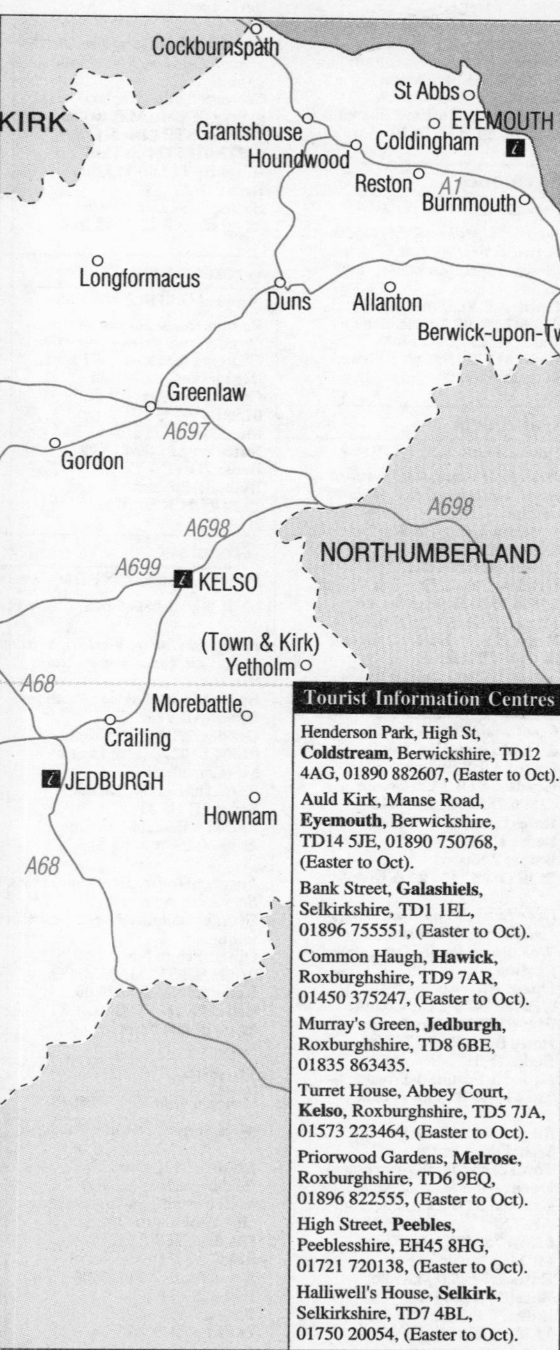

Tourist Information Centres

Henderson Park, High St, **Coldstream**, Berwickshire, TD12 4AG, 01890 882607, (Easter to Oct).

Auld Kirk, Manse Road, **Eyemouth**, Berwickshire, TD14 5JE, 01890 750768, (Easter to Oct).

Bank Street, **Galashiels**, Selkirkshire, TD1 1EL, 01896 755551, (Easter to Oct).

Common Haugh, **Hawick**, Roxburghshire, TD9 7AR, 01450 375247, (Easter to Oct).

Murray's Green, **Jedburgh**, Roxburghshire, TD8 6BE, 01835 863435.

Turret House, Abbey Court, **Kelso**, Roxburghshire, TD5 7JA, 01573 223464, (Easter to Oct).

Priorwood Gardens, **Melrose**, Roxburghshire, TD6 9EQ, 01896 822555, (Easter to Oct).

High Street, **Peebles**, Peeblesshire, EH45 8HG, 01721 720138, (Easter to Oct).

Halliwell's House, **Selkirk**, Selkirkshire, TD7 4BL, 01750 20054, (Easter to Oct).

Allanton

National Grid Ref: NT8654

Allanton Inn

Allanton Inn, *Allanton, Chirnside, Duns, Berwickshire, TD11 3JZ.*
Traditional country inn.
Open: All Year
01890 818260 Mrs Ward
Rates fr: *£23.00*-**£23.00**.
Beds: 1F 1D 2T
(0) (8)

Burnmouth

National Grid Ref: NT9561

Greystonelees Farm House, *Burnmouth, Eyemouth, Berwickshire, TD14 5SZ.*
Comfortable Georgian farmhouse.
Open: All Year
Grades: STB 3 Cr, Comm, AA 3 Q
01890 781709 Mr & Mrs Goff
Rates fr: *£16.00*-**£16.00**.
Beds: 1D 2T
Baths: 2 Private 1 Shared
(5yrs.) (5)

Cavers

National Grid Ref: NT5315

Cavers Garden Farm, *Cavers, Hawick, Roxburghshire, TD9 8LN.*
Comfortable farmhouse in wooded setting. **Open:** All Year
Grades: STB Listed, Comm
01450 377222 Mrs Witten
Rates fr: *£15.00*-**£16.00**.
Beds: 1D 1T **Baths:** 1 Shared

Cockburnspath

National Grid Ref: NT7770

Cockburnspath Hotel, *Cockburnspath, Berwickshire, TD13 5YG*
Family-run C17th coach house.
Open: All Year
01368 830217 Mr Redpath
Rates fr: *£16.00*-**£17.00**.
Beds: 1F 5D 1T 1S **Baths:** 3 Shared

Townhead Farm, *Cockburnspath, Berwickshire, TD13 5YR.*
Traditional Berwickshire working farm. **Open:** Easter to Oct
01368 830465 Mrs Russell
Rates fr: *£14.00*-**£14.00**.
Beds: 1F 1D **Baths:** 1 Shared

Coldingham

National Grid Ref: NT9066

Ship hotel

Melville House, *Eyemouth Road, Coldingham, Eyemouth, Berwickshire, TD14 5NH.*
Victorian house in attractive village.
Open: All Year (not Xmas)
018907 71231 (also fax no)
Mr Lockwood
Rates fr: *£14.00*-**£15.50**.
Beds: 3F 3D 1T 2S **Baths:** 3 Shared
(10)

Westloch Farm, *Coldingham, Eyemouth, Berwickshire,* TD14 5QE.
Renowned for good Scottish hospitality. **Open:** May to Sep
018907 71406 Mrs Scott
Rates fr: *£14.00*-**£14.00**.
Beds: 1D 1T **Baths:** 1 Shared
(4)

Crailing

National Grid Ref: NT6824

Crailing Old School, *Crailing, Jedburgh, Roxburghshire,* TD8 6TL.
Large converted C19th rural school. **Open:** Easter to Oct
01835 850382 Mrs Skea
Rates fr: *£13.00*-**£15.00**.
Beds: 1F 1T **Baths:** 2 Shared
(6)

Duns

National Grid Ref: NT7853

Barniken House Hotel, Allanton Inn

St Albans, *Clouds, Duns, Berwickshire,* TD11 3BB.
Secluded garden, Excellent varied breakfast.
Open: All Year (not Xmas)
Grades: STB 2 Cr, High Comm
01361 883285 Mrs Kenworthy
Fax no: 01361 883 775
Rates fr: *£16.50*-**£19.50**.
Beds: 2D 1T 1S **Baths:** 2 Shared
(11)

Cairnbank, *Sinclairhill Road, Duns, Berwickshire,* TD11 3HR.
Beautiful and comfortable Georgian house.
Open: Easter to Sep
01361 883590 (also fax no)
Mr & Mrs Hughes
Rates fr: *£17.50*-**£15.00**.
Beds: 1D 1T 1S
Baths: 1 Ensuite 1 Shared
(2)

Eshiels

National Grid Ref: NT2739

Brookside, *Eshiels, Peebles, Peeblesshire,* EH45 8NA.
1.25 miles from Peebles on A72.
Open: Easter to Nov
01721 721178 Mrs Dennison
Rates fr: *£13.00*-**£16.00**.
Beds: 1D 1T 1S **Baths:** 1 Shared
(3)

Ettrick Valley

National Grid Ref: NT3018

Kirkbrae House, *Tushielaw, Ettrick Valley, Selkirk,* TD7 5HT.
Ideal base for walking, touring, fishing.
Open: April to October
01750 62208 Mrs Hannay
Rates fr: *£13.00*-**£15.00**.
Beds: 1F 1D 1T
(3)

Ettrickbridge

National Grid Ref: NT3824

Oakwood Farm, *Ettrickbridge, Selkirk,* TD7 5HJ.
Comfortable farmhouse, peaceful countryside.
Grades: STB Listed, Comm
01750 52245 Mrs Nixon
Rates fr: *£13.50*-**£15.00**.
Beds: 1F 1T **Baths:** 2 Shared
(6)

Eyemouth

National Grid Ref: NT9464

Westfield, *Millpark, Eyemouth, Berwickshire,* TD14 5RE.
Modern, spacious house, rural setting.
Open: All Year (not Xmas)
018907 50590 Ms Henderson
Rates fr: *£14.00*-**£14.00**.
Beds: 1D 1T **Baths:** 1 Shared
(2)

Galashiels

National Grid Ref: NT4936

Wakefield Bank, *9 Abbotsford Road, Galashiels, Selkirkshire,* TD1 3DP.
Award-winning B&B in beautiful Victorian house.
Open: Easter to Oct
Grades: STB 2 Cr, High Comm
01896 752641 (also fax no)
Mrs Platt **Rates fr:** *£16.50*.
Beds: 2D 1T **Baths:** 2 Shared
(2)

Ettrickvale, *33 Abbotsford Road, Galashiels, Selkirkshire,* TD1 3HW.
Comfortable, modern semi-detached bungalow.
Open: All Year (not Xmas)
Grades: STB 1 Cr, Comm
01896 755224 Mrs Field
Rates fr: *£14.00*-**£16.00**.
Beds: 1D 2T
Baths: 2 Shared
(2)

Over Langshaw Farm, *Langshaw, Galashiels, Selkirkshire,* TD1 2PE.
Welcoming family farm, superb location.
Open: All Year
Grades: STB 2 Cr, Comm
01896 860244 Mrs Bergius
Rates fr: *£18.00*-**£25.00**.
Beds: 1F 1D
Baths: 1 Ensuite 1 Private

Kings Hotel, *Galashiels, Selkirkshire,* TD1 3AN.
Town centre family-run hotel.
Open: All Year (not Xmas)
Grades: STB 2 Cr, Comm, AA 2 St
01896 755497 (also fax no)
Mr MacDonald
Rates fr: *£26.00*-**£35.00**.
Beds: 1F 1D 4T 1S
Baths: 7 Private
(6)

Gordon

National Grid Ref: NT6443

Cobbles Inn (Kelso), Castle Inn (Greenlaw)

Old School Gallery, *The Old School, Gordon, Berwickshire,* TD3 6LS.
Converted village school, art gallery. **Open:** May to Oct
Grades: STB Listed, Comm
01573 410582 Mrs Holl
Rates fr: *£15.00*-**£15.00**.
Beds: 1F 1T 1S
Baths: 1 Ensuite 1 Private
(2) (4)

Grantshouse

National Grid Ref: NT8065

Renton House, *Grantshouse, Duns, Berwickshire,* TD11 3RP.
Georgian manor set in 7 acres, large rooms.
Open: All Year
01361 850335
Mrs Skivington-Jones
Rates fr: *£15.00*-**£15.00**.
Beds: 2D 1T
Baths: 1 Private 1 Shared

Greenlaw

National Grid Ref: NT7146

Wheatsheaf Hotel, Castle Inn

Bridgend House, *West High Street, Greenlaw, Duns, Berwickshire,* TD10 6XA.
Built 1816 in riverside location.
Open: All Year
Grades: STB 2 Cr, Comm
01361 810270 (also fax no)
Mrs Carruthers
Rates fr: *£18.00*-**£20.00**.
Beds: 1F 1D 2T
Baths: 3 Ensuite 1 Private
(4)

Fogorig House, *Greenlaw, Duns, Berwickshire,* TD11 3RB.
Georgian country house, peaceful setting.
Open: Feb to Nov
01890 840535 Mr & Mrs Gray
Rates fr: *£25.00*-**£25.00**.
Beds: 1F 1D 1T **Baths:** 2 Private
(5) (20)

Hawick

National Grid Ref: NT5015

Sergio's, Aroma Tandoori

Ellistrin, *6 Fenwick Park, Hawick, Roxburghshire,* TD9 9PA.
Victorian villa in large garden.
Open: Easter to Oct
Grades: STB 2 Cr, Comm
01450 374216 Mrs Smith
Rates fr: *£17.00*-**£17.00**.
Beds: 2D 1T
Baths: 3 Ensuite
(3)

Wiltonburn Farm, *Hawick, Roxburghshire, TD9 7LL.*
Open: All Year
Grades: STB Listed, Comm
01450 372414 / 01374 192551
Mrs Shell
Rates fr: *£16.00*-**£17.00**.
Beds: 1F 1D 1T
Baths: 1 Private 1 Shared
(6)
You will be warmly welcomed and cared for on our working hill farm, 2 miles from Hawick. Log fires, cosy rooms & converted barn (containing exclusive designer CASHMERE KNITWEAR at very competitive prices) will make your stay more pleasurable!

7 Beaconsfield Terrace, *Hawick, Roxburghshire, TD9 0HS.*
Warm, welcoming family home.
Open: Jan to Nov
Grades: STB Listed, Comm
01450 374842
Mrs Harker
Rates fr: *£12.00*-**£13.00**.
Beds: 1F 1T
Baths: 1 Shared

Oakwood House, *Buccleuch Road, Hawick, Roxburghshire, TD9 0EH.*
Open: Jan to Oct
Grades: AA 3 Q, Recomm
01450 372896
Mrs Kirkpatrick
Rates fr: *£16.00*-**£20.00**.
Beds: 2D 1T
Baths: 1 Ensuite 1 Shared
(5) (4)
Victorian house just off A7 South, overlooking gardens and bowling greens. Easy walking distance to knitwear shops or beautiful park. Plenty of private parking.

Houndwood

National Grid Ref: NT8463

White Lodge, *Houndwood, Eyemouth, Berwickshire, TD14 5TP.*
Old manse - comfortable, well appointed bedrooms.
Open: All Year (not Xmas)
Grades: STB Listed, Approv
01361 850262
Mrs Blades
Rates fr: *£14.00*-**£16.00**.
Beds: 1F 1D 1T
Baths: 2 Ensuite 2 Shared

Hownam

National Grid Ref: NT7719

Greenhill, *Hownam, Kelso, Roxburghshire, TD5 8AW.*
Country mansion. Foothills of Cheviots.
Open: All Year (not Xmas)
01573 440505 Mrs Harris
Rates fr: *£16.00*-**£17.50**.
Beds: 1D 1T 2S
Baths: 3 Private
(1) (4)

Innerleithen

National Grid Ref: NT3336

Traquair Arms

Corner House Hotel, *Innerleithen, Peebleshire, EH44.*
Recently refurbished small family hotel. **Open:** All Year
Grades: STB 2 Cr, Approv
01896 830818
Rates fr: *£20.00*-**£20.00**.
Beds: 2F 2D 2T **Baths:** 6 Ensuite
(6)

Traquair Bank, *Innerleithen, Peebleshire, EH44 6PS.*
Comfortable farmhouse near River Tweed. **Open:** Apr to Feb
Grades: STB Listed
01896 830425 Mrs Caird
Rates fr: *£17.00*-**£17.00**.
Beds: 1F 1D 1T **Baths:** 2 Shared

Jedburgh

National Grid Ref: NT6520

The Pheasant, The Castlegate

Froylehurst Guest House, *The Friars, Jedburgh, Roxburghshire, TD8 6BN.*
Victorian house in own grounds.
Open: Mar to Nov
Grades: STB 1 Cr, High Comm, AA 4 Q, Select
01835 862477 Mrs Irvine
Rates fr: *£15.50*-**£20.00**.
Beds: 2F 1D 1T **Baths:** 2 Shared
(5) (5)

Kenmore Bank Hotel, *Oxnam Road, Jedburgh, Roxburghshire, TD8 6JJ.*
Victorian house - all bedrooms ensuite. **Open:** All Year
Grades: STB 3 Cr, Comm, AA 3 Q
01835 862369 Mr Muller
Rates fr: *£18.50*-**£29.00**.
Beds: 2F 2D 2T **Baths:** 6 Private
(6)

The Spinney, *Langlee, Jedburgh, Roxburghshire, TD8 6PB.*
Spacious house in own grounds.
Open: Mar to Oct
Grades: STB 2 Cr, Deluxe, AA 5 Q, Prem Select
01835 863525 (also fax no)
Mrs Fry
Rates fr: *£19.00*-**£30.00**.
Beds: 2D 1T
Baths: 3 Private
(9)

Ferniehirst Mill Lodge, *Jedburgh, Roxburghshire, TD8 6PQ.*
Modern guest house in peaceful setting. **Open:** All Year
Grades: STB 2 Cr, AA 2 Q, RAC Acclaim
01835 863279 Mr Swanston
Rates fr: *£21.00*-**£21.00**.
Beds: 3D 5T 1S **Baths:** 9 Ensuite
(10)

Craigowen, *30 High Street, Jedburgh, Roxburghshire, TD8 6AG.*
Centrally located for all amenities.
Open: All Year (not Xmas)
Grades: STB Listed, Comm
01835 862604 Mrs Campbell
Rates fr: *£15.00*-**£15.00**.
Beds: 2F 2D 1T 1S
Baths: 2 Shared
(3)

Kelso

National Grid Ref: NT7234

Cobbles Inn, Queens Head Hotel

Lochside, *Yetholm, Kelso, Roxburghshire, TD5 8PD.*
Victorian country house, beautiful setting.
Open: Apr to Oct
Grades: STB 2 Cr, Comm
01573 420349 Mrs Hurst
Rates fr: *£20.00*-**£22.00**.
Beds: 1D 1T
Baths: 2 Ensuite
(3)

Craignethan House, *Jedburgh Road, Kelso, Roxburghshire, TD5 8AZ.*
Comfortable welcoming home; panoramic views.
Open: All Year
Grades: STB Listed, Comm
01573 224818 Mrs McDonald
Rates fr: *£16.50*-**£16.50**.
Beds: 2D 1T
Baths: 2 Shared
(6)

Inglestone Guest House, *Abbey Row, Kelso, Roxburghshire, TD5 7HQ.*
300 year old town house.
Open: All Year
Grades: STB Listed, Comm
01573 225800 Mrs McArthur
Rates fr: *£18.50*-**£22.50**.
Beds: 1T 1D
Baths: 2 Ensuite 1 Private

Wester House, *155 Roxburgh Street, Kelso, Roxburghshire, TD5 7DU.*
Comfortable, warm, Scottish town house.
Open: All Year (not Xmas)
Grades: STB Listed, Comm
01573 225479 (also fax no)
Ms Hawkins
Rates fr: *£16.00*-**£12.00**.
Beds: 1F 1D 1S
Baths: 1 Private 2 Shared

Black Swan Hotel, *Horsemarket, Kelso, Roxburghshire, TD5 7HE.*
Small, friendly, family-run hotel.
Open: All Year (not Xmas/New Year)
Grades: STB 3 Cr, Comm
01573 224563
Rates fr: *£19.00*-**£25.00**.
Beds: 2F 1D **Baths:** 3 Private

Kirk Yetholm

National Grid Ref: NT8228

***Blunty's Mill,** Kirk Yetholm, Roxburghshire, TD5 6PG.*
Beautiful rural setting in 6 acres.
Open: All Year
Grades: STB 1 Cr, Comm
01573 420288 Mrs Brooker
Rates fr: *£16.00*-**£16.00**.
Beds: 1D 1T **Baths:** 1 Shared
(3) (10)

Kirkton Manor

National Grid Ref: NT2237

***Langhaugh Farmhouse,** Kirkton Manor, Peebles, Peebleshire, EH45 6JF*
Large modernised farmhouse.
Open: All Year
01721 740226 Mrs Campbell
Fax no: 0172 740226
Rates fr: *£18.50*-**£20.00**.
Beds: 1F 1T
Baths: 3 Private 1 Shared
(4)

Langshaw

National Grid Ref: NT5139

***Over Langshaw Farm,** Langshaw, Galashiels, Selkirkshire, TD1 2PE.*
Welcoming family farm, superb location. **Open:** All Year
Grades: STB 2 Cr, Comm
01896 860244 Mrs Bergius
Rates fr: *£18.00*-**£25.00**.
Beds: 1F 1D
Baths: 1 Ensuite 1 Private

Lauder

National Grid Ref: NT5247

Lauderdale Hotel, Eagle Hotel

***The Grange,** 6 Edinburgh Road, Lauder, Berwickshire, TD2 6TW.*
Open: All Year (not Xmas)
Grades: STB 1 Cr, Comm
01578 722649 Mr Gilardi
Rates fr: *£15.00*-**£15.00**.
Beds: 1D 2T **Baths:** 1 Shared
(3)
Large comfortable detached house in own grounds overlooking rolling Lammermuir hills. On A68 road hence ideal for Edinburgh and all of Scottish Border Country.

***Redpath House,** 25 Eas High Street, Lauder, Berwickshire, TD2 6SS*
Open: All Year
Grades: STB Listed, Comm
01578 718795 Ms Henderson
Rates fr: *£15.00*-**£15.00**.
Beds: 1F 1D 1T
Baths: 2 Shared
Bright comfortable family home on Southern Upland Way. Lauder town centre. Fishing on Rivers Tweed and Leader. Good touring base close to Edinburgh and borders.

Legerwood

National Grid Ref: NT5843

***The Smithy,** Legerwood, Earlston, Berwickshire, TD4 6AS.*
Renovated smithy, home cooking.
Open: Apr to Oct
01896 849518 Mrs Pope
Rates fr: *£13.50*-**£13.50**.
Beds: 1D 1T 2S **Baths:** 2 Shared
(4)

Lilliesleaf

National Grid Ref: NT5325

***Plough Inn,** Lilliesleaf, Melrose, Roxburghshire, TD6 9JD.*
Charming C18th rambling inn.
Open: Easter to Oct
Grades: STB 3 Cr, Comm
01835 870271 Mr Hannah
Rates fr: *£24.00*-**£28.00**.
Beds: 2D 2T
Baths: 2 Private 1 Shared
(20)

Longformacus

National Grid Ref: NT6957

***Eildon Cottage,** Longformacus, Duns, Berwickshire, TD11 3NX.*
Converted large cottage.
Open: All Year (not Xmas)
Grades: STB 1 St, Comm
01361 890230 Mrs Amos
Rates fr: *£16.00*-**£16.00**.
Beds: 2F 1T
Baths: 2 Ensuite 1 Private
(2)

Melrose

National Grid Ref: NT5434

***Braidwood,** Buccleuch Street, Melrose, Roxburghshire, TD6 9LD.*
Listed town house, central, friendly.
Open: All Year
Grades: STB 2 Cr, High Comm
01896 822488 Mrs Graham
Rates fr: *£17.00*-**£22.00**.
Beds: 2D 1T
Baths: 1 Private 1 Shared

***Dunfermline House,** Buccleuch St, Melrose, Roxburghshire, TD6 9LB*
Family home of comfort.
Open: All Year
01896 822148 Mrs Graham
Rates fr: *£21.00*-**£21.00**.
Beds: 2D 2T 1S **Baths:** 5 Private

Morebattle

National Grid Ref: NT7234

***Morebattle Tofts,** Morebattle, Kelso, Roxburghshire, TD5 8AD.*
Elegant C18th farmhouse, idyllic rural location.
Open: All Year (not Xmas)
Grades: STB 2 Cr, Comm
01573 440364 Mrs Playfair
Rates fr: *£17.00*-**£16.00**.
Beds: 2D 1T **Baths:** 3 Private
(6)

Mountain Cross

National Grid Ref: NT1547

***Rowallan,** Mountain Cross, West Linton, Peeblesshire, EH46 7DF.*
New bungalow, picturesque, peaceful setting. **Open:** Easter to Oct
01968 660329 Mrs Cottam
Rates fr: *£14.50*.
Beds: 1F 2D **Baths:** 2 Shared
(7) (3)

Newcastleton

National Grid Ref: NY4887

***Yethouse Farm,** Newcastleton, Hawick, Roxburghshire, TD9 0TD.*
Farmhouse and pony-trekking centre.
Open: All Year (not Xmas)
013873 75642 Ms Fraser
Rates fr: *£10.00*-**£10.00**.
Beds: 1F **Baths:** 2 Shared
(4)

Peebles

National Grid Ref: NT2540

***Lyne Farmhouse,** Lyne Farm, Peebles, Peeblesshire, EH45 8NR.*
Open: All Year (not Xmas)
Grades: STB Listed, Comm
01721 740255 Mrs Waddell
Rates fr: *£15.00*-**£18.00**.
Beds: 2D 1T **Baths:** 2 Shared
(5) (4)
Beautiful Georgian farmhouse, with tastefully decorated rooms. Walled garden plus hillwalking and picnic areas on farm. Ideally placed for Edinburgh and picturesque town of Peebles.

***Robingarth,** 46 Edinburgh Road, Peebles, Peeblesshire, EH45 8EB.*
Comfortable attractive welcoming private house. **Open:** All Year (not Xmas)
Grades: STB Listed, Comm
01721 720226 Miss Inglis
Rates fr: *£15.00*. **Beds:** 1D 1T
Baths: 1 Ensuite 1 Private

***Rowanbrae,** Northgate, Peebles, Peeblesshire, EH45 8BU.*
Tasteful Victorian house accommodation. **Open:** Easter to Nov
01721 721630 Mrs O'Hara
Rates fr: *£15.00*-**£17.00**.
Beds: 1F 1D **Baths:** 1 Shared

Selkirk

National Grid Ref: NT4728

County Hotel, Cross Keys Inn, Plough Inn

***Ivy Bank,** Hillside Terrace, Selkirk, TD7 2LT.*
Ivy Bank sits in its own grounds.
Open: All Year (not Xmas)
Grades: STB 1 Cr, Comm
01750 21270 Mrs MacKenzie
Rates fr: *£15.00*-**£16.00**.
Beds: 1D 1T **Baths:** 1 Shared
(4)

Hillholm, *36 Hillside Terrace, Selkirk,* *TD7 4ND.*
Elegant Victorian private home.
Open: Easter to Oct
Grades: STB 2 Cr, Comm, AA 4 Q, Select
01750 21293 Mrs Hannah
Rates fr: *£15.00*-**£22.00**.
Beds: 2D 2T
Baths: 2 Private 1 Shared
(10)

Heatherlie House Hotel, *Heatherlie Park, Selkirk,* *TD7 5AL.*
Privately-owned Victorian mansion house.
Open: All Year (not Xmas)
01750 21200 Mrs Fleming
Fax no: 01750 20005
Rates fr: *£22.50*-**£21.00**.
Beds: 2F 2D 2T 1S
Baths: 6 Ensuite 1 Shared
(12)

St Abbs

National Grid Ref: NT9167

St Abbs Haven

7 Murrayfield, *St Abbs, Eyemouth, Berwickshire,* *TD14 5PP.*
Former fisherman's cottage.
Open: All Year (not Xmas)
Grades: STB Listed
018907 71468 Mrs Wilson
Rates fr: *£14.50*-**£17.00**.
Beds: 1F 1T
Baths: 1 Ensuite 1 Shared

Castle Rock Guest House, *Murrayfield, St Abbs, Eyemouth, Berwickshire,* *TD14 5PP.*
Sea views from all rooms.
Open: Easter to Oct
Grades: STB 3 Cr, High Comm
018907 71715 Mr & Mrs Lutas
Fax no: 018907 71520
Rates fr: *£23.00*-**£23.00**.
Beds: 1F 1D 1T 1S
Baths: 4 Private 1 Shared
(5)

St Boswells

National Grid Ref: NT5930

Whitehouse Farmhouse, *St Boswells, Melrose, Roxburghshire,* *TD6 0ED.*
Large farmhouse, log fires, home baking.
Open: All Year
Grades: STB 2 Cr, High Comm
01573 460343 Mrs Tyrer
Fax no: 01573 46061
Rates fr: *£17.00*-**£20.00**.
Beds: 1D 2T
Baths: 1 Private 2 Shared
(5)

St Mary's Loch

National Grid Ref: NT2420

Tibbieshiels Inn, *St Mary's Loch, Selkirk,* *TD7 5LG.*
Scenic, lochside, historical coaching inn.
Open: All Year (not Xmas)
01750 42231 Mr Brown
Rates fr: *£23.00*-**£26.00**.
Beds: 2F 2D 1T

Town Yetholm

National Grid Ref: NT8128

Greenside, *Main Street, Town Yetholm, Kelso, Roxburghshire,* *TD5 8RG.*
Large Victorian home offers warm welcome in conservation village.
Open: All Year (not Xmas)
01573 420249 Mrs Gowers
Rates fr: *£15.00*-**£15.00**.
Beds: 1F 1D 1T 1S
Baths: 2 Shared
(4)

Traquair

National Grid Ref: NT3334

Traquair Mill House, *Traquair, Innerleithen, Peeblesshire,* *EH44 6PT.*
Authentic comfortable C18th mill house.
Open: Easter to October
01896 830515 Mrs Fremi Hamilton
Rates fr: *£18.00*-**£25.00**.
Beds: 1F
Baths: 1 Private
(4)

Tushielaw

National Grid Ref: NT3018

Kirkbrae House, *Tushielaw, Ettrick Valley, Selkirk,* *TD7 5HT.*
Ideal base walking, touring, fishing.
Open: April to October
01750 62208 Mrs Hannay
Rates fr: *£13.00*-**£15.00**.
Beds: 1F 1D 1T
(3)

Tushielaw Inn, *Tushielaw, Ettrick Valley, Selkirk, Roxburghshire,* *TD7 5HT.*
Traditional country pub, idyllic location.
Open: All Year
01750 62205 Mr Osbourne
Rates fr: *£19.00*-**£19.00**.
Beds: 1F 2D
Baths: 3 Private

Walkerburn

National Grid Ref: NT3537

Willowbank, *13 High Cottages, Walkerburn, Peeblesshire,* *EH43 6AZ.*
Late-Victorian stone house overlooking Tweed.
Open: All Year (not Xmas)
01896 870252 Mrs Barbour
Rates fr: *£15.00*-**£16.00**.
Beds: 1D 2T
Baths: 2 Shared

The George Hotel, *Galashiels Road, Walkerburn, Peeblesshire,* *EH43 6AF.*
Family-run hotel overlooking River Tweed.
Open: All Year
01896 870336 Mrs Forsyth
Rates fr: *£20.00*-**£24.00**.
Beds: 1F 5D 2T
(30)

Yarrow Feus

National Grid Ref: NT3426

Cross Keys

Ladhope Farm, *Yarrow Feus, Yarrow Valley, Selkirk,* *TD7 5NE.*
Lovely, comfortable old farmhouse.
Open: Apr to Oct
Grades: STB Listed, Comm
01750 82216 Mrs Turnbull
Rates fr: *£14.00*-**£13.5014.00**.
Beds: 2D
Baths: 1 Shared

Yetholm

National Grid Ref: NT8128

Cobbles Inn (Kelso)

Greenside, *Main Street, Yetholm, Kelso, Roxburghshire,* *TD5 8RG.*
Large Victorian home offers warm welcome in conservation village.
Open: All Year (not Xmas)
01573 420249 Mrs Gowers
Rates fr: *£15.00*-**£15.00**.
Beds: 1F 1D 1T 1S
Baths: 2 Shared
(4)

Blunty's Mill, *Yetholm, Roxburghshire,* *TD5 6PG.*
Beautiful rural setting in 6 acres.
Open: All Year
Grades: STB 1 Cr, Comm
01573 420288 Mrs Brooker
Rates fr: *£16.00*-**£16.00**.
Beds: 1D 1T
Baths: 1 Shared
(3) (10)

Lochside, *Yetholm, Kelso, Roxburghshire,* *TD5 8PD.*
Victorian country house, beautiful setting.
Open: Apr to Oct
Grades: STB 2 Cr, Comm
01573 420349 Mrs Hurst
Rates fr: *£20.00*-**£22.00**.
Beds: 1D 1T
Baths: 2 Ensuite
(3)

Border Hotel, *The Green, Kirk Yetholm, Yetholm, Kelso, Roxburghshire,* *TD5 8PQ.*
C17th village inn.
Open: All Year
01573 420237 Mr Russell
Rates fr: *£17.00*-**£22.00**.
Beds: 2D 2T
Baths: 2 Shared

Dumfries & Galloway

Tourist Information Centres

Town Hall, **Dalbeattie**, Kirkcudbrightshire, DG5 4JS, 01556 610117, (Easter to Oct).

Whitesands, **Dumfries**, Dumfriesshire, DG1 2SB, 01387 53862.

Gatehouse of Fleet, Markethill, **Castle Douglas**, Kirkcudbrightshire, DG7 2JQ, 01557 814212, (Easter to Oct).

The Old Headless Cross, **Gretna Green**, Carlisle, Cumbria, CA6 5HY, 01461 37834, (Easter to Oct)

Harbour Square, **Kirkcudbright**, Kirkcudbrightshire, DG6 4HY, 01557 30494, (Easter to Oct).

High Street, **Langholm**, Dumfriesshire, DG13 0JH, 01387 380976, (Easter to Oct).

Churchgate, **Moffat**, Dumfriesshire, DG10 9EJ, 01683 20620, (Easter to Oct).

Tolbooth, High Street, **Sanquhar**, Dumfriesshire, DG4 6DZ, 01659 50185, (Easter to Oct).

Port Rodie Car Park, **Stranraer**, Wigtownshire, DG9 7EE, 01776 2595, (Easter to Oct).

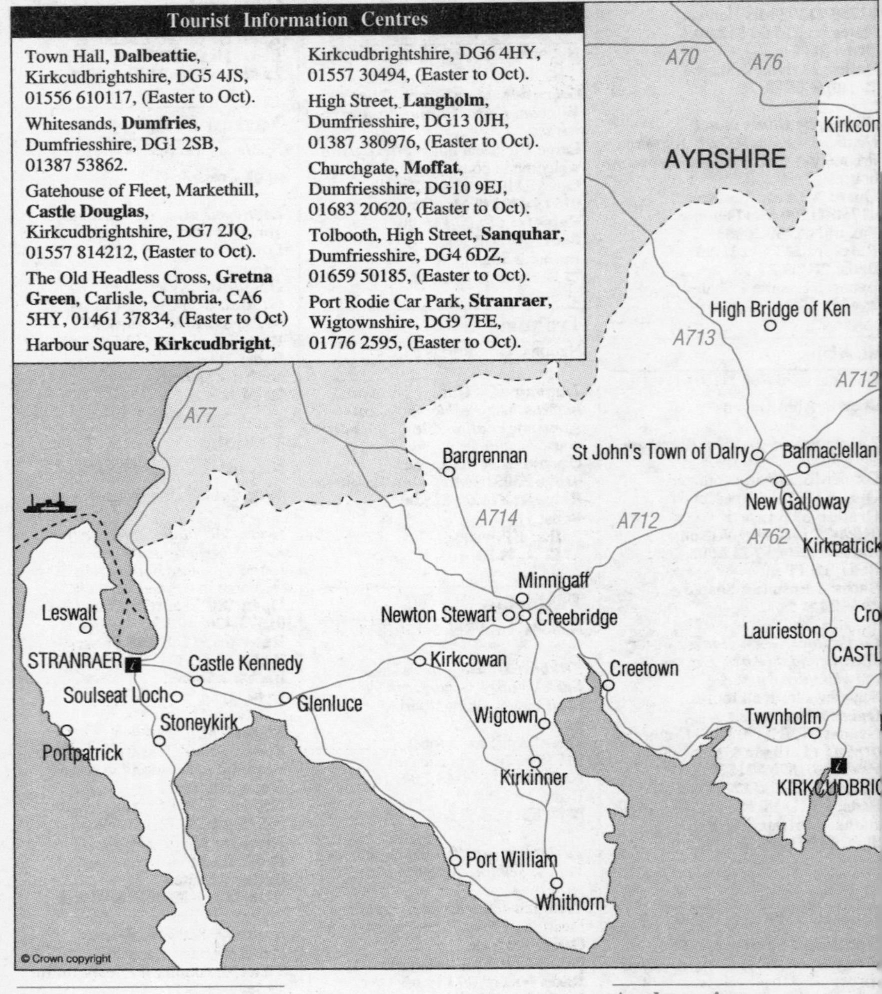

Annan

National Grid Ref: NY1966

Ravenswood Private Hotel, *St Johns Road, Annan, Dumfriesshire, DG12 6AW.*
Red sandstone villa. Family-run.
Open: All Year
01461 202158 Mrs James
Rates fr: *£15.50*-**£16.50**.
Beds: 3F 1D 1T 3S
Baths: 2 Shared

The Craig, *18 St Johns Road, Annan, Dumfriesshire, DG12 6AW.*
Friendly comfortable Victorian private house.
Open: All Year (not Xmas)
01461 204665 Mrs Anderson
Rates fr: *£14.00*-**£14.00**.
Beds: 1F 2T 1S
Baths: 1 Shared
(6 months)

Auchencairn

National Grid Ref: NX7951

Old Smugglers Inn

Rascarrel Cottage, *Auchencairn, Castle Douglas, Kirkcudbrightshire, DG7 1RJ.*
Open: Mar to Oct
Grades: STB 2 Cr, High Comm
01556 640214 Mrs Hendry
Rates fr: *£16.00*-**£20.00**.
Beds: 1D 2T **Baths:** 2 Ensuite 1 Shared
(3)
Superb accommodation in attractive cottage situated on C18th smuggling route. Ground floor bedrooms. Beautiful farm and coastal views. Sea 500 yds. Village 2 miles.

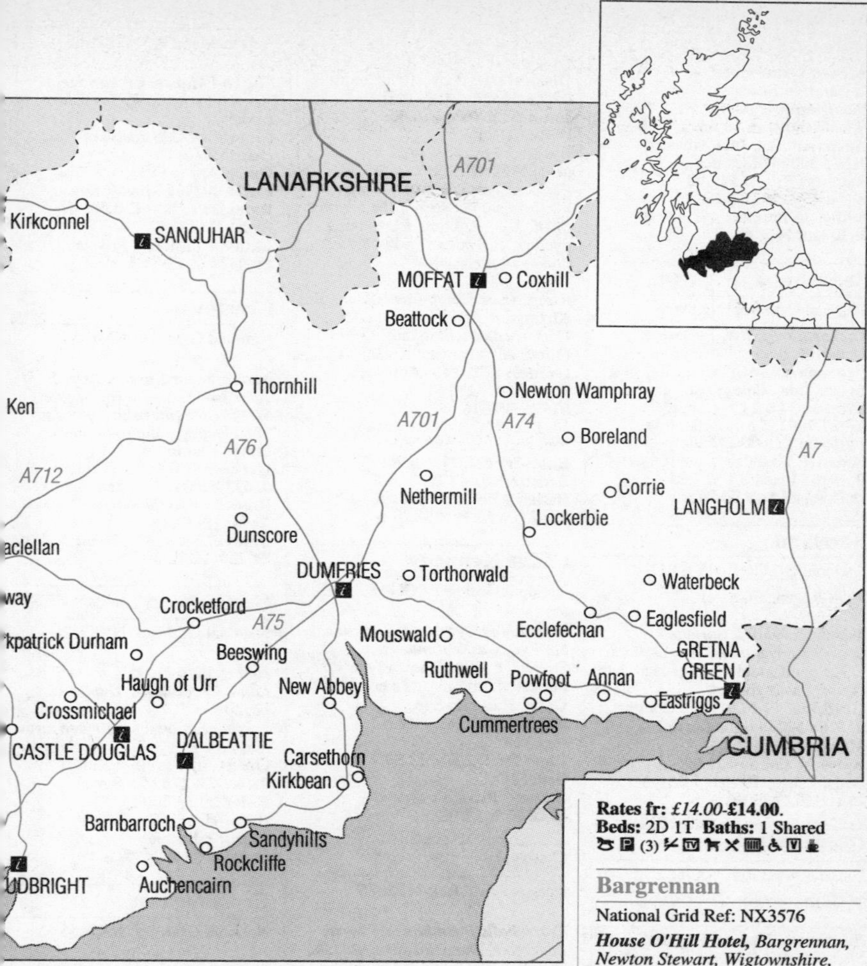

ollin Hill Farm, *Auchencairn, astle Douglas, irkcudbrightshire,* DG7 1QN.
pen: Feb to Nov
rades: STB 2 Cr, High Comm
1556 640242 Mrs Cannon
ates fr: *£18.00*-**£20.00.**
eds: 1F 1D 1T
aths: 2 Ensuite 1 Private
(10) (3)
warm welcome awaits you at ollin Hill. Excellent location for alking, golf, castles, etc. whilst riving scenic country roads is a otorist's dream. Tastefully furished, spectacular sea views.

The lowest **single** *rate is shown in* **bold.**

The Rossan, *Auchencairn, Castle Douglas, Kirkcudbrightshire,* DG7 1QR.
Open: All Year
Grades: STB Listed, Approv
01556 640269 Mrs Bardsley
Rates fr: *£14.00*-**£14.00.**
Beds: 3F **Baths:** 2 Shared
(4)
Homely B&B. Between shore and hills. Hill-walking, bird-watching. Clothes, boots dried overnight. Meat, vegetarian, medical diets. Large garden. Guests return and recommend. STB Listed, Approv.

Balmaclellan

National Grid Ref: NX6579

High Park, *Balmaclellan, Castle Douglas, Kirkcudbrightshire,* DG7 3PT.
Comfortable, traditional farmhouse. **Open:** Easter to Oct
01644 420298 Mrs Shaw
Rates fr: *£14.00*-**£14.00.**
Beds: 2D 1T **Baths:** 1 Shared
(3)

Bargrennan

National Grid Ref: NX3576

House O'Hill Hotel, *Bargrennan, Newton Stewart, Wigtownshire,* DG8 6RN.
Small, family-run C19th hotel.
Open: All Year (not Xmas)
01671 840243 Mrs Allwood
Rates fr: *£17.00*-**£17.00.**
Beds: 2F **Baths:** 2 Private

Barnbarroch

National Grid Ref: NX8456

The Anchor (Kippford), The Mariner (Kippford)

Boundary Cottage, *Barnbarroch, Dalbeattie, Kirkcudbrightshire,* DG5 4QF.
Pretty countrified cottage, surprisingly roomy.
Open: All Year (not Xmas)
01556 620247 Ms Williams
Rates fr: *£15.00.*
Beds: 1F 1D 1T
Baths: 1 Private 2 Shared
(4)

Beattock

National Grid Ref: NT0702

***Auchen Castle Hotel,** & Restaurant, Beattock, Moffat, Dumfriesshire, DG10 9P.*
Country hotel in 50 acres.
Open: All Year (not Xmas)
01683 300407 Mrs Beckh
Rates fr: *£30.00*-**£46.00**.
Beds: 1F 12D 10T 3S
Baths: 26 Ensuite
(40)

Beeswing

National Grid Ref: NX8969

***Locharthur House,** Beeswing, Dumfries, DG2 8JG.*
Georgian house in beautiful countryside. **Open:** All Year
Grades: STB 2 Cr, Comm
01387 760235 Mrs Schooling
Rates fr: *£15.00*-**£15.00**.
Beds: 1F 1D 1T
Baths: 1 Ensuite 1 Shared
(6)

Boreland

National Grid Ref: NY1791

Ravenshill hotel

***Nether Boreland,** Boreland, Lockerbie, Dumfriesshire, DG11 2LL.*
Large comfortable farmhouse.
Open: Easter to Nov
Grades: STB 2 Cr, High Comm
01576 610248 (also fax no)
Mrs Rae
Rates fr: *£18.00*-**£21.00**.
Beds: 2D 1T **Baths:** 3 Private
(12) (3)

Castle Douglas

National Grid Ref: NX7662

Kings Arms

***Barrington House,** 39 St Andrew Street, Castle Douglas, Kirkcudbrightshire, DG7 1EN.*
Open: All Year
01556 502601 Mrs Farley
Rates fr: *£17.00*-**£17.00**.
Beds: 1D 2T 1S
Baths: 2 Shared
(12) (2)
Central Galloway market town. Many golf courses. Ideal for hill-walking, cycling, orienteering, fishing, bird-watching. Beautiful coastline. Numerous places of interest. Residents' lounge. Very warm welcome.

***Corbieton Cottage,** Haugh of Urr, Castle Douglas, Kirkcudbrightshire, DG7 3JJ.*
Delightful country cottage, lovely views. **Open:** All Year (not Xmas)
01556 660413 Mr Jones
Rates fr: *£15.00*-**£16.00**.
Beds: 1D 1T
Baths: 1 Shared
(2)

***Craigvar House,** 60 St Andrew Street, Castle Douglas, Kirkcudbrightshire, DG7 1EN.*
Open: Mar to Oct
Grades: STB 2 Cr, High Comm
01556 503515 Mrs Brierley
Rates fr: *£20.00*-**£26.00**.
Beds: 1D 1T
Baths: 2 Ensuite
(1)
Personally-run Georgian town house in a quiet area of this market town. A perfect base for walking, cycling, birdwatching, history & non-smokers.

***Kings Arms Hotel,** Castle Douglas, Kirkcudbrightshire, DG7 1EL.*
Converted coaching inn.
Open: All Year (not Xmas)
Grades: STB 4 Cr, Approv, AA 2 St, RAC 2 St
01556 502626
Mr Fulton
Fax no: 01556 502097
Rates fr: *£25.00*-**£28.00**.
Beds: 2F 4D 4T 2S
Baths: 9 Ensuite 1 Private
(15)

Castle Kennedy

National Grid Ref: NX1160

***Serendipity Cottage,** (Old Railway Station), Castle Kennedy, Stranraer, Wigtownshire, DG9 8RY.*
Former station-master's house.
Open: Easter to Sep
01776 705206
Mrs Tait
Rates fr: *£12.50*-**£12.50**.
Beds: 1D 1T
Baths: 1 Private 1 Shared

Corrie

National Grid Ref: NY2086

***Corriehalls Farmhouse,** Corrie, Lockerbie, Dumfriesshire, DG11 2NL.*
Farmhouse in beautiful countryside.
Open: All Year
01576 710267
Mrs Deamer
Rates fr: *£12.00*-**£13.00**.
Beds: 1D 1T
Baths: 1 Shared

Coxhill

National Grid Ref: NT0904

***Coxhill Farm,** Old Carlisle Road, Coxhill, Moffat, Dumfriesshire, DG10 9QN.*
Modern, comfortable farmhouse, outstanding views.
Open: All Year (not Xmas)
01683 220471 Mrs Long
Rates fr: *£16.00*-**£20.00**.
Beds: 2D 1T
Baths: 2 Shared

Creebridge

National Grid Ref: NX4165

***The Old Manse,** Creebridge, Newton Stewart, Wigtownshire, DG8 6PU.*
Large Victorian manse of character.
Open: Apr to Oct
01671 402901 Mrs McKay
Rates fr: *£15.00*-**£20.00**.
Beds: 1D 1T
Baths: 1 Ensuite 1 Private
(1) (4)

Creetown

National Grid Ref: NX4758

***Marclaysean Guest House,** 51 St John Street, Creetown, Newton Stewart, Wigtownshire, DG8 7JB.*
1889 local granite-built house.
Open: Mar to Oct
Grades: STB Listed, Comm
01671 820319 Mrs Seal Spiers
Rates fr: *£18.00*-**£20.00**.
Beds: 1D 1T 1S
Baths: 1 Private 1 Shared

Crocketford

National Grid Ref: NX8372

***Henderland Farm,** Crocketford Road, Crocketford, Dumfries, DG2 8QD.*
Large traditional family-run farmhouse.
Open: All Year (not Xmas)
01387 730270 Mrs Smyth
Rates fr: *£15.00*-**£15.00**.
Beds: 1F 1D 1T
Baths: 3 Ensuite
(4)

Crossmichael

National Grid Ref: NX7366

Kings Arms

***Culgruff House Hotel,** Crossmichael, Castle Douglas, Kirkcudbrightshire, DG7 3BB.*
Large Victorian baronial mansion.
Open: All Year
Grades: RAC 2 St
01556 670230 Mr Grayson
Rates fr: *£15.00*-**£17.00**.
Beds: 4F 4D 7T 2S
Baths: 4 Private 4 Shared
(50)

***Blairinnie Farm,** Crossmichael, Castle Douglas, Kirkcudbrightshire, DG7 3BJ.*
Large, comfortable, quiet C17th farmhouse.
Open: May to Oct
01556 670268 Mrs McMorran
Rates fr: *£15.00*-**£17.00**.
Beds: 1D 1T
Baths: 1 Shared
(8) (4)

Cummertrees

National Grid Ref: NY1466

Kirkland Hotel, Golf Hotel

***Huckledale Farm,** Cummertrees, Annan, Dumfriesshire, DG12 5QA.*
Large well-appointed farmhouse.
Open: All Year (not Xmas)
Grades: STB 2 Cr, Comm
01461 700228 Mrs Forrest
Rates fr: *£18.00*-**£22.00**.
Beds: 1F 1D 1T
Baths: 2 Ensuite 1 Private
(6)

Dalbeattie

National Grid Ref: NX8361

***Briardale House,** Haugh Road, Dalbeattie, Kirkcudbrightshire, DG5 4AR.*
Open: Jan to Oct
Grades: STB 3 Cr, Deluxe
01556 611468 / 0850 267251
Mrs Woodworth
Rates fr: *£20.00*-**£28.00**.
Beds: 1F 1D 1T **Baths:** 3 Ensuite
(3)
John and Verna Woodworth invite you to relax in their elegant 3 Crown, Deluxe Victorian house providing modern facilities, comfort, peace and quiet at a very reasonable price. Both professional chefs, our table d'hotel dinner menu offers 3 choices at each course, changing daily. Car parking in our large walled garden. Our visitors' book says it all.

***The Pheasant Hotel,** Maxwell Street, Dalbeattie, Kirkcudbrightshire, DG5 4AH.*
Good food, fine real ales.
Open: All Year
Grades: STB 3 Cr, Comm, AA Listed, 3 Q
01556 610345 Mr Windsor
Rates fr: *£17.50*-**£19.00**.
Beds: 4F 2T 1S
Baths: 6 Private 1 Shared

Dumfries

National Grid Ref: NX9776

Courtyard Bistro, Hill Hotel, Moreig Hotel

***Cairndoon,** 14 Newall Terrace, Dumfries, DG1 1LW.*
Town centre, gracious, quiet home.
Open: All Year
01387 256991 Mrs Stevenson
Rates fr: *£15.50*-**£15.50**.
Beds: 2F 1S **Baths:** 1 Private 1 Shared
(2)

***Moreig Hotel,** 67 Ann Road, Dumfries, DG1 3EG.*
Elegant large sandstone licensed hotel. **Open:** All Year
01387 255524 Mr Black
Rates fr: *£22.50*-**£35.00**.
Beds: 3F 3D 2S **Baths:** 8 Ensuite
(20)

***4 Cassalands,** Dumfries, DG2 7NS.*
Large Victorian private house - central.
Open: All Year (not Xmas)
01387 253701
Mrs Vaughan
Rates fr: *£16.00*-**£16.00**.
Beds: 1D 1T 2S
Baths: 2 Shared
(6)

***Lochenlee,** 32 Ardwall Road, Dumfries, DG1 3AQ.*
Quiet, warm, large Edwardian house.
Open: All Year
01387 265153
Mrs Porteous
Rates fr: *£14.00*-**£13.00**.
Beds: 2F 1S
Baths: 1 Shared

***Selmar,** 41 Cardoness Street, Dumfries, DG1 3AL.*
Small homely Bed & Breakfast.
Open: All Year (not Xmas)
01387 252095 Mrs McKie
Rates fr: *£13.50*-**£13.50**.
Beds: 1F 1T
Baths: 1 Shared

Dunscore

National Grid Ref: NX9186

***Low Kirkbridge,** Dunscore, Dumfries, DG2 0SP.*
Lovely farmhouse, super breakfasts.
Open: All Year (not Xmas)
Grades: STB Listed, Comm
01387 820258 (also fax no)
Mrs Kirk
Rates fr: *£15.00*-**£15.00**.
Beds: 1D 1T
Baths: 2 Shared
(4)

Eaglesfield

National Grid Ref: NY2374

***Cushathill Cottage,** Eaglesfield, Lockerbie, Dumfriesshire, DG11 3JT.*
Farm cottage in secluded rural location.
Open: Apr to Oct
01461 500643 Mrs Sherlock
Rates fr: *£16.00*-**£16.00**.
Beds: 1F 1D
Baths: 1 Shared

Eastriggs

National Grid Ref: NY2466

***Stanfield Farm,** Eastriggs, Annan, Dumfriesshire, DG12 6TF.*
C19th farmhouse.
Open: Easter to Oct
01461 40367 Mrs Mallinson
Rates fr: *£15.00*.
Beds: 1F 2D
Baths: 1 Private 1 Shared
(3)

Ecclefechan

National Grid Ref: NY1974

***Carlyle House,** Ecclefechan, Lockerbie, Dumfriesshire, DG11 3DG.*
C18th house in small village.
Open: All Year (not Xmas/New Year)
Grades: STB Listed, Approv
01576 300322 (also fax no)
Mrs Martin
Rates fr: *£12.50*-**£12.50**.
Beds: 1F 1T 1S
Baths: 2 Shared
(6)

Glenluce

National Grid Ref: NX1957

Glenbay, Ingleneuk

***Bankfield Farm,** Glenluce, Newton Stewart, Wigtownshire, DG8 0JF.*
Large spacious farmhouse.
Open: Easter to Oct
01581 300281 Mrs Stewart
Rates fr: *£18.00*-**£15.00**.
Beds: 1F 1D 1T
Baths: 2 Ensuite 1 Private

***Grayhill Farm,** Glenluce, Newton Stewart, Wigtownshire, DG8 0NS.*
Comfortable family-run beef farm.
Open: Easter to Oct
Grades: STB Listed, Comm
01581 300400 Mrs Marshall
Rates fr: *£15.00*-**£16.00**.
Beds: 1D 1T
Baths: 1 Shared

***Belgrano,** 81 Main Street, Glenluce, Newton Stewart, Wigtownshire, DG8 0PP.*
Large, comfortable, modernised Victorian house.
Open: All Year
01581 300554 Mr Walker
Rates fr: *£16.00*-**£16.00**.
Beds: 1F 1D 1T 1S
Baths: 2 Ensuite 1 Private 1 Shared
(1) (4)

Gretna Green

National Grid Ref: NY3168

Royal Stewart Motel, Solway Lodge Hotel

***Greenlaw Guest House,** Gretna Green, Gretna, Dumfriesshire, CA6 5DU.*
Homely, comfortable, friendly guest house.
Open: All Year (not Xmas)
Grades: STB 2 Cr, Approv, AA 2 Q, Recomm
01461 338361 Ms Adams
Rates fr: *£15.00*-**£17.00**.
Beds: 1F 4D 3T 2S
Baths: 1 Ensuite 1 Private 3 Shared
(12)

***Alexander House,** Gretna Green, Gretna, Dumfriesshire, DG16 5DU.*
Friendly, clean & comfortable.
Open: All Year
01461 337597 Mrs Crosbie
Rates fr: *£15.00*-**£18.00**.
Beds: 1D 1T
Baths: 2 Private

Haugh of Urr

National Grid Ref: NX8066

Laurie Arms

***Corbieton Cottage,** Haugh of Urr, Castle Douglas, Kirkcudbrightshire, DG7 3JJ.*
Delightful country cottage, lovely views.
Open: All Year (not Xmas)
01556 660413 Mr Jones
Rates fr: *£15.00*-**£16.00**.
Beds: 1D 1T **Baths:** 1 Shared
(2)

***Woodburn House,** Haugh of Urr, Castle Douglas, Kirkcudbrightshire, DG7 3YB.*
Former C18th coaching inn.
Open: All Year
Grades: STB Listed, High Comm, AA 2 Cr
01556 660217 Mrs Wormald
Rates fr: *£16.00*-**£19.00**.
Beds: 1F 1D 1T
Baths: 1 Ensuite 2 Private
(0) (6)

High Bridge of Ken

National Grid Ref: NX6191

***2 Muirdrochwood,** High Bridge of Ken, Carsphairn, Castle Douglas, Kircudbrightshire, DG7 1SW.*
Friendly small holding.
Open: All Year (not Xmas)
01644 460226 Mrs Burnie
Rates fr: *£14.00*.
Beds: 1F **Baths:** 1 Shared

Kirkconnel

National Grid Ref: NS7313

***The School House,** Main Street, Kirkconnel, Sanquhar, Dumfriesshire, DG4 6NE.*
In own grounds on A76.
Open: All Year (not Xmas)
01659 67284 Mrs Heywood
Rates fr: *£13.00*-**£13.00**.
Beds: 1F 1D **Baths:** 2 Shared
(4)

Kirkcudbright

National Grid Ref: NX6850

Auld Alliance Restaurant, Serkirk Arms Hotel

***Parkview,** 22 Millburn Street, Kirkcudbright, Kirkcudbrightshire, DG6 4EA.*
Quiet situation, warm welcome guaranteed.
Open: Easter to Oct
01557 330056 Mrs McIlwraith
Rates fr: *£15.00*-**£15.00**.
Beds: 2D
Baths: 1 Shared
(2)

***Gladstone House,** 48 High Street, Kirkcudbright, Kirkcudbrightshire, DG6 4JX.*
'Award Winning', delightful Georgian townhouse.
Open: All Year
Grades: STB 2 Cr, High Comm, AA 4 Q
01557 331734 (also fax no)
Mrs Westbrook
Rates fr: *£27.00*-**£34.00**.
Beds: 3D
Baths: 3 Private
(12)

***Emahroo,** 109a High Street, Kirkcudbright, Kirkcudbrightshire, DG6 4JG.* 'Home from home'.
Open: Easter to Sep
01557 331279 Mrs Durok
Rates fr: *£14.50*-**£16.00**.
Beds: 1D 1T
Baths: 1 Shared
(8)

***Gordon House Hotel,** 116 High Street, Kirkcudbright, Kirkcudbrightshire, DG6 4JQ.*
Comfortable, centrally situated, family-run hotel.
Open: All Year
Grades: STB Listed
01557 330670
Rates fr: *£18.00*-**£18.00**.
Beds: 1F 3D 5T 3S
Baths: 3 Shared

Kirkinner

National Grid Ref: NX4251

Kirkinner Inn

***Jubilee Cottage,** Braehead, Kirkinner, Newton Stewart, Wigtownshire, DG8 9AH.*
1890 traditional 'whinstone' cottage.
Open: All Year
01988 840604 Mrs Boardman
Rates fr: *£14.00*-**£14.00**.
Beds: 2F 1T
Baths: 1 Shared
(2) (5)

Kirkpatrick Durham

National Grid Ref: NX7870

***Glenhill,** Kirkpatrick Durham, Castle Douglas, Kirkcudbrightshire, DG7 3HE.*
Comfortable house in rural village.
Open: Easter to Oct
Grades: STB Listed, Comm
01556 650274
Mrs Mathie
Rates fr: *£14.50*-**£15.50**.
Beds: 1D 1T
Baths: 1 Private 1 Shared
(2)

Langholm

National Grid Ref: NY3684

Crown hotel

***Esk Brae,** Langholm, Dumfriesshire, DG13 0DP.*
Riverside bungalow with beautiful garden.
Open: Easter to Oct
Grades: STB Listed, Comm
013873 80377 Mrs Geddes
Rates fr: *£15.00*-**£15.00**.
Beds: 1D 1T
Baths: 1 Shared
(2)

Laurieston

National Grid Ref: NX6864

Laurie Arms

***Craig of Balmaghie Farm,** Laurieston, Castle Douglas, Kirkcudbrightshire, DG7 2NA.*
Family-run upland farm.
Open: Easter to Oct
Grades: STB 2 Cr, Comm
01644 450287
Mrs Gordon
Rates fr: *£14.00*-**£16.00**.
Beds: 2D 1T
Baths: 1 Private 1 Shared
(3)

Leswalt

National Grid Ref: NX0163

Crown Hotel, Crown Golf Hotel

***Windyridge,** Leswalt, Stranraer, Wigtownshire, DG9 0XL.*
Comfortable country cottage in woodland setting.
Open: All Year
01776 870280 Mrs Rushworth
Rates fr: *£12.50*-**£13.00**.
Beds: 1D 1T **Baths:** 1 Shared
(4)

Lockerbie

National Grid Ref: NY1381

***Ravenshill House Hotel,** Dumfries Road, Lockerbie, Dumfriesshire, DG11 2EF.*
Large Victorian house, Chef proprietor.
Open: All Year (not Xmas)
Grades: STB 3 Cr, Comm, AA 1 St
01576 202882 (also fax no)
Ms Tindal
Rates fr: *£25.00*-**£35.00**.
Beds: 2F 3D 3T
Baths: 7 Ensuite 1 Private
(30)

The lowest **single** *rate is shown in* **bold.**

Minnigaff

National Grid Ref: NX4166

Cree Inn

Flowerbank Guest House, *Minnigaff, Newton Stewart, Wigtownshire, DG8 6PJ.*
Quiet C18th house. River setting.
Open: All Year (not Xmas)
Grades: STB 2 Cr, Comm
01671 402629 Mrs Inker
Rates fr: *£16.50*-**£20.00**.
Beds: 3F 2D 1T
Baths: 3 Ensuite 1 Private 2 Shared
(10)

Moffat

National Grid Ref: NT0805

Morlich House, *Ballplay Road, Moffat, Dumfriesshire, DG10 9JU.*
Open: Feb to Nov
Grades: STB 3 Cr, Comm
01683 220589 Mrs Wells
Fax no: 01683 221032
Rates fr: *£16.00*-**£14.00**.
Beds: 2F 1D 1T 1S
Baths: 4 Ensuite 1 Private
(8)
A superb Victorian country house set in quiet elevated grounds overlooking town and surrounding hills. Just 5 minutes walk from town centre. Rooms are ensuite with colour TV, radio alarm, tea/coffee, direct dial telephone. Evening meal (menu choice).

Hartfell House, *Hartfell Crescent, Moffat, Dumfriesshire, DG10 9AL.*
Splendid Victorian manor house.
Open: Mar to Nov
Grades: STB 3 Cr, High Comm, AA 3 Q
01683 220153 Mrs White
Rates fr: *£18.00*-**£22.50**.
Beds: 2F 3D 2T 2S
Baths: 5 Ensuite 2 Shared
(9)

Ivy Cottage Guest House, *High Street, Moffat, Dumfriesshire, DG10 9HG.*
Open: All Year (not Xmas)
01683 220279 Mrs Holland
Rates fr: *£15.50*-**£17.50**.
Beds: 1F 2D 1T **Baths:** 1 Shared
(2)
A C18th house and gardens of character. Ideal base for touring Galloway and the Borders, or overnight accommodation enroute for the Highlands. TV lounge. Warm welcome.

The Arden House Guest House, *Moffat, Dumfriesshire, DG10 9HG.*
Converted bank.
Open: Easter to Nov
Grades: STB Listed, RAC Acclaim
01683 220220
Rates fr: *£15.50*-**£18.50**.
Beds: 2F 2D 2T 1S
Baths: 4 Ensuite 1 Private 2 Shared

The Lodge, *Sidmount Avenue, Well Road, Moffat, Dumfriesshire, DG10 9BS.*
Peaceful, comfortable Victorian house.
Open: All Year
01683 220440 (also fax no)
Mr Hall
Rates fr: *£16.00*-**£20.00**.
Beds: 1F 1D 1T 1S
Baths: 1 Ensuite 2 Shared
(10)

Fairfield, *Ballplay Road, Moffat, Dumfriesshire, DG10 9JU.*
Homely, beautiful garden. Good food.
Open: Easter to Oct
01683 220769
Miss Denholm
Rates fr: *£13.00*-**£18.00**.
Beds: 1D 1T
Baths: 1 Shared
(2)

Wellview Hotel, *Ballplay Road, Moffat, Dumfriesshire, DG10 9JU.*
Excellent centre to explore Borders.
Open: All Year
Grades: STB 3 Cr, AA 1 St, RAC High Acclaim
01683 220184
Mr Schuckardt
Rates fr: *£27.00*-**£37.00**.
Beds: 4D 2T
Baths: 6 Private
(8)

Black Bull Hotel, *Churchgate, Moffat, Dumfriesshire, DG10 9EG.*
Olde worlde inn.
Open: All Year
01683 220206
Miss Hughes
Rates fr: *£20.00*-**£25.00**.
Beds: 1F 4D 2T 1S
Baths: 6 Private 2 Shared

Woodhead Farm, *Moffat, Dumfriesshire, DG10 9LU.*
Luxuriously furnished farmhouse, wonderful views.
Open: All Year (not Xmas)
Grades: STB 3 Cr, High Comm
01683 220225 Mrs Jackson
Rates fr: *£22.50*-**£25.00**.
Beds: 1D 2T
Baths: 3 Ensuite
(Yes)

Nethermill

National Grid Ref: NY0487

Lochrigghead Farmhouse, *Nethermill, Parkgate, Dumfries, DG1 3NG.*
Comfortable farmhouse, picturesque, good hospitality.
Open: All Year
01387 860381 Mrs Burgoyne
Rates fr: *£14.00*-**£14.00**.
Beds: 1F 1D 1T
Baths: 1 Private 1 Shared
(5)

New Abbey

National Grid Ref: NX9666

Criffel Inn, *2 The Square, New Abbey, Dumfries, DG2 8BX.*
Open: All Year
01387 850244 Mr McAlister
Rates fr: *£20.00*-**£20.00**.
Beds: 2F 1T 2S
Baths: 3 Ensuite 2 Shared
(20)
Small owner-managed hotel set in picturesque New Abbey. Home baking/cooking. Well stocked bar. Ideal base for golf, shooting, fishing, walking or simply relaxing.

New Galloway

National Grid Ref: NX6377

The Smithy Licensed Restaurant, *& Craft Shop, New Galloway, Castle Douglas, Kirkcudbrightshire, DG7 3RN.*
Accommodation in converted 'Smiddy' (blacksmith's).
Open: Mar to Oct
01644 420269 Mr McPhee
Rates fr: *£15.00*-**£15.00**.
Beds: 1D 1T
Baths: 1 Shared
(2)

The Smithy Licensed Restaurant, *& Craft Shop, New Galloway, Castle Douglas, Kirkcudbrightshire, DG7 3RN.*
Converted smiddy attached to restaurant.
Open: Mar to Oct
01644 420269 Mr McPhee
Rates fr: *£15.00*-**£15.00**.
Beds: 1D 1T
(2)

Cross Keys Hotel, *High Street, New Galloway, Castle Douglas, Kirkcudbrightshire, DG7 3RN.*
C18th olde worlde hotel.
Open: All Year (not Xmas)
Grades: STB 2 Cr
01644 420494 Mr Berriman
Rates fr: *£15.50*-**£16.50**.
Beds: 1F 3D 3T 2S
Baths: 3 Private
(1) (7)

Leamington Hotel, *High Street, New Galloway, Castle Douglas, Kirkcudbrightshire, DG7 3RN.*
Family-run comfortable hotel.
Open: Dec to Oct
01644 420327 Mr Dolan
Rates fr: *£16.00*-**£14.00**.
Beds: 3F 3D 1T 2S
Baths: 6 Private 2 Shared
(9)

The lowest *double* rate per person is shown in *italics*.

Newton Stewart

National Grid Ref: NX4065

Crown Hotel, Bruce Hotel

Carty Farm, *Newton Stewart, Wigtownshire, DG8 6AY.*
Farmhouse, one mile Newton Stewart.
Open: All Year (not Xmas)
01671 402570 Mrs Butcher
Rates fr: *£15.00*-**£15.00**.
Beds: 1D 1T 1S
Baths: 1 Shared
(6)

The Stables Guest House, *Corsbie Road, Newton Stewart, Wigtownshire, DG8 6JB.*
Modern comfortable family home.
Open: All Year
Grades: STB 2 Cr, Comm
01671 402157 Mrs Stables
Rates fr: *£16.00*-**£18.00**.
Beds: 4D 1T 1S
Baths: 4 Ensuite 2 Private
(1) (8)

Palakona Guest House, *30 Queen Street, Newton Stewart, Wigtownshire, DG8 6JL.*
Centrally located, comfortable, homely.
Open: All Year
01671 402323 Mr Barlow
Rates fr: *£15.00*-**£15.00**.
Beds: 4F **Baths:** 2 Shared
(3)

Lynwood, *Corvisel Road, Newton Stewart, Wigtownshire, DG8 6LN.*
Original Victorian house, home baking.
Open: All Year (not Xmas)
01671 402074 Mrs Gustafson
Rates fr: *£14.00*-**£14.00**.
Beds: 1F 1D 1T **Baths:** 1 Shared
(3)

Newton Wamphray

National Grid Ref: NY1194

The Red House Hotel, *Newton Wamphray, Moffat, Dumfriesshire, DG10 9NF.*
Small country hotel.
Open: All Year (not Xmas)
01576 470470 Mrs Wilson
Rates fr: *£20.00*-**£20.00**.
Beds: 1D 1T 1S
Baths: 1 Ensuite 1 Shared
(6)

Port William

National Grid Ref: NX3343

Monreith Arms Hotel

Monreith Arms Hotel, *Port William, Wigtownshire, DG8 9SE.*
Village hotel, overlooking harbour.
Open: All Year
01988 700232 Mrs Rogerson
Rates fr: *£19.00*-**£20.00**.
Beds: 3F 3D 3T 3S
Baths: 12 Private

Portpatrick

National Grid Ref: NW9954

Downshire Hotel, Crown Hotel, Mount Stewart Hotel

Blinkbonnie Guest House, *Portpatrick, Stranraer, Wigtownshire, DG9 8LG.*
Modern coastal villa, panoramic views
Open: All Year (not Dec)
Grades: STB 3 Cr, Comm, AA 3 Q, Recomm
01776 810282 Mrs Robinson
Rates fr: *£17.50*-**£18.00**.
Beds: 4D 2T
Baths: 4 Private 2 Shared
(10)

Albony House, *4 Blair Terrace, Portpatrick, Stranraer, Wigtownshire, DG9 8SY.*
Cosy, homely, quiet seaside house.
Open: All Year (not Xmas)
Grades: STB 2 Cr, Comm
01776 810568 Miss Dowell
Rates fr: *£15.00*-**£15.00**.
Beds: 1F 1D 1T 1S
Baths: 1 Ensuite 1 Private 1 Shared

Braefield House, *Portpatrick, Stranraer, Wigtownshire, DG9 8TA.*
Large Victorian house, superb views. **Open:** All Year (not Xmas)
Grades: STB 2 Cr, Comm
01776 810255 Mrs Moffat
Rates fr: *£17.00*-**£17.00**.
Beds: 1F 4D 3T 1S
Baths: 4 Private 1 Shared
(20)

Melvin Lodge Guest House, *South Crescent, Portpatrick, Stranraer, Wigtownshire, DG9 8LE.*
Large Victorian house, sea views.
Open: All Year
Grades: STB 2 Cr, Comm
01776 810238 Mr & Mrs Pinder
Rates fr: *£17.00*-**£17.00**.
Beds: 4F 3D 1T 2S
Baths: 6 Ensuite 2 Shared
(8)

Ard Choille Guest House, *1 Blair Terrace, Portpatrick, Stranraer, Wigtownshire, DG9 8SY.*
Comfortable family-run guest house.
Open: All Year
01776 810313 Mrs Black
Rates fr: *£15.00*-**£15.00**.
Beds: 1F 1S
Baths: 1 Ensuite 1 Shared
(1) (3)

Rockcliffe

National Grid Ref: NX8453

Clonyard House Hotel

Albany, *Rockcliffe, Dalbeattie, Kirkcudbrightshire, DG5 4QQ.*
Magnificent views, quiet, on shore.
Open: All Year (not Xmas)
01556 630355 Mrs Proudlove
Rates fr: *£16.00*-**£18.0**.
Beds: 1D 1T 1S
Baths: 1 Ensuite 1 Private
(3)

Millbrae House, *Rockcliffe, Dalbeattie, Kirkcudbrightshire, DG5 4QG.*
Perfect touring base, near the sea.
Open: Jan to Oct
01556 630217 / 0850 038947
Rates fr: *£16.00*-**£24.00**.
Beds: 2D 3T
Baths: 4 Ensuite 1 Private
(12) (5)

Ruthwell

National Grid Ref: NY0967

Kirkland Country House Hotel, *Ruthwell, Dumfries, DG1 4NP.*
Former manse home, good food.
Open: All Year
01387 870284 Mrs Coatsworth
Rates fr: *£21.00*-**£25.00**.
Beds: 1F 2D 3T
(10)

Sanquhar

National Grid Ref: NS7809

Blackaddie Hotel

Penhurst, *Townhead Street, Sanquhar, Dumfriesshire, DG4 6DA.*
Large sandstone family house.
Open: All Year
Grades: STB Listed, Comm
01659 50751 (also fax no)
Mrs McDowall
Rates fr: *£12.00*-**£12.00**.
Beds: 1F 1D 1T
Baths: 1 Shared

28 High Street, *Sanquhar, Dumfriesshire, DG4 6BL.*
Large, comfortable, informal family flat. **Open:** All Year
Grades: STB Listed, Approv
01659 58143 Mrs Turnbull
Rates fr: *£12.50*-**£12.50**.
Beds: 1D 1T **Baths:** 1 Shared

St John's Town of Dalry

National Grid Ref: NX6281

59 Main Street, *St John's Town of Dalry, Castle Douglas, Kirkcudbrightshire, DG7 3UP.*
Comfortable, friendly accommodation. **Open:** Easter to Oct
01644 430420 Mrs Findlay
Rates fr: *£13.00*-**£13.00**.
Beds: 1D 1T
Baths: 1 Shared

Lochinvar Hotel, *St John's Town of Dalry, Castle Douglas, Kirkcudbrightshire, DG7 3UP.*
C18th ivy-clad hotel.
Open: All Year
01644 430210
Mrs Pennington
Rates fr: *£15.00*-**£17.50**.
Beds: 3F 6D 5T 1S
Baths: 7 Private 2 Shared
(30)

Stoneykirk

National Grid Ref: NX0853

Torrs Warren Hotel, *Stoneykirk, Portpatrick, Stranraer, Wigtownshire, DG9 9DH.*
Family-run country house hotel.
Open: All Year
Grades: STB Listed, Approv
01776 830204 (also fax no)
Mrs Camlin
Rates fr: *£21.00*-**£23.00**.
Beds: 4F 3D
Baths: 4 Private 3 Shared
(0) (30)

Stranraer

National Grid Ref: NX0560

Flemings, L'Aperitif, Crown Hotel

Hartforth, *33 London Road, Stranraer, Wigtownshire, DG9 8AF.*
Centrally situated spacious comfortable accommodation.
Open: All Year
01776 704832 Mrs Hull
Rates fr: *£15.00*-**£15.00**.
Beds: 2F 1D 1T
Baths: 2 Shared
(8)

Jan Da Mar, *1 Ivy Place, London Road, Stranraer, Wigtownshire, DG9 8ER.*
Early C19th townhouse.
Open: All Year
Grades: STB 2 Cr, Comm
01776 706194 Mrs Bewley
Rates fr: *£14.00*-**£16.00**.
Beds: 3F 3T 2S
Baths: 2 Private 2 Shared

Kildrochet House, *Stranraer, Wigtownshire, DG9 9BB.*
C18th Adam dower house.
Open: All Year
Grades: STB 3 Cr, High Comm
01776 820216 Mr & Mrs Whitworth
Rates fr: *£23.00*-**£27.00**.
Beds: 1D 2T
Baths: 2 Ensuite 1 Private
(8)

Windyridge, *Leswalt, Stranraer, Wigtownshire, DG9 0XL.*
Comfortable country cottage in woodland setting.
Open: All Year
01776 870280 Mrs Rushworth
Rates fr: *£12.50*-**£13.00**.
Beds: 1D 1T
Baths: 1 Shared
(4)

2 Birnam Place, *Station Street, Stranraer, Wigtownshire, DG9 7HN.*
Private house.
Open: All Year
01776 703935 Mrs Jameson
Rates fr: *£14.00*-**£14.00**.
Beds: 1F 1T 1S
Baths: 2 Private 1 Shared
(4)

Fernlea Guest House, *Lewis Street, Stranraer, Wigtownshire, DG9 7AQ.*
Comfortable, friendly guest house.
Open: All Year (not Xmas)
Grades: STB 3 Cr, Comm
01776 703037 Mrs Spiers
Rates fr: *£15.00*-**£18.50**.
Beds: 2D 2T
Baths: 2 Ensuite 2 Shared
(10) (5)

Torthorwald

National Grid Ref: NY0378

Tor House Hotel

Smithy House, *Torthorwald, Dumfries, DG1 3PT.*
Ideal base, touring, fishing, yachting.
Open: All Year (not Xmas)
Grades: STB 1 Cr, Comm
01387 750518 Mr Ireson
Rates fr: *£15.00*-**£20.00**.
Beds: 1F 1D 1T
Baths: 1 Private 2 Shared
(4)

Twynholm

National Grid Ref: NX6654

Star Hotel

Glencroft, *Twynholm, Kirkcudbright, Kirkcudbrightshire, DG6 4NT.*
Modern comfortable farmhouse near A75. **Open:** Easter to Oct
Grades: STB 1 Cr, Comm
01557 860252 Mrs Robson
Rates fr: *£14.00*-**£14.00**.
Beds: 1F 1D 1S **Baths:** 2 Shared
(3)

Waterbeck

National Grid Ref: NY2477

Carik Cottage, *Waterbeck, Lockerbie, Dumfriesshire, DG11 3EU.*
Converted byre, 3 miles A74.
Open: Mar to Oct
01461 600652 Mrs Hislop
Rates fr: *£14.00*-**£16.00**.
Beds: 2D 1T
Baths: 1 Private 1 Shared
(6)

Whithorn

National Grid Ref: NX4440

Belmont, *St John Street, Whithorn, Newton Stewart, Wigtownshire, DG8 8PG.*
Open: All Year
01988 500890 Mrs Fleming
Rates fr: *£12.00*-**£16.00**.
Beds: 1D 1T 1S
Baths: 1 Private 1 Shared
Lovely spacious family home in quiet surroundings, ample parking space. Large library. Beautiful area - walking, birdwatching, fishing, golf, historical and archaeological interests. Warm welcome.

All rates are subject to alteration at the owners' discretion.

Baltier Farm, *Whithorn, Newton Stewart, Wigtownshire, DG8 8HA.*
Modern comfortable farmhouse.
Open: All Year (not Xmas)
01988 600241 Mrs Forsyth
Rates fr: *£14.00*-**£14.00**.
Beds: 1F 1D 1T 1S
Baths: 1 Shared

Wigtown

National Grid Ref: NX4355

Bladnoch Inn

Glaisnock House, *20 South Main Street, Wigtown, Wigtownshire, DG8 9EH.*
Town house with licensed restaurant.
Open: All Year (not Xmas)
Grades: STB 2 Cr, Comm
01988 402249
Mr & Mrs Cairns
Rates fr: *£15.50*-**£15.50**.
Beds: 1F 1D 1T 1S
Baths: 1 Ensuite 1 Private 1 Shared

Craigmount Guest House, *High Street, Wigtown, Wigtownshire, DG8 9EQ.*
Comfortable refurbished family home. **Open:** All Year
01988 402291 Mrs Taylor
Rates fr: *£17.00*-**£17.00**.
Beds: 2F 1D 1T 1S
Baths: 2 Private 1 Shared
(10)

Sunnybrae Guest House, *Wigtown, Newton Stewart, Wigtownshire, DG8 9EQ.*
Large private villa.
Open: Easter to October
01988 403306 Mrs Boyd
Rates fr: *£12.00*-**£13.00**.
Beds: 1F 1D 1T 1S
Baths: 1 Shared
(1) (10)

Torhousekie Farm, *Wigtown, Wigtownshire, DG8 9BJ.*
Comfortable farmhouse, all home baking.
Open: All Year (not Xmas)
01988 403202 Mrs Adams
Rates fr: *£13.00*-**£13.00**.
Beds: 1F 1D
(3)

Planning a longer stay? Always ask for any special rates.

Fife

Tourist Information Centres

Scottish Fisheries Museum, **Anstruther**, Fife, KY10 3DQ, 01333 311073, (Easter to Oct).

4 Kirkgate, **Burntisland**, Fife, KY3 9DB, 01592 872667.

Marketgate Museum & Heritage Centre, **Crail**, Anstruther, Fife, KY10 3TL, 01333 450869, (Easter to Oct).

Fluthers Car Park, **Cupar**, Fife, KY15 4BH, 01334 652874

Abbot House, Maygate, **Dunfermline**, Fife, KY12 7NH, 01383 720999, (Easter to Oct).

Queensferry Lodge Hotel, North Queensferry, **Inverkeithing**, Fife, KY11 1JH, 01383 417759.

19 Whyte's Causeway, **Kirkcaldy**, Fife, KY1 1XF, 01333 429464

South Street, **Leven**, Fife, KY8 4NU, 01333 429464.

78 South Street, **St Andrews**, Fife, KY16 9JT, 01334 472021.

Aberdour

National Grid Ref: NT1985

Hawkcraig House, *Hawkcraig Point, Aberdour, Burntisland, Fife, KY3 0TZ.*
Water's edge, old ferryman's house.
Open: Mar to Oct
Grades: STB 3 Cr, Deluxe, AA 5 Q
01383 860335 Mr Barrie
Rates fr: *£21.00*-**£25.00**.
Beds: 1D 1T
Baths: 2 Ensuite
(10) (3)

The Woodside Hotel, *High Street, Aberdour, Burntisland, Fife, KY3 0SW.*
Refurbished Listed building in pleasant village.
Open: All Year
Grades: AA 2 St, RAC 3 St
01383 860328 Mr Austen
Fax no: 01383 860920
Rates fr: *£27.00*-**£47.00**.
Beds: 15D 3T 1S
Baths: 19 Ensuite
(35)

The lowest *double* rate per person is shown in *italics*.

Anstruther

National Grid Ref: NO5603

Haven Restaurant, Dreel Tavern

The Sheiling, *32 Glenogil Gardens, Anstruther, Fife, KY10 3ET.*
Pretty white bungalow near harbour.
Open: Apr to Sep
Grades: STB 1 Cr, Comm
01333 310697 Mrs Ritchie
Rates fr: *£14.00*-**£20.50**.
Beds: 2D **Baths:** 1 Shared
(2)

The Hermitage, *Ladywalk, Anstruther, Fife, KY10 3EX.*
First class accommodation in charming 'East Neuk' town house (c.1817).
Open: All Year
01333 310909 Mrs McDonald
Rates fr: *£20.00*-**£25.00**.
Beds: 3D 1T **Baths:** 2 Shared
(4)

The Spindrift, *Pittenweem Road, Anstruther, Fife, KY10 3DT.*
Imposing Victorian house in picturesque East Neuk.
Open: All Year
01333 310573 Mr McFarlane
Rates fr: *£25.00*-**£32.50**.
Beds: 3F 2D 3T
Baths: 8 Private
(10)

Auchtermuchty

National Grid Ref: NO2311

Forest Hills Hotel, *High Street, Auchtermuchty, Cupar, Fife, KY14 7OP.*
Old inn in village square.
Open: All Year
Grades: STB 3 Cr, Comm
01337 828318 (also fax no)
Mr Van Beuskom
Rates fr: *£25.00*-**£37.00**.
Beds: 2F 4D 2T 2S
Baths: 8 Private 1 Shared

***Viewbank**, 4 Bondgate, Auchtermuchty, Cupar, Fife, KY14 7AF.*
Large Georgian country house.
Open: Mar to Oct
01337 828221 Mrs Morton
Rates fr: *£17.00*-**£20.00**.
Beds: 1D 1T
(4)

Balfarg

National Grid Ref: NO2803

***Tarry-A-While**, 11 Ardgartan Court, Balfarg, Glenrothes, Fife, KY7 6XB.*
Quiet, clean, comfortable, hospitable abode.
Open: All Year
01592 745259 Mrs Sunter
Rates fr: *£13.50*-**£13.50**.
Beds: 1D 1T
Baths: 1 Shared

Boarhills

National Grid Ref: NO5614

***Parkmill**, Boarhills, St Andrews, Fife, KY16 8PS.*
C18th mill and house.
Open: All Year (not Xmas)
01334 880254 Mr & Mrs Frodsham
Rates fr: *£14.00*-**£16.00**.
Beds: 1F 1D 1S
Baths: 1 Shared
(4)

Burntisland

National Grid Ref: NT2386

Inchview Hotel

***The Beach House**, Lochies Road, Burntisland, Fife, KY3 9JX.*
Listed Victorian house overlooking Edinburgh.
Open: All Year
01592 874474 Mr & Mrs McVay
Rates fr: *£20.00*-**£25.00**.
Beds: 2D 1T
Baths: 3 Ensuite

***Gleniffer**, 28 Kirkton Road, Burntisland, Fife, KY3 0BY.*
30 minutes to Edinburgh by car or train.
Open: All Year
01592 873903 Mrs Lawson
Rates fr: *£10.00*-**£13.00**.
Beds: 1F 2S
Baths: 1 Private
(5)

***Inchview Hotel**, 69 Kinghorn Road, Burntisland, Fife, KY3 9EB.*
Beautiful comfortable family-run hotel.
Open: All Year
Grades: STB 4 Cr, Comm, AA 2 St
01592 872239 Mr Black
Rates fr: *£29.50*-**£39.50**.
Beds: 1F 6D 3T 2S
Baths: 12 Ensuite
(15)

Clayton

National Grid Ref: NO4318

***East Lodge**, Clayton, St Andrews, Fife, KY16 9YE.*
Old country lodge in 9 acres.
Open: Easter to Oct
01334 870282 Mr & Mrs Rollo
Rates fr: *£15.00*-**£18.00**.
Beds: 2D 1T **Baths:** 2 Shared
(6)

Cowdenbeath

National Grid Ref: NT1691

***Struan Bank Hotel**, 74 Perth Road, Cowdenbeath, Fife, KY4 9BG.*
Open: All Year
Grades: STB 2 Cr, Comm, AA 3 Q
01383 511057 (also fax no)
Mr Hutton
Rates fr: *£17.00*-**£18.50**.
Beds: 2F 3D 2T 2S
Baths: 6 Ensuite 1 Shared
(6)
A genuine welcome. Comfortable lounge, good food, licensed. Ideal for touring - golf, castles, fishing villages, palaces, Edinburgh, St Andrews, Perth - all within an hour's drive.

Crail

National Grid Ref: NO6107

Balcomie Hotel

***Woodlands Guest House**, Balcomie Road, Crail, Anstruther, Fife, KY10 3TN.*
Open: Feb to Dec
Grades: STB Listed, Approv
01333 450147 Mrs Wood
Rates fr: *£16.00*-**£20.00**.
Beds: 2F 3D
Baths: 2 Shared
(2) (20)
Magnificent setting in 0.5 acre walled gardens; superb views; next to farm and sea; beach 5 minutes; St Andrews 10 minutes; family-run; 20 golf courses closeby.

***Hazelton Guest House**, 29 Marketgate, Crail, Anstruther, Fife, KY10 3TH.*
Your comfort is our concern.
Open: Feb to Nov
Grades: STB Listed, Comm
01333 450250
Mr Brown
Rates fr: *£16.00*-**£16.00**.
Beds: 2F 2D 2T 1S
Baths: 2 Shared

***Selcraig House**, 47 Nethergate, Crail, Anstruther, Fife, KY10 3TX.*
Victorian villa with antique furniture.
Open: All Year
01333 450697 Ms Carstairs
Rates fr: *£15.00*-**£20.00**.
Beds: 2F 1D 2T
Baths: 2 Shared

***Westgarth**, Kirkmay Road, Crail, Anstruther, Fife, KY10 8SE.*
Large old Scottish villa.
Open: Easter to Oct
01333 450289 Mrs Clarkson
Rates fr: *£16.00*-**£16.00**.
Beds: 1D 1T

Cupar

National Grid Ref: NO3714

Eden House Hotel, St Michaels Inn (Leuchars), Guardbridge Hotel (Guardbridge)

***Scotstarvit Farm**, Cupar, Fife, KY15 5PA.*
Picturesque characteristic farmhouse, hearty breakfasts.
Open: All Year
Grades: STB 2 Cr, Comm
01334 653591 Mrs Chrisp
Rates fr: *£16.00*-**£20.00**.
Beds: 1D 1T
Baths: 1 Private

***Todhall House**, Off A91, Cupar, Fife, KY15 4RQ.*
Welcoming, traditional Scottish country home. Close to St Andrews.
Open: Apr to Oct
Grades: STB 3 Cr, High Comm, AA 5 Q, Prem Select
01334 656344 (also fax no)
Mrs Donald
Rates fr: *£22.00*-**£27.00**.
Beds: 2D 1T
Baths: 3 Private
(10) (5)

***20 Drumdryan Place**, Cupar, Fife, KY15 5JJ.*
Modern bungalow in residential area.
Open: All Year (not Xmas)
01334 656378 Mrs Gardner
Rates fr: *£15.00*-**£18.00**.
Beds: 2T
Baths: 1 Shared
(5) (2)

Dairsie

National Grid Ref: NO4117

***Easter Craigfoodie**, Dairsie, Cupar, Fife, KY15 4SW.*
Comfortable farmhouse.
Open: All Year
01334 870286 Mrs Scott
Rates fr: *£15.00*-**£17.00**.
Beds: 2D 1T
Baths: 3 Private

Bringing children with you? Always ask for any special rates.

Dunfermline

National Grid Ref: NT1087

Roadhouse Public House, Saline Hotel

***The Halfway House Hotel,** Main Street, Kingseat, Dunfermline, Fife,* *KY12 0TJ.*
Open: All Year
Grades: STB 3 Cr, Comm, RAC 2 St
01383 731661
Mr & Mrs Pegg
Fax no: 01383 621274
Rates fr: *£20.00*-**£30.00**.
Beds: 3D 9T
Baths: 12 Private
(80)
Modern business/tourist hotel. Close to Junction 3 M90 Motorway, Edinburgh city centre 30 minutes away. Restaurant and bar meals available. Proprietors Ann and Vic Pegg.

***Broomfield Guest House,** 1 Bloomfield Drive, Dunfermline, Fife, KY12 7DZ.*
Large Victorian comfortable guest house.
Open: All Year (not Xmas)
01383 732498
Mrs Taylor
Rates fr: *£19.00*-**£16.00**.
Beds: 2F 1D 1T 2S
Baths: 5 Ensuite 1 Private
(8)

***Pitreavie Guest House,** 3 Aberdour Road, Dunfermline, Fife, KY12 4PB.*
Ideally situated comfortable guest house.
Open: All Year
01383 724244
Mr & Mrs Walker
Rates fr: *£16.50*-**£17.50**.
Beds: 1F 1D 2T 2S
Baths: 2 Shared
(6)

***Bowleys Farm,** Roscobie, Dunfermline, Fife, KY12 0SG.*
Spacious, comfortable C19th farmhouse.
Open: Easter to Nov
Grades: STB 1 Cr, Comm
01383 721056
Mrs Fotheringham
Rates fr: *£16.00*-**£18.00**.
Beds: 2F
Baths: 1 Shared
(10)

***Lynn Farm,** Dunfermline, Fife, KY12 9LR.*
Working farm with panoramic views.
Open: Easter to Oct
Grades: STB 2 Cr
01383 852261
Mrs Cousar
Rates fr: *£15.00*-**£20.00**.
Beds: 1F 2T
Baths: 2 Private

Dysart

National Grid Ref: NT3093

***Royal Hotel,** Townhead, Dysart, Kirkcaldy, Fife, KY1 2XQ.*
Friendly C18th coaching inn.
Open: All Year
Grades: STB Listed
01592 654112 Mrs Di Marco
Rates fr: *£17.00*-**£19.50**.
Beds: 1F 3D 6T
Baths: 2 Shared
(16)

***Norview,** 59 Normand Road, Dysart, Kirkcaldy, Fife, KY1 2XP.*
Clean, comfortable, detached Edwardian house.
Open: All Year
01592 652804 Mrs Linton
Rates fr: *£11.00*-**£11.00**.
Beds: 1D 2T **Baths:** 1 Shared

Elie

National Grid Ref: NO4900

Ship Inn, The Toft

***Milford House,** 19 High Street, Elie, Leven, Fife, KY9 1BY.*
Large Victorian house.
Open: All Year
Grades: STB 2 Cr, Comm
01333 330567 Mr Cowan
Rates fr: *£15.00*-**£20.00**.
Beds: 2D 1T
Baths: 1 Ensuite 2 Private

***Ingleside,** 39 Park Place, Elie, Leven, Fife, KY9 1DH.*
Self-contained cottage in gardens.
Open: All Year
01333 330418 Mrs Birrell
Rates fr: *£15.00*-**£20.00**.
Beds: 1D **Baths:** 1 Private

Falkland

National Grid Ref: NO2507

Warbecks, Covenanter Bistro

***Templelands Farm,** Falkland, Fife, KY15 7DE.*
Modern comfortable farmhouse, tasty food.
Open: Easter to Oct
Grades: STB 1 Cr, Comm
01337 857383 Ms McGregor
Rates fr: *£15.00*-**£17.00**.
Beds: 1F 1D 1S
Baths: 2 Shared
(4)

***Ladieburn Cottage,** High Street, Falkland, Fife, KY7 7BZ.*
Centre of picturesque historic village.
Open: All Year
01337 857016 Mrs Heather
Rates fr: *£15.00*-**£18.00**.
Beds: 1F 1T
Baths: 2 Private

Freuchie

National Grid Ref: NO2806

***Little Freuchie,** Freuchie, Cupar, Fife, KY7 7HU.*
Well-situated, comfortable farmhouse.
Open: Easter to Oct
01337 857372
Mrs Duncan
Rates fr: *£15.00*-**£17.00**.
Beds: 1F 1T
Baths: 2 Shared
(2)

Glenrothes

National Grid Ref: NO2701

Brewers Fayre

***3 Taylor Drive,** Glenrothes, Fife, KY7 4EX.*
Modern, detached private house.
Open: All Year (not Xmas/New Year)
01592 752692 Mrs Allan
Rates fr: *£13.00*-**£13.00**.
Beds: 1T 1S
Baths: 1 Shared
(2)

***27 Duncan Road,** Glenrothes, Fife, KY7 4HS.*
Cottage-type house.
Open: All Year
01592 756791
Mr & Mrs Guy
Rates fr: *£12.00*-**£12.00**.
Beds: 1D 1S
(2)

Guardbridge

National Grid Ref: NO4519

Guardbridge Hotel

***Guardbridge Hotel,** Old St Andrews Road, Guardbridge, St Andrews, Fife, KY16 0UD.*
C18th inn with railway memorabilia.
Open: All Year (not Xmas)
01334 839337
Mrs Bayliss
Rates fr: *£20.00*-**£20.00**.
Beds: 1D 2T 1S
Baths: 1 Shared

***The Larches,** 7 River Terrace, Guardbridge, St Andrews, Fife, KY16 0XA.*
Large, comfortable, converted memorial hall.
Open: All Year
Grades: STB 1 Cr, AA 2 Q, Recomm
01334 838008 (also fax no)
Mrs Mayner
Rates fr: *£16.00*-**£21.00**.
Beds: 1F 1D 2T
Baths: 2 Shared

Hillend

National Grid Ref: NT1483

Granary (Dalgety Bay)

***National Activity Centre,** Fordell Firs, Hillend, Dunfermline, Fife, KY11 5HQ.*
Superb bunkhouse and campsite.
Open: All Year (not Xmas)
01383 412704
Mr Barnes
Rates fr: *£5.00*-**£7.00**.
Beds: 7F 2D
(7) (100)

Inverkeithing

National Grid Ref: NT1382

***The Roods,** 16 Bannerman Avenue, Inverkeithing, Fife, KY11 1NG.*
Set in quiet gardens, excellent transport links.
Open: All Year
Grades: STB 3 Cr, High Comm, AA 3 Q
01383 415049
Mrs Marley
Rates fr: *£19.00*-**£22.00**.
Beds: 1D 1T
Baths: 2 Ensuite
(4)

***Borland Lodge Private Hotel,** 31-33 Boreland Road, Inverkeithing, Fife, KY11 1DA.*
Modern well-appointed hotel.
Open: All Year
Grades: STB 3 Cr, Comm
01383 413792
Mr Milton
Fax no: 01383 410872
Rates fr: *£18.50*-**£29.00**.
Beds: 2F 7D 3T 14S
Baths: 26 Private
(21)

***Forth Craig Hotel,** 90 Hope Street, Inverkeithing, Fife, KY11 1LL.*
Modern, purpose-built, family hotel.
Open: All Year
01383 418440
Mrs Guthrie
Rates fr: *£17.50*-**£20.00**.
Beds: 2D 1T 2S
Baths: 5 Private
(8)

Kennoway

National Grid Ref: NO3502

Burns Tavern

***Woodlands Cottage,** Cupar Road, Kennoway, Leven, Fife, KY8 5LR.*
Modernised, comfortable, one-level cottage.
Open: All Year
01333 350520 Ms MacKay
Rates fr: *£17.50*-**£15.00**.
Beds: 1D 1T
Baths: 1 Shared

Kilrenny

National Grid Ref: NO5704

***Rennyhill House,** Kilrenny, Anstruther, Fife, KY10 3JF.*
C18th farmhouse in own grounds.
Open: Jan to Dec
01333 312234 Mrs Wotherspoon
Rates fr: *£17.50*-**£24.50**.
Beds: 1F 1D 1T
Baths: 3 Private
(6)

Kinghorn

National Grid Ref: NT2686

Longboat Inn, Kingswood Hotel

***Craigo-Er,** 45 Pettycur Road, Kinghorn, Fife, KY3 9RN.*
Large Victorian house. Sea views.
Open: All Year
01592 890527 Mrs Thomson
Rates fr: *£16.50*-**£16.50**.
Beds: 1D 2T
Baths: 2 Shared

***The Anchorgate,** 55 Pettycur Road, Kinghorn, Fife, KY3 9RN.*
Excellent base for St Andrews, Edinburgh.
Open: Jan to Dec
01592 890245 Mr & Mrs McArthur
Rates fr: *£15.00*-**£15.00**.
Beds: 1F 1D 1T
Baths: 1 Ensuite 1 Shared

Kingsbarns

National Grid Ref: NO5912

Cambo Arms Hotel

***Kingsbarns Bed & Breakfast,** 3 Main Street, Kingsbarns, St Andrews, Fife, KY16 8SL.*
Converted farmhouse, modern facilities.
Open: Apr to Oct
Grades: STB 2 Cr, Comm
01334 880234 Mrs Hay
Rates fr: *£18.00*-**£22.00**.
Beds: 2D 1T
Baths: 3 Ensuite
(2)

Kingseat

National Grid Ref: NT1290

***The Halfway House Hotel,** Main Street, Kingseat, Dunfermline, Fife, KY12 0TJ.*
Modern business/tourist hotel. Close to Junction 3 M90 Motorway.
Open: All Year
Grades: STB 3 Cr, Comm, RAC 2 St
01383 731661 Mr & Mrs Pegg
Fax no: 01383 621274
Rates fr: *£20.00*-**£30.00**.
Beds: 3D 9T
Baths: 12 Private
(80)

Kirkcaldy

National Grid Ref: NT2791

Kingswood Hotel (Kinghorn), Victoria Hotel, Smithy's

***Crawford Hall,** 2 Kinghorn Road, Kirkcaldy, Fife, KY1 1SU.*
Open: Feb to Nov
01592 262658 Mrs Crawford
Rates fr: *£14.00*-**£15.00**.
Beds: 1F 1T
Baths: 1 Shared
(4)
Large rambling house, once local manse. Set in lovely gardens. 2 minutes from beach - 10 minute walk to town centre. Comfortable rooms, substantial breakfast.

***143 Victoria Road,** Kirkcaldy, Fife, KY1 1DQ.*
Large former Victorian manse. Sea views.
Open: All Year
Grades: STB 1 Cr, High Comm
01592 268864 / 0585 215059 Mr & Mrs Cairns
Rates fr: *£16.00*-**£16.00**.
Beds: 1D 1T 1S
Baths: 1 Shared
(12) (4)

***Cameron House,** 44 Glebe Park, Kirkcaldy, Fife, KY1 1BL.*
Comfortable, friendly, central, good food.
Open: All Year (not Xmas)
01592 264531 Mrs Nicol
Rates fr: *£14.00*-**£14.00**.
Beds: 1F 1D
Baths: 1 Shared

***Cherrydene,** 44 Bennochy Road, Kirkcaldy, Fife, KY2 5RB.*
Comfortable large Victorian family home.
Open: All Year
Grades: STB 2 Cr, Comm
01592 202147 Mrs Nicol
Rates fr: *£15.00*-**£18.00**.
Beds: 1F 1D 1S
Baths: 2 Ensuite
(3)

***32 Glebe Park,** Kirkcaldy, Fife, KY1 1BT.*
Victorian terraced. Central, quiet location.
Open: All Year (not Xmas)
01592 264656 Mrs Brown
Rates fr: *£13.00*-**£14.00**.
Beds: 1T 1S
Baths: 1 Shared
(5)

The lowest *double* rate per person is shown in *italics*.

Lammerlaws

National Grid Ref: NT2386

Inchview Hotel

Inchcape Guest House, *1 South View, Lammerlaws, Burntisland, Fife, KY3 9BS.*
Large Victorian private house.
Open: All Year
01592 873270 Mrs Sharp
Rates fr: *£15.00*-**£15.00**.
Beds: 1F 1T 1S

Leuchars

National Grid Ref: NO4521

Milton Farm, *Leuchars, St Andrews, Fife, KY16 0AB.*
Charming Georgian farmhouse in 500 acres.
Open: All Year (not Xmas)
01334 839281 Mrs Black
Rates fr: *£20.00*.
Beds: 1F 2D 1T
(10) (6)

Leven

National Grid Ref: NO3800

Burns Tavern (Kennoway)

Duniface Farm, *Windygates, Leven, Fife, KY8 5RH.*
Comfortable farmhouse - ideal holiday base.
Open: All Year
01333 350272 Mrs Hamilton
Rates fr: *£14.00*-**£16.00**.
Beds: 1D 1T
Baths: 1 Shared

Forth Bay Guest House, *Promenade, Leven, Fife, KY8 4HZ.*
Very comfortable large Victorian house.
Open: All Year
01333 423009 Mrs Hamilton
Rates fr: *£12.50*-**£12.50**.
Beds: 2F 2D
Baths: 3 Ensuite 2 Shared
(5)

Lower Largo

National Grid Ref: NO4102

Crusoe Hotel, *2 Main Street, Lower Largo, Leven, Fife, KY8 6BT.*
Open: All Year
Grades: STB 3 Cr, Comm
01333 320759 Mr Jurgensen
Rates fr: *£33.05*-**£53.45**.
Beds: 1F 6D 4T 2S
Baths: 13 Ensuite
(25)
Friendly family-run hotel at waters edge in Lower Largo, birthplace of Alexander Selkirk, Daniel Defoe's Robinson Crusoe (exhibition in hotel). Bar and restaurant meals daily.

Markinch

National Grid Ref: NO2901

Laurel Bank Hotel

Havilah, *2 Balgonie Place, Markinch, Glenrothes, Fife, KY7 6AB.*
Clean comfortable accommodation. Golf centre.
Open: All Year (not Xmas)
01592 758392 Mr Scott
Rates fr: *£16.00*-**£16.00**.
Beds: 2F 1T

Wester Markinch Cottage, *Balbirnie Estate, Markinch, Glenrothes, Fife, KY7 6JN.*
Extended Victorian cottage.
Open: All Year
01592 756719 Ms Tjeransen
Rates fr: *£17.50*-**£15.00**.
Beds: 1D 2S
Baths: 1 Private 1 Shared
(6)

Laurel Bank Hotel, *1 Balbirnie Street, Markinch, Glenrothes, Fife, KY7 6DB.*
Modern family-run hotel.
Open: All Year
Grades: STB 3 Cr, Comm
01592 611205 Mr Drummond
Rates fr: *£21.00*-**£28.00**.
Beds: 2F 1D 5T 3S
(30)

Shythrum Farm, *Markinch, Glenrothes, Fife, KY7 6HB.*
Comfortable farmhouse, 1 mile from Markinch.
Open: All Year (not Xmas)
Grades: STB 2 Cr, Comm
01592 758372 Mrs Craig
Rates fr: *£16.00*-**£16.00**.
Beds: 1F 1T
Baths: 1 Ensuite 1 Shared
(3)

Newburgh

National Grid Ref: NO2318

Baiglie Inn, Aberargie, Burnside Hotel, Abernethy Hotel

200 High Street, *Newburgh, Cupar, Fife, KY14 6DZ.*
Comfortable converted Georgian property.
Open: All Year
01337 840606 Mrs Menzies
Rates fr: *£15.00*-**£15.00**.
Beds: 1F 1D
Baths: 2 Shared
(1)

Easter Clunie, *Newburgh, Cupar, Fife, KY14 6EJ.*
Traditional, stone-built, comfortable farmhouse.
Open: Easter to Oct
Grades: STB 2 Cr, Comm
01337 840218 Mrs Baird
Rates fr: *£14.00*-**£14.00**.
Beds: 1D 2T
Baths: 1 Ensuite 2 Private
(3) (3)

Ninewells Farm, *Woodriffe Road, Newburgh, Cupar, Fife, KY14 6EY.*
Quiet comfortable farmhouse, panoramic views (warm welcome).
Open: April to Oct
Grades: STB Listed, High Comm
01337 840307 (also fax no)
Mrs Baird
Rates fr: *£16.00*-**£20.00**.
Beds: 1D 1T
Baths: 2 Shared
(9) (3)

Peat Inn

National Grid Ref: NO4509

Pitscottie Inn

West Mains Farm, *Peat Inn, Cupar, Fife, KY15 5LF.*
Comfortable farmhouse near St Andrews.
Open: Easter to Oct
Grades: STB Listed, Comm
01334 840313 Mrs Grant
Rates fr: *£13.00*-**£15.00**.
Beds: 1D 1T
Baths: 1 Shared

Pittenweem

National Grid Ref: NO5402

The Anchor Inn, *42 Charles Street, Pittenweem, Anstruther, Fife, KY10 2QJ.*
Meals served all day.
Open: All Year
Grades: STB Listed, RAC Listed
01333 311326 Miss Chung
Rates fr: *£18.00*-**£18.00**.
Beds: 1F 2D 1T
Baths: 1 Shared
(40)

Lawside Cottage, *Easter Kellie Farm, Pittenweem, Anstruther, Fife, KY10 2RF.*
Modernised farm cottages, quiet, scenic.
Open: Mar to Nov
01333 720249 Mrs Howden
Rates fr: *£14.00*-**£20.00**.
Beds: 1F **Baths:** 1 Shared
(4)

Rosyth

National Grid Ref: NT1083

Gladyer Inn, *Ridley Drive, Rosyth Dunfermline, Fife, KY11 2BT.*
Family-run 2 Star hotel.
Open: All Year
Grades: AA 2 St, RAC 2 St
01383 419977 Mr Innes
Fax no: 01383 411728
Rates fr: *£22.50*-**£28.50**.
Beds: 1F 4D 16T
Baths: 21 Private
(97)

The lowest **single** *rate is shown in* **bold**

Saline

National Grid Ref: NT0292

The Saline Hotel, *West Road, Saline, Dunfermline, Fife, KY12 9UN.*
Private and comfortable. Chalet accommodation.
Open: All Year
01383 852798
Miss Gordon
Rates fr: *£17.50*-**£20.00**.
Beds: 3T
Baths: 3 Ensuite
(20)

St Andrews

National Grid Ref: NO5116

Guardbridge Hotel, Playfairs Bar, Dolci Vita (Strathkinness), Restaurant 33

Edenside House, *Edenside, St Andrews, Fife, KY16 9SQ.*
St Andrews 3 miles, waterfront, golfing, birdwatching.
Open: Easter to Oct
Grades: AA 4 Q, Select
01334 838108
Dr Mansell
Fax no: 01334 838493
Rates fr: *£20.00*-**£25.00**.
Beds: 3D 6T
Baths: 9 Ensuite
(10)

Aslar House, *120 North Street, St Andrews, Fife, KY16 9AF.*
Elegant and comfortable Victorian townhouse.
Open: All Year
Grades: STB 2 Cr, High Comm
01334 473460
Mrs Pardoe
Fax no: 01334 477540
Rates fr: *£24.00*-**£25.00**.
Beds: 2D 2T 1S
Baths: 5 Ensuite
(5)

Abbey Cottage, *Abbey Walk, St Andrews, Fife, KY16 9LB.*
C18th cottage with walled garden.
Open: All Year (not Xmas)
Grades: STB 1 Cr, Comm
01334 473727
Mrs Coull
Rates fr: *£17.00*-**£17.00**.
Beds: 1D 2T
Baths: 1 Ensuite 2 Private
(3)

Bell Craig Guest House, *8 Murray Park, St Andrews, Fife, KY16 9AW.*
Comfortable and attractive guest house.
Open: All Year
Grades: STB 2 Cr, Comm, AA 3 Q, RAC High Acclaim
01334 472962 (also fax no)
Mr Black
Rates fr: *£16.00*-**£26.00**.
Beds: 2F 3D 1T
Baths: 6 Ensuite

1 Kilrymont Place, *St Andrews, Fife, KY16 8DH.*
Welcoming and comfortable family home.
Open: All Year (not Xmas)
01334 472335
Mrs W J Chenery
Rates fr: *£13.00*-**£13.00**.
Beds: 1T 1S
Baths: 1 Shared
(10) (1)

Romar Guest House, *45 Main Street, Strathkinness, St Andrews, Fife, KY16 9RZ.*
Imposing modern bungalow, panoramic views.
Open: All Year
Grades: STB 1 Cr, Comm, AA 3 Q, RAC Acclaim
01334 850308 (also fax no)
Mrs Patterson
Rates fr: *£16.00*-**£16.00**.
Beds: 1F 1D 1T 2S
Baths: 3 Private 1 Shared
(5)

2 King Street, *St Andrews, Fife, KY16 8JQ.*
Friendly welcome, fairly central, quiet.
Open: All Year
Grades: STB Listed
01334 476326
Mrs Allan
Rates fr: *£14.00*-**£18.00**.
Beds: 1D 1T
Baths: 1 Shared
(1)

Amberside Guest House, *4 Murray Park, St Andrews, Fife, KY16 9AW.*
Popular Victorian friendly guest house.
Open: All Year
01334 474644
Mr Wood
Rates fr: *£18.00*-**£18.00**.
Beds: 2F 2D 2T 1S
Baths: 5 Private 1 Shared

Spinkstown Farmhouse, *St Andrews, Fife, KY16 8PN.*
Two miles from St Andrews on A917 coast road to Crail.
Open: All Year (not Xmas)
Grades: AA 4 Q
01334 473475 (also fax no)
Mrs Duncan
Rates fr: *£18.00*-**£18.00**.
Beds: 2D 1T
Baths: 3 Private
(4)

12 Newmill Gardens, *St Andrews, Fife, KY16 8RY.*
Modern, comfortable, quiet, private house.
Open: All Year
Grades: STB Listed
01334 474552
Mrs Irvine
Rates fr: *£14.00*-**£18.00**.
Beds: 1D
Baths: 1 Private
(1)

Linton, *16 Hepburn Gardens, St Andrews, Fife, KY16 9DD.*
Spacious Edwardian villa overlooking park.
Open: Easter to Oct
Grades: STB 2 Cr, High Comm
01334 474673 Mrs Pumford
Rates fr: *£17.00*.
Beds: 2D 1T
Baths: 1 Private 1 Shared
(3)

Parkland Hotel & Restaurant, *Double Dykes Road, St Andrews, Fife, KY16 9DS.*
C19th castellated building.
Open: All Year (not Xmas)
Grades: STB 3 Cr, Comm, AA 2 St, RAC 2 St
01334 473620 Mr MacLennan
Rates fr: *£25.00*-**£30.00**.
Beds: 2F 1D 5T 7S
Baths: 8 Private 3 Shared
(15)

Cadzow Guest House, *58 North Street, St Andrews, Fife, KY16 9AH.*
Elegant Victorian town house.
Open: Feb to Nov
Grades: RAC Acclaim
01334 476933
Mrs Small
Rates fr: *£15.00*-**£20.00**.
Beds: 1F 4D 2T 1S
Baths: 6 Private 1 Shared

St Monans

National Grid Ref: NO5201

Mayview Hotel, Cabin Bar

Inverforth, *20 Braehead, St Monans, Fife, KY10 2AN.*
Comfortable homely accommodation, home baking.
Open: Easter to Oct
Grades: STB Listed, Comm
01333 730205
Miss Aitken
Rates fr: *£17.50*-**£17.50**.
Beds: 1D 2T
Baths: 1 Shared
(8)

Strathkinness

National Grid Ref: NO4616

Pitscottie Inn (Pitscottie)

Romar Guest House, *45 Main Street, Strathkinness, St Andrews, Fife, KY16 9RZ.*
Imposing modern bungalow, panoramic views.
Open: All Year
Grades: STB 1 Cr, Comm, AA 3 Q, RAC Acclaim
01334 850308 (also fax no)
Mrs Patterson
Rates fr: *£16.00*-**£16.00**.
Beds: 1F 1D 1T 2S
Baths: 3 Private 1 Shared
(5)

Glasgow & District

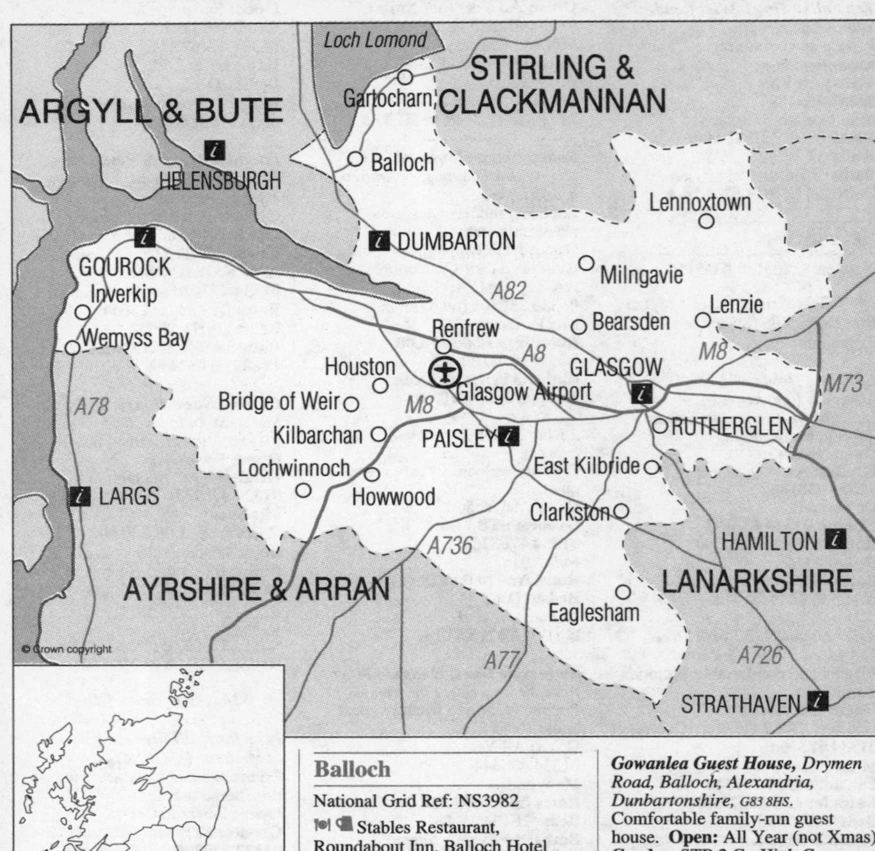

Tourist Information Centres

A82 Northbound, Milton, **Dumbarton**, G82 2TD, 01389 42306, (Easter to Oct).

35 St Vincent Place, **Glasgow**, G1 2ER, 0141 204 4400.

Pierhead, **Gourock**, Renfrewshire, PA19 1QS, 01475 39467, (Easter to Oct).

Town Hall, Abbey Close, **Paisley**, Renfrewshire, PA1 1JF, 0141 889 0711.

Balloch

National Grid Ref: NS3982

Stables Restaurant, Roundabout Inn, Balloch Hotel

***Glyndale,** 6 McKenzie Drive, Balloch, Alexandria, Dunbartonshire, G83 8HL.*
Open: All Year
Grades: STB Listed, Comm
01389 758238 Mrs Ross
Rates fr: *£15.00*-**£17.00**.
Beds: 1D 1T
Baths: 1 Shared
(2)
Comfortable family home within easy reach of Loch Lomond and Balloch Station. Ideal base for Glasgow, Stirling, Trossachs areas. 25 minutes from Glasgow Airport.

***Oakvale,** Drymen Road, Balloch, Alexandria, Dunbartonshire, G83 8JY.*
Beautiful family home - pretty rooms.
Open: All Year
01389 751615 Mrs Feltham
Rates fr: *£16.00*-**£20.00**.
Beds: 2D 1T **Baths:** 3 Ensuite
(4)

***Gowanlea Guest House,** Drymen Road, Balloch, Alexandria, Dunbartonshire, G83 8HS.*
Comfortable family-run guest house. **Open:** All Year (not Xmas)
Grades: STB 2 Cr, High Comm, AA 4 Q, Select
01389 752456 Mrs Campbell
Fax no: 01389 710543
Rates fr: *£18.00*-**£22.00**.
Beds: 2D 2T **Baths:** 4 Ensuite
(4)

***Montrose Cottage,** Ballagan, Balloch, Alexandria, Dunbartonshire, G83 8NB.*
Country cottage 1 mile outside Ballock.
Open: All Year (not Xmas)
01389 750194 Mrs Hendry
Rates fr: *£14.00*-**£14.00**.
Beds: 1D 1T
(4)

***Anchorage Guest House,** Balloch Road, Balloch, Alexandria, Dunbartonshire, G83 8SS.*
Detached cottage. **Open:** All Year
01389 753336 Mr Bowman
Rates fr: *£15.00*-**£20.00**.
Beds: 1F 2D 2T **Baths:** 4 Private
(6)

Bearsden

National Grid Ref: NS5742

Kilmardinny Guest House, *Milngavie Road, Bearsden, Glasgow, G61 3DH.*
Large modern house.
Open: All Year (not Xmas)
Grades: STB Listed
0141 943 1310 Mr Somerville
Rates fr: *£15.00*-**£16.00**.
Beds: 3D 1T 4S
Baths: 8 Shared
(20)

Bridge of Weir

National Grid Ref: NS3965

Trust Inn

Pannell Farm, *Kilbarchan Road, Bridge of Weir, Renfrewshire, PA11 3RN.*
Farmhouse close to Glasgow Airport.
Open: All Year
01505 612480 Mrs McIntyre
Rates fr: *£15.00*-**£15.00**.
Beds: 1F 1D 1S
Baths: 1 Private 1 Shared
(10)

The Gryffe Inn, *Main Street, Bridge of Weir, Renfrewshire, PA11 3NR.*
Comfortable inn located in village.
Open: All Year
01505 613023 Mrs Mitchell
Rates fr: *£22.50*-**£22.50**.
Beds: 2D 4T
Baths: 2 Ensuite
(14)

Dumbarton

National Grid Ref: NS4075

Abbotsford Hotel

Kilmalid House, *17 Glen Path, Dumbarton, G82 2QL.*
Large Victorian manse. Overlooking castle.
Open: All Year
01389 732030 Mr & Mrs Muirhead
Rates fr: *£16.00*-**£16.00**.
Beds: 1F 2D 1S
Baths: 1 Shared
(12)

The Gable, *1 Sutherland Drive, Dumbarton, G82 3NT.*
Clean, comfortable, warm, friendly home.
Open: All Year
01389 732223 Mrs Larkin
Rates fr: *£15.00*-**£18.00**.
Beds: 1D 1T 1S
Baths: 1 Shared
(1)

The lowest **single** *rate is shown in* **bold.**

National Grid References are for villages, towns and cities - *not* for individual houses.

Eaglesham

National Grid Ref: NS5752

Annecy, *60 Montgomery Street, Eaglesham, Glasgow, G76 0AU.*
Attractive cottage in conservation village.
Open: Nov to Sep
01355 302413 Mrs Margetts
Rates fr: *£18.00*-**£20.00**.
Beds: 1D 1T 1S
Baths: 1 Private 1 Shared

East Kilbride

National Grid Ref: NS6354

11 Markethill Road, The Village, *East Kilbride, Glasgow, G74 4AA.*
1920 detached sandstone house.
Open: All Year (not Xmas)
01355 231547 Mrs Gibb
Rates fr: *£15.00*-**£20.00**.
Beds: 4T
Baths: 2 Shared

Gartocharn

National Grid Ref: NS4286

Clachan Inn

Ardoch Farm, *Gartocharn, Dunbartonshire, G83 8ND.*
Open: All Year (not Xmas)
01389 830279 Mr & Mrs Morgan
Rates fr: *£18.00*-**£28.00**.
Beds: 1D 2T
Baths: 1 Ensuite 2 Private
(5)
Set in 130 acres, peaceful rural setting, spectacular view of Loch Lomond. Ideal base for West Coast, Edinburgh, Glasgow, Stirling and Clyde steamers within easy reach.

Mardella Farm, *Old School Road, Gartocharn, Loch Lomond, Alexandria, Dunbartonshire, G83 8SD.*
Welcoming, happy atmosphere. Ducks galore!
Open: All Year
Grades: STB Listed, AA 4 Q, Select
01389 830428 Mrs MacDonell
Rates fr: *£18.50*-**£23.00**.
Beds: 2F 1D
Baths: 1 Ensuite 1 Shared
(5)

Glasgow

National Grid Ref: NS5965

Oachard Park Hotel, Bellahoustow Hotel

Kirkland House, *42 St Vincent Crescent, Glasgow, G3 8NG.*
Open: Mar to Oct
Grades: STB Listed, Comm
0141 248 3458 (also fax no)
Mrs Divers
Rates fr: *£25.00*-**£25.00**.
Beds: 1F 2D 3T 2S
Baths: 6 Private 2 Shared
(1)
City-centre guest house with excellent rooms on beautiful Victorian Crescent in Finnieston (Glasgow's 'little Chelsea'). Short walk to Scottish Exhibition Centre, Museum-Art Gallery, Kelvingrove Park and all West End facilities. Glasgow International Airport 10 minutes. Members of the Harry James Society.

23 Dumbreck Road, *Glasgow, G41 5LJ.*
Large Victorian private house.
Open: Apr to Sep
Grades: STB Listed, Comm
0141 427 1006
Mrs Sinclair
Rates fr: *£18.00*-**£20.00**.
Beds: 1D 1T 1S
Baths: 2 Shared
(5)

Holly House, *54 Ibrox Terrace, Glasgow, G51 2TB.*
Open: All Year
Grades: STB Listed, Comm
0141 427 5609 (also fax no)
Mr Divers
Rates fr: *£20.00*-**£25.00**.
Beds: 1F 1D 1T 2S
Baths: 5 Ensuite
(10) (6)
Situated in an early Victorian tree-lined terrace in the city centre, near Glasgow Airport, Ibrox Stadium, Burrel Gallery, 10 minutes to SEC. Family owned.

4 Holyrood Crescent, *Glasgow, G20 6HJ.*
Large Victorian private town house.
Open: Apr to Sep
Grades: STB 1 Cr, Comm
0141 334 8390
Mrs Adey
Rates fr: *£15.00*-**£18.00**.
Beds: 1F 1D 1T
Baths: 2 Shared

10 Forres Avenue, Giffnock, *Glasgow, G45 6LJ.*
Private house in quiet suburb.
Open: All Year (not Xmas)
Grades: STB 1 Cr, Comm
01850 440234 / 0141 638 5554
Mrs Davies
Rates fr: *£17.00*-**£17.00**.
Beds: 2D
(4)

Kelvingrove Hotel,
944 Sauchiehall Street, Glasgow, G3 7TH.
Open: All Year
Grades: STB 2 Cr
0141 339 5011 Mr Wills
Fax no: 0141 339 6566
Rates fr: *£19.00*-**£22.00**.
Beds: 4F 7D 5T 4S
Baths: 18 Private 1 Shared
Centrally located family-run hotel, set in Glasgow's fashionable West End. Close to pubs, clubs, art galleries, museums, University, shops, rail and bus links - all within walking distance.

The Terrace House Hotel,
14 Belhaven Terrace, Glasgow, G12 0TG.
Friendly family-run West End hotel.
Open: All Year
Grades: STB 3 Cr
0141 337 3377 (also fax no)
Ms Black
Rates fr: *£29.00*-**£45.00**.
Beds: 4F 5D 3T 3S
Baths: 15 Private

16 Bogton Avenue, *Glasgow, G44 3JJ.*
Red sandstone terraced private house.
Open: All Year (not Xmas)
Grades: STB 1 Cr, Comm
0141 637 4402 Mrs Paterson
Rates fr: *£18.00*-**£18.00**.
Beds: 1T 2S **Baths:** 2 Shared
(2)

Botanic Hotel, *1 Alfred Terrace, By 625 Gt Western Road, Glasgow, G12 8RF.*
Large Victorian private house.
Open: All Year
Grades: STB 2 Cr, High Comm, AA 3 Q
0141 339 6955 Mr Soldani
Rates fr: *£21.00*-**£25.00**.
Beds: 1F 4D 5T 1S
Baths: 7 Private 4 Shared

Park House, *13 Victoria Park Gardens South, Glasgow, G11 7BX.*
Large Victorian private home.
Open: All Year
Grades: STB 3 Cr, High Comm
0141 339 1559 (also fax no)
Mrs Hallam
Rates fr: *£25.00*-**£27.50**.
Beds: 1F 3D 1T
Baths: 4 Private 1 Shared
(4)

National Grid References are for villages, towns and cities - *not* for individual houses.

The lowest *double* rate per person is shown in *italics*.

Albion Hotel, *405-407 North Woodside Road, Glasgow, G20 6NN.*
Ideal for seeing Glasgow.
Open: All Year
0141 334 8159 (also fax no)
Mrs Doull
Rates fr: *£25.00*-**£35.00**.
Beds: 2F 6D 4T 4S
Baths: 16 Private
(10)

Glasgow Airport

National Grid Ref: NS4863

Myfarrclan Guest House, *146 Corsebar Road, Glasgow Airport, Paisley, Renfrewshire, PA2 9NA.*
Peaceful, quality, high comfort experience.
Open: All Year
Grades: STB 3 Cr, Deluxe, AA 5 Q, Prem Select, RAC Acclaim
0141 884 8285 (also fax no)
Mr Farr
Rates fr: *£25.00*-**£35.00**.
Beds: 2D 1T
Baths: 2 Ensuite 1 Private
(2)

Gourock

National Grid Ref: NS2477

Anchorage Hotel, *1 Ashton Road, Gourock, Renfrewshire, PA19 1BY.*
Excellent for touring Clyde coast.
Open: All Year
01475 632202 Mr Keenan
Rates fr: *£25.00*-**£25.00**.
Beds: 1F 5D 4S
Baths: 10 Ensuite
(4)

Houston

National Grid Ref: NS4066

The Houston Inn, *North Street, Houston, Johnstone, Renfrewshire, PA6 7HF.*
A pleasant country local.
Open: All Year
01505 614315 Mr McKean
Rates fr: *£20.00*-**£25.00**.
Beds: 2F 2S
Baths: 1 Shared
(25)

The lowest *double* rate per person is shown in *italics*.

Howwood

National Grid Ref: NS3960

Howwood Inn, *Main Road, Howwood, Johnstone, Renfrewshire, PA9 1BQ.*
Open: All Year
01505 703119
Mrs Donnelly
Rates fr: *£18.00*-**£18.00**.
Beds: 1F 1D 2T 1S
Baths: 2 Shared
(50)
Comfortable family-run C18th coaching inn. Ideal touring base for hill-walking, bird-watching and water sports at Lochwinnoch. 10 minutes drive from Glasgow Airport.

Kilbarchan

National Grid Ref: NS4063

Trust Inn, Gryffe Arms (Bridge-of-Weir)

Gladstone Farmhouse,
Burntshields Road, Kilbarchan, Johnstone, Renfrewshire, PA10 2PB.
Welcoming farmhouse ten minutes from airport.
Open: All Year
Grades: STB Listed, Comm
01505 702579
Mrs Douglas
Rates fr: *£15.00*-**£15.00**.
Beds: 1F 1D 1T
Baths: 1 Ensuite 1 Shared
(6)

Lennoxtown

National Grid Ref: NS6277

Glazert Country House Hotel,
Lennoxtown, Glasgow, G65 7DJ.
Family-run country hotel.
Open: All Year
Grades: STB 3 Cr, Comm
01360 310790 (also fax no)
Mr McConnell
Rates fr: *£20.00*-**£34.00**.
Beds: 1D 4T
Baths: 5 Private

Lenzie

National Grid Ref: NS6572

Golden Pheasant (Auchinloch)

16 Laurel Avenue, *Lenzie, Glasgow, G66 4RU.*
Ideal for Glasgow & district.
Open: All Year
0141 776 1634
Mr & Mrs Martyn
Rates fr: *£17.50*-**£22.00**.
Beds: 1D 1T
Baths: 1 Ensuite 1 Private
(2)

ochwinnoch

ational Grid Ref: NS3559

Mossend Hotel, Gateside Inn
Beith), Gable End Restaurant

***ast Lochead,** Lochwinnoch,
enfrewshire, PA12 4DX.*
pen: All Year
rades: AA 4 Q
1505 842610 (also fax no)
Irs Anderson
ates fr: *£25.00*-**£35.00**.
eds: 1F 1T
aths: 1 Ensuite 1 Private
(6)
ountry house overlooking Barr
och. Beautiful location, yet 15
inutes from Glasgow Airport.

***pringfield,** North Kerse,
ochwinnoch, Renfrewshire,
A12 4DT.*
17th modernised mill cottage,
5 mins Glasgow Airport.
pen: All Year
rades: STB Listed, Comm
1505 503690 Mr & Mrs Rothney
ates fr: *£16.00*-**£16.00**.
eds: 1D 1T 1S
aths: 2 Shared
(6)

ilngavie

ational Grid Ref: NS5574

Allander Bar

***Vestview,** 1 Dougalston Gardens
outh, Milngavie, Glasgow, G62 6HS.*
Modern detached, unique, comfort-
ble, convenient to West Highland
Vay.
pen: All Year
rades: STB 2 Cr, Comm
141 956 5973 Mr & Mrs McColl
ates fr: *£18.00*-**£20.00**.
eds: 1F 1D 2T
aths: 3 Ensuite
(6)

***13 Craigdhu Avenue,** Milngavie,
Glasgow, G62 6DX.*
Traditional family house, warm
welcome.
Open: Mar to Oct
0141 956 3439 Mrs Ogilvie
Rates fr: *£15.00*-**£16.00**.
Beds: 1F 1T **Baths:** 1 Shared
(3)

***Grainneag House,** 55 Drumlin
Drive, Milngavie, Glasgow, G62 6NF.*
Large, modern, family house.
Open: All Year (not Xmas)
0141 956 6681
Rates fr: *£15.50*-**£15.50**.
Beds: 2D 1T
Baths: 1 Private 1 Shared
(2)

Paisley

National Grid Ref: NS4863

***Accara Guest House,**
75 Maxwellton Road, Paisley,
Renfrewshire, PA1 2RB.*
Townhouse near Glasgow airport.
Open: All Year
Grades: STB 1 Cr, Comm
0141 887 7604 Mrs Stevens
Rates fr: *£16.00*-**£16.00**.
Beds: 1F 1D 1T 1S
Baths: 2 Shared

***Myfarrclan Guest House,**
46 Corsebar Road, Paisley,
Renfrewshire, PA2 9NA.*
Peaceful, quality, high comfort
experience.
Open: All Year
Grades: STB 3 Cr, Deluxe,
AA 5 Q, Prem Select,
RAC Acclaim
0141 884 8285 (also fax no)
Mr Farr
Rates fr: *£25.00*-**£35.00**.
Beds: 2D 1T
Baths: 2 Ensuite 1 Private
(2)

Renfrew

National Grid Ref: NS4966

Wallace Bar

***Renfrew Guest House,** 4 West
Avenue, Renfrew, PA4 0SZ.*
Very comfortable semi-detached
villa.
Open: All Year (not Xmas)
Grades: STB Listed, Approv
0141 561 1920 / 886 4350
Mrs McHugh
Rates fr: *£15.00*-**£18.00**.
Beds: 1D 1T **Baths:** 1 Shared
(5) (4)

Rutherglen

National Grid Ref: NS5862

***49 Kingsknowe Drive,** Rutherglen,
Glasgow, G73 2AB.*
Traditional bungalow bed &
breakfast.
0141 647 8464 Mrs Boyle
Rates fr: *£14.00*. **Beds:** 1D 1T

Wemyss Bay

National Grid Ref: NS1968

***Beachcliff,** Undercliff Road,
Wemyss Bay, Renfrewshire,
PA18 6AN.*
Private beach. Walled gardens,
panoramic views.
Open: Easter to Oct
01475 520955 Mrs Burns
Rates fr: *£18.00*-**£18.00**.
Beds: 2D 3T **Baths:** 2 Shared
(10) (15)

Planning a longer stay? Always ask for any special rates.

Highland

Tourist Information Centres

Aviemore, 01479 810363
Bettyhill, 01641 521342
Carr Bridge, 01479 841630
Daviot, 01463 772203
Dornoch, 01862 810400
Durness, 01971 511259
Fort Augustus, 01320 366367
Fort William, 01397 703781
Gairloch, 01445 712130
Glenshiel, 01599 511264
Grantown on Spey, 01479 872773
Helmsdale, 01431 821640
Inverness, 01463 234353
John O'Groats, 01955 611373
Kingussie, 01540 661297
Kyle of Lochalsh, 01599 534276
Lochcarron, 01520 722357
Lochniver, 01871 844330
Nairn, 01667 452753
North Kessock, 01463 731505
Ralia, 01540 673253
Spean Bridge, 01397 712576
Strathpeffer, 01997 421415
Strontian, 01967 402131
Thurso, 01847 892371
Ullapool, 01854 612135
Wick, 01955 602596

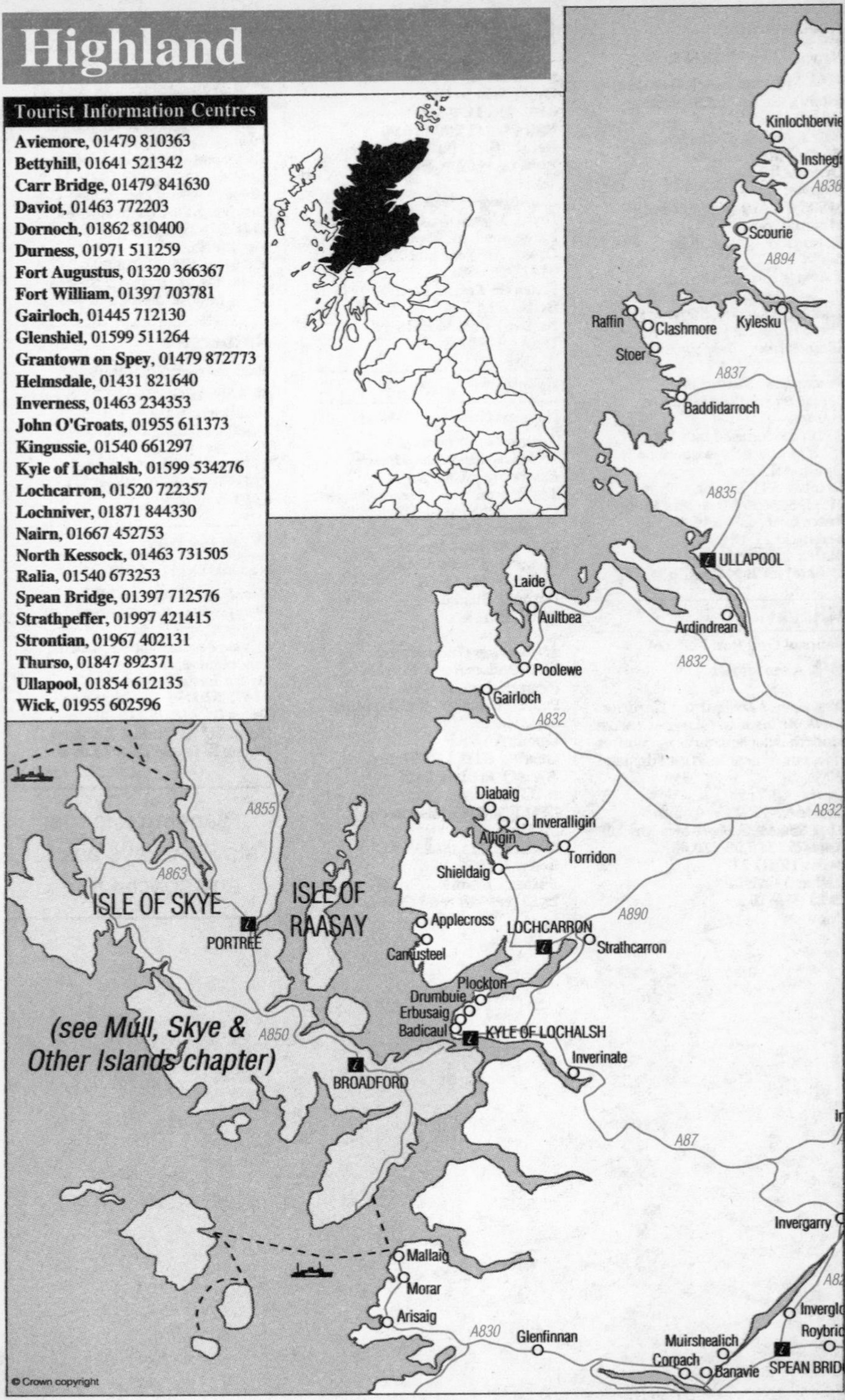

(see Mull, Skye & Other Islands chapter)

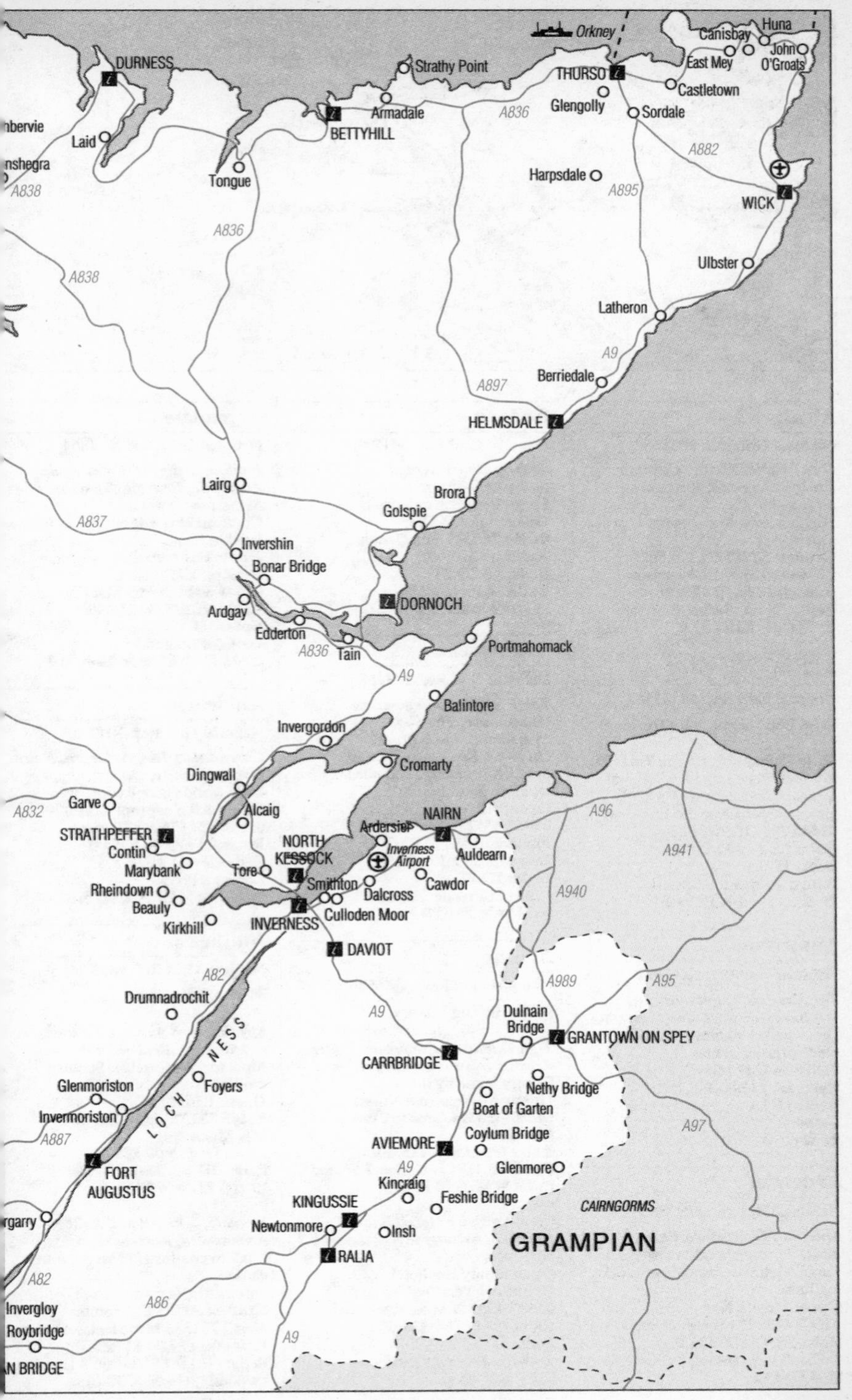
Orkney
DURNESS
Strathy Point
THURSO
Canisbay
Huna
East Mey
John O'Groats
Castletown
Armadale
BETTYHILL
Glengolly
Sordale
A836
Laid
Tongue
A838
A882
Harpsdale
A895
WICK
A836
A838
Ulbster
Latheron
A9
Berriedale
A897
HELMSDALE
Lairg
Brora
Golspie
A837
Invershin
Bonar Bridge
Ardgay
DORNOCH
Edderton
Portmahomack
A836
Tain
A9
Balintore
Invergordon
Cromarty
Dingwall
Garve
A832
Alcaig
NAIRN
Ardersier
STRATHPEFFER
NORTH KESSOCK
Inverness Airport
Auldearn
Contin
Marybank
Tore
Cawdor
Rheindown
Smithton
Dalcross
Beauly
Culloden Moor
Kirkhill
INVERNESS
DAVIOT
A96
A941
A940
A82
Drumnadrochit
A9
A989
A95
Dulnain Bridge
GRANTOWN ON SPEY
LOCH NESS
CARRBRIDGE
Foyers
Nethy Bridge
Glenmoriston
Invermoriston
Boat of Garten
A887
Coylum Bridge
AVIEMORE
A97
FORT AUGUSTUS
A9
Glenmore
Kincraig
KINGUSSIE
Feshie Bridge
CAIRNGORMS
Newtonmore
Insh
GRAMPIAN
RALIA
A82
A86
Invergloy
Roybridge
A9

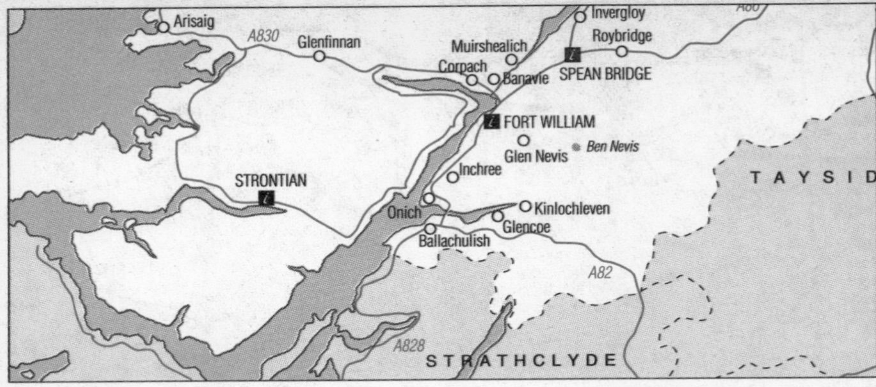

Alcaig

National Grid Ref: NH5657

***Dun Eistein,** Alcaig, Conon Bridge, Dingwall, Ross-shire, IV7 8HS.*
Highland country cottage.
Open: Apr to Oct
Grades: STB 1 Cr, Comm
01349 862210 Mrs Morrison
Rates fr: *£14.50*-**£20.00**.
Beds: 1F 1D **Baths:** 2 Private
(3)

Alligin

National Grid Ref: NG8358

Ben Damph Bar (Torridon)

***Baile Thormoid,** Alligin, Torridon, Ross-shire, IV22 2HB.*
Modern bungalow with superb views. **Open:** April to End-Oct
01445 791325 Mrs Finan
Rates fr: *£15.00*-**£18.00**.
Beds: 1D 1T
Baths: 1 Private 1 Shared
(2)

Applecross

National Grid Ref: NG7144

***The Kennels,** Applecross, Strathcarron, Ross-shire, IV54 8ND.*
Quiet stalker's house. Wild deer.
Open: Easter to Oct
01520 744247 Mrs Griffin
Rates fr: *£12.00*-**£12.00**.
Beds: 1F 1S
Baths: 1 Shared
(2)

Ardersier

National Grid Ref: NH7855

***Milton of Gollanfield Farm,** Ardersier, Inverness, IV1 2QT.*
Large Victorian farmhouse, working farm.
Open: May to Nov
01667 462207 Mrs MacBean
Rates fr: *£15.00*-**£16.00**.
Beds: 2D 1T **Baths:** 2 Shared

Ardgay

National Grid Ref: NH5990

***Ardgay House,** Ardgay, Sutherland, IV24 3DH.*
Large Victorian country house.
Open: April to Oct
01863 766345 Mrs Denton
Rates fr: *£16.00*.
Beds: 1F 3D 2T
Baths: 4 Private 1 Shared
(7)

Ardindrean

National Grid Ref: NH1588

***Taigh na Mara Vegetarian Guesthouse,** The Shore, Ardindrean, Loch Broom, Ullapool, Ross-shire, IV23 2SE.*
Scottish vegetarian secluded lochside guest house.
Open: All Year
01854 655282 Mr Weston
Fax no: 01854 655292
Rates fr: *£19.50*-**£26.50**.
Beds: 2D 1T
Baths: 1 Private 1 Shared

Arisaig

National Grid Ref: NM6586

The Old Library

***Tigh Dobhran,** Camus-an-T'allen, Arisaig, Inverness-shire, PH39 4NU.*
Family home by the sea.
Open: All Year (not Xmas)
01687 450314 (also fax no)
Mrs Hutchens
Rates fr: *£15.00*-**£15.00**.
Beds: 1F 1D 1T **Baths:** 2 Shared

***Croc Na Faire Hotel,** Back of Keppoch, Arisaig, Inverness-shire, PH39 4NS.*
Small family-run hotel.
Open: All Year (not Xmas)
01687 450249 Miss MacDonald
Rates fr: *£17.00*-**£17.00**.
Beds: 3D 2T 2S
Baths: 2 Private 1 Shared

Armadale

National Grid Ref: NC7864

***Poulouriscaig,** 169 West End, Armadale, Bettyhill, Thurso, Sutherland, KW14 7SA.*
Comfortable croft bungalow one level.
Open: Easter to Oct
Grades: STB Listed
01641 541269 Mrs MacKay
Rates fr: *£13.00*-**£15.00**.
Beds: 1D
Baths: 1 Shared
(0) (2)

Auldearn

National Grid Ref: NH9155

***Covenanters Inn,** Auldearn, Nairn, Inverness-shire, IV12 5TG.*
Olde worlde country inn.
Open: All Year (not Xmas)
01667 452456 Mr Harrison
Rates fr: *£23.00*-**£35.00**.
Beds: 2F 4D 2T
Baths: 8 Private
(70)

Aultbea

National Grid Ref: NG8789

Aultbea Hotel

***Strathdale,** 8 Aultbea, Aultbea, Achnasheen, Ross-shire, IV22 2JA.*
Modern, comfortable, Scottish croft house.
Open: Easter to Oct
01445 731373 (also fax no)
Mrs MacAskill
Rates fr: *£15.00*-**£20.00**.
Beds: 1D 1T **Baths:** 1 Shared
(11) (3)

***Sandale,** 5 Pier Road, Aultbea, Achnasheen, Ross-shire, IV22 2JQ.*
Modern comfortable house with garden.
Open: All Year (not Xmas)
Grades: STB 3 Cr, Comm
01445 731336 Mrs MacLennan
Rates fr: *£19.00*-**£19.00**.
Beds: 1F 1D 1T **Baths:** 3 Ensuite
(8) (3)

Aviemore

National Grid Ref: NH8912

Old Bridge Inn, Winking Owl

***Ardlogie Guest House,** Dalfaber Road, Aviemore, Inverness-shire, PH22 1PU.*
Quiet street. Views to Cairngorms.
Open: All Year
Grades: STB Listed, Comm
01479 810747
Rates fr: *£18.00*.
Beds: 4D 1T
Baths: 4 Ensuite 1 Private
(3)

***Waverley,** 35 Strathspey Avenue, Aviemore, Inverness-shire, PH22 1SN.*
Modern comfortable bungalow.
Open: All Year (not Xmas)
01479 811226 Mrs Fraser
Rates fr: *£15.00*-**£16.00**.
Beds: 1D 1T
Baths: 1 Ensuite 1 Private
(8)

***Ravenscraig Guest House,** Aviemore, Inverness-shire, PH22 1RP.*
Family-run guest house.
Open: All Year
Grades: STB 2 Cr, Comm, AA 3 Q, RAC Acclaim
01479 810278
Mr Thompson
Rates fr: *£20.00*-**£20.00**.
Beds: 2F 5D 4T 1S
Baths: 12 Ensuite
(14)

***Kinapol Guest House,** Dalfaber Road, Aviemore, Inverness-shire, PH22 1PY.*
Modern, quiet, central, mountain views.
Open: All Year
Grades: STB 1 Cr, Comm
01479 810513 (also fax no)
Mr & Mrs Hall
Rates fr: *£14.00*-**£16.00**.
Beds: 2F 3D
Baths: 2 Shared
(4)

***Richeldis,** 21 Muirton, Aviemore, Inverness-shire, PH22 1SF.*
Modern, detached bungalow in village.
Open: All Year
Grades: STB Listed, Comm
01479 811074 Mrs Edmondson
Rates fr: *£13.00*-**£15.00**.
Beds: 3T
Baths: 1 Shared
(4)

***Alt-na-Craig House,** 131 Grampian Road, Aviemore, Inverness-shire, PH22 1RL.*
Victorian house - restaurant, bars, garden.
Open: All Year
01479 810378 Mrs Whelan
Rates fr: *£18.00*-**£18.00**.
Beds: 2F 6D 4T
Baths: 7 Ensuite 2 Shared
(12)

***Lynwilg House,** Aviemore, Inverness-shire, PH22 1PZ.*
Spacious, award winning, 1920s country house.
Open: Jan to Oct
Grades: STB 3 Cr, High Comm
01479 811685 (also fax no)
Mrs Cleary
Rates fr: *£28.00*-**£30.00**.
Beds: 2D 1T 1S
Baths: 3 Ensuite 1 Private
(10) (10)

***Sonas,** 19 Muirton, Aviemore, Inverness-shire, PH22 1SF.*
Ideally situated to explore Highlands/ski.
Open: All Year (not Xmas)
01479 810409 Mrs Clark
Rates fr: *£14.00*-**£17.50**.
Beds: 2D 1T
Baths: 2 Shared
(10) (3)

***A`anside Guest House,** Off Grampian Road, Aviemore, Inverness-shire, PH22 1QD.*
Peaceful location with lovely views.
Open: All Year
01479 810871 Mrs Roberts
Rates fr: *£15.00*-**£20.00**.
Beds: 2F 4D 1T 1S
Baths: 6 Ensuite 2 Shared
(8)

Baddidarroch

National Grid Ref: NC0822

***The Albannach,** Baddidarroch, Lochinver, Lairg, Sutherland, IV27 4LP.*
Characterful C19th house by sea.
Open: All Year except Jan & Feb
Grades: STB 3 Cr, High Comm
01571 844407 Mr Craig
Rates fr: *£28.00*-**£44.00**.
Beds: 2D 2T
Baths: 4 Private
(6)

Badicaul

National Grid Ref: NG7529

Tingle Creek Hotel

***The Nest,** Badicaul, Kyle of Lochalsh, Ross-shire, IV40 8BB.*
Modern comfortable bungalow with panoramic views of Isles of Skye and Raasay.
Open: Mar to Oct
01599 534612 Mrs Hedge-Holmes
Rates fr: *£14.00*-**£15.00**.
Beds: 1D 1T
Baths: 1 Shared
(3)

Balintore

National Grid Ref: NH8675

***Balintore Hotel,** Balintore, Tain, Ross-shire, IV20 1UA.*
Family seaside country hotel & hostel.
Open: All Year
01862 832219 Mr Mercer
Rates fr: *£15.00*-**£15.00**.
Beds: 1F 2D 1T
Baths: 4 Ensuite

Ballachulish

National Grid Ref: NN0858

Glencoe Hotel

***Fern Villa Guest House,** Ballachulish, Argyll, PA39 4JE.*
Open: All Year
Grades: STB 3 Cr, Comm, AA 4 Q
01855 811393 Mr Chandler
Fax no: 01855 811727
Rates fr: *£18.00*-**£23.00**.
Beds: 3D 2T
Baths: 5 Ensuite
(5)
A warm welcome awaits you in this village setting surrounded by spectacular mountains and lochs. All rooms ensuite. Dinner home made. Non-smoking.

***Riverside House,** Ballachulish, Argyll, PA39 4JE.*
Modern comfortable family house.
Open: Easter to Oct
Grades: STB 2 Cr, Comm
01855 811473 Mrs Watt
Rates fr: *£15.00*-**£18.00**.
Beds: 2D 1T
Baths: 1 Ensuite 2 Shared
(5) (4)

***Inverlaroch,** Albert Road, Ballachulish, Argyll, PA39 4JR.*
Modern, comfortable, spacious, homely bungalow.
Open: All Year (not Xmas)
01855 811726 Mrs Castles
Rates fr: *£15.00*-**£30.00**.
Beds: 1F 2D
Baths: 3 Private
(3) (5)

Banavie

National Grid Ref: NN1177

Moorings Hotel

***Taormina,** Banavie, Fort William, Inverness-shire, PH33 7LY.*
Modern bungalow in quiet situation.
Open: Apr to Oct
Grades: STB 1 Cr, Comm
01397 772217 Mrs McInnes
Rates fr: *£14.00*-**£14.00**.
Beds: 1F 1D 1T 1S
Baths: 2 Shared
(4)

***Grianan,** 4 Lochiel Crescent, Banavie, Fort William, Inverness-shire, PH33 7LZ.*
Modern, comfortable bungalow.
Open: Easter to Oct
Grades: STB 1 Cr, Comm
01397 772659 Mrs Maclean
Rates fr: *£13.00*-**£20.00**.
Beds: 3D
Baths: 1 Shared
(5) (3)

Algarve Badabrie, *Banavie, Fort William, Inverness-shire, PH33 7LX.*
Magnificent situation within 3 miles of Fort William.
Open: Easter to Oct
Grades: STB 2 Cr, High Comm
01397 772461 Mrs McIntyre
Rates fr: *£17.00*-**£18.00**.
Beds: 2D 1T 1S
Baths: 1 Private 2 Shared
(3)

Fordon, *Badabrie, Banavie, Fort William, Inverness-shire, PH33 7LX.*
Modern house with beautiful views.
Open: All Year
01397 772737 Mrs Wilkinson
Rates fr: *£12.00*-**£12.00**.
Beds: 2F 1D 1T 1S
Baths: 1 Private 2 Shared
(6)

Beauly

National Grid Ref: NH5246

Caledonian Hotel, *The Square, Beauly, Inverness-shire, IV4 7BY.*
Hub of the village for 300 years.
Open: All Year
Grades: STB 2 Cr, Approv
01463 782278 (also fax no)
Mr Campbell
Rates fr: *£17.50*-**£20.00**.
Beds: 3F 3D 3T
Baths: 9 Ensuite
(2)

Wester Moniack Farm, *Kirkhill, Beauly, Beauly, IV5 7PQ.*
Highland hospitality at its best.
Open: All Year
Grades: STB Listed, Comm
01463 831237 Mrs Munro
Rates fr: *£13.00*-**£15.00**.
Beds: 1F 1D
Baths: 1 Shared

Berriedale

National Grid Ref: ND1222

Mulberry Croft, *2 East Newport, Berriedale, Caithness, KW7 6HA.*
Working croft with panoramic views.
Open: All Year (not Xmas)
01593 751245 Mrs Steven
Rates fr: *£14.00*-**£14.00**.
Beds: 1F 1T
Baths: 1 Shared
(3)

Bettyhill

National Grid Ref: NC7071

Shenley, *Bettyhill, Thurso, Caithness, KW14 7SS.*
Homely Bed & Breakfast with sea view.
Open: Easter to Oct
01641 521421 Mrs Allan
Rates fr: *£12.50*-**£12.50**.
Beds: 2T
Baths: 2 Shared
(5) (0)

Boat of Garten

National Grid Ref: NH9418

Boat Hotel, Heatherbra (Nethybridge)

Heathbank - The Victorian House, *Drumuillie Road, Boat of Garten, Inverness-shire, PH24 3BD.*
Open: Dec to Oct
Grades: STB 3 Cr, High Comm, AA 5 Q, Prem Select
01479 831234 Mr Burge
Rates fr: *£24.00*-**£24.00**.
Beds: 1F 4D 2T
Baths: 7 Ensuite
(12) (8)
Cooking with imagination, style, flavour. Chef/proprietor (member Association Culinaire Francaise) awarded 'Taste of Scotland'. Conservatory dining-room. Enchantingly beautiful characterful Victoriana-filled bedrooms. Two four-posters, even a sunken bathroom!

Locheil, *Boat of Garten, Inverness-shire, PH24 3BX.*
Small friendly B & B.
Open: All Year
Grades: STB 1 Cr, Comm
01479 831603 Mrs Davison
Rates fr: *£14.00*-**£14.00**.
Beds: 1D 1T 2S
Baths: 1 Shared
(5)

Ryvoan Guest House, *Kinchurdy Road, Boat of Garten, Inverness-shire, PH24 3BP.*
Open: All Year
Grades: STB 3 Cr, High Comm, AA 4 Q, Select
01479 831654
Mr & Mrs Whiston
Rates fr: *£18.00*-**£18.00**.
Beds: 2D 1T
Baths: 2 Ensuite 1 Shared
(6)
Beautifully furnished Victorian house in wooded gardens with red squirrels overlooking Cairngorms. Cosy lounge with log fire and library of books. Home cooking. Optional dinners. Vegetarians welcome.

Mullingarroch Croft, *Boat of Garten, Inverness-shire, PH24 3BY.*
Comfortable bungalow in rural setting.
Open: Feb to Oct
01479 831645 Mrs Grant
Rates fr: *£14.50*-**£14.50**.
Beds: 2D 1S
Baths: 1 Shared
(3)

Bringing children with you? Always ask for any special rates.

Glen Sanda, *Street Of Kincardine, Boat of Garten, Inverness-shire, PH24 3BY.*
Modern bungalow with view.
Open: All Year
Grades: STB 2 Cr, High Comm
01479 831494 Mrs Lyons
Rates fr: *£17.50*-**£17.50**.
Beds: 2D 1T
Baths: 3 Private
(3)

Steornabhagh, *Deshar Road, Boat of Garten, Inverness-Shire, PH24 3BN.*
Comfortable bungalow in garden setting.
Open: All Year (not Xmas)
01479 831371 Mrs Cunningham
Rates fr: *£19.00*-**£19.00**.
Beds: 1F 1D 1T **Baths:** 3 Ensuite
(2) (6)

Avingormack Guest House, *Boat of Garten, Inverness-shire, PH24 3BT.*
Rural location with stunning views.
Open: All Year
01479 831614 Mrs Ferguson
Rates fr: *£17.50*-**£19.50**.
Beds: 1F 2D 1T
Baths: 2 Private 2 Shared
(8)

Bonar Bridge

National Grid Ref: NH6191

Kyle House, *Dornoch Road, Bonar Bridge, Ardgay, Sutherland, IV24 3EB.*
Superb old Scottish guest house.
Open: Feb to Oct
Grades: RAC Listed
01863 766360 Mrs Thomson
Rates fr: *£17.50*-**£17.50**.
Beds: 1F 2D 2T 1S
Baths: 2 Private 1 Shared
(4) (6)

Rowanlea, *12 Airdens, Bonar Bridge, Ardgay, Sutherland, IV24 3AS.*
Modern croft house, spectacular views. **Open:** Easter to Oct
01863 766440 Mrs Lowe
Rates fr: *£15.00*-**£15.00**.
Beds: 1F 1D 1S
Baths: 1 Private 1 Shared
(6)

Brora

National Grid Ref: NC9004

Ar Dachaidh, *Badnellan, Brora, Sutherland, KW9 6NQ.*
Open: All Year
01408 621658 (also fax no)
Ms MacDonald
Rates fr: *£13.50*-**£13.50**.
Beds: 1D 1T 1S
Baths: 1 Shared
(10) (3)
Traditional croft house in quiet rural setting. Ideal for golfing, fishing, walking or touring. Lochs, brochs and castles abound. Come and sample our highland hospitality.

***Non Smokers Haven,** Tigh Fada, Golf Road, Brora, Sutherland,* *KW9 6QS.*
Open: All Year (not Xmas/New Year)
Grades: STB 2 Cr, Comm
01408 621332 (also fax no)
Mrs Clarkson
Rates fr: *£16.50*-**£16.50**.
Beds: 1D 2T
Baths: 1 Ensuite 2 Private
(5) (10)
Quality accommodation. Prime location, splendid views, peat fire and central heating. Fine food, home baking, large garden with pitch & putt and croquet. Plenty parking.

***Clynelish Farm,** Brora, Sutherland,* *KW9 6LR.*
Large Victorian farmhouse (1865).
Open: Apr to Oct
Grades: STB 2 Cr, Comm
01408 621265 Mrs Ballantyne
Rates fr: *£17.00*-**£18.00**.
Beds: 1F 1D 1T
Baths: 2 Private 1 Shared
(6)

***Sutherland Arms Hotel,** Brora, Sutherland,* *KW9 6NX.*
Small, comfortable, family-run hotel.
Open: All Year
01408 621209 Mr Munro
Rates fr: *£22.50*-**£22.50**.
Beds: 2F 2T 2S
Baths: 2 Shared
(5)

Camusteel

National Grid Ref: NG7042

Applecross Inn, Flower Tunnel

***Camustiel,** Camusteel, Applecross, Strathcarron, Ross-shire,* *IV54 8LT.*
Modern private comfortable house.
Open: All Year
01520 744229 Mrs Gillies
Rates fr: *£15.00*-**£15.00**.
Beds: 2D
Baths: 2 Shared
(4)

***Raon Mor,** Camusteel, Applecross, Strathcarron, Ross-shire,* *IV54 8LT.*
Modern croft house. Wonderful views.
Open: May to Oct
01520 744260 Mrs Thompson
Rates fr: *£14.00*.
Beds: 2D 1T **Baths:** 1 Shared

Canisbay

National Grid Ref: ND3872

***Bencorragh House,** Upper Gills, Canisbay, John O'Groats, Wick, Caithness,* *KW1 4YB.*
Working croft with panoramic views.
Open: Apr to Oct
Grades: AA 3 Q, RAC Acclaim
01955 611449 Mrs Barton
Rates fr: *£17.00*-**£22.00**.
Beds: 1F 2D 1T
Baths: 4 Ensuite
(5) (15)

Carrbridge

National Grid Ref: NN9022

The Cairn Hotel, Rowanlea Bar

***Cairn Hotel,** Main Road, Carrbridge, Inverness-shire,* *PH23 3AS.*
Open: All Year (not Xmas)
Grades: STB 3 Cr, Comm
01479 841212 Mr Kirk
Fax no: 01479 841362
Rates fr: *£16.00*-**£16.00**.
Beds: 2F 2D 1T 2S
Baths: 4 Ensuite 1 Shared
(20)
Enjoy log fires, real ale, malt whiskies, affordable food and weekend entertainment in this family-owned village centre hotel. Reductions for children and longer stays.

***Craigellachie House,** Main Street, Carrbridge, Inverness-shire,* *PH23 3AS.*
Warm comfortable Victorian house, village centre.
Open: All Year
Grades: STB 2 Cr, Comm
01479 841641 Mrs Pedersen
Rates fr: *£15.00*-**£15.00**.
Beds: 2F 2D 2T 1S
Baths: 3 Private 2 Shared
(8)

***Cruachan,** Carrbridge, Inverness-shire,* *PH23 3AA.*
Modern bungalow.
Open: All Year
Grades: STB 2 Cr, Comm
01479 841609 Mrs Campbell
Rates fr: *£13.00*-**£14.00**.
Beds: 1T 1S 1D **Baths:** 1 Private
(12) (5)

***Carrmoor Guest House,** Carr Road, Carrbridge, Inverness-shire,* *PH23 3AD.*
Licensed, family-run, warm welcome.
Open: All Year
Grades: STB 3 Cr, RAC Acclaim
01479 841244 (also fax no)
Mrs Stitt
Rates fr: *£17.00*-**£19.00**.
Beds: 1F 2D 2T
Baths: 5 Ensuite
(5)

***Mariner Guest House,** Station Road, Carrbridge, Inverness-shire,* *PH23 3AN.*
Modern, comfortable, friendly. Quiet area.
Open: Dec to Oct
01479 841331 Mrs Handley
Rates fr: *£18.00*-**£21.00**.
Beds: 2F 2D 2T
Baths: 6 Private 1 Shared
(2) (6)

Castletown

National Grid Ref: ND1967

***Clydesdale Bank House,** Main Street, Castletown, Thurso, Caithness,* *KW14 8TP.*
Family-run comfortable guest house.
Open: All Year
01847 821656 Mrs Munro
Rates fr: *£15.00*-**£15.00**.
Beds: 1F 1D 5T
Baths: 7 Ensuite 1 Private
(3)

***St Clair Arms Hotel,** Castletown, Thurso, Caithness,* *KW14 8TP.*
Small, friendly, family-run hotel.
Open: All Year
01847 821656 Mrs Munro
Rates fr: *£25.50*-**£27.00**.
Beds: 1F 8D 11T 5S
Baths: 25 Ensuite
(6)

Cawdor

National Grid Ref: NH8449

Cawdor Tavern

***Dallaschyle,** Cawdor, Nairn, Nairnshire,* *IV12 5XS.*
Modern house in rural setting.
Open: All Year
Grades: STB Listed, Comm
01667 493422 Mrs MacLeod
Rates fr: *£16.00*-**£20.00**.
Beds: 1F 1D
Baths: 1 Shared
(2) (4)

Clashmore

National Grid Ref: NC0331

***Solus na Mara,** Clashmore, Lochinver, Lairg,* *IV27 4JQ.*
Bright, cosy, welcoming croft house.
Open: All Year (not Xmas)
01571 855396 Mrs Shannon
Rates fr: *£13.50*-**£13.50**.
Beds: 1F 1T **Baths:** 1 Shared
(4)

Contin

National Grid Ref: NH4555

***Achilty Hotel,** Contin, Strathpeffer, Ross-shire,* *IV14 9EG.*
Characterful Highland hotel, beautifully restored.
Open: All Year
Grades: STB 3 Cr, AA 2 St
01997 421355 Mr Vaughan
Rates fr: *£17.50*-**£22.50**.
Beds: 3F 4D 5T

Bringing children with you? Always ask for any special rates.

Corpach

National Grid Ref: NN0976

The Neuk, *Corpach, Fort William, Inverness-shire, PH33 7LR.*
Modern comfortable privately-run house. Home-cooking.
Open: All Year
Grades: STB 2 Cr, Comm
01397 772244 Mrs McCallum
Rates fr: *£16.00*-**£22.00**.
Beds: 1F 2T
Baths: 3 Ensuite
(6)

Clintwood, *23 Hillview Drive, Corpach, Fort William, Inverness-shire, PH33 7LS.*
Modern villa in the village of Corpach.
Open: Easter to Oct
01397 772680 Mrs Macleod
Rates fr: *£20.00.*
Beds: 2F 2D
Baths: 4 Ensuite
(3)

Coylum Bridge

National Grid Ref: NH9110

Bridge Inn, Cairgorm Hotel

Avalon, *Coylum Bridge, Aviemore, Inverness-shire, PH22 1RD.*
Modern country setting, wonderful walks.
Open: All Year
01479 810158 Mrs McCombie
Rates fr: *£17.00*-**£17.00**.
Beds: 1D 1T
Baths: 2 Ensuite 1 Shared
(2) (3)

Cromarty

National Grid Ref: NH7867

7 Church Street, *Cromarty, Ross-shire, IV11 8XA.*
Traditional Scottish townhouse with stepped gable.
Open: All Year (not Xmas)
01381 600488 Mrs Robertson
Rates fr: *£14.00*-**£14.00**.
Beds: 1D **Baths:** 1 Private

Culloden Muir

National Grid Ref: NH7345

Culloden Moor Inn

Westhill House, *Westhill, Culloden Muir, Inverness, IV1 2BP.*
Open: Mar to Oct
Grades: STB 1 Cr, Comm
01463 793225 Mrs Honnor
Fax no: 01667 454509
Rates fr: *£18.00*-**£18.00**.
Beds: 1F 1T 1S
Baths: 2 Ensuite 1 Shared
(4)
In spectacular position 1 mile from Culloden Battlefield, 3 miles from Inverness. Tim and Janet Honnor welcome you to their spacious modern family home.

Culdoich Farm, *Culloden Muir, Inverness, IV1 2EP.*
Warm welcome in C18th traditional farmhouse.
Open: May to Oct
01463 790268 Mrs Alexander
Rates fr: *£15.00.*
Baths: 1 Shared
(4)

Dalcataig

National Grid Ref: NH4017

Glenmoriston Arms Hotel

Burnside, *Dalcataig, Glenmoriston, Inverness, IV3 6YG.*
Modern bungalow, tranquil woodland, 1 mile from Loch Ness.
Open: Easter to Oct
Grades: STB 2 Cr, Comm
01320 351262 Mr & Mrs Douglas
Rates fr: *£16.50*-**£16.50**.
Beds: 2D 1S
Baths: 2 Ensuite 1 Private
(3)

Dalcross

National Grid Ref: NH7748

Cawdor Tavern

Easter Dalziel Farm, *Dalcross, Inverness, IV1 2JL.*
Victorian farmhouse, superb central location.
Open: All Year
Grades: STB 1 Cr, High Comm, AA 3 Q, Recomm
01667 462213 Mrs Pottie
Rates fr: *£16.00*-**£20.00**.
Beds: 2D 1T **Baths:** 2 Shared
(10)

Daviot

National Grid Ref: NH7239

Deerstalker

Torguish House, *Daviot, Inverness, IV1 2XQ.*
Open: All Year
01463 772208 Mr & Mrs Allan
Fax no: 01463 772308
Rates fr: *£16.00*-**£20.00**.
Beds: 3F 3D 2T
Baths: 5 Ensuite 1 Private 2 Shared
(20)
Torguish: Former manse set in quiet rural area, once the childhood home of late author Alistair McLean, who wrote novels such as 'Guns of Navarone', etc.

Glenashdale, *Daviot, Inverness, IV1 2EP.*
Warm welcome assured. No smoking.
Open: All Year (not Xmas)
Grades: STB 2 Cr, High Comm
01463 772221 Mrs Kinnear
Rates fr: *£17.50*-**£25.00**.
Beds: 2D 1T
Baths: 3 Private
(3)

Daviot West

National Grid Ref: NG8160

Deerstalker (Daviot)

Crofthill, *Daviot West, Inverness, IV1 2XQ.*
Modern rural family home.
Open: Easter to Sep
01463 772230 Mrs Lees
Rates fr: *£16.00*-**£20.00**.
Beds: 1D 1T
Baths: 2 Ensuite
(4)

Diabaig

National Grid Ref: NG8160

Croft No 3, *Diabaig, Torridon, Achnasheen, Ross-shire, IV22 2HE.*
Modern, secluded bungalow, log fire.
Open: All Year (not Xmas)
Grades: STB Listed, AA Listed, Recomm
01445 790240
Miss Ross
Rates fr: *£13.50*-**£13.50**.
Beds: 1F 1D 1T 1S
Baths: 1 Shared
(9) (5)

Ben Bhraggie, *Diabaig, Torridon, Achnasheen, Ross-shire, IV22 2HE.*
Comfortable cottage in seaside village.
Open: Easter to Nov
01445 790268
Mrs Ross
Rates fr: *£12.50*-**£12.50**.
Beds: 1D 1T
Baths: 1 Shared
(3)

Upper Diabaig Farm, *Diabaig, Torridon, Achnasheen, Ross-shire, IV22 2HE.*
Comfortable farmhouse beside hill lochs.
Open: Easter to Sep
01445 790227
Mrs Peacock
Rates fr: *£14.00*-**£14.00**.
Beds: 1D 2T
Baths: 1 Shared
(12) (6)

Dingwall

National Grid Ref: NH5458

Donati's Restaurant

18 Millcraig Road, *Dingwall, Ross-shire, IV15 9PZ.*
Quiet, comfortable, friendly family home.
Open: Feb to Nov
Grades: STB 1 Cr, Comm
01349 862194
Mrs Duffus
Rates fr: *£13.00*-**£17.00**.
Beds: 2D 1T
Baths: 2 Shared
(2)

Dornoch

National Grid Ref: NH8089

Eagle Hotel, Own Hotel, Mallin House Hotel

Achandean, *Meadows Road, Dornoch, Sutherland, IV25 3SF.*
Open: Dec to October
Grades: STB 2 Cr, Comm, RAC Listed
01862 810413 (also fax no)
Mrs Hellier
Rates fr: *£18.00*-**£23.00**.
Beds: 2D 1T
Baths: 2 Ensuite 1 Private
(3)
Large, comfortable bungalow. Secluded central position. Off-road parking. Excellent touring. Walks, beach, golf, relaxing. One hour above Inverness. Request brochure. Reknowned for our hospitality in this lovely area.

Rosslyn Villa, *Castle Street, Dornoch, Sutherland, IV25 3SR.*
c.1890, attractive, detached family house.
Open: All Year
01862 810237 Mrs Miles
Rates fr: *£16.00*-**£16.00**.
Beds: 1D 1T 1S
Baths: 2 Ensuite 1 Private
(1)

Mallin House Hotel, *Church Street, Dornoch, Sutherland, IV25 3LP.*
Modern, comfortable family-run hotel.
Open: All Year
Grades: STB 3 Cr, Comm
01862 810338 Mr & Mrs Holden
Fax no: 01862 810810
Rates fr: *£26.00*-**£30.00**.
Beds: 1F 3D 4T 2S
Baths: 10 Ensuite
(24)

Burnside Guest House, *Shore Road, Dornoch, Sutherland, IV25 3LS*
Friendly, comfortable, centrally situated accommodation.
Open: Mar to Nov
01862 810919 Mrs Sharkey
Rates fr: *£16.00*-**£18.00**.
Beds: 1F 1D 2T 1S
Baths: 1 Private 1 Shared
(5)

Trevose Guest House, *The Square, Dornoch, Sutherland, IV25 3QF.*
Comfortable old sandstone house.
Open: Easter to Oct
Grades: STB 2 Cr, Comm
01862 810269 Mrs Mackenzie
Rates fr: *£16.50*-**£25.00**.
Beds: 2F 1D 1T
Baths: 2 Private 2 Shared

The lowest **single** *rate is shown in* **bold.**

Ardencaple, *11 Gilchrist Square, Dornoch, Sutherland, IV25 3HG.*
Comfortable cottage, heated throughout.
Open: Easter to Oct
01862 811024 Miss MacLean
Rates fr: *£14.00*-**£15.00**.
Beds: 3T
Baths: 1 Private 1 Shared
(1)

Drumbuie

National Grid Ref: NG7731

Tingle Creek

Glenmarvin, *Drumbuie, Kyle of Lochalsh, Ross-shire, IV40 8BD.*
Modern crofthouse, picturesque village.
Open: All Year
01599 544380 Mrs Finlayson
Rates fr: *£18.00*.
Beds: 2F **Baths:** 2 Private
(3)

Drumnadrochit

National Grid Ref: NH5029

Ben Leva Hotel, Fiddlers Cafe, Drumnadrochit Hotel

Riverbank, *West Lewiston, Drumnadrochit, Inverness, IV3 6UL.*
Modern architect-designed bungalow.
Open: All Year
Grades: STB 2 Cr, Comm
01456 450274 Mr MacGregor
Rates fr: *£13.00*-**£16.00**.
Beds: 2D 1T
Baths: 1 Private 1 Shared
(5)

Carrachan House, *Milton, Drumnadrochit, Inverness, IV3 6UA.*
Comfortable home. Good touring centre.
Open: All Year (not Xmas)
01456 450254 Mrs MacKenzie
Rates fr: *£14.00*-**£15.00**.
Beds: 1F 2D 1S
Baths: 2 Shared
(4)

Borlum Farm, *Drumnadrochit, Inverness, IV3 6XN.*
Comfortable farmhouse overlooking Loch Ness.
Open: All Year
Grades: STB 2 Cr, Comm, AA 5 Q
01456 450358 (also fax no)
Capt & Mrs MacDonald
Rates fr: *£19.00*.
Beds: 1F 2D 2T
Baths: 2 Private 1 Shared

Glen Rowan Guest House, *West Lewiston, Drumnadrochit, Inverness, IV3 6UW.*
Comfortable riverside house, village setting.
Open: All Year (not Xmas)
Grades: STB 2 Cr, Comm, AA 3 Q
01456 450235 Mrs Harrod
Rates fr: *£14.50*-**£25.00**.
Beds: 1D 2T
Baths: 3 Private

Dulnain Bridge

National Grid Ref: NH9924

Auchendean Lodge, *Dulnain Bridge, Grantown on Spey, Moray, PH26 3LU.*
Comfortable Edwardian country house hotel.
Open: All Year
01479 851347
Mr Kirk
Rates fr: *£21.50*-**£22.50**.
Beds: 4D 2T 2S
Baths: 5 Private 3 Shared
(15)

Balnacrive Guest House, *Dulnain Bridge, Grantown on Spey, Moray, PH26 3LT.*
Set off from road with large gardens.
Open: All Year
01479 851228
Miss Kay
Rates fr: *£16.00*-**£18.00**.
Beds: 2F 2D 1S
Baths: 2 Shared
(10)

Durness

National Grid Ref: NC4067

Caberfeidh Guest House, *Durness, Lairg, Sutherland, IV27 4QA.*
Central for all local attractions.
Open: May to Sep
01971 511215
Ms Marsham
Rates fr: *£14.00*-**£14.00**.
Beds: 2F 2T 2S
Baths: 1 Shared
(6)

Port Na Con House, *Durness, Durness, Loch Eriboll, Lairg, Sutherland, IV27 4UN.*
Converted harbour store.
Open: Mar to Oct
Grades: STB 2 Cr, High Comm, AA 3 Q
01971 511367 (also fax no)
Mrs Black
Rates fr: *£16.50*-**£22.50**.
Beds: 1F 2D 1T
Baths: 1 Ensuite 1 Private 1 Shared
(0) (6)

National Grid References are for villages, towns and cities - *not* for individual houses.

East Mey

National Grid Ref: ND3074

Castle Arms Hotel

Glenearn, *East Mey, Thurso, Caithness, KW14 8XL.*
Open: Easter to Oct
Grades: STB Listed
01847 851608 Mrs Morrison
Rates fr: *£14.00*-**£16.00**.
Beds: 2F 1D
Baths: 1 Private 1 Shared
(5) (4)
House overlooks Castle Mey, Dunnet Head, Orkney Islands. 10 minutes from John O'Groats and Orkney Ferry. Tea and coffee in rooms. Licensed restaurant opposite. French, German spoken.

Edderton

National Grid Ref: NH7184

Ardmore Lodge Hotel, *Edderton, Tain, Ross-shire, IV19 1LB.*
Modern comfortable family hotel.
Open: All Year
01862 821266 Mrs Robbins
Rates fr: *£17.50*-**£19.00**.
Beds: 1F 2D 2T 4S
Baths: 1 Private 3 Shared
(40)

Erbusaig

National Grid Ref: NG7629

Old School House Restaurant, *Erbusaig, Kyle of Lochalsh, Ross-shire, IV40 8BB.*
C19th schoolhouse in idyllic setting. **Open:** Easter to Oct
Grades: STB 3 Cr, Comm
01599 534369 (also fax no)
Mr & Mrs Cumine
Rates fr: *£19.00*-**£25.00**.
Beds: 1D 1T **Baths:** 2 Private
(15)

Feshie Bridge

National Grid Ref: NH8504

Loch Insh Watersports Boat House

Balcraggan House, *Feshie Bridge, Kincraig, Kingussie, Inverness-shire, PH21 1NG.*
Wildlife, walks and cycle routes abound.
Open: All Year
01540 651488 Mrs Gillies
Rates fr: *£25.00*-**£25.00**.
Beds: 1D 1T
Baths: 2 Ensuite
(10) (2)

Fort Augustus

National Grid Ref: NH3709

Lovat Arms Hotel

Sonas, *Fort Augustus, Inverness-shire, PH32 4DH.*
Modern, comfortable bungalow with lovely views.
Open: All Year (not Xmas)
Grades: STB 2 Cr, High Comm
01320 366291 Mrs Service
Rates fr: *£13.00*.
Beds: 1F 1D 1T
Baths: 3 Ensuite
(3)

Appin, *Inverness Road, Fort Augustus, Inverness-shire, PH32 4DH.*
Modern detached bungalow.
Open: Easter to Oct
Grades: STB 2 Cr, Comm
01320 366541 Mr Nairn
Rates fr: *£13.00*-**£15.00**.
Beds: 2D 1T
Baths: 1 Ensuite 1 Shared
(3)

Old Pier House, *Fort Augustus, Inverness-shire, PH32 4BX.*
Beautiful location beside Loch Ness.
Open: Easter to Oct
01320 366418 Mrs MacKenzie
Rates fr: *£20.00*-**£30.00**.
Beds: 1F 1D 1T
Baths: 3 Private
(10) (7)

Fort William

National Grid Ref: NN1073

Pat's Bar, Grogg & Gruel Pub & Restaurant, Moorings Hotel, Crannog Seafood

Distillery House, *Nevis Bridge, North Road, Fort William, Inverness-shire, PH33 6LH.*
Open: All Year
Grades: STB Listed, High Comm, AA 4 Q, RAC Acclaim
01397 700103 Mrs McLean
Fax no: 01397 702980
Rates fr: *£20.00*-**£20.00**.
Beds: 1F 3D 2T 1S
Baths: 7 Ensuite
(7)
Highly commended guest house ideally set at the entrance to Glen Nevis 50 yds from the end of the West Highland Way & 1 mile from the path to Ben Nevis.

Rhu Mhor Guest House, *Alma Road, Fort William, Inverness-shire, PH33 6BP.*
Traditional guest house.
Open: Easter to Oct
Grades: STB Listed, Comm, AA 1 Q
01397 702213
Mr MacPherson
Rates fr: *£17.00*-**£17.00**.
Beds: 1F 3D 3T
Baths: 2 Shared
(7)

Innseagan Holidays, *Achintore Road, Fort William, Inverness-shire, PH33 6RW.*
Open: Easter to Oct
Grades: STB 3 Cr, High Comm
01397 702452
Mr Maclean
Fax no: 01397 702606
Rates fr: *£19.95*-**£29.95**.
Beds: 15D 8T 1S
Baths: 21 Private 3 Shared
Situated in its own grounds on the shores of Loch Linnhe yet only 1.5 miles from the centre of Fort William. Cocktail bar. Full colour brochure available.

Abrach, *4 Caithness Place, Fort William, Inverness-shire, PH33 6JP.*
Modern house in elevated position.
Open: All Year (not Xmas)
Grades: STB 2 Cr, Comm
01397 702535
Mr & Mrs Moore
Rates fr: *£13.50*-**£15.00**.
Beds: 1F 1D 1T 1S
Baths: 2 Ensuite 2 Shared
(6)

Algarve Badabrie, *Banavie, Fort William, Inverness-shire, PH33 7LX.*
Open: Easter to Oct
Grades: STB 2 Cr, High Comm
01397 772461
Mrs McIntyre
Rates fr: *£17.00*-**£18.00**.
Beds: 2D 1T 1S
Baths: 1 Private 2 Shared
(3)
Magnificent situation within 3 miles of Fort William. All rooms have Central Heating. Tea making facilities, parking, hotel, and restaurants nearby. Warm welcome.

Ben View Guest House, *Belford Road, Fort William, Inverness-shire, PH33 6ER.*
Ideally situated close to all services and leisure centre, excellent touring base. Reading and TV lounges. Ample parking.
Open: Mar to Nov
Grades: STB 2 Cr, Comm, AA 3 Q, Recomm
01397 702966
Mrs Smith
Rates fr: *£18.00*-**£18.00**.
Beds: 1F 8D 1T 1S
Baths: 8 Ensuite 1 Private 2 Shared
(16)

Hillview Guest House, *Achintore Road, Fort William, Inverness-shire, PH33 6RW.*
Modernised croft house, family-run.
Open: All Year (not Xmas)
Grades: STB 2 Cr, Comm
01397 704349
Mrs Burton
Rates fr: *£16.00*-**£19.00**.
Beds: 1F 3D 1T 1S
Baths: 4 Ensuite 1 Shared
(5) (7)

'Bardnaclavan', *17 Sutherland Avenue, Fort William, Inverness-shire, PH33 6JS.*
Quiet panoramic situation. Centre 1 mile.
Open: Easter to October
Grades: STB Listed, Comm
01397 704678 Mrs Cameron
Rates fr: *£14.00*-**£15.00**.
Beds: 1F 1T 1S
Baths: 1 Shared

Heston, *Corpach, Fort William, Inverness-shire, PH33 7LT.*
Comfortable house with magnificent views.
Open: Easter to Oct
Grades: STB 2 Cr, Comm
01397 772425 Mrs Wynne
Rates fr: *£16.00*-**£17.00**.
Beds: 1F 1D 1T
Baths: 2 Ensuite 1 Shared
(3) (3)

Corrieview, *Lochyside, Fort William, Inverness-shire, PH33 7NX.*
Comfortable modernised croft house.
Open: All Year (not Xmas)
Grades: STB 2 Cr, Comm
01397 703608 Mrs Turner
Rates fr: *£15.00*-**£15.00**.
Beds: 2D 1T
Baths: 2 Ensuite 1 Private
(6)

Daraich Guest House, *Cameron Road, Fort William, Inverness-shire, PH33 6LQ.*
Stone house overlooking Loch Linnhe.
Open: All Year
01397 702644 Mrs Denney
Rates fr: *£16.00*-**£15.00**.
Beds: 1F 1D 1T 1S
Baths: 2 Shared
(4)

Guisachan Guest House, *Alma Road, Fort William, Inverness-Shire, PH33 6HA.*
Modern, friendly, clean, comfortable house.
Open: All Year (not Xmas)
01397 703797 (also fax no)
Mr & Mrs Rosie
Rates fr: *£18.00*-**£20.00**.
Beds: 3F 6D 5T 2S
Baths: 15 Ensuite 1 Private
(4) (15)

Dorlin, *Cameron Road, Fort William, Inverness-shire, PH33 6LJ.*
Modern bungalow overlooking Loch. **Open:** All Year
Grades: STB 2 Cr, Comm
01397 702016 Mrs Macdonald
Rates fr: *£18.00*.
Beds: 2D
Baths: 2 Ensuite
(2)

Voringfoss, *5 Stirling Place, Fort William, Inverness-shire, PH33 6UW.*
Detached house with large garden.
Open: All Year
Grades: STB 2 Cr, High Comm
)1397 704062 Mr & Mrs Fraser
Rates fr: *£17.00*-**£17.00**.
Beds: 2D 1T
Baths: 3 Ensuite
(5)

Avondale, *Union Road, Fort William, Inverness-shire, PH33 6RA.*
Large Victorian private house.
Open: All Year (not Xmas)
01397 702025
Mrs MacPherson
Rates fr: *£14.00*-**£14.00**.
Beds: 1F 1D 2T
Baths: 1 Shared
(4)

Glenlochy Guest House, *Nevis Bridge, Fort William, Inverness-shire, PH33 6PF.*
Between town centre and Ben Nevis.
Open: All Year
Grades: STB 2 Cr, Comm, AA 3 Q, Recomm
01397 702909 Mrs MacBeth
Rates fr: *£15.00*-**£17.00**.
Beds: 1F 4D 5T
Baths: 8 Private 1 Shared
(14)

Lochview Guest House, *Heathercroft, Argyll Terrace, Fort William, Inverness-shire, PH33 6RE.*
Quiet location, superb views.
Open: Easter to Oct
Grades: STB 2 Cr, Comm, AA 3 Q
01397 703149 (also fax no)
Mrs Kirk
Rates fr: *£18.00*-**£25.00**.
Beds: 5D 2T 1S **Baths:** 8 Private
(8)

The Grange, *Grange Road, Fort William, Inverness-shire, PH33 6JF.*
Large Victorian luxury town house.
Open: Nov to Sep
Grades: STB 2 Cr, Deluxe, AA 5 Q, Prem Select
01397 705516 Mrs Campbell
Rates fr: *£26.00*-**£52.00**.
(6) (4)

Crolinnhe Guest House, *Grange Road, Fort William, Inverness-shire, PH33 6JF.*
Large Victorian private house.
Open: Easter to Nov
Grades: STB 2 Cr, Deluxe
01397 702709 Ms MacKenzie
Rates fr: *£27.00*-**£34.00**.
Beds: 4D 1T
Baths: 3 Private 2 Shared
(6)

Ashburn House, *Achintore Road, Fort William, Inverness-shire, PH33 6RQ.*
Large Victorian private house.
Open: Feb to Nov
Grades: STB 2 Cr, Deluxe, AA 5 Q, RAC High Acclaim
01397 706000 (also fax no)
Mr Henderson
Rates fr: *£20.00*-**£20.00**.
Beds: 4D 1T 2S
Baths: 6 Private 1 Shared
(8)

Foyers

National Grid Ref: NH4920

Foyers Bay House, *Lower Foyers, Foyers, Inverness, IV1 2YB.*
Modernised Victorian villa with cafe/restaurant.
Open: All Year
01456 486624 Mrs Panciroli
Rates fr: *£17.50*.
Beds: 1D 2T
Baths: 3 Private

Gairloch

National Grid Ref: NG8076

Myrtle Bank Hotel, Old Inn

Duisary, *24 Strath, Gairloch, Ross-shire, IV21 2DA.*
Traditional, modernised croft house. Superb views.
Open: Apr to Oct
Grades: STB 2 Cr, Comm
01445 712252
Miss MacKenzie
Rates fr: *£15.00*-**£16.00**.
Beds: 1F 1D 1T
Baths: 1 Private 1 Shared
(10)

Kerrysdale House, *Gairloch, Ross-shire, IV21 2AL.*
Comfortable C18th guest house - peaceful setting.
Open: Easter to Oct
Grades: STB 2 Cr, Comm
01445 712292 Mrs MacRae
Rates fr: *£18.00*-**£25.00**.
Beds: 2D 1T
Baths: 2 Ensuite 1 Private
(3)

Slioch, *Gairloch, Ross-shire, IV21 2DB.*
Peaceful situation scenic views.
Open: May to Sep
01445 712110 Mrs MacKay
Rates fr: *£14.00*.
Beds: 2D **Baths:** 1 Shared
(4)

Horisdale House, *Strath, Gairloch, Ross-shire, IV21 2DA.*
Purpose built for scenic views.
Open: May to Oct
Grades: STB 2 Cr, High Comm, AA 4 Q, Select
01445 712151 Ms Strack
Rates fr: *£17.50*-**£18.00**.
Beds: 1F 1D 1T 2S
Baths: 1 Private 2 Shared
(7) (10)

The Mountain Restaurant & Lodge, *Strath Square, Gairloch, Ross-shire, IV21 2BX.*
Unique, lively restaurant. Themed accommodation.
Open: Apr to Oct
Grades: STB 2 Cr, Comm
01445 712316 Mr Rudge
Rates fr: *£19.95*-**£39.90**.
Beds: 2D 1T
Baths: 3 Ensuite

Burnbridge House, *Shore Street, Gairloch, Ross-shire, IV21 2BZ.*
C19th converted cottage.
Open: All Year (not Xmas)
01445 712167 (also fax no)
Mrs Cuthbertson
Rates fr: *£14.00*-**£20.00**.
Beds: 1F 1D 1T
Baths: 2 Shared
(8) (6)

Garve

National Grid Ref: NH3961

Garve Hotel, Inchbae Lodge Hotel, Achilty Hotel

Birch Cottage, *Station Road, Garve, Ross-shire, IV23 2PS.*
Traditional Highland cottage, modernised.
Open: All Year
Grades: STB 2 Cr, High Comm
01997 414237 Mrs Hayton
Rates fr: *£14.00*-**£15.00**.
Beds: 2D 1T
Baths: 3 Private
(1) (4)

The Old Manse, *Garve, Ross-shire, IV23 2PX.*
Former free church manse c.1860.
Open: All Year (not Xmas)
Grades: AA 3 Q, Recomm
01997 414201
Mr & Mrs Hollingdale
Rates fr: *£15.00*-**£15.00**.
Beds: 2D 1T
Baths: 1 Private 1 Shared
(6)

Glen Nevis

National Grid Ref: NN1272

Cafe Beag

Achintee Farm, *Glen Nevis, Fort William, Inverness-shire, PH33 6TE.*
Open: All Year
Grades: STB 2 Cr, Comm
01397 702240 Mr & Mrs Young
Rates fr: *£14.00*-**£14.00**.
Beds: 3D 1T 1S
Baths: 2 Private
(15)
Beautiful setting at the start of Ben Nevis Footpath and end of West Highland Way. The perfect base for touring, walking, skiing and climbing.

Glencoe

National Grid Ref: NN1058

Glencoe Outdoor Centre, *Carnoch House, Glencoe, Ballachulish, Argyll, PA39 4HS.*
Comfortable bunk-bedded rooms, converted lodge.
Open: All Year
01855 811350 Mr Williams
Fax no: 01855 811644
Rates fr: *£13.00*-**£13.00**.
Beds: 6F 1T
Baths: 2 Shared
(1) (15)

Glencoe Hotel, *Glencoe, Ballachulish, Argyll, PA39 4HW.*
Open: All Year (not Xmas)
Grades: STB 4 Cr, Comm, AA 2 St
01855 811245
Mr MacConnacher
Fax no: 01855 811687
Rates fr: *£24.00*-**£34.00**.
Beds: 9D 6T
Baths: 15 Ensuite
(30)
Situated in Glencoe village on the A82, this well-appointed family-run West Highland hotel offers the traveller the best in Scottish fayre and hospitality. All rooms have private facilities. Please phone for our colour brochure and current tariff.

Dunire Guest House, *Glencoe, Ballachulish, Argyll, PA39 4HS.*
Modern bungalow in large garden.
Open: Jan to Oct
Grades: STB 2 Cr, Comm
01855 811305 Mrs Cameron
Rates fr: *£14.00*.
Beds: 3D 2T
Baths: 5 Private
(10)

Scorrybreac Guest House, *Glencoe, Ballachulish, Argyll, PA39 4HT.*
Secluded large modern bungalow.
Open: Dec to Oct
Grades: STB 2 Cr, Comm, AA 3 Q
01855 811354 Mr Mortimer
Rates fr: *£14.50*-**£17.00**.
Beds: 3D 3T
Baths: 5 Ensuite 1 Private
(7)

Glenfinnan

National Grid Ref: NM8980

Craigag Lodge Guest House, *Glenfinnan, Inverness-shire, PH37 4LT.*
Old Victorian shooting lodge.
Open: All Year
01397 722240 Mr & Mrs Scott
Rates fr: *£15.00*-**£18.00**.
Beds: 1F 1D 1T
Baths: 1 Shared
(5) (4)

Glengolly

National Grid Ref: ND1066

Pentland Hotel

Shinval, *Glengolly, Thurso, Caithness, KW14 7XN.*
Modern house with large garden in quiet location, minutes from town.
Open: Jan to Dec
Grades: STB 2 Cr, Comm
01847 894306 Mrs Sinclair
Rates fr: *£14.50*-**£14.50**.
Beds: 1F 1D 1T
Baths: 1 Ensuite 2 Shared

Glenmore

National Grid Ref: NH9709

Old Bride Inn (Aviemore), Scott House Hotel (Kingussie)

Cairn Eilrig, *Glenmore, Aviemore, Inverness-shire, PH22 1QU.*
Bungalow, panoramic views of Cairngorms.
Open: All Year
Grades: STB Listed, Comm
01479 861223 Mrs Ferguson
Rates fr: *£14.00*-**£18.00**.
Beds: 1F 1T
Baths: 1 Shared
(2)

Glenmoriston

National Grid Ref: NH2912

Glenmoriston Arms Hotel

Burnside, *Dalcataig, Glenmoriston, Inverness, IV3 6YG.*
Open: Easter to Oct
Grades: STB 2 Cr, Comm
01320 351262 Mr & Mrs Douglas
Rates fr: *£16.50*-**£16.50**.
Beds: 2D 1S
Baths: 2 Ensuite 1 Private
(3)
Modern bungalow in tranquil woodland setting at end of country road. 1 mile from Loch Ness. Easy access for east or west coast.

Golspie

National Grid Ref: NH8399

Golf Links Hotel, *Church Street, Golspie, Sutherland, KW10 6TT.*
Small, friendly, family-run hotel.
Open: All Year
01408 633408 Mrs Burns
Rates fr: *£25.00*-**£25.00**.
Beds: 3D 5T
Baths: 8 Private

Kirkton Farm House, *Golspie, Sutherland, KW10 6TA.*
Comfortable, family-run farm-house.
Open: May to Sep
01408 633267 Mrs Murray
Rates fr: *£14.00*-**£20.00**.
Beds: 1D 1T **Baths:** 1 Shared
(4+)

Grantown on Spey

National Grid Ref: NJ0327

Craighynne Hotel

Garden Park Guest House, *Woodside Avenue, Grantown on Spey, Moray, PH26 3JN.*
Victorian house in a garden.
Open: Mar to Oct
Grades: STB 3 Cr, Comm, AA 4 Q, Select, RAC Acclaim
01479 873235 Mr Pattinson
Rates fr: *£20.50*-**£20.50**.
Beds: 2D 3T **Baths:** 5 Private
(6)

Crann-Tara Guest House, *High Street, Grantown on Spey, Moray, PH26 3EN.*
Comfortable Victorian town house.
Open: Jan to Oct
Grades: STB 1 Cr, Comm
01479 872197 Mr & Mrs Logan
Rates fr: *£16.00*-**£16.00**.
Beds: 3F 1T 1S
Baths: 2 Shared

Parkburn Guest House, *High Street, Grantown on Spey, Moray, PH26 3EN.*
Family-run guest house.
Open: All Year
Grades: STB 2 Cr, Comm
01479 873116 Mrs Herbert
Rates fr: *£16.00*-**£20.00**.
Beds: 2D 2T
Baths: 2 Private 1 Shared

2 Mossie Road, *Grantown on Spey, Moray, PH26 3HW.*
Modern, comfortable, bungalow. Rural setting.
Open: Easter to October
01479 872076 Mrs Lawson
Rates fr: *£14.00*-**£15.00**.
Beds: 1D 2T
Baths: 1 Private 2 Shared

Harpsdale

National Grid Ref: ND1356

The Bungalow, *Bachmore Farm, Harpsdale, Halkirk, Caithness, KW12 6UN.*
Modern comfortable friendly farmhouse.
Open: All Year
Grades: STB 3 Cr, High Comm
01847 841216 Mr & Mrs Waters
Rates fr: *£17.00*-**£17.00**.
Beds: 1F 1D 1T
Baths: 3 Ensuite

Helmsdale

National Grid Ref: ND0215

Bunillidh Restaurant

Kerloch, *67 Dunrobin Street, Helmsdale, Sutherland, KW8 6JX.*
Converted fisherman's cottage.
Open: All Year
01431 821396 Mrs Smith
Rates fr: *£13.00*-**£13.00**.
Beds: 1D 1T 1S
Baths: 2 Shared

Broomhill House, *Helmsdale, Sutherland, KW8 6JS.*
Comfortable crofthouse, panoramic seaview.
Open: Apr to Oct
Grades: STB 3 Cr, Comm
01431 821259 Mrs Blance
Rates fr: *£16.00*-**£19.00**.
Beds: 2D 1T
Baths: 2 Ensuite 1 Shared

Fir Brae, *189 Marrel, Helmsdale, Sutherland, KW8 6HU.*
Modernised, traditional croft house.
Open: Mar to Nov
01431 821223
Mrs Grainger
Rates fr: *£12.50*-**£12.50**.
Beds: 1F 1T 1S
Baths: 1 Shared

Hazelbank, *West Helmsdale, Helmsdale, Sutherland, KW8 6HH.*
Converted croft house.
Open: All Year
01431 821427 Mrs MacRae
Rates fr: *£13.00*-**£15.00**.
Beds: 1D 1T
Baths: 1 Private 1 Shared

Alderwood, *157 West Helmsdale, Helmsdale, Sutherland, KW8 6HH.*
Comfortable family home in the country.
Open: All Year (not Xmas)
01431 821538 Mrs Clegg
Rates fr: *£14.50*-**£14.50**.
Beds: 1F 1T
Baths: 1 Ensuite 1 Private

Huna

National Grid Ref: ND3673

John O'Groats

Haven Gore, *Huna, Wick, Caithness, KW1 4YL.*
Open: All Year (not Xmas)
01955 611314 Mrs Green
Rates fr: *£14.00*-**£14.00**.
Beds: 1F 1D 1T
Baths: 1 Shared
Near the sea overlooking Orkney Islands only 2 miles from the John O'Groats-Orkney Ferry, which makes daily return trips.

Inchree

National Grid Ref: NN0263

Glendevin, *Inchree, Onich, Fort William, Inverness-shire, PH33 6SE.*
Large private house, quiet location.
Open: Easter to Oct
01855 821330 Mrs McKay
Rates fr: *£12.50*-**£14.00**.
Beds: 2D 2T
Baths: 1 Private 2 Shared

Foresters Bungalow, *Inchree, Onich, Fort William, Inverness-shire, PH33 6SE.*
Swedish-type bungalow.
Open: Apr to Oct
01855 821285
Mrs Maclean
Rates fr: *£13.00*-**£15.00**.
Beds: 1F 2T
Baths: 1 Shared

Insh

National Grid Ref: NH8101

Bothan Airigh, *Insh, Kingussie, Inverness-shire, PH21 1NU.*
Newly-built croft-type detached house & gardens.
Open: All Year
01540 661051 Mrs McAdam
Rates fr: *£12.50*-**£12.50**.
Beds: 1F 1D 1T
Baths: 2 Shared

Inshegra

National Grid Ref: NC2455

Old School Restaurant & Guest House, *Inshegra, Kinlochbervie, Lairg, Sutherland, IV27 4RH.*
Modern comfortable building. Glorious views.
Open: All Year (not Xmas)
Grades: STB 3 Cr, Comm
01971 521383 (also fax no)
Mrs Burt
Rates fr: *£20.00*-**£26.00**.
Beds: 1F 1D 4T
Baths: 4 Private 2 Shared

Inveralligin

National Grid Ref: NG8457

Heather Cliff, *Inveralligin, Achnasheen, Ross-shire, IV22 2HB.*
Open: Feb to Nov
01445 791256
Mrs Rose
Rates fr: *£15.00*-**£15.00**.
Beds: 1F 1D 1S
Baths: 1 Shared
Enjoy the magnificent scenery of the North-West Highlands. Walk, climb or just relax in well fed comfort. All rooms face south over Loch Torridon.

Invergarry

National Grid Ref: NH3001

Invergarry Hotel, Glengarry Castle Hotel

Lundie View Guest House, *Invergarry, Inverness-shire, PH35 4HN.*
Open: All Year
Grades: STB 3 Cr, High Comm
01809 501291 (also fax no)
Mr & Mrs Davies
Rates fr: *£15.00*-**£17.50**.
Beds: 1F 3D 1T
Baths: 4 Ensuite 1 Private
Set in the heart of the Great Glen, Lundie View is ideal for touring, walking, climbing or just relaxing. We pride ourselves on our hospitality and home cooked meals and would be delighted to welcome you to our home.

***Ardfriseal,** Mandally Road, Invergarry, Inverness-shire, PH35 4HR.*
Peaceful situation. Lovely walks - farmhouse.
Open: Easter to Nov
Grades: STB 1 Cr, Comm
01809 501281 Mrs Fraser
Rates fr: *£14.50*-**£20.00**.
Beds: 2D 1T
Baths: 1 Shared

***Lilac Cottage,** South Laggan, Invergarry, Invergarry, Inverness-shire, PH34 4EA.*
Warm welcome in comfortable accommodation.
Open: All Year
Grades: STB Listed, Comm
01809 501410 Mrs Jamieson
Rates fr: *£13.00*-**£15.00**.
Beds: 1F 1D 1T
Baths: 1 Shared
(6)

***Tigh Na Car Ruadh,** Invergarry, Inverness-shire, PH35 4HG.*
Artistic log bungalow. Mountain views.
Open: All Year (not Xmas)
01809 501359
Mr MacKenzie-Rogers
Rates fr: *£13.00*-**£13.00**.
Beds: 1T **Baths:** 1 Shared
(2)

***1-2-3 Nursery Cottages,** Invergarry, Inverness-shire, PH35 4HL.*
Traditional stone cottage.
Open: All Year
Grades: STB 1 Cr, Comm
01809 501297 Mr & Mrs Buswell
Rates fr: *£14.00*-**£17.00**.
Beds: 1F 1D 1S
Baths: 1 Private 1 Shared
(4)

***Invergarry Hotel,** Invergarry, Inverness-shire, PH35 4HG.*
Atmospheric, family-run Highland inn.
Open: All Year (not Xmas)
Grades: STB 3 Cr, Comm
01809 501206 Mr MacCallum
Fax no: 01809 501 236
Rates fr: *£23.00*-**£28.00**.
Beds: 1F 5D 3T 1S
Baths: 10 Ensuite
(20)

Invergloy

National Grid Ref: NN2288

Corriegour Hotel

***Riverside,** Invergloy, Spean Bridge, Inverness-shire, PH34 4DY.*
Secluded Lochside woodland gardens.
Open: Jan to Nov
Grades: STB 2 Cr, High Comm
01397 712684 Mrs Bennet
Rates fr: *£18.00*-**£25.00**.
Beds: 1F 1D
Baths: 2 Private
(2)

Invergordon

National Grid Ref: NH7168

***Craigaron,** 17 Saltburn, Invergordon, Ross-shire, IV18 0JX.*
Converted fisherman's C19th seafront cottage.
Open: All Year (not Xmas)
Grades: STB 2 Cr, Comm
01349 853640 Mrs Brown
Rates fr: *£16.00*-**£18.00**.
Beds: 4T 1S
Baths: 3 Private 1 Shared
(6)

Inverinate

National Grid Ref: NG9221

Dornie Hotel, Clachan Bar (Dornie)

***Foresters Bungalow,** Inverinate, Kyle of Lochalsh, Ross-shire, IV40 8HE.*
Open: Easter to Sep
01599 511329 Mrs MacIntosh
Rates fr: *£15.00*-**£20.00**.
Beds: 2D
Baths: 1 Ensuite 1 Private
(3)
Situated on the shores of Loch Duich on the main A87, with superb views of the Kintail Mountains, an excellent base for hill-walking.

***Mo Dhachaidh,** Inverinate, Kyle of Lochalsh, Ross-shire, IV40 8HB.*
Modern house with superb views.
Open: All Year (not Xmas)
Grades: STB 1 Cr, Comm
01599 511351 Mrs Croy
Rates fr: *£15.00*-**£15.00**.
Beds: 1F 1T 1S
Baths: 1 Shared
(4)

Invermoriston

National Grid Ref: NH4116

***Georgeston,** Invermoriston, Inverness, IV3 6YA.*
Modern bungalow.
Open: All Year
Grades: STB 2 Cr, Comm
01320 351264 Mrs Greig
Rates fr: *£13.00*.
Beds: 2D 1T
Baths: 1 Ensuite 1 Shared
(3)

National Grid References are for villages, towns and cities - *not* for individual houses.

Please respect a B&B's wishes regarding children, animals & smoking.

Inverness

National Grid Ref: NH6645

Craigmonie Hotel, The Waterside, Dow's Diner, Loch Ness House Hotel, Mairten Lodge, Nico's Bistro, Heathmount Hotel

***St Anns House Hotel,** 37 Harowden Road, Inverness, IV3 5QN.*
Open: Feb to Oct
Grades: STB 3 Cr, Comm, AA 3 Q, RAC Acclaim
01463 236157 (also fax no)
Rates fr: *£22.00*-**£19.50**.
Beds: 1F 2D 2T 1S
Baths: 5 Ensuite 1 Private
(4)
Friendly, small, clean, family-run hotel, 10 minutes walk from town centre, bus and rail stations. Restricted licence. Guest lounge. Lovely gardens. Brochure available.

***Ardgowan,** 45 Fairfield Road, Inverness, IV3 5QP.*
Comfortable Victorian house 10 minutes town.
Open: All Year
Grades: STB 2 Cr, Comm
01463 236489 Mrs Shields
Rates fr: *£16.00*-**£17.00**.
Beds: 1F 1D 2T 1S
Baths: 1 Ensuite 2 Shared
(5)

***Laggan View,** Ness Castle Fishings, Dores Road, Inverness, IV1 2DH.*
Open: All Year
Grades: STB 3 Cr, Comm, AA 4 Q, Select
01463 235996 Mrs Saggers
Fax no: 01463 711552
Rates fr: *£18.00*-**£20.00**.
Beds: 1F 1D 1T
Baths: 2 Ensuite 1 Private
(4)
Attractive, centrally-heated house surrounded by beautiful garden in rural setting, only 3 miles from town centre on B862. Walks through woods and by river.

***Cedar Villa,** 33 Kenneth Street, Inverness, IV3 5DH.*
Modern, comfortable old stone house. **Open:** All Year
Grades: STB 2 Cr, Comm
01463 230477 (also fax no)
Mrs Flaherty
Rates fr: *£13.00*-**£13.00**.
Beds: 3F 1D 2T 1S
Baths: 4 Private 2 Shared

Kendon, *9 Old Mill Lane, Inverness, IV2 3XP.*
Open: Mar to Nov
Grades: STB 2 Cr, Comm
01463 238215 Mrs Kennedy
Rates fr: *£19.00.*
Beds: 2D 1T
Baths: 3 Ensuite
(4)
Family bungalow in peaceful location with large garden and private parking. All rooms ensuite with TV and tea/coffee facilities. Totally non-smoking. Excellent restaurants nearby.

Taransay, *Lower Muckovie Farm, Inverness, IV1 2BB.*
Bungalow on farm, magnificent views.
Open: All Year (not Xmas)
Grades: STB 2 Cr, Comm, AA 4 Q, Select
01463 231880 Mrs Munro
Rates fr: *£17.00*-**£23.00**.
Beds: 1F 1T
Baths: 1 Ensuite 1 Private
(5) (3)

Eskdale House, *41 Greig Street, Inverness, IV3 5PX.*
Open: All Year
Grades: STB 3 Cr, Comm, AA 3 Q, Recomm
01463 240933 Mrs Mazurek
Rates fr: *£15.00*-**£18.00**.
Beds: 2F 2D 1S
Baths: 3 Private 2 Shared
(4)
A warm welcome awaits you in our home. 5 minutes from train and bus station. Ideal centre for touring Highlands. Traditional home cooking. Car parking.

Tanera, *8 Fairfield Road, Inverness, IV3 5QA.*
Warm, comfortable, friendly family house.
Open: All Year (not Xmas)
01463 230037 Mrs Geddes
Rates fr: *£14.00*-**£18.00**.
Beds: 2D 1T
Baths: 1 Ensuite 2 Private 1 Shared
(10) (3)

Strathmhor Guest House, *99 Kenneth Street, Inverness, IV3 5QQ.*
Open: All Year
01463 235397 Mr & Mrs Reid
Rates fr: *£13.50*-**£16.00**.
Beds: 2F 1D 1T 1S
Baths: 2 Ensuite 2 Shared
(6)
Warm welcome awaits at refurbished Victorian home. Comfortable bedrooms and guest lounge. Short walk into town. Theatres, restaurants, leisure centre, golf course and fishing nearby.

The lowest **single** *rate is shown in* **bold.**

Torridon Guest House, *59 Kenneth Street, Inverness, IV3 5PZ.*
Open: All Year
01463 236449 Mrs Stenhouse
Rates fr: *£13.00*-**£14.00**.
Beds: 3F 1T
Baths: 2 Ensuite 1 Shared
(5) (4)
Comfortable, family-run house, 5 minutes from town centre, good food, good beds, and a warm welcome assured.

Hebrides, *120a Glenurquhart Road, Inverness, IV3 5TD.*
Non-smoking guest house with parking.
Open: All Year
Grades: STB 2 Cr, High Comm, AA 4 Q
01463 220062
Mrs MacDonald
Rates fr: *£18.00.*
Beds: 2D **Baths:** 1 Private
(3)

68 Lochalsh Road, *Inverness, IV3 6HW.*
Open: All Year (not Xmas)
Grades: STB Listed, Comm
01463 223020 (also fax no)
Mrs Matheson
Rates fr: *£14.00*-**£16.00**.
Beds: 1F 1D 1T 2S
Baths: 2 Ensuite 3 Shared
(5)
Family-run guest house, 10 mins walk from town centre. Ideal touring base for Loch Ness. See the dolphins in the Moray Firth & much more.

Crown Hotel, *19 Ardconnel Street, Inverness, IV2 3EU.*
Clean, warm, friendly. Excellent breakfast.
Open: All Year (not Xmas)
Grades: STB 2 Cr, Comm
01463 231135 (also fax no)
Rates fr: *£16.00*-**£18.00**.
Beds: 2F 2D 1T 2S
Baths: 3 Private 2 Shared

7 Broadstone Avenue, *Inverness, IV2 3LE.*
Comfortable modern home, ideally located.
Open: All Year (not Xmas)
Grades: STB 2 Cr, Comm
01463 225728
Mrs Sinclair
Rates fr: *£15.00*-**£25.00**.
Beds: 1F 2D 1T
Baths: 3 Ensuite

31 Clachharry Road, *Inverness, IV3 6RA.*
Comfortable accommodation overlooking Caledonian canal.
Open: Easter to Sep
01463 235954
Mrs MacDonald
Rates fr: *£12.50.*
Beds: 1D **Baths:** 1 Shared

Bunillidh, *47 Montague Row, Inverness, IV2 3RD.*
Close to town centre, riverside, theatre.
Open: All Year (not Xmas)
Grades: STB Listed, Comm
01463 225079
Mrs Mcclorey
Rates fr: *£12.00*-**£14.00**.
Beds: 1F 1D 1S
Baths: 1 Ensuite 1 Shared

Edenview, *26 Ness Bank, Inverness, IV2 4SF.*
Victorian home on River Ness.
Open: Mar to Oct
Grades: STB 2 Cr, Comm
01463 234397
Mrs Fraser
Rates fr: *£18.00*-**£22.00**.
Beds: 1F 1D 1T
Baths: 2 Ensuite 1 Private
(4)

Doinard Guest House, *39 Old Edinburgh Road, Inverness, IV2 3HJ.*
Large Victorian guest house.
Open: All Year
Grades: STB 2 Cr, High Comm, AA 4 Q, Select
01463 233557
Mrs Fraser
Fax no: 01463 710526
Rates fr: *£18.00*-**£25.00**.
Beds: 2D 1T
Baths: 3 Private
(12) (10)

Malvern, *54 Kenneth Street, Inverness, IV3 5PZ.*
Large detached Victorian house.
Open: All Year
Grades: STB 2 Cr, Comm, AA 3 Q
01463 242251 Mrs McKenzie
Rates fr: *£15.00*-**£15.00**.
Beds: 2F 1D 1T
Baths: 2 Ensuite 1 Shared
(7) (6)

5 Muirfield Gardens, *Inverness, IV2 4HF.*
Comfortable accommodation and warm welcome.
Open: All Year (not Xmas)
Grades: STB 1 Cr, Comm
01463 238114
Mrs MacDonald
Rates fr: *£14.00*-**£18.00**.
Beds: 2D 1T
Baths: 2 Shared
(3)

Winmar House Hotel, *Kenneth Street, Inverness, IV3 5QG.*
Family-run, 5 minutes from town centre.
Open: All Year (not Xmas)
Grades: STB 2 Cr, Comm
01463 239328 (also fax no)
Mrs Maclellan
Rates fr: *£15.00*-**£20.00**.
Beds: 3F 3D 3T 1S
Baths: 3 Ensuite 3 Private 2 Shared
(10)

Ivybank Guest House, *28 Old Edinburgh Road, Inverness, IV2 3HJ.*
Delightful C19th house with tower.
Open: All Year
01463 232796 Mrs Cameron
Rates fr: *£16.00*-**£16.00**.
Beds: 3D 1T 1S
Baths: 2 Private 1 Shared
(13) (8)

St Vincents, *12a Diriebught Road, Millburn, Inverness, IV2 3QW.*
Modern house, comfortable spacious rooms.
Open: All Year
Grades: STB 2 Cr, Comm
01463 224717 Mr & Mrs Campbell
Rates fr: *£17.00*.
Beds: 1F 1D 1T
Baths: 2 Ensuite 1 Private
(4)

Carbisdale, *43 Charles Street, Inverness, IV2 3AH.*
Large comfortable Victorian family home. **Open:** All Year
Grades: STB 1 Cr, Comm
01463 225689 (also fax no)
Mrs Chisholm
Rates fr: *£14.00*-**£14.00**.
Beds: 2D 1T
Baths: 2 Shared

Invershin

National Grid Ref: NH5796

Trading Post Bistro (Bonar Bridge)

Gneiss House, *Balchraggan, Invershin, Lairg, Sutherland, IV27 4ET.*
Happy, homely, comfortable ensuite bungalow.
Open: All Year (not Xmas)
Grades: STB 2 Cr, High Comm
01549 421282 (also fax no)
Mrs Brinklow
Rates fr: *£15.00*-**£20.00**.
Beds: 1F 1D 1T **Baths:** 3 Ensuite
(3)

John O'Groats

National Grid Ref: ND3773

Bencorragh House, *Upper Gills, Canisbay, John O'Groats, Wick, Caithness, KW1 4YB.*
Working croft with panoramic views.
Open: Apr to Oct
Grades: AA 3 Q, RAC Acclaim
01955 611449
Mrs Barton
Rates fr: *£17.00*-**£22.00**.
Beds: 1F 2D 1T
Baths: 4 Ensuite
(5) (15)

The lowest *double* rate per person is shown in *italics*.

Kincraig

National Grid Ref: NH8305

Loch Inch Restaurant, Kith & Kin Inn, Boathouse Restaurant

Grampian View, *Kincraig, Kingussie, Inverness-shire, PH21 1NA.*
Elegant well-maintained Victorian house.
Open: All Year
Grades: STB 2 Cr, Comm
01540 651383
Mrs Neck
Rates fr: *£17.00*-**£17.00**.
Beds: 2D 2T 1S
Baths: 5 Private
(5)

Kirkbeag, *Milehead, Kincraig, Kingussie, Inverness-shire, PH21 1ND.*
Converted C19th church, quiet location.
Open: All Year
Grades: STB Listed, Comm
01540 651298
Mrs Paisley
Rates fr: *£15.00*-**£19.00**.
Beds: 1D 1T
Baths: 2 Shared
(6)

Ossian Hotel, *Kincraig, Kingussie, Inverness-shire, PH21 1QD.*
Family -run hotel in beautiful village.
Open: Feb to Dec
Grades: STB 4 Cr, Comm
01540 651242
Mrs Rainbow
Fax no: 01540 651633
Rates fr: *£18.50*-**£18.50**.
Beds: 2F 3D 2T 2S
Baths: 9 Private
(20)

Braeriach Guest House, *Kincraig, Kingussie, Inverness-shire, PH21 1QA.*
River and mountain views, extremely comfortable.
Open: All Year
Grades: STB 3 Cr, Comm
01540 651369
Mrs Johnson
Rates fr: *£18.00*.
Beds: 1F 2D 1T
Baths: 4 Ensuite
(4)

March House Guest House, *Feshiebridge, Kincraig, Kingussie, Inverness-shire, PH21 1NG.*
Outstanding location, delicious fresh food.
Open: Dec to Oct
Grades: STB 3 Cr, High Comm
01540 651388 (also fax no)
Mrs Hayes
Rates fr: *£18.00*-**£20.00**.
Beds: 1F 2D 3T
Baths: 5 Ensuite 1 Private
(8)

Balcraggan House, *Feshie Bridge, Kincraig, Kingussie, Inverness-shire, PH21 1NG.*
Wildlife, walks and cycle routes abound.
Open: All Year
01540 651488
Mrs Gillies
Rates fr: *£25.00*-**£25.00**.
Beds: 1D 1T
Baths: 2 Ensuite
(10) (2)

Insh Hall, *Kincraig, Kingussie, Inverness-shire, PH21 1NU.*
100 yards from beach.
Open: All Year
01540 651272
The Secretary
Fax no: 01540 651208
Rates fr: *£11.50*.
Beds: 10F 10T
Baths: 20 Ensuite
(15+)

Kingussie

National Grid Ref: NH7500

Scot House Hotel, Tipsy Laird

The Osprey Hotel, *Kingussie, Inverness-shire, PH21 1EN.*
Open: All Year
Grades: STB 3 Cr, Comm, AA 1 St
01540 661510 (also fax no)
Mr Burrow
Rates fr: *£23.00*-**£23.00**.
Beds: 3D 3T 2S
Baths: 6 Ensuite 2 Private
(8)
Small hotel in Area of Outstanding Natural Beauty, offering warm welcome, ensuite accommodation and award-winning food. Ideal base for touring, walking, golf, fishing, etc.

Bhuna Monadh, *85 High Street, Kingussie, Inverness-shire, PH21 1HX.*
Recently refurbished Listed building.
Open: All Year
Grades: STB 2 Cr, Comm
01540 661186 / 0385 931345
Ms Gibson
Rates fr: *£16.00*-**£16.00**.
Beds: 1D 1T
Baths: 2 Ensuite
(5)

Arden House, *Newtonmore Road, Kingussie, Inverness-shire, PH21 1HE.*
Comfortable Scottish Victorian villa.
Open: All Year (not Xmas)
Grades: STB 1 Cr, Comm
01540 661369 (also fax no)
Mrs Spry
Rates fr: *£17.00*-**£17.00**.
Beds: 1F 3D 1T 1S
Baths: 1 Ensuite 2 Shared

Glengarry, *East Terrace, Kingussie, Inverness-shire,* *PH21 1JS.*
Traditional stone villa, attractive gardens.
Open: All Year
Grades: STB 2 Cr, High Comm
01540 661386
Mr & Mrs Short
Rates fr: *£17.00*-**£19.00**.
Beds: 2D 2S
Baths: 1 Ensuite 1 Shared
(4)

Ruthven Farmhouse, *Kingussie, Inverness-shire,* *PH21 1NR.*
Spacious house in landscaped grounds.
Open: All Year
01540 661226
Mrs Morris
Rates fr: *£15.00*-**£15.50**.
Beds: 2D 1T
Baths: 3 Private
(10) (7)

St Helens, *Ardbroilach Road, Kingussie, Inverness-shire,* *PH21 1JX.*
Elegant Victorian private house.
Open: All Year
Grades: STB 2 Cr, High Comm
01540 661430
Mrs Jarratt
Rates fr: *£22.00*-**£38.00**.
Beds: 2D 1T
Baths: 3 Private
(4)

Greystones, *Acres Road, Kingussie, Inverness-shire,* *PH21 1LA.*
Secluded Victorian family home.
Open: All Year
Grades: STB Listed, Comm
01540 661052
Mr & Mrs Johnstone
Fax no: 01540 662162
Rates fr: *£16.00*-**£16.00**.
Beds: 1F 1D 1T
Baths: 2 Shared
(1mth) (6)

Kinlochbervie

National Grid Ref: NC2455

Old School Restaurant & Guest House, *Inshegra, Kinlochbervie, Lairg, Sutherland,* *IV27 4RH.*
Modern comfortable building. Glorious views.
Open: All Year (not Xmas)
Grades: STB 3 Cr, Comm
01971 521383 (also fax no)
Mrs Burt
Rates fr: *£20.00*-**£26.00**.
Beds: 1F 1D 4T
Baths: 4 Private 2 Shared
(12)

Kinlochleven

National Grid Ref: NN1861

Edencoille, *Garbhien Road, Kinlochleven, Argyll,* *PA40 4SE.*
Friendly, comfortable Bed & Breakfast. **Open:** All Year
Grades: STB 1 Cr, Comm
01855 831358 Mrs Robertson
Rates fr: *£15.00*-**£20.00**.
Beds: 1F 2T **Baths:** 2 Shared
(3)

Macdonald Hotel and Camp Site, *Fort William Road, Kinlochleven, Argyll,* *PA40 4QL.*
Modern hotel - two bars, restaurant. **Open:** Mar to Dec
01855 831539 Mr Macdonald
Rates fr: *£18.00*-**£25.00**.
Beds: 1F 4D 5T
Baths: 8 Private 2 Shared
(30)

Mamore Lodge Hotel, *Kinlochleven, Argyll,* *PA40 4QN.*
Victorian lodge on eyrie-like perch 650 foot above the village.
Open: All Year
01855 831213 Mr Bush
Rates fr: *£16.00*-**£21.00**.
Beds: 2F 5D 6T 1S
Baths: 15 Ensuite 2 Shared
(50)

Kirkhill

National Grid Ref: NH5545

Wester Moniack Farm, *Kirkhill, Inverness,* *IV5 7PQ.*
Highland hospitality at its best.
Open: All Year
Grades: STB Listed, Comm
01463 831237 Mrs Munro
Rates fr: *£13.00*-**£15.00**.
Beds: 1F 1D **Baths:** 1 Shared

Boe Roy Inn, *Kirkhill, Inverness,* *IV5 7PX.*
Modern, updated former inn.
Open: All Year (not Xmas)
Grades: STB 4 Cr, Comm, AA 2 St
01463 831296 Mr MacKay
Rates fr: *£22.50*-**£25.00**.
Beds: 2F 4D 2T 2S
Baths: 10 Private
(80)

Kyle of Lochalsh

National Grid Ref: NG7627

Tingle Creek Hotel

The Nest, *Badicaul, Kyle of Lochalsh, Ross-shire,* *IV40 8BB.*
Open: Mar to Oct
01599 534612 Mrs Hedge-Holmes
Rates fr: *£14.00*-**£15.00**.
Beds: 1D 1T
Baths: 1 Shared
(3)
Modern comfortable bungalow with panoramic views of Isles of Skye and Raasay. Hearty breakfast and very warm welcome.

Kylesku

National Grid Ref: NC2233

Newton Lodge, *Kylesku, Lairg, Sutherland,* *IV27 4HW.*
Lovely new small hotel, spectacular scenery.
Open: Easter to mid-Oct
Grades: STB 3 Cr, High Comm, AA 4 Q
01971 502070 Mr & Mrs Brauer
Rates fr: *£26.00*-**£26.00**.
Beds: 4D 3T
Baths: 7 Private
(12)

Laid

National Grid Ref: NC4159

Choraidh Croft, *94 Laid, Laid, Loch Eriboll, Lairg, Sutherland,* *IV27 4UN.*
Modern bungalow on working farm.
Open: Easter to Oct
01971 511235 Mrs Smith
Rates fr: *£13.00*-**£13.00**.
Beds: 1F 1T
Baths: 1 Private 1 Shared
(14)

Laide

National Grid Ref: NG8992

The Old Smiddy Guest House, *Laide, Gairloch, Achnasheen, Ross-shire,* *IV22 2NB.*
Open: Mar to Nov
Grades: STB 3 Cr, High Comm
01445 731425 (also fax no)
Mr & Mrs MacDonald
Rates fr: *£24.00*-**£24.00**.
Beds: 1F 1D
Baths: 1 Ensuite 1 Private
(6)
Enjoy spectacular scenery by daylight, returning to genuine Highland hospitality offered by Steve and Kate, who personally ensure the highest standards in imaginative home cooking and accommodation.

Ocean View Hotel, *Sand, Laide, Achnasheen, Ross-shire,* *IV22 2ND.*
Small family hotel.
Open: All Year
Grades: STB 3 Cr, Approv
01445 731385
Mr Cunningham
Rates fr: *£15.00*-**£15.00**.
Beds: 3D 2T 2S
Baths: 7 Ensuite
(40)

Cul Na Mara, *Sand Passage, Laide, Achnasheen, Ross-shire,* *IV22 2ND.*
Modern comfortable Highland house.
Open: All Year (not Xmas)
Grades: STB 2 Cr, High Comm
01445 731295 Mr Hart
Rates fr: *£19.00*-**£29.00**.
Beds: 1F 1D
Baths: 2 Ensuite
(2) (4)

Lairg

National Grid Ref: NC5806

Nip Inn

***Carnbren**, Lairg, Sutherland, IV27 4AY.*
Modern chalet bungalow.
Open: Mar to Nov
01549 402259 Mrs MacKenzie
Rates fr: *£15.00*-**£22.00**.
Beds: 2D 1T
Baths: 1 Ensuite 1 Shared
(3)

***Tordarroch**, Main Street, Lairg, Sutherland, IV27 4DB.*
Comfortable bungalow with magnificent view.
Open: Easter to Oct
01549 402235 (also fax no)
Mrs Macdonald
Rates fr: *£16.00*.
Beds: 1F 1D 1T
Baths: 1 Ensuite 1 Shared
(3)

***Windy Heights**, Tomich, Lairg, Sutherland, IV27 4DQ.*
Modern, comfortable house with view. **Open:** Easter to Oct
01549 402282 (also fax no)
Mrs Young
Rates fr: *£15.00*-**£18.00**.
Beds: 1F 1D 1T
Baths: 1 Ensuite 1 Shared
(5) (4)

***Strathwin**, Lairg, Sutherland, IV27 4AZ.*
Modern bungalow overlooking little Loch Shin.
Open: May to Oct
01459 402487 Mrs Paterson
Rates fr: *£13.50*-**£14.00**.
Beds: 2D 1T
Baths: 1 Shared

***Ambleside**, Lochside, Lairg, Sutherland, IV27 4EG.*
Recently built bungalow overlooking Loch Shin.
Open: Apr to Oct
01549 402130 Mrs Fraser
Rates fr: *£15.50*-**£19.50**.
Beds: 1F 2D
Baths: 3 Ensuite
(3)

Latheron

National Grid Ref: ND1933

Latheroncoheel Hotel

***Upper Latheron Farm**, Latheron, Caithness, KW5 6DT.*
Farmhouse in Highlands. Riding available.
Open: May to Oct
Grades: STB Listed, High Comm, AA 3 Q
01593 741224 Mrs Sinclair
Rates fr: *£14.00*-**£16.00**.
Beds: 1F 1D 1T
Baths: 1 Shared
(6) (6)

***Tacher**, Latheron, Caithness, KW5 6DX.*
On A895 (Thurso). Modern, comfortable farmhouse.
Open: May to Sep
Grades: STB 2 Cr, Comm
01593 741313 Mrs Falconer
Rates fr: *£14.00*-**£16.00**.
Beds: 1F 1D 1T
Baths: 1 Ensuite 1 Shared
(8)

Lochcarron

National Grid Ref: NG8939

Rockvilla Hotel

***Aultsigh**, Croft Road, Lochcarron, Strathcarron, Ross-shire, IV54 8YA.*
Ideal base for climbing, sightseeing. **Open:** All Year
Grades: STB Listed, Comm
01520 722558 Ms Innes
Rates fr: *£15.00*-**£16.00**.
Beds: 2D 1T **Baths:** 2 Shared
(4)

***Corrack**, Main Street, Lochcarron, Strathcarron, Ross-shire, IV54 8YB.*
Comfortable, central, lochside family home.
Open: All Year (not Xmas)
01520 722647 Mrs Coppock
Rates fr: *£13.50*-**£15.00**.
Beds: 2T 1S **Baths:** 2 Shared
(2)

Mallaig

National Grid Ref: NM6796

Marine Hotel

***Marine Hotel**, Mallaig, Inverness-shire, PH41 4PY.*
Family-run 'Taste of Scotland' hotel. **Open:** All Year (not Xmas)
Grades: STB 3 Cr, Comm, AA 2 St, RAC 2 St
01687 462217 Mr Ironside
Fax no: 01687 462821
Rates fr: *£24.00*-**£25.00**.
Beds: 2F 5D 9T 3S
Baths: 19 Private
(2)

***Seaview**, Mallaig, Inverness-shire, PH41 4QS.*
Comfortable near train/ferry services overlooking harbour.
Open: All Year (not Xmas)
Grades: STB Listed, Approv
01687 462059 Mrs King
Rates fr: *£12.00*-**£15.00**.
Beds: 1D 1T **Baths:** 2 Shared
(4)

***Spring Bank Guest House**, East Bay, Mallaig, Inverness-shire, PH41 4QF.*
Tastefully improved early Victorian house.
Open: All Year (not Xmas)
01687 462459 Mr Smith
Rates fr: *£13.00*-**£13.00**.
Beds: 1F 1D 1T 1S
Baths: 1 Shared

Marybank

National Grid Ref: NH4853

Achilty Hotel (Contin)

***Birchgrove**, Arcan, Birchgrove, Marybank, Muir of Ord, Ross-shire, IV6 7UL.*
Modernised, comfortable country house.
Open: Easter to Oct
01997 433245 Mrs Bell
Rates fr: *£14.00*-**£14.00**.
Beds: 1F 1D 1T
Baths: 1 Shared
(3)

Morar

National Grid Ref: NM6793

Marine Hotel (Mallaig)

***Sunset**, Morar, Mallaig, Inverness-shire, PH40 4PA.*
Comfortable family guest house.
Open: All Year
Grades: STB 1 Cr, Approv
01687 462259
Mrs Clulow
Rates fr: *£12.50*-**£14.00**.
Beds: 1F 2D 1T
Baths: 1 Shared
(5)

***Glengorm**, Morar, Mallaig, Inverness-shire, .*
Guest's quote - 'Home from Home'.
Open: All Year
Grades: STB 1 Cr, Comm
01687 462165 Mrs Stewart
Rates fr: *£13.00*.
Beds: 1D 1T
Baths: 1 Shared
(4)

Muirshealich

National Grid Ref: NN1380

***Strone Farm**, Muirshealich, Banavie, Fort William, Inverness-shire, PH33 7PB.*
Well appointed rural farm house.
Open: Jan to Sep
01397 712773 Mrs Cameron
Rates fr: *£14.00*-**£17.00**.
Beds: 2D 1T
Baths: 2 Private
(3)

Nairn

National Grid Ref: NH8856

Newton Hotel

***Braeval Hotel**, Crescent Road, Nairn, Ross-shire, IV12 4NB.*
Small family-run seaside hotel.
Open: All Year (not Xmas)
Grades: STB 3 Cr, Comm
01667 452341 Mr & Mrs Gordon
Rates fr: *£25.00*-**£25.00**.
Beds: 1F 2D 2T 2S
Baths: 7 Ensuite

Alltan Donn House, *Alton Burn Road, Nairn, Ross-shire, IV12 5NB.*
Luxury accommodation in mansion house. **Open:** All Year (not Xmas)
01667 455728 Mrs Galliard
Rates fr: *£20.00*-**£20.00**.
Beds: 2D 1T **Baths:** 3 Private
(20)

Ardgour Hotel, *Seafield Street, Nairn, Nairn-shire, IV12 4HN.*
'Home from home' excellent value.
Open: All Year
Grades: STB 2 Cr, Comm
01667 454230 Mr Dunlop
Rates fr: *£22.50*-**£20.00**.
Beds: 3F 2D 3T 2S
Baths: 8 Ensuite 2 Private
(12)

Bracadale House, *Albert Street, Nairn, Ross-shire, IV12 4HF.*
Large Victorian private house.
Open: Easter to Oct
01667 452547 **Rates fr:** *£18.00*.
Beds: 2D 1T
Baths: 1 Ensuite 2 Private
(3)

Nethy Bridge

National Grid Ref: NJ0020

Mount View Hotel & Highland Game Restaurant, *Nethy Bridge, Inverness-shire, PH25 3EB.*
Open: All Year
Grades: STB 3 Cr, Comm
01479 821248 (also fax no)
Mrs Parkins
Rates fr: *£15.00*-**£15.00**.
Beds: 4F 1T 2S
Baths: 6 Ensuite 1 Shared
(24)
Situated in the beautiful Spey Valley overlooking the Cairngorms and Abernethy Forest. Many attractions for all interests and age groups. Phone for brochure and menus.

Aultmore House, *Nethy Bridge, Inverness-shire, PH25 3ED.*
Large Edwardian manor house.
Open: Easter to Oct
Grades: AA 4 Q, Select
01479 821473 Mrs Edwards
Rates fr: *£17.50*-**£17.50**.
Beds: 2D 2T 1S
Baths: 2 Private 2 Shared
(12) (20)

Newtonmore

National Grid Ref: NN7199

Braeriach Hotel, Glen Hotel

Craigellachie House, *Main Street, Newtonmore, Inverness-shire, PH20 1DA.*
Relaxed, comfortable, former C19th inn.
Open: All Year (not Xmas)
Grades: STB 1 Cr, Comm
01540 673360 Mrs Main
Rates fr: *£15.50*-**£16.50**.
Beds: 1F 1D
Baths: 1 Shared
(4)

Greenways, *Golf Course Road, Newtonmore, Inverness-shire, PH20 1AT.*
Central stone house, overlooking golf course.
Open: All Year (not Xmas/New Year)
Grades: STB 1 Cr, Comm
01540 673325 Mrs Muir
Rates fr: *£13.00*-**£13.00**.
Beds: 1D 1T 1S
Baths: 1 Shared
(12) (6)

Woodcliffe, *Laggan Road, Newtonmore, Inverness-shire, PH20 1DG.*
Comfortable, traditional stone villa.
Open: All Year (not Xmas)
Grades: STB Listed, Comm
01540 673839
Mrs Morrison
Rates fr: *£14.00*-**£14.00**.
Beds: 1F 1D
Baths: 1 Ensuite 1 Private
(6)

Pines Hotel, *Station Road, Newtonmore, Inverness-shire, PH20 1AR.*
Country house in large gardens.
Open: Apr to Oct
01540 673271
Mr & Mrs Raw
Rates fr: *£23.50*-**£23.50**.
Beds: 2D 3T 1S
Baths: 6 Ensuite
(6) (^)

Ben-Y-Gloe, *Fort William Road, Newtonmore, Inverness-shire, PH20 1DG.*
Comfortable, family-run private house.
Open: All Year
01540 673633 Mrs Ferrie
Rates fr: *£15.00*-**£20.00**.
Beds: 2D 1T
Baths: 3 Private
(12) (3)

Eagle View, *Perth Road, Newtonmore, Inverness-shire, PH20 1AP.*
Traditional stone-built house.
Open: All Year
01540 673675
Mrs Tonkin
Rates fr: *£14.00*-**£20.00**.
Beds: 2D 2T
Baths: 4 Private
(8)

North Kessock

National Grid Ref: NH6548

Bochie Muir, *Drumsmittal, North Kessock, Inverness, IV1 1XF.*
Ideal base to tour Highlands.
Open: All Year (not Xmas)
01463 731615
Mrs Howie
Rates fr: *£15.00*-**£20.00**.
Beds: 1F 1D 1T
Baths: 3 Private
(6)

The lowest **single** *rate is shown in* **bold.**

Onich

National Grid Ref: NN0261

Cuilcheanna House , *Onich, Fort William, Inverness-shire, PH33 6SD.*
Open: Apr to Oct
Grades: STB 3 Cr, Comm
01855 821226 Mr Scott
Rates fr: *£22.00*-**£32.00**.
Beds: 5D 2T
Baths: 7 Ensuite
(7)
Peacefully situated overlooking beautiful Loch Linnhe, small country house hotel with origins in 17th century. Magnificent views, good walking. Excellent food, member of Taste of Scotland. Licensed.

Tom Na Creige, *Onich, Fort William, Inverness-shire, PH33 6RY.*
Comfortable modern house overlooking loch.
Open: Jan to Nov
01855 821405 Mr Collins
Rates fr: *£16.00*-**£24.00**.
Beds: 2D 2T
Baths: 4 Ensuite 2 Shared
(8)

Plockton

National Grid Ref: NG8033

Plockton Hotel, Creag Nan Darrach Hotel

Tomacs, *Frithard, Plockton, Ross-shire, IV52 8TQ.*
Comfortable semi-detached house.
Open: All Year (not Xmas)
Grades: STB 2 Cr, Comm
01599 544321 Mrs Jones
Rates fr: *£15.00*-**£18.00**.
Beds: 1F 1D 1T
Baths: 1 Ensuite 1 Private 1 Shared

Creag Nan Darach Hotel, *Innes Street, Plockton, Ross-shire, IV52 8TW.*
Highland hospitality in beautiful surroundings.
Open: All Year
Grades: STB 3 Cr, Comm
01599 544222 Mr Rae
Fax no: 01599 544487
Rates fr: *£24.00*-**£24.00**.
Beds: 2F 3D 1T 1S
Baths: 5 Ensuite 2 Private
(7)

Right on the border? Look at the neighbouring county, too

***1 Camus An Arbhair**, Plockton, Ross-shire, IV52 8TQ.*
Panoramic view over Loch Carron.
Open: Easter to Oct
01599 544396 Mrs Finlayson
Rates fr: *£16.00*-**£25.00**.
Beds: 2D **Baths:** 1 Shared
(2)

***2 Frithard Road**, Plockton, Ross-shire, IV52 8TQ.*
Modern comfortable 'home from home'.
Open: All Year
Grades: STB 2 Cr, Comm
01599 544226 Mrs Cameron
Rates fr: *£14.50*.
Beds: 1F 2D
(8)

***Plockton Hotel**, Harbour Street, Plockton, Ross-shire, IV52 8TN.*
Local village inn of character.
Open: All Year
01599 544274
Rates fr: *£24.00*-**£29.00**.
Beds: 4D 2T 1S
Baths: 6 Ensuite 1 Private

***An Caladh**, 25 Harbour Street, Plockton, Ross-shire, IV52 8TN.*
Seafront cottage overlooking Plockton Bay.
Open: All Year
01599 544356 Mrs Rowe
Rates fr: *£15.00*.
Beds: 2D 1T
Baths: 2 Private 1 Shared

***Craig Highland Farm**, Plockton, Ross-shire, IV52 8UB.*
Cottage on rare breeds farm.
Open: Easter to Oct
01599 544205 Mrs Heaviside
Rates fr: *£13.00*-**£14.00**.
Beds: 1F 1D 1T **Baths:** 1 Shared
(2)

Poolewe

National Grid Ref: NG8580

***Corriness Guest House**, Poolewe, Ross-shire, IV22 2JU.*
Traditional Scottish late-Victorian house.
Open: Apr to Oct
01445 781262 Mrs Newsham
Rates fr: *£23.00*-**£23.00**.
Beds: 3F 1D 1T 1S
Baths: 6 Private
(10) (15)

Portmahomack

National Grid Ref: NH9184

***The Oyster Catcher**, Main Street, Portmahomack, Tain, Ross-shire, IV20 1YB.*
Acclaimed food and westerly sea views. **Open:** Mar to Jan
01862 871560 Mrs Edwards
Rates fr: *£15.00*-**£15.00**.
Beds: 1F 1D
Baths: 1 Ensuite 1 Shared
(5)

***Caledonian Hotel**, Portmahomack, Tain, Ross-shire, IV20 1YS.*
Spectacular views, on the beach.
Open: All Year
01862 871345 Mr Mutch
Rates fr: *£22.50*-**£24.00**.
Beds: 4F 5D 8T 1S
Baths: 18 Private

Raffin

National Grid Ref: NC0132

Caberfeidh Restaurant (Lochinver)

***The Cottar House**, Raffin, Lairg, Sutherland, IV27 4JH.*
Quiet, comfortable, overlooking The Minch.
Open: May to Sep
01571 855274 (also fax no)
Mrs Hardwick
Rates fr: *£13.50*-**£16.00**.
Beds: 1D
Baths: 1 Shared
(1)

Rheindown

National Grid Ref: NH5147

***Rheindown Farm**, Rheindown, Beauly, Inverness-shire, IV4 7AB.*
Farmhouse, overlooking village. Outstanding views.
Open: Mar to Oct
Grades: STB 1 Cr, Comm
01463 782461 Mrs Richie
Rates fr: *£14.00*-**£18.00**.
Beds: 1F 1D
Baths: 1 Shared

Roybridge

National Grid Ref: NN2781

***Station House**, Roybridge, Inverness-shire, PH31 4AG.*
Comfortable bungalow in quiet location.
Open: Apr to Oct
01397 712285 Mrs Grieve
Rates fr: *£13.50*.
Beds: 1D 1T
Baths: 2 Shared
(3)

Scourie

National Grid Ref: NC1544

Scourie Hotel

***Badcall Stoerview**, Scourie, Lairg, Sutherland, IV27 4TH.*
Open: Easter to Dec
01971 502411 Mrs MacKay
Rates fr: *£14.00*-**£20.00**.
Beds: 1F 1D 1T
Baths: 1 Shared
(4)
Every room with its own spectacular view of Badcall Islands and mountains. Close to fishing, boat trips, climbing, wildlife, hill walking. Plus our farm.

***Minch View**, Scouriemore, Scourie, Lairg, Sutherland, IV27 4TG.*
Modern comfortable croft house. Home cooking.
Open: Easter to Oct
01971 502010 Mrs MacDonald
Rates fr: *£14.00*-**£14.00**.
Beds: 2D 1T
Baths: 2 Shared

Shieldaig

National Grid Ref: NG8153

***Tigh Fada Croft**, 117 Doiraonar, Shieldaig, Strathcarron, Ross-shire, IV54 8XH.*
Comfortable modern quiet croft house.
Open: All Year
01520 755248 Mrs Calcott
Rates fr: *£13.50*-**£13.50**.
Beds: 1F 1D 1T **Baths:** 2 Shared

Smithton

National Grid Ref: NH7145

***3a Resaurie**, Smithton, Inverness, IV1 2NH.*
Open: All Year (not Xmas)
Grades: STB 2 Cr, Comm
01463 791714 Mrs Mansfield
Rates fr: *£15.00*-**£15.00**.
Beds: 2D 1T
Baths: 1 Ensuite 1 Shared
(3)
Quiet residential area. 3 miles east of Inverness. Adjacent to farmland. Views to Moray Firth and Ross-shire Hills. Home baking. High tea. Evening meals.

Sordale

National Grid Ref: ND1461

***Sordale House**, Sordale, Halkirk, Caithness, KW12 6XB.*
C19th farmhouse, oak-beamed bedrooms.
Open: All Year (not Xmas)
01847 831270 Mrs Rodgers
Rates fr: *£14.00*-**£16.00**.
Beds: 1D 1T **Baths:** 2 Shared
(4)

Spean Bridge

National Grid Ref: NN2281

***Old Pines Restaurant with Rooms**, Spean Bridge, Fort William, Inverness-shire, PH34 4EG.*
Open: All Year
Grades: STB 3 Cr, High Comm
01397 712324 Dr & Mrs Barber
Fax no: 01397 712433
Rates fr: *£25.00*-**£25.00**.
Beds: 2F 2D 2T 2S
Baths: 8 Private
(12)
'Best Small Hotel in Britain' - Judith Chalmers Holiday Care Awards. Winners of the 'Taste of Scotland Classic Scotch Lamb Challenge 1995'. 'A Very Special Place'.

***Tirindrish House,** Spean Bridge, Inverness-shire, PH34 4EU.*
Large, comfortable, historic Highland house.
Open: Easter to Oct
Grades: STB 3 Cr, Comm
01397 712398 (also fax no)
Mrs Wilson
Rates fr: *£17.00*-**£17.00**.
Beds: 2D 1T
Baths: 1 Ensuite 2 Private
(4)

***Coire Glas Guest House,** Spean Bridge, Inverness-shire, PH34 4EU.*
Friendly, comfortable, licensed guesthouse.
Open: Jan to Oct
Grades: STB 3 Cr, Comm, AA 2 Q
01397 712272
Mrs MacFarlane
Rates fr: *£14.00*-**£16.00**.
Beds: 2F 4D 4T 1S
Baths: 8 Private 2 Shared

Stoer

National Grid Ref: NC0328

***Cruachan Guest House,** Stoer, Lochinver, Lairg, Sutherland, IV27 4JE.*
Former Victorian manse.
Open: Apr to Oct
01571 855303 Miss Gould
Rates fr: *£17.00*-**£17.00**.
Beds: 1D 2T
Baths: 1 Ensuite 2 Shared
(4)

***Stoer Villa,** Stoer, Lairg, Sutherland, IV27 4JE.*
Large, traditional stone-built villa.
Open: All Year
01571 855305 Mrs Spykers
Rates fr: *£13.00*-**£17.50**.
Beds: 1D 2T
Baths: 1 Shared
(5)

Strathcarron

National Grid Ref: NG9442

***Coulags,** Strathcarron, Ross-shire, IV54 8YU.*
Comfortable traditional style country cottage.
Open: April to Nov
01520 766233 Mrs MacKay
Rates fr: *£12.00*-**£15.00**.
Beds: 1F 1D
Baths: 1 Shared
(3)

Strathpeffer

National Grid Ref: NH4858

Brunstane Hotel

***Linnbhor,** Park Road, Strathpeffer, Ross-shire, IV14 9BY.*
Open: All Year
01997 421528 Mrs MacLean
Rates fr: *£14.00*-**£16.00**.
Beds: 1F 3D 4T 1S
Baths: 7 Private 2 Shared
(9)
Superior Edwardian guest house situated in the Victorian spa village of Strathpeffer, in the heart of the Scottish Highlands. Ideal as a base to tour from.

***Scoraig,** 8 Kinnettas Square, Strathpeffer, Ross-shire, IV14 9BD.*
Quiet location in Victorian village.
Open: All Year
Grades: STB Listed, Comm
01997 421847
Mrs MacDonald
Rates fr: *£13.00*-**£12.00**.
Beds: 1F 1D 1T 1S
Baths: 1 Private 2 Shared
(5)

***Francisville,** Strathpeffer, Ross-shire, IV14 9AX.*
Homely accommodation in Victorian villa.
Open: Easter to Oct
Grades: STB 1 Cr, Comm
01997 421345
Mrs MacKenzie
Rates fr: *£13.50*-**£15.00**.
Beds: 1F
Baths: 1 Private
(4) (2)

***Craigvar,** The Square, Strathpeffer, Ross-shire, IV14 9DL.*
Overlooking square in spa village.
Open: Easter to Oct
Grades: STB 2 Cr, Deluxe, AA 4 Q
01997 421622 Mrs Scott
Rates fr: *£17.00*-**£23.00**.
Beds: 2D 1T
Baths: 3 Ensuite
(4)

Strathy Point

National Grid Ref: NC8167

***Catalina Guest House,** Aultivullin, Strathy Point, Caithness, KW14 7RY.*
Open: All Year
Grades: AA 4 Q, Select
01641 541279
Mrs Salisbury
Fax no: 01641 541314
Rates fr: *£15.00*-**£20.00**.
Beds: 1T
Baths: 1 Private
(2)
'Simply the Best!', 'Splendid', 'Fantastic!' are typical comments from our guests with their own private wing, set amongst the wild splendour of the Far North.

Strontian

National Grid Ref: NM8161

***Loch Sunart Hotel,** Strontian, Acharacle, Argyll, PH36 4HZ.*
Idyllic C18th lochside hotel with spectacular views.
Open: Easter to Oct
01967 402471 Mrs Renton
Rates fr: *£26.00*-**£26.00**.
Beds: 1F 6D 3T 1T
Baths: 10 Ensuite 1 Private
(2) (30)

Tain

National Grid Ref: NH7881

Morangie Hotel, Royal Hotel

***Carringtons,** Morangie Road, Tain, Ross-shire, IV19 1PY.*
Large Victorian house facing sea.
Open: All Year (not Xmas)
Grades: STB 2 Cr, Comm
01862 892635 Mrs Roberts
Rates fr: *£13.00*-**£18.00**.
Beds: 2F 2D 2T
Baths: 2 Ensuite 2 Shared
(6)

***Rosslyn,** 2 Moss Road, Tain, Ross-shire, IV19 1HQ.*
Large Victorian private house.
Open: All Year
Grades: STB 2 Cr, Comm
01862 892697
Mrs Anderson
Rates fr: *£15.00*-**£15.00**.
Beds: 1F 1T
Baths: 2 Ensuite
(4)

***23 Moss Road,** Tain, Ross-shire, IV19 1HH.*
Comfortable family-run home. Home baking.
Open: All Year
Grades: STB 2 Cr, Comm
01862 894087 Mrs McLean
Rates fr: *£14.00*-**£14.00**.
Beds: 1D 1T 1S
Baths: 1 Ensuite 2 Shared
(2) (3)

***Dunbius,** Morangie Road, Tain, Ross-shire, IV19 1PV.*
Modern, accomodating, relaxing, warm, friendly.
Open: All Year
Grades: STB 2 Cr, Comm
01862 893010 (also fax no)
Mrs Ross
Rates fr: *£15.00*-**£20.00**.
Beds: 2D 1T
Baths: 3 Ensuite
(8)

***Heatherdale,** 2 Well Street, Tain, Ross-shire, IV19 1HJ.*
Modern comfortable house, home-baking.
Open: All Year (not Xmas)
01862 894340 Mrs Fraser
Rates fr: *£16.00*-**£18.00**.
Beds: 1D 1T
Baths: 2 Ensuite

Langsdale, *Newton, Tain, Ross-shire, IV20 1RU.*
Modern comfortable bungalow, country location.
Open: All Year (not Xmas)
01862 892244 Mrs Penfold
Rates fr: *£11.00*-**£11.00**.
Beds: 1D 1T
Baths: 1 Shared
(6)

Thurso

National Grid Ref: ND1168

Pentland Hotel, Sandra's Snack Bar, Northern Sands Hotel (Dunnet), The Viking Bowl

Shinval, *Glengolly, Thurso, Caithness, KW14 7XN.*
Open: Jan to Dec
Grades: STB 2 Cr, Comm
01847 894306 Mrs Sinclair
Rates fr: *£14.50*-**£14.50**.
Beds: 1F 1D 1T
Baths: 1 Ensuite 2 Shared
Modern house with large garden in quiet location, minutes from town. Ideal for bird watching, walking, and families with children. Phone or write for brochure.

1 Granville Cresent, *Thurso, Caithness, KW14 7NP.*
Modern bungalow, quiet residential area.
Open: All Year (not Xmas)
Grades: STB 2 Cr, Comm
01847 892993 Mrs Murray
Rates fr: *£16.00*-**£18.00**.
Beds: 2T
Baths: 1 Ensuite 1 Private
(2)

Garth House, *Castletown, Thurso, Caithness, KW14 8SL.*
Recently restored gentleman's residence.
Open: All Year
Grades: STB 2 Cr, High Comm
01847 821429
Mr & Mrs Garfield
Rates fr: *£18.00*-**£18.00**.
Beds: 1D 1T
Baths: 2 Private
(6)

Carlingwark, *5 Mears Place, Thurso, Caithness, KW14 7EW.*
Modern, comfortable bungalow.
Open: May to Oct
Grades: STB 1 Cr, High Comm
01847 894124 Mrs Fisher
Rates fr: *£15.50*-**£15.50**.
Beds: 1D 1T 1S
Baths: 2 Shared
(8) (3)

Ivordene, *Janetstown, Thurso, Caithness, KW14 7XF.*
Modern, comfortable farmhouse.
Open: All Year
01847 894760 Mrs MacIvor
Rates fr: *£13.00*-**£13.00**.
Beds: 1F 1D 2T 1S
Baths: 2 Shared

The St Clair Hotel, *Thurso, Caithness, KW14 7AJ.*
Friendly town centre family hotel.
Open: All Year
Grades: AA 2 St
01847 896481
Mrs Munro
Rates fr: *£22.50*-**£25.00**.
Beds: 11D 13T 12S
Baths: 29 Private 7 Shared
(5)

Station Hotel, *Princes Street, Thurso, Caithness, KW14 7DH.*
Friendly, family-run, centrally situated hotel.
Open: All Year
01847 892003
Mr Munro
Fax no: 01847 896481
Rates fr: *£25.50*-**£27.00**.
Beds: 2F 6D 11T 2S
Baths: 21 Ensuite
(3)

9 Couper Street, *Thurso, Caithness, KW14 8AR.*
Small homely B&B minutes from beach, river, shop, Orkney ferry, and station.
Open: All Year (not Xmas)
01847 894529
Mrs Oag
Rates fr: *£13.00*-**£13.00**.
Beds: 1D 1T 1S

Central Hotel, *3 Traill Street, Thurso, Caithness, KW14 8EJ.*
Close to all amenities.
Open: All Year
01847 893100 / 893129
Mr Cardosi
Rates fr: *£18.50*-**£21.00**.
Beds: 6T 3D 1S
Baths: 10 Ensuite

Tongue

National Grid Ref: NC5956

77 Dalcharn, *Tongue, Lairg, Sutherland, IV27 4XU.*
Open: All Year
01847 611251
Mrs MacIntosh
Rates fr: *£13.00*-**£15.00**.
Beds: 1F 1D 1T
Baths: 1 Shared
(3)
Croft cottage set in quiet valley. Families welcome. Phone for brochure.

Tongue Hotel, *Tongue, Lairg, Sutherland, IV27 4XD.*
Refurbished Victorian Highland hotel.
Open: Easter to end-Sept
Grades: STB 3 Cr, Comm, AA 2 St
01847 611206
Miss Stoltman
Rates fr: *£25.00*-**£25.00**.
Beds: 2F 12D 4T 1S
Baths: 17 Private
(25)

Rhian Cottage, *Tongue, Lairg, Sutherland, IV27 4XJ.*
Secluded cosy crofthouse. Panoramic views.
Open: All Year (not Xmas)
01847 611257 Mrs MacKay
Rates fr: *£18.00*-**£25.00**.
Beds: 1F 1D 1T
Baths: 2 Ensuite 1 Private
(6)

Tore

National Grid Ref: NH6052

Kilcoy Arms

Fiveways, *Tore, Muir of Ord, Ross-shire, IV6 7RY.*
Modern bungalow, welcome always assured.
Open: Easter to Oct
01463 811408 Mrs MacKenzie
Rates fr: *£13.00*-**£14.00**.
Beds: 1F 1D 1T **Baths:** 2 Shared

Torridon

National Grid Ref: NG9056

Heather Cliff, *Inveralligin, Torridon, Achnasheen, Ross-shire, IV22 2HB.*
Open: Feb to Nov
01445 791256 Mrs Rose
Rates fr: *£15.00*-**£15.00**.
Beds: 1F 1D 1S
Baths: 1 Shared
(4)
Enjoy the magnificent scenery of the North-West Highlands. Walk, climb or just relax in well fed comfort. All rooms face south over Loch Torridon.

Ulbster

National Grid Ref: ND3240

Lochside, *Ulbster, Caithness, KW2 6AA.*
Nursery on site, convenient Orkney.
Open: All Year (not Xmas)
01955 651320 Mrs Clarke
Rates fr: *£14.00*-**£14.00**.
Beds: 2F 1S **Baths:** 1 Shared
(6)

Ullapool

National Grid Ref: NH1294

Morefield Motel, Scottish Larder, Harbour Lights Hotel

Taigh na Mara Vegetarian Guesthouse, *The Shore, Ardindrean, Loch Broom, Ullapool, Ross-shire, IV23 2SE.*
Scottish vegetarian secluded lochside guest house.
Open: All Year
01854 655282 Mr Weston
Fax no: 01854 655292
Rates fr: *£19.50*-**£26.50**.
Beds: 2D 1T
Baths: 1 Private 1 Shared

Fyffe House, *Pulteney Street, Ullapool, Ross-shire, IV26 2UP.*
White washed traditional highland home.
Open: Easter to Nov
01854 612452 Mrs MacRae
Rates fr: *£14.50*-**£16.50**.
Beds: 2D 1T
Baths: 1 Private 1 Shared
(3)

Rivendell, *Garve Road, Ullapool, Ross-shire, IV26 2SX.*
Large detached comfortable house. Lovely views.
Open: Apr to Oct
01854 612081 Mrs Jeffers
Rates fr: *£16.00*-**£16.00**.
Beds: 2D 1T 1S
Baths: 2 Ensuite 1 Private 1 Shared
(12) (4)

The Bungalow, *Garve Road, Ullapool, Ross-shire, IV26 2SX.*
Family home overlooking Loch Broom.
Open: May to Sep
Grades: STB 1 Cr, Comm
01854 612233 Mrs Sykes
Rates fr: *£14.00*-**£20.00**.
Beds: 1D 1T
Baths: 1 Private 1 Shared
(3)

Eilean Donan Guest House, *14 Market Street, Ullapool, Ross-shire, IV26 2XE.*
Comfortable quality accommodation. Central location.
Open: All Year
Grades: STB 2 Cr, Comm
01854 612524 Mr Hall
Rates fr: *£14.00*-**£15.00**.
Beds: 1F 2D 2T
Baths: 3 Ensuite 1 Shared
(6)

The lowest *double* rate per person is shown in *italics*.

The lowest **single** *rate is shown in* **bold.**

Dronman Guest House, *Garve Road, Ullapool, Ross-shire, IV26 2SX.*
Modern family-run guest house.
Open: All Year
Grades: STB 2 Cr, High Comm, AA 4 Q
01854 612333 Mrs MacDonald
Rates fr: *£19.00*.
Beds: 2F 3D 2T
Baths: 7 Private
(7)

Oakworth, *Riverside Terrace, Ullapool, Ross-shire, IV26 2TE.*
Modern centrally heated detached bungalow.
Open: All Year (not Xmas)
01854 612290 Mrs Downey
Rates fr: *£17.00*.
Beds: 3D
Baths: 3 Private
(12) (3)

The Sheiling Guest House, *Garve Road, Ullapool, Ross-shire, IV26 2SX.*
Modern, comfortable, lochside house.
Open: All Year (not Xmas)
Grades: STB 2 Cr, High Comm, AA 4 Q
01854 612947 Mr MacKenzie
Rates fr: *£20.00*-**£20.00**.
Beds: 4D 3T
Baths: 7 Private
(7)

3 Vyner Place, *Ullapool, Ross-shire, IV26 2XR.*
Modern, comfortable house (mod cons).
Open: Easter to Sep
01854 612023 Mrs MacRae
Rates fr: *£11.00*.
Beds: 1F 1D
Baths: 1 Shared
(2)

Wick

National Grid Ref: ND3650
Mackays Hotel, Waterfront

Greenvoe, *George Street, Wick, Caithness, KW1 4DE.*
Spacious house with panoramic views.
Open: All Year (not Xmas)
Grades: STB Listed, High Comm
01955 603942 Mrs Johnston
Rates fr: *£14.00*-**£14.00**.
Beds: 1D 1T 1S **Baths:** 2 Shared
(5)

The Clachan, *South Street, Wick, Caithness, KW1 5NH.*
Family-run private house.
Open: All Year (not Xmas)
01955 605384 Mrs Bremner
Rates fr: *£18.00*-**£25.00**.
Beds: 2D 1T **Baths:** 3 Private

Belhaven, *Port Dunbar, Wick, Caithness, KW1 4JJ.*
Modern villa overlooking sea.
Open: All Year
01955 605902 Mrs Gunn
Rates fr: *£14.00*-**£17.00**.
Beds: 1F 1T 1S **Baths:** 2 Shared

Dunelm, *7 Sinclair Terrace, Wick, Caithness, KW1 5AD.*
Quiet private house, near town centre. **Open:** All Year
01955 602120 / 605791
Mrs Coghill
Rates fr: *£15.00*-**£15.00**.
Beds: 1F 1D 1T 1S
Baths: 1 Ensuite 3 Private

Hebron, *Beaufoy Street, Wick, Caithness, KW1 5QG.*
Large comfortable Victorian house.
Open: Easter to Oct
01955 603515 Mrs Gunn
Rates fr: *£13.00*-**£15.00**.
Beds: 1F 1T **Baths:** 1 Shared

Lanarkshire

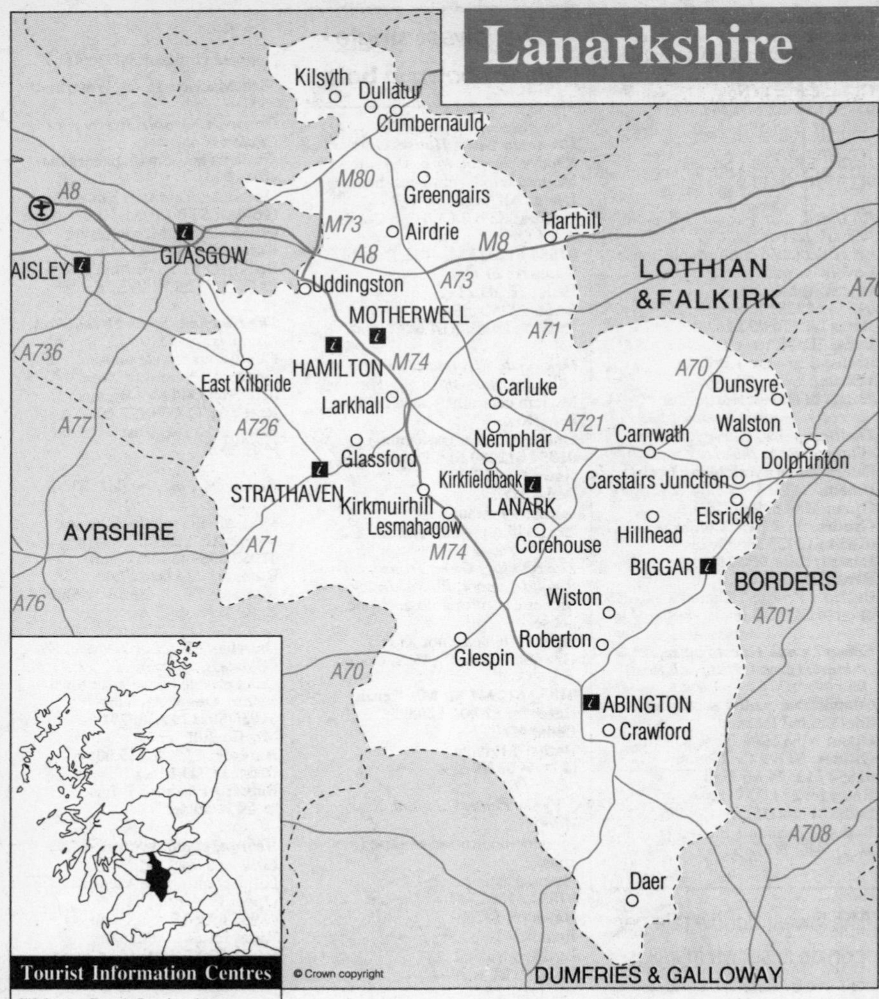

Tourist Information Centres

Welcome Break Service Area, A74 North, **Abington**, Biggar, Lanarkshire, ML12 6SD, 01864 502436, (Easter to Oct).

155 High Street, **Biggar**, Lanarkshire, ML12 6DL, 01899 221066, (Easter to Oct).

The Time Capsule, Buchanan Street, **Coalbridge**, 01236 431133

Road Chef Services, M74 (North), **Hamilton**, Lanarkshire, 01698 285590

Horsemarket, Ladyacre Road, **Lanark**, Lanarkshire, ML11 7LQ, 01555 661661.

Abington

National Grid Ref: NS9323

Townfoot, *Roberton, Abington, Biggar, Lanarkshire, ML12 6RS.*
Rolling hills with lovely views.
Open: All Year
01899 850655 Mrs Craig
Rates fr: *£14.00*-**£14.00**.
Beds: 1F 2T **Baths:** 1 Ensuite 1Shared
(6)

Abington Hotel, *Carlisle Road, Abington, Biggar, Lanarkshire, ML12 6SD.*
Friendly family-run hotel in beautiful countryside.
Open: All Year **Grades:** STB 3 Cr
01864 502467 Mr MacBride
Rates fr: *£19.95*-**£33.50**.
Beds: 3F 10D 8T 7S
Baths: 27 Private

Glentewing Farm, *Abington, Biggar, Lanarkshire, ML12 6ST.*
Stone-built comfortable farmhouse.
Open: Easter to Oct
01864 504221
Mrs Hyslop
Rates fr: *£19.00*-**£19.00**.
Beds: 1D 1T
(2)

Kersdale, *2 Edinburgh Road, Abington, Biggar, Lanarkshire, ML12 6SA.*
Small comfortable family home.
Open: All Year
01864 502323
Mrs Wales
Rates fr: *£12.00*-**£15.00**.
Beds: 1F 1T 1S
Baths: 1 Private 2 Shared
(6)

Airdrie

National Grid Ref: NS7665

Rosslee Guest House, *107 Forrest Street, Airdrie, Lanarkshire, ML6 7AR.*
Former church manse.
Open: All Year
01236 765865 Mr McFadzean
Rates fr: *£17.50*-**£17.50**.
Beds: 1F 3T 2S
Baths: 3 Private 2 Shared
(8)

Biggar

National Grid Ref: NT0437

Elphinstone Hotel

Lindsaylands, *Biggar, Lanarkshire, ML12 6EQ.*
Beautiful country house, peaceful setting.
Open: Mar to Nov
Grades: STB 3 Cr, High Comm
01899 220033 / 221221 Mrs Stott
Fax no: 01899 221009
Rates fr: *£23.00*-**£26.00**.
Beds: 2D 1T
Baths: 2 Ensuite 1 Private
(6)

Woodgill, *12 Edinburgh Road, Biggar, Lanarkshire, ML12 6AX.*
Friendly and welcoming family home. **Open:** Easter to Oct
01899 220324 Mrs Brown
Rates fr: *£15.00*-**£14.00**.
Beds: 1D 1T 1S
(4)

Carluke

National Grid Ref: NS8450

12 Moorside Street, *Carluke, Lanarkshire, ML8 4EJ.*
Semi-detached comfortable relaxed house.
Open: All Year (not Xmas)
01555 773597 Mrs Carr
Rates fr: *£13.00*-**£13.00**.
Beds: 1D 1T **Baths:** 1 Shared

Carnwath

National Grid Ref: NS9846

Wee Bush

Kings Inn Farm, *Carnwath, Lanark, ML11 8LL.*
Quiet country farmhouse, beautiful views.
Open: All Year
Grades: STB Listed
01501 785213 Mrs Orr
Rates fr: *£16.00*-**£20.00**.
Beds: 1F 1D
Baths: 2 Private

The lowest *double* rate per person is shown in *italics*.

National Grid References are for villages, towns and cities - *not* for individual houses.

Carstairs Junction

National Grid Ref: NS9545

Station Hotel, *6 Strawfrank Road, Carstairs Junction, Lanark, Lanarkshire, ML11 8PP.*
Comfortable, licensed family hotel.
Open: All Year
01555 870376 Mr Wilson
Rates fr: *£17.00*-**£20.00**.
Beds: 5T
Baths: 2 Private 1 Shared
(12)

Corehouse

National Grid Ref: NS8843

The Tavern

Corehouse Home Farm, *Corehouse, Lanark, Lanarkshire, ML11 9TQ.*
Quiet farm near nature reserve.
Open: All Year
Grades: STB 2 Cr, Comm
01555 661377 Mrs Hamilton
Rates fr: *£16.00*-**£20.00**.
Beds: 2F 1D
Baths: 3 Ensuite
(6)

Crawford

National Grid Ref: NS9520

Field End Guest House, *The Loaning (opp. Church), Crawford, Biggar, Lanarkshire, ML12 6TN.*
Recommended world wide. Always welcome.
Open: All Year (not Xmas)
Grades: STB 3 Cr, AA 2 Q, RAC Acclaim
01864 502276 Mr Poole
Rates fr: *£15.00*-**£20.00**.
Baths: 3 Private
(6)

Cumbernauld

National Grid Ref: NS7573

Kameron's Brasserie

Ben Ledi, *68 Lammermoor Drive, Cumbernauld, Glasgow, G67 4BE.*
Modern detached villa.
Open: All Year (not Xmas)
Grades: STB Listed, Comm
01236 721307 Mrs Abercrombie
Rates fr: *£16.50*-**£16.50**.
Beds: 3T **Baths:** 1 Shared
(4)

Daer

National Grid Ref: NS9512

Nunnerie Farm, *Daer, Elvanfoot, Biggar, Lanarkshire, ML12 6TJ.*
Friendly working farm.
Open: Mar to Oct
01864 505224 Mrs MacArthur
Rates fr: *£20.00 (inc meal)*-**£20.00**.
Beds: 1D 1T
Baths: 1 Shared

Dullatur

National Grid Ref: NS7476

Castlecarry House Hotel

Dullatur House, *Dullatur, Glasgow, G68 0AW.*
Georgian mansion house c.1740.
Open: All Year
Grades: STB 2 Cr, Comm
01236 738855 Mrs Moore
Rates fr: *£17.50*-**£18.50**.
Beds: 1F 2T
Baths: 3 Private
(6)

Dunsyre

National Grid Ref: NT0748

Dunsyre Mains, *Dunsyre, Carnwath, Lanark, Lanarkshire, ML11 8NQ.*
Comfortable farmhouse, picturesque countryside.
Open: All Year
Grades: STB 1 Cr, Comm
01899 810251 Mrs Armstrong
Rates fr: *£15.00*-**£17.00**.
Beds: 1F 1D 1T
Baths: 2 Shared
(0) (Farmyard)

Elsrickle

National Grid Ref: NT0643

Elphinstone Hotel

Howburn Farm, *Elsrickle, Biggar, Lanarkshire, ML12 6QZ.*
Comfortable farmhouse lovely views. Friendly.
Open: All Year (not Xmas)
01899 810276 Mrs Barrie
Rates fr: *£14.00*-**£16.00**.
Beds: 1F 1T **Baths:** 1 Shared
(0) (6)

Glassford

National Grid Ref: NS7247

Avonlea, *46 Millar Street, Glassford, Strathaven, Lanarkshire, ML10 6TD.*
Comfortable, homely accommodation in country village.
Open: Jan to Nov
Grades: AA 2 Q
01357 521748 / 521369
Miss Rankin
Rates fr: *£16.00*-**£19.00**.
Beds: 2T **Baths:** 1 Shared
(7)

Glespin

National Grid Ref: NS8127

Colebrooke Arms

West Glespin Farm, *Glespin, Douglas, Lanark, Lanarkshire, ML11 0SQ.*
Homely farmhouse. Friendly farmers - come.
Open: Jun to Oct
01555 851349 Mrs Shanks
Rates fr: *£17.50*-**£17.50**.
Beds: 1F 1D 1T
Baths: 2 Shared
(6)

Greengairs

National Grid Ref: NS7870

Easter Glentore Farm, *Slamannan Road, Greengairs, Airdrie, Lanarkshire, ML6 7TJ.*
Best B&B award-winner.
Open: All Year
Grades: STB 2 Cr, High Comm
01236 830243 Mrs Hunter
Rates fr: *£18.00*-**£21.00**.
Beds: 3D
Baths: 1 Ensuite 1 Shared

Hamilton

National Grid Ref: NS7255

The Gills

Glenmhor House, *6 Bent Road, Hamilton, Lanarkshire, ML3 6QB.*
Large, traditional sandstone dwelling.
Open: All Year
01698 423293
Ms McCabe
Rates fr: *£16.00*-**£18.00**.
Beds: 1F 1T 1S
Baths: 1 Shared
(0) (3)

Harthill

National Grid Ref: NS9064

Blair Mains Farm, *Harthill, Shotts, Lanarkshire, ML7 5TJ.*
Small working farm midway Edinburgh/Glasgow.
Open: All Year
01501 751278
Mrs Ireland
Rates fr: *£16.00*-**£16.00**.
Beds: 1F 1D 2T 4S
Baths: 4 Shared
(12)

Kilsyth

National Grid Ref: NS7178

Coachman Hotel

Fairfield, *Glasgow Road, Kilsyth, Glasgow, G65 9JZ.*
Attractive, quality accommodation & food.
Open: All Year (not Xmas)
01236 825745 Mrs Clark
Rates fr: *£17.00*-**£17.00**.
Beds: 1D 1T 1S
(1)

Kirkmuirhill

National Grid Ref: NS7943

Star Inn (Lesmahagow), Waterside Restaurant (Strathaven)

Dykecroft Farm, *Kirkmuirhill, Lesmahagow, Lanark, ML11 0JQ.*
Modern, friendly farmhouse. Beautiful views.
Open: All Year
Grades: STB Listed, Comm, AA 2 Q
01555 892226 Mrs McInally
Rates fr: *£16.00*-**£18.00**.
Beds: 2D 1T **Baths:** 2 Shared
(4)

Larkhall

National Grid Ref: NS7650

Shawlands Roadhouse Hotel, *Ayr Road, Canderside Toll, Larkhall, Lanarkshire, ML9 2TZ.*
Small family-run hotel.
Open: All Year
01698 791111 Mr Dowling
Rates fr: *£18.00*-**£25.00**.
Beds: 4D 16T 1S
Baths: 21 Ensuite
(80)

Lesmahagow

National Grid Ref: NS8139

Star Inn, Poachers Rest, Waterside Restaurant

Auldtoun Farm, *Lesmahagow, Lanark, Lanarkshire, ML11 0JT.*
Large comfortable farm house.
Open: All Year
01555 892910 Mrs Muirhead
Fax no: 01555 892710
Rates fr: *£15.00*-**£18.00**.
Beds: 1F 1D 1T
Baths: 1 Ensuite 1 Shared
(8)

Dykecroft Farm, *Kirkmuirhill, Lesmahagow, Lanark, ML11 0JQ.*
Modern, friendly farmhouse. Beautiful views.
Open: All Year
Grades: STB Listed, Comm, AA 2 Q
01555 892226 Mrs McInally
Rates fr: *£16.00*-**£18.00**.
Beds: 2D 1T
Baths: 2 Shared
(4)

Nemphlar

National Grid Ref: NS8544

Knowetop, *Hall Road, Nemphlar, Lanark, ML11 9JE.*
Spacious, modern, detached country house.
Open: All Year
01555 665786
Mrs Mckelvie
Rates fr: *£14.00*-**£16.00**.
Beds: 1F 1T
Baths: 1 Shared
(8)

Roberton

National Grid Ref: NS9428

Townfoot, *Roberton, Biggar, Lanarkshire, ML12 6RS.*
Rolling hills with lovely views.
Open: All Year
01899 850655
Mrs Craig
Rates fr: *£14.00*-**£14.00**.
Beds: 1F 2T
Baths: 1 Ensuite 1 Shared
(6)

Strathaven

National Grid Ref: NS7044

Waterside, Strathaven Hotel

Cloverhill Farm, *Strathaven, Lanarkshire, ML10 6ST.*
Open: Mar to Nov
01357 300414 (also fax no)
Mrs Morrison
Rates fr: *£15.00*-**£15.00**.
Beds: 1F 1T
Baths: 1 Shared
(4) (4)
A hearty Scottish breakfast and a warm welcome are assured at this modern comfortable farmhouse. Conveniently situated for business or touring on A726, 0.5 mile from Strathaven.

Haroldslea, *3 Kirkhill Road, Strathaven, Lanarkshire, ML10 6HN.*
Comfortable detached house - attractive area.
Open: All Year
Grades: STB Listed, Approv
01357 20617
Mrs Goodwillie
Rates fr: *£15.00*-**£16.00**.
Beds: 1F 1D
Baths: 1 Private
(1) (3)

***pemhor,** West Kype Farm,*
rathaven, Lanarkshire, ML10 6PR.
odern bungalow on farm.
pen: All Year
rades: STB Listed, Comm
357 29831 Mrs Anderson
ates fr: *£14.00*-**£15.00**.
eds: 1D 1T
aths: 1 Shared
(0) P (20) TV

ddingston

ational Grid Ref: NS6960

Redstones Hotel

***orthcote Guest House,** 2*
olmbrae Avenue, Uddingston,
lasgow, G71 6AL.
arge Victorian private house.
pen: All Year
698 813319 (also fax no)
rs Meggs
ates fr: *£14.00*-**£14.00**.
eds: 1F 1D 1S
aths: 1 Shared
P (3) TV

Walston

National Grid Ref: NT0545

***Walston Mansion Farmhouse,** Walston, Carnwath, Lanark, Lanarkshire, ML11 8NF.*
A farmhouse that's 'home from home'.
Open: All Year
Grades: STB 3 Cr, Comm, AA 3 Q
01899 810 338 Mrs Kirby
Fax no: 01899 810338
Rates fr: *£13.00*-**£13.00**.
Beds: 1F 1D 1T
Baths: 2 Private 2 Shared
P (6) TV V

Bringing children with you? Always ask for any special rates.

The lowest **single** *rate is shown in* **bold.**

Wiston

National Grid Ref: NS9532

***Wiston Place,** Wiston, Biggar, Lanarkshire, ML12 6HT.*
Peaceful homely C17th farmhouse.
Open: All Year (not Xmas)
01899 850235 Mrs Mccaskie
Rates fr: *£12.50*-**£12.50**.
Beds: 1F 1T **Baths:** 1 Shared
P TV

***Greenhill Farm,** Wiston, Biggar, Lanarkshire, ML12 6HU.*
Comfortable farmhouse in beautiful location.
Open: All Year (not Xmas)
01899 850232 Mrs Ross
Rates fr: *£12.50*-**£15.00**.
Beds: 1D 1T **Baths:** 1 Shared
P (6) TV V

Lothian & Falkirk

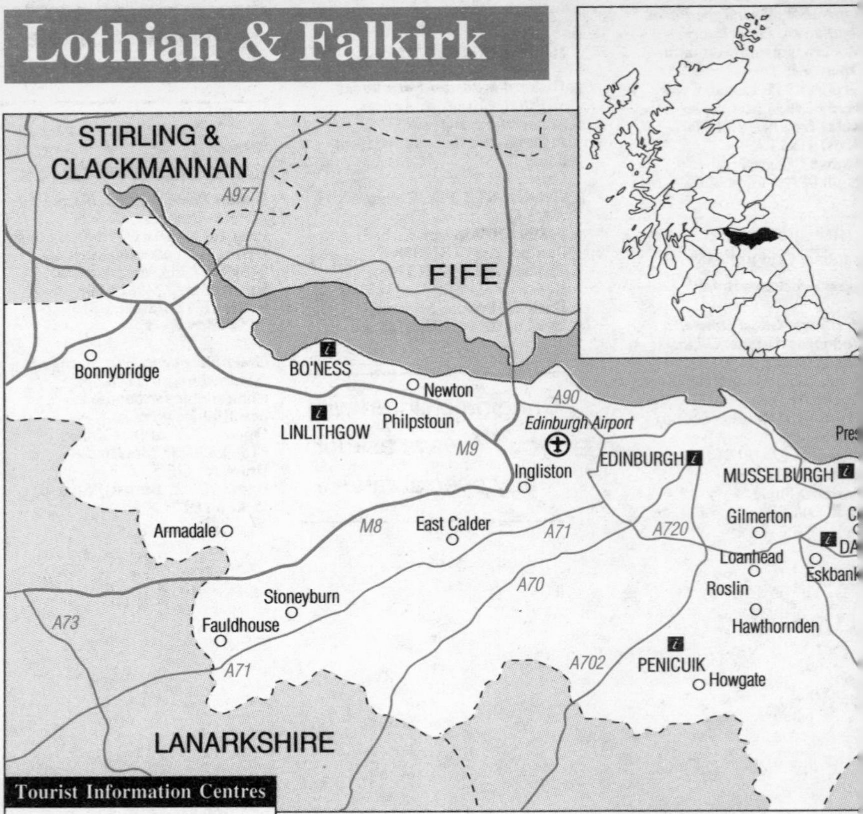

STIRLING & CLACKMANNAN
FIFE
A977
Bonnybridge
BO'NESS
Newton
LINLITHGOW
Philpstoun
A90
Edinburgh Airport
M9
Ingliston
EDINBURGH
MUSSELBURGH
Armadale
M8
East Calder
A71
A720
Gilmerton
Loanhead
Eskbank
Roslin
A70
Stoneyburn
Fauldhouse
A73
Hawthornden
A71
A702
PENICUIK
Howgate
LANARKSHIRE

Tourist Information Centres

Hamilton's Cottage, **Bo'ness**, West Lothian, EH51 0NG, 01506 826626, (Easter to Oct).

The Library, Polton Street, **Bonnyrigg**, Midlothian, EH19 3DQ, 0131-660 6814.

The Library, White Hart Street, **Dalkeith**, Midlothian, EH22 1AE, 0131 660 6818.

143 High Street, **Dunbar**, East Lothian, EH42 1ES, 01368 63353.

3 Princes St, **Edinburgh**, 0131 557 1700.

Burgh Halls, The Cross, **Linlithgow**, West Lothian, EH49 7AH, 01506 844600

Brunton Hall, Ladywell Way, **Musselburgh**, East Lothian, EH21 6AF, 0131 665 6597, (Easter to Oct)

Quality Street, **North Berwick**, East Lothian, EH39 4HJ, 01620 2197

The Library, 3 Bellman's Road, **Penicuik**, Midlothian, EH26 0AB, 01968 72340, EH

Forth Bridge Visitor Centre, **Hawes Pier**, West Lothian, EH30 9TB, 0131 319 1118, (Easter to Oct).

Armadale

National Grid Ref: NS9368

Strathalmond Hotel

Tarrareoch Farm, *Armadale, Bathgate, West Lothian, EH48 3BJ.*
250-year-old comfortable farmhouse.
Open: All Year (not Xmas)
01501 730404 Mrs Gibb
Rates fr: *£12.50*-**£15.00**.
Beds: 3T **Baths:** 2 Shared
(8)

Bolton

National Grid Ref: NT5070

Tweedale Arms

Fieldfare, *Upper Bolton Farm, Bolton, Haddington, East Lothian, EH41 4HL.*
Modern comfortable farmhouse.
Open: All Year
Grades: STB 2 Cr, Comm
01620 810346 Mrs Clark
Rates fr: *£15.00*-**£18.00**.
Beds: 1F 1D 1T
Baths: 1 Private 2 Shared

Bonnybridge

National Grid Ref: NS8380

Castrechery House Hotel

Bandominie Farm, *Walton Road, Bonnybridge, Stirlingshire, FK4 2H*
Comfortable farmhouse with nice views. **Open:** All Year
Grades: STB Listed, Comm
01324 840284 Mrs Forrester
Rates fr: *£15.00*-**£16.00**.
Beds: 2D 1T

Carfrae

National Grid Ref: NT5769

Goblin Ha Hotel, Tweedale Arms Hotel (Gifford)

Carfrae Farm, *Carfrae, Haddington, East Lothian, EH41 4L*
Quiet, comfortable farmhouse. Lovely garden. **Open:** May to Oc
Grades: STB Listed, High Comm
01620 830242 Mrs Gibson
Fax no: 01620 830320
Rates fr: *£18.00*-**£25.00**.
Beds: 2D 1T 1S
Baths: 1 Private 1 Shared
(10) (6)

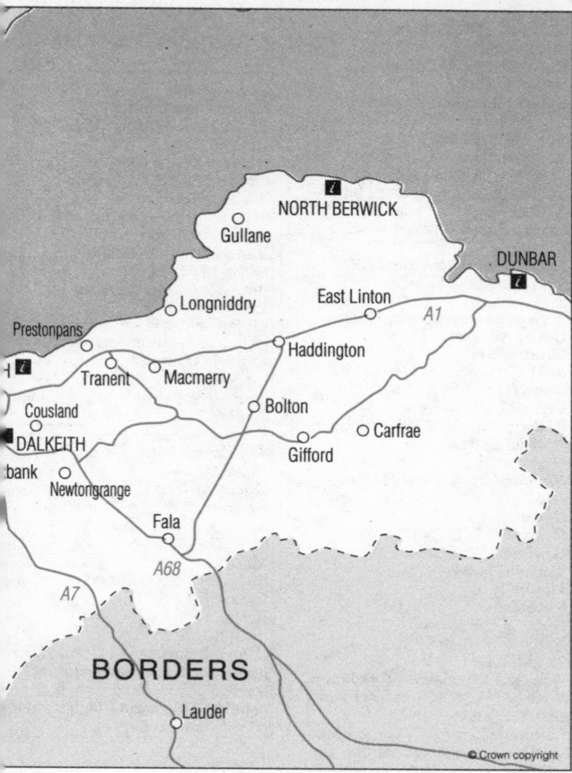

Cousland

National Grid Ref: NT3768

County Hotel

Hadfast Road, Cousland, Dalkeith, Mid Lothian, EH22 2NU.
Modern house with beautiful views.
Open: All Year
0131 663 1294
Mrs Stevenson
Rates fr: *£14.00*-**£16.00**.
Beds: 2D 1T
Baths: 2 Ensuite 1 Private
(3)

Please respect a B&B's wishes regarding children, animals & smoking.

Bringing children with you? Always ask for any special rates.

Dalkeith

National Grid Ref: NT3467

Justinlees Inn, County Hotel

Rathan House Self Catering and B&B, *45 Eskbank Road, Eskbank, Dalkeith, Mid Lothian,* EH22 3BH.
Open: All Year (not Xmas)
Grades: STB Listed, Comm
0131 663 3291 (also fax no)
Mr & Mrs MacRae
Rates fr: *£22.00*-**£22.00**.
Beds: 1F 1T **Baths:** 2 Ensuite
(1) (7)
Set in beautiful leafy conservation area. Edinburgh bypass 2 minutes. Huge elegant refurbished family suite. Safe large walled garden, croquet lawn. Excellent ensuite facilities.

Belmont, *47 Eskbank Road, Dalkeith, Midlothian,* EH22 3BH.
Spacious Victorian house and garden.
Open: All Year (not Xmas)
Grades: STB Listed
0131 663 8676 (also fax no)
Mrs Jarvis
Rates fr: *£17.00*-**£18.00**.
Beds: 2D 1T
Baths: 1 Private 1 Shared
(10)

Woodcot, *22 Bonnyrigg Road, Eskbank, Dalkeith, Midlothian,* EH22 3EZ.
Attractive detached Victorian family house.
Open: All Year (not Xmas)
0131 663 2628 Mrs Blair
Rates fr: *£15.00*-**£15.00**.
Beds: 2F
(4)

Dunbar

National Grid Ref: NT6778

Hillside Hotel

Cruachan Guest House, *East Links Road, Dunbar, E. Lothian,* EH42 1LT.
Friendly private house on beach.
Open: All Year
Grades: STB 1 Cr, Comm
01368 863006
Mr & Mrs McVicar
Rates fr: *£15.00*-**£15.00**.
Beds: 2F 1D 1T 1S
Baths: 1 Private 1 Shared
(6)

Battleblent Hotel, *West Barns, Dunbar, E. Lothian,* EH42 1TS.
Family-run country house hotel.
Open: All Year
01368 862234 Mr Ferguson
Rates fr: *£21.00*-**£24.50**.
Beds: 1F 1D 3T 2S
Baths: 7 Private
(20)

St Laurence Guest House, *North Road, Dunbar, E. Lothian,* EH42 1AU.
Large comfortable Edwardian house.
Open: All Year (not Xmas)
Grades: STB 2 Cr, Comm
01368 862527
Mrs Diggory
Rates fr: *£14.00*-**£14.00**.
Beds: 2D 1T
Baths: 2 Ensuite 1 Private
(4)

Pay B&Bs by cash or cheque. Be prepared to pay up front for one night stays.

St Helens Guest House, *Queens Road, Dunbar, E. Lothian,* EH42 1LN.
Near beach and golf course.
Open: Jan to Oct
01368 863716 Mrs Scott
Rates fr: *£14.00*-**£15.00**.
Beds: 1F 1D 4T 1S
Baths: 2 Private 2 Shared
(4)

Courtyard Hotel & Restaurant, *Woodbush Brae, Dunbar, E. Lothian,* EH42 1HB.
Converted fisherman's waterside cottages.
Open: All Year
01368 864169 Mr Bramley
Rates fr: *£23.50*-**£24.50**.
Beds: 1F 3D 1T 2S
Baths: 2 Private 1 Shared

East Calder

National Grid Ref: NT0867

Midcalder Inn, Midcalder

Overshiel Farm, *East Calder, Livingston, West Lothian,* EH53 0HT.
Traditional stone-built farmhouse.
Open: All Year
Grades: STB 2 Cr, Comm, AA 3 Q
01506 880469 Mrs Dick
Fax no: 01506 883006
Rates fr: *£16.00*-**£20.00**.
Beds: 1D 2T
Baths: 2 Ensuite 1 Shared
(6)

East Linton

National Grid Ref: NT5977

Stonelaws, *East Linton, E. Lothian,* EH40 3DX.
Large Georgian farmhouse, antiques and log fires.
Open: Easter to Oct
01620 870234 Mrs Miller
Rates fr: *£17.00*-**£17.00**.
Beds: 1D 1T **Baths:** 1 Shared

Edinburgh

National Grid Ref: NT2773

Cafe Royal, Suffolk Hall Hotel, March Hall Hotel, Navaar House, Tatlers (Leith), Allison Hotel, Kings Wark

Dickie Guest House, *No 22, East Claremont Street, Edinburgh,* EH7 4JP.
Open: All Year (not Xmas)
Grades: STB 2 Cr, Comm
0131 556 4032 Mrs Dickie
Fax no: 0131 556 9739
Rates fr: *£23.00*-**£25.00**.
Beds: 1F 1D 1T 1S
Baths: 2 Private 1 Shared
B&B at Eileen Dickie's Victorian terraced town house close to Princes Street. Excellent breakast choice - fresh Scottish produce. Unrestricted street parking.

St Margarets Guest House, *18 Craigmillar Park, Edinburgh,* EH16 5PS.
Open: All Year
Grades: STB 2 Cr, Comm, AA 3 Q
0131 667 2202 (also fax no)
Mrs Brown
Rates fr: *£16.00*-**£25.00**.
Beds: 3F 3D 2T
Baths: 4 Ensuite 1 Private 1 Shared
(1) (7)
Victorian house of character. Dining room with French doors leading to garden. Situated on A701/A772. 10 minutes drive to Princes Street. Private carpark.

Joppa Rocks Guest House, *99 Joppa Road, Edinburgh,* EH15 5BP.
A very comfortable guest house.
Open: All Year
Grades: STB 2 Cr
0131 669 8695 Mrs Garvie
Rates fr: *£17.50*-**£17.50**.
Beds: 2T 1S
Baths: 2 Ensuite 3 Shared

Highland Park Guest House, *16 Kilmaurs Terrace, Edinburgh,* EH16 5DR.
Open: All Year (not Xmas)
Grades: STB 1 Cr, Comm
0131 667 9204
Mrs Kelly
Rates fr: *£15.00*-**£16.00**.
Beds: 2F 2T 2S
Baths: 2 Shared
Quiet residential area off Dalkeith Road (A7/A68) convenient for city centre. Friendly service. Comfortable rooms. Frequent bus services. Unrestricted parking. For information contact Cathy Kelly.

Lindsay Guest House, *108 Polwarth Terrace, Edinburgh,* EH11 1NN.
Our guests keep coming back!
Open: All Year (not Xmas)
Grades: STB Listed, Comm, AA 2 Q, RAC Acclaim
0131 337 1580
Mr Lawrie
Fax no: 0131 337 9174
Rates fr: *£22.50*-**£22.50**.
Beds: 1F 3D 2T 2S
Baths: 3 Ensuite 2 Shared
(8)

Templehall Hotel, *77 Promenade, Joppa, Edinburgh,* EH15 2EL.
Open: All Year
Grades: STB 2 Cr, Comm
0131 669 4264 Mr Wilson
Rates fr: *£20.00*-**£20.00**.
Beds: 1F 4D 1T 1S
Baths: 4 Ensuite 1 Private 1 Shared
Located on the beach in a residential suburb of Edinburgh. Ten minutes from city centre by car or regular bus services. Excellent bar and meals.

Rowan Guest House, *13 Glenorchy Terrace, Edinburgh,* EH9 2DQ.
Open: All Year (not Xmas)
Grades: STB 1 Cr, Comm, AA 2 Q, Recomm
0131 667 2463 (also fax no)
Mr & Mrs Vidler
Rates fr: *£19.00*-**£20.00**.
Beds: 2F 3D 2T 2S
Baths: 3 Ensuite 2 Shared
(2)
Elegant Victorian house in quiet, leafy conservation area, with easy access to centre, University, all roads south. Breakfast includes porridge and freshly baked scones. Parking.

44 Gilmore Place, *Edinburgh,* EH3 9NQ.
Open: All Year
Grades: STB 1 Cr, Approv, AA 1 Q, RAC Listed
0131 229 9932
Mr Cran
Rates fr: *£14.00*-**£22.00**.
Beds: 3F 3D 3T 1S
Baths: 3 Shared
(10)
Central Edinburgh - car park, 10 minute walk to Castle and Princes Street. Fully restored town house built in 1770, offers a high standard of accommodation.

Lorne Villa Guest House, *9 East Mayfield, Edinburgh,* EH9 1SD.
Victorian town house.
Open: All Year
Grades: STB Listed, Comm
0131 667 7159 (also fax no)
Mr McCulloch
Rates fr: *£18.00*-**£18.00**.
Beds: 1F 2D 3T 2S
Baths: 3 Ensuite 1 Private 4 Shared
(6)

Classic Guest House, *50 Mayfield Road, Edinburgh,* EH9 2NH.
Open: All Year
Grades: STB 2 Cr, High Comm, AA 4 Q, RAC High Acclaim
0131 667 5847
Mrs Mail
Fax no: 0131 662 1016
Rates fr: *£18.00*-**£25.00**.
Beds: 1F 2D 1T 1S
Baths: 4 Private 1 Shared
Friendly, family-run, Victorian house, totally non-smoking. Personal service, Scottish hospitality. On main bus routes. Perfect for exploring the Capital. Warm welcome awaits, excellent value.

Claymore Guest House, *68 Pilrig Street, Edinburgh, EH6 5AS.*
Open: All Year (not Xmas)
Grades: STB 2 Cr, Comm
0131 554 2500 (also fax no)
Mrs Dorrian
Rates fr: *£17.50*-**£17.50**.
Beds: 2F 2D 2T
Baths: 4 Private 2 Shared
Personally-run centrally situated Victorian house, offering a warm welcome with comfortably appointed bedrooms and including a generous Scottish breakfast. Near to all popular attractions.

Edinburgh House, *11 McDonald Road, Edinburgh, EH7 4LX.*
Central family-run Bed & Breakfast.
Open: All Year
Grades: STB 3 Cr, Comm
0131 556 3434
Mrs Rooney
Rates fr: *£16.00*-**£20.00**.
Beds: 1F 1D 3T
Baths: 3 Private

Ivy Guest House, *7 Mayfield Gardens, Edinburgh, EH9 2AX.*
Open: All Year
Grades: STB 2 Cr, Comm, AA 3 Q, Recomm, RAC Acclaim
0131 667 3411
Mr Green
Rates fr: *£17.00*-**£18.00**.
Beds: 3F 3D 2T
Baths: 6 Ensuite 2 Private
(8)
Quiet, family-run guest house, centrally located and close to all Edinburgh's major cultural attractions. A hearty Scottish breakfast and a warm welcome is assured.

17 Hope Park Terrace, *Edinburgh, EH8 9LZ.*
Fifteen minutes walk city centre.
Open: All Year
Grades: STB Listed, Approv
0131 667 7963
Mrs Frackelton
Rates fr: *£18.00*-**£20.00**.
Beds: 2D
Baths: 1 Shared
(10)

Villa Nina Guest House, *39 Leamington Terrace, Edinburgh, EH10 4JS.*
Open: All Year
Grades: STB Listed, Comm, AA 2 Q
0131 229 2644 (also fax no)
Mr Cecco
Rates fr: *£15.50*.
Beds: 1F 2D 2T
Baths: 3 Private 2 Shared
Very comfortable Victorian terrace-house situated in quiet residential part of city yet 15 minutes walk Princes Street, Castle, theatres. TV in all rooms. Private showers. Full cooked breakfast.

Planning a longer stay? Always ask for any special rates.

Sunnyside Guest House, *13 Pilrig Street, Edinburgh, EH6 5AN.*
Open: All Year
Grades: STB 1 Cr, Comm
0131 553 2084 Mr Wheelaghan
Rates fr: *£14.50*-**£14.50**.
Beds: 1F 4D 2T 2S
Baths: 3 Ensuite 1 Private 2 Shared
Beautiful Georgian family-run guesthouse. An easy atmosphere and ample breakfast. 0.5 miles from city centre. 10 minutes to Playhouse Threatre and restaurants. Own key.

Zetland Guest House, *186 St Johns Road, Edinburgh, EH12 8SG.*
Open: All Year
0131 3343898 Mr Stein
Rates fr: *£16.00*-**£18.00**.
Beds: 1F 3D 3T 2S
Baths: 2 Shared
(7)
Large Victorian house in residential area on the west side of Edinburgh on the A8. Off-street parking. Excellent bus service to city centre.

Leamington Guest House, *57 Leamington Terrace, Edinburgh, EH10 4JS.*
Family-run Victorian house.
Open: All Year
Grades: STB 2 Cr, Comm, AA 2 Q, Recomm
0131 228 3879 Mrs Hodkinson
Fax no: 0131 221 1022
Rates fr: *£20.00*-**£20.00**.
Beds: 3F 2D 1T 2S
Baths: 2 Private 3 Shared

Dukes of Windsor Street, *17 Windsor Street, Edinburgh, EH7 5LA.*
Open: All Year (not Xmas)
Grades: STB Listed, Comm
0131 556 6046 (also fax no)
Mr Manson
Rates fr: *£25.00*-**£25.00**.
Beds: 1F 4D 4T 1S
Baths: 10 Private
Luxury B&B, all rooms ensuite. In quiet, central location near historic monuments, stations, good pubs and restaurants, theatre and shops.

All details shown are as supplied by B&B owners in Autumn 1996.

The lowest **single** *rate is shown in* **bold.**

Cree House B&B , *77 Mayfield Road, Edinburgh, EH9 3AA.*
Open: All Year
Grades: STB Listed, Comm
0131 667 2524 Mr Miles
Fax no: 0131 668 4455
Rates fr: *£16.00*-**£16.00**.
Beds: 1F 1D 3T 2S
Baths: 3 Shared
Warm hospitality assured in comfortable Victorian terraced house on bus route to city centre. Convenient for University. Colour TV and tea/coffee in all rooms.

Camore Hotel, *7 Links Gardens, Leith, Edinburgh, EH6 7JH.*
Views overlooking historical Leith links. **Open:** All Year
Grades: STB 2 Cr, Comm
0131 554 7897 (also fax no)
Mrs Forest
Rates fr: *£19.00*-**£25.00**.
Beds: 2F 1D 3T 4S
Baths: 3 Shared

Dene Guest House, *7 Eyre Place, Off Dundas Street, Edinburgh, EH3 5ES.*
Open: All Year
Grades: STB 2 Cr, Approv
0131 556 2700 Mr McDougall
Fax no: 0131 557 9876
Rates fr: *£18.50*-**£18.50**.
Beds: 2F 2D 3T 3S
Baths: 2 Private 2 Shared
Situated in Edinburgh's famous New Town, this charming Georgian town house offers a warm welcome and a convenient location for all the Capital's main attractions.

Gifford House, *103 Dalkeith Road, Edinburgh, EH16 5AJ.*
Comfortable refurbished friendly guest house. **Open:** All Year
Grades: STB 2 Cr, Comm
0131 667 4688 Mrs Dow
Rates fr: *£18.00*-**£21.00**.
Beds: 2F 2D 1T 1S
Baths: 7 Ensuite

Angusbeag Guest House, *5 Windsor Street, Edinburgh, EH7 5LA.*
Open: All Year
0131 556 1905 J Armstrong
Rates fr: *£19.50*-**£25.00**.
Beds: 2F 1D
Baths: 1 Private 1 Shared
(1)
Georgian Guest House, with three letting bedrooms, 3 minutes Playhouse Theatre, 10 mins from Princes Street, Railway Station, Airport buses, bus station. 0131 556 1905.

Many rates vary according to season - the lowest are shown here.

Cruachan Guest House, *53 Gilmore Place, Edinburgh, EH3 9NT.*
Open: All Year
Grades: STB 2 Cr, Comm
0131 229 6219 (also fax no)
Mrs Gibson
Rates fr: *£17.00*-**£18.00**.
Beds: 1F 1D 1T 2S
Baths: 2 Ensuite 2 Shared
Janette promises you a warm welcome at this very homely non-smoking guest house with full Scottish breakfast. Only ten minutes walk from city centre.

Torivane Guest House, *1 Morton Street, Edinburgh, EH15 2EW.*
Comfortable friendly seaside residence.
Open: All Year (not Xmas)
Grades: STB 2 Cr, Comm
0131 669 1648 Mr Fraser
Rates fr: *£14.00*-**£14.00**.
Beds: 1D 1T 1S
Baths: 1 Ensuite 1 Shared
(6)

Sheridan Guest House, *1 Bonnington Terrace, Edinburgh, EH6 4BP.*
Open: All Year
Grades: STB 2 Cr, Comm
0131 554 4107
Mr Blackhall
Rates fr: *£18.00*-**£28.00**.
Beds: 1F 1D 6T
(1)
Elegant Georgian town house with ample street parking, frequent bus service, 10 minutes from city centre. Elegant Residents Lounge and spacious dining room where a hearty full Scottish breakfast is served. Tastefully furnished bedrooms, some with full private ensuite facilities.

Lauderville Guest House, *52 Mayfield Road, Edinburgh, EH9 2NH.*
Stone-built Victorian town house.
Open: All Year
Grades: STB 2 Cr, High Comm
0131 667 7788 / 667 4005
Mrs Marriott
Fax no: 0131 667 7788
Rates fr: *£18.00*-**£25.00**.
Beds: 1F 3D 2T
Baths: 4 Ensuite 2 Shared

Forthview, *45 Moira Terrace, Edinburgh, EH7 6TD.*
Edwardian house with restful atmosphere.
Open: All Year
Grades: STB 1 Cr, Comm
0131 657 2912 Ms Craig
Rates fr: *£20.00*-**£20.00**.
Beds: 3T 1S
Baths: 4 Ensuite 1 Shared
(12)

Parklands Guest House, *20 Mayfield Gardens, Edinburgh, EH9 2BZ.*
Comfortable Victorian guest house.
Open: All Year
Grades: STB 2 Cr, Comm, AA 3 Q
0131 667 7184 Mrs Drummond
Fax no: 0131 667 2011
Rates fr: *£22.00*-**£30.00**.
Beds: 1F 3D 2T
Baths: 5 Ensuite 1 Private
(1)

Barony House, *4 Queens Crescent, Edinburgh, EH9 2AZ.*
Victorian detached villa, residential area.
Open: All Year
Grades: STB Listed, Comm
0131 667 5806 Mrs Berkengoff
Rates fr: *£18.00*-**£18.00**.
Beds: 3F 1D 2T 2S
Baths: 3 Private 2 Shared
(4)

17 Crawfurd Road, *Edinburgh, EH16 5PQ.*
Victorian family home, friendly welcome.
Open: May to Sep
0131 667 1191
Ms Simpson
Rates fr: *£14.50*.
Beds: 1D 1T
Baths: 2 Shared
(1)

6 Dean Park Crescent, *Edinburgh, EH4 1PN.*
Central, warm, comfortable Victorian home.
Open: All Year
0131 332 5017
Mrs Kirkland
Rates fr: *£16.50*-**£17.50**.
Beds: 2F 1D 1T 1S
Baths: 1 Ensuite 2 Shared

Acorn Guest House, *70 Pilrig Street, Edinburgh, EH6 5AS.*
Large Victorian private guest house.
Open: All Year (not Xmas)
Grades: STB 1 Cr, Comm
0131 554 2187 Mrs Waters
Rates fr: *£15.00*.
Beds: 2F 2D 1T
Baths: 1 Ensuite 2 Shared

The lowest **single** *rate is shown in* **bold.**

Craigelachie Hotel, *21 Murrayfield Avenue, Edinburgh, EH12 6AU.*
Elegant Victorian town house hotel.
Open: All Year
Grades: STB 1 Cr, Comm
0131 337 4076 / 337 2619
Mr Oag
Fax no: 0131 313 3305
Rates fr: *£22.50*-**£25.00**.
Beds: 3F 1D 2T 2S
Baths: 3 Ensuite 2 Shared
(1)

20 Restalrig Gardens, *Edinburgh, EH7 6HZ.*
Terraced house 10 minutes by bus centre.
Open: All Year
Grades: STB Listed, Comm
0131 661 3762
Mrs Ferguson
Rates fr: *£15.00*.
Beds: 2F 1D 1T
(2)

21 Dean Park Crescent, *Edinburgh, EH4 1PH.*
Outstanding comfort in Georgian quarter.
Open: May to Sep
Grades: STB 2 Cr, Comm
0131 332 3096
Ms Toynbee
Rates fr: *£19.50*-**£19.50**.
Beds: 1F 1D 1S
Baths: 3 Ensuite
(3)

Aries Guest House, *5 Upper Gilmore Place, Edinburgh, EH3 9NW.*
Small, central, friendly guest house.
Open: All Year
Grades: STB Listed, Approv
0131 229 4669 Mrs Robertson
Rates fr: *£13.00*-**£15.00**.
Beds: 4D 1T 1S
Baths: 2 Shared

Fala

National Grid Ref: NT4361

Juniper Lea Hotel

Fala Hall Farm, *Fala, Pathhead, Midlothian, EH37 5SZ.*
Comfortable, unusual C16th farmhouse.
Open: All Year (not Xmas)
Grades: STB Listed, Comm
01875 833249
Mrs Lothian
Rates fr: *£15.00*-**£18.00**.
Beds: 1F 1D
Baths: 1 Shared
(3)

Bringing children with you? Always ask for any special rates.

Fauldhouse

National Grid Ref: NS9360

East Badallan Farm, *Fauldhouse, Bathgate, West Lothian,* *EH47 9AG.*
Farmed by Storry's since 1729.
Open: All Year (not Xmas)
01501 770251 Mrs Storry
Rates fr: *£16.00*-**£20.00**.
Beds: 1F 1T
Baths: 1 Shared

Gifford

National Grid Ref: NT53676

Tweedale Arms Hotel (Gifford)

Long Newton Rowan Park Farm, *Gifford, Haddington, E. Lothian,* *EH41 4JW.*
Modern farmhouse - furnished to high standard.
Open: Feb to Oct
Grades: STB Listed, High Comm
01620 810327
Mrs Whiteford
Rates fr: *£17.00*-**£20.00**.
Beds: 1F 1D 1T
Baths: 1 Private 2 Shared
(5) (5)

Gilmerton

National Grid Ref: NT2968

137 Drum Street, *Gilmerton, Edinburgh,* *EH17 4RJ.*
Newly built, ideally situated minutes from city centre.
Open: All Year
0131 664 9548 Mrs Baigan
Rates fr: *£18.50*-**£35.00**.
Beds: 1F 1D 1T 1S
Baths: 5 Ensuite
(16)

Gullane

National Grid Ref: NT4882

Old Clubhouse, La Poitiniere, Golf Hotel

The Bents, *Hill Road, Gullane, E. Lothian,* *EH31 2BE.*
Very close to golf and beach.
Open: All Year
01620 842229 Mrs Morson
Rates fr: *£20.00*-**£20.00**.
Beds: 1F 1T
Baths: 1 Shared

Faussethill House, *Main Street, Gullane, East Lothian,* *EH31 2DR.*
Large Edwardian private house.
Open: Mar to Dec
Grades: STB 2 Cr, High Comm, AA 4 Q, Select
01620 842396 (also fax no)
Mr & Mrs Nisbet
Rates fr: *£20.00*-**£26.00**.
Beds: 1D 2T
Baths: 2 Ensuite 1 Private
(4)

Hopefield House, *Main Street, Gullane, East Lothian,* *EH31 2DP.*
Lovely family home with garden.
Open: Easter to Oct
01620 842191
Mrs Knight
Rates fr: *£20.00*-**£20.00**.
Beds: 1D 3T
Baths: 3 Ensuite 1 Private
(6)

Cruachan, *The Beeches, Off Muirfield Park, Gullane, East Lothian,* *EH31 2DX.*
Comfortable, friendly, excellent, guests say.
Open: All Year
01620 842033 Mrs Lynch
Rates fr: *£14.00*-**£14.00**.
Beds: 2T
Baths: 1 Shared

Haddington

National Grid Ref: NT5173

Goblin Ha'

Eaglescairnie Mains, *Haddington, E. Lothian,* *EH41 4HN.*
Superb farmhouse on working conservation-farm.
Open: All Year (not Xmas)
Grades: STB 2 Cr, Comm
01620 810491 (also fax no)
Mrs Williams
Rates fr: *£18.00*-**£20.00**.
Beds: 2D 1T
Baths: 2 Ensuite 1 Shared
(6)

Schiehallion, *19 Church Street, Haddington, E. Lothian,* *EH41 3ES.*
Beautiful family home - friendliness renowned.
Open: All Year
Grades: STB 2 Cr, Comm
01620 825663 Ms Richards
Rates fr: *£19.00*-**£22.00**.
Beds: 21D 1T
Baths: 1 Ensuite 1 Shared
(6)

Barney Mains Farm House, *Haddington, E. Lothian,* *EH41 3SA.*
Beautiful Georgian farmhouse, spectacular views.
Open: Mar to Nov
01620 880310 Mrs Kerr
Rates fr: *£15.00*-**£17.00**.
Beds: 1D 2T
Baths: 2 Shared
(6)

Hawthornden

National Grid Ref: NT2963

Glenlea, *Hawthornden, Lasswade, Midlothian,* *EH18 1EJ.*
Large Victorian private house.
Open: All Year (not Xmas)
0131 440 2079 Mrs Noble
Rates fr: *£13.50*.
Beds: 1F 2D
Baths: 2 Shared
(10)

Bringing children with you? Always ask for any special rates.

Howgate

National Grid Ref: NS9135

Snooty Fox, Leadburn Inn

Waltower Farm, *Howgate, Penicuik, Midlothian,* *EH26 8PY.*
Open: All Year (not Xmas)
01968 672277 Mrs Marwick
Rates fr: *£16.00*-**£20.00**.
Beds: 1F 1D 1T
Baths: 1 Private 1 Shared
(4)
Country house in mature garden. Family farm, large sitting room with log fire, conservatory. Electric blankets. Excellent restaurants nearby. 10 miles from Edinburgh, Borders, airport.

Ingliston

National Grid Ref: NT1372

Royal Highland Lodge, *Ingliston, Newbridge, Midlothian,* *EH28 8NB.*
Motorway lodge, budget price accommodation.
Open: All Year
0131 333 4331 Mr & Mrs Reid
Rates fr: *£17.50*-**£25.00**.
Beds: 28T 6S
Baths: 36 Ensuite

Linlithgow

National Grid Ref: NS9977

Torphichin Inn

Woodcockdale Farm, *Lanark Road, Linlithgow, West Lothian,* *EH49 6QE.*
Modern farmhouse. Phone now!
Open: All Year
01506 842088
Mrs Erskine
Rates fr: *£16.00*-**£19.00**.
Beds: 1F 1D 1T 1S
Baths: 4 Ensuite

Wester William Craigs, *Linlithgow, West Lothian,* *EH49 6QF.*
Modern country house - quiet location.
Open: All Year (not Xmas)
01506 845470 Mrs Millar
Rates fr: *£17.50*-**£20.00**.
Beds: 1D 1T
Baths: 1 Ensuite 1 Private

The lowest *double* rate per person is shown in *italics*.

National Grid References are for villages, towns and cities - *not* for individual houses.

11 Jocks Hill Crescent, *Linlithgow, West Lothian, EH49 7BJ.*
Modern chalet bunaglow.
Open: All Year (not Xmas)
01506 842866 Mrs Sprot
Rates fr: *£16.00*-**£18.00**.
Beds: 1F 1D 1T **Baths:** 2 Shared
(2)

Loanhead

National Grid Ref: NT2765

Inveravon House Hotel, *9 Inveravon Road, Loanhead, Mid Lothian, EH20 9EF.*
Large Victorian house.
Open: All Year
0131 440 0124 Mr Potter
Rates fr: *£20.00*-**£25.00**.
Beds: 3F 5D 2T 3S
Baths: 13 Ensuite
(20)

Longniddry

National Grid Ref: NT4476

The Spiney, *Old School lane, Longniddry, Longniddry, Prestonpans, E. Lothian, EH32 0NQ.*
Secluded modern bungalow.
Open: Feb to Nov
01875 853 325 Mrs Playfair
Rates fr: *£14.00*-**£16.00**.
Beds: 2D 1T
Baths: 1 Ensuite 1 Shared
(2)

Musselburgh

National Grid Ref: NT3573

Ravelston House Hotel, Woodside Hotel

5 Craighall Terrace, *Musselburgh, Mid Lothian, EH21 7PL.*
Detached bungalow, good bus/train services.
Open: Easter to Oct
Grades: STB Listed, Approv
0131 665 4294 Mrs Douglas
Rates fr: *£16.00*-**£18.00**.
Beds: 1F 1D **Baths:** 1 Shared
(4) (1)

17 Windsor Park, *Musselburgh, Mid Lothian, EH21 7QL.*
Modern semi-detached, private parking. **Open:** All Year
Grades: STB Listed, Comm
0131 665 2194 (also fax no)
Mr Wilson
Rates fr: *£19.00*-**£16.50**.
Beds: 1F 1D 1T
Baths: 1 Ensuite 2 Shared
(2)

Craigesk, *10 Albert Terrace, Musselburgh, Mid Lothian, EH21 7LR.*
Attractive villa, overlooking golf course.
Open: All Year
Grades: STB 1 Cr
0131 665 3344 Miss Mitchell
Rates fr: *£16.00*-**£16.00**.
Beds: 2F 2T 1S
Baths: 2 Shared
(4)

Newtongrange

National Grid Ref: NT3464

Bryans Farm, *Newtongrange, Dalkeith, Mid Lothian, EH22 4SS.*
Large Victorian comfortable farmhouse.
Open: All Year
0131 660 5079
Mr Conlon
Fax no: 0131 663 3058
Rates fr: *£15.00*-**£15.00**.
Beds: 2F 1D 1T 2S
Baths: 3 Shared

North Berwick

National Grid Ref: NT5585

Pointgarry Hotel, Nether Abbey Hotel, Tantallon Inn

Dalrymple Guest House, *12 Quality Street, North Berwick, E. Lothian, EH39 4HP.*
Open: All Year
Grades: STB 1 Cr, Comm
01620 892529 Mr Nichol
Rates fr: *£16.50*-**£16.50**.
Beds: 1F 2D 5T
Baths: 4 Shared
(7)
Original old coaching house 2 minutes walk harbour & beaches & town centre. Superb base for golfing, ornithology, historic attractions, trains to Edinburgh. Good restaurant, substantial breakfasts.

Golf Hotel, *34 Dirleton Avenue, North Berwick, E. Lothian, EH39 4BH.*
Large, converted, family holiday house.
Open: All Year
Grades: STB 1 Cr, Approv
01620 892202 (also fax no)
Mr Searle
Rates fr: *£24.00*-**£24.00**.
Beds: 4F 5T 3S
Baths: 9 Private 2 Shared
(20)

Planning a longer stay? Always ask for any special rates.

Kharg, *5 West Bay Road, North Berwick, E. Lothian, EH39 4AW.*
Seaside bungalow adjacent golf course.
Open: Easter to Sep
01620 894576 (also fax no)
Mrs Mcqueen
Rates fr: *£15.00*-**£15.00**.
Beds: 2D 1S
Baths: 1 Shared
(6)

County Hotel, *High Street, North Berwick, E. Lothian, EH39 4HH.*
Cosy family-run hotel. Warm, friendly atmosphere.
Open: All Year
Grades: STB 3 Cr, Comm
01620 892989 (also fax no)
Mrs Tait
Rates fr: *£22.50*-**£22.50**.
Beds: 1F 3D 3T 1S
Baths: 7 Ensuite 1 Private
(6)

Seabank, *12 Marine Parade, North Berwick, E. Lothian, EH39 4LD.*
Stone built house, sea views.
Open: All Year
Grades: STB Listed, Comm
01620 892884
Mrs Gray
Fax no: 01620 895561
Rates fr: *£15.50*-**£18.00**.
Beds: 1F 3D 1T
Baths: 2 Shared
(5)

The Studio, *Grange Road, North Berwick, E. Lothian, EH39 4QT.*
Refurbished historic building, tastefully decorated.
Open: All Year
Grades: STB 2 Cr, High Comm
01620 895150
Mrs Ramsay
Fax no: 01620 895120
Rates fr: *£20.00*-**£25.00**.
Beds: 1D **Baths:** 1 Private
(2)

The Moorings, *15 Dirleton Avenue, North Berwick, E. Lothian, EH39 4AX.*
Victorian house close to golf and sea.
Open: April to Oct
01620 892178
Mr & Mrs Musselbrook
Rates fr: *£16.00*.
Beds: 1F 2T
Baths: 1 Shared
(All) (3)

Penicuik

National Grid Ref: NT2360

Leadburn Inn, Snooty Fox

Dykeneuk Cottage, *Peebles Road, Penicuik, Midlothian, EH26 8PN.*
Country cottage with alpine garden.
Open: May to Sep
01968 675885 Mrs Hobbs
Rates fr: *£15.00*-**£18.00**.
Beds: 1T **Baths:** 1 Private
(2)

Philpstoun

National Grid Ref: NT0476

Pardovan House, *Philpstoun, Linlithgow, West Lothian, EH49 7RU.*
Detached stone country house.
Open: Easter to Sep
01506 834219 Mr & Mrs Baker
Rates fr: *£16.00*-**£14.00**.
Beds: 1F 1T 1S
Baths: 1 Private 1 Shared
(3)

Prestonpans

National Grid Ref: NT3874

Ellerslie, *Station Road, Prestonpans, E. Lothian, EH32 9EP.*
Comfortable Scottish hospitality.
Open: All Year (not Xmas)
01875 810110 Mrs Murray
Rates fr: *£15.00*-**£17.00**.
Beds: 2T 1S
Baths: 1 Shared
(3)

Roslin

National Grid Ref: NT2763

The Old Waterhouse, *Rosslyn Castle, Roslin, Midlothian, EH25 9QB.*
Comfortable converted Edwardian waterhouse.
Open: Easter to Sep
0131 440 2318 Mrs Stephen
Rates fr: *£15.00*-**£15.00**.
Beds: 1D
Baths: 1 Private
(1)

All rates are subject to alteration at the owners' discretion.

Stoneyburn

National Grid Ref: NS9762

Croftmalloch Inn

1 Cannop Crescent, *Stoneyburn, Bathgate, West Lothian, EH47 8EF.*
Large detached countryside villa.
Open: All Year
01501 762659 Mrs Gray
Rates fr: *£15.00*-**£20.00**.
Beds: 1F 1D 1T 1S
Baths: 1 Private
(3)

Tranent

National Grid Ref: NT4072

Rosebank Guest House, *161 High Street, Tranent, E. Lothian, EH33 1LP*
Large converted C18th house.
Open: All Year
01875 610967 Mr & Mrs Harrison
Rates fr: *£14.00*-**£15.00**.
Beds: 1F 3D 1T **Baths:** 1 Shared
(1) (5)

Mull, Skye & Other Islands

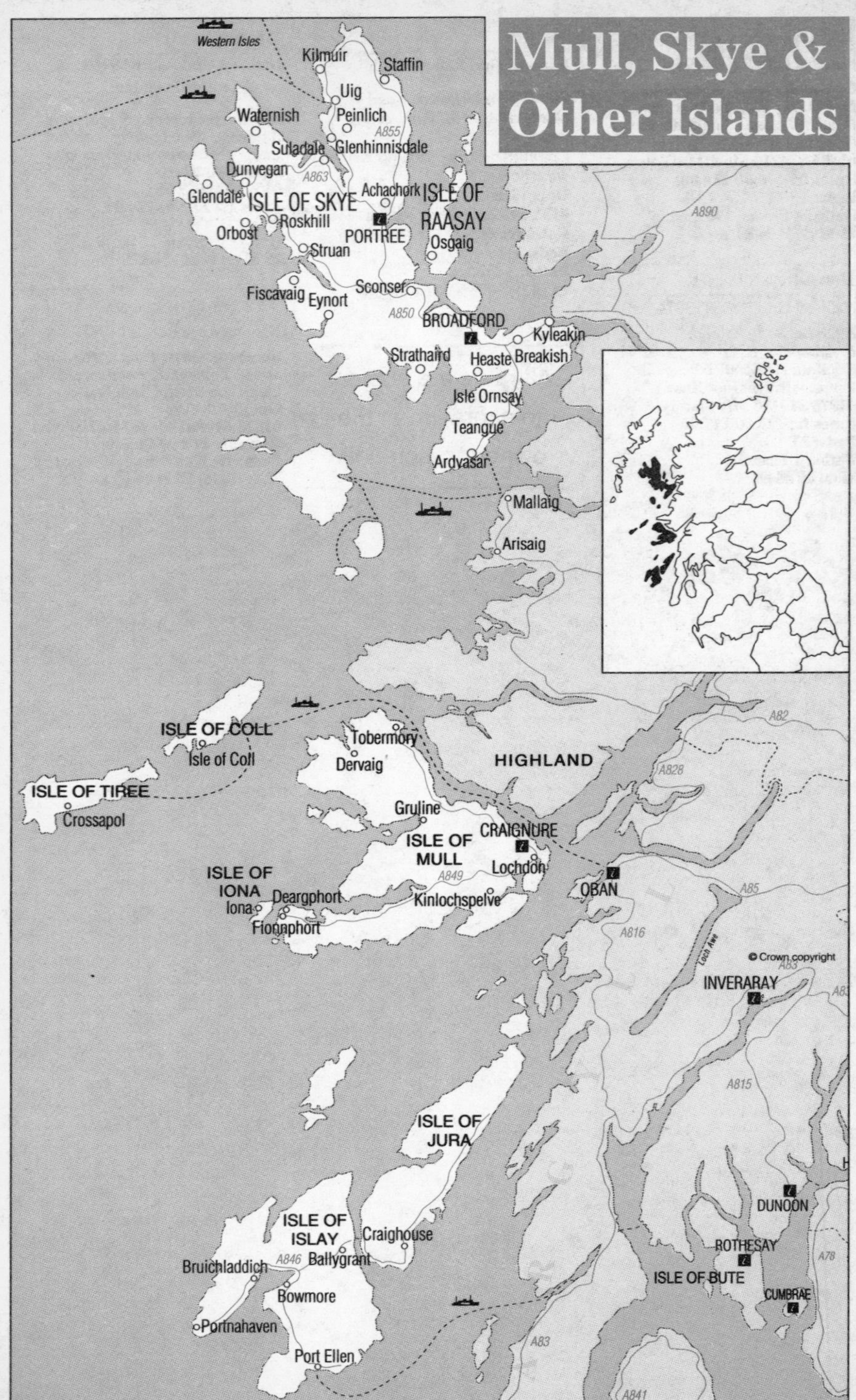

Tourist Information Centres

The Square, Bowmore, Isle of Islay, PA43 7JH, 01496 810254.

Car Park, **Broadford**, Isle of Skye, IV49 9AB, 01471 822361.

The Pierhead, **Craignure**, Isle of Mull, PA65 6AY, 01680 812377.

Stuart Street, **Millport**, Isle of Cumbrae, KA28 0AN, 01475 530753.

Meall House, **Portree**, Isle of Skye, IV51 9BZ, 01478 612137.

Main Street, **Tobermory**, Isle of Mull, PA75 6NU, 01688 302182.

Coll

National Grid Ref: NM1955

Garden House, *Isle of Coll, PA78 6TB.*
Surrounded by bird reserve. Old walled garden.
Open: All Year
01879 230374 Mrs Graham
Rates fr: *£16.00*-**£16.00**.
Beds: 1F 1D 1T 1S
Baths: 1 Shared
(6)

Iona

National Grid Ref: NM2724

Argyll Hotel, *Isle of Iona, Argyll, PA76 6SJ.*
Open: Easter to Oct
Grades: STB 3 Cr, Comm
01681 700334 Fax no: 01681 700510
Rates fr: *£37.00*-**£32.00**.
Beds: 1F 4D 4T 8S
Baths: 15 Ensuite 2 Shared
Relaxing, friendly hotel on the seashore. Cosy lounges with open fires. Cottage-style bedrooms. Spacious dining-room. Freshly prepared meals from local ingredients: also vegetarian. Recommended by many leading guides.

Islay — Ballygrant

National Grid Ref: NR3966

Ballygrant Inn & Restaurant, *Ballygrant, Isle of Islay, PA45 7QR.*
Open: All Year
Grades: STB 1 Cr, Comm
01496 840277 (also fax no)
Mr Graham
Rates fr: *£20.00*-**£20.00**.
Beds: 1F 1D 1S
Baths: 1 Shared
(20)
Family-run comfortable island inn on Hebridean island of Islay. Famous for malt whisky and wildlife. Excellent food (utilising local produce). Bar meals and dinners.

Islay — Bowmore

National Grid Ref: NR3159

Lochside Hotel, *Shore Street, Bowmore, Isle of Islay, PA43 7LB.*
Excellent value accommodation, food and whisky!
Open: All Year
01496 810244 Mrs Birse
Rates fr: *£20.00*-**£20.00**.
Beds: 1F 1D 1T 5S
Baths: 8 Ensuite

Islay — Bruichladdich

National Grid Ref: NR2661

Anchorage, *Bruichladdich, Isle of Islay, PA49 7UN.*
Idyllically situated on Lochside.
Open: Easter to Oct
01496 850540
Mrs MacDonald
Rates fr: *£14.00*-**£14.00**.
Beds: 2D 1T
Baths: 1 Shared
(5) (3)

Islay — Port Ellen

National Grid Ref: NR3645

Tighnargaman, *Port Ellen, Isle of Islay, PA42 7BX.*
Family home overlooking Bay.
Open: All Year (not Xmas)
01496 302345 Mr & Mrs Kent
Rates fr: *£18.00*-**£25.00**.
Beds: 1D 2T
Baths: 1 Ensuite 1 Private 1 Shared

Islay — Portnahaven

National Grid Ref: NR1652

Glenview House, *Church Street, Portnahaven, Isle of Islay, PA47 7SL.*
Excellent hospitality, quiet, relaxing holidays.
Open: All Year (not Xmas)
01496 860303
Mrs MacLean
Rates fr: *£14.50*-**£17.50**.
Beds: 1F 1D 1T
Baths: 1 Shared

Jura — Craighouse

National Grid Ref: NR5267

Jura Hotel

7 Woodside, *Craighouse, Isle of Jura, PA60 7YA.*
Comfortable, friendly island hospitality.
Open: Mar to Sep
01496 820379 Ms Boardman
Rates fr: *£16.00*-**£18.00**.
Beds: 1F 1D 1T
Baths: 1 Shared
(12)

Mull — Craignure

National Grid Ref: NM7136

Craignure Inn, Ceilidh Place

Fois An Lolaire, *Craignure, Isle of Mull, PA65 6AY.*
Modern bungalow. Ideal walkers, bird-watchers.
Open: All Year (not Xmas)
Grades: STB Listed, Comm
01680 812423 Mrs Allan
Rates fr: *£16.00*-**£18.00**.
Beds: 1D 1T
Baths: 1 Shared
(6)

Rainbow End, *5 Kirk Terrace, Craignure, Isle of Mull, PA65 6AZ.*
Real Scottish hospitality, 10 mins pier. **Open:** May to Sep
01680 812491 (also fax no)
Mrs Cameron
Rates fr: *£16.50*-**£16.50**.
Beds: 1F 1S **Baths:** 1 Shared
(2)

Gorsten Farm House, *Loch Don, Craignure, Isle of Mull, PA64 6AP.*
Highest standards and spectacular sea views.
Open: All Year (not Xmas)
Grades: STB Listed
01680 812332 Mrs Auld
Rates fr: *£18.00*-**£25.00**.
Beds: 1D 2T **Baths:** 3 Ensuite
(4)

Inverlussa, *Craignure, Isle of Mull, PA65 6BD.*
Warm spacious elegant relaxed home. **Open:** Apr to Oct
Grades: STB Listed, High Comm
01680 812436 Mrs Wilson
Rates fr: *£15.00*-**£15.00**.
Beds: 1F 1D 1T
Baths: 1 Private 1 Shared
(20)

Mull — Deargphort

National Grid Ref: NM3025

Red Bay Cottage, *Deargphort, Fionnphort, Isle of Mull, PA66 6BP.*
Isolated, modernised home with restaurant.
Open: All Year (not New Year's Day)
01681 700396 Mr Wagstaff
Rates fr: *£15.50*-**£15.50**.
Beds: 1D 2T **Baths:** 2 Shared
(0) (10)

Mull — Dervaig

National Grid Ref: NM4352

Ardbeg House Hotel, *Dervaig, Tobermory, Isle of Mull, PA75 6QJ.*
Large Victorian house set in 1.5 acres.
Open: All Year
01688 400254 (also fax no)
Mr Shilling
Rates fr: *£19.00*-**£19.00**.
Beds: 2F 2D 2T 1S
Baths: 3 Private 4 Shared
(12)

National Grid References are for villages, towns and cities - *not* for individual houses.

***Antium Farm,** Dervaig, Tobermory, Isle of Mull, PA75 6QW.*
Traditional stonebuilt farmhouse.
Open: Easter to Oct
01688 400230 Mrs Boa
Rates fr: *£15.00*-**£20.00**.
Beds: 1F 1D 1T
Baths: 1 Shared
(1) (3)

***Achnacraig,** Dervaig, Tobermory, Isle of Mull, PA75 6QW.*
Stone farmhouse, stupendous views, circling buzzards.
Open: Mar to Oct
01688 400309
Mrs Smith
Rates fr: *£15.00*-**£15.00**.
Beds: 1F 1T 1S
Baths: 2 Shared
(5) (8)

Mull — Fionnphort

National Grid Ref: NR9064

***Bruach Mhor,** Fionnphort, Isle of Mull, PA66 6BL.*
Comfortable modernised croft house.
Open: All Year (not Xmas)
01681 700276 (also fax no)
Mrs Heald
Rates fr: *£15.00*-**£15.00**.
Beds: 1F 1D 1T
Baths: 2 Shared
(3)

***Seaview,** Fionnphort, Isle of Mull, PA66 6BL.*
Traditional Scottish granite house.
Open: All Year (not Xmas)
01681 700235
Mrs Noddings
Rates fr: *£12.00*-**£15.00**.
Beds: 2D 2T
Baths: 1 Private 3 Shared
(6)

Mull — Gruline

National Grid Ref: NM5440

***Torlochan,** Gruline, Isle of Mull, PA71 6HR.*
Small croft with a varied collection of animals.
Open: All Year (not Xmas)
01680 300380
Mrs McFarlane
Rates fr: *£16.0*-**£16.00**.
Beds: 1D 1T 1S
Baths: 1 Shared
(4)

Mull — Kinlochspelve

National Grid Ref: NM6526

***Barrachandroman,** Kinlochspelve, Lochbuie, Isle of Mull, PA62 6AA.*
Luxurious converted barn, superb scenery.
Open: All Year
Grades: STB 3 Cr, High Comm
01680 814220 (also fax no)
Mrs Railton Edwards
Rates fr: *£20.00*-**£20.00**.
Beds: 2D 1T
Baths: 1 Ensuite 1 Private
(6)

Mull — Lochdon

National Grid Ref: NM7333

***Old Mill Cottage Guesthouse & Restaurant,** Lochdon, Isle of Mull, PA64 6AP.*
Quiet situation, wealth of wildlife.
Open: All Year (not Xmas)
01680 812442 Mrs Smith
Rates fr: *£23.50*-**£30.00**.
Beds: 1D 1T **Baths:** 2 Ensuite

Mull — Tobermory

National Grid Ref: NM5055

Western Isles Hotel, MacDonald Arms

***The Cedars,** Dervaig Road, Tobermory, Isle of Mull, PA75 6PY.*
Detached bungalow, separate B & B facilities.
Open: All Year (not Xmas)
01688 302096 Mr Bettley
Rates fr: *£14.00*-**£18.00**.
Beds: 1D 1T **Baths:** 1 Shared
(4)

***Harbour House,** Main Street, Tobermory, Isle of Mull, PA75 6NU.*
Guest house overlooking Tobermory Bay.
Open: All Year (not Xmas)
01688 302209 Mrs MacLean
Rates fr: *£18.00*-**£18.00**.
Beds: 2F 3D 3T 2S
Baths: 2 Private 3 Shared
(10)

***Fairways Lodge,** Tobermory, Isle of Mull, PA75 6PS.*
Modern lodge on golf course.
Grades: STB 2 Cr, High Comm, AA 4 Q
01688 302238 (also fax no)
Mr & Mrs McAdam
Rates fr: *£31.00*-**£31.00**.
Beds: 1F 1D 2T 1S
Baths: 5 Private
(6)

***Tobermory Hotel,** 53 Main Street, Tobermory, Isle of Mull, PA75 6NT.*
Situated on Tobermory's waterfront. **Open:** All Year
01688 302091 Mr Sutton
Rates fr: *£25.00*-**£40.00**.
Beds: 2F 7D 4T 4S
Baths: 9 Private 8 Shared

***Callicvol,** 8 Strongarbh, Tobermory, Isle of Mull, PA75 6PR.*
Value for money B&B.
Open: All Year
01688 302396 Mr Henderson
Rates fr: *£11.00*-**£14.00**.
Beds: 2D 1T
Baths: 1 Shared
(3)

***Staffa Cottages Guest House,** Tobermory, Isle of Mull, PA75 6PL.*
Converted Victorian terrace cottages.
Open: All Year
01688 302464 Mrs Chadwick
Rates fr: *£20.00*.
Beds: 3D 2T
Baths: 5 Private
(10) (8)

Raasay

National Grid Ref: NG7627

***Churchton House,** Isle of Raasay, Kyle of Lochalsh, Ross-shire, IV40 8NX.*
Open: All Year
01478 660260 Mr Brown
Rates fr: *£17.00*-**£17.00**.
Beds: 2D 1T 1S
Baths: 3 Ensuite
(4)
Churchton House on the beautiful unspoilt Isle of Raasay with views of the Cuillins of Skye. Perfect island for walking or cycling. Fine wildlife.

***6 Osgaig Park,** Isle of Raasay, Kyle of Lochalsh, Ross-shire, IV40 8PB.*
Modern, comfortable croft house.
Open: All Year
01478 660207
Mrs Mackay
Rates fr: *£14.00*-**£14.00**.
Beds: 1D 1T
Baths: 1 Shared

Skye — Achachork

National Grid Ref: NG4745

***Creag An Fhithich,** 10 Achachork, Achachork, Portree, Isle of Skye, IV51 9HT.*
Modern farmhouse with panoramic views.
Open: Easter to Nov
01478 612213
Ms MacDonald
Rates fr: *£15.50*-**£15.50**.
Beds: 1F 1D 1T 1S
Baths: 2 Shared
(6)

Planning a longer stay? Always ask for any special rates.

All rates are subject to alteration at the owners' discretion.

Skye — Ardvasar

National Grid Ref: NG6203

Home Leigh, *Ardvasar, Isle of Skye, IV45 8RU.*
Modern house with well-equipped rooms.
Open: Feb to Nov
01471 844361 (also fax no)
Mrs Houlton
Rates fr: *£15.00*-**£13.00**.
Beds: 3T 1S
Baths: 3 Ensuite 1 Shared
(6)

Skye — Breakish

National Grid Ref: NG6823

Crofters Kitchen

Strathgorm, *15 Upper Breakish, Breakish, Isle of Skye, IV42 8PY.*
Spacious modern house overlooking sea .
Open: All Year (not Xmas)
01471 822508 Mrs Graham
Rates fr: *£15.00*-**£17.00**.
Beds: 1F 1D 1T
Baths: 2 Ensuite 1 Private
(6)

Langdale House, *Waterloo, Breakish, Isle of Skye, IV42 8QE.*
Modern double bungalow, centrally heated.
Open: Mar to Nov
01471 822376
Mrs Macgregor
Rates fr: *£20.00*-**£27.00**.
Beds: 2D 2T
Baths: 4 Ensuite
(4)

Skye — Broadford

National Grid Ref: NG6423

Ptarmigan, *Harrapool, Broadford, Isle of Skye, IV49 9AQ.*
Idyllic setting beside seaside.
Open: All Year (not Xmas)
01471 822744 Mrs Macphie
Fax no: 01471 822745
Rates fr: *£25.00*-**£35.00**.
Beds: 2D 1T
Baths: 3 Ensuite 1 Shared
(7)

Westside, *Elgol Road, Broadford, Isle of Skye, IV49 9AB.*
Comfortable modern bungalow.
Open: All Year
01471 822320
Mrs Robertson
Rates fr: *£18.00*-**£17.00**.
Beds: 1D 1T 1S
Baths: 2 Ensuite 1 Private

Tigh Na Mara, *Lower Harrapool, Broadford, Isle of Skye, IV49 9AQ.*
Quiet traditional seaside croft house.
Open: May to Oct
01471 822475 Mrs Scott
Rates fr: *£14.00*.
Beds: 1F 1T **Baths:** 1 Private

Skye — Culnaknock

National Grid Ref: NG5162

Glenview Inn

Half of Five, *Breckery, Culnaknock, Portree, Isle of Skye, IV51 9JH.*
Open: All Year (not Xmas)
01470 562263 Mr Downes
Rates fr: *£15.00*-**£20.00**.
Beds: 1D 1T
Baths: 1 Shared
(7) (2)
Modern croft bungalow set in 6 acres of mixed woodland. Outstanding sea and mountain views. Ideal peaceful location for relaxing, unwinding, fishing, walking, birdwatching, photography.

Skye — Dunvegan

National Grid Ref: NG2543

Old Schoolhouse Restaurant, Chimneys Restaurant

Roskhill Guest House, *Roskhill, Dunvegan, Isle of Skye, IV55 8ZD.*
Open: All Year
Grades: STB 3 Cr, Comm, AA 3 Q, Recomm
01470 521317 Griffith
Rates fr: *£15.50*-**£25.50**.
Beds: 1F 3D 1T
Baths: 3 Ensuite 1 Shared
(5) (6)
Cosy crofthouse beautifully situated for touring this historic island, walking, climbing, bird watching. Delicious home cooking served in stone walled dining room with log fire and resident's bar.

Orbost Farmhouse, *Orbost, Dunvegan, Isle of Skye, IV55 8ZB.*
Beautifully situated farmhouse.
Open: All Year
Grades: STB 1 Cr, Comm
01470 521479 (also fax no)
Mrs MacDonald
Rates fr: *£15.50*-**£15.50**.
Beds: 1F 1D
Baths: 1 Shared
(6)

Silverdale, *14 Skinidin, Dunvegan, Isle of Skye, IV55 8ZS.*
Excellent accommodation, splendid sea views.
Open: All Year (not Xmas)
Grades: STB 2 Cr, High Comm
01470 521251 Mrs Gracie
Rates fr: *£18.00*.
Beds: 1F 21D
Baths: 3 Ensuite
(5) (5)

Planning a longer stay? Always ask for any special rates.

Skye — Eynort

National Grid Ref: NG3826

The Blue Lobster, *3 Forestry Cottages, Eynort, Isle of Skye, IV47 8SG.*
Simple, friendly, informal, amongst hills.
Open: All Year
01478 640320 Mr Van Der Vliet
Rates fr: *£15.00*-**£15.00**.
Beds: 1F 1D 4T
(4)

Skye — Fiscavaig

National Grid Ref: NG3234

The Old Inn (Carbost)

Ivanhoe, *19 Fiscavaig, Fiscavaig, Carbost, Isle of Skye, IV47 8SN.*
Open: All Year
01478 640360 Mrs Wood
Rates fr: *£14.00*-**£14.00**.
Beds: 2D **Baths:** 1 Shared
Warm welcome. Comfortable accommodation, perfect setting for shore or hill-walking. Situated overlooking Fiscavaig Bay, across Loch Bracadle to MacLeod's Tables. Unwind and relax.

Skye — Glendale

National Grid Ref: NG1749

Strupag Cafe

Bailleboideach, *4 Lephin, Glendale, Dunvegan, Isle of Skye, IV55 8WJ.*
Modern crofthouse overlooking Outer Hebrides.
Open: Easter to Sep
Grades: STB Listed, Comm
01470 511376 (also fax no)
Mrs Kernachan
Rates fr: *£14.50*-**£19.50**.
Beds: 1D 2T **Baths:** 1 Shared
(4)

Skye — Glenhinnisdale

National Grid Ref: NG4057

Ferry Inn

Garybuie, *4 Balmeanach, Glenhinnisdale, Uig, Portree, Isle of Skye, IV51 9UX.*
Warm, comfortable house, scenic glen. **Open:** Easter to Oct
Grades: STB Listed, Approv
01470 542310 Mrs Wilson
Rates fr: *£15.00*-**£16.00**.
Beds: 2F 1D 1S **Baths:** 2 Shared
(6) (3)

Mile End House, *Glenhinnisdale, Uig, Portree, Isle of Skye, IV51 9UX.*
C19th house in quiet glen.
Open: All Year (not Xmas)
Grades: STB Listed, Comm
01470 542331 Mrs Butler
Rates fr: *£15.00*-**£15.00**.
Beds: 1F 1D 1T
Baths: 1 Shared
(6)

Skye — Heast

National Grid Ref: NG6417

Faite, *6 Heast, Heast, Broadford, Isle of Skye, IV49 8QF.*
Bungalow in scenic rural location.
Open: Easter to Oct
01471 822268 Mrs Mackinnon
Rates fr: *£15.00*-**£15.00**.
Beds: 1D 1T 1S
Baths: 1 Private 1 Shared
(4)

Skye — Isle Ornsay

National Grid Ref: NG6912

Isle Ornsay Hotel

6 Duisdale Beag, *Isleornsay, Isle of Skye, IV43 8QU.*
Quiet, modern croft house.
Open: Easter to Sep
Grades: STB 2 Cr, Comm
01471 833230 Mrs MacDonald
Rates fr: *£15.00*-**£18.00**.
Beds: 2D 1T
Baths: 3 Private
(3)

Skye — Kilmuir

National Grid Ref: NG3870

1 Herbusta, *Kilmuir, Portree, Isle of Skye, IV51 9YX.*
Highland hospitality, panoramic sea views.
Open: Easter to Sep
01470 552229 Mrs Beaton
Rates fr: *£12.00*-**£12.00**.
Beds: 1F 1D
Baths: 1 Shared

Skye — Kyleakin

National Grid Ref: NG7526

Dunringell Hotel, *Kyleakin, Isle of Skye, IV41 8PR.*
Country house in wooded garden.
Open: Mar to Oct
Grades: STB 3 Cr, Comm
01599 534180 Mr MacPherson
Fax no: 01599 534460
Rates fr: *£21.00*-**£21.00**.
Beds: 7F 6D 2T 3S
Baths: 10 Private 4 Shared
(20)

The lowest **single** *rate is shown in* **bold.**

Skye — Orbost

National Grid Ref: NG2543

Old Schoolhouse Restaurant (Dunvegan)

Orbost Farmhouse, *Orbost, Dunvegan, Isle of Skye, IV55 8ZB.*
Beautifully situated farmhouse.
Open: All Year
Grades: STB 1 Cr, Comm
01470 521479 (also fax no)
Mrs MacDonald
Rates fr: *£15.50*-**£15.50**.
Beds: 1F 1D
Baths: 1 Shared
(6)

Skye — Peinlich

National Grid Ref: NG4158

Peinlich, *Peinlich, Glenhinnisdale, Portree, Isle of Skye, IV51 9UY.*
Beautiful surroundings, near River Hinnisdal.
Open: Easter to Oct
Grades: STB 2 Cr
01472 542406
Mrs Nicolson
Rates fr: *£13.00*-**£13.00**.
Beds: 1F 1D 1T
Baths: 2 Shared

Skye — Portree

National Grid Ref: NG4745

Portree House Hotel

Creag An Fhithich, *10 Achachork, Achachork, Portree, Isle of Skye, IV51 9HT.*
Open: Easter to Nov
01478 612213 Ms MacDonald
Rates fr: *£15.50*-**£15.50**.
Beds: 1F 1D 1T 1S
Baths: 2 Shared
(6)
Modern farmhouse with panoramic views. Situated 2 miles north of Portree. Ideal for touring the North & West of the island. Warm welcome. Full Scottish breakfast. Also TV lounge for guests' use.

Foreland, *Stormyhill Road, Portree, Isle of Skye, IV51 9DT.*
Central for hillwalkers and climbers. **01478 612752**
Mrs Montgomery
Rates fr: *£16.00*-**£20.00**.
Beds: 1F 1D 1T **Baths:** 2 Shared
(5)

Treetops, *Camastianavaig Braes, Portree, Isle of Skye, IV51 9LQ.*
Modern bungalow overlooking the sea.
Open: May to Sep
01478 650218 Mrs Goddard
Rates fr: *£14.00*-**£16.00**.
Beds: 1D 1T
Baths: 1 Shared
(7) (2)

Skye — Roskhill

National Grid Ref: NG2744

Roskhill Guest House, *Roskhill, Dunvegan, Isle of Skye, IV55 8ZD.*
Cosy crofthouse beautifully situated for touring this historic island.
Open: All Year
Grades: STB 3 Cr, Comm, AA 3 Q, Recomm
01470 521317 Griffith
Rates fr: *£15.50*-**£25.50**.
Beds: 1F 3D 1T
Baths: 3 Ensuite 1 Shared
(5) (6)

Skye — Sconser

National Grid Ref: NG5131

Sconser Lodge, Sligachan Hotel

Sgoirebreac, *Sconser, Isle of Skye, IV48 8TD.*
Modern, comfortable croft house.
Open: All Year (not Xmas)
01478 650322 Mrs Nicolson
Rates fr: *£13.50*-**£15.00**.
Beds: 2D 1T
Baths: 2 Shared
(4)

Sgurr Mhairi, *29 Sconser, Sconser, Isle of Skye, IV48 8TD.*
Modern crofthouse. Spectacular lochside scenery.
Open: All Year (not Xmas)
01478 650334 Mrs Maclean
Rates fr: *£15.00*-**£15.00**.
Beds: 2D 1T
Baths: 1 Ensuite 1 Shared
(1) (4)

Skye — Staffin

National Grid Ref: NG4867

Glenview Inn, Flodigarry Hotel, Oystercatcher

Gracelands, *5 Glasphein, Staffin, Portree, Isle of Skye, IV51 9LZ.*
Open: Easter to Nov
01470 562313
Mrs Nicolson
Rates fr: *£13.50*-**£15.00**.
Beds: 1F 1D
(3)
Spacious comfortable rooms with fantastic sea and hill views. Marvellous hill-walking, climbing area. Access to sandy beach. Good food served in local restaurants, hotel.

Benview, *12 Clachan, Staffin, Portree, Isle of Skye, IV51 9JX.*
Hospitable 'home from home' accommodation.
Open: All Year
01470 562328 Mrs MacLeod
Rates fr: *£16.00*.
Beds: 2F 1D
Baths: 1 Ensuite 1 Shared
(3)

Skye — Stenscholl

National Grid Ref: NG4868

Tigh Cilmartin, *Stenscholl, Staffin, Portree, Isle of Skye, IV51 9JS.*
Listed Georgian manse by river.
Open: All Year
01470 562331 Mrs Poole
Rates fr: *£14.00*-**£14.00**.
Beds: 2D 1T
Baths: 1 Ensuite 1 Shared
(6)

Skye — Strathaird

National Grid Ref: NG5317

Strathaird House, *Strathaird, Broadford, Isle of Skye, IV49 9AX.*
Open: Easter to Sep
Grades: STB Listed, Approv
01471 86626901444 452990 (o/s)
Mr Kubale
Fax no: 01471 866269
Rates fr: *£20.00*-**£22.00**.
Beds: 3F 1D 1T 2S
Baths: 4 Shared
(6)
Friendly country guest house near Elgol. Walk to the mountains and sea and enjoy good food, wine and a fireside library. Self-catering annexe also available.

Skye — Struan

National Grid Ref: NG3448

Seaforth, *Coillore, Struan, Isle of Skye, IV56 8FX.*
Comfortable, family-run private house.
Open: Easter to Oct
01470 572230 Mrs Mackinnon
Rates fr: *£14.00*-**£15.00**.
Beds: 1F 1D 1T
Baths: 2 Shared
(4)

The Anchorage, *9 Eabost West, Struan, Isle of Skye, IV56 8FE.*
Modern comfortable crofthouse, panoramic views.
Open: Jan to Dec
Grades: STB 3 Cr, Comm
01470 572206 Mrs Campbell
Rates fr: *£15.00*-**£20.00**.
Beds: 2D 1T
Baths: 2 Ensuite 1 Private
(4)

Skye — Suladale

National Grid Ref: NG3753

1 Suladale, *Suladale, Portree, Isle of Skye, IV51 9PA.*
Modern bungalow on croft.
Open: All Year (not Xmas)
Grades: STB 2 Cr, Comm
01470 582202 Mrs Wright
Rates fr: *£13.00*-**£13.00**.
Beds: 2D 1S
Baths: 1 Private 1 Shared
(4)

Skye — Teangue

National Grid Ref: NG6609

Alltan, *Teangue, Isle of Skye, IV44 8RF.*
Good views and good food.
Open: Easter to Oct
01471 844342 Mr Shaw
Rates fr: *£15.00*-**£20.00**.
Beds: 2D 1T
Baths: 2 Shared
(4)

The lowest **single** *rate is shown in* **bold.**

Skye — Uig

National Grid Ref: NG3963

Uig Bay Bistro

Braeholm, *Uig, Portree, Isle of Skye, IV51 9XX.*
Homely croft house near ferry.
Open: All Year (not Xmas)
Grades: STB 1 Cr, Comm
01470 542396 (also fax no)
Mrs Morrison
Rates fr: *£16.00*-**£16.00**.
Beds: 1D 1T
Baths: 1 Shared
(2)

Skye — Waternish

National Grid Ref: NG2658

Lismore, *1 Camuslusta, Waternish, Isle of Skye, IV55 8SE.*
Converted crofter's cottage, scenic outlook.
Open: Easter to Oct
01470 592318
Mrs Dame
Rates fr: *£14.50*-**£17.50**.
Beds: 1F 1D
Baths: 1 Shared
(6)

Tiree — Crossapol

National Grid Ref: NL9943

The Sheiling, *Crossapol, Scarinish, Isle of Tiree, PA77 6UP.*
Croft house facing beach.
Open: Easter to Sep
Grades: STB Listed, Comm
01879 220503 Mrs Cameron
Rates fr: *£16.00*-**£16.00**.
Beds: 1T 1S
Baths: 1 Shared
(4)

Orkney

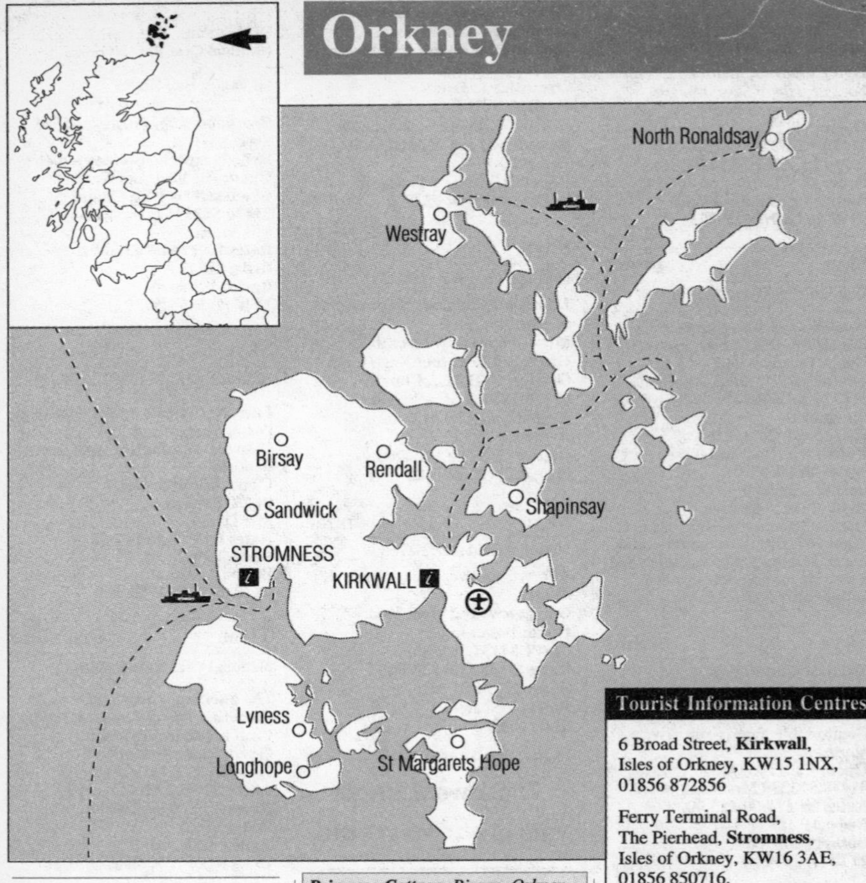

Tourist Information Centres

6 Broad Street, **Kirkwall**, Isles of Orkney, KW15 1NX, 01856 872856

Ferry Terminal Road, The Pierhead, **Stromness**, Isles of Orkney, KW16 3AE, 01856 850716.

Birsay

National Grid Ref: HY2825

Barony Hotel, Smithfield Hotel (Dounby), Merkister Hotel (Dounby)

Fiddlers Green, *Link House, The Palace, Birsay, Orkney, Isles of Orkney, KW17 2LX.*
Open: All Year
01856 721221 Rates fr: *£15.00*-**£15.00**.
Beds: 1F 1D 1T
Baths: 3 Ensuite
(5)
Unbeatable sunsets on Atlantic Coast, sea views, sea birds and seals. Free trout fishing 2 minutes. Archaeology on the doorstop - walkers' paradise - Fiddlers Green (sailors' haven).

The lowest **single** *rate is shown in* **bold.**

Primrose Cottage, *Birsay, Orkney, Isles of Orkney, KW17 2NB.*
Open: All Year
Grades: STB 2 Cr, Comm
01856 721384
Mrs Clouston
Rates fr: *£13.00*-**£13.00**.
Beds: 1F 1D 1S
Baths: 2 Ensuite 1 Shared
(4)
Quiet country cottage overlooking Marwick Bay close to RSPB reserves 'The Loons' and 'Marwick Head'. Ideal for birdwatching, trout fishing and quiet clifftop walks.

Heatherlea, *Birsay, Orkney, Isles of Orkney, KW17 2LR.*
Comfortable house overlooking Boardhouse Loch.
Open: Apr to Oct
Grades: STB 1 Cr, Approv
01856 721382
Mrs Balderstone
Rates fr: *£15.50*-**£15.50**.
Beds: 1D 1T
Baths: 1 Shared
(2) (2)

Kirkwall

National Grid Ref: HY4510

Queen's Hotel

Polrudden Guest House, *Peerie Sea Loan, Kirkwall, Isles of Orkney, KW15 1UH.*
Family-run new guest house.
Open: All Year (not Xmas)
Grades: STB 3 Cr, Comm
01856 874761 Mrs Thornton
Rates fr: *£20.00*-**£25.00**.
Beds: 2F 5T **Baths:** 7 Ensuite
(7)

Orkrest, *Annfield Crescent, Kirkwall, Isles of Orkney, KW15 1NS.*
Bed & Breakfast overlooking bay and islands.
Open: Apr to Oct
Grades: STB 1 Cr, Comm
01856 872172 Mrs Tonge
Rates fr: *£15.00*-**£16.00**.
Beds: 1D 2T
Baths: 1 Shared
(4)

***Craigwood,** Cromwell Road, Kirkwall, Isles of Orkney, KW15 1LN.*
Modern comfortable private house.
Open: All Year
Grades: STB Listed, Comm
01856 872006 Mr & Mrs Linklater
Rates fr: *£15.00*-**£16.00**.
Beds: 1D 1T 1S
Baths: 2 Shared
(4)

***Briar Lea,** 10 Dundas Crescent, Kirkwall, Isles of Orkney, KW15 1JQ.*
Large Victorian private house.
Open: All Year
Grades: STB Listed
01856 872747 Mrs Flett
Rates fr: *£15.00*-**£15.00**.
Beds: 2T 2S
Baths: 2 Shared
(0) (6)

***Elderwood,** 4 Park Loan, Kirkwall, Isles of Orkney, KW15 1PU.*
Modern bungalow in quiet cul-de-sac.
Open: All Year
Grades: STB 1 Cr, Comm
01856 872657
Mrs Omand
Rates fr: *£14.00*-**£14.00**.
Beds: 1D 1T
Baths: 1 Private

***Kemuel,** Bignold Park Road, Kirkwall, Isles of Orkney, KW15 1PT.*
Modern, comfortable & friendly home.
Open: Easter to Sep
01856 873092 Mrs Golding
Rates fr: *£14.00*-**£14.00**.
Beds: 1D 1T 1S
(2)

Longhope

National Grid Ref: ND3191

***Burnhouse,** Longhope, Hoy, Isles of Orkney, KW16 3PA.*
Spectacular views, welcoming family farmhouse.
Open: All Year (not Xmas)
Grades: STB 1 Cr, Comm
01856 701263 Mrs Budge
Rates fr: *£15.00*-**£15.00**.
Beds: 1F 1T
Baths: 2 Shared
(6)

Lyness

National Grid Ref: ND3094

***Stoneyquoy,** Lyness, Hoy, Isles of Orkney, KW16 3NY.*
Award-winning farm, brochure available.
Open: All Year (not Xmas)
Grades: STB 2 Cr, Comm
01856 791234 (also fax no)
Mrs Budge
Rates fr: *£16.00*-**£18.00**.
Beds: 1D 1T
Baths: 2 Ensuite
(4)

North Ronaldsay

National Grid Ref: HY7553

***North Ronaldsay,,** Bird Observatory, North Ronaldsay, Orkney, Isles of Orkney, KW17 2BE.*
Unique environmentally-aware holiday centre.
Open: All Year (not Xmas)
Grades: STB 2 Cr
01857 633200 A E Duncan
Fax no: 01857 633207
Rates fr: *£16.00*-**£16.00**.
Beds: 2D 2T
Baths: 1 Private 1 Shared
(6)

Rendall

National Grid Ref: HY3920

***Millbrig Farm,** Rendall, Orkney, Isles of Orkney, KW17 2EX.*
Orcadian family farm overlooking sea.
Open: May to Oct
01856 761254 Mrs Harvey
Rates fr: *£12.00*-**£12.00**.
Beds: 1F

Sandwick

National Grid Ref: HY2519

Smithfield Hotel (Dounby)

***Netherstove,** Sandwick, Stromness, Isles of Orkney, KW16 3LS.*
Modern, comfortable farmhouse, panoramic views.
Open: Easter to Oct
Grades: STB 1 Cr, Comm
01856 841625 (also fax no)
Mrs Poke
Rates fr: *£15.00*-**£16.00**.
Beds: 1D 1T
Baths: 2 Shared

Shapinsay

National Grid Ref: HY5017

***Girnigoe,** Shapinsay, Orkney, Isles of Orkney, KW17 2EB.*
Traditional, warm, comfortable farmhouse.
Open: All Year
01856 711256 Mrs Wallace
Rates fr: *£12.50*-**£12.50**.
Beds: 1D 1S
Baths: 2 Shared

St Margarets Hope

National Grid Ref: ND4493

***Murray Arms Hotel,** St Margarets Hope, Orkney, Isles of Orkney, KW17 2SP.*
Recently restored small village hotel.
Open: All Year
01856 831205 Mrs Sutherland
Rates fr: *£20.00*-**£20.00**.
Beds: 2D 1T 2S
Baths: 5 Ensuite
(4)

The lowest *double* rate per person is shown in *italics*.

Stromness

National Grid Ref: HY2509

Ferry Inn

***Oakleigh Hotel,** 76 Victoria Street, Stromness, Isles of Orkney, KW16 3BS.*
Friendly, traditional hotel. Near ferry.
Open: All Year (not Xmas)
01856 850447 Ms Woodford
Rates fr: *£22.00*-**£22.00**.
Beds: 1F 2D 2T 1S
Baths: 6 Ensuite

***Ferry Inn,** John Street, Stromness, Isles of Orkney, KW16 3AD.*
Small, family-run, friendly.
Open: All Year (not Xmas)
Grades: STB 3 Cr, Comm
01856 850280
Mrs Dennison
Fax no: 01856 851332
Rates fr: *£17.00*-**£17.00**.
Beds: 6F 5D 5T 1S
Baths: 13 Private 1 Shared
(0)

Westray

National Grid Ref: HY4446

***Pierowall Hotel,** Westray, Orkney, Isles of Orkney, KW17 2BZ.*
Possibly the best fish & chips you've ever tasted.
Open: All Year
01857 677472 J & M Fergus
Rates fr: *£13.00*-**£16.50**.
Beds: 1F 2D 3T **Baths:** 2 Shared
(6)

***Cleaton House Hotel,** Westray, Orkney, Isles of Orkney, KW17 2DB.*
Victorian manse now country hotel.
Open: All Year
Grades: STB 3 Cr, High Comm
01857 677508
Mr Stout
Rates fr: *£25.00*-**£30.00**.
Beds: 1F 2T 2D
Baths: 5 Ensuite
(18)

National Grid References are for villages, towns and cities - *not* for individual houses.

Perthshire & Kinross

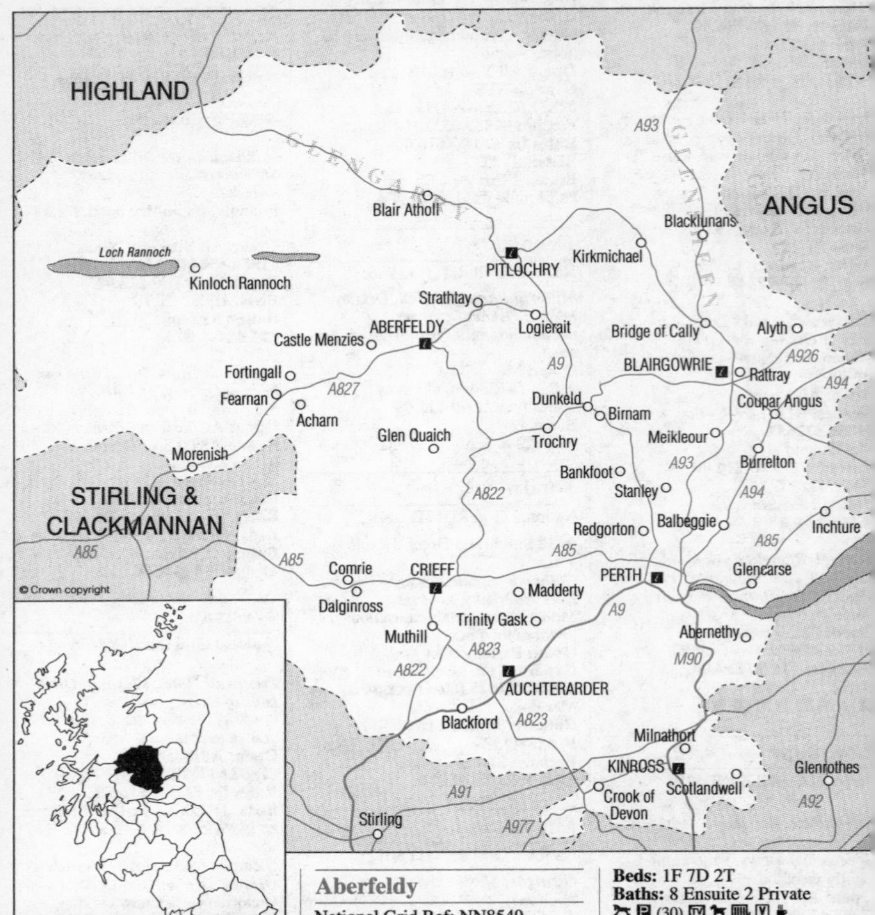

Tourist Information Centres

The Square, **Aberfeldy**, Perthshire, PH15 2DD, 01887 820276.

90 High Street, **Auchterarder**, Perthshire, PH3 1BJ, 01764 663450.

26 Wellmeadow, **Blairgowrie**, Perthshire, PH10 6AS, 01250 872960.

Town Hall, High Street, **Crieff**, Perthshire, PH7 3HU, 01764 652578.

Kinross Service Area, Junction 6, M90, **Kinross**, Kinross-shire, KY13 7BE, 01577 863680, (Easter to Oct).

45 High Street, **Perth**, Perthshire, PH1 5TJ, 01738 638353.

22 Atholl Street, **Pitlochry**, Perthshire, PH16 5BX, 01796 472218

Aberfeldy

National Grid Ref: NN8549

Scottish Bistro, Aileen Chraggan Hotel

2 Rannoch Road, *Aberfeldy, Perthshire, PH15 2BU.*
Large modern bungalow, comfortable and friendly.
Open: Easter to Oct
Grades: STB Listed, Comm
01887 820770 Mrs Ross
Rates fr: *£15.00*-**£15.00**.
Beds: 2D 1T
Baths: 1 Shared
(4)

Balnearn House, *Aberfeldy, Perthshire, PH15 2BJ.*
Outstanding - not to be missed.
Open: Easter to Oct
Grades: STB 2 Cr, Comm
01887 820431 Mr MacLaurin
Rates fr: *£18.50*-**£22.50**.
Beds: 1F 7D 2T
Baths: 8 Ensuite 2 Private
(30)

South Lodge, *Castle Menzies, Aberfeldy, Perthshire, PH15 2JD.*
Comfortable, converted C18th lodge.
Open: All Year (not Xmas)
Grades: STB Listed, High Comm
01887 820115 Mrs Bolam
Rates fr: *£16.00*-**£17.00**.
Beds: 1D 1T
Baths: 1 Ensuite 1 Private
(4)

Tomvale, *Tom of Cluny, Aberfeldy, Perthshire, PH15 2JT.*
Modern comfortable farmhouse.
Open: All Year (not Xmas/New Year)
Grades: STB Listed
01887 820171 Mrs Kennedy
Rates fr: *£15.00*-**£16.00**.
Beds: 1F 1D **Baths:** 1 Shared

***Carn Dris,** Aberfeldy, Perthshire, PH15 2LB.*
Large Edwardian private guest house.
Open: Mar to Oct
01887 820250 Mrs Bell Campbell
Rates fr: *£18.23*-**£18.23**.
Beds: 2D 1T
Baths: 1 Private 1 Shared
(10) (4)

***Callwood Cottage,** Aberfeldy, Perthshire, PH15 2ND.*
HIghland cottage in idyllic setting.
Open: All Year (not Xmas/New Year)
01887 830310 Mrs MacIntosh
Rates fr: *£17.00*-**£25.00**.
Beds: 2D
Baths: 1 Ensuite 1 Private
(4)

***Boisdale,** Old Crieff Road, Aberfeldy, Perthshire, PH15 2DH.*
Welcoming, traditional Bed & Breakfast.
Open: Jun to Sep
01887 820278 Mr & Mrs Steven
Rates fr: *£15.00*-**£15.00**.
Beds: 1D 1T
Baths: 1 Shared
(14) (3)

***Dunolly House,** Taybridge Drive, Aberfeldy, Perthshire, PH15 2BL.*
Spacious Victorian dwelling house.
Open: All Year
01887 820298 Mr Hermiston
Rates fr: *£14.00*-**£11.00**.
Beds: 6F 6D 2T 1S
Baths: 3 Private 5 Shared
(15)

Abernethy

National Grid Ref: NO1816

***Gattaway Farm,** Abernethy, Perth, PH2 9LQ.*
Large Georgian/Victorian farm-house.
Open: All Year
Grades: STB 3 Cr, Comm
01738 850746 (also fax no)
Mrs MacKenzie
Rates fr: *£17.50*-**£19.00**.
Beds: 1D 2T
Baths: 3 Ensuite
(6)

Acharn

National Grid Ref: NN7543

Croft-Na-Caber Hotel

***Old School House,** Acharn, Aberfeldy, Perthshire, PH15 2HS.*
Converted schoolhouse near Loch Tay.
Open: Easter to Oct
Grades: STB 2 Cr, Comm
01887 830307 (also fax no)
Mrs Brodie
Rates fr: *£18.00*-**£25.00**.
Beds: 2D 1T
Baths: 2 Ensuite 1 Shared
(10)

Alyth

National Grid Ref: NO2448

***Alyth Hotel,** Commercial Street, Alyth, Blairgowrie, Perthshire, PH11 8AF.*
Comfortable C18th family-run inn.
Open: All Year
Grades: STB 3 Cr, Comm, AA 2 St, Recomm
01828 632447 Mr Marshall
Rates fr: *£15.00*-**£22.50**.
Beds: 5F 2D 5T
Baths: 8 Private

Auchterarder

National Grid Ref: NN9412

Golf Inn, Collearn Hotel

***Nether Coul,** Auchterarder, Perthshire, PH3 1ET,*
Modernised C18th toll house.
Open: All Year
Grades: STB 2 Cr, Comm
01764 663119
Mr & Mrs Robertson
Rates fr: *£15.00*-**£15.00**.
Beds: 1F 1T
Baths: 2 Private
(5)

***10 The Grove, Collearn,** Auchterarder, Perthshire, PH3 1PT.*
Small modern house.
Open: All Year
01764 662036 Mrs McFarlane
Rates fr: *£12.50*-**£14.00**.
Beds: 1T
(1) (1)

Balbeggie

National Grid Ref: NO1629

MacDonald Arms Hotel

***Andante,** 3 Armadale Crescent, Balbeggie, Perth, Perthshire, PH2 6EP.*
Quietly located, modern, comfort-able bungalow.
Open: All Year (not Xmas)
01821 640606 Mr & Mrs Dickson
Rates fr: *£15.00*-**£15.00**.
Beds: 1T 1S
Baths: 1 Ensuite 1 Shared
(2)

Bankfoot

National Grid Ref: NO0635

***Blair House,** Main Street, Bankfoot, Perth, Perthshire, PH1 4AB.*
Gateway to Highlands. Ideal tour-ing spot.
Open: All Year
01738 787338 Mrs McKay
Rates fr: *£16.00*.
Beds: 1D 1T
Baths: 2 Private 1 Shared
(3)

Birnam

National Grid Ref: NO0341

Birnam Hotel, Atholl Arms

***Heatherbank,** Guthrie Villas, St Marys Road, Birnam, Dunkeld, Perthshire, PH8 0BJ.*
Open: All Year (not Xmas)
01350 727413 Mrs Flatley
Fax no: 01350 727552
Rates fr: *£13.00*-**£20.00**.
Beds: 2D 1T
Baths: 1 Shared
(3)
Warm welcome, friendly service, spacious house carefully main-tained in Victorian character, set in small village surrounded by beauti-ful hills, woodlands, rivers, walks and historic buildings.

***The Waterbury Guest House,** Murthly Terrace, Birnam, Dunkeld, Perthshire, PH8 0BG.*
Victorian rectory with modern comforts.
Open: All Year (not Xmas)
01350 727324 Mrs Ross
Rates fr: *£16.00*-**£16.00**.
Beds: 1F 2D 2T 1S
Baths: 2 Shared
(6)

***Bheinne Mhor,** Perth Road, Birnam, Dunkeld, Perthshire, PH8 0DH.*
Elegant Victorian turreted private house.
Open: All Year (not Xmas)
01350 727779 Mrs Buxton
Rates fr: *£19.00*-**£19.00**.
Beds: 1D 2T
Baths: 2 Ensuite 1 Private
(5)

Blackford

National Grid Ref: NN8908

Blackford Inn, Blackford Hotel

***Yarrow House,** Moray Street, Blackford, Auchterarder, Perthshire, PH4 1PY.*
Large family home, pretty gardens.
Open: All Year (not Xmas)
Grades: STB 2 Cr, Comm, AA 2 Q, Recomm
01764 682358 Mrs Robertson
Rates fr: *£15.00*-**£15.00**.
Beds: 1F 1T 1S
Baths: 1 Ensuite 1 Shared
(3)

Blacklunans

National Grid Ref: NO1460

***Blair View,** Blacklunans, Glenshee, Blairgowrie, Perthshire, PH10 7LP.*
Large modernised farmhouse.
Open: All Year (not Xmas)
01250 882260 Mrs Hardy
Rates fr: *£14.50*-**£14.50**.
Beds: 1F 2T
Baths: 1 Ensuite 1 Private
(4)

Blair Atholl

National Grid Ref: NN8765

Atholl Arms Hotel

Dalgreine, *Off St Andrews Crescent, Blair Atholl, Pitlochry, Perthshire,* PH18 5SX.
Attractive comfortable guesthouse.
Open: All Year
Grades: STB 2 Cr, Comm, AA 4 Q, Select
01796 481276 Mrs Sherrington
Rates fr: *£15.00*-**£15.00**.
Beds: 1F 2D 2T 1S
Baths: 3 Private 1 Shared
(6)

Baile Na Bruaich, *Glen Fender, Blair Atholl, Pitlochry, Perthshire,* PH18 5TU.
Family house, outstanding mountain views. **Open:** Easter to Oct
01796 481329 Mrs Thomson
Rates fr: *£16.50*-**£16.50**.
Beds: 1D 1T 1S **Baths:** 1 Shared
(0) (4)

Lauchope House, *The Terrace, Bridge Of Tilt, Blair Atholl, Pitlochry, Perthshire,* PH18 5SX.
Large 1900 stone-built private house. **Open:** Easter to Oct
01796 481200 Mrs McFarlane
Rates fr: *£14.50*-**£14.50**.
Beds: 1F 1D
Baths: 1 Private 1 Shared
(3)

Blairgowrie

National Grid Ref: NO1745

Angus Hotel Bar, Burrelton Park Inn, Woodside Inn

Norwood House, *Park Drive, Blairgowrie, Perthshire,* PH10 6PA.
Open: All Year
Grades: STB 1 Cr, Comm, AA 3 Q
01250 874146 Mr & Mrs Grant
Rates fr: *£15.00*-**£15.00**.
Beds: 1F 1D 1T **Baths:** 1 Shared
(4)
Family-run Victorian house. Our comfortable bedrooms are all very well equipped. Warm and friendly atmosphere. Ideal base for touring, golfing, walking. Off-street parking.

Garfield House, *Perth Road, Blairgowrie, Perthshire,* PH10 6ED.
Attractive Victorian private house.
Open: Easter to Oct
01250 872999 Mrs Mary
Rates fr: *£14.50*-**£14.50**.
Beds: 1D 1T 1S **Baths:** 1 Shared
(3)

Dryfesands, *Burnhead Road, Blairgowrie, Perthshire,* PH10 6SY.
High quality haven for non-smokers.
Open: All Year
Grades: STB 3 Cr, Deluxe
01250 873417 (also fax no)
Mrs Cowan
Rates fr: *£23.00*-**£28.00**.
Beds: 2D 1T **Baths:** 3 Ensuite
(14) (4)

The Laurels Guest House, *Golf Course Road, Rosemount, Blairgowrie, Perthshire,* PH10 6LH.
Converted C18th farm house.
Open: Jan to Nov
Grades: STB 3 Cr, High Comm, AA 3 Q
01250 874920
Mr & Mrs McPherson
Rates fr: *£18.50*-**£18.50**.
Beds: 2D 3T 1S
Baths: 4 Ensuite 2 Shared
(10) (6)

Dunmore, *Newton Street, Blairgowrie, Perthshire,* PH10 6HT.
Great touring, golfing and skiing area. **Open:** All Year
01250 874451
Mrs Paterson
Rates fr: *£15.50*-**£15.50**.
Beds: 1F 1D 1T 2S
Baths: 2 Shared
(3)

Shocarjen, *The Green, Burrelton, Blairgowrie, Perthshire,* PH13 9NU.
Modernised comfortable house, friendly village.
Open: All Year
Grades: STB 2 Cr, Comm
01828 670223 (also fax no)
Mrs Beattie
Rates fr: *£16.50*-**£19.00**.
Beds: 2F 1D
Baths: 3 Ensuite

Scottish Centres, *Belmont Centre, Meigle, Blairgowrie, Perthshire,* PH12 8TQ.
Residential outdoor education centre.
Open: Easter to October
01899 221 115
Lamb
Fax no: 01899 220644
Rates fr: *£12.10*-**£12.10**.
Beds: 36F
Baths: 7 Shared
(8) (20)

Duncraggan, *Perth Road, Blairgowrie, Perthshire,* PH10 6EJ.
Beautiful 1902 house with turret.
Open: All Year
Grades: STB 1 Cr, Comm, AA 3 Q, Recomm
01250 872082 / 872098
Mrs McClement
Rates fr: *£18.50*-**£18.50**.
Beds: 2D 1T 1S
Baths: 2 Ensuite 1 Private 1 Shared
(0) (6)

Eildon Bank, *Perth Road, Blairgowrie, Perthshire,* PH10 6ED.
Detached family house, near town.
Open: All Year (not Xmas)
01250 873648
Mrs Murray
Rates fr: *£14.00*-**£15.00**.
Beds: 2D 1T
Baths: 1 Ensuite 1 Shared
(2) (4)

Millbank, *Upper Mill Street, Blairgowrie, Perthshire,* PH10 6AG.
Peaceful, centrally located comfortable townhouse.
Open: All Year (not Xmas)
01250 873304 Mrs Miller
Rates fr: *£13.00*-**£13.00**.
Beds: 1F 1D 1T
Baths: 1 Shared
(3)

Bridge of Cally

National Grid Ref: NO1451

Bridge of Cully Hotel, Corriefodly

Tigh Na Bruaich, *Bridge of Cally, Blairgowrie, Perthshire,* PH10 7JL.
Homely cottage in beautiful surroundings. Skiing.
Open: All Year (not Xmas)
01250 886237 Mrs Jacobs
Rates fr: *£17.00*.
Beds: 1D 1T
Baths: 1 Shared
(4)

Bridge Of Cally Hotel, *Bridge of Cally, Blairgowrie, Perthshire,* PH10 7JJ.
The pub with good grub.
Open: All Year (not Xmas)
01250 886231
Mr McCosh
Rates fr: *£17.50*-**£20.00**.
Beds: 1F 3D 4T 1S
Baths: 6 Private 2 Shared

Burrelton

National Grid Ref: NO2037

Burrelton Park Inn, Woodside Inn

Shocarjen, *The Green, Burrelton, Blairgowrie, Perthshire,* PH13 9NU.
Modernised comfortable house, friendly village.
Open: All Year
Grades: STB 2 Cr, Comm
01828 670223 (also fax no)
Mrs Beattie
Rates fr: *£16.50*-**£19.00**.
Beds: 2F 1D
Baths: 3 Ensuite

Castle Menzies

National Grid Ref: NN8349

Aileen Chraggan Hotel

South Lodge, *Castle Menzies, Aberfeldy, Perthshire,* PH15 2JD.
Comfortable, converted C18th lodge.
Open: All Year (not Xmas)
Grades: STB Listed, High Comm
01887 820115 Mrs Bolam
Rates fr: *£16.00*-**£17.00**.
Beds: 1D 1T
Baths: 1 Ensuite 1 Private
(4)

Comrie

National Grid Ref: NN7722

Comrie Hotel

St Margarets, *Braco Road, Comrie, Crieff, Perthshire, PH6 2HP.*
Large Victorian family house.
Open: Mar to Nov
01764 670413 Mr & Mrs Paterson
Rates fr: *£15.00*-**£15.00**.
Beds: 1D 2T **Baths:** 1 Ensuite 1Shared
(3) (4)

Comrie Hotel, *Comrie, Crieff, Perthshire, PH6 2DY.*
Traditional stone-built property, Comrie centre.
Open: Easter to Nov
01764 670239 (also fax no)
Mr Herron
Rates fr: *£20.00*-**£29.00**.
Beds: 3D 6T 2S **Baths:** 11 Private
(14) (26)

Coupar Angus

National Grid Ref: NO2240

Ennerdale Hotel, Burrelton Park Hotel

St Catherines Croft, *14 Union Street, Coupar Angus, Blairgowrie, Perthshire, PH13 9AE.*
Large Victorian private house.
Open: All Year
Grades: STB 2 Cr, Comm
01828 627753 Mr & Mrs Broadley
Rates fr: *£15.00*-**£16.00**.
Beds: 1F 1D 1T 1S
Baths: 2 Ensuite 1 Shared
(5)

Crieff

National Grid Ref: NN8621

Locke's Acre, Satchmo's Bistro, Oakbank Inn, Glenturret Distillery, Arouthie Hotel

Gwydyr House Hotel, *Comrie Road, Crieff, Perthshire, PH7 4BP.*
Open: Feb to Dec
Grades: STB 2 Cr, Comm, AA 2 Q, RAC Acclaim
01764 653277
Mr Hodge & Mr A Garrido
Rates fr: *£25.00*-**£30.00**.
Beds: 2F 3D 3T 1S
Baths: 6 Ensuite 2 Shared
(4) (15)
A handsomely converted Victorian villa with informal gardens. The hotel offers modern day comforts, yet retaining the character of a past era. All rooms are well equipped and most ensuite. Own car park. Quiet location with superb views. 5 minutes walk to town centre.

Somerton House, *Turret Bank, Crieff, Perthshire, PH7 4JN.*
Large, modern private house.
Open: All Year
Grades: STB 2 Cr, Comm
01764 653513 Mrs Sloan
Fax no: 01764 655028
Rates fr: *£17.50*-**£20.00**.
Beds: 1F 1D 1T **Baths:** 3 Private
(5)

Concraig Farm, *Muthill Road, Crieff, Perthshire, PH7 4HH.*
Comfortable farmhouse on arable farm. **Open:** Easter to Oct
Grades: STB Listed, Comm
01764 653237
Mrs Scott
Rates fr: *£16.00*.
Beds: 2D 1T **Baths:** 1 Shared
(3)

Galvelbeg House, *Perth Road, Crieff, Perthshire, PH7 3EQ.*
Situated at the beginning of the Grampians.
Open: All Year (not Xmas)
01764 655061
Mrs Davies
Rates fr: *£19.00*-**£19.00**.
Beds: 1F 2D 1T 1S
Baths: 4 Ensuite 1 Private
(6)

Keppoch House Hotel, *Perth Road, Crieff, Perthshire, PH7 3EQ.*
Family-run hotel offering friendly service.
Open: All Year
01764 654341
Mr Brown
Rates fr: *£15.00*-**£15.00**.
Beds: 1F 5D 4T 1S
Baths: 5 Private 1 Shared
(25)

Bell House, *1 Broich Terrace, Crieff, Perthshire, PH7 3BD.*
Large Victorian private house.
Open: All Year
01764 654689
Mr & Mrs MacLellan
Rates fr: *£14.00*-**£14.00**.
Beds: 2D 1T
Baths: 2 Shared
(3)

Crook of Devon

National Grid Ref: NO0300

High Gables, *Crook of Devon, Kinross, KY13 7HR.*
Large, comfortable house in attractive village.
Open: All Year
01577 840578
Mrs Alsof
Rates fr: *£13.50*-**£16.00**.
Beds: 1F 1T 1D 1S
Baths: 1 Private 1 Shared

Dalginross

National Grid Ref: NN7721

Comrie Hotel (Comrie)

Millersfield, *Dalginross, Comrie, Crieff, Perthshire, PH6 2HE.*
Comfortable modern bungalow peaceful setting.
Open: All Year (not Xmas)
01764 670073
Mrs Rae
Rates fr: *£16.00*-**£16.00**.
Beds: 1D 1T
Baths: 2 Shared
(12) (2)

Dunkeld

National Grid Ref: NO0242

Merryburn Hotel, *Station Road, Dunkeld, Perthshire, PH8 0DS.*
Upgraded comfortable family-run hotel.
Open: All Year
01350 727216 Mr Ormerwood
Rates fr: *£20.00*-**£20.00**.
Beds: 1F 2D 3T 2S
Baths: 2 Shared
(10)

Fearnan

National Grid Ref: NN7244

Farleyer House, Croft-na-Caber

Easter Auchtar, *Fearnan, Aberfeldy, Perthshire, PH15 2PG.*
Open: Feb to Nov
Grades: STB 3 Cr, Comm
01887 830316
Mrs Clapham
Fax no: 01887 830380
Rates fr: *£20.00*-**£25.00**.
Beds: 1F 1D 1T
Baths: 3 Ensuite
(3) (8)
Friendly family house, converted C19th farm building in 2 acre garden among dramatic Scottish hills between Fearnan and Fortingall villages. Most outdoor activities available.

Tigh An Loan Hotel, *Fearnan, Aberfeldy, Perthshire, PH15 2PF.*
Overlooking Loch Tay.
Open: Easter to Oct
Grades: STB 2 Cr, Comm
01887 830249
Mr Kelloe
Rates fr: *£24.00*-**£24.00**.
Beds: 1F 2D 2T 3S
Baths: 3 Private 2 Shared
(20)

Fortingall

National Grid Ref: NN7347

Garth House, *Fortingall, Aberfeldy, Perthshire, PH15 2NF.*
Turreted baronial manor house.
Open: All Year
01887 830515
Mr Lodge
Rates fr: *£17.50*-**£35.00**.
Beds: 1D 1T
Baths: 1 Private

Fendoch, *Fortingall, Aberfeldy, Perthshire, PH15 2LL.*
Traditional country cottage.
Open: All Year
Grades: STB 2 Cr, Comm
01887 830322
Mrs Tulloch
Rates fr: *£14.00*-**£14.00**.
Beds: 1F 1D 1T
Baths: 3 Private
(5)

Glen Quaich

National Grid Ref: NN8538

Tirchardie Farm, *Glen Quaich, Amulree, Dunkeld, Perthshire, PH8 0DE.*
Old-fashioned farmhouse.
Open: All Year
01350 725266 Mrs Simpkins
Rates fr: *£11.50*-**£11.50**.
Beds: 1F 1D 1T 1S
Baths: 2 Shared
(8)

Glencarse

National Grid Ref: NO1921

Clashbenny Farm, *Glencarse, Perth, PH2 7NW.*
Large Georgian farmhouse.
Open: All Year (not Xmas)
01738 860239 Mrs Lawrie
Rates fr: *£15.00*-**£15.00**.
Beds: 1D 1T 1S
Baths: 2 Shared
(5) (6)

Inchture

National Grid Ref: NO2828

Inchturf Hotel

Old School House, *Main Street, Inchture, Perth, Perthshire, PH14 9RN.*
Listed old school house.
Open: All Year (not Xmas)
01828 686275 Mrs Howard
Rates fr: *£15.00*-**£15.00**.
Beds: 1F 2D
Baths: 1 Ensuite 1 Shared
(2)

Kinloch Rannoch

National Grid Ref: NN6658

Bunrannoch House, *Kinloch Rannoch, Pitlochry, Perthshire, PH16 5QB.*
Former hunting lodge, beautiful setting.
Open: All Year (not Xmas)
Grades: STB 3 Cr, Comm
01882 632407 Mrs Skeaping
Rates fr: *£18.00*-**£16.00**.
Beds: 2F 3D 2T
Baths: 5 Private 2 Shared
(10)

Kinross

National Grid Ref: NO1102

107 High Street, *Kinross, Fife, KY13 7AQ.*
Semi-detached. Established 25 years.
Open: All Year
01577 863374 Mrs McBain
Rates fr: *£14.00*-**£15.00**.
Beds: 2F 1S
Baths: 1 Shared

Lochleven Inn, *6 Swansacre, Kinross, Fife, KY13 7TE.*
Local friendly inn (public bar).
Open: All Year (not Xmas)
01577 864185 Mr McGregor
Rates fr: *£17.50*-**£17.50**.
Beds: 1F 1T
Baths: 2 Private
(0) (2)

Grouse and Claret Restaurant, *Heatheryford, Kinross, Fife, KY13 7NQ.*
Peaceful 40 acres. Restaurant (Taste of Scotland)
Open: All Year
01577 864212 Mrs Futong
Fax no: 01577 864920
Rates fr: *£21.50*-**£24.50**.
Beds: 2D 1T **Baths:** 3 Private
(5) (25)

Hatchbank House, *Kinross, Fife, KY13 7LF.*
Georgian farmhouse in beautiful countryside.
Open: All Year
01577 850214 Mrs Muirhead
Rates fr: *£20.00*-**£25.00**.
Beds: 2T
Baths: 2 Private
(10)

East Brackley House, *Kinross, Fife, KY13 7LU.*
Enjoyable country house living.
Open: Jun to Aug
01577 862252 Mr Linton Smith
Rates fr: *£16.00*-**£20.00**.
Beds: 2D
Baths: 1 Private 1 Shared
(6)

Kirkmichael

National Grid Ref: NO0860

Kirkmichael Hotel

The Log Cabin Hotel, *Glen Derby, Kirkmichael, Blairgowrie, Perthshire, PH10 7NB.*
Open: All Year (not Xmas)
Grades: STB 3 Cr, Comm, RAC 2 St
01250 881288 Ms Ibbitson
Fax no: 01250 881402
Rates fr: *£21.50*-**£25.00**.
Beds: 4F 3D 2T
Baths: 9 Ensuite
(12)
Alan and Margaret Ibbitson invite you to their unique secluded log home, with panoramic views where wildlife abounds. Central location for touring/many holiday activities.

Cruachan, *Kirkmichael, Blairgowrie, Perthshire, PH10 7NZ.*
Luxury character property overlooking river.
Open: All Year (not Xmas)
01250 881226 (also fax no)
Mrs Kirk
Rates fr: *£13.50*-**£13.50**.
Beds: 3F
Baths: 1 Ensuite 1 Shared
(3)

Ardlebrig, *Kirkmichael, Blairgowrie, Perthshire, PH10 7NY.*
Friendly family hospitality.
Open: All Year (not Xmas)
Grades: STB Listed, Comm
01250 881350 Mr & Mrs Mills
Rates fr: *£14.00*-**£14.00**.
Beds: 1F 1T 1S
Baths: 1 Shared
(5) (3)

Curran House, *Kirkmichael, Blairgowrie, Perthshire, PH10 7NA.*
Traditional Scottish country house.
Open: Jan to Nov
Grades: STB 2 Cr, Comm
01250 881229
Mr & Mrs Van Der Veldt
Rates fr: *£14.00*-**£14.00**.
Beds: 2D 1T
Baths: 1 Private 1 Shared
(0) (3)

Logierait

National Grid Ref: NN9751

Logierait Hotel, *Logierait, Ballinluig, Pitlochry, Perthshire, PH9 0LJ.*
Historic inn, situated on the A827.
Open: All Year
01796 482423 Miss Ojelade
Rates fr: *£16.50*-**£21.50**.
Beds: 2F 2T **Baths:** 3 Private
(5) (14)

Madderty

National Grid Ref: NN9521

Raith Farm, *Madderty, Crieff, Perthshire, PH7 3RJ.*
Small, friendly farmhouse.
Open: Easter to Oct
01764 683262 Mrs Scougall
Rates fr: *£18.00*-**£20.00**.
Beds: 2F **Baths:** 2 Ensuite

Meikleour

National Grid Ref: NO1539

Tay Farm House, *Meikleour, Perth, PH2 6EE.*
Charming comfortable Georgian country house.
Open: All Year
01250 883345
Rates fr: *£17.50*-**£20.50**.
Beds: 1F 2T **Baths:** 3 Ensuite
(5)

Milnathort

National Grid Ref: NO1204

Balgeddie Toll, The Lamond Inn

Hattonburn Farmhouse, *Milnathort, Kinross, Fife, KY13 7SA.*
Modernised C19th red sandstone farmhouse.
Open: All Year
01577 862362 Mrs Todrick
Rates fr: *£15.00*-**£15.00**.
Beds: 1D 1T **Baths:** 2 Private
(10)

Newlands Farm House, *Milnathort, Kinross, Fife, KY13 7EL.*
Stylish private suite of rooms.
Open: All Year (not Xmas)
01577 863422 Mrs Trevor
Rates fr: *£20.00*-**£23.00**.
Beds: 1D **Baths:** 1 Ensuite
(3)

Morenish

National Grid Ref: NN5935

Morenish Lodge Highland Hse Ht, *Morenish, Killin, Perthshire, FK21 8TX.*
Beautifully situated, traditional country hotel.
Open: Apr to Sep
01567 820258 Mr Naylor
Rates fr: *£25.00*-**£25.00**.
Beds: 1F 5D 6T 1S
Baths: 13 Private
(4) (16)

Muthill

National Grid Ref: NN8616

Highfield, *104 Willoughby Street, Muthill, Crieff, Perthshire, PH5 2AE.*
Unspoilt, detached Victorian sandstone villa.
Open: All Year
01764 681340 Mrs Stewart
Rates fr: *£13.00*-**£15.00**.
Beds: 1F 2T
Baths: 1 Shared
(6)

Perth

National Grid Ref: NO1123

Letham Farmhouse Hotel, Moncrieff Hotel, Lovat Hotel, Royal George Hotel

The Gables Guest House, *24 Dunkeld Road, Perth, Perthshire, PH1 5RW.*
Open: All Year
Grades: STB 2 Cr, Comm, AA 2 Q
01738 624717 (also fax no)
Ms Tucker
Rates fr: *£18.00*-**£19.50**.
Beds: 2F 1D 1T 4S
Baths: 3 Ensuite 1 Shared
(7)
Family-run licensed guest house, ideal touring base. Close to A9 and town centre. Private parking. Warm welcome, comfortable rooms and traditional home cooking.

Achnacarry Guest House, *Pitcullen Crescent, Perth, Perthshire, PH2 7HT.*
Attractive surroundings. Warm, friendly atmosphere.
Open: All Year
Grades: STB 2 Cr, High Comm, RAC Acclaim
01738 621421 Mrs Cowan
Fax no: 01738 444110
Rates fr: *£18.00*-**£20.00**.
Beds: 2F 1D 1T
Baths: 3 Private 1 Shared
(5) (7)

Fingask Farm Rhynd, *Perth, Perthshire, PH2 8QF.*
Open: Easter to Oct
Grades: STB Listed, Comm
01738 812220 Mrs Stirrat
Rates fr: *£15.00*-**£15.00**.
Beds: 1D 1T 1S
Baths: 2 Shared
(5)
Comfortable furnished farmhouse in landscaped garden. Peaceful part of central Perthshire - a haven for the tourist - with a wide range of leisure and sporting opportunities.

Auld Manse Guest House, *Pitcullen Crescent, Perth, Perthshire, PH2 7HT.*
Victorian villa, warm welcome guaranteed.
Open: All Year
Grades: STB 1 Cr, Comm
01738 629187 Mrs Rennie
Rates fr: *£16.00*-**£16.00**.
Beds: 1F 2D 1T 1S
Baths: 2 Ensuite 1 Shared
(5)

Huntingtower House, *Crieff Road, Perth, Perthshire, PH1 3JJ.*
Open: Feb to Dec
Grades: STB 1 Cr, Comm
01738 624681 Mrs Lindsay
Rates fr: *£15.00*-**£15.00**.
Beds: 1D 2T **Baths:** 1 Shared
(10) (3)
Charming country house with large secluded garden, near Perth. Easy access to main routes throughout Scotland. Delicious breakfast served. A friendly welcome is assured.

Castleview Guest House, *164-166 Glasgow Road, Perth, Perthshire, PH2 0LY.*
Large detached Victorian villa.
Open: Feb to Dec
Grades: STB 1 Cr, AA 3 Q
01738 626415
Mr & Mrs Dawson
Rates fr: *£18.00*-**£25.00**.
Beds: 1F 1D 1T **Baths:** 3 Ensuite
(5)

The Darroch Guest House, *9 Pitcullen Crescent, Perth, Perthshire, PH2 7HT.*
Victorian semi - friendly relaxed atmosphere.
Open: All Year
Grades: STB 2 Cr, Comm
01738 636893 Mr & Mrs Hirst
Rates fr: *£15.00*-**£15.00**.
Beds: 1F 1D 2T 2S
Baths: 3 Ensuite 1 Shared
(8)

Parkview Guest House, *22 Marshall Place, Perth, Perthshire, PH2 8AG.*
'B' Listed Georgian town house.
Open: All Year
01738 620297 Mr Farquharson
Rates fr: *£16.00*-**£18.00**.
Beds: 4F 1T
Baths: 3 Private 1 Shared
(4)

2 Pitcullen Crescent, *Perth, Perthshire, PH2 7HT.*
Comfortable, well-appointed accommodation. **Open:** All Year
Grades: STB 2 Cr, Comm, AA 3 Q, RAC Acclaim
01738 627261 Mrs Gray
Rates fr: *£15.00*-**£15.00**.
Beds: 1F 2D 1T 1S
Baths: 2 Private 2 Shared
(6)

Inchview, *25 Marshall Place, Perth, Perthshire, PH2 8AG.*
Large Victorian town house.
Open: All Year
Grades: STB Listed
01738 629610 Mrs Young
Rates fr: *£16.00*-**£16.00**.
Beds: 1F 1D 2T 1S
Baths: 4 Ensuite

Beeches, *2 Comely Bank, Perth, Perthshire, PH2 7HU.*
Family-run Victorian house.
Open: All Year
Grades: STB 3 Cr, AA Listed , RAC Listed
01738 624486 Mrs Smith
Rates fr: *£16.00*-**£16.00**.
Beds: 1D 1T 2S
Baths: 2 Private 2 Shared
(6)

Richmond House, *50 Glasgow Road, Perth, Perthshire, PH2 0PB.*
Pleasant half-villa, central situation.
Open: All Year (not Xmas)
Grades: STB Listed
01738 627548 Mr Normand
Rates fr: *£14.50*-**£17.00**.
Beds: 1F 1D 1T 1S
Baths: 1 Private 1 Shared

Brae Lodge, *140 Glasgow Road, Perth, Perthshire, PH2 0LX.*
Comfortable family home.
Open: All Year (not Xmas)
01738 628473 Mr Muir
Rates fr: *£15.00*-**£18.00**.
Beds: 1F 1D **Baths:** 2 Shared
(2)

Dunallan Guest House, *10 Pitcullen Crescent, Perth, Perthshire, PH2 7HT.*
Well appointed superior Victorian villa.
Open: All Year
Grades: STB 2 Cr, Comm
01738 622551 Mrs Brown
Rates fr: *£18.00*-**£17.00**.
Beds: 1F 1D 2T 3S
Baths: 4 Ensuite 1 Shared
(7)

Abercrombie, *85 Glasglow Road, Perth, PH2 0PQ.*
Beautiful Victorian town house.
Open: All Year
Grades: STB Listed, High Comm
01738 444728 Mrs Dewar
Rates fr: *£16.00*-**£20.00**.
Beds: 2D 1T **Baths:** 3 Ensuite
(2) (4)

Fernlea, *37 Needless Road, Perth, Perthshire, PH2 0LE.*
Comfortable family house.
Open: All Year (not Xmas)
01738 627766 Mrs Davidson
Rates fr: *£13.00*-**£13.00**.
Beds: 1F **Baths:** 1 Shared

Aran Guest House, *1 Pitcullen Crescent, Perth, Perthshire, PH2 7HT.*
Comfortable, friendly guest house.
Open: All Year
Grades: STB 2 Cr, Comm
01738 634216 Mrs Walker
Rates fr: *£14.00*-**£16.00**.
Beds: 1F 1D 1T 1S
Baths: 1 Private 1 Shared
(6)

Lochiel House, *Pitcullen Crescent, Perth, Perthshire, PH2 7HT.*
Beautifully appointed Victorian guest house.
Open: All Year
Grades: STB 2 Cr, Comm
01738 633183 Mrs Buchan
Rates fr: *£16.00*-**£16.00**.
Beds: 2D 1T
Baths: 1 Ensuite 2 Shared
(0) (4)

Grampian Hotel, *37-41 York Place, Perth, Perthshire, PH2 8EH.*
14-bedroom Victorian-style hotel.
Open: All Year
01738 621057 Mr Anderson
Rates fr: *£25.00*-**£35.00**.
Beds: 5F 4D 5T **Baths:** 14 Private
(10)

Heidl Guest House, *43 York Place, Perth, Perthshire, PH2 8EH.*
Central family-run guest house.
Open: All Year (not Xmas)
01738 635031
Mr & Mrs McMahon
Rates fr: *£13.00*-**£17.00**.
Beds: 1F 2D 4T 3S
Baths: 1 Private 2 Shared
(3)

Pitlochry

National Grid Ref: NN9458

Acarsaid Hotel, Pine Trees Hotel, Atholl Arms Hotel, Old Smithy, The Old Armoury

Westlands Of Pitlochry, *160 Atholl Road, Pitlochry, Perthshire, PH16 5AR.*
Open: All Year
Grades: STB 4 Cr, Comm, AA 2 St, RAC 2 St
01796 472266 Mr Mathieson
Fax no: 01796 473994
Rates fr: *£24.50*-**£24.50**.
Beds: 2F 6D 6T 1S
Baths: 15 Private
(30)
Beautifully presented stone-built hotel run by resident owners Andrew & Sue Mathieson. All rooms have facilities. Cocktail bar and restaurant have appealing menus including vegetarian.

Craig Dubh Cottage, *Manse Road, Moulin, Pitlochry, Perthshire, PH16 5EP.*
Open: Mid-April to mid-Oct
01796 472058 Mrs Bright
Rates fr: *£13.50*-**£13.50**.
Beds: 1D 1T 2S
Baths: 1 Ensuite 1 Shared
(3)
A family home where we welcome B&B guests. One mile from the town centre with a large garden, at the end of a quiet lane.

Balrobin Hotel, *Higher Oakfield, Pitlochry, Perthshire, PH16 5HT.*
Quality accommodation, affordable prices. **Open:** Apr to Oct
Grades: STB 3 Cr, High Comm, AA 2 St, RAC 2 St
01796 472901 Mr Hohman
Fax no: 01796 474200
Rates fr: *£25.00*-**£25.00**.
Beds: 1F 12D 2T 1S
Baths: 16 Private
(10) (16)

Tigh-Na-Cloich Hotel, *Larchwood Road, Pitlochry, Perthshire, PH16 5AS.*
Open: All Year
Grades: STB 3 Cr, Comm
01796 472216 (also fax no)
Mrs Hawley
Rates fr: *£20.00*-**£18.00**.
Beds: 1F 4D 5T 2S
Baths: 10 Ensuite 1 Shared
(12)
Lovely Victorian house, friendly informal atmosphere, comfortable licensed accommodation, good food and wine. Peaceful gardens, great views, free parking, easy access town, theatre and golf.

Grove Cottage, *10 Lower Oakfield, Pitlochry, Perthshire, PH16 5DS.*
Victorian house with lovely views.
Open: All Year
01796 472374 Mrs Hawkes
Rates fr: *£14.00*-**£15.00**.
Beds: 1D 1T 2S
Baths: 2 Private 1 Shared
(4)

Tigh-Nan-Eilan, *28 Tomcroy Terrace, Pitlochry, Perthshire, PH16 5JA.*
Open: Easter to Oct
01796 473039 (also fax no)
Mrs Young
Rates fr: *£15.00*-**£20.00**.
Beds: 1D 1T **Baths:** 1 Shared
(2)
In a rural setting with views to the hills all around, yet only a few minutes drive from the town centre. 'A Scottish welcome'.

Adderley Private Hotel, *23 Toberargan Road, Pitlochry, Perthshire, PH16 5HG.*
A small family-run hotel.
Open: All Year (not Xmas)
Grades: STB 3 Cr, Approv
01796 472433 Mr McGhie
Rates fr: *£21.00*-**£21.00**.
Beds: 2F 3D 1T 1S
Baths: 7 Private
(8)

Kinnaird House, *Kirkmichael Road, Pitlochry, Perthshire, PH16 5JL.*
Open: All Year
Grades: STB 2 Cr, High Comm
01796 472843 Mr & Mrs Norris
Rates fr: *£18.00*-**£25.00**.
Beds: 2D 1T
Baths: 3 Private
(7)
Spacious, comfortable, clean accommodation in superb surroundings. Friendly and relaxing. Members of 'The Scottish Quality Collection'. Scottish Tourist Board - 2 Crowns Highly Commended 87% 1996.

Tir Aluinn Guest House, *10 Higher Oakfield, Pitlochry, Perthshire, PH16 5HT.*
Victorian private house. Excellent views.
Open: All Year
Grades: STB Listed
01796 472231 Mrs Walker
Rates fr: *£13.00*-**£15.00**.
Beds: 1F 2D 1T
Baths: 2 Ensuite 2 Private
(Yes)

Briar Cottage, *Wellbrae, Pitlochry, Perthshire, PH16 5HH.*
Open: Easter to Oct
01796 473678 Mrs Scott
Rates fr: *£14.50*-**£25.00**.
Beds: 1D 2T
Baths: 2 Shared
(3)
Bright modern house. Family-run. Suitable for disabled. Quite location 5 minutes walk from town centre. A warm welcome awaits you.

Carra Beag Guest House, *16 Toberargan Road, Pitlochry, Perthshire, PH16 5HG.*
Comfortable, good food, lovely view.
Open: All Year
Grades: STB 3 Cr, Approv
01796 472835
Mr McGhie
Rates fr: *£16.00*-**£16.00**.
Beds: 2F 4D 3T 3S
Baths: 9 Private 1 Shared
(15)

Lynedoch, *9 Lettoch Terrace, Pitlochry, Perthshire, PH16 5BA.*
Stone-built with adjoining annexe.
Open: Mar to Oct
01796 472119
Mrs Williamson
Rates fr: *£15.00*-**£15.00**.
Beds: 2D 1T
Baths: 2 Shared
(3)

Planning a longer stay? Always ask for any special rates.

***Wester Knockfarrie,** Pitlochry, Perthshire, PH16 5DN.*
Large Victorian villa, beautiful views.
Open: Easter to Nov
01796 472020 Mrs Spaven
Rates fr: *£18.00*.
Beds: 2D 1T
Baths: 3 Private
(3)

***Tigh-Na-Lnol,** 11 West Moulin Road, Pitlochry, Perthshire, PH16 5EA.*
Modern bungalow in quiet village.
Open: All Year (not Xmas)
01796 482240 (also fax no)
Mrs Davidson
Rates fr: *£13.00*-**£13.00**.
Beds: 1F 1T
Baths: 1 Shared
(2)

***8 Darach Road,** Pitlochry, Perthshire, PH16 5HR.*
Situated in quiet district.
Open: All Year
01796 472074 Weyda-Wernick
Rates fr: *£12.50*-**£16.00**.
Beds: 1D
Baths: 2 Shared
(3)

***Poplars Hotel,** 27 Lower Oakfield, Pitlochry, Perthshire, PH16 5DS.*
Quiet Victorian house. Home cooking.
Open: Easter to Oct
Grades: STB 3 Cr, Comm
01796 472129 Mr Pollock
Rates fr: *£18.00*-**£19.00**.
Beds: 3F 3D 2T
Baths: 8 Private 1 Shared
(15)

***Ferrymans Cottage,** Port-na-Craig, Pitlochry, Perthshire, PH16 5ND.*
Cosy old ferryman's riverside cottage.
Open: Easter to Nov
01796 473681 Mrs Sanderson
Rates fr: *£16.00*-**£16.00**.
Beds: 2F 1S
Baths: 1 Private 1 Shared
(7)

Rattray

National Grid Ref: NO1845

***Brightview,** High Street, Rattray, Blairgowrie, Perthshire, PH10 7DL.*
'Home from home'.
Open: All Year
01250 875018 Mrs Koppel
Rates fr: *£13.00*-**£15.00**.
Beds: 1F 1D 1T
Baths: 1 Shared
(1) (5)

Redgorton

National Grid Ref: NO0828

The Linnat, Bank Inn

***Pitmurthly Farm,** Redgorton, Luncarty, Perth, Perthshire, PH1 3HX.*
Quiet, delightful farmhouse near Perth.
Open: All Year
Grades: STB 2 Cr, High Comm
01738 828363 Mrs Smith
Rates fr: *£15.00*-**£15.00**.
Beds: 1D 1T 1S
Baths: 1 Private 1 Shared

Scotlandwell

National Grid Ref: NO1801

***6 Bankfoot Park,** Scotlandwell, Kinross, KY13 7JP.*
Modern house in rural setting.
Open: All Year
01592 840515 Mrs Wardell
Rates fr: *£16.00*-**£16.00**.
Beds: 2T
Baths: 1 Private 1 Shared
(3)

Stanley

National Grid Ref: NO1133

The Inn

***Newmill Farm,** Stanley, Perth, Perthshire, PH1 4QD.*
Traditional stone-built farm house.
Open: Jan to Oct
01738 828281 Mrs Guthrie
Rates fr: *£16.00*-**£17.50**.
Beds: 1F 1D 1T
Baths: 2 Private 1 Shared

***Stanley Farm,** Stanley, Perth, PH1 4QQ.*
Friendly, comfortable farmhouse.
Open: Easter to Oct
Grades: STB 1 Cr, Comm
01738 828334
Mrs Howden
Rates fr: *£14.00*-**£16.00**.
Beds: 1F 1D
Baths: 2 Shared

Bringing children with you? Always ask for any special rates.

Strathtay

National Grid Ref: NN9053

***Ballinduin Bothy,** Strathtay, Aberfeldy, Pitlochry, Perthshire, PH9 0LP.*
Recently converted farmhouse, superb views.
Open: Apr to Oct
01887 840460 Mrs Orr
Rates fr: *£16.00*-**£16.00**.
Beds: 3T
Baths: 3 Private

Trinity Gask

National Grid Ref: NN9618

***Lawhill House,** Trinity Gask, Auchterarder, Perthshire, PH3 1JA.*
Open: All Year (not Xmas)
01764 683288 Mrs Buchanan
Rates fr: *£20.00*-**£20.00**.
Beds: 1D 2T
Baths: 2 Shared
(10)
Peaceful, secluded, exceptional views. Surrounded by famous golf courses, riding, fishing, walking, historic interest. Dinner parties, simple meals, adaptable, welcoming hospitality. Creature comforts, log fires.

Trochry

National Grid Ref: NN9740

Atholl Arms, Royal Hotel, Amulree Hotel

***Borelick,** Trochry, Dunkeld, Perthshire, PH8 0BX.*
Open: Easter to Oct
01350 723222 (also fax no)
Mrs Brooiles
Rates fr: *£14.00*-**£16.00**.
Beds: 1F 1T
Baths: 2 Shared
No crowns, no stars, just our home. All our welcome to our small farm of mainly rare breeds, in the Perthshire Hills.

***Scotston,** Trochry, Amulree, Dunkeld, Perthshire, PH8 0ED.*
Comfortable, centrally heated old farmhouse.
Open: All Year
01350 725225 Mrs Lush
Rates fr: *£13.50*-**£13.00**.
Beds: 1F 1D
Baths: 1 Private 1 Shared

Shetland

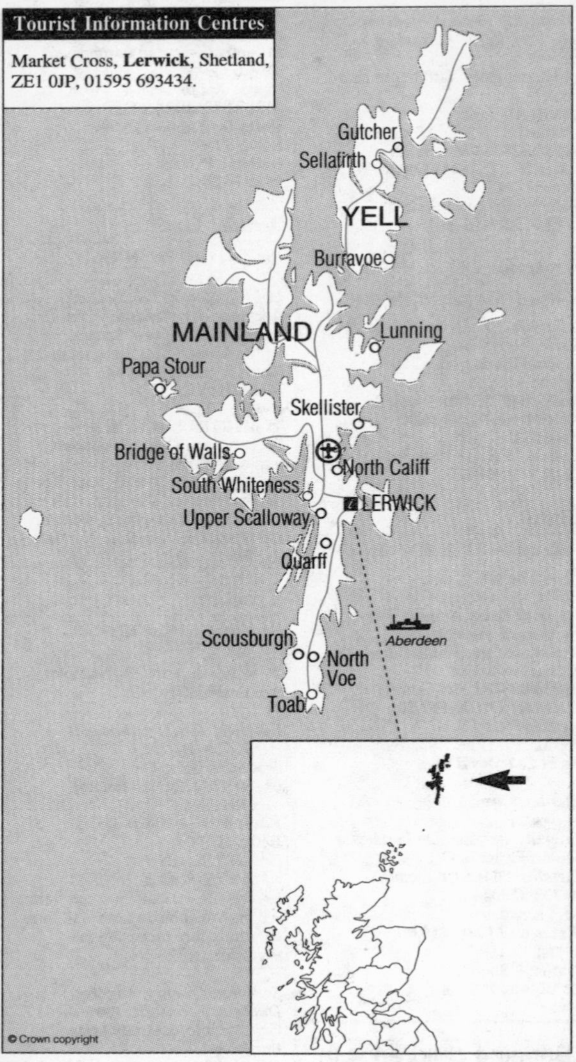

Bridge of Walls

National Grid Ref: HU2651

Hogan, *Bridge of Walls, Shetland,* *ZE2 9NT.*
Modernised crofthouse, warm, comfortable.
Open: All Year
01595 809375 Mrs Leask
Fax no: 01595 809475
Rates fr: *£14.00*-**£14.00**.
Beds: 1F 1D 1S **Baths:** 1 Shared
(8)

Burravoe

National Grid Ref: HU5279

Hillhead, *Burravoe, Yell, Shetland,* *ZE2 9BA.*
Relaxing croft house with panoramic views.
Open: June to Mar
Grades: STB Listed, Comm
01957 722274 Mrs Leask
Rates fr: *£14.00*-**£14.00**.
Beds: 1D 1T
(4)

Gutcher

National Grid Ref: HU5499

Post Office, *Gutcher, Shetland,* *ZE2 9DP.*
Friendly, rural stone-built house.
Open: All Year (not Xmas)
01957 744201 Mrs Tulloch
Rates fr: *£13.00*-**£13.00**.
Beds: 1F 1D 2T
Baths: 2 Shared
(10)

Lerwick

National Grid Ref: HU4741

Candlestick Maker, Queens Hotel

The Old Manse, *9 Commercial Street, Lerwick, Shetland,* *ZE1 0AN.*
1685 house in conservation area.
Open: All Year
Grades: STB 1 Cr, Comm
01595 696301 Mrs Irving
Rates fr: *£18.00*-**£20.00**.
Beds: 1F 2T
Baths: 1 Shared

Whinrig, *12 Burgh Road, Lerwick, Shetland,* *ZE1 0LB.*
Private bungalow. Quiet residential area.
Open: All Year (not Xmas)
Grades: STB 2 Cr, High Comm
01595 693554 Mrs Gifford
Rates fr: *£16.00*-**£18.00**.
Beds: 1D 2T
Baths: 1 Private
(3)

Woosung, *43 St Olaf Street, Lerwick, Shetland,* *ZE1 0EN.*
Central, close to all amenities.
Open: All Year
01595 693687 Mrs Conroy
Rates fr: *£16.00*-**£19.00**.
Beds: 2T
Baths: 1 Shared

95 King Harald Street, *Lerwick, Shetland,* *ZE1 0ER.*
Very central; close all amenities.
Open: All Year
01595 692330 Mrs Kelly
Rates fr: *£15.00*-**£15.00**.
Beds: 2T 1S
Baths: 1 Shared

Bringing children with you? Always ask for any special rates.

Albany House B&B, *50 St Olaf Street, Lerwick, Shetland, ZE1 0EN.*
Very central residential area.
Open: All Year
01595 692468
Rates fr: *£16.00*-**£18.00**.
Beds: 2T **Baths:** 2 Private

Breiview, *43 Kantersted Road, Lerwick, Shetland, ZE1 0RJ.*
Modern guest house, good cooking.
Open: All Year
01595 695956 Mr Glaser
Rates fr: *£20.00*-**£24.00**.
Beds: 1F 2D 3T
Baths: 6 Private
(6)

Lunning

National Grid Ref: HU5067

Skeo Green, *Lunning, Vidlin, Shetland, ZE2 9QB.*
Converted double croft house.
Artist's studio.
Open: All Year
01806 577302 Mrs Ford
Rates fr: *£14.00*-**£14.00**.
Beds: 1T
(3)

North Califf

National Grid Ref: HU4446

Norbreck, *North Califf, Gott, Shetland, ZE2 9SF.*
Comfortable modern house.
Open: All Year (not Xmas)
01595 840315 Mrs Blance
Rates fr: *£11.00*-**£11.00**.
Beds: 1T 1S
(10)

North Voe

National Grid Ref: HU3915

Columbine, *North Voe, Dunrossness, Shetland, ZE2 9JG.*
Comfortable modern bungalow.
Open: All Year
01950 460582 Mrs Reeve
Rates fr: *£15.00*-**£16.00**.
Beds: 1T
Baths: 1 Private

Planning a longer stay? Always ask for any special rates.

Papa Stour

National Grid Ref: HU1660

Northouse, *Papa Stour, Shetland, ZE2 9PW.*
Stone-built island croft on seashore. **Open:** All Year
01595 873238 Mrs Holt-Brook
Rates fr: *£14.00*-**£15.00**.
Beds: 1F 1T 1S
Baths: 1 Private 1 Shared

Quarff

National Grid Ref: HU4235

The Sparl, *Wester Quarff Road, Quarff, Shetland, ZE2 9EY.*
Family home in picturesque valley.
Open: All Year (not Xmas)
01950 477301 Mrs Laurenson
Fax no: 01950 477577
Rates fr: *£14.00*-**£14.00**.
Beds: 1D 1T **Baths:** 2 Shared
(2)

Scousburgh

National Grid Ref: HU3717

Colsa, *Scousburgh, Dunrossness, Shetland, ZE2 9JG.*
Comfortable family home with beautiful views.
Open: All Year (not Xmas)
01950 460503 Ms Murdoch
Rates fr: *£13.50*-**£13.50**.
Beds: 1D **Baths:** 1 Ensuite
(2)

Sellafirth

National Grid Ref: HU5297

Westerhouse Croft, *Sellafirth, Yell, Shetland, ZE2 9DG.*
Beautifully situated on working croft. **Open:** Apr to Oct
01957 744203 Mrs Hamilton
Rates fr: *£13.00*-**£13.00**.
Beds: 1F 1D **Baths:** 1 Shared

Skellister

National Grid Ref: HU4654

The Knowes Guest House, *Skellister, South Nesting, Shetland, ZE2 9PP.*
Small, friendly country guest house. **Open:** All Year
Grades: STB Listed, High Comm
01595 890204 / 0831 586 963
Mrs Jenner
Rates fr: *£18.00*-**£18.00**.
Beds: 1F 1D 1S**Baths:** 1 Shared
(4)

South Whiteness

National Grid Ref: HU3844

Hallibrig, *Easthouse, South Whiteness, Shetland, ZE2 9LL.*
Modern working croft on SSSI.
Open: All Year
01595 840518 Dr Watt
Rates fr: *£18.00*-**£20.00**.
Beds: 1F 1T
Baths: 2 Ensuite

Toab

National Grid Ref: HU3811

Black's, *Toab, Virkie, Shetland, ZE2 9JL.*
Modern, comfortable farmhouse.
Open: All Year (not Xmas)
01950 460710 Mrs Black
Rates fr: *£12.50*-**£13.00**.
Beds: 2T 1S
Baths: 2 Shared
(10)

Upper Scalloway

National Grid Ref: HU4039

Broch Guest House, *Upper Scalloway, Lerwick, Shetland, ZE1 0UP.*
Comfortable guest house.
Open: All Year (not Xmas)
01595 880767
Mrs Young
Rates fr: *£17.00*-**£19.00**.
Beds: 3D
Baths: 3 Ensuite
(3)

Yell

National Grid Ref: HU5190

Hillhead, *Burravoe, Yell, Shetland, ZE2 9BA.*
Relaxing crofthouse with panoramic views.
Open: June to Mar
Grades: STB Listed, Comm
01957 722274
Mrs Leask
Rates fr: *£14.00*-**£14.00**.
Beds: 1D 1T
(4)

Bringing children with you? Always ask for any special rates.

Stirling & Clackmannan

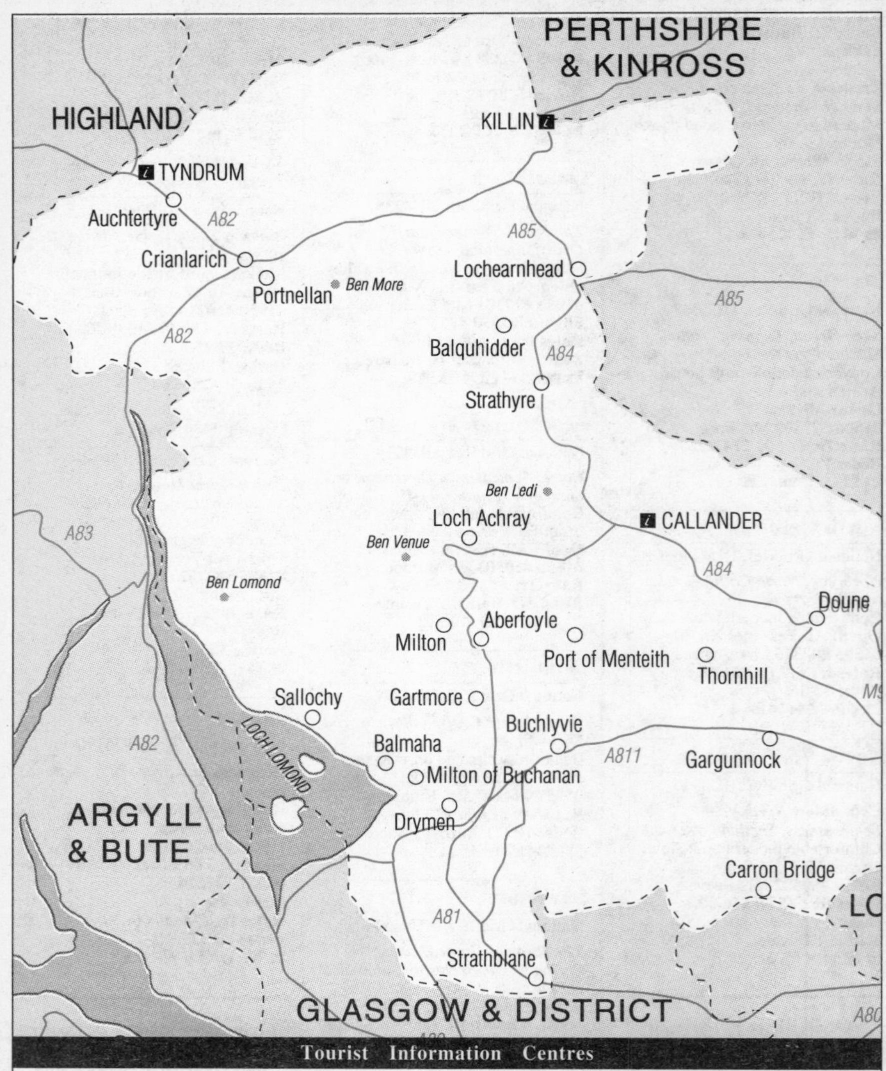

Tourist Information Centres

Main Street, **Aberfoyle**, Stirling, Stirlingshire, FK8 3UG, 01877 382352, (Easter to Oct).

Rob Roy & Trossachs Visitor Centre, Ancaster Square, **Callander**, Perthshire, FK17 8AD, 01877 330342, (Easter to Oct).

Stirling Road, **Dunblane**, Perthshire, FK15 9EY, 01786 824428, (Easter to Oct).

The Steeple, High Street, **Falkirk**, Stirlingshire, FK1 1EJ, 01324 620244.

Main Street, **Killin**, Perthshire, FK21 8UH, 01567 820254, (Easter to Oct).

Pine 'n' Oak, Kincardine Bridge, **Airth**, Falkirk, Stirlingshire, KY2 8JJ, 01324 831422, (Easter to Oct).

41 Dumbarton Road, **Stirling**, Stirlingshire, FK8 2QJ, 01786 475019.

Clock Mill, Upper Mill Street, **Tillicoultry**, Clackmannanshire, FK13 6AX, 01259 52176, (Easter to Oct).

Main Street, **Tyndrum**, Crianlarich, Perthshire, FK20 8RY, 01838 400246, (Easter to Oct).

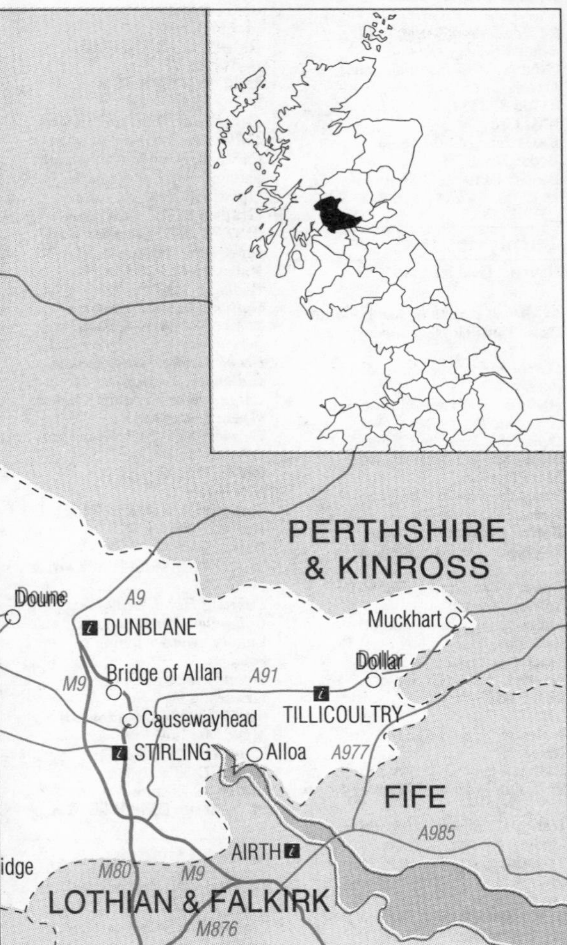

Aberfoyle

National Grid Ref: NN5200

Old Coach House Inn, Inverard Hotel

Mayfield, *Main Street, Aberfoyle, Stirling,* *FK8 3UQ.*
Large Victorian private house in centre of Aberfoyle.
Open: All Year (not Xmas)
Grades: STB Listed, Comm
01877 382845 Mrs Oldham
Rates fr: *£16.00*-**£16.00**.
Beds: 2D 1S
Baths: 3 Ensuite
(4)

Tigh na Cruinn, *Manse Road, Aberfoyle, Stirling,* *FK8 3XF.*
Picturesque bungalow in woodland setting.
Open: Easter to Oct
01877 382760 Mrs Marnie
Rates fr: *£16.00*-**£16.00**.
Beds: 1D 1S
Baths: 1 Ensuite 1 Shared
(3)

The lowest *double* rate per person is shown in *italics*.

Alloa

National Grid Ref: NS8993

Claremont Lodge Hotel, *Kellie Place, Alloa, Clackmannanshire,* *FK10 2OW.*
Open: All Year
Grades: STB 3 Cr, Comm
01259 214575 (also fax no)
Mr McGregor
Rates fr: *£27.50*-**£32.00**.
Beds: 3D 3T 2S
(20)
Family-run hotel, nice and central. Easy reach of at least 12 golf courses. On the Mill Trail, and near 'Braveheart' country.

Alva

National Grid Ref: NS8897

Johnstone Arms Hotel

Johnstone Arms Hotel, *48 Stirling Street, Alva, Clackmannanshire,* *FK12 5EA.*
Open: All Year
Grades: STB Listed
01259 762884
Mr Cairns
Rates fr: *£18.00*.
Beds: 6
Baths: 2 Ensuite
(14) (8)
100-year-old coaching house extensively refurbished, nestling at the foot of the Ochil Hills. Ideal for hill walking, golf, fishing, horse-riding, etc. Also music at week-ends. Large parties welcome.

Auchtertyre

National Grid Ref: NN3529

Auchtertyre Farm, *Auchtertyre, Tyndrum, Crianlarich, Perthshire,* *FK20 8RU.*
Modern comfortable farm bungalow.
Open: All Year
01838 400251
Mrs Baillie
Rates fr: *£15.00*-**£15.00**.
Beds: 2F
Baths: 1 Shared

Balmaha

National Grid Ref: NS4290

Clachen Inn

Critreoch, *Rowardennan Road, Balmaha, Glasgow,* *G63 0AW.*
Lochside family home. Beautiful view.
Open: Easter to October
Grades: STB 2 Cr, Comm
01360 870309 Mrs MacLuskie
Rates fr: *£18.00*-**£24.00**.
Beds: 2D 1T
Baths: 1 Ensuite 2 Private
(6)

Bay Cottage, *Balmaha, Glasgow, G63 0JQ.*
Comfortable and homely cottage.
Open: Mar to Oct
01360 870346 (also fax no)
Mrs Bates
Rates fr: *£18.50*-**£18.50**.
Beds: 2F 1D 1T 1S
Baths: 3 Private 2 Shared
(4)

Moniack, *Balmaha, Glasgow, G63 0BY.*
Modern newly-built house.
Open: All Year
01360 870357 / 870388 Mrs Fraser
Fax no: 01360 870350
Rates fr: *£20.00*-**£25.00**.
Beds: 1D 1T
Baths: 1 Private 1 Shared
(6)

Mar Achlais, *Milton of Buchanan, Balmaha, Glasgow, G63 0JE.*
Rural setting near Loch Lomond.
Open: All Year (not Xmas)
Grades: STB 2 Cr, Comm
01360 870300 Mr Nichols
Rates fr: *£17.00*-**£27.00**.
Beds: 1F 1D
Baths: 2 Ensuite
(2)

Dunleen, *Balmaha, Glasgow, G63 0JE.*
Modern, comfortable bungalow near Loch Lomond.
Open: May to Oct
01360 870274 Mrs MacFadyen
Rates fr: *£16.00*-**£20.00**.
Beds: 1D 1T
Baths: 1 Shared
(2)

Balquhidder

National Grid Ref: NN5320

Kingshouse Hotel

Calea Sona, *Balquhidder, Lochearnhead, Perthshire, FK19 8NY.*
Comfortable stone house, wonderful views.
Open: All Year (not Xmas)
Grades: STB 2 Cr, Comm
01877 384260 (also fax no)
Mrs Blain
Rates fr: *£21.00*-**£25.00**.
Beds: 1D 1T
Baths: 1 Ensuite 1 Private
(4)

Monachachyle Mhor, *Hotel/farmhouse, Balquhidder, Lochearnhead, Perthshire, FK19 8PQ.*
C18th restaurant in own 2000 acres.
Open: All Year
Grades: STB 3 Cr, AA 2 St, 2 Rosettes
01877 384622 Mrs Lewis
Fax no: 01877 384305
Rates fr: *£28.00*-**£38.00**.
Beds: 3D 2T 5D
Baths: 10 Ensuite
(12)

Bridge of Allan

National Grid Ref: NS7997

Westerton Arms

94 Henderson Street, *Bridge of Allan, Stirling, FK9 4HA.*
Ground floor Victorian house.
Open: Easter to Nov
01786 832334
Miss Grew
Rates fr: *£16.00*-**£18.00**.
Beds: 2F 1D 2T
Baths: 1 Private 2 Shared
(4)

Buchlyvie

National Grid Ref: NS5793

Rob Roy Inn, Buchlyvie Inn, Cross Keys Hotel (Kippen)

Gartinstarry, *Buchlyvie, Stirling, FK8 3PD.*
Historic laird's house, peaceful, comfortable.
Open: All Year (not Xmas)
01360 850252 (also fax no)
Mrs Fleming
Rates fr: *£20.00*-**£20.00**.
Beds: 2T
Baths: 1 Ensuite 1 Private
(5) (2)

Upper Gartinstarry, *Buchlyvie, Stirling, FK8 3PD.*
Large country house, quiet location.
Open: All Year (not Xmas)
Grades: STB 2 Cr, Comm
01360 850309
Mrs Golding
Rates fr: *£18.00*-**£22.00**.
Beds: 2F
Baths: 1 Ensuite 1 Private
(10)

Wester Auchentroig, *Buchlyvie, Stirling, FK8 3PB.*
Traditional farmhouse in tranquil setting.
Open: Easter to Oct
01360 850404 (also fax no)
Mr & Mrs Duff
Rates fr: *£14.50*-**£14.50**.
Beds: 1F 1T
Baths: 1 Private 1 Shared

Callander

National Grid Ref: NN6307

Craigroyston, *4 Bridge Street, Callander, Perthshire, FK17 8AA.*
Family-run, comfortable, good food.
Open: All Year
Grades: STB 2 Cr, Comm
01877 331395
Mr & Mrs MacLeod
Rates fr: *£18.00*-**£20.00**.
Beds: 1F 1D 1S
Baths: 3 Ensuite

Auchinlea, *Ancaster Road, Callander, Perthshire, FK17 8EL.*
Quietly situated bungalow near town.
Open: All Year
01877 330769
Mrs McKenzie
Rates fr: *£15.00*-**£17.00**.
Beds: 1D 1T
(1)

East Mains House, *Bridgend, Callander, Perthshire, FK17 8AG.*
C18th mansion house, mature garden.
Open: All Year
Grades: STB 2 Cr, Comm
01877 330535 (also fax no)
Mr & Mrs Thompson
Rates fr: *£18.00*-**£18.00**.
Beds: 1F 3D 1T
Baths: 4 Ensuite 1 Shared
(7)

Brook Linn Country House, *Callander, Perthshire, FK17 8AU.*
Large Victorian country house.
Open: Easter to Oct
Grades: STB 3 Cr, High Comm, AA 4 Q, Select
01877 330103
Mrs House
Rates fr: *£20.00*-**£16.00**.
Beds: 2F 3D 1T 1S
Baths: 7 Private
(1) (10)

Lubnaig Hotel, *Leny Feus, Callander, Perthshire, FK17 8AS.*
Luxury award-winning private hotel.
Open: Easter to Oct
Grades: STB 2 St
01877 330376 (also fax no)
Mr & Mrs Low
Rates fr: *£25.00*-**£30.00**.
Beds: 5D 5T
Baths: 10 Ensuite
(7) (10)

Carron Bridge

National Grid Ref: NS7483

Carron Bridge Hotel, *Carron Bridge, Denny, Stirlingshire, FK6 5JG.*
Very comfortable family-run hotel.
Open: All Year
01324 823459
Mr Scott
Rates fr: *£17.50*-**£25.00**.
Beds: 1F 2T
Baths: 3 Ensuite

All details shown are as supplied by B&B owners in Autumn 1996.

Causewayhead

National Grid Ref: NS8095

Silver Tassie

***28 Airthrey Road,** Causewayhead, Stirling, FK9 5JS.*
Large well-decorated family house.
Open: All Year (not Xmas)
01786 461747 Mrs McIntosh
Rates fr: *£16.00*-**£22.00**.
Beds: 2F **Baths:** 1 Shared
(4)

Crianlarich

National Grid Ref: NN3825

Rod & Reel Restaurant

***Tigh-na-Struith,** Crianlarich, Perthshire, FK20 8RU.*
Open: All Year
01838 300235 Mr & Mrs Chisholm
Rates fr: *£16.00*-**£16.00**.
Beds: 2F 3D 1T
Baths: 1 Ensuite 2 Shared
Friendly guest house set in four acres of grounds on the banks of the River Fillan. Each room has superb views of the Crianlarich Mountains.

***Ben More Lodge Hotel,** Crianlarich, Perthshire, FK20 8QS.*
Family-run hotel beneath Ben More. **Open:** All Year
Grades: STB 3 Cr, Comm
01838 300210 Mr Goodale
Rates fr: *£26.00*-**£27.00**.
Beds: 2F 8D 1T
Baths: 11 Ensuite
(50)

***The Lodge House,** Crianlarich, Perthshire, FK20 8RU.*
Modern comfortable country house.
Open: Mar to Dec
Grades: STB 3 Cr, High Comm, AA 3 Q
01838 300276 Mrs Ferries
Rates fr: *£25.00*-**£25.00**.
Beds: 1F 3D 2T
Baths: 6 Ensuite
(10)

***Alit Chaorain Country House,** Crianlarich, Perthshire, FK20 8RU.*
Very atmospheric home with log fires.
Open: Easter to Oct
Grades: STB 3 Cr, Comm
01838 300283 Mr McDonald
Rates fr: *£33.00*-**£43.00**.
Beds: 4D 4T
(10)

***Glenardran Guest House,** Crianlarich, Perthshire, FK20 8QS.*
Comfortable late Victorian guest house.
Open: All Year
01838 300236 Mr Champion
Rates fr: *£17.00*-**£19.00**.
Beds: 3D 2T 1S **Baths:** 1 Shared
(6)

Dollar

National Grid Ref: NS9698

***Strathallan Hotel,** Chapel Place, Dollar, Clackmannanshire, FK14 7DW.*
Booker's 'Best in Britain' Award.
Open: All Year
01259 742205 Mr Boyd
Rates fr: *£25.00*-**£40.00**.
Beds: 2F 1T
(12)

Doune

National Grid Ref: NN7301

Red Lion Hotel

***Inverardoch Mains Farm,** Doune, Dunblane, Perthshire, FK15 9NZ.*
Traditional farmhouse on working farm. **Open:** Easter to Oct
01786 841268 Mrs Anderson
Rates fr: *£16.00*-**£18.00**.
Beds: 1F 1D 1T
Baths: 1 Private 1 Shared

Drymen

National Grid Ref: NS4788

Clachan

***East Drumquhassle Farm,** Gartness Road, Drymen, Glasgow, G63 0DN.*
Quiet comfortable, excellent food, rural.
Open: All Year
Grades: STB Listed, Comm
01360 660893 Mrs Cross
Rates fr: *£17.50*-**£18.50**.
Beds: 1F 1D
Baths: 1 Ensuite 1 Private
(4)

***Buchanan Arms Hotel,** Main Street, Drymen, Glasgow, G63 0BG.*
Former coaching inn, luxury leisure club.
Open: All Year
Grades: STB 4 Cr, Comm, AA 3 St, RAC 3 St
01360 660588 Mr Kernohan
Rates fr: *£46.00*-**£46.00**.
Beds: 3F 10D 30T 9S
Baths: 52 Ensuite
(100)

***Ceardach,** Gartness Road, Drymen, Glasgow, G63 0BH.*
Converted 250-year-old smithy.
Open: All Year (not Xmas)
01360 660596 (also fax no)
Mrs Robb
Rates fr: *£12.50*-**£15.00**.
Beds: 2D 1T
Baths: 1 Shared
(0) (3)

The lowest **single** *rate is shown in* **bold.**

Always telephone to get directions to the B&B - you will save time!

***Winnock Hotel,** The Square, Drymen, Glasgow, G63 0BL.*
C17th country inn.
Open: All Year
Grades: STB 4 Cr, Comm, AA 2 St, RAC 3 St
01360 660245 Mr Warnes
Rates fr: *£19.50*-**£32.00**.
Beds: 6F 12D 16T 4S
Baths: 38 Private
(60)

Dunblane

National Grid Ref: NN7801

***Westwood,** Doune Road, Dunblane, Perthshire, FK15 9ND.*
Highly Commended by STB.
Open: Mar to Nov
01786 822579 Mrs Duncan
Rates fr: *£18.50*-**£25.00**.
Beds: 2D 1T
Baths: 3 Private
(6)

Gartmore

National Grid Ref: NS5297

Black Bull

***Ardshiel,** Main Street, Gartmore, Stirling, FK8 3RJ.*
Attractive old manse, friendly welcome.
Open: All Year (not Xmas)
01877 382457 Mrs Glasse-Davies
Rates fr: *£14.50*-**£15.00**.
Beds: 1D
Baths: 1 Ensuite
(1)

Killin

National Grid Ref: NN5732

Bridge of Lochay Hotel

***Dalchenna,** Craignavie Road, Killin, Perthshire, FK21 8SH.*
Riverside view, edge of village.
Open: Jun to Sep
01567 820281 Mrs Willison
Rates fr: *£14.00*-**£14.00**.
Beds: 1D 1S
Baths: 1 Shared

***Craigbuie Guest House,** Main Street, Killin, Perthshire, FK21 8UH.*
Large Victorian villa.
Open: All Year
01567 820439 Mrs Hagan
Rates fr: *£14.00*-**£14.00**.
Beds: 3F 2D 2T
Baths: 2 Shared
(5) (7)

Fernbank, *Main Street, Killin, Perthshire,* *FK21 8UW.*
Large Edwardian private house.
Open: Easter to Oct
01567 820511 Mr & Mrs Holms
Rates fr: *£14.00.*
Beds: 1D 2T
Baths: 1 Private 1 Shared
(3)

Loch Achray

National Grid Ref: NN5106

Brig O' Turk Tea Room

Corrie A'an, *Loch Achray, Trossachs, Callander, Perthshire,* *FK17 8HX.*
Open: All Year (not Xmas)
01877 376216 Mrs Lindsay
Rates fr: *£18.00*-**£25.00**.
Beds: 2D 1T
Baths: 2 Ensuite 1 Private
(3)
Unique country house in the heart of Rob Roy country. All rooms with Loch views. Interesting interior design and collections in this Scots-owned home.

Lochearnhead

National Grid Ref: NN5823

Clachan Cottage Hotel, *Lochside, Lochearnhead, Perthshire,* *FK19 8PU.*
Converted and extended crofts.
Open: Easter to Dec
01567 830247 Mr Low
Rates fr: *£25.00*-**£25.00**.
Beds: 2F 10D 9T
Baths: 21 Private
(60)

Milton

National Grid Ref: NN5001

The Byre Inn

Creag Ard House B&B, *Milton, Stirling,* *FK8 3TQ.*
Spectacular views, Loch, mountains, forests.
Open: All Year
Grades: STB 2 Cr, Comm
01877 382297 Mr Carter
Rates fr: *£17.50*-**£20.00**.
Beds: 3D 3T 1S
Baths: 4 Private 1 Shared
(1) (10)

Milton of Buchanan

National Grid Ref: NS4290

Mar Achlais, *Milton of Buchanan, Balmaha, Glasgow,* *G63 0JE.*
Rural setting near Loch Lomond.
Open: All Year (not Xmas)
Grades: STB 2 Cr, Comm
01360 870300 Mr Nichols
Rates fr: *£17.00*-**£27.00**.
Beds: 1F 1D
Baths: 2 Ensuite
(2)

National Grid References are for villages, towns and cities - *not* for individual houses.

Muckhart

National Grid Ref: NS9998

Leys Farm, *Muckhart, Dollar, Clackmannanshire,* *FK14 7JL.*
Modern, comfortable farmhouse. Wonderful views.
Open: All Year
01259 781313 Mr & Mrs Wilson
Rates fr: *£15.00*-**£15.00**.
Beds: 2F 1D 1T
(6)

Port of Menteith

National Grid Ref: NN5801

Crown Hotel

Collymoon Pendicle, *Port of Menteith, Perthshire,* *FK8 3JY.*
Idyllic country house beside river.
Open: Easter to Oct
Grades: STB 1 Cr, Comm
01360 850222 Mrs Tough
Rates fr: *£15.00*-**£15.00**.
Beds: 1F 1D 1S
Baths: 1 Shared
(5) (4)

Inchie Farm, *Port of Menteith, Stirling,* *FK8 3JZ.*
Traditional farmhouse on lakeside.
Open: Easter to Oct
Grades: STB 1 Cr, Comm
01877 385233 Mrs Erskine
Rates fr: *£14.00*-**£17.00**.
Beds: 1F 1T
Baths: 1 Shared
(4)

Portnellan

National Grid Ref: NN4125

Portnellan Lodges, *Portnellan, Crianlarich, Perthshire,* *FK20 8QS.*
Accommodation in luxury individual lodges.
Open: All Year
01838 300284 Mrs Taylor
Rates fr: *£18.00*-**£40.00**.
Baths: 11 Private
(20)

Planning a longer stay? Always ask for any special rates.

Sallochy

National Grid Ref: NS3895

5 Forest Cottage, *Sallochy, Rowardennan, Glasgow,* *G63 0AW.*
Forest village near Ben Lomond.
Open: All Year
01360 870320
Mrs Fraser
Rates fr: *£18.00*-**£18.00**.
Beds: 1D 1T
Baths: 1 Ensuite, 1 Shared

Stirling

National Grid Ref: NS7993

Hogs Head, Hollybank Restaurant, Terraces Hotel

12 Princes Street, *Stirling,* *FK8 1HQ.*
Open: All Year
01786 479228 (also fax no)
Mrs Cairns
Rates fr: *£17.00*-**£18.00**.
Beds: 2T 2S
Baths: 2 Ensuite 2 Shared
(14)
Town centre, 4 minutes from bus and railway stations, personal service always, long established and friendly.

19 Barnsdale Road, *St Ninians, Stirling,* *FK7 0PT.*
Conveniently situated, comfortable Victorian villa.
Open: All Year
01786 461729 (also fax no)
Mrs Pain
Rates fr: *£14.00*-**£17.00**.
Beds: 1F 1D 1T
Baths: 1 Private 1 Shared
(3)

Linden Guest House, *22 Linden Avenue, Stirling,* *FK7 7PQ.*
Open: All Year
01786 448850 Miss McGuinness
Rates fr: *£16.50*-**£22.50**.
Beds: 1F 1D 1T
Baths: 1 Shared
(2)
Close to town centre and providing friendly service. Ideal base for touring central Scotland and beyond. Satellite/colour TV, tea/coffee making facilities in all rooms.

Whitegables, *112 Causewayhead Road, Stirling,* *FK9 5HJ.*
First class service and breakfast.
Open: All Year
Grades: AA 3 Q
01786 479838 Mr & Mrs Black
Rates fr: *£18.00*-**£20.00**.
Beds: 1F 1D 1T 1S
Baths: 4 Ensuite
(8)

The lowest **single** *rate is shown in* **bold.**

15 Albert Place, *Stirling, FK8 2RE.*
Detached Victorian house near town.
Open: Easter to Oct
01786 475175
Mrs Allan
Rates fr: *£16.00*-**£20.00**.
Beds: 1F 1D
Baths: 1 Shared
(2)

Tiroran, *45 Douglas Terrace, Stirling, FK7 9LW.*
Modern house, quiet residential area.
Open: Easter to Oct
Grades: STB 1 Cr, High Comm
01786 464655
Mrs Thomson
Rates fr: *£16.00*.
Beds: 1D 1T
Baths: 1 Shared
(2)

27 King Street, *Stirling, FK8 1DN.*
Comfortable spacious town centre accommodation.
Open: All Year
01786 471082 (also fax no)
Mr & Mrs Macgregor
Rates fr: *£15.00*-**£18.00**.
Beds: 1D 1T 1S
Baths: 1 Private 1 Shared
(2)

Strathblane

National Grid Ref: NS5679

Kirkhouse Inn

The Kirkhouse Inn, *Strathblane, Glasgow, G63 9AA.*
Small, friendly hotel - good food.
Open: All Year
Grades: STB 5 Cr, Comm, AA 3 St
01360 770621
Mr De Banzie
Rates fr: *£25.00*-**£35.00**.
Beds: 6D 7T 2S
Baths: 15 Private
(100)

Strathyre

National Grid Ref: NN5617

Ben Sheann Hotel, *Strathyre, Callander, Perthshire, FK18 8NA.*
Open: All Year
01877 384609 Mr Morton
Rates fr: *£18.50*-**£18.50**.
Beds: 3F 3D 2T 1S
Baths: 2 Ensuite 2 Shared
(15)
This Victorian former railway hotel has a beautiful location in the small village of Strathyre, at the gateway to the Scottish Highlands. Ideal for touring from. The hotel has a reputation for warm hospitality and excellent cuisine.

Coire Buidhe, *Strathyre, Callander, Perthshire, FK18 8NA.*
Former mill. Value for money.
Open: All Year (not Xmas)
Grades: STB Listed, Approv
01877 384288 Mr & Mrs Reid
Rates fr: *£14.00*-**£15.00**.
Beds: 2F 2D 2T 2S
Baths: 1 Private 3 Shared
(6)

The Inn At Strathyre, *Main Street, Strathyre, Callander, Perthshire, FK18 8NA.*
Comfortable friendly C18th inn.
Open: All Year
Grades: STB 3 Cr, Approv
01877 384224 Mr La Piazza
Fax no: 01877 384224 / 384344
Rates fr: *£18.00*-**£25.00**.
Beds: 4D 3T
Baths: 7 Private
(5) (15)

All rates are subject to alteration at the owners' discretion.

Thornhill

National Grid Ref: NS6699

Corshill Cottage, *Thornhill, Stirling, FK8 3QD.*
Blacksmiths' cottage set in 1-acre attractive gardens.
Open: Easter to Sep
01786 850270 Ms Fitches
Rates fr: *£19.00*-**£25.00**.
Beds: 2D 1T **Baths:** 3 Private

Tillicoultry

National Grid Ref: NS9197

Wyvis, *70 Stirling Street, Tillicoultry, Clackmannanshire, FK13 6EA.*
Converted Victorian mill-worker's cottage.
Open: All Year
01259 751513 Mrs Goddard
Rates fr: *£16.00*-**£20.00**.
Beds: 1T
Baths: 1 Private

Tyndrum

National Grid Ref: NN3330

Glengarry Guest House, *Tyndrum, Crianlarich, Perthshire, FK20 8RY.*
Victorian villa with fabulous views.
Open: All Year
Grades: STB 3 Cr, Comm
01838 400224 Mrs Cunningham
Rates fr: *£14.00*-**£17.00**.
Beds: 1F 1D 1T
Baths: 1 Shared
(4)

Dalkjell, *Tyndrum, Crianlarich, Perthshire, FK20 8RY.*
Modern bungalow in 1 acre.
Open: All Year (not Xmas)
01838 400285 Mrs Coffield
Rates fr: *£17.00*.
Beds: 1D 2T **Baths:** 1 Shared

Western Isles

Tourist Information Centres

Pier Road, **Lochboisdale**, Isle of South Uist, PA81 5TH, 01878 700286, (Easter to Oct).

Pier Road, **Lochmaddy**, Isle of North Uist, PA82 5EU, 01876 500321, (Easter to Oct).

4 South Beach Street, **Stornoway**, Isle of Lewis, PA87 2XY, 01851 703088.

Pier Road, **Tarbert**, Isle of Harris, PA85 3BQ, 01859 502011, (Easter to Oct).

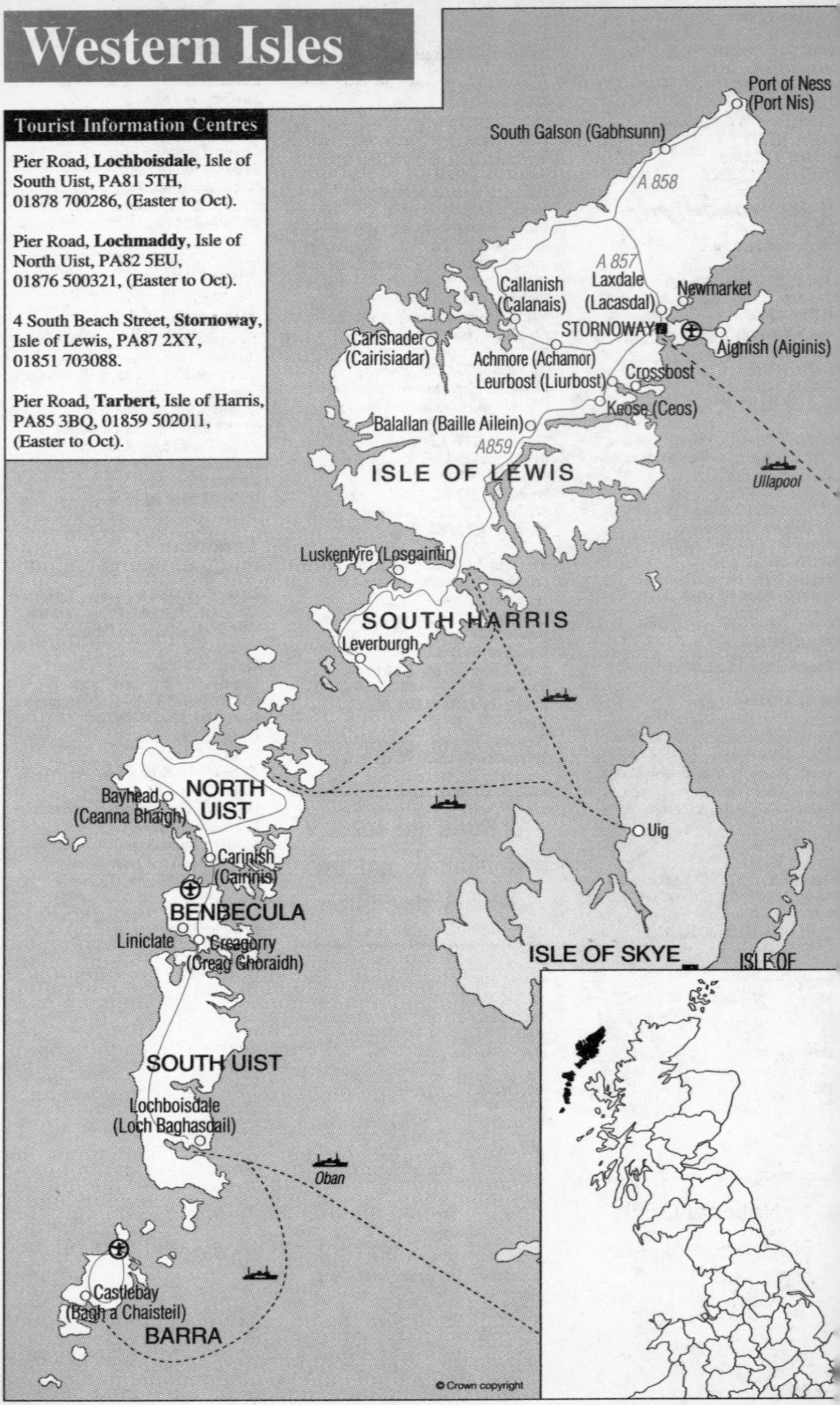

Achmore (Achamor)

National Grid Ref: NB3128

***Lochview,** 35b Achmore, Achmore (Achamor), Lochs, Isle of Lewis, HS2 9DU.*
Ideally situated for touring island.
Open: All Year (not Xmas)
Grades: STB 1 Cr, Comm
01851 860205 Mrs Golder
Rates fr: *£15.00*-**£15.00**.
Beds: 2D 1T
(6)

Aignish (Aiginis)

National Grid Ref: NB4832

***Ceol-Na-Mara,** 1a, Aignish (Aiginis), Point, Isle of Lewis, HS2 0PB.*
Modern house, friendly and welcoming.
Open: All Year
Grades: STB 1 Cr, Comm
01851 870339 Mrs MacDonald
Rates fr: *£15.00*-**£17.00**.
Beds: 1F 1D 1T
Baths: 2 Shared
(3)

Balallan

National Grid Ref: NB2920

***Clearview,** 44 Balallan, Balallan, Isle of Lewis, HS2 9PT.*
Modern bungalow in elevated location.
Open: All Year (not Xmas)
Grades: STB 1 Cr, Comm
01851 830472 Mr & Mrs Mackay
Rates fr: *£15.00*-**£15.00**.
Beds: 1F 1D
Baths: 1 Shared
(6)

Balallan (Baille Ailein)

National Grid Ref:

***Penamber,** 55 Balallan, (Baille Ailein), Lochs, Isle of Lewis, HS2 9PT.*
Ideal base Harris/Lewis, flyfishing.
Open: Apr to Oct
01851 830351 Mrs Smith
Rates fr: *£14.00*.
Beds: 1D 1T
Baths: 1 Ensuite 1 Shared
(4)

National Grid References are for villages, towns and cities - *not* for individual houses.

Bayhead

National Grid Ref: NF7468

***Old Shop House,** Ceann a Bhaigh, Bayhead, Lochmaddy, North Uist, HS6 5DS.*
Comfortable, friendly with traditional cooking.
Open: All Year
01876 510395 Mrs Nicholson
Rates fr: *£13.50*-**£13.50**.
Beds: 1T 1D
Baths: 1 Ensuite 2 Shared
(4)

Callanish (Calanais)

National Grid Ref: NB2135

***Eshcol Guest House,** 21 Breascleit, Callanish (Calanais), Isle of Lewis, HS2 9ED.*
Ensuite facilities. Callanish Stones nearby.
Open: Mar to Oct
Grades: STB 3 Cr, High Comm, AA 4 Q, Select
01851 621357 Mrs MacArthur
Rates fr: *£23.00*-**£25.00**.
Beds: 1D 2T
Baths: 3 Private
(7) (12)

Carinish (Cairinis)

National Grid Ref: NF8259

***Bonnieview,** 19 Cairinis, Carinish (Cairinis), Lochmaddy, North Uist, HS6 5HN.*
Comfortable crofthouse with lovely views.
Open: All Year
01876 580211 Mrs Morrison
Rates fr: *£15.00*-**£18.00**.
Beds: 1D 1T
Baths: 2 Ensuite

Carishader (Cairisiadar)

National Grid Ref: NB0933

***1 Cairisiadar,** Carishader (Cairisiadar), Uig, Isle of Lewis, HS2 9ER.*
Comfortable crofthouse, sea views, walks.
Open: All Year
01851 672239 Mrs MacKay
Rates fr: *£14.00*-**£14.00**.
Beds: 1D 1T
Baths: 1 Shared
(3)

Castlebay

National Grid Ref: NL6698

Craigard Hotel

***Grianamul,** Bagh a Chasteil, Castlebay, Isle of Barra, HS9 5XD.*
Recently refurbished, near ferry.
Open: All Year (not Xmas)
01871 810416 Mrs MacNeil
Rates fr: *£18.00*-**£18.00**.
Beds: 1F 1D 1T
Baths: 3 Ensuite

High season, bank holidays and special events mean low availability *anywhere.*

***Tigh-na-Mara,** Bagh a Chasteil, Castlebay, Isle of Barra, HS9 5XD.*
2 miles from ferry terminal.
Open: Easter to Oct
01871 810304 Mrs MacLean
Rates fr: *£18.00*-**£18.00**.
Beds: 1D 2T 2S
Baths: 3 Ensuite
(6)

Creagorry

National Grid Ref: NF7948

Dark Island Hotel, Orosay Inn

***Dunfarquhar,** Creag Ghoraidh, Creagorry, Isle of Benbecula, HS7 5PY.*
Comfortable croft house.
Open: All Year (not Xmas)
01870 602227 Mrs MacSween
Rates fr: *£16.00*-**£16.00**.
Beds: 3F 1T
Baths: 1 Shared
(7) (12)

Crossbost

National Grid Ref: NB4331

***44 Crossbost,** Crossbost, Isle of Lewis, HS2 9NP.*
Modern comfortable country house.
Open: All Year
Grades: STB Listed, Comm
01851 860340 Ms MacLeod
Rates fr: *£15.00*-**£15.00**.
Beds: 1F 1T
Baths: 1 Shared
(2)

Keose (Ceos)

National Grid Ref: NB3521

***Handa,** 18 The Glebe, Keose (Ceos), Lochs, Isle of Lewis, HS2 9JX.*
Modern, comfortable, home. Good food!
Open: May to Oct
01851 830334 Mrs Morrison
Rates fr: *£16.00*-**£22.00**.
Beds: 2D 1T
Baths: 1 Private 1 Shared
(4)

The lowest **single** *rate is shown in* **bold.**

Anglesey

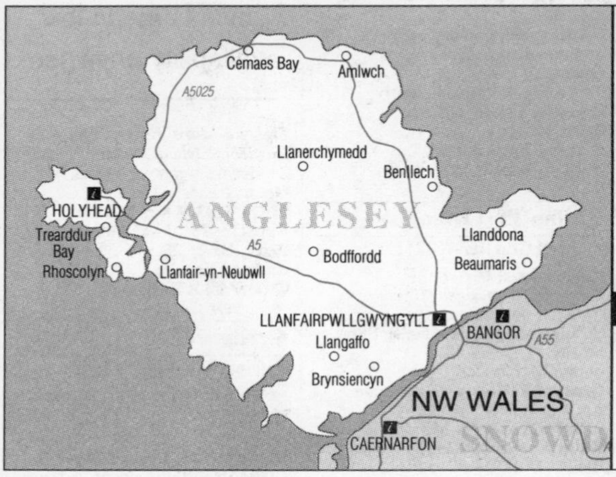

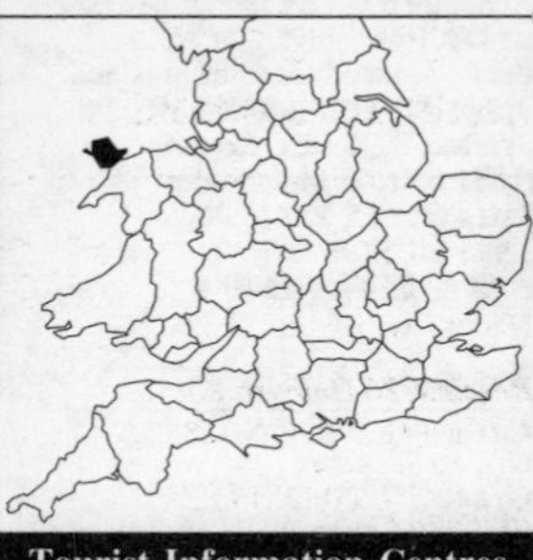

Tourist Information Centres

Marine Square, Salt Island Approach, **Holyhead**, LL65 1DR, 01407-762622.

Station Site, **Llanfairpwllgwyngyll**, Gwynedd, LL61 5UJ, 01248-713177.

Amlwch

National Grid Ref: SH4493

Bryn Arfor Guest House, *Amlwch, Anglesey, LL68 9DU.*
Fabulous coastal location overlooking Bull Bay.
Open: All Year (not Xmas)
Grades: WTB 2 Cr, High Comm
01407 831493
Mr & Mrs Clays
Rates fr: *£15.00*-**£15.00**.
Beds: 2F 2D 2T 2S
Baths: 4 Private 2 Shared
(8)

Beaumaris

National Grid Ref: SH6076

Mor Awel, *Beaumaris, Anglesey, LL58 8NP.*
Large Victorian guest house.
Open: All Year
Grades: WTB 2 Cr, Comm
01248 490826
Mrs Thomas
Rates fr: *£12.50*-**£14.50**.
Beds: 1F 1D 1T
Baths: 1 Private 2 Shared
(4)

Plas Cichle, *Beaumaris, Anglesey, LL58 8PS.*
Period farmhouse in 200 acres.
Open: Mar to Oct
Grades: WTB 2 Cr, High Comm
01248 810488
Mrs Roberts
Rates fr: *£19.00*-**£24.00**.
Beds: 1F 2D
Baths: 2 Ensuite 1 Private
(5) (4)

Benllech

National Grid Ref: SH5182

Woodlands Guest House, *Bangor Road, Benllech, Tyn-y-Gongl, Anglesey, LL74 8PU.*
Very comfortable, welcoming Edwardian home.
Open: All Year (not Xmas)
Grades: WTB 3 Cr, High Comm
01248 852735 Mrs Corbett
Rates fr: *£18.00*-**£20.00**.
Beds: 2F 2D 2T **Baths:** 6 Private
(8)

Bay Court Hotel, *Beach Road, Benllech, Tyn-y-Gongl, Anglesey, LL74 8SW.*
200 yds from sandy beach.
Open: All Year
Grades: WTB 3 Cr, AA 2 St, RAC 2 St
01248 852573 Mr Threfall
Fax no: 01248 852606
Rates fr: *£18.00*-**£18.00**.
Beds: 4F 10D 3T 5S
Baths: 10 Private 3 Shared
(60)

Golden Sands Hotel, *Benllech, Tyn-y-Gongl, Anglesey, LL74 8SP.*
Modern, overlooking beach.
Open: All Year
01248 852384 Mrs Littlemore
Rates fr: *£16.50*-**£18.50**.
Beds: 4F 4D 2T 1S
Baths: 9 Private

Belvoir, *8 Lon Fferam, Benllech Bay, Tyn-y-Gongl, Anglesey, LL74 8RL*
Pleasant, friendly home near sea.
Open: Mar to Oct
01248 852907 Mrs Evans
Rates fr: *£15.00*-**£25.00**.
Beds: 1D 1T **Baths:** 2 Private
(2)

Brynsiencyn

National Grid Ref: SH4867

Penrhos Arms (Llanfairpwll)

Fron Guest House, *Brynsiencyn, Llanfairpwllgwyngyll, Anglesey, LL61 6TX.*
Traditional high class farmhouse accommodation.
Open: All Year (not Xmas)
Grades: WTB 2 Cr, High Comm
01248 430310 Mr Geldard
Rates fr: *£14.50*-**£16.00**.
Beds: 3D
Baths: 1 Private 1 Shared
(4)

Cemaes Bay

National Grid Ref: SH3694

Woburn Hill Hotel, *High Street, Cemaes Bay, Anglesey, LL67 0HU.*
Small hotel in fishing village.
Open: All Year
Grades: WTB 2 Cr, Comm
01407 711388 Mrs Potter
Rates fr: *£17.50*-**£22.50**.
Beds: 3F 1D 2T 1S
Baths: 5 Ensuite 1 Shared
(10)

National Grid References are for villages, towns and cities - *not* for individual houses.

Please respect a B&B's wishes regarding children, animals & smoking.

Holyhead

National Grid Ref: SH2482

***Roselea,** 26 Holborn Road, Holyhead, Anglesey, LL65 2AT.*
Open: All Year
Grades: WTB Listed, Comm
01407 764391
Mrs Foxley
Rates fr: *£14.00*-**£16.00**.
Beds: 1F 1D 1T
Baths: 1 Shared
Homely guesthouse near ferry, beaches, golf-course & sailing. Pleasant family atmosphere & guaranteed hospitality. All rooms furnished to high standard. Early/late arrivals/departures.

***Wavecrest,** 93 Newry Road, Holyhead, Anglesey, LL65 1HU.*
Ideal for Ferry - open 24 hours.
Open: All Year (not Xmas)
Grades: WTB 3 Cr, Comm
01407 763637
Mr Hiltunen
Rates fr: *£12.00*-**£12.00**.
Beds: 3F 1T
Baths: 2 Private 2 Shared

***Hendre,** Porth Y Felin Road, Holyhead, Anglesey, LL65 1AH.*
Old manse full of character.
Open: All Year (not Xmas)
Grades: WTB 3 Cr, Deluxe, AA Listed
01407 762929
Rates fr: *£17.50*-**£20.00**.
Beds: 2D 1T
Baths: 3 Private
(6)

Llanddona

National Grid Ref: SH5779

Owain Glyndwr

***Tyn Pistyll,** Beach Road, Llanddona, Beaumaris, Anglesey, LL58 8UN.*
A beautiful quiet country residence.
Open: All Year
Grades: WTB 2 Cr, High Comm
01248 811224 (also fax no)
S H Peacock
Rates fr: *£18.50*-**£20.00**.
Beds: 2D 1T
Baths: 2 Ensuite 1 Private
(5)

Llanerchymedd

National Grid Ref: SH4184

***Trer Ddol Farm,** Llanerchymedd, Anglesey, LL71 7AR.*
C17th farmhouse of great character.
Open: All Year
Grades: WTB 3 Cr, High Comm
01248 470278 Mrs Astley
Rates fr: *£18.00*-**£23.00**.
Beds: 1F 1D 1T **Baths:** 3 Ensuite
(0) (10Yes)

***Llwydiarth Fawr,** Llanerchymedd, Anglesey, LL71 8DF.*
Secluded Georgian mansion.
Open: All Year (not Xmas)
01248 470321 Mrs Hughes
Fax no: 0248 470540
Rates fr: *£22.50*-**£22.50**.
Beds: 1F 1D 1T 1S
Baths: 4 Private

Llanfair-yn-Neubwll

National Grid Ref: SH3076

Valley Hotel, Bull Hotel

***Ty Gwrthyn,** Llanfair-yn-Neubwll, Holyhead, Anglesey, LL65 3LD.*
Country guest house. Sea views.
Open: All Year
Grades: WTB 2 Cr, Comm
01407 741025 Mrs Montgomery Croft
Rates fr: *£16.00*-**£20.00**.
Beds: 1F 1D 2T **Baths:** 3 Ensuite
(8)

Llangaffo

National Grid Ref: SH4468

***Plas Llangaffo,** Llangaffo, Gaerwen, Anglesey, LL60 6LR.*
Quiet, comfortable farmhouse accommodation.
Open: All Year
Grades: WTB Listed
01248 440452 Mrs Lamb
Rates fr: *£14.50*-**£15.00**.
Beds: 1F 2D 2T **Baths:** 2 Shared
(8)

Rhoscolyn

National Grid Ref: SH2675

***The Old Rectory,** Rhoscolyn, Holyhead, Anglesey, LL65 2SQ.*
Open: All Year (not Xmas/New Year)
Grades: WTB 3 Cr, High Comm, AA 3 Q
01407 860214 Mr Wyatt
Rates fr: *£22.00*-**£24.00**.
Beds: 4D 1T **Baths:** 5 Ensuite
(6)
Peacefully situated Georgian house close to sandy bay & coastal walks. Central heating & resident's licence. Bedrooms ensuite with facilities & colour TV. Brochure available.

Trearddur Bay

National Grid Ref: SH2578

Trearddur Bay Hotel, Beach Hotel

***Moranedd Guest House,** Trearddur Road, Trearddur Bay, Holyhead, Anglesey, LL65 2UE.*
Large comfortable house near sea.
Open: All Year
Grades: WTB Listed, RAC Listed
01407 860324 Mrs Wathan
Rates fr: *£14.00*-**£14.00**.
Beds: 2F 3T 1S
Baths: 2 Shared

Cardiganshire

Tourist Information Centres

Terrace Road, **Aberystwyth**, SY23 2AG, 01970 612125.

High St, **Borth**, SY24 5HY, 01970 871174, (Easter to Oct).

Theatr Mwldan, Bath House Road, **Cardigan**, SA43 2JY, 01239613230.

Church St, **New Quay**, 01545 560865, (Easter to Oct).

Market Hall, **Newcastle Emlyn**, 01239 711333, (Easter to Oct).

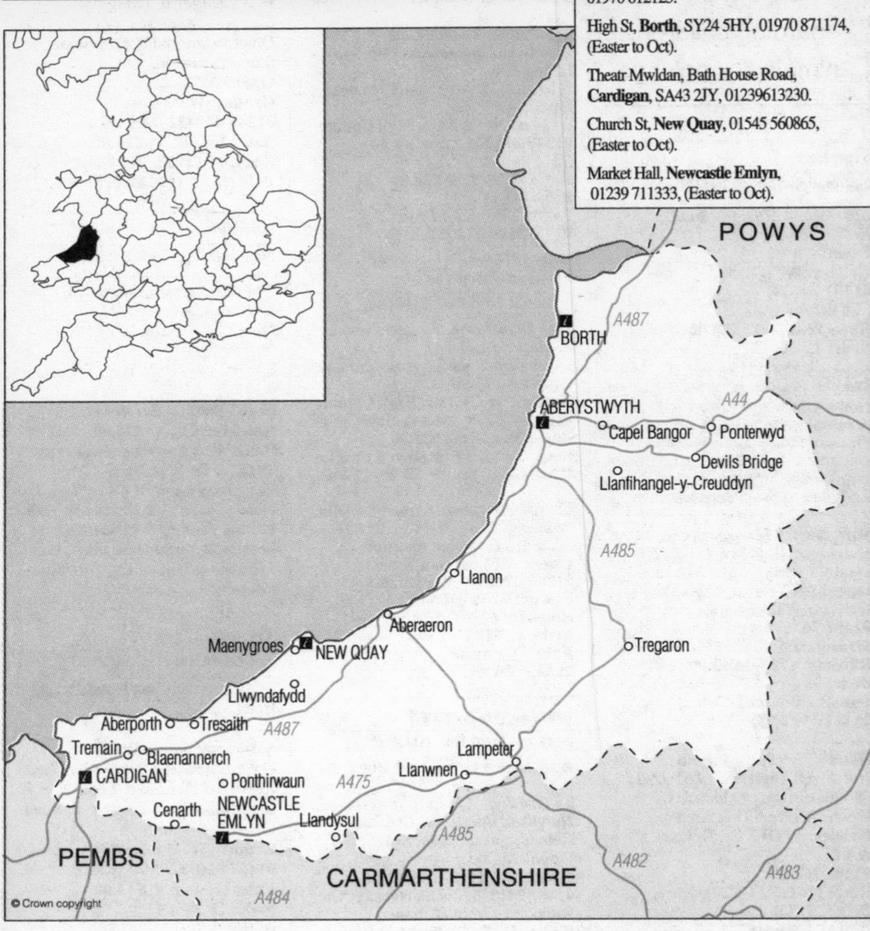

Aberaeron

National Grid Ref: SN4562

Royal Oak, Prince of Wales

Moldavia, *7/8 Belle Vue Terrace, Aberaeron, Ceredigion, SA46 0BB.*
Quiet harbourside setting, stunning views!
Open: All Year
Grades: WTB 2 Cr, High Comm
01545 570107 (also fax no)
Mrs Raw-Rees
Rates fr: *£18.00*-**£18.00**.
Beds: 1F 2D 1T 2S
Baths: 2 Private 1 Shared
(3)

The lowest **single** *rate is shown in* **bold.**

Bringing children with you? Always ask for any special rates.

Monachty Arms Hotel, *Market Street, Aberaeron, Ceredigion, SA46 0AS.*
Centrally situated friendly family-run hotel.
Open: All Year
Grades: WTB 3 Cr, Comm
01545 570389 Mr Howells
Rates fr: *£21.50*-**£24.00**.
Beds: 2F 3D 1T 2S
Baths: 5 Ensuite
(5)

Llys Aeron Guest House, *Lampeter Road, Aberaeron, Ceredigion, SA46 0ED.*
Comfortable, cheerful, Georgian family house.
Open: All Year
Grades: WTB Listed
01545 570276
Mrs Osborne
Rates fr: *£12.50*-**£16.00**.
Beds: 1F 1T 1S
(1) (8)

Planning a longer stay? Always ask for any special rates.

Morawel, *Quay Parade, Aberaeron, Ceredigion, SA46 0BT.*
Lovely character Georgian harbourside house.
Open: All Year (not Xmas)
01545 570120 Mrs Griffiths
Rates fr: *£16.00*-**£18.00**.
Beds: 1F 3D 2T 1S
Baths: 3 Ensuite 1 Private 3 Shared
(6) (7)

Aberporth

National Grid Ref: SN2651

Ffynonwen Country Guest House, *Aberporth, Cardigan, SA43 2HT.*
Ex-farmhouse, family-run, fishing.
Open: All Year
Grades: WTB 3 Cr, High Comm, AA 3 Q
01239 810312
Mr & Mrs Duckworth
Rates fr: *£22.00*-**£22.00**.
Beds: 3F 2D 1T
Baths: 5 Private 1 Shared
(30)

Aberystwyth

National Grid Ref: SN5881

Sinclair Guest House, *43 Portland Street, Aberystwyth, Ceredigion, SY23 2DX.*
Immaculate relaxing accommodation centrally situated.
Open: All Year (not Xmas)
Grades: WTB 3 Cr, High Comm
01970 615158 (also fax no)
Mr & Mrs Ward
Rates fr: *£22.50*-**£27.50**.
Beds: 1D 2T
Baths: 3 Ensuite
(2)

Helmsman, *43 Marine Terrace, Aberystwyth, Ceredigion, SY23 2BX.*
Seafront guest house.
Open: All Year (not Xmas)
Grades: WTB 2 Cr
01970 624132 (also fax no)
Mrs Meyler
Rates fr: *£15.00*-**£15.00**.
Beds: 4F 3D 2T 1S
Baths: 4 Private 2 Shared
(4)

Yr Hafod, *1 South Marine Terrace, Aberystwyth, Ceredigion, SY23 1JX.*
Comfortable sea front guest house.
Open: All Year
Grades: WTB Listed, High Comm, AA 3 Q
01970 617579 Mr Evans
Rates fr: *£17.00*-**£17.00**.
Beds: 2F 3D 2T 2S
Baths: 2 Shared
(1)

The lowest *double* rate per person is shown in *italics*.

Right on the border? Look at the neighbouring county, too

Garreg Lwyd Guest House, *Bow Street, Aberystwyth, Ceredigion, SY24 5BE.*
Comfortable, excellent breakfast, private parking.
Open: All Year (not Xmas)
01970 828830 Mrs Edwards
Rates fr: *£14.00*-**£15.00**.
Beds: 1F 2D 1T 1S
Baths: 1 Shared
(Any)

Brendan Guest House, *19 Marine Terrace, Aberystwyth, Ceredigion, SY23 2AZ.*
Listed Victorian seafront house.
Open: All Year (not Xmas)
01970 612252 Mrs Williams
Rates fr: *£16.00*-**£18.00**.
Beds: 3D 2T 2S
Baths: 4 Private 1 Shared

Blaenannerch

National Grid Ref: SN2449

Craig Y Nos Guest House, *Blaenannerch, Cardigan, SA43 2AL.*
Spacious, comfortable modern house.
Open: All Year (not Xmas)
01239 811348 Mrs Baldwin
Rates fr: *£13.00*-**£13.00**.
Beds: 1F 1D 1T
(4)

Borth

National Grid Ref: SN6089

Glanmor Hotel, ***High Street,*** *Borth, Ceredigion, SY24 5JP.*
Small & friendly seaside hotel.
Open: All Year
Grades: WTB 2 Cr, Comm, AA Listed, RAC Listed
01970 871689 Mr Elliot
Rates fr: *£19.50*-**£19.50**.
Beds: 3F 2D 1T 1S
Baths: 2 Private 2 Shared
(6)

Capel Bangor

National Grid Ref: SN6580

Tynllidiart Arms, Maesbangor Arms, Halfway Inn

Aelybryn Guest House, *Capel Bangor, Aberystwyth, Ceredigion, SY23 3LR.*
Comfortable family-run guest house. **Open:** All Year
Grades: WTB 1 Cr, High Comm
01970 880681 Mrs Jones
Rates fr: *£16.00*-**£16.00**.
Beds: 2D 1T
Baths: 1 Shared
(3)

Tycam Farm, *Capel Bangor, Aberystwyth, Ceredigion, SY23 3NA.*
Modern comfortable farmhouse Rheidol Valley.
Open: Jan to Nov
Grades: WTB 2 Cr
01970 880662 Mr Rowlands
Rates fr: *£36.00*.
Beds: 1D 1T
Baths: 2 Ensuite
(2)

Cardigan

National Grid Ref: SN1746

Eagle Inn

Maes-A-Mor, *Park Place, Gwbert Road, Cardigan, SA43 1AE.*
Edwardian house, family-run non-smoking home.
Open: All Year
Grades: WTB 2 Cr, Comm
01239 614929 (also fax no)
Mr Jones
Rates fr: *£13.50*.
Beds: 2F 3D 2T
Baths: 3 Private
(4)

Cenarth

National Grid Ref: SN2641

Three Horseshoes

Y Garreg Lwyd, *Cenarth, Newcastle Emlyn, Ceredigion, SA38 9RB.*
Delightful former farmhouse cottage.
Open: All Year
Grades: WTB Listed, High Comm
01239 710230
Mrs Daly
Rates fr: *£13.00*-**£20.00**.
Beds: 1D 1T
(2)

Devils Bridge

National Grid Ref: SN7376

Mount Pleasant, *Devils Bridge, Aberystwyth, Ceredigion, SY23 4QY.*
Open: All Year
Grades: WTB 3 Cr, High Comm
01970 890219 Mr & Mrs Sherlock
Rates fr: *£19.00*-**£24.00**.
Beds: 2F 2D 2T
Baths: 5 Ensuite 1 Private
(10) (6)
Mount Pleasant: established 14 years, this tip-top accommodation set amidst beautiful scenic countryside. Ideal for the country-lover & touring mid-Wales. Phone for brochure.

All rates are subject to alteration at the owners' discretion.

National Grid References are for villages, towns and cities - *not* for individual houses.

***Erwbarfe Farm,** Devils Bridge, Aberystwyth, Ceredigion, SY23 3JR.*
Large welcoming comfortable farmhouse.
Open: Apr to Sep
01970 890251 Mrs Lewis
Rates fr: *£16.00*-**£25.00**.
Beds: 1F 1D
(4)

***Hafod Arms Hotel,** Devils Bridge, Aberystwyth, Ceredigion, SY23 3JL.*
Georgian with Victorian tea room.
Open: Feb to Dec
01970 890232 Mr Greedy
Rates fr: *£20.00*-**£25.00**.
Beds: 1F 9D 8T 2S
Baths: 15 Ensuite 3 Shared
(12) (10)

Lampeter

National Grid Ref: SN5848

Kings Head

***Pantycelyn Farm Guest House,** Llanwnen, Lampeter, Ceredigion, SA48 7LW.*
Open: Jan to Dec
Grades: WTB 2 Cr, High Comm
01570 434455
Mrs Jenkins
Rates fr: *£15.00*-**£15.00**.
Beds: 1D 1T 1S
Baths: 3 Ensuite
(4)
In peaceful countryside, an ideal base for Cardigan Bay, Teify Valley, Cambrian Mountains & Cardiganshire's many attractions. Ensuite bedrooms, genuine home cooking, ample local information.

***Haulfan,** 6 Station Terrace, Lampeter, Ceredigion, SA48 7HH.*
Small friendly guest house.
Open: All Year (not Xmas)
Grades: WTB Listed, High Comm
01570 422718
Mrs Williams
Rates fr: *£15.00*-**£15.00**.
Beds: 1F 1D 1S

Bringing children with you? Always ask for any special rates.

Llandysul

National Grid Ref: SN4140

***Pellorwel,** Bwlch Y Groes, Llandysul, Ceredigion, SA44 5JU.*
Glorious food, ambience & location.
Open: All Year (not Xmas)
01239 851226 Mrs Austwick
Rates fr: *£13.50*-**£13.50**.
Beds: 1D 1T 2S
Baths: 1 Shared

Llanfihangel-y-Creuddyn

National Grid Ref: SN6777

Halfway Inn

***The Halfway Inn,** Devils Bridge Road (A4120), Llanfihangel-y-Creuddyn, Aberystwyth, Ceredigion, SY23 4NE.*
Relax with old-fashioned personal service.
Open: All Year
01970 880631 Mr Roger
Rates fr: *£19.50*-**£29.00**.
Beds: 1D 1T
Baths: 2 Private

Llanon

National Grid Ref: SN5166

White Swan

***The Barn House,** Llanon, Aberystwyth, Ceredigion, SY23 5LS.*
Converted barn in landscaped gardens.
Open: All Year
Grades: WTB 1 Cr, Comm
01974 202581 Mrs Rees
Rates fr: *£15.00*-**£15.00**.
Beds: 2T 2S
Baths: 2 Shared
(6)

***Plas Morfa Hotel,** Heol Y Mor, Llanon, Aberystwyth, Ceredigion, SY23 5LX.*
Comfortable, tastefully converted coastal brewery.
Open: All Year
01974 202415 Ms Pearsall
Rates fr: *£24.00*-**£26.00**.
Beds: 1F 2D 1T 4S
Baths: 8 Private
(100)

Llanwnen

National Grid Ref: SN5347

***Pantycelyn Farm Guest House,** Llanwnen, Lampeter, Ceredigion, SA48 7LW.*
In peaceful countryside, ideal base for Cardiganshire.
Open: Jan to Dec
Grades: WTB 2 Cr, High Comm
01570 434455 Mrs Jenkins
Rates fr: *£15.00*-**£15.00**.
Beds: 1D 1T 1S
Baths: 3 Ensuite
(4)

All details shown are as supplied by B&B owners in Autumn 1996.

Llwyndafydd

National Grid Ref: SN3755

***Ty Hen Farm Hotel Cottages &,** Leisure Centre, Llwyndafydd, New Quay, Ceredigion, SA44 6BZ.*
Working farm indoor heated pool.
Open: All Year
Grades: WTB 3 Cr, AA Listed, RAC Recomm
01545 560346 (also fax no)
Mr Kelly
Rates fr: *£19.00*-**£19.00**.
Beds: 2D 3T
Baths: 5 Private
(50)

Maenygroes

National Grid Ref: SN3858

***Arwerydd,** Maenygroes, New Quay, Ceredigion, SA45 9RH.*
Charming 1840 cottage, picturesque seaviews.
Open: Easter to Oct
01545 560401
Rates fr: *£14.50*-**£17.50**.
Beds: 3D
Baths: 2 Shared
(6)

New Quay

National Grid Ref: SN3859

***Brynarfor Hotel,** New Road, New Quay, Ceredigion, SA45 9SB.*
Open: Mar to Oct
Grades: WTB 3 Cr, Comm, AA 3 Q, RAC Acclaim
01545 560358 Mr Jewess
Fax no: 01545 561204
Rates fr: *£20.00*-**£25.00**.
Beds: 3F 2D 1T 1S
Baths: 7 Ensuite
(10)
Overlooking Cardigan Bay where dolphins play in marine heritage coastal waters. Brilliant walks in NT coastal areas. Hotel 5 minutes walk to beaches. Brochure on request.

Planning a longer stay? Always ask for any special rates.

Please respect a B&B's wishes regarding children, animals & smoking.

Newcastle Emlyn

National Grid Ref: SN3040

Maes Y Derw Guest House, *Newcastle Emlyn, Ceredigion, SA38 9RD.*
Open: All Year
Grades: WTB 2 Cr, Comm
01239 710860 (also fax no)
Mrs Davies
Rates fr: *£16.00*-**£16.00**.
Beds: 1F 2D 1T 1S
Baths: 1 Ensuite 2 Private 2 Shared
(10)
Large Edwardian house set in mature grounds offering luxurious comfort & homely friendly atmosphere. Licensed bar, guest lounge, evening meals - 1996 Les Routiers Casserole Award Winners for good food & good hospitality.

Ponthirwaun

National Grid Ref: SN2645

Penwern Fach Holiday Cottages, *Ponthirwaun, Cardigan, SA43 2RL.*
Open: All Year
01234 710694
Mrs Adamson
Rates fr: *£15.00*-**£15.00**.
Beds: 1D 1T 1S
Baths: 1 Shared
Bed & Breakfast or self catering, we supply either. Close by, there are beaches, riding, fishing, golf, sailing, woolen mills, craft centres, railways & much more.

Ponterwyd

National Grid Ref: SN7480

Dyffryn Castell Hotel, *Ponterwyd, Devils Bridge, Aberystwyth, Ceredigion, SY23 3LB.*
Old coaching inn,
Open: All Year (not Xmas)
01970 890237
Rates fr: *£20.00*-**£22.00**.
Beds: 6F 2D 1T
Baths: 6 Ensuite 1 Shared
(60)

Tregaron

National Grid Ref: SN6759

Lluest Guest House, *Lampeter Road, Tregaron, Ceredigion, SY25 6HG.*
Open: All Year (not Xmas)
Grades: WTB 2 Cr, High Comm
01974 298936 Mrs Bull
Rates fr: *£15.00*-**£15.00**.
Beds: 2D 1T 1S
Baths: 1 Ensuite 1 Shared
(5)
Large Victorian house, rambling gardens, foot of Cambrian Mountains. Good for bird watching, walking, fishing. Within easy reach of coast, lakes, rivers. Beautiful scenery abounds.

Talbot Hotel, *The Square, Tregaron, Ceredigion, SY25 6JL.*
Olde worlde comfortable family atmosphere.
Open: All Year (not Xmas)
Grades: WTB 2 Cr
01974 298208 Mr Williams
Rates fr: *£21.00*-**£25.00**.
Beds: 1F 6D 7T
Baths: 4 Ensuite 4 Shared
(6)

Neuaddlas, *Tregaron, Ceredigion, SY25 6LG.*
Central for coast, mountains & nature reserve. **Open:** All Year
Grades: WTB 3 Cr, Comm, AA 3 Q
01974 298905 Mrs Davies
Rates fr: *£16.50*-**£16.50**.
Beds: 1F 1D 2T
Baths: 3 Private 1 Shared
(10)

Fro Villa, *Doldre, Tregaron, Ceredigion, SY25 6JZ.*
Traditional stone cottage.
Open: All Year (not Xmas)
01974 298817
Mrs Whiting
Rates fr: *£13.00*-**£13.00**.
Beds: 1F 1D
Baths: 1 Shared
(1)

Glanbrennig Guest House, *Tregaron, Ceredigion, SY25 6QS.*
Tranquil, in own grounds.
Open: All Year (not Xmas)
01974 298825
Mrs Cutter
Rates fr: *£16.50*-**£18.50**.
Beds: 1F 1D 1T 1S
Baths: 4 Ensuite

Tremain

National Grid Ref: SN2348

Gogerddan Arms

Trellacca Guest House, *Tremain, Cardigan, SA43 1SJ.*
Beautiful house. Ideal touring base.
Open: All Year (not Xmas)
01239 810730
Mrs Garland
Rates fr: *£15.00*-**£15.00**.
Beds: 1D 1T 2S
Baths: 2 Ensuite 1 Shared
(3)

Tresaith

National Grid Ref: SN2751

Iscoed, *Tresaith, Cardigan, SA43 2JG.*
Excellent food, 5 mins to Beach.
Open: Jan to Dec
Grades: WTB 3 Cr
01239 810030
Mrs Harris
Rates fr: *£18.00*-**£21.00**.
Beds: 1F 1D 1T
Baths: 3 Ensuite
(6)

Carmarthenshire

Tourist Information Centres

Lammas Street, **Carmarthen**, Dyfed, SA31 3AQ, 01267 231557.
Heritage Centre, Kings Road, **Llandovery**, Dyfed, SA20 0AR, 01550 70693,
Arddulias Pont, Junction 49, M4, **Llanedy**, Sa4 1FP, 01792 883838
Central Library, Vaughn Street, **Llanelli**, SA15 3AS, 01554 772020

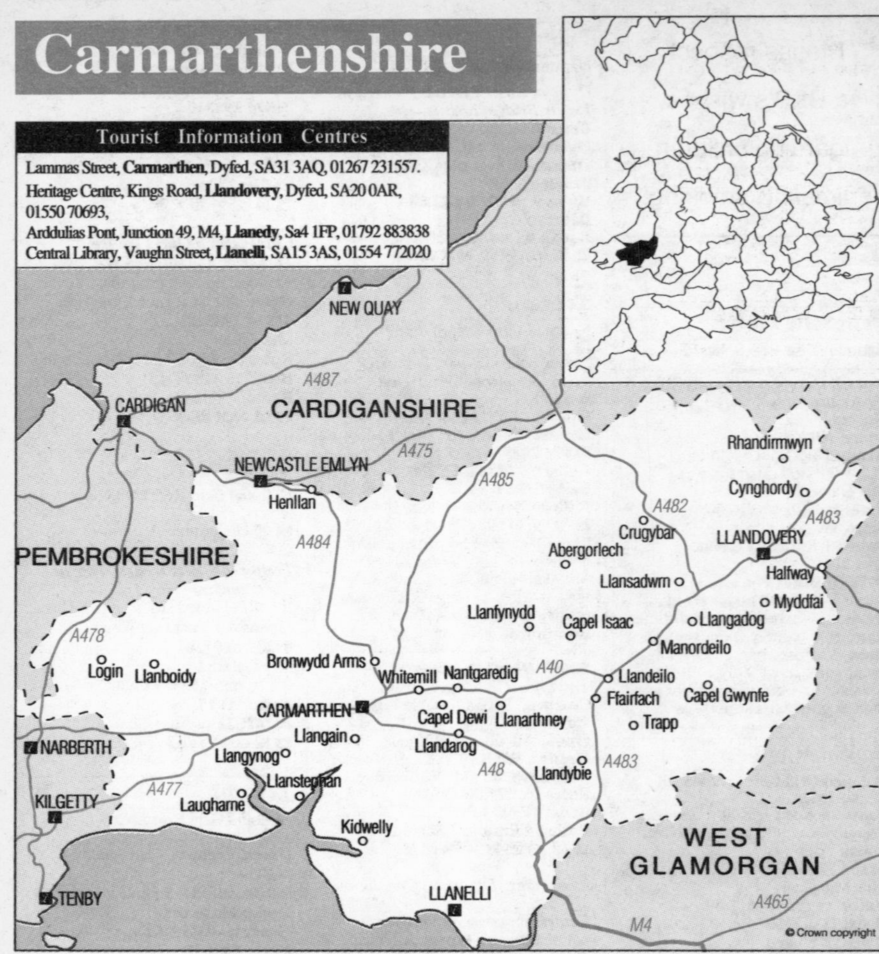

National Grid References are for villages, towns and cities - *not* for individual houses.

Abergorlech

National Grid Ref: SN5230

***2 Llwyncelyn,** Abergorlech, Carmarthen, SA32 7SJ.*
Comfortable guest house.
Open: All Year
01558 685109 Mrs Mallett
Rates fr: *£15.00*-**£16.50**.
Beds: 1D

Capel Dewi

National Grid Ref: SN4720

***Farm Retreats,** Capel Uchaf Farm, Capel Dewi, Carmarthen, SA32 8AY.*
Large, traditional, comfortable secluded farmhouse, New Forest.
Open: All Year
Grades: WTB 3 Cr, High Comm, AA 4 Q, RAC High Acclaim
01267 290799
Mrs Burns
Fax no: 01267 290002
Rates fr: *£23.50*.
Beds: 2D 1T
Baths: 2 Ensuite 1 Private
(5)

***The lowest* single rate *is shown in* bold.**

Capel Gwynfe

National Grid Ref: SN7222

***Pencrug Farm,** Capel Gwynfe, Llangadog, Carmarthenshire, SA19 9RP.*
Traditional Welsh farmhouse.
Open: All Year (not Xmas)
Grades: WTB Listed
01550 740686 Mrs Fleming
Rates fr: *£12.00*-**£12.00**.
Beds: 1D 2T **Baths:** 1 Shared
(4)

Capel Isaac

National Grid Ref: SN5827

***The Manse Organic Farmhouse,** Capel Isaac, Llandeilo, Carmarthenshire, SA19 7TN.*
Secluded organic working farm by river.
Open: All Year
Grades: WTB 2 Cr, Comm
01558 668873 Mr & Mrs Smith
Rates fr: *£14.00*-**£14.00**.
Beds: 1D 1T **Baths:** 2 Private
(10) (6)

Carmarthen

National Grid Ref: SN4120

Fox & Hounds, Coracle Tavern

The Boars Head Hotel, *Lammas Street, Carmarthen, SA31 3AZ.*
Open: All Year
Grades: WTB 3 Cr
01267 222789 Mr Williams
Fax no: 01267 222289
Rates fr: *£20.00*-**£30.00**.
Beds: 1F 6D 4T 3S
Baths: 12 Ensuite 2 Shared
(15)
Situated in the thriving market town of Carmarthen. Close to beaches, leisure activities, Oakwood Park, golf & fishing. Central for Irish Ferries. A warm welcome.

Trebersed Farmhouse, *Travellers Rest, St Peters, Carmarthen, SA31 3RR.*
Friendly, welcoming, working dairy farm.
Open: All Year (not Xmas)
Grades: WTB 2 Cr, High Comm
01267 238182 Mrs Jones
Fax no: 01267 223633
Rates fr: *£17.00*-**£19.00**.
Beds: 1F 1D 1T
Baths: 3 Ensuite

Y Dderwen Fach, *98 Priory Street, Carmarthen, SA31 1NB.*
Central C17th town house.
Open: All Year (not Xmas)
Grades: WTB Listed
01267 234193 Mr & Mrs Bowyer
Fax no: 01267 235766
Rates fr: *£13.00*-**£14.00**.
Beds: 1D 1T 2S
Baths: 2 Ensuite 1 Shared

Plas Farm, *Llangynog, Carmarthen, SA33 5DB.*
Ideal touring base. Spacious farmhouse.
Open: All Year (not Xmas)
Grades: WTB 2 Cr, Comm
01267 211492 Mrs Thomas
Rates fr: *£15.00*-**£16.00**.
Beds: 1F 1D 1T
Baths: 1 Ensuite 2 Shared
(4)

Pantygwyn Farm, *Whitemill, Carmarthen, SA32 7ES.*
Restored Welsh farmhouse.
Open: All Year (not Xmas)
01267 290247 Mr Giles
Rates fr: *£20.00*-**£28.00**.
Beds: 1F 1D 1T
Baths: 3 Private
(10)

Planning a longer stay? Always ask for any special rates.

Crugybar

National Grid Ref: SN6537

Glanrannell Park Hotel, *Crugybar, Llanwrda, Carmarthenshire, SA19 8SA.*
Informal country house hotel.
Open: Easter to Oct
Grades: WTB 3 Cr, High Comm, AA 2 St
01558 685230 Mrs Davies
Fax no: 01558 685784
Rates fr: *£36.00*-**£41.00**.
Beds: 2F 3D 3T
Baths: 8 Private
(20)

Cynghordy

National Grid Ref: SN8042

Llanerchindda Farm, *Cynghordy, Llandovery, Carmarthenshire, SA20 0NB.*
Very comfortable farmhouse, wonderful views.
Open: All Year
Grades: WTB 2 Cr, Comm
01550 750274 Mr Bointon
Fax no: 01550 750300
Rates fr: *£22.00*-**£22.00**.
Beds: 1F 4D 4T 1S
Baths: 10 Private
(12)

Ffairfach

National Grid Ref: SN6221

Torbay Inn

Tycefn Tregib, *Ffairfach, Llandeilo, Carmarthenshire, SA19 6TD.*
Open: All Year (not Xmas)
Grades: WTB 2 Cr, High Comm
01558 823942
Mrs Evans
Rates fr: *£17.00*-**£17.00**.
Beds: 1F 1D 1T
Baths: 2 Ensuite 1 Private
(0) (6+)
Spacious converted stone barn provides excellent friendly accommodation in peaceful wooded grounds. 10 minutes walk village, buses, BR. Stabling & bike hire available. Brochure.

Halfway

National Grid Ref: SN8232

Goyallt Farm, *Halfway, Llandovery, Carmarthenshire, SA20 0SD.*
Modern, comfortable farmhouse. Ideal walking.
Open: Easter to Oct
01550 720604
Mrs Davies
Rates fr: *£15.00*-**£15.00**.
Beds: 1F 1D 1S
Baths: 1 Shared

Henllan

National Grid Ref: SN3540

Brynhawen, *Bryngwenith, Henllan, Llandysul, Carmarthenshire, SA44 5UA.*
Small, friendly country guest house.
Open: All Year (not Xmas)
01239 858908 Mrs Smith
Rates fr: *£12.50*-**£12.50**.
Beds: 2D 1T
(6)

Kidwelly

National Grid Ref: SN4006

Anthony's Hotel

Castle Farm, *Castle Road, Kidwelly, Carmarthenshire, SA17 5BQ.*
Large, comfortable Victorian farmhouse.
Open: All Year
01554 890321 Mrs Lane
Rates fr: *£15.00*-**£15.00**.
Beds: 1F 1D 2T
Baths: 1 Ensuite 2 Shared

Laugharne

National Grid Ref: SN3010

Hurst House, *Laugharne, Carmarthen, SA33 4RS.*
Unique Listed C18th country house.
Open: All Year (not Xmas)
01994 427235
Mrs Bradley-Watson
Rates fr: *£15.00*-**£15.00**.
Beds: 1D 1S
Baths: 1 Ensuite 1 Shared
(6)

Hall Down Farm Guest House, *Laugharne, Carmarthen, SA33 4QS.*
200-year-old farmhouse.
Open: All Year (not Xmas)
01994 427452
Mr & Mrs Best
Rates fr: *£15.00*-**£17.00**.
Beds: 2F 3D
Baths: 1 Private 2 Shared
(8) (10)

Llanarthney

National Grid Ref: SN5320

Golden Grouse

Central House, *Llanarthney, Carmarthen, SA32 8JE.*
Comfortable family home, log-fires, home-cooking.
Open: All Year
01558 668595
Mr & Mrs Prater
Rates fr: *£12.50*-**£12.50**.
Beds: 1F 1T 1S
Baths: 1 Shared
(3)

Llanboidy

National Grid Ref: SN2123

Castell Pigyn Farm, *Llanboidy, Whitland, Carmarthenshire, SA34 0LJ.*
Comfortable farmhouse in peaceful area.
Open: All Year (not Xmas)
Grades: WTB 3 Cr, High Comm
01994 448391 Mrs Davies
Fax no: 01994 448 755
Rates fr: *£19.00*-**£19.00**.
Beds: 1F 1D 1T
Baths: 2 Ensuite 1 Private

Llanddarog

National Grid Ref: SN5016

Coedhirion Farm, *Llanddarog, Carmarthen, Carmarthenshire, SA32 8BH.*
Very conveniently situated modern farmhouse.
Open: All Year
01267 275666
Rates fr: *£18.00*-**£20.00**.
Beds: 2D 1S
Baths: 2 Ensuite 1 Private
(6)

Llandeilo

National Grid Ref: SN6222

White Hart

Brynawel Guest House, *19 New Road, Llandeilo, Carmarthenshire, SA19 6DD.*
Comfortable family-run guest house.
Open: All Year (not Xmas)
01558 822925 Ms Jenkins
Rates fr: *£14.50*-**£19.00**.
Beds: 2D 2T 1S
Baths: 3 Private 1 Shared
(6)

Llandovery

National Grid Ref: SN7634

The Drovers

Cwmgwyn Farm, *Llandovery, Carmarthenshire, SA20 0EQ.*
C17th farmhouse - luxurious accommodation.
Open: Easter to Oct
Grades: WTB 2 Cr, High Comm
01550 720410 Mr & Mrs Lewis
Fax no: 01550 720262
Rates fr: *£20.00*-**£20.00**.
Beds: 2D 1T
Baths: 3 Ensuite
(1) (3)

Llanerchindda Farm, *Cynghordy, Llandovery, Carmarthenshire, SA20 0NB.*
Open: All Year
Grades: WTB 2 Cr, Comm
01550 750274 Mr Bointon
Fax no: 01550 750300
Rates fr: *£22.00*-**£22.00**.
Beds: 1F 4D 4T 1S
Baths: 10 Private
(12)
Very comfortable farmhouse with wonderful views over Towi Valley & Brecon Beacons. Log-fires, library, underfloor heating, licensed, drying room, tea/coffee, TV/satellite all rooms. Famous homemade cooking. Badger & fox watching at night.

Llwyncelyn Guest House, *Llandovery, Carmarthenshire, SA20 0EP.*
Charming stone-built guest house.
Open: All Year (not Xmas)
Grades: WTB 1 Cr, Comm, AA 3 Q
01550 720566 Mr & Mrs Griffiths
Rates fr: *£17.00*-**£19.00**.
Beds: 1F 2D 2T 1S
Baths: 2 Shared
(12)

Kings Head Inn, *Market Square, Llandovery, Carmarthenshire, SA20 0AB.*
Olde world with modern conveniences.
Open: All Year
01550 720393
Mr & Mrs Madeira Cole
Rates fr: *£22.00*-**£26.00**.
Beds: 2D 2T
Baths: 4 Private
(4)

Llandybie

National Grid Ref: SN6115

Glynhir Farm, *Glynhir Road, Llandybie, Ammanford, Carmarthenshire, SA18 2TD.*
Historic mansion in parkland setting.
Open: All Year
01269 850438 Mrs Jenkins
Rates fr: *£21.00*-**£21.00**.
Beds: 1F 4D 1T 1S
Baths: 2 Ensuite 1 Private 1 Shared

Llanfynydd

National Grid Ref: SN5527

Troedyrhiw Guest House, *Llanfynydd, Carmarthen, SA32 7TQ.*
Wonderful countryside, wonderful food.
Open: Apr to Oct
Grades: WTB 2 Cr
01558 668792 Mrs Moore
Rates fr: *£19.00*-**£19.00**.
Beds: 2D 1T
Baths: 3 Private
(3)

Llangadog

National Grid Ref: SN7028

Cynyll Farm, *Llangadog, Carmarthenshire, SA19 9BB.*
Friendly working dairy farm.
Open: All Year (not Xmas)
Grades: WTB Listed
01550 777316 Mrs Dare
Rates fr: *£14.50*-**£14.50**.
Beds: 1F 1D

Pen-Y-Bont, *Llangadog, Carmarthenshire, SA19 9EN.*
Country house in streamside setting.
Open: All Year (not Xmas)
Grades: WTB 2 Cr, High Comm
01550 777126 Mrs Myers
Rates fr: *£18.00*-**£18.00**.
Beds: 2D 1T
Baths: 1 Ensuite 2 Private
(0) (8)

Llangain

National Grid Ref: SN3815

Pantydderwen, Mansion House

Glog Farm, *Llangain, Carmarthen, SA33 5AY.*
Comfortable, convenient town & sea.
Open: All Year
Grades: WTB 2 Cr
01267 241271
Mr & Mrs Rodenhurst
Rates fr: *£20.00*-**£20.00**.
Beds: 2F 1D 1T
Baths: 3 Ensuite 1 Private
(10)

Llangynog

National Grid Ref: SN3316

Fox & Hounds

Plas Farm, *Llangynog, Carmarthen, SA33 5DB.*
Ideal touring base. Spacious farmhouse.
Open: All Year (not Xmas)
Grades: WTB 2 Cr, Comm
01267 211492 Mrs Thomas
Rates fr: *£15.00*-**£16.00**.
Beds: 1F 1D 1T
Baths: 1 Ensuite 2 Shared
(4)

The Wern Inn, *Llangynog, Carmarthen, SA33 5HS.*
Large country inn.
Open: All Year
01267 241678 Mr Coffin
Rates fr: *£14.00*-**£15.00**.
Beds: 1F 2D
Baths: 3 Private
(20)

The lowest *double* rate per person is shown in *italics*.

Llansadwrn

National Grid Ref: SN6931

Myrtle Hill Guest House, *Llansadwrn, Llanwrda, Carmarthenshire, SA19 8HL.*
Lovely old farmhouse, magnificent views.
Open: Mar to Oct
Grades: WTB 2 Cr, Comm
01550 777530 Mr & Mrs Barrett
Rates fr: *£19.00*-**£19.00**.
Beds: 3D
Baths: 3 Ensuite
(8)

Llanstephan

National Grid Ref: SN3510

The Castle

Brig-Y-Don, *The Green, Llanstephan, Carmarthen, SA33 5LW.*
Large Victorian beach house.
Open: All Year
Grades: WTB Listed
01267 241349 Mr & Mrs Gibson
Rates fr: *£15.00*-**£15.00**.
Beds: 3T
Baths: 2 Private 1 Shared
(4)

Login

National Grid Ref: SN1623

Plash Inn

Maencochyrwyn, *Login, Whitland, Carmarthenshire, SA34 0TN.*
Attractive farm. Delicious traditional breakfast.
Open: Apr to Oct
01994 419283 Mrs Worthing
Rates fr: *£14.00*-**£14.00**.
Beds: 1F 1T 1S **Baths:** 1 Private
(2)

Manordeilo

National Grid Ref: SN6626

Dolau Farm, *Manordeilo, Llandeilo, Carmarthenshire, SA19 7AZ.*
Ccomfortable farm house. Lovely view. **Open:** Easter to Oct
01558 823224 Mrs Thomas
Rates fr: *£15.00*-**£15.00**.
Beds: 2D 1T

Myddfai

National Grid Ref: SN7730

Erwlas, *Myddfai, Llandovery, Carmarthenshire, SA20 0JB.*
Modern, comfortable bungalow, quiet location.
Open: All Year (not Xmas)
01550 720797 Mrs Holloway
Rates fr: *£13.00*-**£13.00**.
Beds: 1D 1T **Baths:** 1 Shared

Nantgaredig

National Grid Ref: SN4921

Cwmtwrch Hotel, *Nantgaredig, Carmarthen, SA32 7NY.*
Country house hotel & swimming pool.
Open: All Year (not Xmas)
Grades: WTB 3 Cr
01267 290238 Jenny Willmott
Fax no: 01267 290808
Rates fr: *£25.00*-**£38.00**.
Beds: 1F 3D 2T
Baths: 6 Private
(30)

Cothi Bridge Hotel, *Nantgaredig, Carmarthen, SA32 7NG.*
Family-run country hotel.
Open: All Year
Grades: WTB 3 Cr, AA 2 St
01267 290251 Mrs Jones
Fax no: 01267 290156
Rates fr: *£24.00*-**£35.00**.
Beds: 1F 7D 3T 2S
Baths: 10 Private 2 Shared
(0) (30)

Rhandirmwyn

National Grid Ref: SN7843

Bwlch-Y-Ffin, *Rhandirmwyn, Llandovery, Carmarthenshire, SA20 0PG.*
Comfortable farmhouse with incredible views.
Open: All Year (not Xmas)
01550 760311 Mr & Mrs Williams
Fax no: 01550 760339
Rates fr: *£15.00*-**£15.00**.
Beds: 1D 2T
Baths: 1 Shared
(12)

Royal Oak Inn, *Rhandirmwyn, Llandovery, Carmarthenshire, SA20 0NY.*
Open: All Year
Grades: WTB 1 Cr, AA 3 Q
01550 760201 Mr Alexander
Fax no: 01550 760332
Rates fr: *£20.00*-**£20.00**.
Beds: 1F 1D 1T 2S
Baths: 3 Ensuite 2 Shared
(25)
Many recommendations. Friendly village inn with a fabulous location overlooking the unspoilt Towy Valley. Ensuite accommodation, real ales, log fires and good value interesting food.

Trapp

National Grid Ref: SN6518

Cennen Arms

Morning Watch, *Trapp, Llandeilo, Carmarthenshire, SA19 6TR.*
Brecon National Park coach house.
Open: Feb to Nov
01558 823464 Ms Jones
Rates fr: *£17.00*-**£18.00**.
Beds: 1D 1S
Baths: 1 Ensuite
(5) (3)

Whitemill

National Grid Ref: SN4621

Penyfedw, *Whitemill, Carmarthen, SA32 7HJ.*
Luxury farmhouse at basic rates.
Open: All Year (not Xmas)
01267 290759 Mrs Ratti
Rates fr: *£15.00*-**£18.00**.
Beds: 1F 1D 1S
Baths: 1 Private 1 Shared
(8)

Many rates vary according to season - the lowest are shown here.

Denbigh & Flint

Tourist Information Centres

Autolodge, Gateway Services (A55), **Ewloe**, Deeside, CH7 6HE, 01244 541597.

Town Hall, Castle Street, **Llangollen**, LL20 5PD, 01978 860828.

Scala Cinema, High St, **Prestatyn**, LL19 9LH, 01745 854365, (Easter to Oct).

The Children's Village, Promenade, **Rhyl**, LL181HZ. 01745 355068.

Ruthin Craft Centre, Park Rd, **Ruthin**, LL15 1BB, 01824 703992.

The Guildhall, Lambpit Street, **Wrexham**. LL11 1WN, 01978 292015.

Afonwen

National Grid Ref: SJ1371

***Ddol Ucha,** Afonwen, Mold, Flintshire, CH7 5UN.*
C17th coach house by nature reserve.
Open: Feb to Dec
01352 720125 Mrs Morris
Rates fr: *£16.00*-**£16.00**.
Beds: 1D 1T
(5) (6)

Bodfari

National Grid Ref: SJ0970

***Fron Haul,** Sodom, Bodfari, Denbigh, LL16 4DY.*
The lovely Vale of Clwyd.
Open: All Year
Grades: WTB 2 Cr, High Comm
01745 710301
Ms Edwards
Rates fr: *£16.00*-**£16.50**.
Beds: 1F 1D 1T
Baths: 2 Shared
(12)

Caerwys

National Grid Ref: SJ1272

***Plas Penucha,** Caerwys, Mold, CH7 5BH.*
Large farmhouse with attractive garden. **Open:** All Year
Grades: WTB 3 Cr, High Comm
01352 720210 Mrs Price
Rates fr: *£17.50*-**£17.50**.
Beds: 2D 2T
Baths: 2 Private 1 Shared

Chirk

National Grid Ref: SJ2937

Waterside Restaurant

***Sun Cottage,** Pentre, Chirk, Wrexham, LL14 5AW.*
Oak-beamed character cottage, spectacular riverscape.
Open: All Year (not Xmas)
01691 774542 Mrs Little
Rates fr: *£15.00*-**£15.00**.
Beds: 2F 1S
Baths: 1 Private
(10) (2)

Bringing children with you? Always ask for any special rates.

Pedlar Corner, *Colliery Road, Chirk, LL14 5PB.*
Edwardian cottage with beautiful garden.
Open: All Year (not Xmas)
01691 772903 Mrs Berry
Rates fr: *£14.00*-**£14.00**.
Beds: 2T
Baths: 1 Shared
(10) (3)

The Lodge, *Halton, Chirk, Wrexham, LL14 5BG.*
Charming Listed Georgian mansion in mature grounds.
Open: All Year
01691 774424 Mr Davenport
Rates fr: *£17.50*-**£20.00**.
Beds: 1F 4D 1T 4S
Baths: 2 Ensuite 2 Private
(20)

Clwyd Gate

National Grid Ref: SJ1658

Clwyd Gate Inn

Ffynnon Y Berth, *Clwyd Gate, Llanarmon yn Ial, Mold, CH7 5TA.*
Working farm in idyllic setting.
Open: Apr to Oct
01824 780298 Ms Davies
Rates fr: *£15.00*-**£15.00**.
Beds: 1F 1T
Baths: 1 Private 1 Shared

Bwlch Uchaf, *Clwyd Gate, Llanbedr Dyffryn Clwyd, Ruthin, Denbighshire, LL15 1YF.*
Old Welsh farmhouse.
Open: All Year (not Xmas)
01824 780229 Mrs Gates
Rates fr: *£15.50*-**£15.50**.
Beds: 1D 1T
Baths: 1 Shared

Corwen

National Grid Ref: SJ0743

Central Hotel & Restaurant, *The Square, Corwen, LL21 0DE.*
Situated on the River Dee on the A5. Licensed - good foods.
Open: All Year (not Xmas)
01490 412462 Mr Piccone
Rates fr: *£19.50*-**£19.50**.
Beds: 2F 4D 3T 1S
Baths: 9 Ensuite 9 Private

The lowest *double* rate per person is shown in *italics*.

Corwen Court Private Hotel, *London Road, Corwen, LL21 0DP.*
Converted old police station/court-house.
Open: Mar to Nov
Grades: AA 3 Q
01490 412854
Mr & Mrs Buckland
Rates fr: *£14.00*-**£13.00**.
Beds: 4D 6S
Baths: 4 Private 2 Shared

The Powys House Estate, *Corwen, LL21 9EG.*
Country house in large gardens.
Open: All Year (not Xmas)
01490 412367 Mrs Quinn
Rates fr: *£17.00*-**£22.00**.
Beds: 1F 1D 1T
Baths: 3 Private
(5) (5)

Cynwyd

National Grid Ref: SJ0541

Fron Goch Farmhouse, *Cynwyd, Corwen, Denbighshire, LL21 0NA.*
Superb food & charming views.
Open: All Year
Grades: WTB 3 Cr
01490 440418 Mrs Stille
Rates fr: *£19.00*-**£19.00**.
Beds: 1F 1D 2T 2S
Baths: 3 Private 2 Shared
(6)

Denbigh

National Grid Ref: SJ0566

Brookhouse Hill Tavern

Cayo Guest House, *74 Vale Street, Denbigh, LL16 3BW.*
Large Victorian guest house.
Open: All Year (not Xmas)
Grades: WTB 3 Cr, AA 2 Q
01745 812686 Mrs MacCormack
Rates fr: *£16.00*-**£16.00**.
Beds: 2D 3T
Baths: 4 Private 1 Shared

College Farm, *Denbigh, Denbigh, LL16 4TT.*
Modern farmhouse, warm Welsh welcome.
Open: Mar to Nov
01745 550276 Mrs Parry
Rates fr: *£15.00*-**£17.00**.
Beds: 1F 1D
Baths: 1 Shared
(6)

Dyserth

National Grid Ref: SJ0578

Two Hoots Bed & Breakfast, *4 Bod Hamer, Cwm, Dyserth, Rhyl, LL18 5SL.*
Modern, small, comfortable, homely.
Open: All Year (not Xmas)
01745 570226 Mr & Mrs Tong
Rates fr: *£12.50*-**£12.50**.

The lowest *double* rate per person is shown in *italics*.

Flint

National Grid Ref: SJ2472

Red Lion

Oakenholt Farm, *Oakenholt Lane, Flint, CH6 5SU.*
Lovely C15th farmhouse on dairy farm.
Open: All Year (not Xmas)
Grades: WTB 2 Cr
01352 733264 Mrs Hulme
Rates fr: *£15.00*-**£18.00**.
Beds: 1F 1D 1T
Baths: 2 Shared

Garth

National Grid Ref: SJ2542

Cefn y Fedw Farm, *Panorama Walk, Garth, Trevor, Llangollen, LL14 1UA.*
Working hill farm. Also campsite.
Open: May to Feb
01978 823403 Mrs Roberts
Rates fr: *£16.00*.
Beds: 1F 2D 2T
Baths: 2 Private 1 Shared
(6)

Glanyrafon

National Grid Ref: SJ0242

Llawr Betws Farm, *Glanyrafon, Corwen, LL21 0HD.*
Modern, comfortable farmhouse.
Open: All Year
01490 460224 Mr Jones
Rates fr: *£12.00*-**£12.00**.
Beds: 2F 1D 1S
Baths: 1 Private

Glyn Ceiriog

National Grid Ref: SJ2038

Golden Pheasant Hotel, *Glyn Ceiriog, Chirk, Llangollen, LL20 7BB.*
Open: All Year
Grades: WTB 4 Cr, Comm, AA 3 St
01691 718281 Ms Lawson
Fax no: 01691 718479
Rates fr: *£25.00*-**£25.00**.
Beds: 3F 7D 6T 2S
Baths: 19 Ensuite
(45)
C18th country hotel/traditional inn in unspoilt valley. 15 minutes main road. Well-stocked bar. Bar meals. Restaurant. Picturesque views across valley. Children/pets welcome.

Gwernaffield

National Grid Ref: SJ2064

Maes Garmon Farm, *Gwernaffield, Mold, CH7 5DB.*
Idyllic, luxurious C17th farmhouse.
Open: All Year
Grades: WTB 2 Cr, High Comm
01352 759887 Mrs Cook
Rates fr: *£16.00*-**£18.00**.
Beds: 2D 1T 3S
Baths: 3 Ensuite
(8) (10)

Halkyn

National Grid Ref: SJ2171

Britannia Inn

1 The Barracks, *Halkyn, Holywell, CH8 8DL.*
Open: All Year
01352 781146 Mrs Jackson
Rates fr: *£17.00*-**£21.00**.
Beds: 1F 2D
Baths: 1 Ensuite 1 Shared
(6) (5)
1867 Miners' cottage with history on 2000 acres common land. Magnificent views. Ideal walks, horse-riding. Easy reach A55 Chester, coastal resorts. A lovely cup of tea awaits you!

Hanmer

National Grid Ref: SJ4539

Buck Farm, *Hanmer, Whitchurch, SY14 7LX.*
Tudor farmhouse, serving excellent food.
Open: All Year
Grades: WTB 1 Cr, Comm
01948 830339 Ms Williams-Lee
Rates fr: *£17.00*-**£17.00**.
Beds: 2D 1T
Baths: 2 Shared
(12)

Hawarden

National Grid Ref: SJ3165

Bridge Inn

St Deiniols Ash Farm, *Hawarden, Deeside, CH5 2BR.*
'Stars tell you the story'.
Open: All Year (not Xmas)
Grades: WTB 3 Cr, High Comm
01244 534215 Mrs Connah
Rates fr: *£19.50*-**£23.50**.
Beds: 1F 1D 1T
Baths: 3 Ensuite

The Coach House, *Hawarden, Deeside, CH5 3DH.*
A place to find peace.
Open: All Year (not Xmas)
Grades: WTB 1 Cr
01244 532328 Mrs Jacks
Rates fr: *£17.00*-**£17.00**.
Beds: 2D 2S
Baths: 1 Shared
(10) (4)

Holywell

National Grid Ref: SJ1875

Greenhill Farm, *Holywell, CH8 7QF.*
C15th farmhouse, overlooking Dee estuary.
Open: Mar to Oct
Grades: WTB 2 Cr, AA 2 Q
01352 713270 Mr & Mrs Jones
Rates fr: *£16.50*.
Beds: 1F 1D 1T
Baths: 1 Private 2 Shared
(6)

Llanarmon Dyffryn Ceiriog

National Grid Ref: SJ1532

Gwynfa Guest House, *Llanarmon Dyffryn Ceiriog, Llangollen, LL20 7LF.*
Friendly, excellent food, picturesque village.
Open: Feb to Nov
Grades: WTB 2 Cr, High Comm
01691 600287 Mr Oldaker
Rates fr: *£16.00*-**£16.00**.
Beds: 1F 2T
Baths: 1 Private 1 Shared
(3) (7)

Ty Gwyn, *Llanarmon Dyffryn Ceiriog, Llangollen, LL20 7LD.*
Old Victorian cottage.
Open: All Year (not Xmas)
01691 600229 Mrs Jones
Rates fr: *£12.00*-**£12.00**.
Beds: 1F 1D 1T
Baths: 1 Shared

Llandegla

National Grid Ref: SJ1952

Crown Hotel

Raven Farm, *Llandegla, Wrexham, LL11 3AW.*
Converted C15th drover's inn/farm.
Open: Easter to Sep
01978 790224 Mrs Surrey
Rates fr: *£15.50*-**£15.50**.
Beds: 1F 3D 1T 2S
Baths: 1 Private 1 Shared
(10) (6)

Saith Daran Farm, *Llandegla, Wrexham, LL11 3BA.*
Dairy farm near Horseshoe Pass.
Open: Mar to Oct
Grades: WTB 2 Cr
01978 790685 Mrs Thompson
Rates fr: *£18.00*-**£18.00**.
Beds: 1D 1T
Baths: 2 Private
(5) (4)

The Hand and Handy stores, *Llandegla, Wrexham, LL11 3AW.*
C16th former drovers' inn.
Open: All Year (not Xmas)
01978 790337 Mr Carlisle
Rates fr: *£15.50*-**£15.50**.
Beds: 1F 2D
Baths: 1 Private 1 Shared
(40)

Please respect a B&B's wishes regarding children, animals & smoking.

Llandyrnog

National Grid Ref: SJ1065

Pentre Bach, *Llandyrnog, Denbigh, LL16 4LA.*
C18th farmhouse.
Open: All Year (not Xmas)
01824 790725 Mr & Mrs Carrington-Sykes
Rates fr: *£16.00*-**£20.00**.
Beds: 1D 1T
Baths: 2 Private
(6)

Llanfair Dyffryn Clwyd

National Grid Ref: SJ1355

Fox & Hounds

Plas Uchaf, *Graigadwywynt, Llanfair Dyffryn Clwyd, Ruthin, LL15 2TF.*
C15th manor house, beams, panelling.
Open: All Year
Grades: WTB 2 Cr, High Comm
01824 705794 Mr Jones
Rates fr: *£17.00*-**£17.00**.
Beds: 1F 1D 1T
Baths: 3 Ensuite
(1) (4)

Eyarth Station, *Llanfair Dyffryn Clwyd, Ruthin, LL15 2EE.*
Converted old railway station.
Open: All Year
01824 703643 Mrs Spencer
Fax no: 01824 707464
Rates fr: *£19.50*-**£21.00**.
Beds: 2F 2D 2T
Baths: 6 Private
(3)

Gorffwysfa, *Llanfair Dyffryn Clwyd, Ruthin, LL15 2UN.*
Large Victorian country private house.
Open: All Year (not Xmas)
01824 702432 Mrs Horrocks
Rates fr: *£18.00*-**£18.00**.
Beds: 1F 1D 1T
Baths: 2 Ensuite 1 Private

National Grid References are for villages, towns and cities - *not* for individual houses.

Llanfihangel Glyn Myfyr

National Grid Ref: SH9949

Crown Inn, White Lion, Saracens Head

The Old Rectory, *Llanfihangel Glyn Myfyr, Cerrigydrudion, Corwen, LL21 9UN.*
Luxury retreat in beautiful countryside.
Open: All Year (not Xmas)
01490 420568 / 0850 241795
Mrs Hughes
Rates fr: *£20.00*-**£22.00**.
Beds: 3F
Baths: 1 Shared
(6)

Llangollen

National Grid Ref: SJ2141

Sun, Trevor Inn, Jenny Jones, Woolpack, Wynstay

The Old Vicarage Guest House, *Bryn Howel Lane, Llangollen, Denbighshire, LL20 7YR.*
Open: All Year
Grades: WTB 2 Cr, High Comm
01978 823018 (also fax no)
Mrs Woolley
Rates fr: *£17.00*-**£25.00**.
Beds: 2F 1D 1T
Baths: 4 Ensuite
(6)
Spacious Georgian country house. Quiet exclusive location. Overlooking river. Prize-winning gardens. Natural stream. Picture front cover official Wales BB Guide 1996. Self-catering available.

Ty'n-Y-Wern Hotel, *Maesmawr Road, Llangollen, Denbighshire, LL20 7PH.*
Converted farmhouse with superb views.
Open: All Year
Grades: WTB 3 Cr, RAC 2 St
01978 860252 (also fax no)
Mr Sargeant
Rates fr: *£21.00*-**£32.00**.
Beds: 1F 4D 5T
Baths: 10 Private
(30)

The Grange, *Grange Road, Llangollen, Denbighshire, LL20 8AP.*
Attractive country house in town.
Open: All Year (not Xmas)
01978 860366 Mrs Evans
Rates fr: *£19.00*-**£25.00**.
Beds: 1F 1D 1T
Baths: 3 Ensuite
(3)

All rates are subject to alteration at the owners' discretion.

Many rates vary according to season - the lowest are shown here.

Glanafon, *Abbey Road, Llangollen, Denbighshire, LL20 8SS.*
Open: All Year (not Xmas)
Grades: WTB 2 Cr
01978 860725
Mrs Collinge
Rates fr: *£16.00*-**£16.00**.
Beds: 1F **Baths:** 1 Private
(2)
We are a small family-run B&B specialising in Welsh hospitality for over 10 years with one large room available for guests in our Victorian house.

Hillcrest Guest House, *Hill Street, Llangollen, Denbighshire, LL20 8EU.*
Large Victorian private guest house.
Open: All Year (not Xmas)
Grades: WTB Listed, High Comm, AA 3 Q, Recomm, RAC Acclaim
01978 860208 Mrs Lloyd
Rates fr: *£20.00*.
Beds: 2F 3D 2T **Baths:** 7 Private
(10)

Oakmere, *Regent Street, Llangollen, Denbighshire, LL20 8HS.*
Spacious country house set back from road in own grounds.
Open: All Year
Grades: WTB 2 Cr, High Comm
01978 861126
Mrs Knibbs
Rates fr: *£19.00*.
Beds: 2F 2D 2T
Baths: 4 Ensuite 2 Private
(8)

Dinbren House, *Dinbren Road, Llangollen, Denbighshire, LL20 8TF.*
Large country house in large gardens.
Open: All Year
Grades: WTB 2 Cr
01978 860593
Ms Lewis
Rates fr: *£15.00*-**£15.00**.
Beds: 1F 1D 1T
Baths: 2 Private
(0) (6)

Tyn Celyn Farmhouse, *Tyn Celyn Tyndwr, Llangollen, Denbighshire, LL20 8AR.*
Spacious, oak-beamed, comfortable farmhouse.
Open: All Year (not Xmas)
01978 861117
Mrs Bather
Rates fr: *£17.50*.
Beds: 1F 1D 1T
Baths: 3 Private
(3)

Llangynhafal

National Grid Ref: SJ1263

Golden Lion

Cygnet, *Llangynhafal, Denbigh, Denbighshire, LL16 4LN.*
Open: All Year (not Xmas)
Grades: WTB 3 Cr, Deluxe
01824 790322 (also fax no)
Mrs Edwards
Rates fr: *£20.00*-**£25.00**.
Beds: 1F 1D 1T
Baths: 3 Private
(0) (10)
Situated below the Clwydian Hills, close to C15th church & inn hosting Welsh singing. Magnificent views of the Vale of Clwyd. Ruthin 4 miles.

Esgairlygain, *Llangynhafal, Ruthin, Denbighshire, LL15 1RT.*
Converted stone barn in C16th farmhouse courtyard.
Open: All Year
Grades: WTB 3 Cr
01824 704047 Mrs Henderson
Rates fr: *£16.00*-**£17.50**.
Beds: 1F 1D 1T
Baths: 3 Private

Llantysilio

National Grid Ref: SJ1847

Sun Inn

Hendy Isa, *Llantysilio, Llangollen, Denbighshire, LL20 8DE.*
Country house in picturesque location.
Open: All Year
Grades: WTB 2 Cr, High Comm
01978 861232 Mr Jefferys
Rates fr: *£15.00*-**£20.00**.
Beds: 4F
Baths: 4 Private
(8)

Marford

National Grid Ref: SJ3656

Brackenwood, *67 Wynnstay Lane, Marford, Wrexham, LL12 8LH.*
Welcoming friendly house. Landscaped garden.
Open: All Year
Grades: WTB 2 Cr, High Comm, AA 3 Q, RAC Listed
01978 852866 Mrs Lyon
Fax no: 01978 852065
Rates fr: *£15.00*-**£18.00**.
Beds: 1F 2D 1T 3S
Baths: 4 Ensuite 3 Shared
(10)

Right on the border? Look at the neighbouring county, too

Mold

National Grid Ref: SJ2363

Bryn Awel Hotel

Heulwen, *Maes Bodlonfa, Mold, CH7 1DR.*
Large, secluded, luxurious modern house.
Open: All Year (not Xmas)
Grades: WTB 2 Cr, High Comm, AA 3 Q
01352 758785 Mrs Hollywell
Rates fr: *£17.00*-**£17.00**.
Beds: 1F 1S **Baths:** 2 Private
(3)

Northop Hall

National Grid Ref: SJ2468

Brookside House, *Northop Hall, Mold, CH7 6HR.*
Comfortable accommodation - 'home from home'.
Open: All Year
01244 821146 Mrs Whale
Rates fr: *£16.00*-**£20.00**.
Beds: 1F 1D 1T
Baths: 1 Private 1 Shared

Pentre Celyn

National Grid Ref: SJ1453

Llainwen Ucha, *Pentre Celyn, Ruthin, Denbighshire, LL15 2HL.*
Modern, comfortable farmhouse. Sleeps 6.
Open: All Year (not Xmas)
Grades: WTB Listed
01978 790253 Mrs Parry
Rates fr: *£14.00*-**£15.00**.
Beds: 1F 1D 1S
Baths: 1 Shared
(3)

Pentre Halkyn

National Grid Ref: SJ2072

Glany Artron

The Hall, *Lygan Y Wern, Pentre Halkyn, Holywell, CH8 8BD.*
Self-contained C18th cottage. Lovely grounds.
Open: All Year
Grades: WTB 2 Cr, High Comm, RAC Listed
01352 780215 Mrs Vernon
Fax no: 01352 780187
Rates fr: *£16.00*-**£15.00**.
Beds: 1F 1D 2T 1S
Baths: 1 Private 2 Shared
(0) (6)

National Grid References are for villages, towns and cities - *not* for individual houses.

Bringing children with you? Always ask for any special rates.

Prestatyn

National Grid Ref: SJ0682

Roughsedge House, *26/28 Marine Road, Prestatyn, Denbighshire, LL19 7HG.*
Large family-run guest house.
Open: All Year
Grades: WTB 2 Cr, Comm, AA 2 Q, Recomm
01745 887359 Mrs Kubler
Fax no: 01745 852883
Rates fr: *£15.00*-**£15.00**.
Beds: 2F 4D 2T 2S
Baths: 3 Private 3 Shared
(3)

Traeth Ganol Hotel, *41 Beach Road West, Prestatyn, Denbighshire, LL19 7LL.*
Luxury well-appointed seafront location.
Open: All Year
Grades: WTB 3 Cr, High Comm
01745 853594
Mr & Mrs Groves
Fax no: 01745 886687
Rates fr: *£24.00*-**£30.00**.
Beds: 6F 1D 1T 1S
Baths: 9 Private
(9)

Rhewl

National Grid Ref: SJ1844

Sun Inn

Dee Farm, *Rhewl, Llangollen, LL20 7YT.*
Old stone farmhouse, very comfortable.
Open: Feb to Nov
Grades: WTB 2 Cr, Comm
01978 861598 Mrs Harman
Fax no: 01978 861187
Rates fr: *£17.00*-**£17.00**.
Beds: 2T 1S **Baths:** 3 Ensuite
(7) (6)

Rhyl

National Grid Ref: SJ0181

Links Guest House, *20 Beechwood Road, Rhyl, LL18 3EU.*
Modern, comfortable guesthouse, close to beach.
Open: All Year
Grades: WTB 3 Cr, High Comm, AA 3 Q, Recomm
01745 344381 (also fax no)
Mrs Mariner
Rates fr: *£14.00*-**£16.00**.
Beds: 3F 4D 2S
Baths: 6 Ensuite 1 Private 1 Shared
(5)

Normaz Guest House, *19 Aquarium Street, Rhyl, LL18 1PG.*
Clean, comfortable, licensed guest house.
Open: All Year (not Xmas)
Grades: WTB Listed
01745 334761
Mrs Harper
Rates fr: *£12.00*-**£12.00**.
Beds: 3F 2D 1T 1S
Baths: 1 Private 2 Shared

Carlton House, *25 Palace Avenue, Rhyl, LL18 1HS.*
Small, friendly guest house.
Open: Easter to Oct
Grades: WTB 1 Cr
01745 350257
Mrs Twist
Rates fr: *£12.50*-**£13.00**.
Beds: 2F 2D
Baths: 1 Shared

Snowdon House, *46 River Street, Rhyl, LL18 1PT.*
Friendly, comfortable guest house.
Open: All Year
01745 331786
Mrs Roberts
Rates fr: *£10.00*.
Beds: 3F 1D 1T
Baths: 2 Shared
(3)

Rossett

National Grid Ref: SJ3657

Alyn Hotel

Corner House Farm, *Parkside, Rossett, Wrexham, LL12 0BW.*
Luxury holiday houses Wrexham & Chester.
Open: All Year
Grades: WTB Listed
01829 270452
Mrs Coop
Rates fr: *£18.00*-**£19.00**.
Beds: 1F 1D 1T
Baths: 2 Private 2 Shared

Ruthin

National Grid Ref: SJ1258

Golden Lion

Esgairlygain, *Llangynhafal, Ruthin, Denbighshire, LL15 1RT.*
Open: All Year
Grades: WTB 3 Cr
01824 704047
Mrs Henderson
Rates fr: *£16.00*-**£17.50**.
Beds: 1F 1D 1T
Baths: 3 Private
Converted stone barn within courtyard of C16th farmhouse. Delightful views. Guests lounge, safe parking, refreshments on arrival. Convenient for Chester, North Wales, Snowdonia, Llangollen & coast.

St Asaph

National Grid Ref: SJ0374

Pen-Y-Bryn Farm, *Boderw, St Asaph, Denbighshire, LL17 0LF.*
Comfortable farmhouse in peaceful surroundings.
Open: All Year (not Xmas)
01745 583213 Mrs Williams
Rates fr: *£13.00*-**£13.00**.
Beds: 1F 1D 1S **Baths:** 2 Private
(6)

Tremeirchion

National Grid Ref: SJ0873

Farmers' Arms

Pen Y Graig, *Tremeirchion, St Asaph, LL17 0UR.*
Large, modern, comfortable country house.
Open: All Year (not Xmas)
01745 710253 Mr & Mrs Jackson
Rates fr: *£15.00*-**£15.00**.
Beds: 3T
(10)

Ffynnon Beuno, *Tremeirchion, St Asaph, LL17 0UE.*
Comfortable farmhouse of historical interest.
Open: All Year (not Xmas)
01745 710475 Mrs Pierce
Rates fr: *£15.00*-**£12.00**.
Beds: 1D 1S
Baths: 1 Private 1 Shared

Waen

National Grid Ref: SJ0969

Bryn Clwyd, *Waen, Bodfari, Denbigh, LL16 4BT.*
Quaint cottages combined into one.
Open: Feb to Nov
01745 710357 Mrs Parry
Rates fr: *£14.00*-**£14.00**.
Beds: 1D 1T 1S
Baths: 1 Shared

Whitehurst

National Grid Ref: SJ2840

Plas Offa Farm, *Whitehurst, Chirk, Wrexham, LL14 5AN.*
C17th farmhouse, inglenook fireplace.
Open: All Year (not Xmas)
01691 773760 Ms Mullen
Rates fr: *£15.00*-**£20.00**.
Beds: 2F 2D
Baths: 4 Private 2 Shared

Please respect a B&B's wishes regarding children, animals & smoking.

Wrexham

National Grid Ref: SJ3350

Squire Yorke

Littleton, *24 Bersham Road, Wrexham, LL13 7UP.*
Convenient town centre, buses, trains. **Open:** All Year (not Xmas)
Grades: WTB 1 Cr
01978 352867 Mrs Evans
Rates fr: *£15.00*-**£15.00**.
Beds: 1F 1S **Baths:** 1 Shared
(10)

Plas Eyton, *Wrexham, LL13 0YD.*
3 acre smallholding. Gardens. Parking. **Open:** All Year
01978 820642 Mrs Davies
Rates fr: *£12.00*-**£12.00**.
Beds: 1F 1D 1T 2S
Baths: 2 Shared
(10)

Llangollen

National Grid Ref: SJ2141

1 Bodwen Villas, *Hill Street, Llangollen, Denbighshire, LL20 8HE.*
Homely family-run guest house.
Open: All Year
Grades: WTB 2 Cr, Comm
01978 860882 Mrs Lewis
Rates fr: *£13.50*-**£15.00**.
Beds: 1F 1D
Baths: 1 Ensuite 1 Shared

The Glamorgans

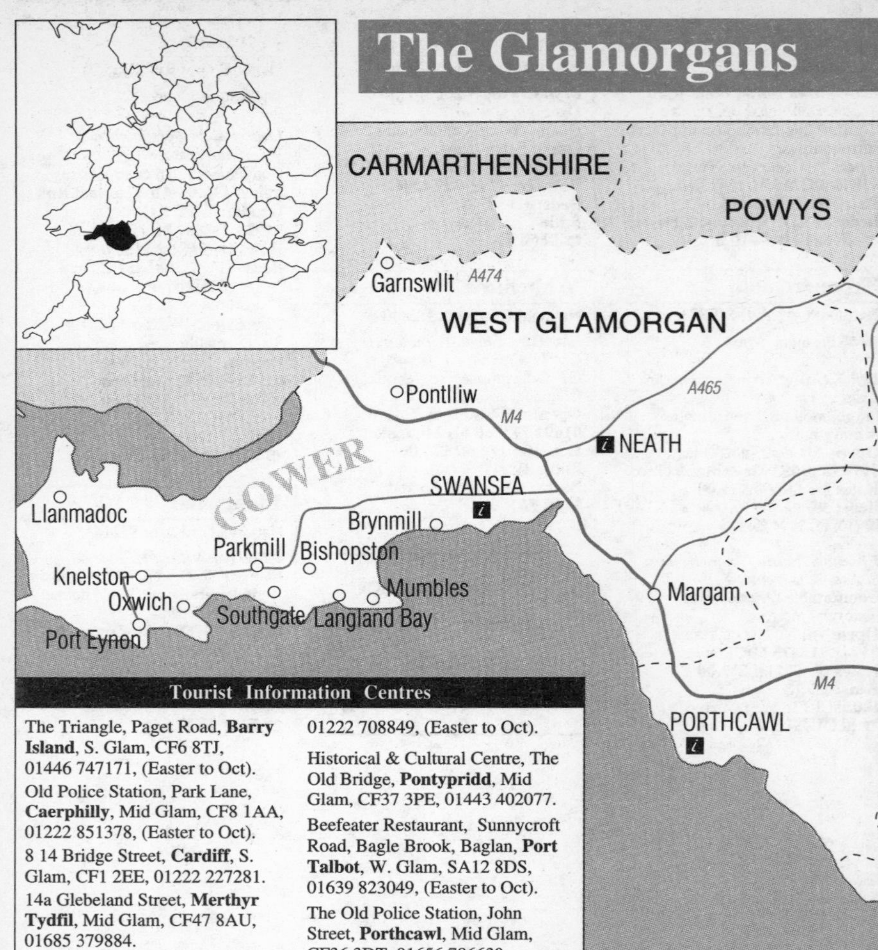

Tourist Information Centres

The Triangle, Paget Road, **Barry Island**, S. Glam, CF6 8TJ, 01446 747171, (Easter to Oct).

Old Police Station, Park Lane, **Caerphilly**, Mid Glam, CF8 1AA, 01222 851378, (Easter to Oct).

8 14 Bridge Street, **Cardiff**, S. Glam, CF1 2EE, 01222 227281.

14a Glebeland Street, **Merthyr Tydfil**, Mid Glam, CF47 8AU, 01685 379884.

Aberdulais Basin, Aberdulais, **Neath**, W. Glam, SA10 8ED, 01639 633531, (Easter to Oct).

Pont Nedd Fechan, Glynneath, **Neath**, W. Glam, SA11 5NR, 01639 721795, (Easter to Oct).

The Esplanade, Penarth Pier, **Penarth**, S. Glam, CF6 2AU, 01222 708849, (Easter to Oct).

Historical & Cultural Centre, The Old Bridge, **Pontypridd**, Mid Glam, CF37 3PE, 01443 402077.

Beefeater Restaurant, Sunnycroft Road, Bagle Brook, Baglan, **Port Talbot**, W. Glam, SA12 8DS, 01639 823049, (Easter to Oct).

The Old Police Station, John Street, **Porthcawl**, Mid Glam, CF36 3DT, 01656 786639.

PO Box 59, Singleton Street, **Swansea**, W. Glam, SA1 3QG, 01792 468321.

Pont Abraham Services: M4, Junction 49, Llanedi, **Pontardulais**, Swansea, W. Glam, SA4 1FP, 01792 883838.

Aberdare

National Grid Ref: SO0002

***Baverstock Hotel,** Heads Of The Valley Road, Aberdare, Mid Glam,* CF44 0LX.
Modern, comfortable hotel.
Open: All Year
01685 386221
Miss Austin
Rates fr: *£24.00*-**£24.00**.
Beds: 2F 27D 17T 6S
Baths: 53 Private
(40)

***Green Meadow Riding Centre,** Dare Valley Country Park, Aberdare, Mid Glam,* CF44 7PT.
Comfortable friendly farmhouse.
Open: All Year (not Xmas)
Grades: WTB 1 Cr
01685 874961 Mrs Williams
Rates fr: *£15.00*-**£18.00**.
Beds: 1D 1T 1S **Baths:** 2 Shared

The lowest **single** *rate is shown in* **bold.**

Bargoed

National Grid Ref: ST1499

***Parc Hotel,** Cardiff Road, Bargoed, Mid Glam,* CF8 8SP.
Comfortable, convenient, home from home.
Open: All Year
Grades: WTB 3 Cr, Comm
01443 837599 / 839828 Mr Butler
Rates fr: *£25.00*-**£27.50**.
Beds: 6F 4S
Baths: 12 Private
(12)

Bringing children with you? Always ask for any special rates.

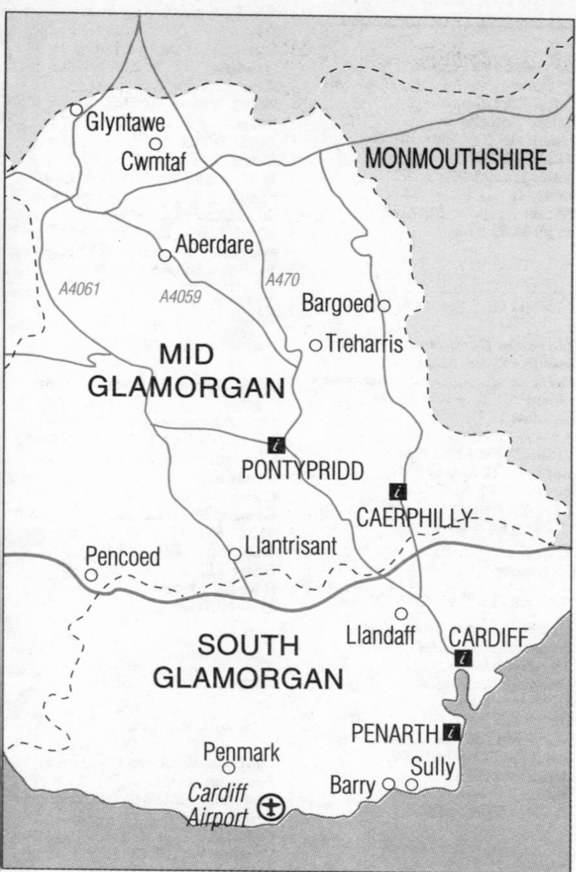

Barry

National Grid Ref: ST1871

Ship Hotel

***Anglesea Guest House**, 9 Romilly Road, Barry, Barry, S Glam, CF62 6AZ.*
Small, late-Victorian guest house.
Open: All Year (not Xmas)
01446 749660 Mr Griffith
Rates fr: *£14.00*-**£14.00**.
Beds: 1F 1T 1S
Baths: 1 Shared
(4)

The lowest *double* rate per person is shown in *italics*.

Planning a longer stay? Always ask for any special rates.

Bishopston

National Grid Ref: SS5788

Plough & Harrow

***Kerensa**, 31 Headland Road, Bishopston, Swansea, SA3 3HD.*
Modern private house, ideal walkers.
Open: All Year
01792 234676 Mrs Rae
Rates fr: *£12.50*-**£15.00**.
Beds: 1D 1T **Baths:** 1 Shared
(12) (2)

Brynmill

National Grid Ref: SS6392

***Ael Y Bryn Private Hotel**, 88 Bryn Road, Brynmill, Swansea, SA2 0AS.*
Comfortable family-run hotel.
Open: All Year
01792 466707 Mr Stapleton
Rates fr: *£16.00*-**£17.50**.
Beds: 3F 2T 2S
Baths: 6 Ensuite
(2)

Caerphilly

National Grid Ref: ST1586

Travellers' Rest, Court House, Moat, Black Cock

***Watford Fach**, Watford Road, Caerphilly, Mid Glam, CF83 1NE.*
C17th farmhouse (longhouse).
Open: All Year (not Xmas)
Grades: WTB 1 Cr
01222 851500
Mr & Mrs Fahey
Fax no: 01222 865021
Rates fr: *£16.00*-**£16.00**.
Beds: 3F 2D 1T 2S
Baths: 5 Ensuite 3 Shared
(10)

***Dugann**, Springfield Bungalow, Rudry Road, Caerphilly, Mid Glam, CF83 3DW.*
Lovely bungalow, lawned gardens, quiet.
Open: All Year
01222 866607
Mrs Powell
Rates fr: *£16.00*-**£20.00**.
Beds: 1F 1D **Baths:** 1 Private
(4)

Cardiff

National Grid Ref: ST1677

Halfway Hotel, Soachers' Lodge

***Rambler Court Hotel**, 188 Cathedral Road, Pontcanna, Cardiff, S Glam, CF1 9JE.*
Open: All Year
01222 221187 (also fax no)
Ms Oxley & L Cronin
Rates fr: *£14.00*-**£16.00**.
Beds: 4F 3T 2S
Baths: 4 Private 2 Shared
Friendly family-run hotel, ideally situated in a tree-lined conservation area, 10 minutes walk to the city centre. Good local restaurants & pubs.

***Clayton Hotel**, 65 Stacey Road, Roath, Cardiff, S Glam, CF2 1DS.*
Excellent family-run homely hotel.
Open: All Year (not Xmas)
01222 492345 Mr Milliner
Rates fr: *£14.00*-**£14.00**.
Beds: 1F 2D 3T 4S
Baths: 4 Private 1 Shared
(3) (6)

Annedd Lon Guest House, *3 Dyfrig Street, Pontcanna, Cardiff, S Glam, CF1 9LR.*
Large Victorian private house.
Open: All Year
01222 223349 Mrs Tucker
Rates fr: *£18.00*-**£18.00**.
Beds: 1F 1D 1T 1S
Baths: 2 Ensuite 2 Shared

Austins, *11 Coldstream Terrace, Cardiff, S Glam, CF1 8LJ.*
Small, friendly, city centre hotel.
Open: All Year
Grades: WTB 2 Cr, RAC Listed
01222 377148 Mr Hopkins
Rates fr: *£14.00*-**£16.00**.
Beds: 1F 5T 5S
Baths: 3 Private 2 Shared

Domus Guest House, *201 Newport Road, Roath, Cardiff, S Glam, CF2 1AJ.*
Clean, friendly, family-run guest house.
Open: All Year (not Xmas)
Grades: AA 2 St
01222 473311 Mrs Barrett
Rates fr: *£18.00*-**£18.00**.
Beds: 1F 3D 3T 2S
Baths: 2 Private 2 Shared
(10)

Tanes Hotel, *148 Newport Road, Roath, Cardiff, S Glam, CF2 1DJ.*
Open: All Year (not Xmas)
Grades: RAC Listed
01222 491755 / 493898
Mrs Mladenovic
Fax no: 01222 491755
Rates fr: *£15.00*-**£17.00**.
Beds: 4F 3D 6T 9S
Baths: 3 Private 5 Shared
(4) (10)

Preste Garden Hotel, *181 Cathedral Road, Pontcanna, Cardiff, S Glam, CF1 9PN.*
Modernised, comfortable, ex-Norwegian consulate.
Open: All Year (not Xmas)
01222 228607 Mr Nicholls
Rates fr: *£15.00*-**£18.00**.
Beds: 1F 3D 3T 3S
Baths: 10 Private
(2)

Wynford Hotel, *Clare Street, Cardiff, S Glam, CF1 8SD.*
Privately owned, city centre hotel.
Open: All Year (not Xmas)
Grades: WTB 2 Cr
01222 371983 Mr Popham
Fax no: 0222 340477
Rates fr: *£19.00*-**£25.00**.
Beds: 3F 4D 11T 2S
Baths: 4 Private 16 Shared
(15)

All rates are subject to alteration at the owners' discretion.

Bringing children with you? Always ask for any special rates.

Bon Maison Guest House, *39 Plasturton Gardens, Pontcanna, Cardiff, S Glam, CF1 9HG.*
Large Victorian house.
Open: All Year (not Xmas)
01222 383660 Mrs George
Rates fr: *£15.00*-**£17.00**.
Beds: 1F 2D 1T
Baths: 2 Private 2 Shared

Cwmtaf

National Grid Ref: SO0013

Llwyn-On Guest House, *Cwmtaf, Merthyr Tydfil, Mid Glam, CF48 2HT.*
Hotel standards, guest house prices.
Open: All Year (not Xmas)
Grades: WTB 3 Cr, AA 4 Q, Select
01685 384384 Mrs Evans
Rates fr: *£24.00*-**£18.00**.
Beds: 2D 1T 1S
Baths: 3 Private 1 Shared
(3)

Garnswllt

National Grid Ref: SN6209

Mount Pleasant Guest House, *Pontardulais Road, Garnswllt, Ammanford, SA18 2RT.*
Mountain position, comfortable accommodation.
Open: All Year
01269 591722 Mrs Carter
Rates fr: *£14.00*-**£16.00**.
Beds: 2F 1D 1T 1S
Baths: 2 Private 1 Shared
(6)

Glyntawe

National Grid Ref: SN8416

Dderi Farm, *Glyntawe, Penycae, Swansea, W. Glam, SA9 1GT.*
C15th comfortable farmhouse.
Open: All Year (not Xmas)
01639 730458 Mrs Williams
Rates fr: *£16.00*-**£17.00**.
Beds: 1F **Baths:** 1 Ensuite

Knelston

National Grid Ref: SS4688

Stoney Forge Guest House, *Knelston, Reynoldston, Swansea, SA3 1AR.*
Heart of the Gower Peninsula.
Open: Mar to Oct
01792 390920 Mrs Davies
Rates fr: *£15.00*-**£15.00**.
Beds: 1F 2D
Baths: 1 Ensuite 1 Shared

Langland Bay

National Grid Ref: SS6087

Wittemberg Hotel, *2 Rotherslade Road, Langland Bay, Swansea, SA3 4QN.*
Open: All Year (not Jan)
Grades: WTB 3 Cr, AA 1 St, RAC Acclaim
01792 369696 Mr Thomas
Rates fr: *£21.00*-**£28.00**.
Beds: 2F 8D 1S
Baths: 10 Ensuite 1 Shared
(10)
Family-run hotel with friendly relaxed atmosphere, ample parking. 80 yds beach, ideal location to explore Gower Peninsula yet only 5 miles west of Swansea.

Llandaff

National Grid Ref: ST1577

Churchills, Plymouth Arms

Plas-Y-Bryn, *93 Fairwater Road, Llandaff, Cardiff, S Glam, CF5 2LG.*
Comfortable Edwardian semi on outskirts.
Open: All Year
Grades: WTB Listed, High Comm
01222 561717 Mrs Lougher
Rates fr: *£17.00*-**£17.50**.
Beds: 2T 1S
Baths: 1 Shared

Llanmadoc

National Grid Ref: SS4493

Britannia Inn

Tallizmand, *Llanmadoc, Gower, Swansea, SA3 1DE.*
Tastefully furnished residence near beach.
Open: All Year
Grades: WTB 3 Cr, High Comm
01792 386373 Mrs Main
Rates fr: *£16.00*-**£19.00**.
Beds: 1F 2D 1T 1S
Baths: 2 Private 1 Shared
(0) (5)

Bryn-Y-Mor, *Llanmadoc, Gower, Swansea, SA3 1DE.*
Spacious, non-smoking, parking, highly commended.
Open: Mar to Oct
01792 386603 Mrs Hughes
Rates fr: *£15.00*-**£18.00**.
Beds: 1F 1D 1T
Baths: 1 Ensuite 1 Private
(4)

Britannia Inn, *Llanmadoc, Gower, Swansea, SA3 1DB.*
C17th village inn.
Open: All Year (not Xmas)
01792 386624 Mr Downie
Rates fr: *£22.50*-**£30.00**.
Beds: 2D 1T
Baths: 3 Private
(30)

Llantrisant

National Grid Ref: ST0483

***The Black Prince,** Llantrisant Common, Llantrisant, Pontyclun, S Glam, CF72 8BR.*
Modern, licensed facilities, swimming pool.
Open: All Year
01443 227723 Mr Long
Rates fr: *£17.00*-**£23.00**.
Beds: 12F 20D 8T
Baths: 40 Private

Margam

National Grid Ref: SS7887

***Ty N-Y-Caeau,** Margam, Port Talbot, W Glam, SA13 2NW.*
C17th vicarage in fields.
Open: Feb to Nov
Grades: WTB 2 Cr, Comm
01639 883897
Mrs Gaen
Rates fr: *£18.00*-**£22.00**.
Beds: 1F 2D 4T
Baths: 6 Private 1 Shared
(2) (8)

Mumbles

National Grid Ref: SS6187

The Pilot, George, Beefeater, West Cross Inn

***The Coast House,** 708 Mumbles Road, Mumbles, Swansea, W Glam, SA3 4EH.*
Friendly, family-run guest house.
Open: All Year (not Xmas)
Grades: WTB 2 Cr, High Comm
01792 368702
Mrs Clarke
Rates fr: *£16.00*-**£18.00**.
Beds: 2F 3D 1S
Baths: 4 Ensuite 1 Shared
(0)

***Rock Villa Guest House,** 1 George Bank, Mumbles, Swansea, W Glam, SA3 4EQ.*
Pleasant family-run guest house.
Open: All Year (not Xmas)
Grades: WTB Listed, High Comm, RAC Acclaim
01792 366794
Mrs Thomas
Rates fr: *£15.00*-**£19.00**.
Beds: 2F 2D 2T
Baths: 4 Private 2 Shared
(3)

***Tides Reach Guest House,** 388 Mumbles Road, Mumbles, Swansea, W Glam, SA3 5TN.*
Elegant, seafront town house.
Open: All Year (not Xmas)
Grades: WTB 2 Cr
01792 404877
Mrs Maybery
Rates fr: *£16.50*-**£20.00**.
Beds: 2F 4D 2T
Baths: 5 Private 2 Shared
(7)

***Carlton Hotel,** 654 656 Mumbles Road, Southend, Mumbles, Swansea, W Glam, SA3 4EA.*
Family-run, friendly, near everything.
Open: All Year
01792 360450 (also fax no)
Mr Lovelock
Rates fr: *£18.00*-**£22.00**.
Beds: 3F 7D 8T 3S
Baths: 11 Private 2 Shared

Neath

National Grid Ref: SS7497

The Highlander

***Victoria Guest House,** 10 Victoria Gardens, Neath, W Glam, SA11 3BE.*
Large Victorian private house.
Open: All Year
Grades: WTB 1 Cr
01639 636233
Mr & Mrs Riando
Rates fr: *£14.00*-**£16.00**.
Beds: 1F 1D 2T 1S
Baths: 1 Shared

***Cwmbach Cottages,** Cwmbach Road, Neath, W Glam, SA10 8AH.*
Beautiful surroundings, high standards.
Open: All Year
Grades: WTB 3 Cr, High Comm, AA 4 Q
01639 639825 / 641436
Mrs Morgan
Rates fr: *£18.00*-**£20.00**.
Beds: 1F 3D 1T
Baths: 5 Private
(6)

Oxwich

National Grid Ref: SS4986

***Woodside Guest House,** Oxwich, Gower, Swansea, SA3 1LS.*
Converted C17th cottage.
Open: All Year (not Xmas)
Grades: WTB 3 Cr, Comm, AA 3 Q, Recomm
01792 390791
Mr Workman
Rates fr: *£18.00*.
Beds: 1F 3D 1T
Baths: 4 Private 1 Shared
(1) (8)

Parkmill

National Grid Ref: SS5489

***Parc Le Breos House,** Parkmill, Gower, Swansea, SA3 2HA.*
Large Victorian farmhouse; extensive grounds.
Open: All Year
01792 371636
Mrs Edwards
Rates fr: *£17.00*-**£17.00**.
Beds: 8F 2D 1S
Baths: 9 Ensuite 2 Private
(12)

Penarth

National Grid Ref: ST1871

***Raisdale House Hotel,** Raisdale Road, Penarth, S Glam, CF6 2BN.*
Fine example of Victorian splendour.
Open: All Year
Grades: WTB 4 Cr
01222 707317 Mr Wheeler
Rates fr: *£22.50*-**£25.00**.
Beds: 2F 6D 5T 3S
Baths: 16 Private

***Westbourne Hotel,** 8 Victoria Road, Penarth, S Glam, CF64 3EF.*
Open: All Year
Grades: WTB 2 Cr
01222 707268 Mrs Hardiman
Rates fr: *£19.00*-**£20.00**.
Beds: 1F 2D 1T 5S
Baths: 3 Ensuite 3 Private 3 Shared
(4)

Pencoed

National Grid Ref: SS9581

***Chatterton Arms,** 2 Hendre Road, Pencoed, Bridgend, Mid Glam, CF35 5NW.*
Modern, comfortable public house.
Open: All Year
01656 860293 Mrs Perks
Rates fr: *£18.00*-**£18.00**.
Beds: 3T **Baths:** 1 Shared

Penmark

National Grid Ref: ST0568

***The Cottage,** Penmark, Barry, Penarth, S Glam, CF62 9BP.*
C16th tastefully furnished residence. **Open:** All Year
01446 710327
Rates fr: *£17.00*-**£20.00**.
Beds: 1F 1D 2T
(3)

Pontlliw

National Grid Ref: SN6101

***Hathaway Guest House,** 87/89 Swansea Road, Pontlliw, Swansea, SA4 1EF.*
Convenient, comfortable, with tavern opposite.
Open: All Year
01792 891777 Mrs Davies
Rates fr: *£14.00*-**£15.00**.
Beds: 2F 2T 1S
Baths: 3 Shared
(6)

Many rates vary according to season - the lowest are shown here.

National Grid References are for villages, towns and cities - *not* for individual houses.

Pontypridd

National Grid Ref: SN0433

***Market Tavern Hotel,** Market Street, Pontypridd, Mid Glam, CF37 2ST.*
Small, town centre hotel.
Open: All Year (not Xmas)
01443 485331
Mrs Wallace
Fax no: 01443 406784
Rates fr: *£14.00*-**£24.00**.
Beds: 2D 6T 3S
Baths: 11 Private

Port Eynon

National Grid Ref: SS4685

***Culver House Hotel,** Port Eynon, Gower, Swansea, SA3 1NN.*
100 yards from high water.
Open: All Year
Grades: WTB 3 Cr, High Comm, AA 1 St
01792 390755 Mrs Still
Rates fr: *£19.50*-**£19.50**.
Beds: 3F 3D 1T 3S
Baths: 10 Private
(7)

Porthcawl

National Grid Ref: SS8277

Rose & Crown

***Rockybank Guest House,** 15 De Breos Drive, Porthcawl, Mid Glam, CF36 3JP.*
First guest house off Junction 37 (M4).
Open: All Year (not Xmas)
Grades: WTB 2 Cr, High Comm
01656 785823
Mrs Lewis
Fax no: 01656 771744
Rates fr: *£17.00*-**£23.00**.
Beds: 1F 1D 1T
Baths: 3 Private
(6)

***Rossett House,** 1 Esplanade Avenue, Porthcawl, Mid Glam, CF36 3YS.*
Small Victorian private house.
Open: All Year (not Xmas)
Grades: WTB 2 Cr
01656 771664
Rates fr: *£15.00*-**£18.00**.
Beds: 1F 2T
Baths: 2 Ensuite 1 Shared
(2)

***Haven Guest House,** 50 New Road, Porthcawl, Mid Glam, CF36 5DN.*
Modernised Edwardian family guest house.
Open: All Year
Grades: WTB 2 Cr
01656 788706 Mrs Seage
Rates fr: *£16.00*-**£18.00**.
Beds: 3F 1D 1S
Baths: 4 Private 1 Shared

***Picton Villa,** 14 Picton Avenue, Porthcawl, Mid Glam, CF36 3AJ.*
Comfortable Victorian house, off seafront.
Open: All Year
01656 786386 Mrs Owen
Rates fr: *£16.00*-**£16.00**.
Beds: 1F 2D 1T 1S
Baths: 1 Private 1 Shared
(4)

Southgate

National Grid Ref: SS5588

Beaufort Arms, Gower Inn, Valley Hotel, Plough & Harrow

***Heatherlands,** 1 Hael Lane, Southgate, Gower, Swansea, W Glam, SA3 2AP.*
Open: Jan to Nov
Grades: WTB 2 Cr, High Comm
01792 233256 Mrs Churchill
Rates fr: *£18.00*-**£20.00**.
Beds: 2D 1T
Baths: 1 Ensuite 2 Private
(8) (4)
Spacious immaculate residence near see cliffs. Short walk Pubbles & Three Cliffs Bay. 3 bedrooms: 2 doubles & 1 twin. 1 ensuite, 2 private bathrooms.

Sully

National Grid Ref: ST1568

Sully Inn

***Ardwyn,** 53 Cog Road, Sully, Penarth, S Glam, CF64 5TE.*
Detached comfortable house, pleasant gardens.
Open: All Year (not Xmas)
Grades: WTB 2 Cr
01222 530103 (also fax no)
Mrs Robinson
Rates fr: *£17.00*-**£17.00**.
Beds: 2T 1D 2S
Baths: 2 Ensuite 1 Shared
(6) (6)

Always telephone to get directions to the B&B - you will save time!

Swansea

National Grid Ref: SS6494

The Pilot, The George, Beefeater, Rat & Carrot, Wig & Pen, Cross Inn

***The Bayswater Hotel,** 322 Oystermouth Road, Swansea, SA1 3UJ.*
Open: All Year (not Xmas)
Grades: WTB 1 Cr, Approv
01792 655301 Mr Ahern
Fax no: 01792 643463
Rates fr: *£13.00*-**£16.00**.
Beds: 2F 2D 1T 1S
Baths: 2 Ensuite 1 Shared
Comfortable, homely guest house overlooking Swansea Bay. All rooms have CTV. Ensuite rooms available. Close to all city amenities & Gower beaches. Mini breaks available.

***Rock Villa Guest House,** 1 George Bank, Mumbles, Swansea, W Glam, SA3 4EQ.*
Pleasant family-run guest house.
Open: All Year (not Xmas)
Grades: WTB Listed, High Comm, RAC Acclaim
01792 366794
Mrs Thomas
Rates fr: *£15.00*-**£19.00**.
Beds: 2F 2D 2T
Baths: 4 Private 2 Shared
(3)

***Harlton Guest House,** 89 King Edward Road, Brynmill, Swansea, SA1 4LU.*
Comfortable guest house.
Open: All Year
Grades: WTB 1 Cr
01792 466938
Mr Drinning
Rates fr: *£10.00*-**£10.00**.
Beds: 2T 5S
Baths: 1 Shared

***The Lyndale Hotel,** 324 Oystermouth Road, Swansea, SA1 3UJ.*
Seafront. Walking distance city centre.
Open: All Year
Grades: WTB Listed
01792 653882
Ms Williams
Rates fr: *£12.00*-**£15.00**.
Beds: 1F 1D 4T 1S
Baths: 2 Shared
(2)

***Mirador Guest House,** 14 Mirador Crescent, Uplands, Swansea, SA2 0QX.*
Large Victorian town house.
Open: All Year
Grades: WTB 1 Cr
01792 466976
Mr Anderson
Rates fr: *£16.00*-**£16.00**.
Beds: 1F 2D 2T 1S
Baths: 1 Ensuite 2 Shared

Jezreel, *168 Bishopston Road, Swansea, SA3 3EX.*
Detached, small, friendly guest house.
Open: Easter to Nov
Grades: WTB 1 Cr
01792 232744 Mrs Jones
Rates fr: *£14.00*-**£14.00**.
Beds: 2D 1T
Baths: 1 Shared
(1) (6)

Osprey Guest House,
244 Oystermouth Road, Swansea, SA1 3UH.
Sea front - nearest city centre.
Open: All Year (not Xmas)
01792 642369 Mrs Ellis
Rates fr: *£14.00*-**£15.00**.
Beds: 2F 2D 4T 2S
Baths: 3 Shared
(6)

Uplands Court Guest House,
134 Eaton Crescent, Uplands, Swansea, SA1 4QR.
Family-run business.
Open: All Year
Grades: WTB 2 Cr, Comm, RAC Listed
01792 473046 Mr Gray
Rates fr: *£17.00*-**£17.00**.
Beds: 2F 2D 4S **Baths:** 3 Shared

Crescent Guest House,
132 Eaton Crescent, Uplands, Swansea, SA1 4QR.
Edwardian town house overlooking bay. **Open:** All Year (not Xmas)
01792 466814 Mrs Convey
Rates fr: *£18.00*-**£23.00**.
Beds: 1F 2D 2T 1S
Baths: 6 Ensuite
(5)

The lowest **single** *rate is shown in* **bold.**

Treharris

National Grid Ref: ST1097

Fairmead, *24 Gelligaer Road, Treharris, Nelson, Mid Glam, CF46 6DN.*
A warm welcome & friendly atmosphere.
Open: All Year
Grades: WTB 2 Cr, High Comm
01443 411174 Mrs Kedward
Rates fr: *£17.50*-**£17.50**.
Beds: 2D 1T
Baths: 2 Private 1 Shared
(5)

Monmouthshire

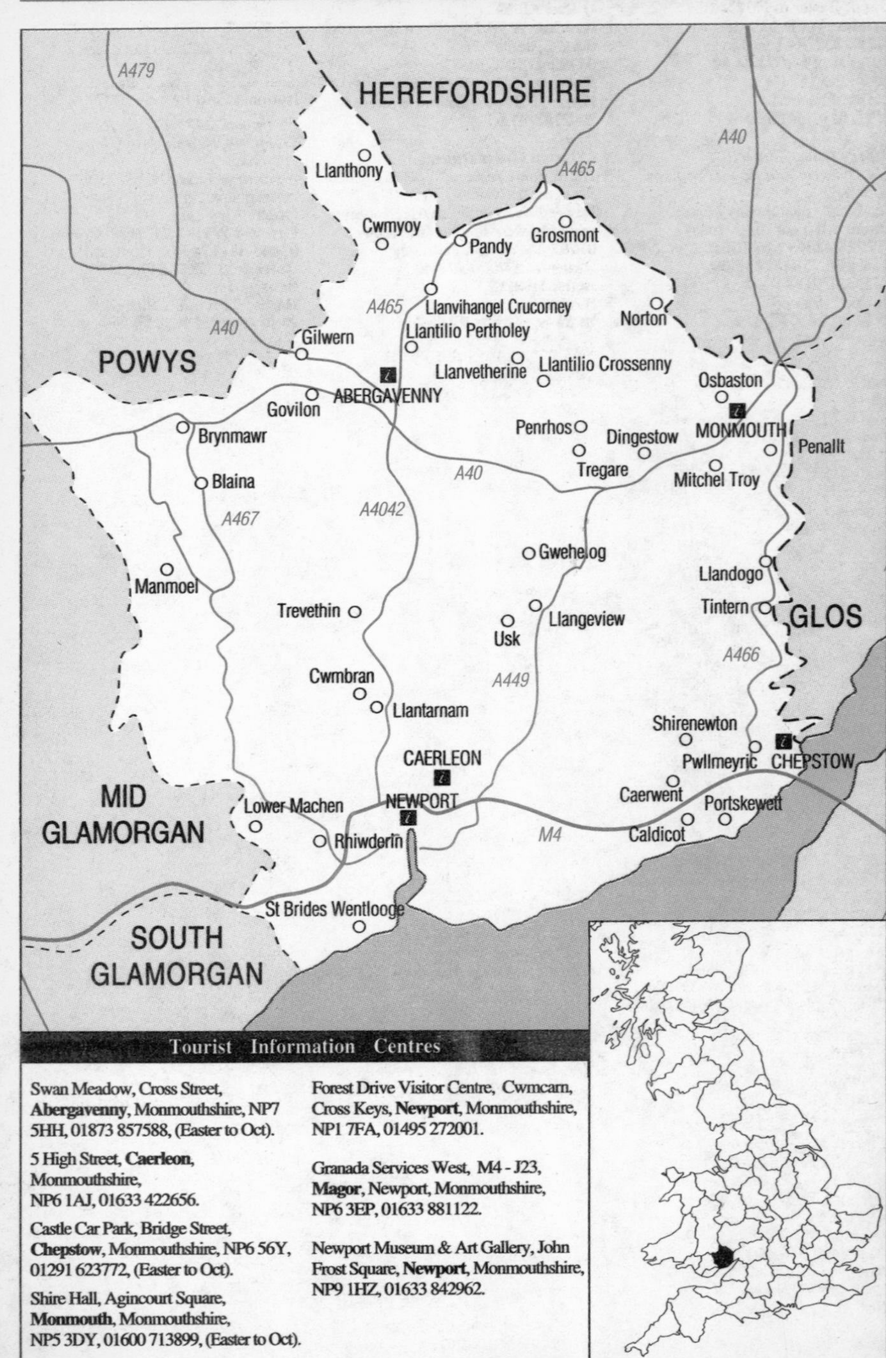

Tourist Information Centres

Swan Meadow, Cross Street, **Abergavenny**, Monmouthshire, NP7 5HH, 01873 857588, (Easter to Oct).

5 High Street, **Caerleon**, Monmouthshire, NP6 1AJ, 01633 422656.

Castle Car Park, Bridge Street, **Chepstow**, Monmouthshire, NP6 56Y, 01291 623772, (Easter to Oct).

Shire Hall, Agincourt Square, **Monmouth**, Monmouthshire, NP5 3DY, 01600 713899, (Easter to Oct).

Forest Drive Visitor Centre, Cwmcarn, Cross Keys, **Newport**, Monmouthshire, NP1 7FA, 01495 272001.

Granada Services West, M4 - J23, **Magor**, Newport, Monmouthshire, NP6 3EP, 01633 881122.

Newport Museum & Art Gallery, John Frost Square, **Newport**, Monmouthshire, NP9 1HZ, 01633 842962.

Abergavenny

National Grid Ref: SO2914

Walnut Tree Inn

The Wenallt, *Gilwern, Abergavenny, Monmouthshire, NP7 0HP.*
Open: All Year
Grades: WTB 3 Cr, AA 3 Q, RAC Listed
01873 830694 Mr Harris
Rates fr: *£15.00*-**£18.00**.
Beds: 1F 8D 4T 8S
Baths: 6 Private 2 Shared
(20)
C16th Welsh longhouse in 50 acres in Brecon Beacons National Park. Oak beams, inglenook log fire places. Ideal for touring, walking. Home cooked meals.

The Guest House, *Mansel Rest, 2 Oxford Street, Abergavenny, Monmouthshire, NP7 5RP.*
Licensed restaurant, central to town. **Open:** All Year
Grades: WTB 1 Cr
01873 854823 Mrs Cook
Rates fr: *£16.00*-**£18.50**.
Beds: 3F 5D 5T 2S
Baths: 3 Shared
(10)

Pentre House, *Brecon Road, Abergavenny, Monmouthshire, NP7 7EW.*
Pretty, small, Georgian country house in wonderful gardens.
Open: All Year
Grades: WTB 1 Cr, High Comm
01873 853435 (also fax no)
Mrs Reardon-Smith
Rates fr: *£15.00*-**£18.00**.
Beds: 1F 2D
Baths: 2 Shared
(6)

Ty'r Morwydd House, *Pen-y-Pound, Abergavenny, Monmouthshire, NP7 5UD.*
Georgian house wedded to modern accommodation.
Open: All Year (not Xmas)
01873 855959 Mrs Senior
Fax no: 01873 855443
Rates fr: *£12.50*-**£17.00**.
Beds: 19T 31S **Baths:** 19 Shared
(30)

Blaina

National Grid Ref: SO1908

Bridge End

Chapel Farm, *Blaina, Monmouthshire, NP3 3DJ.*
C15th renovated farmhouse. Working farm.
Open: All Year
Grades: WTB 2 Cr, Comm
01495 290888 Mrs Hancocks
Rates fr: *£16.00*-**£18.00**.
Beds: 1F 1D
Baths: 1 Ensuite 1 Private 1 Shared

Lamb House, *Westside, Blaina, Abertillery, Monmouthshire, NP3 3DB.*
Detached homely house, beautiful garden.
Open: All Year
01495 290179 Mr Chandler
Rates fr: *£15.00*-**£15.00**.
Beds: 2D 1T
Baths: 2 Private 1 Shared
(5)

Brynmawr

National Grid Ref: SO1811

The Bridge End

Hafod Farm, *Brynmawr, Monmouthshire, NP3 4BU.*
Friendly, comfortable, working farmhouse.
Open: All Year
01495 310379 Mrs Thomas
Rates fr: *£12.50*-**£12.50**.
Beds: 1F 1D 1T
(2) (4)

Caerwent

National Grid Ref: ST4690

Roadside Cottage, *Caerwent, Chepstow, Monmouthshire, NP6 4AZ.*
Small cottage. 'Home from home'.
Open: Mar to Oct
01291 420184 Mrs Goulding
Rates fr: *£18.00*-**£20.00**.
Beds: 1D 1T
Baths: 1 Shared
(12) (2)

Caldicot

National Grid Ref: ST4788

Deepweir Hotel, *Pill Row, Caldicot, Newport, Monmouthshire, NP6 4JD.*
Open: All Year
01291 430500 Mrs Plant
Fax no: 01291 430550
Rates fr: *£24.00*-**£32.00**.
Beds: 2F 4D 4T 2S
Baths: 12 Private
(30)
Only 4 miles from Severn Crossing and motorway. Spacious ensuite accommodation. Quiet gardens. Ideal for visitors to the South Wales Coast.

Chepstow

National Grid Ref: ST5393

Grape Escape

Lower Hardwick House, *Mount Pleasant, Chepstow, Monmouthshire, NP6 5PT.*
Beautiful Georgian house, walled garden.
Open: All Year
01291 622162 Mrs Grassby
Rates fr: *£15.00*-**£14.00**.
Beds: 2F 1D 1T 1S
Baths: 1 Private 2 Shared
(12)

Langcroft, *71 St Kingsmark Avenue, Chepstow, Monmouthshire, NP6 5LY.*
Modern family friendly home.
Open: All Year
Grades: WTB Listed
01291 625569 (also fax no)
Mrs Langdale
Rates fr: *£15.00*-**£15.00**.
Beds: 1D 1T 1S
Baths: 1 Shared
(2)

Upper Sedbury House, *Sedbury Lane, Sedbury, Chepstow, Newport, Monmouthshire, NP6 7HN.*
200-year-old superior country house.
Open: All Year (not Xmas)
Grades: WTB 2 Cr, Comm
01291 627173 Mrs Potts
Rates fr: *£16.50*-**£18.50**.
Beds: 1F 1D 1T
Baths: 1 Private 1 Shared

Cobweb Cottage, *Belle Vue Place, Streep Street, Chepstow, Monmouthshire, NP6 5PL.*
Quiet, secluded, comfortable period cottage.
Open: All Year (not Xmas)
01291 626643 Mrs Warren
Rates fr: *£16.50*-**£18.00**.
Beds: 1D 1T **Baths:** 1 Shared
(5) (6)

Cwmbran

National Grid Ref: ST2894

The Greenhouse

Springfields, *371 Llantarnam Road, Llantarnam, Cwmbran, Monmouthshire, NP44 3BN.*
Large welcoming Victorian private house.
Open: All Year
Grades: WTB 2 Cr, Comm
01633 482509 Mrs Graham
Rates fr: *£16.00*-**£16.00**.
Beds: 3F 3D 3T 1S
Baths: 6 Private 2 Shared
(16)

Cwmyoy

National Grid Ref: SO2923

Skirrid Inn

Gaer Farm, *Cwmyoy, Abergavenny, Monmouthshire, NP7 7NE.*
Peaceful farm. Rare breed animals.
Open: All Year (not Xmas)
Grades: WTB 2 Cr, Comm
01873 890345 Mrs Judd
Rates fr: *£18.00*-**£20.00**.
Beds: 1D 1T **Baths:** 2 Ensuite
(10) (4)

The lowest *double* rate per person is shown in *italics*.

Dingestow

National Grid Ref: SO4510

The Lilacs, *Dingestow, Monmouth, NP5 4DZ.*
Country cottage off beaten track.
Open: All Year (not Xmas)
01600 740686 Mrs Clark
Rates fr: *£12.50*-**£12.50**.
Beds: 1D 2S
Baths: 1 Shared
(1)

New House Farm, *Dingestow, Monmouth, NP5 4EB.*
Comfortable farmhouse on working farm.
Open: All Year
01600 740245 Mrs Smith
Rates fr: *£15.00*-**£18.00**.
Beds: 3F 1D

Lower Pen-y-Clawdd Farm, *Dingestow, Monmouth, NP5 4BG.*
Old converted cider mill.
Open: All Year
01600 740223 Mrs Bayliss
Rates fr: *£15.00*-**£16.00**.
Beds: 1F 1D 1T
Baths: 1 Shared
(1) (10)

Gilwern

National Grid Ref: SO2414

The Wenallt, *Gilwern, Abergavenny, Monmouthshire, NP7 0HP.*
C16th Welsh longhouse, oak beams, inglenook.
Open: All Year
Grades: WTB 3 Cr, AA 3 Q, RAC Listed
01873 830694 Mr Harris
Rates fr: *£15.00*-**£18.00**.
Beds: 1F 8D 4T 8S
Baths: 6 Private 2 Shared
(20)

Govilon

National Grid Ref: SO2613

Lion Inn

Lion Inn, *Old Stable Restuarant, Merthyr Road, Govilon, Abergavenny, NP7 9PT.*
Comfortable family-run inn.
Open: All Year
01873 830404 (also fax no)
Mr Archer
Rates fr: *£15.00*-**£18.00**.
Beds: 1F 1T
Baths: 1 Private 1 Shared

High season, bank holidays and special events mean low availability *anywhere.*

Grosmont

National Grid Ref: SO4024

Lawns Farm, *Grosmont, Abergavenny, Monmouthshire, NP7 8ES.*
Beautiful old C17th farmhouse.
Open: Mar to Oct
01981 240298
Mr & Mrs Ferneyhough
Rates fr: *£18.00*-**£15.00**.
Beds: 1F 1D1T **Baths:** 3 Ensuite

Gwehelog

National Grid Ref: SO3804

Hall Inn

Oak Farm, *Gwehelog, Usk, Monmouthshire, NP5 1RB.*
Comfortable self contained cottage.
Open: All Year (not Xmas)
01291 672830 Mrs Dean
Fax no: 01291 673569
Rates fr: *£16.00*-**£16.00**.
Beds: 1F **Baths:** 1 Private

Little Mill

National Grid Ref: SO3202

Pentwyn Farm, *Little Mill, Pontypool, Monmouthshire, NP4 0HQ*
C16th Welsh longhouse.
Open: All Year (not Xmas)
01495 785249 Mrs Bradey
Rates fr: *£14.00*-**£19.00**.
Beds: 1F 1D 1T **Baths:** 3 Private
(4) (10)

Llandogo

National Grid Ref: SO5204

Sloop Inn

The Sloop Inn, *Llandogo, Monmouth, NP5 4TW.*
Traditional hostelry with modern facilities.
Open: All Year (not Xmas)
Grades: WTB 3 Cr, RAC Listed
01594 530291 Ms Evans
Rates fr: *£19.00*-**£25.00**.
Beds: 1F 2D 1T
Baths: 4 Ensuite

Llangeview

National Grid Ref: SO3700

The Rat Trap, *Chepstow Road, Llangeview, Usk, Monmouthshire, NP5 1EY.*
Olde worlde charm & service with high standards.
Open: All Year
Grades: WTB 3 Cr, Comm
01291 673288
Mr & Mrs Rabaiotti
Fax no: 01291 673305
Rates fr: *£25.00*-**£42.50**.
Beds: 1F 5D 4T 3S
Baths: 13 Private
(40)

Llantarnam

National Grid Ref: ST3093

The Greenhouse

Springfields, *371 Llantarnam Road, Llantarnam, Cwmbran, Monmouthshire, NP44 3BN.*
Large welcoming Victorian private house.
Open: All Year
Grades: WTB 2 Cr, Comm
01633 482509 Mrs Graham
Rates fr: *£16.00*-**£16.00**.
Beds: 3F 3D 3T 1S
Baths: 6 Private 2 Shared
(16)

Llanthony

National Grid Ref: SO2827

Half Moon

The Half Moon, *Llanthony, Abergavenny, Monmouthshire, NP7 7NN.*
Small, friendly country hotel.
Open: All Year (not Xmas)
01873 890611 Mrs Smith
Rates fr: *£17.50*-**£20.00**.
Beds: 1F 4D 2T
Baths: 2 Shared
(5)

Llantilio Crossenny

National Grid Ref: SO3914

Three Crown

Treloyvan Farm, *Llantilio Crossenny, Abergavenny, Monmouthshire, NP7 8UE.*
Converted C17th farmhouse.
Open: Mar to Nov
Grades: WTB 1 Cr
01600 780478 Mrs Watkins
Rates fr: *£12.00*-**£14.00**.
Beds: 1F 1T
Baths: 1 Ensuite 1 Shared

Little Treadam Farm, *Llantilio Crossenny, Abergavenny, Monmouthshire, NP7 8TA.*
C16th Welsh farmhouse.
Open: All Year (not Xmas)
01600 780326 Mrs Ford
Rates fr: *£18.00*-**£20.00**.
Beds: 1D 2T
Baths: 3 Private

Llantilio Pertholey

National Grid Ref: SO3116

Wern Gochlyn Farm, *Llantilio Pertholey, Abergavenny, Monmouthshire, NP7 8DB.*
Working farm with C12th farmhouse.
Open: All Year
01873 857357 Mr Sage
Rates fr: *£15.00*-**£18.00**.
Beds: 1F 1D **Baths:** 2 Private
(1) (7)

Llanvetherine

National Grid Ref: SO3617

Great Tre-Rhew Farm, *Llanvetherine, Abergavenny, Monmouthshire, NP7 8RA.*
Ancient farmhouse on working farm.
Open: All Year (not Xmas)
Grades: WTB Listed
01873 821268 Ms Beavan
Rates fr: *£15.00*-**£15.00**.
Beds: 1F 1D 1T **Baths:** 2 Shared
(8)

Llanvihangel Crucorney

National Grid Ref: SO3220

Skirrid Inn, Crown Inn

Penyclawdd Farm, *Llanvihangel Crucorney, Abergavenny, Monmouthshire, NP7 7LB.*
Comfortable farmhouse in Black Mountains.
Open: All Year
Grades: WTB Listed, AA 3 Q
01873 890591 Mrs Davies
Rates fr: *£15.00*-**£15.00**.
Beds: 1F 1D
Baths: 1 Shared
(0) (4)

The Skirrid Mountain Inn, *Llanvihangel Crucorney, Abergavenny, Monmouthshire, NP7 8DH.*
Historic C12th country inn.
Open: All Year
01873 890258 Mrs Gant
Rates fr: *£20.00*-**£25.00**.
Beds: 1F 2D **Baths:** 3 Private
(20)

Lower Machen

National Grid Ref: ST2288

Hollybush Inn

The Forge, *Lower Machen, Newport, NP1 8UU.*
Comfortable C18th cottage.
Open: All Year
Grades: WTB Listed
01633 440226 Mrs Jones
Rates fr: *£15.00*-**£16.00**.
Beds: 1F 1D 1T **Baths:** 1 Shared
(3)

Mamhilad

National Grid Ref: SO3003

Horseshoe Inn

Ty-Cooke Farm, *Mamhilad, Pontypool, Monmouthshire, NP4 8QZ.*
Spacious C18th farmhouse near Monmouthshire-Brecon Canal.
Open: Mar to Nov
Grades: WTB Listed, Comm, AA 2 Q
01873 880382 Mrs Price
Rates fr: *£16.00*-**£18.00**.
Beds: 1F 1D 1T

National Grid References are for villages, towns and cities - *not* for individual houses.

Manmoel

National Grid Ref: SO1703

Wyrloed Lodge, *Manmoel, Blackwood, Monmouthshire, NP2 0RN*
Large lodge house in countryside.
Open: All Year
01495 371198
Mrs Gittins
Rates fr: *£16.00*-**£16.00**.
Beds: 1F 1D 1T
Baths: 1 Private
(4)

Mitchel Troy

National Grid Ref: SO4910

Church Farm Guest House, *Mitchel Troy, Monmouth, NP5 4HZ.*
C16th beamed former farmhouse.
Open: All Year
Grades: WTB 2 Cr, Comm, AA 3 Q
01600 712176 Mrs Ringer
Rates fr: *£17.00*-**£17.00**.
Beds: 2F 3D 2T 1S
Baths: 6 Private 2 Shared
(8)

Monmouth

National Grid Ref: SO5012

Riverside Inn, French Horn, Green Dragon

Wye Avon, *Dixton Road, Monmouth, NP5 3PR.*
Large stone Victorian private house.
Open: All Year (not Xmas)
01600 713322 Mrs Cantrell
Rates fr: *£15.00*-**£15.00**.
Beds: 1F 1D 1S
Baths: 1 Shared

Riverside Hotel, *Cinderhill Street, Monmouth, NP5 3EY.*
Outstanding converted C17th coaching inn.
Open: All Year
Grades: WTB 4 Cr, High Comm, AA 2 St
01600 715577 Mr Dodd
Rates fr: *£20.00*-**£25.00**.
Beds: 2F 6D 9T
Baths: 17 Private
(1) (50)

Troy Lodge, *Monmouth, NP5 4HX.*
Comfortable annexe with own sitting-room.
Open: All Year (not Xmas)
01600 715098
Mr & Mrs Bennett
Rates fr: *£17.50*-**£13.50**.
Beds: 1D 1T
Baths: 1 Private 1 Shared
(5) (2)

Red Lion House, *16 Drybridge Street, Monmouth, NP5 3AD.*
C18th town house - central town.
Open: All Year (not Xmas)
01600 713633
Mrs Frost
Rates fr: *£13.00*.
Beds: 1D 2T

Newport

National Grid Ref: ST3188

Six Bells

The West Usk Lighthouse, *Lighthouse Road, St Brides Wentlooge, Newport, Monmouthshire, NP1 9SF.*
Open: All Year
Grades: WTB 2 Cr
01633 810126 / 815860
Mr & Mrs Sheahan
Rates fr: *£24.00*-**£40.00**.
Beds: 3D 1T 1S
Baths: 3 Private 1 Shared
(10)
Real lighthouse situated between Newport & Cardiff, overlooking the Bristol Channel. All rooms wedge-shaped. Waterbed & 4-poster ensuite rooms. Flotation tank for deep relaxation. Different.

Caerleon House Hotel, *61 Caerau Road, Newport, Monmouthshire, NP9 4HJ.*
Small Victorian private hotel.
Open: All Year
01633 264869
Mrs Grundy
Rates fr: *£19.00*-**£25.00**.
Beds: 1F 1D 3T 2S
Baths: 7 Private
(8)

Knoll Guest House, *145 Stow Hill, Newport, Monmouthshire, NP9 4FZ.*
Large Victorian house of character.
Open: All Year
01633 263557
Rates fr: *£16.00*-**£21.00**.
Beds: 2F 3D 3T 2S
Baths: 5 Ensuite 4 Private 2 Shared
(6)

Anderley Lodge, *216 Stow Hill, Newport, Monmouthshire, NP9 4HA.*
Converted Victorian house.
Open: All Year
01633 266781 (also fax no)
Mr Smith
Rates fr: *£16.00*-**£19.00**.
Beds: 1D 1T 1S

Norton

National Grid Ref: SO4420

Bell

Brook Cottage, *Norton, Skenfrith, Abergavenny, Monmouthshire, NP7 8UB.*
Converted chapel in rural Wales.
Open: All Year (not Xmas)
Grades: WTB Listed
01600 750319
Miss Finn
Rates fr: *£13.00*-**£14.50**.
Beds: 1F 1D 1S
Baths: 1 Shared
(3)

Osbaston

National Grid Ref: SO5014

Caseta Alta, *15 Toynbee Close, Osbaston, Monmouth, NP5 3NU.*
Comfortable 'upside-down' house, glorious views.
Open: All Year (not Xmas)
01600 713023
Mrs Allcock
Rates fr: *£13.00*-**£18.50**.
Beds: 2D 1T 1S
Baths: 1 Private 1 Shared
(8) (2)

Pandy

National Grid Ref: SO3322

Paddy Inn, Park Hotel

Old Castle Court Farm, *Pandy, Abergavenny, Monmouthshire, NP7 7PH.*
C13th farmhouse, mountain walks nearby.
Open: All Year (not Xmas)
01873 890285
Mrs Probert
Rates fr: *£11.00*-**£12.00**.
Beds: 1F 1D 1T 1S
Baths: 1 Private 2 Shared
(2) (10)

Ny Newydd Farm, *Pandy, Abergavenny, Monmouthshire, NP7 8DW.*
Victorian farmhouse in Black Mountains.
Open: All Year (not Xmas)
Grades: WTB Listed, Comm
01873 890235
Mrs Evans
Rates fr: *£14.00*-**£15.00**.
Beds: 1D 2T
Baths: 1 Shared
(20)

Brynhonddu, *Pandy, Abergavenny, Monmouthshire, NP7 7PD.*
Large C16th-C19th country house.
Open: All Year
01873 890535 Mrs White
Rates fr: *£14.00*-**£16.00**.
Beds: 1F 1D 1T
Baths: 1 Shared
(5) (6)

Rhos Rhudd, *Pandy, Abergavenny, Monmouthshire, NP7 8DW.*
Old Welsh stone cottage.
Open: All Year (not Xmas)
01873 890703 Mrs Bray
Rates fr: *£12.00*-**£12.00**.
Beds: 1F 1D 1T
Baths: 1 Shared
(1) (2)

Penallt

National Grid Ref: SO5210

Cherry Orchard Farm, *Lone Lane, Penallt, Monmouth, Monmouthshire, NP5 4AJ.*
Georgian farmhouse in Wye Valley.
Open: All Year
Grades: WTB Listed
01600 714010 (also fax no)
Mrs Beale
Rates fr: *£15.00*-**£15.00**.
Beds: 2D 1T
Baths: 1 Shared
(6)

Penrhos

National Grid Ref: SO4111

Bottom Farm, *Penrhos, Raglan, Monmouthshire, NP5 2DE.*
C15th farmhouse, working farm.
Open: Feb to Nov
01600 780216 Mrs Watkins
Rates fr: *£13.00*-**£13.00**.
Beds: 1D 1T
Baths: 1 Shared
(10)

Portskewett

National Grid Ref: ST4988

Victorian Farmhouse, *Leechpool House, Portskewett, Monmouthshire, NP6 4TR.*
Large rural Victorian farmhouse.
Open: All Year
01291 423230 Mrs Langford
Rates fr: *£15.00*-**£17.50**.
Beds: 2F
Baths: 1 Shared
(5)

Rhiwderin

National Grid Ref: ST2687

Rhiwderin Inn

Pentre Tai Farm, *Rhiwderin, Newport, Monmouthshire, NP1 9RQ.*
Lovely Welsh sheep farm.
Open: Feb to Nov
Grades: WTB 2 Cr, High Comm
01633 893284 Mrs Proctor
Rates fr: *£18.00*-**£22.00**.
Beds: 1F 1D 1T
Baths: 2 Private 1 Shared
(6)

Shire Newton

National Grid Ref: ST4793

Tredegar Arms

Parsons Grove, *Earlswood, Shire Newton, Chepstow, Monmouthshire, NP6 6RD.*
Top-quality accommodation, country house.
Open: All Year (not Xmas)
Grades: WTB 2 Cr, High Comm
01291 641382 (also fax no)
Mrs Powell
Rates fr: *£17.00*-**£25.00**.
Beds: 2F **Baths:** 2 Ensuite
(10)

Skenfrith

National Grid Ref: SO4520

The Bell

Brook Cottage, *Norton, Skenfrith, Abergavenny, Monmouthshire, NP7 8UB.*
Converted chapel in rural Wales.
Open: All Year (not Xmas)
Grades: WTB Listed
01600 750319 Miss Finn
Rates fr: *£13.00*-**£14.50**.
Beds: 1F 1D 1S **Baths:** 1 Shared
(3)

St Brides Wentlooge

National Grid Ref: ST2982

Church House Inn, Elm Tree, Six Bells

Chapel Guest House, *Church Road, St Brides Wentlooge, Newport, Monmouthshire, NP1 9SN.*
Comfortable accommodation in converted chapel.
Open: All Year
Grades: WTB 2 Cr, Comm
01633 681018 (also fax no)
Mr Bushell
Rates fr: *£16.00*-**£17.00**.
Beds: 1F 1D 1T
Baths: 2 Ensuite 1 Private
(10)

The West Usk Lighthouse, *Lighthouse Road, St Brides Wentlooge, Newport, Monmouthshire, NP1 9SF.*
Real lighthouse overlooking the Bristol Channel.
Open: All Year
Grades: WTB 2 Cr
01633 810126 / 815860
Mr & Mrs Sheahan
Rates fr: *£24.00*-**£40.00**.
Beds: 3D 1T 1S
Baths: 3 Private 1 Shared
(10)

Tintern

National Grid Ref: SO5300

Royal George Hotel

The Old Rectory, *Tintern, Chepstow, Monmouthshire, NP6 6SG.*
Welcoming, comfortable, early-Victorian house.
Open: All Year
Grades: WTB 1 Cr
01291 689519
Mrs Taylor
Rates fr: *£15.00*-**£15.00**.
Beds: 1F 1D 2T 1S
Baths: 1 Shared
(5)

The lowest **single** *rate is shown in* **bold.**

The Wye Valley Hotel, *Tintern, Tintern, Chepstow, Monmouthshire, NP6 6SQ.*
Beautiful unspoilt location, excellent cuisine.
Open: All Year (not Xmas)
Grades: WTB 4 Cr, Comm
01291 689441 Mr Miller
Fax no: 01291 689440
Rates fr: *£24.50*-**£35.00**.
Beds: 2F 6D 1T **Baths:** 9 Ensuite

Valley House, *Raglan Road, Tintern, Chepstow, Monmouthshire, NP6 6TH.*
C18th detached house in picturesque valley.
Open: All Year (not Xmas)
Grades: WTB 2 Cr, Comm, AA 3 Q, RAC Highly Acclaim
01291 689652 Mr & Mrs Howe
Fax no: 01291 689805
Rates fr: *£18.00*-**£26.00**.
Beds: 2D 1T **Baths:** 3 Private

Tranch

National Grid Ref: SO2600

Ty Shon Jacob Farm, *Tranch, Pontypool, NP4 6BP.*
Peacefully situated with magnificent views.
Open: All Year
Grades: WTB 2 Cr, Comm
01495 757536 Mrs Harris
Rates fr: *£17.00*-**£17.00**.
Beds: 2T 1D
Baths: 2 Ensuite 1 Private
(10)

Tregare

National Grid Ref: SO4110

Court Robert, *Tregare, Raglan, Monmouthshire, NP5 2BZ.*
C16th country house, large rooms.
Open: All Year (not Xmas)
01291 690709 Ms Paxton
Rates fr: *£13.00*-**£15.00**.
Beds: 2F **Baths:** 1 Shared

Trevethin

National Grid Ref: SO2800

The Horseshoe

Ty'r Ywen Farm, *Lasgarn Lane, Trevethin, Pontypool, Monmouthshire, NP4 8TT.*
Open: All Year (not Xmas)
01495 785200 (also fax no)
Mrs Armitage
Rates fr: *£20.00*-**£30.00**.
Beds: 3D 1T
Baths: 4 Ensuite
Remote C16th farmhouse in Brecon Beacons National Park. 30 mile views down Usk Valley. Honeymoon suite with jacuzzi, splendid walks, exciting, access road.

The lowest *double* rate per person is shown in *italics*.

North West Wales

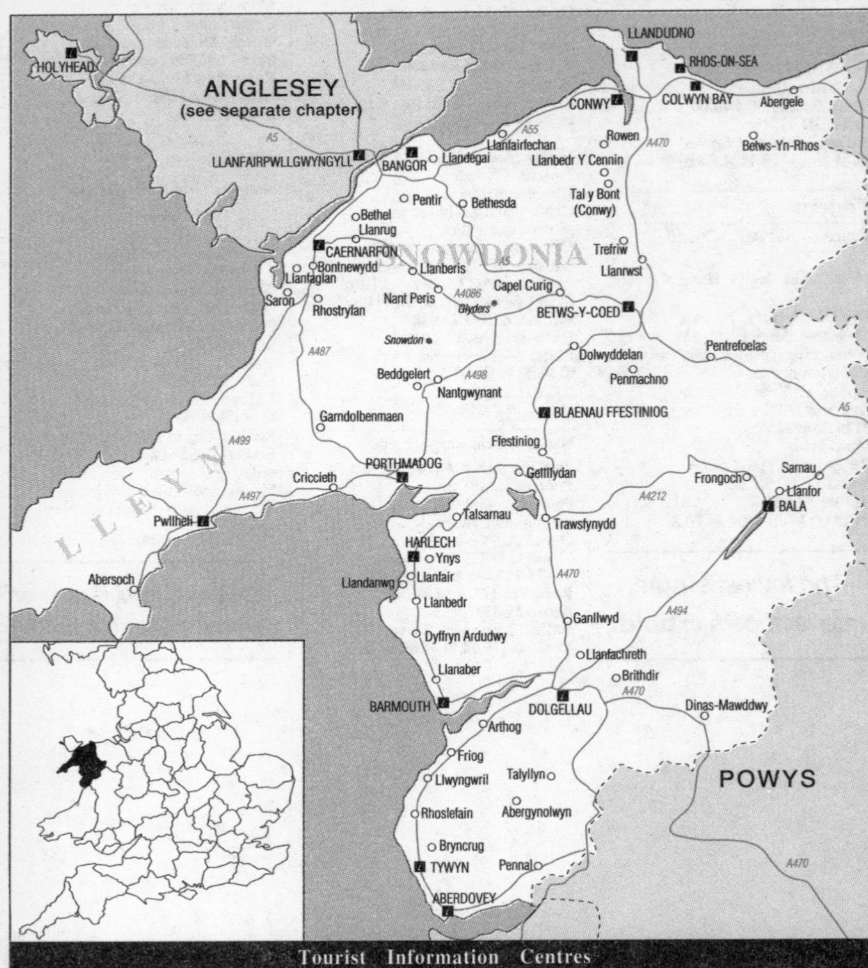

Tourist Information Centres

The Wharf Gardens, **Aberdovey**, LL35 0ED, 01654 767321, (Easter to Oct).

Penllyn Pensain, **Bala**, LL23 7SR, 01678 521021, (Easter to Oct).

Little Chef Site, ASS/S, Llandygai, **Bangor**, LL57 4BG, 01248 353934, (Easter to Oct).

The Old Library, Station Road, **Barmouth**, LL42 1LU, 01341 280787, (Easter to Oct).

Royal Oak Stables, **Betws-y-coed**, LL24 0AH, 01690 710426.

Isallt, High Street, **Blaenau Ffestiniog**, LL41 3HD, 01766 830360, (Easter to Oct)

Oriel Pendeitch, Castle Street, **Caernarfon**, LL55 2PB, 01286 672232.

40 Station Road, **Colwyn Bay**, Denbigh & Flint, LL29 8BU, 01492 530478

Castle Buildings, Castle Street, **Conwy**, LL32 8LD, 01492 592248, (Easter to Oct).

Eldon Square, **Dolgellau**, LL40 1PU, 01341 422888, (Easter to Oct).

Gwyddfor House, High Street, **Harlech**, 01766 870658, (Easter to Oct).

1-2 Chapel Street, **Llandudno**, LL30 2YU, 01492-876413.

High Street, **Porthmadog**, LL49 9LP, 01766-512981.

Min-y-Don, Station Square, Pwllheli, LL53 5HG, 01758 613000,

The Promenade, **Rhos on Sea**, Colwyn Bay, Denbigh & Flint, LL29 8HH, 01492-548778, (Easter to Oct).

High Street, **Tywyn**, LL36 9AD, 01654-710070, (Easter to Oct).

berdovey

ational Grid Ref: SN6196

Penhelig Arms

reswylfa , Balkan Hill, berdovey, LL35 0LE.
pen: Easter to Oct
rades: WTB 2 Cr
654 767239 (also fax no)
Irs Billingham
ates fr: *£19.50*-**£19.50**.
eds: 2D 1T
aths: 3 Ensuite
(4)
ecluded period house set in nowdonia National Park with uperb views over Cardigan Bay. uxury accommodation with piano ounge & fragrant Victorian arden. Phone for brochure.

***odfor Hotel,** Sea Front, berdovey, LL35 0EA.*
arge Victorian hotel on sea front.
pen: All Year (not Xmas)
654 767475 Mr Evans
ax no: 01654 767679
ates fr: *£18.80*-**£22.50**.
eds: 1F 5D 6T 4S

***ossa Guest House,** Penrhos, berdovey, LL35 0NR.*
amily-run guest house.
pen: Mar to Oct
rades: WTB 2 Cr, High Comm, A 2 Q, Recomm
654 767545 Mr Rowley
ates fr: *£16.00*-**£20.00**.
eds: 1F 4D
aths: 4 Ensuite 1 Private
(4) (3)

***ne Trefeddian Bank,** Aberdovey, L35 0RU.*
omfortable Edwardian house. anoramic views.
pen: Mar to Oct
rades: WTB 1 Cr, High Comm
654 767487 Mrs Jones
ates fr: *£14.00*-**£15.00**.
eds: 3D 1S
aths: 1 Shared
(3)

***artref Guest House,** Aberdovey, L35 0NR.*
pacious, detached, overlooking ardigan Bay.
pen: All Year
rades: WTB 2 Cr, AA Approv
654 767273 Mr Williams
ates fr: *£17.00*-**£17.00**.
eds: 1F 3D 2T 1S
aths: 4 Private
(8)

***yddyn Rhys Farm,** Aberdovey, L35 0PG.*
reathtaking views of Dovey stuary & Cardigan Bay.
pen: All Year (not Xmas)
654 767533 Mrs Jones
ates fr: *£14.00*-**£15.00**.
eds: 2D 1S
aths: 1 Private 1 Shared
(8) (6)

Abergele

National Grid Ref: SH9477

***Dolhyfryd Lodge Hotel,** Rhuddlan Road, Abergele, LL22 7HL.*
Purpose-built, modern, very comfortable.
Open: All Year
01745 826505 Mrs Beattie
Rates fr: *£16.25*-**£27.00**.
Beds: 1F 2D 5T 2S
Baths: 10 Private
(20)

Abergynolwyn

National Grid Ref: SH6706

Railway Hotel

***Tanycoed Uchaf,** Abergynolwyn, Tywyn, LL36 9UP.*
Open: Easter to Oct
01654 782228 Mrs Pugh
Rates fr: *£13.00*-**£13.00**.
Beds: 1D 1T 1S
Baths: 1 Shared
(6)
Tanycoed is situated on the B4405 between Abergynolwyn & Dolgoch Falls. Talyllyn gauge railway runs through our land. Ideal for a walking holiday.

***Riverside Guest House,** Abergynolwyn, Tywyn, LL36 9YR.*
Homely accommodation in scenic area.
Open: All Year (not Xmas)
01654 782235 Mr Bott
Rates fr: *£13.00*-**£13.00**.
Beds: 1F 1D 1T 1S
(3) (2)

Abersoch

National Grid Ref: SH3128

***Angorfa Guest House,** Lon Sarn Bach, Abersoch, Pwllheli, LL53 7EB.*
Only the best.
Open: All Year (not Xmas)
Grades: WTB Listed
01758 712967 (also fax no)
Mrs Stanworth
Rates fr: *£13.00*.
Beds: 1F 1D 2T
Baths: 2 Private 2 Shared

***Tudor Court Hotel,** Lon Sarn Bach, Abersoch, LL53 7EB.*
A converted sea captain's residence.
Open: All Year
01758 713354 Ms Jones
Rates fr: *£20.00*-**£25.00**.
Beds: 2F 5D 3T 1S
Baths: 8 Private 2 Shared
(16)

The lowest **single** *rate is shown in* **bold.**

Arthog

National Grid Ref: SH6414

Fairbourne Hotel, Ponderosa

***Craig Wen Guest House,** Arthog, LL39 1BQ.*
Open: All Year (not Xmas)
Grades: WTB 3 Cr, Comm
01341 250482 Mrs Ameson
Rates fr: *£14.50*-**£17.00**.
Beds: 1F 3D 2T 1S
Baths: 3 Private 2 Shared
(20)
Situated in 42 acres woodland & pasture reaching down to Mawddach estuary. Ideal for walkers, mountain climbers & bird watchers. Ensuite & disabled bedrooms also available. Choice of breakfast.

***Cyfannedd Uchaf Guest House,** Arthog, LL39 1LX.*
We offer peace and tranquillity.
Open: May to Sep
Grades: WTB 1 Cr, High Comm
01341 250526 Mrs Tovey
Rates fr: *£17.00*-**£17.00**.
Beds: 2D 1T
Baths: 1 Ensuite 1 Shared
(14) (4)

Bala

National Grid Ref: SH9236

Nevaddy Cyfnod, White Lion, Bryter Inn

***Melin Meloch Guest House,** Llanfor, Bala, LL23 7DP.*
Open: Feb to Dec
Grades: WTB 2 Cr, High Comm
01678 520101
Rates fr: *£19.50*-**£23.00**.
Beds: 1F 3D 2T 2S
Baths: 4 Ensuite 2 Private 1 Shared
(5) (8)
Historic picturesque watermill & granary. Standing in lovely water gardens with mill ponds. Friendly relaxed country house atmosphere. Home cooking. Ideally situated for touring.

***Frondderw Private Hotel,** Stryd-Y-Fron, Bala, LL23 7YD.*
Period mansion in own grounds.
Open: Mar to Nov
Grades: WTB 3 Cr, Comm, AA 2 Q
01678 520301 Mr Jones
Rates fr: *£15.00*-**£15.00**.
Beds: 3F 2D 2T 2S
Baths: 4 Private 2 Shared
(10)

***Traian,** 95 Tegid Street, Bala, LL23 7BW.*
Real Welsh welcome, traditional breakfast. **Open:** All Year
Grades: WTB Listed, Comm
01678 520059 Mrs Jones
Rates fr: *£13.00*-**£13.00**.
Beds: 2F 1S **Baths:** 1 Shared

Bronwylfa Guest House, *Llandderfel, Bala, LL23 7HG.*
Large Victorian house, tranquil setting.
Open: All Year (not Xmas)
Grades: WTB 2 Cr, Deluxe, AA 3 Q, RAC High Acclaim
01678 530207 / 530395
Mrs Andrews
Rates fr: *£16.00*-**£22.00**.
Beds: 1F 2D 2T
Baths: 3 Ensuite 1 Private
(Any) (8)

Cwm Hwylfod, *Cefn-Ddwysarn, Bala, LL23 7LN.*
400-year-old farmhouse on working hill farm.
Open: All Year (not Xmas)
01678 530310 Mrs Best
Rates fr: *£14.00*-**£14.00**.
Beds: 1F 2T
Baths: 2 Shared
(2) (6)

Bangor

National Grid Ref: SH5771

Old Glan, Fat Cats

Swn Y Nant Guest House, *Caernarfon Road, Bangor, LL57 4BT.*
Open: All Year
Grades: WTB 2 Cr, Comm
01248 670792 Mr Harding
Fax no: 01248 671140
Rates fr: *£16.00*-**£17.00**.
Beds: 4F 3D 2T 1S
Baths: 3 Private 3 Shared
(30)
Modern, comfortable, converted farm buildings with ducks, geese, chickens, pigs, sheep, etc. Ideal for children. Many tame animals.

The Guest House, *32 Glynne Road, Bangor, LL57 1AN.*
Well-situated, homely & happy.
Open: All Year (not Xmas)
Grades: WTB Listed
01248 352113 Mrs Roberts
Rates fr: *£12.50*-**£12.50**.
Beds: 2D 2S **Baths:** 1 Shared

Yr Elen, *Bryn, Llandegai, Bangor, LL57 4LD.*
Bungalow, convenient Snowdonia, Anglesey, Ireland.
Open: Mar to Oct
Grades: WTB 1 Cr
01248 364591 Mrs Hughes
Rates fr: *£14.00*-**£25.00**.
Beds: 1F 1D
Baths: 1 Shared
(4)

Many rates vary according to season - the lowest are shown here.

Abbeyfield Hotel, *Tal y Bont, Bangor, LL57 3UR.*
Family-run hotel, high standard accommodation.
Open: All Year (not Xmas)
Grades: WTB 4 Cr, Comm, AA 2 St, RAC 2 St
01248 352219
Mr Newman
Fax no: 01248 362913
Rates fr: *£22.50*-**£25.00**.
Beds: 1F 2D 3T 4S
Baths: 10 Ensuite
(40)

Eryl Mor Hotel, *2 Upper Garth Road, Bangor, LL57 2SR.*
Outstanding sea & countryside views.
Open: All Year
Grades: WTB 3 Cr, High comm
01248 353789
Mr Williams
Fax no: 01248 354042
Rates fr: *£16.00*-**£19.00**.
Beds: 4F 9D 6T 5S
Baths: 16 Private 8 Shared

Goetre Isaf Farmhouse, *Caernarfon Road, Bangor, LL57 4DB.*
Imaginative farmhouse cooking. Outstanding garden.
Open: All Year
01248 364541
Mr Whowell
Fax no: 0248 364541
Rates fr: *£13.00*-**£15.00**.
Beds: 1D 2T
Baths: 1 Private 1 Shared
(12)

Barmouth

National Grid Ref: SH6115

Bryn Melyn Hotel, *Panorama Road, Barmouth, LL42 1DQ.*
Open: Feb to Nov
Grades: WTB 3 Cr, High Comm, AA 2 St, RAC 2 St
01341 280556
Mr Clay
Fax no: 01341 280276
Rates fr: *£24.00*-**£29.00**.
Beds: 2F 4D 3T
Baths: 9 Ensuite
(5) (9)
Delightful small hotel, informal atmosphere, in idyllic position on mountainside with stunning views of river, mountains & sea. Ideal for exploring all of Snowdonia.

Wavecrest Hotel, *8 Marine Parade, Barmouth, LL42 1NA.*
Sea front, licensed traditional hotel.
Open: Easter to Dec
Grades: WTB 3 Cr, High Comm, AA 2 St
01341 280330 (also fax no)
Mr & Mrs Jarman
Rates fr: *£16.00*-**£16.00**.
Beds: 4F 4D 2S
Baths: 7 Private 2 Shared
(2)

Tal-Y-Don Hotel, *High Street, Barmouth, LL42 1DL.*
Spacious rooms, good breakfasts & welcoming.
Open: All Year (not Xmas)
01341 280508
Mrs Davies
Rates fr: *£13.00*-**£20.00**.
Beds: 3F 4D 3T
Baths: 4 Ensuite 2 Shared

Lawrenny Lodge Hotel, *Barmouth, LL42 1SU.*
Family-run hotel, quiet location.
Open: Mar to Dec
Grades: WTB 3 Cr, Comm
01341 280466 Mr Barber
Rates fr: *£18.00*-**£18.00**.
Beds: 1F 4D 2T 1S
Baths: 7 Ensuite 1 Shared
(9)

The Sandpiper, *7 Marine Parade, Barmouth, LL42 1NA.*
Sea front guest house.
Open: Easter to Oct
Grades: WTB 2 Cr, High Comm
01341 280318
Mr & Mrs Palmer
Rates fr: *£13.50*-**£14.50**.
Beds: 4F 5D 2S
Baths: 6 Private 2 Shared

Plas Bach, *Glandwr, Barmouth, LL42 1TG.*
Exceptional comfortable stone-built guest house.
Open: All Year
01341 281234 Mrs Michael
Rates fr: *£25.00*-**£25.00**.
Beds: 3D
Baths: 3 Ensuite

Beddgelert

National Grid Ref: SH5948

Plas Colwyn Guest House, *Beddgelert, Caernarfon, LL55 4UY.*
Stone-built house overlooking river.
Open: All Year (not Xmas)
01766 890458
Mrs Osmond
Rates fr: *£15.00*-**£15.00**.
Beds: 2F 2D 1T 1S
Baths: 3 Ensuite 3 Shared
(5)

Bethel

National Grid Ref: SH5265

Arosfa, *Bethel, Caernarfon, LL55 1UN.*
Comfortable private house, mountain views.
Open: All Year
01248 671249
Mrs Giblin
Rates fr: *£13.00*-**£13.00**.
Beds: 1F 1D 1T
Baths: 1 Shared
(1) (5)

ethesda

ational Grid Ref: SH6266

Vaynol Arms

oys of Life Country Park, *ethesda, Bangor, LL57 4YW.*
Iodern luxury house in
nowdonia.
pen: All Year (not Xmas)
1248 602122
Irs Robinson
ates fr: *£15.00*-**£20.00**.
eds: 1F 1D 1T
aths: 2 Shared
(6)

etws-y-Coed

ational Grid Ref: SH7956

Royal Oak, Stables Bar,
y Gwyn

airy Glen Hotel, *Betws-y-Coed, L24 0SH.*
pen: Feb to Nov
rades: WTB 3 Cr, High Comm,
A 1 St, RAC 1 St
1690 710269 (also fax no)
Ir Ball
ates fr: *£20.00*.
eds: 2F 4D 3T 1S
aths: 8 Ensuite 2 Shared
(12)
amily-run 300 year old small
otel overlooking River Conwy in
ational Park amongst mountains
forest. Warm & friendly wel-
ome with home cooked menus

berconwy House, *Llanrwst Road, etws-y-Coed, LL24 0HD.*
lighly rated, comfortable, quiet,
elaxing.
pen: All Year
rades: WTB 3 Cr, High Comm,
A 4 Q, Select, RAC Acclaim
1690 710202 (also fax no)
Ir Muskus
ates fr: *£22.00*-**£25.00**.
eds: 4D 4T
aths: 8 Private
(10)

ron Celyn Guest House, *lanrwst Road, Betws-y-Coed, L24 0HD.*
ovely Victorian house. Superb
ituation.
pen: All Year
rades: WTB 3 Cr, High Comm
1690 710333
Ir & Mrs Boughton
ax no: 01690 710111
ates fr: *£18.00*-**£17.00**.
eds: 1F 2D 1T 1S
aths: 3 Ensuite 1 Shared
(8)

Fron Heulog Country House, *Betws-y-Coed, LL24 0BL.*
Open: All Year
Grades: WTB 3 Cr, High Comm
01690 710736 (also fax no)
Mr & Mrs Whittingham
Rates fr: *£18.00*-**£20.00**.
Beds: 3D 2T 1S **Baths:** 6 Ensuite
(12)
'The Country House in the Village!' Warm welcome; friendly hospitality. Snowdonia's ideal centre - tour, walk, relax. Excellent modern accommodation - comfort, warmth, style. 'More home than hotel!

Mount Pleasant, *Holyhead Road, Betws-y-Coed, LL24 0BN.*
Clean, comfortable, non-smoking Victorian house.
Open: All Year
Grades: AA 2 Q, Recomm
01690 710502
Mrs Melling
Rates fr: *£15.00*-**£18.00**.
Beds: 4D 1T
Baths: 2 Ensuite 1 Shared
(4)

Swn Y Dwr, *Pentrefelin, Betws-y-Coed, LL24 0BB.*
'Home from home'. Riverside location.
Open: All Year
01690 710648
Mrs Mcgregor
Rates fr: *£17.00*.
Beds: 2D 1T
Baths: 3 Ensuite
(4)

Argoed Guest House, *Trefriw, Betws-y-Coed, LL27.0TX.*
3 miles outside Betws, beautiful views.
Open: Mar to Oct
Grades: WTB 2 Cr
01492 640091
Mr & Mrs Booth
Rates fr: *£15.00*-**£15.00**.
Beds: 2F 2D 1T
Baths: 1 Private 1 Shared
(5)

The Ferns, *Holyhead Road, Betws-y-Coed, LL24 0AN.*
Value for money.
Open: All Year (not Xmas)
Grades: WTB 3 Cr, High Comm, AA 3 Q, Acclaim
01690 710587 (also fax no)
Mr Roobottom
Rates fr: *£18.00*-**£20.00**.
Beds: 2F 6D 2T 1S
Baths: 7 Private 2 Shared
(10) (9)

Royal Oak Farm Cottage, *Betws-y-Coed, LL24 0AH.*
Picturesque C17th farmhouse, riverside setting.
Open: All Year (not Xmas)
Grades: WTB 2 Cr
01690 710760 Mrs Houghton
Rates fr: *£15.00*-**£18.00**.
Beds: 2D 1T **Baths:** 3 Private

Bryn Bella Guest House, *Llanrwst Road, Betws-y-Coed, LL24 0HD.*
Friendly guest house overlooking village.
Open: All Year
Grades: WTB Listed, High Comm
01690 710627 Mrs Fakhri
Rates fr: *£16.00*-**£18.00**.
Beds: 2D 2T
Baths: 3 Private 1 Shared
(1) (5)

Royal Oak Farmhouse, *Betws-y-Coed, LL24 0AH.*
Old water mill in 5 acres.
Open: All Year (not Xmas)
Grades: WTB 2 Cr
01690 710427 Mrs Houghton
Rates fr: *£15.00*-**£15.00**.
Beds: 2D 1T
Baths: 1 Ensuite 2 Shared
(10)

Betws-Yn-Rhos

National Grid Ref: SH9073

Wheatsheaf Inn

The Wheatsheaf Inn, *Betws-Yn-Rhos, Abergele, LL22 8AW.*
Lovely C17th village inn/re staurant.
Open: All Year
Grades: WTB 3 Cr
01492 680218 Mr Perry
Rates fr: *£20.00*-**£20.00**.
Beds: 1F 2D 1T 1S
Baths: 5 Private
(36)

Blaenau Ffestiniog

National Grid Ref: SH7045

The Don Guest House, *High Street, Blaenau Ffestiniog, LL41 3AX.*
Large Victorian house.
Open: All Year (not Xmas)
Grades: WTB 2 Cr
01766 830403 (also fax no)
Mr Cotton
Rates fr: *£13.00*-**£18.00**.
Beds: 1F 2D 2T
Baths: 1 Ensuite 1 Shared
(3)

Afallon Guest House, *Manod Road, Blaenau Ffestiniog, LL41 4AE.*
Comfortable family-run guest house.
Open: All Year (not Xmas)
Grades: WTB 1 Cr, Comm
01766 830468 Mrs Griffiths
Rates fr: *£13.00*-**£13.00**.
Beds: 1D 1T 1S
Baths: 1 Shared
(4)

Brithdir

National Grid Ref: SH7618

***Y Goedlan,** Brithdir, Dolgellau, LL40 2RN.*
Victorian vicarage in peaceful countryside.
Open: Feb to Nov
01341 423131 Mrs Evans
Rates fr: *£15.00*-**£17.00**.
Beds: 1F 1D 1T
Baths: 1 Shared
(4)

***Llwyn Talcen,** Brithdir, Dolgellau, LL40 2RY.*
Country house in rhododendron gardens. **Open:** All Year
01341 450276 Mrs Griffiths
Rates fr: *£15.00*-**£15.00**.
Beds: 2D 1S
Baths: 1 Ensuite 1 Shared
(5)

Bryncrug

National Grid Ref: SH6003

Peniarth Arms

***Cynfal Farm,** Bryncrug, Tywyn, LL36 9RB.*
Open: All Year (not Xmas)
Grades: WTB 2 Cr, High Comm
01654 711703 Mrs Evans
Rates fr: *£16.00*-**£17.00**.
Beds: 2D 1T
Baths: 2 Ensuite 1 Private
(1) (3)
Mixed working farm, magnificently situated with panoramic views of mountains & sea. Spacious ensuite bedrooms, TV and tea/coffee facilities. Steam train runs below farm.

Caernarfon

National Grid Ref: SH4862

Prince of Wales

***Pengwern Farm,** Saron, Llanwnda, Caernarfon, LL54 5UH.*
Open: Feb to Nov
Grades: WTB 3 Cr, Deluxe, AA 5 Q, RAC Listed
01286 831500 / 0378 411780
Mr & Mrs Rowlands
Fax no: 01286 831500
Rates fr: *£20.00*-**£25.00**.
Beds: 1F 2D 1T **Baths:** 3 Private
(3)
Charming spacious farmhouse of character, beautifully situated between mountains & sea. Unobstructed views of Snowdonia. Well appointed bedrooms, all with ensuite.

***Cae Garw,** Cadnant Valley Caravan Park, Llanberis Road, Caernarfon, LL55 2DF.*
Modern, comfortable, well-equipped.
Open: All Year
01286 673196 Mrs Noon
Rates fr: *£14.00*-**£14.00**.
Beds: 1D 1T **Baths:** 1 Shared
(4)

***Princes Of Wales Hotel,** Bangor Street, Caernarfon, LL55 1AR.*
Former coaching inn - centrally located. **Open:** All Year
Grades: WTB 3 Cr
01286 673367 Ms Parry
Fax no: 01286 676610
Rates fr: *£17.50*-**£17.50**.
Beds: 3F 8D 6T 4S
Baths: 19 Private 2 Shared
(1) (6)

Capel Curig

National Grid Ref: SH7258

Cobdens Hotel

***Bryn Glo Cafe,** Capel Curig, Betws-y-Coed, LL24 0DT.*
Clean, comfortable cottage. Easy access. **Open:** All Year
Grades: WTB 1 Cr
01690 720215 Mrs Cousins
Rates fr: *£14.50*-**£16.50**.
Beds: 1F 1D 1T
Baths: 1 Private 1 Shared
(3)

***Llugwy Guest House,** Capel Curig, Betws-y-Coed, LL24 0ES.*
Centre of village, near Snowdon.
Open: All Year
Grades: WTB 1 Cr, Comm
01690 720218 Mr Davies
Rates fr: *£14.00*-**£16.50**.
Beds: 2F 2D 1T 2S
Baths: 1 Shared
(10)

***Bryn Derwen,** Capel Curig, Betws-y-Coed, LL24 0EL.*
Victorian family home. Mountain views.
Open: All Year (not Xmas)
Grades: WTB 1 Cr
01690 720312 Mrs Cousins
Rates fr: *£14.50*-**£16.50**.
Beds: 1F 1D 1T
Baths: 1 Shared
(7) (4)

***Tyn-Y-Coed Hotel,** Capel Curig, Betws-y-Coed, LL24 0EE.*
Fully licensed hotel & restaurant.
Open: All Year
01690 720331 Mr Wainwright
Rates fr: *£22.50*-**£27.00**.
Beds: 4F 6D 4T
Baths: 14 Private

Colwyn Bay

National Grid Ref: SH8678

Toad Hole

***Cabin Hill Hotel,** College Avenue, Colwyn Bay, LL28 4NT.*
Quiet residential area 150 yds promenade.
Open: All Year
Grades: AA 3 Q, RAC Acclaim
01492 544568 Mr Bransby
Rates fr: *£17.00*-**£15.00**.
Beds: 2F 5D 2T 1S
Baths: 7 Ensuite 2 Private

***Grosvenor Hotel,** 106-108 Abergele Road, Colwyn Bay, LL29 7PS.*
Stone built Victorian house.
Open: All Year (not Xmas)
Grades: WTB Listed, AA Listed, RAC Listed
01492 531586 (also fax no)
Mr Wood
Rates fr: *£17.90*-**£17.90**.
Beds: 4F 2D 4T 7S
Baths: 2 Ensuite 4 Shared
(14)

***Norbury Guest House,** 22 Hawarden Road, Colwyn Bay, LL29 8NA.*
Family-run guest house, personal attention.
Open: All Year (not Xmas)
Grades: WTB 2 Cr
01492 531520
Mr & Mrs Bates
Rates fr: *£11.50*-**£11.50**.
Beds: 4F 3S
Baths: 2 Shared

***Clevedon Hotel,** 20 Hawarden Road, Colwyn Bay, LL29 8NA.*
Large Victorian private house.
Open: All Year
Grades: WTB 1 Cr
01492 532194
Mr Roberts
Rates fr: *£11.00*-**£11.00**.
Beds: 5F 5D 3T 2S
Baths: 4 Shared
(1) (6)

***Glyndwr Hotel,** 11 Marine Road, Colwyn Bay, LL29 8PH.*
Comfortable ensuite well equipped rooms.
Open: All Year (not Xmas)
Grades: WTB 3 Cr
01492 533254 Mr Ross
Rates fr: *£17.50*-**£20.00**.
Beds: 2F 6D 2T
Baths: 7 Private 1 Shared
(10)

***Meadowcroft Hotel,** Llannerch Road East, Colwyn Bay, LL28 4DF.*
Private hotel under personal supervision.
Open: All Year (not Xmas)
01492 548375
Mr & Mrs Phillips
Rates fr: *£18.00*-**£18.00**.
Beds: 2F 2D 2T 1S
Baths: 7 Private

Conwy

National Grid Ref: SH7777

***Glan Heulog Guest House,** Llanrwst Road, Conwy, LL32 8LT.*
Victorian house near castle/town.
Open: All Year
Grades: WTB 3 Cr, AA 3 Q
01492 593845 Mr Round
Rates fr: *£13.00*-**£15.00**.
Beds: 1F 3D 2T 1S
Baths: 4 Ensuite 1 Shared
(8)

Bryn Derwen, *Woodlands, Conwy, LL32 8LT.*
A warm welcome to a gracious home.
Open: All Year (not Xmas)
01492 596134 Mrs Matthews
Rates fr: *£12.50*-**£12.50**.
Beds: 3D 1T 1S
Baths: 1 Private 3 Shared
(8)

Criccieth

National Grid Ref: SH5038

Craig Y Mor Guest House, *West Parade, Criccieth, LL52 0EN.*
Large Victorian house, tastefully upgraded. **Open:** Mar to Oct
Grades: WTB 3 Cr, High Comm
01766 522830 Mr Williamson
Rates fr: *£19.00*-**£19.00**.
Beds: 4F 2D
Baths: 6 Private
(6)

Muriau, *Criccieth, LL52 0RS.*
C17th gentleman's residence, secluded garden.
Open: Apr to Oct
Grades: WTB 3 Cr, High Comm, AA Listed
01766 522337 Mrs Thomas
Rates fr: *£15.00*-**£15.00**.
Beds: 3D 1T
Baths: 3 Ensuite 1 Shared
(8)

Mor Heli Guest House, *Min Y Mor, Criccieth, LL52 0EF.*
Large Victorian sea front.
Open: All Year (not Xmas)
01766 522802
Rates fr: *£15.00*-**£15.00**.
Beds: 2F 2D 1T 2S
Baths: 4 Private 4 Shared

Dinas-Mawddwy

National Grid Ref: SH8514

Dolbrodmaeth Inn

Buckley Pines Hotel, *Minllyn, Dinas-Mawddwy, Machynlleth, Powys, SY20 9LP.*
Country hotel recommended by Camra Real Ale.
Open: All Year (not Xmas)
Grades: WTB 3 Cr, Comm
01650 531261 Mrs Farr
Rates fr: *£17.50*-**£16.50**.
Beds: 1F 4D 5T 1S
Baths: 5 Private 2 Shared
(40)

The Dolbrodmaeth Inn, *Dinas-Mawddwy, Machynlleth, Powys, SY20 9LP.*
Tranquil riverside setting. Interesting menus.
Open: All Year
Grades: WTB 3 Cr
01650 531333 Mr & Mrs Williams
Rates fr: *£15.00*-**£20.00**.
Beds: 1F 3D 3T
Baths: 5 Ensuite 2 Shared

Dolgellau

National Grid Ref: SH7217

Cross Foxes Inn, Dylanwad Da, The George, Royal Ship

Ivy House, *Finsbury Square, Dolgellau, LL40 1RF.*
Open: All Year
Grades: WTB 3 Cr, Comm
01341 422535 Mrs Bamford
Fax no: 01341 422689
Rates fr: *£18.00*-**£20.00**.
Beds: 1F 3D 2T
Baths: 3 Private 3 Shared
Attractive country town accommodation & licensed restaurant with a welcoming atmosphere & good homemade food. All rooms have TV & tea/coffee making facilities.

Gwanas Farm, *Dolgellau, LL40 2SH.*
Spacious Georgian farmhouse, sheep farm. Also self-catering available.
Open: All Year (not Xmas)
Grades: WTB 1 Cr, Comm
01341 422624 (also fax no)
Mrs Evans
Rates fr: *£15.00*-**£17.00**.
Beds: 1F 1D 1T **Baths:** 2 Shared
(8)

Arosfyr Farm, *Penycefn Road, Dolgellau, LL40 2YP.*
Homely farmhouse, panoramic mountainous views.
Open: All Year (not Xmas)
Grades: WTB Listed
01341 422355 Mr Skeel Jones
Rates fr: *£14.00*-**£18.00**.
Beds: 1F 1D 1T

Penbryn Croft, *Cader Road, Dolgellau, LL40 1RN.*
Residence of historical interest.
Open: All Year (not Xmas)
01341 422815 Mrs Jones
Rates fr: *£15.00*-**£18.00**.
Beds: 3D 3T

Glyn Farm House, *Dolgellau, LL40 1YA.*
Farmhouse overlooking picturesque Mawddach Estuary.
Open: Easter to Nov
Grades: WTB 2 Cr, AA 2 Q, RAC Listed
01341 422286 Mrs Price
Rates fr: *£14.50*-**£17.50**.
Beds: 3D 1T 1S
Baths: 1 Private 1 Shared
(6)

National Grid References are for villages, towns and cities - *not* for individual houses.

Dolygader Guest House, *Barmouth Road, Dolgellau, LL40 2YT.*
Comfortable well-established family business.
Open: All Year
01341 422379 Mrs Davies
Rates fr: *£15.00*-**£15.00**.
Beds: 2D 1T
Baths: 1 Shared
(4)

Bryn Rodyn Guest House, *Maescaled, Dolgellau, LL40 1UG.*
Secluded C17th Welsh longhouse.
Open: All Year
Grades: WTB 1 Cr, Comm
01341 423470 Mr Jones
Rates fr: *£16.00*-**£20.00**.
Beds: 1D 2T
Baths: 1 Shared
(4)

Esgair Wen Newydd, *Garreg Feurig, Llanfachreth Road, Dolgellau, LL40 2YA.*
Bungalow, mountain views. High standards.
Open: All Year (not Xmas)
Grades: WTB Listed, High Comm
01341 423952 Mrs Westwood
Rates fr: *£16.50*-**£18.50**.
Beds: 2D 1T
Baths: 1 Shared
(3) (3)

Dolwyddelan

National Grid Ref: SH7352

Dolwyddelan Pub

Eirianfa Guest House, *15-16 Castle Road, Dolwyddelan, LL25 0NX.*
Comfortable guest house, good food.
Open: All Year (not Xmas)
Grades: WTB 3 Cr, Approv
01690 750360 (also fax no)
Mrs Salt
Rates fr: *£12.00*-**£20.00**.
Beds: 2D 1T
Baths: 3 Private
(12)

Bryn Tirion Farm, *Dolwyddelan, Conwy, LL25 0JD.*
C12th Dolwyddelan Castle - 100 yds on the farm, beautiful valley.
Open: All Year (not Xmas, Boxing Day, New year)
Grades: WTB Listed
01690 750366 Mrs Price.
Rates fr: *£15.00*.
Beds: 1F 1D 1T
Baths: 1 Shared

Elens Castle Hotel, *Dolwyddelan, LL25 0EJ.*
C18th coaching inn.
Open: All Year
Grades: WTB 3 Cr, AA 2 St
01690 750207 Mr Ratcliff
Rates fr: *£12.00*-**£12.00**.
Beds: 1F 5D 2T 1S
Baths: 1 Shared
(40)

All details shown are as supplied by B&B owners in Autumn 1996.

Dyffryn Ardudwy

National Grid Ref: SH6022

***Byrdir,** Dyffryn Ardudwy, LL44 2EA.*
Traditional Welsh stone farmhouse.
Open: Easter to Sep
01341 247200 Mrs Jones
Rates fr: *£16.50*-**£16.50**.
Beds: 2F 2D 1T 1S
Baths: 4 Ensuite 1 Private

***Ystumgwern Hall Farm,** Dyffryn Ardudwy, LL44 2DD.*
C16th luxury farmhouse, barn conversion.
Open: All Year
01341 247249 Mrs Williams
Fax no: 01341 247171
Rates fr: *£18.00*-**£20.00**.
Beds: 4F 1D 1T 1S
Baths: 7 Ensuite

Ffestiniog

National Grid Ref: SH7041

The Grapes (Maentwrog)

***Tyddyn Pant Glas,** Ffestiniog, Blaenau Ffestiniog, LL41 4PU.*
Self-contained annexe - superb views.
Open: All Year (not Xmas)
Grades: WTB 2 Cr
01766 762442 Mrs Langdale-Pope
Rates fr: *£15.00*-**£20.00**.
Beds: 1D
Baths: 1 Ensuite

***Morannedd Guest House,** Blaenau Road, Ffestiniog, Blaenau Ffestiniog, LL41 4LG.*
Comfortable guest house with mountain views.
Open: All Year
Grades: WTB 2 Cr, Comm
01766 762734 (also fax no)
Mrs Lethbridge
Rates fr: *£17.00*-**£16.50**.
Beds: 1F 1D 2T 1S
Baths: 4 Private 1 Shared

All rates are subject to alteration at the owners' discretion.

Friog

National Grid Ref: SH6112

Fairbourne

***Sea View Guest House,** Friog, Fairbourne, LL38 2NX.*
Georgian house in peaceful area.
Open: All Year
Grades: WTB 3 Cr, Comm
01341 250388 Mr Andrews
Rates fr: *£15.50*-**£15.50**.
Beds: 4F 3D 1T
Baths: 7 Private 1 Shared

***Einion House,** Friog, Fairbourne, LL38 2NX.*
Comfortable C18th licensed guest house.
Open: All Year (not Xmas)
01341 250644 Mr Waterhouse
Rates fr: *£15.50*-**£15.50**.
Beds: 4D 2T 1S
Baths: 6 Private 1 Shared

Frongoch

National Grid Ref: SH9039

Plas Yn Dre

***Ferm Fron-Goch,** Frongoch, Bala, LL23 7NT.*
Beautiful historic farmhouse.
Open: All Year (not Xmas)
Grades: WTB 3 Cr, High Comm
01678 520483 Mrs Davies
Rates fr: *£13.00*.
Beds: 1D 2T
Baths: 3 Private

***Rhydydefaid Farm,** Frongoch, Bala, LL23 7NT.*
Traditional Welsh stone farmhouse.
Open: All Year (not Xmas)
Grades: WTB 2 Cr, High Comm
01678 520456 (also fax no)
Mrs Davies
Rates fr: *£15.00*-**£16.00**.
Beds: 2D 1T
Baths: 2 Ensuite 1 Shared

Ganllwyd

National Grid Ref: SN7223

***Tyn Y Groes Hotel,** Ganllwyd, Dolgellau, LL40 2NH.*
Former C16th coaching inn.
Open: All Year
Grades: WTB 3 Cr, RAC Acclaim
01341 440275 Mr & Mrs Ruthwell
Rates fr: *£21.50*-**£21.00**.
Beds: 1F 4D 1T 2S
Baths: 8 Private

The lowest **single** *rate is shown in* **bold.**

Garndolbenmaen

National Grid Ref: SH4944

***Cefn Uchaf Farm Guest House,** Garndolbenmaen, Porthmadog, LL51 9PJ.*
Comfortable, large farm guest house.
Open: Mar to Nov
01766 530239 Mr & Mrs Easton
Rates fr: *£15.00*-**£15.00**.
Beds: 5F 1D 2T
Baths: 3 Private 2 Shared

Gellilydan

National Grid Ref: SH6839

Bryn Arms

***Gwynfryn,** Gellilydan, Blaenau Ffestiniog, LL41 4EA.*
Detached comfortable, clean, quiet period house.
Open: All Year (not Xmas)
Grades: WTB 1 Cr, Comm
01766 590225 Mrs Jones
Rates fr: *£13.00*-**£13.00**.
Beds: 1F 1D 1S
Baths: 1 Shared

***Tyddyn Du Farm,** Gellilydan, Blaenau Ffestiniog, LL41 4RB.*
Enchanting C17th farmhouse, delicious cooking.
Open: All Year (not Xmas)
01766 590281 Mrs Williams
Rates fr: *£16.00*.
Beds: 1F 2D 1T 1S
Baths: 3 Private 2 Shared

Harlech

National Grid Ref: SH5831

***Lion Hotel,** Harlech, LL46 2SG.*
2 bars & restaurant. Double rooms ensuite.
Open: All Year
Grades: WTB 3 Cr, Comm
01766 780731 Mr Morris
Rates fr: *£18.00*-**£20.00**.
Beds: 4D 1T 1S
Baths: 5 Private

***Tyddyn Y Gwynt,** Harlech, LL46 2TH.*
Central for beach & countryside.
Open: All Year
Grades: WTB 1 Cr
01766 780298 Mrs Jones
Rates fr: *£14.50*-**£14.50**.
Beds: 1F 1T **Baths:** 1 Shared

***Aris Guest House,** Harlech, LL46 2SL.*
Wonderful views, food & welcome.
Open: All Year
Grades: WTB 2 Cr
01766 780409 Mr Owens
Rates fr: *£15.00*-**£15.00**.
Beds: 1F 1D 1T 1S
Baths: 1 Ensuite 1 Shared

Castle Cottage Hotel, *Pen Llech, Harlech, LL46 2YL.*
Comfortable C16th hotel.
Open: March to Jan
Grades: WTB 3 Cr, High Comm, AA 4 Q, RAC High Acclaim
01766 780479 Mr Roberts
Rates fr: *£25.00*-**£23.00**.
Beds: 3D 1T 2S
Baths: 4 Private 2 Shared

Llanaber

National Grid Ref: SH6017

Fronoleu Hall, *Llanaber Road, Llanaber, Barmouth, LL42 1YT.*
Well-appointed coastal private house.
Open: Easter to Oct
01341 280491
Mrs Amison
Rates fr: *£15.00*-**£16.00**.
Beds: 1F 2D 1T 1S
Baths: 2 Ensuite 3 Shared
(8)

Llanbedr

National Grid Ref: SH5826

Gwynfryn Farm, *Llanbedr, LL45 2NY.*
C17th farmhouse in Snowdonia.
Open: Easter to Oct
01341 241381 Mrs Howie
Rates fr: *£15.00*-**£17.00**.
Beds: 1F 1D 1T 1S
Baths: 2 Private
(4)

Llanbedr Y Cennin

National Grid Ref: SH7569

Ye Olde Bull Inn

Church House, *Llanbedr Y Cennin, Conwy Valley, Conwy, LL32 8JB.*
Lovely beamed C16th cottage.
Open: All Year
Grades: WTB 1 Cr, High Comm
01492 660521 Mrs Pavey
Rates fr: *£17.00*-**£20.00**.
Beds: 2D **Baths:** 1 Shared
(3)

Llanberis

National Grid Ref: SH5760

Gwynedd Hotel

Beech Bank Guest House, *High Street, Llanberis, Caernarfon, LL55 4EN.*
Open: All Year (not Xmas)
Grades: WTB 1 Cr
01286 870414 Mrs Watson
Rates fr: *£14.00*-**£16.00**.
Beds: 1F 2D 1T
Baths: 1 Shared
(6)
Situated at quiet end of village, overlooking lakes & mountains. Walking distance to Snowdon Mountain Railway. All rooms H & C and CH.

Gwynedd Hotel, *Llanberis, LL55 4SU.*
Open: All Year
Grades: WTB 3 Cr, Comm
01286 870203 Mr Banks
Fax no: 01286 871636
Rates fr: *£16.00*-**£22.00**.
Beds: 3F 4D 2T 2S
Baths: 10 Private 1 Shared
(1)
Set at the foot of Snowdon, opposite Lake Padarn, offering magnificent surroundings for watersports, walks, fishing & picnics. Cosy bar & elegant restaurant offering a variety of menus.

Glyn Afon Hotel, *High Street, Llanberis, Caernarfon, LL55 4HA.*
Family-run hotel, licensed restaurant.
Open: All Year
01286 872528
Mrs Litton
Rates fr: *£15.00*-**£16.00**.
Beds: 2F 4D 2T
Baths: 2 Private 2 Shared
(4)

Mount Pleasant Hotel, *High Street, Llanberis, Caernarfon, LL55 4HA.*
Friendly, family-run, cosy bar.
Open: All Year
Grades: WTB 2 Cr
01286 870395 (also fax no)
Mrs Waterton
Rates fr: *£14.50*-**£14.50**.
Beds: 2F 3D 2S
Baths: 1 Ensuite 2 Shared
(8)

Gallt Y Glyn Hotel, *Llanberis, Caernarfon, LL55 4EL.*
Comfortable hotel magnificent views.
Open: All Year (not Xmas)
Grades: WTB 2 Cr, AA 1 St
01286 870370
Mrs Rayment
Rates fr: *£16.50*-**£18.50**.
Beds: 1F 5D 3T
Baths: 5 Ensuite 2 Shared
(12)

Alpine Lodge Hotel, *1 High Street, Llanberis, Caernarfon, LL55 4EN.*
All modern facilities, licensed, credit cards.
Open: All Year
Grades: WTB 3 Cr, Comm, AA 3 Q
01286 870294 (also fax no)
Mr Davies
Rates fr: *£18.50*-**£29.00**.
Beds: 2F 2D 2T
Baths: 2 Private
(2) (10)

Right on the border? Look at the neighbouring county, too

Llandanwg

National Grid Ref: SH5628

Llanbeds

Glan-Y-Gors, *Llandanwg, Harlech, LL46 2SD.*
Comfortable guest house near beach.
Open: All Year
Grades: WTB 1 Cr, High Comm
01341 241410 Mrs Evans
Rates fr: *£12.00*-**£12.50**.
Beds: 1F 1D 1T
Baths: 1 Shared
(6)

Llandegai

National Grid Ref: SH5970

Nant Y Fedw, *2 Tre Felin, Llandegai, Bangor, LL57 4LH.*
Charming beamed country cottage.
Open: All Year (not Xmas)
01248 351683 Mrs Davies
Rates fr: *£15.00*-**£18.00**.
Beds: 1F 1D 1T
Baths: 2 Private
(3)

Llandudno

National Grid Ref: SH7881

Hilary Hotel, *32 St Davids Road, Llandudno, LL30 2UL.*
Open: Apr to Nov
Grades: WTB 3 Cr, High Comm
01492 875623
Mr & Mrs Fisher
Rates fr: *£15.00*-**£20.00**.
Beds: 4D 2T 1S
Baths: 7 Ensuite
(4)
A spotlessly clean 'no-smoking' small hotel catering for the over 25s. Set in one of Llandudno's loveliest areas. Convenient for shops, restaurants, promenades, stations.

Hollybank Hotel, *9 St Davids Place, Llandudno, LL30 2UL.*
Charming Edwardian non-smoking guest house.
Open: Easter to Oct
Grades: WTB 3 Cr, High Comm, AA 4 Q, Select
01492 878521 / 01244 674920
Mrs Antrobus
Rates fr: *£19.00*-**£24.00**.
Beds: 2F 3D 2T
Baths: 7 Ensuite
(4)

High season, bank holidays and special events mean low availability *anywhere*.

St Hilary Hotel, *Promenade, Llandudno, LL30 1BG.*
Open: Feb to Nov
Grades: WTB 3 Cr, High Comm, AA 3 Q, RAC Acclaim
01492 875551 Mr Probert
Rates fr: *£15.00*-**£15.00**.
Beds: 4F 4D 3T
Baths: 8 Private 3 Shared
Situated on Llandudno's main promenade overlooking the bay and Great Orme headland. Offering excellent accommodation & great value for money. Brochure/tariff available on request.

Rose Tor Hotel, *120/124 Upper Mostyn Street, Llandudno, LL30 2SW.*
Centrally situated, beautifully furnished hotel.
Open: All Year (not Xmas)
Grades: WTB 4 Cr, High Comm, AA 2 St
01492 870433 Mrs Cotton
Rates fr: *£19.75*-**£22.50**.
Beds: 3F 20D 1T
Baths: 24 Ensuite

Plas Madoc Private Hotel, *60 Church Walks, Llandudno, LL30 2HL.*
Open: Easter to Oct
Grades: WTB 3 Cr
01492 876514 Mrs Lawrence
Rates fr: *£19.00*-**£19.00**.
Beds: 3D 2T 1S **Baths:** 6 Ensuite
(5)
A homely 'no-smoking' hotel, run by the Lawrence family accommodating only adults, assuring you of a high standard of service. Close to town centre.

Karden Hotel, *16 Charlton Street, Llandudno, LL30 2AA.*
Comfortable caring hotel. Ideally situated.
Open: All Year
Grades: WTB 2 Cr, Comm, RAC Listed
01492 879347 Mrs Steward
Rates fr: *£13.00*-**£13.00**.
Beds: 4F 4D 2S **Baths:** 4 Private

Oakwood Hotel, *21 St Davids Road, Llandudno, LL30 2UH.*
Value for money our priority.
Open: All Year
Grades: WTB 2 Cr, High Comm
01492 879208 (also fax no)
Mrs Cockburn
Rates fr: *£13.50*-**£13.50**.
Beds: 3F 3D 3T 1S
Baths: 3 Private 2 Shared

White Lodge Hotel, *Central Promenade, Llandudno, LL30 1AT.*
Victorian seafront luxury hotel.
Open: All Year
Grades: WTB 3 Cr, High Comm, AA 2 St, RAC 2 St
01492 877713 Mr Rigby
Rates fr: *£21.50*-**£27.00**.
Beds: 4F 5D 3T **Baths:** 12 Private
(4) (10)

Bringing children with you? Always ask for any special rates.

Epperstone Hotel, *15 Abbey Road, Llandudno, LL30 2EE.*
Highly Commended, superb value for money.
Open: Feb to Dec
Grades: WTB 4 Cr, Deluxe, AA 1 St, RAC 1 St
01492 878746 Mr & Mrs Drew
Fax no: 01492 871223
Rates fr: *£25.00*-**£25.00**.
Beds: 5F 2T 1S **Baths:** 8 Private
(0) (8)

Westdale Hotel, *37 Abbey Road, Llandudno, LL30 2EH.*
Friendly, family-run private hotel.
Open: All Year (not Xmas)
Grades: WTB 2 Cr, High CommRAC Listed
01492 877996
Rates fr: *£15.50*-**£15.50**.
Beds: 5F 4D 1T 2S
Baths: 3 Ensuite 2 Shared
(4)

Llanfachreth

National Grid Ref: SH7522

Ty'ny Groes (Ganllwyd)

Heulwen, *Llanfachreth, Dolgellau, LL40 2UT.*
Large, comfortable, modern bungalow. **Open:** Easter to Oct
Grades: WTB 2 Cr
01341 423085 (also fax no)
Mrs Watts
Rates fr: *£14.50*-**£16.00**.
Beds: 2D 1T
Baths: 2 Private 1 Shared
(4)

Llanfaglan

National Grid Ref: SH4760

Harp Inn (Llandwrog)

The White House, *Llanfaglan, Caernarfon, LL54 5RA.*
Quiet country house, magnificent views.
Open: Mar to Nov
Grades: WTB 2 Cr, High Comm
01286 673003 Mr Bayles
Rates fr: *£17.50*-**£20.00**.
Beds: 2D 3T
Baths: 3 Ensuite 2 Private
(8)

All details shown are as supplied by B&B owners in Autumn 1996.

Llanfair

National Grid Ref: SH5729

Llew Glas (Llanbedr)

Ty Mawr Guest House, *Llanfair, Harlech, LL46 2SA.*
Open: All Year (not Xmas)
01766 780446 Mrs Jarvis
Rates fr: *£13.50*-**£16.00**.
Beds: 1F 1D 1T
Baths: 1 Private 1 Shared
(8)
A delightful C16th stone house with 2 detached self-catering cottages set in own grounds overlooking Cardigan Bay. Guest lounge, gardens & warm welcome.

Llanfairfechan

National Grid Ref: SH6874

The Towers, *Promenade, Llanfairfechan, LL33 0DA.*
Magnificent old Victorian manor-house.
Open: All Year (not Xmas)
01248 680012 Mrs Goodey
Rates fr: *£17.50*-**£20.00**.
Beds: 2F 2D 1T
Baths: 2 Private
(8)

Llanfor

National Grid Ref: SH9336

Melin Meloch Guest House, *Llanfor, Bala, LL23 7DP.*
Historic picturesque watermill & granary.
Open: Feb to Dec
Grades: WTB 2 Cr, High Comm
01678 520101
Rates fr: *£19.50*-**£23.00**.
Beds: 1F 3D 2T 2S
Baths: 4 Ensuite 2 Private 1 Shared
(5) (8)

Llanrug

National Grid Ref: SH5462

Lakeside, *Llanrug, Caernarfon, LL55 4ED.*
Secluded country home, private lake.
Open: All Year
01286 870065 Mrs Kane
Rates fr: *£18.00*-**£25.00**.
Beds: 1F 1D 1T
Baths: 1 Private 1 Shared
(3)

Llanrwst

National Grid Ref: SH8061

Bron Eirian, *Town Hill, Llanrwst, LL26 0NF.*
Victorian house in elevated position.
Open: All Year
01492 641741 Mrs Gibson
Rates fr: *£16.00*-**£20.00**.
Beds: 2D 1T
Baths: 3 Private
(10) (5)

Bodnant Caravan Park, *Nebo Road, Llanrwst, LL26 0SD.*
Comfortable oak-beamed farmhouse B&B.
Open: All Year (not Xmas)
01492 640248 Mrs Kerry-Jenkins
Rates fr: *£12.50*-**£12.50**.
Beds: 1D 2S **Baths:** 1 Shared

Llwyngwril

National Grid Ref: SH5909

Pentre Bach Guest House, *Llwyngwril, Dolgellau, LL37 2JU.*
Mid Wales Cook of Year.
Open: All Year (not Xmas)
Grades: WTB 3 Cr, High Comm
01341 250294 Mr & Mrs Smyth
Fax no: 01341 250885
Rates fr: *£19.00*-**£19.00**.
Beds: 2D 1T
Baths: 3 Ensuite
(4)

Bryn Y Mor Guest House, *Fairbourne Road, Llwyngwril, LL37 2JQ.*
Victorian house overlooking sea.
Open: Easter to Nov
01341 250043 Mrs Webb
Rates fr: *£15.00*.
Beds: 1F 1D 1T
Baths: 3 Ensuite
(6)

Nant Peris

National Grid Ref: SH6058

Vaynol Arms

3 Gwastadnant, *Nant Peris, Caernarfon, LL55 4UL.*
Friendly welcome in magnificent scenery.
Open: All Year
Grades: WTB Listed
01286 870356 Mr Cumberton
Rates fr: *£13.00*-**£13.00**.
Beds: 3D 1T 1S
Baths: 1 Shared
(16)

Nantgwynant

National Grid Ref: SH6250

Pen-Y-Gwryd Hotel, *Nantgwynant, Caernarfon, LL55 4NT.*
The home of British mountaineering.
Open: Jan to Nov
Grades: WTB 2 St
01286 870211 Mrs Pullee
Rates fr: *£20.00*-**£20.00**.
Beds: 1F 10D 6T 1S
Baths: 5 Ensuite 1 Shared

Penhelig

National Grid Ref: SN6368

Maybank Hotel & Restaurant, *4 Penhelig, Penhelig, Aberdovey, LL35 0PT.*
Recommended by leading good food.
Open: 14th Feb to 2nd Jan
01654 767500 Mr Massey
Rates fr: *£20.00*-**£25.00**.
Beds: 1F 2D 2T
Baths: 5 Ensuite 1 Private

Penmachno

National Grid Ref: SH7950

Ty Coch Farm, *Penmachno, Betws-y-Coed, LL25 0HJ.*
Modern, comfortable farmhouse, good food.
Open: All Year (not Xmas)
Grades: WTB 3 Cr
01690 760248 Mrs Morris
Rates fr: *£16.00*-**£18.00**.
Beds: 2F 2D
Baths: 4 Ensuite

Penmachno Hall Hotel, *Penmachno, Betws-y-Coed, LL24 0PU.*
Former rectory in lovely valley.
Open: All Year (not Xmas)
Grades: WTB 3 Cr, High Comm, AA 4 Q, Select, RAC Acclaim
01690 760207 Mr Cutler
Rates fr: *£25.00*-**£30.00**.
Beds: 1D 3T
Baths: 4 Private
(20)

Pennal

National Grid Ref: SH6900

Gogarth Hall Farm, *Pennal, Machynlleth, Powys, SY20 9LB.*
Enchanting farmhouse with panoramic views.
Open: All Year
Grades: WTB 3 Cr, High Comm
01654 791235 (also fax no)
Mrs Breese
Rates fr: *£12.50*-**£16.00**.
Beds: 1F 1D
Baths: 2 Ensuite 1 Private
(6)

Pentir

National Grid Ref: SH5667

Rainbow Court Guest House, *Village Square, Pentir, Bangor, LL57 4UY.*
Delighful converted village store.
Open: All Year (not Xmas)
Grades: WTB 3 Cr
01248 353099
Mrs Lorrimer Riley
Rates fr: *£13.50*-**£18.50**.
Beds: 1F 1D 1T
(3)

Tros Y Waun Farmhouse, *Pentir, Bangor, LL57 4EF.*
Modern / old working farmhouse.
Open: All Year
01248 364448 Mrs Price
Rates fr: *£12.50*-**£12.50**.
Beds: 1F 1D 1T 1S
Baths: 1 Private 1 Shared

Pentrefoelas

National Grid Ref: SH8751

Geler Arms, Ty Gwyn (Betws-y-Coed)

Maesgwyn Farm, *Pentrefoelas, Betws-Y-Coed, LL24 0LR.*
C17th farmhouse.
Open: Easter to Nov
Grades: WTB Listed, High Comm
01690 770668 Ms Jones
Rates fr: *£15.50*-**£16.00**.
Beds: 1F 1D **Baths:** 1 Private

Porthmadog

National Grid Ref: SH5638

35 Madog Street, *Porthmadog, LL49 9BU.*
Modern terraced house.
Open: All Year (not Xmas)
01766 512843 Mrs Skellern
Rates fr: *£12.00*-**£12.00**.
Beds: 1F 1D 1T 1S
Baths: 2 Shared
(2)

Pwllheli

National Grid Ref: SH3735

Victoria Hotel

Seahaven Hotel, *West End Parade, Pwllheli, LL53 5PN.*
Seafront location.
Open: All Year (not Xmas)
Grades: AA 1 St
01758 612572 Mr Theakston
Rates fr: *£17.00*-**£21.00**.
Beds: 3F 6D 2T 2S
Baths: 5 Private 2 Shared
(3)

Llys Gwyrfai Guest House, *14 West End Parade, Pwllheli, LL53 5PN.*
Comfortable, friendly, Victorian seafront house.
Open: All Year (not Xmas)
Grades: WTB 3 Cr
01758 614877 (also fax no)
Mrs Thomas
Rates fr: *£16.00*-**£17.00**.
Beds: 2D 1T
Baths: 3 Private

Yoke House Farm, Pwllheli,
LL53 5TY.
Attractive Georgian farmhouse.
Open: Easter to Oct
01758 612621
Rates fr: *£16.00*-**£16.00**.
Beds: 1D 1T
Baths: 1 Shared
(10) (5)

Rhos-on-Sea

National Grid Ref: SH8381

Ship Hotel, Nino's, Toad Hall

Sunnyside, 146 Dinerth Road, Rhos on Sea, Colwyn Bay, LL28 4YF.
Open: Easter to Nov
01492 544048 Mrs Pryce
Rates fr: *£13.00*-**£13.00**.
Beds: 1D 1T
Baths: 1 Shared
Central for beaches & mountains, situated between Llandudno & Colwyn Bay. A warm welcome, good food & comfy beds. Phone for details.

National Grid Ref: SH8678
Sunnydowns Hotel, 66 Abbey Road, Rnos-On-Sea, Conwy, LL28 4NU.
Comfortable family-run hotel.
Open: All Year
Grades: WTB 4 Cr, Comm
01492 544256 Mr Willington
Fax no: 01492-543223
Rates fr: *£20.00*-**£25.00**.
Beds: 3F 5D 5T 2S
Baths: 15 Ensuite
(10)

Rhostryfan

National Grid Ref: SH4957

Peniarth Arms (Bryncrug)

Bodowen, Rhoslefain, Tywyn, LL36 9SF.
Old stone house, beautiful views.
Open: Easter to Oct
Grades: WTB 1 Cr, High Comm
01654 710996 Mrs Bowles
Rates fr: *£13.50*-**£17.50**.
Beds: 1D 1T
Baths: 1 Shared
(5) (2)

The lowest **single** *rate is shown in* **bold.**

Hafoty, Rhostryfan, Caernarfon, LL54 7PH.
Awarded 'Best Accommodation in Wales'.
Open: Feb to Nov
01286 830144
Mrs Davies
Rates fr: *£20.00*-**£25.00**.
Beds: 1F 3D 1T
Baths: 4 Ensuite
(10)

Rowen

National Grid Ref: SH7571

Gwern Borter Country Manor, Rowen, Conwy, LL32 8YL.
Idyllic mountain setting, beautiful grounds.
Open: All Year
01492 650360
Mr Powell
Rates fr: *£17.00*-**£24.00**.
Beds: 1F 2D
Baths: 3 Private
(20)

Sarnau

National Grid Ref: SH9739

Penybryn, Sarnau, Bala, LL23 7LH.
'Home-from-home' in beautiful Welsh countryside.
Open: All Year
01678 530297
Mr Jones
Rates fr: *£13.00*-**£15.00**.
Beds: 4D 2T 1S
Baths: 2 Private 2 Shared
(3) (8)

Saron

National Grid Ref: SH4658

Pengwern Farm, Saron, Llanwnda, Caernarfon, LL54 5UH.
Charming spacious farmhouse of character.
Open: Feb to Nov
Grades: WTB 3 Cr, Deluxe, AA 5 Q, RAC Listed
01286 831500 / 0378 411780
Mr & Mrs Rowlands
Fax no: 01286 831500
Rates fr: *£20.00*-**£25.00**.
Beds: 1F 2D 1T
Baths: 3 Private
(3)

Tal y Bont (Conwy)

National Grid Ref: SH7668

Lodge Motel, Tal y Bont (Conwy), Conwy, LL32 8SD.
Modern rural hotel, family-run.
Open: All Year
01492 660766
Mrs Baldon
Rates fr: *£25.00*-**£33.95**.
Beds: 10D
Baths: 10 Private

Talsarnau

National Grid Ref: SH6135

Estuary Motel Y Traeth, Talsarnau, LL47 6TA.
Purpose-built family-run motel.
Open: All Year
01766 771155 Mrs Crowley
Rates fr: *£19.00*-**£23.00**.
Beds: 2F 4D 2T 2S
Baths: 10 Shared
(16) (40)

Talyllyn

National Grid Ref: SH7109

Dolffanog Fach, Talyllyn, Tywyn, LL36 9AJ.
Open: All Year (not Xmas)
Grades: WTB 2 Cr, High Comm
01654 761235 (also fax no)
Mrs Pughe
Rates fr: *£17.00*-**£18.00**.
Beds: 1F 1D 1T
Baths: 3 Ensuite
(8)
Stone-built with modern conveniences situated at the foot of Cader Idris with lovely views of Talyllyn Lake. Warm Welsh welcome with good home cooking.

Dolffanog Fawr, Talyllyn, Tywyn, LL36 9AJ.
Open: All Year (not Xmas)
Grades: WTB 3 Cr, High Comm, AA 4 Q, Select
01654 761247
Mr & Mrs Coulter
Rates fr: *£21.00*-**£36.00**.
Beds: 2D 2T
Baths: 4 Ensuite
(6)
Breathtaking scenery with views to lake & mountains. Excellent home cooking. Beautifully furnished ensuite rooms with all facilities & many extras for your comfort.

Trawsfynydd

National Grid Ref: SH7035

Bryn Celynog Farm, Cwmprysor, Trawsfynydd, Blaenau Ffestiniog, LL41 4TR.
Homely accomodation on working farm.
Open: All Year
Grades: WTB 2 Cr, High Comm
01766 540378 (also fax no)
Mrs Hughes
Rates fr: *£17.00*-**£17.00**.
Beds: 1F 1D 1T
Baths: 1 Ensuite 1 Shared
(4)

All rates are subject to alteration at the owners' discretion.

Old Mill Farm House, *Fron Oleu, Trawsfynydd, Blaenau Ffestiniog, LL41 4UN.*
Ensuite lake & mountain views.
Open: All Year
Grades: WTB 2 Cr
01766 540397 (also fax no)
Mrs Bain
Rates fr: *£19.00*-**£20.00**.
Beds: 3F 2D 2T
Baths: 7 Ensuite
(0) (10)

Trefriw

National Grid Ref: SH7863

Argoed Guest House, *Trefriw, Betws y Coed, LL27 0TX.*
3 miles outside Betws, beautiful views.
Open: Mar to Oct
Grades: WTB 2 Cr
01492 640091
Mr & Mrs Booth
Rates fr: *£15.00*-**£15.00**.
Beds: 2F 2D 1T
Baths: 1 Private 1 Shared
(5)

Crafnant House, *Trefriw, LL27 0JH.*
100-year-old Victorian residence in Conwy Valley.
Open: All Year
01492 640809 Mr Eaton
Rates fr: *£16.00*-**£17.50**.
Beds: 1F 3D 1T **Baths:** 5 Private
(8)

Tywyn

National Grid Ref: SH5800

Peniarth Arms

Hendy Farm, *Tywyn, LL36 9RU.*
Large comfortable farmhouse near town.
Open: All Year (not Xmas)
Grades: WTB 2 Cr, High Comm
01654 710457 Mrs Lloyd -Jones
Rates fr: *£14.75*-**£17.50**.
Beds: 2D 1T
Baths: 2 Ensuite 1 Private

The Arthur Hotel, *6 Marine Parade, Tywyn, LL36 0DE.*
Comfortable family hotel, facing sea. **Open:** Feb to Dec
Grades: WTB 3 Cr, Comm
01654 712146 Mr Harrison
Rates fr: *£21.00*-**£24.00**.
Beds: 3D 3T 2S
Baths: 8 Private

Monfa Guest House, *Pier Road, Tywyn, LL36 0AU.*
Large Victorian house near sea.
Open: Easter to Sep
01654 710858 Mr Bray
Rates fr: *£15.00*-**£15.00**.
Beds: 1F 3D 1T **Baths:** 5 Private
(8)

Ynys

National Grid Ref: SH5935

Gwrach Ynys, *Ynys, Talsarnau, LL47 6TS.*
Deluxe accommodation. Cater for vegetarians.
Open: Apr to Oct
Grades: WTB 3 Cr, Deluxe
01766 780742 Mrs Williams
Fax no: 01766 781199
Rates fr: *£22.00*-**£22.00**.
Beds: 3F 2D 1T 1S
Baths: 6 Private 1 Shared
(8)

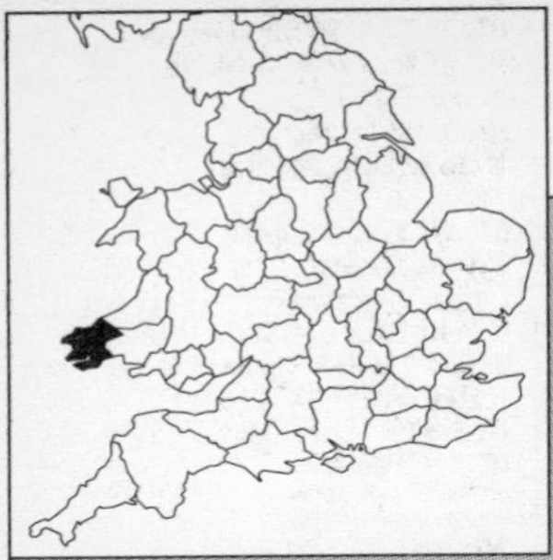

Pembrokeshire

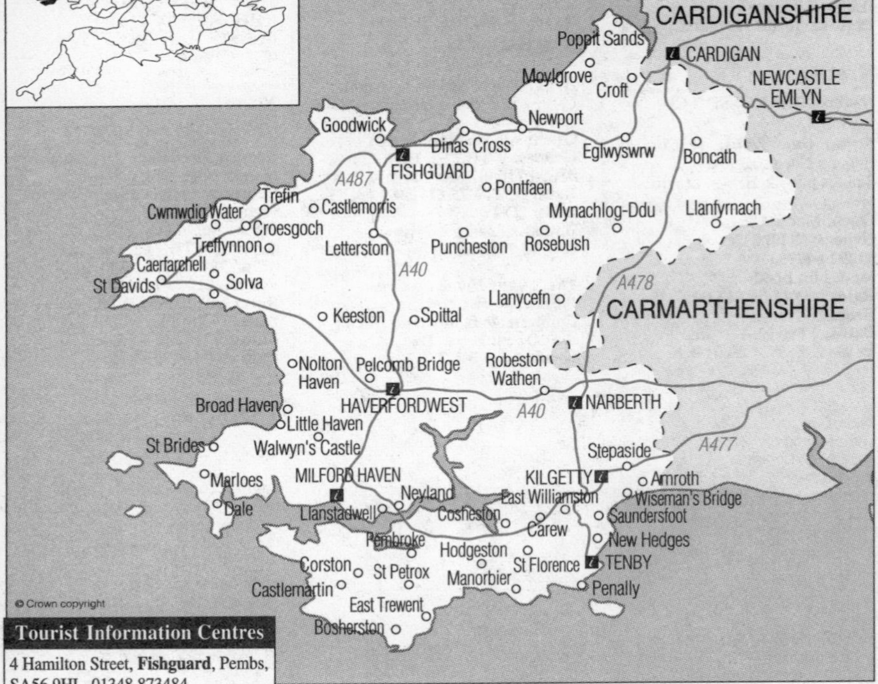

Tourist Information Centres

4 Hamilton Street, **Fishguard**, Pembs, SA56 9HL, 01348 873484.

Old Bridge, **Haverfordwest**, Pembs, 01437 763110,

Kingsmoor Common, **Kilgetty**, Pembs, SA68 0YA, 01834 813672, (Easter to Oct).

94 Charles Street, **Milford Haven**, Pembs, SA73 2HL, 01646 690866, (Easter to Oct).

Town Hall, **Narberth**, Pembs, SA67 7ER, 01834 860061, (Easter to Oct).

The Croft, **Tenby**, Pembs, SA70 8AP, 01834 842402, (Easter to Oct).

National Grid References are for villages, towns and cities - *not* for individual houses.

Amroth

National Grid Ref: SN1607

Beach Haven, *Amroth, Narberth, SA67 8NG.*
Family-run guest house & Post Office.
Open: Easter to Nov
01834 813310
Miss Evans
Rates fr: *£14.00*-**£14.00**.
Beds: 2F 2D 1T
Baths: 2 Shared

Boncath

National Grid Ref: SN2038

Awel-Y-Grug, *Boncath, Pembrokeshire, SA37 0JP.*
Large Victorian Welsh slate house.
Open: 4 -11
Grades: WTB 3 Cr, High Comm
01239 841260 Mrs Vaughton
Rates fr: *£20.00*-**£20.00**.
Beds: 1D 2T 1S
Baths: 2 Ensuite 2 Shared 1 Private

Bosherston

National Grid Ref: SR9694

School House, *Bosherston, Pembroke, SA71 5DN.*
Victorian village cottage.
Open: All Year (not Xmas)
01646 661269 Mrs Strudwick
Rates fr: *£13.00*-**£13.00**.
Beds: 1D 1T
Baths: 1 Shared
(2)

Broad Haven

National Grid Ref: SM8613

Ringstone Guest House, *Haroldston Hill, Broad Haven, Haverfordwest, Pembrokeshire, SA62 3JP.*
Beach, windsurfing, bird islands, coastal walks.
Open: All Year (not Xmas)
01437 781051 Mrs Morgan
Rates fr: *£16.00*-**£17.00**.
Beds: 1F 2D 1T
Baths: 4 Private
(2) (7)

Caerfarchell

National Grid Ref: SM7926

Hamilton House, *Caerfarchell, Solva, Haverfordwest, SA62 6XG.*
Charming C19th character cottage.
Open: Easter to Oct
01437 721264 Mrs Griffiths
Rates fr: *£13.50*-**£13.50**.
Beds: 1D
Baths: 1 Private
(4) (2)

Carew

National Grid Ref: SN0403

Carew Inn

Carew Inn, *Carew, Tenby, Pembrokeshire, SA70 8SL.*
Opposite Carew Castle, beautiful location.
Open: All Year (not Xmas)
01646 651267 Mr Hinchliffe
Rates fr: *£12.50*-**£15.00**.
Beds: 1D
Baths: 1 Shared
(20)

Old Stable Cottage, *Carew, Tenby, Pembrokeshire, SA70 8SL.*
Grade II Listed building, inglenook fireplace.
Open: Mar to Nov
01646 651889 Mrs Fielder
Rates fr: *£22.50*-**£35.00**.
Beds: 1F 1D 1T
Baths: 3 Ensuite
(5) (1)

Castlemartin

National Grid Ref: SR9198

Court Farm, *Castlemartin, Pembroke, SA71 5HE.*
Large comfortable farmhouse, huge breakfasts!
Open: All Year
01646 661228
Mrs Alderman
Rates fr: *£13.50*-**£15.00**.
Beds: 1F 1D
Baths: 1 Shared

Chapel Farm, *Castlemartin, Pembroke, SA71 5HW.*
Large comfortable farmhouse overlooking sea.
Open: All Year (not Xmas)
01646 661312
Mrs Smith
Rates fr: *£15.00*-**£15.00**.
Beds: 1F 1T
Baths: 1 Shared
(10)

Gupton Farm, *Castlemartin, Pembroke, SA71 5HW.*
Friendly, comfortable farmhouse.
Open: All Year (not Xmas)
01646 661268
Mrs Watkins
Rates fr: *£14.00*-**£14.00**.
Beds: 1F 1D **Baths:** 1 Shared
(6)

Castlemorris

National Grid Ref: SM8934

New Mill, Tregwynt, *Abermawr, Castlemorris, Haverfordwest, Pembs, SA62 5UX.*
Open: Easter to Sep
Grades: WTB 2 Cr, Comm
01348 891637 Mrs Holloway
Rates fr: *£18.00*-**£21.00**.
Beds: 1D 2T
Baths: 1 Ensuite 2 Private
(3)
New Mill, once a water mill, is a small farm in a delightful setting a few minutes walk from unspoilt beaches. Guest lounge. Quality meals.

Corston

National Grid Ref: SR9299

Corston House Hotel, *Axton Hill, Corston, Hundleton, Pembroke, SA71 5HB.*
Comfortable, spacious, homely Georgian house.
Open: All Year
01646 661220 Mrs Remmington
Rates fr: *£15.00*-**£17.00**.
Beds: 3F 5D 1T 4S

Cosheston

National Grid Ref: SN0003

Ferry Inn

The Old Rectory, *Cosheston, Pembroke Dock, SA72 4UJ.*
Large former rectory.
Open: All Year (not Xmas)
01646 684960 Mrs Bailey
Rates fr: *£15.00*-**£15.00**.
Beds: 1F 1D 1T 1S
Baths: 2 Shared
(4)

Croesgoch

National Grid Ref: SM8230

Artramont Arm, Square & Compass

Bank House Farm, *Abereiddy Road, Croesgoch, Haverfordwest, Pembrokeshire, SA62 6XZ.*
Open: All Year (not Xmas)
Grades: WTB Listed
01348 831305 Mrs Lloyd
Rates fr: *£14.00*-**£16.00**.
Beds: 1D 1T **Baths:** 1 Shared
(10) (2)
Idyllically set near coastal path, 0.5 mile from A487 at Croesgoch & Fishguard-St Davids bus route. TV lounge. Groups of 2-5 people preferred. Welsh welcome.

The lowest *double* rate per person is shown in *italics.*

The lowest *double* rate per person is shown in *italics.*

Maes y Ffynnon, *Penygroes, Croesgoch, Haverfordwest, Pembrokeshire, SA62 5JN.*
Modern large bungalow, private grounds.
Open: Apr to Sep
Grades: WTB 1 Cr, Comm
01348 831319
Mrs Evans
Rates fr: *£16.50*-**£18.50**.
Beds: 1F 1T
Baths: 2 Ensuite
(4)

Bryn, *Croesgoch, Haverfordwest, Pembrokeshire, SA62 6ND.*
Peacefully situated, beautiful farmhouse home.
Open: Easter to Aug
01348 831384
Mrs Jenkins
Rates fr: *£15.00*-**£15.00**.
Beds: 1D 1S
Baths: 1 Private

Trearched Farm, *Croesgoch, Haverfordwest, Pembrokeshire, SA62 5JP.*
C18th Listed farmhouse.
Open: All Year
01348 831310 Mrs Jenkins
Rates fr: *£15.00*-**£15.00**.
Beds: 2D 2T 2S

Croft

National Grid Ref: SN1541

Croft Farm, *Croft, Cardigan, Pembrokeshire, SA43 3NT.*
Small friendly family-run farm.
Open: All Year (not Xmas)
01239 615179
Mr & Mrs Gow
Rates fr: *£15.00*-**£15.00**.
Beds: 2D 1T
Baths: 2 Ensuite 1 Private
(3)

Cwmwdig Water

National Grid Ref: SM8030

Cwmwdig Water Guesthouse, *Berea, Cwmwdig Water, Haverfordwest, Pembrokeshire, SA62 6DW.*
Converted old oak-beamed farmhouse.
Open: All Year (not Xmas)
01348 831434 Mr Evans
Rates fr: *£18.00*-**£18.00**.
Beds: 5D 5T 2S
Baths: 5 Private 3 Shared

Dale

National Grid Ref: SM8005

Point Farm, *Dale, Haverfordwest, Pembrokeshire, SA62 3RD.*
Comfortable farmhouse on coastal path.
Open: All Year (not Xmas)
01646 636254 Mrs Webber
Rates fr: *£15.00.*
Beds: 1D 2T 1S
Baths: 2 Ensuite 1 Shared
(8)

Dinas Cross

National Grid Ref: SN0039

Fron Isaf Farm, *Dinas Cross, Newport, Pembs, SA42 0SW.*
Small working farm with sea views.
Open: All Year (not Xmas)
Grades: WTB Listed
01348 811339 Mr & Mrs Urwin
Rates fr: *£18.00*-**£18.00**.
Beds: 1D 1T
Baths: 1 Shared
(2) (3)

East Trewent

National Grid Ref: SS0097

East Trewent Farm, *East Trewent, Freshwater East, Pembroke, SA71 5LR.*
Beautifully converted stone-built farm buildings.
Open: All Year
01646 672127 Mr Ireland
Rates fr: *£15.50*-**£15.50**.
Beds: 2D 2T 1S
Baths: 2 Ensuite 3 Shared

East Williamston

National Grid Ref: SN0904

Cross Inn

Urshalim, *East Williamston, Tenby, Pembrokeshire, SA70 8RU.*
Bungalow, large garden, heated pool.
Open: All Year (not Xmas)
Grades: WTB 1 Cr, Comm
01834 813828 Mrs Reese
Rates fr: *£12.50*-**£15.00**.
Beds: 1D 1T
Baths: 1 Private 1 Shared
(2)

Eglwyswrw

National Grid Ref: SN1438

The Pear Tree, *Eglwyswrw, Crymych, Pembrokeshire, SA41 3UP.*
Converted farmhouse in peaceful surroundings.
Open: Easter to Oct
Grades: WTB 2 St
01239 891385
Ms Moore
Rates fr: *£20.00*-**£22.00**.
Beds: 1D 1T
Baths: 2 Private
(4)

Fishguard

National Grid Ref: SM9537

Rose & Crown, Glendower, Hope & Anchor, Farmhouse Kitchen, Royal Oak

The Beach House, *Fishguard Harbour, Fishguard, Pembs, SA64 0DH*
Open: All Year
Grades: WTB 2 Cr, Comm
01348 872085 / 875491
Mrs Wagstaff
Rates fr: *£13.50*-**£13.50**.
Beds: 3F 2D 3T 2S
Baths: 4 Ensuite 4 Private 2 Shared
(10)
Seafront guest house on Fishguard Harbour (village location), Approved & Commended by WTB. Splendid bay views.
Open 24 hours. Visa, Mastercard & Eurocard.
Ensuites. Friendly. On the Coastal Path.

Coach House Cottage, *Glendower Square, Goodwick, Fishguard, Pembs, SA64 0DH.*
Delightfully converted C18th mill & coachhouse.
Open: All Year (not Xmas)
01348 873660
Mrs Maxwell-Jones
Rates fr: *£13.00*-**£13.00**.
Beds: 1T
Baths: 1 Shared

Cartref Hotel, *13-19 High Street, Fishguard, Pembs, SA65 9AW.*
Convenient, friendly town hotel.
Open: All Year
Grades: WTB 3 Cr, AA 2 St, RAC 2 St
01348 872430 (also fax no)
Mrs Bjorkquist
Rates fr: *£18.00*-**£17.00**.
Beds: 2F 2D 2T 6S
Baths: 6 Ensuite 2 Shared
(5)

Seaview Hotel, *Seafront, Fishguard, Pembs, SA65 9PL.*
Friendly family-run hotel on seafront.
Open: All Year
Grades: WTB 3 Cr
01348 874282 (also fax no)
Mrs Wren
Rates fr: *£20.00*-**£25.00**.
Beds: 2F 6D 4T 4S
Baths: 16 Private
(1) (50)

Inglewood, *13 Vergam Terrace, Fishguard, Pembs, SA65 9DD.*
Comfortable, spacious mid-terrace dwelling house.
Open: All Year (not Xmas)
Grades: WTB 1 Cr, High Comm
01348 873475
Mrs Lewis
Rates fr: *£13.50.*
Beds: 2D 1T
Baths: 1 Shared
(12)

Rhos Felen, *Scleddau, Fishguard, Pembs, SA65 9RD.*
Family-run Country house.
Open: All Year
01348 873711 Mr Solomon
Fax no: 01348 873 711
Rates fr: *£16.00*-**£24.00**.
Beds: 1F 1D 1T
Baths: 1 Private 1 Shared
(0) (40)

Cri'r Wylan, *Pen Wallis, Fishguard, Pembs, SA65 9HR.*
Peaceful, fantastic view, good breakfast.
Open: All Year (not Xmas)
Grades: WTB 1 Cr, High Comm
01348 873398 Mrs Nicholas
Rates fr: *£15.00*-**£16.00**.
Beds: 1D 1T 1S **Baths:** 1 Shared
(4)

Goodwick

National Grid Ref: SM9438

Farmhouse Kitchen

Ivybridge, *Drim Mill, Dyffryn, Goodwick, Fishguard, Pembs, SA64 0FT.*
Open: All Year (not Xmas)
Grades: WTB 3 Cr, High Comm
01348 875366 / 872623
Mrs Davies
Rates fr: *£19.50*-**£19.50**.
Beds: 1F 3D 1T 1S
Baths: 6 Ensuite
(8)
Pembroke - Ivybridge. All rooms ensuite. Close to Fishguard-Rosslare ferry terminal. Heated pool, bar and spa. Family rooms. All diets catered for. Tel - 01348 875366 & 872623.

Villa Calabria, *New Hill, Goodwick, Fishguard, Pembs, SA64 0DU.*
Sea views; walking. Irish Ferry.
Open: All Year (not Xmas)
01348 874175 Mrs Trueman
Rates fr: *£14.00*-**£14.00**.
Beds: 1D 1T
Baths: 1 Private 1 Shared
(5) (2)

Bryntirion Guest House, *Glanymor Road, Goodwick, Fishguard, Pembs, SA64 0ER.*
Large Victorian private house.
Open: All Holiday Periods (not Xmas)
01348 872189 Mr Grace
Rates fr: *£13.00*-**£13.00**.
Beds: 1F 1T **Baths:** 2 Shared
(2)

Stanley House, *Quay Road, Goodwick, Fishguard, Pembs, SA64 0BS.*
Comfortable house overlooking Fishguard Bay.
Open: All Year
01348 873024 Ms Hendrie
Rates fr: *£13.50*-**£13.50**.
Beds: 1F 2D 1T 2S
Baths: 2 Shared
(3)

Haverfordwest

National Grid Ref: SM9515

Greenways, *Shoals Hook Lane, Haverfordwest, Pembs, SA61 2XN.*
Quiet retreat, 'home from home'.
Open: All Year
Grades: WTB 2 Cr, High Comm
01437 762345 Mr Tuson
Rates fr: *£20.00*-**£20.00**.
Beds: 1F 3D 3T 4S
Baths: 3 Private 1 Shared

Cuckoo Mill, *Pelcomb Bridge, St Davids Road, Haverfordwest, Pembs, SA62 6EA.*
Working farm in central Pembrokeshire.
Open: All Year
01437 762139 Mrs Davies
Rates fr: *£14.00*-**£14.00**.
Beds: 1F 2D 1T **Baths:** 2 Shared

College Guest House, *93 Hill Street, Haverfordwest, Pembs, SA61 1QX.*
Large Georgian family house.
Open: All Year (not Xmas)
01437 763710 Mr Gerson
Rates fr: *£15.00*-**£16.00**.
Beds: 1D 5T 4S
Baths: 5 Private 2 Shared
(30)

Hodgeston

National Grid Ref: SS0399

Rosedene, *Hodgeston, Pembroke, SA71 5JU.*
Country guest house, adjacent village green.
Open: All Year
Grades: WTB 3 Cr
01646 672586
Mrs Fallon
Rates fr: *£17.50*-**£20.00**.
Beds: 3D 1T **Baths:** 4 Private
(5)

Keeston

National Grid Ref: SM9019

Keeston Kitchen

Keeston Kitchen, *Keeston, Haverfordwest, Pembs, SA62 6ES.*
2.5 miles from Pembrokeshire coast.
Open: All Year
01437 710440 Mrs Hallett
Rates fr: *£16.00*-**£17.50**.
Beds: 1T **Baths:** 1 Ensuite

All details shown are as supplied by B&B owners in Autumn 1996.

Letterston

National Grid Ref: SM9329

Heathfield Mansion, *Mathry Road, Letterston, Haverfordwest, Pembrokeshire, SA26 5EG.*
Georgian country house in own grounds.
Open: Easter to Nov
Grades: WTB 3 Cr, High Comm
01348 840263 Mrs Rees
Rates fr: *£16.50*-**£18.00**.
Beds: 1F 2D
Baths: 2 Ensuite 1 Private
(10)

Little Haven

National Grid Ref: SM8512

The Bower Farm, *Little Haven, Haverfordwest, Pembs, SA62 3TY.*
Friendly farmhouse, fantastic sea views.
Open: All Year (not Xmas)
Grades: WTB 3 Cr, High Comm
01437 781554 Mr Birt-Llewellin
Rates fr: *£18.00*-**£25.00**.
Beds: 1F 1D 1T 1S
Baths: 4 Ensuite
(0) (12)

Llanfyrnach

National Grid Ref: SN2231

Bron-Y-Gaer, *Llanfyrnach, Pembs, SA35 0DA.*
Comfortable accommodation on peaceful smallholding.
Open: All Year
Grades: WTB 2 Cr, Comm
01239 831265 (also fax no)
Mrs Waghorn
Rates fr: *£18.00*-**£18.00**.
Beds: 3F
Baths: 3 Ensuite
(3)

Llanstadwell

National Grid Ref: SM9005

Ferry Inn

Ferry Inn, *Hazelbeach, Llanstadwell, Milford Haven, Pembrokeshire, SA73 1EG.*
Modern riverside village inn.
Open: All Year
01646 600270
Mr & Mrs Philips
Rates fr: *£15.00*-**£15.00**.
Beds: 1F 1D 2T 3S
Baths: 1 Ensuite 2 Shared

The Old Mill, *Hazelbeach, Llanstadwell, Milford Haven, Pembrokeshire, SA73 1EG.*
Converted old mill, comfortable.
Open: All Year (not Xmas)
01646 600150
Mr Johnson
Rates fr: *£12.00*-**£12.00**.
Beds: 2D 4T
Baths: 4 Shared
(10)

Llanycefn

National Grid Ref: SN0923

Ty Newydd Farm, *Llanycefn, Clynderwen, Carmarthenshire, SA66 7XT.*
Comfortable farmhouse with horse-riding.
Open: All Year (not Xmas)
Grades: WTB Listed, Approv
01437 532717 Mrs Dunn
Rates fr: *£13.00*-**£15.00**.
Beds: 1D **Baths:** 1 Shared
(5) (2)

Manorbier

National Grid Ref: SS0697

Castle Inn

Hillgarth, *Manorbier, Tenby, Pembs, SA70 7TN.*
Country house in delightful gardens.
Open: All Year (not Xmas)
01834 871266 Mrs Bell
Rates fr: *£17.00*-**£17.00**.
Beds: 1F 1D 1T
Baths: 1 Ensuite 1 Shared

Fernley Lodge, *Manorbier, Tenby, Pembs, SA70 7TH.*
Recently refurbished Victorian country house.
Open: All Year (not Xmas)
01834 871226 Mrs Cowper
Rates fr: *£18.00*-**£20.00**.
Beds: 1F 2D
Baths: 1 Private 1 Shared
(2) (7)

The Old Vicarage, *Manorbier, Tenby, Pembs, SA70 7TN.*
Stone Victorian Gothic private house.
Open: All Year (not Xmas)
Grades: WTB Listed
01834 871452 / 0421 595858
Mrs McHugh
Rates fr: *£19.00*-**£19.00**.
Beds: 1D 1T **Baths:** 2 Private

Marloes

National Grid Ref: SM7908

Griffin Inn Dale

Greenacre, *Marloes, Haverfordwest, Pembs, SA62 3BE.*
Welcoming, quiet family home.
Open: All Year
01646 636400 Mrs Howe
Rates fr: *£16.00*-**£16.00**.
Beds: 1D 1T 1S **Baths:** 1 Shared
(5)

Foxdale, *Glebe Lane, Marloes, Haverfordwest, Pembs, SA62 3AX.*
Close to Skomer & Skokholm Islands. **Open:** All Year
01646 636243 Mrs Roddam-King
Rates fr: *£15.00*-**£18.00**.
Beds: 2F 3D 2T
Baths: 1 Private 2 Shared
(6)

Milford Haven

National Grid Ref: SM9005

Belhaven House Hotel, *29 Hamilton Terrace, Milford Haven, Pembs, SA73 3JJ.*
Large Georgian private terraced house.
Open: All Year (not Xmas)
Grades: RAC Listed
01646 695983 Mr Henricksen
Fax no: 01646 690787
Rates fr: *£20.00*-**£25.00**.
Beds: 3F 2D 5S
Baths: 2 Private 4 Shared
(8)

Kings Arms, *Hakin Point, Milford Haven, Pembs, SA73 3DG.*
Public house, comfortable, sea views. Close to Marina.
Open: All Year (not Xmas)
01646 693478 Mrs Hutchings
Rates fr: *£15.00*-**£15.00**.
Beds: 2F 1D 3T **Baths:** 3 Private

Cleddau Villa, *21 St Annes Road, Hakin, Milford Haven, Pembs, SA73 3LQ.*
Large Victorian private house.
Open: All Year (not Xmas)
01646 690313 Mr & Mrs Binnion
Rates fr: *£13.00*-**£13.00**.
Beds: 4F **Baths:** 2 Shared

Moylegrove

National Grid Ref: SN1144

Cwm Connell, *Moylegrove, Cardigan, SA43 3BX.*
Converted traditonal stone farm buildings. **Open:** Easter to May
01239 881691 Mr & Mrs Jenkins
Fax no: 01239 881691
Rates fr: *£14.50*-**£14.50**.
Beds: 2T 2D
(4)

Mynachlog-Ddu

National Grid Ref: SN1430

Dolau Isaf Farm, *Mynachlog-Ddu, Clynderwen, Pembrokeshire, SA66 7SB.*
Homely, peaceful, central hill farm.
Open: All Year (not Xmas)
Grades: WTB 1 Cr, Comm
01994 419327 Mrs Lockton
Rates fr: *£16.00*-**£16.00**.
Beds: 2D 1T 1S
Baths: 1 Ensuite 1 Shared
(6)

Trefach Riding Centre/Guest House, *Mynachlog-Ddu, Clynderwen, Carmarthenshire, SA66 7RU.*
Large farmhouse/guest house.
Open: Easter to Oct
Grades: WTB Listed
01994 419457 Mr Smith
Rates fr: *£15.00*-**£15.00**.
Beds: 1F 1D 1T 1S
Baths: 1 Shared
(10) (6)

Yethen Isaf, *Mynachlog-Ddu, Clynderwen, Carmarthenshire, SA66 7SN.*
250-year-old farmhouse, working farm. **Open:** All Year (not Xmas)
01437 532256 Mrs Barney
Rates fr: *£17.00*-**£20.00**.
Beds: 1F 1D 2T
Baths: 1 Private 1 Shared
(6)

New Hedges

National Grid Ref: SN1302

Luigis's

Pen Mar Guest House, *New Hedges, Tenby, Pembs, SA70 8TL.*
A 'Taste of Italy' in Wales.
Open: Dec to Oct
Grades: WTB 3 Cr, High Comm, RAC Acclaim
01834 842435 Mrs Romeo
Rates fr: *£16.00*-**£16.00**.
Beds: 3F 5D 2T
Baths: 6 Private 4 Shared
(10)

Newport

National Grid Ref: SN0539

Llwyngwair Arms, Cnapan Restaurant

Grove Park Guest House, *Pen Y Bont, Newport, Pembs, SA42 0LT.*
Scenic setting, estuary views. 100 yards Pembrokeshire Coast Path.
Open: All Year (not Xmas)
Grades: WTB 3 Cr, High Comm
01239 820122 Mrs King
Rates fr: *£18.00*-**£23.00**.
Beds: 3D 1T
Baths: 2 Private 1 Shared
(3)

Llysmeddyg Guest House, *East Street, Newport, Pembs, SA42 0SY.*
Large Georgian house & flat.
Open: All Year (not Xmas)
Grades: WTB 2 Cr, High Comm
01239 820008 Mr & Mrs Ross
Rates fr: *£19.00*-**£21.50**.
Beds: 2D 2T 2S
Baths: 1 Ensuite 2 Shared
(5)

Hafan Deg, *Long Street, Newport, Pembs, SA42 0TN.*
Quiet, central, modern & warm.
Open: All Year (not Xmas)
Grades: WTB 2 Cr
01239 820301 Mr & Mrs Joseph
Rates fr: *£16.00*-**£16.00**.
Beds: 1D 2T 1S
Baths: 2 Ensuite 2 Shared
(0) (6)

2 Springhill, *Parrog Road, Newport, Pembs, SA42 0RH.*
Listed comfortable house, sea views. **Open:** All Year
Grades: WTB 1 Cr. High Comm
01239 820626 Mr Inman
Rates fr: *£15.00*-**£15.00**.
Beds: 1F 1D 1T **Baths:** 2 Shared
(2)

Cnapan Country House, *East Street, Newport, Pembs, SA42 0WF.*
Comfortable Georgian house, fine food.
Open: Easter to Jan
01239 820575
Rates fr: *£23.00*-**£23.00**.
Beds: 1F 3T 1D
Baths: 1 Shared
(6)

Neyland

National Grid Ref: SM9605

Oddfellow Arms

Y Ffynnon, *45 Honeyborough Road, Neyland, Milford Haven, Pembs, SA73 1RF.*
Comfortable private house, friendly welcome.
Open: All Year (not Xmas)
Grades: WTB Listed
01646 601369 Mr Hawley
Rates fr: *£14.00*-**£14.00**.
Beds: 1D 1T 1S
(1)

Nolton Haven

National Grid Ref: SM8618

Mariners Inn

Nolton Haven Farmhouse, *Nolton Haven, Haverfordwest, Pembs, SA62 4NH.*
Beachside farmhouse, working farm.
Open: All Year (not Xmas)
Grades: WTB Listed
01437 710263 Mrs Canton
Rates fr: *£14.00*-**£14.00**.
Beds: 3F 2D 1T 1S
Baths: 2 Private 4 Shared
(20)

Pelcomb Bridge

National Grid Ref: SM9317

Rising Sun Inn

Rising Sun Inn, *St Davids Road, Pelcomb Bridge, Haverfordwest, SA62 6EA.*
Friendly country inn, family-run.
Open: All Year (not Xmas)
Grades: WTB 2 Cr
01437 765171 Mrs Brown
Rates fr: *£20.00*-**£22.50**.
Beds: 1D 1T 2S
Baths: 2 Private
(12)

All details shown are as supplied by B&B owners in Autumn 1996.

Pembroke

National Grid Ref: SM9801

Watermans Arms, Armstrong Arms

Merton Place House, *3 East Back, Pembroke,* *SA71 4HL.*
Open: All Year
Grades: WTB Listed, Approv
01646 684796
Mrs Pearce
Rates fr: *£15.00*-**£15.00**.
Beds: 2D 2T
Baths: 1 Shared
(6)
Lovely old merchant house, walled garden. Quiet road, centre of Pembroke. Full of books & useful guides. Some French spoken. Civilised creature comforts, small pretty rooms.

High Noon Guest House, *Lower Lamphey Road, Pembroke,* *SA71 4AB.*
Comfortable, cosy, convenient & cheerful.
Open: All Year
Grades: WTB 3 Cr, Comm
01646 683736
Mr Barnikel
Rates fr: *£13.00*-**£15.00**.
Beds: 2F 3D 1T 3S
Baths: 5 Ensuite 2 Shared
(10)

Penally

National Grid Ref: SS1199

Cross Inn, Crown

Crossing Cottage, *Penally, Tenby, Pembs,* *SA70 7PP.*
Secluded house, village outskirts.
Open: All Year (not Xmas)
01834 842291
Mr & Mrs Watts
Rates fr: *£12.50*-**£12.50**.
Beds: 1F 1D 1T
Baths: 1 Shared
(6)

Brambles Lodge, *Penally, Tenby, Pembs,* *SA70 7.*
Family-run guest house.
Open: Easter to Oct
Grades: WTB 1 Cr
01834 842393
Mrs Nightingale
Rates fr: *£13.00*-**£13.00**.
Beds: 7D 1T
Baths: 1 Ensuite 2 Private
(8)

Myrtle House, *Penally, Tenby, Pembs,* *SA70 7PU.*
Victorian cottage, sea views.
Open: All Year (not Xmas)
01834 843623
Mrs Penn
Rates fr: *£12.50*-**£12.50**.
Beds: 1F 1T
Baths: 1 Shared

Pleasant Valley

National Grid Ref: SN1406

Pleasant Valley House, *Pleasant Valley, Stepaside, Narberth, Pembrokeshire,* *SA67 8NY.*
Small detached hotel, own grounds.
Open: Easter to Sep
01834 813607 Mrs Holmes
Rates fr: *£13.50*-**£13.50**.
Beds: 1F 5D 1T 1S
Baths: 3 Private 3 Shared
(4)

Pontfaen

National Grid Ref: SN0234

Tregynon Country, *Farmhouse Hotel, Pontfaen, Gwaun Valley, Fishguard, Pembs,* *SA65 9TU.*
C16th country farmhouse hotel.
Open: All Year
Grades: WTB 3 Cr, High Comm, AA 2 St, RAC High Acclaim
01239 820531 Mr Heard
Fax no: 01239 820808
Rates fr: *£24.00*. **Beds:** 4F 4D
(20)

Poppit Sands

National Grid Ref: SN1548

Webley Hotel

Glan-y-Mor, *Poppit Sands, St Dogmaels, Cardigan, Pembs,* *SA43 3LP.*
Ex-farmhouse with sea view.
Open: All Year
01239 612329 Mrs Sharp
Rates fr: *£12.50*-**£12.50**.
Beds: 1F 1D **Baths:** 1 Shared

Princes Gate

National Grid Ref: SN1312

Angel Inn (Narberth)

Hidden Spring Guest House, *Princes Gate, Narberth, Pembrokeshire,* *SA67 8TF.*
Large country house. Panoramic views. **Open:** Easter to Oct
Grades: WTB 2 Cr
01834 861074 Mr & Mrs Sargeant
Rates fr: *£17.50*-**£17.50**.
Beds: 2D 1T 1S
Baths: 2 Ensuite 1 Shared
(10) (6)

Puncheston

National Grid Ref: SN0029

Penygraig, *Puncheston, Haverfordwest, Pembrokeshire,* *SA62 5RJ.*
Modern comfortable farmhouse, unspoilt area.
Open: Easter to Oct
Grades: WTB 2 Cr, High Comm
01348 881277 Mrs Devonald
Rates fr: *£15.00*-**£15.00**.
Beds: 1F 1D
Baths: 1 Private 1 Shared
(6)

Robeston Wathen

National Grid Ref: SN0815

Canton House, *Robeston Wathen, Narberth, Pembrokeshire,* *SA67 8EP.*
Large peach-coloured country house.
Open: All Year (not Xmas)
01834 860620 Mrs Brown
Rates fr: *£12.50*-**£15.00**.
Beds: 1F 2D 1T 1S
Baths: 5 Shared
(1) (10)

Rosebush

National Grid Ref: SN0729

The Old Post Office, *Rosebush, Clynderwen, Carmarthenshire,* *SA66 7QU.*
The heart of the Preseli Hills.
Open: All Year
Grades: WTB 1 Cr, Comm
01437 532200 Mrs Thomas
Rates fr: *£17.95*-**£17.95**.
Beds: 2D 1T 1S
Baths: 2 Shared
(4)

Saundersfoot

National Grid Ref: SN1304

Royal Oak

Pinewood, *Cliff Road, Wiseman's Bridge, Saundersfoot, Narberth, Pembs,* *SA67 8NU.*
Peaceful; beach 350 yards; views.
Open: All Year (not Xmas)
Grades: WTB 2 Cr, High Comm
01834 811082
Mrs Grecian
Rates fr: *£17.00*-**£17.00**.
Beds: 2D 1T
Baths: 3 Ensuite
(3)

Sandy Hill Guest House, *Tenby Road, Saundersfoot,* *SA69 9DR.*
Large garden with swimming pool.
Open: Mar to Oct
01834 813165
Mr & Mrs Edwards
Rates fr: *£14.00*-**£14.00**.
Beds: 2F 2D 1T
Baths: 3 Private
(3) (7)

Solva

National Grid Ref: SM8024

Royal George, Cambrian Inn, Ship Inn

Pendinas, *St Brides View, Solva, Haverfordwest, Pembs,* *SA62 6TB.*
Modern, comfortable house, glorious sea views.
Open: All Year
01437 721283
Ms Davies
Rates fr: *£15.00*-**£15.00**.
Beds: 2D 1T
Baths: 1 Shared
(3)

***Llanddinog Old Farmhouse,** Solva, Haverfordwest, Pembs, SA62 6NA.*
C16th traditional Welsh farmhouse.
Open: All Year (not Xmas)
01348 831224 Mrs Griffiths
Rates fr: *£16.00*-**£16.00**.
Beds: 1F 1D
Baths: 2 Ensuite
(20)

***River View Cottage,** 6 River Street, Solva, Haverfordwest, Pembs, SA62 6TJ.*
Unique riverside cottage.
01437 721679 Mrs Williams
Rates fr: *£15.00*-**£15.00**.
Beds: 3D 2T 1S
Baths: 1 Private 3 Shared

Spittal

National Grid Ref: SM9723

***Lower Haythog,** Spittal, Haverfordwest, Pembs, SA62 5QL.*
300-year-old farmhouse full of charm & character.
Open: All Year
01437 731279 Mrs Thomas
Rates fr: *£17.50*-**£20.00**.
Beds: 1F 2D 1T
Baths: 4 Private

St Brides

National Grid Ref: SM8010

The Foxes

***Fopston Farm,** St Brides, Haverfordwest, Pembrokeshire, SA62 3.*
Spacious C17th comfortable farmhouse.
Open: All Year (not Xmas)
01646 636271 Mrs Price
Rates fr: *£15.00*-**£15.00**.
Beds: 1F 2T
Baths: 1 Shared
(6)

St Davids

National Grid Ref: SM7525

***Ramsey House,** Lower Moor, St Davids, Haverfordwest, Pembs, SA62 6RP.*
Open: All Year
Grades: WTB 3 Cr, High Comm, AA 4 Q, Select, RAC High Acclaim
01437 720321
Mr & Mrs Thompson
Fax no: 01437 720025
Rates fr: *£23.00*-**£25.00**.
Beds: 4D 3T
Baths: 6 Ensuite 1 Private
(10)
Quiet relaxation exclusively for non-smoking adults. Traditional Welsh cuisine, fine wines, cosy bar. Convenient location for Cathedral/coast path, beaches, attractions. Dinner/B&B £35-£40 pppn, £210-£240 weekly.

***Y Gorlan,** 77 Nun Street, St Davids, Haverfordwest, Pembs, SA62 6NU.*
Family-run guest house close to cathedral.
Open: All Year
Grades: WTB 3 Cr, High Comm, AA 4 Q , RAC High Acclaim
01437 720837 (also fax no)
Mrs Dyson
Rates fr: *£18.50*-**£19.50**.
Beds: 1F 2D 1T 1S
Baths: 5 Ensuite
(2)

***Ty Olaf,** Mount Gardens, St Davids, Haverfordwest, Pembs, SA62 6BS.*
Quiet modern bungalow.
Open: All Year
Grades: WTB Listed, High Comm
01437 720885 Mrs Liggitt
Rates fr: *£13.50*-**£13.50**.
Beds: 1F 1D 1T 1S
Baths: 1 Shared
(3)

***Y Glennydd Guesthouse,** 51 Nun Street, St Davids, Haverfordwest, Pembs, SA62 6NU.*
Comfortable Victorian property.
Open: Feb to Oct
01437 720576
Mr Foster
Rates fr: *£16.50*-**£18.50**.
Beds: 4F 4D 1T 1S
Baths: 7 Ensuite 2 Shared

***Grove Hotel,** High Street, St Davids, Haverfordwest, Pembs, SA62 6SB.*
Regency hotel, bars & restaurant.
Open: All Year
01437 720341
Mrs Pengelly
Rates fr: *£18.00*-**£18.00**.
Beds: 6D 7T 3S
Baths: 16 Private 1 Shared

St Florence

National Grid Ref: SN0801

***The Ark,** St Florence, Tenby, Pembs, SA70 8LN.*
Comfortable small Pembrokeshire cottage.
Open: All Year (not Xmas)
Grades: WTB 2 Cr, High Comm
01834 871654
Mrs Taylor
Rates fr: *£17.00*.
Beds: 2D 1T
Baths: 3 Ensuite
(3)

***Flemish Court,** St Florence, Tenby, Pembs, SA70 8LS.*
Luxury private house.
Open: All Year
Grades: WTB Listed
01834 871413
Mr Taylor
Rates fr: *£13.00*-**£15.50**.
Beds: 2D 1T 1S
Baths: 3 Private 1 Shared
(4)

***Grove Farmhouse,** St Florence, Tenby, Pembs, SA70 8LZ.*
Spacious, tastefully furnished accommodation.
Open: Apr to Sep
01834 871730 Mrs Paice
Rates fr: *£14.50*-**£15.00**.
Beds: 2D 1T
Baths: 2 Shared
(3)

St Petrox

National Grid Ref: SR9795

Armstrong Arms, St Govans Inn

***Home Farm,** St Petrox, West Stackpole, Pembroke, SA71 5BX.*
Comfortable period farmhouse near Bosherston Lake.
Open: Easter to October
01646 661244
Mrs James
Rates fr: *£15.00*-**£17.50**.
Beds: 1F
(10)

Stepaside

National Grid Ref: SN1307

***Merrixton Bungalow,** Stepaside, Narberth, Pembs, SA67 8PJ.*
Comfortable bungalow, panoramic sea views.
Open: Easter to Sep
01834 812002
Mrs Carlan
Rates fr: *£12.50*-**£15.00**.
Beds: 1T
Baths: 1 Ensuite
(2)

Tenby

National Grid Ref: SN1300

Five Arches Tavern

***High Seas,** The Norton, Tenby, Pembs, SA70 8AA.*
Open: Easter to Oct
Grades: WTB 2 Cr, High Comm
01834 843611
Mr MacDonald
Rates fr: *£16.00*-**£16.00**.
Beds: 1F 4D 1T
Baths: 3 Ensuite 2 Private 1 Shared
Georgian town house, retaining many original features, comfortably furnished & close to town centre. It overlooks the beach & most rooms have fine sea views.

All details shown are as supplied by B&B owners in Autumn 1996.

Belgrave Hotel, *The Esplanade, Tenby, Pembs, SA70 7DU.*
Open: All Year
Grades: WTB 1 Cr
01834 842377 Mr Thomas
Rates fr: *£17.50*-**£17.50**.
Beds: 17F 12D 8T 10S
Baths: 44 Private
(12)
Superb position overlooking coastal footpath. South Beach Golf Course open throughout the year. Weekends, midweek bargain breaks, Christmas, New Year. Please ring for brochure.

Clarence House Hotel, *Esplanade, Tenby, Pembs, SA70 7DL.*
Seasonal seafront private residential hotel.
Open: Easter to Sep
Grades: WTB 3 Cr, Comm, AA Listed, 3 Q, RAC Listed
01834 844371 Mr Phillips
Rates fr: *£14.00*-**£17.00**.
Beds: 25D 25T 18S
Baths: 68 Private 5 Shared

Hallsville Hotel, *Victoria Street, Tenby, Pembs, SA70 7DY.*
Superbly situated, comfortable hotel.
Open: All Year
Grades: WTB 2 Cr
01834 842410 / 0500 655307
Mrs Davison
Rates fr: *£12.00*-**£15.00**.
Beds: 4F 4D 2T
Baths: 4 Ensuite 2 Shared

St Oswalds Guest House, *Picton Terrace, Tenby, Pembs, SA70 7DR.*
Large Victorian guest house.
Open: All Year (not Xmas)
Grades: WTB 2 Cr, Comm
01834 842130 (also fax no)
Mrs Davies
Rates fr: *£17.50*-**£20.00**.
Beds: 6D 4T
Baths: 10 Ensuite
(2) (10)

Sunny Bank, *Harding Street, Tenby, Pembs, SA70 7LL.*
Friendly, refreshing luxury, good food.
Open: All Year
Grades: WTB 3 Cr, High Comm
01834 844034 (also fax no)
Mrs Aston
Rates fr: *£16.00*-**£18.00**.
Beds: 2F 2D 1T 1S
Baths: 5 Ensuite 1 Private

Lyndale Guest House, *Warren Street, Tenby, Pembs, SA70 7JX.*
Large terraced Victorian house.
Open: All Year
Grades: WTB 2 Cr
01834 842836
Mrs Percival
Rates fr: *£12.00*-**£12.00**.
Beds: 1F 3D 1T 1S
Baths: 2 Ensuite
(4)

Ripley St Marys Hotel, *St Marys Street, Tenby, Pembs, SA70 7HN.*
Free parking in private garage.
Open: Easter to Oct
Grades: WTB 3 Cr, AA 3 Q Recomm, RAC Acclaim
01834 842837 (also fax no)
Mr Mace
Rates fr: *£19.00*-**£20.00**.
Beds: 4F 5D 3T 2S
Baths: 8 Private 3 Shared
(0) (14)

Ivy Bank, *Harding Street, Tenby, Pembs, SA70 7LL.*
Highly Commended Victorian town house.
Open: All Year (not Xmas)
Grades: WTB 3 Cr, High Comm, RAC Acclaim
01834 842311
Mrs Cromack
Rates fr: *£16.00*-**£32.00**.
Beds: 2F 2D 1T
Baths: 5 Ensuite

Glenthorne, *9 Deer Park, Tenby, Pembrokeshire, SA70 7LE.*
Lovely rooms & warm welcome.
Open: All Year
Grades: WTB 2 Cr
01834 842300
Rates fr: *£14.00*-**£14.00**.
Beds: 4F 3D 1T 1S
Baths: 5 Ensuite 1 Private 3 Shared
(4)

Treffynnon

National Grid Ref: SM8428

Llainpropert Cottage, *Treffynnon, Croesgoch, Haverfordwest, Pembrokeshire, SA62 5JY.*
Comfortable 200-year-old cottage.
Open: Mar to Oct
01348 831135 Mrs Cortis
Rates fr: *£15.00*-**£15.00**.
Beds: 2D 1T
Baths: 1 Ensuite 1 Shared
(7) (4)

Trefin

National Grid Ref: SM8332

Binchurn Farm Guest House, *Trefin, St Davids, Haverfordwest, Pembs, SA62 5.*
Farm guest house with superb sea views.
Open: All Year
01348 831264
Mrs Morgan
Rates fr: *£20.00*-**£25.00**.
Beds: 1F 1D 1S
Baths: 1 Private 1 Shared
(8) (6)

Bryngarw, *Abercastle Road, Trefin, Trevine, Haverfordwest, Pembs, SA62 5AR.*
Modern, sea view guest house.
Open: Easter to Oct
01348 831211
Mr & Mrs Gratton
Rates fr: *£20.00*-**£23.00**.
Beds: 1F 2D 2T
Baths: 5 Private
(10)

Walwyns Castle

National Grid Ref: SM8711

Masons Arms

Barley Villa Guest House, *Walwyns Castle, Haverfordwest, Pembrokeshire, SA62 3EB.*
Modern house in peaceful countryside.
Open: Easter to Oct
Grades: WTB 2 Cr, Comm
01437 781254
Mrs Davies
Rates fr: *£13.50*-**£17.50**.
Beds: 1T 1D
Baths: 1 Ensuite 1 Shared
(4)

Wiseman's Bridge

National Grid Ref: SN1406

Royal Oak

Pinewood, *Cliff Road, Wiseman's Bridge, Narberth, Pembs, SA67 8NU.*
Peaceful; beach 350 yards; views.
Open: All Year (not Xmas)
Grades: WTB 2 Cr, High Comm
01834 811082 Mrs Grecian
Rates fr: *£17.00*-**£17.00**.
Beds: 2D 1T
Baths: 3 Ensuite
(3)

Powys

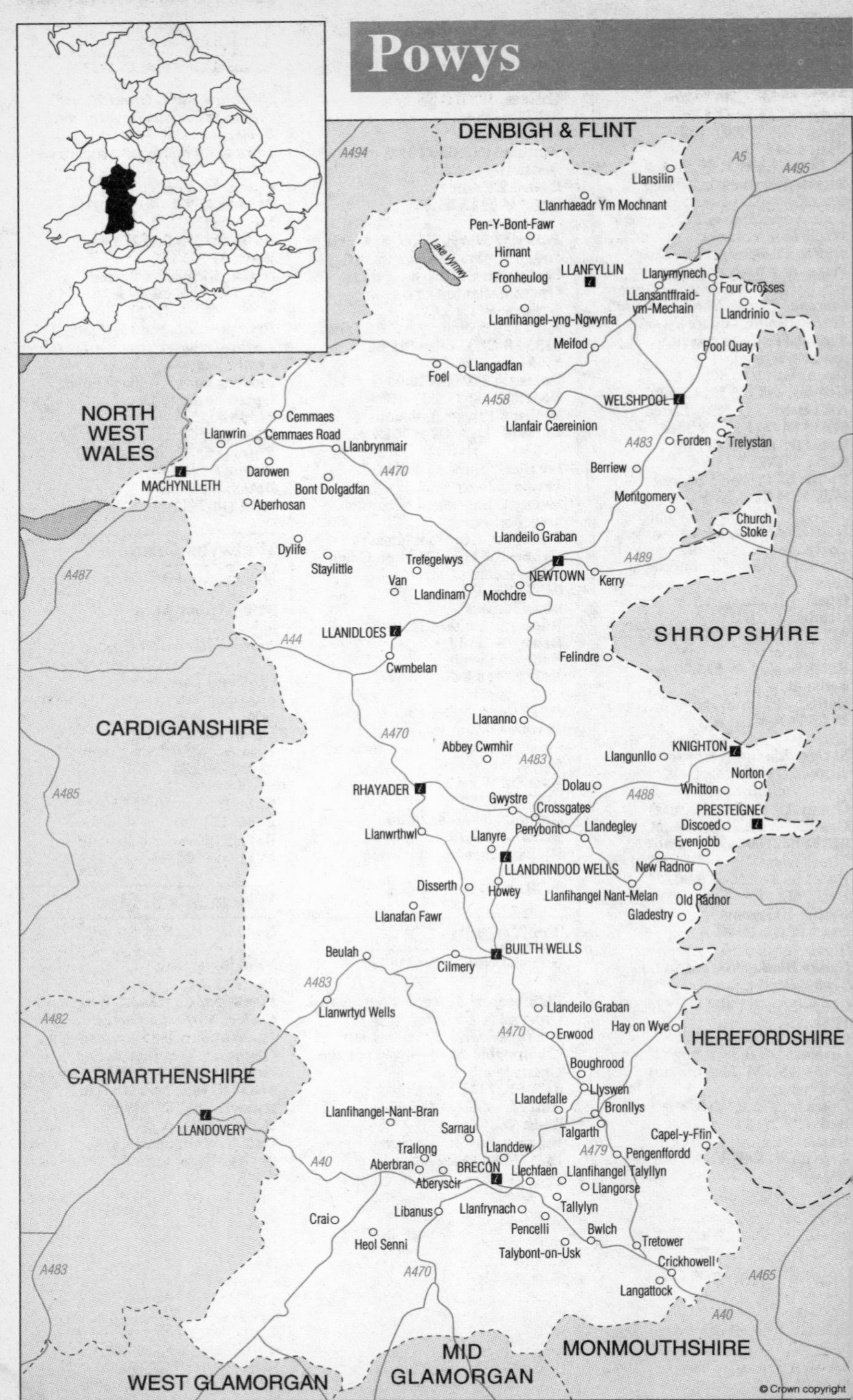

DENBIGH & FLINT
A494
A5
A495
Llansilin
Llanrhaeadr Ym Mochnant
Pen-Y-Bont-Fawr
Lake Vyrnwy
Hirnant
LLANFYLLIN
Fronheulog
Llanymynech
LLansantffraid-ym-Mechain
Four Crosses
Llandrinio
Llanfihangel-yng-Ngwynfa
Meifod
Pool Quay
Foel
Llangadfan
A458
WELSHPOOL
NORTH WEST WALES
Cemmaes
Llanfair Caereinion
Llanwrin
Cemmaes Road
Llanbrynmair
A483
Forden
Trelystan
Darowen
A470
Berriew
MACHYNLLETH
Bont Dolgadfan
Aberhosan
Montgomery
Church Stoke
Llandeilo Graban
Dylife
A487
Staylittle
Trefegelwys
A489
Van
NEWTOWN
Kerry
Llandinam
Mochdre
LLANIDLOES
SHROPSHIRE
A44
Felindre
Cwmbelan
CARDIGANSHIRE
Llananno
A470
Abbey Cwmhir
A483
KNIGHTON
Llangunllo
Norton
A485
RHAYADER
Dolau
A488
Whitton
Gwystre
Crossgates
PRESTEIGNE
Penybont
Llandegley
Discoed
Llanwrthwl
Llanyre
Evenjobb
LLANDRINDOD WELLS
New Radnor
Disserth
Howey
Llanfihangel Nant-Melan
Old Radnor
Llanafan Fawr
Gladestry
Beulah
BUILTH WELLS
Cilmery
A483
Llanwrtyd Wells
Llandeilo Graban
A482
A470
Erwood
Hay on Wye
HEREFORDSHIRE
Boughrood
CARMARTHENSHIRE
Llyswen
Llandefalle
Bronllys
Llanfihangel-Nant-Bran
LLANDOVERY
Sarnau
Talgarth
Capel-y-Ffin
Trallong
Llanddew
A479
Pengenffordd
A40
Aberbran
BRECON
Llechfaen
Llanfihangel Talyllyn
Aberyscir
Llangorse
Libanus
Llanfrynach
Tallylyn
Crai
Pencelli
Bwlch
Heol Senni
Talybont-on-Usk
Tretower
A470
Crickhowell
A483
A465
Langattock
A40
MID GLAMORGAN
MONMOUTHSHIRE
WEST GLAMORGAN
© Crown copyright

Tourist Information Centres

Groe Car Park, **Builth Wells**, Powys, LD2 3BT, 01982 553307,

Craft Centre, **Corris**, Machynlleth, Powys, SY20 9SP, 01654 761244, (Easter to Oct).

The Offas Dyke Centre, West Street, **Knighton**, Powys, LD7 1EW, 01547 528753.

Old Town Hall, Memorial Gardens, **Llandrindod Wells**, Powys, LD1 5DL, 01597 822600.

Unit 2, Vrynwy Craft Centre, **Lake Vrynwy**, SY10 0LY, 01691 870346

Great Oak Street, **Llanidloes**, Powys, 01686 412685, (Easter to Oct).

Canolfan Owain Glyndwr, **Machynlleth**, Powys, SY20 8EE, 01654 702401.

Central Car Park, **Newtown**, Powys, SY16 2 PW, 01686 625580, (Easter to Oct).

The Old Market Hall, Broad Street, **Presteigne**, Powys, LD8 2AW, 01544 260193, (Easter to Oct).

North Street, West Street, **Rhayader**, Powys, LD6 5BY, 01597 810591, (Easter to Oct).

Vicarage Gardens Car Park, **Welshpool**, Powys, SY21 7DD, 01938 552043.

Abbey Cwmhir

National Grid Ref: SO0571

Home Farm, *Abbey Cwmhir, Llandrindod Wells, Powys, LD1 6PH.*
C18th working farm.
Open: All Year (not Xmas)
01597 851666
Mrs Hamer
Rates fr: *£13.00*-**£13.00**.
Beds: 3D
Baths: 1 Private 1 Shared

Aberbran

National Grid Ref: SN9829

Aberbran-Fach Farm, *Aberbran, Brecon, Powys, LD3 9NG.*
C16th farmhouse.
Open: All Year
01874 622929
Mrs Jones
Rates fr: *£17.50*-**£15.00**.
Beds: 1F 1D 1S
Baths: 1 Shared

Abercynafon

National Grid Ref: SO1122

Abercynafon Lodge, *Abercynafon, Talybont-on-Usk, Brecon, Powys, LD3 7YT.*
Family home, quiet, idyllic situation.
Open: All Year
01874 676342 Mrs Carr
Rates fr: *£15.00*-**£17.00**.
Beds: 1D 2T
Baths: 1 Private 2 Shared
(3)

Aberhosan

National Grid Ref: SN8097

Bacheiddon Farm, *Aberhosan, Machynlleth, Powys, SY20 8SG.*
Modern, comfortable farmhouse, lovely scenery.
Grades: WTB 2 Cr
01654 702229 Mrs Lewis
Rates fr: *£17.00*-**£20.00**.
Beds: 3D
Baths: 3 Private

Aberyscir

National Grid Ref: SN9929

Aberyscir Old Rectory, *Aberyscir, Brecon, Powys, LD3 9NP.*
Elegant Victorian stone house.
Open: All Year
01874 623457 Mrs Gould
Rates fr: *£18.00*-**£25.00**.
Beds: 1F 1D 1T
Baths: 3 Private

Berriew

National Grid Ref: SJ1800

Red Lion, Talbot Hotel

Upper Pandy Farm, *Berriew, Welshpool, Powys, SY21 8PW.*
Timbered farmhouse with lovely views.
Open: Easter to Oct
01686 640338 Ms Jones
Rates fr: *£15.00*-**£16.00**.
Beds: 1F 1D 1T
Baths: 1 Ensuite 1 Shared

Beulah

National Grid Ref: SN9251

Trout Inn

Trout Inn, *Beulah, Llanwrtyd Wells, Powys, LD5 4UU.*
Superb ensuite accommodation. Home cooked food.
Open: All Year (not Xmas)
01591 620235 Ms Green
Rates fr: *£25.00*-**£30.00**.
Beds: 1F 2D 2T
Baths: 5 Ensuite
(12) (30)

Bont Dolgadfan

National Grid Ref: SH8800

Cyfeiliog Guest House, *Bont Dolgadfan, Llanbrynmair, Powys, SY19 7BB.*
Comfortable C18th riverside guest house.
Open: All Year
Grades: WTB 2 Cr, Comm
01650 521231
Mr & Mrs Fox
Rates fr: *£15.00*-**£15.00**.
Beds: 1F 1D 1T
Baths: 1 Private 1 Shared
(3)

Boughrood

National Grid Ref: SO1339

Upper Middle Road, *Boughrood, Brecon, Powys, LD3 0BX.*
Quietly situated smallholding. Lovely views.
Open: All Year (not Xmas)
Grades: WTB Listed, Comm
01874 754407 Mrs Kelleher
Rates fr: *£12.50*-**£12.50**.
Beds: 1D 1T 1S
Baths: 1 Shared
(3)

Balangia, *Station Road, Boughrood, Brecon, Powys, LD3 0YF.*
Small house near River Wye.
Open: Easter to Sep
01874 754453
Mrs Brown
Rates fr: *£12.00*-**£12.00**.
Beds: 1F 1T
Baths: 1 Shared

Brecon

National Grid Ref: SO0428

Three Horseshoes Inn, Clarence, George Hotel

Beacons Guest House, *16 Bridge Street, Brecon, Powys, LD3 8AH.*
Open: All Year (not Xmas)
Grades: WTB 3 Cr, Comm, AA 3 Q, RAC Acclaim
01874 623339 (also fax no)
Mr & Mrs Jackson
Rates fr: *£16.50*-**£16.50**.
Beds: 3F 2D 4T 1S
Baths: 8 Private 1 Shared
(8)
Family-run licensed town guest house. TV and tea trays in rooms. Excellent home cooking - Taste of Wales recommended. Ideal touring centre, ample car parking.

Paris Guest House, *28 The Watton, Brecon, Powys, LD3 7EF.*
Family-run C17th guest house.
Open: All Year (not Xmas)
Grades: WTB 1 Cr
01874 624205 Mrs Haines
Rates fr: *£15.00*-**£15.00**.
Beds: 1F 1D 1T 1S

***Lansdowne Hotel,** 39 The Watton, Brecon, Powys, LD3 7EG.*
Open: All Year
Grades: WTB 3 Cr, AA 1 St
01874 623321 Mr Nancarrow
Rates fr: *£23.50*-**£27.50**.
Beds: 2F 4D 2T 2S
Baths: 8 Private 1 Shared
(7)
Family-run hotel situated in Brecon & close to all amenities. Licensed restaurant noted locally for excellent food at reasonable prices. Access, Visa, AE, DC, Mastercard.

***Trewalter House,** Llangorse, Brecon, Powys, LD3 0PS.*
Friendly, peaceful, views, good food.
Open: All Year (not Xmas)
Grades: WTB 3 Cr, High Comm
01874 658442 (also fax no)
Mrs Abbott
Rates fr: *£18.00*-**£28.00**.
Beds: 2D 1T
Baths: 3 Private

***Glanyrafon,** 1 The Promenade, Kensington, Brecon, Powys, LD3 9AY.*
Open: Easter to Oct
Grades: WTB 1 Cr, High Comm
01874 623302 Mrs Roberts
Rates fr: *£15.00*-**£18.00**.
Beds: 2D 1T **Baths:** 2 Shared
(10) (3)
Elegant Edwardian house in quiet position on bank of River Usk. 5 minute walk into town. Highly Commended by Welsh Tourist Board. Warm Welsh welcome.

***Flag & Castle Guest House,** 11 Orchard Street, Llanfaes, Brecon, Powys, LD3 8AN.*
Convenient town/national park, amenities.
Open: All Year
01874 625860 Mrs Jones
Rates fr: *£15.00*-**£16.00**.
Beds: 1F 2D 1T 2S
Baths: 1 Private 2 Shared

***Tir Bach Guest House,** 13 Alexandra Road, Brecon, Powys, LD3 7PD.*
Panoramic view of Brecon Beacons.
Open: All Year (not Xmas)
Grades: WTB 1 Cr, Comm
01874 624551
Rates fr: *£14.00*-**£15.00**.
Beds: 1F 1T 1D
Baths: 1 Shared

***Cambridge House,** St David Street, Llanfaes, Brecon, Powys, LD3 8BB.*
Small family-run guest house.
Open: All Year
Grades: WTB 1 Cr, High Comm
01874 624699 Mr Lomas
Rates fr: *£14.00*-**£15.00**.
Beds: 2D 1T 1S
Baths: 1 Private 1 Shared
(4)

Bronllys

National Grid Ref: SO1435
Honey Cafe

***Bronllys Court,** Bronllys, Brecon, Powys, LD3 0LF.*
Easily accessible farmhouse, hearty breakfasts.
Open: Easter to Oct
Grades: WTB 1 Cr, Comm
01874 711362 Mrs Hopkins
Rates fr: *£14.00*-**£15.00**.
Beds: 1F 3D 2S
Baths: 2 Shared

Builth Wells

National Grid Ref: SO0350
Llanelwedd Arms, Greyhound Hotel

***Bron Wye,** Church Street, Builth Wells, Powys, LD2 3BS.*
Large Victorian semi-detached house.
Open: All Year
Grades: WTB 3 Cr, Comm
01982 553587
Mr & Mrs Wiltshire
Rates fr: *£16.00*-**£16.00**.
Beds: 1F 2D 1T 1S
Baths: 5 Private

***The Owls,** 40 High Street, Builth Wells, Powys, LD2 3AB.*
Family-run licensed guest house, restaurant. **Open:** All Year
Grades: WTB 3 Cr
01982 552518 Mrs Bond
Fax no: 01982 553867
Rates fr: *£16.50*-**£14.00**.
Beds: 1F 3D 1T 1S
Baths: 4 Ensuite 2 Shared
(8)

***Woodlands,** Hay Road, Builth Wells, Powys, LD2 3BP.*
Edwardian house in woodland setting.
Open: All Year (not Xmas)
01982 552354 (also fax no)
Mrs Nicholls
Rates fr: *£20.00*-**£25.00**.
Beds: 5T **Baths:** 5 Ensuite
(4)

***Dollynwydd Farm,** Builth Wells, Powys, LD2 3RZ.*
C17th farmhouse. Situated beneath the Eppynt hills.
Open: All Year (not Xmas)
Grades: WTB 2 Cr
01982 553660 Mrs Williams
Rates fr: *£15.00*-**£15.00**.
Beds: 1D 2T
Baths: 1 Ensuite 1 Private 1 Shared
(12)

The lowest **single** *rate is shown in* **bold.**

Bwlch

National Grid Ref: SO1421

***The Old Rectory,** Cathedine, Bwlch, Brecon, Powys, LD3 7SX.*
Small elegant rectory, idyllically situated.
Open: All Year (not Xmas)
01874 730399 Mrs Bean
Rates fr: *£14.00*-**£16.00**.
Beds: 1D 1T **Baths:** 1 Shared
(14) (6)

***Gilwych Farm,** Bwlch, Brecon, Powys, LD3 7JJ.*
Newly refurbished stables in Brecon Beacons.
Open: All Year **01874 730460**
Rates fr: *£15.00*-**£15.00**.
Beds: 1F 1D 1T
(10)

Capel-y-Ffin

National Grid Ref: SO2531

***The Grange,** Capel-y-Ffin, Abergavenny, NP7 7NP.*
Small Victorian family guest house
Open: Easter to Nov
01873 890215 Mrs Griffiths
Rates fr: *£20.00*-**£20.00**.
Beds: 3F 1D 3T 1S
Baths: 3 Shared
(8) (10)

Cemmaes

National Grid Ref: SH8306

***Penrhos Arms Hotel,** Cemmaes, Machynlleth, Powys, SY20 9PR.*
Late C18th coaching inn.
Open: Easter to Oct
01650 511243
Mr Liggett
Rates fr: *£12.00*-**£12.00**.
Beds: 1F 2D

Cemmaes Road

National Grid Ref: SH8403

***Gwalia,** Commins Coch, Cemmaes Road, Machynlleth, Powys, SY20 8LQ.*
Peaceful, secluded smallholdings, Vegetarian home cooking.
Open: All Year (not Xmas)
01650 511377
Mrs Chandler
Rates fr: *£14.00*-**£14.00**.
Beds: 1F 1T
Baths: 1 Shared

***Cefn Coch Uchaf,** Cemmaes Road, Machynlleth, Powys, SY20 8LU.*
C14th Dovey Valley farmhouse, lovely views.
Open: All Year (not Xmas)
01650 511552
Mrs Harris
Rates fr: *£14.50*-**£14.50**.
Beds: 2D 1T
Baths: 1 Private 1 Shared

Church Stoke

National Grid Ref: SO2794

The Drewin Farm, *Church Stoke, Montgomery, Powys, SY15 6TW.*
C17th farmhouse with panoramic views.
Open: Easter to Oct
Grades: WTB 3 Cr, High Comm, AA 4 Q, Select
01588 620325 Mrs Richards
Rates fr: *£16.00*-**£17.00**.
Beds: 2F **Baths:** 1 Private 1 Shared
(6)

Cilmery

National Grid Ref: SO0051

Prince Llewelyn Inn

Llewelyn Leisure Park, *Cilmery, Builth Wells, Powys, LD2 3NU.*
Jacuzzi, snooker, self-catering available.
Open: All Year
01982 552838 (also fax no)
Mr Johnson
Rates fr: *£14.00*-**£18.00**.
Beds: 2F 1S **Baths:** 2 Shared
(0) (7)

Crai

National Grid Ref: SN8924

Llwynhir Farm, *Crai, Brecon, Powys, LD3 8YW.*
500-acre mixed working farm.
Open: Mar to Oct
01874 636563
Rates fr: *£15.00*-**£16.00**.
Beds: 2D 1S

Crickhowell

National Grid Ref: SO2118

Bell Inn

Dragon Hotel, *High Street, Crickhowell, Powys, NP8 1BE.*
Open: All Year
Grades: WTB 3 Cr, High Comm, AA 2 St, RAC Acclaim
01873 810362 Mr & Mrs Thomas
Fax no: 01873 811868
Rates fr: *£25.00*-**£35.00**.
Beds: 2F 5D 6T 2S **Baths:** 15 Private
(14)
Character C18th hotel in picturesque Crickhowell. Marvellous atmosphere, excellent food/accommodation. Organiser of southern section of Cambrian Way Walkers' Association. Good value walking breaks programme.

White Hall, *Glangrwyney, Crickhowell, Powys, NP8 1EW.*
Comfortable Georgian house, next to restaurant.
Open: All Year **Grades:** WTB 2 Cr
01873 811155 / 840257 Ms Llewelyn
Rates fr: *£15.00*-**£13.00**.
Beds: 1F 2D 1T 1S
Baths: 2 Private 1 Shared
(3)

Hafod Swn-Y-Dwr, *The Dardy, Crickhowell, Powys, NP8 1PU.*
C18th canalside property - superb views.
Open: All Year
01873 810821
Mr Williams
Rates fr: *£17.50*-**£26.00**.
Beds: 1F 2D
Baths: 2 Ensuite 1 Private
(5)

Crossgates

National Grid Ref: SO0864

Guidfa House, *Crossgates, Llandrindod Wells, Powys, LD1 6RF.*
Licensed Georgian guest house.
Open: All Year
Grades: WTB 3 Cr, High Comm, AA 4 Q, Select
01597 851241
Mr Millan
Fax no: 01597 851875
Rates fr: *£24.00*-**£21.00**.
Beds: 2D 3T 2S
Baths: 5 Private 2 Shared
(10)

Park Motel, *Crossgates, Llandrindod Wells, Powys, LD1 6RF.*
Conveniently situated, comfortable motel/restaurant.
Open: All Year (not Xmas)
Grades: WTB 2 Cr, Comm
01597 851201
Mr & Mrs Sipple
Rates fr: *£18.00*-**£18.00**.
Beds: 7D
Baths: 7 Private
(20)

Cwmbelan

National Grid Ref: SN9481

Glyngynwydd, *Cwmbelan, Llanidloes, Powys, SY18 6QQ.*
Beautifully restored traditional C17th farmhouse.
Open: All Year
01686 413854
Mrs Davies
Rates fr: *£17.50*-**£20.00**.
Beds: 3D
Baths: 1 Private 2 Shared
(12)

Darowen

National Grid Ref: SH8201

Cefn Farm, *Darowen, Machynlleth, Powys, SY20 8NS.*
Quiet, comfortable, modernised old farmhouse.
Open: All Year (not Xmas)
Grades: WTB 2 Cr
01650 511336
Mr Lloyd
Rates fr: *£15.00*-**£15.00**.
Beds: 1F
Baths: 1 Private
(3)

Discoed

National Grid Ref: SO2764

Woodwinds, *Discoed, Presteigne, Powys, LD8 2NW.*
Clean modern house in superb location.
Open: All Year (not Xmas)
01547 560302
Mrs Ambridge
Rates fr: *£15.00*-**£15.00**.
Beds: 1F 1D 2T
Baths: 2 Private 1 Shared
(3)

Disserth

National Grid Ref: SO0350

Disserth Mill, *Disserth, Builth Wells, Powys, LD2 3TN.*
A sun trap by stream.
Open: Easter to Oct
01982 553217
Mrs Worts
Rates fr: *£15.00*-**£18.00**.
Beds: 2D 1T
Baths: 1 Shared
(4)

Dolau

National Grid Ref: SO1467

Glan Yr Afon, *Dolau, Llandrindod Wells, Powys, LD1 5TB.*
Comfortable house in beautiful countryside.
Open: Easter to Oct
01597 851677 Mrs Ruell
Rates fr: *£13.00*-**£13.00**.
Beds: 1D 2T
(4)

Dylife

National Grid Ref: SN8694

Star Inn

Star Inn, *Dylife, Staylittle, Llanbrynmair, Powys, SY19 7BW.*
Traditional country inn, log fires, real ales.
Open: All Year
01650 521345 Mrs Ward -Banks
Rates fr: *£17.00*-**£17.00**.
Beds: 1F 3D 1T 2S
Baths: 2 Private 1 Shared

Erwood

National Grid Ref: SO0942

Erwood Inn

Orchard Cottage, *Erwood, Builth Wells, Powys, LD2 3EZ.*
Cottage charm, modern comforts, River Wye.
Open: All Year
Grades: WTB 2 Cr, High Comm
01982 560600 Mr & Mrs Prior
Rates fr: *£15.50*-**£19.00**.
Beds: 1F 1D 1T
Baths: 1 Private 1 Shared
(5)

The Old Vicarage, *Erwood, Builth Wells, Powys,* *LD2 3DZ.*
Spacious Edwardian former vicarage.
Open: All Year
Grades: WTB 1 Cr, Comm
01982 560680
Mrs Williams
Rates fr: *£13.00*-**£13.00**.
Beds: 1F 1D 1T 1S
Baths: 1 Shared
(0)

Evenjobb

National Grid Ref: SO2662

The Barn, Old Barland, *Evenjobb, Presteigne, Powys,* *LD8 2SH.*
Secluded, idyllic Victorian barn conversion.
Open: All Year (not Xmas)
01547 560402
Mr & Mrs Smith
Rates fr: *£17.50*-**£17.50**.
Beds: 4D 1T
Baths: 2 Ensuite 2 Shared

Felindre

National Grid Ref: SO1681

Trevland, *Felindre, Knighton, Powys,* *LD7 1YL.*
Spacious, comfortable & quiet bungalow.
Open: All Year
01547 510211
Mrs Edwards
Rates fr: *£15.00*-**£15.00**.
Beds: 2F 1D 1T
Baths: 2 Ensuite 1 Shared
(4)

Foel

National Grid Ref: SH9911

Cann Office Hotel

Lluest Fach, *Foel, Llangadfan, Welshpool, Powys,* *SY21 0PB.*
Secluded smallholding, comfortable walkers' barns.
Open: All Year (not Xmas)
Grades: WTB Listed
01938 820351
Miss Wallace
Rates fr: *£15.00*-**£15.00**.
Beds: 1F 1T
Baths: 1 Shared
(4)

Forden

National Grid Ref: SJ2200

Railway Inn

Church House, *Forden, Welshpool, Powys,* *SY21 8NE.*
Pretty Georgian house & garden.
Open: All Year
01938 580353
Mrs Bright
Rates fr: *£14.50*-**£14.50**.
Beds: 1F 1D 1T
Baths: 2 Shared

Railway Inn, *Forden, Welshpool, Powys,* *SY21 8NN.*
100-year-old black-and-white inn.
Open: All Year (not Xmas)
Grades: WTB 2 Cr
01938 580237
Mr & Mrs Thomas
Rates fr: *£23.50*-**£18.50**.
Beds: 2D 1T
Baths: 2 Ensuite
(20)

Four Crosses

National Grid Ref: SJ2718

Ty-Coch Bungalow, *Four Crosses, Llanymynech, Powys,* *SY22 6QZ.*
Extensive bungalow, all rooms ground-level.
Open: All Year (not Xmas)
01691 830361 Mrs Lee
Rates fr: *£15.00*-**£15.00**.
Beds: 1D 1T 1S
Baths: 2 Private
(10)

Fronheulog

National Grid Ref: SJ0418

Fronheulog Bungalow, *Fronheulog, Llanwddyn, Oswestry, Shropshire,* *SY10 0LX.*
Top of the hill, lovely views.
Open: Easter to Oct
01691 870662 Mrs Jones
Rates fr: *£12.50*-**£15.00**.
Beds: 1D 1T
Baths: 1 Shared

Gladestry

National Grid Ref: SO2355

Wain Wen, *Gladestry, Kington, Powys,* *HR5 3NT.*
Comfortable farmhouse, gateway to Wales.
Open: Easter to Oct
01544 370226
Mrs Lloyd
Rates fr: *£15.00*-**£15.00**.
Beds: 1F 1T
Baths: 2 Shared
(9) (4)

Gwystre

National Grid Ref: SO0665

Gwystre Inn

Gwystre Inn, *Gwystre, Llandrindod Wells, Powys,* *LD1 6RN.*
Attractive Georgian inn, comfortable rooms.
Open: All Year
Grades: WTB 2 Cr
01597 851650
Mr & Mrs Sherwood
Rates fr: *£15.00*-**£15.00**.
Beds: 1F 2T
Baths: 3 Private
(40)

Hay-on-Wye

National Grid Ref: SO2242

Swan Hotel, Old Black Lion, Hollybush Inn, Kilverts Restaurant

The Seven Stars, *Broad Street, Hay-on-Wye, Hereford,* *01497 820886.*
Open: All Year **(also fax no)**
Mrs Ratcliffe
Rates fr: *£16.50*-**£20.00**.
Beds: 4D 2D 2T 1S
Baths: 3 Ensuite 3 Private
Charming character oak beamed, family-run hotel. Ideally situated in beautiful book town, on the paths of the Wye Valley & Offa's Dyke Path.

Rest for the Tired, *6 Broad Street, Hay-on-Wye, Hereford,* *HR3 5DB.*
C16th black-and-white B&B.
Open: All Year (not Xmas)
Grades: WTB 2 Cr, Comm
01497 820550
Mr Thomas
Rates fr: *£17.00*-**£25.00**.
Beds: 2D 1T
Baths: 3 Ensuite
(4)

Tinto House, *Broad Street, Hay-on-Wye, Hereford,* *HR3 5DB.*
Comfortable Georgian town house.
Open: Easter to Nov
Grades: WTB 2 Cr
01497 820590 Mrs Wheeler
Rates fr: *£17.50*-**£20.00**.
Beds: 1F 1D !T
Baths: 3 Ensuite
(2)

York House, *Cusop, Hay-on-Wye, Hereford,* *HR3 5QX.*
Quietly situated, late Victorian house.
Open: All Year
Grades: AA 4 Q Select, RAC High Acclaim
01497 820705 Mr Roberts
Rates fr: *£22.00*-**£24.00**.
Beds: 2D 2T
Baths: 4 Ensuite
(8) (6)

Fernleigh, *Hardwick Road, Cusop, Hay-on-Wye, Hereford,* *HR3 5QX.*
Large Victorian private house.
Open: Easter to Oct
01497 820459
Mr Hughes
Rates fr: *£14.00*-**£18.00**.
Beds: 2D 1T
Baths: 1 Shared

Lynwood, *Llanigon, Hay-on-Wye, Hereford,* *HR3 5PU.*
Modern bungalow. pleasantly situated.
Open: Easter to Oct
01497 820716 Mrs Davies
Rates fr: *£14.00*-**£14.00**.
Beds: 1D 1T 1S
Baths: 1 Shared
(4)

Heol Senni

National Grid Ref: SN9223

Lion Pub

***Maeswalter,** Heol Senni, Brecon, Powys, LD3 8SU.*
C17th farmhouse in picturesque countryside.
Open: All Year
Grades: WTB 1 Cr, AA 3 Q, Recomm, RAC Acclaim
01874 636629
Mrs Mayo
Rates fr: *£15.00*-**£20.00**.
Beds: 2D 1T
Baths: 1 Private 2 Shared
(1) (10)

Hirnant

National Grid Ref: SJ0522

***Blaen Hirnant Guest House,** Hirnant, Pen-Y-Bont-Fawr, Oswestry, Shropshire, SY10 0HR.*
Tastefully renovated C14th Welsh farmhouse.
Open: All Year (not Xmas)
01691 870330
Mr & Mrs Russell
Rates fr: *£15.50*-**£18.50**.
Beds: 1D 2T
Baths: 3 Private
(5)

Howey

National Grid Ref: SO0558

***Corven Hall,** Howey, Llandrindod Wells, Powys, LD1 5RE.*
Large Victorian country house.
Open: All Year (not Xmas)
Grades: WTB 3 Cr, High Comm
01597 823368 Mrs Prince
Rates fr: *£16.50*-**£22.50**.
Beds: 6F 2D 2T
Baths: 8 Private 3 Shared
(3months) (12)

***Holly Farm,** Howey, Llandrindod Wells, Powys, LD1 5PP.*
Comfortable old farmhouse.
Open: Easter to Nov
Grades: WTB 3 Cr, High Comm, AA 3 Q
01597 822402 Mrs Jones
Rates fr: *£16.00*-**£18.00**.
Beds: 1F 1D 1T
Baths: 3 Private
(6)

***Three Wells Farm,** Chapel Road, Howey, Llandrindod Wells, Powys, LD1 5PB.*
Licensed farm guest house.
Open: All Year (not Xmas)
Grades: WTB 4 Cr, HIgh Comm, AA 4 Q, Select, RAC High Acclaim
01597 824427 Mr Bufton
Rates fr: *£18.00*-**£18.00**.
Beds: 1F 6D 6T 1S
Baths: 14 Private
(10) (20)

***Brynhir Farm,** Chapel Road, Howey, Llandrindod Wells, Powys, LD1 5PB.*
C17th house on working farm.
Open: All Year
01597 822425 Mrs Nixon
Rates fr: *£17.00*-**£17.00**.
Beds: 3D 3T 2S
Baths: 8 Ensuite
(10)

Kerry

National Grid Ref: SO1489

***Greenfields,** Kerry, Newtown, Powys, SY16 4LH.*
Comfortable guest house, good food.
Open: All Year (not Xmas)
Grades: WTB 3 Cr, Comm
01686 670596
Mrs Madeley
Fax no: 01686 670354
Rates fr: *£17.50*-**£17.50**.
Beds: 1D 2T
Baths: 2 Ensuite 1 Private
(4) (8)

***Cefn-Caled Farmhouse,** Kerry, Newtown, Powys, SY16 4NG.*
C13th farmhouse in quiet location.
Open: All Year (not Xmas)
01686 670311
Mrs Jones
Rates fr: *£14.00*-**£14.00**.
Beds: 1D 1T
Baths: 1 Shared
(4)

Knighton

National Grid Ref: SP0356

Horse & Jockey

***The Fleece House,** Market Street, Knighton, Powys, LD7 1BB.*
Converted C18th coaching inn.
Open: All Year
Grades: WTB 2 Cr, Comm
01547 520168
Mrs Simmons
Rates fr: *£18.00*-**£21.00**.
Beds: 6T
Baths: 2 Ensuite 2 Shared

***Cwmgilla Farm,** Knighton, Powys, LD7 1PG.*
Modern comfortable farmhouse.
Open: Easter to Nov
01547 528387 Mrs Davies
Rates fr: *£17.00*-**£18.00**.
Beds: 2D 1S
Baths: 1 Shared
(10) (5)

***Cwm Sanaham Farm,** Knighton, Powys, LD7 1TP.*
Traditional old working farm.
Open: All Year (not Xmas)
01547 528431
Mrs Matthews
Rates fr: *£11.00*-**£11.00**.
Beds: 1F 1D
Baths: 1 Shared

***Pilleth Court,** Whitton, Knighton, Powys, LD7 1NP.*
Listed Elizabethan farmhouse.
Open: All Year (not Xmas)
Grades: WTB 2 Cr, High Comm
01547 560272 Mrs Hood
Rates fr: *£17.00*-**£19.00**.
Beds: 1F 2D 1T
Baths: 1 Ensuite 1 Shared
(9) (6)

Libanus

National Grid Ref: SN9925

Tair Bull Inn

***Tair Bull Inn,** Libanus, Brecon, Powys, LD3 8EL.*
Open: All Year
Grades: WTB 3 Cr, High Comm, RAC 1 St
01874 625849 Mrs Williams
Rates fr: *£18.00*-**£20.00**.
Beds: 1F 3D 1T
Baths: 5 Private
(1) (12)
Small, friendly inn, at the heart of the beautiful Brecon Beacons. Ideal walking or touring base. Car park, packed lunches on request, good food.

Llanafan Fawr

National Grid Ref: SN9655

***Gwern-Y-Mynach,** Llanafan Fawr, Builth Wells, Powys, LD2 3PN.*
Mixed sheep & dairy farm.
Open: All Year
01597 860256 Mrs Davies
Rates fr: *£12.00*-**£12.00**.
Beds: 1F 1S
Baths: 1 Private 1 Shared

Llananno

National Grid Ref: SO0974

***Bwlch Farm,** Llananno, Llandrindod Wells, Powys, LD1 6TT.*
C15th cruck hall house, 8 acres.
Open: Mar to Nov
Grades: WTB 2 Cr, High Comm
01597 840366 (also fax no)
Mr & Mrs Taylor
Rates fr: *£17.00*-**£19.50**.
Beds: 2D 1T
Baths: 2 Ensuite 1 Private

Llanbrynmair

National Grid Ref: SH8902

***Wynnstay Arms Hotel,** Llanbrynmair, Powys, SY19 7AA.*
In a walkers' paradise.
Open: All Year (not Xmas)
01650 521431 Mrs Taylor
Rates fr: *£14.50*-**£14.50**.
Beds: 2F 3D 1T
Baths: 2 Shared

Llanddew

National Grid Ref: SO0513

George Hotel

***The Old Rectory,** Llanddew, Brecon, Powys, LD3 9SS.*
Peacefully situated Victorian private house.
Open: All Year (not Xmas)
Grades: WTB 2 Cr, High Comm, RAC High Acclaim
01874 622058 Mrs Williams
Rates fr: *£18.00*-**£24.00**.
Beds: 1F 1D 1T
Baths: 2 Ensuite 1 Private
(10)

Llandefalle

National Grid Ref: SO1035

***Cilfodig,** Llandefalle, Brecon, Powys, LD3 0NR.*
300-year-old farmhouse.
Open: Easter to Oct
01874 754207 Mrs Evans
Rates fr: *£14.50*-**£14.50**.
Beds: 1F 1D 1S
(4)

Llandegley

National Grid Ref: SO1362

***Ffaldau Country House,** Llandegley, Llandrindod Wells, Powys, LD1 5UD.*
C15th cruck-beamed longhouse.
Open: All Year
01597 851421 Mr Knott
Rates fr: *£20.00*-**£28.00**.
Beds: 2D 2T
Baths: 3 Ensuite 1 Private
(10)

Llandeilo Graban

National Grid Ref: SO0944

***Penygraig Farm,** Llandeilo Graban, Erwood, Builth Wells, Powys, LD2 3YJ.*
C17th farmhouse.
Open: Feb to Nov
01982 560687 Mrs Carpenter
Rates fr: *£12.00*-**£13.00**.
Beds: 2T
Baths: 1 ensuite
(4)

Llandinam

National Grid Ref: SO0288

Lion Hotel

***Trewythen,** Llandinam, Powys, SY17 5BQ.*
Working farm in peaceful surroundings.
Open: Easter to Oct
Grades: WTB 2 Cr, High Comm
01686 688444 (also fax no) Mrs Davies
Rates fr: *£18.00*-**£18.00**.
Beds: 1F 1D 1S
Baths: 2 Ensuite 1 Private

***Lower Gwerneirn Farm,** Llandinam, Powys, SY17 5DD.*
Spacious Victorian farmhouse.
Open: All Year (not Xmas)
01686 688286 Mrs Brown
Rates fr: *£14.00*-**£13.00**.
Beds: 2D 1T

Llandrindod Wells

National Grid Ref: SO0561

Llanerch Inn, The Drovers

***The Cottage,** Llandrindod Wells, Powys, LD1 5EY.*
Open: All Year (not Xmas)
Grades: WTB 2 Cr, Comm
01597 825435 Mr Taylor
Rates fr: *£15.00*-**£17.00**.
Beds: 1F 2D 4T 1S
Baths: 4 Ensuite 1 Shared
Unusual Edwardian (Arts/Crafts) residence. Central location. Superb base for touring all Wales & historic Marches. Mine of useful information. Good French, some German spoken.

***Greylands,** High Street, Llandrindod Wells, Powys, LD1 6AG.*
Open: All Year
Grades: WTB 3 Cr, Comm
01597 822253 Mr MacDonald
Rates fr: *£14.00*-**£15.00**.
Beds: 1F 2D 1T 3S
Baths: 4 Private 1 Shared
Victorian spa town guest house surrounded by the beautiful hills of Mid Wales. Comfortable base for touring, country pursuits & golfing holidays.

***Griffin Lodge Hotel,** Temple Street, Llandrindod Wells, Powys, LD1 5HF.*
Friendly, comfortable, licensed Victorian hotel.
Open: All Year (not Xmas)
Grades: WTB 3 Cr ,High Comm, AA 3 Q, RAC Acclaim
01597 822432 Mrs Jones
Fax no: 01597 825196
Rates fr: *£18.50*-**£21.00**.
Beds: 4D 4T
Baths: 5 Private 3 Shared
(8)

***Three Wells Farm,** Chapel Road, Howey, Llandrindod Wells, Powys, LD1 5PB.*
Open: All Year (not Xmas)
Grades: WTB 4 Cr, HIgh Comm, AA 4 Q, Select, RAC High Acclaim
01597 824427 Mr Bufton
Rates fr: *£18.00*-**£18.00**.
Beds: 1F 6D 6T 1S
Baths: 14 Private
(10) (20)
Three Wells is a licensed farm guest house which overlooks a fishing lake in beautiful countryside. All rooms ensuite. An ideal setting for a romantic break.

***Drovers Arms,** Llandrindod Wells, Llandrindod Wells, Powys, LD1 5PT.*
Comfortable, real ale, great food.
Open: All Year (not Xmas)
Grades: WTB 2 Cr, Comm
01597 822508 Mrs Day
Rates fr: *£15.00*-**£20.00**.
Beds: 1D 1T
Baths: 1 Private
(8) (2)

***Llanerch Inn,** Llanerch Lane, Llandrindod Wells, Powys, LD1 6BG.*
C16th inn with relaxed atmosphere.
Open: All Year
Grades: WTB 3 Cr, Comm
01597 822086 Mr Leach
Fax no: 01597 824618
Rates fr: *£25.00*-**£25.00**.
Beds: 2F 5D 3T 2S
Baths: 11 Ensuite 1 Private
(0) (50)

Llandrinio

National Grid Ref: SJ2817

***Haimwood,** Llandrinio, Llanymynech, Powys, SY22 6SQ.*
C18th riverside farmhouse.
Open: All Year (not Xmas)
01691 830764 Mrs Nixon
Rates fr: *£13.00*-**£13.00**.
Beds: 1D 1T 1S
Baths: 1 Shared
(0) (6)

Llanfair Caereinion

National Grid Ref: SJ1006

***Madogs Wells,** Llanfair Caereinion, Welshpool, Powys, SY21 0DE.*
Astronomy breaks & wheelchair access.
Open: All Year (not Xmas)
Grades: WTB 1 Cr, Comm
01938 810446 Mrs Reed
Rates fr: *£15.00*-**£15.00**.
Beds: 1F 3D 1S
Baths: 1 Shared
(5)

***Cwm Llwynog,** Llanfair Caereinion, Welshpool, Powys, SY21 0HF.*
Cosy C17th farmhouse.
Open: Easter to Oct
Grades: WTB 3 Cr, High Comm, AA 4 Q
01938 810791 Ms Cornes
Rates fr: *£14.00*-**£14.00**.
Beds: 1D 1T
Baths: 1 Private 1 Shared

Always telephone to get directions to the B&B - you will save time!

Llanfihangel Nant Melan

National Grid Ref: SO1858

Red Lion

***Summergill,** Llanfihangel Nant Melan, Presteigne, Powys, LD8 2TN.*
Dormer bungalow surrounded by farmland.
Open: All Year (not Xmas)
01544 350247 Mrs Griffiths
Rates fr: *£12.50*-**£12.50**.
Beds: 2D 1T
Baths: 2 Ensuite 1 Shared
(3)

Llanfihangel Talyllyn

National Grid Ref: SO1128

***Glynderi,** Llanfihangel Talyllyn, Brecon, Powys, LD3 7SY.*
Large Regency house set in 3 acres of mature gardens.
Open: All Year (not Xmas)
01874 658263 Ms Copping
Fax no: 01874 658363
Rates fr: *£18.00*-**£18.00**.
Beds: 2D 1T
Baths: 3 Ensuite
(4)

Llanfihangel-Nant-Bran

National Grid Ref: SN9434

***Penpentre Farmhouse,** Llanfihangel-Nant-Bran, Brecon, Powys, LD3 9NA.*
Modernised centrally-heated farmhouse. **Open:** All Year
01874 636533 Mrs Jones
Rates fr: *£16.00*-**£16.00**.
Beds: 1D 1T **Baths:** 2 Shared

Llanfihangel-yng-Ngwynfa

National Grid Ref: SJ1419

***Cyfie Farm,** Llanfihangel-yng-Ngwynfa, Llanfyllin, Powys, SY22 5JE.*
A touch of something special, off the beaten track.
Open: All Year
01691 648451 Mrs Jenkins
Rates fr: *£18.50*-**£20.50**.
Beds: 1F 1D 1T
Baths: 3 Private

Llanfrynach

National Grid Ref: SO0725

White Swan

***Llanbrynean Farm,** Llanfrynach, Brecon, Powys, LD3 7BQ.*
Beautiful countryside, traditional family farmhouse.
Open: Feb to Nov
Grades: WTB 1 Cr
01874 665222 Mrs Harpur
Rates fr: *£15.50*-**£16.00**.
Beds: 1F 1D 1T
Baths: 1 Private 1 Shared

***Tyfry,** Llanfrynach, Brecon, Powys, LD3 7AX.*
Traditional Welsh farmhouse.
Open: All Year
01874 665232 Mrs Phillips
Rates fr: *£12.50*-**£12.50**.
Beds: 2F 1D
Baths: 2 Shared

Llanfyllin

National Grid Ref: SJ1419

***Gribbin Fach,** Llanfyllin, Powys, SY22 5EN.*
Oak-beamed country-house with cordon bleu cooking.
Open: All Year
01691 648528 Mrs Potts
Rates fr: *£17.00*-**£18.00**.
Beds: 2D 1T
Baths: 1 Private 1 Shared
(1) (5)

Llangadfan

National Grid Ref: SJ0110

***Cann Office Hotel,** Llangadfan, Welshpool, Powys, SY21 0PL.*
Historic posting inn.
Open: All Year (not Xmas)
01938 820202 Mr Lewis
Rates fr: *£18.00*-**£20.00**.
Beds: 3T
Baths: 2 Shared

Llangattock

National Grid Ref: SO2117

Horseshoe Inn

***The Horseshoe Inn,** Beaufort Ave, Llangattock, Crickhowell, Powys, NP8 1PN.*
C17th coaching inn.
01873 810393 Mrs Groves
Rates fr: *£14.50*-**£15.00**.
Beds: 1D 2T
Baths: 1 Shared

Llangorse

National Grid Ref: SO1327

Red Lion

***Red Lion Hotel,** Llangorse, Brecon, Powys, LD3 7TY.*
Friendly C18th village inn.
Open: All Year
Grades: WTB 3 Cr, Comm
01874 658238 Mrs Rosier
Fax no: 01874 658595
Rates fr: *£20.00*-**£25.00**.
Beds: 1F 5D 3T 1S
Baths: 5 Private 5 Shared
(20)

The lowest **single** *rate is shown in* **bold.**

***Trewalter House,** Llangorse, Brecon, Powys, LD3 0PS.*
Friendly, peaceful, views, good food.
Open: All Year (not Xmas)
Grades: WTB 3 Cr, High Comm
01874 658442 (also fax no)
Mrs Abbott
Rates fr: *£18.00*-**£28.00**.
Beds: 2D 1T
Baths: 3 Private

Llangunllo

National Grid Ref: SO2171

***Craig Fach,** Llangunllo, Knighton, Powys, LD7 1SY.*
Renovated, extended, traditional cottage.
Open: All Year (not Xmas)
01547 550605 Mrs Livingstone-Lawn
Rates fr: *£13.50*-**£13.50**.
Beds: 2F 1S
Baths: 1 Shared
(0) (10)

***Lower Cernsuran Farm,** Llangunllo, Knighton, Powys, LD7 1SL.*
C16th Welsh farmhouse, superb views.
Open: All Year (not Xmas)
01547 550219 Mrs Morgan
Rates fr: *£16.00*-**£17.00**.
Beds: 1F 1D 2T **Baths:** 4 Private
(10) (8)

Llanidloes

National Grid Ref: SN9584

***Dol-Llys Farm,** Trefeglwys Road, Llanidloes, Powys, SY18 6JA.*
C17th farmhouse.
Open: All Year (not Xmas)
Grades: WTB 2 Cr, High CommRAC Listed
01686 412694 Mr Evans
Rates fr: *£15.00*-**£17.00**.
Beds: 2D 1T
Baths: 3 Private

***Gorphwysfa Guest House,** Westgate Street, Llanidloes, Powys, SY18 6HL.*
Large Victorian house & garden.
Open: All Year
Grades: WTB 2 Cr
01686 413356 Mrs Lines
Rates fr: *£12.50*-**£12.50**.
Beds: 1F 1D 1T 1S
Baths: 2 Shared
(1yr) (5)

***Lloyds,** Cambrian Place, Llanidloes, Powys, SY18 6BX.*
Quiet, Victorian town-centre hotel.
Open: All Year
Grades: WTB 2 Cr, Comm
01686 412284 Fax no: 01686 412666
Rates fr: *£18.00*-**£16.50**.
Beds: 2D 3T 4S
Baths: 4 Private 3 Shared

Llanrhaeadr-ym-Mochnant

National Grid Ref: SJ1226

***Llys Morgan,** Llanrhaeadr-ym-Mochnant, Oswestry, Shropshire, SY10 0JZ.*
William Morgan translated the Bible into Welsh here in 1588.
Open: All Year
Grades: WTB 3 Cr, Comm
01691 780345 Mrs Morgan
Rates fr: *£16.50*-**£16.50**.
Beds: 1F 3D 1T
Baths: 3 Ensuite 2 Shared
(5)

***Wynnstay Arms Hotel,** Llanrhaeadr-ym-Mochnant, Oswestry, Shropshire, SY10 0JL.*
Small friendly family-run hotel.
Open: All Year (not Xmas)
01691 780210 Mr & Mrs Vaughan
Rates fr: *£17.00*-**£20.00**.
Beds: 1F 2D
Baths: 3 Private
(8)

Llansantffraid-ym-Mechain

National Grid Ref: SJ2120

***Pennygarreg,** Winllan Road, Llansantffraid-ym-Mechain, Llanfyllin, Powys, SY22 6TS.*
C17th black-and-white hillside house.
Open: Feb to Dec
01691 828452 Mrs Willis
Rates fr: *£17.00*-**£19.00**.
Beds: 1F 2T 1S

Llansilin

National Grid Ref: SJ2028

***Lloran Ganol,** Llansilin, Oswestry, Shropshire, SY10 7QX.*
Modern farm in 300 acres.
Open: All Year
Grades: WTB 1 Cr
01691 791287
Mrs Jones
Rates fr: *£13.50*-**£13.50**.
Beds: 1D 1T 1S
Baths: 2 Shared

Llanwrin

National Grid Ref: SH7803

Black Lion

***Mathafarn,** Llanwrin, Machynlleth, Powys, SY20 8QJ.*
Elegant country farmhouse.
Open: All Year (not Xmas)
Grades: WTB 2 Cr, High Comm
01650 511226 Mrs Hughes
Rates fr: *£17.00*-**£17.00**.
Beds: 1D 1T 1S
Baths: 1 Private 1 Shared

Llanwrthwl

National Grid Ref: SN9763

***Dyffryn Farm,** Llanwrthwl, Llandrindod Wells, Powys, LD1 6NU.*
Peaceful, spacious C17th stone farmhouse.
Open: Mid-Mar to Oct
01597 811017 Mrs Tyler
Rates fr: *£16.50*-**£16.50**.
Beds: 2D 1T
Baths: 1 Ensuite 1 Shared
(15) (6)

Llanwrtyd Wells

National Grid Ref: SN8746

Stonecroft Inn

***Neuadd Arms Hotel,** The Square, Llanwrtyd Wells, Powys, LD5 4RB.*
Half-Georgian, half-Victorian hotel.
Open: All Year
Grades: WTB 2 Cr, RAC 1 St
01591 610236 Mr Green
Rates fr: *£20.00*-**£20.00**.
Beds: 1F 5D 6T 8S
Baths: 11 Private 4 Shared
(10)

***Cerdyn Villa,** Llanwrtyd Wells, Powys, LD5 4RS.*
Peaceful, comfortable Victorian family house.
Open: All Year
Grades: WTB 2 Cr
01591 610635 Ms Lomax
Rates fr: *£16.00*.
Beds: 1F 1D 2T
Baths: 2 Private 2 Shared
(6)

***Carlton House Hotel,** Dolycoed Road, Llanwrtyd Wells, Powys, LD5 4SN.*
Bow windowed Edwardian villa.
Open: All Year (not Xmas)
01591 610248 Dr Gilchrist
Fax no: 01591 610242
Rates fr: *£23.00*-**£33.00**.
Beds: 2F 2D 1T
Baths: 5 Private

***Stonecroft Inn,** Dolecoed Road, Llanwrtyd Wells, Powys, LD5 4RA.*
Warm welcome awaits you at traditional country pub.
Open: All Year
01591 610332 Mr Lutman
Rates fr: *£18.00*-**£20.00**.
Beds: 1F 2D
Baths: 1 Ensuite 1 Shared
(20)

Llanymynech

National Grid Ref: SJ2620

***Hospitality,** Vyrnwy Bank, Llanymynech, Powys, SY22 6LG.*
C18th house with unusual features.
Open: Feb to Dec
01691 830427 Mrs Fahey
Rates fr: *£15.00*-**£15.00**.
Beds: 1D 1T 1S
(6)

Llanyre

National Grid Ref: SO0462

***Highbury Farm,** Llanyre, Llandrindod Wells, Powys, LD1 6EA.*
Large spacious farmhouse.
Open: Easter to Oct
Grades: WTB 2 Cr, High Comm
01597 822716 Mrs Evans
Rates fr: *£16.00*-**£18.00**.
Beds: 1F 1D 1T
Baths: 1 Private 1 Shared
(3)

Llechfaen

National Grid Ref: SO0828

***Upper Farm,** Llechfaen, Brecon, Powys, LD3 7SP.*
Modern, comfortable farmhouse.
Open: All Year
01874 665269 Mrs Williams
Rates fr: *£14.50*-**£14.50**.
Beds: 1F 1D 1T **Baths:** 1 Shared

Llyswen

National Grid Ref: SO1337

Griffin Inn, Bridge End Inn

***Lower Rhydness Bungalow,** Llyswen, Brecon, Powys, LD3 0AZ.*
Very comfortable bungalow, 150 acre farm. **Open:** Easter to Dec
01874 754264 Mrs Williams
Rates fr: *£15.00*-**£15.00**.
Beds: 1D 1T 1S
Baths: 1 Shared
(3)

Machynlleth

National Grid Ref: SH7400

White Lion, Glyndwyr Hotel

***Wynnstay Arms Hotel,** Maengwyn Street, Machynlleth, Powys, SY20 8AE.*
Open: All Year
Grades: WTB 4 Cr, Comm, AA 2 St, RAC 2 St
01654 702941 Mr Healing
Fax no: 01654 703884
Rates fr: *£22.50*-**£25.00**.
Beds: 1F 11D 5T 6S
Baths: 23 Ensuite
(36)
Tastefully refurbished C18th coaching inn at the heart of historic market town. Comfortable ensuite accommodation, cosy bar & lounges. Warmest welcome guaranteed.

***Pendre Guest House,** Maengwym St, Machynlleth, Powys, SY20 8EF.*
Georgian house, warm friendly atmosphere.
Open: All Year (not Xmas)
Grades: WTB 2 Cr
01654 702088 Ms Petrie
Rates fr: *£16.00*-**£24.00**.
Beds: 2F 1D 1T
Baths: 2 Private 2 Shared
(3)

Talbontdrain, *Uwchygarreg, Machynlleth, Powys, SY20 8RR.*
Remote, comfortable farmhouse, excellent food.
Open: All Year (not Xmas)
01654 702192 Ms Matthews
Rates fr: *£15.00*-**£12.50**.
Beds: 1D 1T 2S
Baths: 1 Private 1 Shared
(5)

The Glyndwr Hotel, *Doll Street, Machynlleth, Powys, SY20 8BQ.*
Small family-run hotel.
Open: All Year
Grades: WTB Listed
01654 703989 Mrs Duckett
Rates fr: *£15.00*-**£15.00**.
Beds: 1F 1D 1T
Baths: 2 Shared

Awelon, *Heol Powys, Machynlleth, Powys, SY20 8AY.*
Small comfortable private house.
Open: All Year (not Xmas)
Grades: WTB Listed, Comm
01654 702047 Ms Williams
Rates fr: *£14.00*-**£14.50**.
Beds: 1F 1T 1S
Baths: 1 Shared
(2)

Meifod

National Grid Ref: SJ1513

King Head

Pentrego Farm, *Meifod, Powys, SY22 6DH.*
Early C16th black-and-white farmhouse.
Open: All Year (not Xmas)
Grades: WTB Listed
01938 500353 Mrs Watkin
Rates fr: *£16.50*-**£16.50**.
Beds: 2F 1S **Baths:** 2 Private

Mochdre

National Grid Ref: SO0788

Llettyderyn, *Mochdre, Newtown, Powys, SY16 4JY.*
Restored farmhouse. Home baked bread.
Open: All Year
Grades: WTB 3 Cr, High Comm
01686 626131 Mrs Jandrell
Rates fr: *£17.00*-**£20.00**.
Beds: 2D 1T **Baths:** 3 Ensuite

Montgomery

National Grid Ref: SO2296

Little Brompton Farm, *Montgomery, Powys, SY15 6HY.*
Working C17th farm on Offa's Dyke. **Open:** All Year
Grades: WTB 3 Cr, High Comm, AA 4 Q, RAC Listed
01686 668371 Mrs Bright
Rates fr: *£18.00*-**£20.00**.
Beds: 1F 1D 1T
Baths: 2 Ensuite 1 Private

The Manor House, *Pool Road, Montgomery, Powys, SY15 6QY.*
Friendly private house.
Open: All Year (not Xmas)
01686 668736
Mrs Williams
Rates fr: *£15.00*-**£15.00**.
Beds: 1F 1D 1T 1S
Baths: 1 Private
(2)

New Radnor

National Grid Ref: SO2160

Eagle Hotel

Eagle Hotel, *Broad Street, New Radnor, Presteigne, Powys, LD8 2SN.*
Traditional coaching inn & outdoor activities.
Open: All Year
Grades: WTB 1 Cr
01544 350208 Mrs Hoy
Fax no: 01544 350401
Rates fr: *£17.50*-**£20.00**.
Beds: 2F 2D 2T
Baths: 2 Private 2 Shared
(8)

Bache Farm, *New Radnor, Presteigne, Powys, LD8 2TG.*
C17th farmhouse on working farm.
Open: All Year (not Xmas)
Grades: WTB 2 Cr
01544 350680 Mrs Hardwick
Rates fr: *£16.00*.
Beds: 1D 2T
Baths: 1 Private 1 Shared

Newtown

National Grid Ref: SO1191

Pen-Y-Gelli, *Newtown, Powys, SY16 3AH.*
Country house with swimming pool. **Open:** All Year
Grades: WTB 3 Cr
01686 628292 Mrs Hawkins
Rates fr: *£17.50*-**£17.50**.
Beds: 1F 1D 1T
Baths: 3 Private
(5)

Greenfields, *Kerry, Newtown, Powys, SY16 4LH.*
Comfortable guest house, good food.
Open: All Year (not Xmas)
Grades: WTB 3 Cr, Comm
01686 670596 Mrs Madeley
Fax no: 01686 670354
Rates fr: *£17.50*-**£17.50**.
Beds: 1D 2T
Baths: 2 Ensuite 1 Private
(4) (8)

Plas Canol Guest House, *New Road, Newtown, Powys, SY16 1AS.*
Detached family-run guest house.
Open: All Year
Grades: WTB Listed, High Comm
01686 625598 Mrs Burd
Rates fr: *£16.00*-**£16.00**.
Beds: 1F 1D 1T
Baths: 2 Private 1 Shared
(3)

Norton

National Grid Ref: SO3067

Wellingtonia Cottage, *Norton, Presteigne, Powys, LD8 2EU.*
Extended late-Victorian farmworker's cottage.
Open: All Year (not Xmas)
01544 260255 Mrs Hobley
Rates fr: *£13.00*-**£13.00**.
Beds: 1D 1T 1S
Baths: 1 Private 1 Shared
(3)

Old Radnor

National Grid Ref: SO2459

Harp Inn

Bryn Farm, *Old Radnor, Presteigne, Powys, LD8 2RP.*
Working mixed farm, near Offa's Dyke.
Open: All Year
01544 350240 Mrs Price
Rates fr: *£14.00*-**£14.00**.
Beds: 2F 1S
Baths: 1 Ensuite

Trewern Farm, *Old Radnor, Presteigne, Powys, LD8 2RP.*
Large Georgian house, friendly welcome.
Open: Easter to Oct
01544 350255
Mrs Lewis
Rates fr: *£17.50*-**£17.50**.
Beds: 2D 1S
Baths: 1 Ensuite 1 Shared

Pen-Y-Bont-Fawr

National Grid Ref: SJ0824

Green Inn, The Tanal (Llangynog)

Glanhafon, *Pen-Y-Bont-Fawr, Oswestry, Shropshire, SY10 0EW.*
Open: Easter to Oct
Grades: WTB 2 Cr, High Comm
01691 860377 Mrs Evans
Rates fr: *£15.00*-**£18.00**.
Beds: 1F 1D 1T
Baths: 2 Ensuite 1 Private
(3) (4)
Secluded farmhouse in the Upper Tanat Valley, close to Lake Vyrnwy and Pistyl Falls. Working sheep farm. Guests' own lounge. Children welcome. Phone for brochure.

Penyceunant, *Pen-Y-Bont-Fawr, Oswestry, Shropshire, SY10 0PF.*
Undiscovered countryside, walkers/tourist information.
Open: All Year (not Xmas)
Grades: WTB 1 Cr, High Comm
01691 860459
Mrs Francis
Rates fr: *£14.50*-**£16.00**.
Beds: 1F 1D
Baths: 1 Shared
(4)

Glyndwr, *Pen-Y-Bont-Fawr, Oswestry, Shropshire, SY10 0NT.*
Comfortable C17th Welsh stone cottage.
Open: All Year (not Xmas)
Grades: WTB 2 Cr
01691 860430 Mrs Henderson
Rates fr: *£16.00*-**£19.00**.
Beds: 2D 1T
Baths: 3 Private
(3)

Pencelli

National Grid Ref: SO0925

Ty Newydd Farm, *Pencelli, Brecon, Powys, LD3 7LJ.*
C18th Welsh farmhouse.
Open: Mar to Nov
01874 665315 Mrs Griffiths
Rates fr: *£17.50*-**£19.50**.
Beds: 1F 2D 1T
Baths: 4 Private
(100)

Pengenffordd

National Grid Ref: SO1730

Cwmfforest Guest House, *Pengenffordd, Talgarth, Brecon, Powys, LD3 0EU.*
Open: All Year
Grades: WTB 2 Cr
01874 711398 Mrs Turner
Fax no: 01874 711122
Rates fr: *£20.00*-**£20.00**.
Beds: 2T 2S
Baths: 2 Ensuite 1 Shared
(10)
Idyllic sheltered location close to highest Black Mountains peaks. Traditional farmhouse developed for long distance horse-riding holidays; exceptional cooking, evening meals. Host has extensive knowledge of best routes in Mid-Wales.

Penybont

National Grid Ref: SO1163

Severn Arms (Penybont)

Neuadd Farm, *Penybont, Llandrindod Wells, Powys, LD1 5SW.*
Open: All Year (not Xmas)
Grades: WTB 3 Cr, High Comm, AA 4 Q, Select
01597 822571 (also fax no)
Mr & Mrs Longley
Rates fr: *£19.50*.
Beds: 1D 2T
Baths: 3 Ensuite
(10) (6)
Comfortable C16th farmhouse in 92 acres. Guest lounge & dining room with inglenook fireplaces. Ideal for walking & touring mid-Wales. Peacefully situated, scenic views.

The lowest *double* rate per person is shown in *italics*.

The lowest single rate is shown in **bold.**

Pool Quay

National Grid Ref: SJ2511

Severn View, *Pool Quay, Welshpool, Powys, SY21 9JS.*
Georgian manor house, C18th annexe.
Open: All Year (not Xmas)
01938 590464 Mrs Kellaway
Rates fr: *£17.50*-**£17.00**.
Beds: 1F 2D 3S
Baths: 1 Private 1 Shared
(6)

Presteigne

National Grid Ref: SO3164

Willey Lodge Farm, *Presteigne, Powys, LD8 2NB.*
Comfortable C16th farmhouse - working farm.
Open: Easter to Nov
Grades: WTB 2 Cr, Comm
01544 267341 Mrs Davies
Rates fr: *£15.00*-**£15.00**.
Beds: 1D 1T
Baths: 1 Private
(4)

The Cabin Restaurant, *High Street, Presteigne, Powys, LD8 2BA.*
C16th licensed restaurant.
Open: All Year
01544 267068
Mr & Mrs Duggan
Rates fr: *£14.00*-**£14.00**.
Beds: 2T
Baths: 1 Shared

Rhayader

National Grid Ref: SN9768

Crown Inn

Beili Neuadd, *Rhayader, Powys, LD6 5NS.*
Secluded position with stunning views.
Open: All Year (not Xmas)
Grades: WTB 3 Cr, High Comm
01597 810211
Mrs Edwards
Rates fr: *£18.00*-**£18.50**.
Beds: 2D 1T 1S
Baths: 2 Ensuite 2 Private
(8)

Liverpool House, *East House, Rhayader, Powys, LD6 5EA.*
Large pleasant guest house, private car park.
Open: All Year
Grades: WTB 3 Cr
01597 810706 Mrs Griffiths
Fax no: 01597 810356
Rates fr: *£13.50*-**£15.00**.
Beds: 1F 2D 1T 1S
Baths: 3 Ensuite 1 Shared
(6)

Brynteg, *East Street, Rhayader, Powys, LD6 5EA.*
Comfortable Edwardian guest house.
Open: All Year (not Xmas)
01597 810052 Mrs Lawrence
Rates fr: *£14.50*-**£14.50**.
Beds: 2D 1T 1S **Baths:** 4 Private
(4)

Gigrin Farm, *Rhayader, Powys, LD6 5BL.*
Cosy, C17th Welsh farmhouse.
Open: All Year (not Xmas)
Grades: WTB Listed
01597 810243 Mrs Powell
Rates fr: *£15.00*-**£16.00**.
Beds: 2D 1S **Baths:** 1 Shared
(5) (3)

Downfield Farm, *Rhayader, Powys, LD6 5PA.*
Friendly farmhouse.
Open: Feb to Oct
Grades: WTB 1 Cr, Comm
01597 810394 Mrs Price
Rates fr: *£14.00*-**£15.00**.
Beds: 2D 1T **Baths:** 2 Shared
(10)

Sarnau

National Grid Ref: SO0232

Tai'r Bull Inn, Tower Hotel

Cefncoedbach Farm, *Sarnau, Brecon, Powys, LD3 9PT.*
Comfortable farmhouse with lovely views. **Open:** All Year
Grades: WTB Listed
01874 623548 Mrs Powell
Rates fr: *£12.00*-**£14.00**.
Beds: 1F 1D 1T
Baths: 1 Private 2 Shared
(3)

Staylittle

National Grid Ref: SN8892

Maesmedrisiol Farm, *Staylittle, Llanbrynmair, Powys, SY19 7BN.*
Friendly, comfortable, stone-built farmhouse.
Open: All Year (not Xmas)
01650 521494 Mrs Anwyl
Rates fr: *£14.00*-**£14.00**.
Beds: 2F 2D 1T 2S
Baths: 1 Private
(1) (8)

Talgarth

National Grid Ref: SO1533

Mason's Arms Hotel, Castle Inn

Craigend, *The Bank, Talgarth, Brecon, Powys, LD3 0BN.*
Victorian village house - Brecon Beacons National Park.
Open: All Year (not Xmas)
Grades: WTB Listed, Comm
01874 711084 Ms Price
Rates fr: *£15.00*-**£16.00**.
Beds: 2D 1T
Baths: 1 Ensuite 1 Shared
(5)

Castle Inn, *Pengenffordd, Talgarth, Brecon, Powys, LD3 0EP.*
Traditional rural inn.
Open: All Year
01874 711353 Mr Mountjoy
Rates fr: *£18.00*-**£18.00**.
Beds: 1F 2D 1T 1S
Baths: 2 Private 1 Shared
(50)

Talybont-on-Usk

National Grid Ref: SO1122

Travellers' Rest

Llanddety Hall Farm, *Talybont-on-Usk, Brecon, Powys, LD3 7YR.*
C17th Listed country house.
Open: Mar to Dec
Grades: WTB 3 Cr, High Comm, AA 4 Q, Select
01874 676415 Mrs Atkins
Rates fr: *£18.00*-**£21.00**.
Beds: 2D 1T
Baths: 2 Ensuite 1 Private
(10) (5)

Talyllyn

National Grid Ref: SO1027

Glascwm, *Talyllyn, Brecon, Powys, LD3 7SY.*
Large Edwardian country house.
Open: All Year
01874 658649 Mrs James
Rates fr: *£16.00*-**£17.00**.
Beds: 1F 1T 1D
Baths: 2 Ensuite
(4)

Trallong

National Grid Ref: SN9629

Llwynneath Farm, *Trallong, Sennybridge, Brecon, Powys, LD3 8HN.*
Comfortable working farm, warm welcome.
Open: All Year (not Xmas)
01874 636641 Mrs Williams
Rates fr: *£15.00*-**£18.00**.
Beds: 1F 1D **Baths:** 2 Private

Trefeglwys

National Grid Ref: SN9790

The Dingle, *Trefeglwys, Caersws, Powys, SY17 5PN.*
Ground floor rooms, peaceful garden.
Open: Mar to Oct
01686 430451 Mrs Loydall
Rates fr: *£16.00*-**£14.00**.
Beds: 1F 1S
Baths: 1 Ensuite 1 Shared
(5) (2)

Trelystan

National Grid Ref: SJ2603

Chapel House, *Trelystan, Leighton, Welshpool, Powys, SY21 8HX.*
Modernised house with smallholding.
Open: All Year (not Xmas)
01938 580476 Mr & Mrs Owens
Rates fr: *£14.00*-**£14.00**.
Beds: 1F 2D
Baths: 1 Shared

Tretower

National Grid Ref: SO1821

The Firs, *Tretower, Crickhowell, Powys, NP8 1RF.*
Cottage-style country house.
Open: All Year (not Xmas)
01874 730780 Mrs Eckley
Rates fr: *£16.50*-**£18.50**.
Beds: 1F 2D 1T
Baths: 2 Private 1 Shared
(10)

Van

National Grid Ref: SN9587

Esgairmaen, *Van, Llanidloes, Powys, SY18 6NT.*
Modern comfortable farmhouse.
Open: Easter to Oct
01686 430272 Mrs Rees
Rates fr: *£16.00*-**£16.00**.
Beds: 1F 1D
Baths: 1 Private 1 Shared

Welshpool

National Grid Ref: SJ2207

Tynllwyn Farm, *Welshpool, Powys, SY21 9BW.*
Farmhouse on Offa's Dyke & Glyndwr's Way.
Open: All Year
Grades: AA 3 Q, RAC Listed
01938 553175 Mrs Emberton
Rates fr: *£15.00*-**£18.00**.
Beds: 2F 2D 2T
Baths: 1 Ensuite 2 Shared
(20)

Tresi-Aur, *Brookfield Road, Welshpool, Powys, SY21 7PZ.*
Delightful, quiet guest house.
Open: Jan to Nov
Grades: WTB 2 Cr
01938 552430
Mrs Davies
Rates fr: *£14.00*-**£15.50**.
Beds: 1F 1D 1T
Baths: 1 Private
(2)

Lower Trelydan, *Welshpool, Powys, SY21 9PH.*
Black-and-white farmhouse, Listed, historical.
Open: All Year
Grades: WTB 3 Cr, High Comm, AA 4 Q, Select
01938 553105
Mrs Jones
Rates fr: *£19.00*-**£25.00**.
Beds: 1F 1D 1T
Baths: 3 Private

Dysserth Hall, *Powis Castle, Welshpool, Powys, SY21 8RQ.*
Comfortable friendly home. Superb view.
Open: Easter to Nov
01938 552153
Mr Marriott
Rates fr: *£18.00*-**£18.00**.
Beds: 1D 2T 1S
Baths: 2 Private 1 Shared
(8) (12)

Burnt House, *Trelydan, Welshpool, Powys, SY21 9HU.*
Lovely black-and-white house, great food.
Open: Feb to Nov
Grades: WTB 3 Cr
01938 552827
Mrs Wykes
Rates fr: *£17.00*-**£17.00**.
Beds: 1D 1T
Baths: 1 Private 1 Shared

Whitton

National Grid Ref: SO2767

Pilleth Court, *Whitton, Knighton, Powys, LD7 1NP.*
Listed Elizabethan farmhouse.
Open: All Year (not Xmas)
Grades: WTB 2 Cr, High Comm
01547 560272 Mrs Hood
Rates fr: *£17.00*-**£19.00**.
Beds: 1F 2D 1T
Baths: 1 Ensuite 1 Shared
(9) (6)

Location Index

The cities, towns, villages and hamlets listed in this index all have entries in **STILWELL'S DIRECTORY** under their respective regional heading. Features (eg Ben Nevis) or areas (eg Cotswolds) are also listed to point the reader to the relevant chapter. If there is no listing for the place you wish to stay in, the section map for that particular region will show you somewhere else to stay close by.

A — Page no.

C Page no.

D — Page no.

E — Page no.

F Page no.

G Page no.

H Page no.

M	Page no.

N	Page no.

O — Page no.

P — Page no.

Q Page no.

R Page no.

T — Page no.

U — Page no.

Y — Page no.

Z — Page no.

NOT LISTED IN STILWELL'S?

Do you know of a B&B that should be listed in these pages, but isn't? Use this form to recommend the B&B, telling us briefly why you think it merits inclusion.

I nominate the following B&B for inclusion in next year's edition of Stilwell's Britain: Bed & Breakfast. Please print the details.

B&B Owner's Name ....

B&B Address ....

....

B&B Tel No ....

Reasons for Nomination ....

....

....

Nominated by ....

Nominee's Address ....

Send this form to:

Britain: B&B, Stilwell Publishing Ltd, The Courtyard, 59 Charlotte Road, Shoreditch, London, EC2A 3QT.

NOT LISTED IN STILWELL'S?

Do you know of a B&B that should be listed in these pages, but isn't? Use this form to recommend the B&B, telling us briefly why you think it merits inclusion.

I nominate the following B&B for inclusion in next year's edition of Stilwell's Britain: Bed & Breakfast. Please print the details.

B&B Owner's Name ....

B&B Address ....

....

B&B Tel No ....

Reasons for Nomination ....

....

....

Nominated by ....

Nominee's Address ....

Send this form to:

Britain: B&B, Stilwell Publishing Ltd, The Courtyard, 59 Charlotte Road, Shoreditch, London, EC2A 3QT.

NOT LISTED IN STILWELL'S?

Do you know of a B&B that should be listed in these pages, but isn't? Use this form to recommend the B&B, telling us briefly why you think it merits inclusion.

I nominate the following B&B for inclusion in next year's edition of Stilwell's Britain: Bed & Breakfast. Please print the details.

B&B Owner's Name ....

B&B Address ....

....

B&B Tel No ....

Reasons for Nomination ....

....

....

Nominated by ....

Nominee's Address ....

Send this form to:
Britain: B&B, Stilwell Publishing Ltd, The Courtyard, 59 Charlotte Road, Shoreditch, London, EC2A 3QT.

NOT LISTED IN STILWELL'S?

Do you know of a B&B that should be listed in these pages, but isn't? Use this form to recommend the B&B, telling us briefly why you think it merits inclusion.

I nominate the following B&B for inclusion in next year's edition of Stilwell's Britain: Bed & Breakfast. Please print the details.

B&B Owner's Name ....

B&B Address ....

....

B&B Tel No ....

Reasons for Nomination ....

....

....

Nominated by ....

Nominee's Address ....

Send this form to:

Britain: B&B, Stilwell Publishing Ltd, The Courtyard, 59 Charlotte Road, Shoreditch, London, EC2A 3QT.

NOT LISTED IN STILWELL'S?

Do you know of a B&B that should be listed in these pages, but isn't? Use this form to recommend the B&B, telling us briefly why you think it merits inclusion.

I nominate the following B&B for inclusion in next year's edition of Stilwell's Britain: Bed & Breakfast. Please print the details.

B&B Owner's Name ....

B&B Address ....

....

B&B Tel No ....

Reasons for Nomination ....

....

....

Nominated by ....

Nominee's Address ....

Send this form to:
Britain: B&B, Stilwell Publishing Ltd, The Courtyard, 59 Charlotte Road, Shoreditch, London, EC2A 3QT.

NOT LISTED IN STILWELL'S?

Do you know of a B&B that should be listed in these pages, but isn't? Use this form to recommend the B&B, telling us briefly why you think it merits inclusion.

I nominate the following B&B for inclusion in next year's edition of Stilwell's Britain: Bed & Breakfast. Please print the details.

B&B Owner's Name ....

B&B Address ....

....

B&B Tel No ....

Reasons for Nomination ....

....

....

Nominated by ....

Nominee's Address ....

Send this form to:
Britain: B&B, Stilwell Publishing Ltd, The Courtyard, 59 Charlotte Road, Shoreditch, London, EC2A 3QT.

ORDER A COPY FOR A FRIEND OR COLLEAGUE

Yes, I wish to order a copy of

( ) **Stilwell's Directory: Britain - Bed & Breakfast 1997 @ £11.95 (inc. £2 p&p)**

( ) **Stilwell's Directory: Ireland - Bed & Breakfast 1997 @ £6.95 (inc. £1 p&p)**

( ) **Stilwell's National Trail Companion 1997 @ £10.95 (inc. £1 p&p)**

Please make your cheque payable to Stilwell Publishing Ltd. Please send me my copy within 21 days of receipt of this order. Please print details clearly.

Name ....

Address ....

....

.... Postcode ....

Tel No ....

Please send this order form, accompanied by your payment, to:

Copy Sales, Stilwell Publishing Ltd, The Courtyard, 59 Charlotte Road, Shoreditch, London, EC2A 3QT.

Please debit my credit/payment card.

Card no. ....

Expiry date ....

Signature ....

ORDER A COPY FOR A FRIEND OR COLLEAGUE

Yes, I wish to order a copy of

( ) **Stilwell's Directory: Britain - Bed & Breakfast 1997 @ £11.95 (inc. £2 p&p)**

( ) **Stilwell's Directory: Ireland - Bed & Breakfast 1997 @ £6.95 (inc. £1 p&p)**

( ) **Stilwell's National Trail Companion 1997 @ £10.95 (inc. £1 p&p)**

Please make your cheque payable to Stilwell Publishing Ltd. Please send me my copy within 21 days of receipt of this order. Please print details clearly.

Name ....

Address ....

....

.... Postcode ....

Tel No ....

Please send this order form, accompanied by your payment, to:

Copy Sales, Stilwell Publishing Ltd, The Courtyard, 59 Charlotte Road, Shoreditch, London, EC2A 3QT.

Please debit my credit/payment card.

Card no. ....

Expiry date ....

Signature ....

STILWELL'S

Key to Entries

- Children welcome (from age shown in brackets, if specified)
- Off-street car parking (number of places shown in brackets)
- No smoking
- Television (either in every room or in a TV lounge)
- Pets accepted (by prior arrangement)
- Evening meal available (by prior arrangement)
- Special diets catered for (by prior arrangement - please check with owner to see if your particular requirements are catered for)
- Central heating throughout
- Suitable for disabled people (please check with owner to see what level of disability is provided for)
- Christmas breaks a speciality
- Coffee/Tea making facilities

The location heading - every hamlet, village, town and city mentioned in this directory is represented on the local county map at the head of each section.

Use the National Grid reference with Ordnance Survey maps and any atlas that uses the British National Grid. The letters refer to a 100 kilometre grid square. The first two numbers refer to a North/South grid line and the last two numbers refer to an East/West grid line. The grid reference indicates their intersection point.

Penny Hassett

National Grid Ref: PH2096.

Cat & Fiddle, The Bull

Local pubs - these are the names of nearby pubs that serve food in the evening, as suggested by local B&Bs

The Old Rectory, *Main Street, Penny Hassett, Borchester, Borsetshire,* BC2 3QT.
C18th former rectory, lovely garden.
Grades: ETB 2 Cr, Comm.
Tel: **01676 512480.** Mrs Smythe.
Rates fr: *£14.00*-**£16.00**.
Open: All Year
Beds: 1F 1D 1T
Baths: 1 Private 2 Shared
(4) (2)

The figure in *italics* is the lowest 1997 double or twin rate per person per night. The figure in **bold** is the lowest 1997 single rate. Some establishments do not accept single bookings.

Bedrooms
F = Family
D = Double
T = Twin
S = Single

Grades - the English, Scottish and Welsh Tourist Boards (**ETB**, **STB** and **WTB**) have the national Crown rating (**Cr**), in which the range of facilities and services an establishment provides is indicated by "Listed" or 1 to 5 Crowns in ascending order of merit. Jersey in the Channel Islands uses Diamonds (**Di**). An optional quality grading, using the terms Approved (**Approv**), Commended (**Comm**), Highly Commended (**High Comm**) and De Luxe is also used. More details of the national Crown rating and the quality grading can be had from any Tourist Information Centre. The Automobile Association (**AA**) employs two grading systems: the one for hotels uses 1 to 5 Stars (**St**) in ascending order of merit; there is also a B&B rating that uses the letter **Q** (for quality) on a scale of 1 to 4; the highest have 4 Qs and a Selected award (**Select**). For more details, telephone the AA on 01256 20123. The Royal Automobile Club (**RAC**) also uses a Star (**St**) system for large hotels; small hotels and B&Bs obtain the ratings 'Listed' (**Listed**), 'Acclaimed' (**Acclaim**) or 'Highly Acclaimed' (**High Acclaim**). For more details, telephone the RAC on 0181-686 0088.